American Folklore

Garland Reference Library of the Humanities (Vol. 1551)

Advisory Board

American Folklore

An Encyclopedia

Edited by
Jan Harold Brunvand

Garland Publishing, Inc. New York & London, 1996

Library of Congress Cataloging-in-Publication Data

American folklore : an encyclopedia / Jan Harold Brunvand, editor.
          p.   cm. — (Garland reference library of the humanities ; vol.
    1551)
        Includes bibliographical references and index.
        ISBN 0-8153-0751-9 (alk. paper)
        1. Folklore—North American—Encyclopedias.   2. North America—
Social life and customs—Encyclopedias.   I. Brunvand, Jan Harold.
    II. Series.
    GR101.A54   1996
    398.2'0973—dc20   95–53734
                                                                CIP

Cover photo: Henry Ossawa Tanner's "The Banjo Lesson." Courtesy Hampton
University Museum, Hampton, Virginia.

Cover design by Lawrence Wolfson Design, NY.
Picture research by Jacob Love.
Cover research by Marjorie Trenk.

Contents

vii   Preface

ix   Standard Folklore Indexes and
      Classifications

xi   Contributors

1   The Encyclopedia

777   Index

Preface

This volume is a comprehensive general reference work intended for scholars, students, writers, and the general public on "American folklore," which is defined here as North American folklore, including Canadian but excluding, except for a few general topics, the folklore of Native Americans, which will be covered in its own encyclopedia. However, under many topics—immigrant folklore, African American folklore, occupational folklore, genres of folklore—reference to areas outside the United States and Canada was inevitable.

In 1930, Alexander H. Krappe called American folklore "a bad misnomer," asserting that there existed "only European (or African, or Far Eastern) folklore on the American continent." More usefully, in 1978, Richard M. Dorson distinguished between "Folklore in America" and "American Folklore," repeating the call that he had sounded decades before for more attention by folklorists to "the background of American history, with its unique circumstances and environment" and to both the adaptations of older folklore and the creation of new folklore against this historical background. The present encyclopedia affirms that "American folklore" indeed does exist, and it includes in its scope both the older adapted themes and the newer original ones developed within the larger cultural matrix of American history.

The qualifier "American" should be understood in the titles of all of the extensive entries gathered here for folklore genres, folk groups, scholarly approaches, general topics, folk performers, and folklorists. For the latter category—folklore scholars—only those people whose life work has been completed have been included. Living folklorists are not represented. For folk performers, this living-person rule was not applied, although a close association of each performer's work with genuine folk tradition was required. The range of general topics covered runs from traditional areas like folklore scholarship, film and folklore, history and folklore, mass media and folklore, parody in folklore, and public folklore to such leading-edge topics as bodylore, coding in American folk culture, cultural studies, computer folklore, empowerment, organizational folklore, and postmodernism.

Readers interested in a survey of scholarly approaches to American folklore might begin by reading the entries AMERICAN FOLKLORE SCHOLARSHIP: THE EARLY YEARS, CANADIAN FOLKLORE, ETHICS IN FOLKLORE RESEARCH, FIELDWORK, FOLKLIFE MOVEMENT, and MATERIAL CULTURE before turning to the specific "approaches" topics: ANTHROPOLOGICAL, COMPARATIVE, CONTEXTUAL, FEMINIST, FUNCTIONALISM, MARXIST, ORAL-FORMULAIC, PSYCHOLOGY OF FOLKLORE, SEMIOTIC, SOCIOLOGICAL, and STRUCTURAL. Similarly, one might read the general entry REGIONAL FOLKLORE before consulting the specific regional articles: NEW ENGLAND, MIDDLE ATLANTIC, ADIRONDACKS, APPALACHIA, PIEDMONT, MIDWEST, GREAT PLAINS, SOUTH, OZARKS, SOUTHWEST, ROCKY MOUNTAINS, NORTHWEST COAST AND ALASKA, AND GREAT BASIN. Or the general entries ETHNIC FOLKLORE and IMMIGRANT FOLKLORE, STUDY OF, could be read first as an introduction to the entries on ethnic and immigrant groups: AFRICAN, BALTIC, BASQUE, CAJUNS, CHINESE, DUTCH, FILIPINO, FINNISH, FRENCH, GERMAN, GREEK, GYPSIES, HUNGARIAN, IRISH, ITALIAN, JAPANESE, POLISH, ROMANIAN, SCANDINAVIAN, SCOTTISH, SLAVIC, UKRAINIAN, and WENDS.

Of course, every entry and its reference list is an independent entity worth consulting on its own merits, with no prior review of a general topic required. A "see also" line for most entries indicates cross-references to related topics.

The major American folklore genres and occupational folk groups have been included, insofar as reference material exists to document them, but we did not attempt to cover all minor genres, occupations, and hobbies that may have their own distinctive folklore. Thus, there are long essays on such genres as CUSTOM, FOLKSONG, FOLKTALE, GAMES, MYTH, PROVERBS, RIDDLES AND PUZZLES, and SUPERSTITION, but shorter entries on such genres as ANECDOTE, ANTI-LEGEND, CADENCE CHANT, DOZENS, JACK TALES, MNEMONIC DEVICES, PRAYER, RECITATION, and SHIVAREE. Similarly for occupations, we have longer entries for COWBOYS, FARMERS, LOGGERS, RAILROADERS, STEELWORKERS, and the like, but shorter ones for groups like BIKERS, BIRDERS, LAWYERS, MEDI-

CAL PROFESSIONALS, PRINTERS, and WATERMEN.

Readers will find all of the expected arts and crafts of American folk tradition represented here: BASKETMAKING, BLACKSMITHING, COSTUME, NEEDLEWORK, POTTERY, QUILT MAKING, WEAVING, WOOD CARVING, and so on, as well as some perhaps less familiar, like BOATBUILDING, PAPERCUTTING, TATTOOING, and the creations produced by "outsider artists." In like manner, there are, predictably, entries on major musical forms, such as BALLAD, BLUEGRASS, BLUES, CHANTEYS, GOSPEL MUSIC, LULLABY, LYRIC SONG, PLAY-PARTY, SHAPE-NOTE SINGING, SPIRITUALS, and WORK SONG but also less-expected entries on such forms as CONJUNTO MUSIC, COUNTRY MUSIC, ELVIS, FILK MUSIC, JAZZ, KLEZMER, RAP, and ZYDECO.

Each user of this volume, we hope, will find special surprises and pleasures in it. For his own part, the editor confesses to having a special affinity for the entries AUTOHARP, CATFISH, CON ARTIST, COW TIPPING, CURSING, FISHING (SPORT), NUCLEAR LORE, OUIJA, SHEEP CAMP, and UFO LORE, none of which were on the originally planned entry list but all of which yielded fascinating essays in the hands of the experts who wrote them.

American folklore is a large and diversified field with a long and proud tradition of scholarship devoted to its collection and interpretation. This encyclopedia is the first serious attempt to provide a detailed reference source on the field, based on the work of academic folklore specialists. The net was cast widely, but in the confines of a one-volume book much had to be summarized or even omitted. So, besides using the reference lists following many individual entries, the reader is urged to consult such general sources as the following.

General Reference Material

Brunvand, Jan Harold. 1979. *Readings in American Folklore.* New York: W.W. Norton.

———. 1986. *The Study of American Folklore: An Introduction.* 3d. ed. New York: W.W. Norton.

Dorson, Richard M. 1959. *American Folklore.* (Paperback ed. with revised bibliographical notes, 1977.) Chicago: University of Chicago Press.

———. 1964. *Buying the Wind: Regional Folklore in the United States.* Chicago: University of Chicago Press.

———. 1972. *Folklore and Folklife: An Introduction.* Chicago: University of Chicago Press.

———. 1973. *America in Legend: Folklore from the Colonial Period to the Present.* New York: Pantheon Books.

———, ed. 1983. *Handbook of American Folklore.* Bloomington: Indiana University Press.

Dundes, Alan, ed. 1965. *The Study of Folklore.* Englewood Cliffs: Prentice-Hall.

Flanagan, Cathleen C., and John T. 1977. *American Folklore: A Bibliography.* Metuchen: Scarecrow Press.

Haywood, Charles. 1961. *A Bibliography of North American Folklore and Folksong.* 2d. rev. ed. New York: Dover Books.

Leach, Maria, and Jerome Fried, eds. 1950. *Standard Dictionary of Folklore, Mythology, and Legend.* (Rev. ed., 1972.)

Oring, Elliott, ed. 1986. *Folk Groups and Folklore Genres: An Introduction.* Logan: Utah State University Press.

———. 1989. *Folk Groups and Folklore Genres: A Reader.* Logan: Utah State University Press.

Toelken, Barre. 1979. *The Dynamics of Folklore.* Boston: Houghton Mifflin.

Wilgus, D.K. 1959. *Anglo-American Folksong Scholarship Since 1898.* New Brunswick: Rutgers University Press.

Jan Harold Brunvand

Standard Folklore Indexes and Classifications

The following are cited within entries in the short forms shown in brackets.

Aarne, Antti, and Stith Thompson. 1964. *The Types of the Folktale: A Classification and Bibliography.* 2d. rev. ed. Folklore Fellows Communications, No. 184. [Cited as AT, Type, or Tale Type followed by the appropriate number.]

Baughman, Ernest W. 1966. *Type and Motif-Index of the Folktales of England and North America.* Indiana University Folklore Series, No. 20. The Hague: Mouton. [Cited as Baughman Type or Baughman Motif followed by the appropriate letter or number.]

Child, Francis James. [1882–1898] 1965. *The English and Scottish Popular Ballads.* 5 vols. New York: Dover. [Cited as Child followed by the appropriate number, from 1 through 305.]

Coffin, Tristram Potter. 1977. *American Balladry from British Broadsides: A Guide for Students and Collectors of the Traditional Song.* American Folklore Society, Bibliographical and Special Series. Vol. 8. Philadelphia.

Laws, G. Malcolm, Jr. 1957. *American Balladry from British Broadsides: A Guide for Students and Collectors of Traditional Song.* American Folklore Society, Bibliographical and Special Series. Vol. 8. Philadelphia. [Cited as Laws followed by the letter J through Q followed by the appropriate number.]

———. 1964. *Native American Balladry: A Descriptive Guide and a Bibliographical Syllabus.* Rev. ed. American Folklore Society, Bibliographical and Special Series. Vol. 1. Philadelphia. [Cited as Laws followed by the letter A through I followed by the appropriate number.]

Thompson, Stith. 1955–1958. *The Motif-Index of Folk-Literature.* Rev. ed. 6 vols. Bloomington: Indiana University Press. [Cited as Motif followed by the appropriate letter and numbers.]

Contributors

Barbara Allen
Independent Scholar
Cheyenne, WY

R. Gerald Alvey
Professor, Department of English
University of Kentucky

Philis Alvic
Independent Scholar
Lexington, KY

Ruth E. Andersen
Independent Scholar
Austin, TX

John J. Appel
Adjunct Curator
Michigan State University Museum

John Ashton
Professor, Department of Folklore
Sir Wilfred Grenfell College
Canada

Louie Attebery
Professor, Department of English
Albertson College of Idaho

Ronald L. Baker
Chairperson and Professor of English
Indiana State University

Karen Baldwin
Director, ECU Folklore Archive
East Carolina University

Amanda Carson Banks
Library Development
Vanderbilt University

Thomas E. Barden
Director, American Studies Program
University of Toledo

Robert Baron
Folk Arts Program Director
New York State Council on the Arts

Peter Bartis
Folklife Specialist, American Folklife
    Center
Library of Congress

John Bealle
Independent Scholar
Cincinnati, OH

Stephen Dow Beckham
Pamplin Professor of History
Lewis & Clark College

Kristi A. Bell
Archivist, Brigham Young University
    Folklore Archive

Dan Ben-Amos
Professor of Folklore and Folklife
University of Pennsylvania

Richard J. Blaustein
Professor
East Tennessee State University

Betsy Bowden
Professor, Department of English
Rutgers University–Camden

Erika Brady
Associate Professor, Programs in Folk
    Studies
Western Kentucky University

Margaret K. Brady
Associate Professor, Department of
    English
University of Utah

C. Ray Brassieur
Oral Historian/Folklorist, State
    Historical Society of Missouri
University of Missouri–Columbia

Charles L. Briggs
Professor of Anthropology
Vassar College

Simon J. Bronner
Professor, American Studies Program
Pennsylvania State University–
    Harrisburg

David A. Brose
Manager, Folklore Program
John C. Campbell Folk School
Brasstown, NC

Peggy A. Bulger
Folk Arts Director
Southern Arts Federation
Atlanta, GA

Thomas E. Bullard
Independent Scholar
Bloomington, IN

Carol Burke
Associate Dean for Academic Affairs
    and Associate Professor, School of
    Arts and Sciences
Johns Hopkins University

Richard Allen Burns
Assistant Professor of English and
    Folklore
Arkansas State University

John A. Burrison
Professor, Department of English
Georgia State University

Anne Burson-Tolpin
Adjunct Instructor
Essex County College–West Essex
    Campus

Charles Camp
Maryland State Arts Council

Hal Cannon
Founding Director, Western Folklife
    Center
Elko, NV

Sue Spencer Cannon
Independent Scholar
Irvine, CA

Simon J. Carmel
Assistant Professor, Anthropologist,
    National Technical Institute for the
    Deaf
Rochester Institute of Technology

Carole H. Carpenter
Professor, Ontario Folklife Centre/
    Humanities
York University
Canada

John Cash
Folklore Institute
Indiana University

Frances Cattermole-Tally
Independent Scholar
Los Angeles, CA

Vivien T.Y. Chen
Project Director, Smithsonian
    Institution Traveling Exhibition
    Service (SITES)
Smithsonian Institution

Sally C. and Barry E. Childs-Helton
Independent Scholars
Indianapolis, IN

William M. Clements
Professor of English and Folklore
Arkansas State University

Janet M. Cliff
Independent Scholar
San Antonio, TX

Robert Cochran
Director, Center for Arkansas and
    Regional Studies
University of Arkansas

Tristram Potter Coffin
Independent Scholar
Wakefield, RI

John M. Coggeshall
Department of Sociology
Clemson University

David Steven Cohen
Senior Research Associate
New Jersey Historical Commission

Norm Cohen
Independent Scholar
Portland, OR

Kristin G. Congdon
Professor of Art
University of Central Florida

Cecelia Conway
Independent Scholar
Chapel Hill, NC

Kay Cothran Craigie
Independent Scholar
Paoli, PA

Daniel J. Crowley
Professor, Department of Anthropology
University of California–Davis

Keith Cunningham
Professor of English
Northern Arizona University

Larry Danielson
Professor and Chair, Intercultural and
    Folk Studies Department
Western Kentucky University

Frank de Caro
Professor, Department of English
Louisiana State University

Linda Dégh
Distinguished Professor of Folklore
Indiana University

Douglas DeNatale
Manager, Cultural Heritage and
    Technology
New England Foundation for the Arts
Boston, MA

C. Kurt Dewhurst
Director, Michigan State University
    Museum

Sandra K. Dolby
Professor, Folklore Institute
Indiana University

John Dorst
Professor, American Studies Program
University of Wyoming

William A. Douglass
Coordinator, Basque Studies Program
University of Nevada–Reno

Norine Dresser
Retired Faculty, now Independent
    Scholar
California State University–Los
    Angeles

Doris J. Dyen
Steel Industry Heritage Foundation
Homestead, PA

Brenda M. Eagles
Research Librarian, Center for the
    Study of Southern Culture
University of Mississippi

Eric Alden Eliason
Independent Scholar
Austin, TX

Bill Ellis
Associate Professor of English and
    American Studies
Pennsylvania State University–
    Hazleton

David G. Engle
Professor, Department of Foreign
    Languages and Literature
California State University–Fresno

David Evans
Professor of Music
University of Memphis

Barbara Fertig
Savannah History Museum
Savannah, GA

Alta Fife
Independent Scholar
Logan, UT

Gary Alan Fine
Professor of Sociology
University of Georgia

Elizabeth C. Fine
Associate Professor, Center for
    Interdisciplinary Studies and
    Department of Communication
    Studies
Virginia Tech

John Miles Foley
W.H. Byler Professor of Classics and
    English
University of Missouri

Edith Fowke
Independent Scholar
Canada

Robert A. Georges
Professor Emeritus, Folklore and
    Mythology Program
University of California–Los Angeles

Angus Kress Gillespie
Associate Professor, American Studies
    Department
Rutgers University

Janet C. Gilmore
Independent Scholar
Mount Horeb, WI

Stephen D. Glazier
Professor of Anthropology
University of Nebraska

Christine Goldberg
Independent Scholar
Los Angeles, CA

Peter D. Goldsmith
Dean of First-Year Students and
    Adjunct Associate Professor of
    Anthropology
Dartmouth College

Joseph P. Goodwin
Assistant Director, Career Services
Ball State University

Andrea Graham
Director, Folk Arts Program
Nevada State Council on the Arts

Joe S. Graham
Chair, Department of Psychology and
    Sociology (Anthropology)
Texas A&M University–Kingsville

Stephen Green
Sound and Image Librarian
Southern Folklife and Historical
    Collections/Wilson Library
University of North Carolina–Chapel
    Hill

Pauline Greenhill
Associate Professor, Anthropology and
    Women's Studies
University of Winnipeg
Canada

Sylvia Grider
Department of Anthropology
Texas A&M University

Hanna Griff
Assistant Professor
Sanyo Gakuen University
Japan

James S. Griffith
Coordinator, Southwest Folklore
    Center
Special Collections Library
University of Arizona

John A. Gutowski
Professor, Department of English
Saint Xavier University

Sandra G. Hancock
Professor, Department of English
University of Tennessee

Judith Lynne Hanna
Senior Research Scholar
University of Maryland

Gregory Hansen
Associate Instructor
Indiana University

Ilana Harlow
The Folklore Institute
Indiana University

Joseph Harris
Professor, Department of English and
    American Literature
Harvard University

Phyllis A. Harrison
Executive Director, Life on the Sound
Tacoma, WA

Guy Haskell
Professor, Judaic and Near Eastern
    Studies
Oberlin College

Judith Haut
Independent Scholar
Topanga, CA

Elissa R. Henken
Associate Professor
University of Georgia

Jerrold Hirsch
Professor, Division of Social Science
Northeast Missouri State University

Maggie Holtzberg
Director, Folklife Program
Georgia Council for the Arts

Laurel Horton
Independent Scholar
Seneca, SC

Jim Hoy
Professor, Division of English
Emporia State University

Patrick Huber
Department of History
University of North Carolina

Mary Hufford
Folklife Specialist, American Folklife
    Center
Washington, DC

Linda A. Hughes
Visiting Assistant Professor
University of Delaware

Lin T. Humphrey
Independent Scholar
Claremont, CA

Ray Hyman
Professor, Department of Psychology
University of Oregon

Joyce Ice
Assistant Director, Museum of
    International Folk Art
Santa Fe, NM

Alan Jabbour
Director, American Folklife Center
Library of Congress

Bruce Jackson
SUNY Distinguished Professor
State University of New York–Buffalo

Timothy B. Jay
Professor of Psychology
North Adams State College
North Adams, MA

Paula J. Johnson
Maritime Specialist, National
    Museum of American History
Smithsonian Institution

Michael Owen Jones
Professor of Folklore and History
University of California–Los Angeles

Rosemary Joyce
Independent Scholar
Columbus, OH

Ed Kahn
Independent Scholar
Pinole, CA

Joann W. Kealiinohomoku
Independent Scholar
Cross-Cultural Dance Resources
Flagstaff, AZ

Kenneth B. Keppeler
Independent Scholar
Albuquerque, NM

Cheryl L. Keyes
Assistant Professor, Department of
    Ethnomusicology
University of California–Los Angeles

Sojin Kim
University of California–Los Angeles

Alana Paige Kimbel
Student Archivist, Brigham Young
    University Folklore Archive

James W. Kirkland
Professor, Department of English
East Carolina University

Barbro Klein
Associate Professor, Department of
    Ethnology
Stockholm University
Sweden

LuAnne Gaykowski Kozma
Assistant Curator of Folk Arts and
    4-H Specialist
Michigan Traditional Arts Program
Michigan State University Museum

Miles Krassen
Professor, Judaic and Near Eastern
    Studies
Oberlin College

Elon Kulii
Professor, Department of English
North Carolina A&T University

Richard Kurin
Director, Center for Folklife Programs
    and Cultural Studies
Smithsonian Institution

Donald M. Lance
Professor Emeritus of English
University of Missouri

Janet Langlois
Professor, Department of English
Wayne State University

George E. Lankford
Bradley Professor in the Social
    Sciences
Lyon College

Jan Laude
Independent Scholar
Minneapolis, MN

John Laudun
The Folklore Institute
Indiana University

Monica Lawton
Lecturer
University of Pennsylvania

James P. Leary
Faculty Associate, Folklore Program
University of Wisconsin

Wendy Leeds-Hurwitz
Professor, Communication Department
University of Wisconsin–Parkside

William E. Lightfoot
Professor, Department of English
Appalachian State University

Jennifer Livesay
Independent Scholar
Bloomington, IN

Yvonne R. Lockwood
Michigan State University Museum

Michael A. Lofaro
Professor, Department of English
University of Tennessee

Guy Logsdon
Independent Scholar
Tulsa, OK

Terry L. Long
Professor
Ohio State University–Newark

Jens Lund
Independent Scholar
Olympia, WA

Michael Luster
Director, Louisiana Folklife Festival

Richard March
Wisconsin Arts Board

Howard Wight Marshall
Professor, Department of Art History
and Archaeology
University of Missouri

Gail Matthews-DeNatale
Assistant Professor, Institute for
Educational Transformation
George Mason University

Robert McCarl
Professor, Department of
Anthropology
Boise State University

William Bernard McCarthy
Professor of English
Pennsylvania State University–DuBois

Margy McClain
Urban Traditions
Chicago, IL

Ellen McHale
Independent Scholar
Esperance, NY

W.K. McNeil
Folklorist, The Ozark Folk Center
Mountain View, AR

Jay Mechling
Professor, Department of American
Studies
University of California–Davis

Bohdan Medwidsky
Professor, Slavic and East European
Studies
University of Alberta
Canada

Herminia Q. Meñez
Independent Scholar
Los Angeles, CA

Richard E. Meyer
Professor of English
Western Oregon State College

Wolfgang Mieder
Professor, Department of German and
Russian
University of Vermont

Yvonne J. Milspaw
Associate Professor of English and
Humanities
Harrisburg Area Community College

John Minton
Assistant Professor of Folklore
Indiana University–Purdue Univer-
sity–Fort Wayne

Roger Mitchell
Professor Emeritus, Anthropology
University of Wisconsin–Eau Claire

John F. Moe
Fulbright Professor of American
Studies
University of Tampere
Finland

William Lynwood Montell
Professor, Programs in Folk Studies
Western Kentucky University

Eric L. Montenyohl
Independent Scholar
Cary, NC

John Morgan
Instructor in English
University of Missouri–Rolla

Linda Morley
Independent Scholar
Manchester, NH

Patrick B. Mullen
Professor, Department of English
Ohio State University

Peter Narváez
Department of Folklore
Memorial University of
Newfoundland
Canada

Bruno Nettl
Professor, School of Music
University of Illinois

Elliott Oring
Professor, Department of
Anthropology
California State University–Los
Angeles

Blanton Owen
Independent Scholar
Carson City, NV

Beverly Bush Patterson
Folklife Specialist
North Carolina Arts Council

Deirdre M. Paulsen
Consultant, Honors and General
Education
Brigham Young University

Barry Lee Pearson
Professor, Department of English
University of Maryland

Ron Pen
Professor, School of Music
University of Kentucky

Charles L. Perdue Jr.
Professor, Departments of
Anthropology and English
University of Virginia

Burton W. Peretti
Professor, Department of History
Colorado College

Natalie Rainey-Peters
Independent Scholar
Havre de Grace, Maryland

Erskine Peters
Professor, Department of English
University of Notre Dame

Kenneth D. Pimple
Independent Scholar
Bloomington, IN

James Porter
Professor and Chair, Ethnomusicol-
ogy, Folklore and Mythology
University of California–Los Angeles

Nolan Porterfield
Independent Scholar
Bowling Green, KY

Jennifer Post
Curator, Helen Hartness Flanders
    Ballad Collection, Starr Library
Middlebury College

Cathy Lynn Preston
Professor, Department of English
University of Colorado

Michael Preston
Professor, Department of English
University of Colorado

Leonard Norman Primiano
Professor, Department of Religion
Cabrini College

Marie Luise Proeller
Independent Scholar
New York, NY

Colin Quigley
Associate Professor, Department of
    World Arts and Cultures
University of California–Los Angeles

Joan Newlon Radner
Professor, Department of Literature
American University

John M. Ramsay
Retired Director of Recreation
    Extension at Berea College, now
    Independent Scholar
Berea, KY

Richard Raspa
Professor, Wayne State University
Detroit, MI

Robert M. Rennick
Independent Scholar
Prestonsburg, KY

Roger deV. Renwick
Associate Professor
University of Texas–Austin

W. Edson Richmond †
Professor Emeritus
Bloomington, IN

Warren E. Roberts
Professor Emeritus, Folklore Institute
Indiana University

Danielle M. Roemer
Associate Professor
Northern Kentucky University

Bruce A. Rosenberg
Professor, American Civilization
Brown University

Neil V. Rosenberg
Professor, Department of Folklore
Memorial University of
    Newfoundland
Canada

Kent C. Ryden
Assistant Professor, American and
    New England Studies Program
University of Southern Maine

Lynn Moss Sanders
Professor, Department of English
Appalachian State University

Jack Santino
Professor of Folklore and Popular
    Culture
Bowling Green State University

Patricia Sawin
Department of English
University of Southwestern Louisiana

Elizabeth D. Schafer
Independent Scholar
Loachapoka, AL

John Schleppenbach
Professor, Department of Language,
    Literature, and Communication
Quincy University

Adolf E. Schroeder
Professor Emeritus, German Studies
University of Missouri–Columbia

Rebecca Schroeder
Editor, Missouri Folklore Society

Tom Schroeder
Independent Scholar
Kansas City, MO

Anthony Seeger
Curator, The Folkways Collection
Smithsonian Institution

Charlie Seemann
Program Associate, The Fund for Folk
    Culture
Santa Fe, NM

Sharon Sherman
Director of Folklore Program and
    Professor of English
University of Oregon

David P. Shuldiner
Adjunct Assistant Professor, School of
    Family Studies
University of Connecticut

Steve Siporin
Professor, Department of English
Utah State University

Guntis Šmidchens
Visiting Lecturer, Scandinavian
    Department
University of Washington

Moira Smith
Assistant Head of Reference for
    Instructional Services, Richter
    Library
University of Miami

Jean Haskell Speer
Director/Professor, Center for
    Appalachian Studies and Services
East Tennessee State University

David Stanley
Professor, Department of English
Westminster College of Salt Lake City

Shalom Staub
President, CEO, Institute for Cultural
    Partnerships
Harrisburg, PA

Polly Stewart
Professor, Department of English
Salisbury State University

Kay F. Stone
Professor, Department of English
University of Winnipeg
Canada

Ruth Stotter
Director, Certificate-In-Storytelling
    Program
Dominican College
San Rafael, CA

C.W. Sullivan III
Professor, Department of English
East Carolina University

Scott Hamilton Suter
Curator, Shenandoah Valley Folk Art
    and Heritage Center
Dayton, VA

Richard Sweterlitsch
Professor, Department of English
University of Vermont

Michael Taft
Adjunct Professor of Anthropology
    and Archaeology
University of Saskatchewan
Canada

Timothy Tangherlini
Professor, Scandinavian Section
University of California–Los Angeles

David A. Taylor
Folklife Specialist, American Folklife
    Center
Library of Congress

Monica Maria Tetzlaff
Assistant Professor
Indiana University–South Bend

Kenneth A. Thigpen
Associate Professor of English,
    Comparative Literature, and
    American Studies
Pennsylvania State University

Gerald Thomas
Professor, Department of Folklore
Memorial University of Newfoundland
Canada

Jeff Todd Titon
Professor, Department of Music
Brown University

Barre Toelken
Professor and Director, Folklore
    Program
Utah State University

Peter Tokofsky
Professor, Folklore/Mythology
    Program
University of California–Los Angeles

Elizabeth Tucker
Associate Professor of English
Binghamton University

Richard W. Tucker
Professor, English as a Foreign
    Language
George Washington University

Tad Tuleja
Independent Scholar
Naples, NY

Patricia A. Turner
Professor, African American Studies
University of California–Davis

Rory P.B. Turner
Independent Scholar
Baltimore, MD

Diane Tye
Assistant Professor of Folklore
Memorial University of Newfoundland
Canada

John Michael Vlach
Professor and Director, Folklife
    Program
George Washington University

Eleanor Wachs
Commonwealth Folklife Association
Quincy, MA

Thomas Walker
Independent Scholar
St. Paul, MN

Robert E. Walls
Folklore Institute
Indiana University

Barry J. Ward
Professor, Department of English
West Virginia University

Don Ward
Professor Emeritus, Department of
    Germanic Languages
University of California–Los Angeles

K. Marianne Wargelin
Independent Scholar
Minneapolis, MN

Marta Weigle
Professor and Chair, Department of
    Anthropology
University of New Mexico

Rosemary Wells
Independent Scholar
Deerfield, IL

William Westerman
Coordinator, Program for Immigrant
    Traditional Artists
International Institute of New Jersey

Peter White
Professor, Department of English
University of New Mexico

Wm. H. Wiggins, Jr.
Professor, Afro-American Studies
    Program
Indiana University

Henry Willett
Director, Alabama Center for
    Traditional Culture

John Alexander Williams
Director, Center for Appalachian
    Studies
Appalachian State University

Clover Williams
Adjunct Professor
Indiana University

Kathryn E. Wilson
Lecturer
University of Pennsylvania

William A. Wilson
Humanities Professor of Literature
    and Folklore, and Director of
    Charles Redd Center for Western
    Studies
Brigham Young University

Douglas Wixson
Professor of English, Emeritus
University of Missouri–Rolla

Daniel Wojcik
Assistant Professor, Folklore Program
University of Oregon

Charles Wolfe
Professor of English
Middle Tennessee State University

Charles Wukasch
Independent Scholar
Austin, TX

Donna L. Wyckoff
Lecturer, Department of English
Ohio State University

Sally M. Yerkovich
South Street Seaport Museum
New York, NY

Margaret Yocom
Associate Professor, Department of
   English
George Mason University

Katharine Young
Lecturer
University of California–Berkeley

Steve Zeitlin
Director, City Lore
New York, NY

Ed Zotti
Independent Scholar
Chicago, IL

Charles G. Zug III
Professor and Chair, Curriculum in
   Folklore
University of North Carolina

Rosemary Lévy Zumwalt
Professor of Anthropology and Chair,
   Department of Anthropology and
   Sociology
Davidson College

American Folklore

Academe, Folklore of

Folk traditions of the college and university campus. The academic world consists of two principal subcultures—student and faculty—which, like all groups sharing common concerns over long periods of time, have developed constellations of folk belief, custom, folk speech, legend, jocular narrative, and ritual.

The most prevalent folk beliefs among university students (beyond the assumption that a college education leads to a job in "the real world") fall into two arenas of potential anxiety: class attendance and examinations. In both contexts, certain excuses (such as "my grandmother is dying") are believed to be more efficacious than others in obtaining pardon or permission for missing something for which the student has already paid. Virtually universal among American college students in their first two years of university work is the belief that there is a standard waiting period for a professor who does not arrive punctually. The most common system requires students to wait five minutes for an instructor, ten for an assistant professor, fifteen for an associate professor, and twenty for a full professor, although one also hears of ten minutes for a non-Ph.D., twenty for a Ph.D., fifteen for most faculty, all period if necessary for a full professor. This set of beliefs, like most folklore, is not learned from formal authority (indeed, such an obligation has yet to be found in the formal student rules of any American university), but from other members of the folk group: in this case, other students. University students in Germany, by contrast, routinely arrive in the classroom about fifteen minutes *after* the scheduled time, an acknowledged manipulation of time called *der akademische Viertel* (the academic quarter [hour]).

Students facing examinations, especially "finals," try to affect their fortunes or their self-confidence by wearing lucky clothes (such as a shirt that was worn during a previous exam that was successful), carrying amulets, dolls, or special pens, hoping the exam falls on a lucky day (including the seventh, fourteenth, or twenty-first of the month), avoiding normal personal grooming (not combing hair, not shaving, or wearing "grubbies"), abstaining from sex (to conserve brain energy), and knocking loudly on the desk before starting the exam. While these observances may seem superficially to be either naive or simple matters of haste, they all fall into quite ancient categories of psychological tradition. In addition to the student's own talents in the class, which are affected by a number of variables, and in response to the professor's power in the class, which is believed to be wielded inconsistently, the anxious student can obtain confidence or magical help by utilizing a belief system that has been in existence for hundreds of years. In a similar way, members of hazardous occupations (like deep-sea fishermen and firefighters) adopt the beliefs and customs passed on by several generations of coworkers, thus availing themselves of an accumulation of experience, know-how, and psychological aids that they do not have time to discover on their own before being in danger.

Student customs extend far beyond the issues of academic anxiety, however. Collectors of student folklore have noted extensive drinking games ("Cardinal Puff," "Fuzz-Buzz"), theme parties, engagement and marriage rituals (passing a candle around a group of sorority women to announce an engagement), clothing and personal-decoration variations (especially at sports events and at graduation), and the use of obscene songs as unofficial expressions of membership in clubs, fraternities, sororities, and sports teams (especially rugby). At Utah State University (formerly an agricultural college), a student becomes a True Aggie by standing on a small concrete monument formed in the shape of an A and being kissed by someone who is already a True Aggie, at midnight, while the bell in nearby Old Main tolls the hour, preferably on a full moon, and preferably on Homecoming Saturday. It is rumored that another more complex and private ritual produces a "True Blue Aggie," but its details have remained in the dark. At other universities, gates, statues, and fountains are the focal points of similar rituals and observances.

The folk speech of university students abounds with terms that mark the users as insiders: "cutting" or "sluffing" for intentionally missing a class, "cramming" for earnest studying, "Mickey" or "Mickey Mouse" to describe an easy course, "ballbuster" for a difficult course, "brown-nose" for a teacher's pet. Terms like "comps," "finals," "defense," "How much of a load are you carrying?" "What's your GPA?" and the like are readily understood on campus but are usually unintelligible to anyone not a part of the academic group.

Academic legends (stories told as true, but not by someone who was an eyewitness) recall prudish deans of the 1950s who prohibited red dresses and patent leather shoes (responding to overzealous interpretations of *in loco parentis*), obscene or crazy comments by professors in their classes, epic pranks (like the dead horse in the fraternity cellar), and spectacular feats of cheating on final examinations. Professorial arrogance is parodied in the legend of the lecturer who notices most of his students using tape recorders so they won't have to take notes; he responds by sending a graduate assistant to play tapes to them so he will not have to lecture. An absentminded biology professor, getting ready to dissect a frog, pulls out of his backpack the sandwich he thought he ate at lunch. Students playing recordings backward discover satanic messages or hypnotic orders that lead them to suicide (in joking response, other students claim to have played a record of the Mormon Tabernacle Choir backward, obtaining twenty new recipes for Jello salad).

Pranks are another important genre of academic folklore, though it is not always clear whether the pranks actually are carried out, or if they are simply parts of the oral traditions of campus groups. One hears about well-fed cows being left overnight in the offices of unpopular professors and about the dean's car being taken apart and reassembled on the roof of the administration building, but it is easier to find avid narrators than eyewitnesses to these events. Modern legends of student hackers gaining access to academic records and changing friends' grades are matched by newspaper accounts of people who have been caught doing it.

Faculty folklore focuses more on the humor, irony, and occasional disappointments in the life behind the lectern than it does on anxiety and fun. Although there are some jokes about students—like the young woman who says she will "do anything" for a grade and is then told by the professor to try studying, or the joke about the student who almost chokes to death trying to swallow his "crib notes" at an examination—professorial traditions complain about the devices used for cheating on exams, the range of excuses given for being absent (it is noted cynically that final examination week is extremely dangerous for the elderly, since so many grandmothers die then), and the unwillingness of students to learn (teaching is characterized as "casting fake pearls before real swine").

As much as anything, faculty members both instigate and utilize much of the folklore circulating among their students, very likely because they were also students in a previous life. When a professor is late for class, she can be sure that the students will wait for at least ten minutes before daring to leave. If a professor wants to intimidate or astound the students, he can quote from tradition, as when a University of Oregon

English professor asked the women in his Milton class to cross their legs so that the gates of Hell would be closed when they discussed *Paradise Lost,* using a legend he had heard at his own alma mater when he was a student. A music professor at the University of Utah waited until the critical moment (was it twenty minutes?) when his students were about to leave the room, then ceremoniously stepped out of the grand piano while beginning his initial lecture.

Folklore is not found only among the backward, illiterate, and uninformed; it is a vital expressive component in the lives of all ongoing human groups. Academic folklore is a dynamic illustration of the ways in which folklore functions for modern, well-educated, upwardly mobile people whose occupational context places them under particular strains and concerns that are well articulated on the vernacular level.

Barre Toelken

References

Bronner, Simon. 1990. *Piled Higher and Deeper: The Folklore of Campus Life.* Little Rock, AR: August House.

Dorson, Richard M. 1959. The Folklore of College Students. In *American Folklore.* Chicago: University of Chicago Press, pp. 254–267.

Toelken, Barre. 1986. The Folklore of Academe. In Jan Harold Brunvand, 3d ed. *The Study of American Folklore: An Introduction,* New York: W.W. Norton, pp. 502–528.

Academic Programs in Folklore

Folklore programs in the United States and Canada. Folklore courses were introduced at several North American universities in the 1920s and 1930s, and in 1940 Ralph Steele Boggs established the first degree-granting program in folklore, at the University of North Carolina at Chapel Hill, which remains a center for the study of folklore. Awarding both an M.A. degree and a doctoral minor, the curriculum in folklore at North Carolina is designed primarily for graduate students, though undergraduates may create an interdisciplinary degree with a concentration in folklore. Supported by several research collections—including D.K. Wilgus' papers, Archie Green's labor-song collection, the Southern Folklife Collection, the John Edwards Memorial Collection, the American Religious Tunebook Collection, and the Southern Historical Collection—the North Carolina program is especially strong in folksong and Southern folklife studies. Other emphases include African American folklore, ethnographic filmmaking, public-sector folklore, and occupational folklore.

The first Folklore Department in an American college or university was established at Franklin and Marshall University in 1948 by Alfred L. Shoemaker, assistant professor of American folklore. Although called the Department of American Folklore, the program was influenced by European folklife concepts and emphasized the study of Pennsylvania folklore and folklife. Franklin and Marshall's short-lived Folklore Department first appeared in the catalog for 1949–1950 but remained in it only two years. By 1995, Franklin and Marshall offered only a single folklore course, and in the United States only Indiana University and the University of Pennsylvania had Folklore Departments.

Stith Thompson joined the English faculty at Indiana University as director of freshman composition in 1921 and introduced the first folklore course there in 1923. After directing several M.A. theses and doctoral dissertations in folklore for graduate students majoring in English, Thompson established the first American Ph.D. program in folklore, at Indiana in 1949. After Thompson's retirement in 1955, his successor, Richard M. Dorson, guided an expanded folklore program of courses and faculty to departmental status in 1963. Under Thompson's direction, the program emphasized the comparative study of international folktales. Dorson continued to stress coverage of major international cultural areas in the curriculum, but, trained in the history of American civilization, he also added an Americanist orientation to the program. Warren E. Roberts, in 1953 the recipient of the first American doctorate in folklore, introduced a course in traditional arts, crafts, and architecture in 1961 and contributed to widening the range of the Indiana program, which emphasizes theoretical approaches in covering the entire field of folklore studies. An ethnomusicology program within the Department of Folklore and an Archives of Traditional Music strengthen the B.A. program as well as the M.A. and Ph.D. programs in folklore.

The second doctoral program in folklore was established in 1959, at the University of Pennsylvania, by MacEdward Leach. Leach remained on the English faculty at Penn after receiving a Ph.D. in Middle English literature there in 1930 and changed two literature courses into a general folklore course and a ballad course. Penn's interdisciplinary graduate program in folklore first emphasized studies in ballads and folksongs and in folklore and literary relations, but by the time Leach retired in 1966, Penn had a comprehensive program covering the entire range of folklore studies. Influenced by sociolinguistic approaches and the ethnography of communication, the Department of Folklore and Folklife, offering an undergraduate degree and an M.A. in folklore as well as a doctorate, stresses social-scientific approaches to folklore.

Another major center of folklore studies is the folklore and mythology program at the University of California at Los Angeles, where Sigurd B. Hustvedt introduced a graduate course in the traditional ballad in 1933. Wayland D. Hand joined the German faculty in 1937, introduced a general folklore course in 1939, and established an interdepartmental folklore program in 1954. By 1995, UCLA's folklore and mythology program offered more than seventy-five courses, either directly or in conjunction with cooperating departments throughout the university, and awarded interdisciplinary master's and doctoral degrees in folklore and mythology. A research institute, the Center for the Study of Comparative Folklore and Mythology, and other university research centers strengthen UCLA's academic program.

An M.A. in folklore is offered in the Department of Anthropology at the University of California at Berkeley, and an M.A. in folk arts is offered through the Tamburitzans Institute of Folk Arts in the School of Music at Duquesne University. Western Kentucky's program in folk studies, housed in the Department of Modern Languages and Intercultural Studies, offers an undergraduate minor as well as an M.A. degree in folk studies. In Canada, Memorial University of Newfoundland and Université Laval have folklore programs, both awarding doctoral, master's, and undergraduate degrees in folklore. In 1962 Herbert Halpert joined the faculty of Memorial and, encouraged and supported by E.R. Seary, professor and head of the Department of English and place-names scholar, developed a folklore program within the Department of English. In 1968 Halpert established a Department of Folklore that offers a complete line of folklore courses. Three archives support the teaching mission: the *Centre d'études franco-terreneuviennes,* the Centre for Material Culture Studies, and the Folklore and Language Archive. Université Laval, with folklore studies dating from 1944 when Luc Lacourcière was appointed to a chair in folklore, offers undergraduate and graduate degrees in folklore, with emphasis on French folklore in North America, through its *programmes d'arts et traditions populaires* in the *Département d'Histoire.*

Two institutions without formal graduate programs in folklore, Pitzer College and Harvard University, offer B.A. degrees in folklore. Folklore studies at Harvard date from 1856 when Francis James Child began collecting English and Scottish folk ballads from books, broadsides, and manuscripts. Child did not develop separate folklore courses or a folklore program, but he incorporated folklore in his English courses and trained several notable American folklorists, including George Lyman Kittredge, successor to Child's English professorship in 1894. Harvard became the center for the literary study of folklore in North America in the late 19th and early 20th centuries, and the interest in folklore at Harvard was maintained in the 1930s by a group of Americanists, who promoted an interdisciplinary study of American culture to include folk and popular cultures as well as formal culture, and by Milman Parry and Albert Bates Lord, who initiated field research in European oral epics. Harvard remains a center for the comparative study of folklore, because graduate studies in oral literature in allied areas complement Harvard's undergraduate degree program in folklore and mythology, awarded through its Committee on Degrees in Folklore and Mythology.

Over eighty North American colleges and universities offer majors in other disciplines (notably English, anthropology, and American studies) that permit a folklore minor or concentration. These programs range from formal curricula to informal concentrations at all degree levels. For example, an M.A. and a Ph.D. in anthropology or English with a folklore concentration is offered at the University of Texas at Austin. Undergraduate majors as well as graduate majors in anthropology at Texas A&M University also may elect a concentration in folklore. Degrees in folklore at the University of Oregon are coordinated through its folklore and ethnic studies program, in which master's students create their own program of study through an individualized program and doctoral students in English or anthropology may elect folklore as an area of concentration. Through its program in folklore, mythology, and film studies, the State University of New York at Buffalo awards an M.A. in English or humanities and a Ph.D. in English with a folklore and mythology concentration. A concentration in folklore also is available in the Department of Performance Studies at New York University.

George Washington University's folklife program grants an M.A. in American studies or anthropology and a Ph.D. in American studies with a concentration in traditional material culture—a program that takes advantage of the resources of the Smithsonian Institution, the American Folklife Center, and other museums, libraries, archives, and historical societies in the Washington, DC, area. The folklore program at Utah State University is administered through the American studies program, and undergraduate and master's degrees in American studies with a folklore emphasis are offered. Folklore concentrations also are available to history or English majors at Utah State. Master's candidates may elect areas in general folklore, public folklore, or applied history/museology. Ohio State University has offered folklore courses since the 1930s and has a Center for Folklore and Cultural Studies, allowing undergraduate and graduate students a folklore concentration in an interdisciplinary program, which emphasizes folklore and literary relations and narrative theory.

The academic study of folklore has made considerable progress since Boggs established the first folklore program in 1940, but few degree-granting programs in folklore have developed. Most folklore courses are taught in departments other than folklore, typically in English and anthropology departments or in American studies programs in the United States and in anthropology and history departments in Canada.

Ronald L. Baker

References

Baker, Ronald L. 1971. Folklore Courses and Programs in American Colleges and Universities. *Journal of American Folklore* 84:221–229.

———. 1978. The Study of Folklore in American Colleges and Universities. *Journal of American Folklore* 91:792–807.

———. 1986. Folklore and Folklife Studies in American and Canadian Colleges and Universities. *Journal of American Folklore* 99:50-74.

———. 1988. The Folklorist in the Academy. In *One Hundred Years of American Folklore Studies,* ed. William M. Clements, pp. 65–69. Washington, DC: American Folklore Society.

Boggs, Ralph Steele. 1940. Folklore in University Curricula in the United States. *Southern Folklore Quarterly* 4:93–109.

Bronner, Simon. 1991. A Prophetic Vision of Public and Academic Folklife: Alfred Shoemaker and America's First Department of Folklore. *Folklore Historian* 8:38–55.

Bynum, David E. 1974. Child's Legacy Enlarged: Oral Literary Studies at Harvard since 1856. In *Four Generations of Oral Literary Studies at Harvard University.* Publications of the Milman Parry Collection. Cambridge: Center for the Study of Oral Literature, Harvard University.

Dorson, Richard M. 1950. The Growth of Folklore Courses. *Journal of American Folklore* 63:345–359.

———. 1972. The Academic Future of Folklore. In *Folklore: Selected Essays.* Bloomington: Indiana University Press, pp. 295–304.

Leach, MacEdward. 1958. Folklore in American Colleges and Universities. *Journal of American Folklore* (Supplement):10–11.

See also American Studies and Folklore; Canadian Folklore Scholarship; Canadian Studies and Folklore; Folklife Movement; Material Culture

Adirondacks

A five-million acre, mountainous region in northeastern New York, bounded on the north by the Canadian border, on the east by Lake Champlain, on the south by the Mohawk River Valley, and on the west by the Saint Lawrence and Black River Valleys. The Adirondack Mountains constitute part of the Canadian Shield and are not, as popularly perceived, a part of the Appalachian Mountains. About half of the 5,177 square miles is a state forest preserve; much of the area has been designated a state park since 1892, thus limiting development. To many New Yorkers, the region is simply referred to as the "North Country."

The term "Adirondack" is a lexicographer's nightmare. Authorities offer a variety of translations. It is said to be (1) Iroquois for "They of the Great Rock," referring to a tribe of Indians who once lived along the Saint Lawrence River; (2) a Mohawk generic name for the French and the English; or (3) Mohawk for "tree-eaters," the derisive term that Mohawks, or Iroquois as the French called them, used to describe their enemy, the Algonquins. Before European contact, both tribes vied for control of the region because its forests and numerous lakes and streams provided a good source for meat and furs. Trails crisscrossed the region linking its numerous lakes and also to the Saint Lawrence, but there is little evidence of any Native American permanent settlements beyond seasonal camps.

European contact is generally dated from 1609, when the French explorer Samuel de Champlain accompanied an Algonquin war party on its way to attack an Iroquois village on what eventually became known as Lake George. Later in the same century, French and Dutch trappers from Montreal and Albany forayed into the region, but they did not establish permanent communities.

After the American Revolution, however, Vermonters, in particular, and other New Englanders, many of whom received land as payment for their military service, settled around the edges of the Adirondacks. Shortly thereafter, toward the end of the 18th century, logging in the eastern Adirondack region, along the headwaters of the Hudson River, stimulated settlement and development.

The southern Adirondack region would experience growth from a different source. By the late 1810s, tourists from New York City and Boston discovered the recreational value of the Adirondacks. The mineral waters found near Saratoga Springs drew crowds desiring to bathe in and drink the radioactive mineral waters, believing that the natural springs offered cures for numerous ailments. Equally alluring were fishing and hunting within the Adirondack Mountains. The pursuit of health and outdoor recreation provided the bases for a tourist industry that shaped much of the development and settlement patterns in the southern Adirondacks. By the 1840s and 1850s, hotels and rustic "camps" had sprung up throughout the southern Adirondack region. The growth mushroomed so quickly that shortly after the Civil War conservationists banded together in efforts to protect the tourist industry from logging interests that were encroaching from the northern Adirondacks. The heyday of tourism spanned more than three decades, from 1875 to 1910. In 1900, for example, a quarter of a million people visited the Adirondacks in the summer months alone. Many of these either rented camps, stayed in luxurious hotels, or vacationed in their own camp.

In the late 1870s, the area around Saranac Lake began to be touted for its healthy air. Medical doctors recommended extended stays in the region for the treatment of tuberculosis and other lung diseases. Numerous sanatoriums were constructed around the village, drawing thousands of famous and obscure patients, all seeking to breathe the curing Adirondack air.

Out of the tourist industry developed a folk tradition centering on the exploits and heroism of the Adirondack guide. The earliest guides, such as Sabael (ca. 1749–1855) or Mitchell Sabattis (1801–1906) were Abenakis. Local lore and some ethnographic research attributes Native Americans living in the region with producing both the Adirondack guide canoe and the Adirondack packbasket, two important items of Adirondack material culture that are rooted in Abenaki tradition. Eventually, Native American guides were replaced by White guides, some of whom were originally loggers or trappers. Other guides claimed to lead the life of outdoor hermits who spent their entire lives exploring the peaks and rivers of the region. Familiarity with the backwoods country allowed the guides to lead city tourists deep into the Adirondack forests on camping, hunting, mountain climbing, and fishing trips. The 19th-century Romantic impulse of educated city folk to touch the primordial world was adequately served by these guides. In some cases, these stalwart outdoorsman took on the additional responsibility of camping throughout the winter in a tent or an isolated camp helping a tubercular-ridden invalid strengthen his or her lungs and physical stamina, hoping to overcome the dreaded disease.

Popular narratives of the day described how these mountainmen-guides entertained their guests with outlandish tales about their marksmanship and hunting skills. Folk tradition continues to keep alive the memory of Native American and White guides, including among the latter the famous guide Mart Moody (1833–1910). Tales about his outdoor skills and eccentricities are shared among visitors and natives, and they have found their way into local literature, becoming part of the regional lore. The oral traditions about the older guides have become part of the narrative repertory of contemporary guides, and, in some instances, the older tales are even retold in the first person by the present generation of guides.

Despite the surge in tourism and health industries in the second half of 19th century, the interior of the Adirondacks remained largely unexplored. Accurate maps of the whole region were not available until the 1890s. It remained for the Gilded Age a wilderness, a place of mystery that offered potential adventures in uncharted regions. While popular urban icons of the age such as Diamond Jim Brady and Lillian Russell spent their time at the racetrack and spas in Saratoga, only a few miles away an area lay untouched that offered the more adventurous the thrill of visiting an uncharted wilderness.

The northern and western borderlands of the Adirondacks are marked with a very different history of settlement and development. Logging stimulated movement into the region. Vast tracts of pine and hardwood had attracted Canadian lumber interests as early as the mid-18th century when French Canadian loggers harvested the forests along the northwestern fringes of the Adirondacks and floated logs north to the Saint Lawrence River and Montreal. The work was hand-labor intensive, but the promise of a job lured many French Canadian lumbermen and lumberjacks to settle along with their families in the northern and western edges of the Adirondack region. As the industry moved deeper into the mountains in search of more timber, the workers and their families followed, gradually establishing small communities along the rivers and edges of the many lakes. There they cut white pine and either sawed it into timber to be transported south on railroad spurs or floated the logs north to the Saint Lawrence, where they became part of the Canadian market. Despite the efforts of conservationists to block logging throughout the Adirondacks, intensive commercial logging swept across the region. By the early 20th century, logging and several major forest fires had depleted the virgin forests, but many of the workers stayed behind, working in much smaller logging operations that harvested a second growth.

Small communities scattered throughout the region developed chiefly in response to logging, although a few sprung up where there were small-scale iron- or lead-mining interests. The Lake Placid-Lake George-Lake Saranac region developed a skiing industry and has hosted the Winter Olympics on two occasions. Along the western foothills of the Adirondacks, dairy farming emerged as the major industry. In some parts of the region, potato farming, fruit growing and other small cash crop farming developed. The central region, dotted by very small communities, continues for the most part to cater to tourists.

Folklore for the entire Adirondack region has never been comprehensively and systematically collected, although independent researchers have published a moderate range of material about specific counties or occupations in the Adirondacks. These studies suggest that a rich lode of folk traditions might be found in the region.

Native American material is sparsely represented in any collections and appears most frequently in older, uncritical publications. Hoping to appeal to the interests of tourists, some published accounts of local history contain examples of folk speech, proverbs, or tales about eccentric characters and bizarre occurrences. Personal narratives about roughing it in the woods appear alongside traditional tall tales describing the struggles to survive the onslaught of hordes of black flies and voracious mosquitoes or accounts of the superhuman skills of hunters. Along the eastern Adirondacks that border Lake Champlain, 19th-century eyewitness reports, publicized by local tourist interests, provide a historical setting for Lake Champlain monster sightings, a tradition that continues to intrigue tourists and local citizens. Other popularizers have sought to create belief in a Bigfoot-like creature living in the remote recesses of the Adirondacks.

Ethnic humor about the perceived idiosyncracies of French Canadians are commonly told by Adirondack folk. "Canucks" worked in the woods, and their difficulties with the language and the local customs of the dominant Anglo American culture provided situations for local humor and dialect tales. Even in the late 20th century, humor about the French Canadian shoppers and their efforts to avoid paying duty on items purchased in the States constitutes a viable theme in Adirondack and border humor.

The richest body of lore yet tapped in the Adirondacks is from the region's robust logging traditions. The oral recollections of the modern loggers and of the older native population in general are rich in both grass-roots history and folklore of logging. Personal-experience tales mix with traditional tall-tale motifs; the old lifestyles in the logging camps are recalled with nostalgia. Idioms of folk speech still spice the conversations of the men who spent much of their early life working in the bush and living in the camps. With ease, they can recall how, in the evenings, as the exhausted loggers gathered in the "doghouse" (the center of the bunkhouse), the loaders, road hogs, teamsters, and jacks pushed aside their "turkeys" (tightly rolled bundles of clothes) and sat down on "deacon's benches" to swap lies.

Especially prized are tales about the prodigious strength and extraordinary skills of lumberjacks, about marvelous rescues from the dangers of logging, and about accidental injury and death. In cycles of stories, eccentric crew foremen and backwoods strongmen mature into local villains and heroes. Yarns are woven about the dictatorial policies of cooks who demanded total obedience to the unwritten codes of bunkhouse decorum. Many narratives recount practical jokes that initiated unwitting greenhorns into the world of the lumberman or that undermined the authority of a tyrannical foreman. Barroom brawls, which are often the result of grudges that fester in the logging camps or on the job, become sagas peppered with violence and brutality.

In addition to swapping stories, the loggers maintained a rich singing tradition. Ballads such as "The Saranac River" or "Blue Mountain Lake" chronicle the work experiences of local lumbermen. "Tebo" tells how Tebo died while breaking a log jam. But these songs appear to be no more or less popular than such migratory lumber songs as the sentimental "Jam on Gerry's Rock" or "Lumberman's Alphabet." Many of the logging songs collected in the Adirondacks are localized versions of songs that can be found throughout the United States and Canada, wherever the axes of the lumbermen rang through the forests. Collectors in this century also have found a rich tradition of Anglo, Anglo Irish, and French Canadian ballads existing alongside these American logging ballads.

Efforts at revitalizing or maintaining some of the Adirondack folklife traditions seek to tap tourist dollars and to educate local people and visitors about Adirondack life. Woodcrafts, ranging from whittling pine chains, to weaving baskets that recapture traditional Native American patterns, to producing Adirondack chairs and canoes, provide glimpses of traditions that a few years ago could be found only in museums. Oral traditions, especially folksongs, are performed at folk festivals held during the summer and fall months throughout the Adirondacks. Several museums featuring examples of Adirondack folklife, including both arts and crafts, are open to the public. These public events and displays provide new audiences for the traditions of the Adirondacks.

Richard Sweterlitsch

References

The Adirondacks. 1966. *New York Folklore Quarterly* 22:2.

Bethke, Robert D. 1981. *Adirondack Voices: Woodsmen and Lore.* Urbana: University of Illinois Press.

Cutting, Edith E. 1944. *Lore of an Adirondack County.* Ithaca, NY: Cornell University Press.

Thomas, Howard. 1962. *Folklore from the Adirondack Foothills.* N.p.: Prospect Books.

Thompson, Harold W. [1939] 1962. *Body, Boots, and Britches: Folktales, Ballads, and Speech from Country New York.* New York: Dover.

Wessels, William L. 1961. *Adirondack Profiles.* Lake George, NY: Adirondack Resorts Press.

White, William Chapman. 1967. *Adirondack Country.* New York: Alfred Knopf.

African Americans

Known as American Negroes in 1888 when the American Folklore Society (AFS) identified those American ethnic groups whose unique cultural traditions should be documented and preserved. Much debate ensued over the label attached to this group, which presently comprises between 11 and 12 percent of the total U.S. population. As was customary during the late 19th century, the founders of the AFS used the Spanish-derived title "Negro." However, pejoratives such as "darky," "nigger," and "coon" were not uncommon vernacular labels during that era and were often used unashamedly. Turn of the century activist Ida B. Wells-Barnett and her colleagues made the case that "Afro-American" ought to be adopted by the American population. For many, the designation "colored" was considered a polite and acceptable label until the 1960s. In the heyday of the modern civil rights movement, the label "Black" became the one accepted by many members of the group. This name appealed to those who felt that peoples of African descent should embrace their dark complexions and African physical features. Of course, several centuries of mixing between the various ethnic groups of the United States meant that a wide range of skin tones, facial features, and body types were evident in this population. By the 1980s, many began to prefer a designation that specified the country of origin. Since then, "African American" has been the preferred label.

The founders of the American Folklore Society connected Negro folklore with the institution of slavery. They rationalized that efforts to collect Negro folklore must be undertaken before all of those who had experienced slavery died. The presumption seems to have been that traces of slave tradition would not be evident in the repertoires of the descendents of slaves. But even before the formation of the American Folklore Society, African American folklore had aroused the interest of a few talented persons. In particular, the musical traditions of the slaves had triggered the curiosity of individuals such as Lucy McKim Garrison and Thomas Wentworth Higginson, who published collections containing Negro folk music in the 1860s.

Journalist Joel Chandler Harris' fascination with the folktales he had heard as a child led him to publish seven volumes of folktales featuring the exploits of Brer Rabbit, Brer Fox, Brer Alligator, and numerous other animal characters. Three additional volumes were published after Harris' death in 1908. Known as trickster tales, these narratives suggest that the slaves identified with ostensibly powerless heroes who used their verbal dexterity, cunning, and verve to outwit larger, more obviously powerful opponents. Such tales served to educate and entertain African Americans of all ages. Trickster tales and other folk narratives continued to be important to African Americans long after the demise of slavery.

Most late 19th- and early 20th-century folklore research took place in Southern environs. In particular, a chain of islands along the coasts of Georgia and South Carolina known as the Sea Islands proved to be a rich region for fieldwork. Once a popular destination point for slave ships, these islands were inhabited by large numbers of Blacks whose connections with Africa were stronger than those of Blacks elsewhere in the United States. Until well into the 20th century, residents of the Sea Islands spoke distinctive dialects—gullah and geechee—clearly derived from West African language systems. In addition their verbal traditions, their material culture—house types, gardens, textiles, and like artifacts—reflect strong Caribbean and African influences.

In the first decades of the 20th century, the field of folklore began to attract a few trained African American folklorists. Because Black informants were more apt to reveal provocative texts to other blacks, this was a particularly welcome development. The works of Thomas Washington Talley and Arthur Huff Fauset laid significant groundwork for future Black folklorists. However, of the early 20th-century Black folklorists, Zora Neale Hurston emerges as the most significant innovator. In her landmark text *Mules and Men* (1935), she included contextual information as well as the actual tales recited by her rural Black informants. During the folk-belief phase of research for this volume, she underwent the rituals necessary to become a voodoo priestess in New Orleans. Although her creative output was not limited to folklore per se, all of her literary endeavors reflected her appreciation for folklore.

Starting with the Harlem Renaissance, several African American literary figures dabbled in folklore collecting and research. Celebrated poet Langston Hughes published a lengthy volume on Negro folklore. His collection of short stories on the trials and tribulations of Jesse B. Semple contains prodigious quantities of Black folk speech. Most important African American novelists have expressed a profound debt to folklore. Literary giant Ralph Ellison relied heavily on African American folklore in his masterpiece *Invisible Man,* and later in the 20th century, Toni Morrison, Alice Walker, and Terry McMillan acknowledged their reliance on folklore materials for their short stories and novels.

In the 1930s, the Works Progress Administration (WPA) created jobs for unemployed writers and teachers that entailed fieldwork collecting folklore and life histories from elderly ex-slaves. Coordinated by Benjamin A. Botkin, the project was an enormous one, yielding thousands of interviews. Many of the collectors had no formal training and were unaccustomed to thinking of Black traditions as worthy of respect. Rather than quoting the informants word for word, the untrained collectors summarized the tales in their own words. Still, the narratives contain a wealth of information unduplicated in other sources. Responsible folklorists are careful to acknowledge the collecting irregularities when using this data.

From spirituals to gospel, from field hollers to rap, the wide range of African American sacred and secular musical expression has long intrigued folklorists and ethno-musicologists. Like their African ancestors, African Americans considered music an essential component of everyday life. In most African communities, composing and performing music appropriate for each activity was an integral part of spiritual expression. The African impulse to produce and perform music survived the horrendous strains of the Middle Passage and became a mainstay of New World African Americans, who wove their own musical styles with those they heard from the masters. During the slavery era, the slaves' musical aptitude was duly noted by the master class. Thus was born the still pervasive stereotype that holds that Blacks are born musicians who possess "natural rhythm." Slaves are credited with introducing percussion instruments and a forerunner of the banjo with them to the New World. Polyrhythms, frequent use of percussion instruments and antiphonal or call-and-response patterns are distinctive features of African American folk musical expression.

Few academic debates proved more resilient than the one over "survivals" in African American folklore. Whether it is the rhythm of the music, the arrangement of blocks in a quilt, the personality of a hero in a narrative, the first question asked is often, "Where did it come from—Africa or Europe?" In the first decades of folklore research, it was widely assumed that

Street musicians play an accordion and a washboard. Near New Iberia, Louisiana, about 1940. Photo Russell Lee. Library of Congress.

the Middle Passage—the brutal interim spent aboard slave ships between Africa and the Americas—combined with the devastating impact of the seasoning years, had eradicated all traces of African culture from the psyches of slaves, rendering them cultural blank slates. Advocates of this position maintained that slave lore was derived from inept, clumsy imitations of the European forms to which the slaves were exposed. However, as researchers began to scrutinize West African cultures, common denominators between African and African American folklore became increasingly apparent. Africanist William R. Bascom noted numerous motifs and tale types common to West African folktales. Folk-speech specialists such as Lorenzo D. Turner identified many African words and idioms within the English spoken by both White and Black Americans. For folk-music authorities, the emphasis on call-and-response structure and the polyrhythmic organization of African American musical expression signaled its connection to West African types.

Of course, European influences on African American folklore are undeniable. English is the first language of African Americans and, like their African ancestors, African Americans enjoy and value imitation. By the same token, the folklore traditions of Americans of European descent reflect borrowings from Black traditions. Most folklorists agree that African American folk traditions are syncretized. Blacks have retained many West African aesthetic principles and wedded them to those from other cultures to which they have been

exposed. The songs, narratives, jokes, rituals, beliefs, and so forth that result are intrinsically African American.

Throughout the late 19th century and well into the 20th, African Americans migrated from rural Southern roads to urban Northern streets. Folklore continued to function as an essential expression of everyday Black life. Older genres were modified to fit city environments. Bluesmen frequently replaced acoustic instruments with electric ones, and lyrics focused on the challenges posed by urban industrial life. Quilters modified their techniques to include sewing machines. Worship services took place in storefront churches rather than in pine-board ones. Thus, urban life altered but did not diminish the importance of folklore.

African Americans celebrate verbal versatility and have employed a variety of modes of verbal communication to express themselves. Children are urged to hone their oratorical abilities. Girls often begin by chanting the intricate rhymes that accompany "Double-Dutch" jump-roping sessions. Boys and many girls develop their skills by participating in ritual insult-swapping sessions known as "playing the dozens." In some circles, sophisticated verbal artistry is conveyed in toasts—lengthy epic poems featuring the escapades of unlikely Black heroes. Other familiar genres of African American folk speech include signifyin', capping, rapping, loud-talking, and marking. Friendly competition is often the hallmark of these forms as individuals vie for respect by showing off their verbal prowess.

Contemporary legends and rumors are as common among African Americans as they are within the dominant culture. Some cycles, like the Kentucky Fried Rat and the mouse in the Coke bottle, are well known by both Blacks and Whites. But cycles specific to the concerns of African Americans have evolved and are well contained within the group. Businesses that have unorthodox advertising practices and symbolically charged products are often identified in these legends. The notion that "the government" constructs elaborate anti-Black conspiracies is often promoted.

Not all scrutiny of African American folklore has been on verbal forms. In the past several decades, many folklorists have turned their attention to material culture, in particular house types and quilts. Throughout African American rural communities, shotgun houses have been cataloged. The floor plans for these houses line up a back exit behind a front entrance with no wall or structural interference between the two doors. Thus, it is said that if a shot was fired from either the front or rear of the house, the bullet would go straight through, without lodging in the home. These houses are remarkably similar to structures found in many West African communities. There the folk explanation for the floor plan maintains that if the spirit of an ancestor wanders into the home, it will wander out the other side without getting trapped within. Many quilts made by African American women and men vary a great deal from other American quilts. Like many kinds of West African textiles, long, rectangular strips dominate many of the quilts. Conventional symmetry in which a shape or a color is balanced on one side by the same shape or color on the other seems to be less important to African American quilters than to other quilters. Many Black quilters prefer to fool the eye by knowingly constructing asymmetrical arrangements. Synthetic fabrics are used more often in African American quilts than in mainstream quilts, and red is the most frequently used color. Academic attention to African American material culture has triggered interest in the art world. African American quilts, baskets, sculpture, and other artifacts are found and sold in the finest museums and galleries.

African American spiritual life has always been a rich source of folklore. During the slavery era, African Americans combined West African and Caribbean folk-belief practices with Christian beliefs. A system of folk belief known as conjure or hoodoo evolved in many Southern locales. Believers presumed that conjure doctors understood how to use powers contained in nature, and some conjure doctors were accorded the same respect as preachers. Conjure or hoodoo are sometimes confused with voodoo, which is akin to *vaudou* in Haiti. These belief systems stem from Dahomean (present-day Nigeria) sacred practices. Dahomeans traded into slavery were transported to Haiti. Some of these slaves were then traded to New Orleans. Voodoo is an enormously complex system centered on root work and snake worship. In voodoo as well as *santeria* (Cuba and the United States), *candomble* (Brazil and the United States), and *shango* (Trinidad and the United States), African religious principles are syncretized with Christian principles.

More conventional Christian worship is also common in African American communities. Folklorists have been particularly interested in the delivery styles of African American preachers and the status afforded the congregation. African American congregations actively participate in all aspects of the worship service. Preachers frequently chant their sermons, all the while soliciting affirmation and testimony from their listeners. A lively, vocal congregation is the sign of a successful preacher.

Young African Americans often complain about the speed at which the population at large appropriates appealing Black folk expression. Music, clothing, dance styles, and art forms shaped by African Americans are soon adopted by the dominant culture. However, the impulse to transform and invent folk expression is a strong one, and African Americans, like all folk groups, will continue to enjoy an exciting folk culture.

Patricia A. Turner

References

Abrahams, Roger.[1964] 1970. *Deep Down in the Jungle: Negro Narrative Folklore from the Streets of Philadelphia.* Chicago: Aldine.

Dance, Daryl Cumber. 1978. *Shuckin' and Jivin': Folklore from Contemporary Black Americans.* Bloomington: Indiana University Press.

Davis, Gerald L. 1985. *I Got the Word in Me and I Can Sing It, You Know.* Philadelphia: University of Pennsylvania Press.

Dorson, Richard M. 1967. *American Negro Folktales.* New York: Fawcett World Library.

Dundes, Alan, ed. 1990. *Mother Wit from the Laughing Barrel.* Jackson: University of Mississippi Press.

Ferris, William. 1983. *Afro-American Folk Art and Crafts.* Jackson: University of Mississippi Press.

Fry, Gladys-Marie. 1975. *Night Riders in Black Folk History.* Knoxville: University of Tennessee Press.

———. 1990. *Stitched from the Soul: Slave Quilts from the Antebellum South.* New York: Dutton Studio Books.

Hughes, Langston, and Arna Bontemps, eds. 1958. *The Book of Negro Folklore.* New York: Dodd, Mead.

Jones, Bessie, and Bess Lomax Hawes. 1972. *Step It Down: Games, Plays, Songs and Stories from the Afro-American Heritage.* Athens: University of Georgia Press.

Kochman, Thomas. 1977. *Rappin' and Stylin' Out: Communication in Urban Black America.* Urbana: University of Illinois Press.

Levine, Lawrence W. 1977. *Black Culture and Black Consciousness: Afro-American Thought from Slavery to Freedom.* Oxford: Oxford University Press.

Major, Clarence. 1994. *Juba to Jive: A Dictionary of African American Slang.* New York: Penguin Books.

Morgan, Kathryn J. 1980. *Children of Strangers: The Stories of a Black Family.* Philadelphia: Temple University Press.

Roberts, John W. 1989. *From Trickster to Badman: The Black Folk Hero from Slavery to Freedom.* Philadelphia:

University of Pennsylvania Press.

Southern, Eileen. 1983. *The Music of Black Americans: A History.* New York: W.W. Norton.

Turner, Patricia A. 1993. *I Heard It through the Grapevine: Rumor in African American Culture.* Berkeley: University of California Press.

Vlach, John Michael. 1991. *By the Work of Their Hands: Studies in Afro-American Folklife.* Charlottesville: University of Virginia Press.

Wiggins, William H., Jr. 1987. *O Freedom: Afro-American Emancipation Celebrations.* Knoxville: University of Tennessee Press.

See also Banjo; Black English, Blues; Breakdancing; Dozens; Gospel Music; Holler; Jazz; Juke Joint; Juneteenth; Kwanzaa; Minstrel Shows; Mojo; Rap; Sermon, Folk; Shout; Social Protest in Folklore; Spirituals, African American; Stagolee; Stepping; Toast; and the names of individual performers, characters, and scholars

Aging, Folklore and

Traditional expressive culture created around the experience of growing old. During the 1970s, an area of shared interest opened for gerontologists and folklorists, as many in the social sciences abandoned explanatory, scientistic paradigms of aging in favor of interpretive approaches. Gerontologists, in search of predictable patterns and processes, theorized aging largely as a social problem: The elderly "disengage" by mutual agreement (disengagement theory), or they actively resist disengagement (activity theory), or they form a discrete subculture in an age-stratified society (subculture theory), or they undergo identity crises, precipitated by the loss of former roles (identity crisis theory) (Mullen 1992:10–13). Folklorists, on the other hand, had long assembled collections—of ballads, riddles, tales, and tunes—from the memories of elders, little heeding a pattern linking the culture collected to an elderly consultant's position in the life cycle.

As phenomenological perspectives gained ground in the social sciences, folklorists began to attend more carefully to contexts for performance and collection, and gerontologists, shelving the quest for predictable patterns, began to explore how the elderly construct and interpret their own experience. A mutually engaging domain for folklorists and gerontologists has been opened up by questions about how societies constitute the life cycle through culture, how and why intergenerational communication is staged, and what kinds of culture elders create around the experience of growing old.

The Social and Cultural Organization of Aging

Ways of thinking about and dividing up the life cycle vary over time and across cultures. Folklore generated in America about this progression articulates and comments upon "stages" of life. Anticipating life's stages, children recite them in rhymes and songs: "Solomon Grundy, born on Monday / Christened on Tuesday / Married on Wednesday . . ." or "When I was a baby, a baby, a baby, when I was a baby, this is what I did," which continues through grandmotherhood and death (Huf-

ford, Hunt, and Zeitlin 1987:18). Reflecting on those stages, elders hone hindsight into aphorism: "If you're twenty and not a revolutionary, you have no heart. If you're forty and a revolutionary, you have no mind" or "A fox is smart because he is old, not because he is a fox" or "Snow on the roof doesn't mean there's no fire in the furnace." These fragments hint at multigenerational perspectives on the life cycle, and an underlying ever-present negotiation of the elder's image and role in society.

Biological and social milestones formally separate and define phases of life. Out of tradition, history, personal experience and social relationships, communities fashion rites of passage to signal or precipitate transitions from one stage of life to another: the christening or bris (circumcision rite), the bar mitzvah or confirmation, the graduation, the driver's license, the wedding, the divorce, the baby shower, the retirement banquet, the funeral and associated rituals. Displaying knowledge about nature and society, such rites socially redefine the person passing from preschool to school age, childhood to adolescence, single to married state (and vice versa), career to retirement, life to death.

The notion of the milestone implies gradual progression, or "development," toward a goal. Around experiences common to each stage of life people create and master expressive forms that social scientists have related to "developmental" tasks. Through such cultural practices as jumping rope, children develop physical coordination, social skills, and cognitive proficiency. Children riddling come to terms with cultural categories and learn that the conceptual frames holding reality in place are manipulable. Adolescents on the threshold of greater social responsibility dramatize their concerns in frightening stories about baby-sitting and dating, or through humor about sexuality. Adults in what psychologist Eric Erikson terms their "generative" phase engage again with the early stages of life, but this time from the perspective of parents, teachers, or supervisors, shaping out of symbolic repertoires new realms of lore and custom: bedtime rituals, occupational rites of initiation, narratives of birth and delivery, and ways of celebrating anniversaries, birthdays, and holidays. Throughout this period of life, as physical abilities peak and decline, proficiency with symbolic resources like proverb, narrative, and ritual is apt to increase.

The transition from the social roles and experiences generally associated with mid-life to those associated with old age does not happen automatically or abruptly. Though distinguished by certain kinds of events—the retirement banquet, the birth of grandchildren, the fiftieth high school reunion, the golden jubilee—old age is experienced by many as "one of the great unrealizables," in the words of Simone de Beauvoir. However, the accumulation of experiences common to old age, such as loss of loved ones and diminishing physical abilities, are also linked with cultural practices distinctive to that stage in life, including reminiscing and the rendering of long memories into tangible form.

Reminiscing, a logical practice for those with the longest memories, was until recent decades discouraged in the elderly, because it seemed to betoken a desire to disengage from the present and dwell in the past. However, research since the 1960s suggests that: (1) reviewing one's memories is essential to a major developmental task in later years: life integration (Butler 1968); and (2) folklore is a resource used by elders to give meaning to their lives (Bronner 1984; Hufford, Hunt, and Zeitlin 1987; Kirshenblatt-Gimblett 1989a, 1989b; Mullen 1992). In addition to recasting our perceptions of culture created by elders, this insight has tremendous implications for the practice of folklore, which has traditionally relied on the memories of elderly informants.

The Elderly as Culture Makers

Certain kinds of experience distinguish the elderly from those in earlier stages of life and form the basis for the creation of culture—material, verbal, and ritual—that is distinctive to elders. Looming large in later life is the experience of discontinuity. Ruptures of various kinds cast the social and biological terrain into disarray: the deaths of loved ones and acquaintances, the loss of physical ability, the severance from agendas that held childhood and mid-life in place. Many cultural practices of the elderly—the crafting of new routines, the sociality achieved in senior centers, the revival of skills or traditions acquired in youth—appear especially designed to mend such breaches.

Another experience, shared only with members of one's generational "cohort," is that of having entered the stream of history at the same time and experiencing pivotal moments from a shared position in the life cycle—a position historically unique to that generation. Having participated in history from the same position in the life cycle, elderly contemporaries share understandings to which younger generations are not privy, and these shared understandings and memories are a resource that the culture elders produce with and for each other. Some studies have looked at how elders use tradition to craft sociality: elderly Italian men playing bocce ball (Mathias 1974); Mexicano *viejos* giving voice to elders of bygone days *(viejos)* through *la platica de los viejitos de antes* (Briggs 1988); Hungarian raconteurs fitting personal experiences into traditional tale types over the telephone (Dégh 1969); older women collaborating on quilts that embody overlapping biographies (Beck 1982); jokes and narratives exchanged—over a game of cards or pool or on a tour bus—about memory lapses or other physical problems ("organ recitals," in a coin of Mayer Kirshenblatt) (Hufford, Hunt, and Zeitlin 1987:32). Thus engaging each other, shaping and affirming their generation's reality, elders bestow form and meaning on the inchoate and disquieting aspects of old age. The culture they create defends against isolation and discontinuity, stitching together a community as it gathers disjunct moments in history into a coherent whole.

A related experience is the capacity to see the world from the perspective of multiple generations. "At eighty you can be the age of whoever you talk to," said Ethel Mohammed of Belzoni, Mississippi, when in her eighties (Hufford, Hunt, and Zeitlin 1987:27). "I am all ages simultaneously," wrote Bluma Purmell in her autobiography (Hufford, Hunt, and Zeitlin 1987:56–59). This ability to adopt the perspective of other age groups is a powerful resource for overcoming a devastating sense of "otherness" (Mullen 1992:18). Cultivating empathy in the young, the elder becomes someone who was, and still is, a child or a young man or a new mother, who knows what life's central experiences are like, despite sweeping technological changes.

In recent decades, some folklorists have examined the ways in which elders shape reminiscence into "life review projects." In some cases, elders compose autobiographies, explicitly for grandchildren, organizing their memories on paper or on tape (Hufford 1992:174–188). Other projects take the form of scrapbooks, or organizing the photo album or a chest of keepsakes. Objects featured in folk-art exhibits developed during the 1980s show the hallmarks of self-definitional rites, which Barbara Myerhoff observed in the elderly (Myerhoff 1978). Fashioning autobiography, some elders craft new social roles and networks as well.

Autobiography, which situates the self in narrative, is one way of conferring wholeness on a fragmented array of experience. Some elders begin to reconstitute their past in response to cataclysmic loss—the death of a loved one who was a significant witness in a person's life, premature unemployment, the onset of significant disability, the removal of familiar settings, or recognition of the sheer passage of time. Thus, feeling "like a ship without a rudder" at her husband's death, Ethel Mohammed began a series of embroidered scenes spanning the years of her life (Hufford, Hunt, and Zeitlin 1987:44–45). Other memory projects have been precipitated by life-cycle events or by inexplicable memory surges reported among the very elderly. To celebrate her retirement from a family business in the year of her fiftieth wedding anniversary, Viola Hanscam of Oregon transformed scraps of clothing worn over the years by family members into seven stair rugs, each depicting a threshold event such as a wedding, a birth, a move to a new home (Jones, 1980:85). Bluma Purmell of Philadelphia found her mind flooded with insistent memories from her childhood, and she then saturated canvases with bright paintings of turn-of-the-century farm life in southern New Jersey (Hufford, Hunt, and Zeitlin 1987:56–59).

Memory projects may materialize a world in which an elder took shape but which now exists only in memory. Reconstituting a lost world enables an elderly artist to recover the experiences of that world, to articulate the imprint of the elder's generation on the world at a particular time in history. Crafting a miniature farmyard, carving a set of old-fashioned lumbering tools, modeling scenes from childhood neighborhoods or homelands, displaying collections of tools on barn walls or in home museums, or demonstrating the use of old machinery at festivals, elderly artists materialize aspects of life that exist only in memory and thus show younger witnesses how the world has changed (Beck 1982; Hufford, Hunt, and Zeitlin 1987).

Such projects can provide elders with new social currency, functioning as thresholds for narratives and other forms of enactment that conjure lost worlds in the presence of witnesses. Myerhoff has observed that performing before witnesses is essential to complete the work of self-definition: "Always, self and society are known to the subjects themselves—through enactments" (Myerhoff, 1978:32). Witnesses provide the reflecting surface integral to any definitional rite, affirming that the self portrayed and the self apprehended are one and the same. Interestingly, in a number of remembered worlds, the elder is represented as a young witness to a now vanished way of life. This representation comprises a subtle direction to fresh witnesses of worlds written, collected, carved, narrated, or painted. The elder's self-definitional work becomes a resource for future elders, furnishing models and materials for the perennial task of defining self and community.

As a widespread and patterned means of traditionalizing experience, memory projects invite serious folkloristic study. Recent studies of memory projects challenge traditional perspectives on folk art, which have excluded memory projects as too personal, too nontraditional, or too eclectic for consideration. In another quarter, folk-art collectors and historians have obscured the material culture of the elderly through interpretations that excise autobiographical and historical meanings (Kirshenblatt-Gimblett 1988:148).

This pattern of constructing intergenerational ties challenges dominant assumptions about cultural transmission. Traditional skills, which according to conventional wisdom are "passed on from generation to generation," are not, in fact, so automatically transferred. The link-chain effect of grandparents teaching grandchildren is echoed in the elder's exploration of life's earlier stages for skills and memories to take up in later years. The common pattern of a cultural hiatus in mid-life fosters an impression that traditions are "dying" along with their elderly practitioners. Repeatedly we see retirees revive skills to which they were exposed in childhood, such as fiddling, basketry, gardening, and needlework (Jabbour 1981; Hawes 1984), but the recycled skill need not take the form of a canonical tradition to fit this pattern. Nontraditional materials and idioms may be used in the traditionalizing labor of shaping life's experiences into meaningful form. The active role of younger witnesses in stimulating such practices among elders seems to support Margaret Mead's assertion that cultural survival depends on the simultaneous participation of three generations (Mead 1972:311).

Such insights about witnessing shed new light on the folklorist's traditional reliance on the elderly. For folklorists and anthropologists seeking information about vanishing traditions, elderly individuals were ideal informants for documenting "culture at a distance." Sifting through the memories of elders for vanished customs, sayings, narratives, songs, and so forth, early folklorists were able to assemble collections that effectively displaced autobiographical contexts of origin. Only recently have folklorists and anthropologists come to appreciate their role as witnesses to the life stories jointly constructed in the ethnographic interview, itself a worthy topic for further investigation.

Mary Hufford

References

Beck, Jane. 1982. *Always in Season: Folk Art and Traditional Culture in Vermont.* Montpelier: Vermont Council on the Arts.

Briggs, Charles. 1988. *Competence in Performance: The Creativity of Tradition in Mexicano Verbal Arts.* Philadelphia: University of Pennsylvania Press.

Bronner, Simon. 1984. *Chain Carvers: Old Men Crafting Meaning.* Lexington: University Press of Kentucky.

Butler, Robert N. 1968. The Life Review: An Interpretation of Reminiscence in the Aged. *Psychiatry* 26 (1):65–76.

Dégh, Linda. 1969. Two Old World Narrators in an Urban Setting. In *Kontakte und Grenzen: Festschrift für Gerhard Heilfurth.* Göttingen, Germany.

Hawes, Bess. 1984. Folk Arts and the Elderly. In *Festival of American Folklife Program Book,* ed. Thomas Vennum. Washington, DC: Smithsonian Institution.

Hufford, Mary. 1992. *Chaseworld: Foxhunting and Storytelling in New Jersey's Pine Barrens.* Philadelphia: University of Pennsylvania Press.

Hufford, Mary, Marjorie Hunt, and Steven J. Zeitlin. 1987. *The Grand Generation: Memory, Mastery, Legacy.* Washington, DC: Smithsonian Institution Travelling Exhibition Service; Seattle: University of Washington Press.

Jabbour, Alan. 1981. Some Thoughts from a Folk Cultural Perspective. In *Perspectives on Aging: Exploding the Myth,* ed. Priscilla Johnston. Cambridge: Ballinger.

Jones, Suzi. 1980. *Webfoots and Bunchgrassers: Folk Art of the Oregon Country.* Salem: Oregon Arts Commission.

Kirshenblatt-Gimblett, Barbara. 1988. Mistaken Dichotomies. *Journal of American Folklore* 101:140–155.

———. 1989a. Authoring Lives. *Journal of Folklore Research* 26:123–149.

———. 1989b. Objects of Memory: Material Culture as Life Review. In *Folk Groups and Folklore Genres: A Reader,* ed. Eliot Oring. Logan: Utah State University Press.

Mathias, Elizabeth. 1974. The Game as Creator of the Group in an Italian American Community. *Pennsylvania Folklife* 4:22–30.

Mead, Margaret. 1972. *Blackberry Winter: My Earlier Years.* New York: William Morrow.

Mullen, Patrick. 1992. *Listening to Old Voices: Folklore, Life Stories, and the Elderly.* Bloomington: Indiana University Press.

Myerhoff, Barbara. 1978. *Number Our Days.* New York: Simon and Schuster.

See also Life History

Almanac

Annual compendium of calendar, weather, astronomical, astrological, and navigational charts eventually expanded to include miscellaneous entertainments and information on a broad range of topics. Almanacs as we recognize them evolved in the late Middle Ages in order to provide useful charts and information about the movements of celestial bodies and the tides. By the 16th and 17th centuries, astrology and belief in the ability to prognosticate weather based on the movements of the heavenly bodies received wide acceptance among the educated, and charts reflecting both became staples in most almanacs.

The first book printed in colonial America was an almanac, written by Captain William Pierce and published by Stephen Daye in 1639, at Cambridge, Massachusetts. By the end of the century, the number and variety of almanacs published by colonial presses increased dramatically up and down the Atlantic seaboard.

Driven by fierce competition, 18th-century printers broadened what they included in their almanacs and made outrageous claims about the superiority of their almanacs over all others. The Man of Signs showing the impact of the celestial bodies on the vital organs of human beings became standard in 18th-century almanacs. James Franklin and Nathaniel Ames, two Boston printers, added snippets of news events and short moralizing essays. James' brother Benjamin Franklin, using the pseudonym Richard Saunders, edited from 1732 to 1758 *Poor Richard's Almanac,* perhaps one of the best known American almanacs. It was packed with proverbs—some of his own coining, but most drawn from other sources—practical recommendations for farmers and domestics, and detailed descriptions of American customs and traditions.

Gradually, printers incorporated popular jests and current comic anecdotes into their almanacs. Immigrants, women, lawyers, and politicians were common targets. Medical formulas for curing beasts and humans became usual features, while other publishers added thrilling tales of frontier explorations, Indian captivities, and eyewitness accounts of marvelous events and strange occurrences. Homespun poetry, humorous and tragic anecdotes, popular legends and ballads, political speeches, notable quotations, patriotic essays, and cracker-barrel philosophy found their way into almanacs, alongside the weather predictions, schedules of the tides, and astrological charts.

Almanac publishers also targeted particular audiences. The almanacs directed at farmers were very successful, and one of them, the *Farmer's Almanac,* founded in 1792, endures today. Although much has been added to it, it retains many of the features of the earliest almanacs, including astrological charts, weather predictions, proverbs, and jests. Other shorter-lived, special-interest almanacs, including the *Lady's Almanac,* the *Temperance Almanac,* the *New England Anti-Masonic Almanac,* and those devoted to various religious and political causes, such as the *Christian Almanac* and the *Whig Almanac,* appeared and disappeared almost yearly. Virtually every state had its own almanac.

One of the more notable specialized almanacs featured Davy Crockett. Appearing first in 1835, two years after the publication of Crockett's *Life,* and continuing until 1856,

Title page of Davy Crockett's Almanack *for 1836. In the mid-1800s, humorous almanacs surged in popularity. Library of Congress.*

its various authors packed the series with tall tales and graphic illustrations about the incredible adventures of the real and a fictitious Crockett. This almanac played a significant role in transforming this backwoodsman, politician, and soldier of fortune into a culture hero.

By the 19th century, almanacs had become important conduits of popular culture and cheap literature. But late in the century, publishers began calling books of facts almanacs. Addressed to urbanites, these publications dropped the astrological and navigational information and ceased publishing material drawn from folklore and popular culture. In their place, publishers provided statistical information about business and industry, news summaries of major national and international news events, and factual data about government, entertainment, and sports.

At the end of the 20th century, only a few of the earlier kind of almanacs exist, maintaining a publishing tradition that saw its heyday in the 18th and 19th centuries when almanacs captured in print current popular culture and folk traditions.

Richard Sweterlitsch

References

Dodge, Robert K. 1987. *Early American Almanac Humor.* Bowling Green, OH: Bowling Green State University Popular Press.

Dorson, Richard M., ed. [1939] 1977. *Davy Crockett: American Comic Legend.* Westport, CT: Greenwood.

Kittredge, George Lyman. 1904. *The Old Farmer and His Almanack.* Boston: William Ware.

Sagendorph, Robb. 1970. *America and Her Almanacs.* Dublin, NH: Yankee; Boston: Little, Brown.

Stowell, Marion Barber. 1977. *Early American Almanacs: The Colonial Weekly Bible.* New York: Burt Franklin.

See also Franklin, Benjamin; Weatherlore

American Folklife Center

A national research, archival, and programming center established in 1976 within the Library of Congress (LC) in Washington, DC, by Public Law 94–201, the American Folklife Preservation Act. The center's congressional mandate to "preserve and present American folklife" has led to a variety of field projects, publications, public programs, and exhibitions, and its Archive of Folk Culture is the largest and most comprehensive North American ethnographic collection of folk music, folklore, and folklife.

The center was created after several years of congressional debate regarding its value, location, and functions, and a lobbying effort supported by the American Folklore Society and organized by folklorist Archie Green. The effort also resulted in the creation of the folk and traditional arts program of the National Endowment for the Arts, and it coaxed the National Endowment for the Humanities into greater recognition of the field. The center is overseen by a board of trustees, and its budget is from federal appropriations supplemented by private funds.

The center undertakes projects that document folk cultural traditions in the field. Such projects continue the tradition of the center's Archive of Folk Culture, which since 1928

In addition to projects around the country, the American Folklife Center sponsors events close to home, like demonstrations of singing and dancing in front of the Library of Congress. Washington, DC, 1995. Photo J. W. Love. Courtesy of the photographer.

has used fieldwork to generate collections. In the archive's early history, documentation focused on musical traditions and used sound recordings as the primary medium. The center's fieldwork includes verbal traditions, dance, ceremony, material culture, traditional knowledge and skills, and "way of life." Documentary media include not only sound recordings but still photography and other visual media.

Center publications range from research tools to policy studies, from bibliographies and discographies to compact discs and a videodisc, from informational booklets to exhibition catalogs. Two series, *Publications of the American Folklife Center* and *Studies in American Folklife,* are ongoing, and a third, *Folklife Annual,* produced five editions between 1985 and 1990. Other center publications have appeared in cooperation with private-sector presses and media companies. *Folklife Center News* (1977–) publishes articles on center activities and essays on the field.

Center exhibitions have ranged from modest displays to major traveling exhibitions with book-length catalogs, such as *The American Cowboy* (1983) or *Old Ties, New Attachments: Italian American Folklife in the West* (1992). Public events include a summer concert series, winter workshops and demonstrations, periodic lectures, symposia, and scholarly conferences. The center's tradition of technological experimentation began with its archive. Just as Robert Winslow Gordon experimented with a portable disc-cutting machine in the early 1930s, the center produced a videodisc *(The Ninety-Six Ranch)*

Logo of the American Folklife Center, Washington DC.

in the 1980s and has pioneered in using the Internet to share information and collections digitally in the 1990s.

Reference services are available in both the archival collections and the general subject areas of folklore and folklife. In addition to direct access to the collections, visitors to the Folklife Reading Room find a selection of the LC's publications pertaining to folklore and folklife, listening and viewing facilities, and extensive vertical files covering persons, organizations, and subject areas. Reference services are available by telephone, correspondence, or electronic mail. *Folklife Sourcebook* lists information regarding the national field. The center is accessible through LC MARVEL, the Library of Congress' Internet address: lcmarvel@seq1.loc.gov. A recorded telephone service, Folkline, provides information on events, jobs, and other subjects (202-707-2000). Address inquiries to American Folklife Center, Library of Congress, Washington, DC 20540–8100, or call 202-707-6590 (offices) or 202-707-5510 (Folklife Reading Room).

Alan Jabbour

References

Hardin, James. 1990. The Role of the American Folklife Center: Preserving and Presenting the Nation's Traditional Culture. *Library of Congress Information Bulletin* 49 (June 4):203–207.

See also Archive of Folk Culture

American Folklore Scholarship: The Early Years

Collection and study of American folklore from the beginning to the 20th century. In a sense, American folklore scholarship began almost simultaneously with the European discovery of the New World. Friar Ramon Pane accompanied Christopher Columbus on his second voyage in 1493 for the express purpose of collecting all the "ceremonies and antiquities" of the Taino Indians, a tribe that has long been extinct. Three years later, in 1496, Pane's little book, *On the Antiquities of the Indians,* appeared. This moralistic view of Indian folklore written from a Christian standpoint included narratives, beliefs, and accounts of rituals. In its emphasis upon the Indian and his quaintness, Pane's volume is typical of most of the works dealing with American folklore that followed it over the next four centuries.

While there were other collectors of American folklore after Pane, it was the 19th century before anyone envisioned a field of study in which folklore would be the central concern. Henry Rowe Schoolcraft (1793–1864) was the first American to set forth a systematic concept for a discipline of folklore. His first suggestions in this regard were presented in *Algic Researches* (1839), a collection of American Indian narratives Schoolcraft gathered during several years as an Indian agent on the northwestern frontier. His ideas were more fully presented in later publications. Basically, Schoolcraft envisioned a total science of man, albeit one that focused on the "rude nations," in which folklore played an important part. Schoolcraft's new discipline had four main objects of inquiry: (1) physical type of man; (2) material existence, by which he meant what is now called material culture; (3) intellectual existence, including music and poetry, oral tales and legends, medical knowledge, and mythology; and (4) geographical phenomena affecting or modifying the above features. These elements were to be determined through examination of numerous types of data, including art remains, dictionaries, grammars, place names, skulls, mummies, histories by European travelers, missionary translations, works ascribed to natives, "authentic traditions of all ages and countries," natural history, and mythology. Although much more than folklore was included in this new field of study, Schoolcraft nevertheless considered oral and material tradition basic and essential to the whole. Mythology was particularly significant because it contained the framework of the philosophy and religion of the "rude nations" and gave character to their songs and poetry.

Schoolcraft's "new" science involved both field observation and library work, emphasized the American Indian, and was survivalistic. Oral traditions were regarded as fossils of an earlier day that were still preserved and functioning though rapidly disappearing. Like the bones of extinct or ancient species of animals, they were far removed from civilization. This concept of folklore made the collection of such materials urgent, because those gathering them were retrieving from "the oblivion of past generations matter for thought and reflection for the future."

Although Schoolcraft is correctly designated the "father of American folklore," he made little contribution to his chosen field beyond the information he collected. Like most of his contemporaries, he considered himself primarily a collector, but a few scholars active at the same time were primarily theorists. The two most important of these were Horatio Emmons Hale (1817–1896) and Daniel Garrison Brinton (1837–1899), America's premier solar mythologists. Both were indebted to the German-born scholar Max Müller (1823–1900), who maintained that all myths could be linked to the sun and the solar cycle. While Hale basically accepted the "disease of language" thesis that Müller used to dismiss any factual basis for myth and legend, he was convinced that such traditions often originated historically. In numerous books, such as *Myths of the New World* (1868) and *American Hero-Myths* (1882), Brinton reached essentially the same conclusion as Müller, differing from the European master in not relating all myths to the sun; in several instances, he found connections with the moon or with lightning. Brinton saw a need to study the influence of myths on both the individual and the national mind, but he realized that the state of collections often made this kind of analysis difficult, if not impossible. Both Brinton and Hale championed a theoretical viewpoint that was never very popular in America and is now the most soundly rejected of all past folklore theories, and neither of these men had any students. What is more, solar mythology was a theoretical school characterized by disunity rather than unity. Most proponents acted as if they were unaware of the contributions of others holding the same views. So, although Hale and Brinton became significant individuals in folklore study, neither exerted much influence on future generations of folklorists.

Based purely on folklore collecting, few Americans of the 19th century were more important than John Wesley Powell (1834–1902). As head of the Bureau of Ethnology (after 1894, the Bureau of American Ethnology) from its founding in 1879 until his death, Powell was responsible for publishing most of the major collections of American Indian folklore that appeared in print during that twenty-three year span. Congress established the bureau primarily to carry on research already begun, but from the outset Powell intended more. He thought of the agency as the focal point around which all American Indian studies would be centered. Toward this goal, he implemented a research program that included detailed bibliographic compilations, new field studies, the development and circulation of questionnaires, and publication of *Annual Reports* and *Bulletins.*

Powell belonged to the evolutionary school that saw all society developing through four levels of progress. Three of these stages—savagery, barbarism, and civilization—were already realized, but in the future an additional level, that of "enlightenment," would be achieved. He expounded his views in a large number of prolix and dense publications, but these writings are of interest to 20th-century readers only as historical curiosities. Powell's real importance is as the overseer of several folklore works issued in twenty-three *Annual Reports* prepared under his direction. The authors of these works include many of the best-known 19th-century students of American Indian folklore: Erminnie A. Smith, Washington Matthews, James Owen Dorsey, James Mooney, John G. Bourke, Alice Fletcher, and Frank H. Cushing, among others. Most of these studies were consistent with Powell's view of folklore as survivals from a lower stage of culture.

Throughout the 19th century great attention was accorded Indian folklore; prior to 1900 relatively little work was done with the lore of other groups. Even such a significant cultural group as African Americans was virtually ignored until the second half of the 19th century. Two major assumptions prevalent in American society contributed to this neglect: first, that the Black man was incapable of any thought or expression worthy of serious study, and, second, that Whites knew everything worth knowing about the slaves who lived inside White society. In the mid-19th century, this paternalistic view was considerably altered, and, in large part because of the controversy over slavery, an intellectual curiosity of the part of Whites toward the Negro emerged.

Occasional references to African American folklore started appearing beginning in the 1830s. One of these, a letter by Lucy McKim (1842–1877) in *Dwight's Journal of Music* in 1862, is often cited for first bringing slave songs to public attention, although that claim can be disputed. Not until the post–Civil War years was the first extensive collection of Negro folklore published, and it came about largely through the efforts of a classical scholar who was a pioneer in both Black dialect and song studies. William Francis Allen (1830–1889) was a native of Massachusetts who spent two years in the South with the Freedmen's and Sanitary Commissions after the Civil War. During his stay in South Carolina and Arkansas, Allen collected Negro songs, and he eventually met Charles Pickard Ware (1840–1921) and McKim, both of whom had also collected songs. The three soon met other collectors and combined their material to produce *Slave Songs of the United States* (1867).

For a pioneering work, this volume set a high standard and was unusual in that it contained musical settings for each of its 136 texts. The authors also considered regional characteristics of Negro folk music, a topic overlooked by most of their successors. They paid attention to the situations in which songs were performed, another subject that few collectors of their time considered. Admirable as it is, *Slave Songs of the United States* does have flaws, perhaps the most glaring being the ethnocentric judgments that Allen, Ware, and McKim occasionally make. For example, Negro music is judged as being either civilized or barbaric rather than seen as a musical system with its own set of values. Despite its limitations, the book brought Black folklore, or the musical part of it, to widespread public view and whetted the interest in collecting, analyzing, and performing Negro folk music that has never since abated.

Nearly two decades after the appearance of *Slave Songs of the United States,* the first extensive account of African American secular music was published. In 1886 George Washington Cable (1844–1925), primarily remembered as a local-color novelist, produced two articles for *Century* magazine dealing with Creole Negro folksong and dance. In these essays, Cable touched on two topics that were controversial for many years thereafter. One was the dispute over the banjo and its use by Black musicians, Cable flatly stating that "it is not the favorite musical instrument of the negroes of the Southern States of America." The second dispute was over the idea that Negro songs had originated in Africa, a view that received little challenge from Cable's American contemporaries but was firmly opposed by some foreign writers, like the Englishman Richard Wallashek. The most damaging attack on the theory of African origins came many years later with the publication of Newman Ivey White's *American Negro Folksongs* (1928).

In the same decade that Cable's articles appeared, a second kind of Negro folklore came to public attention, one that all commentators at the time agreed was of purely African origin. This body of Black lore was the animal tale, as handed down from generation to generation by word of mouth. These tales gained widespread prominence in 1880 through the efforts of Georgia journalist Joel Chandler Harris (1848–1908). Harris had heard African American folktales most of his life, but the immediate impetus for his writing on the subject was a December 1877 article, "Folklore of the Southern Negroes," in *Lippincott's* magazine. Taking exception to author William Owens' efforts, Harris produced his own book, *Uncle Remus: His Songs and His Sayings* (1880), which was received as a literary and folklore masterpiece. Harris claimed he was an accidental author and an unintentional folklorist, but there is little doubt that his various publications had a profound affect on the subsequent collecting of African American folktales.

Harris was sometimes uncomfortable being regarded as

an authority on folklore, but he was not reticent about offering theories. At least two that he included in his Uncle Remus volumes were accepted unquestioningly by most later students of African American lore: that the folktales of Blacks were of remote African origin and did not betray European influences, and that Negro folktales had not been influenced by those of the American Indian, as John Wesley Powell and others had suggested. On the latter point, Harris was supported by no less an authority than folktale scholar Thomas Frederick Crane (1844–1927), who, in an 1881 review article, concluded that the idea of Blacks borrowing narratives from the tribesmen was "an hypothesis no one would think of maintaining." Eighty-four years later, in 1965, Alan Dundes offered further support for this view, although he was more temperate in his claims than Crane. Among other points, Dundes noted that "many folklorists have assumed, wrongly in my opinion, that all African origins must be in West Africa." He then pointed out that many slaves came from East Africa, where the hare, an important figure in African American folktales, is the principal trickster figure. Dundes asserted that the burden of proof was mainly on those making the claim that Blacks borrowed their trickster tales from the American Indian.

Richard M. Dorson (1916–1981), one of the most prolific American folklorists, offered the first significant challenge to the thesis of African origins of black folktales. Working with a corpus of over one thousand folktales he collected in the 1950s from Negroes born in the South, Dorson concluded that "this body of tales does not come from Africa" or "from any one place but from a number of dispersal points." What's more, he argued that the animal tales, such as those recorded by Harris, "are of demonstrably European origin." Although basing his conclusions on the best available modern reference works, such as motif indexes, Dorson's argument fell largely on deaf ears.

Two basic approaches to folklore coexisting in the late 19th century were the anthropological and the literary. Largely because of the influence of William Wells Newell (1839–1907) and Franz Boas (1858–1942), the American Folklore Society (AFS), established in 1888, was oriented toward the anthropological approach. These two men were the major forces in the early years of the AFS, Boas maintaining that role for half a century. They were united in their view of folklore as a division of the broader science of anthropology, and both wanted to make anthropology and folklore more professional. Newell thought that amateurs would undoubtedly continue to be active in folklore, but he believed they should adhere to rigorous scholarly standards. He sided with Boas on the anthropological emphasis of the American Folklore Society, thinking that in so doing he would both distinguish himself from the nonprofessionals interested in folklore and simultaneously increase the scholarly output of the *Journal of American Folklore (JAF)* by filling it primarily with anthropological data. This alliance also added the weight of the European academic tradition, represented by Boas, to Newell's attempts to professionalize folklore.

Boas also benefited greatly from his relationship with Newell and the AFS. He had a genuine interest in folklore as a significant aspect of anthropology, and he needed the society as a power base through which he could propound his ideas. Moreover, the *JAF* was an excellent publishing outlet for his students because, unlike the anthropological journals, it allowed him control over the form and timing of the publication of articles. Actually, the American Folklore Society was virtually Boas' last hope for gaining professional clout, because it was the only organization that indicated some interest in him and his approach to anthropology. He had earlier attempted unsuccessfully to obtain positions of influence in the American Association for the Advancement of Science and the Bureau of American Ethnology. Newell, however, was grateful to have him as an ally, and he gave him virtually a free hand in AFS matters.

Perhaps the main reason Newell found Boas appealing is that Boas offered a more comprehensive and systematic approach to folklore than had existed before, one that he ultimately illustrated in his studies, theoretical papers, and field collecting projects. A major element in Boas' approach to folklore was good fieldwork, gathering material firsthand with extensive interviews. This emphasis was a bold step away from his earlier influences; 19th-century European scholars, representatives of the tradition in which Boas was trained, generally held a negative attitude toward fieldwork, regarding it as mere collecting and, thus, far removed from true scholarship, defined as the comparison, analysis, and interpretation of materials.

To Boas, good fieldwork consisted of accurately recording data and finding the best informants. Ideally, the collector should seek out someone who knew and could relate data on every aspect of village life. He usually relied on a single informant from a community, an approach unusual in his day, but one adopted later by his students. Boas also helped popularize the practice of amassing data with no particular problem in mind and with no clear idea of what was to be gained in the end. This approach resulted from his belief that each culture possesses its own concepts, categories, and biases, and that to arrive at a true understanding of another culture it was essential for scholars to collect vast quantities of reliable material in the native language. Myths and tales thus gathered would be preserved for all time as undistorted expressions of the culture, containing all of the keys necessary to understand that society. By poring over accurately recorded texts, one would arrive at new theories and new problems to be solved. In other words, the data would direct the interpretation.

Much of Boas' field methodology is considered faulty by modern standards, but he did record an enormous amount of useful data and, more than most scholars of his day, tried to view Western civilization as only one, not *the,* standard of reference. Furthermore, he realized the limitations of personal observation, and he was convinced that people see what they expect to see and interpret what they see in the light of their previous experiences. Boas insisted on accuracy in recording data and on limiting research to problems that could be solved by observable facts. He also made fieldwork, at least among "exotic" groups, popular and acceptable in a way it had never been before. Finally, his emphasis on the value of presenting accurately transcribed texts was important at a time when folktales were often published as literary products, without care for their original form.

Boas was not opposed to making theoretical pronouncements, but he was cautious about offering them. Indeed, he maintained that collecting numerous folktales from contiguous peoples and plotting the distribution of their "elements"—by which he meant something roughly akin to motifs—must precede any theoretical work. He failed to explain, however, how much collecting and mapping were needed before one could justifiably begin theorizing. It is also unclear exactly what Boas meant by theory in folklore, for he never demonstrated by example his ideas in this regard. He often referred to statements of a psychological kind, but his only detailed discussions are of historical processes.

Boas' thinking about folklore is most completely set forth in the mammoth volume *Tsimshian Mythology* (1916). In this book, especially its prefatory essay, he emphasizes proper recording and presentation of texts, offering the then novel suggestion that folklorists should not limit their work to "star" informants or to the "correct" version of an item when variants occurred and such versions affected transmission of the tale. Unfortunately, neither Boas nor his disciples followed this idea, which is still not common practice in folklore fieldwork. The book is also important because it sets forth Boas' concept of folktales as a "reflector of culture," a point only hinted at previously but restated in several later writings. This thesis led Boas to think of tales as a type of cultural autobiography; he overlooked the possibility that an oral literature might not mirror all aspects of life equally.

From a scholarly standpoint, there were both positive and negative results of Boas' decades-long influence in the American Folklore Society. His insistence on good objective fieldwork and accurate presentation of data, caution about theorizing based on faulty or insufficient material, professionalization of the field of folklore, and production of folklore fieldworkers and support for their research and publications are on the positive side. Moreover, his students constitute a veritable Who's Who of anthropological folklorists, including, among others, A.L. Kroeber, Elsie Clews Parsons, Robert H. Lowie, Paul Radin, Martha Warren Beckwith, Ruth Benedict, Melville Jean Herskovits, Gladys Reichard, Ruth Bunqel, and Melville Jacobs.

One negative aspect of Boas' influence was an overemphasis on American Indian folklore. While he recognized that other peoples had oral traditions, he showed little interest in nonaboriginal subjects. For example, he refused to allow Vance Randolph to do a dissertation topic dealing with Ozark mountaineers, preferring instead to direct him toward a West Coast Indian tribe. Rather than follow Boas' suggestion, Randolph left graduate school. Boas' bias permeated American Folklore Society publications during the more than three decades that Boasian folklorists were editors of the *Journal of American Folklore*. Throughout this period, virtually every issue of the quarterly contained at least one article or collection of tribal myths or tales, all following the Boasian model whereby texts are presented with little or no attention given to the informants, context, or style. There was, of course, nothing wrong with the collection of American Indian traditions, merely with the journal's imbalance. The net effect was to reinforce a view held by many that folklore existed only in places and among peoples outside the mainstream of civilization.

Boasian scholarship can be faulted on several other counts. Boas had no intellectual interest in informants except as repositories of oral traditions, a lack of concern derived from his orientation toward the past. He focused entirely on bygone traditions, or what has come to be called "memory culture." Having thus given up any concern for the present, he saw no need to learn much about the living bearers of a tradition. Moreover, his belief in a superorganic concept of culture made any interest in those who preserve and pass on folklore irrelevant; the recording of texts was all that one needed. Boas was certainly not the only person holding such views, but he was one of the most influential adherents. This attitude held sway among folklorists long after Boas' death in 1942 and only began to change in the mid-1960s.

Some other aspects of Boas' thinking about folk traditions did not bode well for the future development of an independent discipline devoted to the study of folklore. He believed that it was important to collect and study oral traditions because primitive man is our ancestor, and folklore, as a reflector of culture, offers important insights into primitive thought. Through a rigorous study of tribal lore and culture, one could eventually arrive at what he called "original nature." Thus, folklore, or the "primitive arts" as Boas sometimes called it, had importance only as a means to an end. Many of his contemporaries and scholarly descendants had essentially the same outlook.

Ultimately, Boas' significance in the history of American folklore is that he effectively presented a systematic way of dealing with his materials. He offered a method for recording oral traditions that promised to lead eventually to the formation of folklore theories based on sound scholarship. That his ideas were adopted by numerous other scholars was in no sense a small achievement.

During the late 19th century, the literary approach to folklore was championed primarily by the Chicago Folk-Lore Society and its moving force, Fletcher S. Bassett (1847–1893), a retired lieutenant in the U.S. Navy. An independently wealthy man, Bassett had been forced into retirement in 1882 by ill health, whereupon he moved to Chicago and devoted the remaining years of his life to private scholarship. In 1891 he persuaded more than sixty people to attend the inaugural meeting of the new society, and for the next couple of years it was a viable organization devoted to pursuing the idea of folklore as an art form totally independent of its cultural milieu.

Bassett's goal was to display folklore in an engaging manner. The folklorist should approach his data as a man of letters rather than one who enshrouded his materials in a coldly clinical scientific style. Because those in charge of the *Journal of American Folklore* were opposed to this idea, it was necessary to create a new folklore publishing outlet, so in July 1892 the *Folk-Lorist,* the official publication of the Chicago Folk-

Lore Society, appeared. Bassett also produced the *Folk-Lore Manual* (1892) so that interested parties would know how to go about collecting lore. This publication elucidates Bassett's concept of folklore more than any other source. Like many of his contemporaries, he believed that "the fast-decaying traditions of our native tribes and of the negroes and mixed races are the most important, and work among them, will, perhaps, bring the most abundant results." He shared the view of folklore as data that were rapidly disappearing, but, unlike other scholars of the day, he maintained that oral traditions existed among all classes of human beings, not just among primitive and uncivilized people. He even suggested that railroading, telegraphy, and photography were three professions in which folklore could be found in abundance.

The Chicago Folk-Lore Society's crowning achievement was the International Folk-Lore Congress held at the 1893 Columbian Exposition in Chicago. This gathering of scholars from around the world was intended to be of interest to the general public as well as to academics. Although the meeting got off to a good start with a huge audience attending the first session, attendance by both the audience and the academic participants dwindled after the first day. Even the Chicago newspapers commented on the failure of speakers to show up. A greater problem for the society was Bassett's death shortly after the congress ended. In fact, his loss was fatal to the organization, because no one filled his role. Probably the main reason for this situation is that, except for Bassett, the other resident members were folklore dilettantes. In 1898 the *International Folk-Lore Congress of the World's Columbian Exposition*, containing papers from the 1893 congress, appeared, but by that time the society was, for all practical purposes, defunct.

With the demise of the Chicago Folk-Lore Society, the idea that folklore was a thing worthy of study in itself also ceased to be an actively espoused concept for nearly a half century. Ironically, though, the literary view of folklore won in a sense because most 20th-century folklorists were either trained or influenced by Stith Thompson (1885–1976) of Indiana University, and Archer Taylor (1890–1973) of University of California, Berkeley, who, while not following the literary approach advocated by the Chicago Folk-Lore Society, were literary folklorists nonetheless.

By the 1880s, folklore investigations of the American Indian were in full swing, even though by then the Native American had been examined by investigators of traditional culture for almost four centuries. After so long a time, seemingly every aspect of tribal culture would have received adequate consideration, but there was still one feature of Indian society that lacked intensive examination—music. This situation was soon rectified by a number of people, the first being Theodor Baker, a native of New York City who obtained a Ph.D. from the University of Leipzig with a dissertation based on songs he collected from Senecas in New York State and from members of various tribes at the Training School for Indian Youth at Carlisle, Pennsylvania. This volume was published in 1882 as *Über die Musik der nordamerikanischen Wilden* (On the Music of the North American Savages). Sev-

enty-one melodies were printed, thirty-two of which were analyzed in some detail, but, despite the serious tone of Baker's book and its landmark importance in the history of ethnomusicology, it has remained obscure and little used. Baker's later lack of interest in Indian music and the fact that his volume was published in German both played a part in its general lack of recognition.

Far better known is the work of Alice Cunningham Fletcher (1838–1923), an erudite and urbane Bostonian, who almost reached middle age before starting work in ethnomusicology. Fletcher struggled to overcome her reaction to Indian music as "screeching cacophony" and her own preconceived ideas concerning "savage" music; she later admitted that she had been enslaved by her previous racially biased training. By 1891 she received a fellowship that enabled her to devote the rest of her life to her Indian studies, the best known of her publications being *A Study of Omaha Music* (1893). This work was also the major result of her collaboration with John Comfort Fillmore (1843–1898), who used the study to set forth his theory of primitive music. His was an elaborate, evolutionary scheme that proposed a single line of development for all cultures, based on the study of a specific culture. All music was constructed along "harmonic" lines, folk music differing from art music only in the manner of development. Therefore, all attempts to reduce primitive melodies to scales had to consider the natural harmonies involved. So convinced was Fillmore of this "natural harmonic basis" that he provided harmonizations with the melodies he printed, not merely to make the music more "pleasing" to Western ears, but also to indicate the "true nature" of the tunes.

Fillmore never wavered from his theory, and it found acceptance among scholars primarily because it elevated Indian music to an artistic form worthy of respect. At the time, there was a prevailing attitude that the aborigines had no musical sense or genius, particularly when compared to the Negro. The Fillmore-Fletcher work, however, belied this, pointing out that all musics were essentially the same, just in different stages of development. After Fillmore's death, Fletcher did not publicize his theory, perhaps because her own interests were more general. She produced one other major work, *The Hako: A Pawnee Ceremony* (1904).

Jesse Walter Fewkes (1850–1930) is important as the first American to utilize the phonograph in fieldwork, when in 1890 she used the then new invention to collect songs and tales of the Passamaquoddy tribe in Maine. A short time later, Frances Densmore (1867–1957), destined to become one of the most famous ethnomusicologists of her time, began her work with a collection of Chippewa music. At first she produced mainly popular works, but later she became a thoroughgoing scholar. Like many other ethnomusicologists, she also began to work in isolation from other published materials, as if no one else had ever written on the topics she treated.

Few collectors of Indian music had plans as ambitious as Natalie Curtis Burlin (1875–1921), who wanted to produce a book representative of all North American Indian music. Realizing this was an impossible task, she opted for one hundred forty-nine songs from eighteen tribes in *The Indians' Book* (1907). She hoped the volume would demonstrate the "latent capabilities" of a people "utterly unlike any other in the world." Further, she thought that Indian music would provide the art musician with "a new and vigorous art impulse" because the tribe members unconsciously tried "to make beautiful the things of daily living." This possibility made it imperative that her publication be of a popular nature.

A number of classical composers essentially agreed with Burlin that Indian music could be utilized as the basis of artistic compositions. Among the leaders of this movement were Arthur Farwell (1872–1952), establisher of Wa-Wan Press, a venture committed to works developing in "interesting fashion" any indigenous folk music, Charles Wakefield Cadman (1881–1946), and Arthur Nevin (1871–1943). These, and other composers, arranged collections of Indian melodies, inspiring a movement that continued well into the 20th century and eventually included consideration of much more than just Indian music.

Another aspect of music received consideration when Francis James Child's ten-volume collection, *The English and Scottish Popular Ballads,* appeared in 1882 to 1898. Child (1825–1896) saw this as a work of cultural archaeology because he was convinced that ballad singing was a dead art. He was rescuing the cream of the crop from oblivion; hence the *The* in his title. Ironically, this summing up of the English and Scottish ballad tradition was done before any of the substantive work in Anglo folksong and ballad collecting had been done. In effect, Child motivated that fieldwork; it was almost as if collectors were intent on proving him wrong about ballad singing being a lost art. Consequently, for approximately fifty years after his final volume appeared, most fieldworkers set about recording variants and versions of Child ballads, *and little else.* An exception to this trend was Cecil Sharp (1859–1924), an Englishman who traveled the southern Appalachians from 1916 to 1918 collecting all manner of songs that were of English derivation. Another exception was Vance Randolph, the most famous of Ozark folklorists, who spent approximately three decades collecting ballads and folksongs from Ozark mountaineers. Even Randolph, who thought everything sung by a folksinger was important, gave the highest priority to Child ballads, reserving the first volume of his mammoth *Ozark Folksongs* (1946–1950) to these gems.

The study of American dialect began in the 19th century, although, unlike other areas of folklore scholarship, this movement was an outgrowth of neither the Romantic movement nor anthropology, but philology. Most of those who investigated American dialect were ignorant of, or even uninterested in, other genres of oral tradition, a situation not unusual in the history of American folklore studies, so often a history of disunity rather than unity. For his *A Vocabulary or Collection of Words and Phrases which have been supposed to be peculiar to the United States of America* (1816), John Pickering (1777–1846) deserves credit as the first American dialectologist. More important, however, was John Russell Bartlett (1805–1886), whose *Dictionary of Americanisms* (1848) was a scholarly best-seller, appearing in two subsequent editions in 1859

and 1877. Bartlett's theory of dialects depicted them as originating in two ways. First, local language developed from the propinquity of nationalities speaking different tongues borrowing words and phrases from one another. A more fruitful and permanent source was migration, and its effects could be seen in England, where "the immigrations of various nations into Great Britain from the Saxons down to the period of the Norman conquest are yet distinctly marked in the dialects of that country." Thus, one could know beforehand exactly when and where variations from standard language could occur, important because Bartlett thought it only a matter of a few generations until the United States would witness a proliferation of dialects as marked as those of Great Britain.

Bartlett's collection and that of his protege Maximilian Schele De Vere (1820–1898), who produced *Americanisms: The English of the New World* (1871), were gathered mainly from printed sources. This was not the case with Benjamin Homer Hall's *A Collection of College Words and Customs* (1851), a potpourri including everything from folk terms to an explanation of the Dudleian Lecture, an anniversary sermon preached at Harvard University, to a discussion of Harvard's merit system. Of course, Hall had to rely mainly on oral sources because many of the "odd words and queer customs" he sought were not written down. Even though he directed his attention to the unusual and the uncommon, Hall deserves credit not only for compiling one of the early works on dialect, but also for producing the first book dealing with college folklore.

In 1890, two years after the founding of the American Folklore Society, the American Dialect Society was established. Almost from the outset, one of the society's goals was to produce a dictionary that would provide "a complete record of American speech forms." Toward this goal, word lists from various areas of the United States appeared in virtually every issue of *Dialect Notes,* the organization's journal. Even so, more than one hundred years later the envisioned dialect dictionary has yet to appear, a testament to the difficulty of the task. What society members had in mind was something akin to Joseph Wright's six-volume *English Dialect Dictionary* (1898–1905), but the problems in this country are different from those encountered by Wright. Americans are more fluid, both geographically and socially, than Europeans, making the development of an extensive local speech more difficult. Distinctions between dialect and standard speech are also less rigid in the New World; regional terms frequently appear in the usage of the educated; "illiterate" features repeatedly crop up in the works of local-color novelists. Compilers of general dictionaries have usually recognized these facts and included in their compilations a number of dialectal terms. America is also much larger, both geographically and demographically, and less homogeneous than England. Furthermore, when Wright started work, much of the labor had already been done in the form of published glossaries of English county dialects, and, in addition, local correspondents were available for consultation whenever needed.

Dialectologists made the same kinds of errors other folklorists committed, the basic one being an overcommitment to collecting and an undercommitment to gathering material in context. Motivated by a desire to recover every item of dialect before it was lost or by some other equally charitable goal, most collectors found little time or need to do more than provide a listing of materials. In one regard, however, dialectological work was ahead of most other folklore collecting done prior to the 20th century. Dialectologists never confined their subject matter to a savage or peasant state of society or, in fact, to any single group of people. They rightly saw it as belonging to all classes and periods of society. Had work in the many areas of folklore been more unified at the time, other scholars might have benefited from this attitude.

One final group of scholars active in the late 19th and early 20th centuries that deserve mention are what might be called "the overseas folklorists." These were men like Charles Godfrey Leland (1824–1903), Jeremiah Curtin (1835–1906), and Lafcadio Hearn (1850–1904), who were peripatetic scholars who spent so much time in other parts of the globe that they never had time or opportunity to develop strong followings at home. Still, their contributions are significant in the history of American folklore studies, for their large number of publications, if nothing else.

Work in the various areas of folklore studies mentioned in this survey continued in the 20th century. These later works are covered in other entries of this encyclopedia, so are not repeated here.

W.K. McNeil

References

Bassett, Fletcher. [1885] 1971. *Legends and Superstitions of the Sea and of Sailors.* Detroit: Singing Tree Press.

Bisland, Elizabeth, ed. 1906. *The Life and Letters of Lafcadio Hearn.* Boston: Houghton Mifflin.

Crane, Thomas Frederick. 1888. The Diffusion of Popular Tales. *Journal of American Folklore* 1:8–15.

Darrah, William Culp. 1951. *Powell of the Colorado.* Princeton, NJ: Princeton University Press.

Dundes, Alan. 1973. African Tales among the North American Indians. In *Mother Wit from the Laughing Barrel: Readings in the Interpretation of Afro-American Folklore.* Englewood Cliffs, NJ: Prentice-Hall, pp. 114–125.

Fillmore, John Comfort. The Harmonic Structure of Indian Music. *American Anthropologist* 1:297–318.

Goldschmidt, Walter, ed. 1959. *The Anthropology of Franz Boas.* Menasha, WI: American Anthropological Association.

Hale, Horatio. 1890. "Above" and "Below": A Mythological Disease of Language. *Journal of American Folklore* 3:177–190.

Hofmann, Charles. 1968. *Frances Densmore and American Indian Music: A Memorial Volume.* New York: Museum of the American Indian.

Judd, Neil. 1967. *The Bureau of American Ethnology: A Partial History.* Norman: University of Oklahoma Press.

Powell, John Wesley. 1895. The Interpretation of Folklore. *Journal of American Folklore* 8:97–105.

Wallashek, Richard. 1893. *Primitive Music: An Inquiry into the Origin and Development of Music, Songs, Instruments, Dances, and Pantomimes of Savage Races.* London: Longmans, Green.

See also American Studies and Folklore; Applied Folklore; Canadian Folklore Scholarship; Canadian Studies and Folklore; Comparative Approach; Contextual Approach; Cultural Studies; Ethnomusicology; Folklife Movement; Functionalism; Immigrant Folklore, Study of; Material Culture; Oral-Formulaic Approach; Performance Approach; Postmodernism; Psychology and Folklore; Semiotic Approach; Sociological Approach; Structural Approach

American Folklore Society

A scholarly association that exists to further the discipline of folklore studies. The society was founded in Boston in 1888 by such luminaries as Francis James Child, William Wells Newell, Daniel Garrison Brinton, and Franz Boas, with its principal emphasis directed toward the publication of a "scientific" journal and the convening of an annual meeting.

Generations of scholarly theories and approaches are reflected in the society's publications, revealing the sometimes partisan leanings of its members toward folklore as literature or folklore as a subfield of anthropology. The *Journal of American Folklore (JAF)* has been published quarterly since 1888. It includes articles, notes, and commentaries; reviews of publications, films and videotapes, audio recordings, and exhibitions and events; and obituaries. The *Centennial Index* (1988; vol. 101, no. 402 of *JAF*) provides a serial listing of all *Journal* entries from 1888 to 1988, with author, title, and subject indexes.

Additional publications of the society include a Memoir Series of book-length monographs (1894–1975), a Bibliographical and Special Series (1950–1978), and a New Series (1980–). Titles in the New Series, judged by a publications series editor and outside readers to be outstanding in the field, are issued with the imprimatur of the American Folklore Society through various university presses.

The *American Folklore Society Newsletter* has been published bimonthly since 1971. This publication carries official news and reports of the society's business, as well as a wide range of information relevant to the field generally. Regular features include listings of academic meetings, publication news, job notices, grant announcements, a cooperation column, prizes, and information on electronic media. Special features include columns on computer applications in folklore study, career opportunities, the status of funding for folklore in federal agencies, and folklore studies outside the United States. The preliminary program of each year's annual meeting is published in the August issue of the *Newsletter*.

In recent years, the society has moved beyond the early dichotomy between literary and anthropological folklorists. It provides a common forum for folklorists working in academic settings and those working in the "public sector," a term broadly applied to folklorists working in nonacademic positions such as federal, state, and local government agencies (such as arts or humanities funding agencies) or private nonprofit organizations (such as museums or historical organizations). The need to bridge the academic and public sectors has prompted the society to sponsor an annual public-sector internship for a graduate student to gain experience working in a public-sector agency and a public-folklorist-in-residence program, which places experienced public folklorists in an academic setting to pursue individual research and interact with faculty and students. The residency program was developed in cooperation with Indiana University's Folklore Institute. Future partners for this residency program include Utah State University and Western Kentucky University.

The society's annual meeting takes place in October in cities throughout the continental United States and occasionally Canada. The five-day gathering offers panels, forums and workshops, film and video screenings, book exhibitions, special events, and tours of folkloristic interest. The society offers several prizes to honor outstanding work in African American folklore studies, public folklore, and Francophone folklore studies. Additionally, sections of the AFS, which are interest groups of society members, offer separate prizes. In 1995, there were approximately thirty such sections, addressing folklore genres (such as dance, folk arts, folk belief, folk narrative, foodways, and music), folklore of particular folk groups (such as African, American Indian, Baltic, British, Catholic, children, gay and lesbian, Italian, Jewish, Latino, occupational, and women), and professional issues (such as computer applications, graduate students, journals, social justice, and public programs). Sections meet at the annual meeting. Many of them sponsor sessions, offer prizes, and issue newsletters or journals of their own. Several sections maintain electronic bulletin boards, as does the society itself, available via a gopher at the University of Texas–Pan American.

The American Folklore Society is governed by an executive board composed of nine members plus the president and the president-elect, as set forth in the society's by-laws. An executive secretary-treasurer is responsible for the day-to-day administration of the society's business. The society's papers and records are archived at Utah State University's Library, Special Collections Division. These archives are indexed and are accessible for research.

Additional information about the society can be obtained by contacting the American Folklore Society, 4350 North Fairfax Drive, Suite 640, Arlington, VA 22203.

Shalom D. Staub

References

Clements, William M., ed. 1988. *One Hundred Years of American Folklore Studies: A Conceptual History.* Washington, DC: American Folklore Society.

Dwyer-Shick, Susan. 1979. *The American Folklore Society and Folklore Research in America, 1888–1940.* Ph.D. diss., University of Pennsylvania.

Newell, William W. 1888. On the Field and Work of a Journal of American Folk-Lore. *Journal of American Folklore* 1:3–7. Reprinted in *Journal of American Folklore* 101:56–59, 1988.

Zumwalt, Rosemary Lévy. 1988. *American Folklore Scholarship: A Dialogue of Dissent.* Bloomington: Indiana University Press.

See also American Folklore Scholarship: The Early Years

American Studies and Folklore

Scholarly connection interpreting traditions shaped by experiences and settings in the United States. American studies arose during the 1930s with folklore research as an important component. This interdisciplinary academic movement strove to interpret American society in a national perspective by combining American history, literature, and culture. The driving mission of identifying a national tradition led many American-studies scholars to folklore research, which had been used in Europe to examine the cultural basis of regions and nations.

A basic split occurred in early American-studies scholarship between those examining a distinctively national folklore, thus underscoring the case for an American exceptionalism, and those emphasizing the adaptation of international folk traditions on the American scene, thus suggesting a multicultural society. Since the 1980s, the argument has shifted to issues of multiple identities held by Americans, often expressed through folklore and the processes of cultural production.

Before Harvard University established the first formal degree-granting program for American studies in 1936, a substantial shelf of American-studies scholarship using folklore research had emerged. Constance Rourke (1885–1941) published *American Humor* in 1931 and cited American folklore—including traditionally learned tall tales and legends of tricksters and "ringtailed roarers"—as the distinguishing influence on American literary humor. Rourke believed that a distinctive American folklore formed out of the special circumstances of the new nation, such as its frontier. This folklore influenced the rise of an American literature based on vernacular characters such as James Fenimore Cooper's Leather-stocking and traditional themes such as "rags to riches" and the "noble and ignoble savage." In fact, she observed that the American tradition—in art, architecture, and literature—overall contained a unity of folk or vernacular spirit. For Martha Warren Beckwith (1871–1959), formerly a colleague of Rourke's at Vassar College, American society was too diverse and derived too greatly from foreign sources to describe as a single tradition. Established as America's first chair of folklore at Vassar, Beckwith outlined many living ethnic and religious "strains in the process of creating an American cultural life" in *Folklore in America* (1931).

Henry Nash Smith, the first graduate of Harvard's History of American Civilization program, examined folklore sources of Edward Eggleston and Mark Twain, among other American fiction writers, in his dissertation, which led to the influential book *Virgin Land* (1950). In his work, Smith introduced an American-studies approach of "myth, symbol, and image," drawn largely from folkloristic ideas of the consciousness-building powers of cultural mythology, and he used the development of the American West, an interest he credited to Texas folklorist J. Frank Dobie (1888–1964), to demonstrate his approach. American "myths," scholars such as Smith and Russell Nye held, were not narrative texts in the usual sense; they were driving concepts or "collective representations" that unified Americans; examples were Smith's "myth of the garden" (power of Americans to transform wilderness and desert into a new Eden-like garden) and Nye's "myth of superabundance" (popular belief that resources are endless in America).

Smith suggested that historical patterns such as the westward movement were influenced by such myths and the lore and literature that arose from them. Philip D. Jordan pointed out, for example, that terms such as "manifest destiny" in the American experience were folk mottos of crucial themes that characterized the "essential narrative of this nation" (Jordan 1946). Such themes included westward movement, immigration, and industrialization. To this list, Nye added character traits of individualism, free enterprise, and progressivism that are evident in the nation's emergent folklore.

Smith encouraged the folklore research of Richard M. Dorson (1916–1981), a fellow graduate student at Harvard, who went on to become the strongest voice within folklore studies for building a relation to American studies. As director of Indiana University's Ph.D.-granting Folklore Institute, Dorson guided many students (he claimed he directed more than 200 dissertations) and devoted many books, especially *American Folklore* (1959), *American Folklore and the Historian* (1971), *America in Legend* (1973), *Man and Beast in American Comic Legend* (1982), and two special issues of the *Journal of the Folklore Institute* (1978, 1980) to the conceptualization of "American folklore" as opposed to "folklore in America." His work followed an agenda set out in "A Theory for American Folklore" presented in 1957 at the first joint meeting of the American Studies Association and the American Folklore Society (see Dorson 1978). He called attention to a unique set of historical forces—exploration and colonization, Revolution and the establishment of a democratic republic, westward movement, immigration, slavery and the Civil War, and industrialization and technology—that "shaped and created new folklore, or new adaptations of old folklore themes" peculiar to American society.

Dorson argued, for example, that the case of Davy Crockett required the perspective of both folklore and American studies. The frontier, he wrote, not only bred "new species of men and new institutions remote from European influences, but it cradled folk heroes and released a flood of legends" (Dorson 1971:32). Other "unique" heroes he described were Mike Fink the Keelboatman, Mose the Bowery B'hoy, Sam Patch the Mill Hand, Yankee Jonathan the Countryman, and Gib Morgan the Oil Field Liar. The folklore of these figures represented a new national consciousness. In *America in Legend,* he fashioned a history of the United States that followed the development of American folklore. The "religious impulse" represented by lore of providences, witchcraft, and judgments characterized the colonial period. The democratic impulse represented by ring-tailed roarers and folk heroes characterized the early national period. In the later na-

tional period, the economic impulse dominated and fostered lore of cowboys, lumberjacks, miners, oil drillers, and railroaders. In the contemporary period, Dorson concentrated on the folklore of youth culture and its "humane impulse."

Besides helping to frame a history or narrative of the United States, the connection of folklore to American studies held a methodological and theoretical significance. In the introductory textbook *Folklore and Folklife* (1972), Dorson divided the folklore of the Old and New Worlds for analytical purposes. Espousing a nationalistic approach, Dorson asserted that "the folklore of each New World country needs to be analyzed in terms of its ethnic-racial and historical ingredients" (Dorson 1972:44). In addition, he emphasized "special historical and environmental factors that have shaped traditions." Accordingly, in the *Handbook of American Folklore* (1983), Dorson further organized folklore in relation to American studies. At the outset are "American Experiences" followed by "American Cultural Myths" and "American Settings." These categories lead to a consideration of "American Entertainments" and "American Forms and Performers" as preludes to the "Interpretation of Research."

Folklore, Dorson and others argued, was especially convincing evidence because it represented deep-seated values and long-standing beliefs held by a society. Alan Dundes, who had studied with Dorson, especially developed the concept of "folk ideas as units of world view" and examined folk ideas basic to American national character. For example, he made a case for the future orientation of Americans as well as their reliance on the number three (Dundes 1980). He called for American studies to be more comparative and cross-cultural in its use of folklore as evidence of national character.

As the historically oriented Constance Rourke had her detractor in Martha Beckwith, so, too, did Dorson have challenges from folklorists seeking less of a nationalistic connection to American studies. Collections such as *Folklore in America* (1966), edited by Tristram Potter Coffin and Hennig Cohen, and *Folklore on the American Land* (1972), edited by Duncan Emrich (1908–1977), emphasized the continuities of folklore in America with sources elsewhere rather than the existence of a distinctive "American folklore." Jan Harold Brunvand's introductory textbook *The Study of American Folklore* (1968) took a middle ground in the debate covering both folklore traditions "found in" America and those "originated" there.

Writing in *American Quarterly,* Richard Bauman and Roger D. Abrahams with Susan Kalcik (1976) reiterated the split between American folklore and folklore in America and surveyed the familiar categories of region, ethnicity, race, occupation, and genre. They closed with attention to "a social interactional perspective, centering around the notion of performance," that they believed was modifying the traditional organizing principles of American folklorists. Influenced by anthropological approaches to linguistics and communication, in this perspective researchers observed varying individual "performances" of traditional behavior influenced by the immediate sociocultural context. The performance-centered approach led to more consideration of the lives of individual

American folk performers and artists from a wide range of backgrounds and the processes for learning and expressing folklore under various American conditions. Thus, Bauman, Abrahams, and Kalcik pointed to studies of biography, repertoire, and performance style of folk performers leading to increased interest in "community, locale, and personal experience as formative influences" in diverse American contexts.

In the attention to community and personal experience, scholars implied a shift in the mission of American studies from one of uncovering, in Rourke's words, the "common storage of experience and character," usually centered on literary arts, to one of seeking to describe American lives and identities, centered on everyday cultural practice. This shift suggested leaving behind the issue of whether American traditions were created or imported (seen as a process, they are both), and moved to the complex use of traditions by and for individuals in various settings that are part of American life. Additionally, inquiry followed the ways that Americans carry multiple identities through their lives and the patterns of forming, expressing, and manipulating those identities. This kind of inquiry opened American Studies to global applications, since these identities are in question when Americans or American expressions enter into surroundings outside the United States.

If there has been a trend since the 1970s, it has been that writing on folklore in American studies appeared more "ethnographic." The basis of fieldwork using interview and observation to describe the communication of symbols among people in contemporary cultural scenes became increasingly important. The ethnographic orientation of folklife and material culture with its uncovering of cultural persistence and diversity was notably added to the folkloristic relation to American studies (Bronner 1992; Glassie 1968). With the addition of folklife and material culture, a rejuvenation of the historical component of tradition was evident, thus forming a new folkloristic synthesis of art, literature, culture, and history (Bronner 1986). Rather than trying to describe America as a whole, scholars turned more attention to describing the complexity of American scenes and people that influence, and have influenced, the sense of the whole and its parts. Thus, studies of Louisiana Cajuns, Pennsylvania Germans, city firefighters, and corporate humorists were all "American studies" that connected to cultural studies in parts of the United States and abroad. Implying the importance of social identities, these studies were complemented by a movement in folklore and folklife research to consider the importance of settings and practices they suggest (schools, workplaces, and leisure spots, for example) within the common scenes of American life.

Particularly in its emphasis on the processes of "tradition" in sociocultural context, folklore and folklife research significantly contributed to American studies by identifying longstanding values and beliefs inherent in socially shared expressions that connect to individual lives as part of the American experience. Judging from the keywords in American studies to describe American life, during the 1970s the anthropological and folkloristic "culture" replaced the humanistic "civilization." The increasing use of folkloristic terms such as "tradition," "narrative," and "folkways" in American studies suggests a more behavioral understanding of American experiences (see Jones 1982). Examining the symbolism of American images and artifacts from wildlife to the New Jersey Turnpike, American-studies scholars have included folklore as a means to analyze the rhetorical meaning of ways that Americans present themselves (Gillespie and Mechling 1987; Gillespie and Rockland 1989).

Another indication of the scholarly appeal of folklore in American studies has been the rise of folklore and folklife courses in American-studies programs and departments from a few in 1971 to 13 percent of all folklore courses offered in the United States in 1986. The previous domination of ballad and song gave way to American folklore and folklife as the dominant folkloristic subject taught in American colleges (26 percent) just behind the introductory course (Baker 1971, 1986). Indiana University allows for a joint Ph.D. degree in folklore and American studies, and George Washington University offers a folklife program within the American studies Ph.D. Other American studies Ph.D.-granting institutions, such as the University of Pennsylvania, the University of New Mexico, Bowling Green State University, and Michigan State University, have strong folkloristic components.

In American studies, folklore studies are used to demonstrate the persistence and diversity of America's social groups and the interplay between folk and popular cultures. In the area of folksong, for example, where previously studies of British-American balladry dominated, significant new research has considered the theme of railroads in American country music (Cohen 1981) and the cultural meanings of blues (Oliver 1984). Ethnic folk music received its due in American studies with studies of klezmer, polka, and Cajun music. In keeping with the trend toward community and personal experience, many of the newer titles use the keyword of "makers" to draw attention to individual performers in the process of cultural production. Other identities such as age, gender, disability, and sexual preference are the subjects of study in other genres such as legend, humor, and proverb. With the influence of folklife study, American-studies scholarship also has studies that explore a number of different expressions, tangible and intangible, in the round of everyday life within communities.

Besides expanding the range of folklore to folklife concerns of material culture and community life, researchers increasingly seek out the multiple cultures that interact in an American commonwealth. American folklorists increasingly ask questions about the influences of tradition on the behaviors and identities that Americans take on in many settings, organizational and physical, in the United States and abroad. The guiding problem for the relation of folklore and folklife research to American studies no longer revolves exclusively around the simplistic opposition of imported and emergent traditions, an opposition that in its formation seeks to create an American exceptionalism. Instead, the main problem statement concerns the rhetorical uses of traditions from various perspectives—the individual, the community, the region, the nation. The goal of interpreting cultural process and social context historically and ethnographically undergirds many new American studies of traditions. The promise of these studies is their inquiry into the adaptive nature of everyday lives and the ways that these lives represent the American experiences.

Simon J. Bronner

References

Baker, Ronald L. 1971. Folklore Courses and Programs in American Colleges and Universities. *Journal of American Folklore* 84:221–229.

———. 1986. Folklore and Folklife Studies in American and Canadian Colleges and Universities. *Journal of American Folklore* 99:50–74.

Bauman, Richard, Roger D. Abrahams, and Susan Kalcik. 1976. American Folklore and American Studies. *American Quarterly* 28:360–77.

Bronner, Simon J., ed. [1985] 1992. *American Material Culture and Folklife.* Logan: Utah State University Press.

———. 1986. *Grasping Things: Folk Material Culture and Mass Society in America.* Lexington: University Press of Kentucky.

———. 1993. Exploring American Traditions: A Survey of Folklore and Folklife Research in American Studies. *American Studies International* 31.

Bronner, Simon J., and Stephen Stern. 1980. American Folklore vs. Folklore in America: A Fixed Fight? *Journal of the Folklore Institute* 17:76–84.

Cohen, Norm. 1981. *Long Steel Rail: The Railroad in American Folksong.* Urbana: University of Illinois Press.

Dorson, Richard M. 1976. *The Birth of American Studies.* Bloomington: Indiana University Press.

———. 1978. Folklore in America vs. American Folklore. *Journal of the Folklore Institute* 15:97–112.

———, ed. 1980. The America Theme in American Folklore. *Journal of the Folklore Institute* 18, nos. 2–3.

Dundes, Alan. 1980. *Interpreting Folklore.* Bloomington: Indiana University Press.

Georges, Robert A., special ed. 1989. Richard M. Dorson's Views and Works: An Assessment. *Journal of Folklore Research* (Special Issue) 26, no. 3.

Gillespie, Angus K., and Jay Mechling, eds. 1987. *American Wildlife in Symbol and Story.* Knoxville: University of Tennessee Press.

Gillespie, Angus K., and Michael Aaron Rockland. 1989. *Looking for America on the New Jersey Turnpike.* New Brunswick, NJ: Rutgers University Press.

Glassie, Henry. 1968. *Pattern in the Material Folk Culture of the Eastern United States.* Philadelphia: University of Pennsylvania Press.

Hufford, Mary. 1991. *American Folklife: A Commonwealth of Cultures.* Washington, DC: American Folklife Center.

Jones, Michael Owen. 1982. Another America: Toward a Behavioral History Based on Folkloristics. *Western Folklore* 41:43–51.

Jordan, Philip D. 1946. Toward a New Folklore. *Minnesota History* 27:273–280.

Nye, Russell B. 1966. *This Almost Chosen People: Essays in the History of American Ideas.* East Lansing: Michigan State University Press.

Oliver, Paul. 1984. *Songsters and Saints: Vocal Traditions on Race Records.* Cambridge: Cambridge University Press.

See also Academic Programs in Folklore; Canadian Studies and Folklore

Anansi

Also "Ananse," "Anancy," and "Nansi," the spider trickster of West and Central Africa. Anansi is so popular a character in this great body of tales that, even when he does not appear, they are called *Anansesem* (Ananse stories) by the Akan-speakers of Ghana and the Côte d'Ivoire. Although Anansi usually has spider characteristics, to make matters even more complicated for scholars he can also turn into a human, and conversely, other animals such as a rabbit, a fox, and a hare sometimes take over his role in popular stories. Indeed, he was first known to most European Americans as the trickster Brer Rabbit in Joel Chandler Harris' 19th-century literary retellings of African (and non-African) Uncle Remus stories. Although Anansi stories and other African tales have been collected and published since the first quarter of the 19th century, they reached a wider non-African audience through Cronise and Ward's *Cunny Rabbit, Mr. Spider, and the Other Beef* (1903), Beckwith's *Jamaica Anansi Stories* (1924), and Rattray's comprehensive collection, *Akan-Ashanti Folk-Tales* (1930).

Known from Senegal to Angola in Africa, and throughout the African Diaspora in the Caribbean, northern South America, and the United States, Anansi is 'Ti Malice in Haiti, Boy Nasty and B'Rabby in the Bahamas, Nansi in Curaçao, Aunt Nancy and Miss Nancy on the Carolina/Georgia Coast, and he can be a girl, a boy, or an old man or woman rather than a spider. In the Anglophone Caribbean, particularly Jamaica and Trinidad, his stories are often told as an entertainment during the overnight rituals associated with wakes for the dead; in Suriname, they are told only at night during wakes.

Most commonly, Anansi is a wily, cunning spider with human abilities such as speech, who uses his insect characteristics such as his sticky web, his eight feet, and his ability to descend rapidly from a ceiling, to attain his goals or save his life. He plots and plans, using every kind of clever and amoral duplicity to satisfy his greed, but he is sometimes outwitted or bested by other animals. Some stories explain how spiders were created, while others feature Anansi as a kind of culture hero who steals the sun for humankind and tricks the sky god into giving him these stories.

One of the most famous Anansi stories is how he tricked Tiger through cajolery, while pretending to be ill and weak, into letting him ride him complete with saddle, bridle, and whip. In another, a farmer catches thieving Anansi by putting a tar baby, or gumdoll, in his field. When the doll does not answer Anansi's greeting, he slaps it and his hand sticks, then he kicks it when it won't release his hand, so when the farmer catches him, he beats him flat, thus explaining how spiders came to be flat. Although many of the tales are adult in content, and far from edifying in their trickery, their tremendous range of character and action explains why they have kept their appeal and are constantly being "retold" by writers of children's books. Even so, African American artist John Biggers, in *Ananse: The Web of Life in Africa* (1962), sees Ananse as depicting ". . . every kind of hero. There is an Ananse story for every situation in life. God gave Ananse the meaning of order."

Daniel J. Crowley

References

Bascom, William. 1992. *African Folktales in the New World.* Bloomington: Indiana University Press.

Anecdote

Single-episode, believed folk narrative, especially one centering on a particular individual. The word originally meant "things unpublished or secret" and referred to the actions and sayings of famous people that were not included in their official biographies. Anecdotes often focus on things said in a particularly witty or effective way, such as the line attributed to British Prime Minister Winston Churchill when told by a female member of Parliament that, if he were her husband, she would poison his tea. "Madam," he is said to have answered, "if I were your husband I would drink it." As this example illustrates, anecdotes are typically humorous, but they should be distinguished from jokes, which are understood to be fictive by their tellers and hearers. In effect, anecdotes are to legends as jokes are to folktales, shortened or crystallized equivalents; unlike many legends, however, they do not involve the supernatural.

The folk anecdote has parallels in the written literary tradition that go back at least to the great 14th-century English anthology of illustrative stories of the Roman emperors, called the *Gesta Romanorum,* which was printed in Latin. Such "ana," or published collections of anecdotes, grew to great popularity in 17th- and 18th-century Europe, where they focused primarily on famous living personalities rather than historical ones.

The usual subject matter of serious anecdotal narratives, whether folk or published, is revealed in the headings Stith Thompson's *Motif Index of Folk-Literature* (1955–1958) gives for the genre—social types and relationships, wise and unwise conduct, and rewards and punishments. The subject matter of humorous anecdotes includes such things as great lies, ludicrous mistakes, escapes, exaggerations, tricks, practical jokes, and especially the well-put or stinging verbal comebacks of clever people.

While anecdotes often concern famous individuals—generals, politicians, kings, actors, and the like—some ordinary individuals gain folk fame based solely on their sayings and deeds that generate anecdotes among their group. The exploits of one Charlie Ferg, for example, which constitute a local genre of folklore in southwest Wisconsin's Ocooch Mountains, are basically a set of this ne'er-do-well's one-line responses to judgments against him by community moralists. In one narrative, Charlie stumbled by a group of church members on his way home from a tavern one night, and a deacon asked him if he had found Jesus. "Why no, Deacon," he replied, "I didn't know he was lost!"

Besides their entertainment value, both folk and literary anecdotes of this type often serve moral purposes as well, as the following narrative about Thomas Jefferson shows. It was collected by Works Progress Administration (WPA) workers in Virginia in the 1930s: "Jefferson with one of his friends was in a town near Washington while he was president and met an old colored an' weather-beaten slave, who bowed nearly to his knees to him. The President in turn bowed to him and spoke kindly to him and drew him into conversation. He saw that the military officer with him did not like the idea of his talking to the old negro so kindly, so he said 'Shame on you my man, I would not want an aged slave to have more manners than I. And furthermore, he was more polite to me than you are to disapprove of my behavior.'" Testimony to the folk nature of this anecdote is the fact that it is printed in Booker T. Washington's *Up from Slavery* attributed to George Washington and in Benjamin A. Botkin's *Treasury of Southern Folklore* (1949) attributed to Robert E. Lee. While, as this indicates, anecdotal narratives do float, they tend to attach themselves to individuals of similar characteristics, such as the "great gentlemen" named above, or to men such as Albert Einstein and Bertrand Russell as representing the type of "the genius." Both men are said to have been approached by beautiful women to have sex with them—to bear a child with "my body and your brains." Each man is said to have replied, "What if [it] turns out the other way around?"

There are vast numbers of folk, popular, and literary anecdotes in circulation. Perhaps the anecdote is such an active genre of narrative in American society because of its brevity and focus on individual personality, both of which are amenable features to contemporary culture.

Thomas E. Barden

References

Barden, Thomas E., ed. 1991. *Virginia Folk Legends.* Charlottesville: University of Virginia Press.
Botkin, Benjamin A., ed. 1949. *Treasury of Southern Folklore.* New York: Crown.
Leary, James, ed. 1991. *Midwestern Folk Humor.* Little Rock, AR: August House.

See also Local-Character Anecdote

Anglo Americans

Arguably the largest and most influential group of Americans sharing an ethnic heritage, yet for that very reason the least self-identified and least likely to be perceived as an ethnic group. The predominance of the English among the earliest American settlers; the consequent distance in time between many contemporary English-surnamed Americans and their original English emigrant ancestors; the extensive adoption and adaptation of English beliefs, practices, institutions, and language in the United States; enmity between Great Britain and America throughout the 19th century; and the universal tendency of dominant social groups to perceive themselves as the norm and only others as "ethnic" have all militated against identification of Anglo Americans as a culturally distinct group within American society. Americans of English descent have more cultural sanction than persons of other backgrounds to consider themselves simply "American" rather than "Anglo American." Similarly, English folkways that have survived in the United States have been reidentified as American rather than English.

In comparison to their likely numbers by some measures, Anglo Americans are under-represented as a self-identified ethnic group. Indeed, they are nearly invisible in the United States today. Ascertaining the size of any ethnic population is necessarily problematic and the process is especially complex in a country like the United States where the philosophy of the melting pot (although periodically challenged by xenophobia and prejudice) has made intermarriage among the many different emigrant groups relatively easy, so most citizens trace a multi-ethnic ancestry. More importantly, in any country, ostensibly objective measures like the sources of surnames or even the national origin of ancestors (if discoverable) may not correspond with the determinative factor, the individual's self-identification as a member of a particular group. Individuals who identify themselves as members of an ethnic group must perceive that this will confer benefits that will more than compensate for the disadvantages of being seen by others as "ethnic," that is, non-mainstream.

For persons of English descent in the United States, except for very recent arrivals, there is and has been little need or reward for identifying oneself as Anglo American. In the 1990 Census, respondents were asked to report the ancestry group or groups with which they most closely identified. Out of the total U.S. population of 248,709,873, 32.7 million people claimed English ancestry (13%), the third largest group after German: 57.9 million (23%), and Irish: 38.7 million (15.5%). Another 12.4 million (5%) said their ancestry was "American." Given the preponderance of the English among early emigrants and thus among the longest-settled American families and the preponderance of English surnames in many parts of the country, it appears that Americans with English ancestry are less likely to see that as a significant part of their current identity than do those with ancestral connections to other nationalities. In folklore fieldwork, researchers commonly find that persons asked to identify their ethnic heritage will name other ancestry (regardless of the extent to which they actually retain the traditional practices of a particular ethnic group), but if their background is mostly English (or to a lesser extent from the rest of the British Isles) they will label themselves "plain white American."

During the 17th century English emigrants formed the great majority of arrivals in the American colonies. Protestant dissenters fled the religious persecution that was not legally rescinded in England until 1689. In the southern colonies, farm laborers, domestic servants, and artisans seeking to improve their fortunes could make a start in the new world without capital by going into indentured service. Not until the 1680s did increased importation of African slaves displace English emigrants for plantation work. During the 18th century, the balance of emigration shifted so that the number of French, Germans, Scots, and Scotch-Irish arriving in the colonies together exceeded the number of new English arrivals. Population grew fastest during this period in the middle colonies and by the end of the colonial period more than half the inhabitants of Pennsylvania were not of English birth, but in most areas the English still formed between 60 percent and 80 percent of the white population. In the course of one hundred and seventy years of colonial rule the English language as well as many aspects of English common law, the tradition of representative government, the acceptance of multiple Protestant sects, and English trade practices became firmly ensconced. Despite modifications required by new circumstances, the heritage of the majority of inhabitants and the continued colonial linkages with Great Britain assured the establishment of an essentially English culture.

The struggle for American independence, the Revolutionary War, and the bitter War of 1812 not only severed the legal connection between mother and daughter countries, but ushered in a century of enmity and rivalry between the United States and Britain. It was only during World War II that the special relationship between the two countries, which now feels timeless and inevitable, was reestablished. Alexis de Toqueville, chronicling the unique character of Americans and their democratic experiment, remarked that it was difficult to imagine a more intense hatred than that of Americans for England. The similarity of worldview and shared cultural heritage remained, but the 19th century was the time in which Americans set out to forge a separate cultural identity. Americans envied English eminence both in commerce and in culture and desired to supplant their mother/rival in both. In the realm of commerce, England could and did place obstacles in America's path. While resenting the interference, American business sought its own success by emulating the English model and establishing duplicate institutions. In the realm of culture, in contrast, Americans rejected the English heritage. "Our day of dependence, our long apprenticeship to the learning of other lands, draws to a close," wrote Ralph Waldo Emerson in "The American Scholar" (1837). And Walt Whitman, in the 1855 Preface to *Leaves of Grass,* predicted that America would inspire new poets to create a new and superior literature, neither partisan nor nationalistic nor parochial, but built on healthy, natural models. Developments in the course of the century fostered general awareness of a distinct American language and a distinct American brand of humor as well as a desire not only to create arts to represent the American landscape and society but to do so in a distinct and appropriate American style (see Spencer 1957 and Crapol 1973).

In such a climate, American citizens of English ancestry tended to jettison any lingering sense of ethnic affiliation and to identify themselves as purely "American" and their accomplishments as contributions to American society. Entries in

Rebecca King Jones, noted for singing a fine version of the English ballad "Barbara Allen." Crab Tree Creek, Piedmont region, North Carolina, 1941. Photo Frank Warner. American Folklife Center.

this volume on other American ethnic groups enumerate the names of group members who played important roles in the development of American society. The same might be done for Anglo Americans, from the scholars of early New England to the Founding Fathers to the most influential authors of the new American literature to 19th-century industrialists and

Suffragists, except that all of these consciously acted not as members of an ethnic subgroup, not as persons of English extraction, but as Americans centrally defining what America and Americans should be.

The hatred of England that flourished during the 19th century was focused, however, on the British government and

British commercial interests. Individual English men and women who emigrated to the U.S. in several economically-influenced waves were rarely penalized or judged too harshly because of their place of origin. Commonality of language, religion, customs, and institutions made for ease of contact and rapid acceptance and intermarriage between English emigrants and native-born Americans. In rural areas in the Midwest, English colonies and churches rarely survived with that identity for more than a generation or two unless there was a substantial influx of additional English people to the same area. Fast-growing western cities offered the English opportunities for upward mobility that also militated against ethnic organizing. In eastern cities St. George's Societies were longer-lived, but were relatively uninfluential as well as limited to a small elite. Only in the mining and industrial districts of the East were the English successful in founding institutions (often to distinguish themselves from the Irish), but these trade unions, cooperatives, and lodges were inherently more class- than ethnicity-based, so those that throve quickly lost their all-English character. English workers also were more likely than other emigrants to move up in the class hierarchy, which further discouraged the maintenance of strong ethnic ties. By the end of the century the English had a far less organized social institutional life than the other large emigrant groups of the time, the Irish and Germans (see Erickson 1972 and 1980).

Along with more formal institutions like English legal practices, many English crafts and folkways were transported to this country and many survive. Those that have been retained as mainstream traditions, however, have mostly been stripped of their ethnic associations. Who now recalls that Christmas carolling was originally an English practice? Even in rural communities where more elements of traditional English culture were preserved for longer, practitioners of the traditional arts came to see them as American after a few generations. Folklore scholars may recognize a North Carolina version of "Barbara Allen" as an originally English text and tune given a few American details, but neither the singer from whom it was collected nor the general public with whom it has been popularized by revivalist performers is likely to think of it as anything but American. The same can be said for many ballads, songs, and fiddle tunes from the British Isles, as well as Jack Tales, quilting techniques, split white oak basketry, and the contra dancing developed from English country dancing. Contemporary folklore theory would argue that a practice adapted and perpetuated in a new country should be regarded as a part of the folklore of that country rather than only of the source country. Customs from other sources have also undergone a similar Americanization process: consider the African banjo and the German Christmas tree. Nevertheless, English customs and crafts seem most readily detached from their origins, perhaps because they are associated instead with an internal pseudo-ethnic group, Appalachian people.

In the late 19th and early 20th centuries, there was a resurgence of interest among middle- and upper-class Americans in the preservation of English bloodlines and old English traditions in the United States and an interest in Appalachia as a repository of both. This concern was constructed, however, so as to emphasize the supposed superiority of the English heritage (social and genetic) with which most "mainstream" Americans would implicitly identify themselves without explicitly connecting the elite, professional, and business classes of the North and Midwest with poor Appalachian mountaineers nor in any sense classifying the bulk of Americans of English descent as an Anglo American ethnic group equivalent to other ethnics. As western European emigration slowed and increasing numbers of poor immigrants from eastern and southern Europe arrived in the United States toward the end of the 19th century, xenophobic and racist elements complained of the "pollution" of the American genetic pool and advocated the uplift and incorporation of Appalachian people because they could supply a fresh stream of citizens of "the very best American type," (that is, of Anglo-Saxon genetic heritage).

A number of the philanthropic efforts aimed at improving the lot of Appalachian people were based on the assumption that these people (until touched by recent modern influences) had retained an essentially old English culture and would thrive if they could be restored as an Anglo American folk enclave. Appalachian scholars now see these schemes as misguided, especially to the extent that they sought to "return" mountain inhabitants to a mythical simple, wholesome, pre-industrial English rural lifestyle. Attempts to get contemporary mountaineers to carve and weave and dance English ritual dances and sing only the old songs impeded the people's own efforts to acquire the skills necessary to advance in a changing marketplace. This construction of events in the mountains also obscured political awareness that the supposed "corruption" of a rural folk by modern culture was a less serious problem than the depredations of huge timber and mining companies that exploited local resources without regard for the well-being of the inhabitants. While the antique quality of Appalachian culture was celebrated, those who made a good living from the culture were the musicians who parlayed their skills into the uniquely American form now known as Country Music (see Whisnant 1983).

The nascent field of American folklore study played a part in the identification and paradoxical definition of Anglo American culture in the late 19th century. The English ballad scholar Cecil Sharp and others following his lead discovered remnants of English traditional music in the Appalachians, thereby bolstering the public sense that this was a bastion of Anglo American culture. At the same time, folklorists drew a distinction between English folklore in America and folklore from other sources. The lead article in the first issue of the *Journal of American Folklore* (1888) advocated:

The collection of the fast-vanishing remains of Folk-Lore in America, namely:
(a) Relics of Old English Folk-Lore (ballads, tales, superstitions, dialect, etc.).
(b) Lore of Negroes in the Southern States of the Union.

(c) Lore of the Indian Tribes of North America (myths, tales, etc.).

(d) Lore of French Canada, Mexico, etc.

It was entirely in keeping with the theories of the day to regard folklore as something produced only in Europe or only by peasants and thus as something that existed in America only in the form of survivals that could not last. Notably, however, the *JAF* statement of purpose identifies African Americans, Native Americans, French Canadian Americans and Mexican Americans as peoples possessing as a group their own proper (and living) lore. In contrast, Anglo Americans are not named and "Relics of Old English Folk-Lore" are presented as existing entirely independently of any folk community. There might be English lore existing among the general population, but that did not make these people (unless they were Appalachian mountaineers) Anglo American ethnics or Anglo American folk.

One should also note that in practice the term "Anglo American" is not necessarily restricted to persons of English descent. In general usage and even in scholarly usage it is often employed as a more euphonious alternative to "British American." Thus "Anglo American folksongs" includes songs of Scottish and possibly Irish origin. Likewise works on the migration of English, Scots, Irish, and Scotch Irish settlers into the Appalachian region sometimes differentiate the streams but often lump the groups as Anglo American. In Texas and the Hispanic Southwest, the abbreviated version, "Anglo," is applied to indicate any person of other than Hispanic descent and may thus be used to refer not only to European Americans of other than English descent, but also to African Americans.

The invisibility of Anglo Americans is a complex political and historical phenomenon, resting equally on the predominance of English cultural influences in the formative years of the nation, the need of the daughter country to create a separate identity from her mother, and the tendency of dominant groups to see themselves as unmarked and others as ethnic. Even today, with the upsurge of ethnic pride movements and the institutionalization of anti-racist practices, a curious relation to the English component of our national heritage persists. Not only in Canada, where the linkages to English culture are more recent and obvious (see Greenhill 1994), but also in the United States, the mainstream implicit assumption of superiority rests to a considerable, if diminishing, extent on identification with the original English cultural and genetic heritage, while this identification must be erased or denied and people of English background must be cast as non-ethnic to preserve their rights to dominate the society.

Patricia E. Sawin

References

Crapol, Edward P. 1973. *America for Americans: Economic Nationalism and Anglophobia in the Late Nineteenth Century.* Westport, CT, and London: Greenwood Press.

Erickson, Charlotte J. 1972. *Invisible Immigrants: The Adaptation of English and Scottish Immigrants in Nineteenth-Century America.* Coral Gables, FL: University of Miami Press.

———. 1980. English. In *Harvard Encyclopedia of American Ethnic Groups.* Cambridge, MA: Harvard University Press, pp. 319–336.

Greenhill, Pauline. 1994. *Ethnicity in the Mainstream: Three Studies of English Canadian Culture in Ontario.* Montreal & Kingston, London, Buffalo: McGill-Queen's University Press.

Reddy, David, Riki Saltzman, Bob Stone, and Debbie Fant. 1991. "Rediscoveries": African-American and Anglo-Celtic-American Traditions in Florida. In *Thirty-Ninth Annual Florida Folklife Festival.* Bureau of Florida Folklife Programs, pp. 6–10.

Spencer, Benjamin T. 1957. *The Quest for Nationality: An American Literary Campaign.* Syracuse, NY: Syracuse University Press.

U.S. Department of Commerce, Economics, and Statistics Administration, Bureau of the Census. 1993. *Statistical Abstract of the United States 1993: The National Data Book,* 113th ed.

Whisnant, David E. 1983. *All That Is Native and Fine: The Politics of Culture in an American Region.* Chapel Hill: University of North Carolina Press.

See also Appalachia; Ethnic Folklore; Irish Americans; Scottish Americans; Welsh Americans

Animals

Fauna of North America and their related lore. At every level of American culture, from the casual joke or Saturday morning cartoon to the serious novel or scientific monograph, animals—especially wild animals—have always exerted a special imaginative appeal. Scholarly work by American folklorists demonstrates that, throughout our history, symbolic uses of distinctively American wild animals have expressed national attitudes about such crucial matters as politics, race, gender, sex, and danger.

The folkloristic sources of the ideas, images, and stories about wild animals are many, but we may distinguish seven types: conversational genres, oral narratives, children's literature, popular culture, performances, elite culture, and scientific writing.

First are the shorter conversational genres most central to our commonsense knowledge of the world. These are the jokes, proverbs, riddles, superstitions, and so on that constitute much of the everyday discourse by Americans about wild animals. Embedded in and expressed by these genres are "folk ideas," the basic units of belief about objects in the world. For example, jokes about armadillos often involve people unwittingly eating them; the underlying idea is that armadillos are not edible. Likewise, jokes about alligators often involve people being eaten by them; the underlying idea is that alligators are dangerous. Proverbial expressions, including the humorous versions such as "It's hard to soar with eagles when you work with turkeys" or ". . . up to your ass in alligators," similarly encode metaphorical connections between folk ideas about animals and human social situations.

Also a folk genre is oral narrative, the second source of ideas about wild animals in America. This genre includes the true "stories" people pass on to explain to one another the meaning of a wild animal. It is also the category that has been treated to the most folklore scholarship. Myths are the longest genres of this sort, and there are many Native American myths involving such animals as the coyote, armadillo, or bear. For some animals, there exist folktales from Native American, African American, and European traditions. We also find "encounter stories" (relating the narrator's encounter with a wild animal) among amateurs and professionals alike. A park ranger is as likely to have a repertoire of stories as is a tourist-attraction announcer or a hunter holding forth in a local tavern.

The third source of ideas about wild animals is children's literature, the printed stories and accompanying illustrations that provide a repertoire of ideas and images for making sense of all sorts of animals. Some children's literature is little more than a printed version of the traditional oral narratives, and some is original. Authors of children's books seem especially disposed to use animal characters in lieu of human ones. Like the folk genres, this written, visual source of ideas is powerful because its influence begins so early in the creation of the child's map of the everyday world. It is powerful, too, because of its visual component, the illustrations accompanying the children's stories. All the more powerful is the transformation of animal illustrations into three-dimensional toys, such as the Teddy Bear or Winnie-the-Pooh. Thus, a persistent problem for the rangers at Yosemite and Yellowstone National Parks is that Americans tend to approach real bears as if they were the storybook kind. Rangers refer to this phenomenon as "the Bambi complex"—which suggests the fourth main source of ideas about wild animals.

Popular culture (also known as mass-mediated culture or commercial culture) is an increasingly important locus of such ideas and images. Included in this category are postcards, souvenirs, cartoons, comics, television commercials, print advertising, theatrical films, and mass-circulation magazines. Popular culture provides a repertoire of stories and images accessible to a wide audience, crossing gender, ethnic, and social-class divisions. Popular materials from commercial culture can be found in abundance from the Warner Brothers cartoon character Wile E. Coyote to advertisements for Wild Turkey bourbon to a theatrical film like *Alligator* (1980).

The fifth source of ideas, images, and stories is the performances that involve somehow an interpretation of a wild animal. These are the participatory drama-like events that include tourist attractions, festivals, museum and zoo programs, hunting expeditions, cooking and foodway events, and the like. Oldest in this category are the Native American performance rituals and dances that involve the armadillo, the coyote, the bear, and the rattlesnake. The snake handling in certain religious communities is a related phenomenon.

The sixth source of our notions about animals is elite culture, the body of literature and fine arts that is the usual subject matter of humanistic study. Fine painting, poetry, novels, and short stories in America often feature wild animals as central symbols in the imaginative landscape of their fictive worlds. But even here folk ideas are often present, though recast in more elegant language. Herman Melville's white whale and William Faulkner's bear are only the best known cases. Poets Gary Snyder and Simon Ortiz find the coyote an especially attractive figure, and novelist Thomas Pynchon uses the alligators-in-the-sewers legend for his own artistic purposes in his novel *V.* In American elite art, we can trace the iconography of American wildlife from the earliest European renditions through the likes of John James Audubon and John Singer Sargent up to the present.

It will surprise some to learn that scientific discourse is the seventh source of American ideas about wild animals. So accustomed are we to think of scientific writing as "fact," opposed to folk and popular "fiction," that we fail to appreciate how cultural is the history of American scientific writing about wild animals. Some scientific writing is the source of, or at least perpetuates, the oldest folk ideas about animals, and, even when a scientific treatise takes space in its historical account to "debunk" the "myths and fallacies" about the animal, the author is acknowledging tacitly that the starting point for American understanding of the beast is a repertoire of folk and popular beliefs concerning it.

Angus Kress Gillespie

References

Bateson, Gregory. 1979. *Mind and Nature: A Necessary Unity.* New York: Dutton.

Douglass, Mary. 1982. *Natural Symbols: Explorations in Cosmology.* New York: Pantheon.

Gillespie, Angus Kress, and Jay Mechling, eds. 1987. *American Wildlife in Symbol and Story.* Knoxville: University of Tennessee Press.

Wilson, David Scofield. 1978. *In the Presence of Nature.* Amherst: University of Massachusetts Press.

See also Catfish; Coyote; Fable; Fishing (Commercial); Fishing (Sport); Groundhog Day; Hunting; Jackalope; Opossum; Trapping

Anniversaries

Annual rites of passage celebrated privately or publicly according to cultural preferences. Anniversaries represent cyclical time measurement; the most common anniversaries are wedding and birthday celebrations and commemorations of important historic dates, especially centennials of significant events.

Wedding anniversaries are traditionally recognized with gifts of flowers and special items. Popular beliefs endorse specific gifts to bring good luck according to how many years the couple has been married. Materials such as metals and minerals symbolize the couple's marriage commitment in terms of years. Following German tradition, these anniversaries are frequently referred to by the gift given, such as "silver anniversary."

The commonly accepted anniversary gifts for significant

anniversaries are these: one year, paper; five years, wood; ten years, tin; fifteen years, crystal; twenty years, china; twenty-five years, silver; thirty years, pearl or ivory; thirty-five years, coral; forty years, ruby; forty-five years, sapphire; fifty years, gold; fifty-five years, emerald; sixty and seventy-five years, diamond.

The most prominent anniversaries celebrated include the silver, golden, and diamond weddings. Less significant anniversaries also have prescribed gifts, although these are infrequently observed. They include, two years, cotton; three years, leather or muslin; four years, silk; six years, iron; seven years, copper or wool; eight years, electrical appliances; and nine years, pottery.

Anniversary gifts may be practical, luxurious, and even silly variations of the prescribed anniversary motifs. Any items composed of the material for the designated anniversary, such as clothing, tools, toys, or other household goods, are given. Most couples celebrate anniversaries of their nuptials privately, but anniversaries of royal and celebrity couples often receive great publicity and ceremony with political overtones.

Additional anniversary traditions include burning a tall, white memory candle that smells like lily of the valley, a traditional wedding flower. Presented at the wedding reception, a candle burned only annually may last through the golden anniversary. Some women display or wear their wedding gowns at anniversary parties, and the original wedding party and guests may be invited to attend, along with the official who performed the ceremony. Portions of the wedding cake are often saved to eat at anniversary parties (and at christenings) to symbolize that the marriage has lasted and matured.

Birthday anniversaries are celebrated annually for children with parties, presents, and games. Traditions such as spanking once for each year and an extra pat to grow on as well as pinch day, kiss day, and the like are observed. Elaborate birthday celebrations are staged for significant stages of maturity, such as turning twenty-one, reaching full adulthood, or forty years of age, marking the beginning of middle age.

Anniversaries of historic events, usually commemorating military battles, tend to generate patriotic traditions, including the placement of flags in significant locations, such as on graves for Decoration Day. These anniversaries are also occasions for the preservation of historic sites, the commercialization of the event with commemorative items, or the reiteration of folklore glorifying national heroes like George Washington or Abraham Lincoln.

Anniversaries of death dates are sometimes mentioned in commemorative newspaper ads, and they enter modern folk culture with the common tales of "The Vanishing Hitchhiker," often a young woman picked up near a cemetery, who is attempting to return home on the anniversary of her death.

Elizabeth D. Schafer

References

Baker, Margaret. 1977. *Wedding Customs and Folklore.* Vancouver: David and Charles.

Johnston, William M. 1991. *Celebrations: The Cult of Anniversaries in Europe and the United States Today.* New Brunswick, NJ, and London: Transaction Publishers.

See also Birthdays

Anthropological Approach

Folklore as anthropologists have studied it—as part of culture. In the 19th century, when folklore was established as a subject worthy of investigation, the orientation of American scholars to its study was greatly influenced by the presence of the American Indian. The collection of American Indian mythology was deemed a proper enterprise for those interested in folklore. On the Continent, the study of folklore was defined as the study of the peasant populations of Europe, while the study of American Indians or other non-European peoples, who were classified as savages or primitives, was considered to be the domain of the ethnologists. The differing orientation was critical for the development of American folklore scholarship since it designated the study of native peoples as a suitable subject for folklore as well as for anthropology.

American anthropologists, in carving out their discipline, developed a more restricted definition of folklore than did scholars in literature, but a more inclusive view of the folk. Folklore was given a specific place within anthropology, that of oral literature. Anthropologists, who traditionally worked in cultures without writing, could not designate folklore as that which was oral, since that would include *all* aspects of culture. As Erminie Voegelin elaborated the point, orally transmitted prose and verse forms were "myths and tales, jests and anecdotes, dramas and dramatic dialogues, prayers and formulas, speeches, puns, riddles, proverbs, and song and chant texts" (Voegelin, 1949–1950:403). William R. Bascom simply designated the same area as "verbal art" (Bascom 1955). The folk could be Euro-American, African American, or Native American, though the anthropological folklorist usually studied the latter to the exclusion of the two former groups. Significantly, the anthropological folklorists, merely by their choice of the group to be studied, had succeeded in broadening the concept of "folk" to include a non-European component.

The anthropological folklorists studied folklore as a part of culture—a way of learning more about the culture history, as with Franz Boas, or a way of learning more about the patterns of culture, as with Ruth Benedict. For the anthropological folklorists, the questions were not directed to folklore per se, but rather to culture: What is the nature of culture? and How is this reflected in the folklore?

Deemed crucial for the anthropological folklorists was the collection of detailed narrative texts. The goal was twofold: first, to make an accurate record of the language; and, second, to study the culture as it was reflected in the narratives. Boas' work on Northwest Coast Indian cultures is an example. In *Chinook Texts* (1894), *Tsimshian Mythology* (1916), *Kutenai Tales* (1917), and *Kwakiutl Culture as Reflected in Mythology* (1935), Boas recorded the narratives phonetically in the native language, and translated them interlineally. The texts were, as Gladys Reichard remarked, "Boas' self-built monument."

The anthropological folklorists were likely to compile their material by focusing either on a single culture or on several cultures. They might also study a single aspect of folklore as it was manifested in several cultures. Elsie Clews Parsons'

Pueblo Religion (1939) and Benedict's "The Concept of the Guardian Spirit in North America" (1923) exemplify this comparative approach. On occasion, the anthropological folklorist focused on a genre of folklore. For example, Paul Radin wrote *The Trickster: A Study in American Indian Mythology* (1955), and Benedict produced two volumes on *Zuñi Mythology* (1935). However, Radin's and Benedict's works were not intended as investigations of folklore genres—a concept that was not used by the anthropological folklorists—but rather as explorations in cultural patterning.

The emphasis on cultural patterns was critical for the shift that took place in American anthropology, a shift from an earlier focus on detailed description to a focus on theme and meaning. Thus, folklore manifested certain themes that resonated in other areas of culture as well. In Benedicts' terms, it was part of the personality of the culture. Benedict, Radin, and Melville Jacobs were the innovators in this approach to folklore. Their contributions had an impact that continues to reverberate in folklore theory. The three were characterized by Robert H. Lowie as scholars of folklore who were "not averse to psychoanalytic interpretation" (Lowie 1960:467). Together they sparked the psychological interpretation of folklore. This innovation in folklore studies combined three approaches: the psychological, the cultural, and the folkloristic.

Rosemary Lévy Zumwalt

References

Bascom, William R. 1955. Verbal Art. *Journal of American Folklore* 68:245–252.

Dundes, Alan. 1966. The American Concept of Folklore. *Journal of the Folklore Institute* 3:226–249.

Lowie, Robert H. 1960. Contemporary Trends in American Cultural Anthropology. In *Selected Papers in Anthropology*, ed. Cora du Bois. Berkeley: University of California Press, pp. 461–471.

Reichard, Gladys. 1943. Franz Boas and Folklore. In *Franz Boas, 1858–1942*, ed. A.L. Kroeber. Memoirs of the American Anthropological Association, No. 61. Menasha, WI: American Anthropological Association, pp. 52–57.

Voegelin, Erminie. 1949–1950. Folklore. In *Funk and Wagnalls Standard Dictionary of Folklore, Mythology, and Legend*, ed. Maria Leach. New York: Funk and Wagnalls.

Zumwalt, Rosemary Lévy. 1988. *American Folklore Scholarship: A Dialogue of Dissent*. Bloomington: Indiana University Press.

See also American Folklore Scholarship: The Early Years; Contextual Approach; Functionalism; Psychology and Folklore; Sociological Approach

Anti-Legend

A term proposed in 1930 by Andre Jolles in his book *Einfache Formen* and brought into use in American folklore scholarship by Linda Dégh. In her examination of the processes of legend formation, Dégh utilized the metaphor of a conduit. Within a network of legend tellers, what she called the "legend conduit" circulates numerous oral versions of a given legend. Having determined that narrators will hold an array of attitudes ranging from acceptance through skepticism to outright opposition, she argues that those at the negative end of the spectrum are likely to transform the story into an anti-legend; that is, they will attempt to undermine the credibility of the story in order to impugn its veracity and to mock those who might be inclined to find the story worthy of retelling as true. Tactics used include rationalizations, alternative explanations, and the citation of supposed higher authorities. A committed narrator's judgment might even be questioned, and his or her belief might be mocked as silly superstition.

Since humor is one of the most effective means of challenging a fervent belief, some legend narratives are transformed into jokes or comical narratives. Often these stories, resembling catch tales or shaggy-dog stories, will turn on a surprise ending that catches the listener off guard. Having lured listeners into the story by the presentation of a series of plausible situations or credible details, in the end the "punch line," frequently a pun or a parody of a well-known saying, reveals that the whole narrative was fallacious and the listener an unsuspecting dupe. For example, a story of an encounter with a ghostly revenant that pursues the narrator as he or she attempts an escape might conclude at the seemingly most harrowing moment with the eerie creature grabbing its victim only to say: "Tag you're it." Or a mysterious voice crying out in mournful tones: "One black eye" might be stopped with the smart-aleck retort: "You better shut up or you'll have *two* black eyes." The warnings offered by such tales are manifold; listeners are not only informed that the veracity of a particular belief (ghostly or spirit apparitions) is suspect, but they are further encouraged to dismiss legends altogether as foolish tales. The anti-legend, then, challenges both legend content and the social significance of the narrative genre as well. The efficacy of such attempts to overturn entrenched beliefs is questionable. The public appetite for tales of mysterious apparitions, strange voices in the night, and other baffling events continues to be insatiable. Indeed, many of these tales are essentially anti-legends minus the comical ending. Within the flow of the legend conduit, an anti-legend can readily be transformed into a belief tale.

John Michael Vlach

References

Dégh, Linda, and Andrew Vazsonyi. 1971. Legend and Belief. *Genre* 4:281–304.

Vlach, John Michael. 1971. One Black Eye and Other Horrors: The Case for the Humorous Anti-Legend. *Indiana Folklore* 4:95–140.

See also Ghost Stories

Appalachia

Physiographic region embracing West Virginia and parts of eighteen other Eastern and Southern states. Appalachia, in cultural history, includes three hundred counties covering most of West Virginia and the Blue Ridge and parts of Alabama, Georgia, Kentucky, Tennessee, Maryland, North and South Carolina, and Virginia. The region is also called the Southern Highlands, the Upland South, and (in colonial history), the Back-country. Richard M. Dorson called Appalachia "folklore's natural habitat." "Of all of the distinctive regions in the United States," he wrote, "the one most customarily linked with folklore is the southern Appalachians." The idea that Appalachia is a reservoir of American folk culture originated with the local-color movement of travel and fiction writers of the late 19th century and persisted through the development of folklife studies as a professional enterprise. By the close of the 20th century, the centrality of Appalachia in the definition and study of folklife had receded, but folklife forms still provide icons that set apart the region from other parts of the United States. Lacking conventional political boundaries and regionwide economic or social institutions of the sort that help define regions such as New England or the West, Midwest, or South, Appalachia is nearly always represented in popular culture by some sort of reference to folklife, usually folk music or crafts.

Nineteenth-century writers created an inventory of cultural expression and deviant behaviors that signified Appalachian "otherness" to metropolitan audiences; these included speech and dialect, log architecture, folk music and dance, handicrafts, woodcraft, superstitions and religious practices, moonshining, illiteracy, and a reliance on "folk justice," most dramatically in a series of "mountain feuds" given sensational coverage by the metropolitan press. Four influential books of the early 20th century both critiqued and codified this repertory and marked out paths that later generations of professional folklorists would follow in the region. Emma Bell Miles' *The Spirit of the Mountains* (1905) offered a sympathetic and contextual portrait of mountain people, with emphasis on the expressive culture of religious, social, and domestic life and on the role of women as "repositiories of tribal lore—tradition and song, medical and religious learning." Horace Kephart's *Our Southern Highlanders* (1913) elaborated upon Miles' portrayal of men as the bearers of outdoor traditions associated with farming, hunting, and woodcraft and attempted to balance the sensationalism that journalists had attached to the subjects of moonshining and the so-called mountain feuds. John C. Campbell's *The Southern Highlander and His Homeland* (1921) offered a magisterial survey of Appalachian geography, history, and culture, into which was incorporated the folksong researches of his wife (and posthumous editor) Olive Dame Campbell. *English Folk-Songs from the Southern Appalachians* (1917) was the product of collaboration between Olive Dame Campbell and Cecil Sharp, an English folklorist who made three extensive collecting expeditions (1916–1918) and gathered 1,600 folk songs in North Carolina, Virginia, West Virginia, Tennessee, and Kentucky.

Meanwhile, academic interest in ballad texts made the second and third decades of the 20th century a "golden age" of folksong collecting in the mountains, with such active collectors as C. Alphonse Smith and Arthur Kyle Davis, Jr. in Virginia, Frank C. Brown in North Carolina, E.C. Perrow, Josiah H. Combs, and Hubert G. Sherin in Kentucky, and John Harrington Cox in West Virginia. Cox's *Folk Songs of the South* (1925) established a model for the academic publication of folksongs, which was reinforced by the expanded publication of Sharp's collection in two volumes in 1932. State folklore societies established in Kentucky and North Carolina in 1912, Virginia in 1913, and West Virginia in 1915 grew out of the collectors' focus on folksongs, as did the establishment of the first folk festivals in the region, at Asheville, North Carolina, in 1928 and White Top Mountain, Virginia, in 1931. The development of recording equipment made it possible to focus upon tunes as well as texts, and anxiety that radio and the burgeoning recording industry would somehow dilute the purity of "authentic" folk expression lent urgency to this project. Robert Winslow Gordon began his ambitious scheme to create a national collection of recorded folksongs with an expedition to western North Carolina in 1925. His subsequent success in establishing the Archive of American Folk Song in the Library of Congress allowed him to claim in 1930 that "The Government recognizes the hill-billy and the American Negro as the basis of American folk-song and music." Gordon's successors at the Library of Congress and other federal agencies during the 1930s expanded the scope of collecting in the region, adding topical songs to the canon, along with mining and other occupational folksongs and folklore. Two additional influential works that appeared in the 1930s were George Pullen Jackson's *White Spirituals of the Southern Uplands* (1933) and Allen Eaton's *Handicrafts of the Southern Highlands* (1937). Eaton's work led to the creation of the Southern Highlands Handicraft Guild and an offical outlet for mountain crafts along the Blue Ridge Parkway near Asheville.

In addition to codifying genres and contexts for folklife study in Appalachia, Miles, Kephart, and the Campbells also amplified two other tendencies that shaped the perception of Appalachia as a cultural region. One was the habit of generalizing about the entire southern Appalachian region, regardless of the geographic limits of a given investigator's research. Kephart, for example, spent almost all of his time in the mountains in or near Swain County, North Carolina, but he did not hesitate to echo Miles' claim that "throughout the highlands . . . our nature is one, our hopes, our loves, our daily life the same. . . . "The mountaineers are homogenous so far as speech and manners and experiences and ideals can make them" (Kephart 1913) he wrote, an assertion that belied careful distinctions drawn elsewhere in his and Miles' work between prosperous "valley people," "the average hillman," and impoverished "branch-water people." This tendency reinforced the presumption that, no matter how carefully a researcher's conclusions were qualified or how sharply the research might be focused upon a particular genre or on the folklife of a particular locality or even of a particular family, they would be interpreted as documentation of a regional folk culture. Thus, Leonard Roberts wrote in introducing his *Sang Branch Settlers: Folksongs and Tales of a Kentucky Mountain Family* (1974) that "the fundamental conclusion is that, although a geopolitical history of Appalachia has not yet been written, perhaps never can be or need not be written, the

The Faust family at work in front of their house. Anderson County, Tennessee, 1910. Library of Congress.

region's oral literature and folkways reveal it to be a rich repository of British and European culture."

John C. Campbell's more systematic approach to regional analysis led him to emphasize the importance of "constant qualification" in generalizing about the mountains, but he (and particularly Olive Dame Campbell) contributed to a second tendency—an instrumental view of folklife, valuing it in relation to its usefulness in advancing other projects, such as the "folk school" established in Brasstown, North Carolina, by Campbell in her husband's memory in 1925 as the centerpiece in a program of rural uplift. Earlier, at Berea College in Kentucky and in numerous settlement schools established in the region between 1895 and 1925, educators and missionaries had created "fireside industries" and instructional programs in handicrafts and folk music and dance as an adjunct of moral instruction and vocational education. During the 1930s, conservatives promoted folk festivals as engines of economic development and the preservation of "Anglo-Saxon" culture, while liberals and radicals incorporated folk music into the tool kit of labor organizers and expanded collecting under the auspices of the employment programs of the Works Progress Administration (WPA). Federal agencies such as the

Tennessee Valley Authority, Great Smoky Mountains National Park, and the Blue Ridge Parkway used folk artifacts such as log buildings and hand tools to create quaintly flattering frames to showcase their modernizing activities, while systematically driving mountain people from their homes and destroying artifacts (such as frame buildings of Cades Cove or the gasoline-powered generating equipment of Mabry's Mill) that conflicted with the image of Appalachia as a folk culture.

After World War II, Appalachian folk music was adapted to the needs of the urban folk-music revival of the 1940s and 1950s and the construction of alternative lifestyles for disenchanted young people during the 1960s. In the 1970s, folk music became a favorite tactic of community organizers, while Eliot Wigginton's Foxfire program of Rabun Gap, Georgia, reintroduced folklife study and publication as a pedagogical tool in remote mountain settings. Inspired in part by the commercial success of the Foxfire publications, folk festivals expanded to embrace crafts and storytelling as well as a variety of traditional and commercial musical genres and became a standard component in tourism promotion in most of the Appalachian states.

This instrumentalism—and the consumerism that has

often grown out of it—presented a challenge to professional folklorists who believed, with Thelma James, that "the truest values of folklore are entertainment for the participants or . . . materials for cultural studies by the scholar." Students of Appalachian folklife during the postwar era, and particularly since the 1960s, have responded to this challenge in two ways. Some have rejected the policing of boundaries between folk and popular culture by exploring and documenting the interpenetration of folk and popular genres, as in the work of Archie Green on coal-mining songs and D.K. Wilgus, Bill C. Malone, Neil V. Rosenberg, and Robert Cantwell on the folk roots of commercial country music. Another response has been to expand beyond research on music, crafts, and tales in favor of genres that do not lend themselves to "commoditization." Examples are Jeff Todd Titon's (1988) and Thomas Burton's (1993) studies of religious music, preaching, and worship as folk performance, Michael Ann Williams' (1991) reconstruction of vernacular housing as the patterning of interior and exterior space rather than as a set of architectural artifacts and building techniques, Lynwood Montell's study of "folk justice" and interpersonal violence, and the growing number of studies that explore the African American roots of Appalachian cultural forms. The work of Williams, Montell, and Patrick Mullen are examples also of the increasing influence of oral history in folklife scholarship and of a renewed interest in topics, such as the gender and age-related dimensions of folk culture, that were first raised by Emma Bell Miles in the early 20th century. At the same time, folklife research is of increasing interest to scholars in other disciplines. A notable example is historian David Hackett Fischer's *Albion's Seed: Four British Folkways in America* (1989), which defines Appalachia as one of four colonial hearths of American culture and defines its culture, both in its transplantation from Great Britain and Ireland and in its evolution in the United States, almost exclusively in terms of folkways such as speech, dress, gender relations, marriage customs, and child-rearing practices, foodways, naming practices, domestic architecture, religion, superstitions, plus the familiar triad of illiteracy, moonshining, and feuds. This ambitious work also exemplifies another trend: that of defining the core of Appalachia in a broader cultural region that extends across the entire Upland South to the Ozarks, north Texas, and the Anglo-American component of the desert Southwest. While such a view is controversial, it is likely to ensure that the pivotal role that folklife has played in studies of Appalachia as an American region will continue for many decades to come.

John Alexander Williams

References

Burton, Thomas. 1993. *Serpent-Handling Believers.* Knoxville: University of Tennessee Press.

Campbell, John C. 1921. *The Southern Highlander and His Homeland.* New York: Russell Sage Foundation.

Campbell, Olive Dame, and Cecil Sharp. 1917. *English Folk-Songs from the Southern Appalachians.* New York: Putnam.

Jones, Michael Owen. 1989. *Craftsman of the Cumberlands: Tradition and Creativity.* Lexington: University Press of Kentucky.

Kephart, Horace. 1913. rev. ed. 1922. *Our Southern Highlanders.* New York: Macmillan.

Malone, Bill C. 1993. *Singing Cowboys and Musical Mountaineers: Southern Culture and the Roots of Country Music.* Athens: University of Georgia Press.

McNeil, W.K., ed. 1989. *Appalachian Images in Folk and Popular Culture.* Ann Arbor, MI: UMI Research Press.

Sharp, Cecil. 1932. *English Folk-Songs from the Southern Appalachians.* 2 vols. New York: Oxford University Press.

Titon, Jeff Todd. 1988. *Powerhouse for God: Speech, Song, and Chant in an Appalachian Baptist Church.* Austin: University of Texas Press.

Whisnant, David E. 1983. *All That Is Native and Fine: The Politics of Culture in an American Region.* Chapel Hill: University of North Carolina Press.

Williams, Michael Ann. 1991. *Homeplace: The Social Use and Meaning of the Folk Dwelling in Southwestern North Carolina.* Athens: University of Georgia Press.

Applied Folklore

An approach that advocates the use of folklore materials to foster social, economic, and political change. The targeted constituency includes communities, work environments, and institutions such as schools, churches, and hospitals. Applied folklore used the paradigms of applied anthropology as a model, and each grew out of the social and political milieu of the mid- to late 1960s.

During the later 1960s and early 1970s, a group of folklorists formed an Applied Folklore Section within the American Folklore Society, to share concepts in the formation of theories, techniques, and methodologies. As with applied anthropology, members of the Applied Folklore Section labored hard toward an acceptable definition that would adequately represent the paradigms within which those involved would operate. In 1971 a Middle Atlantic Conference on Folk Culture was held in Pittsburgh, the main theme of which was applied folklore. The following definition was used at this conference: ". . . the utilization of the theoretical concepts, factual knowledge, and research methodologies of Folklorists in activities or programs meant to ameliorate contemporary social, economic, and technical problems." This definition called directly for change and implicitly placed the folklorist as a necessary catalyst in fostering that change.

Clearly, inherent within the first definition of applied folklore are problems of one's personal orientation and bias. For instance, *who* would identify these "contemporary social, economic, and technical problems?" In addition, the rhetoric did not define the role of the communities, institutions, or structures involved as an equal agent in the process of decision making and implementation.

During the 1971 Conference on Folk Culture, Richard Bauman presented his proposal for the establishment of a Center for Applied Folklore. Although pursued for a short period by a handful of devoted folklorists, such a center has

After finishing fieldwork in Chicago, Elizabeth Mathias (right) leads a folklife workshop for members of the Italian community there. Chicago, 1977. Photo Carl Fleischhauer. American Folklife Center.

never materialized. There were, of course, those who stood in strong opposition to the very idea of applying folklore outside of the academic arena. Among those who stood in opposition was the late Richard M. Dorson, who believed strongly that the role of the folklorist was within the academic arena. Dorson advocated that research, publication, and teaching were the mainstays of the folklorist, and he further contended that scholarship suffered when extra activities outside of the academic environment pulled scholars away from their accepted duties. Dorson's views on applied folklore (and later, public-sector folklore), softened after he directed a research project among mill workers in Gary, Indiana, in the 1960s.

Just as there were definite possibilities for "cultural dynamite" inherent within the definition of applied folklore, so were there also inherent problems within Dorson's (and others') objections. Implicit within the thinking of those who opposed applied folklore was the belief that scholarship was for a chosen few and that the larger audiences comprised of the "general public" had no direct role in the applications of scholarship. Those who favored applied folklore did not stand in opposition to solid scholarship; they wished to place the results of their education and research into some practical use to foster positive action and change while testing the validity and soundness of theories from folkloristics.

During the next few years, the strivings of those persons involved in applied folklore were diffused through dichotomies that arose between the two camps of thought, and the

very definition of applied folklore was softened. A new rhetoric arose that relegated the role of applied folklore to an exercise that took the folklorist from the activities of research, publication, and teaching into "activities" outside the academic arena. These "activities" were broadly defined, and absent was the stronger rhetoric pertaining to the active pursuit of social, economic, or political change.

Historically, there were earlier movements that embodied the strivings of the applied folklorist of the late 1960s to 1970s. When folk schools were first formed in the early 20th century, for example, their founders directly stated the desire to improve social, economic, and political conditions for their community members and constituents. The Highlander Folk School of Tennessee served as a training ground for Dr. Martin Luther King, Jr. and Sister Rosa Parks in their activities involving peaceful protest and civil disobedience. In the 1930s, the John C. Campbell Folk School of Brasstown, North Carolina, instituted woodcarving and cooperative farming activities (with training in new farming technologies) in a desire to empower the members of the community while increasing their economic status. Placed in the context of the original definition for applied folklore, these folk schools wished to institute a change in the lives of their constituents that would "ameliorate economic and technological problems."

Into the 1990s, the things that the applied folklorists strove toward have been reached to some degree within public-sector folklore. Early in the movement of applied folklore, one of its defining characteristics was a desire to expand folk-lorists' roles and responsibilities into venues outside of the academic arena. With the establishment of state, regional, and local folk-arts programs, the folk-arts program at the National Endowment for the Arts, the American Folklife Center at the Library of Congress, and the Festival of American Folklife as presented by the Smithsonian Institution, many folklorists are employed outside of university and college contexts. Most of these would define themselves as public-sector folklorists. In addition, there has been a related movement termed "cultural conservation," which advocates much collaborative research, publication, and programming activities among persons employed within a diversity of public and private institutions. One may ask, however, if the persons who embody these positions strive to institute social change or solve perceived social inadequacies, in the original meanings of the applied-folklore movement. In addition, the same question must be asked about public-sector folklore as is posed above regarding the definition of applied folklore: Do the people or communities involved in the activities of the public-sector folklorist necessarily want or desire the increased visibility, empowerment, and attention that comes to them as the result of these public programs? Further, upon whose terms are these public programs and their related activities envisioned and implemented? The ethical and theoretical problems inherent within public-sector work (as an extension of applied folklore) are numerous.

Despite the visibility and attention given to public-sector folklore and cultural conservation, applied folklore in its original meanings and definitions continues to be carried forth. David Hufford, for example, actively utilizes folklore theory and techniques in his work within medicine and hospitals, with an objective toward implementing changes in certain structures and systems. The Highlander Folk School continues as a center for the study of environmental pollution, with very active protest activities implemented to institute change. In 1985 folklorist Leslie Prosterman edited a special issue, entitled "Practicing Folklore," for the journal *Practicing Anthropology,* a publication of the Society of Applied Anthropology. The issue was devoted to then current activities in applied folklore, illustrating its continued vitality. Thus, some of the goals that fueled the original proponents of applied folklore continue to motivate folklorists, sometimes couched in the current activities within the public sector and cultural conservation.

David A. Brose

See also Cultural Conservation; Ethics in Folklore Research; Folk Schools; New Deal and Folk Culture; Public Folklore

April Fools' Day

The first day of April, an unofficial holiday observed in northern Europe and North America with pranks, innocent fibbing, and practical jokes. It is also known as All Fools' Day and, in Scotland, as Huntigowk Day, from the custom of sending the gullible on "gowk-hunting" missions—the gowk, or cuckoo, being an emblem of simpletons (for other European anteced-

ents, see Dundes 1989). In America, too, fools' errands are traditional, with the unwary being sent for sky hooks or pigeon's milk. Children delight in mildly aggressive mischief (salting the sugar bowl, placing "Kick me" signs on friends' backs) and in various forms of creative deception, from gluing coins to the sidewalk to "Made you look" lies ("There's a spider on your shoulder!"). Also perennial are telephone gags. A friend might be told, "Call this number and ask for Mr. Lion," only to discover that he has reached the local zoo.

Adults, too, engage in subversive raillery. Hennig Cohen and Tristram Potter Coffin (1987) recount office pranks in which a fellow worker is told his girl friend is pregnant, and a scofflaw is "arrested" for parking violations. The day is a special boon for hoaxing journalists. The British media have run stories on Italy's "spaghetti harvest" and on a marathon runner who, misreading the rules, intends to run nonstop for twenty-six days. College newspapers announce the firing of the faculty. The April 1, 1985, issue of *Esquire* magazine carried George Plimpton's biography of ballplayer Sidd Finch, a Zen enthusiast with a 168-mile-per-hour fastball.

The day's association with bootless errands has suggested many historical prototypes, including the flight of Noah's dove, Jesus' shuttling between judges at his trial, and Ceres' search for the echo of Proserpine's crying. The holiday has also been linked to the medieval Feast of Fools, the Hindu festival of Holi, and the unstable, "fooling" weather of early spring. The most probable origin, though, is calendrical. In 1582 France's Julian calendar gave way officially to the Gregorian, shifting New Year's Day from March 25 to January 1. But the official policy was slow to drive out habit. For years the conservative and the forgetful continued the custom of exchanging calls and gifts on April 1, the octave of the traditional New Year's Day. Their error made them Europe's first "April fools," or *poissons d'avril* (from the belief that "April fish" are easily deceived).

Functionally, the mild mayhem of April Fools' Day is a vernacular form of "symbolic inversion" quite appropriate to the season of the vernal equinox. The day has been called a "calendrical rite of passage" that allows for a temporary "reversal of power" (Dundes 1989). Like other inversive holidays such as Halloween, it operates under an unwritten protocol that periodically tolerates the impermissible. Hence the impunity of the April 1 jokester. When he signals a joke with the formula "April Fool!" the recipient must respond nonaggressively. Folk wisdom claims that a loss of temper may ensure the victim "real" bad luck. That April fooling is a means for managing disorder is also evident in the custom, now defunct, of sending anonymous love letters, "all in fun," to those whom one was afraid to approach directly (Harder 1961).

Finally, computer users have their own April Fool practical jokes designed for them, such as the shareware program that alarms the user by announcing the presence of water in the hard drive, then turns your computer into a spin drier. Bogus announcements of April Fools' Day computer viruses have also occurred.

Tad Tuleja

References

Babcock, Barbara, ed. 1978. *The Reversible World: Symbolic Inversion in Art and Society.* Ithaca, NY: Cornell University Press.

Challfont, Fran E. 1987. April Fool Jokes: A Look into the Heritage of WHIMSY. In *WHIMSY V: World Humor and Irony Membership Yearbook,* ed. Don L. Nilsen and Aileen Pace Nilsen. Tempe: Arizona State University Press, pp. 8–11.

Cohen, Hennig, and Tristram Potter Coffin, eds. 1987. *The Folklore of American Holidays.* Detroit: Gale.

Dundes, Alan. 1989. April Fool and April Fish: Towards a Theory of Ritual Pranks. In *Folklore Matters.* Knoxville: University of Tennessee Press, pp. 98–111.

Harder, Kelsie B. 1961. Just an April Fool. *Tennessee Folklore Society Bulletin* 27:5–7.

See also Prank

Architecture, Vernacular

Artifacts and landscapes built in communities according to time-tested but flexible customs and generally without the services of professional architects; also called "traditional architecture" and "folk architecture." Like other features of folk tradition, vernacular architecture involves a swirl of inherited ideas and skills in contact with changing fashions and models from sources outside of the community's shared aesthetic. This kind of building combines sensible habits with variations that meet the community's expectations and ideals.

The much mythologized rural, small town, and "main street" America continues to be the focus of many studies in vernacular building. Typically, main street was built and rebuilt by generations of pioneers or early builders and then by entrepreneurs and businessmen who worked to establish a secure, prominent position for their community in the economy of the state, region, and nation. Many a town got its start as a small service community for commercial mining or timbering employees, farmers, or river tradesmen. The town may have further evolved with the coming of the railroad, a tourist and recreation enterprise, a new factory, or an interstate highway. The majority of historic buildings in any town or region are vernacular, or traditional, buildings. It is that kind of commonplace built environment that conserves the essence of a town's special history. At the end of the 20th century, we are beginning to appreciate everyday architecture and to see the messages ordinary buildings convey. Understanding and conserving all kinds of buildings and places will be important if future citizens are to comprehend history accurately and in context.

For the past fifty years, new commercial architecture and reconstructions of downtown buildings have mostly tried to imitate icons from other regions of the nation (witness the long-running Williamsburg, Virginia-derived "Colonial Revival" style). Projects have eradicated and thus denied the authentic traditions of cultural regions with distinctive folk traditions; when the threads of local personality are severed, the fragile connections of local heritage are lost.

Vernacular buildings usually (but not always) express patterns of ethnic and regional character. Vernacular architecture often has localized and regional patterns based on familiar traditions in design, construction, decoration, and use that have evolved over generations. It often, but rarely exclusively, employs local building materials. Scholars study these patterned resemblances through space and time, charting the tenacity of ideas as well as the dynamics and changes that always occur in cultural heritage. Researchers have sorted the many varieties of vernacular buildings into *types.* This typology, or placing building types into categories based on *form,* demonstrates their genealogies and helps illustrate their formal evolution through time, sometimes through centuries of use and movement. Form (floor plan, layout, height) is important in traditional building because form is relatively stable over time and space, and scholars can use form to devise categories and assist in investigations of cultural diffusion.

Type differs from *style* in architecture. Type is an important element in the study of vernacular architecture. A building's type—floor plan, placement of chimney or stove, roof form, height—is very stable over time. Distinct patterns of vernacular buildings can be charted and mapped through time and space, and we are sometimes able to detect the probable origin for types of buildings we had previously thought to simply be "American." Matters of construction, use, and decoration of vernacular buildings are also very important and are the subject of scholarly research and interpretation.

Most stores, roads, houses, bridges, barns, warehouses, gas stations, and so on are the result of the dynamics and processes of vernacular design in the place where they were imagined and constructed for the needs of routine life, work, and commerce. When people have choices, they select types and styles in dwellings that reflect a number of forces. Choices may be made to present an impression to the neighborhood, to express well-being and success and participation in the fashion trends of the day.

Among the best-known types of American vernacular houses are British Isles-based types such as the single-cell (or "single pen") house, varieties of double-pen houses (such as the hall and parlor and the saddlebag subtypes), the I house, the Georgian cottage and house, and the foursquare house of the Midwest, along with the French Creole house, the *Ern-haus,* or "hall-kitchen" house, built by German-speaking immigrants, and the shotgun house. All but the shotgun house are based on postmedieval European spatial traditions; the shotgun house, a long narrow one-story house with its door or front in the gable that faces the street, has its origins in West African communities and in a sequence of evolution that took place in the Caribbean and the Mississippi River Basin around New Orleans. There are a dozen or so major barn types in America, among them the English barn type familiar in the East and the transverse-crib barn type, a widely distributed Midwest and Southern type typical of the 19th century. These house and barn types were erected in all manner of traditional construction materials, from adobe and sod to brick and stone, and in the various forms of horizontal and vertical log and wooden frame construction.

Sharecroppers' house. Asheville, North Carolina, late 1800s or early 1900s. Library of Congress.

In the context of vernacular architecture, style pertains to visual elements of decoration and ornament that buildings exhibit. One can place buildings in a category of style by studying these surface qualities. In vernacular architecture, style has little to do with a building's functions or its use of interior space. Stylistic periods change through time as fashions change in the context of popular design and taste, often as influenced by a small number of designers, artists, or architects whose ideas are widely disseminated in the media. One of the problems with classifications of styles and periods is that the categories are fuzzy and easily abused. For example, "Classical" applies equally to an 18th-century English brick house in the Virginia tidewater, a New England church facade, and a suburban shopping mall storefront in Los Angeles.

Vernacular buildings may also display flashes of the style and ornaments of the age, such as "Georgian," "Greek Revival," "Gothic," "Mission Revival," or "Colonial Revival." These broadly popular styles reflect national changes in taste. Stylistic ornament is characteristically applied as a sort of mask or Sunday clothes, put on the form of an otherwise ultraconservative vernacular house. The special architectural style that dresses up a vernacular building is a vital element in the building's social and cultural context.

Symbols are important. For example, we have inherited a deep-seated concept that Greek- and Roman-looking clas-sical columns lend dignity if not a look of success and power to the front of a 19th-century farmhouse or the entry on a new suburban banking facility. Americans love grand columns and Classical pediments, whether realized in massive limestone on the county courthouse or made of flat vinyl and nailed as a decorative motif up and around the porch of a ranch-style house.

Students of vernacular architecture concoct long lists of questions to ask about the subject. In addition to the questions inherent in the remarks above, two more may be mentioned: Why do things last after their supposed original function changes or ends? Are they survivals from earlier periods or other places? Take, for example, the large fireplace in the new suburban house. Its original function gone (cooking hearth and heating), the fireplace continues to be built because a hearth has symbolic values for millions of people—and offers the correct place for some American families' ritual hanging of the Christmas stockings.

Studying vernacular architecture gives us entry into broader areas of behavior and cultural expression. People live in environments, whether haphazard ones or planned, and not merely in buildings. We build these environments, and their relationships with other environments are important. Vernacular buildings often reflect an intention to conform to accepted values in the community, resulting from hallowed (and some-

To store vegetables and canned goods, the Jarvis family uses this cellar. Alleghany County, North Carolina, 1978. Photo Lyntha Scott Eiler. American Folklife Center.

times moribund) traditions in design rather than from fashionable or futuristic academic architects. Folk builders naturally and often reuse parts of old structures or entire structures as they expand and tinker with their landscapes and people take advantage of local climate and terrain. To be conservative is not necessarily to be old-fashioned or resistant to change.

Traditional builders acquire competence through apprenticeship and imitation of admired models and artisans rather than through institutionalized classes or schools of design. Design values are imbedded in the community's traditions and worldview. Rather than being called an "architect," the designer of a country store, a gas station, a Philadelphia row house, a railroad-crossing shack, or a coal-mine tipple was likely to be called a builder, a contractor, a craftsman, a bricklayer, a carpenter, a stone mason, or another such term.

One of the features of vernacular design that differentiates it from high-style design is the degree to which the client and other members of the community participate in the architectural process. Forms are often familiar; neighbors understand what is being built and why. The contractor knows similar buildings, and his work is attuned to the needs of the client. This sometimes means there is less room for creativity in the job than in high-style design, but that is expected in the processes of traditional building. People apply decorative details

and variations to give the building special character.

Vernacular buildings range from the prehistoric Native American dwellings of natural materials to the vertical-log-walled houses of French settlers in the Mississippi Valley and the vast barns of the Pennsylvania farm; from the fine Georgian and Federal I houses of early times to the split-foyer suburban house of the 1970s and 1980s. Vernacular building is well represented in structures that may seem to be high-style but exhibit strong elements of local and ethnic cultural heritage, such as the Victorian town house, the community school building, the mail-order-catalog bungalow, and the county courthouse.

We can help guide changes in our built environments through planning, zoning, efforts in historic preservation, and cultural conservation. We may, in fact, select buildings, artifacts, and memories that we deem important in a community's heritage. The remembered story of how the electric company forced people off the fertile river bottomland to build the hydroelectric project or the flood-control reservoir, or the chair made by the itinerant carpenter, or the log house that once served as a stagecoach stop—these memories and artifacts become heirlooms of value. Thus it is that scholars of traditional building look at architecture, landscape, and landmarks as palpable, tangible manifestations of culture, both high-style and vernacular. For vernacular design, one of the best ways to study culture is by direct examination and analysis of the built environment, because material things are stable and expressive vessels for communication of ideas. We need to look at structures that embody the citizens' sense of place and of history in both conscious ways (statues in the cemetery, public-school design, churches) and unconscious ways (farmstead layout, vernacular houses' symmetry). People who study buildings need to help manage and direct the forces of progress if they are to help leave a usable history to those who follow.

Howard Wight Marshall

References

Carter, Thomas, and Bernard L. Herman, eds. 1989–1991. *Perspectives in Vernacular Architecture.* Vols. 3–4. Columbia: University of Missouri Press.

Cummings, Abbott Lowell. 1979. *The Framed Houses of Massachusetts Bay, 1625–1725.* Cambridge: Harvard University Press, Belknap Press.

Glassie, Henry. 1975. *Folk Housing in Middle Virginia: A Structural Analysis of Historical Artifacts.* Knoxville: University of Tennessee Press.

Hubka, Thomas. 1984. *Big House, Little House, Back House, Barn.* Hanover, NH: University Press of New England.

Jordan, Terry G., and Matti Kaups. 1989. *The American Backwoods Frontier.* Baltimore: Johns Hopkins University Press.

Marshall, Howard Wight. 1981. *Folk Architecture in Little Dixie: A Regional Culture in Missouri.* Columbia: University of Missouri Press.

Martin, Charles. 1984. *Hollybush: Folk Building and Social Change in an Appalachian Community.* Knoxville: University of Tennessee Press.

Upton, Dell, and John Michael Vlach, eds. 1985. *Common Places: Readings in Vernacular Architecture.* Athens: University of Georgia Press.

Williams, Michael Ann. 1991. *Homeplace: The Social Use and Meaning of the Dwelling in Southwestern North Carolina.* Athens: University of Georgia Press.

See also Art, Folk; Crafts; Cultural Landscape; Folklife Movement; Material Culture; Vernacular

Archive of Folk Culture

The archival arm of the American Folklife Center. The Archive of Folk Culture was founded in 1928 within the Music Division of the Library of Congress. Originally named the Archive of American Folk-Song, it represented an early institutional commitment to documentation and research in the area of the American folksong. Its first head was Robert Winslow Gordon, and during the 1930s it flourished under the direction of John and Alan Lomax, building a large collection of field recordings and manuscripts from all regions of America and becoming a national center for documentation of American folk traditions. Later heads included Benjamin A. Botkin, Duncan Emrich, Rae Korson, Alan Jabbour, and Joseph C. Hickerson. In 1978 the archive became part of the American Folklife Center, and in 1980 it was renamed the Archive of Folk Culture to reflect the makeup of its ethnographic collections.

In 1941 the first of a long-lived series of albums appeared from the archive's collections, presenting documentary recordings of folk music and folklore. The series pioneered in using sound recordings to present folk culture to a broad audience, and commercial companies producing documentary recordings in later decades owe much to the archive's early published series. The archive was also the basis for creation of the library's Recording Laboratory in 1941, and during the same period Alan Lomax experimented with field documentaries and hosted programs on radio.

Collecting concentrated on American folk music in the archive's early years, but Alan Lomax took a step toward making the collections international by visiting the Bahamas in 1935 and Haiti in 1937. His documentary work also led to experiments with artistic biography in sound, involving verbal interviews as well as musical performances of artists such as Aunt Molly Jackson, Huddie Ledbetter (Lead Belly), Woodrow Wilson "Woody" Guthrie, and Ferdinand "Jelly Roll" Morton. By the later 1930s, the office helped launch the term and concept "oral history." In the 1940s, under Botkin and more strongly under Emrich, the emphasis on verbal and other traditions grew, and for a period in the 1950s the unit was renamed the Folklore Section. Korson strengthened the archive's ties to ethnomusicology, and during her tenure the worldwide holdings were strengthened.

Under the aegis of the American Folklife Center, the archive collections have been significantly increased by ethnographic field projects. These collections include every medium of documentation and cover the full subject-matter gamut of folklore and folklife. In 1994 the archive held more than one million items, including 600,000 manuscripts, 200,000 color and black-and-white still photographs, 50,000 sound recordings, 200,000 ephemera, and lesser numbers of moving-image documentation, computer discs, and other media. Roughly three-fourths of the collections are from the United States, including materials from every state. The international and older domestic collections are primarily musical, whereas ethnographic collections from Folklife Center projects are strong in material and verbal culture and in occupational and ethnic traditions from both rural and urban areas. U.S. collections range from American Indian materials to documentation of the most recent immigrant traditions.

Alan Jabbour

References

Bartis, Peter Thomas. 1982. *A History of the Archive of Folk Song at the Library of Congress: The First Fifty Years.* Ann Arbor, MI: UMI Research Press.

Green, Archie. 1985. The Archive's Shores. *Folklife Annual 1985.* ed. Alan Jabbour and James Hardin. Washington, DC: Library of Congress, pp. 60–73.

Kodish, Debora G. 1978. A National Project with Many Workers: Robert Winslow Gordon and the Archive of American Folk Song. *Quarterly Journal of the Library of Congress* 35 (October):218–233.

Lloyd, Timothy. 1992. *The Archive of Folk Culture: The National Collection of American and World Folklore.* Washington, DC: American Folklife Center, Library of Congress, 16 pp.

See also American Folklife Center

Archives, Folklore

Depositories of collected folklore materials, including tapes, transcripts, photos, films, material-culture items, and so forth. Folklore-archive materials reflect different folklore genres as they are practiced among different peoples and in different geographic areas. Folklore archives have existed in Europe since the 1800s; however, not until 1928 was the Archive of Folk Culture founded in the United States. Housed in the Library of Congress, the Archive of Folk Culture benefited from Works Progress Administration (WPA) projects, in the 1930s and 1940s, and more recently has sponsored folk studies in various areas of the nation. Though technically a national archive, the Archive of Folk Culture does not function as comprehensively as its European counterparts. As a result, a folklore scholar in the United States needs to be familiar with smaller archives throughout the country.

While there are archives affiliated with state folk-arts councils, the majority of folklore archives in the United States are connected to universities. Often starting in boxes that eventually take over the office of a folklore professor, archives need their own space to be effectual. Such archives rapidly expand, composed primarily of materials submitted by students to fulfill class requirements, as well as items collected by professional folklorists. Collecting leads logically to archiving, which in turn fosters research.

Students visiting folklore archives are able to see how their collections are used by other students and scholars. However, archivists generally do not allow students unlimited access to an archive. A folklore archivist secures archive materials so that no precious information is lost. Some archives have material that is restricted, and limitations are often put upon documents folklorists use for personal research. In addition, the informant and the collector may also place restraints on material. Despite such restrictions, a well-organized and extensive archive will contain a wealth of easily procurable material.

Maintaining an archive is a never-ending process. A folklore archive needs to have folklore material readily available in order to be useful for scholarly research by both the student and the folklore professional. Ideally, folklore archives should be used by scholars of varying disciplines, creating camaraderie rather than competition. The magnitude of material submitted to an archive requires organization by diligent archivists to see that items are available and that the archive runs smoothly.

Well-organized submissions and careful use of archive materials are essential in developing a well-run archive. However, no matter how well organized or well supported an archive is, its success hinges, ironically, upon both the flexibility and the consistency of methods employed by the archivists.

The first step in building an archive is to gather a large enough body of material to warrant a collection and from which to be able to draw valid conclusions. Some archives contain private collections of one person's life research. Other archives, such as those in the public sector, contain material collected from the community, while archives at universities and colleges often contain items collected by students.

One of the most critical tasks in establishing and maintaining an archive is that of preservation. The archivist must be aware of the types of paper used, the boxes in which they are stored, the manner of storing recorded tapes, and the temperature and humidity of the archive, among other things. If an archive has hundreds of narratives about the fishing community in a given area, but stores copies on low-quality paper, that collection may be useless within twenty years because the printing may begin to fade or the paper to crumble.

Once the material in the archives is in good condition and ready to be filed, a system must be established so that patrons and employees can easily access this material. The best possible system depends on the nature of the collections and on the needs of the users. One traditional method of narrative classification is represented by the Aarne-Thompson Type Index and the Thompson Motif-Index. Another way to classify material, not limited to narrative, is described in William A. Wilson's 1993 article, "Mormon Folklore: Cut from the Marrow of Everyday Experience." There is no one technique perfect for every archive, and types of indexes vary from one archive to the next.

Until recently, most archives compiled their indexing systems on a series of index cards, similar to a card catalog in a library. As computers have become more popular and more readily available, archives across the country have begun to index their material on computer.

With a system of indexing in place, the archivist must evaluate the collection and determine the best placement of each item. This step is one of the most time-consuming and often most frustrating for the archivist. Most items slide easily into the niches devised for them, but there are many that resist classification. This is why the archivist is forced to keep constantly informed of current scholarship and genre classification issues. As time passes, genres are interpreted and perceived differently, and adjustments are made to definitions.

At all times, the archivist must keep in mind that the archive is only valuable if a researcher can easily access the material. Patrons of a folklore archive can maximize their research time by having a specific topic in mind, with key words and phrases that will help the archivist locate the needed material. The more information provided the archivist, the more he or she will be able to help in research. Flexibility is also important because folklore is not always classified as one might expect.

Those collecting material that will eventually be archived should contact the particular archive intended as the recipient in order to find out what format to use and what contextual information to include. In this way, archive contributions will be more valuable. There are several ways to find an archive in a specific area. The *Folklife Source Book,* available through the American Folklife Center at the Library of Congress, has

*Folklorist Blanton
Owen numbers his
slides taken in 1978
for the American
Folklife Center's Blue
Ridge Parkway
Folklife Project.
Photo Margaret
Counts. American
Folklife Center.*

an extensive list of archives in the United States. Those who have Internet access can find a list through the Library of Congress LC Marvel gopher.

> Kristi Bell
> Alana Paige Kimbel

References

Archive Sources. 1989. In *Folklore, Folklife*. Washington, DC: American Folklore Society, pp. 17–18.

Bartis, Peter, and Hillary Glatt. 1993. *Folklife Sourcebook: A Directory of Folklife Resources in the United States*. 2d ed. Washington, DC: American Folklife Center.

Camp, Charles, ed. 1989. *Time and Temperature*. A Centennial Publication of the American Folklore Society. Washington, DC: American Folklore Society.

Wilson, William A. 1993. Mormon Folklore: Cut from the Marrow of Everyday Experience. *BYU Studies* 33 (3):521–541.

See also Archive of Folk Culture; Fieldwork

Art, Folk

Objects of aesthetic expression usually appreciated for their traditional aspects. Most artworks identified as folk come from traditional cultures and are learned in a nonacademic face-to-face interchange. While folk art often seems to be synonymous with ethnic art (Hmong storycloths, Amish quilts, or Mexican American death carts), it also comes from traditional communities held together by ties related to occupation, region, religion, generation, politics, economics, or family. While there is a continuing debate over precisely how to define folk art, generally speaking, most scholars agree that the boundaries for art categories such as folk, fine, tourist, ethnic, or popular are fluid.

Since the beginning of the 20th century, folk-art study in the United States has been influenced by antique collecting, European class structures, museum practices, modernist perspectives of fine art, and varying approaches to the study of all art within different academic disciplines. In the United States, folk art's "beginnings" (which ignored the work of Native Americans, classifying it as "primitive") were first identified with new immigrants who continued their European traditions. These new citizens often settled in communities with others from their country of origin. While there was sharing among varying cultural groups, thereby somewhat changing the weaving, the basket, the carving, or the pottery, many traditional practices of ritualistic use or content remained.

Originally, the creator of folk art was usually seen as a rural, nonliterate, poor, and isolated individual. This approach probably grew out of the European way of identifying folk artists as peasants. Holger Cahill, who was influential in folk art's early study, believed that the great period of American folk art covered the second quarter of the 17th century up to the third quarter of the 19th century.

It was not until the early part of the 20th century that American folk art gained recognition outside of the community of origin. The first "discovery" came from members of the group we call fine artists. Artists such as Peggy Bacon, Alexander Brook, Charles Demuth, Yasya Kuniyoshi, Robert

Garden-of-Eden tree made by Lithuanian-American wood-carver Vilius Variakojis; a snake's head emerges from the base of the trunk. Chicago, 1977. Photo Jonas Dovydenas. American Folklife Center.

Night-sky tree made by Lithuanian-American wood-carver Vilius Variakojis. Chicago, 1977. Photo Jonas Dovydenas. American Folklife Center.

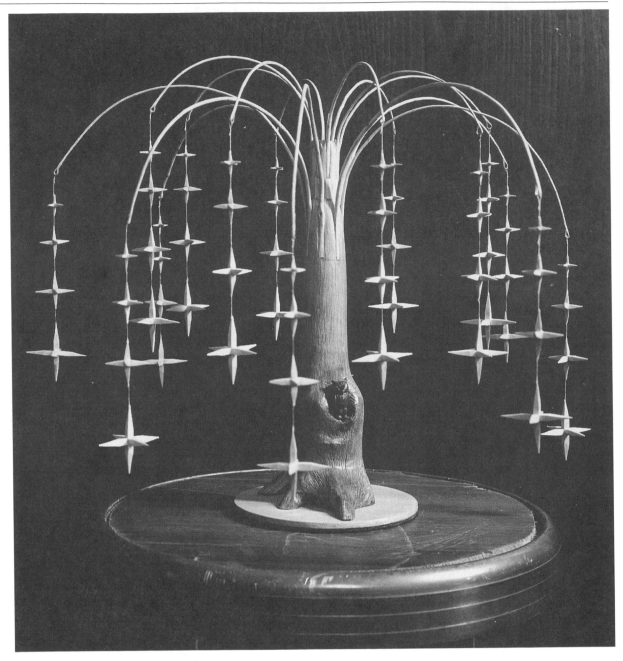

Laurent, Elie Nadelman, and William Zorach appreciated both the immediacy and the directness of the work as well as the kinds of materials that were used, often wood and iron. Besides these artists, early collectors included the Rockefellers, the Kaplans, and the Lipmans. Little attention was paid to documentation of the artists or their contexts, thereby encouraging the idea of folk art as anonymous. Edith Halpert and Cahill are credited with initiating widespread public acceptance of folk art and the collecting of it as "proper" artistic expression. By "proper," they meant that they viewed folk art as objects with aesthetic value based on formalist approaches, rather than objects coming from traditional communities that functioned in ritualistic or utilitarian ways.

In the 1920s, artists and collectors would flock to rural Maine in the summer to gather paintings, carvings, weather vanes, gravestones, and ship and architectural carvings. Ameri-

cans were interested in having a separate identity from Europe, and they believed that folk art would help us understand our own cultural heritage. In addition, as the United States became more industrial, many citizens wanted to keep the past alive. They theorized that if the folk arts continued to thrive, important elements of the past would continue. The notion prevailed that the best folk art was that which was old.

For many years, *Art in America* and *Antiques* were the only periodicals that would publish articles on folk art. Because collector Jean Lipman was the editor of *Art in America* from 1940 to 1971, articles about folk art were encouraged. Alice Winchester, another early-20th-century collector, was the editor of *Antiques* for many years. This magazine was largely responsible for stimulating and maintaining an interest in folk art (viewed as closely aligned with antiques) during that time. In 1950, an issue of *Antiques* was published that solicited definitions for the term "folk art" from people who had either written about it, collected it, or exhibited it. Most of the writers were "art-" oriented people (as opposed to folklore-, history-, or anthropology-oriented people), and they described folk art from the object point of view (as opposed to a context perspective). However, even among these writers, there did not seem to be much of a common focus.

The first widely acclaimed collection of American folk art was begun in the 1920s by Abby Aldrich Rockefeller with the help of Edith Halpert, who was then the director of the Downtown Gallery in New York. This collection is housed at the Abby Aldrich Rockefeller Folk Art Center in Williamsburg, Virginia. Electra Havemeyer's collection began as early as 1910 when she married J. Watson Webb. In 1947, the Webbs founded the Shelburne Museum in Shelburne, Vermont. During this period, Eleanor and Mabel van Alstyne also developed a strong collection, which they gave to the Smithsonian Institution in 1964. Jean Lipman's collection was bought by Stephen C. Clark in 1950 for the New York Historical Association in Cooperstown, and Henry F. du Pont made his home into the Henry Francis du Pont Winterthur Museum in Winterthur, Delaware. His house is full of many folk-art masterpieces. Henry Ford's extensive collection is in the Henry Ford Museum in Dearborn, Michigan, which also includes some folk art. More recently, Herbert Hemphill gave his extensive collection to the Smithsonian, and Michael and Julie Hall made a gift of their folk art to the Milwaukee Art Center in Wisconsin.

The first public folk-art exhibition, organized by Gertrude Vanderbilt Whitney, was in 1924 at the Whitney Studio Club in New York City. Since then, the momentum and interest in exhibiting folk art have been building. In 1932 the Museum of Modern Art in New York City exhibited a show called *American Folk Art: The Art of the Common Man in America, 1750–1900.* Included were oil paintings on glass, cookie molds, wood and metal sculptures, plaster ornaments, ships' figureheads, toys, carved wooden cigar-store Indians, weather vanes, decoys, metal stove plates and figures, and ornamental eagles and roosters. The majority of works in this show and other early ones were from New England. The idea of folk art as art by the common, everyday person persevered. Because of the enthusiasm for these kinds of objects by antique collectors, many handmade objects that had been called "antique" were now being called "folk."

The Depression years brought about the Works Progress Administration (WPA). This federal program funded not only the collection of ballads and other oral folklore, but also an assemblage of art objects from rural areas. It also helped create hundreds of day and evening art classes at schools and community groups across the country. Art was seen as important and necessary, and for people everywhere, including folk artists, the sense that art was a worthwhile activity was promoted.

The *Index of American Design* is one of the most comprehensive documentations of 18th- and 19th-century arts and crafts. It was one of many projects initiated in the spirit of

Florence Cheek stands with her quilt "on the order of Trip Around the World." Traphill, North Carolina, 1978. Photo Pat Mullen. American Folklife Center.

Franklin D. Roosevelt with the expressed intent of giving the nation a sense of wholeness and the "common" people a sense of pride and worthiness during troubled times. This book was edited in 1950 by Erwin O. Christensen, and it recorded 22,000 art representations, many of them considered folk art.

In the 1950s and 1960s, researchers began to look to the South and West as the idea of what could be considered folk art expanded. In 1970, Herbert Hemphill organized the exhibition *Twentieth-Century Folk Art and Artists* at the Museum of American Folk Art in New York City. This show was notable because it appeared to be the first time 20th-century American folk art (beyond the realm of painting) had been so broadly explored by a major institution. Folk art began to lose some of its close identity with antiques. This exhibit included wood carving, *santos* of the New Mexican religious tradition, neon road signs, toys, decoys, fabric and needlework pieces, assemblage pieces, and photographs showing examples of fantasy gardens and environments, storefront art, graveyard

art, and scarecrows. It made folk art appear abundant and important in 20th-century America. Additionally, folk art appeared to be alive and well all over the country.

In 1974 another major show, curated by Alice Winchester, took place at the Whitney Museum of American Art in New York City. It was called *The Flowering of American Folk Art, 1776–1876,* and it is credited by some as the first exhibition to survey "the entire range of folk art," which is and was, of course, an impossible task. It is interesting to note that the popular magazine *Art News* critiqued the catalog book, written by Jean Lipman, as disturbingly having more focus on biography than stylistic analysis. The art object, clearly, was being more connected to the artist, and the idea of folk art as anonymous art was fading.

In the 1970s, as state and regional arts councils flourished, geographical regions began to research and curate shows. These shows were usually coordinated by folklorists, trained to see folk art as a traditional process rather than as an isolated object to be viewed against a white wall and appreciated for its formalistic design elements. The cultural community in which an artist lived and worked was determined to be important to the understanding and appreciation of the artistic process and, in turn, the way the product was understood and appreciated. The *Early Art in the Genesee Valley* exhibit in 1974 concentrated on one region in New York state. It was set up to reveal "the social function of arts during the eighteenth and nineteenth centuries in the Genesee Valley by the display of artifacts locally manufactured or locally owned." This show emphasized that the objects exhibited were to return to people and houses instead of museums. In other words, the objects functioned within the daily lives of individuals and communities, and, therefore, their return was viewed as important.

The 1978 Michigan Folk Art Show, organized by C. Kurt Dewhurst and Marsha MacDowell at Michigan State University, identified folk artists in four different ways that incorporated both conservative definitions focusing on tradition and community belonging, and individual expression and the influence of technology. This approach was an attempt to incorporate a broad enough definition to include both the traditional and the vernacular artist. However, in general, subsequent folk-art shows coordinated by folklorists holding positions as state folk-arts coordinators, attempted to define folk art as more traditionally bound. Additionally, they made attempts to portray the meanings and functions of the objects in people's lives. Good examples of these types of exhibitions were those held in 1980 in Oregon (coordinated by Suzie Jones) and in Utah (by Hal Cannon).

Within the last few decades, folk-art publications and exhibitions have come from two major directions. Generally speaking, museums utilize the art-historical approach, which has traditionally looked at the folk-art object from an aesthetic perspective. When folklorists are involved with the research and display, the exhibit direction becomes more contextual. Also, some curators and art historians lean toward a folkloric approach to folk art. Probably the three most active museums in exhibiting and publishing works on folk art have been the Museum of American Folk Art in New York City, the Winterthur Museum in Delaware, and the Abby Aldrich Rockefeller Museum in Williamsburg, Virginia.

Most of the fifty states have folk-art coordinators, who have not only surveyed their regions for folk art and exhibited the works, but also often coordinate folk festivals in an effort to educate the public on the relationship among the artist, the object, and the artist's community. Publications resulting from these programs emphasize the cultural community, the ways the object is used and appreciated, and the values and beliefs that are communicated. Folk-arts coordinators have also been active in developing folk arts in education programs, in which folk artists are employed to teach about local traditions. These programs, like many folk-art projects, are often funded by the Folk Arts Division of the National Endowment for the Arts. Apprenticeship awards, folklore fieldwork, and other folkloric activities are also often supported by this federal agency.

As the 20th century comes to an end, avenues for communication have increased, and competition over the study of folk art has blossomed, but there remains a lack of consensus on the definition of folk art. Over the last one hundred years, many words and phrases have been used to define folk art, many of which are demeaning, classist, racist, colonialist, and just plain narrow-minded. Among the terms used are: simplistic, provincial, childlike, a dying art form, copied, antique, nonacademic, unsophisticated, naive, primitive, untrained, unprofessional, handiwork, utilitarian, art by isolates, outsider, grass-roots, and peasant art.

In 1977 the Henry Francis du Pont Winterthur Museum held a conference on American folk art with Scott Swank as chair. It was an attempt to have scholars from different areas (university professors, museum directors, collectors, and specialists in folklore and material culture) analyze traditional views on folk art and look for new ones. At the same time, there was a folk-art show on display at the Brandywine River Museum. The show was developed in conjunction with the Winterthur Museum and expressed some of the new directions its curators wished to pursue with folk art. The new (and old) perspectives, which were discussed at the conference and at the exhibit, stirred controversy among attendees. The result was perhaps more confusion, less consensus, and increased alienation among groups interested in the study of folk art. The 1980 anthology *Perspectives on American Folk Art*, edited by Ian M.G. Quimby and Swank, was a result of these events.

Since the early 1970s, folklorists have become increasingly interested in folk art. Early folklore scholars who led the way include Louis Jones from Cooperstown, New York; Michael Owen Jones (1989), who did an early extensive study on a chairmaker in the Kentucky mountains; Henry Glassie, who studies vernacular architecture; and John Michael Vlach, who continues to do studies in African American folk art and material culture. While anthropologists have studied folk art in far-off places, they have, generally speaking, neglected folk-art study in the United States. Because of anthropology's absence in American folk-art study, folklore's late entry, and museum collectors' earlier hold on the approach to folk art, there remain conflict in defining folk art, political turf guarding of funding sources, and general disagreement over what objects to study as folk and how to study them.

In many respects, it is the folkloric approach to the study of art that permits an emphasis to be placed on the holistic creative process. Whereas a fine-art perspective usually entails a product-boundaried approach in its categorization, a folklorist will study many aspects of the creative process, often focusing on that which is traditional. One of the most often identified areas of tradition a folklorist will emphasize in defining a work as "folk" is how the tradition is learned. The tradition, then, is identified in the process of passing on certain community values and beliefs from one generation to another during the learning process. Examples would be Leon "Peck" Clark, a Mississippi basket maker who learned to weave from a community member; George Lopez of Cordova, New Mexico, a sixth-generation *santos* carver whose children also carve; or the African American families from Mt. Pleasant, South Carolina, who weave baskets in similar ways to their

African ancestors. Folklorists say that folk art cannot be learned in academic settings; it is the informality of the process and the community-based values passed on that makes the work "folk." This process of defining folk art becomes problematic when one begins looking at more formal apprenticeship programs such as those in which the traditional boatbuilder in Mississippi is taught. While the boats and the artists are said to be traditional, the learning mode has been formalized. Or, in the case of orthodontists trained at the University of Washington to learn soldering skills by making art, when many of these students graduate they continue to make soldered sculptures, often informally sharing them with their former fellow students and other local orthodontists.

Some folklorists like to emphasize the tradition that exists in the creative process. For example, one Canadian Northwest Coast Indian carver learns his craft from his father by working on his own totem pole, imitating each move he sees his father make. As a result, the two poles are basically identical. Michael Owen Jones recognizes that more often the ideas, techniques, and skills that are passed on from one individual to another incorporate some change. However, there is a tendency toward conformity in these procedures. In fact, most folklore scholars agree that new tools and updated technology might also be used in the re-creation of a folk piece. For example, if an Oregon logger who learned traditional carving techniques from other loggers decided to switch to a chain saw, the artwork and creative process would still be considered "folk." On the other hand, one must recognize that artists who are academically trained also employ certain traditional techniques and skills they learn in the classroom. These skills may have to do with the way to wedge clay or how to pull a pot from the potter's wheel, but traditional creative processes are certainly passed on.

The most product-oriented way of looking at folk art is to find tradition in the content of the object. In other words, a carved piece of scrimshaw made by a Newfoundland fisherman should have on it a traditional motif in order for the work to be considered "folk." Folk-art totem poles are made with traditional images of whales, ravens, or bears, and quilts are created from traditional patterns passed down from mother to daughter. However, in fine art, there is also tradition in the content of art objects. For example, in European paintings, the still-life bowl of fruit is ubiquitous, as is the reclining female nude. Many artists make a series of similar works that explore one topic or idea. For example, Alberto Giacommetti spent many years making the same thin, standing figures over and over again.

Some scholars look to the style of an art object for traditional aspects. Certainly there is no one style that can be used to identify all folk art. However, there are stylistic traditions within folk-art expressions. Hmong storycloths are often embroidered on a blue background with bright colors reflecting similar scenes of villages and animals. Loggers carve similar kinds of chains and fans, and Pueblo potters utilize traditional clays, surface design elements, and firing practices to produce pottery recognizable to their region. In like fashion, fine artists, too, are grouped with those who share similar ideas

about style. The Impressionists have stylistic similarities as do the Cubists, the Expressionists, and the Futurists.

Many folk-art survey books organize themselves around the form of the object. There are chapters on quilts, wood carvings, scrimshaw, weather vanes, gravestones, or circus figures. This also poses problems in differentiating folk-art classification systems since fine-art and popular-art books might also be organized in the same manner. In other words, there is nothing exclusive about the form of a quilt that makes it automatically folk art. Clearly, today many quilts are made that are categorized as fine art for a variety of reasons. Additionally, many artists today use traditional practices and re-create them in innovative ways. Such is the process of New York artist Miriam Schapiro.

Folklorists often look for tradition in the context of an object to determine if it is folk art. The question is raised, is dulcimer making "folk" when carried out in the Ozarks, but not when done in California? Does the tradition somehow exist in the human and physical environment as an extension of the individual? The difficulty lies in determining whether or not a certain set of values, attitudes, and beliefs is a part of the artist's context. But as folk art is continually changing, how much change is acceptable within its boundaries is not easily stated. Potters in the Central and Western states learned new skills and techniques from ceramicists who, traveling west from the southeastern states, brought with them a unique alkaline form of glazing, wheel-turned handles, and the groundhog kiln; decoys were made by White settlers who imitated the Indians' bird lures; and quilt patterns have been shared among diverse groups of women, although the names are often changed to fit specific local beliefs.

When folklorists study folk art, they inevitably look to how it is used within its context. Some scholars theorize that folk art is often so ingrained in the lives of everyday people that it is not differentiated from other activities, thereby defusing any need to refer to it as art. New England samplers were commonplace between 1620 and 1860; quilts, in many communities, were often made for every room of the house; and weaving rooms were part of every plantation until 1785. Likewise, Native American baskets were (and on some reservations still are) made for hauling loads, storage, winnowing, sifting, and even housing rattlesnakes. However, this definitional approach is problematic because popular forms such as comics, television, and movies, and fine-art forms such as park sculptures and elite architecture, also have their place in our everyday lives. Another way this issue has been approached is to say that much folk art is utilitarian. However, as Ruth Bunzel has pointed out, many traditional cultures also make art simply to gratify the aesthetic impulse. One example is the bone and ivory carvings of the Eskimos. Another categorization problem is that often the traditional artist makes a decision to create for the collector. When carver Lem Ward from Crisfield, Maryland, makes a decoy that ends up on a collector's shelf somewhere outside Ward's community, is it no longer folk art?

Some folklorists suggest that tradition resides not so much in the object itself as in the extension of the premises and assumptions that are shared and transmitted over time and space within a small community of people. However, it is clear that elite artists in many ways share common jargon, values, aesthetics, and folk tales. As much as fine artists are often viewed as isolates, studies like Howard Becker's *Art Worlds* (1982) clearly demonstrate the collaborative process of all artwork. Nonetheless, as Jones (1987) points out, the idea of "the folk" is misleading. When we discuss aesthetics, we realize that one person's values will not necessarily agree with another's, because we all belong to several folk groups at one time. The importance of tradition in the appreciation process should not be dismissed, however, just because of the difficulties in understanding it. As with the other aspects of folk art discussed, although problems exist definitionally, the manner in which the object is appreciated and the community accepts it are primary aspects in understanding folk art. For many folk artists, to have an identity and acceptance with the rest of the folk group is important. If an artist is seen as a renegade, his or her art begins to be viewed in the category of fine art.

Besides the importance of tradition, there are several other factors that go into defining a work of art as "folk": folk art is intended to be used in everyday life among members of a small, close group; it functions as a remembrance of the past or as a demonstration of respect for elders; it is made by persons who do not call themselves artists as readily as creators from other art groups do; and the artist and/or group members use a different language structure from the art school- or university-trained artist to talk about their work.

Kristin G. Congdon

References

Ames, Kenneth L. 1977. *Beyond Necessity: Art in the Folk Tradition.* New York: W.W. Norton.

Andrews, Ruth, ed. 1977. *How to Know American Folk Art.* New York: Dutton.

Cahill, Holger. 1932. *American Folk Art: The Art of the Common Man in America, 1750–1900.* New York: W.W. Norton.

Ferris, William, ed. 1983. *Afro-American Folk Art and Crafts.* Boston: G.K. Hall.

Glassie, Henry. 1989. *The Spirit of Folk Art: The Girard Collection at the Museum of International Folk Art.* New York: Harry N. Abrams.

Jones, Michael Owen. 1987. *Exploring Folk Art: Twenty Years of Thought on Craft, Work, and Aesthetics.* Ann Arbor, MI: UMI Research Press.

———. 1989. *Craftsman of the Cumberlands: Tradition and Creativity.* Lexington: University Press of Kentucky.

Thompson, Robert Farris. 1983. *Flash of the Spirit: American and Afro-American Art and Philosophy.* New York: Vintage Books.

Vlach, John Michael, and Simon J. Bronner, eds. 1986. *Folk Art and Art Worlds.* Ann Arbor, MI: UMI Research Press.

See also Crafts; Folk Museums; Folklife Movement; Index of American Design; Material Culture; Outsider Art; Paper Cutting; Tattooing

Asch, Moses (1905–1986)

Founder and director of Folkways Records, the prototype of small, independent folk-music record companies. Asch was born in Warsaw, Poland, to a family of Jewish writers, scholars, and revolutionaries; his father was Sholem Asch, the most widely read Yiddish author in the years between the World Wars. From him Asch acquired a profound sense of the importance of artistic independence. Asch was first schooled outside Paris, and then in the New York City public schools after the family immigrated to the United States in 1915. Although he never finished high school, he spent two years in a German *hochschule* studying electronics and radio technology. Upon returning to New York in 1925 he worked in the radio business, later establishing his own company, Radio Laboratories, and branching into the field of public address systems before entering the commercial recording market in 1941.

Asch's first records were of Jewish liturgical music (cantorials) for his "Asch" label. He initially ventured beyond the Jewish field by recording the African American singer Huddie Ledbetter (Lead Belly) in 1941. Although he found financial success recording jazz artists during World War II (and until the bankruptcy of his second recording company, Disc, in 1947), it was also during the war that he began recording those singers and instrumentalists who became the pantheon of American folk music, including Woody Guthrie, Cisco Houston, Pete Seeger, Sonny Terry, and Josh White.

Asch established Folkways Records and Service in 1948 with his secretary, Marion Distler, and ran it until his death in 1986. While often imperious, he was also revered by many because of his insistence upon principles of artistic, cultural, and historical worth that were often at odds with the commercial constraints of the record business.

Peter D. Goldsmith

References

Shelton, Robert. 1960. Folkways in Sound; or, The Remarkable Enterprises of Mr. Moe Asch. *High Fidelity* (June):42–44 ff.

Sherman, Tony. 1987. The Remarkable Recordings of Moses Asch. *Smithsonian* 18 (5):110–121.

Young, Israel. 1977. Moses Asch, Twentieth Century Man. Parts 1–2. *Sing Out!* 26 (1–2):2–6, 25–29.

See also Folkways Records; Revivalism

Auctions

Method of selling in which the price or value of merchandise is set by the buyer through a competitive bidding process. The bidding may be accomplished through written, oral, or gestural responses to offers, and most often follows an ascending price pattern. The auction process provides an efficient vehicle for the redistribution of large quantities of varied merchandise and for setting a market value on items of unknown or variable value. Most auctions are led by an auctioneer, who functions as the intermediary between buyer and seller and who generally plays a large role in organizing and conducting the sale. Except in the case of some charity auctions, auctioneers conducting sales are trained, licensed professionals.

The auction process involves a wide variety of merchandise and situations: real estate, personal property, full estates including both real and personal property, livestock, automobiles, and fish and produce (from fresh-cut flowers to tobacco). Those auctions serving a wholesale market, where goods are purchased for resale, generally attract professional or semiprofessional buyers. Folklorists most often study community-based auctions that involve the general public: estate sales, local livestock sales, and sale barns or auctions held on a regular basis at a fixed location where individuals bring lots of merchandise to be sold by the auctioneer. Such sales offer particularly fertile ground for folkloristic inquiry, in part because the social process and the economic process are so closely intertwined.

One initial task in the investigation of any auction is to identify, through the collection of quantifiable data, the actual demographics of the community present at the sale. The distance a participant traveled to attend the sale; the relationship among participants, the auctioneer, and the owner of the merchandise; the methods through which a participant learned of a sale; and the participant's reasons for attending a sale—these are some of the factors that help describe the social dynamics of this economic process.

Folkloristic inquiry identifies a number of areas in which the interaction of auction participants creates and maintains traditions that further define the economic process of buying and selling. The ways in which goods are exhibited for sale, the order in which items are sold, the kinds of goods that are not sold (for example, some auctioneers will not sell a Bible at auction) and whether that decision is based on personal preference or state law, the operation of food concessions (who sells what and why) at a sale, and the manner in which a sale is advertised to the public are all factors frequently determined by community-based tradition and precedent.

The verbal artistry of the auction process—perhaps the most easily recognized, most familiar, and most investigated aspect of the auction sale—is also shaped by community-based tradition. Though most auctioneers attend training schools where they receive some instruction in crying or chanting a sale, skillful auctioneers perfect this art through the lengthy traditional process of observation and imitation—through working with, and around, other successful auctioneers. The smooth patter combines the repetition of a current bid with the request for a higher bid, frequently interspersed with nonsense syllables that enhance the singsong rhythm of the chant. Most auctioneers punctuate their sales with jokes, stories, and personal exchanges with individuals in the crowd, all of which serve to keep people involved in the sale and to bolster the atmosphere of community and play that permeates the general sale. Community-based values and experiences shape these exchanges, which help the auctioneer balance the need to push

Matt Burnett conducts an auction. Near Woolwine, Virginia, 1978. Photo Blanton Owen. American Folklife Center.

the bid higher with the need to maintain a personal rapport with buyers.

Narratives told about auctions comprise yet another traditional genre that sheds much light on the nature and meaning of the auction sale. Frequently told as personal narratives or as the experiences of the infamous friend of a friend, these tales and anecdotes educate auction attendees about the specifics of the auction process and its role—both actual and perceived—in a community. Stories regarding unintentional (and generally outrageous) purchases accomplished through a wave to a friend or the scratch of an ear, and stories involving great treasures uncovered through the purchase of junk merchandise (the sofa or baking soda can stuffed with bills), circulate regularly in any community where auctions are held. The latter story is particularly interesting in that generally the marvelous treasure is returned to the estate—a remarkable act of generosity underscoring the perception of the auction as a community-based and equitable means for the redistribution of property.

Phyllis Harrison

References
Aibel, Robert, Ben Levin, Chris Musello, and Jay Ruby. 1984. *A Country Auction: The Paul V. Leitzel Estate Sale.* 16mm. University Park: Pennsylvania State University Audio-Visual Services. Color Film and Videotape.
Cohen, D. *Going, Going, Going.* Portland, OR: Raspberry Wood Productions. Videotape.
Ferris, Bill. [1977]. *Ray Lum: Mule Trader.* Memphis, TN: Center for Southern Folklore. Multimedia Package.
Harrison, Phyllis. 1979. Indiana Auctioneering: No Two Sales the Same. *Indiana Folklore* 12:101–119.
Jansen, William Hugh. 1956. Down Our Way: Who'll Bid Twenty? *Kentucky Folklore Record* 2:113–121.
Marsh, Anne, and William Aspinall Jr. 1971. Harold E. Leightley: Portrait of an Auctioneer and His Craft. *Keystone Folklore Quarterly* 16:133–150.

Austin, Mary Hunter (1868–1934)

Writer best known for nonfiction and fiction works on nature and native cultures in California and the Southwest. Born and raised in Carlinville, Illinois, she moved to central California in 1888. In 1892 she began a prolific career pursued in Carmel's art colony after 1905, in New York City and Europe, and in Santa Fe's art colony from 1924 until her death.

A mystic and naturist with a college degree in sciences, Austin developed her environmentalism in arid and semiarid regions and was active in the Western conservation movement, including campaigns against the Boulder Dam project in the 1920s. An antimodernist, she proposed ecologically and artistically integrated "folk-life" as the antidote for American rootlessness, and native village socialism as an alternative to 1920s European communism. Her regionalism highlights the sociocultural contributions of women, Hispanics, and especially Indians to an envisioned "multiethnic democracy" grounded in authentic indigenous expressions. In 1925 Austin helped organize both the Indian Arts Fund and the Spanish Colonial Arts Society in Santa Fe, New Mexico.

Austin wrote and lectured about folktales, folk drama, and various other folk arts, but her most extensive folklore research focused on Amerindian song/poetry, a model for poetic evolution in all societies and the measure for true American poetry because of its attunement to a set of rhythms peculiar to the American environment. The crucial "landscape line" involves melody, emotion, and ideation. She did song and tale translations/reexpressions, criticizing both anthropological and literary folklore collectors and translators for exercising too little or too much "creative intelligence." Although never fully accepted by either ethnologists or literati, Austin was influential in publicizing the Indian cultures she primarily championed.

Marta Weigle

References
Austin, Mary. 1903. *The Land of Little Rain.* Boston and New York: Houghton Mifflin.
———. 1923. *The American Rhythm: Studies and Reexpressions of American Songs.* New York: Harcourt, Brace.
———. 1924. *The Land of Journeys' Ending.* New York and London: Century.
———. 1934. *One-Smoke Stories.* Boston and New York: Houghton Mifflin.
Blend, Benay. 1988. Mary Austin and the Western Conservation Movement, 1900–1927. *Journal of the Southwest* 30:12–34.
Fink, Augusta. 1983. *I-Mary: A Biography of Mary Austin.* Tucson: University of Arizona Press.

Autoharp

A type of zither played by pushing down chord bars. It was designed by Karl August Gutter in Markneukerchen, Germany, in 1884 and first manufactured in the United States in 1885 by Charles F. Zimmerman.

The autoharp consists of a wooden sound box with thirty-six to thirty-eight strings tuned to either a chromatic or a diatonic scale. From three to twenty-one movable bars, called chord bars, are suspended across the strings. The bars have felt pads attached, and these pads are spaced on the chord bar so that when they are pressed against the strings, certain strings are dampened. The undampened strings make up the notes of a designated chord. By pushing down a series of chord bars and strumming or plucking the strings, either a musical accompaniment or a melody can be played.

In 1871 Zimmerman patented a system of numerical musical notation. To promote its use, he designated a stringed instrument that he called an "autoharp" and patented in 1882. However, when he began manufacturing the instrument in 1885, it deviated greatly from his original design and more closely resembled the *volkszither* patented in England by Karl Gutter. It is thought that Zimmerman used Gutter's design because it was easier to manufacture.

Autoharps have been manufactured by several different companies since then. A popular instrument between 1892 and 1897, with 300,000 produced, it declined in popularity until the 1950s when Oscar Schmidt International began promoting the instrument to school music programs. This promotion and the 1960s "folk revival" spurred its continuing popularity.

The development of the autoharp as a folk instrument was molded by publications. There have been few autoharp teachers, so people learned to play from self-instructional books included with their instrument. The earliest of these was *Collection of Popular Figure Music for C.F. Zimmerman's Miniatur* [sic] *Autoharp,* published in 1885.

Depictions of playing the autoharp in the 1890s show it lying flat on a tabletop or on a horizontal stand. The strings were plucked or strummed below the chord-bar assembly. The manuals of the 1890s instructed the student to do rhythm accompaniment strums with the thumb and first finger and pluck melody strings with the first finger. The autoharp was used mostly for accompaniment and acquired the nickname "idiot zither" because it was so easy to play in that way.

In the 1890s, the autoharp began to be played as a melody instrument. Between 1895 and 1897, Aldis Gery toured the United States with the Victor Herbert Band playing popular tunes on a "Concert Grand" autoharp. Around 1900 the autoharp was introduced to the Southern mountain region through mail-order catalogs and door-to-door sales. It was also the "mountain piano" of rural missionaries.

Mike Seeger documented several playing styles of the early 1900s on the 1965 recording *Mountain Music Played on the Autoharp.* All of the players laid the autoharp on their laps or on a table. They played the strings below the chord bars. Their repertoires consisted of waltzes, hymns, and simple reels. Neriah Benfield from North Carolina played melody notes with the back of his first fingernail plucking the string in a frailing banjo style. Accompaniment was done with the thumb or first finger. Ernest Stoneman from Virginia plucked the melody string with his first finger and simultaneously plucked a bass harmony note with his thumb. Accompaniment was done by the thumb or the first finger moving back and forth across the strings. On September 6, 1924, Stoneman made the first record using the autoharp. Sara Carter popularized lap-style playing when she played rhythm accompaniment on the autoharp with the Carter Family from 1927 to 1943. This style of playing was common until the 1950s.

In the 1950s, Maybelle Carter, who played guitar with the Carter Family, began performing on the autoharp holding it upright against her chest. This made it easier to play into a microphone. She also began playing the strings above the chord bars, which gave the instrument a softer sound. This style became known as the "Appalachian style," and by the 1970s it had almost completely replaced lap-style playing. Meg Peterson authored several instructional books in the 1960s that illustrated this new style.

Prior to the 1970s, autoharp strings were tuned to a chromatic scale. Then Bryan Bowers, a popular performer, began tuning his strings to a diatonic scale. This allowed him to double tune some strings to the same tone, much like a twelve-string guitar. Tuned this way, the autoharp produced a fuller sound. Bowers still played in a traditional "closed-chord style," pushing a chord bar against the strings for every melody note played. Ron Wall developed a method of playing with diatonic tuning in an "open-chord style," in which some of the melody strings are played without any chord bars being depressed. Now autoharps are tuned to many different scales, and they are played in both open- and closed-chord styles.

The most comprehensive review of autoharp history is Becky Blackley's *The Autoharp Book* (1983), which includes descriptions of all autoharp models from 1885 to 1983. In 1963, A. Doyle Moore published the first scholarly paper on its history.

The first magazine for autoharp players was *Autoharpoholic,* published by Becky Blackley beginning in 1980. Other magazines and newsletters that followed were *Autoharp Teachers Digest, Autoharp Quarterly,* and *Autoharp Clearinghouse.*

The autoharp's appearance has not changed much since 1885, and instructional books and magazines still influence its development. A recent trend has been the organization of autoharp contests, clubs, and festivals. Autoharp performers play jazz, blues, Celtic music, and New Age music, in addition to the traditional American music.

Tom Schroeder

References

Moore, A. Doyle. 1963. The Autoharp: Its Origin and Development from a Popular to a Folk Instrument. *New York Folklore Quarterly.* Reprinted in *Folkstyle Autoharp,* ed. Harry Taussig. New York: Oak Publications, 1967, pp. 10–20.

Schroeder, Tom. 1991. In the Beginning: Five-Year Review. *Autoharpoholic* 12:6.

Seeger, Mike. 1965. Liner notes of *Mountain Music Played on the Autoharp.* Folkways Records FA 2365.

Stiles, Ivan. 1991. The True History of the Autoharp. *Autoharp Quarterly* 3:3–6.

See also Carter Family; Revivalism

B

Ballad

A song composed in stanzas sung to a repeating tune that recounts a short, usually single-episodic, tale of complication, climax, and resolution. Since it tells a story, the ballad exhibits certain traits common to other narrative forms of folklore like epic song and fairy tale: It concentrates on the leading character, features two interacting protagonists to a scene (seldom more than three actors in the whole drama), and is a solo performance piece, though it may have a refrain or a chorus for group participation.

Of the several forms of American folksong, ballads have received the bulk of scholarly attention, and of that bulk the Anglo American ballad has received the largest share. It is to the Anglo American tradition, therefore, that this entry is pertinent, though many of the generalizations also apply to Mexican American traditions (especially the romance and corrido genres) and to some African American traditions. Indeed, one of the ballad types discussed below, the blues ballad, is found in the repertoires of both Black and White folksingers. At the most general level, we customarily distinguish four subtypes of ballad in Anglo American culture: the medieval, or Child, ballad, the broadside ballad, the blues ballad, and the parlor ballad.

The medieval ballad is the oldest. It emerged somewhere in Europe in the late Middle Ages, was fully established as a popular song type in Britain by the late 15th century, and flourished in Scotland especially up to the late 1600s. After 1700, however, almost no new songs were made in the style, though many of the existing ones remained popular in British oral tradition; not surprisingly, many were brought to America and incorporated into our everyday singing occasions. When, more than a hundred years ago, the American scholar Francis James Child set out to make a comprehensive survey and catalog of the British Isles tradition of this medieval ballad type, he could find a total of 305 distinct ballads in the documentary record, some reprinted in old songbooks and street-poetry flyers ("broadsides"), some in published anthologies of songs gathered from oral tradition, and still others in unpublished manuscripts and field notes of 18th- and 19th-century folksong collectors. Child brought together in a single exhaustive work, *The English and Scottish Popular Ballads* (1882–1898), all of the versions he could find in his library and archival research, assigning each ballad a number for easy identification and comparison. Most of the 305 he found in several versions from different sources, the number of versions reflecting just how popular any particular ballad had been, how often it had been printed, and how often it had been collected from oral tradition. In honor of Child's seminal work, ballad scholars have given his name to the genre.

In its British tradition, the Child ballad encompassed a range of topics, which can be conveniently divided into four categories: (1) magical and marvelous (the stories that turn on supernatural agency, some grounded in pre-Christian beliefs, some in Christian ones); (2) romantic and tragic (which turn on everyday domestic affairs, mostly love relationships); (3) historical and legendary (ballads on actual events, such as a battle or a crime, or on historical-like topics, such as an exploit of Robin Hood); and (4) humorous. The ballads of the second group, romantic and tragic, are the ones that best transcend cultural and historical specifics and display a more general appeal; they are the kind most likely to be found in pan-European tradition and, similarly, are the ones most likely to have made the transatlantic crossing and become popular in America.

The specific features that distinguish the Child ballad from its more recent relatives constitute its particular *way* of telling a story. For instance, Child-ballad style tends to be impersonal; that is, not only is the story in third person but it seldom proselytizes. In other words, it doesn't include specific instructions in its text as to how a listener should react to, or evaluate, the personalities and events in its story. It prefers to just present the facts, and one must infer feeling and moral value from what the characters say and do.

The Child ballad also tends to be less expository than the broadside style; it virtually plunges into the heart of its tale, with very little lead into the complication, and ends just as suddenly after the climax has been reached and a resolution swiftly achieved. It tells its tale dramatically, almost acting it out rather than relating it—for example, by often not ascribing its dialogue to a specific speaker. It just gives the speech, and the speaker is implied. Even its imagery is dramatically exaggerated—hair bound with gold, horses shod with silver, roses and briars growing over dead lovers' graves and entwining, and so on. Yet another trait the Child ballad shares with a nonnarrative song genre, the lyric is a strong reliance on stylized, formulaic verse. Certain stanzas appear again and again in different ballads, creating a kind of reservoir of reusable epithets to cover similar situations. Suicides, for example, will usually be described with some variant of "He put the sword handle against the wall / The point against his breast," a bedtime with "The day being gone, the night coming on / While all men were asleep." Then there is a recurring metrical trait: Child-ballad verse is most commonly of two strophic types, a four-line stanza accented 4/3/4/3 or a two-line stanza accented 4/4.

Though, like all folklore, Child ballads adapt to their environments, contexts, and even settings of performance so that we frequently find variations that localize, modernize, rationalize, or jocularize some old-fashioned or simply too unfamiliar content, a further feature of the type is that modern-day versions still more often than not retain a premodern ambience to their content. Thus, many American versions of these old British ballads still talk about lords and ladies, castles, and ghosts. Finally, perhaps the most striking trait of all, in their structure the Child ballads incorporate a feature most prominent in non-storytelling catalog songs and combine it with storytelling purpose to achieve a highly redundant style of narrative progression that relies heavily on repetition, both exact and incremental, on twofold and threefold parallelisms, and on framing structures that imbed and nest constituent parts within each other in an overall design of great formal symmetry and balance. The repetitions and parallelisms tend to freeze the story, as it were, by lingering on an action for several stanzas before moving on to pause at the next tableau (a technique sometimes called "leaping and lingering").

An excerpt from a Missouri version of Child 81 will illustrate several of these aforementioned traits. Lord Arnold has just surprised Little Matthy Groves in bed with his wife:

> "And it's how do you like my fine feather-bed,
> And it's how do you like my sheets?
> And it's how do you like my gay ladie
> That lies in your arms and sleeps?"

> "Very well do I like your fine feather-bed.
> Very well do I like your sheets
> But much better do I like your gay ladie
> That lies in my arms and sleeps."

> "Now get you up, little Matthy Groves,
> And all your clothes put on;
> For it never shall be said in Old England
> That I slew a naked man."

> "I will get up," said little Matthy Groves,
> "And fight you for my life,
> Though you've two bright swords hanging by your
>   side
> And me not a pocket knife."

> "If I've two bright swords by my side,
> They cost me deep in purse,
> And you shall have the better of the two
> And I will keep the worse."

> The very first lick that little Matthy struck
> He wounded Lord Arnold sore.
> But the very first lick that Lord Arnold struck
> Little Matthy struck no more.

The broadside ballad style, which succeeded the medieval type in popularity and which remained vital as a compositional model up to the end of the 19th century in the song traditions of North American regional and occupational groups (logging, ranching, coal mining, seafaring), though it lost popularity in more urban centers a bit earlier, coalesces as a distinct type in Britain after 1700. "Broadside" refers to the method by which many of this type of song made their initial appearance: cheaply printed on single sheets of paper and sold at street corners, market stalls, and fairs by itinerant peddlers. The songs tended to be on actual topics—sensational crimes, military victories, accidents and disasters that claimed many lives—but were often imaginary as well, *especially* when the topics were about courtship and love relations in general.

The conventions of the broadside style can be contrasted with those of the older Child style. For example, the broadside way of telling a story in sung verse tends toward subjectivity; often in first person, often featuring the narrator as an actual participant in the drama, often explicitly passing judgment or loading with sentiment the circumstances related, broadside style has certain similarities with the lyric song. The broadside style is also more expository; in what is often a very journalistic way, it specifies details of time, place, personnel, motive, and so forth that tell more about what's going on, providing an explanatory as well as an interpretive context for its events in a way the Child ballad generally eschews. And broadside ballads aren't as dramatic: Word use is closer to conventional language than is the stylized, exaggerated word use of the older form, and dialogue is ascribed to its speaker rather than just given.

Broadsides are less formulaic than Child ballads, not necessarily in their plots but in the language—their epithets, lines, and stanzas; we don't find as many "floating" verses reused to say essentially the same thing in different ballads. Many broadsides also feature a metrical pattern that extends the shorter ballad stanza considerably to 7/7/7/7 (that is, seven stresses per line in a four-line stanza), though this particular trait seems to be much indebted to the Irish strand of broadside traditions in the New World. Finally, the structure of the broadside style reflects its greater dependence on print for its composition and diffusion, for it does not display nearly the

internal redundancy—the catalog trait—of the more highly patterned Child style. The broadside style is more linear and chronologically continuous from stanza to succeeding stanza, with less repetition, parallelism, framing, and "leaping and lingering."

Illustrative of the broadside style are the first five stanzas of a ballad on a murder in Sullivan County, Missouri, in 1894:

> About one mile from Brown town, at the foot of Jenkins' hill,
> Took place this awful murder by the Taylors, George and Bill.
> Gus Meeks' wife and children were taken from the [their] home,
> Were taken by those Taylors to meet their fatal doom.
>
> They wrote to Gus Meeks a letter telling him to be ready at ten
> And try to leave the country to save his grace [disgrace] from them.
> How little did he think them those Taylors, George and Bill,
> That night would murder his family upon the Jenkins hill.

> But the hand of Providence came to little Nellie and said [Nellie's aid],
> Ere the break of morning safe escape she made.
> She came out of her straw-made grave and to Carter's house she came
> And told this mournful story, that adds to our country's shame.
>
> She stood before the doorway with that awful gash in her head;
> While she sobbed and wept most bitterly these were the words she said:
> "Some very cruel men last night came and took us from our bed.
> They shot our papa and mama, and thought us three were dead.
>
> "They put us in our wagon and took us to our straw-made grave.
> How little did they think them their sad little Nellie would save!
> But Providence was against them; the righteous hand was there
> And willed against those murders little Nellie's life to spare."

G. Malcolm Law Jr. has cataloged broadside ballads in American tradition, placing them in two logical divisions for the purpose: ballads that originated in the British Isles (Laws 1957), and ballads that were made on this continent and treat what are more or less distinctive North American experiences (Laws 1964). Some topics are common to both kinds: for instance, ballads of war, of sailors and the sea, of crime and criminals. More interesting are the differences. In general, broadside ballads originating in Britain and Ireland that took root in American singing tradition heavily favor what the Child ballads that flourished here favor—stories of love affairs that had no actual historical event behind them (stories about parents opposing their childrens' choice of mate, and stories of lovers who employ some disguise or trick in the machinations of courtship were particularly popular)—while ballads made in the United States and Canada tend to favor male occupational experiences, principally of the outdoor, laboring kind (such as cowboying and lumbering), as well as the more sensational sort of topic that Laws places in categories of "murder ballads" and "ballads of tragedies and disasters." These topics are not unknown in British ballads that diffused to America; they simply are not as numerous, as patterned, and as interrelated as indigenous ballads on the same subject and so were incorporated into other categories. The primary value of Laws' catalogs are not as typologies, however, but as systematizations: He gives each ballad an identificatory letter-and-number combination for ease of identification—thus, for example, "The Meeks Family Murder" given above is Laws F28.

Unlike the Child and broadside models, the third way of telling a story in song found in Anglo American folk tradition, the blues ballad, is home grown, though similar forms can be found in other cultures, such as Irish Gaelic. Indeed, in both its genesis and its life history, the model is as much an African American one as it is Anglo American. As its name implies, the type emerges from the fusing of the ballad's narrative way of articulating images in sung verse (predominantly a White tradition) with the lyric song's emotive way (in this case, chiefly the Negro lyric style). Like a broadside ballad, though often in a somewhat impressionistic and elliptical way, a blues ballad's topic is situated in an actual event and features an array of specific characters, settings, materials, and actions; like the lyric, however, the song is unified by a heightened mood of lament or celebration rather than by a story line, often drawing as well from a pool of formulaic imagery:

> They took him to that cemet'ry
> In a rubber-tired hack,
> They took him to that cemet'ry
> But they did not bring him back.

As far as plot is concerned, the blues ballad is not as linear and continuous as the broadside, favoring the more tableau style of the Child ballad, moving forward to be sure but from striking scene, to dramatic confrontation, to evocative speech in a sequence that is often as much associational as it is chronological. We also often find in blues ballads the repetitions, parallelisms, and other symmetries intrinsic to the Child style:

> Sol Matting he lied a-sleeping,
> Poor boy was sleeping so sound,
> When the fire took place in the deck-room
> The night the Bicera burned down.

> Chorus: O! the Bicera she hollered,
> O! the Bicera she moaned;
> The City St. Louis did answer
> The night the Bicera burned down.

> When she left St. Louis
> She had five hundred men;
> When she got to New Mattick
> She hadn't but a hundred and ten.

> Ain't that a pity,
> Ain't it a sin and a shame,
> The fire took place in the deck-room
> The night the Bicera burned down.

> The Bicera was a fine boat.
> O! the Bicera she moaned;
> But when she got to New Mattick
> O! the Bicera was gone.

> The Bicera was a fine boat,
> Her smoke stacks painted brown,
> When the fire took place . . .
> . . . .

> O! Sol Molting [*sic*] he whooped and he hollered,
> Sol Molting he hollered so strong;
> When the fire took place in the deck-room
> Poor Sol Molting was gone.

Like many African American recreational-song genres, but unlike Anglo American, Child, and broadside ballads, the blues ballad in performance was usually dependent on instrumentation, the singer accompanying himself or herself on banjo or guitar, and instrumental breaks between groups of stanzas were common.

While the Child and the broadside ballad types are widely recognized and studied by folksong scholars, there is less consensus on the status of the blues ballad and, consequently, less scholarly literature on the subject. This is even truer of the fourth ballad type, the parlor, or sentimental, ballad (itself one kind of the more general parlor song, which may come in ballad or in lyric manifestations). The parlor ballad has forebears in Britain that go back several centuries, but those found in American domestic singing tradition by modern-day folksong collectors are mostly of late-19th-century origin, originally popularized in some formal milieu or other, such as a variety hall, a traveling minstrel show, a Chautauqua, or a temperance society meeting, and widely disseminated through songsters and sheet music. As a result, a parlor ballad's composer is often known to us, which is rarely the case with blues ballads, virtually never with broadside and Child ballads.

The distinctiveness of parlor-ballad poetry (tunes tend to be quite distinctive as well) seems to lie in the generally bourgeois sensibility that informs it. Parlor songs in general display more conventionally genteel, refined, elevated feeling and morality, often indeed to the point that, to the outsider, their patriotism appears jingoistic, their virtues pious, their sentiments maudlin. While their composers were undoubtedly more knowledgeable in formal poetic techniques, so that alongside other traditional ballad types parlor ballads appear less formulaic in language and content, more unified in plot and theme, more regular in meter and rhyme, more heterogeneous in verse formats, they do not project to the academic sensibility a world honestly experienced and represented. Plot and character seem contrived, the evocation of emotion manipulative:

I saw a man at early dawn
Standing by the grogshop door.
His eyes were sunk, his lips were parched;
I viewed him o'er and o'er.

Refrain. I viewed him o'er and o'er,
His eyes were sunk, his lips were parched;
I viewed him o'er and o'er.

His little girl stood by his side,
And as to him she said,
"Father, mother lies sick at home,
And sister cries for bread."

Refrain: And sister cries for bread, etc.

He staggered off up to the bar,
Where he had been before,
And faltering to the landlord said,
"Oh, give me one glass more."

Refrain: Oh, give me one glass more, etc.

The landlord arose at his command
And filled the liquid bowl.
He drank while wife and children starved
And ruined his own soul.

Refrain: And ruined his own soul, etc.

Like other kinds of parlor songs, parlor ballads seem dependent on the premise that song should be ennobling, uplifting, or educational; hence they are invariably grounded in value orientations and worldviews that seem indebted to middle-class aspirations and the idea of polite society. Although lumbermen sang them in bunkhouses and sailors at the forecastle, the "parlor" rather than the "porch" seems to us their natural setting for folk performance, the piano rather than the banjo their appropriate supporting instrument. But in the quotidian contexts of their performance, they were no less real for all that, as meaningful and functional to those who sang them as was an outlaw blues ballad to a Louisiana penitentiary inmate, a murdered-pregnant-sweetheart broadside ballad to an Indiana farmwife, or a Child ballad about lords and ladies astride silver-shod steeds and living richly passionate lives to an Appalachian mountaineer.

Roger deV. Renwick

References

Coffin, Tristram Potter. 1977. *The British Traditional Ballad in North America.* rev. ed. with a supplement by Roger deV. Renwick. Austin: University of Texas Press.

Ellis, Bill. 1979. "The 'Blind' Girl" and the Rhetoric of Sentimental Heroism. *Journal of American Folklore* 91:657–674.

Laws, G. Malcolm, Jr. 1957. *American Balladry from British Broadsides: A Guide for Students and Collectors of Traditional Song.* Bibliographical and Special Series Vol. 8. Philadelphia: American Folklore Society.

———. 1964. *Native American Balladry. A Descriptive Guide and a Bibliographical Syllabus.* rev. ed. Bibliographical and Special Series Vol. 1. Philadelphia: American Folklore Society.

Wilgus, D.K., and Eleanor R. Long. 1985. The Blues Ballad and the Genesis of Style in Traditional Narrative Song. In *Narrative Folksong: New Directions. Essays in Appreciation of W. Edson Richmond,* ed. Carol L. Edwards and Kathleen E.B. Manley. Boulder, CO: Westview, pp. 437–482.

See also Bronson, Bertrand Harris; Child, Francis James; *Corridos*; Folksong

Baltic Peoples in the United States

Lithuanian, Latvian, and Estonian Americans. Each is a distinct ethnic group and maintains a unique language and culture. The 1990 U.S. Census reported 812,000 persons of Lithuanian ancestry, 100,000 Latvians, and 27,000 Estonians. The largest Baltic communities may be found in New York City, Chicago, and Los Angeles, while Toronto is a center of Baltic activities in Canada. For Baltic immigrants, the reasons for leaving the homeland define the kinds of group traditions that will be maintained in America. A brief historical overview of the waves of Baltic immigration, therefore, provides a good introduction to Baltic American folklore today.

Baltic *economic immigrants* began arriving while the territory of today's Baltic republics was still part of the Russian Empire. They arrived in America seeking the opportunities offered by expanding American industry—finding work, for example, in textile mills, furniture factories, and steel mills. The largest numbers of Baltic immigrants came from rural Lithuania, settling in the coal-mining towns of Pennsylvania, the industrial cities of the Northeast, and in Chicago, which is believed to have the largest population of Lithuanians outside Lithuania. Around 1880, Latvian and Estonian immi-

grants also began to establish communities in New York City, Boston, Philadelphia, and Chicago.

Having no Social Security system, the immigrants organized social-welfare societies and lodges to provide for themselves in illness and after death. They founded church congregations to continue the mainstream religious customs of their homelands (Lutheran for Estonians and Latvians, Catholic for Lithuanians), singing the songs and reciting the prayers that maintained their faith in the old country. At the turn of the century, *religious persecution* by the Russian government stimulated another, albeit much smaller, wave of emigration, when groups of Estonian and Latvian Baptists left for the religious freedom of America.

After Estonia, Latvia, and Lithuania became independent in 1918, emigration took place largely for economic reasons, tapering off in the mid-1930s with the end of the economic Depression in Europe. The founding of the three independent states found echoes in Baltic American patriotic societies, which sent aid to their war-torn homelands in the early 1920s, petitioned the U.S. government to give political recognition to the three states, and popularized the culture of Lithuania, Latvia, and Estonia among the American public—for example, in exhibits at the World's Fair Expositions in Chicago and New York City.

Baltic socialists arrived in the United States both legally and illegally after the failed Revolution of 1905, finding refuge in America from arrest and execution in Russia. Socialist organizations fostered a lively intellectual culture, establishing libraries of books from the homeland, theater troupes, and even schools with instruction in the native language. They maintained the political traditions of their class in the Baltics, actively participating in the American socialist movement. Their ideology conflicted with that of the Baltic American religious and patriotic organizations, and the political divisions within each group sometimes ended in violent confrontations.

World War II caused the massive emigration of Baltic *political refugees*. Estonia, Latvia, and Lithuania were occupied and annexed in 1940 by the Soviet Union and remained under Soviet rule after the war. Persons living in the Baltics were not allowed to leave the USSR, but several hundred thousand had fled to the West during the war. The refugees were unwilling to return to the Stalinist terror in their homelands, and lived in temporary displaced-persons (DP) camps before they dispersed around the globe from 1948 to 1950. Some 100,000 were allowed to settle in the United States.

The Baltic political refugees organized communities with a mission that was both cultural and political. They had left their homelands, not as emigrants seeking a better life, but as exiles whose goal was the preservation of the Baltic cultures and the continuation of the battle for political independence lost in 1940 (see Carpenter 1988). They purchased churches, community centers, and rural retreats as "miniature homelands" to substitute for their countries imprisoned behind the Iron Curtain, and they established weekend schools, summer camps, Scouts, folk-dance troupes, and other youth activities to pass their language and culture on to American-born generations. National organizations held public demonstrations and lobbied the American government for policies favorable to renewed Baltic independence. It was the conscious maintenance of an identity as political exiles that brought about the blossoming of Baltic ethnic traditions in the United States after the early 1950s.

The most recent wave of Baltic immigrants began with the breakup of the USSR. When the former Soviet borders began opening in the 1980s, the first to emigrate were political dissidents expelled by the government. Later, a new trickle of Baltic economic immigrants began entering the United States. Baltic Americans have recently been moving to the Baltic, too, and cultural and social ties between the American ethnic groups and the three homelands are expanding.

Language has provided the main force of cohesion and survival in the communities and traditions of the Baltic immigrants. The emergence of language loyalty among Lithuanians, for example, caused them to break away from the Polish-speaking congregations they had joined in the 19th century. Most Baltic immigrants followed the pattern of assimilation typical of American immigrants, with the second, American-born, generation not speaking the language of their grandparents. As the language died with the immigrant generation, many folklore traditions were also forgotten.

Archaic folklore that immigrants remember from life in the Baltic countryside has been collected, for example, by Jonas Balys, who in 1949 and 1950 recorded more than one thousand Lithuanian songs, tales, legends, and riddles from prewar immigrants. A blind Latvian immigrant, Janis Plavnieks, told traditional folktales, anecdotes, personal-experience narratives, riddles, puzzles, and songs to his folklorist granddaughter, Inta Gale Carpenter (1980). Much remains to be done, however, in the study of archaic Baltic folklore in the United States. The folksong collections of Balys, Elena Bradunas, and others deserve much further analysis. Much priceless material has been lost with the passing away of Latvian and Estonian immigrants.

Material traditions also survive tenaciously among immigrants. A Lithuanian garden rarely lacks rue (*ruta*, Ruta graveolens), a green-leafed plant believed to be the young woman's companion; a sprig of rue is likewise an important part of the Lithuanian bride's dress. Berry plants and trees in the Baltic garden are often traditional favorites, which are not common in mainstream American gardens: Gooseberries, raspberries, red and black currants, apple trees, birches, and lindens, for example, have long been loved by Baltic farmers, poets, and immigrants alike.

Food traditions reflect both urban and rural roots. Meat preserved in aspic (Es. *sült*, La. *galerts*, Li. *drebucai*) was a popular food in both cities and countryside, and older immigrants still enjoy it with horseradish or vinegar. Their grandchildren, however, often dislike the mere idea of eating meat jelly. Both in America and in Latvia, the *klingeris*, a large, pretzel-shaped bread flavored with cardamom, colored with saffron, and decorated with almonds and powdered sugar, has been present at urban Latvian birthday celebrations for several generations. At Christmas, Estonians prepare *verivorst* (blood sausage), recalling the winter holiday traditions of their rural ancestors. Estonians and Latvians alike bake small bacon buns (Es. *pirukas*, La. *pirags*) on special occasions. Lithuanians prepare a rich variety of foods from rural tradition, including *cepelinai* (potato dumplings filled with meat) prepared from what Baltic Americans usually agree is the staple food of their nations: the potato.

Folklore also emerged out of the immigrant experience, in the clash and merging of two foreign cultures. Immigrants both follow and transform the old-country tradition of the death announcements printed in native-language newspapers. The name of the departed is printed in bold type, surrounded by a black border. Along with the birth and death dates and names of surviving family members, excerpts from poems, folksongs, and hymns are included to reveal the individual's personality and traditional attitudes toward death. Many of these memorials refer to the sorrow of life in a foreign country (America) and to dreams of the faraway Baltic homeland.

A similar immigrant tradition is found in American cemeteries having Lithuanian, Latvian, or Estonian sections. Tombstones reveal a personal side of immigrant traditions, expressing religious convictions and attachment to the homeland in epitaphs and ornate traditional carvings. In any Baltic American cemetery, some epitaphs are written in the native tongue, others in English, still others in a mixed language. Whether they reveal a longing for the homeland with phrases from patriotic poems, or a longing for eternity with quotations from church songs and the Bible, the stones cluster together in a declaration of the ethnic identity and community cohesion of their makers.

The merging of individual and ethnic identity appears in other traditions as well. The folk art of a Lithuanian immigrant, Joseph Mender, synthesized many identities and ideologies. Long ago, he learned to make wooden canes from tree branches from his grandfather in Lithuania. The figures and words he carved and painted on these canes, and an enormous collection of miniature pictures he drew, reveal a complex identity based on a composite of memories from childhood in Lithuania, the Catholicism of his relatives, socialist ideology strengthened during work in an American factory, and pre-Christian Lithuanian religion as described in the books he avidly read in his home in upstate New York (Biella and Lux 1990).

Baltic communities consciously maintain customs that foster ethnic unity. The three National Independence Days (Estonia, February 24; Latvia, November 18; Lithuania, February 16) are often considered most important to the communities as a whole and are celebrated at assemblies featuring speeches by both community leaders and local politicians and concerts. Soon after World War II, a day of national mourning was established on June 14 to commemorate the date in 1941 when the Soviet government began the deportation of hundreds of thousands of Baltic citizens to Siberia. In church and at home, Baltic Americans also celebrate Christian holidays (Christmas, Easter, Catholic Mardi Gras for Lithuanians) according to the traditions they have inherited from their homelands. Midsummer night, June 23, is held outdoors according to peasant traditions, with large bonfires, beer, and songs. Latvian non-Christian religious groups called *Dievturi*, and the Lithuanian *Romuva*, revive the pre-Christian customs of the seasonal cycle.

Cultural displays place ethnic traditions in the open, defining to the members of the group as well as outsiders what it means to belong to that group. Unlike the folklore of immigrants, who made traditional foods because they were tasty and easy to prepare, or sang songs to express their emotions, the ethnic groups usually ascribe a meaning of ethnic identity to nearly all forms of Baltic folklore.

What has been called folklorism, the conscious use of folklore as an ethnic or national symbol, has roots in the three Baltic cultures that reach back two centuries. The German philosopher Herder, who praised the beauty of the folksongs of the Estonian, Latvian, and Lithuanian serfs, established national symbolism still maintained by Baltic Americans. They continue the modern singing traditions of the 19th-century Baltic national movements, in which songs collected from oral tradition were arranged for performance by massive choirs on stage. Most dramatic are the national song festivals, at which choirs from across the continent perform together in a single choir of up to a thousand singers.

Baltic American festivals include many other ethnic traditions. Handmade clothes have been meticulously studied and copied from ethnographic publications from the 19th century. Handcrafted jewelry replicates pieces found in archaeological digs in the Baltic. Amber, which has for centuries been washing up from the Baltic Sea onto the western beaches of Lithuania and Latvia, is the favorite stone in necklaces and brooches. Musical instruments derived from Baltic folk tradition, in particular the Estonian *kannel,* Latvian *kokle,* and Lithuanian *kankles* (all variations of a zither-like instrument) are played on stage or displayed in exhibits of folk art. Many Baltic folklore traditions continue in America, in the cultural displays put on at international festivals, as well as in the more personal context of family gatherings such as weddings or funerals.

Guntis Šmidchens

References

Aun, Karl. 1985. *The Political Refugees: A History of Estonians in Canada.* Toronto: McClelland and Stewart.

Balys, Jonas, ed. 1977. *Lietuviu dainos Amerikoje: Lithuanian Folksongs in America.* Second Collection. Silver Spring, MD: Lietuviu Tautosakos Leidykla.

Biella, Peter, and Karen Lux. 1990. *God's Mother Is the Morning Star: The Life and Art of Joseph Mender.* 30 min. [Philadelphia]: Documentary Film. Videorecording.

Carpenter, Inta Gale. 1980. *A Latvian Storyteller: The Repertoire of Janis Plavnieks.* New York: Arno Press.

———. 1988. *Being Latvian in Exile: Folklore as Ideology.* Ph.D. diss., Indiana University.

Kezys, Algimantas, ed. 1977. *A Lithuanian Cemetery: St. Casimir Lithuanian Cemetery in Chicago, Ill.* Chicago: Lithuanian Photo Library.

Kundzins, Pauls. 1979. *Latviesu immigracijas sākumi Albertas province Kanādā un Karla Plavina seta.* N.p.: Gauja.

Van Reenan, Antanas J. 1992. *Lithuanian Diaspora: Königsberg to Chicago.* Lanham, MD: University Press of America.

Banjo

A plucked-string instrument with a neck, hollow round sound chamber, thin (animal skin or plastic) covering, and bridge. Often considered the emblem of the Southern mountaineer, the banjo actually arrived in this country with Africans in the 18th century, became an integral part of the exchange between Southern Blacks and Whites, and inspired indigenous American music before the mid-19th century.

The banjo brought to the Americas is related to the Wolof *halam* and the Mandingo *bania* still played in 20th-century Africa. Early written records prove that slaves, including Wolofs, either brought the gourd instrument with them from Africa or reconstructed the "banjar" with local materials as early as 1740. Early paintings and drawings clearly identify the short, drone string of the instrument. For almost a century, only African Americans played the banjo; it echoed the traditions of their homeland and paced their songs and dances at community gatherings. A drum-banjo ensemble dominated performances in the Louisiana area, but in the Upland South, an older stronghold of the tradition, individual banjo performances accompanied by clapping or other percussive improvisations persisted tenaciously, especially after the end of the 18th century, when laws curtailed drumming in the East.

In the middle of the 19th century, White Americans became fascinated with the Black banjo tradition. In the Southern mountains, at dances and celebrations far from the popular stage, the African American "short-thumb-string" banjo and the complexly rhythmic "thumping," or downstroke, playing style took hold. Black banjo players lived on the mountain frontier by 1800, and the ancestors of mountain Whites had earlier contact with Black musical traditions in the Piedmont. Before 1850 and increasingly during the musical exchange of the Civil War, musicians began to set the African banjo, now often adapted to have a smooth wooden neck and a wooden-rimmed open back, ringing with the European fiddle. This interchange was especially energetic among African Americans and Celtic Americans. White interest in the African American gourd banjo resulted in the innovation or popularization of the fiddle-banjo ensemble and later in the old-time string bands finally documented on records in the 1920s and 1930s.

By 1840 White fascination with the banjo had also led to the invention of stage minstrelsy (Whites in blackface devoted to the imitation—often a caricatured parody—of Blacks). Minstrelsy moved from the circus ring to its own stage and became one of the first and most applauded indigenous expressions of popular culture. The development of the five-string, wooden-rim banjo extended the instrument's rhythmic range to include greater melodic possibilities and added durability useful to traveling performances. The minstrel tradition later stimulated a flourishing of classical parlor and orchestral styles and of ragtime picking. The 19th-century banjo exchange also shaped the 20th-century innovations of the

Roby Monroe Hicks plays a banjo he has made. Beech Mountain, North Carolina, 1938. Photo Frank Warner. American Folklife Center.

tenor banjo (played with a plectrum in quartets and jazz bands) and the bluegrass banjo, which emerged with its finger-picking styles at the time of the increasing industrialization of the South during World War II. While classical, jazz, and ragtime styles dispersed, the most vital folk styles, downstroking and up-picking, remained strong, close to their roots in the rural South. Two-finger up-picking, acquired from Blacks by minstrels before 1865, also emerged in the rural South. These developments laid the groundwork for the hard-driving, syncopated, bluegrass style popularized by Earl Scruggs and others.

While the old-time five-string folk banjo tradition was still strongly shared by Blacks and Whites during the last half of the 19th century, the complex trading of song material between these musicians gave rise to a distinct genre of American folk music—the banjo song. Although initially and predominantly influenced by African American tastes, the diverse and continuing exchange of these songs came to reflect the influences of both traditions. Old-time African American banjo playing began to decline in the first decade of the 20th century, soon after inexpensive guitars became readily available and at the time that Jim Crow laws became increasingly restrictive for Blacks. Shaped by the banjo-song genre, the songster qualities of the guitar, and industrial encroachment,

a growing sense of African American community resistance began to emerge in the blues. But still today, in the performance of both White and Black old-time musicians, the echo of the old African American banjo rings. The instrument itself—the fretless, short-drone-string banjo—its "thumping," downstroke playing style, its special tunings, and its repertoire of lyric banjo songs persist among both Southern Whites and some Blacks. These same traditions were influential in the folk revival popularized by Pete Seeger, the New Lost City Ramblers, and Southern bands like the Hollow Rock String Band and the Highwoods.

Though other Europeans, some of whom were German, made five-string banjos and contributed to the availability and influence of the instrument in the 19th century, banjo musical exchange seems to have taken place primarily in the rural South between two especially gifted groups: African Americans, including Wolofs, and Celtic Americans, many of whom were Scots-Irish and Irish. The fact that the interchange flourished in the 1840s supports this pattern, for at that time the Irish who emigrated to escape the potato blight began to reinvigorate and diversify the Scots-Irish fiddle tradition and other musical trading. Ireland was one of the early places toured by the first full minstrel band in 1843, and Black banjo pickers still play certain traditional fiddle pieces quite old in Ireland.

The honor of "inventing" the five-string banjo has often rested with Joel Sweeney, a Southern mountain boy of Irish descent who learned to play from Black slaves about 1830 and later became one of the earliest and most influential minstrels. Although Sweeney could have added a fifth string (now called the fourth string) and a wooden rim to the banjo, he definitely popularized these innovations, which served the melodic needs of White performers. He did not, however, add the shortened thumb string (now called the fifth string), which served the musical needs of downstroking ("thumping" or clawhammer) and arrived in the Americas with the ancestors of 20th-century Black musicians like Dink Roberts, John Snipes, and Odell and Joe Thompson.

Some have argued that mountain Whites learned directly from minstrels, but the few reports available tend to identify this early exchange as examples of early minstrels "catching" material from Blacks and White Upland Southerners. The fact that Sweeney himself became a minstrel accounts for considerable folk transmission to the formative players of minstrelsy. That mountain Whites learned directly from Blacks seems apparent from the fact that present-day southern Blacks and Whites share certain special tunings and techniques that are not emphasized and often not even described in the mid-19th-century minstrel banjo instructors. In short, the interest of White mountain musicians and minstrels in African American banjo traditions led to a lively exchange that indelibly shaped indigenous American folk music and still flourishes as the 20th century draws to a close.

Cecelia Conway

References

Bailey, Jay. 1972. Historical Origin and Stylistic Developments of the Five-String Banjo. *Journal of American*

Folklore 95:58–65.

Cohen, John, and Mike Seeger, eds. 1964. *New Lost City Ramblers Songbook.* New York: Oak Publications.

Conway, Cecelia. 1995. *African Banjo Echoes in Appalachia.* Knoxville: University of Tennessee Press.

Epstein, Dena J. 1977. *Sinful Tunes and Spirituals: Black Folk Music to the Civil War.* Urbana: University of Illinois Press.

Heaton, Cherrill P. 1971. The Five-String Banjo in North Carolina. *Southern Folklore Quarterly* 35:62–82.

Lornell, Kip. 1974. Pre-Blues Banjo and Fiddle. *Living Blues* 18:25–27.

Webb, Robert Lloyd. 1984. *Ring the Banjar! The Banjo in America from Folklore to Factory.* Cambridge: MIT Museum.

Winans, Robert. 1976. The Folk, the Stage, and the Five-String Banjo in the Nineteenth Century. *Journal of American Folklore* 89:407–437.

See also Bluegrass; Macon, David Harrison "Uncle Dave"; Minstrel Shows; Seeger, Pete

Barbeau, Marius (1883–1969)

Canada's leading folklorist. Barbeau's contribution to Canadian folklore can hardly be overestimated. *The Dictionary of Literary Biography* (92:13–16, 1990) gives an extensive bibliography and describes his career.

He worked at the National Museum from 1911 until his death, and the Canadian press once summed up his work thus:

> He gave the national Museum a collection of 195 Eskimo songs, more than 3,000 Indian, close to 7,000 French-Canadian, and 1,500 old English songs. Many of them are still on the old tube-like records that came off his Edison recorder. . . . "I would need two lives to process all my research," he once said.

The work he achieved in one lifetime was almost unbelievable. In an age of increasing specialization, he ranged over the whole field of folklore and anthropology, collecting, studying, and describing Indian myths, ceremonials, language, music, arts, and culture; French Canadian folktales, folksongs, art, games, handicrafts, and architecture; and Anglo-Canadian songs and art. His books include two novels reflecting Indian life. A prolific writer, and completely bilingual, he published fifty major books, as many more pamphlets and monographs, and 700 articles in a hundred different periodicals ranging from scientific journals to popular magazines and daily papers. His home was a miniature museum of Indian and French Canadian folk art.

In 1947 Luc Lacourcière wrote, *"Monsieur Barbeau a consacre sa vie et ses etudes a nos traditions populaires. Grace a lui, le folklore canadien occupe sa place dans l'etude scientifique des traditions comparees,"* and in 1950 F.J. Alcock, curator of Canada's National Museum, wrote the following:

> Dr. Barbeau has been responsible for the development of folklore research in Canada, and the wealth of folklore material in the possession of the national Museum of Canada was largely collected by him and the numerous students to whom he has transmitted his enthusiasm for this type of study.

Barbeau was a Fellow of the American Folklore Society, and he served as president and associate editor of the *Journal of American Folklore,* for which he prepared ten special Canadian issues. He founded the Canadian Folk Music Society in 1956 and organized the 1961 International Folk Music Council conference in Quebec.

The list of honors he received would fill a page. They include the Gold Medal of the Royal Society of Canada, honorary degrees from the Universities of Montreal, Laval, and Oxford, and the title of Companion of the Order of Canada, the highest honor Canada bestows.

His major books from the National Museum include *Totem Poles* (1950–1951), *Haida Carvers in Argillite* (1957), *Huron-Wyandot Traditional Narratives* (1960), and three massive volumes of French-Canadian songs: *Le Rossignol y chante* (1962), *En roulant ma boule* (1982), and *Le Roi boit* (1984).

Barbeau was no ivory-tower scholar: He tried to preserve and promote folklore in every way he could. He lectured to many groups, wrote popular books and articles, appeared on radio and television, and made several records. His personal charm comes across in *My Life in Recording Canadian-Indian Folk-Lore* (Folkways Records 3502), in which he sings and beats an Indian drum.

Edith Fowke

Barnicle, Mary Elizabeth (ca. 1898–1979)

Educator and folklorist. Barnicle was an energetic and enthusiastic collector-educator whose work in the area of Appalachian folklife has not been fully appreciated. A Bryn Mawr graduate specializing in medieval English literature, Barnicle taught at New York University from the early 1930s to the late 1940s. While teaching folklore there, she fell under the influence of John Lomax's work and organized a field trip to Georgia, Florida, and the Bahamas to collect folklore in 1935. (These recordings are on deposit at the Library of Congress' Archive of Folk Culture.)

In 1935 she met her husband-to-be, Tillman Cadle, a Kentucky miner and union activist, who had come to New York to visit his friend, Jim Garland, who had suffered a serious mining injury. In 1938 and thereafter, Cadle accompanied Barnicle on a series of recording trips in Kentucky. Her last teaching position was at the University of Tennessee in 1949–1950, but she left there under a cloud, following political problems with a very conservative English Department. Just as she was leaving the university, Barnicle was informed that 200 of her cherished field recordings, which had been on deposit in a campus office, had been misplaced. Deeply hurt by what she and Cadle regarded as the suspicious circumstances of the recordings' disappearance, she lost interest in any further fieldwork.

In 1983, on the shelves of the radio station at the University of Tennessee at Knoxville, folklorist Willie Smyth stumbled upon a cache of 150 recordings that had been made by Barnicle between 1938 and 1949 in the Pineville, Kentucky, area. The 1986 LP recording based on this find is an excellent sampling from her field recordings, together with extensive biographical information.

Norm Cohen

References

Smyth, Willie. 1986. *It's Just the Same Today: The Barnicle-Cadle Field Recordings from Eastern Tennessee and Kentucky, 1938–1949.* Tennessee Folklore Society LP TFS 108.

Barrick, Mac E. (1933–1991)

Major collector of regional folklore in central Pennsylvania and analyst of proverbs, beliefs, jokes, and traditional tools. Barrick graduated from Dickinson College in his native Carlisle, Pennsylvania, in 1955; he went on to the University of Illinois for his M.A. and the University of Pennsylvania for his Ph.D. He taught Spanish and folklore at Villanova University, Lycoming College, and Dickinson College, and after 1968 at Shippensburg University. Barrick compiled a major regional archive of folklore from central Pennsylvania, which is housed at the Center for Pennsylvania Culture Studies at Pennsylvania State University at Harrisburg. He died in 1991.

Barrick's collections of central Pennsylvania folklore began in the 1960s; drawing on these materials, he developed detailed articles on proverbs, riddles, rhymes, legends, tales, anecdotes, autograph verses, language, games, medicine, and beliefs. In these articles, he showed his mastery of textual analysis from both comparative and contextual points of view. With his knowledge of foreign languages, Barrick scoured books from international libraries to annotate his sources. He appropriately wrote the chapter "Folklore and the Verbal Text" for the American Folklore Society's bicentennial publication, *100 Years of American Folklore Studies* (1988). Barrick developed a series of articles on popular joke cycles and regional folk humor, and he offered one of the first inquiries into photocopied and typescript humor as folklore.

Barrick was avidly interested in preindustrial tools and folk crafts within the context of rural economy and community life. He developed this interest with studies of fishing spears (1972), hay knives (1983), corn knives and husking pegs (1970), scrapers (1979), folk toys (1979), and log houses (1986). In central Pennsylvania, much of his collecting was from the Pennsylvania "Dutch," descendants of German settlers who came to Pennsylvania during the late 18th and early 19th centuries. He expanded his knowledge of German American traditions across the country, and his research led to his book *German American Folklore* (1987). He also worked in Spanish folklore, documenting proverb usage in medieval Spain and Portugal and folklore in the work of Miguel de Cervantes and other writers.

Barrick was twice elected president of the Pennsylvania Folklore Society. He served on the editorial board of *Pennsylvania Folklife* and was an original member of the Folklife Advisory Council for the Pennsylvania Heritage Affairs Commission.

Simon J. Bronner

References

Barrick, Mac E. 1963. Proverbs and Sayings from Cumberland County. *Keystone Folklore Quarterly* 8:139–203.
———. 1985. "Welcome to the Clothes": Changing Proverb Function in the Spanish Renaissance. *Proverbium* 2:1–19.
———. 1994. *Lewis the Robber: A Pennsylvania Folk Hero in Life and Legend.* Terre Haute, IN: Hoosier Folklore Society.

Barry, Phillips (1880–1937)

Most important of the post-Child generation of American ballad scholar-collectors, whose theory of communal re-creation eventually laid to rest the communal theory of ballad origins. Barry based his scholarly writing on both library research and fieldwork and "was the first Anglo-American scholar to investigate traditional song in all its aspects: text, tune, performance, and transmission" (Wilgus 1959:68). Barry brought to his endeavors the unique combination of vast learning, superb academic training, and a comprehensive understanding of musicology. He was a great stimulus to the critical study of the ballad, and his notions of the genre were prescient and far reaching, still exerting their influence on the field.

Educated at Harvard University in the years immediately after Francis James Child, Barry studied folklore, theology, and classical and medieval literature, maintaining a long relationship with his mentors, George Lyman Kittredge, Kuno Franke, and Leo Wiener. This lent him meaningful credibility as a private scholar of independent mind and means, for Barry enjoyed both the respect of the academy and the freedom to devote his time and energies exclusively to scholarship. At the start of his career, the very definition of a ballad was far from settled (the terms "folk-song," "ballad," and even "folk music" were used interchangeably). Despite increasingly strident attacks, Francis Barton Gummere's theory of communal origins held sway. Through extensive fieldwork, exacting documentation, gradual publication, and continual analysis of a growing body of American folksong items, Barry and his peers presided over the sorting out of definition, style, transmission, and other vexing matters left unclear by the great library-centered scholars of the preceding century.

A dedicated collector, Barry followed fieldwork leads from family, friends, and associates, moving beyond these personal networks by placing notices in local newspapers, the *Boston Transcript,* among others. He kept in close contact with other collectors and scholars, contributing both insights and examples to the work of such learned colleagues as H.M. Belden and encouraging hosts of amateur collectors, especially in New England.

Barry's pursuit of American folk music, beginning in 1903, bore fruit in a steady harvest of folksong texts and melodies, primarily from northern New England and the Maritimes, a region that, until his pioneering work, was thought devoid of migratory ballads. Publishing his results, in such journals as the *Journal of American Folklore, American Speech,* and *Modern Language Notes,* initially he was adding Northeast examples to a growing compendium of American folksong texts. His first article, "The Lord Randall Ballad in America" (1903), presents six texts and three melodies of Child 12 and includes a few comments comparing Barry's collected examples to versions already in print. He was soon working out his ideas, bit by bit, in headnotes to texts and melodies and in a number of ballad histories, making important theoretical advances. His responses and reactions to ideas of other ballad scholars appear throughout his writings, in lively discussions or brief statements like fine tunings, always confidently asserted. Typically, his gracefully written, succinct, and erudite commentaries illumine matters large and small, so that, taken together, they comprise a thorough treatment of his subject.

Working in the era of discovery of American folksongs, Barry ushered in the modern age of ballad studies. Among the more recognized of his accomplishments is his demonstration that songs of the folk, rather than being products of "dancing throngs" composing communally, are instead compositions of "individual invention plus communal re-creation," a term he introduced in 1907 in an instructive musicological discussion contrasting "traditional" and "composed" airs. He considered the notion to be the very crux of the issue of origins. A song is traditional, he claimed, if it is composed by the folk, first as an individual composition, then communally re-created through the process of transmission. "It should be understood," he stated at the end of his career, "that *communal re-creation* must include not merely the cumulative effect of accidental and partly conscious change made by many folk singers over a long period of time, but also sudden, marked and perfectly intentional changes by folk singers who are also folk composers, and have . . . retold an old ballad story in more or less new wording of their own."

A number of Barry's other contributions are at least as far reaching, and perhaps of greater significance. Fieldwork with singers stretched his understanding of the genre, and he daringly followed their lead in shaping both his conclusions and his methodology. His was a sophisticated understanding of structural and aesthetic aspects of folksinging. For him, folksongs were the union of text and air (the whole text and the whole melody), completely interdependent. Although Barry's analysis of texts "actually outweighs his analysis of tunes" (Wilgus 1968), his pioneering discussion of traditional singing style and sets of tunes anticipated the great musicological treatments of folksong melodies published by the subsequent generation of folk-tune scholars. He insisted that other collectors search for tunes and treat them properly. Furthermore, he remained faithful to his early declaration that "to a folk-singer, words and music together make the ballad he sings. The one is not felt to exist without the other."

As evidence accumulated, Barry saw ballad tradition as a mixture of old and new pieces, all subject to communal re-creation. He edged toward including older popular pieces of known authorship into the rubric of folksong, stating boldly that whatever a folksinger sings "from memory" and "for the sheer joy of singing" is traditional. The idea was abhorrent to purists among his contemporaries, but Barry asked, "Why make a distinction when the folk makes none?" The effect of communal re-creation on such songs of commercial origin as "Casey Jones" supports his claim.

Just as prescient was his assertion, ventured in a discussion of Irish folksongs, of the "fact that folk-song is in reality an idea," of which, by tracing its history, "we can get but the process of actualization." This is a revolutionary shift in understanding the nature of a ballad. Elsewhere, he clarified his meaning: "No longer is a ballad a static narrative of an event or situation," but it is a "process . . . one by which a simple event in human experience of subjective interest, narrated in simple language, set to a simple melody is progressively objectivated." Barry also challenged the pervasive attitude that folk tradition is the product of illiteracy, pointing out that the printed ballad often stimulated tradition. He went so far as to claim "illiteracy" to be "a negative factor in ballad tradition . . . inhibit[ing] its survival," thereby including the ballad printer among the folk engaged in re-creation.

Late in his life, Barry wrote of an "instinct" he had felt when he started collecting, "to go to the folk-singers . . . [for] evidence in solving the . . . problems of balladry." It is entirely possible that the incidence of a few folksongs in his own family's tradition gave him a glimmer of the process of transmission he later articulated, thus accounting for the intuition that more than thirty years later he reflected upon as "instinct."

Barry was a scrupulous editor who wrote in a style accessible to a general audience, and his mentorship of talented amateur collectors, some of whose work he greatly enhanced by outright collaboration, is also noteworthy. He shared his prodigious learning, introduced the resources of other scholars, provided models for documenting and archiving, and gave editorial guidance. A number of exceedingly well-edited mid-century New England collections of ballads and folksongs bear his stamp.

Barry mentored and collaborated extensively with Fannie Hardy Eckstorm and Mary W. Smyth in Maine and Helen Hartness Flanders in Vermont, among others. Eloise Hubbard Linscott paid him posthumous tribute in her *Folksongs of Old New England,* published in 1939. Of all New England collectors who were his contemporaries, only Edith Sturgis makes no mention of a significant debt of gratitude to Barry, and her *Songs from the Hills of Vermont* was a parochial effort unconnected to any ballad studies network.

A long interest in starting a separate professional American society for folksongs led Barry to found the Folk-Song Society of the Northeast. From 1930 on, he published the greater portion of his collections and commentary under its aegis in the *Bulletin of the Folk-Song Society of the Northeast,* which ceased publication at his death. (There is an annual of broader scope, *Northeast Folklore,* the publishing arm of the Northeast Folklore Society, which, in turn, was founded in the 1960s as a tribute to Phillips Barry by Edward M. Ives at the University of Maine, Orono.)

Linda Morley

References

Barry, Phillips. [1930–1934] 1960. Ed. and principal contrib. *Bulletin of the Folk-Song Society of the Northeast*. Introduction by Samuel P. Bayard. Philadelphia: American Folklore Society.

———. 1939a. *Folk Music in America*. New York: National Service Bureau.

———. 1939b. *The Maine Woods Songster: Fifty Songs for Singing*. Cambridge, MA: Powell.

Barry, Phillips, Fannie H. Eckstorm, and Mary W. Smyth, eds. 1929. *British Ballads from Maine*. Critical Notes by Phillips Barry. New Haven, CT: Yale University Press.

Flanders, Helen Hartness, Elizabeth Flanders Ballard, George Brown, and Phillips Barry, eds. 1939. *The New Green Mountain Songster*. New Haven, CT: Yale University Press.

Wilgus, D.K. 1959. *Anglo-American Folksong Scholarship since 1898*. New Brunswick, NJ: Rutgers University Press.

Bascom, William R. (1912–1981)

The leading American Africanist of his generation, specializing in art, folkloristics, and the Yoruba people of southeastern Nigeria. An early graduate student of Melville Jean Herskovits, Bascom shared his interest in the comparative study of religion, art, and folklore throughout Africa and its Diaspora. Beginning fieldwork in Nigeria in 1937, he learned the difficult tonal Yoruba language.

After wartime governmental research in Nigeria and Micronesia, Bascom and his Cuban-born wife, Berta, his lifelong coworker, began their studies of the Shango cult, *santeria,* and divination practices of Yoruba origin in Cuba and elsewhere in the New World. *Continuity and Change in Africa Cultures,* which he edited with Herskovits in 1959, is a reference text so popular that it has been reprinted eight times. In 1957 he left Northwestern University, Evanston, Ill., to become the founding director of the Lowie (now Phoebe A. Hearst) Museum of Anthropology at the University of California, Berkeley, where his brilliant exhibitions of African art produced several fine catalogs and a popular text. Continuing his interest in Yoruba religion first developed in his dissertation on cult groups, he produced the magisterial *Ifa Divination: Communication between Gods and Men in West Africa* in 1969, which won the Pitre Prize, plus follow-up studies on the Shango cult of the Yoruba god of thunder and lightning as it spread throughout the New World, and a parallel study of the spread of Ifa divination.

Although he described himself as "an anthropologist who does folklore," Bascom's contributions were invaluable in a number of papers showing the interplay between myth, narrative, and divination. His two addresses as president of the American Folklore Society, "Four Functions of Folklore" (1954) and "Verbal Art" (1955), along with other major papers displaying his outstanding skill in careful and clear description and analysis in preference to theory, were collected as *Contributions to Folkloristics* just after his death in 1981. He was interested in diffusion theory, as in his major survey article on "Folklore Research in Africa" published in the *Journal of American Folklore* in 1964, as well as in the aesthetics of narration, as shown in *African Dilemma Tales* (1975). Edited by Alan Dundes in 1992, his posthumous *African Folktales in the New World* is Bascom's final triumphant blast in the decades-long battle with Richard M. Dorson, who held that he had never collected a tale of African origin from his many African American informants, only European, Native American, or Asian tales, and that "Anansi (the popular African trickster) fails to set foot in the United States." Bascom published numerous tales unquestionably from Africa but told in the Americas, including Anansi stories from the United States. The book also brings up important and embarrassing questions about diffusion and independent invention so long unanswered that contemporary scholars simply eschew them.

Daniel J. Crowley

References

Bascom, William R. 1944. *The Sociological Role of the Yoruba Cult-Group*. Memoirs of the American Anthropological Association No. 63. Menasha, WI: American Anthropological Association.

———. 1947. *Ponape* [now Pohnpei]: *A Pacific Economy in Transition*. Vol. 8 of *Economic Survey of Micronesia*. Honolulu: U.S. Commercial Co.

———. 1967. *African Arts: An Exhibition at the Lowie Museum*. Berkeley: University of California Press.

———. 1972. *Shango in the New World*. Occasional Publications of the African and Afro-American Research Institute No. 4. Austin: University of Texas Press.

———. 1973. *African Art in Cultural Context*. New York: W.W. Norton.

———. 1980. *Sixteen Cowries: Yoruba Divination from Africa to the New World*. Bloomington: Indiana University Press.

Ottenberg, Simon, ed. 1982. *African Religious Groups and Beliefs; Papers in Honor of William R. Bascom*. Meerut, India: Folklore Institute.

Baseball

A form of "rounders"; America's national game for nearly 150 years. Baseball is played formally and informally as "hardball," "softball," "stickball," "wiffle ball," "monkey move-up," "one old cat," and in dozens of other forms. Almost all Americans have played some version of it, watched it, and read about it, and most Americans are exposed to its lore and language more often than they realize. Baseball has also sunk deep roots in Japan and Latin America.

Baseball players are from disparate regional and ethnic backgrounds. They come together only for practices, games, and road trips, then go their separate ways. White, Black, Latino, they are literate and subject to the same popular culture that America at large shares. Moreover, they read the people who write about the game, and they talk to the people who broadcast it. Thus, they are not a clear-cut folk group, although they have a certain homogeneity, and an occupa-

THE AMERICAN NATIONAL GAME OF BASE BALL.
GRAND MATCH FOR THE CHAMPIONSHIP AT THE ELYSIAN FIELDS, HOBOKEN, N. J.

tional lore has developed among and about them. This lore may be divided into three parts.

First is the lore brought to the game by the players from their varied backgrounds. This lore is drawn on as needed and, even if modified to fit the occupation, differs little from the same lore beyond the game. The number thirteen is unlucky on the diamond as at home. Second is the lore that grows up within the game itself. Dizzy Dean strolls over to the opposing dugout, asks each starter what pitch he prefers, then, throwing only the pitches requested, hurls a shutout. Third is the lore that sportswriters, radio and television personnel, and sometimes fans create about baseball, much of which filters back to the players. The proverb "Nice guys finish last," erroneously attributed to Leo Durocher, is a case in point.

Because most ballplayers come from literate backgrounds, they have no need for the major forms of folk tradition: for religious stories like myths (they have their Christianity or Islam or other religions), for songs, ballads, and love lyrics (they have radios, televisions, and cassette players), nor for full-blown legends chronicling the history of their cultures. What one finds, therefore, are anecdotal legends and jokes, proverbial lore, superstitions, and especially a vigorous body of folk speech.

Baseball's most famous tale is about George Herman "Babe" Ruth, the true hero of the game. Supposedly, this superman, at the plate in the fourth inning of the third game of the 1932 World Series against star pitcher Charlie Root, had two strikes on him when he pointed to the centerfield stands and on the next pitch hit a home run to the exact spot

indicated. Eyewitnesses agree that Ruth did raise his finger after the second strike, but Root insisted until he died that all Ruth was doing was illustrating his taunt: "You still need one more, kid!" Nevertheless, the "indicator home run" story is known wherever baseball is known and has pretty much hardened into fact. Ruth, who was by far the most charismatic player to play the game, is also the hero of numerous anecdotes: He drinks all night, then smashes three homers when hung over; he earns more than President Hoover and rationalizes it on the grounds that he had a better year than the "prez";' he eats and wenches in a fashion that would exhaust Hercules.

But there are other heroes and other tales. Rube Waddell loads the bases on purpose, calls in the outfield, and strikes out the side. Lefty Gomez comments on his fastball at the end of his career: "I'm throwing as hard as I ever did; they just aren't getting there as fast." Such anecdotes wander, attaching themselves to whatever hero is before the camera at the moment. Who was the player who hit one for the sick child? Who was the pitcher so mean he "low-bridged" his mother at a church softball game? Who was the batter thrown out of the game because he told the umpire he was sick, ". . . sick of bad calls"?

Many stories take the form of tall tales or outright jokes. Satchel Paige is known to throw so hard he can get strikeouts without releasing the ball: He simply winds up, the catcher slaps his glove, and the duped umpire yells "Strike!" the batter blinking in agreement. A dog runs onto the field and grabs a grounder, forcing Honus Wagner to pick up the animal and heave him to first for the out. Gaylord Perry throws an illegal spitball that is so loaded it sprays both the batter and the umpire.

Although baseball has developed a number of beliefs and superstitions—such as the seventh-inning stretch and the prohibition against telling a pitcher he has a no-hitter going—most such material is highly personal. Players who always cross a baseline right-foot-first, or who pick up every scrap of paper in the dugout, or who wear lucky clothes and carry amulets are acting no differently than any human faced with a critical situation. Nor is most of this material unique to the game. The bad luck associated with a black cat, and the good luck associated with four-leaf clovers, the rabbit's foot, and not shaving on the day of a game, are superstitions known everywhere in America.

Baseball's proverbs and proverbial sayings are much more apt to rise from the occupation itself. Besides the famous "Nice guys finish last," there are true proverbs like "Don't pitch a country boy high" (Don't throw fastballs to a rookie), truisms like "Southpaws are crazy," conventional phrases like "Stick it in his ear," and popular comparisons like "Loose as a goose" or "Loosey goosey." Much of this material is part of the cant of the game and is a vital part of American speech. Even the least interested know the meaning of words and phrases like "rookie," "bench warmer," "rooter," "beanball," "southpaw," "bush-league," "pinch hit," "out in left field," or "out of my league," even if they have no idea of the meaning of a "can of corn" (easy fly ball), a "gopher ball" (a pitch a batter can "go for"), or a clothesline (line drive).

Sportswriters and announcers, mingling with the players, have been instrumental in spreading such folk-say. One of their efforts has resulted in the widely used malapropisms attributed to former catcher, coach, and manager Yogi Berra: "It's not over 'til it's over," "It's *déjà vu* all over again," and (at an event honoring him), "Thanks for making this night necessary." Some writers and announcers have had true literary talent or flair: Ring Lardner, Gilbert Patton, Edward Stratemeyer, Grantland Rice, Paul Gallico, Ernest Thayer, and James Thurber, to name a few. In magazines and newspapers, these men created an entire lore about the game. Tales of Lardner's Jack O'Keefe in *You Know Me, Al;* Patton's Frank Merriwell, Stratemeyer's Baseball Joe, Thayer's Casey of Mudville, and Thurber's midget in *You Could Look It Up* (which inspired Bill Veeck to send midget Eddie Gaedel to bat in a major league game) are as much a part of baseball's lore as stories about Ruth, Waddell, or Dean.

Tristram Potter Coffin

References

Coffin, Tristram Potter. 1971. *The Old Ball Game: Baseball in Folklore and Fiction.* New York: Herder and Herder.
———. 1975. *The Illustrated Book of Baseball Folklore.* New York: Seabury.
Ludwig, H.A. 1986. *Baseball Lingo.* Cleveland, OH: Lingo.
McCue, Andrew. 1991. *Baseball by the Books: A History and Complete Bibliography of Baseball Fiction.* Dubuque, IA: William C. Brown.
Okrent, David, and Steve Wulf. 1989. *Baseball Anecdotes.* New York: Oxford University Press.

Basketmaking

An ancient traditional technique of shaping natural material into a container form. Using one of three methods—plaiting, weaving, or coiling—basket makers have created hundreds of shapes and sizes over the centuries. Their products, probably used in every society in the world, have functioned in myriad ways: as silos, sheds, vehicles, boats, furniture, garments, roofs, shoes, hats, targets, decorations, strainers, cradles, coffins, ceremonial objects, trays, houses, fans, creels, and tools. Baskets have been used as containers to hold such things as gourds, eggs, bottles, canes, weapons, milk, apples, mush, berries, water, money, cosmetics, and firewood.

Traditional basketry has been produced in every size, from tiny thimble cases to giant fish-storage baskets. The range of sizes and shapes is usually dictated by function, and the raw materials by ecology. Leaves, vines, and reeds are used in tropical areas, grasses and low-growing plants in arid regions, and split wood and bark in woodland areas.

In the Orient, elegance of design, attention to detail, and perfection of craftsmanship have produced some of the most exquisite baskets in existence. In Africa, where materials are plentiful and artful decoration is an accepted part of daily life, basketry has always been an important craft, and remains so today. There is still a Basketmakers' Guild in London, and traditional (though now usually poorly made) baskets have become a popular tourist item in Europe and elsewhere. Baskets made by Native Americans are known throughout the world for their diversity of design and technique, their beauty, and their ancient history (baskets discovered in Utah have been dated from 7,000 B.C.). Researchers believe that Native Americans had well over a hundred general and specific uses for basketry.

Among the colonists in the United States, traditional basketry began with simply importing European baskets and using indigenous versions. Those who later wove baskets for themselves and for sale followed their own native traditions (as they would with all of their folkways), adapting local materials where necessary. However, they often copied or modified the materials, forms, and techniques used by their neighbors as well (including Native Americans, other immigrants, and Africans).

Basketry was usually a "side" profession with American immigrants, since it lent itself so readily to a spare-time occupation. Some producers became established as professionals in a few sections of the country; and sometimes whole families kept a business going, taking wagonloads of baskets around the countryside to sell. Usually, however, output was reserved for family and near-neighbor consumption.

Several traditional American groups—religious, ethnic, racial, and regional—have been renowned for their basket artistry. The Shakers were justly famous for all of their fine products, among them an astounding variety of basket types. They manufactured quantities of baskets of sound construction and elegant simplicity that were sold outside the community in the early and mid-19th century. The Pennsylvania

Walter Handy with basketmaking materials and his baskets. Claudeville, Virginia, 1978. Photo Blanton Owen. American Folklife Center.

"Dutch" (German) immigrants, who settled primarily in the southeastern portion of that state, continued to make their traditional baskets from coiled rye straw (sometimes wheat and oat straw as well), round willow rods, and flat oak splints. They produced a wide array of functional forms, made almost entirely by part-time workers, usually on winter evenings. African Americans living in the coastal regions, especially in South Carolina, made coiled sweet-grass baskets that closely resemble those produced in Africa. Baskets from the Southern Appalachian Highlands demonstrate a continuity in form, since ribbed baskets were and are their best-known type. Ash, oak, elm, maple, hickory, and various barks were used, though

white oak became the prevalent wood used in that region and in the Ozarks, along with young shoots of willow, a variety of vines, and other tough-fibered plant materials.

Finding and identifying baskets made today in a traditional manner and locating their makers is not easy, though it is possible with diligent research. In the case of old baskets, correlating them with their makers is virtually impossible. Basket makers almost never signed their works, nor did they keep records. City directories, Census records, and other standard historical documents seldom uncover basket weavers; they simply were not listed, since the craft was nearly always a side profession. House and farm inventories, store records, and oral tradition have been the most fruitful, albeit limited, sources for uncovering their history.

In the mid-19th century, machine-made baskets decimated a once thriving business in the United States, and younger men turned to other trades instead. (There are few reports of White women basket makers, only "helpers," which may simply reflect a bias on the part of writers.) The Arts and Crafts movement in the 19th century helped avoid a total decline of craftsmanship during the Industrial Revolution. In the early 20th century, the Rural Handicrafts movement also came to the fore, supporting crafts as art, as recreation, and as a source of rural income, especially for residents of the Southern Appalachian Highlands. This type of activity was interrupted by World War II, and for several decades basket-making declined precipitously. More recently, with the wave of nostalgia for the "good old days," along with a revolt against our society's plastic, disposable lifestyle, basketmaking has experienced such a resurgence that the few remaining traditional weavers cannot meet increasing demand for their products.

Baskets had, of course, been a necessary adjunct to a number of important occupations, such as farming, fishing, hunting, the production of cheese, honey, and cotton, and the wood industries. They were used in numerous household activities and were popular gift items, too. But those early baskets were nearly all woven with function as the primary consideration. Recently, instead of being used only for functional purposes, baskets have acquired a new role as decorative objects. Contemporary artists utilize traditional techniques, but with a freedom from the constraints of the usual form-dictated-by-function, which allows for innovative, artistic approaches. Still, for many who learned in the traditional way by example, either in a family or a community setting, there is little experimentation, and the old ways are considered the best (and also the best *sellers*).

Preparing the wood splints for plaiting and weaving is one of the most difficult aspects of basketmaking. It entails finding a tall, healthy tree, straight and relatively knot free (or other suitable, easier material), chopping it down, and then splitting it into sections. After the bark is removed, the wood, after being started with a knife, is pulled into long strips with the hands. The strips continue to be pulled apart by hand, until they are the desired thinness.

At this point, those artisans making flat splints scrape and smooth the wood on their laps on a shaving horse, using a sharp knife. Those making round splints or rods (a rare technique today) have several more steps to perform. First they pull a one-fourth- to one-half-inch splint through a series of metal dies set into a board. The board is secured and the dies are filed sharp; as the splint is pulled through the die with pliers, it is neatly shaved. A rod of the desired diameter is achieved by pulling it through successively smaller holes.

There are three types of basket construction: plaiting, weaving, and coiling.

Plaiting consists of working flat materials in two opposite directions, interweaving them at right angles in either an over one/under one pattern, or an over two/under two pattern.

When *weaving*, the basket maker works warps or stakes, held together by wefts. In one type of weaving, wickerwork, a single weft is woven through the stakes; in twining, two or more wefts are twisted and locked around the stakes. Weaving can be done with either flat or round splints.

When constructing a plaited or woven basket, the maker constructs a bottom first. In plaiting, splints are laid out, usually on the floor or on a table, and then interwoven into a bottom of the desired shape. These splints are then bent up at each side and plaited in an over/under pattern with splints running at right angles to form the sides of the basket. A rim is bound on, and a handle is then inserted and lashed into place.

In weaving, the bottom resembles a spider web, with spokes radiating from a circular core. When using flat splints, those spokes are pulled or bent up to become uprights for the sides. When making round-rod baskets, new rods are inserted into the bottom and bent up for the stakes around which the weavers are manipulated.

Coiling consists of winding a round bundle of tightly gathered material—usually a type of grass or straw—into a spiral and sewing it together at regular intervals with a binder. The binder can be either a long strand from the bundle itself, or a different material altogether. Collecting materials for this method is less arduous than for the other two methods of basketry, since sweet grass, pine needles, palmetto, and rush, for example, are easier by far to harvest than trees.

A basket is begun by gathering and knotting a handful of central fiber into a bundle of the desired diameter (often one-fourth inch), then wrapping a portion tightly with a flexible binder. Turning the coil clockwise (usually), the maker forms a continuous spiral, using a needle or an awl to girdle the grass with one stitch, and then attach it to the preceding row with another. Shape is dictated by the placement of the subsequent coils in relation to those preceding them.

It must be emphasized that, as technical as a description becomes, it suggests only a few of the steps involved in these often arduous processes. As basket maker Dwight Stump of Hocking County, Ohio, admitted, sometimes the work becomes tedious. One day, chuckling, he commented:

> At times I have a notion to quit. Like everything, it gets monotonous. Sometimes I have to stop and do something else, mebbe two, three months. Then I wonder how I'd go to make baskets, and I go back to makin' baskets again. Yeah, it's like an old basket maker used to tell me, "When you get in the Basket makers' Row once, it's hard to get out." I don't know why, it just kind of grows on a person. You get attached to it. (Joyce 1989)

Rosemary O. Joyce

References

Davis, Gerald L. 1976. Afro-American Coil Basketry in Charleston County, South Carolina: Affective Characteristics of an Artistic Craft in a Social Context. In *American Folklife*, ed. Don Yoder. Austin: University of Texas Press, pp. 151–184.

Harvey, Virginia. 1974. *Techniques of Basketry.* New York: Van Nostrand Reinhold.

Irwin, John Rice. 1982. *Baskets and Basket Makers in Southern Appalachia.* Exton, PA: Schiffer.

James, George Wharton. [1909] 1972. *Indian Basketry.* New York: Dover.

Joyce, Rosemary O. 1989. *A Bearer of Tradition: Dwight Stump, Basketmaker.* Athens: University of Georgia Press.

Lasansky, Jeannette. 1979. *Willow, Oak, and Rye: Basket Traditions of Pennsylvania.* University Park: Pennsylvania State University Press.

Law, Rachel Nash, and Cynthia W. Taylor. 1991. *Appalachian White Oak Basketmaking: Handing Down the Basket.* Knoxville: University of Tennessee Press.

Marshall, Howard Wight. 1974. Mr. Westfall's Baskets: Traditional Craftsmanship in Northcentral Missouri. *Mid-South Folklore* 2:43–60. Reprinted in *Readings in American Folklore,* ed. Jan Harold Brunvand. New York: W.W. Norton, 1979, pp. 168–191.

Teleki, Gloria Roth. 1975. *Baskets of Rural America.* New York: Dutton.

Will, Christoph. 1985. *International Basketry: For Weavers and Collectors,* trans. Edward Force. Exton, PA: Schiffer.

Wright, Dorothy. 1983. *The Complete Book of Baskets and Basketry.* 2d ed. Newton Abbott, England: David and Charles.

Basque Americans

Immigrants (and their descendants) from the western Pyrenees and Cantabrian seacoast region of southern France and northern Spain. Long regarded as the quintessential sheepherder of the American West, Basques entered the region as a part of the California gold rush. Many came from southern South America, where, by the early 1800s, Basques were heavily engaged in sheep husbandry on the pampas under frontier conditions. Thus, despite the common belief that Basques were transplanting a Pyrenean skill to the American West, the pattern of sheep transhumance that emerged throughout the region was based more upon a South American than a European model.

By the 1850s, some Basques, disillusioned with mining, had turned to sheep husbandry in southern California, either leasing land from the dons or moving to the edges of European settlement. The typical pattern was for a sheepman to send back to Europe for a kinsman or fellow villager who would work for him for a few years. The herder would take his wages in ewes, running them alongside those of his employer. Once his own band was sufficiently large to be self-supporting, he would head out in search of unoccupied range. By the turn of the century, Basques were present in the open-range districts of all thirteen Western states.

In their guise as itinerant sheepmen ("tramps" to their detractors), Basques were vilified as usurpers. Moving ceaselessly about the public lands, and with no possessions other than a pack animal, gear, dogs, and a sheep band, the itinerants, by their very existence, challenged the local arrangements of settled livestock ranchers (cattlemen and sheepmen alike). Technically, grazing was open to all on a first-come basis, though in reality the ranchers regarded the public lands adjacent to their holdings as their private domain. The tactics used to harass the itinerants varied from local legislation extending grazing rights one or two miles beyond private fence lines (subsequently declared unconstitutional), to intimidation and outright violence such as the destruction of a sheep camp, the shooting of the sheep, or the roping and dragging of the herder himself. Such confrontations lent litigation to the courts and copy to the newspapers.

Of greater significance was the itinerant sheepman's role as a catalyst in the region's land-use legislation. With creation of the national forests, newspaper headlines heralded "Sheepmen Get Basques Excluded." In the first years after establishment of Yosemite National Park, it was necessary to use Army troops to patrol its precincts in order to keep itinerant Basque sheepmen off their traditional summer range. The desire to exclude the itinerants also informed legislation in the 1930s that ordered the remaining public lands into grazing districts, subsequently under the jurisdiction of the Bureau of Land Management (BLM). Whether regarding access to summer range in the national forests or winter range controlled by the BLM, livestock allotments were henceforth to be awarded solely to U.S. citizens, with commensurate deeded land and in consultation with advisory boards consisting of local ranchers. Exclusion of the itinerants could not have been more complete. Thus, in a negative sense, Basques may be regarded as key architects of the land-use policies on the public domain of the American West.

Restrictive immigration policies enacted by the U.S. Congress in the 1920s limited Basque immigration. Based upon a national-origins quota, after 1924 only 131 Spaniards were to be admitted annually and most of Europe's Basques resided in Spain. By World War II, most of the Basque herders had either died, retired, or returned to Europe. The manpower shortage of the war years exacerbated the labor crisis in the sheep industry. Consequently, a pattern emerged in which Basques contrived to reach an American port, jump ship, and make their way to a sheep ranch. The rancher then lobbied his congressman to introduce special legislation legalizing the herder's status as an emergency measure. Through these so-called Sheepherder Laws, 383 Basques were accorded permanent residency.

The practice was both cumbersome and inadequate. In 1950 Senator Patrick McCarran of Nevada, an ex-sheepman, framed legislation to facilitate the recruitment and introduction of Basque sheepherders into the United States. The sheepmen formed the Western Range Association to facilitate the program. Between 1950 and the 1970s, several thousand Basques worked in the American West on three-year herding contracts (designed specifically to prevent them from qualifying for permanent residency, which would enable them to abandon herding). By the 1970s, sheep numbers on the open range were plummeting due to greater restrictions in response to budding environmentalism and trends in the world mar-

Sheep camp, with commissary wagon, tender's trucks, and herder's horses. Near Panaca, Lincoln County, Nevada, 1988. Photo Blanton Owen. Nevada State Council on the Arts.

ket for sheep products. At the same time as Europe's postwar economy improved, Basques became unwilling to work for the relatively low sheepherder wages. The Western Range Association redirected its recruitment efforts toward Latin America. By the mid-1990s, there were only a few hundred sheepherders left in the American West, and they were much more likely to be Mexican, Peruvian, or Chilean than Basque.

Throughout their nearly century and a half in the American West, the Basque immigrants were more sojourners than settlers. Few, if any, of the young men who left the Pyrenees came with the intention of remaining either in herding or in this country. Rather, their idea was always to make a stake and return to Europe to retire a farm mortgage, purchase a property, or start a small business. However, in each cohort of immigrants a few changed their minds, buying or homesteading a ranch property or possibly establishing a small business in town.

The demographic profile of Basque immigration (dominated by young, single males) and the seasonality of the labor demand within the sheep industry (roughly half of the herders were laid off after the lambs were shipped in the fall and two summer bands were combined into a single winter one) favored establishment of Basque boarding houses throughout the open-range districts of the American West. With the spread of the transcontinental railroad and its branches, the typical Basque "hotel" was situated close to the train station. Newly arrived immigrants, met at the dock in New York City by a representative of Valentin Aguirre's *Casa Vizcaína* hotel and then sent westward with their destination pinned on their lapels, would descend wide-eyed from the train anxious to spot the promised ethnic haven.

For the herder, the hotel was an address, a place to store his town clothes when out on the range, and his rifle, saddle, and gear when on a visit back to his homeland. Each hotel was a part of a wider intelligence network regarding job opportunities (usually, though not exclusively, in the sheep industry) and therefore served as an employment agency. The hotel was a base of operations for the vacationing herder out for a fling on the town. It was a convalescent home for an injured herder;

a retirement home for the family-less one.

The hotel keeper, usually an ex-herder himself, was translator, banker, confidant, and even father figure for his clients. Rather unwittingly, he also held the key to the formation of the Basque American community. He required kitchen and domestic help and activated his ties in the old country to bring over single women for service. In the single-male atmosphere of the Basque hotel, few of the women remained unattached for long. Thus, each hotel provided a tiny, if steady, trickle of women who married men prepared to abandon herding (since the occupation was inimical to family formation) and settle down. Others sent back or went back to Europe for brides. In short, out of each cohort of the intending sojourners a few changed their minds and became permanent settlers in the American West. Over time, there came to be a few dozen or even hundred Basques in each of the region's open-range districts.

For the Basque Americans, the hotels were the center of social life as well. It was there that they practiced their language, learned about the Basque country, and shared an occasional meal with the boarders, served family style at a common table. It was there that on weekends they joined the herders in dancing the *jota* to the strains of an accordion. It was there that more than one Basque American woman met her future spouse, thereby extending a pattern of endogamy into the second generation of the Basque American experience. In short, for Old World Basques and Basque Americans alike, the Basque hotel was the key ethnic institution, indeed practically the only one until the second half of the 20th century.

By the 1950s, there were the faint stirrings of Basque American ethnic pride. In 1949 Boise Basques formed a club, Euskaldunak, Inc. (Basques, Inc.), and in 1951 they built a clubhouse in the downtown area that functions to this day. In 1957 Robert Laxalt published his book *Sweet Promised Land,* the story of his father's life as a sheepman in Nevada and California and his return visit to his natal village. The work was widely read and critically acclaimed, instantly providing the Basque Americans with their literary spokesman.

In 1959 a Sparks, Nevada, casino operator, married to an Idaho Basque, decided to sponsor a national Basque festival. The venue proved fortuitous, since western Nevada was the one part of the American West where the largely Bizkaian population of eastern Oregon, southern Idaho, and northern Nevada overlapped with the mainly French and Navarrese Basque populations of California, eastern Nevada, Utah, Colorado, Wyoming, and Montana. The organizing committee embraced the spectrum of European Basque regional distinctions and bridged the Old World/New World-born generational gap as well. The hundreds of letters Laxalt had received from Basque Americans throughout the American West, thanking him for depicting their family's saga by describing his own, served as the vital link for bringing together the heretofore isolated fragments of what ultimately became a Basque American community of regional scope.

The first festival was an "invention" in the sense that its organizers combined certain Old World and New World elements into a pastiche unlike anything previously celebrated on either side of the Atlantic. In the process, they established a model that continues to be emulated.

In the aftermath of the first festival, Basque clubs proliferated in California, Nevada, and Idaho, most founded to sponsor a folk-dance group and to organize a local festival. Today there is a Basque festival cycle that is truly a movable feast, weekend-long celebrations that begin in late spring and shift venues throughout the region until late summer. Each festival likely entails a public dance, possibly a Basque-language mass, given by an ambulatory Basque chaplain, performances by the local club's dance group in folk costume (and possibly one or more visiting ones as well), athletic contests (stone lifting, woodchopping, weight carrying and tug-of-war), possibly sheep dog trials and a sheep-hooking contest, and a Western-style barbecue featuring lamb, "Basque beans," sourdough bread, and copious amounts of red wine.

Thus, like many other hyphenated Americans, by the 1960s and 1970s Basques were engaged in public display of their heritage. In this regard, they were a part of the broader "roots" phenomenon, though not to be confused with "ethnic revival," since Basque Americans were developing unique forms of group expression rather than reviving previously forsaken ones.

The wider public's interest in the Basques was furthered by several factors. There was the aura surrounding them as Europe's mystery people, a prehistoric group of undetermined origin speaking a language unrelated to any other human tongue. There was their sheepherding legacy with its appeal to a world grown weary with urban malaise and easily seduced by the imagery of the stoic figure leading a life of splendid isolation amidst the spectacular setting of Western deserts and mountains. Consequently, the Basque sheepherder and his colorful descendants of the rural West became the popular subjects of film documentaries, articles, and newspaper stories.

The creation of Basque American culture was furthered by the establishment, in 1967, of a Basque studies program at the University of Nevada, Reno. Its Basque Book Series, published through the University of Nevada Press, provided additional substance to Basque American identity. The program sponsored summer and year-long study courses in the Basque country, attended by many Basque Americans who returned to assume leadership roles within their local Basque club or dance group. In 1972 several clubs formed North American Basque Organizations, Inc. (NABO), an overarching structure that facilitates contacts both among its members and with Europe.

Under NABO's auspices, Basque Americans hold periodic summer music camps where children are taught to play the traditional *txistu* (flute). NABO sponsors national *mus* (a card game) and *pelota* (handball) tournaments and sends its representative to international competitions. NABO has also facilitated the North American tours of European Basque performing artists (dance groups, singers and *bertsolariak,* or versifiers). NABO has twenty-six member clubs, located mainly in California, Nevada, and Idaho.

At the closing of the 20th century, then, there are many manifestations of Basque American culture. The Basque hotels, some of which evolved into dinner rather than boarding houses, are popular eating places for Basque Americans and non-Basques alike. They, in turn, have made Basque cuisine famous throughout the region (as well as an alcoholic beverage called the Picon Punch). Associational life among Basque Americans has never been more robust. The annual festival cycle attracts thousands of participants and considerable media coverage, and it has converted the Basques (somewhat ironically) into one of the region's highest-profiled ethnic groups. Sporadically, there are even more impressive happenings such as the *Jai Aldi* cultural festival sponsored in 1990 by Boise Basques. It included several days of film, lectures, and performances (including some by European artists) and attracted about ten thousand participants.

At the same time, as with all immigrant cultures, questions cloud the future prospects of the Basque American experience. In August 1989, on a hillside near Reno, Nevada, 2,500 people gathered to dedicate the National Monument to the Basque Sheepherder. The sculpture itself is an abstract, rather than figurative, rendering of a herder carrying a lamb. The instant controversy that it engendered among Basque Americans is itself evidence of the dilemma facing the group. Continued Basque immigration from Europe has been all but interdicted, the sheep industry is faltering, as is the occupational association of Basques with it, and fewer Basque Americans retain their ancestral tongue or seek Basque marriage partners. Thus, the survival of the group is at issue as well as the real substance of the response of the 47,956 persons who self-identified as Basque ethnics in the 1990 U.S. Census.

And what were the tangible marks left upon the physical and cultural landscapes of the American West by the presence of the Basque sheepherder? Not surprisingly, the traces are faint. Given the lack of fully formed family units in the Basque immigrant experience, which would have provided mature repositories and carriers of Old World Basque culture, it is scarcely surprising that the descendants of those who departed Europe as single young males or females have essentially had to create Basque American cultural reality in the New World context. Consequently, the attempts to collect among Basque Americans folksongs, stories, sayings, medicinal practices, religious beliefs, and the like have turned up fragmentary evidence at best—and then largely from Old World-born informants. Similarly, Basques have left practically no architectural evidence, whether domestic or religious, of their presence. Rather, visible display of ethnic identity is essentially restricted to the family escutcheon, a wood carving of an Old World motif and a few books on Basque topics displayed in one's living room.

Perhaps fittingly, the real evidence of the region's Basque presence is to be found in the mountains. There the herders built ovens for their bread making and erected stone cairns, *harri-mutillak,* or "stone boys" in their language, both to wile away the boredom-filled hours and to humanize an unremittingly natural landscape. It is also there that the herders converted groves of aspens into veritable living galleries and message banks of images and statements.

Referred to technically as dendroglyphs, the tree carvings document the inner thoughts of men thrust into a situation of near total social isolation in a foreign land. Thus, there are the nostalgic images of the farmhouse or village church back home, the pining verse dedicated to the girl left behind, or the patriotic statement regarding one's region *Viva Navarra* or Basque nationalism *Gora Euskadi*. There are the complaints about one's boss or the neighboring herder over the hill. There are the pornographic images of nubile women and *crise de coeur* of sexual frustration. Finally, there is the simple record of a man's name and the date, which convey his presence to future herders. Such were the graphic means employed by the Basque herder to countermand the human fear of total anonymity.

William A. Douglass

References

Baker, Sarah. 1972. *Basque American Folklore in Eastern Oregon.* M.A. thesis, University of California, Berkeley.

Douglass, William A., and Jon Bilbao. 1975. *Amerikanuak: Basques in the New World.* Reno: University of Nevada Press.

————, and Richard H. Lane. 1985. *Basque Sheepherders of the American West: A Photographic Documentary.* Reno: University of Nevada Press.

Laxalt, Robert. [1957] 1984. *The Basque Hotel.* Reno: University of Nevada Press.

————. 1957. *Sweet Promised Land.* Reno: University of Nevada Press.

Mallea, Jose. 1992. History That Grows on Trees: Basque Aspen Carving in Nevada. *Nevada Historical Society Quarterly* 35:21–39.

Paris, Beltran, and William A. Douglass. 1979. *Beltran: Basque Sheepman of the American West.* Reno: University of Nevada Press.

See also Sheepherder

Bassett, Fletcher S. (1847–1893)

Moving force behind the Chicago Folk-Lore Society. Bassett was born in Adams County, Kentucky, the year after the word "folklore" was coined, and was initially a military man, running away from home during the Civil War to enlist in the 108th Illinois Volunteers. He later enrolled in the U.S. Naval Academy and, after graduation, spent thirteen years in naval service. In 1882 ill health forced him into retirement, and he then moved to Chicago and devoted the remainder of his life to private scholarship.

Bassett's *Legends and Superstitions of the Sea and of Sailors* [1885] 1971, was a disappointing work, almost totally secondhand, although the topic is one that he knew firsthand. The book received enough favorable publicity to justify a second edition in 1892, but it has no real bearing on Bassett's status in folklore. His reputation rests mainly on his organizational abilities, specifically his key role in founding the Chicago Folk-Lore Society (CFS). The inaugural meeting of this organization was held on December 12, 1891, and it soon became popular both as an agency for the collection of regional data and as a philosophical and organizational alternative to the American Folklore Society (AFS). For a brief period, the Chicago society was a formidable rival to the older society, but with Bassett's death on October 19, 1893, the Chicago Folk-Lore Society soon lost steam, and it passed into oblivion in 1904. It did bring about the establishment of a fund to award an annual Chicago Folklore Prize, which continues to the present.

The two societies were at odds over the question of whether the study of folklore properly belonged to the field of anthropology or literature. The AFS opted for the anthropology side, while the CFS chose the literary view. Bassett and William Wells Newell, the American Folklore Society's intellectual leader, clashed over the International Folklore Congress of 1893 that Bassett organized. Held at the Columbian Exposition in Chicago, it did bring folklore much favorable publicity by showcasing many important scholars from around the world. At the same time, the anthropological meeting supported by Newell was a failure. This small victory, however, was the Chicago Folk-Lore Society's last hurrah.

Bassett was in one sense a good organizer because he successfully brought together a large number of people to form an organization. In another sense, though, he was a poor organizer because he dominated the Chicago Folk-Lore Society so completely that after his death the association was leaderless. He also failed by recruiting a membership that was mainly made up of dilettantes.

W.K. McNeil

References

Bassett, Fletcher S. [1885] 1971. *Legends and Superstitions of the Sea and of Sailors.* Detroit: Singing Tree Press.

————. [1892] 1973. *The Folk-Lore Manual.* Darby, PA: Norwood Editions.

The Folk-Lorist. [1892–1893] 1973. Philadelphia: Norwood Editions.

McNeil, W.K. 1985. The Chicago Folklore Society and the International Folklore Congress of 1893. *Midwestern Journal of Language and Folklore* 11:5–19.

Baughman, Ernest Warren (1916–1990)

Folklorist and professor of American and British folklore and American literature. Baughman was a Fellow of the American Folklore Society and a collector of Southwestern folktales, legends, jokes, rhymes, proverbs, and superstitions.

Born in Manson, Iowa, September 10, 1916, Baughman received his B.A. from Ball State Teachers College in Muncie, Indiana, in 1938, started teaching and collecting local folklore in Muncie, in 1939, and received his M.A. from the University of Chicago that same year. From 1942 to 1948, he continued graduate studies at Indiana University under Stith Thompson and served as a teaching assistant and later instructor. He received his doctoral degree in folklore in 1953 when he finished his dissertation. It was published in 1966 as *A Type* and *Motif Index of the Folktales of England and North America* (Indiana University Folklore Series No. 20) and was Baughman's greatest academic achievement.

In addition to his massive *Index,* Baughman published short articles and reviews in journals, including the *Journal of American Folklore, Midwest Folklore, Western Folklore, Southern Folklore Quarterly, New Mexico Historical Quarterly,* and the *New Mexico Folklore Record,* which he edited off and on from 1952 to 1979. He also did the scholarly annotations for Vance Randolph's *Sticks in the Knapsack and Other Ozark Folktales* (1958), and contributed annotations for Herbert Halpert's *Folktales of the New Jersey Pines* (1973) and Randolph's *Pissing in the Snow* (1976), the latter a controversial collection of bawdy tales from the Ozarks. Baughman also did significant work in American literature, publishing in 1967 a notable article in *New England Quarterly,* "Public Confession and the Scarlet Letter," that was reprinted in the Norton Critical Edition of *The Scarlet Letter* in 1978.

Baughman served as president of the New Mexico Folklore Society in 1957 and was named to the New Mexico Folklore Society Roll of Honor in 1976. Throughout his professional career, he served on various committees on the executive board of the American Folklore Society (AFS), and he was named an AFS Fellow in 1971.

During his career at the University of New Mexico, Baughman collected over 2,000 tales and 20,000 3 x 5 index cards from students that recorded riddles, rhymes, proverbs, superstitions, jokes, and legends. This collection, more than ten cubic feet of printed material, is housed in the Special Collections Department of Zimmermann Library at the University of New Mexico. An avid fisherman, summertime resident of Telluride, Colorado, and renowned humorist, Baughman was considered by many in the field as a helpful and thorough colleague who practiced collection, indexing, and annotation in the traditional form of scholarly folklore research.

Peter White
Kenneth B. Keppeler

Beck, Earl Clifton (1891–1977)

Collector of Michigan lumberjack songs. Nebraska-born Beck began studying Michigan lumberjacks in the 1930s. He collected their songs, stories, and dances through the 1940s, urging the seventy- and eighty-year-old former lumber workers to let him collect and publish the material before it disappeared. Beck taught English and folklore at Central Michigan University, where he also chaired the English department. In addition to his passion for teaching, Beck's love was collecting songs in the woods. He once described his fieldwork as "high adventure," adding that "it has given me unforgettable experiences, vigorous days in the out of doors, and some most interesting friends." He compiled various portions of the collection in three books, *Songs of the Michigan Lumberjacks* (1942), *Lore of the Lumbercamps* (1948), and *They Knew Paul Bunyan* (1956), all published by the University of Michigan Press.

Beck was as much a promoter and educator as he was a field collector. Not content simply to write books, he pursued numerous opportunities to present his informants and their traditions to public audiences. The group he helped form—The Michigan Lumberjacks—first performed at the 1934 National Folk Festival in St. Louis. Beck acted as their manager and toured with the Lumberjacks around the state and nation over the next twenty years, appearing at trade shows and school assemblies and even on national radio broadcasts. In 1959, when the Library of Congress produced the recording *Songs of the Michigan Lumberjacks,* Beck edited the liner notes.

Beck was a founding member of the Michigan Folklore Society, president of the Michigan Education Association, and vice president of the Michigan Academy of Science, Arts, and Letters. After retiring from Central Michigan University in 1958, he traveled extensively, occasionally performing lumberjack-song programs. He published a book of memoirs—*It Was This Way*—in 1963. In 1989, he was posthumously awarded a Michigan Heritage Award.

LuAnne Gaykowski Kozma

Beckwith, Martha Warren (1871–1959)

Anthropologist and folklorist who played a major role in the compilation and analysis of Hawaiian mythology. In addition, she conducted important research on American Indians (Mandan, Hidatsa, and Oglala), Jamaicans, Portuguese residents of Goa, regional folklore in the United States (Dutchess County folklore; folklore of college students), and African Americans. Beckwith served as president of the American Folklore Society from 1932 to 1933.

Born January 19, 1871, in Wellesley Heights, Massachusetts, she spent much of her childhood in the Hawaiian Islands, primarily the island of Maui. She earned her B.A. in English from Mount Holyoke College, taught literature for many years, and did not begin her formal training in anthropology and folklore until she was in her mid-thirties. She earned her Ph.D. in anthropology under Franz Boas at Columbia University in 1918. Beckwith was appointed research professor of the Folklore Foundation at Vassar College in 1920 and remained in that position until her retirement from Vassar in 1938.

An indefatigable fieldworker, she made numerous trips to Jamaica between 1919 and 1922. In the summer of 1926, Beckwith gathered folktales at the Pine Ridge Indian Reservation in South Dakota, and in 1927 she worked among Portuguese settlers in India. Her primary contributions are her long-term studies of Hawaiian creation chants and myths and her many useful translations of Kepelino, Kamakau, and other 19th-century Hawaiians whose writings described the later period of the Hawaiian monarchy. Her classic study *Hawaiian Mythology,* representing more than thirty years of exhaustive research, was not published until 1940. In addition to her research on Hawaii, she also conducted pioneering work in the field of Hawaiian ethnobotany and ethnopharmacology. She spent the last years of her life collecting and classifying Hawaiian herbal remedies.

The publication of *Black Roadways: A Study of Jamaican*

Folklife in 1929 was the culmination of a series of notable papers on Jamaican folklore that included analyses of proverbs, children's games, Christmas Mumming, and animal stories. The book received a number of favorable reviews, including an extended review in 1930 by Melville Jean Herskovits in the *Journal of American Folklore* (43:332–338), which praised *Black Roadways* as "the first ethnographic study of the life of any New World Negro which, to my knowledge, has been attempted." In his review, Herskovits took Beckwith to task for what he saw as her inadequate attention to individual behavior and for ignoring variation within Jamaican culture. Nevertheless, he concluded that *Black Roadways* is a landmark study that provides a firm foundation for future research.

References evidencing Beckwith's keen interest in Gaelic literature and Celtic folklore appear throughout her publications. Trained in both anthropology and English literature, Beckwith attempted to bridge the gap between these two disciplines and met with considerable success. An example of an article combining the methods of literature and folklore is her 1924 essay "The English Ballad in Jamaica: A Note upon the Origins of the Ballad Forms," which appeared in *Publications of the Modern Language Association* (39:455–483). Beckwith died on January 28, 1959, at the age of eighty-eight. She is buried on Maui.

Stephen D. Glazier

References

Beckwith, Martha Warren. 1923. Signs and Superstitions Collected from American College Girls. *Journal of American Folklore* 36:1–15.

———. 1940. *Hawaiian Mythology.* New Haven, CT: Yale University Press.

Luomala, Katherine. 1962. Martha Warren Beckwith: A Commemorative Essay. *Journal of American Folklore* 75:341–353.

Belden, Henry Marvin (1865–1954)

Ballad and song scholar, editor, and teacher. Belden was born in Wilton, Connecticut, into an old New England family of modest means. He graduated from Trinity College in Hartford, Connecticut, and taught at a private training school for West Point candidates until a small inheritance from his grandmother enabled him to begin graduate work in English at Johns Hopkins University in 1889. In 1893 he spent a year at the University of Nebraska, where he met Louise Pound, who became a lifelong friend and ally in ballad scholarship. After a year at the University of Strassburg to complete his thesis, he received his doctorate, and in 1895 he accepted a position at the University of Missouri in Columbia, a place he had never heard of but where he was to spend the rest of his life.

In 1903 Belden learned from his students that traditional balladry and song, thought no longer extant by Francis James Child, flourished in Missouri, and the collection and study of song became his major interest. He organized the Missouri Folk-Lore Society in 1906, and in 1908 he spent a semester at the British Museum to study broadside ballads. His successful collecting in Missouri and enthusiastic reports of his find-

ings at meetings and in German and American journals brought him to national attention, and he served as president of the American Folklore Society in 1910 and 1911. He spent 1916 and 1917 at Harvard University, working on his collection, and, believing it complete, he left a copy to be published by the American Folklore Society as part of the anticipated volume on Missouri folklore. World War I brought an end to plans for publication then and eventually to the Missouri Folk-Lore Society. Archer Taylor, then at Washington University in St. Louis, was elected secretary in Belden's place in 1920, but no further meetings were held. The long-time president and supporter of the society, Mary Alicia Owen, who was to provide the African American and Native American materials for the Missouri volume, died in 1934, and with her any hope for publication of a collection of Missouri folklore.

Although influenced to some extent by the scholarly views of his time, Belden was a pioneer in his study of broadside and Native American balladry, at first for clues to problems of ballad definition and origin, later because he became intrigued with tracing the songs and the events that inspired them. He was very early in recognizing the importance of collecting music with text and urged collectors to note data on the singer and his or her source for the song. He took part, with Louise Pound, in the "Ballad Wars," standing masterfully against Francis Barton Gummere's theory of communal origin. His *Ballads and Songs Collected by the Missouri Folk-Lore Society,* finally published in the University of Missouri Studies series in 1940, was widely praised for its scholarly notes and careful editing, but critized, ironically, for not providing more music by a critic who was perhaps not aware of how early the songs had been collected.

Into his mid-eighties, Belden worked with Arthur Palmer Hudson to edit the ballad and folksong volumes of *The Frank C. Brown Collection of North Carolina Folklore,* published in 1952 when he was eighty-seven, bringing to the task an undiminished enthusiasm and energy in spite of failing eyesight.

Rebecca B. Schroeder

References

Belden, H.M., ed. 1940. *Ballads and Songs Collected by the Missouri Folk-Lore Society.* University of Missouri Studies Vol. 15, No. 1. Columbia: University of Missouri. Reprint, with foreword by Edward Weatherly. Columbia: University of Missouri Press, 1955, 1973.

Belden, Allen, ed. 1976. Autobiographical Notes. In *A Belden Lineage, 1066–1976.* Washington, DC.

Pentlin, Susan, and Rebecca B. Schroeder. 1986–1987. H.M. Belden, The English Club, and the Missouri Folk-Lore Society. *Missouri Folklore Society Journal* 8–9:1, 1–42.

Benedict, Ruth (1887–1948)

Anthropologist and folklorist. First a student of Elsie Clews Parsons at the New School for Social Research in New York City, Benedict went on to study with Franz Boas at Columbia University where she completed her doctorate in anthropology on "The Concept of the Guardian Spirit in North America."

Benedict brought to her work in the social sciences a background in the humanities. Her undergraduate degree from Vassar College in 1909 had been in literature. She remained throughout her life a poet, publishing under the pen name of Ann Singleton. Benedict was conscious of her dual approach to anthropology and folklore. In December 1947, she delivered an address as the outgoing president to the American Anthropological Association on "Anthropology and the Humanities," in which she maintained that not only were the humanities compatible with the study of anthropology, they were necessary for the vitality of the discipline (Benedict 1948).

Benedict stressed the importance of studying a culture holistically, with folklore as a vital component. She is remembered primarily for *Patterns of Culture* (1934), in which she discussed individual cultures as "personality writ large." In *Zuñi Mythology* (1935), Benedict undertook an intensive examination of a single body of myths and folktales from a culture where "folklore [was] a living and functioning culture trait."

Benedict taught courses in folklore and anthropology at Columbia from 1926 until her death in 1948. From 1925 to 1939, she was editor of the *Journal of American Folklore,* and of the *Memoirs* of the American Folklore Society. She served as president of the American Ethnological Society (1927–1929), and of the American Anthropological Association (1946–1947). During World War II, Benedict worked for the Office of War Information, where she began her research on Japanese national character that resulted in *The Chrysanthemum and the Sword* (1946).

Rosemary Lévy Zumwalt

References

Benedict, Ruth. 1948. Anthropology and the Humanities. *American Anthropologist* 50:585–593.

Briscoe, Virginia Wolf. 1979. Ruth Benedict: Anthropological Folklorist. *Journal of American Folklore* 92:445–476.

Mintz, Sydney. 1981. Ruth Benedict. In *Totems and Teachers,* ed. Sydel Silverman. New York: Columbia University Press, pp.141–168.

Modell, Judith Schachter. 1983. *Ruth Benedict: Patterns of a Life.* Philadelphia: University of Pennsylvania Press.

Berea College

Private liberal arts college founded by abolitionists in Kentucky in 1855. Berea College makes use of folk culture in addressing the intellectual, social, and spiritual needs of the people of America's Southern Highlands. Christianity provides the unifying belief at Berea, and folk culture provides a basis for different people to collaborate with one another, each enriching the life of the other. There were also economic considerations in the founding of Berea College.

Early emphasis was on the handcrafts of America's Southern Highlands, from which the college takes 80 percent of its students. Weaving and woodworking were developed as student "industries" through which some students could earn their college expenses. Broomcraft, pottery, and wrought iron were added later, along with many other types

of work opportunities. Enrollment is limited to those from low-income situations, no students pay tuition, and all students are required to contract for a labor assignment. The college even has a dean of labor.

A Homespun Fair, Appalachia's first craft fair and model for many others, ran concurrently with commencement in 1896 and is portrayed in a PWA (Public Works of Art)-sponsored mural by Frank Long in the Berea post office. The college became instrumental in marketing efforts and in the formation of the Southern Highland Handicraft Guild in 1928–1929 and the Kentucky Guild of Artists and Craftsmen in 1961.

Members of Berea College's Music Department took an early interest in ballads and regional music. Cecil Sharp (1859–1924), the English collector, visited the campus in 1916 and 1917 while collecting English ballads and folksongs in the United States. The Mountain Collection of the Hutchins Library at Berea College has extensive material on Appalachian music. Recent additions of sound archives of traditional music from field and commercial recordings and radio programs dating to the early days of country music are in the process of being made available to scholars and the public.

Interest in other folk arts, especially dance, developed in cooperation with the Council of Southern Mountain Workers and the University of Kentucky in a program that supported itinerant recreation leaders. In 1936 Berea College undertook full responsibility for Recreation Extension, and the Mountain Folk Festival was organized. Christmas Country Dance School was opened in 1938, and the Berea College Country Dancers, a performing troupe, was organized in the same year.

The college dancers feature Kentucky Set Running, a democratic, peasant, or "country" dance from 16th-century Britain. The dance was well preserved in eastern Kentucky and other Appalachian communities from whence it evolved into the American square dance.

Leonard Roberts, a 1939 graduate of Berea College, did pioneering work in contextual collecting of eastern Kentucky folktales, riddles, and songs. A robust craft industry has grown up in the city surrounding the college, and the State Legislature of the Commonwealth of Kentucky passed a joint resolution in 1988 designating Berea as the "folk arts and crafts capital of Kentucky."

John M. Ramsay

References

Alvic, Phylis. 1993. *Weavers of the Southern Highlands: Berea.* Murray, KY: Published by the author.

Barker, Garry. 1991. *The Handcraft Revival in Southern Appalachia, 1930–1990.* Knoxville: University of Tennessee Press.

Peck, Elizabeth Sinclair. 1982. *Berea's First 125 Years, 1855–1980.* Lexington: University Press of Kentucky.

See also Appalachia; Crafts; Weaving

Bigfoot

North American version of the traditional wild-man figure, named for the immense footprints it purportedly leaves. In

Canada this creature is called Sasquatch, an anglicization of a Coast Salish Indian term. Stories of Bigfoot and its spoor are among the best-known belief legends on the continent, particularly in the Pacific Northwest among loggers and Native Americans.

While scattered reports of strange humanoid creatures and people who had "gone wild" in the woods have circulated since colonial times, it was not until the late 1950s that this legendary figure was routinely associated with a specific name and American region. Its origins are unclear but almost certainly stem from a fusion of ancient European wild-man traditions with Northwest Native American beliefs in hairy simian-like humanoids.

In the Northwest particularly, the creatures are described by Euro-Americans in rather mundane terms. All are said to be covered by hair, with a heavy build and ape-like face, and to emit an intolerable stench. Adults can be eight feet in height, while juveniles are much smaller; females often have large pendulous breasts. They have no speech, but communicate by grunts, whistles, and unearthly screams. They remain elusive through both their intelligence and their agility over rough terrain. At worst, they are only mischievous, never dangerous to humans, and are seen only because of their curiosity or sheer human good fortune. Sightings typically consist of people briefly seeing them at the edge of a forest clear cut or running across a road. More recently, as the legend has extended to regions outside the Northwest (and receives attention through sensationalistic tabloid headlines, movies, television commercials, and the like), the creatures frequently are linked with UFOs and the world of the paranormal—magical associations that presumably allow them to survive undetected in more densely populated areas. The Northwest, however, is where the legend is most consistently manifested through periodic sightings and investigations of footprint discoveries. The creature's purported existence is also acknowledged in several small tourist-oriented festivals in Northern California. Among loggers, Bigfoot is the subject of both jokes and serious discussion, depending on social contexts. Some loggers engage in the playful practice of fabricating realistic footprints in an attempt to deceive others and reinforce a sense of the forest's potential for mystery.

The legend of Bigfoot has become popular during the recent ascendancy of environmental concerns and seems to reflect a reevaluation of humanity's place in the natural world more than a fear of wildness. For loggers, the legend serves as a symbolic defense of their controversial livelihood, projecting into the future the continued existence of endless forests hiding elusive monsters. However, for Native Americans, with tribes as diverse as the Hopi, Lakota Sioux, and Cree experiencing periodic waves of Bigfoot sightings during times of social crisis, the legendary creature serves as a Pan-Indian being whose appearance represents a spiritual warning of the need for tribal unity and traditional values and beliefs.

Robert E. Walls

References

Halpin, Marjorie, and Michael Ames, eds. 1980. *Manlike Monsters on Trial: Early Records and Modern Evidence.* Vancouver: University of British Columbia Press.

Hunter, Don, with René Dahinden. 1993. *Sasquatch/ Bigfoot: The Search for North America's Incredible Creature.* Toronto: McClelland and Stewart.

Milligan, Linda. 1990. The "Truth" about the Bigfoot Legend. *Western Folklore* 49:83–98.

Bikers

Persons whose individuality and social identity are in good measure expressed through motorcycle riding, modification, and decoration. In some senses, anyone who "rides" is a biker, but those who ride only occasionally are motorcycle "owner-operators" or "enthusiasts" to those who understand a narrower, gender- and brand-chauvinistic notion that "a biker is a *guy* with a *Harley* who rides a *lot*." Bikers ride as often as they can and express an aesthetic of "the ride" through dress and bike modification or decoration; through customary ways of being on the road, at the track, and in parked array; and through participation in large ritualized gatherings—rallies and races, rides, or runs.

Men and women who ride are harassed by media-maintained images of bikers as rough, raunchy, paunchy, boozy males covered with hair and "tatts" (tattoos), dressed in worn denim, weathered leathers, and glinting chains, astride large, loud (typically Harley-Davidson) cycles, roaring two abreast along highways in packs of a dozen or more—mavericks, at best, or dangerous, unsavory misfits. Male bikers, members of clubs whose "colors" and "attitude" (club insignia and demeanor) purposefully resemble those of "outlaw" organizations like the Hell's Angels, Pagans, Banditos, and the Family *are* the reference for this "citizen" or "straight" nonrider image of bikers. This outlaw persona of bikers developed in the United States since the 1940s, fertilized by film images like *The Wild One* (1953) featuring Marlon Brando and Lee Marvin in Stanley Kramer's portrayal of bikers as reckless, rebellious threats to ordinary folks, inspired by the 1947 "riot" during the Hollister, California, Independence Day motorcycle races, when the Booze Fighters rampaged the town, then posed for *Life* magazine photographs. In biker legend, "Hollister" is the genesis for the outlaw image and for the "one percenter" designation, worn as a jacket patch ("1%") by outlaw bikers, distinguishing them from the other ninety-nine percent of law-abiding motorcyclists—members of the national Motor Maids Inc. or a chapter of Women on Wheels (WOW), members of Stoney Lonesome MC in Columbus, Indiana; the Orphans MC in Lemoyne, Pennsylvania; the BMW Rim Riders of Arizona in Scottsdale; the Copper Kettle Soul Riders in eastern North Carolina, or the Idontknow MC in Central Islip, New York. In 1994, *American Motorcyclist* reported that six million persons in the United States owned motorcycles and 200,000 were members of the seventy-year-old American Motorcyclist Association.

Within the majority, bikers continue a process of esoteric discrimination that conflates cycle brands, engine types, models and production years, factors for vehicle modification, regularity of use, length and level of the biker's experience, a biker's affiliation with a motorcycle group, and the biker's gender. Some bikers distinguish "American-made" (Harley-Davidson) and "import" (Japanese manufacture) motorcycles, derisively termed "rice-burners." Harley bikers joke about pranking an "import" owner by throwing a handful of rice under the cycle, and telling the other biker, "Hey, you got a leak." Conversely, Harleys are called "John Deeres" or "tractors" by bikers who characteristically ride hunched forward in racing posture astride brightly colored "crotch rockets," aerodynamically snub-nosed and all fairing. "Harley owners wear black leathers, so the oil won't show" is a snide reference to a purported tendency for Harleys to leak, and aspersions concerning Harleys' unreliability are various—a Harley road repair kit needs only "a hammer and a pickup truck with tie downs."

Bikers dress for safety and comfort, but also for theater. Leathers, helmets, face guards, and boots protect from cold, wind, flying debris, and contact with the road —"going down" or "dropping the bike." Leather or denim vests and jackets are bedecked with souvenir patches or pins commemorating specific rallies and runs, and memorial patches for bikers killed in collisions with automobiles. An affiliated biker will "fly" the club "colors" on a vest or jacket back—an embroidered symbol emblem centered between curved "rockers" that name the club (top rocker) and the club's location (bottom rocker). The Christian Motorcyclists Association center patch shows praying hands at the base of a cross, and the rockers read, "Riding For" (top) "The Son" (bottom). Though not members, a few women fly the colors of fraternal clubs with additional appliqués declaring them to be "Property of . . ." some male member whose biker name—like "Nub" or "Jake"—completes the "property tag" message. T-shirts abound, naming biker clubs or far-flung bars, dealerships, rides, or rallies the wearer has visited. Helmets reflect biker attitudes toward their compulsory use; they are the smallest "token" helmet the law will allow; they bear sticker messages— "Let Those Who Ride Decide" or "Helmet Laws Suck"; and, for festive occasions, imaginative parody helmets appear for slow-ride parade wear—aluminum colanders and stew pots; "Visigoth" helmets with fur and horns. A Harley "shovelhead" owner wears a shovel blade fixed to his visor cap; and owners of Indian motorcycles may wear full feather war bonnets.

Bikers identify with their motorcycles in various ways. They individualize engine performance or body styling through "chopping," "customizing," or "trick" work, and they sometimes refer to themselves and others by their "rides"— "I'm the '48 panhead chopper," or "He's the '88 Softail." Motorcycle paint decorations are like biker tattoos: they follow the contours of the cycle body—gas tank, fenders, luggage pods—and are self-conscious, symbolic expressions of the individual biker's "attitude." Individualized motifs and murals are configured by traditional patterns: (1) symbols of death and violence (skulls, stilettos dripping blood, Vietnam combat helicopters above the legend "A Great Day to Die"), speed and power (flames, lightning bolts), magic and fantasy (bearded sorcerers, dragons), femininity and nature (pink ribbon bows, peacock feathers, bees, hummingbirds, and flowers), machismo and nature (nude cartoon women, eagles, snakes, a Native American brave in loincloth, bareback on his

horse, solemnly scanning a desert vista above the legend "The Last Ride"); (2) portraits of persons as significant to the biker as his or her cycle, such as first-born sons and wives; and (3) legends alone—"Loud Pipes Save Lives," "Live to Ride–Ride to Live." "Rat bikes," a perverse alternative in the mode of cycle as identity extension, are often oil caked and corroded, assembled from mismatched parts, with elaborate use of coat hanger wire and steel alloy cans for patch; rat bikes may also be decorated with assemblages of found objects—antlers, turtle shells, jingle bells, pieces of vintage Chevy, raccoon tails, shopping carts, and whatever.

Bikers find companionship and safety in numbers; solo riders are most vulnerable to being stranded by cycle malfunction or being "downed" in accidents caused by automobile drivers. If a touring "full dresser," weighing hundreds of pounds, breaks down or that biker goes down, more than one person is needed to turn it "rubber side down, shiny side up" and push the machine to a sheltering overpass. Where possible, cyclists ride two abreast to force passing automobiles to use the adjacent lane and to make themselves more visible, day or night. Or bikers do road runs in staggered single file for their own visibility and, again, to encourage car and truck drivers to pass without crowding. Bikers greet each other on the road with customary gestures, rather than horn noises—a subdued right hand "thumbs up," a raised right fist, a modest helmet bob and hand wave, or a flamboyant, "tall in the saddle" turning wave. Bikers set their cycles to go when they park, in paramilitary closed ranks, all leaned into the same kickstand angles, facing the exit route. Customary parking renders individual motorcycles less vulnerable to damage from automobiles and signals biker group identification and control. In any parked array, "bike looking" is expected and managed by protocol— avoid coming within two feet of a bike whose owner is not standing next to it; never lean over a bike, lest studs or chains accidentally scratch; point, but never touch, lest a ring or wrist zipper cause harm, or a concealed razor blade purposely cut a wire; and speak only admiring words—never bad mouth: "People know their faults; you comment on the good things; it's etiquette."

Local communities of bikers draw together for holiday and theme runs, often with charity fund-raising as "license" to assemble and ride in large numbers. A HOG (Harley Owners Group) Strut or Honda Hoot features brand-bike trophy shows; a Poker Run or Carnival Run involves a series of stops along a route at which bikers draw cards for poker hands or play carney games of chance; a Toy Run is a parade of bikers with assorted large pink plush elephants, archery sets, Raggedy Ann 'n' Andy dolls, and bright plastic ride toys bungeed to their bikes, riding two abreast through town, often with police escorts giving bikers right of way by blocking automobile traffic at intersections. Biker day events or week-long rallies involve competitive cycle shows, stunt or skill driving or racing events, and games—the helmet toss, plank ride, weenie bite. Regional events draw 6,000 bikers to such as the Golden Aspen Rally in Ruidoso, New Mexico. A weekend of treacherous ice- and snow-covered-mountain road riding is the reason for the Elephant Ride in the Colorado Rockies in February. Since the 1950s, the Black Hills Motorcycle Rally in Sturgis, South Dakota, and Daytona, Florida, Bike Week have become national gatherings, attended by more than 50,000 (motorcycles)—event counts are important; bikes are tallied first, then people.

Biker festivals as large as Sturgis or Daytona, or as significant to the local biker community as the annual Saturday-before-Thanksgiving Toy Run in Greenville, North Carolina, give context for understanding the attraction to motorcycling that biker folklife artistic forms provide, and some of the reason bikers spend so much time on and with their cycles and with others who ride. Diversity and individuality are important to bikers, tolerance and camaraderie are necessarily complementary, but, in the end, the ride is most important, as a Texas biker with fifty-two years experience pointed out during one Golden Aspen Rally: "I did 100,000 [miles] last year, and this motorcycle's not a year old and it's got 75,308. I ride a motorcycle every chance I get. Fresh air, in the wind, the people—that's why I ride."

Karen Baldwin

References

Baldwin, Karen. 1993. "Bring a Toy and Leave Your Attitude at Home": A Festival View of Biker Folklife. *North Carolina Folklore Journal* 40:1–18.

Borhek, J.T. 1989. Rods, Choppers, and Restorations: The Modification and Recreation of Production Motor Vehicles in America. *Journal of Popular Culture* 22:97–107.

Burns, John. 1991. Born to Be Mild. *Cycle* 42 (January):64–69.

Dorrance, John. 1986. Brotherhood of the Black Hills: Sturgis. *Cycle* 37 (December)44–49, 67.

Gutkind, Lee. 1973. *Bike Fever*. Chicago: Follett.

Hopper, Columbus B., and Johnny "Big John" Moore. 1983. Hell on Wheels: The Outlaw Motorcycle Gangs. *Journal of American Culture* 6:58–64.

Johnson, David. 1993. Family Affair: Four Men, One Dream: Harley-Davidson at 90; 1903–1993. *Cycle World* 60 (September).

Krakauer, Jon. 1993. A Hog Is Still a Hog, but the "Wild Ones" Are Tamer. *Smithsonian* 24 (8):88–99.

Sagnier, Thierry. 1974. *Bike! Motorcycles and the People Who Ride Them*. New York: Harper and Row.

Walle, Alf H. 1985. Harley Davidson: The Renegade Image Free at Last. *Journal of American Culture* 7:71–76.

Billy the Kid (1859–1881)

The American West's most famous outlaw. Gaining notoriety as a vigilante in New Mexico, William H. Bonney (his best-known alias) became a legend in his own lifetime thanks to embroidered stories in the *Police Gazette* and dime novels. After his death at the hands of Pat Garrett, the legend evolved until he became not the sour rebel of the lawman's recollection but a friend to the poor and a romantic charmer. The "good bad man" gloss, introduced by Walter Noble Burns ([1926] 1973), was sustained in popular fiction, radio and

Billy the Kid, with carbine. Library of Congress.

television treatments, and dozens of Hollywood serials and feature films.

According to Garrett, Billy was born in New York City, moved West with his family as a child, killed a man for insulting his mother when he was twelve, and murdered twenty more before he died—one for every year of his life. Scholars today believe that his given name was Henry McCarty and that the body count of his victims was greatly exaggerated. Well documented is his part in the 1870s Lincoln County, New Mexico, range feud between cattleman John Chisum and Lawrence Murphy. As a Chisum "regulator," Billy apparently killed the murderers of Chisum's ally John Tunstall as well as a Murphy sheriff, William Brady; engaged in two major shoot-outs with rival gunmen; and took his pay for services rendered in rustled cattle. Surrendering in hope of a pardon, he spent two brief spells in jail but escaped both times, gunning down another two lawmen in his second flight. Sheriff Pat Garrett finally cornered him near Fort Sumner, New Mexico and shot him to death from cover of darkness at a friend's ranch.

The Kid's legend was variously elaborated over time. For a generation after Garrett's 1882 biography, he was the embodiment of violent disorder, a social evil that only violence could subdue. In the 1920s and 1930s, a more ambivalent figure emerged, as Americans used to bootleg gin and bread lines evinced a "mixed response" to a "loss of faith in traditional explanations" (Tatum 1982:90). By the postwar era, as shown in Arthur Penn's film *The Left-Handed Gun* (1957), the Kid became a reflection of social malaise, "an alienated, troubled youth" pitted tragically against "regimented middle class society" (Tatum 1982:133). Through these changes, heroic motifs continued to resonate. His mysterious birth, his touted affection for the oppressed, and his death at the hands of a faithless friend made the outlaw a Southwestern model of the mythical victim. The mythical parallels fed stories, told into the 1940s, that he had magically survived Garrett's ambush and was still alive.

Hollywood treatments of the legend, in addition to Penn's film, included King Vidor's *Billy the Kid* (1930), Howard Hughes' *The Outlaw* (1943), Marlon Brando's *One-Eyed Jacks* (1961), and Sam Peckinpah's *Sam Garrett and Billy the Kid* (1973). The score for the Peckinpah film featured Bob Dylan's country-style dirge "Knockin' on Heaven's Door," a late addition to a body of musical elegies that included "Bilito" corridos as well as English-language ballads.

Tad Tuleja

References

Burns, Walter Noble. [1926] 1973. *The Saga of Billy the Kid*. New York: Ballantine.

Dykes, J.C. 1952. *Billy the Kid: The Bibliography of a Legend*. Albuquerque: University of New Mexico Press.

Garrett, Pat, with Ash Upson. [1882] 1965. *The Authentic Life of Billy the Kid*. Norman: University of Oklahoma Press.

Steckmesser, Kent. 1965. *The Western Hero in History and Legend*. Norman: University of Oklahoma Press.

Tatum, Stephen. 1982. *Inventing Billy the Kid: Visions of the Outlaw in America, 1881–1981*. Albuquerque, NM: University of New Mexico Press.

Birders

Persons whose hobby is to identify and study birds in nature, usually with the aid of optical equipment. North American birders number in the millions, making birding as popular as hunting or fishing. Birders interact via cultural forms incorporating speech and nonverbal utterances, narratives, customs, ritual, dress, tools, and technology.

Until the early decades of this century, birders were more likely to "collect" specimens by shooting in order to identify birds "in the hand." The availability of high-quality optics and improvement in methods and guides for field identification have transformed birders from shooters to sighters. "A bird in the bush is worth two in the hand" is a purposeful parody, and was the motto of *Bird-Lore,* the first journal of the National Audubon Society. Landmarks in the history of bloodless birding include the 1900 founding of the Christmas Bird Count by Frank M. Chapman, the 1934 publication of Roger Tory Peterson's *A Field Guide to the Birds,* the 1968 establishment of the American Birding Association, and the 1984 advent of the World Series of Birding, a fund-raising bird-a-thon, sponsored by the New Jersey Audubon Society.

North Americans use "birder" and "birding" more likely than "bird-watcher" and "bird-watching," and examples of usage include: "Where did you bird fall migration?" "Have you birded Attu?" and "I'm birding Churchill in June." More particularly, one might go "owling," "hawking," or on a "rail romp," depending on the "target" species; "wire-birding" is done while birders are driving. Identifying a bird by "jizz," a composite of features such as general impression, size, and shape, is possible only by skilled birders who can, for instance, "call" birds at great distance, distinguishing a male "Coop" (Cooper's Hawk) from a female "Sharpie" (Sharp-Shinned Hawk) in an autumn sky of migrating raptors. "Pishing," done by birders of all levels of expertise, is onomatopoeic of the sound made to flush birds from cover. The word might be used as in, "He pished up a Song," meaning that a Song Sparrow flushed to investigate the pishing. In the field, birders often use abbreviated common names like "Buffy" for Buff-Breasted Sandpiper, "T.V." for Turkey Vulture, and "Maggie" for Magnolia Warbler.

Most birders acknowledge the significance of the life list, a list of all species of birds identified by one person. "Life birds," or "lifers," are birds sought for inclusion on that list, and "hard-core listers" will travel great distances to gain sightings of species reported by the North American Rare Bird Alert, a subscription "hot line" information phone service operated by Houston's Audubon Society. Any day's birding might produce sightings of "nice" birds (good examples of species) or "good" birds (rare or difficult sightings for an area or season). Birds the birder is not able to identify qualify as "LBJs" (little brown jobs) or "LBBs" (little brown birds).

Birders dress functionally to protect themselves and their equipment from environmental conditions, such as tick bites, cold, rain, and salt spray. Each birder customizes outfits of preferred equipment and clothing, but general rules apply: Wear dull rather than bright colors; Wear nothing to flap in the wind or make noise as one moves. Certain birders also wear clothing and emblems to display their ornithophilic interest: bird club or birder event T-shirts, multipocketed vests decorated with bird club and birding "hot spot" embroidered patches, and narrow-brimmed hats festooned with tiny bird pin souvenirs of American Birding Association conventions. Birders' automobiles bear bird club window decals and bumper sticker messages of "Caution! Sudden Stops! We're bird-watchers." Custom license tags name a favorite or unusual species with perhaps abbreviated or coded spelling: ELF OWL, KISKA-D, HOOPOE, BLUJAY, MERLIN!, BL GRSB (Blue Grosbeak).

Birders operate within a hierarchy of expertise and preference that distinguishes "dickie birders" and backyard birders from hawk watchers and birders with life lists of North American sightings exceeding 600 or 700 species. Binoculars are ubiquitous among birders, and any birder also may use a tripod-mounted spotting scope for magnification at greater distances than "binocs" or "binos" will handle. Customarily, birders share scope views, and once a bird is "in the scope" the owner steps back and offers the view to others. Birding may be a solo or ensemble enterprise, but birders who "list" prefer to bird with at least one other person of equal expertise for sighting verifications. Custom is for a birder who has sighted a bird to "call" the identification for others' benefit, naming at least species, sex, location or flight direction, and continue to call, until others "have" the sighting. Built into that custom is the expectation for accuracy, so those with the greatest expertise are likely to call first. Birders narrate their experiences and exchange information about "hot spots" (locations with avifaunal variety) and identification "tips," the sharing based on a democratic sense of group identity. Birders greet by inquiring about each others' sightings, and in these exchanges birders estimate the quality of sightings claimed based on unspoken, indirect evaluations of the claimant's expertise.

Birders' expressed values include conservation of birds and preservation and creation of habitats, cooperative sighting and continuous study, benign interruption of birds' natural life, scrupulously honest and exquisitely detailed reporting. High competition is a feature of Big Day events, wherein birders compete to identify the greatest number of birds within twenty-four hours. Christmas Bird Counts are informally competitive for numbers of individual birds and species identifications as well as for numbers of participants and modes of transportation used to accomplish counts. The World Series of Birding involves sponsored teams competing in Big Day fashion for the highest number of species identified during this spring-migration event. Ceremonial closure at birder events is the "countdown," wherein the checklist is read aloud and birders respond aloud, "yes" or "no," for each species named, composing a corporate list. In the countdown, beginning or unsuccessful birders can share in the expertise of the assemblage, understanding the meaning of the birder proverb: "Even the worst day birding is the best day you'll ever have."

Karen Baldwin

References

Connor, Jack. 1988. *The Complete Birder: A Guide to Better Birding.* Boston: Houghton Mifflin.

Dunne, Pete. 1992. *The Feather Quest: A North American Birder's Year.* New York: Penguin Books.

Harrison, George H. 1979. *The Backyard Bird Watcher.* New York: Simon and Schuster.

Kastner, Joseph. 1986. *A World of Watchers.* New York: Alfred Knopf.

Komito, Sanford. 1990. *Birding's Indiana Jones: A Chaser's Diary.* N.p.

Leahy, Christopher. 1982. *The Birdwatcher's Companion: An Encyclopedic Handbook of North American Birdlife.* New York: Bonanza Books.

Peterson, Roger Tory. 1957. *The Bird Watcher's Anthology.* New York: Harcourt, Brace.

Sill, Ben L., Cathryn P. Sill, and John C. Sill. 1993. *Beyond Birdwatching: More Than There Is to Know about Birding.* Atlanta: Peachtree.

Terres, John K., ed. 1991. *The Audubon Society Encyclopedia of North American Birds.* New York: Wings Books.

Birthdays

Annual celebrations of the anniversary of the date of someone's birth, sometimes marking significant points in the life cycle. Birthdays are celebrated most often in a family setting, but also at school and in the workplace. The birthdays of prominent citizens may be commemorated publicly in either an official or a casual ceremony, and the media often mention the birthdays of well-known people. Whatever the contexts for celebrating a birthday, in American tradition one expects to have a cake (or other special food) decorated with lighted candles (one for each year of the honoree's life), the singing of the birthday song, and (following the honoree's blowing out the candles) gifts from the guests.

Birthday traditions include the custom of associating certain gems with one's birthdate ("birthstones"), the lore of astrology, the sending of birthday cards, literary birthday references (such as Humpty Dumpty's "un-birthday present" in Lewis Carroll's *Through the Looking-Glass* [1872]), and national holidays associated with birthdays (President's Day and Christmas). There are also numerous folk beliefs and customs associated with birthdays, such as that "the best day to start a business is on your birthday," "a child that cries on its first birthday will have an unlucky life," and "if a slice of the birthday cake tips over on the plate, that person will never marry."

But the main focus of folkloristic investigation of American birthday celebrations is the birthday party itself, with its much varied routines involving cake, candles, song, and gifts. (At children's parties there is also usually a ritual spanking of the honoree and the playing of traditional games like "Pin the Tail on the Donkey.") Family celebrations of birthdays usually begin at age one and may continue, more or less "complete," until the end of a person's life. Special emphasis tends to fall on the first birthday, the thirteenth (becoming a teenager), the sixteenth ("sweet sixteen"), the eighteenth (driving, drinking, and perhaps draft age), the twenty-first ("adulthood"), and the following decade years (especially the 40th). Often these milestones are marked by special foods, speeches, gifts, or even commemorative advertisements in the newspaper ("Lordy, Lordy! / Look who's forty!").

As the person grows older, the correct number of candles may be rationalized by using number-shaped candles, designating each candle as meaning five or ten, or spelling out the number with candles. Interpreting the ubiquituous candle-blowing rite, Theodore Humphrey suggests, "The breath of the honoree becomes symbolic of the divine afflatus, the life-giving and sustaining force of the universe, and by breathing it over this culturally encoded symbolic food, the cake, the birthday honoree endows it with magic power." The standard "belief" is that the honoree makes a secret wish before blowing out the candles; if he or she extinguishes all of the candles in one puff, the wish will come true.

"Happy Birthday to You," the birthday song in English, was originally published in 1893 with the title "Good Morning to All"; it is probably the most frequently sung song in the United States, especially if one includes the common parodies sung by children (such as, "Happy birthday to you / You live in the zoo . . ."). Other nations have their own traditional

A postcard for a birthday boy, 1916. Collection J.W. Love.

songs, such as the Danish one that begins "*I dag er det (Jans) fødselsdag*" (Today is [Jan's] birthday).

Birthday gifts (as well as cake decoration, a party theme, and the like) often reflect the occupation or hobby of the honoree. Gifts may also mark the life-cycle points (such as liquor for one who comes of age), and special attention is often paid to the fortieth birthday, which may have a "mourning" theme since the honoree is now "over the hill." The typical celebration includes a black cake, funereal decor, and geriatric gifts. (Remember, too, that Jack Benny never allowed himself to become more than thirty-nine years old.) Gift wrappings may or may not be saved for reuse, according to family custom, each unwrapped gift may be bumped on the honoree's head before being opened while a rhyme is recited ("Heavy, heavy hangs over your poor head . . . "), and possibly a wish is made for the giver.

Among the many other variations on, and additions to, the birthday routine practiced in American families are these: a "date with daddy" for the birthday girl; birthday parties held for pets or dolls; conference calls with absent family members, with everyone singing "Happy Birthday" together; butter put on the nose of the birthday person; kidnapping of the honoree for a birthday breakfast; surprise birthday parties; commemorative newspaper ads on the birthdays of deceased family members, and small items baked into the birthday cake

that supposedly have divinatory significance.

Thus, birthdays inspire ceremonies that unite a family or a peer group—even if some members are separated by distance—in order to focus upon and honor the person who has reached one more year of age. The celebration may set up new relationships for a brief time (like "Queen" or "Boss" for the day), and birthdays are linked whenever possible with stages in the life cycle, especially leaving infancy, achieving maturity, and reaching middle age.

Jan Harold Brunvand

References

Humphrey, Theodore C. 1991. A Family Celebrates a Birthday: Of Life and Cakes. In "*We Gather Together": Food and Festival in American Life,* ed. Theodore C. Humphrey and Lin T. Humphrey. Logan: Utah State University Press, pp. 19–26.

See also Anniversaries; Custom; Family Folklore

Black English

Pronunciations, vocabulary, and grammatical forms used primarily by African Americans; also known as *Vernacular Black English* or *African American Vernacular English* (AAVE). AAVE is primarily associated with lower- and working-class African American oral culture but may be used by speakers from any social level. Black English is not limited to particular age groups, though there are generational differences in the incidence of some features. Many African Americans never use AAVE, and others use it only in informal conversations with other African Americans. Some speakers use only a few features of AAVE, whereas others use most of them. Virtually all phonological and grammatical features of AAVE are used in other varieties of Southern speech, but they are used much more frequently by African Americans—evidence that AAVE developed alongside other varieties of English in the American South. With the migration of Southerners into industrial and urban centers after World War II, AAVE has expanded geographically, with urban varieties developing usage patterns that are noticeably different from those of more conservative rural varieties. Features originating in rural varieties of AAVE were caricatured in popular entertainment prior to the 1960s, and since the 1970s urban AAVE has frequently been used in television, popular music, and stand-up comedy.

When linguists began seriously studying AAVE in the 1960s (and popularized the term Black English), they noted similarities between the vernacular language of African Americans and pidgin and creole languages. Gullah, a regional dialect spoken on the coastal islands of South Carolina and Georgia where rural African Americans lived in relative isolation until the 1930s, has many characteristics in common with pidgins and creoles of West African origin, but the vernacular language of 20th-century African Americans in communities where there is social interaction among a broad range of Black and White cultural groups has much more in common with other varieties of Southern American English. Because the first generation of African Americans learned English as a second language, a substratum of West African phonological, grammatical, and lexical forms remained in African American English for several generations—just as a substratum of Germanic, Romance, or Slavic influence remained for several generations in the speech of immigrants from Europe. As successive generations of African Americans became further removed from African language and culture, and as they interacted more with Anglo Americans, African features declined in their speech.

AAVE is "r-less"; that is, *r* after a vowel is either not pronounced (homophones: *door* and *dough)* or is pronounced "uh" (homophones: *boa* and *bore).* The sounds spelled with *th* alternate among several pronunciations: the voiced fricative alternates with [d] and [v] *(that, dat, bruvuh);* the voiceless fricative alternates with [t] and [f] *(nothin/ nut'n/ nuffin).* Older speakers of Gullah and AAVE who had little contact with other dialects during their youths may never produce the "th" sounds with the tip of the tongue between the teeth. Other characteristics of AAVE include word-initial stress (PO-lice, IN-surance); elision of initial unstressed syllables *(remember —> 'member);* special pronunciations of certain words *(ask* as *axe, aunt* with the vowel of *dawn);* typical "Southern" pronunciation of the "long *i"* in *time* as *tahm* and use of an *ao* diphthong in *caught;* special meanings for certain words *(passed =* "died"); repetition of the subject in pronoun form *(My sister she like the color red);* frequent use of *ain't (I ain't got any);* and other nonstandard usages such as multiple negation and nonstandard verb forms *(It don't make no difference).* All of these dialect features also occur in the folk speech of White Americans in the South.

The features of AAVE phonology that most differentiate it from other varieties of English are the lack of consonant combinations at the ends of words and the suppression of final consonants in general *(desk—> dess, cold—> cole—> coe).* These features affect the inflectional system of the dialect. The regular plurals and possessives of nouns and the tense forms of regular verbs in standard English have final consonant combinations that are often truncated in AAVE *(her sister's friends —> her sister friend; he walks—> he walk; it rained—> it rain).* Some linguists have attributed these forms to pidgin or creole influences, implying that the lack of strongly articulated final consonants in AAVE derives from the fact that many of the languages of Africa have consonant combinations at the beginnings of words but few final consonants.

Salient in AAVE are special uses of verb forms, particularly the verb *be.* Where standard English may contract *is* and *are,* AAVE has no verb *(He drivin' too fast; You right;* but: *I'm right; I know he is).* Other special verb forms that linguists have documented as being widespread in AAVE are "habitual *be"* *(He be doin' that all the time),* "perfective *done" (He done lef' already),* "remote-time *been" (I been finish that book),* and "double modals" *(We may can get together, but might can't settle everything).* All of these structures except "completive *been"* and some combinations of double modals occasionally occur in the folk speech of many White speakers in the South. The use of AAVE rarely causes problems in understanding for Americans familiar with the dialect, but exclusive use of AAVE

for personal communication adds to the challenges that young African Americans face in learning to write and speak standard language in school.

Urban varieties of AAVE have made substantial contributions to popular American vocabulary, from terms like *jazz, cool,* and *rap* to contemporary usages associated with urban gangs (such as *bad* meaning "good"). Urban AAVE is innovative in its vocabulary, but because of the negative stigma attached to AAVE most of these usages remain in the realm of slang.

Because language is a powerful social instrument, AAVE has proven to be useful to African American communities in maintaining group identity. Recent research has indicated that, rather than being reduced by the prevalence of mass communication and public education, the primary features of AAVE enjoy a vigorous life. African American stand-up comics and rap artists capitalize on AAVE pronunciations, grammatical forms, and expressions to evoke desired responses from their audiences, just as any verbal artist uses certain features of dialect to indicate social class, level of education, ethnicity, and rural versus urban origin.

Donald M. Lance

See also Folk Speech

Blacksmithing

A venerable folk technique for molding iron and steel. The blacksmith heats a selected piece of metal to an extremely high temperature on a forge (approximately 1,500°F) and then shapes it into his desired form by the force of repeated hammer blows as the metal is drawn across the surface of an anvil. For more than four millennia these three elements—fire, hammer, and anvil—have constituted the core of the blacksmith's business even though the usual blacksmith shop is filled with hundreds of tools, including numerous types of tongs, punches, chisels, drills, and wrenches. Blacksmiths are so named because they work with iron, the so-called black metal; all other metal workers are then collectively referred to as "white smiths."

The oldest known examples of worked iron, which date to about 2000 B.C. were found in the Near East. Blacksmithing spread so rapidly from the eastern Mediterranean that by 1000 B.C. the craft was well entrenched in central Europe as well as in Asia and Africa. During Europe's Middle Ages, blacksmiths came to be recognized as the pivotal artisans among all of the skilled trades. They not only produced useful articles necessary for the efficient operation of every household such as cooking utensils and fireplace gear, but they also made the tools employed by all of the other craftsmen. They provided hammers, saws, and drill bits for carpenters, chisels for stone cutters, trowels for masons and plasterers. And when these tools became worn or were broken, they were brought back to the smithy to be mended. Farmers, of course, looked to local blacksmiths for plows, shovels, hoes, pitchforks, and other implements used to raise and process their crops. In maritime settings, smiths provided all manner of "boat iron" as well as chains, anchors, and fishing hooks. Land transpor-

Threading a pipe at a blacksmith shop. San Augustine, Texas, 1939. Photo Russell Lee. Library of Congress.

tation might come to a halt without the assistance of blacksmiths, who could provide shoes for horses' hooves, iron tires for wooden wheels, and the gear needed to hitch animal teams to their wagons. Since the preindustrial era was the "age of iron," the blacksmith was necessarily an ubiquitous figure. Indeed, even now "Smith" remains the most common surname among people of English descent.

Given the fact that there is no evidence of iron working in North America before the arrival of European settlers, the American tradition for blacksmithing is clearly descended from Old World precedents. Indeed, the tools and techniques that American blacksmiths employ as well as the types of objects they produce differ very little from European models. The sickle-like corn knives found in the Northeastern section of the United States, for example, derive from European short-handled scythes. The lightweight swing plows that early pioneers used to navigate around the tree stumps that littered their newly cleared fields, while often seen as evidence of homegrown American ingenuity, were based on a 16th-century English prototype that had its ultimate origins in Holland. In Pennsylvania, blacksmiths made strap hinges shaped in the form of rams' horns or cocks' heads and etched into them hearts, flowers, stars, and various geometric insignias. These bits of hardware were one of the means by which the highly decorative Germanic tradition in folk art was preserved. The Hispanic tradition for ironwork that flourished in the Southwest is seen in distinctive gear used by the horsemen who tended the cattle that were left to forage out in the open. The spurs and branding irons that are now regarded as standard features of the Old West and cowboy culture were actually imports from the Iberian Peninsula. Moving across the country, one finds finally very little in American blacksmithing that is uniquely American. Rather, as with much material folk culture in the United States, there is a diversity of expression. It is the plurality of blacksmithing traditions that is most emblematic of the American experience.

Gathered under the title of blacksmith are several distinct metal trades: the farrier, who cares for horses' hooves and provides them with protective metal shoes; the wheelwright, who builds wooden wheels and fashions iron tires for their rims; the wainwright, who builds wagon bodies and equips them with the needed iron parts; the angle smith, who supplies structural iron for buildings; the toolmaker, who makes and repairs various metal implements; and the ornamental ironworker, who designs and builds decorative gates, fences, and window grills. In urban areas, an artisan might specialize in only one of these branches of ironwork, but the rural blacksmith could be called upon to perform all of these tasks. In the era before industrialization, a blacksmith was required to master several of the ironworking trades. But as more and more hardware was produced in factories, the demand for the blacksmith's skills was progressively reduced. Changes in our basic modes of transportation during the 20th century eliminated the need for most blacksmiths. With no horses to shoe or wagons to build or iron tires to repair, many artisans simply ended their careers. Others held on by turning to repair work. From being a creator or maker, these artisans became salvage or service craftsmen and often worked on broken car bodies.

The ornamental field, however, is one area of ironwork in which traditional smithing practices continue to thrive because factory production techniques cannot as yet successfully duplicate the effects of handwrought decoration. In the Charleston, South Carolina, area, for example, relatively young men carry on today under the watchful eye of Philip Simmons, an active octogenarian whose craftsmanship is rooted in a genealogy stretching back to the early 19th century (Vlach 1992). In Simmons' opinion, there is more than enough work in his city for four or five blacksmithing operations. During the late 1920s, when Simmons faced declining prospects for future employment, he took heart in the advice of his teacher who had told him, "Don't worry boy, there will always be work for a blacksmith." Turning to ornamental ironwork proved to be his salvation, and the steady flow of requests from local customers for gates and fences has allowed him to perpetuate his blacksmithing skills. But in the late 20th century, clearly the utilitarian dimensions of blacksmithing have been overshadowed by aesthetic motives as a craft tradition has been transformed primarily into a mode for artistic expression.

John Michael Vlach

References

Aston, James, and Edward B. Story. 1941. *Wrought Iron: Its Manufacture, Characteristics, and Applications.* Pittsburgh: A.M. Byers.

Robins, Frederick William. 1953. *The Smith: The Traditions and Lore of an Ancient Craft.* London and New York: Rider.

Southworth, Michael, and Susan Southworth. 1978. *Ornamental Ironwork: An Illustrated Guide to Its Design, History, and Use in American Architecture.* Boston: David R. Godine.

Vlach, John Michael. 1992. *Charleston Blacksmith: The Work of Philip Simmons.* rev. ed. Columbia: University of South Carolina Press.

Weygers, Alexander G. 1974. *The Modern Blacksmith.* Princeton: Van Nostrand Reinhold.

Bluegrass

A form of string-band and vocal music with strong ties to Southern folk music traditions. It emerged within country music in the 1940s. Embraced in the late 1950s by folk-music enthusiasts who saw it as modern Southern mountain folk-music, it was the focus of a revival movement beginning in the mid-1960s that stimulated the rise of bluegrass festivals, clubs, magazines, and related businesses. Now well established as a music culture, bluegrass can be found in a range of contexts extending from full-time international commercial enterprise in the domain of popular culture to part-time local grass-roots involvement in the domain of folk culture.

Bluegrass takes its name from the band of its principal architect, Bill Monroe. A member of the influential Grand Ole Opry radio show on WSM in Nashville, Tennessee, since 1939, Kentuckian Monroe assembled a particularly influential version of his Blue Grass Boys in the years following World War II. It included mandolinist and tenor singer Monroe; guitarist and lead singer Lester Flatt, banjoist Earl Scruggs, fiddler Chubby Wise, and bassist Howard Watts ("Cedric Rainwater"). The copying of the instrumental and vocal styles, and the repertoire, of this band of self-accompanied vocalists initiated the development of bluegrass as a musical genre.

Today the music is perceived as the result of the intention of Monroe, and of those musicians who played with or emulated him, to modernize the Southeastern string-band folk-music traditions that were known as "old-time" music (although this term is used in other parts of North America to refer to many different local, regional, and ethnic folk traditions). The primary instruments—fiddle, guitar, five-string banjo, mandolin, and bass—as well as the repertoire and melodic structures of bluegrass reflect a continuity with this past. So does the strong insistence by bluegrass musicians that the instruments used be acoustic rather than electric. Modernization, then, occurred in the realm of what might best be termed "arrangement," as bluegrass developed its own musical rules and traditions concerning the roles of individual musicians in producing its sounds. Considerable emphasis is placed in bluegrass vocals upon the singing of harmony parts, and a number of intricate patterns of harmonic arrangement have become accepted as part of the traditions of the music. Instruments are used to support vocals and provide musical interludes between periods of singing, as in many other contemporary popular forms. But the role of instruments in bluegrass reflects the high proportion of instrumental pieces in the repertoire and a concomitant expectation of instrumental virtuosity. This is accentuated by a stress on speed: Most bluegrass performances are at a brisk tempo that is particularly noticeable in those items of the repertoire that come from other music cultures. Also stressed is the choice of keys for singing that place the singers' voices in high pitches. Bluegrass listeners often pay as much attention to the musical textures (high-pitched vocal harmonies, dense instrumental patterns) and the instrumental interludes in vocal pieces as to the words themselves.

The bluegrass repertoire has, in its general profile, remained remarkably constant. Newly composed pieces alternate with older songs taken from popular sources, particularly country music, and from the oral traditions of the performers. Secular love and story songs (often with duet or trio refrains), gospel songs (generally sung by quartets), and instrumental pieces (usually featuring fiddle, banjo, and mandolin soloing in the jazz mode) all follow the same source patterns. While full-time professional groups are expected to create new and distinctive repertoires, the part-time followers of the music, who constitute the majority of those involved with it, typically perform a repertoire of songs and tunes based on the most popular items in the repertoires of the early influential bands—like "Foggy Mountain Breakdown" by Flatt and Scruggs, "Little Cabin Home on the Hill" by Bill Monroe, "Rank Strangers" by the Stanley Brothers, and "Love Please Come Home" by Reno and Smiley—and the many others more popular in recent times. As is frequently the case with folk traditions of many kinds, the origins and histories of specific items are often not known fully (if at all), and this information may not be considered very important. At the hundreds of annual bluegrass festivals and similar events, informal jam sessions attract as much attention as formal performances on stage. In these sessions, the familiar repertoire facilitates music making between both friends and strangers.

In its early years, bluegrass was most popular with rural working-class people from the southern Appalachians and other parts of the Upland South. Its popularity within the folk-music revival of the 1950s and 1960s attracted middle-class youth from outside that region. The bluegrass revival and the growth of festivals in the 1960s and 1970s broadened the audience still further. In the 1990s, bluegrass bands could be found in many parts of Europe and in Japan, New Zealand, and Australia. Like jazz, it is recognized as a musical genre that is characteristically American but also accessible to adventurous musicians from other cultures. And as with jazz and other established musical genres, it has developed its own politics of style, with various combinations of repertoire and performance practices described as "traditional," "progressive," "newgrass," "new acoustic," and so forth.

Until the late 1980s, all of the influential bluegrass musicians were men. By 1990 a growing number of influential women stars were altering that pattern, following the success of singer and fiddler Alison Krauss and her band Union Station. Although bluegrass repertoire and musical style reflect the influences of African American music, there are few Black bluegrass musicians.

Neil V. Rosenberg

References

Cantwell, Robert. 1984. *Bluegrass Breakdown*. Urbana: University of Illinois Press.
Rosenberg, Neil V. 1985. *Bluegrass: A History*. Urbana: University of Illinois Press.

See also Banjo; Country Music; Fiddle Music; Monroe, Bill; Revivalism

Blues

Folksong and music genre highly influential in popular music. Blues first came to public notice around the beginning of the 20th century. The precise time and place cannot be identified, but its appearance is associated with a growing spirit of individualism in the African American community, especially in the generation born in the first decades of freedom. Early centers of the blues were rural and small town "juke joints" and house parties, country picnics, saloons, levee, lumber, and railroad camps, railroad stations, hobo jungles, parks and street corners, medicine, minstrel, and vaudeville shows, and urban "rent parties."

The music's core audience and its most prominent practitioners have been African Americans with a rural Southern background. Blues was especially popular in regions of new agricultural development, such as the Mississippi Delta, Louisiana's Caddo Lake, and south Florida, among landless sharecroppers and migrant farm workers and among recent rural migrants to the Southern and Northern cities. The creation and performance of blues quickly became a means of making extra money and even a full-time living, and the music began to appear on the professional stage during the first decade of the 20th century, in sheet music during the next decade, and by 1920 on phonograph records. The music's popularity spread to other segments of the African American community, to White Americans in the South and elsewhere, and eventually worldwide. Over the course of approximately 100 years, blues has persisted as a folk music, developed as a popular music, and exerted enormous influence on many other types of popular music.

It is difficult to offer a concise definition of the blues, yet certain prevalent characteristics can be noted. The most common verse form is the three-line stanza, in which the first line is repeated, followed by a final line that differs in content but rhymes. Sometimes a single line is sung three times or the final line does not rhyme, and there are two-line, four-line, and other forms as well. Usually each line is contained within four musical measures, so that the common three-line form occupies twelve measures (the so-called "twelve-bar blues"). The use of a musical instrument is integral to the blues, however, and it serves to punctuate and respond to the vocal lines. Thus, the voice is not heard throughout a blues performance, and there are phrases and sometimes whole choruses that are purely instrumental. A typical three-line blues stanza might run as follows:

Got the blues and can't be satisfied
(instrumental response)
Got the blues and can't be satisfied . . . *(instrumental response)*
If I keep these blues, gonna catch a train and ride . . . *(instrumental response)*

In some folk blues, the performers play a series of instrumental "riffs" following the lines of verse. These are short repeated melodic-rhythmic phrases. Most male blues singers and most folk blues singers of both sexes play their own instrumental accompaniment, usually a guitar, piano, or harmonica. Many female blues singers and some male singers of popular blues do not play an instrument. In some folk and many popular blues, the singer's instrument is supplemented by other instruments.

The scale of most blues differs from the Western diatonic scale in having a flexibility of pitch at certain steps of the scale, most notably the third and seventh and sometimes the fifth and other steps. Notes that are sounded within these flexible tonal ranges are commonly known as "blue notes," although they can be found in many other genres of African American folk and popular music besides blues. Blue notes can occur as microtonal variants of these scale steps within a single performance, as neutral pitches, as slides, as waverings, and as the simultaneous sounding of different variants of the scale step (such as major and minor). On instruments, blue notes can be achieved by "bending" techniques on the guitar and harmonica, by the "slide" guitar technique with the use of a bottleneck or knife, and by the rapid alternation or simultaneous playing of major and minor notes on the piano. In pentatonic tunes, blue notes are often especially prominent and lend these pieces a strongly non-Western character.

Most folk blues do not use harmonies more complex than the basic tonic, subdominant, and dominant chords and their variant seventh chords. Some folk blues, particularly those from Mississippi and adjacent states, have even less harmonic development or are entirely modal in character. Over the years, popular-music forms, such as jazz, have introduced more complex harmonies into blues, and these are especially apparent in many popular blues since the 1940s. Like most African American music, blues utilizes a full range of tonal qualities, both vocal and instrumental. Rough and smooth, percussive and melodic sounds are frequently mixed in the same performance, and the overall aesthetic of performers and audiences encourages this variety.

Most blues lyrics deal with the common events of everyday life, especially relations between men and women, from the purported point of view of the singer. They may or may not reflect the singer's actual life or feelings, but they generally represent a dramatic projection of these, so that the singer creates a larger-than-life persona during performance, even when singing the composition of someone else. The songs discuss human relationships in very frank terms, yet with colorful language, poetic imagery, and dramatic exaggeration. They describe and celebrate the temporary ups and downs of life, frequently juxtaposing themes of retention and rejection, staying (or returning) and leaving, praise and abuse, boasting and self-pity. Overall, they display an attitude of dissatisfaction with the status quo, with long-term relationships, or with permanent situations of any kind.

For singers and audiences, whose lives were often characterized by economic drudgery, limited mobility, and an ascribed social inferiority, blues offered an imaginative playground full of excitement, changes, and opportunities. Many blues singers and some members of their audiences have tried to make this playground a reality in their lives, in a limited, if not a full, sense. Besides relations between men and women, other prominent blues themes are travel, agricultural and industrial work, poverty and unemployment, sickness and death, alcohol and drugs, gambling, luck and magic, crime and punishment, and current events—either notable occurrences in the singer's life or regional or national events as they affect the singer and audience (for example, natural disasters, wars, government policies). While the term "blues" suggests songs characterized by unremitting pathos, there is actually considerable humor and irony in blues lyrics, and the overall function of the music is cathartic and therapeutic for performers and audience. A number of blues songs reinforce a context of dance and celebration, and some are purely instrumental performances designed for virtuoso display or dance accompaniment.

As a new type of folk music, blues rapidly developed a large body of lyric phrases, verses, and couplets, melodic phrases and lines, and instrumental phrases and techniques that were shared by performers. Whole songs with their vocal and instrumental parts were not usually transmitted relatively intact, as in the case of ballads. Instead, performers fashioned blues by drawing from the common pool of lyric and musical elements. Sometimes a "core" combination of one or more verses, a melody, and an instrumental part would be transmitted, to which the singer would add further verses. Depending on their creativity and individual propensities, singers would introduce original elements into their blues songs. Even the same performer might vary a blues tune considerably from one performance to another, and some blues songs are unique combinations of the moment, either from traditional elements, or original material, or some blending of the two. The transmission of elements and exchange of ideas often occur in a local tradition, so that blues in a single community displays a certain commonality of content and style. Individual local traditions blend to

Blues legend John Lee Hooker teams up with guitarist Carlos Santana to shoot a video for their song "The Healer," ca. 1989. American Folklife Center.

form regional traditions (such as Delta blues, Piedmont blues), and these in turn blend to form the overall folk-blues tradition. Crosscutting these relationships are the influence of popular blues and the mass media, particularly phonograph records, and the prestige of performers who become popular "stars" and songs that become "hits." " Popularity affects blues by spreading songs and ideas quickly to many people over long distances, but also by freezing and canonizing certain songs, performances, and styles. Thus, the popularizing tendency simultaneously introduces creative and original elements to the tradition while serving to homogenize the tradition by excluding and reducing the prestige of less popular expressions.

The basic vocal material of folk blues is derived from the tradition of field hollers, a type of worksong sung by a soli-

tary worker in the fields or in other occupations requiring nonrhythmic manual labor. Chanted prayers and sermons may also have contributed to the style of blues singing, but they have less in common with blues in their lyric content than do the secular hollers. The flexibility and spontaneity of the hollers were given form by a variety of other folksong and folk-music genres, particularly the folk ballad. By the 1890s, a three-line ballad form had come into existence in the African American community and among musicians working in a mixed Black-White environment. Many ballads utilizing this form were about characters who lived outside the law and organized society, such as "Stagolee," "Frankie and Albert," and "Railroad Bill." These ballads were usually instrumentally accompanied in performance, and their form consisted of a rhymed couplet followed by a one-line refrain. This form was easily transformed to the common AAB verse structure of the blues. It is significant that the origins of the blues form incorporate a tension between songs associated with onerous work and songs about characters who defied the work ethic and did as they pleased. Other folk-music genres contributed to the blues as well; spirituals, group worksongs, and children's songs were part of the general musical background to which most folk-blues singers were exposed.

Instrumental and instrumentally-accompanied music, such as folk ragtime, banjo and fiddle tunes, and fife and drum music, all contributed to the blues, particularly certain rhythmic patterns and the use of riffs. The folk-blues tradition is also a reservoir for many older folk musical instruments, such as a one-stringed zither using the slide technique, the one-string (or washtub) bass, the jug, kazoo, washboard, and spoons—all instruments derived from African prototypes, using American materials of construction or common household objects. In general, the stylistic, technical, and aesthetic features of the blues are predominantly African, while its formal features (such as strophic organization, three-chord harmony, and primary accompanying instruments) come from the European musical tradition. Its content, of course, reflects cultural patterning, individual creativity, and time, place, and events.

The popularization of blues began almost as soon as folk blues was created. Traveling professional and semiprofessional folk performers included increasing numbers of blues in their repertoires, and medicine show, tent show, and vaudeville performers incorporated them into their stage acts in the first decade of the 20th century. In the next decade, blues became popular on the Black vaudeville circuit, and songs were published in sheet-music form as early as 1912. Songs like W.C. Handy's "Memphis Blues" (1912) and "St. Louis Blues" (1914) became national hits and for the first time gave White Americans outside of the South access to this music. In 1920 Mamie Smith became the first Black singer to make a blues record. Hundreds of records by her and other vaudeville-stage singers like Bessie Smith, Ma Rainey, and Ida Cox, were issued through the end of the 1920s and the demise of vaudeville. Most of these stage singers were women, usually accompanied by a pianist or a small jazz group. Meanwhile, beginning in 1926, large numbers of self-accompanied folk-blues singers, mostly male, were recorded. Among these were guitarists Blind Lemon Jefferson, Blind Willie McTell, Tommy Johnson, Charlie Patton, and Memphis Minnie McCoy, and pianists Pine Top Smith and Roosevelt Sykes. Also recorded at this time were various duos, trios, and other small groups, such as jug bands, string bands, skiffle bands, and hokum bands. Many of the recordings of these folk-blues singers and combos were made on location in Southern cities, such as Atlanta, Memphis, and Dallas.

In the 1930s and up to World War II, recording activity was almost entirely concentrated in Chicago and New York, and only three companies accounted for the vast bulk of all record releases. A "star" system arose, particularly among resident Chicago blues artists, and performers like Big Bill Broonzy, Washboard Sam, and Tampa Red had hundreds of releases, often accompanying one another on records. The homogeneity that resulted was offset somewhat by the continued recording of new Southern folk-blues artists like Robert Johnson and Blind Boy Fuller. Another development of the 1930s was the addition to blues combos of typical jazz instruments, such as trumpet, clarinet, saxophone, and drums. By the 1940s, jazz and popular music influenced many blues singers. Some were known as blues "shouters," such as Big Joe Turner, while others, like Charles Brown and Ivory Joe Hunter, were crooners.

Many independent regional record companies sprang up in the late 1940s and early 1950s and recorded a variety of new types of blues. There was a brief upsurge of folk-blues recording activity, spurred largely by the novelty of the electric guitar and the creativity of artists such as John Lee Hooker and Lightnin' Hopkins. Small electric urban blues bands were also recorded at this time, especially in Chicago under the leadership of such figures as Muddy Waters and Howlin' Wolf. The most pervasive development of this period, however, was the creation of a new jazz-influenced electric lead guitar style. This style, which features the bending of strings, was pioneered by Texas guitarist T-Bone Walker and adapted further by B.B. King of Memphis. In the 1950s, gospel-influenced "soul" blues singing became popular, and the electric bass and organ were introduced.

In the 1960s, White performers began to define themselves as blues artists, reviving and adapting a range of styles from solo folk blues to electric blues bands. A blues revival of international proportions began, which has included the African American community, characterized by the rediscovery of older performers and the discovery of new ones, the development of a concert, festival, and club circuit, and the creation of blues societies, awards programs, fan and collector magazines, and newsletters.

In addition to having a history and development of its own, blues has influenced many other forms of popular music in the 20th century. The first commercially published blues was essentially a new type of multistrain ragtime music, whose innovations were the introduction of the three-line strain, a semblance of blue notes, and a greater seriousness in the lyrics. These traits, along with the improvisational quality of blues, would ultimately lead to the decline of ragtime. The blues form, blue notes, and improvisation were at the heart of early jazz and the performances of such jazz pioneers as King Oliver, Louis Armstrong, and Jelly Roll Morton. Swing bands, like those of Benny Goodman and Count Basie, relied heavily on blues, and in the 1940s blues was central to the music of innovative beboppers like Charlie Parker and Thelonious Monk as well as that of the Dixieland revivalists. Blues has been an important component of most jazz movements ever since.

Many of the innovative stars of country music, such as Jimmie Rodgers, Bill Monroe, and Hank Williams, learned directly from African American blues musicians. Rodgers in particular, often called the "Father of Country Music," is best known for his blues with yodeling refrains. The "Father of Gospel Music," Thomas A. Dorsey, was a successful blues composer and performer before he became prominent in gospel music in the 1930s. Blues helped introduce instrumental accompaniment, blue notes, and improvisation to gospel music, and a number of prominent gospel artists, such as Roebuck "Pops" Staples, have had prior blues careers. Most of the early rock and roll hits of Elvis Presley, Chuck Berry, Little Richard, and others were blues songs. Blues continued to be an important part of rock music in the 1960s in the surf music of the Beach Boys, the sound of many British rock groups, psychedelic rock, and the "soul" music of artists like Ray Charles and James Brown. Blues has remained an important part of rock music in the "heavy metal" sound and has also entered many American ethnic traditions, including Midwestern polka music, Texas-Mexican *norteño* music, and Louisiana Cajun music. The Creoles of southwestern Louisiana have developed a special form of blues and blues-influenced music known as zydeco, featuring the accordion. Blues has also influenced the work of composers like George Gershwin, poets like Langston Hughes and Sterling Brown, and writers like Zora Neale Hurston.

Blues scholarship began shortly after the music was created and even before it took on a recognizable identity as "blues." Early folklorists like Howard W. Odum and John Lomax made collections of blues in the South in the first and second decades of the 20th century. Because of the highly fluid nature of blues, they eschewed the comparative scholarship of the ballad collectors and concentrated their analysis instead on the blues lyrics as reflections of African American daily life and character. This sociological type of analysis has been continued in the writings of Paul Oliver on popular commercial blues. Musicians W.C. Handy and John Jacob Niles published collections of folk and popular blues in the 1920s, and blues was included in the collections of Negro folk music compiled by Dorothy Scarborough, Howard W. Odum and Guy Benton Johnson, and Newman Ivey White. Since the 1930s, significant collections of folk blues have been made by Zora Neale Hurston, Alan Lomax, Harry Oster, David Evans, William Ferris, and others. The historical and discographical study of popular blues was an outgrowth of jazz studies and has been carried on largely outside the discipline of folklore by researchers like Paul Oliver and Samuel Charters, who helped pioneer this approach in the 1940s and 1950s. Much of this work is centered on interviews and biographical portraits of artists who participated in the music's commercial development. This work now accounts for the bulk of writing about blues. Cultural-contextual study of folk blues has been carried out by William Ferris, Alan Lomax, and others, while musicological and textual analysis of the workings of the folk-blues tradition has been done by Jeff Titon, David Evans, and Peter van der Merwe. Much of the blues scholarship in recent years has combined some of these approaches and interests.

David Evans

References

Evans, David. 1982. *Big Road Blues: Tradition and Creativity in the Folk Blues.* Berkeley: University of California Press.

Ferris, William. 1978. *Blues from the Delta.* Garden City, NY: Anchor.

Harris, Shelton. 1979. *Blues Who's Who.* New Rochelle, NY: Arlington House.

Hart, Mary L., Brenda M. Eagles, and Lisa N. Howorth. 1989. *Blues: A Bibliographic Guide.* New York: Garland.

Lomax, Alan. 1993. *The Land Where the Blues Began.* New York: Pantheon.

Oliver, Paul. 1963. *The Meaning of the Blues.* New York: Collier.

———. 1969. *The Story of the Blues.* London: Barrie and Rockliff.

———, ed. 1989. *The Blackwell Guide to Blues Records.* Oxford: Basil Blackwell.

Oster, Harry. 1969. *Living Country Blues.* Detroit: Folklore Associates.

Titon, Jeff. 1977. *Early Downhome Blues: A Musical and Cultural Analysis.* Urbana: University of Illinois Press.

Van der Merwe, Peter. 1989. *Origins of the Popular Style: The Antecedents of Twentieth-Century Popular Music.* Oxford: Clarendon.

See also Holler; Jazz; Juke Joint; and names of various artists

Boas, Franz (1858–1942)

Anthropologist and folklorist. After receiving his doctorate in physics at Kiel, Germany, in 1881, Boas left for Baffinland, where he conducted fieldwork among the Eskimo (1883–1884). Through his fieldwork among the Tsimshian, Bella Coola, Tlingit, and Bella Bella, Boas came to view mythology, as he wrote in his diary, as "a useful tool for differentiating and judging the relationship of tribes" (Rohner 1966:159). In his work on folklore, Boas was concerned with an accurate recording of texts, and with an analysis of the texts either for linguistic purposes or for reconstruction of culture history through a study of the distribution of motifs. Boas' interest in folklore was apparent from his earliest publication, "Sedna und die religiösen Herbstfeste" (1884), to *Chinook Texts* (1894), *Tsimshian Mythology* (1916), *Kutenai Tales* (1917), and *Kwakiutl Culture as Reflected in Mythology* (1935).

Boas exerted a critical influence on the organizational framework of anthropology and folklore through professional societies and the development of university and museum programs. In the course of his editorship (1908–1924), and that of his colleagues and students, Boas was able to exert influence on the tone, character, and content of the *Journal of American Folklore*. As Regna Darnell notes, Boas necessarily and "deliberately built up a counter power-bloc to the Bureau [of American Ethnology], in large part through the American Folklore Society and the American Ethnological Society" (Darnell 1969:875). Boas trained the first two generations of anthropologists and anthropological folklorists.

By establishing authority over university research and instruction in anthropology, and by maintaining control of the

Journal of American Folklore, Boas brought to fulfillment his initial plan for folklore that he had formulated in the 1890s: that folklore should be kept under the wing of anthropology. The course set by Boas was changed in 1940, with the reorganization of the American Folklore Society, which was instituted to ensure a sharing of power between the literary and the anthropological folklorists.

Boas' legacy to folklore studies lies in his advocacy of fieldwork and of recording and publishing texts in the native language, and in respect for the integrity and value of each individual culture.

Rosemary Lévy Zumwalt

References

Darnell, Regna. 1969. *The Development of American Anthropology, 1879–1920: From Bureau of American Ethnology to Franz Boas.* Ph.D. diss., University of Pennsylvania.

Dwyer-Shick, Susan. 1979. *The American Folklore Society and Folklore Research in America: 1888–1940.* Ph.D. diss., University of Pennsylvania.

Jacobs, Melville. 1954. Folklore. In *The Anthropology of Franz Boas,* ed. Walter Goldschmidt. Memoirs of the American Anthropological Association No. 89. Menasha, WI: American Anthropological Association, pp. 119–138.

Rohner, Ronald P. 1966. Franz Boas: Ethnographer of the Northwest Coast. In *Pioneers of American Anthropology: The Uses of Biography,* ed. June Helm. Seattle: University of Washington Press, pp. 149–222.

Zumwalt, Rosemary Lévy. 1988. *American Folklore Scholarship: A Dialogue of Dissent.* Bloomington: Indiana University Press.

Boast

Hyperbolic exaggeration used to impress listeners with the alleged superiority of the speaker. The boast or the brag is related to the tall tale because both forms depend upon exaggeration. Unlike the tall tale, the true boast lacks narrative elements. Typically, it hinges upon preposterous comparisons, outlandish exaggerations, and the flamboyant oratorical skills of the speaker. It is folk expression that allows speakers to impress all listeners with their alleged boldness, strength, and cunning. But seldom is the braggart taken seriously because of the boast's outrageous hyperbole. "I am a Mississippi snapping turtle: have bear's claws, alligator's teeth, and the devil's tail; can whip any man, by G-d," brags one ringed-tailed roarer.

Boasting about physical strength and endurance appears in epic poetry as an obligatory part of the self-imaging that pugnacious heroes create about themselves. Primitive warriors such as Beowulf and chivalrous knights like Charlemagne boasted in lengthy speeches about their skills in combat. In the 19th-century United States, the heroic brag assumed comic dimensions. It found a suitable home along the frontier, where braggadocio reflected the young nation's expansive exuberance and self-confidence.

Travelers reported that colorful boasts and bragging duels were part of the social customs throughout the old Southwest, and these brags eventually became staples in popular literature of the day. Both Mike Fink and Davy Crockett became national heroes partly because of almanacs and newspapers stories written about them, and both allegedly were archetypal masters of brag. In the 1836 *Crockett Almanac,* Davy modestly proclaims: "I am a raal ringtailed roarer of a jaw breaker, from the thunder and lightning country, down east. I make my breakfast on stewed Yankee and pork steak, and by way of digestion, rinse them down with spike nails and epsom salts; I take dinner of roast goose, stuff'd with wild cats and onions; I sup on nothin but wind. . . . I can out-eat, out-drink, out-work, out-grin, out-snort, out-run, out-lift, out-sneeze, out-sleep, out-lie anything in the shape of a man or beast, from Maine to Louisiana" (quoted in Dorson 1977: xv–vi). And Mike bellows: "I'm a half wild horse and half cock-eyed alligator and the rest o' me is crooked snags an' red-hot snappin' turtle. I can hit like the fourth-proof lightnin' an' every lick I make in the woods lets in an acre o' sunshine. I can out-run, out-jump, out-shoot, out-brag, out-drink, an' out-fight rough-an'-tumble, no holts barred, ary man on both sides of the river from Pittsburgh to New Orleans an' back ag'in to St. Louiee" (quoted in Blair and Meine 1933:105–106).

Semantically, 19th-century boasts depend on imagery grounded in similes and metaphors shaped by life on the frontier. The emphasis is on masculine feats of courage and brute strength. Self-comparisons to forest and swamp animals such as alligators, snapping turtles, bears, raccoons, and snakes hardly outshine metaphors related to powerful natural phenomena including hurricanes, tornadoes, floods, and windstorms. In the brag, muscle and brawn outmatch brains and reason. Boastful proclamations are peppered with allusions to superhuman combats with gargantuan beasts, human and otherwise. Rhetorically, most brags are structured around monosyllabic nouns and verbs that were exaggerated by compounds and strung together into bombastic flourishes. Authors trying to reproduce the nuances of frontier boasts were forced to use phonetic spellings and fractured grammar. Strategically, big talkers sought to entertain all bystanders and to outbrag all opponents with their quick wit and shocking comparisons. While boasts may exaggerate the truth, they are testimonies to the splendid imagination and verbal dexterity of these ring-tailed roarers. Few of these comic braggarts are ever asked to prove their rhetoric true.

The vernacularism of frontier speech and the long-winded loquacity of frontier and riverboat men attracted the attention of 19th-century writers. Easterners provided a ready market for a literature based on tall tales and brags, and American humorous literature was born. James K. Paulding, Augustus Baldwin Longstreet, Thomas Bangs Thorpe, and especially Mark Twain elevated the traditional oral boast to grandiose heights. Gradually, the comic boast in 19th-century literature lost its popular appeal as American literary tastes shifted away from the writings of local colorists.

But the boast has not diminished in oral tradition. Among young Black Americans, for example, "sounding" is a session of verbal boasting in which the participants, mouth-to-mouth as it were, try to better one another through their imaginative deployment of formulaic taunts and brags. In addition, modern rap and street-music lyrics, with their themes of sexual prowess and armed strength, popularize through commercial conduits the brag and reintroduce it to a whole new generation of urban Americans. In some folk contexts, brags sometime serve as invective taunts, and their abusive nature may lead to a fight. Barroom brawls may be preceded by verbal duels that consist of the protagonists hurling insults and brags at one another.

Bragging may also a found as a part of occupational lore, as when workers boast to naive bystanders about their particular on-the-job expertise. Researchers have shown that the lore of lumberjacks, cowboys, oil drillers, and smoke jumpers is rich with exaggerated boasts.

Richard Sweterlitsch

References

Abrahams, Roger D. 1970. *Deep Down in the Jungle: Negro Narrative Folklore from the Streets of Philadephia.* Chicago: Aldine.

Blair, Walter. 1937. *Native American Humor, 1800–1900.* New York: American Book.

Blair, Walter, and Franklin J. Meine. 1933. *Mike Fink.* New York.

Dorson, Richard M. 1959. *American Folklore.* Chicago: University of Chicago Press.

———. [1939] 1977. *Davy Crockett: American Comic Legend.* Westport, CT: Greenwood.

Hyde, Stuart. 1955. The Ring-Tailed Roarer in American Drama. *Southern Folklore Quarterly* 19:171–178.

Leary, James P. 1976. Fists and Foul Mouths: Fights and Fight Stories in Contemporary Rural American Bars. *Journal of American Folklore* 89:27–39.

Thompson, William F. 1934. Frontier Tall Talk. *American Speech* 9:187–199.

See also Crockett, Davy; Fink, Mike

Boatbuilding

Traditional construction of watercraft, and the related folklore of vernacular boats. Boats are a conspicuous, highly significant class of artifacts in maritime communities. Because of this, traditional boatbuilding practices and associated traditions have been the focus of studies by folklorists and other cultural investigators. These studies, which generally deal with vernacular watercraft, frequently analyze how the design, construction, and use of boats reflect boatbuilders' responses to local environmental factors and requirements for work, recreation, transportation, and other functions. Some studies endeavor to chart cultural zones on the basis of the spatial distribution of boat construction techniques, designs, terminology, and other data.

Vernacular boats are cultural artifacts produced by craftsmen who follow the rules and techniques of local, often community-based boatbuilding traditions. Most traditional boatbuilders (invariably men) have learned their trade in an informal manner characterized by an emphasis on observation and imitation rather than verbal instruction. Typically, youngsters in maritime communities will watch their fathers or other men build boats and sometimes assist them with simple tasks. If their interest in boatbuilding remains strong, they acquire more advanced skills as they grow older. When opportunities are available, some become apprentices to established professional builders. Depending on local circumstances, having acquired the basic skills some build boats on a part-time basis while remaining engaged in one or more other economic activities, or become full-time boatbuilding specialists working either in their own shops or in the shops of other full-time professionals.

In general, the vernacular boat designs from which local builders choose are fairly limited. They usually consist of those that have been built and used in the area over the generations—that is, younger builders rely on the tested designs handed down to them by their predecessors. The basic elements of these designs are often preserved in the form of devices such as molds, templates, and half-hull models, along with traditional measurement formulas and other types of knowledge required to translate designs into actual boats. Over time, as they build more and more boats, builders sometimes add small improvements to the traditional designs. If these changes are deemed successful, they usually enter the local design canon and are passed along to subsequent generations of boatbuilders.

Innumerable examples of vernacular boat types can be found along the rivers, lakes, and seacoasts of North America and throughout the world. North American examples range from multipurpose aboriginal craft, such as Alaskan skin boats; to commercial fishing craft, such as the Maine lobster boat, the Lake Michigan fish tug, and the Northwest Coast bow picker; to recreational craft, such as the Southern jon boat, the Reelfoot Lake (Tennessee) stumpjumper, and the Rangeley (Maine) guide boat. Vernacular boats are of interest to folklorists because, like songs, stories, quilts, and other traditional expressive forms, they exhibit continual variation over time and space and reflect the values of the people who create and use them.

Early studies of the folklore of sailors, fishermen, and other maritime peoples tended to be more concerned with customs and beliefs associated with boats than with boats themselves and the details of their design, construction, and use. Beliefs thought to invoke good or bad luck—many of which can still be found in maritime communities—have been especially well documented. These beliefs include taboos against whistling or uttering certain words on board; bringing certain people, animals, or objects aboard; beginning a voyage on a certain day; and painting a boat with certain colors. Beliefs about actions thought to bring good luck include using certain types of wood for specific boat parts, placing a silver dollar under a vessel's mast, launching a newly built boat according to a set ritual, placing statues of saints and other religious artifacts on board, and participating in blessing-of-the-fleet ceremonies. Early studies also considered the rich and unique nomenclature of boatbuilders, including regionally distinctive terms as well as those in widespread use.

Most studies explicitly about vernacular boats have concentrated on the materials and construction practices used to fashion them, along with their shapes or "lines." The builder and his cultural milieu are generally of secondary concern. Consequently, boats are often analyzed from the writer's cultural perspective, not the perspective of the boat's builder; and their features are described with the standard terminology of naval architecture, not the terms used in the areas where the boats are built and used. One particularly influential practitioner of this approach was Howard I. Chapelle (1901–1975), a naval architect and maritime historian who was a curator of transportation at the Smithsonian Institution in Washington, DC. He authored many books on the design of American boats and ships, boatbuilding techniques, and regional boat types. In addition, he was a catalyst for the preservation of American watercraft. His book *American Small Sailing Craft* (1951) is especially noteworthy because it documents over 100 vernacular boat types, most located on the Atlantic and Gulf Coasts, between Maine and Texas. Based largely on Chapelle's own prodigious field research, the book presents a wealth of empirical data on the boats he describes, including line plans and tables of offsets that can be used to build actual boats. Still the only survey of such scope, *American Small Sailing Craft* established a model for persons interested in documenting North American vernacular watercraft and, to a certain extent, established a canon of vernacular boat types. Even more important, this book was instrumental in awakening interest in American vernacular boats.

Since at least 1970, there has been a movement to revive wooden boats in the United States that has emphasized the construction of many vernacular watercraft, including many documented by Chapelle, by amateur and professional builders. Other manifestations of this revival include the founding of small schools for the building of wooden boats, the establishment of small boatbuilding shops, and the organization of several annual wooden-boat festivals. The wooden-boat revival, which has analogues in other craft-revival movements, has received little scholarly attention.

Outside classic maritime communities—generally the most alluring research areas for folklorists—one can also find traditions associated with boatbuilding. Especially prominent are stories about amateurs' boatbuilding projects that did not work out as planned. Common themes include ambitious projects that were never finished, and projects that resulted in boats built in places (often a garage or a basement) from which they could be removed only by cutting a new opening in a wall. Another sort of tradition related to boatbuilding can be seen in a number of communities, situated on the banks of rivers, that have instituted river festivals and other local celebrations. Among other activities, these events feature boat races involving competing teams rowing outlandish vessels of their own design and construction.

In recent years, a small number of folklorists and other scholars have used an ethnographic approach for the study of vernacular boats. In essence, their work endeavors to document and analyze the intricacies of traditional watercraft design, construction, and use within regional cultural contexts. Relying heavily on interviews and observations in the field, these recent studies have investigated the meaning of boats from the perspectives of boatbuilders, boat users and other residents of maritime communities. Especially prominent in this approach is the assumption that, in order to understand the cultural significance of the vernacular boat, one must view it as part of a dynamic process and not as an isolated artifact.

David A. Taylor

References

Johnson, Paula J., and David A. Taylor. 1993. Beyond the Boat: Documenting the Cultural Context. In *Boats: A Manual for Their Documentation,* eds. Paul Lipke, Peter Spectre, and Benjamin A.G. Fuller. Nashville: American Association for State and Local History, pp. 337–356.

Taylor, David A. 1992. *Documenting Maritime Folklife: An Introductory Guide.* Publications of the American Folklife Center No. 18. Washington, DC: Library of Congress.

See also Fishing (Commercial); Maritime Folklore; Watermen

Boatright, Mody Coggin (1896–1970)

Folklorist. A native Texan educated in Texas (B.A. from West Texas State Teachers College, M.A. and Ph.D. from the University of Texas), Mody Boatright spent his entire career in Texas as a teacher of English. After brief appointments at West Texas State Teachers College and Sul Ross State Teachers College, he became an instructor at the University of Texas in 1926; he retired from there forty-three years later, having served in all academic ranks and as department head. He served as secretary-editor of the Texas Folklore Society from 1943 to 1964, succeeding his friend and colleague J. Frank Dobie. He was elected a Fellow of both the American Folklore Society and of the Texas Folklore Society.

A lifetime spent in Texas did not make Boatright parochial or narrow in outlook, even though he focused his folklore research on Texas topics, including cowboys and pioneers *(Tall Tales from Texas Cow Camps* [1934] and *Folk Laughter on the American Frontier* [1949]). His most important work dealt with the folklore of oil prospecting and production *(Folklore of the Oil Industry* [1963], *Gib Morgan: Minstrel of the Oil Fields* [1945]), and with collaborator William A. Owens he wrote *Tales from the Derrick Floor* (1970), a pioneering piece of oral history. His best-known work, however, is his groundbreaking essay *The Family Saga* (1958), in which he defined and described this distinctive narrative genre.

Sylvia Ann Grider

References

Boatright, Mody. 1958. *The Family Saga and Other Phases of American Folklore.* Urbana: University of Illinois Press.

Speck, Ernest B., ed. 1973. *Mody Boatright, Folklorist: A Collection of Essays.* Austin: University of Texas Press.

Bodylore

Ways of thinking, speaking, and moving that embody cultural notions of personhood; the study of such corporeal dispositions and their symbolic import. The body, corporeality, embodiment, the self, thought, mind, and the relationships among them are construed differently in different cultures. Each culture engenders practices and discourses that encode its own understandings of what it is to be a body. Consider, in this vein, the nature of embodiment in American culture.

The American body is, from its inception, a cultural artifact, not a natural object. No brute, material, literal, physical, biological *given* precedes our conceptions of it. Experience of the body, and the conceptions that inform it, comes into being with embodiment. For instance, the body American that biomedicine invents is instantiated in its practices. No other more fundamental body lies beyond medical discourse. Rather, the medical body simply is the body as it is experienced in medicine (Young 1993).

The body is not merely culturally shaped; rather it takes shape, it comes into being, it materializes, within a culture. Beyond the discourses into which the body is inscribed—in which it takes shape and is experienced—is neither the Platonic form of the body nor its crude substance. The body is constituted by its discourses. The real body is not lurking behind the medical textualizations that humanize as well as dehumanize it (Ritchie 1993). The American body, the ethnic body, the gendered body, *my* body is *the* body. It might be clearer to think of multiple embodiments, shifts in the ontological status of the body, instead of hypothesizing a fundamental, essential, or prior body. The proliferating lore of the body investigated under the aegis of bodylore makes visible this cultural construction.

The term *bodylore* was coined by Katharine Young for the 1989 American Folklore Society meetings to position the body as a locus of inquiry in folklore. Bodylore condenses into one subfield an array of folkloristic interests in such corporeal matters as the uses of obscene-photocopy lore in American corporations (Roemer 1994); initiations, both sacred initiations into Cuban American *Santeria* (Mason 1994) and the profane initiations of the bachelor party (Williams 1994); issues of the flesh and the spirit with respect to the bodies of clergywomen (Lawless 1994); the sensual properties of Native American pots (Babcock 1994); kinaesthetic analysis of Hasidic body movement in a New York synagogue (Sklar 1994); American women's tattooing traditions (Attie, Monroe, and Wellner 1989); the analogy between President John F. Kennedy's corpse and the body of the king (Zelizer 1993); American quilts as corporeal discourses (Przybysz 1993); rituals of purification in American spas (Slyomovics 1993); and body metaphors in American folklore (Neustadt 1994). These inquiries are by no means new wrinkles. The body has been explicitly examined in American folklore in movement analysis, gender studies, gesture or body language, feminist theory, studies of ritual and taboo, cosmological systems, creation myths, clothing, food, manners, and elsewhere, and implicitly examined in studies of bodily practices from folk speech

to the law. Bodylore puts forward as the central term of discourse a metaphysical idea that hovers in the background of these studies: the body.

Close examination makes it clear that the body is not simply the inarticulate, uninflected, primordial ground of its discourses. The discourses invent the body. In American spas, for instance, the body is regarded as a continent object sealed off from the threat of contaminating influences by its skin (Slyomovics 1993). In European spas, by contrast, the skin is regarded as a pervious membrane through which benign influences pass into the body. The body in water appears as the incarnation of a cultural disposition. Likewise, consider the peculiarly American inflection of the king's body as the body politic given to Kennedy's corpse (Zelizer 1993). Over the course of its several examinations, the condition of the body is perceived to reflect the condition of the society. And American quilts, taken as the quintessence of femininity, have been reconstituted by feminist theorists as *ecriture feminine,* in Helene Cixous' term, women's genres that carry the possibility of dismantling the category of the feminine (Przybysz 1993). Quilts materialize a shifting sense of the self in American culture.

Persons participate in multiple discourses and experience their bodies differently in each. Transferring from one discourse to another, in the gesture phenomenologists call realmshift, can entail a transformation of bodily state. In the traditional hazing on the eve of their weddings, American bachelors are obliged to experience their bodies as at once intensely sexualized and emasculated, so that they find themselves acutely aware of their corporeal selves at just the moment of their transformation (Williams 1994).

The body itself appears in different material densities in American culture. It may be solidified by medical discourse, the male gaze, or the bourgeois sensibility, each of which is concerned to construct the body as a kind of object in order to preserve, respectively, detachment, otherness, or propriety. This solidification of the body is not unique to these discourses. Medicine, for instance, is a condensation of our cultural drift toward the objectification of the body and its estrangement from the subject (Young 1993). We are all heir to Cartesian dualism. In other discourses, the metaphysical idea of the body may not have material instantiation. Spirit bodies, for instance, are etherealized enough to permit such New Age phenomena as astral projection—or, the self may be able to slough off the substance of the body, either transiently, in out-of-body experiences, or persistently, in the form of ghosts.

The obtrusiveness of the corporeal self is at issue with respect to the religious body in which spirituality, conceived as a rarification of the flesh, is set against sexuality, conceived as a manifestation of the flesh. This issue is especially acute in the face of the increasing ordination of American women, whose bodies are taken incorrigibly to obtrude their sexuality (Lawless 1994). Shifts in the material constitution of the body in these different discourses challenge any presumption of its inherent substantiality.

The body incorporates, corporealizes, culture. For that rea-

For paying audiences in the 1800s and early 1900s, strongmen—like this one, posing in 1914—gave demonstrations of power and physique. Library of Congress.

son, entering into a new discourse requires educating the body. Irritants in his ablutions make the initiate into *santeria* uncomfortably aware of his scalp just as he is about to receive an *oricha*, a deity who rules the head (Mason 1994). Bodily inscriptions attest to this corporealization of culture. Literal inscriptions on the body's surface, body painting, tattoos, surgical incisions, and likewise their erasure through such practices as shaving, pluck-ing, bleaching, or surgical excisions, literalize the sense in which culture is metaphorically inscribed on the body. The intent of face painting in American practice, for instance, appears to materialize the imaginary, to *make up* the face. Tattoos, supple-ments of the body as well as apertures into it, both exscribe and overwrite the inscription of culture on the body (Attie, Mon-roe, and Wellner 1989). Breaches of the boundaries of the body constitute transgressions. In a doubling of this transgressiveness, obscene-photocopy lore, itself an expression of what Mikhail Bakhtin calls the grotesque body, is deployed as an assault against the corporate body in which it is produced (Roemer 1994). Breaches of body taboos, by implication, locate the boundaries of the proper body.

But the body is not just inscribed into its discourses; it takes up its discourses. Gestures and postures modulate into attitudes and inclinations, at once the imprints of external pressures on the body and the expression of internal states out of the body. Immersing oneself bodily in the practices of Hasidic Jews provides us intelligence of a corporeal kind about the nature of the religious life (Sklar 1994). The rhythms of ritual may arouse emotion in the body or emotion may tran-spire as a body rhythm. From the outside, the body appears as a perceptible object; from the inside, as an experiential lo-cus. Body image is composed at the intersection between vi-sual apprehension and kinesthetic sensation.

The body is the source as well as the site of discourses. It has been made the scale for separating discourses of the minute from discourses of the magnificent (Stewart 1984). Body puns, body metaphors, and body symbols inform the body of state, the corporate body, and nature of knowledge. The predominance of visual metaphors in epistemological discourse since the Enlightenment has sustained the estrange-ment of perceiver from perceived in Western thought. Lingual metaphors reincorporate thought as bodily knowledge (Neu-stadt 1994). Corporeal discourses extruded off the body in-vest corporeality in material culture as well. The pots Native American women produce bodily are also held to reproduce them bodily, so that objects take on the sensuous properties of subjects (Babcock 1994).

Bodylore relates investigations of the cosmological body of myth, of ritual acts, religious bodies and body taboos, of emotion, spirituality, and intellection as bodily phenomena, of bodily substances and insubstantial bodies, of the fluid body, the solid body, and the spirit body, of the domesticated body and the transgressive body, of the private body and the body politic, to ongoing investigations of the body in other fields of inquiry.

Katharine Young

References

Attie, Barbara, Nora Monroe, and Maureen Wellner.
    1989. *Skin and Ink*. New York: Women Make Mov-ies. Film.
Stewart, Susan. 1984. *On Longing: Narratives of the Minia-ture, the Gigantic, the Souvenir, the Collection*. Balti-more: Johns Hopkins University Press.
Young, Katharine, ed. 1993. *Bodylore*. Knoxville: University of Tennessee Press. (Examples in this entry are cited from essays by Jane Przybysz, Susan Ritchie, Susan Slyomovics, Katharine Young, and Barbie Zelizer.)
Young, Katharine, and Barbara Babcock, eds. 1994 *Journal of American Folklore* (Special Issue) Vol. 107, No. 423, pp. 1–196. (Examples in this entry are cited from es-says by Barbara Babcock, Elaine Lawless, Michael Ma-son, Kathy Neustadt, Danielle Roemer, Deirdre Sklar, and Clover Nolan Williams.)

See also Feminist Approaches to Folklore; Tattooing

Boggs, Ralph Steele (1901–1994)

Teacher, bibliographer, and pioneering student of Latin Amer-ican folklore and folkloristics. Born in Terre Haute, Indiana, Boggs became interested in folklore at the University of Chi-cago, where he studied with Archer Taylor and earned his Ph.D. in Spanish in 1930. His dissertation on the folktales of Spain was published in *Folklore Fellows Communications* the same year.

He had particularly strong ties with the University of North Carolina (UNC) at Chapel Hill, where he taught from 1929 until 1950 when he accepted a post at the University of Miami. During his first year in Chapel Hill, he introduced the first folklore course taught at the university. In the 1930s, he began to forge ties with faculty members who shared his folk-loric interests—Guy Benton Johnson (sociology), Arthur Palmer Hudson (English), Frederick Koch (drama), Urban Tigner Holmes (romance languages), Jan P. Schinhan (music), and Richard Jente (German). By 1940 Boggs had established the university's curriculum in folklore, the first folklore gradu-ate program in the United States.

His outreach continued at the University of Miami, where Boggs taught from 1950 until his retirement in 1967. There he developed extensive contacts with Latin American folklorists. He served as director of the Hispanic American Institute and developed that into the university's International Center.

Boggs founded the periodical *Folklore Americas* and the journal *North Carolina Folklore,* and he was the author of 150 books and articles on folklore and Spanish literature. When *Southern Folklore Quarterly* began publication in 1937, he was asked to compile an annual bibliography of publications on folklore, a task that he continued for twenty-two years.

Boggs and his wife, Edna Garrido de Boggs, herself the author of studies of Dominican folklore, remained profession-ally active long after his retirement. They donated to the UNC library his books, recordings, and most notably his seventy-six volumes of *Biographic Documentation* that include corre-spondence with leading folklorists in the United States, Eu-rope, and especially Latin America.

Beverly Patterson

References

Boggs, Ralph Steele. 1981. Reminiscences on the Prenatal Care and Birth of the Curriculum. *Newsletter,* Curricu-

lum in Folklore. Chapel Hill: University of North
Carolina at Chapel Hill, pp. 1–3.
(Patterson, Daniel W.) 1990. Boggs Donates Recordings
and Papers. *Newsletter,* Curriculum in Folklore.
Chapel Hill: University of North Carolina at Chapel
Hill, p. 1.

Botkin, Benjamin A. (1901–1975)

Folklorist; best known for his annotated anthologies of folk-lore from oral tradition and print sources and for his early advocacy of applied folklore and multicultural studies. Botkin was educated at Harvard University (M.A., 1920, magna cum laude), Columbia University (M.A., 1921), and the University of Nebraska (Ph.D., 1931). He founded and edited the regional annual *Folk-Say* (1929–1932). "Folk-say" is a term Botkin "coined in 1928 to designate unwritten history and literature in particular and oral, linguistic, and floating material in general."

He went to Washington DC on a Julius Rosenwald Fellowship in 1937 to do research at the Library of Congress in Southern folk and regional literature. From 1938 to 1941, he was, successively, national folklore editor of the Federal Writers' Project, cofounder and chairman of the Joint Committee on Folk Arts of the Works Progress Administration (WPA), and chief editor of the Writers' Unit of the Library of Congress Project; in 1941 he became a Library of Congress Fellow in Folklore (Honorary Fellow 1942–1956). In 1942 he was named head of the library's Archive of Folk Song.

In 1945, while president of the American Folklore Society, Botkin resigned from the library and moved to New York to devote himself to writing full time. About that time, his interest shifted from rural to urban folklore, work helped by a Guggenheim Fellowship in 1951. Botkin's first book was *The American Play-Party Song* (1937), a study of frontier game songs. *Lay My Burden Down: A Folk History of Slavery* (1945), based on WPA interviews with ex-slaves, is one of the key documents in the development of oral history. His other books were annotated collections of regional or occupational folklore culled from oral, printed, and archival sources. The first and best known of these was *A Treasury of American Folklore* (1944).

Botkin's background and interests were broadly humanistic. He knew folklore, but he also knew literature, politics, and music. His brother was a painter, his cousins George and Ira Gershwin, a composer and a lyricist. Botkin himself published poetry before he published folklore, and he continued publishing it for many years. When asked his occupation, Botkin responded "Writer," not "Folklorist." Botkin saw the study of folklore as part of the study of culture rather than a field of independent value in its own right. He was less interested in survival folklore (which was the focus of concern of many of his contemporaries in the field) than in multiculturalism, urban folklore, occupational folklore, and especially applied folklore, which he said was "folklore for understanding and creating understanding."

Bruce Jackson

References
Botkin, B.A. [1937] 1963. *The American Play-Party Song.*
New York: Frederick Ungar.
———. ed. 1944. *A Treasury of American Folklore: Stories,
Ballads, and Traditions of the People.* New York:
Crown.
———, ed. 1945. *Lay My Burden Down: A Folk History of
Slavery.* Chicago: University of Chicago Press.
———, ed. 1947. *A Treasury of New England Folklore: Stories,
Ballads, and Traditions of the Yankee People.* New
York: Crown.
Hirsch, Jerrold. 1987. Folklore in the Making: B.A. Botkin.
Journal of American Folklore 100:3–38.
Jackson, Bruce. 1976. Benjamin A. Botkin, 1901–1975.
Journal of American Folklore 89:1–6.
———. 1986. Ben Botkin. *New York Folklore* 12:23–32.
Widner, Ronna Lee. 1986. Lore for the Folk, Benjamin A.
Botkin and the Development of Folklore Scholarship
in America. *New York Folklore* 12:1–22.

Breakdancing

Or "breaking"—a specific genre of competitive, physically demanding, injury-risky, artistically inventive, pyrotechnic acrobatic and gymnastic dance movements. These include head spins from a headstand with hands in the air; back spins with legs tucked up and held by arms; "baby swipes," or handstands in which the legs scissor sharply across each other and the hips spiral with the legs; "suicides," or no-hands forward flips landing flat on the back; and "hand glides," in which one hand supports the body while the other propels the body in a spin.

Breakdancing developed in the 1970s and came to public attention from the Bronx borough of New York City in the early 1980s. The undocumented early history is wreathed in legend. Similar to dances in other parts of the United States, breakdancing extended African traditions of male youth competition, innovation, self-expression and male bravura, comment on current life, and warrior dances. During the late 1960s, immigrant West African dancers and musicians began performing and teaching in American public schools and for professional and amateur dancers; some Black Americans traveled to Africa to bring back traditions to teach and perform. Also influencing the development of breakdance were West Indian rapping (rhythmic spoken or chanted musical accompaniment), the Afro-Brazilian martial art of *capoiera*, the African American dance repertoire, including the Lindy and the Charleston, and mainstream culture. The legendary Black singer James Brown's athletic, frenetic dancing to his 1969 hit song "Get on the Good Foot" catalyzed experimentation with movement forms in which "b-boys," young Black and Hispanic dancers, became proficient.

Concerned with increasing inner-city gang violence, Afrika Bambaataa encouraged breakdancing as a peaceful alternative. He founded the Zulu Nation, a loose confederation of Bronx dance crews. Intensely competitive dance "battles" occurred between warring factions. This spread to localities from New York to California. Breaking was a way to be Number One without "blowing somebody away," in some instances killing. However, police sometimes arrested breakdancers, thinking they were fighting. Dancers were banned from city streets and shopping malls for causing disturbances and attracting undesirable crowds. Occasionally, a dance battle escalated into actual violence.

Breakdancers and onlookers form an impromptu circle, and each performer has a brief turn in the ring. Common breakdancing choreographic segments are robot-like movements and other mime sequences known collectively as "electric boogie." Movements include the wave, the tick, the mannequin, the walls, the King Tut (miming figures in Egyptian hieroglyphics), popping (isolating body parts in robot-like segmentation), pop-locking (locking joints in place between movements in exaggeration for comic effect), glides, *huevos* (dancers walk on the toes of shoes one size larger than usual and stuffed with newspaper), moon walks (shifting weight from one leg to the other and sliding backward), athletic steps such as "uprocking" (mimed fighting and insults) and "top-rocking" (standing and performing foot movements), breaking, and shaming through mimed insults between dancers.

Ghetto breakdancers express personal style and gain a sense of power while also conveying flamboyant, energetic group identity, values, and aesthetics. The dance is the most recent part of the former underground hip-hop social and political youth movement with its wild-style graffiti art, special slang and clothing, and rap music. Breakdancing music is played on a recorded disco rhythm track. Common rap themes are personal self-aggrandizement and comments about women, the police, and society. There are a few female breakdancers.

Media obsession with breakdancing popularized it nationwide. The ABC *20/20* television news show aired young street-gang members settling disputes through dance. *Mademoiselle, Time, Rolling Stone, People, Newsweek,* and the *Washington Post* all ran pieces that spotlighted breakdancing. Burger King and Pepsi ads on television showed breaking. The first hip-hop feature film, *Wild Style* highlighted breakdancers, as did the film *Beat Street.*

Outstanding breakdancers gained financial rewards through performing on the street, in theaters, at birthday parties and bar mitzvahs, through club bookings and international tours, and on television and film. They gave classes at college campuses, grade schools, exercise studios, and recreation centers.

The media hype eventually altered breakdancing's form and meaning. The circular format became linear, the style became standardized with less improvisation, and acrobatics overshadowed the "freeze" (a held, often seemingly impossible position of personal and group expression). Like many popular dances, breakdancing became part of the formalized history of Black folklore. By the 1980s, street kids believed that breaking no longer belonged to them and went on to create new dances.

Judith Lynne Hanna

References

De Shane, Nina. 1988. Breakdance, Young Warriors in the Inner City. *Play and Culture* 1:258–266.

George, Nelson, Sally Banes, Susan Flinker, and Patty Romanowski. 1985. *Fresh: Hip Hop Don't Stop.* New York: Random House, pp. 79–113.

Hanna, Judith Lynne. 1986. Interethnic Communication in Children's Own Dance, Play, and Protest. In *Interethnic Communication,* ed. Young Y. Kim. Vol. 10 of *International and Intercultural Communication Annual* Newbury Park, CA: Sage, pp. 176–198.

———. 1987. *To Dance Is Human.* Chicago: University of Chicago Press.

Brewer, John Mason (1896–1975)

Texas' most prominent Black writer and one of the nation's leading black folklorists. Brewer (who published as J. Mason Brewer) was the first Black member of the Texas Folklore Society and the first Black to serve as vice president of the American Folklore Society. In 1954, he also became the first African American member of the Texas Institute of Letters after Theta Sigma Phi recognized him as one of twenty-five best Texas authors following one of his most notable publications, *The Word on the Brazos: Negro Preacher Tales from the Brazos Bottoms of Texas* (1954).

Born in Goliad, Texas, Brewer received his early education in the Black public schools in Austin and then earned a B.A. degree in 1917 from Wiley College in Marshall, Texas. He served as a French interpreter for the American Expediting Forces (AEF) in 1918 before turning to teaching and later becoming a principal in Fort Worth, Texas. Brewer later wrote stories and poems that he published in both a Colorado oil company's trade journal and a national journal, *American Negro.* Before returning to Texas, Brewer briefly held a professorship at Clafflin College in Orangeburg, South Carolina, and then was a professor in 1926 at Huston-Tillotson College in Austin, where he met University of Texas Professor J. Frank Dobie, who encouraged him to collect and publish African American folklore. In 1950 Brewer earned an M.A. from Indiana University; he then earned an honorary doctorate a year later from Paul Quinn College, a Methodist College in Waco, Texas.

Like Zora Neale Hurston, Brewer employed Black dialects when documenting stories he collected from his informants. A regular contributor to the annual publications of the Texas Folklore Society, Brewer's earliest collection of African American slave tales appeared as the lead chapter in *Tone the Bell Easy* (1932), under the title "Juneteenth." His most notable works include *Aunt Dicy Tales* (1956), *Dog Ghosts and Other Negro Folk Tales* (1958), *Worser Days and Better Times* (1965), and an anthology, *American Negro Folklore* (1968), for which he received the Chicago Book Fair Award in 1968 and the Twenty-first Annual Writers' Roundup award for one of the outstanding books written by a Texas author in 1969. Besides the recognition he received from folklorists as the best storyteller of Black folklore anywhere in America, Brewer also lectured at Yale University, the University of Texas, Duke

University, the University of Colorado, and the University of Arizona.

After several years of teaching at Livingston College in Salisbury, North Carolina, Brewer returned to Texas and was a distinguished visiting professor at East Texas State University in Commerce from 1969 until his death on January 24, 1975. The following year, Brewer appeared in *Who's Who in America*.

Richard Allen Burns

References

Abernethy, Francis Edward. 1992. *The Texas Folklore Society: 1909–1943*. Vol. 1. Publications of the Texas Folklore Society No. 51. Denton, University of North Texas Press.

Byrd, James W. 1967. *J. Mason Brewer, Folklorist*. Austin, TX: Steck-Vaughn.

Brewster, Paul G. (1898–?)

Folksong and folk-game scholar. Born in Stendal, Indiana, he earned a B.S. degree from Oakland City College in Indiana in 1920 and an M.A. from the University of Oklahoma in 1925. Most of Brewster's teaching career was at Tennessee Technological University.

American folklorists are mostly familiar with Brewster's folksong scholarship. His historic-geographic emphasis, conclusions, collection techniques, presentation style, and perceptions of who constitutes "the folk" and what constitutes "folklore" are typical of his better contemporaries.

Brewster's sixty-five publications on folk games are likewise typical of his time. However, his continual, extensive, and intensive research in this genre is atypical and, thus, ultimately more significant to folklore studies. While adding little theoretically to the study of games, Brewster's *American Nonsinging Games* (1953) is probably his most important work because it does not focus on games with music as many preceding studies had.

Brewster published on a wide variety of other genres, including folk medicine, riddles, narratives, jokes, and rituals, and on such exotic topics as snake handling and fire walking. During the middle of the 20th century, Brewster became better known internationally than in America by often co-writing works with foreign folklorists, having these works published overseas, and writing about such people as Czechoslovaks, Hungarians, East Indians, Nigerians, Malaysians, Egyptians, Russians, Iranians, and Tibetans, among others.

Although Brewster, along with Robert E. Allen, was a founding member of the Hoosier Folklore Society in 1937, he was not a member of the American Folklore Society. Instead, he belonged to the Gypsy Lore Society (a folk group on which he never published) and the American Dialect Society.

Despite Brewster's early promise, competent scholarship, and more than 100 publications, he never completed his Ph.D. in folklore at Indiana University, he lacked professional advancement, and he shifted to international contacts in mid-career. American folklorists tend to explain these anomalies through multiple and inconsistent stories—none verifiable—usually involving some type of scandal. Thus, the folklorist himself, in this case, has become the subject of folklore.

Janet M. Cliff

References

Brewster, Paul G. [1940] 1981. *Ballads and Songs of Indiana*. New York: Folklorica.

———. [1952] 1976. *Children's Games and Rhymes*. New York: Arno.

———. 1953. *American Nonsinging Games*. Norman: University of Oklahoma Press.

———. 1953. *The Two Sisters*. Folklore Fellows Communications No. 147. Helsinki.

Bridger, Jim (1804–1881)

Mountain man, trapper, explorer, guide, storyteller. As a teenager, Bridger ran away from a blacksmith's apprenticeship in St. Louis to join William Ashley's fur-trapping expedition. For the next twenty years, he roamed and explored the vast territory from northern New Mexico to the Canadian border. He became the first White man to see the Great Salt Lake after braving the rapids of the Bear River in a skin canoe, and he also was among the first to report on the natural wonders of Yellowstone country.

Bridger and a few associates challenged the near monopoly of larger fur-trapping interests in the West. Men willing to work for substantially reduced wages clamored for the opportunity to join the famous Jim Bridger. When the fur market declined in the early 1840s, he established Fort Bridger on the Oregon Trail in southwestern Wyoming. The fort supplied many immigrants heading West, including the first Mormon (Latter Day Saints) pioneers, whom Bridger led into the Great Salt Lake Valley.

Bridger fell out with the Saints when they suspected him of stirring up the Indians. In 1853 Mormon militiamen seized and plundered Fort Bridger. It is no surprise, then, that in 1857–1858 Bridger eagerly guided Colonel Albert Sidney Johnson's expedition to crush an ostensible Mormon rebellion.

In his later years, his health and eyesight failed him; he died near Kansas City, Missouri, in 1881.

Bridger's life reflected the mixing of cultures and turbulent times of the early frontier era. Though illiterate, he spoke Spanish, French, and several Indian languages. He was initiated into the Crow tribe, and his third marriage, to an Indian woman, made him a son-in-law to the Shoshone head chief Washakie. He was a believer in Indian religion and magic, and he adopted many Native American customs, including taking the scalps of the men he slew.

Jim Bridger is both the source and the subject of some of the American West's most famous folklore. He was a renowned storyteller, but many fantastic tales that he never told as truth—and often never actually told at all—were ascribed to him by later Westerners. Two examples are the tale of a petrified forest where petrified birds would sing songs that could not be heard (because they were petrified), and the tale of a stream that was cool at the bottom and boiling on top, where if one caught a fish and brought it up slowly, it would be cooked and ready to eat when pulled out of the water. His serious descriptions of natural features were always accurate, and his incredible geographic knowledge was invaluable to map makers.

Bridger's name became immortalized not only through his place in American folklore as "King of the Mountain Men" but also by the Bridger Mountains, Bridger Pass, and the Bridger National Forest in Wyoming.

Eric Eliason

References

Alter, J. Cecil. 1962. *Jim Bridger.* Norman: University of Oklahoma Press.

Vestal, Stanley. 1946. *Jim Bridger, Mountain Man: A Biography.* New York: William Morrow.

Bronson, Bertrand Harris (1902–1986)

Ballad scholar, musicologist, and professor of English at the University of California, Berkeley, from 1927 to 1970. While Bronson's career as a scholar (he would have said "student") of English literature cannot be overlooked (he did important studies on Chaucer, Joseph Ritson, Samuel Johnson, and the Enlightenment), his essential contributions to the study of folklore might be symbolized by the title of his 1969 collection of essays: *The Ballad as Song.* The founders of American folkloristics emphasized folksongs as cornerstone artifacts in the budding discipline, but paradoxically they most often treated the material as "folk poetry." Francis James Child, for example, gave only a handful of tunes to accompany the hundreds of texts in his *English and Scottish Popular Ballads.*

In his *Traditional Tunes of the Child Ballads* (1959–1972), Bronson set out to track down all of the extant tunes associated with ballads from Child's corpus. The resulting four-volume monument of scholarship not only provides us a cornucopia of melodies and texts, of references to popular discs and archival recordings, but also—because Bronson included texts to the melodies—outdoes Child himself. In other research, Bronson pioneered the use of computers in musicological research as early as the 1940s and developed a scheme of melodic classification (the "mode star").

By insisting that folksongs are to be sung, Bronson played an important role in legitimizing the folksong revival and in preparing the way for folklore's later emphasis on performance studies. It is folly, Bronson argued, to tear text and tune asunder, or to divest either of their reasons for being: folksingers, musicians, and audiences in performance contexts.

David G. Engle

References

Bronson, Bertrand Harris. 1949. Mechanical Help in the Study of Folk Song. *Journal of American Folklore* 62:81–86.

Green, Archie. 1987. Bertrand Harris Bronson, 1902–1986. *Journal of American Folklore* 100:297–299.

Hand, Wayland. 1983. Foreword. In *The Ballad Image:*

Essays Presented to Bertrand Harris Bronson, ed. James Porter. Los Angeles: Center for the Study of Comparative Folklore and Mythology, UCLA, pp. ix–xii.

Broonzy, Big Bill (1893–1958)

Blues singer. William Lee Conley Broonzy was born in Scott, Mississippi, to a family of seventeen children, but he grew up on a farm near Pine Bluff, Arkansas. There he learned violin from an uncle, Jerry Belcher, and later became proficient on the guitar and mandolin. In his early teens, he started entertaining at local parties and picnics. Then, after a brief stint in the army during World War I, Broonzy worked as a musician in Little Rock clubs until he moved to Chicago in 1920.

In the Windy City, Broonzy met a large number of musicians and worked with several of them in local clubs. Still, it was six years before he made his first record; thereafter he had at least one session a year until 1957. During those thirty-one years, he recorded a variety of sides ranging from country and dance pieces ("Saturday Night Rub," "Guitar Rag") to hokum blues ("Somebody's Been Using That Thing") to Bluebird blues ("You Know I Gotta Reason") to protest material ("Black, Brown, and White").

Broonzy's recording career had three distinct phases. The decade 1926 to 1936 was largely given over to hokum (light-hearted sides featuring lyrics filled with sexual metaphors and including jokes and verbal interplay), and also to rags. The period 1936 to 1942 was the Bluebird period, an era when he recorded formulaic blues for the Bluebird label. These records usually featured small groups often made up of bass, piano, drums, trumpets, clarinets, or saxophones. In the late 1940s, Broonzy became a favorite on the New York City "folk" circuit, and he emphasized a very diverse repertoire, including ballads, gospel numbers, and contemporary songs, as well as blues. This new audience was primarily White, and their acclaim probably led to the 1955 publication of a ghostwritten autobiography, *Big Bill Blues* (rev. ed. 1964). Broonzy continued playing concerts in Europe and America until illness forced him to halt those activities in 1957. He died of cancer the following year.

Broonzy was one of the most frequently recorded of blues singers and is noteworthy as a link between the country and the urban blues traditions. His generosity, wit, support of younger singers, and his considerable talents, combined to make him one of the most popular of all blues musicians.

W.K. McNeil

References

Charters, Samuel. 1959. *The Country Blues.* New York: Rinehart.

Oliver, Paul. 1969. *The Story of the Blues.* London: Barrie and Jenkins.

Brother Jonathan

A caricature of the American common man, popular from the late 1700s until the mid-19th century. Brother Jonathan descends from Yankee Doodle and sires Uncle Sam. His fictive life spans the years from the end of the American Revolution to shortly after the Civil War, when he appears in hundreds of political cartoons, in countless humorous anecdotes printed in almanacs and jest books, in popular verse, and most importantly in American theatrical comedies.

During the heyday of his popularity in the first half of the 19th century, he was a major American icon whose crude ruralisms reflected backwoods demeanors of American settlers. He came into prominence when into his hands the spirit of Jacksonian democracy placed the political reins of a fledgling nation. Over the course of his life, he took on many guises. As a manservant, Jonathan was fiercely loyal to his master and country; as a shrewd peddler, he profited from his customer's dull wit; as a cracker-barrel philosopher, his backwoods simplicity and practicality confounded sophisticated politicians. He rolled up his sleeves and tore into challenges that faced the young nation and sought to present a strident warning to any power, foreign or internal.

Brother Jonathan received his formal introduction to American audiences in Royall Tyler's successful comedy *The Contrast* (1787). In the play, Brother Jonathan is transplanted from the Vermont backwoods to the streets of New York City, where he encounters alluring prostitutes, the mysteries of the theater, and the stilted affectations of urban sophisticates. Although Tyler pokes at Jonathan's naivete, his honest simplicity serves as a foil against the foppish mannerisms and shallow pretenses of city dwellers. In later plays, the figure of Brother Jonathan prides himself on his strong individualism and fierce nationalism. Through him, the American nation presented itself to the world.

During the second war of independence (War of 1812), Jonathan took up the banner of patriotism, extending his popularity across the seaboard states and the burgeoning frontier. Playwrights in particular re-created Jonathan in many of their dramatic productions, representing the American everyman, fiercely independent, stubborn, and sly. Between acts of other dramas, actors who were posed as Brother Jonathan dressed in the outfits of country bumpkins recited. They extended monologues complete with satire and country vernacular speech. Eventually, Jonathan figured in cartoons and in almanac humor.

Nearing mid-century, the image of Brother Jonathan began to lose its freshness and its popular appeal. Jonathan was depicted more and more as an ordinary American, less identified with his New England roots. Gradually, he began to appear as a reactionary, who offered tirades against immigrants and progressive political movements. Shortly after the Civil War, the figure of Brother Jonathan had outlived its usefulness, and only occasionally did he appear in British magazines as a caricature of Americans in general.

Richard Sweterlitsch

References

Dorson, Richard M. 1940. The Yankee on the Stage: A Folk Hero of American Drama. *New England Quarterly* 13:467–493.
———. [1946] 1969. *Jonathan Draws the Long Bow.* New York: Russell and Russell.

Matthews, Albert. 1901. Brother Jonathan. *Transactions of the Colonial Society of Massachusetts* 8:94–126.
———. 1935. Brother Jonathan Once More. *Transactions of the Colonial Society of Massachusetts* 32:374–386.
Morgan, Winifred. 1988. *An American Icon: Brother Jonathan and American Identity.* Newark: University of Delaware Press.

Brown, Frank Clyde (1870–1943)

Folklorist, teacher, and collector of North Carolina folklore. Born in Harrisonburg, Virginia, Brown made his home in Durham, North Carolina, after earning an A.B. degree in 1893 from the University of Nashville, Tennessee, and his M.A. and Ph.D. degrees in 1902 and 1908, respectively, from the University of Chicago. At Trinity College (now Duke University), he began a lifelong career as professor of English and also taught classes in folklore.

An energetic organizer, he responded to the urging of John Lomax, president of the American Folklore Society, to establish a local group to collect, preserve, and publish North Carolina folklore. At its first meeting in 1913, the North Carolina Folklore Society elected Brown secretary-treasurer, a post he held until he died. From its beginning, the society planned to publish a collection of North Carolina folklore under Brown's supervision, and Brown inspired numerous contributors to help him amass a state collection that remains one of the largest of its kind. He himself traveled extensively throughout the state recording folksongs.

The publication of *The Frank C. Brown Collection of North Carolina Folklore* (1952–1964) did not occur until after his death. Brown had firmly resisted publication, often citing incompleteness even though the collection reached gargantuan proportions—more than 38,000 items from more than 650 contributors. With Professor Newman Ivey White as general editor, and a distinguished team of specialized editors, Duke University Press posthumously published the seven-volume collection that bears Brown's name. It reflects genres considered important at the time but omits many folklore forms current in the state. All materials related to the Brown Collection are deposited in Duke University's Perkins Library.

Beverly Patterson

References

White, Newman Ivey. 1952. General Introduction. *The Frank C. Brown Collection of North Carolina Folklore.* Vol. 1. Durham, NC: Duke University Press.

Bunyan, Paul

Giant, fictitious logger capable of Herculean deeds and perhaps America's best-known folk hero, a demigod symbolic of American aspirations and identity. His protean manifestations include the oral traditions of loggers, literature written for children, advertising symbols, honorific statues, and community festivals and pageants. The name probably originates from a 19th-century logger who actually worked in Canada or the United States, although an unlikely phonetic link to the popu-

Bronze plaque in the municipal park, erected by the Chamber of Commerce, Oscoda-AuSable, Michigan, before 1951. American Folklife Center.

lar but diminutive French trickster figure Bon Jean has been suggested.

Folklorists and popular writers have adduced some evidence of the existence of Bunyan tales among late-19th-century loggers in eastern Canada and the American Northeast and Upper Midwest. However, the first description of a Paul Bunyan tale in print did not occur until journalist James

McGillivray wrote several essays entitled "The Round River Drive" for Upper Midwest newspapers in 1906 and 1910. In 1914, William B. Laughead, an advertising executive for the Red River Lumber Company, a large logging firm known for its eccentric advertising strategies, initiated a publicity campaign and a series of publications featuring the exploits of Paul Bunyan. Booklets of Bunyan stories and colorful illustrations were distributed by the company free of charge for decades; no attempt was made to copyright the figure of Bunyan; and the company vigorously encouraged its adoption outside the industry by writers in order to enhance its own name recognition. Laughead was the author of the booklets' stories, which he freely admitted were literary embellishments of a small amount of oral tradition he had encountered over a decade before in the logging camps around Bemidji, Minnesota.

Laughead's tales clearly draw upon the outrageous character and motifs of American tall tales, with all of their comic extravagance. The giant logger himself is depicted as a leader of men, incredibly strong and hardworking, and blessed with an innate sense of entrepreneurial ingenuity. To accompany Bunyan, Laughead fabricated or reinvented a complete cast of larger-than-life characters, often with a distinctly Scandinavian flavor: Babe, Paul's giant Blue Ox, was joined by such logging camp companions as Johnny Inkslinger, camp clerk; Big Ole, the blacksmith; Sourdough Sam, the cook; and Shot Gunderson, Paul's foreman. The stories often had an etiological theme: Paul dug the Great Lakes to serve as Babe's water hole; the Mississippi River sprang forth when Paul's water tank leaked. Other tales revolved around superhuman deeds: to shoe Babe, who was seven ax handles wide between the eyes, required the ore of an entire Minnesota iron mine; to expedite logging, Paul and Babe simply hauled entire sections of forestland to where trees could be cut as if shearing sheep; a winter of blue snow was caused by Paul swearing a blue streak after hitting his thumb with a sixteen-pound hammer.

Through the 1920s and 1930s, other writers built on Laughead's foundation with their own literary embellishments. Ida V. Turney, Esther Shephard, James Stevens, and many other authors wrote articles and books, first for adults but then almost exclusively for a juvenile audience. By the end of World War II, Bunyan had been incorporated into virtually all aspects of popular and elite art, including plays, vocal and instrumental music, ballets, murals, and paintings, the poetry of Robert Frost and Carl Sandburg, and even an operetta by W.H. Auden and Benjamin Britten. On a regional level, tales of Bunyan as a master driller in the Texas oil fields circulated in local oral tradition. In the Upper Midwest and Pacific Northwest, community festivals and pageants celebrated local lumbering heritage with tributes to Bunyan and the average working logger. Respected men and women were selected to serve as honorary Paul and Pauline Bunyans, representing the social order of married model employees in the new paternalistic company towns that replaced transient logging camps.

The fascination with Paul Bunyan continues in local and popular culture. As the subject of television cartoons and children's books, he is in the late 20th century more likely to be portrayed as a reformed, ecologically minded woodsman who loves wilderness than as a rapacious destroyer of nature's forests. Giant statues of Bunyan—with his classic muscular build, beard, plaid shirt, and stocking cap—delight tourists in areas that have had logging-dominated economies. Folklorists still record the occasional Bunyan tale from older loggers and woodsmen, although such stories almost certainly derive from literary texts. Those same workers are now more likely to write songs and poems that highlight Paul's abilities as both a logger and a tree planter. Community festivals still feature honorary Paul Bunyans and Bunyanesque loggers participating in local competitions of occupational skills.

Interpretations abound of Paul Bunyan's significance to American culture. Folklorist Richard M. Dorson argued that Bunyan was pure "fakelore," a spurious, commercialized creation that belonged in the pantheon of other contrived American "folk heroes": Pecos Bill, the cowboy; Joe Magarac, the steelworker; Febold Feboldson, the Nebraska plainsman. Most folklorists agree that such big, powerful, efficient workers of our industrial age were symbolic embodiments of the heroic virtues of American identity, models of resilient rugged individualism, and symbols of America's mastery over nature. Folklorist Alan Dundes believes that Bunyan, as a giant, indefatigable industrial worker, was a concise assertion of early-20th-century national identity and strength and thus fulfilled a national psychic need, appearing when America suffered from an acute national inferiority complex, before becoming an acknowledged superpower. Paul Bunyan's significance also lies in how he was used in relationship to the labor force from which he purportedly originated. Bunyan's emergence through corporate sponsorship during a period of intense labor unrest early in the 20th century, and the accompanying explosion of imagery and concocted narrative in publications loggers read (including local newspapers and trade journals), made woodsmen well aware of his presence. Paul Bunyan became a quintessential model for labor, a paragon of conformity to an unattainable work ethic—for Paul Bunyan represents the single, male, superproductive laborer for whom the work and its attendant lifestyle are their rewards, who is able to shun all notions of social mobility for the pride of group membership and the nobility of toil. Bunyanesque loggers do not quit or complain and, by extension, do not revolt. Labor, management, and the nation thus collaborated in containing and ennobling the American logger, a proud producer of American consumable natural resources, a hero of free enterprise.

Robert E. Walls

References

Dorson, Richard M. 1956. Paul Bunyan in the News, 1939–1941. *Western Folklore* 15:26–39, 179–193, 247–261.

Fowke, Edith F. 1979. In Defense of Paul Bunyan. *New York Folklore* 5:43–51.

Haney, Gladys J. 1942. Paul Bunyan Twenty-Five Years After. *Journal of American Folklore* 55:155–168.

Hoffman, Daniel. G. 1983. *Paul Bunyan: Last of the Frontier Demigods*. Lincoln: University of Nebraska Press.

C

Cadence Chant

Folk rhyme used in the military to coordinate the marching of soldiers. Also termed cadence calls, their two basic tempos correspond to the two main speeds of march, quick time and double time, but rhythmic variation is possible. George G. Carey noted six distinct metric patterns for double-time chants alone in studying cadence calls in the Army's 101st Airborne Division. Since any song lyric in 2/2, 2/4, or 4/4 time can be appropriated for use in the chants in performance, the possible variation in rhyme schemes is great. And since, like sea chanties, track-lining songs, and field hollers, cadence chants help time the physical actions of a group and lessen the energy they expend, it is not surprising that they have the same pattern of oral delivery—a solo line with a choral response. Also not surprisingly, the words "left" and "right" often appear as the appropriate foot touches down, as in: Solo (leader): "You had a good home but you left." Group (soldiers): "You're right!"

The subject matter of the chants varies from approval to criticism of military life and may function to build esprit de corps, complain about conditions and treatment, or lament the loss of civilian niceties; the variation here usually depends on whether the solo leader is a private soldier, an officer or a noncommissioned officer (NCO), a draftee, or a volunteer. The folk character Jody, a mythical civilian who takes advantage of soldiers' absence to appropriate their cars, clothes, and girlfriends or wives, appears in many cadence chants.

Thomas E. Barden

References

Burke, Carol. 1989. Marching to Vietnam. *Journal of American Folklore* 102:424–441.

Carey, George G. 1965. A Collection of Airborne Cadence Chants. *Journal of American Folklore* 78:52–61.

Cajuns

Descendants of French-speaking Acadians who settled in south Louisiana after being deported by the British from Nova Scotia, formerly known as L'Acadie. "Cajun" is a corruption of *Acadien,* or *Cadien,* the French term that former inhabitants of L'Acadie and their descendants called themselves. The term "acadie" derives from a Micmac word rendered in French as *cadie* (land of plenty). Permanent settlement of Acadia began during the first decade of the 17th century, and Acadians were among the first European immigrants to develop a distinct North American identity (Brasseaux 1987:161–172).

Acadian folk culture emerged as French and Native American traditions blended and adaptations to a special maritime environment were forged. Acadians were also affected by 150 years of colonial conflict between France and England. After the Treaty of Utrecht in 1713, which ceded Acadia to Britain, the Acadians became French neutrals, and Acadia was renamed Nova Scotia. Their fate was ultimately sealed when they refused to sign an unconditional oath of allegiance to England, which would have required them to give up their Catholic religion and take up arms against their kinsmen and Indian allies. *Le Grand Dérangement,* the Acadian deportation from Noval Scotia, which began in 1755 and continued until the Treaty of Paris in 1763, put an end to hostilities between France and England. Between 2,500 and 3,000 exiled Acadians arrived in Louisiana between 1764 and 1803 and tried to reestablish their former society.

In the 1990s, the core Cajun population resides in south Louisiana within a more or less triangular-shaped region with its apex near Alexandria. However, communities of migrant Cajuns have resettled in east Texas, California, and elsewhere in the United States. In the face of complex social, cultural, and demographic transformation, Cajuns maintain a sense of group identity and continue to display a distinctive set of cultural expressions nearly two-and-one-half centuries following their exile from Acadia.

Popular and stereotypical images have long tended to skew representations of Cajun history and culture. Henry Wadsworth Longfellow's popular poem *Evangeline,* originally published in 1847, inspired romantic depictions of Cajuns as pious, peace-loving, pastoral peasants carrying forth timeless

French traditions. Louisiana writer Felix Voorhies' *Acadian Reminiscences: The True Story of Evangeline* (1907), another telling of the Acadian tragedy featuring characters with believable local Cajun names, inspired local interest and ethnic pride. During the 1920s, young girls dressed in peasant maiden "Evangeline" costumes helped campaign for the establishment of a national shrine; Longfellow-Evangeline State Park was eventually established in St. Martinsville (Brasseaux 1988). Before and after the 1955 bicentennial of the Acadian exile, political leaders like Dudley LeBlanc and Roy Theriot helped advance a growing Cajun revival by reenforcing the connection between Cajun identity and the Acadian saga. Popular notions about Cajun identity thus tended to ignore the dynamic sociocultural realities of the 19th and 20th centuries. But, in retrospect, however inaccurate these representations may seem, they appear mild compared to some of the misrepresentations proliferating at the end of the 20th century as a result of the unbridled commercialization of Cajun "chic" by entrepreneurs in the food, music, entertainment, and tourism industries. In the 1900s popular culture, Cajuns seem to be alternately presented as swamp-dwelling, homicidal outcasts or as humorous, wine- and hot sauce-guzzling chefs.

Recent scholarship has presented more complete and balanced views of Cajun culture. Historian Carl A. Brasseaux, in *The Founding of New Acadia,* explores social history in early Louisiana Cajun settlements. In order to survive in Spanish Louisiana, Cajuns made great adjustments to new environmental and social factors. They learned to live in a diverse society populated by European, African, Asian, and West Indian immigrants, Louisiana Creoles, and Indians. They

learned about slavery and some became slaveholders. Brasseaux's *Acadian to Cajun: Transformation of a People, 1803–1877* (1992) demonstrates how 19th-century changes, like those resulting in the formation of separate and distinct Cajun socioeconomic classes, affected Cajun folklife and contributed to the development of modern Cajun society. He also investigates the darker sides of Cajun violence and racism before and after the Civil War.

Most misunderstandings concerning the genealogical "purity" of Louisiana Acadian-Cajun stock have been addressed by scholars. With regard to ancestral origin, modern-day Cajuns are far from homogenous, if indeed any group of Acadians ever was. In *The People Called Cajuns: An Introduction to an Ethnohistory* (1983), James Dormon discusses the complex demographic history of Louisiana Cajuns and the difficulties of trying to define them in terms of Acadian ancestry. The ancestors of 18th-century Acadian immigrants to Louisiana included peoples from various parts of France, native Micmacs, some Scots, Basques, and others of assorted European ancestry. Once in Louisiana, Acadians intermarried and/or mixed with neighboring Native Americans, foreign immigrants, and native Louisiana-born people of German, French, Spanish, African, Asian, and other origins. Living side by side with families named Thibodeaux, Breaux, and Hebert are Cajuns named Abshire, McGee, Reed, Walker, Brown, Rodriguez, and Schexnayder.

Neither does Cajun material culture represent, to any significant degree, the diffusion and survival of forms from ancient L'Acadie. For example, Acadians arriving in Louisiana borrowed from existing folk architectural patterns, innovating and expanding as needed (Ancelet, Edwards, and Pitre 1991;

Edwards 1986). After several generations, their raised houses, with full incised galleries, were practically identical to other Creole houses of Louisiana much different from those in their pre-expulsion villages. Malcolm Comeaux has identified and described the typical Louisiana Cajun barn *(hangar)* (Comeaux 1989). Its features do not resemble maritime Acadian or French barns. Comeaux postulates that the Cajun barn, with its characteristic square floor plan and identifying incised and enclosed gable-front entrance, was borrowed from neighboring German farmers who were already established along the Mississippi River before the Acadians arrived in Louisiana. Acadians certainly brought boatbuilding skills from their maritime homeland, but Louisiana Cajun watercraft bear few resemblances to those of Nova Scotia. In the case of the sailing lugger, the most common Louisiana fishing boat used by coastal Cajuns throughout the 19th century, the sailing rig may have remained constant, but the shape and construction of the hull, the internal arrangement of space, and the entire superstructure evolved with input from Italian, Dalmatian, and Canary Island fishermen into a form distinctive to the northern Gulf Coast (Brassieur 1990).

Many elements of Cajun expressive culture can best be understood in terms of creolization, the dynamic process of cultural blending that occurs when diverse populations interact. Cajun foodways certainly represent a blend. The ideas, if not the specific recipes or ingredients, for stews and sauces thickened with *roux*, seafood *courtboullion, ettouffé, boudin, andouille, chaudin* (stuffed pork stomach), *crêpes, beignets,* and other Cajun culinary items were transplanted to Louisiana from France and Acadia. Corn dishes like *macquechoux* (stewed fresh corn), *sagamité* (hominy-grits) and *couche-couche* (skillet-fried cornmeal), *filé* (ground sassafras leaves), *tasso* (dried or smoked meat), along with dishes prepared from native fish and game, fruits, and vegetables, all represent contributions to Cajun cuisine from Native Americans. Gumbo and jambalaya are African in origin. Okra (called *gumbo févi* in Cajun French) was imported from western Africa, where it is called *guingombo.* Cayenne and other hot peppers, native to the Americas, represent Spanish and Afro-Caribbean influences. The Cajun preference for rice as a staple began to develop toward the end of the 19th century. The widespread consumption of crawfish, an activity now popularly linked with Cajun identity, is a relatively new trend in Cajun cuisine (Comeaux 1972).

Cajuns are perhaps best known by their music and, like most other features of Cajun culture, it, too, represents a dynamic blending of diverse elements. Barry Jean Ancelet characterizes Cajun music as "a blend of German, Spanish, Scottish, Irish, Anglo American, Afro-Caribbean, and American Indian influences with a base of western French and French Acadian folk tradition" (Ancelet 1989:1). Unaccompanied French folksongs and ballads, as well as instrumental dance music, came to Louisiana from France, either through Acadia, by way of other parts of French America, or more directly from the European continent. These older forms blended with rhythmic and percussive elements, syncopation and singing styles brought to Louisiana from Africa, Anglo American folk music and song traditions, and popular European and American musical trends to influence the development of Cajun music. Changes in instrumentation, beginning with the introduction of the diatonic accordion, and later the steel guitar, electric guitar and bass, and full drum set transformed Cajun music during the 20th century. The musical duets of White fiddler Dennis McGee and Black accordionist Amadé Ardoin, recorded in the late 1920s to 1930s, characterize the metamorphosis then occurring in Cajun dance music.

A strong Americanizing trend, reflected in Cajun music by an increasing use of English lyrics and by the strong influence of nationally popular country string-band music, like that produced by Bob Wills and the Texas Playboys, typified the 1930s and 1940s. In place of the accordion, the steel guitar, electric guitar and bass, and full trap drum set joined the violin to became preferred instruments. However, a renewal of older musical forms featuring accordion and French lyrics began during the late 1940s and was aroused, according to Ancelet, by the need among returning World War II veterans to hear homemade music (Ancelet 1989). Iry LeJeune, a young accordionist from Point Noir, led the vanguard of excellent bandleader-accordionists that included Lawrence Walker, Nathan Abshire, Aldus Roger, and Austin Pitre.

During the 1960s, with the rising popularity of rock and roll and rhythm and blues, and with the subsequent reinvasion of this music from England by groups like the Beatles and the Rolling Stones, Cajun music increasingly became the music of the older generations. The work of folklorists, music producers, and musicians from both inside and outside Cajun culture reversed this trend. In 1964 traditional Cajun musicians Gladius Thibodeaux, Vinesse LeJeune, and Dewey Balfa performed at the Newport Folk Festival, where they awakened the world to the excitement of Cajun music. Balfa became an effective spokesperson, and the recordings he made with his brothers and other musicians serve as models to aspiring young Cajun artists. In 1974 the first Tribute to Cajun Music Festival was held in Lafayette; this festival continues to provide the opportunity to honor older heroes and a stage where younger musicians are brought to light. The phenomenal international, national, and local successes of Zachary Richard, Michael Doucet and Beausoleil, Wayne Toups, Bruce Daigrepont, Steve Riley, and many other younger musicians and groups has propelled Cajun music into widespread popularity. The amazing and unprecedented rise in popularity of Cajun music during the 1980s, both inside and outside of the culture, appears to carry forth with no abatement, and another generation of young virtuoso performers is proudly taking its place on the bandstand.

Mardi Gras (literally "Fat Tuesday," also known as Shrove Tuesday) is another element of Louisiana folk culture that has profited along with the growing Cajun cultural revitalization. Mardi Gras is tied to ancient folk Catholic (and earlier pre-Christian) annual ritual cycles and shares features with other New World French questing rituals such as *La Chandeleur,* practiced in the French Canadian Maritimes; *La Guillonnée,* practiced in Missouri and Illinois; and various Carnival fêtes of the Caribbean. Features shared by these "begging quests" include disguise, suspension (or inversion) of ordinary rules of behavior, a traditional chant or song, rewards for performance, a leader and a band of followers, a round of house-to-house visits, at least the threat of pranks, and ritual "begging." Beyond these basic similarities, the Mardi Gras ritual of each Cajun community in Louisiana has its own distinguishing features with regard to song texts, traditional role-playing, costumes, specific rules for participation, and modes of transportation (Ancelet, Edwards, and Pitre 1991). Although, like Cajun music, Mardi Gras is growing in popularity both within and without the culture, it is much more than a popular tourist attraction. From pre-event preparation to concluding communal gumbo, Mardi Gras continues to promote Cajun community cohesion and ethnic pride.

Cajun storytelling, particularly that performed in Cajun French, represents a vital aspect of cultural expression that has not received popular recognition on the same level with Cajun music or food, since it is inaccessible to most American audiences. In *Cajun and Creole Folktales: The French Oral Tradition of South Louisiana* (1994), Ancelet provides an excellent compilation of Cajun oral material that renders Louisiana dialects legible to readers of standard French and also provides English translations. Ancelet sorts his collection into animal tales, magic tales, jokes, lies and tall tales, Pascal stories, legendary tales, and historical tales; he pays particular attention to the context and language of events, as well as the repertoires and life stories of the storytellers. By presenting material from White Cajuns and Black Creoles together in one volume, Ancelet reminds us of the inextricable blend of expressive forms that make up Louisiana French life and lore. Another advantage of Ancelet's work emerges from the extensive comparative notes provided for each piece. Through these annotations, the reader is connected with the work of earlier collectors and their collections of French material from Louisiana and elsewhere in the French-speaking world.

In spite of the overwhelming Cajun cultural revitalization that has been unfolding during the past few decades, questions concerning cultural continuity revolve around language retention. The oral French language spoken by Cajuns, which includes a range of distinctive local variation, was dominant in many communities in south Louisiana at the turn of the 20th century. The Progressive Era policies of the Theodore Roosevelt presidency, particularly those that established mandatory English-language education throughout the United States, severely altered this situation. Cajun children were punished for speaking French on the school grounds, and Cajuns who spoke no English, or those who spoke with a heavy accent, were often ridiculed and held as the butt of jokes. The powerful stigma that developed among native speakers of Cajun French prohibited many parents from teaching French to their offspring. In 1968 the Council for the Development of French in Louisiana (CODOFIL) was established to help salvage a dying language. Its activities, particularly with regard to the promotion of Cajun music, contributed to the cultural revitalization, but the fate of Louisiana French language is far from secure. Within the last several years, a few south Louisiana parish school systems have initiated French-language-immersion curriculums for elementary schoolchildren. This approach has attained local popularity and success, but in the 1990s it is not widely available to Cajun children. In the meantime, while Cajun pride swells in many aspects of life, spoken French is becoming increasingly rare among Cajuns under forty years of age.

Since the late 18th century, Acadians and their descendants have adapted to new environmental conditions, adopted many American, European, Native American, African and Asian cultural traditions, and made innovations when necessary and desirable. Late-20th-century Cajun culture is certainly distinct, but it is also dynamic and difficult to define. Perhaps Cajuns are best characterized by their amazing adaptability to change, combined with a lively capacity to reinterpret and reshape cultural expressions to suit their own purposes, principles, and preferences.

C. Ray Brassieur

References

Ancelet, Barry Jean. 1989. *Cajun Music: Its Origins and Development.* Lafayette: Center for Louisiana Studies, University of Southwestern Louisiana.

Ancelet, Barry Jean, Jay Edwards, and Glen Pitre. 1991. *Cajun Country.* Jackson: University of Mississippi Press.

Brasseaux, Carl A. 1987. *The Founding of New Acadia.* Baton Rouge: Louisiana State University Press.

———. 1988. *In Search of Evangeline: Birth and Evolution of the Evangeline Myth.* Thibodaux, LA: Blue Heron.

Brassieur, C. Ray. 1990. The Louisiana Sailing Lugger: Survival of Traditional Form and Method. *Transactions of the Pioneer America Society* 13:23–33.

Clark, Andrew Hill. 1968. *Acadia: The Geography of Early Nova Scotia to 1760.* Madison: University of Wisconsin Press.

Comeaux, Malcolm. 1972. *Atchafalaya Swamp Life: Settlement and Folk Occupations.* Louisiana State University Geoscience Publications No. 2. Baton Rouge.

———. 1989. The Cajun Barn. *Geographical Review* 79 (1):47–62.

Edwards, Jay. 1986. *Louisiana's Remarkable French Vernacular Architecture, 1700–1900.* Monograph of the Fred B. Kniffen Cultural Resources Laboratory, No. 1. Baton Rouge: Department of Geography and Anthropology, Louisiana State University.

LeBlanc, Dudley. 1966. *The Acadian Miracle.* Lafayette, LA: Evangeline.

See also French Canadians; French in the United States; *Guillonée;* Zydeco

Campa, Arthur Leon (1905–1978)

Authority on the culture of the American Southwest. Professor Campa was associated with the University of Denver as chairman of the Department of Modern Languages and Literature from 1946 until his retirement in 1972.

Born in Mexico, where his father was a Methodist missionary (killed by Pancho Villa in 1914), Campa grew up on a west Texas ranch, earning his B.A. and M.A. degrees from the University of New Mexico and his Ph.D. degree from Columbia University.

His advanced work in cultural anthropology prepared him to collect and interpret materials from his own region, and his knowledge of the traditions of *le gente,* his own people, provided him with inestimably rich resources for scholarly work. His magnum opus—*Hispanic Culture in the Southwest* (1979), published posthumously—was the product of fifty years of research. In it he showed that all aspects of culture, including the traditional materials of *le gente*—or, as a rural Anglo might translate the expression, "the folks"—are processes and products of a locale and a region. In addition to many articles appearing in popular and scholarly publications, Campa wrote *Spanish Folkpoetry in New Mexico* (1946) and *Treasure of Sangre de Cristos* (1962) and edited *The Brand Book* (1966).

Together with Levette Davidson and John Greenway, Campa helped bring the American folklore program of the University of Denver to national prominence in the 1950s. For a discussion of folklife studies in the American West, see the Foreword by Wayland D. Hand in *Idaho Folklife: Homesteads to Headstones* (University of Utah Press, 1985) edited by Louie W. Attebery.

Louie W. Attebery

Campbell, Joseph (1904–1987)

Mythologist and literary scholar. Campbell is best known for his study of repetitive plot patterning in heroic tales cross-culturally, *The Hero with a Thousand Faces* (1949), and the four-volume *The Masks of God* series on the world's mythologies (1959–1968). A professor of literature at Sarah Lawrence College in Bronxsville, New York, from 1934 to 1972, Campbell took a universalist approach, positing that mythology is essential for human persistence and that myths are understandable only in terms of panhuman psychological processes and principles.

Campbell attributed the contemporary increase in, and pervasiveness of, violence, civil unrest, and dysfunctional family and other social relationships to the domination of science and a consequent rejection of mythology because of its imaginative nature. He insisted that science and mythology seem incompatible only when myths are viewed as factual historical narratives. When conceptualized as a creative and symbolic phenomenon that has its sources in the human psyche, however, mythology is not only seen as compatible with science, but its restorative and integrative potential also becomes apparent. In the late 1980s, Campbell discussed these views at length with journalist Bill Moyers in a popular six-hour Public Broadcasting System television series, for which there was an accompanying and derivative book (1988).

Campbell's conception of, and approach to, mythology are often compared with those of psychoanalyst C.G. Jung. Scholars disagree about the extent to which Campbell may have been influenced by, or derived his own ideas from, Jung, but Campbell was explicit in his concurrence with many of Jung's views, crediting him in particular with recognizing that "the imageries of mythology and religion serve positive, life-furthering ends" (1972:13).

Robert A. Georges

References

Campbell, Joseph. 1972. *Myths to Live By.* New York: Viking.

Campbell, Joseph, with Bill Moyers. 1988. *The Power of Myth,* ed. Betty Sue Flowers. New York: Doubleday.

Segal, Robert Alan. 1987. *Joseph Campbell: An Introduction.* New York: Garland.

Campbell, Marie Alice (1903–1980)

Collector of southern Appalachian folklore and professor of folklore. Campbell was born in Tamms, Illinois. Influenced by John C. Campbell's *The Southern Highlander and His Homeland,* she accepted a position at the Hindman Settlement School at Caney Creek, Knott County, Kentucky, and then one at the Gander School in Letcher County, Kentucky, during the periods 1926–1927, 1930–1931, and 1933–1934. It was at Caney Creek in the summer of 1926 that she began to collect the traditions of her neighbors.

In 1932 Campbell graduated from Southern Illinois University with a bachelor's degree in education; in 1937 she received her Master of Arts in English from George Peabody College. She taught English, folklore, and creative writing at West Georgia College and Peabody College and at Alabama Laboratory School and Carollton High School in Georgia. She also made home visits for the Kentucky Crippled Children's Commission in the summers.

A recipient of Julius Rosenwald and Guggenheim Fellowships, Campbell completed her Ph.D. in folklore and comparative literature from Indiana University in 1956. She taught at Glassboro State College in New Jersey, Bowling Green State University in Ohio, and the University of Massachusetts at Amherst. Along with numerous articles, she wrote *Cloud-Walking* (1942) and *Tales of the Cloud-Walking Country* (1958), two collections of southern Appalachian folktales; *Folks Do Get Born* (1946), a study of birthing practices based on interviews with African American midwives; and *A House with Stairs* (1950), a novel about an Alabama African American family during the Civil War. Campbell often did not publish verbatim versions of the traditional material she collected; her strength lies in her early recognition of the importance of presenting a folktale's context.

Margaret R. Yocom

References

Yocom, Margaret R. Forthcoming. Marie Campbell. In *Notable American Women Folklorists,* ed. Susan Kalcik and William McNeil. Publications of the American Folklore Society.

Campbell, Olive Dame (1882–1954)

Ballad collector, founder of John C. Campbell Folk School, cofounder of Southern Highland Handicraft Guild, and second executive secretary of the Council of the Southern Mountains. Though for three decades a powerful influence on social agencies working in Appalachia, Olive Dame Campbell is best known among folklorists for discovering the Appalachian ballad tradition and bringing English folklorist Cecil Sharp to collect it.

Born in Medford, Massachusetts, Campbell came to the South in 1907, when she married John C. Campbell. The following year, her husband accepted a Russell Sage grant to survey agencies working in the mountain South. She dated her interest in ballads from hearing student Ada B. Smith sing "Barbry Allen" at the Hindman Settlement School, December 3, 1908. Having gathered more than sixty ballads, she persuaded Cecil Sharp to come make a more systematic collection. On three tours, in 1916, 1917, and 1918, Sharp and Maud Karpeles spent a total of forty-six weeks. The outcome was the 1932 *English Folk Songs from the Southern Appalachians*.

After the death of her husband in 1919, Campbell succeeded to his position on the Council of the Southern Mountains and finished his book *The Southern Highlander and His Homeland*. Having spent fourteen months touring Scandinavian folk schools established on the Grundtvig model, Campbell in 1925 founded the John C. Campbell Folk School at Brasstown, North Carolina. The school and the Southern Highland Handicraft Guild, which she also helped establish, were influential in developing a distinctive southern Appalachian style in handicrafts created for the marketplace.

William Bernard McCarthy

References

Campbell, Olive Dame. 1928. *The Danish Folk School: Its Influence in the Life of Denmark and the North.* New York: Macmillan.

Whisnant, David E. 1983. *All That Is Native and Fine.* Chapel Hill: University of North Carolina Press.

Camplore

The oral, customary, and material traditions found in groups camping outdoors, especially in residential summer camps for children and youths. While humans have been telling stories and singing songs around campfires for eons, American camplore is best seen as arising at the end of the 19th century, when the urbanization of the United States transformed the "outdoors" into a site for escape, recreation, and renewal. This view of the outdoors, popular at a time when Americans worried that their wilderness was disappearing, was a piece of the Progressive Era (late 1800s to 1917) ideology lying behind natural-conservation movements. Tourist camps, organized campgrounds at national parks, private hunting and fishing camps, church camps, and summer residential camps arose in the 1890s and the early 20th century, serving the recreational needs of the urban and suburban middle and upper classes. Youth movements, from the Young Men's Christian Association (YMCA) to the Boy Scouts and Girl Scouts of America, created organized summer camps and published guidebooks aimed at assisting adults in creating campfire programs and other customs for the campers. Private summer camps for families, but especially for children, grew through the century, and in the 1950s part of a typical suburban middle-class childhood was packing off to summer camp for up to two months.

The residential summer camp, where campers live in relative isolation over a period ranging from days to months, serves as the model of an institutional setting for camplore. Campers typically live, sleep, bathe, and eat together, reproducing the experience of the homeworld and creating the sorts of intimate, shared experiences that can lead to shared folk traditions. Thus, camplore often includes the "everyday" genres and texts one finds in family folklore, such as nicknaming, personal-experience narrating, joking, and practical joking.

The nature of camplore will vary considerably, depending upon the larger purpose of the organization. Secular camps, run as businesses or as social-service organizations, will tend to create a camp culture with many of the features of American public culture. A camp sponsored by a religious organization will bring to the official camp program ideas, symbols, and activities particular to that faith. A camp sponsored by a youth organization, such as the Boy Scouts or the Girl Scouts, will bring to the camp's official culture still a different set of public symbols, customs, and expectations. Regardless of the official agenda, campers also bring their own folk cultures and expectations to the camp experience. The resulting folk culture of any camp, therefore, owes its character to the interaction between official organizational goals and the dynamics of the folk cultures the campers bring with them.

Camps will also differ significantly by the demographic characteristics of the campers. The cultures of family camps, with a range of ages, will differ significantly from those of camps designed for a narrow age group. Single-sex camps will vary considerably from coeducational camps, just as the folk cultures of girls' cabins will differ from the folk cultures of boys' cabins at the same camp. Some campers might bring with them folk traditions associated with ethnic cultures, and the effect of those traditions upon camp culture will depend upon the minority or majority status of the ethnic folk culture at the camp.

Just as in families, campers honor (and sometimes "invent") folk customs around routine, but symbolically important, events, such as meals. An eating group might honor the tradition of waiting for everyone to finish eating before beginning dessert, but food fights (or other forms of playing with food) can be just as traditional. Campers often have special folk names for familiar foods ("bug juice" for Kool Aid) and belief legends featuring the contamination of food or drink (the story that the kitchen staff puts saltpeter in the iced tea to dampen adolescent male sexual desire).

Sharing sleeping quarters (typically tents or cabins) gives rise to traditions solidifying the smaller folk-group identity. Thus, a sleeping group might decorate their living space in some traditional way, might develop folk dress to indicate group membership, or might play traditional games. Solidarity is also tested and served by living-group traditions of joking and practical joking, which include such well-known pranks as "shortsheeting," moving a sleeping camper, placing a sleeping camper's hand in warm water to induce urination, and so on. The classic Snipe Hunt, in which a victim is tricked into engaging in an elaborate (and eventually humiliating) hunt for a nonexistent creature, is one of the more complex examples of camp pranks.

Camplore also includes traditions beyond the everyday. Campfire programs, for example, are usually performed at special times and in special places, heightening the participants' sense that this activity is extraordinary. Campfire programs typically combine two or more of the following elements: songs, stories, skits, games, and contests. The songs may range from the traditional folksong or spiritual to songs written for the particular camp. Perennial favorites of the first sort include "My Darling Clementine" and "Michael, Row the Boat Ashore." Some traditional songs ("chain songs") permit the campers to inject into the formulaic verses new lyrics specific to the camp and the campers. Campfire stories may range from the oral performance of written stories, to the local belief legend. Local belief legends told at campfires usually are meant to frighten the younger campers, so these legends resemble adolescent urban legends in their narrative conventions. These stories of ghosts, deranged killers of campers, and others are told with the usual details of place and names meant to induce belief in the audience. Sometimes the campfire legends are of the humorous kind ("anti-legends"), beginning seriously but ending with a punch line depending upon a bad pun or a sudden movement or shout meant to frighten the listeners.

Scouts and other organizations encourage small-group skits (or folk dramas) at campfires. Campers may draw upon published versions of these skits or invent their own. Skits are meant to be humorous, but sometimes skits resemble practical jokes and the humor is at the expense of a camper who gets doused with water or suffers some other indignity. Like skits, games and contests are meant to be fun.

Interpretations of the meanings of camplore must take into account the particulars of organizational goals, gender, age, social class, ethnicity, and so on. But folklorists value camplore because the camp creates an intense, family-like setting that is more diverse than a family. Interpreters of camplore assume that the camp's separation from routine, everyday life makes it a "safer" setting for people (especially children and adolescents) to explore what it means to be a member of a group through the stylized performances of folklore. The camplore of children and adolescents usually displays the parody and nonsense characteristic of their other folklore, which empowers the children by providing symbolic resistance against the socializing pressures brought by adults. The content of camplore often reflects the social and psychological anxieties brought from everyday life. Thus, food-contamination jokes and campfire stories about maniacal killers roaming the woods provide young people with conventional, stylized narratives that help them deal with anxieties about their changing bodies, about safety, about abandonment, and about similar psychological matters.

Jay Mechling

References

Bronner, Simon J. 1988. *American Children's Folklore*. Little Rock, AR: August House.
Ellis, Bill. 1981. The Camp Mock-Ordeal: Theater as Life. *Journal of American Folklore* 94:486–505.
———. 1982. "Ralph and Rudy": The Audience's Role in Re-creating a Camp Legend. *Western Folklore* 41:169–191.
Leary, James P. 1973. The Boondocks Monster of Camp Wapehani. *Indiana Folklore* 6:174–190.
Mechling, Jay. 1980. The Magic of the Boy Scout Campfire. *Journal of American Folklore* 93:35–56.
———. 1984a. High Kybo Floater: Food and Feces in the Speech Play at a Boy Scout Camp. *Journal of Psychoanalytic Anthropology* 7:256–268.
———. 1984b. Patois and Paradox in a Boy Scout Treasure Hunt. *Journal of American Folklore* 97:24–42.

Canadian Folklore (Anglophone)

English-language folklore of Canada. Until the 1950s, Canada lagged behind other countries in its study of many types of folklore. Those folklore items that existed were collections or descriptions; analysis came more recently.

The Jesuits and early explorers noted Indian beliefs, tales, and customs in their writings, and anthropologists began to study the various tribes. Such research has continued, and the native peoples are the most thoroughly researched of Canada's various ethnic groups.

Second to the wealth of Indian lore was that of the French Canadians. Visitors, travelers, early writers, and voyagers recorded French Canadian customs, tales, and songs. In 1865 Ernest Gagnon published the first major Canadian folksong collection, *Chansons populaires du Canada*. An early English report of habitant life was W.P. Greenough's *Canadian Folk-Life and Folk-Lore* (1897). Then in the early 20th century, Marius Barbeau began his pioneering work; this led to the folklore section of the National Museum of Canada with its archive of folk materials. His disciple, Luc Lacourcière, established folklore archives at Laval University, and the collection and study of French Canadian folklore flourished.

Little Anglo-Canadian lore appeared until the 20th century except folklife descriptions in diaries, autobiographies, histories, and pioneer accounts. The best known of these early books are Anna Jameson's *Winter Studies and Summer Rambles in Canada* (1839), Catherine Parr Trail's *The Backwoods of Canada* (1836), and Susanna Moodie's *Roughing it in the Bush* (1852).

The latter part of the 19th and the early 20th centuries saw some collecting, but little organized work. Early folklore societies were started but soon died out.

Some collectors—Alexander Chamberlain, George Patterson, and Alice Leeson—published a few items in the *Journal of American Folklore*, the best being Patterson's series on Newfoundland dialect (1895–1897).

In 1895 the *Family Herald* and *Weekly Star* started its "Old Favourites" song page that included some folksongs, and Newfoundlanders John Burke and James Murphy published small songbooks in the early 1900s. This indicates the genre—folksong—that was to dominate Anglo-Canadian folklore for most of the 20th century.

W. Roy Mackenzie was the first important Anglo Canadian collector. He published some Nova Scotia songs in the *Journal of American Folklore* in 1908 and 1910 and went on to describe his collecting in *The Quest of the Ballad* (1918). This is a fascinating description of how he went about his search, and of the singers from whom he got a remarkable number of songs. Later he published the first major Anglo Canadian folksong volume, *Ballads and Sea Songs from Nova Scotia* (1928). His carefully researched notes make this still an important book; he was one of the first collectors to trace broadside references.

Carrie Grover's *A Heritage of Song*, composed of items learned from her parents in Nova Scotia, is another important early collection.

Canadian folklore collecting and publishing flourished in the early 1930s. Helen Creighton, who followed Mackenzie's lead in Nova Scotia, became the first in English Canada to cover more than one genre. In addition to songs, her major field, she collected tales, superstitions, games, riddles, proverbs, and customs, assembling the largest Anglo Canadian collection of any individual; it remained unequaled until Memorial University's folklore students began collecting in the 1970s.

Between 1932 and 1988, Creighton published ten important books—six of songs, covering not only the Anglo-Canadian but also the French Canadian and Gaelic material in Nova Scotia. Her *Bluenose Ghosts* and *Bluenose Magic* were the first major Canadian collections of beliefs and superstitions. She also published folklore of the German Canadian settlers of Lunenburg and issued two Folkways records, *Folk Music of Nova Scotia* (no. 1006), and *Maritime Folk Songs* (no. 4307). Her autobiography, *A Life in Folklore* (no. 1975), describes her long career.

When Creighton began collecting in Nova Scotia, Mary L. Fraser, a Catholic nun, was also collecting for her doctoral dissertation. Published in 1931 as *Folklore of Nova Scotia*, it gave many popular superstitions, with reports of second sight, ghosts, forerunners, fairy lore, and mermaids and stories of the devil.

Many of the early collectors in English-speaking Canada came there from Britain or the United States. An American, Arthur Huff Fauset, was collecting for his dissertation at the same time as Fraser. He worked with Nova Scotia's Black population, and in 1931 he published *Folklore from Nova Scotia*, the first, and by the mid-1940s almost the only, book about the lore of African Canadians. It contained the first large collection of folktales reported in Canada, ranging from *Märchen* through jokes, tall tales, local stories, and legends.

While these collectors were working on the mainland, two Americans and an Englishwoman were collecting in Newfoundland. When Elisabeth Bristol (later Greenleaf) came up from Vassar College in New York state to teach at the Grenfell Mission Summer School, she was fascinated by the Newfoundland singers, and she returned with a musicologist,

Grace Yarrow (Mansfield), to record their songs. In 1933 Harvard published their *Ballads and Sea Songs of Newfoundland*, the first, and still one of the best, volumes from the island. (Later Greenleaf published some Newfoundland riddles in the *Marshall Review*.)

At the same time as the Vassar women, Maud Karpeles came from England to collect in Newfoundland. She was prompted to go there by the British collector Cecil Sharp, who had hoped to go himself after their 1916–1918 trips to collect southern Appalachian folksongs, but his death intervened. She published some songs with piano accompaniment in 1932, but her complete *Folk Songs from Newfoundland* did not appear until 1971. It was large but not as valuable as the 1933 Greenleaf-Mansfield book; Karpeles was interested only in the old British songs she found, and she ignored Newfoundland's rich local tradition.

An early factor that helped preserve and spread Newfoundland songs was the series of small songsters issued by Gerald S. Doyle, a St. John's merchant, who used them as an advertising device. The first appeared in 1927, followed by four editions from 1940 to 1978.

The first Canadian to investigate Newfoundland songs was Kenneth Peacock, who worked for the National Museum. Between 1951 and 1961, he made six field trips, and in 1965 he published a massive, three-volume *Songs of the Newfoundland Outports*, the largest Canadian collection to date. Much later the Newfoundland record company Pigeon Inlet issued some of these songs (no. 7319).

Another American, MacEdward Leach, spent the summer of 1960 collecting in Labrador for the National Museum, and in 1965 he published *Folk Ballads and Songs of the Lower Labrador Coast*. He collected some songs on the island that he put on a Folkways record (no. 4075), and some Celtic tales from Cape Bretoners.

Fifteen years later Shannon Ryan and Larry Small published *Haulin' Rope and Gaff: Songs and Poetry in the History of the Newfoundland Seal Fishery*, emphasizing the strong maritime tradition that Mackenzie and Greenleaf had stressed earlier. In 1985 Genevieve Lehr published *Come and I Will Sing You*, 125 songs collected in the previous decade. Awaiting publication is Kenneth Goldstein's huge collection of Newfoundland songs, amassed through repeated summer excursions to the island and Labrador.

The first New Brunswick collector was Louise Manny. Although she did not collect as extensively as Creighton, she did much to preserve the local songs. Inspired by Lord Beaverbrook, she began collecting from the Miramichi lumbermen. Soon she started a regular radio program featuring local singers, and in 1958 she launched the Miramichi Folk Festival, named for the river that was the center of New Brunswick's lumber trade. This festival was unique in North America in that it featured only traditional singers. Manny's work resulted in a book, *Songs of Miramichi* (1968), and two records, *Folksongs of the Miramichi* (Folkways 4053) and *Marie Hare of Strathadam, New Brunswick* (Folk Legacy FSC 9). These emphasized local songs of the northern lumbermen; Helen Creighton's *Folksongs of Southern New Brunswick* (1971) has more older British ballads.

Later, Carole Spray produced a useful tale collection, *Will O' the Wisp: Tales and Legends of New Brunswick* (1979).

Prince Edward Island was neglected until Edward Ives from the University of Maine extended his collecting into the Canadian Maritimes. He published some Canadian items in journals in the 1950s and 1960s and devoted the 1963 issue of *Northeast Folklore* to "Twenty-one Folksongs from Prince Edward Island." Randall and Dorothy Dibblee published *Folksongs from Prince Edward Island* in 1973, and Sterling Ramsay published *Folklore Prince Edward Island* in 1976.

Ives found that singers in the Maine and New Brunswick woods had very similar repertoires. His Canadian collecting continued over forty-odd years, resulting in important studies of three Maritime singer-composers: *Larry Gorman: The Man Who Made the Songs* (1964), *Lawrence Doyle: The Farmer-Poet of Prince Edward Island* (1971), and *Joe Scott: The Woodsman-Songmaker* (1979). More recently he published *Folksongs of New Brunswick* (1989).

Meanwhile, in 1962, another American, Herbert Halpert, came to Memorial University in St. John's, Newfoundland, and in 1968 he founded the first, and by the mid-1990s the only, Anglo Canadian Folklore Department. He also established the Memorial University of Newfoundland Folklore and Language Archive, known as MUNFLA. At first the staff comprised scholars from the United States and Britain. Newfoundlanders were added as they graduated, but by 1995 it was still rather heavily staffed with Americans and Britishers, including Neil V. Rosenberg, Gerald L. Pocius, J.D.A. Widdowson, David Buchan, Martin Lovelace, and Paul Smith. Canadians include Gerald Thomas, Wilfred Wareham, and Lawrence Small.

Some of MUNFLA's publications are *A Regional Discography of Newfoundland and Labrador, 1904–1972* (1975) by Michael Taft; *Folklore and Oral History* (1978), edited by Neil Rosenberg; and *Canadian Folklore Perspectives* (1978), edited by Kenneth Goldstein; the latter is a group of essays relating folklore to the search for a Canadian identity.

Since Memorial's founding, collecting and research have flourished. For the first time, folklorists have made an extensive study of the varied folklore of one region, building up a vast archive. Their most important publications so far (1995) are the first detailed study of a Canadian custom, *Christmas Mumming in Newfoundland* (1969), edited by Halpert and George M. Story; and the huge *Dictionary of Newfoundland English* by Story, W J. Kirwin, and Widdowson (1977). Other valuable books are *Studies in Newfoundland Folklore: Community and Process* (1978), which contains sixteen essays on various aspects of tradition, edited by Gerald Thomas and Widdowson, and Colin Quigley's pioneer study, *Close to the Floor: Folk Dance in Newfoundland* (1985).

An interesting volume in the university's Folklore and Language Series is Halpert's *A Folklore Sampler from the Maritimes* (1982). It contains narratives, beliefs, dites, proverbial sayings, and childlore, collected by Mount Allison University students in Sackville, New Brunswick, when Halpert held the Winthrop Pickard Bell Chair of Maritime Studies there. It is particularly valuable for Halpert's detailed bibliographic essay on the folktale in English.

A more general series published by Newfoundland's Institute of Social and Economic Research (ISER) includes some folklore books. One of the most important is Widdowson's study of threats, *"If You Don't Be Good": Verbal Social Control in Newfoundland* (1977). Others of interest are Joseba Zulaika's *Terranove's The Ethos and Luck of Deep-Sea Fishermen*, Tom Philbrook's *Fisherman, Logger, Merchant, Miner: Social Change and Industrialism in Three Newfoundland Communities*, and Gerald L. Pocius' *Living in a Material World: Canadian and American Approaches to Material Culture*.

In 1991 ISER published Barbara Rietl's fascinating account of *Strange Terrain: The Fairy World of Newfoundland*, and Garland published Peter Narváez's compilation of *The Good People: New Fairylore Essays*, a broader international survey. The superstitions documented in those studies are treated in Gary Butler's important analysis, *Saying Isn't Believing: Conversation, Narrative, and the Discourse of Belief in a French Newfoundland Community* (1990).

Narváez collected songs of Newfoundland's Buchans miners, and Breakwater issued them on a record, *Come Hell or High Water* (1001). Breakwater also published studies of Newfoundland folklife by Victor Butler, Hilda Murray, Helen Porter, and Audrey Tizzard, and a study of Newfoundland's Scottish Gaelic traditions, Margaret Bennett's *The Last Stronghold* (1989).

The fiddle is Canada's major folk instrument, and many great fiddlers have made records. Newfoundland's Emile Benoit (Pigeon Inlet 732 and 7311), and Rufus Guinchard (Pigeon Inlet 737 and Breakwater 1002) are excelled only by Canada's greatest fiddler, Quebec's Jean Carignan (Folkways 3531, 3532, Philo 2001, 2012, 1014).

The Highland Scots who settled Cape Breton preserved their Gaelic traditions to a greater extent than Scots elsewhere in Canada. The first important study was Charles W. Dunn's *Highland Settler: A Portrait of the Scottish Gael in Nova Scotia* (1968). Later, Gaelic songs appeared in two large volumes, Donald A. Fergusson's *Fad Air Falbh As Inse Gail: Beyond the Hebrides* (1977), and Margaret MacDonnell's *The Immigrant Experience: Songs of the Highland Emigrants in North America* (1982). In 1976 John Shaw and Rosemary Hutchison collected on the island, producing two Topic records, *Gaelic Tradition in Cape Breton* and *Cape Breton Scottish Fiddle* (12TS353 and 12TS354).

Three important collections of Cape Breton tales appeared in both the original Gaelic and English translations. The earliest and most general is Calum MacLeod's *Stories from Nova Scotia* (1974). (MacLeod later coauthored *Gaelic Songs in Nova Scotia* with Helen Creighton.) The others are studies of two tale-tellers' repertoires: *Luirgean Eachainn Nill: Folktales from Cape Breton*, told by Hector Campbell and translated by Margaret MacDonell and John Shaw (1982); and *Tales until Dawn: The World of a Cape Breton Gaelic Story Teller* (1987) by Joe Neil MacNeil, translated by John Shaw.

Meanwhile, John C. O'Donnell was studying another part of Cape Breton folklore, that of the miners. He organized a choir, Men of the Deeps, which became widely known through cross-country concerts and international tours, and aired its songs on several Waterloo records. In 1992 he published a comprehensive volume, *"And Now the Fields Are Green": A Collection of Coal Mining Songs in Canada*. In addition to older songs from Britain and the States, it gives many composed by the Cape Breton miners.

In addition to Nova Scotia, Scots settled in Quebec's Eastern Townships, and the National Museum published a study of them, *Cultural Retention and Demographic Change: Studies of the Hebridean Scots* (1980); it contains an important article on folktales by Margaret MacDonnell.

Except for the native collections, little folklore was reported from Canada west of Quebec until the middle of the 20th century. In 1918 the *Journal of American Folklore's* special issue had small general Anglo Canadian collections from Ontario by W.J. Wintemberg, F.W. Waugh, and Eileen Bleakney. Wintemberg also collected from the Pennsylvania Germans around Waterloo, and his *Folk-Lore of Waterloo County, Ontario* appeared in 1950. George Elsmore Reaman's *The Trail of the Black Walnut* (1957) was one of several historical accounts of this group, and an irregular journal, *Canadian-German Folklore*, started in 1961.

During the 1950s and 1960s, Edith Fowke produced documentary folksong programs on the Canadian Broadcasting Corporation (CBC), using commercial records. Audience inquiries for Canadian songs led her and Richard Johnston to compile *Folk Songs of Canada* (1954), drawing upon the collections of Greenleaf, Creighton, and Barbeau. Next they published *Chansons de Quebec/Folksongs of Quebec* (1957), which gave singable English translations of some popular French Canadian songs. *More Folk Songs of Canada* followed in 1967.

For many years, singer Alan Mills had a weekly CBC program; he made numerous records and toured extensively in Canada and the United States, doing much to make Canadian songs known. Another singer, Ed McCurdy, also had CBC programs and made some records of Canadian songs along with many American ones.

Mills and Fowke collaborated on various CBC programs, Fowke writing the scripts that Mills narrated and sang. One series resulted in a book, *Canada's Story in Song* (1965), and a two-record Folkways set (no. 3000). In 1985 Fowke updated and enlarged it as *Singing Our History*. These were designed for use in the schools.

Noting the lack of songs from west of Quebec, Fowke began looking for some in Ontario and discovered many fine singers around Peterborough: Mary Towns, Vera Keating, and Tom Brandon, among others. When she continued her collecting farther north, she found O.J. Abbott, one of Canada's finest traditional singers.

Some of the Peterborough singers appeared on *Folk Songs of Ontario* (Folkways 4005), O.J. Abbott on *Irish and British Songs from the Ottawa Valley* (Folkways 4051), and Tom Brandon on Folk Legacy No. 10.

Ontario's Scottish settlers preserved fewer songs than the Irish, although some survived in eastern Ontario's Glengarry County. The best singer there was Grace Fraser, who had a large repertoire of both Scottish and Irish songs.

In Toronto C.H.J. Snider, an authority on nautical matters, had collected many Great Lakes songs; he and Stanley Baby, whose father had been a captain on sailing ships back in the 1870s, liked to meet with other sailors and their wives for singing sessions. From them Fowke got material for *Songs of the Great Lakes* (Folkways 4018).

Most Ontario songs came from the Irish settlements in Peterborough and the Ottawa Valley, and from men who had worked in the lumber camps. Irish colonists had brought many Irish songs, and local Ontario songs described work in the camps or accidents in the woods or on the drives.

Traditional Singers and Songs from Ontario (1965) featured seven singers whose songs came mostly from the British Isles. The native Canadian songs appeared later in *Lumbering Songs from the Northern Woods* (1970) and *Lumbering Songs from the Ontario Shanties* (Folkways 4052), the first Canadian book and record devoted to one occupation. In 1973 a more general selection, *The Penguin Book of Folk Songs*, with a record, *Far Canadian Fields* (Leader 1067) gave a cross-section of Canadian songs from coast to coast.

Later Fowke collected from LaRena Clark, another good traditional singer who knew an enormous number of songs, with many rare ones. *LaRena Clark: Canadian Garland* (Topic 12T140) and *A Family Heritage: LaRena Clark's Story and Songs* (1993) document some of these.

From songs, Fowke went on to collect children's lore, publishing *Sally Go Round the Sun: 300 Games, Rhymes, and Songs of Canadian Children*, with a record, in 1969; *Ring around the Moon: 200 Songs, Tongue Twisters, Riddles, and Rhymes*, in 1977; and *Red Rover, Red Rover: Children's Games Played in Canada*, in 1988.

She also compiled several general anthologies. *Folklore of Canada* (1976) is a collection of folklore items grouped as "The Native Peoples," "Canadians," "Anglo-Canadians," and "Canadian Mosaic"; it gives tales and songs from all groups, plus parlor games, foodways, riddles, jokes, square-dance calls, autograph verses, vernacular speech, and folkways.

Folktales of French Canada (1982) gives English translations of tales from Barbeau's "Contes populaires canadiens" in the *Journal of American Folklore* between 1916 and 1940. *Tales Told in Canada* (1986) is a selection of Indian myths, animal tales, Märchen, jokes, anecdotes, formula tales, legends, and personal-experience narratives from a variety of sources. Oxford Press published Fowke's general survey, *Canadian Folklore*, in 1988.

Roy Clifton, an Ontario dance caller, recorded three records of square and other folk dances with a local group (Folkways 8825, 8826, and 8827).

Sheldon Posen collected extensively among the Irish Canadians around Chapeau, Quebec, and published a book about their best known song "The Chapeau Boys" in 1988.

Pauline Greenhill has researched and written of family photographs, folk drama, mock weddings, and shivarees. Her most important work to date (1995) is a study of recitations in a community context, published as *True Poetry: Traditional and Popular Verse in Ontario* (1989).

Ontario customs and folk arts and crafts are documented in many books and articles. Mary-Lou Patterson and Michael Bird have published extensively on the art of the Mennonites around Waterloo; Katherine B. Brett described women's costumes in early Ontario; Dorothy and Harold Burnham have written of quilts, textiles, and handweaving; and Edna Staebler describes the Mennonite foodways in several books, beginning with *Food That Really Schmecks* in 1968.

Edwin C. Guillet's *Early Life in Upper Canada* (1933), John Kenneth Galbraith's *The Scotch* (1964), and John J. Mannion's *Irish Settlements in Eastern Canada* (1974) are useful studies of folklife.

Because western Canada was settled later, collecting there has been, and still is, very spotty. Before the 1940s, the only publications were some limited studies of minority groups, place-name collections, and articles, pamphlets, and books of pioneer life. Since then a few more significant items have appeared, although the coverage of Anglo Canadian material is still poor. Most collecting in the four western provinces has been of other ethnic groups.

Among the limited publications dealing with English or French is Kay Stone's *Prairie Folklore* (1976), which she assembled from her students' papers at the University of Winnipeg. As she notes, it is "an extensive gathering of recent material from Manitoba, from simple children's skipping rhymes to lengthy fairy tales."

In the 1960s Barbara Cass-Beggs published *Eight Songs of Saskatchewan*, and Seven Metis *Songs of Saskatchewan* with translations. More recently Robert Cosbey wrote an excellent small book, *All in Together, Girls: Skipping Songs from Regina, Saskatchewan* (1980), and Michael Taft wrote *Discovering Saskatchewan Folklore: Three Case Studies* (1983), discussing a storytelling session in a rancher's home, a pilgrimage to a shrine at St. Laurent, and lace making in a Belgian family.

In the *Alberta Historical Review* (Autumn 1962), John C. Higinbotham described "Western Vernacular" as he heard it in the 1880s. Grant McEwen published books of prairie farming and ranching. He also produced *Eye-Opener Bob* (1957), the story of the legendary Robert Chambers whose one-man paper, the *Calgary Eye-Opener* (1901–1922), won him fame as a prairie Mark Twain.

In Alberta and British Columbia, folklorists have reported many tall tales. An American, Robert Gard, published a short-lived *Alberta Folklore Quarterly* in 1946–1947, and a book, *Johnny Chinook: Tall Tales and True from the Canadian West;* Herbert Halpert collected "Tall Tales and Other Yarns from Calgary, Alberta," when he was stationed there during World War II; and Michael Taft published *Tall Tales of British Columbia* in 1983.

The most significant Anglo Canadian book from the western provinces to date (1995) is *Songs of the Pacific Northwest* (1979), which Philip J. Thomas collected and researched; it contains some songs from oral tradition and some found in archives, with detailed notes relating the songs to British Columbia's history.

Canada is a multicultural country, and the National Museum's Canadian Centre for Folk Culture Studies has assembled folklore materials from more than fifty different groups. Apart from those whose native language is English or French, the three largest groups are the Pennsylvania Germans, the Ukrainians, and the Doukhobors.

The major Pennsylvania-German settlement was in Ontario; most of the other ethnic groups settled in the west. The Ukrainian Canadians first came out to Manitoba in the 1890s and were followed by others after World War I and later. In Manitoba, by far the largest number of publications have featured Ukrainian songs and tales. Florence R. Livesay published a pioneer volume, *Songs of Ukraina,* in 1916. In 1958 J. Dzobko published *My Songs: A Selection of Ukrainian Folksongs in English Translation.* J.B. Rudnyc'kyj made an extensive collection of Ukrainian folklore, *Ukrainian-Canadian Folklore: Texts in English Translations,* and compiled two volumes of *Readings in Canadian Slavic Folklore* (1961).

The National Museum (which later became the Canadian Museum of Civilization) contracted for and published many books on ethnic communities, mostly from the West. In 1970 it published Robert B. Klymasz's *The Ukrainian Winter Folksong Cycle* and *The Ukrainian Immigrant Folksong Cycle in Canada,* and in 1973 *Folk Narrative among Ukrainian-Canadians in Western Canada,* Canada's first major collection of folktales.

Other important folklore publications were Kenneth Peacock's *Twenty Ethnic Songs from Western Canada* (1965), *Songs of the Doukhobors* (1970), and *A Garland of Rue: Lithuanian Folksongs of Love and Betrothal* (1971).

Papers on folkways in the museum's mimeographed Mercury Series include Rolf W. Brednich's *Mennonite Folklife and Folklore* (1977), Robert Blumstock's *Bekevar: Working Papers on a Canadian Prairie Community* (1979), and Linda Dégh's *People in the Tobacco Belt* (1975).

More specific topics were Charles Sutyla's *The Finnish Sauna in Manitoba* (1977), Ban Seng Hoe's *Structural Changes of Two Chinese Communities in Alberta* (1976), Gordon Cox's *Folk Music in a Newfoundland Outport* (1979), and Gerald L. Pocius' *Textile Traditions in Eastern Newfoundland* (1979). Ellen Karp edited *Many Are Strong among the Strangers* (1984), a collection of Canadian immigrant songs. A more important publication was Carole Carpenter's *Many Voices: A Study of Folklore Activities in Canada and their Role in Canadian Culture* (1979), a lengthy general survey and analysis.

Many works deal with folk art and material culture. Jean Francois Blanchette, Rene Bouchard, and Gerald L. Pocius compiled a useful bibliography of "Folk Material Culture in Canada, 1965–1882" for *Canadian Folklore canadien*'s special issue, "People and Things" (1982). A few outstanding books it lists are David Zimmerly's *Contextual Studies of Material Culture* (1978), Michael Bird's *Canadian Folk Art: Old Ways in a New Land* (1983), and *From the Heart: Folk Art in Canada* from the National Museum.

The first *Bibliography of Canadian Folklore in English* (1981), edited by Fowke and Carpenter, is fairly complete up to 1980. The bibliographies in Fowke's *Canadian Folklore* (1988) are smaller but somewhat more up-to-date.

Fowke and Carpenter also collaborated on *Explorations*

in Canadian Folklore (1985). It contains some analytic articles: Barbara Kirshenblatt-Gimblett's study of Montreal's Jewish community, "A Parable in Context"; Robert Klymasz's report on the ethnic joke; and Carole Carpenter's "The Ethnicity Factor in Anglo-Canadian Folkloristics."

Folklore Studies in Honour of Herbert Halpert (1980), edited by Goldstein and others, contains articles on a wide variety of subjects.

Canada's two major folklore organizations are the Canadian Folk Song Society, which Barbeau organized in 1960; and the Folklore Studies Association of Canada, launched in 1976. They started the two major folklore journals: the annual *Canadian Folk Music Journal* in 1971 and *Canadian Folklore canadien* in 1979. Both societies publish quarterly bulletins. Also important is *Culture and Tradition,* published annually by Laval and Memorial students since 1976.

The journal *Ethnomusicology* had a special Canadian issue in September 1972, *Canadian Ethnic Studies* had a special issue on "Ethnic Folklore in Canada" in 1975, and the *Laurentian University Review* featured "Folklore and Oral Tradition in Canada" in February 1976.

The Canadian Folk Music Society recently joined with the Canadian ethnomusicologists to become the Canadian Society for Music Traditions (CSMT). Its most useful function is operating a CSMT Mail Order Service (#510, 1701 Centre St. NW, Calgary, Alberta, T3E 8A4) whose folk-music catalog lists more than 300 records (CDs, cassettes, and LPs) and books of Canadian folk music.

Edith Fowke

Canadian Folklore Scholarship

Study of folklore in Canada. There is a distinctive pattern to the folklore studies of and in Canada that reflects more the unique geographical and historical factors that have strongly influenced the nation's economic, political, and cultural development than intellectual trends or imperatives derived from within the discipline itself. The scholarship is decidedly selective in genres and groups studied and, despite its relative abundance, continues to have little impact on either cultural scholarship and policies in most of Canada or the field of folklore around the world.

The preponderance of folklore scholarship concerns that part of Canada east of the head of the Great Lakes—that is, the oldest in terms of settlement and the richest in the traditional lore associated with distinctive subsistence-oriented, conservative and inward-focused groups, or folk. Especially in Quebec and Newfoundland, where large numbers of people lived effectively as peasants long into the 20th century, local culture was identified with folklore until well past World War I. These circumstances drew foreigners seeking folk traditions to the region to study them and prompted the local intelligentsia aiming to foster identity or achieve sociopolitical goals to focus attention upon them. The resultant valorization of folklore is evident in the academic folklore programs that exist only within this area and in the significance of folklore to the cultural politics not only of Quebec, but also of fishermen, Gaelic speakers, and other cultural groups within the region.

West of the Great Lakes and in the northern territories, native traditions continue to dominate the scholarship as they did to the virtual exclusion of most other folklore until 1971, when multiculturalism became Canada's official cultural policy and work on a diversity of groups became a sociopolitical necessity. Some groups had earlier produced scholars of their own traditions (such as Jaroslav Rudnyc'kyj and Robert Klymasz among the Ukrainians), but cultural outsiders (including many foreign scholars) are responsible for much of this multicultural work.

Franz Boas was particularly influential in focusing attention on Canada's West, especially the Northwest Coast natives, which he and his followers studied intensively. With the postcolonial demand for reclamation of voice, more of the scholarship throughout Canada is the work of native people or close collaborations sought by them (for example, Wendy Wickwire's work with Harry Robinson to produce *Write It on Your Heart* [1989] and *Nature Power* [1992]). Cultural politics is, then, a key influence on the direction and focus of contemporary scholarship.

The greatest strength of Canadian folklore scholarship is that concerned with French Canadian traditions, which has a breadth, depth, and cultural significance unmatched by any work elsewhere in Canada. Virtually every genre, from folk language to children's toys, costume to belief, is represented in the literature—an exception to the general pattern in the country. The impact of this extensive scholarship on the field of folklore is somewhat limited owing to language and the insularity of many Quebecois scholars who have connected more with other Francophone cultural scholars than with the mainstream North American and international folklore movement. A preservationist tendency toward collection and a long-standing political activism through culture have combined to encourage collection in preference to theoretical studies, resulting in extraordinary archives, admirable catalogs and numerous published collections. French Canada has not produced much in terms of scholarship seminal to the evolution and development of the broader discipline, but then, neither has Canada as a whole.

Few Canadians number among the key figures in folklore over time (among, for example, the Fellows of the American Folklore Society). One major contemporary scholar, Barbara Kirshenblatt-Gimblett, retains Canadian citizenship despite decades of American residence and includes Canadian material within her studies of Jewish traditions. Canada and Canadian folklore have been significant to the work of numerous prominent scholars, including Boas, MacEdward Leach, Herbert Halpert, E.D. Ives, J.D.A. Widdowson, David Hufford, and Kenneth Goldstein.

The next greatest strength of the Canadian works rests in collections and descriptive works of musical traditions (almost exclusively song or fiddle music), primarily produced by foreigners (including Maud Karpeles, Elisabeth Greenleaf and Grace Y. Mansfield, N.N. Puckett, as well as Leach and Ives) or other outsiders to the traditions they specifically studied (such as Kenneth Peacock in Newfoundland and Helen Creighton among rural Nova Scotians).

Until recently, it was most typical of Anglo Canadian folklorists to focus attention on groups outside their own, so that the mainstream traditions are still neglected in the scholarship and undervalued in the culture, a circumstance reflected in the absence of national texts and analyses or scholarly compendiums comparable to the *Oxford Companion to Australian Folklore* (1993). Works on Canadian traditions (including many of Edith Fowke's books such as *Sally Go Round the Sun* [1969] and *Tales Told in Canada* [1986]) generally target a popular readership. The best of majority-group Anglo Canadian studies are focused works on a genre or aspect of tradition (such as Pauline Greenhill's *True Poetry* [1989] on folk and popular verse in Ontario or Fowke's much earlier *Traditional Singers and Songs from Ontario* [1965]).

Many genres are virtually absent from the historical studies (for instance, riddles, proverbs, dance, and instrumental music apart from fiddling), and others are present but maligned (particularly legend). Contemporary work by ethnomusicologists and dance ethnographers addresses the paucity of thorough scholarship on traditional music and movement and also applies the studies to cultural problems (for example, the dynamics of heritage cultural instruction in multicultural milieus). Owing to the prominent role of historians as interpreters of Canadian culture, cultural scholars long actively ignored legend and personal/community narrative in favor of genealogy and other documentable accounts. Helen Creighton's most popular (and arguably her best) work, *Bluenose Ghosts* ([1957] 1976), probably reinforced rather than countered this negative attitude through its concentration on supernatural legend. Much recent work by oral historians, a certain emphasis on the contemporary legend at Memorial University in St. John's, Newfoundland (especially the work of Paul Smith and Diane Goldstein), and individual fine studies such as Gary Butler's *Saying Isn't Believing* (1990) have contributed to a greater appreciation of oral narrative generally, particularly legend.

Material-culture traditions, formerly the province of antiquarians and collectors, are now the subjects of solid academic study (for instance, studies of textile traditions, folk-art sculpture, and painting). The establishment of the Textile Museum in Toronto, the material culture studies emphasis at Memorial, and a national journal, *Material History Bulletin*, were significant steps to giving folklife studies academic credibility. Strong earlier work by architectural historians (such as Alan Gowans, *Building Canada* [1966]) had included substantial structures of interest to folklorists, but much tangible heritage of common Canadians remained ignored until recently.

Simultaneously a significant strength and a serious recent problem in scholarship is the emphasis on multiculturalism, especially as it has influenced the Canadian Centre for Folk Culture Studies (CCFCS). The demand to show appropriate scholarly interest in the diversity of Canada's population following the adoption of official multiculturalism led the CCFCS to contract numerous studies of the traditions among various cultural minorities. These studies emphasized the retention of imported traditions rather than their interaction with and adaptation into a Canadian cultural milieu. Much data—oral and material—were collected and are important in mounting the many multicultural exhibitions at the new Museum of Civilization in Ottawa (formerly the National Museum of Canada), such curatorial work now being the primary occupation of the CCFCS staff. The contribution to folklore scholarship of this multicultural research has been limited, though, since it was not connected with the ongoing international movements in applied and public folkloristics and cultural conservation. Nor has the scholarship impacted significantly on the development of multicultural theory or methodological approaches for studying or interpreting multicultural milieus. Further, with few exceptions, the studies were product- rather than process-oriented and, since they were not matched by comparable study of mainstream Canadian traditions, did more to serve political ends than the development of cultural studies in the country.

Such a pragmatic approach to folklore tends to underlie much of its serious study, at least that done by Canadians or supported by Canadian institutions. Given the prevailing elitist, product-oriented definition of culture combined with an association of folklore with marginal or delimited groups, folklore scholarship tends to remain neglected except when and where it is directly associated with a sociopolitical imperative. Consequently, traditions of the mainstream have not been collected systematically because it was never politically necessary or, more recently, politically correct to do so. The central folklore-studies organization responded to political need rather than scholarly direction. Typically, it has reacted to cultural legislation rather than forging ahead intellectually, with the result that it has never been at the forefront of the discipline and has neither political clout nor scholarly presence. That is not to say that individuals and the institution have not had influence; quite the contrary.

Once termed "The Dean of Canadian Folklorists" and certainly the single most influential scholar of folk traditions in Canada, Marius Barbeau profoundly affected the nature of Canadian folklore scholarship through his position as director of the National Museum's folklore activities (and eventually of its Folklore Division, the precursor to the CCFCS) as well as through the prodigious work he instigated on French Canadian and native traditions. From the eight Canadian numbers of the *Journal of American Folklore* Barbeau edited (between 1916 and 1950), through the financial assistance and collegial support he offered and the political and cultural connections he brokered, Barbeau orchestrated much of the Canadian research (almost all of Helen Creighton's work, for instance). A prolific writer, an avid collector, and a powerful personality, Barbeau was yet not a truly meticulous scholar of the modern scientific anthropological school. Consequently, he was unable throughout his long career to engender much academic respect for folk material and its study within the broad scholarly community outside of Quebec.

A most notable characteristic of the scholarly work on folklore in Canada is the extent to which it lacks an academic base. Folklorists such as W. Roy Mackenzie left Canada in the early years of the 20th century to find academic employment, a trend that continues. A significant proportion of the most prominent Canadian folklorists have not been associated with academic institutions (for instance, Louise Manny in New Brunswick) or have had rather limited connections (such as Creighton's position as dean of women at King's University in Halifax) that relied more on personal associations (such as Marius Barbeau's with Luc Lacourcière at Laval University) than actual scholarly affiliation. Only where folklore has been directly linked to specific cultural studies has the scholarship developed much beyond marginality in academe. The inclusion of folklore and ethnology within le Centre d'études sur la langue, les arts et les traditions populaires des francophones en Amérique du Nord (CELAT) at Laval ensures the academic legitimacy of studying folk culture as part of *la patrimoine*, a matter of considerable consequence in the ongoing struggle for Quebec independence. Similarly, interest in promoting Newfoundland studies at Memorial University led to the hiring of Herbert Halpert in 1962 to establish the folklore program and archive, now the largest in the Commonwealth. Le Centre d'études acadiennes at l'Université de Moncton likewise was born (in 1970) out of sociopolitical circumstances that dictated a focus on local folk traditions, considered to be underappreciated and threatened by the mainstream culture and, therefore, singularly important to the process of effecting social and political change. Elsewhere in Canada, folklore remains largely an academic frill with little perceived probability for development except, possibly, in interdisciplinary area or group-oriented studies.

The establishment of the Folklore Studies Association of Canada in 1975 and its journal, *Canadian Folklore canadien*, was a hopeful sign for scholarly folklorists. The organization has raised the academic profile of folklore through meetings with the Learned Societies of Canada and some limited lobbying of government funding groups and university departments. However, no significant increase in academic positions for folklorists has ensued, and the organization has failed to protect a separate category and juries for folklore funding from the Social Science and Humanities Research Council, the primary agency for such academic funding in Canada. Outside of Quebec, there is effectively no public employment for scholars trained in folklore studies nor much hope of there being any in the foreseeable future—a sure sign of the inertia within the discipline and its continuing rather limited status in Canada.

Carole H. Carpenter

References

Carpenter, Carole Henderson. 1979. *Many Voices: A Study of Folklore Activities in Canada and Their Role in Canadian Culture*. Ottawa: National Museums of Canada.

Fowke, Edith. 1988. *Canadian Folklore*. Toronto: Oxford University Press.

Fowke, Edith, and Carole Henderson Carpenter, comps. 1981. *A Bibliography of Canadian Folklore in English*. Toronto: University of Toronto Press.

Greenhill, Pauline, and Jean-Claude Dupont, eds. 1986–1987. Canadian Folklore Studies. *Association for Canadian Studies Newsletter* 8:4, 1–34.

See also Canadian Folklore (Anglophone); Canadian Studies and Folklore; French Canadians

Canadian Studies and Folklore

Study of folk traditions shaped by experiences and settings in Canada. Within the context of Canadian studies, folklore does not figure prominently either as a discipline or as an aspect of culture. Yet, interest in folklore throughout the country over time directly reflects a concern with identity of immediate relevance to Canadian studies.

Academic concern with folklore in Canada predates any Canadian-studies movements, in that scholarly interest in folk speech was important in the rise of French Canadian nationalism in the decade preceding the rebellions of 1837 in both Upper and Lower Canada. Folklife as well as the lore was intertwined with the Romantic nationalism prominent in Quebecois intellectual life throughout the remainder of the 19th century, with the direct consequence that such material has, until quite recently, been equated primarily with *les Canadiens,* or the native peoples.

Inasmuch as study of that which is *in* Canada may be termed Canadian studies, there is a case for the centrality of folklore based upon studies of Canada's First Nations. From the records of the Jesuit and other missionaries through exploration accounts, travelers' journals, and eventually ethnographic studies, the oral traditions of the indigenous people loom large in the literature. Postcolonial discussions devalue much of this material, yet, whatever its failings, it certainly succeeded in focusing attention on folklore as survivals—cultural remnants of a doomed race or, in the case of the French Canadians, remembrances of a backward, peasant existence.

The Anglophone intelligentsia (primarily in Upper Canada [Ontario after 1867] and the Maritimes) conceived of folklore in a decidedly British and cultural-imperialist mode. In the minds of this ruling elite, such material was necessarily connected with underdeveloped and uncultivated people. Hence, it was not to be revered and studied as primary documentation of pioneer times, but to be overcome and discarded in favor of *real* (that is, high) culture. Nationalism smacked liberally of colonialism, and a colonial mentality flourished whereby people generally believed that the best in anything was not to be found in Canada; therefore, what was in Canada could not be valorized. Consequently, colonial traditions merited little attention and definitely no dedicated scholarly attention.

The first blossoming of Canadian nationalism—the Canada First movement founded in 1868—involved and stimulated the high arts, inspiring the Confederation poets prominent in the latter half of the 19th century and, by extension, the landscape artists known as the Group of Seven, who achieved an iconographical position in the Canadian imagination soon after their first exhibition in 1920. Folklore was, if anything, denounced except for a brief period at the turn of the century in Ontario under the influence of David Boyle, the first archaeologist with the Ontario Provincial (later

Royal Ontario) Museum and a powerful figure in the Canadian intellectual community. An immigrant from Argyllshire, Scotland, Boyle recognized the significance of folklore in his own life and argued for its serious study and preservation. As a result, in 1908 he and a small congenial group founded the Canadian Folk-Lore Society (modeled after the Folk-Lore Society in Britain and destined to die with him in 1911). Boyle also wrote and lectured on folklore to the erudite and used a popular medium (a newspaper column) to reach a wider audience, the foundation of a recurring pattern in Anglophone Canada. Further, Boyle proclaimed the necessity of developing a national consciousness through folklore and, to this end, wrote the text for the young country's first color-illustrated children's book, *Uncle Jim's Canadian Nursery Rhymes for Family and Kindergarten Use* (1908). Commonly dismissed as doggerel, the verses are blatantly nationalistic and heavily influenced by folk (mainly Scots) tradition while antithetical to children's own folklore owing to their overt didacticism.

This period witnessed the rise in eastern Canada of regional studies based around folklore. Marius Barbeau began his monumental work on French Canadian tradition, concentrating on song, and nurtured a band of dedicated collectors, chief among whom was E.-Z. Massicotte. Scholars *In Quest of the Ballad* (to use the title of W. Roy Mackenzie's 1919 book documenting his part in this intellectual phenomenon) began to search out the Maritimes and Newfoundland, producing publications that entrenched folklore in the scholarly study of those regions while perpetuating the mainstream Anglo-Canadian idea of folklore being the property of others, not themselves, denying folklore any centrality in the study of the national Canadian culture, which, general opinion had it, had yet to develop.

Imperial concerns preempted much focus on Canada within the scholarly community through the first two decades of the 20th century. Following World War I, the impact of immigration necessitated an approach to Canadian culture and its study recognizing the (essentially folk) traditions maintained by the many immigrants. A surge of interest in folklore ensued, influenced by the national music theory popular in 19th-century Europe and the Romantic nationalism revolving around folk traditions in many countries at the time that, like Canada, were young as nation states (Finland, Germany, and Ireland, for example). Folklore became linked through public policy and in the popular culture with the newcomers in our midst: It was a means to develop links among all Canadians as well as a way to showcase the contribution of immigrants to the emerging culture. J. Murray Gibbon, general publicity agent for the Canadian Pacific Railway, organized a series of festivals, held at the railway's famed hotels during the late 1920s, expressly to celebrate diversity and promote unity among Canadians through mutual appreciation of tradition. He thereby established the pattern for a parade of such events that continues to the present despite growing opposition from minority-group members and mainstream Canadians alike to this "song and dance" approach to culture (see Bissoondath 1994; Hryniuk 1992). Gibbon, along with Barbeau and the important Canadian mu-

sician, Sir Ernest Macmillan, strived for cultural cohesion through the supposed international language of music—Gibbon and Barbeau published books of song for Canadians to sing; Macmillan and Barbeau collected together; and Macmillan arranged folk music to be performed that, through his prominence, found its way into most Canadian classrooms and, therefore, into the Canadian sensibility in the 1930s through the 1950s.

Easily to mid-century, in scholarly circles, Canadian studies meant almost exclusively history and literature except in Quebec, where folklore was entrenched at Laval University with Luc Lacourcière's appointment there in 1944. The prevailing approaches to these dominant studies were antithetical to folk traditions, emphasizing constitutional and legislative history and the British connections of Canadian (as a colonial) literature.

Broader cultural concerns moved into the purview of Canadian studies as a result of several federal studies, beginning with the Royal Commission on National Development in the Arts, Letters, and Sciences (known as the Massey Commission) which in 1950 reported significant Canadian accomplishment to that point (especially in the visual arts) worthy of recognition and study. Canadian institutions subsequently focused more on national production, one significant example being the folksong programming on the national public radio, the Canadian Broadcasting Corporation (CBC), which was Edith Fowke's inaugural folklore work.

As Canada approached its 1967 centennial, interest in things Canadian heightened along with a demand for cultural symbols with which to identify and products to exhibit. This search into "Canadianness" coincided with the Royal Commission on Bilingualism and Biculturalism. Originally charged in 1963 with reporting on the state of, and means to promote, bilingualism and biculturalism in the country, the commission produced a massive report that was directly responsible for the creation of Canada's multicultural policy. One immediate consequence was an increased evidence of both study and display of minority-group traditions throughout the culture. Folklore work blossomed; the staff at the Canadian Centre for Folk Culture studies mushroomed. Canadian studies, which had been growing in academic institutions, embraced ethnic studies, which necessarily involved folklore studies. A major journal, *Canadian Ethnic Studies,* produced a special issue on "Ethnic Folklore in Canada" edited by Robert Klymasz in 1975. More post-secondary universities across the country sought folklorists.

Yet another spur to the development of folklore within Canadian studies was the 1976 report of the Symons Commission on Canadian-studies (1972–1974), *To Know Ourselves,* which specifically recommended the establishment of many more folklore courses throughout the nation. Several Canadian-studies programs (such as those at Mt. Allison University, Trent University, and the University of Waterloo) subsequently hired folklorists.

The Folklore Studies Association of Canada, (FSAC), incorporated in 1975, first met in June 1976 at the Learned Societies of Canada annual meeting and subsequently joined the Learned Societies in part to raise the profile of folklore studies within Canadian studies generally. A greater presence for folklore came from the FSAC's lobbying effort, but even more from its journal, *Canadian Folklore canadien,* which enjoys a fine reputation and good circulation.

The Association for Canadian Studies regularly welcomes presentations by folklorists and, in 1986, devoted a special extended section or "Dossier," of its *Newsletter* to "Canadian Folklore Studies." In 1990 the Association for Canadian Studies in Australia and New Zealand requested its premier panel on folklore, The Leading Edge: Folklore Studies in Contemporary Canada, involving Carole H. Carpenter, Ronald Labelle and Gerald L. Pocius. This and similar connections have furthered scholarly links among Canadianists as well as folklorists.

Folklorists have held two research chairs in Canadian Studies: Herbert Halpert, the Winthrop Pickard Bell Chair at Mt. Allison University in New Brunswick (1979–1980), and Carole H. Carpenter, the John P. Robarts Chair at York University in Toronto (1994–1995). Given the few endowed positions in Canadian studies, this recognition of folklore studies is particularly indicative of its growing acceptance in Canadian academe generally.

Folklore programs and courses are threatened by the financial situation and consequent retrenchment throughout Canadian academe. The interdisciplinarity of both folklorists and their studies protects them within some programs, but the contemporary situation for folklore in Canadian studies is further vexed owing to cultural politics in Canada and the threat of Quebec separatism. The decrease in funding by major government agencies necessitated by fiscal restraint has eliminated special juries for folklore projects and thereby diminished the discipline's presence in the cultural bureaucracy. Multicultural projects have faced similar reduction in funding, especially given the intense debate over the validity of bolstering heritage traditions of minorities to the detriment of facilitating their access to the mainstream. Formerly the bastion of multicultural folklore studies, the Canadian Centre for Folk Culture Studies operates primarily as a repository and springboard for mounting exhibitions, sponsoring only that research directly required for specific exhibits.

The possibility of Quebec's separation from the rest of Canada poses a significant intellectual problem involving redefinition of the culture. If, as is sometimes argued, Canada is evolving into the first postmodern borderless state rather than merely disintegrating, then its nature as a collective of communities held together by a distinctive national sensibility will favor folklore studies.

The focus in neither of Canada's postgraduate folklore-studies programs reflects a nationalistic orientation. Scholars at Laval have always concentrated on Francophone North Americans, showing little interest in comparative or intercultural analysis involving other Canadians. Combined with a majority of Canadian Francophones among the scholars, this inward orientation encourages the social application of folklore, heightening appreciation of the material and its study as significant to the culture. The program at Memorial University of Newfoundland originally aimed at involving substantial numbers of native Newfoundlanders studying regional traditions, but over the years it has taken on an increasingly international character that directs attention further away from Canadian folklore and its study. Public-folklore activities have not, as a result, grown out of this academic base.

Changes in the public perception of Canadian culture must precede any appreciable alteration in the position of folklore within Canadian studies: An acceptance of grass-roots culture, of culture as a way of life, of intangible heritage as significant must become part of the cultural concept. The Ontario Heritage Policy Review (OHPR) (1987–1990) proposed such a redefinition as a key aspect of *A Strategy for Conserving Ontario's Heritage* (the report of the OHPR, 1990), but by 1995 the proposed policy had not been ennacted.

Given the state of flux in Canada, the nature of Canadian studies is bound to change. Folklore has occupied a certain position within Canadian studies to date; its importance will most likely increase in the future, whatever happens to the country.

Carole H. Carpenter

References

Bissoondath, Neil. 1994. *Selling Illusions: The Cult of Multiculturalism in Canada.* Toronto: Penguin.

Carpenter, Carole Henderson. 1979. *Many Voices: A Study of Folklore Activities in Canada and Their Role in Canadian Culture.* Ottawa: National Museums of Canada.

Greenhill, Pauline, and Jean-Claude Dupont, eds. 1986–1987. Canadian Folklore Studies. *Association for Canadian Studies Newsletter* 8:4, 1–34.

Hryniuk, Stella, ed. 1992. *Twenty Years of Multiculturalism: Successes and Failures.* Winnipeg: St. John's College Press.

Lacourcière, Luc. 1961. The Present State of French-Canadian Folklore Studies. In *Folklore Research around the World,* ed. Richard M. Dorson. Bloomington: Indiana University Press, pp. 86–95.

See also Canadian Folklore (Anglophone); Canadian Folklore Scholarship; French Canadians

Canal Lore

Traditions associated with waterways dug across land to facilitate transportation. The push for canal construction in the United States in the 19th century came from growing American trade and agriculture. The Erie Canal in New York, completed in 1825, made the Great Lakes accessible to ships from the Atlantic Ocean. It also established New York City as the commercial and financial center of the nation. The success of the Erie Canal led to a boom in canal construction in the Middle Atlantic States and the Great Lakes region. However, starting in the 1830s, the railroad began to take the place of the canal as the major carrier of goods in the United States. Canals declined because shippers could move goods faster by railroad than by canal.

When canals were in their prime, they were not restricted

to the carrying of freight. For the business of transporting passengers, special boats called "packets" were constructed. In addition to freight boats and packets, there were department-store boats, showboats, and missionary boats.

In the early days, canals offered a chance for adventure and for travel. Many colorful characters—including farm workers, loggers, and adventurers of all sorts—were attracted to a lifestyle characterized by its lack of customary restrictions. Far from home, heavy-drinking canal boaters could do as they pleased without incurring the disapproval of their neighbors. Because of the frequent feuds and fighting, early canallers acquired a reputation for rowdyism. However, with the passage of time, things settled down to a more commonplace existence.

A typical canal barge might have an owner-captain who would be assisted by his wife, who ran the galley, and a mule tender, plus a boy who helped with the mules that pulled the barge from the towpath. Mules set the pace for progress along the canal; twenty-five miles a day was a fair rate. Mules were ideally suited for the work; they were long lived and sure footed. They also had great powers of endurance; twelve-hour days were common in the industry, and it was generally a six-day week, with only Sundays off.

The work of the canaller had a definite annual cycle. In November the boat captain would begin to prepare for laying up for the winter. He would want to get his boat out of the water before freeze-up, which could damage the boat. By Thanksgiving the canal would already be closed for the winter, so both the Thanksgiving and the Christmas holidays were observed at home, not on the canal. Necessary repair work could be done during the winter.

In the spring, canal boaters would get their equipment in order for the long, productive summer boating season. Memorial Day was a well-observed holiday with picnics and get-togethers. The Fourth of July was celebrated with parades and fireworks at the small towns along the canal. Gradually, summer would turn to fall, and the cycle would be repeated.

Some folklorists and oral historians have collected work-experience narratives from old canallers. These reminiscences of the past are typically first-person accounts replete with hearsay, rumor, and gossip. The old canal boaters relate stories of harassing apprentices, surviving floods, thwarting crimes, tricking weighmasters, avoiding missionaries, and breaking in mules.

More structured than the work-experience narratives are the tall tales, which were very popular among the canal boaters. The tall tales are often based on the boasting accomplishments of strongman heroes overcoming remarkable obstacles. The collected legends show that many canallers feared the dead and believed in spirits. Legends grew out of local tragedies, curious shapes of natural scenery along the canal, and from encounters with outlaws.

Sad to say, most projects to collect canal folklore were launched in the 20th century after canals had already declined. Although our knowledge is sketchy, we do know that some of the canallers carried fiddles, accordions, banjos, and harmonicas on their boats. After a long trip, they could relax and enjoy homemade music. In addition to making music on Sundays, their regular day of rest, canal boaters did have other occasional leisure opportunities. They might be able to make music on a weekday when their boat was tied up at a dock to be loaded, or because there was some obstacle to navigation blocking their passage.

Whenever possible, they would stop off at a canal-side saloon to have a few drinks, play the fiddle, and sing some songs. The songs grew out of their work environment. For example, there were many bridges passing over a canal to permit farmers to cross from one side to the other. Typically, these bridges were very low. If a canaller were inattentive, he might get a bump on the head. The mule driver was supposed to call out "Low bridge!" to warn the others when he spotted a bridge. This helps explain the refrain from "The Erie Canal," America's best-known canal folksong: "Low bridge, ev'rybody down! / Low, bridge, for we're going thru a town."

The canal ballads come largely from the second half of the 19th century, and they have all of the stereotyped attitudes and situations of that genre. One well-known ballad tells of an ill-fated romance between a mule driver and a lock tender's daughter. Another tells of a jealous lock tender who murdered his wife for her affair with a canal boatman. Still others deal with haunted houses along the canal, fights, and stabbings.

Though the Golden Age of the canal has come and gone, it has not been entirely forgotten. Some American communities along the once mighty canal system, having restored portions of their original canals along with the associated structures, hold nostalgic annual festivals to commemorate that earlier era. Such festivals typically feature a mix of music, crafts, and canal rides. They may also present historical and educational exhibits. A particularly effective exhibit is the actual construction of a canal boat, with the boatbuilder and crew on hand to discuss work on the boat and answer questions for festival goers.

Angus Kress Gillespie

References

Bourne, Russell. 1992. *Floating West: The Erie and Other American Canals.* New York: W.W. Norton.

Garrity, Richard. 1977. *Canal Boatman: My Life on Upstate Waterways.* Syracuse, NY: Syracuse University Press.

Korson, George, ed. 1949. *Pennsylvania Songs and Legends.* Baltimore: Johns Hopkins University Press, pp. 258–288.

Kytle, Elizabeth. 1983. *Home on the Canal.* Cabin John, MD: Seven Locks.

Yoder, C.P. 1972. *Delaware Canal Journal.* Bethlehem, PA: Canal.

See also Nye, Pearl R.

Cansler, Loman D. (1924–1992)

Collector of Midwestern folklore and folksong, scholar, and traditional singer. Cansler was born in Dallas County, Missouri, into a family of singers and music lovers. He served in the U.S. Navy during World War II and entered the University of Missouri in Columbia in 1946, without, as he later wrote, the benefit of a high school education. Exploring the university library, he soon discovered that among the songs published by H.M. Belden in *Ballads and Songs Collected by the Missouri Folk-Lore Society* and Carl Sandburg in *The American Songbag* were many he had heard his family and neighbors in Dallas County sing. While still at the university, he began collecting folklore and folksongs from his family and fellow students and researching the origins of the songs.

After receiving a B.S. from Missouri in 1949 and a master's in education in 1950, Cansler became a high school teacher and counselor, first for two years in Fayette in central Missouri and later in north Kansas City. He acquired a tape recorder in 1954 and for a number of years spent summers camping with his family to seek out traditional songs and other folklore, working primarily in Missouri but also collecting in Kansas, Illinois, and other Midwestern states. He spent a summer at the Indiana University Folklore Institute in 1962, and in 1968 he represented Missouri at the National Folklife Festival in Washington, DC.

One of Cansler's primary interests was songs by known authors, particularly those originating in his native state, and he documented the lives and work of several Missouri songwriters. His contributions to folksong and folklore research in the Midwest were substantial and include articles in folklore and other journals and two albums of songs for Folkways, *Folk Songs of Missouri* (1959) and *Folksongs of the Midwest* (1973), both accompanied by extensive notes on the songs and contributors.

Following his retirement from North Kansas City High School in 1982, Cansler worked in the Missouri Valley Room of the Kansas City Public Library and devoted himself to transcribing and organizing his collection, which with field notes, published and unpublished articles, and other materials, has been deposited in the University of Missouri Western Historical Manuscript Collection in Columbia. His work was profiled in a video, *Down in Missouri with Loman Cansler*, produced in 1982 by the University of Missouri.

Rebecca B. Schroeder

References

Cansler, Loman D. 1954. Boyhood Songs of My Grandfather. *Southern Folklore Quarterly* 19:177–189.

———. 1964. Madstones and Hydrophobia. *Western Folklore* 23:95–105.

———. 1967. Walter Dibben, an Ozark Bard. *Kentucky Folklore Record* 81–89.

———. 1968. Midwestern and British Children's Lore Compared. *Western Folklore* 27:1–18.

———. 1970. He Hewed His Own Path. *Studies in the Literary Imagination* (Georgia State University) 3:36–63.

———. 1976. The Last of the Big Cattle Drives. *Heritage of Kansas* 9:10–19.

———. 1991–1992. The Fiddle and Religion. *Missouri Folklore Society Journal* 13–14:31–43.

Carmer, Carl Lamson (1893–1976)

Author and collector of Southern and New York folklore. A native New Yorker descended from Dutch farmers, Carmer graduated from Hamilton College in Clinton, N.Y., and Harvard University. He wrote poetry about upstate New York, and in 1921 he accepted a position teaching poetry classes at the University of Alabama.

His six years in Alabama were the apex of his career. Interested in folk dancing and singing, he accompanied students and friends, including Ruby Pickens Tartt, who introduced him to Afro-American oral traditions, on treks through Alabama back roads. Visiting both shacks and mansions, Carmer observed a lynching, tasted moonshine, and listened to storytellers. In a journal, he recorded local lore, fiddle songs, and unique characteristics of his adopted state, which he called the "strange country."

Leaving Tuscaloosa in 1927, Carmer planned to pen a scholarly article on Southern folklore but instead produced a collection of poetry, *Deep South* (1930), and *Stars Fell on Alabama* (1934), a portrait of Alabama cultural history that describes baptizings and foot washings, Ku Klux Klan rallies, and other eccentricities of the Deep South, especially documenting Black Belt plantation life. Although criticized by Northern reviewers for romanticizing antebellum customs, and by Southern readers for reporting about racial violence, Carmer attained national recognition as a folklorist.

A member of the New York State Folklore Society, Carmer focused on Hudson Valley folklore, writing books such as *Listen for a Lonesome Drum* (1936) and editing albums of regional songs. On his radio program, *Your Neck of the Woods,* Carmer discussed national folk heroes and myths.

Elizabeth D. Schafer

References

Carmer, Carl Lamson. 1956. *American Folklore and Its Old-World Backgrounds.* New York: Compton.

Raines, Howell. 1980. The "Strange Country." *Virginia Quarterly Review* 66:294–305.

Carrière, Joseph Médard (1902–1970)

Collector of Midwestern French folklore and comparative scholar of North American French language and customs. A native French speaker born in Curran, Ontario, Carrière studied French literature and romance languages at Laval University; Marquette University; the Sorbonne, Paris; and Harvard University (Ph.D. 1932). He became a naturalized U.S. citizen in 1936 while serving as assistant professor at Northwestern University. In 1942, Carrière moved to the University of Virginia, where he finished his career as a distinguished professor.

In 1934 Carrière began a series of visits to Old Mines, Missouri, where he found six hundred French-speaking families. Using a wax cylinder recorder, he collected a number of folksongs and tales. Of the seventy-three folktales he collected, sixty-five were told by French-speaking barite miner Joseph Ben Coleman. Published in 1937, his collection of folktales, rendered in Creole dialect, and analyzed by tale type and motif, was later republished, along with English translations and comments by Rosemary Hyde Thomas (1981).

Carrière's work among the Midwestern French is embodied in phonological-historical treatises of Missouri French dialect, a published collection of Indiana French folksongs, reports documenting French folk customs, and a range of perspectives he used in comparative analyses of North American French culture.

Carrière's leadership capabilities, especially in cross-cultural and cross-disciplinary situations, were called upon frequently: He served as president of the American Folklore Society (1946–1947); president of the American Association of Teachers of French (1948–1950); trustee of the Institute Français of Washington, DC (1950–1971); Officier d'Acadamie Française (1938); and corresponding member of many professional organizations. He was awarded a Medal de L'Acadamie Française in 1948 for activities in French literature and cultural relations, and he received the French title of Chevalier de la Legion d'Honneur in 1950.

C. Ray Brassieur

References

Carrière, Joseph Médard. 1937. *Tales from the French Folklore of Missouri.* Northwestern University Studies in the Humanities No. 1. Evanston and Chicago: Northwestern University Press.

———. 1941. The Phonology of Missouri French: A Historical Study. *French Review* 14 (5):410–415; (6):510–515.

———. [1946] 1973. Introduction and Notes to *Folk Songs of Old Vincennes,* by Cecilia Ray Berry. Chicago: H.T. FitzSimons.

———. 1946. The Present State of French Folklore Studies in North America. *Southern Folklore Quarterly* 10:219–226.

Thomas, Rosemary Hyde. 1981. *It's Good to Tell You: French Folktales from Missouri.* Columbia: University of Missouri Press.

Carson, Fiddlin' John (1868–1949)

Highly influential folk musician who made commercial recordings of 200 sides between June 19, 1923, and February 28, 1934. One hundred and sixty-nine performances were issued. His 1923 recording of "The Old Hen Cackled and the Rooster's Going to Crow" and "The Little Old Log Cabin in the Lane" were the first country recordings directly marketed to a country audience and, therefore, mark the beginning of the commercial country-music industry.

Much of Carson's early life is shrouded in mystery; not even the date and place of his birth are certain. Dates from 1868 to 1874 are given in various sources, but March 23, 1868, is the birth date most often accepted. He was born either in Cobb or Fannin County, Georgia; records that would definitely prove one or the other no longer exist. Not surprisingly, there is also debate about when he learned to play; some accounts say at age five, others have it at age eleven. According to tradition, he acquired the nickname "Fiddlin' John" at

an early age from Fiddlin' Bob Taylor, later governor of Tennessee, who met the youth at a political rally. Although the nickname stuck for the rest of his life, his closest associates usually called him "Fiddler" rather than "Fiddlin' John."

As a young man, Carson moved to Atlanta, where he worked at a variety of jobs and became a fixture at fiddle contests. Within a few years, he became the best-known country artist in Atlanta, a fact not lost on Polk Brockman, a local distributor for the Okeh label. Brockman persuaded his company to record Carson, and the success of those records led to numerous other sessions over the next eleven years. His first six sessions consisted mostly of solo performances, but on April 15, 1925, he made his last solo record. Thereafter he recorded with a band, usually consisting of his fiddle, two guitars, and a banjo. His daughter, Rosa Lee, generally billed as "Moonshine Kate," frequently supplied banjo and guitar work as well as vocals on these recordings.

Carson's repertoire consisted of pre-20th-century secular folksongs (like "Bachelor's Hall"), wordless fiddle tunes (like "Billy in the Low Ground"), minstrel show songs (like "Bully of the Town"), 19th-century popular, non-minstrel songs (like "After the Ball"), 20th-century pop songs (like "Darkstown Strutters' Ball"), religious songs (like "At the Cross"), and 20th-century folk-style songs (like "The Death of Floyd Collins"). Of these categories, the pre-20th-century secular folksongs made up the largest portion of Carson's repertoire, and religious songs were the smallest portion. By the mid-1930s, Carson's style was considered *passé* and, as a result, his recording career ended. That he was unwilling to alter his style to suit changing tastes indicates that he was typical of most folksingers, who are conservative in such matters. Indeed, it seems likely that his style of singing and playing changed little since the 1880s; thus, listening to his recordings offers a chance to hear the sort of music many Americans, particularly those in the South, liked in the late 19th century.

After his recording career ended, Carson was awarded political patronage jobs as elevator commissioner (meaning he occasionally ran the elevator in the Georgia State Capitol) and game warden at large by Gene Talmadge in appreciation for Carson's help in his gubernatorial campaign. Carson died December 11, 1949.

W.K. McNeil

References

Carson, Fiddlin' John. ca. 1973. *The Old Hen Cackled and the Rooster's Going to Crow.* Rounder Record 1003.

Daniel, Wayne W. 1990. *Pickin' on Peachtree: A History of Country Music in Atlanta, Georgia.* Urbana: University of Illinois Press.

Wiggins, Gene. 1987. *Fiddlin' Georgia Crazy: Fiddlin' John Carson, His Real World, and the World of His Songs.* Urbana: University of Illinois Press.

Carter Family

Highly influential pioneer hillbilly singing group who recorded more than 250 songs between 1927 and 1941. From their recording debut and throughout the Depression, their

The Carter Family in the early years. Left to right: Maybelle, A.P., Sara. American Folklife Center.

music continued to sell. A.P., Sara, and Maybelle Carter became a model for country music, singing old ballads, sentimental pieces, humorous songs, Victorian parlor songs, religious songs, and ballads, and a few of their own compositions. In the late 1930s, they went to Del Rio, Texas, broadcasting from 1936 to 1942 over XERA, the most powerful radio station in the world. The trio disbanded in 1943, following their final radio work over WBT in Charlotte, North Carolina.

The group influenced generations of country musicians, who built on both their style and their repertoire. While their music was a simple blend of vocals with guitar and either a second guitar or autoharp accompaniment, their unique harmonies and syncopation set the stage for bluegrass and other styles of country music that adhered most strongly to traditional songs and sounds. Their repertoire and style influenced another generation of musicians during the folksong revival.

The Carter Family was made up of Alvin Pleasant Delaney Carter (A.P.), his wife, Sara, and her first cousin, Maybelle. A.P. Carter was born in Scott County, Virginia, on April 15, 1891, the oldest of eight children. He inherited a rich store of music, including ballads and religious songs. His maternal uncle, a music teacher, taught A.P. a good deal about singing

as well as how to read shape notes. Carter also sang bass in a church choir as early as 1913.

Sara was born Sara Elizabeth Dougherty in Wise County, Virginia, on July 21, 1898. After her mother died when she was two, she was raised by her aunt and uncle, Melinda and Milburn Nickles, who lived in Scott County on the other side of Clinch Mountain from the Carters. She grew up with a wealth of traditional music. At an early age, Sara learned to play the autoharp, then banjo, and guitar.

The third member of the trio was Maybelle Addington, born near Nicklesville, Scott County, on May 10, 1909. Maybelle grew up within a quarter of a mile of Sara and early on showed an interest in the music of the community. She soon mastered the autoharp, banjo, and finally the guitar.

In 1914, while selling fruit trees, A.P. Carter visited a distant relative and met Sara, who was singing "Engine 143" and accompanying herself on the autoharp. This meeting was followed by more visits and letters back and forth. They married on June 1, 1915. A.P. brought his new bride back to Maces Spring, Virginia, where his family lived. Sara brought a few pieces of furniture, several quilts, and a dozen pullets and a rooster that her aunt had given her.

A.P. and Sara now began taking their home music throughout the local community. They played with other musicians in the area and occasionally made more formal appearances such as a performance they gave at the Newhope Methodist Church on Christmas in 1915. Despite their musical popularity, A.P. made his living by farming, selling fruit trees, carpentry, and other rural occupations. Over the years, visits to see Sara's relatives were frequent. As Maybelle grew up, she joined in their music making.

The trio crystallized after Maybelle's marriage to Ezra, A.P.'s brother, in 1926. Now, for the first time, they all lived in the same community. They performed throughout the area. From time to time, they played at schoolhouses or other meeting places for money. A.P. did the promotions. The personnel of the group was quite fluid. If one member of the family could not be there, other relatives filled in. A.P. always served as emcee and introduced his wife, then Maybelle, and, finally, any other family members who might be performing that night. He always stressed the family relationships when introducing the members. The musical aggregate was so informal that when Sara and A.P. auditioned for a Brunswick talent scout, Maybelle bore no hard feelings from being left out.

In 1927, Ralph Sylvester Peer set up a temporary recording studio in the state-line city of Bristol, Tennessee/Virginia. A.P. probably learned of the auditions through an article or advertisement in the Bristol *News Bulletin,* and the trio decided to try out. Maybelle was pregnant with her first child, and A.P. and Sara brought along their baby, Joe, as well as eight-year-old Gladys to baby-sit. Sara remembered being embarrassed by her country clothes and entering the makeshift studio by the fire escape to avoid being seen. Maybelle recalled asking A.P. if she should bring along her guitar.

This was homespun music. The Carters sang into a microphone in the same way they had to friends, but the media of recordings and later radio took the Carters' music to far and distant places they had never dreamed of singing. Their first recording, made on August 1, 1927, was a traditional song, "Bury Me under the Weeping Willow." The trio sang with Maybelle's guitar and Sara's autoharp. The first day, they recorded four songs. The next day, they recorded two more selections, including "Single Girl, Married Girl," a traditional lament on which Sara sang solo, accompanied by her autoharp and Maybelle's guitar. Peer recognized her singing talent, commenting: "As soon as I heard her voice . . . that was it."

After this initial session, the Carters, like most of the others who recorded for Peer during his nine-day recording expedition, returned to their normal lives. But the Carters met with unanticipated success. Over the next fourteen years they were called back into the recording studios eighteen more times. Their recordings were distributed in Australia, Canada, England, India, Ireland, and South Africa as well as the United States.

Despite the sale of their records, the Carter Family continued a simple rural life with occasional appearances in nearby Tennessee, Virginia, Kentucky, and North Carolina. Booking was informal. A fan might write them a personal letter and ask if they could do a performance and work out the details. At these shows, not only did they perform, they also learned and obtained leads on new songs. In order to augment their repertoire, A.P., especially, kept on the lookout for new material. Their original repertoire consisted of songs they knew and a few numbers that A.P. had written. When the supply was exhausted, A.P. became a sort of folksong collector. Stories abound about him searching out obscure material and having a sixth sense about where he might find songs that could be adapted to the Carter style.

By about 1930, personal appearances had come to an end. Regular employment took Maybelle and her husband to Washington, DC; A.P. journeyed to Detroit to work as a carpenter. But the group always came together to rehearse new material for recording sessions. Another deterrent to personal appearances was the tension that was developing between A.P. and Sara, which led to separation in early 1933 and finally divorce.

After the separation, the Carters continued to record. In 1936, Peer, who continued to manage the family as well as publish their songs, arranged for them to broadcast over radio station XERA. The studios, in Del Rio, Texas, transmitted from across the border in Mexico. This work gave the Carter Family an exposure they would otherwise never have enjoyed because the station broadcast their daily shows into all forty-eight states as well as numerous foreign countries. By 1938 their radio work took a new twist as they stopped making live broadcasts and moved to San Antonio, where they made transcription disks of their shows, broadcasting the transcriptions from several border stations.

In 1939 Sara married A.P.'s cousin, Coy Bayes. Sara and Coy moved to California, but she returned for recordings and other work until the group finally disbanded in 1943. After that time, Sara lived in the Sierra foothills of California until her death in 1979. A.P. returned to Maces Spring and lived with his daughters until his death in 1960.

Maybelle, now bitten by the show business bug, moved to Richmond, Virginia, where she and her daughters worked on the WRVA Old Dominion Barn Dance before moving on to the Grand Ole Opry in Nashville, where Mother Maybelle and the Carter Sisters enjoyed a successful career for many years. She died in 1978.

The Carter Family music expressed their collective musical taste, but the imagination to record clearly belonged to A.P. Even after the breakup of the original group, he always hoped he would find a way back into the music business. Although A.P. had helped build the foundation of modern country music, he simply could not alter his offerings in the way the commercial music world demanded. Maybelle, on the other hand, made the transition into commercial Nashville music. She sensed the required changes and accommodated. Sara loved the music but did not care one way or the other about the music business. The Carter Family was elected to the Country Music Hall of Fame in 1970.

Although the Carter Family recorded a number of traditional pieces, they are nevertheless the name associated with many of the songs they recorded. Among their best-known pieces are their theme song, "Keep on the Sunny Side," as well as "Worried Man Blues," "Wildwood Flower," and "Wabash Cannonball."

The original Carter Family has been silent since 1943, but descendants into the third generation are still actively performing on stage and recordings.

Ed Kahn

References

Atkins, John. 1975. The Carter Family. In *Stars of Country Music,* by Bill C. Malone and Judith McCulloh. Urbana: University of Illinois Press, pp. 95–120.

Carter, Janette. 1983. *Living with Memories.* [Hiltons, VA]: Carter Family Memorial Music Center.

Green, Archie. 1961. The Carter Family's "Coal Miner's Blues." *Southern Folklore Quarterly* 25:226–237.

Kahn, Ed. 1970. *The Carter Family: A Reflection of Changes in Society.* Ph.D. diss. UCLA.

Cassidy, Butch (Robert LeRoy Parker) (1866–ca. 1908?)

Western outlaw and subject of legends. Cassidy (an alias) was born to Mormon pioneer stock in southern Utah and became the leader of the Wild Bunch, a group of rustlers who graduated to robbery of banks, mines, and trains in the 1890s, frequently hiding out in remote parts of Wyoming and Utah. Their migratory ways, the obsessive pursuit of them by the Pinkertons, and their specialization in attacking the most feared and hated institutions in the West led to a wide range of Robin Hood-like legends. After fleeing in 1902 with Harry Longabaugh ("The Sundance Kid") and Etta Place to South America, where they began a series of bank and gold-shipment robberies, Cassidy and Longabaugh were reported killed in a battle with Bolivian troops about 1908, but persistent stories of sightings—one dated 1958, when Cassidy would have been ninety-two—suggest that they somehow escaped to the United States.

In keeping with the Robin Hood motifs, most legends turn on Cassidy's defiance of the power of government and industry, on his trickster-like wit and intelligence, on his ability to escape death and frequently reappear, and on his compassion for the weak, the poor, and the downtrodden. Supposedly, Cassidy never killed anyone, spared the lives of bank and railroad-express clerks, rode through a snowstorm with medicine for a sick child, and gave away large sums of plunder. In one frequently repeated tale, Cassidy heard that a poor widow was about to lose her ranch to foreclosure. The Wild Bunch rode into town, held up the bank, delivered the full amount of the mortgage to the widow, waited until the banker had collected from her, then held him up again. Similar tales have been told of Robin Hood, Jesse James, and Sam Bass.

Other legends concern buried treasure throughout his range, secretive visits to his aged mother, and sightings of him with Pancho Villa, Wyatt Earp, and scores of old friends. Many of these recent legends have gained material from a dozen books published since 1938 and from popular television shows and films beginning with George Roy Hill's *Butch Cassidy and the Sundance Kid* (1969). The entire corpus suggests the increasing influence of modern media on oral narrative and their growing interdependence.

David H. Stanley

References

Betenson, Lula Parker, and Dora Flack. 1975. *Butch Cassidy, My Brother.* Provo, UT: Brigham Young University Press.

Pointer, Larry. 1977. *In Search of Butch Cassidy.* Norman: University of Oklahoma Press.

Steckmesser, Kent L. 1966. Robin Hood and the American Outlaw: A Note on History and Folklore. *Journal of American Folklore* 79:348–355.

———. 1982. The Three Butch Cassidys: History, Hollywood, Folklore. In *American Renaissance and American West,* ed. Christopher S. Durer et al. Proceedings of the Second University of Wyoming American Studies Conference. Laramie: University of Wyoming Press, pp. 149–155.

Catfish

In America, eight edible species of the family *Ictaluridae.* Three species *(Ictalurus melas, natalis,* and *nebulosis)* are called "bullheads." They are the most common and prevalent catfish on the North American continent. Bullhead fishing with improvised gear and bait is a childhood tradition over much of North America.

More important in traditional culture are four species called simply "catfish," or "cats." They are the channel cat *(I. punctatus),* the blue cat *(I. furcatus),* the white cat *(I. catus),* and the flathead, yellow, or mudcat *(Pylodicits olivaris).* All are common in the South and (excepting the white cat) the Midwest. Local taxonomies include additional "folk" species, such as the "coalbolter" and the "boneless cat."

Catfish never achieved the importance to Native Americans that they later reached among some Whites and African Americans. Only the Arikara of the northern Plains and the Cherokee of the Southeast made them an important part of their diet. A'yu[n]ini, or Swimmer's, mid-19th-century North Carolina Cherokee manuscript includes a prayer to induce large blue cats to the hook.

Catfish are associated with popular stereotypes of lazy or relaxing rural Southerners or Midwesterners sitting by a riverbank or pond with a pole. Cats are popularly believed to be scavengers and are, therefore, not considered fit food by many people, especially farm families. However, the barefoot kid fishing for catfish or bullhead in the old swimming hole is also part of rural Southern and Midwestern nostalgia. Another sentimental image is the poor man catching catfish on his trotline. Riverbank tramp characters in literature and popular culture, such as Cormac McCarthy's Suttree and "Catfish John" in the bluegrass song by Bob McDill and Allen Reynolds, are closely associated with catfish.

Catfish's reputation as a bottom feeder has made it a despised food fish for some, especially those who revere clear-coldwater game fish. Captain Frederick Marryat's 19th-century description of the Mississippi River declared that "it contains the coarsest and most uneatable of fish, such as the catfish," to which Mark Twain replied, "the catfish is a plenty good enough fish for anybody."

The paramount commercial fish in Southern and Midwestern rivers are young channel cats, known as "fiddlers," when under about fifteen inches. Fully grown, they can reach over sixty pounds and four feet, but such large ones are extremely rare today. Fiddlers are easy to distinguish from other young catfish because of their spotted skin. At the eight- to ten-inch range, they have the best flavor and texture. Fiddlers are reputed to be the most delicious fish in the rivers.

Fiddlers are also the chief crop of both the commercial catfish farms and the "pay-and-fish" ponds that have proliferated in the American South. Mississippi is the leading catfish-farming state. Most commercially sold catfish, retailed in supermarkets and eaten in restaurants, are fiddlers, but connoisseurs consider farm- and pond-raised fiddlers inferior. They claim that commercial feed "makes them taste like alfalfa" and that they are soft and mushy due to lack of the muscle tone that they would have, were they fighting current in a river.

Flatheads (yellow cats, mudcats) are called *goujon* by Cajuns and "cushawn" by Lower Mississippi Anglos. They grow large, up to six feet and more than 120 pounds. Three- and four-footers are still caught. Combined with its habit of hiding in hollow logs and old tiles and culverts, the flathead's unsavory looks have caused it to be maligned. Thus the use of the term "flatheads" to describe bottomland bandits and riverbank squatters, and Huckleberry Finn's description of his father as of "no more breeding than a mudcat."

Channels, flatheads, and especially blues can achieve enormous size, and this quality has helped make catfish an important part of local folklore in many areas where the fish are native. Monster and horror legends about extremely large catfish abound, usually concerning flatheads or blue cats. Monstrous flatheads are reputed to inhabit oxbows, cutoffs, or backwaters, tempting anglers for years. A number of cutoffs and oxbows in river country have their legendary monster cats, often bearing a name. One is "Cut-Off John," who has defied anglers for generations, hiding in the Ribeyre Island Cutoff, an oxbow lake across the Wabash River from New Harmony, Indiana. The flathead's large mouth and its habit of hiding, with its mouth open, ready to swallow anything swimming past, has made it the typical "monster catfish" of legend, despite the fact that blue cats run larger.

Big flatheads have reputedly been caught with various contents in their stomachs, including outboard motors, cats, dogs, and piglets. There are a number of legends of them swallowing humans, or at least pulling unsuspecting humans into the river where they then drown. A Moravian missionary reported such an incident on the Ohio River in 1780. Others are quite current, including the persistent rumor of a large flathead caught at the mouth of the Tradewater River on the Ohio, by Caseyville, Kentucky, which contained a human baby. This supposedly occurred during the 1970s. In Troy, Indiana, local fishermen tell of a ten-year-old boy who was pulled under and eaten by a giant catfish while wading for

mussels. A fisherman near Metropolis, Illinois, reportedly drowned after being dragged underwater by the hooks of his own trotline, trying to unhook a giant catfish. Many river folk believe that very large catfish, hardly ever encountered by fishermen, live in deep holes in the river for decades. There are also legends of huge catfish living at the bases of dams, who prey on divers inspecting or performing maintenance.

By way of comparison, it is worth noting that the giant catfish of legend is not only a creature of North America. The Eurasian catfish, or wels *(Siluris glanis),* which has reached fifteen feet and over 600 pounds, has been documented to swallow humans, livestock, and small watercraft.

Part of the lore of the giant flathead includes the practice of catching them by "tickling," "noodling," or "hogging." This practice, which is a traditional display of machismo among young men who live near the river, consists of reaching into hollow logs or under floating debris or overhanging banks to locate a hiding catfish. In some accounts, the tickler strokes the fish, causing it to relax, before grabbing it. Often it is immediately seized, by the lip or gill cover, and hauled ashore. Some ticklers will even thrust a hand down the fish's throat and grab the gill cover from inside. Flatheads have no teeth, but they do have an abrasive surface on the inside of their lips. A Tolu, Kentucky, man proudly displayed a bracelet-like callus on his wrist from his many tickling adventures. Needless to say, tickling is a risky sport in waters where snapping turtles live.

The flathead's hiding habits help some fishermen trap it by setting out culvert pipes with one end beaten shut. A line with a float is attached to the open end and the fisherman need only pull up the rope every few days to discover and remove what may be hiding inside. Big cats are also caught on large-hooked lines baited with everything from bologna to liver to squirrel guts. The most common techniques for catching all species of catfish commercially are the trotline, the hoop net, and the box trap, baited with a strong-smelling bait, such as waste cheese. Fish poachers have used dynamite, fireworks (such as "cherry bombs" and M80s), and telephone magnetos to catch large quantities of catfish illegally.

Despite its negative image, the flathead is a high-quality table fish. Many consider it superior to the more popular channel cat. Its better quality is ascribed to its purely carnivorous diet, which presumably makes it less subject to off-flavors found in more omnivorous species. A minstrel song once popular in Illinois, "The Darkey and the Catfish," sings its praises:

Don't talk to me o' bacon fat
Or taters, coon, or possum,
For when I'se hooked a yaller cat,
I'se got a meal to boss 'em.

The blue cat is the largest species in the river. During aboriginal times, blue cats ran to six feet in length and probably more than 200 pounds. Native Americans told Fathers Joliet and Marquette stories of man- and canoe-eating monsters that lived in the Midwestern rivers. Marquette's own canoe encountered a fish that struck it with such force that he first thought the fish was a tree trunk. Huck and Jim caught one over 200 pounds. One of the largest ever recorded was a 150-pound behemoth shipped to the Smithsonian Institution in Washington, DC, from the Missouri River in 1879, and there were claims that river had produced a 315-pounder earlier in that century.

Legends and tall tales about blues sometimes describe them weighed down with tackle from previous encounters. A Wabash River fisherman claims to have landed on a trotline a big blue cat with so many hooks and sinkers stuck in it that it was sold to a scrap-metal dealer. A look through family photo albums of river folk often reveals many photos of people, frequently fishermen's children, standing beside a large blue cat hanging on an overhead hook.

A somewhat confusing catfish is the "coalbolter" or "niggerlipper." Midwestern fishermen consider it a separate species, as did biologists until the 1940s. (They called it *I. anguilla*, the "eel or willow cat.") Now it is considered a variant of the channel cat. "Niggerlippers," as they are commonly called, at least by Whites, are a late spawn run of channel cat, with distinctive genetic characteristics. They have no spots, and a more massive head than ordinary channel cats.

People with little experience with catfish often erroneously believe that the barbels, the whisker-like feelers around the fish's snout, are venomous. The three spines that extend from a catfish's dorsal fin and gill covers can injure, and they do contain a slightly venomous, or at least irritating, substance to which some people react very painfully. The folk cure is to rub the wound with slime from elsewhere on the fish's body. The Arikara used a local sagebrush species as an antidote for catfish venom. Fishermen sometimes encounter the tiny catfish called the tadpole madtom or "polliwog" *(Noturus gyrinus)* whose dorsal spine contains a painful venom.

The importance of catfish in the Kentuckian pioneer diet is noted in the writings of Harriet Simpson Arnow. Catfish are usually breaded with a spiced cornmeal-and-flour mixture and deep-fat fried, the smaller ones whole, the larger ones as steaks. Some individuals living near the rivers are reputed to be especially fond of eating big catfish. Sometimes large cats are barbecued in the fashion typical of the Upper South and Lower Midwest, which consists of slow roasting over a charcoal fire to which green hickory blocks have been added.

The spoonbill, paddlefish, or spooney *(Polyodon spathula)* are no relation to the catfish family, but they count as a catfish in the markets of the lower Midwest and Upper South. They have catfish-like flesh and no bones and are sold as "boneless cat." They are a very unusual looking fish, with a shark-like body and an oar-like snout one-third the length of the entire fish.

Rare enough to be endangered in most localities, spoonbill are still commercially fished in a few areas. They also have their place in local legend. Called a "living fossil," they have teeth only when very young. The toothless adults are plankton feeders and are almost never caught by anglers, except when accidentally snagged. They can grow to six feet and 200 pounds, but even eighty-pounders are rare today. Commer-

cial fishermen regularly catch four-footers in the fifty-pound range. Their large size, shark-like shape, and bizarrely formed head have also been a source of monster-fish legends.

Perhaps because of their odd appearance and unfamiliarity to the casual angler, spoonbill are thought by many to be inedible. A Cave-in-Rock, Illinois, fish, market customer expressed loud revulsion as a fisherman hauled in a tub of freshly caught spoonbill. "You'll never catch me eating one of those!" he exclaimed with disgust, and promptly purchased thirty pounds of frozen, dressed, packaged boneless cat for a family reunion. The spoonbill fishery industry in the 1940s wasted many fish in the quest for spoonbill caviar. Caspian caviar was then unavailable due to World War II, and New York restaurants bought caviar from Midwestern and Southern rivers. Boneless cat are filleted and deep-fried and served as fish sandwiches.

Catfish are also the focus of local boosterism in a number of Southern and Midwestern communities. "Catfish Capitals of the World," complete with annual catfish festivals, include Belzoni, Mississippi; Paris, Tennessee; Petersburg, Indiana; and Toad Suck, Arkansas.

Jens Lund

References

Kaukas, Dick. 1980. What Really Lives in the Ohio?: "Sure We Have Monsters Down There." *Louisville Times. Saturday Scene* Magazine Section. September 6, pp. 3–4, 22.

Lund, Jens. 1995. *Fisher Folk of the Lower Ohio Valley.* Lexington: University Press of Kentucky.

Madson, John. 1984. To Catch This Fish, Put Hand in Mouth, Hang on—and Pull. *Smithsonian* 15 (September): pp. 54–63.

McClane. A.J. 1974. *McClane's Field Guide to Freshwater Fishes of North America.* New York: Holt, Rinehart, and Winston.

Young, Dianne M. 1989. Catfish. In *Encyclopedia of Southern Culture,* ed. Charles Wilson Reagan and William Ferris. Chapel Hill: University of North Carolina Press, pp. 378–379.

See also Fishing (Sport)

Cemeteries

Sites of interment, concentrated repositories of unique material artifacts (gravemarkers), and focal points for a wide variety of traditional practices. The concept and physical siting of cemeteries in America follows a distinctive evolutionary pattern closely linked to changing standards in taste and cultural values. Unlike their European (primarily British) counterparts, the earliest organized burial sites in the colonies did not, as a general rule, surround church structures and thus were not commonly known as "churchyards." Instead they were called, in the more generically descriptive terms, "burying ground," "burial ground," or "graveyard." The term "cemetery" itself, deriving from the Greek word for sleeping chamber, would not gain general currency until the early 19th century, eventually

to be challenged in the 20th century by the even more euphemistic "memorial park."

Community burial grounds in New England and other areas of early American settlement, though they often had recognizable perimeters, generally lacked formal patterns of internal organization and—other than the gravemarkers themselves—overtly decorative qualities. Markers were arranged rather haphazardly, with scant attention to precise alignment, and their placement within the yard was more often a reflection of death date than familial or social status. Formal pathways, secondary plantings, and other decorative alterations to the landscape were infrequently employed, all of this symbolically in keeping with prevailing attitudes toward death, which viewed it as a grim necessity untempered by elements of sentimentality or, for that matter, undue hopes for a blissful afterlife.

By the early years of the 19th century, burial grounds situated within burgeoning urban areas were becoming filled to capacity and were viewed as both eyesores and health hazards. These factors, combined with, on the one hand, a practical desire to utilize valuable urban real estate in a more profitable manner, and, on the other, aesthetic and philosophical considerations deriving from European Romanticism, helped create a radically new concept in cemetery design and function. Located outside existing urban boundaries, on sites specifically chosen for their topographical and horticultural qualities, these new "rural" cemeteries, characterized by their tasteful blending of splendid monuments with other natural and ornamental features, became sentimentalized landscapes of memory, often functioning as the forerunners of urban parks, and would set the tone for cemetery design into the next century.

The last phase of this evolutionary process—and that which has come to dominate 20th-century cemetery design—is the "memorial park," a generally nondescript landscape featuring markers set flush to the ground surface and a minimum of plantings or other decorative features. Along with these developments has come the trend of memorial parks serving as "one-stop shopping" centers for funerary purposes, one convenient location where all necessary services—mortuary, burial (or crematory), floral, monumental, even nonsectarian religious—can be arranged in a single transaction. To many, such places would seem to epitomize not only late-20th-century Americans' obsession with convenience, but also the enormous distance they have contrived to place between themselves and the fact of death itself.

While the majority of cemeteries in America have always been municipally or privately controlled operations, a sizable proportion of them were initially created, and in many instances are still maintained, by various fraternal, religious, and ethnic groups. Though they share many of the features of the "mainstream" cemeteries, these sites, owing to the specialized nature of their clientele, frequently exhibit a number of highly unusual and meaningful qualities, particularly with regard to gravemarker iconography and ritual funerary and remembrance patterns. Nowhere is this more evident than in the large number and wide variety of ethnic cemeteries found in America, wherein it is possible, among other things, to chart the shifting balance over time between patterns of cultural retention and assimilation.

Traditional practices associated with cemeteries, one of their least-studied features, are widespread and vary considerably along historical, regional, and ethnic lines. The evolution of the typical American funeral—particularly its gravesite elements—from the elaborate processions of the Puritans and highly codified mourning behaviors of the Victorians to the essentially sanitized ceremonies of the late 20th century serves as one telling indication of historic changes in the manner in which Americans have chosen to ritualize this significant rite of passage. Among the more interesting of regional patterns in cemetery-related ritual is the practice, widespread throughout much of America's Upland South areas, of Decoration Day, an annual time of cleaning, repair, and decoration closely allied to concepts of familial and community solidarity. Ethnic groups provide some of the most interesting and colorful of all such traditions. Frequently annual in occurrence and centered around familial customs of ancestor worship, these ethnic traditions include practices ranging from Louisiana Cajun grave painting to the cemetery-specific elements of such festivals as *Ching Ming* (Chinese), *O Bon* (Japanese), and *La Dia de los Muertos* (Mexican).

Finally, cemeteries provide the stimulus and focal point for an astounding variety of traditional practices, beliefs, and even narrative forms prominent in American folklore. From proverbial utterances such as "whistling past the graveyard" to superstitions and popular beliefs (such as "When a grave sinks early, another will follow soon") to blues and other musical forms (like John Lee Hooker's "Graveyard Blues"), cemeteries function as a metaphorical context for a number of elements of folk wisdom and sentiment. Legends of all sorts, ranging from traditional ghostlore to accounts of weeping sculpted angels and telephones in mausoleums, feature cemeteries as their primary setting. Sad to say, even destructive forms of behavior such as cemetery vandalism may be viewed as essentially folkloric activities, especially when practiced—as is most frequently the case—by age- and gender-specific groups as rituals of initiation, bonding, and status enhancement.

In America, as elsewhere, cemeteries are outdoor museums—of history certainly, but also of art, architecture, ethnicity, regionalism, and a host of other elements of cultural evolution. For the folklorist, they represent a substantial body of readily available resources whose full potential has been barely explored.

Richard E. Meyer

References

Farrell, James J. 1980. *Inventing the American Way of Death, 1830–1920.* Philadelphia: Temple University Press.

Jackson, Kenneth, and Camillo José Vergara. 1989. *Silent Cities: The Evolution of the American Cemetery.* New York: Princeton Architectural Press.

Linden-Ward, Blanche. 1989. *Silent City on a Hill: Landscapes of Memory and Boston's Mount Auburn Cemetery.* Columbus: Ohio State University Press.

Meyer, Richard E., ed. 1992. *Cemeteries and Gravemarkers: Voices of American Culture.* Logan: Utah State University Press.

———. 1993. *Ethnicity and the American Cemetery.* Bowling Green, OH: Bowling Green State University Popular Press.

Sloan, David Charles. 1991. *The Last Great Necessity: Cemeteries in American History.* Baltimore: Johns Hopkins University Press.

See also Epitaph; Gravemarkers

Center for the Study of Southern Culture

First institution established for the interdisciplinary study of the American South. Founded in 1977 at the University of Mississippi, the center has had only one permanent director so far (1995), folklore scholar William R. Ferris. In 1995 the associate director was Ann J. Abadie, and faculty included Charles R. Wilson and Ted Ownby (history), Robert Brinkmeyer (English), and Lisa N. Howorth and Thomas Rankin (art). The curriculum offers core courses in Southern studies and cross-listed courses in history, English, anthropology, sociology, music, art, political science, Afro-American studies, and women's studies, culminating in B.A. and M.A. degrees in Southern studies.

The center publishes a quarterly newsletter, the *Southern Register,* and several magazines, including *Old Time Country, Rejoice!,* and *Living Blues,* the major American blues serial. It sponsors an interdisciplinary journal, *Crossroads;* has underwritten several reference books, including the *Encyclopedia of Southern Culture* (1989), edited by Wilson and Ferris; and has published several other books.

The center cosponsors annual conferences, including the Faulkner and Yoknapatawpha Conference, the Chancellor's Symposium in Southern History, and the Oxford Conference for the Book, as well as individual symposiums and weekly presentations that are open to the public. Graduate students in Southern studies have conducted folklore fieldwork for the National Park Service and the Woodruff Foundation.

The Center for the Study of Southern Culture is housed in the restored Barnard Observatory, one of three antebellum buildings on the University of Mississippi campus in Oxford.

Brenda M. Eagles

Chanteys

Songs sung to accompany work in maritime settings. The practice of singing while at work was historically a widespread phenomenon crossing cultural boundaries from Greece to the Hebrides and extending to virtually every corner of the earth. In all of sub-Saharan Africa, including the area from Senegal to Angola, from which most of the American slaves were taken, songs were sung by individuals to accompany a variety of tasks, including ironwork and weaving. More typically, group tasks, such as agricultural work and the rowing of boats, utilized the overlapping call-and-response singing style, the leader calling or singing a phrase and then joining the other workers in a completing chorus. The Limba of Sierra Leone sang while hoeing in their rice seed. In work collectives in Dahomey (modern Benin), known as *dokpwe,* workers used such a style while kneading earth for walls, laying thatch, and hoeing, and there were other cooperative labor systems—such as the *kurum* of Cameroon, the *ku* of Liberia, and, in the New World, the *coumbite* and *societe* of Haiti and the fishing people of Nevis and Tobago—in which the people utilized singing to accomplish their work, be it catching fish or moving houses.

Many of these tasks, in fact, both in Africa and the Caribbean, were water-related, from the growing of rice, to fishing, to transportation. West African dugout canoes, or pirogues, have been shown to have contributed to the evolution of the Native American canoe, and West African men, such as the Kru of Liberia, were acknowledged masters of both boat construction and boat handling. The early presence of the Wolof of Senegal aboard European ships may have contributed to the high instance of Wolof-derived words that have survived in New World English, and men of African descent were to be quite prevalent aboard sailing ships and those that came after.

The use of chanteys (or shantys) aboard European and New World ships seems to draw heavily on West African influence as well. While there was at least a Celtic precedent for maritime worksongs, the African call-and-response pattern, such as that still used by the boatmen of the Zaire (Congo) River, seems to have had a strong effect on the evolution of the New World chantey. The word itself, depending on the choice of spelling, may derive either from the imperative form of the French verb *chanter* (to sing) or from the singing heard from or during the moving of the waterside huts, or "shantys," another French-derived word from *chantier* (a timberyard or shipyard). Neither spelling occurs until the middle of the 19th century, and chanteying as we know it may date from as little as a generation before that.

The first mentions of songs we can identify with this classic chanteying tradition are drawn from shore-based occupations of New World Blacks, including the songs of the boatmen who worked the waters of the Caribbean and the Southeastern United States. Like their African forebears—or, indeed, as they themselves may have done before being transported—the New World boatmen sang as they rowed, utilizing the call-and-response pattern and, occasionally, the beat of a drum. Much remarked upon in the coastal waters of South Carolina, the sound and style of these workers were very similar to those heard on the coast of Ghana in the 1790s.

The songs of the boatmen on the South Carolina coast also seem to have added to this a high proportion of Christian spiritual songs, including "On Canaan's Happy Shore," "Roll, Jordan, Roll," "Run, Mary, Run," and "Drinking Wine, Drinking Wine."

The African worksong tradition also adhered to other mainland and coastal occupations. The Black firemen aboard steamboats sang at their work as did the stevedores and roustabouts of the Southern ports. Near the shore, agricultural workers sang at their labors, and so did the mule skinners and those who worked constructing and maintaining the railroad tracks. Workers in tobacco warehouses, oyster-shucking and crab-picking houses, and those under confinement—whether slaves marching in shackles or prisoners behind bars—all frequently used singing to make their work go better. All of these precedents combined to create the chanteys used by the menhaden fishermen who worked the waters from New Jersey to Texas. Catching the oily menhaden for industrial applications, these fishermen were the last actively to use chanteys. The invention of the power block, a mechanical net-puller, in the mid-1950s all but eliminated the old songs, but older fishermen continued to sing them for pleasure into the 1990s.

Michael Luster

References

Abrahams, Roger D. 1974. *Deep the Water, Shallow the Shore: Three Essays on Shantying in the West Indies.* Publications of the American Folklore Society Memoir Series Vol. 60. Austin: University of Texas Press.

Doerflinger, William Main. 1990. *Songs of the Sailor and Lumberman.* rev. ed. Glenwood, IL: Meyerbooks.

Hugill, Stan. 1984. *Shanties from the Seven Seas: Shipboard Work-Songs and Songs Used as Work-Songs from the Great Days of Sail.* 2d (abridged) ed. London: Routledge and Kegan Paul.

See also Fishing (Commercial); Maritime Folklore; Worksong

Chase, Richard (1904–1988)

Collector and performer of Jack tales, folksongs, and dances. Chase's family was from New England, but his father established a nursery near Huntsville, Alabama, and Richard grew up there. He went to local schools and, as he put it, a school in Tennessee "for problem boys." At age twenty, Chase was in Boston, where he learned about the Pine Mountain Settlement School in Kentucky. There he discovered ballads and the work of folksong collector Cecil Sharp. He had found his calling. For the rest of his life, he collected, performed, and taught various forms of folklore to audiences around the country.

In the mid-1920s, Chase attended Harvard University for two years and also took courses in progressive education with Marietta Johnson in Greenwich, Connecticut, and Fair Hope, Alabama. During this period, he worked off and on as a performer-teacher of folksongs and dances. In 1929 he graduated from Antioch College in Ohio with a B.S. in botany. He married in 1930 and then spent two or three years in Europe, where he developed contacts with the English Folk Dance and Song Society.

In 1935 Chase was hired to teach folksongs at a teachers' conference in Raleigh, North Carolina, and, from a student there, he learned for the first time about Jack tales (essentially, European-derived Märchen [fairy tales] that feature a young man, Jack, as the main protagonist). Chase began collecting, performing, and publishing Jack tales, collected primarily from members of the Ward family of Beech Mountain, North Carolina. Six tales were published in *Southern Folklore Quarterly* beginning with Volume I, Number 1 in

1937 and continuing into 1941.

In late 1940, Chase learned through the Ward family that there were Jack tales to be found in Wise County, Virginia. About a year later, he was employed by the Works Progress Administration (WPA) Virginia Writers' Project to put together a book on Wise County folklore, but the goal was shortly changed to emphasize folktales. For various reasons—in part because the Writers' Project ended—the Wise County book was never published, but thirty-four Wise County tales, fifteen of which were Jack tales, were included (in whole or part) in Chase's three books: *The Jack Tales* (1943), *Grandfather Tales* (1948), and *American Folk Tales and Songs* (1956).

Chase also began working with the White Top Mountain folk festival in North Carolina in 1934 and remained with it until its demise in 1941. The next year he moved to a small farm in Albemarle County, Virginia. His life and travels between 1942 and his death in 1988 are too complex to delineate here. Suffice it to say that, in that period, he lived, traveled, and performed in various places in Virginia, North Carolina, and California, moving back to his original hometown of Huntsville, Alabama, about 1983.

Richard Chase is best seen as an editor of folklore, using his creativity to put together several versions of each Jack tale when he told it or when he published it. His collated versions were widely popular and are frequently told by professional storytellers; and a few appear to have been picked up by traditional tale-tellers.

Charles L. Perdue Jr.

References

Perdue, Charles L., Jr., ed. 1987. *Outwitting the Devil: Jack Tales from Wise County Virginia.* Santa Fe, NM: Ancient City.

Child, Francis James (1825–1896)

Ballad editor, literary scholar, and a founder of the American Folklore Society. One of eight children in the family of a sailmaker in Boston, Child graduated from Boston Latin School and Harvard College, where he subsequently became a tutor, first in mathematics, then in history and political economics. After study at the Universities of Berlin and Göttingen, he was appointed Boylston Professor of Rhetoric and Oratory and, finally in 1876, Harvard's first professor of English.

Renowned as a scholar, revered as a teacher, and admired as an administrator, when he was in Germany Child became a great admirer of the brothers Grimm and was thoroughly imbued with the scholarly techniques of the German philologists, whose methods, relatively new to the United States, he adhered to for the rest of his life. These methods allowed him to edit *The Poetical Works of Edmund Spenser* and to publish a volume modestly entitled *Observations on the Language of Chaucer's Canterbury Tales,* perhaps the first truly scientific analysis of the Middle English language. In addition, he lectured and wrote extensively on the works of Shakespeare, taught courses on the full range of English literature, and was constantly involved in the teaching of what today would be called composition. Among his students and colleagues were such influential scholars as George Lyman Kittredge, Francis Barton Gummere, and Phillips Barry.

Despite the excellence of his literary work, Child is known primarily for his edition of the five-volume work titled *The English and Scottish Popular Ballads* ([1882–1898] 1965). Child's approach to ballads was governed by his training in the methods of German philologists. Unlike such predecessors as Percy, Scott, and Jamieson, who also looked upon ballads as a part of the English literary heritage, Child subjected ballad texts to the same rigorous scrutiny he had applied to the poetry of Spenser and the language of Chaucer. In addition to reproducing every text exactly as he found it, Child attempted in his notes to set each text in its own narrative tradition and sought narrative parallels internationally, a practice followed in Scandinavia by such editors as Svend Grundtvig. Indeed, so close are the editorial techniques employed by Child in *The English and Scottish Popular Ballads* and Svend Grundtvig in *Danmarks gamle Folkeviser* (1853) that one must see Child and Grundtvig as intellectual collaborators, a fact borne out by their correspondence (Hustvedt 1930). Moreover, neither Child nor Grundtvig was a field collector, and Child's edition of 305 ballad types, which he saw as definitive, derived with very few exceptions from manuscripts or books, as do most of Grundtvig's 539 Danish types.

The English and Scottish Popular Ballads has served in the English-speaking world as the definer of the ballad genre: Ballads are what appear in Child! Though folklorists often decry Child's dependence upon manuscripts and printed materials, though ethnomusicologists lament his lack of attention to music, and though popularists question his apparent notion that ballad singing was dead when he began his editorial work, there is absolutely no doubt that Francis James Child laid the groundwork for ballad study in the 20th century.

W. Edson Richmond

References

Child, Francis James. [1882–1898] 1965. *The English and Scottish Popular Ballads.* 5 vols. New York: Dover.

———. 1902. Ballads. *The Universal Cyclopedia.* New York: Appleton.

———. [1930] 1972. *Letters on Scottish Ballads from Professor Child to W.W.* Norwood, PA: Norwood Editions.

James, Thelma. 1933. The English and Scottish Popular Ballads of F.J. Child. *Journal of American Folklore* 46:51–68.

Leach, MacEdward, and Tristram P. Coffin. *The Critics and the Ballad.* Carbondale: Southern Illinois University Press, pp. 12–19.

Hustvedt, Sigurd Bernhard. 1930. Francis James Child and Other Americans; and Appendix A: The Grundtvig-Child Correspondence. In *Ballad Books and Ballad Men.* Cambridge: Harvard University Press, pp. 205–229, 241–300.

Children

A folk group defined, primarily, by age. From the first encounters with their peers until the time they begin to experience puberty, children create and pass on traditional lore—oral, customary or social, and material. While they are aware of sexual and racial differences and, to an extent, ethnic and national differences (all of which show up in their lore), children transmit their folklore quite freely within their group. Children's folklore is the traditional material created and transmitted by children up to about age twelve; after that, they are adolescents, and their lore changes as they attempt to put childhood behind them.

The family is the first folk group within which children learn traditional materials. The various rituals practiced at mealtime, bathtime, and/or bedtime, on holidays, for birthdays and other anniversaries, during the different seasons, and at any other times when the family regularly gathers form some of the initial ways in which a child's world is structured. A child soon learns that different families have different traditional practices, and children discuss these differences with their parents and peers.

Once children begin to associate with their peers without direct adult supervision, they begin to learn their own group's folklore, which often has been passed down to the present through centuries of generations. That folklore comprises three broad categories: (1) *oral,* those items from individual words to complete stories that make up children's discourse; (2) *customary,* those traditionally established practices, whether simple superstitions or complex games, by which two or more children interact; and (3) *material,* all of those concrete items, like paper airplanes and snow forts, that children learn to build during their preteen years.

As children interact in the sandbox or the backyard, at day care or kindergarten, they use words that have specific meaning within their age group. Some of their earliest oral folklore consists of words like "doo doo," to refer to feces, or "doo doo head," an insult, which they have made up themselves. At one time, it was common for children to use the word "fish" as a derogatory adjective, as in "Those are really fish sneakers!" to indicate an unacceptable pair of sneakers (a discount-store brand rather than a fashionable name brand, for example). Certain pranks may have their own names; a "wedgie" or "melvin" describes the act of pulling someone else's (usually a male's) underpants up sharply by the rear waistband. As children become aware of conformity, they have special epithets and insults for the nonconformers who tattle ("Tattle tale, tattle tale . . ."), lie ("Liar, liar, pants on fire . . ."), cry ("Cry baby, cry . . ."), allow their underwear to show ("I see London, I see France . . ."), leave a zipper down ("XYZ," that is, "Examine your zipper"), or engage in other behavior disapproved of by the group.

With increasing age comes a concomitant development in language skills and oral folklore. Children ask traditional riddles ("What's black and white and red/read all over?") and tell jokes ("There was this kid, Johnny . . .") that have been around for generations. The category of riddle joke combines the two. The riddle joke—whether about polacks, dead babies, morons, teachers, parents, elephants, famous people, or a host of other topics—indicates not only the child's increasing capacity for humor, but also his or her participation in a tradition (continuing the moron or Helen Keller jokes) and additions to that tradition (space shuttle disaster or Dolly Parton jokes). These forms of humor, along with parodies of everything from "The Star-Spangled Banner" to "Joy to the World" and a good deal of gross or obscene humor, show both an increasing sophistication of wit as well as a willingness to either mock adult society or violate its rules—perhaps in preparation for the greater independence of puberty.

Children also tell folktales that are often transmitted in situations in which there is little or no adult supervision, but they are about the dangers of such situations. Children at a slumber party or sleepover will, generally after the supervising adults have gone to bed, tell ghost stories and participate in various rituals with ouija boards, mirrors, and other mediums through which they attempt to contact the supernatural. Older (but still preteen) girls who are baby-sitting or are baby-sitters may relate stories such as the one about the threatening telephone call discovered to be coming from an upstairs phone. Boys or girls in summer camps tell, or are told by counselors and then pass on, ghost stories—usually set in the same locale as the camp. The absence of protecting adults (in the usual family ratio) makes the stories scarier.

Customary folklore helps children structure their own activities without adult intervention. Counting-out rhymes ("One potato, two potato . . ." or "Eeny, meeny, miney, mo . . .") allow children to pick the first "It" person for the game, the one who must suffer the punishment of being "It" without having been caught. The various tagging, hiding, chasing, and capturing games all have rules established by tradition that can vary from neighborhood to neighborhood. Whether "It" counts by fives to fifty or tens to one hundred, whether the hiders must hide more than five feet or more than ten feet from the seeker's goal ("Anybody around my goal is it!"), and whether or not the house counts in wood tag are matters for which group tradition provides a rule or an answer. Hundreds of jump-rope rhymes, ball-bouncing rhymes, hand-clapping rhymes, and other game rhymes (for example, "The farmer in the dell . . .") provide the structures for games dating back many generations.

Customary behavior also guides children through the world in other ways. Some items are learned from both the family and the peer folk group. A child might learn the traditional birthday song from parents, but only his or her peers will teach the equally traditional parody ("Happy Birthday to you, you live in the zoo . . ."). Other holiday customs may be a similar combination of family and peer traditions. Children also have a variety of folk beliefs or superstitions, from the popular "Step on a crack, break your mother's back" to various omens of, or practices for, luck before the baseball or soccer game or before a test at school, as well as beliefs (many of which they share with adults) having to do with good and bad luck. Girls, mostly, have a variety of ways (twisting apple stems or peeling apples while reciting the alphabet) to discover the initials or name of the boy they will marry or to discover the number of children they will have. There are also clubs, some secret, with their requisite initiation ceremonies, wherein children gather in groups, united against whatever may come their way.

The category of material culture encompasses the least-studied aspect of children's folklore. Perhaps this is because some of the most obvious items in that group are made of the least-durable substance—paper. The most ubiquitous of these is the paper airplane, constructed in a variety of sizes and shapes from clean notebook paper as well as returned test papers or homework. Paper is also used for boats, fortune-telling devices, bracelets and chains, drinking cups, "poppers" (which make a loud noise when the teacher is not looking), various animals (some derived from origami patterns), footballs (to play with in study hall), game boards (for "hangman" or "battleships"), puppets and "cootie" catchers, cone-shaped missiles (launched in the updraft from the hot-air heaters), and rubberband-fired spitwads—to name a few. Most of these constructions, along with snappers made from hairpins and various other devices, are found more often in schoolrooms than anywhere else.

Outside of the school, children are equally creative, and they have more materials with which to work. Some of their creations may come from seasonally available materials: sand castles, hideouts, and tree houses in the summer; snow forts, snow angels, sled runs, and snowballs in the winter. Boys, mostly, make guns, knives, slingshots, bows and arrows, spears, lances, and quarterstaffs out of available pieces of wood. Boys and girls alike make "motors" for their tricycles and bicycles out of old playing cards or other pieces of cardboard. Girls, mostly, make friendship bracelets out of thread with bits of metal or beads woven in. In our modern, high-tech society, some children still make traditional string figures and "conkers" (a British term for horse chestnuts with string through them), a testament to the endurance of some folklore.

A century of scholarship, during which a number of folklorists have found children's folklore a rewarding field of study, has shaped the current awareness and study of the subject. One of the first to study children's lore, and also the first editor of the *Journal of American Folklore,* was William Wells Newell, whose *Games and Songs of American Children* (1883) was the first major study of American children's folklore. In some ways, especially in his focus on games and songs, Newell set the tone for much subsequent study of children's folklore. Shortly after Newell's book, Henry C. Bolton published *The Counting-out Rhymes of Children: Their Antiquity, Origin, and Wide Distribution: A Study in Folk-Lore* (1888). Newell and Bolton started a trend in children's folklore that, in many ways, culminated in such encyclopedic studies as Roger Abrahams' *Jump-Rope Rhymes: A Dictionary* (1969), his *Counting-out Rhymes: A Dictionary* (1980), Iona and Peter Opie's *Children's Games in Street and Playground* (1969), and their *The Singing Game* (1985). Between Newell's and the Opies' books, there were several variations on the main theme. Stewart Culin's "Street Games of Boys in Brooklyn, N.Y." (1891) was a study of a specific region and a specific kind of game, and it certainly pointed toward Alan Milberg's book *Street Games* (1976). Other variations included articles and books that were not exercises in scholarship but collections of games and songs for children, such as Charles Weir's *Songs the Children Love to Sing* (1916) and *Songs to Sing to Children* (1935). Children's games and songs (and other folklore) were also included in such expansive studies as *The Frank C. Brown Collection of North Carolina Folklore* (1952–1964) (especially Volume 1 edited in part by Paul G. Brewster), and Carl Withers' *Plainville USA* (1941) and subsequent works.

As the study of songs and games continued, the study of children's folklore in general began to broaden. Among the few examples that must stand for a great many books and articles, Brewster's *American Nonsinging Games* (1953) was the first large study of nonsinging games. The 1950s also saw the publication of Iona and Peter Opie's *The Lore and Language of Schoolchildren* (1959), which gives nearly as much space to customary behavior as to oral traditions. Martha Wolfenstein's *Children's Humor: A Psychological Analysis* (1954) is important for the depth of analysis her narrow focus allowed, and John McDowell's *Children's Riddling* (1979) is similarly tightly focused, both in region and in genre. Mary and Herbert Knapp's *One Potato, Two Potato: The Secret Education of American Children* (1976) helped open the way for serious consideration of children's gross and obscene humor. Margaret K. Brady's *"Some Kind of Power": Navajo Children's Skinwalker Narratives"* (1984) looks at Native American children's lore, and Bessie Jones' and Bess Lomax Hawes' *Step It Down: Games, Plays, Songs and Stories from the Afro-American Heritage* (1972) looks at the lore of African American children. Simon J. Bronner's *American Children's Folklore* (1988) continues and balances most of these trends; he deals with a wide variety of children's folklore (including one of the few substantial surveys of material traditions available), makes some cogent, in-depth analyses, and provides an excellent bibliography.

C. W. Sullivan III

References

Dargan, Amanda, and Steven Zeitlin. 1990. *City Play.* New Brunswick, NJ: Rutgers University Press.

Fowke, Edith. 1988. *Red Rover, Red Rover: Children's Games Played in Canada.* Toronto: Doubleday Canada.

Mechling, Jay. 1986. Children's Folklore. In *Folk Groups and Folklore Genres,* ed. Elliott Oring. Logan: Utah State University Press, pp. 91–128.

Sutton-Smith, Brian. 1981. *The Folkstories of Children.* Philadelphia: University of Pennsylvania Press.

Turner, Ian, June Factor, and Wendy Lowenstein. 1978. *Cinderella Dressed in Yella.* 2d. ed. Richmond, Australia: Heinemann Educational Australia.

Withers, Carl. 1948. *A Rocket in My Pocket: The Rhymes and Chants of Young Americans.* New York: Holt, Rinehart, and Winston.

See also Camplore; Family Folklore; Games; Halloween; Tongue Twisters; Tooth Fairy; Toys, Folk

Chinese Americans

A diverse community of immigrants from China, and their descendants, distinguished by ethnic, regional, and class variations. The Chinese American population ranges from newly

In American cities, an elaborate archway often marks the location of Chinatown. Washington, DC, 1995. Photo J. W. Love.

arrived immigrants to families who have been established in the United States for several generations.

The majority of the earliest Chinese immigrants came from Guangdong Province in southeast China. Fleeing from war and inflation, and enticed by news of discovery of gold in California in the 1840s, more than 300,000 arrived between 1850 and 1882, settling in California, Oregon, Washington, Idaho, Montana, and Colorado. Chinese laborers played a crucial role in the development of the West, reclaiming marshes, mining minerals, farming, fishing, and building tunnels, bridges, and roads, as well as the Central Pacific Railroad that made large-scale transcontinental travel possible. Among the immigrants was a small group of merchants—wealthier and better educated than the majority who were peasants—who held more social and economic power in the new society.

Racial discrimination and an economic crisis in California contributed to an anti-Chinese movement that severely restricted Chinese immigration, naturalization, and legal rights of Chinese Americans, culminating in the passage of the Exclusion Act of 1882. The exclusion acts were not repealed until 1943. As hostility intensified during the 1880s and 1890s, Chinese immigrants left rural areas and congregated in larger towns; many of these settlements later became "Chinatowns."

Nineteenth-century Chinese American society was primarily a bachelor community. A network of kinship and village ties formed the basis of a social structure that substituted for the traditional family unit. Family associations brought together people with the same surname, while district associations brought together members from the same geographical region in China. The association lodge functioned as a multi-service community center and the focus of a surrogate family.

Religion provided spiritual comfort to lonely men living in a foreign and often hostile land. Most practiced folk beliefs that sought the protection and assistance of various gods and patron deities with whom they were familiar from south China. The creation of a relatively homogeneous concentrated community made possible the retention and adaptation of Chinese cultural practices. The traditional Chinese worldview was a combination of elements of folk belief with Daoist, Buddhist, and Confucian teachings. This included belief that those in the spirit world have the power to intervene and to assist in the affairs of the living, and that there exists a continuum and an interdependency between the dead and the living. Prayers were addressed to ancestors, seeking assistance in curing diseases, averting calamities, and bringing prosperity and happiness to descendants. In return, spirits of the deceased needed to be nurtured, ritually fed, and made to feel a part of the living world. The seasonal festivals helped strengthen this bond.

From the late 1880s through the turn of the century, dozens of temples—from wayside shrines and simple wooden structures in rural communities to large and elaborate com-

munity temples—were built throughout the West, in Hawaii, and in such Eastern cities as New York and Philadelphia. Many reflected the use of Chinese geomancy, or *feng-shui* (wind and water), and were situated near water sources or at the edge of settlements.

When an individual wanted to communicate with the deities, seek guidance, protection, or success in his business venture, or express appreciation for good fortune, he visited the temple. Incense sticks to purify the air, candles to illuminate, and paper money for use in the spirit world were burned as offerings to the patron deity. In addition, temples offered fortune-telling services. Businesses maintained small altars for Guan Gung, regarded by merchants as a god of wealth and fidelity in business transactions. Patron deities were based on historical individuals who had led exemplary lives and were later deified. For example, Guan Gong was a warrior known for his loyalty and popularized through the Ming-dynasty novel *Romance of the Three Kingdoms*; Tien-Hou (Empress of Heaven) lived from A.D. 960 to 987 in Fujian Province, and was later known for her spiritual ability to guide seafarers safely home through storms.

The early immigrants brought genres of Cantonese folksongs, including the *muk-yu* (wood-fish) cantefable (or chantefable) form. Marlon K. Hom describes its structure and content:

Chantefables were performed by a storyteller who chanted in rhymes, sometimes interspersed with spoken speech, and accompanied by musical instruments—a string instrument, a small bell, a pair of wooden clappers, a wooden block, or simply the clapping of hands. The muk-yu chantefable consists of stories derived from historical figures and popular legends. While some pieces are humorous and entertaining, many are melancholic complaints about hardship and suffering, loneliness, and separation. The emigration of the Cantonese native to the United States provided additional topics, particularly on the sorrow and lamentation of forsaken wives left behind at home. One common feature among these chantefables is a didactic and moralistic overtone. (Hom 1989)

Seasonal festivals, based on the lunar calendar, were important social events for Chinese Americans. Most important of these was the New Year; it marked a time of renewal, a time to clear debts, visit friends and relatives, drive away bad spirits, and usher in good luck for the coming year. Local communities organized parades that staged lion and dragon dances amid thundering firecrackers, instrumental bands, floats, banners, and lantern processions. Chinese American merchants held open house, preparing a table of treats for the larger American community. Smaller festivals that were observed included Quin Ming (pure and bright) rites for the deceased in April, Dragon Boat races commemorating patriot Chu Yuan in June, and mid-autumn family reunions in September. Special foods were associated with each festival, and several festivals had public as well as private dimensions, being expressions of both community and ethnic pride. At the same time, communities made it clear that they had become part of American life, so they participated in pan-American events such as July fourth parades.

Annual birthday celebrations for the principal deity of a community temple featured offerings to the deity, a procession in which a figure of the deity was paraded through the streets, and an opera performance to entertain both the deity and the public. The town of Point Alones in Monterey Bay, California, held an annual Ring Game honoring the God of Wealth, from 1894 to 1904. The climax of the event was the firing of "bombs" (woven bamboo rings) into the air from a giant firecracker and the ensuing struggle for the rings by large crowds. It was believed that whoever secured a ring was blessed with luck and wealth for the coming year. The Marysville, California annual temple festival during the second lunar month celebrated the birthdays of both Bok Kai and a regional earth god, marking the emergence of a dragon from slumber to oversee rains bringing forth a new agricultural season. The Ghosts Festival in the eighth lunar month aimed to appease the wandering souls of those who died without a proper burial because they had died far away from home, had left no descendants, or had died violently. If left unattended, these spirits could harm the living. Occasionally, communities also held a *jiao* ritual, such as occurred after a natural disaster hit Sacramento, California, to appease and dispel ghosts that caused such happenings.

The funerals of early Chinese pioneers were swift and simple. As communities gained stability, numbers, and wealth, the funerals resembled those practiced in south China—with ritual offerings, professional mourners, public processions, and annual grave visits. While many dead were buried in Chinese sections of American cemeteries, it was believed that their spirits would not be at rest after death without the proper and regular ministrations of their families. Twice a year, during Quin Ming in the spring and the Ghosts Festival in the autumn, family and district association members swept graves, planted flowers, burned incense, and offered food and drink to nourish the spirits of the deceased. Usually, after a period of seven years, graves were opened, the bodies exhumed, and bones packed and shipped to China for permanent reburial in native villages. An adaptation of Cantonese mortuary rites, this practice of reinterment in China continued until World War II.

Chinese herbal medicine was practiced, and specialists such as "Doc Hay" of John Day, Oregon, established successful medical practices, restoring patients to the proper "physical balance." Apothecaries, walls lined with drawers containing herbs, were staffed with herbalists to dispense prescriptions for customers.

Chinese opera, a dramatic form that combines elements of movement, dialogue, singing, and combat, was probably the most popular entertainment among the Chinese working class. Throughout the 1860s, there was at least one theater operating full time in San Francisco's Chinatown; in 1897 the first building was constructed specifically for Chinese theater. Opera clubs later served as centers for social and recreational activities. Visiting troupes featuring well-known actors were booked into theaters for one week to ten days; local opera-club members fleshed out the rest of the cast or provided musical accompaniment. Amateur participation in performances as a personal means of artistic expression still has an extensive tradition in China. The 20th century saw the growth of amateur musical clubs and ensembles, such as the Nam Chjung Musical Society located in San Francisco, in which Cantonese opera continues to be performed and practiced today. More than a dozen music clubs practicing Cantonese opera, Peking opera, and instrumental music exist in the San Francisco Bay area.

Several factors contributed to the diminished practice of traditional religions and festivals after the 1920s. With the emergence of a new republic in China in 1911 that replaced 2,000 years of dynastic rule, Chinese American leaders sought to construct a new image of the Chinese as a "modern" and "progressive" community. As American-born Chinese became urbanized and acculturated, they struggled with the challenge of maintaining their ethnic heritage while adapting to the mainstream of American culture.

The abolition of the discriminatory immigration-quota system and the enactment of the 1965 Immigration Act increased immigration sharply from Taiwan and Hong Kong, bringing in more students and middle-class families. Since the normalization of U.S. relations with the People's Republic of China in the 1970s, people have also emigrated from mainland China, as well as ethnic Chinese refugees coming from southeast Asian countries. These new immigrants have revitalized Chinese American communities, increased the demand for cultural activities, and enriched the membership of cultural organizations by introducing new and diverse talent, repertoires, and regional styles.

The rising ethnic awareness of the 1960s fueled the creation of numerous community-based organizations. New immigrants filled the ranks of instrumental music, opera, folk-dance, shadow-theater, and choral and visual-arts organizations, either as participants, audience members, or educators. In some cases, patrons have recruited and sponsored master performers for long-term residencies of coaching and directing positions.

In more recent years, several Chinese American cultural organizations have developed folklife programs within their research, exhibition, and public-program initiatives. The Asian American Art Centre in New York, for example, exhibited wood-block prints of Chinese door gods in the 1980s and hosted lunar New Year workshops featuring folk artists teaching such crafts as paper cutting, wood-block printing, and dough-figure construction. Impetus for such programs comes from concern about how contemporary art is connected to the past and to a community, a tradition, or a lifestyle.

The Chinatown History Museum in New York City salvaged a Cantonese opera collection—instruments, costumes, scripts, and props used by the Chinese Musical and Theatrical Company since the 1930s—that was just being thrown out. Museum staff recorded oral histories from club participants, and they cataloged and conserved the collection. In its earlier years, the museum documented the occupational folklife of laundry workers. San Francisco's Chinese Culture Center has organized exhibitions of Chinese folk arts and lunar New Year programs. The Chinese Historical Society of America, in addition to mounting exhibitions, has published books and a periodical, *Chinese America: History and Perspectives*, that include aspects of the folklife of early Chinese Americans.

The arrival of traditional artists increased community access not only to high-quality performances, but also to apprenticeships and educational programs. Zhushan Chinese Opera Institute, based in the Washington, DC, area, for example, offers opera classes to young people enrolled on weekends in Chinese American language schools.

The recognition of master folk artists through the National Heritage Fellowships of the National Endowment for the Arts' folk-arts program—Ng Shueng-Chi, Toissan *muk-yu* folk singer, and Liang-xing Tang, pipa player—has provided visibility and support to community programs, while federal, state, and local grants to organizations make it possible for scholars to participate in research-based public programs that engage both Chinese- and English-speaking audiences.

Chinese American seasonal festivals continue to be practiced—both family-based and public celebrations—the most important of which is the lunar New Year. In 1990 the Los Angeles Chinese American community produced a Moon Festival as part of the larger Los Angeles Festival that brought attention to the multiethnic nature of the city, reviving a tradition last practiced in 1947. The festival featured performances by martial-arts, folk-dance, opera, and instrumental ensembles; it included folk artists' workshops, mooncake demonstrations, and storytelling. The festival culminated in a harvest-moon banquet, with a lantern procession and a moon-viewing party via telescopes placed in a schoolyard. While the program was a marker of ethnic identity, it also introduced a new element of cross-cultural programming. Storytellers, for example, introduced audiences to repertoires of tales about the moon from several diverse cultural traditions and perspectives. Chinese Americans' folk practices will continue to change as they negotiate their ethnic identity and relate it to the larger complex American society.

Vivien T.Y. Chen

References

Hom, Marlon K. 1989. A Muk-yu from Gold Mountain. *Chinese America: History and Perspectives 1989*. Chinese Historical Society of America, pp. 17–18.

Hoy, William. 1948. Native Festivals of the California Chinese. *Western Folklore* 7:240–250.

Lydon, Sandy. 1985. *Chinese Gold: The Chinese in the Monterey Bay Region*. Capitola: Capitola Book.

Ma, L. Eve Armentrout. 1988. Chinese Traditional Religion in North America and Hawaii. *Chinese America: History and Perspectives 1989*. Chinese Historical Society of America.

Slovenze-Low, Madeline. 1991. On the Tail of the Lion: Approaches to Cross-Cultural Fieldwork with Chinese Americans in New York. In *Creative Ethnicity: Symbols and Strategies of Contemporary Ethnic Life*, ed. Stephen Stern and John Allan Cicala. Logan: Utah State University Press, pp. 55–71.

Christensen, Abigail Mandana ("Abbie") Holmes (1852–1938)

Collector of African American folklore of the South Carolina Sea Islands. Born in Massachusetts, Holmes moved to South Carolina with her abolitionist parents during the Civil War. She published stories and a book of African American dialect tales in the 1870s and 1890s and was a proponent of the African origins of Southern Black folklore.

Holmes heard the stories of Br'er Rabbit and the others of "de beastises" told by formerly enslaved African Americans as she matured into adulthood in Beaufort, South Carolina. While a student at Mount Holyoke Female Seminary, she published "De Wolf, de Rabbit, an' de Tar Baby" in a Massachusetts newspaper in 1874. Thereafter, she contributed several tales in the Sea Island dialect to the New York *Independent*. After she married in 1875, she wrote under the name Mrs. A.M.H. Christensen. In 1892 Christensen published a collection of dialect stories entitled *Afro American Folk Lore Told Round Cabin Fires on the Sea Islands of South Carolina*. She belonged briefly to the American Folklore Society and wrote a paper on African American spirituals and shouts that was read at the 1893 World's Columbian Exposition in Chicago and published in the *Journal of American Folklore* the following year.

Christensen believed she should use the profits from the sale of her book on behalf of African Americans. Starting with a modest sum, she worked with other Whites and Blacks to found the Port Royal Agricultural School for African Americans in 1902. Christensen was also an early advocate of women's suffrage, temperance, and socialism.

Monica M. Tetzlaff

Christeson, Robert Perry (1911–1992)

Fiddler, fiddle-tune collector, and scholar. Christeson was born in Dixon, Pulaski County, Missouri, at a point in time and space, as he noted, in which old-time fiddling and square dancing flourished and were integral components of social life. He was drawn to the fiddle as a young boy, and as a teenager he schooled himself in the characteristics of Missouri old-time fiddling by attending dances in Dixon and surrounding communities.

After working his way through the University of Missouri in Columbia, Christeson worked as an assistant county agent, county agent, and a resettlement administrator, and in other offices in northeast and southeast Missouri and the Ozarks region, learning about fiddling styles in different areas of the state. Service in the U.S. Army during World War II and as a statistician in the Livestock Reporting Section of the U.S. Department of Agriculture took him away from Missouri for almost three decades, but at every opportunity he returned to his study of Missouri fiddle music. He began his historic field collection in 1948 by recording Bill Driver, a black fiddler he had first heard two decades before.

In 1970 Christeson returned to his home state and settled in Auxvasse in Callaway County. His retirement years were devoted to preparing his fiddle-tune collection for publication and promoting old-time Missouri fiddling. Both his first volume of fiddle tunes, accompanied by an album of forty-one field recordings, and the second volume were highly praised for the quality of the editing and the significance of the material.

Although reluctant to play his fiddle unless he felt up to his own exacting standard, Christeson shared his enthusiasm and knowledge at a number of festivals and workshops during the 1970s and 1980s. His work as collector, old-time fiddler, and scholar was largely responsible for the renaissance of old-time Missouri fiddling that has occurred since the mid-1980s. Toward the end of his life, he participated in the production of *Now There's a Good Tune,* the award-winning album in the Masters of Missouri Fiddling

Series published at the University of Missouri.
Rebecca B. Schroeder

References

Christeson, Robert Perry, ed. 1973. *The Old-Time Fiddler's Repertory.* Vol. 1. Columbia: University of Missouri Press.

———, ed. 1976. *The Old-Time Fiddler's Repertory.* Historic Field Recordings of Forty-One Traditional Tunes, with Commentary by R.P. Christeson. Columbia: University of Missouri Press.

———, ed. 1984. *The Old-Time Fiddler's Repertory.* Vol. 2. Columbia: University of Missouri Press.

Christmas

Christian holy day and secular holiday. The early Christian church was ambivalent about celebrating the birth of Jesus. Some church leaders, in fact, disapproved of acknowledging the occasion at all. Moreover, since canonical accounts do not

Labels for Christmas presents. Used in Lake Worth, Florida, in the 1930s. Collection J. W. Love.

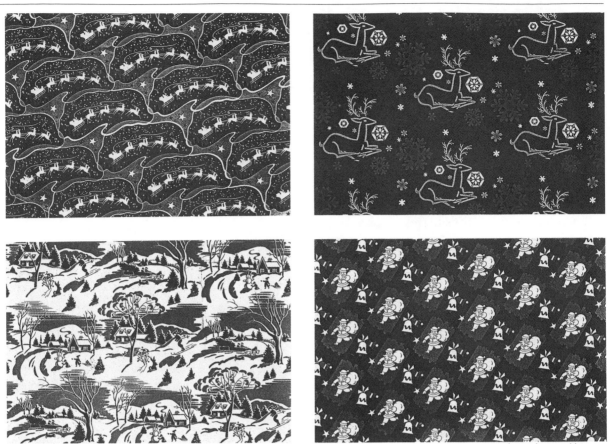

By the end of the Great Depression, the use of special wrappings for Christmas presents was becoming common. Wrapping-paper designs by Donald Jameson, Chicago, 1940s.

specify a date or even season for Jesus' birth, early celebrations occurred at various times. Eastern churches began to focus their observances on January 6, now the Feast of the Epiphany, which commemorates the visit of the Magi to the infant Jesus and is still sometimes referred to as "Little Christmas." The Western church, though, selected December 25 to commemorate the nativity, probably because the date coincided with winter-solstice celebrations. That date has become generally accepted throughout Christendom, except among adherents of the old Julian calendar, who observe Christmas on January 7. For most modern Americans, the Christmas season actually begins several weeks before December 25 and climaxes during the week between that date and New Year's Day.

The first Christmas observance in what is now the United States probably occurred in Jamestown, Virginia, in 1607. The New England Puritans were less hospitable to the holy day, and, in fact, Massachusetts temporarily outlawed its observance. Such regional differences have continued to figure in American Christmas traditions, even though nationwide customs now dominate the celebration. The varied ethnic heritages represented in the United States also contribute to some diversity in American Christmas festivities.

That Christmas has been recognized as a holiday by federal and state governments since the 19th century has contributed to the development of a nationwide Christmas culture, adapted, in part, from specific regional and ethnic traditions.

Customs focus overtly on Christmas' religious significance and on its more generally festive aspects. An example of the former is the nativity scene. Though some courts have ruled that placing nativity scenes in public places violates the constitutional prohibition of government-sponsored religion, many businesses, churches, and residences (either on the front lawn or in a special place indoors) display figures of Jesus' parents, the child himself, animals appropriate to a stable setting, angels, shepherds, and the Magi. Most nativity scenes use statues, but churches may have amateur actors assume the roles for at least a few nights during the Christmas season.

A widely known custom with fewer religious overtones involves the Christmas tree, reputedly brought to America by Hessian soldiers during the Revolutionary War. Using a decorated evergreen as the centerpiece for a home's holiday decorations became widespread during the mid-19th century and received official sanction when President Franklin Pierce erected a Christmas tree in the White House in 1856. Other widely practiced Christmas customs in the United States, religious and secular, include exchanging gifts, identifying Santa Claus as the festive spirit of the season, mailing greeting cards, holding special public programs such as parades, and attending special church services.

Though many have spread to other parts of the country, distinctly regional traditions also continue to characterize American Christmas celebrations. For example, such customs as fox hunts on Christmas morning, the greeting phrase

"Christmas gift," and fireworks developed in the Old South, where the season provided unwonted respite from labor even for slaves. In Louisiana, bonfires continue to be lit on Christmas Eve. In the west Texas community of Anson, an annual Cowboys' Christmas Ball commemorates an event first held in 1885.

In the Southwest, Hispanics and Latinos continue to practice ethnic Christmas customs. They decorate with *luminarias* (lighted candles set in sacks of sand), perform folk plays such as *Los Pastores* that combine traditional piety with broad comedy, and participate in *Las Posadas,* which dramatizes the search by Mary and Joseph for shelter. Among Germans in Pennsylvania, children have traditionally awaited the arrival of the Belsnickel, a figure who, like the more widely known Santa Claus (probably a Dutch import), brings gifts to those who have behaved themselves. But he also carries a switch to punish the naughty. Ethnic foods figure into Christmas menus. For Italian Americans, the Christmas Eve vigil has required dinners consisting of an odd number of meatless dishes, eel being a special favorite. Italian American bakers also prepare festive cookies such as *biscotti, pignollati,* and *cuccidati* for the holiday season.

National Christmas traditions have replaced some holiday practices that once flourished in regional and ethnic communities. Examples include the mummers' plays, which survived in pockets of British settlement such as the southern Appalachians, and some folk carols. Many communities, though, have begun to revive and preserve distinctive customs to complement the national Christmas culture, which they view as lacking in spirituality and oriented toward material consumption.

William M. Clements

References

Barnett, James H. 1954. *The American Christmas: A Study in National Culture.* New York: Macmillan.

Flynn, Tom. 1993. *The Trouble with Christmas.* Buffalo, NY: Prometheus.

Golby, J.M., and A.W. Purdue. 1986. *The Making of the Modern Christmas.* Athens: University of Georgia Press.

Kane, Harnett T. 1958. *The Southern Christmas Book: The Full Story from Earliest Times to the Present: People, Customs, Conviviality, Carols, Cooking.* New York: David McKay.

Samuelson, Sue. 1982. *Christmas: An Annotated Bibliography.* New York: Garland.

See also Solstices, Summer and Winter

City Lore

New York Center for Urban Folk Culture. City Lore is the first organization in the United States dedicated specifically to the documentation, preservation, and presentation of urban folk culture. The organization had its genesis in 1978 when a group of New York City-based folklorists founded the New York City chapter of the New York Folklore Society and in the following years sponsored a series of conferences on urban culture:

The Folklore of New York City (1979), *The Folklore of Urban Public Spaces* (1980), and *The Folk Culture of the Bronx* (1981).

In 1986 Steven Zeitlin, then president of the chapter, worked to incorporate the group under the name *City Lore,* and he became its first director; Barbara Kirshenblatt-Gimblett became the first board president. Unlike the statewide folklore society from which it emerged, City Lore had the mission to document urban culture exclusively. In exhibitions such as *City Play* and *"Welcome to Your Second Home": New York City's Ethnic Social Clubs,* the organization has explored a number of themes characteristic of the urban environment. These themes, some of which were originally mapped out by Kirshenblatt-Gimblett in her essay "The Future of Folklore Studies in America: The Urban Frontier," include the folk imprint on the built environment, customizing mass culture, and the process of traditionalizing as it continually transforms urban cultures.

City Lore is conceived as a collaborative effort through which folklorists, anthropologists, historians, and filmmakers apply for grants and develop projects on urban folk culture and cultural history. It has explored urban phenomena such as graffiti, New York's memorial walls, the history and culture of Coney Island, lawn shrines, city-based gospel music, Christmas lights, and urban pageantry, including the Italian *giglio* celebration and the West Indian Carnival. City Lore advocates for endangered local establishments and cultural sites crucial to their communities; houses a leading photographic archive of urban ethnic culture, primarily by photographer Martha Cooper; sponsors the annual City Lore Festival of Folk Cultural Film and Video, a major showcase for films on American folklore and folklife; honors grass-roots contributions to folk culture with the People's Hall of Fame awards; and has taken a leading role in folk arts and education, organizing the conference "Folk Arts in the Classroom" for the National Endowment for the Arts in 1993.

City Lore is located at 72 East First Street, New York, New York 10003; its telephone number is 212–529–1955.

Steven Zeitlin

See also Education, Folklife in; Film and Folklore; Urban Folklore

Civil War

War between the Union (North) and Confederacy (South), 1861–1865. Traditional processes, genres, and contexts of folkloric creativity arose out of the American Civil War, or "War between the States," experience. Songs like "Dixie," legends and family narratives, and commemorative forms have left their mark on American folk culture to the present day. An event as powerfully definitive as the American Civil War is bound to make an enormous impact on a people's expressive culture. In the Civil War period, folk expressive traditions were richly intertwined with popular literate traditions of the day. This is particularly true in the area of music but also holds for narrative and verbal art.

The musical culture of the Civil War period was strong and varied. In this era before the age of mechanical reproduction, the majority of people engaged in music making. People drew both from the continuing unwritten folk musical traditions they were part of and also from the popular music of the day with its lively sheet-music and broadside industry. What people actually sang, played, and danced to was a blend from these sources.

Probably the most famous songs to come out of the war were the rallying songs and anthems of the conflict; "Dixie," "The Bonnie Blue Flag," "John Brown's Body," "Maryland, My Maryland," "Marching through Georgia," and "The Battle Cry of Freedom" are some of the best known. All of these songs were original compositions (often based on traditional melodies) that were quickly embraced by participants, who modified and changed the words to better express their perspectives on the situations they found themselves in. Thus, Union soldiers sang "Northern" versions of "Dixie," and Southern women sang an adaptation of "The Bonnie Blue Flag" called "The Homespun Dress" that expressed the hardships of the time from a woman's perspective and has remained popular in the folk tradition.

The rival army camps were fertile grounds for folkloric musical creativity. "All Quiet along the Potomac," "Lorena," "When Johnny Comes Marching Home Again," "Home Sweet Home," "Tenting on the Old Camp Ground," and other tragic and sentimental songs were widely sung. Other songs had less serious themes, including the humorous "Goober Peas" and the drinking song "Drink It Down." Glee clubs, impromptu string bands, minstrel troupes, and military brass bands performed regularly in the camps. The routines of camp life, reveille, dinner calls, sick calls and musters were all subject to parody and witty musical embellishment. In the Northern Army, the different ethnic groups such as Germans, Italians, and Irish contributed to the musical mix with songs from their own traditions.

The war also proved to be a rich source of material for the Anglo American ballad tradition. Several ballads have been collected that recount aspects of the naval action surrounding the *Monitor* and the *Merrimac.* "The Battle of Shiloh" adapts a traditional British ballad, "The Heights of Alma," to comment on the glories and horrors of that engagement. "Fare You Well My Darling" recounts the sad farewell of a soldier from his wife.

For Black Americans, the war had a different significance than for their White counterparts. In the Black tradition, the Civil War stood as a redemptive moment, the long awaited call to freedom. This is humorously marked in a line from an improvised worksong recorded by anti-slave activists in Port Royal, South Carolina: "De Northmen Dey's Got Massa Now, Glory Hallelujah." For Blacks, narratives focused on emancipation and the countless scenes at the end of the war when their freedom was announced. In dozens of oral histories of former slaves, this scene is recounted and signals a turning point in both collective and personal history.

For White participants, oral forms were more varied, reflecting a greater range of experiences. The camps once again were the point of origin of much of this folklore. Although much of the folk humor of the war remains undocumented because of the sensibilities of this period, a good deal remains, found in the many letters, diaries, and reminiscences that were written. "Here's your mule" became a standard joke in the Southern camps, a greeting whose origin lies in the wit of a soldier who pointed out a bedraggled comrade in his tent to another soldier searching for his animal. Soldiers "fined" each other "muggins," bottles of whiskey, for making cracks about the privations of camp life.

The process of legend dissemination began to be greatly influenced by print media in this period. Colorful incidents focusing on the great leaders of the period—Lincoln, Lee, Grant, Sherman, Stuart, McLellan—were circulated orally in the camps and picked up on by reporters, who further embellished them and broadcast them to the larger public where again these stories were retold. In the context of the camps, where spare time, lack of solid information, and anxiety intermingled, rumors enjoyed a vigorous life. Assassination plots, peace, and foreign intervention were favorite topics of speculation.

Particularly in the regions where the war was fought, legends have persisted about incidents of the war. Personal-experience narratives became family narratives and legends fueled by the powerful themes of ambivalence of loyalty, personal hardships, and acts of courage. Many of these narratives focus on the strength of women in the face of the horrors and injustice of war. A common theme of these stories is the bravery or guile of household members responding to raiders and bushwhackers. Many a great aunt has been celebrated for taking the law into her own hands at the rough treatment her household received.

Along with these verbal forms, the memory and meaning of the war continued in other genres. For Blacks coming from the east Texas area, Juneteenth celebrations are important commemorations of emancipation. Veterans of the war donned their uniforms, marched in parades, and encamped at battlefields on important holidays and anniversaries of battles. Civil War reenacting, a recent form, provides opportunities for folkloric creativity and has become a tradition in its own right, interacting with preserved spaces, history education, movies, and video documentaries like Ken Burns' PBS (Public Broadcasting System) series *The Civil War* to keep the war alive as part of the national imagination. Finally, the Confederate battle flag has become a powerfully contested symbol reflecting the continuing struggles for cultural definition in contemporary society.

Rory P.B. Turner

References

Anderson, Jay. 1984. *Time Machines: The World of Living History.* Nashville: American Association for State and Local History.

Botkin, Benjamin A. 1960. *A Civil War Treasury of Tales, Legends, and Folklore.* New York: Random House.

Heeps, Willard Allison. 1960. *The Singing Sixties: The Spirit of the Civil War Days Drawn from the Music of the Times.* Norman: University of Oklahoma Press.

Silber, Irwin. 1960. *Songs of the Civil War.* New York: Columbia University Press.

Turner, Rory P.B. 1990. Bloodless Battles: The Civil War Reenacted. *TDR* (Tulane Drama Review) 34:123–136.

Wiggins, William H., Jr. 1982. "They Closed the Town up, Man!": Reflections on the Civic and Political Dimensions of Juneteenth. In *Celebration: Studies in Festivity and Ritual,* ed. Victor Turner. Washington, DC: Smithsonian Institution, pp. 284–295.

Wiley, Bell Irvin. [1943] 1978. *The Life of Johnny Reb: The Common Soldier of the Confederacy.* Baton Rouge: Louisiana State University Press.

Coding in American Folk Culture

Communicating through a set of signals—words, forms, behaviors, signifiers of some kind—that protect the creator from the consequences of openly expressing particular messages. (This specialized definition is distinct from the use of "code" simply to designate the system of language rules through which communication is possible.) Coding occurs in the context of complex audiences, in situations in which some of the audience may be competent to decode the message, but others—including those who might be dangerous—are not competent (or not willing) to do so.

Although coding may be undertaken as play (children's "pig latin," for instance) or to preserve privacy (signals between lovers, or immigrant elders using their mother tongue when children are around), much coding takes place in situations of significant risk. The traditional creations and performances of dominated cultures often contain covert expressions of resistance—ideas, beliefs, experiences, feelings, and attitudes that the dominant culture would find disturbing or threatening if expressed in more overt forms. Slave songs may express a secret wish for freedom; a gay man's conversation may conceal his assertion of sexual preference; a wife's knitting may covertly protest her husband's assumption that his activities are more significant than hers.

Three kinds of coding—explicit, complicit, and implicit—may be distinguished. In cases of explicit coding, the presence of a code is obvious even to those who cannot decipher it—a dangerous matter in situations of great risk. A letter written in cipher, for instance, announces itself as containing a secret, and thus can invite efforts to decode. In situations of complicit coding, however, the existence of a code is concealed from those outside of the coding group. The code and its uses are collectively determined ahead of time (passwords, code names, a sheet hanging on a clothesline to indicate safe passage on the underground railway) or are drawn from esoteric experience and adopted on the spot (a lesbian's naming of a local women's bar; a Jewish American's conversational use of a Yiddish word). Complicit coding is consciously employed among members of a folk group united by a shared culture and a shared sense of threat.

Both explicit and complicit acts of coding are manifestly intentional, undertaken knowingly and purposefully. However, coding need not be deliberate. In the third type, implicit coding, even the existence of a coded message is arguable and may be denied by the creator; not only the message, but coding itself is concealed and may be subconscious.

Implicit coding thus raises complex questions about intentionality and about the interpretations that may be constructed both by the original receiving community and by outside observer-analysts such as folklorists. A woman who sews a quilt patch in which Sunbonnet Sue, a traditional pattern figure representing feminine submissiveness, diligence, and innocence, is swallowed by a snake may dismiss her creation as "just a joke"; inferring from contextual knowledge rather than the quilter's assertion, however, an audience might see an encoded message of feminist resistance to a traditional stereotype. The interpretation of implicit coding often presents a dilemma, since there is neither the signaling of an intention to code nor any open complicity in a coding system; in fact, the performance is meant to pass for an uncoded activity. With careful and respectful scholarship grounded in the specific cultural context of the performance, however, it is feasible to posit at least the possibility that an act of coding has occurred. A context for concealed coding (complicit or implicit) exists when, for a particular individual or folk group, there exists a situation of oppression, dominance, or risk; when there is some kind of opposition to this situation that cannot safely be made explicit; and when there is a community of potential "listeners" from which one would want to protect oneself. However, the identification and interpretation of implicit coding must ultimately remain an act of inference—inference that has potentially serious consequences for individuals and communities and should not be undertaken without care.

The coded status of individual texts and performances will often remain ambiguous, and different audiences may disagree as to their interpretation. Nevertheless, it is possible to designate the following strategies of expression that lend themselves to the complicit or implicit coding of messages:

Appropriation: adapting to the purposes of oppressed culture forms or materials normally associated with the dominant culture (example: Native American "riffs on the White world" through adaptation of traditional beadwork to decorate such popular mainstream items as baseball caps, Bic pens, and Bingo markers).

Juxtaposition: ironic arrangement of texts, artifacts, or performances so that they develop additional, often tendentious, levels of meaning (example: a wife braiding a foot-wiping rug for the front doorway from pieces of her husband's old suits).

Distraction: strategies that drown out, or draw attention away from, the subversive power of a message (examples: singing lyrics expressing fear or protest in a soothing lullaby; "passing" as a member of the mainstream—a gay man in the military, for instance, emulating masculine stereotypes and taking part in "locker room" talk).

Indirection: the many ways in which, as Emily Dickinson put it, one can "tell all the truth but tell it slant." Perhaps the most common strategy of coding, indirection includes metaphor, impersonation, hedging, and metonymy (examples: Mexican American women telling legends of vaginal serpents as metaphoric expressions of sexual fears; Kentucky mountain women singing traditional Anglo American ballads as impersonal lessons about how to outsmart men; lesbians making metonymic inquiries about the sexual orientation of strangers by asking if they have been to the Michigan Women's Music Festival).

Trivialization or *Minimalization*: strategies that understate, minimize, or "normalize" the subversive power of a message, sometimes by employing forms that the dominant culture considers to be unimportant, innocuous, or irrelevant (Examples: telling a joke to express criticism; downplaying the seriousness of conversation by giving it a traditionally disparaging label, such as "gossip," or "woman-talk").

Incompetence: expressing resistance to the dominant culture's expectations by claiming or demonstrating incompetence at activities conventionally associated with one's oppressed culture; associated with underclasses of workers whose labor power is being exploited (Example: a woman claiming she "can't cook").

Joan N. Radner

References

Babcock, Barbara, ed. 1978. *The Reversible World: Symbolic Inversion in Art and Society.* Ithaca, NY: Cornell University Press.

Gates, Henry Louis, Jr. 1988. *The Signifying Monkey: A Theory of Afro-American Literary Criticism.* New York: Oxford University Press.

Levine, Lawrence W. 1977. *Black Culture and Black Consciousness: Afro-American Folk Thought from Slavery to Freedom.* New York: Oxford University Press.

Radner, Joan Newlon, ed. 1993. *Feminist Messages: Coding in Women's Folk Culture.* Urbana and Chicago: University of Illinois Press.

See also Children; Gay Men; Lesbians; Semiotic Approach; Social Protest in Folklore

Cold War

Period of an incessant nuclear-arms race between the United States and the Soviet Union. The detonation of atomic bombs over Hiroshima and Nagasaki in Japan in August 1945 froze international politics into what became known as the Cold War. The post–World War II era presented the everyday reality of nuclear warfare and ushered in decades of terror, tension, and anxiety that permeated American popular culture and folklore. A policy of secrecy encouraged rumors and legends.

Although sparked by the A-bomb, the Cold War matured in the 1950s with the outbreak of the nonnuclear Korean War. During this decade, an "Iron Curtain" separated East Europe from the democratic West. Political crises in Hungary, the Suez, and Lebanon, as well as the erection of the Berlin Wall, escalated the Cold War, and possibilities of World War III loomed ominously.

Atomic weaponry symbolized the Cold War era. Both the United States and the Soviet Union stockpiled thousands of intercontinental missiles, prepared to launch them in a policy of immediate massive retaliation. Sophisticated technology, including radar, computers, and nuclear-powered submarines, complemented the weaponry.

Cold War culture, dominated by technological-oriented themes, stressed dehumanization, surrealism, alienation of individuals, and the absurdity of a military government with too much power. Good versus evil permeated the lore of the postwar period.

In what has been called the "folklore of capitalism," Americans became a consumer society, enjoying the affluence of the 1950s. Ranch houses, suburbs, and education financed by the GI Bill symbolized the mythic "American Dream" of prosperity, security, and a perfect society. The baby boom assured the demographics considered necessary for supremacy in the world.

Americans clung to past traditions to counter insecurities and uncertainties; for example, a major weapon systems, the Minuteman missle, were named after historical precedents. Americans embraced conformity, while in the Soviet Union a propagandistic pseudofolklore, praising the Soviet government and Joseph Stalin, disseminated official Communist ideology.

Many Cold War stories involved military themes, as civilians pondered such questions as whether the United States would be invaded by Cuban dictator Fidel Castro after the Bay of Pigs fiasco. The capture by the Soviets of U2 pilot Gary Powers in 1960 spurred rumors about America's spy-plane capability. The secrecy of the American military program led to exaggerated speculations about the types and size of weaponry both sides possessed.

Nuclear consciousness pervaded American folk popular culture. Radioactive warning signs, the silhouette of Three Mile Island, and pictures of mushroom clouds represented the hysteria of the Atomic Age. Bartenders concocted atomic cocktails, and children purchased atomic rings and played A-bomb games on the playground. Popular magazines printed cartoons and jokes about the bomb, and Cold War slang terms such as "Ground Zero," "bikini," and "Catch-22" entered American jargon.

Examples of "Grandma's Pantry," as the home bomb shelters were sometimes termed, proliferated. The Soviet Union's detonation of an atomic bomb in 1957 spurred doomsday-oriented stories in which the threat of nuclear war was often compared to an attack by carnivorous animals. Folktale themes stressed unbeatable power not peaceful coexistence. The mythical red button and the telephone hotline in the president's office became the focal point of holocaust scenarios, especially during the 1962 Cuban missile crisis. Rumors of secret underground bomb shelters in the Pentagon and the White House suggested that the government would abandon the common people. Atomic monsters, whether mutations or metaphorical imagery, represented the fears of the Nuclear Age.

It might be said that aspects of folk culture in the 1960s became the counterculture, incorporating peace signs, psychedelic art, hippie clothes, and protest songs that were more or less "folk." Antiwar protests, sit-ins, and the free-speech movement fought authority. The Vietnamese War's folk culture included decals and bumper stickers, depicting peace symbols and American flags, either placed with respect on construction helmets or worn on the seat of the pants by war protesters. This war for self-determination entered the American consciousness by being shown on television daily, and, of course, the soldiers fighting in Vietnam developed their own brand of wartime folklore.

The Camelot administration of President John F. Kennedy (1961–1963), who admonished Americans to discover "what you can do for your country," introduced new themes of lore, and conspiracy theories abounded to explain the president's assassination in November 1963 as well as the deaths of other prominent people, including actress Marilyn Monroe. Activism and the social programs of the 1960s War on Poverty inspired new bohemian and beatnik folk culture by singers thought of by the public as traditional folk singers, such as Joan Baez.

The 1957 Soviet Sputnik satellite spurred the creation of NASA (National Aeronautics and Space Administration) and the American effort to explore space. The United States landed men on the moon, a fact disputed by some who claim the television footage was actually filmed secretly on earth. The Space Age encouraged numerous UFO (unidentified flying object) sightings and movies, and even defense programs adopted such pop-cult space themes as "Star Wars."

During Cold War flare-ups in the 1970s and 1980s, nostalgia for the 1950s revived folklore from that period, but the later decades reintroduced affluence, materialism, and narcissism, with an accompanying body of modern folklore. Jokes and anecdotes about Watergate, the "third-rate burglary" that led to the impeachment of President Richard M. Nixon in 1974, materialized at office water coolers. Legends of folk saints, miracles, and answered prayers resurfaced as Middle East conflicts and terrorism brought new dimensions to the Cold War. Yellow ribbons represented Americans anxiously awaiting the return of loved ones held hostage in Iran or fighting in the Gulf War in 1991, and red ribbons symbolized the loss of murdered children and also AIDS victims. POW-MIA ("prisoner of war" or "missing in action") bracelets signified the hope that rumors of lost prisoners in Asia being located were true.

During the period of the Cold War, graffiti painted on the Berlin Wall and stories about East-to-West escapes persisted as expressions of resistance, but with the fall of the Berlin Wall in 1989 and the collapse of the Soviet Union, the Cold War thawed considerably, having established a folklore tradition to initiate the 21st century.

Elizabeth D. Schafer

References

Boyer, Paul. 1985. *By the Bomb's Early Light: American Thought and Culture at the Dawn of the Atomic Age.* New York: Pantheon.

Lipsitz, George. 1981. *Class and Culture in Cold War America: "A Rainbow at Midnight."* New York: Praeger.

Mieder, Wolfgang. 1990. "It's Five Minutes to Twelve": Folklore and Saving Life on Earth. *International Folklore Review: Folklore Studies from Overseas* 7:10–21.

Santino, Jack. 1992. Yellow Ribbons and Seasonal Flags: The Folk Assemblage of War. *Journal of American Folklore* 105:19–33.

Whitfield, Stephen J. 1991. *The Culture of the Cold War.* Baltimore: Johns Hopkins University Press.

See also Nuclear Lore

Columbus Day

October 12, a legal holiday in most of the United States, commemorating the landing of Christopher Columbus in the Bahamas in 1492; now usually observed on the second Monday of October. Christopher Columbus was rarely mentioned in American chronicles before the era of the American Revolution. Then between 1775 and 1792, he emerged as a full-fledged American hero, the central figure in a national-origin myth that stressed America's separateness from Europe and the expansive future that seemed open to the "new and rising empire" of the United States. American nationalists of the 1790s created the Columbus Day observance, erected the first Columbus monuments, and scattered the admiral's name in both its latinized and feminized forms across the national map. Succeeding generations embedded his story in admiring biographies and in schoolbooks and enshrined it in poetry and art. Most schoolchildren know the rhyme, "In fourteen hundred and ninety-two / Columbus sailed the ocean blue."

The fact that Columbus never set foot in North America and died unaware of its existence meant that he was not identified with any one state or section of the country. This made him all the more suitable as a symbol of the revolutionary generation's aspiration to national unity and continental expansion. The late 19th century saw the emergence of Columbus as a hero of cultural pluralism, as Irish Catholics and Italian Americans emphasized religious and ethnic dimensions in Columbus' story that earlier generations of Yankee admirers had more or less overlooked. Italian Americans took the lead in this work, but they had important assistance from the Knights of Columbus, an Irish Catholic fraternal organization founded in New England and renamed in Columbus' honor in 1882, and from the "Americanist" wing of the nation's Roman Catholic hierarchy, bishops who worked to reform the American church and to promote the church as an assimilating agency training immigrants for democratic citizenship. As a result, the celebration of ethnicity became the dominant theme in the Columbian tradition during the 20th century.

Italians, as is well known, did not bring national, but rather regional, identities to the Americas, and so it was the Ligurians among them who began the refashioning of Columbian traditions. First in New York (1866) and then in San Francisco (1869), Ligurian immigrants rallied their *connazionali* to the process of "italianizing" the Yankee Columbus Day, turning it from an occasion of solemn assemblies and oratory into a festival of parades and banquets. Columbus became an ethnic hero—and his holiday an amalgam of a tra-

Joseph Cervetto, Jr., plays Columbus at the annual Columbus Landing Ceremony. Aquatic Park, San Francisco, California, 1989. Photo Ken Light. American Folklife Center.

ditional Italian Saint's Day festival and an Anglo American patriotic ceremony. For an immigrant community fragmented by class, region, dialect, and personal and political rivalries, Columbus Day became a means of creating a pan-Italian identity. The annual parades and the once-in-a-lifetime drive to raise money to erect a Columbus statue became fixtures of Italian American communities.

Angelo Noce, a Ligurian who served as the Italian consul first in San Francisco and later in Denver, is credited with winning the first establishment of Columbus Day as an official holiday, in 1907 in Colorado. The long lists of sponsoring oraganizations typically inscribed on Columbus statues testifies to the tenuous character of the unity that the parades and statues achieved, but as Italian Americans prospered, and their leaders gained political and economic influence, Columbus Day became a national holiday, first by presidential proclamation (1934), then by congressional action (1968; effective 1971), which changed the holiday from October 12 to the second Monday in October. The format of the observance—parades, speeches, banquets, and ceremonies focused on Columbus statues—remained the same, but with declining public participation or interest as the fifth Columbian centenary approached in 1992.

The quincentenary highlighted rival ethnic claims to Columbus Day. In New York, Puerto Ricans and other Hispanics had begun celebrating October 12, in common with the rest of Latin America, as *El Dia de la Raza*. In 1988 Congress expanded "Hispanic Heritage Month," traditionally anchored on the Mexican national holiday of September 15, into mid-October, taking in Columbus Day

as a gesture to Hispanics of non-Mexican descent. No specific rituals were associated with the movement, although cities with large Hispanic populations, such as Miami and San Antonio, established festivals focused on October 12 and/or the federal holiday. In San Francisco, the traditional Columbus Day ceremonies expanded to take in Asian Americans, who had, in fact, come to outnumber Italian Americans in the traditionally "Italian" North Beach neighborhood. Noting the ethnic diversity of the occasion, the *San Francisco Chronicle* commented in 1984 that the Columbus Day parade in that city had become as "Italian as guacamole pizza."

The most provocative challenge to the celebratory character of Columbus Day came from Native Americans, or from Whites claiming to speak for them. In 1976, for example, student protesters from Stanford University disrupted the mock landing of Columbus in San Francisco's Aquatic Park, a ritual that dated back to the days when the "discoverer" would come ashore from an immigrant fishing boat. The fear of further disruption led the organizers of the mock landing to abandon the practice of having Whites dressed as Indians welcome Columbus, in favor of hiring Native Americans from California and later from Mexico to play this role. After demonstrators prevented the landing altogether in 1992, the ritual was abandoned. Native American protests in other cities have been characterized by inventive desecrations of Columbus statues or by counterparades that identify Columbus as the agent of enslavement and genocide.

It remains to be seen whether these new ethnic challenges will transform Columbus Day as fully as Italian Americans did a century ago. In 1993 San Francisco's Columbus Day parade attracted little attention, notwithstanding that the day officially had become *El Dia de la Raza* / Day of Concern for Indigenous People." Although some voices have been raised in favor of abandoning the holiday altogether, it seems more likely that the holiday will evolve in the direction of consumerism, not ethnicity. If one of the items consumed on Columbus Day is ethnic food, whether of Hispanic or Italian origin, that will serve merely to distinguish the holiday from other similar observances such as Labor Day, Memorial Day, or Presidents' Day.

John Alexander Williams

References

Bushman, Claudia. 1992. *America Discovers Columbus: How an Italian Explorer Became an American Hero.* Durham, NH: University Press of New England.

Speroni, Charles. 1948. The Development of the Columbus Day Pageant of San Francisco. *Western Folklore* 7:325–335.

———. 1955. California Fishermen's Festivals. *Western Folklore* 15:77–83.

Williams, John Alexander. 1993. The Columbus Complex. In *Old Ties and New Attachments: Italian American Folklife in the West,* ed. David Taylor and John Alexander Williams. Washington, DC: American Folklife Center.

Combs, Josiah H. (1886–1960)

Professor of modern languages and folklorist with special interest in Appalachian dialect and folk music. Combs was born January 2, 1886, at Hazard, Perry County, Kentucky, and grew up in a large singing family in nearby Hindman in Knott County. In 1902, when Combs was sixteen years old, he attended the newly established Hindman Settlement School. The school's founder, Katherine Pettit, took an interest in local balladry, and she noted a number of songs from the young Combs. These were eventually forwarded to Harvard University scholar George Lyman Kittredge, who included them in an article in the *Journal of American Folklore* in 1907. Thus, Combs contributed indirectly to one of the earliest published collections of folksongs from the Southern Uplands.

In 1905 Combs entered Transylvania University in Lexington, Kentucky. His contact there with Dr. Hubert Shearin led to joint publication of *A Syllabus of Kentucky Folk-Songs* (1911). This was followed by *The Kentucky Highlanders from a Native Mountaineer's Viewpoint* (1913), and in 1915 Combs edited an anthology of Kentucky poetry.

From 1911 to 1918, Combs taught languages and literature at high schools and colleges in Kentucky, Tennessee, Virginia, and Oklahoma. He also found opportunities to perform Kentucky folk music for sophisticated city audiences, using an Appalachian-plucked dulcimer to accompany his lecture-recitals.

Military service in World War I took Combs to Czechoslovakia (1920–1921) after which he returned to the United States to teach French and Spanish at West Virginia University (1922–1924). He next studied at the Sorbonne in Paris, taking his Ph.D. summa cum laude in 1925 with a dissertation entitled *Folk-Songs du Midi des États-Unis.*

Combs has most often been associated with Kentucky folksong study, yet he was equally passionate about the study of language. His facility with Greek, Latin, French, Spanish, Italian, German, Old English, and Middle English was supplemented by an extensive knowledge of Old and Middle English literature. He was especially interested in showing connections between folk speech in America and earlier English forms, and he was an enthusiastic collector of locally created words and expressions.

Combs eventually settled in Forth Worth, Texas, to teach at Texas Christian University. Although he maintained his interests in folk music, languages, and literature, he was largely outside the ken of folklorists until Wilgus contacted him in the late 1950s. Unfortunately, Combs died suddenly on June 2, 1960, only a few days before Wilgus was to visit him to tape record the tunes of items in Combs' ballad collection. Subsequently, Wilgus edited a long overdue English translation of *Folk-Songs du Midi des États-Unis* (Folk-Songs of the Southern United States), which apeared in the American Folklore Society's Special Series in 1967.

Combs was an individual whose insights reflected both the immediacy of his family roots and the mediating distance of scholarly analysis. As Wilgus later pointed out, Combs tended to be both defensive and self-critical when discussing his native Appalachian region. His scholarship reflected "sturdy common sense along with his intimate knowledge of . . . folk culture."

Combs is buried at Fort Sam Houston National Cemetery in San Antonio, Texas, and his ballad collection is housed at Berea College in Kentucky as part of the papers of D.K. Wilgus.

Stephen Green

References
Combs, Josiah H. [1925] 1967. *Folk-Songs of the Southern United States*, ed. D.K. Wilgus. American Folklore Society Special Series. Austin: University of Texas Press.

———. 1960. The Highlander's Music. *Kentucky Folklore Record* 6:108–122.

Combs, Josiah, and Hubert Shearin. 1911. *A Syllabus of Kentucky Folk-Songs.* Lexington, KY: Transylvania.

Kahn, Ed. 1960. Josiah H. Combs, 1886–1960. *Kentucky Folklore Record* 6:101–103.

Wilgus, D.K. 1957. Leaders of Kentucky Folklore: Josiah H. Combs. *Kentucky Folklore Record* 3:67–69.

———. 1960. The Josiah H. Combs Collection of Songs and Rhymes. *Kentucky Folklore Record* 6:125–136.

Comparative Approach

The practice of comparing substantial numbers of cognate items of folklore to establish their similarities, differences, and probable course of development. Comparison has always been characteristic of folklore studies. Whether we consider the interest in foreign cultures that flourished during the Renaissance, the citation of parallel texts beginning with the Grimm brothers, the interest in cultural evolution championed by late-19th-century anthropologists, or the stemmatic model of the historic-geographic method to be the beginning of "modern" folklore scholarship, we find that more or less rigorous comparison has always been essential. Only through careful comparisons of superficially similar traditional forms can the relative contributions of replication and variation, or the likelihood of independent origins (polygenesis), be assessed. In addition, comparison of traditions in adjacent cultures can identify particular developments that have occurred in each culture or subculture.

Anthropologists have argued that, because comparison is essential to human thought, there is no single comparative approach (Lewis 1970; cf. Boas 1940:270–280). Folklore does not suffer from this ambiguity. Here, "comparative" is a technical term, borrowed from philology, as evidenced in such phrases as Antti Aarne's title *Leitfaden der vergleichenden Märchenforschung* (Guide to Comparative Folktale Study, [1913]). Insofar as they are practicing the comparative method, folklorists restrict their comparisons to variants of a single tradition: Their purpose is to define that tradition.

The Historic-Geographic Method. The study of Indo-European linguistics began in 1786 when Sir William Jones established the relationship of Sanskrit to Greek and Latin. On the basis of the similarities among these languages, a parent language was inferred. The simplicity and objectivity of this approach made it seem both suitable and desirable for the reconstruction of early forms of oral traditions.

Intrigued by work of Elias Lönnrot, who "reconstructed" the Finnish epic *The Kalevala* from ballads and songs, Julius Krohn began, in the latter part of the 19th century, to codify procedures for reconstructing oral traditions based on philological principles: The variant texts should be analyzed to see how they led back to a single original text (in German, the *Urform;* in English, the "archetype"). At this time, scholars were arguing about the diffusion of traditional literary forms, including folktales: Some believed that it was primarily prehistorical, while others thought that most of it occurred during the Middle Ages. Julius' son Kaarle Krohn set out to test the idea that European folktales came from India in historical times by reconstructing the original forms of individual tales and, at the same time, determining their original homes and their paths of migration. His method was called historic-geographic because early (literary) variants are arranged historically and later (oral) variants are grouped geographically, in order to achieve the reconstruction as objectively as possible. Ideally, the versions of the tale will fall into a stemmatic pattern—all of the later forms of the tale can be seen to have developed from the hypothetical original form. This stemmatic pattern is analogous to that used by philologists to reconstruct the Indo-European language.

This method works very well for traditions, like language, that change slowly or in regular patterns. It is most useful for folktales that are relatively stable, like "The Clever Peasant Girl" (AT 875), "The King and the Abbot" (AT 922), and "The Kind and Unkind Girls" (AT 480). For tales that are subject to more variation, the method is more difficult to use. The original form of the tale is less obvious, and may even be the subject of a debate. Kaarle Krohn's *Übersicht über einige Resultate der Märchenforschung* (Survey of Some Results of Folktale Study) (1931) offers an alternative historical development for several tales. Nevertheless, the fact that scholars using the method assembled large numbers of variants and paid careful attention to their contents advanced the respectability of folklore studies as an academic discipline.

The American folklorist Stith Thompson contributed greatly to the success of the historic-geographic method. His *Motif Index* (1995) and his revisions of Aarne's *The Types of the Folktale* (Aarne and Thompson 1964) helped considerably to make the large numbers of variants necessary for historic-geographic studies easily available. Since this classification began with European tales, and since the Americas are peripheral regions of European culture, folklorists studying American folktales have not taken full advantage of the possibilities the method offers. Yet, regardless of whether it is able to establish an archetype for a particular tale, the method often discovers features that are unique to particular regions. Thus, the tale "The Taming of the Shrew" (AT 901) has developed an American joke form (Brunvand 1991:213–228).

Two other genres to which the historic-geographic method has been applied successfully are the ballad and the riddle. Following Svend Grundtvig's work on Danish ballads *(Dan-*

marks gamle Folkeviser, beginning in 1853), Francis James Child classified English ballads, adding notes that are useful even for tale studies. Neither of these scholars attempted the rigorous laying out of variants and careful reconstruction of the original text that Krohn advocated, but they did comment on the relationships among their texts, noting which were derived from which. Thus, these notes were the foundation of 20th-century historic-geographic ballad studies (Taylor 1927–1928). In addition to his many historic-geographic studies of folktales, Aarne wrote several historic-geographic studies of riddles, which are interesting because they identify regional characteristics.

The method depends on the scholar's ability to find variants. Genres that have defied indexing, such as legend, where the texts are too variable, are difficult if not impossible to study in this way. In the case of simple material, such as folk beliefs and single narrative motifs, each item is too brief to permit conclusions about its history. Based as it is on the idea of texts being diffused from a single place of origin, generally by land routes through territory inhabited by settled populations, the method is not suitable for Old World traditions brought to America by immigrants from different countries. In this case, Old World ethnic origins, not the location in America, may be the appropriate criteria for the arrangement of variants. Nor is the method suitable for modern traditions that are carried by national or international media, or even in letters or telephone conversations; in such cases, geography is irrelevant to the development of the item.

The Comparative Approach in America. While the American folklorists Thompson and Archer Taylor were prominent in the development of the indexes that are essential to the historic-geographic method, less-stringent comparative approaches have characterized the study of folklore in America. For example, annotators of folktales, such as Herbert Halpert and Leonard Roberts, in comparing American variants to their European counterparts, have occasionally remarked on peculiarly American alterations to certain tales.

American ballads and proverbs have received more attention. For her comparative study of "The Maid Freed from the Gallows," Eleanor Long (1971) found that grouping the texts according to their verbal correspondences was more helpful than using their places of origin. Tristram Potter Coffin (1977) noticed that American ballads tend to be shorter and more lyrical than their British antecedents. They concentrate on the climax of the story and replace some of the supernatural motifs with rationalistic ones. Ballads composed in America have also been cataloged according to story types (Laws 1964), which has aroused some opposition from those who believe that indexing ballad themes would be more effective (Wilgus 1970). Since, for practical reasons, folklore indexes must be made before each entry can have been thoroughly studied, they often separate items that are, in fact, interconnected. While such lapses do not necessarily prevent the indexes from leading to the relevant material, they make them cumbersome and they are often considered defects.

Taylor was instrumental in advancing proverb scholarship to the point where comparative studies (both American and international) could be accomplished. American proverbs have been collected more thoroughly from literary sources than from oral ones. Comparative studies show that some become more stylized with time, evolving into forms with more pronounced poetic features such as rhythm, rhyme, and well-defined structure (Taylor 1975; Mieder 1987:157–228).

Taylor, in his *English Riddles from Oral Tradition* (1951), annotated English (including Anglo American) riddles with references not only from Europe but also from other parts of the world; however, subsequent studies of riddles have been more interested in their structures and functions than in their types and variations. Finding-lists of children's rhymes (Abrahams 1969; Abrahams and Rankin 1980) provide access to that material. In the case of superstitions, however, indexing has been frustrated by the variety of combinations of motifs. Many superstitions are spread rather evenly throughout the country rather than confined to particular regions.

In the realm of material culture, comparative research has managed to do well even in the absence of indexes. Comparisons of artifacts reveal cultural regions within the United States, sometimes showing how European forms were altered as they were adapted to the requirements and fashions of America (Glassie 1968).

For studies of oral tradition of preliterate cultures, a geographic arrangement of the material is often feasible. Franz Boas took such an approach to the study of Native American folklore. He was interested in the regions that such studies reveal and in the borrowing, lending, and adaptation of culture elements. Thompson (1965) followed up his early interest in Native American folktales by using the geographic pattern of one tale to determine its history, as a test case to prove that the historic-geographic method would indeed work even without old variants.

The comparative approach has been important in the study of the origins of African American folklore. Melville Jean Herskovits, following Boas' example, pursued what he called "the comparative study of cultures within a given historic stream" (Herskovits 1956:141), as opposed to the global comparative approach of earlier anthropologists such as Tylor and Frazer. Richard M. Dorson (1967) was able to cite European antecedents for many folktales told by African Americans. As more African folktales, and indexes to folktales, have been published, many of those same tales can be seen to have African antecedents as well. If this situation makes it seem as though origins are wherever you look for them, that is not the fault of the comparative method, but rather of the imperfect state of folklore collection and classification.

In the 1920s and 1930s, the historic-geographic method was presented as *the* method of folklore scholarship (Krohn 1971). Its present advocates have come to believe that other approaches can supplement it to good effect. Beginning in the 1960s, it became unfashionable and was quickly overtaken by other methods. Several of these, however, including structuralism (in which a single pattern is found in several different items) and the oral-formulaic approach (in which type-scenes and story types replace motifs and tale types), are derived at least in part from folklore's comparative approach or from its

antecedents or cognates in other disciplines such as linguistics and classics. Also at about the same time, many American folklorists became interested in genres of folklore that had not been indexed: They were too new (such as jokes and toasts) or too variable (such as legends). Since variants could not be located, comparative studies were impossible.

Even so, as long as folklore studies continue, the comparative approach will not become obsolete because tradition can not be defined without careful comparison. While the particular details of traditional items such as folktales and riddles are usually culture specific, more general features are often found in diverse cultures. Thus, the comparative approach is well suited to showing basic, common beliefs and traditions held jointly by people of many different cultures. With it, folklorists can explore both the unity and the diversity of mankind.

Christine Goldberg

References

Aarne, Antti, and Stith Thompson. 1961. *The Types of the Folktale.* FFC 184. Helsinki.

Abrahams, Roger D. 1969. *Jump-Rope Rhymes: A Dictionary.* American Folklore Society Bibliographical and Special Series, Vol. 20. Austin: University of Texas Press.

Abrahams, Roger D., and Lois Rankin. 1980. *Counting-out Rhymes: A Dictionary.* American Folklore Society Bibliographical and Special Series Volume 31. Austin: University of Texas Press.

Boas, Franz. 1940. *Race, Language, and Culture.* New York: Macmillan.

Brunvand, Jan Harold. 1991. *The Taming of the Shrew.* New York: Garland.

Coffin, Tristram Potter. 1977. *The British Traditional Ballad in North America.* rev. ed. with Supplement by Roger deV. Renwick. Austin: University of Texas Press.

Dorson, Richard M. 1967. *American Negro Folktales.* Greenwich, CT: Fawcett.

Glassie, Henry. 1968. *Pattern in the Material Folk Culture of the Eastern United States.* Philadelphia: University of Pennsylvania Press.

Herskovits, Melville J. 1956. On Some Modes of Ethnographic Comparison. *Bijdragen tot de Taal-, Land en Volkenkunde* 112:129–148.

Krohn, Kaarle. 1971. *Folklore Methodology,* trans. Roger L. Welsch. Austin: American Folklore Society, Bibliographical and Special Series, Vol. 21.

Laws, G. Malcolm. 1964. *Native American Balladry.* Folcroft, PA: Folcroft.

Lewis, Oscar. 1970. Comparisons in Cultural Anthropology. In *Anthropological Essays.* New York: Random House, pp. 90–134.

Long, Eleanor. 1971. *"The Maid" and "The Hangman."* Folklore Studies No. 21. Berkeley: University of California Press.

Mieder, Wolfgang. 1987. *Tradition and Innovation in Folk Literature.* Hanover, NH: University Press of New England.

Taylor, Archer. 1927–1928. Precursors of the Finnish Method of Folk-Lore Study. *Modern Philology* 25:481–491.

———. 1975. *Selected Writings on Proverbs,* ed. Wolfgang Mieder. Folklore Fellows Communications No. 216. Helsinki.

Thompson, Stith. 1946. *The Folktale.* New York: Dryden.

———. 1955. *The Motif Index of Folk Literature.* rev. ed. 6 vols. Bloomington: Indiana University Press.

———. 1965. The Star-Husband Tale. In *The Study of Folklore,* ed. Alan Dundes, Englewood Cliffs, NJ: Prentice-Hall, pp. 414–474.

Wilgus, D.K. 1970. A Type-Index of Anglo-American Traditional Narrative Songs. *Journal of the Folklore Institute* 7:161–176.

Computer Folklore

Folklore either about computers and those who use them, or folklore that circulates among those who use computers, especially by means of the technology or based upon specific features of the technology. Computer folklore is not yet well documented. Folklore about computers dates back to the late 1940s, with the exoteric perspective representing computers as more than human, sometimes literally divine, as this example illustrates:

> IBM had just installed its newest computer at the Massachusetts Institute of Technology (MIT), and a number of campus notables gathered for its unveiling. Members of the group were requested to submit questions that they thought would test the huge machine. An astronomer submitted a question about the size of the universe, and a physicist asked the number of black holes in the universe. Both seemed satisfied with the answers given.
>
> Finally, a philosopher asked the ultimate question: "Is there a God?" The computer operators fed this question to the computer, and after several minutes of computation, the computer printed out its answer: "There is now!"

A variant of the omniscient-computer joke begins the same way, but the third person's father had died recently, and so he asked where his father was. To this the computer did not answer "in heaven" or "in hell" as expected, but rather "in Wisconsin." When the third person provided the information that his father had died three days earlier, the computer's immediate reply was: "The man who married your mother died three days ago. Your father is fishing in Wisconsin." (The same joke, however, circulated many years ago about a fortune-telling scale.)

In the 1950s and early 1960s, early attempts at computer translation were hugely unsuccessful, presumably resulting in such computer-as-idiot jokes as this: Did you hear about the computer-translation project? The computer translated "out of sight, out of mind" into "invisible idiot!"

The exoteric view of computers remains bifurcated, with computers either supremely able or inhumanly stupid, demanding payment of debts of $00.00 or converting change for an $8.39 breakfast to $83,900.00 Such accounts seem to be on the wane due to the improvement of the technology and the increase in the popular understanding of how computers operate.

Those who work with computers have an insider's perspective that does not tolerate apocryphal tales about the machines' capabilities. "Garbage in, garbage out" (or GIGO), rarely heard today, reflects insiders' shifting the onus for computer failure onto data-entry operators and, perhaps less commonly, onto programmers. Nonetheless, those inside the technology long told stories about larger-than-life exploits of individuals, whether, in the era of mainframe computing, about individuals who had a cot at the local computing center so that they could work all night or, with the advent of interactive computing, about all-night "hacking." These stories, which may be contrasted with the omniscient computer, were almost always accurate in technical details.

Nearly everyone knows the account of the founding of Apple Computer, and the later success of Microsoft's Bill Gates is told, and reported in newspapers, with the same larger-than-life rhetoric of hero legends. Conversely, there is a traditional demonizing rhetoric—for example, about contemporary hackers who threaten national security—just as there was, and remains, a rhetoric about computer viruses and their authors.

One way of outlining a history of computer folklore is to consider the development of various aspects of the technology, because printers and other "output devices" have often been put to "folk" uses, much as office photocopy machines have been used to reproduce the traditional items called Xeroxlore or photocopylore. Especially in the 1960s and 1970s, the computer printouts that festooned the walls of many system analysts' offices were, in their complexity, markers of technical expertise and, through their use of exotic devices such as color printers, markers of access to those devices. Less-expert programmers had to settle for simple nudes and comic characters, such as the ubiquitous representations of the cartoon dog Snoopy. Interest in traditional graphic images, even simple ones, continues. The accompanying "Kilroy" and "Granny" graphic come from the signature blocks of computer users' electronic mail messages:

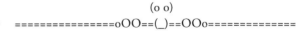

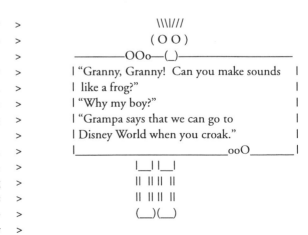

Indeed, even Xeroxlore is circulated widely on the Internet, the most accessible being texts that are easily represented by strings of alphanumerics. "The Complete Set of Blonde Jokes" (more than 400 jokes comprise the file) begins:

Q: What do you call a blonde with half a brain?
A: Gifted!

The following item, titled "WHY ASK WHY?" contains a lengthy series of seeming paradoxes and contradictions, beginning:

Why do you need a driver's license to buy liquor when you can't drink and drive?
Why isn't phonetic spelled the way it sounds?
Why are there interstate highways in Hawaii?

But computer folklore is more than jokes, tales, and Xeroxlore adapted to a new medium. In the late 1970s, a computer game, "Adventure," was developed as a project in artifical intelligence. It was quickly appropriated by experienced computer programmers across the country for their own recreational use. Other computer games proliferated, and eventually many of them, including "Adventure," were commodified for popular consumption.

Computer "viruses" were developed in the context of artificial intelligence in the early 1970s at MIT and elsewhere. Innocent enough in an environment of stand-alone computers, these programs proved highly destructive on networked computers in the late 1980s and early 1990s.

Much computer folklore reveals the extent to which the transmitters of that folklore are elite computer users, with access to increasingly sophisticated technology. Considered over time, technical computer folklore has "trickled down," with massive imitation of the original few programs. Computer folklore—whether traditional items such as chain letters or computer games and viruses—that is copied and communicated by this means poses many difficulties to the industry. Computer viruses, of course, may be understood as direct threats, but computer games and even chain letters may consume so much time and space that they are treated as similar threats to the efficient operating of computer networks. Like the "little moron" jokes that were so popular during World War II that they interfered with the wartime production at many factories, the popularity of computer folklore also results in its proscription in many workplaces.

Michael J. Preston

References

Dorst, John. 1990. Tags and Burners, Cycles and Networks: Folklore in the Telectronic Age. *Journal of the Folklore Institute* 27:179–190.
Jennings, Karla. 1990. *The Devouring Fungus: Tales of the Computer Age.* New York: W.W. Norton.

See also Organizational Folklore; Xeroxlore

Con Artist

A swindler who, with criminal intent, gains the trust of strangers, usually through an assumed identity and carefully staged charades. Con games often depend on the victim's belief that she or he stands to profit dishonestly by cheating the con artist or some third party; the third party is usually the con artist's partner—though the victim is unaware of the partnership. Related terms include "confidence game," "con man/woman," "confidence man/woman."

One classic confidence game still in regular use is the "pigeon drop," in which the "roper" (the partner who "ropes in" the victim) strikes up a casual acquaintance with the potential victim in a public place, such as a town square or a shopping mall. The "pigeon" (victim, also known as a "mark," "sucker," "apple") is led to discover a "lost" wallet with no identification but a great deal of money. The "inside man" (the second partner) appears and provides expert advice: The money will be legally theirs to split if it is not claimed in one month. In the meantime, they should leave it with a reputable lawyer (the roper names one), along with earnest money, a deposit equal to, say, 10 percent of the amount found. The roper and the pigeon both contribute their share, names and addresses are exchanged, and the roper and the inside man make off with the pigeon's deposit.

The term *confidence man* was coined in 1847 in a *New York Herald* article describing a man (later identified as Wm. Thompson) who would approach a stranger on the street and ask whether the latter had enough confidence to entrust Thompson with his watch. The victim, thinking Thompson was an acquaintance not at the moment recognized, would comply, and the confidence man would walk off laughing. The term quickly gained popularity, eventually spreading internationally, and by 1856 Herman Melville published a novel titled *The Confidence-Man: His Masquerade.* The con artist has since appeared in many guises in literature, on the stage, and in motion pictures.

Many scholars have argued that the con game not only originated in the United States, but that it is a peculiarly American phenomenon and that the con artist is an American folk hero—our version of Robin Hood. Con artists are often depicted as charming, fast-talking rogues preying only on unsavory characters who deserve to be fleeced. The immorality of the confidence man's actions is mitigated by his choice of victims and overshadowed by his personal charm and impressive capabilities, not the least of which is a keen insight into human nature.

Con artists may be seen as folk heroes because they embody some fundamentally American characteristics. Con artists depend on their ability to assume false identities, an ability enhanced by America's social and geographic mobility. Furthermore, their readiest victims are people who believe that the world is characterized by promise, that it is full of wealth to be had for the taking—people who believe in the possibility of getting something for (virtually) nothing. The great bounty of America helped foster this attitude, especially in the expansive years before the Civil War.

Like many criminal types, con artists comprise their own

subculture, complete with traditions, values, and their own jargon. Some further terms for confidence games include "the broads," "the wire," "the rag," "the hype," and "the tat." Several terms describe props, strategies, and moves within a game: The "convincer" is money the mark is allowed to win before being swindled; a "cackle bladder" is a rubber bladder filled with fake blood (in early days with chicken blood, hence its name) and used to fool the mark into thinking one of the con artists has been killed; "to blow off" is to get the mark to leave the scene of the crime (the cackle bladder is often used to blow off the mark); and "to put the mark on the send" is to send him or her to get more money to lose to the con artists. A "short con" is any con game in which the mark is taken for only the amount of money he or she is carrying; a "big con" is any confidence game in which the mark is put on the send (see Maurer 1974).

The "sting" is the moment when the mark's money is taken, and *to sting* is to take money from a pigeon. Popularized in the Academy Award-winning 1973 film *The Sting* starring Robert Redford and Paul Newman, the term has become widely used to describe covert and duplicitous operations by law-enforcement officials intended to catch criminals in the act of breaking the law. Thus, in an ironic twist, in so-called "sting operations," police officers or FBI (Federal Bureau of Investigation) agents emulate con artists to capture criminals.

Kenneth D. Pimple

References

Goldhurst, William. 1979. *Our Own Confidence Man: A Study of His Origins and Development in Our National Literature.* Gainesville, FL: Mister Print.

Lindberg, Gary H. 1982. *The Confidence Man in American Literature.* New York: Oxford University Press.

Maurer, David W. 1974. *The American Confidence Man.* Springfield, IL: Thomas.

Conjunto Music

A folk-music tradition that emerged in south Texas in the late 1920s and moved into its popular culture form beginning in the late 1940s. Manuel Peña's *The Texas-Mexican Conjunto: History of a Working-Class Music* (1985) provides the definitive history of this musical form. The music's forms and instruments were brought into the region from the Matamoros, Mexico, area beginning in the late 19th century. Central to *conjunto* music is the accordion, which become the preferred instrument in working-class *tejano* music. It was readily available and relatively inexpensive, particularly the one-button models from Germany and Italy, which were available duty-free in Reynosa.

Two basic types of music were popular at the time, music to listen to and music to dance to. Early *conjunto* music was popular at dances partly because it was instrumental rather than sung music, which was common in cantinas and in the *bailes de negocio* (dances where men paid their partners to dance, often women of the street), both of which carried a social stigma among the family-oriented *mexicanos*. Too, the *conjunto*—composed of the accordion, accompanied by a *tambora de rancho* (a folk instrument like a drum) or a handmade *bajo sexto* (a twelve-stringed instrument)—was affordable for those who wanted to hire musicians for a *baile decente* (decent dance), such as those held at weddings, anniversaries, and other such events. Early in the 1930s, the *bajo sexto* replaced the *tambora de rancho*. The common dance music included the polka, the schottische, the mazurcas, the *vals bajito* (redowa), and the *huapango*.

Like many folk traditions, *conjunto* music became a boundary marker between folk groups, in this case not only between Anglos and *tejanos*, but also between working-class *tejanos* and those in the middle or upper class, who preferred the music of the *orchestra típica* (composed of mostly stringed instruments) or singing duets or trios accompanied by guitars.

Beginning in the late 1920s and early 1930s, recording companies began issuing *conjunto* music to sell to members of *la raza* not only in Texas but in California and the rest of the Southwest, as well as the areas where migrant workers had settled, like Detroit and Chicago. They also became popular performers on the Spanish-language radio stations throughout the Southwest and beyond. These performers were folk musicians who made their living working at various jobs and playing part-time. Their popularity and fame spread as a consequence of this exposure on radio and record.

The most important accordion players and shapers of the *conjunto* music of this era included Narciso Martínez, Santiago "Flaco" Jiménez, Bruno Villarreal, José Rodríguez, and Lolo Cavazos, among others.

Beginning in the later 1940s, *conjunto* music evolved from a folk into a popular musical form. It remained one of the most popular music forms among the working-class Mexican Americans in Texas and beyond. The electric bass replaced the *bajo sexto*, and drums were added. Eventually, some groups replaced the accordion with the new electronic keyboard. *Conjunto* music continues to be popular among working-class Mexican Americans.

Joe S. Graham

References

Paredes, Américo. 1976. *A Texas-Mexican Cancionero.* Urbana: University of Illinois Press.

Peña, Manuel. 1981. The Emergence of *Conjunto* Music, 1935–1955. In *"And Other Neighborly Names": Social Process and Cultural Image in Texas Folklore,* ed. Richard Bauman and Roger Abrahams. Austin: University of Texas Press, pp. 280–299.

———. 1985. *The Texas-Mexican Conjunto: History of a Working-Class Music.* Austin: University of Texas Press.

Strachwitz, Chris. 1975. Jacket notes of *Texas-Mexican Border Music.* Vol. 4. Arhoolie Records.

———. 1978. Jacket notes of *Texas-Mexican Border Music.* Vol. 13. Arhoolie Records.

Conroy, Jack (1898–1990)

Novelist, storyteller, editor, industrial-folklore collector. Born in a coal-mining camp near Moberly, Missouri, Conroy grew up in a work community called Monkey Nest, where orality and the customs of immigrant miners (Irish, British, Italian) meshed with labor-union activism. Shortly before World War I, "Monkey Nest" vanished, victim of a new industrial order and cheaper sources of energy. It appeared that the folk culture of preindustrial communities might vanish, too, in the tide of proletarianization, but Conroy observed that this culture took new forms in factories, shops, and mills. Apprenticing in the Wabash Railroad shops, Conroy practiced his writing skills as secretary of the union local. After the defeat of the 1922 Great Railroad Strike, Conroy worked in auto factories and steel mills until 1930 when the Great Depression cast millions of workers loose to survive as best they could. Drawing upon the transformed folk culture of industrialized workplaces and his own experiences, Conroy wrote sketches and short stories for magazines such as the *American Mercury*, encouraged by editors H.L. Mencken and Mike Gold (*New Masses*). Skilled at transforming folk narrative into literary sketches, Conroy received acclaim from both conservative and radical critics in the early 1930s.

Founding editor of the *Anvil*, which published Erskine Caldwell, Nelson Algren, Meridel Le Sueur, and Richard Wright, Conroy later joined the Illinois Writers' Project in Chicago, where he participated in conceptualizing and collecting industrial folklore. Drawing from this work, Conroy and the Black novelist Arna Bontemps wrote a number of very successful children's stories. They received the James L. Dow Award for their collaborative work on Black social history, which drew in part from Conroy's earlier research as a Guggenheim Fellow. Among his honors were an NEA (National Endowment for the Arts) artist's grant; an honorary doctorate from the University of Missouri, Kansas City; and the Literary Times Award from the state of Illinois.

The populist-radical impulses that animate Conroy's novels, folk narratives, and sketches express the grief, joy, and dignity of working-class people, translated into new factory settings. Humanitarian conviction and generosity of spirit illuminate the work of this remarkable man.

Douglas Wixson

References

Conroy, Jack. [1933] 1991. *The Disinherited*. Introduction by Douglas Wixson. Columbia: University of Missouri Press.

———. 1935. *A World to Win*. New York: Covici-Friede.

———. 1942. *The Fast Sooner Hound*. New York: Houghton Mifflin.

———. 1966. *Anyplace but Here*. New York: Hill and Wang.

———. 1979. *The Jack Conroy Reader*. Ed. David Ray and Jack Salzman. New York: Burt Franklin.

———. 1985. *The Weed King and Other Stories*. Introduction by Douglas Wixson. Westport, CT: Lawrence Hill.

Wixson, Douglas. 1984. Jack Conroy and Industrial Folklore. *Missouri Folklore Society Journal* 6:61–68.

———. 1994. *Worker-Writer in America: Jack Conroy and the Tradition of Midwestern Literary Radicalism, 1898– 1990*. Urbana: University of Illinois Press.

Conspiracy Theories

Notions of history and society holding that certain unexplained events, as well as human suffering and powerlessness, result from the machinations of secretive groups whose surreptitious aim is to wield power through deceit and violence.

The attempt to expose and combat ostensible conspiracies is a particularly American pastime. In fact, the United States is the only Western nation in which conspiracy to commit a crime is prosecutable as a crime in and of itself. This infatuation with conspiratorial activity articulates the American values of democratic openness and antielitism.

Some schools of conspiracy theory address a single event, such as the deaths of Abraham Lincoln, John F. Kennedy, or Marilyn Monroe. Others do not settle for identifying trivial cabals, but propose the existence of worldwide networks that form the center of a conspiratorial worldview that allows its adherents to make sense of the whole world and all of its events in a manner not unlike a religious belief system. Indeed, conspiratorialism and religious belief are often inexorably intertwined. The devil is often regarded as the source of all conspiracy, and God is the protector of those conspired against.

America's first great conspiracy concern involved this sort of religious dimension. The Puritans regarded the pope in Rome as the biblically prophesied anti-Christ who would aspire to world domination in the last days—an idea that would never leave some segments of American folk consciousness. Since colonial America had few Catholics, Puritan anti-Catholicism found few tangible targets. In the 1820s, when William Morgan was allegedly murdered by Freemasons for exposing their secret rites, anti-Masonry became so popular that it formed the basis for an influential political party. Later in the 19th century, as hundreds of thousands fled Ireland and eastern and southern Europe for the United States, anti-Catholicism reemerged reinvigorated by the presence of living, breathing Catholics. Nativist politicians decried Catholic allegiance to the Vatican as treasonous, and lurid tales of the diabolical deeds of monks and nuns saturated the popular press. As the 20th century began, Communism (often associated with eastern European immigration) began to emerge as the main conspiratorial threat to American culture.

During the second Red Scare of the 1950s, the John Birch Society—whose name is almost synonymous with conspiracy theory-ism—regarded U.S. Senator Joseph McCarthy (ironically, a Catholic) of Wisconsin as a folk hero. Curiously, despite its vehement anti-Communism, the John Birch Society identified the same groups that leftists identified (and continue to identify) as the key players in the worldwide conspiracy game—the United Nations, the World Bank, the International Monetary Fund, and big-money capitalists.

Conservative Protestants—long the instigators of conspiracy accusations—found themselves in the late 20th century on the receiving end of conspiratorial accusations as they mounted campaigns to influence local and national politics.

Today, Americans can pick from a smorgasbord of paranoias. None of the traditional conspirators ever really disappeared; they just faded into the background as new ones more resonant with modern concerns emerged.

Conspiracy theories can be seen as "folk social science" and "folk history" that attempt to accomplish the same goals as their mainstream academic counterparts—providing meaningful and accurate explanations for conditions in the world. Conspiracy theories do this outside respected forums and styles of discussions and through such folkloric media as the fringe press and oral transmission.

Conspiracy theory-ism is a thriving industry whose various manifestations support numerous bookstores, magazines, and symposiums. Conspiracy theorists form communities of "true disbelievers"—subcultures of intellectual dissent from official, mainstream cultural analysis.

The great irony of conspiracy theory-ism in America is that it is often those groups most caught up in exposing the conspiracies of others that themselves behave in the most conspiratorial manner. Anti-Masons would meet in secret groups to denounce the secrecy of Freemasonry and conspire to destroy its adherents. The fleetingly influential nativist "Know Nothing" political party got its name from the fact that it began as a secret society whose members would disclaim any knowledge of the organization. The Ku Klux Klan has long been warning against conspiracies to strip "real" Americans of their constitutional freedoms, while at the same time conspiring behind white sheets and secret meetings to deprive African Americans, Jews, and Catholics of their civil rights.

Eric Eliason

Contextual Approach

Refers to the general and the specific background of a composition or a structure and, in the verbal arts, also to the parts preceding and following a given section. The term "context" is from the Latin *contextus,* stem of *contexere,* meaning to "weave together." William R. Bascom has proposed that any functional analysis requires an adequate description of the social context of folklore, including the time and place for the telling of specific forms; the identity of the narrators and the composition of the audience, as well as the relationship of the narrator to the text; the use of dramatic and rhetorical devices in performance; audience participation; folk classification of traditional genres and the people's attitudes toward them (Bascom 1954). Since speakers understand their folklore through the knowledge of these details, any interpretation of a tale, a song, a proverb, a riddle, or any other genre of folklore must account for them as well. The meaning of a text, a melody, or a design is its meaning in context.

The deliberate shift, or the accidental transference, of any folklore text to a different literary, historical, or cultural context grants it a new meaning. When a composer employs a folk tune or an author refers to, rewrites, or even reproduces verbatim a folktale, they bestow upon them new meanings, of which, their being considered traditional expressions is a part. When a tale that has a worldwide distribution becomes a part of the repertoire of one more society, its members interpret it in terms of their own culture, history, religion, and worldview, and when immigrants use their folklore in their new country they convey in their telling and singing their longing for their homeland—a meaning these tales and melodies do not have in their country of origin.

Of all folklore methods, the contextual approach is most specifically a challenge to the comparative approach. It seeks to interpret folk ideas, customs, tales, and songs not in terms of their similarities to the forms and subjects of folklore of other nations, but in their integration with the life, thought, language, and actions of the people that perform, observe, and act upon them in their own society and time. A valid interpretation is, therefore, an interpretation of a text in context.

Contrary to the views of some scholars, the contextual approach does not assume that there is an opposition between text and context. Rather, its basic supposition is that folklore exists in a contextual state. Therefore, some scholars prefer to treat the entire context as if it were a literary text. Each situation is a unique integrated whole. While no two contexts are alike in speaking or singing, people follow cultural rules and social patterns that are discoverable and that reveal the dynamics and the poetics of folklore in society.

Folklore forms differ in their dependency upon their context for their interpretation. The briefer the form and the more stable its text is, the higher is its contextual dependency; conversely, the longer and consequently the more variable a text is, the lower its contextual dependency appears to be. The meaning of proverbs, for example, is highly context-dependent, whereas tales, even epics, that have a wider range for textual variations retain stability of meaning in a variety of contexts. Such an observation applies mostly to the immediate context of performance, but not to the context of culture at large, the influence of which is very pervasive.

Proverbs are quotations from tradition. Their speakers intend to resolve an immediate social conflict by summoning into the situation the authority of the past. Their use, therefore, is prevalent in situations of traditional litigation, informal mediation, and pedagogical conversation. By their very use, these speakers claim authority. Riddles, on the other hand, contrast with proverbs in form and context. Their users are mostly children and youth rather than the elderly. They instruct but without morals. When adults pose them, they do so in situations of entertainment or even rites of passage rather than social conflict. In African societies, riddles serve to instruct pubescent initiates, while in earlier European and Asian cultures they were part of courting behavior and wedding ceremonies. Riddles often invoke humor rather than judgment, play and fantasy rather than ethical values, as proverbs do.

Among the narrative genres, ballad singing has been seen in the context of entertainment. In 18th- and 19th-century Scotland, farmhands performed ballads during work and in leisure and festive times. Literature attests to ballad singing on the streets and in the marketplaces in the urban centers of England even earlier, and, together with recitation, ballads have been the main staple of male pub singing. Their broad range of textual variations appears to be performer- rather than context-dependent.

Contextual analysis of folktales has focused upon the roles

of narrators, either itinerant or resident, their repertoire, the telling events, the narration of specific genres, the social interaction in narrating situations, and the poetics of performed tales. A contextual approach to storytelling reveals a correlation between audiences, locations, and subject matters. People are more likely to tell competitive stories in the workplace and in all-male gatherings; whereas the place of tales about existing or attained family harmony is around the hearth.

A common methodological error in the analysis of the context of folklore involves its treatment as if it were another item to be collected. With full realization of its significance, students would set out "to collect context." However, unlike the texts of folklore genres, context is not a collectible. It may be observable, or at least partially so, and therefore should be carefully recorded, but in and of itself it is not as tangible as a text or a picture is. The information about the context of folklore performance has to be integrated with the verbal, visual, or musical communication of folklore in order to offer an adequate basis for the interpretation of an event.

Bronislaw Malinowski, the anthropologist who was among the first to draw attention to the importance of context in the understanding of language and folklore, distinguished between *context of culture* and *context of situation* (Malinowski [1923] 1946). The context of culture is the broadest framework for the perception and interpretation of folklore. It comprises the knowledge shared by the speakers, their conventional behavior and ethical principles, their history, their beliefs, and their speech metaphors and genres. In contrast, the situation is the narrowest, most direct, context for folklore performance and, therefore, a key for its interpretation. It comprises a speaker, a musician, or a designer (sender), a message in the appropriate medium, and a listener or viewer (a receiver). While at first glance this model for a context of situation may appear a simplistic truism, its significance becomes apparent by pointing out that any understanding of folklore can be achieved only through the analysis of the relationship between the sender, the message, and the receiver. The deciphering of the intricate relations and nuanced attitudes, past experiences, mutual perceptions, and purposes of speaking is the key for its interpretation. It elucidates the use and the significance of a particular fable, story, proverb, melody, or design, as they occur in social interaction in a particular time and place. The context of situation is an interactive arena in which the speakers' age, status, and gender gain symbolic significance in their communication. Similarly, the code, style, and measure, the intonation and dramatization, the genre and its conventions, the time and place of performance, and the gender of the performer convey meanings. In the totality of the situation, the different components interact upon one another, having the capacity to redefine and renegotiate constantly the framework for communication. Within the context of situation, there is a correlation between the semantic values of the various components. For example, old age implies authority and traditionality and is appropriate for the speaking of proverbs, but not for riddling, which challenges the established order and for which youth is more suitable. In an interactive context of situation, age itself and,

for that matter, other parts are negotiable.

Methodologically, the study of a context of situation may present researchers with an apparently insurmountable problem: The very presence of a folklorist in such a context changes the composition of the group. The sender may address his message as much to the folklorist, the outside observer, as to the addressees. As a solution to this dilemma, Kenneth S. Goldstein proposed the situational construction of an "induced natural context," in which the researcher arranges for the exchange of folklore forms in their conventional circumstances in the society "as if" it occurs naturally, and then stays in the background and observes (Goldstein 1964). Such a staging of events may succeed on some occasions and fail on others. The folklorist's dilemma points to the most important change that the focus on context introduced into folklore research. This is a shift from collecting forays into different countries, the countryside, or even a specific ethnic group in an urban setting and toward prolonged fieldwork. Although even fieldwork of a long duration may involve similar questions, the requirement for a sustained presence in a society exposes the researcher to a broad range of social situations in which folklore forms occur in the life of the community.

Context is a value-free concept, and no one contextual situation is privileged over any other. Therefore, any situation constitutes its own context, regardless of its approximation to any imagined or authentic researcher-free performance. The presence of a folklorist in a recording situation adds to its meaning as well. Any narrator or singer can use the folklorist to enhance his position in the community or to present him with the traditions with which he and his community identify.

The contexts in which people perform folklore forms in their own society are *events*. An event is a culturally defined context to which a community allocates forms of discourse and which have known rules and conventions for folklore performance. It is possible to violate the rules of an event, but not those of a context. No utterance can be out of context because any new situation has its own context within or outside the cultural system of communication. Furthermore, if such a violation is deliberate and meaningful, it implies a higher degree of context dependency, because the performance acquires its significance from being counter to traditional conventions and rules. The performance of folklore forms can be within their culturally defined events or outside their boundaries, but they can never be out of context.

Dan Ben-Amos

References

Bascom, William R. 1954. Four Functions of Folklore. *Journal of American Folklore* 67:333–349.

Bauman, Richard. 1983. The Field Study of Folklore in Context. In *Handbook of American Folklore*, ed. Richard M. Dorson and Inta Gale Carpenter. Bloomington: Indiana University Press, pp. 362–368.

Ben-Amos, Dan. 1971. Toward a Definition of Folklore in Context. *Journal of American Folklore* 84:3–15. Reprinted in *Toward New Perspectives in Folklore*, ed.

Américo Paredes and Richard Bauman. American Folklore Society Bibliographical and Special Series, Vol. 23. Austin: University of Texas Press.

———. 1982. *Folklore in Context: Essays.* New Delhi: South Asian Publishers.

———. 1993. "Context" in Context. *Western Folklore* 52:209–226.

———. 1994. The Induced Natural Context in Context. In *Fields of Folklore: Essays in Honor of Kenneth S. Goldstein,* ed. Roger Abrahams. Bloomington, IN: Trickster.

Dewey, John. 1931. Context and Thought. *University of California Publications in Philosophy* 12:203–224.

Dundes, Alan. 1964. Texture, Text, and Context. *Southern Folklore Quarterly* 28:251–265.

Goldstein, Kenneth S. 1964. *A Guide for Field Workers in Folklore.* Hatboro, PA: Folklore Associates for the American Folklore Society.

Goodwin, Charles, and Alessandro Duranti. 1992. Rethinking Context: An Introduction. In *Rethinking Context: Language as an Interactive Phenomenon,* ed. Alessandro Duranti and Charles Goodwin. Cambridge: Cambridge University Press, pp. 1–42.

Hymes, Dell. 1962. The Ethnography of Speaking. In *Anthropology and Human Behavior,* ed. T. Galdwin and W.C. Sturtevant. Washington, DC. Anthropological Society of Washington, pp.13–53. Reprinted in *Readings in the Sociology of Language,* ed. Joshua Fishman. The Hague: Mouton, 1968, pp. 99–138.

Malinowski, Bronislaw. [1923] 1946. The Problem of Meaning in Primitive Languages. In *The Meaning of Meaning,* ed. C.K. Ogden and I.A. Richardsk. New York: Harcourt, Brace, and World, pp. 296–336.

Scharfstein, Ben-Ami. 1989. *The Dilemma of Context.* New York: New York University Press.

Wilgus, D.K. 1973. The Text Is the Thing. *Journal of American Folklore* 86:241–252.

Wolf, George S. 1989. Malinowski's "Context of Situation." *Language and Communication* 9:259–267.

Young, Kathrine. 1985. The Notion of Context. *Western Folklore* 44:115–122.

See also Performance Approach

Corridos

Mexican American folk ballads popular throughout the Southwest from the 1830s to the 1930s. Passed from singer to singer, most folk *corridos* are anonymous, telling a story considered important to the local people. *Corrido* conventions include the formal opening and the *despedida,* or formal close, and the sixteen-syllable-line quatrain rhyming *abcb.* The central focus is to tell a good story, and specific facts are not too important. The story jumps from scene to scene, drawing on imagery from the *vaquero* life, from horse racing, and from cockfighting. The language is simple and direct, in contrast to the pseudoliterary language of the broadside ballad *(corrido* written and sold on the streets of larger cities in Mexico), of-

ten borrowing such terms from English as *cherife* (sheriff) and *rinche* (meaning law-enforcement officer, particularly the Texas Ranger).

The themes of the early *corridos* included fights with Indians, *vaquero* experiences, and various tragedies of importance to the local people. In Texas the border conflict beginning in 1836 and continuing into the 1930s was the focus of many *corridos.* Such border heroes as Juan Nepomuceno Cortina, Catarino Garza, Jacinto Treviño, and others were important because of their standing up to the Anglos (usually law-enforcement officers). Gregorio Cortez emerged as the idealized Mexican American folk hero, a border man who stood up for his rights against the Anglo law-enforcement officers, "with his pistol in his hand."

The ancestors of the *corrido* include the Spanish *romance,* a narrative ballad form brought into the Southwest by the first Spanish settlers and colonists in California, Arizona, New Mexico, southern Colorado, and Texas. The *verso* or *copla* (a short, lyrical stanza) was cultivated in some areas prior to the rise of the *corrido.* The *décima* (a ten-line stanza) of oral tradition, found in the American Southwest as well as Mexico, also came with the early Spanish settlers and would compete with the *corrido* in the 19th century. The *corrido* century in Texas (1836 to the 1930s) corresponds to the period of serious border conflict, and many compositions dealt with the struggle to establish the Republic of the Rio Grande and with the guerilla warfare against Zachary Taylor's troops.

One of the earliest border *corridos* in its complete form is the "Corrido de Kiansas," dating to the late 1860s or early 1870s, which tells of the experiences of *vaqueros* on a trail drive to Kansas in this period. Fifty years later, this *corrido* would serve as a model for the "Corrido de la Pensilvania," in which the men involved were not *vaqueros* but rather builders of railroads.

Beginning in the 1850s, the *corrido* form emerged in Greater Mexico, replacing the *décima* as the most important ballad form. A number of these were brought into the American Southwest. The dominant themes included personal or family relationships, love tragedy, and filial disobedience, as is found in "El Hijo Disobediente."

In the late 1920s in Texas, record companies began making 78-rpm records of many of these folk *corridos,* and the *corrido* slowly moved from a folk-music form to a popular-culture form, in which the text does not go through the process of being passed from singer to singer and being shaped to the cultural ideals and values of the community. The *corridos* recorded after the assassination of President John F. Kennedy, for example, were similar in many ways to the earlier broadside *corridos* in the Southwest. *Corridos* continue to be a significant form in popular music. On ranches and in many small communities along the Rio Grande, one can still hear the old folk *corridos* as well, indicating that the tradition continues.

Joe S. Graham

References

Boatright, Mody, ed. 1946. *Mexican Border Ballads and Other Lore.* Publications of the Texas Folklore Society,

No. 21. Dallas: Southern Methodist University Press.

Dickey, Dan W. 1978. *The Kennedy Corridos: Study of the Ballads of a Mexican American Hero.* Austin: University of Texas Press.

Hague, Eleanor. 1917. *Spanish-American Folk-Songs.* New York: American Folk-Lore Society.

Mendoza, Vicente T. 1954. *El corrido mexicano.* Mexico: Fondo de Cultura Económica.

Paredes, Américo. 1958. *"With His Pistol in His Hand": A Border Ballad and Its Hero.* Austin: University of Texas Press.

———. 1976. *A Texas-Mexican Cancionero: Folksongs of the Lower Border.* Urbana: University of Illinois Press.

Robb, John D. 1954. *Hispanic Folk Songs of New Mexico and the Southwest: A Self-Portrait of a People.* Albuquerque: University of New Mexico Press.

Strachwitz, Chris. 1974a. Liner notes of *Corridos Part I, 1930–1934.* Folklyric LP 9005.

———. 1974b. Liner notes of *Corridos Part II, 1929–1936."* Folklyric LP 9005.

See also Ballad

Cortez, Gregorio (1875–1916)

Legendary Mexican American folk hero during an era of violence against Mexican Americans in south Texas in the early 20th century. While his popularity was greatest during the first three decades of the century, many older Mexican Americans in the region, particularly those on south Texas ranches, continue to hold him in high regard.

Cortez was born on a ranch just south of the Rio Grande on June 22, 1875. His family crossed into Texas and moved to the Austin area in 1887. For several years, he and his older brother, Romaldo, worked together on farms in Karnes and Gonzalez counties. In 1900 they rented land to farm for themselves.

Gregorio Cortez became a folk hero as a consequence of his standing up for his rights, "with his pistol in his hand," against the Karnes County sheriff and two deputies who had come to arrest him for horse thievery, of which he was not guilty. Mexican Americans of this period were not given the due process of law accorded Anglos. They were often shot or beaten and arrested with little or no chance of consequences. Unaware that Gregorio Cortez was carrying a pistol, the sheriff pulled his pistol and shot Cortez's brother, Romaldo, seriously wounding him. He also shot at Gregorio, but missed, and Gregorio shot him three times.

During the following chase, several hundred men in a number of posses pursued Gregorio, who walked more than 120 miles and rode three mares more than 400 miles. He was surrounded on occasion, but escaped. After ten days and a number of heroic efforts, Gregorio was betrayed by one of his own kind and captured by a Texas Ranger. He was returned to San Antonio, Texas, where he was placed in prison to await trial. During this period of the chase, more than 200 Mexican Americans were killed, many as part of a fictional "Cortez gang."

Cortez was tried and found guilty three times, but the Texas Court of Criminal Appeals overturned the convictions. Then he was convicted for killing Sheriff Glover and sentenced to life in prison. He entered the Huntsville Penitentiary on January 1, 1905, and was paroled by the governor of Texas on July 7, 1913. He died of an apparent heart attack in 1916.

During the chase and the trial, Gregorio Cortez's name was in the newspapers on a regular basis, often in stories revealing the typical Anglo prejudices against Mexican Americans of this period. The response among the Mexican Americans was the opposite—Gregorio Cortez became a hero. With his pistol in his hand, he had stood up to the Anglos and their mistreatment of Mexican Americans, and in essence he had defeated them. Through his skill as a horseman and his skill with weapons, he had outsmarted hundreds of law-enforcement officers until he was betrayed by El Teco, one of his "friends."

Many legends grew around Gregorio Cortez and his heroic acts, and both broadside ballads and true folk ballads (both called *corridos)* about him were composed and sung during the next forty or so years.

Joe S. Graham

References

Paredes, Américo. 1958. *"With His Pistol in His Hand": A Border Ballad and Its Hero.* Austin: University of Texas Press.

Costume, Folk

Any manner of stylizing, marking, or manipulating the appearance of the human body with culturally understood symbols and forms in a way that articulates an individual's identification with a community. Folk costume usually refers to the dress of ethnic groups, subcultures, or other small groups, but it also can characterize the adornment practices common in any locality. The term "costume" includes not only clothing, but also other body adornment practices such as jewelry, cosmetics, hairstyling, masking, tattooing, and scarification, and can refer to everyday adornment as well as dramatic, ritual, or festival costuming. Themes in American folk-costume study include the outward articulation of identity through costume by diverse cultural groups, the interaction and creolization of costume forms in New World contexts, and the pluralistic legacy of such encounters in contemporary costume styles.

Folklorists who discuss adornment have concentrated on costume's socializing force and its relationship to the maintenance of individual and group identities. According to Don Yoder (1972), folk costume expresses identity in a symbolic way; functioning as an outward "badge" of community identity and expressing an individual's manifold relationships to and within that community. In many 19th-century religious sects, such as the Amish, Mennonites, and Shakers, fashion is rejected in plain-dress articulated group separation from mainstream society by embodying the principles of sectarian doctrine and enacting a "hedge" against the temptations of the

world. Thus, folk costume promotes group solidarity and maintains personal and group boundaries as individuals embody a community by reshaping their bodies in keeping with group values.

American society has been characterized by a plethora of traditions of dissent or differentiation articulated through costume and bodily adornment. In what Elizabeth Wilson has termed "oppositional dress" (Wilson 1985), the body is transformed into a site of struggle by disaffected subcultures as they attempt to define themselves as a social body by redefining the appearance and meaning of their physical bodies. The costume aesthetic of such groups is often formed through processes of appropriation or the manipulation of normative costume forms in a new, or nonnormative, fashion. Nineteenth-century feminists seeking equality, for example, clothed their demands in masculine attire, advocating dress reform and appropriating men's-style jackets and ties for women's professional costume. Twentieth-century youth subcultures appropriate normative or fashionable costume signs and reassemble them within the terms of an alternative aesthetic. During World War II, African American and Latino youths articulated their discontent by adopting an exaggerated form of men's suits known as the zoot suit. This suit, characterized by its brightly colored fabric, drape jacket, wide pleated trousers, and prominent accessories, defied wartime rationing and engendered clashes with American servicemen. The suit was clearly at issue as a symbol of minority self-definition disenfranchised from patriotic, mainstream America.

Oppositional dress has also characterized postwar sub-

cultures. During the 1960s, countercultural hippies confounded gender distinctions (in long hair and untidiness) and appropriated both working-class clothing (such as denim Levis) and "sacred" American symbols (such as the flag) in clothing that functioned as a form of protest against conventional norms and values. This same tendency toward adornment as protest is present in the practices of contemporary punks and anarchists, who refuse mainstream consumption by wearing secondhand clothing reassembled with images of transgression and violence (rips, crosses, and multiple body piercings). In all of these cases, subcultures define themselves in part through costume by appropriating recognizable symbols and reworking their meanings within the terms of an alternative aesthetic. The juxtaposition of seemingly conflicting meanings in dress highlights and articulates the larger social conflicts addressed by such groups.

In local and regional New World settings, costume, like other aspects of material folklife, bears the signs of historical contacts, struggles, and exchanges between different cultures' understandings about adornment and the body. The design and meaning of new creolized vernacular forms emergent from the localized confluence of different traditions are particularly relevant issues for the study of American folk costume. Many specifically American types of costume emerged from the interaction of diverse costume traditions in dialogue with indigenous materials and environments. Recognizable forms in Western regional costume, for example, are creolized forms resulting from the interaction of different traditions of dress. The costume of mountain men who charted new Western territory—fringed buckskin coats, breeches and shirts, fur "coonskin" hats, and thick, colorful blanket jackets—was an adaptation of Native American costume forms suitable for native environments and constructed with indigenous materials. The occupational costume of the American cowboy was also the result of the interaction of various cultural forms in dialogue with the demands of occupation and environment. Many of the recognizable elements of the classic American cowboy costume, such as spurs, hat, boots, and chaps, were the result of cultural exchanges between working Anglo and Mexican cowboys, known as *vaqueros. Vaqueros* were known by their wide-brimmed hats, short jackets, colorful neckerchiefs, red sashes, elaborate spurs, and protective leather leggings, known as *chaparreras* (flared leather trousers with side buttons) and *armas* (wide leather coverings that lay across a rider's lap and legs). Texas cowboys adopted and adapted neckerchiefs, wide-brimmed hats and an abbreviated form of *armas*, or *armitas*, which became known as chaps and are still closely identified with American cowboys. These Western frontier costumes illustrate both a deep connection between the appearance of individuals and their identities as types on the American social landscape, as well as the dynamism typical of New World costume forms and cultural environments.

The cultural effects of enslavement and the forced migration of African peoples to the New World also engendered new creolized forms of bodily style and practice emergent from the collision and renegotiation of different cultural notions about

Taking the train was once a formal outing. Silver Spring, Maryland, 1943. Photo Ann Rosener. Library of Congress.

the body in African and European cultures. For example, new forms of African American hairstyling emerged involving African techniques of braiding in distinctly American styles as well as a variety of new forms constructed through straightening, waving, and recurling techniques, such as the "conk." Kobena Mercer refers to these styles as "ethnic signifiers" that reflect African understandings about hair while creating new styles not present in African cultures, styles specific to the concerns and complex cultural heritage of African Americans (Mercer 1987). Such creole forms are invariably politicized in the context of historical displacement, inequality, and cultural hierarchy.

Although Americans celebrate few costume-centered holidays, costumes play an important role in several American festive occasions. Many American ethnic groups dress in folk costumes to observe holidays, and ethnic costuming also plays an important role in the performance of ethnic identity during folk festivals and folk-art performances for outsiders. The folk costumes of eastern and central European ethnic groups are often codified versions of past peasant festival styles from the culture of origin. Dance performances and parades, in particular, are important occasions for sporting ethnic costume.

Unlike ethnic-festival costuming, which aims to make social identity clear and recognizable, other festival costumes center on the confusion or distortion of identity and the tak-

ing on of new, fictional, or performative roles. During Halloween, for example, children invert social distinctions by playing adult roles and taking on the identities of role models or fantasy figures. In addition, the boundaries between the human and the supernatural worlds are broken in costumes that represent spirit figures such as ghosts, witches, and figures of horror and in mischievous behavior such as pranks and housebreaking. In carnival contexts, such as Mardi Gras, a key feature of costumes is their excess. Elaborate and expensive, these carnival costumes exaggerate and distort the features and proportions of the body and extend its boundaries. This exaggeration and excess contribute to the sense of spectacle and a carnivalesque celebration of the excesses of the body and its pleasures. Masquerade and cross-dressing are major mediums for inversion and other renegotiations of social boundaries, common at such times when individuals try on new roles or identities, and the barriers between individuals are broken down during a period of license and transgression.

Folklorists studying costume traditions in any community need to discern what identities are being produced, maintained, or contested through costume forms, as well as the multiple cultural influences that shape costume forms in any locality. They need to understand how individuals appropriate new ideas from fashion of other cultural groups and integrate them into their wardrobes within the terms of a specific local, regional, or cultural aesthetic (including cut, color, accessory, or rules of assemblage). In addition, costume study is increasingly linked to the study of bodylore, and folklorists need to tease out the subtle bodily understandings of any given cultural group and see costume as an integral part of the everyday, habitual practices through which the body—its appearance, sensations, and boundaries—is managed and understood in any culture. In this context, costume must be understood in relation to other aspects of a culture, such as food consumption, healing practices, deportment, gesture, and speech—all practices that stylize the body, associate it with cultural attributes, and convey the substances of diverse American identities.

Kathryn E. Wilson

References

Banner, Lois. 1983. *American Beauty.* Chicago: University of Chicago Press.

Cosgrove, Stuart. 1988. The Zoot Suit and Style Warfare. In *Zoot Suits and Secondhand Dresses: An Anthology of Fashion and Music,* ed. Angela McRobbie. Boston: Unwin Hyman, pp. 3–22.

DeMarly, Diana. 1986. *Working Dress: A History of Occupational Costume.* New York: Holmes and Meier.

Kidwell, Claudia Brush, and Valerie Steele, eds. 1989. *Men and Women: Dressing the Part.* Washington, DC: Smithsonian Institution.

McClellan, Elizabeth. 1904. *Historic Dress in America, 1607–1870.* Philadelphia: G.W. Jacobs.

Mercer, Kobena. 1987. Black Hair/Style Politics. *New Formations* 3:33–54.

Reedstrom, E. Lisle. 1992. *Authentic Costumes and Characters of the Wild West.* New York: Sterling.

Wilson, Elizabeth. 1985. *Adorned in Dreams: Fashion and Modernity.* Berkeley: University of California Press.

Yoder, Don. 1972. Folk Costume. In *Folklore and Folklife: An Introduction,* ed. Richard M. Dorson. Chicago: University of Chicago Press, pp. 295–324.

———. 1990. Sectarian Costume. In *Discovering American Folklife: Studies in Ethnic, Religious, and Regional Culture.* Ann Arbor, MI: UMI Research Press, pp. 143–171.

See also Bodylore; Tattooing

Country Music

A commercial music form and business with roots in vernacular music, popular music of the 19th and early 20th centuries, and religious music. Vernacular music had been popular throughout the rural United States from the earliest days of the country, and some of this regional material was captured on phonograph records as early as 1922. By 1923 record companies began to send talent scouts through the South to search out regional musicians whose music would have a special appeal within their own part of the country. The result led to "race records," appealing to a regional Black audience, and "hillbilly" music, designed to appeal to a regional White audience.

In the early days of recording rural White vernacular music, traditional songs, ballads, instrumentals, and religious material provided a large percentage of the repertoire. As the artists exhausted this material, they began to compose new material in the mold of the old. The shift in styles was gradual and for years reflected the musical styles the musicians had known from childhood. Innovation came partly from normal musical growth and change, partly as a result of the pressure a commercial music industry imposed on the artists. On the earliest commercial disks, before the advent of electrical recordings in 1926, the emphasis was on string-band music from the Southeast part of the country. A few Western artists were captured on wax, but few recordings were made west of Dallas in these early years.

New York had long been the center of the popular-music business as well as the recording industry. Talent scouts fanned out from there. Despite the early emphasis on rural recording acts, the first huge country hit was by a classically trained tenor from Texas with the stage name of Vernon Dalhart. His 1924 release of "The Prisoner's Song" and "The Wreck of the Old '97" became an instant million-selling record and ushered in an era of commercial disaster ballads. While Dalhart and others working in the same style performed such topical ballads, many of the songs actually were written by Southern songwriters who had learned how to fashion these ballads after a traditional model. Some of these songs entered into tradition. In subsequent years, folklorists who knew nothing of their commercial origins collected these songs.

In 1927 a field expedition to Bristol, on the Tennessee-Virginia line, yielded two of the most important early artists: Jimmie Rodgers and the Carter Family. The success and influence of these artists lasted for years and continues today. Rodgers and the Carters both extended the influence of African American musical songs and styles into country music. The Carters additionally established harmonies and rhythm that had a marked influence on later bluegrass music. A generation of singers, including Hank Snow, Ernest Tubb, and Gene Autry, began their careers as Rodgers imitators.

In the years following the stock market crash of 1929 and the ensuing Depression, the record industry shrank to a fraction of what it had been in its peak year of 1929. By 1935, when the industry began its recovery, it had a different flavor. No longer were traditional musicians providing the mainstay of the stable of artists, and no longer were traditional songs providing the bulk of the repertoire. Rather, a fully commercial product evolved out of the roots that had taken hold a decade earlier. New musical forms were developing. Western artists emerged, and a new musical form known as Western Swing took shape. Artists like Milton Brown and, later, Bob Wills defined this new musical style that reflected a strong influence of both jazz and the blues superimposed on Texas fiddle music. Recordings were still coming from temporary recording studios set up in major centers, including Dallas and Atlanta.

During the mid- and late 1930s, the Western film emerged as a major genre. The Western, perhaps defining the mythology of the United States, became a powerful influence in both music and film. Singing cowboys like Gene Autry and Roy Rogers, as well as others who followed their lead, took center stage. These artists, on film and recordings, spawned a large repertoire of songs that imitated or mirrored music sung on the cattle range. Los Angeles began to develop as a recording center, and new Western artists like the Sons of the Pioneers gained exposure on both film and records.

World War II produced a number of changes in the country-music market. As soldiers from all parts of the country mingled, musical preferences merged and tastes moved into a more nearly national market. Furthermore, this period saw the rapid movement from rural to urban life. After the war, urban centers began to emerge as major markets for what had been previously seen as a rural commodity. The merging of Eastern and Western musical markets and styles gave birth to the hyphenated country-western music label. The cross fertilization was all-encompassing. Western wear, borrowed from the movies, became the preferred style of dress even for Southeastern singers. Nearly the whole country-music industry embraced the cowboy image as Southeastern musicians tried to discard the hillbilly stereotype.

Nashville, Tennessee, was originally one of many regional music centers, but certainly not the most important one. Cincinnati, Atlanta, Chicago, Richmond, Dallas, and Los Angeles were equally important as markets that shaped the development of country music. The Grand Ole Opry, begun in Nashville in 1925, was one of many influential radio barn dances. Although not the first such show, in time it emerged as the most important of these shows and was carried live throughout the nation on the NBC network. After the end of World War II, Nashville began to emerge as a recording center as stars of the Opry provided a focus for recording activity. Gradually, Nashville attracted the supporting industry of music publishers, professional songwriters working in the country vein, and artists hoping to gain a foothold in the business.

While the older string bands of the 1920s and 1930s were largely things of the past, they left their influence in a number of ways. The country musicians of the 1940s and 1950s often featured fiddles and guitars. But the emphasis had changed from a band that often included vocals to a lead singer with a backup band. Outstanding artists like Roy Acuff and, later, Hank Williams utilized these instruments and typified this trend. Many of the bands from this period also included an electric steel guitar. While this instrument had its origin as a Hawaiian steel guitar, the addition of an amplifier and electric pickup better suited many bands that made personal appearances in rowdy honky tonk bars. Microphones and amplification inevitably changed the character of country music. The electric steel guitar bridged both Western and Eastern music. The Dobro, an unamplified instrument, descended from the Hawaiian steel guitar. It was featured as a centerpiece of Roy Acuff's band.

The Dobro also found its way into some bluegrass bands, especially that of Lester Flatt and Earl Scruggs. While Nashville moved further and further from the traditional roots of old-time string bands, Bill Monroe began to experiment in the early 1940s with a musical form descended from these bands. This style of country music became known as bluegrass, named after Bill Monroe's home state of Kentucky and his 1940 band called the Blue Grass Boys. While bluegrass has generally not been as popular as more commercial brands of country music, in many ways it has been the one branch of country music in which traditional songs and instrumentals have survived. Bluegrass music seldom utilizes amplified instruments and stresses close harmonies.

In the mid-1950s, an older style of popular music began to give way to newer rock and roll, influenced by African American forms. Radio stations began to feature this new music that appealed to a younger audience, leaving many of the older fans with no music that sounded familiar to them. Increasingly, this audience turned to contemporary country music, which, in turn, moved closer and closer to the expectations of its audience. During this period, country-music radio outlets expanded dramatically, and this music captured a large urban following previously not interested in country music. A smooth sound developed that left out fiddles and steel guitars and incorporated drums and lush arrangements. Jim Reeves and Eddy Arnold typified this period.

From the mid-1930s forward, Los Angeles and other centers in Southern California have consistently been a counterbalance to the Eastern centers of country music. In the years after World War II, Southern California made significant contributions to the development of country music as artists from the East migrated West. In the 1960s, Bakersfield emerged as a major force in the development of country music, with artists like Buck Owens and Merle Haggard.

Since the mid-1960s, country music has gone in a number of related directions. On the one hand, traditional country music featuring steel guitar and fiddle has flourished with a new breed of younger country artists interested in "traditional" sounds. On the other hand, a new breed of crossover country music has developed. This music, marked by highly amplified instruments and elaborate stage presentations, has made inroads into the wider-pop music market. Garth Brooks is the most successful of these artists at this writing (1995).

The history of country music is marked by a movement from traditional material to commercial product and from regional to national markets. Nevertheless, country music has remained especially popular in regions that have ties to a rural past. One of the hallmarks of country music from the beginning has been a focus on an idealized life that never was. As country music became popular in the cities, there was a strong trend that idealized rural values from which many in the audience came or with which they identified. The past has always been portrayed as a better time in which values of old were paramount. A longing for the past has been present throughout the history of country music. In recent years, this has often translated into conservative political values, leading some observers to identify country music with middle-America, blue-collar values. In fact, it is a descendant of a populist theme that was found in the earliest days of the industry.

To understand the history of country music, one must not only focus on the recorded documents, but also examine the history of radio broadcasts of this music. In the earliest days, regional music was presented to a regional audience on a regular basis. Artists would broadcast to a local audience and then tour the area making personal appearances. After "working out" an area, they would move on to another regional radio station and repeat the pattern. Gradually, recordings replaced the live broadcasts as a national market emerged. Today, there is little left of regional presentation. Television shows, once regional rather than local, are for the most part national. Radio shows increasingly rely on commercial recordings selected from national popularity charts. Several cable channels present country music, but these channels are distributed nationally even though they enjoy more popularity in certain regions of the country.

Ever since American soldiers took country music around the world during World War II, there has been increasing international interest in it—to the point that country music has become truly international in appeal, with fans throughout the world. Even the biggest record companies are international in both ownership and distribution. The regional music of the South has evolved into an international musical form.

Scholarship in country music developed slowly. A group of nonacademic researchers who worked independently of any academic discipline or institution ferreted out information about the early years of the country-music industry. These free-lance scholars conducted the initial and best early research into discography and biography of the earliest artists. They gained their first voice with the formation of the John Edwards Memorial Foundation (JEMF), which sought to bring them together with country-music musicians, industry representatives, and academic folklorists who were interested in this area of inquiry.

The music industry, following on the heels of the JEMF, established the Country Music Foundation. Located in Nashville and supported by the music industry, the foundation houses the largest collection of materials documenting the history and development of the country-music industry. The archives of the John Edwards Memorial Foundation are housed in the Southern Historical Collection at the University of North Carolina, Chapel Hill.

Ed Kahn

References

Ginell, Cary. 1994. *Milton Brown and the Founding of Western Swing.* Urbana: University of Illinois Press.

Malone, Bill C. 1985. *Country Music U.S.A.* rev. ed. Austin: University of Texas Press.

See also Bluegrass

Courlander, Harold (1908–)

Historian, essayist, ethnomusicologist, novelist, poet, dramatist, editor, and folklorist who played a major role in compiling and popularizing African American, Hopi, and Afro-Caribbean folktales. Born September 18, 1908, in Indianapolis,

Courlander earned his B.A. from the University of Michigan in 1931. His professional career included nine years (1945–1954) as an editor at the United States Information Agency's Voice of America and more than fifteen years as an analyst at the United Nations. He served as editor of *United Nations Review* from 1956 to 1959.

Courlander was an indefatigable fieldworker; his first publication was a play, *Swamp Mud,* published by Blue Ox Press in 1936. This was followed by a vast outpouring of novels, poems, folklore collections, and nonfiction works as well as nine record albums for which Courlander served as collector, editor, and compiler. His record albums—most of which were taken from field recordings made in Haiti, Cuba, and Ethiopia—were distributed by the Folkways Ethnic Library Series and are still available from Smithsonian-Folkways Recordings. By any standard, Courlander's productivity is phenomenal; especially in light of the fact that he held nine-to-five jobs for most of his career. His writing and research were largely confined to weekends, mornings, and evenings.

Courlander is author, editor, or coeditor of more than thirty volumes of folktales, which cover such diverse geographical regions and cultural areas as the Southern United States, the American Southwest, Haiti, the Dominican Republic, Cuba, Nigeria, Ghana, Ethiopia, Indonesia, and the Pacific islands. His publications are difficult to categorize. They are not strictly anthropological monographs, folklore, or journalistic treatments, but fall between these genres. All of his published works have enjoyed wide distribution in the United States and abroad and are featured in the catalogs of both commercial and university presses.

He has also experienced a degree of notoriety. After much soul-searching, Courlander brought a successful copyright infringement suit against novelist Alex Haley in 1978. Haley ultimately paid him more than $500,000, acknowledging that portions of Haley's *Roots* had been taken from Courlander's 1967 novel *The African.*

Perhaps Courlander's best-known publication is *The Drum and the Hoe: Life and Lore of the Haitian People* (1960; new ed. 1985), which James G. Leyburn hailed as "a fine example of bookmaking and a tribute to Courlander's perceptive respect for the culture." Also notable are *The Fourth World of the Hopis* (1971) and *People of the Short Blue Corn: Tales and Legends of the Hopi Indians* (1970), which vividly portray Hopi myth and history. The author visited northern Arizona reservations in 1968, 1969, and 1970 and began extensive conversations with Hopi elder Albert Yava. These conversations culminated in *Big Falling Snow* (1978), a well-received attempt to accurately represent Hopi religious beliefs and practices from a native's point of view.

His novel *The Bordeaux Narrative* (1990) skillfully examines the universe of voodoo through the eyes of a late-19th-century Haitian peasant who sets off to rescue a brother who has been turned into a zombie. As Stephen D. Glazier (1992) notes, *The Bordeaux Narrative* serves as an "excellent vehicle for its author's vast knowledge of Haitian folklore as well as an opportunity to demonstrate his keen eye for ethnographic detail." In this—as in all of his publications—Courlander sees himself first and foremost as a storyteller preserving cultural legacies from one generation to the next.

Stephen D. Glazier

References

Glazier, Stephen D. 1992. Review of *The Bordeaux Narrative* by H. Courlander. *Anthropology and Humanism Quarterly* 17:105–106.

Johnson, Abby Arthur. 1984. The Big Old World of Harold Courlander. *Midwest Quarterly* 25:450–470.

Leyburn, James G. 1961. Review of *The Drum and the Hoe* by H. Courlander. *American Sociological Review* 26:300.

Cousin Jack Stories

Brief, generally fictitious, humorous narratives involving 19th-century immigrants from Cornwall who followed the hard-rock mining occupation acquired in the old country. Although some attribute the term "Cousin Jack" to the habit of 'cussin'," more link it to chain migration: A Cornishman with a job in a mine would invariably recommend his "Cousin Jack" when a vacancy opened. Cornishwomen were known as "Cousin Jennies."

As in life, the Cousin Jacks of jokes were miners who might fancy a drink despite their Methodism. Their wives were inclined toward temperance and the baking of saffron buns and pasties (meat-and-potato turnovers). Men and women alike spoke a dialect marked by elongated vowels, a missing *g* in present participles, and the paradoxical coupling of an absent *h* at a word's beginning and its inclusion before vowels. Jokes commonly turned on dialect, as in the case of a miner beset by a growling dog. The owner reckons Towser is wagging his tail and will not bite. Cousin Jack replies: "'E's waggin' 'is tail at one hend and barkin' at the hother. I doan't naw which of 'is hends to believe."

Charles E. Brown first gathered this and other Cousin Jack stories in Wisconsin's lead-mining region in the 1930s. The stories have also been documented in Colorado, Minnesota, Montana, and especially in the "copper country" of Michigan's Upper Peninsula, where they persist.

James P. Leary

References

Bancroft, Caroline. 1944. Cousin Jack Stories from Central City. *Colorado Magazine* 21:51–56.

Brown, Charles E. 1940. *Cousin Jack Stories: Short Stories of the Cornish Lead Miners of Southwestern Wisconsin.* Madison: Wisconsin Folklore Society.

Dorson, Richard M. 1948. Dialect Stories of the Upper Peninsula: A New Form of American Folklore. *Journal of American Folklore* 61:113–150.

———. 1952. *Bloodstoppers and Bearwalkers: Folk Traditions of the Upper Peninsula.* Cambridge: Harvard University Press, pp. 103–122, 286–287.

Leary, James P. 1991. *Midwestern Folk Humor.* Little Rock, AR: August House, pp. 73–78, 234–235.

Rowse, A.L. 1969. *The Cousin Jacks: The Cornish in America.* New York: Scribners.

Cow Tipping

Prank allegedly popular at colleges in rural areas of the United States, in which students tip over sleeping cows standing in the fields. Stories about cow tipping have circulated since the 1970s and probably earlier, but it has never been definitely established that the practice actually occurs. Cow tipping is celebrated not only in oral tradition but also on greeting cards and T-shirts.

Skeptics, including many farmers, argue that an adult cow, at upwards of 1,000 pounds (455 kg), is too big to tip, and further that cows, unlike horses, do not sleep standing up, although they may doze on their feet while grazing. However, syndicated newspaper columnist Cecil Adams (Return of the Straight Dope) (1994) reported a claim by a former student at Albion College in Albion, Michigan, that she had participated in a cow-tipping episode as a freshman in about 1980. After a party one evening, the woman and several others had traveled to a farmer's field and watched as two male members of the group crept up on a sleeping cow and tipped it over. The startled cow scrambled to its feet, and the predictable hijinks ensued. The woman could supply no corroborating witnesses, and despite Adams' appeals, no participants in similar stunts stepped forward.

The feasibility of cow tipping could be quickly determined experimentally, but the scientific community has been unaccountably lethargic in this respect, and the matter awaits its Madame Curie.

Ed Zotti

Cowboy Poetry

Poetry claimed by ranching people in the American West. It tells their story, represents their lives, chronicles their history, and elucidates their feelings. Cowboy poetry was born on the long trail drives of the mid- to late-19th century, when large groups of men enlisted in the unfamiliar and dangerous occupation of moving cattle on horseback through the wild lands of the Western frontier. Though this poetic tradition is stronger today than ever, there have been many changes in its form and content. In the early days, cowboy poems were either published or memorized for oral recitation. They took the ballad form with simple rhyme and rhythm schemes. Today ranching men and women write and recite poems in every modern form, yet great respect is given to older traditions, including the old-time recitation style.

It is curious that one occupation, that of a cowboy, is so charged with mythic qualities. There is a wealth of expression—written and told, sketched and painted, braided and sewn—in a single, relatively uncommon occupation. There are no historic narratives from the original cowboy days, the trail drives following the Civil War, that fully explain the chemistry of an incredibly diverse lot of men brought together, in the wilderness, relying on each other and animals for long and trying odysseys. From this experience came an amazing amalgam of life that forever would identify Americans—a jazz of Irish storytelling and lore, Scottish seafaring and cattle tending, Moorish and Spanish horsemanship, European cavalry, African improvisation, and a reluctant observation of Native

American survival that can be heard and seen in this way of life even today.

Most singing in the old times was unaccompanied. Ballads were performed with little regard for strict rhythm; singing was closer to storytelling. In other words, the line between song and recitation may have been less distinct in earlier times. To understand this, notice the older Pentecostal preaching styles, which teeter between song and oration. The drama of the story dictated the rhythm more than some cosmic metronome did.

In discussing cowboy poetry, it is difficult to isolate the life of cowboys from their expressive existence, which simply reflects the life. In chronicling the poetry of cowboys, the word follows the trail of history. Before the century's turn, poetry and song tended to contain the nostalgia of the Victorian era and a loneliness from the trail for loved ones back home. Songs and poems such as "Bury Me Not on the Lone Prairie" were predominant. In the earliest ballads, there was also a plea for respect, as in this song from the 1860s, "The Western Pioneer":

> The cowboy's name is butchered by the papers in the
>   East,
> And when we're in the city we're treated like the beast.
> But in our native country our name is ever dear,
> And you bet we're always welcome by the western pio-
>   neer.

By the 1880s, romance had entered the stories. One of the earliest published examples is the poem "Lasca" written by an English theatre critic, Frank Desprez, and published in the *Montana Stock Growers Journal* in 1888. This work, one of the most widely recited cowboy poems yet today, enjoyed wide distribution in American society, not only around the campfire but in Victorian parlors and chautauqua programs. It began:

> I want free life and I want fresh air,
> And I sigh for the canter after the cattle,
> The crack of a whip's like shots in battle,
> The medley of horns and hoofs and heads
> The wars and wrangles and scatters and spreads
> And dash and danger and life and love
> And Lasca! Lasca used to ride. . . .

Lawrence Chittendon, the first to publish a widely distributed book of cowboy poems, had a hit with "The Cowboy's Christmas Ball." Written in cowboy dialect, it is one of a few poems in his 1893 collection *Ranch Verses* that is not rife with Victorian stuffiness and sentimentality. A caricature of a cowboy dance, it was embraced by ranch folks and entered the folk tradition. By the early part of the 20th century, John Lomax had collected versions of the poem with melodies. Lomax recognized that the poem had been improved by the folk process; he wrote, "One night in New Mexico a cowboy sang to me, in typical cowboy music, Larry Chittendon's entire 'Cowboy's Christmas Ball'; since that time the poem has often come to me in manuscript form as an original cowboy song. The changes—usually, it must be confessed, resulting in bettering the verse—which have occurred in oral transmission, are most interesting."

When Lomax published his second collection of cowboy songs in 1920, *Songs of the Cattle Trail and Cow Camp,* he compiled a book full of poems that he claimed had been "set to music by the cowboys, who, in their isolation and loneliness, have found solace in narrative or descriptive verse devoted to cattle scenes." Unlike his groundbreaking collection, *Cowboy Songs and Other Frontier Ballads* (1910), there is no musical notation to these songs. Most of the verse in this second edition never had music; yet, curiously, Lomax claimed these poems as songs.

By the 1920s books of cowboy poems, cowboy recordings, and cowboy novels were spreading like prairie fire. The cowboy image was set on its own course, a course of music, filmmaking, and literature that as the years passed strayed increasingly from the reality of ranch life.

If there was a Golden Age of cowboy poetry, it was between the turn of the century and 1930, when cowboys who had lived the life on a fenceless range celebrated their culture. This was before the popular cowboy image was buried by the onslaught of popularizers. There was a genuine, though sentimental, celebration of the lifestyle. Poets like Curley Fletcher put the kinetic beauty of a bronco ride to words in " The Strawberry Roan"; Bruce Kiskaddon, who self-published a book of poems in 1924, the year before he quit cowboying and moved to Los Angeles to be a bellhop, wrote poems like "The Old Night Hawk," which have been favorites of ranch folks ever since:

> I can see the East is gettin' gray.
> I'll gather the hosses soon;
> And faint from the valley far away
> Comes the drone of the last guard's tune.
>
> Yes, life is just like the night-herd's song,
> As the long years come and go.
> You start with a swing that is free and strong,
> And finish up tired and slow.

Most widely published heroes of cowboy poetry from this golden age led lives with some position in society. Badger Clark, S. Omar Barker, Gail I. Gardner, and Henry Herbert Knibbs all were educated or were ranch owners. They had first-hand cowboy experience; yet they could take an outsider's view as well.

By the early 1980s, when folklorists began a concerted effort to document cowboy poetry and music, the commercial cowboy fire had burned out, and the ranching community was adamantly suspicious of any interpretations of their culture by outsiders. At the same time, most were shy in presenting their story to a larger world. The art of the ranching community was an insider's affair, but this is no longer the case. Into the 1990s, true renaissance of cowboy arts is under way. It is powered by great pressure on a way of life foreign to the modern world. Grazing on the open lands of the West is being challenged by thirsty cities, recreationists, and environmentalists. Beyond a cry from the wilderness, beyond the mere nostalgic look at a vanishing past, there is strength and knowledge in this poetry, story, and song worthy of attention.

By 1995 there are more than 150 poetry gatherings in small Western towns, all spawned by the largest event of its kind, the Cowboy Poetry Gathering in Elko, Nevada. More than 500 books of ranch poetry have been published in the past century, as well as a handful of journals and magazines that print the work. The stories, songs, and poems that come out of this new movement recognize loss. They protest the modern world, offering advice to a disintegrating society. They make us laugh with the ridiculous, and they span the human experience of life and livelihood on the ranch. They tell stories that illustrate traditional values, about land and environment, about animal intelligence, about neighboring, cooperation, and about new sexual roles. Like most folk art, the themes are inherently best appreciated by insiders, but among the hundreds of men and women on ranches who write and recite poetry, there are some who have reached out to tell their stories to wider audiences. Several best-selling anthologies and recordings of this poetry have been released since the mid-1980s.

Hal Cannon

References

Cannon, Hal, ed. 1985. *Cowboy Poetry: A Gathering*. Salt Lake City: Peregrine Smith.

———. 1990. *New Cowboy Poetry: A Contemporary Gathering*. Salt Lake City: Peregrine Smith.

Cannon, Hal, and Thomas West, eds. 1993. *Buckaroo: Visions and Voices of the American Cowboy*. New York: Simon and Schuster.

Jordan, Teresa. 1994. *Graining the Mare: The Poetry of Ranch Women*. Salt Lake City: Peregrine Smith.

Miller, Warren, ed. 1994. *Cattle, Horses, Sky, and Grass: Cowboy Poetry of the Late 20th Century*. Flagstaff, AZ: Northland.

See also Gardner, Gail I.; Lomax, John Avery; Recitation

Cowboys

Mythical heroes of the Western United States, their image synonymous with ethics, integrity, loyalty, and rugged individualism. The cowboy's Hollywood, television, and literary romanticized image is a god-like figure, justified in administering punishment and death to those who are evil or are perceived to be evil, dishonest, or immoral. The 20th-century cowboy does believe in loyalty and independence and lives Western ethical values; he enjoys a limited amount of the romanticized image. Yet, the real working cowboy, past and present, bears only a partial resemblance to the image. The men and women who, indeed, do work cattle and horses live and work in the cold, heat, dust, rain, mud, and manure, and often they face pain, injury, and death; it is not romantic work, and the cowboy has not always enjoyed a mythical image.

The original "cow boy" was merely a boy who tended cows, but during the American Revolution, bands of Tory (loyalist) guerrillas and irregular cavalry, raiding mostly in Westchester County, New York, stole cows and other goods and called themselves cowboys. The next known usage was when Texas became a republic; a band of wild young men chased longhorns and Mexicans and called themselves cowboys, as did early Western outlaws. Even modern-day usage of the word occasionally implies a wild outlaw type or has a derogatory meaning such as "Reagan's cowboys." The mythical cowboy image came from the trail drives northward out of Texas following the Civil War; however, there were men who tended cattle long before the Texas trail herd/open range industry emerged.

Cattle and horses were introduced to the North American continent in Mexico by the Spanish. Settlers on the East Coast also brought cattle and horses, but the methods of tending, the tools, and the terminology used in the American West came from the Spanish and from Mexico. In Mexico and what is now the Southwestern United States, they tended, on horseback, large herds of cattle on wide open ranges, much different from the herd size and topography worked by settlers in the East and the Southeast. The story of the "hired man on horseback" in the Western Hemisphere, including Hawaii, is told by Richard W. Slatta in *Cowboys of the Americas* (1990), and, indeed, cowboys are working men on horseback hired by cattlemen-ranchers.

The terms "cattleman" and "rancher" imply ownership, not cowboy skills; the large ranch cattleman is confronted with the business of producing beef, decision making, buying and selling, profit or loss, hiring and firing, keeping up with scientific care and breeding of cattle, watching and working the "futures" market, and numerous other ownership problems. In fact, the modern-day cattleman may spend more time at a computer than working cattle on horseback. Yet, this does not imply that ranch owners have limited cowboying skills, for many past and present cattlemen were and are excellent cowboys. Smaller-ranch owners usually work side-by-side with their hired men, but it is the hired man on horseback who became the romantic cowboy myth.

As the range-cattle industry moved northward out of Mexico through Texas toward the Northern Plains states, the men on horseback rarely called themselves cowboys. They were cowmen, cowpunchers, cowhands, cowpokes, and other similar appellations, for most were young and did not want to be called "boys." They were men living a "wild and woolly," often dangerous, life on horseback in the wide open spaces—a life that gave them a sense of independence, an ethic of loyalty, and a belief in rugged individualism. Those men who served as the post–Civil War origins for the myth were mostly Southerners who migrated to Texas seeking a new life, and they carried strong English-Scottish traditions, particularly in their songs. But the Anglos were not the only cowboys in Texas.

Southern African Americans also migrated West, some escaping slavery before the war and others seeking a new life after the war. While most were hired for menial tasks, a few

became cooks and even fewer were given leadership responsibilities. There were African Americans who became ranchers with large land and cattle holdings, particularly along the coastal area of Texas, but generally the Anglos did not fight the Civil War to become trail-drive companions or bunkhouse pals with former slaves, and Black traditions, including music, made very little impact on cowboy culture. The greatest cultural influence came from Mexican *vaqueros*.

The Americanization of Spanish is part of basic cowboy lingo. *La reata* (the rope) became lariat, while *reata* indicates a rawhide rope. *Dar la vuelta* (to take wraps around an object) became dally-welta, or dally roping, which means that the roper dallys the reata or lariat around the saddle horn until the cow is under control; this is the opposite of "tying hard and fast," which means the lariat is tied to the saddle horn (the song "Windy Bill" tells the problem of tying hard and fast). *Chaparreras* (leg armor or leather leggings to protect the rider from thorns and brush) was Americanized to chaps. *Remotha* (remount) became remuda, a herd of extra horses, for on roundup and trail herding a horse needed two days' rest after a hard day's work. *Rodea* became rodeo, a cowboy contest, and there are other Americanized Spanish-Mexican words that are frequently heard.

A different strain of *vaquero* moved northward through California into Nevada and Oregon, and slowly the Americanization of the word *vaquero* became buckaroo. While they,

too, were hired men on horseback, their style of clothing and tools varied slightly from cowboys of Texas and the Plains states, but their dedication to raising beef and to working horses was equal to the Texas strain of cowboys.

The Western saddle (no matter what style or region) and its decorations, the Western spur with its varied designs, the lariat and the method of roping from horseback, the organized open-range roundup, protective gear for horseman and horse, and other aspects of the range-cattle industry were greatly influenced by Spanish crafts and traditions. However, the general language, foodways, songs and music, basic clothing, and other lifeways were Anglo.

Another ethnic grouping of cowboys has basically been ignored by historians, folklorists, and image makers—the American Indian. It is wrong to categorize them into the umbrella term "American Indian," for they are as diverse in language, culture, and traditions as is all of Europe. Each tribe had its own lore and history of contact with horses and eventually cattle. Raiding Spanish horse herds not long after they were introduced into their region, the Apaches were the earliest horsemen among the Indians, and the Five Civilized Tribes (nations of Cherokee, Choctaw, Chickasaw, Creek, and Seminole) were probably the earliest cattle herdsmen. Following their forced removal into Indian Territory (Oklahoma) in the 1820s and 1830s, particularly the mixed-blood members reestablished their businesses. By the 1840s and 1850s, herds of cattle were grazing in the Nations, and when Texas cattlemen drove herds up the old Texas Trail through eastern Indian Territory to Missouri, Indian cattlemen often joined the drive. Unfortunately, many of those drives were unprofitable, and they created a hatred of Texas cattle through the spread of Texas fever among the herds along the trail.

As buffalo were slaughtered and as ranching and farming spread throughout the West and into Canada, a few surviving Plains Indian tribes slowly turned to cattle raising for subsistence. Their successes, failures, and problems are told by Peter Iverson in *When Indians Became Cowboys* (1994).

Cowboys versus Indians has been a common theme in dime novels, Western novels, movies, and television, when, in fact, there was limited conflict between them. In early-day Texas and occasionally in other areas, there were some problems and conflicts, but cowboys and Indians have much in common. They love and respect the Earth and depend upon it for life, and their love and respect for horses is mutual. Especially in Oklahoma, ranchers, cowboys, and Indians are often one in the same, for full-blood and mixed-blood Indians own ranches and work their cattle. Following the Civil War, land was leased to cattlemen, and many Indians developed their own herds, some growing to as many as 15,000 head of cattle.

In 1867, when the cowboys who became the myth drove their herds toward Kansas, they crossed the Red River into the Chickasaw Nation and then crossed the Cheyenne-Arapaho Reservation into the Cherokee Outlet (owned by the Cherokee Nation). The Chickasaws, Choctaws, and Cherokees organized their own cattle associations to register brands and combat rustling, and they were cowboys who carried Anglo cowboy traditions as well as Indian traditions.

Cowboy traditions did not appear overnight, for as with other occupations the idiom (even with Spanish-Mexican influence) and clothing styles required time to become relatively standardized and traditional. Existing evidence indicates that songs and poems in the cowboy idiom using cowboys as the theme were not sung or recited prior to 1870; perhaps the exception is the granddaddy of cowboy songs, "The Old Chisholm Trail," since it is structured with disconnected couplets and a refrain.

Cowboy ballads and lyrical songs that slowly came out of the trail-drive experience received little non-cowboy attention until the turn of the century, and were generally touted to be songs from Texas with no known authorship. While Nathan Howard "Jack" Thorp compiled the first collection of cowboys songs, it was John Lomax's *Cowboy Songs and Other Frontier Ballads* (1910) that became the standard collection and also standardized lyrics, but scholarly research in the last half of the 20th century has identified the writers of many of the great and popular traditional ballads and songs as being non-Texans. These include Jack Thorp (New Mexico), Curley Fletcher (California and Nevada), Charles Badger Clark Jr. (Arizona and South Dakota), D.J. O'Malley (Montana), and many others.

The mythical cowboy also is often depicted as a singer with a guitar. Yet, few cowboys past or present have been singers, and only a few have had good voices. There also are other misconceptions about singing cowboys. The image of riding a horse at full run and singing a song to quell a stampede indicates a lack of experience with riding and singing, for not only is it impossible to sing under those conditions, but also thousands of stampeding cattle could not have heard a melodic voice, even an operatic voice at full volume. When old-time cowboys shouted, "Sing out to them," they were telling other cowboys to yell or make loud sounds. Songs were not written or sung to the gait of a horse, for each horse has individual gait characteristics and some are stiff-legged animals. Also, nearly 50 percent of the older cowboy songs are in waltz time, and not many horses have a $^3/_4$ rhythm gait.

The guitar was not a popular musical instrument in the United States until after the turn of the century. There may have been an occasional guitar in a bunkhouse, but it was too bulky to carry on a trail drive. It became associated with the cowboy in the 20th century through radio, recordings, and movies. The instrument most often heard was the fiddle, followed in popularity by the banjo, and the harmonica was as scarce as the guitar. In fact, if a cowboy sang, it was usually as an unaccompanied vocalist.

Among 19th-century cowboys, the most popular songs were sentimental and music-hall songs, traditional ballads, a few hymns, and, particularly, bawdy songs. A few cowboy- and outlaw-themed songs made their way through the cow camps, but the bulk of songs about cowboys were written in the 20th century.

Clothing varied slightly from region to region, simply because of the variation in climate, but a neckerchief was standard. In dry, dusty areas, it was used to cover the nose and mouth to filter out dust; in colder regions, its primary purpose was for warmth. With the passage of time, the neckerchief became decorative as well as utilitarian; in Texas the bandanna was known as a "wipe." In states such as Montana and Wyoming, the colorful silk neckerchief was, and is, a "tuf rag" or a "wild rag" and is still used for warmth and decoration; in Texas, Oklahoma, New Mexico, and warmer regions, the neckerchief is rarely used among working cowboys.

Chaps also had and have regional variation in style. The Mexican *vaqueros* wore tight leggings; in Texas the "bat wing," or chaps with flaps made of thick leather, became the popular style. In colder states, chaps made of Angora goatskin or bearskin were popular, for they were warmer and the hair shed rain better than the all-leather chaps. However, Angora chaps became identified with "dudes." In California and Nevada, the smaller chaps (known as chinks) that cover the upper leg instead of the entire leg were the style, and by the latter part of the 20th century chinks had spread in popularity throughout the Western states.

Other regional variations in the working-cowboy world exist. The most common belief, even though it is not necessarily true, is that cowboys from colder regions are better rough stock riders, and that cowboys in the warmer climates are better ropers. This was a strong belief among cowboys who followed the rodeo circuit when rodeo cowboys were also working cowboys, not professional athletes.

The 20th century saw many changes in the cowboy world. Feedlots, where cattle are gathered to fatten before being shipped to the slaughterhouse, grew in demand and size and required cowboys to tend them. The number of feedlot cowboys has grown, and in regions where grass is abundant and supports more cattle on smaller tracts of land, the size of a cow spread is smaller. In these areas, it is not uncommon to see the cowboy-owner drive his truck to the pasture, honk the horn, and the cattle come to be fed. The use of three-wheelers instead of horses is practiced on some ranches. No matter how they move around the ranch, working cowboys still have to tend cattle—feed them, doctor them, pull calves, and do other tasks involved in cattle raising, working any time of day or night in all kinds of weather. It is not romantic work.

Since the beginning of the trail drives and range-cattle industry, each generation has stated that the real cowboy dies with that generation. There are scholars and writers who have predicted the death of cowboying as a way of life, and even though the myth makers and the image shapers have created a romantic mythical cowboy there still are real working cowboys. Cattle have to be cared for, and as long as people eat beef there will be real working cowboys.

Guy Logsdon

References

Dary, David. 1981. *Cowboy Culture: A Saga of Five Centuries.* New York: Alfred Knopf.

Dobie, J. Frank. 1941. *The Longhorns.* Boston: Little, Brown.

————. 1952. *The Mustangs.* Boston: Little, Brown.

————. 1964. *Cow People.* Boston: Little, Brown.

Durham, Philip, and Everett L. Jones. 1965. *The Negro Cowboys.* New York: Dodd, Mead.

Jordan, Teresa. 1982. *Cowgirls: Women of the American West.* Garden City, NY: Doubleday.

Logsdon, Guy. 1989. *"The Whorehouse Bells Were Ringing" and Other Songs Cowboys Sing.* Urbana: University of Illinois Press.

Roach, Joyce Gibson. 1990. *The Cowgirls.* 2d ed. Denton: University of North Texas Press.

Ryan, Kathleen, ed. 1989. *Ranching Traditions: Legacy of the American West.* Photos by Kathleen Jo Ryan. New York: Abbeville.

Taylor, Lonn, and Ingrid Maar, eds. 1983. *The American Cowboy.* Washington, DC: American Folklife Center.

Ward, Fay E. 1987. *The Cowboy at Work: All about His Job and How He Does It.* Norman: University of Oklahoma Press.

See also Cowboy Poetry; Rodeo

Cox, John Harrington (1863–1945)

American folksong collector and editor, educator, doyen of the West Virginia Folk-Lore Society. Cox was born May 27, 1863, in Madison County, Illinois. Educated at Illinois State Normal, Brown, and Harvard Universities, he advanced to full professor of English philology at West Virginia University in Morgantown, where he resided from 1903 until his death on November 21, 1945. His book *Folk-Songs of the South* (1925) signaled the maturation of academic folksong collection and publication in the United States.

Cox came to folksong through an interest in medieval narrative poetry. In 1913 he spearheaded the formation of the West Virginia Folk-Lore Society, with himself as president, archivist, and editor; as he would later allow, "the activities of the Society centered in its President." Indeed, the society's one notable achievement was the publication of Cox's *Folk-Songs of the South,* based on his 1923 Harvard dissertation and the source of the foregoing quotation.

Notwithstanding its various precursors, *Folk-Songs of the South* was truly the first of the major regional collections of American folksong; any shortcomings aside, it remains one of the best. Although the book follows the then almost obligatory "Child-and-other" organization (assigning, that is, first place to older British ballads), it also includes a remarkable variety of other migratory and local songs and song types. Overwhelmingly textual in emphasis (there are only twenty-nine tunes for the 446 texts), and with virtually no information on sociocultural functions or performance settings, it nonetheless features some data on the singers and their communities. Despite his implicit acceptance of oral transmission as final proof of "folk" status, Cox simultaneously admitted considerable evidence for the traditional role of popular print. His cogent yet often extensive headnotes are models of the folksong scholarship of their day.

Some of the book's imbalances were redressed in two subsequent volumes, *Folk-Songs Mainly from West Virginia* (1939) and *Traditional Ballads Mainly from West Virginia* (1939), which were reprinted together in 1964. However, *Folk-Songs of the South* is and will rightly remain the basis of Cox's reputation as a seminal American folklorist.

John Minton

Coyote

Animal of the canine family, a Western Native American trickster figure, and a person of mixed blood. Scientifically classified as *Canis latrans* (barking dog), the animals are popularly known by the Spanish name *coyote,* originally borrowed from the Nahuatl *coyotl* and later appropriated into English, wherein they were first called "prairie wolves." The trickster Coyote predominates in traditions of Northwest coastal and interior, California, Southwest, and Southern Plains tribes and is also found in Meso-America. As a social classification, "coyote" derives from the Spanish colonial *casta* system, a legal plan to categorize and stratify a polyethnic society. In the American Southwest, the term came to designate Spanish and Indian or Black, and later Anglo and Indian or Hispano and Mexican, mixture.

Originally native to open plains in North America, the nineteen recognized subspecies of coyote are now usually "edge animals" that migrate to various "edge" terrains after human encroachment onto their natural, range territory. Widely distributed in all states west of the Mississippi River and from

Alaska to Costa Rica, in the American West the prolific coyote is often considered a destructive carnivore. The first printed description of "the Spanish fox" or "the Adipus (jackal)" appears in Francisco Hernández's 1651 *History of the Animals and Minerals of New Spain*. Its scientific name was assigned by American zoologist Thomas Say during an 1820s expedition to the Rocky Mountains. Natural-history–folklore accounts include Mark Twain's 1861 encounter with "cayote," described in Chapter 5 of *Roughing It* (1872), and J. Frank Dobie's *The Voice of the Coyote* (1949), but much more systematic, integrative work remains to be done before the biological and cultural "animal" can be fully articulated.

Coyote stories proliferate in folklorists', anthropologists', and linguists' Native American collections and translations since the 19th century. Often bowdlerized, such texts have been variously classified, usually etically, as humorous anecdotes, jokes, animal tales, folktales, legends, and/or myths—epic or episodic narratives involving a sacred and/or secular "trickster-transformer–culture hero" (Ricketts 1966). William Bright anthologizes Native American oral traditions and English-language literary texts by Indian, Latino, and Anglo writers to present a "natural history" of mythic Old Man Coyote as wanderer, *bricoleur*, glutton, lecher, thief, cheat, outlaw, spoiler, loser, clown, pragmatist, (horny) old man, and survivor (Bright 1993). Like Bright's, most studies establish Coyote as generically male and transformatively female or sometimes hermaphroditic, partly reflecting bias in available collections and interpretations, which generally overlook or obscure emic understandings wherein Coyote may be considered generically female or equally engendered and empowered by either sex.

As trickster, Coyote remains anomalous: a powerful, paradoxical, polysemic, liminal figure who is at once ambiguously animal and human, social and antisocial, deity and mortal. Barbara Babcock ([1975] 1985) argues for the generativity of this fundamental ambivalence and contradiction in the bewildering profusion of trickster tales. Coyote's "foolish" antistructure challenges the structured world and creates multiple reconfigurations and illuminations of it.

Careful ethnographic and performance study reveals Coyote's great variety and complexity. Folklorists studying Navajo Coyote stories have tried to distinguish between sacred texts about a Holy Person deity and secular tales of Trotting Coyote, but Barre Toelken (1971:204) found Navajos make no distinction between Ma'i (Coyote) the animal, the power in all coyotes, the narrative character, and the mythological symbol of disorder. Ma'i is an "enabler" whose humorous but serious stories, Yellowman (one of Toelken's sources) states, are told to children so "they will grow up to be good people" and to adults because "through the stories everything is made possible" (Toelken and Scott 1981:80). Telling stories in properly performed Navajo language creates reality, and Toelken distinguishes four levels of meaning in Coyote narratives from the Navajo perspective: entertainment, moral or evaluative, medicinal, and witchcraft. The first two are appropriate subjects of conversation and inquiry by Navajos and folklorists; the last two are crucial and esoteric for Navajos and should not

be broached by outsiders (Toelken 1987).

Borderlands Mexican folk narratives more commonly depict Coyote as trickster-dupe than mediating figure, according to Theresa Meléndez. Spanish and non-Spanish speakers on both sides of the border class as *coyotes*: smugglers illegally transporting people for profit, migrant-labor contractors, black-market Mexican money vendors, and fraudulent attorneys with no legal training, while "a woman who is accused of tempting and deceiving men is called a *coyota* (which a civil liberties organization of prostitutes convening in San Francisco has picked up as its name, COYOTE: 'Call Off Your Old Tired Ethics')" (Meléndez 1987:224). The colonial term *coyote* has come to designate mixed bloods or the *mestizo* generally, may be used derogatorily or affectionately, and now can simply indicate the indigenous or native.

Marta Weigle

References

Babcock, Barbara. [1975] 1985. "A Tolerated Margin of Mess": The Trickster and His Tales Reconsidered. In *Critical Essays on Native American Literature,* ed. Andrew Wiget. Boston: G.K. Hall, pp. 153–185.

Bright, William. 1993. *A Coyote Reader*. Berkeley: University of California Press.

Meléndez, Theresa. 1987. The Coyote. In *American Wildlife in Symbol and Story,* ed. Angus K. Gillespie and Jay Mechling. Knoxville: University of Tennessee Press, pp. 203–233.

Ricketts, Mac Linscott. 1966. The North American Indian Trickster. *History of Religions* 5:327–350.

Toelken, Barre. 1971. *Ma'i Joldloshi:* Legendary Styles and Navaho Myth. In *American Folk Legend: A Symposium,* ed. Wayland D. Hand. Berkeley: University of California Press, pp. 203–211.

———. 1987. Life and Death in the Navajo Coyote Tales. In *Recovering the Word: Essays on Native American Literature,* ed. Brian Swann and Arnold Krupat. Berkeley: University of California Press, pp. 388–401.

Toelken, Barre, and Tacheeni Scott. 1981. Poetic Retranslation and the "Pretty Languages" of Yellowman. In *Traditional American Indian Literatures: Texts and Interpretations,* ed. Karl Kroeber. Lincoln: University of Nebraska Press, pp. 65–116.

See also Trickster

Crafts

Objects made by hand from materials in the local environment that reflect established norms and techniques within a community, transmitted through informal channels such as word of mouth or demonstration. Crafts produce traditional homemade objects that are primarily functional but may be decorative as well.

The etymology of the word "craft" links it to notions of strength, power, force, and virtue. Only in English does it transfer to conceptions of skill, art, or some skilled occupation. Even then, as Simon J. Bronner points out, crafts remain

Eighth-graders Zollie M. Brooks, Lucenda Harvard, Pearlie M. Leurs, and Susie Vinson make corn-husk mats. Flint River Farms, near Montezuma, Georgia, 1939. Photo Marion Post Wolcott.

objects that have both physical and intellectual consequences; they extend ideas and feelings into three-dimensional form (Bronner 1986).

In preindustrial America, crafts fulfilled a need to make things for oneself rather than rely on outside suppliers. People made what they needed to solve the practical problems of shelter, food, clothing, transportation, and entertainment. Tools and textiles, baskets and pots, boats and buildings, toys and musical instruments all were made by hand according to community traditions of pattern, process, and style. Products of the craftperson's hands were judged by community norms. The process of craft production was sometimes a community event, such as a quilting bee or a barn raising; sometimes it demanded the solitary work of wood carving, weaving, or silversmithing. Crafts were a social force in the life of colonial and pioneer communities.

As the United States industrialized in the mid- to late 19th century, the need for handcrafted items declined as manufactured goods, readily available in stores and catalogs, solved the problems of domestic life. With increasing urbanization and availability of commercialized goods came a wave of nostalgia in which rural life and its handmade artifacts came

to represent a kind of Romantic idealism and moral purity that seemed lacking in urban life.

The renewed interest in crafts in America was influenced by the Arts and Crafts movement in England that began in the mid-19th century. John Ruskin decried the sameness and tedious perfection of manufactured goods and argued for the essential humanity of handcrafted artifacts in *The Stones of Venice* (1851). Ruskin's rules for craft called for (1) the classical notion of *invention* in the making of articles rather than the industrial ideal of identical fabrication, (2) the irregularity of hand-finished artifacts over the exact finish produced by machines, and (3) the stamp of individuality working within a tradition rather than rigid imitation or copying of forms and styles.

Ruskin's work influenced William Morris, a young Oxford student, who ultimately created his own firm for the creation of craft and craft designs in decorative art in the 1860s. By 1888 England had a Guild and School of Handicraft and an Arts and Crafts Exhibition Society; this was, incidentally, the same year the American Folklore Society came into being.

Interest in Ruskin's and Morris' ideas of decorative arts as a moral force surfaced in America by the 1870s. Decorative ceramics, built on the tradition of functional folk pottery, became popular with socially prominent young women in urban centers who organized clubs and exhibitions for their work throughout the 1870s and 1880s. Lucie-Smith argues in *The Story of Craft* (1981:223) that this early interest in pottery provides a glimpse of the wide spectrum of American attitudes toward crafts, including the involvement of amateurs, especially women; a willingness to borrow ideas from many sources; an interest in experimentation for its own sake rather than for utility; a strong business sense about craft marketing; and an interest in craft, not only for its own sake, but as a medium of education.

By the turn of the century, handicraft clubs and guilds, arts and crafts centers, and magazines such as *Handicraft* and *The Craftsman* (devoted to William Morris) flourished throughout the United States. *The Craftsman* praised the art, work, and lives of preindustrial people and suggested that modern Americans could simplify their lives by owning native crafts and thereby identifying with "the people" (Boris 1987:217).

This suggestion promoted interest in crafts produced by ethnic minorities within America, particularly Native Americans, and cultural minorities such as Appalachian mountaineers. For example, in 1879 John Wesley Powell, a self-taught anthropologist and charter member of the American Folklore Society, lobbied for a national agency to study Native American culture. His work resulted in formation of the Bureau of American Ethnology (BAE) that documented Indian life.

Many crafts were on the decline in their native communities in the industrial and commercial boom of the late 19th century, but entrepreneurial educators and social reformers encouraged their revival with missionary zeal. They believed, in fact, that crafts embodied the ideal of culture and uplift they hoped to bring to what they believed were their more primitive, impoverished brethren.

In Appalachia, for example, President William Goodell Frost of Berea College in Kentucky recognized the quality and potential market value of crafts, particularly handweaving, and started a work-study program at the college called the Fireside Industries in 1893 (Barker 1991). Frost took a horseback tour of students' homes in southern Appalachia that year and saw handcrafted baskets, chairs, coverlets, crockery, and other items that he thought had market potential with the college's New England supporters. In 1896 he organized the first Homespun Fair at Berea to encourage craft production in the region.

Frost's efforts were quickly emulated throughout the region at Allanstand Cottage Industries, Biltmore Industries, Penland School, and the John C. Campbell Folk School in North Carolina, the Pi Beta Phi School (Arrowmont) in Tennessee, and Hindman and Pine Mountain Settlement Schools in Kentucky. By the late 1920s, the craft movement in Appalachia had attracted the interest of Allen Eaton of the Russell Sage Foundation in New York City, long a proponent of the value and virtues of crafts. Eaton had promoted interest in crafts from all types of rural and ethnic groups throughout America in his work with the American Country Life Asso-

Ambrose Roanhorse, Navajo silversmith. American Folklife Center.

ciation and the American Federation of Arts.

Eaton helped the various craft cooperative groups throughout Appalachia form the Southern Highland Handicraft Guild in 1930. The goals of the guild included preservation of mountain craft work and creation of national markets for the crafts as a step toward economic independence for the people of Appalachia. In the 1930s, the guild offered several regional and national exhibitions of mountain crafts, and Eaton published his comprehensive and influential *Handicrafts of the Southern Highlands* (1937).

As David Whisnant (1983) points out, the story of crafts in Appalachia evolved into a story of cultural intervention in which forces outside the local communities shaped the processes, design, production, and marketing of what had been traditional craft work into craft work for widespread commercial consumption (Whisnant 1983). The idea of using crafts as an educational and moral force, as well as an economic boon, also reflected the educational and moral values of middle-class America and not necessarily the values associated with handmade work in the local community.

The saga of craft development in Appalachia was repeated among numerous Native American groups, Eskimos, African Americans, and Pennsylvania Germans. The Arts and Crafts movement in America in the late 19th and early 20th centuries associated crafts with vanishing rural life, so that crafts seemed to be survivals or precious relics of an earlier, simpler, more idyllic life. This led to a self-consciousness in craft production that altered the natural cultural impulses for craft artistry and caused the place of craft in urban life largely to be ignored.

The Depression years of the 1930s fostered attention crafts as a way to recognize the contributions of immigrant groups in America and to increase self-esteem among all Americans hard hit by the economic crash. Allen Eaton followed his work in Appalachian crafts with exhibitions and a book on immigrant contributions to American life (Eaton 1932). President Franklin D. Roosevelt, through the mechanism of the Works Progress Administration (WPA), put writers, artists, and musicians to work recording all manner of American life, including crafts. The massive Index of American Design contained thousands of drawings of handicraft utensils, carousel animals, scrimshaw carvings, and similar objects (Green 1977:5). Other federal agencies, such as the Extension Division of the U.S. Department of Agriculture and the Division of Subsistence Homesteads in the Department of Interior, encouraged the production of crafts to provide domestic necessities and supplement family incomes during the lean years of the Depression and its aftermath.

Interest in crafts was subsumed by the heightened industrial production of the war years of the 1940s and the increasing emphasis on science and high technology in the postwar 1950s. Handcrafted work seemed irrelevant in a world of atomic bombs, television, and ventures into space. But the 1960s brought a backlash to mass consumerism and what seemed to be increasingly dangerous technological developments.

Folk music provided anthems for the 1960s and ushered in a new era of interest in making folk instruments and handcrafted clothing. The principles of cultural pluralism and ecological harmony that guided the 1960s and 1970s foregrounded the contributions of America's minority groups, including women, African Americans, Native Americans, Hispanics, religious minorities, and rural people in general, and fostered a resurgence in craft production among these groups. Popular books such as the Foxfire series created appreciation for making and studying traditional crafts in a vast public audience. A shift in emphasis among some folklorists from the study of "folklore" to the more inclusive "folklife' helped launch such ventures as the Festival of American Folklife in 1967, a festival that featured craft demonstrations on the national mall in Washington, DC, creation of a folk-arts program in the National Endowment for the Arts in 1974; and passage of the American Folklife Preservation Act of 1976 that created the American Folklife Center at the Library of Congress.

Contemporary interest in handcrafted items has never waned since the fertile period of the 1960s and 1970s. Among folklorists, crafts are studied and documented with particular attention to the cultural context in which they are created. Much craftsmanship has become increasingly tied to standards set by distant and alien markets. For example, Hmong textile work changed from traditional geometric patterning to narrative storycloths with subtitles in English when refugees left Southeast Asia for the cities of the United States. These changes were responses to demands of the Western marketplace (Conquergood 1992).

Another significant change in craft work is the continual blurring of the line between craft and fine art (Lucie-Smith 1981:277). Many craft artists have ambitions for their work to be judged by the same criteria as fine art, with little reference to the utilitarian qualities of the craft, and often based on conceptions drawn from avant-garde art. Some critics have suggested that the category of craft is no longer meaningful when it can embrace those who still visibly embrace a traditional craft in their own communities and artist-craftspersons who create craft for pure contemplation. Others suggest that craft must embrace both the amateur and the trained artist-craftsperson because both represent a "necessary antonym" to industrial society and visible reminders of where industry originates.

As Bronner argues, the handmade object in contemporary life more than ever draws symbolic and social attention to itself as it raises questions of purpose, celebrates control of some aspect of life for its maker, and, for a mass society, gives a tangible reminder of involvement (Bronner 1986:8, 216).

Jean Haskell Speer

References

Barker, Garry G. 1991. *The Handcraft Revival in Southern Appalachia, 1930–1990*. Knoxville: University of Tennessee Press.

Boris, Eileen. 1987. The Social Ideas of the Arts and Crafts Movement. In *"The Art That Is Life": The Arts and Crafts Movement in America, 1875–1920*, ed. Wendy Kaplan. Boston: Little, Brown, pp. 208–222.

Bronner, Simon J. 1986. *Grasping Things: Folk Material Culture and Mass Society in America*. Lexington: University Press of Kentucky.

Conquergood, Dwight. 1992. Fabricating Culture: The Textile Art of Hmong Refugee Women. In *Performance, Culture, and Identity*, ed. Elizabeth C. Fine and Jean Haskell Speer. Westport, CT: Praeger, pp. 207–248.

Eaton, Allen. 1932. *Immigrant Gifts to American Life*. New York: Russell Sage Foundation.

Green, Archie. 1977. Foreword. In *Folklife and the Federal Government*, ed. Linda C. Coe. Washington, DC: American Folklife Center, pp. 1–9.

Lucie-Smith, Edward. 1981. *The Story of Craft*. Ithaca, NY: Cornell University Press.

Whisnant, David. 1983. *All That Is Native and Fine: The Politics of Culture in an American Region*. Chapel Hill: University of North Carolina Press.

See also Art, Folk; Basketmaking; Blacksmithing; Index of American Design; Needlework; Outsider Art; Paper Cutting; Pottery; Quilt Making; Toys, Folk; Weaving; Wood Carving

Crane, Thomas Frederick (1844–1927)

Professor of Romance philology, founding member of the American Folklore Society, and the leading representative of European folklore scholarship in the United States for several decades. From the 1870s until his death, Crane published articles, books, and scores of reviews in literary and scholarly journals that remain valuable resources for folklorists.

Crane's reviews of *Folklore Fellows Communications* Vols. 1–21 (Crane 1916) introduced this important series to American folklorists and helped Antti Aarne, an early Finnish folklorist, gain a professorship in Finland. His review of Joel Chandler Harris' *Uncle Remus* tales and their parallels provided important evidence for the African origin of African American narrative. In an 1883 paper on "Mediaeval Sermon-Books and Stories" and his 1890 critically and comparatively annotated edition of *The Exempla of Jaques de Vitry,* Crane surveyed the field of exempla research and established the significance of these religious tales as stores of cultural information. This work set off a new field of research in Europe and, later, the United States. Other publications on exempla, Italian folktales and customs, French folksongs and the tales of the brothers Grimm remain models of comparative folklore scholarship.

Upon invitation from William Wells Newell, Crane served on the editorial board of the *Journal of American Folklore* from 1888 to 1892 and contributed a survey of European folktale theory to the first issue. But Crane seems to have played a minor role in steering the further course of the journal, which failed to publish a notice of his death.

Peter Tokofsky

References

Crane, Thomas Frederick. 1881. Plantation Folk-Lore: Review of Joel Chandler Harris' *Uncle Remus. Popular Science Monthly* 18:824–833.
———. 1916. *Folklore Fellows Communications,* Vols. 1–21. *Romanic Review* 7:110–125.
———. 1925. Bibliography of the Writings of T.F. Crane. In *Liber de Miraculis: Sanctae dei Genitricis Mariae.* Ithaca, NY: Cornell University Press.

Creighton, Helen (1899–1989)

Folklore collector and disseminator. Creighton was a regionalist who documented and promoted the folklore of Canada's Maritime Provinces, especially her native Nova Scotia. Her primary interest was Anglo Canadian folksong, but she also collected other genres and from other groups.

Born into an upper-middle-class family, Creighton first became interested in folklore as a young woman trying to establish a career in journalism. A self-taught collector, she was influenced initially by the English Folk Song and Dance movement but, after attending Indiana University's Folklore Institute in 1942, was aware of developments in American folkloristics.

From 1928 she collected folklore and published sixteen books without university affiliation and with limited institutional support. In 1943 the Rockefeller Foundation provided her with Library of Congress recording equipment; the National Museum (now the Canadian Museum of Civilization) made her an adviser from 1947 to 1964, supplying her with a tape recorder from 1949 on. She is remembered as a skilled fieldworker, eclectic in scope and sensitive to community dynamics.

Creighton was innovative as a popularizer, using print and broadcast media to publicize folklore. Her work also inspired many adaptations including *Sea Gallows,* a ballet performed by Montreal's Les Grands Ballets Canadiens (1958) and *The Celtic Mass for the Sea,* an orchestral work by composer Scott MacMillan for Symphony Nova Scotia (1988). Creighton helped shape provincial and regional identity, and one folksong she collected, "Nova Scotia Song," is the Nova Scotian anthem.

She received many public honors, including six honorary degrees and the Order of Canada (1976). Dartmouth, Nova Scotia, operates her former home as a museum and since 1990 holds an annual folklore festival in her memory. Despite her public appeal, however, she has had little impact on Canadian folklore studies, since folklorists were slow to appreciate her work.

Diane Tye

References

Creighton, Helen. [1932] 1966. *Songs and Ballads from Nova Scotia.* New York: Dover.
———. 1950. *Traditional Songs from Nova Scotia.* Toronto: Ryerson.
———. 1957. *Bluenose Ghosts.* Toronto: Ryerson.
———. 1961. *Maritime Folksongs.* Toronto: Ryerson.
———. 1968. *Bluenose Magic.* Toronto: Ryerson.
———. 1975. *A Life in Folklore.* Toronto: McGraw-Hill Ryerson.

Crimelore

A widespread theme in oral tradition concerning the individuals who violate the laws, either within the society they live in or within the context of the folkloric form in which they appear, and, of the victims who are affected by their unlawful actions. Crimelore is as widespread in the American folk tradition as it is within many aspects of contemporary society. Crime themes appear in almost every genre of folklore, but particularly in balladry and folksong, tales about legendary outlaws, and in contemporary urban legends. Crimelore, too, has its own esoteric components found in the folk speech or jargon of criminals, stories about "confidence men" or swindler-tricksters, as well as the personal-experience stories about criminal activities told by incarcerated prisoners and victims of urban crime.

Oral tradition is filled with stories about notorious

criminals and their exploits. These include stories about outlaws of the 19th-century Wild West, such as Jesse James, and gangsters of the 20th century, such as the robber-murderer John Dillinger of Indiana and Al Capone, the crime boss of Chicago, who sold illegal liquor during Prohibition. In contemporary times, stories have circulated about mass murderers, such as ringleader Charles Manson of the 1960s; Albert DeSalvo, the Boston Strangler; and Jeffrey Dahmer, the cannibal murderer, among others. While these murderers become widely known via the media, stories about them often circulate in local communities and become part of the crimelore already circulating in that locale. Two examples of pre-media age localized tales that are still part of each community's lore would be that of Belle Gunness of LaPorte, Indiana, and Lizzie Borden of Fall River, Massachusetts. Also known as the Lady Bluebeard, Gunness was believed to have murdered her family and several mail-order husbands and to have buried their remains in her backyard; the remains were discovered on her property after a fire in 1908. Lizzie Borden was known to have murdered her parents on August 2, 1892. The popular children's song circulates in Fall River today:

> Lizzie Borden took an axe,
> Gave her father forty whacks.
> And when Lizzie was all done,
> She gave her mother forty-one.

One subtype of crimelore involves white-collar crime. This lore includes stories found in the workplace relating to office workers—from petty thieves to insider junk-bond traders (such as Ivan Boesky) whose actions could topple financial markets. Recently included as white-collar criminals are computer hackers who violate laws by pirating software and illegally transmitting software over computer bulletin boards. Stories are passed on about brilliant "electronic burglars" such as Robert Morris, who in 1988 achieved notoriety when he wrote a computer program that halted an important computer network.

In the Anglo American tradition, ballads about outlaws and outlaws regarded as heroes by the folk have circulated widely and are well known. Ballads that deal with criminal activities fall into two types: those that explain the outlaw's escapades and are sung by a narrator who claims to have known of the outlaw's adventures; and those in which the central character, the criminal, relates his own tale of how he turned against the law and was later caught by the authorities. An example is "The Ballad of Jesse James." Missouri-born James was one of the most sought after bank and train robbers in his day. Along with his gang of twenty-two, he committed more than twenty-five robberies for a booty exceeding $600,000. James was murdered in 1882 by a member of his own gang, Robert Ford, who was tempted by the $10,000 reward for James' capture. He also wanted to be immortalized as the "man who killed Jesse James." The ballad refers to James' alias, "Mr. Howard," and describes the murder:

> Jesse James was a lad that killed many a man.
> He robbed the Danville train.
> But that dirty little coward that shot Mr. Howard
> Has laid poor Jesse in his grave.
> It was Robert Ford, that dirty little coward,
> I wonder how he does feel;
> For he ate of Jesse's bread and slept in Jesse's bed
> And he laid poor Jesse in the grave.

While some ballads recount the exploits of outlaws, others relate events of historic import, such the assassination of President James Garfield on July 2,1881, by Charles Guiteau, who was hanged for his crime on June 30, 1882. In the well-known folksong "The Ballad of Charles Guiteau," the narrator, Guiteau, atones for his crime. Ballads of this sort are often categorized as the "criminal's good night," a ballad feature in which the criminal feels remorse for his unlawful actions. His "good night" is usually sung on the eve of his execution. In the following verse, Guiteau laments his fate:

> My name is Charles Guiteau,
> My name I'll ne'er deny.
> I leave my aged parents
> In sorrow for to die
> But little did they think,
> While in my youthful bloom,
> I'd be taken to the scaffold
> To meet my earthly doom.

One of the most widely circulated murder ballads is about a young woman named Pearl Bryant of Greencastle, Indiana. She was beheaded by Scott Jackson, the father of her illegitimate unborn baby, and his accomplice, Alonzo Walling; both were executed in 1897. In some locales in Indiana, the ballad remains in oral tradition along with a legend concerning her ghost returning to the murder site. One ballad stanza explains the crime:

> A horrible crime was committed,
> Soon was brought to light,
> For parents to look on their headless girl,
> 'Twas a sad and dreadful sight.

Contemporary stories about crime are told by incarcerated men and women in prison and by criminals on the street. In these narratives about dangerous exploits, the stories are often filled with insider jargon, or folk speech used for nicknames, events, and everyday items. For example, the phrase "a songbird doing time in the Big House" describes a prison informer who has been sentenced to a federal prison. The use of everyday speech within prison, the prison culture, and the exploits of prisoners have been collected from prisoners by folklorists, most notably by Bruce Jackson.

Crime is a major issue in the everyday lives of many Americans, and so they create a folkloric form to deal with the anxiety of the possibility of being a crime victim. Most recently, crime-victim stories have been collected from urbanites who are constantly bombarded about crime by reports on television news, newspaper headlines, and stories that urbanites tell to one another about crime-victim events. These crime-victim stories, describing muggings, rapes, murder, and other physical assaults, are highly structured narratives that explicate a confrontation between an offender and his victim. Often, the teller describes where the event took place and the action between the story's characters. Narrators often complete the narrative with an explanation of how the event was resolved and a coda, or comment, about the event or a general comment about the overwhelming intrusion of crime into daily life.

Crime-victim stories are told for several reasons. They impart crime-prevention skills, or "street smarts," telling urbanites about safe and unsafe locales so they can adjust their mental maps of their urban environment. They reinforce the theme of bystander apathy: There are few Good Samaritans in the city. Following is an example of a crime-victim narrative as told by a New Yorker emphasizing the bystander motif and the premonition that crime is an interruption to daily life:

> My friend was walking down the street one evening. She saw these four kids coming toward her and she said, . . . she was thinking to herself. . . . "Why not go across the street? You know, 'cause you never know." But she started thinking why should she do that because there are just four kids walking down the street. Well, they got her! One had a knife and took her money and all that. (Wachs 1988)

Recently there has been a constant debate whether violence on television or in other forms of media (or folklore), promotes more violence in our culture, especially among teenage males. This issue has surfaced again with the acceptance of "rap" or "gangsta" music, a narrative, musical form relative to the African American toast. Both of these spoken forms have common themes of violence, particularly against women, and rationalization for breaking laws. More, too, is heard about youth gangs, particularly those found in urban ghettos of large cities, whose members wear their own colors (or uniforms), stake out their own boundaries, and take on new personas or nicknames.

Eleanor Wachs

References

Hafner, Katie, and John Markoff. 1991. *Cyberpunk: Outlaws and Hackers on the Computer Frontier.* New York: Simon and Schuster.

Langlois, Janet. 1985. *Belle Gunness: The LadyBluebeard.* Bloomington: Indiana University Press.

Wachs, Eleanor. 1988. *Crime Victim Stories: New York City's Urban Folklore.* Bloomington: Indiana University Press.

See also Outlaw; Personal-Experience Story; Prison Folklore; Urban Folklore

Crockett, Davy (1786–1836)

Famous frontiersman, Tennessee and U.S. congressman, defender of the Alamo, and legendary folk hero. Born in Greene County in east Tennessee on August 17, 1786, Crockett was an unknown backwoods hunter with a talent for storytelling until his election to the Tennessee legislature in 1821 as the representative of Lawrence and Hickman Counties and to the U.S. House of Representatives in 1827. He had promoted himself as a simple, honest country boy who was an extraordinary hunter and marksman, someone who was on all levels a literal "straight shooter."

Political notoriety gave his image a life of its own by the 1830s, and Crockett became the model for Nimrod Wildfire, the hero of James Kirke Paulding's play *The Lion of the West* (1830) as well as the subject of articles and books. Tales swirled about him so thickly that Crockett said he was compelled to publish his autobiography *(A Narrative of the Life of David Crockett of the State of Tennessee)* ([1834] 1973) to counteract the outlandish stories printed under his name as the *Sketches and Eccentricities of Colonel David Crockett of West Tennessee,* published in 1833. Taken up by the anonymous Boston hack writers who spun out tall tales for the Crockett Almanacs (1835–1856), the fictional Davy expanded his role as a legendary backwoods screamer. He could "run faster, jump higher, squat lower, dive deeper, stay under longer, and come out drier, than any man in the whole country," save the world by unfreezing the sun and the Earth from their axes, and ride his pet alligator up Niagara Falls.

Crockett's "corrective" *Narrative* can also be viewed as the first presidential-campaign biography, since he was being touted by the Whigs as the candidate who would oppose Andrew Jackson's handpicked successor, Martin Van Buren. Crockett's defeat in his bid to be returned to Congress in 1835 ended his presidential ambitions, and, temporarily disenchanted with politics and his constituents, he made the now famous remark: "You may all go to hell and I will go to Texas." His last surviving letters spoke of his confidence that Texas would allow him to rejuvenate his political career and finally make his fortune. He intended to become land agent for the new territory and saw the future of an independent Texas as intertwined with his own.

He and his men joined Colonel William B. Travis in the defense of the Alamo, and Travis wrote that, during the first bombardment, Crockett was everywhere in the Alamo "animating the men to do their duty." The siege of thirteen days ended on March 6, 1836, when the Alamo was overrun. Crockett and five or six other survivors were captured. Several Mexican officers asked that the prisoners be spared, but Santa Anna had the prisoners bayoneted and then shot.

Many thought that Davy deserved a better end and provided it, from thrilling fictions of his clubbing Mexicans with his empty rifle until cut down by a flurry of bullets or bayonets or both, stories that undergirded the movie portrayals by Fess Parker and John Wayne, to his survival as a slave in a salt mine in Mexico. No matter what the past or future directions of the legends of Davy Crockett, however, it is clear that his popularity in the media from his time forward guarantees his continuing preeminence in the American mind as

Davy Crockett. Engraving by Charles Gilbert Stuart, after a painting by John Gadsby Chapman. Library of Congress.

the heroic representative of frontier independence and virtue.

Michael A. Lofaro

References

Crockett, David. [1834] 1973. *A Narrative of the Life of David Crockett of the State of Tennessee,* ed. James A. Shackford and Stanley J. Folmsbee. Knoxville: University of Tennessee Press.

Lofaro, Michael A., ed. 1985. *Davy Crockett: The Man, The Legend, The Legacy, 1786–1986.* Knoxville: University of Tennessee Press.

Shackford, James A. 1986. *David Crockett: The Man and the Legend.* Chapel Hill: University of North Carolina Press.

Culin, Stewart (1858–1929)

Best known as a pioneer in traditional game research, particularly of Native American and East Asian peoples. Culin was an early president, in 1897, of the American Folklore Society and a founding member, in 1902, of the American Anthropological Association. He served as director of the University of Pennsylvania Museum of Archaeology and Paleontology from 1892 to 1903 and subsequently as curator of ethnology at the Brooklyn Museum's Institute of Arts and Sciences.

Fieldwork in Korea, Japan, China, and India was the basis for his *Korean Games, with Notes on the Corresponding Games of China and Japan* (1895, reprinted in 1958 as *Games of the Orient).* A comprehensive collection that remains an important reference, this work also makes readers aware of the many similarities among the world's traditional games and the important part games play in all societies.

Culin's most ambitious and enduring publication is his descriptive and classificatory *Games of the North American Indians* (1907, reprinted in 1975), in which he addresses questions about game implements and playing techniques, the relationships between games and other aspects of culture, the history and geographical distribution of selected games, and the nature of the similarities discernible in American Indian games and those of other (particularly Asian) peoples.

Between 1889 and 1900, Culin also published (in the *Journal of American Folklore* and the *American Anthropologist)* seminal essays on Hawaiian (Culin 1889) and Filipino (Culin 1900) games and on American immigrant and urban folklore, including, a Sicilian marionette theater in New York City; Chinese American dice, domino, and gambling games; African American sorcery; and urban-American boys' street games.

Robert A. Georges

References

Culin, Stewart. 1899. Hawaiian Games. *American Anthropologist,* n.s., 1:201–247.

———. 1900. Philippine Games. *American Anthropologist,* n.s., 2:643–656.

Cults

As understood by most Americans, deviant religious groups that pose a threat to society. Some such groups, such as the Reverend Sun Myung Moon's Unification Church (the "Moonies") are large, well-organized offshoots of Christianity; others, like Charles Manson's "Family" or Jim Jones' People's Temple, were small, short-lived dissident groups prone to violence (Melton 1986; Saliba 1990).

During the 1970s, many alternative religions were assumed to be cults gaining tight psychological control to brainwash teenagers they attracted. Deprogramming, a form of kidnapping and confrontational dialogue, became a popular form of attempting to remove adolescents from such groups. However, formal studies have shown that there is little value in such practices (Bromley and Richardson 1983). Nevertheless, a Gallup Poll conducted in the late 1980s characterized "cults" as the most despised groups in America.

Rumors and legends about minority religions have circulated since ancient times, the most notorious being the Blood Libel, in which the members of a cult are said to be kidnapping children, murdering them during a religious rite, and then cannibalizing their flesh and blood (Dundes 1991). First attached to Christians during Nero's reign, it was later used by the church to justify the persecution and mass execution of Jews, witches, and members of heretical sects. In 19th-century America, it was attached to Catholics, and after a mentally ill woman claimed to have been a former nun who was forced to "breed" babies for ritual murder, a nationwide wave of attacks on Catholic priests, convents, and churches followed (Billington 1938).

More recently, anticult rumors have been attached to "satanists," who in addition to committing ritual murder and cannibalism, secretly abuse children, force women to breed babies, and brainwash teenagers into committing suicide. The members of a cult may be said to commit murder or mutilation as part of an initiation rite, similar to the practices of youth gangs often thought to rob, mutilate, or kidnap women at shopping malls. They may use holidays like Halloween as opportunities to abduct and murder children. In one especially widespread legend, satanists are said to need a "blonde-haired, blue-eyed virgin" for a specific sacrifice, often on a Friday the Thirteenth.

The FBI (Federal Bureau of Investigation) has never been able to document any child abduction or murder as a satanic cult sacrifice, but believers attribute this to the influence of satanists in positions of power. Procter and Gamble, for many years, has been accused of giving money to cults—first the "Moonies," later devil-worshipers—and their logo supposedly contains satanic imagery (Fine 1992). Similar rumors have been attached to other corporations, such as Ray Kroc's fastfood chain, McDonalds; Liz Claiborne's clothing and cosmetics firm; and recording corporations responsible for producing "heavy metal" rock music.

Social scientists blame such legends on the defensive posture of traditional Christianity (Richardson, Best, and Bromley 1991). Nevertheless, sincere belief in satanic cults continues to circulate among law-enforcement agents (Hicks 1991). The presence of such narratives has influenced some groups and criminals to commit real acts of abuse and violence (Ellis 1989), so that anticult lore has, ironically, helped bring into being the danger it feared.

Bill Ellis

References

Billington, Ray Allen. 1938. *The Protestant Crusade, 1800–1860.* New York: Macmillan.

Bromley, David, and Richardson, James T., eds. 1983. *The Brainwashing-Deprogramming Controversy.* New York: Edwin Mellen.

Dundes, Alan, ed. 1991. *The Blood Libel Legend: A Casebook in Anti-Semitic Folklore.* Madison: University of Wisconsin Press.

Ellis, Bill. 1989. Death by Folklore: Ostension, Contemporary Legend, and Murder. *Western Folklore* 8:201–220.

Fine, Gary Alan. 1992. *Manufacturing Tales: Sex and Money in Contemporary Legends*. Knoxville: University of Tennessee Press.

Hicks, Robert D. 1991. *In Pursuit of Satan: The Police and the Occult*. Buffalo, NY: Prometheus.

Melton, J. Gordon. 1986. *Encyclopedic Handbook of Cults in America*. New York: Garland.

Richardson, James T., Joel Best, and David G Bromley. 1991. *The Satanism Scare*. New York: Aldine de Gruyter.

Saliba, John A. 1990. *Social Science and the Cults*. New York: Garland.

Victor, Jeffrey S. 1993. *Satanic Panic: The Creation of a Contemporary Legend*. Chicago: Open Court.

See also Religion, Folk

Cultural Conservation

The protection of cultural resources, broadly defined as "community life and values," in managing change and development. The term appears rarely in the literature before an American Folklife Center report (Loomis 1983) that defines it as "a concept for organizing the profusion of public and private efforts that deal with traditional community cultural life." The center prepared the report for the Department of the Interior in response to a congressional request for information on the status of government policy and "intangible cultural resources." In addition to stressing the need for greater coordination among government agencies with cultural mandates, the report recommended a more inclusive, flexible, case-by-case approach to identifying cultural resources and determining their significance. It also called attention to the unexploited potential of existing legislation, such as the National Environmental Policy Act of 1969, the National Historic Preservation Act of 1966, and the American Folklife Preservation Act of 1976.

Following the report's publication, the term "cultural conservation" began to appear at conferences and festivals, and with increasing frequency in publications, as public-sector folklorists, state historic-preservation officers, and others involved with cultural planning explored its implications and published the results of their programs and discussions (Feintuch 1987; Howell 1990; Hunt and Seitel 1985; Hufford 1994). The cultural-conservation report led to increased cooperation between the National Park Service and the American Folklife Center, and various states began implementing cultural-conservation programs and initiatives, such as the state of Maryland's Office of Cultural Conservation.

The concept has come under criticism from some quarters as a potential form of mystification (Kirshenblatt-Gimblett 1988). Historically, the scientific collection and classification of culture belonging to a putative unself-conscious "folk" has, in effect, silenced the politically powerless in decision making. Moreover, inventorying endangered traditions as if they are natural objects can serve to conceal the shaping hands and political agendas behind the inventories (Whisnant 1983). However, *history* is an essential tool for cultural construction, and development—whether of highways or wilderness—alters the course of history. In so doing, development often rearranges social relations together with the practices expressive of those relations. Where the course of history is at issue, consultation with its authors is critical. To many of its proponents then, the concept of cultural conservation essentially holds out the promise of democratizing the planning process and of broadening public access to the forces and policies shaping cultural change.

Mary Hufford

References

Feintuch, Burt. 1987. *The Conservation of Culture: Folklorists and the Public Sector*. Lexington: University Press of Kentucky.

Howell, Benita, ed. 1990. *Cultural Heritage Conservation in the South*. Athens: University of Georgia Press.

Hufford, Mary, ed. 1994. *Conserving Culture: A New Discourse on Heritage*. Urbana: University of Illinois Press.

Hunt, Marjorie, and Peter Seitel. 1985. Cultural Conservation. In *1985 Festival of American Folklife*, ed. Thomas Vennum Jr. Washington, DC: Smithsonian Institution, pp. 38–39.

Kirshenblatt-Gimblett, Barbara. 1988. Mistaken Dichotomies. *Journal of American Folklore* 101:140–155.

Loomis, Ormond. 1983. *Cultural Conservation: The Protection of Cultural Heritage in the United States*. Washington, DC: American Folklife Center.

Whisnant, David. 1983. *All That Is Native and Fine: The Politics of Culture in an American Region*. Chapel Hill: University of North Carolina Press.

Cultural Landscape

A natural landscape shaped by people; essentially, the physical stage for human behavior. Cultural landscapes result from the same forces involved in creation of any vernacular artifact. The "place" may be as large as a river valley or as small as a kitchen garden.

Study of cultural landscapes has been the domain of geographers and material-culture-oriented folklorists. Geographer Carl Ortwin Sauer developed the concept in the 1920s, and geographer Fred Kniffen's articles made vernacular and folk buildings a focus in analyzing landscapes. Cultural landscape is a subject explored by scholars in many fields; writers such as Estyn Evans, W.G. Hoskins, Henry Glassie, William Tishler, David Lowenthal, Pierce Lewis, J.B. Jackson, Paul Groth, and Reynar Banham have made contributions to understanding cultural landscape, and most specialists in vernacular architecture include it in their studies. Jackson's founding of the journal *Landscape* in 1951 and his essays (see Jackson 1984) have made the study of cultural landscape a permanent field crossing disciplinary boundaries.

Howard Wight Marshall

References

Deetz, James. 1976. *In Small Things Forgotten: The Archaeology of Early American Life*. Garden City, NY: Anchor.

Glassie, Henry. 1968. *Pattern in the Material Culture of the Eastern United States.* Philadelphia: University of Pennsylvania Press.

Jackson, J.B. 1984. *Discovering the Vernacular Landscape.* New Haven, CT: Yale University Press.

Jordan, Terry G., and Matti Kaups. 1989. *The American Backwoods Frontier.* Baltimore, MD: Johns Hopkins University Press.

Meinig, D.W., ed. 1979. *The Interpretation of Ordinary Landscapes: Geographical Essays.* New York: Oxford University Press.

Stilgoe, John R. 1982. *The Common Landscape of America, 1580–1845.* New Haven, CT: Yale University Press.

Zelinsky, Wilbur. 1973. *The Cultural Geography of the United States.* Englewood Cliffs, NJ: Prentice-Hall.

See also Architecture, Vernacular; Art, Folk, Crafts; Material Culture; Vernacular

Cultural Studies

Interdisciplinary, transdisciplinary, and often counterdisciplinary project to describe, analyze, and theorize the ways in which cultural practices are entangled with, and within, relations of power. Taking much of its impetus from the works of Raymond Williams *(Culture and Society, 1780–1950* [1958] and *The Long Revolution* [1961]), Richard Hoggart *(The Uses of Literacy* [1958]), and E.P. Thompson *(The Making of the English Working Class* [1963]), cultural studies, as an institutionalized discipline, began with the founding of the Center for Contemporary Cultural Studies at Birmingham, England, in 1964. Since then, cultural studies has become an international set of discursive practices in which culture is viewed as a site of serious contest and conflict over meaning. *How* meaning is made, *what* meaning is made, *who* makes meaning, and *for whom* are explored through borrowings from Marxist—in particular revisionist (sometimes called "neo-" or "post-") Marxist—writings on class; feminist writings on gender; postcolonialist writings on race, ethnicity, and nation; lesbian- and gay-studies writings on sexuality; and poststructuralist writings on language and other signifying systems. Folkloristics intersects with cultural studies when folklorists position folklore within the politics of cultural production—in other words, when folklorists address how folklore is shaped by, and in turn shapes, sociocultural power relations.

Rejecting the traditional humanities' equation of "culture" with "high culture," cultural studies instead accepts a more anthropologically based definition of culture made available in part by the "culture-as-text" metaphor developed in the writings of Roland Barthes *(Mythologies* [1957, 1972]) and Clifford Geertz *(The Interpretation of Cultures* [1973]). As Lawrence Grossberg and colleagues have explained, "All forms of cultural production need to be studied in relation to other cultural practices and to social and historical structures" (Grossberg, Nelson, and Treichler 1992). Thus, cultural studies is "committed to the study of the entire range of a society's arts, beliefs, institutions, and communicative practices" (1992). But unlike anthropology, cultural studies has developed out of an analysis of modern industrialized societies—hence its practitioners' early interests in class-based power relations (later expanded to include those of gender, ethnicity, race, nation, and sexuality) as well as the production, marketing, and consumption of popular forms of expressive and material culture, and the vernacular uses of those forms (drugstore romances and novels, journalistic writing, advertising, comics, film, television, video, various forms of music with mass and/or subcultural appeal, the fashion industry, the aesthetic arrangements of household items, as well as sporting events and such festive occasions as carnival).

Key to discussions of the popular have been Theodor Adorno's theory of the anesthetizing, and thereby dominating, effect of "mass culture" and what he calls the "culture industry" (the commodification and industrialized reproduction of cultural artifacts); Louis Althusser's explanation of how ideology (as a system of representations) positions people as "subjects" in a way that actually "subjects" (subordinates) them to the interests of the ruling classes; and Antonio Gramsci's understanding of "hegemony," a term he uses to mean both domination and the process of negotiation and consensus-formation in which culture is a site of struggle between accurate and just representations of self and misrepresentations by others. The differences among these theorists, as well as among those who invoke their theories, resides in a conflict over how much credibility one is to ascribe to individual or personal agency, whether none or some.

For those who argue "some," poststructural insights deriving variously from the writings of Jacques Lacan, Jacques Derrida, Roland Barthes, Michel Foucault, and Julia Kristeva are used to deconstruct and thereby decenter formalist readings of culture that, in alignment with traditional "humanism," presuppose a "center" (sometimes conceived as an author) that organizes and regulates cultural meaning. Cultural "texts" or "sites" are instead seen as incorporating differing modes of signification (or, according to Mikhail Bakhtin, multiple voices) that conflict with each other, thereby providing a means of dismembering rhetorics that otherwise seek to dominate or control meaning. Thus, reader-response theoreticians argue that consumers' uses of cultural products become of importance because consumers may appropriate products and refashion them to meet their own personal and group needs.

Folkloristics intersects with cultural studies, as Charles L. Briggs and Amy Shuman note in their 1993 "New Perspectives" issue of *Western Folklore,* when it follows Américo Paredes' challenges of the 1970s "to place questions of the politics of culture at the heart of the discipline of folklore." This means, on the one hand, "understanding that folklore is already (in Derrida's terms) a politics of culture" and, on the other hand, understanding that the discipline of folkloristics is, through its representational practices, also a politics of culture.

Exploring folklore as a politics of culture, Barbara Babcock has explained how Cochiti women "have contrived to tell stories" through their pottery about men's storytelling, thereby subverting "masculine discursive control" and disturbing "the distribution of [local] power profoundly" (Babcock 1993), while Mark E. Workman has discussed folk-group tropic constructions of self and otherness in relation to differing group and personal responses to AIDS (Workman 1993). Jay Mechling, noting children's appropriations of television cartoon characters as part of their unstructured play, has exhorted folklorists to explore the ways in which people negotiate private and group readings of popular culture (in Briggs and Shuman 1993), while Susan Davis has argued that such forms of public culture as parades, although frequently used to assert the dominant culture's ideological agendas, may be used by a subordinate group "as vehicles for protest as well as for historical commemoration" (Davis 1986). John Dorst has described the traditionalizing practices of Chadds Ford, an elite suburb in southeastern Pennsylvania, which in a postmodern turn inscribes and markets itself through "pamphlets, brochures, glossy travel magazines, gallery displays, postcards, tourist snapshots, amateur art, styles of interior decoration, and suburban architecture and landscaping" (Dorst 1989). And José Limón has historicized and localized the study of the social contradictions of race, class, and gender in Mexican American social poetry (Limon 1992).

Disclosing folkloristics as a politics of culture, others have addressed the ways in which the discipline has been, from its early foundation in Romantic nationalism, participatory in the dominant culture's appropriations of folk culture as a means of enhancing hegemonic ideological agendas. Richard Bauman, for example, has described the ways in which Henry Rowe Schoolcraft's early 19th-century publications (Schoolcraft has been described as "the Father of American Folklore and Anthropology") appropriated Ojibway narratives for the construction of an "authentic" Anglo American literature by erasing their individual tellers and the particularity of their performance contexts, thereby attributing them collectively to the Ojibway Nation, and by rewriting them to fit better an Anglo European literary aesthetic. In turn, Schoolcraft's publications became the source material for parts of Henry Wadsworth Longfellow's popular poem *The Song of Hiawatha* (1855), one of Longfellow's attempts to create a national American epic. Thus, the production of a hegemonic popular American literary voice (Anglo and male) entailed the appropriation (decontextualization and recontextualization) of a subordinate group's cultural traditions that, through hegemonic representational practices, misrepresented, thereby erasing, individual Ojibway voices (Briggs and Shuman 1993). Similarly, John W. Roberts has argued that folkloristic representational practices participated in the construction of a hegemonic equation between "authentic" African American experience and the traditions of the poor in the rural South, an equation that erased those African American experiences that were urban or middle-to-upper class (in Briggs and Shuman 1993).

Other folklorists (like their anthropological colleagues James Clifford, George E. Marcus, and the other contributors to *Writing Culture: The Poetics and Politics of Ethnography* [1986]) have begun to disclose and reevaluate the scientific essentialism of folkloristic paradigms and methods, both the fallacy of scientific objectivity and the subject-object relations constructed with the discourse of older participant-observation positionings (Collins 1990). We have begun to address not only the disciplinary and broader sociocultural effects of folklorists' participation in the construction (through professional writings, museum displays, and popularized "folk" festivals) of the dominant culture's "quintessential others," the "folk," but also folklorists' participation in the construction of folklore's others—modern, elite, popular, and mass culture as well (Briggs and Shuman 1993; Stewart 1991). And folklorists have begun to evaluate the ways in which the discipline is enmeshed within the socioeconomic politics of its supporting institutions: universities, arts councils, historical societies, and the like (Kirshenblatt-Gimblett 1988).

At a time when anyone's right to represent and thereby construct an "other" is being called into question, folklorists' self-reflexive turns mark a willingness, as Briggs and Shuman have noted, to take responsibility for our discipline by disclosing and evaluating the conceptual problems inherent in our constructions of "folk" culture (Briggs and Shuman 1993). "Meaning," for folklorists who participate in cultural studies' discursive practices, is not situated in a "transhistorical" aesthetics independent of economic, social, or political conditions. It is allied with Louis Althusser's definition of ideology as "lived practice" and, thus, is contextualized by historically specific economic, social, and political conditions and the ways in which these conditions interact at the "local," "larger than local," and global levels.

Cathy Lynn Preston

References

Babcock, Barbara A. 1993. "At Home, No Women Are Storytellers": Potteries, Stories, and Politics in Cochiti Pueblo. In *Feminist Messages: Coding in Women's Folk Culture,* ed. Joan Newlon Radner. Chicago: University of Illinois Press, pp. 221–248.

Briggs, Charles and Amy Shuman, eds. 1993. Theorizing Folklore: Toward New Perspectives on the Politics of Culture. *Western Folklore* (Special Issue) 52:2,3,4.

Collins, Camilla A., ed. 1990. Folklore Fieldwork: Sex, Sexuality, and Gender. *Southern Folklore* (Special Issue) 47:1.

Davis, Susan. 1986. *Parades and Power: Street Theatre in Nineteenth-Century Philadelphia.* Berkeley: University of California Press.

Dorst, John D. 1989. *The Written Suburb: An American Site, an Ethonographic Dilemma.* Philadelphia: University of Pennsylvania Press.

Grossberg, Lawrence, Cary Nelson, and Paula Treichler, eds. 1992. *Cultural Studies.* New York: Routledge.

Kirshenblatt-Gimblett, Barbara. 1988. *Mistaken Dichotomies. Journal of American Folklore* 101:140–155.

Limón, José E. 1992. *Mexican Ballads, Chicano Poems: History and Influence in Mexican-American Social Poetry.* Berkeley: University of California Press.

Stewart, Susan. 1991. *Crimes of Writing: Problems in the Containment of Representation.* New York: Oxford University Press.

Workman, Mark E. 1993. Tropes, Hopes, and Dopes. *Journal of American Folklore* 106:171–183.

See also Feminist Approaches to Folklore; Marxist Approach; Postmodernism

Curanderos

Folk healers in the Mexican American community. Folk medicine remains important among Mexican Americans throughout the Southwest and beyond. Similar to other folk medical systems, the Mexican American folk medical system consists of three levels: *remedios caseros* (household remedies), *barrio* (neighborhood) healers (including the *partera,* or lay midwife; the *sobador[a],* or folk chiropractor; and the *yerbera[o],* or herb specialist—all part-time healers), and the *curandero(a),* who has received a *don de Díos* (gift from God) to heal the sick. The *curandero(a)* is the only healer in this society who is believed to have the power to heal cases of *brujerá* (witchcraft). In addition, the healer is thought to have all of the knowledge about folk healing that those in the two other levels of healing possess.

Some *curanderos* serve local communities, while others serve larger regional communities, and some even the international community. In south Texas, for example, Don Pedrito Jaramillo of Los Olmos, who died in 1907, was widely sought for his services by people from throughout the region and beyond, including some Anglos. El Niño Fidencio of Espinazo, Nuevo Léon (Mexico), who died in 1938, continues to have a large following of espirituistas (spiritualists) throughout the region on both sides of the border. Teresita Urrea of the state of Chihuahua, Mexico, had a very large following in several Mexican states as well as in New Mexico, Arizona, and California.

Some of these healers achieve the status of folk saints— that is, they are treated as though they were saints, though they are not canonized by the Catholic Church. Their photographs appear on home altars throughout the region, and their followers believe that one day the Catholic Church will canonize them, as it has other healers.

The *curandero* is assumed to have a knowledge of medicinal herbs and the skills to treat such folk illness syndromes as *mal de ojo* (an illness that is caused by looking at someone or something in excess admiration), *susto* (an illness caused by fright), *empacho* (an illness caused by eating too much raw or very rich foods), *caída de la mollera* (fallen fontanel in infants), and others. Other healers in the culture can deal with these illnesses, but the *curandero,* because of his gift from God, has the power to heal cases of witchcraft, which healers in the other levels cannot treat.

It is not uncommon to find some confusion as to who is a *curandera* and who is a *bruja* (witch). Some clearly understand that the *curandero(a)* can do only good and cannot cause harm, and that the *bruja,* who has made a pact with the devil, can only cause harm, but can do no good. Such confused labeling plays an important role in *Bless Me, Ultima,* the novel by Rudolfo Anaya that explores a young man's understanding of the *curandera,* Ultima, who has come to live with his family in New Mexico.

Because of the conflict with the worldview of the dominant majority, there is a correlation between education, social class, birthplace, and language preference and the acceptance or rejection of certain parts of the folk medical system. The *curandero(a)* level is usually the first to be rejected, in part because it is at greatest variance with the worldview of the macroculture. Recent surveys in south Texas indicate that around 90 percent of the Mexican Americans living in rural areas continue to rely on herbal remedies, and as many as 29 percent of the women have used *parteras* (lay midwives) to assist with childbirth, but belief in and use of *curanderos* has dropped significantly since the 1950s.

Joe S. Graham

References

Clark, Margaret. 1970. *Health in the Mexican-American Culture: A Community Study.* Berkeley: University of California Press.

Dodson, Ruth. 1951. Don Pedrito Jaramillo: The Curandero of Los Olmos. In *The Healer of Los Olmos and Other Mexican Lore,* ed. Wilson M. Hudson. Publications of the Texas Folklore Society, No. 24. Dallas, TX: Southern Methodist University Press.

Graham, Joe S. 1985. Folk Medicine and Intracultural Diversity among West Texas Mexican Americans. *Western Folklore* 44:168–193.

Kiev, Ari. 1968. *Curanderismo: Mexican-American Folk Psychiatry.* New York: Free Press.

Madsen, William. 1964. *The Mexican-Americans of South Texas.* New York: Holt, Rinehart, and Winston.

Romano, Octavio. 1965. Charismatic Medicine, Folk Healing, and Folk Sainthood. *American Anthropologist* 67:1151–1173.

Rubel, Arthur J. 1966. *Across the Tracks.* Austin: University of Texas Press.

Saunders, Lyle. 1954. *Cultural Difference and Medical Care: The Case of the Spanish-Speaking People of the Southwest.* New York: Russell-Sage Foundation.

Trotter, Robert T., II, and Juan A. Chavira. 1981. *Curanderismo.* Athens: University of Georgia Press.

See also Medicine, Folk

Cursing

Offensive, abusive, or opprobrious language used to express anger or to wish harm to another. Cursing and swearing are general terms for colloquial expressions that are differentiated on the basis of a speaker's intention.

Ancient curses were intended to cause harm on the basis of a primitive or magical form of thinking, as if the invocation or curse would come true by saying it, as in *go to hell* or *be damned.* Modern swearing allows speakers to intensify a variety of thoughts and emotions but is most commonly associated with forms of verbal aggression, frustration, anger, or surprise. Cursing is frequent and pervasive in American speech, and it appears in forms of humor, folk stories, rock and roll and rap music, theater, jokes, sex talk, slang, shoptalk, verbal dueling games (the dozens), and sporting events.

In folk language, swearing categories include profanity, blasphemy, epithets, insulting or name calling, ethnic-racial slurs, scatology, and obscenity. Profanities are secular or irreligious uses of sacred words *(holy shit)*, while blasphemy is a direct attack on religious figures or thought *(screw the pope)*. Epithets are expressions of frustration without targets, as when one hits a thumb with a hammer *(son of a bitch!)*. Insults and name calling are words targeted at wrongdoers and are based on animal names *(jackass)*, references to deviancy *(queer)*, gender-related terms *(slut)*, and comments about physical appearance *(lardass)*, mental functioning *(retard)*, or regional stereotypes *(briar hopper)*. Ethnic-racial slurs denote physical, mental, or food-related characteristics of a minority group *(taco bender)*. Scatological cursing is based on terms for body parts, products, and processes *(shit)* and is one of the early types of childhood cursing and humor. American obscenities are pointedly sexual *(fuck)* and are subject to censorship.

Cursing is controlled by contextual constraints, such as social-physical setting, speaker-listener relationships and status, intended meaning of the message, and communication channel. Curse words and phrases range from mild euphemisms *(gosh darn)* to explicit sexual referents *(fuck* or *cunt)* and are mainly based on British English terms, although other foreign terms are borrowed *(schmuck)*. Cursing occurs frequently in personal conversations but is censored in print and electronic media through the application of literary or broadcast standards and policies. It can be legally restricted when construed as a form of sexual harassment, fighting words, or obscenity.

Episodes of swearing appear across all age ranges, geographic locations, professions, and economic strata. In public, men swear about twice as much as women, and teenagers more than children or the elderly. Cursing is erroneously thought to be associated with lack of control, education, or vocabulary by those who seek to maintain spoken-language standards. However, cursing follows conventional semantic and syntactic language rules and is based on a logical method of expressing emotional thoughts.

Timothy B. Jay

References

Jay, Timothy B. 1992. *Cursing in America.* Philadelphia: John Benjamins.

See also Folk Speech

Custom

An activity performed with such regularity that it is considered expected behavior or a part of social protocol. Simply put, a custom is the usual way of doing things. Ethnographers consider custom part of the daily lives of a particular group of people; folklorists, in practice, consider custom part of the group's folkways and folk beliefs. When they take on the authority of law, customs are often called "mores." Customs such as shaking hands when greeting people, offering a polite "God bless you" when someone sneezes, or "knocking on wood" are found virtually throughout the United States and elsewhere. People learn these and other customs sometimes by word of mouth—that is, the knowledgeable members of the folk group simply tell the uninitiated what is expected in particular situations. Parents play a major role in continuing customs by telling children when and how certain practices are appropriate in particular contexts. At other times, custom is learned by imitation—that is, by repeating the actions of those who are more experienced and familiar with the "way things are done." Being part of a folk group means practicing the customs of the group.

The study of national customs is generally beyond the concern of specific folklore studies. Folklorists instead limit themselves to collecting and analyzing customs maintained within discrete folk groups. For example, the agricultural and religious customs of the Pennsylvania Dutch as well as the customs found among Cajun folk receive considerable attention from folklorists.

A review of the major folklore collections and bibliographies reveals that American folklorists seldom treat "custom" per se, but consider it linked with other genres or with particular folk groups. They may refer broadly, for example, to rural or urban folk customs, or more specifically to religious customs, customs associated with various trades and professions, and children's play customs. The term "folkways" is often used analogously with custom and often refers to rural customs and practices, especially those closely affiliated with agriculture and animal husbandry.

Customs are divided in folklore studies into several categories: those linked (1) to the calendar (practices associated with certain dates or times of the year); (2) to rites of passage (practices associated with important events in the human life cycle); (3) to significant social events (festivals and large group celebrations); and (4) to folk belief (practices that result from holding certain beliefs). The division serves purposes of cataloguing, since rarely do these divisions not overlap.

Folk calendar customs in the United States are not as common as they are in Europe. While many Americans celebrate calendar holidays nationally, such as the Fourth of July or Thanksgiving Day, they maintain regional and familial traditions that distinguish the way in which one group of people commemorates these holidays from the ways of other groups. Although folklorists may not focus their attention on Thanksgiving Day as a national harvest celebration, they research regional and family customs that develop as part of celebrating Thanksgiving. The preparation of unique foods that are served at the Thanksgiving meal, who performs what activities associated with preparing and serving the meal and cleaning up afterward, when and where the meal is to be served, and so forth are often determined by family custom. Among some folks in rural parts of Vermont, New Hampshire, Maine, and upstate New York, it is a custom on Thanksgiving for the men and boys in an extended family to spend the morning and early afternoon outside deer hunting while the women prepare the traditional meal. In some families, this is the occasion for the younger children in the company of their father, uncles, and

The Lemuel Smith family says grace before supper. Carroll County, Georgia, 1941. Photo Jack Delano. Library of Congress.

older brothers to make their first hunt. More often than not, no animals are shot this day, thus stressing the social dimension of this Thanksgiving Day custom.

The calendar offers other opportunities for practicing different customs. Vermont gardeners customarily sow vegetable and flower seeds indoors on Town Meeting Day, the first Tuesday of March. Across the nation, school-age youngsters play pranks on their peers on April 1, April Fools' Day. Ringing in the New Year may be replaced by shooting in the New Year among German and Italian Americans. Some U.S. calendar customs, such as sending Father's Day and Mother's Day cards or giving candy on St. Valentine's Day are supported more by commercial interests than by folk tradition.

Calendar customs that draw upon the coordinated participation of large groups of people are often studied as festivals and celebrations. Native Americans gather annually for national powwows, during which festivals they share, reinvigorate, and revitalize their traditional customs. Many state and

national folk festivals are hybrid products of a surging interest in folk traditions and the availability of major funding; they would probably not exist on the scale they do without federal and state support and a large professionally oriented organization behind them.

Rites of passage mark major transitions in the life of an individual, and customs associated with them are important ways for folk groups to recognize the changes. From conception to death, folk groups have produced an enormous number of customs that measure the growth and development of their members. Deciding on the name of a child may be left up to the whim of parents, or family or ethnic custom may dictate that the parents follow the custom of naming the child after an ancestor or relative. The custom of giving the birthday child a punch on the arm for every year of age is common among children throughout the United States. Customarily the tooth fairy trades candy or money for the children's baby teeth when they fall out. Although this tradition may have had ancient roots in

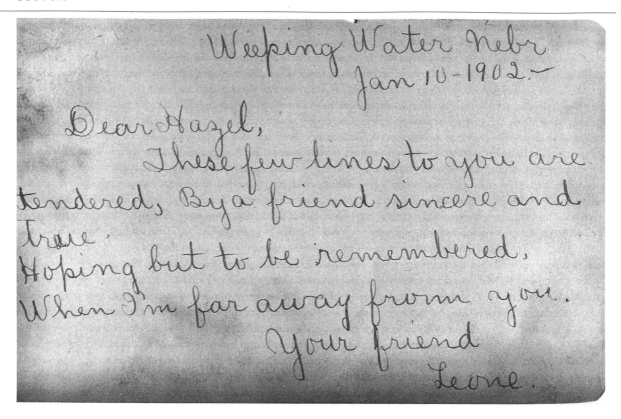

Weeping Water Nebr
Jan 10-1902.—

Dear Hazel,
These few lines to you are tendered, By a friend sincere and true.
Hoping but to be remembered,
When I'm far away from you.
Your friend
Leone.

superstition, the custom as practiced in most of the United States simply marks the transition of the child into adulthood and promotes a safe and easy way for the parents to dispose of the unwanted teeth. Numerous customs associated with marriage persist in the United States. Among some Mexican Americans, it is customary for a group of the young man's friends to visit the young girl's family to ask permission for the courtship to begin. Decorating cars after a wedding and parading through the bride and groom's neighborhoods immediately after the wedding ceremony remains a part of some community and ethnic traditions. In some parts of the South and Midwest, the marriage celebration includes the custom of disrupting the newlyweds' first night with a surprise shivaree. Customs associated with death are equally widespread. Some families consider it customary to stop their clocks to mark the time that someone in the house died. In parts of the South, pottery and medicine bottles decorate graves. Large meals held after a funeral customarily celebrate life. Survivors maintain the grave site of relatives and decorate it on the anniversary of their death or for particular calendar celebrations.

Folk festivals provide the opportunity for a large degree of community involvement. The Scottish American Highland Games held annually in New Hampshire provide the opportunity for descendants of Scottish families to celebrate their heritage. The women prepare the customary dishes of Scotland; the children, dressed in kilts, perform the Highland dances; and the men compete in games of testing their strength. Folks in backwater communities of Louisiana celebrate Mardi Gras following old customs unlike those practiced in the massive, more commercialized Mardi Gras celebration in New Orleans. Among many Italian Americans,

December 26 is Visiting Day: You customarily leave your front door open, set out drinks on a table near the door, and arrange for viewing the gifts you received on Christmas; then you visit your neighbors' homes, calling on folks who themselves may be out making other visits. The custom provides the opportunity to show your generosity to your friends and to display signs of your own prosperity.

Some customs are closely associated with folk belief, making it sometimes difficult to distinguish custom and ritual. But the two, at least in the abstract, are different. Ritual is usually performed in order to affect the future. Customs, in the abstract, are not practiced to influence the future. To break custom can bring questioning, criticism, or censure from members in the folk community. The practice of dressing a male infant in blue and a female infant in pink partly derives from a primitive European belief that the color blue protects infants from harm. While the belief itself generally has died out in the United States, many Americans follow the practice because "that's the way things are done." They are unaware of the custom's origin in folk belief, or, if they are aware of it, they do not necessarily subscribe to the belief, but they continue the custom anyway because it is expected of them.

In the broadest sense, much of folklore is itself a part of custom, because folklore is appropriate and oftentimes expected behavior in certain contexts. By custom, an ill person seeks advice from the herb doctor; custom tells the Native American storyteller to wait until winter to tell certain tales; the singer frames the performance of a song with customary opening and closing formulas. While remedies, tales, and songs are not necessarily considered customs, the practice of each may be decided by folk custom.

As folklorists look at folk traditions in the work place, they discover a whole range of customs. Richard M. Dorson's research among lumberjacks in the Upper Peninsula of Michigan discerned a code of behavior that prescribed a number of customs. For example, the jack, after spending months in the woods, was by custom expected never to walk away from a fight, to be courteous toward women, and to spend all of his wages on drinks for himself and his fellow lumberjacks. Lumberjacks also hold their own carnivals at which they customarily compete in various games that demonstrate their logging skills. In other occupations, custom dictates a hierarchy on the assembly line, with new workers often expected to do the unpleasant tasks. The customary coffee break provides both white- and blue-collar workers with a time for gossip, sharing stories, and playing practical jokes. In this context, too, new workers learn more about the social and work protocols expected of them.

Determining when a traditional craft should be undertaken may also be bound with custom. In some regions of the United States, it is a custom for a young girl to complete her first quilt—usually a doll-sized one—before reaching puberty. The finished quilt is stored in her hope chest until she marries, and eventually it is used to bundle her first child.

Families may have their own customs, such as parents sitting at the head of the table at main meals or the youngest child opening the first gift on Christmas morning. Eating the main meal in the early afternoon on Sundays is by custom different from the practice during the week, when the main meal is served in the evening. Among Vermonters who tap their own maple trees and boil their own syrup, it is a custom to celebrate the first of the family's maple-sugar crop by using it to make sugar-on-snow, which is customarily served with dill pickles and plain doughnuts.

The study of folk custom has not developed per se as strongly in American folklore scholarship as it has in Europe, but with the increasing interest in folklife studies, more attention will be given to custom.

Richard Sweterlitsch

References

Brewster, Paul G., ed. 1952. Beliefs and Customs. In *The Frank C. Brown Collection of North Carolina Folklore,* ed. Newman Ivey White. Vol. 1. Durham, NC: Duke University Press, pp. 222–282.

Hand, Wayland D. 1970. Anglo-American Folk Belief and Customs: The Old World's Legacy to the New. *Journal of the Folklore Institute* 7:136–155.

Smith, Robert Jerome. 1972. Festivals and Celebrations. In *Folklore and Folklife: An Introduction,* ed. Richard M. Dorson. Chicago: University of Chicago Press, pp. 159–172.

Summer, William Graham. [1907] 1960. *Folkways.* New York: Mentor Books.

See also April Fools' Day; Christmas; Folkways; Foodways; Shivaree; Thanksgiving Day; Tooth Fairy; Valentine's Day

D

Dance, Folk

Stylized movements of individuals, couples, or larger groups in traditional patterns, usually performed to musical accompaniment. In modern folkloristics, dance is generally understood as a panhuman but nonuniversal type of structured movement system involving the creative use of the human body in time and space in a manner that formalizes and intensifies kinesthetic experience and communication through culturally distinct idioms distinguished as such within particular societies. This is a perspective developed by such anthropology-of-dance theorists as Adrienne Kaeppler and Drid Williams. The adjective "folk" is applicable to any dance idiom transmitted through traditional processes, but the term "folk dance" is identified most closely with dances thought to express group identity, especially those idioms with a history of rural, peasant practice seen to represent ethnic and national identities.

Folk dance has a variety of manifestations: It can be found as an unselfconscious practice of vernacular forms, or it may appear as elaborately choreographed and staged representations of such forms; it may also be practiced as a more or less formally organized recreational activity. "Popular" dance forms—social dances of more recent provenance and associated with mass-mediated modes of transmission—are often contrasted with folk forms, even though popular dances are clearly traditional in their transmission and varied in their practice. The term "vernacular" dance is gaining acceptance as a more inclusive term that situates a dance practice among nonprofessionals in community settings, as characterized by Susan Elke Spalding and Jane Harris Woodside in *Communities in Motion* (1995).

The term "folk dance" achieved currency late in the 19th century in comparison with other folklore genres, being considered then as a lesser aspect of folk custom. The connotations of the term are closely related to the study of traditional vernacular dance forms in Europe. Its particular connotations, popular associations, and uses, however, vary widely in relation to circumstances in different countries. In the United States and Canada, "folk dance" is often associated, and sometimes conflated, with terms such as "ethnic," "popular," "traditional," and "vernacular"; indeed, folklorists have turned their attention to all of these phenomena. Not surprisingly, given its tangled history and diverse manifestations, many dance researchers have turned away from the generic term "folk dance," choosing instead to consider their subject matter more broadly; dance idioms move easily between various cultural strata, and it makes little sense to draw these boundaries too firmly.

Many definitions emphasize, as did that of Gertrude Kurath, a key figure in American dance research, its communal nature, magico-religious function, and connection with "life's crucial cycles." Such characterizations invoke conceptions of folkore as a survival of hypothesized earlier stages of cultural evolution or of particular historical periods and Romantic nationalist concepts of the spirit of a people located in imagined anonymous communal expressions. To some degree, these concepts persist and inform folk-dance study, particularly among those who carry on its "revival"—that is, the selfconscious practice of folk forms in recreational and representational contexts.

As folklorists reconceptualized their subject matter later in the 20th century, emphasizing its functions in culture, folk dance, too, was redefined. Alan Lomax attempted to relate various measures of dance-movement characteristics to broad features of cultural history on a worldwide scale in his "choreometrics" project (Lomax 1968). Joann Wheeler Kealiinohomoku, as part of her effort to influence the study of dance from an anthropological perspective, emphasized the vernacular character of folk dance, thus subsuming social and popular dance forms while excluding "art" and "classical" forms, and further specifying that folk dance include both "first and second existence" practice. This distinction she took from Felix Hoerburger, who adapted these terms to distinguish dance that has an "integral part in the life of a community" from that which is no longer "functional" but is rather the property of "a few interested people." Folk-dance study,

Cloggers at the Georgia Mountain Fair. Hiawassee, Georgia, 1980s. American Folklife Center.

Hoerburger argued, was often necessarily concerned with the latter, partricularly in America where first-existence dance was, he believed, practically nonexistent. Hoerburger thought first-existence dance to be the field of folklore research; second-existence, that of "cultivation." Most took his distinction to imply a devaluation of second-existence practices and to suggest that researchers cleave to what little first-existence material they could find. Similarly, until recently in America, folkloristic perspectives have been most often brought to bear on vernacular dance idioms, both traditional and popular, often mass-mediated forms, and only somewhat grudgingly on the "second-existence" practices of recreational clubs and theatrical presentation, and then usually as an occasion for criticism. These latter phenomena have recently been somewhat rehabilitated as the study of "folklorism" has been articulated in its own terms and become more acceptable.

Given the somewhat discontinuous assortment of dance practices brought together by the history of folkloristics, we might better characterize folk-dance study by its research perspectives than by its subject matter. Folk-dance research methods include dance collection and analysis of form and structure, usually applied in order to classify and trace patterns of diffusion and change. These techniques, highly developed in Europe, had an influence in America as well, but were generally not applied here as systematically. The technically sophisticated system of Labanotation, for example, which was widely adopted in Europe, is rare in American publications, where notation is primarily provided only for use by teachers

in educational and recreational settings. Indeed, almost all American collections of this type lack even basic scholarly apparatus. Contemporary researchers, such as Lee Ellen Friedland, have reviewed the unpublished papers of collectors to glean information about their methods and to render their works more useful. Methods for the documentation and analysis of dance events, propounded by American dance ethnologists in the 1970s in works such as *New Dimensions in Dance Research: Anthropology and Dance* (1974), edited by Tamara Comstock for the Committee on Research in Dance, were subsequently employed in many folk-dance studies. Analysis of dance *events* rather than merely *dances* serves both to situate dancing within a particular cultural system and to focus attention on the communicative processes enacted in dance performance.

Despite confusion over the precise application and scope of the term, "folk dance" in America certainly includes the dances of many cultural traditions, including those identified with the early Anglo American settlers (sometimes presented as "the" American folk dance), some African American dance idioms, and the dance traditions of immigrant groups, particularly Europeans. Perhaps less popularly conceived as "folk," but equally treated by folklorists in the late 20th century, are vernacular popular idioms of social dance among the numerous subcultural groups in our diverse society. Even these groupings cannot be made too distinct, however, for if American folk dance is characterized by anything, it is the interaction of many different cultural streams. It is not possible here to compile, much less fully explore, a complete accounting of folk dance in America; rather, this survey characterizes some general features of dance practice, with a focus on dance forms of particular interest and importance in the history of folk-dance study.

In purely choreographic terms, one can identify several systems of expressive-movement resources in use among American folk dances. The disposition of dancers in space, their arrangement in various formations, often called "sets," and their subsequent movement in relation to one another, traveling particular paths from place to place within these sets, in patterns often called "figures," constitutes one significant domain of movement articulation and a resource, deriving primarily from the northern and western European dance heritage brought to the New World by several groups of settlers, on which dancers have drawn in the process of reconfiguring their dance traditions to meet changing circumstances. The more dance-like of childrens' singing games and the adult play-parties practiced in communities where religion forbade "dancing" generally fall into this category.

The similarity of some square-dance figures to those of childrens' games led some to see these dances as survivals of "ancient fertility rites." In the late 20th century, it seems more reasonable to consider these common figures as particular manifestations of an underlying structural aspect of western European dance-movement systems. Although dancers may move through figures as individuals, the basic building block of the dance set is usually the mixed-sex couple; couple dancing is, of course, one of the most widespread European structural forms. Dances in which men and women move together performing movement sequences that articulate their relationship to one another, usually holding one another, or moving around each other in various ways, sometimes facing, sometimes side by side, at times far apart, and at times close together, have been a rich resource in the development of American vernacular dance, particularly in interaction with African American movement concepts. Finally, the structuring of dance movement in fixed sequences of footwork, or steps, is also a common European movement structure. It coexists and combines with other structuring principles, such as the spatial organization of dancers, in various ways in particular idioms. As in couple dancing, "step" dancing (understood as the articulation of rhythm by the feet) has been a movement idiom in which European and African cultural streams have produced a fruitful confluence. The "line dancing" usually performed to country music, documented in Betty Casey's *Dances across Texas* (1985) is a good example of such an amalgamation of different structuring principles in a popular social dance idiom.

One genre of figure dance, the square dance, is perhaps the most studied of American folk-dance forms. It is, in fact, a whole complex of related forms and events, a source of confusion since a square-dance event may include performances of other dances. The square dance is generally associated with Anglo American settlers and has often been treated as the quintessentially "American" folk dance. The identification of the square dance, particularly that typical of the Southeastern

American states, as an isolated, rural survival of ancient English dance forms is attributable to Cecil Sharp and his influential publication of *The Country Dance Book Part V: The Running Set* (1918), collected in Kentucky, and the successful work of the American Folk Dance Society that he founded—which continues as the Country Dance and Song Society—in promoting his agenda for dance revival. This dance, on the contrary, has been shown to have been but one example of an American circular-formation figure dance reflecting the shared European heritage of the settlers of the southern Appalachians who created and perpetuated it. The dance is performed by a small number of couples, usually from four to six, in small kitchens typical of its informal performance, well into the 20th century. The couples are arranged in a circle, and the dance has two parts: group figures for the entire set, such as circling in a ring or exchanging partners around the set in various patterns, which alternate with two-couple figures performed successively as one couple travels around the set performing figures with each of the other couples in turn. These figures are of several types and are composed of such movements as turning, or swinging, one's partner or one's "opposite"; one couple tracing a figure eight or other pattern as they dance around the other couple, who stand relatively still; or dancing around one another, while turning under each other's arms in various patterns without letting go of each others' hands.

Many such figures were collected and published in literally hundreds of instructional square-dance books; unfortunately, for scholarly purposes, very few of these collections were adequately documented. Some study of the distribution of figures has nevertheless been attempted, but the diffusionary picture has probably been muddied beyond recovery by the overlay of subsequent dance developments. Comparison with documentation of other far-flung but related dance traditions, such as the one described by Colin Quigley in *Close to the Floor: Folk Dance in Newfoundland* (1985), shows this figure dance form to be widespread.

In the Northeastern states, in a milieu documented by Elizabeth Aldrich in *From the Ballroom to Hell* (1991), continuing interaction of rural practice with popular dance forms of the urban ballrooms, such as the longways country dance and the quadrille, resulted in a genuinely "square" formation dance for four couples. They performed rather different figures in facing pairs; these usually involve crossing the set or exchanging partners in various ways. These dances retained their popularity in rural New England and have become a resource for several revivals in the 20th century.

Elizabeth Burchenal in 1917 published American Country Dances from New England. She was the most influential pioneer of the "international" folk-dance movement of that period in the United States, publishing many national collections for use in educational and recreational contexts. Henry Ford drew on this material in his campaign to promote old-time dancing in the 1920s. Ralph Page promoted the New England "contra" dance, a figure dance performed in longways formation—that is, by lines of men and women facing each other "up and down the hall," as the dance callers would say. So-called longways country dances "for as many as will" were

Parade-dance at the Crow Fair. Montana, 1979. Photo Michael Crummett. American Folklife Center.

perhaps the most popular social dance form of the colonial era, and the formation retained its popularity into the 20th century in parts of New Hampshire and Vermont, an environment evoked in Beth Tolman and Ralph Page's *The Country Dance Book* (1937). Contra dancing again became the focus of a revival movement in the 1960s and 1970s, this time associated with the counterculture and "back-to-the-land" attitudes of that era. Its practice has spread across the United States and overseas, joining the ranks of other loosely networked affinity groups that have coalesced around folk-dance idioms.

The Southeastern and Northeastern square-dance traditions seem to have interacted during westward migrations to generate the traditional Western square dance, a hybrid form utilizing a four-couple set along with a succession of two-couple figures. In the 1930s, Lloyd Shaw was a key figure in the development of modern Western square dancing, responsible for many innovations as he worked with teams of exhibition dancers, publishing descriptions in his 1939 book *Cowboy Dances*. Since the 1950s, square dancing has developed an increasingly standardized and complex repertoire of figures through an organized nationwide network of recreational clubs, distinct from the older regional traditions. It is these groups that launched, in the 1980s, a legislative campaign to have the square dance declared the "national American folk dance," harking back in their arguments to the oldest concepts of "folk" as national expression. The response of

the professional folklore community was unanimous in opposition. The counterarguments and range of examples brought forward suggest the scope of what might reasonably be considered American folk dance. African American tap dancers, Hispanic *folklorico* organizers, Lindy Hoppers, Swing dancers, and Native Americans, among others, testified that their dance traditions were not represented by "square dancing," and that no matter how *American* that form indeed might be, as an expressive form resulting from a particular history it could not represent all American histories.

Among the histories of these "other" Americans to be found in folk dance, that of the African Americans looms particularly large. It is well covered in Lynne Emery's *Black Dance from 1619 to Today* (1988). The conditions of slavery in the United States, of course, were not conducive to the perpetuation of African cultural forms. African religion with its incorporation of music and dance was particularly repressed, but American slaves perpetuated the spirit of African sacred dance under the guise of Protestantism in the form of the "shout." Often performed as a ring, but also found as individual religious expression, the shout is marked by a shuffling step in which legs were not crossed and heels did not leave the floor. At the same time individual dancers expressed themselves freely in a wide range of body movement and vocalization performed with a clapped and sung accompaniment. Practiced at religious meetings in the Deep South, it built up tremendous energy during the course of a night's performance.

The context of slavery and subsequent African American life in the Caribbean was quite different, allowing for more continuity with African practice. In this region, dance is an integral part of such hybrid religious systems as *santeria* and *vodoun,* in which divine spirits "mount" participants and identify themselves through distinctive dance movements. Pioneer researcher and influential African American dancer Katherine Dunham did much to draw attention to these traditions in works such as *Dances of Haiti* ([1947] 1983). In some places, European figure dancing was adapted into these African American expressive-movement systems, as described in Jay Dobbin's *The Jombee Dance of Montserrat: A Study of Trance Ritual in the West Indies* (1986). The African American experience is also well represented in the secular realm of games, plays, and dances, such as those recorded by Bess Lomax Hawes from Georgia Sea Islander Bessie Jones in her collection *Step It Down* (1972). In general, African dance traditions in America were radically reconfigured in response to oppression, through processes described by Roger D. Abrahams in *Singing the Master: The Emergence of African American Culture in the Plantation South* (1992). Paradoxically, however, certain aspects of the African movement resources have come to permeate American vernacular popular dance. *Jookin': The Rise of Social Dance Formations in African-American Culture* (1990) by Katrina Hazzard-Gordon and *Jazz Dance: The Story of American Vernacular Dance* by Marshall and Jean Stearns (rev. ed. 1994) explore this history in detail. Contemporary African American urban dance idioms move quickly between the vernacular social dance contexts of the streets, mass-media projections that have a global reach, and back again into local practice. "Popular Dance in Black America," a 1983 special issue of the *Dance Research Journal of the Congress on Research in Dance,* provides a good introduction to this subject.

The European and African dance-movement cultures that met in America were quite different. The European forms—articulated in spatial patterns and fixed step patterns, performed in an erect, uplifted posture with little torso articulation—contrast fundamentally with the bent posture and grounded focus of the West African idioms, in which individual improvisation on basic movement motifs, and group-soloist interactions, contrast with the paired male-female organization of European couple and figure dances. These two systems combined in the domain of popular entertainment and social dance to produce many American vernacular forms, including tap dancing in several guises and an endless stream of couple-dance forms from the turn of the 20th century—the cakewalk, through the later Charleston, Lindy Hop, and jitterbug—into the era of unattached-partner dances such as the twist, disco, and subsequent "rock" styles.

Tap dance is one, albeit itself diverse, genre of percussive step dancing. As suggested above, this dance idiom is one in which African and European elements intermingled freely, moving as well easily and frequently through popular, traditional, social, and theatrical contexts. Folklorists have generally been most interested in its vernacular social manifestations, Mike Seeger and Ruth Pershing's *Talking Feet* (1992) providing the best overview of its southern Appalachian manifestations as clogging, flatfoot, and buck dancing. More detailed folkloristic studies of particular dancers and their communities have explored the meanings attached to the contrastive styles suggested by these different terms. Like the square dance, with which stepping may be combined in different ways, this dance idiom has also been strongly associated with Appalachian identity and developed as an exhibition form. *Communities in Motion* (1995), edited by Susan Elke Spalding and Jane Harris Woodside, provides a comprehensive treatment of the dynamics of vernacular dance traditions in the American Southeast. Its articles reach beyond an isolated view of the region or a segregated treatment of Black, White, and Native American traditions to suggest the complexity of community interaction at work in these dance traditions. While Native American dance is outside the consideration of this encyclopedia, it should be noted that dance moves across this cultural border as well—a process explored in depth in Craig Mishler's *The Crooked Stovepipe: Athapaskan Fiddle Music and Square Dancing in Northeast Alaska and Northwest Canada* (1993).

When considering the European dance heritage in America it is important to note that this tradition includes much besides the ideologically dominant discourse of Anglo American heritage. The French have long been settled in North America and, indeed, remain a majority in Quebec and a significant minority elsewhere in the Canadian Maritimes and parts of Louisiana, where a distinctive Cajun regional culture has evolved. French dance tradition in the Northeast, based on the figure-dance quadrille, cotillion, and country (or contra) dance forms, is most thoroughly described in Simon Voyer's *La danse traditionelle dans l'est du Canada: Quadrilles et Cotillons* (1986). Clearly the dances of the French shared much with those of the Scots, Irish, and English among whom they lived, and mutual borrowing and adaptation produced a distinctive French Canadian amalgam. The Quebecois separatist movement inspired a surge of interest in French tradition, which found expression in exhibition ensembles, mentioned in Richard Handler's *Nationalism and the Politics of Culture in Quebec* (1988). Among the Cajuns in Louisiana, contact and exchange with African American culture has produced a couple-dance idiom in waltz and two-step rhythms emphasizing improvisation, strongly influenced by mid-20th-century vernacular couple-dance forms. Cajun dance has become fashionable as a genre of recreational social dance practiced nationally within the framework of its own networked affinity group. While Cajun music is well documented, dance is represented only in less formal publications, such as Jerry Duke's *Dances of the Cajuns* (1987).

Spanish American folk-dance culture, reflecting another early European presence in America, is strong in the Southwest and has remained distinct despite its many shared features. The incorporation of some widespread features of European ceremonial-dance forms carried by the Spanish settlers and missionaries into religious contexts in this region's tricultural milieu has received the most scholarly attention. Flavia Champe describes in *The Matachines Dance of the Upper Rio Grande* (1983) examples of a dance complex found among both Spanish and Indian communities throughout the U.S. southwest and northern Mexico. Practiced as a Christmas or Saint's Day observation, the dance is part of a dramatic enactment. It employs a double file of men in costume who perform weaving and "combat" figures common in the historical European matachine dances, along with accompanying clowns, both threatening and humorous, and other characters. Once seen as an example of acculturation resulting from Spanish domination, recent research explores the degree to which the matachines dance has been incorporated into Native American traditional formats of movement expression. Spanish American secular social dance traditions employ both 19th-century figure- and couple-dance forms, but they are not much documented in vernacular practice apart from the influence of the *folklorico* movement, which employs primarily Mexican dance forms to represent Mexican American identity. In the 1990s, research is under way on such urban vernacular popular dance forms as the *quebradita,* a modernization of traditional couple dancing closely associated with chicano youth in Southern California. Latin American popular dance idioms, themselves often African influenced, are common in contemporary social dance. Marta Savigliano's *Tango and the Political Economy of Passion* (1995) treats the international history and complex cultural transformations of one such genre.

Specific European dance traditions are found in many regions of the United States and Canada where immigration patterns have led to ethnic concentrations. Polka music and dance, for example, are widespread, with significant centers of activity in Milwaukee, Chicago, and Buffalo, New York. Derived from central European couple dancing and processed through 19th-century ballroom practice, the polka was reclaimed and reinvigorated among 20th-century American immigrant communities as a working-class expression and later marketed as a musical commodity. It is maintained as both a vernacular community expression, open to many influences from 20th-century popular couple dancing, and as a networked affinity-group practice more concerned to maintain a distinct polka tradition. As with many musical-dance idioms, polka-music culture has been better documented than the dance, but much can be gleaned from sources such as Charles Keil's *Polka Happiness* (1992).

In Canada, where the action of an ethnic "melting pot" ideology was less pronounced, the dance traditions of European groups, such as the Ukrainians of the prairie provinces, are firmly entrenched. These have gone through several stages of development in the New World and exist in several distinct contexts explored in Andrei Nahachewsky's detailed study of *The Kolomyika: Change and Diversity in Canadian Ukrainian Dance* (1991). He identifies distinctive types of *kolomyika,* often paralleled among other European ethnic-community dance traditions in America: early social, national, childrens', spectacular, and contemporary social manifestations. We might add to this list recreational "international folk dance" adaptations. The interactions among such different contexts is a central issue in understanding the contemporary practice of European folk dance in particular. Elsie Dunin is one of the

few scholars to have addressed her work to these issues in detail in relation to a particular immigrant community, South Slavs in California, where vernacular social dance events are intergenerational affairs in which different repertoires and dance styles are constantly negotiated among the participants. While this is a largely unregulated process occurring in the immigrant community, Irish dance in America on the other hand, is dominated by control exercised through a system of dance competitions, *claled feis,* and dance-teacher certification, run by an Irish Commission. Such organized and codified Irish dancing has largely supplanted informal vernacular practice.

The dance traditions of Asian immigrants have been even less studied. Brought into folkloristics generally through their "ethnic" associations, some of these are religious in character, such as the Japanese Buddhist *bon odori* dance introduced in California in the 1940s, a communal dance of celebration now widely practiced by Buddhist congregations throughout the United States. Another example is the performances of Korean female shamans, sometimes for ritual, sometimes for ethnic display. Other Asian American dances are derived from "classical" court forms, such as Indian Bharata Natyam, widely taught to young women among South Asians in the United States and Canada, or the Cambodian court dance preserved by refugee artists in the United States. A few such dances are emerging hybrid vernacular forms, such as that danced to *bhangra,* a genre of world music that originated in England and is recorded internationally and "mixed" by disc jockeys for social occasions among young, usually second- and third-generation, South Asians.

Dance remains one of the least systematically studied forms of folk expression in America. This lamentable situation is changing, however, with the increasing availability of new technologies to aid documentation and the growing recognition of the dancing body as a significant site of knowledge, power, and expression susceptible to analysis. As researchers acknowledge "folk dance" in its limited sense as only one domain of cultural production amenable to folkloristic approaches, and as they look beyond it to encompass the tremendous vitality of dance practice in America, the future of dance studies looks to be exciting.

Colin Quigley

References

Burns, Thomas A., with Doris Mack. 1978. Social Symbolism in a Rural Square Dance Event. *Southern Folklore Quarterly* 42:295–328.

Dunin, Elsie. 1989. Migrations and Cultural Identity Expressed through Dance: A Study of Dance among South Slavs in California. In *Migrations in Balkan History,* ed. Nikola Tasic and Dusica Stosic. Belgrade: Institute for Balkan Studies, Serbian Academy of Sciences and Arts, pp. 161–170.

Feintuch, Burt. 1981. Dancing to the Music: Domestic Square Dances and Community in South-Central Kentucky, 1880–1940. *Journal of the Folklore Institute* 18:49–68.

Freidland, LeeEllen. 1995. Social Commentary in African-

American Movement Performance. In *Human Action Signs in Cultural Context: The Visible and the Invisible in Movement and Dance,* ed. Brenda Farnell. Metuchen. NJ: Scarecrow, pp. 136–157.

Hast, Dorothea. 1993. Performance, Transformation, and Community: Contra Dance in New England. *Dance Research Journal* 25:21–32.

Hoerburger, Felix. 1965. Folk Dance Survey. *Journal of the International Folk Music Council.* 17:7–8.

———. 1968. Once Again on the Concept of "Folk Dance." *Journal of the International Folk Music Council* 20:30–32.

Kealiinohomoku, Joann Wheeler. 1972. Folk Dance. In *Folklore and Folklife: An Introduction,* ed. Richard M. Dorson. Chicago: University of Chicago Press, pp. 381–404.

Kurath, Gertrude Prokosch. 1949. Dance: Folk and Primitive. In *Standard Dictionary of Folklore, Mythology, and Legend,* ed.Maria Leach and Jerome Fried. New York: Funk and Wagnalls.

Lomax, Alan. 1968. Folk Song Style and Culture. Washington, DC: American Association for the Advancement of Science Publication No. 88.

Quigley, Colin. 1994. A Hearing to Designate the Square Dance the American Folk Dance of the United States: Cultural Politics and an American Vernacular Dance Form. In *Seventeenth Symposium of the Study Group on Ethnochoreology 1992 Proceedings: Dance and its Socio-Political Aspects, Dance and Costume,* ed. Irene Loutzaki. Nafplion, Greece: Peloponnesian Folklore Foundation, pp. 87–88.

Rodriguez, Sylvia. 1994. Defended Boundaries, Precarious Elites: The Arroyo Seco Matachines Dance. *Journal of American Folklore* 107:248–267.

See also Bodylore; Breakdancing; Play-Party; Polka; Powwow; Shout; Stepping

Davidson, Levette Jay (1894–1957)

American folklorist and university professor. Levette (accent on the first syllable) Davidson was associated with the University of Denver from 1922 to 1957, and during this thirty-five-year tenure he led a productive life as a teacher, an administrator, and a scholar. He died of cancer in the spring of 1957.

Born in Eureka, Illinois, Davidson earned his A.B. degree from Eureka College in 1915, two A.M. degrees from the University of Illinois in 1916 and Harvard University in 1917, and his Ph.D. degree from the University of Michigan in 1922. He was a member of Phi Beta Kappa.

In 1922 he joined the English faculty of the University of Denver, becoming a full professor in 1929, beginning his long tenure as chair in 1940, serving as acting chancellor of the university in 1953, then returning to his departmental duties and continuing to direct the Western Folklore Conference, a responsibility he held for a decade and a half. This annual series of meetings attracted scholars and artists of the first magnitude, including Wilson O. Clough, LeRoy Hafen,

Marjorie Kimmerle, Harold G. Merriam, Louise Pound, Frank Waters, S.I. Hayakawa, John Jacob Niles, Archer Taylor, and many others.

Davidson was member of the Modern Language Association, the American Dialect Society, and other professional organizations. The author of many books and articles, Davidson is remembered especially for his *Literature of the Rocky Mountain West, 1803–1903* (with Prudence Bostwick) (1939); *Rocky Mountain Tales* (with Forrester Blake) (1947); and *Guide to American Folklore* (1951). This last work was one of the earliest and most useful systematic approaches to the collection and interpretation of American folklore and retained that distinction until 1968.

When Arthur Leon Campa and John Greenway were brought into his program, Davidson made the University of Denver one of the national centers for the study of American folklore.

Louie W. Attebery

Davis, Arthur Kyle, Jr. (1897–1972)

Folk ballad and Victorian-literature scholar. He was born in Petersburg, Virginia, and received his B.A. from the University of Virginia in 1917. He completed his Ph.D. in literature there in 1924 and was a Rhodes Scholar at Baliol College, Oxford. He joined the English department at Virginia in 1924 and became a protege of Professor C. Alphonso Smith, who had founded the Virginia Folklore Society in 1913 and encouraged its members to collect folksongs. When Smith died in 1924, Davis became president of the society and began editing the Child ballads in its holdings.

In 1929 he published *Traditional Ballads of Virginia,* which included more than 400 versions of 150 Child ballads with meticulous notes and annotations. It was heralded for its scholarship and for demonstrating the continued existence of a performed-Child-ballad tradition in America. In his career at Virginia, he instituted a folklore curriculum, presided over the Virginia Folklore Society, and published two more books of Virginia folksong materials, *Folksongs of Virginia* in 1949 (an index of the society's nonballad materials with no texts) and *More Traditional Ballads of Virginia* in 1960 (50 further Child canon texts). He was assisted on the latter by Paul Clayton Worthington, who, as Paul Clayton, sang a number of the Virginia ballads on recordings for Folkways Records and other labels in the early 1960s. Davis was the Virginia representative to the *Dictionary of American Popular Beliefs and Superstition* and also did research on the letters and papers of the English poet Matthew Arnold. He died in Charlottesville, Virginia, in 1972.

Thomas E. Barden

Deaf Folklore

Term coined in 1977 for the folklore shared by a unique minority of people with hearing loss in their linguistic and cultural community. Folklore includes stories, jokes, riddles, anecdotes, beliefs, games, and other genres traditionally passed from one person to another or from one generation to the next by "word of mouth." However, in the Deaf Community—or

"Deaf World"—folklore is combined inextricably with the traditional transmission "by sign of hands."

There are approximately two million deaf people in the United States, and about 450,000 minimally interact among themselves inside the core of the Deaf Community. In the past, some psychologists, physicians, sociologists, and other researchers viewed deafness as a pathological or a medical disability. However, in the late 20th century, deaf people portray deafness as a strongly cultural phenomenon; they do not regard themselves as a category of specially disabled persons. They argue that they feel fine and can do anything except hear. Their deafness is often called an "invisible physical handicap," in contrast to the obvious presence of blind people with their guide dogs and white canes, amputees with missing limb parts, and paraplegics moving on wheels anywhere in public.

The salient features of deaf culture that has been traditionally passed on for many years are: American Sign Language (ASL); deaf clubs and local, state, and national associations of the deaf; newsletters, magazines, and newspapers for the deaf and books about notable deaf people; videotapes of storytellers for deaf children and adults; strong endogamous marriages among deaf partners; community theaters and the National Theater of the Deaf; local and national sports tournaments and the World Summer and Winter Games for the Deaf; residential schools for the deaf and Gallaudet University in Washington, DC, and the National Technical Institute for the Deaf in Rochester, New York; assistive devices, including baby-cry signalers, flashing and/or vibrating alarm clocks, doorbells, and phones, hearing dogs, TV closed-captioners, and teletext phone devices.

There are more than 200 deaf clubs in the United States; people attend mostly on weekends for social life, business meetings, workshops or lectures, watching captioned films, playing games, seeking mates, exchanging gossip, celebrating holidays, and telling public and private stories and jokes. Also, many deaf clubs sponsor teams or events in bowling, softball, racquetball, basketball, touch football, and golf in which members participate once or twice a week. Often, more than one deaf club exists in a large city; for instance, there are three clubs in Washington, DC, two clubs in Philadelphia, and more than thirty-five clubs in metropolitan New York City. This indicates the cultural diversity of people with different personal, educational, and occupational backgrounds in the Deaf Community.

As part of this cultural diversity, there are *signers,* who use sign language, finger spelling and gestures; and *oralists,* who don't use sign language but speak and lipread. Some people are born deaf, while others are born hearing and become deaf later. Common causes of deafness are childhood diseases (measles, mumps, scarlet fever, and the like), heredity, birth defects, physical injury, or exposure to excessive noise. Some deaf individuals attend residential schools for the deaf; others go to mainstreamed public schools or special day-schools. Ninety percent of deaf people have hearing parents. The deaf children of deaf parents carry the core of deaf culture since it is inheritedly transmitted from one generation of deaf individuals to another. Furthermore, 95 percent of deaf people

tend to marry other deaf partners, and about 10 percent of deaf parents have deaf children.

Also in the Deaf Community are other groups of people with a minimal degree of hearing loss. These include hearing-impaired people who can use their residual hearing through amplification to such degree that they are able to carry on oral communication with a minimum of difficulty. Another group includes deafened persons who have functioned in the hearing world for many years before they lose their hearing through aging, accident, war, heredity, or illness and continue to do so afterward.

Many deaf Americans use ASL. Different from the spoken English language, it is a strongly visual, intricately structured and autonomous language with its own vocabulary, syntax, grammar, and idioms. Hand and arm movements, facial expression, and body positions make up the grammar of ASL. Like other languages, ASL has various regional dialects across the United States.

A "universal sign language" does not exist among deaf people around the world, but there is great diversity of national sign languages, just as there are different spoken languages. There are at least 100 different national sign-language dictionaries; however, through frequent personal contacts, deaf people from different countries are able to understand one another through the use of International Signs or "Gestuno" at the World Congresses of the Deaf and the World Games for the Deaf, as well as at other international conferences or events.

Deaf folklore includes deaf jokes, anecdotes, riddles, signlore (sign play including manual alphabet and numbers stories, sign poetry, "catch" sign riddles, sign puns, name signs, and many other forms), personal-experience narratives, games, and lore about notable deaf persons. Some individuals collect deaf cartoons, which depict deaf characters or comment on some attribute of hearing loss; deaf cartoons have appeared in both deaf and hearing publications. All of these genres depict the strong revelation of deaf culture and heritage that stimulate deaf children's and adults' pride in their own identity.

In general, the common sites of storytelling transmission throughout the nation have been the networks of residential schools and colleges for the deaf, deaf clubs, homes with deaf families, camps, parties and picnics, athletic events, fraternal and political associations of the deaf's conventions and banquets, deaf friends' houses, and work places with deaf coworkers.

A sample of a typical deaf jokes told in the Deaf Community is this one: A lumberjack walked into a forest, went to a tree, and started to cut it down with his ax. When the tree was ready to fall he yelled, "Timber!" and the tree came crashing down. He did the same thing with a second tree. Then he started to cut down a third tree, but when he yelled, "Timber!" the tree did not fall. The lumberjack was perplexed. He cut some more and yelled, "Timber!" again. Still no success; the tree remained standing. He tried once more but he had no luck, so he decided to phone a tree surgeon to come and check the tree. After his diagnosis, the tree surgeon told the lumberjack, "The tree is deaf." The man then knew what to do, and he asked the doctor to move aside. Facing the tree, the lumberjack started to finger spell "T-I-M-B-E-R!" to it. Sure enough, when he finished the word, the tree came crashing down!

The following example demonstrates how deaf characters in jokes or anecdotes frequently tend to find a way to solve a problem in the hearing world: After being married, a young man and woman started to drive their car on their long honeymoon trip. They drove all day until, very late at night, they felt tired and stopped at a motel. Exhausted, the wife fell onto a bed and immediately fell asleep. But the husband was thirsty, so he went out to find a soda machine. He was on his way back to his room when he realized that he had forgotten the room number. He was confused by all of the similar motel doors down the hallway, and he pondered how to get back to his room. Then he got an idea; he walked to his car and blew the horn several times. The lights went on in all of the motel rooms except one, and, thus, he found his own room because his wife could not hear the horn.

In typical signlore or sign play, signers creatively combine hand shapes and movements to create twisted signs or sign puns and other humorous changes of words, sometimes as a part of supposed IQ tests. For instance, in a typical sign pun, the combination of a closed fist resting on the forehead and a snappy opening of the forefinger upward means that one understands, but if the little finger is flipped it means one understands a little. Another sign pun for the word "understand" is this: the combination of a left open palm facing downward in front of one's body and the movement of two straight fingers (forefinger and middle finger) of the right hand touching beneath the left palm. It refers to the word: "under" and "stand" (two fingers designate for a person to stand). Thus, it also denotes "understand," but in a completely different way. Signers have invented humorous name signs for presidents, including Nixon, Carter, Ford, and Reagan. For example, one formerly signed the "N" hand shape alongside one's nose, denoting Nixon's long nose bridge, but after the Watergate crisis one moved the same hand shape across his or her chin, denoting a "liar!" For President Ford, one places the "F" hand shape on the forehead, denoting Ford's Band-Aid on his forehead resulting from bad falls. As for President Reagan, one places the "R" hand shape over one's head, depicting Reagan's hairdo, or both the "R" hand shapes rub together, denoting his being a former movie star. A new sign for him was invented after Reagan was shot. The sign was the tip of the "R" hand shape touching one's side, indicating where the president was shot. Moreover, there are variations of the popular "I love you" sign (both the middle finger and the third finger closed to the palm with the thumb, forefinger, and little finger open in front to a viewer). This combined sign indicates the "I" with the little finger, "L" with both the forefinger and the thumb, and "Y" with the thumb and the little finger. Two humorous examples are: when one uses the combined sign of ILY and rotates only the forefinger in midair, it refers to "I always love you"; and when one flicks the forefinger tip several times with his or her facial expression (one eyebrow lifts up with the question mark on the face), it means "Do you love me?" Historically, this ILY sign probably dates back to 1895 or possibly earlier.

A typical riddle reflecting the topic of deafness is this: Ten blackbirds were sitting on a telephone line; a hunter came and shot at them. Nine flew off and one stayed. Why? Answer: Nine blackbirds were hearing; one was deaf. Another example is: A riddler asks, "Why do deaf people make the best lovers?" Answer: They can't say no in the dark.

Deaf people tell legends about notable deaf people, such as Dummy Hoy, a celebrated deaf baseball pitcher who invented the umpire signs, and Deaf Erastus Smith of Texas, General Sam Houston's chief scout and spy. The legends also cover some hearing individuals who involved themselves with deaf people, such as children of deaf parents or teachers at schools for the deaf or at Gallaudet University. The late FBI Director J. Edgar Hoover is sometimes said to have had deaf parents and to have known sign language, but no evidence supports this claim.

Another popular national deaf legend is about the supposed finger-spelled "A" and "L" hand shapes on the statue of Abraham Lincoln at the Lincoln Memorial site in Washington, DC. Deaf people feel inspired with the revelation of this symbol because Lincoln signed the charter in 1894 to establish a new deaf college, now Gallaudet University in Washington, DC. The Lincoln statue was created by the celebrated hearing sculptor Daniel French, who had finished the statue of Gallaudet, the founder of the first school for the deaf in Hartford, Connecticut, and of Alice Cogswell, the first deaf pupil of Gallaudet. But evidence does not exist in any of French's personal diaries that he purposely sculpted the finger-spelling hands of Lincoln after having become familiar with the manual alphabet of deaf people when he worked on the Gallaudet statue. Deaf people keep spreading this legendary story among young and old deaf individuals throughout the country in order to express pride about the supposed subtle example of finger spelling and to commemorate the involvement of notable hearing people with deaf people.

Some negative stories told by deaf individuals tend to criticize the hearing world, as in this personal-experience narrative: Two young deaf men were conversing in sign language on a public bus. An awestruck stranger sitting behind them wrote a note asking, "Can you read?" One of the deaf men, disgusted at this question, took out an expensive pen and wrote on the note: "No, I can't, but can you write?" Another powerful negative joke is a typical example of some deaf people's hostile attitude toward the predominant hearing society: One day three gentlemen were on a train—a hearing Russian man, a hearing Cuban man, and a deaf man. Suddenly, the Russian opened a window and threw a half-full bottle of vodka out. The deaf man wrote a note asking why he had thrown the bottle away instead of saving it to drink later. The Russian explained, "At home I have PLENTY of vodka bottles! No need to worry about." Later, the Cuban threw half of his expensive cigar out of the train window, and the deaf man wrote a note asking why he had thrown half of the long cigar away. The Cuban explained, "At home I have PLENTY of Cuban cigars! No need to worry about." Then a few minutes later, the deaf man threw a hearing passenger out of the train window. Bewildered, both the Russian and the Cuban rushed to ask him why he had done that, and he responded in a note saying, "At home I have PLENTY of hearing people!" This story seems to demonstrate how much the deaf man wishes to have more deaf people around him for convenient communication and for better social life. Many hearing people, the story suggests, don't understand or respect deaf people and their culture.

The genres of deaf folklore traditionally passed on among deaf people by "sign of hands" reflect the unique cultural and linguistic features and the strongly shared "deaf identity" within the deaf world surrounded by the predominantly hearing world.

Simon J. Carmel

References

Baldwin, Karen. 1982. The Lumberjack and the Deaf Tree: Images of the Deaf in Folklore Narrative. *Kentucky Folklore Record* 28:6–11.

Bragg, Bernard, and Eugene Bergman. 1981. *Tales from a Clubroom.* Washington, DC: Gallaudet College Press.

Gannon, Jack R. 1981. *Deaf Heritage: A Narrative History of Deaf America.* Silver Spring, MD: National Association of the Deaf.

Hall, Stephanie A. 1991. Door into Deaf Culture: Folklore in an American Deaf Social Club. *Sign Language Studies* 73:421–429.

Hodgson, Edwin A. 1891. *Facts, Anecdotes, and Poetry Relating to the Deaf and Dumb.* New York: Deaf Mutes' Journal (Gallaudet University Archives, Washington, DC).

Jacobs, Leo M. 1989. *A Deaf Adult Speaks Out.* 3d ed. Washington, DC: Gallaudet University Press.

Klima, Edward S., and Ursula Bellugi. 1979. Wit and Plays on Signs. In *The Signs of Language.* Cambridge: Harvard University Press, pp. 319–339.

Padden, Carol, and Tom Humphries. 1988. *Deaf in America: Voices from a Culture.* Cambridge: Harvard University Press.

Rutherford, Susan D. 1981. Funny in Deaf—Not in Hearing. *Journal of American Folklore* 96:310–323.

Supalla, Samuel J. 1992. *The Book of Name Signs: Naming in American Sign Language.* San Diego, CA: DawnSignPress.

See also Gestures

Densmore, Frances (1867–1957)

Early student of American Indian music. Frances Densmore began field collecting around the turn of the century. A native of Red Wing, Minnesota, Densmore spent most of her long life in her hometown. At an early age she displayed an interest in, and an aptitude for, music; at Oberlin College she took a degree in music with the intention of becoming a teacher. Later she studied under Leopold Godowsky and won acclaim for her piano and organ performances as well as her lectures on Wagnerian opera. But in 1892, when she heard John Comfort Fillmore speak on American Indian music, and shortly thereafter when she chanced to meet Alice Fletcher, the course of her life's work was changed. Densmore soon started giving lectures and lecture recitals on Indian music; and in 1901 she began doing fieldwork, her initial efforts being among the Chippewas near her home. Later her interests expanded to other groups, and eventually she amassed more than 2,400 songs, a collection now housed in the Smithsonian Institution. From 1907 until her death, she was associated with the Bureau of American Ethnology.

Densmore's early efforts were evolutionary and heavily influenced by the work of Fletcher and Fillmore, but her later work became increasingly independent. Not only did she avoid theoretical considerations, she also ignored other writings on ethnomusicology. Her notes clearly indicate that the people she interviewed in her fieldwork were every bit as exciting to her as their music. Densmore considered herself to be a musical archaeologist, digging up the songs of yesterday but, unlike some collectors with similar aims, avoiding hasty work and a sense of urgency that might antagonize informants. She preferred showing respect for these people as individuals, an attitude that helped develop a relaxed relationship with those from whom she collected.

Her first publications were primarily popular accounts, but Densmore's later writings were of a more scholarly nature. Her studies generally combined a musicological analysis of melodies, their cultural setting, methods of making valid written transcriptions, and the historic and social significance and function of specific songs. She constantly refined and improved her techniques of recording and analysis. Despite her rigorous methodical approach, Densmore's accomplishments have been better received in musical than in folklore or anthropological circles. This was possibly due to the musical complexities of her highly specialized studies. She received honorary degrees from her alma mater, Oberlin College, and from Macalaster College; her work served as the basis for Alberto Bimoni's opera *Winona.* Densmore is also said to have inspired Charles Wakefield Cadman to write compositions with Indian themes.

W.K. McNeil

References

Densmore, Frances. [1910] 1913. *Chippewa Music I and Chippewa Music II.* Bureau of American Ethnology, Bulletins No. 45 and No. 53. Washington, DC: U.S. Government Printing Office.

Hofmann, Charles. 1968. *Frances Densmore and American Indian Music: A Memorial Volume.* New York: Museum of the American Indian, Heye Foundation.

Lurie, Nancy Oestreich. 1966. Women in Early American Anthropology. In *Pioneers of American Anthropology: The Uses of Biography*, ed. June Helm. Seattle: University of Washington Press, pp. 68–72.

Dialect Story

Traditional narrative juxtaposing the regional, or class, or ethnic dialect of some comic stock character with standard American English. Humorous stories emphasizing dialect

For Frances Densmore, on a visit to the Smithsonian Institution, the Blackfoot singer Mountain Chief interprets in sign language the words of a song. Washington, DC, 1916. American Folklife Center.

have circulated both orally and in print since America's linguistically diverse beginnings. Eighteenth-century comic almanacs regularly offered the unconventional locutions of stereotypical rural Yankees, Western frontiersmen, American Indians, Blacks, and Dutch or German, French, Irish, Jewish, and Welsh characters. Similar publications flourished in the 19th century, while writers like Mark Twain and Joel Chandler Harris also integrated jocular dialect into "local-color" fiction.

By the early 20th century, immigrant Italian, Scandinavian, and Slavic characters had joined the comic parade through oral tradition, joke books, the vaudeville stage, and sound recordings. Sometimes intended for a mainstream American audience assuming superiority over some ill-spoken "other," the dialect stories of folk and popular culture were just as often produced by and for particular dialect speakers who valued their community's unassimilable verbal peculiarities.

In 1948, although mindful of the genre's lineage, Richard M. Dorson nonetheless pronounced the dialect story "a new form of American folklore." Dorson's stance, following fieldwork in the Upper Peninsula of Michigan, was based less upon dialect texts than upon their sociocultural context. The egalitarian polyglot culture of Indian and immigrant farmers, miners, and loggers in the Upper Peninsula rendered "Yoopanese," a babel of "foreign"-inflected English, the region's lingua franca. Subsequent generations of "Yoopers," raised with the vernacular yet schooled in standard American English, continue to invoke "the lexical and grammatical errors, the special intonations" of their elders through dialect stories.

James P. Leary

References

Blair, Walter, and Raven I. McDavid Jr., eds. 1983. *The Mirth of a Nation: America's Great Dialect Humor.* Minneapolis: University of Minnesota Press.

Corenthal, Michael. 1984. *Cohen on the Telephone: A History of Jewish Recorded Humor and Popular Music, 1892–1942.* Milwaukee, WI: Yesterday's Memories.

In a lifeboat, survivors of the sinking of the Titanic *seek the safety of the rescueship* Carpathia. *North Atlantic Ocean, 1912. Library of Congress.*

Dodge, Robert K. 1987. *Early American Almanac Humor.* Bowling Green, OH: Bowling Green State University Popular Press.

Dorson, Richard M. 1948. Dialect Stories of the Upper Peninsula: A New Form of American Folklore. *Journal of American Folklore* 61:113–150.

Leary, James P. 1991. *Midwestern Folk Humor.* Little Rock, AR: August House.

Springer, George T. 1932. *Yumpin' Yiminy: Scandinavian Dialect Selections.* Long Prairie, MN: Hart.

Disaster Folklore

The lore created in response to natural or human-made disaster. Events such as floods, earthquakes, hurricanes, tornadoes, or toxic chemical spills can permanently alter cultural landmarks and the natural landscape, rupturing the common body of knowledge crucial for everyday patterns of communication and living.

Common activities, such as driving, cooking, eating, and washing become major tasks following a disaster. While struggling to reestablish accustomed lifeways, disaster victims may also grapple with the alien bureaucracies of state and federal agencies as they seek emergency aid. Survivors struggle to build new life understandings out of nightmarish experiences that often defy their previously held assumptions about life order (Erikson 1976). Folklore helps victims make meaning of their disaster experience, wresting a new order from surrounding chaos. Psychological research with trauma victims indicates that the shared narratives and traditions that people create to cope with disaster play a crucial role in recovery. Story swapping encourages a renewed sense of partnership, countering the sense of loneliness that is often associated with widespread disorder (Ochberg 1993:780–81).

Disaster folklore is not limited to the lore created by victims. Outsiders, intrigued and disturbed by the news of a major disaster, often respond by creating sick jokes that make light of others' misfortune (Oring 1987; Simons 1986; Smyth 1986).

Although each disaster generates its own unique body of folklore, commonalities encourage the generation of jokes and legends that can float from disaster to disaster. For example, South Carolinians jokingly referred to 1989's Hurricane Hugo as a "four-billion-dollar blow job." Following Hurricane Andrew, Floridians sported T-shirts that described their experience in similar terms.

Some regions are especially prone to certain types of disasters: earthquakes on the West Coast, tornadoes and floods in the Midwest, hurricanes along the East Coast. In these instances, disaster folklore is integrated into regional lore, shaping notions of regional identity (Danielson 1990).

There are at least six phases of the disaster experience: warning and preparation, the disaster event, postdisaster damage assessment, cleanup and rebuilding, the first anniversary, and historification. Each disaster phase generates a new set of folklore.

Warning and Preparation. Many disasters strike without warning, yet even unexpected disasters are presaged by a body of lore that admonishes humans to "expect the unexpected." Preparation lore includes homemade emergency kits; traditional methods for securing person and property, such as taping windows before a hurricane or constructing a tornado shelter; preternatural warnings, such as the appearance of the "Greyman" before violent storms in South Carolina or apparitions foretelling the loss of a loved one; and family stories of past disasters used as exemplars to prepare future generations for intermittent catastrophes. Some predisaster rituals are designed to flaunt danger, such as bacchanalian "hurricane parties."

The Disaster Event. Lore associated with the unfolding of a disaster event usually resembles disjointed and fantastic dream narratives. Some stories may boast of heroic or creative rescue. Disaster stories from this phase are fantastic accounts of personal experience, often embellished as they are later shared with other survivors (Ward 1991).

Damage Assessment. In the aftermath of a disaster, survivors evaluate present confusion within the frame of lost order. Documentation necessitated by insurance or relief-fund claims, which might include photos of fallen trees, crushed cars, or ransacked buildings, is often used to create homemade disaster "shrines." Pictures tacked up on an entry wall may remain for years after the completion of repairs as a testimonial to the magnitude of the disaster experience. Owners of property prone to flooding may permanently mark and date annual water highs for all passersby to see.

Cleanup and Rebuilding. An often lengthy and uncomfortable process, cleanup generates stories that are grounded in situational humor, like the family without plumbing who develops humorous narratives about sharing bath water. Resentment toward long waiting lines, unscrupulous outsider repair firms that exploit survivors, and the morass of bureaucratic relief-agency paperwork may generate aggressive joking. FEMA (Federal Emergency Management Agency) jokes often circulate freely in federally declared disasters. Conspiracy theories, coupled with wishful thinking, may spontaneously transform into urban legends, such as the claim that federal authorities downgraded a 1994 California earthquake from its true Richter-scale reading because a reading greater than 7.0 allegedly would have exempted survivors from paying income tax.

The First Anniversary. The one-year anniversary, often a time of reflection, may be marked with community celebrations that applaud survivor recovery and ceremonies that honor the memory of victims. It is often at this time that disaster lore begins to become integrated within the fabric of local history.

Historification. As years pass, trauma stories, jokes, legends, and other traditional artifacts of disaster are pooled, transformed, and fashioned into traditional accounts that reassimilate the chaos of disaster within the larger historical understanding of the community. As accounts become normalized, the disruption in communication is healed.

Disaster lore is folklore in the making, a response to a systemic breakdown requiring the regeneration of patterns of communication. Careful examination of disaster folklore elucidates the process a community undergoes when it breaks down and must regenerate itself.

Gail Matthews-DeNatale
Doug DeNatale

References

Bendix, Regina. 1990. Reflections on Earthquake Narratives. *Western Folklore* 49:331–347.

Danielson, Larry. 1990. Tornado Stories in the Breadbasket: Weather and Regional Identity. In *Sense of Place: American Regional Culture,* ed. Barbara Allen and Thomas J. Schlereth. Lexington: University Press of Kentucky.

Erikson, Kai. 1976. *Everything in Its Path: Destruction of Community in the Buffalo Creek Flood.* New York: Simon and Schuster.

Matthews-DeNatale, Gail. 1993. Bent, but Not Broken: Hurricane Hugo, Video, and Community-Centered Learning. In *Images of the South,* ed. Karl Heider. Athens: University of Georgia Press.

Ochberg, Frank. 1993. Post-Traumatic Therapy. In *International Handbook of Traumatic Stress Syndromes,* ed. John Wilson. New York: Plenum.

Oring, Elliott. 1987. Jokes and the Discourse on Disaster. *Journal of American Folklore* 100:276–286.

Simons, Elizabeth Radin. 1986. The NASA Joke Cycle: The Astronauts and the Teacher. *Western Folklore* 45:261–277.

Smyth, Willie. 1986. Challenger Jokes and the Humor of Disaster. *Western Folklore* 45:243–260.

Ward, Carol. 1991. *In the Eye of the Hurricane: Women's Stories of Reconstruction.* 47 min. Clemson, SC: Clemson University English Department. Videorecording.

See also Nuclear Lore

Dixon, Willie (1915–1992)

Blues songwriter. Born in Vicksburg, Mississippi, Dixon first learned religious songs from his mother, a self-taught poet. His father preferred the secular world of the blues. After studying quartet singing, Dixon joined the Union Jubilee singers and performed on the radio in Mississippi. Moving to Chicago in 1936, he became a boxer and worked with several musical groups—The Five Breezes, The Four Jumps of Jive, and The Big Three Trio, the latter the most commercially successful, performing a sophisticated three-part-harmony version of the blues. Later in life, Dixon worked with Memphis Slim and other, more down-home groups in order to showcase his own compositions.

A gifted musician, vocalist, producer and all-around blues businessman, Dixon is best remembered for his songs, blues classics that included "Back Door Man," "Big Boss Man," "Little Red Rooster," "I'm Your Hoochie Man," and "Wang Dang Doodle," which he fed to Chicago stars Howling Wolf, Jimmy Reed, Muddy Waters, and KoKo Taylor.

A charismatic spokesman for the blues, Dixon set up the Blues Heaven Foundation to promote and preserve his chosen art form. His autobiography *I Am the Blues* (1989), was not an empty boast. His credentials included more than half a century of influence in the blues business.

Barry Lee Pearson

Dobie, J. Frank (1888–1964)

Folklorist. Dobie was so well known and so influential in the world of Texas letters that he was known as "Mr. Texas." With a B.A. from Southwestern University in Georgetown, Texas, and an M.A. from Columbia University in New York City, Dobie spent most of his professional career, from 1914 until 1947, as an on-again, off-again teacher of English at the University of Texas at Austin. Outspoken and liberal, he was frequently at odds with the university administration; nevertheless, although he never received a Ph.D., in 1933 he was promoted to full professor. His most lasting contribution to the University of Texas was the development of his pioneering course, "Life and Literature of the Southwest."

An avid promoter and popularizer of Texas lore, especially legends, Dobie served as editor and secretary of the Texas Folklore Society from 1922 to 1942. His stated goal was "to open the eyes of the people to the richness of their own tradition." Much to the consternation of later, professionally trained folklorists, he continually modified, rewrote, and "improved" the materials he collected from oral tradition.

His most significant publications, aside from the innumerable newspaper articles, magazine essays, and other journalistic pieces, are his more than twenty books dealing with Texas people and Texas lore. His first book, *A Vaquero of the Brush Country* (1929), a biographical study of a Texas cowman, received national recognition, as did *Coronado's Children* (1930), a collection of legends of buried treasure. Other significant works, which can be classified as natural history as well as folklore, include *The Longhorns* (1941), *The Voice of the Coyote* (1949), *The Mustangs* (1952), and *Cow People* (1964).

Sylvia Ann Grider

References

Bode, Winston. 1965. *A Portrait of Pancho: The Life of a Great Texan.* Austin, TX: Pemberton.

1988. *Southwestern Historical Quarterly.* Special issue about J. Frank Dobie and Walter Prescott Webb. 92:1.

Tinkle, Lon. 1978. *An American Original: The Life of J. Frank Dobie.* Boston: Little, Brown.

Dorson, Richard M. (1916–1981)

Folklorist and historian. Dorson earned three degrees in American civilization from Harvard University, and he taught at Harvard (1943–1944) and Michigan State University (1944–1957). In 1957 Dorson succeeded Stith Thompson as head of the Indiana University folklore program; he transformed the program into the Folklore Institute in 1963 and directed the institute until his death. Dorson's many other professional contributions included serving as editor of the *Journal of American Folklore* (1959–1963), president of the American Folklore Society (1966–1968) and of the Fellows of the American Folklore Society (1971–1972), and founder (1963) and editor of the *Journal of the Folklore Institute* (later renamed the *Journal of Folklore Research).*

Chief among Dorson's strongly held views was his insistence that American folklore be studied in terms of the unique history and culture of the United States. He outlined this approach in a now classic essay (Dorson 1959) and first exemplified it in *American Folklore* (1959). Dorson's pioneering fieldwork-based study of African American folklore, *Negro Folktales in Michigan* (1956), uncovered a rich vein of narrative traditions. It included an antebellum-based cycle of stories about the competitive interactions between the White Old Master and the Black slave-servant John. Dorson also focused

attention on immigrant folklore, initially in a series of essays and in his 1952 book, *Bloodstoppers and Bearwalkers: Folk Traditions of the Upper Peninsula.* He demonstrated that folklore can be expressive of interethnic group contacts and relationships within American society (Dorson 1981), as well as of continuities and changes in the Old World–folklore heritage of members of individual immigrant groups. Fieldwork Dorson conducted in coastal Maine, Michigan's Upper Peninsula, and the industrial cities of northern Indiana served as bases for numerous books and essays that explore matters central to an understanding of regional and urban cultures in the United States.

While it was his principal focus, Dorson did not limit his inquiries to the study of American folklore. He wrote a major history of British folklore studies (Dorson 1968), and he edited volumes of important papers on Japanese (Dorson [1963] 1972) and African (Dorson 1972a) folklore and on folklore research in eighteen continents, countries, and other geographical areas outside the United States (Dorson 1961). He participated in and organized numerous international meetings, including a 1973 conference at which folklorists from four continents and thirty-one countries made presentations. (Dorson edited twenty-three of the papers for publication in *Folklore in the Modern World* [1978].) Concerned as well with the need for accurate and comprehensive teaching and research materials, Dorson also edited an important folklore textbook (Dorson 1972b) and a *Handbook of American Folklore* (Dorson 1983).

Dorson's convictions that folklore study should be fieldwork based and carried out in accordance with the highest scholarly standards made him an outspoken critic of purveyors of what he called "fakelore" (Dorson 1976). He also demonstrated repeatedly to colleagues in allied disciplines how their investigations could benefit from a knowledge of folklore and familiarity with folklorists' methods and findings. Thus, in addition to being a devoted student, documenter, analyst, and teacher of folklore, Dorson was an outspoken proponent of scholarly standards and a dedicated advocate for his discipline as well.

Robert A. Georges

References

Dorson, Richard M. 1959. A Theory for American Folklore. *Journal of American Folklore* 72:197–215.

———, ed. 1961. Folklore Research around the World: A North American Point of View. *Journal of American Folklore* 74:287–260. Reprinted under the same title as Indiana University Folklore Studies Series No. 16. Bloomington: Indiana University Press.

———, ed. [1963] 1972. *Studies in Japanese Folklore.* Port Washington, NY: Kennikat.

———. 1968. *The British Folklorists: A History.* Chicago: University of Chicago Press.

———, ed. 1972a. *African Folklore.* Bloomington: Indiana University Press.

———, ed. 1972b. *Folklore and Folklife: An Introduction.* Chicago: University of Chicago Press.

———. 1976. *Folklore and Fakelore*. Cambridge: Harvard
University Press.

———. 1981. *Land of the Millrats*. Cambridge: Harvard
University Press.

Georges, Robert A., ed. 1989a. Richard M. Dorson's Views
and Works: An Assessment. *Journal of Folklore Research*
26:1–80.

———, ed. 1989b. Richard Dorson. *Western Folklore* (Special Section). 48:325–374.

Ozzie Waters witches wells. Concord, California, 1940. American Folklife Center, Cowell Collection (WPA).

Dowsing

A means for locating underground water with a forked twig
or a divining rod. The dowser holds a branch of the twig in
each hand and walks over a plot of land until the rod reacts
by rotating in his or her hand. The practice originated for
locating underground minerals in Germany around the beginning of the 15th century. Baron de Beausoleil (1576–1643)
and his wife popularized the practice for finding water early
in the 17th century, and the practice became widespread
throughout Europe by the end of the century.

German and English settlers in North America brought
dowsing with them. The written record on dowsing in North
America is sparse before 1800; after that date, however, newspapers, magazines and other literature suggest widespread use
of dowsing to find water, minerals, hidden treasures, natural
gas, lost animals, and other objects. The prototypical dowser
uses a forked twig to find underground water while walking
over a plot of land. From the beginning, however, variations
appeared in both Europe and the United States. E.Z. Vogt and
Ray Hyman found that the peach tree was the single most
popular source for the forked twig, with willow the second
most popular (Vogt and Hyman 1979). Other sources were
cherry, apple, persimmon, hickory, plum, pear, elder, birch,
and maple trees. Metal rods and wire are frequently used in
place of wooden rods. Dowsers also use crowbars, pitchforks,
horsewhips, commercially made devices, and pendulums.

The object of the search also varies widely. Most frequently it is underground water. Other underground substances, such as gold, oil, ores, hidden pipes, and archaeological objects, have been targets. During the Vietnam War,
American Marines used the divining rod to look for underground tunnels used by the enemy. As far back as the 17th
century, some dowsers began using the rod to search for objects above the ground, such as criminals, missing persons, and
lost animals. Typically, dowsers search for their targets on site.
Increasingly, however, dowsers have claimed success in dowsing for water and other objects over a map rather than on the
actual site.

Although members of the American Society of Dowsers
and writers on the subject prefer to call the practice "dowsing,"
the term "water witching" is more widely used among the rural
practitioners in the United States. The term "water divining"
is also popular, mainly in the Southeast. Vogt and Hyman also
found the following terms in use: switching, water smelling,
channel surveying, water finding, doodlebugging (most typically in relation to finding oil), and water prophesying.

The typical dowser in the United States charges a small

fee or nothing. He or she operates in rural areas and views the
practice in pragmatic terms. For these dowsers, the practice
has no occult connection. The members of the American
Society of Dowsers, which was founded in 1960, on the other
hand, tend to come from urban areas and treat dowsing as one
of several occult techniques.

The evidence that dowsing "works" is merely anecdotal.
The many tests of dowsing that use objective baselines for
comparison have consistently found that dowsers do no better than chance. The proponents of dowsers denounce these
tests as unfair because they place the dowser in an unfamiliar
and hostile setting. Such objections occur mainly after the
negative results have been reported.

Vogt and Hyman argued that the rod moves through
involuntary muscular action—ideomotor action. The principle is the same as that involved in the pendulum, Ouija
board, and table tilting. Today many proponents of dowsing
agree that the rod moves because of involuntary muscular
movements of the dowser. They insist that this response is
triggered by a dowsing signal—one that comes directly from
the underground water or that comes to the dowser through
some form of extrasensory perception.

The involuntary movement of the dowsing instrument
is quite compelling, and the experience creates a strong belief
in the dowser. Believers use a variety of excuses to dismiss failures, such as interference from radio waves and inept drilling,
and they dismiss the consistently negative findings from scientific studies as due to the limitations of science rather than
to the invalidity of dowsing.

Vogt and Hyman's 1956 survey estimated that there were

25,000 dowsers in the United States. The typical dowser, they found, discovered his or her "powers" by watching a dowser in action. Usually, the process went something like this: Although skeptical, the observer accepted the dowser's invitation to try the rod. To the observer's surprise and consternation, the rod turned in his or her hands when the observer reached the location that the dowser had previously designated. The observer knew that he or she had not consciously made the rod dip. Not knowing about ideomotor action, the observer became a believer both in dowsing in general and in his or her ability to dowse.

Ray Hyman

References

Bird, C. 1979. *The Divining Hand: The 500-Year-Old Mystery of Dowsing.* New York: Dutton.

Hitching, F. 1977. *Pendulum: The Psi Connection.* Glasgow, Scotland: Fontana.

Vogt, E.Z., and Ray Hyman. 1979. *Water Witching U.S.A.* 2d ed. Chicago: University of Chicago Press.

Dozens

Short for "playing the dozens," a predominantly Black male cultural form of verbal dueling most widely known as "sounding," "the dozens," and "the dirty dozens." Other names for it, which vary regionally, include "signifying" or "sigging" (Chicago), "joning" (Washington, DC), "woofing" (Philadelphia), and "capping" (West Coast). The object of the contest, usually performed in front of an audience, is to artistically hurl insults, or "snaps," against one's opponents; the loser either backs down, runs out of insults and is therefore humiliated, or responds to verbal attacks with physical violence. From an examination of ethnographic data to support their claims, folklorists have subdivided the verbal art form into "signifying," which refers to a speaker directly insulting his or her target, and "dozens," which apply to insults toward the victim's family members, most often the mother. Sometimes "sounding" refers to the initial exchanges, "signifying" to personal insults, and "the dozens" to insults on relatives. However, "sounding" can also refer to ritualized insult against a relative, while for somebody to "sound on" somebody else refers to a ritualized attribute of that person. In short, the above synonyms describe a verbal activity that can take on a wide range of meanings. H. "Rap" Brown, a 1960s civil rights leader, wrote in his autobiography: "The real aim of the Dozens was to get a dude so mad he'd cry or get mad enough to fight" (354). Moreover, Brown pointed out, "some of the best Dozens players were girls"; therefore, the game is not necessarily gender specific, although the content of the insults may be quite different.

The earliest essay devoted to the subject and its origins appeared in 1939 in the first volume of *American Image*, a psychoanalytic journal, in which John Dollard examined material from his study of Black adolescents in Southern and Northern cities. One of his informants explained that "the dirty dozens" (as opposed to "the dozens") include references to the victim's mother, sisters, father, and brothers (Dollard [1939] 1994). Roger Abrahams cites another possible source that suggests the term "the dozens" may have originated in reference to the bad luck of rolling a twelve in craps; however, Abrahams cites among other possible origins Mack McCormick, who, in the liner notes "to his record *Unexpurgated Songs of Men* gives the most compelling source, a formulaic song routine about the subject which began 'I fucked your mother one . . .' going up to twelve" (Abrahams [1963] 1970: 261). On the other hand, Quincy Jones, in his foreword to *Snaps* (Percelay, Ivey, and Dweck 1994), understood through oral tradition that the term "dirty dozens" came from slavery. After the Atlantic crossing, auctioneers grouped the twelve most sickly looking slaves and sold them at a bargain rate. Says Jones, "The only thing even more degrading than slavery was to be part of this group. Insulting your mama was meant to make you feel as low as one of the dirty dozens" ([1993] 1994:8).

African ethnographic literature strongly suggests an African origin for "the dozens." For example, William Schecter reported verbal contests of this kind existing among the Ashanti (in Percelay, Ivey, and Dweck 1994:28). Similarly, Alan Dundes reminds us of a 1951 study of the Gusii (a Bantu people) by Philip Mayer, which describes verbal dueling among same-age boys engaging in a common initiation ceremony and who referred to one another's mothers pornographically (Dundes [1973] 1994:296–297). Participants (both audience and contestants) give such extreme license to one another that they usually allow participation only among those with whom it is safe to play. Generally speaking, "sounding" is an in-group process; when it occurs across group lines, its antagonists mean to provoke a fight (Labov 1972:304).

According to Abrahams, "sounding" is what crowds of boys do, and when they are just entering puberty they experiment with words and concepts they have overheard from adults. Although the contest is usually short, a definite pattern emerges, as in the following interchange taken from Abrahams' *Deep Down in the Jungle: Negro Narrative Folklore from the Streets of Philadelphia*:

> I hear your mother plays third base for the Phillies
> Your mother is a bricklayer, and stronger than your
>   father.
> Your mother eats shit.
> Your mother eats shit and mustard. (1970:48)

As the boys grow older, "the vilification of the mother is changed to sexual matters, the contests become more heated and the insults more noteworthy" (1970:48). The following, also from Abrahams' study, exemplify such vilification as adolescents insult one another:

> I fucked your mother on an electric wire.
> I made her pussy rise higher and higher.
>
> I fucked your mother between two cans.
> Up jumped a baby and hollered, "Superman."

At least my mother ain't no doorknob, everybody gets
   a turn (1970:49).
Effeminacy or homosexuality of the father or brother may also
appear as common subjects, such as the following:
   Least my father ain't pregnant in the stomach.
   Least my brother ain't no store; he take meat in the
      back (1970:50).

As Abrahams and other researchers have noted, certain
contrastive linguistic features outline the rules of the game
(Abrahams [1962] 1994:301). When Abrahams wrote on the
topic in 1962, he observed the following features: (1) participants rely upon formulaic patterns; (2) the patterns often
contain rhyme; and (3) speech rhythms change from natural
ones to ones that conform to the formula. Furthermore, William Labov identified specific patterns from Black adolescents
living in Harlem in the mid-1960s. Constructions Labov analyzed included: "Your mother is (like) . . ." ("Your mother look
like Flipper"); "Your mother got . . ." ("Your mother got a
putty chest"); "Your mother so ——— she ———" ("Your
mother is so old she got spider webs under her arms"); "Your
mother raised you on . . ." ("Your mother raised you on ugly
milk"); "I went to your house . . . (I went to your house to ask
for a piece of cheese. The rat jumped up and say, 'Heggies
["dibbs" or "halfsies"], please'")" (Labov 1972:276–283).

By the 1990s, hip hop had influenced the ritualized entertainment, while rhymed couplets of earlier "dozens" often
emerged as one-liners: "Your mother is so stupid, she thought
Boyz II Men was a day-care center," and "Your mother is so
dumb, she couldn't pass a blood test." Exhibiting several similarities with those constructions Labov identified, these last
two examples come from the more recent collection of ritual
insults in *Snaps* (Percelay, Ivey, and Dweck 1994). Certainly
not as analytical as Labov's study, *Snaps* nevertheless provides
not only a brief history of "the dozens," but also offers seventeen types of ritual insults that come from both folklore and
popular culture, such as fat snaps ("Your mother is so fat, she
broke her arm and gravy poured out"—from the movie *White
Men Can't Jump*); stupid snaps ("You're so dumb, you think
Taco Bell is a Mexican phone company"); ugly snaps ("If ugliness was a crime, you'd get the electric chair"); old snaps
("Your mother is so old, she knew Burger King when he was
just a prince"); and, of course, sex snaps ("Your mother is like
an elevator—if you push the right button she'll go down on
you").

Within these evolving guidelines for ritual insults, contestants not only develop important linguistic skills that require creativity, wit, and humor, but they also learn self-con-
trol. Moreover, as researchers have pointed out, "the dozens"
are also, to a much lesser extent, played by females as well as
White males, though their functions and content are decidedly quite different. Dollard and Abrahams, whose data come
from Black males, have provided the most classic interpretations of "the dozens." Dollard explained them in light of race
relations and displaced aggressions among Blacks. Abrahams
thought of them as a reflection of tensions emerging from the

Black family structure, from which eventually "black males
find themselves in a totally male environment in which the
necessity to prove one's masculinity (and to reject the feminine principle) recurs constantly (Abrahams 1970:54). Because the young boy cannot openly attack his own mother
either to himself or to others, he creates a play situation that
enables him to attack some other person's mother, thereby
"exorcising" his mother's influence (Abrahams 1970:55). By
playing "the dozens," the combatants not only develop defense
mechanisms, but each also builds up his own self-image and
affirms his own masculine characteristics. Despite their compelling arguments, such explanations do not provide how "the
dozens" might function among females; nevertheless, Dollard,
Abrahams, and the additional authors cited below merit the
attention of any scholar wishing to pursue further inquiries
into "playing the dozens."
Richard Allen Burns

References
Abrahams, Roger. [1962] 1994. Playing the Dozens. In
   *Mother Wit from the Laughing Barrel: Readings in the
   Interpretation of Afro-American Folklore,* ed. Alan
   Dundes. Jackson: University Press of Mississippi, pp.
   295–309.
———. [1963] 1970. *Deep Down in the Jungle: Negro Nar-
   rative Folklore from the Streets of Philadelphia.* Chicago:
   Aldine.
Brown, H. Rap. [1969] 1994. Street Smarts. In *Mother Wit
   from the Laughing Barrel: Readings in the Interpretation
   of Afro-American Folklore,* ed. Alan Dundes. Jackson:
   University Press of Mississippi, pp. 353–356.
Dollard, John. [1939] 1994. The Dozens: Dialectic of Insult. In *Mother Wit from the Laughing Barrel: Readings
   in the Interpretation of Afro-American Folklore,* ed. Alan
   Dundes. Jackson: University Press of Mississippi, pp.
   277–294.
Dundes, Alan, ed. [1973] 1994. *Mother Wit from the Laugh-
   ing Barrel: Readings in the Interpretation of Afro-Ameri-
   can Folklore.* Jackson: University Press of Mississippi.
Jackson, Bruce. 1974. *"Get Your Ass in the Water and Swim
   Like Me": Narrative Poetry from Black Oral Tradition.*
   Cambridge: Harvard University Press.
Kochman, Thomas. 1970. Toward an Ethnography of
   Black American Speech Behavior. In Afro-American
   Anthropology: Contemporary Perspectives, ed. Norman
   E. Whitten Jr. and John F. Szwed. New York: Free
   Press, pp. 145–162.
Labov, William. 1972. Rules for Ritual Insult. In *Rappin'
   and Stylin' Out: Communication in Urban Black
   America,* ed. Thomas Kochman. Chicago: University
   of Illinois Press, pp. 265–314.
Levine, Lawrence. [1977] 1980. *Black Culture and Black
   Consciousness: Afro-American Folk Thought from Slavery
   to Freedom.* New York: Oxford University Press.
Majors, Richard, and Janet Mancini Billson. 1992. Playing the
   Dozens. Chapter 8 in *Cool Pose: The Dilemmas of Black
   Manhood in America.* New York: Lexington, pp. 91–102.

Mitchell-Kernan, Claudia. [1971] 1973. Signifying. In *Mother Wit from the Laughing Barrel: Readings in the Interpretation of Afro-American Folklore*, ed. Alan Dundes, Jackson: University Press of Mississippi, pp. 310–328.

Percelay, James, Monteria Ivey, and Stephen Dweck. 1994. *Snaps: "If Ugliness Were Bricks, Your Mother Would Be a Housing Project" . . . and More Than 450 Other Snaps, Caps, and Insults for Playing the Dozens.* New York: William Morrow.

Wepman, Dennis, Ronald B. Newman, and Murray B. Binderman. 1976. *The Life: The Lore and Folk Poetry of the Black Hustler.* Philadelphia: University of Pennsylvania Press.

Drama, Folk

A theatrical performance given for a specific and cohesive group of people, wherein the actors and the audience are conscious of both their roles in the performance and their shared identity as group members. The form that the drama takes varies, the most common being performances by human actors; but folk dramas also rely upon pantomime, puppetry, shadow figures, or any combination of these forms.

These dramas range from informal, even spontaneous, performances to highly elaborate, well-planned, and rehearsed productions; from one-person monologues to large casts; from improvised lines to written dialogue. The more elaborate forms of folk drama include songs, costuming, and stage props, while the simplest are little more than a single actor in street clothes ad-libbing to a one-member audience. What all folk dramas have in common, however, are (1) at least one role-playing performer, (2) a plot, storyline, or coherent scene, and (3) an established "distance" between actors and audience, such as a stage or a space specifically cleared or marked for the theatrical production.

Folk dramas are often performed as part of religious rituals and festivals and, in this context, usually have their roots in Old World theater. The reenactment of stories from the Old and New Testament, of saints' lives, or of hero tales from legendry and myth, or the dramatic interpretation of some important point of religious dogma or philosophy made up the bulk of medieval European mystery plays, passion plays, miracle plays and combat dramas, and immigrants have brought these ancient forms of drama from Europe to North America. Among the earliest of these migratory folk dramas were the Spanish *pastorelas*: plays that recounted and celebrated the birth of Christ, not only through the retelling of the New Testament story, but also through scenes of combat between St. Michael and Lucifer over the soul of the infant Jesus and comic scenes depicting shepherds and other peasants. These plays, as well as other dramas of Spanish origin, continue to delight and instruct Christmastime audiences in churches, halls, outdoor squares, and homes in Hispanic communities, especially in the Southwest.

English and Irish immigrants brought Christmas mumming dramas to the New World: Troupes of actors would house-visit in their communities during the holiday season and perform combat dramas wherein St. George (or some other heroic character) would fight with and defeat The Turkish Knight (or some other, usually non-Christian, figure); The Doctor would often revive The Turkish Knight, who would then pledge his loyalty to the hero. These ritual combats between good and evil were most commonly performed in Newfoundland and in the West Indies, although by the mid-1990s such productions were rare, except as performed by professional and semiprofessional actors in the context of folkrevival.

Perhaps the most common Christmas folk drama, however, is the school Christmas concert. All over North America, schoolchildren, under the direction of their teachers, perform elaborate stage productions before family and neighbors. Often these dramas relate to Christmas themes, either retelling the story of Christ's birth or acting out a visit from Santa Claus, but many of these productions include secular skits, usually comic or melodramatic, on a wide variety of themes. Of course, at other times of the year schools put on dramas, and whereas these productions are staged primarily for the benefit of the students, their parents, and members of the immediate community, they are a part of the folk-drama tradition. Likewise summer camps, scouting troops, and other organized activities for children are a venue for skits and other forms of folk drama.

Easter pageants, which retell the story of the crucifixion of Christ, are common among the church services of several ethnic and immigrant groups (for example, Hispanic Americans and German Americans), as well as among community groups. Similarly, a number of African American churches include folk dramas in their yearly cycle of services, most of which are morality plays of the Everyman or Faustian type. For example, the congregation of the Northside New Era Baptist Church of Indianapolis, Indiana, has produced *In the Rapture,* while *Heaven Bound* has been part of the Easter celebrations of African American churches in Georgia and South Carolina (among other places), and *The Old Ship of Zion* is a mainstay of churches in many parts of North America. In all of these African American productions, the devil, as a comic trickster figure, battles with the forces of righteousness for the soul of a mortal.

A similar transplant from the Old World is the *purimshpil,* which forms a part of the celebration of the Jewish festival of Purim. Especially among Hasidic Jews, congregations will perform either the story of Esther, Mordecai, King Ahasuerus, and the villainous Haman (taken from the Book of Esther), or some other Old Testament story; the Bobover Hasidic community of Brooklyn, New York, for example, has retold the story of Abraham and Isaac as part of its Purim celebrations.

Because folk drama demands a certain intimacy between actors and audience (all of whom are a part of the same group—for example, a single church congregation or a cohesive ethnic community), most of these ritual dramas include local, secular themes within their productions—themes that relate more directly to community life than do the larger biblical or religious themes of the dramas. Current events, local characters, politics, and community in-jokes, as well as the shared knowledge and understanding of movie stars, television shows, and other aspects of popular culture, are all grist for the folk-drama mill. This intimacy also allows considerable flexibility during dramatic performances: ad-libbing, interjections from the audience, and even roughhousing between the actors and members of the audience are all characteristic of folk drama.

The one exception in ritual drama is its use in certain rites of passage, where the traditionality (and, therefore, inflexibility) of the performance is paramount in fulfilling the rite. The best example of this form of theater is the initiation drama performed by Freemasons: The acting out of the murder of Hiram Abif must be done without any variation in the plot or script from one performance to the next (although variation does occur in costuming, props, and other peripheral matters).

While religious rituals act as a venue for many forms of folk drama, the secular world provides even more opportunities for such performances. Although little documented, occupational groups often perform skits during company picnics and other such get-togethers; these skits are almost always comedies and parodies involving the reenactment (in exaggerated form) of everyday work, workplace characters and stereotypes, and interactions between workers and the outsiders with whom they must deal. For example, health workers in one hospital produced a drama made up of interlocking skits that, among other things, portrayed an anesthesiologist as a samurai warrior, commented on malpractice insurance, and made fun of hyperactive patients. Such skits are usually irreverent and esoteric, and they can be quite shocking to unknowledgeable outsiders.

Of a more serious nature, labor groups have used drama to protest unfair working conditions. As a means of raising the consciousness of workers or setting the proper emotional tone before or during a strike-action, union organizers sometimes produce in-group dramas in which workers can act out their frustrations with management and rehearse their demands. This same form of drama sometimes becomes "street theater," when it is performed in public as part of a strike or a labor demonstration. Chicano farm workers in California have been especially adept at this form of drama, but some of the same strategies have found a place among political demonstrators and protest movements throughout North America.

Folk drama functions most clearly as a way of raising consciousness and developing self-awareness in the context of group psychotherapy, where a group member, under the guidance of a therapist, will sometimes create a personal, autobiographical drama, using some members of the therapy group as supporting actors, while the rest of the group acts as audience for the performance. This therapeutic method is called psychodrama. Group gestalt therapy also makes use of theatrical conventions in its treatment of patients. Self-help groups, as well, make use of drama, as when, for example, graduating students and unemployed workers perform mock interviews in preparation for entering (or reentering) the workplace.

Skits performed within the context of a region or a family are also forms of folk drama. For example, mock wedding dramas are quite common in various parts of North America. Often involving cross-dressing, bawdiness, and local satire, these parodies of the traditional wedding ceremony take several forms. In small Saskatchewan prairie towns, for example, cross-dressed performers will honor a couple's milestone wedding anniversary (usually the twenty-fifth) with a mock wedding that includes humorous incidents from the couple's past; in North Carolina (among other places), men's volunteer fire departments will produce womenless weddings as a community fund-raiser; especially in the Southern states, church socials sometimes include a Tom Thumb wedding, a parody in which children perform the roles.

A more elaborate type of community folk drama involves the retelling of the history of a region. In such dramas, often performed outdoors, local people reenact, for the benefit of their neighbors, the European settling of their community, important local historical events, or local legends. For example, since the early 1960s the people of Big Stone Gap, Virginia, have produced *Trail of the Lonesome Pine,* which tells the story of industrialization and the clash of cultures in their area in the 1890s. As with much ritual folk drama, certain people or families in the region will sometimes take responsibility for a specific role in the drama, with the part handed down from one generation to the next.

Of course, any form of community drama performed by locals and directed toward members of that community is folk drama. Even the plays of Shakespeare and other masterpieces from the world of popular and elite theater enter the repertoires of local actors and become transformed into folk drama. As in other forms of folklore, there is a constant interplay and interchange between folk drama and other theatrical traditions.

The dividing line between folk drama and other kinds of drama, however, is not always clear. For example, folk-play movements (such as the Carolina Playmakers) employ writers to construct dramas about regional history and traditions, and these plays are usually presented to people from the region, but the actors, directors, and writers may not all be from the area, and these dramas travel, rather than stay in any one community; thus, there is not the intimacy between actors and audience usually associated with folk drama. Likewise, local dramas performed on radio and television (such as local radio performances of Pennsylvania German dialect plays) cannot achieve the intimacy and shared performance of their live counterparts.

Many kinds of popular theater are related to folk drama, especially traveling shows that play in small communities. Chautauquas, circuses, tent shows, medicine shows, magic shows, and minstrel shows relate to folk drama in their use of traditional material, their incorporation of local knowledge into their performances, and their evocative and nostalgic natures. Dramas such as professional wrestling and Punch and Judy puppet shows play out the same combat between good and evil, comedy and tragedy, which is at the heart of the ritual dramas described above. Professional ethnic theater (such as Yiddish theater), of necessity, makes use of shared traditions and esoteric knowledge. But in all of these cases, the intimacy demanded of folk drama is diluted by too great a social distance between actors and audience.

Yet folk drama also dilutes its intimacy when played before outsiders. For example, performers of African American morality dramas travel far from their congregations to play before general audiences, while community historical dramas cater to tourists and other outsiders. Even audiences for local mock-wedding dramas, school Christmas concerts, and occupational skits often include outsiders who might be unfamiliar with local dramatic aesthetics and traditions, and who may not understand in-joke references in the scripts. Thus, folk-drama actors often play to two audiences at the same time—insiders and outsiders—which results in their productions being partly folk and partly popular. All drama lies on a continuum of intimacy, with "pure" folk drama being the most intimate and "pure" popular drama being the most distant.

By the same token, not all folklore that has dramatic qualities is folk drama. For example, games and play often demand role-playing, but there is no clear separation between audience and actors in this context. There are many masking traditions (Halloween house visits, Mardi Gras, and parades, for example) in which performers play roles and are certainly separated from their audience, and in which costuming can be quite elaborate, but there is no coherent, narrative structure nor set of scenes in such performances. Pranks include many elements of folk drama, yet the dupes—the main performers in pranks—are unaware of their status as actors, and thus they do not consciously distance themselves from their audience.

But there is a continuum here from conscious drama to unconscious drama. The school clowns who, in front of their classmates, spontaneously imitate and caricature their teachers are performing dramas in perhaps only a semiconscious way; the nurse who uses an anatomically correct puppet to explain operations to young patients might be a conscious actor, but the children might not be consciously aware of their roles as an audience. While the boundaries of folk drama might be unclear, at the center of this tradition is an intimacy and shared consciousness of purpose among actors, directors, writers, stagehands, and audience.

Michael Taft

References

Burson, Anne C. 1980. Model and Text in Folk Drama. *Journal of American Folklore* 93:305–316. Occupational Drama.

Charyk, John C. 1985. *The Biggest Day of the Year: The Old-Time Christmas School Concert*. Saskatoon: Western Producer-Prairie Books.

Cohen, Hennig, and Tristram Potter Coffin, eds. 1991. *The Folklore of American Holidays*. 2d ed. Detroit: Gale. Purimshpil, pp.103–111.

George, Louise Wright. 1952. Shakespeare in La Ceiba. *Shakespeare Quarterly* 3:359–365.

Glassberg, David. 1990. *American Historical Pageantry: The Uses of Tradition in the Early Twentieth Century*. Chapel Hill: University of North Carolina Press.

Greenhill, Pauline. 1988. Folk Drama in Anglo-Canada and the Mock Wedding: Transaction, Performance, and Meaning. *Canadian Drama/L'Art dramatique canadien* 14:169–205.

Huerta, Jorge A. 1982. *Chicano Theater: Themes and Forms*. Ypsilanti, MI: Bilingual Press/Editorial Bilingüe.

Richards, Deborah Bowman. 1979–1981. A Bibliographic Essay on Afro-American Folk Drama. *Ohio Folklife: Journal of the Ohio Folklore Society* 6:37–55.

Stowell, Bonnie. 1970. Folk Drama Scholarship in the United States: A Selective Survey. *Folklore Annual of the University Folklore Association* 2:51–66.

See also Fiesta; Mummers

Dulcimer

A fretted instrument of the box-zither family, variously known as the "Appalachian dulcimer," "mountain dulcimer," "lap dulcimer," "plucked dulcimer," or "Kentucky dulcimer." Characteristically, the dulcimer features three or four strings stretched along a fingerboard that runs the length of an hourglass- or teardrop-shaped hollow sound box. The Appalachian dulcimer is a southern Appalachian folk instrument unrelated to the similarly named "hammered dulcimer," which is a trapezoidal board zither whose strings are struck with hammers.

With origins in northern European instruments such as the German *scheitholt*, the Scandinavian *langeleik* and *hummel*, and the French *épinette des Vosges* brought by German immigrants to the Shenandoah Valley, the dulcimer's characteristic design was developed in areas of southwestern Virginia and eastern Kentucky at the beginning of the 19th century. Even though the instrument itself appears to have no direct antecedent in the British Isles, the musical repertoire consisting of lyric and frolic songs, ballads, and dance tunes reflects the Scots-Irish heritage of the Southern Appalachian Highlanders who fashioned the instrument to accommodate their musical aesthetic. The distinctive melody with drone accompaniment texture of the dulcimer may be a more gentle echo of similar bagpipe style and timbre.

As the dulcimer is a material artifact of folk culture, there is considerable variation in the design, dimensions, and materials of the instruments crafted by different artisans. Customary physical features usually include: (1) an hourglass- or teardrop-shaped sound box approximately 32 inches long and 2 inches deep with a softwood belly (pine or spruce) and hardwood sides and back (cherry, maple, or black walnut); (2) a hardwood fingerboard, whose underside is hollowed out to transmit sound and then mounted over the vertical axis of the sound box; (3) a strum depression approximately 5 inches long scooped out toward the base of the fingerboard; (4) a scale of eighteen diatonically arranged wire frets spanning the length of the fingerboard (each fret extends across the width of the fingerboard although originally the frets lay only under the melody string); (5) variously shaped sound holes cut into the top plate of the sound box (hearts and violin-like "F" holes are common); (6) a peg box with tuning devices (friction pegs and machine heads are common) for each string, located above the nut at the head of the instrument; and (7) fastening devices below the bridge at the base of the dulcimer.

On the Ala-Sippi Dulcimer Association's Dulcimer Day, Juanita Keys plucks a dulcimer while Charles Keys bows a saw; behind them sits a technician. Tishomingo, Mississippi, 1987. American Folklife Center.

Musicians usually play the dulcimer seated, with the instrument laid across their lap and the melody strings located closest to them. Pitches are obtained by depressing the string over the fret with fingers or a short stick called a "noter" or "fretter." Traditionally, only the melody strings were noted to create melodies and countermelodies, with the other strings resonating as an open drone. As the dulcimer has diatonic rather than chromatic frets, various tunings are used to accommodate the different modes, such as Ionian, Aeolian, and Dorian.

Sound is created by strumming the instrument with fingers or a plastic pick (originally feather quills and twigs), although several historical instances of bowed dulcimers have been documented as well. Modern dulcimer technique has been expanded to include chording, chromaticism, note bending and vibrato, elaborate finger picking, and the use of various electronic effects. Because of the gentle tone and soft dynamic response, the dulcimer has traditionally been used in intimate settings as a solo instrument or as an accompaniment for voice. Since the 1950s, however, recording technology and amplification have provided the instrument with great flexibility in arrangement and performance.

Historically, dulcimer building and performance activity appear to have been limited to small extended-family enclaves within the mountains during the 19th century. However, dulcimer-related activity increased markedly at the beginning of the 20th century concurrent with the establishment of the settlement schools. According to David Whisnant, the instrument represented the genteel "Bradley-Furman" version of Appalachian culture that the settlement schools were attempting to inculcate. Whisnant wrote that ". . . the shadowy and presumably ancient origin of the dulcimer was appealing; its plaintive, simple sound was congruent with prevalent assumptions about 'Elizabethan' culture in the mountains; and perhaps best of all, the instrument was physically unsuited to playing the lively banjo tunes that were insinuating themselves into more and more mountain households" (Whisnant 1983:98). In particular, the Hindman Settlement School in Knott County, Kentucky, played a central role in the dissemination of the dulcimer both inside and outside Appalachia through the building and marketing activity of "Uncle" Ed Thomas (1850–1933) and Jethro Amburgey (1895–1971).

Spreading forth from its regional settlement school base, the dulcimer experienced a sharp increase in visibility and popularity concurrent with the folk revivals of the 1930s through the 1960s. Sparked by the public performances, recordings, and publications of performers such as John Jacob Niles, Paul Clayton, Frank Noah Proffitt, I.D. Stamper, and, especially, Jean Ritchie, the instrument experienced a "revival" of popularity that brought it out of regional obscurity and into widespread national consciousness. Today there is a national network of builders, players, teachers, dulcimer clubs, and festivals, and a quarterly journal, *Dulcimer Players News,* devoted to dulcimer-related activity.

While many performers and craftspeople seek to preserve traditional style and practice, others are actively expanding the dulcimer in new directions. Late-20th-century performers such as Robert Force, Lois Hornbostel, and David Schnaufer have stretched the repertoire and technique far beyond the instrument's folk origins. Correspondingly, builders have modified the instrument's basic design to incorporate chromatic frets, scalloped fingerboards, and MIDI (musical instrument digital interface) electronics to accommodate innovative performance techniques.

Ron Pen

References

Alvey, R. Gerald. 1984. *Dulcimer Maker: The Craft of Homer Ledford.* Lexington: University Press of Kentucky.

Eaton, Allen W. 1937. *Handicrafts of the Southern Highlands.* New York: Russell Sage Foundation.

Ritchie, Jean. 1963. *The Dulcimer Book.* New York: Oak.

Seeger, Charles. 1958. The Appalachian Dulcimer. *Journal of American Folklore* 71:40–51.

Smith, L. Allen. 1980. Toward a Reconstruction of the Development of the Appalachian Dulcimer: What the Instruments Suggest. *Journal of American Folklore* 93:385–396.

———. 1983. *A Catalogue of Pre-Revival Appalachian Dulcimers.* Columbia: University of Missouri Press.

Smith, Ralph Lee. 1986. *The Story of the Dulcimer.* Cosby, TN: Crying Creek.

Whisnant, David E. 1983. *All That Is Native and Fine.* Chapel Hill: University of North Carolina Press.

See also Niles, John Jacob; Proffitt, Frank Noah; Ritchie, Jean

Dusenbury, Emma Hays (1862–1941)

Blind Arkansas singer of traditional ballads and songs. Born in Georgia, Emma Hays moved with her family to Arkansas in 1872. She learned many of her songs during the eight years she lived with her family in Baxter County; these were years of hard work but also of church meetings, play parties, and Sunday afternoon song sessions. In the late 1880s, Emma married Ernest Dusenbury, an itinerant worker with a taste like hers for music and dancing—"I wasn't blind in my heels, nohow." They had one daughter, Ora. Four years after her marriage, a prolonged fever left her blind. In 1907 the family settled to farming near Mena, Arkansas. Ernest suffered a crippling accident ten years later, but he lived until 1933.

Apparently discovered by Professor F.M. Goodhue of Commonwealth College in Mena, between 1930 and 1936 Emma Dusenbury sang for collector Vance Randolph, author John Gould Fletcher, composer and Arkansas Symphony Director Laurence Powell, and collectors John Lomax and Mrs. Sidney Robertson, among others. Randolph printed twenty Dusenbury songs in *Ozark Folksongs,* including fine versions of Child 13 and 49 and an unusual tune for Child 289. Lomax, in a two-day marathon, recorded eighty-two songs. Robertson recorded forty-three, including approximately seven songs also recorded by Lomax. The Lomax and Robertson recordings now reside in the Library of Congress. Dusenbury's large repertoire is representative of the southern mountain tradition, though especially strong in ballads and other early and rare items. Emma Dusenbury sang for the Arkansas State Centennial celebration at Little Rock in 1936. Five years later, she died and was buried by the county.

William Bernard McCarthy

References

Cochran, Robert. 1983. Sweet Emma. *Arkansas Times.* November, pp. 46–48. (Followed by a reprint of John Gould Fletcher's brief memoir, The Ozark Singer.)

McNeil, William K. 1980. Introduction. *Ozark Folksongs Collected and Edited by Vance Randolph.* Columbia: University of Missouri Press, pp. 14–15.

Dutch Americans

Immigrants and their descendants from the Dutch-speaking Netherlands and certain adjacent provinces. These include Flemish-speaking Belgium, *Plattdeutsch* (Low German)-speaking Germany, Frisian-speaking Friesland (the Netherlands), and others, including even Scandinavians who were culturally considered "Dutch" in 17th-century New Netherland.

True Dutch Americans should not be confused with the "Pennsylvania Dutch," who are actually *Deutsch* (the German word for "German"). The confusion comes from the fact that two hundred years ago the Dutch language was called *Nederduits* (the Dutch word for "Low German") or simply *Duits.* In modern Dutch, the name of the language is *Nederlands* or *Hollands.* But the latter term also causes confusion, since it is common for the Dutch to refer to their country as Holland even though that term properly refers to only the two provinces of North and South Holland.

Dutch immigration to North America came in two waves: first the approximately 100,000 immigrants and their descendants who came to colonial North America by 1790; and, second, the more than 250,000 Netherlanders who immigrated during the 19th century. The first wave of immigrants settled primarily in the Hudson River Valley, Long Island, and northern New Jersey. About half of the people in the colonial migration came, not from the Netherlands itself, but from provinces adjacent to the Netherlands. The second wave settled primarily in the Midwest, clustering in towns such as Holland and Grand Rapids, Michigan; Pella and Orange City, Iowa; Cedar Grove, Wisconsin; and Edgerton, Minnesota.

In the 20th century, these Midwestern Dutch communities developed what folklorist Richard Dorson termed "presentational" folk festivals, in which a highly romantic and stereotyped image of Dutch traditions was presented primarily for tourists. These festivals featured tulip gardens, re-creations of Dutch windmills, wooden shoe dancing, and street scrubbing.

Similarly, the folklore of the colonial Dutch population was satirized in the writings of Washington Irving in such short stories as "The Legend of Sleepy Hollow" and "Rip Van Winkle," published in *The Sketch Book* (1819–1820) and his facetious *A History of New York* (1809), written under the pseudonym Diedrich Knickerbocker. Irving's caricature of Dutch folk traditions was so influential that the term Knickerbocker came to mean a native New Yorker—hence the name New York Knicks for the professional basketball team.

The term "Dutch" itself, in American slang, has taken on a negative meaning, as in "Dutch treat" (which is not a treat at all), "Dutch uncle" (which refers not to an uncle, but to someone who scolds), and "Dutch courage" (which means false courage, especially under the influence of alcohol).

Little remains of genuine Dutch American folklore, but it is possible to reconstruct from written sources the traditions that were transplanted by the settlers of New Netherland in the 17th century and survived through the end of the 19th century, especially in the rural, farming areas.

Two distinct dialects of spoken Dutch developed in New York and New Jersey, one called "Jersey Dutch" and the other "Hudson-Mohawk Dutch" or simply de Tal (literally, "the language"). Each dialect contained English and Native American loan words, Algonquian words in Jersey Dutch and Iroquoian in Hudson-Mohawk Dutch. In addition, there developed among free Blacks and slaves in the Dutch American culture area a distinct variant of the dialect. These spoken dialects survived into the opening decades of the 20th century. The last known speaker of Jersey Dutch died in the 1940s.

The same creolization of Dutch and English culture that occurred in the language is also evident in the folk music and dance. In 1787, the Scottish American physician Alexander Coventry noted in his diary that the Dutchmen he observed in a tavern near Catskill, New York, sang in both English and Dutch. He wrote: "Mr. Demun from Esopus, was singing a Bagatelle; first he sang it in Dutch, and then he sang it in English. Then Peter Yates sang what is called 'The Song.' . . . Then he sang 'The Debtor,' also several Dutch songs. . . ." Later, in 1802, Coventry accompanied Jeremiah van Rensselaer and the latter's two sisters on a wagon ride, and he noted, "When we came to the wagon again Mr. V.R. desired me to take a seat at his side, which I did and had the pleasure of the young ladies sing a number of songs, of which several were Scottish." Coventry also noted that the Dutch farmers of the Upper Hudson Valley were fond of dancing reels, another cultural borrowing from the British Isles.

Notwithstanding these cultural borrowings, a Dutch folksong tradition survived through the end of the 19th century. Several of these songs from Ulster County, New York, were written down about 1907 by local historian Benjamin Myer Brink. One such song was De Pruttelarij Voerman

("The Grumbling Wagoner"):

> Eens had ik mijn wagen verhuurd, en dat aan oude
>   wijven,
> Toen zij op der kermis kwamen, gigen zij aan't kijven;
> Nooit meer wil ik het wagen, ouder wijven in mijn
>   wagen.
> Rijdt wat an, wagen, wagen. Rijdt wat an, voerman.

> (Once had I my wagon hired, and that to old gossips,
> Soon as they reached the fair, all began to scold;
> No more will I hire the wagon, have old hags in my
>   wagon.
> Ride on wagon, wagon. Ride on, wagoner.)

The song continues with verses about *oude mannen* (old curmudgeons), *oude dochters* (old maids), and *oude heeren* (old lords). In each case, the wagoner resolves never again to transport that group of people in his wagon, until in the last verse, he takes *jonge dochters* (young women) to the fair:

> Eens had ik mijn wagen verhuurd, en dat aan jonge
>   dochters.
> Toen zij op de kermis kwamen werden zij al verkocht
>   er;
> Verkocht al hier, verkocht al daar.
> Jonge dochters is goede waar.
> Ik wil wel laden op mijn wagen van de jong dochter.
> Rijdt wat an, wagen, wagen. Rijdt wat an, voerman.

> (Once had I my wagon hired, and that to young
>   women.
> Soon as they reached the fair, every one was taken;
> Were purchased here, were purchased there.
> Young women are good wares.
> I will load up my wagon with young women.
> Ride on, wagon, wagon. Ride on, wagoner.)

The references in the song to the agricultural fair *(kermis)*, a tradition that did not survive the 17th century in America, and to the old lords *(oude heeren)*, an aspect of European social structure that did not come to America, indicate a survival in the folk memory of the culture of the old country. The attitudes toward young women expressed in the song, which depart from the strict Calvinist teachings of the Dutch Reformed Church, suggest that folk attitudes do not always correspond with the official doctrines of the church.

Some of the folklore that survived the longest was that which was learned the earliest—namely, children's folklore. One nursery rhyme in particular, "Trip a Trop a Troontjes," has been collected in the Netherlands, South Africa, and Bergen County, New Jersey, as recently as the 1930s:

> Trip a trop a troontjes,
> De varkens in de boontjes.
> De koetjes in de klaver,
> De paarden in de haver.

De eenjes in de water-plas,
De kalf in de lange grass;
So grott mijn kleine poppetje was.

(Trip a trop a troontjes,
The pigs are in the bean vines.
The cows are in the clover blooms,
The horses in the oat fields.
The ducks are in the waterpond,
The calf is in the long grass;
So tall my little baby was.)

Much of Dutch American folklore was related to farming, which is not surprising considering the fact that the Dutch American farmers were the main bearers of this folk tradition, the urban merchants having quickly acculturated to the dominant English ways after the English conquest of New Netherland in 1664. There were Dutch rhymes that were recited to ensure a good crop:

Klip, klop, bovenop,
Zet je hoed al aan je kop.
Draaie, vleie, drie maal zaaie,
Pluk de veere van de kaaie.

(Klip, klop, bovenop,
Set your hat on your head.
Turn, go, three times sow,
Pick the ferry from the quay.)

Other sayings were folk remedies to cure sick livestock. For example, if a horse had worms, you should take the animal into the yard and stroke its abdomen while repeating the charm, *"Marie demoeder's Heere, ghing over de land. Se had drie worme in d'r hand. De een wat wit, nander swaatm, de derde was rood. Soo gha je dood."* ("Mary, mother of the Lord, went over the land. She had three worms in her hand. The one was white, another black, and the third was red. So you shall die.") If a horse had the hiccups, you stroked it three times and turned it around by its head in the sun, while saying, *"De heiligh seght: Joseph ghing over'n Akker. Daar vond hy drie worme. De een swaart, nander bruin, de derde was rood. Je sal starveghan dood."* ("The saint says: Joseph went over the field. There he found three worms. One was black, another was brown, the third was red. You shall drop dead.") The invocation of "Mary, mother of the Lord," "the saint," and "Joseph" in these charms is evidence of Catholic survivals in the folk beliefs of the Protestant Dutch. Folklorist Don Yoder has noted similar survivals of Catholicism among the Pennsylvania Germans.

Distinctive Dutch American customs were associated with Shrove Tuesday, Easter, Whitsunday, and Saint Nicholas Day. Some of these customs, which survived through the 19th century, were observed by slaves and free Blacks living in New York and New Jersey.

The main traditional activity associated with Shrove Tuesday (the day before Ash Wednesday and the beginning of Lent) was "riding the goose." This custom consisted of riding on horseback past a greased goose suspended by a rope and trying to pull off its head. The Dutch Reformed Church disapproved of this custom, and the Director General and Council of New Netherland repeatedly banned it, but to no avail. There is no evidence, however, that the custom of riding the goose persisted past the 17th century.

The Dutch name for Easter was Paas, which the White Dutch and their slaves celebrated for two days. As with other European groups, colored eggs, symbolizing Christ's resurrection, were part of the Dutch American Easter festival. Another part was the preparation of *Paas* cakes, made from a batter of eggs and flour, fried on an iron "spider" (a skillet with legs).

Pentecost, or Whitsunday, was known as Pinkster among the Dutch Americans. Its religious significance was to commemorate the appearance of the Holy Ghost to the Apostles after Christ's crucifixion. In its folk manifestation, it became a springtime carnival festival, celebrated by both Blacks and Whites for two days. In the early 19th century, Blacks in Albany and from the surrounding countryside would assemble on the day following Pinkster under the leadership of a slave known as King Charles. Dressed in the costume of a British soldier, he would lead what was described as a "Guinea dance" to the accompaniment of fiddle, flute, fife, Jew's harp, drums, banjo, and the tabor. From contemporary descriptions, it seems that Pinkster in Albany was an Afro-Dutch celebration with certain African cultural survivals. Thus, it was akin to the carnival celebrations in New Orleans, the Caribbean, and South America. Ironically, Pinkster survived longer among the Blacks than the Whites. In 1874 local historian Gabriel Forman wrote that on Long Island "poor Pinckster [*sic*] has lost its rank among the festivals, and is only kept by the negroes; with them, however, especially on the west end of the island, it is still much of a holiday."

Saint Nicholas is the patron saint of Amsterdam, and his Saint's Day is celebrated in the Netherlands on December 6. He appears on the eve of the holiday dressed as a bishop on horseback and accompanied by his servant, Zwarte Piet (Black Peter). Children receive gifts in their shoes, which they set out overnight. There is some doubt, however, whether this Saint's Day was ever celebrated in Dutch colonial America. In the 19th century, St. Nicholas became associated with the holiday of Christmas, in part because of Washington Irving's description of St. Nicholas in *A History of New York*. Some Dutch Americans retained the custom of placing gifts in children's shoes, but on Christmas, not St. Nicholas Day. Thus, a Dutch patron saint was associated with a holiday that was German in origin and English by adoption, resulting in another example of the cultural syncretism that occurred among the Dutch in America.

David Steven Cohen

References

Brink, Benjamin Myer. 1902. *The Early History of Saugerties, 1660–1825.* Kingston, NY: R.W. Anderson and Sons.

Cohen, David Steven. 1984. In Search of Carolus Africanus

Rex: Afro-Dutch Folklore in New York and New Jersey. *Journal of the Afro-American Historical and Genealogical Society* 5:149–162.

———. 1992. *The Dutch-American Farm.* New York and London: New York University Press.

Furman, Gabriel. 1874. *Antiquities of Long Island.* New York: J.W. Bouton.

Prince, John Dyneley. 1910. The Jersey Dutch Dialect. *Dialect Notes* 3:459–484.

Rodes, Sara Puryear. 1956. Washington Irving's Use of Traditional Folklore. *Southern Folklore Quarterly* 19:143–153.

Van Loon, L.G. 1938. *Crumbs from an Old Dutch Closet: The Dutch Dialect of Old New York.* The Hague: Martinus Nijhoff.

White, Shane. 1989a. Pinkster: Afro-Dutch Syncretization in New York City and the Hudson Valley. *Journal of American Folklore* 102:68–75.

———. 1989b. Pinkster in Albany, 1803: A Contemporary Description. *New York History* 70:191–199.

E

Easter

Christian holy day and holiday. Commemorations of Jesus' resurrection have figured in the liturgical calendar since the beginnings of Christianity. The problem of choosing a date for the celebration vexed the early church as it tried to resolve differences between the Jewish lunar calendar that determined the date for Passover, during which, according to the New Testament, the crucifixion and resurrection occurred, and the solar calendar of the Roman world. Relying solely on Passover itself meant that Easter might fall on any day of the week, but both Eastern and Western branches of Christianity agreed that the festival should occur only on Sundays. The two major Christian traditions also agreed that the date should be the first Sunday following the full moon that appears on or after the vernal equinox. This means that the actual date for Easter may range from March 22 to April 25. The Eastern church has also specified that Easter must occur after the beginning of Passover. Consequently, its observance may fall one to five weeks later than the celebrations of Western Christendom. While important in its own right, the date for Easter also affects the timing of other holy days, including Good Friday, Ascension Day, and Pentecost.

Since it is more specifically religious than Christmas, Easter has received less secular recognition. However, in some parts of the United States, schools' spring vacations may be scheduled to incorporate the week preceding Easter. Formerly, even public schools arranged holidays for the Friday preceding and the Monday following Easter weekend.

The move away from official governmental sanction of Easter has not retarded development of a national Easter culture, which centers primarily on extrareligious elements of the holy day, many of which probably derive from pre-Christian fertility symbolism in Europe. The gift-bearing Easter bunny and Easter egg hunts and rolls (one of which occurs on the White House lawn) need not reflect Easter's religious significance, but can suggest the reawakened fecundity of spring. This seasonal focus has also made Easter a time for purchasing and wearing new clothing in bright and pastel colors to contrast with the somber hues of winter attire.

For Christians who observe the Lenten season, Easter represents the end of a forty-day period of self-denial. Even though the strict fasting and abstinence that once characterized Lent have been mitigated, Easter continues to provide a sense of release and relief. Consequently, in addition to their attendance at worship services (perhaps the only time in the year some may go to church), Christians pay considerable attention to the Easter meal, which is likely to feature a festive meat dish such as roast turkey or baked ham with new spring vegetables. Ethnic foodways have also focused particular attention on Easter. Italian Americans, for example, bake braided and glazed Easter breads that contain whole hard-boiled eggs, or Easter pies made from riccotta cheese and wheat or rice.

Other ethnically distinctive features of American Easter celebrations include bonfires set on the hills surrounding Fredericksburg, Texas, by German Americans and reenactments of Christ's Passion among Hispanic *penitentes* in northern New Mexico. The Yaquis of southern Arizona have developed an elaborate dramatization of the conflict of good and evil that climaxes at Easter. On each Friday during Lent, figures representing Roman soldiers and Pharisees search for Christ, their menace softened by comic touches. They finally find him (represented by a crucifix) on Holy Thursday, crucify him the next day, and try to commandeer the church on Saturday. Repelled by members of church organizations and traditional Yaqui figures such as deer dancers, the evil forces unmask to receive blessings and initiate the festive joy that culminates in the announcement of Christ's resurrection on Sunday.

Ethnicity at Easter also finds expression through egg decorating. Though commercial dyes for eggs have long been available, people—especially from eastern European heritages—may still decorate eggs in traditional ways. Polish Americans, for example, begin by drawing a design incorporating the phrase "Happy Easter" (which requires sixteen letters in Polish) on an uncooked egg. Boiling the egg with purple

Easter parade on the boardwalk. Atlantic City, New Jersey, about 1905. Library of Congress.

or brown onion skins fixes the design. The eggs, called *pisanki,* provide the symbolic main course for Easter dinner and figure in a friendly competition. When two persons hit the ends of their *pisanki* together, the person whose egg remains intact wins the opponent's cracked egg.

Other decorative traditions that figure into American Easter observances include displays of greenery and flowers, which, like bunnies and eggs, reflect the day's religious significance and its relationship to the birth imagery of spring.

William M. Clements

References

Bratkowski, Joann. 1984. "*Wesolego Alleluja* = Happy Easter." In *The Charm Is Broken: Readings in Arkansas and Missouri Folklore,* ed. W.K. McNeil. Little Rock, AR: August House, pp.169–172.

Caplow, Theodore, and Margaret Holmes Williamson. 1980. Decoding Middletown's Easter Bunny: A Study in American Iconography. *Semiotica* 32:221–232.

Cohen, Hennig, and Tristram Potter Coffin, eds. 1991. *The Folklore of American Holidays.* 2d ed. Detroit: Gale.

Griffith, James S. 1988. *Southern Arizona Folk Arts.* Tucson: University of Arizona Press.

Newall, Venetia. 1971. *An Egg at Easter: A Folklore Study.* London: Routledge and Kegan Paul.

Eaton, Allen (1878–1962)

Leader in the handicrafts movement in the United States in the early 20th century. Eaton organized many important ex-

hibits of arts and crafts and wrote what remain the definitive studies of craft work in the United States before 1935. In the 1920s, Eaton worked with the Russell Sage Foundation and the American Federation of Art designing a series of exhibits on the arts and crafts of the homelands of Europe, which led to his book *Immigrant Gifts to American Life* (1932). Eaton then turned his attention to the crafts of the southern Appalachian Mountains, helping organize the Southern Highland Handicraft Guild and producing his most widely known book, *Handicrafts of the Southern Highlands* (1937).

Prior to his full-time involvement in craft work, Eaton served four terms in the Oregon House of Representatives and was an arts educator on the faculty of the University of Oregon. In 1917 Eaton was forced to resign from the university for his association with a pacifist group thought to be pro-German and disloyal to the American war effort. Many believed that Eaton was the victim of mass hysteria and intolerance. This event catapulted him into his zealous support for the artistic expression of unsung, denigrated, persecuted groups throughout the United States. During World War II, for example, he studied the art of Japanese citizens in internment camps, resulting in his book *Beauty behind Barbed Wire: The Arts of the Japanese in Our War Relocation Camps* (1952), published after his retirement from the Russell Sage Foundation in the late 1940s. Eaton was working on another book when he died in 1962.

Eaton elevated the level of public discourse about folk art in the United States, helped forge a more democratic and culturally plural concept of art, and prodded the government and other important social institutions to be more culturally egalitarian.

Jean Haskell Speer

Eckstorm, Fannie Hardy (1865–1946)

Collector of Native American and Anglo American folklore. Eckstorm was born in Brewer, Maine, in 1865, educated at Abbott Academy and Smith College, and spent most of her adult life exploring aspects of Maine history and culture. Her research and publications on the social, cultural, and linguistic history of the state led her to be regarded as an authority on Native American lore, language, and natural history, lumbering life in northern Maine, and the Anglo American folksong traditions of Maine.

Eckstorm wrote extensively on Native American history, legends, and material culture, especially on the Penobscots of Maine. With a particular interest in Maine Indian nomenclature, she published *Indian Place-Names of the Penobscot Valley and the Maine Coast* (1941). Her articles and lectures on Native American culture culminated in the publication of *Old John Neptune and Other Maine Indian Shamans* (1945).

Eckstorm's interest in life in the Maine woods—particularly the life of the river drivers who worked for the lumber industry along the Penobscot River—provided the impetus for *The Penobscot Man* (1904) and *David Libbey: Penobscot Woodman and River-Driver* (1907).

In the 1920s, Eckstorm began an active period of song collecting. She contributed to *Songs and Ballads of the Maine*

Lumberjacks (1924) and to *The Maine Woods Songster* (1939), both edited by Phillips Barry, and she was coauthor of *Minstrelsy of Maine* (1927) and *British Ballads from Maine* (1929). Her collections preserved both British- and American-derived ballads and songs found in family traditions of the 19th and early 20th centuries.

In 1930 Eckstorm and Phillips Barry founded the Folk-Song Society of the Northeast. She contributed to nearly all of the twelve volumes of the *Bulletin of the Folk-Song Society of the Northeast* during its eight-year existence (1930–1937) with articles providing interpretive and analytical information on songs. Fannie Eckstorm died in 1946 at age 81 in Brewer, Maine.

Jennifer C. Post

References

James, Edward T., ed. 1971. *Notable American Women, 1607–1950: A Biographical Dictionary.* Cambridge: Harvard University Press, Belknap Press, pp. 549–551.

Whitten, Jeanne Patten. 1975. *Fannie Hardy Eckstorm: A Descriptive Bibliography.* Orono, ME: Northeast Folklore Society.

Williams, Donald H. 1985. Lady of the Woods: Some Correspondence of Fannie Hardy Eckstorm. *Colby Library Quarterly* 21:28–33.

Eddy, Mary O. (1877–1967)

Folksong collector and researcher. Born in Wayne County, Ohio, Eddy grew up in Perryville in Ashland County, where her maternal ancestors had been early settlers. She graduated from Wooster College in 1898 and taught high school in Canton, Ohio, for many years.

As a graduate student at the University of Chicago from 1915 to 1917, she took Albert H. Tolman's course on "Ballad and Epic Poetry" and discovered that she could contribute significantly to his collection of ballads and folksongs. At first among family and friends in Perryville and later through her students in Canton, she began her major collection of the traditional songs of northern Ohio, at first only as a contributor to Tolman. In an article published in 1916 in the *Journal of American Folklore (JAE),* Tolman attributed several of the ballads to Eddy, and in the 1922 *JAF* in an article prepared in 1917 that took up the whole October–December issue, he listed her as joint author, noting that most of the songs and almost all of the airs had come from her and calling attention to her efforts to collect "all the folksongs surviving in tradition in the state of Ohio."

Following Tolman's death in 1928, his papers and manuscripts were scattered, but Eddy continued working on her collection. In 1934 or 1935, she sent her manuscript to Harvard University English professor and folklorist George Lyman Kittredge, but it was returned unopened. She published *Ballads and Songs from Ohio* at her own expense in 1939. Representing the song literature collected in a limited geographical area over a long period of time (and including some pieces from scrapbooks and other written sources), *Ballads and Songs* was praised at the time of its publication for its many

fine airs and meticulous editing.

The published collection did not contain all of the songs Eddy had found. A copy of an early manuscript in two volumes in the John H. White Collection at the Cleveland Public Library, and of its "Supplement Number I" in the Houghton Library at Harvard, constitute a more complete collection. Eddy continued her research in folksong and published a number of articles on hymns and broadsides in the 1940s and 1950s.

Rebecca B. Schroeder

References

Eddy, Mary O. [1939] 1964. *Ballads and Songs from Ohio,* with Introduction by D.K. Wilgus. Hatboro: Pennsylvania Folklore Associates.

———. 1939. *Ballads and Songs from Ohio.* Harmonized for Piano Accompaniment by Le Roy James Wakefield. Cleveland: WPA.

———. 1943. Some Early American Hymns. *Southern Folklore Quarterly* 7:119–129.

———. 1946. Three Early Hymn Writers. *Southern Folklore Quarterly* 10:177–182.

———. 1952. William Reily's Courtship. *Midwest Folklore* 2:113–118.

———. 1953. Twenty Folk Hymns. *Midwest Folklore* 3:35–45.

Education, Folklife in

Programming of folklife-studies and folk-arts presentations in elementary and secondary schools. There are four essential approaches to folklife-in-education [FIE] programming: (1) in-residence projects coordinated by a folklorist, (2) seminars for schoolteachers, (3) production of educational materials, and (4) assembly programs or field trips featuring traditional culture. Recently, academic interest in folklife in education has focused on its role in cultural conservation, theories of learning, multicultural education, and educational reform.

Despite the variety of forms of FIE, there are common incentives for incorporating folklife studies in curricula; many children are interested in folklife for the same reasons adults are. They enjoy learning about family history and sharing family traditions. They value the study of local history and culture. They appreciate the opportunity to hear music that is rarely heard in commercial venues and to see artists whose work is often unknown to the wider community. Many students also recognize the appeal of a conversation with a talented, knowledgeable person. Folklorists have responded to these interests through FIE programs that introduce students and teachers to valuable education resources that are readily available but often overlooked.

Professional folklorists began working in school systems in 1976 through grant support from the folk-arts program of the National Endowment for the Arts (NEA). Modeled after artist-in-education programs developed by the NEA, these in-residence projects allow folklorists to research a community's folk culture, then present the local traditions and tradition bearers to students. Through programs across the nation, folklorists have coordinated performances and demonstrations by tradition bearers, thereby providing many students with their first exposure to old-time fiddling, Japanese origami, traditional boat building, and hundreds of other traditional activities. FIE programs have evolved from show-and-tell presentations by local folk artists to sophisticated projects that use folklife as a resource for teaching many facets of a school's curriculum.

Teachers have used folklore in their classrooms independent of FIE programs. Notable was Rachel Davis Dubois, who developed a program of "intercultural education" during the 1920s. Her approach focused on studies of immigrant and ethnic groups through research on ethnic culture, assembly presentations by tradition bearers, field excursions by students, and student presentations of their research. Another success is the Foxfire Project created by B. Eliot Wigginton in 1967. His Rabun Gap High School students researched the local traditions of north Georgia and published the magazine *Foxfire*, eventually amassing enough material to publish the *Foxfire Book* Series. The project has continued to grow, and the Foxfire Fund supports an array of programs, including the Skyline Teachers Network, an approach allowing teachers in urban schools to adopt the Foxfire methods.

Methods and theories from FIE programs have inspired teachers across the nation to use folklife in their instruction. Consequently, various folk-arts agencies offer seminars and workshops that train teachers to incorporate folklore in lessons. Seminars sponsored by the Smithsonian Institution, the National Endowment for the Arts, and state folk-arts programs have covered topics from Native American folk culture to the folklore of schoolchildren. Although teachers regularly give these projects highly positive evaluations, few folklorists have advanced to the next step of establishing academic positions for folklorists in colleges of teacher education.

Folklorists have long recognized that school districts provide an incredible potential audience for the materials they produce, and a wide variety of curricular resources awaits wider distribution. Many of these resources have been developed within FIE programs, and various journals and newsletters routinely publish bibliographies of teacher guides, curriculum resources, film and video productions, recordings, and learning kits. Although the market for folklorists' media and instructional materials is growing, many of these resources have been lost in the overload of educational materials distributed to school administrators and teachers.

Recognizing both the educational setting and the potential audience that schools provide, folklorists have developed a final approach to FIE programming: school assemblies for folk performers and field trips to public events. Deemed attractive and cost-effective to school administrators, these programs have perhaps served the largest number of schoolchildren. Students regularly attend children's days at folk festivals, and many schools are venues for traditional musicians. Although this type of programming provides many students with their first exposure to public folklife programs, the educational impact of the hit-and-run approach is limited. A folklorist's interpretive comments can appear overly pedantic, and teachers often find it

difficult to introduce the event to the students in a meaningful manner because they have little exposure to folklife studies. A critical evaluator would find it disconcerting that this form of FIE programming is the only one that receives its primary funding from the school system rather than from grants or financial support from a folk-arts agency.

As FIE projects and approaches are continually developed and refined, researchers have begun to examine the value and benefits of continuing folklife studies in the classroom. The vital need for FIE projects becomes increasingly evident, for research has shown FIE's value to the field of folklore and to the educational community. FIE emerges as a valuable resource for multicultural education and as a vital agent for cultural conservation. Educators have noted FIE's value for enhancing language-arts instruction and its importance to art and music education. Both folklorists and educators are studying how the discipline's methodology can serve as an aid to instructional techniques.

Many folklorists working in FIE programs have become acutely aware of the cultural basis of education and have begun studying the worldview of the educational community itself. Although the transmission of culture through formal education appears antithetical to a folklorist's interest, folklorists' perspectives and skills prepare them to examine social and political implications of education. Developing and continuing the dialogue between folklorists and educational theorists could greatly enhance both fields of study. Folklorists have much to learn from educators, and folklorists' perspectives, methods, and theories have great potential for developing innovative approaches for improving children's education.

Gregory Hansen

References

Belanus, Betty, ed. 1985. *Folklore in the Classroom*. Indianapolis: Indiana Historical Bureau.

Dubois, Rachel Davis. 1945. *Build Together Americans: Adventures in Intercultural Education for the Secondary School*. New York: Hinds, Hayden, and Eldredge.

MacDowell, Marsha. 1983. *Folkpatterns*. East Lansing: Michigan State University Museum.

Nusz, Nancy, guest ed. 1991. Folklife in Education. *Southern Folklore* (Special Issue) 48:3–94.

Wigginton, B. Eliott. 1985. *Sometimes a Shining Moment: The Foxfire Experience*. Garden City, NY: Anchor/Doubleday.

Elvis (1935–1977)

Elvis Aaron Presley, "The King" of American rock and roll. His performance style evolved from its roots in Southern rhythm and blues music, heard in such tunes as "Hound Dog" and "Blue Suede Shoes," to the "crooning" sound of a Las Vegas show singer, as in "Love Me Tender." Viewed by many as a uniquely American folk hero, Elvis was regarded during his lifetime as the embodiment of the traditional Horatio Alger "rags to riches" success story with strong Robin Hood overtones. He rose above his childhood poverty in the South to become a worldwide musical sensation and a B-movie star,

Elvis Presley in "Jailhouse Rock." *Library of Congress.*

lavishing gifts of cars and jewelry on his family, associates, and fans.

While the process of heroic creation was begun during his lifetime through favorable media accounts and careful publicity that emphasized his devotion to family, country, and God, the most defining element in the reshaping of Elvis from star to American folk hero came with his unexpected death in 1977 at his home of Graceland in Memphis, Tennessee. Tens of thousands of fans went to mourn and continue to do so, making Graceland the most visited home in the United States after the White House (Gregory and Gregory 1992:219). His death not only revealed an attention and devotion that is unsurpassed, it stimulated a recasting and a retelling of his life story with the imputation of greater deeds and the expurgation of lesser ones. Furthermore, traditions have developed that, along with King Arthur, Barbarossa, and the Magyars, Elvis is not dead. This belief, largely supported by the tabloid press, rests on traditional American beliefs surrounding the misspelling of a name on a gravestone, mysterious phone calls from Elvis to various fans, and the numerous accounts of "Elvis sightings" in malls, burger restaurants, and airports throughout the United States. These sightings have become a stock motif for comic strips, comedy routines, and television shows.

Perhaps the most culturally revealing aspect of the Elvis phenomenon however, is his posthumous rise to become a semireligious figure. This deitific regard can be seen in the language followers use to describe Elvis and their feelings about him, the reverence with which they flock to Graceland, and the tales that recount his healings of illness, blindness, and sorrow through dreams and his music. The inscriptions written on the wall surrounding Graceland best sum up this quasi-religious quality Elvis has achieved in American culture: "Elvis, we believe always and forever"; "Elvis, you are my God and my King"; "Elvis, every mountain I have had to climb, you carried me over on your back."

Many theories—ranging from postwar feelings of alienation from government and religion to the growing voice of discontent of the baby-boom generation—have been presented to explain this phenomenon. The fundamental question of why society chose Elvis above other famous and lost figures of the same period like Marilyn Monroe and James Dean, however, remains unanswered. In the years following his death, Elvis Presley has become a folk hero backed by a large body of modern American legend, song, iconography, and humor.

Amanda Carson Banks

References

Gregory, Neal, and Janice Gregory. 1992. *When Elvis Died: Media Overload and the Origins of the Elvis Cult*. New York: Pharos.

Harrison, Ted. 1992. *Elvis People: The Cult of the King*. London: Fount.

Marcus, Greil. 1991. *Dead Elvis: A Chronicle of a Cultural Obsession*. New York: Doubleday.

Moody, Raymond. 1989. *Elvis after Life*. New York: Bantam.

Empowerment

A process of enablement or permission in which power is given by those who have it to those who do not. The term emanates from social and economic theory rooted in Marxist thought. In the 20th century, following from the writings of educators like Paulo Freire and postmodernist thinkers like Foucault and Habermas, the term has also become common in culture theory. Empowerment in the context of folklore studies implies a revolution against the cultural domination and economic exploitation practiced by popularizers, critics, scholars, dealers, and collectors who claim authority as "legitimate" interpreters of folk culture. It further implies a return of cultural authority and even, at times, economic and political power to the "disempowered" folk.

The notion that the folk have been disempowered or effectively stripped of control over their own cultural traditions rests on several assumptions. First, the collecting, anthologizing, museumizing, or otherwise commercializing of folk art and lore by the dominant culture involves a removal of these forms of expression from their proper context and function in the folk community. Second, in decontextualizing and appropriating the material products and performance traditions of the folk minority, the dominant culture reinterprets, redefines, and often alters these forms, both in content and value. Third, the dominant culture thus asserts its hegemony over both the products and the producers through an institutionalized process of patronage and assimilation of folk traditions into the popular and elite traditions of the dominant society.

Misperception and misrepresentation play important roles in disempowerment. When mass-produced andirons depicting George Washington are termed folk art solely because of their relative antiquity or association with our "national heritage" there is an implicit assumption that collectors and critics can "discover" folk art in the absence of any identifiable folk. When New Mexican *santos* are sold and collected as "primitives," their original significance as devotional objects is diminished. Such distortions signal a failure to reference folk groups or a tendency to deem their intentions irrelevant, thus giving primacy to the "aesthetic" of the dominant culture.

Empowerment advocates call for a democratization of culture through the transfer of power and cultural authority from the holders of cultural capital to the producers, the folk communities themselves. Commentators such as Kenneth L. Ames (1977), Nelson Graburn (1976), and Sally Price (1989) have shown how hegemonic forces influence not only the appreciation, but also the production, of folk art. They have maintained that cultural products cannot be understood independent of their function within the folk community of their provenance and that such communities are the true arbiters of the value and meaning of those products.

Empowerment advocates have also asserted that an empowered folk should exert considerable control over how their art is defined, displayed, and marketed, and that folk communities should be the beneficiaries of any cultural or economic capital generated through the exchange of their literary, musical, or artistic work with the dominant culture. This aspect of empowerment is perhaps most concretely realized in an activist strain of folklore studies known as the public-folklore movement. Public folklorists have emphasized not only the preservation of traditional arts and practices, but also the continued support of folk communities, even as these communities are transmuted by changing social, economic, and political realities. Though wary of the effects that their intervention as interpreters and advocates may have on the artists and their art, public folklorists work through government and other organizations to provide advice, awards, and opportunities to exhibit.

The career of Louisiana cane carver David Allen offers an example of empowerment in public folklore. With the help of folklorist Susan Roach, this artist rose from local to national recognition largely through presentations at folk festivals such as those sponsored by the Louisiana Folklife Program and the National Endowment for the Arts. Through his eventual participation in the National Folklife Festival, Allen came to recognize the monetary and cultural worth of his work and his own membership in a community of African American carvers. This elevated status and self-esteem worked changes in Allen and his art, but it also provided him with the means and motivation to explore his craft and perpetuate it through teaching.

While the cry for empowerment of the folk may be construed as humanistic in its emphasis on the makers rather than the made, it may also be seen as condescending because it assumes that folk traditions do not have the vitality to survive in and of themselves but must be rescued by advocates from the academic or cultural elite. Perhaps in response to this implication, the term "self-empowerment" has come into use. Self-empowerment implies that the disempowered can empower themselves by recognizing and asserting their own self-worth and by refusing to accept the imposed "authorized" or "canonical" version of the meaning of their own cultural products.

Richard W. Tucker

References

Ames, Kenneth L. 1977. *Beyond Necessity.* Winterthur, DE: Winterthur.

Baron, Robert, and Nicholas R. Spitzer, eds. 1992. *Public Folklore.* Washington, DC: Smithsonian Institution.

Graburn, Nelson. 1976. *Ethnic and Tourist Arts: Cultural Expressions from the Fourth World.* Berkeley: University of California Press.

Price, Sally. 1989. *Primitive Art in Civilized Places.* Chicago: University of Chicago Press.

Emrich, Duncan B.M. (1908–1977)

Folklorist. Although he wrote many articles and eleven books on folklore, Emrich is best remembered in folklore circles for the decade he spent as head of the Folk Song and Folklore Archives at the Library of Congress in Washington, DC. Born in Turkey to missionary parents, he moved with his family to New England during World War I. Emrich won a scholarship to Phillips Exeter Academy and went on to receive college degrees from Brown, Columbia, and Harvard Universities,

and the University of Madrid. At Harvard he studied under the noted scholar George Lyman Kittredge. After receiving his Ph.D., Emrich began his teaching career at Columbia. Three years later, he moved to the University of Denver, then in 1943 he entered the U.S. Army. He worked in Army Intelligence, won a Croix de Guerre for his action in France, and, as a member of General Dwight D. Eisenhower's staff, prepared an account of the war in Europe.

After the war, Emrich moved to Washington, DC, where he became head of the American Folk Song and Folklore Archives, a position he held until 1955. After that he served as a cultural affairs officer at American embassies in several countries, including Greece and India, frequently collecting folklore in his spare time. In 1966 Emrich returned to Washington as an officer in the United States Information Agency. In 1969, after a twenty-six-year hiatus, he returned to the classroom as adjunct professor of American folklore at American University in Washington. There in 1976 he established a fund to support an annual lecture series. At the time of his death the following year, he was, coincidentally, working on a book on the folklore of death.

Emrich was a collector, compiler, and popularizer of folklore rather than a theorist. These approaches are seldom appreciated by scholars, especially those who regard theorizing as the only acceptable way to treat folklore. But the negative reviews many of his books received were not wholly attributable to lack of theory; there were some genuine problems with Emrich's publications. For example, he rarely distinguished between items from folk tradition and those from popular culture, since he reasoned that popular-culture materials had undeniable appeal to the folk and thus rightly belonged in books on folklore. Moreover, Emrich thought that the inclusion of such material made his books more interesting to the general public, and he considered that audience just as important as the scholarly one. Whatever their flaws, volumes like Emrich's *American Folk Poetry* (1974) and *Folklore on the American Land* (1977) introduced folk traditions to many people who had never before opened a book about folklore.

W.K. McNeil

References

Beck, Horace. 1978. Obituary for Duncan Emrich. *Journal of American Folklore* 91:701–703.

Epitaph

Inscription on a tombstone. The custom of inscribing tombstones came to the United States with European settlers. Typically, gravemarkers are artifacts with both visual and verbal components that together not only comment about the deceased in particular or death in general, but also make general observations reflective of cultural attitudes toward dying and death. Students of funerary art and customs commonly distinguish between the visual elements and verbal inscriptions and refer to the latter as epitaphs.

The comparative study of epitaphs found on American gravemarkers provides insights into collective attitudes toward death. The most simple include the name (or initials) of the deceased and often the date of death. These modest inscriptions function minimally to identify the deceased and to perpetuate his or her memory.

The occasion of erecting a graveyard monument provides survivors with an opportunity to inscribe additional comments. The earliest tombstones followed funerary custom that required the inscriber to include in addition to the name and age of the deceased, something about the dead person's position in life, the manner of his or her death, and some praiseworthy quality or deed. It was not uncommon that the tombstone was embellished with symbols of death, sometimes arranged to frame the epitaphs. As the spirit of egalitarianism grew in America, epitaphs changed. Formulaic expressions of loss and salvation appeared with increasing frequency. They range from verses drawn from scripture or other devotional texts ("I am the resurrection and the life"), to short prayers ("May she rest in peace," sometimes abbreviated to R.I.P.), terse expressions of grief ("Gone, but not forgotten"), succinct statements about the deceased's position in life ("Loving husband"), and bleak admonitions about death ("As I am now, so you must be / Prepare for death and follow me").

Originality is not an imperative for epitaphs. By the late 18th century, booklets with epitaphs suitable for every occasion were marketed to memorial inscribers. These and more elaborate and less formulaic epitaphs continue to provide extended discourses on the value of life and the inevitable reality of death. Those with a religious theme point to salvation in the next world for the righteous and condemnation for the evildoer.

For some people, ready-made inscriptions could not reflect their appropriate, personalized sentiments. They sought to capture in original epitaphs something about the life of the deceased. Thus we find an inscription such as this one on the gravestone of a Milford, Connecticut, minister: "During his ministry / He enjoyed 7 revivals / Admitted 716 members / Baptized 1117 and / Buried 1126 of his flock." Other epitaphs explain the circumstances that caused the death. Consider this inscription on the tomb of a Pelham, Massachusetts, man whose wife poisoned him: "Think my friends when this you see / How my wife hath dealt by me / She in some oysters did prepare / Some poison for my lot and share / Then of the same I did partake / And nature yielded to its fate." One young lady's accidental death prompted this epitaph: "Ellen Shannon / Who was fatally burned / March 21, 1870 / by the explosion of a lamp / filled with 'R.E. Danforth's / Non-Explosive / Burning Fluid.'"

Humorous epitaphs have attracted particular attention and have been the bases for a number of regional epitaph collections. In Enosburg, Vermont, the grave of Anna Hopewell reminds all visitors: "Here lies the body of Anna / Done to death by a banana / It wasn't the fruit that laid her low / But the skin of the thing that made her go."

Until recently, research into American epitaphs has been most intense in New England, where elaborate and simple gravestones dating back as far as the earliest colonial settlements survive relatively intact. By examining them chronologically, scholars have gained some insights into changing attitudes toward death and religion. Isolated collections of epitaphs found in other parts of the country can be found in regional journal articles.

Richard Sweterlitsch

References

Ludwig, Allan I. 1966. *Graven Images: New England Stonecarving and Its Symbols*. Middletown, CT: Wesleyan University Press.

Mann, Thomas C., and Janet Greene. 1968. *Sudden and Awful: American Epitaphs and the Finger of God*. Brattleboro, VT: Stephen Green.

Meyer, Richard E., ed. 1989. *Cemeteries and Gravemarkers: Voices of American Culture*. Ann Arbor, MI: UMI Research Press.

———, ed. 1993. *Ethnicity and the American Cemetery*. Bowling Green, OH: Bowling Green State University Popular Press.

Vovelle, Michel. 1980. A Century and One Half of American Epitaphs, 1660–1813: Toward the Study of Collective Attitudes about Death. *Comparative Studies in Society and History* 22:534–547.

Wallis, Charles L. 1954. *Stories on Stone: A Book of American Epitaphs*. New York: Oxford University Press.

See also Gravemarkers

Esoteric-Exoteric Factor in Folklore

A concept introduced by American folklorist William Hugh Jansen in 1959 to characterize the ways that folklore expresses attitudes about group traits and reveals the dynamics of intergroup perceptions and beliefs. The *esoteric* factor consists of a group's folklore about itself and what it supposes others think of it. This would include, for example, the traditional narratives, beliefs, and jokes expressed by group members that depict the group's self-image and perceived traits (such as pride, independence, or frugality), as well as what group members assume outsiders think of their group ("They think we are arrogant, aloof, and stingy"). *Exoteric* folklore consists of the ideas and images that one group has about another group—for instance, stereotypes and *blason populaire* (traditional slurs). It also includes what one group "thinks that other group thinks it thinks" ("They think that we all think that they are greedy and treacherous").

Jansen stated that esoteric folklore is based on the specialized knowledge of a group and serves to preserve that knowledge and strengthen a sense of group identity. Exoteric folklore, on the other hand, not only expresses intergroup conflict but may serve to define a sense of one's own group by contrasting "them" with "us." Jansen proposed four general "statements" about the esoteric-exoteric factor: (1) The smaller the group, the stronger the esoteric element in its folklore; (2) the more distinctive the group, the more likely the occurrence of exoteric folklore about it; (3) the larger and more self-confident the group, the weaker the esoteric element in its folklore; but (4) great size and self-confidence in a group are not necessarily deterrents to the development of exoteric folklore about that group.

Jansen's ideas about the esoteric-exoteric factor have been used primarily by folklorists interested in ethnic jokes and slurs, stereotyping, legends and rumors, and ways these expressions reflect intergroup dynamics.

Daniel Wojcik

References

Basso, Keith H. 1979. *Portraits of "The Whiteman": Linguistic Play and Cultural Symbols among the Western Apache.* Cambridge: Cambridge University Press.

Dundes, Alan. 1987. *Cracking Jokes: Studies of Sick Humor Cycles and Stereotypes.* Berkeley: Ten Speed.

———. 1991. *The Blood Libel Legend: A Casebook in Anti-Semitic Folklore.* Madison: University of Wisconsin Press.

Hall, Edward T. 1959. *The Silent Language.* Garden City, NY: Doubleday.

Jansen, William Hugh. 1959. The Esoteric-Exoteric Factor in Folklore. *Fabula: Journal of Folktale Studies* 2:205–211. Reprinted in *The Study of Folklore,* ed. Alan Dundes. Englewood Cliffs, NJ: Prentice-Hall, 1965, pp. 43–51.

Turner, Patricia A. 1993. *I Heard It through the Grapevine: Rumor in African–American Culture.* Berkeley: University of California Press.

Espinosa, Aurelio Macedonio (1880–1958)

Pioneer scholar of Spanish American and Spanish folklore and dialectology. A native of the San Luis Valley in southern Colorado and a multilingual academician, Espinosa initiated folklore and language study in Hispanic northern New Mexico and southern Colorado and did extensive work on Spanish folktales.

After receiving a University of Chicago doctorate in Romance languages and literatures with a minor in Indo-European comparative philology, Espinosa joined the Romanic Languages Department at Stanford University in 1910 and there did his influential teaching and prolific research until retiring in 1947. Beginning in 1902 and intermittently until the 1950s, he conducted folklore fieldwork in northern New Mexico and southern Colorado; as it was done in formerly Spanish, coastal California between 1911 and 1919; in Spain, during a 1920 expedition. Among the founders of the Société Internationale de Dialectologie Romane (1909), the American Association of Teachers of Spanish (1917), and the Linguistic Society of America (1925), Espinosa was also active in the American Folklore Society, serving as president in the years 1923–1924.

A disciplined, language-oriented folklorist, Espinosa collected and published a variety of verbal genres from Hispanic America. He contributed to comparative ballad studies but accomplished most in folktale scholarship by developing a classification of Spanish folktales, tracing American ones' peninsular roots and Iberian ones' Oriental origins, and comparing them with other European and Native American traditions. Much contemporary criticism focuses on Espinosa's assertion of Spanish origins and hegemony for Southwest Hispanic folklife without adequate sociohistorical consideration of the region's complex, inter- and intracultural dynamics. Nevertheless, Espinosa is recognized as an exemplary linguist and literary folklorist who opened significant new areas of study.

Marta Weigle

References

Espinosa, A.M. 1910–1916. New Mexican Spanish Folklore: Parts 1–11. *Journal of American Folklore* 23:395–418, 24:397–444, 26:97–122, 27:105–147, 28:204–206, 319–352, 29:505–535.

Espinosa, Aurelio M. 1930–1946. *Estudios sobre el español de Nuevo Méjico.* 2 vols. Buenos Aires: Biblioteca de Dialectología Hispanoamericana, Instituto de Filología, Universidad de Buenos Aires.

———. 1946–1947. *Cuentos populares españoles, recogidos de la tradición oral de España.* 3 vols. Madrid: Consejo Superior de Investigaciones Cientificas.

———. 1953. *Romancero de Nuevo Méjico.* Madrid: Revista de Filología Española-Anejo LVIII.

———. 1985. *The Folklore of Spain in the American Southwest: Traditional Spanish Folk Literature in Northern New Mexico and Southern Colorado,* ed. J. Manuel Espinosa. Norman: University of Oklahoma Press.

Ethics in Folklore Research

A code of conduct for responsible and fair treatment of the human subjects of folklore research. As humanists and as social scientists, researchers in folklore have sought to gather significant information while respecting the integrity of their informants. This dual focus upon data collection and human rights has generated compelling ethical dilemmas. Regulations for the protection of human research subjects in the United States have been implemented since the late 1970s; nonetheless, fieldworkers have had considerable leeway to apply the dictates of their own consciences. Manuals for fieldworkers, from Kenneth S. Goldstein's *A Guide for Field Workers in Folklore* (1964) to Bruce Jackson's *Fieldwork* (1987), have placed increasing emphasis upon ethical issues. Primary concerns include the fieldworker's self-presentation, methodology, ownership of material, reciprocity, protection of informants' identities, and respect for sensitive issues.

Recent controversies on ethics have reflected evolving definitions of the folk. Cultural anthropologists and folklorists in the late 19th and early 20th centuries tended to view their informants as data sources quite different from themselves, requiring careful manipulation and propitiation. More recent researchers have tended to see their informants as fellow human beings who become partners in a shared fieldwork enterprise. As Robert A. Georges and Michael Owen Jones point out in their book *People Studying People,* "fieldworker and subject are first and foremost human beings" (Georges and Jones 1980:3). With this common humanity as a central premise, ethical considerations have become crucial for successful fieldwork.

Before fieldwork begins, the researcher must make choices that have ethical dimensions. Choices of subject, site, and informant population may involve consideration of sensitive social and political issues. The researcher's presentation of himself or herself to the group can be completely honest or somewhat manipulative. "Role-playing," sometimes recommended for folklore students, calls for introducing oneself as a "student," "teacher," "collector of local history," or other personage. While such a term may be accurate to some extent, it limits the informant's perception of what the researcher is trying to accomplish. If the chosen term is not accurate, it makes the researcher vulnerable to accusations of falsehood. As Bruce Jackson says, "getting the information isn't important enough to warrant going undercover and lying to people" (Jackson 1987:263).

How the researcher chooses to record information also has ethical implications. If handwritten notes are the chosen method, the researcher runs the risk of getting an incomplete or misleading version of what the informant said. While tape recorders are much more accurate, it is easy to conceal their usage; folklorists must think carefully about being open with their informants. Video cameras are less easy to conceal and are appealing because of the range of audiovisual information they capture. However, the collector may find that some informants are reluctant to give permission for its use, since visual images fully reveal one's identity. Obtaining permission for recording information is always important, no matter what method is used. At the time of the interview, Edward D. Ives recommends, the researcher should explain how long tapes will be preserved and what sort of access people will have to them, in an archive or otherwise. Getting a signed release at the end of the interview is crucial, with any restrictions on future usage specified by the informant (Ives 1980:51).

The question of ownership has undergone much revision since folklore research began. Whether an informant ultimately owns the story, song, or joke he or she has shared with a collector and what the collector has the right to do with that material are complex issues. With recordings of traditional or semitraditional songs and music, debates about ownership have become especially intense. Litigation about ownership of the song of television personality Barney the Dinosaur, roughly based on the folksong "This Old Man," gained media attention in 1994. Ideas about ownership of traditional materials and their offshoots continue to evolve as precedents build in an increasingly litigious society.

Closely related to the ownership question is the issue of reciprocity. If informants indeed own their material, what sort of compensation should they receive? Judgments vary from Goldstein's preference for nonfinancial assistance and compensation for wages lost to Jackson's case-by-case determination of payment "on the basis of the relationships among the people involved, the money available, and the realities of the situation" (Jackson 1987:269). If the fieldworker makes a substantial sum of money from something that an informant provided, it seems only fair to share some of that money with the person who made it possible. However, variations in research situations have brought about many different responses to the payment issue.

Another aspect of fairness to informants is disclosure of their identities. Some folklorists prefer to use pseudonyms or just informants' first names, in order to protect their privacy. Others believe that pseudonyms are not sufficient to protect privacy, so other identifying details should be changed as well. The need for protection of informants varies according to the kind of material collected; for example, tellers of dirty jokes tend to be more concerned about being identified than sharers of traditions about the weather. No matter how innocuous the material may seem, researchers must be scrupulous about respecting the preferences of their informants. If no specific preferences are given, researchers simply use their best judgment. Jackson recommends that fieldworkers apply the Golden Rule, "Do unto others as you would have them do unto you," to all fieldwork questions that do not have a clear, immediate answer.

Yet another layer of ethical complexity comes from consideration of informants who cannot fully consent to sharing information. Children, for example, may enjoy telling dirty jokes to researchers but may then regret having done so when they are older. While parents have the legal right to give permission for their children to be involved in a research project, some advocates of children do not believe that this is fair. Mentally disabled individuals and others whose judgment is affected by illness or stress may not be able to give full consent either. Each researcher must decide how to handle such situations until litigation provides more definite rules.

As discussion of ethics continues, researchers develop guidelines for appropriate conduct. The drafting of a "Statement on Ethics" for the American Folklore Society in 1986 caused much debate. Although the resolution of many ethical issues is still unclear, it is quite clear that ethics will be a prime topic for folklorists' discussion in the future.

Elizabeth Tucker

References

Georges, Robert A., and Michael Owen Jones. 1980. *People Studying People: The Human Element in Fieldwork.* Berkeley: University of California Press.

Goldstein, Kenneth S. 1964. *A Guide for Field Workers in Folklore.* Hatboro, PA: Folklore Associates.

Ireland, Tom. 1974. Ethical Problems in Folklore. In *Conceptual Problems in Contemporary Folklore Study,* ed. Gerald Cashion. *Folklore Forum* Bibliographic and Special Series 12:69–74.

Ives, Edward D. 1980. *The Tape-Recorded Interview: A Manual for Field Workers in Folklore and Oral History.* Knoxville: University of Tennessee Press.

Jackson, Bruce. 1987. *Fieldwork.* Urbana: University of Illinois Press.

Smidchens, Guntis, and Robert E. Walls. 1986. Ethics and Fieldwork. *Folklore Forum* 19:117–124.

See also Fieldwork

Ethnic Folklore

Traditional expressive behavior of ethnic groups as they migrate, resettle, and interact with other groups. In the late 20th century in the United States, the term "ethnic" is usually applied to foreign nationality or immigrant groups and is often extended to refer to American Indians, African Americans, and other racial groups, and sometimes to specific religious groups, irrespective of their national background. Initially conceived of as the content of a distinctive ethnic identity—part of the constellation of cultural traits that together distinguish one group from another—ethnic folklore is now generally defined in terms of its role in the creation, maintenance, and negotiation of cultural boundaries between groups. Such negotiation of group boundaries always involves the display of a range of shared cultural traditions, or folklore.

The folklore of ethnic groups has been a prominent concern of American folklorists since the inception of the American Folklore Society (AFS). In fact, the 1888 AFS charter mentions the traditions of American Indians, African Americans, and other ethnically distinct communities as particularly appropriate sources of data for folklorists.

Like their European precedents, the first studies of the folklore of American ethnic groups were collections of "survivals." The assumption behind these collections of songs, stories, superstitions, and other Old World forms was that these treasures would somehow be lost as soon as acculturation (specifically, linguistic acculturation) had taken place. The task of the folklorist, then, was to document these Old World traditions before they disappeared during the process of Americanization. Initially, British ballads, songs, and folktales were the foci of such studies that concentrated on recovering these relics of British countryside traditions especially in the Upland South, New England, and the Ozarks. As Roger D. Abrahams has pointed out in his thorough discussion of the history of American ethnic folklore scholarship in the *Harvard Encyclopedia of American Ethnic Groups* (1980), a hierarchy of forms and even items was established in the late 19th and early 20th centuries, but actual collections of such items in North America wasn't carried out extensively until the 1920s and 1930s. These collections, several of them conducted under the auspices of the Works Progress Administration (WPA), focused primarily on determining the oldest and most widespread texts of ballads and folktales and estimating how widely they might be found and in what range of versions and variants.

A wide range of ethnic-folklore research has been conducted employing this kind of antiquarian approach to the collection and analysis of ethnic lore of groups as diverse as Pennsylvania Germans, Louisiana French, and Southwestern Mexican Americans. Such studies have served primarily to document the conservative, traditional preservation of Old World ethnic traditions in these often isolated communities.

Studies of Native American folklore developed along somewhat similar lines. In the 19th century, the collection of Native American folklore, however, also was put into the service of developing a kind of nationalistic sentiment. Native American lore was collected in order to identify distinctly "American" cultural roots that might serve to distinguish the young nation. These collections soon provided indexes of the rate of survival of Native American cultural forms, since, unlike the study of the folklore of Euro-American ethnic groups,

there were no previous baseline studies of precontact narratives, songs, and rituals available.

Other scholars, particularly those studying Euro-American folklore, combined similar collecting techniques with a somewhat different analytic perspective. In these studies, the collected texts served as indexes not only of the degree of preserved ethnicity, but also of the degree of "assimilation" of the particular ethnic group. Conducted primarily in culturally conservative communities in which ethnic distinctiveness was highlighted, this kind of ethnic-folklore research compared the collected material to Old World repertoires in order to gauge the various stages in the process of acculturation. The clear assumption was that the more Americanized an individual ethnic group became, the fewer vestiges of Old World forms would remain, and, in time, ethnic differences in American culture would simply disappear. Following the work of early-20th-century historians and social scientists interested in ethnicity, then, folklorists viewed ethnic communities as living laboratories in which the processes of assimilation and acculturation could be observed and analyzed firsthand. Such studies served to highlight the selective maintenance of traditional forms and practices within particular ethnic communities.

A similar perspective also has been used to suggest, however, that African and American Indian repertoires or styles have been eliminated in the process of colonization. This deculturation perspective is most frequently identified with African Americanists E. Franklin Frazier and Robert Park, although it was maintained by other collectors of African American lore until well into the 1960s. Such a Eurocentric position has been easily rebutted by a number of prominent scholars who have demonstrated a strong maintenance of African expressive forms, styles, and performance patterns in the United States. The work of Melville Jean Herskovits (cf. Herskovits 1942) has been particularly influential in formulating a more complex model of the ways ethnic-folklore forms function as indicators of degree of acculturation. Herskovits distinguished three modes of continuity and adaptation: (1) straight *retention;* (2) *reinterpretation,* in which forms are maintained in new environments with new uses and meanings; and (3) *syncretism,* in which similar elements of two or more cultures merge. This attention to the cultural dynamics of intergroup contact in which expressive forms change and emerge redirected scholarly attention away from folklore items themselves and toward an analysis of the various factors affecting the use of these forms as displays of ethnicity.

Most 20th-century folklore studies on ethnicity have focused on the changes in ethnic groups and their lore that come about as the result of cultural contact. In his influential *American Folklore* (1959), Richard M. Dorson formulated a set of questions that served as guidelines for folklorists interested in the lore of ethnic groups for at least the next ten years: "What happens to the inherited traditions of European and Asiatic folk after they settle in the United States and learn a new language and new ways? How much of the old lore is retained and transmitted to their children? What parts are sloughed off, what intrusions appear, what accommodation is made between Old Country beliefs and the American physical scene? These are the large questions that confront the assessor of immigrant folk traditions" (Dorson 1959).

Many folklorists took up Dorson's call for studies of immigrant traditions that would answer these questions. A fine example of such acculturation studies is Robert A. Georges' work with the Tarpon Springs, Florida, Greek community in which he analyzed the ways narratives, rites of passage, and holiday celebrations help to maintain the traditional belief system of these fairly isolated transplanted Greek fishermen. Georges demonstrated both the survival and the reinforcement of Greek traditions in this one small American community. Folklorists have continued to document both persistence and change in the ethnic traditions of immigrant groups. Barbara Kirshenblatt-Gimblett's study of traditional storytelling in a Toronto Jewish community, Robert Klymasz's study of Ukrainian folklore in Canada, and Elli Köngäs-Maranda's analysis of Finnish American lore, for example, document the various factors effecting change in ethnic traditions in the New World.

European models of ethnological research have formed the basis for the "acculturation model" research of folklorists like Linda Dégh, who has called for case studies that will provide an analysis of the assimilation process as it affects groups in contiguous and intermittent contact over a period of time. This process of "cultural adjustment" requires the observation of transgenerational folkloric expression as various ethnic groups come in contact with one another. Dégh has continually suggested that the determination of ethnic boundaries and the examination of intercultural borrowing should be the focus of research on ethnic folklore.

In this insistence on the analysis of the process of ethnic interaction, Dégh's work (cf. Dégh 1975) is representative of the ways in which American ethnic-folklore scholarship since World War II has moved away from a concern with "survivals" of Old World forms as the cultural content of ethnic groups and toward an understanding of the processes of ethnic-boundary maintenance or negotiation. Like their European colleagues, American folklorists have drawn extensively on the work of Norwegian ethnographer Fredrik Barth in making this shift in theoretical emphasis. Barth's *Ethnic Groups and Boundaries* (1969) proposed an understanding and definition of ethnic groups based not on the identification of a cluster of culture traits for each particular ethnic group, but rather on the *process* that that group and others use to separate and define the group itself. Barth argued that the focus for the analysis of ethnicity should be "the ethnic boundary that defines the group, not the cultural stuff that it encloses." This simple but powerful notion of boundaries has proven to be one of the most theoretically useful in clarifying the ways in which ethnic identity is articulated and actively negotiated in interaction within and between ethnic groups. Such a perspective points clearly to the influence of contextual variability on ethnic identity: As social, economic, and political conditions change, so may systems of ethnic identification.

Attention to the role of folklore in the process of boundary making was first articulated by William Hugh Jansen in "The Esoteric-Exoteric Factor in Folklore" (1959). Jansen discussed the range of factors associated with boundary making and maintenance as they are revealed in oral narrative. His work suggests that by examining the folklore of a group's own self-image as well as that of its images of other groups, one might better understand the role folklore plays in the creation, negotiation, and maintenance of ethnic boundaries. While Jansen's work focused primarily on the ways in which folklore operates as a "function of shared identity," binding groups together, Richard Bauman has pointed out that differential identities and asymmetrical relationships can also be the basis for folklore performance (Bauman 1971). Américo Paredes, for example, has explored the relationship between "gringos" and "greasers" in the joking behavior of Mexican Americans as dramatizations of real social inequities. Roger D. Abrahams also has suggested that folklore performances may additionally operate as a means of distinguishing separate or even antagonistic segments within the same ethnic community, as Alan Dundes' work on Jewish American humor demonstrates.

As members of ethnic groups negotiate the construction, manipulation, and exploitation of boundaries between themselves and others, they draw on a wide range of cultural and linguistic resources in multiple cultural repertoires. In her 1983 essay "Studying Immigrant and Ethnic Folklore," Barbara Kirshenblatt-Gimblett suggested that a special feature of the folklore of ethnicity is a heightened awareness of cultural diversity and self-reflexivity so that the relevant research questions become: "To what extent, how, and to what effect is folklore used to make cultural comparisons and to mark cultural distinctiveness? How is folklore used to define cultural differences, incongruities, and convergences? What are the nature and content of these comparisons, of this marking or foregrounding?" Attention to these questions required a shift from studying the lore of a particular named group to an examination of the settings, social occasions, and events in which boundary negotiation is an important activity.

Clearly, this shift in focus was at least partially a response to the new attention to folklore performance in the late 1960s and 1970s. With Dan Ben-Amos' 1971 redefinition of folklore as patterned expressive communication within a group meeting together face-to-face came an emphasis on the folk *group* rather than on solely text-centered analyses, and on the folklore *process* rather than product. For scholars interested in ethnicity, this particular theoretical move opened the discipline in new ways to serious considerations of the ways in which ethnic-group members used folklore in the creation and maintenance of cultural boundaries. In addition, the concept of emergence—that folklore forms, contexts, and performances are constantly emerging—proposed by Dell Hymes and Richard Bauman, helped to undermine the long-held assumption that ethnic folklore traditions gradually and inevitably erode and disappear. Instead, folklorists now focused their attention on the creative, ever-changing ways in which ethnic groups and individuals display their own ethnic identities.

At the same time, rising ethnic consciousness within the United States in the 1960s and 1970s created an increasing public interest in understanding the dynamics of ethnic interaction. Folklorists sometimes found themselves in the position of "ethnicity brokers" as they became involved in the public display of ethnicity in a variety of festival settings ranging from the Festival of American Folklife in Washington, DC, to small, local gatherings. Such festivals became means of dramatizing ethnic persistence in a particular region or community. The process of "going public" raised a whole new set of questions for both folklorists and members of ethnic groups such as: What happens to folklore forms when they are performed within large heterogeneous groups that have come together only to be entertained rather than within close, face-to-face, homogeneous communities with shared cultural values and expectations? What happens when ethnic identification becomes marketable? What is the effect on the ethnic community itself? Is the social base of ethnic folklore completely undermined in such performance contexts? Or are these festival situations simply different occasions on which boundary negotiation takes place, new responses to ethnic persistence in a truly pluralistic society?

During the late 1970s and 1980s American folklore scholars began to extend their analyses of ethnic groups and their lore in taking account of the wide variety of contexts in which ethnicity is constantly negotiated and renegotiated. Many of the articles in the 1977 special issue of *Western Folklore,* "Studies in Folklore and Ethnicity," edited by Larry Danielsen, demonstrate this range of concerns.

Acknowledging that ethnic meaning arises only out of the social interactions of individuals whose expressions of ethnicity may be affirmed, contested, and/or celebrated by other participants, researchers began to examine the interactions of particular ethnic individuals. As Shalom Staub has pointed out in *Yemenis in New York City,* "ethnicity is therefore an identity which resides not within the individual person, or even the particular group, but *between* individuals and *between* groups engaged in social interaction." The 1991 collection of essays on ethnic folklore edited by Stephen Stern and John Allan Cicala, *Creative Ethnicity: Symbols and Strategies of Contemporary Ethnic Life,* is representative of this new direction in ethnic-folklore scholarship. Through an examination of the forms, symbols, strategies, and stylistic resources of the folklore performances of a variety of ethnic individuals and groups, the authors attempt to demonstrate the richness and diversity of ethnicity as it is experienced on a dynamic, personal level.

Scholars interested in the folklore of ethnic groups no longer confine themselves to the task of documenting survivals and chronicling acculturation patterns. Instead, folklorists around the world are attempting to take into account both the broad historical conditions that influence ethnicity as well as the factors affecting specific individual negotiations of ethnic identity as they are played out within particular social interactions. The analysis of creative expressions of negotiations of ethnicity is crucial to an understanding of the ways in which groups and the individuals who comprise those groups continually articulate and reshape the meaning of their own ethnic identifications.

Margaret K. Brady

References

Abrahams, Roger D. 1980. Folklore. In *Harvard Encyclopedia of American Ethnic Groups,* ed. Stephen Thernstron. Cambridge: Harvard University Press, pp. 370–379.

Barth, Fredrik. 1969. *Ethnic Groups and Boundaries: The Social Organization of Cultural Difference.* Boston: Little, Brown.

Bauman, Richard. 1971. Differential Identity and the Social Base of Folklore. *Journal of American Folklore* 84:31–41.

Dégh, Linda. 1975. The Study of Ethnicity in Modern European Ethnology. *Journal of the Folklore Institute* 12:113–129.

Georges, Robert A., and Stephen Stern. 1982. *American and Canadian Immigrant and Ethnic Folklore: An Annotated Bibliography.* New York: Garland.

Herskovits, Melville. 1942. *The Myth of the Negro Past.* New York: Harper.

Jansen, William Hugh. 1959. The Esoteric-Exoteric Factor in Folklore. *Fabula: Journal of Folktale Studies* 2:205–211. Reprinted in *The Study of Folklore,* ed. Alan Dundes. Englewood Cliffs, NJ: Prentice-Hall, 1965, pp. 43–51.

Kirshenblatt-Gimblett, Barbara. 1983. Studying Immigrant and Ethnic Folklore. In *The Handbook of American Folklore,* ed. Richard M. Dorson. Bloomington: Indiana University Press, pp. 39–47.

Klymasz, Robert B. 1973. From Immigrant to Ethnic Folklore: A Canadian View of Process and Transition. *Journal of the Folklore Institute* 10:131–139.

Paredes, Américo. 1959. *With His Pistol in His Hand.* Austin: University of Texas Press.

Royce, Anya Peterson. 1982. *Ethnic Identity: Strategies of Diversity.* Bloomington: Indiana University Press.

See also African Americans; Immigrant Folklore, Study of

Ethnic Stereotypes

Conventional, formulaic, oversimplified conceptions of a group. The noun "stereotype," in this sense, was first used by journalist Walter Lippmann in his Public Opinion (1922). Since then it has been employed by all manner of writers, particularly sociologists and psychologists. The word "stereotype" originated in the printing trade, where it refers to a metal plate that reproduces the original exactly. Combined with the adjective "ethnic," it has served when the older "nationality," "race," or "immigrant" was no longer considered adequate.

Ethnic stereotypes, some inaccurately called "stereotypical slurs," deal with images of reality rather than reality itself. They are the verbal and graphic images of crafty Chinese, beer-swilling Germans, fighting Irish, gesticulating Jews, watermelon- and chicken-stealing African Americans, and lazy Mexican Americans, among others, that have peopled the magazines and stages in American humor and entertainment of the 19th and 20th centuries. Because of the presence of a slight kernel of truth in some stereotypes, any joke alluding to this truth might not please a member of such a group.

Examples: The countless jokes about Scots and Jews may well refer to a commonly observed quality of both people called "thrift," normally deemed a good quality. At what point does thrift become stinginess? And who is the judge? The countless unkind jokes about stinginess may reflect a genuine concern with thriftiness, not a negative quality.

A typical single-group stereotype about Irishmen is: "Whenever there are four Irishmen, there is bound to be a Fifth," alluding to the alleged penchant of the Irish for drinking. Multigroup international stereotypes or slurs usually single out only one trait for each nation.

The crossbreed riddle is another type of international double-slur joke: "What do you get when you cross an Italian with a Mexican?—A gangster on welfare."

Stereotypes stem from the historical and cultural experience of groups, are highly inaccurate, yet generally are, or *were,* based on a smidgen of truth. To ignore such realities can be as bad as exaggerating or denying them.

Not all stereotypes are negative; some are quite complimentary. "The French are great lovers" and "The Chinese are courteous" are samples of stereotypes reflecting well on people. However, they are equally exaggerated generalizations and should not be accepted as the unqualified truth.

Groups also create, or at least contribute to the longevity of, their own stereotype. The Irish are known for praising their own ability to make good politicians. Jews at first did their part in inventing the stereotype of the "JAP," the "Jewish American Princess."

Frequently, the negative import of the joke is determined by who utters the negative item to whom, and who is present. A self-deprecation joke told in the presence of only in-group members becomes a serious insult if told by an outsider or stranger.

Our ideas about stereotypes come not from actual, prolonged contact with other people, but from the stereotypes we learn about them, and these stereotypes are based on folklore—from proverbs, songs, jokes, and other traditional forms.

Stereotypes change slowly in response to altered perceptions, some taking on almost opposite meanings from their original stance. Israeli Jews have moved from reluctant soldiers to bloodthirsty fighters, and the new German stereotype does not depend on beer and *Gemühtlichkeit* as much as the old one did.

John J. Appel

References

Adorno, T.W., et al. 1950. *The Authoritarian Personality.* American Jewish Committee Social Studies Series, No. 3. New York: Harper.

Dundes, Alan. 1987. Stereotypes. In *Cracking Jokes.* Berkeley, CA: Ten Speed, pp. 41–168.

Harding, John. 1968. Stereotypes. In *International Encyclopedia of the Social Sciences,* Vol. 15, ed. David L. Sills. New York: Macmillan.

Helmrich, William B. 1982. *The Things They Say behind Your Back.* Garden City, NY: Doubleday.

See also Jokes; Riddle Jokes

Ethnomusicology

Holistic study of the world's music, primarily from a cognitive, stylistic, performative, and contextual viewpoint. The Dutch scholar Jaap Kunst coined the term "ethno-musicology" in 1950 in order to displace the earlier "comparative musicology," his reason being that the field did not *compare* more than any other. The "ethno-" prefix, however, has been a source of debate. It suggests the study of "ethnic" music other than that of the West, and scholars in Third World areas (for example, sub-Saharan Africa) that have complex unwritten traditions rightly prefer "musicology" for the study of their own music. Despite these problems, the term has been adopted throughout the world, displacing even the German *Musikethnologie* or the French *ethnographie musicale.* This is due primarily to the influence of North American scholarship, which has emanated from the Society for Ethnomusicology, founded in 1955 and its journal, *Ethnomusicology.* The earlier International Folk Music Council (IFMC) in London founded in 1949 (since 1980 renamed the International Council for Traditional Music, or ICTM) displayed in its original title the influence of scholars such as Belá Bartók and Cecil Sharp at the turn of the 20th century. Ethnomusicologists, however, had come in the 1960s to consider folk music suspect as a descriptive category. This was largely because they found the terminology inappropriate for small-scale, Third World societies, but they also attacked it increasingly for its idealized character, and the term gave way to the more neutral "traditional music."

Ethnomusicology (and before 1950, comparative musicology) has normally meant the study of musical traditions outside the Western world. But recent work includes historical and written traditions, within and outside the West, using documentary resources that include sound in addition to writing. More immediately, ethnomusicology in the 1990s involves the study of music as a human activity and thus subsumes all musical traditions, especially living traditions, regardless of geographical area. The African musicologist J.H.K. Nketia has described it quite simply as "a discipline which combines formal and contextual techniques in the scholarly study of music" (Kwabena 1990). The main paradigms in theory and method have come from anthropology and musicology, and the evolution of the discipline has closely paralleled that of anthropology (and folklore when complex societies are involved). Among terms that have been closely linked to the history of both comparative musicology and ethnomusicology in the 20th century, for example, are *"anthropology of music," "musical ethnology," "musical ethnography,"* and *"musical folklore."* Work in psychology, sociology, linguistics, art, dance, and literary criticism has also contributed to the interdisciplinary character of ethnomusicology.

Like folklorists, however, ethnomusicologists can argue that their subject is a discipline rather than a field simply because of its intensive production, over more than a century, of published work that fuses different strands or approaches in

Mexican-American fruitpickers perform for the record. Farm Labor Camp, El Rio, California, 1941. American Folklife Center.

analyzing the central subject matter. While 19th-century scholars such as Guido Adler saw comparative musicology as a subfield of musicology (Adler 1885), many scholars would now reverse this Eurocentric view of ethnomusicology given the rise of popular and especially African American musics, rapidly changing demographics, the crisis in Western art music's harmonic language, and the downturn in the academic demand for musicologists. Ideologically, too, ethnomusi-

cologists tend to reject the assumption that Western music is superior to other kinds. This has to do with their generally egalitarian stance, as a result of which, like many anthropologists and folklorists, they have pointed to the ethical dilemmas of studying the "exotic" other.

Work in ethnomusicology since 1970 has focused on two kinds of problems affecting musical traditions in the past and the present: (1) musical thought and behavior in spe-

For the Federal Cylinder Project, Florida Seminoles Annie Jimmie, Betty Mae Jumper, and Nancy McInturf, and (right) ethnomusicologist Dorothy Sara Lee, study wax-cylinder recordings of Seminole music, 1982. Photo Carl Fleischhauer. American Folklife Center.

cific and often remote, small-scale cultures; and (2) music whose nature has been affected by change of context, tourism, or ideology, or by other factors such as the mass media and the cassette industry. The first kind of study is guided principally by the methods of cultural anthropology or folklore; the second, more by sociological analysis and cross-cultural explanation in aesthetics or semiotics. A third kind of problem involves music learning and perception and is based in the methods of cognitive anthropology or cognitive psychology. All of these approaches have been informed at a deeper level by developments in critical theory (sociology), cultural praxis (anthropology), and hermeneutics (philosophy).

The 18th-century antiquarian interest in cultural evolution that led to the founding of folklore and anthropology as fully fledged disciplines in the 19th century also spurred curiosity about musical behavior. Numerous early collections of "exotic" music were made: Chinese, Canadian Indian, and Finnish examples appeared in Rousseau's *Dic-*

tionnaire de musique (1768). Father Amiot, working as a missionary in China, translated old Chinese musical treatises in his landmark *Mémoire sur le musique des chinois* (1779), and William Jones, an English High Court judge in Calcutta, published a work on the modes of Hindu music (1784). Important sections on indigenous music, drawn from field observation and relatively free from Western bias, were contributed by the French scholar Guillaume-André Villoteau to the twenty-five-volume *Description de l'Egypte* (1809–1826). F.-J. Fétis' *Histoire générale de la musique* (1869) was the first history to insist that music outside the Western tradition, including that of China, Japan, India, and Siberia, should be represented.

By the 1880s, investigation of musical traditions both within and outside the West was given impetus by the invention of the phonograph in 1877. Recorded music could now be played back repeatedly for the purposes of study. This period, then, brought forth publications that were to be highly influential: for instance, A.J. Ellis' "On the Scales riod, then, brought forth publications that were to be highly influential: for instance, A.J. Ellis' "On the Scales of Various Nations" (1885), which proposed dividing the equal-tempered halftone into 100 parts called "cents" in order to make possible the precise comparison of different tonal systems. In the same year, the Viennese scholar Guido Adler prescribed an outline for the scholarly study of music, in which "comparative musicology" was to bring together "the sound products, especially the folksongs of different peoples, lands and territories for the purposes of ethnographic ends, and to group and divide them according to the difference in their nature." In 1886 the German scientist Carl Stumpf published his study, with transcriptions made by ear, of the music of the Bella Coola Indians of British Columbia, a group of whom had visited Germany in the previous year.

With the invention of the phonograph, scholars were able to gather data on musical traditions and to study them intensively. Jesse Walter Fewkes recorded Passamaquoddy and Zuni Indians in 1890, and the songs of the latter were transcribed by Benjamin Ives Gilman and published in the *Journal of American Ethnology and Archaeology* (1891). Europeans were not slow to see the potential of the phonograph, and Béla Vikár (1896) and Evgenija Linyova (from 1897) made field recordings of folksongs from rural peasants in Hungary and Russia, respectively. Later collectors found the phonograph indispensable: Zoltán Kodály (1905), Béla Bartók (1906), and Percy Grainger (1908), for example, used it for various purposes, Kodály and Bartók to demonstrate that the ethnic basis of Hungarian peasant song owed nothing to Gypsy music, and Grainger to reveal the artistry of the English country singer. Grainger's strikingly original transcriptions in the *Journal of the Folk-Song Society* (Grainger 1908) influenced Bartók's own detailed transcriptions of Hungarian, Slovak, Romanian, Serbo-Croatian, Arabic, and Turkish music. These scholars were also composers who saw possibilities for the renewal of Western art music in drawing on folk-music idioms.

Eastern European collectors were among the most assiduous of those making field expeditions after 1900. In Moscow, a Musical-Ethnographic Commission was founded in 1901 and sponsored field expeditions for recording purposes in parts of the Russian Empire, including the Ukraine and Georgia as well as among Mongol and Yakut peoples. Linyova's graphic notation of Russian folk polyphony that she had recorded was a notable attempt to grasp its structural principles. After the Russian Revolution, the study of "folk" or "ethnic" music received strong support from the state, and several notable Soviet scholars emerged: K. Kvitka (1880–1953), for instance, born in the Ukraine, founded and led the Folk Music Bureau at the Moscow Conservatory in 1933 and published important essays on, for instance, calendar songs and folk musicians (cf. Kvitka 1972–1973). One of his students was Moshe Beregovski, who made detailed studies of traditional Jewish music in the Ukraine (Beregovski [1934] 1982). In Hungary and Poland, the important archival centers at Budapest, Warsaw, and Poznan were irreparably damaged in World War II, but postwar field collecting managed to restore knowledge of traditional genres and styles, including several described or recorded earlier by such collectors as Oskar Kolberg in Poland and Bartók and Kodály in Hungary.

In America anthropologists had devoted effort to studying Indian musics: the recordings of Franz Boas (Kwakiutl, 1895), Livingstone Farrand (Quileute, Quinault, 1898), Frank Speck (Creek, Yuchi, 1905), and Joseph K. Dixon (Crow, 1908–1909) were housed at the American Museum of Natural History in New York. These, along with the recordings of Fewkes, who later became director of the Bureau of American Ethnology in Washington, DC, and others made by the Field Museum in Chicago, the Peabody Museum of Harvard University, the Pennsylvania Museum in Philadelphia, and the University of California at Berkeley, served as the basis for important work in ethnomusicology. The influence of Boas at Columbia University and Edward Sapir at Yale University led to work on Eskimo and Native American musics by Frances Densmore, Helen H. Roberts, and George Herzog. Marius Barbeau studied both French Canadian and Canadian Indian musical idioms, and the Museum of Man in Ottawa has continued to sponsor investigation of musical traditions in Canada.

The availability of sound recordings posed the need for archives and laboratories. The Vienna Phonogramm-Archiv was founded in 1899, the Musée Phonographique in Paris in 1900, and the Phonogramm-Archiv of Berlin, active from 1905, had its beginnings with Stumpf's collecting in 1900. The Berlin archive became the most significant of these for the future of ethnomusicology because it was systematically linked to research into the world's music under the tutelage of Erich M. von Hornbostel, who served as director from 1905 to 1933. A circle of workers at the Berlin archive included some who would later emigrate with the coming of Nazism: George Herzog, Mieczyslaw Kolinski, and Klaus Wachsmann. Also associated with the archive were Marius Schneider and Walter Wiora, who continued the "comparative" basis of the archive's work in contrasting ways: Schneider on musical prehistory (1946) and the distribution of polyphony (1934), Wiora on the comparative study of European folk music (1953). Another colleague of Hornbostel was Curt Sachs, who, although he had training in musicology and taught at the University of Berlin, was an ambitious historian of art. Sachs collaborated with Hornbostel on a major project dealing with musical instruments, the "Systematik der Musikinstrumente" (Hornbostel and Sachs 1914, Eng. trans. 1961). Later, after immigrating to the United States, he compiled learned works on dance, music, and instruments that enshrined the concepts of comparative musicology.

After World War II, however, the premises of comparative musicology fell into disrepute. The Berlin School's work had an undeniable bias of cultural evolutionism built into it, and even Sachs came to question notions of "progress" in music in his book *The Wellsprings of Music* (1962), which was prepared for posthumous publication by his younger colleague, Jaap Kunst. By this time, functionalist anthropology, itself a reaction against post-Darwinian ideas, had begun to influence the discipline, and the study of single music cultures displaced comparative endeavors. Kunst, a notable specialist in Indonesian music who had also studied his own Dutch folk music, succeeded Sachs as honorary president of the Society for Ethnomusicology and Vaughan Williams as president of the International Folk Music Council. Kunst was also was the teacher of Mantle Hood, who later became a leading figure in the development of ethnomusicology after 1960. Hood was to introduce a generation of students to the discipline through an Institute for Ethnomusicology at the University of California, Los Angeles. Hood's concept of "bi-musicality," in which performance was taught by native instructors, was central to his notion of how his students could arrive at a meaningful knowledge of "non-Western" musical idioms (Hood 1960). At UCLA, Hood enlisted the services of Charles Seeger, whose philosophical bent as a musicologist offered a foil to his experimental work with the Melograph Model C, a device for portraying a melodic line more precisely as well as its tone-color. Like other scholars, Seeger thought that Western notation was inadequate to describe the complex fluctuations of music from oral tradition. Following Seeger's lead, melographic studies of vocal and instrumental music emerged, although his claim that the Melograph could somehow portray "musical events" was called into question.

Charles Seeger was also motivated by ideological concerns: to promote egalitarianism and to educate young Americans musically along a broad front of acquaintance with diverse idioms. His writings reflect these concerns (cf. Seeger 1977). Some of his goals have been brought nearer fruition in and through the performance careers of his famous children, Pete and Peggy, and by the Lomax family. In particular, Alan Lomax, son of the folklorist John Lomax who recorded cowboy songs, has produced several works of importance, especially the collaborative *Folk Song Style and Culture* (1968), which set forth the idea of cantometrics, a cultural and musical scale for constructing profiles of song style around the world. A later version was geared to music education through the use of cassette tapes (Lomax 1976), and Lomax also made a film on the cross-cultural analysis of dance (1975). With the classification of melody types and tonal structures put forward by Kolinski (1961), Lomax's attempt represents one of the few to evolve a cross-cultural methodology in ethnomusicology after 1960. It has not escaped criticism, in particular for ethnocentrism and inadequate data bases.

A parallel development reflecting the dominance of anthropological thought in North American ethnomusicology, and particularly its paradigms of cultural relativism and functionalism, is found in the work of Willard Rhodes (Peyote music), Richard Waterman (African influence on Black music), and David McAllester. Studies of Navaho music by McAllester typically stress the cultural values that are expressed therein (cf. McAllester 1954). The figure who was to emerge with the greatest status from this orientation, however, was Alan Merriam, whose *The Anthropology of Music* (1964) set the standard in American work for several decades. Merriam was less concerned with the technical analysis of music than with probing the cultural values that scholars could discern in field

studies of musical life. Merriam proposed a feedback model for music (concepts, sound, behavior) that was new and dynamic. Merriam's musical analysis, however, did not match his brilliance as a theorist. He delineated his own fieldwork with the Flathead Indians of Montana in a later, less successful book that relied on such conservative techniques as intervallic description and statistical analysis of the music (Merriam 1967). Most recently, Merriam's model has been modified to include elements of theory and method drawn from the interpretive anthropologist Clifford Geertz.

One other influential anthropologist of music, the English scholar John Blacking, began his career with field studies of the Venda people of the Transvaal. Coming into conflict with the South African authorities, Blacking left to take up a chair of anthropology at Belfast in Northern Ireland. Where Merriam's work tends to mask ideological issues, Blacking's writing carries a strong ideological flavor, and his book *How Musical Is Man?* (1973) set the tone for a new exploration of ethical questions in ethnomusicology. By the mid-1970s, the conventional methods of the discipline (objectivist field collecting, transcription, classification) had suffered under concerted intellectual attacks from anthropology. Methods of transcription and classification such as those developed by Bartók (Bartók and Lord 1951) receded in importance, and major compilations of traditional tunes, such as those by B.H. Bronson (1959–1972) and T. Knudsen, S. Nielsen, and N. Schiørring (1976), marked, with the work of W. Danckert (1970) and Wiora in Germany, a diminution of interest in comparative scholarship. In contrast, Blacking brought an array of concerns to the field: the description of music, the ethnography of musical performance, the anthropology of the body, meaning and value in music, and ethics. His teaching at Belfast attracted students from Third World countries because of his insistence on the scrupulous regard of the scholar for coworkers, and it inculcated a strong sense of the reflexivity that was permeating anthropology during the 1970s and 1980s.

By the mid-1970s, ethnomusicologists had begun to question their methods with some prompting from the intellectual Left. The expropriation of musical traditions by Western collectors and scholars, through recordings and expository texts, emerged as a thorny issue in the 1970s and 1980s. Research in Africa, the Americas, Australia, and the Pacific raised ethical dilemmas in studying the music of indigenous peoples given the brutal colonialist politics that had dispossessed or displaced them. Critics questioned the role of the ethnomusicologist in evaluating music cultures through the "objectivity" prized by an older generation of fieldworkers such as Constantin Brailoiu (1981) or George List (1974).

At the same time, the influence of Marxists such as the Italian social philosopher Antonio Gramsci found its way into studies of popular music in Western society. As a result, ethnomusicologists, with folklorists and cultural historians, were drawn to scrutinize the politics of culture, a dynamic that often takes the form of tension between socialist and nationalist ideologies. One semiotically based study of propagandistic song by Vladimir Karbusicky (1972) demonstrates how the proponents (Nazis, Communists) often use similar musical and textual means.

Some of this had been prefigured in the work of the sociological Frankfurt School (Adorno, Horkheimer, Marcuse), which dealt with the place of music in an industrial society. Sociologists of "popular music" have examined the role of media and mass-produced musical culture, continuing thereby the tradition stemming from the Frankfurt School. This perspective has tended to rely, however, on the semiotic analysis of music and society rather than the reflexive study of individuals. The romantic pastorialism of the folk-music revival in Europe, moreover, was dismissed by these scholars for the reason that "folk music" was a regressive kind of musical idiom. The flowering of the folk revival in the 1950s and 1960s, first in Britain and Ireland, then in Italy, Germany, and Scandinavia, was a development that had serious political consequences. Stimulated by Alan Lomax's brand of populism, the revival initially encouraged resistance to the commercialization of popular music but later gave way to issues of regionalism, political empowerment, and gender. Symposiums on ideology and tourism, as influences on traditional music, posed these as two pressing issues in the 1980s. The twin themes of ideology and cultural policy, often as reactions to tourism or the need for an imagined past, have generated studies of musical applications—for example, on Ireland by E.O, Henry (1989), on Sweden by O. Ronström (1989), and on Switzerland by S. Bolle-Zemp (1990). Another study by J.K. Cowan (1990) has analyzed the ideological intertwining of music, dance, and politics in Greece.

The anthropological legacy of Merriam and Blacking found its way into several studies of small-scale societies: S. Feld's work on the Kaluli people of Papua, New Guinea (1982, 2d ed. 1990), R. Stone's on the Kpelle of Liberia (1982), and A. Seeger's on the Suyá of Brazil (1987). This research, based on intensive fieldwork, exemplifies the close attention to musical concepts and behavior by an ethnomusicology that is cogently influenced by theory and method in anthropology. Because of that influence, its practitioners often appear to prefer the terms "musical anthropology" or "anthropology of music" to "ethnomusicology." The value of these works lies in their detailed exposition of music and musical concepts as symbolic of social formations, though they do tend to portray the societies as somewhat homogeneous. The "restudies" that occurred in anthropology have begun to filter into ethnomusicology, such as Nazir Jairazbhoy's recent restudy of the fieldwork in India of his teacher, the Dutch scholar Arnold Bake, in the 1930s (Jairazbhoy 1991). A scrutiny of the discipline's history, indeed, seen as a split between "anthropology of music" and "comparative musicology," was at the heart of a recent conference.

Perhaps the most surprising development in recent times has been the exploration of western art music by ethnomusicologists who, in the past, had shunned this as part of a European cultural dominance they regarded with suspicion. The German scholar Walter Wiora initiated the study of European folk music as a source for art-music composition (Wiora 1957). But the historical division between "folk-music study" and "ethnomusicology" began to break down in the 1970s, mainly under pressure from key figures such as Charles Seeger, Frank Harrison, and Gilbert Chase. The conceptual divorce of "European music" from "non-Western music," part of ethnomusicology's debt to anthropology, has gradually begun to move toward resolution in a few publications. Scholars began to realize that if ethnomusicology is the study of "world music" rather than of "non-Western music," then they must include Western art music in such a scheme. Further, John Blacking had emphasized the biology of music making in his later work, a topic that involves the nature of musical intelligence cross-culturally (Blacking 1992). This area of investigation overlaps to some degree with the traditional concerns of "systematic" musicology: perception and cognition, the computer analysis of time series, and tone measurement. This more "musicological" move within ethnomusicology has come partly from Europe, where traditions of ethnographic research have not always been as strong as they were in North America.

Organology has been a major part of ethnomusicology ever since Hornbostel and Sachs set forth their program for the systematic comparison of musical instruments. Various alternative schemes of classification have been set forth since, for example by Hood (1971) and Kartomi (1990). Tonometric analysis using Ellis' system of cents is still used, though with modification. African and Indonesian music has often been the focus of such research because of its scale formations. The Study Group on Folk Musical Instruments of the IFMC (ICTM) has produced numerous volumes of conference proceedings, mainly on European folk cultures. These studies have explored instruments from other perspectives, such as use, manufacture, or musical concepts. The new subfield of musical archaeology, significant for the relationship between historical, systematic, and ethnomusicology, has relied mainly on the analysis of musical instruments to suggest the use of music in pre- and early history. Similarly, the ICTM study groups on analysis and systematization, dance choreology, and so on have tended to show the interdisciplinarity of a great deal of work in ethnomusicology. And the institutionalization of the field has lately come under scrutiny from a number of viewpoints.

A significant venture in this regard was the founding, by John Blacking, of the European Seminar in Ethnomusicology (ESEM) in 1981. The seminar, which came into existence for reasons of financial support for scholars unable to travel to meetings in North America, has met regularly and published its conference proceedings. An allied development has been the emergence of European journals for the study of traditional music, such as *Culturi musicale* (1985–), *Cahiers de musiques traditionnelles* (1988–), and the *British Journal of Ethnomusicology* (1992–). Recent issues have included work by scholars from the former Soviet Union as well as studies of Central Asian music by East Europeans. While the dream of a Europe united politically has faded in the agony of Bosnia, the breakup of the Soviet Union has opened up possibilities for cooperative research. The question raised by some Europeans, of whether there is a "European" or an "American" mode of ethnomusicology, draws boundaries that are largely nonexistent. The discipline has always benefited from the scholarly exchange of views. The Society for Ethnomusicology, the International Council for Traditional Music, and the ESEM include members from many countries, and the council has met in locations that are worldwide. In Africa, the Americas, Asia, and Europe, researchers have continually sought international contact in the study of musical cultures, including their own. Symposiums on orality and literacy in music, for example, or tourism and music have taken place in Japan and Jamaica, respectively. Indeed, the question of whether there is an "inside" view of a particular music (as opposed to an "outside" one) is moot, since scholars now tend to believe that every view of the music has some value, whatever the angle of perception. The subjectivity of individual musical experience, in other words, has begun to influence the evaluation of all kinds of music in terms of its production and consumption.

In the late 1970s, ethnomusicologists felt the need to move beyond a "hard-core" musical ethnography that had emerged earlier in the decade. This was largely the result of a growing dissatisfaction with cultural relativism and with describing single cultures in depth as if they had no relation to the outside world. The dissatisfaction also arose, in part, from the information explosion and increasing cultural contact among the world's peoples through radio, television, and cassette recordings. It was less a premature return to the vexed question of musical "universals," which had been a recurring if unresolved theme during the 1970s (see *Ethnomusicology*, Vol. 15, 1971). At the same time, the influence of European literary and philosophical movements began to find its way into ethnomusicology, principally that of phenomenology, hermeneutics, and Marxist social anthropology. The work of Pierre Bourdieu, Paul Ricoeur, and others resonates sympathetically with the influence of Geertz and other anthropologists who emphasize the need for a greater self-consciousness on the part of the social researcher. Semiotics, on the other hand, has been less influential in ethnomusicology, largely because of the abstractedness of its musical analysis. As a corrective, Blacking called for exploring a range of "ethnic perceptions" in the semiotics of music (Blacking 1981). Some attention, however, has been paid to the iconic properties of music. Folkloristics, in contrast, which had pioneered the study of individual tradition bearers in the 19th century and had foregrounded the analysis of context, events, and artistic performance in the 1970s, continues to have an effect on ethnomusicological thinking. The influence of sociolinguistics, palpable in folklore studies, has found its way into ethnomusicology—for example, in P. Hopkins' analysis of the musical and symbolic codes that permeate playing of the Hardanger fiddle in Norway (Hopkins 1986).

Since the mid-1980s, some scholars have directed their attention toward synthesis in ethnomusicological theory and method. An account of the discipline's recent history by R.M.F. Joseph (1988) drew attention to four "converging models" in ethnomusicology, derived from (1) semiotics, (2) folkloristics, and (3) sociolinguistics (performance and context studies), and (4) cognitive semantic anthropology. J.H.K. Nketia had already advocated integrating objectivity and experience in ethnomusicological studies in order to avoid the conceptual dichotomies set up by divorcing music sound from music behavior, or the social from the musical (Nketia 1985). Like Nketia, Blacking has called for a "reintegration of musicology" that relies to some extent on cognitive processes in fashioning a "human science of the tonal art." Dropping the indefensible "ethno-" prefix, this integrated musicology will forge its own theory and methods by explaining the facts of music making in all known societies. The task is "to discover in each case what is irreducibly musical and to what extent musical factors are paramount." Following the phenomenologist Alfred Schutz (1951), Blacking believes that individuals have the capacity for "making musical sense of the world" and can transform abstract structures of cognition and affect into social and cultural forms. How this musical "tuning-in" becomes conceptualized and can be reproduced in other contexts, with other meanings, is a major problem for the human sciences that Blacking (1991) believes is not peculiar to music. Similar, if more abstract statements, have come from East European ethnomusicologists who take a broadly anthropological, comparative, and synthesizing stance in the study of "man, culture, cosmos" (Karbusicky 1990) or "culture, text, man" (Zemtsovsky 1993). While ethnomusicology still acknowledges its debt to anthropology, a paradigm based on musical performance as a potent symbol of human intentionality seems to be at the forefront of the discipline. An ethnomusicology that aims at synthesis through a comparative study of performance is, therefore, the central concern of the 1990s.

James Porter

References

Adler, G. 1885. Umfang, Methode, und Ziel der Musikwissenschaft. *Vierteljahrschrift für Musikwissenschaft* 1:5–20.

Bartók, B., and A.B. Lord. 1951. *Serbo-Croatian Folk Songs.* New York: Columbia University Press.

Baumann, M.P. 1992. The Ear as Organ of Cognition: Prolegomenon to the Anthropology of Listening. In *European Studies in Ethnomusicology: Historical Developments and Recent Trends,* ed. M.P. Baumann, A. Simon, and U. Wegner. Wilhelmshaven: Florian Noetzel Verlag, pp. 123–141.

Becker, J. 1986. Is Western Art Music Superior? *Musical Quarterly* 72 (3):341–359.

Becker, J., and Alton Becker. 1981. A Musical Icon: Power and Meaning in Javanese Gamelan Music. In *The Sign in Music and Literature,* ed. W. Steiner. Austin: University of Texas Press, pp. 203–215.

Bengtsson, I. 1967. On Melody Registration and "Mona." In *Elektronische Datenverarbeitung in der Musikwissenschaft,* ed. H. Heckmann Regensburg: Gustav Bosse, pp. 136–174.

Beregovski, M. [1934] 1982. Jewish Folk Music. In *Old Jewish Folk Music,* ed. and trans. Mark Slobin. Philadelphia: University of Pennsylvania Press, pp. 19–43.

Blacking, J. 1981. The Problem of "Ethnic" Perceptions in the Semiotics of Music. In *The Sign in Literature and Music*, ed. Wendy Steiner. Austin: University of Texas Press, pp. 184–194.

———. 1991. Towards a Reintegration of Musicology. In *Proceedings of the Second British-Swedish Conference on Musicology: Ethnomusicology, Cambridge, 5–10 August 1989*, ed. A. Buckley, K. Edström, P. Nixon. Gothenburg: University of Gothenburg, pp. 61–69.

———. 1992. The Biology of Music-Making. In *Ethnomusicology: An Introduction*, ed. H. Myers. New York: W.W. Norton, pp. 301–314.

Boiles, C. 1983. Processes of Musical Semiosis. *Yearbook for Traditional Music* 14:24–44.

Bolle-Zemp, S. 1990. Institutionalized Folklore and Helvetic Ideology. *Yearbook for Traditional Music* 22:127–140.

Brailoiu, C. 1981. *Problems of Ethnomusicology*, trans. A.L. Lloyd. Cambridge: Cambridge University Press.

Bronson, B.H. 1959–1972. *The Traditional Tunes of the Child Ballads*. 4 vols. Princeton, NJ: Princeton University Press.

Brook, B., et al., eds. 1972. *Perspectives in Musicology*. New York: W.W. Norton.

Cowan, J.K. 1990. *Dance and the Body Politic in Northern Greece*. Princeton, NJ.: Princeton University Press.

Crossley-Holland, P., ed. 1974. *Selected Reports in Ethnomusicology*. Vol. 2. No. 1. Los Angeles: Institute of Ethnomusicology (Melograph Issue).

Danckert, W. 1970. *Das europäische Volkslied*. Bonn: H. Bouvier.

Feld, S. 1982. *Sound and Sentiment: Birds, Weeping, Poetics, and Song in Kaluli Expression*. 2d ed. 1990. Philadelphia: University of Pennsylvania Press.

Gourlay, K. 1978. Towards a Reassessment of the Ethnomusicologist's Role in Research. *Ethnomusicology* 22:1–36.

Grainger, P. 1908. Collecting with the Phonograph. *Journal of the Folk-Song Society* 3 (3):147–169.

Henry, E.O. 1989. Institutions for the Promotion of Indigenous Music: The Case for Ireland's Comhaltas Ceoltoiri Eireann. *Ethnomusicology* 33:67–95.

Hood, M. 1960. The Challenge of Bi-Musicality. *Ethnomusicology* 4:55–59.

———. 1971. *The Ethnomusicologist*. New York: McGraw-Hill. 2d ed. 1982. Kent, OH: Kent State University Press.

Hopkins, P. 1986. *Aural Thinking in Norway: Performance and Communication with the hardingfele*. New York: Human Sciences Press.

Hornbostel, E.M. von, and C. Sachs. 1914. *Systematik der Musikinstrumente. Zeitschrift für Ethnologie* 46:553–590. Reprinted as Classification of Musical Instruments, trans. A. Baines and K.P. Wachsmann. *Galpin Society Journal* 14:3–29, 1961.

Jairazbhoy, N.A. 1991. The First Restudy of Arnold Bake's Fieldwork in India. In Comparative Musicology and Anthropology of Music: Essays on the History of Ethno-musicology, ed. B. Nettl and P.V. Bohlman. Chicago: University of Chicago Press, pp. 210–227.

Joseph, R.M.F. 1988. Ethnomusicology: Towards the Holistic Study of Music. *Bulletin of the IFMC* (UK Chapter) 19:2–28; 20:4–19

Karbusicky, V. 1972. *Ideologie im Lied, Lied in der Ideologie*. Cologne: Hans Gerig.

———. 1990. *Kosmos-Mensch-Musik: Strukturalistische Anthropologie des Musikalischen*. Hamburg: R. Kramer.

Kartomi, M.J. 1990. *On Concepts and Classification of Musical Instruments*. Chicago: University of Chicago Press.

Keil, C. 1979. *Tiv Song*. Chicago: University of Chicago Press.

Kingsbury, H. 1988. *Music, Talent, and Performance: A Conservatory Cultural System*. Philadelphia: Temple University Press.

Knudsen, T., S. Nielsen, and N. Schiørring, eds., 1976. *Danske Gamle Folkeviser*. Vol. 11. (tunes of the Danish ballads).

Kolinski, M. 1961. Classification of Tonal Structures. *Studies in Ethnomusicology* 1:38–76.

Kunst, J. 1950. *Musicologica*. Amsterdam: Royal Tropical Institute.

Kvitka, K. 1972–1973. *Izbrannye Trudy* [Selected Works], ed. V. Hoshovsky. Moscow: Soviet Composer.

List, G. 1974. Folk Music Fieldwork: Recording Traditional Music. In *Folklore and Folklife: An Introduction*, ed. R.M. Dorson. Chicago: University of Chicago Press, pp. 363–379, 445–463.

Lomax, A. 1968. *Folk Song Style and Culture*. Washington, DC: American Association for the Advancement of Science.

———. 1976. *Cantometrics*. Berkeley: University of California Press.

McAllester, D. 1954. *Enemy Way Music*. Cambridge: Peabody Museum Papers, Vol. 41, No. 3.

Merriam, A.P. 1967. Ethnomusicology of the Flathead Indians. Chicago: Aldine.

———. 1977. Definitions of "Comparative Musicology and "Ethnomusicology": An Historical-Theoretical Perspective. *Ethnomusicology* 21:189–204.

Middleton, R. 1991. *Studying Popular Music*. Milton Keynes, England: Open University Press.

Nattiez, J-J. 1975. *Fondements d'une sémiologie de la musique*. Paris: Union génerale d'éditions.

Nettl, B. 1983. *The Study of Ethnomusicology: Twenty-Nine Issues and Concepts*. Urbana: University of Illinois Press.

———. 1989. Mozart and the Ethnomusicological Study of Western Culture. *Yearbook for Traditional Music* 21:1–16.

Nettl, B., and P.V. Bohlman, eds. 1991. *Comparative Musicology and Anthropology of Music: Essays on the History of Ethnomusicology*. Chicago: University of Chicago Press.

Nketia, J.H.K. 1985. Integrating Objectivity and Experience in Ethnomusicological Studies. *World of Music* 27:3–19.

———. 1990. Contextual Strategies of Inquiry and Systematization. *Ethnomusicology* 34:75–97.

Porter, J. 1993. Europe. In *Ethnomusicology: Historical and Regional Studies*, ed. H. Myers, New York: W.W. Norton, pp. 215–239.

Qureshi, R.B. 1987. Musical Sound and Contextual Input: A Performance Model for Musical Analysis. *Ethnomusicology* 31:56–86.

Rice, T. 1986. Toward the Remodeling of Ethnomusicology. *Ethnomusicology* 31:469–488 (with responses).

Ronström, O. 1989. Making Use of History: The Revival of the Bagpipe in Sweden in the 1980s. *Yearbook for Traditional Music* 21:95–108.

Schneider A., and A.E. Beurmann. 1990. Notes on the Acoustics and Tuning of *gamelan* Instruments. In *Performance in Java and Bali: Studies of Narrative, Theatre, Music, and Dance*, ed. B. Arps. London: School of Oriental and African Studies, pp. 197–218.

Schneider, M. 1934. *Geschichte der Mehrstimmigkeit*. Vol. 1. Berlin: J. Bard.

———. 1946. *El origen musical de los animalos-simbolos en la mitología y la escultura antiguas*. Barcelona.

Schutz, A. 1951. Making Music Together: A Study in Social Relationship. *Social Research* 18 (1):76.

Schuursma, A.B. 1992. *Ethnomusicology Research: A Select Annotated Bibliography*. New York: Garland.

Seeger, A. 1987. *Why Suyá Sing: A Musical Anthropology of an Amazonian People*. Cambridge: Cambridge University Press.

Seeger, C. 1977. *Studies in Musicology, 1935–1975*. Berkeley: University of California Press.

Sharp, C. 1907. *English Folk-Song: Some Conclusions*. London: Simpkin, Novello.

Shepherd, J., P. Virden, G. Vulliamy, and T. Wishart. 1977. *Whose Music? A Sociology of Musical Languages*. New Brunswick, NJ.

Slobin, M. 1991. *Subcultural Sounds: Micromusics of the West*. Hanover, NH: University Press of New England.

Stockmann, D. 1979. Die Transkription in der Musikethnologie: Geschichte, Probleme, Methoden. *Acta Musicologica* 51:204–245.

Stone, R. 1982. *Let the Inside Be Sweet: The Interpretation of Music Events among the Kpelle of Liberia*. Bloomington: Indiana University Press.

Stumpf, C. 1886. Lieder der Bellakula-Indianer. *Vierteljahrschrift für Musikwissenschaft* 2:405–426.

Sugarman, J.C. 1989. The Nightingale and the Partridge: Singing and Gender among Prespa Albanians. *Ethnomusicology* 33:191–215.

Tokumaru, Y., and O. Yamaguti, eds. 1986. *The Oral and the Literate in Music*. Tokyo: Academia Music.

Vaughan, K. 1990. Exploring Emotion in Sub-Structural Aspects of Karelian Lament: Application of Time Series Analysis to Digitized Melody. *Yearbook for Traditional Music* 22:106–122.

Vetter, R. 1989. A Retrospect on a Century of Gamelan Tone Measurements. *Ethnomusicology* 33:217–227.

Wiora, W. 1953. *Europäischer Volksgesang*. Cologne: Arno Volk. Eng. trans. 1966. *European Folksong: Common Forms in Characteristic Modification*. New York: Leeds.

———. 1957. *Europäische Volksmusik und abendländische Tonkunst*. Kassel: J.P. Hinnenthal.

Zemtsovsky, I. 1993. Text, Kultur, Mensch: Versuch eines synthetischen Paradigmas. In *Festschrift zum 60. Geburtstag von Wolfgang Suppan*. ed. B. Habla. Tutzing: H. Schneider, pp. 113–128.

Etymology, Folk (Popular)

A process by which people either (1) mispronounce or change the pronunciations of foreign or strange-sounding words to make them more similar to, or compatible phonologically with, other words in their lexicons, or (2) explain from hearsay evidence how particular words originated.

"Woodchuck" is a transformation by folk etymology from the Ojibwa or Cree word for that animal (*otchig* and *otcheck*, respectively) and has nothing to do with wood or chuck(ing). The Spanish *cucaracha* (wood louse) evolved by folk etymology into "cockroach," an insect that has no relationship to either a rooster (cock) or a freshwater fish (an early, and still alternate, meaning of roach). Because of folk etymology, "sparrow grass" once (mid-17th through the mid-19th century) competed with "asparagus" as the name of a common vegetable, and "chaise lounge" now vies with the original French *chaise longue* as the designator for a long reclining chair.

Folk etymology is also used to identify hypothetical explanations—usually presented in story form—for word derivations. After the spelling of *surloin* (a cut of meat from an animal's hindquarter) was changed to "sirloin," someone created, and others perpetuated, the tale that an enthusiastic English king once knighted a loin of beef, his country's national dish, dubbing it *"Sir Loin."* Another story illustrating folk etymology attributes the origin of *gringo* to a misperception that occurred in 1846–1848 when Mexicans, hearing American soldiers repeatedly singing the Robert Burns song "Green Grow the Rashes, O," heard the first two words as one and subsequently identified Americans as *gringos*.

Robert A. Georges

References

Greenough, James Bradstreet, and George Lyman Kittredge. 1905. *Words and Their Ways in English Speech*. New York: Macmillan, pp. 330–344.

See also Folk Speech

F

Fable

An animal tale with a moral, according to folklorists. Ben Edwin Perry, the authority on Aesopic tradition, preferred an ancient Greek definition that captures the fable's essentially rhetorical genius: "a fictitious story picturing a truth." According to Perry, the fable is an artistic form that can include stories from any of several genres, with human, animal, or inanimate objects as their characters. Its defining quality is its use of narrative metaphor to make a point. Most fables teach worldly wisdom and shrewdness, not moral values or good conduct (cf. Perry 1965).

Fables have a long history, both oral and literary. Aesop, a Thracian slave (later a freedman) who lived on the island of Samos in the sixth century B.C., told his stories, which have Semitic antecedents, orally. Beginning in the fourth century B.C., collections of prose fables attributed to Aesop were used by rhetoricians. In the Middle Ages, Greek, Latin, Indian, and other fables circulated in collections called beast epics, with Renard the Fox and similar characters. European (and thus Euro-American) fable tradition comes, therefore, from many different cultures.

Fables with sound moral lessons have long been considered suitable reading material for children. Most fables, however, are satiric rather than preceptive. These include La Fontaine's *Fables* (1668 Eng. trans. 1954) and James Thurber's *Fables for Our Time* (1940) and *Further Fables for Our Time* (1956). Some of Thurber's fables are modern inventions, while others are variants of Aesopic tales; many include proverbs as their morals. For example, one about journalists in a rush to publish is called "The Sheep in Wolf's Clothing;" in another, "The Tortoise and the Hare," the hare wins the race, and the moral is: "A new broom may sweep clean, but never trust an old saw."

American oral tradition transmits fables as proverbs (sour grapes, the lion's share, don't count your chickens before they're hatched). In addition, satiric animal fables are recounted orally, especially in African American tradition. In one, a fox trapped the deer who had been raiding his garden. The deer sang beautifully, and tricked the fox, who wanted to

hear better, into letting him escape. According to the narrator, "There's people just like that, these confidence men. . . . There's a lesson in all these stories" (Dorson 1967:96–97).
Christine Goldberg

References
Blackham, H.J. 1985. *The Fable as Literature*. London and Dover, NH: Athlone.
Carnes, Pack. 1985. *Fable Scholarship: An Annotated Bibliography*. New York: Garland.
———, ed. 1988. *Proverbia in Fabula: Essays on the Relationship of the Proverb and the Fable*. Sprichwörterforschung Vol. 10. Bern: Peter Lang.
Daly, Lloyd W. 1961. *Aesop without Morals*. New York and London: Thomas Yoseloff.
Dorson, Richard M. 1967. *American Negro Folktales*. Greenwich, CT: Fawcett.
The Fables of La Fontaine. [1668] 1954. trans. Marianne Moore. New York: Viking.
Perry, Ben Edwin, ed. 1965. *Babrius and Phaedrus*. Loeb Classical Library. London: William Heinemann; Cambridge: Harvard University Press.

Fairies

The supernaturally powered "little people" of European folklore. Apart from the generically distinct, ubiquitous Tooth Fairy, described by one scholar of the subject as "America's only [indigenous] fairy," beliefs and customs concerning fairies from European tradition appear sparse in most parts of North America. A wealth of documentation from Atlantic Canada, however, in the form of informational testimonies, place names, personal-experience narratives and local legends, has revealed a vital, living heritage of transplanted and adapted Irish, Scottish, English, and French *(lutin)* fairylore in that region.

The variety of fairy behaviors depicted in such accounts render any single definition of "fairy" lacking. In part, this diversity of meanings reflects the complex etymological development of the Modern English term "fairy" from conceptually related terms in Latin *(fatua, fatum)*, Old French *(fee)*, Old English *(fagan, faege)*, and Middle English *(fay, fairye)*. As it has developed in Britain and continues to evolve in the English-speaking world, "fairy" is a generic term that has incorporated the meanings of many regional supernatural rivals such as "boghost," "phooka," "boobagger," "bugalug," "thurse," "shuck," "Sidhe," and "Tylwyth Teg." Today this associative, subsuming process goes on, with creatures such as elves, pixies, goblins, and *lutin* often being thought of as "kinds" of fairies. Interestingly, many informants who participate in living fairy traditions refuse to use the term. Because of a traditional taboo against saying "fairy" aloud, fairies on both sides of the Atlantic are often referred to with a variety of euphemisms, including the "good people," "those people," and simply "them."

It has been argued that the 20th-century meaning of "fairy" as a male homosexual developed in the United States in the late 19th century, but at least one student has contended that such usage occurred in Britain as early as the 16th century with the advent of the small, delicate, effeminate fairy of literary tradition.

Contemporary students of fairylore in Atlantic Canada have interpreted fairies as representing challenging, "significant other" societies of liminal personae possessing supernatural powers that can be used for evil or good. Fairies have been described as being between heaven and hell (fallen angels), between the dead and the living (restless dead), or spatially dwelling between purity (a mortal's home or home community) and danger (deep woods, barrens, bogs, cliffs) in areas such as barns, gardens, and berry grounds. Thus, fairy limnality has demanded that mortals be cautious, observe taboos, and practice defensive and remedial magic.

Sometimes portrayed in oral tradition as a diminutive race living in groups or in solitude, but rarely in pairs, fairies dress in all manner of garb (red suits, flowing gowns) and engage in both festive (dancing, playing musical instruments, feasting, riding horses [*lutin*]) and solemn (funerals) activities. Verbal depictions of fairies in Atlantic Canada have been influenced by mass culture, but they usually have not included the diaphanous-winged, dainty fairy images of literature and popular culture.

The presence of fairies has often involved extraordinary natural circumstance (such as "fairy winds") or psychological influence more than actual visible, physical interaction. In Newfoundland, for instance, to be "in the fairies," "fairy-led," "led astray," or "taken astray" refers to a form of disorientation sometimes resulting in getting lost in dangerous areas, frequently while berry picking or cutting wood in a forest. While in this mental state, an individual may experience being in one place and then in another without temporal or spatial transition. One of the most popular counteractant magical practices in such circumstances has been to reverse one's fate by turning articles of clothing (cap, shirt, or coat) inside out.

In other circumstances, physical disorders have been attributed to fairies, again often without actual human-fairy encounters. The fairy "blast" in Newfoundland, parallel to the European "elf shot," is a wound that commonly becomes tumorous. It is inflicted by angry fairies in contexts in which individuals intrude on fairy territory or cross fairy paths. Narrators maintain that when medical doctors have lanced such tumors they have found objects such as feathers, pins, straw, hair, and teeth. Similarly, changeling accounts cite the presence of an abnormal, often old, fairy "child"; yet, as a rule, the "normal" fairy abductors of the human child are not caught in the act. It is relevant in this regard that recent interpretations of European changeling traditions stress the parental importance of such beliefs in assigning moral responsibility for the advent of disabled infants to fairy activities rather than to personal deficiencies.

While all of these fairylore phenomena have clear European antecedents, perhaps the greatest distinction between Old and New World fairylore is the spatial emphasis of the latter, a characteristic that has expressed the need of dealing with potential tragedies of getting lost or encountering mortal dangers in vast wilderness areas through magico-religious means. Orally circulated accounts concerning dangerous zones, and the tragic encounters of specific individuals with fairies in such places that have resulted in permanent physical stigma (awkward demeanor, disfigurement, premature aging, lameness, speech impairment) or psychological disability ("strange" behavior, retardation, "sinful" tendencies, insanity) have served as geographical warnings on the cognitive maps of community residents. In addition, they have left moral imprints as cautionary tales and served as agents of social control. As such, fairylore has maintained traditional values by stressing the importance of subordinating individual desires to collective needs (obedience to community norms) and the necessity of yielding to the wisdom of generational pressures (the admonitions of one's elders concerning fairies as threatening figures). Strong community beliefs in fairies have also provided opportunities for some individuals, as in the case of changeling "parents," to coalesce with fairies by using fairy explanations in order to avoid the sanctions, embarrassment, and shame of other, more condemning traditional interpretations (such as the "cursed child"—a child cursed by the sins of its parent[s]). Relatedly, oral accounts reveal the possibility that fairy explanations have been used as alibis to mask a variety of deviant behaviors such as extreme tardiness, premarital sexual relations, infidelity, incest, child molestation, wife battering, and sexual assault.

In Atlantic Canada in the late 20th century, fairy beliefs are often relegated to the recent past or thought of as moribund. Informants cite a variety of causes for the demise of fairy traditions, including the advent of roads, cars, electric light, television, and other contemporary electronic media. Some students of fairylore maintain, however, that fairies have not disappeared; they have simply transformed into the growing numbers of "little green" inhabitants of unidentified flying objects (UFOs) who continue their traditional practice of abducting humans with impunity. Others observe that for centuries there have been reports of fading fairy traditions and that the idea of the fairies' disappearance itself is part of the fairylore belief complex.

Peter Narváez

References

Briggs, Katharine M. 1967. *The Fairies in Tradition and Literature*. London: Routledge and Kegan Paul.

Halpert, Herbert. 1958. Legends of the Cursed Child. *New York Folklore Quarterly* 14:233–241.

Hand, Wayland. 1981. European Fairy Lore in the New World. *Folklore* 92:141–148.

Narváez, Peter. 1987. Newfoundland Berry Pickers "In the Fairies": The Maintenance of Spatial and Temporal Boundaries through Legendry. *Lore and Language* 6 (1):15–49.

———, ed. 1991. *The Good People: New Fairylore Essays*. New York: Garland.

Rieti, Barbara. 1991. *Strange Terrain: The Fairy World in Newfoundland*. Social and Economic Studies No. 45. St. John's: Institute of Social and Economic Research, Memorial University of Newfoundland.

Widdowson, J.D.A. 1977. *If You Don't Be Good: Verbal Social Control in Newfoundland*. Social and Economic Studies No. 21. St. John's: Institute of Social and Economic Research, Memorial University of Newfoundland.

See also Tooth Fairy

Fairs

Exhibitions, held on an annual basis, usually lasting up to a week, featuring livestock, agricultural, and domestic products along with commercial displays, midways, and entertainment. Modern fairs have their roots in the European trade fairs and markets of the Middle Ages in which farmers and merchants offered their wares for sale. In the United States, Elkanah Watson is generally credited with initiating agricultural fairs and promoting agricultural societies in 18th-century New England for the purpose of disseminating information to farmers and improving agricultural practices. In the 19th century, state departments of agriculture began to provide funds in support of prizes or premiums to be given to exhibitors for the best produce, crops, and animals shown at county fairs. Agricultural exhibitions and livestock shows continue as major aspects of fair activities in the late 20th century. Run by volunteer boards of directors elected by stockholders or shareholders, fairs are organized into various departments headed by superintendents.

Fairs in the United States may be described as local festivals, which have predictable schedules and are marked by expressive public forms such as parades, rituals, and competitions that serve educational, social, economic, and symbolic functions. Typical fair events include tractor pulls, harness racing, dairy and beef cattle shows, shows of other livestock (swine, sheep, poultry, goats), demonstrations of sheep shearing, carding, and spinning, fire department and farm equipment parades, beauty contests, demolition derbies, and auto thrill shows.

Fairs foster a sense of place and regional identity and encourage a feeling of pride in the occupational skills associated with agriculture and farm work. Adults enter open-class competitions at county fairs, while young people involved in the Future Farmers of America, Junior Grange, and 4-H Clubs participate in various restricted classes, where they receive recognition for their achievements and learn both formally and informally from adults and peers what is expected of them

Making baskets at the Georgia Mountain Fair. Hiawassee, Georgia, 1980s. American Folklife Center.

in this setting. The judging process promotes set standards, such as uniformity, neatness, style, and appearance, by which animals, crops, canned and baked goods, and needlework are measured. Judges examine exhibits, provide comments to exhibitors, and reinforce the shared values that define blue-ribbon winners, who then are eligible for competition at the state-fair level.

The agricultural components of county fairs are paralleled by commercial displays featuring local businesses, such as banks, feed stores, and car dealers; civic and charitable organizations ranging from Rotary and Kiwanis Clubs to the American Heart Association and the Red Cross; county, state, and federal government agencies having to do with agriculture, land use and management, rural life, health and social services; and political parties and their candidates, especially in election years.

These community-based sections of county fairs contrast with the entertainment provided by the carnival midway, which consists of rides, sideshows, and games of skill and chance—attractions and amusements from outside the local area. The sociability that characterizes the agricultural and commercial departments is replaced by a less familiar, more surrealistic atmosphere on the midway, which depicts the transient and the ephemeral against the agricultural interests that are distinctly rooted to the land.

Agricultural fairs have always combined a dual nature with a multiplicity of voices and symbols emphasizing progress and technology while at the same time presenting a nostalgic view of a romanticized rural past. The tensions and contradictions between an impulse for change versus a need for stability, between emerging and ongoing traditions, between various participants and fair audiences, and the relationships of animal and human, of human and machine, of rural and urban—all find expression against the backdrop of the fair.

Joyce Ice

References

Neeley, Wayne Caldwell. 1935. *The Agricultural Fair.* New York: Columbia University Press.
Prosterman, Leslie Mina. 1982. *The Aspect of the Fair: Aesthetics and Festival in Illinois County Fairs.* Ph.D. diss., University of Pennsylvania.

See also Farmers

Fakelore

"The presentation of spurious and synthetic writings under the claim that they are genuine folklore" (Dorson 1971:9). As the study of folklore struggled to define itself and its field of interest, the term "fakelore" was coined and defined as above by Richard M. Dorson in 1950. Fakelore is the product of writers, not the product of the folk and folklore process. What triggered Dorson's campaign was the appearance of Benjamin A. Botkin's anthology *A Treasury of American Folklore* in 1994, which received critical acclaim in the popular press and in folklore circles.

Dorson coined the term to show his outrage. He was concerned that publications such as the *Treasury* present themselves as compendiums of true folklore when, from Dorson's perspective, they were at their best superficial and at their worst "uncritical encomiums" that catered to the marketplace and not to a true presentation of what folklore is. Dorson sought to undermine the respectability of what he perceived as the vulgarization of the study of folklore and of folklore material itself. Publications that pretended to be folklore and lacked verification of their authenticity or any scholarly apparatus that might be used to shore up their claims to authenticity needed to be denounced. He intended the term "fakelore" to "become a rallying cry against the distortion of a serious subject" (Dorson 1950). The critical need was to educate the public about the true nature of folklore and to shore up the scholarly integrity of fledgling folklore-studies programs that were at the time beginning to appear on American university campuses.

Now that the study of folklore is firmly established in academia, folklorists are looking again at the material once labeled "fakelore" with a different purpose. Terms such as "folklure" and "folklorismus" seek to legitimize scholarly interest in the commercialization of folklore for mass-marketing and tourism purposes. Links between popular culture and folklore can be explored once the actual province of each had been understood within the discipline of folklore.

Richard Sweterlitsch

References

Denby, Priscilla. 1971. Folklore in the Mass Media. *Folklore Forum* 4:113–121.
Dorson, Richard M. 1950. Folklore and Fakelore. *American Mercury* 70:335–343.
———. 1971. Fakelore. In *American Folklore and the Historian.* Chicago: University of Chicago Press, pp. 3–14.
Sullenberger, Tom E. 1974. Ajax Meets the Jolly Green Giant: Some Observations on the Use of Folklore and Myth in American Mass Marketing. *Journal of American Folklore* 87:53–65.

See also Bunyan, Paul; Folklore; Lovers' Leaps; Magarac, Joe; Pecos Bill

Family Folklore

Traditional behavior learned through oral transmission and/or customary example and shared among family members who may or may not consciously regard it as important or distinctive to their family life. A diverse range of genres constitutes family folklore, including family stories, proverbial expressions, songs, nicknames, customs, rituals, foodways, and folk arts and crafts. Some of these traditions may have been observed by past generations, while others are created and enacted in the course of but one generation. Important factors that affect family folk tradition include ethnicity, regional culture, religion, socioeconomic class, and family size and structure. For example, the number of family members affects the number of times families celebrate family members' birthdays each year, which could influence the nature of the birth-

Four generations of an Italian American family hold a reunion, to which several persons have brought ancestral photographs. Pueblo, Colorado, 1992. Photo Ken Light. American Folklife Center.

day celebration tradition; religious beliefs shape the nature of a family's Passover or Easter observance; and ethnicity and ethnic identity may affect what a family eats and drinks in everyday life and on festive occasions.

Folklore studies of family culture in the past have usually concentrated either on the study of a noteworthy folk tradition practiced within a particular family (for instance, folk pottery or folksong), or on traditional narrative shared among family members, often across generations, about the family past. In the former, folklorists have focused on a specific folk-art tradition performed by the family for the community; in the latter, on personal-experience stories or legends shared within the family unit and dealing with family life and history.

Mody C. Boatright's essay "The Family Saga as a Form of Folklore" (1958) was one of the first American folklore studies to concentrate on family legends based on traditional motifs. Later studies of family folk narrative tend to deal with historical personal-experience stories and their transformation into third-person legendary narrative as one generation passes them on to the next. Past family-folklore studies have also treated family foodways and religious traditions; however, few American folklorists have described and analyzed secular custom and ritual in lengthy, detailed ethnographies. Theodore C. Humphrey's essay "A Family Celebrates a Birthday: Of Life and Cakes" (1991) is one of the few discussions of the birthday celebration in American family life, certainly a widespread tradition with many variations. American sociologists, however, have examined family custom and ritual since mid-cen-

tury, when the James H.S. Bossard and Eleanor S. Boll study of family ritual appeared (1949).

The mass media, new technologies, and commercial merchandising increasingly affect family folklore, but in no way do they discourage it. In fact, sometimes they facilitate the maintenance of traditions or the creation of new ones. For example, an artificial Christmas tree is not a folk artifact in and of itself, but how the tree is decorated (even with commercial ornaments), where it is placed, and the customary music, foods, and behavior associated with its decoration—all make up a holiday folk tradition that is important in many American families. Annual television specials during the Christmas season are by no means "folk theater," but as a family views a particular holiday special year after year, the event becomes a ritualized holiday observance for its members. Changes in camera and video technology affect family photography and the conventional "family photograph album" and "home movie." However, traditional content, themes, and visual images continue to appear in family videos viewed on the television screen and computerized programs of family photographs.

Family members may take for granted many kinds of behavior within the family as "the way we do it," and may not conceptualize the behavior as family folklore because it is so familiar to them. Everyday traditions in family life are as important as the festive traditions that first come to mind. Just as significant as holiday rituals, family reunions, and religious rites of passage in family life are weekday foodways, mealtime prayers, gardening, housekeeping duties and responsibilities, the uses of individual and collective space in the home, and vacation travel customs—all are family traditions that deserve the folklorist's scrutiny.

As social historians and sociologists have revised their conceptualization of the American family in recent years, so have folklorists expanded and reconsidered their conceptualization of family folk tradition. The nuclear-family model—father as breadwinner, mother as homemaker, children nourished by generational continuity—no longer represents the reality of contemporary family life. In fact, most social historians of the American family question whether it was ever as vigorously and positively maintained as commonly believed. The distinction between the "horizontal" family (viewed at any given moment in time) and the "vertical" family (viewed over time across generations) is helpful in clarifying the definition of family, as is the distinction between "family" and "household" (Roush 1994:62, 65–66).

Family counselors, social-work agencies, and the media have increasingly addressed issues of dysfunction, abuse, and emotional trauma within American families, both reflecting and stimulating public discussions of American family life and the politics of family-related legislation. As a consequence, folklorists have initiated studies that range beyond the positivist functionalism of past family-folklore studies, which emphasized the celebratory and focused almost exclusively on issues of positive family identity. In the last decade of the 20th century, they are expanding their definitions of family and the kinds of behavior to be studied as family folk tradition. In addition to the more conventional family-folklore subject matter like family narrative and foodways, new research interests include folk tradition in gay and lesbian families, customary housekeeping and gender roles, disciplinary traditions in the family and their relation to family values, dyadic tradition shared by childless couples, rituals of separation and exclusion, strategies of celebration innovated to meet the constraints of time and energy, the hybridization of customs in blended families, and the divorce story as a family-narrative genre. Such family folklore studies reflect concerns at large in American society about variations in family life.

Larry Danielson

References

Adler, Thomas A. 1981. Making Pancakes on Sunday: The Male Cook in Family Tradition. *Western Folklore* 40:45–54.

Boatright, Mody C. 1958. The Family Saga as a Form of Folklore. In *The Family Saga and Other Phases of American Folklore,* by Mody C. Boatright, Robert B. Downs, and John T. Flanagan. Urbana: University of Illinois Press, pp. 1–19.

Bossard, James H.S., and Eleanor S. Boll. 1949. *Ritual in Family Living.* Philadelphia: University of Pennsylvania Press.

Danielson, Larry, guest ed. 1994. Family Folklore. *Southern Folklore* 51.

Morgan, Kathryn L. 1980. *Children of Strangers: The Stories of a Black Family.* Philadelphia: Temple University Press.

Roush, Jan. 1994. On Teaching Family Folklore: A Cautionary Tale. *Southern Folklore.* (Special Issue) 51:61–71.

Troll, Lillian E., ed. 1988. Rituals and Reunions. *American Behavioral Scientist* (Special Issue) 31:619–716.

Wilson, William A. 1991. Personal Narratives: The Family Novel. *Western Folklore* 50:127–149.

Zeitlin, Steven J., Amy J. Kotkin, and Holly Cutting Baker. 1982. *A Celebration of American Family Folklore.* New York: Pantheon.

See also Anniversaries; Birthdays; and entries on individual holidays

Farmers

People engaged in the growing of crops on farms in whose cultural life the traditions surrounding this engagement play a significant role. The farm is both an economic and a social unit, worked by members of a single family. The traditions of these rural agricultural groups vary depending on geographic region, available resources, and ethnic and religious traditions. The resulting cultural life is a mix of elements both agricultural and nonagricultural, traditional and assimilated.

Farmers have been the object of folklore studies since the beginnings of the discipline, when European scholars described rural folk cultures as unchanging and folklore as "survivals" from earlier cultural stages, "in our time but not of it." For folklorists in North America, the French Canadian *habitants* and the Pennsylvania Dutch were the archetypes of the traditional farmers, members of an industrious culture with customs of European origin. This approach, evolutionist in theory and archaeological in method, emphasized the collection and preservation of farmers' oral literature, customs, and folk music. While it included elements of folklife, it generally neglected material culture. An excellent encapsulation of the aims of the scholarship of the time appears in a report on a farmers' proverb, "Your tongue is hung on a swivel and is loose at both ends" (Smith 1948). Its subject is a member of the family (the wife of the folklorist's own grandfather). Its logic is based on familiarity with the swivel and other farm implements of the day. The "author," who comes from a cultural region where the "habitual use of proverbs" survives, himself has a "gift for language." In one story from New Hampshire, a clergyman congratulates a farmer on his success with a rocky plot of land, saying, "'You and God certainly have done a nice piece of work here.' 'Yeah,' the man answered, "you ought to have seen it when God had it all alone'" (Botkin 1947:172). Under government sponsorship during the 1930s and 1940s, this and other farmers' stories were collected in the field or from older written sources and published in many larger collections of regional folklore.

From the second half of the 20th century, folklore scholars began to move beyond the mere placing of farmers' lore in a historic and geographic context. Spurred by the decline of rural farming communities, and in keeping with the reorientation of their discipline from product to producer, folklorists shifted their focus from the study of traditional farms per se

Farmhouse, built in the 1890s. Weeping Water, Nebraska. Collection J. W. Love.

to the study of local, regional, or ethnically distinct communities of farmers. They forged links with the many academic disciplines whose paths met at the study of farmers' traditional life. They began to deal with the diverse picture of rural traditions in the United States and Canada, the result of many different traditions laid one over the other as immigrant groups arrived to farm the land. Yet, for the most part, folklorists have chosen to focus tightly on a region or a rural craftsperson, leaving larger issues (such as women as farmers) to historians or sociologists. Four areas of study have been perhaps the most productive to folklorists: material culture studies, cultural geography, history (especially oral history), and folklife study. In addition to expanding our picture of rural agricultural traditions, the bridges built between these areas and folklore have meant that the term "farmers" can now include many who formerly were not considered farmers per se, such as women, African Americans, and Native Americans.

Material-culture studies generally have been concerned with the history of a particular craft, or have focused on the craftsperson and his or her tradition. Thus, we can read of rural potters or quilters (or pots or quilts), and only indirectly of the craftsperson as farmer. Yet, material-culture scholars have contributed to our understanding of different farming traditions through study of the physical and cultural characteristics of farm types. The types of farm that became dominant in the United States and Canada carried on the traditions of northwest European colonists. They were conceived of as self-sufficient family units, yet tied to the community through shared religious beliefs and market economy. The chief variants of this type developed along cultural lines. The *habitant's* farms of Quebec stretched along the rivers like towns along roads, forming part of an extended community that included those engaged in river traffic. Among the English and Swiss-German religious groups of Pennsylvania, the farm was conceived as more independent, indeed as the image of an orderly and enduring religious community. Farms were occupied by one family over several generations. Their choice of land, their building style, and the planned diversity of their crops and livestock reflect the desire of these farmers for permanence. The agricultural traditions of the Scotch-Irish conceived of the raising of crops as a part-time occupation, augmented by cottage industry. These farmers chose poorer, cheaper land, often on the hills rather than in the valleys. They were also less inclined to settle permanently.

While the northwest European model was carried westward by settlers of the pioneer period to become predominant in the North American Midwest, the Scotch-Irish tradition prevailed in Appalachia and in the Southern Uplands. Cultural geographical studies have helped trace the migration patterns of these settlers by tracing the spread of variant building traditions, such as those for barns, fences, and farmhouses, or for farm layout and village planning. Some folklorists, using linguistic models, have made detailed examinations of the "grammar" of the aesthetic behind such building traditions to understand the psychology of rural agricultural communities (Glassie 1975).

The diaries of settlers on the frontier and the accounts of those days by their children or grandchildren are mines of information about regional and rural history as well as traditional practices. The process of clearing new land was directed toward establishing the farm and involved the same techniques as farming, such as choice and management of draft animals. Yet, farmers seem to have recognized by 1870 that the farming life their fathers had come to regard as unchanging was, in fact, facing great change (Van Wagenen 1953). Developments such as rail transportation and mechanized farming in the form of harvesters, balers, and especially tractors put pressure on farmers to put aside traditional practice, practical experience, even government incentives and switch to raising a single cash crop. Amish farmers continue to follow a daily and a seasonal cycle of traditional work—feeding livestock, hauling manure, and repairing harnesses and equipment in the winter, and plowing, seeding, and harvesting in the summer—yet the inroads made by mechanization have not left these religious communities untouched (Hostetler 1963).

Scholars of rural agriculture have faced the passing of traditional farming and the decline in the number of farmers by studying the accompanying economic and social changes. Among the methods developed for this was the use of personal interviews to construct an oral history of events. This method has been used to reconstruct and understand life as lived by members of farming communities in Appalachia (Montell 1983) and elsewhere. While some oral-history projects have resulted in scholarly treatments of a community's history, others, such as the *Foxfire* books, have been successful grass-roots efforts to record traditional folkways (Wigginton 1972 and later). In particular, folklife studies and oral histories have enlarged our understanding of the ways in which women contributed as members of farming communities.

Folklorists have broadened their view of farmers by joining farming communities to record the experience of farmers from inside (Welsch 1990). Enough of these books have appeared that they have become a genre, with a necessary focus on region. Working in the public sector, folklorists have also made farmers' lives accessible and more comprehensible to the public. The 1991 Festival of American Folklife in Washington, DC made farm life a major focus. Museums such as the Farmers' Museum at Cooperstown, New York, serve as reconstructed communities for public education and as research facilities, and are geared toward the presentation and understanding of rural folklife and the everyday processes of farm life. At Plimoth Plantation in Massachusetts, archaeological evidence was used to study the material culture and illuminate the folklife of the English Pilgrims. In addition, evidence of unusual diet and house construction not matching the English traditions revealed the presence of Black farmers in Plymouth after the Revolution.

Two trends still hinder the researcher of the traditions of farmers. First, agricultural traditions that coexisted with the dominant farm type are seldom studied beyond the local level, in articles in journals of regional folklore. Few comprehensive studies by folklorists exist that encompass these traditions and their impact (for one such study, see Stilgoe 1991). Second, the majority of studies of rural agricultural people or communities continue to assume the farm and focus on the craft or craftsperson, the storyteller or the storytelling. Folklore about farming itself seems to fly past in snippets in the midst of the study of the community or its products.

John Cash

References

Botkin, B.A. ed. 1947. *A Treasury of New England Folklore.* New York: Crown.

Festival of American Folklife. 1991. Washington, DC: Smithsonian Institution.

Glassie, Henry. 1975. *Folk Housing in Middle Virginia.* Knoxville: University of Tennessee Press.

Hostetler, John A. 1963. *Amish Society.* Baltimore: Johns Hopkins University Press.

Montell, William Lynwood. 1983. *Don't Go up Kettle Creek: Verbal Legacy of the Upper Cumberland.* Knoxville: University of Tennessee Press.

Smith, Grace Partridge. 1948. Notes and Queries: A Yankee Proverb, Vermont Variety. *Journal of American Folklore* 61:392–393.

Stilgoe, John R. 1991. *Common Landscape of America, 1580 to 1845.* New Haven, CT: Yale University Press.

Van Wagenen, Jared, Jr. 1953. *The Golden Age of Homespun.* Ithaca, NY: Cornell University Press.

Welsch, Roger. 1990. *It Ain't the End of the Earth, but You Can See It from Here: Tales of the Great Plains.* New York: Villard.

Wigginton, Eliot, ed. 1972. *The Foxfire Book.* Garden City, NY: Doubleday.

See also Folk Museums, Folklife Movement

Feminist Approaches to Folklore

Decentering of male-centered (androcentric) cultural paradigms in order to make room for female voices and rhetorics. In America the first wave of feminism culminated in 1920 with the passage of the nineteenth Amendment to the Constitution, granting women the right to vote. The second wave began for many women when they read Betty Friedan's *The Feminine Mystique* (1963), Simone de Beauvoir's *The Second Sex* ([1949] 1970), Kate Millett's *Sexual Politics* (1970), or Shulamith Firestone's *The Dialectic of Sex* (1972). Arguing that much of Western civilization is patriarchal (not only male-centered, but also organized and controlled so that women are subordinated to men), these works initiated the process of teaching women to resist the ways in which women are conditioned to participate in their own objectification by, and subordination to, the various relations of power in society.

Feminism happened when women realized that the "personal" was "political," when, as is now frequently noted, "women learned to say 'I.'" By the 1980s, feminism had also learned just how political that "I" could be when poor and working-class women, women of different racial and ethnic identities, and women who were bisexual and lesbian accused the women's movement of the 1960s and 1970s (which had frequently represented women's lives through a use of the communal "we" as if all were Anglo, middle class, and heterosexual) of being essentialistic and appropriative. These voices and the variety of discursive practices variously adapted by feminism (from psychoanalytic, Marxist, poststructuralist, and postmodernist theories) have made feminism of the 1990s a multivocal project.

Although feminism of the 1990s has no single theory or practice, there are points of affinity among feminists. Gender (the traits, whether biologically inherited or culturally constructed, that constitute what is masculine and what is feminine) is understood as being fundamental to lived experience, while the multivocality of that experience (the differences among women according to race, class, age, occupation, religion, sexuality, and the like) is also acknowledged. Sexual inequality is asserted to be a cultural construct. Thus feminism generally seeks (1) through "feminist critique" to disclose the ways in which culture and the rhetorics through which culture is constructed have been shaped and dominated by male perspectives, (2) through ethnographic fieldwork, oral-history projects, and literary history to record present and retrieve past female lives, and (3) through what is termed "gynocriticism" to uncover, discover, and/or develop a female-centered language and theory of aesthetics. From inception, the feminist project has called for both intellectual and political participation. In other words, it has endeavored not only to document and interpret culture, but to transform and create culture as well.

Feminism reached the discipline of folklore in the 1970s. The first issue of *Folklore Women's [Feminist] Communication* was published in the fall of 1973, and two collections of essays focusing on women's experiences followed: *Women and Folklore* (1975), edited by Clair R. Farrer, and an issue of *Frontiers: A Journal of Women Studies* that published a special cluster of essays on the topic "Women as Verbal Artists" (1978). The inscription of women's lives, points of view, and heretofore marginalized genres was to continue throughout the 1980s and into the 1990s. Rosan A. Jordan and Susan J. Kalcik edited and published *Women's Folklore, Women's Culture* (1985), a collection of essays theoretically indebted to Mchelle Zimbalist Rosaldo's (and the other contributors to *Woman, Culture, and Society* [1974]) interest in the separation between domestic or private (female) and public (male) spheres in cultural production. The *Journal of American Folklore* followed with a special issue in 1987 on "Folklore and Feminism," ed. by Bruce Jackson, and the *Journal of Folklore Research* published a special issue in 1988 on "Feminist Revisions in Folklore Studies," edited by Beverly J. Stoeltje, both of which began to more fully theorize women's lives in respect to extant power relations. In 1990 Camilla A. Collins edited a special issue of *Southern Folklore*, "Folklore Fieldwork: Sex, Sexuality, and Gender," which inscribed the transformative effects of feminist discourses on fieldwork relationships, methodologies, and interpretive strategies, thus mapping the extent to which American folkloristics had become a feminized discipline.

While the disclosing of androcentric claims to univer-sality as gendered discourse was to open spaces for female voices, the retrieval and foregrounding of these voices was the central feature of early feminist applications in folklore studies. Until the 1970s, the majority of published fieldwork had been collected by male researchers from male informants and had focused on canonical genres (such as folktale and legend, folksong and ballad), relegating such genres as gossip, anecdote, and personal narrative, frequently associated with women's performances, to marginal status. As Farrer noted in her Introduction to *Women and Folklore*, "the general trend throughout the history of the *Journal* [of American Folklore] has been to rely on data from women for information about health, charms, some games, and various beliefs and customs but in other areas to use women as informants only when men informants were unavailable" (Farrer 1975). To this Marta Weigle added the further observation that not only were important genres overlooked, but such practices "fail to record versions they feel to be 'inferior,' and misconstrue the native system of artistic genres and critical evaluation" (Weigle 1978). Weigle was to go on to foreground the genre of women's gossip-anecdote in relation to folk belief, in particular its ability to engender cosmic order(s), establishing a new paradigm, "gossip as myth," and thereby critiquing hegemonic dichotomies between "the mundane and the theoretical," between "data and theory" (*Spiders and Spinsters* [1982] and *Creation and Procreation* [1988]). In doing so, Weigle began to map the possibilities of what Margaret Mills has more recently referred to as "low theory" in her argument for folklorists "to see how 'experience near' (from our subject's point of view) our theoretical constructions can be" (Mills 1993).

Susan J. Kalcik, working with the structure and aesthetics of women's personal narratives, identified what she called the "kernel story," a story that emerges from the conversational context, the point of which may shift to meet the needs of the conversational group. For example, one woman's brief anecdote about a female student who consciously tried to get lower grades than her boyfriend because he "had threatened to take back his fraternity pin if she continued to get a higher grade-point average than he did" might be expanded upon later by the original narrator or by other women in the group such that it becomes a commentary on either "how men do not like women to display their intelligence" or how "women are stupid to deny their abilities." Eventually, as a traditional piece of the group's repertoire, such kernel stories might be alluded to, "Right, like X's student," in order to support another story. Such storytelling appears to be collaborative in nature, a process of women narrating together, and thus problematizes the disciplinary dominance of monovocal, authoritative modes of storytelling (Farrer 1975).

Analogously, Elaine J. Lawless—working with the life stories of female ministers (*Handmaidens of the Lord* [1988] and *Holy Women, Wholly Women: Sharing Ministries through Life Stories and Reciprocal Ethnography* [1993])—has suggested that women construct their life stories as "deeply-explored blocks of experience" that give to their narratives a "many-layered, multi-textured structure" that is different from the "linear, objective, goal-oriented" stories told by men (Lawless 1991). Furthermore, while documenting how female ministers claim discursive space for themselves in relation to a traditionally male sphere of cultural production by invoking metaphors of nurturing and motherhood, Lawless also began to explore a "reciprocal ethnography" that intensifies the collaborative nature of a subject-subject relationship between ethnographers and the people with whom they work.

The necessity for women to negotiate carefully their discursive spaces as well as the various ways in which this is done has been further explored by Joan N. Radner and colleagues *(Feminist Messages: Coding in Women's Folk Culture* [1993]), who have documented stategic coding practices women use as a means of expressing covert ideas that the dominant culture and, in some cases, they themselves would be adverse to. For example, as Susan S. Lanser has argued, a woman's claim or performance of domestic incompetence (an inability "to cook, bake, knit, sew, or keep a clean house") may function as a coded rejection "not only of the task in question but also of a culturally constructed female role." The woman claims "'I can't' when she means but cannot say 'I won't'" (in Radner 1993).

Moving female experience from the margins to the center of cultural production has meant, on the one hand, describing the function of telephone gossip among two elderly immigrant Hungarian American women as they negotiated performance space and, on the other hand, describing aesthetic differences in performances between female and male family members. It has meant collecting legends and memories from among Mexican American women that disclose the physical and emotional vulnerability of their lives while documenting the possibility that motifs found in both female and male narratives can mean different things depending on the performer's gender. It has meant exploring female verbal aggression and female erotica, an Anglo woman's making of teddy bears, African American women's "rap," Kodiak midwifery, Mormon women's visionary narratives, and a Sicilian American woman's "giving an altar" during a St. Joseph's Day feast. And it has meant listening closely while women perform and/or explain the significance of quilting and rug making or describe the uses and meanings of the interior spaces of the dwellings in which they live and work.

But while documenting women's lives and communicative forms has been a primary focus in feminist applications to folklore, without early and continuing feminist critique the invisible gaps in academic discourse would not have been made visible and thereby open to female voicings of female experiences. Early forms of feminist critique (frequently referred to as the "images of women approach") focused attention on representations of women in androcentric speech and literature (oral and written). In folklore studies, Kay Stone, for example, added her voice to what was to become an onslaught of revisionary treatises on fairy tales, particularly those canonized within American popular culture that represented women as either passive and good or active and evil. More recently, Maria Herrera-Sobek has examined the stereotypical image of Mexicanas and Chicanas in Mexican balladry *(The Mexican Corrido, A Feminist Analysis* [1990]).

By the 1980s, the "culture as text" metaphor, developed in the discourses of cultural studies and symbolic anthropology, made the broad rubric of culture accessible to methods of critique initially developed in literary studies, and textual-critical activities were applied to culture in general. In folklore studies, feminist cultural critique is exemplified by Barbara A. Babcock's analysis of process-commodity relations in respect to the lives of three women (Helen Cordero, a Cochiti potter and inventor of the storyteller doll; Elsie Clews Parsons, a folklorist and feminist of the early 1900s; and the Statue of Liberty). In the essay, Babcock discusses the effects of commodity fetishism on folk artists and material-cultural studies, the invisibility of female academics and their work, and male appropriation of the female body for use as a semiotic object (Jackson 1987). Analogously, Robbie E. Davis-Floyd disclosed the medical establishment's rituals for enculturating women into a "technological model of reality" by means of a paradigm that represents the female body as a defective machine and technology as necessary for successful reproduction (Jackson 1987). M. Jane Young analyzed the actual and symbolic processes of women's reproductive power in Western Puebloan identity (Jackson 1987). And Beverly J. Stoeltje examined the construction and negotiation of female gender in rodeo festivals (1988), while Dianne Dugaw historicized negotiated constructions of gender and sexuality in respect to British and American balladry *(Warrior Women and Popular Balladry, 1650–1850* [1989]).

Whether working from an essentialist, biologist definition of gender, from a constructionist definition of gender, or from a more mediated position; whether exploring the separation between domestic (female) and public (male) spheres of cultural production or the significance of "mothering" and an ensuing "ideology of reproduction"; or whether emphasizing oppression or repression, raising consciousness or exploring the unconscious, disclosing power relations or exploring pleasure—American feminist applications to folklore have had a salient affect on the discipline. This has been felt most strongly in discussions of fieldwork.

Where older models of ethnography were governed by the essentializing discourse of scientific objectivism and an implicit empiricism that constructs the scientist as subject and that which is studied as object, contemporary feminist (female and male) fieldworkers discuss subject-subject relations that emphasize contiguity and reciprocity, acknowledge the ethnographer's subjectivity and the ethnographic subject's agency, accept the decentering effects of multivocality, and court a dialogic discourse. Where older models of ethnography were governed, as Debora Kordish has disclosed (Jackson 1987), by themes of colonialist conquest and penetration or, as Miriam Camitta has suggested, by a male model invoking a "sharp delineation of the self from the other" defined by "separation and autonomy" (Collins 1990), contemporary ethnography has begun to explore themes of surrender and of affiliation and connectedness. Because representational practices construct and thereby create culture, researchers in a feminized folkloristics now must ask, along with Gayatri Chakravorty Spivak, "not merely who am I? but who is the other woman [man]? How am I naming her [him]? How does she [he] name me?" (*In Other Worlds: Essays in Cultural Politics* [1988]). To this Margaret Mills has cogently added that we must also "ask for *whom* we are translating [disclosing meaning] and to what end?" (Collins 1990).

Cathy Lynn Preston

References

DeCaro, F.A. 1983. *Women and Folklore: A Bibliographic Survey.* Westport, CT: Greenwood.

Lawless, Elaine J. 1991. Women's Life Stories and Reciprocal Ethnography as Feminist and Emergent. *Journal of Folklore Research* 28:35–60.

Mills, Margaret A. 1993. Feminist Theory and the Study of Folklore: A Twenty-Year Trajectory toward Theory. *Western Folklore* 52:173–192.

Weigle, Marta. 1978. Women as Verbal Artists: Reclaiming the Daughters of Enheduanna. *Frontiers: A Journal of Women Studies* 3:1–9.

See also Coding in American Folk Culture; Gender and Folklore; Postmodernism

Festival

A time set aside for celebration. The American festival of the late 20th century can be traced to earlier religious revival meetings, political gatherings, and Saturday night dances. Annually there are more than 3,000 festivals held in the United States, so the student of festivals is confronted with a bewildering variety of events. At the most basic level, there are homegrown, grass-roots festivals organized by and for a particular community.

Since even grass-roots festivals involve considerable planning to bring together people and resources, they must be calendared events. Many of them come from the older agricultural year and are structured around a particular crop such as the watermelon, peanut, or eggplant—whatever is of economic and symbolic importance to the particular community. Such planned-for events contrast with the everyday, notably the workaday, world. Ceremonial events underscore the special, nostalgic, traditional nature of the festival. Festivities suggest evoking the spirit of fun, of entertainment, play, and games.

Sometimes these basic homegrown festivals evolve in order to make the event understandable and appealing to outsiders. Then, as organizers discover that they can attract wider audiences and greater profits, they typically work actively to attract tourists and consumers. The resulting event may still have folk roots, but it tends to move in the direction of mass popular culture.

The oldest grass-roots festival in the United States is the Fiesta de Santa Fe, which seems to have started in 1715. The term "folk festival" came into use much later; one of the first uses was in 1892 to describe performances of traveling musicians in Virginia. By the early 1900s, "folk festival" had been used in other areas of the country to describe the performances of immigrants. Large-scale folk festivals are a 20th-century development. In 1927 Bascom Lamar Lunsford (1882–1973), a small-town lawyer interested in the old-time music in his area, began the Mountain Dance and Folk Festival in Asheville, North Carolina, to celebrate southern Appalachian music and dance. His festival differed little from other fiddle contests that began during the same decade, but his title showed that this event was, in part, aimed at tourists. Yet, much of the original audience for the festival was composed of people who knew the performers because they were friends and neighbors.

Later, the brilliant and eccentric Sarah Gertrude Knott (1895–1984), a woman of considerable energy and vision, chartered the National Folk Festival in St. Louis, Missouri. Along with her business manager, Major M.J. Pickering (1883–1957), she held the first National Folk Festival there in 1934. This festival differed significantly from the festival originated by Lunsford. For one thing, it was multicultural, rather than monocultural. Among the performers at Knott's festival were American Indians, French singers, cowboy singers, Mexican American musicians, sacred-harp singers, singers of sea chanteys, lumberjacks, costumed dancers of different ethnic origins, and an Afro-American choir. Knott included both "survival" performers (those whose performances represented an unbroken chain of tradition from their own family and community) and "revival" performers (those who learned performance skills from a culture other than their own). The term "revival" persists, but few "revival" performers are reviving anything from their own culture, and there is little evidence that the "revived" art continues in its new family.

The National Folk Festival, founded in 1934, is the oldest consecutive folk festival in the United States. It is produced by the National Council for the Traditional Arts, a private, nonprofit corporation. In the early years, the festival moved from city to city, depending on the vicissitudes of financing. Sponsoring cities included New York, Philadelphia, Chattanooga, Chicago, Cleveland, and Washington, DC. For a time in the 1970s and early 1980s, the festival seemed to have found a permanent home at Wolf Trap Farm Park in Vienna, Virginia. However, it has once again moved from place to place. The decision to move about this time was made not so much for financial reasons as ideological ones. Organizers reasoned that once communities hosted the National Folk Festival, they would be in a good position to start up their own local celebrations. Recent locations under this plan have included the Akron-Cleveland area of Ohio; Lowell, Massachusetts; Johnstown, Pennsylvania; and Chattanooga, Tennessee.

Because folk festivals require dedication, time, and energy, as well as money, few have had the staying power of the National Folk Festival. For example, the Pennsylvania Folk Festival was launched with good intentions and high hopes in the 1930s. George Korson (1899–1967), a journalist and collector of folklore in Allentown, Pennsylvania, put on a small festival featuring anthracite-coal miners in 1932. This success-

During the annual Santa Rosalia Festival, men carry the saint's statue through the streets. Monterey, California, 1989. Photo Ken Light. American Folklife Center.

ful festival came to the attention of the president of Bucknell University, who invited Korson to come to Lewisburg as director of the newly created Pennsylvania Folk Festival. Like the National Folk Festival, Korson's festival performers included ethnic dancers, occupational groups, and American Indians. Although Korson held festivals at Bucknell in 1936 and 1937, the Pennsylvania Folk Festival could not overcome the combined effects of the Depression and World War II gas rationing.

Once the war was over, there was increased leisure and tourism, spurred in part by plentiful gasoline that cost only 15 cents a gallon. One of the striking developments of the postwar period was the monocultural festival, celebrating a single minority culture in a particular region. For example, in 1950 a group of professors from Franklin and Marshall College started the Kutztown Folk Festival in Pennsylvania, celebrating the folk culture of the Pennsylvania "Dutch" (Germans). Although the more secular Pennsylvania Germans support the festival both as participants and as visitors, the Amish and the Mennonites, who are depicted, do not. The festival is particularly strong in crafts such as bread baking, chair caning, and blacksmithing. It also includes dramatic creations that purport to show the religious strife that led to immigration, and dramatic skits featuring mock trials, hangings, and weddings. These costumed skits are, however, highly romantic in concept. Other monocultural festivals include the Cajun Festival at Abbeville, Louisiana, and the annual Crow Fair at Crow Agency, Montana.

A postwar festival with national scope was the Newport Folk Festival in Rhode Island, created after the popular group the Kingston Trio drew large crowds at the 1958 Newport Jazz Festival. In the late 1950s and early 1960s, the Newport Folk Festival featured popular folk celebrities along with traditional performers. The stars helped attract large audiences. However, many who attended had no interest in tradition and came only to hear the stars.

The Festival of American Folklife has loomed over all other festivals since its inception in 1967. Run by the Smithsonian Institution, it is presented on the National Mall in Washington, DC. Originally planned for a week in early October, the festival is now scheduled to coincide with the Fourth of July holiday every year. In the 1970s, fieldworkers for the festival traveled far and wide to identify participants. Some original fieldwork continues and helps ensure the high quality and authenticity of the exhibits and performances. Innovative techniques for presenting traditional folk performers have been developed. Although a few urban folksong revivalists are presented, the emphasis is on traditional folk performers, not only in music, but also in the areas of occupational skills, foodways, crafts, and narratives.

Over the years, the Smithsonian staff has come up with a number of fresh categories for presenting folk culture. One such innovation was the "featured state" program, which started in 1968 with Texas. This device is primarily a way to obtain funding through state legislatures, but it also stimulates fieldwork and challenges folklorists to find new ways to present their findings. For example, in 1982 when Oklahoma was the featured state, a racetrack was set up on the Mall to showcase the excitement of quarter-horse racing. In 1983 when New Jersey was the featured state, a replica of the Atlantic City boardwalk was erected. Similarly, in 1992 when New Mexico was featured, a full-scale adobe house was built. These large-scale structures are created in an attempt to suggest context and to show work skills.

There are numerous folk experiences at the job site, whether blue-collar or white-collar, and these have been grist for folklorists since the 1930s. The Third National Folk Festival, held in Dallas in 1936 as part of the Texas Centennial, offered demonstrations in various work skills. These were expanded in a series the Smithsonian launched in 1971 with a program featuring the folklife of construction workers. Since then, they have presented the folklife of meat cutters, bakers, garment workers, carpenters, cowboys, farmers, stone masons, sheet-metal workers, seafarers, taxi drivers, firefighters, and others. Some of these programs have resulted in publications and documentary films.

In part spurred by the post-1965 increase in federal and state funding for cultural programs and in part encouraged by the example of the Festival of American Folklife, more American colleges and universities began sponsoring folklife festivals in the early 1970s. Some festivals, like the New Jersey Folk Festival at Rutgers University founded in 1975, have evolved from the presentation of hobby crafters and revival performers toward featuring more traditional and ethnic artists. Others, like the Blue Ridge Folklife Festival at Ferrum College in Virginia, emphasized precommercial musical idioms and rich craft traditions from their very beginnings.

Part of what is new is the widespread acceptance of the term "folklife," which was rejected by some early festival organizers such as Sarah Gertrude Knott, who considered it condescending and manipulative. Those who like the term believe it allows them to show facets of culture other than music and dance.

Whatever the origins of these festivals may be, folklorists are increasingly attending them, planning them, and studying them. Yet, the scholarly literature on folk festivals is surprisingly sparse. What little study has been done tends to have been done by folklorists who themselves have had some festival management experience. Understandably, these studies have been addressed to other folklorists who share concerns about such issues as authenticity and the politics of culture. The primary concern of the professional folklorist has been to find and to showcase authentically traditional participants.

For the festival director, the festival is a statement of taste and a managerial challenge. For the staff, a festival represents hard work, a chance to meet old friends, and an opportunity to have intimate backstage access to traditional artists. At its best, the festival is to tradition bearers, both musicians and craftspeople, a validation and affirmation of their art and of their culture. It is somewhat harder to say just what the festival means to its audience. It is clear that entire cities can be drawn into folk celebrations. In 1992 the city of Lowell, Massachusetts, had as many as 186,000 people at its weekend Lowell Folk Festival (a continuation of the National Folk Festival's 1987–1989 stay in that city). That festival, located in the middle of an industrial downtown, enjoyed support from nearly every segment of the population.

Some critics of folk festivals have suggested that most festival goers are not really attentive or knowledgeable about what they are seeing and hearing. Indeed, folklorist Charles Camp has argued that a tourist audience can be counted on to respond positively to *any* exhibit or performance, including a "dead monkey." What Camp was suggesting was that public taste could be excited by anything out of the ordinary and that crowd psychology can be counted on to lure more and more people regardless of the actual merits of the attraction.

If festival audiences will be entertained by anything, what do festivals accomplish that is different from other entertainment? The key here, most folklorists say, is that audience attention is not a relevant index for the festival's success, value, and justification. The important thing to focus on is the festival's impact on the artists. What do folk artists derive from festival participation? It is something much more important than money—a sense of pride and a validation of their art and their culture. Exit interviews with both musicians and craftspeople, with few exceptions, typically confirm that their festival experience gives them renewed confidence, enthusiasm, and pride, which they take back to their home communities.

Fans of folk festivals note that they are expected to meet higher criteria than any other public-performance event. No one expects a symphonic performance to improve the lifestyle and community values the performing artists, but folklorists constantly look for such positive benefits for folk communities at folk events. This seems as much a misunderstanding of performance as it is an affirmation of the positive values of folk performance.

Angus Kress Gillespie

References

Bauman, Richard, Patricia Sawin, and Inta Carpenter. 1992. *Reflections on the Folklife Festival: An Ethnography of Participant Experience.* Bloomington, IN: Folklore Institute.

Camp, Charles, and Timothy Lloyd. 1980. Six Reasons Not to Produce a Folk Festival. *Kentucky Folklore Record* 26:67–74.

Falassi, Alessandro. 1987. *Time out of Time: Essays on the Festival.* Albuquerque: University of New Mexico Press.

Wilson, Joe, and Lee Udall. 1982. *Folk Festivals: A Handbook of Organization and Management.* Knoxville: University of Tennessee Press.

Wolf, Thomas. 1979. *Presenting Performances: A Handbook for Sponsors.* Cambridge: New England Foundation for the Arts.

Yoder, Don. 1974. Twenty-Five Years of the Folk Festival. *Pennsylvania Folklife* 22:2–7.

See also Festival of American Folklife; Fiesta; Mummers; Na-

Noenoe Lewis, Kau`i Zuttermeister, and Hau`oli Lewis perform a hula `auana. *Festival of American Folklife, Smithsonian Institution, Washington, DC, 1984. Photo Adrienne L. Kaeppler. Courtesy of the photographer.*

tional Folk Festival; Powwow; Revivalism; Rodeo; Saint's Day; Solstices, Summer and Winter

Festival of American Folklife

A living exhibition of folklife traditions produced every summer for about two weeks around the Fourth of July by the Smithsonian Institution, outdoors on the National Mall in Washington, DC. The festival is organized by the Smithsonian Institution's Center for Folklife Programs and Cultural Studies as part of its mission to research, present, and conserve the skills, knowledge, aesthetics, and wisdom of grass-roots cultures.

Since its inception in 1967, the festival has featured more than 16,000 musicians, artists, performers, craftspeople, workers, cooks, storytellers, ritual specialists, practitioners of folk medicine, and other exemplars from numerous ethnic, tribal, regional, and occupational cultures. It typically includes daily and evening programs of music, song, dance, celebratory performance, crafts demonstrations, cooking demonstrations, storytelling, illustrations of workers' culture, and narrative sessions for discussing cultural issues. The festival is free to the public and annually attracts up to 1.5 million visitors. As the largest annual cultural event in the U.S. capital, it receives considerable media attention. It has often energized efforts of featured tradition bearers and organizations to continue their own research, education, cultural conservation, and advocacy work. The festival is documented and has stimulated the pro-

duction of other publications and educational products.

The festival was founded by Ralph Rinzler in 1967 under Smithsonian Secretary S. Dillon Ripley and Division of Performing Arts Director James Morris. It was part of a larger effort by Ripley to make the National Mall more accessible to the American public and to make the Smithsonian's programs more exciting and engaging. Rinzler developed the model of a research-based festival from his work at the Newport Folk Festival in Rhode Island and the ideas of Alan Lomax, Charles Seeger, Don Yoder, and others. It was an instant hit in its first year, drawing approximately 400 visitors and the praise of the Washington press. Congressional support followed, as the festival, drawing inspiration from the civil rights movement, represented many people and communities not usually given national attention. Its popularity encouraged the development of the folk-arts program at the National Endowment of the Arts, the American Folklife Center at the Library of Congress, and several state programs. The festival was a centerpiece of the U.S. Bicentennial in 1976, lasting for three months and involving thousands of participants.

The festival developed ways to present cultural traditions, including the concept of researched and curated programs organized around such ideas as the African Diaspora, Old Ways in the New World, occupational cultures, featured states, countries and regions, and various themes, such as cultural conservation. To date (1995), the festival has featured exemplary tradition bearers from 53 nations, every region of the United States, scores of ethnic groups, more than 100 American Indian groups, and some 60 occupational groups. The annual event typically includes several distinct international, regional-state, occupational, and thematic programs. The strongest feature of the festival is its attempt to foreground the voices of tradition bearers as they demonstrate, discuss, and present their cultures. At the festival, tradition bearers, local scholars, and Smithsonian curators speak for themselves, with each other, and to the public. The festival encourages visitors to participate—to learn to sing, dance, eat the foods, and converse with people represented in the program. Like other Smithsonian exhibits, the festival includes museum-quality signs, photo-text panels, a published program book and catalog, learning centers, museum shops, and food concessions. It also attempts to create a physical context for the traditions represented. The event has included, among other things, a horse racecourse (from the Washington Monument to the U.S. Capitol Building), an Indian village with 40-foot-high bamboo and paper statues, a Japanese rice paddy, and a New Mexican adobe plaza.

The festival annually costs about $2 million to produce and is supported by a combination of federal appropriations, state and foreign-country contracts, foundation grants, corporate and in-kind gifts, and concessions income. Diana Parker, who succeeded Rinzler as festival director in 1982, supervises a staff of about 80 and about 100 volunteers a day who work on the festival.

The festival is a research-based production, over the years drawing on the efforts of more than 700 folklorists, cultural anthropologists, ethnomusicologists, and numerous other academic and lay scholars. Research for the event and documentation of it have resulted in complex community-level collaborations, training, and a documentary archival collection held at the Smithsonian and disbursed back to various local institutions. These resources have been used for various publications by fellows, visiting scholars, and the Smithsonian's own folklife-studies series; for Smithsonian Folkways recordings; and for various other educational products.

The festival has had strong impacts on policies, scholarship, and on folks "back home." Many U.S. states and several nations have remounted festival programs and used them to generate laws, institutions, educational programs, documentary films, recordings, museum and traveling exhibits, monographs, and other cultural activities. In many documented cases, the festival has energized local and regional tradition bearers and their communities, and thus helped conserve and create cultural resources. It has provided models for the Black Family Reunion, the Los Angeles Festival, and other major civic cultural presentations, including America's Reunion on the Mall for the Clinton Inaugural.

The festival generates a great deal of publicity and has positively affected cultural tourism in many places. In 1994 it was named the "Top Event in the U.S." by the American Bus Association as a result of a survey of regional tourist bureaus—thus joining previous winners that include the Olympics and the World Expo. The festival has also been the subject of numerous books, documentary films, and scholarly articles.

Richard Kurin

See also Rinzler, Ralph Carter; Smithsonian Institution Center for Folklife Programs and Cultural Studies

Fiddle Music

Traditional music played on a bowed stringed instrument. The fiddle has been in America since European settlement, and its cultural significance is magnified by its prominence in so many different regional and ethnic styles throughout the continent. Fiddle tunes are the backbone of the dance repertoire in many American traditions, and the fiddle has been pressed into other uses as well. Though fiddle music ebbed in favor during the mid-20th century, by the later part of the century the instrument enjoyed a resurgence. The American traditions within which the fiddle is central are variegated, yet not so different as to preclude a remarkable cross-cultural sharing in which the fiddle is instrumental.

The word "fiddle" has long and deep English roots; indeed, the word is cognate with "violin," since the Italian *violino* is, in effect, "little *viol*," and *"viol"* is simply "fiddle" in Romance guise. To musicians in North America, "fiddle" and "violin" are essentially synonymous terms, though the former is apt to be informal and the latter formal. Yet, people persist in inquiring whether the two terms signify different instruments, or at least different musical styles. The sense that the words signify something different reveals a sort of cultural clutter that a little history may illuminate.

Fiddle-like instruments have existed in Europe, Asia, and Africa for millenia. Central Asia, the original domain for the cultivation of the horse, may also be the original domain for the fiddle with its horsehair bow. The modern violin originated in the 16th and 17th centuries in northern Italy, where a cluster of famed instrument makers settled upon a design for the violin that proved vastly popular. The Italian violin spread northward through Europe, displacing other varieties of fiddles as it took hold. By the early 18th century it had established itself as a court instrument in Great Britain, and by the late 18th century the success of a number of violin manufactories, which produced the new violins in quantity, made the instrument accessible to ordinary people. It thus emerged as the central instrument in a revolution in instrumental music and popular dance that swept the British Isles in the later 18th century. That cultural revolution parallels rather neatly the larger social and political revolutions that transformed the English-speaking world in the later 18th century.

Americans often think of American fiddle music as simply continuing and elaborating on the British styles and repertoire. To an extent this is true, but the reality is more complex. The modern repertoires and styles of fiddling in the English-speaking world, and indeed in much of northern and central Europe, took shape in the late 18th and early 19th centuries. During this period, every region participated in the revolution in instrumental music and dance, yet each region developed a particular style and repertoire influenced by its own cultural norms and values. Thus, the modern styles of Scotland, Ireland, England, Quebec, and Maritime Canada, New England/New York/Pennsylvania, and the Piedmont/Appalachian region of the Upper South arose in the same general era. Though the flow of culture was largely from the British Isles to America, these regional styles can best be described, not in terms of ancestry and descent, but as cultural cousins.

There is a classic form to instrumental tunes (and for the most part this means fiddle tunes) in the cultural style that has predominated since the 18th century. A typical tune has two sections (or "strains"), each having a duration of eight or sixteen beats (or "steps," in terms of dance). The strains are subdivided into shorter melodic sections ("phrases"), which may correspond to phrasing in the dance steps. In theory, all of the phrases could be made up of musically distinct material (abcd), but in practice the weaving of similar melodic material into different phrases (similar to rhyme and assonance in verbal art) is aesthetically attractive and aids the memory as well (such as, abac). The first strain is played, then repeated; next, the second strain is played, then repeated; then the entire tune is repeated. The same tune may be repeated in this way until the dance is over, or the music may move from one tune to another in medley fashion.

The relationship of instrumental music to dance is profound. The origin and history of virtually all of the many genres of American fiddle tunes are bound up in dance forms that arose in the later 18th or early 19th century in the British Isles or continental Europe and spread rapidly to the Americas. The reel, a quick-paced instrumental tune in 2/4 or 4/4 originally associated with group dancing in lines (longways), dates from before the late 18th century but became the dominant genre in the new repertory. The jig, which also predates the Revolution but developed a large and complex repertoire soon after, has a structure and rhythm similar to the reel but uses 6/8 meter. The slip jig, popular in Irish music but less common in other regions, uses 9/8 meter. The hornpipe—not the earlier hornpipe genre but a bold new form of the late 18th century—is usually in 4/4 but at a slower pace than the reel; it marks the advent of the modern solo fancy dance, and its phrases or strains characteristically close with three crisp eighth notes, echoing the steps of the dancer.

The beginning of the 19th century brought couple dancing and an array of associated genres to the Americas. First was the 3/4-time waltz, which arrived from Europe via England as the century began. The 1840s brought two new dances of central European provenance, the schottische (a German dance inspired by the European Romantic rage for things Scottish) and the polka. Both were fashionable ballroom dances, yet their enduring popularity in America (especially in the North and Midwest) was buttressed by the simultaneous immigration of German and other ethnic populations from central Europe.

By the mid-19th century, new dances emerged together with clusters of new instrumental repertoire. The clog was the first of a parade of new solo fancy dances leading ultimately to tap dancing in the 20th century. The Negro jig and other adaptations owing to the popular influence of the minstrel stage revealed a more homegrown American trend in dance and instrumental music. By the end of the century, ragtime augured a 20th century of successive dance styles, with a debt to both African American traditions and popular culture, which radiated through and left an imprint on American fiddling.

Though fiddling and dancing seem inextricably intertwined, traditional fiddling has made use of other musical genres in America. The march is a well-known item in many fiddlers' repertoires. Marching is a form of dancing, but the relationship to fiddling goes deeper: Throughout the 19th century, many fiddlers in the United States were also fifers in local fife-and-drum corps, and there was thus a great degree of crossover between fiddling and fifing repertoires. The fiddle also came to be closely associated (especially in the American South) with a class of lyric folksongs that are spritely, playful, allusive, and occasionally obscene. Verses from these songs are often performed by solo fiddlers or ensembles along with the instrumental tune.

Such "instrumental songs"—that is, songs associated with instrumental music, as opposed to the older solo lyric song tradition—may be an element in what might be termed the gradual emancipation of fiddling from dance. So was the use of fiddles to mimic the human voice in slow airs, hymns, and other songs. But for whatever reason, the fiddle, while never losing its connections to dancing, prompted the evolution of a repertoire of tunes that are maintained and performed solely to be listened to. Whether on a back porch, in a saloon, or on a stage, the fiddle became a concert instrument in folk tradition just as it did in popular and elite music.

Several regional styles of fiddling emerged in America, and their broad outline has persisted despite the cultural flux and interchange of the 20th century. The performance style on the fiddle varies most in bowing patterns. Bowing, as fiddlers attest, is the essence of fiddling, and the way one handles the bow defines one's style. In particular, whether one plays each note with a separate bow stroke or joins together more than one note in the same bow stroke ("slur"), and what pattern of slurs and separate strokes are used, creates the musical texture that, in regular recurrence, is called style.

In any region there is a wide variety of bowing styles—fiddling provides room at the local level for stylistic variety, and most localities boast fiddlers who perform at various levels of technical proficiency and stylistic elaboration. But there are larger patterns of stylistic consistency that define regional and subregional styles. In Canada and the Northern United States, the bowing styles reflect a preference for separate bow strokes, and slurs tend to group the notes into twos or fours. In the Southern United States, particularly in the Upper South, there is a preference for bowing patterns that syncopate the musical texture—groupings of notes in a complex fabric of threes and twos, stylized anticipations of the beat, and other devices closely resembling the syncopations characteristic of 20th-century American popular music. The resemblance is not fortuitous, for evidence suggests that these patterns of syncopation first emerged in Southern fiddling, then spread into other zones of folk and popular music.

In the 19th century, both Whites and Blacks participated in Southern fiddling, shaping together the emergent regional style. The syncopated patterns are an African American contribution to folk fiddling—and ultimately, through fiddling, to the popular musical idiom of the civilization at large. This is only the most dramatic example of an ethnic contribution to American fiddling. The early regional styles were all syntheses of an ethnically heterogeneous population assembled from various parts of the British Isles, northern Europe, Africa, the Caribbean, and perhaps even American Indian cultures. The cultural syntheses in fiddling can be said to represent an infusion of ethnic elements into the new regional cultures of America.

Later immigrants also left their mark in fiddling. The Irish immigrants after 1850, populating both urban areas and rural regions, brought the new Irish style with them and influenced both style and repertoire, especially in Canada and in urban areas of the Northern United States. The German immigration similarly had an impact on Midwestern fiddling, and German and Jewish musicians contributed to traditional fiddling styles in another way through their major influence upon American popular and "classical" music, which in turn had an impact on rural folk styles. By the 20th century, immigration had less influence on rural areas and the regional styles rooted there, but urban neighborhoods continued to sustain a wide variety of ethnic musics depending on the fiddle. Since the diffusion of the Italian violin was not limited to Europe and the Americas, but included North Africa, the Middle East, and Asia as well, contemporary immigrants from those parts of the world have brought with them not only a host of fiddling traditions but several that already utilized the modern violin.

The repertoire of American folk fiddling is vast and varied. Tunes are not simply musical fodder, to be shaped and reshaped as fancy directs. Rather, they are treated like precious artifacts, to be acquired, preserved, and rendered faithfully. Most fiddlers do not compose tunes, but some do, both by conscious composition and by using traditional unconscious devices like dreams. The repertoire multiplies both by the addition of new tunes and by the gradual differentiation of tune variants until they become new tunes. The process of differentiation is aided by the wide variation in tune titles and the periodic experimentation with recasting tunes in different "keys," enabling tune variants ultimately to stand side by side in the same regional repertoire.

The repertoire of all of the older regions dates from the 18th century. Though a few tunes may be older, they are not older in their modern instrumental form. The 19th century greatly swelled the repertoires of all of the larger regions of the English-speaking world, but the American regional styles seemed to expand their repertoires exponentially. The Northern and Southern styles are paralleled by Northern and Southern repertoires with surprisingly little overlap until the modern media fostered interregional sharing. The Northern repertoire was to an extent sustained by a vigorous print culture for fiddle tunes. In the South, where musical literacy was confined to the church and the cosmopolitan parlor, printed music had virtually no influence on the larger course of tradition. Meanwhile, the repertoires of Canadian fiddling traditions, including the French traditions, were deeply influenced by the pervasive influence of Irish fiddling.

The older British American fiddling tradition is essentially a solo tradition. By the 19th century, however, the fiddle began to appear in ensembles. Southern tradition generated and lent to popular music the fiddle-banjo ensemble, the banjo being an originally African instrument that took root in the Upper South. Elsewhere, the fiddle began to be accompanied by the pianoforte or the accordion. With the migration of the guitar from parlor to porch in the 20th century, fiddle-and-guitar duos became popular, especially in the South. In general, the fiddle has been part of every kind of ensemble, including jazz bands, and almost always maintains a lead role. The traditions of Southern string bands, bluegrass, and Western Swing bands have perhaps led to the fullest integration of fiddling into a larger ensemble context.

Despite the ubiquity of the Italian violin as a model and the omnipresence of inexpensive store-bought violins (Sears Roebuck Company distributed violins from its catalog by the early years of the 20th century), homemade fiddles have never disappeared from the American scene. From Southern gourd fiddles through the cigar-box fiddle (really a device for children), some homemade fiddles have kept alive the ancient idea of the fiddle as a modest and structurally variable bowed instrument. Meanwhile, other makers have adopted and adapted the Italian model, and their handiwork is readily encountered at fiddlers' conventions throughout the United States. Often the local repairer of fiddles is also an occasional maker of new instruments. It is a testimony both to the popularity of fiddling and to the cross-cultural fascination with the shape, form, and resonance of a violin that violin making continues to thrive as a home art.

The titles of American fiddle tunes are a rich domain for creative expression. Some, like "Bonaparte's Retreat" and "Hull's Victory," commemorate historical events (especially battles) and personages. Many, especially in the South, commemorate places, geographic features, natural phenomena, or the vibrancy of the seasonal round ("Waynesboro," "Three Forks of Cheat," "Forked Deer," "Frosty Morning"), conveying through the fiddler's repertoire, publicly announced, a celebration of sense of place and way of life. Some are named after local persons, including other fiddlers or authors of tunes. Many are named after women. Many are playful, and some of these are obscene ("Dog Shit a Rye Straw"), with the associated obscene verses in turn generating playful title substitutions ("The Dog in Difficulty"). With some regularity, the titles are rhythmic and assonant in a way that seems to evoke the music itself. All in all, American fiddle tune titles, with their knack for celebration, evocation, and playfulness, amount to a sort of imaginative triumph in the art of naming.

As a popular and imagination-provoking instrument, the fiddle is the subject of an array of associated lore. Stories connecting the fiddle with the devil are widespread, and its association with the devil has perhaps prevented its adoption for religious services, even in churches in which electric guitars and drums are safely in the fold. In the South and sometimes elsewhere in America, fiddlers insert rattlesnake rattles into their fiddles. There are legends surrounding the fiddle or in which a fiddle is central. Among fiddlers, the music connects up memory in a thousand ways, and fiddlers often pepper their performances with associated stories and anecdotes that amount to a sort of running contextualization of their art.

The fiddle has historically been a man's instrument; though a few women have always played the fiddle, the late 20th century provided the first generation with numerous women fiddlers of the finest caliber within their regional or ethnic traditions. Hence, much of the lore surrounding the instrument is a sort of men's lore, and some men describe the fiddle itself in feminine terms. It remains to be seen how the character of that lore may shift as women become central to the perpetuation of fiddling as an art.

The fiddling contest, a traditional cultural event honoring fiddling, has a documented history spanning two centuries in America. In the 20th century, fiddlers' conventions, incorporating the fiddling contest but broadening to include a variety of musical and dance traditions, have been popular throughout the country. Also notable in the 20th century (though largely absent in the South) is the sprouting up of dozens of state and regional fiddlers' associations, which sponsor conventions, publish newsletters, sell records, tapes, and souvenirs, and otherwise provide a modicum of modern organization and "networking" to fiddlers and fiddling enthusiasts. The continuing popularity of fiddlers' conventions and fiddle records, and the renascence of dance styles that employ fiddle music, seem to assure that the fiddle will maintain its central role in American folk music in the decades to come.

Alan Jabbour

References

Bayard, Samuel Preston. 1944. *Hill Country Tunes: Instrumental Folk Music of Southwestern Pennsylvania.* Memoirs of the American Folklore Society, Vol. 39. Philadelphia: American Folklore Society.

———. 1982. *Dance to the Fiddle, March to the Fife: Instrumental Folk Tunes in Pennsylvania.* University Park and London: Pennsylvania State University Press.

Blaustein, Richard J. 1971. *Traditional Music and Social Change: The Old-Time Fiddlers Association Movement in the United States.* Ph.D. Diss. Indiana University.

Jabbour, Alan. 1971. *American Fiddle Tunes.* LP with Accompanying Booklet. AFS L62. Washington, DC: Library of Congress.

Wells, Paul F. 1978. *New England Traditional Fiddling: An Anthology of Recordings, 1926–1975.* LP with Accompanying Booklet. JEMF 105. Los Angeles: John Edwards Memorial Foundation.

See also Banjo; Bluegrass; Christeson, Robert Perry; Dance, Folk; Hoedown; Polka; Stubblefield, Blaine "Stub"; Zydeco

Fieldwork

Observing and documenting people where they are and doing what they do, one of the three major modes of acquiring primary information in the social sciences. (The other two—statistical surveys and decontextualized interviews or performances—are rarely used in primary folklore studies.) Fieldwork information is gathered with various media: notebooks, film and video cameras, and audio recorders. Fieldworkers may be after material in active tradition (things people do now) or material in passive tradition (things they know and recognize, and may even have an aesthetic for, but wouldn't, unless solicited, perform or utter). Fieldworkers may join in the events going on ("participant observation"), or they may pretend to be totally outside them (but, except for large community events, like festivals and parades, it is difficult for a fieldworker to be totally invisible). They may be active in their pursuit of information (interviewing, asking for items, asking for explanations), or they may be passive (waiting, observing, recording).

Fieldwork is the key research act for most scholarship in folklore, anthropology, and oral history. More than thirty years ago, Richard M. Dorson wrote, "What the state paper is to the historian and creative work to the literary scholar, the oral traditional text is—or should be—to the student of folklore" (Dorson 1964:1). Although few folklorists now would limit the field-gathered information to "texts," and many wouldn't agree on what the word "text" means any more, Dorson's observation still holds true.

Some folklore studies use preexisting print or electronic media as the source of primary information (studies of the apparent scope, character, and function of folklore materials in commercial advertising or political speeches, say, or folklore in the works of Homer, Shakespeare, or Mark Twain, or folklore on the Internet), but such studies are predicated on ideas of folklore derived from fieldwork. The hypothetical and theoretical work by Milman Parry and Albert Bates Lord on the nature of Homeric performance and composition was extrapolated from their extensive fieldwork among Serbian epic singers. They were able to assert that certain aspects of classical texts were grounded in folklore performance and transmission only because their fieldwork let them understand the character of such performance and transmission.

Even folklore scholars whose work is totally theoretical are dependent for the substance underlying their generalizations and speculation on the fieldwork of others. It would be difficult, if not impossible, to theorize cogently and relevantly about the meaning of folklore in a community unless someone had first gathered information about what folklore exists in that community and what functions the folklore has. Comparative folklore studies (texts or behaviors from different places or times compared for differences in aesthetic or functional aspects) are predicated on the quality and scope of field-gathered material.

Folklorists doing fieldwork may be after specific genres

Supported by Bob Fulcher's knees, Terry Eiler videotapes Mr. and Mrs. Josh Easter as they prepare apples for drying, assisted by folklorist Wally Macnow (left). Surry County, North Carolina, 1978. Photo Lyntha Scott Eiler. American Folklife Center.

or kinds of folk behavior: ballads, recipes, survivals of older traditions in modern communities, modern folkways in technological communities, the nature of folk performance. But it is difficult to know the social meaning of an item of performance without knowing about the conditions of performance. One interprets, for example, the place and function of ballads in a community differently if there are many people in that community who sing many long ballads on a regular basis to a wide local audience that knows and enjoys such ballads, or if the performers sing their songs only when collectors come in from the outside to solicit them. The words and tunes may be the same, but what we make of them will vary. One may analyze and value a particular ballad text differently if it was learned from a book, a recording, a school chum, or a grandparent.

Early folklorists often examined texts alone, much as some literary scholars examine texts of poems as freestanding items. Examination of folklore texts without consideration of collateral information now is rare. Only fieldwork can gather the items, provide information for identifying folk genres, and locate the character of folklore performance in ordinary life.

It is not just that scholars are more sophisticated now about the questions that might be asked; it is also that the equipment available now frees the fieldworker to ask more sophisticated or multidimensional questions. When fieldworkers had to take down all words by hand, approximations of texts or tunes were sufficient. Now that machines capture the words and music, fieldworkers examine context. They examine not just the joke, but who tells which jokes to whom and under what circumstances. How are the jokes interpreted?

What part do those jokes play in the social event going on? How does that redaction of that joke relate to others made of the same words? Is the meaning the same if the context is different? What is the relation between observer and observed? The reflexive movement in field sciences in recent years (cf. Clifford and Marcus 1986) is predicated on a technology that could document the observer at the same time it documented the observed.

Fieldwork has always been a technology-driven endeavor. The kinds of questions one asks of field-gathered material are predicated on the kinds of information that can be gathered in or brought home from the field. Fieldworkers approaching complex events will define their options differently if they have at their disposal and know how to use effectively and efficiently various kinds of image and sound recorders. Fieldworkers studying material culture have different questions and, therefore, may incorporate different technologies than fieldworkers interested in narrative tradition or matters of custom or belief. Fieldworkers trying to document the folklife of a community may need a wider range of technical expertise than fieldworkers focusing on genres or items.

Nineteenth- and early-20th-century folklorists depended on simple recording devices and techniques: notebooks, memory, sound cylinders, and disks. They used bulky devices to record musical performances on cylinders and then on large flat disks. Such machines were capable of recording only a few minutes of performance before they had to be wound up and supplied with a new recording surface. Unless the recordist struck a tuning fork or other device of known frequency at the beginning or ending of the recording, there was no way for a listener to know exactly what speed these recordings were to

During spring branding, Linda Gastañaga interviews Dennis Brown, foreman of the Circle A Ranch. Humboldt County, Nevada, 1978. Photo Carl Fleischhauer. American Folklife Center.

be played. Listeners, therefore, never knew if they were hearing the recording at the right tempo or pitch. Because the equipment was so bulky, movement was difficult and performers often had to be brought to where the machine was located. Cameras used large glass plates and required a great deal of light or a long static time to work.

What the great folklorists of the 19th and early 20th centuries provided us were not so much records of performances, but rather interpretations or versions of performances: They were not only editors of what they found, but also participants in the line of performers they documented. When, say, Vance Randolph spent an evening listening to stories or songs and then went home and wrote up the stories he had heard or sat at the piano and worked out tunes of songs he had heard, he was doing exactly what many folk performers do.

Fieldworkers in the 1990s can gather more complex field documents because they have at their disposal instruments that provide a record of transient detail impossible a half-century ago:

Small automated 35 mm cameras weighing less than a pound zoom from wide-angle to telephoto, focus and set apertures automatically, using film capable of making images in moonlight.

Video cameras easily held in one hand record high-quality images in low light with high-fidelity stereo sound on tapes and rechargeable batteries each lasting two hours. Some of these cameras have stabilization electronics that compensate for horizontal and vertical shake, which means deep zoom shots that only a few years ago were impossible without a tripod can now be done on the fly.

Audio recorders controlled by crystals, the tapes from which are therefore replicable on any crystal-controlled machine anywhere, and, for the really sophisticated, Digital Audio Tape (DAT) machines with real-time coding, produce recordings of great accuracy and dynamic range.

A fieldworker can go out with a full complement of this new equipment—video camera, still camera, crystal-controlled audio recorder, enough tape for a dozen hours of video and sound recording, and enough film for hundreds of separate images—in a shoulder bag.

The effects of all of this technology are multifold. First, the fieldworker is capable of acquiring enormously more information than was ever possible previously. Before mechanical means of reproduction were available, every documentation of even the simplest text was at best an approximation, what someone could write down about an event that could never be redone exactly. With early means of reproduction, it was possible to get crude audio recordings and photographic images made in a narrow range of situations. With modern equipment, it is possible to get extremely accurate sounds and images in a wide range of situations.

Second, the fieldworker has been freed of the need to concentrate on the capture of items (the machines do that very well) and thus allowed to consider more complex questions, such as the way various parts of performance or enactment interrelate or minute complexities of performance itself. The performance analyses of Dennis Tedlock (1983), for example, are impossible without accurate recordings that can be listened to again and again on equipment that lets the analyst find exact moments in performance.

Third, the problem of how to get information has been replaced by what is to be done with the great mass of information so easily acquired. A 19th-century collector of ballads or narratives had no difficulty managing information back home: It was easy enough organizing the songs and stories and providing simple annotations giving the specifics of performance. A 20th-century fieldworker coming home with videotapes, audiotapes, and photographs of a complex event has a far more difficult job of documentation, storage, and analysis. Those machines that are so good at getting information weigh us down with the information they provide.

In the field, the researcher looks at a world of nearly infinite possibility: so many songs, dances, stories, images, recipes, redactions, processes, interactions, moments, movements, facial expressions, and body postures. Once home, the researcher deals with a world of specific and limited possibility: the kind, quality, and range of information brought home, no more, no less. What isn't in the notes, on the film or tapes, or in memory is gone. Subsequent analysis will be predicated not on what existed out there in real life, but on what made it back. Since field documents may be used in studies never envisioned by the fieldworker at the time of the fieldwork, and since analysis may occur long after memory has had time to impose its con-

fusions, proper documentation is of key importance in all fieldwork projects. Without notes on who was doing what and under what conditions the documentation and event occurred, sound recordings, videotapes, and photographs may in time be virtually useless.

Fieldworkers also deal with the problem of preservation. A large portion of the audio cylinders made early in the 20th century have turned to carbon dust. No one knows how long information on audiotapes and videotapes will last. Audiotapes made in the 1960s often have problems in the 1990s of the recording material pulling away from the backing. Notes made with felt-tip pens fade. The most lasting form of documentation is graphite pencil on acid-free paper. Such paper is enormously resistant to decay (left alone, it lasts centuries), and the graphite particles are imbedded in the paper fiber and are not subject to fading or oxidation.

The immediate result of fieldwork is the acquisition of various kinds of documentary materials. A long-term result is involvement in a range of ethical questions and responsibilities. To whom does the material one brings home from the field belong? What obligations are there to privacy and ownership? Who is owed what if material is used in a book, or a recording, or documentary film? What obligations obtain toward other collectors working in the same area or on the same materials? Fieldwork is only one part of a complex series of personal, intellectual, and ethical acts and decisions.

Bruce Jackson

References

Clifford, James, and George Marcus, eds. 1986. *Writing Culture: The Poetics and Politics of Ethnography.* Berkeley: University of California Press.

Dorson, Richard M. 1964. Collecting Oral Folklore in the United States. In *Buying the Wind: Regional Folklore in the United States.* Chicago: University of Chicago Press, pp. 1–20.

Finnegan, Ruth. 1992. *Oral Traditions and the Verbal Arts: A Guide to Research Practices.* London and New York: Routledge.

Georges, Robert A., and Michael O. Jones. 1980. *People Studying People: The Human Element in Fieldwork.* Berkeley: University of California Press.

Goldstein, Kenneth S. 1964. *A Guide for Field Workers in Folklore.* Hatboro, PA: Folklore Associates.

Ives, Edward E. 1964. *The Tape-Recorded Interview: A Manual for Field Workers in Folklore and Oral History.* Knoxville: University of Tennessee Press.

Jackson, Bruce. 1987. *Fieldwork.* Urbana: University of Illinois Press.

Jackson, Bruce, and Edward D. Ives, eds. 1996. *The World Observed: Reflections on the Fieldwork Process.* Urbana: University of Illinois Press.

Tedlock, Dennis. 1983. *The Spoken Word and the Work of Interpretation.* Philadelphia: University of Pennsylvania Press.

At a fiesta, a man tries to knock down dolls in a booth. Taos, New Mexico, 1940. Photo Russell Lee. Library of Congress.

See also Contextual Approach; Ethics in Folklore Research; Folklife Movement; Material Culture; Oral-Formulaic Approach; Performance Approach

Fiesta

Structured celebration at which much traditional behavior is observable. The Spanish word *fiesta* means "celebration," "party," or "feast." In traditional Mexican and Mexican American culture, a fiesta is a Catholic religious celebration, often taking place on a Saint's Day or some other holy day. Although each fiesta is unique to its particular time and place, most fiestas share some or all of a cluster of traditional activities.

Mass is usually celebrated in the morning or early afternoon of a feast day. A procession often follows Mass. The image of the saint being honored is carried out of the church, through some of the streets of the community, and back again into church. In some communities, elaborate temporary decorations are placed along the route where the procession is to pass. These include homemade lanterns of colored paper, floral arches, and designs applied to the street surface itself.

Ritual dancers and musicians may accompany the procession, or may perform in the churchyard at any point during the day. These dances may or may not include elements of ritual drama. Examples of such dances and ritual dramas include the dances of *los Indios, los Matachines,* and *los Aztecas,* and the dramas of *la Conquista* and *los Moros y Cristianos.* Ritual performers may come from distant towns to dance at an important fiesta, while smaller fiestas may only attract local dancers and musicians.

Commercial activity also has a place at community fiestas. All sorts of sacred and secular trinkets may be purchased at temporary stalls that have been set up in the plaza in front of the church. Horse races and other traditional sports as well as gambling are often fiesta activities. Feasting, either sponsored by the church organization or made possible through the sale of foods at stalls, is also an important part of fiesta behavior. This feasting often includes the consumption of alcoholic beverages. Finally, many fiestas include a social dance as an important, culminating event.

In many communities, especially those with indigenous roots, the fiestas are organized and paid for by an elaborate hierarchy of officials who change regularly. Another strategy for raising the necessary money is to lease space in the plaza or streets to merchants.

In the 1980s, the *Fiesta de San Lorenzo* (St. Laurence, martyr, August 10) in Clint, Texas, began with a morning mass. After mass, the statue of the saint was carried on a large circuit of streets around the church, accompanied by musicians playing and singing traditional religious songs and by Matachines dancers. Matachines also danced in front of and beside the church after the procession. Meanwhile, in the plaza in front of the church, traditional festive foods were sold from stalls operated by local individuals and charitable organizations. Other stalls offered trinkets and games of skill. A dance took place in the evening.

Other fiestas will have other characteristics, and may last for several days, attracting pilgrims from great distances. All share some or all of the cluster of traditional activities outlined above.

James S. Griffith

References

Toor, Frances. 1947. *Mexican Folkways*. New York: Crown, pp. 170–260.

Fife, Austin E. (1909–1986)

Folklorist with a particular interest in Mormon folklore, cowboy and Western songs, and material culture. The grandson of Mormon pioneers, Fife grew up in Utah and Idaho. His academic training was in French language and literature at Stanford and Harvard Universities, and most of his professional career was in this field. A student of Aurelio M. Espinosa, he became interested in folklore and pursued the study of it as an avocation, eventually becoming an acknowledged expert.

Fife held academic appointments at Occidental College, Indiana University, with the U.S. Air Force (as a historian) and the U.S. Department of Education, at UCLA, and at Utah State University. He received a Fulbright grant to lecture on American folk music in France in 1950, a Guggenheim Fellowship for the study of cowboy and Western songs in 1959, a National Endowment for the Humanities Senior Award in 1971, and a Distinguished Service Award at Utah State University (USU) in 1976. Fife was a Fellow of the American Folklore Society and of the Utah State Historical Society, elected to both in 1968.

In 1972 he established the Fife Folklore Archive at USU with the gift of his private library, his field notes on Mormon folklore and on cowboy and Western songs, his acetate and tape recordings, and his slides and photographs of material culture—primarily fences, hay derricks, stone houses, mailboxes, and gravestones. Many of his early recordings of folk music and lore are deposited in the Library of Congress in Washington, DC. In addition to several published books, often written in collaboration with his wife, Alta S. Fife, he wrote many articles for folklore and historical journals.

Alta S. Fife

References

Delarue, Paul. 1956. *The Borzoi Book of French Folk Tales*, trans. Austin E. Fife. New York: Alfred Knopf.

Fife, Austin E. 1988. *Exploring Western Americana*. Ann Arbor, MI: UMI Research Press.

Fife, Austin E., and Alta S. Fife. [1956] 1980. *Saints of Sage and Saddle*. Salt Lake City: University of Utah Press.

———. 1969. *Cowboy and Western Songs*. New York: Clarkson N. Potter.

———. 1970a. *Ballads of the Great West*. Palo Alto, CA: American West.

———. 1970b. *Heaven on Horseback*. Logan: Utah State University Press.

Thorp, N. Howard. 1966. *Songs of the Cowboys*. Variants, Commentary, Notes and Lexicon by Austin E. and Alta S. Fife. New York: Clarkson N. Potter.

Filipino Americans

Immigrants (and their descendants) from various ethnolinguistic regions of the Philippines, especially the Ilocos, Tagalog, and Visayan Provinces. The largest Filipino communities in the United States started in Hawaii and California during the first quarter of the 20th century while the Philippines was an American territory. The influx of thousands of predominantly young, single, male agricultural workers during that time has been augmented since the mid-1960s by even larger numbers of immigrants, including entire families and professionals of both sexes, who reside with their descendants, in urban centers throughout the country. Filipino American folklore reflects the marked differences in the American experience of these two waves of immigrants.

The early immigrants, known as "old-timers" (abbreviated as "O.T." in Filipino folk speech), were lured to the Western states by "drummers" of shipping lines, and by photographs, enclosed in glowing letters from relatives and friends, showing young *Pinoys* (Stateside Filipinos) sporting tailor-made *Amerikana* suits, silk shirts, wing-tip shoes, and Panama or Stetson hats. From their poverty-stricken villages, young men caught in the "Hawaiian Fever," or, in dreams of an "Eldorado" in California, sought passage on the Dollar Lines, bringing with them no more than their basket of clothes, with perhaps a bottle of shrimp or fish paste to flavor their monotonous diet aboard the ships.

These ocean journeys, along with more journeys on land, still are the subject of storytelling by the elderly *manong*, as the old-timers are called. The narrator vividly reviews the routes of his occupational life—cutting sugarcane and harvesting pineapples in Hawaii; following the crops from Washington state to Mexicali while picking hops, thinning lettuce, planting celery, "stooping for the green gold" of asparagus, harvesting grapes, strawberries, and apricots; then returning north to the canneries and to the salmon-fishing season in Alaska. Drifting to the cities in winter, exiled in cheap hotels in Chinatown or "Manilatown," his dreary life was punctuated with brief forays into gambling casinos, pool halls, taxi-dance halls, and brothels.

Since miscegenation laws forbade marriage to White women, and few Filipinas immigrated, he remained a bachelor. At labor camps, he bunked with other lonely unmarried men. With them, he enjoyed boxing, cockfighting, and other male sports. Racial attacks, which, for instance, killed a bunkmate during the anti-Filipino riots in Watsonville, California, in 1930, ensured his isolation at work and at play.

From the *Alaskero* to the *Hawaiiano*, Filipino migrant workers share a common repertoire of personal narratives, as well as legends, jokes, and folk speech. Legends feature a migrant worker who does the work of ten grape pickers and eats the tortilla and pork chops prepared for forty men. Dialect stories, jokes about the immigrant greenhorn (such as the Pinoy who drew a map of the kitchen when told to mop the kitchen floor), and protest tales about the labor foreman or the ship's captain (whose vengeful Filipino steward served him coffee brewed with the latter's smelly socks) follow traditional structures and motifs but revolve around their work life. Still to be documented from the workers themselves are the stories of houseboys, waiters, bellhops, and other service workers among the early immigrants, as well as the experiences of

latter-day housekeepers, garage attendants, nurses, and office workers in Filipino American communities everywhere.

The folklore of the new immigrants, unlike that of the bachelor pioneers, revolves around the family, the church, and community organizations—institutions designed for the preservation and transmission of cultural traditions. The home is the main transmitter of cultural identity. Stories from their own childhood are retold by the older to the younger generation. In many Catholic homes, the altar, with its assemblage of favorite Catholic saints' statues, serves as a reminder of family unity.

Rites of passage such as baptisms, birthdays, weddings, anniversaries, and funerals, which reunite relatives and friends from far and near, reinforce kinship ties. Ritual kinship established by cosponsorship of godchildren at baptisms and weddings extends the interdependent unit. The Filipino definition of family is flexible and adaptive. Those without families, like the early immigrants, become ritual or fictive "aunts" and "uncles."

The Filipino sense of community likewise is elastic and expansive. It is rooted in an ever-widening circle of *kababayan* (people who come from the same place). A Filipino may belong to several different clubs—one composed of his covillagers or townspeople, another consisting of province mates, and still another, which comprises his whole region. His strong attachment to his place of origin is a key theme in the proliferation of community clubs around which social activi-

ties revolve. Most of these clubs sponsor town and provincial fiestas in honor of their respective patron saints.

Community celebrations are marked by the usual cultural displays characteristic of many other ethnic festivities. Unlike family affairs, which usually are exclusively Filipino, community festivals are intended for other groups as well. Foodways, folk dances and music, as well as a selected array of traditional arts and crafts, are associated with various celebrations from saints' feast days to national holidays. Although family affairs often are gastronomic feasts, public events tend to have a scaled-down, stereotyped menu with the favorite triumvirate of *pancit* (a noodle dish), *lumpia* (a kind of egg roll), and *adobo* (chicken or pork stewed in spices and vinegar). Along with these foods, folk dances, especially the *tinikling* bamboo dance (also taught as a recreational activity in public elementary schools), the music of the *rondalla* (string band), and the folk art of making the *parol* (festival lantern) have become stereotyped features of community festivals.

Parades and processions, traditionally held during national holidays and religious feasts, respectively, have turned as well into presentations of ethnic cultural heritage. In addition to the American-style drum-and-bugle corps and floats bearing city dignitaries, parades often feature Filipinos costumed as northern Luzon hill tribes, Mindanao Muslims, and Christian lowlanders—ethnocultural categories promoted by local and visiting dance troupes as an instance of cultural richness and diversity. Also highly popular is the *Santacruzan* (a religious procession of community club beauty queens who represent important titles of the Virgin Mary). Traditionally held in May, the *Santacruzan* has become a regular feature of many other community events, including those held during city-sponsored cultural-heritage months. Community celebrations, while continuing to be reunions of compatriots, also have become collective expressions of ethnic pride and identity.

The family, the church, and community clubs, along with ethnic-heritage schools that teach folk dances, music, and arts and crafts, are the active preservers and purveyors of tradition for new generations of Filipino Americans.

Herminia Q. Meñez

References

Almirol, Edwin B. 1985. *Ethnic Identity and Social Negotiation: A Study of a Filipino Community.* New York: AMS.

Bulosan, Carlos. 1943. *American Is in the Heart: A Personal History.* New York: Harcourt, Brace.

Cordova, Fred. 1983. *Filipinos: Forgotten Asian Americans: A Pictorial Essay, 1763–circa 1963.* Dubuque, IA: Kendall/Hunt.

Meñez, Herminia Q. 1980. *Folklore Communication among Filipinos in California.* New York: Arno.

Takaki, Ronald. 1989. *Strangers from a Different Shore: A History of Asian Americans.* New York: Penguin Books.

Filk Music

The musical tradition of science fiction (SF) and fantasy fans. "Filking" occurs at science-fiction conventions ("cons") and creates a specialized social context and identifying role (the "filker") for its practitioners. It fuses elements of traditional folk, folk-revival, and popular music with lyrics oriented toward SF, space, and political parody. Participants define filk as "music played in a filk room," and a filk room as "a place where you play filk music." This circular definition precisely defines the music and its social context for participants who share the music and fellowship.

In the 1950s, fans actively interested in folk music, especially folk-revival styles, began bringing instruments (primarily guitars) to cons to play for their own amusement. During this period, a typo in a fanzine transformed a "folk sing" into a "filk sing," and the unique term was adopted immediately. Early filk gatherings drew fewer than ten people, who knew few songs, and who performed for each other in hotel rooms, furnace rooms, stairwells, and service halls. Gradually, filkers began writing original lyrics set to known tunes and, later, to original tunes as well. An early example is the traditional "Eddystone Light," a song about a lighthouse keeper, updated and transformed to "Asteroid Light."

In the late 1970s and early 1980s, filkers began demanding time and space at conventions to play music. Today almost all cons feature filking, and by 1993 seven annual conventions devoted to filking had emerged in the United States, Canada, and Great Britain. Filk's popularity has grown to include several filk fanzines, computer bulletin boards, and at least seven cottage-industry studios that produce and sell both live and studio-recorded tapes and CDs. As performers and recordings became more professional, filk received radio air play nationally and internationally, especially on novelty music programs like "Dr. Demento."

Filking normally takes place at cons on Friday and Saturday nights, in a room or rooms set aside for it, beginning about 10:00 P.M. and often lasting until dawn. Filk concerts have become common, spotlighting a performer or group, and "jamming" is also becoming popular. The instrumentation has expanded from acoustic guitar and voice to include almost any instrument, including both ethnic and electric/electronic instruments. Performing duos, trios, and groups are becoming common. Topics include SF texts (both literary and media-derived), current events, the SF community, personal experiences, and jobs, especially those in high-tech fields. Spaceflight and hope for the future are common themes. Leslie Fish's "Hope Eyrie" (a tribute to the first moon landing) has become a filk-room anthem, sung unanimously in complex harmony: "The Eagle has landed, / Tell your children when. / Time won't drive us down to dust again."

At least three distinctive regional styles of filk performance exist in the United States, with some overlap. "Singalong" (East Coast) involves participants singing from songbooks directed by a song leader. "Chaos" (Midwest) is a free-associating flow of musical styles, moods, and themes, governed primarily by implicit etiquette. "Bardic circle" (West Coast) follows a formal code of "pick, pass, or play." Performing ability ranges from beginner to professional, but imaginative writing (especially lyrics) and good filk-room manners are valued above sheer technique.

In filk the social context is as important as the music; self-expression, play, and sharing are paramount. This aesthetic is shown by the absence of a fixed distinction between performers and audience. Participants may sing along on choruses or during entire tunes, make jesting comments, and participate in "schtick." Many fans prefer live filk tapes to studio tapes because these remind them of the supportive social atmosphere of the filk room.

Sally C. Childs-Helton
Barry E. Childs-Helton

Film and Folklore

A field of study within the discipline of folklore; films used to document or present folklore. Films that are edited to be shown to an audience are called "folkloric films" by Sharon R. Sherman. Video is often subsumed under "film and folklore," and with its increasing use, "folklore and video"—or perhaps "folkloric videos"—may become a commonplace term, perhaps incorporating film within its definition, much as film now does for video.

Like the documentary "films of fact" shot in the 1900s, some American folkloric films are made up of short clips of interesting phenomena captured for posterity. Other folkloric films have a heavily narrated expository style similar to documentaries made prior to World War II and lasting through the 1960s. Certain folkloric films utilize either a *cinéma vérité* or a *post vérité* approach that combines synchronous sound or voice-over with linear depictions of folklore as events (including interactions, performances, and creative processes). Yet other films are reflexive and intersubjective, incorporating the filmmaker as one of the subjects.

Many folklorists who use film are tied to the models adopted by their documentary-film forerunners and to the conceptual premises of past folklore scholars. Thus, in folkloric films, the rural often takes precedence over the urban, and the past assumes greater importance than the contemporary. For example, John Cohen searched for Child ballads in Appalachia and documented folksinging in *The High Lonesome Sound* (1962); Les Blank documented little-known peoples in the once isolated regions of America, such as Cajuns and Creoles in the Louisiana Bayo, in *Dry Wood and Hot Pepper* (1973) and *Spend It All* (1970); and Bill Ferris presented musicians in rural Mississippi in *Gravel Springs Fife and Drum* (1971). However, these filmmakers have examined contemporary activities and the urban scene as well. Usually, they began with a Romantic stereotypic notion of the folk for their initial films and then recognized a need to broaden the definition of their work as their film corpus grew.

Folklore filmmakers most interested in texts often employ the techniques of narration and montage, showing the viewer the means by which representation is achieved. The montage structure employed in such films as Ferris' *I Ain't Lying* (1975) and *Made in Mississippi* (1975), and in Blank's food films (such as *Garlic Is as Good as Ten Mothers* [1980], provides a means for discovering what the filmmaker thinks about the subject being documented. For historic-reconstruction films, such as Pat Ferrero's *Hearts and Hands* (1987), the narration may be assembled from the words of journal, diary, and letter writers.

Although many folkloric films document a community, such as Blank's *Zivili* (1987) about Serbian Americans, frequently American folklore filmmakers choose a biographical "Everyman" to represent the group. Blank, in several films, (such as *Yum, Yum, Yum: A Taste of Cajun and Creole Cooking* (1990); has Marc Savoy explain aspects of being a Cajun; Jorge Preloran looks at Luther Metke as an exemplar of both the elderly and the log-cabin builder in *Luther Metke at 94* (1979); Ferris documents James Thomas as a bluesman and a storyteller in *Delta Blues Singer* (1969) and *I Ain't Lyin'* (1975); and Sherman presents *Kathleen Ware: Quiltmaker* (1979) and chainsaw sculptor Skip Armstrong in *Spirits in the Wood* (1991). Such folklore filmmakers have documented people as both cultural or artistic representatives and as unique personalities.

For folklorists, *cinéma vérité* (film truth), with its sync-sound portable cameras, provided a fieldwork opportunity to document events from beginning to end and to test the theoretical perspectives about folklore as human behavior established the late 1960s. Long takes and sync-sound filming became the rage. At last, the people being studied could speak for themselves and provide their own functional analyses without the imposition of a narrator or scholar. The focus on the individual shown in such documentary films as *Showman*

(1962), a portrait of movie mogul Joseph E. Levine, by Charlotte Zwerin and Albert and David Maysles; and *Don't Look Back* (1967), a D.A. Pennebaker film on Bob Dylan, became examples for folklorists of how filmmakers might document individuals to arrive at the "truth."

Those films that acknowledge their power to seemingly represent experience *and* reveal the means by which they do so go beyond the ideals of *cinéma vérité* into the openly subjective realm of what Sherman has named *"post vérité,"* in which the art form of the documentary is a given. Whereas *cinéma vérité* was art masquerading as objectivity, *post vérité*, unmasks the illusion of objectivity and displays it. For example, in *Gimme Shelter* (1970), a documentary of the Rolling Stones concert tour of America, flashbacks confuse what is "real"; in *Woodstock* (1970), an observational camera style is fused with split-screen images, sound mixes, and rhythmic shots chosen for their balance with the audio track. The long takes disappear into edited rhythms, as they do in Roberta Cantow's folkloric film *Clotheslines* (1981). The interview, abhorred by *cinéma vérité* for proclaiming the constructed nature of film, may occupy a central role in *post vérité*, as in such folkloric films as Tom Davenport's *A Singing Stream* (1987), Judy Peiser's *All Day, All Night: Memories from Beale Street Musicians* (1990), and Paul Wagner's *The Grand Generation* (1993). For *Paris Is Burning* (1991), Jennie Livingston creates a *post vérité* film from a melange of interviews, *cinéma vérité* techniques, and inter-titles.

In the United States, for the most part, *cinéma vérité* films were used to tell the stories of the "other people," those without access to media production. With *post vérité*, the "others" may become the cinematic weavers of their own stories, directly addressing the camera as the "experts." In recognizing the blatancy of film as art, *post vérité* films may also cross into the realm of reflexivity. For example, Zulay Saravino takes over the making of a film about her culture and turns it into one about her own transcultural experiences in America and Ecuador in *Zulay, Facing the 21st Century* (1993). In the film, Saravino shows herself editing the film about herself.

Unlike documentary films that look at people within the filmmaker's own society, films that Sherman calls "ethnodocumentary" are a specific type of documentary film that tends to document the "other"—people who are conceptualized as being unlike the film team or the ethnographer. As ethnographers become less concerned with cultural overviews and more interested in *events* in culture (a feast, a funeral, a festival), their films have become more like folkloric films. The folkloric film focuses primarily on traditional behavior, documenting many of the most fundamental features of our lives and ranging widely from rituals, ceremonies, and folk art, to folk narrative and folksong, to the lore of various peoples bonded by ethnicity, age, gender, family, occupation, recreation, religion, and region. The folklorist, as Richard M. Dorson has pointed out, often conducts fieldwork at the folklorist's "back door." Many folkloric filmmakers have, indeed, examined traditions in their own locales, sometimes even among their own families.

Differences of major emphasis and locale set the folkloric

film apart from other documentary-film traditions, although *any* film having folklore content might aptly be called a "folkloric film." Just as anthropologists define certain films as "ethnographic" when they successfully elucidate anthropological approaches, the true folkloric film may be defined as one whose content deals primarily with topics that folklorists study and whose intent is to meet the dictates of folkloristic research and teaching. Such films include ones created by folklorists themselves or by nonfolklorists who are filmmakers or videographers recording folklore. Put simply, the point of these films is to document folklore, no matter who is making them.

A unique twist to the study of film and folklore is the popular use of folklore as the primary plot line or unifying thread for commercial feature films. *The Serpent and the Rainbow* (1988), for example, exploits the practices of voodoo. The urban legend about a baby-sitter frightened by a telephone caller is the basis for *When a Stranger Calls* (1979). The film *Avalon* (1990) plays upon family and ethnic narratives to structure the larger narrative of family and ethnic-neighborhood dissolution in the America of the 1940s through the 1960s, using one family as exemplar. *When Harry Met Sally* (1989) relies on the courtship narratives of many different couples as a transition device.

Memorable in its re-creation of folklore is *Candyman* (1993), in which a folklore graduate student conducts research on the legend or horror tale of "The Hooked-Arm Man," who has scared teenagers in lovers' lanes for decades. In this film, the legend comes to life, and the man with the hook torments the graduate student. With the popularity of Jan Harold Brunvand's books on urban legends, this genre of folklore is familiar to a vast audience, and thus viewers have undoubtedly seen the irony.

Nonacademic feature films in general release often incorporate folklore as a detail—for example, a woman singing "Barbara Allen" (Child 84) in *The Piano* (1993). Animated films, such as *Anansi the Spider* and *John Henry*, are targeted at the educational market. But the folkloric films perhaps the most popular with general audiences are Walt Disney's animated *Märchen* [fairy tales]. From *Snow White and the Seven Dwarfs* (1937) to *Cinderella* (1950) and *Beauty and the Beast* (1991), the Walt Disney Studio has presented a number of "Disneyized" folktales to huge audiences. Viewers may accept these renditions as the original tales, an idea reinforced by the same images repeated in spin-off products such as books, dolls, games, and other toys.

Folklore becomes a thematic wellspring for films. Folk beliefs about vampires and werewolves have spawned a whole genre of horror films. Folk-like heroes and plots emerge in stories created or adapted from books by screenwriters, films such as *The Never-Ending Story* (1984), *The Princess Bride* (1987), and *Friday the 13th* (1980). Other visual forms of popular culture appropriate themes such as "the quest," "journey," or "adventure" found in folktale and epic, reconfiguring them in video and computer games.

The video camera, like the movie camera before it, has changed the way people document their lives. In essence, what filmmakers and videographers choose to record in both pro-

fessional films and "home movies" or amateur videos often involves presenting a vision of the self by documenting the central aspects of life, such as rites of passage (birthdays, bar mitzvahs, graduations, weddings); calendrical and religious holidays (Christmas, Passover, Mardi Gras); and performance events (from children's sports to ethnic festivals). Folkloric films also create biographies of individual folk artists, documenting the traditional processes in which they are engaged (for example, play activities, folksinging, craft creation). These subjects form the key narratives of the folkloric film and the folkloric video, which build upon these "narratives of life" by explaining how such events and processes function in the lives of those depicted.

Sharon R. Sherman

References

Collier, John, Jr. [1967] 1986. *Visual Anthropology: Photography as a Research Method.* Revised and Expanded with Malcolm Collier. Albuquerque: University of New Mexico Press.

Heider, Karl. 1976. *Ethnographic Film.* Austin: University of Texas Press.

Hockings, Paul, ed. 1975. *Principles of Visual Anthropology.* The Hague: Mouton.

Jacobs, Lewis, ed. 1979. *The Documentary Tradition.* 2d ed. New York: W.W. Norton.

Nichols, Bill. 1991. *Representing Reality: Issues and Concepts in Documentary.* Bloomington: Indiana University Press.

Rollwagen, Jack R., ed. 1988. *Anthropological Filmmaking: Anthropological Perspectives on the Production of Film and Video for General Audiences.* Chur: Harwood Academic Publishers.

Rosenthal, Alan, ed. 1988. *New Challenges for Documentary.* Berkeley: University of California Press.

Ruby, Jay, ed. 1982. *A Crack in the Mirror: Reflexive Perspectives in Anthropology.* Philadelphia: University of Pennsylvania Press.

Sherman, Sharon R. 1991. Visions of Ourselves: Filming Folklore, Present and Future. *Western Folklore* 50:53–63.

Waugh, Thomas, ed. 1984. *"Show Us Life": Toward a History and Aesthetics of the Committed Documentary.* Methuchen, NJ: Scarecrow.

See also Fieldwork; Mass Media and Folklore; Popular Culture and Folklore

Fink, Mike

Riverboatman and legendary folk hero. Mike Fink was probably born in Pittsburgh, Pennsylvania, during the last quarter of the 18th century. He evidently lived a colorful life as a boatman on the Ohio and Mississippi Rivers. He is thought to have died around 1823 as a result of a personal feud. Although he does not appear in conventional histories of the early 19th century, there is some indication that he was for several decades a well-known individual around whom anecdotes and legends clustered, expanding his personality into an image of an exclusively American backwoods hero. Associated with this image was a personality characterized by rough ways and exaggerated speech and behavior, which appealed to the American aesthetic conscience of the middle part of the 19th century. Constance Rourke referred to this type as "The Gamecock of the Wilderness." Mike's exuberant and explosive ways were too confined by civilization to make either comfortable around the other. But at a distance the backwoodsman seemed amusing and even intriguing. It was as if a new, white-skinned, noble savage had emerged. Richard M. Dorson described these characters as "nineteenth-century Ring-tailed Roarers, bullies, brawlers, and daredevils," who could shoot farther, jump higher, dive deeper, and come out drier than any man this side of Roaring River. Walter Blair characterized Mike Fink as "half horse and half alligator" (Blair and Meine 1956).

Alphonso Wetmore's three-act farce *The Pedlar,* written in 1821, gives the first known reference to Mike Fink, who appears in the play as a stereotype of the uncouth boastful river man. Mike Fink is known today almost exclusively from similar printed sources of subliterary works of the 19th century, including almanacs and sporting journals. Many of the writers who produced these stories about Mike Fink claimed oral sources for their accounts. Several of the Davy Crockett almanacs contain anecdotes about Mike Fink, usually referring to "the celebrated Mike Fink" and always carrying the assumption that the reader has heard of the "Roarer." Writers of these backwoods tales and other humorous regional sketches often credited an eyewitness as a source for their creative journalism, although some of the writers actually heard their basic facts from narrators who told them orally as anecdotes. Mike Fink was known during the early 19th century in a vigorous oral tradition and was once a "folk" hero.

Certain episodes about Mike Fink recur. Mike demonstrates prowess with his rifle by shooting a cup of whiskey off the head of another boatman, or in some cases the head of his wife. Sometimes the compliment is returned by another sharpshooter. This practice even plays a part in his own death, by most accounts, when he shoots at the cup on the head of his protégé after a disagreement and either accidentally or intentionally shoots him dead. Mike is then killed in revenge by the boy's friend or relative. Other common episodes include shooting the scalp lock off an Indian's head and removing a Negro's protruding heel by a surgically precise shot.

In some ways, Mike Fink is of the same ilk as Davy Crockett. Mike appears in several episodes of the Crockett almanacs, having some encounters with Davy himself. Dorson showed that Davy's portrayal in the almanacs sets him in an early American "Heroic Age." Mike Fink's portrayal sets him in this same age. His vainglorious boasting and self-confident challenges are quite similar to those of Crockett. They both are "Roarers." While Mike can match Davy in some heroic aspects—he can boast as well, fight as fiercely, and his rifle is a match for Davy's—he lacks Davy's heroic qualities in others.

In later accounts, Mike is drawn to be even less heroic.

Beginning in 1850, most stories written about Mike's fights had him defeated, his colorful braggadocio now turned to bluster. The circulation of Mike Fink legends diminished greatly with the advent of the Civil War, partly due to the changing sensibilities of the American people, no longer amused by the inglorious aspects of his death and the more negative presentation of his character. Later, the life of the keelboatman that Mike Fink personified was no longer relevant to a modern age of transportation.

In the 20th century, Mike Fink lived again, but in a dubious resurrection. Colonel Henry Shoemaker, who wanted to turn Mike into a regional folk hero by stressing his Pennsylvania origins, claimed to have heard oral tales about Fink, but his claims have been widely discounted. Writers of children's books and compilers of bedside companions cleaned up the distasteful elements of Mike Fink's character and included him along with Davy Crockett in quaintly worded stories about "folk"-type heroes. But once again, Mike Fink was overshadowed by Davy Crockett, this time as a popular culture hero. Though Davy could be toned down to suit the bland tastes of the popular markets, including Disney portrayals as "king of the wild frontier," Mike Fink appeared only as a minor character.

Kenneth A. Thigpen

References

Blair, Walter, and Franklin J. Meine. 1933. *Mike Fink: King of Mississippi Keelboatmen.* New York: H. Holt.
———. 1956. *Half Horse, Half Alligator: The Growth of the Mike Fink Legend.* Chicago: University of Chicago Press.
Dorson, Richard M. 1959. *American Folklore.* Chicago: University of Chicago Press, pp. 202–214.
Hoffman, Daniel. 1965. *Form and Fable in American Fiction.* New York: Oxford University Press, pp. 56–78.
Rourke, Constance. 1931. *American Humor: A Study of the National Character.* New York: Harcourt, Brace, pp. 37–69.

Finnish Americans

People whose ancestral origins in North America include family members who came from Finland and the Finnish-speaking sections of Russia, Norway, and Sweden. Most come from western Finland and are known simply as Finnish Americans or Finnish Canadians. However, Finnish Americans include people identified also as Finland Swedes, Finland Sami, Finland Karelians, Finnish Laestadians, and Finnish American Indians. All but the Finnish American Indians reflect separate folk communities also in Finland. These subgroups share a Finnish cultural geography, although the Finland Swedes speak Swedish and the Finland Sami speak Sami.

Finnish people participated in American colonial history, both in the New Sweden colony in Delaware after 1638 and in the Russian colony in Alaska in the 1840s. The Delaware Finnish colonists introduced a wooden log cabin dwelling using a dovetailed corner construction method whose influence intrigues 20th-century historical geographers. In Alaska

Finns worked as carpenters and other skilled craftsmen. Finnish influences remaining in Alaska include the Sitka Lutheran Church and the carpentry work done by Finns on the Russian bishop's house, the most significant remaining building from the Russian American era. Sitka Finns later helped form Finnish communities along the Northwest Coast, in Seattle, Astoria, and San Francisco.

Modern Finnish American immigration to the United States began in 1864 and continued until 1924, when the immigration gates effectively closed to Finnish immigrants. By that time, 300,000 immigrants had settled in the United States. Finnish Canadian immigration began as second-stage migration from the States in the 1880s. Immigration directly to Canada from Finland began around the turn of the 20th century. After 1924 Finnish immigration to North America shifted to Canada until the Depression effectively halted most migration. Although some post–World War II Finnish immigrants entered the United States, most went to Canada, swelling urban Finnish communities in Thunder Bay, Toronto, and Montreal. At the beginning of the 1990s, 658,870 Americans identified themselves as Finnish Americans and 100,000 Canadians identified themselves as Finnish Canadians.

Most Finnish immigrants between 1864 and 1930 were general workers, people familiar with agricultural and unskilled labor but unfamiliar with industrial work or urban life. Men worked in the mining, lumbering, and fishing industries, and they joined railroad and dock work gangs. Before 1892 women who came largely joined their husbands or brothers; they provided essential services like room and board, shopkeeping, and managing the small farms they started with their husbands. After 1892, when the immigrants were largely young and single men and women, women came to do domestic work in the major cities while men found work in the steel industry, in logging, and in the coal-, iron-, and copper-mining fields, primarily in the Upper Midwest and the mountain states. Artisans such as stone carvers, carpenters, painters, tailors, and jewelers joined this later migration, but the professional people who came were few, mostly journalists, teachers, ministers, political activists, and adventurers. In spite of the distances separating the sexes, Finnish immigrants primarily married other Finnish immigrants, using newspapers ads and national summer festivals to meet.

The earliest Finnish immigrants, primarily Laestadians from northern Finland, around the Tornio River, and from northern Norway, arrived in 1864 to homestead prairie lands in south central Minnesota and in 1865 to work in the copper mines in Michigan. The first Finnish American communities, Cokato, Minnesota, and Hancock, Michigan, originated from these two groups of immigrants, whose letters home encouraged others to follow. By 1887, around 21,000 had arrived. Most 19th-century Finnish American urban communities formed in the Upper Peninsula of Michigan, in Minnesota, and in the Pacific Northwest. Finnish immigrants homesteaded in Minnesota, South Dakota, and along the Columbia River in Oregon and Washington. Urban communities originating with Finnish sailors also existed in San Francisco, New York City, and Boston. Immigrants created a prairie homestead community in New Finland, Saskatchewan, in 1889 and an urban community in Nanaimo, British Columbia, by 1890.

As immigration expanded, Finns moved across the northern tier of the United States. The permanent Finnish American settlements formed three regions—East, Midwest, and West—which further subdivided into twelve subregions: (1) New England and upper New York state; (2) New York City; (3) West Virginia, western Pennsylvania, and northeast Ohio; (4) southern Lake Michigan, including Detroit and Chicago; (5) the copper country, or the Keweenaw Peninsula, on Lake Superior in Michigan; (6) the iron-mining and cutover region of northern Michigan and Wisconsin; (7) the Minnesota Iron Range and the cutover lands adjacent; (8) western Minnesota and the Dakotas; (9) Rocky Mountain states (particularly Montana, Wyoming, and Idaho); (10) Oregon and Washington; (11) San Francisco and Northern California; and (12) Southern California and Arizona. Each region developed distinctive features based on variables such as where the immigrants came from in Finland, the time and place the region was settled, the employment options, and forms of interactions with American neighbors. In the 1990s, more than half of all Finnish Americans continue to live in the Midwest regions.

Migration between regions affected the cultures that developed. Many Finnish Americans, for example, trace their family's origins in the United States to Michigan's Keweenaw Peninsula, from which they then continued to migrate to other Finnish American settlements throughout the nation. Thus, the Copper Country developed a reputation (which continues) as the *pesäpaika* (nesting place) of Finnish America. In addition, from very early days Finnish Americans would settle farmsteads and maintain a seasonal migration pattern with a nearby urban area. For example, a rural area like Naselle, Washington, developed a symbiotic connection to Astoria, Oregon; Cokato, Minnesota, developed a similar relationship with Minneapolis/St. Paul; and Tapiola, Michigan, with Hancock. Later, mining regions in northern Minnesota developed connections to Duluth and Minneapolis, just as Upper Peninsula mining and rural communities developed connections to Detroit, Milwaukee, and Chicago. Thus, rural settlements maintained an urban perspective, and tradition dictated where children migrated when they left the farms.

Within these regions, Finland Swedes concentrated in Massachusetts, New York City, Michigan, Wisconsin, Minnesota, Oregon, Washington, and California. Sami peoples settled predominantly in Michigan, Minnesota, the Dakotas, Oregon, and Washington. Finnish American Indians live primarily in northern Minnesota and in the Upper Peninsula of Michigan. Since the late 1950s, an additional region has emerged in Florida, particularly around Lake Worth/Lantana and Tampa/St. Petersburg, where Finnish Americans and Finnish Canadians joined Finnish nationals in search of the sun. During the winter, temporary residents transform Lake Worth/Lantana into the largest urban Finnish American community in the country, a curious contemporary recreation of the earlier Finntowns that dotted the Finnish American regions across the nation.

Permanent Finnish Canadian settlements formed three regions—the east, the prairie provinces, and the far west. These communities, largely begun after the Finnish American communities, reflect a different set of variables based on place of origin, time of settlement, and employment options. Furthermore, differences between Canadian and American social and political climates make the Canadian cultural regions even more distinct. Almost two-thirds of Finnish Canadians settled in Ontario. The second-largest group settled in British Columbia. Farming communities in Alberta, Saskatchewan, and Manitoba also developed. In the 1990s, these regions continue to define the Finnish Canadian population.

A rich body of Finnish American lore with regional and individual variants confirms this cultural geography. Part of that lore grows out of the strong Finnish American and Finnish Canadian institutions the immigrants created in their communities—churches, temperance societies, workers' halls, cooperatives, and benefit societies. The arts, particularly community theater, bands, and choirs, flourished at regular local programs and at regional and national festivals. Hall life included dances and sports exhibitions. In the larger communities, such activities attained high standards, often involving professionals hired to organize and direct. Largely literate, Finnish immigrants valued education and the power of the word. The proverb "Suomalainen uskoo sanan voimann" (A Finn believes in the power of the word) encouraged the immigrants to create lending libraries, self-education study groups, and a rich Finnish-language newspaper, serial, and book-publishing life. The *nyrkkilehti* (fist newspaper) was a spontaneous creation that occurred in many immigrant enclaves. This handwritten immigrant newspaper circulated among friends and local organizations, providing a colorful honest record of immigrants' lives.

These institutions, even though effectively separating Finnish immigrants from other Americans, helped them adjust and fit into American culture. The Finnish cooperative movement illustrates how this worked. Cooperation was a central value to the Finnish immigrant, illustrated in the many informal cooperative efforts, like the *talkoo työ* (work bee), which built the immigrants' early churches, halls, houses, and outbuildings. The cooperative spirit promoted efforts at communal living, the best known being Kreeta, Michigan, a collective farming community on Drummond Island in Lake Huron, and Sointula (meaning Harmony), the utopian colony (infamous also because stories implied that the colony had practiced free love), offshore from Vancouver Island in British Columbia, 1901–1904. By the end of the 19th century, however, the Finns had begun to create formal Finnish cooperative solutions to consumer issues particularly suited to Finns living in an American culture.

What they created out of these efforts, finally, was the largest working retail cooperative in America: the Central Cooperative Exchange, later renamed the Central Cooperative Wholesale, an organization that united scattered retail and general-merchandise stores across the Upper Midwest. Their initiative also created an enduring Midwest oil company, the Minnesota-based Mutual Life Insurance Company, and the

Workers Credit Union of Fitchburg, Massachusetts. Nonetheless, the cooperatives emphasized Finnish solutions for Finnish immigrants, and non-Finns defined it as clannish behavior, part of the reason for the continuing reputation for clannishness that Finns have with the general American public who know them.

Finnish American cooperatives took different forms: in urban areas, cooperative boarding houses, restaurants, groceries, general merchandise, and apartment buildings; in rural areas, groceries, retail, and general-merchandise stores. Started as buying clubs, they became full-fledged businesses as strikes and other labor conflicts made buying difficult. In farming communities, the "co-op," as it was called, gave new meaning to the proverb "oma tupa, oma lupa" (Your own cottage, your own freedom). Origin stories for these rural co-ops tell often how the co-op began after the local merchant promised to pay a certain price for timber or farm produce, then reneged one too many times on the agreement. Cooperatives stopped such exploitation and encouraged the immigrants to make communal consumer decisions that created an intimate ethnic environment where even Brooklyn, New York, cooperative apartment buildings came complete with humorous Finnish nicknames (Köngäs 1964.)

In spite of the rich yet separate cultural life, Finnish immigrants never created a united community to speak to the larger North American world. Finns divided into numerous factions, some emphasizing spiritual issues, and others emphasizing politics and economics. Most Finnish immigrants had been members of the Church of Finland (Lutheran), but in the United States the Lutherans split into three branches, as well as smaller groups of Methodists, Pentecostals, Congregationalists, and Unitarians. Similarly, while many immigrants, particularly those who came after 1892, were politically progressive and organized nationally as Socialists in 1906, by 1914 the Wobblies left the Federation to form their own group, the Industrial Workers of the World. After 1917 the Social Democrats split away from those who were joining the Communist Party. Finally, in 1929, the Central Cooperative split away from the Communists. All of this proved once again that "If you have four Finns in a room, you'll get four separate organizations."

Stories about these factions usually refer to two general categories—"Church Finns" and "Hall Finns" or, using Finland's Civil War of 1917–1918 as the source for the categories, "White Finns" and "Red Finns." Rhetoric aside, all groups participated in some form of the cooperatives, and most were active in unions. When strikes occurred, Finnish halls often served as strike headquarters for all ethnic groups. In this latter context, Finns developed reputations for troublemaking in the community, and non-Finns developed stories that talked about the Finns "brazenly marching down the street carrying a red flag." This non-Finn lore about the "radical Finns" worked in counterpoint to Finnish America's own lore about the *sisu* (bravery or stubborn determination) that drove the Finnish workers on against incredible odds.

Finns, the first and largest foreign-language unit in the Socialist Party of America, remained 17 percent of the membership in 1917. In the late 1920s, they accounted for more than 40 percent of the Communist Party. For both their labor activities and these political connections, other Americans racially attacked the Finnish Americans. Although Finns had earlier developed reputations for hard drinking and fighting, that reputation took racist overtones when labor troubles began. Epithets like "Finn-LAND-er" and "dumb Finn" were common, and vigilante attacks occurred. The double racism implicit in statements that Finns were Mongolian and, therefore, Asian hurt so deeply that one Finnish American group still needed to refute the issue in its 1957 book publication, *Finlandia: The Racial Composition, The Language, and a Brief History of the Finnish People*. All sorts of slurs practiced in Finnish American cultural regions continued well into the 1970s (Jarvenpa 1976).

In the 1990s, Finnish Americans often tell about this racism practiced against Finns, racism that either they experienced or know occurred, and they counter the racist attacks with a repertoire of materials based in ethnic pride. They will speak about the Delaware Colony, a body of lore that incorporates the beliefs that John Morton, one of the original signers of the Declaration of Independence, was, in fact, a Finn, and that the American log cabin begins with Finnish log construction dating back to Delaware. They will speak of the ancient folk epic, the *Kalevala*, and the ancient folk instrument, the *kantele*. They will speak of Finland's modern heroes, of the athlete Paavo Nurmi and the composer Jean Sibelius. They will speak of Finland's honesty—"the only country to pay their war debt"—and of Finland's *sisu*—a small nation fighting the Russians alone in the 1939–1940 Winter War.

In addition to the institutional and politically motivated lore, Finnish Americans developed lore about the immigrant work life. This includes richly detailed stories about Finnish domestics working for wealthy Yankee employers like John Pillsbury, who learned to like *puuro* (Finnish porridge) from his Finnish cook; jokes built around Finnish *mainarit* (miners) who use words like *horiop* (hurry up), *vastu märe* (what's the matter), and *sanomapits* (son of a bitch); and even tall tales about Finnish loggers like Otto Walta in northern Minnesota (Karni 1967). Large oral collections of such Finnish American lore exist at Wayne State University in Detroit; at the Immigration History Research Center, University of Minnesota; at the Finnish Heritage Center, Suomi College, Hancock, Michigan; at the Minnesota Historical Society, St. Paul, Minnesota; and at the Iron Range Research Center, Chisholm, Minnesota.

Finnish Americans themselves recognized early the need to collect their own oral traditions in a written form. Salamon Ilmonen collected the origin stories of countless local Finnish American individuals, families, and communities across the country and published them in a series of volumes from 1919 to 1939, all in Finnish. Excerpts from some of these, for example in Minnesota, are available in English translations made during the WPA (Works Progress Administration) period of the 1930s and 1940s. In addition to Ilmonen, Viljami Rautanen collected the origin stories of the churches, and Elias Sulkkonen compiled the origin stories of the workers' move-

ment within the Finnish American community. After World War II, members of the aging immigrant generation began to publish their own community and regional histories, some as chapbooks, others as monographs. After the 1970s, second-generation Finnish Americans have been prolific authors of memoirs and family histories. In the 1980s, the Immigration History Research Center at the University of Minnesota became the repository of a largely third- and fourth-generation collective effort, the Minnesota Finnish American Family History Project with histories of more than 100 families. The emphasis throughout these efforts has been to record the collective ethnic culture rather than to promote achievements of the individual because "Oma kehu haisee" (Self-praise smells putrid).

In spite of this rich ethnic lore born in the Finnish American immigrant experience, most folklore fieldwork among Finnish Americans has emphasized survivals of folklore from the old country. Finnish Americans were the exotic people living under the shadow of the enormous Finnish folk collections developed and maintained in Finland. The collections of verbal materials from which Elias Lönnrot created the Finnish national epic, the *Kalevala* (1835), led early collectors of Finnish Americana to look for similar treasure troves among the Finnish Americans. Marjorie Edgar, the semiprofessional folklorist collecting in Minnesota in the 1930s, looked specifically for surviving Finnish folklore items. Likewise, Richard M. Dorson, in the mid-1940s, went looking for *Märchen* (fairy tales) among the Upper Peninsula Finnish Americans. However, Finnish American immigrants largely represented folk groups from western Finland, and the *Kalevala* had been assembled from the collected oral traditions of folk groups in the more remote regions of eastern Finland. In actual fact, Finnish Americans learned about the *Kalevala* more in America, becoming familiar with it because Anglo Americans expressed interest in this aspect of their culture (Wargelin Brown 1986).

Collectors have never stopped turning to the Finns for survival folklore, and they have continually discovered and documented a broad variety of old-country verbal and material-culture traditions embedded in Finnish American life. Dorson, for example, found old-country stories about the *noita* (healer) and the *tietäjä* (seer), as well as jokes and tall tales from western Finland, when he collected in the Upper Peninsula of Michigan in the 1940s (Dorson 1952). Ten years earlier, Marjorie Edgar had collected music, proverbs, and charms, all survivals of Finnish folklore from fieldwork conducted in Minnesota. Throughout the 1950s, 1960s, and 1970s, as the immigrant institutions disappeared, it was the vernacular log construction that people valued and saved (Lockwood 1990:24–31). In the 1980s, folklorists discovered in Minnesota how strong the Finnish tradition of bread making remained, particularly *rieska* (unleavened rye bread) and *pulla* (cardamom-flavored coffee bread). Equally important were the daily ritual of coffee drinking and the habit of entertaining at the *kahvi pöytä* (coffee table) (Kaplan, Hoover, and Moore 1986).

Museums with Finnish American collections attest to the

interest in old-country survivals. A number of open-air museums include Finnish Americans' folk buildings. Old World Wisconsin maintains two farmsteads. Embarrass, Minnesota, maintains an entire historic district created from a farming community. The Honka homestead in Arnheim, Michigan, and the Wirtanen farmstead near Duluth, Minnesota, provide examples of small backwoods farmsteads. The National Historic Register identifies similar buildings and living sites throughout the regions of Finnish America. Museum collections of Finnish American material objects, while few, emphasize survival materials as well. The Nordic Heritage Museum in Seattle, Washington, and the Finnish Heritage Center at Suomi College, Hancock, Michigan, have largely undocumented collections. The Cokato, Minnesota, city museum includes a good view of 19th-century Finnish American homestead life. Peoples' created museums throughout Finnish American regions will also display old-country survivals. The Michigan State University Museum has a significant collection, professionally documented, of materials that include both old-country and Finnish American objects.

The one survival that attracts everyone's attention is the sauna, the Finnish steam bath. Already in the earliest non-Finn stories told about the Finns are references to the sauna, that strange custom brought with the immigrants. It attracted the interest of the average citizen as well as the professional researcher. Looking for survival folkways, the late-20th-century researcher discovers that the sauna remains, in many minds, the primary folkway survival from Finland, practiced by the immigrants and continued by the third, fourth, and even fifth generations. Immigrant homesteaders, legends record, built their sauna before cabins. As traditional believers in natural health care, immigrants used the sauna for massage and cupping (bloodletting done with small animal horns inserted in the back); immigrant women gave birth in the sauna with the assistance of traditional midwives. The sauna kept the immigrants clean and healthy. Finnish men, coming home from the logging camps, would head straight for the sauna to get rid of lice or bedbugs.

Later generations have not continued all of these early practices, but they maintain a strong belief in the healing power of the sauna. If a person is sick, he or she takes a sauna. A Finnish proverb still repeated says "Jos ei sauna ja viina ja terva auta niin se tauti on kuolemaksi"(If a sauna, whiskey, and tar salve don't make you well, death is imminent). Not only is the sauna good medicine for respiratory and circulatory problems, it can relax stiff muscles, cure aches and pains, and relieve stress. Finnish Americans know how to pronounce the word (SOW-nah) and how to create *löyly* (steam from the hot rocks) and practice the rituals for taking a sauna. The saunas in suburban basements and at the lakeshore attest to the importance that the sauna retains (Lockwood 1978).

Other traditions maintained are less visible to the outsider (and thus less documented by collectors) yet remain markers of the survival of Finnish folkways. Particularly important are berry picking, hunting, trapping, woodworking (carpentry, furniture making, carving), and fiber working (knitting, crocheting, embroidery, lacework, and weaving).

Rag-rug weaving and rag rugs used in the home have become a signature piece for Finnish Americans, a practice noticed in an exhibition developed by the Michigan State University Museum in 1990.

Music, too, has been a source of survival folklife. Some have wished the survival had been the ancient Finnish folk instrument, the *kantele,* and the immigrant community did have some *kantele* players. However, the musical instruments of choice for immigrants were fiddles and accordians, and they remain the instruments of those who maintain the traditions (Gallmann 1982; Leary 1988). Some people, like legendary accordianist, Viola Turpeinen, and Art Moilanen, violinist and 1990 National Heritage Fellow, took these forms and adapted them to American audiences (Leary 1988; Lockwood 1990). All of these traditions are enjoying a revival as third- and fourth-generation Finnish Americans have rediscovered the traditional Finnish American musical repertoire and have created musical groups with names like *Koivun Kaiku* (Song of the Birches), a *kantele* group, and *Ameriikan Pojat* (Boys of America), a brass-band ensemble. A few Finnish American choral groups continue from their origins in the immigrant communities, but most Finnish American choral singing, like the bands, has disappeared.

Finnish Americans maintain several Finland-based holidays. On December 6, many communities commemorate Finnish Independence Day, December 6, 1917. During the Christmas season, Christmas parties *(pikku joulu)* occur. *Laskiainen* (a celebration of, and participation in, winter sports activities) is traditionally Shrove Tuesday. The Smithsonian Institution film *At Laskiainen in Palo, Everyone Is a Finn* (1983) reveals something of how Finnish holidays have been adopted by the larger non-Finnish community. Some communities also celebrate Kalevala Day (February 28) programs in honor of the Finnish epic. Midsummer celebrations, complete with *ikokkoî* (large fire) burning in the night during the parties, are held during the summer.

Separate from survivals, Finnish American folklore created in the United States and collected by professional folklorists begins with Dorson, in the 1940s, who recognized the dialect stories told by both first- and second-generation Finnish Americans (Dorson 1948). This has been a continually fruitful field, even published by Finnish-American folk authors like Hap Puotinen and Jingo Viitala Vachon. *(Tradition Bearers,* a 1987 film by Michael Loukinen, includes a segment on Vachon.) More recently, folklorists like Yvonne Lockwood have examined unique folk traditions created in the United States, such things as the "pasty," a meat pie eaten by Cornish miners and adopted and adapted by the Finns (Lockwood 1990). Likewise, Marsha Penti has examined a national Finnish American summer festival, FinnFest USA. Beginning from the Finnish American immigrant tradition of large summer festivals, FinnFest USA, held annually, alternates among the various Finnish American regions (Lockwood 1990).

Finnish Americans have created a new culture revolving around the Finnish word *sisu,* a unique characteristic of Finns. While the word is known and used in Finland, the term takes new meaning in the Finnish American community, a badge of honor found on sweatshirts, hats, and coffee mugs. It has become an explanation for the Finnish American's stoicism, independent spirit, and stubbornness, part of a special ethnic mystique called upon in difficult situations, part of a mantra recited by Finnish Americans: "Sauna, Sisu, and Sibelius," the three S's that describe Finnish American culture.

Finally, one completely Finnish American folkloric invention has been St. Urho, an invented Finnish saint reputed to have driven the ubiquitous grasshoppers out of Finland. St. Urho has become the reason for a holiday commemorated in many Finnish American communities. Finnish Americans have managed to get the day declared an official day of commemoration in all fifty states in the nation as well. Not surprisingly, the day is celebrated March 16, the day before St. Patrick's Day, and has inspired a collection of broad dry-wit poems and songs, a color code of purple and green, and an excuse for greeting cards, parades, and parties. Sources indicate that the origins of the elaborated ethnic joke are in the state of Minnesota. Finnish Americans use it as a day that permits pranks and good times (Lockwood 1987).

One of the early Finnish American factions, were the Laestadians, who continue to maintain a conservative Finnish American lifestyle, based in early Finnish American experiences. Laestadians, who practice a form of Lutheranism based in active use of the Finnish language and circumpolar spiritualism rooted in Sami culture, live separate from, but within, traditional Finnish American cultural regions. As a group, they help validate a separate Finnish cultural life that continues to be practiced in the communities where they live. One faction, known as the *Esikoisuus* (the first born), visibly distinguishes themselves through clothing and hairstyle choices. Most, however, are unique only in that they tend to create a separate community with their own cultural activities.

Among the other smaller Finnish folk groups, little if any collecting has been done from Finland Swedes specifically. Recent efforts to recognize Sami Finns have resulted in the beginning of a new effort to study and collect their heritage. Their quarterly journal, *Baiki,* has become a good source for information. The Karelian Finns, eastern Finland Finns who emigrated from Finland after World War II when Karelia was taken over by the Russians, have had little scholarly attention given to their traditions. Neither have the Finnish American Indians, largely Chippewa descendants of Finnish American fathers or mothers. Their Finnish American lore relates mostly to stories of interracial relations with their Finnish American relatives and their own personal experiences with such Finnish folklife as saunas.

K. Marianne Wargelin

References

Dorson, Richard M. 1948. Dialect Stories of the Upper Peninsula: A New Form of American Folklore. *Journal of American Folklore* 61:113–150.

———. 1952. Finns. In *Bloodstoppers and Bearwalkers: Folk Traditions of the Upper Peninsula.* Cambridge: Harvard University Press, pp. 123–149.

Gallmann, Matthews. 1982. Matti Pelto: Finnish American Button Accordion Player. *Midwestern Journal of Language and Folklore* 8:43–47.

Jarvenpa, Robert. 1976. Visual Expression in Finnish-American Ethnic Slurs. *Journal of American Folklore* 89:90–91.

Kaplan, Anne R., Marjorie A. Hoover, and Willard B. Moore. 1986. The Finns. In *The Minnesota Ethnic Food Book.* St. Paul: Minnesota Historical Society Press, pp. 142–162, 346–357.

Karni, Michael G. 1967. Otto Walta: Finnish Folk Hero of the Iron Range. *Minnesota History* 40:391–402.

Kaups, Matti. 1981. Log Architecture in America: European Antecedents in a Finnish Context. *Journal of Cultural Geography* 2:131–153.

Köngäs, Elli Kaija. 1964. Nicknames of Finnish Apartment Houses in Brooklyn, N.Y. *Journal of American Folklore* 77:80–81.

Leary, James. 1988. Reading the "Newspaper Dress": An Exposé of Art Moilanen's Musical Traditions. In *Michigan Folklife Reader,* ed. C. Kurt Dewhurst and Yvonne R. Lockwood. East Lansing: Michigan State University Press, pp. 205–223.

Lockwood, Yvonne Hiipakka. [1977] 1978. The Sauna: An Expression of Finnish-American Identity. *Western Folklore* 36:71–84. Reprinted in *Folklore and Ethnicity,* ed. Larry Danielson. Los Angeles: California Folklore Society.

———. 1987. Immigrant to Ethnic: Symbols of Identity among Finnish-Americans. In *Folklife Annual 1986,* ed. Alan Jabbour and James Hardin. Washington, DC, pp. 93–107.

Lockwood, Yvonne Hiipakka, guest ed. 1990. Finnish American Folklife. *Finnish Americana* (Special Issue) 8.

Lockwood, Yvonne Hiipakka, with William G. Lockwood. 1991. Pasties in Michigan: Foodways, Interethnic Relations and Cultural Dynamics. In *Creative Ethnicity,* ed. Steven Stern and Allan Cicala. Logan: Utah State University Press.

Sutyla, Charles. 1977. *The Finnish Sauna in Manitoba.* Ottawa: National Museums of Canada, Canadian Centre for Folk Culture Studies.

Wargelin Brown, K. Marianne. 1986. The Kalevala as Western Culture in Finland and America. *Finnish Americana* 7:4–12.

Fishing (Commercial)

Capturing fish in great quantities for the purpose of trade and profit. Fishing in contemporary North America is highly regulated by state and federal governments and generally categorized as commercial or sports. Sports fishing is perceived as primarily recreational, with the fish becoming both object of play and fellow player, and the consumption of fish caught often being a subordinate concern to play, meditation, or socializing. Comparatively, commercial fishing is viewed as work, with cash ultimately exchanged for the fish. Here fish is a commodity expected to be consumed in a number of ways by distant consumers, not necessarily the commercial fisher.

Commercial fisherman Charles Herrin of Jacksonville, Florida, empties a trawlnet full of shrimp and fish onto the afterdeck of his boat, 1986. Photo David A. Taylor. American Folklife Center.

Where sports fishing may be chiefly an individual pursuit for the purpose of seeking individual and perhaps social pleasures, commercial fishing can be likened to farming, with individuals, but more often small crews of workers, performing a public service. Oppositions of pleasure versus work, quality versus quantity, non-consumption versus consumption, and individual versus common good characterize official and, to a large extent, unofficial conceptualizations of modern fisheries. Confounding these distinctions, however, are the majority of commercial fishers who say they pursue their work mainly for the pleasure and challenge of it, and sports fishers who persistently catch in quantity to exchange fish informally with family, friends, and neighbors.

Increasingly forgotten is subsistence fishing—that pursued in order to survive, whether through the direct consumption of fish or through trade of fish. Now lumped under sports fishing and restricted in commercial fishing to the trade but not the consumption of fish, subsistence fishing historically integrates the two fishing arenas, overcomes many of the definitional oppositions, and implies a total cultural experience, as well as symbolic and socioeconomic systems, in which fishing plays a part.

A simpler, broader definition of commercial fishing based on fishing intensity and trade reflects its connection to subsistence fishing and enhances cross-cultural and cross-fishery comparisons. For folklorists, thus, commercial fishing is best seen as fishing that results in catching more fish than a fisher can use and that, therefore, inspires trade. It covers a wide range of fishing operations, from the sports or tribal fisher who systematically catches a daily limit and exchanges it fresh or preserved with family, friends, and neighbors; to the person who fishes with a commercial license part of the year with or without a crew, perhaps in a small open boat powered by an outboard motor; to people who fish with crews of one to eight year-round in a mid-size diesel-powered boat; to people who fish on big processing ships in large crews of as many as twenty, who sometimes stay at sea for months at a time.

Generally, commercial fishers come from families, neighborhoods, or shoreside communities where experiences and work on, or adjacent to, bodies of water are common. By observation, word of mouth, and experience they learn a wide variety of attitudes, skills, and behaviors related to water and fishing. Practicing keen observational skills, they learn to identify and name the desirable and undesirable species of available fish, and learn personality traits and habits of specific kinds of fish and even of specific individual fish. Commercial fishers acquire knowledge of the fishing grounds, learning to visualize the underwater terrain, learning the names for commonly known underwater features, and memorizing landmarks along shore to use in triangulation to position themselves on the water and their fishing gear under the water. They use the behavior of birds, weather phenomena, and the color and character of water to predict weather changes and movements of fish. They also learn to watch and identify the behavior of other fishers in order to protect their own fishing spots; determine another fisher's fishing spots, equipment, and related success; and come to the rescue in case of an emergency. Since their watchful, secretive occupational style often appears deceptive, commercial fishers reinforce exoteric stereotypes of themselves as untrustworthy and unlawful.

Dedicated fishing people additionally share a wealth of traditional knowledge regarding the design, construction, maintenance, and manipulation of fishing equipment—from lures and jigs to nets, from skiffs to ships—all carefully calibrated to the locale. Familiar with a basic repertoire of knots for building fishing gear and securing equipment, fishers often associate skill with knots with fisherly competence. Secondarily, their knots provide an individual signature for the identification of gear. With well-designed, properly knotted gear, a fisher also learns how to place it most effectively with respect to fish behavior, water and weather conditions, and the capabilities of the fishing boat. Critical to the placement of gear in most fishing operations are communication and coordination with others, learning rhythm, timing, and speed while running boats, handling gear, and removing fish from the gear.

Once fish are caught, fishers handle and process them using a variety of traditional techniques related to type of fish, weather conditions, market demand, and transportation concerns. Back ashore, fishers participate in several marketing networks to sell fish most effectively, gaining access to these networks and learning negotiation skills from others and through experience. People who avidly pursue fish generally consume more fish, more types of fish, and more parts of fish than do those whose experiences with fish are more limited.

Accordingly, they practice a greater repertoire of methods for handling, preserving, and preparing fish for home consumption, and they regularly include fish on the menu for social occasions, private and public.

While commercial fishers share a basic repertoire of customs, subsets of other traditions depend on the size of the fishing operation and the extent to which a fisher makes a living from fishing. Typically, the smallest operations are broadly and well-integrated into shoreside communities; practitioners share maritime knowledge that is widespread within the shoreside community; and because they do not venture far offshore they exhibit neither highly exclusive occupational traditions nor strongly proscriptive superstitious behaviors surrounding their work on the water. The larger, more specialized, and more full-time the fishing operation, the more likely it takes place at some distance from home, in an environment perceived to be dangerous or different enough from land-based and near-shore locations that it requires special training, equipment, and support. Practitioners generally belong to specialized occupational communities within a greater maritime community separate from the broader shoreside and land-based society. They pass highly esoteric occupational knowledge among themselves and restrict access to membership. They often adhere to occupational rituals and proscriptive superstitious behaviors, and their entire family acts as a support system for the work pursued. Because of the location of work, specialized routines and schedules, family dynamics and interfamily dependence—all oriented toward the water—intensive, larger-scale commercial fishing can be seen as an occupation that fosters a distinctive subculture. Exoteric stereotypes often flourish in adjacent communities signifying the otherness of this subculture.

Larger fishing operations break down again into two types according to size. The smaller, what some anthropologists call "artisanal" fisheries, are small businesses in which people make most of their living from fishing; in which family members, neighbors, and friends make up the work force and women, children, and elders are involved in shoreside activities; and in which each fisher practices a diversity of skills, having both the opportunity and the necessity to learn each angle of the business. These fishers perpetuate esoteric stereotypes of the strongly independent, individualistic, self-sufficient, professional fisher, and they actively tell personal-experience narratives that express attitudes about work, an addiction to fishing, and views of fisheries bureaucrats, sportsfishers, pleasure boaters, and other commercial fishers.

In the largest ventures, what might be called *corporate* fisheries, job specialization increases, the hierarchy of jobs and management structures are stricter and more complex, crew backgrounds and onshore experiences are more diverse, and the involvement of women, children, and elders is restricted to social, political, and relief organizations that support fishing. Since fishers spend so much time with one another, isolated on board, they tend to create a complete social order in microcosm on the ship, in effect leading two separate lives, one with their family ashore, and the other with their "family" at sea.

Because specialized commercial fishing appears to promote a common occupational pattern regardless of where it occurs, it has been said to transcend ethnicity. Yet within most maritime communities where commercial fishing is pursued, a variety of fisheries and scales of operation coexist based on fish sought, gear used, intensity of fishing effort, and related management structures. Fishery divisions often follow ethnic and family lines, with fishers jockeying for position across and within groups, establishing a hierarchy of fishing operations informed by the status of fish sought and ethnic preferences in equipment, fishing terrain, group dynamics, and fish-handling techniques. While perhaps subordinate to an overall occupational pattern, ethnic and family variations are common, as are conflicts among the various ethnic and family groups. Esoteric stereotypes establish the differentiation in networks and fishing philosophies and styles. Finally, wherever commercial fishers occur, they complement occupational groups that serve them and other water-related and land-based groups. These often conflicting groups form a diversified maritime community, not unlike agrarian counterparts, offering a universe of traditions to examine from myriads of theoretical perspectives.

As fish disdain national boundaries, commercial fishing challenges the bounds of definitional constructs and, like fish to fishers, lures folklorists ever farther and deeper.

Janet C. Gilmore

References

Acheson, James M. 1988. *The Lobster Gangs of Maine.* Hanover, NH: University Press of New England.

Gilmore, Janet C. 1986. *The World of the Oregon Fishboat: A Study in Maritime Folklife.* Ann Arbor, MI: UMI Research Press.

Johnson, Paula J., ed. 1988. *Working the Water: The Commercial Fisheries of Maryland's Patuxent River.* Charlottesville: University of Virginia Press.

Mullen, Patrick B. 1978. *"I Heard the Old Fisherman Say": Folklore of the Texas Gulf.* Austin: University of Texas Press.

Orbach, Michael K. 1977. *Hunters, Seamen, and Entrepreneurs: The Tuna Fishermen of San Diego.* Berkeley: University of California Press.

Poggie, John J., and Carl Gersuny. 1974. *Fishermen of Galilee: The Human Ecology of a New England Coastal Community.* University of Rhode Island Marine Bulletin Series, No. 17. Kingston: University of Rhode Island Press.

Taylor, David A. 1992. *Documenting Maritime Folklife: An Introductory Guide.* Publications of the American Folklife Center, No. 18. Washington, DC: Library of Congress.

Turgeon, Laurier, ed. 1990. Identité Maritime Identity. *Canadian Folklore canadien* 12:2.

See also Boatbuilding; Fishing (Sport); Great Lakes; Maritime Folklore; Watermen

Fishing (Sport)

Recreational activity the popularity of which transcends racial, ethnic, social, and economic boundaries. Remarking on the curious allure of angling, folklorist and fisherman Andrew Lang suggested that "the passion, or instinct, being in all senses blind, must no doubt be hereditary. It is full of sorrow and bitterness and hope deferred, and entails the mockery of friends, especially of the fair. But I would as soon lay down a love of books as a love of fishing" (Lang 1891:7).

The assumption that fishing as a pastime affords pleasure to its participants as well as amusement to observers is so deeply entrenched in American folklore that it is necessary to remind oneself that fishing as a traditional sport is by no means a cultural universal, or even a historical constant in the traditions feeding our own. Anglo Saxon documents indicate that fishing in that era was regarded as primarily practical, deep-sea fishing being especially feared; only quite late in the Middle Ages does one find accounts such as that of the 15th-century prioress of the convent at Sopwell, Dame Juliana Berners, *On Fysshynge wyth an Angle* (1496), in which practical advice is mingled with commentary on the spiritual value of fishing as an aid to relaxation, concentration, and virtuous contemplation—values associated with fishing that recur throughout the British and Anglo American literature on fishing from Izaak Walton to the latest issue of *Field and Stream*. African American folklore is rich in the lore of fishing for pleasure as well, but it is more difficult to trace the roots of these in African tradition.

Despite the abundance of written and other media pub-

lications at all levels of sophistication concerning fishing, it is an activity learned initially almost invariably by example and direct tutelage, ensuring that the body of knowledge held by any one angler will have a strong and often conservative traditional component. The activity offers a curious combination of characteristics from the standpoint of cultural analysis: Although often pursued in solitude and intrinsically personal and isolated in nature, it contains several elements of performance. At the most primary level, the angler presents a deceptive performance for the fish that, if convincing enough, results in a catch. At the secondary level, the angler presents himself or herself to others using an array of expressive forms that define him or her as a member of one or several subgroups of anglers, and that account for triumphs or explain away defeats.

Although fishing for pleasure in the United States is not limited to a particular class or group of individuals and all generalizations are dangerous, it is possible to speak of types of American anglers in terms of certain "folk taxonomies." Fly fishermen, for example, are understood to pursue a technique considered rarefied and a bit arcane, with an elaborate esoteric vocabulary, garb, and history all of its own. Its roots are deep in the aristocratic British angling tradition, although the demands of American stream terrain and species have brought about some characteristic innovations in custom and practice. At the other end of the continuum is the image of the bait fisherman—the barefoot kid with a cane pole (now more likely graphite) and a can of worms wending his simple way to the local fishin' hole, innocently delighted to bring home a mess of obliging bluegill. The powerful American tendency toward organization and competition can be observed in the rather recent phenomenon of groups of bass fishermen engaged in day-long fishing tournaments, vying for substantial cash prizes. One group of anglers large in number but neglected in traditional images of fishing in America is that of women—despite the example of Dame Juliana, their status remains marginalized and their stereotype remains tainted by the imputation of incompetence or dumb luck.

American fishing folklore offers folk taxonomies of fish as well as fishermen. Unlike the British tradition's relatively consistent distinction between "rough" fish and "game" fish, American categories are as diverse as the American communities of fishermen. Folk nomenclature reflects this diversity: *Pomoxis annularis* and *nigromaculatus,* for example, known most commonly as white and black crappie, go by at least fifty other regional and local names, including goggle-eye, papermouth, banklick, lamplighter, Dolly Varden, and sac-a-lait. From the fierce, elusive muskellunge and the glamorous trout, to lowly bottomfeeders such as carp and catfish, each variety of fish is characterized according to appetite, temperament, appearance, and savor by the communities of anglers who seek or reject them.

Customary folklore concerning fishing is extensive, providing some support for the theory that ritual and belief practices are especially strong where an activity's outcome is uncertain. It is by far the aspect of sport fishing most thoroughly documented by folklorists. Portents of good and poor fishing days involving observation of the weather, animal behavior, and lunar cycles are common: The latter can be found in any contemporary almanac or popular fishing magazine. Luck is attributed to the presence or absence of numerous factors, the variables of which encompass virtually every aspect of the fisherman's circumstances and behavior except those controlled by skill, experience, and observation.

Fishing folklore is by no means limited to the practice itself: Verbal lore concerning fabulous catches represents a whole category of exaggerated narrative, highly formulaic and entertaining in content, with skeptical reaction from the audience an expected part of the performance. Perhaps in response to this automatic skepticism, many fishermen nowadays document their more impressive catches by photographs in which the poses and composition are consistent in pattern—a practice that has largely taken the place of the older, more expensive tradition of taxidermy.

Erika Brady

References

Hand, Wayland Debs. 1964. *Beliefs and Superstitions.* Vol. 7 of *The Frank C. Brown Collection of North Carolina Folklore.* Durham, NC: Duke University Press, pp. 470–483.

Hand, Wayland Debs, Anna Casetta, and Sondra B. Thiederman. 1981. *Popular Beliefs and Superstitions: A Compendium of American Folklore from the Ohio Collection of Newbell Niles Puckett.* Boston: G.K. Hall, pp. 1025–1029.

Lang, Andrew. 1891. *Angling Sketches.* London: Longmans, Green.

Poggie, John J., Jr., and Carl Gersuny. 1972. An Interpretation of Fishermen's Folklore in a New England Community. *Journal of American Folklore* 85:66–72.

See also Catfish; Fishing (Commercial); Hunting

Flanders, Helen Hartness (1890–1972)

Foremost collector and editor of Vermont folk-music traditions and founder of the Helen Hartness Flanders Folk Music Collection at Middlebury College. A conscientious, enterprising, and intelligent woman, Flanders undertook her collecting in May 1930 for the Vermont Commission on Country Life, which had the 150th anniversary of Vermont's statehood (1941) in mind. The avocation of a lifetime began as an exercise to record Vermont heritage for the benefit of all Vermonters. The wife of Ralph Edward Flanders, a wealthy businessman who served Vermont in the U.S. Senate, she began documenting old songs and melodies in the living memory of Vermont descendents of early settlers, gaining an understanding of folk tradition in the process. Between May and December 1930, she recorded a small, yet impressive, body of early New England songs and music, including rare ballad texts with their tunes. Of that first season, Flanders said, "before undertaking Prof. Peach's challenge, I had never even heard a traditional song." That she found immediate satisfaction in fieldwork is evident from her assessment of that effort: "Desire in this quest mounts readily to passion. The fascination of this lore continues; its excitement is cumulative."

Flanders ventured upon the ballad-hunting scene at a most fortuitous time. American ballad scholars and collectors had broken new ground over the preceding quarter-century; had figured out an appropriate categorization, definition, and catalog of American ballads; and had fostered great interest among a small but dedicated band of ballad enthusiasts. New England had just attained its due as a repository of migratory ballads, and, although the active tradition was fast declining, tradition bearers were numerous enough to impart a respectable, even enviable, repertoire of Old World and New World pieces. Music annotation and analysis had become an important component of folksong fieldwork, and Phillips Barry had demonstrated the importance of the informant and the setting in documenting folk tradition.

In the tight circle of New England balladry, Flanders soon crossed paths with Barry. She benefited greatly from his mentoring, improving the scope of her fieldwork, applying appropriate archiving principles to her data, and getting to know everyone of importance in folk-music studies. She placed articles in newspapers (those of Springfield, Massachusetts, and Narragansett, Rhode Island, for example), greatly increasing her list of informants and correspondents. In 1939 she invited Alan Lomax of the Library of Congress for a week of recording her informants for the library and for her Archive of Vermont Folk Music, then at Smiley Manse, her home in Springfield, Vermont.

As her material came to the attention of ballad scholars,

Flanders received many inquiries about specific items, enough to know that her collection had value within academe. This fact was a motivating force behind moving her archive to Middlebury College. (The college also boasted a ballad specialist on its faculty and a ballad course in its curriculum.) In February 1941, she established the Helen Hartness Flanders Collection there, containing New England folksongs, ballads, and folk tunes collected by her or under her direction. Disk records, dictaphone cylinders, typescripts of each recording, and items sent by her correspondents numbered about 2,000 items. A dozen years later, the collection accommodated close to 10,000 items. Flanders had large aspirations for the archive. She envisioned Middlebury students learning to sing (thereby, she naively assumed, perpetuating the tradition), then returning to their home regions to collect like materials. The college indicated its intention of integrating the archive not only in literature courses, but also in history, music, and even the social sciences.

Flanders took delight in introducing informants to the public. In July 1940, she invited Lena Bourne Fish of Jaffrey, New Hampshire, to Middlebury's Bread Loaf College to present her songs to an audience of students, faculty, and townspeople. In February 1948, she delivered the Louis Charles Elson Memorial Lecture at the Library of Congress, where she presented Elmer George and Asa Davis of Vermont and Charles Finnemore of Maine to sing some of the ballads they had recorded for her.

Flanders began publishing out of her collection for local readers very early on, producing, in 1931, *Vermont Folk-Songs and Ballads,* with music transcriptions by George Brown, a cellist from Melrose, Massachusetts. With Barry's professionalism as a guide, she produced *The New Green Mountain Songster* (1939), the first scholarly treatment of items from her collection. George Brown again supplied musical transcriptions, and her daughter, Elizabeth Flanders Ballard, took an active role. The volume was a success, reaching both a popular and a scholarly audience. Barry's introduction and annotations contributed a high order of scholarship, and the inclusion of short pieces, play parties, and dance materials found resonance in the lives of her rural New England readers.

Flanders hired musicologist Marguerite Olney to be her assistant, and they collaborated on the highly readable miscellany *Ballads Migrant in New England* (1953), which included an Introduction by Robert Frost. Olney became the first archivist of the Flanders Collection at Middlebury and annotated the long-playing recording *Eight Traditional British-American Ballads from the Helen Hartness Flanders Collection of Balladry and Folk Music* (1953).

Through her association and collaboration with professional ballad scholars, Flanders brought a depth to her fieldwork and related activities she could not have achieved on her own. She was admirably open to the guidance of veteran fieldworkers while never abandoning the original impulse of her efforts—to preserve Vermont's heritage for the benefit of all Vermonters. After Barry's death in 1937, Tristram Potter Coffin, a young scholar who had expressed an early admira-

tion for Flanders' ballad collection, worked closely with her. Together they produced four scholarly volumes of Child ballads. Coffin wrote the headnotes, and Bruno Nettl provided musical transcriptions and notations.

Working in an era when a spirit of competition dogged the field, Flanders succumbed to a bit of bean counting. She was tweaked occasionally about including examples of spurious folk origins to inflate the breadth of her collection, especially in the area of the treasured Child ballads. While there is some evidence for this, the proportion of suspect items is minuscule. Flanders was influenced, one assumes, by the entrenched bias of the academic ballad scholars, even as the field was trying to move beyond the ballad-aristocracy mindset. This was an abiding problem for the amateur collector, who was often far more successful in garnering tradition than were the scholars but whose understanding of the tradition was usually rather shallow. To her credit, Flanders vaulted this gap by gaining the respect and collaboration of scholars among the most eminent of the time. Helen Hartness Flanders reached for the highest standards and achieved them.

Linda Morley

References

Flanders, Helen Hartness. 1934. *A Garland of Green Mountain Song.* Northfield, VT.

———, comp. and ed. 1960–1965. *Ancient Ballads Traditionally Sung in New England: From the Helen Hartness Flanders Ballad Collection Middlebury College, Middlebury, Vermont.* 4 vols. Critical Analysis by Tristram P. Coffin. Music Annotations by Bruno Nettl. Philadelphia: University of Pennsylvania Press.

Folk Ideas

Culturally held beliefs that are constituent parts of the larger worldview of a culture. (Worldview refers to the total manner in which the members of a culture see the nature of the universe and their place in it.) The term was coined in 1972 by Alan Dundes and has not been widely used by other folklorists.

Dundes proposed the term because he thought that worldview was such a broad concept that students of culture needed a way to refer to smaller "units" of it. He also hoped that "folk ideas" would replace the misuse of the term "myth" (which, to folklorists and anthropologists, means a type of narrative) to refer to the grand, controlling ideas of a culture (as in the "myth of the frontier"), a usage adopted by literary critics and others. The term "folk ideas" was not meant to refer to a specific genre of folklore but rather to concepts that might be embedded in various kinds of folklore or even in other, nonfolkloric cultural expressions, including literature and the mass media.

Dundes suggested that folk ideas included such "cultural axioms" as the American notion of unlimited good (there is no limit on the amount of something that can be produced or obtained) and the American belief that all persons have equal opportunity. The idea of unlimited good might be expressed, for example, in the folk expression, "There's plenty more where that came from." A culture may have contradictory folk ideas.

Folk ideas are related to folk stereotypes (such as those about ethnic groups), but Dundes saw the former as less consciously conceived than the latter.

Frank de Caro

References

De Caro, Frank. 1992. New Orleans, Folk Ideas, and the Lore of Place. *Louisiana Folklore Miscellany* 7:68–80.
Dundes, Alan. 1972. Folk Ideas as Units of Worldview. In *Toward New Perspectives in Folklore,* ed. Américo Paredes and Richard Bauman. Austin: University of Texas Press and the American Folklore Society, pp. 93–103.

Folk Museums

Museums displaying artifacts of traditional life, often in a park-like, rural, or "village" setting. The origin of the folk museum has been generally credited to museums established in Scandinavia in the late 19th century. Artur Hazelius' idea of the folk museum led to what is known today as the Nordiska Museet and Skansen (meaning open-air museum) in Stockholm. In his earliest museum exhibit work at the 1878 World's Fair in Paris, Hazelius is said to have "arranged his exhibits as stage sets with one side open facing the public, the figures arranged in highly emotional tableaux similar to the way it is done at a waxworks." Bernard Olsen, founder of the Danish Folk Museum, found Hazelius' method of exhibition unsatisfactory when he saw it at the World's Fair in Paris in 1878. He preferred the approach that the Dutch had employed, a complete room that one could walk into and where "each single thing came from old houses and stood in its accustomed position." Olsen later recalled: "In contrast to the Swedish manner the effect was stirring, and from the moment I entered the room, it was as if one were in another world—far away in time and space from the crowded, modern exhibition. It was clear to me this is how a folk museum should be."

These early reflections on the proper approach and organization of the folk museum were shaped also by the national Romanticism of northern Europe. Later, in 1891, Skansen, the first open-air museum, was founded in Stockholm, where old farmsteads and community buildings from Sweden and Scandinavia were saved, moved, and then reerected. Both the Nordiska Museet and Skansen provided the impetus for other nations and smaller community efforts in the development of folk museums.

These early folk museums fostered the concept of the open-air or outdoor museum and the spread of ethnological research in Great Britain and then to Canada and the United States. Folklife museums in the late 20th century explore a variety of approaches to the investigation and understanding of human social organization and stress the holistic nature of a traditional culture on all levels of society.

The concept of the open-air museum was utilized as a model for American museums such as the Farmer's Museum in Cooperstown, New York; Colonial Williamsburg, Virginia;

Old Sturbridge Village, Massachusetts; and the Henry Ford Museum, Dearborn, Michigan. In Europe the influence of the Skansen model led to the growth of additional open-air museums on into the 20th century. Among the major museums were the Welsh Folk Museum, St. Fagans, Wales; Osterreichische Freilichtmuseum, Stubing, Austria; and Schleswig-Holsteinisches Freilichtmuseum, Kiel, Germany. The growth of these open-air museums encouraged the development of smaller complexes across Europe, the United States, and Canada.

The open-air museum as a folk museum was designed to provide a focal point for the study, collection, and interpretation of national, regional, and local culture. The emphasis has been primarily on the assembly of buildings in a new interpretive setting where the cultural life of a particular place in time is re-created. Over the years, museum staffs have enhanced the presentation of the cultural life of the nation, region, or locale by involving traditional artists and performers, tradition bearers, and interpreters, as well as re-creating the patterns of daily life by utilizing animals, plants, gardens, and features of the natural world to re-create a more natural context.

The idea of the folk museum has evolved to be a conceptual approach to various specific cultural traditions. The folk-museum movement has been spurred by the scholarly desire to depict the history and lifeways of average families, typical communities, and everyday life. The result has been the creation of living history farms, museums linked to occupational traditions—such as those of miners, textile workers, or ironworkers—urban museums featuring tenement-house life or immigrant communities, and museums that serve to present local ethnic and cultural traditions.

Folklife as a discipline has contributed substantially to the development of these new community-based museums. With the goal of re-creating a living museum experience where the visitor encounters authentic contexts for learning, folklorists have played critical roles in re-creating everyday life and the historical processes that make a particular culture. The use of oral-history fieldwork, the involvement of informants as presenters, and the attention to the complexity of community-based culture are critical elements in providing an effective and accurate learning environment.

An extension of the folk museum has been the emergence of the folk festival as a short-term living museum. The Smithsonian Institution's annual Festival of American Folklife in Washington, DC, has established a model in which folk arts, occupational traditions, and regional culture are presented with exhibit-like sets to evoke the original context. Professional ethnomusicologists, folklorists, and other cultural specialists are engaged as researchers and presenters to enhance the educational presentations. This approach has been adapted by other museums and cultural organizations in the creation of state and local folklife festivals.

In the later 20th century, folklife exhibits (continuing and temporary) and folklife collections have been developed by many art museums, history museums, and natural cultural history museums. Early open-air museums such as Colonial

Williamsburg and Old Sturbridge Village have been followed by, among others, the Museum of International Folk Art in Santa Fe, New Mexico; the Museum of American Folk Art in New York City; and the Museum of Civilization in Ottawa, Canada—as well as museums devoted to specific cultural groups—all featuring folk traditions and emphasizing the folk process as well as the products of folk culture.

Folklife-museum interpretation has made a substantial contribution to museum interpretive theory as it is practiced today. The contextual approach to folklife stresses the expressive behaviors of tradition bearers. This approach has influenced the interpretive educational approach of history museums, leading to more hands-on activities, special demonstrations, and a wide array of museum-sponsored festivals and creative restagings of special cultural events and activities.

The growth of folk museums has been truly extraordinary over the past century. The Association of European Open Air Museums produces a guide to more than 350 open-air museums in twenty-one European countries. Community-based folk museums are also being established at a rapid rate. Legislation such as the federal Native American Grave Protection and Repatriation Act has led to an explosion of tribal museums in the United States. Meanwhile, major history, natural history, and art museums are recognizing folk arts as valued materials to collect and present. This development has enabled museums to achieve more representative collections of their communities and thus attract broader audiences. The folk museum movement continues to thrive as the basis of independent freestanding museums as well as a scholarly force that has shaped museology in Europe, North America, and now in other parts of the world.

C. Kurt Dewhurst

References

Anderson, Jay. 1984. *Time Machines: The World of Living History.* Nashville: American Association for State and Local History.

Bronner, Simon J., ed. 1982. *American Material Culture and Folklife: A Prologue and Dialogue.* Logan: Utah State University Press.

———, ed. 1987. *Folklife Studies from the Gilded Age: Object, Rite, and Custom in Victorian America.* Ann Arbor, MI: UMI Research Press.

Hall, Patricia, and Charlie Seemann, eds. 1987. *Folklife and Museums: Selected Readings.* Nashville: American Association for State and Local History.

Higgs, J.W.Y. 1963. *Folklife Collection and Classification.* London: Museums Association.

Jenkins. J. Geraint. 1972. The Use of Artifacts and Folk Art in the Folk Museum. In *Folklore and Folklife: An Introduction,* ed. Richard M. Dorson. Chicago: University of Chicago Press.

Loomis, Ormond. 1977. *Sources on Folk Museums and Living History Farms.* Bloomington, IN: Folklore Forum Bibliographic and Special Series.

See also Festival; Folklife Movement; Material Culture

Folk Schools

The English translation (sometimes "folk college") of the Danish words *Folkehojskole* or *Hojskole.* In their various uses, the terms carry social, philosophical, educational, and political meanings, with certain paradigmatic relationships to the applied folkloristics of the mid- and later 20th century.

The folk-school movement was envisioned and inspired by Nikolaj Frederik Severin Grundtvig (1783–1872). Grundtvig was a theologian who loved Danish history and people and harbored a deep concern that everyone have access to education. In the years following 1830, this goal became an immediate necessity as the result of political change. South of the Danish border, a new German state was emerging, and it became Grundtvig's desire that Danes reawaken to spirituality and strength of the individual self while promoting strength in national character. In publications of the early and mid-19th century, Grundtvig wrote passionately regarding the need for the *Folkehojskole.* A new movement was also beginning to spread throughout Denmark replacing Rationalism with Romantic nationalism. These shifts in worldview changed the dominant school of thought in the literary, visual, and performing arts. Coinciding with these movements was one that advocated that people take the spiritual concerns and matters of the church into the people's own hands, much the same as the "Great Awakening" religious movement functioned in the United States during the 18th century. Grundtvig, influenced by all of these intellectual currents, was an advocate for the children of rural farm families, whom he wished to see acquire technical skills in a noncompetitive environment, while having their physical and spiritual needs enhanced. Thus, the *Folkehojskole* was viewed as an informal institution that would enrich the body, mind, and spirit while fostering independent thinking by enlightened, courageous, and conscientious citizens.

The first Danish *Folkehojskole* was founded in south Jutland on November 7, 1844, and was called *Rodding Hojskole.* By 1870 a total of fifty-two such schools had been founded, and by the late 20th century hundreds had been founded throughout Denmark, many of which are still in existence.

In England in the late 19th century a related movement to found "settlement schools" emerged. The settlement-school idea arose from desires, articulated by prominent persons of the time, to improve the lives of the poor (Charles Dickens, 1812–1870), to eliminate inhumane working conditions in factories (Robert Owen, 1771–1858), and to create a more even distribution of wealth (John Stuart Mill, 1806–1873). In 1884 Toynbee Hall was established as a settlement school in east London. This school has been characterized by Allen Davis as "the culmination of a diverse reform movement, closely allied with Romanticism, that sought to preserve humanistic and spiritual values in a world dominated by materialism and urban industrialism," all concepts that were dear to the thinking of Grundtvig as well.

During the late 19th century in the United States, a generation of people, many of them women, left formal educational institutions in the Northeast after completing their educations and emigrated into regions of the Appalachians to perform "cultural work" among the indigenous people. Part of this work included the establishment of cottage industries in the arts and functional crafts, and this practice helped usher in an arts-and-crafts revival in Appalachia, the impact of which is still felt in mountain communities.

The concept of the folk school in the United States, drew from the forces of the craft revival in Appalachia, the settlement-school concept in Britain, and the Danish *Folkehojskole*. During the early 20th century, New England native Olive Dame Campbell began to travel in the Appalachian Mountains with her husband, John C. Campbell, who was working on a social survey of Appalachian life for the Russell Sage Foundation. During her travels in which she implemented some of the first and most scientific ballad collecting in Appalachia, she formulated the desire to found such a school in the region. With folksong and folk-dance collector Cecil Sharp of England, she collaborated on *English Folk Songs from the Southern Appalachians* (1917). She was also a founding member of the Southern Highland Handicraft Guild, and thus instrumental in the revival of folk craft in Appalachia.

In 1925, after traveling and studying the folk high schools in Denmark, Olive Campbell and Margaret Butler of the Hindman Settlement School in Kentucky founded the John C. Campbell Folk School in Brasstown, North Carolina. Until her retirement in the mid-20th century, Campbell codirected the school and taught her students concepts of enlightenment for the body, soul, and spirit through nature studies, the construction of folk art and functional craft with an emphasis upon *process* over *product*, and the awakening of the inner self through music and dance in a spirit of noncompetitive interaction among a diverse cross-section of the populace.

As the 21st century approaches, the John C. Campbell Folk School serves more than 3,000 students per year. More than an educational institution, the school also maintains an archive and a collection of art and craft objects, presents weekly concerts that celebrate the musical traditions of the community and region, sponsors community dances that focus on local and regional dance styles, and maintains an ongoing folklore program, which documents and makes visible the intrinsic folklife of the region through a wide variety of publications and public programs.

During the 20th century, other such folk schools were established, but their emphasis has shifted as cultural, educational, and spiritual concerns have changed. The Highlander Folk School of Tennessee, for instance, became a training ground for social protest and civil disobedience during the late 1950s and 1960s. It was at the Highlander Folk School that Sister Rosa Parks and Dr. Martin Luther King Jr. were trained. In the mid-1990s, the Highlander Folk School is involved in environmental studies and related applied protest activities regarding environmental waste and pollution. The Hindman Settlement School of Kentucky, founded on the English settlement-school model and closely related to the folk-school movement, has evolved into an educational institution specializing in dyslexia-related reading disorders among children and young adults.

Thus, the humanitarian concepts and aspirations toward holistic education continues with a very few folk schools still in operation in the United States; of them, the John C. Campbell Folk School is the longest in continuous operation upholding the original strivings of the Danish *Folkehojskole*.
David A. Brose

References

Davis, Allen. 1967. *Spearheads of Reform: The Social Settlements and the Progressive Movement, 1890–1914*. New York: Oxford University Press.

Folk Speech

Vernacular pronunciations, grammatical forms, and expressions associated with rustic or old-fashioned members of a culture. Folk *speech*, like folk*lore*, is transmitted from one generation to another within oral traditions of a culture rather than through public communications media or educational or institutional precept. It is associated primarily with the working class in both agrarian and industrial settings, particularly when spoken with a strong regional accent. Folk speech may be used by anyone, but it is most commonly associated with individuals who are past middle age, who have relatively little formal education, or whose income is well below the national average. Because folk speech persists through many generations, it contains many archaisms and is often used in folk sayings.

Many of the pronunciations, words, grammatical forms, and syntactic structures that are regarded as folk speech originated in earlier stages of a language and have been retained in some or many dialects for centuries. For instance, double or triple negatives and the use of *ain't* (*He ain't never done nuthin like that before*) derive from the use of augmented negation in Old and Middle English and the contraction of *are not / am not* and *have not / has not* (with later loss of *h* and weakly articulated *v* and *s*) in Early Modern English. Folk usages may also develop from nonhistorical forms of untraceable origin, such as *He ain't do that* ("He didn't do that") in African American Vernacular English. Some folk speech is found in all dialects of a language, such as double negatives and *ain't*, whereas other folk usages are specific to certain regions, such as the use of *y'all* in the American South. Folk forms may develop in English as a second language and be retained after acculturation, as in the German and Polish American use of *ainna / enna* (from *ain't it*) as a tag question (*Hot today, ainna?*) used by residents of Milwaukee and South St. Louis. Occasional folk usages can be traced through millennia, such as the Chicano Spanish verb form *semos* for standard *somos* (we are), traceable to variant usage in Rome when Augustus Caesar used *simus* rather than *sumus*.

In the United States, the regions that were settled by native speakers of English before 1800—New England, the Southeast, Appalachia—are known for their folk speech, such as "Down East" language in Maine or "hillbilly" talk in Tennessee and northern Georgia. The Upland South, the Mississippi Delta, and the Ozark Mountains were settled by immigrants from lowland and upland areas of the Southeast and thus use folk speech forms derived from the language of their linguistic ancestors in the South Atlantic states. The Midwest and the West attracted a greater variety of immigrants and consequently a mixing of cultural and linguistic traditions; also, public education was widely available within two generations after these areas were settled, thereby widening the influence of "book language" on local speech. Thus, the expression "folk speech of Kansas" would have a much narrower range of reference than "folk speech of Maine" or "folk speech of Alabama."

The folk language of African Americans in the South developed through oral culture, not just during the time of slavery but well into the 20th century. Because of limited educational and economic opportunities prior to the last quarter of the 20th century, African Americans not only have had less access to "book language," but also have lived in social environments that contribute to the development of vernacular speech that is substantially different from the language of Americans who have economic, social, and political power. During Southern migrations to urban areas in the first half of the 20th century, folk speech forms in Black English vernacular spread across America (such as the uninflected *be* in *He always be tellin me somethin new*). Because Black folk speech originated in Southern states, the expression "folk speech of African Americans in California" would be relatively meaningless, whereas "folk speech of African Americans in the Mississippi Delta" is very meaningful.

Nonstandard verb forms are particularly salient in folk speech. In interviews for the *Linguistic Atlas of the United States and Canada* (see Editor's Note) in New England, the Upper Midwest, the Atlantic states, and the Gulf states, a substantial number of Americans said *he don't* rather than *he doesn't*, particularly older speakers with less than a high school education. Similar results were found by fieldworkers for the *Dictionary of American Regional English* (Cassidy et al. 1985–; henceforth *DARE*). Most of the nonstandard verb forms that are regarded as folk speech derive directly or indirectly from regularization processes that were well under way in Early Middle English (ca. 1250). In Old and Middle English, the suffixes of past-tense verbs and past participles were weak (added a suffix with *d* or *t: talk / talked, say / said, buy / bought*) or strong (changed the root vowel but did not add *d* or *t: know / knew / known, find / found / found*). Virtually all new verbs that have entered the language since Late Middle English use the regular weak inflections (add *d* or *ed)*, and many of the older verbs have changed their form (*boughten —> bought*). Present-day folk use of *knowed* and *growed* reflects the tendency for Early Modern English speakers to use the new form of suffixation, whereas *holp* and *clomb* reflect retention of an old form. Past-tense verbs like *he writ* and *he drunk* derive from strong verbs that used different root vowels in singular and plural forms *(he wroot / thei writ; he drank / thei drunk)*; in the 18th and 19th centuries, authors of dictionaries and school grammars favored

one of the competing forms but the "folk" often continued to use other form. Folk usages such as *hit* (it), *betwixt, three foot high / go three mile down the road*, and many pronunciations (for example, *sech* for *such*) also have historical explanations.

Folk usages do not necessarily derive from Middle English (1100–1500) or Early Modern English (1500–1700) grammatical forms. The present-day use of past-tense forms as past participles *(it was wrote that way; he should have went home)* developed in Modern English after the loss of distinction between past-tense and past-participle forms. Though these verbs are considered "wrong" by educators, they persist in oral contexts and thus are part of folk speech. The past-tense forms *dove* and *snuck,* following the older vowel-change forms of the past tense, apparently developed during the 19th century *(Webster's Dictionary of English Usage)*. In the late 20th century, writers tend to use *snuck* only for humorous effect or to suggest rural or unsophisticated speech, but both *dived* and *dove* are used widely in print. The competing past-tense forms of *dive* have regional distributions, with *dove* predominant in Atlas data from Northern states and *dived* predominant in data from Southern states. The distribution of *div* in Atlas surveys was similar to that of other archaic forms (thus folk speech)—namely, in northeastern New England and the Upper South and in the speech of African Americans.

Pronoun forms play a prominent role in folk speech. Throughout medieval and Renaissance Europe, the second-person-plural pronouns *vous* (French), *Sie* (German), and *ye / you* (Late Middle English) were used for singular reference in formal social contexts, and the singular forms *tu, du, thou / thee* were reserved for informal contexts. After *you* had become established as a singular form in Early Modern English, *you all* and *you ones* developed as folk plural forms. Over time, these forms were contracted to *y'all* and *youens*. Folk forms also developed in the possessive pronouns in Late Middle English as *my / mine* and *thy / thine* developed from Middle English *min* and *thin*. The *n* was elided when these words were modifiers of nouns beginning with consonants, and the longer forms were used in modifiers before vowels and in the pronoun form *(mine eyes, they are mine)*. In Southern and Midland dialects in 14th-century England, the *n* came to be associated with the pronoun form and was added to other possessive pronoun forms *(your eyes, they are yourn; his eyes, they are hisn)*. In Northern and East Midland dialects in 14th-century England, *s,* by analogy to noun forms, was often used to mark the possessive pronoun *(your eyes, they are yours; her eyes, they are hers)* (Mossé 1952:59–60). In Old and Middle English, none of these possessive pronouns had ever used *s*. The East Midland form, which would have been used in the London area, became the preferred form in printed documents. In interviews for *The Linguistic Atlas of the Gulf States* in the 1970s, *yourn* was used twenty-three times and *hisn* forty-two times. In vernacular Black English, *s* is often added to the pronoun *mine* in emphatic usage, particularly by young speakers *(What's mines is mines!)*.

Loan transfers and borrowings in the speech of immigrant groups have become part of American folk speech, such as *schlep* and *Are you coming with?* from Yiddish influence. Elements of foreign accent often remain in speech well after acculturation, such as *dese tings* in urban Italian American settings in the East; *dis* and *dat* in the speech of Midwesterners of German ancestry; and the Scandinavian American pronunciation *rench* for *range* in the Iron Range of Minnesota. These usages are usually regarded as *ethnic dialect;* they are passed from one generation to another by processes that keep other elements of folk culture alive.

During the 1960s and 1970s, when national attention was focused on the education of children from impoverished homes, linguists used the term *social dialect* to refer to the language of socioeconomic and ethnic groups in America. Social dialects include not only the "nonstandard" language of minorities (Hispanics, Blacks) and poor Whites, but also language typically used by speakers of higher social status in certain contexts, such as the language of sales personnel in elegant shops catering to the rich. In this sense, Standard English is the dialect that educated people use in semiformal and formal social contexts.

Authors often use folk speech to indicate that a character is uneducated, rustic, or old-fashioned. Generally, an author uses only a few folk-dialect items, just enough to evoke the intended impression. Writers often spell words to give the impression of folk pronunciations, such as *duz, sez, wuz,* and *wimmin.* These spellings are known as *eye dialect.* In most standard varieties of English, *does, says,* and *women* are pronounced *duz, sez,* and *wimmin,* and in rapid speech *was* is pronounced *wuz* under weakened stress. Even though these spellings accurately represent standard as well as folk pronunciations, the "misspellings" give the impression of rusticity or low level of education.

Though slang and argots are transmitted through oral traditions, they are not folk speech because their use is limited to groups with specialized interests or to generations younger than middle age. Slang terms tend to be shortlived: What was *neat* in the 1950s became *cool* in the 1960s, *rad* in the 1980s, and *fly* in the 1990s. Such terms are used primarily by younger speakers and experience short lives, but *pot, dope,* and *crack* as terms for illegal drugs have become candidates for standard usage in public discussions of drugs in print and electronic media. If these latter terms continue to be used for several generations after other terms have replaced them, they, too, may be considered folk speech at some time in the future.

Though folk speech is generally associated with nonstandard usage, such as the examples used so far, much of our everyday language derives from oral traditions and, in this sense, is folk speech. For example, *soda, pop, tonic,* and *dope* are used in conversation to refer to carbonated soft drinks. *Tonic* occurs primarily in New England and *dope* in the Southeast, whereas the other two terms are used throughout the country, though with some regional distribution (*pop* in Kansas City and *soda* in St. Louis). In formal written contexts, *soft drink* is preferred because the conversational terms are considered informal. Young people may introduce terms that later will be regarded as folk speech. For instance, most of the informants in the *Atlas* and *DARE* surveys had regional variants for *dragon fly* (such as *snake doctor, snake feeder, darning needle*), and interviews during the 1960s and 1970s found that young speakers had added *helicopter bug.* Some everyday terms have regional distributions that are rarely noted by anyone except dialectologists. For example, in *DARE* interviews, *armful* is common in Northern and Eastern states whereas *armload* is more common in Southwestern and Western states.

Though many competing grammatical forms and all conversational vocabulary ultimately derive from oral traditions, some are sanctioned by usage mavens, and others are not; whether a particular form would be considered folk speech depends on who is "passing judgment," who uses the form, and the circumstances under which it is used. In a school setting, *He knowed just where it was—three mile down the road,* would be considered "incorrect," and perhaps quaint, but the same sentence spoken by the pupil's grandfather would be considered folk speech. *I seen him,* spoken by an elegantly dressed office worker would be considered "uneducated," but the same phrase in the speech of a laborer digging a ditch for a sewer pipe would be considered working-class folk speech. English professors who use the phrase in any social context would be committing a gaffe, but animal husbandry professors who use it in conversations with pig farmers might be merely using the folk speech of those with whom they communicate in their profession.

Donald M. Lance

References

Cassidy, Frederic G., et al. 1985, 1991. *Dictionary of American Regional English.* Vol. 1, A–C. Vol. 2, D–H. Cambridge: Harvard University Press, Belknap Press.

Mossé, Fernand. 1952. *A Handbook of Middle English,* trans. James A. Walker. Baltimore: Johns Hopkins University Press.

Webster's Dictionary of English Usage. 1989. Springfield, MA: Merriam-Webster.

In 1929 plans were made for a series of surveys for the *Linguistic Atlas of the United States and Canada.* By the mid-1990s, three completed atlases had been published: Hans Kurath et al. (1939–1943). *The Linguistic Atlas of New England.* 3 vols., in 6 parts. Providence, RI: Brown University; Harold B. Allen. 1973–1976. *The Linguistic Atlas of the Upper Midwest.* 3 vols. Minneapolis: University of Minnesota Press; Lee Pederson et al. 1986–1992. *The Linguistic Atlas of the Gulf States.* 7 vols. Athens: University of Georgia Press. Three books have been published on *Atlas* data collected in the area from Maine to eastern Georgia that was settled before 1800: Hans Kurath. 1949. *A Word Geography of the Eastern United States.* Ann Arbor: University of Michigan Press; E. Bagby Atwood. 1953. *A Survey of Verb Forms in the Eastern United States.* Ann Arbor: University of Michigan Press; Hans Kurath and Raven I. McDavid Jr. 1961. *The Pronunciation of English in the Atlantic States.* Ann Arbor: University of Michigan Press.

Public Law 94-201
94th Congress, H. R. 6673
January 2, 1976

An Act

To provide for the establishment of an American Folklife Center in the Library
of Congress, and for other purposes.

*Be it enacted by the Senate and House of Representatives of the
United States of America in Congress assembled,* That this Act may
be cited as the "American Folklife Preservation Act".

DECLARATION OF FINDINGS AND PURPOSE

SEC. 2. (a) The Congress hereby finds and declares—
(1) that the diversity inherent in American folklife has contributed greatly to the cultural richness of the Nation and has
fostered a sense of individuality and identity among the American
people;
(2) that the history of the United States effectively demonstrates that building a strong nation does not require the sacrifice
of cultural differences;
(3) that American folklife has a fundamental influence on the
desires, beliefs, values, and character of the American people;
(4) that it is appropriate and necessary for the Federal Government to support research and scholarship in American folklife in order to contribute to an understanding of the complex
problems of the basic desires, beliefs, and values of the American
people in both rural and urban areas;
(5) that the encouragement and support of American folklife,
while primarily a matter for private and local initiative, is also
an appropriate matter of concern to the Federal Government;
and
(6) that it is in the interest of the general welfare of the Nation
to preserve, support, revitalize, and disseminate American folklife traditions and arts.
(b) It is therefore the purpose of this Act to establish in the
Library of Congress an American Folklife Center to preserve and
present American folklife.

DEFINITIONS

SEC. 3. As used in this Act—
(1) the term "American folklife" means the traditional expressive culture shared within the various groups in the United
States: familial, ethnic, occupational, religious, regional; expressive culture includes a wide range of creative and symbolic forms
such as custom, belief, technical skill, language, literature, art,
architecture, music, play, dance, drama, ritual, pageantry, handicraft; these expressions are mainly learned orally, by imitation,
or in performance, and are generally maintained without benefit
of formal instruction or institutional direction;
(2) the term "Board" means the Board of Trustees of the
Center;
(3) the term "Center" means the American Folklife Center
established under this Act;

Excerpt from the law that defined "American folklife" and established the American Folklife Center.

See also Black English; Cursing; Etymology, Folk (Popular)

Folklife Movement

Scholarly approach beginning in the 19th century emphasizing the "folk cultural" or holistic study of everyday practices,
artifacts, and expressions in community context. The roots of
the movement date to the use of the Swedish word *folkliv*
(folklife) in 1847, when it appeared in a Swedish book,
Folklivet i Skytts harad (The Folklife of the Jurisdictional District of Skytt). By 1878 it was used in the title of a new periodical, *Svenska Landsmal och Svenskt Folkliv* (Swedish Dialects

and Swedish Folklife). The German equivalents of folklife were
Volksleben and *Volkskunde,* which regularly appeared after
1806. *Volkskunde* was variously defined, but a significant
meaning for it emerged emphasizing everyday life and tradition of individuals and communities in ethnic-regional contexts. Richard Weiss defined *Volkskunde* in 1946 as "the study
of the interrelationships between the folk and folk-culture, in
so far as they are determined by community and tradition"
(Weiss 1946:11). Influenced by German and Swedish models of folklife research, Don Yoder proposed that folklife study
in American scholarship "is oriented toward holistic studies of

culture regionally delimited and toward 'life,' the life of the society under study and of the individual within that society" (Yoder 1976:4).

The first general book on American folklife, *Zur Amerikanischen Volkskunde* (1905) was written by Karl Knortz (1841-1918) and was translated into English as *American Folklore* in 1988. Early English-language folklife titles included Heli Chatelain's "African Folklife" (1897), William Greenough's *Canadian Folk-Life and Folk-Lore* (1897), and Martha Warren Beckwith's *Black Roadways: A Study of Jamaican Folk Life* (1929). In addition to folklife, terms such as "folk culture" and "regional ethnology" also are used to refer to holistic studies of traditional societies, particularly of regional-ethnic groups. From its relatively minor role in English American folklore scholarship during the late 19th century, folklife study has gained prominence in the United States, particularly after World War II.

The English scholarly approach of "folklore" inherited by the founders of the American Folklore Society was to limit the materials of folklore to oral tradition and to emphasize the organization of the subject by genres. Concentrating on the accumulation of narrative texts, English American scholars often constructed histories of literary types and themes. Folklife scholars expanded the cultural materials under study to all products of tradition, including rituals, customs, crafts, architecture, clothing, furnishing, and art. They also included the mental aspects of culture, such as concepts of shelter, settlement, space, and time. They organized the subject by cultures or culture areas and attempted to integrate the many aspects of culture in a regional or community context, taking into account cultural patterns, historical and geographical conditions, and social changes and movements. Using the active social references of "life" and "culture" as keywords, they examined their subject as a living tradition and, therefore, applied a combination of sociological, ethnographic, and historical methods.

German, Swedish, and Irish scholars used folklife and folk-culture research particularly in relation to enclosed peasant societies. Rooted in place and conducting their lives according to tradition, peasants appeared to live in a community-bound folk culture. Because such cultures were considered stable over time but variable over space, they were examined to map the extent of regional and ethnic influence and relationships of cultures to one another. Within the communities, scholars analyzed the integrative functions of traditions within a society. Comparing the patterns of customs, narratives, architecture, and crafts, folklife scholars also sought to uncover guiding concepts (also called "base concepts" or "worldview") of space, behavior, and time. In some nations, peasant societies were considered to constitute the cultural roots of the nation, and uncovering such concepts was thought to offer insights into the social patterns of national societies.

In the United States, European-type peasant societies were thought not to exist, but folklife scholarship found adherents particularly among Pennsylvania German researchers, who found the model appropriate to studying the community and regional variations within an ethnic-agricultural settlement. The Pennsylvania German folklife scholars emphasized the formation of traditional community life. As early as 1882, Phebe Earle Gibbons brought together descriptions of language, religion, festivals, quiltings, farming, holidays, and manners and customs to discuss communities of Pennsylvania Germans (Gibbons 1882). In 1888 Walter James Hoffman departed from the typical contents of the *Journal of American Folklore* by including considerations of foodways, architecture, and custom alongside speech and narrative (Hoffman 1888). In 1900 F.J.F. Schantz published *The Domestic Life and Characteristics of the Pennsylvania-German Pioneer* under the imprint of the Pennsylvania German Society, and up to World War II, Pennsylvania German researchers such as John Baer Stoudt, Preston Barba, and Thomas Brendle made substantial contributions to the study of Pennsylvania German folklife.

The big boost for the folklife movement in the United States came in 1948 when Alfred L. Shoemaker, who had studied folk culture in Germany, Switzerland, Ireland, and Sweden, established the first Department of Folklore in the United States at Franklin and Marshall College in Lancaster, Pennsylvania, and organized it around a folklife approach. With Don Yoder and J. William Frey, he directed the Pennsylvania Dutch Folklore Center, which published the *Pennsylvania Dutchman* (subtitled *Devoted to Pennsylvania Dutch Folk-Culture*) and held seminars on the "Folk Culture of the Pennsylvania Dutch Country" (intended for "serious students of American folk-life"). In addition, the center compiled an archive called the "folk-cultural index," organized what came to be America's largest folk festival, and began the Pennsylvania Folklife Museum. Shoemaker published studies in folk culture, including books on the Pennsylvania barn and on Christmas and Easter customs. "The center" Don Yoder recalled, "was based on European models and its purposes included the collecting, archiving, and disseminating of scholarly information on every aspect of the Pennsylvania German culture. In 1956, under the influence of the European *Volkskunde* and folklife (regional ethnology) movements, we changed the title of our organization to the Pennsylvania Folklife Society and the name of the periodical published by our society from the *Pennsylvania Dutchman* to *Pennsylvania Folklife*. In this way we felt that we might do justice to all of Pennsylvania's ethnic groups" (Yoder 1982: 18). Inspired by the appearance of *Ulster Folklife* in 1955, *Pennsylvania Folklife* became the first in the United States with "folklife" in its title.

In 1963 Yoder proclaimed the "folklife-studies movement" to be launched, and he called for research in regions outside Pennsylvania and applications in colleges, museums, and historical societies. At the University of Pennsylvania, Yoder became part of the first Ph.D.-granting institution with folklife in its title—the Department of Folklore and Folklife. Influenced by events in Pennsylvania, the Cooperstown graduate program, granting the M.A. degree in American folk culture with required courses in folklife research (sponsored jointly by the New York State Historical Association and the State University of New York at Oneonta from 1964 to 1979), was established by Louis C. Jones. In the Midwest, the Folk-lore Institute at Indiana University included folklife courses taught by Warren Roberts. In 1965 Jones helped bridge European and American folklife (Wildhaber 1965), research by publishing a translation of European *Volkskunde* scholar Robert Wildhaber's bibliography of American folklife (Wildhaber 1965), and further communication was heralded in 1967 by the publication of "An Approach to Folklife Studies," by Scottish folklife specialist Alexander Fenton, in the Pennsylvania journal *Keystone Folklore*.

A major contribution of folklife research to the English American model of folklore scholarship was a broadening of scope to include material culture. Norbert F. Riedl in 1965 made a special plea for the use of German *Volkskunde* research and its use of material evidence in American scholarship. In 1968 Henry Glassie, a product of the Cooperstown and Pennsylvania programs, demonstrated the appropriateness of folklife and material-culture research for a diverse American society in *Pattern in the Material Folk Culture of the Eastern United States*. On the basis of diffusion patterns evident from architecture, food, and craft, Glassie identified regional cultures emanating from four historic cultural "hearths" on the Eastern seaboard: North, Mid-Atlantic, Lowland South, and Upland South. Whereas Glassie emphasized historical development of regional cultures, more of the ethnographic approach to the individual in folk art and material culture was evident in the work of Michael Owen Jones, who studied at Indiana University and later taught in the Ph.D. program at UCLA. From the 1960s to the 1980s anthologies appeared—such as *Forms upon the Frontier* (1969), edited by Austin E. and Alta S. Fife and Henry Glassie; *Folklore and Folklife* (1972), edited by Richard M. Dorson; *American Folklife* (1976), edited by Don Yoder; and *American Material Culture and Folklife* (1992), edited by Simon J. Bronner—including both historical and ethnographic approaches to folklife and covering a broad range of groups, communities, and regions in North America. The scope of folklife research extended to Louisiana Cajuns, inner-city Blacks, Mexican Americans in northwest Mexico, African Americans from the South Carolina Sea Islands, and upstate New York Yankees. Indicating this expanded scope, a Ph.D. folklife program was established in the American Civilization Department at George Washington University in the nation's capital.

In addition to making inroads into American academe, folklife became well established in the public sector during the 1960s and 1970s. Begun in 1967, the Festival of American Folklife on the National Mall in Washington, DC, led to the formation of the Office of Folklife Programs at the Smithsonian Institution in 1977. In 1974 the National Endowment for the Arts developed its folk-arts program to award grants for the presentation of community-based traditional arts and artists. In 1976 the American Folklife Preservation Act was passed establishing the American Folklife Center in the Library of Congress. The act defined folklife as "the traditional expressive culture shared within the various groups in the United States: familial, ethnic, occupational, religious, regional" and directed the center to "preserve and present

American folklife" through programs of research, documentation, archival preservation, live presentation, exhibition, and publication. As a result of these developments, the folklife movement is especially evident in the public sector. Of the forty-four public programs listed in the 1992 American Folklore Society directory, thirty-seven use folklife, folk culture, or folk arts in their titles. Museums employing folklife research, sometimes called "folk museums," representing regional and ethnic cultures abound. Many museums such as Old World Wisconsin or the Museum of Frontier Cultures present outdoor village settings and demonstrate customs and practices of traditional cultures.

The folklife movement during the 1990s has been successful in introducing ethnographic concerns for individual and community contexts into American folkloristic practice. It has broadened the scope of the materials that folklorists study. Folklife has become an addendum rather than a replacement or umbrella term for text-based folklore research; as the titles of Dorson's textbook *Folklore and Folklife* (1972) and the University of Pennsylvania's Department of Folklore and Folklife indicate, it is frequently paired with, but second to, folklore in descriptions of the studies that folklorists undertake. Contrary to the agenda of the pioneer American folklife scholars, "folklore" has not been categorically subsumed by folklife. One indication is the handling of the potential confusion between folklore and folklife in Jan Harold Brunvand's influential textbook *The Study of American Folklore* (1968, 1978, 1986). While conceptually defining folklife broadly as "the full traditional lore, behavior, and material culture of any folk group, with emphasis on the customary and material categories," Brunvand, under the heading of "Folklife and Folklore," nevertheless invoked "current usage" in his narrower operational characterization of folklife "to mean only customary and material folk traditions, even though there is good reason to substitute the word immediately and permanently for the much-abused term 'folklore.'" (Brunvand 1986:401).

While widely employed, the keyword of "folklife" often lacks clarity, for it may be used loosely for the concern for context or the use of material evidence, or more specifically for an interpretation using the sociocultural idea of traditions serving integrative functions in a community. Folklife research originally claimed a distinction years ago because it focused on local social context and behavior in contrast to the kind of literary treatment that sought the global view of tradition. Yet, built into the folklife effort was the assumption that data could become comparative, even quantifiable, and that the role of the researcher was to systematically compile data and interpret the patterns of everyday life for individuals and their communities across time and space. Europeans had a head start, pioneer American folklife scholars opined, but with the rapidly growing vigor of American folklife studies, they imagined that traditional culture on the American continent could be charted and analyzed. The message of the the 1990s has been that, while promising, carrying out the social philosophy of accounting for each traditional community and activity in nations as complex as the United States and Canada is immense and problematic. In addition, the important psychological concern for investigating individual lives in the practice of tradition brings even more burden to this great task. Attempts to coordinate folklife research in the form of a cultural atlas for the United States have not been successful, and efforts to organize team research in communities has been all too infrequent.

The lobbying efforts of the American folklife movement has taken different turns. In the mid-1990s, there is still an active discussion of a single term—folklore, folklife, folk culture, regional ethnology—to describe what American folklorists do. Whether folklore is paired with folklife or subsumed under folklife implies certain strategies and directions for American students of tradition. Another point of discussion is the adaptation of folklife methods typically oriented toward bounded rural communities to diverse urban and postindustrial settings. The ethnography of organizations such as corporate cultures, boys' groups, and universities suggested by Michael Owen Jones, Gary Alan Fine, Jay Mechling, and others addresses large issues of how and why subcultures are created. Another issue is the role of the individual adapting to communities by negotiating between personal creativity and social tradition (Bronner 1992). This aspect is especially important to American folklife researchers commonly working within a field with mobile social networks, individuals with multiple cultural heritages and identities, and extended, often temporary, communities. The applications of folklife activity in public settings continues to be another concern of the new folklife movement, and new uses of folklife besides museums and historical societies in areas of education, human services, and government are actively being pursued (Jones 1993).

Simon J. Bronner

References

Bronner, Simon J., ed. 1987. *Folklife Studies from the Gilded Age: Object, Rite, and Custom in Victorian America.* Ann Arbor, MI: UMI Research Press.

———. 1989. Folklife Starts Here: The Background of Material Culture Scholarship in Pennsylvania. In *The Old Traditional Way of Life: Essays in Honor of Warren E. Roberts,* ed. Robert E. Walls and George H. Schoemaker. Bloomington, IN: Trickster, pp. 283–296.

———. 1990. The Fragmentation of American Folklife Studies. *Journal of American Folklore* 103:209–214.

———. 1991. A Prophetic Vision of Public and Academic Folklife: Alfred Shoemaker and America's First Department of Folklore. *Folklore Historian* 8:38–55.

———, ed. 1992. *Creativity and Tradition in Folklore: New Directions.* Logan: Utah State University Press.

Erixon, Sigurd. 1950. An Introduction to Folklife Research or Nordic Ethnology. *Folk Liv* 14:5–15.

Fenton, Alexander. 1973. The Scope of Regional Ethnology. *Folk Life* 11:5–14.

Fine, Gary Alan. 1987. *With the Boys: Little League Baseball and Preadolescent Culture.* Chicago: University of Chicago Press.

Gibbons, Phebe Earle. 1882. *"Pennsylvania Dutch" and Other Essays.* 3d. ed. Philadelphia: J.B. Lippincott.

Hines, Donald M. 1972. The Development of Folklife Research in the United Kingdom. *Pennsylvania Folklife* 21:8–20.

Hoffman, W.J. 1888. Folklore of the Pennsylvania Germans. *Journal of American Folklore* 1:125–135.

Hufford, Mary. 1991. *American Folklife: A Commonwealth of Cultures.* Washington, DC: American Folklife Center.

Hultkrantz, Ake. 1960. *General Ethnological Concepts.* Copenhagen: Rosenkilde and Bagger.

Jones, Michael Owen. 1975. *The Handmade Object and Its Maker.* Berkeley: University of California Press.

———. 1985. *Exploring Folk Art: Twenty Years of Thought on Craft, Work, and Aesthetics.* Logan: Utah State University Press.

———, ed. 1993. *Putting Folklore to Use.* Lexington: University Press of Kentucky.

Jones, Michael Owen, Michael Dane Moore, and Richard Christopher Snyder, eds. *Inside Organizations: Understanding the Human Dimension.* Newbury Park, CA: Sage.

Knortz, Karl. 1988. American Folklore, trans. by Helga B. Van Iten and James Dow. *Folklore Historian* 5:1–43.

Loomis, Ormond H. 1983. *Cultural Conservation: The Protection of Cultural Heritage in the United States.* Washington, DC: Library of Congress.

Riedl, Norbert F. 1965. Folklore vs. *Volkskunde:* A Plea for More Concern with the Study of American Folk Culture on the Part of Anthropologists. *Tennessee Folklore Society Bulletin* 31:47–53.

———. 1966. Folklore and the Study of Material Aspects of Folk Culture. *Journal of American Folklore* 79:557–563.

Roberts, Warren E. 1988. *Viewpoints on Folklife: Looking at the Overlooked.* Ann Arbor, MI: UMI Research Press.

Weiss, Richard. 1946. *Volkskunde der Schweiz: Grundriss.* Erlenback and Zurich: Eugen Rentsch Verlag.

Wildhaber, Robert. 1965. A Bibliographical Introduction to American Folklore. *New York Folklore Quarterly* 21:259–302.

Yoder, Don. 1963. The Folklife Studies Movement. *Pennsylvania Folklife* 13:43–56.

———. 1982. Folklife in Pennsylvania: An Historical Survey. *Keystone Folklore,* n.s., 1:8–20.

———. 1990. *Discovering American Folklife: Studies in Ethnic, Religious, and Regional Culture.* Ann Arbor, MI: UMI Research Press.

See also Art, Folk; Crafts; Folk Museums; Folklore; Material Culture; Vernacular

Folklore

Word coined in 1846 (to replace the term "popular antiquities") by English scholar William J. Thoms, who defined it as "*the Lore of the People . . .* [comprising] the manners, customs, observances, superstitions, ballads, proverbs, etc. of the olden time." To some degree, the antiquarian tone and the open-ended enumerative format of Thoms' concept of folklore has remained, while at the same time the word has acquired several new connotations and faces competition from such terms as "folklife," "expressive culture," "traditional culture," "verbal arts," and "vernacular culture." The greatest divergence in the 20th century from the original concept of Thoms and his times concerning folklore has been to remove the emphasis on the rural and the past in order to include now as well the "lore" of the modern, the urban, and the technologically advanced times.

The English word "folklore" itself gained international currency having its counterparts in such forms as *Volkskunde* in German and *folkeminne* in Norwegian. In English, folklore inspired compounds like folktale, folksong, folklorist (one who studies folklore), and folkloristics (the field of folklore study), as well as the negative term fakelore. The British Folk-Lore Society, founded in 1878, and the American Folklore Society, in 1888, both continue to this day. Still, there is considerable debate (especially in the United States) about exactly what parts of culture the word "folklore" refers to, and there is much disagreement on the wording of a suitable definition of the word. As a result, the editors of the *Standard Dictionary of Folklore, Mythology, and Legend* (1949) simply allowed each of twenty-one contributors to submit his or her own definition, and all of these statements were published in lieu of an agreed-upon common definition. But, as American folklorist Kenneth Goldstein suggested, "Despite variance of opinion, there is a certain core of materials which all definitions recognize as belonging to folklore."

The three common features of the numerous cultural elements (including proverbs, tales, songs, dances, games, toys, foods, fences, and so forth) that are included in most folklorists' concepts of what comprises folklore are: (1) that these elements are transmitted orally or by means of informal demonstration; (2) that these elements are traditional in form and content; and (3) that these elements (as a result of their traditional circulation) always exist in different versions, or "variants." Secondarily, in a minimal definition of folklore, most folk-traditional elements of culture are anonymous as to origin, and they tend to become formularized in the ways that they are performed or expressed. Similar concepts of folklore prevail in the wording of most definitions of the word, including, for example, Jan Harold Brunvand's definition, Robert A. Georges' ("continuities and consistencies in human behavior . . . [expressed] during face-to-face interaction" [1980]), and Barre Toelken's ("tradition-based communicative units informally exchanged in dynamic variation through space and time" [1979]). Another viewpoint, however, is that of Elliott Oring, who wrote in 1986: "At this point, a definition is not really necessary. The field is still being mapped and any hard and fast definition is likely to prove partial, idiosyncratic, or inconsistent."

Beginning in the 1950s the European folklife movement (named after the Swedish word *folkliv*) began to strongly influence American folklore studies, inspiring more attention to customary and material traditions instead of primarily oral

traditions. For example, Richard M. Dorson had written in 1959: "'Folklore' usually suggests the oral traditions channeled across the centuries through human mouths. In its flexible uses folklore may refer to types of barns, bread molds, or quilts; to orally inherited tales, songs, sayings, and beliefs; or to village festivals, household customs, and peasant rituals. The common element in all these matters is tradition." But in 1968, taking these ideas further, Dorson admitted that "my own view of the subject matter of the folklorist has shifted somewhat from the established genres to what might be called the unofficial culture."

In 1976, a major piece of national legislation supporting folklore study was enacted, The American Folklife Preservation Act, which established in the Library of Congress the American Folklife Center. The short definition of "American folklife" quoted in the act was "traditional expressive culture shared within the various groups in the United States: familial, ethnic, occupational, religious, regional . . . mainly learned orally, by imitation, or in performance, and . . . generally maintained without benefit of formal instruction or institutional direction. . . ."

In the 1960s, a strong behavioral, or performance- and communications-oriented, movement influenced younger American folklorists, whose statements of their "new perspectives" on the theory and practice of folklore research found expression (among other places) in 1972 in a special issue of the *Journal of American Folklore*. Distilling the essence of this approach in a concise phrase, Dan Ben-Amos proposed as a definition, ". . . artistic communication in small groups." The major influence of the behavioral approach is a shift in focus from recording merely the items of folklore and their histories to analyzing the processes and functions involved in the events in everyday life during which folklore is performed. Echoing most of the varying approaches to folkloristics of the past and present, the American Folklore Society itself, in a booklet published in 1984, declared: "We now speak of folklore/folklife as song and story, speech and movement, custom and belief, craft and ritual—expressive and instrumental activities of all kinds learned and communicated directly or face-to-face in groups ranging from nations, regions, and states through communities, neighborhoods, occupations, and families."

Although the aspect of constant variation of folk materials and folk expressions is something that is not always stated directly in their formal definitions, the scholars' interest in different "versions" and "variants" is amply demonstrated in many of their published studies. In a booklet written by folklife specialist Mary Hufford, titled *American Folklife: A Commonwealth of Cultures*, published in 1991 by the American Folklife Center, the importance of folklore variation—changes in both form and in function—is emphasized in a paragraph that begins: "Traditions do not simply pass along unchanged."

In the 1980s, influenced by such movements as Marxism, feminism, postmodernism, and cultural studies, American folkloristics made yet another change of direction, this time toward what is often referred to as "the culture of politics" (or "the politics of culture"). The introduction (published in 1993 in *Western Folklore*) to a 1992 American Folklore Society symposium that reviewed the "new perspectives" of twenty years before states simply that "folklore as a discipline is concerned with the study of traditional, vernacular, and local cultural productions." The editors further suggest that folkloristics examines "the ways in which traditionalizing (identifying aspects of the past as significant in the present) [is] a dynamic cultural process." But the editors also warn that some people ". . . have challenged the authority of any nation, group, gender, or class to represent the experience of an-Other." Thus, these contemporary folklorists allude to the political nature of current folklore study in the United States. No longer does it seem politically correct to define folklore (even jokingly), as one American folklorist did in 1973, as ". . . what folklorists study," since we must now be aware of who is studying whose traditions, plus how, why, and for whose advantage the study is being conducted.

Jan Harold Brunvand

References

Briggs, Charles, and Amy Shuman, guest eds. 1993. Theorizing Folklore: Toward New Perspectives on the Politics of Culture. *Western Folklore* (Special Issue) 52 (2–4):109–400.

Brunvand, Jan Harold. 1986. The Field of Folklore. In *The Study of American Folklore*. 3d ed. New York: W.W. Norton, pp. 1–15.

Dorson, Richard M. 1959. A Foreword on Folklore. In *American Folklore*. Chicago: University of Chicago Press, pp. 1–6.

Dundes, Alan, ed. 1965. *The Study of Folklore*. Englewood Cliffs, NJ: Prentice-Hall, pp. 1–51.

Folklore [21 definitions]. 1949. In *Standard Dictionary of Folklore, Mythology, and Legend,* ed. Maria Leach and Jerome Fried. New York: Funk and Wagnalls.

Oring, Elliott. 1986. On the Concepts of Folklore. In *Folk Groups and Folklore Genres*. Logan: Utah State University Press, pp. 1–22.

Paredes, Américo and Richard Bauman, eds. 1972. *Toward New Perspectives in Folklore*. Austin: University of Texas Press.

See also American Folklore Scholarship: The Early Years; Cultural Studies; Fakelore; Folklife Movement; Postmodernism

Folklore and American Literature

Study of the relationships between American folklore and American literature, these relationships involving both of the disciplines and their materials. It is difficult to separate the discipline of American folklore from that of American literature because the two fields developed from common interests and an overlapping group of scholars. Their early histories are inevitably bound together. Academic training in folklore was begun in the United States at Harvard University by Francis James Child and George Lyman Kittredge, scholars of language and literature. The American Folklore Society, formed in 1888, began only five years after the creation of the Modern Language Association of America and included several literary scholars and writers, among them Mark Twain, Joel Chandler Harris, and Edward Eggleston, as charter members. The study of folklore for some time was widely accepted as a key component to the study of any national literature, modern or classical; as a result, folklore courses in the late 20th century are still most often taught in university Departments of Language and Literature. Over time, both disciplines have grown. Folklore, like linguistics, comparative literature, computer science, and other 20th-century offspring of well-established academic areas, has come to generate its own disciplinary identity. Nevertheless, the American Folklore Society and the Modern Language Association of America still have a number of close ties, many common members, and similar interests among the memberships.

As for the materials themselves, almost inevitably scholars have begun their task by considering folklore and by trying to differentiate it from literature. Even though folklore is related to many other disciplines—from art and architecture to music and recreation—literature has remained the key one. Scholars have proposed at least three different means to distinguish the materials.

One viewpoint is that while literature is an art, folklore is more like a craft; in other words, folklore is literature minus the art. This may be fairly characterized as an elitist view of literature, although American folklore's historical pursuit of marginal peoples—rural, poor, immigrants, and others—and their folklore has certainly contributed to this perception. This view denies that folk arts are art at all, and tends to be fundamentally socioeconomic- and class-based; that is, the wealthy can afford (both in money and time) art, while the working class may not, and the poor and isolated cannot, and therefore they have none. Conversely, rural and poor peoples have folklore, while urban, educated, and wealthy Americans do not.

American folklorist Alan Dundes has proposed that "we are all folk," and this conception is particularly appropriate for the United States, a country founded upon democracy, equality, and freedom. This viewpoint has ramifications as to who has art, including verbal art. No longer is art necessarily elite, something necessary to import into rural and impoverished communities; indeed, folklorists, anthropologists, and other scholars have turned their attention to "indigenous" arts or folk arts that arise from, and already exist in, traditional communities. Also, American folklorists have worked for more than a generation to document and study urban folklore. Nevertheless, artistic status and significance are granted more easily to formally trained performers in tuxedos and evening dresses on a concert stage than to traditional blues singers performing in a nightclub or storytellers on a porch. In American culture, however, fine storytellers are, in fact, "verbal artists." Similar cases can be made for wood-carvers, clock makers, quilters, potters, and other folk performers—art is fundamental to them all. In fact, one of the similarities between American folklore and American literature is that historically they are *not* class-based. American authors have come from all groups and classes, and the same is true for American folklore. All classes and groups in America have art, literature, and folklore, even if they have not all yet been studied adequately.

A second viewpoint—the belief that folklore and literature are fundamentally and clearly separable, according to one criterion or another—has led to a number of dividing lines, none of which finally stand up to scrutiny. Perhaps the most commonly used is that of *medium;* that is, folklore is oral, while literature is written. Some scholars from both literature and anthropology see this as a firm dividing line and then consider folklore as simply the precursor of literature, because cultures developed oral communication before writing. Thus, for example, H. Monro and Nora K. Chadwick's monumental study *The Growth of Literature* (3 vols. 1932–1940) views folklore (including ballads, romances, and epic) as the predecessors to written works of literature in cultures around the world. To be sure, oral folklore did precede written literature, but oral folklore has not died out over the thousands of years since writing or even the hundreds of years since printed books have been available. Nor have literary works necessarily developed in all cultures that have developed writing and print. Thus, to depict the distinction as unidirectional and evolutionary based on technological development is misleading and simplistic. Indeed, oral traditions have persisted, and new traditions have been created; they are all thriving well into the era of electronic communication.

Further complicating the matter is that the line drawn according to the medium of transmission is no longer widely accepted. Folklorists have accepted and studied a number of traditional written forms, including graffiti, and literary scholars have moved away from the criterion of writing. After all, there are still thousands of different languages active within the United States. Is it accurate to conclude that so many cultures have no literature? If by "literature" one means written works of artistic merit, then yes, but more and more literary scholars have adopted the term "oral literature" as a means of acknowledging and accepting oral performances as works of artistic merit and significance as well. As a result, the claim that medium provides a clear distinguishing line between folklore and literature is no longer valid.

A number of other criteria for distinction between folklore and literature have been proposed, most based upon a gross generalization from a few select, but not always representative, examples. For example, attempts have been made to differentiate the materials according to *permanence:* that is, folklore is fluid and transitory, while literature, because it is fixed in print, is permanent. Here one must consider what is meant by permanent. While it is true that most folklore is transitory in the sense of its orally performed characteristics, one must recall that oral genres and even specific texts can be traced back several thousand years. The texts of many literary works are hardly as "fixed" as some literary scholars represent, and their reputation or place in the culture can change just as dramatically and quickly as oral performances. Thus, permanence has not turned out to be a wholly satisfactory or clearly distinguishable characteristic. Another criterion proposed has been the *orientation:* folklore expresses the traditional within a culture, while literature (as art) forsakes the

traditional for the creative and innovative. To be sure, folklore does capture traditional aspects of a culture, but each performer invigorates the traditional with his or her own creative use in performance, and literature certainly has its own traditional elements. Therefore, literature and folklore cannot be fairly characterized as though one looks forward while the other looks backward; they are both complex artistic forms combining traditional elements with innovation in performance. Still other scholars have attempted to separate them according to what might be termed *ownership:* Literature is signed and identified, while folklore is anonymous. This may be due more to convention and copyright law than anything else, but, even so, it is not completely true. Many literary works, such as Walt Whitman's *Leaves of Grass,* were published anonymously, while in many cultures certain stories are told only by (and thus, in effect, "owned by") a particular performer. Others have suggested *complexity* as a distinguishing criterion: Literature's style and structure is more complex than folklore's. This distinction depends in large part upon which works one selects as representative examples of literature and folklore. Furthermore, it depends on how scholars account for all of the different levels of complexity—including metrics, structure, and style. Finally, some scholars persist in asserting that folklore and literature are distinguished by *who creates it;* that is, folklore is created by groups, while literature is generated only by individuals. Folklore scholars long ago dismissed the notion of folklore being created by groups. Individuals generate performances for others, whether they read or listen in groups or individually.

In general, the attempt to create neat and simple dichotomous categories for folklore and literature has led to frustration. In fact, the boundaries between folklore and literature are neither natural nor secure. Any number of works are problematic. What does one call *The Odyssey,* Grimm's *Household Tales,* or Joel Chandler Harris' *Uncle Remus: His Songs and Sayings?* Are these examples folklore, oral literature, orally based literature, literature based upon folklore, or simply literature itself? Perhaps one key to understanding that cultural expressions can be either—and even both—and that the interaction between folklore and literature is necessarily fluid and complex lies in realizing that folklore and literature are different kinds of cultural products, valued essentially by different groups.

Literature, at least until quite recently, has been viewed primarily as a written product (although in the 1990s this is being revised to include oral forms for many cultures) whose value and significance are not limited to the ethnic and national group from which it comes; that is, the artistic merit and human values expressed are not specific or unique to one culture. Indeed, in some cases it has been readers from other cultures around the world who have called attention to particular artists' works, rather than readers within the author's native group. In contrast, folklore is a wider category (in that it includes more than verbal forms), but the value and significance of traditions are fundamentally within or between particular cultures. As a result, outsiders may see folklore as exotic, quaint, or even disturbing in contrast to their own familiar artistic expressions. Both folklore and literature, therefore, function as artistic and significant cultural expressions for their respective audiences.

Particular examples of folklore—proverbs, songs, tales, legends—have been recorded, transcribed, printed, and distributed to become part of American literature. Examples range from American Indian myths and folktales to Anglo American ballads and folksongs. The original oral tradition may continue independent of, and perhaps wholly oblivious to, the written product. Similarly, a work of literature can help generate an oral tradition while the original written work remains intact. Biographical narratives about famous American figures—from George Washington and John F. Kennedy to Lizzie Borden and Marilyn Monroe—have helped create or spread stories into oral tradition. Further, a written tradition may interact with an oral tradition in any number of different ways. In fact, the history of American culture provides many rich opportunities for case studies of the interaction between folklore and literature.

The study of the relationships between American folklore and American literature is complex at least partly because any artist, whether oral or a writer, takes some cultural knowledge and combines it with creativity and inspiration, and thus inevitably reshapes the raw material. There are often differences, sometimes quite major, between one work and another. One might consider the difference in form and style between traditional American Indian tales, Henry Rowe Schoolcraft's *Algic Researches* (1839), and, finally, Henry Wadsworth Longfellow's *Hiawatha*. Connections between folklore and literature in general, and specific texts in particular, may seem obvious, but folklorists have learned to assess relationships very carefully. Richard M. Dorson proposed that scholars studying the relationships of folklore and literature consider at least three kinds of evidence (biographical, internal, and corroborative) before asserting any direct connection (Dorson 1957). *Biographical evidence* would include pertinent data that an author did indeed know about a particular culture and information about how he came to know it firsthand. Longfellow, for example, never lived among American Indians as preparation for writing *Hiawatha*, nor did he live among Cajuns before he wrote *Evangeline*. On the other hand, George Washington Cable grew up and lived much of his early life in New Orleans and was employed by the U.S. Census Bureau for work across southern Louisiana. His representations of Cajuns and Creoles, while not always flattering to those cultures, are at least based on his personal experiences. Dorson's *internal evidence* involves evaluating whether a particular product (tale, song, proverb, joke, and the like) is set in an appropriate context for the particular culture and community represented. If the writer faithfully depicts the scene, this adds evidence that the writer does indeed have firsthand knowledge of the culture and its folklore. Finally, *corroborative evidence* consists of proof that the particular material (a story, proverb, joke, custom) has had an independent traditional life. This requires checking other appropriate collections to confirm the existence of this item in oral tradition. For instance, examining collections of Cajun folk history and legends will produce virtually no evidence for an oral version of *Evangeline*. On the other hand, Mark Twain recalled a traditional ghost legend ("The Golden Arm") told to him in his youth and wrote Joel Chandler Harris to ask if he knew the story as well. Harris had not heard it, but he later collected it and used it as the basis for a tale in *Nights with Uncle Remus,* while Twain used his version for part of the essay "How to Tell a Story"—and alternated between the two versions in his performances on the lecture circuit.

The history of American literature is inevitably and deeply tied to American folklore. Early American writing clearly contains numerous examples of folklore and stands as an expression of Americans' peculiar concerns and experiences. Illustrations abound in Richard M. Dorson's *America Begins: Early American Writing* (1950), a sourcebook of American colonial writings. The volume contains selections from many familiar colonial authors: John Josselyn, Increase and Cotton Mather, John Smith, John Winthrop, and others. However, Dorson groups the readings not by author and work but according to issues and themes pertinent to those encountering the New World: voyages to the New World, natural wonders, remarkable providences, Indians (including captivity stories), witchcraft, and so forth. By doing this, Dorson illustrates the colonists' lifestyles and culture as manifest in both their folklore and the written accounts. These early American writings are strongly rooted in American folklore and New World experiences.

Over the next century and a half, however, prominent American writers looked more to the Old World for models, especially literary models. Forms popular in France, Germany, and England became the norm for American writers—the essay, short story, and romance among prose forms, for example. With those forms came their concerns, including class distinctions and the development of refinement and taste.

By shortly after the Civil War, at least one prominent writer spoke up to criticize American literature—specifically, for forsaking American folklore and American themes. In fact, Walt Whitman, in *Democratic Vistas* (1877), claimed that so far there was virtually no American literature. He recognized that the heart of any national literature was what made that particular culture different and unique—especially its experiences and its peculiar genres. Whitman denounced earlier American writers for following Old World themes and Old World forms, such as the romance. He argued that American writers instead should pay attention to American experiences, such as the Civil War. He pointed out that the national character of Old World countries was best found and expressed in their ballads (part of their folklore), and that the goal for American writers was to find the appropriate forms for this in the New World. To be sure, Whitman's contribution to American literature is not at all limited to this stance. His free verse broke the tradition of English metrics and offered opportunities to future generations of writers, and for much of his career he wrote powerfully about America and his love of it (including "I Hear America Singing," "Song of Myself," and many other works). Still, Whitman is remarkable in his outspoken views about the importance of America (the New

World); its folklore, its themes, and its forms of American literature were to develop as something more than an emulation of Old World authors and styles.

Whether one attributes the change to Whitman or not, American literature changed during the 19th century and moved to incorporate and depict American experiences, themes, and issues, including the Civil War, slavery and racial prejudice, opportunities for economic success, the woman's changing role in society, and the Vietnam War, among others. New forms—such as slave narratives and other kinds of life stories—became important sources. Many American writers, from Horatio Alger and Edward Albee to John Barth and T.S. Eliot, from William Faulkner and Sylvia Plath to William Styron and Eudora Welty, have used folklore in some ways in their writings. Clearly, the focus on the American experience, including its particular themes, issues, and folklore, has had a major impact on American literature.

Literary critics, however, have sometimes associated folklore primarily with regional literature. In their view, folklore consists primarily of regional dialects, folk humor, and peculiar character types and is chiefly found in humorous writings of the Old Southwest and New England. The impact of folklore is much broader than this and is by no means limited to regional literature. In fact, the finest works of American Literature are deeply rooted in American folklore; including Herman Melville's *Moby Dick,* Twain's *The Adventures of Huckleberry Finn,* Ralph Ellison's *Invisible Man,* Faulkner's *Absalom, Absalom.* Several writers specifically address the importance of folklore in American life. Huckleberry Finn, for instance, learns far more about life and how to live among others from the runaway slave Jim than from his book-learned friend Tom Sawyer. Jim's lessons, often on signs and customs but occasionally using personal narratives, are often humble, but always heartfelt, and it is his respect and affection to which Huck ultimately responds.

In the past, the primary focus and methodology for studies in folklore and literature lay in the identification of items of folklore within works of literature. Over the last several decades, scholars have urged that both identification and interpretation be part of the process: that is, if folklore is indeed part of a written work, how and why is that relevant? How does the folklore influence the audience's associations and perceptions? Most recently, the area of folklore and literature has expanded to include the complex interactions between the two related expressive forms. This includes not just the identification of, and relationships between, particular texts, but also the choices that artists make when creating a work in a particular medium or tradition. In some cases, issues such as form (genre), style, structure, and tone may be just as significant as the text. Quite a few American writers, including Washington Irving, Nathanial Hawthorne, Twain, and others have used the fairy tale *(Märchen)* form—not a traditional *American* oral form—for a wide range of purposes. James Thurber's "The Girl and the Wolf," for example, parodies the form. More recently, authors have turned to this form in an attempt to redraw the distinctions in the roles in traditional tales. Because the study of folklore and literature involves expressive forms that are fluid and that interact with each other, this area has also grown to include the relationships of orality and writing in general. The study of oral performance, composition, aesthetics, and repertoire has become inevitably connected to the study of writing, print, and electronic media. In many contemporary cultures, performers must choose from among several media and many forms. Those studying the relationships between folklore and American literature can contribute to a better understanding of how artists make their choices and how creativity can be expressed and manipulated.

Eric L. Montenyohl

References

Brown, A. LaVonne, and Jerry W. Ward. 1990. *Redefining American Literary History.* New York: Modern Language Association of America.

Dorson, Richard M. 1957. The Identification of Folklore in American Literature. *Journal of American Folklore* 70:1–8.

Dundes, Alan. 1965. The Study of Folklore in Literature and Culture: Identification and Interpretation. *Journal of American Folklore* 78:136–142.

Jones, Steven Swann. 1984. *Folklore and Literature in the United States: An Annotated Bibliography of Studies of Folklore in American Literature.* New York: Garland.

Rosenberg, Bruce A. 1991. *Folklore and Literature: Rival Siblings.* Knoxville: University of Tennessee Press.

See also American Folklore Scholarship: The Early Years; American Studies and Folklore; Harris, Joel Chandler; Hurston, Zora Neale; Twain, Mark; Whittier, John Greenleaf

Folk-Say

A term coined by Benjamin A. Botkin and first publicly used as the title of the regional literary anthology he created and edited from 1929 to 1932 while teaching at the University of Oklahoma. The *Folk-Say* volumes contained literature of the folk, literature about the folk, and discussions of the meaning of the terms "folk" and "lore." Throughout a long career, Botkin continued to use the term and to elaborate on its meaning. After a lifetime of studying folklore, he wrote,

"My dual interest in the folk values of literature and the literary values of folklore, with which *Folk-Say* began, did not end with the series but continued to grow and expand in a number of directions, interregional and interdisciplinary, with special emphasis on the interrelations of written and unwritten traditions and history and sociology."

Given both the academic and the popular understanding of the term "folklore" in 1929 (and later), Botkin thought he needed a new word to cover the cultural phenomena he wanted to examine and to encourage. From the beginning, the word "folk-say" was associated with Botkin's belief in the value of regional folk traditions, in interdisciplinary approaches to the study of the folk and their lore, in an acceptance and celebration of American diversity, and in a role for the student of folklore in promoting intercultural understanding and a cultural renaissance through the study and appreciation of folklore. By using the term "folk-say," Botkin also wanted to call attention in particular to the relationship between oral and written literature (between "folk-say and book-say," as he once put it), and in general to the constant interaction he saw in the modern world among folk, popular, and high culture. The very term "folk-say" described a contemporary activity and, therefore, constituted an implicit rejection of the idea that folklore was a vanishing survival of an early stage in humankind's evolution that was destined to disappear with progress.

Botkin coined folk-say, he later wrote, "not as a substitution for 'folklore,' but as an extension of it." He wanted a word "possessing a wider and fresher connotation, not fixed by academic usage." Botkin thought folk-say emphasized "*folklore as literature* rather than as science," called attention to the "*oral, linguistic, and story-telling . . . aspect of folklore and its living as well as anachronistic phases*," focused on "*literature about the folk as well as literature of the folk*" (emphasis in original), and, unlike the word "folklore," did not have the ambiguous "double sense of the material and its study." (This last explanation is the same as that given in defense of the term "folkloristics," a subject of more recent debate.)

When Botkin became folklore editor of the New Deal's Federal Writers' Project (FWP) (1938–1939), he saw an opportunity to present folk-say to a larger audience than he had previously. As in the *Folk-Say* anthologies, his idea involved experimenting with ways of offering this material to a diverse American audience. Looking back at his work on the FWP, Botkin wrote: "Next to collection, the most important problem was presentation. In the attempt to reach a large audience, we emphasized the folk-say (oral, linguistic, and story-telling) aspects of folklore." He also noted a shift in emphasis from his use of the term during his Oklahoma period. Earlier he had employed folk-say to indicate his rejection of evolutionary anthropology's view of history and the role of studying folklore as a relic useful in reconstructing earlier stages in human history. Working on the FWP, Botkin wrote, he had moved from a primary concern with folk-say as literature to an exploration of folk-say as history. A direct connection runs through the mix of materials that Botkin included in the *Folk-Say* volumes, his encouraging creative writers on the FWP Living Lore units he created to listen actively to ordinary folk-say, and the editorial procedures that governed his selection of materials for his later work, such as *A Treasury of American Folklore* (1944) and his other regional and topical folklore treasuries.

Richard M. Dorson's 1950 neologism "fakelore" attacked not only the legitimacy of the materials Botkin called folk-say, but also the role Botkin advocated that folklorists play in the larger culture. Botkin, nevertheless, or perhaps in response, reiterated the idea that the term "folk-say," indicated not only a new definition of the material to be studied, but also a new role for the folklorist and a new relationship between the folklorist and the layman. At a time when his critics, such as

Dorson, regarded interdisciplinarity as a threat to their effort to establish folklore as a respected discipline in the academy, Botkin insisted that a proper study of folk-say was inherently interdisciplinary.

Botkin gave a central place to the history of his use of the term "folk-say" in his 1953 essay "Applied Folklore: Creating Understanding through Folklore," a major theoretical statement about the role of the folklorist and the utilization of folklore (Botkin 1953). In this article, Botkin noted that while working on the FWP, "folk-say came to mean what the folk have to say not only for but about themselves, in their own way and in their own words," what he began to call "own stories" and folk history. He had viewed it as his responsibility as a folklorist to see that the FWP shared with other Americans what it had learned from the folk-say it had recorded. In an unpublished 1967 conference paper that constituted an intellectual biography of his ideas about folklore, Botkin declared, that "in the interdisciplinary and intercultural folklore studies of the Federal Writers' Project, I made the workers' and their informants social problems so much mine that 'living lore,' folk-say, myths, and symbols came alive for me in a very personal and practical way and I acquired not only a social point of view but a liberal social education" (Botkin 1967a).

In a 1967 article, Botkin commented on the history of folk-say in American dictionaries (Botkin 1967b). He reported that the term had been noted for the first time in the *American Collegiate Dictionary* in 1947 and in the *Random House Dictionary of the English Language* in 1966. In both cases, there was a narrow emphasis on sayings of the people. In the 1990s, lexicographers largely ignore Botkin's neologism. Nevertheless, the term reflects not only the outlook of a prominent American folklorist, but also an important phase in the history of American folklore studies. Although the use of the term has narrowed and declined, the values that Botkin advocated in his use of folk-say are now shared by many folklorists.

Jerrold Hirsch

References

Botkin, Benjamin A. 1931. Folklore and Folk-Say. *American Speech* 31:404–406.

———. 1946. Living Lore on the New York City Writers' Project. *New York Folklore Quarterly* 2:252–263.

———. 1947. Tall Yarns Re-Spun in the American Manner: How Our Professional and Folk Narrators Made Good Stories Better. *Philadelphia Inquirer Books*. August 24.

———. 1953. Applied Folklore: Creating Understanding through Folklore. *Southern Folklore Quarterly* 17:199–206.

———. 1958. We Called It "Living Lore." *New York Folklore Quarterly* 14:189–198.

———. 1967a. Applied Folklore: A Semantic-Dynamic Approach. Unpublished Manuscript.

———. 1967b. Folklore in and out of the RHD. *New York Folklore Quarterly* 23:67–69.

Hirsch, Jerrold. 1987. Folklore in the Making: B.A. Botkin. *Journal of American Folklore* 100:1–38.

See also Botkin, Benjamin A.; Fakelore

Folksong

Traditional sung verse that exhibits characteristics shared by other kinds of folklore. Its natural performance settings are customary occasions of group work, leisure, ritual, and play; its participants' social identities remain overwhelmingly those of neighbor, kin, or workmate and are not displaced by the personae of singer and audience member; it is social rather than personal in meaning and function; it enjoys a strong and direct relevance to "real life"; it displays continuity over time along with adaptability to each context of performance; and it relies heavily on stylized form and reusable content. Song traditions matching this depiction have decreased enormously in vitality since the late 19th century, particularly in Anglo American culture, as we have handed over what was once a kind of everyday practice to professional surrogates and become chiefly consumers of song rather than users of song, seldom participating in singing occasions keyed to the habits of daily life. Consequently, the picture sketched here is largely a historical one.

In their portrayals of the genre, folksong scholars have embraced a number of categorical schemes: by topic (for instance, songs about war, songs about thwarted lovers), by geography (folksongs of Indiana, folksongs of the South), by origin (imported songs, indigenous songs), and by culture group (songs of the cowboys, of the lumbermen), among others. For an overview of the present sort, however, the most frequently employed distinctive features have been the verses' poetic conventions, without reference to the music of songs, to the circumstances of their performance, or to singing style. In such an overview, folksong is a way of articulating a topic in sung verse, and over time several such "ways" have jelled into fairly distinct—but not mutually exclusive—models. We can recognize three such ways or models as dominant in Anglo American folksong tradition: the catalog, the lyric, and the ballad.

Even though probably the oldest of the three, the catalog has been least analyzed by folklorists. Indeed, we do not even possess a commonly agreed-upon name for the type, usually subsuming it under more empirically observable categories like lullabies, play-party songs, local songs, and so on, thereby masking the commonality of such pieces under a mishmash of disparate traits—functional, situational, and geographical, among others. But there is great formal unity throughout the type that these more parochial divisions disguise: In essence, the topic is held suspended in time and space and its component parts inventoried or listed (hence catalog). For example, members of a team of lumbermen are named and portrayed one by one (a common kind of catalog song, and not confined to occupational groups either, that are often called "moniker songs"), or if the topic is an individual rather than a group, his or her most salient traits are menued:

I wouldn't have an old maid;
I'll tell you the reason why:

Her neck's so long and stringy
I'm afraid she'd never die.

I wouldn't have a preacher;
I'll tell you the reason why:
He's always in the pulpit
A-preachin' chicken pie.

I wouldn't have a lawyer
I'll tell you the reason why:
He's always in the courthouse
Swearin' many a lie.

Similarity and/or contiguity among parts is a striking feature of catalog songs, not only in the portrayal of those parts (as in the consistently unfavorable depictions above), but even in actual verbal repetition. Indeed, some catalog songs, especially the cumulative (like "Old MacDonald Had a Farm") and dialogic (like "Soldier, Soldier Will You Marry Me?" or "Where Have You Been All the Day, Billy Boy?") kinds, depend for much of their effect on repetition. As these examples suggest, whenever song is linked with physical action, especially in group activity—game playing, dancing, manual labor, ritual custom—more than likely the catalog will be the preferred model.

The second major genre of Anglo American traditional song is the lyric, the most recognizable surface feature of which is its subject matter: the emotional reaction of a protagonist (often the song's first-person "speaker") to a past experience rather than the nature of the experience itself. The lyric song articulates its topic by linking its images in a more sophisticated way than the catalog's listing method: Topic-parts are interrelated by imaginative associations of shared mood, texture, implication. For example:

Come all ye fair and tender ladies,
Be careful how you court young men.
They're like bright stars in a summer morning,
They first are here and then they're gone.

While many sacred songs follow the format, secular songs predominate in the traditional lyric repertoire; in these songs, sorrow and bitterness at a failed love affair are by far the most common emotions. Lyric songs in general, but particularly lyric love songs, are deeply symbolic in that their images connote strongly contrasting ideas like superfluity and dearth, amplification and abatement, movement and stasis:

Oh, love is sweet and love is charming
And love is pleasant when it's new.
But love grows cold as love grows older,
And fades away like the morning dew.

The third folksong model common in Anglo American community-singing tradition is the ballad. The ballad is like a tale in sung verse: It tells a story, and so links its stanza-images, or topic component parts, in a narrative way—actions result in reactions; causes are followed by effects; decisions lead to their implementation, and so on, all unified by a small cast of interacting characters and a chronologically unfolding "plot." Folksong collectors have found four ballad subtypes prominent in American folk tradition, two inherited from Old World culture, one homegrown, and one whose flowering was more or less transatlantic. These are, respectively: the medieval, or Child, ballad (so called to honor Francis James Child, the great 19th-century authority on the genre), the broadside ballad, the blues ballad, and the parlor ballad. The Child type is the oldest, emerging in Europe in the late medieval period and remaining a usable model for new songs up to the late 1600s. More than 100 songs of this type have been found in 20th-century American singing tradition, all diffused to this country from the British Isles and more often than not retaining their premodern ambience (they often feature dramatis personae who possess titles, live in castles, and ride finely accoutered steeds). Child ballads are most notable within the ballad model for their internally symmetrical, balanced, parallelistic form, often very like the catalog but, of course, telling a story rather than just listing parts of the topic's anatomy:

> She had not been on sea three weeks,
> I am sure it was not four,
> Until fair Ellender began to weep,
> And she wept most bitterly.
>
> "Oh, do you weep for your house carpenter,
> Or do you weep for your gold,
> Or do you weep for your sweet little babe
> Whom you never will see any more?"
>
> "I neither weep for your gold," said she,
> "Neither do I weep for your store,
> But I do weep for my house carpenter and sweet little
>   babe
> Whom I never will see any more."
>
> She had not been on sea three weeks,
> I am sure it was not four,
> Until the ship sprang a leak
> And sank to rise no more.

The broadside ballad, is of more recent vintage, its emergence associated with the issuing of songs (invariably just the words) on single sheets of paper for sale on street corners, and at market stalls and country fairs. As folklorists use the word, "broadside" denotes primarily a style of song that coalesced in 18th-century Britain (though, once again, it was a pan-European form and followed European culture's diffusion to other continents). It tells its simple tale more concretely than its older relative, the Child ballad, specifying the journalistic variables of who, what, where, when, how, and why; it is more linear, sequential, and not as repetitive in its plot development; and it betrays its relatively modern history by portraying a more varied society in which working- and middle-class people are invariably the main protagonists:

> My name is Daniel Martin,
> I'se borned in Arkansas;
> I fled from those base rebels
> Who fear not God or law.
>
> I left my aged father
> And my beloved wife;
> I'se forced to go to Rollie
> For to try to save my life.
>
> I jined in Phillip's regiment—
> I'm not ashamed to tell—
> My colonel and my officer
> They treated me mighty well.
>
> I served four months at Rollie
> Through sleet, snow, and ice,
> And next received my orders:
> Go meet old Sterling Price.

The third ballad type is of American origin, though similarities to its way-of-telling-a-story-in-sung-verse can be found in other cultures. We call this type the blues ballad, and it fuses traits from African American song traditions, especially catalog and lyric types like worksongs and spirituals, with Anglo American song traditions, most notably (but not exclusively) the broadside ballad. The blues ballad holds up in sharp relief striking, dramatic scenes selectively chosen from its topic at large, unifying them with a common mood of celebration or lament, but, in ballad-like manner, the images generally follow a chronological sequence, though in a more fits-and-starts than cause-and-effect progression. And like so many broadside ballads—especially the indigenous American ones—a blues ballad is invariably based on an actual event in the region's immediate past and does allude to people, places, and actions in a quasi-journalistic way, though so impressionistically and elliptically that someone unfamiliar with the historical event would be quite unable to reconstruct it in any detailed way from the song:

> My father was a gambler, he learnt me how to play,
> My father was a gambler, he learnt me how to play,
> Saying, "Son, don't go a-begging when you hold the
>   ace and tray,
> When you hold the ace and tray."
>
> Chorus:
> Hang me, O hang me, and I'll be dead and gone,
> Hang me, O hang me, and I'll be dead and gone;
> I wouldn't mind the hangin', it's bein' gone so long,
> It's layin' in the grave so long.
>
> They took me down to old Fort Smith as sick as I
>   could be,
> They took me down to old Fort Smith as sick as I
>   could be,
> They handed me a letter saying "Son, come home to me,"
> Saying, "Son, come home to me."

The fourth ballad type is the parlor (or sentimental) ballad. Ballads of this type collected from American folk tradition often (but not always) date from the late 19th century and are traceable to known composers, many of whom copyrighted their compositions and issued them on sheet music. Parlor ballads exhibit a self-consciously "literary" style of more formal—and less formulaic—diction, greater unity and continuity of plot, stricter regularity in meter and rhyme, and especially more extravagant expressions of sentiment than do other ballad types, even the broadside ballad:

> Oh, the sun was setting in the west,
> And it fell over the lingering way,
> To the branches of the forest,
> Where a wounded cowboy lay.
> Neath the shade of a palmetto
> And beneath the sultry sky,
> Far away from his loved old Texas
> They laid him down to die.
>
> His comrades gathered round him
> To hear what he might say,
> And the tears rolled down each manly cheek
> As his life-blood ebbed away.
> One loved friend and companion
> Was kneeling by his side
> Trying to stop the life-blood flowing,
> But alas, in vain he tried.

In sum, parlor ballads, like the parlor songs in general that entered folk tradition, apparently exemplify bourgeois sensibility, worldview, ethic, and taste.

We must remember that, like all folklore, folksongs were constantly being adapted by those who sang them to their children, their playmates, their neighbors, their comrades-in-arms, and so forth in the course of everyday life. Thus, a song may have followed chiefly ballad conventions in one enactment, chiefly lyric in another. The models, in short, are not mutually exclusive straitjackets; indeed, most songs invariably draw upon not just one way, but two and even more ways, of articulating their topics, even though one way will generally predominate. It is that quality of variability more than any other that has consistently stimulated scholarly interest in folksong.

Roger deV. Renwick

References

Abrahams, Roger D., and George Foss. 1968. *Anglo-American Folksong Style*. Englewood Cliffs, NJ: Prentice-Hall.

McNeil, W.K. 1988. *Southern Folk Ballads,* 2 vols. Little Rock. AR: August House.

Posen, I. Sheldon. [1988] 1993. *For Singing and Dancing and All Sorts of Fun*. Ottawa: Well Done Books.

See also Ballad; Blues; Filk Music; Lullaby; Lyric Song; Spirituals, African American; Worksong

Folktale

A fictional narrative varied in length and rich in symbolic and metaphorical meaning, oral in origin but now found more often in printed collections. The term "folktale" is often used loosely to describe all forms of traditional narratives, from brief jokes and anecdotes to lengthy adventure tales. Here the term applies only to the more complex narratives, the wondertales *(Märchen),* of European origin that were brought from Europe to the New World in oral and printed form by successive waves of settlers. This kind of story is popularly known as a fairy tale, though this is not an accurate description of its content or significance.

The broader definition of folktale is more current in Europe, where comparable terms refer to oral fictitious stories in general. In the New World, the generic use of "folktale" is often not appropriate; hence, the narrower definition is more useful. For example, "folktale" is not a suitable description of aboriginal narratives, many of which are more appropriately viewed as sacred or historical legends.

Folktales are filled with fantastic creatures, events and objects, but their main characters are ordinary people (lazy Jack, clever Polly, common farmers, among others) who are the recipients of wondrous bean trees, cups that never empty, or the granting of three wishes. Such tales have been regarded either as escapist fantasies that take one out of reality, or as profound metaphors that carry one deeper into an inner reality. There is continuing controversy over their suitability for children, given their fantastic nature as well as the violence often a part of these tales. It should be noted that while fairy tales now appear mostly in books intended for children, the original oral tales were and are more often directed to adult listeners, though children were not necessarily excluded.

Many of these stories still exist orally in the United States (notably in regions of the South) and in Canada (in Quebec and the Maritime Provinces). These regions were among the first colonized and farmed by Europeans and their descendants in the 17th and 18th centuries. Many early settlers were from England, Scotland, Ireland, and France; hence, folktales from the British Isles and France exist to this day in these older rural regions of both the United States and Canada, though much diminished. In later decades, settlers from other parts of Europe, and from non-European areas as well, added their own wealth of oral narratives to the growing treasury of New World folktales. Changes in social and economical environments and the loss of original languages have taken a heavy toll on folktales in the New World, but they persist.

Folktales arise in an oral tradition; thus, one cannot identify original or authoritative texts. There are as many texts of any particular folktale as there are people who have told it over many generations. Widespread stories like "Cinderella" and "Beauty and the Beast," for example, have countless variants, each as original and authoritative as any other, although the aesthetic quality of a text also depends on the artistry of the individual teller. This rich variety is reflected in the titles of contemporary folktales from five different North American collections. "Beauty and the Beast," one of the most widely collected tales, has eighteen separate titles, including "Bully Bornes," "The Pretty Girl and Her Lost Children," and "White Bear Whittington." Even more popular is the clever and often lazy young man known as "Jack" or "Little Jack" in English-speaking tradition and "Ti-Jean" in French tradition, the protagonists of stories still told in the 1990s. Despite the wealth of such stories, modern reworkings of folktales still focus on popular European tales instead of New World counterparts such as the Kentucky variant of "Cinderella," called "The Girl Who Could Do Any Job of Work."

Each folktale has an author, since active tellers reframe stories from their own experiences. Unfortunately, some collectors failed to include the names of those who told the stories, which gave rise to the notion that folktales were anonymous, communal creations. This is an inaccurate reflection of the skill and sophistication of excellent narrators, the best of whom are comparable to authors of written literature. Even in the New World, where storytelling traditions often did not survive the passage across the ocean and the hard life that followed, there are still a number of skilled traditional narrators with a rich legacy of folktales handed down in family and community settings. The Hicks and Ward families from North Carolina, for example, have kept alive tales from their ancestor Council Harmon (1807–1896). Many of these family stories were collected and then rewritten by popularizer Richard Chase, who claimed them as his own property (cf. Chase 1943, 1948). Other North American collectors have been more careful in crediting the individual tale-tellers themselves.

Collections of New World folktales, unlike those of Europe, date from the middle decades of the 20th century. European collectors were initially inspired by the works of the Grimm brothers in Germany in the early 19th century, a time when the United States was still a young nation and Canada was not yet a unified country. Thus, the nationalism that fueled European collecting found different expression in the New World; regional, ethnic, and racial considerations were more significant motivators in North American collecting.

There was a resurgence of interest in folktales in libraries and schools in the early part of the 20th century, drawing largely on the stories of Charles Perrault, the Grimm brothers, and Hans Christian Andersen. The more recent rekindling of interest in the early 1970s grew from this earlier book-oriented tradition but has blossomed to include stories from oral, printed, and electronic media. This new form of storytelling parallels, but does not arise from, the older oral tradition. Each has unique social and communal needs, aesthetic patterns, and performance contexts. The older oral storytelling usually exists in small family and community groups already familiar with both tellers and tales, and this tradition rests firmly on oral tales brought from Europe by their ancestors. The newer storytellers, still reliant largely on written tradition, are individual artists generally independent of a particular community; many perform for large audiences not directly connected with the tellers or their tales.

Kay F. Stone

References

Baughman, Ernest W. 1966. *Type and Motif Index of the Folktales of England and North America*. The Hague: Mouton.

Campbell, Marie. 1958. *Tales from the Cloud Walking Country*. Bloomington: Indiana University Press.

Chase, Richard. 1943. *The Jack Tales*. Boston: Houghton Mifflin.

———. 1948. *Grandfather Tales*. Boston: Houghton Mifflin.

Fauset, Arthur Huff. 1931. *Folklore from Nova Scotia*. Philadelphia: American Folklore Society.

Fowke, Edith. 1979. *Folktales of French Canada*. Toronto: NC Press.

Gardner, Emelyn. 1937. *Folklore from the Schoharie Hills, New York*. Ann Arbor: University of Michigan Press.

MacNeil, Joe Neil. 1987. *Tales until Dawn: The World of a Cape Breton Gaelic Story-Teller*. Kingston and Montreal: McGill-Queen's University Press.

Randolph, Vance. 1952. *Who Blowed up the Church House?* New York: Columbia University Press.

———. *The Devil's Pretty Daughter*. New York: Columbia University Press.

Roberts, Leonard. 1955a. *South from Hell-ferSartin*. Berea: Council of Southern Mountains.

———. 1955b. *Up Cutshin and down Greasy*. Lexington: University Press of Kentucky.

———. 1969. *Old Greasybeard*. Detroit: Folklore Associates.

Thompson, Stith. 1946. *The Folktale*. New York: Holt, Rinehart and Winston.

See also Anecdote; Fable; Jack Tales; Jokes; Legend; Myth; Storytelling; Tall Tale; Urban Legend; Yarn

Folkways

Habitual actions, such as manners, customs, usages, and mores. An expanded sense of the term includes values and meanings in an attempt to describe the complex interlocking parts of a cultural system. Folkways might best be thought of as cultural artifacts, actions that due to their repeatability have the stability of objects. An example might be as simple as the custom in the United States of shaking hands when first greeting someone; the same encounter in France would require the mutual kissing of both cheeks.

Folkways as a term first appeared in 1906 with the publication of American sociologist William Graham Sumner's book of the same name (Sumner [1906] 1960). The term has remained in circulation mostly among historians and sociologists, especially those who work within the American context, having never really attracted much attention from folklorists. Folkways research is most often focused at the national or regional level and often emphasizes instances of ethnocentrism, the belief that one's own practices are right and natural and those of another culture are wrong or illogical. The anthropologist Edward Hall's many books focus on just such issues.

Sumner conceived of folkways as being the result of instincts becoming customary: Basic drives for food or shelter come to be satisfied in particular ways accepted by the group. Children or other novices learn mostly through imitation and less often through instruction. Even in instruction, however, the reasons for a particular action remain largely unknown to both teacher and pupil. In some sense, folkways challenge conventional understandings of meaning

Charlie Landfried works an old wheel on a new wheelstand. Limestone, Montana, 1979. Photo Michael Crummett. American Folklife Center.

as explicit; the meaning of habitual actions is in the actions themselves, repeated through space and time. If asked, most people will not be able to tell why they cross themselves whenever they pass a cemetery, yet the action in itself has significance—it gives comfort, connects the individual with a particular perspective on death, and/or pays respect to the dead.

An enumeration of things that could be considered as folkways includes: (1) speech: conventions of writing or speaking as well as pronunciation, vocabulary, syntax, grammar, and inflection (such as the different forms of the second-person plural in the United States, including "you guys," "y'all," "You 'uns," and the like; (2) housing: what kind of homes people build as well as how they live in them; (3) family: parenting responsibilities, marriage customs, and social relations between family members; and (4) food: what people eat and how they eat it, special feasting or fasting occasions (note the term "foodways"). The list could be much longer, and it could include folkways of sex, religion, magic, dress, sports, work, and more. Readers examining particular studies would find that they only augment this list.

Folkways should not be taken as standing in opposition to modernity, as habits of limited use and practiced unconsciously. As some scholars have made clear, the more advanced a society becomes in material terms, the stronger its folkways become, concretized in technologies and sometimes required by institutions (Fischer 1989:10). For example, the fondness of Cajuns for such foods as crawfish is only redoubled by the establishing of modern crawfish-farming methods.

John Laudun

References

Fischer, David Hackett. 1989. *Albion's Seed: Four British Folkways in America.* New York: Oxford University Press.

Sumner, William Graham. [1906] 1960. *Folkways: A Study of the Sociological Importance of Usages, Manners, Customs, Mores, and Morals.* New York: Mentor Books.

See also Custom; Foodways

Folkways Records

Recording company founded by Moses Asch and Marian Distler in 1949, the third record company Asch had started. The earlier Asch and Disc labels had ended in bankruptcy, but Folkways was a success by almost any standard. Between 1949 and 1986, Asch issued more than 2,000 LP titles on the Folkways label (the early 78-rpm albums were all reissued on LP). Folkways was a key participant in the folk-music revival from the 1940s on, and it published many titles recorded, compiled, or annotated by folklorists, ethnomusicologists, and anthropologists.

The record business has always been dominated by a few major recording companies with their own distribution systems. National in scope and corporate in organization, they usually left the smaller niche markets to smaller companies until those markets proved profitable enough to invest in. The small companies used other forms of distribution and sold to targeted audiences. Folkways was one such relatively small company. Its market consisted largely of libraries and the urban middle class; its editorial policy was the opposite of corporate—based on the vision of a remarkable individual, Moses Asch, and a group of collaborators who advised him. Raised in an international, politically-active, urbane, literary home, Asch created a company that was international in scope, included hundreds of albums of literature, and captured the intense creativity of the diverse musical, literary, and political activities of his times.

Several key features distinguished Folkways Records from most other niche-market record companies. First, Folkways did not specialize in any given genre or ethnic group: its recordings ranged from the last chanters in Tierra del Fuego to African polyphony, Appalachian fiddle players, rural blues singers, American Indian chanters, John Cage and electronic music, and a large number of children's artists. The Folkways catalog included hundreds of spoken-word albums in dozens of languages, natural sounds, and documentaries of current events from the McCarthy era to Watergate, with a strong series on the civil rights movement. Second, every Folkways record had some kind of pamphlet inserted in the jacket. These notes varied from a few sheets with song lyrics to fifty or more tightly printed pages with extensive descriptions of context and style. This format was ideally suited for bringing unfamiliar material before the public, as well as for schools and libraries. Third, once a record was published, it was not deleted from the catalog. This was extremely rare in an industry that traditionally focused on hits and deleted slow-selling items without compunction. Asch not only kept Folkways records in print, he sometimes published recordings that the major labels had not kept in print in order to bring the music of earlier periods to a new audience—as in the famous *Anthology of American Folk Music* (1952) compiled by Harry Smith, which influenced many folk-revival musicians, folklorists, and others.

Moses Asch was ahead of his times in his interest in wedding print, visual media, and sound into a single package—which today would be labeled "multimedia." He was a partner in Oak Publications, which published songbooks of many Folkways artists. He was involved with *SingOut!* magazine in the early years. Some of his "liner notes" became separate books—as in his instruction albums. At one time he called his operation "Record, Book, and Film Sales."

Folkways published recordings that other companies would not touch for political, economic, or other reasons. Throughout the 1950s and 1960s, Folkways published blacklisted performers—among them Pete Seeger, with fifty-four albums on Folkways—and the only known recordings of Jose Miguels, a Communist Portuguese poet living in exile. Folkways would publish recordings for which sales projections were minimal partly because Asch wanted to represent the whole world, and partly because he estimated that no matter what the recording, he could sell about 400 copies. If he kept the costs low enough (and he was well known for doing so), he could publish almost anything. This was one reason he published so many field recordings—they were inexpensive to produce, and they were recordings of music made in a more natural context than that of a recording studio.

During the 1960s, the success of the folk-music revival

Women arrange dishes of food for St. Joseph's Day at St. Therese's Roman Catholic Church. Pueblo, Colorado, 1990. Photo Myron Wood. American Folklife Center.

turned a niche market into a hit market. This brought both the major companies and new independent record labels into the field. With their larger royalties and wider distribution, they attracted many artists who earlier might have published on Folkways. In the 1970s and 1980s, a similar process occurred with music from other parts of the world ("Worldbeat"). Folkways survived as a label characterized by field recordings and largely supported by its sales of recordings for children.

Although some Folkways titles are more enduring than others, the Folkways Records catalog came to include a vast number of highly significant recordings. Largely through the efforts of Ralph Rinzler, Folkways Records was acquired by the Smithsonian Institution, which committed itself to keeping all of the recordings in print, in 1987. In addition to the master tapes and associated rights, the Smithsonian acquired the business papers and files of the company. The collection is housed in the Smithsonian's Center for Folklife Programs and Cultural Studies, which archives the papers, maintains the entire collection in print on cassette, and started Smithsonian/Folkways Recordings in 1988 to reissue selected Folkways titles as well as new projects. The center subsequently acquired two other small record labels, Cook and Paredon. A free catalog of Folkways recordings, as well as those of Cook and Paredon, may be obtained by writing the Center.

Anthony Seeger

See also Asch, Moses; Revivalism; Smithsonian Institution Center for Folklife Programs and Cultural Studies

Foodways

The intersection of food and culture. Foodways entered the stream of American folklore studies during the 1880s—the decade that saw the founding of the American Folklore Society and the holding of the Cotton Centennial Exposition. The development of foodways as a subdiscipline of folklore has retained the stamp of identity placed upon the discipline by the odd circumstances of its origin. Briefly recounted, these circumstances revolve around Lafcadio Hearn, a struggling journalist and traveler, who in 1879 sought to supplement a meager writing income by opening a small restaurant in New Orleans, which he advertised as "the cheapest eating house in the South." The restaurant closed in short order, Hearn's silent partner and cook taking off with the little cash Hearn had raised to open its doors.

In order to pay the debts incurred by this failed venture, Hearn turned to William Coleman, a friend and bookshop proprietor. Hearn pitched Coleman on the idea of publishing several small books on New Orleans life and tradition to be sold to visitors expected at the Cotton Centennial Exposition, an event of World's Fair scale planned for New Orleans in 1884. Hearn was chiefly looking for an opportunity to publish a collection of proverbs, the fruit of his ongoing, self-guided explorations of New Orleans' Creole culture. Coleman agreed to publish the proverbs, but only if Hearn agreed to write an additional collection of Creole recipes. Misfortune continued to plague Hearn's ventures, as printing delays prevented the books from reaching bookstores until 1885, by which time the exposition and its thousands of tourists had left town. The two books—*Gombo Zhebes* and *La Cuisine*

Canned goods in the home of Florence Cheek. Traphill, North Carolina, 1978. Photo Pat Mullen. American Folklife Center.

Creole—were published to poor sales and reviews.

La Cuisine Creole met its author's claim as the only work in print that described the methods of New Orleans' Creole cooks. But for folklorists and others who, in the decades to follow its publication, were to value detailed, firsthand accounts of traditional expression, particularly among America's racial minorities, *La Cuisine Creole* came to represent the tangible, visible part of an otherwise invisible world, mixing African, Caribbean, and European cultures. *La Cuisine Creole* clarified Hearn's sketches of street life, transcriptions of street vendors' cries, and collected proverbs.

However, Hearn's choice of food as the expressive "medium" through which to communicate the cultural "message" of Creole tradition served over time to distance this body of work from his other ethnographic writings. Even as Hearn's stature as an ethnographer rose among American folklorists, the medium of foodways, which had proven so successful in his depiction of Creole life, failed to find the same scholarly acceptance as custom, music, dance, or verbal folk genres.

In 1884 the term "foodways" was not in English currency. A stowaway among European folk-cultural concepts that made their way into American scholarly usage a half-century later, "foodways" owes its intellectual identity to "folklife." The efforts of American folklorists such as Don Yoder and Warren Roberts to broaden the range of genres touched by tradition was at first largely perceived as a modest correc-

tive—an attempt to change folklore's rules of evidence by adding material culture to the verbal and customary expressions that formed the academic canon at the time. While folk craft, folk architecture, folk costume, and other material genres did gain a heightened degree of professional respect as the result of the folklife movement, foodways gained the most, and for reasons that had more to do with imported ethnology than with food. The European theoretical emphasis upon "common" culture—the ordinary structures of everyday life—found in foodways a bridge to American folklore studies and an opportunity to contribute to those intellectual trends in postwar America that sought to widen the category of people considered "folk."

Interestingly, the demand for a culture-based understanding of food within the social sciences had been articulated in America far more eloquently and forcefully than in Europe, largely due to the efforts of Margaret Mead and her colleagues at the National Research Council's Committee on Food Habits. In the late 1930s and early 1940s, Mead worked with a large contingent of anthropologists, home economists, sociologists, and nutritionists to develop profiles of cultural food preferences. The strongest of these preferences, called "food habits," became the data upon which statistical projections of required foodstuffs and the hypothetical effects of wartime rationing could be calculated. The data proved more hypothetical than the theories that prompted its collection, but Mead succeeded in demonstrating the utility of applied anthropology and the close association among foodways, cultural identity, and community.

In the late 1970s, foodways also proved to be the vessel for a revised model of tradition in culture that combined two emergent concepts unrelated to any particular genre: first, an expanded notion of "context," and, second, increased attention upon folk expression as "symbol making." Unlike other genres, foodways were seldom anonymous: The intentions of a person producing food to eat and the expectations of the people consuming it were either evident or easily documented. Field research that focused upon foodways was as likely to plumb the cultural significance of the names of foods as to document the tools or techniques used to prepare it. Similarly, what folk informants identified as traditional about a food could range from the occasion for which it was prepared, to the origin of special ingredients, to customs that invested food with luck.

As a consequence, almost as soon as foodways came to be recognized within the enterprise of folklore, the new genre branched out in nearly as many directions as there were researchers. Not surprisingly, the patterns of this new work reflect accepted folkloristic approaches to identity and community: age, ethnicity, gender, locale, occupation, religion. In an inclusive discipline, foodways became the most inclusive and least-disciplined genre.

In this regard, at least, foodways research enjoys the benefits of a broad definition and suffers few of the negative consequences. The term "foodways" has come to mean the intersection of food and culture. Lines of research, analysis, comparison, or theory that approach this intersection or pro-

Chefs assemble food for a Samoan-American lu'au. Carson High School, Carson, California, 1974. Photo J.W. Love.

ceed from it are generally viewed with equal acceptance. There is no mission for foodways research—no priority list of work to be done and no palpable displeasure about the absence of one. In some respects, it has been of benefit to foodways as an emerging discipline that no single sector of the broad subject has come to dominate discussion: The production of foodstuffs, patterns of marketing and processing, cookery, the sale of foods in commercial venues, and even the customs and manners associated with eating have garnered equivalent scholarly attention.

What have emerged as defining characteristics of American foodways research are, first, a serious tone of voice, and, second, high regard for imaginative description. The first of these characteristics distinguishes foodways scholarship from the voluminous output of popular and promotional writings about food that flood the nation's book racks, magazines, and newspapers. The second is, ironically, a recognition that good writing about food and culture turns up frequently in virtually every corner of the literary marketplace.

One useful way of surveying the work that contemporary scholars have brought to the study of American foodways is to examine what this body of work contributes to folklore's preoccupation with community.

Food and Age. With the exception of oral-history work, foodways research is less likely to focus upon the food-related customs or behavior of a single age group. Foodways pays respect to community elders—from the matriarch who presides over Thanksgiving dinner to the sage Lake Erie fisherman whose skills in spotting fish suggest a third eye—but probably less so than other disciplines. When cooking or eating is involved, the attention is more likely to be focused upon household members personally involved in these enterprises, and less likely to focus upon people either too young or too old to actively participate.

Food and Ethnicity. Foodways has been identified as ethnicity of last resort—the last bit of ethnic difference to be shed in America's rush to assimilation. One might expect this view to attract greater numbers of scholars interested in the display of ethnicity, but the opposite is more nearly true. The loss of singing, craft, costume, and other traditions seems more acute when "all" that is left is an occasional meal that conjures the preimmigrant past. Nonetheless, foodways is probably the most available, quantifiable, and comparable information offered to today's students of ethnic community.

Food and Gender. Unlike other subdisciplines, which have seen new research into gender-based roles, styles, and notions of tradition, American foodways scholarship has paid little attention to the ways in which foodways represent gender. Folklorist Thomas Adler's useful speculations on sexual provinces in cookery and meal schedule are a noteworthy exception (cf. Adler [1981] 1983), but they have not inspired further inquiry. The constant reinforcement of popular stereotypes depicting farmers as men, cooks as women, and eaters as families may discourage a closer examination of the varied activities associated with foodways and a more particular look at who does what—and why.

Food and Locale. "Regional foodways" represents the consummation of the long-sought marriage of folklore and geography, and the demonstration of functionalist theories about how culture conserves nature. In theory, at least, it follows (in a backwards sort of way) that if people are what they eat, and they eat where they are, they are where they are. An Iowa farm family sitting down to a groaning table of vegetables, fresh from the garden, and home-cured ham; a warming Maine chowder, simmered from the day's catch; Maryland crab cakes;

Boston baked beans; a Rhode Island clambake; Texas chili—each of these images conjures a connection between a place, its native foodstuffs, local styles of cookery, and—in some cases—social events that encapsulate several of these elements.

As vernacular culture, the stuff of images and advertisements, this notion of regional foodways is demonstrably "authentic." There are more pictures of dancing red crabs on restaurant marquees in Baltimore than in Phoenix; more log cabin–lettered roadside billboards advertising barbecue in the Blue Ridge than in the Catskills. But while these culinary animations do proscribe regions in a somewhat coherent way, their coherence does not derive from agriculture, horticulture, or aquaculture. Worse, these images often conceal shifts in what people are actually growing, cooking, and eating.

Food and Occupation. Some of the best folklore research on occupational traditions belongs under the broad rubric of "foodways" but predates the folklife movement. Folklorists' attention to fishermen, farmers, and cowboys begins before the turn of the century and has been nourished by continued interest in customs, beliefs, worksongs, and stories that configure the worker, the worker's peers, a job, and the dangers that bind them. As the notions of occupation and occupational folklore have diversified, the appeal of these few occupations has remained strong to scholars. Integrating research about them into foodways studies requires little more than recognition of the appetites and market forces that have historically driven these occupations, and willingness (not yet in evidence) to apply the high standards of prior research to other food-related occupations.

Food and Religion. The range of associations between food and religion is extensive—from dietary rules that limit what a member of a particular faith may eat, to the symbolic connection between nutritional and spiritual sustenance, to the frequent use of food events such as church suppers and bake sales as fund-raisers and social events benefiting religious groups. Religious communities are seldom formed *because* of their attitudes toward foods, but they may come to be known by, and differentiated from, other communities as a consequence of food-related beliefs, rituals, or other practices. Such is certainly true for Jewish kosher-food practices, Muslim dietary laws, and Catholic abstention from meat on Fridays—the source of the derogations "fisheater" or "mackerel snapper."

More than anything else, American foodways are characterized by the marketplace—a plethora of choices and patterns of consumption that respond to impulse, trend, season, or times. Such whimsy leads many folklorists to look past much of consumer behavior in search of those aspects of food-related culture more deeply rooted in the kinds of communities listed above, or elsewhere. Table manners seem to survive passing fashions that affect the foods being eaten. The foods prepared for special occasions—birthday dinners, Thanksgiving, religious holidays, Fourth of July picnics, and such—also seem more resistant to change. But to invest too much importance in these seeming constants is to place too heavy a burden upon them for "carrying on" the broad legacies we assign them. Important food events have symbolic value because they are important in the first place, and many, if not all, of the participants are aware of what is symbolically being "said" when a Thanksgiving turkey is carved or birthday-cake candles are blown out.

The seriousness that anthropologists brought in the late 1930s and early 1940s to the study of food habits offers an indication of key questions American foodways research must tackle. What does the term "food habit" mean in a consumerist society? Where is significance located in the twisted trail from field to table? Tradition is no less active in decision making about what seed to plant in a suburban backyard garden or the choice of a pizza venue. The study of American foodways holds the promise of offering an approach to folklife in its broadest sense and widest reference—a scholarly enterprise that locates significance in common experience and cultural variety.

Charles Camp

References

Adler, Thomas. 1981. Making Pancakes on Sunday: The Male Cook in Family Tradition. *Western Folklore* 40:45–54. Reprinted in *Foodways and Eating Habits: Directions for Research,* ed. Michael Owen Jones, Bruce Giuliano, and Roberta Kress. Los Angeles: California Folklore Society, 1983, pp. 45–54.

Camp, Charles. 1989. *American Foodways.* Little Rock, AR: August House.

Cussler, Margaret, and Mary L. de Give. 1952. *'Twixt the Cup and the Lip: Psychological and Socio-Cultural Factors Affecting Food Habits.* New York: Twayne.

Gutierrez, C. Paige. 1992. *Cajun Foodways.* Jackson: University of Mississippi Press.

Kirlin, Katherine S., and Thomas M. 1991. *Smithsonian Folklife Cookbook.* Washington, DC: Smithsonian Institution.

Neustadt, Kathy. 1992. *Clambake: A History and Celebration of an American Tradition.* Amherst: University of Massachusetts Press.

Sokolov, Raymond. 1981. *Fading Feast.* New York: Farrar, Strauss, Giroux.

Vennum, Thomas, Jr. 1988. *Wild Rice and the Ojibway People.* St. Paul: Minnesota Historical Society Press.

Fortier, Alcée (1856–1914)

Collector of Louisiana French folklore. Born in St. James Parish, Louisiana, son of a sugar planter, Fortier was a member of a prominent Creole family. In 1884 he became professor of French at the University of Louisiana, which later became Tulane University, and he spent his academic career there. He was an important figure in New Orleans educational and intellectual circles, and a school, a park, and a street in the city are named after him.

His own French heritage and devotion to French culture influenced his interest in collecting folklore, though he had other scholarly interests. His principal contribution to folklore is his book *Louisiana Folk-Tales* (1895), the second volume published in the American Folklore Society's Memoir

Series. The tales it contains were collected by Fortier and two of his nieces from Creole-speaking African Americans, and they were published in both English and French. He also published an article on customs and superstitions in the first volume of the *Journal of American Folklore,* drawn mostly from his childhood memories of African American life on his family plantation, and he made a field trip to the Acadian country in 1890.

Fortier was a talented organizer who in 1892 established the Louisiana Association of the American Folklore Society, one of several branches of the national society and the only one located in the South. For several years, this organization played a role in the cultural life of New Orleans, and a number of prominent educators, writers, and community leaders were members who collected and discussed folklore. Fortier was also active in the national society, becoming its president in 1894.

Frank de Caro

References

Crombie, Jeanne F. 1972. Professor Alcée Fortier, 1856–1914. *Louisiana Historical Quarterly* 60:v–x, 1–62.

De Caro, F.A. 1985. A History of Folklife Research in Louisiana. In *Louisiana Folklife: A Guide to the State,* ed. Nicholas R. Spitzer. Baton Rouge: Louisiana Folklife Program and Center for Gulf South History and Culture, pp. 11–34.

Jordan, Rosan Augusta. 1992. Folklore Study in New Orleans' Gilded Age: The "Louisiana Association." *Louisiana Folklore Miscellany* 7:2–22.

Foxfire

Magazine and educational project. In 1966 Eliot Wigginton began teaching ninth- and tenth-grade English at the Rabun Gap-Nacoochee School, a private religiously oriented institution in the Appalachian Mountains of northwestern Georgia. His failure to interest students in the conventional curriculum encouraged him to seek new pedagogical methods. Publishing a magazine appealed to the students, who determined that at least part of its subject matter would involve the region's folkways, particularly those that seemed to be in danger of disappearing. Consequently, the first issue of *Foxfire,* which appeared in 1967 and sold out of two 600-copy printings, supplemented the standard fare of student-published literary magazines with material on local folk beliefs and traditional remedies. These were illustrated with photographs and drawings, the entire production being the work of students under Wigginton's direction.

The local reception of the first issue of *Foxfire* encouraged Wigginton and his students to plan a second. Gradually, short articles on such subjects as soap making, planting by the signs, butter churning, and ghost stories dominated the contents of the magazine, which within a year had become a quarterly. Special issues on topics such as the "old-time religion" and log-cabin building also appeared. Several other special issues of *Foxfire* have surveyed the history and culture of mountain communities near Rabun Gap. Publicity by the local and state press, as well as awards from state education associations, resulted in notices in national newspapers and magazines, and by 1970 *Foxfire* had achieved considerable recognition. Wigginton emphasized student involvement in every stage of the magazine's production and distribution: researching (usually through interviews) and writing the articles, editing, developing layouts, soliciting subscribers, and determining costs, for example.

In 1972 Wigginton edited the first anthology of material from *Foxfire.* The commercial success of *The Foxfire Book* (with more than two million copies sold) contributed to public awareness of the magazine and helped ensure the financial stability of the Southern Highlands Literary Fund (later the Foxfire Fund), the organizational base that Wigginton had developed for his project. Moreover, *Foxfire's* reputation attracted the attention of the Washington-based Institutional Development and Economic Affairs Service (IDEAS), which sought funding to encourage other schools from around the country to undertake similar programs that allowed high-school students to write pieces, usually based on interviews with family members and neighbors, about local history and folklore. The first *Foxfire*-inspired magazine started under the auspices of IDEAS was *Hoyekiya,* published by Lakota students on the Pine Ridge Reservation in South Dakota. Other projects that have imitated *Foxfire* include *Loblolly* (Gary, Texas), *Salt* (Kennebunkport, Maine), and *Nanih Wayah* (Neshoba County, Mississippi), all of which emphasized regional culture. In terms of visibility, among the most successful of *Foxfire's* imitators has been *Bittersweet,* begun in 1973 by Ellen Gray Massey in Lebanon, Missouri. Two anthologies of material from this Ozark-oriented student magazine have been published (cf. Massey 1978).

The successes of *Foxfire* and *The Foxfire Book* have also generated a considerable publishing phenomenon. By the mid-1990s, the original anthology had been followed by nine other collections of material originally published in the magazine, most edited by Wigginton; a cookbook featuring Appalachian foodways; a volume on Christmas customs; a book on toys and games from the region; a biographical study of Aunt Arie Carpenter, one of the principal sources from whom Wigginton's early students collected their information on Appalachian folkways; and several books by Wigginton detailing his pedagogical philosophy and methodology (Wigginton 1975, 1985). Some of these were originally published locally by the Foxfire Press and reprinted by national presses. For a time, *Foxfire* had its own record label, and the Foxfire String Band, comprised of student musicians, appeared on the Grand Ole Opry and at the Knoxville, Tennessee, World's Fair. Moreover, *Foxfire* has inspired a play of the same name written by fantasy novelist Susan Mary Cooper and actor Hume Cronyn. The play opened in New York City in 1983 with Cronyn and Jessica Tandy heading the cast.

Since becoming aware of Wigginton's project, academic folklorists have had mixed feelings about *Foxfire.* On one hand, many have recognized that having high-school students collect folklore provides rich possibilities both for the students, who thereby have the opportunity to learn more about their own heritages, and for the study of folklore, which may benefit from

As part of the Foxfire *project, students reconstruct a house. Rabun Gap, Georgia, 1974. American Folklife Center.*

As part of the Foxfire *project, students reconstruct a house. Rabun Gap, Georgia, 1974. American Folklife Center.*

the data so collected. Wigginton's students, for instance, have documented the material culture of their community, a complement to the record of folksong and folk narrative that folklore collectors have been making in the Appalachians for almost a century. Moreover, the positive reputation of *Foxfire* has contributed to an educational climate to which folklorists involved in public-sector work have responded. For example, programs funded in part by local, state, and federal arts councils, whose support may have been easier to obtain because of the publicity surrounding *Foxfire,* have brought tradition bearers into classrooms to demonstrate their skills.

At the same time, though, many folklorists deplored the antiquarian emphasis in *Foxfire,* which seems to equate folklore exclusively with a way of life that is growing increasingly obsolete. Though Wigginton's students often did not even use the term "folklore" to refer to what they were gathering from their neighbors, reviewers of the magazine and the anthologies have usually identified the publications' contents as folklore, thus reinforcing one popular view of the term's meaning. Folklorists have also criticized the nostalgic romanticism in the methods and presentation of the material in *Foxfire,* a tone derived in part from Wigginton's unfamiliarity with the formal study of the subject. To his credit, Wigginton responded to the criticisms of folklorists by attempting to involve them in his work. Richard M. Dorson, for example, wrote an afterword for *Foxfire 4,* which came out in 1977, and folklorists such as Edward D. Ives, Joseph Hickerson, and Ralph Rinzler have served on the magazine's advisory board. George Reynolds, who had taken a master's degree in folk studies at Western Kentucky University, joined Wigginton's staff in

1976. Respondents to critics of *Foxfire* have also stressed that the project's intention has been to employ cultural journalism to teach basic communications skills, not to teach folklore research methods.

William M. Clements

References

Dorson, Richard M. 1973. The Lesson of *Foxfire*. *North Carolina Folklore Journal* 21:157–159.

Massey, Ellen Gray, ed. 1978. *Bittersweet Country*. Garden City, NY: Anchor/Doubleday.

Puckett, John L. 1989. *Foxfire Reconsidered: A Twenty-Year Experiment in Progressive Education*. Urbana: University of Illinois Press.

Wigginton, Eliot, ed. 1972. *The Foxfire Book: Hog Dressing, Log Cabin Building, Mountain Crafts and Foods, Planting by the Signs, Snake Lore, Hunting Tales, Faith Healing, Moonshining, and Other Affairs of Plain Living*. Garden City, NY: Anchor/Doubleday.

———. 1975. *Moments: The Foxfire Experience*. Kennebunkport, ME: IDEAS/The Foxfire Fund.

———. 1985. *Sometimes a Shining Moment: The Foxfire Experience*. Garden City, NY: Anchor/Doubleday.

See also Education, Folklife in

Franklin, Benjamin (1706–1790)

Statesman, scientist, inventor, publisher, and author. His untiring energy and keen mind made Franklin one of the most influential members of 18th-century America. In addition to his numerous diplomatic and entrepreneurial accomplishments, he also was much interested in his average fellow citizens. It was for them that he published his instructive and entertaining almanac for twenty-five years from 1733 to 1758. His sense of humor, his practical advice, and his pragmatic worldview made these annual publications of twenty-four to thirty-six pages a major success. Under the pseudonym of Richard Saunders, the *Poor Richard's Almanack* was published in editions of more than 10,000 copies each year, setting new standards for the moralistic, pragmatic, and entertaining content of similar publications.

While Franklin included short folk narratives, weather superstitions, and various other folkloric texts, he was primarily interested in providing his compatriots with proverbial wisdom. Contrary to popular belief, he coined hardly any new proverbs but copied them from major English proverb collections. Of greatest influence was his essay titled "The Way to Wealth" that appeared in the last almanac, of 1758 (cf. Gallacher 1949). This short essay contains 105 proverbs culled from the previous issues of the almanac, and the wisdom contained in them became the proverbial philosophy of virtue, prosperity, prudence, and, above all, economic common sense that guided the population of this young nation. These five proverbs appear to be his own: "Three removes is as bad as a fire," "Laziness travels so slowly, that poverty soon overtakes him," "Sloth makes all things difficult, but industry all easy," "Industry pays debts, while despair increases them," and "There will be sleeping enough in the grave." The name of Benjamin Franklin or at least the popular pseudonym "Poor Richard" became attached to many traditional folk proverbs. While Franklin originated few new proverbs, he deserves much credit in popularizing old proverbs as pragmatic American wisdom.

Wolfgang Mieder

References

Barbour, Frances M. 1974. *A Concordance to the Sayings in Franklin's "Poor Richard."* Detroit: Gale.

Gallacher, Stuart A. 1949. Franklin's "Way to Wealth": A Florilegium of Proverbs and Wise Sayings. *Journal of English and Germanic Philology* 48:229–251.

Meister, Charles W. 1952–1953. Franklin as a Proverb Stylist. *American Literature* 24:157–166.

Mieder, Wolfgang. 1989. Benjamin Franklin's "Proverbs." In *American Proverbs: A Study of Texts and Contexts*. Bern: Peter Lang, pp. 129–142.

Newcomb, Robert. 1957. *The Sources of Benjamin Franklin's Sayings of Poor Richard*. Ph.D. diss., University of Maryland.

See also Almanac; Proverbs

French Canadians

Immigrants and their descendants from France—*Canadiens*. North America was discovered by the Venetian John Cabot in 1497, sailing for Henry VII of England. In 1534 Jacques Cartier began the first of three voyages of discovery on behalf of François I of France, but it was not until 1604 that the first serious attempt was made to implant French settlers in the New World. Port-Royal, in Acadia, was founded in 1604–1605; the future city of Quebec, by Samuel de Champlain in 1608.

Colonization was slow at first; in 1671 there were no more than 500 colonists in Acadia, 300 of these at Port-Royal, on the Bay of Fundy. By 1663 there were 3,000 settlers in the three centers of Montreal, Quebec, and Three Rivers, along the St. Lawrence River. The two colonies were separated by a considerable distance and were administratively distinct. The distinction was enhanced by the origins in France of the settlers; the majority of French Canadians had come from the Ile-de-France, Normandy, and nearby provinces; most Acadians came from the center-west provinces of Saintonge, Aunis, and Poitou. The French spoken in Quebec is quite distinct from that of the Acadians of Canada's Atlantic Provinces (Nova Scotia, New Brunswick, Prince Edward Island, and Newfoundland).

Wars between France and England led first to the loss of Acadia, definitively ceded to England by the Treaty of Utrecht in 1713, and then to the loss of New France as a result of the Seven Years War, sealed by the Treaty of Paris in 1763. When that war broke out in 1756, there were no more than 64,000 settlers in New France, compared to the million or so in the

English colonies. Yet in the 150 years or so of French colonization, *voyageurs* (canoe men) and *coureurs de bois* (woods runners) had opened up the land west of the English colonies, explored the Mississippi, established numerous posts, including New Orleans in 1718, and laid claim to the vast western lands known collectively as Louisiana.

From 1763 until the 1960s, the survival of French culture in Canada was greatly influenced by the Catholic Church, whose priests defended their flocks against cultural attack by the English in whatever province they might be. French Canadian *voyageurs* and *coureurs de bois* had been to the fore in opening up the West, pushing ever forward from the earliest decades of the 18th century, so that by the end of the 19th century important French communities were found in northern Ontario, in Manitoba and Saskatchewan, and to a lesser extent in Alberta and British Columbia. Their presence was felt, too, in many American states of the Midwest and Far West.

Apart from the Atlantic Provinces of Canada and along the Lower St. Lawrence River, where the fishery naturally remained a dominant aspect of culture, farming was always a central activity of French Canadians, supplemented by work in the lumber woods, still a major industry in eastern Canada. The Catholic Church was to maintain its influence in Quebec until the "Quiet Revolution" of the 1960s; it controlled education and influenced all areas of life. It was, however, an agent of conservatism, which perhaps explains in part why an intellectual elite did not begin to emerge in Canada until the middle of the 19th century; it also explains the force of oral tradition as a potent agent of cultural maintenance, and why, in most French Canadian settled areas of Canada, folklore in its many forms has remained a vibrant force in the social fabric.

An awareness of tradition as a unifying, cohesive factor of French Canadian civilization began to emerge only in the 1860s, with the writings of Joseph-Charles Taché and Philippe Aubert de Gaspé; they wrote with understanding and sensitivity about, in Taché's case, the life and legends of the lumbermen; in Aubert de Gaspé's, the seigneurial and peasant life in Quebec.

Their writings were, understandably enough, of a literary rather than an ethnographic bent, but they helped define the emerging sense of identity of the Quebecois *habitant* (settler). A further impulse in this direction was given by the publication of the first truly folkloristic work to appear in Quebec, Ernest Gagnon's *Chansons populaires du Canada* (1865). Gagnon was ahead of his time in that he noted the melodies of the 100 or so songs he wrote down, as well as information on his informants.

Gagnon's achievement was not to be followed up, however, for another fifty years or more, although he had brought to public attention what was to prove to be one of the richest folksong traditions in the French-speaking world.

Folk tradition was neglected very largely between Gagnon and the advent of Marius Barbeau on the folklore scene in Canada in 1914; apart from the occasional literary adaptations in family magazines of traditional materials, and the abortive Canadian branch of the American Folklore Society founded in Montreal by Honoré Beaugrand in 1892, the only work of note was by the American travel writer William Parker Greenough, whose *Canadian Folk-Life and Folk-Lore* (1897) is a remarkable survey of many aspects of peasant life of the period. Probably the first book published in North America to include the term "folk-life" in its title, the work is still worth reading for its sympathetic historical background, and its evocation of the customs, stories, songs, occupations, and character of the French Canadians.

Marius Barbeau (1883–1969) had an enormous impact on the organized collection and study of folklore in Canada, not only in the Francophone regions but also among Anglophone Canadians and native peoples. Attached to the National Museum of Canada in Ottawa, following a meeting with Franz Boas in 1913 Barbeau began a lifetime of collecting, in the course of which he not only amassed more than 7,000 French Canadian folksongs, but also influenced several generations of French Canadian scholars in folklore.

It was Barbeau who brought to the attention of folklorists the incredible richness of the French folk narrative tradition in Canada, publishing whole series of *Märchen* (fairy tales) in the pages of the *Journal of American Folklore,* of which he was an associate editor for many years. His interests were all-encompassing, however, as his more than 600 articles and books, in both French and English, attest. He explored and documented such diverse aspects of folk culture as clothing, foodways, housing, furniture, weapons, domestic utensils, games, formulas, customs and beliefs, and folk art and imagery, in addition to his collections of folktales, legends, anecdotes, songs, and music; folksongs, however, were closest to his heart, and he published four major collections of them, in addition to numerous scholarly articles.

Most of his work was in his native province of Quebec, and it was there, either directly or indirectly, that he set the course of future research in French Canadian folklore. His foremost disciple was Luc Lacourcière (1910–1989), who began teaching folklore at Laval University in 1944 and organized the Archives de Folklore there. Lacourcière collected extensively in Quebec and New Brunswick, his chief interest being in folktales; his goal was to publish a definitive catalog of French folktales found in North America, and, while largely complete, it remained unpublished at his death.

Lacourcière's main influence was through his teaching; he supervised several generations of Quebec folklorists in their research and influenced many more Francophone scholars, Acadians and Franco-Americans alike. The Publications of the Archives de Folklore Series, which he edited, remains a major contribution to the readily available folklore documentation of Quebec; it has a preponderance of works, usually theses or dissertations in origin, dealing with aspects of folk narrative, although six of the twenty-five volumes to have appeared by 1991 formed the bulk of Conrad Laforte's massive *Catalog de la Chanson folklorique française,* a work attempting to impose a logical order on the whole corpus of French folksong from around the world.

Though song and narrative were Lacourcière's main concerns, like Barbeau his interests extended beyond oral folklore; one of his students, Jean-Claude Dupont, who was to succeed him at the head of folklore studies at Laval, has devoted much of his professional career to the study of the material culture of Quebec life and was responsible for giving a new emphasis to folklore studies at Laval. While scholarly and popular works on French folktales continued to appear—notably a series edited by Lacourcière's student Jean-Pierre Pichette, begun in 1978—Dupont instituted in 1981 a new series at Laval called Ethnologie de l'Amérique française, under the aegis of the newly formed CELAT *(Centre d'études sur la langue, les arts et les traditions populaires des francophones en Amérique du Nord);* this series was broader in scope than that of the Archives de Folklore, including volumes on leather-working traditions, traditional religious iconography, domestic heating, dance, forestry and woodworking, domestic and community life, vernacular architecture, and children's folklore, as well as volumes on aspects of the folksong and narrative traditions. Dupont's early research was in the art and technology of the blacksmith.

The emphasis given to narrative by Lacourcière is nonetheless evident not only in the volumes that appeared in the Archives de Folklore Series, but also those edited by his student Jean-Pierre Pichette. Catherine Jolicoeur, Germain Lemieux, Hélène Bernier, Nancy Schmitz, and Jean-Pierre Pichette in the former series; Jean-Claude Dupont, Conrad Laforte, Clément Legaré, Bertrand Bergeron and Gérald Aucoin in the series Mémoires d'Homme—all have published collections of narratives even when, as is the case for Dupont and Laforte, their reputations were made in material culture and folksong, respectively.

Folksong studies have remained central to Laval-generated scholarship; works by Russell Scott Young, Dominique Gauthier, Conrad Laforte, Donald Deschênes, Charlotte Cormier, Madeleine Béland, and others testify to the longstanding influence of Marius Barbeau, quite apart from the intrinsic interest of the songs themselves. Besides material-culture studies, areas such as custom and belief, foodways, folk speech, and other genres have been less well studied than narrative and song. As is often the case, some kinds of research are entirely dependant on the interests of one individual; thus for several years, Madeleine Doyon-Ferland was alone in the study of material culture, children's lore and games, and dance; latterly, Simone Voyer for dance, Jean Simard for folk art and religion, and Jean DuBerger in narrative and popular culture have broadened the scope of published research. In the Laval tradition, studies by these scholars have been chiefly comparative and historical in emphasis.

Mention should be made here that while Laval scholars have naturally been preoccupied with Francophone traditions, they have not totally eschewed non-Francophone traditions in Quebec; Nancy Schmitz's work among the Quebec Irish is a case in point. Acadian scholars, of course, have always been only too well aware of the realities of living in a bilingual culture; this was underlined by the Acadian Catherine Jolicoeur who, during her presidency of the Folklore Studies Association of Canada *(l'Association canadienne d'ethnologie et de folk-*

lore), readily switched from one language to the other.

The fact that Canada is a bilingual nation has required cooperation between French and English scholars, if only for the necessary federal funding; such cooperation began formally in 1976 with the first volume of an annual journal entitled *Culture & Tradition* (the ampersand being bilingual), put together by students of the folklore programs at Laval and Memorial Universities. It was followed in 1979 by the organ of the national association, *Canadian Folklore canadien,* which generally includes an equal number of articles in French and English.

A scholar much influenced by Lacourcière was Robert-Lionel Séguin (1920–1983), whose path diverged however from that of his illustrious colleague. As much as Lacourcière was a scholar of oral traditions, so Séguin was of material culture. With his base at the University of Quebec at Three Rivers, Séguin labored to produce a portrait of the whole of daily Quebecois life from the 17th through the 20th centuries, his writings dealing with topics as diverse as farm equipment in the 17th and 18th centuries, mills and barns, costume, entertainments, toys, witchcraft, utensils, swearing, work techniques, and customary life. Séguin also founded and edited the *Revue d'Ethnologie du Québec.* Beginning in 1975, the series included twelve issues before its demise in 1980. In his Introduction to Volume 1, Séguin stressed the growth of interest in Quebec in ethnohistoric research, suggesting it to be a logical path in the search for his people's identity.

This approach to the study of folklore has been the unifying thread of folklore studies in Quebec and, indeed, in French-speaking Canada as a whole. While it was not explicit in the writings of Barbeau and Lacourcière, at least not to the point of it becoming part of the French Canadian folklorist's credo, subsequent generations have certainly stressed more and more openly their interest in their traditional heritage as the key to their identity—as Quebecois, or Acadians, or Franco-Ontarians, or French Newfoundlanders.

This was in part a consequence of the "Quiet Revolution" of the 1960s, which saw the rejection on the part of younger generations of many traditional values and institutions, and an assertion, within the larger Canadian context, of their distinctiveness. The more extreme adherents to this position took up the cause of Quebec nationalism and began pursuing the goal of a separate and independent Quebec state. Many turned to the study of folklore and ethnology to find the roots and nature of their cultural distinctiveness, and at Laval University, where folklore studies had been established since 1944, they found a ready-made resource. The general preoccupation with the past led ultimately to the absorption of folklore as a distinct discipline into the larger field of history; folklorists trained at Laval now take their degrees in history, with specialization in *Arts et Traditions populaires.*

Lacking the same unified political status as the province of Quebec, Acadians have not followed the same path. While by the mid-1990s they constituted up to 30 percent of the population of New Brunswick, Acadians in Nova Scotia and Prince Edward Island have nowhere near the same substantial minority, with populations of Francophones below 10 percent. The Acadian element in Newfoundland, even when taken together with other groups of French speakers, constitutes less than 1 percent of the province's population.

Here again the influence of, first, Marius Barbeau and then Luc Lacourcière was significant. The former had influenced the Acadian journalist Joseph-Thomas Leblanc, who used his newspaper, *L'Evangéline,* to collect 1,200 Acadian folksongs in the 1930s. Another pioneer collector of Acadian folklore was Anselme Chiasson who, with his cousin Br. Daniel Boudreau, published five modest but significant series of folksongs between 1942 and 1979; his 1961 study of the history and traditions of Cheticamp, in Cape Breton Island, his home community, was widely praised for its exploration of a hitherto little known Acadian enclave. Chiasson subsequently published a volume on the folklore of the Magdalen Islands in 1980, covering many aspects of the social, material, and spiritual life of the inhabitants.

Lacourcière's influence on Acadian folklore studies went back, in fact, to Chiasson's initial work in 1942; Chiasson was in touch with Marius Barbeau, and Barbeau had sought Lacourcière's advice on a problem raised by Chiasson. But Lacourcière's greatest influence was as a teacher, not only of Quebecois folklorists, but also of many of the major Acadian scholars from the 1950s onward. Indeed, Jean-Claude Dupont, the Quebec native who succeeded Lacourcière at Laval, taught at the University of Moncton before returning to Laval, his research there leading to two major studies of Acadian tradition (Dupont 1977, 1978a).

Well before Dupont's work in Acadia, Lacourcière had collected there, and drew to him the first academically trained Acadian folklorists—notably, Catherine Jolicoeur, whose 1963 dissertation supervised by Lacourcière, on Acadian phantom vessel legends, was subsequently published in the *Archives de Folklore* Series (Volume 11, 1970); Antonine Maillet, whose celebrity as an author has cloaked her studies in folklore, which have nonetheless informed her fictional writings; and Lauraine Léger, whose study of traditional sanctions in Kent County, New Brunswick, was a novel departure from the more common preoccupations with song, narrative or material culture.

The most significant development for Acadian culture was the creation, in 1963, of the Maritime Provinces' only Francophone university at Moncton, New Brunswick, and, more specifically still, the foundation of its *Centre d'études acadiennes* (Cea) in 1970. The Cea has been geared to the amassing of every available document in the world relative to the history of the Acadians, but from the start oral traditions were not neglected; important contributions from Anselme Chiasson, Charlotte Cormier, and Ronald Labelle (both taught by Lacourcière), as well as by collectors already named, have made of the Cea a major folklore archive of Acadian traditions. Labelle, a Quebec native, currently directs the center, but his training has been invaluable in instituting major research projects on oral history, foodways, and folk medicine, among others.

The leading Acadian folklorist in Prince Edward Island, Georges Arsenault, was also trained by Lacourcière. Besides an important volume on Acadian ballads published in 1980, he authored a unique study of Candlemas festivities on the island in 1982. Significant collections have also been made in Acadia by Vivian Labrie and Robert Bouthillier, chiefly of tales and songs; by Dominique Gauthier, of songs; by Marielle Boudreau and Melvin Gallant of foodways, by Gallant of tales; and, on Cape Breton Island, by Gérald Aucoin of tales. The most important work to date on the Acadians of southern Nova Scotia remains Alain Doucet's little known study of the oral literature of the St. Mary's Bay region, published in 1965.

The handful of French villages on the coast of Newfoundland's Port-au-Port Peninsula represent a quite different set of historical circumstances than those pertaining to the Quebec or Acadian French. The original French settlers were, in the main, deserters from the 19th-century French fishery prosecuted on Newfoundland's West Coast, coming from Brittany, Normandy, and other maritime regions of France, as well as from St. Pierre and Miquelon, off Newfoundland's South Coast. Intermarrying with Acadians from Cape Breton Island who began settling nearby regions at the same period, the Port-au-Port French, despite their infinitesimally small numbers (less than 3,000), have maintained a remarkably rich tradition of folktale, folksong, music, and other traditions in the face of constant pressures to assimilate to the dominant Anglophone majority. Their French culture is one of the few in eastern Canada not to have been explored in depth by Quebec scholars; work there has been based at Memorial University of Newfoundland, led by Gerald Thomas and a small number of his students. In light of his training, the differences of approach between French Canadian and Anglo Canadian folklorists is apparent in Thomas' 1983 study of the folktale tradition and Gary Butler's 1990 analysis of supernatural beliefs.

Ontario, traditionally considered the heartland of English Canada, nonetheless has a Francophone population of approximately 450,000, which makes it by far the largest such minority in any of the Canadian provinces and territories. Ontario is also the site of the national capital, Ottawa, where the National Museum of Canada (now the Canadian Museum of Civilization) is situated. The museum has always had a significant role to play in folklore studies in Canada, and the attention paid to French Canada, while less in the late 20th century than in the past, has been important.

It was Barbeau, who was attached to the National Museum, who launched research on French Canadian traditions on a systematic basis; apart from his own extensive collecting and publishing, he influenced many researchers in the first half of the 20th century and was a key figure in promoting Lacourcière's career at Laval. In addition, the museum provided support of various kinds for institutional and independant researchers, and has created a large and important archive. Major development of the Folklore Section was made by Barbeau's successor at the museum, Carmen Roy. A native of the Gaspé Peninsula, she is the author of the *Littérature orale en Gaspésie* (1955), which was derived from her 1953 doctoral dissertation from the Sorbonne in Paris and was a major survey of a region but little explored at the time. She also made a survey in 1966 of the French islands of St. Pierre and Miquelon, which has not received the recognition it deserves.

The one person who stands alone in the collection and publication of Franco-Ontarian folklore is Germain Lemieux, S.J. In the late 1940s and early 1950s, Lemieux was collecting local history and traditions for the *Société historique du Nouvel-Ontario,* and upon meeting Luc Lacourcière in 1950, he was little by little beguiled into pursuing graduate studies at Laval. There he completed both his M.A. and his Ph.D. degrees, his dissertation being the comparative analysis of an international tale type, versions of which he had collected in the French region of northern Ontario. His collecting continued with renewed vigor, and in 1972 his work *Les jongleurs du billochet,* which served as an introduction to subsequent volumes of folktales, was published. Volume 1 of a proposed thirty appeared in 1973, as a publication of the Centre Franco-Ontarien de folklore of the University of Sudbury. Volume 29 appeared in 1990. The series is quite remarkable, not only for the large number of tales included, but for Lemieux's effort to provide both a scholarly transcription of his texts and a more accessible standardized version following.

Much of Lemieux's work is being continued by the embryonic Folklore Department of the University of Sudbury, where Jean-Pierre Pichette, Lacourcière's last doctoral student, has a program in place that emphasizes field collections. Its archive is an important addition to archives of French culture in Quebec and the Atlantic Provinces. Franco-Ontarians themselves are for the most part the descendants of 19th-century Quebec settlers, whose traditions they brought with them.

The present-day province of Manitoba was claimed for France as early as 1738; but even after the English conquest of French Canada in 1763, English commercial interests employed large numbers of French Canadians there. By the beginning of the 19th century, there were as many as 6,000 or 7,000 French Canadians implanted there, many of whom married native women, which facilitated the maintenance of peace in the region. There was a slow but continuous immigration of Quebec natives into the Red River area; by 1871, half of the population of what was to become St. Boniface, opposite Winnipeg, was described as *Métis* (those with a French father and an Indian mother). However, the Manitoba Act of 1870, which brought the province into the Canadian Confederation, also ushered in an influx of settlers from Ontario and a gradual decline of French rights.

The erosion of French culture in Manitoba has had numerous opponents from the days of Louis Riel and his abortive rebellion. Its chief defender in the late 20th century is the *Centre d'études franco-canadiennes de l'Ouest,* organized by Annette Saint-Pierre and Robert Painchaud in 1975. As its name implies, its concern is with French language and culture in all of the Western Provinces. Relatively few works of interest to folklorists have been published, for want of qualified scholars, with the notable exception of Marcien Ferland's *Chansons à répondre du Manitoba* (1979).

French Canadian folklore scholarship can be characterized in the following ways: First, as one would expect, it is most solidly based in Quebec, chiefly at Laval University; it has several subsidiary bases, both in Quebec and in the Atlantic provinces, chiefly at Moncton. The farther west one moves, the less well entrenched it is as a subject for academic study. Second, folklore is used by French Canadians as an important tool in the preservation of their cultural heritage, and in some circles as a justification or an illustration of their distinctive identity (and, therefore, of their right to political distinctiveness). Third, folklore studies have been largely historical and comparative in nature, in part because that approach was the dominant one everywhere until the 1960s, and in part because since the 1960s folklore has acquired the cultural-political function noted previously.

Gerald Thomas

References

Bouchard, René, ed. 1983. *La vie quotidienne au Québec: Histoire, métiers, techniques et traditions: Mélanges à la memoire de Robert-Lionel Séguin.* Quebec: Presses de l'Université du Québec.

Dionne, René, ed. 1983. *Quatre siècles d'identité canadienne.* Montreal: Bellarmin.

Dupont, Jean-Claude. 1977. *Héritage d'Acadie.* Ottawa: Leméac.

————. 1978a. *Histoire populaire de l'Acadie.* Ottawa: Leméac.

————, ed. 1978b. *Mélanges en l'honneur de Luc Lacourcière. Folklore français d'Amérique.* Ottawa: Leméac.

Labelle, Ronald, and Lauraine Léger, eds. 1982. *En r'montant la tradition: Hommage au père Anselme Chiasson.* Moncton: Les Editions d'Acadie.

Thomas, Gerald. 1983. *Les Deux Traditions: Le conte populaire chez les Franco-Terreneuviens.* Montreal: Bellarmin.

Toye, William, ed. 1983. *The Oxford Companion to Canadian Literature.* Toronto: Oxford University Press, pp. 40–42, 264–267.

See also Cajuns; Canadian Folklore Scholarship; French in the United States; *Guillonée*

French in the United States

Immigrants and their descendants who came to the United States directly from France or indirectly through Canada or the West Indies. The history of the French in the United States is complicated by several factors: shifting political boundaries on the North American continent from the 17th through the 19th centuries, the mobility of different French-speaking populations, and their various degrees of acculturation and senses of identity. The study of French folklore and folklife in the United States is further complicated by the variety of sources available, ranging from romanticized local histories to scholarly histories and ethnographies of specific groups. French, French Canadian, Franco-American, and American researchers also have had distinctive theoretical perspectives on the French experience in America, although the 1994 retrospective conference "L'Ethnologie des Francophones en

Amérique du Nord, 1944–1994: Bilan et Perspectives" at Laval University in Quebec City symbolizes a critical rapprochement.

This entry briefly traces French vernacular culture in the United States through folklife studies growing out of the initial exploration and settlement in 17th- and 18th-century New France; *Métis* culture; 19th-century French Canadian immigration; Acadians in New England; and current Franco-American identity issues.

New France

Through their explorations, 17th-century fur traders, *coureurs de bois* (woods runners), *voyageurs* (canoe men), explorers for the Crown, Jesuit missionaries, and the colonial military expanded the territory of New France, centered in Quebec City and Montreal (founded by Samuel de Champlain in 1608 and by Maisonneuve in 1643, respectively) to what is now a large part of the continental United States. They explored the Great Lakes and the Mississippi and its tributaries, the Missouri and the Ohio, and established fur trading posts, military forts, and missions at strategic points along these waterways. They paved the way for French Canadian settlements, which grew up around these sites in the 18th century. These settlements were relatively small—the total population of New France has been estimated at only 60,000 *habitants* (settlers) by 1760. Yet, a case can be made for French folk cultural influence extending into the 20th century, despite France's loss of its colonial empire and the subsequent loss of the French language among *habitant* descendants.

France ceded to the British by treaty in 1763 the Upper Midwest, that area north and west of the Ohio River that would become the Northwest Territory by ordinance of the U.S. Congress in 1784. It ceded to the Spanish the vast Louisiana Territory which the Americans later obtained in 1803. Detroit, which was founded in 1701, New Orleans in 1718 and St. Louis in 1764 are just a few examples of the 3,000 places in the United States whose names still mark the outlines of what was once New France.

The *voyageurs* have a special place in American folklife study. Although their image is part of the romanticization of the frontier, an earlier generation of scholars—notably, French Canadian folklorist Marius Barbeau and American historians Theodore Christian Blegen and Grace L. Nute—traced these boatmen's distinctive folk patterns, especially their *chansons* (songs). The *chansons*, like other worksongs, apparently helped the *voyageurs* paddle in unison and build morale and identity through two centuries: first, for the French fur-trading monopolies; then for the North West Company; and, finally, for the American Fur Company. Typically, novice boatmen, called *mangers de lard* (pork eaters), brought manufactured goods from Montreal to a point on the north shore of Lake Superior, now Grand Portage, Minnesota, to exchange for furs. The experienced boatmen, called *hivernants* (winterers), traveled there from far-flung posts in the interior with pelts for the manufactured goods in return. The *hivernants* shared their repertoires, polished by long winter nights of singing and fiddling, with the less experienced men before returning to their posts to begin the cycle anew.

Yet, their songs also connected the *voyageurs* to *habitant* culture because they usually selected and adapted 17th-century traditional tunes and lyrics also sung in settlements throughout New France. Barbeau writes that folksongs were "as familiar as barley-water to the home-keeping villagers of Quebec, Acadia, Detroit and Louisiana." Marcel Bénéteau, a researcher at Laval University, has found, for example, that this folksong tradition was extant in the Detroit River region settlements the 1940s (Bénéteau 1991). French families, whom he has interviewed on both sides of the border since the 1980s, have given him "scribblers," or handwritten books, with song texts. They have also remembered songs sung at *viéllees* (traditional evening gatherings), as well as at weddings and other celebrations whose versions date back to this early period. Both *voyageurs* and *habitants* once sang "A La Claire Fontaine" (At the Clear Fountain), now called the unofficial anthem of French Canada, and the familiar "Alouette" (The Lark), for instance.

Other *habitant* folklore and folklife has been recorded in states created from the old Northwest Territory—Illinois, Indiana, Michigan, Minnesota, Ohio and Wisconsin—and from those states once part of the Louisiana Territory—Louisiana and Missouri, in particular. These works suggest that distinctive verbal arts, social folk customs, and material culture, once based in the French colonial agricultural and mercantile economy and Catholic religious structure, are, for some, cultural memories and, for others, ongoing or revived traditions in these localities.

M.C.W. Hamlin, writing *Legends of le Détroit* in 1884, noted *les peurs* (horror stories) about *la chasse galerie* (the phantom canoe), *le feu follet* (fairy lights), and *le loup garou* (the werewolf) as well-remembered narratives among French families "on the strait" between Lakes Michigan and Erie. WPA (Works Progress Administration) folklife researchers recorded these same stories as memory culture in 1930s Vincennes, Indiana. Folklorist Ron Baker edited their findings in his *French Folklife in Old Vincennes* (1979). Baker discusses Vincennes' strategic position in New France from the 1730s; as a fort, then a village, it was located at the confluence of the Wabash and Ohio Rivers and so allowed water access from Detroit to New Orleans. French Canadian folklorist Joseph Médard Carrière also recorded *contes* (classic wonder tales) about the hero 'Tit Jean (Little John) in the 1930s from residents in Old Mines, Missouri, a village dating from the 1760s that was orginally made up of French colonials who had come from France or from the Illinois Territory, which had gone to the British. In the mid-1990s, folklorist C. Ray Brassieur is continuing folklife study among Missouri Creoles.

In his article "The Lingering Shadow of New France," Dennis Au notes that the French custom of *charivari* (shivaree) is still practiced in Monroe County, Michigan, in what was once the River Raisin settlement of the 1780s, augmented by French families leaving Detroit once British rule was established there (Au 1987). Mary Agnes Starr found the same tradition in some Wisconsin French communities in her *Pea Soup and Johnny Cake* (1981), noting that the custom of making noise outside newlyweds' home was once a sign of community disapproval of an inappropriate marriage (for example, one spouse was much older, too recently bereaved or not a Catholic), but was now just one more prank played by friends on the new couple. Traditional Christmas suppers after Midnight Mass and New Year's gift giving and blessings are other customs not only surviving but also evolving within families on the eve of the 21st century.

Baker and Au outline *habitant* material culture, including settlement and agricultural patterns. The "ribbon farm," in which houses cluster at river's edge and fields stretch out in long, thin plots behind, occurs often, and there is other typical log-cabin construction and tool use. They also note foodways legacies, including use of outdoor bakeovens, construction of traps and trapping techniques, and a variety of dishes for everyday and festival use. Au traces muskrat eating, for example, still current in some parts of Michigan and Ohio, to the *voyageurs*, who learned the techniques for trapping the animal and preparing it from the Native American groups originally in the area. These muskrat-eating French call themselves and their patois "Mushrat French" to distinguish themselves from the Quebecois and continental French.

Métis (*Michif* or *Mechif*) Culture

The *Métis* are descendants of 17th-century French *voyageurs* and/or 18th-century Scottish and Irish trappers and Native American women. As almost all settlements in New France included interracial marriages, conducted either according to "the customs of that country" or according to Quebecois tradition, many of those who trace their ancestry to that colonial period are "of mixed blood." Many French Canadians who immigrated to the United States in the 19th and 20th centuries to work in the lumber camps also married Native American or *Métis* spouses.

Métis communities in Canada have a stronger sense of a distinctive ethnic grouping than do those in the United States, perhaps because *Métis* Louis Riel led an 1869 rebellion in what is now Manitoba and a second in 1885 in what is now Saskatchewan and has been memorialized in folk ballads. *Michif* or *Mechif* are the terms used more often in the United States for those of mixed ancestry. Individuals in the United States may define themselves as *Métis, Michif*, or *Mechif*, French, or French Canadian, or as Native American. Aunt Jane Godreau, interviewed by folklorist Richard M. Dorson in Michigan's Upper Peninsula in the 1940s, for example, was French Canadian and Ojibwa (Dorson 1948). Her repertoire of anecdotes, legends, and jokes about "half breeds" and Dorson's comment that she lived in one of the "half breed" villages along the shores of Lake Superior suggest that she could have been defined as *Métis* or *Michif*, although she was either self-identified or identified by Dorson as a *canadienne* in his *Bloodstoppers and Bearwalkers* (1952).

Filmmaker Michael Loukinen and his consultants found that the fiddlers they documented in the 1991 ethnographic film *Medicine Fiddler* defined themselves ethnically in all of these ways. Although the focus of the film is on Native American and *Métis* incorporation of a European instrument and musical styles into blended but distinctive repertoires, the French or French Canadian strands emerge through the accompanying booklet edited by folklorist James Leary (Leary 1992). Fiddlers define an older style of playing as "the old fur-trading way" since it was the French *voyageurs* who first introduced fiddles and step dancing to native peoples at trading posts and weddings. French Canadians continued the traditions in lumber camps and taverns. The fiddlers also recognized specific tunes, such as "Red River Jig" and "White Fish on the Rapids," as French contributions.

Nineteenth-Century French Canadian Immigration

So many French Canadians left Quebec Province for the United States between the 1840s and the 1920s that *La Belle Province* was said to have lost one-third of its population, and communities in the United States dating from colonial New France were designated "Old French" to distinguish them from the new. As indicated above, many Quebecois came to work in the white-pine lumber industry in New England and the Upper Midwest. Folklore researchers have noted French Canadian traditions in the lumber camps and towns from Maine to Michigan, reminiscent of the *voyageur* traditions two centuries before and connected to the folklife in contemporary Quebecois camps. Loggers shared similar *contes* and *légendes* at *des veillées d'cahiers* (evening gatherings in the camps) and often brought them home to kitchen hearths through the 1940s. Dorson, with French folklorist Ariadne Felice in Michigan, French Canadian folklorist Jean-Claude Dupont in Michigan, Vermont, and New York, and American folklorist Horace P. Beck in Maine, found, for example, that loggers supplemented the older stories and songs with newer genres of tall tales about extraordinarily strong men. Dorson also recorded a new genre of dialect stories performed by French Canadian and Franco-American raconteurs in Michigan's Upper Peninsula from the 1940s that commented humorously on language differences and issues of acculturation and identity (Dorson 1948).

Even more Quebecois (many, but not all, farm families) emigrated to work in New England industrial centers, especially in textile mills, shoe factories, and construction companies. French-Canadian sections of towns and cities, called *Petits Canadas* (Little Canadas) sprang up in Connecticut, Maine, Massachusetts, New Hampshire, Rhode Island, and Vermont. Researchers at the French Institute at Assumption College in Worcester, Massachusetts (cf. Quintal 1983), and at the Franco-American Resource Opportunity Group at the University of Maine at Orono, for example, have documented the social, political, and historical dimensions of these diverse communities. They have found that Little Canadas had fluctuating populations since many residents moved freely back and forth between the United States and Canada. Some residents repatriated; others moved out as they acculturated to American life. Although Little Canadas no longer exist geographically, a great percentage of New Englanders are of French Canadian descent so that folk-cultural matrices remain within Franco-American contexts.

Folklorists and folklife specialists have documented

French Canadian folk cultures and Franco-American folklife in mill towns and former mill towns. Brigitte Lane's comprehensive study *Franco-American Folk Traditions and Popular Culture in a Former Milltown,* based on her fieldwork in the 1980s, traces aspects of ethnic urban folklore and the dynamics of folklore change in Lowell, Massachusetts (Lane 1990). Lane finds, as Dorson did earlier for Michigan's Upper Peninsula lumber towns, that the older French Canadian genres, often Quebecois cultural survivals, are memory culture with symbolic implications, while the newer joking forms as well as immigrant stories and personal-experience narratives are current in Lowell. These newer narratives have a self-reflexive quality, playing on Franco-American understandings of language maintenance and change.

The Lowell Folklife Project, sponsored by the American Folklife Center at the Library of Congress in 1987–1988 with folklorists Peter Bartis as director and Doug DeNatale as field coordinator, was designed to document Lowell's then-current cultural traditions (cf. Bartis 1988; DeNatale 1988). Researchers found that Franco-Americans, one of the oldest groups represented in the study, negotiated their own ethnic awareness juxtaposed with Irish, Greek, Portuguese, Puerto Rican, and Cambodian communities in a folklore of ethnicity. The fieldwork data are available at the Library of Congress.

The American Folklife Center's 1979 Rhode Island Folklife Project included a Franco-American component as well. Folklorist Jerry Johnson focused on folksinger and tradition bearer Roméo Berthiaume, then living in the former mill town of Woonsocket. Berthiaume, whose family had moved back and forth between Quebec and Rhode Island and who had worked in the mills, recalled the family *veillées* in both countries as instrumental in developing his love of French Canadian cultural traditions. He once said that his repertoire of 350 songs helped him express feelings that were "dear to those who are interested in our ethnic background." He also wrote his own songs, short stories, and plays, which extended his Franco-American cultural expression. Field research material is also available at the Library of Congress (Lane 1990:145–148).

Franco-American storyteller Michael Parent draws on his memories, personal-experience narratives and family stories of growing up in Lewiston, Maine, for his performances and writing as well. His award-winning audiotape *Sundays at Grandma's House (Dimanches chez memère)* (1988) evokes memories of family life within a bilingual-bicultural mill town, as does his piece "Olive and Bidou" in *Lives in Translation: An Anthology of Contemporary Franco-American Writings* (1991) edited by writer Denis Ledoux. Both Berthiaume's and Parent's work confirm what folklorist Julien Olivier told Lane in a 1982 interview: "Qu'il y ait une culture qui est surtout une culture orale, pour moi c'est du folklore aussi." ("Where there's a culture that is completely oral, then, for me, it's also folklore") (Lane 1990:154). Olivier's work on Franco-American traditions in New England, directed toward education of young people in confirming their ethnic and regional identity, is a relatively early example of putting folklore to use (cf. Olivier 1979).

Acadians in New England

When the Maine state legislature funded the creation of the Acadian Archives *(Archives Acadiennes)* at the University of Maine at Fort Kent in 1989 and the U.S. Congress passed the Maine Acadian Culture Preservation Act in 1990, these official acts sanctioned a cultural identity long recognized in the state's Upper St. John River Valley, located in the northernmost county of Aroostook. Acadians, many from Brittany and Normandy, had settled in a region the French called "Arcadie" or "Acadia" after a Micmac name for what is now Nova Scotia, New Brunswick, and Prince Edward Island. Their principal settlement of Port-Royal (now Annapolis, Nova Scotia) had been founded by Samuel de Champlain in 1605 before he moved up the St. Lawrence River to found Quebec in 1608.

The British and the French contested claims to Acadian lands for a century and a half. The British governor in Nova Scotia deported many Acadians in 1755, questioning their allegiance in the impending war with France. Some settled in the Upper St. John River Valley, while others went down the Mississippi River to Louisiana, where they became known as Cajuns. At the conclusion of the French and Indian war in 1763, more Acadians from Cape Breton and Ile St. Jean (later Prince Edward Island settled in the valley as well. *La Grande Dérangement,* as the Acadian Diaspora is called, lasted officially from 1755 to 1763, but its cultural significance remains among Acadians in the late 20th century. The Acadians were joined by French Canadians from Quebec by 1831. Although the Acadian cultural presence is more strongly marked in this region, its French language and culture draw from both groups. Once the international boundary line between New Brunswick and Maine was established in 1842, more settlers moved across the border to augment the communities in the United States.

A number of folklorists have noted Acadian and blended-French folklife in the Upper St. John River Valley in the 19th and 20th centuries. The bibliography *Folklore and Folklife in the Upper Saint John Valley* (1994), prepared by folklorist Lisa Ornstein, director of the Acadian Archives *(Archives Acadiennes),* shows that French folklorist Geneviève Massignon, French Canadian folklorist Luc Lacourcière, Acadian folklorist Catherine Jolicouer, and Franco-American folklorist Roger Paradis have been among those who have documented the folk arts of the region. Paradis' article, "Franco-American Folk-Lore: A Cornucopia of Culture," based on a series of lectures at the University of Maine at Fort Kent, looks at the connections between folklore and history—for example, in evaluating some of the region's historical legendry, including that about *la guerre des sauvages* (the French and Indian War) and the Acadian Diaspora—within his argument for critcally recognizing this French regional folk culture (Paradis 1974).

Paradis also briefly summarizes *la coutume* (social folk customs) of the early settlers, which include domestic arts and crafts such as foodways, weaving and embroidery, medicine making for the women, and lumbering, farming, hunting, and trapping skills for the men. The American Folklife Center's 1990–1991 Maine Acadian Cultural Survey, with folklorists

David A. Taylor as director and C. Ray Brassieur as field coordinator, documented their retention and change in the valley in the late 20th century (Brassieur 1991). Foodways traditions, which Brassieur notes are both Acadian and regional, are especially long lasting. *Pâté chinois* (a shepherd's pie made of mashed potatoes, ground meat, and corn) and "JoJo potatoes" (batter-fried potatoes), reflect the major agricultural crop of the region. Buckwheat *ployes* (thin pancakes) are a regional specialty as are *tourtières* (meat pies, originally Quebecois, made for special occasions).

Out migration to southern New England to work in the textile mills drew many Acadians from the St. John Valley in the late 19th and 20th centuries as it had the Quebecois. Acadian communities, therefore, are scattered throughout the New England states, especially in Connecticut and Massachusetts. Brassieur writes that the connections between the valley and these communities continue, evidenced most clearly in a whole system of summer family reunions, the annual Acadian Festival Family Reunion being a more public sign of the private get-togethers.

Franco-American Identity Issues

Patrice Higonnet, writing about French immigration to the United States from the time of the English colonies to the late 20th century, in the *Harvard Encyclopedia of American Ethnic Groups* (1980), states that most emigrés did not maintain a cultural identity and that most came as middle- or upper-middle-class individuals whose culture it was to assimilate to American values. This acculturation process was especially true of the French Huguenots, or French Protestants, such as Paul Revere's father, who identified with English Protestants more readily than with the French Catholic regime that had deported them when the Edict of Nantes granting religious freedom was revoked in 1685. Elliott Barkan, writing in the same encyclopedia about French Canadians in the United States, notes that the movement from French Canadian to Franco-American to American is the most common one, and inevitable once the French language is lost. James Parker suggests that a French American identity is a mythic one, in his *Ethnic Identity: The Case of the French Americans* (1983).

Given the sense among these scholars that a Franco-American identity is not a viable one, how folklife specialists and the communities they have studied see these issues is instructive. Roger Paradis, speaking of French culture in Maine in 1974, said that "within a few years, Franco-American folk-lore as a folk culture, at least in its traditional form, may have ceased to exist" (Pardis 1974:44). Franco-American folklorist Julien Olivier and French folklorist Brigitte Lane, speaking of Quebecois in New England, agree that the old social structures have been changing since the 1940s and that traditional folklore forms are endangered, but they also agree that new forms and adaptations are emerging, many of them closer to popular culture, so that the definition of "Franco-American folklore" needs expansion. Folklorists C. Ray Brassieur and Dennis Au, speaking for the Old French and Creole communities in the Midwest, see that submerged identities and corresponding folk cultural behavior can

exist regardless of communities' self-perceptions. Lane concludes her 1990 study with the hope that "as ethnic pride seems to be thriving among the Franco-Americans" so ethnic rediscovery and folklore revivals will follow. She writes, "Obviously the battle for *'notre langue, notre foi, et nos coutumes'* [our language, our faith, and our customs] is not over, even if it is assuming today new and different dimensions within the group itself" (Lane 1990: 462).

Janet L. Langlois

References

Au, Dennis. 1987. The Lingering Shadow of New France: The French-Canadian Community of Monroe County, Michigan. In *Michigan Folklife Reader*. ed. C. Kurt Dewhurst and Yvonne Lockwood. East Lansing: Michigan State University Press.

Bartis, Peter T. 1988. Center Launches Lowell Study. *Folklife Center News* 10 (Winter):1,5.

Beck, Horace P. 1957. Lumbering. In *The Folklore of Maine*. Philadelphia and New York: Lippincott.

Bénéteau, Marcel. 1991. *Vielles chansons du Détroit* (Old French Songs of the Detroit River Region). Cassette produced for the Essex County Historical Society, Windsor, Ontario, Canada.

Blegen, Theodore Christian. 1966. *Voyageurs and Their Songs*. St. Paul: Minnesota Historical Society.

Brassieur, C. Ray. 1991. The Long Hard Road to Madawaska: Acadian Cultural Retention in Maine's Upper Saint John Valley. *Folklife Center News* 13 (Fall):4–13.

DeNatale, Doug. 1988. Lowell Fieldwork Completed. *Folklife Center News* 10 (Summer):1–3.

Dorson, Richard M. 1948. Dialect Stories of the Upper Peninsula: A New Form of American Folklore. *Journal of American Folklore* 61:119–123.

Dupont, Jean Claude. 1986. *Légendes de l'Amérique francaises*. 2d. ed. Quebec.

Hamlin, Marie Caroline Watson. [1884] 1977. *Legends of le Détroit*. Detroit: Gale.

Lane, Brigitte Marie. 1990. *Franco-American Folk Traditions and Popular Culture in a Former Milltown: Aspects of Ethnic Urban Folklore and the Dynamics of Folklore Change in Lowell, Massachusetts*. New York: Garland.

Langlois, Janet L. 1985. A Brief Look at French-Canadian and Franco-American Folklore. *Michigan's L'Habitant Heritage: Journal of the French-Canadian Heritage Society of Michigan* 6:1–5, 24.

Leary, James, ed. 1992. *Medicine Fiddle: A Humanities Discussion Guide* (to Michael Loukinen's 1991 film of the same name). Marquette: Northern Michigan University Press.

Ledoux, Denis, ed. 1991. *Lives in Translation: An Anthology of Contemporary Franco-American Writings*. Lisbon Falls, ME: Soleil.

Nute, Grace L. [1931] 1955. *The Voyageurs*. St. Paul: Minnesota Historical Society.

Olivier, Julien. 1979. *D'La boucane: Une introduction au folklore franc-américaine de la Nouvelle-Angleterre.* Cambridge, MA: National Assessment and Dissemination Center for Bilingual/Bicultural Education.

Paradis, Roger. 1974. Franco-American Folklore: A Cornucopia of Culture In *Vers l'évolution d'une culture,* ed. Céleste Roberge. Orono, ME: Franco-American Resource Opportunity Group, University of Maine at Orono.

Quintal, Claire, ed. 1983. *The Little Canadas of New England.* Papers presented at the Third Annual Conference of the French Institute, Assumption College, Worcester, MA. 1982.

See also Cajuns; Carrière, Joseph Médard; French Canadians; *Guillonée*

Friday the Thirteenth

A date—occurring from one to three times a year—widely believed to be unlucky. Although widespread, the notion that Friday the Thirteenth is unlucky has received surprisingly little attention from scholars. Aside from entries on "Friday" and "thirteen" in the major collections of popular beliefs and superstitions, one must turn to the news media to find published references to the persistence of the belief.

The association of Friday the Thirteenth with bad luck is the result of a complex interaction of ancient folk beliefs. Friday has long carried negative connotations, in great part because, according to Christian tradition, Christ was crucified on a Friday. In addition, Friday was a holy day in many early cultures. Work was considered inappropriate or was even prohibited on Fridays in such societies. This tradition persists in the belief that one should not begin a project on a Friday unless it can be completed the same day. (Some people attach this belief to Friday the Thirteenth.) In addition, early Christian missionaries associated the holy day of pagan people with evil.

The number thirteen, although considered a lucky number in some cultures (for example, the Chinese, the Hebrews, and some Central American Indians), is widely believed to be unlucky. To some people, twelve symbolized completion; thus, thirteen represented excess. Thirteen people were present at the Last Supper—Jesus and his twelve disciples—one of whom was to betray him.

Various cultures have told stories of gods and goddesses or magical beings who attend a banquet for twelve guests. An uninvited thirteenth guest arrives and wreaks havoc. (Loki kills Baldur in Norse mythology; Eris tosses a golden apple inscribed "For the Fairest" into the midst of the Greek deities, which eventually leads to the Trojan War; the thirteenth fairy at the celebration of Sleeping Beauty's birth curses the child.)

Triskaidekaphobia, the fear of the number thirteen, manifests itself in many ways. Numerous contemporary tall buildings have floors numbered one through twelve, followed by fourteen. At least one major airline (no longer in business) did not use thirteen on gates, on rows of seats, or in flight numbers.

Rose Cade, Queen of the Lemons, points to a reminder of her nomination as the "Swat the Jinx" girl. Southern California, 1920. Library of Congress.

People often cite examples of negative events associated with the number thirteen. The lunar mission Apollo 13 suffered an explosion on April 13, 1970 (a Monday) and had to return to Earth earlier than planned. Of course, not all instances of thirteen are believed to be unlucky in America. Consider the thirteen stars and other occurrences of thirteen on the seal of the United States, or the extra item in a baker's dozen.

With many negative associations, the number thirteen, when combined with an evil day—Friday—has come to be considered especially unlucky. Some people claim that Friday the Thirteenth is unlucky for all except those born on such a day. In contrast, others believe:

> A child born on Friday the thirteenth must carry with him a rabbit's foot from a rabbit killed at midnight by a cross-eyed farmer. Otherwise, it will bring bad luck to the family. If he loses the rabbit's foot, he will die. (Puckett, item 3865)

Just as people can cite examples of the negative influence of the number thirteen, so do the media play up the connotations of Friday the Thirteenth. An immensely popular series of movies, *Friday the 13th* and its numerous sequels, began in 1980. The films spawned a television series as well. The movies center on a fiend—Jason in most of them—who murders teenagers with bloody glee.

Consider also the following three examples from October 13, 1989, that were discussed by major newspapers in relation to Friday the Thirteenth. The Dow Jones Index dropped 190 points in that day's final hours of trading. The next Friday the Thirteenth, in April 1990, the market was closed. (Of course, it was also Good Friday.)

The American Cancer Society had planned to hold a medieval festival in Saratoga Springs, New York, on that Friday. After complaints from fundamentalist Christians about the day's evil associations, the rhyme of "medieval" with "evil," and plans to include fortune-telling at the event, the society dropped the theme in favor of a costume ball. The date was not changed.

Finally, the media widely reported the threat supposedly facing personal computers in the United States: a computer "virus" dubbed Friday the Thirteenth. Although the virus was expected to destroy the data in many computers, few people reported actual attacks.

Ironically, the persistence of fear of Friday the Thirteenth may be due in large part to the media's keeping the tradition in the public's consciousness.

Joseph P. Goodwin

References

Wayland, D. Hand, ed. 1964. *Popular Beliefs and Superstitions from North Carolina. The Frank C. Brown Collection of North Carolina Folklore.* Vol. 7. Durham, NC: Duke University Press.

Wayland, D. Hand, Anna Casetta, and Sondra B. Thiederman, eds. 1981. *Popular Beliefs and Superstitions: A Compendium of American Folklore from the Ohio Collection of Newbell Niles Puckett.* Boston: G.K. Hall.

Fuller, Blind Boy (Fulton Allen) (1908–1941)

Piedmont blues artist. Born in Wadesboro, North Carolina, in 1908, Fuller learned guitar as a teenager. By 1935 he had mastered the techniques of the Piedmont tradition, a blues style associated with the Carolinas and Virginia. Solo or working with Gary Davis, Sonny Terry, or washboard player Bull City Red, Fuller recorded a substantial body of work over a six-year span. He was one of the most recorded artists of his time and by far the most popular and influential Piedmont blues player of all time.

Initially discovered and promoted by Carolina entrepreneur H.B. Long, Fuller recorded for ARC, Decca, Vocalian, Okeh, and Columbia. He also served as a conduit to recording sessions, steering fellow blues musicians to the studio. In spite of his recorded output, most of his musical life was spent as a street and house-party musician. Adept at various guitar styles, he could reinterpret or cover other artists' hits. In this sense, he was a synthesizer of styles, parallel to Robert Johnson, his contemporary. Like Johnson, Fuller lived fast and died young.

Fuller was a fine expressive vocalist and a masterful guitar player best remembered for his uptempo ragtime hits "Rag Mama Rag," "Trucking My Blues Away," and "Step It up and Go." At the same time, he was capable of deeper material, as evidenced by his versions of "Lost Lover Blues" and "Mamie." Because of his popularity, he may have been overexposed on records, yet the majority of his songs stayed close to tradition, and his repertoire and style are kept alive by North Carolina and Virginia artists.

Barry Lee Pearson

References

Bastin, Bruce. 1986. *Red River Blues: The Blues Tradition in the Southeast.* Urbana: University of Illinois Press.

Functionalism

A theoretical perspective that attempts to explain folklore and other sociocultural phenomena in terms of their functions or effects on the wider social or cultural system. "Function" is distinguished from "purpose" or "use" in that it does not presuppose any conscious or deliberate intention in bringing these effects about.

The concern with "function" in the social sciences depends on an analogy drawn between biological and social processes. The analogy began with Auguste Comte (1798–1857) and was extended by Herbert Spencer (1820–1903), who argued that, like biological organisms, societies were built up from discrete structures that fulfilled distinct functions. Biological and social life depended on component structures functioning to fulfill the needs of the organism. Emile Durkheim (1858–1917) emphasized the importance of both causal and functional analysis in the understanding of social facts. Causal analysis focused upon the antecedents of a particular social institution, whereas functional analysis concentrated on the contribution that institution made to the larger social system of which it was a part. For Durkheim, the ultimate contribution, and the one he emphasized in virtually all of his analytical works, was the reinforcement of "collective sentiments" and the strengthening of those bonds essential to holding society together.

A.R. Radcliffe-Brown (1881–1955) and Bronislaw Malinowski (1884–1942) both read Durkheim, and each introduced a type of functionalism into anthropological theorizing. Radcliffe-Brown directly followed Durkheim, focusing on the structure of social relations and the contribution of these structures to the integration of society. When the function of a particular structure in integrating the society could be shown, that structure was, in effect, explained. For example, Radcliffe-Brown regarded the taboos against eating dugong, pork, and turtle observed by expectant parents in the Andaman Island as standardized expressions that symbolized the significance and importance of the reproductive event to the parents and the community. The care and concern required in observing such ritual prohibitions establish and fix those fundamental values that bind a society together.

Malinowski attempted to present a theory of society based on needs that had to be fulfilled if a society were to endure. There were the basic biological needs —nutrition, reproduction, bodily comforts, safety, movement, growth, and health— that every culture had to satisfy, at least minimally, if it were to survive. The satisfaction of these basic needs, however, creates derived cultural needs that demand economic systems, mechanisms of social control, education, and political organizations for their fulfillment. Culture itself depends upon the fulfillment of *symbolic* or *integrative* needs. Knowledge ensures the continuity of experience within society. Magic and religion provide intellectual, emotional, and pragmatic means to deal with chance and the inevitability of human death, while myth explains and validates a society's institutions. The particular institutional forms that might fulfill basic, derived, or symbolic needs would necessarily vary from society to society, but these needs would have to be met by all societies in some way. The contribution of an institution to meeting a basic, derived, or integrative need constitutes its function.

Functionalism was introduced into folklore by anthropologists. William R. Bascom (1912–1981), in his essay "Four Functions of Folklore," enjoined folklorists to pay more attention to the social and cultural contexts of folklore and to the functions which folklore fulfilled in society (Bascom 1954). Drawing directly on Malinowski's work, Bascom defined and illustrated four particular functions of folklore. The first was *escape;* that is, escape in fantasy from the restrictions and frustrations imposed on the individual by his or her society or environment. For example, Zuni folktale motifs concerning the abandonment of children might permit the expression of a resentment against children that the Zuni could not express more directly. The second function was *validation;* folklore could be used to justify the rituals and institutions of the society. A myth might be used to justify a particular ritual, or a proverb might be used to validate why a particular course of action was the correct or appropriate one. The third function was *education.* Folklore could inculcate the values of the society in the younger generation. Folktales frequently illustrate moral principles and describe the consequences of failing to strictly obey them. The role of folklore in education was noted as particularly important in nonliterate societies in which all education was conducted orally or through customary example. The fourth function was *social control;* folklore could be used to reward and punish individuals in order to ensure conformity to group standards. A traditional song, riddle, or proverb could be recited to express disapproval or to ridicule someone who had violated a social norm. Bascom recognized that these four functions were not the only functions of folklore. Nevertheless, he saw these as the most important ones. Each could contribute to the maintenance of a cultural system through time.

During the late 1950s and 1960s, a number of folklore essays began to appear with the term "function" in their titles. Alan Dundes reprinted a series of essays on function—including Bascom's 1954 essay—in his anthology *The Study of Folk-* *lore* (1965), thereby introducing a burgeoning generation of folklore students to the functional perspective. Function became a basic element in the teaching of folklore analysis. American folklorists made particular use of the psychological function of escape in their efforts to explain seemingly irrational behaviors and fanciful narrative motifs and episodes.

Fishing superstitions, dowsing, ethnic humor, cruel jokes, lullabies, and whaling songs are some of the forms of American folklore that have been examined from a functional perspective. For example, superstitions among Texas coastal fisherman were studied by Patrick B. Mullen (Mullen 1969). Despite their employment of the latest in communications and fishing technologies, coastal fishermen would not sail with women on board, they would not bring black suitcases or utter the word "alligator" on board, nor would they turn a hatch cover upside down. Following Malinowski, Mullen claimed that such superstitions were the fishermen's response to the anxiety engendered by the dangerous and uncertain conditions of their enterprise. The superstitions functioned to reduce this anxiety by giving the fishermen a sense of mastery of forces over which they had no real control. Mullen's hypothesis was supported by the fact that the more hazardous sea fishery involved twice as many magical beliefs as the safer bay fishery.

By the mid-1970s, the heyday of functionalism had passed. The rationale for functionalist analysis had been undermined in anthropology and sociology. Functional explanations were shown to be illogical, teleological, and grounded in questionable assumptions. At best, they could serve to point out important, if unnoticed, effects of, and interrelations between, a cultural practices, but they explained nothing. In folklore studies, the embrace of functionalism had largely been the embrace of a culturally and socially situated analytic and interpretive paradigm—a paradigm absent in earlier diffusionist and literary approaches to folklore. As emerging structuralist, semiotic, performance, and phenomenological perspectives offered alternatives to, or subsumed, functionalist assessments, functionalism faded as an explicit approach to the analysis and interpretation of folklore.

Elliott Oring

References

Bascom, William R. 1954. Four Functions of Folklore. *Journal of American Folklore* 67:333–349.

Burns, Tom. 1969. Involving the Introductory Student of Folklore in the Functional Analysis of the Material He Collects. *Folklore Forum* 2:13–27.

Hawes, Bess Lomax. 1974. Folksongs and Functions: Some Thoughts on the American Lullaby. *Journal of American Folklore* 87:140–148.

Mullen, Patrick B. 1969. The Function of Magic Folk Belief among Texas Coastal Fishermen. *Journal of American Folklore* 82:214–225.

Oring, Elliott. 1976. Three Functions of Folklore: Traditional Functionalism as Explanation in Folkloristics. *Journal of American Folklore* 89:67–80.

See also Anthropological Approach

Fund for Folk Culture

Nonprofit, publicly supported foundation established in 1991 to help answer the need for increased funding for the field of folk arts and culture. The Fund for Folk Culture (FFC) is dedicated to the preservation, dissemination, study, and appreciation of the multiplicity of folk cultures in the United States and abroad. The fund raises monies from foundations, public-sector sources (such as the National Endowment for the Arts), and private individuals, and then regrants funds to organizations, individuals, and projects in the folk arts and culture. The FFC also provides technical assistance, education and consultation as services to the field.

The fund was created as a vehicle to provide a national, non-profit corporation as a response to the increasing need for a flexible, private organization that could bridge the gap between private-sector funding sources and the growing folk-culture field. In 1990 conversations began between Jillian Steiner Sandrock, who had initiated the now-discontinued folks-arts funding program of the L.J. and Mary C. Skaggs Foundation, and several important individuals in the folk-culture field. These individuals, who formed a Fund for Folk Culture planning committee to assess the feasibility of creating the FFC, included Alan Jabbour, director of the American Folklife Center at the Library of Congress; Joseph T. Wilson, executive director of the National Council for the Traditional Arts; folklorist Archie Green; and cultural historian Raye Virginia Allen. This planning committee for the fund ultimately became the organization's founding board of trustees. The FFC's initial funding came from the National Endowment for the Arts folk arts program, the National Council for the Traditional Arts, the L.J. and Mary C. Skaggs Foundation, and contributions from individuals.

Shortly after its incorporation in 1991, the organization entered into a partnership with the James Irvine Foundation to create and administer a folk-arts regranting program. This was a specialized program to support folk arts and tradition bearers in the state of California, with funding provided by the James Irvine Foundation. In May of the same year, the Lila Wallace-Reader's Digest Fund commissioned the FFC to undertake a national needs assessment for the folk-culture field. Results of this national survey, which involved approximately 900 individuals, led the Lila Wallace-Reader's Digest Fund to launch a major initiative to support the folk arts in the United States. As part of this initiative, the fund made a $1 million grant to the FFC to underwrite the Lila Wallace-Reader's Digest community folklife program. The FFC's first national regranting program, the pilot effort supported community-based activities to preserve, strengthen, and document folklife and folk-arts traditions, as well as to present them to the public in educational and celebratory programs.

A relatively new organization, the Fund for Folk Culture envisions a future in which it will continue and expand state, regional, national, and international technical assistance and grant-making programs and function as an advocate for folk culture in the broader spheres of the arts and humanities, economic development, and education.

Charlie Seemann

See also Public Folklore

G

Games

Recreational, usually competitive, activities with agreed-upon rules that organize play and provide criteria for determining winners and losers (Roberts, Arth, and Bush 1959). Games may be played either alone or with others, and opposition may occur between players or teams or with impersonal obstacles or fortune. The desired outcome or goal is only sometimes achieved. Like play, games are generally voluntary and non-utilitarian, but they are sufficiently systematic in their rules and procedures that they can be repeated by others (Avedon and Sutton-Smith 1971). Sports are generally distinguished from games by the vicarious participation of persons other than the players and a more formal institutional structure.

Like much of the early study of folklore and folklife, serious scholarly interest in games began in the last half of the 19th century and reflected the Romantic impulses of the period. The early collectors combined an interest in identifying patterns of cultural contact and diffusion with an antiquarianist concern for preserving the vestiges of ancient lore. William Wells Newell, a founder of the American Folklore Society who published the first major collection of American children's folklore, *Games and Songs of American Children* ([1883] 1963), reflected both of these concerns.

Like many others at the time, Newell believed that the traditions he was studying were rapidly dying out. This led him to collect the childhood memories of adults rather than the ongoing traditions of contemporary children. He assumed that the further back in time he reached, the richer the traditions would be and the closer he would come to their "original" forms. This perspective characterized most of the work on games well into the 20th century and may still be found in contemporary game collections.

Newell also systematically annotated his collection with similar rhymes and games found in historical documents and in non-English-speaking countries. He argued that cultural diffusion was the only reasonable explanation for these similarities. Early anthropologists like Edward B. Tylor and Stewart Culin, who wrote *Games of North American Indians* (1907),

also studied games for clues to patterns of cultural evolution, contact, and diffusion, and for vestiges of primitive magical practices. They also observed, however, that many children's games mimic culturally important adult activities like hunting and combat, and they proposed that games continue to play an important role in the enculturation of children.

The other major 19th-century English-language collection of children's games, Lady Alice B. Gomme's two-volume work *The Traditional Games of England, Scotland, and Ireland* ([1894, 1898] 1964), also reflected a greater concern for what children's games could tell us about the past than for what they could tell us about the present. She believed that children's games were imitations of adult customs, preserved over centuries only in the play of children. Like Newell, Gomme relied primarily on the recollections of adults, looked for patterns in the geographical distribution of games in the British Isles, and annotated connections with folk customs and similar rhymes and games in historical documents.

American Paul G. Brewster, who published extensively on games from many parts of the world beginning in the late 1930s (see bibliography in Avedon and Sutton-Smith 1971:162–164), continued the diffusionist and antiquarianist tradition. His *Children's Games and Rhymes* (1953) represents the most extensive early collection of children's games in the United States.

While interest in the origins and diffusion of games has continued, studies of children's games are no longer primarily driven by the belief that they are historical documents to be preserved and deciphered. Educator Dorothy Mills Howard, who began collecting games in the early 1930s, was a pioneer in studying the ongoing traditions of contemporary children and collecting games directly from children themselves. The changing focus of games studies is most evident, however, in the work of Iona and Peter Opie, who began collecting children's folklore in the British Isles in the 1950s, and Brian Sutton-Smith, who studied games in New Zealand in the late 1940s and the early 1950s and, later, games in the United States.

Criticizing "shelfloads of books . . . instructing children

Checkers, played with bottle caps. Red Bank, near Florence, Alabama, about 1937. Library of Congress.

in the games they ought to play . . . [or] instructing adults on how to instruct children in the games they ought to play," the Opies used extensive surveys of schoolchildren to "record games children in fact play . . . of their own accord when out of doors, and usually out of sight" (Opie and Opie 1969:v). In their *Children's Games in Street and Playground* (1969) and *The Singing Game* (1988), and in Iona Opie's *The People on the Playground* (1993), they documented a rich and dynamic body of ongoing tradition. The remarkable historical preservation and broad geographical distribution they found in children's games were strong evidence for the vitality and continuity of children's lore in Great Britain. Children's games were far more than hollow vestiges of the past, and they did not appear to be in immediate danger of extinction.

The Opies were influenced by Sutton-Smith, who had documented a similarly vital and dynamic body of children's games, but while the Opies focused on continuity in childhood traditions, he focused on how they changed over time.

Sutton-Smith set out to place contemporary New Zealand children's games in historical context by collecting from both children and adults and by extensively reviewing historical documents. He used newspapers and radio to solicit written accounts, conducted interviews, surveyed hundreds of

college students, visited and collected reports from schools, and observed children's play at one school over a period of two years. In *The Games of New Zealand Children* (1959, reprinted in 1972 in his *Folkgames of Children),* Sutton-Smith organized his material historically within game type, contrasting the games played between 1870 and 1920 with those played between 1920 and 1950. *A History of Children's Play: The New Zealand Playground, 1840–1950* (1981) extended the historical record back to the English settling of New Zealand in 1840.

In these works, Sutton-Smith documented the explosion of traditional games that accompanied the introduction of compulsory schooling in the last half of the 19th century, and "the taming of the playground" (Sutton-Smith 1972:13) that occurred as adult supervision of playgrounds increased in the early 20th century. Rougher types of play decreased, even as more active types of play increased among girls. He showed how, especially from 1920 on, the influence of organized sports and recreation for children and the increasing presence of commercial toys led to the loss of traditional games. Many that survived were relegated to younger children, especially to girls.

Sutton-Smith also outlined a developmental progression from the choral and simple central-person games (like ring-around-a-rosy, hide-and-seek, and various forms of tag) played by children younger than ten years old to the more complex competitive and team games (like king of the mountain, marbles, hopscotch, dodgeball, and keep-away) played by older children. He proposed that dramatic, central-person games were popular among younger children because they replicated children's common experiences of family relationships. At the same time, he believed, they helped children master the give-and-take with peers necessary for the more complex competitive games of later years.

This early work launched Sutton-Smith on the most varied and persistent career of any researcher in the area of children's games in the United States. An educator and developmental psychologist by training, he has brought to his work an interdisciplinary perspective often guided more by the social sciences than by folklore. Over the years, he has drawn on historical, anthropological, developmental, and psychological theory and methods to explore children's games and game involvement. His *Folkgames of Children* (1972) covers topics as diverse as the "it" role in children's games, sex differences in play choices, historical changes in American children's game preferences, and adolescent kissing games.

Numerous collections of games have appeared since these pioneering works. Many are small local or regional collections that are widely scattered through the literature (Sutton-Smith, Mechling, Johnson, and McMahon 1994 presents an extensive bibliography of children's folklore, including games). Other collections, like Roger D. Abrahams' *Jump-Rope Rhymes: A Dictionary* (1969) and (with Lois Rankin) *Counting-Out Rhymes: A Dictionary* (1980), are compilations of texts associated with particular game types. More general collections of American children's folklore, like Mary and Herbert Knapp's *One Potato, Two Potato: The Secret Education of American Children* (1976) and Simon J. Bronner's *American Children's Folklore* (1988), also include sections on children's games.

There is no single, complete, and broadly accepted system for classifying games. Collectors have employed literally dozens of different game categories, and different collectors have categorized the same games in different ways. Some, like Gomme, simply presented their games alphabetically by title. Others, like Newell, ordered their collections in part around themes like love, history, and mythology.

Most collectors have relied on similarities in game structures or actions to group their games into categories and subcategories. Some of the more common categories of traditional games are: singing games (like London bridge), counting-out games (like one potato, two potato), chasing games (like tag), catching games (like prisoner's base), seeking games (like hide-and-seek), leader or central-person games (like Mother, may I? or statues), daring games (like truth or dare), guessing games (like odd or even), fortune-telling games (like cooties), dueling games (like the dozens), acting games (like fox and chickens), pretending games (like cops and robbers), ball games (like dodgeball or foursquare), rhythmic games (like jump rope, hand-clapping and ball-bouncing games), gambling games or games of chance (like dice), parlor games (like charades or tic-tac-toe), games of skill (like jacks, marbles, hop-

scotch, or string games), and board or table games (like chess and various card games). Many other categories can be found in the literature, and it is likely that new types of games, like video games and fantasy role-play games, will eventually expand them still further.

Since the 1960s, cross-cultural studies have used a much simpler scheme for classifying games. In "Games in Culture," anthropologist John M. Roberts and his colleagues categorized games based upon whether their outcomes depended on physical skill, chance, strategy, or some combination of these elements. They went on to demonstrate that the types of games played in different cultures are related to various dimensions of cultural complexity and evolution, and to variations in child-rearing practices (Roberts, Arth, and Bush 1959).

According to these analyses (reviewed in Chick 1984), complex cultures have more complex games and more types of games than simpler cultures. Games of physical skill (like races, hopscotch, and many marble games) seem to be very ancient. They are the most widespread among world cultures and appear at all levels of cultural complexity. In contrast, games of strategy (like checkers, go, and tic-tac-toe) appear to have developed later and are common only in societies with complex political and social structures. Games of chance (like bingo and a variety of dice and fortune-telling games) are more common in societies characterized by environmental uncertainty, regardless of the degree of social complexity. Further, these analyses found that games of physical skill were associated cross-culturally with training children for high levels of achievement; games of strategy, with high obedience training; and games of chance, with training for high levels of responsibility. Combination games (like football which relies on both physical skill and strategy, and poker, which combines elements of strategy and chance) show even more complex and interactive patterns of relationship to childhood socialization practices.

Roberts and his colleagues explained these connections by proposing a "conflict-enculturation hypothesis" of game involvement. They believed that societal demands for particular qualities induce conflicts in children, who are then drawn to activities like games that allow them to explore and master these conflicts in a playful, buffered environment. From this perspective, games are "expressive models" of important cultural qualities and a medium through which children are gradually enculturated to core values and behaviors.

In the 1960s and 1970s, Roberts and his colleagues also extended this model to adult involvement in games like eight-ball pool, tennis, trapshooting, and soccer. In a series of ethnographic studies (reviewed in Chick 1984), they explored why individuals choose and abandon particular games, and how novice and expert players differ in their patterns of involvement in particular games. These are some of the very few studies of adult games in American culture outside of the context of sport.

Studies of the games of non-Anglo American children are also less common. A notable exception is Bessie Jones and Bess Lomax Hawes' *Step It Down: Games, Plays, Songs, and Stories from the Afro-American Heritage* (1972). This is a compilation of children's lore drawn from Bessie Jones' experiences growing up in Georgia and the Georgia Sea Islands in the early 20th century. It includes many types of games, including baby games, clapping, jumping, and skipping games, singing and ring plays, dances, house plays, and outdoor games.

In her introduction, Hawes notes that almost all of the games reported by Bessie Jones are group activities involving music and dance. She reflects on how these games differ from the more individual, competitive games common in Anglo American culture, noting that many are miniature dramatic "plays" that publicly dramatize the conflicts and confrontations inherent in Afro-American life.

Comparisons like this of the games played by different groups within American society are rare. The only major exception is the games played by boys and girls. Game researchers have long noted gender differences in children's games (reviewed by Hughes in Hollis, Pershing, and Young 1993:130–148). Boys and girls largely play in separate play groups and play different types of games throughout childhood, especially in the school settings where most children's games have been observed and collected.

A number of differences have been noted in the games typically played by boys and girls. Boys' games (like baseball, cowboys and Indians, and more recently video games) have been characterized as more complex, competitive, active, and aggressive than girls' games. They more often involve physical contact, larger and outdoor spaces, larger and more mixed-age play groups, and well-defined outcomes with clear winners and losers. In contrast, girls' games (like hopscotch, jump rope, and clapping games) have been characterized as simpler and more passive, cooperative, and verbal. They more often involve indirect competition among individuals rather than teams, smaller and more indoor spaces, smaller play groups (often twos or threes), more waiting in line, turn-taking, and sustained cooperative, choral activity (like clapping or skipping) rather than clear winners and losers.

It has been suggested that these differences prepare boys and girls for different adult roles. The small, intimate play groups common among girls, and the more cooperative, verbal, and passive quality of their play, has been associated with preparing girls for traditional domestic roles. The more active, aggressive, and competitive qualities of boys' team games and sports have been similarly associated with preparation for work roles.

One of the interesting questions in games study is whether recent changes in adult gender-role expectations, and attempts to increase girls' participation in sports, will result in changes in the games girls and boys play. At least since the 1920s, boys appear to have been narrowing their game choices largely to ball games and other sports-related activities, while girls have increased their involvement in more active games and their interest in games previously played mostly by boys. It is not clear, however, how much girls' spontaneous game participation has actually changed.

Folklore studies have recently moved away from analysis of isolated texts like game descriptions or rhymes toward more in-depth analysis of the contexts in which folk groups create and communicate traditional culture. Folklorist Kenneth S. Goldstein (in Avedon and Sutton-Smith 1971:167–178) was an early advocate of ethnographic field studies of how games are actually played. He proposed that games, with their easily stated rules, were ideal for studying how folklore is expressed, performed, transmitted, circulated, and used.

Goldstein also pointed out that there are often important differences between the stated rules of games and the actual rules used by their players. As a result, he proposed, many studies of games may be based on inaccurate classifications. To illustrate, Goldstein described how children in a working-class neighborhood of Philadelphia played the game of counting-out. While commonly classified as a game of chance, many of the players Goldstein observed actually played it as a game of strategy. Among other things, they chose rhymes with different numbers of beats depending on the number of players or tagged on additional rhymes when the outcome was not the one they wanted ("My mother told me to . . .").

Following Goldstein, folklorist and developmental psychologist Linda Hughes has explored contrasts between game rules and the rules actually used by players (in Sutton-Smith, Mechling, Johnson, and McMahon 1994). She conducted a two-year-long ethnographic study of how one girls' play group played the game of foursquare (in Hollis, Pershing, and Young 1993:130–148), describing how social relationships influenced how players elaborated, interpreted, modified, and selectively ignored the stated rules of their game. She also described a way of competing among these players that differed in important ways from the individual competition specified by the rules of the game.

Several in-depth ethnographic studies of the dynamics of social life in particular play groups and children's understanding of their own games have been conducted on school playgrounds. Andy Sluckin focused on children's folklore in two English primary schools. In *Growing Up in the Playground* (1981), he described the games his children played, but also how they included and excluded each other from play groups, gained entry into the game and particular game roles, started and resolved disputes, made and maintained friendships, and negotiated status in the play group and relations between the sexes. Folklorist Ann Richman Beresin (in Sutton-Smith, Mechling, Johnson, and McMahon 1994) conducted a year-long ethnographic study of recess at an elementary school serving an ethnically diverse, working-class neighborhood in a large American city. Relying primarily on children's interpretations of videotapes of their own play, she explored the complex social worlds children construct on the playground and in their games.

There are also a number of in-depth studies of children's play and games outside of school settings. Anthropologist and sociolinguist Marjorie H. Goodwin studied the play of African American children in the neighborhoods of Philadelphia. In *He-Said-She-Said* (1990), she analyzed how boys and girls organize their play groups and games. In *Shared Fantasy* (1983), sociologist Gary Alan Fine explored the gaming culture of players of fantasy role-play games like dungeons and dragons. In *With the Boys* (1987), Fine examined the world of little league baseball from the players' perspectives.

City Play (1990), by Amanda Dargan and Steven Zeitlin, represents another type of contextual study of games. They used fieldwork and historical research in the neighborhoods of New York City to explore how the urban environment shapes, and is exploited for, play; how play has varied with class, ethnicity, and gender; and how it has changed with a changing environment and cast of players.

One of the most interesting issues in games study is how changes in society will affect children's traditional games. During the 20th century, children's play has been increasingly brought under adult supervision and direction and channeled into organized sports and recreation programs. More and more schools are shortening recess or confining it to children of the same age. Some are even proposing to eliminate it altogether. At the same time, safety concerns in many neighborhoods are limiting children's opportunities for spontaneous play and exploration, and television and video games are competing for children's time and attention. All of these ongoing changes in American society will continue to affect when, what, how, and with whom children play. What the effects will be, whether they will be positive or negative for children, and how they will further alter children's repertoires of traditional games remains to be seen.

Linda A. Hughes

References

Avedon, Elliott M., and Brian Sutton-Smith. 1971. *The Study of Games.* New York: John Wiley.

Chick, Garry E. 1984. The Cross-Cultural Study of Games. *Exercise and Sport Sciences Reviews* 12:307–337.

Hollis, Susan T., Linda Pershing, and M. Jane Young, eds. 1993. *Feminist Theory and the Study of Folklore.* Urbana: University of Illinois Press.

Roberts, John M., M.J. Arth, and R.R. Bush. 1959. Games in Culture. *American Anthropologist* 61: 597–605.

Sutton-Smith, Brian, Jay Mechling, Thomas W. Johnson, and Felicia McMahon, eds. 1994. *Children's Folklore: A Sourcebook.* New York: Garland.

See also Children; Toys, Folk

Gardner, Emelyn Elizabeth (1872–1967)

Folklore collector and educator. Born in central New York state, Gardner devoted most of her professional life to teaching students at Wayne State University in Detroit, Michigan. Her pioneering work with immigrant folklore in urban Detroit is the foundation for the Folklore Archives at Wayne State University, which Gardner founded in 1939 with collections of Armenian, Italian, Polish, and Finnish lore.

Gardner became interested in the folklore of rural New York state through the tales told by a laborer on her father's central New York farm. Trained originally to teach high school, Gardner taught for five years in rural Schoharie County, New York. After receiving an A.B. from the University of Chicago in 1902, and inspired by the then-current literary approaches to folklore scholarship, Gardner returned to Schoharie County to collect its folklore. This material formed the basis for her master's thesis (University of Michigan, 1915) and was published in book form as *Folklore from the Schoharie Hills, New York* (1937).

Gardner joined the faculty at Ypsilanti State College; in 1918 she moved to Wayne State University, where she spent the remainder of her professional career. During her twenty-four years of teaching folklore and children's literature at Wayne State, Gardner inspired many students to pursue the study of folklore and to collect the folklore of their own communities.

Gardner's collecting has been lauded for its inclusiveness and scope. While criticized for the absence of some contextual information, her *Ballads and Songs of Southern Michigan* (1939), compiled with her student Geraldine Jencks Chickering, was noteworthy for its time for the addition of biographical information on informants and the thoroughness of documentation.

Ellen McHale

Gardner, Gail I. (1892–1988)

Cowboy poet, author of "Sierry Petes, or, Tying Knots in the Devil's Tail." Born in Prescott, Arizona Territory, Gardner attended Dartmouth College (1911–1914), then returned to Prescott, where he operated a small cow outfit until 1960. He served as postmaster of Prescott from 1936 to 1957.

His first poem, "The Sierry Petes, or Tying Knots in the Devil's Tail," was written in 1917 and set to music by fellow Prescott cowboy Bill Simon. It deals in a humorous fashion with an incident in which Gardner and another cowboy went into Prescott for what they later described as a "little whizzer," and met and subdued the devil on their way back to camp.

Gardner sang this song at an annual rodeo at Jimmy Minotto's ranch near Prescott in the 1920s. The next year, he came up with another original song, "The Moonshine Steer," concerning the difficulties a couple of cowboys had trying to work cattle after chancing upon a hidden still and sampling its contents. For the next several years, a performance of a new poem by Gardner was an expected event at Minotto's gathering. In 1935, tired of writing his verses out for cowboys, Gardner published twelve of his poems in the booklet *OREJANA BULL for COWBOYS ONLY.* The seventh edition, published by the Sharlot Hall Museum of Prescott in 1987, was still in print in 1955.

Gardner always claimed to have written his poems solely to amuse cowboys. They continue to serve this purpose. "The Sierry Petes" is the best-known cowboy song among working cowboys, while several others of his poems have been collected from cowboy singing and recitation tradition.

James S. Griffith

References

White, John I. 1975. *Git Along, Little Dogies: Songs and Songmakers of the American West.* Urbana: University of Illinois Press, pp. 117–125.

Gay Men

A subculture comprising openly homosexual men of as many different tastes and interests as mainstream American culture. Folklorists have published little research on the traditions of gay men. In addition to conducting fieldwork, people interested in pursuing gay folklore as a research topic must glean corroborative examples from studies in history, sociology, cultural anthropology, and other disciplines—like Esther Newton's *Mother Camp: Female Impersonation in America* (1972)—as well as from such works of gay fiction as Armistead Maupin's *Tales of the City* series (1978–1990).

Despite the risk of overgeneralizing, one can make certain broad statements about gay men's folklore. First, the gay subculture shares many of its traditions with White male culture, not surprising since ethnic groups are represented in the gay subculture in the same proportions as they appear in the mainstream.

Gay folklore exists in most genres—jokes, narratives, contemporary legends, beliefs, proverbs, folk speech, customs, costumes, arts and crafts, and so on. (There is also evidence of a defunct folksong tradition in the sung lines, "God save us nelly queens" and "Wait 'til your son turns nelly!") Distinctions between genres are sometimes difficult to make when one is studying gay folklore, especially because humor suffuses almost all of the material. In addition, the gay subculture has developed at least two genres of its own—drag, or female impersonation, and camp.

Camp, as described in the only book-length study of gay men's folklore, "is an attitude, a style of humor, an approach to situations, people, and things . . . assertively expressed through exaggeration and inversion, stressing form over content, deflating pomposity, mocking pretension, and subverting values" (Goodwin 1989:38–39). For example, in the early 1980s, a folder in the vertical file labeled "Homosexual Drag" at the internationally renowned Alfred C. Kinsey Institute for Research on Sex, Gender, and Reproduction at Indiana University contained a flyer announcing the Miss Gay Philadelphia Drag Ball and several programs for the Vienna Boys Choir. Whoever slipped the programs into the folder was implying by this camp gesture that the choirboys were gay and in drag, mocking the presumed sweetness, innocence, and purity that the public associates with the young singers.

Gay men's traditions differ from mainstream folklore in several ways—most notably, where performances occur, the strategies for which the items are used, and the themes contained in the material. Because homosexuality has for centuries been reviled in Western societies, gay men have been forced to meet clandestinely. As a result, most gay men restrict their use of overtly gay traditions to private settings such as gay bars and parties in people's homes. Some larger cities have gay neighborhoods in which performances are more open. Because of its highly esoteric nature and its frequent reliance on ambiguity, much of the folklore of gay men can function for identification and communication in nongay settings.

Gay men can use their jokes and other esoteric references to suggest their homosexuality to one another in public. Gay folklore also functions to help maintain group cohesion within

In the late 20th century, responding to a growing need for information, Lambda Rising and other gay and lesbian bookstores established themselves in communities across the country. Washington, DC. Drawing by James M. Labonski, 1993. Courtesy of Deacon Maccubbin and Jim Bennett.

the subculture and to cope with conflict, both in gay society and between the gay and straight worlds. The following joking exchange illustrates these functions:

My mother made me a homosexual.
If I get her the yarn, will she make me one, too?

Freudian psychoanalytic theory maintains that homosexuality is caused by a distant father and a dominant or close-binding mother. These two lines play with that notion, suggesting also that homosexuality is a status to be desired.

Gay folklore often has sexual overtones. This quatrain can serve as a humorous cohesive device or as a potential "pick up" line:

Friends may come, and friends may go,
And friends may peter out, you know,
But I'm your friend through thick or thin—
Peter out, or peter in.

In addition, gay men may use their traditions publicly to defy their oppressors and to express contempt for heterosexual society. Oppressed groups often invert traditions that their enemies have used against them in this way. Thus, an activist group has assumed the name Queer Nation. Gay men and lesbians are increasingly demonstrating and chanting, "We're here! We're queer! Get used to it!" The subculture has coopted the hateful word "queer," imbued it with pride, and hurled it back in the face of the oppressive mainstream.

Gay folklore addresses many themes of concern to gay men. In addition to expressing group membership, defiance, and pride, the traditions express fears, fantasies, friendship, and much more. The racism and sexism of the straight world are also reflected in gay men's folklore. Frequently, the underlying theme is power—either having it or being subjected to it. Just as sexism and racism—regardless of the sexual orientation of the person using the material—are expressions of one's presumed power over someone else, so inversion is an attempt to reclaim power that oppressors have tried to claim as their own.

Gay folklore is a rich area for research. In addition to much-needed studies of a general nature, such topics as the folklore of people with multiple oppressions (being gay and African American, or deaf and gay, for example), the folklore of AIDS (both esoteric and exoteric), and the folklore of younger gay men, who have come of age during the plague years (that is, during the AIDS epidemic), await the attention of folklorists.

Much of the folklore of AIDS, for example, comprises legends and rumors about the origins and transmission of the HIV virus assumed to cause acquired immune deficiency syndrome. The various AIDS jokes that circulated widely during the 1980s were primarily heterosexist jokes aimed at the gay male subculture. (The jokes had a brief circulation among gay men as well.) An exception is the following:

Do you know what the most difficult thing about having AIDS is?

Trying to convince your mother that you're part Haitian.

(Soon after AIDS was "discovered," the Centers for Disease Control included Haitians with gay men and intravenous drug users as the primary groups at risk.)

This esoteric joke addresses the anxiety of coming out to one's family and friends, a prospect potentially more frightening than enduring a devastating terminal illness.

Such traditions offer insights into the lives and concerns of a substantial segment of American society. A rich field awaits those willing to venture into it.

Joseph P. Goodwin

References

Bronski, Michael. 1984. *Culture Clash: The Making of a Gay Sensibility.* Boston: South End.
Dynes, Wayne. 1990. *Encyclopedia of Homosexuality.* New York: Garland.
Goodwin, Joseph P. 1989. *More Man Than You'll Ever Be: Gay Folklore and Acculturation in Middle America.* Bloomington: Indiana University Press.
Katz, Jonathan Ned. 1976. *Gay American History: Lesbians and Gay Men in the U.S.A.* New York: Avon.
———. 1983. *Gay-Lesbian Almanac: A New Documentary.* New York: Harper and Row.
Read, Kenneth E. 1980. *Other Voices: The Style of a Male Homosexual Tavern.* Novato, CA: Chandler and Sharp.
Rodgers, Bruce. 1972. *Gay Talk: A (Sometimes Outrageous) Dictionary of Gay Slang.* (Originally published as *The Queen's Vernacular.*) New York: Paragon.

See also Gender and Folklore; Lesbians

Gayton, Anna Hadwick (1899–1977)

Anthropologist and folklorist who played a major role in compiling and analyzing California Indian mythology. Born September 20, 1899, in Santa Cruz, California, Gayton served as book review editor for the *Journal of American Folklore,* as vice president of the American Folklore Society, and was elected its president in 1950. In addition, she made significant contributions in the areas of textile research, California ethnography, and Peruvian archaeology.

All of Gayton's higher education was taken at the University of California, Berkeley, from which she was the first woman to receive a Ph.D. in anthropology, in 1928. Her dissertation dealt with the narcotic plant *Datura* and was written under the direction of Professors A.L. Kroeber and Robert H. Lowie. She also carried out extensive ethnographic research between 1925 and 1930 on the Yokuts and Mono of the southern San Joaquin Valley, and published nine essays between 1929 and 1948 dealing with Yokut and Mono myth and oral tradition. In her monumental "Yokuts and Western Mono Myths" (coauthored with Stanley S. Newman), Gayton provides a thorough synopsis and in-depth analysis of 214 myths and tales, 55 of which had not been published previously (Gayton and Newman 1940). Her treatment is notable for its keen attention to narrative styles.

Gayton married anthropologist Leslie Spier in 1931. She followed Spier in his teaching career at Yale University and the University of New Mexico and did not resume her own professional career until 1948, when she was recruited to fill a position in the Department of Decorative Arts at Berkeley. During her tenure at Berkeley, Gayton published numerous articles on textile analysis and worked to further the University of California folklife program. She was a pioneer advocate of comparative folklore studies. In "Folklore and Anthropology" (presented in 1946 and published in 1947), she cogently argues that American folklorists should look beyond American Indian myths to include Oceanic, African, and Asiatic myths, and should undertake comparative, analytic studies on already collected and published materials (Gayton 1947). For Gayton the greatest need was for research on the roles of myth in all cultures. In terms of her own folklore research, Gayton's various studies of religious festivals celebrated among Azorean Portuguese in Gustine, California, are a major triumph. Toward the end of her Berkeley career, she conducted primary research in Gustine and the Azores, publishing three important essays on the Festa da Serrata (cf. Gayton 1948). In her last publications, she carefully chronicles the creation of ritual and sacred space and provides a pioneering discussion of the impact of culture and tourism on living folk traditions. Gayton died on September 18, 1977, in Santa Cruz.

Stephen D. Glazier

References

Boyer, Ruth M. 1978. Anna Hadwick Gayton, 1899–1977. *Journal of American Folklore* 91:834–841.

Gayton, Anna Hadwick. 1947. Folklore and Anthropology. *Utah Humanities Review* 2:26–31.

———. 1948. The Festa da Serrata at Gustine. *Western Folklore* 7:251–265.

Gayton, Anna Hadwick, and Stanley S. Newman. 1940. Yokuts and Western Mono Myths. *Anthropological Records* 5:1–109.

Gender and Folklore

The traditional cultural expression of maleness and femaleness. In folklore, gender is expressed in interpersonal, familial, and communal behavior; public and private ritual; speech and song; music; foodways; costume; vernacular architecture and domestic space; and religious and other forms of belief (medical, political, and the like). Men and women may have particular physical attributes that distinguish them as human beings, but their biological forms are not the sole constituents of their gender. Gender also consists of the social construction of sexual identity within a particular cultural context. Categories of gender are culturally defined, shaped, and imbued with significance and sets of expectations. Gender, therefore, is a central organizing category for experience; it emerges at various times and in various situations as a salient marker by which people identify themselves. It is one of the basic ways in which people encounter and interpret the world as individuals and differentiate community membership.

Folklore, as the expressive elements of a culture, not only manifests, but also helps construct and determine rules, behaviors, and ideas within particular cultures relating to men's and women's sense of themselves and their interrelationships. Specific folkloric activities can be recognized as distinguishing markers of gender within a given culture. In fact, expressive forms (for example, speech acts, material culture, and customary behavior) are almost always particularly gendered. In the United States, midwifery, women's laments, quilting, gossiping, foodways, altar making, narrating personal experiences, ballad singing, egg decorating, experiencing Marian apparitions, recounting prophetic visions of Mormon women, and private home liturgizing are often considered by both the general public and folklorists as spheres of American female creative activity, while the occupations and lore of lumberjacks, firefighters, truck drivers, policemen, race-car drivers, cowboys, and rodeo riders; *fraktur* painting; "hex"-sign painting; decoy carving; ship building; stone and wood carving; fox hunting, joke telling; preaching styles; toasting; and "doing the dozens" are usually perceived as spheres of American male creative activity.

In American society, gender roles are reinforced by various forms of cultural expression, including television, radio, cinema, theater, music, newspapers, magazines, and billboards. The roles that American culture generates and reinforces create a situation of single-sex, specifically male, domination through idealized notions of gender. Historically, there has been resistance from women to these idealized roles. The feminist movement in North America has called attention to what women consider male dominance and an androcentric perspective within everyday life and academic scholarship. In an effort to equalize the power available to both sexes and to bring women's voices into public discourse, gender scholars have launched a critique of the role of gender in American culture. Gender for them is located fundamentally within a set of power relations. This critique has led folklorists to a greater consideration of the potential of gender as an identifiable, defining and analyzable category in their fieldwork.

Feminist folklorists have argued that patriarchal structures, hegemony, and pedagogical agendas, all informed by gender, have facilitated the exclusion of specific expressive forms from the discipline. Studies of femininity and masculinity and hierarchies within occupational, leisure, religious, family, private, and public culture have led to a reevaluation of the field of folklore and folklife as informed by a new conceptualization of gender. This new scholarly orientation has led to an expansion of what should be considered significant forms of folklore. For example, gossip, which was once considered a trivial and insignificant feminine speech act, has been recognized by folklorists as a uniquely female collaborative device in women's everyday lives as opposed to male hierarchical ways of speaking. Additionally, the personal-experience narrative has also been identified as a gendered form of communication in America, meaning that within this genre, first identified in the 1970s, there are male and female ways of communicating such narratives. While men tell stories that bear similarities to "tall tales" told for entertainment value, women's personal-experience narratives are told for instructional purposes.

Work has also been done on the contestative potential within the traditional religion of Pentecostal women pastors in the Midwest. These women use their skills of oral performance to outline their "calling" to serve the community as pastors. This presentation of self allows them to break with the traditional admonition of fundamentalist Christianity that women not concern themselves directly with church affairs. These women are wresting religious power from a socioreligious context that traditionally denies their full participation. As such, their activity is a criticism of that order and its culture of denial to women. It is also, strangely enough, a confirmation of the spirit of Pentecostalism, because these women, as living exceptions to the rule, possess both an ability and the blessing from their God to preach and be pastors to their communities.

Within the folklife of the American people, there are identifiable traditions that dichotomize gender, creating standards of culturally expected behavior for men and women. Specifically, within ritualized life-cycle events there are clear expectations about gender roles. A rich example of the social

In single-sex organizations, crossdressing is an American tradition. Women at the last ball of the season. Young Women's Christian Association, Chicago, 1912.

and cultural reinforcement of gender can be found within traditions surrounding American wedding ceremonies. The cultural construction of gender can be seen in the "customs" that surround public and private marriage events. Traditionally, the participation of the bride's family and the groom's family is shaped by gender, and it reflects the expected "roles" of the marrying couple. Throughout the planning of the wedding, various sources such as family members, clergy and other religious professionals, etiquette books, and "bride magazines" are influential in providing details regarding expected cultural behaviors. The serenading by the groom on the eve of the wedding, the duty of hosting the rehearsal dinner, the "dollar dance" with the bride at the wedding reception (where a guest gives a dollar to the bride in exchange for a dance), the cutting of the cake, the throwing of the bouquet, and removing the garter from the bride are traditions specific to the American ethnic wedding that are focused on a particular gender. Within religious wedding rituals, there remains in American weddings a strong emphasis on gender and cultural expectations that were received from various regional and ethnic bridal customs. For example, based on European Christian bridal custom, often the father of the bride or a close male relative "gives away" the bride, walking her down the center aisle at the beginning of the religious ceremony in the church and giving her at the altar to the man who is to be her husband. In traditional Roman Catholic ceremonies, the bride can also be presented to the Virgin Mary at her altar while the

congregation prays for her to be a good wife and mother.

Another traditional activity associated with customary gendered behavior and "folk" religion in the United States is the creation by women of "holy corners" and home altars as places of honor within the domestic environment. Within the Christian tradition, this custom has been particularly associated with women as they create a site in their homes for intercessory prayer. On a covered table, in a nook, or even on top of a television set, through an assemblage of religious images such as mass-produced small prints, self-made and decorated images, statues, rosaries, photographs of loved ones, flowers, and votive candles, the woman expresses the vitality of her faith and its connection to her family and community life. Home-altar building, however, is also a significant aspect of American religious life outside of the Christian context, as demonstrated, for example, by the practices of contemporary paganism and witchcraft, or Wicca. In these cases, both women and men independently construct their own sacred spaces for spiritual and ritual purposes, assembling them from a variety of perceived religious objects from nature, family, and the cosmos. There is a quality to these sacred spaces specifically relevant to the gender of the creators. Still, the activity of creating altars from an assemblage of unrelated objects is not gender specific, but is an expressive form shared by both men and women.

The activity of making something out of nothing takes place for both men and women in the private as well as the public sphere. For example, evidence of a male public folk aesthetic has been observed by folklorists in the craftsmanship of the community of Italian American stone masons who built and decorated many of the public buildings found in the United States. Stonecutters, stonemasons, and woodworkers are all excellent examples of men engaged in the process of producing public artifacts, the skills for which have been passed on to them because of their gender. Men and women, consequently, have access to different traditions of information based on their gender. Men traditionally take apprenticeships to carve stone, lay bricks, and fit pipes, while women are traditionally taught to embroider in the home, or learn to roll pierogies within the context of the Slavic American parish community.

The community or public emphasis of women's creative activity is manifest most clearly in foodways in the United States, where the production and consumption of food is often organized in gender-specific ways. Foodways is a realm of activity traditionally associated with female culture. Oriented toward the family and community, women are socialized to express their creativity, status, and location in the household through the medium of food. Gender roles can be seen at the center of the home economy and relate directly to the division of labor within it. For example, in a *Tejano* (Mexican Americans in Texas) migrant-worker community, women call on the financial, familial, cultural, and social resources of their community to prepare a labor-intensive meal of tamales for their husbands. The activity of producing volumes of tamales as a community of women reinforces family ties and simultaneously affirms the identity of this

This poster, recruiting seamen during World War II, tells a tale of gender. Benton Harbor, Michigan, 1940. Photo John Vachon. Library of Congress.

community as an ethnic group in the United States.

A problematical aspect of the folkloristic study of gender has been discerning those less clearly defined occasions of traditional cultural activity in which both genders participate. Some spheres of creativity are very clearly defined while others are fluid, shared by each gender, and engage each other in a dialogue of sorts. Urban legends, rap songs, recitations, joking, cross-dressing, tattooing, body piercing, graffiti, photocopied and computer-based texts, and other forms of traditional and contemporary folklore are being perceived in a new light. For example, customary behaviors such as male "stag" parties are mirrored in the bachelorette parties and "Chippendale Clubs" (in which male exotic dancers perform) that emerged in the 1970s in response to, and as the counterpart of, the traditionally male bachelor party. Similarly, shared forms of gendered socializing are found in leisure occasions at college and university fraternities and sororities at which lengthy repertoires of drinking songs are circulated, the content of which is often explicitly sexual.

Any consideration of folklore forms shared by men and women necessitates the consistent questioning and deconstructing of traditional gender dichotomies that are continuously present in the American experience and interpretation of reality. A primary example of blurred gender and sexual boundaries can be found in the complex culture of the Ameri-

can gay and lesbian community. This community tests the limits of America's understanding of gender expectations by engaging in expressive forms of speech, dress, action, and body movement that traditionally have been assigned by members of the opposite sex to each other. Gay men accentuate specific qualities associated with male gender roles especially in social contexts where they encounter other gay males, such as a "leather" bar. They can also invert such masculinity and denigrate feminine qualities through the use of camp behavior. A particularly rich example of the blurring of gender boundaries can be found in the American gay and lesbian community's support of the Names Project/AIDS Quilt. The creation of this quilt to commemorate those individuals who have died because of acquired immune deficiency syndrome (AIDS) involves the participants in an activity commonly recognized as a female domain—quilting. The quilt purposely creates a memorial primarily for men that is transient in nature. The organic nature of the quilt perfectly accommodates the potentially unending numbers of deaths of community members from the disease. In this case, a gendered sphere was borrowed by a man, Cleve Jones, using a female expressive form to memorialize and personalize the loss of life. The medium of this memorial tests the expectations Americans may have about the materials used, the stability of location, and the accessibility of a memorial to Americans who have died in a battle. As the number of AIDS deaths has grown, the quilt has changed to represent males and females, homosexuals and heterosexuals, with gender being superseded by the experience of disease.

The intersection of other markers of human identification such as race and class with gender has emerged as problematic for the contemporary folklorist. The folkloristic representation of a group simply on the basis of gender is difficult if not impossible because of the possibility of these other factors influencing and even superseding gender. Fieldworkers are increasingly aware of the difficulty of representing people even if they share the same sex or sexual orientation. The Fieldworkers' academic status naturally infringes upon folklorists' ability to represent individuals and groups who are in subordinate positions of power. Gender is inextricably linked to the power differentials within a particular culture because gender involves the process of defining men and women. Understanding who dictates that process and how it is worked into the everyday lives of men and women is especially important for folklorists and all individuals working on the culture of everyday life. The lesson of the feminist critique that women's lives have been erased in past scholarship and need to be rediscovered and celebrated through ethnographic research does not mean that men's lives are adequately characterized by patriarchal stereotypes. The care that needs to be given to the study of women's lives and folkloric expressions needs also to be lavished on male culture and male folklore and folklife to prevent an unreflective view of what actually constitutes the uniqueness of that culture.

Gender-specific and overtly gendered folklore forms seem to occur within the realm of material culture and "activity" more than in the domain of oral expressive forms. While the content of the jokes, stories, and songs told by men and women often differs, the divergence of genders within material objects of folklore is more clearly defined. Perhaps in the right context, a man or a woman might perform an oral genre, or have knowledge of an oral genre, regardless of his or her gendered "right" to perform it in the public or private sphere. However, creating physical evidence of experimentation within a gendered sphere of activity to which one is not culturally privileged, such as whittling, quilting, or beadwork, may often be deemed too risky for it may raise issues of gender competency, critique, and ownership. Consequently, the material genres maintain their gendered status and characteristics over time.

It is impossible to consider American folklore and folklife, its form, function, or meaning, without reflecting on the role of gender. The production, maintenance, and transmission of various American folklore forms are gendered. The ways in which cultural expectations are constructed and fulfilled speak to the ideology of gender that communities and individuals create and transmit. Within the North American context specifically, a process of experimentation about gender that is potentially both radical and destabilizing has been taking place throughout the 20th century. Folklore forms have often represented the crossing of traditional gender lines. The future of American folkloristics in the study of gender lies in exploring the ongoing deconstruction of gender boundaries and their reformation along new paradigms of male and female identity and senses of self.

Monica Lawton
Leonard Norman Primiano

References

Bacon-Smith, Camille. 1992. *Enterprising Women: Television Fandom and the Creation of Popular Myth.* Philadelphia: University of Pennsylvania Press.

Blincoe, Deborah, and John Forrest, eds. 1993. Prejudice and Pride: Lesbian and Gay Traditions in America. *New York Folklore* 19:1–244.

Brown, Linda Keller, and Kay Mussell, eds. 1985. *Ethnic and Regional Foodways in the United States: The Performance of Group Identity.* Knoxville: University of Tennessee Press.

Burke, Carol. 1992. *Vision Narratives of Women in Prison.* Knoxville: University of Tennessee Press.

Hollis, Susan Tower, Linda Pershing, and M. Jane Young. 1993. *Feminist Theory and the Study of Folklore.* Urbana: University of Illinois Press.

Hufford, Mary T. 1992. *Chaseworld: Foxhunting and Storytelling in New Jersey's Pine Barrens.* Philadelphia: University of Pennsylvania Press.

Lawless, Elaine J. 1988. *Handmaidens of the Lord: Pentecostal Women Preachers and Traditional Religion.* Philadelphia: University of Pennsylvania Press.

Matthiessen, Peter. 1986. *Men's Lives.* New York: Vintage.

Noyes, Dorothy. 1989. *Uses of Tradition: Arts of Italian Americans in Philadelphia:* Philadelphia Folklore Project, Samuel S. Fleisher Art Memorial.

Stahl, Sandra Dolby. 1989. *Literary Folkloristics and the Personal Narrative.* Bloomington: Indiana University Press.

Tannen, Deborah. 1990. *You Just Don't Understand: Women and Men in Conversation.* New York: Ballantine.

See also Feminist Approaches to Folklore; Gay Men; Lesbians

German Americans

Descendants of the largest U.S. immigrant group. The long history of German settlement in America reflects centuries of religious, political, and social turmoil in the German-speaking countries of central Europe. The Protestant Reformation generated a number of fervent religious movements throughout Europe, led by those who believed that Reformation leaders had stopped far short of true reform. The rise of the Anabaptists in the 16th century, and the Pietists and Radical Pietists in the 17th and 18th centuries, demonstrated a pervasive longing in post-Reformation Europe for religious freedom. After the Augsburg Accord of 1555 gave the princes of the provinces and the governments of the free cities the right to introduce the Reformation into their territories, religious choice had remained in the hands of the rulers of the patchwork of small principalities and kingdoms that constituted Germany. While not actually stated by the accord, "whoever rules determines the religion" became the established practice,

Dancers at the Donauschwaben Club. Chicago, 1977. Photo Jonas Dovydenas. American Folklife Center.

causing continuing unrest as mystics, visionaries, and intellectuals rebelled against the rigid conformity enforced by the established churches and governments. Religious persecution, political oppression, heavy taxation, and compulsory military service led to massive German emigration during the 18th century, both to the east (to the Russia of Catherine the Great) and to the west (to the "New World" with its promise of freedom and opportunity).

The Napoleonic Wars and a series of failed revolutions led to another surge in German emigration in the first half of the 19th century, both to Russia, where Wuerttembergers and others established the Black Sea colonies at the invitation of Czar Alexander I, and to America, where immigrants began to move west with the frontier. Promotional literature and letters home promised free or cheap land in the "Far West," low or no taxes, and an absolute freedom undreamed of in Europe. A wave of "Amerika-Fever" swept Germany, and sto-

ries of hardships and failed plans did little to discourage those who saw America as the answer to worsening problems of overpopulation, poverty, and oppression at home.

In 1608 German glassmakers had been among the first group of non-English brought to the Jamestown Colony by the Virginia Company. Conflicts with the English settlers soon developed. Apparently dissatisfied with conditions in the colony, the German craftsmen, with a Swiss, joined with the American Indian chief Powhatan, leading Captain John Smith to coin the "damned Dutch-men" epithet (based on the mispronunciation by English speakers of *Deutsch,* or German) that was to echo in broadsides and songs during both the Revolutionary and Civil Wars. Later in the 17th century, as the vision of America became more firmly rooted in the European imagination, individuals or small groups of Germans began to settle along the East Coast. The first permanent group settlement in America was established in Pennsylvania in 1683, when German Mennonites and Quakers from the Lower Rhine established Germantown. During Queen Anne's reign (1702–1714), the British government promoted German immigration, and Germans continued to arrive in increasing numbers during the first half of the 18th century. Benjamin Franklin, who had established a German newspaper in 1732, was complaining by the 1750s that Pennsylvania was becoming a German colony. At the outbreak of the Revolutionary War, a third of Pennsylvania's population was German, and substantial settlements had been established in Georgia, Maryland, the Carolinas, New York, and elsewhere.

Thoughout American history, political and religious refugees from Germany have had a substantial impact on the cultural, political, and social development of their adopted country. With the support of the large numbers of immigrants who left home for purely economic reasons, German intellectuals, religious leaders, and exiled revolutionaries have at times been able to gather enough political power in many states to affect local and national affairs. *Turnvereine* (athletic societies dedicated to the principle of "a sound mind in a sound body") were established in Germany by Friedrich Ludwig Jahn after the defeat of Prussia by Napoleon in 1806. Brought to the United States by former revolutionaries, particularly the "Forty-Eighters" (often university-educated intellectuals who participated in the 1848 revolutionary movements in Germany and, as a result, had to fleee to avoid prosecution and imprisonment), Turner societies became convenient vehicles for organizing political action as well as providing athletic and cultural activities. The power German immigrants gained, their great numbers, and the tenacity with which they held to their language and social customs have often been viewed with alarm by other Americans.

The concept of the "melting pot," Michel Guillaume de Crevecoeur's vision of Americans as individuals of all nations "melted into" a new race of men, has been fixed in the national political consciousness since colonial times and has continued to pervade American political rhetoric, particularly during times of national crisis. However, most German immigrants came to the United States not to assimilate into another culture but to have the freedom to practice the religion of their choice and preserve for their children the language they treasured. They established churches, schools, newspapers, and organizations toward that end.

Historic events sometimes beyond their control have not made their Germanness easy to accept. The use of impressed (and often kidnapped) young Hessian men by King George III to put down the rebellion in the American colonies inspired numerous revolutionary broadsides and songs about the "Hessian mercenaries." Even during the Revolutionary War, however, as they were to do later, Germans presented a dilemma for patriotic-song makers. On the one hand, there were many who fought against the British, including General Nicholas Herkimer and his four battalions recruited in New York's "German Flats." On the other hand, there were the fearful Hessians. Versions of the broadside "Saratoga" include both salutes to "Herkimer's brave soldiers" and complaints about British General John Burgoyne's German troops: "To plunder and to mur-

der was solely their intent." The "Song of the Vermonters" with its anti-German sentiment, published anonymously but finally acknowledged by John Greenleaf Whittier, persisted in the oral tradition in New England for a century and a half, as ballad collector Helen Hartness Flanders found.

The terms "Hessians" and "Dutchmen" were revived by Civil War song makers and lingered in the folk memory through the second half of the 20th century. German participation on the Union side was substantial, and Northern songs celebrated "the loyal sons of Germany," while Southern broadsides raged against the "hireling Hessian knaves" and the "bloody Dutch." Even the pro-German Civil War broadsides had a tendency to satirize German accents, food preferences, and an affinity for lager beer ("I Goes to Fight Mit Sigel," "De Goot Lager Bier").

Following the Civil War, the German practice of the "Continental Sabbath" continued to offend many Anglo Americans, and a movement to prohibit theater performances and other social activities enjoyed by Germans on Sunday inspired "blue laws" to bring Germans into step with their neighbors. It was the German affinity for wine and beer, their concept of the tavern as a center for community and family activities, and their enthusiastic celebrations of holidays, both their own and American patriotic holidays, that most often brought them into disfavor with their English neighbors. "The Hell Bound Train," collected by Vance Randolph in the Ozarks, expresses a prevailing view in many areas: "The tank was full of Lager beer / And the devil himself was the Engineer." As World War I approached, supporters of Prohibition reminded voters in southwest Missouri that a vote for Prohibition was a vote against the Kaiser, and state Councils of Defense set out to abolish "enemy languages" in churches and schools.

The degree to which German immigrants and their descendants assimilated into the mainstream American culture at various times is a matter of dispute among cultural historians. Acculturation did, of course, take place even in the areas with the heaviest German population. New German immigrants to Pennsylvania in the 1830s, imbued with the romantic notion then prevailing in Germany that everything characteristically German ought to be preserved, were so offended by the Americanization of the old immigrants in Philadelphia that they formed a German Settlement Society to establish a colony in the West that would be "German in every particular." Naming the planned colony Hermann for the old Germanic hero who had defeated the Roman legions in the Teutoburger Wald in A.D. 9, and with streets and sites for churches, promenades, and parks already in mind, society members moved to an isolated site on the Missouri River 80 miles west of St. Louis. For many decades, from the 1840s to World War I, they were able to achieve their dream of a Golden Age of German culture in America, with German churches and schools, musical groups, a theater, and a thriving wine industry that inspired a succession of festivals and celebrations.

Whether articulated, as with the founders of Hermann, the leaders of intentional communities, and such ambitious groups as the well-educated members of the Giessen Emigration Society, whose aim was to establish a German state in the

Far West, or simply as a matter of course, German immigrants proceeded to cluster into settlements and enclaves of their kind ("herding together," as Franklin had said) and began transplanting their language and cultural habits to the new environment. This did not simply mean German, but Bavarian, Westphalian, Rhinelander, or Hannoverian. The strong local folk tradition and local pride that survived German unification under Bismarck (and continues to thrive) was maintained in the United States and resulted in numerous benevolent, musical, and social clubs in urban areas based on provincial origin. Chain migration led to rural settlements of immigrants from the same area who preserved their regional customs and dialects for generations. The language they spoke was central to their identity. Most communities maintained their dialects as the "social" language, although High German was used in the churches and schools. As new immigrants arrived in established communities throughout the 19th century, language and traditions were reinvigorated and became more firmly entrenched. This massive and continuing immigration served to transplant a multiplicity of German religious and traditional practices in many parts of the United States. The arrival of the "Germans from Russia," Catholics, Lutherans, and Mennonites, who began to emigrate after the American Civil War when Czar Alexander II instituted universal conscription, brought to the Plains states old beliefs, customs, and practices preserved for almost 100 years in Russia. Healing and magic practices, songs, and sayings took root in many isolated communities.

Ironically, religious controversy among the Germans continued in America as new groups arrived and new churches were established. George Rapp's Harmonists, who came to Pennsylvania from Wuerttemberg in 1804, moved to Indiana in 1814, and went back to Pennsylvania in 1824, and suffered a Great Schism in the 1830s when some Harmonists followed the charismatic Count Leon to Louisiana and some went with Wilhelm Keil to Missouri. William Nast, founder of the German Methodists, was stoned by his compatriots in Cincinnati when he preached his new faith, and traditional Lutheran and German Reformed Church leaders protested the formation of the evangelical *Kirchenverein des Westens* on the Missouri frontier, ridiculing its leaders and launching personal attacks on its pastors in St. Louis newspapers. The Germans from Russia formed their own churches and held tightly to their own customs, partly because they were not welcomed by other German Americans.

The class system caused some difficulties among early immigrants, but often the "bond of common memories" from home, seemingly always stronger than the bond of common American experience, overcame the class distinctions. In many towns in the Missouri Rhineland, the doctor, lawyer, butcher, baker, and their wives and children took part in the German theater performances sponsored by the *Turnverein* or other societies. The Turner societies generally became less political after the Civil War period and sponsored diverse cultural and social events such as poetry readings, theatricals, and concerts rather than military drills. Athletic competitions continued, but in the 1990s some Turners report that about the only exercise at meetings is bending the elbow. In 1995, about eighty Turner societies still existed.

The customs maintained most faithfully by German Americans were church and family centered. Both Catholic and Protestant groups preserved pre-Lenten, Easter, and Christmas traditions into the 20th century: *Wurstjäger* (sausage hunters) sang Rhenish begging songs current in early-19th-century Germany when they went out to collect food for the community pre-Lenten feast in American communities. In Protestant communities, children went from door to door begging for *Fettküchli*. Easter was celebrated with both religious ceremony and bonfires. Holy palms are still placed in homes as a protection against lightning. St. Nicholas Day was celebrated primarily by Catholic groups, who transplanted different customs from various provinces in Germany and Austria to settlements in America. On December 6, St. Nicholas visited homes in rural Catholic communities accompanied by "Black Peter" or the devil in chains. It was an experience that not many adults recalled with pleasure, accompanied as it was by the rattling of chains and the frightening prospect of recalling a year's transgressions. In communities where St. Nicholas did not actually appear, children put out their shoes with gifts for the expected visitors. Sometimes curious adaptations and confusions of customs occurred. In a German community in south Louisiana, children put out rice for Santa's reindeer on December 6. In the Bethel colonies in Missouri and Oregon, a tradition of a Black Santa developed, and on Christmas Eve in some communities children were visited by the *Christkindl*, a female figure. The *Christkindl* in affluent St. Louis homes was considerably more benevolent than the stern Kris Kringle who visited Bethel. The custom of wedding inviters, who composed invitations in German verse to recite at neighboring homes, was one of the folk traditions that persisted in many rural communities. Those who accepted the wedding invitation pinned a ribbon on the inviter's staff or jacket and provided him with the expected refreshment. *Maifeste, Schützenfeste,* harvest celebrations, and "Shooting in the New Year" were a part of pre–World War I German American community life and were sometimes revived after the War. A *Schützenverein* in eastern Missouri held its competition, crowned its king, and enjoyed the customary ball into the 1950s.

The book burnings, vandalism, and attacks on German Americans during World War I served to diminish the use of their language in public and curtail the exuberant festivals, but such actions did not extinguish them altogether. The events of the 1930s and World War II led to a further diminution of public cultural activities, but family and sometimes community customs continued. The American Bicentennial in 1976 and the celebration of the Tricentennial of German group settlement in America in 1983 encouraged a revitalization of the German American spirit, but language barriers continue to discourage the kind of extensive collection and study of German folklore that resulted in the preservation of major collections of African American and Anglo American folklore in the early 20th century. Only in Pennsylvania has German folklore been consistently collected, published, and studied, although the Germans from Russia, both the Volga River and the Black Sea groups, have extensively documented their history and folklore since World War II.

Yet, in many areas of the United States, the influence of German immigrants can be seen in the distinctive churches, townscapes, and farm buildings that remain. Early communal and other intentional settlements have been preserved, often as tourist attractions, and serve as reminders of the long history of the search for religious freedom. German foods, which once inspired satire, are part of the American diet, and many holiday customs, including the Christmas tree and Christmas music, have been adopted by all Americans. More language has been lost than is remembered, but newly established Low German Theater performances draw large local audiences, and singing societies are still popular in the cities. Many German American communities are trying to preserve, revitalize, and promote their German heritage, often with such activities as "Wunderbar Days," "Gesundheit Festivals," and *Strassenfeste*. *Oktoberfeste* and *Wurst* (sausage) festivals attract German Americans and others for traditional food and drink. German Americans are still perceived as Germans and perceive themselves as German. As the 20th century nears its close, they make up almost one-fourth of the U.S. population.

Adolf E. Schroeder

References

Arends, Shirley Fischer. 1989. *The Central Dakota Germans: Their History, Language, and Culture.* Washington, DC: Georgetown University Press.

Barrick, Mac E. 1987. *German-American Folklore.* Little Rock, AR: August House.

Coburn, Carol K. 1992. *Life at Four Corners: Religion, Gender, and Education in a German-Lutheran Community, 1868–1945.* Lawrence: University Press of Kansas.

Faust, Albert Bernhardt. 1909. *The German Element in the United States.* Boston: Houghton Mifflin.

Gerlach, Russell. 1976. *Immigrants in the Ozarks.* Columbia: University of Missouri Press.

Rippley, La Vern. [1970] 1980. *Of German Ways.* New York: Barnes and Noble.

Wittke, Carl. 1939. *We Who Built America.* Cleveland: The Press of Western Reserve University.

See also Pennsylvania Germans ("Dutch")

Gerould, Gordon Hall (1877–1953)

Medievalist, litterateur, folklorist. Born in Goffstown, New Hampshire, Gerould was educated at Dartmouth College (A.B. 1899) and Oxford University (B.Litt. 1901). In 1901 he was appointed reader in literature at Bryn Mawr College; in 1905 he was named preceptor at Princeton University, where in 1938 he became Holmes Professor of Belles Lettres and from 1942 to 1946 he served as chairman of the Department of English.

He was a member of the Medieval Academy and also served as a vice president of the Modern Language Association of America.

Known to folklorists primarily through two of his books—*The Grateful Dead: The History of a Folk Story* (1908) and *The Ballad of Tradition* (1932)—he taught the full range of English literature and published a definitive study of saints' legends (Gerould 1916), translations of *Beowulf* and *Sir Gawain and the Green Knight,* as well as *How to Read Fiction* (1934) and *The Patterns of English and American Fiction* (1942). He also published four novels.

The Grateful Dead served as a model for folktale study among students of literature and was influential in the development of the "historic-geographic" school of folktale study. *The Ballad of Tradition* was the first explicit statement of the theory of communal re-creation, and for four decades it served as a substitute for the introduction that Francis James Child never wrote to *The English and Scottish Popular Ballads* (1882–1895). It remains the most influential of all introductions to the ballad genre.

W. Edson Richmond

References

Gerould, Gordon Hall. 1916. *Saints' Legends.* Boston: Houghton Mifflin.

———. 1952. *Chaucerian Essays.* Princeton, NJ: Princeton University Press.

Gestures

A metalanguage with distinctive features, categories, and functions. The story of the man who would not be able to talk if he could not use his hands is no joke; gestures are essential in communication. When a multilingual person switches from one spoken language to another, the accompanying gestures switch also. Even within the same language, gestures vary according to context. Gestures used at a church differ from those used at a bowling alley.

Gestures are made by articulating body parts, including limbs, torso, and face, in isolation or in combination. Gestures are shaped by four dimensions—three spatial extensions plus time—textured by varying dynamics. Though fleeting, gestures' impact exceeds the time of execution. Gestures linger in the "mind's eye" of the receiver and remain within the human transmitter in neurological, chemical, and cognitive ways that are not fully understood. Gestures are kinesthetically sent but visually received. As ideas are often clarified to both the listener and the speaker when they are spoken aloud, so information and feelings are confirmed to both viewer and performer when they are embodied in gestures.

The shapes of gestures are partly delineated by apparel, paraphernalia, and environment. In some transplanted European and Mexican folk dances, women gesture decoratively with their arms while their fingers grasp their skirts. The skirts and held objects such as rattles are gesture modifiers. Gestures by hands that hold or manipulate items differ from those of unencumbered hands. Bare or shod feet with, say, slippers, boots, or sandals, differentially define the kinds and qualities of leg and foot gestures. Likewise, whether the ground space is hard floor or soft sand affects leg and foot gestures.

Most gestures are learned. Involuntary gestures, shared

universally with all human beings include grinning, flailing, flinching, shielding, jerking, and empathic mirroring. They are comparable to vocalics of laughing, babbling, grunting, whimpering, squeaking, or imitative echoing.

All humans share the same potential for gestures, just as all humans are capable of uttering the same sounds, but the range of gestures and vocalizations is species specific. When selected, codified, and habituated, gestures and vocalizations are culture specific and comprise a repertoire (with idiosyncratic flavorings). Even ad hoc gestures adapt movements from the repertoire.

Gestures bridge the mind-body dichotomy. Gestures reinforce, augment, give nuances, sometimes supplant, even occasionally nullify oral language. If someone says, "no," but simultaneously nods affirmatively, the gesture prevails. The cliché that actions speak louder than words, thus, has credence.

A constant in human life, gestures are incorporated in both ordinary and extraordinary experiences. Although all gestures are meaningful in some way, their intent differs. They can express emotions or be emotionally neutral. They can perform tasks or be useless. They can emphatically communicate or phatically conform. They can be spectacular or taken for granted. They can be significant by their very existence or in the breach. Gestures can energize or be wasted. They can establish or remove boundaries. Gestures can be communal, private, or intimate. Whatever their reasons, they are part of all human life at all times.

Gestures function variously as signs, signals, symbols, and signatures. Gestures can serve as punctuation, such as raised eyebrows to indicate a question. Gestures can reinforce an idea. For example, raising the first and middle fingers to form a "V" signifies "Victory;" lifting only the middle finger is a vulgar insinuation. Gestures can even evoke the unseen or invite metaphysical intervention, such as lifing both hands above the head with the palms facing up to invoke a heavenly blessing, or crossing the first two fingers or knocking on wood for luck and protection.

Vocational gesture idioms reveal identity while affecting the course of action, such as signaling in the stock exchange, at auctions, by umpires at baseball games, or by train conductors to move trains. The latter is an example of changing gestures, because walkie-talkies have replaced hand gestures and the swinging of a lantern.

Idiosyncratic gestures, such as nervous habits of finger tapping or hair twisting, can become signatures of an individual. Sometimes symbolic gestures are restated in other media. For example, in some dances Hopi male dancers hook their fingers over the uplifted curved fingers of the dancer on either side, a gesture that expresses brotherhood. That gesture is graphically replicated by hooked half circles drawn on a dancer with body paint.

Whether or not a gesture consciously communicates, it can be "read," but only by those who are literate in the gesture code. For example, a Midwesten Euro-American who asks a Southwestern Native American where something is may be perplexed or even insulted when the Native American pro-

trudes his lower lip in reply, a traditional way to point.

The smile is a universal human facial gesture, but the meaning ascribed to it varies by culture, subculture, and situation. For Japanese Americans, a smile with a bow is etiquette and does not indicate an emotion. The U.S. gestural repertoire includes smiles of pain, irony, joy, shame, modesty, humor, cynicism, imbecility, flirtation, cruelty, triumph, and even disassociation. Young Hawaiian and Native American women and older Japanese American women self-consciously cover their smile with their fingertips.

Gestural greetings are made by everyone, but their expressions are culture specific. For example, mainstream Americans associate direct eye contact and a firm handshake with strength of character. Native Americans, however, associate direct eye contact and a firm handshake with arrogance and disrespect. They greet each other with eyes slightly averted and gently clasp hands or touch fingertips. African Americans and others who wish to be "cool" alternately grasp one another's thumbs. Members of fraternities signify their membership with esoteric handshakes. In polite Euro-American society, a lady proffers her hand before a gentleman extends his. Likewise, an older person initiates a handshake with someone who is younger. Respect is shown by allowing the lady or the older person to determine whether or not they will touch the other party.

Salutatory embraces and kisses in the United States are also determined by gender, age, status, and cultural backgrounds. Many American women greet each other with an embrace and a kiss on the cheek. But male-to-male, or male-to-female greetings with embraces and kisses are selective, lest those gestures violate propriety. American men seldom greet one another with a kiss. Often they do not even kiss their own sons after they outgrow babyhood. However, men who follow Latin traditions kiss each other repeatedly on first one cheek then the other. Hawaiians of both sexes greet each other by an embrace and gentle nose-to-nose touches, on first one side then the other. Older Japanese Americans traditionally greet each other with a bow instead of physical contact.

Embodied ideas and feelings often include a complex of gestures. A person who reads a script over the radio uses gestures even though he or she is not seen by the radio audience. The person who wears a mask replicates the mask's expression gesture on his or her own face. Those invisible facial gestures accompany the visible bodily gestures. Interactive gestures often produce empathy, as exemplified by the mother who opens her own mouth while spoon-feeding her infant.

Some gestures need an exterior context in order to be deciphered. For example, a forward outstretched arm with the palm of the hand facing down can be, variously, a blessing, a request to be recognized, or a Nazi salute. In contrast, enchained gestures often create their own context. The American Sign Language for the deaf and Plains Indian sign language are enchained systems. Although those gestural languages are codified, the messages are not fixed. Similar to conversational oral speech, the content is extemporaneous, unique, and requires semantic interpretation.

However, signed messages may be stereotypical and redundant, especially at formal events. With a choreographed and fixed routine, based on Plains Indian sign language, pantomiming the song "Go My Son" is a popular performance piece for young Native American women. Enclaves of Tibetan lamas in exile are located in several areas of the United States. They all perform the same prayers and psalms, which interface chanting with esoteric *mudras* (gestures).

Mudras are used, also, in Bharatanatyam, a Hindu dance form that is attracting many students throughout the United States. The *mudras* have ascribed denotations, but, depending on the dynamics of performance, the connotations vary. A series of paragestures—that is, the "same" gestures modified to alter affect—can present such diverse emotions as longing, anticipation, impatience, jealousy, and pleasure, all differing facets of a base metaphor.

Hawaiian hula gestures interpretively illustrate the semantics of texts that characteristically have more than one meaning—literal, double entendre, and *kaona* (soul). Because specific glosses are not assigned to them as they are to *mudras,* hula gestures cannot be read as a sign language. However, combined with the texts, hula gestures teach, celebrate, and confirm the Hawaiian cultural legacy while they arouse emotions in both the performers and the audience.

When gestures are speech surrogates, they transmit information and interpretation without buttressing words. For example, the Yaqui Indian ritual performers called *chapayeka* do not speak while they are wearing their masks. Simple pantomime communicates basic ideas and provides comic relief. But when a *chapayeka* passes by a sacred icon, such as a crucifix, he twists and shakes his hips rapidly two or three times. That gesture causes clusters of deer or pig hooves on his belt to swish audibly. When several *chapayeka* pass by a sacred icon, in single file and one after the other, the ripple of trembling sounds reminds the onlookers of the divine metaphor.

Gestures reveal the human condition. Storytellers and actors borrow conventionalized gestures to indicate gender, age, health, class, role, and character in their representations. With an astute use of gestures, a storyteller can eliminate much oral exposition. Fingers slightly separated on hands that move gracefully, a clenched fist that pounds the table, rigid fingers that claw at the air, and trembling flaccid hands—all evoke differing images.

Within the American gesture repertoire, there are many variables, such as gender, age, health, ethnicity, values, mores, economics, status, role, education, vocations, worldview, attitude, circumstances, and geographical region. The gestural repertoire, as dynamic as the United States itself, experiences timely changes with new cultural infusions, technologies, professions, and models for living.

Despite its multivariables, there is a standard American gesture repertoire (comparable to Standard American English but not formally acknowledged) that has been tacitly incorporated through common usages. Consistently displayed and reinforced in the television medium, it has become normative. Its primary antecedents are European, but additions and modifications make it uniquely American.

Gesture studies in the United States have focused on theory and methods, specific subcultures, and anecdotal accounts. There is no formal mapping of U.S. gestures and gestural dialects as Desmond Morris and colleagues provided for western and southern Europe and the Mediterranean (Morris, Colbert, Marsh, and O'Shaughnessy 1979).

Ubiquitous and important as both causes and effects in human communications, gestures are critical to the study of folklore and folklife.

Joann W. Kealiinohomoku

References

Benthall, Jonathan, and Ted Polhemus, eds. 1992. *The Body as a Medium of Expression.* New York: Dutton.

Birdwhistell, Ray L. 1970. *Kinesics in Context.* Philadelphia: University of Philadelphia Press.

Hewes, Gordon W. 1973. Private Communication and the Gestural Origin of Language. *Current Anthropology* 14:5–24.

Lamb, Warren. 1965. *Posture and Gesture.* London: Gerald Duckworth.

McNeill, David. 1992. *Hand and Mind.* Chicago: University of Chicago Press.

Morris, Desmond, Peter Colbert, Peter Marsh, and Marie O'Shaughnessy. 1979. *Gestures: Their Origins and Distribution.* New York: Stein and Day.

See also Deaf Folklore

Ghost Stories

Tales, legends, and personal-experience stories about revenants, informally called ghosts, creatures that return from the realm of the dead to help or harass the living. Popular among both children and adults, ghost stories have circulated widely in print and in the mass media, as well as in oral tradition. Some narratives are linked to specific places—often the scene of the person's death—while others are more generalized.

In some early ghost stories told by Native Americans, the revenant is a skeleton (motif E422.1.11.4) that can heal injuries, frighten travelers, and shift its shape. Most ghost stories of more recent vintage feature ghosts that closely resemble living people. Their purposes in returning to Earth include completing unfinished business, getting revenge, revealing how they died, and disclosing the site of hidden treasure (motif E545.12).

Young children's ghost stories tell of sudden noises that signal the revenant's appearance. Aarne-Thompson (AT) tale types 326, "The Youth Who Wanted to Learn What Fear Is," and 366, "The Man from the Gallows," provide the frameworks for many children's narratives. The hero of stories based on AT 326 must vanquish a ghost that announces its presence with such frightening cries as "One black eye!" and "Bloody fingers!" In variants of AT 366 that include "The Stolen Liver" and "The Golden Arm," a dismembered corpse seeks revenge. Mark Twain explains the art of timing the catch ending of "The Golden Arm" in his essay "How To Tell a Story." This folktale has frightened generations of campers and slumber-party participants. Published collections of ghost stories by

Maria Leach, Alvin Schwartz, and others have reinforced children's awareness of oral traditional patterns.

One of the ghosts best known to American children and adults is the vanishing hitchhiker (motif E332.3.3.1). In circulation since the 1890s, this legend has many subtypes, in all of which a spectral hitchhiker disappears. Proof of the ghost's identity often comes from an object left behind: a blanket or a sweater, for example, that may be discovered draped over a tombstone. Sometimes the hitchhiker is a young girl who died a year or more ago; other times it is Jesus Christ, returning to tell people about the approach of the final judgment. The earliest vanishing-hitchhiker stories, collected in New York, tell of the ghost of a girl jumping up behind a young man on a horse. In Hawaii one incarnation of the vanishing hitchhiker is the volcano goddess Pele. Linkages also exist between the hitchhiker and *La Llorona,* the weeping female ghost of Mexican folklore. The vanishing-hitchhiker legend has inspired scenes in several movies, including *Pee Wee's Big Adventure* (1985) and *Mr. Wrong* (1984). The legend has also developed a connection to conjuring games. Mary Whales, an accident victim said to be a hitchhiker at the site where she died, becomes the object of a game involving a mirror. Ritually repeating "Mary Whales, I believe in you," the player tries to summon Mary, who may reach out to scratch her summoner.

Places with a reputation for being haunted draw visitors who may tell ghost stories before, during, and after their pilgrimages. Cemeteries and haunted houses are among the most frequent destinations, especially for adolescent visitors. Legends about deranged individuals who killed themselves and others—and might still be awaiting further victims—provide raw material for dramatic enactments by groups. Buildings such as the House of Blue Lights in Indianapolis become famous locally; it is somewhat rare for haunted houses to achieve national recognition. The great popularity of the movie *The Amityville Horror* (1979), bolstered by newspaper accounts and oral legends about a house in Amityville, New York, provides one compelling example of the fascination exerted by haunted houses.

Ghost stories also arise in connection with high-risk occupations. In the South and West, stories of miners' ghosts are common; these ghosts may frighten people but frequently come back to help other miners. Big John and Jeremy Walker of West Virginia are two miners celebrated in local legendary. Similarly, flight attendants, firefighters, and others who have died in the course of their work may become the central characters of stories, often warning others to avoid potentially fatal situations.

While some ghost stories focus on helpful acts and others on malevolent behavior, certain narratives present revenants that simply want to do some of the same things they did while living. Residents of an old Victorian house in New York speak of hearing the ghost of the house's former owner carrying wood upstairs, as he did every evening when he was alive. Similarly, summer residents of an old house in Maine describe hearing seven footsteps in the parlor at midnight, speculating that a ghost has unfinished business there. Per-

sonal-experience narratives like these may become legends as friends of the tellers repeat them; alternatively, they may have more limited circulation within family folklore.

Dreams and visions of ghosts often provide the basis for ghost stories. Sometimes people find omens in visions and dreams; other times they find comforting indications that the spirit of a loved one is near. Stories about dreaming of a relative close to the time of that person's death, for example, may become very significant to the dreamers and those who hear their narratives.

More research needs to be done on the interrelationships among personal-experience stories, legends, and folktales about ghosts. The popularity of movies such as *Poltergeist* (1982) and *Ghostbusters* (1983) shows that ghostlore continues to flourish in the mass media. As more extensive studies of oral, printed, and mass-media ghost stories emerge, we will have a better understanding of this art form's evolution in our complex society.

Elizabeth Tucker

References

Brown, Dee. 1979. *Folktales of the Native American.* New York: H. Holt, pp. 155–168.

Browne, Ray B., ed. 1976. *"A Night with the Hants" and Other Alabama Folk Experiences.* Bowling Green, OH: Bowling Green State University Popular Press.

Brunvand, Jan Harold. 1981. *The Vanishing Hitchhiker: American Urban Legends and Their Meanings.* New York: W.W. Norton.

Dégh, Linda. 1980. The House of Blue Lights in Indianapolis. In *Indiana Folklore: A Reader,* ed. Linda Dégh. Bloomington: Indiana University Press. pp. 179–195.

Jones, Louis C. 1959. *Things That Go Bump in the Night.* New York: Hill and Wang.

Langlois, Janet. 1980. "Mary Whales, I Believe in You." In *Indiana Folklore: A Reader,* ed. Linda Dégh. Bloomington: Indiana University Press, pp. 196–224.

Montell, William Lynwood. 1975. *Ghosts along the Cumberland.* Knoxville: University of Tennessee Press.

Musick, Ruth Ann. 1965. *The Telltale Lilac Bush.* Lexington: University Press of Kentucky.

Twain, Mark. 1897. *How to Tell a Story and Other Essays.* New York: Harper's.

Gordon, Robert Winslow (1888–1961)

Folksong collector. A native of Maine, Gordon became interested in ballads during courses at Harvard University. After graduation in 1910, Gordon briefly taught at the University of California at Berkeley, where he directed graduate students' theses on folksongs. Disliking institutional expectations, Gordon attempted to balance his popular and scholarly interests and returned to Harvard for advanced studies.

Harvard's Sheldon Fellowship provided Gordon funds to collect Southern folksongs during the early 1920s. Gordon built his own portable recording equipment for his Appalachian fieldwork and was one of the first folklorists to use this equipment in the Southern mountains and to interview a hillbilly singer. Basing his fieldwork from Asheville, North Carolina, Gordon recorded more than 1,000 cylinders of songs and photographed unusual folk architecture. In 1926 Gordon moved to his wife's hometown, Darien, Georgia, and initiated fieldwork to preserve African American folk traditions, especially ex-slaves' accounts, spirituals, and chants, along coastal Georgia and South Carolina.

Gordon chose to use pulp magazines, not scholarly publications, to discuss his work. As column editor of "Old Songs Men Have Sung" in *Adventure* magazine from 1923 to 1927, he acquired several thousand songs. Unlike other scholars who sought obscure folksong origins, Gordon focused on determining the precise historical events that inspired each song.

Gordon consulted for the RCA Victor Talking Machine Company in copyright lawsuits, most notably regarding "The Wreck of the Old 97." He testified in court about dating textual evidence by studying ballad versions. He also wrote a series of articles about folksongs in the Sunday *New York Times Magazine* from January 2, 1927, to January 22, 1928. In 1938 the Works Progress Administration's federal theater project published a compilation of these articles.

In 1928 Gordon was named the first archivist of the Archive of American Folk Song at the Library of Congress. His private collection formed the nucleus of the archive, and he acquired and indexed collections overlooked by scholars. In 1933, however, the library dismissed Gordon for erratic work habits.

Gordon performed clerical and editorial duties for several government agencies, collecting folksongs in his spare time. He participated in the American Folklore Society and at folksong festivals but never published a scholarly book or an article in folklore journals, and he remained on the periphery of his profession. His most lasting professional contribution was his extensive collection gathered through rigorous fieldwork.

Elizabeth D. Schafer

References

Allen, Lucy H. 1977. *Manuscript Collections Acquired and/or Indexed by Robert Winslow Gordon in the Archive of Folk Song.* Washington DC: Library of Congress, Music Division, Archive of Folk Song.

Cohen, Norm. 1974. Robert W. Gordon and the Second Wreck of "Old 97." *Journal of American Folklore* 87:12–38.

Gordon, Robert Winslow. 1931. The Negro Spiritual. In *The Carolina Low-Country*, eds. Augustine T. Smythe, et al. New York: Macmillan, pp. 191–222.

———. 1938. *Folk-Songs of America.* New York: National Service Bureau.

Kodish, Debora. 1986. *Good Friends and Bad Enemies: Robert Winslow Gordon and the Study of American Folksong.* Urbana: University of Illinois Press.

Rosenberg, Neil V., and Debora Kodish. 1978. *"Folk-Songs of America": The Robert Winslow Gordon Collection, 1922–1932.* Washington, DC: Library of Congress. AFS L68. Sound Recording.

Gospel Music

A 19th-century development in Protestant hymnody growing out of the evangelical movement's emphasis on emotion, conversion, and the believer's personal relation to Jesus. Gospel hymns usually exhibit a verse-chorus structure (eight measures to each), set to two contrasting melodies. The lyrics, almost always written in the first person, emphasize the loving relationship between the Christian and Jesus and dwell on the felt joys of salvation. The first verse and chorus of "Will the Circle Be Unbroken" offers a familiar example:

> There are loved ones now in glory
> Whose dear faces we often miss.
> When you close your earthly story,
> Will you join them in their bliss?
>
> Chorus: Will the circle be unbroken
> By and by, Lord, by and by.
> There's a better home awaiting
> In the sky, Lord, in the sky.

Anglo American gospel hymnody includes a Midwestern and a Northern urban tradition that drew on Victorian sentimental popular song and "correct" singing styles. Fanny Crosby was the most prolific early composer in this tradition, which was popularized by Ira Sankey and continued to be associated with the mass meetings and revivalism practiced by such evangelists as Dwight L. Moody, Billy Sunday, and Billy Graham. In the South, a regional tradition arose that drew on shape-note hymnody and on African American camp-meeting songs. In the early 20th century, gospel publishing houses such as James D. Vaughan and later Stamps-Baxter turned out hundreds of these songs annually. Many became part of the hymnals used in evangelical Baptist and Pentecostal denominations throughout the South, and the repertoire may still be heard there in bluegrass as well as popular gospel groups.

African American composers began writing music for gospel songs around the turn of the 20th century, and they have been sung by soloists, quartets and other small groups, and massed choirs. Among the most important composers were Thomas A. Dorsey (considered "The Father of Black Gospel Music") and W. Herbert Brewster (the greatest poet). Dorsey's best-known song is "Precious Lord," while Brewster's most famous are "Move up a Little Higher" and "Our God Is Able." In the Black communities, gospel is both a performing style and a repertoire of music. The style embodies ecstasy, improvisation, repetition, elaboration, dress, gesture, posture, and other features characteristic of African diaspora culture and music, and the same improvisatory scale and mode used in spirituals, blues, and jazz. Black gospel music is sung in worship services, at special gospel concerts, in religious pageants, and recently in the theater. It has had considerable influence on secular Black genres such as blues, soul music, hard bop, funk, and hip hop.

Jeff Todd Titon

References

Cusic, Don. 1990. *The Sound of Light.* Bowling Green, OH: Bowling Green State University Popular Press.

Reagon, Bernice Johnson. 1992. *We'll Understand It Better By and By: Pioneering African American Gospel Composers.* Washington, DC: Smithsonian Institution.

See also Shape-Note Singing; Spirituals, African American

Gossip

Conversational genre of moralistic and speculative talk about persons usually not present, the persons who engage in this talk, and the speech events of such interaction. Max Gluckman influenced its anthropological study by proposing rule-governed gossip and scandalizing as both hallmark and duty of small-group membership, functioning to bound struggles, maintain unity, and distinguish that group from others (Gluckman 1963). He acknowledges it as an art, but only more recent work has elaborated the performance and narrative skills required in this catalytic social process.

Because gossip deals informally and privately in particulars, personalities, and personal relationships, it is often considered a form of resistance to dominant, official, public culture—the province of those unable to address issues openly. Women are popularly believed to be gossips, a definition first noted in 1566: "A person, mostly a woman, of light and trifling character, esp. one who delights in idle talk; a newsmonger, a tattler" (Oxford English Dictionary [*OED*]). However, in Old English *godsibb* meant "god-related," ritually established relationships between godparents, while Middle English usage designated familiar acquaintances of either sex, especially a woman's female friends invited to attend her at childbirth. Samuel Johnson gives as his third dictionary definition of gossip: "One who runs about tattling like women at a lying-in." By Victorian times, emerging male medical specialists forbade female gossips during labor because they were too "noisy." Certainly men, too, are gossips, and the gender, age, and social status of both gossipers and their subjects must be determined ethnographically.

Gossip as both negatively and positively valued conversation was recognized by 1811: "Idle talk; trifling or groundless rumour; tittle-tattle. Also, in a more favourable sense: Easy, unrestrained talk or writing, esp. about persons or social incidents" *(OED).* Scholars have viewed it as an informal means of teaching morality, maintaining social control and solidarity, managing reputations, negotiating covertly, exchanging information, expressing sociability itself, and entertainment. Gossip's powerful, ambivalent potential may be seen, for example, in its association with both witchcraft and traditional healing, the latter to aid diagnosis and treatment of social factors in illness. Jörg R. Bergmann claims its "equivocal-contradictory character" (publicly deplored, privately practiced) stems from being "a structural part of private information" that "violates the precept of discretion and respects it at the same time . . . insofar as a mutual friend is initiated into the secret and thereby a new secret created" (Bergmann 1993:149, 150, 152).

Until more ethnographic studies are undertaken, neither the universality of gossip nor its variety can be assessed. Ethnographies of speaking gossip are problematic in both fieldwork and presentation because the art of gossip—its performance and ethnoaesthetics—is by nature private, elusive, and situationally specific. Still, like more publicly valued narrative forms such as myth, epic, and legend, gossip should be considered significant storying that informs and enlivens social life in a range of groups.

Marta Weigle

References

Bergmann, Jörg R. 1993. *Discreet Indiscretions: The Social Organization of Gossip,* trans. John Bednarz Jr., with Eva Kafka Barron. New York: Aldine de Gruyter.

Gluckman, Max. 1963. Gossip and Scandal. *Current Anthropology* 4:307–316.

Haviland, John Beard. 1977. *Gossip, Reputation, and Knowledge in Zinacantan.* Chicago: University of Chicago Press.

Levin, Jack, and Arnold Arluke. 1987. *Gossip: The Inside Scoop.* New York: Plenum.

Spacks, Patricia Meyer. 1985. *Gossip.* New York: Alfred Knopf.

Yerkovich, Sally M. 1976. *Gossiping; or, The Creation of Fictional Lives, Being a Study of the Subject in an Urban American Setting Drawing upon Vignettes from Upper-Middle-Class Lives.* Ph.D. diss. University of Pennsylvania.

See also Rumor

Graffiti

Writings and inscriptions found on public walls and other surfaces. The term is derived from the Italian verb *graffiare* (to scratch) and the noun *graffio* (a scratching). The word "graffiti" is commonly used in English as a singular noun. Central to the contemporary application of the term is the implication that graffiti writing is an illicit activity; it exists in contrast to "official" inscriptions or informational graphics. Essentially, graffiti is a form of visual communication via the built and natural environments. As a subject of academic inquiry, graffiti is generally perceived as reflecting not simply the idiosyncratic concerns and values of individual writers, but also the broader concerns of particular social groups and society at large.

Among the diverse phenomena characterized as graffiti are prehistoric petroglyphs, inscriptions in the Roman catacombs, anonymous messages on the walls of public lavatories, love vows carved into the bark of trees, spray-painted territorial markings of contemporary gangs, and colorful letters and figures painted on the sides of New York City subway trains. Scholars from different disciplines have addressed the content of messages, the social groups who write the messages, and the aesthetic aspects of the practice. Some researchers have photographed and collected colorful examples into "art" volumes, while others have analyzed the texts as exhibitions of emotional

Urban graffiti. Washington, DC, 1995. Photo J. W. Love.

repression and wish fulfillment, interpreted the phenomena as indicators of social decay and the perpetrators as deviant, described its generation as a highly thoughtful means of communication, or used ancient inscriptions as historical evidence.

The first American scholarly treatment of graffiti was Allen Walker Read's *Lexical Evidence from Folk Epigraphy in Western North America* (1935). Read, a linguist, collected graffiti from the walls of public lavatories in the Western United States and Canada and used these examples to illustrate the difference between dictionary and vernacular usages of certain words. Thirty-one years later, folklorist Alan Dundes similarily collected graffiti but pursued psychological questions about why so much graffiti appeared in men's rooms. Coining the term "latrinalia," Dundes attributes the phenomena to the infantile smearing impulse and repressed male anal creativity (Dundes 1966). Other scholars have collected phrases from walls to generally reveal the prevalence of folk humor and folk speech in the form of traditional sayings, puns, and word games.

In many instances, graffiti can be a public forum, for it is, as one scholar insightfully characterized it, "gregarious" (Smith 1986:104). Graffiti can attract or prompt additional graffiti—often in direct response to what is already written on a surface. Chains of remarks and one-upsmanships will proliferate—advice may be requested and suggested, political views debated, or performances of verbal art displayed.

Particularly ubiquitous is graffiti that marks a person's presence—"I was here"—or actions at a certain site. One such famous inscription is the carved beech tree in Tennessee that indicates "D. Boon Cilled A. Bar in ThE YEAR 1760." During World War II, a graffiti line drawing of a figure peering over a wall proliferated, accompanied by the claim "Kilroy was here." This inscription is reported to have been found in the most inaccessible and far-flung places: under the *Arc de Triomphe,* on the torch of the Statue of Liberty, at the base of the Marco Polo bridge, and so forth. It is rumored that Kilroy was the brainchild of an infantry sergeant who sought to daunt the Air Force troops who often bragged of their prowess. Thus, every time Air Transport Command members set up base in a different country, they would be greeted by an inscription indicating that Kilroy had preceded them to that destination.

The signature—the name—is the central element in the graffiti most prevalent in urban public spaces in the 1990s. "Tags," idiosyncratically penned nicknames, are etched with a sharp piece of metal, scribbled with a wide-tipped marker, or painted with a spray can on walls, trees, mailboxes, and windows. The objective of tagging is to demonstrate ingenuity and mobility, with the individual marking as many surfaces as possible. Taggers are not concerned with form and style so much as "getting up" or "getting around," a project that resonates with the spirit of "Kilroy." While "tagging" is practiced around the country, the first tagger of renown was TAKI 183, a teenager named Demetrius from 183rd Street in New York City.

The esoteric graffiti of social or cultural groups has also been documented. For example, "hobos," the nomadic men who travel the country often via railroad boxcars, developed a means of written, symbolic communication that was chalked onto walls and fences to provide fellow travelers with messages that warned, for instance, of bad dogs or indicated the homes of "kind hearted ladies." Mexican American youth in Southern California and the Southwest sometimes append the term *"con safos"* abbreviated as "cs" or "c/s" to their graffiti inscriptions to protect claims of identity, love, or territory.

The originators of "New York style," the colorful combinations of words and images that first appeared on the New York subways in the 1970s, sought fame through style and technique rather than profusion. A number of arts organizations formed to promote graffiti as an art, several artists became recognized for their graffiti-style work, and for a while graffiti attracted the attention of the gallery art world. These developments introduced the discussion of whether to term these productions "graffiti" or "graffiti art." Graffiti writers themselves distinguish between different categories of graffiti: "pieces," short for masterpieces, indicate the more complicated designs; "throw-ups" refer to the lettering of initials or nicknames in a logotype configuration; and "tags" are the speedily applied name inscriptions. "Wild style" is the term used to describe lettering using stylized forms that seem unreadable. Over time, styles have been honed and tools and techniques developed for shaping letterforms and using color, and "style wars" have become a means by which preeminence is achieved. Graffiti writers sometimes form working groups, or "crews," for self-protection and collaboration. Around all of the writers, a social world has emerged with its own mores, visual and verbal languages, and criteria for judging artistic excellence.

Graffiti styles can be regional. Writers from different parts of a city or in different cities across the country develop distinct styles. On the West Coast and in the Southwest, Old English (Gothic) is a style of graffiti lettering often found in Mexican American neighborhoods. Since at least the 1940s, Chicano youth have painted their names or nicknames in Old English on public surfaces, reportedly as a means of instilling on their names the same honor and formality associated with the letterforms as used on diplomas and other official documents. Considered a classic, Old English continues to be a popular lettering form in Los Angeles and is sometimes referred to as "cholo style," "West Coast style," or "old style."

Though in the late 20th century the term graffiti tends to provoke discussions about crime, vandalism, and distinctions between graffiti and graffiti art, it still refers to a broad range of human expressive inscriptions. Immigrants from Europe and Asia left poems and messages on the walls of the detaining centers of Ellis Island and Angel Island; "Croatan" was the enigmatic word hastily carved on a pole in 1590, the final trace of the mysterious "lost" colony of Roanoke, North Carolina. These examples may also be characterized as graffiti, and thus they underline the many potential angles for investigating this subject.

Sojin Kim

References

Castleman, Craig. 1982. *Getting up: Subway Graffiti in New York.* Cambridge: MIT Press.

Dundes, Alan, ed. 1966. Here I Sit: A Study of American Latrinalia. *Kroeber Anthropological Society Papers* 34:91–105. Reprinted in *Analytic Essays in Folklore.* The Hague: Mouton, 1975, pp. 177–191.

Grider, Sylvia. 1975. Con Safos: Mexican-Americans, Names, and Graffiti. *Journal of American Folklore* 88:132–142. Reprinted in *Readings in American Folklore,* ed. Jan Harold Brunvand. New York: W.W. Norton, 1979, pp. 138–151.

Howorth, Lisa N. 1989. Graffiti. In *Handbook of American Popular Culture.* New York: Greenwood, pp. 549–565.

Lachmann, Richard. 1988. Graffiti as Career and Ideology. *American Journal of Sociology* 94:229–250.

Reisner, Robert. 1971. *Graffiti: Two Thousand Years of Wall Writing.* Chicago: Henry Regnery.

Romotsky, Jerry, and Sally R. 1976. *Los Angeles Barrio Calligraphy.* Los Angeles: Dawson's Book Shop.

Silver, Tony, and Henry Chalfant. 1983. *Style Wars.* Distributed by New Day Films. Film.

Smith, Moira. 1986. Walls Have Ears: A Contextual Approach to Graffiti. *International Folklore Review* 4:100–105.

Gravemarkers

Monuments at gravesites to mark the spot of burial and commemorate the person departed. The erecting of gravemarkers is one of humanity's most ancient practices and has produced over the centuries artifacts of extraordinary beauty and cultural significance. In America the primary material for the fashioning of gravemarkers has always been stone, and the evolution of gravemarker style is inextricably keyed to three periods in which a particular type of stone dominated: slate (late 17th through 18th centuries), marble (19th century), and granite (20th century).

American art, it may be said, had its origins in the graveyard. Following several decades in which gravemarkers were fashioned of wood or roughly shaped fieldstone, the discovery of deposits of high-grade slate in the greater Boston area led to the adoption of this highly workable material as the memorial stone of preference among folk craftsmen in the communities of eastern Massachusetts. There, Puritan theological concepts became transformed into grim yet exceptionally beautiful folk artifacts that featured winged skulls, crossbones, and even whole skeletons, as well as various secondary death symbols (coffins, hourglasses, picks and shovels) in the tympanum (top central) area of the erect, tablet-style markers. Intricate vegetative or geometric designs frequently decorated the side and bottom borders, while Latin inscriptions such as *Memento Mori* (Remember Death) or *Hora Fugit* (The Hours Fly) served as effective counterparts to the visually dominant mortality symbolism. Epitaphs similarly echoed these grim themes, the most popular featuring variations on this well-known quatrain:

> Hearken stranger, as you pass by,
> As you are now so once was I,
> As I am now so you shall be,
> Prepare for Death and follow me.

The passage of years would temper the grim severity of early American gravestone iconography, though slate remained the dominant medium (its only significant competition being the red sandstone favored in the Connecticut River Valley area of central New England). Carvers in the early 18th century gradually abandoned most overt mortality symbolism in favor of elements more suggestive of hope and eternal bliss. One of the most striking visual indicators of this shift is the manner in which the winged-skull motif, the most prevalent of gravestone symbols from the Puritan period, gradually metamorphosed into the winged cherub's head found on so many 18th-century markers. Gaining in popularity throughout this same period was another, far less emotionally charged visual emblem—the neoclassically inspired urn and willow motif. Verbal inscriptions reflected these trends also, with harsh reminders of imminent death giving way to prospective sentiments emphasizing eternal rewards or retrospective testimonials to earthly character and achievements.

Among the many changes that dominated American cultural life in the 19th century, there arose radically new concepts in cemetery design and function, and, concomitantly, in the material artifacts that fill the cemetery landscape. Marble (with some competition from the visually similar limestone) would come to be viewed as the ideal stone for the monuments designed to occupy these sites, its greater adaptability to three-dimensional sculpture and larger scale, along

A gravemarker decorated for All Saints' Day: at the center of the beadwork is a photograph under glass. New Roads, Louisiana, 1938. Photo Russell Lee. Library of Congress.

with the dazzling whiteness of its surface, making it far more appropriate than slate to the aspirations and cultural values of an aggressively expanding nation.

Though the modestly scaled, erect tablet would remain a staple of gravemarker design during this period, marble's versatility encouraged experimentation with ever larger and more elaborate forms, particularly when markers were created for wealthy patrons. The culmination of this trend may perhaps best be seen in the massive and richly decorated mausoleums, often inspired by "Revival-style" (Classical, Gothic, Near Eastern) architecture, which appear near the end of the century. The skills of gravestone carvers naturally expanded in accordance with these new fashions, though the ability to incise precise designs and lettering on the face of memorials would always remain the primary test of a given craftsman's talents. Near century's end, the popularity of marble was challenged briefly by a type of manufactured metal marker known as "white bronze" (actually a zinc alloy), which could be cast in a variety of forms and touted virtual indestructibility as its chief selling point.

Decorative symbolism on 19th-century gravestones is enormously rich and varied, the most commonly recurring motifs being the hand with upraised index finger (signifying resurrec-

tion), the weeping willow (a generic mourning emblem), and clasped hands (a contextually specific figure with several explanations). Also dating from this period are a number of images specifically associated with children, women, various occupations, and fraternal groups. Epitaph styles, especially late in the century, became increasingly unctuous and exhibit some of the least desirable qualities of bad Victorian poetry.

In the early 20th century, marble gave way to granite, a very dense stone prized initially for its durability and later as well for its range of color possibilities. Initial attempts to work decorative motifs upon the surface of this material were crude and aesthetically suspect, though with the application of new technologies, particularly stencil sandblasting and, more recently, laser etching, a seemingly endless number of artistic possibilities have become available to the designers of contemporary gravemarkers. At the same time, the increasing separation of these designers from the actual working of their medium raises interesting theoretical questions concerning the folkloristic nature of the craft and its products.

In keeping with late-20th-century American lifestyles and philosophies, both the visual and the verbal elements emerging with ever increasing frequency on markers since the 1960s have tended to place strong emphasis upon the individual and upon things of this life, particularly occupational and recreational interests. The dominant form of the 20th-century gravemarker has been that of the horizontal slab, placed flush with the ground surface, though recent decades have witnessed a noticeable resurgence of upright configurations.

There have, of course, always been gravemarkers fashioned of materials other than stone, a phenomenon perhaps most commonly associated with the practices of certain ethnic groups. Whether conceived as expressions of cultural preference or economic expediency, these artifacts of metal, wood, concrete, and a host of other substances are not only among the most beautiful and interesting of American gravemarkers but also retain most strongly the characteristics of a true folk-art form.

Richard E. Meyer

References

Benes, Peter. 1977. *The Masks of Orthodoxy: Folk Gravestone Carving in Plymouth County, Massachusetts, 1689–1805.* Amherst: University of Massachusetts Press.

Chase, Theodore, and Laurel K. Gabel. 1990. *Gravestone Chronicles: Some Eighteenth Century New England Carvers and Their Work.* Boston: New England Historic Genealogical Society.

Forbes, Harriette Merrifield. 1927. *Gravestones of Early New England and the Men Who Made Them, 1633–1800.* Boston: Houghton Mifflin.

Jordan, Terry G. 1982. *Texas Graveyards: A Cultural Legacy.* Austin: University of Texas Press.

Ludwig, Allan I. 1966. *Graven Images: New England Stonecarving and Its Symbols, 1650–1815.* Middletown, CT: Wesleyan University Press.

Markers: Journal of the Association for Gravestone Studies. 1980.

McDowell, Peggy, and Richard E. Meyer. 1994. *The Revival Styles in American Memorial Art.* Bowling Green, OH: Bowling Green State University Popular Press.

Tashjian, Dickran, and Ann Tashjian. 1974. *Memorials for Children of Change: The Art of Early New England Stonecarving.* Middletown, CT: Wesleyan University Press.

See also Cemeteries; Epitaph

Great Basin

Region of the American West where water flows to neither the Pacific nor the Atlantic Ocean but stays within the region, having no outlet to the sea. Other criteria to define the region include geology, flora, and its indigenous culture. The chief physical characteristics are that it is an extremely arid land of alternating mountain ranges and valleys called "basin and range." The Great Basin includes almost the entire state of Nevada, portions of California east of the Sierra, southeastern Oregon, southern Idaho and the western third of Utah (in some descriptions, also tiny corners of Arizona or Wyoming). Anthropologists use a cultural definition of the Great Basin, which also varies but generally includes the traditional lands of the Paiute, Shoshone, Bannock, Ute, and Washoe tribes, a region that covers an area larger than the physical Great Basin and extends into western Wyoming and Colorado and northern Arizona. This essay focuses on the physiographic-hydrologic Great Basin region as it is most commonly understood and accepted by the general public.

The Great Basin is a high and dry land, with an average annual rainfall of just 7 inches. The valleys, or basins, average 4,000 to 5,000 feet in elevation, with the peaks often more than 11,000 feet, and the two highest in Nevada just over 13,000. The land is rugged, poor in water, but rich in minerals, a fact crucial to understanding its history and culture.

The original human inhabitants of the Great Basin were mainly the Paiute, Shoshone and Washoe tribes. The Paiute to the west, and the Shoshone to the east, have very similar cultures, languages, and traditions. The Washoe, in far western Nevada and the Lake Tahoe region, belong to a different language group and have somewhat different traditions. All of these tribes lived in small family bands and were seasonally nomadic, a necessity brought on by the harsh, barren environment. Winters were spent in the valleys and summers in the foothills and mountains; survival depended on the ability to hunt and to gather plant foods.

Material arts were very limited, with a willow-basketry tradition the most distinctive aspect of the culture, one that continues. In the 1990s, the living basket makers are mostly elderly and are members of the last generation to be raised traditionally, speaking their native languages and familiar with traditional plants and foods. There is a heartening interest, though, in passing on those traditions, and more young people seem to be asking their elders to teach what they know.

The Great Basin tribes have a singing tradition that was originally unaccompanied but that is now commonly performed with hand-drum accompaniment. The songs are sung for dances and during hand games to distract the opposing team. Traditional celebrations, once called "fandangos," include the annual Pine Nut Festival in September to bless the nuts before the harvest. Other contemporary community events include rodeos and intertribal powwows.

The earliest non-native people to venture into the forbidding Great Basin landscape were usually just passing through on their way somewhere else. After the explorers came parties of gold seekers heading for California in 1849, most of them following the Humboldt River through northern Nevada, and only a few staying to establish supply posts. Several parties of Mormon settlers were sent out from Utah in the early 1850s, and the town of Genoa at the base of the Sierra near Lake Tahoe lays claim to being Nevada's oldest settlement, founded as Mormon Station in 1851. Although those early settlers were recalled by Brigham Young in 1857, Mormons today are a significant element of the Great Basin population and culture, especially in Utah and eastern Nevada.

Nevada had its own mineral rush a decade after California's when the Comstock Silver Lode was discovered and the town of Virginia City established. Many people rushed back over the Sierra from California in search of riches, and at its peak in the 1870s Virginia City had a cosmopolitan population of more than 30,000. Numerous other small towns rose and fell with the fortunes of their mines, but many of them today are no more than ghost towns populated by legends of greatness. Many of the miners came from Cornwall in England and brought such traditions as a belief in Tommyknockers, little mischievous creatures who lived in the mines and stole lunch food, but also warned miners of impending dangers. Underground mining is almost a lost art, but a specialized occupational language, and the skills involved in prospecting and working ore, live on in a few independent miners.

A modern mining bonanza in northern and central Nevada has once again sent the state into the upper reaches of its periodic boom-bust cycle. These huge open-pit operations involve skills more akin to construction work than traditional underground mining, but some of the language survives, as well as the historical connection the workers feel for the industry that established the state.

Farming and cattle ranching followed shortly on the heels of the discovery of gold and silver, since all of those miners needed to be fed. The valleys of western Nevada were relatively well watered, although even the Native Americans had constructed irrigation ditches to help encourage some wild plant foods; settlers from Germany, Italy, and later Portugal began raising produce, hay for horses, and dairy and beef cattle to supply the booming mining camps. The northern and eastern parts of Nevada, and up into Oregon and Idaho, were much drier, but large cattle operations, often with corporate owners from Texas or California, soon began moving their herds in and establishing huge ranches—in the arid climate, it takes about 108 acres to support one cow and her calf. The ranchers also started cultivating and irrigating the natural hay fields along rivers and creeks, since winter feeding was a necessity. Basque herders were brought in to tend sheep, and they led an isolated and nomadic life following their herds.

A distinctive cow-working culture developed in the Great Basin, derived from the Spanish *vaquero* traditions that had evolved in California and suited to the dry, open country and the vast territories to be covered on horseback. Cowboys, called "buckaroos" (the name also derived from *vaquero*), are known for their skill on horseback and for their extravagant style of dress and horse gear. They wear large hats, bright scarves (called "wild rags"), and knee-length chaps (called "chinks"); they use silver-mounted bits and spurs, braided rawhide reins, and twisted horsehair ropes (called "mecarties"). All of these accoutrements have practical origins, but they have been taken beyond practicality in the buckaroo tradition. The recently rediscovered tradition of cowboy poetry seems always to have been a part of Great Basin cow culture as well, along with the better-known singing traditions, with origins in Victorian literary culture and a literate cowboy work force. With thousands of acres of open-range cow country still existing, the Great Basin remains the home of a vibrant cowboy and ranching culture, despite the pressures of modern life.

In tandem with the development of mining and ranching cultures in the Great Basin came the railroads, first the transcontinental, whose Central Pacific line from San Francisco ran along the Humboldt River route through northern Nevada in 1868. From this main line ran numerous spurs reaching many of the mining cities such as Eureka, Ely, Austin, and Virginia City and serving as shipping points for cattle to markets east or west. Most of the towns in northern Nevada along the modern Interstate 80 got their start as railroad towns, including Elko, Winnemucca, and Reno, continuing a long tradition of the Great Basin being a place people passed through on their way to somewhere else.

Las Vegas, at the edge of the Great Basin, was also first established as a railroad town at the late date of 1905, when the line from Los Angeles to Salt Lake City came through. It did serve as a supply hub for some outlying mining camps in southern Nevada and northern Arizona, but, consistent with Nevada's pattern, it was primarily the main street of saloons, gambling halls, and hotels that made it an amusing stopping place en route elsewhere. Nevada's hot, dry, rugged nature did not have much to offer travelers until gambling was legalized again after a ten-year hiatus in 1931, when Reno started its rise as a tourist destination; Las Vegas' growth spurt started after World War II and the evolution of the Southern California automobile culture.

At the closing of the 20th century, gambling and tourism are Nevada's biggest industry, while other areas of the Great Basin without the lure of "gaming" (the industry's preferred term for gambling) still rely on ranching and mining—and this includes the majority of Nevada. The whole culture of gambling is rich with tradition—good- and bad-luck beliefs, specialized language, and legends of mob involvement, to name a few. A thriving entertainment industry accompanies the gambling culture, and showgirls, magicians, lounge acts, and even prostitutes (working legally and illegally) have rich subcultures that add to the Great Basin stew.

Another major presence in the Great Basin from its earliest times has been the federal government, which owns, as an example, 87 percent of the land in Nevada. Irrigation projects, Bureau of Land Management (BLM) grazing lands, National Forests, military practice areas and bombing ranges, a Department of Energy lab in Idaho, and the Nevada Test Site for nuclear weapons are all examples of the strong, and often resented, federal occupancy of the arid West. As much as Westerners take pride in their independence, their way of life would not be possible without the role of the federal government—if only for the fodder it provides for stories about inept BLM rangers, secret UFO research facilities, mutant creatures in the tunnels at the Test Site, and window-shattering overflights by military jets.

One major role played by the federal government in the Great Basin is in the capture and distribution of the region's scarce water. Irrigation projects in the 1920s made possible much of western Nevada's farming economy, and Hoover Dam (Boulder Dam to the locals) was a major boost to southern Nevada's economy during the Depression, and makes possible the tremendous growth of Las Vegas and Los Angeles. Water has always been a revered commodity in the desert, and the frequent appearance of the Paiute-Shoshone syllable "pah," meaning water, in place names and tribal names reflects this. Many stories of the Paiute and Shoshone people concern water sprites. Stories of hidden underground lakes, a tunnel connecting Lake Tahoe and the water in the Virginia City mines, thefts of water from irrigation ditches, mysterious disappearing underground rivers, and devastating flash floods testify to the power of water in the nation's driest region.

Like the rest of America, the desert West has always been seen as a land of opportunity, and immigrants from around the world have been a part of its culture for more than 100 years. These include Irish and Chinese railroad laborers, miners from England and Ireland, storekeepers and farmers from Italy and Germany, and Basque sheepherders. In fact, in the late 19th century Nevada had the highest foreign-born population of any state in the union. Early on, most of these immigrants were European, and they assimilated quickly into the culture of the surrounding community and occupational groups, but the Chinese, Mexicans, and Native Americans were not so accepted. In the late 20th century, the Hispanic population—which is diverse, coming from Central and South America and the Caribbean as well as Mexico—is growing rapidly throughout the region, in ranching communities as well as big cities. Other non-European immigrants are primarily moving to the cities—Las Vegas in particular—in search of work in the booming economy. The cities of the West are the ultimate in community-defying suburban sprawl and alienating economic conditions, exacerbated in Nevada by the twenty-four-hour lifestyle and the shift work required to make it possible, so the conditions necessary to maintain traditions and a sense of history and community are sorely lacking. Still, the folk arts and cultures of these new residents, whether from Thailand, Paraguay, Ethiopia, the Philippines, or Lebanon, are present, although people are struggling to keep folk traditions a part of their daily lives.

The Great Basin is both the most rural and the most urban area of the country. Well over 80 percent of Nevada's population lives in Reno or Las Vegas, and Las Vegas is one of the fastest-growing cities in the country in the 1990s. The vast majority of the land in the Great Basin, however, is thinly settled. Although people speak of "rural" Nevada, many of the small towns there are not rural in the traditional sense of being agricultural, but rather are historically urban and industrial cities because of the mining influence. They may be small and isolated today, but they retain more of an urban sensibility than a rural one. The Great Basin's ranching communities are communities in the cultural rather than the geographic sense. Ranchers living hundreds of miles apart know each other and keep up with each other's doings more regularly than neighbors on the same street in Las Vegas ever do.

The folk culture of the Great Basin has been strongly shaped by the region's harsh climate and geography, probably more so than in other areas because it is so limiting and unforgiving. The strongest human-made influence in the region is legal gambling in Nevada; were it not for the chance to win money with no effort, there would be little reason for outsiders ever to stop on their way through. Those who live in the Basin have had to adapt to its reality and have developed unique traditions that make the most of what it has to give.

Andrea Graham

References

Ahlborn, Richard, and Howard W. Marshall. 1981. *Buckaroos in Paradise*. Lincoln: University of Nebraska Press.

Brunvand, Jan Harold. 1968. Folklore of the Great Basin. *Northwest Folklore* 3:17–32.

Cannon, Hal, ed. 1985. *Cowboy Poetry: A Gathering*. Salt Lake City, UT: Peregrine Smith.

Carter, Thomas, and Carl Fleischhauer. 1988. *The Grouse Creek Cultural Survey: Integrating Folklife and Historic Preservation Field Research*. Washington, DC: Library of Congress.

Clark, Thomas. 1987. *The Dictionary of Gambling and Gaming*. Cold Spring, NY: Lexic House.

D'Azevedo, Warren L., ed. 1986. *Great Basin*. Vol. 11 of *Handbook of North American Indians*. Washington, DC: Smithsonian Institution.

Graham, Andrea, ed. 1994. *Neon Quilt: Folk Arts in Las Vegas*. Carson City: Nevada State Council on the Arts.

Graham, Andrea, and Blanton Owen. 1988. *Lander County Line: Folklife in Central Nevada*. Reno: Nevada State Council on the Arts.

Hadley, C.J. 1993. *Trappings of the Great Basin Buckaroo*. Reno: University of Nevada Press.

McPhee, John. 1980. *Basin and Range*. New York: Farrar, Straus, and Giroux.

Taylor, David A., and John Alexander Williams, eds. 1992. *Old Ties, New Attachments: Italian-American Folklife in the West*. Washington, DC: Library of Congress.

See also Basque Americans; Cowboys; Mormon Folklore; Sheepherder

Great Lakes

Lakes Huron, Ontario, Michigan, Erie, and Superior (remembered by the acronym HOMES), bordering the states of New York, Pennsylvania, Ohio, Michigan, Indiana, Illinois, Wisconsin, and Minnesota on the U.S. side and the province of Ontario on the Canadian side. Folklore of the Great Lakes is widely varied in content and form and includes folk beliefs, legends, tall tales, customs, festivals, rhymes, proverbs, foodways, folk architecture, and more—the full range of expressive culture found in any area of the country. Each state or province has its own unique lore about the lakes, but there is also folklore that extends from one end of the Great Lakes to the other.

For instance, old-timers on all of the lakes talk about the effects of pollution and how at an earlier time the lakes were much clearer than they are today. Commercial fishermen tell stories about being able to see huge schools of fish at great depths, and they complain about the extinction of certain species that used to be abundant. Massive efforts have been made since the 1970s to clean up the lakes, and they have been largely successful, but the folklore continues to project a Golden Age of purer water and more abundant fish populations.

Occupations connected to the inland seas have folklore that can be found on all five Great Lakes. Workers on the large freighters that carry iron ore, grain, coal, petroleum, and steel on the lakes have a body of occupational folklore that binds them together. Great Lakes sailors have a number of superstitions—for example, it is bad luck to have a woman on board a ship, and it is bad luck to whistle on the ship—beliefs that they share with seafarers worldwide. The freighters sail the Great Lakes from April until December, when ice and winter storms make navigation difficult if not impossible. Workers on freighters face the hazards of storms, ice, fog, and other potential disasters. The most famous freighter accident on the Great Lakes was the sinking of the *Edmund Fitzgerald* on Lake Superior. Singer-songwriter Gordon Lightfoot's popular ballad "The Wreck of the Edmund Fitzgerald" is in the tradition of earlier Great Lakes ballads such as "The Persian's Crew," "Red Iron Ore," and "The Beaver Island Boys."

Other occupational groups on the Great Lakes have their own folklore. For instance, commercial fishermen have traditional knowledge and techniques about making and mending fishing nets. They tell personal-experience narratives that help define them as individuals who have strong identities as fishermen. On Lake Erie, commercial fishermen tell of the hardships of fishing—long hours, hard work, and low pay—that often cause them at some point in their lives to quit fishing and go to work in factories on shore. Invariably, they get tired of being indoors and punching a time clock and return to the lake. "Fishing gets in your blood," they say as a means of explanation.

Many outdoor occupations along the Great Lakes have similar attitudes toward their work. Loggers in the forests of northern Michigan, Wisconsin, Minnesota, and Ontario also see themselves as freedom-loving, independent outdoorsmen who have an almost mystical attachment to their jobs. According to Edith Fowke, Ontario loggers tell stories about the giant lumberjack hero Paul Bunyan, but Richard M. Dorson claimed that Paul Bunyan stories are mainly used for advertisements and local promotions that have caused Paul Bunyan to become strongly associated with the woods around the northern side of the Great Lakes. There are Paul Bunyan festivals, woodchopping and logrolling contests, wood carvings, and outdoor dramas throughout the region, and many of these events are directly tied to tourism.

Tourism and folklore have a strong connection in the Great Lakes, especially in resort areas. The use of local or regional folklore to promote tourism can itself revive dormant folk traditions or, as seems to be the case with Paul Bunyan, create an image of a folk hero in the popular imagination. In Vermilion, Ohio, on Lake Erie, a boutique has kept alive the memory of an old local-character fisherman named Jib Snyder with a statue of him outside the shop. The commercial fishermen tell stories about Jib Snyder that contradict the noble "old salt" image of the statue. According to them, he was an alcoholic who could not navigate his own boat, who was regularly thrown in jail, and who had to be taken to the hospital to be given his annual bath. Thus, the folklore of a small group may differ markedly from the popular tourist representations of the group. There are likely to be touristic uses of folklore wherever there are resort areas, including Mackinac Island on Lake Huron, Sleeping Bear Dunes on Lake Michigan, and Isle Royale on Lake Superior.

Most of the resort areas are located in less populated areas, but there is also folklore associated with cities on the Great Lakes—Toronto, Hamilton, Buffalo, Cleveland, Gary, Chicago, Milwaukee, and Duluth. These cities are populated by a cross section of the major ethnic groups in North America, and each group has its own body of folk traditions. From West Indian festivals in Toronto, Polish American foodways in Buffalo, Italian American folk beliefs in Cleveland, Hungarian American storytelling in Gary, African American blues music in Chicago, German American beer halls in Milwaukee, and Serbian American folk dance in Duluth, there is a rich tradition of ethnic folklore throughout the Great Lakes region. Cleveland's West Side Market, which is only a few blocks from Lake Erie, contains stands selling foods from many ethnic traditions, and the people selling and buying these goods represent every ethnic group in the city; the market is a virtual microcosm of ethnic America. The audience listening to blues musician Buddy Guy at the Checkerboard Lounge on the South Side of Chicago is mainly Black, but there are usually a handful of White people there, often German or French tourists.

American Indian folklore is found in both urban and rural areas on the Canadian and U.S. sides of the Great Lakes, and, in fact, the political boundary has often been ignored by Indian tribes with members on both sides of the border. According to Robert B. Klymasz, the Iroquois have an annual border-crossing parade and festival that is meant to transcend the idea of national borders and reinforce Indian identity (Klymasz 1983). The celebration includes the selling of Indian crafts and foods so that again there is an element of tourism,

but a political function seems more important in this case. Their identity is more closely linked to the Great Lakes region than to either country.

There is both a folklore of the Great Lakes and folklore in the Great Lakes region; the first kind reflects the region itself and includes legends and ballads such as "The Wreck of the Edmund Fitzgerald" and stories about water purity in a Golden Age. The second kind includes most of the ethnic folklore, which would be the same or similar to ethnic folklore in other regions of the United States or Canada. Some folklore seems to be both in and of the Great Lakes; Paul Bunyan is strongly associated with the region, but there is also Paul Bunyan lore in the Pacific Northwest, taken there by loggers who migrated from one region to another. The occupational folklore of commercial fishermen is linked to the particular lake where they fish because their personal narratives are set on that lake and mention specific place names; on the other hand, their occupational narratives have similar patterns to stories of fishermen in other parts of the United States and Canada. The folklore of the Great Lakes is as complex and varied as the size and diversity of the region suggest it would be.

Patrick B. Mullen

References

Dorson, Richard M. 1981. *Land of the Millrats.* Cambridge: Harvard University Press.

Klymasz, Robert B. 1983. Folklore of the Canadian-American Border. In *Handbook of American Folklore,* ed. Richard M. Dorson. Bloomington: Indiana University Press, pp. 227–232.

Lloyd, Timothy, and Patrick B. Mullen. 1990. *Lake Erie Fishermen: Work, Identity, and Tradition.* Urbana: University of Illinois Press.

See also Beck, Earl Clifton; Bunyan, Paul; Fishing (Commercial); Midwest; Walton, Ivan

Great Plains

The vast west-central section of North America, stretching from Texas into Canada, comprising one of the world's largest grasslands. Once termed "The Great American Desert" because of the paucity of trees, much of the native prairie sod of the Great Plains has been turned into farmland, resulting in a more positive nickname, "The Bread Basket of America." The region remains, as well, the major cattle-raising area of the continent. Both farming and ranching have contributed significantly to the folklore of the region.

As with many geographical regions, the precise boundaries of the Great Plains are imprecise. Using the broadest interpretation, which would include much of the original tallgrass prairie of the midcontinent, the eastern fringes of the Plains extend into parts of Missouri, Iowa, and Minnesota, while the western boundary is more clearly demarcated by the Rocky Mountains. Major river drainages include the Rio Grande in the south and the Missouri and its tributaries to the north. All or parts of thirteen states and three Canadian provinces lie within the region: Texas, New Mexico, Oklahoma,

Calendar for 1898
By Frederic Remington
PUBLISHED BY R. H. RUSSELL, NEW YORK

Colorado, Kansas, Missouri, Iowa, Nebraska, Wyoming, South Dakota, Minnesota, North Dakota, Montana, Alberta, Saskatchewan, and Manitoba.

Although the general appearance of the Plains is to the unskilled eye featureless, in truth the landscape is varied. Native plant life ranges from the sagebrush and mesquite of the Southwestern Plains, to the native tall-grass prairies of the Eastern Plains, to the shortgrass of the Canadian Plains, while major agricultural crops range from cotton in Texas, to corn, sorghum, and soybeans in the Central Plains, to winter wheat in the Southern and Central Plains, to spring wheat and flax in the Northern Plains. Geographically, the rolling vistas of the Plains are broken by numerous broken landforms—the Palo Duro Canyon of Texas, the Osage Hills of Oklahoma, the Flint Hills of Kansas, the Sandhills of Nebraska, the Black Hills of South Dakota, the Badlands of North Dakota, the Bearpaw Mountains of Montana, the Bighorn Mountains of Wyoming, and the Cypress Hills of Saskatchewan, to name some of the more obvious.

In the pre-Columbian era, the expanses of the Great Plains were filled with game—bison, elk, antelope, deer, bear, wolves, panthers—and were home to native peoples whose lifestyles ranged from nomadic hunters to village agriculturists. The Spanish colonization of the Southwestern Plains, beginning in the 16th century, caused a great change in the folkways for those Plains Indians that acquired the horse. Such tribes as the Pawnee and Mandan continued to farm and live in earthen lodges for part of the year, then go on extended buffalo hunts, while other tribes such as the Cheyenne and Sioux gave up farming completely to become true horse nomads. A distinguishing feature of indigenous Plains cultures was the sundance, a religious ritual that was present in one form or another in every Plains tribe.

European cultural influences in the Great Plains began with the Spanish explorers in the south and with the French fur traders in the north. Much of the U.S. portion of the Great Plains was acquired in the Louisiana Purchase of 1803. Early explorers such as Lewis, Clark, Pike, and Long were not impressed with the economic potential of the region, which, along with its comparative aridity, caused it to be one of the last regions of the continent to be settled by Euro-Americans. Its late-20th-century reputation as "flyover" or "drive-across" country mirrors the attitudes of traders who crossed the Plains on the Santa Fe Trail, of settlers bound for the Pacific Northwest on the Oregon Trail, or of mountain men and fur traders who plied the Missouri in the first half of the 19th century, none of whom became permanent settlers.

The Kansas-Nebraska Bill of 1854, which opened the Central Plains to settlement with the provision of popular sovereignty on the issue of slavery, resulted in "Bleeding Kansas," a pre–Civil War conflict that brought elements of both Southern and New England cultures into the territory. Settlement by farmers on the Central Plains after the Civil War was encouraged by the Homestead Act of 1867. At the same time, Texans on the Southern Plains were beginning to organize cattle drives to Kansas on a vast scale—several million head over a twenty-year period—an enterprise that would result in the creation of America's greatest folk hero, the cowboy.

Among the cowboy's many contributions to folklore are a distinctive work attire (wide-brimmed felt hat, high-heeled boots, neckerchief, chaps), equipment (spurs, saddle, lariat rope, chuck wagon), methodology (roping, bronc riding, roundups, trail drives), and sport (rodeo). A significant contribution to the body of American legend derives from the exploits of such cowtown lawmen as Wild Bill Hickok, Wyatt Earp, Bat Masterson, and Bill Tilghman, while, in the tradition of Robin Hood, Great Plains outlaws such as Billy the Kid, Cole Younger, Sam Bass, and Belle Starr have been romanticized and glorified. On a more mundane level, tales and stories relating to the dangers, attractions, and excitement of ranch work are traditional among working cowboys. Much of this narrative material has, for well over a century, been fashioned into verse and song. While public recitations of cowboy poetry have only recently come into fashion, cowboy songs have long been a staple of American folk music and balladry. Some, such as "The Old Chisholm Trail," are trail-driving songs, sung by lone cowboys to relieve the tedium of daily work. Others, such as "When the Work's All Done This Fall," are campfire or bunkhouse songs, sung on occasions of leisure to entertain one's fellow cowhands. Still others, such as "I Ride an Old Paint," are work songs, night-herding songs sung to keep a trail herd of longhorns at rest—and the cowboy awake.

The Great Plains farmer, too, has had a distinctive impact on American folklore, from the image of the covered wagon, to the sodbusting plow, to the statues of "The Madonna of the Plains" that can be found in towns throughout the region. Conflict between homesteaders and cattlemen over the use of the Plains sometimes resulted in legendary conflicts, such as the Johnson County War in Wyoming. Among the beliefs fostered by the attempts to settle the semiarid Plains was that rain would follow the plow, that planting trees would increase rainfall, and that clouds would form from the smoke of railroad steam engines, thus causing more rain to fall. Actually, annual rainfall tends to vary significantly over much of the Plains, which can result in a string of good years followed by a long-lasting period of drought. Widely variable weather, in fact, is a hallmark of Plains life and provides the basis for much Plains folklore, including rainmaking, forecasting, superstition, and humor. A body of tornado lore permeates the Southern Plains, while jokes about sudden and drastic temperature swings (such as the farmer skinning the ox that died of heat exhaustion only to have its yoke-mate freeze to death before he finished the task) can be heard throughout the region.

One of the most colorful symbols of pioneer farm life on the Plains was the sod house, an architectural necessity resulting from the lack of economically available wood or stone for building, particularly on the High Plains (generally speaking, that area west of the 100th meridian). Using a special plow, a farmer would turn over furrows of native sod, then cut them into building blocks to be laid up as walls for houses, sheds, and fences (thus the expression, "ugly as a mud fence"). Sod houses were well insulated, being warm in winter and cool in summer. If the roof, however, was made of sod, it would not only leak but would continue to drip long after rain had ceased falling. Moreover, insects, mice, and snakes often lived in the walls. Thus one of the first signs of affluence in a pioneering Plains family was the building of a frame house.

As with the cowboy, farming songs from the Great Plains form a major subgenre in American folk music. Some, such as "Sweet Betsy from Pike," originated with travelers on the Oregon Trail, while others, such as "The Lane County Bachelor," reflect the rigors of homesteading on the sod-house frontier. Boom and bust are reflected in a song with variants ranging from "Kansas Land" to "Saskatchewan Land," in which life on the Plains is either praised for its rich agricultural rewards or damned for the drought and the heat that have reduced the unfortunate homesteader to poverty. A song considered by some to be the most beautiful of all American folk lyrics is "Home on the Range," which originated on the farming frontier of north-central Kansas in 1873, then was spread throughout the West by cowboys, before becoming a standard popular song in the 1920s.

Other major occupational folk groups in the Great Plains include, or have included, miners (for gold in the Black Hills of South Dakota or for lead and zinc in the Little Balkans of southeast Kansas and northeast Oklahoma), railroaders and railroad builders, and oil-field workers. Some of the major oil fields in the country have been found in the Great Plains (Texas, Oklahoma, Kansas, North Dakota, Wyoming), resulting in all of the traditional raucousness and lore associated with boom towns.

Ethnic plurality in the Great Plains was greatly enhanced in the later 19th century by the practice of the railroads in promoting immigration from Europe. Among the many groups that have made permanent homes in the Southern and Central Plains, alongside the earlier settlers of British heritage, are Mennonites (including Amish), Volga Germans, and Czechs, while the Northern American Plains were heavily settled by Scandinavians, as well as Hutterites, Germans, and central Europeans. The Canadian Plains, in addition to residents of British origin, have many pockets of central Europeans and Ukrainians, as well as the French and Indian *Métis*. A sizable population of American Indians still lives in the Plains, many on reservations. In the decades following the Civil War, many ex-slaves from the South moved into the Central Great Plains in a migration known as the Exoduster movement. Chinese laborers were often used in railroad construction on the Northern Plains, while Mexican laborers were imported for the same type of work in the Southern Plains. In the recent past, large populations of Southeast Asians have come into the Central and Southern plains to work at meatpacking plants. The influence of minorities, including African Americans and Jewish settlers, was relatively common in pioneer Plains life, despite popular belief to the contrary.

Folk arts in the Great Plains have been influenced by ethnicity as well as by geography. Many traditional crafts that arrived with settlers, such as *kraslice* (egg decorating), tatting, and quilting, have been continued. Other crafts that have developed in the region, such as saddle making and spur making, can be traced back to the cattle drives of the late 19th century. Influential pioneer saddlers such as Frazier, Gallatin, Meanea, and Collins, for instance, were located in the North-Central Plains in order to take advantage of cowboys when they were paid at the end of a trail drive. For the same reason, early boot makers, such as Charles Hyer of Olathe, Kansas, reputed to be the first to make a distinctive pair of cowboy boots, were often located in or near the shipping centers or market towns of Kansas.

In addition to the folksongs of the farmer and the cowboy that developed on the Great Plains, settlers often brought with them their own musical traditions. Thus, mariachi music and *corridos* can be found in the Southwestern Plains of Texas and New Mexico, while the dance music of the Germanic and Slavic settlers tended to run from Texas into Canada. In terms of effect on popular music, the Great Plains can be seen as the home of Western Swing in the south to Lawrence Welk in the north, not to mention the influence of cowboy songs on country-western music.

Distinctive forms of material culture in the Great Plains, in addition to sod houses, include barns of varying designs and sizes, hay sheds (some of them "hay barracks" with movable roofs), corncribs, cotton gins, silos, and grain elevators. The cattle guard, a gate substitute made by spacing metal bars over a pit in the roadway that is now found on every continent, was first developed as a device of Great Plains folk technology. Post rock, a layer of easily worked limestone found in north-central Kansas, is used extensively for fence posts and construction of bridges and houses.

Among the many folk monuments in the Great Plains are

the Garden of Eden in Lucas, Kansas (a concrete sculpture garden reflecting the populist leanings of its creator, S.P. Dinsmoor); the fifteen-foot-tall jackalope statue in Douglas, Wyoming; the giant cowboy outside the Big Texan Steakhouse in Amarillo; the huge fiberglass pheasant in Huron, South Dakota; and Salem Sue, a giant Holstein cow statue in North Dakota.

James F. Hoy

References

Abernethy, Francis Edward. 1979. *Built in Texas*. Waco, TX: E-Heart.

Friesen, Gerald. 1984. *The Canadian Prairies: A History*. Toronto: University of Toronto Press.

Hoy, Jim, and Tom Isern. 1987. *Plains Folk: A Commonplace of the Great Plains*. Norman: University of Oklahoma Press.

Koch, William E. 1980. *Folklore from Kansas*. Lawrence: University Press of Kansas.

Pound, Louise. 1959. *Nebraska Folklore*. Lincoln: University of Nebraska Press.

Sackett, Samuel, and William E. Koch. 1961. *Kansas Folklore*. Lincoln: University of Nebraska Press.

Taft, Michael. 1983. *Discovering Saskatchewan Folklore: Three Case Studies*. Edmonton: NeWest.

Webb, Walter Prescott. 1931. *The Great Plains*. New York: Ginn.

Welsch, Roger. 1972. *Shingling the Fog and Other Plains Lies*. Chicago: Swallow.

Greek Americans

Immigrants from Greece and their American-born descendants. Greek sailors may have been aboard Christopher Columbus' ships when he discovered America; and Greeks were recruited along with Italians in the late 18th century to work in the vineyards and orchards of Florida's New Smyrna colony. But people from Greece did not immigrate to the United States in large numbers until the second decade of the 20th century. The nearly 200,000 who reached America's shores between 1911 and 1920 settled principally in large East Coast and Midwestern cities such as Boston, New York, Pittsburgh, and Chicago.

Poverty, political oppression, and natural disasters motivated Greeks to emigrate during the late 19th and early 20th centuries. Many came to the United States only to earn and save enough money to be able to return home and buy land. Like other "new immigrants" from southern and eastern Europe, however, most Greeks remained in America and made their living not from the soil, but by working in factories and operating small businesses instead.

Because of quotas, fewer than 1,000 Greeks a year entered the United States from the 1920s through the 1950s. But the numbers swelled again beginning in 1965. More than 120,000 Greeks were admitted to the country in the decade that followed. Unlike their unskilled predecessors, many of these immigrants were educated professionals who moved quickly and easily into positions as teachers, doctors, and engineers.

Greek immigrants come from a country with a long history and rich variety of folk traditions. The mythology that mirrored and reinforced the ancient Greek pagan belief system lives on in the customs and folk narratives of Christian Greeks. Features of the landscape, sociopolitical institutions, and historical events give rise to an ever-evolving body of legendry and song. Isolation and resourcefulness led to the development, and contribute to the perpetuation, of a rich and varied handicraft tradition that manifests itself most notably in woven goods, embroidery, and metalwork. Preparing traditional foods, making music, and dancing are integral parts of life-cycle and calendrical events in all of the areas of Greece from which people emigrate.

Greek immigrants have always done what is necessary to adapt to life in the United States. They learn English and speak it when required or appropriate. They acquire the education, skills, and know-how to make a living. They participate in leisure activities that preoccupy other Americans. But much folklore of the Greek homeland remains relevant in the United States, and it often takes on added importance in a multicultural society. Folklore serves Greek immigrants and their American-born descendants as a means of remembering, and making their children aware of, their history and cultural background. It also facilitates their interactions, both with fellow Greeks and with others interested in their homeland and culture.

Greek Americans express their heritage at such public events as ethnic festivals principally through foodways, music making, and dancing. Foods traditionally prepared and regularly expected in Greek American homes and at special events include egg-lemon soup *(sóopah ahvghohlémohnoh)*, stuffed grape leaves *(dohlmathákya)*, roasted or skewered lamb *(ahrnée)*, rice pilaf *(peeláfee)*, cheese pie *(teeróhpeetah)*, salad *(saláhtah)*, bread *(psohmée)*, resin-flavored wine *(retséenah)*, and pastry made with filo dough, chopped nuts, and honey *(baklahváh)*.

Greek American musicians performing folk music play a combination of string, wind, and percussion instruments—usually a violin, clarinet, lute, drum, and sometimes (but with ever-decreasing frequency) a *santoúri,* a trapezoid-shaped dulcimer played with two covered wooden mallets. The *bouzoúki,* a long-necked, mandolin-like stringed instrument, has increasingly become an integral part of, and the lead instrument in, Greek American folk-music ensembles. Electric amplification is also common for performing groups in the 1990s, most of which play American popular, as well as Greek folk, music.

Both live and recorded music accompany traditional circle and line dancing in which Greek Americans participate. When musicians are present, they usually follow the lead dancer, complementing and accenting his or her movements instrumentally. The person leading the open-circle *syrto* pulls the chain of dancers along, holding hands and moving counterclockwise with dragging and shuffling steps. The popular *kalamatiano* is another open-circle dance characterized by springing steps rather than foot dragging, with a lead dancer leaping and whirling about as the followers hop and skip behind him or her. The *hassapiko* is another fast-paced, carefree

The John Georganas family. Des Plaines, Illinois, 1977. Photo Jonas Dovydenas. American Folklife Center.

dance, done in an open circle with hands on shoulders and movement counterclockwise. The *vari hassapiko*, by contrast, is a slow chain dance, done with hands on shoulders and movement to the right with the body bent slightly forward. Steps are catlike, and legs are tense and moved sharply. Numerous variations of these and other folk dances not only persist, but also continue to evolve in the United States, and new variants feed back to the homeland and influence traditional dancing in Greece as well.

While traditional foodways, music making, and dancing are overt behaviors that invite public observation and even participation, much of the folklore of Greek Americans manifests itself only in small-group gatherings and private rituals. A fatalistic worldview that some scholars trace back to ancient Greece is common among Greek Americans, many of whom protect themselves from unwanted changes in their fates by prefacing future-oriented statements with "if God wills" and taking precautions against the evil eye *(mátiasma)*. Spitting three times in the direction of a person or animal one admires averts ill effects of inadvertently looking admiringly at the object of praise, and wearing blue beads with small eye shapes painted on them protects oneself from the consequences of jealous or excessive admiration. Garlic is another effective evil-eye preventive, whether eaten in whole cloves, worn on one's person, or included in traditional utterances that accompany one's compliments (such as *"Skórdho sta mátia su"* [Garlic in your eyes].

Stories about the consequences of being overlooked are told to illustrate and reinforce the belief in the evil eye. One concerns a narrator's pretty baby sister upon whom an aunt inadvertently cast the evil eye "because she didn't have any saliva in her mouth that day to spit the baby." The child died shortly thereafter. Another recounts an eyewitness' report of a huge rock breaking into "six, seven pieces" and a pony dropping dead immediately after a woman capable of casting the evil eye had praised each (Georges 1980:80–83).

Because of the pervasiveness of the belief in the evil eye, numerous diagnostic and curing rituals that immigrants learned in Greece are practiced traditionally in the United States as well. One involves dropping olive oil into a plate containing water and looking to see if the oil forms eye shapes. Another requires one to flick cloves into an open flame, mentioning, each time a clove is flicked, the name of a person with whom the afflicted had come into contact immediately prior to his or her being stared at. When a clove pops, the person whose name is associated with it is pronounced the culprit. Treatments range from having the victim drink from the other side of a cup or glass from which the suspect has drunk, to anointing the overlooked with ashes from an herb such as chamomile or basil that crackles when it is burned.

Traditional beliefs and rituals based on, and suggested by, the Greek Orthodox religion are also numerous and varied. Like those in their ancestral homeland, many Americans of Greek descent venerate figures in the religious pantheon—particularly the Virgin Mary and various saints. Saints' icons are displayed not only in churches, but also in homes and occupational environments (in cars and trucks, aboard merchant ships, on animals utilized in one's work). Icons are used traditionally in diagnosing and curing maladies; and they are the foci of home altars, before which people not only regularly pray, but also make requests for saintly intervention and assistance. That such requests are frequently granted is attested by the miniature likenesses of human limbs, hearts, eyes, and such *(tágmata)* that one sees adorning or surrounding icons in Greek Orthodox churches and shrines (Teske 1980). Further attestation comes from the recounting of personal experiences about saintly interventions being responsible for miraculous cures, survivals from natural disasters, financial turnarounds, and career and economic successes.

In addition to telling stories about evil-eye incidents and saintly assistance, Greek Americans also recount personal experiences associated with immigration and the challenges of adapting to life in a new land. Many such tales are humorous, such as that about the non-English-speaking Greek who asks a friend to teach him a few English words so he can get something to eat in a restaurant. The words he learns are *apple pie and coffee*. "Every day for all meals I had *apple pie and coffee*," the man reports. Anxious to try something else, the man asks his friend to teach him some more words and is told to order *a sandwich with eggs and ham*. When he first orders this, he's asked how he wants the eggs cooked. Unable to respond, the man orders apple pie and coffee again instead.

Another story concerns a Greek who finds an Italian produce store he likes. His visual cue for locating the market is the pile of watermelons on the sidewalk by the entrance. The Greek shops at the store regularly. But one day he cannot find it because the season has changed, and there is no longer a pile of watermelons outside to enable him to locate it (Gizelis 1974:132–133, 139). More sober narratives illustrate both the overt and covert discrimination that Greeks (like other immigrants) experience in the United States because of the sound of their native language, their appearance, or their ignorance of American customs and laws.

Also a part of the narrative repertoires of many Greek immigrants and some of their American-born descendants are entertaining fictional tales, most told less frequently today in the United States than in the past. The trickster figure Nastradin Hodja is the protagonist of one cycle of still enjoyed humorous tales, many of which Greeks share with other peoples from southeastern Europe, the Middle East, and North Africa. Frequently, Hodja is depicted as stupid or naive, as when he ignores the warning of a passerby and continues to sit on the outside of a tree branch he is sawing. When he cuts through the branch and falls to the ground with it, Hodja acknowledges the accuracy of the advice (Tale Type 1240. "Man Sitting on Branch of Tree Cuts It Off"). Other tales portray Hodja as cleverly outwitting or triumphing over antagonists. For instance, when refused entry to a vizier's banquet to which he has been invited because of the way he is dressed, Hodja goes home, puts on his finest garments, returns, and is immediately granted entrance to the banquet hall and seated beside the host. When the soup course is served and the guests begin to eat, Hodja dips first one and then the other of the flowing sleeves of his robe into the soup, saying, "Eat, sleeves, eat. It is you who were invited, not I." (Tale Type 1558. "Welcome to the Clothes") (Georges 1980:110–114).

Persisting in the late 20th century mostly in the memories of older Greek immigrants to the United States is a body of folklore concerning ominous supernatural beings, which is on the wane in Greece as well. When prompted, some Greek Americans will still tell frightening stories about the *vrykólakas*, a nondecomposed corpse that leaves its grave, usually at night, to engage in acts that range from the mischievous to the violent. They also recall hearing about individuals' encounters with *neraídhes*, tall, graceful women adorned in flowing white dresses, who steal babies from their cradles and leave adults who encounter them unable to speak. Some can also describe the *kalikánzari*, dwarf-like beings who appear at Christmastime and engage in such mischievous tasks as overturning furniture and leaving things in household kitchens in general disarray. But most Greek Americans who remember such supernatural beings have little concern about, or interest in, them today. Such beings and stories about them are from a different era and native to a country that now seems different as well.

Robert A. Georges

References

Dorson, Richard M. 1957. Tales of a Greek-American Family on Tape. *Fabula* 1:114–143.

Georges, Robert A. 1980. *Greek-American Folk Beliefs and Narratives*. New York: Arno.

Gizelis, Gregory. 1974. *Narrative Rhetorical Devices of Persuasion: Folklore Communication in a Greek-American Community*. Athens: National Centre of Social Research. Reprinted as *Narrative Rhetorical Devices of Persuasion in the Greek Community of Philadelphia*. New York: Arno, 1980.

Papanikolas, Helen Zees. 1970. Toil and Rage in a New Land: The Greek Immigrants in Utah. *Utah Historical Quarterly*. (Special Issue) 38 (2):100–204. 2d. rev. ed., 1974.

Teske, Robert. 1980. *Votive Offerings among Greek-Philadelphians*. New York: Arno.

Greenway, John (1919–1991)

Folklore scholar, teacher, writer, and performer. Greenway was born John Groeneweg in Liverpool, England, but became a U.S. citizen. Educated at the University of Pennsylvania, he received his doctorate there with a thesis that was later printed as the now standard work *American Folksongs of Protest* (1953). After a brief period as an English teacher at Rutgers University and the University of Denver, he switched to anthropology, teaching in that department at the University of Colorado through most of his career.

A versatile scholar and brilliant writer, he published books, monographs, and articles on subjects ranging from a handbook on James Joyce's *Ulysses*, to *Folklore of the Great American West* (1969), to studies and bibliographies in his specialty, the Australian aborigine. He edited or authored nineteen books; his complete bibliography is available in *Contemporary Authors*, IX (First Revision), p. 366. Two of his books, both published in 1964, were widely read: *The Inevitable Americans* and *Literature among the Primitives*.

Greenway also edited the *Journal of American Folklore* (1964–1968) as well as *Southwestern Lore* (1959–1963) and *Western Folklore* (acting editor, 1960–1961).

During the late 1950s and early 1960s, Greenway was active as a folksinger, making a number of records of protest songs and frequent concert appearances.

Tristram Potter Coffin

References

Coffin, Tristram Potter. 1992. Obituary and "A Reminiscence." *Journal of American Folklore* 105:208–210.

Greenway, John. 1963. *Bibliography of the Australian Aborigines and the Native Peoples of Torres Strait to 1959.* New York: Angus and Robertson.

———. 1972a. *Down among the Wild Men: The Narrative Journal of Fifteen Years Spent Pursuing the Old Stone Age Aborigines of Australia's Western Desert.* New York: Atlantic-Little, Brown.

———. 1972b. *The Last Frontier.* New York: Dodd, Mead.

Groundhog Day

February 2, when the groundhog supposedly comes out of its burrow to check the weather. If the sun shines and the groundhog sees its shadow, there will be six more weeks of winter; if the day is cloudy or rainy, winter will come to an early close.

Groundhog Day originated in Europe, where Candlemas Day on February 2 marked the vernal equinox and the beginning of the growing season. In France the bear supposedly returned to its hole for forty days if the sun shone, while in Germany the badger did the same thing. One could expect a good planting season if the animal showed that winter would end soon.

In America local variations have placed Groundhog Day on either February 2 or February 14. Some traditionalists in Missouri, Arkansas, and Illinois have insisted that February 14 is the proper date, although an edict of the Missouri Legislature made Groundhog Day official in that state on February 2.

Groundhog Day is not a complex or sentimental holiday in the United States, but local traditions have made it memorable in some areas. In Punxsutawney, Pennsylvania, for example, the groundhog named "Punxsutawney Phil" is a minor celebrity whose picture and behavior become newsworthy on this one day of the year. Sometimes people gather for a Groundhog Day dinner. The movie *Groundhog Day* (1993) gave the holiday an unusual degree of commercial recognition; normally, however, Groundhog Day is a low-key and pleasant reminder of agrarian routines that have become increasingly distant from urban society.

Elizabeth Tucker

References

Cohen, Hennig, and Tristram P. Coffin, eds. 1987. *The Folklore of American Holidays.* Detroit: Gale, pp. 57–58.

Hand, Wayland D., ed. 1964. *Frank C. Brown Collection of North Carolina Folklore.* Vol. 7. Durham, NC: Duke University Press, pp, 214–215.

Wardle, H. Newell. 1919. Note on the Ground-Hog Myth and Its Origin. *Journal of American Folklore* 32:521–522.

Guillonée

French New Year's Eve questing ritual performed by costumed revelers; also, the particular song sung by these revelers. A wide range of popular and scholarly beliefs concerning its origin persists. Recent evidence supports Celtic derivation of *guillonée* from Breton *eginane,* which refers to cereal germ, or seed (Postic and Laurent 1986). Variants of this questing ritual are found in Celtic strongholds of Great Britain, throughout northern and western France, and in northern Spain.

In North America, *guillonée* is practiced in Quebec and in the Mississippi Valley, where it has continued uninterrupted since colonial times. The annual quest is particularly popular in the towns of Prairie du Rocher, Illinois, and Ste. Genevieve, Missouri. Performance of the Mississippi Valley *guillonée* has transformed rapidly in the 20th century as a result of social changes and loss of native French linguistic competence.

North American versions of the song all begin similarly:

> Bon soir le maître et la maîtresse et tout le monde du logis.
> Pour le dernier jour de l'année la guillonée vous nous devez.
>
> (Good evening master and mistress and all who reside here.
> On this last day of the year you owe us the *guillonée.)*

The following two lines, in some form, also occur in most variants:

> On vous demande seulement la fille ainée.
> On lui ferons faire bonne chère, on lui ferons chauffer les pieds.
>
> (We ask you only for the oldest girl of the house.
> We will see that she becomes a dear sweetie, we will warm her feet.)

These lyrics suggest the *guillonée's* association with communal reciprocity and the coming-of-age of young women. Related French American mumming rituals include *La Chandeleur* of the French Canadian Maritimes; Mardi Gras of rural Louisiana; and various *Carnival* fêtes of the Caribbean.

C. Ray Brassieur

References

Carrière, Joseph Médard. 1937. *Tales from the French Folklore of Missouri.* Northwestern University Studies in the Humanities, No. 1. Evanston, IL: Northwestern University Press.

Dorrance, Ward A. 1935. *The Survival of French in the Old District of Ste. Genevieve.* University of Missouri Studies, Vol. 10, No. 2. Columbia: University of Missouri Press.

Gagnon, Ernest. 1880. La Ignolée. In *Chansons Populaire Du Canada.* 5th ed. 1908. Montreal: Beauchemin, pp. 199–200.

Postic, Fanch, and Donatien Laurent. 1986. Eginane, au gui l'an neuf? Une enigmatique quête chantée. *Armen* 1:42–56.

Primm, Wilson. 1900. New Year's Day in the Olden Time of St. Louis. *Missouri Historical Society Collections* 2:12–22.

Thomas, Rosemary Hyde. 1978. La Guillonée: A French Holiday Custom in the Mississippi Valley. *Mid-South Folklore* 6:77–83.

Gulf War

American military engagement in the Persian Gulf area during the first half of 1991. The United States was part of a multinational force opposing the August 1990 invasion of Kuwait by Iraq. Despite the short duration of the conflict, the dominant military power of the United States and its allies, and the high-tech nature of the warfare, typical wartime folklore quickly appeared.

Already in late 1990, when the United States had troops in the area as a show of force ("Operation Desert Shield"), a rumor swept the country that the Pentagon, in anticipation of bloodshed to come, had special-ordered massive numbers of caskets to be shipped to Saudi Arabia. The alleged orders escalated from an early rumor of 10,000 to 23,000 eventually to as many as 40,000 or 50,000. "Those rumors are baloney," one U.S. military spokesman said, while a Gannett News Service report in December 1990 concluded, "The casket story has bounced from sea to shining sea with enough strength for it to be nominated as an 'urban legend.'"

On January 16, 1991, President George Bush ordered active U.S. engagement in the conflict to begin ("Operation Desert Storm"), commanded by General Norman Schwarzkopf. "No war or run-up to war is complete without its tales of atrocity," an article in the *Nation* stated on February 4, 1991; the article went on to show that "the single most publicized atrocity was untrue." The story, widely repeated by politicians and the press, was that Iraqi troops entering Kuwait City had raided hospitals, removing more than 300 premature babies from incubators, which were then shipped to Baghdad. Amnesty International, at first accepting the report, inquired further after the end of the war in April 1991 and "found no reliable evidence that Iraqi forces had caused the deaths of babies" by such means or in such numbers.

A homefront horror story described an injured Gulf War veteran telephoning his parents from the hospital to ask if he might bring home a wounded comrade who was both blind and a multiple amputee. The parents said no, that this would be too much of a burden on them, so their son killed himself, since he was describing his own injuries. The vet realized that his parents would never be able to accept him again in his condition.

Many other rumors, tales, and warnings relating to the Persian Gulf War circulated by word of mouth, on radio talk shows, and over the Internet. A frequent theme was "amazing coincidences"—things that may have happened in reality but were modified and exaggerated as the tales were repeated. Typically, an American soldier opens a letter or a package of cookies addressed to "Any Soldier" and finds that it was sent by a relative of his as part of an organization's "support our troops" effort. Another common notion was that an Iraqi prisoner spoke fluent American English, wore American clothing, and was eager to be "captured," since he was a U.S. citizen who happened to be visiting relatives in Baghdad when the war broke out. A group calling itself Mothers against Saddam Hussein (MASH) warned that return addresses should be removed from discarded envelopes containing mail from home, because the enemy was collecting addresses from the trash to target American families for terrorist attacks. Stateside, yellow ribbons were widely displayed as symbols of support for our troops.

The advanced electronic weaponry employed in the Gulf War produced its own folklore, including accounts of incredible accuracy that were contradicted by other reports of failures of equipment or errors in strategy. One amusing story claimed that on an island in the Gulf that was controlled by the enemy, the Iraqis had put up wooden decoys of military vehicles and installations, hoping to fool the American bombers. Supposedly, after Air Force intelligence recognized the trick, the bombers retaliated by dropping decoy bombs onto the decoy targets.

Anti-Iraqi riddle jokes by the hundreds were circulated, picturing the enemy as inept, ill trained and poorly supplied, and hopelessly outclassed in the conflict. Some examples:

What do Hiroshima, Nagasaki, and Baghdad have in common?
Nothing, yet.

How do you get 100 Iraqis on a twenty-passenger bus?
Throw in an MRE. ("Meals ready to eat," American combat rations, disliked by our troops, but allegedly superior to anything the enemy had to eat.)

What do the Iraqis use sandpaper for?
Maps.

Why is it so easy to teach Iraqi pilots how to fly?
Because you don't have to teach them how to land.

Newspaper editorial cartoons satirizing or criticizing Saddam Hussein, Iraq's president (referred to by President Bush as "The Butcher of Baghdad"), were recopied and posted, while numerous anonymous photocopied drawings and fliers appeared. A favorite was a poster for the "Baghdad Air Show of 1991," which advertised the bombardment of the Iraqi capital as being merely an aerial firepower demonstration. One cartoon showed an American fighter jet chasing a camel-riding Hussein out of Kuwait with the caption (borrowed from a cigarette ad) "I'd fly 7,000 to Smoke a Camel." There were several variations of the "weapons versus camels" theme, including one that showed a supposed Iraqi mobile Scud missile launcher consisting of a camel with the missile in its mouth, having its testicles struck with a mallet. Another cartoon was in the form of a dart board inviting the player to choose the punishment for Saddam Hussein's war crimes; each subsection of the board offered another bizarre torture, including "Feed him to the Israelis."

Israel had agreed to remain passive in the face of missile attacks and the fear of chemical warfare from Iraq. This unaccustomed wartime role spawned numerous grim jokes, such as:

What is Israeli roulette?
Three gas masks and four people in a sealed room.

What does Scud stand for?
Saddam Comes Again Damn-it!
Hey, but Scud is spelled with a "U."
True, but Saddam doesn't know English.

What's the similarity between Scuds and married love making?
Both start at the frequency of five times a night and finish with one time every five nights.

The abrupt end of the conflict in April 1991 with the Iraqi government accepting allied surrender terms was followed by widespread charges that high-tech American weapons used in the Gulf War had not performed as perfectly as the government claimed. An aura of folklore cloaked the subject, as, for example, in NBC News commentator John Chancellor's remarks (published in the *New York Times*) that the war had created "facts misperceived, truth bent out of shape, and a fog of myth and misconception."

Jan Harold Brunvand

References

Nevo, Ofra, and Jacob Levine. 1994. Jewish Humor Strikes Again: The Outburst of Humor in Israel during the Gulf War. *Western Folklore* 53:125–146.
Santino, Jack. 1992. Yellow Ribbons and Seasonal Flags: The Folk Assemblage of War. *Journal of American Folklore* 105:19–33.
Wukasch, Charles. 1992. The Folklore of the Gulf War. *Tennessee Folklore Society Bulletin* 55:158–159.

Gummere, Francis Barton (1855–1919)

Literary theoretician, philologist, medievalist. Gummere was born in Haverford, Pennsylvania, the son of the then president of Haverford College. He received his A.B. from Haverford in 1872, and in 1875 he was awarded an A.M. from Haverford and an A.B. from Harvard College, where he had studied under Francis James Child. He then went on to study at the Universities of Strasbourg, Berlin, and Freiburg, from which he was granted a Ph.D. magna cum laude.

Though he taught for a few years at two different preparatory schools and was an instructor for the academic year 1881–1882 at Harvard, where he was a colleague of George Lyman Kittredge, he spent most of his academic career as professor of English at Haverford College (1887–1919). He was also the fifteenth president of the Modern Language Association of America.

Gummere devoted his scholarly life to the study of the origins of literature. Thoroughly indoctrinated in the methodological techniques of the German philologists, he theorized that at one time in history poetry was the product of everyman, the theory on which two of his books—*Germanic Origins* and *The Beginnings of Poetry*—are based. He became the principal proponent of the theory of communal origins for the traditional ballad, a theory based upon his understanding of the concepts promulgated by the brothers Grimm, especially those of Jacob, and by his interpretation of a statement that Gummere attributed to them, *"das Volk dichtet."* From its introduction in 1897 until the 1930s, the theory served as an often misinterpreted foundation for ballad scholarship.

W. Edson Richmond

References

Gummere, Francis Barton. 1897. The Ballad and Communal Poetry. *Child Memorial Volume, Harvard Studies and Notes in Philology*, 5:40–56.
———. 1897. *Old English Ballads*. Boston: Ginn.
———. 1903–1904. Primitive Poetry and the Ballad. *Modern Philology* 1:193 202, 217–234, 373–390.
——— 1907. *The Popular Ballad*. Boston and New York: Houghton Mifflin.

Guthrie, Woody (1912–1967)

Singer of traditional songs, songwriter, poet, novelist, artist, and a major influence in the urban folk revival, the folk-rock movement, and social-protest song writing. Born on July 14, 1912, and named after the Democratic presidential nominee Woodrow Wilson, Guthrie was the third of five children born to Charley and Nora Guthrie in Okemah, Oklahoma; his parents were a popular, prosperous couple with the prospect of a successful small business and good middle-class family life. Charley was a Texan who entered Indian Territory (now Oklahoma) as a cowboy, and Nora was the daughter of a schoolteacher who had come to the territory from Kansas. As a child, Woody heard his father sing cowboy songs and his mother play the piano and sing "old" ballads.

When Woody was approximately six years old, unforeseen and misunderstood problems hit the family with destructive force. His older sister died from burns, and his mother exhibited symptoms of Huntington's disease. However, the family, the community, and Woody's friends believed her to be losing her mind. The family slowly disintegrated. Charley lost land holdings, cattle, and other collateral, and Nora's illness intensified.

A few months before his fifteenth birthday, Woody had to become self-sufficient, for his father was severely burned and his mother was committed to the Oklahoma Hospital for the Insane, where she later died. Charley was taken to Pampa, Texas, where relatives nursed him back to health, but Woody remained in Okemah and for a few months lived in a club-

Woody Guthrie in 1943. Photo Al Aumuller for the New York World-Telegram. *Library of Congress.*

house that he and friends had built. For the next two years, he stayed with different families during the school year and hitchhiked or hoboed his way to south Texas to stay with friends during the summer. He made living money by picking up junk in back alleys, washing and polishing spittoons to pay rent on a shoe shine stand, selling newspapers, and working at other odd jobs.

In high school, Woody sang in the choir, was the "joke editor" for the school annual, and often entertained fellow students with his harmonica, his wit, and his jig-dancing skills. He was a popular student, but in 1929 at the end of his junior year in Okemah High School, Woody joined his father in Pampa. The following year, the drought and dust storms started, and they lasted through the entire decade. Even though he later became known as the "Oklahoma Dust Bowl Balladeer," it was Pampa, where he experienced his Dust Bowl years, that provided inspiration for many songs. These and subsequent events in Woody's life are described in his autobiographical novel *Bound for Glory* (1943).

While in Pampa, his uncle, Jeff Guthrie, and other friends taught Woody to play the guitar, fiddle, banjo, and mandolin; he played in a Junior Chamber of Commerce cowboy band, worked for a bootlegger, and painted signs, but mostly he played at dances and entertained with his uncle. In October 1933, he and Mary Jennings married; unfortunately for Mary, Woody was more interested in making music, writing, and traveling than in providing for a family. For a few months, Woody, Mary, and his uncle and aunt traveled with a small medicine show, but when the owner went broke they had to return to Pampa. There, in 1935, Woody wrote a few poems and parodies of popular songs that still survive as evidence of his early writing interests.

In November 1935, their first child, a daughter, was born, but Woody still had no motivation for steady work. When he made money from singing, he often gave it to someone he thought needed it more than he—his childhood experiences had instilled a compassion for the poor and downtrodden. A few months before a second daughter was born in July 1937, Woody's wanderlust drove him westward to California.

He stayed with relatives in the Los Angeles area and started playing music with his cousin, Jack Guthrie, who played a variety of stringed instruments and sang in the style of Jimmie Rodgers. Woody developed a musical style similar to the Carter Family, so he and Jack did not sing as a duo but played backup music for each other. In August 1937, Jack arranged a radio show for them over KFVD, Hollywood, and they quickly attracted a following of fans. Jack had to leave the show for work that would support his family, so Woody and Maxine "Lefty Lou" Crissman, a young lady whose family was close to Jack and had taken Woody as a friend, became a musical team. The "Woody and Lefty Lou Show" drew thousands of fan letters over a few months' time and made a little money for them.

His family joined him in California, and a few months later Woody and Lefty Lou accepted a lucrative offer to broadcast for XELO in Tijuana, Mexico. Woody's propensity for saying what he believed, often with humor, angered Mexican officials, and in a short time they were banned from Mexico. Woody returned to KFVD, where he became acquainted with a radical news commentator, Ed Robbins. Through Robbins, Woody became interested in left-wing political and social activities and attended activist meetings along with movie stars and other lesser-known individuals seeking solutions for Depression-era problems. He soon was writing a column "Woody Sez," in the style of his hero Will Rogers, for the Communist newspaper *People's World*.

During the approximately eighteen months he sang at KFVD, Woody wrote "Oklahoma Hills," "Philadelphia Lawyer," "Do, Re, Mi," "Ship in the Sky," and many other songs and became acquainted with the man who became his traveling and recording companion, Cisco Houston.

In 1939 with his actor friend Will Geer, Woody traveled to New York City, where he met Alan Lomax, Pete Seeger, and others influential in what became the urban folk revival. In 1940 Lomax invited him to Washington, DC, where Woody recorded songs for the Library of Congress, and one month later in New York City, he recorded his *Dust Bowl Ballads* for RCA Victor, later recording a few songs for smaller companies. In 1941 he and his family traveled to Portland, Oregon, where he wrote twenty-eight songs in twenty-eight days for the Bonneville Power Authority, including "Roll on, Columbia" and "Pastures of Plenty."

The early 1940s were important creative years during which Woody wrote "So Long, It's Been Good to Know You," "Tom Joad," "This Land Is Your Land," and *Bound for Glory* and started his second family with Marjorie Mazia. He sang and recorded with the Almanac Singers and appeared on numerous radio shows, such as *Pipe Smoking Time, Pursuit of Happiness, We the People, Cavalcade of America,* and *Back Where I Come From*. During this time, he and Cisco Houston joined the Merchant Marine and were on three torpedoed ships, and as World War II neared its end he was drafted into the Army, where he spent less than one year.

In 1944 Woody met Moses Asch, the founder of Asch Records and Disc Records, and started a recording friendship that lasted until 1950. During those six years, Woody recorded approximately 200 sides, possibly more, for Asch. The master recordings that survive are in the Asch/Folkways Collection now owned by the Smithsonian Institution. Not only did he record his own songs, but he also recorded numerous traditional and country songs, most of which he knew before becoming a participant in the folksong scene. He used and/or adapted melodies from this vast storehouse of songs for many of his tunes.

By 1950 Woody was showing symptoms of Huntington's disease, the genetic illness that killed his mother, and, as had happened with his parents, his personal and family life slowly disintegrated. His wandering increased as his creativity decreased, and he and Marjorie divorced. A short-lived third marriage also ended in divorce after Woody was finally hospitalized in 1955.

In his productive years, writing was an obsession with Woody, words flowed onto paper as easily as speech from his mouth—almost in a stream-of-consciousness style. His prose, poems, and song lyrics were laced with humor and vivid description. When he was inspired, or occasionally was paid, to write about a topic, an event, or a person, he would sit at the typewriter for hours, writing until all thoughts and inspiration were on paper, and usually a body of songs or poems would be written. His inspiration might come from a newspaper article, a movie, a conversation, or just from observing people.

Equal to his obsession with writing, Woody was a voracious reader who wrote his interpretations, reactions, and beliefs in the margins of the books he read. From the Okemah Public Library to the New York City Public Library, wherever he went, he obtained books to read. He knew world and U.S.

history; he knew the theories of political and economic science; and he knew the Bible extremely well. He was capable of adjusting his grammar and speech to please the individual or crowd to whom he was speaking, but he always preferred to play the role of the "Grapes of Wrath Okie."

He wrote well over 1,000 songs—songs that document the Dust Bowl decade and problems confronted by migrant agriculture workers, children's songs, peace and war songs, cowboy and hobo songs, union and work songs, and love songs; and during his short creative period of approximately fifteen years, he also wrote three novels, short stories, newspaper columns, magazine articles, and hundreds of letters and drew hundreds of illustrations for his songs and books. After approximately thirteen years of hospitalization, Woody Guthrie died on October 3, 1967.

During his hospitalization and following his death, fame and recognition grew through numerous musical tributes to him and through the efforts of Pete Seeger, who usually included a Guthrie song in his concerts. Marjorie Guthrie, his second wife (although divorced from him) lectured about and lobbied for Huntington's disease research, making Woody an international symbol of the effects of the disease. Arlo Guthrie, the older son born to Woody and Marjorie, also gained fame as a folk and topical singer/songwriter with his satirical "Alice's Restaurant" and his rendition of Steve Goodman's "The City of New Orleans"; he also includes songs by his father in his concerts and recordings, and he and Pete Seeger have given numerous concerts and recorded together and have appeared at many Woody Guthrie tributes. Woody Guthrie's reputation as a multitalented, creative man continues to grow long after his death.

Guy Logsdon

References

Guthrie, Woody. 1976. *Seeds of Man: An Experience Lived and Dreamed.* New York: Dutton.

———. 1988. *"Roll on, Columbia:" The Columbia River Songs,* ed. Bill Murlin. Portland, OR: Bonneville Power Administration.

———. 1990. *Pastures of Plenty: A Self-Portrait,* ed. David Marsh and Harold Leventhal. New York: Harper Collins.

———. 1992. *Woody Guthrie Songs,* ed. Judy Bell and Nora Guthrie. New York: TRO Ludlow Music.

Klein, Joe. 1980. *Woody Guthrie: A Life.* New York: Alfred Knopf.

WOODY GUTHRIE RECORDINGS

Guthrie, Woody. 1940. *Library of Congress Recordings.* Issued in 1964 by Elektra Records EKL-271/272, with Notes by Alan Lomax, Robert Shelton, and Woody Guthrie. Sound Recordings. Reissued in 1988 by Rounder Records 1041/2/3. Compact Discs/Cassette Tapes.

———. 1940. *Dust Bowl Ballads.* Victor Records P–27 and P–28. Sound Recordings. Reissued in 1964 by RCA Victor LPV–502. Reissued in 1988 by Rounder Records 1040. Compact Disc/Cassette Tape.

———. 1994. *Long Ways to Travel: The Unreleased Folkways Masters, 1944–1949,* comp. Jeff Place and Guy Logsdon, annotated by Guy Logsdon. Smithsonian/ Folkways Recordings SF 40046. Compact Disc/Cassette Tape.

Gypsies

A popular misnomer (derived from "Egyptian") referring to an ethnic group of Indian origin numbering more than one million in the United States and about ten million worldwide. Linguistic observation in late-18th-century Europe led to the discovery of the Gypsies' Indian roots. North American Gypsy populations all speak some form of Romani, an Indian language similar to Sanskrit with overlays from Persian, Armenian, Byzantine Greek, South Slavic, Romanian, and several Romance languages. Gypsies call themselves *Rom* or *Roma* and those outside their own ethnic group *gazhe* or some variant of the term. Comprised of several subgroups with distinct histories, the *Roma* share a core culture consisting of the Romani language and an intuited cosmology of structural oppositions (God/devil, good/evil, purity/pollution, *Roma/gazhe*). This worldview informs many Romani traditions, particularly a strict boundary maintenance between *Roma* and *gazhe*.

After their departure from India (sometime before A.D. 900), the *Roma* dispersed into many countries, where they were generally feared, persecuted, or executed because of their unfamiliar appearance, language, customs, and religious beliefs. Records documenting their arrival in eastern Europe in the Middle Ages emphasize the *Roma's* dark hair and complexion as symbolic of incarnate evil. They often suffered when Christians misidentified them as Muslims, especially during the late medieval period when Christendom was threatened by Islamic invaders.

Paradoxically, while the *Roma* were frequently persecuted as unbelievers in Christian countries, they were often forced to worship outside the established church when they became Christians. In much of Europe, Gypsies were prohibited from entering Catholic churches until the late 19th century. At the close of the 20th century, many *Roma* in the United States are folk Catholics, practicing a syncretistic religion that draws some (more ancient) elements from Zoroastrianism and Hinduism (such as animal sacrifice, herbal healing, use of household shrines) and others from Eastern Orthodox Catholicism (such as monotheism, belief in the efficacy of prayer and the saints' intercession, and celebration of the saints' days and festivals of the Eastern Orthodox calendar). Several thousand North American *Roma* have joined the significant Romani evangelical movement and consider themselves "born-again" Christians.

In the 1990s, the *Roma* are a little-known group in the Americas but constitute the largest non-White minority in Europe. In each European country where a Romani group has settled without the recent threat of expulsion or extermination (such as France, Spain, and the British Isles), their language and culture have altered under the influence of those of the host nation. In Great Britain, they are called Romanichals and speak Anglo-Romani (which retains much of the lexicon but little of the grammar and syntax of earlier Romani). In Spain they are known as Gitanos and speak Caló. Romani subgroups have developed distinct identities, and representatives of those European populations have emigrated to the Americas at different times for varying reasons. In the United States, scholars have focused on one such Romani subgroup: the Kalderash (Russian Coppersmiths). Ancestors of American Kalderash lived in Russia until the late 19th and early 20th centuries, and, as a result, Kalderash Romani contains many Russian and Slavic loan words and combining forms.

Linguistic assimilation is probably the least oppressive of the negative forces that the *Roma* have historically endured. Throughout their millennium-long diaspora, they have withstood not simply marginalization (perhaps in part a natural result of their own cultural prohibitions on interaction with outsiders), but also persecution and even genocide. They were enslaved for more than 500 years (until 1864) in the Balkans, and more than half a million were exterminated in the Nazi regime's Final Solution. While Romani-Americans do not suffer the intense persecution apparently endemic to many European countries, they face widespread stereotyping and prejudice. Organizations active in combating persecution of *Roma* include the International Romani Union (which sends a delegate to the United Nations) and the Romani Congress. After then Prime Minister Indira Gandhi officially recognized the *Roma* as an expatriate Indian population, the Indian government was able to assist in financing the first world Romani Congress, which was held in 1971 and included several Indian delegates.

As the stereotypical "Gypsies," the Romani people have inspired a huge body of expressive culture and oral tradition. The word "Gypsy" has developed into a synonym for a range of stock characters and fanciful beings of American folklore and popular culture: the clever trickster, the happy-go-lucky vagabond, the irresponsible itinerant, the mysterious soothsayer, and the picturesque free spirit. Elite and popular art, literature, and music—from the Victorian era to modern-day Hollywood—have used the Gypsies collectively as a convenient vehicle for fantasies of freedom, escape, and licentiousness.

While the Gypsies of folk and popular culture are largely irrelevant to actual North American Romani life, one point of intersection is fortune-telling, still a source of livelihood for some Romani-American families who make solid commercial use of their secure traditional identity as psychics, astrologers, palm readers, and Tarot-card readers. An outstanding example of the successful marketing of expressive culture, this ubiquitous element of the colorful stereotype of Gypsy life is likely to endure for another thousand years in spite of frequent legal and religious prohibition. Fortune-telling—like other exoteric entertainment functions of the Gypsies—is rooted in the *Roma*'s proficiency in absorbing, transporting, and marketing folk and popular culture throughout their history. Various Romani groups possess rich oral-performance traditions not limited to their skills in fortune-telling: Folk and popular music, folktales, myths, legends, proverbs, riddles, jokes, memorates, and other folkloric forms have been observed in contemporary Romani performance tradition in Europe and North America.

Over the centuries, the *Roma* have survived through fortune-telling and other forms of entertainment, agricultural work, metalwork and munitions manufacture, horse trading, and other similarly portable, flexible occupations. Many modern-day Romani-Americans pursue careers in industry and the professions, while others have selected more traditional means of livelihood such as fortune-telling; auto-body and fender repair, boiler repair, re-tinning, copper-plating, metal recycling, and other metalwork; and used-car sales (perhaps a descendant of horse trading). Many of the older generation of Romani-Americans were once migrant agricultural workers, a form of livelihood still common to the Romani population in the British Isles but rare among *Roma* in the United States in the 1990s.

Romanologists disagree as to when and why the *Roma* left India. Until recently, the predominant hypothesis identified modern-day *Roma* as descendants of 10,000 Luri musicians given to the ruler of Persia by his brother, the sovereign of India, in A.D. 439. However, recent research in India itself has exposed evidence that the *Roma*'s exodus from India may have occurred somewhat later, perhaps in the 8th or 9th century. According to this theory—promulgated at first by a few scholars but now gaining more extensive acceptance—the Indian forbears of modern-day Roma were a group of Rajput warriors and their camp followers who moved westward into Persia for reasons associated with the Indo-Persian wars and later, instead of returning to India, continued traveling farther and farther west.

Ruth E. Andersen

References

Acton, Thomas. 1974. *Gypsy Politics and Social Change.* London: Routledge and Kegan Paul.

Frazer, Angus. 1993. *The Gypsies.* Oxford: Basil Blackwell.

Gropper, Rena C. 1975. *Gypsies in the City: Culture Patterns and Survival.* Princeton, NJ: Darwin Press.

Hancock, Ian F. [1981] 1985. *Land of Pain: Five Centuries of Gypsy Slavery.* Ann Arbor, MI: Karoma.

———. 1987. *The Pariah Syndrome: An Account of Gypsy Slavery and Persecution.* Ann Arbor, MI: Karoma.

Kenrick, Donald, and Grattan Puxon. 1972. *The Destiny of Europe's Gypsies.* New York: Basic Books.

Sutherland, Anne. 1975. *Gypsies: The Hidden Americans.* New York: Macmillan.

Tong, Diane. 1989. *Gypsy Folktales.* New York: Harcourt Brace Jovanovich.

Yoors, Jan. 1967. *The Gypsies.* New York: Simon and Schuster.

H

Halloween

October 31, the eve of the Christian feast of All Saints, or All Hallows, which is November 1. The day is known also as All Hallows' Eve, the Eve of All Saints' Day, All Hallow Even, or Hallowe'en; the terms "mischief night," "cabbage night," and "devils' night" are sometimes associated with the holiday.

May 13 had been established as a feast for St. Mary and the Martyrs by Pope Boniface IV in A.D. 610, in order to honor all Christians who had died for their faith but were not officially recognized. In A.D. 731, All Saints' Day was established on November 1 by Pope Gregory III. The evening prior to the feast, the Eve of All Hallows, or All Hallow Even, has become known as Hallowe'en or Halloween. Many scholars have noted the apparent continuity of traditions with the ancient Celtic quarter day known as Samhain, November 1, and have suggested that the church fathers were attempting to redirect the religious devotion of that day toward a Christian feast while redefining the customary behavior in a Christian context. This would account for the continuity of activities such as mumming (performing, often in costume, in return for gifts of food and drink,) along with the belief that the evening was a time of wandering spirits.

Samhain (pronounced Sah-win) was the first day of both winter and the Celtic New Year and was also a time for the souls of the dead to pass into the otherworld. Little is actually known of Samhain; it is referred to in Irish sagas written down between the 9th and 12th centuries, hundreds of years after the times to which they refer. Although oral versions of these narratives would certainly have been much older than these sources, the written narratives are not contemporaneous with the festival itself. According to these sagas, Samhain is the principal festival of the four quarter days, each of which begins a new season. Dead souls were believed to be traveling; people left offerings for them; bonfires were lit; and, eventually, mumming traditions developed. Around A.D. 1006, the church declared November 2 as All Souls' Day. This day is in recognition of the souls of all of the faithful departed who had died during the previous year. In this way, it is closer in spirit to the Celtic Samhain than is All Saints' Day.

Through its missionaries, the church also redefined the beliefs along with the rituals and practices of the peoples it converted. The spirits associated with Samhain, once thought to be wild and powerful, were now taught to be something worse: They were evil. The church maintained that the gods and goddesses and other spiritual beings of traditional religions were diabolical deceptions, that the spiritual forces that people had experienced were real but were manifestations of the devil, the Prince of Liars, who misled people toward the worship of false idols. Thus, the customs associated with All Hallows Eve included representations of ghosts and human skeletons—symbols of the dead—and also of the devil and other creatures said to be malevolent and evil. A direct link between Samhain and Halloween has never been demonstrated, however, and is disputed by some scholars.

Marginal, supernatural creatures such as fairies and witches have been associated with Halloween over the centuries. The traditional British ballad "Tam Lin" (Child 39) gives a detailed account of the belief in the great fairy rides on Halloween, while the day is said by many to be the highest feast day of the year for witches. The association of Halloween with the souls of the dead continues to be very strong. In parts of Ireland in the late 20th century, Halloween is thought to be a night when the spirits of departed ancestors return and visit their households. Frequently, people leave their hearth burning and set out plates of food or drink.

As a seasonal turning point, Halloween has always been related to the agricultural and pastoral cycles as well. By this date, crops should be harvested and livestock brought in from pasture. The seasonal and organic relationships are manifested in the frequent uses of apples, nuts, and turnips (pumpkins in North America) in the games and rituals associated with Halloween. Many of these reflect the day's liminal status as an annual and seasonal day of transition, in which barriers between this world and the world of spirits are lifted. Often, the games are divinatory in nature. For instance, in one popular game, nuts are named for two individuals and set near a hearth

"THE PUMPKIN EFFIGY."—[DRAWN BY L. W. ATWATER.]

"The Pumpkin Effigy." Engraving, after a drawing by L.W. Atwater. Harper's Weekly, *23 November 1867. Library of Congress.*

where they are "burned," or heated by the flame. If the nuts crack and explode, the couple cannot expect a long or happy relationship. If the nuts roast quietly, the opposite is true. In other divinatory rituals, apples are used to foretell future spouses. Such games are many, and frequently involve the use of an edible item, harvested at about this time of year, to foretell the future. In fact, the connection between harvested fruits and nuts and Halloween is so strong that Halloween is often called Nutcrack Night in Ireland.

Other games and customs also are divinatory. In some it is said that the participants call forth the devil for knowledge of the future. More often than not, these events provide the subject matter for frightening stories told among family and friends at Halloween. In all of this can be seen the combining of various elements associated with Halloween: ideas of spirits and other supernatural beings roaming, the association of these with evil in the Christian era, the use of harvest symbolism, along with traditions of food, stories, bonfires (fireworks in Northern Ireland), and other family and community gatherings. In addition to all of these, possibly inspired by beliefs in malevolent beings lurking about, or perhaps due to the liminality of the day, pranking has long been a part of Halloween activities. In Ireland, these are done usually for several weeks in advance of Halloween, as is Halloween rhyming (begging for fruit or money, like pranking done by children). Halloween night itself is usually given over to family celebrations.

Halloween beliefs and customs were brought to North America with the earliest Irish immigrants, first the Ulster Protestants, commonly referred to as Scots-Irish, then by the great waves of Irish immigrants fleeing the famines of the first half of the 19th century. Known in the North American continent since colonial days, by the middle of the 20th century Halloween had become largely a children's holiday. More recently, however, Halloween has grown dramatically in popularity in the United States. Adults have begun celebrating it in great numbers with masquerade parties, elaborately decorated houses and yards, campus festivities, and urban street celebrations all around the country. As a large-scale, outdoor, costumed adult street festival, Halloween has become reminiscent of Carnival and Mardi Gras. Both the street festivals and the assemblages of symbolic elements used to decorate houses and commercial establishments, however, are consistent with Halloween tradition and history. Harvest images such as jack-o-lanterns are seen alongside personifications of death, such as ghosts and skeletons, and evil, such as devils and witches. Alongside the manifestations of ancient fears are representations of contemporary monsters and plagues as well, drawn from popular entertainments, politics, and current events.

Although Halloween is not a national holiday in the United States, it is widely celebrated. Different groups perceive it in different ways, and many people are uncomfortable with its imagery of devils, witches, and demons. Others see this as merely playful, while still others see these images as reflecting a history of suppression and distortion of non-Christian religious practices. In spite of its controversial nature, Halloween has grown to become second only to Christmas as a major annual participatory festival. Despite its connection with the church calendar as the eve of All Saints' Day, many people believe Halloween to be nondenominational in nature. Despite the vast quantities of advertising and commerce surrounding it, many also believe that Halloween is noncommercialized. It is celebrated at the end of the 20th century as a time when threatening images and ideas are paraded and parodied, when taboo behavior is tolerated and even encouraged. Halloween in America is a festival of inversion that still speaks not only of death but of contemporary life as well.

Jack Santino

References

Babbatyne, Leslie Pratt. 1990. *Halloween: An American Holiday, An American History.* New York: Facts on File.

Linton, Ralph, and Adele Linton. 1950. *Halloween through Twenty Centuries.* New York: Henry Schuman.

Santino, Jack. 1994. *All around the Year: Holidays and Celebrations in American Life.* Urbana: University of Illinois Press.

———. 1994. *Halloween and Other Festivals of Death and Life.* Knoxville: University of Tennessee Press.

Hand, Wayland D. (1907–1986)

Folklorist and Germanist. Born on March 19, 1907, in Auckland, New Zealand, where his parents had immigrated, Hand returned as a young child with them to the United States and eventually settled in Utah, where he spent his early years. After graduating from high school, Hand went in 1927 on a Mormon mission to Germany, where he remained for almost three years, developed an interest in German literature and culture, and became fluent in German. After his return, he studied German at the University of Utah, from which he received his B.A. in 1933 and his M.A. in 1934. He then went to the University of Chicago, where he earned his Ph.D. under Archer Taylor with a thesis *The Schnaderhüpfel: An Alpine Folk Lyric,* which was published by the University of Chicago Press in 1936.

After teaching German for one year at the University of Minnesota, Hand joined the faculty of German Languages at UCLA, where he remained for the remainder of his career and where he developed an interdepartmental teaching program and research institute in folklore—the Center for the Study of Comparative Folklore and Mythology. He also built up the folklore collection in the University Research Library to become the best of its kind in the world. In 1941, together with Archer Taylor, he founded the California Folklore Society. From 1947 to 1951, he was editor of the *Journal of American Folklore* and later assumed the same position for *Western Folklore* (1954–1966). He was president of the American Folklore Society from 1957 to 1958 and of the California Folklore Society from 1969 to 1970.

Hand conducted field research among miners in Montana, Utah, and California, publishing his findings in a series of articles from 1941 to 1946. He also published a *Dictionary of Words and Idioms Associated with Judas Iscariot* (1942). In addition, he authored many articles on such wide-ranging topics as the Mormon legends of the three Nephites, German proverbs in Los Angeles, folksongs, and folk customs. However, it was in the area of popular belief and superstition in which Hand made his greatest and lasting impact. Assembling materials collected from the field and culled from thousands of publications, both scholarly, ephemeral, and popular, he compiled the UCLA Archive of Popular Beliefs and Superstition. Hand's classification system developed through the years formed the basis of his edited works, including the two-volume *Popular Beliefs and Superstitions from North Carolina* (1961–1964), the three-volume *Popular Beliefs and Superstitions: A Compendium of American Folklore from the Ohio Collection of Newbell Niles Puckett* (1981), and *Popular Beliefs and Superstitions from the Anthon S. Cannon Collection of* [Utah] *Folklore* (1984). Hand's system became the model upon which archives of belief materials have been arranged around the world. For the North Carolina collection, he was awarded the Giuseppi Pitrè International Folklore Prize in 1965. In 1972 the government of Finland inducted him as a Knight First Class in the Order of the Lion.

Hand also published extensively on the related topic of folk medical practices, calling the attention of scholars to such practices as "crossing water," "measuring," "magical divestment and transference of disease," "passing through," "plugging," and healing with the "dead man's hand." Most of these essays and others were compiled in a single volume, edited by Hand, titled *Magical Medicine* (1980).

On October 22, 1986, while changing planes in Pittsburgh on a trip from Detroit, where he was enlisting help for his projected *Encyclopedia of American Popular Belief and Superstition,* to Baltimore, where he was to participate in the annual meeting of the American Folklore Society, Hand died of sudden cardiac arrest. His UCLA coworkers are continuing work on his *Encyclopedia.*

Donald J. Ward

Handcox, John L. (1904–1992)

African American songwriter, poet, and organizer for the Southern Tenant Farmers Union (STFU) in Arkansas and Missouri in 1936–1937. In the spring of 1936, having escaped from a possible lynching in eastern Arkansas for his efforts in organizing sharecroppers and farm workers who were being evicted from their homes, Handcox wrote "We're Gonna Roll the Union on" and "There Is Mean Things Happening in This Land." During this time, he became known as "The Sharecropper Troubadour" (Mitchell 1979). In March 1937, while on a fund-raising tour for the Socialist Party in the Northeast, Handcox recorded eight songs and poems at the Library of Congress (Library of Congress Recording AFS 32/37–39). His songs have frequently been published in anthologies of American folk music. "Raggedy, Raggedy Are We" was popular at STFU meetings, and "Roll the Union on" remains a popular song at union meetings and on picket lines.

Handcox moved to Oklahoma in 1937 and then to San Diego, California, in 1942, working primarily as a carpenter and having no contact with union activists, although Pete Seeger had tried to locate him. Reunited with his old friends in 1980, Handcox resumed his writing and performing of poems and songs about labor issues. He performed in Washington, DC, every year from 1980 to 1991, as well as at fes-

tivals and gatherings in other locations. In 1985 he was interviewed at the Library of Congress on his labor activities and his music (AFS 241111). In 1989 the Labor Heritage Foundation gave the first annual Joe Hill Award to Handcox for his contributions to labor.

Donald M. Lance

References

Mitchell, H.L. 1979. *Mean Things Happening in This Land: The Life and Times of H.L. Mitchell, Cofounder of the Southern Tenant Farmers Union.* Montclair, NJ: Allenheld, Osmun.

Schroeder, Rebecca B., and Donald M. Lance. 1993. John L. Handcox: "There Is Still Mean Things Happening." In *Songs about Work: Essays in Occupational Culture for Richard A. Reuss,* ed. Archie Green. Special Publications of the Folklore Institute, No. 3. Bloomington: Indiana University Press.

Handy, W.C. (1873–1958)

Popularizer of blues, sometimes called "Father of the Blues." Although an enormously important figure in the history of American music, William Christopher Handy's full career has never been investigated objectively, and his own statements and writings are the main sources of information. Handy helped develop his own legend, and his accounts sometimes differ in detail or are not entirely congruent with data from other sources.

Handy was born and raised in Florence, Alabama, the son and grandson of Methodist ministers. Although he grew up in the midst of African American folk music, he initially rejected it to pursue the formal study of music and a career in popular music. During the late 1890s, he was leader and cornet player in a minstrel band that traveled in the United States, Mexico, and Cuba. Around 1903 he took a position as leader of a band associated with a Black fraternal organization in Clarksdale, Mississippi. There he turned his attention to folk music, especially the new blues form, after observing its growing popularity in the Delta region. By 1907 Handy had a similar position as band leader in Memphis. His band was hired in support of the 1909 mayoral campaign of E.H. Crump, during which it introduced an arrangement of a folk tune called "Mister Crump." Handy added blues strains to this tune and published it in 1912 as "The Memphis Blues," the first song to use the word "blues" in its title. This was followed by the publication of "Jogo Blues," "St. Louis Blues," "Yellow Dog Blues," "Joe Turner Blues," "The Hesitating Blues," "Beale Street Blues," "Loveless Love," and others, all of which drew material and inspiration from folk-music sources.

In 1917 Handy made his first commercial recordings as a band leader, and he continued to record sporadically through the 1930s. In 1918 he moved to New York City, where he increasingly concentrated his activities on music publishing and solidifying his reputation through public appearances, writings, and collaborations. Beginning in the 1920s, Handy gradually shifted his attention to the publication of his arrangements of Negro spirituals, also treating African and Latin

W.C. Handy in 1941. Photo Carl Van Vechten. Library of Congress.

American themes and creating works of "serious" music with various collaborators. He was honored during his lifetime with the dedication of a park in his name on Beale Street in Memphis in 1933 and the erection of a statue there after his death.

In the 1920s Handy was interviewed by folklorist Dorothy Scarborough as her main authority on the origins and meaning of the blues. Handy published an anthology of his own and other songwriters' blues compositions (Handy 1926), later revised and expanded. He also published a survey of Negro composers (Handy 1938) and his autobiography. Over the years, he collaborated with many prominent musical, artistic, literary, and business figures and was a leading participant in the Harlem Renaissance of the 1920s. Handy is significant as a great composer who recognized and utilized folk traditions and as the first major popularizer of the blues. Throughout his career, he upheld and defended the dignity of African American folk music and did much to promote the works of its purveyors and popularizers.

David Evans

References

Handy, W.C. 1926. *Blues: An Anthology*, with Introduction and Notes by Abbe Niles. New York: A. and C. Boni. rev. ed. 1949. *A Treasury of the Blues*. New York:

Charles Boni.

——. 1938. *Negro Authors and Composers of the United States*. New York: Handy Brothers Music.

———. 1941. *Father of the Blues*, ed. Arna Bontemps. New York: Macmillan.

———. 1980. *Father of the Blues: A Musical Autobiography*. DRG SL 5192. Sound Recording.

Harris, Joel Chandler (1848?–1908)

Author best known for his collections of tales told by Uncle Remus. Harris is arguably one of the earliest and most significant collectors of African American folktales. His Uncle Remus works exemplified and helped popularize American folklore at the time when Americans began to organize scholarly folklore societies.

Harris grew up in poverty in Georgia. From 1862 to 1866, he worked as a printer's apprentice on a nearby plantation. After the Civil War, he worked as a typesetter and editor for newspapers in Macon, Forsyth, and Savannah. In 1876, fleeing a yellow fever epidemic in Savannah, Harris moved his family to Atlanta, where he accepted a job as associate editor of the *Constitution*. He stayed with that newspaper until he retired in 1900.

Although he worked daily for the newspaper, Harris is best remembered for his other writing. He wrote a wide range of works, from historical romances to children's stories. The most significant for both folklore and literature are those African American folktales in the Uncle Remus collections. From 1876 to 1879, Harris created a series of humorous sketches for the *Constitution*. Their success began with the development of the character of Uncle Remus—especially his past on the plantation—in "Uncle Remus as a Rebel," later revised and reprinted as "A Story of the War." In 1879 Harris returned Remus to the plantation and had him tell stories to the young son of the plantation's owners. Those animal tales, about Brer Rabbit, Brer Fox, and the other animals, were so popular that Harris collected these newspaper columns and published them in *Uncle Remus: His Songs and Sayings* ([1880] 1881). Harris wrote in the Introduction that the tales were not his own but were recollected from his youth on the plantation and verified as still in oral circulation. American folklorists, struggling to describe what American folklore was and why it was important, quickly recognized the book's value.

Harris followed this collection with others in 1883, 1889, 1892, 1905, and 1907, with posthumous volumes appearing in 1910, 1918, and 1948. He was careful to distinguish folktales—those still in oral circulation—from others. The folktales became Uncle Remus tales; other narratives were used in different ways, some of them appearing in his Thimblefinger Series of children's books. Harris did not write only of middle Georgia or African American culture either. He published a number of books with stories about north Georgia "crackers," for instance, and Remus swaps tales with storytellers from other regions and traditions, including several who tell their tales in gullah.

Harris insisted that he was only a "cornfield journalist,"

Joel Chandler Harris, sitting on the front porch of his home, Wren's Nest, in 1900. Library of Congress.

but he was hardly naive about folklore. He was a member of the (English) Folk-Lore Society and a charter member of the American Folklore Society in 1888. His Introduction to *Nights with Uncle Remus* (1883) proved that he had read widely in folktale scholarship and knew the issues of the day. He had quit the American Folklore Society by 1892, however, apparently rebuffed by its leaders' call for "scientific" study.

Harris also edited several popular collections that remain valuable records, especially *American Wit and Humour* (1907) and the seventeen-volume *Library of Southern Literature* (1909–1923). He was one of many American writers who have utilized folklore in their work. Harris had a profound impact because his Uncle Remus works exemplified to a wider culture exactly what American folklore was, how it was transmitted, and why it was important to record.

Eric L. Montenyohl

References

Baer, Florence. 1980. *Sources and Analogues of the Uncle Remus Tales.* Folklore Fellows Communications No. 228. Helsinki: Suomalainen Tiedeakatemia.

Bickley, R. Bruce. 1978. *Joel Chandler Harris: A Reference Guide.* Boston: G.K. Hall.

———. 1987. *Joel Chandler Harris.* Athens: University of Georgia Press.

Henry, John

Legendary African American folk hero, renowned mostly in song for competing with a steam hammer in laying railroad track. John Henry should not be confused with John, also the hero of many African American tales called the "Old Marster and John tales."

Origins of the John Henry legend are often linked to the Big Bend Tunnel built in West Virginia in the early 1870s. Despite meticulous research, scholars have given up hope of determining the truth of John Henry's exploits. Most folklorists now agree that the impact of the tale—a Black workingman defeating a modern machine—lies in the fact that the story can be proved neither true nor false. Any truth has been obscured by the reality of Black laborers in the South, born slaves or into a South struggling against Reconstruction. Antebellum naming practices would have given John Henry either no last name or the last name of his former owner. Research by Guy Benton Johnson found at least eleven John Henrys and reason to believe there were many more (Johnson 1929:12).

Tunneling—the setting for the John Henry story—is, of course, hard, demanding, and dangerous work. At the time, the Big Bend Tunnel was the longest of its kind, and it stretched beyond the limits of what safety and technological measures would have been available. Tunnels were hot and dusty; miners died from silicosis, heat prostration, rock slides, premature blasts, or even from sheer exhaustion. The most dangerous work was at the heading, where a small section was cut out in order either to cut down the remaining rock or to blast it out with explosives. John Henry was said to be a driver, one who pounded steel drills into the rock face in order to bore the holes for the explosives. The "shaker" named in many versions of the John Henry narratives was the man who held the steel drill—a steel rod a little larger than an inch in diameter and anywhere from 2 to 14 feet in length. The shaker's job was to turn and shake the drill to keep its cutting edge clear. Keeping a rhythm with the man who was swinging a 40-pound block of steel at him was extremely important; thus, the song about John Henry was an integral part of the songs a worker like John Henry most likely would have sung himself, and vice versa.

Most John Henry narratives, whether in story or song, contain at least these ingredients: his infant prophecy, his love for a woman, his test against the machine, his victory, and his death. Of course, not every instance must contain all of these parts, nor must it limit itself to them. Another common aspect is the formal style of most of the songs, which have the last line of each verse repeated, as in this stanza:

John Henry said to his Captain,
"A man ain't nothin' but a man,
And before I'll let your steam drill beat me down,
I'll die with this hammer in my hand, Lord, Lord,
I'll die with this hammer in my hand."

The focal point of the John Henry story is the contest between man and machine, in which the man wins but dies from exhaustion. Contests between drivers were common, and it seems only logical that the idea, if not in fact at least in fiction, be extended to the products of the Industrial Revolution. There is no record of any such race ever having taken place, but drill manufacturers were pressing their machines into operation everywhere, challenging the work forces of skilled laborers. Such a concern with technology explains not only the rapid spread of the ballad across geographic and racial distances, but also its recurring popularity and significance for contemporary audiences.

John Laudun

References

Johnson, Guy B. 1929. *John Henry: Tracking Down a Negro Legend.* Chapel Hill: University of North Carolina Press.

Lead Belly (Huddie Ledbetter). *Shout On.* Folkways Records FT 31030. Washington, DC: Smithsonian Institution.

Williams, Brett. 1983. *John Henry: A Bio-Bibliography.* Westport, CT: Greenwood.

Henry, Lorenzo ("Len") (1852?–1946)

North Idaho tall-tale teller; regional Münchhausen figure. Although he was described in his obituary in the Lewiston *Idaho Morning Tribune* as "a great storyteller," only four short examples of Henry's tales were published the year following his death. His repertoire of "windies" survived in oral tradition of the area until collected in the early 1960s by Jan Harold Brunvand and his students at the University of Idaho. One hundred sixteen versions of sixty-seven distinct stories were told to the fieldworkers by twenty-eight informants. The tales either matched well-known traditional types and motifs (about half of the stories) or came from Henry's creative imagination working with frontier themes like hunting, fishing, and farming. Typical of Münchhausen narrators, Henry told his lies in the first person, developing the persona of a trickster and skilled outdoorsman.

Little is known of Henry's life except that his family originated from Pennsylvania German stock, that he was probably born in Kansas City, that he migrated to Idaho in the 1860s, and that he had married a Nez Perce woman and moved to Indian land near Lapwai and Sweetwater, Idaho, in the 1890s. As a "Squawman," Henry may have been the object of scorn, but his skills as a narrator overcame the stigma, and he was remembered by former neighbors and friends as a likeable, entertaining, quick-witted person. One informant remarked that Len could tell stories "anytime, anyplace, anywhere"; another commented, "He always had something, no matter what you brought up . . . and later on he'd tell the same story exactly the same way" (Brunvand 1985).

More likely, however, Henry, like other tall-tale tellers, adapted the style and content of his stories to different audiences. For example, the story about his dog getting stuck on a curve of a winding mountain road after Henry had guided a large horse-drawn wagon along the same route without difficulty was told by several informants, each asserting that he or she was repeating the tale exactly as Henry told it. But details differed among narrators as to the number of horses, the kind of dog, where the wagon was going, and how Henry rescued his stuck dog

Henry was best known for such familiar tales as "The Frozen Echo," "The Popcorn Freeze," "The Sprouting Buggy Whip," "The Snake-Bit Hoe Handle," and "The Wonderful Hunt" (Tale Type 1890). His other stories bragged up his own abilities as a rider, roper, or shooter. (He once bought just two rifle shells, commenting, "Your damn game laws only allow me one deer and one elk"; and he claimed that he had shot a horse that was falling down a cliff, to put the creature out of its misery, seven times before it hit the ground—using his six-shooter!)

One anecdote about Henry's quick wit reveals adaptive borrowing of a motif. He was watching someone tune a car engine one time, and he accidentally put his hand on a spark-plug of the running engine. He pulled his hand quickly away, and the man asked, "Did it shock you, Len?" The storyteller replied, "Nope, I was too quick for it." The remark is an updating of the punch line of a traditional story about a man who picks up a hot horseshoe, drops it at once, and claims, "It just don't take me long to look at a horseshoe" (Brunvand 1987).

Jan Harold Brunvand

References

Brunvand, Jan Harold. 1985. Len Henry: North Idaho Münchausen. In *Idaho Folklife: Homesteads to Headstones*, ed. Louie W. Attebery. Salt Lake City: University of Utah Press, pp. 120–128.

———. 1987. The Looking-at-a-Horseshoe Catch-Phrase. *Indiana Folklore and Oral History* 16:61–63.

Dorson, Richard M. 1982. Len Henry. In *Man and Beast in American Comic Legend*. Bloomington: Indiana University Press, pp. 139–143.

Henry, Mellinger Edward (1873–1946)

Collector of American folksong and balladry, teacher of English, and avid outdoorsman. Henry was born in 1873 at Mount Pleasant, Pennsylvania. He graduated from Brown University in the class of 1899 and pursued additional studies at Harvard and Columbia Universities. From 1906 until 1937, he taught high-school English in Patterson and Jersey City, New Jersey. On August 3, 1921, Henry was married to Florence Stokes of Atlanta, Georgia.

The Henrys were vacationing in the North Carolina mountains in 1923 when they attended a lecture on balladry given by Prof. C. Alphonso Smith. Inspired, they soon began collecting songs from people they met during their regular summer trips to the Blue Ridge and Great Smoky Mountains. Henry took down the words to songs (and later concerned himself with researching variants and sources), while Florence Henry, being musically trained, was able to notate the tunes.

Once the nucleus of a collection was established, Henry sought to put the materials into perspective by corresponding with other folksong scholars. Among those offering encouragement and information were George Lyman Kittredge, Robert Winslow Gordon, Fannie Hardy Eckstorm, Louise Pound, Arthur Palmer Hudson, Guy Benton Johnson, and Mary O. Eddy.

Although Henry was interested in the literary aspects of ballad poetry and the effects of oral transmission, he was more than an armchair scholar. His enthusiasm for song collecting was second only to his passion for hiking and mountain climbing, and he belonged to numerous mountain clubs in the East. Through editorials, articles, and lectures, he encouraged the opening of the Blue Ridge Mountain region for vacationers through the creation of trail networks for hikers and climbers. He admired, and felt an affinity with, many of his informants whom he perceived as living the outdoor life. Ironically, as the National Park Service began to take an interest in the region, several of Henry's singer-informants found themselves forced to sell their land and relocate as a result of the establishment of the Great Smoky Mountains National Park in the 1920s.

Henry was a founding member of the Southeastern Folklore Society and took an active role in festivals, including the White Top Folk Festival in southwest Virginia.

In 1931 and 1932, a substantial portion of the Henrys' collection appeared in two installments in the *Journal of American Folklore* (Henry 1931, 1932). A book, *Songs Sung in the Southern Appalachians*, was published in 1934 and was supplemented in 1938 by *Folk Songs of the Southern Highlands*. These works offered careful documentation of sources and broke away from the organizational model of "Child ballad and other" followed by many earlier works. The inclusion of song fragments as well as music notation was a credit to the Henrys' understanding of the needs of folksong study.

Henry's contributions to folksong scholarship exemplified what was possible by an amateur collector. Over the course of three decades, he climbed mountains in the Appalachian chain from Maine to Georgia and, in the process, made friends with many excellent folksingers in the Southern Highlands, including members of the now well-known Harmon and Hicks families.

Henry died at Englewood, New Jersey, on January 31, 1946, and was buried in West View Cemetery, Atlanta, Georgia. Florence Henry donated her husband's papers and ballad collection to the John Hay Library at Brown University.

Stephen Green

References

Green, Stephen. 1989. *Mellinger Edward Henry: Papers, 1910–1946: An Inventory and Index of American Folksong Materials*. Providence, RI: John Hay Library.

Henry, Mellinger. 1931. More Songs from the Southern Highlands. *Journal of American Folklore* 42:254–308.

———. 1932. Still More Ballads and Folksongs from the Southern Highlands. *Journal of American Folklore* 45:1–176.

———. 1937. *A Bibliography of American Folk-Songs*. London: Mitre.

Henry, Florence Mellinger. 1959. The Ballad-Hunting Henrys. *North Carolina Folklore* 7:32–34.

Hudson, Arthur Palmer. 1946. [Mellinger Henry Obituary]. *Journal of American Folklore* 59:316.

Herskovits, Melville Jean (1895–1963)

Africanist and anthropologist. Born in Bellefontaine, Ohio, on September 10, 1895, Herskovits was elected president of the American Folklore Society in 1945 and served as editor of *American Anthropologist* from 1949 to 1952. A man of many interests, he was recognized widely for his strong commitment to humanistic anthropology and for his concern with the total range of human cultural behavior. Herskovits made significant contributions to folklore as well as physical anthropology, ethnology, culture contact, ecology, economic anthropology, material culture, art and aesthetics, applied anthropology, African American studies, and African studies. A pioneer in African American studies in the United States, he was one of the first anthropologists to scientifically trace links between Africa and the New World. With the publication of his seminal *The Myth of the Negro Past* (1941), he single-handedly formulated what was to become a major focus of worldwide scholarly inquiry and debate. In recognition of his many accomplishments, Herskovits was appointed to the first chair of African studies in the United States, at Northwestern University in 1961.

Herskovits studied at Hebrew Union College and at the

University of Chicago, where he earned his B.A. in history in 1920. He received his M.A. (1921) and Ph.D. (1923) degrees in anthropology at Columbia University under Franz Boas. His dissertation dealt with the cattle complex in East Africa. He also studied at the New School for Social Research with anthropologist Alexander A. Goldenweiser and economist Thorstein Veblen. After briefly teaching at Howard University, Herskovits spend the remainder of his long academic career at Northwestern University, where he influenced several generations of researchers, among them William R. Bascom, James W. Fernandez, Daniel Crowley, Richard Waterman, Richard M. Dorson, and George Eaton Simpson (cf. Simpson 1973).

Ably assisted by his wife and professional collaborator, Frances S. Herskovits, he conducted fieldwork in Suriname, sub-Saharan Africa, Haiti, Brazil, and Trinidad. His research in Suriname and Africa—primarily funded by folklorist Elsie Clews Parsons—resulted in the publication of two important folklore volumes: *Suriname Folk-lore* (1936) and *Dahomean Narrative: A Cross-Cultural Analysis* (1958). *Dahomean Narrative* offered a critique of then current theories of myth from the perspective of the authors' field experiences as well as native Dahomean categories distinguishing myths (*hwenho*) from tales (*heho*). This study also contains an intriguing analysis of sibling rivalry and the Oedipal complex in an African society. The Herskovitses also made major contributions to ethnomusicology, recording both singing and instrumental music from Suriname, Dahomey, Ashanti, Nigeria, Togoland, Trinidad, and Brazil as well as providing thorough documentation of dance and drumming in Haitian *vodun* and Trinidadian *shango*. A major theoretical contribution to folklore is Herskovits' 1946 presidential address to the American Folklore Society, "Folklore after a Hundred Years: A Problem of Definition," in which he posits a useful distinction between "folk literature" and "folk custom" and suggests that folklorists confine their interests to the former category. Herskovits died on February 25, 1963, in Evanston, Illinois.

Stephen D. Glazier

References

Simpson, George Eaton. 1973. *Melville J. Herskovits*. New York: Columbia University Press.

Herzog, George (1901–1983)

Ethnomusicologist, anthropologist, and folklorist. Born in Hungary, Herzog studied in Berlin with E.M. von Hornbostel, immigrated to the United States in 1925, and completed his Ph.D. at Columbia University under Franz Boas. Beginning in 1926, he made repeated trips over two decades to do ethnomusicological fieldwork among Native American peoples, including Pueblo, Pima, Yuman, Comanche, and Navajo peoples, recording songs and studying their sociocultural contexts. From 1930 to 1931, he studied the verbal art and linguistic signaling systems of the Jabo in Liberia.

Herzog held two Guggenheim Fellowships and was involved in the founding and development of several scholarly organizations. From 1932 to 1948, he served on the faculty of Columbia University, and from 1948 until his early retirement in 1958 for reasons of health, at Indiana University. At both institutions he was responsible for pioneering the establishment of leading programs in ethnomusicology.

More than anyone else, Herzog is credited with establishing ethnomusicology (called "comparative musicology" before 1950) in the United States. He fashioned a holistic but unified style of research from the methods of Hungarian folk-music research developed by Béla Bartók, the comparative studies of the Berlin ethnomusicologists, and cultural anthropology as taught by Boas. He was further influenced by the Finnish school of folkloristics, as represented in the United States by Stith Thompson, and by Bloomfieldian linguistics.

Herzog's most influential publications date from the 1930s and include the earliest detailed comparative work, the recognition of tribal musics as systems of thought, the use of music in ethnohistory, the relationship of language and music, and historical stratification in music. Exhibiting a great variety of interests, his substantive contributions appeared exclusively as articles in folklore and anthropology journals.

Bruno Nettl

References

Herzog, George. 1936. *Jabo Proverbs from Liberia: Maxims in the Life of a Native Tribe*. Oxford: Oxford University Press.

Herzog, George, and Harold Courlander. 1947. *The Cow-Tail Switch and Other West African Stories*. New York: H. Holt.

Krader, Barbara. 1956. George Herzog [bibliography]. *Ethno-Musicology Newsletter* 6 (January):11–20.

Nettl, Bruno, and Philip V. Bohlman, eds. 1991. *Comparative Musicology and Anthropology of Music: Essays on the History of Ethnomusicology*. Chicago: University of Chicago Press.

Hicks-Harmon Families

An enormous extended-family complex noted for its large number of active bearers of Appalachian folklore. Emanating from "the Beech," the area on and near Beech Mountain in Avery and Watauga Counties, North Carolina, dozens of members of these families have for nine generations contributed both directly and indirectly to several important studies of American folklore, performing folktales (especially Jack tales), legends, lyrical folksongs, ballads, instrumental tunes, religious music, dances, and woodcrafting, and passing along folk customs and folk beliefs.

The parents of David Hix (later Hicks) (ca. 1719–ca. 1792) are assumed to have moved from England (one scholar suggests from Somersetshire) to Richmond, Virginia, during the late 17th century. It is known that in 1778 or so Hicks moved his family from the North Carolina Piedmont to the Upper Watauga River area in the northwestern part of the state, located near the crest of the Blue Ridge Mountains. David's son Samuel (known in the region as "Big Sammy") (ca. 1753–1835) built a home near his father in the fertile valley now known as Valle Crucis. Both Samuel and his son "Little

Sammy" (ca. 1800–?) were extraordinarily talented performers of folk traditions, especially music and Jack tales. This British folklore was perhaps intermingled with German traditions when Big Sammy's daughter Sabra (1785–?) married Andrew Harmon (1789–1814).

Andrew was the grandson of George Hermann (1710–1787), who had moved to America from Mittelfranken, Germany, about 1725, and the son of Cutliff Harmon (1748–1838), who settled in the Upper Watauga area in 1789. Among the children of Andrew and Sabra was Council (1807–1896), who became the major conduit for the transmission of a substantial body of Hicks-Harmon folklore.

When Council was seven years old, his father dead and his mother moved from the region, he was accepted into the household of his grandfather Big Sammy, where he absorbed the rich folklore of the Hickses. Council reported in his later years that he had learned his lore from his mother, Sabra Hicks, and his grandfather, who could have been either Big Sammy or Cutliff Harmon. Existing evidence suggests, however, that the Hickses were the source of Council's repertoire, although it is tempting to entertain the notion that the Hermanns were familiar with the stories that were to be included in the Grimm brothers' *Nursery and Household Tales* first published in 1812.

"Old Counce" Harmon eventually became a master storyteller, musician, and dancer who liked to drink and have a good time. In fact, he was "churched" (brought before the congregation and publicly expelled) on several occasions. Many of Counce's progeny assimilated the old man's traditions and went on to become gifted performers.

For example, during the last few years of his life, Old Counce lived with his daughter Sarah and her husband, A.J. Ward. The Ward children, especially Roby Monroe (1875–1944) and Miles (1877–1956), spent many hours listening to Counce's stories, later becoming, along with Miles' son Marshall (1906–1981) and the brothers Ben and Roby Hicks, primary contributors to folklorist Richard Chase's three books on Appalachian folklore: *The Jack Tales* (1943), *The Grandfather Tales* (1948), and *American Folk Tales and Songs* (1956).

Counce's grandson Reverend Lee Monroe Presnell (1876–1963), along with several other members of the Hicks-Harmon families, was featured on the excellent recordings produced by Sandy Paton and Lee B. Haggerty on Folk-Legacy Records, *The Traditional Music of Beech Mountain, North Carolina* (1964, 1965).

The Hicks and Harmon families were united once again when Council's son Goulder (ca. 1844–?) married Little Sammy's daughter Nancy Jane Hicks (ca. 1844–?). Their son Samuel (ca. 1869–?) and his wife, Pollyanna (ca. 1874–?), both absorbed the family traditions, and they were "discovered" in 1928 by Mellinger Henry. Many of this couple's songs are included in Henry's *Folk-Songs from the Southern Highlands* (1938).

The first member to share family traditions with a folklorist, however, was Council's granddaughter Jane (Mrs. Eugene) Gentry (1863–1925), who in 1916 contributed sixty-four songs (more than any other informant) to the seminal collection *English Folk Songs from the Southern Appalachians* (1932) by Cecil Sharp and Maud Karpeles. Sharp ignored Jane Gentry's fund of folktales, but in 1923 Isabel Gordon Carter collected fifteen stories from her (most of them Jack tales), which were published in 1925 as "Mountain White Folk-Lore: Tales from the Southern Blue Ridge" (*Journal of American Folklore* 38:340–374). This important piece of scholarship provides unadulterated narrative texts from the Beech, predating Richard Chase's modified composites by eighteen years. Moreover, Jane Gentry's daughter Maud (Mrs. Grover) Long (1893–1984) also became an accomplished singer and storyteller, recording her lore for the Library of Congress in 1947 (released as AAFSL47, Jack tales; and ASFSL21, songs).

All during this time the strong body of Hicks traditions continued to flourish. For example, Fanny Hicks (1837–1914), Big Sammy's granddaughter, passed on her immense repertoire of songs to her granddaughter Nora (1886–1953), who later contributed to *The Frank C. Brown Collection of North Carolina Folklore*.

Perhaps the most propitious event in the development of Hicks-Harmon family folklore occurred when Little Sammy's grandson Samuel III (1848–1929) married Old Counce's daughter Rebecca (1842–1919), once again crossbreeding the families' traditions. From this union came Ben, Andy, and Roby, who became immersed in the folklore of both families. Ben, his son Nathan and granddaughter Ray, Andy's daughter Rena (who married Nathan), and Roby, along with his wife, Buna Vista, and their son Stanley, have contributed to several major folklore collections, including the Chase books, the Foxfire books and records, Thomas G. Burton's *Some Ballad Folks* (1978), and Frank and Anne Locher Warner's collection of folksongs. Stanley (1911–1989) and Ray (1922–) have become the most widely known disseminators of the Hicks-Harmon lore, having appeared often at local and national concerts and festivals and, along with Marshall Ward, serving as the subjects of Cheryl Oxford's excellent study *"They Call Him Lucky Jack": Three Performance-Centered Case Studies of Storytelling in Watauga County, North Carolina* (Ph.D. diss., Northwestern University, 1987). Among their many honors was the National Heritage Fellowship award, given to both in 1983.

Aside from Ray Hicks, a superb storyteller and undisputed master of Jack-tale performances, the Hicks-Harmon traditions are being kept alive at the dawn of the 21st century by Frank Proffitt Jr. and Orville Hicks. Proffitt (1946–) inherited the lore of both his mother, Bessie (Ray Hicks' sister), and his father, Frank, the celebrated folk musician. His narrative style influenced primarily by his uncle Ray, Proffitt appears regularly in public telling Jack tales and other stories and performing folksongs on the dulcimer and fretless banjo, including his father's famous rendition of "Tom Dooley." Orville (1951–) is the son of Gold and Sarah Hicks, Council Harmon's granddaughter, who taught him around fifty stories, about half of them Jack tales. Orville Hicks also performs regularly for schools, colleges, and other local and national programs. In recent years, he has absorbed a great

deal about storytelling from Ray Hicks, and he enjoys the
master's blessing as his heir apparent.

William E. Lightfoot

References

Harmon, Terry L. 1984. *The Harmon Family, 1670–1984:
The Genealogy of Cutliff Harmon and His Descendents.*
Boone, NC: Minor's Publishing.

Hicks, John Henry, Mattie Hicks, and Barnabas B. Hicks.
1991. *The Hicks Families of Western North Carolina.*
Boone, NC: Minor's Publishing.

Thompson, James W. 1987. The Origins of the Hicks Family Traditions. *North Carolina Folklore Journal* 34:18–28.

See also Jack Tales

Hill, Joe (1879–1915)

Songwriter and satirist, poet and performer, romantic drifter
with a vision. Hero and martyr for America's radical labor
movement, Hill was Born Joel Hägglund in Gälve, Sweden,
on October 7, 1879. After immigrating to America, Joe became involved in radical unionism and helped pioneer the use
of protest songs as instruments of social change. Two of his
best-known songs are "Casey Jones: The Union Scab," a
parody of the folksong, and "Pie in the Sky," (Hill coined this
phrase; it became the popular title of his song "The Preacher
and the Slave," an anthem calling for the betterment of the
workingman's lot in this life, not the next).

Through his skills as composer and performer, Hill became an influential member of the Industrial Workers of the
World (popularly known as the IWW or the Wobbly Party),
and he guided that organization's recruitment and propaganda
strategies toward public singing events. IWW cultural performances had the look and feel of evangelical revivalism—a fact
underscored by Hill's coupling of his lyrics with traditional
and popular gospel tunes. The IWW advocated direct action
(slowdowns, strikes, purposefully poor workmanship) to take
over the means of production rather than the political negotiation favored by the American Federation of Labor (AF of L).
The IWW held that the interests of workers could never be
reconciled with those of management. Unlike other unions,
the IWW was far ahead of its time in promoting racial equality. Although they eschewed violence, Wobblies were widely
regarded as instigators behind many of the terrorist attacks that
fueled the Red Scare of the early 20th century.

While the Wobblies remained a political force at the
fringes of power in America, the appealing humor and witty
sarcasm of Hill's songs caused the movement to gain recognition beyond what its membership roles might suggest. Hill
inspired others to compose folksongs about him even as he
continued to produce his own. In the later 20th century, Hill's
memory has been perpetuated by American folk singers—
notably, Pete Seeger and Woody Guthrie.

Hill's immortality as a folk hero was sealed on November 19, 1915, when he was executed in Utah for murdering a
Salt Lake City merchant, but the fairness of Hill's trial was a
matter of heated and public debate. National figures such as
Samuel Gompers, Helen Keller, and Woodrow Wilson raised
voices on his behalf, but to no avail. Hill's parting words of
protest were, "Don't waste any time in mourning—organize!"

Eric Eliason

References

Smith, Gibbs M. 1984. *Joe Hill.* Salt Lake City, UT: Peregrine Smith.

History, Folk

A body of oral narratives told by people about themselves.
Such narratives articulate the feelings and attitudes of individuals and groups about the events and persons described.
Folk history is thus people history—history from a personal
view. It is intricately tied with the subjectivity of those who
talk about it, and it is very often history from the bottom up—
history in which the people themselves become their own
chroniclers.

One school of thought holds that firsthand information
about the past should be labeled oral history, and that secondhand or traditional information about the past is folklore.
Another viewpoint regards oral history and folklore as alike
in their use of the spoken word as a medium of expression.
Folk history and oral history, as defined by folklorists, are
indeed one and inseparable. The methodology is the same, and
may be divided into three component parts. The first is folk
history as *firsthand,* or *eyewitness,* history. This is history based
on a testimony that says, "I was there, I saw or took part in
the action, and this is the way I recall what happened." Eyewitness accounts have been used by folk historians since the
Greeks began the practice more than 2,500 years ago. Ancient
Hebrews used both firsthand and traditional oral accounts
even earlier to produce much of the Old Testament.

Contemporary eyewitness testimonies offer insights into
all aspects of local life and culture, including, for example,
African American attitudes toward their insecure status prior
to desegregation; senior citizens' feelings about retirement,
economic well-being, and life in nursing homes; and the way
people of all ages feel about their roles in society.

The second component of folk history comprises the
information provided by narrators who are one or more generations removed from what is being described. They know
of an event or topic, not because they were there personally,
but because they talked with someone who was. The information thus narrated is *secondhand.* It may not be as trustwor-
thy as a firsthand account, but it is historically valuable when
interpreted with care. Valuable sources of secondhand folk
history might include children of parents and grandparents
who crossed the ocean to America, great grandchildren of
Black slaves, children whose parents lived through the throes
of the Great Depression of the 1930s, and the grandchildren
of Jewish or Lebanese entrepreneurs who began their careers
peddling their wares across the South and Midwest.

The third variety of folk history consists of *oral historical traditions.* This is a large, often unwieldy, but fruitful corpus of information. Included are traditional accounts based

in fact, traditions based on hearsay, and those that merely express what people wish had happened. Whether oral traditional stories are proven fact, unverifiable hearsay, or wish fulfillment, all are worthy of being recorded, as living generations may learn much about previous generations from narratives told repeatedly in family and community circles. This form of folk history is often our only meaningful link with the past.

It may be that any group's oral historical traditions are microcosms of national history and that these oral kernels could provide insight into the attitudes of the American people both now and a century or more ago toward the major events of the day. In this regard, the context or setting of the narration becomes as important as the narrative text itself. The attitude toward the truth of history is as important as the bit of truth conveyed. Granted, most local oral traditions are not oriented to the nation's capital. Indeed, most oral historical texts are inner-directed, being mainly concerned with family and community affairs and with the role of the individual in community perspective. Thus, the major thrust of folk history is directed toward gathering verbal documents that can be used as source materials in the study of community life and thought.

In reconstructing folk history, the researcher defines local geographical and/or cultural boundaries in accordance with the concepts held by the people who live there, since their statements and feelings about their way of life may differ sharply from those of outsiders. Since folk history is necessarily oral, it is not to be found in archives and libraries, except in unpublished manuscripts that are, themselves, generally based on oral accounts. Thus, obtaining folk history calls for (1) conducting as many tape-recorded interviews as necessary with carefully chosen interviewees of varying age, sex, and race; (2) obtaining written permission from all narrators to use materials contained in the taped interviews; (3) organizing the information gathered in each interview according to chronological and topical categories; and (4) interpreting what people say in accordance with their own concepts of what is historically significant. The folk historian must also be familiar with published information and archival collections relating to the community or subject under study, using these materials as corroborative evidence when testing oral information for validity.

The historical data contained in oral narratives, whether personal, secondhand, or traditional, permit researchers to interpret significant topics of any human group in light of the totality of its history. Any facet of history, contemporary or earlier, is worthy of being recorded and preserved if the living generations treasure it enough to talk about it. Folk history is valuable to researchers because of the manners in which it reveals people's feelings about themselves in relation to their families, their communities, and to the land itself.

In addition to people's associations with generations past, they also have knowledge of buildings and other tangible objects on the culture landscape because of personal identification with them, or because of local stories that contain mention and description of these physical objects. The reasons human beings retain information of historical interest often explain as much about the people as the kernels of truth contained in their oral recollections. The recollections themselves explain history; the reasons for passing along these accounts orally explain the mind of the community and its people and help set it apart from surrounding communities.

Advantages of tape recording folk histories include (1) having available the exact words uttered by the narrator, as pauses and vocal inflections frequently say as much as words; (2) capturing the speaker's colloquial and dialectical tone of voice; (3) obtaining individual views, which may be at variance with what is commonly accepted, about contemporary and past local history; (4) obtaining new and exciting kinds of evidence; and (5) filling in gaps detected in formal historical records.

Imperfections inherent in oral folk history are readily apparent. Yet, in the skilled hands of properly trained researchers, oral texts can be weighed carefully so as to separate the core of historical truth from the intrusive folk motifs and migratory legends that are often used to polish good stories and make them even better for a listening audience.

In orientating themselves to this distinct type of local history, researchers learn to place stress on the large number of Americans, living or dead, whose lives were and are shaped by folk concepts, customs, beliefs, and traditional patterns of living. The story of these people, submerged and unknown to the world at large, represents a whole new area of historical research and writing.

Numerous exemplary studies are based on American folk, or "grass-roots," history. These include, in addition to the works listed as references below, Kai T. Erikson's *Everything in Its Path: Destruction of Community in the Buffalo Creek Flood* (1976), which documents local response to the cataclysmic flood in 1972 that devastated a West Virginia community; Sherna Gluck's *From Parlor to Prison: Five American Suffragists Talk about Their Lives* (1976), which explores the life experiences of five women deeply involved in the women's suffrage movement of the late 19th and early 20th centuries; Tamara Hareven and Randolph Langenbach's *Amoskeag: Life and Work in an American Factory City* (1978), comprising the social history of textile-mill workers in Manchester, New Hampshire; Edward D. Ives' *Joe Scott: The Woodsman-Songmaker* (1978), a book set in the lumberwoods of Maine with emphasis on a local songmaker and what his song creations meant to him and others; William Lynwood Montell's *Killings: Folk Justice in the Upper South* (1986), which affords a penetrating look at homicidal behavior and prevailing attitudes and values surrounding violent deaths in a Kentucky-Tennessee border area; and Kathryn L. Morgan's *Children of Strangers: The Story of a Black Family* (1980), which provides keen insight into the strategies used by Blacks raising their families in a White-dominated society.

William Lynwood Montell

References

Allen, Barbara, and Lynwood Montell. 1981. *From Memory to History: Using Oral Sources in Local Historical Research.* Nashville: American Association for

State and Local History.

Botkin, Benjamin A. 1945. *Lay My Burden Down: A Folk History of Slavery.* Chicago: University of Chicago Press.

Fry, Gladys-Marie. 1975. *Night Riders in Black Folk History.* Knoxville: University of Tennessee Press.

Montell, William Lynwood. 1970. *The Saga of Coe Ridge: A Study in Oral History.* Knoxville: University of Tennessee Press.

Thompson, Paul. 1978. *Voices from the Past: Oral History.* Oxford: Oxford University Press.

Wilson, William A. 1973. Folklore and History: Fact Amid the Legends." *Utah Historical Quarterly* 41:40–58. Reprinted in *Readings in American Folklore*, ed. Jan Harold Brunvand. New York: W.W. Norton, pp. 449–466.

See also Life History

Hoedown

Both a vigorous rural dance and the musical accompaniment for it. Any discussion of the term involves both the history of American folk and popular dance *and* the story of American popular and folk instrumental music.

The *Dictionary of American Regional English* lists the word under the main entry "Breakdown" as a synonym along with "shindig." The first appearance of "breakdown" is in a text from 1819. The OED (*Oxford English Dictionary*), however, locates "breakdown" in 1864 and "hoedown" as early as 1860. Richard Hopwood Thornton's *An American Glossary* (1912, 2d. ed. 1962) does not include "breakdown" but has three entries for "hoe-down."

What appears to be fairly clear respecting the dance tradition is that quite early, perhaps by the last quarter of the 18th century, a style of dancing heavily influenced by Blacks, rapid and vigorous in execution, and identified with gatherings of rural people had developed. It was variously called a breakdown or a hoedown.

A note on the "raftsman passage" from Chapter 16 of the *Adventures of Huckleberry Finn* is enlightening. The text describes a keelboat crew in a moment of recreation:

> Next they got out an old fiddle, and one played, and another patted juba, and the rest turned themselves loose on a regular old-fashioned keelboat breakdown. They wouldn't keep that up very long without getting winded. . . .

Both dances were of Negro origin: juba, much like a vigorous tap dance to a clapping accompaniment; and breakdown, a sort of shuffling dance to a fast beat. Bruce R. Buckley describes the juba as "an African jig-type step with elaborate variations, including stiff-legged shuffles and hops" (Buckley 1968:140).

It is likely that the widespread clogging-step dancing-jigging among the English, Scottish, and Irish immigrants to the New World provided a stimulus that enabled Blacks to accommodate this European tradition to their own usages, among which the juba was prominent. In notes accompanying a 1976 Library of Congress issue of *American Fiddle Tunes,* Alan Jabbour identifies the reel as the same as a breakdown. Thus, another stimulus was the set dance—reels, quadrilles, and square dances often accompanied by the fiddle in 2/4 or 6/8 time.

As for the music to which the hoedown was danced, Robert Perry Christeson's two-volume *The Old-Time Fiddler's Repertory* offers about 200 tunes in musical notation with key signatures and time indications, identifying them as breakdowns, quadrilles, and "pieces." Here, indeed, are most of the favorites of both dancers and fiddlers: "Soldier's Joy," "Devil among the Tailors," "Hell among the Yearlings," "Gray Eagle," "Tom and Jerry," "Mississippi Sawyer," and many more, not to mention breakdowns identified by number rather than title (Christeson 1973–1984).

It is not uncommon for fiddlers to refer to these tunes as square-dance tunes, quadrilles, or simply dance tunes. What some fiddlers play in 2/4 time, others play in 6/8. And the variations in the names of the tunes show the same folk process of dynamic variation apparent in the execution of the tunes: "Forked Deer," "Forked Horn Deer," "Forky Horn Deer," "Durand's Hornpipe," "Durang's Hornpipe," "Durango Hornpipe," and so on.

In the absence of solid evidence, folk etymologists have supplied engaging, imaginative, and perhaps even accurate ways of accounting for the terms "hoedown" and "breakdown." By some it is suggested that a certain configuration in the dancing of a quadrille is called a breakdown. Why it is not called something else is not clear. Another explanation is that in performance a fiddler breaks the piece down into its most musical components of melody and rhythm and concentrates upon them, an explanation not unlike the familiar "emotional core" of which a ballad consists. Another explanation holds that both terms refer to a work stoppage. When a breakdown in some part of a work process occurred or when an essential piece of equipment was broken—a wagon made immobile because of a broken coupling pole or "reach," for instance—there was a corresponding moment of leisure until the equipment could be repaired. During this lull, the hoes (perhaps a metonym for all hand implements) were laid down, and the juba and step dancing-jigging-clogging were performed.

Yet another folk etymologist suggests that in performing a breakdown-hoedown the dancers' improvisations included imitations of wielding a hoe. A final explanation claims that the expression "hoedown" conveyed the idea of speed. Thus, rapid dancing would have that term applied to it. If this last explanation seems either ingenuous or ingenious, one might reflect upon the last stanza of "Dixie":

> Dar's buckwheat cakes and Injun batter,
> Makes you fat or a little fatter:
> Look away, look away, look away, Dixie Land!
> Den *hoe* it *down* and scratch your grabble,
> To Dixie's land I'm bound to trabble;
> Look away, look away, look away, Dixie Land!

Square dancing on Saturday night. Weslaco, Texas, 1942. Photo Arthur Rothstein. Library of Congress.

Make haste, line four of this mid-19th century song says, using the words in verb form, hurry it up, dig out, and get yourself back to Dixie.

If today's "Flint Hill Special" and "Foggy Mountain Breakdown" are representative, the present notion of a breakdown or hoedown features strong rhythm, a driving banjo or banjo-fiddle lead, and speedy execution, appropriate for clogging but probably too fast for a square dance.

Louie W. Attebery

References

Attebery, Louie W. 1979. The Fiddle Tune: An American Artifact. In *Readings in American Folklore*, ed. Jan Harold Brunvand. New York: W.W. Norton, pp. 324–333.

Buckley, Bruce R. 1968. "Honor Your Ladies": Folk Dance in the United States. In *Our Living Traditions: An Introduction to American Folklore*, ed. Tristram Potter Coffin. New York: Basic Books, pp. 134–141.

Christeson, R.P. 1973–1984. *The Old-Time Fiddler's Repertory.* 2 vols. Columbia: University of Missouri Press.

Quigley, Colin. 1985. *Close to the Floor: Folk Dance in Newfoundland.* St. Johns, Newfoundland: Memorial University.

See also Dance, Folk; Fiddle Music

Holler

A brief loud melodic phrase characterized by highly stylized vocal techniques including yodel-like glottal snaps, falsetto, staccato, blue notes (in African American tradition), and various other techniques employing a wide tonal compass. The holler characteristically employs vocables, or meaningless syllables, rather than words and is performed without instrumental accompaniment. Musical and entertaining in form, the holler is generally performed outdoors and may also be performed to communicate as signals, animal calls, greetings between farmers, and by vendors announcing their presence. Because they are individually stylized vocal performances bearing the unique style of the individual performer, hollers are a musical oddity that do not readily lend themselves to written description. Performances may range from a gently rising melismatic whooping sound to an energetically hooted falsetto rendition of a popular hymn.

Although hollers and hollering are documented in both Caucasian and African American traditions, most references to the holler occur in publications by collectors and scholars treating them as idiomatic material closely related to worksongs and blues. One of the earliest descriptions appears in 1856 in Frederick Law Olmstead's *A Journey in the Southern Slave States,* in which he described shrill music "whoops" of Negro laborers as "Negro jodeling" and "Carolina yells." Numerous other writers in the first half of the 20th century viewed the holler in relationship to the development of early blues, often pointing to characteristic wordless moan-like refrains and advancing the view that the holler is an antecedent to the blues. Contemporary thinking de-emphasizes the romanticized view that the holler is a pre-blues form and suggests that hollering was one among a familiar stock of vocal techniques from which performers borrowed.

The term "holler" also subsumes a broad range of stylized vocal performances that share many common elements. Remarkably similar performances have been reported as cattle calls, street cries and shouts, and the shantyman's "sing-outs."

Although hollers are rarely performed in the 1990s, there is broad public recognition of the term due to the continued media coverage of the annual Spivey's Corner Hollering Contest since its beginning in North Carolina in 1969. During the contest's early years several participating traditional performers appeared on national television and radio programs.

Peter Bartis

References

Bartis, Peter T. 1973. An Examination of the Holler in North Carolina White Tradition. *Southern Folklore Quarterly* 39:209–217.

Browne, Ray B. 1954. Some Notes on the Southern "Holler." *Journal of American Folklore* 67:73–77.

Courlander, Harold. 1963. *Negro Folk Music U.S.A.* New York: Columbia University Press.

Odum, Howard W., and Guy B. Johnson. 1926. *Negro Workaday Songs*. London: Oxford University Press.

Olmstead, Frederick Law. 1856. *A Journey in the Southern Slave States with Remarks on Their Economy*. New York: Dix and Edwards.

Howard, Dorothy Mills (1902–)

Teacher and folklorist. Howard was a pioneer and innovator in the study of children's folklore. In her 1938 doctoral dissertation, *Folk Rhymes of American Children,* she collected directly from children, rather than from adults recollecting their childhoods, as her predecessors such as William Wells Newell had done. She insisted throughout her long career that the children themselves must be the focus of research regarding children's traditions.

The eminent British folklorists Iona and Peter Opie contacted her early in their careers, and she was a strong influence on the development of their theories and techniques regarding the collection, documentation, and analysis of children's folklore.

After teaching for a time in public school, Howard spent the rest of her career as an English professor at Frostburg State College in Maryland, serving also as department head. She retired in 1967 and then served as a consultant for the Tri-University Project in children's playlore of the University of Nebraska, New York University, and the University of Washington. From 1954 to 1955, she was awarded a Fulbright Fellowship to study and collect children's folklore in Australia, a subject on which she published widely and an interest she continued for the rest of her career. Most of her publication was in the form of articles in scholarly and professional journals. She published three books, one an autobiographical study of her own childhood, *Dorothy's World: Childhood in Sabine Bottom, 1902–1910* (1977); another (with Eloise Ramsey) a critical and descriptive bibliography for use in elementary and intermediate schools, *Folklore for Children and Young People* (1952); and the last one the documentation of the life of a Mexican village boy, *Pedro of Tonala* (1989).

Sylvia Ann Grider

References

Grider, Sylvia Ann. 1994. Dorothy Howard: Pioneer Collector of Children's Folklore. *Children's Folklore Review* 17:3–17.

Hudson, Arthur Palmer (1892–1978)

Folklorist, teacher, and editor of folklore collections. Hudson was born in Attala County, Mississippi. He earned his B.S. and M.A. degrees (1913, 1920) from the University of Mississippi and taught there. After a second M.A. (1925) from the University of Chicago, and a Ph.D. (1930) from the University of North Carolina, he accepted a position at the University of North Carolina, where he taught folklore and British romantic literature. He received a Kenan Professorship in 1951.

Hudson became aware of folklore as an academic field from E.C. Perrow, his freshman English instructor at the University of Mississippi, and he formed his scholarly approaches in subsequent study with Louise Pound and Archer Taylor at the University of Chicago. His motivation for folklore research probably derived from experiences he described in an autobiographical sketch, "An Attala Boyhood" (Hudson 1942), and is most clearly seen in his published lecture series, *Folklore Keeps the Past Alive* (1962).

Although his books are clearly a product of their time, *Folksongs of Mississippi and Their Background* (1936), *Humor of the Old Deep South* (1936), and *Folklore in American Literature* (1958) show him to be a meticulous editor of texts. With H.M. Belden, he edited the two volumes of song texts in *The Frank C. Brown Collection of North Carolina Folklore* and was probably the best of many editors who collaborated on that work.

Hudson succeeded Frank C. Brown as secretary-treasurer of the North Carolina Folklore Society and guided it for more than twenty years. During that time, he edited the society's journal, *North Carolina Folklore*.

From 1950 until 1963, Hudson served as head of the curriculum in folklore at the University of North Carolina. At the close of his teaching career, he donated his materials to the University of Mississippi and the University of North Carolina. The latter collection formed the nucleus of the university's Southern Folklife Collection, one of the nation's major folklore archives.

Beverly Patterson

References

Howell, A.C. 1956. *The Kenan Professorships*. Chapel Hill: University of North Carolina Press, pp. 269–270.

Hudson, A.P. 1942. An Attala Boyhood. *Journal of Mississippi History* 4:59–75, 127–155.

Patterson, Daniel W., ed. 1965. *Folklore Studies in Honor of Arthur Palmer Hudson*. Chapel Hill: North Carolina Folklore Society.

Humor

A distinct form of communication involving comical or amusing ideas and situations. The study of humor arose late in the consciousness of folklorists. Although early folklorists collected humorous materials, they did so because that humor was encapsulated in recognized traditional genres—tales, ballads, proverbs, riddles—not because of any interest in humor per se. Wilhelm and Jacob Grimm included numerous humorous tales in their *Kinder und Hausmärchen* (1812–1816) because these tales, alongside those of magic and adventure, were alive in the mouths of the folk. The interest of the 19th-century English folklorists in "folk wit" was an interest in proverbs and riddles as a repository of old "wisdom," not humor. Francis James Child included humorous texts in *The English and Scottish Popular Ballads* (1882–1898) because they met his criteria for traditional narrative song.

When the historic-geographic, or Finnish, method came to dominate folklore study in the first half of the 20th century, humor was regarded as something embedded in a traditional text whose origins and routes of diffusion might be reconstructed. Humorous tales, like magic tales, were classified and comparatively scrutinized according to this method. Humorous tale types and motifs were cataloged in the great international and regional indexes. The historic-geographic approach gave further impetus to the collecting of humorous texts, and thousands were published in journals and regional collections in both Europe and the United States, but no interest was expressed by folklorists then in how humor might be defined, how humorous texts were structured, or what their communicative possibilities might be.

Folklorists were awakened to these possibilities by American social and literary historians. As early as 1838, it had been suggested that the originality and distinctiveness of American literature lay in its unique style of humor, but it was only after Frederick Jackson Turner focused attention on the role of the frontier in shaping American institutions and character that historians began to explore American humor with any degree of seriousness. Jennette Tandy's *Crackerbox Philosophers in American Humor and Satire* (1925) and Frank J. Meine's *Tall Tales of the Southwest* (1930) were the first volumes to bring a portion of 19th-century humor to the attention of scholars, but it was Constance Rourke's *American Humor* (1931) that set out to delineate, through the scrutiny of comic figures—the Yankee, the backwoodsman, the Negro—and forms—the monologue, the rhapsody, and the tale—the outlines of an American humor and national character that profoundly influenced the shape of American literature.

Richard M. Dorson (1916–1981), often referred to as the "Dean of American Folklore," was trained within this intellectual milieu. Dorson's publishing career began with *Davy Crockett: American Comic Legend* (1939), which was merely a selection of the "better" stories in the Crockett almanacs. Nevertheless, Dorson regarded this humor—as did other historians—as a comic mythology that was at once vigorous and robust and that captured the confidence and boldness of those who settled the vast American wilderness. In *Jonathan Draws the Long Bow* (1946), Dorson again set out to capture aspects of national character and historical circumstance in the traditions—supernatural as well as humorous—of New England from a variety of subliterary sources.

From Dorson's point of view, the short span of American history did not allow the creation of the kind of heroic legendry found in the Old World. American mythology was fragmented and scattered, rather than a consistent and sober whole. Fashioned in an age of unbelief, American mythology could only be an assortment of humorous episodes about scalawags, fools, and other comic types. Nevertheless, Dorson came to see these heroes as the embodiment of a democratic impulse—one of the four great impulses, in his view, that conditioned the development of American character and culture. On the whole, folklorists regarded American humor as an expression of democratic optimism born in the confident rejection of European and Eastern manners and gentility. They tended to see the humor in a more positive light than historians who seemed more attuned to undercurrents of darkness and despair.

Although students of American humor recognized that the true roots of 19th-century American humor were oral, there was little choice but to establish the character of this bygone era from newspapers and other subliterary sources. Nevertheless, only Dorson was concerned to demonstrate that such sources were genuine repositories of orally circulated traditions. He was careful to call attention to the descriptions of oral storytelling in this subliterature and to identify the traditional narratives that appeared in their pages. Dorson collected folklore in rural American communities and encountered oral humor firsthand. He severely criticized social and literary historians for failing to recognize the spurious character of much of what had been promoted as America's comic mythology. Too often the materials were what Dorson called "fakelore"—ersatz compositions of boosters and promoters—rather than genuine American folklore. Dorson and other American folklorists remained keen to record and document the persistence of frontier humor—particularly tall lying, practical joking, exaggerated metaphor, and dialect stories—in oral tradition, attending not only to documenting the texts but also to occasionally characterizing their styles of performance as well.

Another major influence on folklorists' approach to humor came from psychology via anthropology. In 1905 Sigmund Freud published *Jokes and Their Relation to the Unconscious,* in which he argued that jokes and other forms of humor were, like dreams, vehicles for the expression of otherwise unacceptable sexual and aggressive thoughts. Freud's theory of jokes was part and parcel of his psychoanalytic psychology, which held that socially unacceptable impulses were repressed and achieved expression only indirectly through disguised representations. Freud's theory was enormously influential, and numerous books were written about folklore and humor from a psychoanalytic perspective—although not by folklorists. Folklorists continued assiduously to collect, catalog, and publish humorous texts from oral tradition with little or no commentary or interpretation. Anthropologists, however, in their fieldwork, encountered joking relationships, trickster figures, and ritual clowning. The fact that such humor—often of the most outrageous and obscene kinds—organized relations between kin and proved central to an assortment of mythological and ritual expressions required explanation. In some instances, anthropologists found that explanation in psychoanalytic theory.

Alan Dundes (1934–) single-handedly brought the psychoanalytic perspective to the attention of American folklorists. His interpretations of scores of myths, legends, tales, rituals, artifacts, and jokes made the perspective seem more prominent in the discipline than it, in fact, was. Dundes' interest in humor centered on joke cycles—elephant jokes, Polish jokes, quadriplegic jokes, Jewish American Princess (JAP) jokes, and the like—prominent in the United States in the latter decades of the 20th century. Generally, Dundes viewed these jokes as providing a socially sanctioned outlet for the expression of forbidden thoughts. Thus, the elephant was a symbol of the Black person against whom the jokes permitted certain symbolic aggressions—aggressions that could no longer be openly expressed in a the post–civil rights era. Dead-baby jokes, with their graphic images of mutilation and destruction, served to express a hatred of babies aroused by guilt over abortion. JAP jokes allowed for the expression of ambivalent attitudes toward the redefinition of women's roles. On the one hand, the Jewish American Princess expressed women's discontent with traditional domestic demands, particularly cooking and sex. On the other, she symbolized the resentment against feminist dogma that a woman abandon house and home in favor of business and career. Dundes' interpretations often presume the underlying hostility of humor and the requisite identification of groups against whom that hostility is directed. Yet they remain sensitive to the sociohistorical conditions in which such jokes emerge and are told. The targets of aggression are not constant; they are a function of time and place.

Dundes' joke interpretations have been particularly influential in folklore, and the presumption of aggression runs through a good deal of folklorists' interpretations of humor. Nevertheless, recent perspectives have emphasized the close analysis of humorous texts and performance contexts without the presumption that the humor is motivated by the desire to attack or degrade. Some scholars have urged that more attention be paid to the structure of humor and the way information is encoded within that structure. Humor demands the perception of an "appropriate incongruity"—that is, the perception of a relationship of two incongruous semantic domains that are somehow made to seem appropriately linked. The examination of the incongruous semantic categories and the way that they are made appropriate may lead to alternative understandings of the meaning of some of the contemporary jokes whose interpretations have frequently been based on details of plot and character. Thus the question-and-answer joke from the 1960s, "What do you call a Negro with a Ph.D.?"—"Nigger," cannot immediately be regarded as motivated by racial hatred. The joke depends upon the incongruity that someone with a Ph.D. degree who deserves a title of respect such as "Doctor" or "Professor" earns only an odious racial epithet, but this incongruity can be recognized as ap-

propriate if one accesses the information that there are individuals for whom race is a stigma that no achievement can overcome. Hearers of this joke need not believe this to be the case; they need only recognize that such a view exists. Whether the joke is motivated by racial hatred or is, in fact, a critical comment on the racist character of a society where Blacks cannot succeed no matter what they do, cannot be determined from the text alone. That determination can be made only if something of the context of the joke is known, such as who is telling it to whom and under what conditions.

Joke texts are ambiguous; they are usually capable of bearing more than a single interpretation. Sometimes even the most detailed contextual data may not be sufficient to resolve the ambiguity. Nevertheless, close attention to the incongruous semantic categories and the means by which they are made appropriate may alert interpreters to a range of potential messages encoded within particular humorous texts and repertoires.

Recently, there has been greater emphasis placed on the study of folklore performance, including humor performance. These approaches regard an oral performance as a verbal work of art and attend to the full range of devices and techniques by which this art is accomplished. Performance approaches also regard this art as created in performance and thus scrutinize the dynamics of the social event within which it is created. Performance approaches have paid close critical attention to instances of tall lying, comic anecdotes, and the recounting of practical joking, highlighting their aesthetic structures, the manipulation of point of view, the use of quoted speech, the employment of meta-narration, as well as how such techniques and devices contribute to the narrative as a tactical social accomplishment.

As it stands in the mid-1990s, the primary contribution of folklore to the study of humor does not lie in the advancement of a particular theoretical perspective or interpretive methodology. Rather it lies in the relentless collection and publication of humorous materials from folk sources, the classification and cataloging of these materials in indexes and finding lists, and the insistence that the contexts of performance are crucial to understanding the meanings and uses humor.

Elliott Oring

References

Bauman, Richard. 1986. *Story, Performance, and Event: Contextual Studies of Oral Narrative.* Cambridge: Cambridge University Press.

Bluestein, Gene. 1962. "The Arkansas Traveler" and the Strategy of American Humor. *Western Folklore* 21:153–160.

Boatright, Mody C. 1946. *Folk Laughter on the American Frontier.* New York: Macmillan.

Clark, William Bedford, and W. Craig Turner, eds. 1984. *Critical Essays on American Humor.* Boston: G.K. Hall.

Dorson, Richard M. 1973. *America in Legend: Folklore from the Colonial Period to the Present.* New York: Pantheon.

Dundes, Alan. 1987. *Cracking Jokes: Studies of Sick Humor*

Cycles and Stereotypes. Berkeley, CA: Ten Speed Press.

Mintz, Larry, ed. 1988. *Humor in America: A Research Guide to Genres and Topics*. New York: Greenwood.

Nilsen, Don L.F. 1993. *Humor Scholarship: A Research Bibliography*. Westport, CT: Greenwood.

Oring, Elliott. 1992. *Jokes and Their Relations*. Lexington: University Press of Kentucky.

See also Anti-Legend; Jokes; Parody in Folklore; Riddle Jokes; Tall Tale

Hungarian Americans

Immigrants and their descendants from Hungary. The self-designation of Hungarians as *Magyar*, their country as *Magyarország*, originates from the Ugric period and describes their tribal position at the time they separated from their Finno-Ugric language kin, and blended with Central Asian nomadic Turks. According to legend, under the leadership of chieftain Árpád seven tribal chiefs pledged brotherhood by letting their blood flow together and invaded the Carpathien Basin in A.D. 896. Over the centuries, however, the romantically conceptualized "Oriental" *Magyar* culture blended into its central European neighborhood and at the time emigration from Hungary began, 40 percent of Hungarian arrivals belonged to ethnic minorities.

The Hungarian American subculture is a small but heterogeneous part of the patchwork of American ethnics. In itself it does not stand out as a solidly knit community united by conspicuous folkloric identity features, but is more characterized by fragmentation in its display of cultural consciousness, due to Hungary's ethnic heterogeneity and hereditary class hierarchy.

Opening the telephone directory of any American town or industrial area, Hungarian presence is easy to detect by listings such as Szabó (tailor), Kovács (Smith), Varga (cobbler), Kocsis (coachman), and other surnames that indicate occupations. Other names feature physical character, mood, or temper, such as Kiss (small), Nagy (large), Joó (good), and Balogh (awkward), or the geographical region of origin, such as Szegedi (from Szeged) and Veszprémi (from Veszprém). The multinational character of Hungarians is indicated by such common names as Magyar, Tóth (Slovak), Németh (German), Oláh (Romanian), or Horváth (Croatian). Revealing of the same is the fact that people often keep their foreign-sounding names (spelled in Hungarian), like Resetár, Lakcsik, Sisák, Hoffer, or Duczer.

Others may not be so easy to identify as *Magyars*. In the desire to preserve their original names, some anglicize the spelling, (Sillaghe for Szilágyi); those who want to assimilate may simply translate their names into English, like Mr. Shepherd (Juhász) and Mrs. King (Király) did. Dialing any of these listings, however, may lead to different meanings of Hungarianness. We might reach a newcomer who strives for acceptability, a veteran custodian of Hungarian values surviving his succumbing generation, the conscious or unconscious preserver of a selected set of traditions, the young seeker of roots who makes a pilgrimage to Hungary and relearns the forgot-

For a lunchtime audience on the steps of the Library of Congress, members of Tisza Ensemble demonstrate Hungarian dancing. Washington, DC, 1995. Photo J.W. Love.

ten mother tongue, or the person whose Hungarian family name is the only connection to the ancestral past.

Regardless of the individual's place in the timetable of the immigration process, Hungarians never represented a large number in America, nor has their presence greatly fluctuated. In the peak years between 1907 and 1910, two million Hungarian job seekers came to the United States. *Magyars* are shown sporadically and in low and slowly declining numbers in the censuses between 1910 and 1980, in larger cities, townships and industrial counties of the Eastern United States—today there are about 1.8 million Americans in the United States who claim to be of Hungarian ancestry.

A historical overview of the emergence of the Hungarian American subculture must review the period primarily from 1870 to 1956. Emigrant groups of diverse nationality and social status migrated from Hungary to the United States for different reasons, a fact that explains their lack of solidarity.

The first arrivals were exiles of the failed 1848–1849 revolution against the Hapsburg rule, numbering 800 to 900 people who settled in fifteen locations. They dispersed soon to urban centers where they joined other elite emigrés: patriotic, politically conscious intellectuals and businessmen. They launched the symbols that would later form the core of a constructed Hungarian American ethnic identity.

As the second wave, mass emigration began in the 1870s and affected mostly the agricultural population. Until World War I, more than two million people crossed the ocean. In 1882, when steamship agents offered to book passage for a group of thirty-two villagers of County Sopron to bring them to South Bend, Indiana, as laborers for Studebaker's wagon factory and Oliver's plow plant, the farmhands displayed good entrepreneural skills, mobility, and readiness to sacrifice for a better future. They accepted the worst labor- and living-conditions in order to save every penny, return home, and become prosperous farmers. These single, transitory male workers were no "immigrants." Austere communal living kept them within the institution known as the "boarding family" headed by "the lady," wife of a fellow worker and acquaintance from the old country, who provided room and board to young men. With the passing of time and conditions changing, temporary workers had to decide whether to stay or to return. Staying meant breaking out from isolation, learning the language and basic skills, settling with family, and changing loyalty from the homeland to the land of choice.

When political and economic situations in Hungary and the United States forced people to stay where they happened to be, shortly before World War I, several enclaves of peasant settlers emerged in the United States. The emigrants, including ethnic minorities originating from historic Hungary and *Magyars* speaking regional dialects, together established a specific Hungarian American culture. In spite of the diversity of regional Hungarians, with their uneven representation of cultural dialects, religions, and loyalties, four generations of peasant immigrants—the foreign-born, and their first-, second-, and third-generation American-born offspring—comprised the largest, most conspicuous group that established the image and identity of the Hungarian American as it is known today. The group as a whole was nicknamed *öreg Amerikások* (veteran Americans) and represents the main culture-bearing community of Hungarians. However, this population group, totaling about 450,000, never settled anywhere in mass and never created a solid, closed ethnic residency. (Even in Cleveland, the legendary "American Debrecen," stronghold of Hungarian Protestants in America, Hungarians accounted for less than 10 percent of the residents.) People were spread out in the suburban regions of industrial towns, making their living from heavy industry. Only 1 percent ever returned to farming, like the founders of Árpádhon (The Home of Árpád) in Louisiana. This unique settlement of strawberry farmers was established in 1896, the 1,000th anniversary of the birth of Hungary, and romantically named after the nomadic land taker Árpád, although the settlers were of mixed ancestry. Tired of industrial labor in Detroit, South Bend, Akron, Ohio, and other company towns, Hungarian, Slovak, Croatian, German, and Ukrainian peasant emigrants from historic Hungary together, forged the farming community of Árpádhon and invented a Hungarian identity, symbolized by songs and dances celebrating the harvest of their crops.

The third category of emigrants was composed of professionally trained people who began to arrive from Hungary after World War I. They did not join the settling trend of peasants and did not seek companionship with them. Traditionally, peasantry constituted a solid subculture in Hungary and was isolated from the elite, not only as servants (the poor and powerless isolated from the rich and powerful), but also by different standards of education, worldview, language, and the arts. Urban elite emigrés included educated professionals; Jewish intellectuals (who left Hungary between the two World Wars, fearing anti-semitism); and those who left after the end of World War II (displaced military men, politicians, old nobility, and determined emigrants fearful of Communism). Concentrated in large cities—New York, Chicago, Cleveland, Pittsburgh, Los Angeles—these emigrés represent only a symbolic community whose members host cultural events and attend commemorative programs and banquets related to political-patriotic causes. The offspring of these displaced persons no longer claim a Hungarian identity. Many of the so-called "freedom fighters" who fled during the 1956 revolution were not politically motivated but took the opportunity to seek freedom from Communist rule. These newcomers were mostly young people, ready for a new career. Working-class Hungarians opened their purses and hearts to assist them, but the sponsors' enthusiasm soured because their wards targeted higher education not factory jobs; a world's difference separated peasant thrift and the goals of these immigrants, who soon vanished in the mainstream.

In Hungary, peasant culture developed more regionally than nationally. Whereas individuals were efficient in local folk education and loyal to local tradition, they were ignorant of the overall national culture established by school education. Immigrants, at the outset, continued their loyalty to native local heritage and maintained regional identities even after they were forced to disperse and intermingle. Consciousness of Hungarian national identity and its symbols, however, began to infiltrate local-identity features quite early. The Romantic nationalist image of the late 19th century was recast to fit the nostalgic mood of elite expatriates. This image was stronger and more attractive to the masses of homesick immigrants than more divisive, less prestigious ancestral peasant traditions. The new image helped the peasant folk unify through a set of standardized, homogenized identity symbols representing "the noble Hungarian nation" that embraced them only in exile.

The construction of a homogenized Hungarian American culture was conveyed by social, beneficent, and religious organizations whose regional chapters followed the guidance of their national or global headquarters. Enthusiastic clergymen assumed leadership in the promotion of a standardized patriotic-national culture that replaced the inherited local and regional customs, demeaned as stigmas of backwardness. Calendar and life-cycle rituals were supplemented by Hungarian and American patriotic commemorative celebrations, supervised by elite community leaders and filling the ethnic recreational needs of the settlers, who were eager to learn and improve themselves in the new situation. The sensation of a newly acquired dignity by former farmhands made it easier for them to blend into the mainstream.

While the imported repertoire of regional folk costumes, dances, music, and foodways was suppressed and moved from the public to the private area of consciousness and later to complete oblivion, a unanimously accepted stock of new Hungarian American forms emerged and became important symbols of Hungarianness. Among these are the *magyar ruha*

(Hungarian dress, a fabricated festive costume); the *Csárdás* pair dance; Gypsy music; a few popular folk and imitation-folk melodies; and a menu of holiday dishes limited to stuffed cabbage, *gulyás,* chicken *paprikás, kolbász* (smoked sausage), *csiga* and other homemade noodles, *kalács* (milk bread), *kifli* (horns with walnut filling), *rétes* (strudel), and *palacsinta* (crepe)—none of which can be missing from weddings, funerals, associational banquets, church feasts, March Fifteenth (commemorating the 1848 War of Independence) and July Fourth picnics, and the most enduring feasts—the Wine Harvest Dance and the pig-slaughter dinner. The minutes of organizing associations, photo-illustrated yearbook reports, and locally compiled cookbooks inform the carbon-copy similarity of these rituals across Hungarian America.

If prior to 1914 the emigrant elite suppressed regional peasant traditions, the 1956 "freedom fighter" generation temporarily assumed leadership in the revival of ethnic arts. The ambition to teach dances, songs, and crafts, to organize festivals, and to teach the grandchildren of immigrants the forgotten language was motivated by the teachers' own needs. The political-ethnic revival movement, claiming recognition of a multi-ethnic America, activated latent awareness of folk traditions, resulting in the revitalization of fading forms of folklore. It energized the new immigrant intelligentsia and reached out to the young generation of American-born enthusiasts.

In the preliminary stage as "birds of passage," the migrant, temporary workers lived in isolation between two worlds. Their life is well documented in mournful lament poetry, songs, fictitious letters, anecdotes, and amateur skits caricaturing the hardships of adjustment of greenhorns. Without a conscious effort to give up old values, however, assimilation began by learning elementary skills, new concepts, and idioms of the English language, changing habits of eating and clothing, operating appliances, and so forth. When small neighborhoods emerged, they seemed perfect cells to accommodate cultural heritage on a broad base. Similar to other European labor migrants, Hungarians formed their self-sufficient settlements between 1907 and the 1930s. Bankers, lawyers, doctors, food merchants, innkeepers, mail carriers, and pawnshop owners served the immediate needs of patrons in the native neighborhoods of cities, while local chapters of basic Hungarian American institutions—benevolent fraternities, political clubs, and churches—also began to take shape, providing for the physical and spiritual welfare of the community.

The parishes had an overall strong influence on the maintenance of ethnic loyalty and cultural preservation. Nevertheless, while the majority religion of Hungarians is Roman Catholic (ca. 65 percent), the Americanized Protestant denominations of the minority (ca. 25 percent) churches became the centers of cultural and social life. Not only did the church organize life-cycle and calendar rituals, patriotic, political, and civil festivities, and entertaining programs, it also offered education to both children and adults in language, history, literature, and folklore, such as handicraft, dancing, and singing.

The ethnic enclave, an irrational, nostalgic imitation of the hometown, was founded by the immigrant generation seeking temporary shelter in the alien world. Within it, essential values could be maintained while members also built the bridge to the future; it provided help to adjust to the industrial environment, the multilingual neighborhood, and the mainstream.

As long as the ethnic enclaves existed with a majority of the immigrant generation, they were culture-forming and culture-maintaining entities with masters of ceremonies leading traditional customs and practices. Habitat and housing patterns, interior decoration, use of space, religious symbols, vegetable and flower gardens, and the gossip bench in front of the house all corresponded to old-country forms. But as Old World values shifted to a new Hungarian American consciousness with the passing of the generations, there emerged a new brand of ethnic folklore, rooted in the old, but addressing contemporary issues of everyday life. Old stories about bewitching, magic, and healing were replaced by American-style ghost stories and local-character anecdotes highlighting funny cases of ignorance and smartness, tricksters, and dupes in the community. Greenhorn housewives use gesture language in the grocery store; the judge grants citizenship to the numbskull thought to be witty; a smart "Hunkey" peddler outwits other ethnics; an ignorant waitress serves marshmallow instead of mushroom soup; and a short-witted Bible-class student mistakes Pittsburgh for Bethlehem as Christ's birthplace because both are in Pennsylvania.

The ethnic community eventually outlived its usefulness, as the children and grandchildren of immigrants, born in the diaspora, found the environment restrictive. For the first American-born generation, the meaning of ethnicity and loyalty to heritage is different from that of the foreign born. It is an option to choose, retain, and develop images and emblems of ethnicity or reject them completely. In their cultural spectrum, ethnic heritage occupies only a small compartment reserved for special occasions. The ethnic images are select elements displayed more for the general public than for insiders. What is chosen for these occasions is spectacular, attractive, and classy, taken more from the national than from the regional heritage as a more usable item in status-promoting social activities. While everyday life—home decoration, eating habits, and the like—no longer contain traces of homeland ethnicity, a few display items appear prominently at festival occasions, particularly in the performance of dance and music, the wearing of costumes, and the preparation of special dishes. When the International Institute of Indianapolis invited local ethnics to introduce their specialties to the public in 1986, Hungarian women were dressed in *Matyó* (a regional group of northern Hungary) blouses with black skirts and boots mass-produced and exported from Hungary. They served potato stew in paprika with green salad and sang sentimental pseudo-folksongs. This hybrid revival appears as a response to the national appeal of ethnic Americans; it is a conscious self-stereotyping, a message to others, but also a nostalgic gesture toward the in-group and an attempt to preserve elements of a distant past that the new generations do not understand.

The Hungarian-by-choice may be a member of a totally integrated family. The American-born children of the 1956 freedom fighters seem not susceptible to the festival movement propagated by both American and Hungarian agencies. Lacking roots and continuity, however, the movement is superficial, following the performance guidelines given by agencies to amateur performing groups throughout the United States. Ethnicity may be active or latent, depending on circumstances; it may be recalled or completely forgotten.

The accidents of history, the lasting isolation of Hungarian Americans from the old country, the peculiarity of the language belonging to the Finno-Ugric family, and the ideological, social, and cultural segmentation of the immigrant generations, singly and together, have contributed to the discoloration of the modern-day Hungarian American identity.

Linda Dégh

References

Dégh, Linda. 1966. Approaches to Folklore Research among Immigrant Groups. *Journal of American Folklore.* 79:551–556.

———. 1977–1978. Grape-Harvest Festival of Strawberry Farmers: Folklore or Fake? *Ethnologia Europaea* 10:114–131.

———. 1980. The Ethnicity of Hungarian-Americans. *Congressus Quintus Internationalis Fenno-Ugristarum.* Turku. Part 4, pp. 225–290.

Fejös, Zoltán. 1993. *A chicagói magyarok két nemzedéke, 1890–1940* [Two Generations of Chicago Hungarians, 1890–1940]. Budapest: Középeurópai Intézet.

Hoppál, Mihály. 1989. Ethnic Symbolism: Tradition and Ethnicity in a Hungarian and an American-Hungarian Community. In *Folklór Archivum* nr. 18. Budapest: Néprajzi Kutatócsoport, pp. 155–184.

Lengyel, Emil. 1948. *Americans from Hungary.* Philadelphia and New York: Lippincott.

Puskás, Julianna. 1982. *Kivándorló magyarok az Egyesült államokban, 1880–1940.* [Emigrant Hungarians in the United States, 1880–1940]. Budapest: Akadémiai Kiadó.

Szántó, Miklós. 1984. *Magyarok Amerikában* [Hungarians in America]. Budapest: Gondolat.

Vázsonyi, Andrew. 1978. The Cicisbeo and the Magnificent Cuckold: Boardinghouse Life and Lore in Immigrant Communities. *Journal of American Folklore* 91:641–656.

Hunting

The seeking and taking of game animals in a variety of ways. Over time, hunters have evolved stylized modes of pursuit and capture, to which they may attach social and moral significance. Until recently, most anthropological studies of hunting focused on subsistence societies exotic to the investigator, while materials collected by folklorists largely comprised accidental texts—hunting songs, tall tales about hunting, and related lore about animals—gathered in the course of building collections of tales, songs, superstitions, and folk speech.

Hunting is, indeed, abundantly indexed in symbolic discourse, flashing through everyday speech in sayings like "hot on the trail" or "that dog won't hunt" (said of a bad idea). Songs like "Rabbit in a Log," and "Groundhog," which allude to traditional techniques of harvesting and preparing game, are standard fare in bluegrass and old-time music repertoires. In more elaborate figures, hunting has inspired children's games ("hare and hounds"), square-dance maneuvers ("chase the rabbit"), virtuoso imitations of fox chases on fiddle, bagpipes, harmonica, and banjo, and that paramount practical joke, the snipe hunt.

However serious attention to hunting as a form of symbolic interaction in modern society, exemplifying what Victor Turner called the "liminoid phenomena" of complex industrial societies, has been sparse. Only in the 1990s have scholars begun to explore how, through hunting as ritual performance, American hunters come to terms with social and natural hierarchies, and their own positions within them (Hufford 1992; Marks 1992). In the United States, the Civil War roughly divides historically distinctive phases in hunting. Before the Civil War, hunting was part of rural life, providing a pleasurable break from routine as well as putting food on the table. After the Civil War, an industrializing, urbanizing nation—grappling with the detachment of civilization from nature and the separation of livelihoods from the land—radically restructured access to game. As the frontier ebbed toward closure, hunters' associations lobbied for regulations protecting wildlife from market gunners and wilderness from the whims of irresponsible landowners (Ives 1988; Marks 1992). This had the effect of removing game from local control and of pitting backwoodsmen and farmers, who deemed hunting necessary to their ways of life, against urban, elite men of means, for whom hunting offered a form of respite from the modernizing world. The battle lines having been drawn, game became a different kind of cash crop—luring metropolitan dollars into the pockets of seasonal guides and other providers and institutionalizing a running conflict between game wardens and poachers. Stock narratives of poachers as heroes and wardens as buffoons have flourished ever since within thriving traditions of local resistance (Hufford 1992; Ives 1988).

Social relations continue to take shape around the political production and stylized acquisition of wildlife, which varies not only regionally but across the social spectrum. For instance, on the outskirts of Middleburg, Virginia, red foxes race over rolling hills, pursued by packs of pedigreed hounds, followed in turn by red-coated women and men leaping fences on half-bred "hunters." In the mountains of Tennessee, "one gallus" hunters pause in their conversations around ridgetop campfires to decipher the voices of unseen hounds, "singing" on the trails of gray foxes. In West Virginia in the spring, a solitary man dressed in camouflage, his back against a tree, coaxes hen-like calls from a small wooden box to entice a wary gobbler. In December, fathers, sons, uncles, nephews, grandsons, and neighbors, encamped for a week in southern New Jersey gun clubs, organize "deer drives" to flush bucks out of patches of woodland. Each winter, in marshlands along the routes of migratory waterfowl, some gunners conceal themselves with retrievers in duck blinds and eye the skies over their decoy spreads for signs of descending ducks. Others (traditionally a clientele of high social status) are propelled in railbird skiffs by local guides looking not only for railbirds but also for opportunities to perform rites of reversal on their wealthy patrons. "You couldn't hit the side of a barn, Admiral!" said Albert Reeves, a "mudwalloper" from south Jersey, recalling with relish an incident from his guiding career (Parsons 1987).

Such acts of engaging with game are portals on myriad domains built around the central idea of sportsmanship, an idea combining principles of conservation with a gentleman's code of honor. Hunting as the stylized enactment of sportsmanship is thus distinguished from hunting as the mere taking of food for livelihood. Sportsmen, as stewards of wilderness, are enjoined to take no more than their fair share and to retrieve and use any animals they cripple or kill. In a curious twist, the sportsman on the post-frontier hunts not because he needs to, but because his hunting is *needed* in order to protect what remains of wildlife and wilderness. From the sportsman's perspective, hunters' license fees support the land, and their vigilance and discipline keep the stock culled and the species healthy.

While principles of sportsmanship guide the construction of hunting domains, possibilities for enacting sportsmanship and debates about what constitutes it in practice are endless. The ideal of sportsmanship is debated and played out in class ways. Cast as a gentleman's code of honor in an aristocratic setting, the ideal is recast among working men to embody egalitarian principles of honesty, loyalty, fair play, and fellowship.

Domains of hunting are as varied as the communities of sportsmen taking shape around their chosen species. Each domain orders its denizens, categorizing animal players as quarry, allies, and "trash"—players that interfere with the hunt by distracting hounds or competing with hunters for quarry. For coon hunters, "trashing" describes the behavior of a hound diverted by rabbits, possum, or deer. English-style fox hunters call this behavior "rioting," intolerable in the pedigreed hounds of their subscription packs. Hilltoppers, working-class fox hunters who breed their own hounds, contend that pedigree is no guarantee of superior performance, that a "potlicker" with the proper disposition and training can "get out there and do the job" just as well. For working-class hunters whose packs consist of individually owned hounds, the hunting pack can be a study in egalitarian principles of fair competition, honoring the leader, and sharing the leadership. Thus, hunters explore the underpinnings of social hierarchy, justifying or challenging them through discourse about animals (Hufford 1992; Marks 1992).

What distinguishes hunting from other secular rituals in industrial societies is the use of animals, ostensibly to enhance the hunters' grasp of nature and the human position in it. At the heart of hunting rests a paradoxical relationship between hunters and their quarry. Jose Ortega y Gassett argues that the hunter and the hunted must be located at a precise distance from each other on the zoological scale (Ortega y Gassett 1972:124). Maintenance of that distance is crucial to tenets of sportsmanship, whereby hunters relinquish their superiority to give the quarry a competitive edge. Thus, they limit their capacity to kill animals by rules that make practices like hunting during breeding seasons, shooting into a flock of feeding waterfowl, or "spotting" (using lights at night) or "dogging" (pursuing with dogs) for deer illegal. Lowering their status in the animal kingdom, hunters ingeniously seek to enter and inhabit the ordinarily uninhabitable. Imagining themselves from the perspective of their quarry, hunters may contrive to blend with the landscape through camouflage clothing, use of animal scent, decoys, deceptively designed watercraft (such as the Barnegat Bay "sneakbox"), temporary "blinds," sink boxes, and tree stands that stud the landscape, as well as permanent cabins and camps.

Animal helpers, especially dogs, help define and sustain a precise distance on the zoological scale. Through breeding and training, hunters shape hounds to meet regionally distinctive conditions for hunting particular quarry. Walker hounds bred to tree racoons and pursue foxes in mountainous terrain are deemed less well suited to conditions on the Atlantic coastal plain than Maryland hounds (Hufford 1992). Hunters preferring the chase over the kill favor hounds bred to follow the trail on the ground rather than on the wind. Mountain Feist dogs are bred to follow the movements of squirrels by eye through treetops. Blocky and compact English Labs are "wrestlers," shaped to storm hedgerows in search of downed pheasants. Bushy-tailed "decoy dogs" (Nova Scotia duck-tolling [luring] retrievers) are designed to lure ducks for waterfowlers. This breed is modeled after foxes seen cavorting about on banks, using their tails to lure their prey within snatching range.

In conversations and in writing, hunters constitute their quarry and assign meaning to the zoological distance they traverse through empathy, pitting their mental acuity and physical stamina against the intelligence or guile of a most worthy adversary. Hunting domains are staged on the margins, in areas set aside for time-out activities. Not surprisingly, the quarries centered within these marginal worlds often emerge in narratives as paradoxical, anomalous creatures—protagonists of stock tales of tricksters subverting the hunt: the turkey who steals the call box; the flock of ducks departing with the decoys; the buck that melts into the swamp; or the fox that loses a pack of dogs by running through a flock of sheep.

Hunting domains persist as enclaves of wholeness in a world fragmented by industrial expansion. Such worlds are powerful resources for identity building, conferring wholeness and authenticity on their inhabitants. Over time, hunters become historical personages in their domains, evaluated as sportsmen and comrades. Their abilities, personality quirks, and accomplishments may be registered in nicknames, place names, names for hounds, CB handles, and narratives of hunting exploits and blunders.

While maintaining their own perspective, hunters paradoxically must aspire to the quarry's point of view, for, as Ortega y Gassett observes, "the pursuer cannot pursue if he does not integrate his vision with that of the animal" (Ortega y Gassett 1972:124). The ability to "think like a duck" (fox / quail / racoon / bear / squirrel / railbird / or deer), necessary for successful hunting, lends itself to the formation of human identity. As James Fernandez argues, in order to gain identity, humans must first "become objects to themselves, by taking the point of view of 'the other,' before they can become subjects to themselves" (Fernandez 1983:35). Animals provide what he calls primordial metaphors. In line with "taking the animal other," hunters often sport images of their quarry on caps, bumper stickers, mailboxes, stationary, and t-shirts. Regionally distinctive quarry thus become resources for regional identity.

Though deemed avocational, hunting is cast as a true career through language. Hunters speak of the "calling" that continually draws them into a world that takes a lifetime to complete. In some traditions, hunting practices mark the transition from one stage of life to another. A boy killing his first buck may be ritually sprinkled with the animal's blood, while hunters past their prime commonly eschew killing, having proven themselves in youth and mid-life, as multipronged buck "racks" mounted over domestic hearths attest. Mock shaming rituals keep the pressure on those not old enough for this dispensation. A hunter smitten with "buck fever" may be conscripted into the "shirttail club," whose members are required to yield up a shirttail for failing to shoot at a deer within range or for firing and missing.

The recurrent aspects of hunting provide continuity over long lives and offer elderly hunters an organizing principle for their life stories. A famous example is Siegfried Sassoon's *Memoirs of a Foxhunting Man* (1944), but examples abound in sportsmen's magazines (such as *Hunter's Horn,* which Duncan Emrich once said deserves a spot on every folklorist's bookshelf), as well as in memoirs, written and tape-recorded for posterity (Hufford 1992). In these stories, a normative pattern of maturation emerges, as the autobiographer details the mastery of tradition and the concomitant molding of a disciplined, other-centered sportsman from a self-centered youth eager for trophies of conquest.

The world of hunting is a potent conversational resource, engendering sociality among hunters away from the field. Through narrative, hunters constitute a world in which they appear as characters who exercise sportsmanship and fellowship (or whose exercise of sportsmanship is vigorously debated by those present at the storytelling.) This fellowship is generally a fellowship of men, shaped through conversational practices in which quarry are not the only tricksters. Positioned at the margins of everyday life, the sociality of hunting conjures a prankish milieu in which men trick each other. Just as the sociality of men hunting includes a fair amount of teasing and practical joking, so does the sociality of hunters narrating, telling stories termed "lies" because exaggeration is expected. Tall tales, such as "The Wonderful Hunt" (Tale Type 1890), constitute a form of practical joke designed to dupe the gullible hearer. As the hunter in the story may get the better of a colleague, or as an animal pulls one over on a human, so the narrator hopes to bag his

listeners, who must in turn be "good sports" about being "taken in." On the other hand, pranksters and liars are expected to exercise restraint and not take undue advantage of the unsuspecting. Thus, the necessary exercise of sportsmanship in dealing with animals spills over from narrated worlds into human affairs.

Mary Hufford

References

Bauman, Richard. 1986. *Story, Performance, and Event.* New York: Cambridge University Press.

Emrich, Duncan. 1972. Hound Dog Names. In *Folklore on the American Land.* Boston: Little, Brown.

Fernandez, James. 1983. *Persuasions and Performances: The Play of Tropes in Culture.* Bloomington: Indiana University Press.

Hufford, Mary. 1990. "One Reason God Made Trees": The Form and Ecology of the Barnegat Bay Sneakbox. In *A Sense of Place: Essays on American Regional Cultures,* ed. Barbara Allen and Thomas J. Schlereth. Bowling Green: University of Kentucky Press.

———. 1992. *Chaseworld: Foxhunting and Storytelling in New Jersey's Pine Barrens.* Philadelphia: University of Pennsylvania Press.

Ives, Edward D. 1988. *George Magoon and the Down East Game War.* Urbana: University of Illinois Press.

Marks, Stuart. 1992. *Southern Hunting in Black and White: Nature, History, and Ritual in a Carolina Community.* Princeton, NJ: Princeton University Press.

Ortega y Gassett, Jose. 1972. *Meditations on Hunting.* New York: Scribner's.

Parsons, Gerald. 1987. Commercial Hunting of Freshwater Railbirds: An Ethnographic Perspective. Paper delivered before the Maryland Ornithological Association, Upper Marlboro, MD.

Turner, Victor. 1977. Variations on a Theme of Liminality. In *Secular Ritual,* ed. Sally Falk Moore and Barbara Myerhoff. Amsterdam: Van Gorcum, pp. 37–52.

See also Animals; Fishing (Sport); Trapping

Hurston, Zora Neale (1891–1960)

Anthropologist, essayist, novelist, dramatist, and folklorist who played a major role in compiling and analyzing African American and Afro-Caribbean folktales. Born January 7, 1891, in Eatonville, Florida—the first incorporated black township in the United States—Hurston enrolled at Howard University in 1918. Her first published story, "John Redding Goes to Sea," appeared in the Howard University literary magazine *Stylus* in 1921. In 1925 Hurston moved to New York City, where she became a part of the Harlem Renaissance movement and entered Barnard College. She earned her B.A. from Barnard in 1928, and continued her studies at Columbia University under anthropologist Franz Boas. It was Boas who encouraged her to return to the South to collect folklore, with funding from New York socialite Osgood Mason. *Mules and Men* (1935) is a representative collection of materials she gathered in Florida and Alabama between 1929 and 1931. It also includes a revised and expanded version of Hurston's celebrated essay "Hoodoo in America," which had appeared four years earlier in the *Journal of American Folklore* (44:318–418). *Mules and Men* illustrates its author's concern for what Henry Louis Gates termed "the figurative capacity of Black language" (Gates 1990:294) a concern reflected in all of Hurston's books.

The year 1937 saw the publication of her most critically acclaimed novel, *Their Eyes Were Watching God,* considered an accurate and insightful depiction of African American folk beliefs, manners, and speech patterns of the period. This was followed in 1938 by a collection of folktales from Jamaica and Haiti entitled *Tell My Horse.* Part travelogue, part ethnography, *Tell My Horse* provides a detailed and vivid description of the ceremonial aspects of voodoo, with special attention to the role of spirit possession. *Tell My Horse* also stands as one of the most engaging and accessible introductions to Haitian voodoo.

Commissioned by her publisher, J.P. Lippincott, her autobiography, *Dust Tracks on the Road,* appeared in 1942. It has been suggested that this book may contain as much folklore as biography. For example, Lillie P. Howard points out that there is considerable speculation as to whether she even gives her correct date of birth (Howard 1980:13). Nevertheless, always the ethnographer, Hurston in *Dust Tracks on the Road* successfully positions herself as a mediator between the Black folk community and her largely White reading audience. She masterfully represents herself within the context of African American folk traditions.

Her last novel, *Seraph on the Suwanee,* which dealt with psychological and emotional problems of a working-class Southern White woman, was published in 1948. Biographers have noted that Hurston's career declined precipitously thereafter. In the 1950s, she worked as a librarian and a maid before suffering a serious stroke in 1959. She died in obscurity on January 28, 1960, at the Saint Lucie County Welfare Home in Fort Pierce, Florida, and was buried in an unmarked grave.

Stephen D. Glazier

References

Gates, Henry Louis. 1990. Zora Neale Hurston: A Negro Way of Saying. In *Tell My Horse.* New York: Harper and Row, pp. 289–299.

Hemenway, Robert E. 1977. *Zora Neale Hurston: A Literary Biography.* Urbana: University of Illinois Press.

Howard, Lillie Pearl. 1980. *Zora Neale Hurston.* Boston: Twayne.

Hyatt, Harry M. (1896–1978)

Folklore collector and Episcopal clergyman. Hyatt was the son of an Illinois state senator and grew up in Quincy, Illinois, on the Mississippi River across from Hannibal, Missouri.

After advanced religious studies at Oxford University, Hyatt became interested in missionary work and produced a scholarly text on the Coptic Church of Abyssinia in 1928. His wife, Alma, a prominent businesswoman, supported his in-

Zora Neale Hurston in 1938. Photo Carl Van Vechten. Library of Congress.

terest in folklore fieldwork. With the help of his sister Minnie, who lived in Quincy (Adams County), Hyatt began the regional folklore collection that he hoped would exceed the 4,000 entries in a similar Kentucky work. The first edition contained 11,000 entries, while the revised edition contained more than 16,000 items, an effort folklorist Richard M. Dorson described as the most intensive single collection of American superstition.

From 1936 to 1940, Hyatt collected materials in the Eastern and Southern states on hoodoo, conjuration, witchcraft, and rootwork. The hoodoo collection involved beliefs in witchcraft predominantly among African Americans, and it included interviews with nineteen hoodoo doctors and more than 1,600 informants. The five-volume collection, based on more than 3,000 recording cylinders, is more than 5,000 pages in length (Hyatt 1970–1978). Dorson described this collection as the greatest feat of collection in African-American folklore.

Hyatt received many honors, including appointment as an officer of the French Academy. He expressed great pride, as a nonacademic folklorist, in his recognition, in 1972, by the American Folklore Society for his contributions to folklore fieldwork collection.

John Schleppenbach

References

De Caro, Francis A. 1974. Hyatt's Hoodoo Odyssey: A Review Article. *Louisiana Review* 3 (1).

Dorson, Richard M., and Michael Bell, eds. 1979. Harry

Middleton Hyatt. *Journal of the Folklore Institute* (Special Issue). 16 (1–2).

Hyatt, Harry. 1935. *Folklore of Adams County, Illinois.* Quincy, IL, and New York: Memoirs of the Alma Egan Hyatt Foundation.

———. 1970–1978. *Hoodoo-Conjuration-Witchcraft-Rootwork: Beliefs Accepted by Many Negroes and White Persons These Being Orally Recorded among Blacks and Whites.* 5 vols. Quincy, IL, and New York: Memoirs of the Alma Egan Hyatt Foundation.

I

Immigrant Folklore, Study of

Study of the importation of folk traditions by foreign nationals who immigrate to the United States, settle, and form their own communities. As Andrew M. Greely observes, "the immigrants brought many pieces of cultural baggage with them when they came to the New World. Art, political styles, religious perspective are but a few such pieces. But none was as important as the 'how' of being a family. It provided a stable continuous pattern of development in the new surrounding" (Greely 1974). As part of this cultural baggage, old-country folklore becomes crucial to the foundation of New World settlements; it is intimate, like a family, and it allows the foreign-born pioneers to establish their new national identity model and pass it on to their American-born children.

Immigrant folklore is distinguished from the folklore of earlier English, Scottish, German, French, and Spanish colonists who populated large regions of the American continent between 1607 and 1850; these earlier pioneers were culture builders on uninhabited virgin land that inspired them to create their own regional dialect of a commonly formed basic American folklore. But the immigrants who streamed into the United States in masses from impoverished countries of Europe and Asia after the Civil War, and who kept coming until World War I, landed on civilized grounds and sought employment in the labor forces of established cities, industrial areas, and rural areas. Under such conditions, their folklore developed betwixt and between the mainstream in small enclaves close to the workplaces where the processes of transgenerational transformation passed through the ethnic stage and ended up in cultural integration, persisting only in a "symbolic ethnicity" (Gans 1979) of personal choice, thus conforming to the governmental "melting pot" policy of the time.

Mass immigration to the United States uprooted bankrupt small farmers and farm workers from their peasant existence in Europe. Their exodus coincided with the introduction of large-scale commercial farming and the construction of cities and heavy industry where they found employment. Immigrants' success depended on their ability to adjust to new labor conditions and to the multinational environment; they had to adapt to a lifestyle suitable for establishing social relationships. The immigrants' cultural knowledge—peasant self-sufficiency, worldview, and oral and ritual artistry—helped them to cope in the new situation, but at the same time it prolonged their reliance on a heritage that kept them alienated from their homeland and isolated in their new colony from other colonists. As Oscar Handlin aptly observed, the immigrants knew ". . . they would not come to belong. . . . The only adjustment they had been able to make to life in the United States had been one that involved the separateness of their group, one that increased their awareness of the differences between themselves and the rest of the society" (Handlin 1951:285).

The folklore of the immigrant generation, disjointed bits and pieces of an archaic cultural system, since the 1880s attracted the attention of American folklorists as fascinating and exotic. Items of foreign origin surviving in American towns keep appearing on the pages of folklore journals up to this day, and they cover a broad field. Superstitions, curses, magical medicine, evil-eye beliefs, witchcraft, weatherlore, proverbs, riddles and nursery rhymes, stories and myths, customs and rituals (weddings, baptisms, and funerals), celebrations of holidays (such as Easter and Christmas) abound. Scholarly presentations of arts, crafts, and costume could fill volumes, proving the continued interest in the folklore repertoire of the unacculturated alien population. However, the contents of most of the so-called "memory culture" items in folklore collections remain unrepresentative of either the old or the new country; rather, they are evidence of alienation from both. One example is the collection made from a Finnish immigrant woman from Vermont, who after forty-three years in America told her stories for the first time, upon direct questioning by the folklorist (Köngäs 1960). Another example is that of a traditional Macedonian *guslar* (singer of epic verse) in Gary, Indiana, who recited his lengthy epic at a Croatian *tamburitza* festival while eager young dancers barely concealed their disdain. On another occasion, a seventy-four-year-old east Chi-

Peter Boro, immigrant from Croatia, plays his gusla. San Mateo, California, 1940. American Folklife Center, Cowell Collection (WPA).

cago woman, president of the Ladies Aid Society of the Hungarian Reformed Church, remarked, "I am a guest in America for sixty years."

Yet, the heritage of an imported folklore residue of immigrants must determine the future formation of the folklore of American ethnic subcultures. It also determines either the survival or the demise of ethnic identity. Greely and William C. McCready's investigation of the persistence of Old World cultural heritage among children and grandchildren of Irish Catholics and Italians goes back to the roots of the traditions. They argue that the present behavior of American ethnic groups would be difficult to understand without knowing something about the cultural background of their country of origin (Greely and McCready 1975:229). A field study of a Hungarian farming community founded ninety-four years ago on the Great Plains, by settlers from two different regional subcultures in the old country, showed that loyalty to different regional identities rather than to the common national one can maintain long-term hostilities and lead eventually to assimilation (Dégh 1980).

The flow of peasant immigration from Europe and Asia was stopped by World War I, but new waves soon followed as new political and economic conditions forced people to leave their countries of origin and seek their fortunes in North America. Emigrants and exiles came from all over the world, so that the earlier argument for the dominance of Europeans

in the racial-ethnic composition of Americans had to be reconsidered. Likewise, the Anglo-centric cultural model changed to recognize multiculturalism. Over the last decades, the schedule of immigrant timetables accelerated as the number of arrivals grew, and the speed of transgenerational acculturation began to change. New population groups keep showing up on the borders of the United States almost daily, seeking admittance to a safe haven and deliverance from political upheavals, "ethnic cleansing," genocide, and hunger. In the 1990s, Asian, South American, and African immigrants outnumber European arrivals, and under given conditions their adjustment to American life is smoother and faster than that of their European predecessors.

The latest wave of immigrants skipped the bird-of-passage stage and settled for good from the start. They may form large self-contained urban or suburban settlements where their native language, religious philosophy, and imported cultural values may be maintained. An informed public may support continuation of the immigrants' heritage. The ideological spheres of folklore are manifested not only in private, but also in the public representation of identity via spectacular customs, rituals, and artistic displays aimed partly at the outside world. This is a far cry from the situation of groups such as unskilled European laborers in the West Virginia mining towns, or workers in the company towns of the Midwest. We cannot yet measure the transgenerational ethnic process of acculturation of the folklore of current immigrants to mainstream America, because time has been too short to judge the future.

Each wave of immigration and each category of arrivals need to be examined separately, considering the origin, culture, and status of the immigrants, the motivation for their immigration, and the intercultural contacts they make in their settlements. Changing governmental policies toward immigrants have greatly influenced retention or extinction of imported folklore. The masses of peasants arriving at the receiving port of Castle Garden in the 19th century, and later at Ellis Island, were regarded as inferior aliens—"illiterate peasants who differ greatly in enterprise and intelligence from the average American citizen," wrote one observer in 1907, adding that they settle "in communities by themselves, where they continue to speak their native languages and are slow to assimilate American ideas." Governmental agencies always saw these miserable creatures as candidates for happiness in the new country, depending upon their ability to assimilate. Schools for immigrants were established, in hope of soon helping them forget the tortured memories of their homes of birth and embrace the opportunity to become Americans fast. So-called "International Institutes," founded in the 1920s and 1930s in large industrial cities, receiving great numbers of immigrants were the only government-sponsored organizations that encouraged folk-art programs. These had the purpose of stilling the pain of homesick immigrants. In the early 1970s, following the civil rights movement, the tide turned from speedy enforcement of acculturation toward a politically conceived multiculturalism.

The idea of a "nation of immigrants" became the leitmotiv

for Washington's celebration of America's Bicentennial in 1976, with the attendance of all contributing nations. In preparation for the program of "Old World—New World" unity, the Smithsonian Institution hired trained folklorists to collect folklore materials from ethnic American communities (the New World) in order to provide for the performance of spectacular programs or exhibits and demonstrations of arts and crafts on the National Mall. The Smithsonian also invited folk-art ensembles from the countries of origin (the Old World) in order to renew ties between compatriots on American soil in front of a national audience. While new fieldwork enriched archival holdings, creating a gold mine for future research, it did not induce innovative scholarly study of immigrant and ethnic folklore, and it did not generate any new theories. Instead, it opened the way to public-sector propagation of folklore, turning traditional performers into merchants of heritage, functioning to entertain a nostalgic urban-industrial audience that eagerly consumed defunct folkloric symbols of the past in abstracted, condensed, and simulated forms on the stage. The 1976 Washington festival started the series of summer folklife festivals sponsored by the Smithsonian Office of Folklife Programs. It is no longer limited to immigrant folklore, but the original idea behind the program has not changed. The aim is still to present the life of the American folk—natives, races, regionals, ethnics, and immigrants together—following the politics of multiculturalism. The high rating of the recently arrived immigrants' imported folklore—that of the Hmong, the Vietnamese, Cubans, the Yuruba, and Bosnians, for example—may help extend its lease on life, with the assistance of the American Folklife Center's team of folklore fieldworkers and managers.

European scholars saw America as a relic area where foreign nationals, detached from their mother culture, would be able to preserve long-forgotten treasures of their homeland. Between 1916 and 1918, Cecil Sharp visited the southern Appalachian region in search of surviving British balladry. He "often pictured in imagination what it would have been like to have been born a few centuries earlier, when English folksong was the common musical expression of old and young alike. And it seemed almost like a miracle when he discovered that England of his dreams in the United States of America . . ." (Karpeles 1967:140). In 1962 Norwegian folklorist Reidar Christiansen noted that North America "consists of people from practically every European country. . . . All arrived with their store of tradition," but they were "absorbed within a generation or two," emerging as Americans two generations later (Christiansen 1962:15). He suggested that British tradition is fundamental to American culture, absorbing others, and that the English pattern appears to be the main strain in American folklore (Christiansen 1962:122–123).

American folklorists also accepted the characterization of American folklore as essentially *Anglo*-American, and they viewed the process of Americanization of aliens as assimilation to the Anglo-American model. Richard M. Dorson's distinction between colonial, regional, and immigrant cultures remained consistent with the melting-pot idea, yet Dorson's determination to find and characterize folklore in the urban-industrial settlements of the Calumet region of the Midwest

led him to experience a multicultural coexistence of ethnics with other entities, regional, racial, and occupational (Dorson 1981). Dorson's description of the position of ethnic individuals within their groups, their behavior, community involvement, and display of their identity in terms of their folklore opened new perspectives to immigrant folklore study in a multicultural society.

American folklore as a scholarly field emerged from European antecedents, borrowing and applying methods and theories to specific New World conditions. From a cultural-historical perspective, Dorson proposed a new field that studies folklore in emergence within the course of American history—a contextual study of "American folklore vs. folklore in America" (Dorson 1978). The outline of his proposal was provided in the chapters of his book *American Folklore* in 1959, and he established an innovative university curriculum at Indiana University to train specialists in that field and to have them test the validity of his assumptions in their term papers and doctoral dissertations. Dorson's immigrant folklore was only a part of what he wanted to explore. The monographic studies Dorson directed between 1961 and 1977 researched folklore in the immigrant-community contexts of Greek, Finnish, Yiddish, Sephardic, Danish, Swedish, Ukrainian, Italian, Mexican, and Romanian settlements; they were conducted by native ethnographers—ethnic Americans and immigrants themselves. This innovative series had its own strengths and weaknesses. Lacking experience, linguistic competence, and a balanced familiarity with both Old World backgrounds and immigrant conditions, the authors were guided only by common sense and their findings. They highlighted the most conspicuous and most attractive features, finding almost incredible evidence of the preservation of archaic songs and customs. Yet, the variety of case studies revealed the differential roles that immigrant lore can play in the lives of the settlers. They also revealed that the maintenance of heritage does not necessarily foster ethnic survival, though invented identity markers may substitute for it in the construction of ethnic awareness by the first American-born generation. The questions that the studies raised opened vistas for the study of ethnicity: What motivates people to settle? What happens to the inherited tradition after they leave their country, settle in an unfamiliar place, learn a new language and new skills? How and in what ways can their imported anachronistic folklore be maintained after the passing of the first generation? What is the contribution of immigrant lore to an all-American folklore?

With reference to the study of acculturation and assimilation of immigrants and their descendants by anthropologists, sociologists, and historians, Stephen Stern reviewed the publications of Dorson, his disciples, and other folklorists up to 1975. Stern criticized them for focusing on the nature and function of the immigrant generation's heritage and the potentials of its survival (Stern 1977). Calling this "survivalistic perspective" one that is "based on preconceived notions of what the materials of ethnic folklore studies were to be, namely Old World immigrant forms of expression," Stern charged that researchers ignored the development of new forms and the creativity of American-born ethnics and idealized the importations from the Old World; any noticeable alteration, folklorists would refer to with terms like "demise" or "contamination" (Stern 1977:12). A misapplication of Alan Dundes' "devolutionary premise" (Dundes 1969) was used to argue against the rigorous analysis of immigrant folklore—imported baggage that exhibited natural variations between devolution and revolution, contamination, revitalization, wear and tear. All folklore has its life trajectory from inception to high tide, ebb, and demise; at the end of the cycle, new forms emerge from the remains of the old. This is what Stern misconceives as survivalist belief, but the replacement of dysfunctional older forms is a natural and healthy process that opens the door for the production of new folklore. This process belongs to the ethnic stage, not to the study of the immigrant generation. The student of immigrant folklore has to reach back to the roots of the immigrants' baggage and to experience and follow its functions within its own context and authority. Only such focused research can solidify the basis of studying the total cycle of the folklore process from immigration to ethnicity and integration.

Linda Dégh

References

Bauman, Richard, Patricia Sawin, and Inta Gale Carpenter. 1992. *Reflections on the Folklife Festival: An Ethnography of Participant Experience.* Bloomington, IN: Folklore Institute.

Bodner, John. 1985. *The Transplanted: A History of Immigrants in Urban America.* Bloomington: Indiana University Press.

Christiansen, Reidar Th. 1962. *European Folklore in America.* Oslo: Universitetsforlaget.

Dégh, Linda. 1980. Folk Religion as Ideology for Ethnic Survival: The Hungarians of Kipling, Saskatchewan. In *Ethnicity on the Great Plains,* ed. F.C. Luebke. Lincoln: University of Nebraska Press. pp. 129–146.

Dorson, Richard M. 1978. American Folklore vs. Folklore in America. *Journal of the Folklore Institute* 15:97–111.

———. 1981. *Land of the Millrats: Urban Folklore in Indiana's Calumet Region.* Cambridge: Harvard University Press.

Dundes, Alan. 1969. The Devolutionary Premise in Folklore Theory. *Journal of the Folklore Institute* 6:5–19.

Gans, Herbert J. 1979. Symbolic Ethnicity: The Future of Ethnic Groups and Cultures in America. *Ethnic and Racial Studies* 2:1–19.

Georges, Robert A., and Stephen Stern. 1982. *American and Canadian Immigrant and Ethnic Folklore: An Annotated Bibliography.* New York: Garland.

Greely, Andrew M. 1974. *Ethnicity in the United States: A Preliminary Reconnaissance.* New York: Wiley and Sons.

Greely, Andrew M., and William C. McCready. 1975. The Transmission of Cultural Heritages: The Case of the Irish and the Italian. In *Ethnicity: Theory and Experience,* ed. Nathan Glazer and Daniel P. Moynihan. Cambridge: Harvard University Press, pp. 209–235.

Handlin, Oscar. 1951. *The Uprooted: The Epic Story of the Great Migration That Made the American People.* New York: Grosset and Dunlap.

Karpeles, Maud. 1967. *Cecil Sharp: His Life and Work.* Chicago: University of Chicago Press.

Köngäs, Elli-Kaija. 1960. Immigrant Folklore: Survival or Living Tradition? *Midwest Folklore* 10:117–124.

Stern, Stephen. 1977. Ethnic Folklore and the Folklore of Ethnicity. *Western Folklore* 36:7–32.

See also Anglo Americans; Baltic Peoples in the United States; Basque Americans; Chinese Americans; Dutch Americans; Ethnic Folklore; Filipino Americans; Finnish Americans; French Canadians; French in the United States; German Americans; Hungarian Americans; Irish Americans; Italian Americans; Japanese Americans; Mexican Americans; Pennsylvania Germans ("Dutch"); Polish Americans; Romanian Americans; Scandinavian Americans; Scottish Americans; Slavic Americans; Ukrainian Americans; Welsh Americans; Wends (Sorbs) in the United States

Independence Day

National and state holiday celebrated each July 4 (hence often called "the Fourth of July"). The Second Continental Congress voted for independence from England on July 2, 1776. Two days later, the group ratified the Declaration of Independence, which John Hancock, president of the congress, and Charles Thomson, secretary, then signed. The first celebration of these events occurred on July 2, 1777, when Philadelphians sounded bells and lit bonfires and fireworks. Though contemporary sentiment favored retaining July 2 as the festive date, July 4 soon supplanted the anniversary of the actual vote for independence.

Factional displays by Republicans and Federalists marked Independence Day until about 1820, when observances shifted to nonpartisan celebrations of American freedom. That focus, though, yielded to increasing stress on recreation and amusement, manifested especially in noisy, dangerous fireworks. By the early 1900s, injuries resulting from fireworks had reached such proportions that Independence Day became known as the "Barbarous Fourth." In response to what they viewed as degeneration of the holiday and to the growing presence of non-English-speaking immigrants, reformers successfully shifted the emphasis to a generalized Americanism, which foregrounds points of common concern across partisanly political, ethnic, and regional lines.

The federal government and all of the states and territories recognize Independence Day. Public observances usually feature parades, martial music, decorations using national colors and symbols, bell ringing, fireworks, and speech making. Precedents for these activities may be found in mid-19th-century celebrations such as those in frontier Nebraska. These might begin with a dance on July 3. Another dance—this one outdoors—took place on the afternoon of the Fourth itself, with still another scheduled for the evening. The day commenced with bell ringing and fireworks, and a mid-morning parade with military escort set an appropriate

Independence Day parade. Mayville, North Dakota, 1908. Photo J.C. Jansrub. Library of Congress.

tone. In addition to orations on patriotic topics, the morning's schedule might include vocal soloists and a reading of the Declaration of Independence.

In addition to dancing, the afternoon program, which followed an elaborate feast, usually featured ball games and horse races. Other competitions included three-legged races, potato races, sack races, and greased-pole climbings. Perhaps a picnic would conclude the daylight festivities before more dancing began, which could last until the next morning.

Family-oriented celebrations of Independence Day, which lack overt patriotic trappings, involve trips to recreational areas such as lakes or parks. Picnic menus include foods (for example, hamburgers and hot dogs) easily prepared on outdoor grills, summertime beverages such as lemonade and beer, and hand-cranked ice cream. In addition to gossip and storytelling, celebrants may use the day for swimming, fishing, or informal sports such as softball. Neighborhood observances and block parties often center on collaborative meals, each household providing a dish to be generally shared. Frequently, family and neighborhood gatherings adjourn at dusk so that participants can watch community-wide fireworks displays.

Independence Day festivities often evince distinctive ethnic or regional flavors. Italian Americans, for instance, may stage bocce tournaments. Western communities schedule rodeos for the date. Native Americans are likely to hold pow-wows and other events reflecting tribal or pan-Indian identity on July 4.

William M. Clements

References

Cohen, Henning, and Tristram Potter Coffin, eds. 1991. *The Folklore of American Holidays*. 2d. ed. Detroit: Gale.

Cohn, William H. 1976. A National Celebration: The Fourth of July. *Cultures* 3 (2):141–156.

Hatch, Jane M., ed. 1978. *The American Book of Days*. 3d. ed. New York: H.W. Wilson.

Pound, Louise. 1959. *Nebraska Folklore*. Lincoln: University of Nebraska Press.

Samuelson, Sue, and Ray Kepner. 1984. Bocce Ball Meets Hacky-Sack: A Western Pennsylvania Independence Day Gathering. *Keystone Folklore* 3 (2):26–35.

Index of American Design

A collection of approximately 22,000 renderings of objects of folk and popular manufacture made before 1890, housed at the National Gallery of Art in Washington, DC. Many works of folk art and craft can be viewed there in the form of highly realistic watercolor renderings. The Index of American Design was one of the many innovative projects sponsored by President Franklin D. Roosevelt's New Deal, and when proposed in 1935 it was suggested that, in addition to employing hundreds of out-of-work draftsmen, the Index would preserve a record of past American achievement, inspire new design, and serve as a reference work for scholars. However, the project proved to be most successful mainly as an unemployment relief effort.

Because Index administrators fell far short of their anticipated goal of 100,000 images, they never made any serious moves toward assembling the numerous illustrations into the authoritative encyclopedia on early American material culture that they had promised. Furthermore, initial claims of high scholarly standards and a keen focus on interpretation were relinquished when Constance Rourke, then one of the country's foremost cultural historians, was dismissed from the project's administrative staff in 1936. The Index was then transformed essentially into an exercise in fine-art skill and collector taste. Index plates were selected principally on the basis of their appearance, and little attention was paid to the social or historical relevance of the object depicted. Consequently, coverage of many genres, media, technologies, regions, social and ethnic groups, and periods is, at best, spotty. While the images in the Index of American Design are often beautiful to look at, they reveal more about New Deal artists than they do about the history of American folk art and craft.

John Michael Vlach

References

Cahill, Holger. 1950. Introduction. In *The Index of American Design,* by Erwin O. Christensen. New York: Macmillan, pp. ix–xvii.

Vlach, John Michael. 1985. Holger Cahill as Folklorist. *Journal of American Folklore* 98:148–162.

———. 1988. The Index of American Design: From Reference Tool to Shopper's Guide. In *Wood and Woodcarvings from the Index of American Design,* ed. Helen A. Harrison. East Hampton, NY: Guild Hall Museum, pp. 7–14.

See also Art, Folk; Crafts; Material Culture; New Deal and Folk Culture

Irish Americans

Descendants of those who made up the earliest major U.S. immigrant group; their lore and traditions; stereotypes of them. Ireland's exceptionally rich folklore tradition was revitalized in the late 19th and early 20th centuries by a vigorous nationalist movement and literary revival. Little rural Irish folk tradition carried over into the Irish American context, however, except as a kind of quaintness—shillelaghs and leprechauns decorating St. Patrick's Day cards, for example, or a few items from the originally extensive stock of Irish proverbs, toasts, and blessings. Probably the most famous examples of the latter are "May you be in heaven a half-hour before the devil knows you're dead," and the longer one beginning "May the road rise with you and the wind be always at your back. . . ."

The Irish in America have retained a remarkable degree of ethnic identity and communal tradition based largely on the surviving racial memory of Ireland itself, which remains a kind of mythic, pastoral homeland in the group's consciousness, even for generations who were not born there and who, for the most part, have never even visited "the old sod." Much of the Irish American cultural identity was centered in traditional Roman Catholicism, however, and in the old stable neighborhood structure of the American city, neither of which are any longer a significant cohesive influence. In the late 20th century, the group is having to remind itself of its kinship and traditions in order to rekindle its sense of Irishness and to avoid disappearing further into American mass culture. Con-

sequently, there is a trend among Irish Americans to take whatever small measures they can to reinforce their traditions—sending their children, especially daughters, to Irish step-dancing classes, for instance. And there is a greater tendency than formerly to drink Guinness Stout, the Irish national brew. Once available only in a few big city bars, it is now popular enough to be nationally distributed. The Irish American Cultural Institute, headquartered in St. Paul, Minnesota, is one of a number of organizations working for the preservation of Irish American ethnic tradition. The institute publishes a quarterly journal, *Eire-Ireland.*

In the 1990 Census, roughly forty million Americans, one out of six, identified themselves as having some Irish ancestry. For many the Irish connection was immediate and clear; for others it may have been remote, guessed at on the basis of a surname or word-of-mouth family tradition. The likelihood of a contemporary American's having Irish forebears is considerable, given the historical fact of extensive Irish immigration to America, particularly in the 1820s through the 1850s.

There was significant earlier immigration, however, voluntary and forced, as far back as the American colonial period. The 1630s through the 1650s were decades of extraordinary political upheaval in Ireland, of devastating British invasion, and a great many Irish refugees were shipped to work as servants on American plantations. Many others were exiled into penal servitude in the West Indies, from where they ultimately made their way to the Carolinas. (An enduring anti-British sentiment has been a defining trait of Irish American culture, especially up to World War II.)

During the same period, and through much of the 18th century, there was a second major immigration, this time of Ulster Presbyterian Irish (largely of Scots ancestry), the stock from which many notable later Americans derived, William and Henry James, Andrew Jackson, and Stephen Foster among them. (Foster's bittersweet, nostalgic songs, it is often pointed out, markedly reflect the influence of Thomas Moore's *Irish Melodies,* and in 1828 Jackson was hailed as the first Irish American president by Catholic and Protestant Irish alike.) The northern Irish settled mainly in the Southern Atlantic colonies and eventually moved, along with much of the earlier Irish population of the area, west into the Appalachian Mountains and heavily into the Southern and border states. The term "hillbilly," in fact, is thought to have been coined with reference to the Appalachian Ulster Irish, many of whose folk songs celebrated "King Billy" (William of Orange), the popular Protestant Irish hero whose forces defeated those of the Roman Catholic James II at the historic Battle of the Boyne in eastern Ulster in 1690.

These early Irish Americans constitute a people of notable folkloric importance, a primary influence on Southern and mountain culture. Their influence in the area of traditional music has been widely remarked by music historians. Standard Southern string and bluegrass numbers frequently represent variations on traditional Irish jigs, hornpipes, and reels, and bluegrass fiddling clearly harkens back to the Irish country music brought to America by these early settlers—as do the related dance forms. The American folk tune "Cotton Eyed

Irish Americans enjoy a ceili *at the Garden of Eden, Bogan High School. Chicago, 1977. Photo Jonas Dovydenas. American Folklife Center.*

Joe," for instance, is a variation on the Irish tune "The Mountain Top," and the Irish "Battle of the Boyne" became "Buffalo Gal." The extent of this influence was commented on at the Grand Ole Opry's sixtieth anniversary celebration by Ricky Skaggs, who had just just returned from an Irish tour (McWhiney 1988:120–122). Such borrowing continued through the Civil War—"When Johnny Comes Marching Home Again" is a cheerful reworking of the mournful Irish folk song "Johnny I Hardly Knew Ye." Still later, the Irish, a significant portion of the U.S. frontier troops, transformed the lively Irish jig "Garryowen" into the stirring march that became the Seventh Cavalry theme.

Most often when the term "Irish American" is used, it is with the American Irish Catholic population in mind, the descendants of Irish immigrants who came in great waves to America especially during the potato famine of the mid-19th century (two million arrived between 1840 and 1860). Irish American culture is also typically thought of in terms of its urban expression—associated with Boston, Philadelphia, Chicago, and New York in particular (26 percent of New York's population in 1850 had been born in Ireland). The American Irish population has always been much more dispersed than that; early on, New Orleans was an Irish port of entry second only to Boston, and canal, mine, and railroad work particularly led a great many to the Midwest and West ("In eighteen hundred and forty-one / I put me corduroy breeches on / I put me corduroy breeches on / To work upon the railway" went one American Irish worksong). Still, the major cultural focus has, in fact, historically been urban in character.

The typical immigrant's agricultural experience in Ireland had often been unpleasant, associated with tenant farming or sharecropping on rather meager plots. As a result, the Irish often tended not to be drawn to farming as a way of life in America. The inclination of so many Irish to cluster in Northeastern cities can also be ascribed to a kind of sea mystique; many were loath to settle very far from the ocean, a great reminder of home for these North Atlantic island people. Gathering at the oceanside (New York's shore at Far Rockaway, for example, was known as "the Irish Riviera") was a kind of folk-cultural imperative that went beyond the obvious recreational considerations. Saltwater's healing qualities were highly touted by the Irish—the virtues of eating kelp and periwinkles, for instance—as were the agricultural virtues of seaweed. Families often brought seaweed back to the city from the beaches for use as fertilizer in their urban gardens, a carryover from the farming tradition in Ireland.

The significance of the enormous Irish Catholic influx into the United States was not lost on the native WASP (White Anglo-Saxon Protestant) population, whose reaction was decidedly negative and sometimes even violent. (The designation "Scotch-Irish" gained currency at the turn of the century in the United States as a code word whereby Protestant Irish could identify themselves as non-Catholic.) The burning of an Ursuline convent in Charleston, Massachusetts, in 1834, the later Philadelphia and Louisville anti-Irish riots, and attempts to set Lowell and Lawrence, Massachusetts, Irish Catholic neighborhoods afire in the 1850s were the most visible and dramatic expressions of WASP American anti-Irish bigotry. For a long time, tales of these events, as well as of the potato famine itself and the notorious "No Irish need apply" notices that accompanied newspaper job ads in the 19th century, were part of this ethnic group's oral tradition. They reminded younger Irish Americans of where they had come from, tending to make them cognizant of each step in the group's remarkable political and social ascendancy (John F. Kennedy and Grace Kelly being the culture's particular exemplars in that regard).

On the other hand, the Irish adapted extraordinarily well to American life. Speaking English as their first or at least second language as a rule—those who spoke Irish abandoned it perforce early on—and not being notably "foreign" in appearance were advantages. Their exemplary service and high casualties in the American Civil War helped a great deal. (In fact, the most compelling images we have of that war were recorded by an Irish American photographer, Matthew Brady, and the most renowned American sculptural works of the same era—statues of Lincoln, Farragut, Sherman, and others—were those of the Irish-born Augustus Saint-Gaudens.) Mainstream American culture was eventually somewhat taken by "Irish charm," a process helped along by the extensive Irish American stage and music-hall presence epitomized by George M. Cohan. During the same period, two Irish Americans, Mack Sennett and Hal Roach, were creating American silent-screen comedy virtually by themselves.

A certain Irishness eventually became part of the popular culture—reflected over the years in songs like "I'll Take You Home Again Kathleen," "Peg O' My Heart," and "When Irish Eyes Are Smiling," in parish-life movies of the 1940s like *Going My Way* and *The Bells of St. Mary's*, or the long-popular Sunday "Jigs and Maggie" comic strip, *Bringing up Father*. Even the once abundant "Pat and Mike" jokes were generally rather benign, not intended as ethnic slurs. And as early as the late 19th century, Currier and Ives issued a series of Irish landscapes among their otherwise exclusively American ones, an indication of how much an element of Americana the Irish had already become.

But the American Irish also resisted assimilation. Their early experience of prejudice made them somewhat guarded and determined to look out for themselves. They maintained a kind of folk network whereby new arrivals were assisted in finding positions on the police and fire departments, trolley lines, and in the railroad yards and post offices of the major cities. It was a network that typically began with young single women coming to the United States (700,000 between 1885 and 1925 alone) to work as domestic servants, establishing living quarters, and then sending money home to bring their brothers, sisters, and cousins over. From this base, Irish Americans made it their business to master American city politics in a way no other ethnic group was able to do, to the point that they became synonymous with the urban political "machine" and the era of the big-city bosses and legendary mayors, most of whom were folk heros in Irish American neighborhoods—James M. Curley in Boston, "Honest John" Kelly and Jimmy Walker in New York, Richard J. Daly in Chicago, Tom Pendergast in Kansas City, and so on. From there, they moved to the national political stage, and by 1961, a water-

shed year, the Irish American presence in national politics was so extensive that members of this ethnic group occupied the presidency itself as well as the posts of attorney general, Senate majority leader, House majority leader, and Democratic national chairman. Even into the early 1990s, the House majority leader, Tom Foley, was an Irish American and the Senate leader, George Mitchell, was the grandson of an Irish immigrant on his father's side.

As noted, Irish Americans invested an enormous part of their cultural energies in the traditional Catholic Church. The Irish Catholic parish was a mainstay of their ethnic identity. The parish structure complemented, and was to some extent continuous with, the neighborhood-based Irish political structure in the cities. The Catholic Church in America, once the great Irish immigration of the 1800s was accomplished, became an essentially Irish American institution. The Irish took great pride in that fact, as well as in the educational system they were instrumental in building, one that soon ranged from quality parish schools to first-class universities nationwide. Much of the American Irish cultural identity derived from the group's having in common an elaborate, ornate, highly ritualized, and hierarchical religious life, one that differentiated them radically from the Protestant mainstream culture. (Protestant Irish Americans, by contrast, tended to be quickly assimilated.)

A good deal of Irish American folk culture, too, stemmed from the community bonds, the group ties forged and reinforced by a body of shared cultural-religious references—a complex system that included holy days, indulgences, confession, fasting, and what, to outsiders at least, was a female deity. The rigorous and puritanical Catholic school system provided a tradition of "war stories," usually based on Irish Catholicism's rather severe sexual prohibitions. Perhaps the best known of such tales is that the nuns would prohibit girls from wearing skirts with patent leather shoes lest the shiny black surface might serve to mirror their underwear. Another is that the nuns would circulate among "dancing" couples at grade- and high-school dances insisting that the pairs leave "room for the Holy Ghost" between them. Some contemporary stand-up comics—notably, George Carlin—still use such material based on their experiences in an Irish Catholic school environment.

Part of the considerable Irish presence in sports derived from the Catholic connection, too—University of Notre Dame football, from its earliest days, has served as a focal point of Irish American sports legend (though due to Notre Dame's image as a megapower of almost professional status, some of that allegiance has fallen to another Irish Catholic institution, Boston College). The religious connection resonated in various ways locally, too. In Chicago, for instance, the allegiance of Irish Americans for a long time was to the White Sox, founded by Charles Comiskey, one of their own, as against the "Protestant" Cubs founded by a WASP, Phillip K. Wrigley. But the American Irish presence in sports has been remarkable even aside from the Catholic context. They, along with German Americans, dominated the early days of American baseball history; it has been pointed out that the Mudville nine roster in "Casey at the Bat" (1888), for example, is a markedly Irish one: "Casey," "Cooney," " Flynn," " Jimmy Blake" (McCaffrey 1992:26–27).

And Irish Americans at one time dominated boxing in all weight classes, almost to the degree African Americans have in the late 20th century. John L. Sullivan, the first great Irish American folk hero, won his heavyweight bare-knuckle title from the Irishman Paddy Ryan, fought his most famous defense against the Irish American Jake Kilrain, and ultimately lost the title to the Irish American Jim Corbett. Two other epic moments in Irish American boxing lore, both rehearsed endlessly in neighborhood bars for decades, were the Dempsey-Tunney "long count" bout (though both fighters were Irish Americans, Tunney, being Catholic, was the ethnic favorite here) and the first Billy Conn-Joe Louis fight. Louis had won the title from the Irish American Jimmy Braddock, and Conn appeared to be taking it back into Irish American hands as he had Louis badly beaten for twelve rounds. But those rounds would mark the final end of the Irish heavyweight glory days: Conn walked into a Louis left hook in the thirteenth, and the lights went out.

Something of the 19th-century WASP anti-Irish caricature can be seen (though in a less mean spirited form) in a contemporary American ethnic joke like the following: "What is an Irish seven-course meal?" Answer: "A potato and a six-pack." Implicit in the joke, of course, is the image of the Irish as drunken and devoid of cultural sophistication. It leaves out only a third element of the stereotype—that of the Irish as endlessly combative ("the fighting Irish"). It must be acknowledged that Irish Americans have sometimes nurtured these stereotypes themselves, allowing, for instance, St. Patrick's Day, for the most part a quiet religious holiday in Ireland, to become an Irish American festival associated with alcoholic excess and embarrassing schlock such as green beer, "Kiss-Me-I'm-Irish" buttons, and "Top o' the mornin'" T-shirts. Another example of the same sort of self-parody is the pugnacious imp, clay pipe in mouth, who decorates the Notre Dame marching band's bass drum.

Irish American cuisine is rather limited compared with that of some other American ethnic groups. Corned beef and cabbage is an Irish American creation, one unknown in Ireland itself, where corned beef is unheard of or occurs only as an unappetizing canned item akin to Spam. Corned beef and cabbage probably began as an Irish American variation on the common Irish meal made up of cabbage, boiled bacon, and potatoes. So-called "Irish stew" is likewise an Irish American creation, one substituting beef for lamb and employing potatoes to a degree the Irish do not in this dish. A predilection for oatmeal and for oats generally as the grain of choice was also traditionally characteristic of Irish American cooking. Daily consumption of many cups of strong tea was the rule in households for the first generation or two, but coffee generally supplanted it after that. Perhaps most notable among traditions carried over from Ireland, the closest thing to Irish American "soul food," is Irish soda bread. A simple, hard-crusted and delicious bread, it is made from buttermilk, raisins, baking soda, and flour (and sometimes caraway seeds).

Irish grandmothers and mothers have traditionally shown their daughters how to make this bread (it is thought to be not easily transmittable via written recipe), and it is not uncommon for it to have survived three and four generations in a family. Irish American clubs in some cities still sponsor soda-bread competitions.

Another way in which the American Irish have attempted to resist being entirely absorbed into American mass culture is through the employment of traditional Irish names in naming their children. Bridget, Eileen, Nora, Maureen, Deirdre, Cathleen, and Mary-Margaret, for instance, have been common for girls; Sean, Dennis, Patrick, Kevin, Brian, and so forth for boys. But these distinctly Irish names have been taken over by the American culture at large in many cases. Back in the 1960s, the name "Kevin," for example, was virtually a guarantee of its bearer's Irishness, not so in the 1990s. Irish Americans in recent years have sometimes gone to the unmistakably Irish name "Brendan" to mark their sons' heritage, but even that name has begun to be used more broadly and figures in time to lose its ethnic specificity, too.

John Morgan

References

Blessing, Patrick J. 1992. *The Irish in America: A Guide to the Literature and the Manuscript Collections.* Washington, DC: Catholic University Press of America.

Callahan, Bob. 1989. *The Big Book of American Irish Culture.* New York: Viking Penguin.

Clark, Dennis. 1991. *Erin's Heirs: Irish Bonds of Community.* Lexington: University Press of Kentucky.

Griffin, William D. 1990. *The Book of Irish Americans.* New York: Random House.

Marman, Ed. 1992. *Eire-Ireland: A Comprehensive Index, 1966–1988.* Publication of the Irish American Cultural Institute Vol. 27, No. 1. St. Paul, MN: Irish American Cultural Institute.

McCaffrey, Lawrence J. 1992. *Textures of Irish America.* Syracuse, NY: University of Syracuse Press.

McWhiney, Grady. 1988. *Cracker Culture: Celtic Ways in the Old South.* Tuscaloosa: University of Alabama Press.

Miller, Kerby A. 1985. *Emigrants and Exiles: Ireland and the Irish Exodus to North America.* New York: Oxford University Press.

Nolan, Janet A. 1989. *Ourselves Alone: Women's Emigration from Ireland, 1885–1920.* Lexington: University Press of Kentucky.

Potter, George W. 1974. *To the Golden Door.* Westport, CT: Greenwood.

See also St. Patrick's Day

Irving, Washington (1783–1859)

The most popular American author of the pre–Civil War era. Irving was born in New York City, the son of a Scottish father and an English mother. As a youth, he was an avid reader and a competent writer. Indeed, he was so skilled that he of-

Washington Irving. Engraving by James S. King (1852–1925). Library of Congress.

ten wrote compositions for his classmates in exchange for their help in solving his arithmetic problems, the latter a task that he detested. He was an adventurous youth, at fifteen exploring the Sleepy Hollow region that became the scene of one of his best-known stories. Two years later, he sailed up the Hudson River on his own voyage of discovery. Irving studied law in college, although he never seriously practiced that profession. At age nineteen, using the pen name Jonathan Oldstyle, he began wrting newspaper letters, and two years later, in ill health, he began a two-year trip to Europe. After his return, with his brother William Irving and James Kirke Paulding, Irving started the periodical *Salmagundi,* modeled after Addison and Steele's *Spectator* and Goldsmith's *Citizen of the World.* Some scholars believe that Irving's contributions to *Salmagundi* contain the germs of almost everything he did afterward.

In 1809 Irving's fiancee, Matilda Hoffman, died at age eighteen. Irving outlived her by fifty years, remaining a bachelor and reportedly carrying her Bible with him wherever he traveled. The year 1809 was also significant in Irving's life because his masterpiece, "Diedrich Knickerbocker's" *History of New York,* appeared that year. Ten years later, *The Sketch Book* (1819) appeared, containing "Rip Van Winkle" and "The Legend of Sleepy Hollow," his two most famous stories. And in 1822, *Bracebridge Hall* was published, followed two years later by *Tales of a Traveller.* Like *The Sketch Book,* these volumes contain short stories, essays, and sketches, many suggestive of the *Spectator's* contents. These important books were all written while Irving was living in Europe, where he had moved in 1815. During his stay overseas, he lived in England and Spain, serving as secretary of the American legations in London and Madrid. By the time he returned to America in 1832, Irving had completed the major portions of his life's literary work.

Although Irving made extensive use of folklore in several of his major works, his concerted effort at collecting folklore was slight, consisting solely of noting popular sayings and beliefs wherever he traveled. He had some familiarity with American storytelling habits, but when creating fictional tales he relied as much on German, English, and Spanish folklore as on American traditions. For example, both "Rip Van Winkle" and "The Legend of Sleepy Hollow" are set in America, but their plots are largely derived from German sources. The former story was taken from narratives about Peter Klaus, and the latter was based on headless-horseman tales found in Johann Karl August Musaeus' *Volksmärchen der Deutschen* (German Folktales). Nevertheless, Irving was more than just a copier of narratives printed by others (although in his day he was accused of plagiarism); instead, he utilized his creative genius to make these tales his own.

The most important literary influence on Irving's use of folklore was Sir Walter Scott, whom Irving met in 1817 and who had impressed a generation of readers and authors both with his formal studies and collections of folklore and with his use of folklore in his fiction. Irving was one of Scott's earliest and most popular disciples. He was also acquainted with German folklorist Karl Böttiger, who often advised him on folklore topics. Irving's occasional use of Native American folklore in his writings has been overlooked by some critics but overestimated by others.

W.K. McNeil

References

Allen, Patrick F., ed. 1983. Washington Irving's *Hearthside Tales.* New York: Union College Press.

Hoffman, Daniel G. 1965. *Form and Fable in American Fiction.* New York: W.W. Norton.

Pochmann, Henry A. 1930. Irving's German Sources in *The Sketch Book. Studies in Philology* 27: 477–507.

Italian Americans

Immigrants from Italy and their descendants; inheritors of Old World traditions who maintained and transformed their customary regional practices in the New World. Some Italian Americans see themselves as descendants of Romans and the Italians of the Renaissance. However, Italian immigrants brought to America their own folk traditions—rich customs that varied from north to south, province to province, and village to village. The immigrant journey was an odyssey of change and adaptation. Villagers moved beyond their regionalism to identify themselves in the United States first as Italians, then later as Italian Americans. Their traditional practices represent that cultural odyssey. Folk crafts and architecture, foods, wines, and stories, along with customary veneration of saints and other festivals, are prime markers of Italian American identity.

Italians have been in America since the time of Columbus. In the 16th, 17th, and 18th centuries, under Spanish or French companies, they sailed to the Western Hemisphere as adventurers, navigators, and cartographers. They came as fur traders, trappers, priests, and soldiers wandering the American wilderness. Alfonso and Enrico Tonti, at the end of the 1690s, were explorers who accompanied LaSalle. Enrico was known as "Iron Fist," for the legend that arose about the iron prosthesis that replaced the hand he lost during an expedition

During the annual parade of the St. Joseph Athletic Association, men move a statue of Saint Joseph through the streets. Chicago, 1977. Photo Jonas Dovydenas. American Folklife Center.

on the American continent. He was the second governor of a fort that eventually became the city of Detroit. Filippo Mazzei, a doctor, was a friend of Thomas Jefferson. Folk narratives observe his political influence on Jefferson and the American Revolution. These early Italians, while influential, were few in number and came as isolated individuals. Mass migrations did not begin until the 19th century. Between 1820—date of the first official American Census to count immigrants—and 1880, almost 50,000 Italians entered the United States. The peak period was between 1880 and 1920. More than four million Italians entered, more than any other European group except Germans, who came at about the same time.

Until 1880 almost all immigrants were from the richer, industrialized northern Italian provinces—Liguria, Lombardy, and Piedmont—attracted, for the most part, by the opportunities in the West. Among the immigrants were skilled craftsmen, small businessmen, as well as farmers, who brought their folk beliefs and customs and adapted them to the new environment. While they came as individuals and families, in general there were not enough of them to support a Little Italy, a whole Italian quarter maintained by internal institutions. The merchants, tailors, lawyers, doctors, and so on arrived in the Eastern United States at a later date. Nonetheless, Italians imprinted their legacy on the West in such obvious industries as food and wine and left their marks on the landscape. Some came to the state of Washington and, using their village planting and harvesting techniques, cultivated a strain of onion renowned today as the Walla Walla sweet. Folk stories identify the local legendary character Pete Pieri as the Italian who brought the parent strain of the sweet onion from Corsica. Italians also came to Colorado, Utah, Wyoming, and Nevada to work as miners and charcoal burners. Some were involved in the formation of the miners' unions and joined the confrontations between laborers and owners. Since mining work was seasonal, Italian immigrants and their families survived by producing much of their food on their land, except for staple items like coffee and salt. They modified the uniform wheat and oat fields with Italian-style vegetable, spice, and fruit gardens that included zucchini, broccoli, garlic, oregano, and basil as well as peach, plum, apricot, and walnut orchards. They dotted the High Desert landscape with outbuildings behind the main house—chicken coops, rabbit hutches, goat and hog pens—to raise animals that they slaughtered and cured according to Old World recipes. They enacted other folk traditions by building canning sheds to preserve the vegetables they grew in conformity with ancient practice. They built outdoor domed brick ovens for baking bread like the ones found in Alpine Mountains.

Some immigrants went on to California to work as longshoremen and fishermen in the maritime industry or to purchase land near San Francisco to plant vegetables and vineyards. Originally, Italians ran these truck gardens and vineyards in the traditional way as family enterprises. On their property, some built finely crafted stone houses based upon the symmetrical three-part villas of northern Italy. Eventually, some of the farms and wineries grew to become large corporations, like Del Monte, Italian Swiss Colony, and Gallo Brothers, and realized the American Dream of success.

Other immigrants who went to the West ruptured the physical and occupational stereotypes surrounding Italian immigrants. Here were pioneers who became cowboys in Paradise Valley, Nevada, buckaroos who wore goatskin chaparajos and silver-mounted spurs. On quarter horses, they herded cows and carried sixty-five-foot rawhide ropes to lasso the animals. They spoke Italian at home, Shoshone with Native Americans, and English with other ranchers. They started out by building mud-and-willow prairie cabins to house their growing families. Eventually, they bought ranches and lived the immigrant dream of owning their own land. They became entrepreneurs and transformed themselves into the most vivid symbol of the American West, the cowboy.

After 1880, 80 percent of the immigrants were from the poorer, agrarian regions of south Italy—the *Mezzogiorno*: Abruzzo-Molise, Campania, Apulia, Lucania, Calabria, Sardinia, and Sicily. Almost all were *contadini* (peasants). While a few had owned land, the majority were sharecroppers and day laborers who saw themselves as no more than beasts, like mules or bison. They cursed the land that sentenced them and their families to live on the edge of starvation. What pushed more than 15,000 immigrants a day to America some years was the culmination of natural and social calamities in south Italy that smothered the peasant's will to continue *la miseria*—the unbearable pain of poverty and virtual serfdom that had been their legacy for hundreds of years. Excessive taxation continued, as did the abuses by wealthy landowners and capricious local governments. In the end, it was the collapse of vineyards and silk crops, and the cholera epidemic of the 1880s, that finally drove many to emigrate.

More than 90 percent of Italians came in chain migrations, beginning with single males. One villager would find a job, then send back for family members or *paesani* (fellow villagers), who joined him for the work. Usually, single men came "as birds of passage," living in inexpensive boarding houses, hoping to save enough money to return to Italy to buy and farm land and to reap the prosperity of ownership. Only after the first decade of the 20th century did intact families in great numbers make the journey. Italian immigrants then settled in Little Italies in large American cities, close to kin or *comare* and *compare* (friends through godparenting), *paesani*, and others from the same southern region. Approximately 70 percent of Italian immigrants settled in the Northeast, 16 percent in the Midwest, 10 percent in the West, and 4 percent in the South. In the 1990s, almost 90 percent of Italian Americans live in metropolitan areas.

South Italians carried their own regional traditions to the New World. *Campanilismo* is the term defining that ethos. It means that all of the important things in life lie within the sound of the village church bell. In burgeoning American cities like New York, Philadelphia, and Boston, immigrants transplanted their villages to urban neighborhoods, and *Campanilismo* thrived. The newly arrived joined settled *paesani* in congested flats, row houses, or tenements. They found work mostly as unskilled laborers in the expanding manufacturing, railroad, and coal industries in the East.

In Detroit men boarded crowded streetcars for the long ride to the Dodge assembly plant or the Ford Rouge plant. To pass the time, they joked and played the village game of *morra*, an intense contest requiring lightning reflexes and aggressive confidence. As two men stand face to face, each throws down one arm and extends any number of fingers, then guesses and yells in Italian the sum total of digits extended by both players. It is a game of strategy, and the best players display an esteemed trait in peasant culture—composure in the face of pressure. During hot summer evenings, women would sit on stoops in Chicago, Brooklyn, and elsewhere to gossip in familiar local dialects and share remedies for *malocchio* (the evil eye), the pervasive Mediterranean belief in the power of envy to control human destiny. For calendar holidays like Christmas and Easter, local Italian food merchants, like Giglio's in Detroit and Termini's in south Philadelphia, helped maintain the food practices of the Italian American community against impersonal commercial transitions. Familiar village foods, like *baccala* (cod), *prosciutto* and *capocollo* (ham), *soppressata* (sausage)—all *roba buona* (fresh food)—would be displayed with *cassata* and *sfogliatelle* (Sicilian and Neapolitan pastries). The neighborhood's *Campanilismo* helped Italian Americans survive the upheaval of immigration and begin the process of acculturation.

While there are obvious deficiencies in seeing the village as the world, there are also many strengths. What sustained these immigrants as they uprooted themselves from the land, and cut the cords binding them to family, was their folklore. Oral traditions guided them through the trials of immigration as it had through transitions in the village. Folk stories—fairy tales as well as humorous anecdotes about priests, pretentious townsfolk, and ignorant stepmothers—entertained and at the same time instructed the listeners, both children and adults, in how to deal with the dread of loss and the pain of rejection, how to summon the courage to confront fear, deception, and cruelty, all of these being universal Old and New World experiences. The stories encoded the collective wisdom of the community and provided keys to solving the problems of daily living.

The story of "Little Peter," for example, was a popular one in Italian American communities. This tale is an example of a characteristic European narrative form—the *Märchen* (fairy tale). It has retained in the United States the stylistic and thematic features of the Italian original. This story represents the transplantation of an Old World tradition in the American context. Under various names, "Little Peter" is a folktale found all over the world, part of a cycle of narratives that involves a child encountering an ogre. The young boy Peter grows up impoverished in a household with only one parent— a common experience, as many mothers died in childbirth and fathers perished in accidents or were away working in another country. The story reflects the community's code for survival: respect and spontaneity. The plot turns on Little Peter's failure to listen to his mother. In the forest, he is trapped by a witch and thrust into a sack to serve as her dinner later that evening. Peter's quick wit, however, allows him to outsmart the witch and fill the sack with rocks. When the witch returns home, she and her husband gleefully empty the sack of stones into a boiling pot. The sudden splash of water causes the flames to leap to the witches' clothing and eventually consume them. Peter, who has been peeping down the chimney all the while, is elated. He takes the chest of gold from their house, returns to his family, and, like a respectful son, shares the wealth with his mother and siblings. The tale dramatizes for the audience the qualities that allowed Peter to deal successfully with a threatening situation, overcome his poverty, and live happily ever after.

In addition to the fairy tales, Italian Americans generated stories to combat stereotypes of themselves. Films have frequently portrayed American criminals as being Italian, and some newspapers and journals have depicted Italians as criminals and anarchists. Some epithets endure, such as "wop" and "guinea"; a cycle of "dago jokes" and numskull stories continues to circulate. One common figure is the "spaghetti bender," who offends others by emitting the strong scent of garlic or by consuming traditional holiday delicacies such as roasted goat's head and chicken-feet soup.

In opposition, Italian Americans tell stories about the culinary incompetence of traditional adversaries, such as the Irish in the East and the Mormons in the West. These stories deride the folly of substituting catsup for genuine tomato sauce and of determining when pasta is cooked by throwing a fork full of noodles against the wall. These anecdotes show that those who ridicule Old World village foods lack the culinary sophistication to produce dishes that excite the palate in dramatic textures, aromas, and tastes. In an ironic twist, pizza has "Italianized" Americans who have incorporated it into their national food repertoire. This peasant Italian food represents the ultimate assimilation of an ethnic tradition. Eating with hands from a communal dish, always on the edge of violating table etiquette—pulling too much hot melted cheese into strands that stretch like rubber—creates instant informality, affinity, and fun. Americans tend to include pizza affectionately in a range of social situations: as a main course in a casual dinner, as a way to get to know someone informally, as a way to celebrate important events. Even pasta has become an American institution. The late-20th-century popular trend to eat healthy foods has focused on pasta as a premier source of nutrition.

Another aspect of Italian American life is the public veneration of saints in festivals. St. Joseph's Day, a feast that originated in Sicily as a way to feed the poor, enacts in the New World the basic peasant theme of reciprocity, to render a gift for a favor. A supplicant will petition the saint for a miraculous cure or for the solution to an overwhelming problem. In exchange the petitioner promises to build an altar of food as an expression of gratitude. If the petition has been answered, then on St. Joseph's Day, March 18, the supplicant displays in his or her home, after weeks of preparation, an altar containing an astounding abundance of meatless products. It is a fusion of Italian and American cookery—braided Easter breads, *frittate* (omelets), and *cannoli* (custard pastries), vying with non-Italian snacks like cherry winks, snarkles, and peanut butter cookies. In some cases, the host feeds 500 or more people. The veneration of saints in homemade altars renews ties with the past, with Italian American society, and now with the larger Catholic parish. In some communities, St. Joseph's Day altars have been adopted by other ethnic groups, who incorporate their own traditional foods in its display.

The most prominent and official Italian American festival is the Columbus Day celebration. Columbus Day is an icon for Italian Americans. It is both a national holiday honoring Christopher Columbus as an American hero as well as an Italian American festival celebrating Italian rather than village or regional identity. Many celebrations follow the tradition established by Italian immigrants of the past. In the morning is a Mass eulogizing the Italian navigator and his discovery of the Western Hemisphere for millions of Europeans. Then follows a parade of Italian American fraternal organizations and sodalities behind a float carrying a statue of Columbus. The speeches at the parade's destination, usually at an important civic location, follow the laying of a wreath at the monument by prominent Italians and political leaders. The festivities and the dinner afterward have helped bond the Italian American community and visibly proclaim their contribution to American society.

As Italian Americans assimilate into the middle class, much of their folk identity disappears. Whether, as some scholars argue, American ethnicity for those of European ancestry is in a twilight phase or whether ethnic identity is continually reinvented in consensual forms is an interesting academic question. There is a more personal issue, however. For Italian Americans, what remains after they have abandoned language, food, neighborhood, and religious traditions is a faint stirring in the heart of a world based on village and neighborhood culture. It is a view of life unfolding most humanely in the web of close relationships in the family and community, a web where people develop and mature not in the private space of solitude but along public lines in daily connections with others.

Richard Raspa

References

Bianco, Carla. 1974. *The Two Rosettos*. Bloomington: Indiana University Press.

D'Ariano, Regina, and Roy D'Ariano. 1976. *ItaloAmerican Ballads, Poems, Lyrics, and Melodies*. Parsons, WV: McClain Print.

Del Guidice, Luisa, ed. 1993. *Studies in Italian American Folklore*. Logan: Utah State University Press.

Gans, Herbert. 1962. *The Urban Villagers*. Glenco.

Lopreato, Joseph. 1970. *Italian Americans*. New York: Random House.

Malpezzi, Frances M., and William M. Clements. 1992. *Italian-American Folklore*. Little Rock, AR: August House.

Mangione, Jerre. 1981. *Mount Allegro*. 2d. ed. New York: Columbia University Press.

Mathias, Elizabeth, and Richard Raspa. 1985. *Italian Folktales in America: The Verbal Art of an Immigrant Woman*. Detroit: Wayne State University Press.

Noyes, Dorothy. 1989. *Uses of Tradition: Arts of Italian Americans in Philadelphia*. Philadelphia: Samuel S. Fleisher Art Memorial and Philadelphia Folklore Project.

Taylor, David, and John Alexander Williams, eds. 1992. *Old Ties, New Attachments: Italian-American Folklife in the West*. Washington, DC: Library of Congress.

Williams, Phyllis. 1938. *South Italian Folkways in Europe and America: A Handbook for Social Workers, Visiting Nurses, School Teachers, and Physicians:* New Haven, CT: Yale University Press.

See also Columbus Day

Ives, Burl (1909–1995)

Folksinger, actor. The son of Illinois tenant farmers, Ives learned traditional ballads from his grandmother, played banjo in high school, and built a repertoire of American song in the 1930s on an extended tramp throughout North America. Settling in New York City in 1937, he did stage and radio work until 1940, when CBS gave him his own show and the sobriquet "The Wayfaring Stranger." From this show and his work in the Broadway folk cavalcade *Sing Out, Sweet Land* (1944), Ives became the best-known exponent of American folksong until the advent of the folksong revival in the 1950s and 1960s. With lively arrangements of such old-time numbers as "The Foggy Foggy Dew," "The Big Rocky Candy Mountain," and his signature tune, "Blue Tail

Burl Ives in 1955. Photo Carl Van Vechten. Library of Congress.

Fly," he fulfilled what he later identified as his life's purpose—to promote the "shared heritage" of "native American folk music."

Ives also achieved success as an actor and a country music singer. He won an Oscar for his work in *The Big Country* (1958), although he is better remembered for his screen portrayal of Big Daddy in *Cat on a Hot Tin Roof* (1958), a role he had created on Broadway in what critic Walter Kerr called "Rabelaisian contribution." His country career peaked in 1962, with three songs topping the country charts, and "Funny Way of Laughin'" earning a Grammy. Ives' dedication to traditional song was also evident in his editing of several songbooks, including the popular *Burl Ives Songbook* (1953).

He died on April 14, 1995, Good Friday, at the age of eighty-five.

Tad Tuleja

References

Ives, Burl. 1948. *Wayfaring Stranger*. New York: McGraw-Hill.

———. 1962. *Song in America: Our Musical Heritage*. New York: Duell, Sloan, and Pearce.

J

Jack Tales

A cycle of long, fictional oral prose narratives focusing on the episodic adventures of a "youngest-best" teenage trickster-hero named Jack as he negotiates an ultimately successful quest for maturity and prosperity. A typical Jack tale begins with the unlikely hero leaving home either to escape mistreatment or "to seek his fortune." Because he is either kind to a stranger or simply lucky, Jack acquires a magic object, supernatural ally, or supranormal skill that, when combined with his persistence, native wit, courage, creative imagination, ability to deceive, and propensity for attracting good luck, helps him perform a series (usually three) of seemingly impossible tasks or tests and conquer a formidable opponent. Having been rewarded with material wealth and, often, a beautiful wife, Jack returns to his home as an adult with elevated status in the community.

Jack tales originate from an international inventory of traditional narrative types and motifs, with American texts deriving generally from European stories about an ordinary young man—named Hans in Germany, Jock or Jake in Scotland, and Jack in England and Ireland—behaving heroically. In these stories, Jack is usually either a generic name for the protagonist or a boy characterized as a dependent, immature numskull. But in America, Jack became a cunning, self-reliant, occasionally amoral trickster, especially as he was conceptualized in Appalachia.

While early collectors uncovered Jack tales throughout the Eastern United States, including several from African Americans, the cycle eventually settled in Appalachia (especially in eastern Kentucky, southwestern Virginia, and northwestern North Carolina), becoming consistent with that region's folk-cultural worldview. Stories from the rich repertoire of the Hicks-Harmon families of Watauga and Avery Counties, North Carolina, were collected by Isabel Gordon Carter in 1923 and by Richard Chase in the 1930s and 1940s. Chase's texts, which appeared in *The Jack Tales* (1943), *The Grandfather Tales* (1948), and *American Folk Tales and Songs* (1956), were actually composites, however, collated from several different performances and contami-nated with Chase's editorial changes and creations: words deleted and substituted, episodes added from other sources, and titles altered. Leonard Roberts, on the other hand, was a responsible folklorist who began collecting Jack tales in the mid-1940s in his native Kentucky, many of them from the Couch family in Harlan and Leslie Counties. In the early 1940s, James Taylor Adams and James M. Hylton recorded twenty Jack tales in Wise County, Virginia, as part of the Works Progress Administration's (WPA) Virginia Writers' Project, including several from Gaines Kilgore, that area's most active storyteller.

Chase's books were quite popular and have clearly influenced the repertoires of such contemporary narrators as Ray and Stanley Hicks, Maud Long, Marshall Ward, Frank Proffitt Jr., and Orville Hicks. But, in a sense, this borrowing from printed sources has always been a part of the folk process. Many orally performed texts are remarkably close to those in the Grimm brothers' collection, so it seems reasonable to assume that the ancestors of Appalachian performers—the Hickses, Harmons, Kilgores, and Couches—may have been familiar with the popular *Nursery and Household Tales,* which was first published in 1812 and went through numerous subsequent editions.

William E. Lightfoot

References

Carter, Isabel Gordon. 1925. Mountain Folk-Lore: Tales from the Southern Blue Ridge. *Journal of American Folklore* 38:340–374.

McCarthy, William B., ed. 1994. *Jack in Two Worlds: Contemporary North American Taletellers.* Chapel Hill: University of North Carolina Press.

McGowan, Thomas, ed. 1978. Jack Tales. *North Carolina Folklore Journal* (Special Issue) 26:49–143.

Perdue, Charles L., Jr., ed. 1987. *Outwitting the Devil: Jack Tales from Wise County, Virginia.* Santa Fe: Ancient City Press.

Roberts, Leonard W., ed. 1955. *South from Hell- fer-Sartin:*

Kentucky Mountain Folk Tales. Lexington: University Press of Kentucky.

See also Chase, Richard; Folktale; Hicks-Harmon Families; Ward, Marshall

Jackalope

Mythical beast of the Great Plains and Rocky Mountains combining a jackrabbit's body with deer spike antlers or antelope horns. The jackalope is a favorite subject for picture postcards and, in its mounted state, as a taxidermist's joke, it is often found on barroom, filling station, or cafe walls in the Mountain-Plains region.

The origins of the American jackalope tradition are obscure, although much of the initial activity seems to have centered in Wyoming. The National Jackalope Society, based in Sheridan, sells jackalope hunting licenses and bumper stickers. Douglas, which boasts a large jackalope statue, bills itself as the "Home of the Jackalope," largely because two local taxidermists, Doug and Ralph Herrick, began to make and sell jackalopes in the 1930s. One of the earliest reports of a mounted jackalope is from a store in Buffalo, Wyoming, in the early 1920s. Legend credits the first sighting of a jackalope to mountain man Roy Ball, back in 1829.

The American jackalope is not unique; tales of horned rabbits have been collected in Africa, Mexico, and Central America, where a Mayan legend recounts how the god Chinax felt pity for the rabbit, who had been created with horns but had lost them to the trickster deer. In compensation the god stretched the rabbit's ears so that it could hear its enemies coming and enlarged its hind legs so that it could outrun them.

In Europe the *wolpertinger,* said to have been among the animals in Hannibal's menagerie, has long been a staple of Bavarian folklore. This creature, purportedly a member of the marten family, often has a rabbit or a weasel body with hog tusks, bird fore feet and rabbit hind feet, hawk wings, fox tail, deer antlers, and a coxcomb in the forehead. Saliva from the *wolpertinger* is said to stimulate hair growth, while impotence can be cured by sipping nectar through a *wolpertinger's* shankbone, then urinating across a stream against the current. Similar in appearance to the *wolpertinger,* the French *dahu* is often the prey in a practical joke, similar to an American snipe hunt, in which a credulous youth is taken into the woods on a winter night with a lantern, a sack, and a baton while his companions ostensibly go off to drive the *dahu* toward him but in reality repair to the nearest tavern.

Jackalopes are said to be extremely shy, but when stirred to anger they will charge viciously (at speeds in excess of 65 miles per hour) and can be brought down only with a buffalo gun. The warrior rabbit of Nebraska and South Dakota has pheasant wings and tail, in addition to horns. In the Southwest, the beast is often termed an "antelabbit," while in the North Woods it is called the "Jack-pine Jackelope." Jackalopes can mimic the human voice, early reports mentioning a French accent. They usually sing at night during thunderstorms, often echoing the songs of night-herding cowboys. Jackalopes mate only during flashes of lightning, and their

milk, like patent medicine, is said to cure a host of afflictions.

Despite its fabulous nature, there is a basis in fact for the jackalope. A viral infection, Shope's papillomas, causes warty skin growths on cottontail rabbits. These growths, physiologically similar to the outer sheath of the horn of a pronghorn antelope, sometimes resemble horns.

James F. Hoy

References
Dance, Peter. 1975. *Animal Fakes and Frauds.* Maidenhead, Berkshire: Sampson Low, pp. 114–115.

Dorson, Richard M. 1982. *Man and Beast in American Comic Legend.* Bloomington: Indiana University Press, pp. 50–54.

Kirein, Peter. 1968. *Der Wolpertinger Lebt.* Munich: Karl M. Lipp.

Jackson, George Pullen (1874–1953)

Collector and scholar of religious folksong. Professor of German at Vanderbilt University, Jackson discovered a rich body of music sung throughout the South and preserved in songbooks. He became the first major scholar to describe, classify, and trace the origins of this vast repertoire, originally in *White Spirituals in the Southern Uplands* ([1933] 1965), a study of shape-note hymnody.

His most controversial assertion—expressed in *White and Negro Spirituals* (1943) and elsewhere—opposed the prevailing theory of African origins by stating that "Negro spirituals" derived directly from "White spirituals" transmitted to African Americans primarily through camp meetings and revivals. Jackson's reliance on printed texts, his emphasis on melody and lyric to the exclusion of contextual factors as well as rhythm and vocal embellishment, and his reluctance to concede any substantial African influence have since been vigorously attacked as erroneous, even racist, most scholars in the late 20th century preferring a theory of syncretism, hybridization, and exchange.

Born in New England and reared in the South, Jackson came to the study of religious folksong through attending and participating in singing conventions and mining old hymnals, which resulted in three collections: *Spiritual Folk-Songs of Early America* (1937), *Down-East Spirituals* (1942), and *Another Sheaf of White Spirituals* (1952).

Jackson's research demonstrated origins of spirituals in British and American religious verse and in secular folk tunes; traced diffusion from New England to the South; established the vital roles of evangelism, revivalism, singing schools, and the camp meeting; demonstrated common origins by grouping tunes into what he called "tune families"; and created a typology of folk hymns, revival spirituals, and religious ballads. He was also an active organizer of singing events and an early advocate for introducing American folk music in public schools.

David H. Stanley

References
Epstein, Dena J. 1982. Myths about Black Folk Music. In *Folk Music and Modern Sound,* ed. William Ferris and

Mary L. Hart. Jackson: University of Mississippi Press, pp. 151–160.

Wilgus, D.K. 1959. The Negro-White Spirituals. In *Anglo-American Folksong Scholarship since 1898.* New Brunswick, NJ: Rutgers University Press, pp. 344–364 et passim.

Yoder, Don. [1933] 1964. Introduction. *White Spirituals in the Southern Uplands,* by George Pullen Jackson. Hatboro, PA: Folklore Associates, pp. i–xv.

Jackson, Mary Magdalene (Garland; "Aunt Molly") (1880–1960)

Union activist and folksinger. During the 1930s, Jackson was an important advocate for the unionization of the Appalachian coalfields. Her appearances at labor rallies featured original protest songs that were closely tied to the melodic shape and balladic form of traditional Appalachian music.

Molly Jackson, the daughter of coal miner, preacher, and union activist Oliver Perry Garland and Deborah (Robinson) Garland, was born in Clay County, Kentucky, in 1880. The family, of Scotch-Irish and Cherokee lineage, stretched back seven generations in Clay County. As described by Molly:

> They cut down trees and built their own log cabins, they cleared their own land, they built their own fences, and split their own rails, they built their own church houses, and their schools out of logs, they raised their own corn, that fattened their own hogs, they caught possums and coons with their own dogs, they owned the stuff that they worked and raised—I still say them were the good old days (Greenway [1953] 1977:253).

As a five-year-old child, Molly was already engaged in caring for her younger siblings and assisting her father on picket lines and at union meetings. Molly's mother died of tuberculosis in 1886, and eleven months later her father married Sarah Lucas with whom he had an additional eleven children, including well-known union activists Sarah Elizabeth Ogan Gunning (1910–1983) and Jim Garland (1905–1978).

At the age of fourteen, Molly married Jim Stewart, a coal miner, and she bore two children while training as a midwife and working as a nurse in a Clay County Hospital. In 1912 her husband's poor health required a move to Florida, but five years later Stewart died in a mining rockslide accident. Returning to Kentucky, Molly married another miner, Bill Jackson, and moved to Harlan County, where she worked as a midwife, delivering 884 babies by her own reckoning.

During the Depression years Aunt Molly Jackson, as she became popularly known, totally dedicated herself to labor organization on behalf of the National Miners' Union. In this cause, she gave speeches and performed her powerful protest songs such as "I Am a Union Woman" (1931), "Kentucky Miner's Wife" (1932), and "Dreadful Memories" (1935), which was also claimed by her half-sister Sarah. "Poor Miner's Farewell," written three months after the death of her brother Richard in a mining accident, was widely disseminated through inclusion in the *Red Song Book* published in 1932 by Workers Library Publishers.

Jackson's activity caused her to be blacklisted by the mine operators in 1931, and subsequently she was compelled to divorce her husband so that he could continue to work in the mines. That same year, The National Committee for the Defense of Political Prisoners sent a delegation (including authors Theodore Dreiser and John dos Passos) to Kentucky to focus attention on the poverty and starvation in the coal camps. Influenced both by the hearings and the advice of folklorist Mary Elizabeth Barnicle, Aunt Molly decided to extend her efforts outside the Appalachian region. In December 1931, accompanied by Jim Garland and Sarah Ogan, she traveled to New York City and made her first public appearance in front of an audience of 21,000 at the Coliseum.

Aunt Molly spent the next five years traveling on behalf of labor, despite serious injuries sustained in a bus accident in Ohio. In 1936 she settled in New York City with her final husband, Gustavos Stamos. She died on August 31, 1960, in Sacramento, California, where she was buried.

Aunt Molly Jackson's use of folksong as a political weapon compelled her to tread that fine line separating tradition from innovation. Her songs were always modeled on folk sources, but the composition was dictated by utilitarian function rather than folkloric context. Jackson's own definition of folksong, as she wrote it, provides the best description of her role as a traditional singer in the modern world. "This is what a folk song realy is the folks composes there own songs about there own lifes an there home folks that live around them" (Greenway [1953] 1977:8).

Ron Pen

References

Ardery, Julia S., ed. 1983. *Welcome the Traveler Home: Jim Garland's Story of the Kentucky Mountains.* Lexington: University Press of Kentucky.

Green, Archie. 1972. *Only a Miner.* Urbana: University of Illinois Press.

Greenway, John. [1953] 1977. *American Folksongs of Protest.* New York: Octagon Books.

Jackson, Aunt Molly. 1991. *The Songs and Stories of Aunt Molly Jackson.* Folkways Records FH 5457.

Lomax, Alan, Archie Green, and D.K. Wilgus, eds. 1961. Aunt Molly Jackson. *Kentucky Folklore Record* (Special Memorial Issue) (October-December):129–176.

James, Jesse Woodson (1847–1882)

Civil War guerilla and postwar robber who has frequently been cast as an American Robin Hood. Born into a staunch pro-slavery family in rural northwestern Missouri, James was raised amidst the border conflict between Union and Confederate forces. In 1864—soon after the torture of his stepfather and the jailing of his mother and sister by the local militia—Jesse James followed his older brother Frank (1843–1915) into the ranks of "Bloody Bill" Anderson's irregular cavalry. Strife continued after the Civil War as Missouri's Radical Republican government denied amnesty to persons who had acted under Confederate orders.

Although precise dates and motives are disputed, the James brothers became linked with bank robberies as early as 1866. They carried a price on their heads after the 1869 plunder of a Gallatin, Missouri, bank in which an unresisting cashier, Captain Sheets, was murdered—presumably for his part in the wartime death of Bill Anderson. Over the next dozen years, the Jameses and a gang of pistol-wielding, hard-riding ex-guerillas were implicated in bank and train robberies not only in Missouri, but throughout the Midwest. Their 1876 attack on the bank in Northfield, Minnesota, proved disastrous. While Frank and Jesse escaped, a posse killed and captured several gang members.

Thereafter the James brothers were largely in hiding, although numerous robberies were attributed to them. On April 3, 1882, living under the name of Mr. Howard in St. Joseph, Missouri, Jesse was fatally shot in the back of the head by a cousin, Robert Ford. Missouri's Governor Crittendon,

under political pressure for harboring an outlaw, had conspired with Ford and quickly granted him amnesty.

Several ballads soon circulated, the most popular of which recounted notable robberies, lauded Jesse's courage, pitied his family, and condemned Robert Ford as "the dirty little coward who shot Mr. Howard." By 1882 the James gang's sixteen years at large had already generated considerable legendry, news stories, and imaginative popular "histories." A torrent of largely fictitious "dime novels" followed.

While detractors labeled Jesse a criminal continuing his wartime pursuits out of pure meanness, more numerous defenders dubbed him an avenger of cruelties inflicted by Missouri's militia and bankers. The oral tradition from Jesse's home territory typically presented the outlaw as a bold and gallant Robin Hood. He gives money to a poor widow so that she can save her home from a banker who plans to foreclose; after the payment, Jesse steals the money back. Always deferent to women, Jesse is also the devout leader of a Baptist choir. An artist with pistols, he monitors his pursuers in disguise, then shoes his horse backward to confuse them. Ubiquitous stories even claim that Jesse James did not die at all. Several pretenders to his identity sustained this notion into the mid-20th century.

Since the 1883 production of J.J. McCluskey's *The Bandit King,* the Robin Hood version has been reprised often on stage and in films, perhaps the most notable of which, *Jesse James* (1939), cast Tyrone Power as the Missouri outlaw. Meanwhile, the oft-recorded "The Ballad of Jesse James" persists in the repertoires of old-time country musicians.

James P. Leary

References

Breihan, Carl W. 1953. *The Complete and Authentic Life of Jesse James.* New York: Frederick Fell.

Croy, Homer. 1949. *Jesse James Was My Neighbor.* New York: Duell, Sloan, and Pearce.

Randolph, Vance. 1980. *Ozark Folksongs.* Vol. 3. Columbia: University of Missouri Press.

Settle, William A. 1966. *Jesse James Was His Name.* Columbia: University of Missouri Press.

Wellman, Paul I. 1961. *A Dynasty of Western Outlaws.* Garden City, NJ: Doubleday.

James, Thelma Grey (1899–1988)

Teacher, collector, and archivist of urban folk traditions. Born and raised in a Quaker family in Detroit, Michigan, James joined folklorist Emelyn Elizabeth Gardner in 1923 as a junior lecturer in the English Department at the Colleges of the City of Detroit, later to become Wayne State University. James had received her B.A. in 1920 and her M.A. in 1923 from the University of Michigan. She took graduate courses there and at the University of Chicago in the historic-geographic method of folklore scholarship. She was president of the Michigan Folklore Society in 1949–1950 and of the American Folklore Society in 1950–1951. She was elected a Fellow of the American Folklore Society in 1961. She retired from Wayne State University in 1967 after forty-four years of teaching.

James and Gardner, both involved in the settlement-house movement, founded the Wayne State University (WSU) Folklore Archive in 1939. They conducted folklore-collecting projects in the city with students until Gardner's retirement in 1941. James continued collecting projects, supervising student collectors, and archiving urban, ethnic, and occupational traditions until her retirement. Her pioneering recognition of the diversity of urban traditions emerges in an early report to her department chair in which she wrote that she recorded an old-time fiddler, a roof shingler and a singer of Albanian-Macedonian folksongs on Edison wire recordings in one spring term. Although she did not publish many articles about her fieldwork research, her legacy lives on in the WSU Folklore Archive and in publications by her students, such as Susie Hoogasian-Villa's *100 Armenian Tales and Their Folkloristic Relevance* in 1966 and Harriet M. Pawlowska's *Merrily We Sing: 105 Polish Folksongs* in 1983.

Janet L. Langlois

References

James, Thelma G. 1933. Frances J. Child and the English and Scottish Ballads. *Journal of American Folklore* 46:51–69. Reprinted in *The Critics and the Ballad,* ed. Tristram Potter Coffin and Mae Edward Leach. Carbondale: Southern Illinois University Press, 1960.

———. 1948. Folklore and Propaganda. *Journal of American Folklore* 61:311.

Reuss, Richard. 1970. Thelma James Interview. Wayne State University Folklore Archive. Accession No. 1970(155) Tapes 667–668.

Jameson, R.D. (1895–1959)

Teacher, scholar, administrator. Raymond Deloy Jameson (who published under his initials and was known to his friends as Jim) was born in Tennessee and reared by his widowed mother in Ohio. He earned bachelor's and master's degrees at the University of Wisconsin, worked briefly as a newspaperman, and subsequently enjoyed a colorful academic career that spanned the globe. He taught literature, philology, and history in the United States as well as in Europe and Asia, most notably at the University of Peking (1925–1938), where he founded and directed the Orthological Institute of China, devoted to English-language instruction. Returning to the United States in 1938, Jameson joined the staff of the Library of Congress, serving as consultant in comparative literature and as administrator of the Consultant Service. During and after World War II, he was historical officer of the American Red Cross in the Southwest Pacific region, quartered in Australia and later in the Philippines (1942–1948). In his last years, Jameson settled into a relatively quiet life as professor of English at Highlands University in Las Vegas, New Mexico, where he taught until his death shortly before he was scheduled to retire. His widow, Dorothy, donated his papers to the University of California.

Jameson's best-known contributions to folkloristics are in the work of his later years. At Highlands he initiated and supervised an ambitious student collecting project (unfinished at the time of his death) of Hispanic materials from northern New Mexico; he served as book review editor of *Western Folklore* in the five years before his death; and, perhaps most significantly, he contributed dozens of articles, both signed and unsigned, to the *Funk and Wagnalls Standard Dictionary of Folklore, Mythology, and Legend* (1949), including the long surveys "Chinese Folklore," "Romany Folklore," and "Phallism," as well as shorter pieces on subjects ranging from "Adultery" through "Yü Huang." His definition of "Folklore" is among the notorious twenty-one in that same compendium. Two years before his death, he was invited to participate in the Summer Folklore Institute at Indiana University. After his death, he was honored with a memorial issue of *Western Folklore.* Portions of his students' New Mexico collectanea have been published posthumously by the University of California Press (cf. Robe 1977).

Polly Stewart

References

Greenway, John. 1960. R.D. Jameson, 1895–1959. *Western Folklore* 19:153–54.

Jameson, R.D. 1932. *Three Lectures on Chinese Folklore.* Shanghai.

Robe, Stanley L., ed. 1977. *Hispanic Folktales from New Mexico: Narratives from the R.D. Jameson Collection,* with Introduction and Notes by Stanley L. Robe, Foreword by Wayland D. Hand. Berkeley: University of California Press.

Jansen, William Hugh (1914–1979)

Folklorist. A native of Stamford, Connecticut (B.A., Wesleyan University, 1935), and holder of the third-oldest American doctorate in folklore (Indiana University, 1949), Jansen taught in the English Department at the University of Kentucky from 1949 to 1979; he retired one month before his death.

Jansen became an internationally recognized folklorist largely from his work on cultural stereotyping and through the publication of his article on what he termed the "esoteric-exoteric factor" in folklore (Jansen 1959). He also lectured widely abroad, and his other research documented the historical existence of legendary figures—one the subject of a famous Turkish legend, and another the subject of Jansen's doctoral dissertation, published in 1977 as *Abraham "Oregon" Smith: Pioneer, Folk Hero, and Tale-Teller.*

Late in his career, Jansen was recognized for having contributed earlier seminal ideas to the "new folkloristics"—concerning oral folklore, the role of performer and performer-audience relationships, and their imperative correlations with genre, context, and function.

Jansen published fifty articles and served as editor of four state and regional folklore journals. He was a Fellow of the American Folklore Society, and he served as general editor of the society's Bibliographical and Special Series and twice as its vice president. Jansen was a Fulbright Lecturer, a Ford Foundation Fellow, a Fellow of the National Endowment for the Humanities, a member of the International Society for Folk Narrative Research, and a delegate to the American Council of Learned Societies.

R. Gerald Alvey

References

Alvey, R. Gerald. 1980. Obituary: Wm. Hugh Jansen. *Journal of American Folklore* 93:57–59.

Jansen, William Hugh. 1959. The Esoteric-Exoteric Factor in Folklore. *Fabula: Journal of Folklore Studies* 2:205–211. Reprinted in *The Study of Folklore,* ed. Alan Dundes. Englewood Cliffs, NJ: Prentice-Hall, 1965, pp. 43–51.

Ward, William S. 1993. *The English Department, University of Kentucky: An Informal History.* Lexington: University Press of Kentucky, pp. 174–178.

Japanese Americans

American-born descendants of Japanese contract laborers ("sojourners") and immigrants from Japan. Japanese Americans are self-identified by the following terms: the *issei* (from *ichi-,* one or first) are the Japanese immigrants, who, because of government restrictions on Asian immigration, were usually not allowed to become U.S. citizens; the *nisei,* or "second people," are their children, born in the United States and possessing citizenship; the *sansei* are the third generation; and the *yonsei* are the fourth. The *kibei* (*ki* from *kaeru,* to return; *bei* from *beikoku,* America) are those who were born in the United States and are thus citizens of this country, but were taken back to Japan when their families' work contracts were finished; they returned to the United States, often after years of Japanese schooling, in many cases to marry.

Folklore of the *issei* was parallel to that of most immigrants: They retained much of their medicinal lore, ghost stories, food customs, and festivals as living reminders of the country they had left behind. This function was especially important for the Japanese because of the significance of belonging to several interactive sets of insider (*uchi*) relationships: family, clan, village, occupation, prefecture, and country. For the *issei,* their folklore—along with popular and elite genres like music, dance, calligraphy, arts, and language—provided a sense of cultural belonging in a strange and forbidding land. The *nisei* generation was given language instruction, but for them the world of folklore was split into at least two segments: Japanese at home and American in public. The *nisei* thus carried on some of the traditions of their parents, and spoke the dialect they heard at home, but many of the regional and occupational beliefs and customs simply did not fit the new cultural environment. The *sansei* and *yonsei* grew up as Americans with almost no acquaintance with Japanese language (except for names of foods and body parts) and with an even smaller set of traditional observances in their lives.

Just as many of the upwardly mobile *nisei* had taken up classical arts like flower arranging, the tea ceremony, *okoto* music, classical dance *(minyo),* and the singing of classical poetry *(shigin)* during the 1930s and through the relocation years of World War II, the *sansei* and *yonsei* are more recently obtaining formal language training in Japanese. On the surface, it would seem that living Japanese traditions have been replaced with American custom and a self-conscious maintenance of elite arts (parallel to the piano, violin, and dance lessons of their European American neighbors).

But in fact—as is often the case with ethnic folklore—the larger range of traditions has been replaced by a more limited but intensified selection of community expressions. Traditional foods constitute one of these genres: *Sukiyaki* (thinly sliced beef simmered in an open pan along with vegetables, *sake,* sugar, mushrooms, and tofu); *teriyaki* (grilled marinated meats); and *tempura* (vegetables and seafood dipped in batter and deep fried) were not traditional dishes in Japan, where only the wealthy could afford such meats and delicacies. But the ability to cook and offer these foods, especially at important events like weddings, funerals, and festivals, has become an important traditional expression for Japanese Americans. As well, the playing of the *taiko* (a large drum used at festival dances), has become extremely popular among Japanese Americans in Hawaii and on the mainland, and in many Japanese

American communities in the United States there are more young people playing the *taiko* than there are in comparable communities in Japan.

Probably nothing typifies the sense of Japanese American community expression better than *obon,* or *bon-odori* (the *bon* dance; the *o–* prefix is honorific). Celebrated in Japan since the 7th century A.D., *obon* brings the spirits of departed ancestors together with their living families for several days of feasting and dancing. Usually held in the parking lot of a Buddhist church or in a blocked-off city street, the *bon-odori* features dances from different parts of Japan performed by Japanese Americans of all faiths wearing kimonos. Many participants practice the steps for months in advance, but anyone is welcome to join in the dancing during the festival. Traditional foods are sold around the periphery of the dancing (or in the nearby Buddhist church), and demonstrations of *taiko* drumming are given during intermissions. In Japan, *obon* brings people from all over the country back to their home villages and neighborhoods; in America the festival brings Japanese Americans together from various neighborhoods in a celebration of ethnic community.

Probably nothing illustrates the retention of the Japanese sense of *uchi* (insider) custom better than the celebration of *oshogatsu,* New Year. Traditional families rise early on New Year's morning and eat a special fish-based soup called *ozoni,* then spend the rest of the day entertaining close friends and family members with traditional foods (sushi, teriyaki chicken, tempura shrimp).

Funerals provide still another opportunity for the exercise of traditions that bind families together with their larger community: Friends and relatives give *koden,* a note of condolence with a sum of money enclosed (the closer the relationship, the larger the amount). The family of the deceased person notes the name of each donor and the amount given; cards of thanks are sent to all donors, and when someone in any of those families dies, one is obligated to send in a *koden* of the same size. The Japanese custom of *omiyage,* bringing a gift when visiting someone, is widely practiced by Japanese Americans, as is the custom of removing one's shoes when entering a house (a custom based on funerary beliefs in Japan but now functioning as a gesture of polite behavior in the United States).

These traditions, selective as they may be, are accompanied by other expressive forms that are more in the nature of hobbies (many are learned from instruction books, not from the living contexts in which one lives), which nonetheless provide models of Japanese attitudes about number, arrangement, color, and pattern: *origami* (paper folding), *temari* (winding silk threads into decorative balls with complex patterns), *bunka shishu* (embroidery done from one side of the cloth), doll making, sand painting, and flower arranging. All of these arts require the individual to subordinate his or her own talents to the demands of the craft, which does carry certain recognizable traditional features, often from ancient times.

As with all immigrant cultures, the Japanese Americans practice a mix of the old and the modern, traditional and pop, imported and American. The genres of folklore that have been maintained have been intensified (for most, but probably not for all) as a way of experiencing and celebrating cultural identity in a land of diversity.

Barre Toelken

References

Araki, Nancy K., and Jane Horii. 1985. *Matsuri: Festival! Japanese American Celebrations and Activities.* Union City, CA: Heian International.

DeFrancis, John. 1973. *Things Japanese in Hawaii.* Honolulu: University Press of Hawaii.

Fugita, Stephen S., and David J. O'Brien. 1991. *Japanese American Ethnicity: The Persistence of Community.* Seattle: University of Washington Press.

Opler, Marvin K. 1950. Japanese Folk Beliefs and Practices, Tule Lake, California. *Journal of American Folklore* 63:385–397.

Toelken, Barre. 1990. Cultural Maintenance and Ethnic Intensification in Two Japanese American World War II Internment Camps. *Oriens Extremus* 33:69–94.

———. 1994. Dancing with the Departed: Japanese Obon in the American West. *The World and I* (August), pp. 232–243.

Jazz

Twentieth-century musical form, native to North America, characterized by the use of Western band instruments, improvisation, blues harmony, "swinging" rhythm, and other instrumental and vocal practices. Jazz has rich African American musical and oral roots but was also shaped by other traditions, and it has assimilated and adapted to musical cultures around the world since 1917. In the late 20th century, jazz is an esteemed "classical" music, taught in conservatories and presented in concert halls for all ethnic groups, but it retains its importance in African American culture as an expression of spirituality, virtuosity, oral skill, and communal solidarity.

The term "jazz" is obscure in origin. Most commonly it is said to derive from an Afro-Caribbean word meaning "to speed up," but it has also been said to come from jasmine, a performer named Jazbo or Chas. Brown, or the French *chasser* (to hunt or chase). The common spelling in 1910s New Orleans, "jass," suggests to some "ass" or sexual intercourse. The first printed reference to "jazz" music was in the *San Francisco Bulletin* in 1913. In New Orleans at this time, however, it was usually called "ragtime," and well after 1920 many musicians (such as Eddie Condon and Miles Davis) resisted the term "jazz" and associated their music directly with other accepted musical styles.

The music developed most distinctly as an instrumental counterpart of the Mississippi Delta blues after about 1880. Brass bands between New Orleans and Memphis accommodated the harmonies, rhythms, and timbral effects of vocal blues to the limitations of their instruments, making such effects part of their performance styles. The 1886 International Cotton Exposition in New Orleans may have served as the first gathering point for White and Black regional bands that used these new effects. (The White bandleader Jack Laine insisted that he was playing "ragtime" or jazz by that time.) Bands relied on traditional European march and dance music for much of their presentations, but new creative possibilities coalesced into a distinct style. In the plantation regions up-river, unschooled adult's and children's bands such as Kid Ory's Woodland Band probably nurtured the style with first-hand reference to rural blues and church song, while in New Orleans, musicians with a wide variety of backgrounds and educations performed in a growing array of urban settings. White and Black rural migrants swelled the population of New Orleans and other Southern cities, creating a greater demand for dance halls, parks, lawn parties, clubs and secret associations, saloons, brothels, and wedding and meeting facilities—and for music in those locales.

Similar conditions existed in other Southern cities, but in New Orleans, rich musical traditions, the sheer size of the Black migrant population, and highly developed street and club life created the most vibrant early jazz style and the largest corps of musicians. Jazz built bridges between the Creoles of color in the Vieux Carré (such as pianist-leader Jelly Roll Morton) and rural African American migrants uptown (such as trumpeter Louis Armstrong) at a time when Jim Crow laws were classifying members of both groups as second-class citizens. They were generally poor, and jazz served as a language, profession, and medium that drew them together; even Sicilian immigrants found an interest in jazz. In these groups, older "musicianers" such as the Black Latino Lorenzo "Papa" Tio took in students, initiating the apprenticeship tradition in jazz. Some formal institutions, such as the Jones Colored Waifs' Home (attended by Louis Armstrong), also fed this culture. Anglo-Saxon and Irish Catholic musicians, however, remained apart, often expressing a conventional racist disdain for the music of those who often competed with them for unskilled jobs. These Whites developed their own version of swinging ragtime, which came to be called "Dixieland."

Early jazz was both a traditional and a modern product. Kid, or "spasm," bands kept the music rooted in children's folklore. Unlike rural blues, jazz had few associations with spirit religion or *vodun,* but it otherwise retained the role blues had held in the Delta juke joint, as a concomitant of food, dance, gambling, family activities, and nocturnal vice. Few jazz players before 1920 learned to read or write music, preserving aural and visual cues for composition, rehearsal, and performance. In other ways, jazz was a product of the urbanization of Black culture. Jazz in general was part of a male-centered urban sporting life in New Orleans. Women were usually confined to piano playing and singing, perhaps in comformity to the sex roles of Victorian musical culture, and would long play a marginal role in jazz. From the start, male jazz musicians mixed playing with side work, sports such as baseball, nightlife, parading, street advertising, and occasionally such activity as gambling, narcotics, and pimping (although only pianists like Fess Manetta worked regularly in Storyville, the city's red-light district, from 1897 to 1918).

After 1917, jazz rapidly expanded its fame and geographical reach. Restless New Orleans musicians spread post-ragtime music nationwide. Despite their deep attachments to urban folklife, New Orleans musicians were compelled for economic reasons to tour, both on existing vaudeville, minstrel, and medicine-show circuits and on self-arranged trips. Bassist Bill Johnson moved to Los Angeles in 1909, and others soon followed; by 1915 New Orleans musicians were working regularly in Chicago, St. Louis, Houston, and other cities. With these residencies, and the release in 1917 of the first jazz records by the White Original Dixieland Jazz Band (ODJB), ragtime players nationwide (many already toying with blues techniques) responded to the public's enthusiasm and pursued jazz. As the great migration of Southern African Americans commenced during World War I, jazz followed the path of the Illinois Central Railroad from New Orleans to Chicago.

In the 1920s, jazz was one of the first and greatest examples of mass-media folk tradition. Within a few years, recordings spread the music across the world. Instrumental blues musicians gained bookings in every part of the United States, particularly on the coasts, and soon gained invitations to play for aficionados in the hotels of Shanghai, Bombay, Cairo, Paris, and Rio. In 1922 a Soviet musician formed the First Eccentric Orchestra of Russia with Lenin's official approval. Among Whites in Europe and the Americas, Europeanized forms of jazz caught the fancy of youth, whether they were enjoying prosperity (as in America) or fleeing economic ruin in "decadent" protest (as in Weimar Germany). Many future jazz musicians learned their first tunes and styles from records, often before receiving formal instrument training.

The bursting new African American ghettos in Northern cities, especially Harlem and south Chicago, provided even more sizable urban folk settings for jazz. Traditional Black elites in these communities attacked both jazz and the blues as sinful and unsophisticated, but even most of these critics by the late 1920s came to perceive jazz as a staple of the ghetto's leisure culture. Northern cities had many music-education facilities and outlets for the nationwide entertainment industry, which produced both a need for highly trained musicians and public expectations for polished entertainment. Therefore, such New Orleans non-readers as Louis Armstrong and Kid Ory were compelled in the North to learn music reading and visit classical-instrument teachers. Written jazz arrangements (which nevertheless allowed for solo improvisations) became standard by 1930.

Despite this modernizing trend, much of jazz's folk status persisted. The Northern dance hall played much the same social role as the Delta juke joint. Musicians, while more professional-minded, remained young men with passions for urban nightlife, group fraternizing, and "hard" living. They also preserved much of the Southern performer's folk identity. Musicians' superstitions drew upon both Southern traditions and the lore of show business. Pianists played at rent parties, gatherings that charged admission and helped tenants with their bills (as New Orleans fish fries had done before). Musicians played for weddings, funerals, and other social functions, and touring bands sometimes doubled as semipro baseball teams. New dance halls such as Chicago's Savoy accommodated thousands of customers, where the juke-joint milieu was perpetuated and urbanized; courtship, dancing, and sartorial display were altered accordingly. Musicians also engaged in this exciting milieu of sexual adventure, backstage gambling, and fancy clothing. Outsiders were intrigued by the creative slang of jazz players. Jazz jargon, like 1930s "jive," adapted rural African Americanisms to the city. Such idiosyncratic players as tenor saxophonist Lester Young were virtuosi with jargon as well, using it as an extension of their musical creativity. In general, though, despite the claims of White observers, verbal creativity in jazz was limited and carefully tailored to professional needs.

The earliest White jazz musicians partook in much of this culture as well. After 1920 a few Dixieland players from New Orleans, as well as dozens of Whites across America who heard jazz recordings and touring groups, gravitated to Harlem, south Chicago, and south-central Los Angeles to gain professional apprenticeship with Black players. These apprentices formed the core of the "hot" White players of the 1920s (to be distinguished from "sweet" dance-band musicians who disdained the blues-jazz style), including cornetist Bix Beiderbecke, drummer Dave Tough, and saxophonist Bud Freeman. Relations between White and Black players were often cordial, but tensions arose as Whites consistently captured steadier and more lucrative musical employment. As a result, White players' involvement in the culture of the ghetto was usually short lived.

Beginning in the 1930s, jazz became both a nationally popular music and the locus of increasingly defined subcultures. The Depression forced many out of the business, while remaining players became more professionalized. Still, the persistence of Black dance halls and the aggressive preservation of jazz nightclubs by aficionados (especially in New York City) ensured that the now celebrated 1920s milieu and musicians' cohort would be maintained. As before, young African Americans with talent apprenticed in big bands and then graduated into solo and leader roles. Only a few benefited from the limited integration of major White swing bands by such progressive leaders as Benny Goodman, Artie Shaw, and Charlie Barnet. The musicians' union's recording ban (1942–1944), the military draft during World War II, and new club employment restrictions decreased the always meager opportunities of Black players.

At the time, though, Black jazz was reaching a pinnacle of harmonic and rhythmic sophistication. The resulting "bebop" movement of the 1940s and 1950s was a major musical revolution, but it also heightened the public perception of jazz musicians as angry, alienated outsiders who shunned public approval. The barbed comments and irreverent stage antics of such beboppers as Dizzy Gillespie were informed by political militancy, while others (such as Charlie Parker) were perhaps more bedeviled by such personal problems as drug addiction. Many Whites in dance bands emulated bebop's disdain for "squares" and cultivated unorthodox clothing, drug use, and language. While the affectation of the most demonstratively "alienated" players made a deep impression on the Beat writers and other dissatisfied Americans of the 1950s, paving the way for the crucial union of music and social protest in the 1960s, it rarely reflected the artistic vitality of the "hard bop" era. Only the effort of saxophonist John Coltrane to ally his music with pan-Africanist poetics and spirituality signaled a renewed social commitment by African American jazz musicians, which intensified in the 1960s and 1970s with the coming of the Black Power and Black Arts movements. White musicians became even more remote from the jazz-Black ghetto cultural axis during these years of cultural separatism. Only since the 1970s, as jazz became almost entirely a music patronized by concertgoing elites and performed by professionals, have White players shared a common professional culture with the most successful African American musicians.

Jazz is perhaps the most fully developed and diversified American folk music. Its cultural identities and functions are as complex as the 20th-century society in which it has grown and diversified. The study of the folklore of jazz and of jazz as folklore is in its infancy, but early work by Peter Tamony, Peter Spencer, Neil Leonard, and others suggests paths for future research. Existing scholarship, however, demonstrates that the content, timbre, and structure of jazz music and performance, the organization of the musicians' profession and pedagogy, the social functions of jazz performance, and the extramusical practices of musicians and their admirers are all fascinating and important aspects of American folklore of the 20th century.

Burton W. Peretti

References

Becker, Howard S. 1963. *Outsiders: Studies in the Sociology of Deviance.* Glencoe, IL: Free Press.

Kofsky, Frank. 1979. Afro-American Innovation and the Folk Tradition in Jazz: Their Historical Significance. *Journal of Ethnic Studies* 7:1–12.

Leonard, Neil. 1987. *Jazz: Myth and Religion.* New York: Oxford University Press.

Ogren, Kathy J. 1989. *The Jazz Revolution: Twenties America and the Meaning of Jazz.* New York: Oxford University Press.

Peretti, Burton W. 1992. *The Creation of Jazz: Music, Race, and Culture in Urban America.* Urbana: University of Illinois Press.

Sidran, Ben. 1973. *Black Talk.* New York: Da Capo.

Spencer, Peter. 1986. Jazz and the Folk Process. *Sing Out!* 32:20–25.

Tamony, Peter. 1981. Jazz: The Word and Its Extension to Music. *JEMF Quarterly* 16:9–18.

See also Blues; Klezmer Music

Jefferson, Blind Lemon (1893–1929)

Texas singer and guitarist who became the first country blues artist to gain widespread fame as a recording artist. Even in the modern era, Jefferson is, next to Robert Johnson, the most widely recognized name in classic country blues. The 100 or so recordings he made between 1925 and 1929 form an impressive repertoire of traditional and creative song, and Jefferson's colorful life has spawned legends as popular as his songs.

In fact, there are surprisingly few solid historical facts about Jefferson's life and career. He was born near Wortham, Texas, some 60 miles south of Dallas; the 1900 Census for the area lists him as "Lemmon B. Jefferson" and gives a birth date of September 24, 1893—some years earlier than legend has it. It has been generally assumed that he was born blind, but later musicians who knew him suggested he had some degree of sight; certainly his original songs are full of impressive visual images. He received his early vocal training by singing gospel music in local churches, but was soon "busking" at towns on most of the local H and TC railroad that ran north and south, and to Dallas. Contemporaries remember him in the red-light district of Dallas as a "big loud songster" with a tin cup wired on the neck of his guitar. Like many such songsters, he knew and performed a wide variety of songs other than just blues: He later even recorded a variant of the Child ballad "Three Nights Drunk," as well as gambling ballads like "Jack of Diamonds" and 19th-century pop songs like "Begging Back." For a time he traveled with Huddie Ledbetter (Lead Belly), exchanging songs and guitar styles.

In 1925 a friend put him in touch with talent scout Mayo Williams, who worked for Paramount Records. Produced by a Wisconsin chair company, Paramount was one of the cheaper record companies who used inferior shellac and had spotty distribution. It was, nonetheless, one of the companies most receptive to blues singers, and in 1926 Paramount recorded Jefferson doing "Got the Blues" and "Long Lonesome Blues." Released on the same disc, these songs became the first real commercial hits for country blues—so much so that the company wore out the metal stampers for the disc and had Jefferson remake them. Its success meant that Jefferson would have a welcome in the studios for the rest of his life, but also that he would be expected to record mostly blues songs from his vast repertoire.

In the next few years, he recorded definitive versions of many songs that would become blues standards: "See That My Grave's Kept Clean" (1927), "Black Snake Moan" (1927), "Match Box Blues" (1927), "Corinna Blues" (1926), and "Easy Rider Blues" (1927). His surprisingly high voice and his odd, "broke-time" guitar figures forged a distinctive style that soon was known across the South.

Jefferson's professional career is sparsely documented. Reports suggest he traveled around a great deal, into the Mississippi Delta, into Memphis and Nashville, and even into the remote West Virginia coal camps. His death came in the winter of 1929–1930 when, after playing at a house party in Chicago, he somehow got lost and froze to death in the snow. A fellow Paramount artist, pianist Will Ezell, brought the body back to Wortham for burial.

Charles K. Wolfe

References

Evans, David. 1993. Goin' up the Country: Blues in Texas and the Deep South. In *Nothing but the Blues*, ed. Lawrence Cohn. New York: Abbeville, pp 33–87.

Governor, Alan. 1991. Blind Lemon Jefferson. In *Bluesland*, ed. Toby Byron and Pete Welding. New York: Dutton.

Jefferson, Blind Lemon. *Complete Recordings. Vol. 1-4.* Document 5017–5020. Compact Discs.

———. *King of the Country Blues.* Yazoo 1069. Compact Disc/Cassette.

Jersey Devil

A monstrous creature of southern New Jersey, subject of a legend dating from the early 18th century. After more than 250 years in oral circulation, the legend of the "Jersey Devil" has many variations, and not everyone agrees how he looks or behaves.

Most accounts begin with a woman named Jane Leeds, who lived with her husband, Daniel, at the edge of a great swamp near the Mullica River in present-day Atlantic County. Some folks say that she was strange and different; some even said she was a witch. In any event, it is generally agreed that she had twelve children. Understandably, Jane Leeds was tired of cooking and cleaning and child care. Then one day she learned that she was pregnant with her thirteenth child.

In a moment of weakness, according to one account, that night while she was saying her bedtime prayers, she prayed: "Lord, I hope this one's not a child. Let this one be a Devil!" We now know, at least from legends, that this was a mistake, because on that terrible winter's night in February of 1735, when Mother Leed's thirteenth child was born, something awful happened. They say that at first when the child was born, it seemed like a perfectly healthy and normal infant boy with a chubby little baby face and blue eyes. But in less than half an hour, the child grew quickly into a creature the size, some say, of two full-grown men. It had the hairy torso of a powerful man, but in the place of the baby face was the head of a horse with two giant horns growing out of either side. And growing out of its back were two giant, leathery, bat-like wings. In place of human legs, it had the legs and feet of a goat. Most accounts agree that it also had a long serpentine tail.

Most frightening of all, the "Devil" had powerful, hairy arms. At the end of each arm were paws, and at the end of each paw were long, bony claws. Each claw was razor sharp. With a single swipe of his right paw, he slit the throat of the midwife in attendance, who collapsed in a pool of blood. The creature let out a blood-curdling scream and flew up the chimney and escaped into the Pine Barrens, where, according to legend, he has terrified the citizens of south Jersey ever since.

The Jersey Devil remained an obscure regional legend through most of the 18th and 19th centuries, until 1909 when a series of purported "Devil" sightings inspired a Philadelphia businessman to stage a hoax. He painted a kangaroo green, attached fake wings to the helpless creature, and had it exhibited to the public.

The recent history of the Jersey Devil is more in the realm of popular culture than folklore. As people lost their dread of the legendary creature, they started putting his image on T-shirts, postcards, buttons, menus, and so on. There are even Jersey Devil cocktails sold in south Jersey bars.

Angus Kress Gillespie

References

Gillespie, Angus Kress. 1985. The Jersey Devil. *Journal of Regional Cultures* 5:59–73.

McCloy, James F., and Ray Miller Jr. 1976. *The Jersey Devil.* Wallingford, PA: Middle Atlantic.

McPhee, John. 1968. *The Pine Barrens.* New York: Farrar, Straus, Giroux.

Jewish Americans

An American ethnic and religious group, consisting primarily of immigrants fleeing persecution and economic hardship in Europe. Smaller numbers of Jews arrived in America from virtually every country of the world. Jews came with the first European explorers to the New World, and the earliest settlements in America were of Sephardic (Spanish-speaking) Jews after the mass expulsion from Spain in 1492. The Jewish population remained insignificant until the mid-1880s influx of Jews from Germany who established communities in major urban centers. The largest cohort arrived with the mass immigrations from eastern Europe between 1880 and 1920; two million souls in all, primarily impoverished Yiddish speakers from the Russian Pale of Settlement (a Jewish "reservation" in which Jews of the Russian Empire were imprisoned unless granted special permission to live outside).

The dispersion of Jews after the conquest of their ancestral homeland, Israel, by the Roman Empire in 70 C.E. (Common Era, the Jewish equivalent of the Christian A.D., avoiding the confession of faith couched in the term Anno Domini, meaning "Year of Our Lord"), has created a unique cultural phenomenon: a cohesive ethnic group with a shared core culture, tradition, ancestors, history, religion, and language overlaid with the culture, customs, and languages of their host communities. In addition, traditional Jewish culture and religion are inseparable. Jewish law *(halakhah)* is all encompassing, regulating both personal and communal behavior.

The breakdown of traditional Jewish life for the majority of the world's Jews began in the late 18th century with the Enlightenment and the Industrial Revolution in Europe and was accelerated by three pivotal events: the existence of the largest Jewish community in a secular, pluralistic United States; the existence of the second-largest Jewish community in the secular, anti-religious Soviet Union; and the destruction of six million Jews, and many traditional communities, by Germany and its allies during World War II.

This largest Jewish concentration in the United States is characterized, in part, by a heterogeneity that makes it difficult even to define. Whereas Jewish law defines a Jew as a person born of a Jewish mother or one who converts according to that law, many Americans of Jewish descent do not identify themselves as Jews, whereas many of Jewish patriliny do so, and such descent is recognized by the Reform branch of Judaism. Problems of identity such as these make it difficult to determine who the Jewish folk are, and, thus, what is American Jewish folklore.

A 1990 study concluded that there are 5.5 million Americans who identify themselves as Jewish by religion or cultural identity. Of this core population, 76 percent identify by religion, 20 percent by culture, and 3 percent by choice (converts). Seventy-five percent live in urban areas and, as a group, are much more highly educated than the general population and have a lower birthrate. The largest concentration is in the Northeast. Thirty-one percent are married to non-Jews, and Jews constitute about 2 percent of the total American population *(American Jewish Yearbook* 1992).

The heterogeneity and rapid assimilation of American Jewry produced a folklore whose characteristics mirror both this diversity and the interfaces of Jewish culture with life in America. As in other ethnic communities, traditional forms, which most nearly preserve the lore of the old country, can be found in the older Jewish enclaves in the Northeast, especially the greater New York City area. Within the Orthodox and Hasidic communities, such as Williamsburg in Brooklyn and Boro Park in Queens, cultural conservatism and the preservation of Old World culture and language are intertwined with religious belief and serve to fend off the encroachments of a sometimes alluring secular world. Much as the Amish have preserved their German and rural culture as an act of faith, the ultra-Orthodox attempt to preserve their Yiddish and *shtetl* (Jewish trading town of eastern Europe) culture within America's largest urban amalgam. It is in these insular communities that traditional eastern European folk traditions are most zealously guarded and are adapted to protect against the pull of assimilation.

Within traditional Judaism itself, the relationship between the formal religion and the folk religion has been defined by the terms *halakhah* (law), *hagadah* (lore), and *minhag* (custom). This relationship functioned to establish the dynamic interplay among the three elements within a traditional society, one that accepted the primacy of *halakhah* over any external law and in which faith in God was a given. Some modern American forms of Judaism, however, accept neither *halakhah* nor faith in God as tenets; the distinction between formal and folk religion, then, has become more confused, and what lies outside the boundaries of accepted belief and practice has become more controversial.

As complex and changing as the identity of American Jewry is, there is a rich and variegated Jewish culture in America, dynamic and vital, which displays extreme conservatism at the same time it has inspired some of the most radical social, political, and artistic movements in America. A survey of several areas demonstrates the variety of Jewish folkloric expression in the contemporary United States.

Language. The three primary Jewish languages are Yiddish, spoken by the Jews of eastern Europe; Judeo-Spanish (the use of the colloquial term "Ladino" is controversial among scholars), spoken by the Jews of Iberian descent in the countries of their dispersion following the expulsion from Spain and Portugal in 1492; and Hebrew, the holy tongue of Jewish tradition and the language of ancient and modern Israel. Although German was the native language of the Jews who emigrated from Germany between 1840 and 1860, Yiddish was the *mama loshn* (mother tongue) of the majority of the two million migrants to America who arrived during the Great Im-

migration of 1880–1920. During the forty years after the end of the immigration wave, an entire Jewish culture was created, primarily in New York City but in some other cities with large Jewish concentrations as well, including schools, newspapers, musical groups, publishing houses and theaters. With the passing of the first generation, Yiddish serves in the 1990s as the vernacular of the Hasidic communities. As the main immigrant language, however, it continues to serve as an important sentimental link to the fading ethnic culture, in jokes, anecdotes, songs, and the revival of klezmer (small band) music. Yiddish words and phrases have found their way into American English, primarily through the popularity of Jewish comedians such as Milton Berle, Henny Youngman, Jerry Lewis, George Burns, the Marx brothers, and Billy Crystal, many of whom began their careers in the Borscht Belt, the Jewish hotels and resorts in the Catskill Mountains of New York state, which served as the primary vacation getaway for New York City Jews and the training ground for Jewish American actors, singers, and comedians.

Judeo-Spanish serves a similar sentimental link for the small number of Sephardic Jews in America, 50,000–60,000 of whom arrived during the Great Immigration, although it, too, is spoken by very few. With the increasing significance of Israel as a symbolic, cultural, and educational center for American Jews, Hebrew is growing in currency as a second language, and instruction in spoken Hebrew has grown tremendously in the final decades of the 20th century.

Rites of Passage. Ceremonies marking Jewish rites of passage are rich grounds for folkloric expression and have been trans-formed by the American experience, especially the movement for women's rights. On the eighth day after birth, the male child is circumcised in the *brit milah* (or *bris*) ceremony. Some American Jews have instituted a *simkhat bat* (joy of the daughter) ceremony as an equivalent for female children. As this celebration has no rabbinic precedent, it provides opportunities for creative expression.

Since its initiation in 1922 by the Reconstructionist movement (a liberal offshoot of Conservative Judaism), the bat mitzvah ceremony for girls has mirrored the traditional bar mitzvah ceremony for boys. Whereas the traditional bar mitzvah celebrated the thirteen-year-old's entry into legal adulthood and the rights and responsibilities of ritual majority, including the beginning of a lifetime of Jewish learning, the modern bar mitzvah among non-Orthodox Jews often marks the end of Jewish learning, and perhaps the last time the child will engage in formal Jewish study or even enter a synagogue. It has become an often elaborate, materialistic affair, where the gifts received have become the center of focus, and in some cases the reception revolves around a "theme," such as the Wild West, baseball, or a Hawaiian Luau. Such syncretisms mark a particular modern American influence.

Holidays. The most striking change in the folklore of Jewish holidays is the elevation of Hanukkah from a relatively minor historical holiday to a major holiday, mostly as a result of its temporal proximity to, and competition with, the American Christmas. Likewise, certain traditionally more important festivals, such as *Shvu'ot* (Feast of Weeks), have faded in importance. A recent survey indicated that Passover was one of the most widely observed holidays among Jews in America, with secular Jews often emphasizing its theme of universal liberation from oppression. The centerpiece of Passover, the seder meal, lends itself to the creation of family folklore and traditions. Family seder committees have even been formed to help organize the complex arrangements necessary to bring scattered extended families together. Many Jews who cease to attend synagogue on other occasions will continue to attend the High Holidays, Rosh Hashanah (New Year) and Yom Kippur (Day of Atonement), and tickets must be purchased to ensure that the otherwise empty sanctuary is not overwhelmed. Folkloric innovation can also be seen in the feminist revival and reinvention of the Rosh Khodesh (New Moon) ceremony.

Foodways. As in other American ethnic communities, foods from the old country often serve an important role in ethnic identification. Among Jews, foods have a special status, both because of dietary laws *(kashrut)* and the important role of festive meals in the observance of Jewish holidays. The decrease in the observance of the laws of *kashrut* among American Jews has further decreased the continuity of traditional cuisine, and those who do "keep kosher" are not limited to "Jewish" dishes in order to adhere to the law. Among the majority of American Jews, eastern European dishes maintain a ceremonial prominence. Yet, with assimilation, traditional Jewish cuisine has taken on a significance that limits it to specific dishes associated with specific occasions. Some foods, such as bagels with cream cheese and lox, have become stereotypical Jewish foods, even though this particular combination held no special significance in the Old World. Many foods, such as bagels and sweet kosher wine, have become staples of non-Jewish Americans, many of whom are unaware of their Jewish origins. A breakfast sandwich with bacon and egg on a bagel is served by a popular fast-food chain, and Mogen Dovid kosher wine is known by many poor urban dwellers as "Mad Dog Twenty Twenty."

Folklore Genres. The realities of modern American life and mass culture have affected Jewish folklore just as they have affected all immigrant and ethnic lore in the New World. Traditional oral genres, such as the folktale, legend, riddle, and proverb, have been supplanted by the quintessentially American genre, the joke. In fact, the influence of the Borscht Belt comedians on American mass entertainment has had an enduring impact on American culture as a whole. The stand-up comics, once mostly Jewish, have surged in popularity, and there is not an hour of the day that they cannot be seen doing their "schtick" (act) on television. A number of these comedians, including Jerry Seinfeld, Paul Reiser, and Jackie Mason, have developed television situation comedies that have a distinctly Jewish flavor and continue to influence American entertainment and attitudes. Whereas Mason's show emphasized Jewish stereotypes, Seinfeld and Reiser rarely allude to the Jewish underpinnings of their comedy in their shows.

As with other ethnic groups, there exists a large corpus of "Jewish jokes," told by Jews about other Jews and by non-Jews about Jews. Many derogatory stereotypes abound in both, particularly stinginess, the negative characteristics of complaining, frigidity, materialism of the "Jewish American Princess" (JAP), and the overprotectiveness of the "Jewish Mother." More traditional genres persist primarily in the ritual setting; however, there have been a number of revivals of eastern European Jewish folklore, including Yiddish and klezmer music. But the influence of modern Israel is more pervasive, and Israeli folksong and dance have become staples within Jewish community centers and youth groups.

It is not from the particular native lore of immigrant Jews that a persisting American Jewish folklore will develop, but in the adaptation of Jewish law, lore, and custom to the realities of a pluralistic and assimilating popular culture. Smaller, more traditional, and separate communities will continue to exist, preserving much of the Old World culture in their attempt to stave off the outside world. Because many Orthodox Jews have fused the Jewish culture of premodern eastern Europe with the practice of Jewish law, the force of this culture will endure long after the influence of the Old World culture in other ethnic communities has attenuated. Yet, it is in the interstice between the maintenance of a distinct culture and identity and participation in the wider American culture that most contemporary Jewish lore is generated.

Guy H. Haskell

References

Glanz, Rudolph. 1961. *The Jew in the Old American Folklore.* New York: Waldon.

Kirshenblatt-Gimblett, Barbara. 1974. The Concept and Varieties of Narrative Performance in East European Jewish Culture. In *Explorations in the Ethnography of Speaking,* ed. Richard Bauman and Joel Sherzer. New York: Cambridge University Press, pp. 283–308.

Kliger, Hannah, ed. 1992. *Jewish Hometown Associations and Family Circles in New York: The WPA Yiddish Writers' Group Study.* Bloomington: Indiana University Press.

Kugelmass, Jack. 1986. *The Miracle of Intervale Avenue: The Story of a Jewish Congregation in the South Bronx.* New York: Schocken.

———, ed. 1988. *Between Two Worlds: Ethnographic Essays on American Jewry.* Ithaca: Cornell University Press.

Meyerhoff, Barbara. 1978. *Number Our Days: A Triumph of Continuity and Culture among Jewish Old People in an Urban Ghetto.* New York: Simon and Schuster.

Mintz, Jerome R. 1968. *Legends of the Hasidim: An Introduction to Hasidic Culture and Oral Tradition in the New World.* Chicago: University of Chicago Press.

Sherman, Josepha. 1992. *A Sampler of Jewish American Folklore.* Little Rock, AR: August House.

Zenner, Walter P., ed. 1988. *Persistence and Flexibility: Anthropological Perspectives on the American Jewish Experience.* Albany, NY: SUNY Press.

See also Klezmer Music; Passover

John Edwards Memorial Foundation

Folk music archive and research center. John Edwards (1932–1960) was an Australian record collector who developed a passionate interest in American country music of what he called the Golden Age (1924–1939). He not only amassed a respectable collection of 78-rpm recordings, but also carried on correspondence with many old-time artists and published numerous biographical and discographical articles in American, English, and Australian fan magazines. He was killed in an auto accident on Christmas Eve, 1960. He had left a will instructing that his collection—records and all related materials—be used for the "furtherance of serious study, recognition, appreciation, and preservation of genuine country or hillbilly music . . ." and designated his friend, American record collector Gene Earle, as executor. Earle and other of Edwards' American correspondents, Archie Green, D.K. Wilgus, Fred Hoeptner, and Ed Kahn, formed a nonprofit corporation in California—the John Edwards Memorial Foundation (JEMF)—and found a congenial host at the University of California at Los Angeles in the person of Wayland D. Hand, chairman of the Folklore and Mythology Center there.

From 1964 to 1988, the JEMF devoted itself to the preservation and study of country music and related forms of folk-derived musical genres, including blues, Cajun, gospel, western, and various ethnic musics. The foundation's activities included publishing a regular journal, the *JEMF Quarterly;* issuing an occasional special series of bibliographic, discographic, and historical pamphlets; reprinting important articles from scholarly publications; and issuing extensively documented LP sound recordings. Over the years, the JEMF built up a major collection of sound recordings, journals, songbooks, documents, and other ephemera relating to those various musical traditions. In 1988 the JEMF collection was sold to the University of North Carolina at Chapel Hill, where, as the John Edwards Memorial Collection (JEMC), it was incorporated into the Southern Folklife Collection in the Manuscripts Department of the Academic Affairs Library. The JEMF was reorganized as the John Edwards Memorial Forum, with primary purposes to raise funds in support of the JEMC and to support, however possible, the study of traditional, folk, and vernacular music.

Norm Cohen

References

Cohen, Norm. 1991. The John Edwards Memorial Foundation: Its History and Significance. In *Sounds of the South,* ed. Daniel W. Patterson. Chapel Hill: University of North Carolina, pp 113–126.

Johnny Appleseed

Nickname of John Chapman, legendary planter of apple trees. Chapman was a historical figure (1774–1845) who established apple orchards in the early 19th century from his native Massachusetts westward through Pennsylvania, Ohio, and Indiana. He was eccentric for his time, following the visionary teachings of the Swedish philosopher Emanuel Swedenborg and choosing an ascetic life that denied materialism and promoted altruism. His odd lifestyle no doubt generated controversial commentary among the other frontier people. He cared little for his own appearance, dressing in frayed or even tattered clothes; he pierced his flesh as testimony to his spirituality; he argued for humane treatment of all animals; and he spoke about mystical things.

His potential for appeal to modern sensibility has been obscured by two 20th-century treatments. In the first place, his story was exaggerated and distorted by writers of children's books between World Wars I and II, who presented him as a quaint and funny fellow and touted him as "Johnny Appleseed," a genuine American tall-tale hero. In the second, Richard M. Dorson countered that tendency for unrealistic and saccharine writing about American tall-tale characters in general by dismissing those treatments of Johnny Appleseed as purely contrived "fakelore," of the same ilk as the fictions created about Annie Christmas or Paul Bunyan.

Although undoubtedly influenced by both the ersatz literary treatments and Johnny Appleseed's fakelore notoriety, stories about John Chapman do have a continuing role in some local oral traditions, where people can still point to remnants of original Chapman orchards. Some local traditions also attribute more than apple orchards to Chapman. Stands of "native" hemp, or cannabis, are alleged to have been planted by Johnny along with his apple seeds. State historical markers and several local festivals honor John Chapman as "Johnny Appleseed," a pioneer hero. In 1966, as the first issue of the American Folklore Series, a 5-cent U.S. commemorative postage stamp was issued depicting Johnny Appleseed.

Kenneth A. Thigpen

References

Dorson, Richard M. 1959. *American Folklore.* Chicago: University of Chicago Press, pp. 232–236.
———. 1971. Fakelore. In *American Folklore and the Historian.* Chicago: University of Chicago Press, pp. 3–14.
Price, Robert. 1954. *Johnny Appleseed: Man and Myth.* Bloomington: Indiana University Press.

Johnson, Clifton (1865–1940)

Author, illustrator, photographer, and folklore collector. Johnson was born near Hadley, Massachusetts, the son of a small farmer; he left school at age fifteen to work in a bookstore in Northampton. There he acquired a great love for books and pictures, and he decided to be an artist. He spent several winters studying at the Art Students' League in New York City, supporting himself by drawing and writing. By 1885 he had developed a small market for his illustrations, whereupon he returned to the family farm at Hadley, his home for the rest of his life. Five years later, in 1890, he bought a camera and started taking photographs as an aid to his drawing. He showed some photos to a publisher, meaning to suggest the subject matter of drawings he wished to sell, but to Johnson's surprise the publisher bought the photographs. This convinced him that he should write books as a means of selling his photographs, and eventually he wrote, edited, or illustrated more than 100 volumes.

Johnson's titles include *The New England Country, The Farmer's Boy,* a ten-volume American highways and byways series, two county histories *(Historic Hampshire* and *Camden County),* and a book of reminiscences of the Civil War collected from former soldiers on both sides, titled *Battleground Adventures in the Civil War.* Most of his publications contain some examples of folklore, but of most significance to folklorists are his series of fairy-tale books named for American trees *(The Oak Tree Fairy Book, The Birch Tree Fairy Book,* and so forth); *Mother Goose Rhymes My Children Love Best,* which contains otherwise unreported rhymes evidently taken from New England folk tradition; *The Country School in New England, Old-Time Schools and School-Books* ([1904] 1963); and *What They Say in New England* ([1896] 1963). The latter book is important as a pioneer collection of Anglo American sayings, signs, beliefs, rhymes, songs, folktales, and legends.

Clifton Johnson was no theorist or analyst, but rather a knowledgeable writer who, apparently, developed rapport with a wide variety of people. From them he garnered much important material, and he reported it accurately and without "improvements." For that reason, his data are still useful and his works are still worthwhile sources.

W.K. McNeil

References

Johnson, Clifton. [1896] 1963. *What They Say in New England and Other American Folklore.* New York: Columbia University Press.

———. [1904] 1963. *Old-Time Schools and School-Books.* New York: Dover.

Johnson, Guy Benton (1901–1991)

Sociologist and folklorist. Born in Texas, Johnson studied sociology at the University of Chicago before attending the University of North Carolina at Chapel Hill. He spent his first year of doctoral work editing Howard W. Odum's massive collection of African American folksongs. The result was the joint publication by Odum and Johnson of two important early studies of African American secular song (Johnson and Odum 1925, 1926).

In 1929 Johnson published the first full-length study of an American folksong, *John Henry: Tracking Down a Negro Legend.* He continued his studies of African American folk culture at St. Helena Island, South Carolina, and published *Folk Culture on St. Helena Island* in 1930. The book is an early study of the gullah dialect, and Johnson also investigated the origin of the African American spiritual.

After contributing these important works of collection and scholarship to the field of folklore, Johnson returned to his earlier interest in race relations. In 1939 his research contributed to Gunnar Myrdal's study of African Americans, *An American Dilemma,* and from 1944 to 1947 he served as the Southern Regional Council's first executive director. After his retirement from the sociology faculty at the University of North Carolina at Chapel Hill, Johnson and his wife, Guion Griffis Johnson, published a history of the university's Institute for Research in Social Science (Johnson and Johnson 1980).

Johnson considered himself a sociologist rather than a folklorist, but he made important contributions to the field, largely because of his musical knowledge and his interest in African American folksongs as cultural products.

Lynn Moss Sanders

References

Johnson, Guion Griffis, and Guy Benton Johnson. 1980. *Research in Service to Society: The First Fifty Years of the IRSS at the University of North Carolina.* Chapel Hill: University of North Carolina Press.

Johnson, Guy Benton, and Howard W. Odum. 1925. *The Negro and His Songs: A Study of Typical Songs in the South.* Chapel Hill: University of North Carolina Press.

———. 1926. *Negro Workaday Songs.* Chapel Hill: University of North Carolina Press.

Johnson, Robert (1911–1938)

Mississippi Delta blues artist. Possibly America's finest blues poet, Johnson is the best known, if least understood, practitioner of down-home blues. Under the tutelage of various lesser-known musicians, he mastered his local tradition, eventually blossoming into one of the preeminent regional guitar stylists. According to his contemporaries, he possessed a "phonographic" memory that allowed him to re-create the musical phrases and songs he heard on the radio and on phonograph recordings or from other local performers. Influenced by various recording artists, particularly Lonnie Johnson, he expanded the local tradition, creating an innovative personal style. Adept at synthesis, he could cover other artists' songs, but he also possessed the ability to transpose musical phrases or techniques associated with instruments such as the piano to the guitar.

Credited with instrumental innovations—the use of a repeated bass figure as a rhythmic foundation and the turnaround, or "get back," a rhythmic melodic phrase that seamlessly bridges blues verses—Johnson was fiercely jealous of his techniques, and he tried to keep them from other musicians. Nevertheless, these techniques were quickly absorbed into tradition as were many of his compositions. In 1936 and 1937, he recorded twenty-nine songs, including "I Believe I'll Dust My Broom" and "Sweet Home Chicago," both of which showcase his guitar innovations and remain favorites of his traditional audience.

Like his guitar playing, Johnson's songs have the modern feel of single poetic units. Johnson traveled much of the country, ranging from Texas to New York, St. Louis, and Canada. Initially typecast as a naive country musician, he was a musical genius determined to make records. Unfortunately, well-meaning critics, writing for blues-revival audiences, have fostered an image of him as a loner or outsider whose skills derive from supernatural sources rather than from his community traditions and his own artistic vision. These romantic stereotypes helped sell reissues of his recordings in the 1960s and in 1990, but they have also clouded our understanding of Johnson's life and work. In 1994 Robert Johnson's face appeared on a 29-cent U.S. postage stamp, but minus a cigarette that appears in the photo from which the stamp design was derived.

Barry Lee Pearson

References

Charters, Samuel. 1973. *Robert Johnson*. New York: Oak Publications.

Guralnick, Peter. 1989. *Searching for Robert Johnson*. New York: Dutton.

Johnson, Tommy (1896–1956)

Mississippi blues singer and guitarist. Born into a large family near Terry, Mississippi, about 20 miles south of the city of Jackson, Johnson grew up in nearby Crystal Springs. As a teenager, he began learning guitar and African American folksongs from older family members. Before World War I, he began making extended trips northward to Mississippi's Delta region to work on plantations and perform music. There he encountered and learned blues music from such established musicians as Charlie Patton and Willie Brown. His brother, Reverend LeDell Johnson, stated that Tommy claimed to have learned how to play the guitar well by making a pact with the devil. He returned to Crystal Springs and taught blues to his three brothers and other local musicians. For much of the 1920s he participated in the blues activity of Crystal Springs, Jackson, and the Delta, also making frequent trips southward to Tylertown and to Bogalusa and New Orleans, Louisiana. Married four times, he never sustained a stable family life, maintaining the same pattern of rambling and making up to his death. He made commercial recordings of his blues in two sessions for Victor Records in 1928 in Memphis and one session for Paramount Records at the end of 1929 in Grafton, Wisconsin. He was addicted to alcohol, which he consumed in truly legendary fashion all of his adult life, frequently in the form of cooking fuel, shoe polish, hair tonic, or rubbing alcohol. Johnson died of a massive heart attack at the end of an engagement playing music at a house party in Crystal Springs.

Only seventeen recordings by Johnson survive. All but one are blues, and most of these adhere closely to the standard twelve-bar, three-line blues form. They are heavily indebted to a shared tradition of lyric, melodic, and instrumental phrases and ideas, with many correspondences to the phrases and ideas of other blues performers in the local traditions in which Johnson participated. His recordings include three blues performed in alternate takes, another pair recorded almost two years apart, and a song, "Alcohol and Jake Blues," that extends the theme of an earlier recording, "Canned Heat Blues." Both of these latter pieces were personal in nature and dealt with his drinking habits. Most of his other blues dealt with themes of rambling and unstable relationships with women. Because of their heavy reliance on traditional elements and the existence of several alternative versions, Johnson's blues serve as an excellent example of folk processes at work in composition and performance. His seventeen recordings, along with those of his mentors, associates, and many disciples, demonstrate that he varied his pieces considerably during performance.

Johnson interacted with the top level of Mississippi blues artists in the 1920s and 1930s, including Charlie Patton, Willie Brown, Ishman Bracey, Charlie McCoy, Rubin Lacy, and Walter Vincson. The strong influence of his music can be heard in subsequent recordings by Vincson, Willie Lofton, Shirley Griffith, K.C. Douglas, Babe Stovall, Roosevelt Holts, Houston Stackhouse, Boogie Bill Webb, and a host of others, all of whom learned directly from Johnson. Many others learned songs from his commercial records. One of his songs, "Big Road Blues," has been especially widely performed over the years since Johnson recorded it in 1928, while the popular blues-rock group Canned Heat took its name in the 1960s from another of Johnson's blues.

David Evans

References

Evans, David. 1971. *Tommy Johnson*. London: Studio Vista.

———, comp. 1979. *The Legacy of Tommy Johnson*. Matchbox SDM 224. Sound Recording.

Johnson, Tommy. 1990. *Complete Recorded Works in Chronological Order*. Document DOCD–5001. Sound Recording.

Jokes

Humorous oral narratives. The narrative joke—also called the jocular folktale, humorous folktale, humorous anecdote, merry tale, farcical tale, jest, and *Schwank*—is simple in form, earthy in content, ancient in origin, ubiquitous in distribution, and endless in variety. Varieties of narrative jokes include tall tales, catch tales, humorous animal tales, jokes about married couples, jokes about drunks and lazy people, stories about the wise and the foolish, jokes about the clergy and religious figures, jokes about professional or occupational groups, and jokes about contemporary pastimes.

The catch tale or hoax story, such as "The Golden Arm" (Type 366, "The Man from the Gallows"), generally is told as a true story, but it ends abruptly and humorously by tricking the audience with a punch line or by forcing a listener to ask the storyteller a question that elicits a foolish answer. Many kinds of jokes are swapped within joking sessions; however, the catch tale is most effective when it appears spontaneously in a nonjoking context—that is, within the framework of ordinary conversation. The shaggy-dog story—"a nonsensical joke that employs in the punch line a psychological non sequitur, a punning variation of a familiar saying, or a hoax to trick the listener who expects conventional wit or humor" (Brunvand 1963:44)—is an example of the catch tale since it tricks the audience.

Droll folktales in which animals talk and behave like human beings are historically and geographically widespread and survive as children's entertainment in storybooks and cartoons, but in the contemporary oral tradition animal tales generally take the form of off-color jokes rather than children's tales. Stock characters from ancient Indo-European folklore, such as the parrot, and favorite themes of international folktales, such as the Trickster animal, also persist in oral jokes. Breaking a taboo is a common theme in some modern animal jokes, and animals often do things in jokelore that people refrain from doing. American males often project in the behavior of animals deep-seated fears of castration, quick orgasms, disparity in the size of male and female organs, and insatiable females.

Jokes about married couples deal with seduction and adultery; competition between husband and wife; sexual anxieties; sexually unresponsive husbands and wives; wives outwitting their husbands; retorts between husband and wife; wives who withhold intercourse from their husbands to get their way; and the unfaithful, vain, obstinate, mean, or lazy wife. A classical tale of married couples still found in North American oral tradition is "The Taming of the Shrew" (type 901), which, in a joke called "That's Once!" has been reported in well over 300 versions from around twenty-five countries and goes back to at least the Middle Ages.

Stories about the foolish collected in North America sometimes are general numskull tales dealing with absurd ignorance or absurd misunderstandings and are not about any particular place or group; however, more often these tales attribute absurd ignorance or other unfavorable qualities to some specific ethnic or regional group. Such tales are popular nearly everywhere. In England numskull tales are told about the Wise Men of Gotham; in Denmark, about the Fools of Molbo; and in Germany, about the Citizens of Schilda. In North America, the same or very similar numskull jokes may also be told about Little Morons, Irishmen, Blacks, Poles, Jews, Italians, Puerto Ricans, or any ethnic, racial, religious, or regional group. Although many of the numskull tales collected in North America are reworkings of older material, settlement history and location help determine the butt of these tales. For example, absurd ignorance is attributed to Kentuckians in Indiana, Buckeyes or Hoosiers in Kentucky, Aggies (students at Texas A&M University) or Mexicans in Texas, Okies in California, Cajuns in Louisiana, and Newfies in Canada.

In the North American oral tradition, humorous tales of the wise are not as popular as tales of the foolish, though they were common in medieval exempla, Renaissance jestbooks, and Oriental literary collections. Oral humorous tales of the wise often are brief narratives about local characters. Although these anecdotes frequently are attached to real people and have realistic settings, they are versions of common traditional tales told in other locations about other characters. As a character type in rural areas, the farmer sometimes is portrayed as a clever deceiver; however, the folk don't always distinguish clearly between the wise and the foolish, for in folklore the Trickster sometimes is a clever deceiver and other times is a numskull. In modern jokes, the Trickster often does things that most people refrain from doing. These tales frequently serve a cathartic function, providing a socially approved outlet for social repressions.

In contemporary jokes, drunkenness and laziness often are attributed to ethnic, minority groups—drunkenness to Irishmen and laziness to Blacks, for example; however, often these negative traits are not attributed to any particular group. Most jokes about drunks incorporate motifs of absurd misunderstandings: Similar sounding words are mistaken for each other, or one thing is mistaken for another. Apparently, attributing ignorance to drunks is a way of rationalizing foolish behavior. Humorous tales dealing with extreme laziness are widespread and extremely old—popular themes in literary collections of jokes.

Although religious jokes are popular in North American oral tradition, they are by no means a modern invention. In medieval satire, hypocritical and lecherous priests, monks, and friars were stock characters. In the late 20th century, priests and nuns who fail to uphold their vows of poverty, obedience, and chastity remain the butt of similar jokes. With the advent of Protestantism in Europe, the preacher assumed the role of the amorous priest in humorous folktales. Modern North American humorous tales still deal with the preacher's lust for women, but they also deal with his desire for worldly pleasures, including money, liquor, and fried chicken. Likewise, widespread stereotypic traits attributed to Jews—for example, a preoccupation with money, business, professionalism and pro-Semiticism—are found in modern jokes about rabbis and Jews.

In the 1970s, a whole cycle of sick-Jesus jokes developed, mostly in the form of short riddle jokes. Some longer religious narrative jokes about Jesus are varieties of the modern sick joke, which is faddish and sometimes topical. People who appreciate religious jokes are not necessarily agnostics and atheists. On the contrary, they may be religious people who tell tales about God or Jesus to relieve them of the pressure of a too ideal model.

Jokes about professional and occupational groups reflect an age-old tendency of the folk to mock certain trades and professions. Lawyers and physicians, as well as clergymen, have been the subject of satirical folk humor since the Middle Ages and continue to be popular figures in contemporary jokelore. A very general motif in some tales about physicians is "Repartee concerning doctors and patients"; however, many of the jokes about physicians also are forms of contemporary sick humor, and some follow the good news–bad news format.

The female schoolteacher in North American jokelore is a symbol of female dominance as well as a model of moral authority. A dominant figure in the classroom, the schoolmarm is envisioned by schoolboys as also a dominant figure in the bedroom. In schoolboy fantasy, as reflected in jokes, the schoolmarm is the subject of sexual desire and conquest, frequently by a stock character, Little Johnny. More precocious than his schoolmates, Johnny possesses sexual knowledge far beyond what is normal for his age. Sometimes he speaks profanely in inappropriate contexts, but the humor in most of the jokes is based on punning or other wordplay, such as trick names. Usually learned and recited in adolescence, jokes about schoolteachers serve important psychological functions for young males. For instance, they reduce their fear about sex since Johnny always gets the best of a woman considered sexually dominant. Jokes about female schoolteachers also reduce adolescent male hostilities toward the oppressive moral authority of adults since an authority figure, the schoolmarm, is presented as not so very moral.

Other authority figures mocked in jokes are politicians. In political humor, no political party or figure is safe. The folk tell jokes, usually topical, about Republicans and Democrats, about Richard Nixon and John F. Kennedy, about George Wallace and Jesse Jackson, about Dan Quayle and Ross Perot, and about Newt Gingrich and Bill Clinton. Generally, as a class, politicians are distrusted in contemporary jokelore.

Many North American jokes, then, concern sex, ethnicity, religion, and politics and tend to reveal threats, concerns, and anxieties of those who pass them along. North Americans are competitive in play as well as in work, and jokes about contemporary pastimes constitute another class of contemporary jokelore. Humorous tales about golfers, for example, are common and offer relief from pressures brought about by competition on the golf course. There are jokes about novice golfers, women golfers, and golf widows as well as jokes about clerics and religious figures on the golf course, numskulls on the golf course, and frustrations on the golf course. There are even shaggy-dog tales about golf. Jokes about the callous golfer who thinks only of his game are especially popular.

Many narrative jokes told in North America are familiar forms of international humorous folktales, though here they are modified by time, locale, folk tradition, and the individual joke tellers. Jokes about the traveling salesman and the farmer's daughter, for example, are contemporary descendants of old pastourelles that dealt with the seduction of a shepherdess by a roving knight. The traveling salesman is but a contemporary name for the potential interloper, a threat to conjugal rights.

What's more, the influence of popular culture on modern jokelore gives a certain uniformity to the form, content, and theme of humorous folktales throughout North American oral tradition. North Americans live in the midst of a prevailing popular culture spread by the mass media, which influences jokes, just as, more generally, popular culture nourishes, and is nourished by, the folklore. The influence of popular culture on joke telling is not a recent development, though, as formerly jokes were preserved in jestbooks and chapbooks. In the late 20th century, electronic media, including e–mail, as well as an expanded print media spread a much larger variety of jokes, including bawdy material once taboo in mainstream popular culture but fairly common now on the Internet and in popular collections of humor and slick magazines that are readily available in drugstores, supermarkets, and shopping-mall bookstores.

Though all kinds of jokes have been assimilated into popular culture, the narrative joke remains one of the most collectible forms of folk literature in North America. Jokes remain popular because they touch on every aspect of human life, may pop up spontaneously at any time in almost any social context, and are short, thus fitting very well into the fast pace of contemporary urban folklife.

Ronald L. Baker

References

Baker, Ronald L. 1986. *Jokelore: Humorous Folktales from Indiana.* Bloomington: Indiana University Press.

Brunvand, Jan Harold. 1963. A Classification for Shaggy Dog Stories. *Journal of American Folklore* 76:42–68.

Hoffmann, Frank. 1973. *An Analytical Survey of Anglo-American Traditional Erotica.* Bowling Green, OH: Bowling Green State University Popular Press.

Leary, James P. 1991. *Midwestern Folk Humor.* Little Rock, AR: August House.

Legman, G. 1968. *No Laughing Matter: An Analysis of Sexual Humor.* 2 vols. Bloomington: Indiana University Press.

Randolph, Vance. 1976. *Pissing in the Snow and Other Ozark Folktales.* Urbana: University of Illinois Press.

See also Anecdote; Dialect Story; Humor; Local-Character Anecdote, Riddle Jokes; Tall Tale; Trickster

Jones, Hathaway (1870–1937)

Raconteur of tall tales. Born in Roseburg, Oregon, Jones was the son of William Samson Jones and Elizabeth (Epperson) Jones. His parents and grandparents were Oregon Trail pioneers of the 1850s who settled in the Umpqua Valley. William and Elizabeth Jones divorced in 1883. In 1890 Hathaway joined his father at his gold claim at Battle Bar deep in the canyon of the Rogue River. With little education, Jones became a contract mail carrier. He picked up mail at Dothan on the West Fork of Cow Creek and traveled by mule team over fifty miles of mountainous trail to Illahe and Agness on the Rogue River. The mail then began a forty-mile journey by boat to the southwest coast of Oregon. Jones continued in this enterprise for forty-two years.

During his solitary treks through the mountains, Jones developed a rich repertoire of tall tales. His stories included three cycles: stories about his grandfather Ike (a wise old man of the woods), stories about his father, Samson (who possessed phenomenal strength), and stories about himself. In his tales about falling rocks, fantastic snow drifts, gigantic rattlesnakes, fierce panthers, and flying bears, Jones came to terms with the existential threats that lurked on all sides. Jones spun traditional tales, and in several cases he drew upon a motif or an event in a story he had heard from someone else and relocated the tale in the Rogue River wilderness. In 1937 his mule threw Jones over a cliff to his death.

More than fifty of Jones' tales survive, and many are yet told in the wild country of southwestern Oregon. Arthur Dorn began writing down the repertoire when he settled in Agness in the mid-1930s. Dorn worked for the WPA (Works Progress Administration) Oregon Folklore Project. Jones' tales appeared in Nancy Wilson Ross' *Farthest Reach* (1941) and in a 1946 article by Jean Muir in the *Saturday Evening Post.* Stephen Dow Beckham first heard the tales in the 1940s, and between 1965 and 1973 he collected many from informants residing in southwestern Oregon. The Jones stories are one of the largest collections from a single teller of tall tales in the United States.

Stephen Dow Beckham

References

Beckham, Stephen Dow, ed. [1974] 1991. *Tall Tales from Rogue River: The Yarns of Hathaway Jones.* Corvallis: Oregon State University Press.

Riddle, Claude. 1954. In the Hills with Hathaway. In *In the Happy Hills: A Story of Early Day Deer Hunting.*

Roseburg, OR: M-M Printers.

Jones, John Luther ("Casey") (1863–1900)

Railroad engineer, ballad hero. Jones, a Welsh American reared in Cayce, Kentucky, signed his name "Cayce Jones" on most documents, to distinguish himself from the legion of other Welsh American Joneses who also took to railroading as an occupation in the middle of the 19th century. The name was, however, pronounced "Casey," and according to some sources it was newspapermen who changed the spelling to make it consistent with the pronunciation.

In 1888 Jones entered the employ of the Illinois Central (IC) Railroad, and two years later he took over as engineer of the most prestigious run of the railroad: the IC's Cannonball Express, fast passenger train from Chicago to New Orleans. Jones brought with him his distinctive six-chime train whistle (in those days engineers could install whatever type of whistle they wanted), so indeed, as the ballads told,

> The switchman knew by the engine's moans
> That the man at the throttle was Casey Jones.

On Sunday, April 29, 1900, Jones and his fireman, Sim Webb, were due to take charge of the Cannonball in Memphis at a departure time of 11:35 P.M., southbound to Canton, Mississippi. However, the train was 95 minutes late, and Jones, who always had a reputation as a "fast roller," highballed southward, apparently determined to make up lost time. He was nearly back on schedule when his train approached Vaughan, 175 miles south of Memphis. There, because of an unusual combination of circumstances, the caboose of a southbound freight extended past the siding switch and was on the main line in Jones' way. Jones was going too fast to stop. His fireman, Webb, yelled a warning, and Jones told him to jump, while he applied the brakes. Webb did jump, sustaining only slight injuries, but Jones died as his engine plowed into the caboose of the other train.

In 1909 two vaudevillians, T. Lawrence Seibert and Eddie Newton, published a pop song, "Casey Jones (The Brave Engineer)," that quickly became a national hit. The ultimate source of Seibert and Newton's material remains uncertain, but the evidence suggests that they had heard some fragmentary songs or ballads that were composed and sung about Jones by African American railroad workers shortly after the accident. (There are references to songs about Jones as early as 1908, when a complete ballad was published in *Railroad Man's Magazine.*) Hillbilly and blues recordings in the 1920s, as well as field collections from the 1910s and 1920s, suggest that such "pre-Seibert-Newton" versions circulated fairly widely in the decade following the accident; some of them were evidently based on still earlier songs about hobos and railroaders.

Norm Cohen

References

Cohen, Norm. 1981. *Long Steel Rail: The Railroad in American Folksong.* Urbana: University of Illinois Press.

Jones, Louis Clark (1908–1990)

Folklorist noted for his work on murder tales, ghost stories, and folk art, and as founder of the Cooperstown graduate programs, the first American graduate training program emphasizing material culture. Born June 28, 1908, in Albany, New York, Jones graduated from Hamilton College in 1930 and received his doctorate from Columbia University in 1941. His dissertation was published the following year as *Clubs of the Georgian Rakes.* Jones started his career as a teacher at Long Island University in 1931. Later he taught at Syracuse University and at the State College for Teachers in Albany. In 1947 Jones became director of the New York State Historical Association and the Farmer's Museum, a post he retained until his retirement in 1972.

Jones' early folklore interests centered on murder and ghostlore, and he published important work in both areas. His 1936 article "The Berlin Murder Case" traced the story behind a New York murder ballad, and his 1944 "The Ghosts of New York: An Analytical Study" was a groundbreaking examination of the ghostlore of the Empire State. Although Jones never lost interest in either subject, his later works on these topics, such as *Things That Go Bump in the Night* (1959), were in a popular rather than an academic vein.

After 1950 Jones' turned his scholarly sights on American folk art; two of his publications on this subject are *American Folk Art* (1952), coauthored with Marshall Davidson; and *New-Found Folk Art of the Young Republic* (1960), coauthored with his wife, Agnes Halsey Jones. In 1982 Syracuse University Press published *Three Eyes on the Past: Exploring New York Folklife,* a collection of his writings dealing with history, folklore, and material culture.

Jones was much more than just a library scholar; he was also an avid collector of folk art. Largely due to his efforts, the Fenimore House Collection at the New York State Historical Association became one of the outstanding collections in America. He was also largely responsible for establishing the Cooperstown Graduate Programs in 1964. Here a group of thirty students could obtain M.A. degrees in museology or American folk culture. This program was generally recognized as meeting a need for professionalism in both the museum field and American folklife studies. Unfortunately, the American folk-culture program was phased out in 1979, though the museology program continues.

Jones was a Fellow of the American Folklore Society. After a long illness, he died in Haverford, Pennsylvania, on November 25, 1990.

W.K. McNeil

References

Somewhere West of Albany: A Festschrift in Honor of Louis C. Jones. 1975. Cooperstown, NY: New York Folklore Society.

Jones, Louis Marshall ("Grandpa") (1913–)

Singer, banjoist, comedian, longtime member of Grand Ole Opry radio show and Country Music Hall of Fame. A major figure in country music since the 1940s, he is generally credited with keeping alive interest in the five-string banjo and the older frailing playing style in the 1940s and 1950s, and he has been one of the few modern country singers with a keen appreciation of the music's traditional roots.

Jones was born in Niagra, Kentucky, on the Ohio River and grew up hearing the old ballads of his mother and the fiddle tunes of his father. In 1929 he started a radio show in Akron, Ohio, billing himself as "The Young Singer of Old Songs" and featuring his ability to imitate the then popular yodels of Jimmie Rodgers. After a stint on the radio show *Lum and Abner* (as a musician), he began working with Kentucky ballad singer Bradley Kincaid, who became his most important musical mentor. During the mid-1930s, he performed with Kincaid over station WBZ in Boston, finding that rural New Englanders liked their ballads and old songs as much as Southerners did. It was Kincaid who gave Jones his sobriquet "Grandpa"; though Jones was only twenty-two years old, his grouchiness on the early morning show reminded Kincaid of an old man. The familiar Grandpa Jones costume—high-topped boots, fake mustache, and suspenders—was created with help from vaudeville comic Bert Swor.

In 1937 Jones struck out on his own, going first to the powerful station WWVA in Wheeling, West Virginia, and later to the even stronger WLW in Cincinnati. Following Kincaid's lead, Jones issued his own songbooks and offered a varied program of traditional ballads, old-time songs, current country favorites, gospel songs, and even recitations. In his spare time, he learned how to play the clawhammer banjo from Cousin Emmy (Cynthia May Carver), then a popular radio star from south-central Kentucky.

At WLW Jones met three of the most influential musicians in country music history: Alton and Rabon Delmore (songwriters who pioneered close-harmony singing) and Merle Travis (the young guitar player who parlayed western Kentucky choking style into the most popular modern method). Though their tenure at WLW was interrupted by the draft and wartime restrictions, the four influenced one another in countless ways. One endeavor was their organizing of a gospel quartet, the Brown's Ferry Four, which helped popularize classics by writers like Albert Brumley and Cleavant Derricks. Another was their work for King Records, which would emerge after the war as the nation's leading independent company and the one most devoted to vernacular music. Two of Jones' most important songs, "Mountain Dew" and "Rattler," both derived from traditional sources, were recorded on King in 1947, and these won him his national reputation.

After marrying Ramona Riggins, Jones moved to Nashville and began working on the Grand Ole Opry in 1946. Though later jobs at Richmond, Virginia, and Washington DC, intervened, Jones soon became a fixture on the Opry and later (1969) joined the cast of the television show *Hee Haw*. In 1978 he was elected to the Country Music Hall of Fame, and in later years he became one of the leading spokesmen for traditional music in the increasingly commercial Nashville community.

Charles K. Wolfe

References

Jones, Grandpa. *Hall of Fame Series*. MCA MCAD—10549. Compact Disc/Cassette).

———. *Sixteen Greatest Hits*. Hollywood HCD—224. Compact Disc.

Jones, Louis M. "Grandpa," with Charles K. Wolfe. 1984. *Everybody's Grandpa: Fifty Years behind the Mike*. Knoxville: University of Tennessee Press.

Wolfe, Charles. 1982a. *Kentucky Country: Folk and Country Music of Kentucky*. Lexington: University Press of Kentucky.

———. 1982b. The Music of Grandpa Jones. *Journal of Country Music* 8:47–88.

Juke Joint

Small-scale commercial establishment where patrons eat, drink, gamble, and dance to the homemade music of local and itinerant artists. The term is derived from the word "juke," "jook," or "joog," which, among coastal Georgia and South Carolina's gullah African Americans means wild or disorderly. In *Blues off the Record*, British blues historian Paul Oliver described typical country jukes he found in the South in the late 1950s and early 1960s in this way: "Generally they are wood, patched and remade on their balloon frames, but covered sometimes with tar paper and imitation tiles stamped on sheets of roofing felt" (Oliver 1988:45). Alcohol, usually homemade, was an important element of juke joints, especially before modern zoning and licensing laws curbed folk-distilling activities.

Alice Walker's well-known novel *The Color Purple* (1982), much of which takes place in a juke joint named Harpo's after its builder-owner, gives a good sense of the atmosphere of a typical Southern juke joint. As her description indicates, they were built in the backwoods for a reason: "What you building? I ast. Jukejoint, he say. Way back here? No further back than any of the others. . . . Jukejoint spossed to be back in the woods, say Harpo. Nobody be bothered by the loud music. The dancing. The fights. I wain say the killings. Harpo say and the police don't know where to look."

Some scholars have suggested that the term "juke" can ultimately be traced to the West African word *dzugu*, meaning wicked or evil. This connotation is substantiated by folklorist Zora Neale Hurston's descriptions of community attitudes toward juke joints in north Florida in the 1930s, and by comments made by many blues artists about the atmosphere in which they learned and played their music. Hurston defined a "jook" as ". . . a fun house. Where they sing, dance, gamble, love and compose 'blues' songs incidentally" (Hurston 1935:63). Paul Oliver has pointed out that like "barrel house," the term "juke joint" often simply meant a brothel.

While the term is primarily applied to Black establishments, it is also common for Whites to speak of "going jukin'" in referring to bar hopping, especially in the Deep South. The origins of all-Black juke joints lie in the off-road whiskey-distilling shacks of the Reconstruction era; their Golden Age seems to have been from Prohibition through the 1930s; and while they are much rarer since the civil rights era, Birney Imes'

Jitterbugging in a juke joint on Saturday night. Near Clarksdale, Mississippi, 1939. Photo Marion Post Wolcott. Library of Congress.

photographic essays from Mississippi in the late 1980s indicate that they are still a significant aspect of rural Southern Black life (Imes 1990).

The word "juke" has entered common American speech as part of "jukebox," the folk name for coin-operated phonographs that play recordings the customers select. The first documented jukebox was featured at the Palais Royal Saloon in San Francisco in 1899. It was an Edison electric phonograph equipped with four coin slots and extra speakers. These early machines were not called jukeboxes, however, and the term did not come into popular use until the late 1930s, when "race" and swing music achieved a wide audience.

Juke joints have played an important part in Black folk culture in that they provided the situation and context for the creation and dissemination of the down-home blues, a major Black folk music and one of the cornerstones of American popular music. Several factors are relevant to this context.

First, improvisation (and thus individual creativity) was encouraged in juke joints' settings. Events and personalities from the local scene were incorporated into lyrics of already existing couplets and songs. Also, performers were in constant interaction with the patrons. That, along with the practice of "cutting heads," or competing for audiences' attention and loyalty, kept the level of musical and theatrical skill high; one held the stage or gave up. Furthermore, juke joints usually operated on a two-level talent basis: There were traveling musicians who could sustain more or less professional careers because of the extensive circuit of juke joints, and there were local musicians who, while they did not travel, could stay in touch with the best musicians, and with new styles and repertoires, by playing with, or warming up for, those "on the circuit."

When the great migration of Blacks to Northern urban centers took place, beginning in the 1930s and accelerating in the late 1940s, the Southern milieu of the "down-home" juke joints was recapitulated in the small steamy bars of such urban settings as Chicago's South Side, Detroit's Hastings Street, and Toledo's Canton Avenue. In this context, the juke joint began to function as an idea and an ideal, with the atmosphere of the bars both generating and relieving pangs of nostalgia for the juke joints and other positive aspects of the rural Southern setting more than six million Blacks had recently left behind. Next to the Black church, the juke joint, both as an actual locale and as a cultural symbol, has probably served as the most fertile ground for the creation and maintenance of African American folk culture.

Thomas E. Barden

References

Hurston, Zora Neale. 1935. *Mules and Men*. Philadelphia: J.B. Lippincott.

Imes, Birney. 1990. *Juke Joint*. Jackson: University of Mississippi Press.

Oliver, Paul. 1988. *Blues off the Record*. New York: Da Capo.

Palmer, Robert. 1981. *Deep Blues*. New York: Penguin Books.

Juneteenth

June 19; a holiday commemorating the emancipation of the slaves. Juneteenth began on June 19, 1865, when General Gordon Granger landed at Galveston, Texas, with a regiment of Union Army soldiers and read General Order No. 3, which began with these two memorable sentences: "The people of Texas are informed that in accordance with a Proclamation from the Executive of the United States, all slaves are free. This involves an absolute equality of rights and rights of property between former masters and slaves, and the connection heretofore existing between them becomes that between employer and free laborer."

Juneteenth, which was originally celebrated in east Texas, western Louisiana, and southwestern Arkansas, began its expansion beyond these three states soon after its initial celebrations. In the 1800s, a significant number of former slaves, driven by the collapse of Reconstruction, carried the cultural baggage of Juneteenth along with their meager possessions when they began to migrate out of this tri-state area into the Western territories that would eventually become the new states of Oklahoma, Kansas, and Colorado. The second Western mass migration of African Americans from the three original Juneteenth-celebrating states, into Arizona, California, and Washington, was triggered by their flight from the Great Depression of the 1930s and their attraction to good-paying jobs during the World War II era of the early and middle 1940s.

Political actions spawned by the civil rights movement also played a major role in the revitalization and renewed geographical spread of Juneteenth celebrations. In 1979 the Texas state legislature passed House Bill 1016 making Juneteenth the first and only Emancipation celebration to be accorded official state recognition. The bill, which was approved on June 7, 1979, and became a part of Texas law on January 1, 1980, reads in part:

"The . . . 19th day of June . . . of each year, and every day on which an election is held throughout the state, are declared legal holidays, on which all the public offices of the state may be closed and shall be considered and treated as Sunday for all purposes regarding the presenting for payment or acceptance and of protesting for giving notice of the dishonor of bills of exchange, bank checks and promissory notes placed by the law upon the footing of bills of exchange. The 19th day of June is designated "Emancipation Day in Texas" in honor of the emancipation of the slaves in Texas on June 19, 1865.

Since Governor William P. Clements signed this historic bill into law, Juneteenth observances have spread into all regions of the United States, including such nontraditional cities as Washington, DC; Buffalo, New York; Milwaukee, Wisconsin; and Minneapolis, Minnesota.

William H. Wiggins Jr.

References

Wiggins, William H., Jr. 1982. "They Closed the Town up, Man!": Reflections on the Civic and Political Dimensions of Juneteenth. In *Celebration: Studies in Festivity and Ritual*. Washington, DC: Smithsonian Institution.

———. 1987. *O Freedom!: Afro-American Emancipation Celebrations*. Knoxville: University of Tennessee Press.

K

Kirkland, Edwin Capers (1903–1972)

Folksong collector, teacher, and bibliographer. For many years, Kirkland's reputation rested on a monumental bibliography of the folklore of India, which he compiled during several tours of duty there as a cultural officer and consul. During the 1980s, however, after Kirkland's sudden death at the University of Florida, a considerable collection of Southern folksongs gathered by him and his wife, Mary, in the 1930s came to light. Many of these songs had been recorded on disc, with no real help or encouragement from the Library of Congress or other major philanthropic organizations, making the Kirklands pioneers in Southern field recordings. Kirkland was also far-sighted enough to perceive the interplay between commercial mass media and traditional song, and his unpublished collection "Knoxville Folk Songs" showed a sophisticated perception of traditional song in an urban society.

Coming to the University of Tennessee from Northwestern in 1931, Kirkland did most of his collecting between 1935 and 1939. He and his wife traveled with their disc cutter to remote areas of Tennessee, the Carolinas, Kentucky, and north Georgia, in addition to collecting in Knoxville and even within the university community. In the fall of 1946, he moved to the University of Florida, where he worked with Alton C. Morris and helped establish the Florida Folk Festival in White Springs. In the 1960s, he and his wife traveled widely in Europe and the Far East; with the encouragement of Richard M. Dorson, Kirkland compiled his bibliography of the folklore of India, which was published in 1968.

Charles K. Wolfe

References

Kirkland, Edwin C. 1946. Check List of the Titles of Tennessee Folksongs. *Journal of American Folklore* 59:423–476.
———. 1968. *Bibliography of the Folklore of India.* Bloomington: Indiana University Press.
Thomson, Robert. 1984. Edwin C. Kirkland: The Collector and His Methods. *Tennessee Folklore Society Bulletin* 50:95–109.

Wolfe, Charles, Robert Thomson, and Kip Lornell. 1984. The Kirkland Recordings: A Preliminary Checklist. *Tennessee Folklore Society Bulletin* 50:114–126.

Kittredge, George Lyman (1860—1941)

Harvard University English professor and folklorist, a dominant force (arguably *the* dominant personality) in the humanities in America from the turn of the century to World War II. From an old New England family, Kittredge grew up in Barnstable, Massachusetts, and never lost his ties to Cape Cod. He exercised his great literary and linguistic gifts as an undergraduate at Harvard and graduated, summa cum laude with the equivalent of a major in Latin and Greek, in 1882. He taught Latin at Phillips Exeter Academy from 1883 until he moved to Harvard in 1888, except for a honeymoon-study year (1886–1887) in Germany. Kittredge retired from Harvard in 1936, two years short of the fifty years' service of his great mentor, Francis James Child.

In 1904 Kittredge was president both of the Modern Language Association of America and of the American Folklore Society (AFS); he served as first vice president of the AFS from 1911 to 1918 and as assistant or associate editor of the *Journal of American Folklore (JAF)* from 1909 to 1940. He edited several important literary and philological series, and the list of his honors (honorary degrees, distinguished lecture series, and the like), especially in later life, is long.

At Harvard Kittredge is especially remembered as the demanding teacher of "English 2: Shakespeare"; his brilliance, wit, and eccentricities were reflected in college legends and anecdotes. Some are still known among undergraduates, though usually with "this white-bearded old professor" unnamed. Perhaps the best and most representative is Kittredge's purported answer to the impertinent question why he had never taken the Ph.D. degree: "Who would have examined me?" (But see Whiting 1972:xxxi–xxxii on the institutional background of this anecdote.)

Kittredge's bibliography of 383 items includes books edited by him, various reprints, and juvenilia; even so, the list of substantial titles seemed superhuman in its time, the range including English language and literature, especially Chaucer, Malory, and Shakespeare; ballads and folklore; witchcraft; the Greek and Latin classics; Americana, especially concerning settlers of Massachusetts; Old and Middle French; biographical sketches; humor; and more. For folklorists the most obviously important items are Kittredge's work on the final volume of Child's *The English and Scottish Popular Ballads* (1898), his stimulating introductory essay for a one-volume edition of Child (1904), and other ballad articles and collections (such as those that appeared in *JAF* from 1907 to 1926), but he was also instrumental in encouraging many field collectors—notably, John and Alan Lomax. Two of Kittredge's famous books were, in his time, considered to appertain to folklore: *The Old Farmer and His Almanack* (1904) and *Witchcraft in Old and New England* (1929). Kittredge's approach to the Middle English romances also comprised comparative study of popular story-material, ritual, and custom; in addition to articles and notes, there are his substantial monograph on *Arthur and Gorlagon* (1903) and the masterpiece on *Sir Gawain and the Green Knight* (1916).

Joseph Harris

References

Birdsall, Esther K. 1973. Some Notes on the Role of George Lyman Kittredge in American Folklore Studies. *Journal of the Folklore Institute* 10:57–66.

Bynum, David E. 1974. Child's Legacy Enlarged: Oral Literary Studies at Harvard since 1856. *Harvard Library Bulletin* 22:237–267.

Hyder, Clyde Kenneth. 1962. *George Lyman Kittredge: Teacher and Scholar.* Lawrence: University Press of Kansas.

Robinson, F.N., John Livingston Lowes, and J.D.M. Ford. 1991. [Memorial Minute on the Life and Services of] George Lyman Kittredge. *Harvard University Gazette* 37 (April 25, 1942):165–166. Reprinted in *Harvard Scholars in English, 1890 to 1990,* ed. W. Jackson Bate, Michael Shinagel, and James Engell. Cambridge: Harvard University Press, pp. 15–18.

Thorpe, James. 1948. *A Bibliography of the Writings of George Lyman Kittredge,* with an Introduction by Hyder Edward Rollins. Cambridge: Harvard University Press.

Whiting, B.J. 1972. Introduction. In *Chaucer and His Poetry,* by George Lyman Kittredge. 55th anniversary ed. Cambridge: Harvard University Press, pp. vii–xxxvi.

Klezmer Music

Instrumental music played by east European Jews for weddings. The term "klezmer" (plural, *klezmorim*) is a Yiddish term based on the Hebrew words *keley zemer,* which mean "musical instruments." The Yiddish term referred to a musician who was a member of a professional or semiprofessional class whose origins can be traced back at least to the 16th century. Such Jewish instrumentalists, although primarily occupied with providing music for the various stages of Jewish weddings, were often knowledgeable in, and influenced by, non-Jewish east European musical traditions as well. Although it is probable that most early klezmer musicians were musically illiterate, transcriptions of klezmer melodies were published at the beginning of the 18th century.

Originally, klezmer music was played primarily on violins and other stringed instruments as well as on flutes, drums, and a type of cymbalom, called *tsimbl* in Yiddish. While it is difficult to determine the precise nature of klezmer music before the 20th century, vivid literary depiction of *klezmorim* can be found in stories by such authors as Sholom Aleichem, Y.L. Perets, and Anton Chekov that focus on klezmer violinists. Some measure of the klezmer violinist's capability may be judged from the rapid development of a great number of outstanding Jewish violinists from the beginning of the 20th century, once Jews began to be admitted to Western conservatories. Although initially primarily string music, klezmer was decisively affected by the development of the clarinet at the beginning of the 19th century and by the addition of brass band instruments toward the end of that century. By the beginning of the 20th century, the most important instrumentalist in klezmer ensembles had become the clarinet virtuoso.

Klezmer music reached the United States around the turn of the 20th century with the influx of Jewish immigrants from eastern Europe. In the United States, *klezmorim* continued to provide music for Jewish weddings as well as for non-Jewish social occasions, primarily in New York City and Philadelphia, where sizable immigrant Jewish communities developed. As in Europe, these Jewish musicians were known for their flexibility and improvisational skills. In addition to the social events for which *klezmorim* had played for centuries, new opportunities arose for these musicians in the United States, primarily from about 1913 to the 1940s. Increased demand for klezmer music was fostered by the development of the American Yiddish theater, the recording industry, and ethnic radio programs. However, these media required musicians who had the ability to read music. As a result, those who were capable of playing only the old eastern European repertory were relegated to a secondary status.

While klezmer music continued to be played, its most popular and respected instrumentalists disdained the term "klezmer." Ironically, in the heyday of American klezmer music, the term became pejorative, referring specifically to those illiterate, "second-rate" musicians who were not able to adjust to the new American influences, particularly jazz. However, musically literate Jewish musicians were able to find employment in the orchestras of the Yiddish theater, which often included klezmer music as a nostalgic element in its productions. In addition, hundreds of recordings of klezmer music were made for ethnic consumption. The designated audience, while primarily Jewish, also included Greek, Polish, and Ukrainian communities. Often klezmer recordings were released in both Jewish and non-Jewish editions, with tune titles in the language of the targeted community. A third haven for klezmer music and musicians was the ethnic radio programming of station WEVD in New York City, where the largest Jewish community resided. This station was owned by the leading Yiddish daily, *Forverts,* and featured klezmer music not only as program material, but also in its commercials.

From early on, a curious symbiosis existed between klezmer and jazz music. Harry Kandel's 1926 recording, "Jakie Jazz 'Em up," attests to the extent that traditional klezmer ensembles absorbed the rhythms and modalities of the American popular music of the period. Perhaps even more surprising is the Original Dixieland Jazz Band's recording of "Palestina," which consciously imitated klezmer. Klezmer nuances can also be discerned in the music of Benny Goodman. Although Goodman was not a product of klezmer himself, his big band, ca. 1938, featured trumpeter Ziggy Elman, who exploited his klezmer background in several solos, most memorably in the classic "And the Angels Sing." More recently, Don Byron, a professional jazz musician, has distinguished himself as an outstanding klezmer clarinetist, and the Klezmatics, a progressive klezmer ensemble, have drawn on modern jazz elements in creating an innovative style of contemporary klezmer.

Although many outstanding musicians played klezmer music, several deserve particular mention. Two leading orchestra leaders dominated the early recordings. Beginning in 1917, Harry Kandel, a clarinetist centered in Philadelphia, made numerous recordings for Victor. His counterpart for Columbia was Abe Schwartz, a violinist and composer for the Yiddish theater whose klezmer recordings featured the two most important and influential klezmer clarinetists, Naftule Brandwine (1889–1963) and Dave Tarras (1897–1989). Brandwine, was an outstanding virtuoso and improviser whose eccentricities made him the subject of many legends. However, he was soon replaced in his role as premier klezmer clarinetist by the more musically literate, versatile, and reliable Tarras. The latter was able to weather the influences of a variety of popular American musical trends, including jazz and swing music, whose popularity affected the musical demands of the klezmer audience. As a result, Tarras was able to extend his career into the 1960s. In 1984 he was honored with a National Heritage Folklife Award by the NEA (National Endowment for the Arts).

By the 1940s, as the American Jewish community became increasingly acculturated, interest in klezmer music had waned. Toward the end of the 1940s, the arrival of Hasidic survivors of the Holocaust provided a slight lift. Nevertheless, klezmer music was all but moribund by the 1960s: A token klezmer tune might still be played at a typical bar mitzvah or wedding or crop up in the arrangements for a recording of Yiddish theater hits by Theodore Bikel. Only in the early 1970s was there a revival of interest in klezmer music. Sometime after a series of recordings by Argentina-born Israeli clarinetist Giora Feidman, a small number of musicians in California and New York City began to actively pursue their interest in klezmer music. Most of these musicians were products of the folk- and ethnic-music revival. Interest was fostered by exposure to collections of classic 78-rpm recordings of klezmer music at the Judah Magnes Museum in Berkeley, California, and at the Yivo Institute for Jewish Research in New York City. Klezmer enthusiasts in New York were particularly fortunate in locating Dave Tarras, who became a mentor for young klezmer musicians. By the early 1980s, several klezmer groups had formed. These included the Klez-

morim of California, Kapelye in New York City, the Klezmer Conservatory Band of Boston, and an ensemble that featured duets by *tsimbl* player Walter Zev Feldman and Tarras' protégé, Andy Statman, on clarinet. All of these groups were to make influential recordings that stimulated interest in klezmer music throughout the United States. It is important to note that several of these groups included non-Jewish musicians who were attracted to the music for its own sake. However, most of the early participants in the klezmer revival were probably also motivated by the opportunity that the music provided for expressing identity with Yiddish culture. By the 1990s, klezmer music had established itself as a part of popular American culture. Dozens of klezmer bands were active in various parts of the United States. Several of the leading bands had appeared in, or provided music for, such Hollywood movies as *The Chosen*. A number of anthologies of classic 78-rpm recordings had been released, as well as numerous recordings by contemporary klezmer ensembles. In addition, beginning in 1985, Yivo, under the direction of Henry Sapoznik, sponsored an annual Yiddish folk-arts program, "Klez Camp," where Yiddish, klezmer music, and dance were taught and enjoyed.

Miles Krassen

References

Sapoznik, Henry. 1987. *The Compleat Klezmer*. Cedarhurst, NY: Tara Publications.

Shiloah, Amnon. 1992. *Jewish Musical Traditions*. Detroit: Wayne State University Press.

Slobin, Mark. 1982. *Tenement Songs: The Popular Music of the Jewish Immigrants*. Urbana: University of Illinois Press.

Stutschewsky, Joachim. 1959. *Klezmorim (Jewish Folk Musicians): History, Folklore, Compositions*. (in Hebrew). Jerusalem: Bialik Institute.

RECORDINGS

Sapoznik, Henry, ed. 1986. *Klezmer Music, 1910–1942: Recordings from the Yivo Archives*. New York: Global Village.

Sapoznik, Henry, and Michael Schlesinger, eds. 1985. *Jakie Jazz 'Em up: Old-Time Klezmer Music, 1912 to 1926* New York: Global Village.

Schlesinger, Michael, ed. 1988. *Abe Schwartz: Master of Klezmer Music*. Vol. 1. New York: Global Village.

———, ed. 1989. *Dave Tarras*. Vol. 1. New York: Global Village.

Strachwitz, Chris, and Martin Schwartz, eds. 1983. *Klezmer Music: Early Yiddish Instrumental Music, The First Recordings, 1910–1927*. El Cerrito, CA: Arhoolie.

Knortz, Karl (1841–1918)

German American folklorist. One of the most prolific scholars of 19th-century America, Knortz, though little known today, was the first person to write a book devoted to the entire spectrum of American folklore. The reasons for this situation were that he wrote most of his numerous publications in German, that most were published in Germany, that he always remained closer to his German colleagues than to American scholars, and that he was a solar mythologist, a theoretical school that never enjoyed great popularity in the United States.

A native of Prussia, Knortz migrated to the United States in 1863; during the next fifty-five years, he wrote books and articles on folklore, literature, education, and German American relations. Unlike most solar mythologists, Knortz was an avid fieldworker who collected material for his several books during many years spent as a secondary-school teacher and minister in Michigan, Wisconsin, Ohio, Indiana, New York, and Pennsylvania. Knortz's two major aims were to foster ethnic pride among his fellow German Americans and to make American literature better known and appreciated in his homeland. His two most important books to folklorists are *Nachklänge Germanischen Glaubens und Brauche in Amerika: Ein Beitrag zur Volkskunde* (Reminiscences of German Beliefs and Customs in America: A Contribution to Folklore) (1903) and *Zur Amerikanischer Volkskunde* (American Folklore) (1905). The former is one of the best early works on ethnic folklore, and the latter is the first volume purporting to cover the entire field of American folklore.

Knortz's work is in many ways creative and innovative, but as a solarist he was conventional. Myths, in this interpretation, originated in a prescientific era when the only explanations of natural phenomena available were poetic fantasies in which various natural forces were represented as living beings. Over time the original meanings of these tales were lost, and they became generally accepted as factual. Therefore, when people saw or experienced different natural phenomena they were reminded of its corresponding story. Although many solar myths were known in only one society, others (like the Prometheus story) were the property of all civilized people. Although oral tradition helped spread such myths, their widespread occurrence was also due to the efforts of literary artists like Aeschylus and Goethe. In this sense, Knortz was aware that print did not always have an adverse effect on spoken narratives, a view not accepted by most scholars of his day but later widely recognized.

W.K. McNeil

References

Iten, Helga B. Van, and James Dow, trans. 1988. American Folklore. *Folklore Historian* 5 (1).

Knott, Sarah Gertrude (1895–1984)

Founder and program director of the National Folk Festival. Trained in drama, and with no academic grounding in folklore, Knott pursued her lifetime goal to introduce the folk performing arts to the widest American audience. After several years of almost single-handed and often frustrating effort, she staged the first National Folk Festival in 1934 in St. Louis, Missouri. This was followed by annual festivals cosponsored by local groups in more than a dozen other American cities until, in 1971, the national event settled down at the Wolf Trap Farm near Washington, DC. Knott personally produced and staged each festival until her retirement in 1971; there-

after, until her death, she served as consultant to state and community folk-arts programs for the national Folk Festival Association and similar organizations. Over the years, her festivals have become the standard for many similar events throughout the country.

Knott had a vision of national gatherings of peer- rather than producer-selected performers keeping true to their own traditions in an age of standardization and mass audience appeals. Her goal was a better understanding and appreciation of America's diverse ethnic, geographic, and occupational groups through the preservation and perpetuation of their inherited cultural legacies.

Her efforts were much criticized by academic folklorists. They particularly objected to her insistence that only through the medium of regional and national festivals (big shows with large audiences) could the country's traditional legacies survive, and to her failure to see the inconsistency between her "standards of authenticity" and the artificiality of "big show" performances in large auditoriums.

Knott's last years were spent in the preparation of a definitive history and rationale for folk festivals, a work that was never completed to her satisfaction.

Robert M. Rennick

References

Knott, Sarah Gertrude. 1963. Prepared and Supplementary Statements. *Hearings before the Special Subcommittee on the Arts of the Committee on Labor and Public Welfare.* U.S. Senate, 88th Cong., 1st sess. Washington, DC: GPO, pp. 257–261.

Ramsay, John M. 1992. Sarah Gertrude Knott. In *The Kentucky Encyclopedia.* Lexington: University Press of Kentucky, p. 522.

Knox, George (1862–1892)

Northern Maine lumberjack and trickster reputed to have sold his soul to the devil for magical powers. According to some older informants, Knox had joined a circus as a youth and returned with a bag of tricks to play on his more gullible fellow woodsworkers. Often mentioned is his book of tricks, transmuted by the superstitious into a "black book" of devilish contents.

The greater part of the Knox traditions revolves about a Faustian theme. Thirty years of power for thirty dollars was the deal, and then the devil collected his due (no informant was aware that, according to the records, Knox died at age thirty of tuberculosis). This portion of the tradition is the strongest and is replete with black dogs, sacrifices of black cats at crossroads at midnight, and the swearing of oaths of fealty to the "evil one."

Another sizable body of tradition is work oriented, celebrating great feats of strength and tremendous amounts of work accomplished, this often with enchanted lumbering tools. A common tale has Knox sitting on a stump while his ax is industriously chopping down trees. All of this was very secretive; and should someone touch the famous ax, Knox would know and immediately change its handle.

Throughout both segments of the Knox tradition, Knox emerges as a man to be feared and avoided. It was said that Knox always slept alone in the lumber camps, although the general space- and money-saving practice was to have two to a bunk. The reason given was simple: No one wanted to sleep in the same bed with a man of Knox's evil reputation.

The localization of the Knox traditions and their present-day vitality appear related to two circumstances: first, that this region is a stable, long-settled rural area with no in-migration; and second, the great majority of the population belongs to conservative Protestant religions in which the devil has not as yet become an abstraction.

Roger E. Mitchell

References

American Folklore and Legend. In *Reader's Digest*. 1978. Pleasantville, NY, pp. 356–358.

Dorson, Richard M. 1973. *America in Legend: Folklore from the Colonial Period to the Present*. New York: Pantheon, pp. 176–180.

Mitchell, Roger E. 1969. George Knox: From Man to Legend. *Northeast Folklore* 2.

Köngäs-Maranda, Elli (1932–1982)

Folklorist, anthropologist, and poet. Born and raised in a small village in northern Finland, Köngäs-Maranda earned a Ph.D. in folklore at Indiana University in 1963; her dissertation concerned Finnish American verbal traditions. From 1970 until her death, she taught in Canada, first at the University of British Columbia, Vancouver, and thereafter at Laval University in Quebec. She also spent long periods conducting fieldwork among the Lau of Malaita in the Solomon Islands and as a guest lecturer at European universities. In 1978 she was elected a Fellow of the American Folklore Society, one of many honors that she received.

A recurrent theme in Köngäs-Maranda's work is folklore in the contexts of migration and exile. Another is women—as folklore carriers or as scholars. A third is structural analysis; throughout her career, Köngäs-Maranda attempted to locate constant structures among diverse folkloric expressions. While often rigorously formalized, her structural analyses also have poetic force. Several of them are devoted to riddles communicated among Lau women or among Finns in North America. Köngäs-Maranda believed that structural analysis was worth little if the materials were not situated in people's lives.

On many issues, Köngäs-Maranda was a pioneer, and folklorists have not always known how to evaluate her contributions. Yet, her theoretical insights and unusual career continue to capture imaginations, not least among women. The Women's Section of the American Folklore Society annually awards the Elli Köngäs-Maranda Prize for Contributions to the Study of Women and Folklore.

Barbro Klein

References

Dubois-Quellet, Simone, et al., eds. 1982. *Travaux et Inédits de Elli Kaija Köngäs-Maranda*. Quebec: Cahiers du CELAT.

Köngäs-Maranda, Elli. 1980. *Finnish-American Folklore: Quantitative and Qualitative Analysis*. New York: Arno.

Köngäs-Maranda, Elli, and Pierre Maranda. 1971. *Structural Models in Folklore and Transformational Essays*. The Hague: Mouton.

Maranda, Pierre, and Elli Köngäs-Maranda, eds. 1971. *Structural Analysis of Oral Tradition*. Philadelphia: University of Pennsylvania Press.

Korean Americans

Immigrants from Korea and their descendants living in the United States. The first Korean immigrants arrived in Hawaii in 1903 to work on plantations. Because of immigration laws, few Koreans immigrated to the United States until 1965. After 1965 and the easing of immigration restrictions, a wave of Korean immigration began, and by 1977 more than 30,000 Koreans per year were immigrating to the United States. In the 1990s, Hawaii and California continue to have the largest concentration of Korean Americans, and Los Angeles and New York City are the urban centers that have the highest numbers of Korean American households. Among Korean Americans, immigrants who come to the United States as adults are referred to as "first generation," those who come during childhood as "one-point-five" generation, and those who were born in the United States as "second generation." Large numbers of second-generation Korean Americans are having children, and a significant "third generation" is quickly emerging.

In Los Angeles, the Korean American community is centered around Koreatown. While Korean Americans are not the main residents of this area, this section of the city has a remarkable concentration of Korean American–owned businesses that cater to a mainly Korean American clientele. The signage is written in the Korean alphabet *(hangul)*, and the use of space is reminiscent of shopping areas in South Korea. The development of the "swap meet," an amalgamation of privately owned vending booths under one roof is remarkably similar to the Korean markets, the best known of which are *Namdaemun shijang* and *Tongdaemun shijang*, both in Seoul. Koreatown represents a reinterpretation of the traditional Korean business space into the American urban environment. The political associations, parties, and alliances of Koreatown are also reminiscent of neighborhood politics in the large Korean cities, suggesting that political culture among first- and one-point-five-generation Korean Americans is closely linked to that of South Korea.

Korean-language print and broadcast media help Korean Americans maintain a sense of common ethnic heritage and reinforce the use of the Korean language. Many second-generation Korean Americans have learned the Korean language since childhood. In Korean American households, one often hears first-generation parents speaking Korean to their second-generation children, who reply to their parents in English. Many Korean American children attend supplementary language classes on weekends to bolster their language skills. At the university level, there has been a significant increase in the

Transmitting a Korean tradition, Myung Chul Choi teaches a martial-arts class. Silver Spring, Maryland, 1982. Photo Lucy Long. American Folklife Center.

numbers of Korean American students in Korean language, literature, and culture courses.

Churches and other religiously affiliated organizations play a major role in the Korean American community. Many Korean Americans are members of various denominations of the Protestant Church; as in Korea, the church and church organizations are a main focus of social activity. The churches often provide support services for recent immigrants, offer both English- and Korean-language classes, and have various social groups, such as teen groups, senior citizens' groups, and study groups. These groups bolster the development of a church-centered Korean American identity.

Shamanism, one of the best-known elements of Korean religious expression, can also be found in the Korean American communities. Primarily women, shamans often hold rituals to ensure good luck, to help ease the way for a departed spirit, and to discover the cause of chronic illnesses. Elements of shamanism have also carried over into some evangelical Protestant churches with the emergence of the "deaconess," who holds prayer sessions in individual households. Household rituals, designed to placate various spirits and directly linked to Korean shamanism, are practiced by some first-generation Korean Americans. Fortune-telling, geomancy, and matchmaking are also actively practiced by some members of the Korean American communities.

Life-cycle rituals based on Korean traditions are commonly practiced by Korean Americans. Perhaps the most frequently performed of these rituals are the *baekil* ceremony 100 days after a child's birth and the *hwangap* (a celebration held on a person's sixtieth birthday, marking the completion of one full life cycle). Weddings in the Korean American community frequently combine elements from the "traditional" Korean wedding festival, such as dress, and the "Western" wedding ceremony. At times, two ceremonies are held, one Korean and one Western. Among calendrical festivals, Korean Americans are most likely to celebrate *Ch'useok* (the Harvest Moon festival), which is a chance for the extended family to gather. While in Korea, families travel to their *kohyang* (ancestral village) at *Ch'useok,* this is not possible for most Korean Americans. *Chesa* (ancestor-worship rituals) are usually performed during the celebration of *Ch'useok.* The celebration of *chesa* throughout the year is common among first-generation Korean Americans, but less so among the second generation.

Foodways are perhaps the most evident of the Korean American cultural expressions to non-Korean-Americans. One can find Korean restaurants in many American cities serving Korean barbecue *(bulgoki* or *kalbi). Kimch'i* (pickled cabbage) is also available in most urban grocery stores, as are ramen noodles. In many urban areas, one finds Korean-cooking classes, often taught at community centers and often attended by one-point-five- and second-generation Korean Americans eager to learn how to prepare Korean foods. Foods used in ancestor-worship rituals, such as *tt'ok* (rice cake), are readily available in areas such as Koreatown.

Revolving credit associations, known as *kye,* are common in areas where the Korean American population is large. Mostly popular among first-generation Korean Americans, these associations offer the members an opportunity to borrow money interest free from the other association members. Each member pays a certain amount into a general pot every month. Members then take turns borrowing the pooled financial resources of the group. In this manner, many recent Korean American immigrants are able to acquire the capital necessary to establish small businesses. Misunderstandings over the source of this capital have led to tensions in some urban areas between Korean Americans and other groups unaware of the *kye*.

In the late 20th century, as a significant population of second-generation Korean Americans reach adulthood, a burgeoning interest in both Korean culture and the expression of an independent Korean American culture has become evident. At universities, Korean American student associations are common. Besides Korean and Korean American history, these groups often study Korean culture, including expressions such as drumming (*p'ungmul*) and mask dance drama (*t'alch'um*). The riots in Los Angeles in 1992 resulted in massive losses among Korean American merchants. Many second-generation Korean Americans saw the riots as an attack on their community, with a resultant flowering of interest among Korean Americans on Korean and Korean American culture and identity.

Timothy R. Tangherlini

References

Barringer, Herbert R. 1989. *Koreans in the United States: A Fact Book*. Honolulu: Center for Korean Studies, University of Hawaii.

Choy, Bong-young. 1979. *Koreans in America*. Chicago: Nelson Hall.

Kim, Ilsoo. 1981. *New Urban Immigrants: The Korean Community in New York*. Princeton, NJ: Princeton University Press.

Patterson, Wayne. 1976. *The Koreans in North America*. Philadelphia: Balch Institute.

Yu, Eui-Young, Earl H. Phillips, and Eun-Sik Yang, ed. 1982. *Koreans in Los Angeles: Prospects and Promises*. Center for Korean American and Korean Studies, Koryo Institute.

See also Korean War

Korean War

America's first military loss, often dubbed "the Forgotten War" by its veterans and historians. The Korean War barely influenced cultural traditions; thus, folklore of the war is minimal. Rather than preserve the war's heritage, most Americans preferred to cling to traditions from more glorious military precedents such as the World Wars. Military cadence chants, which refer to previous wars, often omit the Korean War, skipping from World War II to Vietnam.

The major popular-culture monument to the Korean War, the movie and television series entitled *M*A*S*H**, portrays many of the basic folklore themes and situations of the Korean War, such as Rosie's Bar and the interaction of Korean civilians and merchants with soldiers.

Not even officially a war—termed a police action by politicians—the Korean conflict was the first test in the chilling Cold War. Common soldiers suffered anger, frustration, and despair at the stalemate resulting from the containment tactics and no-win policy as political and military leadership disagreed about how to conduct the conflict. Feeling betrayed by their leaders and abandoned by Americans, soldiers in Korea established their own culture to cope with their situation.

In July 1950, novice American troops naively believed that the enemy would immediately retreat when it heard the United States was fighting. Instead, North Korean troops advanced, shocking soldiers who were not physically or emotionally prepared for combat. The Korean hills and the monsoon heat and humidity overwhelmed soldiers.

Soldiers in Korea sang lyrics describing their feelings about the military, the enemy, and service in Korea. One machine gunner's ditty revealed the gloom Korean soldiers felt: "The last time I saw Taejon it was not bright and gay. / Today I'm going to Taejon and blow the place away." Other songs eulogized comrades ("There Are No Fighter Pilots Down in Hell") and expressed frustration with commanders ("Give Me Operations"). The popular Korean War song "Itazuke Tower" resurfaced in the Vietnam War as "Phan Rang Tower."

Parodies of songs, such as the British Indian Army's "Bless 'Em All," revealed the comradery of soldiers stuck in the cold and terror of Chosin Reservoir:

> Bless 'em all, bless 'em all.
> The Commies, the U.S. and all:
> Those slant-eyed Chink soldiers
> Struck Hagaru-ru
> And now know the meaning of U.S.M.C.
> But we're saying goodbye to them all.
> We're Harry's police force on call.

Along the main line of resistance, rumors spread about the potential dangers of guerilla attacks, suicidal ambushes, fake surrenders, and enemy soldiers hiding in refugee columns. Soldiers repeated stories of "human wave" attacks by Chinese fanatics and of collaboration by American prisoners of war. Other rumors described the Communists' treatment of prisoners, whom gossip accurately portrayed as suffering cruel torture, interrogation, and brainwashing. United Nations soldiers also worried about Communist agents being purposefully captured as prisoners to spark prison riots. Other rumors concerned Communists taking over the U.S. government. Germ warfare, which the Communists claimed the allies were waging, joined the folk culture of the war through tall tales, cartoons of mutant insects, and displays, including a mouse rigged with a parachute by American prisoners. Rumors about impending peace were always rampant.

Korean soldiers created terminology to cope with their often miserable conditions. During the severe winters of subzero temperatures in the Korean hills, they joked about living in the "Ice Bowl." Faced by overwhelming forces, many troops fled under fire. The term "bugout" designated units who readily retreated, especially the Twenty-Fourth Regiment, which gained a reputation for cowardice in the early stages of the war. Soldiers called the Korean conflict the "yo-yo war" because it never seemed to end, and prominent entrenchments were nicknamed after movie stars or other culturally recognizable names: Jane Russell, T-Bone, Old Baldy, and Porkchop Hills. M*A*S*H* was an acronym for mobile hospitals, and code names for military campaigns (such as Operation Killer) entered the wartime vocabulary.

"R&R" the eagerly anticipated morale-boosting break from the front for rest and recuperation in Tokyo, became known later in the war as "I&I" (intercourse and intoxication) because of the excesses in which jaded soldiers engaged. The "big R," or rotation home, gained by accruing monthly points according to combat duty, created customs that curried staying alive until soldiers had enough points to go home. Low-number men covered for high-point men in dangerous combat, expecting new men to do the same for them in the future.

The *won* (Korean currency), as well as the black market, also entered war lore. Other symbols associated with the Korean War included military C rations, Lucky Strike cigarettes, napalm, and military bunkers. The First Cavalry wore yellow scarves traditionally associated with the cavalry and also representative of the soldiers' wish to return home to loved ones. Soldiers erected signs crudely lettered with mileage to distant home cities and carried homemade regimental signs. They displayed captured Chinese horns and burp guns as well as identifying emblems such as the Garry Owen crest. Folk gestures aided Korean War prisoners who, when photographed for Communist propaganda, gestured with the "Devil's Horns" to protest their incarceration without their captors understanding the code.

Anti-Truman sentiments prevailed in Korea and America, protesting the continuation of the war and President Harry Truman's dismissal of General Douglas MacArthur for wanting to extend the war to China. Near Hoengsong, Marines designed a sign declaring, "Massacre Valley—Scene of Harry S Truman's Police Action. Nice Going Harry." In America, "Punch Harry in the Nose" clubs organized and "Oust President Truman" bumper stickers appeared on cars.

Conflict between the Korean population and the American forces resulted in the Americans using disparaging terms such as "gook" for Koreans. Koreans believed that the spirits of their ancestors followed them, and they exorcised evil spirits by jumping in front of army vehicles. Some GI's, disgusted by what they viewed as the Korean's primitive lifestyle, encouraged their comrades to hit civilians on purpose.

South Korean troops incorporated GI English into their vocabularies. During what they termed their "Civil War," traditional Korean folktales, depicting the God of War and fierce warriors saving Seoul from invasion, proliferated. New themes stressed anti-Chinese folklore and the gallantry and sacrifices of wartime.

As possibilities of armistice neared, American GI's, trying to save every life possible, constructed signs warning, "Drive carefully! The man you hit might be your replacement." The July 27, 1953, truce without victory, however, divided Korea and left such permanent symbols of war folklore as Freedom House, Bridge of No Return, Propaganda Village, and tombstone-like markers, designating the demilitarized zone (DMZ). Speculation about soldiers missing in action and captives who refused repatriation continue to circulate more than forty years later.

Annually, forces of the U.S., the Eighth Army and the Republic of Korea engage in "Team Spirit," military exercises preparing for possible future invasion. Koreans ritually plant trees every April to reforest their battle-scarred hills. The tensions between the governments in Seoul and Pyongyang keep Cold War attitudes simmering and perpetuate rumors of invaders digging tunnels from the North underneath the DMZ.

Elizabeth D. Schafer

References

Blair, Clay. 1987. *The Forgotten War: America in Korea, 1950–1953.* New York: Anchor/Doubleday.

Goulden, Joseph C. 1982. *Korea: The Untold Story of the War.* New York: Times Books.

Knox, Donald. 1985. *The Korean War: An Oral History.* New York: Harcourt Brace Jovanovich.

Toner, James H. 1981. American Society and the American Way of War: Korea and Beyond. *Parameters* 11:79–90.

Wallrich, William. 1957. *Air Force Airs: Songs and Ballads of the United States Air Force, World War One through Korea.* New York: Duell.

Wiltz, John E. 1977. The Korean War and American Society. In *The Korean War: A 25-Year Perspective,* ed. Francis H. Heller. Lawrence: Regents Press of Kansas, pp. 112–158.

See also Cold War; Military Folklore

Korson, George (1899–1967)

Collector of coal-mining folklore. Born into a poor working-class Jewish family in the Ukraine, Korson grew up in Wilkes-Barre, Pennsylvania, where he became a newspaperman and later a folklorist with a national reputation for his pioneer work collecting the stories and songs of coal miners.

Korson took up the study of mining folklore—both in the eastern Pennsylvania anthracite fields in the 1920s and 1930s and in the bituminous fields of the South and Midwest in the 1940s—while he worked as a reporter in Pottsville and Allentown, Pennsylvania, in New Jersey, and as chief editor of Red Cross publications. Korson's books assumed that coal-mining folklore should be presented in the holistic context of a community's way of life.

During forty-three years of full-time journalistic employment, Korson wrote five definitive books on coal-mining folklore, as well as many articles; started the Library of Congress archive of miners' songs and ballads; founded and directed the Pennsylvania Folk Festival; and helped launch the National Folk Festival. He was awarded a Guggenheim Fellowship in 1957, a University of Chicago Folklore Prize in 1961, and was elected a Fellow of the American Folklore Society in 1960.

Though Korson was keenly aware of the problems of

American miners in terms of wages and working conditions, politically he was a liberal-centrist reformer rather than a radical revolutionary. Basically, he believed that strong labor unions were socially desirable to balance the excesses of capitalism.

Angus Kress Gillespie

References

Gillespie, Angus K. 1980. *Folklorist of the Coal Fields: George Korson's Life and Work.* University Park: Pennsylvania State University Press.

Korson, George. 1927. *Songs and Ballads of the Anthracite Miner.* New York: Frederick H. Hitchcock, Grafton Press.

———. [1938] 1964. *Minstrels of the Mine Patch.* Hatboro, PA: Folklore Associates.

———. [1943] 1965. *Coal Dust on the Fiddle.* Hatboro, PA: Folklore Associates.

———. [1949] 1960. *Pennsylvania Songs and Legends.* Baltimore: Johns Hopkins University Press.

———. 1960. *Black Rock: Mining Folklore of the Pennsylvania Dutch.* Baltimore: Johns Hopkins University Press.

Korson, Rae Rosenblatt (1901–1990)

Head of the Archive of Folk Song at the Library of Congress from 1956 to 1969. Born in Morristown, New Jersey, she attended the New Jersey College of Law. She married George Korson in 1926 and took an interest in his folksong research. Both Korsons were caught up in the urban folk consciousness and proletarian renaissance of the 1930s. She began her career at the library in 1941, serving as an assistant to archive heads Benjamin A. Botkin and Duncan Emrich. When Korson became head in 1956, she focused on preserving and organizing the folksong collection. Although her predecessors had been concerned with fieldwork and collecting, Korson directed her efforts toward the orderly processing of the growing collection. As head she developed successful administrative strategies to effectively handle the library staff and officials as well as the collectors, scholars, and performers who used the archive.

Rae Korson helped in the preparation of so many theses, manuscripts, and books on folk music that at one point Austin E. Fife, former president of the American Folklore Society, said that every notable work in the field of folksong since 1944 had some acknowledgment of her help.

During the folksong revival of the 1950s and 1960s, she tactfully balanced the conflicting agendas of political activists associated with that movement and the conservative Library of Congress. In 1970 she received an honorary doctorate of humanities degree from Kings College in Wilkes-Barre, Pennsylvania, for overseeing the organization of her late husband's papers on coal-mining folklore.

Angus Kress Gillespie

References

Gillespie, Angus K. 1980. *Folklorist of the Coal Fields: George Korson's Life and Work.* University Park: Pennsylvania State University Press.

Lesoravage, Alice. 1970. Folklorist's Dream Fulfilled. *Morning Call.* Allentown, Pennsylvania. (October 3), p. 11.

White, John. 1948. Did You Happen to See—Mrs. Rae Korson? *Times-Herald.* Washington, DC. (March 26), p. 2.

Krappe, Alexander Haggerty (1894–1947)

One of the most prolific American folklorists of the early 20th century. Krappe always seemed more European than American in his scholarly work. Born in Dorchester, Massachusetts, he took most of his secondary and undergraduate education in England, Ireland, and Germany, although his graduate training was in the United States, at the Universities of Iowa and Chicago. After receiving his doctorate at age twenty-five, he taught for the next twenty-eight years at a large number of schools, including the Universities of Michigan, Indiana, and Minnesota. Krappe's rather abrasive personality undoubtedly contributed to his frequent job changes, but his obvious intellectual abilities made it possible for him to acquire other positions. An erudite scholar, Krappe was fluent in a variety of languages, including German, Italian, French, Spanish, and Finnish. His areas of expertise were also broad-ranging, including classical literature, anthropology, economics, military and religious history, Provençal literature, Oriental folklore, and European folklore and mythology. At his death, he left manuscripts for books on social anthropology, the origin of the epic, and a translation of the Grimm brothers' *Kinder- und Hausmärchen.*

Krappe's first published book was *The Legend of Roderick, Last of the Visigoth Kings, and the Ermanarich Cycle* (1923), but the volume by which he is best remembered in folklore circles is *The Science of Folklore* (1930), a useful survey of the major genres of international folk tradition. However, in this work Krappe argued that there was no genuine American folklore, merely borrowings from European folklore that soon died out in this country. He further maintained that folksong "originated anonymously, among unlettered folk in times past" and that it "remained in currency . . . as a rule for centuries." Yet, in the same book, Krappe ignored his own definition when he called "My Old Kentucky Home" a folksong, apparently under the mistaken impression that it was composed by some unknown Blacks. This 1853 Stephen Foster composition is a popular song that has always been passed on primarily through the mass media, not in folk tradition. Furthermore, the song was not even a century, much less centuries, old in 1930. Even at that time, Krappe's arguments on the point must have seemed unnecessarily rigid and dated.

W.K. McNeil

References

Krappe, Alexander Haggerty. 1927. *Balor with the Evil Eye.* New York: Columbia University.

Taylor, Archer. 1948. Alexander Haggerty Krappe. *Journal of American Folklore* 61:201–202.

Kurath, Gertrude Prokosch (1903–1992)

Self-identified as an "ethnochoreologist." Kurath was an independent scholar who received foundation support for some of her work. Her first major article about a non-Western dance culture appeared in the *Journal of American Folklore* in 1946. Kurath encouraged others in the fields of folklore, anthropology, dance, and music to conduct research and publish on dance. She served as dance editor of the journal *Ethnomusicology* from 1956 to 1971.

She drew upon her B.A. and M.A. from Bryn Mawr College in history of art and archaeology, studies of several dance forms, music, and her working relationship with anthropologist William Fenton to observe and analyze dances of the Iroquois in her self-styled research. In a seminal article, "Panorama of Dance Ethnology," in *Current Anthropology* in 1960, she synthesized categories for collecting dance data.

Kurath pursued fieldwork among Indian groups in Mexico, the United States, and Canada. She examined popular and sacred dances of African Americans, immigrants, and temporary residents in Michigan. Much of her work focused on the relationship between dance and music. She may have been the first dance scholar to credit her major informant as her coauthor (in *Music and Dance of the Tewa Pueblos*, 1970). Kurath has numerous books, articles, dictionary and encyclopedia entries, reviews of books and records, an Ethnic Folkways Record, dance performances, and dance-drama and pageant productions to her credit (see her bibliography in *Ethnomusicology* 14:114–128, 1970).

Judith Lynne Hanna

References

Kurath, Gertrude Prokosch. 1946. Los Concheros. *Journal of American Folklore* 59:387–399.

———. 1964a. *Dances of Anáhuac: The Choreography and Music of Pre-Cortesian Dances.* Viking Fund Publications in Anthropology No. 38. Chicago: Aldine.

———. 1964b. *Iroquois Music and Dance: Ceremonial Arts of Two Seneca Longhouses.* Bulletin 187. Washington, DC: Bureau of American Ethnology.

———. 1968. *Dance and Song Rituals of Six Nations Reserve, Ontario.* Bulletin 220, Folklore Series No. 4. Ottawa: National Museum of Canada.

Kwanzaa

African American holiday, beginning on December 26, the day after Christmas, and concluding on New Year's Day. Kwanzaa is a Swahili word that means "first fruits of the harvest." In 1966, forty years after Carter G. Woodson, the founder of the Association for the Study of Afro-American Life and History, conceived and celebrated the first National Negro History Week, Maulana "Ron" Karenga, a graduate student at UCLA and an active member of the political and cultural Black nationalist group US, created and led the initial observance of Kwanzaa, as another celebration of African Americans' rich African cultural roots and supportive family and group ties.

Each of the seven days of Kwanzaa is marked by the lighting of a candle and the reflection upon one of the *Nguzo Saba*, the cultural principles that African Americans should live by. These seven red, black, and green candles, which are called *Mishumae saba*, are placed in a *Kinara*, a candelabrum, which symbolizes the African continent and the peoples of Africa. The order in which they are ceremonially lit is as follows: on the first day, the candle of *Umoja* (unity); on the second day, the candle of *Kujichagulia* (self-determination); on the third day, the candle of *Ujima* (collective work and responsibility); on the fourth day, the candle of *Ujamma* (cooperative economics); on the fifth day, the candle of *Nia* (purpose); on the sixth day, the candle of *Kuumba* (creativity); and on the seventh day, the candle of *Imani* (faith).

The altar on which the *Kinara* stands is usually also adorned with a *mazao*, a collection of fruits and vegetables that symbolizes the product of group unity; a *mkeka*, a straw mat that symbolizes respect for tradition; and a *vibunzi*, an ear of corn that symbolizes each child in the family observing the celebration.

Rituals observed during Kwanzaa include the giving and receiving of *Zawadi*, simple handmade gifts that reinforce the value of education and the significance of African culture; and the drinking and pouring of libations to the past, present, and future of African Americans from a *Kikombe cha umoja*, a communal cup. On December 31, the day before the celebration ends, the *Kwanzaa Karamu*, the feast of African unity, is held, which features traditional dishes from Africa and the African diaspora communities of the Caribbean and North and South America. Karenga devised the following five-part program to culminate this feast: (1) *Kukaribisha*, the welcoming of the important guest and elders gathered for the celebration; (2) *Kukumbuka*, the remembering of some cultural theme or principle by a celebrant; (3) *Kuchunguza tena na kutoa ahadi tena*, the reassessment and recommitment of the African American struggle in a short speech by a distinguished guest speaker; (4) *Kushangilia*, communal rejoicing that includes *Tamshi la tambiko*, the offering of a libation statement; *Kikombe cha umoja*, drinking from the unity cup; *Kutoa majina*, the calling of the names of family ancestors and African American heroes; and *Ngoma*, the beating and dancing to drums; and (5) *Tamshi la tutaonana*, the issuing of a farewell statement. Variations of this ritual are observed throughout the United States and Canada.

William H. Wiggins Jr.

References

Copage, Eric V. 1991. *Kwanzaa: An African-American Celebration of Culture and Cooking.* New York: William Morrow.

L

La Llorona

A ghostly female figure, the subject of many legends and *casos* (first-person experience narratives) among Mexican Americans throughout the Southwest and other areas of the United States, as well as Mexico and other Hispanic countries. *La Llorona* haunts waterways like canals, creeks, and rivers, wailing loudly as she searches for the spirits of her children.

Similar beliefs and legends may be found in many countries, but for the Mexican American community, *La Llorona*'s origins lie in Mexico. Tradition has it that an upper-class Spaniard and an Indian peasant maiden fall in love. The man's family refuses to allow him to marry her, so without the blessings of the church, they establish a household and have children. His parents finally persuade him to marry an upper-class Spanish woman to keep the family heritage alive. When he informs the Indian mother, she becomes distraught, and in her anger and desire to punish the Spaniard, she kills their children by drowning them. She is executed, and when she arrives at Heaven's gates, she is told that she must find the spirits of the children she has killed. Thus, she returns and must spend her future searching for her children's spirits along various types of waterways.

The legend takes many specific forms. One version identifies the Spaniard as Hernan Cortés, who led the conquest of the Aztecs. The Indian maiden, known as La Malinche, not only bore Cortés' children but also aided in the conquest by serving as a translator for the Spaniards. She is looked upon as a betrayer of her people, a theme emphasized by many of the more militant Chicanos.

The legend is popular throughout the Southwest and wherever Mexican Americans gather. In one popular form, *La Llorona* is the siren who tempts men who are out drinking and otherwise looking for ways to violate the social norms of the group. They follow her, only to discover when they get close and she turns on them that she has long, sharp fingernails or the face of a horse. The terrified men flee for their lives and swear never to violate these social norms again.

Many first-person experience narratives are told about personal experiences with *La Llorona*. Often these take the form of one hearing a loud wailing at night and seeing *La Llorona*, dressed in white, moving along a creek, river, or canal. Such stories are often used by parents to persuade young people not to go out at night.

A collection (Hawes 1968) of *La Llorona* legends and first-person narratives gathered at a reform school for girls in Los Angeles County, California, portrays the ghost woman as one who has murdered her children and takes the role as a dangerous siren, as a mourning woman, or as a woman dangerous to children. The theme of loss—loss of children, loss of beauty, loss of life—and the theme of mutilation are predominant in these narratives.

The *La Llorona* legend continues to thrive in the Mexican American community in the Southwest, particularly in rural areas.

Joe S. Graham

References

Espinosa, Aurelio M. 1910. New Mexican Spanish Folklore. *Journal of American Folklore* 23:395–418.

Hawes, Bess L. 1968. *La Llorona* in Juvenile Hall. *Western Folklore* 27:153–170.

Kirtley, Bacil F. 1960. *La Llorona* and Related Themes. *Western Folklore* 19:155–168.

Leddy, Betty. 1948. *La Llorona* in Southern Arizona. *Western Folklore* 7:272–277.

———. 1950. *La Llorona* Again. *Western Folklore* 9:363–365.

Pérez, Soledad. 1951. Mexican Folklore from Austin, Texas. In *The Healer of Los Olmos and Other Mexican Lore*, ed. Wilson M. Hudson. Publications of the Texas Folklore Society No. 24. Dallas: Southern Methodist University Press, pp. 73–76.

West, John O. 1981. The Weeping Woman: *La Llorona*. In *The Legendary Ladies of Texas*, ed. Francis E. Abernathy. Publications of the Texas Folklore Society No. 43. Dallas: E-Heart, pp. 31–36.

Labor Day

National and state holiday observed annually on the first Monday in September. Peter J. McGuire of the Brotherhood of Carpenters and Joiners reputedly proposed the idea for Labor Day at a meeting of the the New York Central Labor Union in May 1882. He suggested scheduling a day to honor organized labor in late summer or early fall. Coming in the most pleasant season of the year, this date would also provide needed respite from the work routine since it fell halfway between Independence Day and Thanksgiving. The first observance of Labor Day, occurring later that year in New York City, featured a workers' parade, picnic, concert, and bombastic oratory. Within two years, other Northeastern cities had added their observances. In 1887 Oregon became the first state officially to endorse Labor Day, and Congress approved it as a federal holiday in 1894.

During early observances, unions used Labor Day to dramatize particular grievances through speeches, parades, and labor songs, many of which adapted the folk idiom. Once such concerns had been addressed, the sharply political tone of the holiday diminished. Observances throughout the United States, though, continue to involve some speech making and parades, and Labor Day remains the traditional starting date for presidential campaigns.

Viewed as marking the end of summer, Labor Day has become distinctly recreational. Community picnics, block parties, and family trips to beaches or resorts now characterize this holiday. Moreover, county and state fairs, religious festivals, and family reunions may be scheduled with Labor Day in mind to take advantage of its three-day weekend.

William M. Clements

References

Cohen, Hennig, and Tristram Potter Coffin, eds. 1991. *The Folklore of American Holidays*. 2d. ed. Detroit: Gale.

Hatch, Jane M., ed. 1978. *The American Book of Days*. 3d. ed. New York: H.W. Wilson.

Lacourcière, Luc (1910–1989)

Collector of French Canadian folklore and founder of the Archives de Folklore of Laval University, Quebec, Canada. After studies at Laval University, Lacourcière met the "father of Canadian Folklore Studies," Marius Barbeau, who introduced him to the discipline, trained him, and influenced his appointment in 1944 to the first chair of folklore at Laval University and the creation of the first Folklore Department in Canada.

Between 1942 and 1972, Lacourcière made extensive field collections in eastern Quebec and the three Maritime Provinces of Nova Scotia, New Brunswick, and Prince Edward Island, gathering thousands of folktales and folksongs. He was, however, deeply involved, too, in the teaching of French Canadian literature; his literary and folkloristic interests led him to found two major series, the literary *Nenuphar* (1944) and the *Archives de Folklore* (1946), Volume 25 of which appeared in 1991.

Lacourcière's publications were chiefly in the form of articles in journals or books; his major work, the "Analytical Catalogue of French Folktales in North America," based on historic–geographic principles, was unpublished at his death. Lacourcière devoted his time to teaching, editorial work, and thesis supervision, directing almost 100 M.A. and Ph.D. dissertations, many in folklore, and teaching most of the outstanding Quebec and Franco–American folklorists of the period.

Lacourcière was awarded fellowships by the Carnegie (1939–1940), Guggenheim (1943–1944), and Rockefeller (1956–1957) Foundations; elected a Fellow of the American Folklore Society (1973); made a Companion of the Order of Canada (1970); and, upon its founding in 1976, was made an honorary president of the Folklore Studies Association of Canada.

Gerald Thomas

References

Dupont, Jean-Claude, ed. 1978. *Mélanges en l'honneur de Luc Lacourcière: Folklore français d'Amérique.* Ottawa: Leméac.

Lacourcière, Luc. 1975. Sept contes ou légendes du Canada français. In *Folktales Told around the World*, ed. Richard M. Dorson. Chicago: University of Chicago Press, pp. 429–467.

Thomas, Gerald. 1994. Luc Lacourcière in Newfoundland. *Folklore Historian* 11:5–14.

Larkin, Margaret (1899–1967)

Collector and singer of cowboy songs. Larkin was also a poet, a journalist, a playwright and writer of nonfiction, a trade-union activist, a student of the kibbutz movement in Israel, and a forerunner in the growth of the urban folk revival. Born in Las Vegas, New Mexico, Larkin was reared among cowboy singers and tellers of tales as well as among carriers of Hispanic lore. She attended the University of Kansas, where she earned recognition as a poet, and by 1925 was a member of the "intellectual middle class" arts movement in Santa Fe, where her award-winning play *El Cristo* was published.

Larkin's passion for journalism took her to the East Coast in the late 1920s, and in 1929 while working as press agent for striking textile workers in Gastonia, North Carolina, she met Ella Mae Wiggins, the gifted writer of textile protest "ballets." The murder of Wiggins three weeks after their meeting drove Larkin deep into radical activity. She took her knowledge of Wiggins to New York City, where she wrote articles about Wiggins and her songs, and gave concerts singing those songs. The improvement of working-class life as promised by Communism appealed to her, and in the 1930s she became a leader of the intellectual Left.

Larkin had developed a reputation as a singer of cowboy songs, and when her friend from Santa Fe days Lynn Riggs needed additional songs for his play *Green Grow the Lilacs*, he turned to her. She later became a member of the road troupe, singing cowboy songs during interludes. Larkin compiled her songs into *Singing Cowboy: A Book of Western Songs* ([1931] 1963). Her texts were printed as she had learned them; they were not edited to conform to the Lomax texts, and she wrote realistic and extensive explanatory notes about cowboys and their songs, stressing that cowboy songs were not worksongs and that it was merely a "happy accident" when a song fit the gait of a horse.

Larkin's first husband was Liston M. Oak, a member of the Communist Party and editor of *Soviet Russia Today*. They shared a belief in the power of drama and became founding members of the Theatre Union, the nation's first professional theater organization dedicated as a voice for the working class. Political differences among board members killed the organization in 1937, along with the marriage of Larkin and Oak; however, she had become acquainted with another member of the Theatre Union, playwright Albert Maltz. They were married in 1941 and moved to Hollywood, where Maltz became an award-winning screenwriter. In 1947 Maltz gained notoriety as one of the Hollywood Ten (a group of screenwriters cited for contempt of Congress and blacklisted), and eventually he served ten months in jail.

After his release, the family moved to Cuernavaca, Mexico, and a few years later Larkin's book about a bizarre murder plot in Mexico was published under the title *Seven Shares in a Gold Mine* (1959). She also worked as a free-lance sociological researcher and writer, which earned her the position as editorial assistant to Oscar Lewis in preparing *La Vida* (1966). Larkin's last book, *The Hand of Mordecai* (1966), recounted life on a kibbutz. She died in Mexico City on May 8, 1967.

Guy Logsdon

References

Denisoff, R. Serge. 1971. *Great Day Coming: Folk Music and the American Left.* Urbana. University of Illinois Press, pp. 21, 46.

Green, Archie. 1972. *Only a Miner: Studies in Recorded Coal-Mining Songs.* Urbana: University of Illinois Press, p. 78.

Lawyers

Members of the legal profession, among whom and about whom traditions circulate. Owing in part to media exposure, lawyers have an increasingly public profile. Possibly in response to broadening social and political discussions about the legal profession and its apparent elitism, nonlawyers tell vituperative jokes about lawyers. Although members of the Bar are aware of these jokes, and some may also tell them, attorneys also share occupational lore through their own narrating. This occupational lore includes narratives about federal judges, gender bias, and the foibles of practicing law.

Lawyer jokes and riddles are in wide oral and written circulation, likening lawyers to rats, sharks, and toxic waste. Lawyers are purported to be greedy, to lack compassion, or to possess other inhumane characteristics. One joke in oral circulation directly comments on this lack of positive virtues: A pope upon dying and arriving in heaven is distressed to learn that not only is his heavenly housing for all eternity a mere 4,000-square-foot home, but that the commanding edifice on the hill is for a lawyer. St. Peter tells the protesting pope, "Hey, this is heaven after all! We've got plenty of popes, but we only got one lawyer."

Members of the American Bar Association are aware of the negative images portrayed in lawyer jokes. From discussions during continuing-education classes to informal gatherings, some lawyers debate how to counter the negative images. Following a murderous assault on a San Francisco law office, the president of the California State Bar Association even attempted to find support for legislation giving stiff penalties for repeating lawyer jokes. Significantly, lawyers report that these negative jokes are told directly to them by non-lawyers, unlike other jokes vilifying members of particular ethnic or racial groups. One Los Angeles-based attorney said that before her famous athlete-celebrity client even met her for the first time, the client elicited her answer to the riddle, "What's black and brown and looks good on a lawyer?" (Answer: a rottweiler [Variant: a doberman]).

Attorney-judical relations may range from fractious to collusive, at least as expressed in attorneys' own traditional lore. There are lawyers' jokes that portray federal judges as capricious, willful, and excessively controlling in their courtrooms. In one joke, even God is portrayed as "liking to play federal judge." Attorneys narrate firsthand experiences and friend-of-a-friend narratives about particular individual federal judges; one judge is reputed to have said to an attorney who dared question his ruling: "This is not Burger King. We do not do it your way." On the other hand, criminal lawyers are reputed to have arranged a secret code with certain judges. As one lawyer describes the esoteric signal, a criminal lawyer can alert a judge he needs a continuance because he has not been paid by saying, "I'm sorry, your honor, my witness Mr. Green has not appeared." (Similar codes are used by the medical profession for coded communications in hospitals.)

Attorneys share information through personal-experience narrating as they make the transition from fresh graduates to seasoned lawyers. One rule of thumb is this:

> If the facts aren't on your side, pound on the law.
> If the law's not on your side, pound on the facts.
> If neither the facts nor the law are on your side, pound on the table.

Insurance lawyers deride the stereotypical dress of criminal lawyers (such as diamond pinkie rings) and plaintiff lawyers denigrate the rich lifestyle of the defense. Female attorneys help prepare younger female associates with accounts of their experiences before particular judges, including the judge who yells at female attorneys for wearing open-toed shoes. Some attorneys believe that by sharing these narratives that turn on issues of gender they are beginning to affect attorney-client relationships.

Lawyer-to-lawyer narrating grows because of the nature of the profession and its training. The opportunity for narrating exists because hours are spent waiting in court or at group depositions. In addition, lawyers have learned the importance of narrating to make a case to a jury (see Schrager 1986) as well as to add to their competitive stance vis-à-vis other attorneys. As one practicing lawyer commented, "Lawyers tell stories to other lawyers to enhance their case, their position."

Judith E. Haut

References

Abel, Richard. 1989. *American Lawyers.* New York: Oxford University Press.

Lipson–Walker, Carolyn. 1981. Black-Robed Folklore: The Oral and Customary Traditions of the Supreme Court. *Southwest Folklore* 5:21–41.

Roth, Andrew, and Jonathan Roth. 1989. *Devil's Advocates: The Unnatural History of Lawyers.* Berkeley, CA: Nolo.

Schrager, Samuel. 1986. Trial Lawyers as Storytellers. In *Festival of American Folklife, 1986.* Washington, DC: Smithsonian Institution, pp. 12–16.

Leach, MacEdward (1892–1967)

Scholar, folklore collector, and teacher. Leach, who sometimes gave his birth date as 1896, was born near Bridgeport, Illinois, and educated at the University of Illinois. Originally a medievalist with a master's degree from Johns Hopkins and a doctorate from the University of Pennsylvania, he edited standard editions of the romances *Amis and Amiloun* and *Paris and Vienne*, teaching and writing in medieval studies all of his life.

His fame, however, came as a folklorist at the University of Pennsylvania, where he spent his entire career. Fostered in the study of folklore by Americanist Cornelius Weygandt and his friend ethnologist Frank Speck, Leach developed courses within the Department of English that eventually became the doctoral program in folklore and folklife. He was known as a spellbinding lecturer, encouraging many of his graduate students to become scholars. Folklorists Roger Abrahams, Horace P. Beck, Tristram Potter Coffin, John Greenway, Kenneth Goldstein, G. Malcolm Laws, and a host more were started on their way by Leach.

In his role as secretary-treasurer (1943–1960) and then president (1961–1962) of the American Folklore Society, Leach almost single-handedly nurtured that organization from near collapse to vigor, encouraging local societies as a foundation for the national one, inaugurating the Bibliographical and Special Series to generate revenue, and giving his time whenever and wherever needed.

An avid folklore collector, he did fieldwork, often with Horace Beck, most notably in Virginia, Labrador, and Jamaica. He was twice married, the first time to Alice Mary Doan (Maria Leach), who edited the *Standard Dictionary of Folklore, Mythology, and Legend* (1949), and the second time to Nancy Rafetto.

Tristram Potter Coffin

References

Leach, MacEdward. 1955. *The Ballad Book.* New York: Harper.

———. 1965. *Folk Ballads and Songs of the Labrador Coast.* Bulletin 201, Anthropological Series No. 68. Ottawa: National Museum of Canada.

Leach, MacEdward, and Tristram P. Coffin. 1961. *The Critics and the Ballad.* Carbondale: Southern Illinois University Press.

MacEdward Leach. *Journal of American Folklore (Special Memorial Issue)* 81:97–120, 1968.

Huddie ("Lead Belly") Ledbetter, about 1942. Photo Berenice Abbott. American Folklife Center.

Ledbetter, Huddie ("Lead Belly") (1888–1949)

Probably the best-known Black folksinger in modern American culture. Though many people refer to him as a blues singer, Ledbetter was, in fact, far more than that: He was a traditional songster with a huge repertoire of all kinds of pieces, a pioneering figure in the introduction of folk music to the American public. His colorful life and career have attracted media attention since the mid-1930s, and though he died in 1949, his music and songs have endured better than those of any other traditional performer and have won him honors such as election to the Rock and Roll Hall of Fame. Critics often refer to him as "America's Greatest Black Folksinger," a title few seem to be willing to challenge; certainly, many music fans who cannot name one other blues or folk singer know the name Lead Belly (a nickname given to him by a prison chaplain).

Ledbetter, according to the Census reports, was born on January 15, 1888, on the Jeter plantation near the Caddo Lake area north of Shreveport, Louisiana. This area, right on the Louisiana–Texas line, was then the home of a large rural Black population that included his family, who were sharecroppers; later Ledbetter would recall playing at rural dances where "there would be no White man around for twenty miles." The music he grew up with included old fiddle tunes, play-party games, ballads, field hollers, church songs, and old vaudeville and popular songs; some of these, like "Ha Ha Thisaway," later became staples in his repertoire. Though his first instrument was a "windjammer" (a small accordion), by 1903 he had acquired a guitar and was plying his trade at dances and in local string bands.

In 1904, when he turned sixteen, he made his way to the notorious red-light district of Fannin Street in nearby Shreveport. There he heard jazz and blues and watched the piano players in the bordellos with fascination; he later admitted that he eagerly sought to adapt the left-hand piano runs to his guitar style. He learned more music during years of wandering between 1906 and 1908, absorbing the rich musical brew that was spawning ragtime, jazz, and blues. In 1908 he married Aletha Henderson and moved to the Dallas area. There two important things happened: He heard and bought his first twelve-string guitar (the instrument he would make famous), and he met the legendary bluesman Blind Lemon Jefferson. Though Jefferson was actually Ledbetter's junior by five years, he had had more experience as a full-time musician, and he taught Ledbetter much about the blues itself. Around the Deep Ellum district of Dallas, the two performed until about 1915.

Returning to Harrison County, Texas, Ledbetter began a series of encounters with the law that would alter his life and almost destroy his performing career. In 1915 he was sent to the chain gang on an assault charge, but he escaped and moved to Bowie County under the alias of Walter Boyd. There, in 1917, he was convicted of killing a cousin and wound up at the Sugarland Prison farm in south Texas. By now he was gaining a reputation as a singer and a hard worker in the prisons, a favorite of trusties and guards; he learned and sang songs like "The Midnight Special," and he began to create topical songs about local people and events. When Texas Governor Pat Neff visited the prison, Ledbetter asked to be among the ones to entertain him, and he composed a song to the governor, asking to be pardoned; surprisingly, Neff did so, signing the papers on January 16, 1925. For the next five years, Ledbetter stayed around the Shreveport area, but in 1930 he was convicted again of assault—knifing a prominent local White citizen. This time he was sentenced to a six-to-ten-year term in Angola, arguably the worst prison in America.

It was there, in 1933, that he encountered collector John Lomax and sang for his recording machine songs like "The Western Cowboy" and "Irene," the latter one he had learned from his uncle. A year later, at a second visit, Ledbetter decided to try his pardon-song technique again and recorded a plea to Louisiana Governor O.K. Allen. Though Lomax did leave the disc at the governor's office, and though Ledbetter assumed it had had its effect, when he was released in 1934, it was because of a Depression-related pardon program called "double–good time," not because of the song. He took a job driving for Lomax and helping him as he collected songs in prisons; along the way, he developed a good sense of what a traditional song was and added to his own considerable fund of such songs. (One was "Rock Island Line," which Huddie picked up in an Arkansas camp.)

Lomax took Ledbetter with him to New York City in January 1935, and the result was a sensational round of newspaper stories, newsreels, radio shows, recordings, college concerts, and even a publicity-heavy marriage to a childhood sweetheart from Shreveport, Martha Promise. For the first time, the general American public was being introduced to the concept of a genuine traditional singer. For three months, money and offers poured in, but complex tensions led to an estrangement between Lomax and Ledbetter, and finally the latter returned to Shreveport.

A year later, Ledbetter returned to New York City to try to make it on his own. He found his audience not in the African American fans of the Apollo Theater, but in the young White social activists of the various political and labor movements. Though he felt strongly only about civil rights songs, Lead Belly produced songs on a number of topics, the best of which were "Bourgeois Blues" and "We're in the Same Boat, Brother." His success with radio shows in New York City led to a sojourn in Hollywood, where he tried out for a role in the film version of *Green Pastures* and produced his best commercial recordings, for Capitol. The later 1940s saw more touring, a series of recordings for the Folkways label, and the development of his apartment into a headquarters for the folk movement. Martha's niece Tiny began managing him and, for the first time trying to straighten out his affairs; things were looking up when, in 1949, Huddie was diagnosed with amyotrophic lateral sclerosis (Lou Gehrig's disease). It progressed rapidly, and on December 6, 1949, he died in Bellevue Hospital in New York City. His body was returned to Mooringsport for burial, and a plaque marks his resting place at the rural Shiloh Baptist Church.

Charles K. Wolfe

References

Lead Belly. *The Midnight Special: Library of Congress Recordings Vol. 1*. Rounder CD 1044.

———. *Gwine Dig a Hole to Put the Devil in: Library of Congress Recordings Vol. 2*. Rounder CD 1045.

———. *Let It Shine on Me: Library of Congress Recordings Vol. 3*. Rounder CD 1046.

———. *Huddie Ledbetter's Best*. Capitol CDP 7 92075 2.

———. *Alabama Bound*. RC–BMG 9600-2-R.

Lomax, John A., and Alan Lomax. 1936. *Negro Folk Songs as Sung by Lead Belly*. New York: MacMillan.

Wolfe, Charles, and Kip Lornell. 1992. *The Life and Legend of Leadbelly*. New York: HarperCollins.

Lee, Hector H. (1908–1992)

Collector and scholar of Western folk narrative. Born in Texas but reared in southwestern Utah, as a child Lee heard Mormon pioneer and Paiute stories that eventually sparked his interest in regional folklore. Primarily a college administrator at Chico and Sonoma State Colleges in California throughout his career, Lee published a major study of Mormon legend and several collections of California tales; he also popularized folklore studies in the West as a well-known lecturer, interview subject, and raconteur.

After studies at the Universities of Utah and California, Berkeley, Lee became the first recipient of a doctorate in American civilization at the University of New Mexico with a dissertation later published as *The Three Nephites: Their Substance and Significance in Folklore* (1949). Returning to the University of Utah to teach English and folklore, in 1944 Lee obtained a Rockefeller Foundation grant to establish the Utah Humanities Research Foundation, a folklore archive, and the quarterly journal *Utah Humanities Review* (1947–1949), which featured Western literature and folklore and later evolved into the literary and critical journal *Western Humanities Review*.

Lee's most significant work is represented by his research on Mormon lore. Drawing on his own collecting and the work done by his contemporaries Wayland D. Hand and Austin E. and Alta S. Fife, Lee showed that Mormon folklore reflects the changing circumstances, experiences, and identity of people of Mormon culture and that the Three Nephite legends illustrate the adaptation of old traditions to the new West.

After settling in California in 1947, Lee published four collections: *Tales of California* (1974), *The Bodega War* (1988), *Tales of the Redwood Empire* (1962), and *Heroes, Villains, and Ghosts* (1984). He also hosted television and radio shows and was active in the California Folklore Society, serving as its president from 1973 to 1975.

Stephanie Sherman

Legend

A monoepisodic, localized, and historicized traditional narrative told as believable in a conversational mode. Psychologically, legend is a symbolic representation of folk belief and reflects the collective experiences and values of the group to whose tradition it belongs. Thematically, legends often deal with the supernatural or other remarkable phenomena. These events typically are said to occur in a specific place and time with named characters.

Characterizing the legend genre was begun by Jacob Grimm, who observed that "the folktale is more poetic, the legend is more historical." The view of the legend as historically true informed the majority of legend scholarship throughout the 19th and early 20th centuries. Most studies of legend focused on attempts to isolate the historical kernel of the narrative. Consequently, studies of legend concentrated primarily on the text, ignoring important aspects of the genre, such as the manner of performance.

Legend is characteristically a highly localized narrative. Legend accounts have also been characterized as highly oikotypified. Carl Wilhelm von Sydow introduced the concept of oikotypes (or "ecotypes") to explain differences between similar folk expressions collected from separate tradition group. Through oikotypification, tradition participants change a narrative to fit their needs, adapting it to the cultural and geographical environment in which it is told. The internal reality of the legend account often mimics the external reality of the tradition participants, both culturally and geographically. Because legend narrators wish their accounts to be believable, they are further inclined to situate the account in the immediate geographical area. Thus, a legend told in one area about events closely linked to a specific place can be found in other areas closely linked to entirely different places. For example, one variant of "The Vanishing Hitchhiker" begins: "A traveling man who lived in Spartanburg was on his way home one night . . . ," while another begins: "This friend was driving up Hearst Avenue one night . . . ," (Brunvand 1981:25–26).

The use of historically verifiable personal names, or the reference to people known to the tradition participants, is another characteristic of legend. The inclusion of known individuals in the stories further contributed to the early characterization of the genre as "historical." However, identical stories with different named individuals appear in disparate traditions. Just as place names and topographical features of a story are varied to fit the tradition participants' physical environment, so, too, are proper names and historical referents varied to fit the tradition participants' historical environment. For example, Maurice Alley told the legend of "Buying the Wind" as follows: "Paris Keller was the captain of a vessel, and he got out one day and got becalmed. He was going to the west'ard and wasn't no wind. And he wanted some wind, so he threw a quarter overboard. He wanted to buy a quarter's worth. He said he wished it would blow so hard she wouldn't lug a nail in a paulpost. . . . So he said it commenced to blow; it blowed till it blowed the sails off her . . ." (Dorson 1964:32–33). Richard M. Dorson reports similar variants of the legend that relate how George Beal, Captain Belmore, Nick Bryant, Cam Crowley, and Malcolm Lowell buy the wind in a similar fashion. These examples confirm the tendency of legend-tellers to attribute their accounts to individuals known to the tradition participants. In a study of medieval legends and their modern analogs, Shirley Marchalonis shows how legends extant in the Middle Ages have been updated to fit contemporary times. This process of variation can be labeled "historicization." Therefore, one can propose a modification of the Grimms' earliest characterization of the legend. The legend is not historical narrative, but rather *historicized* narrative.

Much of the believability of the legend resides in the close link between the daily reality of the tradition participants and that found in the legend. In a buried-treasure legend from the Texas Gulf Coast, the narrator uses a familiar setting for the action: ". . . up here on the Tres Palacios River, there was an old trading post . . ." (Mullen 1978:97). This descriptive setting stands in stark contrast to the folktale in which the inner reality of the tale usually bears little or no resemblance to the outer reality of the tale-teller and the audience. Often, phrases such as "This actually happened to a fellow I know . . ." contribute to the presentation of the legend as a believable account, while the well-known "Once upon a time . . ." opening is used in the folktale.

Legend also derives believability from the folk beliefs of the tradition participants. Scholars proposed a subgenre of legend, the "belief legend," as a means for categorizing legends that primarily made use of folk belief, but since legend itself is a believable narrative, it by default reflects folk belief. Consequently, *all* legends can be said to fit the category "belief legend," thus presumably rendering the added appellation "belief" unnecessary. Legend taps already established belief and thereby reinforces those beliefs. Just as legend relies on folk belief, so, too, does folk belief rely on legend. The following account illustrates this close interrelationship: "I was loading ice, threw the hatches off, and one of them flipped over on the deck. My brother came down and told me to never let that happen again, that that damn boat was going to sink. The next night it did. Where he got it from I don't know; that was the first I heard of it" (Mullen 1978:4). This legend incorporates reference to the belief among fishermen of the Texas coast that turning hatch covers upside down leads to calamity. As the complex forces at work in society change people's beliefs and values, the changes become reflected in the legends. If the legend fails to adapt to its new cultural, historical, or geographical environment, it loses its viability in tradition and is no longer told.

An important characteristic of legend is its narrative form—legend tells a story. For an account to be considered a legend, it must include a temporal junction: X *then* Y. The above example of "Buying the Wind" illustrates this point: "And he wanted some wind, so [Temporal Junction] he throwed a quarter overboard." The narrative form sets legend apart from other nonnarrative folk genres and helps distinguish it from simple nonnarrative statements of folk belief such as "If you throw money overboard you can buy some wind."

A legend does not typically include multiple episodes; instead, it relates a single event. Scholars have attempted to provide a structural description of legend narrative without great success. W.F.H. Nicolaisen's structural scheme is perhaps the most successful of the suggested systems, because it allows for great variation and attempts to describe only the most general aspects of legend structure. At the very least, legend can be said to have three structural components. The first of these, the "orientation," sets the stage for the action. The second component, the "complicating action," recounts the event. The third component, the "result," relates what happened as a result of the complicating action. Using this map, one can describe a variant of "The Vanishing Hitchhiker" as follows: "Someone Miss Packard knew, unfortunately, I cannot remember the person's name, was driving on a deserted road towards Holbrook on a cold, rainy night [Orientation]. As she was driving, she saw a figure on the side of the road, soaking wet trying to thumb a ride. She felt sorry for the person, stopped the car, and a young man sat down in the front seat [Complicating Action]. After a long period of silence he said, 'Jesus is coming again.' She turned to look at him, and he was gone [Result]" (Brunvand 1981:39). Often, the complicating action or result of a legend includes an unexpected or supernatural event.

Despite the brevity of the monoepisodic legend account, the legend form is extremely elastic. Legend can be contracted or expanded depending on the requirements of the performative setting. Legend can include numerous allied motifs, detailed description, nuanced actions, and intricate dialogues—or, a legend can be presented in a nearly skeletal form, exhibiting great economy of expression. Because of legend's narrative elasticity as well as the extreme localization and historicization of the accounts, scholars have encountered difficulties in developing useful type indexes of legend collections.

Legend is closely allied to rumor. Rumor, like legend, is performed as a believable account. It, too, is highly localized and closely linked to a particular historical period. The notable difference between rumor and legend is that rumor is not always a narrative. The designation "rumor" can also refer to nonnarrative expressions of folk belief. Therefore, the term "rumor" does not describe a specific genre, but rather a hyperactive transmissionary state. If a legend is repeated frequently within a short time period in a circumscribed area, it can be called a "rumor." Even after the disappearance of the "rumor," the potential for the legend to be told remains.

Study of legend-telling events reveals that legend is more closely linked to "joke" than to "folktale." While folktales are generally told by a single narrator who uses opening and closing formulas to signal the beginning and end of the performance, legends are characteristically told conversationally. Often, jokes appear alongside legends in these settings. This proximity between jokes and legends during performance has lead Linda Dégh to dub the two forms "symbiotic." In the conversational performance of legend, the beginning and the end of the story are rarely clearly defined. Furthermore, participants other than the main narrator interject their own variants into the performance. Legend-telling events often progress in fits and starts, with the position of primary narrator frequently shifting. Often legend arises in the conversational setting as a means for making a point or substantiating a claim, leading to the conclusion that legend may serve various rhetorical purposes.

One of the main areas of study for legend scholars has revolved around the distinction between "memorates" and "fabulates." Von Sydow proposed that firsthand accounts of supernatural events were qualitatively different from accounts in which the narrator was at a greater distance from the narrated events. He labeled firsthand narratives "memorates" and called narratives that placed the narrator at more than two transmissional links from the narrated events "fabulates." According to this theory, memorates could become fabulates when they became part of the tradition of a folk group and lost their firsthand narration. However, field recordings reveal that tradition participants often eliminate transmissional links between themselves and the reported events. Depending on the situation, a narrator can perform a legend as a memorate even though he or she may originally have heard it as a fabulate. Thus, the memorate-fabulate distinction ultimately fails. Narrators are motivated to eliminate numerous transmissionary links in their accounts to bolster the believability of their stories. A story that begins: "A friend of a friend of a friend told me that his friend . . ." has virtually no believability. Since narrators are inclined to reduce the number of transmissionary links between themselves and the narrated events, legend cannot be characterized by the proximity of the narrator to the narrated events.

The reasons people tell legends are linked to psychological factors. Legends organize complex environmental and cultural forces, tap beliefs, and express fears and values common to the tradition participants (see Crane 1977). Telling legends allows people an opportunity to explore their outer reality through the symbolically constructed inner reality of the legend as well as the opportunity to express both anxieties and aspirations. The values and beliefs of the teller and the audience inform the legend account and allow for a narrative negotiation of their concerns.

Contemporary legends have come under close scrutiny particularly among scholars interested in psychology. These legends are often referred to as "modern urban legends." While this term suggests that these legends are different from other legends, because they are both "modern" and "urban," actually many modern legends have counterparts in traditions from the 19th century and before. This suggests that all legends, at some point, were "modern" (see Marchalonis 1976). Therefore, it may be more accurate to refer to these legends as "contemporary." The label "urban," although traditional among folklorists, seems likewise misplaced. Legend narrators adapt their stories to their historical, geographical, and cultural environments. Thus, a story that is set in an urban center by one narrator can often be set in a rural setting by another narrator. There is nothing exclusively "urban" about these contemporary legends.

Timothy R. Tangherlini

References

Brunvand, Jan Harold. 1981. *The Vanishing Hitchhiker: American Urban Legends and Their Meanings.* New York: W.W. Norton.

Crane, Beverly. 1977. The Structure of Value in "The Roommate's Death": A Methodology for the Interpretive Analysis of Folk Legends. *Journal of the Folklore Institute* 14:133–151.

Dégh, Linda. 1976. Symbiosis of Joke and Legend: A Case of Conversational Folklore. In *Folklore Today: A Festschrift for Richard Dorson*, ed. Linda Dégh, Henry Glassie, and Felix Oinas. Bloomington: Indiana University Press, pp. 81–91.

Dorson, Richard M. 1964. *Buying the Wind.* Chicago: University of Chicago Press.

Grimm, Jacob Ludwig Karl, and Wilhelm Grimm. 1816–1818. *Deutsche Sagen.* Berlin: Nicolaische Verlag.

Hand, Wayland Debs, ed. 1971. *American Folk Legend: A Symposium.* Publications of the UCLA Center for the Study of Comparative Folklore and Mythology. Berkeley: University of California Press.

Marchalonis, Shirley. 1976. Three Medieval Tales and Their Modern Analogues. *Journal of the Folklore Institute* 13:173–184.

Mullen, Patrick B. 1978. *I Heard the Old Fishermen Say: Folklore of the Texas Gulf Coast.* Austin: University of Texas Press.

Nicolaisen, W.F.H. 1987. The Linguistic Structure of Legends. In *Perspectives on Contemporary Legend.* Vol. 2, ed. Gillian Bennett, Paul Smith, and D.D.A. Widdowson. CECTAL Conference Papers Series No. 5. Sheffield, England: Sheffield Academic Press, pp. 61–76.

Tangherlini, Timothy R. 1990. "It Happened Not Too Far From Here . . .": A Survey of Legend Theory and Characterization. *Western Folklore* 49:371–390.

Von Sydow, Carl Wilhelm. 1948. *Selected Papers on Folklore.* Copenhagen: Rosenkilde and Bagger.

See also Anecdote; Lovers' Leaps; Memorate; Namelore; Rumor; Urban Legend

Legend Trip

A ritual; teenagers hear a legend about uncanny events said to occur at a particular spot, then visit the site to test the legend. Widespread in many parts of the United States, such trips focus on "spooky" places such as a bridge, an abandoned house, or a remote church or graveyard.

Many types of legend trips are common in the United States. Often a baby is said to have died or been murdered, frequently at a bridge, and its ghost is said to cry at certain times. Or a person—man or woman—was decapitated in an accident, and a ghostly light lingers at the site of the tragedy. Near Maco, North Carolina, generations of teens have come to witness a mysterious light along a railroad track, said to be a headless brakeman looking for his lost head (Walser 1980:50–52). In many places, a headless horseman—or now a headless motorcyclist or little old lady in a VW—rides over back roads at night. In certain graveyards, a monument or statue may carry a curse, so that those who touch or sit on it will soon suffer death or misfortune; if vandalized, the stone will magically heal itself.

Roads used for parking may collect such legends, particularly about a parent figure, crazed or disfigured in some way, who will try to interrupt couples' lovemaking and attempt to murder them or scare them away (Samuelson 1979). In some cases, a mystery animal like a werewolf or goat-man is believed to appear to visitors (Harling 1971), or a strange force is said to pull cars uphill or off railroad tracks (Glazer in Bennett and Smith 1989:165–177). Such legends do not keep teens away from the legendary spots but, paradoxically, function as dares that excite repeated visits to invoke danger.

The visit is usually made by automobile, and illegal drinking, recreational drug use, and sexual experimentation are integral parts of the "trip" (Ellis 1983). Legend trips typically have a three-part structure. First, as the site is often remote from the teens' home neighborhoods, the group will spend time on the way there sharing "origin legends" about why the site is haunted and "proof legends" about spooky things that supposedly happened on previous visits. During these storytelling sessions, participants may add other migratory legends popular among teens: "The Hook," "The Baby-sitter and the Man Upstairs," and the like (Hall in Dégh 1980:225–257).

Second, on arrival, members of the group will dare each other to act out the part of the legend said to put them into danger. Sometimes this may involve no more than turning off the car motor or leaving the security of the vehicle, but many traditions involve further ritual actions. These may include honking the car horn or blinking its lights a certain number of times, calling out the entity's name, sitting on a "cursed" grave marker or stone seat, or walking around a monument backward. In some cases, the tradition may include a dramatic ordeal, such as standing inside a railroad tunnel as a train rushes through. The trip often climaxes when something unexpected happens—a noise, a sudden wind, even a prearranged hoax by friends of one of the group—and the visit often ends with a panicked retreat to the car.

Finally, the group members share their various perceptions of what has happened, and in retrospect the visit may inspire personal-experience narratives that enter tradition as additional "proof legends." Even negative accounts of visits may inspire further visits, but in general the tradition generates a "suspension of disbelief" necessary to create the right mood for future trips.

This ritual is similar to an older British tradition of visiting holy wells and ancient stone monuments on certain dates such as May Day. A number of historical sources note that such visits were characterized by drinking, lovemaking, and brawls (Bord and Bord 1985:56, 75). In modern times, many legends have been collected from youthful British informants, describing visits to sites where the devil (or an evil ghost) could be raised by performing rituals like running around a tomb or megalith or calling out the entity's name. As in American lore, many monuments carry a curse: Anyone who moves or damages them will suffer harm, and the stone will magically move back (Grinsell 1976:64–65). Here, too, such legends seem to have encouraged, not discouraged, ritual visits.

In recent times, evidence left by legend trips has been taken by some American law-enforcement agents as evidence for dangerous cults. Some trips may climax in a party around a bonfire with singing and dancing, and such trips often lead to acts of vandalism, ranging from spray-painted obscene or "satanic" graffiti to destruction of stone crosses and gravestones. In some instances, road-killed animals have been hung in trees as "sacrifices," and groups of teens may frighten each other or adults by dressing in black robes and jumping out in front of cars. Such activities, misunderstood by police, may cause local panics, and some teens may prolong the sensation through hoaxes or by actually performing improvised rites of "devil worship" at legend-trip sites (Ellis, in Richardson, Best, and Bromley 1991:279–295).

Studies of legend-trip participants, however, suggest that the ritual is seen mainly as a form of entertainment, and, in fact, the events narrated and experienced have trivial impact on adolescents' belief systems. Teens are attracted to many other forms of play behavior involving role playing: seances, Halloween costuming and visits to institutional haunted houses, and imaginative games like the Ouija board and Dungeons and Dragons (see Fine 1983). Despite its alarming and frequently damaging aftermath, the legend trip is best understood as part of the "ritual of rebellion" that is a normal part of most adolescents' culture.

Bill Ellis

References

Bennett, Gillian, and Paul Smith, eds. 1989. *The Questing Beast: Perspectives on Contemporary Legend.* Vol. 4. Sheffield, England: Sheffield Academic Press.

Bird, S. Elizabeth. 1994. Playing with Fear: Interpreting the Adolescent Legend Trip. *Western Folklore* 53:191–209.

Bord, Janet, and Colin Bord. 1985. *Sacred Waters: Holy Wells and Water Lore in Britain and Ireland.* London: Grenada.

Dégh, Linda, ed. 1980. *Indiana Folklore: A Reader.* Bloomington: Indiana University Press.

Ellis. Bill. 1983. Adolescent Legend-Tripping. *Psychology Today* (August): 68–69.

Fine, Gary Alan. 1983. *Shared Fantasy: Role-Playing Games as Social Worlds.* Chicago: University of Chicago Press.

Grinsell, Leslie V. 1976. *Folklore of Prehistoric Sites in Britain.* North Pomfret, VT: David and Charles.

Harling, Kristie. 1971. The Grunch: An Example of New Orleans Teen-Age Folklore. *Louisiana Folklore Miscellany* 3:15–20.

Richardson, James T., Joel Best, and David G. Bromley. 1991. *The Satanism Scare.* New York: Aldine de Gruyter.

Samuelson, Sue. 1979. The White Witch: An Analysis of an Adolescent Legend. *Indiana Folklore* 12:18–37.

Walser, Richard. 1980. *North Carolina Legends.* Raleigh: North Carolina Department of Cultural Resources.

See also Legend; Urban Legend

Lesbians

The community of homosexual women whose folk traditions serve to isolate them from the larger community and to encourage cohesion within their group. The folk traditions of lesbians may be examined against the backdrop of the American lesbian movement. This movement has three stages: 1950–1967 was the butch-femme era; 1968–1974 the transitional era; and 1975 into the 1990s is the lesbian-feminist era. The collected folklore falls into three major categories: verbal traditions, customary traditions, and material traditions.

With the development of the lesbian movement in the 1950s, homosexual women became more visible to one another in the lesbian and gay bars. Folk speech was one product of that visibility. The terms "butch" and "femme" refer to lesbian roles predominantly in the White working-class subculture. These roles represent the possibilities of what it means to be a woman. Joan Nestle, an archivist, author, and a femme who came out in the 1950s defines butch-femme relationships as "an erotic partnership serving both as a conspicuous flag of rebellion and an intimate exploration of women's sexuality"

(Nestle 1987:101). An array of variations occurs in folk speech: "butch," for example, gave rise to "soft butch" (a less severe image), "baby butch" (a new lesbian), and "outbutched" (drawing attention to one's self). The terms "dyke" and "queer" are examples of folk speech that during the butch-femme era were derogatory, but in the lesbian-feminist movement have been reclaimed as terms of pride. One example of a new term coming into circulation is "festi-virgin" (one who attends a women's music festival for the first time). Folk speech also identifies those persons outside the lesbian community, as "straights," "hets," and "breeders," for example.

Expressions in circulation in the 1990s include "dykes for days" (seeing a lot of dykes in unexpected places such as the grocery store), and "she goes to my church" (she's a lesbian). Expressions also include initialized terms such as "d.p." (dyke potential).

Word play displays the lesbian communities' verbal humor. Examples include "no homo" (said when the other party did not answer the phone), "gaily forward" (used when giving directions), and "straightening up" (when cleaning the house, to get rid of anything that reveals one's lesbian identity).

During the butch-femme era, one fascinating area of folk speech emerged in the form of naming. A group of butches would give one another masculine names such as "Bob." Butches used these names only when they were in a group by themselves, refusing to use the masculine names in other settings, including at home. This restriction was a caution against revealing one's lesbianism. A masculine name from the group was a sign of affection and signaled acceptance. A group could have only one of each name, so there never could be two "Bobs." All names were short and simple. Using "brother" instead of a name was acceptable. Femmes never received folk names. As a stigmatized minority, lesbians feel special about themselves when using folk speech as they possess something no other minority or majority group possesses. As an insulator from outsiders, the specialized vocabulary is reflective of community mores, reflecting a desire to maintain secrecy.

Coming-out stories of lesbians are often repeated and requested as personal-experience narratives. Coming-out stories reveal one's lesbianism. These narratives are told primarily to other lesbians, often when they are becoming acquainted. Each lesbian has an initial coming-out story, and more follow as she continually declares her lesbian identity to an increasingly wider circle of people. Lesbians often request another's coming-out story, and retelling of coming-out stories reinforces a lesbian's identity.

Festivals are one type of customary folklore celebrated by lesbians. Festivals are especially important as they mark the beginning of the lesbian-feminist era. The Michigan Womyn's Music Festival ("womyn" being a folk spelling used to erase the masculine reference) was the first in 1975, and it continues annually. This occasion marks the first time in history that a large group of lesbians were visible to one another. Thousands of lesbians attended the festival, which featured camping, womyn's music, workshops, and other forms of entertainment. Lesbians from different segments of the population had the chance to meet and compare ideas. Folklore abounds during festivals; they have recently instituted rituals—for example, a conception ritual in which a lesbian is artifically inseminated. Vendors name their booths in womyn-identified language, such as the "womb" (health tent). Festivals like the Michigan one range from the East to the West Coasts.

The three most widely practiced customary celebrations among lesbians are anniversaries, bondings, and baby showers. Lesbians celebrate their relationship on one or two days per year. The most common anniversary marker is the day a couple first made love. A second marker is the day a couple met. Anniversary celebrations are usually quiet, with a dinner at home or in a restaurant where the partners exchange gifts.

Lesbians celebrate bondings as a way to unite couples in the eyes of the lesbian community. The bonding is based on "womyn's spirituality," a spirituality embraced by many lesbians. Guests bring presents, and after the ceremony a potdinner follows with womyn's music and dancing. With more lesbians having babies, baby showers became common celebrations, and lesbians, like all parents, send birth announcements when their babies are born.

Costumes clearly follow the lesbian movement, with each era having a distinct costume type. Costumes fall into three major categories according to one's role: butch, femme, and what is often termed "just me." The latter phrase refers to lesbians who do not follow a stereotyped role and who simply dress as they personally wish.

The original butch-femme costumes were popular in the 1950s and 1960s. Women then wore these costumes only to gay and lesbian bars and to private parties. The butch proudly wore a man's suit, socks, and shoes, while the femme did not wear a costume but wore what a heterosexual woman would wear at the time. One common belief at the time was that a woman could be arrested for cross-dressing if she did not wear at least three pieces of women's clothing. As a result, women would leave home in their everyday clothes and stop near the bar or party to dress. Such a law does not seem to be on record and may be regarded as a form of urban legend. Other items completed the costume, including a pinky ring, a watch worn low on the wrist and turned face down, a large belt buckle worn on the side, and one clip-on earring.

Costume, thus, was what one wore as well as *how* one wore it. Cigarettes were also a feature of the costume, with the butches smoking Marlboros and Winstons; some menthols were considered "too femme." Only gruff lesbians or "diesel dykes" smoked unfiltered cigarettes such as Camels.

During the transition era of the lesbian movement, costume underwent many changes. Butches softened their appearance, and one common costume was jeans, a flannel shirt, bib overalls, and hiking boots. Lesbians referred to this look as "dressed down." Femmes, however, made little change in their costume traditions, except to follow the ever-changing fashions worn by heterosexuals.

With the lesbian-feminist era came further costume changes. The once distinctive butch and femme costumes then became similar and androgynous. Some lesbians wore T-shirts boasting "I Got This Way from Kissing Girls," and extremely baggy pants or "parachute pants" were new choices. Variety in costume became the hallmark of the lesbian-feminist era. Jewelry had always been popular, but now there was a large selection of lesbian-feminist jewelry made by lesbians, such as a "labrys," which looks like a double-headed axe, worn to symbolize one's lesbian identity. The androgynous look signals the increasing acceptance of lesbians into American society, a goal of the lesbian-feminist political era.

As lesbians became more visible to the public through the political process, they modified their costumes to resemble more closely mainstream and middle-class values, but avoided female markers such as high heels and makeup while maintaining marks of membership, especially in jewelry. It may be that the shift to mainstream exemplifies the acceptance of lesbians by American society.

Lesbian folklore changed during the three eras of the lesbian movement, although some changes did not coincide with the specific eras themselves. As time progressed, lesbian folklore became less like "defensive masquerading" and more like "pride in self." Lesbian folklore exists for the most part within the community; in fact, much of it is meaningless outside of this context. Thus, members of the lesbian community have found a method to mark themselves as belonging to a group that encourages group cohesion.

Jan Laude

References

Adam, Barry. 1987. *The Rise and Fall of a Gay and Lesbian Movement.* Boston: Twayne.

Faderman, Lillian. 1991. *Odd Girls and Twilight Lovers: A History of Lesbian Life in Twentieth Century America.* New York: Columbia University Press.

Katz, Johnathan. 1976. *Gay American History: Lesbians and Gay Men in the U.S.A.* New York: Thomas Crowell.

———. 1983. *Gay-Lesbian Almanac: A New Documentary.* New York: Harper and Row.

Krieger, Susan. 1983. *The Mirror Dance: Identity in a Women's Community.* Philadelphia: Temple University Press.

Laude, Jan. 1991. *Folklore as an Instrument of Stigma; Folklore as an Instrument of Liberation: The Case of Lesbian Coding.* Ph.D. diss., Indiana University.

Nestle, Joan. 1987. *A Restricted Country.* Ithaca, NY: Firebrand.

See also Feminist Approaches to Folklore; Gay Men

Life History

A written account of a person's life based on spoken conversations and interviews. This genre has had an awkward history in the discipline of folklore. For many years, folklorists saw storytellers as the bearers of tradition they did not own. Among other folklore texts, life histories were regarded as a collective representation of a group rather than a personal possession of individuals. When folklorists realized that the ballad singer or storyteller was recognized by his or her own community and very much aware of his or her role in the culture, they began to ask questions about the individual lives and the influences on lives, in order to help explain the role of the legend or ballad in the folk group. Thus, the life of the "performer" became important in collecting and evaluating the text (and became a required appendix to all studies). Thus, the study of folklore evolved from studying only the text to integrating the person's life history into the text as well.

A life history may be defined in many ways: It could be told as an oral text or narrative, responding to a prepared questionnaire and interviewer; it could be the product of an intensive analytic conversation between folklorist and informant; or it could come close to spontaneous narration, with the folklorist trying to minimize his or her influence on the natural context and to allow the informant free expression. It may be argued that life history is all three; it starts off as a question-and-answer session, then, as the folklorist feeds questions, conversation follows. The narrator continues to add to the narrative, which is then processed through inspiration and becomes self-reflective. As folklorists recognize this reflexive construction of a life, new interest in this genre has arisen.

As most scholars of life history agree, the success of the interview process then depends on the personalities of the folklorist and the informant, on the framing of questions and the listening to the answers. The folklorist needs to be a sophisticated listener, understanding that memory is selective and that the teller of the life history is a different person than he or she was thirty, twenty, or even three years ago. Often the individual may not realize or want to realize these differences. The life history becomes a curious fiction fused with fact, as people make order out of their memories as they account for who they are in the present. Life histories, then, have much to offer, as they allow the interviewer to go beyond mere facts. The goal of a life history is not to chronicle every last detail, but to affirm the identity of the informant in the act of the telling; what the informant thinks of himself or herself, and why he or she continues to sing ballads, quilt, or use folk medicine to heal others contributes to a broader biographical pattern that transcends any specific culture.

Hanna Griff

References

Dolby Stahl, Sandra. 1977. The Personal Narrative as Folklore. *Journal of American Folklore* 90:9–30.

Titon, Jeff Todd. 1980. The Life Story. *Journal of American Folklore* 93:276–292.

See also History, Folk; Personal-Experience Story

Linscott, Eloise Hubbard (1897–1978)

Collector of New England folksongs, ballads, folk dances, and folk music whose anthology, *Folk Songs of Old New England*, has as its core repertoire the music traditions of her own family. Published to enthusiastic reviews in the heyday of New England ballad studies, Linscott's book stands out for the lively treatment of its contents and its useful organization. At a time when the Child ballad took center stage in serious publications of Anglo American traditional folksongs, Linscott divided her collection into four sections with items ordered alphabetically within each: "Singing Games"; "The Country Dance"; "Sea Chanteys and Fo'castle Songs"; and "Ballads, Folk Songs, and Ditties"—an ordering that met her "sole purpose to preserve the music that abounds in New England." Linscott provided more than 160 tunes, for she wanted "a songbook you can take to the piano when the family gather round and sing." But as an insider to the tradition, she also wanted her descriptions of the singing and dancing to bring the music alive. She hoped to honor the music of her ancestors and at the same time keep it going.

A good singer and musician herself, Linscott knew the music intimately, and her documentary instincts mirrored that of her contemporaries among ballad scholars. Her book contains social information that is lacking in the great majority of prior traditional-music publications. She gives detailed directions for playing a singing game or calling a dance; descriptions of singing style; headnotes on the item's history; and background information on the artists. Linscott took courage from the advice of Phillips Barry. He "was my guide," she once explained. "I had no idea of what I was doing until I met him. To me it was just my family music, nothing of great significance." Apparently, Barry found her closeness to the tradition to be an advantage. "Phillips Barry told me that because I didn't have a professionally trained ear, I could hear things others didn't."

Linscott began collecting because she "couldn't find our songs in any music books." She was a natural fieldworker. On a typical field trip, she "would go to a dance. I would learn the dance that's their favorite by watching and dancing. If it was a good fiddler, I would ask the fiddler to play the tune off the dance floor. I never took anything down the first time. At our family's summer camp there was a woman, 76 years old, I'd write down what she sang and to make it more natural, I'd write down mine, too. It is necessary to realize that folk music cannot be tampered with," she emphasized. "It must be recorded from each individual as accurately as possible." Phillips Barry died before she completed her manuscript, "so I asked his friend, James Carpenter," then teaching at Harvard University, "to write an introduction." Carpenter was an expert in sailor-song traditions, and his essay maintains Linscott's standard of informality.

As so often happens with the publication of scarce material, Linscott's book "jogged many a memory, and [I was] led a merry way to a rich Harvest of Yankee music." She continued collecting, prevailing upon the Library of Congress for the loan of "half-way decent recording equipment." The resulting fieldwork yielded a generous return, including Shaker music, Portuguese music, and Indian songs and dances. Frustrated at her failure to interest publishers in a second volume, she began lecturing at regional music societies, women's clubs, and arts organizations. She would bring informants, and all would dress in colonial or native garb for their performances. She organized two large New England festivals, the first at the Boston Arena and the other at the Boston Garden, at which she proudly presented her favorite artists. "I brought Arthur Walden and Princess Metosanya, the Wampanoag Tribe's last royal princess—all traditional music." She believed that "it was

the first time anything like that was shown in New England."

Born in Taunton, Massachusetts, on the next to the last day of 1897 to a local physician and his wife, Hubbard graduated from Wellesley College in 1920, married businessman Charles Linscott, and moved to Needham, Massachusetts, where she lived until her death in 1978. She described lifelong family evenings when her father would tell Bible stories and then everyone would sing. "My family ran a camp in New Hampshire for forty years," she said. "We often had dances there, and most of the musicians knew a lot of fiddle tunes and dances." Once she started collecting, she said, "people were always very interested in letting me hear their songs."

Having given up her hope of publishing a sequel, Linscott settled for establishing her claim in a brief summary of her unpublished data in the preface to the second edition of *Folk Songs of Old New England*. In addition to her Indian materials, Linscott was particularly proud of having collected from Carrie Grover of Gorham, Maine, "what she didn't sing she played on her fiddle from a repertoire of more than 400 songs," she wrote. Linscott bequeathed her collection to the Archive of Folk Culture at the Library of Congress.

Linda Morley

Editor's Note

Quoted material not from Linscott's book is from the author's 1973 interview with the subject.

Local-Character Anecdote
A brief, usually humorous, narrative describing the odd behavior of an eccentric person well known in his or her community. The local-character anecdote may vary from a lengthy story about an episode in the life of the local character—in which case it borders on the genre of the local legend—to a brief description of a single action that implies a mutual understanding on the part of teller and audience.

Though the term "local-character anecdote" has occasionally been used to describe narratives of the history and behavior of prominent, successful individuals, it is probably best reserved for stories about eccentric, possibly disruptive, individuals who regularly violate community norms of appearance, way of life, and behavior. In contrast to other narrative categories, the term centers not on the ontological status of the narrative—as do "legend," "memorate," or "personal-experience narrative"—but on the narrative's central subject. The anecdotes may, therefore, vary greatly in length, amount of detail and exposition, type of framing devices, and amount of personal commentary by the narrator.

The local character was first defined by Richard M. Dorson on the basis of character traits: low cunning, effrontery, chicanery, verbal cleverness, offbeat talent, shiftlessness, parsimony, degeneracy, stubbornness, stupidity, or gullibility (Dorson 1964:23). Sandra K.D. Stahl has added "grossness" of appearance or behavior (Stahl 1975:286), so it is apparent that narratives of local characters revolve around excess, whether of behavior, living conditions, or appearance, and around conflict between the main character and the community in which he or she lives.

More remarkable, perhaps, is the common occurrence of repetition and reinforcement in these narratives. It is rare for a local character to be defined by only one of these characteristics; more frequently, the character has two or more, often a physical characteristic reinforced by a behavioral one, so that the subject may be unbelievably filthy *and* an enormous eater, may be physically deformed *and* a consummate liar, may dress in castoffs *and* invent bizarre contraptions. These contrastive replications serve to underscore the character's marginal status by simultaneously objectifying his or her physical being while describing behavior that confronts social norms.

The narratives themselves have a clear functionality, whatever the relationship between teller and audience. If told to outsiders, the narrative is likely to be framed by statements critical of the local character that clearly identify the narrator as upholder of community norms, the local character as outsider or deviant (Mullen 1988). Yet, the narratives are also likely to be prefaced by an explanation of the causes of the deviant behavior; local characters are frequently described as having undergone massive physical or psychological trauma through war, accident, disease, or birth defect. In this way, the community may seek to apologize for or rationalize its marginalization of the local character by identifying external causes for the character's behavior.

If told within the community shared by narrator and subject, the local-character anecdote serves to reinforce the shared values of the participants, at the same time continuing to marginalize the local character. In fact, the anecdotes may often be trimmed to the briefest of descriptors so that an anecdote might be as attenuated as "You won't believe what Lefty did this time—carried home all the boards from the outhouse we tore down." Another common opening frame uses an encompassing "it" ("Lefty really did it this time" or "Lefty did it again") to objectify the character further in terms of a set of repetitive behaviors marked by social deviance. In fact, the community may even refer to these capsule anecdotes—which, of course, imply a shared knowledge of the character's background, habits, living and working conditions, and particular set of eccentricities—by the character's name: "Have you heard the latest 'Lefty'?" The local character then becomes, in effect, his or her own set of narratives; to the community, he or she may seem to live in anecdote more clearly than in real life.

Local-character anecdotes bear close resemblance to narratives of trickster figures who confront community standards; the local character's freedom constitutes an implicit critique that reveals simultaneously the value-laden basis of those standards and the potential consequences of departing from them. As trickster, the local character challenges and disrupts by demonstrating the rigidity and artificiality of social norms and by suggesting the possibility of violating them; in this sense, the local character not only proves a mischievous and entertaining source of disruption, but also demonstrates exactly the community's rules for behavior and the interrelationships among those rules.

These functional interpretations are at the center of the scholarship on local-character anecdotes. Where Patrick B.

Mullen (1988) uses theories derived from the sociology of deviance and labeling theory to describe the boundaries drawn between local characters and members of their communities, Diane Tye sees the anecdotes as allowing residents to clarify their "group of shared values" (Tye 1982:47), adding that the narratives are "not only cathartic for residents but . . . reify other guidelines of expected social behavior" (Tye 1987:106). Further, local characters through narrative may act as "agents of social control," guarding against those who may seek inappropriately to advance themselves at the expense of their neighbors (Tye 1987:107).

More subtly, narratives of local characters may, according to Tye (1989), mediate oppositions within the community: individualism versus conformity, homogeneity versus heterogeneity, hospitality versus distrust of outsiders, fear of deviance versus concern for the less fortunate. At the same time, the anecdotes may also provide reassurance for residents that the community is concerned for everyone and will care for them if misfortune occurs.

As Tye (1982) also points out, local characters are capable of recognizing, building upon, and exploiting their status through role-playing, storytelling, stylized performance, or cooperation with other members of the community, who may in turn create performative grounds where the local character can interact with—and possibly embarrass—outsiders. Communities frequently beset with visitors—tourists, salespeople, travelers—may thus use a local character as an ironic symbol of themselves to make fun of the outsider's assumption that everyone in the community behaves in this way.

In structure, the local-character anecdote usually proceeds, as Stahl has said, "from a normal stance to an abnormal extreme stance through the direct channel of one-tracked, almost surreal 'logic'" (Stahl 1975:290). The narrative carries the listener from everyday activity to the unpredictable or bizarre; the local character sets out to buy a loaf of bread but winds up buying cat food for a circus lion. This narrative pattern, then, suggests the escalating consequences of deviation from established patterns of behavior.

Similarly, many local characters have a body of narrative assigned them from sources in other genres (Peck 1992). A local character ("the Champion") known for his lying abilities may have attributed to him the well-established folktale (Tale Type 1920B) in which an acquaintance asks him to tell a lie but is told that there isn't time because a relative is injured, ill, or dead. When the instigator later passes the Champion's house, he sees the healthy relative sitting on the porch with the Champion. In this instance, the local character becomes a center of accretion for local legends and for more widely distributed tales. This process may be especially noticeable after the death or departure of the local character, who may gain with time a quasi-legendary status. The narratives may also focus and concentrate thematic elements so that the local character becomes progressively less eccentric and more purposeful in confronting authority, reinforcing local customs, or gulling outsiders.

In American narrative communities, the local character may be further marginalized by membership in a minority or ethnic group, by gender or age or physical handicap, by education or economic status. The narrative treatment of such persons may then combine with stereotyping to reflect the boundary-making power of narrative and its capacity to isolate as well as to incorporate.

David H. Stanley

References

Baker, Ronald. 1982. *Hoosier Folk Legends.* Bloomington: Indiana University Press.

Dorson, Richard M. 1964. *Buying the Wind.* Chicago: University of Chicago Press.

Mullen, Patrick B. 1988. *I Heard the Old Fisherman Say.* 2d. ed. Logan: Utah State University Press.

Peck, Catherine. 1992. Local Character Anecdotes Down East. *North Carolina Folklore Journal* 39:63–71.

Stahl, Sandra K.D. 1975. The Local Character Anecdote. *Genre* 8:283–302.

Tye, Diane. 1982. The Role of Watson Weaver, Itinerant Pedlar and Local Character, in His Community of Northern Nova Scotia. *Culture and Tradition* 6:40–51.

———. 1987. Aspects of the Local Character Phenomenon in a Nova Scotian Community. *Canadian Folklore canadien* 9:99–111.

———. 1989. Local Character Anecdotes: A Nova Scotia Case Study. *Western Folklore* 48:181–199.

See also Anecdote; Legend; Trickster

Loggers

Or "lumberjacks," hewers of forest trees, men engaged in lumbering. Logger folklore, shaped by both the social structure and experiences of industrial labor and the uncontrollable forces of the natural world, includes the full range of oral narrative and musical traditions; the ritualistic behavior of customs; and the tangible expressions of work-related material culture. Historically, American logger folklore has occurred in rural contexts dominated by skilled male laborers working seasonally under dangerous conditions. Logging has followed a resource-dependent and market-driven migrating frontier of timber production, starting in the 18th-century maritime states and moving over two centuries to the Upper Midwest, the Deep South, and finally the Pacific Northwest. Lumbering continues in all regions, although the Northwest's logging subculture remains the most concentrated social base for occupational traditions.

Three things have profoundly shaped everyday logger life and, by extension, the content and performance of logger folklore. First, the labor force has always been ethnically diverse and discontinuous: Canadian Francophone loggers joined Irish descendants in the Northeast and the Midwest; African Americans joined Whites in the Deep South; and repeated infusions of Scandinavians poured into the woods of the Midwest and the Northwest. Second, the changing social context of work has led to an increasingly fragmented sense of sociability, as isolated, all-male logging camps evolved into company towns characterized by the domestic order of married

employees, which in turn became the dispersed commuter—oriented subculture of the late 20th century. Moreover, divisions exist between union-oriented loggers who work for corporate giants such as Weyerhaeuser and those who work for small, independent, contract loggers whose entrepreneurial activities are often run by family members. Third, logging as commodity production in the outdoor world of forest environments leads to a profession that is inherently dangerous and difficult, as workers must adjust to changing conditions of weather, terrain, and ecosystem. Combined with workers' reactions to popular imagery of the American logger (for example, the public persona of Paul Bunyan), these three factors have shaped occupational traditions that stress the nature of shared work experience and identity and the distinctiveness of logging as a means of employment.

The greatest proportion of logger folklore is verbal in nature and decidedly colorful and poetic in style. Loggers have developed one of the richest occupational jargons known. Names exist for virtually all aspects of the job. People who worked in the woods prior to 1900 usually called themselves "shantyboys," "woodsmen," "loggers," and "lumbermen"; the use of the term "lumberjack" is more recent, with its popularity derived primarily from turn-of-the-century literary and journalistic accounts of the industry. Woodsworkers in the Northwest in the 1990s usually call themselves loggers and, to a lesser extent among themselves, "timberbeasts" or "brush apes." Naming of work technology, job titles, job situations, or specific individuals is often crude, masculine, associated directly or metaphorically with flora and fauna, and occasionally derived from an older lingua franca, such as Chinook jargon. Before the demise of camps, nicknames were universal ("Roughouse Dixon," "Pig-face Joe"). A "bullbuck" is the boss of men who cut trees; a "nosebag" is a lunch bucket; "corks" are boots with spikes in the soles to give secure footing on slippery logs; "Skookum" is Chinook jargon for big, strong, good. Expressions also abound: "Ground so steep even the ants wear cork shoes." Knowledge of this esoteric language is considered crucial for acceptance into the occupational group.

Storytelling has served important functions among loggers, from entertainment, to education, to the expression of worker ideology. In the Northwest, stories are commonly told while "logging," a traditional category of conversational talk in which workers review the history, humor, and business of logging. Personal-experience stories of "close calls" on the job serve to remind workers of the constant perils of the profession, while other narratives detail the heroic feats of loggers who solve work problems through tenacity, brute strength, or ingenuity. Paul Bunyan has, in fact, probably never been a common subject of logger tales, although the Bunyanesque image is pervasive in statues, parades, and community festivals. "Lies" are a category of often humorous stories that are either greatly exaggerated or wholly fictitious sometimes include traditional motifs from tall tales; examples include hunting anecdotes; pranks played on government personnel sent to monitor loggers' activities; and Scandinavian-dialect stories. Tales of the legendary Bigfoot are sometimes considered "lies" since they involve jokes or pranks played on other loggers or

HARPER'S WEEKLY.

WOOD-SAWYERS' TOURNAMENT AT LAFAYETTE, INDIANA.—DRAWN BY C. G. BUSH.—[SEE PAGE 758.]

outsiders (occasionally involving the practice of fabricating large footprints); however, many serious stories of encounters with this hairy, simian-like monster also are told by workers in more private contexts and reflect their concern with the mysteries of wild, forested areas.

Studies and well-annotated collections of logger songs and ballads are legion. While loggers had no tradition of singing during work, there is anecdotal evidence of their leisure-time singing activities, especially in the isolated camps of the Northeast and the Midwest prior to World War I. Of the dozens of songs recorded by folklorists, many appear to be anonymous and traditional, derived from the Irish-influenced song tradition of Maritime Canada; still other songs, as documented by Edward Ives, were written by specific individuals, such as Joe Scott and Larry Gorman, who worked in the Northeastern woods. Stylistically, such music was sung in a loud, hard voice by a single individual, unaccompanied by instruments, and had a declamando ending (a spoken last line). Many of the best singers were said to be of Irish descent, whose repertoires included traditional British broadside and Native American ballads as well as logging-related songs. Thematically, the occupational songs focused on the dramatic events of lumbering, such as accidental drownings on river drives ("The Jam on Gerry's Rock," "Peter Emberly"); nights on the town ("The Green Mountain Boys"); or the general nature of woodswork and camp life ("A Shantyman's Life").

In the late 20th century, the legacy of logger song making as entertainment has practically vanished, a victim of radios, literacy, and the demise of logging camps in favor of private homes. Songs that address the same themes are still written by loggers, but they are released as commercial productions. The expression of sentiment is now likely to be found in written poetry that appears in trade journals and privately printed publications. Older workers in particular have taken the jargon, legends, and customs of the industry to make nostalgic, humorous, or political statements on the realities of everyday life for loggers past and present.

It can be argued that among the customs of logging, the process of learning technical work skills is traditional in the apprentice-like fashion in which new workers watch, imitate, and ask questions of more experienced loggers. Included in this process are the kinds of beliefs and warnings one might expect in a dangerous occupation (such as cold hands or feet the night before work are a sign of death or injury). Other work-site customs include initiation rites, such as sending greenhorns in search of imaginary tools (a "sky hook," a "cable stretcher"). Pranks are commonly played on all members of a work crew, the loggers constantly testing and reinforcing their solidarity and using humor to lessen the tensions of a difficult occupation. One custom occurs in front of entire logging communities and even tourists and resembles the ritualistic events of American rodeos. The "log show" is an occupational festival, featuring parades, foods, music, charity auctions, and especially playful competitions based on the work skills and athleticism of local loggers.

Logger folklore also includes material expressions of work culture. The most conspicuous aspect of Northwest logger identity is their distinctive traditional attire, worn both at work and at various public occasions. No logger is complete without striped "hickory" shirt, "stagged" pants (which have the hems cut off for safety reasons), suspenders, and "cork" shoes. Additionally, dioramas of work settings using finely crafted wood or metal models, and large chainsaw carvings of wood figures have become increasingly popular. Both of these examples of folk art demonstrate technical knowledge and a feeling for form and beauty according to logger aesthetics, expressed through the creator's skills and creativity as derived from work experience.

On an everyday level, participation in the seriousness and humor of logger song making, storytelling, and customs has helped bind together individuals who must work a dangerous job under adverse conditions. Folklore also plays a significant role in negotiating logger identity and ideology, as it articulates traditional occupational values of hard work, independence, and creativity. Logger traditions demand acknowledgement of the importance and distinctiveness of woodswork apart from all other means of employment. With the ascendancy of environmental concerns since the 1960s and 1970s and the activities of loggers under increased public scrutiny, these traditions have assumed a more political role, as songs, customs, and poetry are used with more frequency in public forums to present a positive image of loggers to the outside world, and consequently change public opinion of their controversial profession.

Significant archival collections of logger lore include the Northeast Archives of Folklore and Oral History at the University of Maine, Orono, and the Randall V. Mills Archive of Northwest Folklore at the University of Oregon.

Robert E. Walls

References

Bethke, Robert E. 1981. *Adirondack Voices: Woodsmen and Woodslore.* Urbana: University of Illinois Press.

Dorson, Richard M. 1973. Lumberjacks. In *America in Legend: Folklore from the Colonial Period to the Present.* New York: Pantheon.

Ives, Edward D. 1978. *Joe Scott: The Woodsman-Songmaker.* Urbana: University of Illinois Press.

James-Duguid, Charlene. 1985. Orofino Lumberjack Days. In *Idaho Folklife: From Homesteads to Headstones,* ed. Louie W. Attebery. Salt Lake City: University of Utah Press.

Leary, James P. 1991. Loggers. In *Midwestern Folk Humor.* Little Rock, AR: August House.

Schrager, Samuel, ed. 1991. Folklore. *Forest and Conservation History* (Special Issue) 35:4–30.

Toelken, Barre. 1979. *The Dynamics of Folklore.* Boston: Houghton Mifflin.

Walls, Robert E. 1987. Logger Poetry and the Expression of Worldview. *Northwest Folklore* 5:15–45.

Lomax, John Avery (1867–1948)

American folksong collector and compiler of popular collections of folksongs. Born in Goodman, Mississippi, in 1867, Lomax was the youngest of seven children of James Avery Lomax, a farmer, and Susan (Frances) Copper Lomax, both natives of Georgia. In 1869 the family moved west by wagon, establishing a farm on the Bosque River in central Texas.

Lomax sometimes portrayed himself as a Westerner, sometimes a Southerner, and he sometimes stressed his childhood on his father's small ranch on the Chisholm Trail. He asserted that he was the offspring of "the upper crust of the 'po' white trash', traditionally held in contempt by the aristocracy of the Old South and by their Negro slaves." He grew up singing the camp-meeting hymns of Southern Methodists and listening to cowboy stories and songs.

An avid reader, at age twenty Lomax was able to pursue higher education at a nearby Methodist institution, Granbury College, after selling his pet pony to help pay for his education. He could afford only the one-year program Granbury offered; it is not clear, however, that he wanted to stay longer. Granbury offered courses from grade school through college stressing recitation and rote learning; its rigid rules, Lomax recalled, made the college students feel "just as if they were first graders." Weatherford College, another Methodist institution, regarded Lomax's year at Granbury as adequate preparation for a teaching position. He taught there for six years but remained eager for a broader education and a wider view of the world. In 1895, at the age of twenty-eight, he fulfilled his dream of enrolling at the University of Texas in Austin, where he completed his B.A. in two years.

Lomax struggled to fulfill his scholarly ambitions as he coped with the need to earn a living. Despite his academic achievements, he had to postpone advanced academic training and look for work. Lomax cultivated a wide range of contacts at the University of Texas, and he landed a position as a secretary to the president of the university, which included responsibilities as registrar and steward of men's dormitories. After six years at this position, in 1903 Lomax accepted an appointment as instructor at Texas Agricultural and Mechanical College, where President David F. Houston recognized him as a gifted teacher and promising scholar. Houston helped arrange for Lomax to study at Harvard University for a year and provided that he would receive a third of his salary while on leave. In 1907 Lomax earned an M.A. in English.

While at Harvard, studying with Barrett Wendell and George Lyman Kittredge, Lomax discovered that these men, unlike the educated elite of Texas, valued the indigenous folklore of his native state. They were impressed with the cowboy songs that Lomax had been writing down since childhood, and they arranged for him to receive three summer Sheldon Fellowships from Harvard so he could travel throughout the Western cattle country collecting songs. Lomax wrote letters to editors of newspapers throughout the West announcing his desire to preserve and publish cowboy songs. The extensive correspondence brought him into contact with numerous carriers of cowboy tradition and with first-person accounts of cowboy life and singing.

Lomax's *Cowboy Songs and Other Frontier Ballads* ([1910] 1986) was a path-breaking book that quickly became part of Western lore as it helped spread the oral tradition and led to new variations of familiar songs. The book contributed to the shaping of a national mythos surrounding the cowboy and to the view that Americans had a distinctive national folklore. Former President Theodore Roosevelt, in his Preface, and Barrett Wendell, in his Introduction, added their prestige to Lomax's argument that cowboys represented endangered American values of mobility, freedom, and individualism. They saw in cowboy songs a recapitulation on American soil of processes that had earlier created English ballads.

Lomax tried to make his cowboy materials fit the academic definition of the ballad: a song telling a story, produced by a homogeneous group, without authorship or date, passed on by word of mouth, and impersonal in tone. But it was difficult to make this definition fit, and it became increasingly so as his interests turned to African American song. The dominant assumption was that ballads were no longer being created and that the only ones in America were survivals from elsewhere. Lomax's argument that the term "ballad" could be applied to living materials was a radical attempt to stretch the term.

The critical success of *Cowboy Songs* did not ease Lomax's economic insecurity—nor did his appearances as a popular lecturer and performer of cowboy songs. The presentation of his ideas and research before academic audiences, and his term as president of the American Folklore Society, failed to gain him a university position. Lomax, who had married Bess Bauman Brown of Austin, Texas, in 1904, was still struggling in 1910 to make a living and to support his four children, Shirley, John Avery, Alan, and Bess. The little security he enjoyed ended in 1917, when, in a politically inspired attack on the Austin campus, Texas Governor James E. Ferguson fired Lomax and others at the university. Lomax's Eastern connections once again saved him, and Barrett Wendell Jr. obtained a job for him as a bond salesman in Chicago. In 1919 Lomax returned to the University of Texas as secretary of the ex-student's association. He left in 1925 to become the director of the Bond Department at the Republic Bank in Dallas. Although far removed from folksong collecting, he kept in contact with scholars and amateurs who shared his interest in American folksong.

In 1932 the collapsing American economy cost Lomax his job. Ironically, in the midst of the Great Depression Lomax was able to resume collecting songs and to publish a series of important collections. With a contract from the Macmillan Company, and assistance from the Library of Congress and the American Council of Learned Societies, Lomax returned to the field in 1932, often assisted by his son Alan, on collecting trips that concentrated on the music of Southern Blacks. More than 10,000 recordings of the songs he had collected were deposited in the Library of Congress Archive of American Folk-Song. Drawing on this material, John and Alan Lomax edited *American Ballads and Folksongs* (1934), *Our Singing Country* (1941), and *Folk Song U.S.A.* (1947).

Cultural tensions and contradictions that characterize Lomax's work contributed to both its strength and its weaknesses. Lomax increasingly argued for the creative contribution of African Americans to American folksong, but he could not fully accept the democratic and egalitarian implications of his argument that great art came from the lowest rungs of the social ladder. He used the popular media and the latest technology to collect and disseminate what he had collected, yet he saw himself racing against media and technology as he searched for isolated groups that maintained their lore in "pure" form.

John Lomax was a Romantic nationalist who maintained that American folklore was the creative response of diverse American folk groups to their New World experience, not a vanishing remnant of Old World traditions. Implicitly, Lomax contended that anything that changed African Americans' place in Southern culture would destroy their folklore. Yet, in studying Black folklore, he was choosing to cherish material many White Southerners and Northerners did not value, and in the process of studying this material he pointed the way toward new directions in American folkloristics.

In 1935 John Lomax arranged for the African American folksinger Huddie Ledbetter (Lead Belly) to tour Northeastern cities. This effort took place within a racist context that patronized Lead Belly. Nevertheless, the tour contributed to the folksong revival in New York City, and eventually throughout the nation. Lomax provided an account of Lead Belly's life, a description of the tour, a revealing discussion of his relationship with Lead Belly, and a collection of songs in *Negro Songs as Sung by Lead Belly* (1936).

When in 1936 at nearly age seventy Lomax became the national folklore editor of the Federal Writers' Project (FWP), his view of the world and folklore was well established and clearly stated in the manual given to FWP workers. The manual dismissed folklorists who valued "only what can be traced back to a past for which they have a nostalgia." Instead, it praised folklorists who assume that "creative activity is still functioning." Although the European origins of American culture could not be denied, the FWP, he wrote, was "interested in the mutations and developments wrought by transfer to a new and pioneer land." Lomax insisted that the FWP valued "a recital of the woes of Clementine and her forty-niner parent above those of the Lady Claire." He was determined to collect what he thought of as a distinctive American lore before it was too late. Although national FWP officials shared some of Lomax's positions, they tried to reconcile Romantic nationalism with American pluralism and with modernity in ways he could not.

The American folksong collections that John and Alan Lomax edited together took a new approach to the American folksong tradition. Earlier collections had usually focused on a single genre or a single region, often a single genre within a particular region. The very title of the Lomaxes' first collection, *American Ballads and Folksongs,* reflects the Lomaxes' effort to take a broader view. This collection also reflects John Lomax's Romantic nationalism and his belief that folklore was associated with uneducated and isolated groups. By the time *Our Singing Country* and *Folk Song U.S.A.* appeared, the Lomaxes felt confident that they no longer needed the word "ballad" in their titles. The latter volumes emphasize a functionalist and pluralist approach to American folksong.

Initial scholarly assessments of John Lomax's work stressed the inadequate documentation of sources and the composite texts. Questions about Lomax's methodology are, however, increasingly placed in the larger context of his contribution as a field collector and popularizer. His Southern background, his assumptions about race, his impact on popular culture, and his view of modernity are key areas of inquiry for folklorists and cultural historians who recognize the magnitude of his contribution to folklore studies and his impact on popular attitudes toward American folksong.

Lomax's first wife, who died in 1931, did not live to see the publication of the folksong collections that her husband and son compiled. In 1934 Lomax married Ruby Terrill, a professor of classical languages and dean of women at the University of Texas. While visiting Greenville, Mississippi, in 1948, Lomax died of a cerebral hemorrhage. He was buried in Austin, Texas.

Jerrold Hirsch

References

Filene, Benjamin. 1991. "Our Singing Country": John and Alan Lomax, Leadbelly, and the Construction of an American Past. *American Quarterly* 43:602–624.

Hirsch, Jerrold. 1992. Modernity, Nostalgia, and Southern Folklore Studies. *Journal of American Folklore* 105:183–207.

Lomax, Alan, [1910] 1986. Introduction. In *Cowboy Songs and Other Frontier Ballads*, by John Lomax. New York: Collier, pp. xi–xxxvi.

Lomax, John. 1915. Some Types of American Folk-Song. *Journal of American Folklore* 28:1–17.

———. 1917. Self-Pity in Negro Folk-Songs. *Nation* 105:141–145.

———. 1934. "Sinful Songs" of the Southern Negro. *Musical Quarterly* 20:177–186.

———. 1947. *Adventures of a Ballad Hunter*. New York: Macmillan.

Loomis, C. Grant (1901–1963)

Folklorist and professor of German. Loomis' scholarly concerns varied from the study of popular tradition in literary works to Western American tradition, particularly parodies of folklore. Grant Loomis, as he preferred to be called, was editor of *Western Folklore* from 1949 to 1952 and associate editor for the following ten years. He contributed numerous articles and notes to the journal during that time. He was also associate secretary of the Modern Language Association of America (1952) and was active in many other learned societies.

From 1926 to 1928, Loomis studied in Munich with Professor Max Foerster. His experiences in Germany apparently determined his decision to enter academic life. On his return to the United States, he entered Harvard University and received his Ph.D. in 1933. His dissertation, *Old English Saints' Lives* was written under the direction of George Lyman Kittredge, another teacher who influenced him greatly. Loomis' book *White Magic: An Introduction to the Folklore of Christian Legend*, further developing his dissertation topic, was published in 1948.

Loomis taught German language and literature at Tufts College, Harvard, Radcliffe, and the University of California at Berkeley, where he chaired the German Department from 1957 to 1962. Although he never taught folklore, the field was an important part of his life, and he was a staunch supporter of the California Folklore Society from its beginning in 1941.

He retired as chairman of the German Department in 1962, and he was looking forward to spending more time on his own work. In January 1963, he wrote to Wayland D. Hand, "Two book-length subjects, namely, American Wordplay and Never Say Die, euphemisms for avoidance of that word, are still awaiting attention. I hope I can see to finish them." But Loomis died unexpectedly of a heart problem in March of that year.

Frances Cattermole-Tally

References

Loomis, C. Grant. 1949a. Traditional American Wordplay: The Epigram and Perverted Proverbs. *Western Folklore* 8:248–257.

———. 1949b. Traditional American Wordplay: Wellerisms or Yankeeisms. *Western Folklore* 8:1–21.

———. 1955. Wellerisms in California Sources. *Western Folklore* 14:229–245.

———. 1956a. Bret Harte's Folklore. *Western Folklore* 15:19–22.

———. 1956b. Proverbs in the Farmers Almanac. *Western Folklore* 15:172–178.

———. 1957. Henry David Thoreau: Folklorist. *Western Folklore* 16:90–106.

———. 1958. Mary Had a Parody: A Rhyme of Childhood in Folk Tradition. *Western Folklore* 17:45–51.

———. 1962. American Limerick Tradition. *Western Folklore* 21:153–157.

Lord, Albert Bates (1912–1991)

Slavicist, folklorist, comparatist, and collector of South Slavic oral poetry; co-originator (with Milman Parry) of the oral-formulaic theory. Initially Parry's research assistant in their fieldwork with oral epic singers in the former Yugoslavia from 1933, Lord transformed what had been a laboratory exercise—employing the South Slavic analogy to confirm Homeric oral tradition—into a multidisciplinary field that now treats more than 130 ancient, medieval, and modern traditions. Trained in a variety of areas (A.B. classics, Harvard, 1934; M.A. and Ph.D. comparative literature, Harvard, 1936 and 1949), he focused on South Slavic, ancient and Byzantine Greek, Old English, Old French, Russian, Latvian, Albanian, central Asian, Finnish, and Biblical studies. Through his innovative scholarship, the direction that Parry had mapped out developed far beyond the original conception, taking on an identity as one of the major 20th-century movements in folklore, literature, and anthropology.

In 1949 Lord completed the doctoral dissertation that was to become *The Singer of Tales* eleven years later. In it, he fully elaborated the dynamics of the recurrent phrase, or *formula*, which he defined as "a group of words which is regularly employed under the same metrical conditions to express a given essential idea" (Lord 1960:30), and narrative type-scenes, or *themes*, "groups of ideas regularly used in telling a tale in the formulaic style of traditional song" (Lord 1960:68). He also described *story-patterns*, or tale types, like the Odysseus story known not only in South Slavic but also in Albanian, Turkish, Russian, and other traditions.

The basis for Lord's far-reaching scholarship lay principally in his and Parry's fieldwork in the former Yugoslavia, begun in the years 1933–1935 and continued by Lord in 1950–1951 and later. These collecting expeditions have yielded the ongoing series *Serbocroatian Heroic Songs*, none more important than Lord and David Bynum's edition and translation of *The Wedding of Smailagic Meho* (1974), dictated to Parry and Lord in 1935 by the unlettered master-singer Avdo Medjedovic and totaling 12,311 lines, about the length of the Homeric *Odyssey*.

In addition to these major, seminal works, Lord contributed more than seventy articles in a wide variety of areas, selectively sampled in his *Epic Singers and Oral Tradition* (1991) and exhaustively listed in a 1992 obituary in the *Journal of American Folklore*.

John Miles Foley

References

Foley, John Miles. 1992. Obituary: Albert Bates Lord, 1912–1991. *Journal of American Folklore* 105:157–165.

Lord, Albert B. 1960. *The Singer of Tales*. Cambridge, MA: Harvard University Press.

———. 1991. *Epic Singers and Oral Tradition*. Ithaca, NY: Cornell University Press.

See also Oral-Formulaic Approach

Lovers' Leaps

Widespread subject of local legends, found in many states with remarkably similar plots. Typically, two Indian lovers, often from different tribes, are prevented from marrying because of tribal enmity or taboo; in despair or defiance, one or both commit suicide by jumping off a precipice. Variations occur; at Blowing Rock, North Carolina, for example, the lovers are returned to the ledge by a strong updraft from the undercut cliff, demonstrating the "Great Spirit's" intervention. Charles Skinner lists well-known lovers' leaps associated with such stories, distributed from New England to the Far West. Louise Pound found four such leap sites in Nebraska, a state she admitted is "pretty flat."

Lovers'-leap legends are also common in Europe, and Pound cites two possible Greek prototypes: the story of Sappho, who, spurned by Phaon, leapt to her death from the Leucadian rock (the subject of four *Spectator* essays by Joseph Addison in 18th-century England); and the tragedy of Hero and Leander as treated in Virgil's *Georgics*. Another likely literary influence is Shakespeare's *Romeo and Juliet*, dramatizing the tragic end of "star-crossed" lovers from feuding families.

Pound conjectures that such legends in the United States began with a conspicuous promontory: "In someone's imagi-

nation it became the site of a suicidal leap, and it was given a name that expressed this idea. Next, some local author accounted for the naming by attaching to it a romantic story of the past—the past of our region is Indian—and narrated it in verse or prose. The 'legend' . . . eventually was generally accepted as of Indian tradition" (Pound [1959] 1976:86).

The evolution of "Sautee and Nacoochee," one of Georgia's best-known local legends, is substantially documented in print (see Burrison 1990). It confirms Pound's suspicion of literary origins, but in this case the leap off Mount Yonah is a later addition (1869) by writer George W. Williams, who grew up in that area of White County and who also borrowed the Indian lovers' names from local creeks. Consistent with the earlier version (1854) presented by George White is the mound erected to mark their burial. Williams' account inspired a narrative poem, a school play, and "A Cantata of the Cherokees for Mixed Voices," which, in turn, contributed to the oral tradition.

These tales could be dismissed as romantic Victorian fantasies, but Francis de Caro suggests they may serve the psychological function of assuaging White guilt by "self-destructing" the Native American population. While they are "fakelore" in the sense of purporting to be authentic Indian narratives, many have achieved oral currency and are important symbols of a locale's identity, sometimes exploited for tourism.

John A. Burrison

References

Burrison, John A. 1990. Sautee and Nacoochee: Anatomy of a Lovers' Leap Legend. *Southern Folklore* 47:117–132.

De Caro, Francis A. 1986. Vanishing the Red Man: Cultural Guilt and Legend Formation. *International Folklore Review* 4:74–80

Pound, Louise. 1959 [1976]. "Nebraska Legends of Lovers' Leaps." *Nebraska Folklore*. Westport, CT: Greenwood Press, pp. 79–92.

Skinner, Charles M. [1896] 1969. *Myths and Legends of Our Own Land*. Vol. 2. Detroit: Singing Tree Press, pp. 318–328.

———. 1974 [n.d.]. *American Myths and Legends*. Vol. 2. Detroit: Gale, pp. 249–265.

Lullaby

A song used to lull an infant or toddler to sleep, typically while rocking the child in one's arms or in a cradle or carrier. Apparently a near-universal song type, lullabies are accordingly found in the New World among both Native Americans and more recent arrivals of African, Asian, or European descent. At their simplest, such songs may merely consist of wordless humming or nonsense syllables (the English term "lullaby," and, through it, the verb "to lull," derive from one popular European instance of the latter). More elaborate pieces fulfilling this function can be broadly divided between those items that, in content and usage, are specifically intended for, or identified as, lullabies; and the quite various songs idiosyncratically put to this use by individual singers. Among the better-known English-language examples of the former are

"Rockabye Baby," "All the Pretty Horses," "Sleep, Baby, Sleep," "Hush, Little Baby, Don't Say a Word (The Mockingbird Song)," "Go Tell Aunt Rhody," and "Bye, Baby Bunting." The second category may include virtually any song or song type, though certain items employed after this fashion may, through repeated usage, become associated primarily with the lulling of children. Such has been the case, for instance, with "Two Babes in the Wood," a sentimental ballad originating on 16th-century broadsides.

As befits their function, lullabies are typically sung softly, often in an undertone or whisper, with little expression but considerable repetition. Aside from humming or vocables, their texts tend to emphasize phonemic or formal patterns regarded as restful or soothing (hence the prevalence in English-language lullabies of perfect rhymes, regular meters, alliteration, parallel syntax, and so forth), qualities also pertaining to tunes, tempos, and time signatures; predictably, such highly subjective factors vary considerably from culture to culture. Topically, however, those songs employed primarily as lullabies tend to dwell on a relative few conventional themes, an area that, somewhat surprisingly, seems to exhibit far less cross-cultural variation. So the singer may proffer various bribes or rewards for good behavior or sleep, or, conversely, issue threats or warnings, facetious or otherwise, should the child fail to comply. The song may describe the tranquility of the household or of the world as a whole, or the benign or beneficent activities of other family members (from the inverse perspective, some lullabies lament the mother's hard lot or complain of the father's abuse or neglect), or it might extol the child's appearance or person, predicting a glorious future. Sleep itself may be personified or described as a fabulous, never-never land (this last is balanced by the bogies sometimes enlisted in threats).

Curiously, many if not most lullabies also incorporate seemingly incongruous images of isolation, disorder, violence, or death, exemplified by that best-known of all American cradle songs:

> Rockabye baby, in the treetop,
> When the wind blows the cradle will rock.
> When the bough breaks the cradle will fall,
> And down will come baby, cradle and all

Folklorists have advanced various complementary hypotheses for these ostensibly inappropriate elements, which, after all, are clearly more meaningful for singers than their largely nonverbal auditors (the same can be said, of course, for the lullaby's more benevolent images). According to these interpretations, such figures may vicariously vent the latent hostilities or more general postpartum depression experienced by new mothers, or ease the separation strain eventuated by their infants' growing independence. Or they may more literally reflect conditions in traditional societies characterized by high rates of infant mortality or similar hazards and tragedies. Even under less stressful conditions, this seeming contradiction in the lullaby worldview suggests a fundamental dilemma in parenting—parents' desire, on the one hand, to protect and nurture their children, tempered by their knowledge, on the other, that the world that awaits their young is hardly the stuff of bedtime stories.

Directed in the first place to the needs of children, lullabies thus simultaneously address the practical and the emotional demands of parenting, a versatility probably explaining this genre's remarkably wide provenance and equally remarkable persistence. In fact, while the contemporary urban American context has witnessed the demise of most forms of traditional song, the lullaby, like other songs associated with children and childrearing, has not only survived but thrived, with no signs of falling dormant in the foreseeable future.

John Minton

References

Brakeley, Theresa C. 1950. Lullaby. In *Funk and Wagnalls Standard Dictionary of Folklore, Mythology, and Legend,* ed. Maria Leach. Vol. 2. New York: Funk and Wagnalls, pp. 653–654

Hawes, Bess Lomax. 1974. Folksongs and Functions: Some Thoughts on the American Lullaby. *Journal of American Folklore* 87:140–148. Reprinted in *Readings in American Folklore,* ed. Jan Harold Brunvand. New York: W.W. Norton, 1979, pp. 203–214.

Toelken, Barre. 1986. Context and Meaning in the Anglo–American Ballad. In *The Ballad and the Scholars: Approaches to Ballad Study,* ed. D.K. Wilgus and Barre Toelken. Papers Presented at a Clark Library Seminar, October 22, 1983. Los Angeles: William Andrews Clark Memorial Library, University of California, pp. 29–52.

Lunsford, Bascom Lamar (1882–1973)

Folk musician, folklorist, organizer and director of the Asheville, North Carolina, Mountain Dance and Folk Festival. Known as "the Squire of South Turkey Creek," Lunsford grew up assimilating the folk traditions of his native Buncombe County in western North Carolina. Folklore became a passion for Lunsford, and he spent his life collecting and performing the folksongs and dances of the southern Appalachians. Committed to allaying the "hillbilly" stereotype of mountain people by celebrating the richness of Appalachian culture, Lunsford insisted on performing and presenting only what he considered to be authentic folk arts. In 1928 he brought together dozens of local musicians and dancers to compete for prizes as part of an Asheville civic pageant. Lunsford's festival, the earliest of its kind, was resoundingly successful, and has continued, serving as a model for subsequent folk-cultural display events.

An accomplished fiddler, banjoist, and singer, Lunsford contributed to several folksong collections, recording 303 tunes for Columbia University in 1935, and 317 for the Library of Congress in 1949. He also made a few commercial records, including his famous "Mountain Dew" for Brunswick in 1928 that was popularized in the 1930s by his friends Lulu Belle and Scotty Wiseman.

*Katharine Luomala
in 1982. Photo J.W.
Love.*

Although Lunsford has been criticized for his tendencies toward self-promotion, his authoritarian management of the festival, his fondness for team-precision clog dancing, and his neglect of African American, topical, and bawdy folksongs, he will be remembered for helping validate the identities of Appalachians by preserving, revitalizing, and generating widespread appreciation for their traditional culture.

William E. Lightfoot

References

Gordon, Jonathan, and David Hoffman. 1965. *Music Makers of the Blue Ridge.* National Educational Television. Film.

Hoffman, David. 1989. *Ballad of a Mountain Man: The Story of Bascom Lamar Lunsford.* Varied Directions. Film.

Jones, Loyal. 1984. *Minstrel of the Appalachians: The Story of Bascom Lamar Lunsford.* Boone, NC Appalachian Consortium Press.

Whisnant, David E. 1979–1980. Finding the Way between the Old and the New: The Mountain Dance and Folk

Festival and Bascom Lamar Lunsford's Work as a Citizen. *Appalachian Journal* 7:135–154.

Luomala, Katherine (1907–1992)

A leading authority on Hawaiian and other Oceanic folklore and myth. A Minnesota Finn rather than the Polynesian aristocrat her name and work suggest, Luomala used her field research in then-little-known Gilbert Islands (now Kiribati), Micronesia, to earn a Ph.D. in anthropology at the University of California, Berkeley, in 1933 from Martha Beckwith, Robert Lowie, and Albert Kroeber. Her dissertation was a comparative analysis of how the mythical figure of Maui developed into a demigod. Following fieldwork among the Diegueno in California and the Navaho in the Southwest, she produced her most famous comparative essay, *Oceanic, American, and African Myths of Snaring the Sun* (1940), showing the complexity between diffusion and independent invention of quite similar motifs.

After wartime work in Japanese relocation camps in the United States, Luomala found her *metier* in 1946 combining teaching at the University of Hawaii with extensive field research and publication for the Bernice P. Bishop Museum in Honolulu. Her full-length studies of the trickster Maui, of the fairy-like Menehune, and of other Polynesian myths and chants soon became the basic sourcebooks on these subjects. She displayed the breadth of her interests in ethnobotanical and faunal studies of the Gilbert Islands and Canton Island in the Phoenix Group and, in 1984, a decade after her retirement, in the definitive book on *Hula Ki'i: Hawaiian Puppetry*. A small, intense, blonde, muumuu-clad personage, she had virtually total recall of an immense body of lore known to very few other scholars. Foreshadowing "performance orientation," she stressed the multiple meanings and functions of "oral narrative" (a term she preferred over "folklore"), always presenting the texts richly contextualized and thus bringing that lore alive for readers everywhere.

Daniel J. Crowley

References

Kaeppler, Adrienne, and Arlo Nimmo, eds. 1976. *Directions in Pacific Traditional Literature: Essays in Honor of Katherine Luomala*. Special Publications No. 62. Honolulu: Bishop Museum Press.

Luomala, Katherine. 1936. *Maui the Demigod: Factors in the Development of a Polynesian Hero Cycle*. Berkeley: University of California Press.

———. 1938. *Navaho Life of Yesterday and Today*. Berkeley: Western Museum Laboratories, National Park Service.

———. 1949. *Maui-of-a-Thousand-Tricks: His Oceanic and European Biographers*. Bulletin 198. Honolulu: Bishop Museum Press.

———. 1951. *The Menehune of Hawaii and Other Mythical Little People of Polynesia*. Bulletin 203. Honolulu: Bishop Museum Press.

———. 1955. *Voices in the Wind: Polynesian Myths and Chants*. Special Publications No. 75. Honolulu: Bishop Museum Press.

Luomala, Katherine, et al. 1947. *Special Studies in Polynesian Anthropology*. Bulletin 193. Honolulu: Bishop Museum Press.

Lyric Song

Folksong type that emphasizes emotional reaction to a significant experience, object, or idea rather than the constituent parts of the experience, object, or idea itself. Other types of folksong express emotion but subordinate it to the telling of a story (as do ballads) or to the depicting of a topic's salient features. Songs that concentrate most of their rhetoric and imagery on accentuating feeling and on evoking an affective response constitute a distinct type in Anglo American tradition, as they do in the traditions of most cultures.

To facilitate this discussion, it is helpful to divide lyric songs into two types: sacred and secular. Sacred songs in Anglo American tradition are in large part indebted for their status as folksongs to a phenomenon known as the camp meeting. Emerging in concert with the revivals of fundamental religious fervor that periodically struck 19th-century America, most dramatically in the South, camp meetings attracted large numbers of participants from the vicinity of their outdoor meeting grounds to gather and worship in a style characterized by spontaneous, demonstrative outpourings of spiritual expression. Singing played a dominant role in the events conducted over the course of the often two- and three-day-long meetings; many of the songs were already well-known hymns from earlier Protestant movements—Wesleyanism, for instance—but as time passed more and more were made for camp meetings themselves by amateur and even professional composers. Soon books of sacred songs compiled especially for camp-meeting devotees (their tunes drawn in a distinctive "shape-note" style) began to appear; the popularity of the songbooks in turn increased the popularity of the meetings themselves and the opportunity they afforded to worship in a more personal, more ecstatic way than that encouraged in the formal services of denominational religions. Many of these "White spirituals" became traditional, sung again and again not only in camp meetings (and later "singing conventions") but in everyday home settings as well; of course, some of the sacred songs that entered oral tradition followed other generic models, such as the ballad, but many were of the lyric type.

More common in the Anglo American folksong repertoire than sacred lyric songs were secular lyric songs. Keeping in mind that sacred songs deal with relationships between human beings and their deity, we can divide secular songs into two further logical types: those that treat relationships between their human subjects and society (homeland, political and economic conditions, friends and relatives) and those that treat relationships between individual men and women—in short, love songs. Lyric songs of the first sort address such topics as one's distress at a forced departure from home, despair at lack of employment and consequent poverty, or deathbed grieving for friends and family lost forever. Sometimes the reasons are one's own shortcomings, as in this North Carolina example:

If I had 'a' listened to what mama said
I wouldn't 'a' been here today
A-lying around this old jail house
A-weeping my life away.

Sometimes blame could be laid elsewhere, as in a Canadian example that shows heavy influence from Old World Irish songs of emigration:

Dear Newfoundland with your fisheries failing
Your sons and daughters must leave each fall,
Forced by poverty and cruel taxation
To the shores of Boston, a home for all.

Although with friends I feel sad at parting
My aged parents on the pier will stand
To bid farewell to their sons and daughters
Who now must leave your dear Newfoundland.

It is the second type of secular lyric, though, the type that deals with interpersonal relationships, that is the most popular in tradition and that folklorists normally think of as epitomizing the genre. These are invariably love songs that treat romantic relationships between men and women. That the lyric muse favors this topic is not too surprising, since the type's chief trait is its emotional quality, and a love relationship (with death running a close second) is the human experience most likely to arouse emotions to their highest pitch for expression in song. Moreover, of the two most intense human emotions, joy and sorrow, the lyric song far prefers the latter, and so, in the worldview espoused by the genre, love affairs, while they have their moments of rapture, are invariably causes for grief and despair. Indeed, even the sacred songs, which rejoice and wax ecstatic over the self's eventual union with his or her heavenly family, expend almost as much of their energy on the suffering endemic to the human earthly condition, as "Christian's Hope" illustrates:

> We have our troubles here below,
> We're trav'ling through this world of woe
> To that bright world where loved ones go,
> Where all is peace and love.

And a lyric song's emotional content was evidently matched by its effect on singers and listeners: George Pullen Jackson wrote in his *White Spirituals in the Southern Uplands* that "Christian's Hope" moved its performers so profoundly that "the third stanza is seldom heard. The singers are in sobs and tears before they get to it" (Jackson [1933] 1965).

While the foregrounding of feeling virtually defines the lyric song in the minds of many folklorists, the type exhibits other conventions as well. For example, the point of view in lyric songs is almost always that of the first person. This would seem apposite, since, after all, emotions are interior, subjective, and requiring of great empathy on the singer's part to communicate effectively in performance. The pronominal usage is thus important for rhetorical, psychological, and artistic reasons:

> The pain of love, I know full well,
> No heart can think, no tongue can tell;
> But I'll tell you now in a few short lines
> Love is worse than sickness ten thousand times.

Lyric love songs use almost exclusively the first-person singular; sacred lyric songs will often employ the plural "we," but in general the individual "speaker" seems to dominate there as well:

> I am a poor wayfaring stranger
> While trav'ling thro' this world of woe,
> Yet there's no sickness, toil nor danger,
> In that bright world to which I go.

Another characteristic shared by many lyric songs is a lack of concreteness, which apparently suggests the relative universality of the experiences depicted. In another traditional Anglo American folksong genre, the ballad, protagonists customarily enjoy names, particular social personae, distinct physical settings, certain actions to perform and motives for performing them that, while to a certain extent stylized and often formulaic as is common in folklore, do situate and specify the story of each song, differentiating it from other songs. Lyric songs, in contrast, constitute an extremely homogeneous body: The personnel, their actions, settings, character traits, motives, and so on are frequently the same from song to song. The protagonists seldom have names; in love songs, for example, they are usually just "young girls," "maidens," "young men." Most of the time, their personae are not those of soldier, merchant's daughter, or lumberman but the far more generalized victim and deceiver. Protagonists act in only one way as well, especially in lyric love songs; the world portrayed is monotonic and virtually predetermined so that there are few options in a life plan apparently long since laid out by higher powers:

> So hard is the fortune of all woman-kind!
> They're always controlled and they're always confined,

while

> Young men are false, oh they are so deceiving,
> Young men are false and they seldom prove true.

The case is similar with the religious songs, in which protagonists are identified as sinners, or pilgrims, or travelers, and so forth with but single motives and destinies: to be freed from the torments of this world and to join the heavenly family:

> Oh who will come and go with me?
> I'm on my journey home;
> I'm bound fair Canaan's land to see
> I'm on my journey home.

A further trait of lyric folksongs, once again especially prominent in songs of love relationships, is their employment of formulaic stanzas in demonstrably different songs. Some scholars have dubbed such verses "commonplaces," others "floating stanzas"; apparently they encapsulate so well the ideas they are meant to convey that they cannot be improved upon and so are reused freely from song to song. Again and again, then, we find in lyric songs the image of the little dove flying from pine to pine, of the broken-hearted maiden's wish to be buried with marble stones at head and feet, of the false lover's letter all "twisted and twined." These images, moreover, are carried by very similar wording so that they are formulaic not only conceptually but also verbally, as in the ubiquitous query:

> Oh, who will shoe your pretty little feet,
> And who will glove your hands,
> And who will kiss your red-rose cheeks
> When I'm in a far-off land?

A further distinctive property of the lyric song is its way of interrelating significant images or, to use a more technical term, its "semiotic." While the ballad, as a contrasting example, relates images to each other chronologically and causally in telling a story, the lyric song's semiotic is based on a thematic principle: Different images resonate with each other in connoting the same abstract concept, such as *movement* or *rest*. Take, for example, the following camp-meeting song:

We have our troubles here below,
We're traveling through this world of woe,
To that bright world where loved ones go,
Where all is peace and love.

We're fettered and chained up in clay,
While in this body here we stay;
By faith we know a world above,
Where all is peace and love.

I feel no way like getting tired,
I'm trusting in his holy word,
To guide my weary feet above,
Where all is peace and love.

The unifying theme of freedom from a bondage of the most trying sort is unmistakable, as are the dual emotions of despair of this life's conditions, bliss at the next's.

Secular lyric songs work the same way, though in lyric songs that address general social misfortune, departure from one's terrestrial home—whether because of emigration, imprisonment, or death—is a cause for lament, not for celebration as in sacred songs. In secular songs, themes of exclusion, of confinement, of isolation and their ilk dominate rather than themes of inclusion, of liberation, and of communality. This thematic preference is best seen in love songs, since they are exceptionally rich in imagery: Not only humans, but human artifacts and indeed even nature's flora and fauna represent the same abstract concepts, such as augmentation and diminishment, plenitude and loss, longevity and impermanence, and so forth:

Young girls, take warning, take warning from me;
Don't put your dependence in a green growing tree.

For the leaves they will wither, the roots they will die;
The young boys will leave you, 'cause one has left I.

They will hug you, they will kiss you, they will tell you
     more lies
Than cross ties on the railroads and stars in the skies.

I once had a lover as dear as my life,
And oft did he promise for to make me his wife.

I left my poor daddy against his commands,
I left my poor mother a-wringing her hands.

And now I'm unhappy, I am sick on my bed;
My husband's off gambling; Lord, I wish I was dead.

I'm going away to Georgia, I am going away to roam,
I'm going away to Georgia for to make it my home.

The lyric song of secular persuasion characterized so far in this essay reflected for the most part the ethos of an agrarian culture with communities that were small in size and homogeneous in population; that learned, stored, and transmitted songs orally; that accepted a view of the world as essentially static and deterministic; and that suffered economies not much advanced beyond subsistence level. But folksong collectors have also found in domestic singing repertoires secular lyric songs that exhibit what might be called a postagrarian sensibility. Such songs emerge in significant quantities after the Civil War and are just one branch of what we call "parlor songs," since their aesthetic suggests the "parlor" of the upwardly mobile bourgeoisie rather than the kitchen or field row of the laboring man and woman as the most apposite setting for their performance:

In the little rosewood casket
Resting here upon the stand
Is a package of old letters
Written by a lover's hand.

You may go and bring them, sister,
And set down here upon my bed
And take gently to your bosom
My poor aching, throbbing head.

You have brought them? Thank you, sister.
You may read them o'er to me.
I have often tried to read them,
But for tears I could not see.

When I'm resting in my coffin
And my shroud around me's wound
And my narrow bed is ready
In the pleasant churchyard ground.

Take this package of old letters;
Strew them all around my heart.
But this little ring he gave me
From my finger never part.

I must say farewell my sister;
Place my hands upon my breast.
I am dying. Kiss me, sister.
I am going home to rest.

The most obvious mark of distinctiveness in such lyric songs of the parlor variety as "Little Rosewood Casket" is the more genteel ambience of the world portrayed and the song's more refined phrasing. The composers (many of whom, like the makers of sacred songs, are known to us, since oftentimes their compositions first appeared in some copyrighted commercial form, like sheet music, before passing into folk tradition) were clearly more educated in approved styles of formal song poetics. To the academic observer, the emotional content of parlor songs seems filtered through a somewhat self-conscious, artificial, romanticized sensibility, one that has a dying woman in a most unlikely way ask her sister to "take gently to your bosom / My poor aching, throbbing head" and refer to her burial place as a "pleasant churchyard ground," while her death posture is the exaggeratedly polite hands-crossed-over-breast. One feels intuitively that there is less genuine sorrow here than there is the proper appearance of sorrowfulness.

Despite what seems to the outsider clear differences in prosody and perception, domestic and community singers accepted parlor songs into their repertoires—and the singers' families and neighbors and workmates into their hearts—with as much sincerity and passion as they had adopted lyric songs encapsulating preindustrial values and worldview. And we must acknowledge the continuities between older style and newer style that gain the parlor ditties found in tradition their status as lyric songs in the first place: their privileging of feeling over action and description, their preference for first-person point of view, their lack of journalistic detail, their special type of thematically unified structure. Indeed, parlor lyric songs often exhibit the *same* imagery and associated themes their older agrarian relatives did, as the "going home to rest"

closing line of "Little Rosewood Casket," which could have been lifted directly from a camp-meeting spiritual, attests.

Roger deV. Renwick

References

Belden, Henry M., and Arthur Palmer Hudson, eds. 1952. *The Frank C. Brown Collection of North Carolina Folklore.* Vol. 3. Durham, NC: Duke University Press, pp. 270–377.

Browne, Ray B. 1979. *The Alabama Folk Lyric: A Study in Origins and Media of Dissemination.* Bowling Green, OH: Bowling Green State University Popular Press.

Coffin, Tristram P. 1952. A Tentative Study of a Typical Folk Lyric: "Green Grows the Laurel." *Journal of American Folklore* 65:341–351.

Jackson, George Pullen. [1933] 1965. *White Spirituals in the Southern Uplands.* New York: Dover.

See also Folksong; Gospel Music; Spirituals; African American; Worksong

M

Macon, David Harrison ("Uncle Dave") (1870–1952)

One of the pioneers of commercial country music, and a founding member of Nashville's Grand Ole Opry, Uncle Dave Macon described himself merely as a "banjoist and songster." He was, however, far more than that. He was one of the crucial links between the rural Southern traditional music of the 19th century and the more modern music of the radio and the phonograph. With the possible exception of the Carter Family, he managed to preserve more old songs and picking styles than any other early performer. His exuberant banjo playing, his boisterous singing, and his wonderfully ornate jokes and tales made him a figure of legend in his own right. "Uncle Dave might not have been the best banjo player, or the best singer, but he sure was the best something" ran one familiar joke about him, reflecting on the power of his personality and the influence of his style.

Though casual observers often describe Macon's banjo playing as "frailing," more serious students of the banjo have isolated sixteen separate styles on his records, including a variety of up-picking and two-finger styles. His repertoire—or that part of it preserved on records and by folksong collectors—numbers more than 200 songs, ranging from Native American ballads to 19th-century sentimental fare, from gospel tunes to minstrel-show walkabouts. Recent research has shown that he shared many lyrics and comic pieces with African American singers from the middle Tennessee area.

Macon was born at the hamlet of Smart Station, near McMinnville, Warren County, Tennessee. As a boy, he absorbed many of the songs of the area, but his real fascination with banjo playing came in 1884, when his family moved to Nashville, where they operated a hotel. There Macon was exposed to the many vaudeville and minstrel troupes who boarded in the hotel while playing the town's theaters; many of them featured banjo-playing comedians with intricate picking methods, and Macon was fascinated. By the time he was fourteen years old, his mother had bought him his first banjo. His interest in vaudeville was abruptly cut short, however, when his father was murdered on the streets of Nashville and the family was forced to return to rural Cannon Country.

For the next thirty-five years, Macon worked a farm, raised a family, and ran a mule-drawn freight line. He continued to learn songs, some from traditional sources, others from Tin Pan Alley sheet music his sisters played for him. About 1923, when his freight line was rendered obsolete by Henry Ford's new trucks, he signed a contract with the Loew's Theater chain and took to the stage. His comic songs like "Keep My Skillet Good and Greasy," "Chewing Gum," and "Hill Billy Blues" endeared him to audiences, and in the fall of 1925, when Nashville's radio station WSM opened, he became one of its first regulars. A few months later the station started a regular *Barn Dance* show—a program that would eventually become the Grand Ole Opry—and Macon soon became a mainstay of the show.

Though he was over fifty when he began performing professionally, Macon often worked with younger musicians who were able to match his own musicianship: fiddler Sid Harkreader, instrumentalists Sam and Kirk McGee, singers Alton and Rabon Delmore. From 1924 until 1938, he recorded more than 180 songs for every major record company; these included topical songs like "The Bible's True" (about the Scopes trial), "Rockabout My Sara Jane" (learned from Black roustabouts on the Cumberland River), "Buddy Won't You Roll Down the Line" (an old pro-labor song), "Late Last Night" (a traditional Appalachian piece), and "The Death of John Henry" (not the familiar song, but a blues ballad probably of black origin). About a third of the Macon repertoire was gospel music, as exemplified by his unofficial theme song, "How Beautiful Heaven Must Be."

In his later years, Macon traveled to Hollywood to make a film, *Grand Ole Opry* (1940), appeared on network radio, and even did local television. He continued to appear on the Opry, even with its electric guitars and modern singers, until a few weeks before his death. He left no real protégé to carry on his music, though David "Stringbean" Akeman inherited his banjo and many of his songs. Many of his old records have remained in print on LP into modern times, and festivals like the annual Uncle Dave Macon Days celebration in Murfrees-boro, Tennessee, have become forums for younger musicians who wish to celebrate his music.

Charles K. Wolfe

References

Macon, Uncle Dave. 1985. *Original Recordings, 1925–1935.* County C–521. Cassette.

———. 1992. *Country Music Hall of Fame.* MCA MCAD 10546. Compact Disc/Cassette.

Rinzler, Ralph, and Norm Cohen. 1970. Uncle Dave Macon: A Bio-Discography. JEMF Special Series No. 3. Los Angeles: John Edwards Memorial Foundation.

Wolfe, Charles. 1975. Uncle Dave Macon. In *Stars of Country Music,* ed. Bill C. Malone and Judith McCulloh. Urbana: University of Illinois Press, pp. 40–64.

———. 1977. *Tennessee Strings: The Story of Country Music in Tennessee.* Knoxville: University of Tennessee Press.

Magarac, Joe

Folk hero; the most famous figure in steelworker lore. The last name means "donkey" in Serbo-Croatian. After almost fifty years of scholarly debate on the subject (focusing especially on the ambivalent ethnic elements in the story), it seems possible, from the work of folklorists Richard M. Dorson and Hyman Richman, historian Clifford Reutter and others, that Joe Magarac was a creation not of folk process, but of a professional writer, Owen Francis, in 1931. At least two sources, however, English-literature scholar George Carver and journalist-folklorist George Swetnam, suggest an independent origin of the Magarac legend earlier in the 20th century, within local southwestern Pennsylvania folk tradition.

In the comic-heroic tales related to the Francis story, Magarac is a large, but still human-size immigrant laborer of "solid steel," who was born in an industrial site (an ore mountain, a slag pile, a furnace). He lives at a mill-town boarding house, eats huge quantities of food, especially cabbage, and works twenty-four hours a day. His exploits are based on his great strength, but he is simple and pure of heart. He dies by melting himself down in a Bessemer furnace. In the George Carver stories, Magarac is a supernatural—"as large as occasions demand"—who appears only when needed in order to rescue a worker from a sudden life-threatening disaster on the job.

In any case, it is clear that the proliferation and perpetuation of stories and songs about Magarac can be attributed primarily to eager folklorists and other writers in the 1940s, such as Jacob Evanson and Benjamin A. Botkin, along with steel-company propaganda. Yet, odd things can happen on the way to tradition. In the wrenching process of the steel industry's precipitous decline and restructuring in southwestern Pennsylvania and across the industrial Northeast, the persona of Joe Magarac as the super-strong, proud steel laborer has become immensely important to displaced workers, whose self-esteem and sense of identity have been severely challenged. The 1980s, for example, saw the staging of a mixed-media production titled *Magarac (A Steel Saga)* in the steel

town of Lackawanna, New York (near Buffalo). Residents of Monongahela Valley mill towns continue to talk of erecting a Joe Magarac statue. In 1991 the union-supported Tri-State Conference on Steel established an annual Joe Magarac Award to recognize efforts to promote reindustrialization in southwestern Pennsylvania.

The perhaps "fakelore" hero Joe Magarac may or may not ever have represented folk tradition during the heyday of the steel industry, but the legacy of Joe Magarac the popular icon has gained new significance for former steelworkers as steel's dominance wanes.

Doris J. Dyen

References

Blair, Walter. 1944. Joe Magarac: Pittsburgh Steel Man. In *Tall Tale America: A Legendary History of Our Humorous Heroes.* New York: Coward-McCann, pp. 232–243.

Botkin, Benjamin A. 1944. The Saga of Joe Magarac: Steelman. In *A Treasury of American Folklore.* New York: Crown, pp. 246–254.

Carver, George. 1944. Legend in Steel. *Western Pennsylvania Historical Magazine* 27:129–136.

Reutter, Clifford J. 1980. The Puzzle of a Pittsburgh Steeler: Joe Magarac's Ethnic Identity. *Western Pennsylvania Historical Magazine* 63:31–36.

Richman, Hyman. 1953. The Saga of Joe Magarac. *New York Folklore Quarterly* 9:282–293.

Swetnam, George. 1988. Joe Magarac. In *Devils, Ghosts, and Witches: Occult Folklore of the Upper Ohio Valley.* Greensburg, PA: McDonald/Sward, pp. 43–48.

See also Steelworkers

Maritime Folklore

Traditional cultural expressions of maritime people; includes the lore of groups such as seafarers, fishers, marine pilots, longshoremen, boatbuilders, and seafood processors, whose work takes place on (or relates to work on) bodies of water; and communities located near oceans, bays, rivers, bayous, and lakes, whose residents have a strong cultural or economic relationship with the water. Maritime folklore encompasses a wide range of genres, including custom and belief, weatherlore, ritual, legend, narrative, language, jargon, and song, as well as folklife forms such as technical skill, festival, foodways, and material culture. While certain traditions are widespread and found in many North American maritime communities, there are numerous variants within genres, reflecting particular local, regional, occupational, historical, and ethnic contexts.

The sea can be unpredictable, unforgiving, and fraught with hazards. To guard against such perils, seafarers have long invoked traditional taboos or avoidance behaviors, which function to assuage the psychological stresses of difficult work in a potentially dangerous environment. Adherence to such beliefs shows respect for the traditions of generations past and also serves to relieve anxiety about the many risks and unknowns inherent in living and working at sea. Modern electronic gear reduces some of the unknowns by helping mariners navigate around shoals, locate seafood resources, anticipate the weather, and communicate with one another. The widespread use of such devices has considerably altered the contexts within which older, traditional taboos and customs were most vigorously maintained (although technology itself has inspired new jargon and systems of conventions). Still, in the second half of the 20th century, folklorists have encountered numerous examples of traditional beliefs from people in a wide range of North American maritime communities.

Historically, some of the most widespread superstitions had to do with women and members of the clergy, both of whom were thought to be unlucky passengers aboard ship. While this attitude has softened in many areas, there are lingering feelings of ambivalence toward women or clergymen boarding vessels in certain maritime communities. Another superstition of long standing concerns the harming of sea birds. To kill an albatross is to court disaster, such as befell the Dutch training ship *Kobenhavn,* which disappeared without a trace in the South Atlantic in 1928. As noted in the *New York Times* on August 21, 1938, ten years after the tragedy, the vanishing of the new, steel-hulled ship with modern radio equipment and auxiliary engines was made more poignant by reports that one of the cadets had captured an albatross shortly before departure.

In many regions, putting to sea on Friday is considered bad luck, as is having an umbrella or black suitcase aboard a boat, turning the hatch cover upside down, changing a boat's name, or whistling on board. Fishermen in various regions avoid certain words and foods. Along the Northwest Coast, for example, serving pea soup aboard some fishing boats would be quite a serious blunder. On some fishing vessels out of Florida and Texas, the word "alligator" is taboo, while on a traditional Chesapeake Bay vessel one would avoid black walnuts. Likewise, a traditional fisherman in Florida would not tolerate a speck of green paint on his workboat, while a Chesapeake waterman would shun anything blue on his.

Customs practiced to bring good luck are not as prevalent as avoidance behaviors. Placing a coin beneath the mast of a vessel is one tradition widely employed for good luck. At one West Coast shipyard until well into the 1950s, workers followed a long-standing custom of ensuring a new boat's success by passing around the whiskey bottle during three important stages of construction: at the laying of the keel, after fastening the final plank (called the "whiskey plank"), and again at the launching. In many regions, when launching a new boat it is customary for a woman, often the wife of the builder or owner, to break a bottle of champagne over the bow. In California's San Pedro fishing community, a boat is considered especially lucky if the champagne bottle doesn't break until the third swing over the bow. Some communities call upon a priest to bless the new boat as well. Should trouble arise at the launching—the vessel runs aground or sustains damage—that boat's future is called into question. While a launching ceremony occurs only once during the vessel's lifetime, other ceremonies for luck and success are held at regular intervals. For example, many maritime communities sponsor an annual Blessing of the Fleet. Part ritual and part festival, the ceremony consists of fishermen parading their decorated boats before a clergyman, who confers a blessing upon each for a safe and successful fishing season.

A few ceremonies are conducted at sea, notably those performed when passengers or crew cross certain lines of latitude or longitude for the first time. On the day a ship crosses the equator, one of the ship's company appears attired as King Neptune, before whom the uninitiated, or "pollywogs," must stand and respond to questions. The novices are then treated to the ministrations of a wicked-looking barber, before running the gauntlet between seasoned seamen and, finally, being drenched with water. At ceremony's end, the pollywogs are declared sons of Neptune, or "shellbacks." A similar rite is held when crossing the international date line (180° longitude), at which sailors become members of the Order of the Golden Dragon. One joins the Order of the Bluenose when such a ceremony is held for crossing the Arctic Circle. These ceremonies are conducted aboard U.S. Navy and Coast Guard ships, as well as merchant and some cruise ships.

Because the lives of maritime people are so intimately connected to nature, many have sharpened their abilities to predict weather based on the appearance of the sky, clouds, wind direction, and changes in atmospheric pressure. Observations about the weather that are widely known and shared among members of the group become weatherlore. Some of the best-known examples of maritime weatherlore have been fashioned into ditties such as "Mackerel skies and mares' tails make tall ships carry short sails" and "Red sky at night, sailor's delight; red sky in the morning, sailor's warning." To many mariners, a circle around the moon portends bad weather, while sun dogs (bright, rainbow-like spots on either side of the sun) foretell a weather change. Fishing people can also read the weather in the behavior of local birds, as well as in the creatures they harvest. In Chesapeake Bay, for example, some watermen believe that blue crabs turn especially mean before a storm, biting everything in sight.

Maritime folklore is rich in legends about events at sea and waterborne villains and heroes. One of the best-known legends among North American and European seamen concerns the Flying Dutchman, condemned to sail forever for having invoked the wrath of God by swearing he would make harbor despite a howling gale. The Flying Dutchman's phantom ship haunts the waters around the Cape of Good Hope, and many seamen believe that anyone who sets eyes on her will subsequently die in a shipwreck or be struck blind. Other maritime legends involve mermaids who tempt mariners to their deaths, plundering pirates, shipwrecks and buried treasure, how individuals met their fate at sea, and modern-day sea monsters such as Chessie in the Chesapeake Bay and Champ of Lake Champlain, both seemingly benign creatures that surface periodically.

Members of various maritime occupational groups often tell stories about their own experiences on the water. These personal-experience narratives typically concern close calls with danger when skill and luck saved the day, enormous harvests of fish landed in the past, brushes with the law, and the like. Told time and again, such narratives become highly structured; when performed in various contexts, they serve to express occupational identity and such values as hard work, courage, specialized knowledge, and competence.

Maritime occupations spawned a multitude of specialized terms and phrases that newcomers had to master, for their own successful performance of duties and, in some circumstances, for the ultimate safety of the entire crew. Each part of the vessel, rig, and gear was named, and commands concerning their manipulation had to be understood and swiftly obeyed. As in many other occupations, greenhorns were tested by the seasoned crew and sent on spurious missions, among them to fetch the key to the keelson; to get some red oil for the port light and green for the starboard light; to tell Charley Noble to report to the first mate (Charley Noble is the name for the galley stovepipe); to go down and shine the golden rivet in the shaft alley; to keep a lookout for the mail buoy; or to go below and retrieve a bucket of steam.

Contemporary American English is replete with terms and phrases whose origins lie in the lore of maritime occupations. When confronted with a dilemma in which all alternatives are equally unappealing, a person may say he or she is "between the devil and the deep blue sea." To the crew aboard a wooden sailing ship, this expression described the circumstances of a crewman, hanging from a bosun's chair over the side of the ship, caulking a seam. The "devil" was the outermost seam of the deck planking, where the deck met the ship's side planking. To caulk a seam in the side planking, a man would be sent over "between the devil and the deep blue sea" to do so.

Another common phrase that has nautical origins is "to be taken aback." (When a square-rigged ship was caught by a shift of wind from ahead, the sails would be pressed back flat against the mast, curtailing forward movement.) Quarrelsome individuals are sometimes said to be "at loggerheads." (A "loggerhead" was a knob of iron on a long rod that, when heated, was used to melt pitch or tar for caulking; it was also used as a weapon. A "loggerhead" was also the single large bitt in the stern of a whaleboat, around which the harpoon line was made fast when the whale was harpooned.) Someone wishing to hear the latest "scuttlebutt" is likely unaware that the "scuttlebutt" was the water cask aboard a vessel. As crew members waited their turn for a drink, talk of various kinds, including rumors and gossip, would ensue. Today, to take something to "the bitter end," means forging on to the very limit. Aboard ship, the "bitter end" was the inboard end of the anchor cable attached to the windlass bitts. When the anchor had been let out to the bitter end, there was no more cable available.

Maritime songs were once an important part of the occupational culture of American seafarers. During the heyday of merchant sail and whaling in the 19th century, sailors sang chanteys (worksongs) and fo'c'sle songs, so called because they were sung in leisure time, often in or near the crew's quarters in the forecastle of the ship. Typically, variants of English, Irish, and Scottish ballads, the fo'c'sle songs expressed such subjects as the harshness and loneliness of life at sea, heroes of famous naval engagements, and notorious ships and captains. In contrast, chanteys were sung aboard ship to establish a rhythm for coordinating heavy hoisting work such as furling the sails, raising the anchor, or manning the pumps. When auxiliary steam replaced manpower on the capstans, halyards, and such, the chantey tradition diminished as well.

Two maritime worksong traditions, however, persisted well into the 20th century among African American workers in certain mid-Atlantic fisheries. Crew members employed in the menhaden fishery to haul by hand the heavy, fish-laden purse seines typically sang call-and-response-style worksongs to synchronize their efforts. Meanwhile, in the seafood-processing houses of Chesapeake Bay, workers often turned to singing gospel songs to help relieve the tedium of shucking oysters or picking crabmeat.

Work in American maritime settings has produced rich material-culture traditions as well, the most significant of which are traditional boats. The pirogue of Louisiana, the Columbia River gill-net skiff, Northwest Coast canoes, the Maine lobster boat, the New Jersey garvey and Sea Bright skiff, the Chesapeake skipjack, and the Florida sponge boat are just a few examples of regional boat designs that reflect local water and weather conditions, building materials, intended uses, and cultural norms. Often constructed locally by builders who have had no formal training and who work without plans, vernacular watercraft represent the tremendous diversity of North American maritime material-culture traditions.

Paula J. Johnson

References

Abrahams, Roger D., Kenneth S. Goldstein, and Wayland D. Hand. 1985. *By Land and by Sea: Studies in the Folklore of Work and Leisure Honoring Horace P. Beck on His Sixty-Fifth Birthday.* Hatboro, PA: Legacy Books.

Bassett, Fletcher S. 1892. *Sea Phantoms; or, Legends and Superstitions of the Sea and of Sailors in All Lands and At All Times.* Chicago: Morrill, Higgins.

Beck, Horace P. 1973. *Folklore and the Sea.* Mystic Seaport Marine Historical Association American Maritime Library Vol. 6. Middletown, CT: Wesleyan University Press.

Carey, George G. 1971. *A Faraway Time and Place: Lore of the Eastern Shore.* Washington, DC, and New York: Robert B. Luce.

Colcord, Joanna. 1938. *Songs of American Sailormen.* New York: W.W. Norton.

———. 1945. *Sea Language Comes Ashore.* New York: Cornell Maritime Press.

Johnson, Paula J., ed. 1988. *Working the Water: The Commercial Fisheries of Maryland's Patuxent River.* Charlottesville: University of Virginia Press.

Lloyd, Timothy C., and Patrick B. Mullen. 1990. *Lake Erie Fishermen: Work, Tradition, and Identity.* Urbana: University of Illinois Press.

Mullen, Patrick B. [1978] 1988. *I Heard the Old Fisherman Say: Folklore of the Texas Gulf Coast.* Logan: Utah State University Press.

Poggie, John J., Jr., and Carl Gersuny. 1972. Risk and

Ritual: An Interpretation of Fishermen's Folklore in a New England Community. *Journal of American Folklore* 85:66–72.

Shay, Frank. [1948–1951] 1991. *An American Sailor's Treasury: Sea Songs, Chanteys, Legends, and Lore.* New York: Smithmark.

Taylor, David A. 1992. *Documenting Maritime Folklife: An Introductory Guide.* Publications of the American Folklife Center No. 18. Washington, DC: Library of Congress.

See also Boatbuilding; Chanteys; Fishing (Commercial); Great Lakes; Merchant Seamen; Watermen; Yarn

Marxist Approach

Seeks social and economic patterns that relate to folk-cultural production. A Marxist approach to data presentation and analysis has played a role in the social sciences since the late 19th century; folklorists, however, were more concerned with humanistic than social or political interpretation of data. This directed them away from application of the highly sociopolitical approach that Marxism engendered until fairly recently.

Marxist approaches to the social sciences use as a basis the writings of Karl Marx and Friedrich Engels. Marx's philosophy relates a society's mode of production to its economy and thus to its social structure and culture. The economic base, therefore, is the underlying principle exerting a primary influence on the political, social, and cultural features of a given social group. In capitalist societies, according to this interpretation, the contradictory relationship between labor and capital ultimately becomes restrictive economically, forcing the landless proletariat to rise up, then to dominate. Marx believed that the overthrow of capitalist society by the revolutionary working class would ultimately yield a classless society.

By understanding how culture affects group and individual consciousness, the Marxist scholar also seeks to understand more about the tendency to rebel against ideological manipulation and the resulting development of alternatives to current norms in Western society (Zipes 1984:334). The use of the Marxist approach in the various social-science disciplines and in different countries, each with unique social and historical structures, created a spectrum of interpretive theoretical variations.

The development and use of Marxist ideology in all of the social-science disciplines has been considerably stronger in Europe than in the United States. In Europe there has historically been a keen sense of nationalism and a more developed social-democratic labor movement—thus, greater identification with the Marxist ideology. In the United States, the term "Marxist" has been applied more loosely, referring often simply to a radical or critical approach influenced only generally by Marxist concepts.

The influence of Marxist ideology on American folklore studies has been affected by European folklore research and scholarship in disciplines that folklorists draw from for their theoretical constructs, especially sociology, anthropology, and history. The greatest influence in folklore came from German scholars beginning in the 1920s. There was a resurgence of influence from Europe in the 1960s and 1970s. Yet, even during periods when political radicalism strongly affected the culture and the academic disciplines, when classical Marxism was being applied to research, folklorists tended to remain less committed to these intellectual currents than to other interpretive approaches.

Folk-literature and folk-music studies have been most frequently influenced by Marxist ideas. Loosely defined Marxist principles have been applied by American scholars such as Charles Seeger, Carl Boggs, and Tim Patterson to analyses of traditional musical culture. Jack Zipes has applied the philosophy in his book *Breaking the Magic Spell: Radical Theories of Folk and Fairy Tales* (1979). These scholars and others have each drawn from several European interpreters of Marxist ideology who played an important role in anthropological, sociological, and historical scholarship, especially Antonio Gramsci, Georg Lukács, Walter Benjamin, and Herbert Marcuse.

Jennifer C. Post

References

Boggs, Carl. 1978. The Blues Traditions: From Poetic Revolt to Cultural Impasse. *Socialist Review* 8:115–134.

Limón, José E. 1983. Western Marxism and Folklore. *Journal of American Folklore* 96:34–52.

———. 1984. Western Marxism and Folklore: A Critical Reintroduction. *Journal of American Folklore* 97:337–344.

Patterson, Tim. 1975. Notes on the Historical Application of Marxist Cultural Theory. *Science and Society* 39:257–291.

Porter, James. 1993. Convergence, Divergence, and Dialectic in Folksong Paradigms: Critical Directions for Transatlantic Scholarship. *Journal of American Folklore* 106:61–98.

Roseberry, William. 1991. Marxism and Culture. In *The Politics of Culture,* Brett Williams. Washington, DC: Smithsonian Institution, pp. 19–43.

Seeger, Charles. 1934. On Proletarian Music. *Modern Music* 11:121–127.

Zipes, Jack. 1984. Folklore Research and Western Marxism: A Critical Replay. *Journal of American Folklore* 97:329–337.

Mason, Otis Tufton (1838–1908)

Anthropologist and museum curator. After graduating from Columbia College in Washington, DC, in 1861, Mason became principal of the institution's preparatory school, where he taught a variety of subjects and by 1884 held the title of professor of anthropology. In that year he became curator of ethnology at the Smithsonian Institution, a position he kept until his death. Advocating the centralization of ethnological research, Mason wrote the constitution for the Anthropological Society of Washington, forerunner of the American Anthropological Association. In 1891 he was the third president of the American Folklore Society.

Stressing classification of artifacts, Mason developed exhibits at the Smithsonian Institution that demonstrated human "invention" by assembling objects from diverse cultures that exemplified what he perceived as evolutionary sequences. Basing his findings upon the museum's collections rather than primary fieldwork, he wrote several studies of human inventiveness and of American Indian material culture. His publications emphasized production techniques, the details of which dominated most of his work. During his last decade, Mason's research interests shifted to Southeast Asia, especially Malaysia.

Challenged by Franz Boas' criticisms of his approach to displaying artifacts, Mason moved toward a culture-area focus in the exhibits he arranged for the 1893 Chicago World's Fair. However, he never abandoned an object-centered, evolutionary perspective. In fact, he believed that material objects most effectively demonstrated humanity's progress from savagery to civilization and was attracted to the arts of Southeast Asia because they seemed to represent a stage between the "savage" cultures of America, which had dominated his previous research, and the eastern Mediterranean forerunners of modern European civilizations.

William M. Clements

References

Hinsley, Curtis M. 1981. *Savages and Scientists: The Smithsonian Institution and the Development of American Anthropology, 1846–1919*. Washington, DC: Smithsonian Institution.

Hough, Walter. 1908. Otis Tufton Mason. *American Anthropologist* 10:661–667.

Mason, Otis T. 1891. The Natural History of Folk-Lore. *Journal of American Folklore* 4:97–105.

———. 1894. *Women's Share in Primitive Culture*. New York: Appleton.

———. 1895. *The Origins of Invention: A Study of Industry among Primitive Peoples*. London: W. Scott.

———. 1903. *Aboriginal American Basketry: Studies in a Textile Art without Machinery*. Washington, DC: GPO.

Mass Media and Folklore

The dynamic relationship between the communication content, genres, and styles of traditional folk cultures and those of communication conducted through print and electronic media. Folklore resembles mass communication in that both rely upon conventional formulas for their verbal and visual "narratives," but whereas most folklore communication takes place face to face, mass communication is "mediated" through a channel that permits (almost requires) anonymity between the producers and a mass audience and provides for none of the usual feedback mechanisms possible in face-to-face communication. People tend to express traditional values through folklore, while mass-mediated culture (as a commercial culture) seeks novelty at the same time that it renders novel materials through conventional formulas.

We find folklore in the mass media, as well as mass-media elements in folklore. This dialectical relationship reflects the fact that folklore and mass-mediated culture share the paradox of being simultaneously dynamic and conservative cultural forms.

The makers of mass-media texts frequently appropriate the content, genres, and style of folklore communication toward commercial ends. Folklore may be the basis for what one folklorist has called "folklure," that is, the use of folklore to induce in the advertising audience the desire to consume the advertised product or service. Print and electronic advertising, for example, frequently invoke familiar folk ideas, characters, and narratives, such as giants (Green Giant vegetables), elves (Keebler crackers and cookies), and magical charms (from cereals to cleaning products). Cartoonists and the creators of comic strips often rely upon the audience's familiarity with folklore. Political cartoons sometimes depend upon folk beliefs or folk sayings for their meaning. Gary Larson's single-frame *Far Side* cartoons feature folk beliefs about snakes and other animals and often play upon familiar folk legends (for example, "The Hooked Hand") and narratives (such as Grimms' fairy tales). Bill Watterson's *Calvin and Hobbes* comic strip, featuring a boy and the stuffed tiger (Hobbes) that becomes alive only for him, draws heavily upon the folklore of children.

The print media bring folklore into other sorts of mass public discourse. Journalists are as likely as anyone to use proverbs, folk beliefs, and folk-narrative conventions to make sense of an unfolding story. Columnists such as Ann Landers (syndicated) and Herb Caen *(San Francisco Chronicle)* frequently pass on legends as actual events. Weekly tabloid newspapers (such as *The National Enquirer),* known for their sensationalism, regularly adopt legends as newsworthy stories. Writers of more serious fiction also appropriate folklore for their own authorial purposes, from the everyday conversational genres (jokes, proverbs, teases) to the more elaborate narratives, such as Thomas Pynchon's use of the alligators-in-the-sewers legend in his novel *V* (1963).

Television and theatrical film narratives frequently tap folklore for familiar motifs and stories. The writers of situation comedies make use of legends, superstitions, jokes, pranks, proverbs, and other genres of folklore experienced in everyday life. NBC's highly successful *Cheers,* for example, built an entire episode around a snipe hunt.

The theatrical film *Her Alibi* (1989) used "The Poisoned Cat" urban legend as a plot device, and the genre of horror films has long drawn upon folk legends. The series of "slasher films" (from *Friday the 13th* [1980] and its sequels through *Nightmare on Elm Street* [1985] and its numerous sequels) may be seen simply as cinematic versions of adolescent urban legends ("The Hooked Hand," "The Babysitter and the Man Upstairs"). The most fully realized example of film's appropriation of folklore is the 1992 film *Candyman,* in which two graduate students in search of urban legends come across a supernatural murderer who embodies the legend of "Bloody Mary." That film also incorporates the legend (with roots as old as Chaucer) of the boy castrated in a public bathroom while his worried mother waits outside.

The appropriation of content, genre, and style by one cultural realm from another also flows the other way. People often appropriate elements of mass-mediated communication in their folk cultures. Children, for example, will adopt dramatic roles and costumes (Batman, the Simpsons, Teenage Mutant Ninja Turtles, fairy princesses) from television and film narratives into their own free, imaginative play. Children create parody versions of television commercials and jingles, and at least one troop of Boy Scouts encourages the adolescents to create parody commercials as campfire skits. A few folklorists have even observed children inventing in their free play living versions of the Nintendo games they play on television screens.

Adults are just as likely to appropriate mass-mediated texts into their folklore. Joke cycles, for example, may include fictional characters or actual actors from the mass media. Mass-media events can also provide the occasion for a folk celebration, from the weekly gathering to watch Monday Night Football to the special parties held to watch the last episode of *M*A*S*H* or *Cheers*. Several scholars have addressed the phenomenon of the daytime-serial (the "soap opera") viewer who seems to include the television characters in his or her everyday world of conversations, personal-experience narrating, and so on. Film and television are such pervasive elements in modern American culture that their narratives weave constantly through the narratives of everyday life.

Criticism arising out of modern cultural studies encourages the view that there is a dynamic, dialectical relationship between the mass media and folklore in modern society. Whereas some scholars worry that the mass media, especially television, work to homogenize culture and to destroy more "authentic" folklore, most media critics attribute great power to audiences to resist the effects of mass-mediated content and forms. Audience-response theory (reader-response theory in literary criticism, viewer-response theory in television and film criticism) looks for the active role audiences take in making and negotiating the meanings of a mass-mediated text. Folklore makes up a great deal of the commonsense, taken-for-granted repertoire of meanings audiences have at their disposal for interpreting, accepting, and even resisting the messages of mass-mediated texts.

Jay Mechling

References

Bausinger, Hermann. 1990. *Folk Culture in a World of Technology*, trans. Elke Dettmer. Bloomington: Indiana University Press.

Bird, S. Elizabeth. 1992. *For Enquiring Minds: A Cultural Study of Supermarket Tabloids*. Knoxville: University of Tennessee Press.

Denby, Priscilla. 1971. Folklore in the Mass Media. *Folklore Forum* 4:113–125.

Fiske, John. 1987. *Television Culture*. London: Routledge and Kegan Paul.

Mechling, Jay. 1989. An American Culture Grid, with Texts. *American Studies International* 27(1):2–12.

Schechter, Harold. 1988. *The Bosom Serpent: Folklore and Popular Art*. Iowa City: University of Iowa Press.

Sullenberger, Tom E. 1974. Ajax Meets the Jolly Green Giant: Some Observations on the Use of Folklore and Myth in American Mass Marketing. *Journal of American Folklore* 87:53–65.

See also Film and Folklore; Popular Culture and Folklore; Urban Legend

Material Culture

A term used to designate the interconnection of tangible, human–made forms as an indicator of cultural ideas and traditions. "Material culture" points to patterns among types of human construction such as craft, industry, art, architecture, dress, food, agriculture, settlement, medicine, and furnishing. Although the study of objects and object types is important to material-culture study, the special emphasis in material-culture study is on the way that a material-environment is formed or cultural ideas and traditions are expressed in material form and construction activities. Material culture often refers to social relations among people mediated by objects and, therefore, involves connections to intellectual and social systems in cultures. With the addition of the modifier "folk," the term "material folk culture" is sometimes used to draw specific attention to constructions that are traditionally part of community life, whereas "folk technical culture" or "folk technics" will appear to refer to traditional construction skills known among members of a cultural group. "Material aspects of culture" occasionally appears to designate an analytical category of traditions that is distinct from "verbal" and "social" traditions.

History of Material-Culture Studies in American Folkloristics

The use of material culture in relation to the study of folk traditions dates to the 19th century, when anthropologists/archaeologists divided the data gathered on the world's tribal groups into "intellectual" (oral and written), "social" (human behavior and structure such as kinship and ritual), and "material" (products of work from human hands). This division influenced later folkloristic division of data into "verbal," "social," and "material." British anthropologist A. Lane-Fox Pitt-Rivers as early as 1875 urged the study of material culture as the "outward signs and symbols of particular ideas in the mind." Of special concern to many Victorian anthropologists was the comparison of technology that could help show an evolutionary sequence for the rise of modern civilization from the primitive to the industrial.

Other anthropologists/archaeologists used the idea of material culture to show diffusion from one culture area to another. In separate publications around the turn of the century, Waldemar Bogoras, for instance, made a case for the migration of American Indians from North Pacific Asia to the American Northwest by using folklore and material culture. That a society could represent a distinctive material culture also suggested that tangible forms could designate differences and boundaries among cultural areas or groups.

A scarecrow in rural
North Carolina,
1938. Photo John
Vachon. Library of
Congress.

Nineteenth-century leaders of the American Folklore Society often came from anthropological museums and had an interest in using material as well as oral evidence to show the evolution and diffusion of folk customs and beliefs. They pointed to the way that objects were integral parts of rituals or reflected beliefs held by a group. Presidents of the American Folklore Society such as Otis T. Mason at the Smithsonian Institution wrote about, and mounted exhibitions on, the evolution of invention, and Stewart Culin at the University of Pennsylvania Museum collected gaming and religious objects to show the connection of modern-day play with earlier religious rites. Folklore became separated from material culture in the early 20th century when anthropologists taking over the *Journal of American Folklore* defined the subject matter of folklore narrowly as oral tradition.

In the 1930s, as folklorists began to reestablish their field within academe and draw on German and Scandinavian scholarship in addition to building on British folklore work, material culture worked back into the definition of folkloristic inquiry. Martha Warren Beckwith, who occupied America's first chair of folklore at Vassar College, made a case in *Folklore in America* (1931) for an American folkloristic contribution that explores the "material arts" to study all traditional expression. She pointed out the American situation of possessing a varied mixture of regional, ethnic, and occupational groups (in addition to the aboriginal tribes favored by anthropologists) that have related oral as well as material traditions. Particular interest in connecting oral, social, and material traditions into one study came from Pennsylvania-German scholars who drew on the German *Volkskunde,* or "folklife," movement to interpret the "total culture," giving priority to material and social expressions in everyday life. Alfred L. Shoemaker, a founder of the Pennsylvania Folklife Society in 1924 and professor at Franklin and Marshall College in America's first Department of Folklore, was especially instrumental in promoting "folk culture" and "material culture" as appropriate terms for the study of America's regional-ethnic diversity.

During the 1960s, the growth of American folklife museums and the establishment of a graduate academic program at Cooperstown, New York, in American folk culture (sponsored by the State University of New York and the New York State Historical Association) furthered research in material culture as a folkloristic concept. In major publications such as *Pattern in the Material Folk Culture of the Eastern United States* (1968), by Henry Glassie, and *Forms upon the Frontier* (1969), edited by Austin E. and Alta S. Fife and Henry Glassie, material culture emerged as a special folkloristic concern for long-standing traditions in lasting tangible forms. Building on the ethnological base of material-culture studies, folklorists added perspectives from history, geography, and folklore, especially applied to stable forms such as houses and barns, to bring out the development of regional-ethnic cultures. In later works such as Michael Owen Jones' *The Hand Made Object and Its Maker* (1975) and Simon J. Bronner's *Grasping Things* (1986), folklorists urged the understanding of aesthetic processes and community psychology in the formation of material culture and, therefore, began focusing on art and craft used by individuals negotiating between tradition and creativity.

By the 1980s, every American graduate program in folklore included material culture in its curriculum, and museums offered numerous exhibitions highlighting traditional material culture. During this period, the journal *Pioneer America* changed its name to *Material Culture* under folkloristic editorship, and the *Journal of American Folklore* featured a number of material-culture studies. In several conferences and anthologies devoted to material-culture studies generally (such as *Material Culture Studies in America* [1982], edited by Thomas Schlereth, and *Material Culture Studies: A Symposium* [1985]), edited by Simon J. Bronner), folklorists contributed significantly to theoretical formulations of material culture in several disciplines.

Characterizations of American Material Culture

A variety of perspectives can be discerned in American studies that identify base concepts of American material culture. Drawing on early American historical experience, one view points to contrasts between American Indian, Northern European, and African influences on the American landscape. According to this perspective, in colonial New England and Virginia different material-culture systems came into conflict when English settlers confronted Native Americans. Observers noted that the English system was built on the formation of lines and rectangles; that of many Indian tribes, on a circular basis. English architecture built on a rectangular foundation and human control over the landscape, its conception of time and age was linear, and its settlements were permanent and arranged on a grid with private properties. Indian settlements were mobile and often arranged in circular patterns, their conception of time and age was often cyclical, and tribal architecture was based less on human dominance than on a relationship with nature. Both groups practiced agriculture, and much of the cultural borrowing that occurred between the groups seems to have been in food processes, including tobacco, corn, and maple syrup. Following this model, a view takes form of enslaved Africans in the American South largely acculturating to European American material systems, while strong signs of ethnic maintenance are evident in house interiors, crafts, dress, and foodways. Many critics of this view point out that American Indian, European, and African material cultures were more diverse than the racial alignment of "Red, White, and Black" suggests. This model implies that the European American westward movement fostered a material culture based on the clearing of the forested wilderness and a reliance on wood as the primary component of construction. This movement helped shape a new national identity, assimilate immigrant groups into the aesthetics of a pioneer American society, and encourage the removal of American Indians. According to this view, the first permanent European settlements in the American experience effectively determined the future course of material-culture development.

Another way that American material culture has been represented is by viewing the movement of material culture historically from American ports of entry into the interior. Glassie, for example, posited four main "cultural hearths" on the Eastern seaboard that influenced the formation of "material folk culture regions." The New England hearth, with its strong English stamp, spread north to New Hampshire and Maine and west across New York and Michigan. The Chesapeake–Tidewater hearth influenced the movement of material culture across Maryland and Virginia into the Upland South. The Lowland South hearth featured a strong African influence and worked its way through South Carolina and Georgia into the Deep South. The last hearth to form was in Pennsylvania, where Palatine Germans, Swiss Anabaptists, English Quakers, French Huguenots, and Scots-Irish people influenced the formation of a plural society and a strong inland Pennsylvania-German culture subregion that spread into the Midwest. Because migration patterns did not uniformly move west, a problem occurs in extending this model into the trans-Mississippi and Far West. In addition, many material forms such as quilts and fences may diverge from regional patterns.

The connection among architecture, foods, and crafts in some settlements marked by an ethnic population or geographic location has led to the mapping of material-culture subregions. Material culture has been used to make an argument, for example, for folk regions such as the Mormon Culture Region (Utah and parts of Idaho, Nevada, and Arizona), the Southwest Culture Region (New Mexico, Arizona, and parts of Texas, Nevada, and Colorado), the Ozark Culture Region (Arkansas, Missouri, and part of Illinois), and "Cajun Country" (Louisiana and part of Texas). These regions are usually based on ethnic populations adapting to a landscape with the construction of regionally distinctive material forms.

Another perspective (ethnography) concentrates less on broad historical-geographic patterns than on contemporary observations of localized behavior and communication in a variety of social settings. Using this approach, some authorities have characterized American material culture as heterogeneous, changeful, individualistic, and subject to a variety of social forces, including gender, age, and class in addition to region and ethnicity. This modernistic view of American material culture includes suburban developments, college campuses, summer camps, and city neighborhoods as occasional settings for shared traditions of dress, food, and craft. Children, women, and workers, among other social networks, can form material folk cultures that may be localized to a specific community, organization, or even an individual and can change readily. Studies have focused, for instance, on the created material culture of Freemasons, Boy Scouts, and corporate offices.

In this ethnographic view, Americans inherit or choose identities that they can enact in different settings with reference to an appropriate material culture. They recognize ways of presenting themselves, ways of "doing things" (praxis), to communicate certain values or adapt to social situations and physical settings. Often at issue in such studies is the degree of control humans have over their creations. Some studies question whether traditional forms have symbolic meanings that affect or reflect behavior. An example is whether the emphasis on the rectangle in American material culture in a social setting such as a classroom affects the kind of teaching and participation that takes place. In decisions such as decorating a front yard with consumable items, residents may be indicating their personal control in mass culture by creating designs through arrangement.

Goals of American Material-Culture Study

Using the concept of material culture in folklore studies forces an assessment of physical evidence as well as social and intellectual forces on the formation of cultural traditions. Some scholars have called for mapping American material folk culture by showing the interrelation of traditional material forms in a comprehensive "folk atlas" similar to those available for the countries of Europe. A step toward this goal was the publication of *This Remarkable Continent* (1982), sponsored by the Society for the North American Cultural Survey. Proponents of such an atlas argue that it provides a graphic tool for interpreting the movements and regions that characterize the formation of cultures in the New World. They point out that artifacts in a study of material culture provide lasting, tangible evidence that can be compared and located in space and time. Much of the work to establish typologies of material traditions has been intended to aid this comparativist effort.

Another goal established early in the use of "material culture" has been to identify mental and behavioral processes through ethnographic observation. By studying individuals and groups engaged in constructive activities, scholars intend to identify the reasoning that influences the shape of the human-built environment. Often at issue is the negotiation within cultures between tradition and creativity present in the enhancement of design and technology. This concern has led to considerable effort to identify the symbolic uses and social functions of material constructions by community "actors" performing within specific cultural scenes. The effort has been to explain the shape of the forms with reference to the activities and contexts that led to their formation, use, enhancement, and replacement. Some applications of these interpretations are used to enhance working environments and social therapies.

Material folk culture also has a significant historical role in the evaluation of American everyday life. Material culture is often tied to everyday uses and points to familiar structures. Traditional architectural forms, in particular, remain stable over time and variable over space, thus suggesting a cultural history that marks significant social change when basic structures change. Folklorists and historians, for example, have examined the great impact of railroad transportation in the 19th century on settlement patterns and material culture of the West. Material folk culture also offers historical evidence for groups marginalized in historical scholarship or without a substantial documentary record, including many ethnic groups. Material culture documents the special experiences of such groups within the American scene. Historical explanation is also possible for the confrontation and combination of ideas communicated through material symbols. The historical perception of a division between Northern and Southern material culture can be viewed in an assessment of American sectionalism, or the historical importance of "log cabin" origins as a symbol of national unity in political campaigns can be interpreted.

Although goals of using the concept of "material culture" vary, the idea that traditions are apparent in tangible forms undergirds most approaches to the subject. Material-culture study is an international movement, with American studies contributing to transnational and cross-cultural research. Yet, distinguishing the field in the United States are some special conditions, such as social and geographical diversity, dramatic migrations, and cross-fertilizations, and a relatively recent history as a formerly colonized nation that has experienced cultural transformations of industrialization, incorporation, and urbanization.

Simon J. Bronner

References

Bronner, Simon J. 1985. Visible Proofs: Material Culture Study in American Folkloristics. In *Material Culture: A Research Guide,* ed. Thomas J. Schlereth. Lawrence: University Press of Kansas, pp. 127–53.
———. [1985] 1992. *American Material Culture and Folklife.* Logan: Utah State University Press.
Fife, Austin. 1988. *Exploring Western Americana.* Ann Arbor, MI: UMI Research Press.
Jones, Michael Owen. 1987. *Exploring Folk Art: Twenty Years of Thought on Craft, Work, and Aesthetics.* Logan: Utah State University Press.
Nelson, Marion, ed. 1994. *Material Culture and People's Art among the Norwegians in America.* Northfield, MN: Norwegian American Historical Association.
Pocius, Gerald L., ed. 1991. *Living in a Material World: Canadian and American Approaches to Material Culture.* St. John's, Newfoundland: Institute of Social and Economic Research, Memorial University of Newfoundland.
Roberts, Warren E. 1988. *Viewpoints on Folklife: Looking at the Overlooked.* Ann Arbor, MI: UMI Research Press.
Vlach, John Michael. 1991. *By the Work of Their Hands: Studies in Afro-American Folklife.* Ann Arbor, MI: UMI Research Press.
Wissler, Clark. 1914. Material Cultures of North American Indians. *American Anthropologist* 16:447–505.

See also Architecture, Vernacular; Art, Folk; Crafts; Regional Folklore; Vernacular

McCoy, Minnie ("Memphis Minnie") (1897?–1973)

Vocalist and guitar player widely celebrated as the greatest female singer of country blues. She also composed, played, and sang country, urban, Chicago, and postwar blues on 212 issued sides recorded from 1929 to 1959; she was the winner of the top female vocalist award in the first *Blues Unlimited* readers' poll (1973) and an acknowledged influence on musicians as diverse as Chuck Berry and the Jefferson Airplane.

Born Minnie Douglas in Algiers, Louisiana, she moved with her family in 1904 to Walls, Mississippi (near Memphis, Tennessee), acquired her first guitar in 1905, and left the family farm to perform in Memphis soon after. She toured the South with a Ringling Brothers show during World War I, met "Kansas Joe" McCoy in the 1920s, and first recorded with him for Columbia in New York in 1929 (the year they married).

Like the "down-home" bluesmen, Memphis Minnie composed much of her own material and performed not just on stage and in nightclubs, but also at home, at picnics, for house parties, and on the street. A consummate guitarist, she was a finger-picker with the speed and agility of the country flat-pickers. One of a handful of female performers who expressed sexual themes in the male-dominated world of blues performance, Memphis Minnie—like the classic blues singers—sang openly of the rough realities of life as a working-class Black female. The lyric content of her compositions includes humor and heartbreak, barnyard and kitchen metaphors, voodoo and eroticism, and several masterpieces such as the prototypical "Bumble Bee" (1929) in the venerable blues tradition of sexual double entendre.

Ruth E. Andersen

McTell, Blind Willie (1901–1959)

Georgia blues musician, significant both for his distinctive voice and his innovative guitar work. Born almost totally blind in Thomson, Georgia, on May 5, 1901, McTell learned guitar from his mother when he was thirteen years old. Shortly thereafter he ran away from home to work in various carnival, minstrel, and medicine shows, though not always as a musician. From 1926 on, he hoboed along the East Coast, earning a meager living playing guitar and singing. McTell's recording career lasted from 1927 to 1956, unusually long for a country blues artist of the time. This extensive recording activity was justified because McTell was extremely versatile.

Most of McTell's recordings featured his high, plaintive, nasal vocals and his masterful twelve-string guitar; he was one of the few real masters of that instrument. Some of his notable recordings were "Atlanta Strut," a ragtime dance with imitative, impressionistic guitar breaks and a spoken narrative; "Death Cell Blues," noteworthy for its outstanding lyrics; the ballad "Chainey and Delia," and "Broke Down Engine Blues," a number in which McTell uses the twelve-string guitar both to provide a rhythmic base and to answer the vocal. His material ran the gamut from the pre-blues songster tradition to the best of lyrical blues.

Following a recording session in 1950, McTell drifted into obscurity. In 1956 he resurfaced for a final album, after which he left music permanently. In 1957 he was pastor of Atlanta's Mt. Zion Baptist Church. Two years later, on August 19, 1959, he died of a cerebral hemorrhage at the Milledgeville State Hospital.

W.K. McNeil

References

Bastin, Bruce. 1971. *Crying for the Carolines.* London: Studio Vista.

———. 1986. *Red River Blues: The Blues Tradition in the Southeast.* Urbana: University of Illinois Press.

Charters, Samuel. 1977. *Sweet as the Showers of Rain.* New York: Oak Publications.

Medical Professionals

Occupational category consisting of doctors, nurses, paramedics, and others whose professions involve health care. The folklore of these groups, who often refer to themselves as "health-care professionals," includes slang, jargon-based word play, joking, occupational sayings, mnemonics, folk stereotypes of patients and colleagues, stories, skits, and other festive behaviors. Parallels to much of this material can be found outside the healing professions, but the content of the medical material reflects the work experiences of those who provide health care. Although medical professionals use traditional patterns to create new folklore, much circulates nationally. Some items, such as certain sayings and stereotypes, are more than fifty years old. Overlap exists between the folklore of different subgroups within the healing professions, but the folklore of each varies according to their different training, responsibilities, and position within the hierarchy.

The specialized language of health-care workers is the foundation on which all other genres rest. In addition to formal scientific and technical terminology, medical language includes informal clipped forms, acronyms, and slang usages. Word play based on all of these forms occurs during casual conversations. For instance, medical workers sometimes refer to "Amphoterrible" instead of the toxic drug "Amphotericin B," and the common laboratory abbreviation "WNL," "within normal limits," is said to stand for "we never looked." The suffix "-oma," meaning tumor, may be combined with the word "horrendous," to form "horrendioma," meaning "an unusually sad or mistake-ridden case." Although these examples are traditional, medical workers use similar techniques to create new jokes, often making pointed comments in the process.

Mnemonics are another form of humorous verbal lore that circulates among medical professionals. These fanciful, often bawdy verbal devices are used as aids in memorizing anatomical structures and other necessary medical and scientific information. Medical students, for example, recall structures in the chest by remembering "the five birds of the thoracic cage"—the esophagus, the azygous, the hemizygous, the vagus, and the thoracic duct ("four geese and a duck"). Although the use of mnemonics peaks during the preclinical years, when many students create their own, some are used later to remember elements of proper diagnosis or clinical practice.

Numerous proverbial sayings communicate aspects of medical culture and belief. For example, the saying, "When you hear hoof beats, look for horses, not zebras," reminds students and physicians alike that a patient's symptoms are more likely caused by common illnesses than rare. Another saying, "See one [procedure], do one, teach one" (sometimes parodied as "See one, do one, kill one"), emphasizes the need for medical students to learn quickly from their teachers so that they, in turn, can teach others.

Much of the folklore of health-care professionals revolves around traditional images of different kinds of patients. Patients are stereotyped on the basis of characteristics such as lifestyle, personality, hygiene, mental status, and the perceived seriousness of their illnesses. Among the terms applied to patients are "crock," an old term for a presumed hypochondriac; "turkey," a marginally sick patient; "vegetable" and "gork," both applied to hopelessly comatose patients; "gomer," a senile, and debilitated elderly patient—the term is sometimes said to be an acronym for "Get Out of My Emergency Room,"—and "dirtball," a dirty, often homeless elderly alcoholic male (the term is most common in Veterans Administration and other public hospitals.) The hostility evident in such characterizations reflects not only a sense of moral and social superiority, but also the difficulties and frustrations of dealing with patients who cannot benefit from, or may not even need, the attention they receive, or who refuse to take adequate care of themselves. Overburdened health-care workers often feel that the large amounts of time they must devote to these patients prevent them from giving better care to others.

Other stereotypes deal with the health-care worker's own colleagues, evaluating them in terms of their "typical" personalities and presumed degree of professional competence. Intensive-care and emergency-room nurses, for instance, are said be tough, as are surgical nurses, who must withstand the reputed abrasiveness of surgeons. Internists consider surgeons to be ignorant technicians and are themselves said to be "compulsive," "uptight," and "indecisive" because of their emphasis on diagnostic details and propensity to order tests. The well-known saying, "The internist knows everything and does nothing, the surgeon knows nothing and does everything, the psychiatrist knows nothing and does nothing, and the pathologist knows everything and does everything—but a day too late," expresses many of these stereotypes and hints at the feelings of inadequacy doctors experience when they cannot help their patients.

Narratives about patients, both in the form of serious case histories and informal stories, play an important part in the working lives of health-care professionals. The case histories, that are orally presented on rounds and written in patients' charts, follow a stylized structure that includes some formulaic elements. Very different narrative patterns shape the stories doctors and nurses tell about their patients in other settings. These stories follow standard American conventions for personal-experience narratives and may include imitations of patients as well as other dramatic devices. Most such stories are humorous and, influenced by the folklore of patient stereotypes, focus on the individual's personal idiosyncrasies rather than his or her medical problems.

Experiences in which the normal routine is disrupted form the grist for many narratives. Stories about particularly arduous or otherwise unusual nights on call are common, as are those concerning encounters with members of other departments. Many young doctors tell "first day on night call" stories, which often end with the frightened new graduate responding to an emergency by yelling, "Call a doctor." Medical students tell accounts about pranks played with cadavers during their anatomy course. In most cases, the lifespan of personal-experience narratives in medicine is relatively brief. New events, new patients, and thus new stories constantly replace the old.

Other forms of storytelling found in medicine include oral historical narratives, especially accounts told to students and residents by older doctors about how much harder it was when they were residents, and anecdotes about the "grand old men" of medicine. Stories often coalesce around particularly memorable colleagues—for example, a surgeon known for his outspoken nature and operating-room antics. In teaching contexts, occasional apocryphal stories about the fatal consequences of mistakes are told as cautionary tales for doctors-in-training.

Medical life is punctuated by numerous traditional events, ranging from the daily battery of meetings and ritualized rounds doctors and nurses make on their patients to intermittent events such as going-away parties for staff and long-term hospital patients or seasonal celebrations such as Christmas or graduation parties. Dinners given in June, the end of the medical-training year, sometimes include mock award ceremonies during which members of the community receive facetious honors or symbolic gifts—for example, a ball and chain given to the incoming chief resident. In many places, medical students or residents put on satiric skits poking fun at the foibles of the individuals at the medical center and of the health professions in general. Such skits, which draw on all other genres of medical folklore, allow the students and (vicariously) the audience to air their grievances in a safe setting while creating a sense of community among groups between which there is normally some friction.

Among the most noticeable characteristics of medical folklore are its cynical outlook and black humor. Although popularized by television shows such as *St. Elsewhere* and by Samuel Shem's cult novel *The House of God* (1979), which is based largely on hospital folklore, this humor remains controversial, even among health-care professionals, who object to the way it dehumanizes patients.

But medical humor must be judged within the context in which it is created. Taking care of patients is stressful under the best of conditions. Health-care workers constantly deal with hostile patients and encounter tragic situations that they cannot resolve. Mistakes, sometimes fatal, are easy to make, and even minor procedures cause patients pain. These problems are aggravated by the conditions of overwork and lack of sleep that plague many medical professionals.

Like other occupational groups whose work involves danger, humor is one way in which health-care workers deal with the stresses caused by their jobs. The bravado of medical humor serves as a defense mechanism, a way of denying the anxieties, insecurities, and emotional pain felt by its users. Although they sometimes overstep the bounds of propriety, medical professionals use their humor to handle feelings that might otherwise undermine the equanimity and objectivity they need in order to function.

Anne Burson-Tolpin

References

Burson-Tolpin, Anne. 1989. Fracturing the Language of Biomedicine: The Speech Play of American Physicians. *Medical Anthropology Quarterly*, n.s., 3:283–293.

———. 1993. A "Travesty Tonight": Satiric Skits in Medicine. In *The Doctor and Drama*, ed. D. Heyward Brock. *Literature and Medicine* (Special Issue) 12:81–110.

George, Victoria, and Alan Dundes. 1978. The Gomer: A Figure of American Hospital Folk Speech. *Journal of American Folklore* 91:568–581.

Gordon, David Paul. 1983. Hospital Slang for Patients: Crocks, Gomers, Gorks, and Others. *Language in Society* 12:173–185.

Hufford, David. 1989. Customary Observances in Modern Medicine. *Western Folklore* 48:129–143.

Liederman, Deborah B., and Jean-Ann Grisso. 1985. The Gomer Phenomenon. *Journal of Health and Social Behavior* 26:222–232.

Medicine, Folk

Medical beliefs and practices derived primarily through oral-traditional processes rather than from printed texts or formal academic or clinical training. Because folk medicine—also known as traditional, vernacular, or community medicine—exists outside the "official" medical establishment and the regulatory system that governs nurses, pharmacists, physicians, and other licensed health-care professionals, it has often been marginalized, equated with quackery, or simply dismissed as a curious anachronism—a vestige of an earlier and simpler time. Yet, as folklorists, anthropologists, ethnobotanists, medical specialists, and researchers in other fields have documented, folk medicine is both widespread and active in contemporary America, representing one of many options in a complex and highly diversified health-care system.

One distinctive characteristic of folk medicine is its multiplicity of forms, almost all of which can be subsumed into three main categories: household medicine (home remedies), herbalism and other forms of naturopathic healing, and magical medicine.

Of the three, home remedies are the most recent in origin and the simplest to prepare and use, requiring little specialized knowledge or expertise. Made from ingredients commonly found in the kitchen cabinet, the refrigerator, or the garage, they are for many people the option of first choice for minor ailments and injuries. Some household prescriptions take the form of generalized wisdom, as in the familiar proverb "Feed a cold, starve a fever," while others offer specific practical advice, such as gargling with salt water to ease the irritation of a sore throat, drinking whiskey mixed with sugar or honey as a cough suppressant, putting moistened tobacco on a bee sting or insect bite to reduce pain and inflammation, or pouring kerosene on a cut to prevent infection.

Older and more complex than home remedies are naturopathic cures derived from animals, minerals, and plants. Plant-based preventatives and cures, known collectively as herbalism, have played an especially prominent role in American folk medicine. Herbalism was an integral part of Native American healing systems long before the first European settlers arrived with their own rich naturopathic traditions, and it continues to flourish in many parts of the country, both independently and as a constituent of larger magico-religious systems.

The botanical pharmacopoeia is extensive and varied, furnishing the ingredients for salves, poultices, teas, and other decoctions used to treat a host of illnesses and injuries, ranging from colds and coughs to heart disease, diabetes, and cancer. A particular plant, such as aloe *(Aloe vera)*, may serve a single function, in this instance as a burn ointment, or a plant may have multiple functions, as in the case of sassafras *(Sassafras albidum)*, which is made into a tea and taken internally as a blood purifier or a spring tonic; as a cure for colds, flu, and fevers; as a means of breaking out measles or chicken pox; and as a heart remedy.

While sassafras tea can be made with relative ease simply by boiling the roots in water, the preparation of a number of other medicinal plants such as poke *(Phytolacca americana)* requires specialized knowledge and skill. Indigenous to the Eastern United States, poke has long been used for medicinal purposes, its specific functions dictated by the season at which it is harvested and the part of the plant from which the medication is extracted. The berries, for example, furnish a juice that is reputed to be effective in treating boils and sores. The leaves, when harvested early in the seasonal cycle, provide the chief ingredient in what is commonly referred to as "poke salad," a popular spring tonic and blood purifier. The root itself has traditionally been used to treat stomach cramps and other intestinal problems.

Just as a particular plant may serve a variety of medicinal functions, so, too, might a particular illness be amenable to a multiplicity of treatments. In a recent study of rheumatism cures used by a prominent Appalachian herbalist, for example, two Duke University botanists, John Crellin and Jane Philpott, identified twenty-three different plant ingredients, including the bark of Bowman's root, the cucumber tree, and the yellow poplar; the bark or leaves of the apple, bay, and beech tree; the bark or berries of the prickley ash; the roots of black cohosh, button snakeroot, devil's shoestring, gentian, Indian hemp, joe-pye-weed, Sampson snakeroot, and sassafras; poke root or berries; tops and roots of Queen Anne's lace; angelico root or leaves; ratsvein leaves; skullcap leaves and stem; and hydrangea bark, leaves, and root. Similar findings have been reported for various other illnesses, both in contemporary field studies and in older regional collections such as Wayland D. Hand's *Popular Beliefs and Superstitions* volumes of the *Frank C. Brown Collection of North Carolina Folklore* (1961–1964), Ray Browne's *Popular Beliefs and Practices from Alabama* (1958), Harry Hyatt's *Folklore from Adams County, Illinois* (1935), and Vance Randolph's *Ozark Superstitions* (1947).

While the herbalists still actively practicing such cures may treat hundreds or even thousands of people a year, the tradition has been gradually declining as the once plentiful stocks of indigenous plants needed to sustain it have diminished and reliance on over-the-counter drugs, health foods, and the like has increased. But another ancient form of folk medicine, based on principles of homeopathic and contagious magic, remains strong. Magical medicine—though sometimes aided by home remedies or herbal treatments—depends for its efficacy not on *materia medica* (substances believed to have medicinal properties) but on verbal charms, ritualized actions, and other practices involving the diagnosis, removal, transference, deflection, or infliction of disease by supernatural means.

According to folk-medical belief, certain ailments can be cured by verbal magic alone, as evidenced by the well-known remedy for styes that advises the sufferer to recite the words "Sty, sty, in my eye, go to someone passing by." More typical, however, are cures in which the verbal charms are accompanied by ritual procedures. In the magico-religious tradition known as "talking out fire," for example, the healer recites, in words that appear garbled and incomprehensible to the patient and anyone else who might be present, a charm that summons divine powers to the aid of the sufferer, as in this recently collected example:

There came three angels from the West,
Three angels of the best, Three angels of God.
Go away fire and come frost.
In the name of the Father, Son, and Holy Ghost.

While reciting the charm, the healer blows on the burned area, passes a hand above the surface, or makes direct contact with the wound—gestures that are all based on homeopathic or contagious principles and intended to alleviate pain as well as to reduce scarring.

Similar combinations of charms and rituals are also used to stop the flow of blood from a wound ("bloodstopping"), to cure "thrush" or "thrash" mouth in children, and to "talk off" warts—a malady for which there are numerous other magical cures as well. One simple expedient, based on homeo-

An ad for Dr. Marshall's Headache and Catarrh Snuff, Frank Leslie's Illustrated Newspaper, *5 April 1862. Collection J.W. Love.*

pathic magic, is to tie knots in a piece of string with the number of knots corresponding to the number of warts to be disposed of, and then to throw the string into running water or bury it in a damp place so that the string (and, by symbolic extension, the warts) will decompose quickly. An alternative strategy, based on contagious magic, is to symbolically transfer the warts to another person through an intermediary object such as a coin, which is rubbed on the affected areas and thrown into the road on the assumption that whoever picks up the coin will get the warts as well. Sometimes the receptor is a tree rather than a person. In a practice called "nailing," for example, the wart is pricked with a nail, which is then driven into a tree. An alternative is to rub a piece of cloth or some other material on the wart, then bore a hole in the tree, and insert a wooden plug.

"Plugging," the term commonly used for this practice, may also be combined with a procedure called "measuring" to effect cures for other kinds or problems, such as asthma in children. First, the child stands against a tree or doorjamb while someone draws a line to mark his or her height. Then a hole is bored at exactly that point, and a lock of the child's hair is stuffed into the hole and plugged, the expectation being that when the child grows taller than the mark the asthma will disappear.

When the illness to be treated is believed to have an unnatural origin, a more complex system of countermagic must be employed to combat it. Those who believe, for example, that certain individuals possess an evil eye—the power to inflict serious physical and psychological harm on another

through an intense stare—typically arm themselves with eye-shaped amulets and horn-like charms to symbolically deflect or pierce the invasive eye of the so-called "overlooker" or "fascinator." If, despite these precautions, someone falls victim to the influence of the evil eye, other magical procedures may be used, including blessings and benedictions intended to cancel out the eye's pernicious effects plus various diagnostic and curative rituals performed by someone in the family or community whose powers are commensurate with those of the overlooker.

In cultures in which the evil eye is only one of many supernaturally induced afflictions, the folk-medical response system is especially complex. Participants in such traditions must be careful, for example, about how they dispose of nail parings, hair clippings, items of clothing, or anything else that has been in contact with them lest these materials come into the possession of someone who wishes to do them harm or gain power over them. Even these cautionary measures provide no defense against illnesses inflicted through homeopathic rituals in which a doll or a piece of knotted string is used as a symbolic surrogate for the intended victim. Further complicating the process of diagnosis and treatment is the fact that the symptoms of unnatural illness—lassitude, depression, numbness, skin rash, and the like—are also indicators of many natural illnesses. If these symptoms persist even after treatment with home remedies, herbal cures, over-the-counter medications, or drugs prescribed by a physician, the usual recourse is to enlist the aid of an occult practitioner.

As the foregoing discussion suggests, folk-medical practitioners do not conform to a single prototype. Rather, they are an extremely heterogeneous group that includes men and women of all ages, occupations, classes, and cultures. Some of them dispense medical advice or treatment so infrequently, to such a small number of people, that they have no distinct identity as healers; others are so well known for their medical expertise that people within and outside the community consult them on a regular basis. Some see themselves as agents of a divine power conferred at birth or passed to them at a later stage of life by a tradition bearer who sees in them the spiritual strength and humanistic concern needed to receive the gift; others are believed to have been born evil or to have obtained their powers through sorcery or witchcraft. Some are specialists, practicing a single cure, such as stopping blood, or a single tradition, such as herbalism; others participate actively in all three major branches of folk medicine.

Essential to any meaningful study of folk-medical practitioners is an awareness of their varying roles in the communities to which they belong. In the Cajun culture of southwestern Louisiana, for example, the principal folk practitioners are called "traiteurs," a term that is commonly applied to three very different types of people: magico-religious healers; individuals who dispense home remedies, patent medicines, and herbal cures; and specialists in the occult tradition known in that part of the country as "hoodoo."

Among the Pennsylvania Germans, folk healers are differentiated into two major groups: "powwows," who practice an occult tradition known in German dialect as *brauche,* and herbalists. In practice, however, the boundaries between the two are often blurred because the herbalist's natural cures are often accompanied by verbal charms, and the powwow's magical formulas are frequently complemented by the use of herbs or other naturopathic remedies.

Divisions are more sharply drawn in the ethnomedical system known as *curanderismo,* widely practiced by Mexican Americans in the Southwestern United States. As the name suggests, the central figure in this cultural tradition is the *curandero* (a healer reputed to draw his powers from both the natural world and the spiritual world), but other types of practitioners may also be consulted. These include herbalists, midwives, folk chiropractors, and other benevolent healers as well as sorcerers or witches known as *brujos.*

The same kind of diversity can be seen as well in other ethnomedical systems such as root working or root medicine, a predominantly African American tradition concentrated in the rural South and in many inner city neighborhoods of the Northeast. Participants in this tradition may consult different types of practitioners depending on whether a particular illness is diagnosed as physical or spiritual, natural or unnatural. If symptoms indicate a physical problem resulting from natural causes, the patient's initial response will usually be self-treatment with home remedies or a consultation with an herbalist. If the problem is perceived to stem from some spiritual failing in the patient, he or she may consult with a minister or some other respected religious figure who acts in the capacity of spiritual adviser or family counselor. If, on the other hand, there is some reason to suspect unnatural causation, a root doctor will in all likelihood be called upon to verify that diagnosis, cast counterspells against the rival conjurer, and administer whatever potions might be needed to restore the victim's health.

It is important to keep in mind that in these and other culturally based systems, folk beliefs and practices have by no means displaced official medicine. Rather, they coexist with it, as well as with other forms of alternative medicine such as chiropractic, osteopathy, and acupuncture. The reasons for this phenomenon are numerous and complex.

One factor, certainly, is the scarcity of medical doctors in many parts of the country—particularly in rural areas where the population is too small or too scattered to support a private practice and where the closest hospital or clinic may be located in the next county. It is not surprising, then, that under these circumstances, people would rely on traditional remedies or turn to folk practitioners, many of whom are both accessible and willing to offer advice or treatment on short notice, often in their own homes.

Even when professional medical care is available, many people cannot afford it—a problem that becomes more pronounced with each new increase in the cost of health insurance, hospital treatment, prescription drugs, and everything else connected with the official health-care system. By contrast, a community herbalist will typically charge only enough to cover expenses, and most magico-religious healers adhere to a rigorous taboo system that prohibits any kind of payment or even any expression of thanks on the grounds that their gift comes not from themselves but from God.

Because such practitioners are often members of the patient's own family or community and usually perform their treatments in the familiar environs of the home or workplace, their interactions with patients are also likely to be more informal and less stressful than those that occur in a clinical setting, where the patient may have to wait several hours in a crowded office for a brief consultation with a physician whose caseload often precludes the kind of personal attention offered by his or her folk counterparts.

Moreover, there are certain illnesses for which the sufferer will consult only a folk practitioner because they do not exist in the disease taxonomies of the official medical system. Participants in the *curanderismo* tradition, for example, routinely consult physicians for broken bones, pneumonia, and other natural illnesses, but not for problems such as *mal de ojo* (evil eye) or *mal puesto* (sorcery), which only a cultural insider can fully understand and treat.

While the prominence of folk medicine in individual and community health-care systems can be easily documented, questions about the efficacy of particular treatments and procedures are more difficult to answer because the proof required by participants in folk-medical tradition is very different from that demanded by medical researchers. For members of the former group, the efficacy of a home remedy, an herbal cure, or a magical procedure can be verified through anecdotal or experiential evidence alone. For those in the scientific medical community, on the other hand, no valid conclusions can be drawn without exhaustive laboratory experimentation and rigorously controlled clinical trials.

Sometimes, scientific research corroborates folk belief, as in the case of foxglove *(Digitalis purpurea),* which was prescribed as a heart tonic by community herbalists long before pharmacological studies confirmed its cardiotonic properties. Conversely, some long-standing folk remedies, such as ingesting turpentine for kidney problems, have been shown to pose serious health risks even when taken infrequently and in moderate dosages. For still other remedies, the medical evidence is inconclusive. Sassafras, for example, has been popular as a spring tonic and blood purifier since colonial times, but laboratory experiments have suggested that the plant's main active ingredient, safrole, is a potential carcinogen.

Even more problematic are magico-religious beliefs and practices, which participants in the tradition accept on faith but which are rarely amenable to laboratory or clinical testing. People who have had the fire talked out of a burn, for example, typically attest to the efficacy of the cure by saying that it immediately alleviated the pain they were experiencing and prevented scarring, but testing these claims scientifically is a difficult task because there is no way to quantify pain, to determine whether the burn was severe enough to produce scars if left untreated, or to control for other variables by establishing experimental and control groups.

Whether medical science confirms or condemns a particular folk-medical practice is ultimately less important than whether the patient has faith in the practitioner and the treatment. As long as the latter two conditions prevail, folk medicine will continue to flourish—not as a substitute for mainstream medicine but as one important constituent in a complex, multidimensional health-care system.

James W. Kirkland

References

Crellin, John K., and Jane Philpott. 1990. Vol. 1, *Trying to Give Ease.* Vol. 2, *A Reference Guide to Medicinal Plants.* Durham, NC: Duke University Press.

Dorson, Richard. 1952. *Bloodstoppers and Bearwalkers: Folk Traditions of the Upper Peninsula.* Cambridge, MA: Harvard University Press.

Genitz, Norman, ed. 1988. *Other Healers: Unorthodox Medicine in America.* Baltimore: Johns Hopkins University Press.

Hand, Wayland, ed. 1976. *American Folk Medicine: A Symposium.* Berkeley: University of California Press.

———. 1980. *Magical Medicine: The Folkloric Component of Medicine in the Folk Belief, Custom, and Ritual of the Peoples of Europe and America.* Berkeley: University of California Press.

Hufford, David. 1983. Folk Healers. In *Handbook of American Folklore,* ed. Richard Dorson. Bloomington: Indiana University Press, pp. 306–313.

Kirkland, James, Holly F. Mathews, C.W. Sullivan III, and Karen Baldwin, eds. 1992. *Herbal and Magical Medicine: Traditional Healing Today.* Durham, NC: Duke University Press.

Moerman, D.E. 1986. *Medicinal Plants of the Native Americans.* 2 vols. Technical Reports No. 16. Ann Arbor: University of Michigan Museum of Anthropology.

Yoder, Don. 1972. Folk Medicine. In *Folklore and Folklife: An Introduction,* ed. Richard Dorson. Chicago: University of Chicago Press, pp. 191–215.

See also Curanderos; Mojo

Memorate

A personal-experience narrative about an encounter with the supranormal. In an effort to establish discrete categories for oral prose narratives, Swedish folklorist Carl W. von Sydow suggested the term "memorate" to refer to single-episodic narratives about a supranormal event, told by the actual person who experienced the event (von Sydow [1934] 1948).

Memorates are not fictive accounts but are allegedly true reports of an actual experience that the narrator had. Von Sydow recognized that folk belief may lie at the core of both memorates and legends, but in terms of tradition the two narrative forms were not related. He sought in his taxonomy to distinguish these apparently nontraditional and oftentimes spontaneous narratives from what folklorists at the time considered to be true legends. He insisted that a memorate was not a form of legend because it lacked two essential qualities: It was neither traditional (that is, it did not circulate by word of mouth because by definition it could be told only by the person who had the experience), nor did it possess poetic characteristics (that is, it lacked the stylistic qualities and alterations that appear in traditional legends). If a memorate sparks enough interest among the folk and is repeated by different people, this nontraditional narrative form may become, in von Sydow's taxonomy, a memorial legend. On the whole, however, memorates, he argued, offer passing interest to the folklorist simply because they provide voice to experiences that the folk find engaging.

Since von Sydow's seminal work, folklorists have made considerable effort to exploring the subtleties of this narrative form and to expand upon von Sydow's original ideas. Many folklorists now view memorates as spontaneous narratives growing out of a noteworthy experience happening in an otherwise routine, day-to-day existence. Folklorists distinguish several types of memorates: those that are based on recognized legend motifs or known legends; those that reveal a folk belief or folk custom or folk attitude; and those that lack legend motifs and belief elements but contain other motifs found in other traditional narrative forms such as the tall tale or the historical legend. Moreover, the term "memorate" may also refer to second- and third-hand accounts of the original narrative if the narration suggests fidelity to the primary account.

Memorates, like supernatural or belief legends, recount encounters with supernatural signs, ghosts, and other mystical beings. The motif of a ghost that returns to haunt the place of an accident or the site of a great tragedy appears frequently in American memorates and legends. Revenants returning from the dead to right wrongs or to provide warnings of impending danger to the living are also very popular core motifs. When narrators tell these stories, they reflect current legend traditions, or at the least, they may be lingering, interesting stories about past beliefs.

Memorates that present encounters with psychic experiences are easily collected. Even in America's technocratic society, dreams portend warnings and charms bring good luck. Experiences with both provide the bases for many memorates. People offer detailed, realistic accounts about a miraculous cure they brought about by performing appropriate religious rituals, such as praying novenas, lighting votive candles, or publishing special prayers in the local newspaper. These stories not only validate existing beliefs, but also promote the rituals. Perhaps some folk superstitions and beliefs persist because their effectiveness is confirmed by memorates.

The third kind of memorate centers on such themes as extraordinary skill and strengths. A narrator presents a realistic depiction of an extraordinary experience in which the narrator either saw or demonstrated tremendous personal stamina or outstanding physical strength and cunning. These memorates avoid the outrageous, comic exaggeration found in traditional boasts, but they may be influenced by content and narrative structure of the tall tale and boast. Richard M. Dorson, in his *Bloodstoppers and Bearwalkers,* refers to the men who narrate this kind of story as sagamen (Dorson 1952:249–272).

Memorates did not receive much attention from American folklorists until the publication of an English translation of von Sydow's work. But as simple as the memorate might first appear, it has elicited extensive debate, and von Sydow's original notions about it have been challenged on a number of fronts. For example, von Sydow considered both form and content when he defined the memorate—its form is that of a first-person narrative and its content deals with a specific supranormal event allegedly experienced by the narrator.

Folklorists now question the stipulation that the memorate must be told by the person who actually experienced the happening. Some identify as memorates supranormal experience stories that are told second- and thirdhand if the narrators acknowledge that they personally know the person who experienced the event and credit that person with the experience. Thus, some scholars consider memorates stories of supranormal encounters that have an opening formula such as "My uncle, who never lies, told me this happened to him" or "A friend of my aunt told me this happened to her." This suggests that the "I"–narrator may actually refer to the narrator or may merely function as a rhetorical technique intended to give immediacy, vigor, and a unique validity to the narrative and its contents. Finally, some critics suggest that earlier collectors in their diligence to publish legend texts did not hesitate to transform memorates into third-person legend form.

The supranormal content of personal narratives naturally suggests a relationship among memorates, legend, and folk belief. Folklorists have become interested in understanding the progression from folk belief to protomemorate, to memorate, to belief legend. One theory suggests that the memorate is a personal narrative about a preexisting folk belief maintained within the folk group, and, through repeated tellings, it provides the foundation for a fabulate or a legend text. In other situations, the memorate, with its emphatic reference to a personal experience, functions as an authoritative and convincing narrative expression of a folk belief, having a revitalizing effect on a belief that has begun to lose its currency because of doubts.

For the most part, folklorists have generally rejected von Sydow's suggestion that the memorate is a relatively insignificant narrative form. Moreover, folklorists are moving away from the impulse to place narrative forms, especially legends, into rigidly segregated categories and are beginning to appreciate the fluidity of oral forms and how readily the same narrative can flow from one telling and genre into a different genre at another telling. In the hands of skilled and unskilled narrators alike, the memorate may easily become a fabulate, and a legend may become a memorate. The socio-narrative conduits and contexts through which belief accounts pass permit variations that encourage poetic creativity and narrative license. With increasing interest in modern legend narratives and the personal-experience narrative in particular, folklorists continue to explore the nature of the memorate and refine their understanding of its relationship to other narrative genres and its place in the study of folk narrative.

Richard Sweterlitsch

References

Dégh, Linda, and Andrew Vazsonyi. 1974. The Memorate and the Protomemorate. *Journal of American Folklore* 87:225–239.

Dorson, Richard M. 1952. *Bloodstoppers and Bearwalkers: Folk Traditions of the Upper Peninsula.* Cambridge, MA: Harvard University Press.

Honko, Lauri. 1964. Memorate and the Study of Folk Belief. *Journal of the Folklore Institute* 1:5–19.

Pentikainen, Juha. 1973. Belief, Memorate, and Legend. *Folklore Forum* 6:217–241.

Stahl, Sandra Dolby. 1989. *Literary Folkloristics and the Personal Narrative.* Bloomington: Indiana University Press.

von Sydow, Carl W. [1934] 1948. Categories of Prose Narratives. *Selected Papers on Folklore.* Copenhagen, pp. 60–88.

Woods, Barbara Allen. 1959. *The Devil in Dog Form: A Partial Type-Index to Devil Legends.* Berkeley: University of California Press.

See also Ghost Stories; Legend

Mercer, Henry Chapman (1856–1930)

Scholar of folklore and material culture, museologist, and ceramic-tile maker. Born into a family of some means, Mercer grew up in Doylestown, Pennsylvania, and later returned there, founding the Moravian Pottery and Tile Works and funding and building the Bucks County Historical Museum.

Formally educated in private schools, Mercer graduated from Harvard University in 1879 and was certified to practice law in 1881. His growing interests in ethnology and archaeology, however, checked a career in law, and his publication of *The Lenape Stone* in 1885 established him as a scholar in those fields. Although he explored caves from his native Bucks County to the Yucatan searching for insights into Paleo-Indian culture in America, by 1896 Mercer had turned his attention to the folk culture of his native Pennsylvania and had begun to study the artifacts of everyday life in America. Beginning with the publication of *Tools of the Nation Maker* in 1897, Mercer went on to write more than thirty books and articles on American material folk culture. In his works, he examined not only the tools of the past, but also houses and the origins of their design and construction. In the last thirty years of his life, Mercer amassed a vast collection of artifacts, which he housed in the museum that he erected in Doylestown.

Perhaps the best-known decorative-tile maker of his day, Mercer was also a proponent of the Arts and Crafts Movement of the late 19th century. His greatest significance, however, lies in the role that he played as an early scholar of material folk culture. Mercer was a pioneer in the field, but his achievements have only recently been recognized for their important contribution to the study of traditional artifacts in the United States. Described by Warren Roberts as a "remarkable scholar," Mercer deserves a place beside other eminent students of American folklife.

Scott Hamilton Suter

References

Mercer, Henry Chapman. [1914] 1961. *The Bible in Iron: Pictured Stoves and Stoveplates of the Pennsylvania Germans,* ed. Joseph E. Sanford. Doylestown: Bucks County Historical Society.
———. [1926] 1976a. *The Dating of Old Houses.* Doylestown: Bucks County Historical Society.
———. [1926] 1976b. *The Origin of Log Houses in the United States.* Doylestown: Bucks County Historical Society.
———. 1929. *Ancient Carpenters' Tools.* 5th ed. 1975. Doylestown: Bucks County Historical Society.
Suter, Scott H. 1989. The Clapboards Lifted: Henry Chapman Mercer and the Origin of an American Log Building Style. *Folklore Historian* 6:76–88.

Merchant Seamen

Workers employed in the seagoing transport of cargo or passengers. Often simply referred to as "sailors," merchant seamen are those maritime workers employed in private-sector, commercial shipping—the merchant marine—and are divided into licensed and unlicensed personnel, officers, and crew, respectively. Crews traditionally are multiethnic in composition, depending upon the vessel's nationality, and were frequently separated in earlier periods along ethnic lines into watches (work shifts) and departments (deck, engine, stewards). The folklore of the merchant seaman deals both with the experience common to all ratings in the merchant marine and with boundary maintenance between groups of different rating. The designation "sailor" itself is often claimed to be the rightful epithet and heritage of the unlicensed, deck sailor.

Merchant seamen have a long history predating the world's navies and other forms of industrial or collective labor. Although merchant seafaring persists today amid newer, faster, and cheaper modes of transport, its great romantic era was the 19th century, the so-called Age of Sail. In the transition from sail to steam propulsion in the latter part of the century, organizational and structural change in this industry effected change in the folklore and traditions. The deck sailor was displaced by an engine department, and the worksongs of sailors that accompanied the routines of handling lines and sail have disappeared along with the sailing ship.

While sailors are notorious for storytelling, the best-documented folklore of the merchant seaman are the songs or chanteys, both fo'c'sle songs and halyard chanteys. Fo'c'sle songs are the songs associated with the sailor's leisure time in the crews quarters, known as the fo'c'sle. (A contraction of "forecastle," the fo'c'sle was traditionally located in the forward portion of the vessel under the bow, while officers resided aft.) Halyard chanteys, or simply chanteys, on the other hand, are songs that aided in the performance of work routine—halyard referring to lines for "hauling the yards," the horizontal beams on a square-rigged vessel to which the sails were tied or "bent." Short-haul and long-haul chanteys were apportioned to lighter and heavier tasks, respectively.

Technical nomenclature of merchant shipping is elaborate and provides a source for word lore. Many popular expressions ashore can be traced to sailors and the technology of seafaring. To "pay the devil," for instance, or to be "between the devil and the deep blue sea" refers to a dreaded and devilish maintenance task aboard leaky wooden vessels in which "paying" meant caulking and the "devil" was the outboard seam between planking just above the keel. To tell a "yarn" or simply "to yarn" as a common expression for garrulous storytelling may also have had its origins among seamen, who would spend leisure hours winding "rope-yarns" for stowage and telling stories.

Yarn spinning or storytelling is perhaps the most ubiquitous category of maritime folklore, but while we know much about the recurrent themes of storytelling—the sailor's last ship, his adventures in foreign ports, lost ships, spectral ships, bully captains, and bucko mates—the study of narrative has focused on only a few well-known folktales and legend types, such as the Flying Dutchman, and the tall tale as a narrative form.

In addition to verbal folklore, merchant seafaring has evolved traditions of material culture. Ship models, notably ship-in-bottle models, woodcarvings, and decorative uses of rope and twine, known as "fancy rope work," are leisure activities among seamen as well as maritime enthusiasts with little or no experience of seafaring.

Finally, merchant seafaring produced an extensive folklore of custom and belief. Danish folklorist Henning Henningsen (1961) made a historical and comparative study of one elaborate, customary shipboard practice known as "crossing the line." Ships' crews performed this custom for the initiation of novice seamen into the craft and brotherhood of seafaring. It took place on crossing the equator and involved a cast of characters in a mock court setting, over which a costumed figure representing Neptune, the god of the sea from classical mythology, presided.

The preponderance of superstitions, as with yarns, may be the landsman's most tenacious stereotype of the sailor. If superstition may be defined as apparently irrational belief, the conditions of uncertainty and vulnerability that have always attended seafaring, particularly as concerns weather, help explain the existence of this body of tradition. The life of the common sailor was constantly at the mercy of the weather and frequently that of strict and abusive officers. Superstition may have provided some degree of control and counsel concerning these forces, even as the term raises complicated questions about the psychology and rhetoric of belief. More simply, however, many superstitions of the sea may be categorized in terms of luck and, as such, have persisted into the modern era of seafaring. During World War II, for instance, sailors would designate certain vessels of the merchant marine as lucky or unlucky depending upon how well and whether or not they succeeded in making their destinations when sailing through treacherous waters.

Although the United States continues to have a merchant marine and merchant seamen, several factors have significantly reduced the population and changed the composition of the merchant marine. These include high casualties from World War II; the Cold War expulsion of merchant seamen from an industry that was radicalized during the 1930s; the increased role of government during World War II in the training, licensing, and certifying of a new cohort of merchant seaman; alternative modes for transporting cargoes and passengers; and technological developments that have greatly reduced manning requirements. Some of these factors have affected shipping globally, but other seafaring nations have generally fared better than the United States in maintaining a merchant marine in which traditions of the sea persist and adapt to new conditions and cohorts.

Thomas Walker

References

Beck, Horace. 1973. *Folklore and the Sea.* Middletown, CT: Wesleyan University Press.

Buss, Reinhard J. 1973. *The Klabautermann of the Northern Seas: An Analysis of the Protective Spirit of Ships and Sailors in the Context of Popular Belief, Christian Legend, and Indo-European Mythology.* Berkeley: University of California Press.

Doerflinger, William Main. [1951] 1990. *Songs of the Sailor and Lumberman.* Glenwood, IL: Meyerbooks.

Henningsen, Henning. 1961. *Crossing the Equator: Sailors' Baptism and Other Initiation Rites.* Copenhagen: Munksgaard.

Rediker, Marcus. 1987. *Between the Devil and the Deep Blue Sea: Merchant Seamen, Pirates, and the Anglo-American World, 1700–1750.* Cambridge: Cambridge University Press.

Richmond, W. Edson. 1985. Any Old Port in a Storm: Sea Words Gone Aground. In *By Land and by Sea: Studies in the Folklore of Work and Leisure Honoring Horace P. Beck on his Sixty-Fifth Birthday,* ed. Roger D. Abrahams, Kenneth S. Goldstein, and Wayland D. Hand. Hatboro, PA: Legacy.

Weibust, Knut. 1969. *Deep Sea Sailors: A Study in Maritime Ethnology.* Stockholm: Kungl, Boktryckeriet P.A. Norstedt & Söner.

See also Chanteys; Maritime Folklore; Yarn

Metafolklore

Folklore about folklore, a word coined by Alan Dundes on the analogy of the term "metalanguage," or linguistic statements about language. Dundes suggested that metafolklore and "oral literary criticism" (informants' commentary upon their own folklore) offer ways to elicit the meanings of folklore items directly from the folk themselves.

Metafolklore may occur within one genre—for example, a proverb about proverbs or a joke about joke telling—or it may cross genre lines, as in the following example of a meta-folkloristic joke that alludes both to the "knock, knock" joke cycle and to a familiar proverb:

Knock
Who's there?
Opportunity. (The proverb is "Opportunity knocks but once.)

Another American metafolkloristic joke parodies the traditional traveling-salesman story in which the salesman is usually invited to sleep with the farmer's daughter. In this variation, he is told instead to sleep with the farmer's *son,* to which the salesman responds, "Oh my God, I must be in the wrong joke." The punch line both comments on the nature of the traveling-salesman joke cycle and draws attention to the theme of homosexuality rather than heterosexuality in this variation.

Jan Harold Brunvand

References

Dundes, Alan. 1966. Metafolklore and Oral Literary Criticism. *The Monist* 50(4). Reprinted in *Readings in American Folklore,* ed. Jan Harold Brunvand. New York: W.W. Norton, 1979, pp. 404–415.

Mexican Americans

Those whose ancestry can be traced to Mexico or to Spain through Mexico. Theirs is the most studied folklore of any ethnic group in the United States. Mexican-American history and folk traditions differ significantly from those of Puerto Ricans, Latin Americans, and other Hispanic groups in the United States. Mexican American folklore makes clear the great intracultural diversity found among Mexican Americans in the American Southwest, as well as those of Mexican descent who have settled in such areas as Florida, New York,

Michigan, and Illinois. Although they share many traditions, there is significant diversity.

The ancestors of many of today's Mexican Americans occupied the Southwest—Texas, New Mexico, Arizona, southern Colorado, and California—long before it became a part of the United States in 1848, with the Treaty of Guadalupe Hidalgo. They came from many different parts of Mexico, and their ancestors came from various parts of Spain and mingled with a number of diverse indigenous peoples. Recent immigrants have traditions significantly different from those whose ancestors have lived in the region for centuries. Those living in urban areas have traditions significantly different from those living in rural areas, emphasizing the fact that folklore reflects the values and concerns of those who share it.

The folk architecture and traditional foodways in south and west Texas demonstrate convincingly that Mexican Americans in west Texas have much more in common culturally and historically with Mexican Americans in New Mexico than they do with those in south Texas.

Those of Spanish Mexican ancestry in the Southwest and beyond refer to themselves in a number of different ways, depending upon a number of factors, including region, social class, and historic background. Those in the wealthier classes tend to call themselves Spanish or Hispanic, and sometimes Latinos, while those in the working class often refer to themselves (among themselves) as *mejicanos,* to differentiate themselves from the Anglos or other ethnic groups. When they go into Mexico, they tend to call themselves *mejico-americanos* to differentiate themselves from Mexican citizens. Mexican Americans in south Texas commonly refer to themselves as

tejanos, while those in New Mexico and southern Colorado call themselves *hispanos,* and those in California call themselves *californios.* In more recent times, a small percentage (8 percent–10 percent) of Mexican Americans refer to themselves as chicanos, a term rejected by many others, particularly those in the working class. The term "chicano" is used mostly by those who are political or social activists or those involved in higher education. Mexican Americans have a number of neutral and pejorative labels for Anglos, including *gabachos, americanos,* and *gringos,* the latter being the most pejorative of the more common terms. There are also terms of varying degrees of severity used to label those who are seen as acculturated—*Inglesados* (Englishized), *engabachados, vendidos* (those who have sold out), or *agringados* (*gringo*-ized).

Although folk traditions have changed significantly among Mexican Americans since the mid-18th century, a wide variety of folklore genres continue to be important, some more than others. Studies of Mexican American folklore, beginning in the late 19th century, reflect the interests of scholars as much as the actual richness of types of folklore known among the people. A wide range of genres has been studied: folk narratives, folk music, folk speech, folk medicine, folk arts and crafts, customs and beliefs, architecture, foodways, costume, and folk games and play, among others. Generally speaking, material culture has received less attention than other types, except in New Mexico. Likewise, certain areas of the Southwest have received more scholarly attention than others, most often the result of whether or not scholars interested in folklore lived and worked in the area.

Some Mexican Americans are monolingual Spanish speakers; some are fluently bilingual in English and Spanish, while others are monolingual English speakers. Consequently, Mexican American folklore may be transmitted in Spanish, in Tex-Mex (the regional dialect of Spanish), in English, or in a combination of these.

Among the verbal arts, such genres as folk speech and naming, proverbs, riddles, and folk poetry may be found in almost every community of Mexican Americans throughout the Southwest and beyond. A wide variety of folk-narrative types remain viable wherever Mexican Americans are found. These differ from group to group, as one would expect.

Most Mexican Americans are strongly Roman Catholic, and religious legends related to various saints continue to be important. *La Virgen de Guadalupe* is the subject of a variety of narrative types, including the story of her appearance to Juan Diego as well as numerous more personal narratives about individuals' experiences with her. Among the many other saints who are the subject of local legends are Santo Niño de Atocha, San Juan, and San Antonio. In addition, many legends circulate about such folk saints (those treated as saints by the people but who have not been canonized by the church) as Don Pedrito Jaramillo and El Niño Fidencio, folk healers of considerable reputation in south Texas and beyond.

Supernatural legends and personal-experience narratives about witches are common. Stories about *La Lechuza* (a woman with an owl's face or one who takes on the form of an owl) are common in many areas, as are stories about *La Llorona*, the weeping woman searching for the souls of her children—a punishment for having drowned them after their father betrayed her. *Pata de gallo* stories, about the devil appearing at a dance and severely disfiguring a young lady who disobeyed her parents and slipped off to the dance, are well known in many regions. Stories about vanishing hitchhikers and ghosts of young women appearing at dances or other places are also fairly common.

Some older legends about folk heroes of earlier epochs continue to be told in certain areas; these include stories about Gregorio Cortez in south Texas, Joaquin Murietta in California, and Pancho Villa in New Mexico and west Texas. One also finds legends about lost treasures in many rural areas of the Southwest.

Perhaps the most ubiquitous forms of folk narratives are the *casos, historias, tallas,* and jokes. *Casos* are short, first-person-experience narratives (like cases-in-point) used to illustrate or validate a wide variety of beliefs. *Historias* are "true" stories about local events of interest. *Tallas* are jests that are used to poke fun at someone present at the telling. The term comes from the verb *tallar,* meaning "to rub or chafe." Mexican Americans enjoy a wide variety of jokes, including ethnic jokes, dirty jokes (*chistes colorados*), *agringado* jokes (which reprove those thought to be too anglicized), and many other types.

A recent survey in south Texas reveals a broad variety of folk narratives popular among *vaqueros* (cowboys) in the region. Storytelling in this group is called *hechando mentiras* (telling lies), and these stories cover such topics as horses and horse training, *vaquero* skills, local tragedies (including work-related deaths and serious injuries), and stories about encounters with ghosts, mystery lights, and lost treasures.

While folk music is still found in some areas, in most communities it has been replaced by popular music, which has become widely available on radio, television, and via cassettes and records. Modern *conjunto* music, which evolved from an earlier folk-music form, may be heard on many Spanish-language radio stations wherever there are significant populations of Mexican Americans. Likewise, the *corrido* (folk ballad) became a popular form of recorded and broadcast music, although some still sing the old ballads from earlier periods. Earlier forms, like the *verso* or *copla* (a short, lyrical stanza) and the *décima* (a ten-line stanza), once very common throughout the Southwest, have virtually disappeared.

In the area of customary folklore, the traditions of folk medicine, folk beliefs of various types, rites of passage, and rites of intensification (celebrations) continue to be important in the lives of many. Folk games can still be found in many rural areas, especially among children—games like spinning tops and playing marbles.

Folk medicine continues to be important to many Mexican Americans. Recent scientific surveys in south Texas reveal that about 90 percent of the Mexican American families in that area continue to rely on herbal remedies, and in some communities as many as 29 percent of the women report having used the services of *parteras* (lay midwives). *Curanderos(as)* (the healers par excellence in the culture, who have a *don de Díos,* or gift from God, to heal, particularly cases of witchcraft) can still be found in most larger cities and in many smaller communities where there are high percentages of Mexican Americans.

The rites of passage important among Mexican Americans everywhere include baptisms and the *compadrazgo* (ritual co-parenthood) relationships, the *quinceañera* for young women (a coming-of-age ceremony and celebration at age fifteen), wedding celebrations, and funeral rites. While most of these events require formal Catholic ceremonies, folk beliefs and practices and some specific traditional activities are almost invariably associated with them.

A broad variety of rites of intensification in the form of celebrations in which Mexican Americans celebrate their *mexicanidad,* or Mexicanness, can be found throughout the Southwest and beyond. The most common are *el cinco de mayo* (May 5) and *el diezyseis de septiembre* (September 16) celebrations. Many who celebrate *el cinco de mayo* are not aware that they are celebrating the victory of the Mexican *campesinos* over the French troops at the Battle of Puebla. A broad variety of other Mexican American celebrations include *charreadas* (the Mexican form of the rodeo) and other local activities celebrating local events important to Mexican Americans living in the area.

As to material culture, many folk arts and crafts traditions remain popular. While folk architecture is not produced in most areas, that of earlier eras is still present. For example, while *jacales* are still being built in many parts of Mexico, they have not been constructed in Texas and other parts of the Southwest for several decades. And while adobes are still made and adobe houses are still being built in west Texas and New Mexico, the earlier forms of stone and *sillar* (caliche block) houses once common in south Texas have not been constructed since the late 1800s.

Folk arts and crafts traditions that have continued among Mexican Americans include paper-flower making, piñata making, quilt making, instrument making (particularly of *vihuelas* and *bajo sextos*—instruments important in *conjunto* music or *mariachi* music), saddle making, boot making, and a number of *vaquero* folk-arts traditions, including making objects of rawhide and horsehair—quirts, bridle reins, ropes of various kinds, *chicotes* (cattle whips), hackamores, and so on.

The *vaquero*'s occupation is an excellent example of a folk occupation. One learns the necessary skills—riding, working cattle, roping, branding, and such—by observation and practice over a long period of time. *Vaqueros* hold great respect for those who have mastered these skills, and young *vaqueros* understand that it will take years for them to master them. These skills have been modified over the centuries by new technologies.

Religious folk art continues to play an important role in most areas. The religious folk art found in most Mexican American cemeteries includes handmade decorations, gravemarkers with a number of traditional epitaphs, and a variety of different images of saints, particularly the Virgin of Guadalupe. Likewise, one can find *nichos* or *grutas* (handmade yard shrines) in working-class neighborhoods throughout the Southwest. Home altars can also be found in many working-class homes, although this tradition is much more common among older women than younger ones.

Roadside crosses, documented as early as the 1820s along the Rio Grande, are still found in south and west Texas, as well as in various areas of New Mexico. These *crucitas* are used to mark the place where someone has died, where the spirit departed the body. Families erect these crosses and return to them on a regular basis to conduct private rituals in memory of the departed.

A number of religious folk-art traditions can be found in such areas as New Mexico, where they have existed for centuries. The *santeros (santos* makers) developed a rich tradition of making religious objects, documented by scholars and preserved in several museums in New Mexico. The *retablos* (paintings) and *bultos* (hand-carved statues) have been influenced in recent years by the marketing of these objects to outsiders, mostly tourists, who are not part of the older tradition.

Secular yard art can be found in many working-class Mexican American *barrios* (neighborhoods) in rural areas as well as larger cities. This yard art includes a variety of manners of decorating with plants (including planters made from castoff automobile or truck tires) and clay figurines.

Public folk art can be found in many communities, particularly in the larger cities. The low-rider tradition of remodeling older automobiles (including the installation of hydraulically operated shock absorbers to make them jump up and down) and decorating the cars with a number of traditional artistic designs continues. Two traditions recently brought to the United States from Mexico include the painting of large murals on public buildings and the making of park benches and other public art objects of cement. Both traditions can be found in such larger cities with large Mexican American populations as San Antonio.

Traditional foodways remain popular throughout the Mexican American population. They vary from region to region, and many have been adopted by such popular-culture institutions as fast-food restaurants. Tamales, tacos, tortillas, and pinto beans in a number of forms are common throughout the Mexican American community, both urban and rural. *Tamaladas* (gatherings where women make tamales) are more common in rural areas. *Fajitas* (a dish made of skirt steak), *tripitas* (a dish made of beef intestines), and *pan de campo* (camp bread) remain popular folk foods in south Texas. *Barbacoa de cabeza* (barbecued beef head), *cabrito* (barbecued kid goat), or *cabrito en su sangre* (a kid goat cut up and cooked in its own blood) are common in many rural areas of the Southwest. A dish made of the internal edible parts of *cabritos* (kid goats) is called *machitos* in south Texas, *buriñate* (or *buruñate)* in west Texas, and *burrañate* in New Mexico. One can find a number of traditional pastries (including *buñuelos* and *bizcochos)* served at weddings and other celebrations.

Mexican American folklore will continue to adapt to the changing circumstances in which its bearers find themselves, and these traditions will continue to play an important role in the lives of Mexican Americans.

Joe S. Graham

References

Briggs, Charles L. 1980. *The Wood Carvers of Córdova, New Mexico: Social Dimensions of an Artistic "Revival."* Knoxville: University of Tennessee Press.

Brown, Lorin, Charles L. Briggs, and Marta Weigle. 1978. *Hispano Folklife of New Mexico: The Lorin W. Brown Federal Writers' Manuscripts.* Albuquerque: University of New Mexico Press.

Bunting, Bainbridge. 1974. *Of Earth and Timbers Made: New Mexico Architecture.* Albuquerque: University of New Mexico Press.

Graham, Joe S. 1991. *Hecho en Tejas: Texas-Mexican Folk Arts and Crafts.* Publications of the Texas Folklore Society No. 50. Denton: University of North Texas Press.

Miller, Elaine K. 1973. *Mexican Folk Narrative from the Los Angeles Area.* Austin: University of Texas Press for the American Folklore Society.

Paredes, Américo. 1976. *A Texas-Mexican Cancionero.* Urbana: University of Illinois Press.

Robb, John D. 1980. *Hispanic Folk Music of New Mexico and the Southwest: A Self-Portrait of People.* Norman: University of Oklahoma Press.

Simmons, Marc. 1980. *Witchcraft in the Southwest: Spanish and Indian Supernaturalism on the Rio Grande.* Lincoln: University of Nebraska Press.

West, John O. 1988. *Mexican-American Folklore.* Little Rock, AR: August House.

Railbirding in the marshes of the Middle Atlantic seaboard. Pinelands, New Jersey, 1984. Photo Dennis McDonald. American Folklife Center.

See also Conjunto Music; *Corridos; Curanderos;* Fiesta; *La Llorona;* Social Protest in Folklore; Southwest

Middle Atlantic Region

Label used by analysts largely to identify the area between the South and New England influenced by cultural migrations through Philadelphia, New York, and Chesapeake ports of entry. Some refer to the area as the "Midland." Its historical influence on the development of American culture has been great since central paths of migration through the Middle Atlantic states of New York, Maryland, Delaware, New Jersey, and Pennsylvania influenced the formation of Midwest and Upland South traditions. Yet, as cultural geographers such as Wilbur Zelinsky have noted, it is the least conspicuous of America's regions, either to outsiders or its inhabitants. Examining the regional names that enterprises use to identify themselves, for example, Zelinsky found that Harrisburg, Pennsylvania, was the only metropolis in which inhabitants significantly used the Middle Atlantic label.

Several factors account for the vagueness of the region. European development of the Middle Atlantic area largely occurred a generation or more after other regions of the South and New England. The seaboard area had more of an urban character than regions to the north and south. It also contained far more inner diversity of religions and ethnic groups than the other regions. In addition to Finns and Swedes in the Delaware Valley, and Dutch in the Hudson Valley who began colonies that turned out to be unsuccessful in the area, English, Welsh, Scots-Irish, Cornish, French, Africans, and Ger-

mans entered the varied Middle Atlantic landscape. New York state presents a special problem because of its strong connection to New England (Zelinsky categorized it as a separate "New England Extended" Region), but with a noticeable difference because of Dutch place names and architecture along with strong Irish and some German influence. The most distinctive cultural formation in the Middle Atlantic states is probably the Pennsylvania-German area of settlement extending from central Pennsylvania into western Maryland and Virginia, referred to as the Pennsylvania Culture Region, because it persisted with a shared ethnicity and agricultural base.

The Pennsylvania Culture Region is at the heart of the "Midland" speech area identified by linguistic geographer Hans Kurath in 1949. Cultural geographer Terry Jordan in 1985 also used the Midland label to describe the preponderance of log buildings stretching from Pennsylvania into the Midwest and Upland South. In addition, Henry Glassie in 1968 described a distinctive material culture located in southeastern Pennsylvania and made the claim that it was the most important of all material folk culture regions, because both North and South were influenced by practices that had their New World source in the Pennsylvania Culture Region. He noted that the mix of British traditions in the Delaware Valley and Chesapeake along with the special German influence in south-central Pennsylvania fostered Middle Atlantic material-culture forms such as the "Middle Atlantic farmhouse." This common house contained a symmetrical exterior reminiscent of British Georgian design along with interior features taken largely from German house plans. The distribution of the house extended well beyond the Pennsylvania core to Maryland, New Jersey, western Pennsylvania, Virginia, and West Virginia. Another point of cultural intersection that influenced the formation of a Middle Atlantic material culture is in foodways, where versions of "mush" and "pot pie" characteristic of the Midland represent combinations of German and British traditions.

Some observers have offered that the Middle Atlantic's lack of visibility ironically owes to the Midland contribution to many cultural patterns considered national or "general American." Zelinsky speculates that its very success in projecting its image upon the remainder of the country rendered the source area less conspicuous. Few cultural organizations are devoted to the Middle Atlantic Region, although the Pennsylvania German Society covers Maryland, New Jersey, Ohio, and Virginia in addition to its central Pennsylvania home base. The contents of state folklore journals in New Jersey, New York, and Pennsylvania frequently cover traditions extending over state boundaries, but, significantly to the cultural formation of the region, the largest circulation is claimed by *Pennsylvania Folklife*. The Middle Atlantic Folklife Association, which sponsored the first "Middle States Folklore Conference" in Harrisburg in 1967, and continues to hold annual meetings, represents separate professional state efforts in Pennsylvania, New York, Delaware, Maryland, Virginia, and West Virginia. Although not constituting a "vernacular" region representing cultural self-perception, the Middle Atlantic has an impact on scholarship as an analytical term to describe cultural formations between New England and the South extending west, north, and south from Pennsylvania.

Simon J. Bronner

References

Gastil, Raymond D. 1975. *Cultural Regions of the United States.* Seattle: University of Washington Press.

Glassie, Henry. 1968. *Pattern in the Material Folk Culture of the Eastern United States.* Philadelphia: University of Pennsylvania Press.

Jordan, Terry. 1985. *American Log Buildings: An Old World Legacy.* Chapel Hill: University of North Carolina Press.

Kurath, Hans. 1949. *A Word Geography of the Eastern United States.* Ann Arbor: University of Michigan Press.

Zelinsky, Wilbur. 1973. *The Cultural Geography of the United States.* Englewood Cliffs, NJ: Prentice-Hall.

———. 1980. North America's Vernacular Regions. *Annals of the Association of American Geographers* 70:3–16.

Midwest

Distinguished from surrounding regions—the Great Lakes, the Middle Atlantic, the South, the Great Plains—by a blend of folk cultures brought together through historical settlement patterns. The folk culture of the Midwestern states—including primarily Indiana, Illinois, Iowa, and Missouri—developed as a consequence of waves of migration into these middle states from the major folk-cultural source areas in New England, the Middle Atlantic, the Upland South, and the Lowland South.

The Midwest contains elements of these earlier folk cultures in its material culture and its folk traditions; the influences can be found as a patchwork that often extends outside the Midwest region. Ohio, with its predominantly Middle Atlantic, or Pennsylvania German, folk culture, could be included in the region. The southern parts of the states of Michigan, Wisconsin, and Minnesota, which are predominantly influenced by New England folk traditions, are often included. Also, the Ozark areas of Kentucky and Arkansas could be included. The journal *Midwest Folklore* (formerly *Hoosier Folklore)* often included commentary on material from these areas, and from areas as distant as Nebraska and Kansas. However, Indiana and the three Midwestern states to its west share some common features.

Geographically, the Midwest is Interior Lowland Topography. The inhabitants of the region also share the Midland speech dialect, and they share features of the Midwest Material Culture Region identified by folklorist Henry Glassie. The folk cultures of the North, the Middle Atlantic, and the South overlap and mingle throughout the Midwest region and also extend beyond it. The settlement process involved constant migration, adaptation to changes in technology and popular culture, and adaptation to new waves of immigration. The Pennsylvania bank barn, as one example, found most often in Ohio, can be found with decreasing frequency to the west as far as Wisconsin and Nebraska. As another example, folkways of the Upland South, such as English and Scots-Irish ballads, found their way into the southern half of the Midwestern states of Ohio, Indiana, Illinois, and Missouri.

Some areas within the Midwest have retained the features of just one of the source areas, and some areas retain unique folk cultures from other sources than the four major Anglo American source areas. Features of Native American folk culture, such as the foodways and folk medicine of the Ojibwa and Potowatomi tribes, have persisted into the 20th century. So have features of 18th-century French folk culture. In Illinois and Missouri, for example, French settlers of Norman-Canadian background built log houses with vertical posts. German immigration into the Midwestern states, beginning in the 1850s, produced many communities in the Midwest that have retained folk-cultural features of their homeland.

Traditions of the Amish in Ohio, in the Amana Colony in Iowa, and among Mennonites in Minnesota confirm the continued development of elements of German folk culture in the Midwest. In addition, immigrant communities from many other parts of the world—Poland, Lithuania, Mexico, Southeast Asia—have kept alive folk traditions in urban areas like Chicago, where they have established their own distinctive cultural matrices. These separate folk traditions have persisted within the mainstream of Midwestern folklore, just as Ozark folklore remains as a distinctive region in the southern half of the Midwest states, and just as occupational folklore (railroad lore, mining lore, factory lore, river lore, lumberjack lore) continues within it.

New England folk culture begins to appear in the Midwest with land grants to veterans of the War of 1812. The material traits of this migration can be seen through the northern Midwest: Yankee barns, Greek Revival house types, the saltbox

Vespers at Holy Trinity Russian Orthodox Greek-Catholic Cathedral. Chicago, 1977. Photo Carl Fleischhauer. American Folklife Center.

house, and the temple-form house. New England foodways (including stoneware and pottery), furniture, toolmaking, and stonecarving can be found through the Midwest states. Covered bridges constructed on the Yankee-barn model appear from Indiana to Iowa. The Yankee folk tradition merged in central Indiana and Illinois with folk traditions from Pennsylvania Germans. The Cumberland Road from Baltimore to Vandalia, Illinois, and the Wilderness Trail, from Philadelphia to Boonesboro, Kentucky, opened up the Midwest to Middle Atlantic pioneers; features of their material culture and folk traditions influenced the Midwest states from north to south.

Some Middle Atlantic traditions (folk art such as *frakturs* and folk tools such as yarn reels) have continental European origins, while others (Conestoga wagons, Sgraffito pottery decoration) are newer composite forms. The stone or log houses of Rhine Valley origin, and Georgian-type cabins of British origin, were supplanted by the Pennsylvania German house types. These distinctive houses, often with central chimney and semiunderground cellars, made their way into the Midwest, as did the Pennsylvania bank barn, which had a stone cellar and an earthen bank or ramp to allow vehicles to be drawn to the second level. In the 1850s, homestead opportunities attracted waves of European, mostly German, immigrants, and the Central Illinois Railway encouraged a land-office boom in Illinois. At the same time, steamboats on the Ohio and Mississippi rivers provided Southern markets for the farm products of two million Midwestern farmers.

These developments also furthered migration of Southern Upland and Lowland settlers into the Midwest. The Southern Upland settlers, following the Wilderness Trail to Boonesboro from Virginia and the Carolinas, continued into southern parts of the Midwest states. Settlers from the Lowland South and Appalachia populated the distinctive Ozark Culture Region, with the "Little Egypt" area of Cairo, Illinois, as one focal point and the Arkansas-Missouri border as another. The folk architecture of Southern settlers included log buildings and buildings without stone foundations. These constructions, along with the one-story Hall-and-Parlor house and the two-story Southern I-frame house, appear in the Southern parts of the Midwest states. Machinery, log construction, transverse or single-crib barns, and other elements of Southern material folk culture can be found in the Midwest states as far east as Southern Ohio. Elements of Southern folksongs and folktales can be found with them.

While these distinctive folk traditions from the North, Middle Atlantic, and the South may be present in specific locales in the Midwest, collections of Midwest folklore have tended to identify specific folk traditions within their local context. Modern researchers in folklore in the Midwest have increasingly examined new forms of folk culture as traditional genres of folklore are displaced by popular culture and by social or technological changes. The traditional legends were developed in the 1820s around the exploits of native character types; the Yankee peddler, the Mississippi keelboatman, and the ringtail roarer remained into the 20th century, while the more transient figures of Revolutionary War veteran and "old salt" Atlantic sailor did not typify the Midwest region or occupations. The image of Mike Fink came to represent the folk-hero quality of the Midwestern boatman on the Mississippi, Missouri, and Ohio, just as Davy Crockett represented the heroic folk type of the hunter to woodsman of the new West.

Mark Twain recognized the importance of these heroes to the folk culture of the Midwest when he incorporated set-pieces of river lore in his works. He also captured the superstitions and domestic folklore that Eastern settlers had brought together in a new formulation. In *Tom Sawyer* and in *Huckleberry Finn,* the household superstitions, animal lore, witch lore, and supernatural lore from the Midwest region offered 19th-century readers a new awareness of the transformations wrought by the frontier experience. Twain's treatment included superstitions later recorded by folklorists from both sides of the Mississippi River. These collections, from the early 20th century, offered a compendium of Midwest folk beliefs, a summary of wisdom accorded to American household gods. There were beliefs and sayings that offered the Midwesterner insights into the factors that could influence the conditions of his life—the weather, the condition of livestock and harvest, the comings and goings of neighbors, the uncertainties of courtship and child rearing, the mysteries of death and the supernatural.

The folklore of the Midwest shows a culture rich in awareness of the potential for signs and omens in everyday life. The spirit world manifested itself in ghost stories, witch lore, and various forms of divination. The extent of awareness by informants of conditions allowing for good luck and bad luck may serve as an indication of a passive acceptance of the operation of nonmaterial influences in the world. The extent of references to conjuration and "hoodoo" indicates an even wider belief in the operation of magic and the supernatural. While such beliefs were undoubtedly more widespread in the Deep South, particularly among African American "power doctors," they are also found in the Midwest.

In the Upper Midwest (Michigan, Wisconsin, Minnesota), such Southern influences are harder to find. The supernatural lore of French Canadian *loup-garou* tales, or the Chippewa Wenebojo and Windigo tales, are more common themes than stories of conjure doctors and witchcraft. The heroes of the Upper Midwest are daring figures from the lumber camps, the Upper Peninsula of Michigan mining camps, and the ore boats of the Great Lakes. Also, unique ethnic influences have produced traditions of folk humor, such as the Scandinavian Ole and Lena jokes, which are rarely found south of the Great Lakes region.

After the development of university studies in folklore, and the development of folklore journals in Indiana and Missouri, efforts began to find examples of folkways beyond the traditional genres. Folklorists found material in factories as well as farms, and in cities as well as rural communities. In the countryside of southern Indiana and Illinois, attention was now paid to a variety of entertainment forms and occupational activities. The camp meetings and minstrel shows of the 19th century were gone, with only the Toby shows surviving as a final remnant. The threshing bees and communal farming activities were no longer necessary with the advent of modern technology in farming. The lore of the steamboat, the railroad, and the mining camp likewise began to wane. With traditional folktales and folksongs now in the memories of individuals rather than alive among whole communities, collecting efforts required much more attention to context. Efforts to record the narrative explanations and procedures in traditional activities like cane making, folksong transmission, or storytelling are more important than ever in the collection of Midwestern folklore.

The folklore of the factory, the office, the school, and the mall have become more important in recent years. The features of modern Midwestern life still allow opportunities for serious collectors in a variety of areas: urban legends, joke lore, children's lore, hunting and fishing lore, and more.

John Schleppenbach

References

Botkin, B.A. 1955. *A Treasury of Mississippi River Folklore: Stories, Ballads, Traditions, and Folkways of the Mid-American River Country.* New York: Crown.

Brewster, Paul G. 1940. *Ballads and Songs of Indiana.* Publications in Folklore Series No. 1. Bloomington: Indiana University Press.

Dégh, Linda. 1976. Symbiosis of Joke and Legend: A Case of Conversational Folklore. In *Folklore Today: A Festschrift for Richard M. Dorson,* ed. Linda Dégh, Henry Glassie, and Felix J. Oinas. Bloomington: Indiana University Press, pp. 81–91.

Dorson, Richard M. 1964. *Buying the Wind: Regional Folklore in the United States.* Chicago: University of Chicago Press.

Fischer, David Hackett. 1989. *Albion's Seed: Four British Folkways in America.* New York: Oxford University Press.

Glassie, Henry. 1968. *Pattern in the Material Folk Culture of the Eastern United States.* Philadelphia: University of Pennsylvania Press.

Kramer, Frank R. 1964. *Voices in the Valley: Mythmaking and Folk Belief in the Shaping of the Middle West.* Madison: University of Wisconsin Press.

Zelinsky, Wilbur. 1973. *The Cultural Geography of the United States.* Englewood Cliffs, NJ: Prentice-Hall.

See also Great Lakes

Midwifery

The practice of assisting women during childbirth, generally considered the province of female midwives and a traditional art rather than a modern science. The earlier, primary meaning of midwife is "a woman by whose means the delivery is effected" and later "a woman who is *with* the mother at the birth" (Oxford English Dictionary [*OED*]). During the transition from midwife-managed to physician-managed childbirth, male surgeons or accoucheurs were sometimes known as men-midwives. Once persecuted as witches, female midwives came to be demeaned by the male-dominated medical profession as "old wives"—ignorant, superstitious, and incompetent folk practitioners who endangered their "patients." Midwifery's decline in the United States dates from the 1920s, when the majority of reported births began to be attended by doctors and increasingly took place in a hospital rather than at home.

In preindustrial European society, female healer-midwives played a major role in traditional health systems and a virtually exclusive one in childbirth. Both came under ecclesiastical scrutiny as witchcraft based on alliance with the devil. The medieval Catholic Church's witch-hunting manual, *Malleus Maleficarum* (*The Hammer of Witches,* first of many editions, 1486), devotes Question XI, Part I, to "witch midwives," who "in Various Ways Kill the Child Conceived in the Womb, and Procure an Abortion; or . . . Offer New-Born Children to Devils," and proclaims: "No one does more harm to the Catholic Faith than midwives," who are accused of a range of reproductive-system crimes. In the 16th century, the Church began licensing midwives as part of its stand against popular belief in magic and an effort both to improve medical practice and to make money (Oakley 1976:26).

Until the late 1700s, childbirth in America was a social event attended by female midwives, relatives, and friends; by the 1920s it had become generally a medical event managed by male obstetricians. Trained in England to regard midwifery as part of science, early American physicians imported "new obstetrics," and after the American Revolution, upper-class, urban American women and very gradually others turned to male physicians for delivery. Throughout the 1800s, doctors characterized female midwives as backward and worse, while the term "meddlesome midwifery" was used to indicate excessive medical intervention. Midwives who once had enjoyed considerable status came to be degraded as unskilled, domestic workers, although some still held high social positions locally in the early 20th century, when physicians began active lobbying to curtail or eliminate them while public-health officials argued for their regulation. Greater centralization of maternity care in hospitals and increasing acceptance of childbirth as a pathological process requiring obstetrical management rather than a natural process with female attendants "standing by" meant that many states banned midwifery or so regulated it that traditional practitioners could not meet the new requirements.

Professional midwifery started in the United States during the 1920s. New York City's Maternity Center Association began in 1918, considered starting the first nurse-midwifery training program in 1923, and established it in 1932. Kentucky native Mary Breckinridge, a professional nurse and British-trained midwife, worked with granny midwives in rural areas of her home state, where in 1925 she started the Frontier Nursing Service to show the efficacy of trained nurse-midwives. In 1928 its staff launched the Kentucky State Association of Midwives, later the American Association of Nurse-Midwives. The American College of Nurse-Midwives was founded in 1955, but the College of Obstetricians and Gynecologists did not recognize certified nurse-midwives, registered nurses with additional midwifery training, as primary childbirth attendants until 1971.

Lay midwifery, sometimes also called "empirical" or "nonnurse," encompasses both licensed and unlicensed midwives who practice legally and illegally according to various state's laws. Margaret Reid (1989) traces contemporary lay midwifery in the United States to the West Coast counterculture movement in the 1960s. Although differing from traditional midwives who are more often rural, ethnic or religious minority women whose children are grown, these predominantly White, middle-class women with young children share with granny midwives, Hispanic *parteras,* and other folk practitioners the informal training through apprenticeship, sense of "calling" or vocation, and greater reliance on herbal remedies and noninstrumental techniques. They are also similar to traditional midwives because they share cultural values and epistemological understandings about childbirth with the women they attend.

Ethnographic and biographical accounts of midwives, their practice, and their clientele need more systematic investigation to delineate fully the role of midwife. Recruitment and training, status within their community and/or among its women, relationships with other health-care practitioners, and the perception and evaluation of competence must be considered as well as the social status and personal circumstance of those who choose or are constrained to seek midwives' services. Conceptual frameworks for the full range of ritual and physical techniques employed should also be determined.

Contemporary American pregnancy and childbirth may be viewed as a yearlong rite of passage involving a range of participants and "ritual specialists," according to Robbie E. Davis-Floyd. She distinguishes two contrasting models of childbirth: the technocratic and the wholistic (1992:160–161). The former is male centered, objectified, and doctor directed; the latter, female centered, integrative, organic, and relatively noninterventionist. The midwife acts as nurturer, skillful guide, and assistant, while responsibility for the birthing is the mother's.

The performance of midwifery, the birth event itself, is seldom fully documented. Brigitte Jordan gives an exemplary account of a Mayan midwife's supervision of delivery (1993: 31–41). Everyone in the birth setting participates in "doing a birth," assisting in physical tasks and engaging in speech that ranges from everyday conversation to "stories" about childbirth and death and "birth talk" specifically addressed to the parturient woman. This complex of birth speech figures in an important meaning of gossip or godsiblingship, the talk and interaction of all of those in attendance at childbirth. Performed midwifery may thus be interpreted as a powerful language or mythology.

Marta Weigle

References

Benoit, Cecilia M. 1991. *Midwives in Passage: The Modernisation of Maternity Care.* St. John's, Newfoundland: Institute of Social and Economic Research, Memorial University of Newfoundland.

Buss, Fran Leeper. 1980. *La Partera: Story of a Midwife.* Ann Arbor: University of Michigan Press.

Davis-Floyd, Robbie E. 1992. *Birth as an American Rite of Passage.* Berkeley: University of California Press.

Donegan, Jane. 1978. *Women and Men Midwives: Medicine, Morality and Misogyny in Early America.* Westport, CT: Greenwood.

Dougherty, Molly C. 1978. Southern Lay Midwives as Ritual Specialists. In *Women in Ritual and Symbolic Roles,* ed. Judith Hoch-Smith and Anita Spring. New York: Plenum, pp. 151–164.

Jordan, Brigitte. 1993. *Birth in Four Cultures: A Crosscultural Investigation of Childbirth in Yucatan, Holland, Sweden, and the United States,* 4th ed. Revised and expanded by Robbie Davis-Floyd. Prospect Heights, IL: Waveland.

Litoff, Judy Barrett. 1978. *American Midwives, 1860 to the Present.* Westport, CT: Greenwood.

Oakley, Ann. 1976. Wisewoman and Medicine Man: Changes in the Management of Childbirth. In *The Rights and Wrongs of Women,* ed. Juliet Mitchell and Ann Oakley. Harmondsworth, Middlesex: Penguin Books, pp. 17–58.

Reid, Margaret. 1989. Sisterhood and Professionalization: A Case Study of the American Lay Midwife. In *Women as Healers: Cross-Cultural Perspectives,* ed. Carol Shepherd McClain. New Brunswick, NJ: Rutgers University Press, pp. 219–238.

Susie, Debra Ann. 1988. *In the Way of Our Grandmothers:*

A Cultural View of Twentieth-Century Midwifery in Florida. Athens: University of Georgia Press.

See also Pregnancy and Birth

Military Folklore

Traditions of members of the armed services. Like any folk group, people in the military use lore to indoctrinate rookies; to censure inappropriate behavior; to explain the irrational, and to define members of the group (whether the group be the platoon, the company, the division, even the branch of the service) from nonmembers. Also, like other groups of workers, military units invent their own language. When freshmen, or "plebes," at the U.S. Naval Academy in Annapolis, Maryland, finish their summer basic training, they trade in their "dixie cups" (sailor hats) for "covers" (officer hats) and begin the toughest year in their careers, a year in which "flamers" "ream them out" in front of their peers for minor infractions. Those who receive the harshest abuse are the "shit screens"; those who ingratiate themselves with upperclassmen, the "smacks."

In World War II, a pilot would rev up his "coffee grinder" (plane engine) and, with permission of the "madhouse" (control tower), take off toward his target, where he would either "hang out the laundry" (drop parachutists), drop a few "eggs" (bombs), or make a "split S" (combat maneuver) and then hightail it from the "junior prom" (hot mission), "flak happy" (suffering from combat fatigue), hoping to get home without a "panting virgin" or a "ruptured duck" (injured plane).

One cannot be a full member of a group without speaking the group's language, and the highly formalized speech of drill instructors, in which every insult and every command has been practiced and polished on preceding recruits, begins the initiation. Although the skills taught in basic training change with the introduction of new weapons and new combat techniques, one learns the proper relation to authority largely from traditional material: through the stories of what happened to previous recruits who failed to take orders, through the sometimes brutal boot-camp games designed to test one's mental as well as physical strength, and through the marching chants performed on the parade field. Such chants, cadence calls, or "jodies," as they are referred to by the Army and the Marine Corps, celebrate the need to repudiate the pleasures associated with one's former civilian past and to embrace a martial future (or, more literally, to leave your girl and love your rifle):

> Cindy, Cindy, Cindy Lou
> Love my rifle more than you.
>
> You used to be my beauty queen,
> Now I love my M–16.
>
> Used to go to the county fair,
> Now I don't take you anywhere.
>
> Send me off to Vietnam
> Goin' to get me some Viet Cong.

> With my knife or with my gun
> Either way it's just as fun.

Not only does lore inculcate the values of a military identity, it also serves those in wartime as a preparation for combat. Before going into battle, warriors of all cultures perform rituals (maybe only as simple as a prayer or a cheer). In Vietnam, one unit filled a porcelain toilet bowl with beer, or liquor when they had it, from which, one by one, soldiers sipped their libation before heading out of camp. In Vietnam, troops decorated helmets with political, religious, and personal slogans, carried tokens as good luck charms, fashioned in-country patches, and transformed planes and helicopters into ferocious animals and friendly mascots, or, like their World War II predecessors, adorned them with cheesecake pictures.

While folk practices instill military values, some also provide a way of safely subverting the chain of command. Veteran sailors (or "shellbacks") crossing the equator summon King Neptune from his royal depths in order to initiate, through a series of humiliating rituals, the "pollywogs," as they are called—those on board making their maiden crossing of the equator (especially fresh officers). Such "crossing the line" ceremonies, performed on board ships since the 1600s, ritualistically subvert military hierarchy by installing for a day at least a new command: the costumed sailor as King Neptune, his cross-dressing buddy as Queen Aphrodite, and their royal baby (generally the fattest sailor on board dressed in a diaper). Not nearly as elaborate, yet thematically similar, anecdotes that celebrate the ways in which a crusty chief petty officer teaches arrogant inexperienced lieutenants a lesson circulate widely among enlisted troops.

To explain the irrational or the uncanny, soldiers tell stories of miraculous occurrences, of bullets deflected by Bibles and dogtags, and every war produces its share of angel-helper stories. Typically, an older soldier helps a younger struggling soldier, one too tired or too wounded to keep up with his fellow retreating buddies. Upon waking the next morning, eager to thank his rescuer, the young soldier finds that the one who helped him back to friendly lines never existed or was someone who had himself died in combat months or years before. Phantom soldiers fight in every war. The spirits of downed pilots repeat their distress calls on the anniversary of their death. In one Vietnam account, an army combat soldier fights valorously until one day when he sees himself in VC (Viet Cong) clothing stalking through the bushes. Such radical ambivalence marks the end of his tour of duty.

Members of all branches of the military exchange short-timer calendars, pictures of either a patriotic or a bawdy image intricately divided into 365 shapes that the short-timer progressively colors, one each day until he returns home, the calendar completely filled in. Short-timer sayings ("He's so short he could jump off a dime" and "He's so short he could wipe an ant's ass") and superstitions about the inadvisability of fighting alongside one with less than a month to serve proliferate during times of war.

The Vietnam War, more than any other, produced a constellation of lore associated with the return home. An account often told to sum up the returning vet, his sacrifices unacknowledged, his heroism unhailed by an American population fed up with the war, is the spat-upon story. The war-weary soldier, many accounts claim, taxis into the gate, deplanes, and walks across the tarmac, but instead of hearing the cheers and bands that welcomed his predecessors, he walks through a crowd of jeering people, one of whom spits on him. Although the account defies reality (How many troop transport planes flew into commercial airports?), it is always told seriously. This story epitomized for many the terrible irony of the Vietnam War, but the story predates that war. It was told about Korean War vets whose pain and hardship seemed to many stateside to have been for little. The story penetrated popular culture as well. In the 1950s film *Shock Corridor*, a journalist going undercover in an insane asylum tells a first-person version of this story in order to ensure his disguise as a shell-shocked Korean vet.

Stories of unappreciative civilians spitting on veterans; of soldiers returning home from Vietnam early, only to be shot by their fathers suspecting them to be intruders; of extraordinary draft-evasion attempts that failed; of crazed combat soldiers fashioning necklaces of severed enemy ears—these stories and many more constitute the legendary repertoire of Vietnam.

Carol Burke

References

Burke, Carol. 1992. "If You're Nervous in the Service . . .": Training Songs of Female Soldiers in the '40s. In *Visions of War: World War II in Popular Literature and Culture*, ed. Paul Holsinger and Mary Anne Schofield. Bowling Green, OH: State University Popular Press, pp. 127–137.

Cleveland, Les. 1985. Soldiers' Songs: The Folklore of the Powerless. *New York Folklore* 11:79–97.

Jackson, Bruce. 1990. The Perfect Informant. *Journal of American Folklore* 103:400–416.

Kenagy, S.G. 1978. Sexual Symbolism in the Language of the Air Force Pilot: A Psychoanalytical Approach to Folk Speech. *Western Folklore* 37:89–101.

Sandels, Robert. 1983. The Doughboy: The Formation of a Military Folk. *American Studies* 24:69–88.

See also Civil War; Gulf War; Korean War; Revolutionary War; Vietnam War; World Wars I and II

Miners

Workers who extract minerals from the earth. As an occupational group, miners in America—both the coal miners east of the Mississippi and the hard-rock metals miners of the Western states—have historically been faced by conditions of uncertainty and antagonism both above and below ground. Within the mines themselves, the history of American mining has been punctuated regularly by deaths and injuries due to cave-ins, fires, and floods, and miners have gone to work each day never knowing when the ore body or coal seam was going to bottom out and end their employment. On the surface, miners have frequently done battle with management in the form of industrial action designed to bring about improvements in working conditions. Finally, the health of the industry as a whole, and thus the welfare and future of its workers, has historically depended on the frequently unpredictable vicissitudes of market forces and metals prices. Faced with these conditions, miners through their folklife expressions have traditionally sought ways to imaginatively control their unpredictable work environments, to commemorate the dead and criticize management antagonists, to celebrate their skills and identities as miners, and to achieve and maintain a strong sense of solidarity and mutual purpose.

A large body of folk beliefs, much of it having its origins in European mining traditions, has traditionally governed behavior within the mines in an attempt either to assure safety and success or to forestall accident and failure. These beliefs usually take the form of omens—signs that predict that disaster is in the offing—or ritual behaviors that are followed in order to either help bring about favorable outcomes or prevent unfavorable ones. Thus, Upper Michigan miner Jim Hodge told folklorist Richard M. Dorson in 1946 that he was once rebuked because he "walked in the Negaunee mine once a-whistling," that women were never allowed down the mine, and that "to kill a rat in the mine is worse than murder" because they "know ahead when ground is breaking; they can hear it." In 1989 north Idaho mining man Bill Bondurant described that, prior to a rockburst, "when the rock was working a little bit, you could hear ping, ping, ping; they said that the tommy knockers—trolls—were warning you to get out of there." He also noted that "there used to be a superstition that you'd lose the vein if a woman looked on the vein, but that's—since women have worked in the mines—well, that superstition is pretty well forgotten."

Largely due to the efforts of folklorist George Korson (1899–1967), modern scholars have available to them a large body of coal miners' folksongs from the late 19th and early 20th centuries. Taken together, these songs provide a glimpse from the miners' perspective of what their lives were like in the days when coal was still mined primarily with pick and shovel. It was not uncommon for mine disasters to be commemorated in folksong, and the songs both preserved the memory of the fallen miners and served as a communal reminder of the tenuous nature of work underground. In 1869, for example, 110 workers died in a fire in the Avondale coal mine in Pennsylvania, a tragedy that was quickly captured in a broadside ballad called "The Avondale Mine Disaster," which Korson collected in the 1920s. Its thrust is both historic and elegiac, as two sample verses show:

> On the sixth day of September,
> Eighteen hundred and sixty-nine,
> Those miners all then got a call,
> To go work in the mine;
> But little did they think that day
> That death would gloom the vale
> Before they would return again from
> The mines of Avondale.
>
> . . .

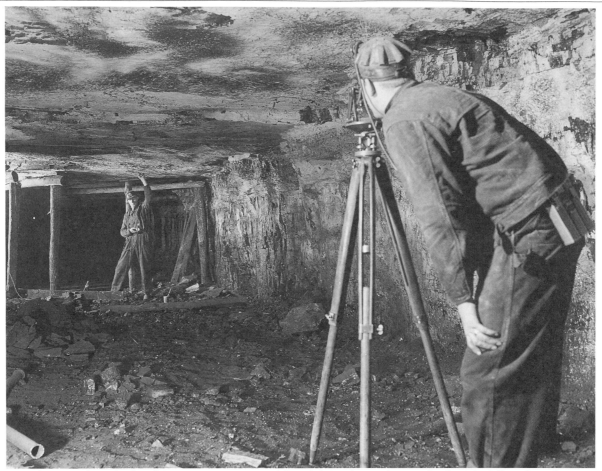

Down the mines at the Pittsburgh Coal Company, engineers survey and plot each day's work. Pennsylvania, 1942. Photo John Collier. Library of Congress.

Now to conclude, and make an end,
Their number I'll pen down—
One hundred and ten of brave stout men
Were smothered underground;
They're in their graves till the last day,
Their widows may bewail,
And the orphans' cries they rend the skies
All round through Avondale!

While mining is still dangerous work, the impulse to remember the fallen in ballads has largely died out in the late 20th century. When ninety-one miners died in a fire in the Sunshine silver mine in Kellogg, Idaho, in 1972, they were commemorated in the form of a monument sculpted by a former miner who had once worked in that mine.

While fully recognizing that their work is dangerous and debilitating, miners have frequently blamed mine owners and management for the high toll that their work has exacted in death and injury. Miners have traditionally seen owners as exploitative antagonists anyway, given at various times and places to blacklisting union miners and requiring that workers live in company houses, shop at company stores, and follow other such restrictive practices. Biting stories circulated about prominent and self-important owners like Marcus Daly, the copper magnate of Butte, Montana, who (so the story went) died and entered heaven only to have God turn to his right and sarcastically say, "Come, Jesus, get up and give Marcus your seat." Korson collected many strike songs from the balladeering 19th and early 20th centuries, as well as ballads describing and assessing the activities of radical labor groups like Pennsylvania's Molly Maguires. Widely shared union-oriented "laborlore," in folklorist Archie Green's term, seems less common in the latter part of the 20th century, or at least it is not as well represented in folklorists' collections.

Not all of miners' folklore, however, has been geared toward coping with death, contingency, and confrontation. An equally strong strain of miners' folklore has focused on celebrating their skills and occupational identity, demonstrating a great deal of pride and faith in themselves and their work. In Western mining camps, hand-drilling contests were for many years a high point of communal Fourth of July celebrations, even after machine drills had taken over the task of boring holes in rock to accept dynamite charges. Korson collected many examples of ballads praising the hard work and indomitable spirit of the coal miner, such as "The Miner Lad":

Nay, don't despise the miner lad,
Who burrows like the mole;
Buried alive, from morn to night,
To delve for household coal—
Nay, miner lad, ne'er blush for it,
Though black thy face be as the pit!

As honorable thy calling is
As that of hero lords;
They owe to the poor miner lad
The ore that steels their swords—
And perils too, as fierce as theirs
In limb and life, the miner shares!

Despite (or, indeed, because of) the difficult conditions under which they have worked, miners have traditionally maintained a sense of communal strength, purpose, and commitment, perhaps related to the traditional attitude that north Idaho mining man Bob Anderson has characterized by saying "Yeah, hope springs eternal, especially in the mining. It's always one foot to a million dollars—the next foot."

Within the workplace, miners have traditionally used several linguistic means to express and maintain a sense of group identity and solidarity. For example, it is common practice in the mining industry for miners to know and refer to each other almost exclusively through nicknames, such as the colleagues about whom Bill Bondurant and Bob Anderson reminisced: Milk Bottle, Rooster-Goose, Screaming Gene, Biffo, Dum-Dum, Little Man, and Red Fred. (Anderson said that many of the names inscribed on the Sunshine miners' memorial are meaningless to him because they are the fallen miners' full names, not their nicknames; he never knew them by their full names.) Such names bind the workers in a mine into a club of sorts, a close-knit fraternity that is separate from the larger world and within which one's most meaningful social identity lies. Beyond the confines of individual mines or communities, miners as a group also share an occupational vocabulary, a set of terms describing their workplace and equipment that outsiders will not understand and that also serves to create and reinforce group cohesion. To an Eastern coal miner, for example, the fine particles resulting from drilling are "bug dust," while waste material is "gob." This vocabulary may have regional variations: The "cage" that carries miners down the shaft in Eastern coal mines is just as likely to be called a "skip" in the Western mountains. Still, this vocabulary is another means through which miners create and proclaim a sense of identity.

Above ground, miners' folklife has also tended to focus on communal situations and gatherings in which talk and song came easily. Korson has written of how ballads were a common part of life in taverns, stores, and other foci of community life in Pennsylvania's coal country. On the Western mining frontier, the saloon was usually one of the first buildings erected, and it quickly became the undisputed social center of the town. By geological necessity, mining has been carried out largely in remote mountainous areas; physically isolated, struggling daily with recalcitrant rock and profit-minded management, miners have perhaps more than other occupational groups been drawn together into mutually supportive communities, and their folklore has consistently reflected this orientation. While mining areas are no longer as isolated as they once were, and while the industry is in decline in many areas of the country, miners continue to feel and express the pride, cohesiveness, and traditional attitudes that have characterized them from the beginning.

Kent C. Ryden

References

Dorson, Richard M. 1952. *Bloodstoppers and Bearwalkers: Folk Traditions of the Upper Peninsula.* Cambridge: Harvard University Press.

Green, Archie. 1972. *Only a Miner: Studies in Recorded Coal-Mining Songs.* Urbana: University of Illinois Press.

———. 1993. *Wobblies, Pile Butts, and Other Heroes: Laborlore Explorations.* Urbana: University of Illinois Press.

Hart, Patricia, and Ivar Nelson. 1984. *Mining Town: The Photographic Record of T.N. Barnard and Nellie Stockbridge from the Coeur d'Alenes.* Seattle: University of Washington Press; Boise: Idaho State Historical Society.

Korson, George. 1938. *Minstrels of the Mine Patch: Songs and Stories of the Anthracite Industry.* Philadelphia: University of Pennsylvania Press.

———. 1943. *Coal Dust on the Fiddle: Songs and Stories of the Bituminous Industry.* Philadelphia: University of Pennsylvania Press.

———. 1960. *Black Rock: Mining Folklore of the Pennsylvania Dutch.* Baltimore: Johns Hopkins University Press.

Preston, Dennis Richard. 1975. *Bituminous Coal Mining Vocabulary of the Eastern United States.* University, AL: American Dialect Society.

Ryden, Kent C. 1993. *Mapping the Invisible Landscape: Folklore, Writing, and the Sense of Place.* Iowa City: University of Iowa Press.

West, Elliott. 1979. *The Saloon on the Rocky Mountain Mining Frontier.* Lincoln: University of Nebraska Press.

Minstrel Shows

An entertainment form in which White male performers blackened their faces in imitation of Negroes to perform what were presented as Black dialect, songs, dances, and jokes. Minstrel shows were popular in America throughout the 19th century and into the early 20th century. While rooted in European music and theater, minstrelsy represented a conscious move in America toward an indigenous entertainment form.

Although minstrelsy enjoyed its greatest popularity during the 19th century, blackface entertainment, which originated in Europe, was performed in America during the early republic period, although American Black life and culture were not used as stage material until the early 1820s. Increasing numbers of performers with cork-blackened faces soon followed, traveling and, initially, performing "Negro" songs and dances during theater interludes or in circuses. One of the most famous, and earliest, of these performers was Thomas D. Rice, who, after observing an elderly Black man dance and sing, adopted the moves and the song, modified both, and created a new act, which premiered in 1828, that featured the song and dance "Jim Crow." By the early 1940s, individual blackface performers began to band together to form minstrel shows.

Opinions differ as to which troupe performed the first minstrel show, although much evidence points toward the February 1843 performance of four blackface performers, Billy Whitlock, Frank Pelham, Dan Emmett, and Frank Brower, who appeared as the Virginia Minstrels. Christy's Minstrels, though, is credited with finding the "ideal minstrel blend" when it combined the rowdiness of the Virginia Minstrels with the sentimentality of Stephen Foster's songs (Toll 1974:38). By the mid-1850s, the three-part minstrel show had evolved and continued to be predominant thereafter. The first part featured the entire minstrel company placed in a semicircle, with the interlocutor, or the straight man, in the center, and flanked by the comic end men, Tambo and Bones. The first part included serious and comic songs, dance, and humor and usually ended with a stump speech, an oration delivered to the audience in Black dialect and filled with malapropisms. The second part, the olio, resembled a variety show and also included a stump speech. The final act was a one-act skit, usually farce and parody.

Minstrelsy had a great and lasting effect on White America's perception of Blacks. One of its earliest appeals was that it offered Whites what they believed were accurate portrayals of Southern Black slaves, with images such as "huge eyes and gaping mouths," shabby and ill-fitting clothes, unique dialect, constant fidgeting, frenzied and eccentric movements in response to music, and an inability to control themselves (Toll 1974:34–36). In contrast to this "foolish" image, the sentimental songs written by Stephen Foster, many of which were performed by minstrel troupes, provided another stereotype of the happy, loyal plantation "darky," such as Old Darky or Old Auntie. Additionally, while earlier portrayals of Blacks demonstrated some variety, later and more successful minstrelsy presented specific stereotypes of Blacks that became firmly entrenched as fact in White consciousness. Blacks were portrayed as intellectually and physically inferior through derogatory characterizations, represented by the happy, carefree, ignorant Southern Black, such as Jim Crow, or the falsely egocentric dandy, such as Zip Coon or Dandy Jim.

Black minstrel troupes appeared occasionally before the Civil War and continued to grow in number and popularity after the end of the war. While Black performers introduced new material to minstrelsy, they generally retained the traditional standards, which often included "blacking up," because they relied on the acceptance of White audiences. One of the earliest and best-known Black minstrels was Master Juba, a dancer who was famous for his rendition of an Irish jig.

The rising popularity of these authentic Black performers as well as the increasing success of other entertainment forms after the Civil War threatened the hold minstrelsy had on the stage. Minstrel troupes responded by expanding in size, traveling extensively, expanding the parts of the show, getting rid of the vulgarity, and even moving away from concentration on Black imitation. Minstrelsy, thus, remained popular through the turn of the century, as is evidenced by the success of Al Jolson, an American blackface entertainer who starred in *The Jazz Singer*, the first full-length film with synchronized sound. Even after its general popularity began to wane, Minstrelsy still drew audiences in rural areas and small towns. It was also used by the WPA (Works Progress Administration), in the 1930s to uplift spirits by providing comedy and laughter to Depression-era Americans, and it was utilized for the same reasons by the USO through World War II. Increasing racial consciousness and the civil rights movement were largely responsible for the virtual demise of minstrelsy by mid-century, although instances of it still appeared as late as the 1970s.

Sandra G. Hancock

References

Boskin, Joseph. 1986. *Sambo: The Rise and Demise of an American Jester.* New York: Oxford University Press.

Nathan, Hans. 1962. *Dan Emmett and the Rise of Early Negro Minstrelsy.* Norman: University of Oklahoma Press.

Toll, Robert C. 1974. *Blacking up: The Minstrel Show in Nineteenth-Century America.* New York: Oxford University Press.

Mnemonic Devices

Verbal or visual formulas or actions used as aids in memorizing and recalling dates, numbers, grammatical rules, formulas, work-related knowledge, or other information considered important but difficult to remember. The term "mnemonic" is derived from the ancient Greek word *mnemonikos,* "of or pertaining to memory," and is related to the name of Mnemosyne, the ancient Greek goddess of memory. Used extensively by preliterate cultures, mnemonics remain common today in educational, scientific, and occupational settings, as well as in everyday life.

Some mnemonic devices involve actions taken to modify an object, which then represents the information to be recalled. The common method of keeping a tally by writing four lines crossed by a fifth is such a device, as is tying a string around one's finger as a reminder.

Some mnemonic systems, including many popularized through books and magazine articles, are based on visualization techniques. For example, in order to remember a new acquaintance's name, one visualizes an image derived from the sound of the person's name. These methods are not strictly traditional, but rather have roots in ancient Greek memory systems.

Most modern mnemonic devices are verbal. Many take the form of short rhymes, phrases, and even songs. For example, many children are introduced to the alphabet through the "ABC Song," memorize the rhyme "Thirty days hath September," and learn the spelling rule "i before e except after c." Numerous traditional rhymes, such as "Rain before seven, clear by eleven" and "Year of snow, fruit will grow," were once used by farmers and sailors to remember agricultural and weather-related knowledge and often incorporated folk beliefs. Even advertising slogans and jingles function as implicit mnemonic devices that keep the name of the product or business in the mind of the hearer.

Verbal mnemonics may also consist of alphabetical or numerical lists of related information. For instance, the "ABC's of emergency care" (airway, breathing, circulation) help doctors, nurses, and paramedics recall the proper order of treatment priorities in their patients. Another medical mnemonic, "the four f's of gall bladder disease" (fat, female, forty, and flatulent), lists characteristics typical of patients with this ailment.

Mnemonics based on various letter-number codes are common. Telephone number mnemonics, for example, consist of short words or phrases created from the letters associated with the appropriate numbers on the telephone dial. Businesses often create telephone mnemonics in which the meaning of the mnemonic word or phrase recalls the nature of the merchandise or services offered.

Many verbal mnemonics take the form of acrostics, sentences in which the initial letters of each word match the first letter of each bit of information to be remembered. For instance, the mnemonics "On old Olympus towering tops, a Finn and German viewed some hops" and "Oh, oh, oh, to taste, touch, and feel a girl's vagina so heavenly," both in circulation among medical students, represent the names and order of the cranial nerves: olfactory, optic, oculomotor, trochlear, trigeminal, abducens, facial, acoustic, glossopharyngeal, vagal, spinal accessory, and hypoglossal. The use of shorter, acronym-like words and phrases is also common. For example, in physics, the name "Roy G. Biv" represents the order of colors of the spectrum: red, orange, yellow, green, blue, indigo, and violet). Many acrostic mnemonics are bawdy and reflect the predominantly male composition of the groups during the time they were created.

Whatever the form of the mnemonic, its underlying technique remains the same. The mnemonic attempts to create within the mind of its user a gestalt, a unified mental construct consisting of both the mnemonic and the information for which it stands. When one remembers the mnemonic, one remembers at the same time the material it encodes. Some mnemonics build image or word patterns linked semantically or through similarity of sound to the information they represent. Others, however, create an association that is purely arbitrary. These mnemonics must be decoded by the user. In either case, stylistic devices such as rhyme, meter, and music may be used to reinforce the linkage of the mnemonic and its referents, making both easier to memorize.

The arbitrary relationship of many mnemonics to the material they represent is the inherent weakness of the genre and the reason for the ambivalence often felt about the more elaborate, fanciful devices. Many people learn them enthusiastically and even create their own, but others find the mnemonics themselves difficult to remember and, therefore, of little value. Although the sexual imagery of the bawdy mnemonics makes them easier to recall than most, many people find that they retain the mnemonic itself far longer than the material it is designed to help them remember.

Anne Burson-Tolpin

References

Brakeley, Theresa C. [1949–1950] 1972. Mnemonic Device. In *Funk and Wagnalls Standard Dictionary of Folklore, Mythology, and Legend,* ed. Maria Leach and Jerome Fried. New York: Funk and Wagnalls, pp. 734–740.

Dundes, Alan. 1961. Mnemonic Devices. *Midwest Folklore* 11:139–147.

Mojo

Amulet, charm object, and more often the belief-practice system of voodoo as known by a significant portion of modern-day African Americans. Scholars and members of the folk community use numerous terms to refer to mojo. The latter group especially, refer to mojo the following terms: "hoodoo," "voodoo," "witchcraft," "conjuration," "fixing," "tricking," and "root working." Similarly, occult practitioners may be called "hoodoo doctors," "mojo doctors," "voodoo doctors," "witch doctors," "conjure doctors," or "root doctors." While the basic belief core of this system has a definite African origin, the etymology of the term "mojo" is uncertain. Norman Whitten (1962) even asserts that the word "mojo" has a North Carolina birth.

The system of mojo tends to encompass almost every facet and institution of African American life. If the husband of an occult believer strays from the path of fidelity, the wife attributes this behavior to mojo (either the magical object or the supernatural system). Likewise, people who are ill and who do not show progress after being treated with scientific medicine are under the influence of root working. Persons involved in games of chance and gambling seek the advice of, and direction from, the renowned mojo doctor. Moreover, the defendant who wants to influence the outcome of his trial wears his mojo (charm) into the courtroom. Mojo especially permeates the blues tradition. Sam "Lightning" Hopkins sings in one of his popular songs:

> I'm going to Louisiana to buy me a Mojo hand
> I'm going to Louisiana to buy me a Mojo hand
> I'm going to *fix* my woman so she can't have no other man.

Although earlier researchers thought that the mojo tradition was specifically a Southern Black phenomenon, later scholars have dispelled that concept. In fact, folklorists now acknowledge that African Americans who migrated from the rural South into the urbanized cities of the United States carried with them their mojo beliefs, practices, and stories. Practitioners in the urban North continue to cure supernatural illnesses and gain occult revenge for ill deeds in traditional ways, but with adaptive modifications. Also, nomenclature for the mojo doctor has changed to avoid possible conflicts with the law. The hoodoo doctor of the South has become a "psychic," a "spiritualist," or a "reader" who is much more commercial than his counterpart.

Elon A. Kulii

References

Cooley, Gilbert E. (Elon A. Kulii). 1975. Root Stories. *North Carolina Folklore Journal* 23:34–36.

Bill Monroe in concert. American Folklife Center.

————. 1977. Root Doctors and Psychics in the Region. *Indiana Folklore* 10:191–215.

Hurston, Zora Neale. 1931. Hoodoo in America. *Journal of American Folklore* 44:317–417.

Hyatt, Harry M. 1970–1975. *Hoodoo, Conjuration, Witchcraft, Rootwork.* 5 vols. Hannibal, MO: Western.

Puckett, Niles Newbell. 1926. *Folk Beliefs of the Southern Negro.* Chapel Hill: University of North Carolina Press.

Snow, Loudell. 1978. Sorcerers, Saints, and Charlatans: Black Folk Healers in Urban America. *Culture, Medicine, and Psychiatry* 2:60–106.

Whitten, Norman E. 1962. Contemporary Patterns of Malign Occultism among Negroes in North Carolina. *Journal of American Folklore* 75:311–325.

Monroe, Bill (1911–)

Singer, mandolinist, and principal creator of bluegrass music. The youngest of eight children in a poor farming family near Rosine in west-central Kentucky, Monroe was raised in a musical household. Formative musical contacts in his youth included his uncle Pendleton Vandiver (with whom he lived as a teenager following his parents' deaths and about whom he later composed one of his most popular songs, "Uncle Pen") and the influential local Black musician Arnold Shultz.

In the early 1930s, Monroe joined several brothers at industrial work in northern Indiana. Soon he began performing with them as mandolinist, singer, and dancer. In 1935 he and older brother Charlie became full-time entertainers. As the Monroe Brothers, they performed on radio in the Carolinas between 1936 and 1938 and placed sixty songs, many of them traditional, on best-selling RCA Victor Bluebird records. By 1938, when he formed his own band, the Blue Grass Boys (named after his home state), Monroe was recognized within the field of country music (then called "hillbilly music") as an innovative mandolinist and powerful vocalist. In 1939 Monroe joined the cast of the Grand Ole Opry, the long-running live radio jamboree at WSM in Nashville, Tennessee. He has been there ever since.

Monroe aimed at preserving and modernizing the old-time traditional music of the rural Upland South. He developed a repertoire that combined the old and the new in instrumental dance and display tunes, secular songs, and religious quartets. During the 1940s through his personal appearances, broadcasts, and recordings (for Victor and Columbia), he popularized his repertoire with a band sound based on earlier Southeastern string-band traditions. Soon other musicians, particularly in Appalachia, were copying him. At first Monroe resented such copying, but by the mid-1960s, following the development of a festival movement that celebrated his musical history, he had accepted the idea that he was "The Daddy of Bluegrass Music" and became comfortable with his role as patriarch and teacher. Monroe's own annual bluegrass festivals, held every June since 1967 at his country-music park in Bean Blossom, Indiana, are widely attended events. Among his many honors are the National Endowment for the Arts' National Heritage Fellowship Award, election into the Country Music Association's Hall of Fame, and the NARAS Lifetime Achievement Award.

Over his career, Monroe has performed and recorded hundreds of folksongs and tunes, helping spread and maintain the traditions in which he has played a significant part. He has also contributed his own compositions, both instrumental and vocal, to oral tradition. And by leading the way in inventing techniques for playing fiddle tunes and blues on an instrument previously utilized for classical and Italian popular musics, he has shaped the development of the mandolin as an instrument used in American folk traditions.

Neil V. Rosenberg

References

Rinzler, Ralph. 1975. Bill Monroe. In *Stars of Country Music*, ed. Bill C. Malone and Judith McCulloh. Urbana: University of Illinois Press, pp. 202–221.

Rooney, James. [1971] 1991. *Bossmen: Bill Monroe and Muddy Waters*. New York: Da Capo.

Monsters

Fabulous beings often compounded of elements from various human or animal forms. Monsters are found in a gray area between zoology and folklore, sometimes called "cryptozoology" (the science of hidden animals), a term coined by the Belgian zoologist Bernard Heuvelmans. Author of key books on the subject, Heuvelmans spent a lifetime collecting and analyzing reports of these creatures that may or may not exist.

Another approach to the subject of monsters is "Fortean," a word coined from the name of the American writer Charles Hoy Fort (1874–1932), who collected and circulated accounts of strange phenomena and experiences, curiosities, mysteries, prodigies, and portents. Just about anything is subject to Fortean investigation: showers of frogs, toenail painters, wild kangaroos in Wisconsin, appearances of the Virgin Mary, crop circles, feral children, and so on. The key element of the Fortean approach is open-mindedness: Strange phenomena are neither uncritically embraced nor automatically dismissed.

In North America, as in the rest of the world, the two basic types of monsters are terrestrial and aquatic. There are dozens of land-based creatures, including the Skunk Ape of the Everglades and Momo the Missouri Monster. A few of them are said to have the ability to fly. In New Jersey, for example, we find periodic reports of the Jersey Devil, an unusual creature with large bat-like wings. And scattered reports from such disparate places as Washington, Texas, and West Virginia have described Mothman, a strange gray winged creature.

Though the idea is regarded with skepticism by the scientific community, some monsters are said to be extraterrestrial visitors. Ever since the 1950s, there have been persistent reports of "little green men" from outer space. Also associated with unidentified flying objects (UFOs) are stories of alleged encounters with men in black, who wear black suits, black hats, and sunglasses.

Of all of the terrestrial monsters, few have had as many reported sightings as the Sasquach, or Bigfoot. The creature has been described as a humanoid about 6 feet tall, almost 3 feet wide, and weighing about 300 pounds. It is said to be covered from head to foot with dark-brown, silver-tipped hair. It was sighted in the early 20th century in Alberta and British Columbia, but more recently it has been spotted south of the Canadian border in Washington, Oregon, and northern California.

Many North American aquatic monsters have affectionate nicknames: Ogopogo, the lake monster of Okanagan Lake in New York; Igopogo of Lake Simcoe near Toronto; Manipogo of Lake Manitoba; Chessie, the Chesapeake Bay sea serpent; Slimy Slim or Sharlie of Payette Lake in Idaho; and Whitey, the White River Monster of Arkansas.

Perhaps the most celebrated aquatic creature is Champ, the monster of Lake Champlain, a lake 125 miles long and 435 square miles in area, between eastern New York State and western Vermont. Most of the reports describe a creature that emerges briefly from the water with several humps on its back and a long snake-like neck supporting a small head. In some ways, Lake Champlain is an excellent place for an unknown animal because of its large size. It is also strikingly deep, reaching 400 feet at its greatest depth. Worldwide, most freshwater-monster reports tend to come from deep, cold-water lakes like this one.

The spirit of open-mindedness governs the International Society of Cryptozoology (ISC), an organization dedicated to the investigation of "all matters related to animals of unexpected form or size, or unexpected occurrence in time or space." Because of the board of the ICS is made up of Ph.D. biologists from respectable academic institutions, their work cannot be readily dismissed. Their goal, quite reasonably, is to attempt to make the inventory of the world's fauna as complete as possible.

Predictably, cryptozoologists have come under heavy criticism from the scientific-rationalistic camp. They have been criticized for straining to find plausible justification for hundreds of would-be animals. Much of the debate centers upon evaluating reports of firsthand sightings. The critics claim that the believers have a tendency to modify supernatural encounters with demons into secular sightings of undiscovered animals. Sorting out the competing claims in this complicated material is difficult and challenging.

Angus Kress Gillespie

References

Cohen, Daniel. 1982. *The Encyclopedia of Monsters.* New York: Dorset.

Dorson, Richard M. 1982. *Man and Beast in American Comic Legend.* Bloomington: Indiana University Press.

Fort, Charles. 1975. *The Complete Books of Charles Fort.* Mineola, NY: Dover.

Heuvelmans, Bernard. 1958. *On the Track of Unknown Animals.* Cambridge, MA: MIT Press.

Meurger, Michel, with Claude Gagnon. 1988. *Lake Monster Traditions: A Cross-Cultural Analysis.* London: Fortean Tomes.

Schultz, Ted, ed. 1989. *The Fringes of Reason: A Field Guide to New Age Frontiers, Unusual Beliefs, and Eccentric Sciences.* New York: Harmony.

See also Bigfoot; Jackalope; Jersey Devil; Vampires

Mooney, James (1861–1921)

Collector and student of American Indian folklore. Mooney started his career as a schoolteacher and later worked as a reporter for a Richmond, Indiana, paper, but since childhood his main interest was the American Indian, and he eagerly sought out every available publication on the subject. In 1885 while visiting Washington, DC, Mooney met John Wesley Powell, who was so impressed with the young man's knowledge that he immediately hired him. Mooney remained with the Bureau of American Ethnology until his death in 1921, dividing his time between library and field researches, the latter being carried out primarily among the Cherokee and the Sioux.

Mooney was interested in the Indians not just as informants, but also as people, and many of his efforts were aimed at improving their lives. For example, he helped bring attention to the alarmingly high death rate of North Carolina Cherokees, and he was instrumental in introducing measures to remedy the situation. His best-known publication, *The Ghost-Dance Religion and the Sioux Outbreak of 1890* ([1896] 1965), also revealed his empathy with the tribesmen. Rather than treat the new religion as a curious oddity, he considered the ghost-dance movement essentially similar to other efforts at cultural revivalism found throughout the world. Wovoka was nothing more than an Indian Joan of Arc.

Although the study is valuable, it does have several flaws. Mooney never really considered the ghost-dance movement of 1870 and its connection with the events of twenty years later. Furthermore, he paid too little attention to the importance of Indian beliefs concerning the return of the dead in starting both ghost-dance movements. Moreover, he overlooked many of the cultural factors giving rise to the ghost-dance religion, focusing only on poverty, oppression, and social dissatisfaction.

The Ghost-Dance Religion has folkloristic importance, but Mooney's most significant folklore volume is *Myths of the Cherokees* ([1900] 1982). This huge collection was recorded between 1887 and 1890 from nine informants. Despite the title, not all of the 126 items are myths, but Mooney thought that all amply made the case that Blacks borrowed tales from the American Indian. He argued that this exchange occurred as a result of miscegenation and the enforced contact of slavery in many Southern colonies, where Indians were kept in servitude and worked side by side with Blacks until the time of the American Revolution. The problem with this line of reasoning is that it upholds the view that Indians borrowed tales from Blacks just as forcefully as the other way around.

Despite entering the dispute about origins (which continued into the second half of the 20th century), Mooney was not primarily a theoretician. His forte was collecting, and he knew it; his collections, however, were always characterized by an ability to see the Indian point of view.

W.K. NcNeil

References

Moses, L.G. 1984. *The Indian Man: A Biography of James Mooney.* Urbana: University of Illinois Press.

Morgan, Gib (1842–1909)

Oil driller known as a Münchausen-like teller of tall tales concerning his adventures working in the oil fields. Containing large doses of exaggeration, Morgan's humorous tales are similar in spirit to those told about the mythical Paul Bunyan and Pecos Bill.

Morgan was born in 1842 in Callensburg, Pennsylvania. In 1859, when Morgan was seventeen years old, the first oil well in the United States was drilled in nearby Titusville. After serving in the Union Army during the Civil War, Morgan got work in the rapidly expanding Pennsylvania oil industry and later wandered the oil fields of the Eastern United States as an itinerant oil driller. He retired in 1892 and, except for occasional visits to family and friends, lived in branches of the National Home for Disabled Soldiers in Indiana, Illinois, and Tennessee from 1894 until his death in 1909. Morgan's stories are tall tales in which he chronicles his fantastic exploits. Although some deal with his prowess as a hunter, farmer, or fisher, most are about his work in the oil fields and require some technical knowledge on the part of the listener. In one story, Morgan claimed to have drilled a well whose oil rig was so big that it had to be hinged to allow the moon to pass. Because it took tool dressers fourteen days to get to the top, he built bunkhouses a day's climb apart on the side of the derrick. Some tales concern Morgan's adventures drilling for oil in South America. There he found his pet, Strickie the Snake, a boa constrictor so long that Morgan used him as a drilling cable. Another group of stories describes Morgan's exploits in the Fiji Islands, where he had been sent by a British syndicate. While drilling there, Morgan encountered layers of buttermilk, champagne, and sweet cream, but not the essence of peppermint he had been hired to find. He almost made a fortune making ice cream out of the cream, but, by the time he had a factory set up, the cream had soured. In Fiji,

Morgan also met Big Toolie, a tool dresser so tall he was able to grease the crown pulleys at the top of the derrick without lifting a foot off the ground.

Many of Morgan's stories are recastings of traditional tales and motifs. His stories are clearly fantastic, although they rely on exaggeration rather than on their hero's claim to supernatural abilities, as sometimes happens in tales about Davy Crockett or other American folk heroes. Morgan's stories reflect the boom-or-bust culture of the early oil industry in America in which the outsize was often close to the norm. His narrative persona is linked to the folk stereotype of the oil driller, the man who supervised the rest of the crew and who was known for his pride in his technical skills, his bravado, and his indifference to the risks of his job. Although Morgan frequently satirized individuals of whom he disapproved, his tales have more in common generically with the traditional tall tale than with other forms of occupational narrative in which themes of conflict between supervisor and subordinate are prominent.

During his lifetime, Morgan was well known as a raconteur. He often held court at a local hotel bar or saloon, telling tales while his audience bought him drinks. His stories were fluid, adaptable, and seemingly spontaneous. He is said to never have told the same story the same way twice. Morgan's fame was at its highest during the years before World War I. After his death, many of the tales told by and about Morgan became attached to Paul Bunyan, a figure well known in the oil fields as well as the forests.

Anne Burson-Tolpin

References

Boatright, Mody C. 1945. *Gib Morgan: Minstrel of the Oil Fields.* Publications of the Texas Folklore Society No. 20. Dallas: Southern Methodist University Press.

———. 1963. *Folklore of the Oil Industry.* Dallas: Southern Methodist University Press, pp.173–192.

Botsford, Harry. 1949. Oilmen. In *Pennsylvania Songs and Legends,* ed. George Korson. Baltimore: Johns Hopkins University Press, pp. 412–422.

Dorson, Richard M. 1973. *America in Legend: Folklore from the Colonial Period to the Present.* New York: Pantheon, pp. 214–226.

Mormon Folklore

One of the richest bodies of religious lore to develop in the United States. The Mormon saga began in the spring of 1820 in Palmyra, New York, when young Joseph Smith, the son of a local farmer, prayed earnestly to discover which of the many churches contending for his membership he should join. According to Smith, God and his son, Jesus Christ, appeared in answer to these prayers and told him he should join no church because all churches then on Earth had lost the essence of the gospel once preached by Christ. In subsequent years, Smith received further visitations from heavenly beings, brought forth a new body of scriptures, and in 1830, under divine direction, "restored" to the Earth the pristine organization originally established by Christ—named the Church of Jesus Christ of Latter-Day Saints, to distinguish it from the early church, but soon nicknamed the Mormon Church by outsiders and insiders alike because of its identification with Smith's new scriptural offering, the Book of Mormon.

"The Joseph Smith Story," canonized and told again and again by an ever-growing number of followers, has to the present day served as the principal charter validating the divine origin of the Mormon Church, but a large body of unofficial, or folk, narratives has also developed and circulated orally among church members, serving equally important functions. These narratives, belonging to the membership at large, will be told on any occasion when a point needs to be emphasized or proven. Thus, the narratives are recounted in Sunday-school classes, in fireside chats, in family circles, in casual gatherings of friends, in carpools as people drive to and from work, and at work itself—in short, in any situation in which Mormons rub shoulders with one another and talk about their lives. Some of the stories are full-blown third-person legends; others are accounts of personal experiences. But all of them are socially based, reveal deep-seated Mormon attitudes and beliefs, and fill significant needs in the lives of both storytellers and their audiences.

The stories cover the full range of Mormon experience, but most can be grouped into three broad categories: (1) those that tie contemporary Mormons to the dramatic events of their collective past; (2) those that testify to the truthfulness of the church's teachings and persuade church members to dedicate themselves fully to the Mormon cause; and (3) those that provide relief through humor from the strictures of an authoritarian theological system.

The Early Church

From the very day Smith made known his remarkable revelation, he and his followers found themselves in conflict with their neighbors and with mainstream America. Their insistence that only the gospel they preached would open the road to salvation, their tendency to establish political and economic control wherever they settled, their attempts to establish a theocratic state, and, later, their practice of polygamy so aroused the hostility of their countrymen that they drove the Latter-Day Saints from New York to Ohio to Missouri and, finally, to Illinois, where in 1844 Joseph Smith paid a martyr's price for his visions of the kingdom of God restored. Two years later, Smith's successor, Brigham Young, led the Mormons to a hoped-for place of peace and refuge in the mountains and deserts of territorial Utah. There they struggled to overcome an unfriendly natural environment, colonized the Great Basin, sent out missionaries to gather in the elect, and set themselves single-mindedly to the task of "building up" a new Zion in preparation for the second coming of the Savior.

Out of this cauldron of struggle and conflict were forged many of the stories Mormons still tell, stories that inculcate in both tellers and listeners a great sense of appreciation for the sacrifices of their forebears and a determination to face present difficulties with courage equal to that of their ancestors.

One such story, typical of many others, tells of a pioneer wagon train caught in a winter storm in Wyoming while trying to reach Utah. With the temperature dropping below zero, one woman huddled next to a little girl as they slept, only to discover in the morning that the girl had frozen to death during the night. The woman's hair had frozen to the girl's stiff body and had to be cut free before the woman could get up. The woman's family kept the scissors used to cut the hair and passed them down from one generation to the next—just as they have passed down the story of the event—to remind family members of sacrifices once made on their behalf and to persuade them to honor their valiant heritage. Similar stories have been circulated in numerous other families. They tell of persecutions, of hardships endured on the trek west, of encounters with Indians, and, in the face of droughts and grasshopper plagues, of attempts to make their new desert home "blossom like the rose."

The stories tell also of the practice of polygamy, which once again put Mormons on a collision course with established society. Initiated by the early 1840s but not exercised openly until the 1850s, the practice of polygamy, or "plural marriage," as the Mormons called it, brought the wrath of Victorian America upon the entire Mormon community and resulted in a series of federal antipolygamy laws. A spate of mainly humorous stories details acts of trickery engaged in by Mormons as they outwitted the callous federal marshals attempting to incarcerate them for "unlawful cohabitation." For example, one good patriarch, summoned to appear before a local magistrate to explain his polygamous activities, asked his wives to wait for him at the cemetery on the outskirts of town. Asked by the judge where his wives were, the man answered truthfully, "In the cemetery, every one." Assuming that the wives were deceased, the judge let the man go. He then stopped by the cemetery, picked up his wives, and returned safely home.

Other stories focus on the heartbreak experienced by plural wives, who had to share their husbands with other women. One poignant and typical account tells of a man about to take a second wife. He, his first wife, and his wife-to-be traveled to town by horse and wagon to have the marriage ceremony performed:

> On the way there the man slept with his first wife in the wagon, and his little fiance slept on the ground under the wagon. But on the way back, the wives reversed positions. The second wife slept with the husband in the wagon, and the first wife slept under them.

The practice of polygamy was officially discontinued by the church in 1890, but stories like this one linger on, engendering among some contemporary Mormon women feelings of sympathy for the pain suffered by their sisters of yesteryear.

The Contemporary Church

As time passed, the world depicted by the stories changed markedly. The horse gave way to the automobile, the rural village to the urban center, and the country lane to the freeway. But one constant remained, tying earlier and contemporary Mormons together—the belief that in times of need God intervenes in the lives of his people. Thus, Mormon folklore, from the beginning, is replete with accounts of miraculous healings, remarkable conversions, rescues from disasters, and the receipt of spiritual guidance.

These themes are often manifest in accounts that comprise one of the best-known legend cycles in American folklore—the legend of the Three Nephites. The Book of Mormon tells of a people who left Jerusalem 600 years before Christ and made their way under God's direction to the New World. Later, following His birth and ministry in the Holy Land, Christ visited this New World people (called Nephites after one of their early leaders), established his church among them after the pattern of the church in Jerusalem, once again chose twelve disciples, and, as he had done with John the Beloved, allowed three of these disciples to "tarry in the flesh," until his second coming to bring people to him. Throughout the Mormon West, stories have circulated telling of the visits of one or more of these ancient disciples, who appear to people in spiritual or physical distress, give assistance, and then miraculously disappear—the remarkable disappearance testifying to the spiritual nature of the visitor. The following story is typical:

> A family consisting of parents and three children were on their way to [a church] conference. They lived on a desert, and it was a hot, dusty ride of two hundred miles to the tabernacle. On the way home the car broke down on a lonely road, which was even more deserted because it was Sunday. The children were hot and hungry, and the poor father could not find the trouble. Just then, two men in white came walking down the road and offered to help. Telling the man to get in his car and start the motor, they lifted the hood. To the family's surprise the car started, and after kissing his wife and hugging his children for joy, he went out to thank the men. They had disappeared.

Whether the assistance given people comes from the Three Nephites or by other means, contemporary Mormon stories of divine intervention tend to cluster around three major themes: missionary efforts, genealogical research, and temple activity. All three themes are closely related. Though Mormons believe that salvation, or exaltation, in the kingdom of God is available only to those who embrace their gospel and participate in its saving ordinances, they also believe that because God is just, he will provide every individual an opportunity to accept or reject this gospel. Hence, Mormons engage in vigorous missionary efforts, attempting to take the restored gospel to "every kindred, tongue, and people." In spite of these efforts, Mormons know that many will have died without ever hearing the message of salvation. So they seek out the names of their dead ancestors and then, in sacred temples, vicariously perform for them saving ordinances like baptism and marriage that must be performed "in the flesh." Those who have been denied an opportunity to hear the gospel in this life will, Mormons believe, have that opportunity in the hereafter. If they accept, and if necessary ordinances have been performed on their behalf by the living, then they will have equal claim on the kingdom with those who have accepted the gospel in this life. In this way, God proves himself no respecter of persons, providing all who have lived the opportunity to accept the gospel of Christ.

Story after story circulating among Mormons reinforces these beliefs and encourages adherence to them. Stories from the mission fields tell of miraculous conversions and of missionaries being saved from angry mobs, starvation, natural disasters, and the dangers of the modern world. The Three Nephites, for example, help missionaries preach at street meetings, calm angry mobs, bring food to hungry missionaries, and pull some of them from flaming pileups on Los Angeles freeways.

Genealogical narratives tell of researchers being led to necessary sources after they have themselves exhausted every possibility. An old man brings a newspaper from another country containing names a researcher has been seeking; a book is accidentally knocked from a library shelf and falls open to a page containing missing information; a man is instructed by a stranger to visit a cemetery where he finds missing family names; another man is instructed to visit a pawnshop, where he finds his genealogical data in a Bible.

Genealogical research culminates in vicarious temple-ordinance activity. And once again stories reflecting and supporting this activity abound. In many of these, as in the following account, the people for whom the ordinances are performed participate in the action of the narrative, thus adding further credence and emotional impact to the story:

This man and woman were going through the temple doing work for the dead, and they got out to Salt Lake, and they had kids. And at the last minute the baby-sitter didn't come, and so they had to take their kids to the temple with them. And they were standing outside the temple waiting to get in, and they didn't know what they were going to do with their kids. There was no one around there they could leave them with, and they didn't know what they were going to do with them. While they were standing there, this strange man and woman came up to them and introduced themselves and said they would tend their kids while they went through the temple. The man and woman tended their kids, and the couple went in and did work for the dead, and that couple tending their kids turned out to be the couple they did the work for. When they came out of the temple, the man and woman were no longer there.

Humor in the Church

Though deeply committed to the theological system that governs their behavior, some Mormons chafe a bit under the need always to yield their own desires to those in authority over them. They cope with this pressure through the saving grace of humor. One cycle of stories providing this relief has gained special prominence. The stories tell of J. Golden Kimball, a crusty old church authority, who had spent his youth on the Idaho frontier and, though he became a church leader, had never succeeded in leaving the language of sheep-herders and cowboys far behind, peppering his sermons with a liberal sprinkling of "damns" and "hells." It was not his swearing, however, that caught the fancy of fellow Mormons—most people raised on the frontier had acquired that habit without Kimball's help; it was his irreverence for the stuffy and the pompous. In story after story, Kimball is juxtaposed alongside a higher and more dour church authority than himself and, in every instance, knocks the props from under him. In one account, for example, Kimball and one of these higher authorities were discussing a church member who was having trouble with the Word of Wisdom (the church health code that forbids the use of alcohol or tobacco). The authority, puffed up in self-righteousness, exclaimed, "Why, I'd rather commit adultery than break the Word of Wisdom." Kimball peered at his companion for a moment over the tops of his wire-rimmed glasses and then screeched in his high-pitched voice, "Wouldn't we all, brother? Wouldn't we all?" Church members who delight in such stories are not trying to overthrow the hierarchical structure of the church; they are simply finding relief through humor from pressures that might otherwise be their undoing.

A second cycle of humorous anecdotes fills another need. The main figure in these stories is not one of the church's central authorities but the local lay leader—the bishop (comparable to pastor) or the Relief Society president (head of the women's auxiliary). Because leadership positions rotate within Mormon wards (congregation), church members know that if they keep their noses relatively clean they may be asked to fill the positions tomorrow they poke fun at today. Hence, there is much less anticlerical bite in these anecdotes than in similar stories from other churches. The narratives reveal instead great sympathy for people struggling to fill positions they did not seek. The humor arises more from the circumstances of being Mormon than it does from the antics of any religious leader. It reminds tellers and listeners alike of their human frailties and eases tensions by allowing them to laugh at themselves. Consider, for example, the story of a bishop who must commit himself to an ideal while pragmatically learning to function in the real world:

A bishop who was conducting a church building fund in his ward preached a sermon from the pulpit one time about being blessed for contributing to the building fund. After his sermon, a member came up to him and said, "Bishop, that was a damned fine sermon." The bishop replied, "Brother, you had better watch the swearing." The member continued, "Yes sir, Bishop, that was such a damned fine sermon that I gave an extra $650 for the building fund." The bishop paused, then said, "Yes, brother, it takes a hell of a lot of money to build a church."

As do most people, Mormons negotiate their way through life by telling stories. Through narratives like those recounted above, they link themselves to, and gain a sense of continuity with, their past; they reaffirm their allegiance to the principles of their gospel and are inspired to live in accordance with them; and when the pressures of day-to-day Mormon living at times become burdensome, they find the means to carry on through humor.

Because religious folklore arises from people's most deeply felt needs, the study of that lore will take us about as close to other human hearts as we are likely to come. This certainly is the case with Mormons, but the attempt to fathom those hearts through the study of Mormon folklore has only just begun. Much study is needed of those stories recounting acts of quiet dedication to duty and service to others; though less dramatic than supernatural tales, these neglected stories are far more pervasive. Likewise, the rich field of Mormon rituals—those repetitive, socializing, patterned activities that turn people into Mormons—is virtually untouched.

Researchers must also turn their attention to new geographic areas. Because of the church's origin in the Eastern United States and its important role in settling the West, we tend to think of Mormonism as an American religion. But the success of the missionary system has transformed the church into a worldwide organization. Of its nearly nine million members, half live outside the United States. In fact, the per-capita percentage of Mormons in Chile is higher than it is in the United States. The 103,000 Japanese Mormons probably do not identify very strongly with the church's pioneer past, and the 22,000 Nigerian Mormons may have rarely heard of the Three Nephites. Yet, Mormons from all corners of the world hold to the revelations of Joseph Smith and to the principles he taught. The task for future research will be to discover how these core beliefs are played out in strikingly different cultures and to illuminate the role of folklore in that process.

William A. Wilson

References

Fife, Austin, and Alta Fife. 1956. *Saints of Sage and Saddle: Folklore among the Mormons.* Bloomington: Indiana University Press.

Lee, Hector. 1949. *The Three Nephites: Substance and Significance of Legend in Folklore.* University of New Mexico Publications in Language and Literature No. 2. Albuquerque: University of New Mexico Press.

Wilson, William A. 1982. On Being Human: The Folklore of Mormon Missionaries. *New York Folklore* 8:5–27.

———. 1985. The Seriousness of Mormon Humor. *Sunstone* 10 (1) 6–13.

———. 1989. The Study of Mormon Folklore: An Uncertain Mirror for Truth. *Dialogue: A Journal of Mormon Thought* 22:95–110.

See also Great Basin; Rocky Mountains

Moser, Artus M. (1894–1992)

Ballad and folktale collector. A native of Swannanoa, North Carolina, Moser first served as an informant for University of Tennessee folklorist Edwin C. Kirkland, to whose influential collection he contributed several ballads. After teaching for a time at Knoxville, he moved on to a series of educational positions in western North Carolina, where he continued to contact, and collect from, local singers and storytellers. Using a portable recording machine borrowed from an Asheville doctor, he made more than 100 field recordings during the late 1930s and early 1940s, including ballads, folksongs, and fiddle tunes. He also recorded a full text of "Jack and the Heifer Hide" from Maud Long, a descendant of the famous Harmon-Hicks families, perhaps the first sound recording of an Appalachian Jack tale.

In 1945 he gave a well-received talk at the University of North Carolina at Chapel Hill, using his recordings as examples, and he was encouraged to bring them to the attention of Duncan Emrich of the Library of Congress. Emrich loaned Moser a more sophisticated portable disk recorder and commissioned him to contact and re-record his informants. The resulting field trip, which occupied the summer and fall of 1946, led to several hundred recordings being added to the Library's Archive of American Folk Song. Moser recorded Maud Long and Asheville revivalist Bascom Lamar Lunsford, along with many other local singers and musicians.

Moser also attended the 1946 Renfro Valley Folk Festival in east Kentucky, where he collected material from participants. Among others, he met Jean Ritchie, whom he recorded for the first time. Many of Moser's disks were issued by the Library of Congress, first as 78-rpm singles then as parts of LP albums illustrating Appalachian folksongs and ballads. Moser was also influential in directing the Library of Congress to Maud Long's folktale repertoire, which she recorded soon after while residing in Washington, DC.

In 1955 Kenneth S. Goldstein recorded Moser's own folksong performances, which were later released on a Folkways LP. During his long retirement, Moser became an accomplished landscape painter; his daughters Joan and Irene Moser also became active in the local folk preservation movement. His papers and recordings are kept in the Moser Family Archives, open by application to his family.

Moser was typical of many Appalachian educators who worked independently to record their culture's folksong and folktale traditions. He received little support from grants or institutions, and he published nothing in the way of formal folklore research; hence, he is little known. Nevertheless, he was a pioneer in using sound recordings to document both text and texture of the performing traditions he contacted.

Bill Ellis

References

Ellis, Bill. 1994. Roots of Revivalism: Maud Long's Jack Tales. In *Jack in Two Worlds,* ed. William Bernard McCarthy. Chapel Hill: University of North Carolina Press.

Goldstein, Kenneth S., ed. 1955. *Artus Moser: North Carolina Ballads.* Sound Recording. Folkways Records FA 2112.

Johnson, Anne, Andy Garrison, Helen Lewis, and Jerry Johnson. 1985. *Artus Moser of Buckeye Cove.* 28 min. Whitesburg: Appalshop. Documentary videorecording.

Mummers

Costumed participants in informal house-to-house visits at Christmastime in Newfoundland (rarely, elsewhere in the New World) or in a massive parade held every New Year's Day in Philadelphia. Origins of both rituals are obscure. Either one may have possibly developed, across the centuries, out of mumming in the British sense of the term: folk plays at winter-solstice time, often performed in house-to-house visits. In America, British mummers' plays sometimes appear in "folk revival" settings. At Pennsylvania State University, for example, the winter holiday party for families of English Department faculty often includes a play in which St. George battles the Turkish Knight, is revived by the doctor, and slays the dragon.

The Newfoundland custom, also known as "mummering" or "janneying," resembles "belsnickling," which was more widely practiced in German American communities through the early 20th century. With local variations, it normally involves a group of adults disguising their appearances and voices. A resident who invites mummers to enter asks ritualized questions about their identities, then requests a musical performance and/or offers food and drink. Symbolically, the custom renders strangers less threatening: Apparent outsiders to the community reveal themselves as insiders after all.

Symbolism appropriate to a large and ethnically diverse city, rather than to isolated villages, appears in the Mummers' Parade, sponsored by Philadelphia since 1900 after two centuries as neighborhood-based, smaller parades. Tens of thousands of marchers spend all year raising ideas and money to construct elaborate costumes—costumes, not floats, for a mummer proves individual prowess by walking the twelve-hour parade route and doing a dance routine as part of a comic club (mostly Irish), a fancy club (mostly Italian), or a string band or a brigade (some with names proclaiming ethnicity, like the Ukrainian American String Band). Each year, each mummers' club enacts a different theme, such as a flower garden, a jailbreak, a carwash, or the Persian Gulf War. Many themes include stereotyped portrayals of ethnic groups other than the club's own. In 1993, for example, three of the top four brigade prizes went to "Singapore Swing," "Nonsense on the Nile," and "Moscow Nights," parodies, respectively, of Chinese, Egyptians, and Russians.

Transplanted folklore, especially large-scale festivals and rituals, survives insofar as immigrants redefine community concerns in reference to their New World situation. British folk drama did not remain relevant. American mummers in the late 20th century actively practice two folk traditions that have continued to grow, to change with the times, and to remain meaningful to generation after generation of Newfoundland neighbors in disguise and mummers proudly strutting up Philadelphia's Broad Street.

Betsy Bowden

References
Brody, Alan. 1970. *The English Mummers and Their Plays: Traces of Ancient Mystery.* Philadelphia: University of Pennsylvania Press.

Halpert, Herbert, and G.M. Story, eds. [1969] (1990). *Christmas Mumming in Newfoundland: Essays in Anthropology, Folklore, and History.* Toronto: University of Toronto Press. 1990.

Welch, Charles E., Jr. 1991. *Oh! Dem Golden Slippers: The Story of the Philadelphia Mummers.* rev. ed. Philadelphia: Book Street Press.

Musick, Ruth Ann (1897–1974)

Collector of West Virginia folklore. Musick was an English professor at Fairmont State College known for documenting ghostlore and immigrant legends in the coalfields of the state. She wrote a weekly column, "The Old Folks Say," for the *Fairmont Times—West Virginian* from 1948 to 1954, and she founded the *West Virginia Folklore Journal* in 1951.

Musick received her doctorate in English and creative writing from the University of Iowa, but most of her academic career was devoted to collecting and preserving West Virginia folklore. She began collecting in 1946 with an emphasis on ballads and folksongs but gradually shifted to folktale and legend.

She received her formal folklore training in a summer Folklore Institute program directed by Stith Thompson at Indiana University. She published many articles and three books of her West Virginia materials: *Ballads, Folk Songs, and Folk Tales from West Virginia* (1960), *The Telltale Lilac Bush* (1965), and *Green Hills of Magic* (1970). An additional book of ghost legends drawn from her collection, *Coffin Hollow and Other Ghost Tales* (1977), was issued after her death.

Musick's books, though popular with general audiences and hence in print since their publication, drew little scholarly attention. This is partly a result of her reliance on written student sources for her materials, and consequently the literary quality of many tales she presented. Even so, she ranks with John Harrington Cox, William Chappell, and Patrick Gainer as indispensable sources of West Virginia state folklore.

Barry J. Ward

Myth

Traditional prose narrative that enables people to discuss preternatural topics. This definition of myth is useful if two conditions are met: First, one must dismiss the current popular notion that a myth is a false belief; and second, one must accept the idea that the creation and transmission of traditional myths is, or was, an attempt to deal with, but not necessarily explain, the unknown.

"Myth" may be one of the most misused words in the language. This stems from Christianity's attempts to discredit competing ancient pantheons, labeling others' beliefs "false mythologies" and calling Christian beliefs "the true religion." The idea of myth-as-false-belief has carried over into secular use and now refers to something a number of people assert as fact that can be shown, usually by reference to scientific analyses, to be false, as in newspaper or magazine articles with titles like "Myths about Cancer" or "Myths about AIDS" that discuss people's incorrect beliefs.

The concept that myth is false belief is further supported by the attitude that people who lived a long time

Images from classical mythology inform American urban architecture. In Washington, DC, this statue of Neptune faces the Capitol. Photo J.W. Love. Courtesy of the photographer.

ago used myth to "explain" natural phenomena, as in the sun being a fiery chariot pulled through the sky; in fact, some basic mythology books end stories with the comment ". . . and that is how the Greeks explained the passage of the sun through the sky." Because we are dealing with people we believe to have been not as advanced as we are—"primitive" people, as we often call them—we are willing to believe that they could have thought that these stories explained natural phenomena. But it is highly unlikely that myths were meant to *explain* anything; it is more likely that they were metaphors—concrete images used to stand for abstract things. The passage of the sun was unexplainable to the ancient Greeks, in astronomical terms, so they used a poetic device to refer to that passage.

If we accept the possibility that myth operates similarly to metaphor, the definition of myth as traditional prose narrative used to discuss preternatural topics begins to clarify its relationship to other areas of folklore. A myth is traditional because it is handed down through the generations, and it is a prose narrative because it tells a complete story. The words "traditional" and "narrative" connect myth with the other major folk narratives, folktale and legend, but the key words in this definition are *preternatural* and *discuss*. Something that is preternatural exists within a natural system but cannot be explained by any method available within that same system; it therefore appears to be beyond, or different from, the natural.

In the myth of the fiery chariot, for example, people observed a natural phenomenon but could not explain what it was or how it did what it did. They could observe its warmth and its sky-spanning movement; therefore, they related it to fire, also warm, and to a chariot, something in which they

traveled long distances. However, because the phenomenon was observable, the Greeks had to talk about it (even if only to their children), and the myth of the fiery chariot allowed them to discuss a phenomenon that they could observe but not explain. We now have the astrophysical, meteorological, and astronomical knowledge to explain the sun's warmth and its apparent passage across the sky.

On a more complex level, the passage of the seasons occasioned narratives in which emotional states were equated with what were for the ancients preternatural phenomenon. In both the Greek (Demeter and Persephone) and the Norse (Freya and her husband) myths, for example, winter occurs because two people who love each other—mother and daughter or husband and wife—are separated. The separation causes the woman (a fertility figure in each case) such sadness that plants stop growing and the weather gets colder; reunion causes warm weather to return and plants to resume their growth. The equation of fulfilled love with spring, and loneliness with winter, creates a metaphor in which emotional states are logically equated with their respective seasons of fecundity or dormancy. Again, the passage of the seasons is a natural, not a preternatural, event for most people today and needs no metaphor by which it may be discussed.

This same definition of myth as a narrative that allows people to discuss preternatural topics can also be applied to narratives that discuss some of what we still consider abstract or philosophical concepts. The problem of disorder (some might say evil) in society has confronted humanity from a very early time. The Scandinavians blamed Loki—half-giant, after all, and therefore at least partly aligned with the forces of chaos—for much of the disorder in Asgard; the Greeks blamed Pandora, whose curiosity led her to open the fatal box. We, today, have made less headway in this area than we have in the area of natural phenomena; we, too, have a variety of "theories" about the causes of evil/disorder/chaos. These theories can be genetic (children can inherit criminal tendencies from parents), sociological (a child who grows up deprived is more likely to become a criminal than one who does not), religious ("the devil made me do it"), situational (the people a person spends time with can lead him or her into trouble), psychological (only insane people commit serious crimes like murder), and popular cultural (violence on television promotes violence in the culture), to name but a few. What most of these theories have in common, and what all of the traditional mythological accounts have in common, is that disorder (chaos) or evil comes from outside; the ancients did not then, and we do not now, like to think that evil is an inherent part of the human condition, and so we create myths or theories to discuss and perhaps account for "where [externally] it comes from."

Myth, then, is metaphor, and it "works" like that other great repository of metaphor, poetry, allowing the user to relate two different items, one often concrete and the other often abstract, or one familiar and local and the other unfamiliar and remote, so that the concrete or familiar-local one helps us understand the abstract or unfamiliar-remote one.

C.W. Sullivan III

References

Campbell, Joseph. 1970–1976. *The Masks of God*. 4 vols. New York: Viking Penguin.

———. 1984. *Myths to Live By*. New York: Bantam.

Stone, Merlin. 1976. *When God Was a Woman*. New York: Harcourt Brace Jovanovich.

See also Folk Ideas

N

Namelore

Names themselves and the traditions surrounding them. Names abound, and most names have their lore. For instance, there probably are well over two million unofficial place names in the United States. These informal names that do not appear on maps truly are folk names, names that people in any region know and use daily. In every region, there are imaginative narratives explaining the origins of most of these folk names as well as many of the 2.5 million official place names in the United States. These fanciful accounts of place naming are legends—stories that natives often believe but that may or may not be factual. Usually, even if these stories had some kernel of truth at their inception, through years of retelling versions have arisen. To the folk who pass them on, place-name legends serve as part of their folk history.

More than any other variety of namelore, place-name legends have been studied by folklorists. Like place-name histories, place-name legends attribute the origins of place names to personal names (sometimes spelled backward), random selection from books (especially the Bible), changes or mistakes made by the post office or others, and incidents, especially those involving supposed utterances of Native Americans, foreigners, and drunks. Tensed, Idaho, supposedly was named for the Desmet mission spelled backward, but, according to local legends, either the post office changed the "m" to an "n" or the telegrapher who wired the name to the post office made a mistake. Incident names include Butcherknife Creek (Oregon) and Bad Axe (Michigan), allegedly named for a knife and broken ax found in those places.

Local pronunciations of place names not only furnish examples of folk speech, but often also inspire place-name legends, such as those about Hymera, Indiana, named for the classical city, Himera. Hymera is pronounced HIGH MARY by some residents, and three legends are based on this pronunciation. One tale says that the postmaster, John Badders, named the town for his unusually tall adopted daughter, nicknamed "High Mary." Another story states that a woman named Mary worked in the post office, and neighbors passing or entering the post office would wave and call, "Hi, Mary!" More recently, it is said that High Mary was a local prostitute who charged high prices. Alum Creek (Ohio), according to local legend, was named for its bitter water, though actually the name comes from the local pronunciation of Elm, which rhymes with "bellum." Although place-name legends may not be accurate in the details they preserve, they reveal other kinds of information. Often they provide an impression of the people who live in a region and use its names, whatever the origin of the names might be; and legends, of course, reveal what the names mean to the folk.

Much neglected by folklorists are place-name jokes—humorous accounts of the origin of names. Lacking contextual information, one can't be certain that stories about the origin of names actually are believed by the folk. Unlike place-name legends, place-name jokes aren't taken seriously by people who pass them along. Accounts of the naming of such places as Perth Amboy, New Jersey, and Sheboygan, Wisconsin, for example, may be jokes. Perth Amboy supposedly received its name when an Indian chief saw the earl of Perth, a Scot, wearing his kilt and remarked, "Perth am girl." "No, Perth am boy," answered the earl. Sheboygan allegedly was named when an Indian with many sons but no daughters announced at the birth of another son, "She boy again." A joke involving Native Americans about the naming of Indianapolis goes: "Do you know how Indianapolis got its name? Well, there was an Indian who put some apples in his teepee for safekeeping. One day he went hunting buffalo, and while he was gone another Indian came by and stole the apples from the teepee. The Indian who did this left the first Indian appleless." Such humorous anecdotes have been reported as legends by collectors who have not determined whether the informant or anyone else in the community believes the tale.

Another kind of informal name is the nickname, which may be applied to anything—including people, pets, guns, houses, and vehicles as well as places. Nicknames often are important for the qualities they attribute to, and the attitudes they reflect about, that which they name. Place nicknames, for example, may influence, among other things, the economic development of a community. Terre Haute, Indiana, received the spontaneous nickname "Sin City" because of its history of gambling and prostitution, and the local Chamber of Commerce has attempted unsuccessfully to combat this negative image with a synthetic nickname, "Pride City." Similarly, "The Big Apple," meaning "something special, out of the ordinary, world class," in the "Empire State" (New York) also was revived by the New York Convention and Visitors' Bureau as the nickname of New York City in 1971 to combat a negative image of the city's violence and bankruptcy. Other nicknames, such as "The City of Brotherly Love" (Philadelphia) in the "Quaker State," project positive images of states and cities. Somewhat related to derogatory nicknames are *blason populaire* and slurring adjectives that incorporate ethnic and place names. Chicken soup is called "Jewish penicillin," and an old work shirt is called a "Puerto Rico Pendleton," for instance.

Place and personal names in other genres—tales, ballads, rhymes, proverbs, sayings, and beliefs—also provide a field of investigation for the folklorist. The ubiquitous "Jack," for example, appears in proverbs, rhymes, and ballads as well as in innumerable English and American "Jack tales," though in ballads Jack usually is a sailor or a servant. In proverbs we find, "All work and no play makes Jack a dull boy," or, more recently, a pun on the name: "All work and no play makes jack [money]."

Some of the most intriguing examples of namelore are found in name magic. According to a proverb, "Speak of the devil, and he will appear"; however, in folk belief naming the devil to his face, as in some versions of the ballad "Riddles Wisely Expounded" (Child 1), causes him to disappear in a blazing flame. Likewise, in the familiar tale "Rumpelstiltskin" (Aarne-Thompson (AT) tale type 500, "The Name of the Helper"), naming the supernatural creature to his face causes him to fall into a rage and tear himself in two. Discovery of the name gives one power over the supernatural creature (motif C432.1).

The magic power of names is common in American folk beliefs, especially those clustering around the main stages of the human life cycle. Thus, to name a child or tell a child's proposed name before it is born is bad luck. If a family has all male children and wants a female, naming the last male "Adam" will assure that the next child will be female. Generally, it is bad luck to name a child after someone who is living; a child should be named after someone who has died, although not for someone who has died tragically or who has died young. If a child is named after a living person, the angel of death may err when seeking the older person and instead take the younger person with the same name. Changing the name of an ill child, though, will confuse the angel of death and spare the child. On the other hand, it is also held in American folklore that a child will have bad luck or even die if his or her name is changed. Although this has changed some since the 1970s, it has been customary in American culture for a married woman to take her husband's last name, but in folk belief it is bad luck for a woman not to change her name when she marries. It is also bad luck for a women to marry a man whose last name begins with the same initial as hers: "Change the name, not the letter / Marry for worse, not for better."

Names arise whenever there is a recurrent relationship between human beings or between human beings and other animals or other things, and lore arises in the same situations; consequently, though neglected, namelore is a rich field of study for the American folklorist.

Ronald L. Baker

References

Baker, Ronald L. 1972. The Role of Folk Legends in Place-Name Research. *Journal of American Folklore* 85:368–373.

———, ed. 1991. *The Study of Place Names.* Terre Haute, IN: Indiana Council of Teachers of English/Hoosier Folklore Society.

Duckert, Audrey R. 1973. Place Nicknames. *Names* 21:153–160.

Hand, Wayland D. 1984. Onomastic Magic in the Health, Sickness, and Death of Man. *Names* 32:1–13.

Mieder, Wolfgang. 1976. International Bibliography of Explanatory Essays on Proverbs and Proverbial Expressions Containing Names. *Names* 24:253–304.

Names (Journal of the American Name Society) (1953–).

Nicolaisen, W.F.H. 1976. Place-Name Legends: An Onomastic Mythology. *Folklore* 87:146–159.

———. 1984. Names and Narratives. *Journal of American Folklore* 97:259–272.

Richmond, W. Edson. 1946. Ballad Place Names. *Journal of American Folklore* 59:263–267.

National Council for the Traditional Arts (NCTA)

A nonprofit organization devoted to the public presentation of the folk arts, especially folk-music performance, with headquarters in Silver Spring, Maryland. The NCTA performs a broad range of services and support for traditional artists. Its officers conceptualize programs, identify artists, and publicize their availability to presenters. They produce and make available recordings for distribution as well as for radio and television broadcast.

The organization started in 1933 as the National Folk Festival Association and produced the first multiethnic folk festival in the nation in 1934 in St. Louis, Missouri. The first National Folk Festival was managed by Sarah Gertrude Knott, who sought expert advice to identify high quality in folk performance.

The public presentation of folklore at festivals was just getting started in the 1930s. The initial festival struggled financially and moved from city to city on an annual basis, but the organizers were dealing consciously with finding the best traditional performers. The National Folk Festival is still organized annually, has been held in twenty-two cities, and moves to a new city every three years.

Since 1972 the organization has been a cooperating association of the National Park Service, helping parks present tribal, folk, and community arts. In 1976 Joseph T. Wilson was recruited as the new executive director of the organization. Under Wilson's leadership, the name was changed to the NCTA, which reflected the desire of the board of directors to broaden its mission.

Thus, the NCTA embarked in 1979 on a program to take folk artists from particular communities on tour to places beyond their normal performance locales. The idea was to create new ways of touring folk artists. For example, the first tours were organized along cultural, ethnic, or occupational themes. In 1979, with the assistance of Mick Moloney of Philadelphia, the NCTA put together a tour of Irish performers called the "Green Fields of America." The NCTA also did an Appalachian tour and a French American tour of performing arts from Louisiana, New England, and French Missouri. There was a Swedish American tour, an Ozark tour, and a cowboy tour.

Some tours have been organized around particular musical instruments. For example, "Masters of the Steel String Guitar" featured six different styles Americans use to play the guitar: blues, Hawaiian, slack key, Dobro, Appalachian, and jazz. Another tour, "Masters of the Folk Violin," showed an equally varied menu of styles: Cape Breton, Appalachian, Texas long bow, Cajun, jazz, and Irish. Other tours in this series include "Masters of the Banjo" and "America's Master Storytellers."

These tours have differed from standard tours in that the NCTA chose not to promote well-known artists. Performers have been chosen instead because they are excellent representatives of particular cultures or musical styles. Audiences are presented with an illustrated booklet that gives some of the history and current context of the art form. An emcee who is knowledgeable about the art form interviews the performers or interprets them to the audience.

In its ongoing efforts to bring traditional music to new performance venues, the NCTA has explored cosponsorship of concerts with a wide variety of community-based presenters such as municipal governments, community colleges, rodeos, ethnic groups, and civil rights organizations.

Angus Kress Gillespie

National Folk Festival

An annual North American event of performing arts and crafts sponsored by the National Council for the Traditional Arts (NCTA) of Silver Spring, Maryland. Performance sites change every three years.

The first National Folk Festival was held in St. Louis, Missouri, in 1934. The idea had originated with Sarah Gertrude Knott, and she served as director of the festival. Major M.J. Pickering was business manager. The term "folk festival" had been used before, but those earlier events had presented single cultures. The festival Knott and Pickering started presented Anglo, Indian, Black, Hispanic, Asian, European, and immigrant culture, as well as regional culture.

Their festival was the first to solicit the help of folklorists, ethnomusicologists, and other serious fieldworkers in presenting performance by authentic folk performers. With this assistance, they originated many of the common techniques used by hundreds of later festivals: crafts displays and demonstrations, comparative workshops, multiple staging, worklore workshops and demonstrations, as well as public discussions by cultural specialists.

The second National Folk Festival was held in Chattanooga, Tennessee, in 1935, and was remarkably like the first one. It was especially rich in central South religious and string-band music. Folklorist George Korson brought a contingent of anthracite coal miners from eastern Pennsylvania.

But there were major differences in scale when the third National was held in Dallas in June 1936. This festival was part of the exposition celebrating the Texas centennial, and it was bigger—six stages instead of one or two, eight days rather than five. It presented bluesmen, Cajun bands, string bands, shape-note singers, Indians, and many ethnic groups.

The National Folk Festival has continued in a nearly unbroken annual chain to present these interactions of folk artists, folklorists, and audiences. The fourth National was held in Chicago in 1937. After that, the National moved to Washington, DC, where it was held from 1938 to 1941. In 1942 it was held in both New York City and Washington, DC.

Festivals in other Eastern and Midwestern urban centers followed until 1971, when the National settled into an eleven-year run at Wolf Trap Farm Park in Vienna, Virginia, near Washington, DC. The National enjoyed this sylvan setting from 1971 through 1982, when the board of directors decided to move on with a basic scheme of rotating on a three-year cycle, with the idea of leaving festivals in place that will continue on their own as local events.

A change in structure came with the 1987–1989 Nationals in Lowell, Massachusetts. Earlier festivals had been sponsored by the NCTA and a single local sponsor. The Lowell festivals emphasized that a local festival would continue from the outset and were cosponsored by the Lowell National Historical Park, the City of Lowell, and the private Regatta Festival Committee. The NCTA was in charge of the programming, but most members were from Lowell. Held downtown on five stages and with parades through the city, these events attracted audiences that ranged from 127,000 to 186,000, the largest in the history of the organization, at a time when most other folk events were losing audiences. The Nationals that have followed in Johnstown, Pennsylvania, and Chattanooga, Tennessee, also have multiple sponsors that include private and governmental bodies and have been large-scale events.

This oldest of multi-ethnic festivals has been staged in twenty cities. It is notable among North American festivals for seeking out folk virtuosos who are authentic carriers of folk or tribal traditions and preferring these originals to interpretations or revival of folk performance.

Angus Kress Gillespie

References

National Council for the Traditional Arts. 1988. *Program Book for the Fiftieth National Folk Festival,* Washington, DC: NCTA.

Wilson, Joe, and Lee Udall. 1982. *Folk Festivals: A Hand-*

book for Organization and Management. Knoxville: University of Tennessee Press.

National Heritage Fellows

Exemplary practitioners of a wide variety of visual and performing folk arts recognized for their achievements by the National Endowment for the Arts (NEA). Approximately twelve National Heritage Fellows are named each year. They come from every region of the United States and represent a remarkable diversity of ethnic, religious, linguistic, and occupational groups.

The program began in 1982; by 1994 there were more than 175 Fellows. A few, like Riley "B.B." King (rhythm and blues musician), Earl Scruggs (bluegrass banjo player), and Arthel "Doc" Watson (Appalachian guitarist and singer), were already well known before being named National Heritage Fellows. But since the Fellows embody particular, locally meaningful traditions, most of them are known mainly within their regional or ethnic groups. Bua Xou Mua, for instance, is a Hmong shaman, dancer, and musician in Portland, Oregon; Mabel Murphy is a quilter from Fulton, Missouri; Ethel Kvalheim a Norwegian *rosemal* painter from Stoughton, Wisconsin; and Valerio Longoria is an accordionist from San Antonio, Texas. There are weavers, like Eppie Archuleta of Alamosa, Colorado; and Jennie Thlunaut of Haines, Alaska; potters, like Helen Cordero of Cochiti Pueblo, New Mexico; and Burlon Craig of Vale, North Carolina; and bobbin-lace makers, like Sonia Domsch of Atwood, Kansas, and Sister Rosalia Haberl of Hankinson, North Dakota. Several National Heritage Fellows are storytellers—Ray Hicks, a Jack tale teller from Banner Elk, North Carolina, and Cleofes Vigil, teller of Hispanic stories, from San Cristóbal, New Mexico, are two. The youngest Fellow to date (1993) is Michael Flatley, an Irish American step dancer selected in 1988 when he was only thirty years old.

The startling diversity of musicians—reflecting the diversity of folk music in America—is hard to communicate other than by enumeration; on one instrument alone, the violin or fiddle, there were eleven different traditional styles represented by 1993; including Howard Armstrong (African American), Kenny Baker (bluegrass), Dewey Balfa (Cajun), Joseph Cormier (Cape Breton), Clyde Davenport (Cumberland), Canray Fontenot (Black Creole), Tommy Jarrell (Appalachian), Simon St. Pierre (French American), Kenny Sidle (Anglo American). Performers of traditional ethnic music, like Nikitas Tsimouris (Greek bagpipe player), Khamvong Insixiengmai (Laotian American singer), and Richard Hagopian (Armenian American *oud* musician), conserve in America outstanding musical traditions that are threatened in their homelands.

The National Endowment for the Arts selects National Heritage Fellows from nominations made by American citizens. Nominations consist of an essay or cover letter describing the artist's career and life, the traditionality of his or her art, its community basis, and other related aspects such as artistic quality and significance. Nominations are accompanied by sample documentation of the artist's performance (audio or video tape recordings) or material art (slides or photos). Letters of support—often from scholars knowledgeable about the particular tradition—are usually solicited by the nominator. A national panel of experts reviews the nominations and makes its recommendations to the presidentially appointed National Council on the Arts. The National Council, in turn, passes its own recommendations to the chair of the National Endowment for the Arts, who makes the final decision. In September, each year's new Fellows are brought to Washington, DC, to receive $5,000 fellowships and to take part in a special recognition ceremony and a concert and display of their work.

Steve Siporin

References:

Hunt, Marjorie. 1991. Masters of Traditional Arts. *National Geographic* 179 (1):74–101.

Siporin, Steve. 1992. *American Folk Masters: The National Heritage Fellows.* New York: Harry N. Abrams.

Needlework

The creation and adornment of items with the use of a needle. Needlework can be divided into two categories: utilitarian, or "plain," needlework consisting of all items necessary for daily survival such as clothing, undergarments, household linens, and bedcoverings; and nonutilitarian, or "fancy," needlework, which is purely decorative and created for enjoyment or display within the home.

Needlework was the core of the early American household. It was done primarily by women, either alone or in a group, and it represented one of their few accepted outlets for creative expression. Since little written history focused on the lives and experiences of women, needlework became a "writing" of sorts, through which women told their personal stories. Throughout American history, a strong connection existed between women's lives and their needlework; as their roles in society changed, so did their needlework.

To the earliest settlers, needlework signified the very survival of the family. After all, members of the family were dependent on the woman of the house to weave the fabric, spin and dye the yarn, sew clothes and blankets, knit stockings and scarves—all by hand—to keep them warm and clothed. Few examples of this early plain needlework survive because the pieces were so valuable that they were used until they literally wore out. Even then, the scraps were saved to make pieced quilts.

Examples of decorative needlework have survived more often because they were not meant for everyday use, but for display. They were often framed or, as in the case of "best" quilts, they were folded and put away and rarely brought out of storage. Skill in decorative needlework showcased a woman's talent and her eligibility for marriage. These skills were passed down from mother to daughter, and later were taught at girls' academies. A young woman would first learn the basic, plain stitches necessary for overseeing a household, then steadily progress to more difficult stitches. But no matter how adept she became at decorative stitchery, she could never forget her

Embroidery by Anna Bilynski, using traditional Ukrainian motifs. Chicago, 1977. Photo Carl Fleischhauer. American Folklife Center.

first lessons in plain needlework because someday her household would depend on them.

The earliest examples of needlework in America closely resemble English traditions, both in design and technique. English settlers brought their needlework with them to the New World in an attempt to retain some of the culture of the homeland they were leaving behind. In Europe, needlework had been a domestic art as far back as the Renaissance, when it was first added to a girl's basic education.

Crewelwork is embroidery of a two-ply worsted wool yarn, called "crewel," on linen. In early America, such embroidery closely resembled traditional English crewelwork, which dated back to the 1500s. Common motifs include vines, flowers, leaping stags, and the tree of life. American women copied these designs from the original crewelwork they brought with them from England or referred to current European pattern books. While crewel yarn was first imported from London to Boston, the colonists soon began to spin and dye the yarn on their own. Yarns dyed with natural earth tones, such as greens and rusts, contrasted well against the natural linen background. Another variation featured yarns of all shades of indigo blues.

Crewelwork was used to decorate many things, from curtains to petticoats, but was most common on bed "furniture," the heavy cloths hung around the bed to provide extra warmth in drafty colonial homes. Elaborate crewelwork designs showed respect for this important item in their homes and the desire of the women to beautify their surroundings.

Canvaswork was another form of early American needlework in the English tradition. Canvaswork is embroidery stitches of thin wool or silk yarn worked with a needle over the entire surface of a canvas background. Each stitch covered only one thread of the canvas, which at that time was more than fifty threads per inch—today's needlepoint material has only about twenty threads per inch. The tight tiny stitches allowed the worker to achieve both a durable textile and intricate details.

Canvaswork was used for seat covers, book covers, fire screens, and pincushions. Large scenes showing men and women partaking of outdoor leisure activities were also popular. These scenes, which often took more than a year to complete, were sometimes referred to as tapestrywork because of their similarity to European tapestries. One version popular in the Boston area in the mid-18th century was called the "Fishing Lady." In the scene, an elegantly dressed woman sits beside a stream, gracefully holding a fishing pole. Examples of this scene are thought to have all been done by students of one Boston needlework-design teacher. Sometimes all canvaswork scenes are referred to as "Fishing Lady," even if the lady herself is not depicted.

By the end of the 18th century, the European look of crewel-and canvaswork was going out of style as America began to define itself. An American style was beginning to appear in needlework—simpler, more creative, less structured, and not married to an ideal technical perfection from which European needlework rarely strayed.

The early years of the 19th century saw the rise of girls' academies, to which all families that could, sent their daughters. These academies taught young girls important feminine skills such as deportment, dancing, and especially needlework. A finished needlework piece, or "accomplishment," acted as a final exam or diploma and was proudly displayed in the family home as a testament to both the girl's talent and the refinement of the household.

Samplers were one of the most common needlework projects done in academies. In a practical sense, samplers are a record of stitches to which a woman can refer back should she ever forget a stitch. During the time of the academies, however, samplers became purely decorative. In Europe samplers tended to be long and thin, with records of stitches in rows. In America, they become shorter and wider, with fanciful borders and text added.

Samplers were usually done in silk thread on a natural linen background, although occasionally a colored background was used. Young girls between the ages of five and nine would begin with simple alphabet samplers. As their skills improved, they would move on to more difficult ones. Between the ages of twelve and eighteen is when girls would usually complete elaborate samplers, which included houses, landscapes, borders, and lengthy text. Texts were often biblical passages or proverbs proclaiming feminine virtues and the benefits of industriousness and piety. All samplers would in-

Embroidery by Anna Bilynski, using traditional Ukrainian motifs. Chicago, 1977. Photo Carl Fleischhauer. American Folklife Center.

clude the name and age of the girl and the date of its completion. A girl might expect to complete two to three samplers during her tenure at an academy.

Once a girl had mastered the sampler, she would move on to more difficult work, called silk-on-silk pictorial embroidery. This included scenes created entirely of silk embroidery on a silk background and represented the most advanced schoolgirl work. Designs were first sketched on the background. Then the entire surface was embroidered, leaving space for faces, arms, and sometimes skies that were later painted with watercolor for a natural effect.

Perhaps the most popular silk-on-silk pictorial was the mourning scene. Mourning scenes followed a common design of bereaved mourners in Empire dress standing around a tombstone or an urn on which the deceased's name and age and any other vital information has been written. A willow tree, a common symbol of death, was often included in these pictures as well.

Other typical motifs included classical or patriotic scenes, biblical stories, and printwork, which involved embroidery of black and grey silk on a white background so the look of a print engraving could be achieved. The girl who could successfully execute a fine piece of printwork was truly skilled and was held in great esteem both in the school and in her community. Printwork was tedious and time consuming, more popular in England but also done in America.

As the 19th century progressed, educational reform began to affect needlework's role in the American woman's life. While girls' academies still flourished, the emphasis now turned to true academic study, and needlework instruction fell behind. Soon, needlework skills ceased to be such a definitive indication of a girl's eligibility for marriage. But while the fine quality of stitchery declined, needlework itself found new significance in the Victorian woman's household.

To the Victorians, home was a special sanctuary. It was the sole responsibility of the woman of the house to create an environment in which good citizens could be raised. Her needlework, or fancywork as it was called, allowed her to decorate and accessorize each room, thereby creating a happy home environment.

Fancywork was created for every room and every purpose. Not restricted to wool or silk thread, the Victorians made use of beads, ribbons, sequins, and lace. Pillows and bookmarks alike were garnished with stitches. An embroidered lambrequin might be used to cover the harsh edge of a mantle, while a cross-stitched motto, such as " Lead Us Not into Temptation," hung in the hallway to instill proper moral tone.

Berlin work, a fad started in Germany, became popular in the mid-19th century. Berlin work is embroidery of wool yarn on canvas. It differs from the canvaswork of the 18th century in that the canvas is of a wider mesh so the stitches were not as delicate, and in it the Victorian aesthetic of bold patterns and bright colors is particularly evident. Preprinted designs on graph paper showed women exactly where the stitches should go and what colors should be used. This let even those women who had not benefited from an academy education create beautiful pieces. Thousands of designs were available from which to choose, among them bouquets of flowers, political portraits such as Washington or Lincoln, and bucolic country scenes.

Late-century needlework included trends such as crazywork, a style that mirrored the Victorians' love for asymmetry. Initially composed of patches of irregular shapes and various sizes in fabrics such as silk, satin, and velvet, crazywork was further embellished with embroidery, applique, and even paint. It was thought to be a result of the strong Eastern influence in America attributable most likely to the Japanese screens, cracked glaze pottery, and other artifacts exhibited at the Philadelphia Centennial Exposition in 1876. Small examples of crazywork include slippers, footstool covers, and even something called a "crazy cushion," which young girls would pass among themselves so each could add a patch. Large examples of crazywork include crazy quilts, which were made throughout the country.

Because of the rise of women's magazines in the second half of the 19th century, such as *Godey's Ladies Book* and later the *Ladies' Home Journal,* needlework was now accessible to a much wider audience. The Victorian era in America was really the first time needlework crossed both class and regional boundaries. Until this time, decorative needlework had been done mostly by women of means who could afford both leisure time and the necessary materials. The Industrial Revolution brought about an increased wealth to the middle class as well as more affordable materials. This meant that more people could participate in needlework.

Much of early American needlework was concentrated in New England and Mid-Atlantic areas. This was due in part to the North's climate being more conducive to long hours indoors, and to the rural nature of the South, where communication was slower and home schooling the norm for a longer period of time. Improvements in transportation and communication, as well as subscriptions to national periodicals, however, brought the country's population closer together. Women from all over, even pioneer women, could keep abreast of the latest needlework trends.

The mass appeal of needlework would begin to decline as the 20th century neared. Increased educational and work opportunities for women took them away from the home in larger numbers. Technological advances such as the sewing machine made social calls with needlework in tow—a popular convention during the 19th century—impossible. Soon it ceased being a social activity. Affordable manufactured clothing and household linens also eliminated the need for women to make these items themselves.

Needlework continued as a hobby. Immigration in the early 20th century brought ethnic groups who established their own needlework traditions in their communities just as the early English settlers had done. Although needlework as a social activity for the majority of American women stopped, the needlework done by women throughout the previous centuries of American history represents the largest and most important contribution by women to American decorative arts.

Marie Luise Proeller

References

Harbeson, Georgiana Brown. 1938. *American Needlework: The History of Decorative Stitchery and Embroidery from the Late 16th to the 20th Century.* New York: Bonanza.

Ring, Betty. 1993. *Girlhood Embroidery: American Samplers and Pictoral Needlework, 1650–1850.* New York: Alfred Knopf.

Swan, Susan Burrows. 1977. *Plain and Fancy: American Women and Their Needlework, 1700–1850.* New York: Holt, Reinhart, and Winston.

Vincent, Margaret. 1988. *The Ladies Worktable: Domestic Needlework in 19th Century America.* Allentown, PA: Allentown Art Museum.

Weissman, Judith Reiter, and Wendy Lavitt. 1987. *Labors of Love: America's Textiles and Needlework, 1650–1930.* New York: Alfred Knopf.

See also Quilt Making

New Deal and Folk Culture

Federal government programs designed to provide employment during the 1930s, creating the first national effort to document and present American folk culture and arts. As a reaction to the desperate economic circumstances of the Great Depression in the United States during the 1930s, President Franklin D. Roosevelt established his "New Deal" for the people, which created many work projects that documented and preserved the folk heritage of the nation and set a precedent for public folklore.

The years of the New Deal comprised a revolutionary era in American thinking. An unprecedented rise in nationalism during the 1930s was coupled with a search for the values that made America great. At the same time, there arose an anti-intellectual movement as the "common man" was pitted against the scholar. The desperate circumstances of the American economy during the 1930s fostered a watershed in intellectual thinking that set the stage for the first experiment in government-sponsored documentation of American heritage and folk culture.

This new interest in American folklore was felt along the entire political spectrum and created a folk revival. The political Right championed a nationalist agenda that extolled the virtues of all things American. Among progressive circles, the Congress of American Writers in 1935 called for literature that was based on folklore and myth to "create an intuitive sense of community among all Americans" and to replace the "proletarian" literature of the past. Among the Communist Left, the impulse toward grass-roots expression within American heritage led to the establishment of the American Music League, formed in 1936 to "collect, study, and popularize American folk music and its traditions." The Roosevelt administration seized upon this infatuation with folk culture and used it to garner support for its program of economic and social self-help, the New Deal. The New Deal embraced the concept of cultural diversity and advocated the value of the common man, two impulses that brought folk culture to the forefront of the American imagination. Nearly all programs of the New Deal administration were influenced by this tidal wave of interest in American folk culture. A notable example is the body of documentary photographs that were taken for the Farm Security Administration (FSA) that captured vividly life during the Great Depression. However, folklore would find its most powerful outlet within the arts programs of the Works Progress Administration (WPA), collectively known as "Federal One."

In an effort to overcome economic and political disaster, Roosevelt, through the WPA arts programs, would seize upon folk culture as the obvious channel to recover a glorious, multifaceted heritage and instill national loyalty. In a 1938 speech, he expressed his feeling that cultural unity could be achieved by using folklore, which "has the elements from which to weave a culture." The theme of "unity through diversity" would become a guiding principle for the New Deal administrators, especially those involved in the WPA Federal One programs.

Federal One consisted of four projects: the Federal Music Project (FMP), the Federal Arts Project (FAP), the Federal Theater Project (FTP), and the Federal Writers' Project (FWP). All four were developed and shaped with the help of folklorists. Herbert Halpert worked for the Federal Theater Project and conducted extensive fieldwork under its auspices. Holger Cahill, a noted authority on American folk art, was

The Folk Music Project, Works Progress Administration. Sidney Robertson, supervisor of fieldworkers, sits by the window, against the partition. University of California, Berkeley, California, 1938. American Folklife Center, Cowell Collection (WPA).

named as the director of the Federal Arts Project in 1935. Under his guidance, the FAP created a national program of civic art that provided public murals and sculpture in cities across the nation. Cahill also conceived of and produced the Index of American Design. The Index, with more than 20,000 watercolor drawings of folk and popular material culture, continues to serve as an invaluable tool in American folk studies.

Ethnomusicologist Charles Seeger was instrumental in emphasizing traditional American music through his work with the Federal Music Project. In an address to the teachers of the FMP on March 21, 1939, Seeger berated the project for lagging behind the other three arts projects in "interpreting America to Americans." He went on to state that "the oral tradition is usually supposed to be dead. On the contrary, America has one of the most vigorous collections of folk music of the day." His early exhortations would bring folk music into the curriculum of the FMP.

Of the four Federal One projects, the Federal Writers' Project was undeniably the most significant to the history of folk studies in America. Created in August 1935, the FWP proposed to put unemployed writers to work, collaborating on publications that would benefit the American people. During its seven-year tenure, the FWP would employ more than 6,500 writers who would produce more than 276 books, 701 pamphlets and 340 "issuances." Most important, the FWP created special work units for folklore, social and eth-

nic studies, and life histories. All three units demanded that workers conduct fieldwork and document the folk culture and heritage of the nation.

The lasting value of the Federal Writers' Project to the field of folklore is less in the production of the American Guide Series and other publications, but in the raw data that was collected in every state of the nation. This fieldwork yielded information on the folklife and traditions of a myriad of cultural groups and regional cultures in the United States. Many folklorists made lasting contributions as employees of the FWP, including Zora Neale Hurston, Herbert Halpert, Alan Lomax, and Stetson Kennedy among others, but a few key people were responsible for the scope and direction of the folklife collection that was accomplished through the Federal Writers' Project.

Morton Royce, as director of the social and ethnic studies unit of the FWP, supervised workers in collecting immigrant and occupational narratives in an interdisciplinary approach to the study of culture. This unit responded to the public's new fascination with America's multicultural roots and published booklets on the ethnic cultures to be found in each state and major city. New Deal historian Ann Banks has suggested that Royce was largely responsible for changing the notion of American culture as a melting pot, into a view of America as a mosaic—each culture retaining a distinct identity, yet contributing to the whole.

The FWP life-histories unit was directed by Southern

writer W.T. Couch. As director of the University of North Carolina Press, Couch actively solicited manuscripts that included direct expressions of Southern folk culture, such as songs, tales, idiom, and the like. In his own book, *Culture in the South* (1934), he shaped his commentary around the traditional Southern values that pervaded everyday life in the region. Couch may have had a lasting effect upon the writers working in his unit in that he insisted upon documentary truth, letting people speak for themselves. In 1936 Sterling Brown was appointed national editor of Negro affairs for the FWP. As such, he was in charge of directing the collection of narratives and life histories from ex-slaves living in Georgia, Florida, South Carolina, and Virginia. This unprecedented research has given us hundreds of firsthand accounts of the institution of American slavery and has provided folklorists with valuable data for contemporary studies.

Also in 1936, John Lomax, at the time serving as curator of the Archive of American Folk Song at the Library of Congress, was appointed as the first national adviser on folklore and folkways for the FWP. Lomax brought to the FWP his combined interests in the rural South, the Negro, and folksong. He worked in cooperation with Brown to establish the Slave Narrative Project and encouraged the collection of folksongs from across the United States.

Lomax resigned as head of the FWP folklore unit in October 1937, but his impact was both lasting and profound. He established the initial interview approach and instructions to fieldworkers (cautioning against editing and using dialect spellings), and he left a legacy of solid work with Southern and rural materials.

At the fiftieth anniversary of the American Folklore Society, held December 27–30, 1937, at Yale University, Federal Writers' Project Director Henry G. Alsberg sought the support of the society to create a permanent folklore unit of the FWP. After presenting his case, Alsberg believed that all he had achieved was a lukewarm resolution that the FWP materials could be put to much better use by professional folklorists.

When Benjamin A. Botkin took over as director of the FWP folklore unit in May 1938, a significant rapprochement occurred. The appointment of Botkin, an academically trained folklorist, brought the academy and the American Folklore Society (AFS) into a dialogue and acceptance of the folklore work of the Federal Writers' Project. Stith Thompson, in his AFS presidential address that year, admitted that the FWP material might prove to be useful, and the society as a whole was relieved to see a "professional" take over.

It was Botkin who, in addition to directing his own unit, had the foresight to forge a fortuitous alliance within the various programs and projects of the New Deal. He established the Joint Committee on the Folk Arts, which brought interested professionals and lay persons together from all four Federal One programs, as well as other government-sponsored initiatives.

Botkin, through his New Deal position, redefined the concept of folklore to embrace previously discounted sources (urban, printed, recorded) and proposed the concept of folklore as "living lore." Botkin himself was influenced by sociologist Howard W. Odum; he would take Odum's notion of society as a biological entity and expand it to develop his own ideas concerning folk culture as a renewable, changeable resource—a functional approach to folk culture. This approach was outlined and defined in Botkin's new FWP handbook, *Instructions to Fieldworkers,* which was given to all folklore-unit supervisors in 1939. Fieldworkers were told to "look everywhere for material," and Botkin emphasized occupational and ethnic materials. He explained and set limits for the parameters of folklore collection to hundreds of FWP employees and subsequently influenced an entire generation of folklorists through this first government-sponsored folklore program. In doing so, he brought his own popular, public perspective to the field of folklore.

Perhaps the most revolutionary notion Botkin proposed was his commitment to help "the folk understand their lore and regain possession of it." Ultimately, Botkin, the humanitarian, was calling for an "applied folklore," in which folklore materials could be used to create understanding and improve the condition of human society. In this thinking, Botkin was a consummate New Dealer—dedicated to bringing about social, political, and economic change through his folklore work with the government.

In addition to the government-sponsored projects of the New Deal, other trends were influencing the course of folk culture and folk studies during the 1930s. Protest as a distinct genre grew out of the Great Depression and was linked with the struggle for labor rights and economic recovery and an emerging struggle for racial equality. Among other impulses, the folk tradition of group singing and ballad making was incorporated into the struggle with the advent of topical songs composed to address specific issues. On a national scale, "folksinging" was now viewed as a universal tool to move people to action. Folklore collectors such as Lawrence Gellert and Alan Lomax were collecting and publishing traditional African American songs that reflected the struggle for freedom, while artists such as Woody Guthrie, Lee Hayes, and Huddie Ledbetter (Lead Belly) were first coming to prominence.

Whether working for the government or struggling from an independent position, folklorists during the New Deal brought their desire for sweeping social and economic reform into the realm of folk-cultural studies. The New Deal era was a time when applied folklore was used as a tool for national recovery and when the public interest in American heritage fueled an unprecedented experiment in government programs to document and preserve the folklore and culture of all Americans. As such, the New Deal was an unparalleled forerunner of the public folklife programs that would emerge in the 1970s.

Peggy A. Bulger

References

Banks, Ann. 1980. *First Person America.* New York: Alfred Knopf.

Billington, Ray Allen. 1961. Government and the Arts: The WPA Experience. *American Quarterly* 13:466–479.

Botkin, Benjamin A. 1939. The WPA and Folklore Research: Bread and Song. *Southern Folklore Quarterly* 3: 7–14.

———. 1958. We Called It "Living Lore." *New York Folklore Quarterly* 14:189–201.

Dwyer-Shick, Susan A. 1975. The Development of Folklore and Folklife Research in the Federal Writers' Project, 1935–1943. *Keystone Folklore Quarterly* 20:5–31.

Halpert, Herbert. 1938. Federal Theater and Folksong. *Southern Folklore Quarterly* 2:81–85.

Hamby, Alonzo L., ed. 1981. *The New Deal: Analysis and Interpretation.* New York: Longman.

Hirsch, Jerrold. 1988. Cultural Pluralism and Applied Folklore: The New Deal Precedent. In *The Conservation of Culture: Folklorists and the Public Sector,* ed. Burt Feintuch. Lexington: University Press of Kentucky, pp. 46–67.

Lash, Joseph P. 1988. *Dealers and Dreamers: A New Look at the New Deal.* New York: Doubleday.

McDonald, William F. 1969. *The Federal Relief Administration and the Art.* Columbus: Ohio State University Press.

See also Index of American Design

New England

Connecticut, Rhode Island, Massachusetts, New Hampshire, Vermont, and Maine, states diverse in their peoples but similar in topography, occupations, customs, and traditions. As a primary region of European contact, New England, like its folklore, can be characterized as multicultural since settlement. The cooperation of indigenous peoples in passing on essential knowledge of the land and its resources eased settlement. The English settlers processed maple sap, added pumpkin, cranberries, and corn meal gruel to their diets, and, along with the French trappers farther north, adopted Native American woods lore and folk cures. Of numerous traditions handed down since contact, some, like the clambake, entrenched themselves regionally. A few, most notably Thanksgiving Day with its attendant foodways, became the custom of the land.

Expansion of settlement led the English along waterways to superior mill sites discovered by hunters, trappers, Indian captives, and early surveyors, and gradually forced the native populations to more remote reservations in northern New Hampshire, Maine, Canada, and interior Connecticut and Vermont, marginalizing for generations those who continued living among White settlers. In the wake of the 1960s civil rights movement, significant numbers of native peoples who had nurtured their heritage through an active network of traditional populations, both on and off tribal lands, shed their anonymity and today preserve and promote many aspects of native tradition both publicly and privately. Wampanoag, for example, tell of Mashaup, the creator giant, who arose one dawn from Cape Cod, his preferred resting place (he could stretch full length, his feet at Providence, hips on Chatham, and head near Sandwich). Mashaup's sodden, sand-filled slippers so angered him that he flung them out to sea where they formed the islands of Martha's Vineyard and Nantucket. New England's tribes, including the Passamaquoddy, Abenaki, Wampanoag, Narragansett, Micmac, and Pequod, are rich in such timeless lore.

In the popular imagination, however, New England is the home of the Yankee, an image based on the official history of the founding of our nation. Obscure in origin, the word "Yankee" applies, in New England, to those English who trace their roots to the Great Migration of the 1630s. Widespread identification of New England as Yankee country arises from the popularity of the Yankee character, that comical schemer and country bumpkin of mid-19th-century theatricals. Quick on the uptake, in storytelling tradition the classic Yankee avoids straight answers; he is a trickster given to wryly innocent verbal putdowns showcasing Yankee shrewdness and the outsider's (or city-slicker's) naiveté. A tourist asks: "Have you lived here your whole life?" The Yankee drawls, "Nawht yet!" "Yankee" also implies trickery, the Yankee trader wily enough to sell wooden nutmegs to unsuspecting housewives; or frugality, as in the proverbial expressions, "Tight as the bark of a tree" and "String too short to be saved." It would not be far fetched to place L.L. Bean's ascent from supplier of sturdy gear and duds for the hunter-trapper to Madison Avenue darling into the Yankee-trader tradition.

The rocky farmlands and seacoasts of New England became a region of villages, towns, and farms, settlements defined by the occupations of their citizens—Cape Cod cranberry growing, New Hampshire and Vermont maple sugaring, Maine lobstering, Rhode Island deep-sea fishing, and Connecticut tobacco farming.

Maritime tradition is tenacious—fishing, lobstering, and boatbuilding being vital to seacoast economy. The whaling tradition of 19th-century Nantucket and New Bedford, Massachusetts, has an extensive folklore. Whaler's scrimshaw, the intricate whalebone carvings of lovers' tokens or whales' teeth incised with marine motifs, are valuable collector's items. Contemporary scrimshanders engrave and ink common animal-bone or polymer substitutes. The high drama of disaster at sea, an all too common feature of maritime history, and the rigors of the sailor's life are well documented in folksong and story and in such mocking ditties as: "Boston, Boston / What do you have to boast on? / Tall steeples, foolish people / And a coast that ships get lost on."

The most prominent aspect of New England government is the town meeting, traditionally occurring the first Tuesday in March. At these open, democratic meetings, townsfolk debate and then vote upon important issues on the town warrant such as taxes, roads, and law enforcement. In the past, a potluck supper and dance followed. In the 1990s, most towns with this form of government conduct general business one evening and school business on another.

Another important political tradition is Election Day, a significant holiday for the Puritan, but even more so for New England's African Americans. In the colonial era, Blacks could assemble freely to elect a Black governor who would serve as the authority for the community that elected him. First in

In the mid-1800s, Boston's championship baseball team earned musical accolades. (A quadrille is a set of square dances for four couples.) Lithograph, John H. Bufford, 1867. Library of Congress.

Massachusetts, and eventually throughout New England, their celebrations included colorful processions, the forerunner to the patriotic parades now a fixture of American holidays nationwide.

Seventeenth- and 18th-century New England is noteworthy for distinctive traditions of gravestone carving reflecting religious beliefs of the early settlers. The unique winged death's head and, following the Great Awakening's lyrical evangelical piety, the cherub soul image, symbolize the transport of the deceased to eternal glory in heaven. Period epitaphs, straightforward messages scattered among New England's graveyards, deliver their comforting words or stark warnings to the living who gaze thereon. Classic is: "Death, the debt to nature due / Which I have paid as so must you." More recently, John Benson, representing the sixth generation of the Benson family, Newport, Rhode Island, stonecutters, designed and fashioned President John F. Kennedy's New England–slate graveside in Arlington National Cemetery in Washington, DC.

Shaping the architecture and landscape of New England, the I-type house is ubiquitous across the Northeast, due in part to the late-20th-century vigorous historic-preservation movement. The extended farmhouse, its outbuildings attractively appended, epitomizes the old regional children's saying, "Big house, little house, back house, barn." White or red clapboard houses, sheds, and barns dot the New England countryside, organize its countless village commons, and crowd its towns and urban neighborhoods. There exists a body of folklore around house, barn, and meeting house raisings, all communitywide events. An example is this partially parodic stanza sung at a 19th-century Connecticut barn raising to the tune of a familiar hymn: "If God to build the house deny, / The builders work in vain. / Unless the Lord doth shingle it / It will blow down again."

With the Industrial Revolution came waves of Quebecois, Irish, Italian, Cape Verdean, Russian, Polish, Greek, and Scandinavian immigrants who provided cheap labor to the burgeoning mill manufactories, somewhat mitigating Yankee influence. With these workers came their values and traditions, along with ethnic social clubs, churches, networks, and neighborhood enclaves. Large communities of Hispanic and Asian immigrants, recently resettled in its metropolitan centers, further diversify New England's population. The startling appearance of the railroad inaugurated numerous items of folklore, including this spirited Massachusetts train riddle from the turn of the 20th century: "Corn stalks twist your hair / Mortar and pestle pound you / Fiery dragons carry you off / Great cart wheels surround you."

The regionwide popularity of dancing, once the culmination of virtually all social gatherings of any size, has dwindled. Neighborhoods and communities held contra dances, generally hiring Yankee and Francophone musicians whose repertoire of English, French Canadian, Irish, and Scottish dance tunes included "St. Anne's Reel" from Quebecois tradition, "Portland Fancy" derived from an Irish reel, and "Soldier's Joy" from the Yankee repertoire. A post–World War II revival of country music and dance traditions, primarily among college-educated newcomers and stabilized by the participation of some old-timers who grew up in the tradition, continues as a popular pastime. In remote rural New England, the barn dance, a meeting ground for young and old of varied ethnicities, thrived until the 1960s, and a few linger even in the 1990s. The music, dance, and foodways of Cape Breton, Scandinavia, Ireland, Asia, and Latin America, among other places, enjoy currency in the active ethnic clubs of New England's cities.

Among popular traditions from the region's immigrants is the annual Blessing of the Fleet in Catholic fishing communities like New Bedford and Marblehead, Massachusetts. An activity once enjoyed by insiders and their local neighbors has become such a popular tourist attraction that it has spawned updated copycat practices like the blessing of a motorcycle fleet in northern New Hampshire. Numerous public processions honor a host of revered Catholic saints on their respective feast days and, among Southeast Asians at their late-winter New Year's celebrations, a fierce, yet benevolent, dragon god dances through the streets of New England's Chinatowns in brilliant red and gold to the raucous accompaniment of Chinese drummers.

A number of social customs continue according to an agricultural calendar: sheepshearings in the spring, agricultural fairs with horse and oxen pulls and timber rolling in the summer, apple and cranberry picking in the fall. All over New England, but especially in New Hampshire and Vermont, late winter's "sugaring off" commences with the tapping of the maples: The sap boils down into various grades of syrup, maple cream, sugar, and candy. Accompanying "sugar-on-snow," a taffy-like treat of thickened maple syrup poured on clean, dry snow and rolled on a fork, are pickles "to cut the sweet" and donuts "to cut the sour."

Two traditional New England meals are the boiled dinner and the bean supper. For the first, pot roast (often corned beef), carrots, potatoes, cabbage, and turnips stew at a simmer for hours. The bean supper, its Saturday night niche promising the cook the relative ease of a Sunday cold lunch, includes frankfurters, steamed molasses brown bread, and beans baked slowly in a pottery crock, the squat bean pot itself a regional icon. Among French Americans, pork pie heads the list of holiday dishes, and, as for baked beans and brown bread, ancestral recipes are family treasures.

Summertime "chowdah" contests attract great crowds who sample myriad variations of the milk-based broth with onions, potatoes, salt pork, and clams. Labor-intensive annual family or community clambakes feature clams, lobsters, and corn on the cob layered with rock weed harvested from local shorelines and steamed in pits atop heated stones. These and other traditional gatherings provide appropriate settings for performances of local music, songs, stories, recitations, and dancing.

The 1888 founding of the American Folklore Society in Cambridge, Massachusetts, marked the formal beginning of the academic study of folklore in the United States. A regional organization for folklore studies, Folklorists in New England (FINE), was founded in Boston in 1980.

Linda Morley
Eleanor Wachs

References

Botkin, Benjamin. 1944. A *Treasury of New England Folk-lore*. New York: Crown.

Eight Traditional British-American Ballads from [the] Helen Hartness Flanders Collection. 1953. Accompanying Notes by Marguerite Olney. Middlebury, VT: Middlebury College.

From Stump to Ship. 1986. Orono, Maine: Maine Folklife Center, University of Maine. Videorecording.

Huntington, Gale. 1964. *Songs the Whalemen Sang*. Barre, MA: Barre Publishing Society.

Ives, Edward D. 1978. *Joe Scott: The Woodsman Songmaker*. Urbana: University of Illinois Press.

Linscott, Eloise Hubbard. 1939. *Songs of Old New England*. New York: Macmillan.

Neustadt, Kathy. 1992. *Clambake: A History and Celebration of an American Tradition*. Amherst: University of Massachusetts Press.

Newell, W.W. [1903] 1964. *Games and Songs of American Children*. New York: Dover.

On My Own: The Traditions of Daisy Turner. 1985. (African American tradition.) Middlebury: Vermont Folklife Center. Videorecording.

Pierson, William D. 1988. *Black Yankees: The Development of an Afro-American Subculture in Eighteenth Century New England*. Amherst: University of Massachusetts Press.

Simmons, William S. 1986. *Spirit of the New England Tribes: Indian History and Folklore, 1620–1984*. Hanover, NH: University Press of New England.

Stories to Tell: The Narrative Impulse in Contemporary New England Folk Art. 1988. Lincoln, MA: DeCordova and Dana Museum and Park.

Newell, William Wells (1839–1907)

Founder of the American Folklore Society. Newell was never president of the AFS, but in several respects he was the organization's most important member. Born in Cambridge, Massachusetts, into one of New England's most affluent families, Newell was named after an ancestor, Reverend William Wells, an English Unitarian minister who sided with the colonists in the Revolutionary War and was forced to move to America. The family's money enabled Newell to obtain an excellent education in private schools and at Harvard College. After graduating from Harvard Divinity School, he spent a brief stint as pastor of a church in Germantown, Pennsylvania, but soon decided that the ministerial life was not for him. He returned to Harvard to obtain a Master of Arts degree in philosophy, then opened a private school in New York that he operated for several years. After his father's death in 1883, he received an inheritance that enabled him to live the remaining twenty-four years of his life as a private scholar.

Although Newell became justly famous in folklore circles, he published relatively little—only four books—on folklore topics. His most important folklore study was his first, *Games and Songs of American Children* ([1883] 1963). This still-useful book achieved many firsts: It was the earliest collection of children's folklore that was systematically compiled and was one of the first large-scale presentations of the games and game songs of English-speaking children. It was also the first annotated comparative study of such data, and it demonstrated that this material belonged to an international tradition. The book, however, is marred by its funerary spirit, a result of Newell's belief that this material would soon be extinct. This assumption also led him to collect the material as "memory culture" from adults rather than from children, who were active bearers of the traditions.

Besides his initial folklore volume, Newell published three books on Arthurian legend, but his significance in folklore's history is largely due to his role as founder and guiding force behind the American Folklore Society during its first two decades. He proposed the initial meeting, held at University Hall, Harvard University on January 4, 1888, at which the society was established, and he served as secretary of the new organization (1888–1906) and editor of the *Journal of American Folklore* (1888–1899). He also sought to make the American Folklore Society a professional society that held rigorous scholarly standards. He thought the field of anthropology offered the best means of achieving this goal, and he thus actively pursued an alliance with Franz Boas of Columbia University in New York City. Newell's efforts in this regard led to Boas exercising great influence in the society's affairs for the first fifty years of its existence. While this assured that the society upheld high scholarly standards, it also inhibited the idea of folklore having importance aside from anthropology.

W.K. McNeil

References

Bell, Michael J. 1973. William Wells Newell and the Foundation of American Folklore Scholarship. *Journal of the Folklore Institute* 10:7–21.

Newell, William. 1888. On the Field and Work of a Journal of American Folklore. *Journal of American Folklore* 1:3–7.

Niles, John Jacob (1892–1980)

Balladeer, collector, and composer. As both a composer of art song and a collector-arranger of traditional material, Niles performed and published original songs, arrangements of folk music, and songs that were newly composed in the style of folk music. These "songs in the style of folk music," including "Black Is the Color," "I Wonder as I Wander," and "Go 'Way from My Window," transformed a core element of traditional music into original song through compositional craft.

Twelve years after his birth in Louisville, Kentucky, Niles moved to rural Jefferson County, where he began collecting and writing music. By 1907 he had completed his first song, "Go 'Way from My Window," which was based on a line of text collected from an African American worker on his father's farm.

In 1909 Niles graduated from DuPont Manual Training High School in Louisville, and began working for the Burroughs Adding Machine Company. In 1917 he enlisted in the aviation section of the Army Signal Corps, serving during World War I as a reconnaissance pilot.

Following the war, Niles studied music at the Schola Cantorum in Paris, the Université de Lyon, and the Cincinnati Conservatory. In 1925 he moved to New York City, where he completed two collections of wartime songs—*Singing Soldiers* (1927) and *Songs My Mother Never Taught Me* (1929)—and also began publishing collections of traditional music, including *Impressions of a Negro Camp Meeting* (1925) and *Seven Kentucky Mountain Songs* (1928).

In 1925 Niles met photographer Doris Ulmann, and between 1928 and 1933 the couple made four trips through the southern Appalachian Mountains to photograph performers and collect music. Many of the ballads recorded during these trips were later published in Niles' *Ballad Book* ([1960] 1970).

During that same period, Niles also initiated a performance career with contralto Marion Kerby. The duo toured throughout the United States and Europe performing Niles' original compositions in addition to his folk arrangements of Appalachian and African American material. By 1933 Niles was concertizing as a solo act and accompanying himself on his original "dulcimers," which more closely resembled eight-string lutes.

After briefly serving as music director at the John C. Campbell Folk School in Brasstown, North Carolina, Niles married journalist Rena Lipetz in 1936 and settled in rural Clark County, Kentucky. At the zenith of his popularity now, Niles was presenting at least fifty concerts annually and recording for RCA's Red Seal label, for Folkways Records, and for Tradition.

Although he maintained an active concert career until 1978, Niles increasingly focused his attention on original composition, completing more than 100 art songs and extended works, such as an oratorio, *Lamentation* (1950), and the *Niles-Merton Song Cycle* (1967–1970). He died at his farm in 1980 and was buried at St. Hubert's Church in Clark County, Kentucky.

Niles collected, arranged, published, and performed traditional material, but he also composed and performed his own songs modeled on folk music. As Niles was both collector and composer, preserver and creator, it was inevitable that these vocations would overlap and create controversy. His adaptation and extension of tradition created confusion and acrimony because folklorists assumed that Niles had plagiarized folk material—while Niles heard his original songs plagiarized by performers who assumed they were folksong.

Ron Pen

References

Burg, David F. 1980. John Jacob Niles. *Kentucky Review* 2:3–10.

Niles, John Jacob. [1960] 1970. *The Ballad Book*. New York: Dover.

Pen, Ronald. 1987. *The Biography and Works of John Jacob Niles*. Ph.D. Diss. University of Kentucky.

Northwest Coast and Alaska

Washington, Oregon, Alaska, and the northern parts of California and Idaho, the area commonly called the Pacific Northwest, a region long regarded as distinct by both residents and outsiders. Physiographically diverse, the area is characterized by a wealth of natural resources, located in environments marked by climatic extremes (aridity east of the Cascade Mountains and considerable moisture west, with arctic conditions prevailing in Alaska). The region was first inhabited by Native Americans 10,000 years ago, with nonnative settlement established relatively recently, in the early 19th century. Since then, the texture of the cultural landscape has included an ethnic mosaic of Latino-Americans concentrated in farming areas east of the Cascades, Asian Americans, and African Americans in urban centers, and Euro-Americans throughout; Native Americans continue to live on and off numerous reservations around the region.

Folklore in the Northwest generally includes any of the oral, customary, and material traditions shared by people who live in the area. However, the most distinctive aspects of Northwest regional lore are those traditions that reveal the intimate links between the region's physical environment and historical context and the resulting sociocultural milieu. As a subsection of the American West, historically subject to the same social forces that precipitated its creation as a political entity (such as colonialism and conflict with native peoples and rapid exploitation of natural resources), the Northwest shares in much of the Western mythos that pervades American popular culture, with Alaska assuming the role of the nation's last "frontier." Therefore, it is not surprising that Northwest regional lore is characterized by expressions of native cultures, the experience of pioneer settlement, and people's close interrelationship with the natural environment.

Native Americans of the Northwest come from six distinct culture areas: Plateau, Great Basin, California, Subarctic, Arctic, and Northwest Coast. The oral literature and material culture of these diverse groups has been well documented by anthropologists and folklorists, perhaps more so than any other area of North America. Such cultures generally recognized at least two types of narrative: myths, which could be told only in the sacred season of winter and featured a world prior to human existence; and historical tales, which featured the present world, with people and supernatural entities. Myths commonly focused on the exploits of specific animal characters that had many human qualities, such as transformers who were serious, purposeful beings that changed the natural landscape and brought culture to the world in preparation of people's arrival. More common were humorous stories of buffoon-like tricksters (often in the form of Raven, Bluejay, or Coyote) who embodied the less admirable qualities of greed, lechery, and conceit but yet, through their power and cunning, still brought incidental benefits to people. Historical tales often portrayed encounters between human and supernatural worlds, often with powerful and malevolent beings such as cannibal ogresses or wild man-like "bushmen." All forms of native oral literature followed specific conventions of plot, motif, repetition, and formula, yet also existed in traditional storytelling contexts wherein each tale could be re-created anew as a dramatic performance, complete with gestures, voice inflections, pauses, stylized speech for individual characters,

Native Americans fish for salmon. Celilo Falls, Columbia River, Oregon, 1941. Photo Russell Lee. Library of Congress.

songs, and interaction between the raconteur and audience.

Native material culture was closely linked to the subjects and themes of oral literature and religious belief. The art of the Northwest Coast is particularly notable, taking such forms as the painting of wood surfaces, the decorative features of basketry, intricately woven textiles such as Tlingit Chilkat blankets, or sculptures of argillite, bone, silver, and wood that included "totem" poles and articulating ceremonial masks. The Subarctic and Plateau are known for their beadwork embroidery of skins with colorful floral designs, while the Arctic features small carvings of ivory figurines.

The wide variety of nonnative ethnic groups that came to the Northwest brought traditions from their homelands. Scandinavians came in great numbers, working as loggers, fishermen, and farmers. Both Swedes and Norwegians brought their recipes for *lutefisk* (dried cod soaked in a lye solution). Norwegians crafted Hardanger fiddles (with elaborate decoration and four extra strings); Swedes continued to begin the Christmas season on December 13, St. Lucia Day, a celebration based on old-country legends; and Finns continued to use saunas for ritual cleansing and healing. Together, many Scandinavians celebrate a *Skandia Midsommerfest* and dance around a flower-bedecked pole to the music of fiddles and accordions, or gather to march in Seattle's annual parade for *Syttende Mai* (May 17), Norwegian Constitution Day. Asian American traditions include festive celebrations of the New Year and the elaborate storycloths and embroidered squares of recent Laotian Hmong refugees. Greeks manage coffeehouses and restaurants in the Puget Sound area; Basques are sheepherders in southeastern Oregon; fishermen of European and Native American descent celebrate Russian Orthodox-influenced weddings and Christmases in Alaska, and Latinos relate stories of nocturnal encounters with the legendary *La Llorona,* a ghostly weeping woman searching for her dead children.

More significant to the study of regional folklore are the distinctive words, actions, and objects that have been shaped by the shared experiences of Northwest life. Northwest oral traditions include a profusion of names, jargons, and expressions wherein pronunciation and understanding conspicuously indicate one's identity as resident or outsider. While many will guess that Webfoots are Oregonians, Sourdoughs are seasoned Alaskans, and bunchgrassers are people who live on the arid side of the Cascades, fewer people are privy to the complex occupational jargons of logging and ranching, or the fact that "side-hill salmon" are, in fact, deer poached out of season, or that "skookum" means strong, big, or fast, according to Chinook jargon, the region's frontier lingua franca. Proverbial expressions aptly describe the local landscape or weather: "Land so poor the jackrabbits have to carry their lunches," or "Fog so thick you could seine a salmon in it." One might recognize that local place names are based on landscape features, historical events, or Chinook jargon, but an outsider might easily mispronounce Puyallup, Willamette, Sequim, or Kwigillingok. Jokes indicate one's familiarity with the sense of humor generated from regional realities, as when western Oregonians remark that ten people fell off their bikes last year and drowned. While folk music of the region largely derives from elsewhere in the country, there are local folksongs that reflect the same sense of humor, such as parodies of the hymn "Beulah Land" that poke fun at the Oregon country's abundant rainfall or of "The Old Settler," who finally gets accustomed to a life amidst "acres of clams."

Folklorists have also documented the tales of, and by, several noted liars, such as Len Henry of northern Idaho and Hathaway Jones and Reub Long of Oregon. These "windies" often employ outrageous falsehoods and traditional motifs from American tall tales to exaggerate the region's natural landscape or frontier heritage, such as the one about an eastern Oregonian who is knocked unconscious by a single desert raindrop and had to have six buckets of sand thrown in his face to bring him around. Even more telling of the Northwest's character are local legends that make concise symbolic statements about regional experience. Heroic rides on horseback to reach a distant doctor, rude Indians that break into homesteader's cabins to steal and eat uncooked foods, cougars that follow children home from school—all reflect attitudes toward the physical isolation of frontier life. The region's legacy of racial prejudice and fear is evinced through stories of tunnels used to smuggle Asian workers after the Chinese Exclusion Act of 1882. Uncertainty about the region's wilderness mysteries has helped foster many stories of the legendary Bigfoot, while anxiety over the unpredictable nature of volcanic activity has facilitated accounts of a prophetic "vanishing hitchhiker" who warns of impending eruptions of Mt. St. Helens. And narratives that portray people's close calls with forest fires, grizzly bears, and "flying by the seat of your pants" air travel all make very personal statements about the ways in which the natural world continues to dominate modern everyday life in the rural Northwest.

The customary folklore of the Northwest includes a wide range of traditional practices ranging from the beliefs (superstitions) that loggers and fishermen have pertaining to good or ill fortune in the workplace, to the traditional techniques of local hunters and trappers, to the gestures and sign language employed by workers in noisy sawmills. Much more prominent, however, are many regional or community festivals. Such structured, regularly scheduled events include local pow-wows where Indian and some nonnative people participate in traditional dancing, singing, and feasting (notably salmon and fry bread) in celebration of tribal persistence and modern pan-Indian identity. Rendezvous, in which costumed mountain men and Indian artisans reenact the region's historical legacy of the frontier fur trade, have become increasingly popular. Even Alaska's Iditarod, a 1,049-mile dogsled race, can be seen as a springtime festival that traditionalizes the "Alaskan spirit" in an attempt to promote modern Alaskan identity and a sense of belonging. Other festivals stem from the dominance of local occupations that exploit the region's natural resources. Lumbering and ranching areas often sponsor log shows and rodeos that feature playful competitions based on the work skills and athleticism of loggers and cowboys ("buckaroos").

Not surprisingly, the material folk culture of the Northwest is dominated by the natural abundance of wood. Until the 1930s, log construction of rural houses, barns, and outbuildings was not uncommon and drew largely upon the traditional forms and construction techniques of the Eastern and Midwestern portions of the country. Perhaps the most distinctive aspects of Northwest folk architecture are the raised caches for food storage in Alaska the widespread "Rocky Mountain log cabin" (with its roof projecting over the gable-end door), and the rather large number of buildings, built by immigrants and based on European models, most notably Finnish log houses, barns, and saunas. Even the more arid sections of the Northwest have many remaining log barns, while some ranches of eastern Oregon still use willow corrals with juniper posts. Also to be considered are distinctive mailbox supports that use old logging, ranching, farming, and fishing equipment to make practical yet aesthetic statements of locality and occupation.

Wood also predominates in traditional arts and crafts, whether it be practical boat construction (the McKenzie River drift boats in Oregon, or the flat-bottom skiffs in Alaska), or the tangible expression of regional aesthetics in carvings of narrative tableaus for Western frontier or logging scenes, or the larger chainsaw carvings of local animals. Also notable is the fine metalwork exhibited in the crafted implements of ranching (custom branding irons, spurs, and bits) or the leatherwork in saddles. Among traditional Northwest foodways, there are innumerable recipes for the preparation and preservation of salmon and shellfish, and for venison, berries, and local edible plants.

As folklorist Suzi Jones has argued, the regionalization of folklore is, in many respects, a rhetorical strategy, a means of making various forms of cultural expression appropriate for a specific audience to make a persuasive statement about regional identity. Such may be the case for the Northwest, the far corner of America, which has long been imagined as distinct, a part of, yet separate from, the classic American West. Euro-American newcomers rationalized pioneer hardships and ethnic conflict in order to claim their place in the nation's farthest "promised land," from the earliest settlers of the 19th century to the separatists of tomorrow—the back-to-the-landers on ecotopian communes, the survivalists and White supremacists, and the many "Lower-Forty-Eight" refugees who seek an alternative way of life homesteading in the Alaskan bush. Regional folklore of the Northwest certainly does comment on the diversity of its cultural landscape, but, more significant, it speaks directly and symbolically to the people's image of themselves: willing to endure the isolation and hardships of a continued "frontier" experience and able to thrive in a natural-resource utopia, where fishermen and farmers, loggers and buckaroos successfully elude the problems of industrial urban life that so dominates other areas of America.

With the exception of Native American traditions, relatively few book-length studies of Northwest folklore have been published, and folklorists have left Alaska virtually untouched. However, the journal *Northwest Folklore* (1965–1969, 1985–) contains numerous informative articles, and at least two textbooks—Jan Harold Brunvand's *The Study of American Folklore* "Len"; and Barre Toelken's *The Dynamics of Folklore* (1979) are infused with examples of Northwest lore. The Randall V. Mills Archives of Northwest Folklore at the University of Oregon remains the largest repository for information on regional traditions.

Robert E. Walls

References

Attebery, Louie W., ed. 1985. *Idaho Folklife: Homesteads to Headstones.* Salt Lake City: University of Utah Press.

Jones, Suzi. 1977. *Oregon Folklore.* Eugene: University of Oregon and the Oregon Arts Commission.

———, ed. 1980. *Webfoots and Bunchgrassers: Folk Art of the Oregon Country.* Salem: Oregon Arts Commission.

Lund, Jens, ed. 1989. *Folk Arts of Washington State: A Survey of Contemporary Folk Art and Artists in the State of Washington.* Tumwater: Washington State Folklife Council.

Suttles, Wayne, ed. 1990. *Northwest Coast.* Vol. 7 of *Handbook of North American Indians.* Washington, DC: Smithsonian Institution.

Toelken, Barre. 1979. Northwest Regional Folklore. In *Northwest Perspectives: Essays on the Culture of the Pacific Northwest,* ed. Edwin R. Bingham and Glen A. Love. Eugene and Seattle: University of Oregon Press and University of Washington Press.

Vick, Ann. 1983. *The Cama-i Book: Kayaks, dogsleds, bear hunting, bush pilots, smoked fish, mukluks, and other traditions of Southwestern Alaska.* Garden City, NY: Anchor.

Walls, Robert E. 1987. *Bibliography of Washington State Folklore and Folklife*. Seattle: University of Washington Press.

See also Bigfoot; Henry, Lorenzo; Jones, Hathaway; Loggers

Nuclear Lore

Folklore of the Atomic Age. The development, use, and proliferation of nuclear weapons fundamentally and irrevocably altered American culture and thought. Advancements in nuclear technology since the 1940s have symbolized military superiority and the promise of a techno-utopian future, but also have fueled fears of global annihilation and evoked widespread fatalism about the future of humanity. The feelings and fears associated with the nuclear era have precipitated various types of folklore, including religious and secular beliefs, legends, songs, folk art, jokes, and speech forms.

Since the dropping of atomic bombs on Hiroshima and Nagasaki in August 1945, the most widespread and persistent folklore associated with nuclear weapons reflects the belief that their use will bring about the end of the world. The folklore about nuclear apocalypse has flourished in both American religious and secular cultures.

Since the 1940s, religious apocalyptists have interpreted the invention of nuclear weapons and the prospect of nuclear war as a fulfillment of divine prophecies, and they have readily incorporated the idea of nuclear holocaust into vernacular religious cosmologies. Premillennialist Christians, for example, frequently regard the symbolic and cryptic language of the Book of Revelation as a prophetic description of a foreordained nuclear apocalypse. The biblical passage "The heavens shall pass away with a great noise, and the elements shall be disintegrated with intense heat; the earth also, and all its works, shall be burned up" (II Peter 3:10) is commonly interpreted as a description of nuclear holocaust. Such beliefs have mythologized and sanctified the threat of nuclear annihilation, by regarding it as a meaningful part of a foreordained, supernatural plan for humanity. In 1991 some premillennialists, watching for the "signs" of imminent doomsday, interpreted the war in the Persian Gulf as the beginning of an "end times" scenario, foretold in the Bible, that would culminate in a nuclear conflagration.

Roman Catholic popular belief during the nuclear era has included prophecies about imminent nuclear apocalypse, often communicated through apparitions of the Virgin Mary. For instance, the "third secret of Fatima," conveyed during a Marian apparition in 1917, is commonly believed to predict nuclear holocaust. A related popular belief is that nuclear annihilation may be averted by the conversion of Russia to Catholicism.

Numerous other religious groups maintain beliefs about nuclear apocalypse, and similar ideas are expressed in New Age prophecies as well as beliefs about the predictions of Nostradamus and Edgar Cayce. Beliefs about the existence of unidentified flying objects (UFOs), which emerged in the 1950s, also seem directly related to nuclear apocalyptic fears. Often characterized by expectations of worldly destruction and salvation, early UFO beliefs frequently assert that extraterrestrials would intervene and save humanity (or a chosen people) from nuclear holocaust.

Unlike religious beliefs about nuclear apocalypse, which promise the salvation of the faithful and a redemptive millennial realm to replace a world destroyed, secular beliefs about nuclear holocaust rarely express such hopes. Popular beliefs and narratives that arose during the Cold War era are often explicitly fatalistic, implying that humanity could not reverse its inevitable path to nuclear destruction. The physicists who worked on the development of the atomic bomb, for instance, were portrayed in narratives as evil geniuses who would ultimately destroy the world because of their obsessive pursuit of power and forbidden knowledge, similar to the legendary Faust character. Speech forms, neologisms, and euphemisms associated with nuclear weapons also seem to reflect feelings of powerlessness and fatalism.

Individual helplessness concerning the uncontrollable destructive power of nuclear weapons is expressed through assorted beliefs about nuclear technology, such as the "Doomsday Button," a red button that supposedly existed in the White House and the Kremlin and that, when pushed, would destroy the world. Even the common use of the expression "the bomb," when referring to the multitude of nuclear warheads that exist, seems to reflect popular perceptions of nuclear weapons as a single, massive, omnipresent force of destruction. Other forms of nuclear lore include beliefs about government secrets concerning the harmful effects of radiation on humans and animals, and the attribution of bizarre weather patterns and natural disasters, such as hurricanes, floods, and unusual heat waves, to nuclear testing.

Jokes about nuclear war and technology are relatively scarce, but those that exist tend to express a sense of ironic inevitability about nuclear doomsday. (What do you do if they drop the bomb? Answer: Hide under a table, put your head between your legs, and . . . kiss your ass goodbye!) A similar sense of gallows humor is expressed in the jokes, narratives, and speech forms created in the aftermath of the accident at the Three Mile Island Nuclear Power Plant near Harrisburg, Pennsylvania, in 1979. (Popular greetings among residents included, "My, you look radiant! and "You're glowing today! [Milspaw 1981:60].) After the disaster, beliefs and rumors about the effects of exposure to radioactivity, such as sterility, genetically mutated offspring, and increased rates of infant mortality, spread rapidly, a reflection of the suspicion that authorities were withholding information, as well as uncertainty about the long-term effects of radiation.

The nuclear disaster that occurred in Chernobyl, Ukraine, in 1986 provoked similar beliefs and rumors, as well as jokes with ironic and macabre themes that expressed anxieties about uncontrollable nuclear technology. (What has feathers, glows in the dark, and cooks by itself? Answer: Chicken Kiev. What do you serve with Chicken Kiev? Answer: A black Russian. What's the weather report from Kiev? Answer: Overcast and 10,000 degrees.)

Although fears of nuclear apocalypse have decreased since

the end of the Cold War, 1990s nuclear lore continues to reflect anxieties about potential nuclear disasters, stemming not only from concerns about nuclear accidents, but also the magnitude and seeming uncontrollability of nuclear weapons and the possibility that such weapons will be developed and used by hostile nations or extremist organizations in the future. Such feelings and fears will no doubt continue to inspire an abundance of folklore in the years ahead.

Daniel Wojcik

References

Boyer, Paul. 1992. *When Time Shall Be No More: Prophecy Belief in Modern American Culture.* Cambridge: Harvard University Press.

Milspaw, Yvonne. 1981. Folklore and the Nuclear Age: The Harrisburg Disaster at Three Mile Island. *International Folklore Review* 1:57–65.

Weart, Spencer R. 1988. *Nuclear Fear: A History of Images.* Cambridge: Harvard University Press.

Wojcik, Daniel. Forthcoming. *Approaching Doomsday: Faith and Fatalism in Contemporary American Apocalyptic Beliefs.* New York: New York University Press.

See also Cold War; Disaster Folklore; UFO Lore

Nye, Pearl R. (1872–1950)

Ohio Canal boat captain, singer, and songwriter. Nye, the fifteenth of eighteen children, was born in Chillicothe, Ohio, on the canal boat *Reform,* which ran between Akron and the Ohio River. Singing was a common entertainment for the Nye family and at canal gatherings, and as early as 1932 Captain Nye began corresponding with archives and libraries about his extensive canal-song collection, written by hand on sheets of yellow paper and pasted together to make long scrolls. In the autumn of 1936, John Lomax received information about him from an Akron journalist and visited him in Akron a week later. In June 1937 he recorded thirty-three of the Nye songs, and in November 1937 Alan and Elizabeth Lomax recorded an additional thirty-nine songs. During the next months, Nye wrote

out hundreds of songs for the Library of Congress, and in May 1938 he sang at Constitution Hall and at a meeting of the American Folk Song Society in Philadelphia. In 1941 his songs were used in a Library of Congress series on the Erie Canal broadcast over NBC, and in 1946 Ohio State University recorded as many of his canal songs as he could recall. A pamphlet, *Scenes and Songs of the Ohio-Erie Canal,* based on these recordings, was published in 1952 (Thomas [1952] 1971).

Captain Nye knew many traditional songs learned from his singing family, but as he grew older and his memory failed, he depended more and more on his own compositions. Among his many compositions describing life on the Ohio Canal, he considered his masterpiece to be "The Old Canal," a work consisting of almost 100 stanzas that named virtually every town, lock, store, and mill along the canal.

The Library of Congress collection of Nye songs includes twenty-three 12-inch discs recorded by the Lomaxes; a film, *Bard of the Ohio Canal;* and microfilm of hundreds of sheets of handwritten songs. Other manuscript materials are in the Ohio State Archaeological and Historical Society in Columbus. More than fifty songs recorded at Ohio State University in the 1940s were somehow lost a number of years ago. However, enough manuscripts and recordings remain to demonstrate that Nye's collection was remarkable in its breadth and scope and preserves many of the traditional songs known on the Ohio Canal.

Rebecca B. Schroeder

References

Hoffman, Daniel. 1953. Review of *Scenes and Songs of the Ohio-Erie Canal. Midwest Folklore* 3:70.

Lomax, John A. 1941. *Adventures of a Ballad Hunter.* New York: Macmillan, pp. 242–244.

Schroeder, Rebecca B. 1973. An Informant in Search of a Collector. *Journal of the Ohio Folklore Society,* n.s., 3:12–28.

Thomas, Cloea, ed. [1952] 1971. *Scenes and Songs of the Ohio-Erie Canal.* Columbus: Ohio State Historical Society.

Occupational Folklore

Expressive culture of the workplace, with special emphasis upon informally learned narrative, skill, and ritual used to determine status and membership in the work group. The earliest investigations of occupational folklore arose from interest in tracing the derivation of words and songs used within particular trades, from seafaring and logging to mining and farming. Later studies expanded into specific traditional crafts, followed by an interest in increasingly industrialized, urban work groups. Contemporary research is devoted to holistic studies of informal work cultures approached as contested landscapes of power, gender, and ethnicity both internally and externally. Occupational folklorists continue to develop methods for negotiating public representations of occupational folklife to outsiders through a variety of presentational formats, from demonstrations of industrial craft to museum exhibitions of skill retention and destruction over time.

The listing of occupational terms and indigenous folksong gave way in American folklore studies to an increased sensitivity toward the way in which these forms reflected historical and cultural change within types of work. John Lomax and Nathan Howard "Jack" Thorp both concerned themselves with cowboy lore, in particular the ways in which the songs and stories of buckaroos reflected a vernacular idiom unique to the frontier. Thorp more than Lomax linked this interest in cowboy lore to its Mexican roots; he also felt no constraints in revising and reshaping the traditional forms he collected from ranchers and buckaroos. Thorp's work of 1908 and 1921 was reprinted and annotated by Austin E. and Alta S. Fife in *Songs of the Cowboys* (1966), while Lomax's *Cowboy Songs and Other Frontier Ballads* (1910) is widely available. Both Thorp and Lomax published in formats that extended the study of occupational folklore beyond the academy into the popular marketplace. They conducted fieldwork at a time when the great cattle drives continued from Southwestern ranches to railheads in Colorado and Montana.

The interest in uniquely American occupations also led regional collectors of folksong into the logging camps, min-

ing regions, and farming areas to collect the indigenous songs and stories of work. Phillips Barry, Fannie Eckstorm, Mary Smyth, and others combed bunkhouses and boarding houses to identify locally recognized singers and storytellers. Although their published anthologies evinced comparative scholarship of some scope, their studies remain somewhat limited because of bowdlerization and the alteration of texts to appeal to local sensibilities. The regional collections also reveal comparative material of some interest between regions (the crosscut saw of the Northeast becomes the "Swede-fiddle" or "misery-whip" of the West); however, these collections did not attempt to place their material in broader occupational contexts.

Following Lomax's published collection in 1910, a young newspaperman in Pennsylvania, George Korson, became interested in the songs and stories of anthracite coal miners. He compiled material from the mining communities of Pennsylvania in *Songs and Ballads of the Anthracite Miner* (1927). Korson's view was that the mine was an occupational, but, more importantly, an industrial, site where workers were isolated from contemporary American society, living in a semiprimitive state and exhibiting an active "folk imagination" that generated a tremendous body of folksong and other lore. As he continued his collecting and publishing of this material, Korson became aware of the unique forms taken by occupational folklore in an industrialized setting. His willingness to shift from a search for specific types of song and story among a peasant-like class of homogeneous workers in the mine patch gave way to an understanding of the complexity and diversity of industrial expression. His ability to make this transition places him in a unique position in American studies of occupational folklore. Korson maintained an interest in publicly presenting miners and their lore through folk festivals and through his recordings and publications at the Library of Congress' Archive of American Folk-Song. He challenged festival organizers who sought to popularize and commercialize these expressive forms by demanding that the miners be presented as skilled workers who performed traditions from their com-

Tim Slate tops tobacco. Claudeville, Virginia, 1978. Photo Carl Fleischhauer. American Folklife Center.

munities rather than as singers and storytellers who happened to be miners.

The impact of ideology on occupational folklore was most dramatically reflected in concepts of social responsibility found in the works of Benjamin A. Botkin and Archie Green. Botkin's experiences as an editor for the Federal Writers' Project in the 1930s led him to recognize the power inherent in publishing the stories and experiences of industrial labor. Botkin sought to present this lore to as many people as possible through books, articles, and dramatizations so that the strength and the pathos of the occupational experience could educate the general public regarding the realities (positive and negative) of American industrial life. Botkin published many "treasuries" of his collections, with the bulk of the occupational material appearing in *Sidewalks of America* (1954) and (with Alvin Harlow) *A Treasury of Railroad Folklore* (1953). Botkin's eclectic collections combined personal-experience narratives of engineers, cab drivers, steelworkers and policemen with material clipped from newspapers and other published sources.

Archie Green's *Only a Miner: Studies in Recorded Coal-Mining Songs* (1972), in the issues it raised and the background of its author, suggests a linkage to the impulses of Botkin and his contemporaries that continues to shape research in occupational folklore. A former shipwright and union activist in San Francisco, Green combined an interest in industrial craftsmanship with an insider's view of the world of work. His book chronicled the role played by recorded music as it is actually received and reinterpreted in mining communities. He illustrated how folklore both shapes and

reflects an occupational worldview that is at once political, linked to work-related concepts of skill and shared knowledge, and in direct opposition to the occupational culture and worldview of owners and managers. Like Korson, Green fought for the accurate presentation of workers' skills and lore in public contexts; largely through his efforts, the Smithsonian Institution has included occupational folklore in the Working Americans section of the Festival of American Folklife since the late 1960s. Green provided a link between the craft traditions of organized labor and the academic study of occupational and labor lore that continues to exert a strong influence on those conducting research in the field. In *Only a Miner,* Green wrote that there is ". . . an observable blurring and overlap in the terms industrial, occupations, labor, or worker when combined with folklore. Hence, industrial lore may be an umbrella term broad enough to cover all job processes as well as urban living, unionism, radicalism, social reform, civil disobedience, and political action" (Green 1972).

Perhaps the most influential comparatist and scholar in the field of occupational folklore was Wayland D. Hand. In his article "American Occupational and Industrial Folklore: The Miner" (Hand 1969), Hand traced the study of mining traditions throughout the Western world and called for additional ethnological comparisons of occupational tradition. Hand's exhaustive comparative research and his initiation of an international dialogue about occupational tradition across cultures provide a potential for more global studies of work culture and its expressive dimensions.

In his treatment of the folklore of miners below and above ground, Hand dealt with a wide range of topics of current concern, including the role of occupational accident accounts in a trade and their relationship to beliefs, customs, and expectations. He also examined the naming and use of tools and skills, the development of clothing and occupational gear, pranks and initiations, jokes and legends, and the impact of occupational culture upon the wider community. Hand maintained in his work with Western miners that in spite of technological change, occupational folklore would continue to form an important part of any work experience.

Although Hand and Green shaped and honed the concepts of occupational and industrial folklore that continue to demarcate the field, there are a number of other influences that directly or indirectly relate to the development of this specialty. These include investigations of political forces or movements that affect or reflect occupational culture, urban studies that include occupational culture in their investigations, studies of a cultural-historic and materialistic nature that focus on work within a specific culture (both folklife and ethnographic), investigations of specific expressive genres (narratives, customs, belief systems, and the like) within occupational settings, and approaches to occupational culture that attempt to apply their findings to specific problems or conflicts within the community and link occupational folklore to political or oppositional strategies for the amelioration of these conflicts.

The political dimension of occupational folklore has been most dramatically expressed in the protest songs and laments generated in the early days of American industrial labor organization. Korson documented the importance of disaster ballads and protest songs sung by men like Con Carbon and Ed Foley about the Avondale mine disaster, the Coal Creek rebellion, and the Ludlow massacre in Colorado. John Green-

way provided the first broad survey of protest songs in his *American Folksongs of Protest* (1953). Greenway refuted the scholarly requirement that all folksongs must be traditional (that is, passed over at least two generations) and must have lost their identity as a consciously composed piece. He found that not only did many mining, lumbering, and agricultural communities recognize poets and songwriters, but these individuals captured cultural history and occupational experience in a compelling manner that resulted in the collective use of these forms over time as traditional documents linked to place.

During the 1950s and 1960s, labor and protest songs moved even further away from the local occupational community, yet their mass-audience impact through radio, television, and records was felt strongly during the civil rights struggles and the antiwar movement. Fully documented by R. Serge Denisoff and Richard Reuss, this era of protest music and folksong revival in urban industrial settings (termed the "proletarian renaissance" by Denisoff), revealed the adaptability of both labor protest tunes and texts to fit the struggles, frustrations, and social contexts of a new generation. This shift from a concentration on occupational folksong text to a closer examination of how that text is consumed by an audience reflects a thematic and a theoretical shift in the production and analysis of these materials.

Thematically the songs of the early days of labor organization (such as "Solidarity Forever" and "Hold the Fort for We Are Coming") are adapted to new audiences and new struggles; folklorists are beginning to appreciate how the material is consumed by wider audiences through the electronic media. As long as the material addresses itself to the beliefs and

Miners' tools. Kern County, California, 1942. Photo Russell Lee. Library of Congress, LC–USW3–3328–D.

cultural concerns of people who derive at least a portion of their social identity from their work, these songs must be considered a significant aspect of occupational folklore. A particular song or style of music—for example, a country-western song about an alienated drifter or angry workers who quit their jobs as a matter of principle for unfair treatment by the boss—can be used as a rhetorical device within the group to make oppositional statements about parallel sentiments or feelings. The seminal work of Américo Paredes and José Limón extends this social and cultural analysis of traditional songs and texts as they emerge from ethnic and class conflict on the Texas-Mexican border. The work of these scholars links the Mexican border ballad *(corrido)* and other cultural forms such as the collective term "chicano" not only to specific historical incidents between Anglos and Mexicanos—more important, they analyze how these expressive forms provide political and personal opportunities for active opposition to Anglo racism and violence toward Mexicanos.

In addition to the literature on labor protest songs and current approaches to urban folklore that relate directly to any consideration of occupational folklife, a body of materials that concerns historical and contemporary work processes and techniques has been generated by folklife scholars, both in the United States and Europe. The concept of "folklife" (German *Volkskunde,* Swedish *folkliv)* is more inclusive than "folklore," embracing the material as well as the verbal and "intangible" elements of traditional expression. Articulated in early articles by Don Yoder and Warren Roberts, the folklife movement gained increased recognition in the work of Henry Glassie, particularly his empirical, cultural-geographic work on large patterns of material expression in the Eastern United States and later in his more critical and reflexive *Passing the Time in Balleymenone* (1982). Glassie not only brings the fieldworker's eye and ear for felicitous detail, but also provides one of the more complete theoretical backgrounds to date (1995) for the relationships among culture, material expression, and worldview as these elements have been experienced over generations of crofters and peat cutters in Northern Ireland.

Other scholarly works in occupational folklore, such as Horace Beck's *Folklore and the Sea* (1973), Tristram Potter Coffin and Hennig Cohen's *Folklore from the Working Folk of America* (1973), Betty Messenger's *Picking up the Linen Threads* (1975), Edward Ives' *Joe Scott: Woodsman Songmaker* (1964)—as well as Ives' other fine biographies of worker-poets—and Patrick B. Mullen's *I Heard the Old Fisherman Say: Folklore of the Texas Gulf Coast* (1978), reflect the comparatist and scholarly treatment of occupational traditions begun by Hand. A more specific study of industrial folklore, completed by Bruce Nickerson in 1974, adapted current theoretical approaches toward folk craft and folk community to an industrial machine shop in New England. Nickerson's linkage of existing models of folklore that were based on the isolation and separation of a community from outside influence, as well as his sensitivity to the variety of expressive forms in the shop, makes his article "Is There a Folk in the Factory?" *(Journal of American Folklore* 1974 87:133–139) a milestone. Research in the Irish textile industry by Betty Messenger and Southern

textile communities by Doug DeNatale and Allen Tullos, extend the work experience into broader political and social constructs of personal identity and collective notions of class.

In 1978 Robert H. Byington edited a special issue of *Western Folklore* titled "Working Americans: Contemporary Approaches to Occupational Folklife," which applied new theories of folklore as communication to the study of work culture. In that issue, Robert McCarl, Roger D. Abrahams, Jack Santino, Archie Green, and Byington illustrate the significance of studying "occupational folklife"—the entire range of expressive behavior in work settings, from the techniques required to succeed and survive on the job to the customs marking passage through the work culture and the verbal arts that provide a context for a range of experiences, both on and off the job.

The model of occupational folklife that forms the basis for that collection of essays was derived from fieldwork designed to produce public presentations of work at the Smithsonian's 1976 Festival of American Folklife. The participation of trade unionists and industrial craftspeople with folklorists in the development of the skills demonstrations and narrative workshops represented more than sixty trades, from meat cutting to firefighting, and from emergency-room technicians to air-traffic controllers. These presentations provided an intensity of meaning for large-scale study and presentation of occupational culture. At a time when de-industrialization, computerization, and robotics were causing massive changes in industry, and the constituencies of organized labor were shifting to adjust to a hostile political climate, this celebration of skill, custom, and verbal art in the contemporary workplace provided a glimpse into a historical plateau of American labor that may not recur.

Following the Smithsonian festival and the research that led to it, a number of folklorists published studies devoted to the analysis of occupational culture in a variety of settings. Jack Santino investigated the linkage of class, ethnicity, and organized labor among Pullman porters; Robert McCarl addressed issues of cultural change among urban firefighters; Maggie Holtzberg-Call documented the ethnohistory of hot-type printers; Paula Johnson and Janet Gilmore portrayed the maritime trades on the eastern shore of Maryland and boatbuilding on the Oregon coast, respectively; and Alicia Gonzales and Suzanne Serrif used feminist and critical theory to analyze the relationships between work technique and changing social relationships within Mexicano culture. Although theoretically and methodologically distinct, all of these documentations of occupational folklife draw upon the ethnographer's goal of cultural holism, while at the same time seeking to portray both the verbal and the non-verbal aspects of patterned communication in the workplace. Contemporary scholars in occupational folklife have retained their attentiveness of work-group values and ethics, and it is within these stratified yet egalitarian social structures that they continue to operate.

The study of occupational folklore in the United States parallels the evolution of folklore methodology in general, from the desire of the early ballad collectors to rescue surviving ballads and songs, to the impact of European-inspired interest in skill and material expression, to the more recent interest in the intersection between work culture, class, ethnicity, and gender. Concurrent with these theoretical and academic interests, occupational folklorists—from Lomax to Green, Korson, and Hand—have maintained an awareness that public presentation of private cultural materials must be negotiated by the researcher with insiders. Public presentations of work culture from studies of firefighters and textile workers by Robert McCarl, museum presentations of slate- and woodsworkers by Catherine Schwoefferman in New York state, and publicly supported exhibitions of transit workers developed by Steve Zeitlin and the organization City Lore in New York City—all such presentations attest to the continued importance of this collaborative posture. Contemporary cultural theories regarding the intersection of power and control inherent within the documentary process suggest that only through a more democratic, egalitarian relationship between folklorist and cultural representative will it be possible to continue the study and presentation of occupational folklore.

Key questions remain concerning the rapid transformation of work as global shifts of capital result in abrupt and sometimes disastrous changes in labor markets. The challenge—for workers, trade unionists, and folklorists—will be to measure these changes as they are reflected in the various human and oppositional forms that they will inevitably create.

Robert S. McCarl

References

Boatright, Mody. 1963. *Folklore of the Oil Industry.* Dallas: Southern Methodist University Press.

DeNatale, Doug. 1993. *The Origins of Southern Mill Culture.* Chapel Hill: University of North Carolina Press.

Denisoff, R. Serge. 1971. *Great Day Coming.* Urbana: University of Illinois Press.

Dewhurst, C. Kurt. 1984. The Arts of Working: Manipulating the Urban Work Environment. *Western Folklore* 63:192–211.

Gonzalez, Alicia Maria. 1981. Guess How Doughnuts Are Made: Verbal and Nonverbal Aspects of the *Panadero* and His Stereotype. In *"And Other Neighborly Names": Social Process and Cultural Image in Texas Folklore,* ed. Richard Bauman and Roger D. Abrahams. Austin: University of Texas Press, pp. 104–123.

Green, Archie. 1993. *Wobblies, Pile Butts, and Other Heroes: Labor-Lore Explorations.* Urbana: University of Illinois Press.

Hand, Wayland D. 1969. American Occupational and Industrial Folklore: The Miner. In *Kontakte und Grenzen: Probleme der Volks-, Kultur-, und Sozial-forschung: Festschrift für Gerhard Heilfurth zum 60 Geburtstag,* ed. Hans Foltin. Göttingen: Verlag Otto Schwartz.

Limón, José E. 1981. The Folk Performance of "Chicano" and the Cultural Limits of Political Ideology. In *"And Other Neighborly Names": Social Process and Cultural Image in Texas Folklore,* ed. Richard Bauman and

Roger D. Abrahams. Austin: University of Texas Press, pp. 197–226.

Lloyd, Timothy, and Patrick B. Mullen. 1990. *Lake Erie Fishermen: Work, Tradition, and Identity.* Urbana: University of Illinois Press.

McCarl, Robert S. 1985. *The District of Columbia Fire Fighter's Project: A Case Study in Occupational Folklife.* Smithsonian Folklife Studies No. 4. Washington, DC: Smithsonian Institution.

Reuss, Richard. 1983. *Songs of American Labor, Industrialization, and the Urban Work Experience: A Discography.* Ann Arbor: Labor Studies Center, University of Michigan.

Santino, Jack. 1989. *Miles of Smiles, Years of Struggle: Stories of Black Pullman Porters.* Urbana: University of Illinois Press.

Serrif, Suzanne. Forthcoming. *Snakes, Sirens, Virgins, and Whores: The Politics of Representation of a Mexican-American Folk Artist.* Philadelphia: University of Pennsylvania Press.

Tullos, Allen. 1989. *Habits of Industry: White Culture and the Transformation of the Carolina Piedmont.* Chapel Hill: University of North Carolina Press.

See also Boatright, Mody Coggin; Botkin, Benjamin A.; Cowboys; Farmers; Folklife Movement; Hand, Wayland D.; Korson, George; Loggers; Maritime Folklore; Medical Professionals; Merchant Seamen; Oilworkers; Organizational Folklore; Printers, Journeymen; Railroaders; Revivalism; Smithsonian Institution Center for Folklife Programs and Cultural Studies; Social Protest in Folklore; Steelworkers; Truckers' Folklore

Odum, Howard Washington (1884–1954)

Sociologist and collector of Southern folk songs. A native of Georgia, Odum was appointed founding chair of the Sociology Department at the University of North Carolina at Chapel Hill in 1920. Odum's "new regionalism" was an important philosophical influence on the intellectual climate of the post-Depression South, and his seminal work, *Southern Regions of the United States* (1936), established his reputation as the leading Southern sociologist of his day.

Odum began collecting African American folksongs while pursuing a master's degree at the University of Mississippi. He subsequently earned Ph.D.s in psychology (Clark University, 1909), and sociology (Columbia University, 1910). In 1911 several issues of the *Journal of American Folklore* featured portions of his psychology dissertation, which is based on transcriptions of the songs he collected in Mississippi.

Odum believed that studies of folklore could increase understanding of African American culture and thus improve Southern race relations. Therefore, his two joint publications with student and colleague Guy Benton Johnson focus on folksongs as cultural products (Johnson and Odum 1925, 1926). Both books are landmark studies of African American secular song as well. Odum also published three "folk novels" based on the repertoire of one of his informants, a wandering laborer named John Wesley Gordon, Odum's "Black Ulysses."

Although Odum's national reputation was based on his influence as a sociologist, his contributions to folklore are equally important because of the number of African American folksongs he collected, his in-depth study of one African American informant, and his focus on the social and psychological function of song in a community.

Lynn Moss Sanders

References

Brazil, Wayne Douglas. 1975. *Howard W. Odum: The Building Years, 1884–1930.* Cambridge: Harvard University Press.

Johnson, Guy Benton, and Howard W. Odum. 1925. *The Negro and His Songs: A Study of Typical Songs in the South.* Chapel Hill: University of North Carolina Press.

———. 1926. *Negro Workaday Songs.* Chapel Hill: University of North Carolina Press.

Odum, Howard Washington. 1928. *Rainbow Round My Shoulder.* Indianapolis: Bobbs-Merrill.

———. 1929. *Wings on My Feet.* Indianapolis: Bobbs-Merrill.

———. 1931. *Cold Blue Moon.* Indianapolis: Bobbs-Merrill.

———. 1964. *Folk, Region, and Society: Selected Papers of Howard W. Odum,* ed. Katharine Jocher, Guy B. Johnson, George L. Simpson, and Rupert B. Vance. Chapel Hill: University of North Carolina Press.

Ohrlin, Glenn (1926–)

America's best-known traditional cowboy singer. Ohrlin was born in Minneapolis, Minnesota. His father, Burt, was a Swedish immigrant who moved to the Twin Cities to work as a house painter. His mother, Alma, was the daughter of Norwegian immigrants. Both parents knew Scandinavian and American songs, and they were their son's earliest source of material. His mother's family, particularly an aunt, Irene Eraker, provided him with several ballads, while his father's sister, Anna Molinder, taught him basic guitar techniques. Music was not Ohrlin's only interest; from early childhood, he wanted to be a rider, and he frequented stables and stockyards to be near horses. In 1940 the family moved to California, and two years later Ohrlin left home to work as a buckaroo in Nevada. In 1943 he started on the rodeo circuit, continuing until the early 1960s, despite suffering a broken back.

During World War II, Ohrlin spent time in Japan where he started learning flamenco guitar from a chicano soldier pal. To this day (1995), he performs a large number of Spanish songs because, he says, the cowboys seem to like them. Despite his growing musical accomplishments, it was the early 1960s before Ohrlin came to the attention of non-cowboy audiences. Then, in 1963, he met folklorist Archie Green, who soon introduced him to the folk-revival audience. Thereafter, Ohrlin appeared at numerous folk festivals and on a large number of commercial recordings. In 1973 he produced *The Hell-Bound Train: A Cowboy Songbook,* a collection of 100 of his favorite songs with extensive commentary by Ohrlin. While the book is an excellent compilation, it by no means covers the gamut of the author's repertoire, which includes traditional ballads, bawdy pieces, GI folksongs, hobo ditties, jukebox hits, and items from song folios and newspapers.

In 1954 Ohrlin moved to the Ozarks, establishing his Rafter O Ranch near Mountain View, Arkansas, a choice dictated largely by economics. Cheap land, low taxes, and free range all played a part in his decision. Ohrlin still performs at folk festivals, concerts, and at the nearby Ozark Folk Center. In addition to singing, he has become well known as a performer of cowboy poetry.

W.K. McNeil

References

Musical Holdouts. 1978. Phoenix films. (In one section of this film, Ohrlin discusses the changing nature of the life of a traditional cowboy.)

Ohrlin, Glenn. *Cowboy Songs.* Philo Records.

———. *Wild Buckaroo.* Rounder Records.

Oilworkers

Workers in the nation's petroleum industry. The jargon, stories, jokes, customs, and songs of oilworkers address the dangerous conditions and long hours of the job, the relative isolation of the work sites, and a strong sense of pride in work among this predominantly male occupational culture. This body of folklore also reflects the technological advancements and larger economic forces that have fundamentally transformed the nature of life and work for oilworkers during the 20th century.

For more than 130 years, American oilworkers have built derricks and tanks, drilled wells, monitored production, constructed pipelines, and refined crude oil, both in this country and abroad. Until the mid-1970s, the United States ranked as the world's leading producer of oil. The nation's petroleum industry dates from 1859, when Edwin L. Drake and his drilling crew struck oil near Titusville, Pennsylvania. Oil exploration and production expanded into New York, West Virginia, Ohio, Indiana, and across the Midwest and Southwest by the turn of the 20th century. During this period, John D. Rockefeller built Standard Oil Company, using technological innovation, bureaucratic management, and large-scale capitalization to achieve a virtual monopoly of the nation's oil-refining industry. Similarly, Gulf Oil Corporation, Phillips Petroleum Company, Sinclair Oil and Refining Corporation, and other major American conglomerates consolidated the holdings of smaller companies and vertically integrated their operations to engage in all phases of petroleum exploration, production, refining, and marketing.

Development of the internal combustion engine and the mass marketing of automobiles created a high demand for gasoline and made petroleum one of the world's major sources of power. After 1900 the center of the nation's petroleum industry shifted to Texas, Oklahoma, and California. The famous discoveries of oil at Spindletop, near Beaumont, Texas, in 1901, and near Henderson, Texas, in 1930, opened the rich

To drill a well, roughnecks use pipe wrenches to screw one piece of drillpipe into another. Kilgore, Texas, 1939. Photo Russell Lee. Library of Congress.

Gulf Coast and east Texas fields, attracting Eastern oil companies, land speculators, and masses of migratory oilworkers, and transforming the Southwest from a rural, agricultural region to an urbanized, industrial one.

Since the early days of the petroleum industry, workers have organized unions to fight for the adoption of an eight-hour workday, higher wages, and worker safety laws. The Oil Field, Gas Well, and Refinery Workers (OFGWRW) union and its successor, Oil Workers International Union (OWIU) have been the major oil unions. Landmark strikes in the labor history of oilworkers occurred at the Standard Oil Company's refinery in Bayonne, New Jersey (1914–1916), in the Gulf Coast oil fields of Texas and Louisiana (1917–1918), at the Mid-Continent Petroleum Corporation's refinery in Tulsa, Oklahoma (1938–1940), at several companies' refineries across the nation (1945–1946), and at the Shell Oil Company's refineries in the Southwest and California (1973).

Historically, production and pipeline workers in the nation's petroleum industry have been chiefly native-born White men and, to a lesser extent, northern and eastern European immigrants. Some Mexicans and African Americans did secure employment in oil-field work, especially during labor shortages and in more recent years. In contrast, refinery workers have constituted a more ethnically and racially diverse group. In the Northeast, they have been primarily of southern and eastern European stock, while rural Whites and Mexicans have predominated in Southwestern refineries. Ex-

cept as secretaries and office staff, women did not generally work in the petroleum industry until the 1970s, when affirmative action and equal-opportunity laws opened the way for their employment.

After World War II, the major petroleum companies expanded oil exploration and production in foreign countries, closing down some American fields. Beginning in the 1950s and accelerating in the 1960s, oilworkers lost jobs as the United States imported more foreign oil and the petroleum industry increasingly automated and mechanized its wells and refineries. In 1974 the then Soviet Union replaced the United States as the world's leading producer of petroleum, and two years later the United States slipped to third behind Saudi Arabia. The discovery of oil at Prudhoe Bay, Alaska, in 1967 and offshore drilling in the Gulf of Mexico and along the California coast created some new jobs in the industry, but in the 1990s the United States, the world's largest consumer of oil, remains heavily dependent on petroleum from the Middle East and other foreign countries.

Documentation of oil-field lore began shortly after the turn of the 20th century, when Clark S. Northrup of Cornell University published two brief articles on the language of oilworkers in the Pennsylvania, New York, and West Virginia fields (Northrup 1903–1904). Generally, however, folklorists and dialect scholars have concentrated on the more recently opened fields of Texas, Oklahoma, and California (Brooks 1928; Dignowity 1927; Pond 1932). During the 1920s and

1930s, John Lee Brooks, Hartman Dignowity, Frederick Pond, and others documented the stories and jargon of the petroleum industry in the Southwest and California (Brooks 1928; Dignowity 1927; Pond 1932). In the late 1940s, Lalia Phipps Boone, a graduate student at the University of Oklahoma, began a comprehensive study of the occupational language of Southwestern oilworkers that resulted in the publication of *The Petroleum Dictionary* (1952). In a 1969 Ph.D. dissertation titled *Lexicon of the Texas Oil Fields,* written at East Texas State University, Elizabeth K. Martin surveyed the changes that had occurred in Texas oil-field speech since Boone's study appeared.

Mody Boatright was the first scholar to systematically collect and analyze the occupational folklore of Southwestern oil-field workers. In 1945 he published his pioneering collection of tales, *Gib Morgan: Minstrel of the Oil Fields.* His classic study, *Folklore of the Oil Industry* (1963), contains lore about the search for oil, accounts of the popular stereotypes of the driller, geologist, and oil promoter, among others, as well as oil-field songs, tall tales, and anecdotes. Boatright's final book, *Tales from the Derrick Floor: A People's History of the Oil Industry* (1970), cowritten with William A. Owens, consists of transcriptions of oral-history interviews that the authors conducted with Texas oil pioneers during the 1950s. Between 1978 and 1985, Roger M. and Diana Davids Olien also recorded an extensive series of interviews that resulted in several books on the social history of the Texas oil industry (Olien and Olien 1982, 1986). The folklore of refinery workers has received little attention from scholars, although, in *America's Working Man: Work, Home, and Politics among Blue-Collar Property Owners* (1984), David Halle explores the importance of religion, ethnicity, and holidays among a New Jersey community of refinery workers and their families.

Between 1900 and 1945, rural Texans and Oklahomans left farms and ranches to find work in the region's oil fields and refineries, while drillers and laborers from Pennsylvania and West Virginia oil patches also flocked to newly opened fields of the Southwest. Migratory workers and their families followed oil booms from field to field in search of economic opportunity and the relatively high wages of the petroleum industry. Oil-field work has traditionally attracted a diverse group of men, including cowboys, farmers, salesmen, and college students, because jobs generally paid better than most unskilled and semiskilled ones. In the Southwest, the largest of the oil fields employed thousands of production and pipeline workers, who worked in small crews monitoring wells and constructing vast networks of pump stations and pipelines that transported crude oil to refineries. Other oil-field workers, such as rig and tank builders and drillers, generally hired out to contractors rather than work directly for petroleum companies. Oil-field work was uncertain and generally short-term employment, as booms quickly turned to busts. Only production and pipeline workers remained after a well began pumping, while drillers, rig builders, and roughnecks (a member of a rotary drilling crew) scurried to the next boom or drifted into other lines of work. Traditional patterns of racism and ethnic discrimination generally blocked employment

for African Americans and Mexicans in the petroleum industry, with skilled and semiskilled jobs reserved almost exclusively for White men.

Throughout its history, oil-field work has been characterized by hard, physically demanding labor, long hours, and harsh conditions at a relatively isolated work site. According to a 1920 Bureau of Labor Statistics report, 75 percent of drillers and production workers in the Southwest and California worked seven days a week, as did 33 percent of pipeliners and 25 percent of refinery workers. Oil-field work, as the expression goes, "teaches you to sweat in freezing weather," and roughnecks worked in rain, sleet, subzero temperatures, high winds, dust storms, and scorching heat. Jobs were also dangerous: Workers could be injured or killed by faulty equipment, open gear boxes and belt drives, a falling load of pipe, electrocution, gas blowouts, and well fires.

In contrast to oil-field work, refinery work was more settled, regimented, and industrialized. The largest refineries employed thousands of workers, who converted crude oil into gasoline, diesel fuel, heating oil, lubricating oils, petrochemicals, and other products. Refinery work was generally hot, dirty, and smelly, but its employees have ranked among the nation's highest-paid industrial laborers since the 1930s. Refineries were usually located within a 100 or so miles of oil fields, including major facilities at Pittsburgh; Cleveland; New York City; Baton Rouge, Louisiana; Hammond, Indiana; and Port Arthur, Texas. Bluegrass pioneers Charlie and Bill Monroe of Kentucky worked in an oil refinery in northwestern Indiana, as did masses of other White Southerners who migrated to Midwestern cities during the Great Depression and World War II. Eastern refinery workers were chiefly Poles, Slovaks, Irish, Germans, and Italians, and predominantly Roman Catholic. Churches served as the cultural and social centers of ethnic neighborhoods, in which working-class communities celebrated baptisms, weddings, ethnic festivals, and holidays (St. Patrick's Day, Columbus Day, and Pulaski Day), attended funerals, played bingo, and sent their children to parochial schools. Wartime expansion of the Gulf Coast petroleum industry opened refinery jobs to working-class Mexican men, but they still faced occupational discrimination and harassment from Anglo foremen and fellow workers. Companies chiefly relegated Mexicans to the unskilled, lowest-paying, and least desirable jobs in plants.

Historically, oilworkers have been one of the least organized groups of industrial workers in the United States. Although earlier unions appeared in the Eastern fields after the Civil War, the first national oilworkers' union, the International Brotherhood of Oil and Gas Well Workers (OGWW) of the American Federation of Labor (AF of L), formed in Ohio and Indiana in 1899. During World War I, the AF of L-affiliated Oil Field, Gas Well, and Refinery Workers Union (OFGWRW), chartered in 1918, organized oilworkers in Kansas, Oklahoma, Texas, and California. Standard Oil Company, Gulf Oil Corporation, and other major petroleum companies refused to bargain collectively with oil unions and practiced antilabor tactics, such as hiring rural White Texans and Mexican immigrants to break strikes in the Southwest. Petroleum companies sponsored corporate welfare programs (pensions, sickness and accident compensation, medical benefits, and company unions) in order to defuse unionization and to generate worker loyalty. As late as 1933, less than one-tenth of the nation's one million oilworkers were organized. One of the greatest periods of union growth occurred between 1933 and 1934, spurred by a series of New Deal labor legislation. The Oil Workers International Union (OWIU), formed in 1936 as an affiliate of the Congress of Industrial Organizations (CIO), organized fields and refineries in the Southwest during the late 1930s. OWIU membership doubled between 1941 and 1946, encouraged by the pro-union policies of the National War Labor Board. In 1955 the OWIU merged with the Gas, Coke, and Chemical Union to form the Oil, Chemical, and Atomic Workers Union (OCAW), and since the 1960s the union has focused chiefly on worker safety and health issues in its organizing campaigns and national contracts.

Before World War II, living conditions in Southwestern oil-field camps and boomtowns were often primitive, uncomfortable, and unsanitary. Families lived in makeshift housing of all sorts, including shacks, tents, trailers, and abandoned railroad cars and buses. Single men sometimes slept in boardinghouses and company bunkhouses. Beginning in the 1920s, some of the major oil corporations provided workers and their families with company housing, which usually consisted of shotgun houses with outdoor toilets. Inadequate water supplies and improper sewage disposal caused outbreaks of dysentery, typhoid, and other diseases. Oil boomtowns were generally overcrowded and bustling places with a few stores, cafes, saloons, and hotels clustered along an unpaved main street. Other common types of boomtown businesses included hamburger stands, chili parlors, filling stations, dance halls, and brothels.

Local farmers and small-town residents frequently looked down upon and ostracized transient oilworkers and their families, calling them "oil-field trash." Participation in churches, social clubs, and school activities served as an important route for oil-working families to achieve the desired level of respectability. Religious denominations of Southwestern oil-field workers included Baptist, Methodist, Church of Christ, Lutheran, and Roman Catholic, and congregations sometimes built churches on land donated by oil companies. The high rate of mobility among oilworkers often meant a series of relocations, adjustments, and hardships, as families withdrew their children from school, packed up their household belongings, and traveled to the next job. In oil-field camps and boomtowns, social and kinship networks were not as strong as those in more settled areas because of the transient nature of oil work. Nevertheless, oil-field people developed close-knit communities, in which neighbors borrowed from one another, relied upon one another for child care, and contributed money or food goods to those families who suffered hard times, sickness, or a death. Oil-field families frequently socialized together at Saturday night house parties and Sunday afternoon barbecues where couples danced to music and drank homemade beer. Others found diversions in dance halls, beer joints, tent shows,

motion pictures shows, and company-sponsored baseball teams. Oil-field culture has greatly admired the values of aggressiveness and toughness symbolized in high school football, a sport that retains an enormous fan following in Texas. Workers also have demonstrated a strong loyalty to the state's college and professional teams, including the University of Texas Longhorns, the Dallas Cowboys, and the Houston Oilers.

Southwestern boomtowns offered workers plenty of amusements on which to spend their leisure time and hard-earned money. Oil-field workers were notorious for their drinking, gambling, fighting, and generally rowdy behavior, but, in some ways, their legendary bouts of drinking on payday helped foster a sense of community and solidarity among them. Occupational custom, for instance, dictated that a roughneck who made a mistake on the job (known as a "boll weevil stunt") had to buy a round of drinks for his crew. But drinking was also often destructive to workers' health and family life, resulting in chronic alcoholism, broken marriages, and countless incidents of domestic abuse. After the repeal of Prohibition in 1933, the Southwestern oil boom spawned the creation of honky tonks and roadside beer joints located on the outskirts of small towns, where working-class patrons could drink, dance, and listen to country-western music. The region's oil-field culture also produced a handful of country-music stars—such as Hank Cochran, Lefty Frizzell, George Jones, and Don Williams—who once worked, or whose fathers worked, as drillers and roughnecks.

Oil-field workers throughout United States possess a distinct occupational language consisting chiefly of technical terms and slang words. The argot of this almost exclusively male culture is peppered with obscene terms and sexual imagery, as in the terms "ass scratchers," "bastard file," "bull prick," "candy ass," "cow's cock," "mother fucker," "pecker neck," "suck ass," and "weed whore." Technological innovation in the petroleum industry has contributed to changes in occupational jargon and to competition between certain groups of workers. For example, as the superior technology of rotary drilling rigs (which employ a revolving drill bit attached to the end of a string of pipe) began after 1901 to replace the older cable-tool method of drilling (which operates by means of a suspended cable that repeatedly lifts and drops a drill bit) in the Southwest and California, the rivalry between rotary drillers and cable-tool drillers sparked a verbal contest of insults. Cable-tool drillers derided rotary drillers as "swivel necks," "chain breakers," and "rig runners," while rotary drillers responded by calling their rivals "jarheads," "rope chokers," and "yo-yo drillers."

Nicknames are also popular among oil-field workers as crew evaluations of a fellow worker. Nicknames, some of them obscene, usually reflect a man's physical appearance, behavior, specific job, work habits, or native city or state (Tiny, Fort Worth Red, Alabama Joe, Mope Pole Slim, Big Hole Bill). State rivalries between oilworkers led to the coining of a host of colorful nicknames as well. During the 19th century, Pennsylvanians referred to West Virginians as "snake-hunters" or later simply as "snakes." West Virginians returned the favor by lampooning Pennsylvanians as "starving owls" or "horse thieves."

Other pejorative labels included "scissorbill" to denote Illinois drillers, "yellow hammer" for Ohioans, and "prune picker" for Californians.

Traditionally, occupational pranks and practical jokes have been a hallmark of oil-field workers. In the late 20th century, seasoned members of a drilling crew still might send an inexperienced man (known as a "boll weevil") to retrieve such fictional tools as "pipe stretchers" or "left-handed monkey wrenches." Roughnecks also perform a host of initiation rites to test the mettle of a new recruit, to demonstrate to him his ignorance of oil-field custom, and—if judged worthy by the other men—to ceremonially induct him into the crew. In one rite, known as "lifting," crew members smear the genitals of an unsuspecting "boll weevil" with a sealing compound used in drilling. Another rite consists of tricking a blindfolded novice into destroying his own safety helmet with an axe. Jokes told by oil-field workers are often scatological and include stereotypical characters such as the roughneck, the driller, the farmer, and the prostitute. According to Jim Harris, contemporary oil-field jokes from the Llano Estacado region of Texas-New Mexico are frequently about Arabs, reflecting the importance of the Middle East in petroleum production (Harris 1982).

The tall tales and stories of the Southwestern oil fields indicate that skill, physical strength, and endurance are prized by workers. Gib Morgan, a cable-tool driller, is the best-known oil-field hero in the Southwest. Morgan, who was born in 1842 in western Pennsylvania, followed the oil boom across the nation during the latter half of the 19th century. Along the way, he told stories of his hair-raising oil-field experiences, and eventually he himself became the protagonist in a family of tall tales once known to many drilling crews throughout the Southwest and California. Paul Bunyan, who came to represent rotary drillers, replaced Morgan as the chief oil-field hero sometime between 1910 and 1920. Tall tales about Bunyan, who was imported from the Northwest woods to the Southwestern oil fields, describe him as a rig builder, pipeliner, or tank builder. John Lee Brooks and other field collectors compiled only fragmentary accounts of Bunyan tales, however. Another oil worker superman, Kemp Morgan, a rotary driller whose sensitive nose allowed him to smell oil underground, appears to be the creation of writers rather than of drillers and roughnecks.

Folklorists and collectors have located only a handful of occupational songs from Southwestern oil-field workers. Mody Boatright collected the full texts of only two songs, an untitled one about a luckless roughneck and another about "The Dying Toolie" (also known as "On the Allegheny Shore"). "There was some singing in the oil fields and attempts were made to compose songs about oil field people and their work," Boatright explained in *Folklore of the Oil Industry,* "but none of the efforts was of sufficient appeal to maintain more than brief and local distribution" (Boatright 1963:155). According to Boatright and Richard M. Dorson, the transient nature of the oil-field work force and its high rate of turnover disrupted any sort of tradition of occupational songs. Several oilworker songs have been preserved on commercial sound recordings, however. There are at least two oil-union songs in existence, although their composer was not himself an oilworker. In 1942 the OWIU commissioned the Almanac Singers, a folksong group of political radicals headquartered in New York City, to write and record two songs "combining union-building strategies with win-the-war sentiments" (Green 1993:210). Woody Guthrie, a member of the group and an Oklahoma native familiar with oil-field work, composed "Boomtown Bill" and "Keep That Oil a-Rolling" for the assignment. Guthrie also wrote another song, probably around this time, called "Boomtown Gallyhouse" about a pipeliner's sexual adventures in a Borger, Texas, brothel. Several songs from the post–World War II era, most of them performed in a country-western style, capture the occupational jargon and nature of work in the Southwestern oil fields. In 1953, for instance, Ramblin' Jimmie Dolan recorded a version of "Tool Pusher on a Rotary Rig" for Capitol Records, while Jimmy Simpson cut "Oilfield Blues" for Republic Records. Former oilworker Alex Zanetis' album *Oil Fields* (1964) contains a dozen songs about work and life in the Southwestern oil fields, including "Roughneck," "Tool-Pusher," and "Wildcats from San Antonio."

Patrick Huber

References

Brooks, John Lee. 1928. Paul Bunyan: Oil Man. In *Follow de Drinkin' Gou'd,* ed. J. Frank Dobie. Texas Folklore Society Publication No. 7. Austin: Texas Folklore Society, p. 44–54.

Dignowity, Hartman. 1927. Nicknames in Texas Oil Fields. In *Texas and Southwestern Lore,* ed. J. Frank Dobie. Texas Folklore Society Publication No. 6. Austin: Texas Folklore Society, pp. 98–101.

Dorson, Richard M. 1973. Oil Drillers. In *America in Legend: Folklore from the Colonial Period to the Present.* New York: Pantheon, pp. 214–234.

Green, Archie. 1993. Woody's Oil Songs. *In Songs about Work: Essays in Occupational Culture for Richard A. Reuss,* ed. Archie Green. Folklore Institute Special Publication No. 3. Bloomington: Indiana University Press, pp. 208–220.

Harris, Jim. 1982. Oil Field Jokes from the Llano Estacado. In *T for Texas,* ed. Francis E. Abernethy. Texas Folklore Society Publication No. 44. Dallas: E-Heart, pp. 213–218.

Northrup, Clark S. 1903–1904. The Language of the Oil Wells. *Dialect Notes* 2:338–346; 373–393.

Olien, Roger M., and Diana Davids Olien. 1982. *Oil Booms: Social Change in Five Texas Towns.* Lincoln: University of Nebraska Press.

———. 1986. *Life in the Oil Fields.* Austin: Texas Monthly Press.

Pond, Frederick R. 1932. Language of the California Oil Fields. *American Speech* 7:261–272.

Winfrey, James W. 1944. Oil Patch Talk. In *From Hell to Breakfast,* ed. Mody C. Boatright and Donald Day.

Texas Folklore Society Publication No. 19. Austin: Texas Folklore Society; Dallas: Southern Methodist University Press, pp. 139–148.

See also Morgan, Gib

Opossum

Small, omnivorous, tree-climbing American marsupial. When in 1608 Captain John Smith described the female opossum as having "a head like a Swine, and a Taile like a Rat, and . . . the bigness of a Cat," further observing that "under her belly she hath a bagge where she lodgeth, carrieth, and suckleth her young," his English audience must have dismissed the account as one more example of the captain's renowned gift for hyperbole. But in this instance, Smith's observations were not exaggerated: from its wide toothy grin to the tip of its scaly prehensile tale, the Virginia opossum *(Didelphis virginiana)* presents an unusual combination of physical and behavioral characteristics securing it a unique place in American folklore. Possessed of more teeth and less cranial capacity relative to its size than any other mammal, subject to a death-like trance when threatened, and adorned with a bifurcated penis in the male and a pouch and double uterus in the female, it is no wonder that the opossum is celebrated in narrative, song, and belief.

It was not only European explorers who marveled at the creature. The name "opossum" (usually shortened to "possum") derives from the Algonquian *apasum,* meaning "bright beast," referring to the striking silvery luster given its pelt by white guard hairs. Choctaw legend explains the size of the creature's mouth as a permanent grimace of pain and embarrassment at having been duped by other animals into singeing the fur off its once-beautiful tail. Joel Chandler Harris drew on African American etiological narrative to offer a different explanation in Uncle Remus' tale "Why Mr. Possum's Tail Has No Hair" and also relates an account of the origin of "playing possum" in "Why Mr. Possum Loves Peace."

Although the opossum is found in most regions of the continental United States, it is symbolically and folklorically most strongly associated with the Southeast, its original habitat. As with traditional esoteric and exoteric attitudes toward the South as a whole, a curious duality suffuses traditional attitudes toward the opossum, who is seen as both foolish and sagacious, vulnerable and persistent, aggressive and defensive, shiftless and resourceful. In Southern Anglo and African American song lyrics, "The possum is a cunning thing, he travels in the dark; / Nothing at all disturbs his mind, till he hears old Ranger bark." The naive yet penetrating wit portrayed in the newspaper cartoon character of Pogo Possum, Walt Kelly's Huck Finn–like denizen of Okefenokee Swamp, effectively represents this complex set of cultural associations.

The vulnerability of the opossum to the forces of industrialization in the form of the automobile is a byword: At truck stops throughout the South, one can purchase novelty items purporting to be "canned roadkill" or "roadkill jerky," with possum invariably listed as a predominating ingredient. In fact, the opossum is hunted and trapped for both its hide and its meat, although neither is considered of high value. As food,

the opossum is treated in the manner of most small furbearers such as raccoon, groundhog, or muskrat: It is braised, roasted, or fricasseed, commonly accompanied by sweet potatoes.

Perhaps the oddest belief associated with the opossum is the once widespread notion that conception is achieved by the male ejaculating into the nostrils of the female, who then sneezes the sperm into her pouch or vagina—a misimpression no doubt suggested by the bifurcate structure of the male organ, and the female's habit of nosing herself in the process of grooming. It has been suggested that this belief may have direct antecedents in a similar set of beliefs, dating at least from classical Greek natural history, concerning the oral gestation of bear cubs, who were believed to be born a formless mass from the female's mouth, then licked into shape.

Erika Brady

References

Hartman, Carl. 1921. Traditional Belief Concerning the Generation of the Opossum. *Journal of American Folklore* 34:321–323.

Schwartz, Charles W., and Elizabeth Schwartz. 1981. *The Wild Mammals of Missouri.* Columbia: University of Missouri Press.

Wilson, Charles Reagan. 1989. Opossum ("Possum"). In *The Encyclopedia of Southern Culture,* ed. Charles Reagan Wilson and William Ferris. Chapel Hill: University of North Carolina Press, pp. 389–390.

Oral-Formulaic Approach

A major approach to the study of oral tradition and of works with roots in oral tradition that prescribes a specialized language or idiom as the basis of composition in performance. Also known as the Parry-Lord theory after its founders, this approach puts a premium on the utility of patterned phraseology *(formulas),* typical narrative scenes *(themes),* and largescale organization *(story-patterns)* in providing ready solutions to the performer's ongoing challenge of maintaining fluent, intelligible composition. In addition to applying the theory to living traditions, chiefly poetry, scholars have retrospectively analyzed ancient and medieval works to determine the extent of their dependence on such paradigms and, in some cases, their "oral" or "literary" character. With typical structures demonstrated in more than 130 separate language areas, the most pressing question has become how to interpret works composed in this specialized idiom.

The oral-formulaic theory began with Milman Parry's pioneering studies of the Homeric epics, the *Iliad* and the *Odyssey,* which reveal systematic patterning behind the recurrence of particular phrases, especially noun-epithet expressions like *podas ôkus Achilleus* ("swift-footed Achilleus") and *thea glaukôpis Athênê* ("goddess bright-eyed Athena"). Instead of explaining the great epics as either conglomerate editions of smaller poems (according to the Analyst school) or as the personal and individual achievements of a single genius (the Unitarian school), Parry argued that a poetic diction as systematized as the language of the Homeric poems must be the legacy of generations of bards, who perfected the idiom over centuries. His fundamental insight was thus that the language of Homer was traditional.

The core of Parry's theoretical proposal was the formula, which he defined as "an expression regularly used, under the same metrical conditions, to express an essential idea" (Parry 1971:13), and which he eventually enlarged beyond the noun-epithet phrase to include any metrically determined unit of Homeric diction. Thus, recurrent expressions for speech-introduction (such as "And so he/she spoke"), for example, were shown to combine with recurrent names for mortals or gods to produce predictable—and, in terms of oral-formulaic theory, useful—hexameter lines.

For Parry, utility in formulaic diction derived from the participation of individual phrases in larger, generative *formulaic systems,* groups of items fitting the same metrical slot that are also related by common semantic and syntactic features. While this aspect of the poetic idiom furnished the composing poet a flexibility in line-to-line construction, the simplicity of the diction was attributed to an overall *thrift*—"the degree in which [a formulaic system] is free of phrases which, having the same metrical value and expressing the same idea, could replace one another" (Parry 1971:276). Formulaic language was, therefore, understood as serving the poet's needs not only in providing ready solutions, but also in productively limiting compositional options.

This approach began as an analytical procedure to prove the traditional nature of ancient Greek texts. But Parry, under the influence of his mentor, Antoine Meillet, and of Matija Murko, a Slovenian academic familiar with South Slavic epic poetry from his own fieldwork, soon added the criterion of *orality* as a necessary implication of the traditional character of verse making. In order to confirm his hypothesis of an oral tradition from which the Homeric poems stemmed, Parry and his assistant, Albert Lord, conducted a large-scale fieldwork expedition to the former Yugoslavia in the period 1933–1935 (continued by Lord in 1950–1951 and later) to study the living phenomenon of the South Slavic oral traditional epic at first hand. They recorded acoustically or by dictation more than a half-million lines of epic from preliterate *guslari* (bards; those who play the *gusle* [a single-stringed lute]), now deposited in the Milman Parry Collection of Oral Literature at Harvard University; Lord and David Bynum have published selective contents in the series *Serbocroatian Heroic Songs* (*SCHS,* 1953–).

Aside from a few shorter papers, Parry did not live to carry out the comparative analyses of Homer and South Slavic epic that he had envisioned. After Parry's death in 1935, Lord assumed responsibility for that planned enterprise and, in fact, moved well beyond the original analogy to make the oral-formulaic theory a truly multidisciplinary undertaking.

The most influential of Lord's writings, in many respects the touchstone for the entire field, is *The Singer of Tales,* completed as his dissertation in 1949 and published in 1960. This book uses the *guslar* in performance as a model for Homer, and also for Anglo-Saxon, Old French, and Byzantine Greek narrative poets. In addition to illustrating formulaic composition in the South Slavic songs, *Iliad* and *Odyssey, Song of Roland, Beowulf,* and *Digenis Akritas,* he also described narrative units called *themes,* or "groups of ideas regularly used in telling a tale in the formulaic style of traditional song" (Lord 1960:68). These included, for example, such typical actions as arming a hero, readying a horse, summoning guests to a wedding or battle, and so on. He also identified *story-patterns* that were coextensive with the work as a whole, the most familiar example being the Return Song, essentially the story of the *Odyssey,* that also appears in Turkish, Bulgarian, Albanian, Russian, medieval English, and other traditions (Lord 1960:99–123, 242–259). At every level, the key concept is multiformity, the mutability of phraseological or narrative patterns within limits, as an aid to composition in performance.

Of Lord's later contributions, Volumes 3–4 (1974) of *SCHS* and *Epic Singers and Oral Tradition* (1991) stand out as exemplary. The first of these consisted of his translation and Bynum's edition of *The Wedding of Smailagic Meho,* a 12,311-line oral epic performed for Parry and Lord in 1935 by the preliterate singer Avdo Medjedovic of Bijelo Polje in Hercegovina. The latter volume is a collection of some of Lord's most wide-ranging and important essays, treating Homer, South Slavic, Finnish, Old English, Bulgarian, and central Asiatic epic.

In the wake of the publication of *The Singer of Tales,* the Parry-Lord theory underwent vigorous translation to Old English (Olsen 1986–1988), Middle English (Parks 1986), Old French (Duggan 1973), Hispanic (Webber 1986), American folk preaching (Rosenberg 1970), Biblical studies (Culley 1986), and scores of other areas; it also continued to expand in ancient Greek (Edwards 1986–1992). A history of the comparative methodology is available in John Miles Foley's *The Theory of Oral Composition* (1988); an annotated bibliography, in his *Oral-Formulaic Theory and Research* (1985), with updates in the journal *Oral Tradition.*

With formulas, themes, and story-patterns identified in traditions worldwide, new questions began to arise about the implications of oral-formulaic theory for interpretation, especially in relation to texts with extensive prior critical histories, such as the Homeric poems. One of the central tenets of the approach as originally stated held that a certain percentage of formulas and formulaic systems constituted proof of the ultimately oral provenance of a given text, independent of any supporting testimony for that claim. The reasoning proceeded from the criterion of utility: If a poet had regular recourse to ready-made diction and narrative patterns, then he or she was composing traditionally, and thus orally. Quantitative measurement of this sort did not take into account the inevitable differences among languages, traditions, or genres, nor did it consider the persistence of the formulaic idiom after the introduction of writing.

Indeed, as the oral-formulaic theory has expanded to more and more traditions, many of them still living, it has become increasingly apparent that an absolute dichotomy of oral versus written does not fit the evidence. Manuscript works that presumably represent freestanding compositions by individual authors still show extensive use of the formulaic language, and different rules govern the structure and texture of formulas and themes from one language to another, or even from one genre to another. Additionally, the issue of performance and all that it entails has come to the fore: Oral tradition presents many channels for communication (linguistic, paralinguistic, and nonlinguistic), only a limited number of which are reflected in what we conventionally reduce to a transcribed text.

Another area in which the theory has been modified is in response to the charge of mechanism—that is, the perception that formulas and themes imprison a verbal artist, restricting originality and diluting expressivity. Although based primarily on literary criteria, not all of them applicable to oral tradition, this objection has stimulated a reexamination of what is meant by the "essential ideas" of formulas and the "typical" content of themes. One proposed answer to the quandary consists of understanding the oral-formulaic idiom as a highly focused species of communication, one that encodes complex information in simple forms within the enabling event of performance and by institutionalized reference to the immanent tradition. By employing this special register of language, in other words, performer and audience (and later writer and reader, if properly prepared) communicate with greatly enhanced economy. Of course, the traditional language cannot accomplish all of the quotidian tasks normally assigned to a much more generalized register, but, as long as audience and reader are fluent in the traditional tongue, its dedicated function promotes a unique economy of expression and reception.

John Miles Foley

References

Culley, Robert C. 1986. Oral Tradition and Biblical Studies. *Oral Tradition* 1:30–65.

Duggan, Joseph J. 1973. *The Song of Roland: Formulaic Style and Poetic Craft.* Berkeley: University of California Press.

Edwards, Mark W. 1986–1992. Homer and the Oral Tradition. *Oral Tradition* 1:171–230, 3:11–60, 7:284–330.

Foley, John Miles. 1985. *Oral-Formulaic Theory and Research: An Introduction and Annotated Bibliography.* New York: Garland.

———. 1988. *The Theory of Oral Composition: History and Methodology.* Bloomington: Indiana University Press.

———. 1990. *Traditional Oral Epic: The Odyssey, Beowulf, and the Serbo-Croatian Return Song.* Berkeley: University of California Press.

———. 1991. *Immanent Art: From Structure to Meaning in Traditional Oral Epic.* Bloomington: Indiana University Press.

———. 1994. *Word: Power, Performance, and Tradition.* Bloomington: Indiana University Press.

Lord, Albert B. 1960. *The Singer of Tales.* Cambridge: Harvard University Press.

Olsen, Alexandra Hennessey. 1986–1988. Oral-Formulaic Research in Old English Studies. *Oral Tradition* 1:548–606, 3:138–190.

Parks, Ward. 1986. The Oral-Formulaic Theory in Middle English Studies. *Oral Tradition* 1:636–694.

Parry, Milman. 1971. *The Making of Homeric Verse: The Collected Papers of Milman Parry,* ed. Adam Parry. Oxford: Clarendon.

Rosenberg, Bruce A. 1970. *The Art of the American Folk Preacher.* New York: Oxford University Press.

Webber, Ruth H. 1986. Hispanic Oral Literature: Accomplishments and Perspectives. *Oral Tradition* 1:344–380.

Organizational Folklore

Folklore about organizations or originating in organizational settings (especially the workplace), and folklore forms as instances of organizing. Organizational-folklore studies emerged in the late 1970s with the growing interest in modern and urban folklore and a broadening of the conception of folk groups to include office personnel and management. In addition, more folklorists found employment in government, discovering firsthand the value of organizational skills and the problems of bureaucracies. And many folklorists began to realize that the bulk of traditions in the organized workplace owe their existence to, and reflect, forces in the organization as a whole.

Urban legends include numerous beliefs and stories about government and big business. Jan Harold Brunvand notes that one of the first examples of urban folklore to be scrutinized for its origins and veracity was "The Wordy Memo." From at least the 1940s to the present, various sources have reported that the Lord's Prayer has 56 words, the 23rd Psalm 118 words, and Lincoln's Gettysburg Address 266 words, but a recent U.S. government directive on pricing cabbage (or fruit) allegedly contains a daunting 26,911 words. Other accounts describe classic foul-ups in paper shuffling, obscure government offices with no current function, and massive military orders. Such stories charge inefficiency, wastefulness, mismanagement, or ineptitude. Even if unfounded in their specifics, the legends point to problems typical of bureaus and the bureaucratic model of organization. Confirmed instances of military suppliers charging outrageous prices for a hammer, a washer, or a toilet seat, and government warehouses glutted with equipment and spare parts, make the legends credible.

Some narratives about business organizations probably originate in actual experiences, according to Gary Alan Fine, who has examined successful lawsuits claiming contamination of bottles of Coca-Cola (and other products) with decomposed mice, putrid peanuts, and so on. Other stories, however, appear to be projections. One subtype of "The Kentucky Fried Rat" legend describes a woman eating fried chicken while watching television at home. Because of the extra crispy coating, it takes her a few bites to realize she is chewing on a rat; a disgruntled employee at the franchise cooked it as a prank. In another subtype, a young man's date dies of strychnine poisoning that had killed the fried rat she unwittingly consumed; unsanitary conditions are to blame. Fine hypothesizes that these narratives "reflect some of the basic anxieties of our times" as America moves from a personalized economy to a bureaucratized, mass-consumption economy. "Because of the impersonality of large institutions," Fine writes, "employees do not feel morally attached to their supervisors or to those served." Rats and mice as contaminants are apt symbols of the decline of community and morality.

Several narrative types concern Third World products. Some report the horror of a customer trying on garments in a discount store and discovering a snake in the arm of an imported coat or sweater. Others allege that Mexican workers urinate into bottles of Corona beer shipped to the United States, giving the beer its bright yellow color and copious foam. Some contend that a finger has been found in a can of *menudo* (Mexican tripe soup). Fine suggests that these accounts express Americans' anxiety over the (dangerous) invasion of foreign goods and the threat to U.S. industry by competitors abroad. (When the contamination rumors surfaced in 1987, Corona beer was the fastest-growing imported brew and quickly becoming a high-prestige product.)

Redemption rumors imply American corporate beneficence: Sending the pull tabs from aluminum cans, tags attached to tea bags, or empty cigarette packages to the corporation allegedly sponsoring the program will result in the purchase of a kidney dialysis machine for a child, an iron lung, a wheelchair, or other medical equipment for a needy person. Fine speculates that such rumors reveal more about the tellers than the organizations—that is, people may be seeking redemption from their own unhealthful habits.

Stories, rumors, and beliefs indicate ambivalence toward business: While some portray corporations as beneficent, others present the corporation as evil. In the late 1970s, rumors spread that Proctor and Gamble's logo (the profile of a man-in-the-moon figure facing left toward thirteen stars) contains satanic symbols, that the company supported demonic cults, and that the founder or a subsequent president had made a pact with the devil. Rumors circulating in the mid-1970s charged that Adolph Coors Company is a Nazi organization. Church's Fried Chicken supposedly is in league with the Ku Klux Klan and sprinkles its food with a substance that causes sterility in Black males. The deceptive corporation is another theme (allegedly Kool-Aid is carcinogenic, Pop Rocks explode, BubbleYum chewing gum is made from spiders' eggs).

Folklore surrounds particular companies. This may be due to the "Goliath effect" (Fine's term), which occurs when a company becomes the symbol for the industry or all business because it is large or familiar. Sometimes, however, a company trait or image lends itself to the generation of folklore. International Business Machines (IBM) Corporation became legendary for its strict dress code, anonymous committees making group decisions, and "strong" corporate culture. A persistent rumor asserts that "IBMers" gather to sing company songs; some people claim to possess or to have seen the songbook. One example of photocopylore purports to be a reprint from IBM Song Book Form No. 30–8798–0–8–12–53–P. It contains the words to "Hail to the IBM" and "Ever Onward." The first song salutes T.J. Watson (IBM's founder), for whom "our voices swell in admiration." The second also honors "our friend and guiding hand." It avows: "We're bound for the top to never fall! / Right here and now we thankfully / Pledge sincerest loyalty / To the corporation that's the best of all!"

In addition to folklore about government, industry, and business, organizational folklore includes traditions generated within institutions. Like individuals everywhere, people in organizations engage in superstitious behavior, especially in times of stress. In November 1983, executives of Japanese-based TDK Corporation (one of the largest manufacturers of audio- and videotapes), asked a Buddhist priest to bless its U.S. headquarters after a run of misfortune (an armed robbery, the death of an employee's child, several automobile accidents, marital discord, and falling corporate profits). The priest sang, burned incense, and said payers. "A blessing cannot hurt," observed one employee. "We can all gain from the experience—if nothing but a common unity."

During the recession in the early 1990s, many people carried talismans with them when making sales pitches and presentations. One banker who had recently joined a company in a Manhattan high rise insisted that he not be assigned an office on the nineteenth floor or be given a phone number with nineteen in it. Adam Rose, vice president of a real estate firm, swapped phones with a colleague so he could have the extension 6789, a number that "has been good to me." When he chaired Mark Cross and Company, George Wasserberger inadvertently arrived at an important meeting wearing one black and one brown shoe; the meeting proved quite successful. In the early 1990s, as president of Stotter Division of Graduate Plastics Company, he intentionally wore mismatched shoes to crucial meetings.

Others have avoided bad luck omens, such as the number thirteen. Brokers and traders noted that 1987, the year of the stock market crash, contained three Friday the Thirteenths (the most that can occur). Although not called superstitions, numerous beliefs and conventional wisdom ranging from what the firm's financial goals should be to how marketing should be done become cherished assumptions on which executives base corporate strategies.

Certain stories cut across organizations and industries. In one, a high-status person breaks a company rule and is challenged by a subordinate (who may or may not be aware of the transgressor's identity); the high-status person does or does not comply (and may react by either complimenting or firing the subordinate). For example, Thomas Watson Jr., the intimidating chairman of IBM's board, wore the wrong clearance badge when embarking on a tour of a security area in the company. His entourage looked on in horror as the young, female supervisor barred his entrance (with trepidation, however, for she recognized him). Watson calmly waited until someone brought him the correct identification. As the story was told at Revlon, the head of the company refused to sign in in the morning like everyone else. Challenged by the new receptionist, Charles Revson inquired if she knew him. When she said no, he told her, "Well, when you pick up your final paycheck this afternoon, ask 'em to tell ya."

"The Rule-Breaking Story" is one of several types found in a wide variety of private and public organizations. Among others are "Is the Big Boss Human?" "How Will the Boss React to Mistakes?" "Can the Little Person Rise to the Top?" and "How Will the Organization Deal with Obstacles?" Positive versions of the stories portray the organization as uniquely good and enable employees to identify with it; negative versions depict the institution as unworthy of its employees. While some stories that are remarkably similar might have originated polygenetically (have multiple origins) because they treat universal concerns, many probably result from monogenesis (single origin) and diffusion through space and time.

Photocopylore proliferates; often the logo of one institution has been cut off, and the document copied onto the letterhead of another organization. Fake memos attributed to the Personnel Office set forth new rules, policies, or procedures. One describes a restroom trip policy involving an accounting and control system to avoid wasted time. Employees receive a limited number of trip credits each month to use the restrooms; these have been equipped with automatic flushing, tissue-roll retraction, and door-opening devices as well as surveillance cameras (to document unauthorized access). The memo concludes by noting that "the college remains strongly committed to finding technical solutions to management problems" and that "we believe our trusted employees will do the right thing when given no other choice!"

Another memo describes a work-force reduction plan, which includes a program called RAPE (Retire Aged Personnel Early). Employees may request a review of their status prior to forced retirement in a phase called SCREW (Study of Capabilities of Retired Early Workers). "All employees who have been RAPE'd and SCREW'd may then apply for a final review" called SHAFT (Study of Higher Authority Following Termination). Employees may be RAPED'd once and SCREW'd twice but "get the SHAFT as many times as [name of the organization] deems appropriate." A popular photocopied item depicts a person with an enormous screw through the torso along with the words: "Work hard and you shall be rewarded." Much photocopylore focuses on stress points in organizational life and areas of strain occasioned by chafing rules, loss of control over individual freedom, the lack of recognition for personal achievement, and the uncertainties or inequities in promotion practices.

Some folklore originates in situations of ambiguity or from feelings of ambivalence. In the railroad, airline, and telephone industries, ambiguity arises from the fact that these occupations are services. Porters, flight attendants, and telephone operators perform in subordinate roles providing obvious or seemingly mundane services. They must work as a team, and they justifiably consider what they do to be important, but sometimes supervisors and the public alike underrate them. Employees must appear pleasant and helpful, no matter their true feelings. Strained relations, interpersonal conflict, and stress may result. According to Jack Santino, people express their dissatisfaction, their "outlaw emotions," through fictive narrative forms such as stories in which a telephone lineman throws a pie in the boss' face or an airline attendent dresses down a captain or spits out a snappy retort to an insulting passenger. The narratives identify and define situations of subordination and hostility and provide symbolic ways of coping with emotions.

Rituals, rites, celebrations, and ceremonials abound. Organizational rites of passage include ceremonies welcoming new employees, celebrations on being promoted, rituals honoring achievement, and ceremonial banquets for retirees. Other rites or rituals range from degradation to enhancement, renewal, conflict reduction, and integration. People celebrate holidays at work, sometimes even minor ones or each others' birthdays. Much can be inferred about "climate" (the tone and tenor of the workplace) from observing what forms and examples of folklore are present or absent.

Jargon, traditional expressions, and oft-used metaphors also reveal feelings, attitudes, values, and assumptions in an organization. Sports, military, and cowboy metaphors have quite different connotations from gardening, family, and music metaphors. Frequent use of such metaphors probably reflects organizational philosophy or leadership style and likely reinforces ways of thinking, behaving, and responding to people and events.

The concept of organizational folklore also includes many folklore forms and examples as instances of organizing. Festivals, parades, religious ceremonies, family reunions, and annual clambakes require organized effort if they are to occur and be judged satisfying. Most family outings, sandlot basebase games, impromptu picnics, and birthday parties are spontaneous organizations. They exemplify organizing in its fundament: people cooperating, channeling resources, and distributing roles and activities for a designated purpose. It scarcely matters that their goals are social and aesthetic rather than pragmatic. What does matter is that they tend to evoke feelings of enjoyment, meaningfulness, and fellowship, while too often the experience of formal organization results in the desire for such feelings and frustration in not having them. In sum, the study of organizational folklore can reveal much about traditional expressive behavior, particular organizations, and the nature of organization.

Michael Owen Jones

References

Brunvand, Jan Harold. 1984. *The Choking Doberman and Other "New" Urban Legends.* New York: W.W. Norton.

Dundes, Alan, and Carl Pagter. 1978. *Work Hard and You Shall Be Rewarded: Urban Folklore from the Paperwork Empire.* Bloomington: Indiana University Press.

Fine, Gary Alan. 1992. *Manufacturing Tales: Sex and Money in Contemporary Legends.* Knoxville: University of Tennessee Press.

Jones, Michael Owen, ed. 1990. Emotions in Work. *American Behavioral Scientist* (Special Issue) 30 (January-February).

———. 1991. Why Folklore and Organization(s)? *Western Folklore* 50:29–40.

Jones, Michael Owen, Michael Dane Moore, and Richard Christopher Snyder, eds. 1988. *Inside Organizations: Understanding the Human Dimension.* Newbury Park, CA: Sage.

Martin, Joanne, Martha S. Feldman, Mary Jo Hatch, and Sim B. Sitkin. 1983. The Uniqueness Paradox in Organizational Stories. *Administrative Science Quarterly* 28:438–453.

See also Occupational Folklore; Urban Legend; Xeroxlore

"The National Ouija Board: You Ask, Ouija Answers." Washington, DC, 1920. Library of Congress.

Ouija

A board game and folk-magic artifact commonly used as a medium for divination and/or communication with discarnate entities. Ouija—a compound of the French and German words for "yes"—was invented in 1892 by American Elijah J. Bond. He sold his patent to William Fuld, "The Father of Ouija," who popularized the product. Fuld sold the patent to the Parker Brothers company in 1966. The game equipment consists of a miniature table with a small window built into the top, and a board with the letters of the alphabet, the numbers zero through nine, and the words "yes" and "no" written on it. Participants rest their fingers on the miniature table, which moves around the board to spell out messages.

Although the Ouija board bears similarities to earlier divinatory devices, it was regarded as a harmless parlor game unrelated to the occult until Pearl Curran, a prominent figure during the World War I–era spiritualism revival, began touting Ouija as a tool for divining the future, finding lost objects, seeking daily advice, and contacting spirits. Soon thousands of Americans were using Ouija to check up on their loved ones fighting in Europe.

Ouija has slipped into association with older, marginalized folk-religious practices, such as dowsing, crystal gazing, and Tarot, engaged in by those not fully exposed to, or fully impressed by, America's chief competing worldviews of scientific thought and orthodox Christianity. Tales of fantastic events and eerie sensations experienced by many who use Ouija boards are common in modern American folklore. Despite being repeatedly debunked by the efforts of the scientific community, and denounced as a tool of Satan by conservative Christians, Ouija remains popular among many (mostly young) Americans. In the midst of these controversies, Parker Brothers maintains that its product is merely a board game.

Serious occultists tend to regard Ouija as a toy that is too "commercial" for their purposes, and many spiritualists have turned to other methods of accessing disembodied beings. Rebellious Christian youth may make up the largest section of the Ouija board market. In some regions of the United States, as many as 50 percent of fundamentalist Christian youth have participated in, or at least observed, the practice of Ouija. Instead of turning to Satan, or becoming mentally deranged and violent—as their pastors warn that they might—these teenagers have frightening encounters with "evil forces" that reconfirm the conservative Christian cosmological notion that the devil and his demons are actual beings who work through such devices. After such experiences, Christian teens rarely tamper with Ouija again, and they gain a renewed commitment to their faith. For Ouija to continue to serve this beneficial function in Christian culture, it must remain marginalized and condemned by the very culture that it benefits.

Eric Eliason

References

Baskin, Anita. 1992. The Redemption of Ouija. *Omni* (December): 101.

Covina, Gina. 1979. *The Ouija Book*. New York: Simon and Schuster.

Outlaw

An often ambiguous legendary figure whose actions, although outside of, or in opposition to, an established power structure's laws, are supported by an ardent constituency. The designations "outlaw" and "criminal" are sometimes synonymous in common speech, but not in American folklore. The Harpe brothers, who slaughtered settlers on the trans-Appalachian frontier; Indiana's Belle Gunness, who murdered immigrant

Norwegian bachelors; North Carolinian Tom Dula, who killed his lover; and Milwaukee's Jeffrey Dahmer, who cannibalized his victims—all have been memorialized in folklore as unequivocally bad. Invoked as threatening figures to control unruly children, or in bloody legends, moralistic ballads, and dark humor, such people are presented, by virtue of their evil or demented actions, as enemies of any social order and obvious criminals.

America's most notable folk outlaws, however, are firmly rooted in, and advocates for, communities with long-standing grievances against the prevailing government. Reviled as criminals by the haves, they are just as forcefully celebrated as heroes by the have nots. Their heroic characterizations often bend reality toward ancient and widely dispersed folk-outlaw traditions.

Folk outlaws have flourished for centuries in stratified societies marked by injustice. European Americans of peasant descent, for example, sustained songs and stories of such Old World outlaws as Willie Brennan, Janosik, Marko Kraljevic, and Robin Hood. As Eric Hobsbawm demonstrates, their composite legend is exemplified most fully by Robin Hood, who is forced into outlawry by injustice, rights wrongs, takes from the rich to give to the poor, kills only in self-defense or for just revenge, never leaves his community, is admired and supported by his people, cannot be killed or captured by fair means, and is not the enemy of just authorities, but of local oppressors (Hobsbawm 1969).

While Robin Hood championed 12th-century Saxon peasants against Norman nobles, America's Robin Hoods had other friends, other foes, other contexts. Jesse James opposed banks and Yankee carpetbaggers in the name of Missouri hillfolk and ex-Confederates. Morris Slater (Railroad Bill) countered racist White bosses in Reconstruction Alabama. Gregorio Cortez defied Texas Rangers against the backdrop of early-20th-century Anglo-Mexican conflict. Pretty Boy Floyd sought vengeance against the banks that foreclosed on "Okie" farmers beset by Dust Bowl and Depression. As individual embodiments of collective resistance, these outlaws became the subjects of folksongs and stories celebrating, and sometimes exaggerating, their courage, marksmanship, humor, cleverness, and gallantry. Their initial local fame, earned at significant historical moments, became amplified through the news media and an array of commercial productions.

The career of John F. Deitz, like those of better-known American outlaws, epitomizes the combination of the Robin Hood pattern, a dramatic sociopolitical context, and the embellishments of journalists and entrepreneurs. A family man and pioneer farmer in northwestern Wisconsin, Deitz ran afoul of the law when he defied a large logging corporation by refusing to allow the sluicing of timber through a dam on his property. From 1906 through 1910, Deitz repeatedly foiled armed posses sent from the county seat by lumber barons and their corrupt local officials. He justified his actions through speeches in nearby communities and letters to regional newspapers that combined fiery rhetoric with earthy humor often cast in verse:

There is a place of great renown
That is known by the name of Hayward town,
Where an evil gang of whiskey bloats
Holds graft by buying Indian votes.

To show what regard they have for the laws,
'Tis even claimed they vote the squaws;
And every squaw that they can hire
They dress her up in male attire.

Surrendering in 1910, after an attack on the farmstead endangered his family, Deitz was sentenced to prison.

There was, however, a prolonged public outcry. Beyond his local following, Deitz won wider attention by symbolizing the Progressive Era's commonfolk sentiment against the greed and might of "robber barons." On Sunday, October 16, 1910, the *New York Times* offered a lengthy illustrated story under the headline "Why Dietz, Outlaw, Defied a State and an Armed Posse." The *Times'* dramatic juxtaposition of the "Lumber Trust" and the "owner of a dam" was echoed in popular culture. Deitz's wounded daughter appeared at packed tent shows with lantern slides; a paperback, *The Defender of the Cameron Dam*, went through several editions; and a melodrama of the same name was "the most popular vehicle on the midwestern circuit." Deitz was eventually pardoned by Wisconsin's governor.

Although John F. Deitz is all but forgotten, folk outlaws have hardly vanished from American life. In the late 20th century, Leonard Peltier, an American Indian activist, resides in prison decades after a reservation gun battle with federal agents. Besides a compact disc of songs in his defense, Peltier is suggested by characters in Louise Erdrich's novel *Love Medicine* (1984) and in the film *Thunderheart* (1992). Vilified by the powers-that-be, Peltier is proclaimed a hero by many native peoples and their sympathizers.

James P. Leary

References

Coates, Robert M. 1930. *The Outlaw Years.* New York: Macaulay.

Hass, Paul H. 1974. *The Suppression of John F. Deitz: An Episode of the Progressive Era in Wisconsin.* Madison: State Historical Society of Wisconsin.

Hobsbawm, Eric J. 1969. *Bandits.* London: Weidenfeld and Nicolson.

Roberts, John W. 1989. *From Trickster to Badman: The Black Folk Hero in Slavery and Freedom.* Philadelphia: University of Pennsylvania Press.

Steckmesser, Kent L. 1968. *The Western Hero in History and Legend.* Norman: University of Oklahoma Press.

See also Billy the Kid; Cassidy, Butch; Cortez, Gregorio; James, Jesse Woodson; Stagolee

Outsider Art

The visual-art products of individuals whose art training and social and economic circumstances lie clearly outside the mainstream art establishment. The term was coined in the 1970s by British scholar Roger Cardinal, who used it to describe the visual art created by inmates in mental institutions. Outsider art is created by self-taught individuals, often inspired by dreams, visions, or religious experiences. Outsider art, connected to neither academic systems of aesthetics nor folk traditions, is created typically to adorn the artist's personal environment and is often obsessive.

Since the late 1970s, outsider art has become particularly popular with gallery owners and art collectors and has been the subject of a number of museum exhibitions. Most of these exhibitions have focused on the work of artists from the Southeastern United States, many of them African American. Among the most recognized outsider artists are Howard Finster (Georgia), Sam Doyle (South Carolina), Moses Tolliver (Alabama), Mary T. Smith (Mississippi), Clyde Jones (North Carolina), Thornton Dial (Alabama), Z.B. Armstrong (Georgia), Charlie Lucas (Alabama), Bessie Harvey (Tennessee), and Royal Robertson (Louisiana).

In academic discourse, outsider art is also labeled visionary, self-taught, idiosyncratic, naive, primitive, found, grassroots, isolate, and folk. There have been continuing debates surrounding the use of the label "folk" to describe art that seems to have no traditional community grounding and surrounding the perceived pejorative connotations of some of the other labels.

Henry Willett

References

Cardinal, Roger. 1972. *Outsider Art.* London: Studio Publishers.

Glassie, Henry. 1989. *The Spirit of Folk Art.* New York: Harry N. Abrams.

Manley, Roger. 1991. Separating the Folk from Their Art. *New Art Examiner* 19 (1):25–28.

Metcalf, Eugene. 1992. American Folk Art and Cultural Meaning. In *North American Material Culture Studies: New Directions,* ed. Gerald Pocius. Canada: Institute for Social and Economic Research.

Patterson, Tom, ed. 1989. *Outsider Art. Arts Journal* (Special Issue) 14 (12).

See also Art, Folk

Owen, Mary Alicia (1850–1935)

Ethnologist, folklorist, and writer. Born in St. Joseph, Missouri, Owen developed a lifelong interest in the folktales she heard in her youth from the African Americans, Native Americans, and other cultural groups in the St. Joseph area. She was educated in private schools and attended Vassar College in 1868–1869. On her return to St. Joseph, she began her writing career with columns on early settlers for the *St. Joseph Saturday Democrat* and later published short stories in *Century* magazine and *Overland Monthly.*

Continuing her collecting activities, Owen worked extensively among the Indian tribes across the Missouri River from St. Joseph, often spending several days at a time with them. Many years later, she wrote in a notebook, now with a collection of her artifacts in the Missouri State Museum in Jefferson City, "I dare say I was a hundred times among the Musquakie between 1881 and 1898. . . . I had much trouble getting my collection. We were always dodging those white idiots the government sent out. They seemed to think dancing was devil worship. Folklore and ethnology had not made much headway then."

After reading Charles Godfrey Leland's *Algonquin Legends of New England* (1884), Owen realized that she had heard some of the same stories in northwest Missouri and northeast Kansas. She sent him a selection of her tales, and Leland encouraged her to continue her work. At his suggestion, she attended the 1891 International Folklore Conference in London, where she presented a paper on "Missouri Negro Traditions," which was enthusiastically received and resulted in the publication of her first book, *Old Rabbit the Voodoo and Other Sorcerers* ([1893] 1969). In preparing her book for publication, she depended on Leland for advice but resisted his pleas not to use dialect so that the tales would be comprehensible to English readers, believing it was important to render the language in which the tales were told as accurately as possible.

Continuing correspondence with the Folk-Lore Society of England about her work among the Native American tribes in the St. Joseph area led to the publication of her second book, *Folk-Lore of the Musquakie Indians of North America and Catalog of Musquakie Beadwork and other Objects in the Collection of the Folk-Lore Society* (1904). Owen was an honorary member of the Sac Indian tribe and of the Folk-Lore Society of England as well as a life member and councilor of the American Folklore Society and active in numerous other societies concerned with folklore research. When the Missouri Folk-Lore Society was established by H.M. Belden in 1906, she became a charter member. She served as president of the society from 1908 until her death in 1935, developed an active St. Joseph group of society members, and presented numerous papers on an eclectic range of subjects at society meetings. She was never able to get together the collection of African American and Native American tales promised Belden, but when his *Ballads and Songs Collected by the Missouri Folk-Lore Society* was finally published in 1940, it was dedicated to her in recognition of her many contributions to the society and her achievements as a folklorist. She was responsible for the collection of a body of tales and the documentation of folk practices that would have been lost without her pioneering efforts.

Rebecca B. Schroeder

References

Allcorn, Mary Elizabeth. 1986. Mary Alicia Owen: Missouri Folklorist. *Missouri Folklore Society Journal* 8–9:71–78.

McNeil, William K. 1980. Mary Alicia Owen: Collector of Afro-American and Indian Lore in Missouri. *Missouri Folklore Society Journal* 2:1–14.

Owen, Mary Alicia. [1893] 1969. *Old Rabbit the Voodoo and Other Sorcerers.* New York: Negro University Press.

————. 1920. Social Customs and Usages in Missouri During the Last Century. *Missouri Historical Review.* 14:176–190.

Ozarks

Eroded mountainous area in the south-central United States. Although most native Ozarkers will likely say there is total agreement on where the geographical boundaries of the Ozarks are, the reality is quite different. There is much disagreement on the region's boundaries, and any two "experts" are likely to provide different boundary lines. This situation results because there are many different means, including geographical, geological, political, and cultural, of determining where boundaries should be drawn. This has resulted in both an exclusive and an inclusive determination of just what land area to include in the Ozarks. If one takes the former tack, the Ozarks consists mainly of most of northern Arkansas and most of southern Missouri. Most scholars, however, consider the Ozarks a much broader area consisting of the above-named areas plus most of eastern Oklahoma, a portion of southeastern Kansas, and most of southwestern Illinois. If one accepts this formulation, it is possible to say that the Ozarks is bounded on every side, more or less, by a river. On the north is the Missouri; on the east, the Mississippi; on the south, the Arkansas; and on the west, the Neoshoa. Setting the boundary lines in this inclusive manner creates a region of more than 60,000 square miles, an area larger than the state of Arkansas.

A question frequently asked is, "Where does the name Ozark come from?" It is easy to answer, because no one really knows. There are a number of theories, mostly involving an anglicization of a French phrase. One argument maintains that "Ozark" is derived from a French phrase *bois aux arc,* meaning "wood for bows." The thesis is that when the first Europeans, the French, came into the region now known as the Ozarks, they found the Indians had bows that were incredibly strong. These were made from the wood of the *bois d'arc* tree, also known as the Osage orange. Soon these Frenchmen began applying the term *bois auc arcs* to the entire region. If one takes the most inclusive definition of the region's boundaries, on a map the Ozarks looks somewhat like an arc. So, it is suggested, the phrase *bois aux arcs* was a pun as well. Over time it became shortened to *aux arcs* and then eventually to *Ozarks.*

A second theory about the origin of the name holds that it comes from a geology book published in 1776 by a German named Abraham Gootlob Werner (1750–1817). Among other things, Werner said that the world had two types of rock: aqueous rock formed by the action of water, and azoic rock formed by the action of fire. According to this hypothesis, when Europeans came into the Ozarks they found much azoic rock in the region. Because on a map the region resembled an arc, it became known as the *azoic arc,* later the *Ozarks.*

A third theory about the origin of the name—the one most people accept—says that it derives from a type of short-hand used by early French settlers. When traveling into a territory, frequently they would note in their journals where they were going by abbreviating long Indian tribal names. For example, they might refer to a hunting expedition as *aux Kans,*

meaning that it was made into the territory of the Kansas Indians. According to this thesis, the terms *aux Arks* and *aux Os* referred to expeditions into the territory of the Arkansas and Osage Indians—the region now known as the Ozarks—and the two terms were eventually anglicized to the present word.

While it is not known where the word Ozark originated, there is no doubt about when it first became widely used to refer to the region; that occurred in the early 19th century. In 1809 an English traveler named John Bradbury became the first person to use the name in print. Six years later, in 1815, government explorer Stephen H. Long was the first to use the term "Ozark Mountains" on a map; for that reason, he is generally credited by historians with making the name official. Yet, Henry Rowe Schoolcraft (1793–1864), "the Father of American Folklore Scholarship," did more to popularize the name outside the region. In 1818–1819 he made a trip into the Missouri and Arkansas Ozarks in search of lead mines, and he kept a detailed diary of his journey. This manuscript, published in London in 1821, contains several references to the region as the Ozark Mountains. After the 1820s, people generally referred to the region simply as the Ozarks.

How can one characterize the culture of the Ozarks? First, the Ozarks is dominated by the culture of the Upland South, being influenced primarily by migration from eastern Tennessee, western North Carolina, eastern Kentucky, southwestern Virginia, and northern Alabama. The major period of movement from those areas into the Ozarks occurred from 1840 to 1860. There were several reasons why this migration occurred at this time, not the least being that the antebellum years were a time when Americans were moving west. In 1790 only 5 percent of the people in the United States lived west of the Appalachian Mountains; by 1850 that number increased to nearly 50 percent. People tend to migrate to places that look much like the place they left, and to those coming from southern Appalachia, the Ozarks was the first place they came to in their trek westward that looked much like the southern Appalachian Mountains they had left. Others came because family members who were in the Ozarks wrote and invited them. Finally, the offer of land grants to descendants of Revolutionary War and War of 1812 soldiers obviously lured many people to the Ozarks.

Although the southern Appalachian mountaineers have been the most influential cultural group in the Ozarks, it is inaccurate to think, as some do, of the Ozarks as Appalachia West. Numerous non-Appalachian cultural groups exist in the region, and there were three major waves of migration into the Ozarks that occurred before 1840. The first, that of the American Indian, began about 12,000 B.C. and continued until A.D. 1835. During that time, there are six periods of Indian migration into the Ozarks, beginning with the Paleo-Indian Period, which lasted from 12,000 B.C. to 8,000 B.C. These earliest tribesmen were roving hunters who sought game in the Missouri and Mississippi River Valleys. About 8,000 B.C. the Dalton Period began, distinguished not only by hunting but by the gathering and preparing of seeds, roots, and fruits for foods. This was followed by the Archaic Period, from approxi-

A man plays a mussel-shell fiddle: two hollowed-out boards, glued together. Lanagan, Missouri, 1930. Photo Vance Randolph. American Folklife Center.

mately 7,000 to 1,000 B.C. During this era, ground stone tools and a greater diversity of chipped tools appeared. Next came the Woodland Period, from 1,000 B.C. to A.D. 900. During this period, the Indians made pottery from clay, crushed bone, or crushed limestone, and they constructed burial mounds. The bow and arrow came into common use, and pipes and ceremonial smoking became widespread. This period was followed by the Mississippian Period that lasted until 1700. Known as the era of the village farmer, this era of Indian occupation consisted of less nomadic, more settled village life. The final era of Indian history in the Ozarks is the Historic Period, from 1700 to 1835, the period of European contact. While most of the tribes who lived east of the Mississippi and traveled west spent some time in the Ozarks, when one speaks today of Ozark Indians one is generally speaking of the Osage, who came into the region about A.D. 800.

Despite the long period of Indian occupation, the Native Americans left little imprint on the cultural landscape of the Ozarks. Some place names, a few folk arts and crafts, and some pseudo-Indian legends constitute the sum of their cultural impact there.

The second major migration into the Ozarks was by Frenchmen in the early 18th century. These migrants, who established permanent settlements in the 1720s, were seeking lead mines and precious metals; they succeeded in the first quest but not in the second. Like the Indians before them, the French left little lasting imprint on Ozarks culture, their main long-term contribution being a number of place names. Not so the Germans, who began moving into the Ozarks in large numbers during the 1830s. Much of this movement was facilitated by the German author Gottfried Duden, who wrote a popular book, *Bericht über eine Reise nach den westlichen Staaten Nordamerikas* (Report on a Journey to the Western States of North America) (1829), that painted an Edenic picture of life in the Missouri Ozarks. Unlike the French and the Indians, the Germans have been considerably influential on modern-day Ozarks culture, although their impact has been greater in Missouri than in other parts of the region. Place names, settlement patterns, agriculture, and religion constitute their major lasting contributions.

Another characteristic of Ozarks culture is that it is rural, far more so than the southern Appalachians, with which the Ozarks is frequently compared. This is not to suggest that there are no urban areas in the Ozarks—clearly there are, the Springfield and Joplin regions in Missouri being two examples; rather, it is to emphasize that the daily tenor of life in the Ozarks is rural. A final characteristic is that Ozarkers have a well-defined sense of place. While there may not be general agreement on exactly where the boundaries of the region lie, there is little doubt about who is and who isn't an Ozarker. One is an Ozarker only if one was born there (preferably his or her parents were also born there), and everyone else is someone "from off." This generally is more of a joking distinction than anything else, but there are some Ozarkers who take such matters very seriously.

Although in stereotype the Ozarks, along with the southern Appalachians, are viewed as *the* places where one encounters folklore, that assumption is both correct and partly wrong. It is correct in that the Ozarks does have much folklore, but it is wrong in that no single place or locale has a corner on folklore; *all* places have folklore, and all are thus fertile grounds for collecting folk traditions. Probably one reason the stereotype exists is because a great deal of folklore has been intentionally collected in the Ozarks since the late 19th century. Even so, the collecting has been spotty, with much more attention given to folksongs and ballads and to folk narratives than to other genres.

The vast majority of the collecting has been carried out by amateurs, hardly surprising since until after World War II there were no academically trained folklorists turned out by American universities. The best known of all Ozarks folklore collectors is Vance Randolph (1892–1980), who, beginning in the early 1920s and continuing until the 1950s, collected material used in approximately twenty books that covered a variety of folklore genres. Calling Randolph an amateur is not to denigrate the quality of his work. He was an amateur only in the sense that he had no formal training in folklore. His various publications are valuable, and were in keeping with scholarly standards at the time of his collecting. The first academically trained folklorist working in the Ozarks was Alexander Haggerty Krappe (1894–1947), who taught at a college in the Missouri Ozarks during the 1940s. Krappe, however, was mainly a theoretician and library scholar, not a fieldworker. In 1960 Herbert Halpert spent a year teaching at the University of Arkansas, Fayetteville, and was the first field-oriented academic folklorist to spend time working in the Ozarks.

W.K. McNeil

References

McNeil, W.K. 1995. *Ozark Country*. Jackson: University of Mississippi Press.

Miller, E. Joan Wilson. 1968. The Ozark Culture Region as Revealed by Traditional Materials. *Annals of the Association of American Geographers* 58:51–77.

Randolph, Vance. 1932. *Ozark Mountain Folks*. New York: Vanguard.

———. 1972. *Ozark Folklore: An Annotated Bibliography*. Columbia: University of Missouri Press.

Randolph, Vance, and Gordon McCann. 1987. *Ozark Folklore: An Annotated Bibliography*. Vol. 2. Columbia: University of Missouri Press.

Rayburn, Otto Ernest. 1941. *Ozark Country*. New York: Duell, Sloan, and Pearce.

Rossiter, Phyllis. 1992. *A Living History of the Ozarks*. Gretna, LA: Pelican.

P

Paper Cutting

Traditional decorative and usually ephemeral cut-paper figures. Paper cutting is a minor folk art in the United States with a long background in foreign traditions. The art probably originated in T'ang dynasty China about A.D. 900 (a date by which paper was surely invented), although some scholars date it as early as the Han dynasty (2nd to 3rd century B.C.).

Today Chinese people produce elaborate cut-paper figures as both patterns for other arts, such as embroidery, and especially as inexpensive, exquisite decorations for ordinary houses during festivals. Using a prepared stencil atop many layers of thin rice paper and a thin knife, folk artists cut many copies at once. The delicate cuttings are then painted, sometimes naturalistically, and are generally fastened to windows, though sometimes to walls or notecards, for a brief show of beauty in a dusty world.

Colloquially known as *chuang hua* (window flowers), they often depict lucky flowers such as the lotus or the peony; red flowers are favored for the Spring Festival (Chinese New Year), and blue or red ones for the annual Moon Festival in autumn. Other favorite subjects are birds or folktale characters like the Eight Immortals or the Rabbit who lives in the Moon.

Paper cutting as a folk art appeared in Europe by the 17th century, where it developed regionally into several distinctive styles. Early examples in German-speaking areas are *Kloisterarbeit* (elaborately cut and painted frames for religious pictures and dictums). In central Europe and North America, similar elaborate *Scherenschnitte* (scissors cuttings) were produced by folding the paper once for bilaterally symmetrical designs, or many times for radially symmetrical designs (snowflakes), and cutting with scissors. Eighteenth-century German examples from both Europe and North America show a continuation of paper cuttings' religious purposes, such as marriage or baptismal certificates *(Taufschein)*. By the 19th century, *Scherenschnitte* was being used for love letters, valentines, patriotic sayings, and as Christmas decorations. Snowflakes were used as doilies and as fancy shelf paper.

Single cuts—silhouettes—of scenes or portraits enjoyed enormous popularity through the 19th century in Europe and America, and their execution as a paper-cutting art was part of every educated person's talents, and certainly part of every middle-class home's decoration.

An especially elaborate version of collage paper cutting called *wycinki* developed in Poland in the mid-19th century. The artist cut either a single figure such as a rooster or a peacock or an elaborate snowflake base, then applied layer after layer of brightly colored paper feathers or flowers to the form, creating brilliant collages. While most were used as wall decorations for the ordinary home, many were particularly designed for Christmas.

Paper cutouts are the favored Christmas decoration for many Scandinavians, especially in Denmark, where at Christmas every windowpane, mantle, and Christmas tree may be covered with decorative red cutouts. Cut from heavy paper with a craft knife, they feature birds, Christmas trees, *nisse* (Christmas elves), candles, and, in Denmark especially, the ubiquitous woven paper hearts. Many are created from two identical cutouts that are fastened together at right angles to form three-dimensional figures. Children learn to make cutouts early in their lives and continue it well into adulthood.

Large paper banners with cutouts of skeletons are found among Mexican folk artists as decorations for the Day of the Dead on All Souls' Day and All Saints' Day in late October and early November. Generally two or more feet square, the *papel picado* is punched out of bright tissue paper with chisels of varying sizes. The artist draws a pattern, places it on the top sheet of a pile, then, working on a fabric-covered table, cuts as many as fifty at a time; some smaller pieces are still cut in the "old style" with scissors. The banners feature skeletal musicians, dancers, and animals cavorting against a paper grid within an elaborate floral frame. In some regions, religious themes of angels and crosses are preferred to the skeletons. During the festival, the banners decorate homes, shops, churches, and special home altars honoring the dead.

Elsewhere in the world, similar traditions of ephemeral decorations or patterns made from paper-like substances are also

"Shakespeare." Paper cutting, 14.5 x 10.5 cm. Ohio, probably 1860s. Collection J.W. Love.

found. There is a tradition of cut birchbark among Ojibwa and Chippewa women, who used the single-folded, symmetrical cutouts as a basis for beadwork designs or occasionally as toys and amusements for children. In all likelihood, similar cut patterns were used as the base for quilled or moosehair embroidery prior to the availability of glass beads. Frances Densmore also reported a tradition of birchbark biting, in which a design was bitten part way into a folded piece of birchbark (Densmore [1928] 1974). When the bark was opened, a symmetrical design—often geometric, but occasionally figural—appeared through a transparent layer of intact bark. These punchouts were used as windows, and the light pouring through them created a pleasant design. Other reported uses of paper and bark cutting among Native Americans include carefully worded reports of sorcery and cut-paper dolls among some Mexican people like the Otomi.

In North America, paper cutting continues as a folk art, as in Christmas snowflakes, children's paper dolls and toys, painting stencils, and needlework patterns, specifically those for appliqué quilt designs. Furthermore, with the revival of interest in traditional arts in the 20th century, many fine artists incorporated paper cutting techniques and patterns into their work. Folk-arts-revival artists reproduce and elaborate upon traditional designs, and laser technology has made mass-produced cut-paper art readily available.

Yvonne J. Milspaw

References

Carmichael, Elizabeth, and Chloe Sayer. 1991. *The Skeleton at the Feast: The Day of the Dead in Mexico.* London: British Museum Press.
Densmore, Frances. [1928] 1974. *How Indians Use Wild Plants for Food, Medicine, and Crafts.* New York: Dover.
Hawley, W.M. 1971. *Chinese Folk Designs: A Collection of 300 Cut-Paper Designs together with 160 Chinese Art Symbols.* New York: Dover.
Hopf, Claudia. 1977. *Scherenschnitte: Traditional Paper-cutting.* Lebanon, PA: Applied Arts Press.
Jablonski, Romana. 1976. *The Paper Cut-Out Design Book.* Owings Mills, MD: Stemmer House.

Parler, Mary Celestia (1905–1981)

Folklorist. Parler is recalled primarily as a longtime teacher of folklore at the University of Arkansas and as the second wife of noted Ozarks folklore collector Vance Randolph. A native of South Carolina, Parler did graduate work at the University of Wisconsin, earning her M.A. in English in 1925. Later she studied for her Ph.D. at the same school and came to the University of Arkansas in 1948, having completed all requirements for the degree but her dissertation. Although she never completed her degree, Parler did yeoman work in folklore during her long stay in Arkansas. A popular teacher, she taught literally thousands of students about folklore. In 1950 she helped found the Arkansas Folklore Society, serving as its secretary for a decade. She was also editor of *Arkansas Folklore,* the society's journal. Parler also did a great deal of field recording, and she established a large archive based on materials contributed by students in her classes.

In 1950 Parler met Randolph, and, although there was mutual attraction, they were not married until 1962. She contributed material to Randolph's books *The Devil's Pretty Daughter* (1955) and *Hot Springs and Hell* (1965), and she helped with the production of *Down in the Holler* (1953), a study of Ozarks folk speech. Parler published relatively little herself, her first effort of an academic nature being "Word-List from Wedgefield, South Carolina," appearing in 1930 in Volume 6 of *Dialect Notes.* One of her main folklore publication outlets was *Arkansas Folklore,* to which she contributed "Folklore from the Campus," ([1958] 1984), one of the earliest articles dealing with oral traditions that circulate among college students. Despite the inclusive title, Parler's essay treats only three genres: proverbs, stories and anecdotes, and beliefs.

In 1954 Parler was featured on CBS-TV in a movie titled *The Search.* This embarrassingly bad film, which was released as *Folklore Research,* is a highly romanticized account of Parler's ballad collecting. In 1975 she retired from teaching, ill health forcing her and her husband to move to a Fayetteville, Arkansas, nursing home. After Randolph's death in 1980, she moved to South Carolina, where she passed away in September 1981.

W.K. McNeil

References

Cochran, Robert. 1985. *Vance Randolph: An Ozark Life.* Urbana: University of Illinois Press.
Folklore Research (Originally aired as *The Search*). 1954. Iowa City: University of Iowa. 28-min. film.

Parler, Mary Celestia. 1958. Folklore from the Campus. Reprinted in *The Charm Is Broken: Readings in Arkansas and Missouri Folklore*, ed. W.K. McNeil. Little Rock, AR: August House, 1984, pp. 25–29.

Parody in Folklore

Verbal or visual art, usually humorous, that imitates and exaggerates features of another item already known to the audience. The parody may ridicule the target item itself and/or its genre, and thereby aspects of the official culture that it represents: established literature, religion, government, education, and the like. The parody item, like all folklore, transmutes into variant forms while being passed from individual to individual in unofficial contexts.

Parody is practiced by most, perhaps all, folk groups. However, American folklorists have so far made no overall statement concerning the concept's importance and implications. A theoretical path has been blazed by Mikhail Bakhtin, analyzing the writings of François Rabelais (d. 1553) in reference to his social context of festivals that mock authority. What Bakhtin wrote in the 1930s, about the vital function of parody in unofficial culture, was first published in the 1960s in what was then the Soviet Union (Bakhtin [1965] 1984. His ideas are just beginning to affect scholarship outside Russia. Papers on Bakhtinian topics first proliferated at the American Folklore Society meeting in 1980, for example, and at the Modern Language Association of America meeting in 1988.

Bakhtin analyzed parody performed by adults, during large-scale folk events like those sometimes staged in the United States—notably, in Philadelphia by mummers. Other parodic folklore created by American adults, although less often collected than that by children and adolescents, would include much Xeroxlore (Dundes and Pagter 1975), adaptations of popular songs (c.f. Burson 1980:311–312), tall tales (c.f. Hurston, [1935]:106–111), and jokes that skew proverbs into punch lines like "People who live in grass houses shouldn't stow thrones" or "I wouldn't send a knight out on a dog like this" (Brunvand 1963:59–61).

Children, however, readily create parodies that folklorists readily collect, document, and publish. As an indication, consider which American folksong might be the most widely performed. "Happy Birthday to You," always learned orally, probably is most often sung. But is it a folksong? It was composed and promptly copyrighted in the late 19th century; its text does not vary in transmission; it attracts parodies itself (". . . You belong in a zoo. . ."). Instead, it may well be that the most actively known American folksong—one of anonymous origins, always transmitted orally within small groups who create textual variations—is a parody of "The Battle Hymn of the Republic." In Grove City, Pennsylvania, in the late 1950s, it was sung thus:

Mine eyes have seen the glory
Of the burning of the school
We have tortured all the teachers
And have broken all the rules
The principals are after us

But we don't give a . . . *HOOT*
Our gang goes marching on
Glory, glory what's it to ya?
Teacher hit me with a ruler
I bopped her o'er the bean with a rotten tangerine
And the juice came pouring down

Researchers in American folklore need not confront most of the problems that have overwhelmed European literary critics since the 17th century, when they began futile efforts to distinguish parody definitively from related terms such as satire, burlesque, irony, lampoon, and travesty—all potentially applicable to contemporary works (Paul Scarron's *Virgile Travesty* [1634]; Samuel Butler's *Hudibras* [1663]; Alexander Pope's *Rape of the Lock* [1712]) as well as to slightly earlier ones (Goliard songs in the 12th and 13th centuries, Geoffrey Chaucer's *Tale of Sir Thopas* in the 14th century), and thence to some of the earliest literature in the Western classical tradition (the mock epic *Battle of the Frogs and Mice*; the plays of Aristophanes). Some American works, such as Mark Twain's *Connecticut Yankee in King Arthur's Court* (1989), bring elements of concurrent oral folklore to enrich parody that participates in the European literary tradition.

The American folk themselves, however, including college-educated folk, would be unlikely to use "parody" or another literary term in reference to their own creations. Thus, American folklorists have the opportunity and the mandate to collect data first, organize second, analyze third, and finally someday propose definitional boundaries based on what the folk do and say rather than on what scholars wish they would do or say.

Betsy Bowden

References

Bakhtin, Mikhail. [1965] (1984). *Rabelais and His World*, trans. Hélène Iswolsky. Bloomington: Indiana University Press.

Bronner, Simon, ed. and comp. 1988. *American Children's Folklore*. Little Rock, AR: August House, pp. 77–81 and passim.

Brunvand, Jan. 1963. A Classification for Shaggy Dog Stories. *Journal of American Folklore* 76:42–68.

———. 1986. *The Study of American Folklore*. 3d. ed. New York: W.W. Norton, pp. 235–237 and passim.

Burson, Anne C. 1980. Model and Text in Folk Drama. *Journal of American Folklore* 93:305–316.

Dane, Joseph A. 1988. *Parody: Critical Concepts versus Literary Practices, Aristophanes to Sterne*. Norman: University of Oklahoma Press.

Dundes, Alan, and Carl R. Pagter. 1975. *Urban Folklore from the Paperwork Empire*. Austin: American Folklore Society.

Hurston, Zora Neale. [1935] 1978. *Mules and Men*. Bloomington: Indiana University Press.

Knapp, Mary, and Herbert Knapp. 1976. *One Potato, Two Potato: The Folklore of American Children*. New York: W.W. Norton, pp. 161–179.

See also Humor; Poetry, Folk; Prayer

Parry, Milman (1902–1935)

Classicist, comparatist, and collector of South Slavic oral epic poetry; co-originator (with Albert Bates Lord) of the oral-formulaic theory. Parry began as a student of the Homeric *Iliad* and *Odyssey* (M.A., University of California, Berkeley, 1923; D. Litt., Université de Paris, 1928), who sought to demonstrate that these epics were the creation not of a single gifted individual but of a centuries-old tradition of verse making. Field expeditions to the former Yugoslavia, specifically to study and record the oral performances of preliterate epic singers *(guslari)*, confirmed his further thesis that such a traditional poetry must also be orally composed and transmitted.

Parry's first crucial insight was that Homer's formulaic diction (for example, noun-epithet phrases like "rosy-fingered dawn" or "swift-footed Achilleus") constituted a specialized, inherited variety of ancient Greek that served the generations of epic singers as a ready medium for tale-telling. Under the particular influence of Antoine Meillet, his mentor at Paris, and Matija Murko, a Slovenian ethnographer who spent his summers studying the *guslari*, Parry evolved a theory that the formula was the touchstone of not only traditional, but also oral, composition.

But Parry was not only a theorist, and it was typical of what he styled his "literary anthropology" that he saw the next step as a journey to what was then Yugoslavia to test his hypothesis in the living laboratory of still extant oral epic song. This fieldwork resulted in acoustic or dictated records of dozens of live performances by singers from various regions.

Parry's groundbreaking explanation of the special idiom of traditional oral epic provided a new and extremely powerful answer to the Homeric Question (Who was Homer? Did he exist? How were his works composed?), and at the same time it eventually gave rise to the interdisciplinary oral–formulaic theory, which has affected more than 130 separate language areas to date.

John Miles Foley

References

Parry, Milman, with Albert B. Lord and David E. Bynum, colls. and eds. 1953–. *Serbocroatian Heroic Songs (Srpskohrvatske junacke pjesme)*. Cambridge: Harvard University Press; Belgrade: Serbian Academy of Sciences.

———. 1971. *The Making of Homeric Verse: The Collected Papers of Milman Parry*, ed. Adam Parry. Oxford: Clarendon.

Parsons, Elsie Clews (1875–1941)

Anthropologist and folklorist. Parsons' early work was in sociology (Ph.D., Columbia University, 1899) with a focus on American family life and feminist issues. In 1912, when her interest shifted to anthropology and folklore, Parsons began making field trips to the Southwest, mainly to the Pueblo Indians. She also embarked on a study of Black narrative folklore in the Caribbean, Nova Scotia, and the Eastern and Southern United States. In 1915, as Leslie Spier, an anthropologist, said, Parsons "fell in" with Franz Boas, and the two worked closely together.

In 1930 Parsons began fieldwork in Mexico (publishing *Mitla, Town of the Souls* [1936]); and in 1940, in Ecuador (*Peguche* [1945]). She journeyed to Spain (1923), and to Egypt and Sudan (1926) in an attempt to find the point of origin for African American folktales. Parsons was a prolific publisher (twenty-eight books, four edited volumes, two translations, and well over 200 articles). Among her works in folklore were *Folk-Lore of the Sea Islands, South Carolina* (1923), *Folk-Lore of the Cape Verde Islands* (1923), *Taos Tales* (1940), and *Pueblo Indian Religion* (1939).

In 1919 Parsons served as president of the American Folklore Society; from 1923 to 1925, as the president of the American Ethnological Society; and in 1941, as the first woman president of the American Anthropological Association. Her support of these scholarly societies was also philanthropic. From 1917 to 1940, she underwrote the cost of publication for almost all of the *Memoirs of the American Folklore Society* and assumed the publication expenses for several issues of the *Journal of American Folklore*. Generous as she was, her fieldwork, publications, and encouragement of others were her main contributions to the field of folklore.

Rosemary Lévy Zumwalt

References

Zumwalt, Rosemary Lévy. 1992. *Wealth and Rebellion: Elsie Clews Parsons, Anthropologist and Folklorist*. Urbana: University of Illinois Press.

Passover

An annual weeklong Jewish holiday commemorating the deliverance of the Jews from bondage in Egypt, their Exodus into the desert, and the journey to the Promised Land—events that occurred more than 3,000 years ago. Passover signals the beginning of spring and a celebration of freedom. In the United States and elsewhere, it customarily combines sanctioned institutional beliefs and practices with folk traditions. The holiday begins with a Seder, a ritual meal, on the eve of the fourteenth of *Nisan* (a month in the Hebrew year, calculated by a lunar calendar, which explains its variation from a fixed secular date). The Seder has an ingrained continuity: According to the Torah, parents have a duty to tell the tale to children, and each Jew must feel as if he or she personally came out of Egypt.

Seder means "order," and participants read from a prayer book, a Haggadah, meaning "telling." The Haggadah contains a blend of instructions, legends, prayers, commentary, questions, and songs set in an order for following the ritual. Although Haggadahs vary in translation and tone, the sequence is constant. Thus, even if as many as five different versions are used at one table, readers recognize the portion of the text being read aloud by other participants.

The origins of Passover were two nature festivals that predate the Exodus. In ancient times, nomadic Jewish shepherds sacrificed a sheep or a goat during the spring lambing season. They smeared the animal's blood on the tent posts to ward off misfortune and ensure good luck for the coming year. This festival, observed within family groups, was called Pesach, derived from "paschal offering."

The agricultural Jews who lived in Palestine celebrated the cutting of the grain in the spring with a Festival of Matsos, or unleavened bread. They first removed all of the fermented dough and old bread made with the *chometz* (leaven) of the preceding year's crop. Then they cut the first new sheaf of grain, the omer, and a priest sacrificed it to God while the entire community attended. Agricultural groups also baked their freshly harvested grain into unleavened cakes eaten in a special ceremony to thank God for the harvest.

These early nature rituals eventually merged to symbolize the exodus of the Jewish people from Egypt—reinterpreting the Pesach sacrifice. The Egyptians suffered ten plagues when the pharaoh refused to release the Jews. For the tenth plague, when the angel of death slew the first-born of the Egyptians, the Jews marked their doors with the blood of the sacrificed animal so the angel would "pass over" their homes. The earlier meaning of the Festival of Matsos now came to symbolize the bread of affliction since the Jews did not have time for their bread to rise when fleeing Egypt.

The seder plate constitutes a table of ritual foods related to the deliverance from Egypt and brings the story of the Exodus into the present. The Pesach sacrifice reemerges as a roasted shankbone (or any roasted meat bone). In addition, a roasted egg *(chagigoh)* symbolizes a second animal sacrificed in Jerusalem. *Charoses* (a nut, cinnamon, wine, and apple mixture) symbolizes the mortar made by Jewish slaves for the pharaoh's buildings in Egypt, and the hope of freedom. Bitter herbs or *moror* (usually horseradish) symbolize the bitterness of the Jews' lives in Egypt. Greens (often parsley, lettuce, or watercress) dipped in salt water (for tears) represent the coming of spring and the hope of redemption. The table setting includes three pieces of matzo, which symbolize: (1) the unleavened bread the Jews took with them upon escaping Egypt; (2) the bread of poverty; and (3) the bread of the simple life in the desert. Participants drink four glasses of wine, which signify the fourfold promise of redemption given by God to the Jewish people: "I will bring you out; I will deliver you; I will redeem you; I will take you to me for a people" (Exodus 6:6–7). (The number "four" is a constant throughout the seder: four glasses of wine, four questions, four sons, four matriarchs of Israel, four promises, and four Pesach symbols.)

A festive meal is served during a break in the Seder. The weeklong prohibitions against leavened foods, and the family's notions of acceptability, determine the "rules" for what may be eaten. Many families serve an egg (a fertility and springtime symbol now often associated with Easter but whose ritual use is ancient) in a bowl with salt water as the first course.

Where the Haggadah lacks commentary, there are opportunities for the creation of folklore. Two examples are the traditions for welcoming Elijah, the prophet, and hiding the Afikomen, or dessert matzo. The table setting includes an empty wine glass that is not filled until the end of the meal for Elijah. (Many Jews refer to any extra chair or place set by accident as Elijah's.) After dinner, the door is opened for Elijah to enter. Families will often relate who Elijah is, and how he will return and announce the coming of the Messiah by visiting families on Passover and taking a sip of wine from the cup reserved for him. The children may be in charge of opening and closing the door and might be joshed about the level of wine diminishing.

The Afikomen must be eaten before the service commences following the meal. During the dinner, as courses are served and cleared, the children often steal this matzo hidden by the Seder leader and rehide it. The hiding and ransoming of the Afikomen follows family tradition, rather than any command in the Haggadah.

The Haggadah also does not proscribe additional prayers, but it is now customary in many families to say an extra prayer for oppressed Jews. The prayer may refer to the pogroms of Russia and Poland, the Holocaust, the Warsaw Ghetto uprising, the establishment of the state of Israel, or the plight of Jews anywhere in the world.

Passover is a metaphor for freedom and survival and serves as a source of ethnic identity. A home-centered festival, Passover, more than any other holiday, is enjoyed by both religious and secular Jews.

Sharon R. Sherman

References

Bokser, Baruch M. 1984. *The Origins of the Seder: The Passover Rite and Early Rabbinic Judaism.* Berkeley: University of California Press.

Fredman, Ruth Gruber. 1981. *The Passover Seder: Afikomen in Exile.* Philadelphia: University of Pennsylvania Press.

Sherman, Sharon R. 1983. *Passover: A Celebration.* 28 min. Eugene: Folklore Program, University of Oregon. Videorecording.

———. 1986. "That's How the Seder Looks ": A Fieldwork Account of Videotaping Family Folklore. *Journal of Folklore Research* 23:53–70.

———. 1988. The Passover Seder: Ritual Dynamics, Foodways, and Family Folklore. In *"We Gather Together": Food and Festival in American Life,* ed. Theodore C. Humphrey and Lin T. Humphrey, Ann Arbor, MI: UMI Research Press, pp. 27–42.

Weinreich, Beatrice S. 1960. The Americanization of Passover. In *Studies in Biblical and Jewish Folklore,* ed. Raphael Patai, Francis Lee Utley, and Dov Noy. Bloomington: Indiana University Press, pp. 329–366.

Patton, Charlie (Charley) (1891–1934)

Mississippi folksinger and guitarist. Of mixed Negro, White, and Indian ancestry, Patton was born in the Mississippi hill country between Vicksburg and Jackson. He was brought north to the Delta shortly after 1900 by his family, who settled on the large Dockery plantation east of the town of Cleveland, Mississippi. He began to learn guitar from neighbors near his birthplace, but he perfected his skills on Dockery's, learning to perform blues and a variety of other types of folksong from local musicians. By 1910 he was performing locally as a paid entertainer. His territory grew to encompass the entire Delta, and by the early 1920s he was the most popular blues performer from this region, a position he retained until his death. He performed all over the Delta, across the Mississippi River in Arkansas and Louisiana, and in places as far away as New Orleans, Memphis, St. Louis, and Chicago, making a substantial income as a working folk entertainer. He also served as a preacher from time to time. His music was equally popular with White and Black audiences.

Patton was married at least eight times and was known as a ladies' man, a braggart and a clown, and a frequenter of rowdy places, yet he was also highly admired for his musical talents, his charisma, and his ability to live well within a physical and social environment characterized by racial and economic oppression and limitation of opportunity. Patton made three recording sessions for Paramount Records in Richmond, Indiana (1929), and Grafton, Wisconsin (1929 and 1930), and one session for Vocalion Records in New York City three months before his death in 1934. He died of heart disease in the Delta town of Holly Ridge, where he had been living for approximately the last two years of his life.

Patton made fifty-six extant recordings under his own name, including alternate takes and rerecording of several pieces, and he played guitar on additional blues by his last wife, Bertha Lee, and fiddler Henry Sims. He was accompanied on second guitar by his longtime partner, Willie Brown, on four pieces, and on fiddle by Sims on several others. About two-thirds of his recorded repertoire consists of blues, but the remainder represents a large cross section of African American folksong. Within this group are ten spiritual recordings, including a sample of his preaching, folk ballads, ragtime tunes, and versions of popular songs. He sang in a heavy, rough voice and often played the guitar in slide style.

Patton's blues are his most famous and influential pieces. They draw musical and lyrical material both from the folk-blues tradition and from Patton's fertile imagination, usually conveying a great sense of conviction, immediacy, and spontaneity. Most of his themes are about the standard blues subjects of man-woman relationships and travel, but they also include prison, violence, bootleg whiskey, and magic. Some of his most remarkable pieces are grounded in personal experience, in which he mentions local people and events, often in a critical manner. These include accounts of the 1927 Mississippi River flood, a dry spell two years later, two jailhouse experiences, his tribulations during a railroad strike in Chicago, and his expulsion by an overseer from Dockery's plantation.

Charlie Patton was probably the first regional role model of the successful blues entertainer in the Delta, a region that has become almost synonymous with the blues. He was multitalented, mobile, independent, outspoken, famous, and respected, by far the most influential Delta blues performer in his lifetime. Beyond the Delta blues tradition, his musical influence greatly affected such diverse figures as Howlin' Wolf, a patriarch of electric Chicago blues; Roebuck "Pops" Staples, a creator of gospel "message" songs; and guitarist John Fahey,

often credited as the progenitor of New Age music.
David Evans

References

Calt, Stephen, and Gayle Wardlow. 1988. *King of the Delta Blues: The Life and Music of Charlie Patton.* Newton, NJ: Rock Chapel.

Fahey, John. 1970. *Charley Patton.* London: Studio Vista.

Patton, Charley. 1992. *The Complete Recorded Works.* Peavine PCD-2255/6/7. Compact Discs.

Sacré, Robert, ed. 1987. *The Voice of the Delta: Charley Patton and the Mississippi Blues Traditions: Influences and Comparisons.* Liège: Presses universitaires de Liége.

Pecos Bill

Fictitious cowboy character with superhuman abilities. Pecos Bill is often alleged to be a genuine folk hero of American cowboys, but both the character and his "saga" were actually created by a writer long after the heyday of open-range cattle raising. The widespread publicity given Pecos Bill occurred in popular culture and advertising rather than folk tradition. Thus, the character is clearly fakelore, not genuine folklore.

In 1923 Edward O'Reilly published the first known Pecos Bill stories, probably inspired by the logger character Paul Bunyan—whom he mentions, spelled as "Bunyon." O'Reilly incorporated some actual Southwestern tall tales into his account, and he claimed to have heard old-timers tell such tales about Pecos Bill, but folklore researchers have never been able to validate this claim. Indeed, Nathan Howard "Jack" Thorp, author of one of the best books of cowboy reminiscences, wrote in his *Pardner of the Wind* (1945): "Cowboys never developed a mythical range rider on the order of Paul Bunyan of the lumber camp, but some of their tales were as tall as the mountains in whose shadows they worked cattle."

O'Reilly wrote that Pecos Bill was born in Texas but fell out of the wagon when his family moved across the Pecos River and into New Mexico, where he was raised by coyotes. After a passing cowboy convinced the boy that he was human and not a "varmint," Bill saddled a mountain lion, used a ten-foot rattlesnake for a quirt, and rode into a cow camp looking for work. Later he raised his horse, Widow-Maker, from a colt, feeding it a diet of nitroglycerin and dynamite; another time he rode an Oklahoma cyclone without a saddle until it rained out from under him.

Pecos Bill fell in love with Slue-Foot Sue when he saw her riding a catfish the size of a whale down the Rio Grande. But when Sue rode Widow-Maker on her wedding day, she was thrown, and the steel spring in her bustle caused her to bounce higher with each fall. After she bounced for three days and four nights, Bill was forced to draw his pistol and shoot her so she would not starve to death. After reporting several other such escapades and heroic feats, O'Reilly concluded that Pecos Bill died by laughing himself to death when he met a man from Boston "wearing a mail-order cow-boy outfit, and askin' fool questions about the West."

Scores of later writers repeated and elaborated upon O'Reilly's stories, often in books written for children, and usually softening the harsher details of killing, drinking, smoking, and carousing in the original. Such details were added to the saga as that Widow-Maker had twenty-seven gaits—twenty-three forward and four in reverse. Some writers even extended Bill's adventures to Australia and Argentina. Advertisers adopted the image of Pecos Bill as emblematic of the old wild West. An illustrated version printed on the back of a box of Kellogg's Cocoa Krispies cereal stated, essentially truthfully, that "few folklore figures can match Pecos Bill's fabulous feats." His greatest fame came when Pecos Bill was featured in the 1948 Walt Disney film *Melody Time* (1948).

The only folklorist to publish Pecos Bill stories was Texan Mody Boatright in a 1934 book, but he readily credited O'Reilly's article as his source. In 1951 New Mexico folklorist Ernest W. Baughman surveyed older ranchers of the Estancia Valley (supposed "Pecos Bill Country") and found that none of them had heard oral stories about Pecos Bill. Brent Ashabranner, in a 1952 article, stated what has never been disputed, that "Pecos Bill is a synthetic product, a character invented by O'Reilly for the purpose of unifying some miscellaneous tall tales around a central character."

Jan Harold Brunvand

References

Ashabranner, Brent. 1952. Pecos Bill: An Appraisal. *Western Folklore* 11:20–24.

Boatright, Mody C. [1934] 1982. *Tall Tales from Texas Cow Camps.* Dallas: Southern Methodist University Press.

Fishwick, Marshall W. 1959. Sons of Paul: Folklore or Fakelore? *Western Folklore* 18:277–286.

O'Reilly, Edward. 1923. The Saga of Pecos Bill. *Century* 106 (6):826–833.

See also Bunyan, Paul; Cowboys; Fakelore

Peddler's Cry

The call, chant, or song of an itinerant merchant, tradesperson, market seller or street vendor. Also referred to as a "street cry." Unlike the lengthy and complex oral prose discourse or "spiel" of the pitchman, auctioneer, or medicine-show performer, the peddler's cry is generally short, metrical, and frequently rhymed. The crier may employ musical pitch, melody, ornamentation, and other forms of vocal embellishment.

Street criers draw upon a stock of traditional verbal and musical formulas that are often specific to their particular trade or mercantile occupation while developing individualistic repertoires and styles that they employ as a means of identification for themselves and their products and services. The primary function of the cry is to announce the appearance of a merchant or tradesperson and attract an audience of potential customers for the goods or services being offered. The advertisement and description of merchandise and proclamation of a selling price may constitute secondary functions. The following examples are from Texas:

> Hot tamales floatin' in gravy,
> Suit ya taste and don't mean maybe

> Watermelons, watermelons,
> Fresh off the vine,
> Get your watermelons,
> A nickel or a dime (Hurley 1953:118, 122).

The peddler's cry constitutes the most overtly expressive component of an entire complex of traditional work techniques. As such its effects may be enhanced by the performer's manipulation of work implements and items of merchandise, gesture, and other traditional semiology, and the use of horns, bells, whistles, musical instruments, and other devices, as performance markers. Street criers may also be recognized by distinct costumes or the lavishly decorated wagons, barrows and stalls from which they ply their trade.

While the cries most commonly heard in the late 20th century are those employed by the vendors of hot dogs, beer, and peanuts in baseball stadiums and similar venues, they belong to a widespread and long-standing tradition of occupational folklife. The first peddlers in America were generally European immigrants who used their success in the trade to finance the later establishment of more permanent and stable business enterprises. Their street cries, derived initially from Old World models, may occasionally be found, with illustrations, among early American broadsides and chapbooks. (Bronner 1976:3; Wright 1927:232–233)

The cries of peddlers and street merchants are immortalized in the literary creations of William Langland and Shakespeare and have inspired the composers of folk, popular, and classical music, from the anonymous creator of the famous Irish "Cockles and Mussels," through the English composer Ralph Vaughan Williams, to George Gershwin, whose *Porgy and Bess* features a variety of African American street cries.

John Ashton

References

Bronner, Simon J. 1976. Street Cries and Peddler Traditions in Contemporary Perspective. *New York Folklore Quarterly* 32:2–15.

Dargan, Amanda, and Steven Zeitlin. 1983. American Talkers: Expressive Styles and Occupational Choice. *Journal of American Folklore* 96:3–33.

Hurley, Elizabeth. 1953. Come Buy, Come Buy. In *Folk Travellers: Ballads, Tales, and Talk*, ed. Mody C. Boatright, Wilson M. Hudson, and Allen Maxwell. Austin: Texas Folklore Society, pp. 115–138.

McGill, Laurilynn. 1971. The Street Cry as an Artistic Verbal Performance. *Folklore Annual of the University Folklore Association* (University of Texas) 3:17–25.

Wright, Richardson. 1927. *Hawkers and Walkers in Early America.* Philadelphia: Lippincot.

Peer, Ralph Sylvester (1892–1960)

Pioneer recording executive and music publisher whose work documented an array of vernacular music. Born in Kansas City, Missouri, Peer, by the age of eleven, developed a fascination with recordings. Upon graduation from high school, he began working for Columbia Phonograph Company, learning every facet of the business. In 1918 he moved over to the small Okeh label and soon became its director of recordings.

In 1920 he authorized the recording of Mamie Smith, a Black songstress popular in Harlem, singing "Crazy Blues." This recording's success began a trend that led to the realization that there was a huge untapped African American market hungry for its own music.

In 1923, eager to find other regional music that would sell on records, Peer initiated the practice of conducting regional expeditions, in which he could find local talent. On his initial field trip, to Atlanta, he discovered Fiddlin' John Carson, the first of many hillbilly musicians that Peer recorded. In succeeding years, Peer combed the South, recording hundreds of rural artists, both Black and White, whose 78-rpm discs complement field recordings made by folklorists during these same years. A major difference is that Peer pushed for fresh material that he could copyright.

Peer eventually pioneered the recording of Latin American music, using the same formula he had worked out for vernacular music in the United States. Peer is largely responsible for the introduction of Latin American music to a northern audience.

Ed Kahn

References

Green, Archie. 1965. Hillbilly Music: Source and Symbol. *Journal of American Folklore* 78:204–228.

Pennsylvania Culture Region

Label used by analysts to describe an area extending from a core in south-central Pennsylvania into western Maryland and Virginia, characterized by connected cultural traditions of Pennsylvania German foodways, religions, architecture, language, and settlement. The region formed from colonial settlement after others had been established in New England, Chesapeake, and the South. Although Pennsylvania German migration came through Philadelphia and the Delaware Valley in the late 17th century, it was inland toward Lancaster and Berks Counties that the cultural region took its distinctive form. The inland region's agricultural lifestyle, ethnic connections, and relative isolation (the area formed into self-sustaining mountain and valley communities) fostered the persistence of a marked regional consciousness, although it was not as well recognized in scholarship as Southern and New England areas. In addition to major influences from Switzerland and the Palatinate Rhineland, the Pennsylvania German settlers adapted customs from English Quakers and Scots-Irish neighbors to develop a New World ethnic-regional hybrid that continues into the present.

Folklorists since the 19th century, many associated with the Pennsylvania-German Society founded in 1891 (a separate Pennsylvania German Folklore Society began operation in 1936), identified the distinctiveness of the "Dutch Country" by describing the ways that oral and material traditions integrated into a regional folklife. Traditions among the Pennsylvania Germans such as hex-sign making, Harvest Home celebrations, Eileschpiggel trickster tale-telling, powwowing (healing), and Schwabian joke telling suggested that the central Pennsylvanians held a unique place in the American cultural landscape. Beginning in the 1940s, cultural geographers used linguistic folk traditions as evidence to definitively map the limits of the region. Although the number of Pennsylvania "Dutch" speakers declined after World War II to less than 100,000, the German dialect had a profound influence on the region's speech. In 1949 Hans Kurath identified a Midland English dialect covering central Pennsylvania, western Maryland, and Virginia between well-recognized Northern and Southern speech areas.

Wilbur Zelinsky found that social traditions such as religion and settlement pattern suggested tighter boundaries than those for speech, but ones nonetheless following the general regional shape of an oval in south-central Pennsylvania extending from Altoona to Allentown and a southwestern extension down the Shenandoah Valley of Virginia (see Zelinsky 1973, 1977). Religious membership in churches of German origin such as Brethren, Lutheran and Reformed, Mennonite, and Amish churches was more concentrated in this region than any other in the United States (another area with similar Pennsylvania German settlement and religious pattern is found in Ontario). Towns in the region usually had a central square or "diamond," dense distribution of houses close to the street, and spacious alleyways. Farmsteads surrounded the towns and typically featured Pennsylvania bank barns and houses that combined German asymmetrical interior plans with English symmetrical exteriors.

In contrast to the one-level English barns set on the ground in New England, Pennsylvania barns have two or three levels with an upper level cantilevered over the lower level on the barnyard side to form an overhang called the forebay. Joseph W. Glass used frequencies of the bank barn to give the most detailed map of the Pennsylvania Culture Region to date (Glass 1986). Subdividing the region according to core, domain, and sphere, based on the model for the Mormon Culture Region in the West, Glass traced the most intensive use of the Pennsylvania barn tradition approximately from Chambersburg to Lancaster, and an encircling domain that takes in much of western Maryland. The sphere of less regional intensity extends down into western Virginia and eastern West Virginia. Henry Glassie made the argument that this sphere is the basis of a wider Middle Atlantic material culture that extended well west and influenced cultural traditions in the Midwest.

Such approaches to finding sharp boundaries of the region focus on historical continuity, and especially architectural evidence. Recent folkloristic investigation into modern-day cultural practice has shown the changing character of the region and probably a fuzzier view of regional culture based more in consciousness than in landscape. While foods served in the region—including chow chow, pot pie, scrapple, and chicken corn soup—offer an image of a wide area of influence, the round of life based on Pennsylvania German customs has moved from the "core" toward southeastern Pennsylvania to the northern edge of the domain in Schuylkill, upper Dauphin, Berks, and Northumberland Counties, where community cohesion continues. Arguments rage over whether the commercial promotion of the Pennsylvania Culture Region, known popularly as the "Dutch Country" in Lancaster County, around the former core has led to the demise or conservation of cultural traditions there. Abundant festivals and exhibitions often allow for celebrations of Pennsylvania regional consciousness to compensate for the loss of Pennsylvania German folklife in daily existence. Indeed, America's largest folk festival is the annual Kutztown Folk Festival devoted to promoting Pennsylvania German folkways, and *Pennsylvania Folklife* boasts the largest circulation for a regional folklife journal. Increasing urbanization and a diversifying mobile population have had a negative impact on maintaining a unified folk-regional integrity, although identification with regional folk customs, such as eating sauerkraut and pork on New Year's Day, and regional folk humor remains strong. Neither Yankee nor Southern, the mix of Pennsylvania German and British traditions in the Pennsylvania Culture Region has had a lasting influence on the ways that people there talk, eat, work, and play.

Simon J. Bronner

References

Bronner, Simon J. 1989. Folklife Starts Here: The Background of Material Culture Scholarship in Pennsylvania. In *The Old Traditional Way of Life,* ed. Robert E. Walls and George H. Schoemaker. Bloomington: Indiana University Press, pp. 283–296.

Glass, Joseph W. 1986. *The Pennsylvania Culture Region: A View from the Barn.* Ann Arbor, MI: UMI Research Press.

Glassie, Henry. 1968. *Pattern in the Material Folk Culture of the Eastern United States.* Philadelphia: University of Pennsylvania Press.

Zelinsky, Wilbur. 1973. *The Cultural Geography of the United States.* Englewood Cliffs, NJ: Prentice-Hall.

———. 1977. The Pennsylvania Town: An Overdue Geographical Account. *Geographical Review* 67:127–147.

See also Pennsylvania Germans ("Dutch")

Pennsylvania Germans ("Dutch")

Descendants of German-speaking immigrants from central Europe, especially the Palatinate Rhineland region of what is now southern Germany and Switzerland, who settled in southeast Pennsylvania from the late 17th to 18th centuries. The concentration of their settlements and the persistence of traditional community life inland helped foster the formation of a cultural region (often called the Pennsylvania Culture Region or, more familiarly, "Dutch Country") that has been maintained to the present day. The core of Pennsylvania German influence lies in south-central Pennsylvania, while the domain covers parts of Maryland, Virginia, New Jersey, and Delaware. The cultural influence of this Mid-Atlantic domain extends into the South and the Midwest of the United States along paths of westward migration and into parts of Canada, particularly Ontario.

Dieses Buch Gehoeret Mir Catharina Kinnig Im iahr 1898 *(This book belongs to me, Catharina Kinnig, in the year 1898). Bookplate, pen and ink and watercolor on laid paper, 17 x 9.5 cm. Artist unidentified. Library of Congress.*

Pennsylvania Germans often refer to themselves as "Dutch" (not to be confused with immigrants from the Netherlands). The term probably derives from old English usage of *Deutsch* before there was a united German nation to include a wide array of settlers from the mouth of the Rhine to its origins in Switzerland. It received reinforcement in the United States, since Dutch approximates *Deitsch* in the dialect used by German speakers from the Palatinate. Although American scholars in the late 19th century encouraged the change to Pennsylvania German, many "Dutchmen" resisted the change because they considered themselves a distinct American group, with sharp contrasts to mid-19th-century German immigrants, and, during the 20th century, to what most Americans considered a bellicose Germany. "Pennsylvania German" has received more widespread acceptance today, but "Dutch," a folk term with the connotation of endearment, is still widely used by people in Pennsylvania of Palatinate Rhineland ancestry to refer to themselves.

The early immigrants to Pennsylvania were a mixed lot that included Palatines, Swabians, Alsatians, Huguenots, Hessians, and Swiss. They mostly held affiliations with the main

Protestant traditions of Lutheran and Reformed churches and were followed by a wave of Mennonite and Amish settlement. Often the distinction is made historically and culturally between the former group, or "church people" (sometimes called "fancy Dutch") and the latter, or "plain sects." The social-religious situation becomes complex in Pennsylvania because of founder William Penn's tradition of religious tolerance and cultural autonomy. Groups including German Schwenkfelders, Seventh Day Adventists, Dunkards, Scots-Irish Presbyterians, and English Quakers wielded influence on the cultural landscape of Pennsylvania. Some small groups that traveled across Pennsylvania, such as Pennsylvania German-speaking Gypsies and Yiddish-speaking Jews (Yiddish and Pennsylvania German are related since they share a source area in the Rhineland), also figure in the ethnic relations within the Pennsylvania Culture Region. In addition, several millennialist communities with German connections emerged in the Pennsylvania Culture Region, including the Ephrata Society and the Moravian Brethren. New religious movements formed in the pluralistic Pennsylvania Culture Region, including the United Brethren, Old Order River Brethren, Evangelical Association, and Churches of God (Winnebrennerian).

Religion also played a significant role historically in the formation of Pennsylvania German identity because of a renewed effort in many central Pennsylvania communities to stress Pennsylvania German ethnicity in response to Methodist revivalism during the early to mid-19th century. Another response of ethnic consciousness in the Pennsylvania Culture Region grew when some synods of the Lutheran and Reformed churches called for use of English over German in services. The church was a central institution in most Pennsylvania German communities and provided schooling (in German) as well as social and spiritual services.

Pennsylvania German settlements were typically concentrated in the inland mountains and river valleys, although some urban centers such as Allentown, Reading, Harrisburg, Lancaster, York, and Lebanon became significant Pennsylvania German cultural hubs. Historically, Pennsylvania Germans were associated with farming and artisan trades. Many Pennsylvania Germans identify themselves by the valleys and counties in which they settled. Some examples of Pennsylvania German valley societies are Mahantango, Hegins, Lykens, Oley, and Lehigh, while significant county combinations that form cultural distinctions made among Pennsylvania Germans are Berks and Lebanon, Dauphin and Schuylkill, Lancaster and York, Cumberland and Adams, and Lehigh and Bucks.

On American soil, Pennsylvania German settlers continued a cultural-unification process that began in the Old World. Although Pennsylvania German culture includes transplants of Old World traditions, it is essentially a new regional-ethnic hybrid that developed distinctively on American soil. This process is evident in the formation of the Pennsylvania German dialect, also called Pennsylvania Dutch or Pennsylfanisch. It is based on dialects from the Rhenish Palatinate with Swiss, French, and English influences. It also has subregional variations, particularly between eastern and western portions of the Pennsylvania Culture Region and between sectarian (Amish, Old Order Mennonite) and nonsectarian speakers. Use of the dialect, once the centerpiece of Pennsylvania German identity, has diminished in the region, although it continues to be taught and used in many plain sects and northern sections of the Pennsylvania Culture Region. Estimated at more than 300,000 in 1950, the number of active Pennsylvania German speakers in 1995 was usually given as less than 80,000. Many nonspeakers of Pennsylvania German in the region display what is known as Pennsylvania German English, familiarly called "a Dutchy" or "central Pennsylvania" accent—the use of phrases in the dialect and rhythms and grammatical formations based on Pennsylvania German patterns.

The number who claim Pennsylvania German ancestry runs into millions and has influenced the spread of many Pennsylvania German traditions into American culture. Among the most familiar traditions are foodways. Pennsylvania German foods, and names for foods, such as sauerkraut, smearcase, pretzels, scrapple *(pannhaas),* corn mush, hot bacon dressing, hot salad, chicken corn soup, chicken pot pie, funnelcakes, rivvel soup, stuffed pig stomachs, *schnitz un gnepp,* and shoofly pies, continue to be popular. Some traditions are tied to holiday observations, such as the eating of *fastnacht* cakes (fried doughnuts), on Shrove Tuesday, and the consumption of pork and sauerkraut for good luck on New Year's Day. Some localized foodways traditions are reminders of variations within Pennsylvania German culture. Pennsylvania German cuisine in Lebanon County, for example, is known for its liberal use of saffron in recipes for noodles, cheese, and bread.

Pennsylvania Germans are known for a number of folk arts, many of which have been revived. *Fraktur,* for example, refers to the art of illuminated manuscripts that flourished between 1750 and 1850 and continued in Amish society to the early 20th century. These manuscripts, typically rendered by a minister who doubled as a schoolteacher, often marked rites of passage such as birth and baptism and marriage. There is a relationship between the structure of the privately illuminated baptismal certificate and the public design of carved gravestones that marked the final rite of passage. Pennsylvania German painted furniture also displays many motifs and designs, such as tulips, hearts, distelfinks, and trees of life common in *fraktur,* as well as the favorite Pennsylvania German colors of red and green (now generally associated with Christmas). Other folk arts associated with Pennsylvania Germans include *Scherenschnitte* (scissors cuttings on paper), decorated earthenware (especially plates and bowls with graffito decoration), "hex sign" painting (colorful geometric designs inside circles used for barn decorations), and embroidered textiles (such as decorative "show towels" meant to be hung over doors).

The extent of Pennsylvania German culture has often been marked by the visible imprint of ethnic architecture on the landscape. Traditions of the Pennsylvania barn and the Pennsylvania house (or Middle Atlantic farmhouse) figure prominently. In contrast to the one-level English barns set on the ground in New England, the Pennsylvania settlers built two-level bank, or forebay, barns (later developing into three levels). An upper level is cantilevered over the lower level on the barnyard side. The overhang is called the forebay (*der Vorschuss* or *der Vorbau* in dialect). On the side opposite the forebay, the barn may be built into a bank or have a ramp. The Pennsylvania German house with three or four rooms (sometimes called the Continental plan in American architectural typology) has German connections (particularly to the *Flurkuchenhaus* [hall-kitchen house]) but has its greatest expression in Pennsylvania. The oldest type is a three-room plan that has an entrance off to the right of the facade. The entrance leads into a long kitchen *(die Kich)* with a central fireplace. On the other side is a front room *(die Stupp* or *die Stube),* and behind it is a smaller sleeping chamber, storage room, or "safest room" *(die Kammer).* English fashion for the classic symmetrical two-story front, with two rooms on each side of a broad central hall, influenced the development of the Pennsylvania house. The house interior retained the Continental plan but adjusted the exterior to the symmetrical arrangement, although usually without stylish trim. Chimneys moved to the gable end, and the house was frequently built in brick and less commonly in frame in addition to the popular stucco and stone. Unlike the classic English plan, the Pennsylvania farmhouse lacked a hallway, and instead had two front doors for entrances. Settlers built the house into a bank with a subterranean cellar (used for cooking and storage of preserved food) and added long porches, sometimes on two levels, around the back. Particularly among many Amish and Old Order Mennonite farmers, the practice of house and barn raising continues according to Pennsylvania German traditions. They also build on to existing homes to create additional self-contained houses for the grandparents *(Grossdaadi Haus),* thus creating a string of different-sized plain white homes.

Beyond the Pennsylvania Culture Region, Pennsylvania German customs of the decorated Christmas tree and the Easter Rabbit have become popular throughout America. The popularity of Groundhog day, or Candlemas on February 2, when sighting of the groundhog's shadow predicts the extent of winter, also owes to Pennsylvania German belief. Other holiday traditions associated with the Pennsylvania Germans are the outdoor decoration of trees with brightly colored eggs at Easter time, Harvest Home celebrations held during the fall in Lutheran and Reformed churches, and Belsnickeling (the Belsnickel is a frightening figure who rang bells, snapped whips, and threw nuts and candy at children) at Christmas. Christmas and New Year's once featured many distinctive beliefs among the Pennsylvania Germans, including leaving food for the Crischtkindel (Christ Child), washing one's face in Christmas dew, playing the role of Belsnickel by teenagers the day after Christmas, and "shooting in the New Year" and performing orally learned blessings at *Wunsching* parties on New Year's Day. Some special customs identify religious subgroups in Pennsylvania German culture. Dunkards are known for foot washing and soups served at "Love Feast" celebrations and the Old Order River Brethren based in Lancaster County have a unique tradition among the plain sects of a bread-baking ritual during its Love Feast weekend celebration.

Pennsylvania Germans have a controversial healing tradition known as powwowing (also referred to as *Braucherei* in the dialect). Many Pennsylvania Germans denounce the practice, and the tradition is in decline, but oral-historical references to Pennsylvania German custom abound with special mention of powwowing practices. Don Yoder has commented that powwowing reflects a Pennsylvania German belief system of the "worldview of the unity of all things, heaven, earth, man, animal, and nature. Within this unity there is a dualism between evil powers, concentrated in the Devil and his voluntary servitors the witches, and good powers, concentrated in God, the Trinity, the saints, and the powwower who is the channel for healing power from source to patient" (Yoder 1990:96). Powwowing in Pennsylvania German culture relies on words, charms, amulets, and physical manipulations applied by special healers to treat animals and humans. The charms contain Biblical and Christian references, printed sources *(The Long Lost Friend* [1819–1820] by John George Hohman is the most frequently mentioned text), and oral tradition. An example is this generally used charm:

> *Die Wasser und dis Feuer,*
> *Die Wasser und dis Feuer,*
> *Die Wasser und dis Feuer,*
> *Die ist eine grosse Dinge,*
> *In dies grosses geheilige Land,*
> *Unser yunge frau Maria,*
> *Father, Son, and Holy Ghost, Amen*

> (This water and this fire,
> This water and this fire,
> This water and this fire,
> This is a big thing,
> In this big holy land,
> Our young lady Maria,
> Father, Son, and Holy Ghost, Amen)

Among the beliefs associated with powwowing is the passage of healing power from woman to man and from man to woman. Reference will also be made to use of a printed blessing called a *Himmelsbrief* to protect the house and person from harm. Many Pennsylvania Germans, not necessarily powwowers, will have a collection of herbal and folk-medical remedies, such as the use of berries, mints, and onions to relieve colds.

The Pennsylvania German folksong tradition includes a form of spiritual that combines English and German and derives from Methodist (including Pennsylvania groups such as the Evangelical Association, Church of the United Brethren in Christ, and Church of God) camp-meeting singing in the Second Awakening after the Revolutionary War. Alfred L. Shoemaker and Don Yoder dubbed this combination of hymns of German Pietism with English-language revival songs of the American Methodists and Baptists that entered oral tradition the "Pennsylvania (Dutch) spiritual," but Albert F. Buffington preferred the label of "Dutchified German spiritual" because of his linguistic analysis that the texts of the songs were neither Pennsylvania German nor Standard German. According to Buffington, the songs approximated the Pennsylvania High German *(Pennsylvaanisch Hochdeitsch)* used by Pennsylvania Germans in their churches and newspapers. In a field collection from the Mahantango Valley area (Boyer, Buffington, and Yoder [1951] 1964), the authors report that the favorite "Dutch" spiritual is "O How Lovely:" *O wie lieblich, wie lieblich / Wie lieblich iss Yeesus! / Er iss mein Erleeser, / Mei Haer un mei Freund* (Oh how lovely, how lovely, / how lovely is Jesus! / He is my redeemer, / My Lord, and my Friend). Its first three verses follow an old German hymn about wise and foolish virgins, and then it shifts to camp-meeting verses of "Oh sisters, be happy . . . It's Jesus in my soul" *(Oh Schweschdre seid dir hallich . . . Siss Yeesus in der Seel).* Yoder hypothesizes that Pennsylvania was a seedbed of American spiritual song and a "transplanting point" where the White spiritual was shared with Blacks and German settlers, with the result that two new types of spiritual arose, the Black spiritual and the Pennsylvania (Dutch) spiritual.

Secular Pennsylvania German folksongs and rhymes, by most accounts, have not thrived as well in contemporary oral tradition as the Pennsylvania spiritual. Finger rhymes, "ABC rhymes," prayers, and lullabies sung in dialect to children figured prominently in the traditional Pennsylvania German childhood. One might chant *Kleiner Finger, Dummer Finger, Langer Finger, Laus Knecker, Haver Stecker* for the different fingers, or *A, B, C, Die Katz leit im Schnee, Der Schnee geht aweg, Die Katz leit im Dreck* for the letters of the alphabet. In the field collection by Boyer, Buffington, and Yoder, adult songs of work and play were reported, especially relating to farm life, courtship and marriage, *snitzing* parties (cutting of apples for making of apple butter), and tavern pastimes. Other secular songs that gained popularity were "Dutchified" versions of English songs such as "Oh, Susanna" and composed comic songs such as *"Die Ford Maschin"* about the shock of the sight of the Model T machines to rural Pennsylvania inhabitants.

The narrative tradition of Pennsylvania Germans is vibrant but has not been widely collected. Reverend Thomas R. Brendle and William S. Troxell were pioneering collectors who issued a representative collection in translation from oral sources (Brendle and Troxell 1944). Among the categories of narrative they found were Eileschpiggel trickster stories, hidden-treasure legends, Parre (preacher) stories, "Stupid Swabians" (also Hessian and "Dumb Dutch") jokes, and legends of the Elbedritsche. The Pennsylvania German Eileschpiggel has a connection to a European trickster figure but tends to be more lovable in Pennsylvania. He is a boastful, impish character who finds ways to outwit the devil. According to one story, for example, a dispute arose as to who was stronger. The devil, to show his strength, tore an immense tree up by its roots and threw it up into the air. Then came Eileschpiggel's turn. He climbed a tree, and the devil asked, "Why are you climbing a tree?" The reply was: "I don't care to waste time in pulling up one tree. I am going to bind the tops of several trees together and then I'll pull them all out at one time." The devil gave up. The hidden-treasure legends also might include pacts with the devil for "seven brothers" in order to receive a

treasure. In various versions, the farmer—or tramp—brings seven suckling pigs, thereby outwitting the devil. The hidden-treasure legends often rely on the belief that buried treasure lies hidden under planks in old barns. A common motif is that a treasure seeker is supernaturally offered riches if he can keep totally silent during the dig, but at the moment he lays eyes on the treasure, he exclaims, "I'm rich," or some other outcry, and the money disappears.

Parre stories depict the preacher as a community folk hero possessing wit, sometimes strength, and an often unexpected earthiness or worldliness. The story is told about Reformed minister Isaac Stiehly who was hard pressed to say a kind word at the funeral of a thief. "Now," said the people, "Stiehly cannot say anything good about the dead." But they were disappointed. He closed his sermon by saying, *"Er hat seine Familie gut besorgt. Er hat sie besorgt bei Tag und bei Nacht"* (He provided well for his family. He provided for them by day and night). Another common theme is the hunting prowess of preachers. Stories of preachers spying a deer or a fox out the window of the church, hunting it quickly, and resuming the sermon are legion. They are also known for repartee, such as the exchange with the famous preacher Moses (Mose) Dissinger, who replied when asked "What are you doing today?" "Today," answered Mose, "I am going to do something the devil never did." "What is that?" asked his friend. "Leave Allentown."

The Stupid Swabian (Hessian or Dumb Dutch) is the Pennsylvania German version of numskull tales known widely in America and elsewhere. There's the commonly heard story, for example, of the Swabians who were building a church in the valley. They cut the logs for the church on the top of a mountain nearby and began carrying them down into the valley. A traveler came along and told them that they could roll the logs down into the valley and he showed them how to do this. Thereupon the Swabians fetched the logs that they had already taken down into the valley, took them back to the top of the hill, and rolled all of them down. Hessian jokes refer to the failure of the Hessians during the Revolutionary War. The story is told about the Hessian commander who led soldiers into the Dutch Country. They came upon a large heap of barnyard manure and at the command of their officer fired upon it. "There is the enemy," he had said when he commanded them to fire.

The Elbedritsche hunting legend and its enactment are the Pennsylvania German version of the snipe hunt. The Elbedritsche is described to young Pennsylvania German boys and girls as a mysterious creature who is caught in the woods with the aid of a sack. The initiate's companions take the youngster to an isolated location and leave him or her with a bag and offer instructions on calling the Elbedritsche. Usually, the initiate is consoled by the explanation that the companions will drive the Elbedritsche toward him or her. Eventually, though, the initiate discovers that he or she is left "holding the bag."

Many observers note that the continuity of Pennsylvania German culture has been disrupted by many factors in the 20th century, including increased mobility, urbanization, and development of the rural landscape (the construction of the Pennsylvania Turnpike and the growth of retail outlets are two frequently mentioned developments that affected the Dutch Country). As early as the mid-19th century, observers noted the loss of Pennsylvania German traditions, especially after compulsory education in English was legislated. Many Pennsylvania German children in the post–World War II baby boom generation noticeably broke ties with the dialect and traditional Pennsylvania German occupations and locations, although they may still maintain foodways and other customary traditions. Amish and Old Order Mennonite groups might maintain community integration characteristic of 19th-century Pennsylvania German life while at the same time developing some traditions that are distinct from the church people (for example, *Ordnung,* dress, quilting, and carriage making), but they, too, face pressures from modernization. They also must cope with state regulation that affects traditional practices such as midwifery, horse-and-buggy travel, and butchering, as well as the group's separate social institutions in education, religion, and labor. Amish migration out of the Pennsylvania core into outlying sections in the Pennsylvania Culture Region and Ohio, Indiana, Missouri, Ontario, New York, and Iowa have in some cases reinvigorated Pennsylvania German culture.

Some contemporary locations for the transmission of narrative and singing traditions are the *Versammling* (gathering) and the *Grundsau Lodch* (groundhog lodge). These social occasions gather Pennsylvania Germans to eat a dinner of traditional Pennsylvania German foods and hear speakers relate stories, particularly folk humor, in dialect. Singing in dialect typically occurs, and often a dialect play will be performed. Other institutions that help maintain the dialect and other traditions are "heritage" or "folk" services provided in dialect, often around the time of Harvest Home. Some churches provide suppers and picnics featuring traditional Pennsylvania German meals such as pig stomach, ham and dandelion salad, pork and sauerkraut, and *schnitz an gnepp.* During the summer, organized family reunions are important social occasions in Pennsylvania German areas. Some radio and television shows in dialect are available in central Pennsylvania, and a few newspapers carry dialect columns. Classes in dialect are offered at several historical societies and schools, and a small program in Pennsylvania German studies is available at Ursinus College (home of the Pennsylvania Folklife Society and the journal *Pennsylvania Folklife*). Several organizations have as their mission the preservation of Pennsylvania German culture, including the Pennsylvania German Society, the Pennsylvania German Cultural Heritage Center, and the Pennsylvania Dutch Folk Culture Society.

Part of the Pennsylvania German core area in Lancaster County has emerged as a major tourist area, and debate can be heard over the effect of this development on Pennsylvania German folk culture. Views of traditional Pennsylvania German practices such as craft, language, and farming are commonly presented to non-Pennsylvania Germans, and folklife plays a significant role in the public programming of this cultural tourism. Ironically, much of the farmland once essential

to Pennsylvania German community life has given way to commercial development around Lancaster, although some scholars respond that the commercial development directs tourists into urban strips away from rural Amish communities. Some critics rail at the misrepresentation of Pennsylvania German life in tourist presentations, such as the conflation of Amish, Mennonite, Brethren, and nonsectarian cultures into a monolithic Pennsylvania German culture. A genre of misplaced "tourist belief" has emerged about Pennsylvania German traditions such as the ideas that "hex signs" warded away witches, that seven sours and seven sweets are standard on the Pennsylvania German table, and that Amishmen painted gates blue to show interested suitors that they had a daughter of marriageable age. Some defenders of cultural tourism, meanwhile, point out the growth of Pennsylvania German ethnic consciousness and spin-off efforts from tourism toward preservation as a result of educational and entertainment programs.

Interest in Pennsylvania German traditions, both outside and within the culture, has fostered an important legacy of folkloristic scholarship. The integration of oral, social, and material traditions within Pennsylvania German communities has attracted scholars to Pennsylvania folk culture. The importance of oral transmission and customary learning in the maintenance of Pennsylvania German life has raised scholarly questions about the traditional systems operating in the community in addition to historical and cultural questions of maintenance and adaptation over the 300 years Pennsylvania Germans have been settled in America. The special relation of community life to the integration of traditions among Pennsylvania Germans influenced the development of the folklife, or folk-cultural, approach championed by Pennsylvania German scholars. In the late 1940s, Alfred L. Shoemaker, J. William Frey, and Don Yoder at Franklin and Marshall College in Lancaster, Pennsylvania, for example, founded the Pennsylvania Dutch Folk Culture Center and the journal *Pennsylvania Folklife*. They also initiated the Pennsylvania Dutch Folk Festival, later to become the Kutztown Folk Festival, held in Kutztown, Pennsylvania, America's largest folk festival. Shoemaker led the nation's first, albeit short-lived, department of folklore, at Franklin and Marshall and stressed a folk cultural approach with special emphasis on folk arts and material culture. Henry Chapman Mercer and the Landis brothers (Henry and George) established museums to preserve and present their collections of Pennsylvania German folk arts and practices (Mercer Museum and Landis Valley Museum, respectively). Reverend Thomas Brendle, a highly respected collector of folk belief, medicine, language, and narrative, had a museum established in his honor at Schaefferstown, Pennsylvania. Essays on the folklore and folklife of Pennsylvania Germans by W.J. Hoffman were featured in the first issues of the *Journal of American Folklore* (1888), and a book-length collection of "The Folklore of the Pennsylvania-German" by Reverend John Baer Stoudt appeared in 1915 as a supplement to the proceedings of the Pennsylvania German Society, founded in 1891. In addition to the folkloristic interest of *Pennsylvania Folklife* and the Pennsylvania Folklife Society in

Pennsylvania German folk culture, a separate Pennsylvania German Folklore Society, with the active leadership of pioneer collectors such as Edwin Fogel and John Baer Stoudt, formed in 1935 and lasted until 1967 when it merged to form the reorganized Pennsylvania German Society (which publishes a book series and the journal *Der Reggeboge* [The Rainbow], edited for many years by Fred Weiser, and since 1992 by Don Yoder, with many features on folk arts and folklife). The special attention given to folklife and material culture in Pennsylvania greatly influenced the spread of these concerns in American folkloristic scholarship generally.

Simon J. Bronner

References

Boyer, Walter E., Albert F. Buffington, and Don Yoder. [1951] 1964. *Songs along the Mahantango: Pennsylvania Dutch Folksongs.* Hatboro, PA: Folklore Associates.

Brandt, Mindy, and Thomas E. Gallagher. 1993–1994. Tourism and the Old Order Amish. *Pennsylvania Folklife* (Winter) 43:71–75.

Brendle, Thomas R., and William S. Troxell. 1944. *Pennsylvania German Folk Tales, Legends, Once-upon-a-Time Stories, Maxims, and Sayings.* Norristown, PA: Pennsylvania German Society.

Brendle, Thomas R., and Claude W. Unger. [1935] 1970. *Folk Medicine of the Pennsylvania Germans: The Non-Occult Cures.* New York: Augustus M. Kelley.

Bronner, Simon J. 1992. "Elaborating Tradition: A Pennsylvania-German Folk Artist Ministers to His Community." In *Creativity and Tradition,* ed. Simon J. Bronner. Logan: Utah State University, pp. 277–326.

Buffington, Albert F. 1965. *"Dutchified German" Spirituals.* Publications of the Pennsylvania German Society Vol. 62. Lancaster, PA: Franklin and Marshall College.

———. 1974. *Pennsylvania German Secular Folksongs.* Publications of the Pennsylvania German Society Vol. 8. Breinigsville, PA: Pennsylvania German Society.

Burke, Susan M., and Matthew H. Hill, eds. 1992. *From Pennsylvania to Waterloo: Pennsylvania-German Folk Culture in Transition.* Waterloo, Ontario: Wilfrid Laurier University Press.

Enninger, Werner, ed. 1986. *Studies on the Languages and the Verbal Behavior of the Pennsylvania Germans.* Vol. 1. Stuttgart: Franz Steiner.

Ensminger, Robert F. 1992. *The Pennsylvania Barn: Its Origin, Evolution, and Distribution in North America.* Baltimore: Johns Hopkins University Press.

Fogel, Edwin Miller. 1915. *Beliefs and Superstitions of the Pennsylvania Germans.* Philadelphia: American Germanica Press.

Long, Amos. 1972. *The Pennsylvania German Family Farm.* Breinigsville, PA: Pennsylvania German Society.

Huffines, Marion Lois. 1980. Pennsylvania German: Maintenance and Shift. *International Journal of the Sociology of Language.* 25:43–57.

———. 1990. Pennsylvania German in Public Life. *Pennsylvania Folklife.* (Spring) 39:117–125.

Kraybill, Donald B. 1989. *The Riddle of Amish Culture.* Baltimore: Johns Hopkins University Press.

Kraybill, Donald B., and Marc A. Olshan, eds. 1994. *The Amish Struggle with Modernity.* Hanover, NH: University Press of New England.

Reed, Henry M. 1987. *Decorated Furniture of the Mahantongo Valley.* Lewisburg, PA: Center Gallery, Bucknell University.

Shoemaker, Alfred L. 1951. *Three Myths about the Pennsylvania Dutch Country.* Lancaster, PA: Pennsylvania Dutch Folklore Center.

Swank, Scott T., with Benno Forman, et al. 1983. *Arts of the Pennsylvania Germans.* New York: W.W. Norton.

Weaver, William Woys. 1986. The Pennsylvania German House: European Antecedents and New World Forms. *Winterthur Portfolio* 21:243–264.

———. 1993. *Pennsylvania Dutch Country Cooking.* New York: Abbeville.

Yoder, Don. 1961. *Pennsylvania Spirituals.* Lancaster, PA: Pennsylvania Folklife Society.

———. 1971. Pennsylvania German Folklore Research: A Historical Analysis. In *The German Language in America: A Symposium,* ed. Glenn G. Gilbert. Austin: University of Texas Press, pp. 76–86.

———. 1990. *Discovering American Folklife.* Ann Arbor, MI: UMI Research Press.

Yoder, Don, and Thomas E. Graves. 1989. *Hex Signs: Pennsylvania Dutch Barn Symbols and Their Meaning.* New York: Dutton.

See also German Americans; Pennsylvania Culture Region; Shoemaker, Alfred L.

Performance Approach

An interdisciplinary perspective that conceives of folklore as artistic communication or performance and seeks to understand folklore through studies that situate it in social life and history. Also referred to as the contextual approach, the communication approach, and performance studies, the performance approach examines a range of aesthetically marked performances, including verbal art and material culture. It includes all of those genres, acts, events, and roles in which people assume responsibility for presentation to an audience. In performance, as Richard Bauman argues, the aesthetic dimension comes to the fore as performers accept responsibility not only for what they do, but also for how they do it. The audience of a performance maintains a dual focus, attending to what is said and done, and how it is accomplished (Bauman [1977] 1984:11) Thus, while performance clearly involves communication, it is an aesthetic mode of communication in which aesthetic features are foregrounded (Fine 1984:58–62).

Performances can be distinguished from other types of communication by textual, stylistic, and contextual features. For example, textual markers such as "Once upon a time . . ." or "Have you heard the one about . . ." signal that a fairy tale or a joke is about to be told. Distinctive intonations or rhythms, or other stylistic traits, as well as special contexts, such as a defined time, place, and audience, also identify performance as aesthetic communication. Dan Ben-Amos, one of the first to conceive of folklore from a performance approach, defines it as "social interaction via the art media" that "differs from other modes of speaking and gesturing" (Ben-Amos 1972:10–11). Certain metacommunicative devices, or signals that communicate *about* the communication, function to frame a performance and thus distinguish it from other modes of communication. These devices serve as keys or signals for performance and include, according to Bauman: (1) special codes, (2) figurative language, (3) parallelism, (4) special paralinguistic features, (5) special formulas, (6) appeal to tradition, and (7) disclaimer of performance ("I'm not a very good joke teller, but . . .") (Bauman [1977] 1984:16–22).

In addition to approaching folklore as artistic communication, performance scholars insist on studying folklore in its social context, simultaneously emerging from and creating a particular social event. Many different and interacting variables influence performance events. The physical setting, such as season, time of day, and location, may stimulate expectations for the performance of certain genres, such as fictional stories or religious narratives. The psychological mood of the setting may further affect the types and styles of performances that emerge. In addition, the kinds of participants and their personalities, relationships, and goals influence the kinds of emerging performances (Fine 1984:62). As these factors change, different expectations for verbal-art performances emerge. These implicit or explicit expectations for performance can be thought of as "ground rules for performance" (Bauman [1977] 1984:28). Despite the existence of such rules for a performance event, particular performances often stretch or violate these rules, creating *emergent* texts, events, and social structures (Bauman [1977] 1984:40–45). In addition to its focus on artistic communication situated in and influencing particular social events, the performance approach emphasizes that folklore is uniquely patterned within specific cultures and variable across cultures.

Scholars who work with a performance approach can be found in many disciplines, including communication, linguistics, folklore, anthropology, sociology, and theater. This multidisciplinary practice reflects the intellectual roots of the performance approach, which were stimulated by research in each of these fields. The emphasis of anthropologists such as Edward Sapir on recording vocal style and Bronislaw Malinowski on recording contextual features, plus the work of linguists of the Prague School in understanding the importance of individual usages of language, helped pave the way for folklorists to examine folklore as a performance in a social context (Fine 1984:25–34). For example, E. Ojo Arewa and Alan Dundes drew on Prague-School theorists Roman Jakobson and Petr Bogatyrev for the conceptual framework of their groundbreaking work, "Proverbs and the Ethnography of Speaking Folklore" (Arewa and Dundes 1964).

The performance approach first emerged as a systematic perspective in folklore studies in the early 1970s, as part of a larger postmodern intellectual movement that embraced the concept of performance as a new paradigm. Stimulated by the interdisciplinary ideas of Kenneth Burke, Erving Goffman, and Gregory Bateson, the social sciences were radically changed by analogies borrowed from the humanities, according to Clifford Geertz. Two of the most powerful analogies, based on drama and game, involved the notion of performance (Geertz 1980:168)

Burke's dramatistic philosophy stimulated comprehensive analytical approaches that took into account not only the work or act, but also the agent who creates or performs it, as well as the agency, the scene, and the purpose. Burke's performance-oriented ideas influenced such folklorists as Brian Sutton-Smith, Bruce Rosenberg, Dell Hymes, and Roger D. Abrahams. Burke also influenced such well-known anthropologists as Victor Turner, James Peacock, and Clifford Geertz, as well as sociologist Goffman. Their works further stimulated a performance approach to the analysis of culture (Fine 1984:35).

In addition to the influence of the drama analogy, the game or play analogy contributed to the new performance paradigm. The most influential applications of the game analogy to the performance paradigm have come from Bateson and Goffman.

In order to explain how beings distinguish between different orders of messages, Bateson introduced the concepts of "frame" and "metacommunication" in his essay "A Theory of Play and Fantasy." Noticing that both animals and humans use signals about signals, or metacommunication, to distinguish messages such as "this is play" from what otherwise might be interpreted as aggression, Bateson argued that such metacommunication serves as an interpretive frame. Such frames help define different orders of messages, such as fantasy, play, and dreams (Bateson 1972).

This concept of frame has provided a useful tool for distinguishing artistic verbal performance from other modes of communication. Much of folklorist Richard Bauman's definition of performance draws on Bateson's notion of frame, as does Barbara Babcock's analysis of metanarration in folk stories (Fine 1984:35–36).

Another important stimulus to the study cultural performances has come from Goffman, who used both dramatistic and game analogies. In *The Presentation of Self in Everyday Life* (1959), he showed how everyday work roles could be interpreted as cultural performance. Ideas from this work, as well as from *Encounters* and *Interaction Ritual* influenced such writers as Hymes, Richard Schechner, Barbara Kirshenblatt-Gimblett, and Bauman. Goffman's *Frame Analysis* (1974) has been especially crucial in shaping Bauman's definition of verbal art as performance (Fine 1984:35–36).

A major intellectual root of the performance approach comes from an area of linguistic anthropology known as the ethnography of speaking. During the early 1960s, Hymes called for an ethnographic study of speaking that would discover the patterns and functions of speaking within specific cultural contexts. He suggested a methodology for this study that begins by identifying a "speech community," or a group of people who share common language and rules for conducting and interpreting speech activities. Within the context of a chosen speech community, the ethnographer describes speech behavior in terms of settings, participants, ends (goals), act sequence, key (tone), instrumentalities (communication channels), norms of interaction and interpretation, and genre (Hymes 1972:35–71). Hymes' work stimulated a number of performance-centered ethnographies within the fields of folklore, communication, and sociolinguistics.

The term "performance approach" should not suggest any simple formula or method for analyzing folklore. Rather, performance scholars in the 1990s recognize the complexity of such terms as text, performance, and context and the dangers of conceiving of them as static objects (Bauman and Briggs 1990:60). Accordingly, performance scholars are studying the processes by which performances are detached from one social situation (decentered or entextualized) and performed in another social situation (recentered, or recontextualized) (Bauman and Briggs:1990:72–78). Such studies necessarily lead beyond the study of a performance in only one time and place to studies of a performance embedded in history. Thus, a given performance might bear traces of earlier performances, texts, and contexts. This historical emphasis promises to reveal additional insights about the relationship of performance to social life and other modes of communication.

Elizabeth C. Fine

References

Arewa, E. Ojo, and Alan Dundes. 1964. Proverbs and the Ethnography of Speaking Folklore. *American Anthropologist* 66 (2):70–85.

Bateson, Gregory. 1972. A Theory of Play and Fantasy. In *Steps to an Ecology of Mind.* New York: Ballantine, pp. 177–193.

Bauman, Richard. [1977] 1984. *Verbal Art as Performance.* Prospect Heights, IL: Waveland.

Bauman, Richard, and Charles L. Briggs. 1990. Poetics and Performance as Critical Perspectives on Language and Social Life. *Annual Review of Anthropology* 19:59–88.

Ben-Amos, Dan. 1972. Toward a Definition of Folklore in Context. In *Toward New Perspectives in Folklore,* ed. Américo Paredes and Richard Bauman. Austin: University of Texas Press, pp. 3–15.

Fine, Elizabeth. 1984. *The Folklore Text: From Performance to Print.* Bloomington: Indiana University Press.

Fine, Elizabeth, and Jean Haskell Speer, eds. 1993. *Performance, Culture, and Identity.* Westport, CT: Praeger.

Geertz, Clifford. 1980. Blurred Genres: The Refiguration of Social Thought. *American Scholar* 49 (Spring):165–179.

Hymes, Dell. 1972. Models of the Interaction of Language and Social Life. In *Directions in Sociolinguistics,* ed. J.J. Gumperz and Dell Hymes. New York: Holt, Rinehart and Winston, pp. 35–71.

See also Contextual Approach

Perrow, Eber Carle (1880–1968)

Professor of English and amateur folklorist known primarily for his collection of folksong texts from the Southeastern United States. Perrow was born in Tye Valley, Virginia, December 7, 1880, and was exposed at an early age to folklore from both Black and White sources. Receiving his B.A. (1903) and M.A. (1905) degrees from Trinity College, he went on to Harvard University, where he studied under George Lyman Kittredge. Perrow earned his Ph.D. from Harvard in 1908, taught briefly at the University of Missouri and elsewhere, and became head of the Department of English at the University of Louisville in 1911.

From his post at Louisville, Perrow compiled folksong materials, relying heavily on his students' contributions and his own memory for texts. Between 1912 and 1915, his "Songs and Rhymes from the South" (270 texts) was published in installments in the *Journal of American Folklore.* Perrow helped found the Kentucky Folklore Society in 1912 and, from 1916 to 1918, served as its third president. Soon after, following medical advice, he retired from the stress of academic involvements and spent his remaining years farming and surveying in the north Georgia foothills. He died at Talking Rock, Georgia, in 1968.

Influenced by the "communalist" theory of ballad origins advanced by Kittredge, Francis Barton Gummere, and others, Perrow demonstrated the existence of what he felt was spontaneous group folksong composition by citing religious revivals and community dances. His own collecting went beyond the literary tradition of English and Scottish popular balladry set forth by his teachers and encompassed a spectrum of lyric folksong, American native balladry, plantation rhymes, dance songs, antislavery songs, and mountain blues.

Perrow, like many others of his generation, tended to view Appalachia as a homogeneous culture just emerging from the 18th century. In his writing, he perpetuated certain cultural stereotypes such as mountaineers' "inborn antipathy toward organized authority." Nevertheless, his "Songs and Rhymes of the South" was one of the first published collections to demonstrate the potential richness of folk music in the Upland South, a richness that was soon after brought to national prominence by the collecting and publishing work of Olive Dame Campbell and Cecil Sharp.

Stephen Green

References

Perrow, E.C. 1957. Background. *Kentucky Folklore Record* 111:31–37.

Wilgus, D.K. 1957. Eber C. Perrow. *Kentucky Folklore Record* 111:29–31.

Personal-Experience Story

A prose narrative relating a personal experience, usually told in the first person, and containing nontraditional content. Unlike most folklore, a personal-experience story is not passed down through time and space and kept alive through variation from one teller to another. Instead, the content of a personal-experience story is based on an actual event in the life of the storyteller. The story may become a repeated and polished item in the repertoire of the person who had the experience and created the story, but, in general, such stories do not enter tradition.

While the content of personal-experience stories is not traditional in the usual sense—that is, one cannot recognize in them known motifs or story plots—still the form, style, and function of such stories are consistent from one story to the next. Thus, one can argue that the genre itself is traditional. Further proof of the traditionality of the genre is found in the many clearly traditional genres that disguise themselves as personal-experience stories—such as tall tales, first-person jokes, and catch tales. Personal-experience stories are found in the oldest recorded literature, such as the ancient Sumerian epic of *Gilgamesh,* in which the hero reports his adventures as pointed narratives, each with a specific, single-episodic plot.

The hallmark of the personal-experience story is that it reports a single event, usually one that would not be considered supernatural. Folklorists use other terms to identify longer stories with a sequence of events, such as life histories, or stories that involve magic healing or the supernatural. Such stories are called memorates, and they usually reflect some traditional belief, even if the experience itself is a personal one. One function of memorates might be to reinforce the traditional beliefs at their base, as in the following (see Stahl 1975) story of seeing the northern lights (aurora borealis) shortly before the American entry into World War II: "Well, the last time that I've seen northern lights that were spectacular was just before World War Two. Course everybody says, you know, that anything phenomenal like that *portends* disaster, and all that sorta stuff. And everybody was wondering what terrible thing was going to happen." (One function of the story could be to maintain the belief in such portents.)

More "secular" personal-experience stories usually serve one of three fairly specific functions: (1) to entertain, (2) to be a cautionary tale or to illustrate the results of certain behaviors, or (3) to present some aspect of the storyteller's character and personal values. Often these functions overlap, as in one teller's story of climbing up into the cupola of their barn while playing hide-and-seek and being unable to get down. The rest of the story in which she finally calls out to her brother and has him stretch across the missing rungs of the ladder so she can crawl over him to safety is entertaining, but it also cautions against rash behavior and reveals something about the teller's character. Thus, it serves a didactic function.

Because of these three broad-based functions, personal-experience stories are found easily in a great variety of contexts—informal contexts, such as bars and coffee shops, family gatherings, work breaks, or parties, and more formal ones as well, such as in sermons, in classrooms, on television talk shows, or in political speeches. But personal-experience stories are not simply unstructured gossip or bragging. In form they are very much like anecdotes—short, single-episodic, often with a kind of punch line or dramatic ending that makes them memorable. Unlike anecdotes, however, personal-experience stories are told by the very person who had the experience. The teller, then, is the one who creates the story, the one who turns an experience into a narrative.

A point of great theoretical interest to folklorists has to do with this process of creating the story. Most folk narratives, such as legends or fairy tales, are assumed to have had an original "creator," an individual who first made up the story, although generally we can no longer trace the story back to find out who that originator was. With a personal experience story, on the other hand, we do know who made the story up, and we can ask some of the questions that so intrigue us about the process of literary creativity. Some researchers are eager to discover what makes an event "story-worthy." Some want to know how different personalities affect the kind of story that grows out of an event. Some want to know how a story changes over time as the teller retells and polishes it. And some want to know which came first, the sense of event or experience or the narrative itself.

The study of the personal-experience story began in Europe with attention to the memorate and the "true story." In American folklore research, one of the earliest scholars to recognize, collect, and publish personal-experience stories was Richard M. Dorson. In 1952 Dorson included a section on "Sagamen" in his book of Upper Peninsula folklore. Dorson recognized the similarity between these nontraditional, anecdotal stories and the tall tales and jocular tales he collected from his informants.

Since then American researchers have become increasingly interested in the personal-experience story and its close neighbors. Some efforts have been made to classify personal-experience stories by theme, as evidenced in books such as Eleanor Wachs' *Crime Victim Stories* (1988). Some scholars, such as Richard Bauman, have offered detailed textual analysis and some fine insights into the wonderfully flexible story-telling style of individual performers. Some, such as this author, have been interested in examining how the cultural frame of reference is used by the teller and the listener to make the story personally meaningful.

Some of the possibilities for attending to the richness of cultural allusion, style, and creativity in the telling of personal-experience stories can be suggested more easily by including a segment of one narrative text. The story below, transcribed in part, was told by Larry Scheiber in 1974 in Huntington, Indiana, to the author and a number of friends. At the beginning of the story, we learn that Larry and his friend "Tiny Wires" had gone cat-fishing using a bucket of chicken blood as bait. They had set the bucket of leftover bait under the trailer that they were sharing that summer. Finally, the stench became so bad that they knew they had to get rid of it. The rotting blood had attracted flies, and the bucket was full of maggots. After a bribe of Mickey's Malt, Larry agreed to drag the bucket out from under the trailer. They decide to throw the whole thing in the river. The story concludes:

> There's a bridge out there, one bridge past Broadway, just a little stony job, about three-foot-high railing. I said, "You drive across that and go *real slow.*" I said, "I'll just heave the whole goddamn mess over the railing, and we'll take off like a big-ass bird." So he's driving real slow and I'm hangin' out the window—this thing's

heavy, man! My ol' Biceps isn't all that big, ya know. I'm holdin' onto that damn bucket. Wires says, "OK, give 'er hell!" So I get my arm underneath it [motions accompanying actions described]—so I [throwing motion]—uhh!—I threw it as hard as I could. Hell, it must've weighed sixty pounds! It made it right to the railing and jumped back. [Motion with hand straight up, and noise—apparent from motions that the contents of the bucket came down all over him] [Laughter and groans] Did you ever just drop a glass of water—see how it shoots up? Hell, I was hangin' out the window or the whole car woulda been full. I'm not kiddin' ya, it just buried me in maggots.

Larry finishes the story by recounting how Wires drove to a car wash and used the high-pressure water to try to get the maggots off his car—with Larry still hanging out the window. But the maggots stuck to the car and had to be removed with a putty knife. The best part of the story, according Larry, was watching Wires try to get the maggots off with a putty knife. He closed with, "Oh God—it was hell! Every time I think of Tiny, I think of that goddamn bucket of maggots."

Larry's story, like so many personal-experience stories, not only instructs and entertains, but also forges a subtle bond between the teller and the listener. The teller reveals something about himself, while the listener learns something about the storyteller. Personal-experience stories serve a number of functions, but perhaps the most telling function is that they invite intimacy, a chance for the teller and the listener to know each other better.

Sandra K. Dolby

References

Bauman, Richard. 1986. *Story, Performance, and Event.* Cambridge: Cambridge University Press.

Dégh, Linda. 1985. When I Was Six We Moved West. *New York Folklore* 11:99–108.

Dorson, Richard M. 1952. *Bloodstoppers and Bearwalkers.* Cambridge: Harvard University Press, pp. 249–272.

Dorson, Richard M., and Sandra K. D(olby) Stahl, eds. 1977. Stories of Personal Experience. *Journal of the Folklore Institute* (Special Double Issue)14 (1–2).

Stahl, Sandra K. Dolby. 1975. *The Personal Narrative as a Folklore Genre.* Ph.D. diss., Indiana University.

———. 1977. The Oral Personal Narrative in Its Generic Context. *Fabula* 18:18–39.

———. 1985. A Literary Folkloristic Methodology for the Study of Meaning in Personal Narrative. *Journal of Folklore Research* 22:45–69.

———. 1988. Contributions of Personal Narrative Research to North American Folkloristics. *Fabula* 29:390–399.

———. 1989. *Literary Folklorists and the Personal Narrative.* Bloomington: Indiana University Press.

See also Crimelore; Life History; Memorate; UFO Lore

Pictorial Tale

A narrative form in which the storyteller draws details of a picture representing narrative descriptions that lead to a surprising ending to the story as shown in the final drawing. In the late 20th century, the form is commonly collected as humorous tales or jokes told by adults to children or children to other children.

In one traditional pictorial tale found commonly in England and America, the figure of a bird is formed from the narrative description of an oval pond (forming the center of the bird's body), cattails at one end of the pond (the bird's tail), a house with one window (the bird's head), a path from the house to the pond (the bird's neck), and two Indians living in tents who came up two paths for water (the bird's feet). A variant commonly collected in the Southern United States describes two men working in a briar patch (forming the feet) who go for water and return (forming the tail), while a father and a son live in a house with a lookout. When the son investigates the noise made by the men, he returns to his father and says "Ain't nothing but a crane, pop." The drawing at this conclusion reveals the figure of a crane. Other animals, sometimes hunted or chased in the tales, are wildcats, ducks, or mice. Pictorial tales also lead to words or landscapes that close out a story. The diagrams are often drawn in the ground, or sketched on chalkboard or paper.

Many of the pictorial tales pose the question, "What's this?" to the details successively being added until the total picture is revealed. Related to this form are riddle jokes using pictorial clues that reveal a spoken answer other than what is expected from the drawing. Often the answer may seem off-color to the child. An example is an Indian teepee to which is added a smokehole and the sun above. With the addition of an arc, the picture becomes: "My dad bending over the tub to wipe it out after he has taken a bath." The pictorial tale is distinguished from a "droodle" by the narrative sequencing found in the tale. The droodle shows a single boxed drawing that gives a clue as to its representation. A common example is two parallel vertical lines with semicircles on them. When the drawer asks, "What's this?" the answer is a bear climbing a tree or a giraffe's neck.

Many American Indian groups have a special form of the pictorial tale in which figures are drawn to represent symbols used in episodes of a story. The symbols are brought together at the conclusion in one encompassing picture. Among the Oglala Dakota, for example, the story of the traveling Indian Wic'o'Wic'aga was collected as a pictorial tale. In this story, he travels westward and sees seven fireplaces, and then comes to a valley in which he sees seven camps. He continues and sees a large camp with seven teepees on each of which is drawn a different picture. The one on the end has no picture, and Wic'o'Wic'aga is instructed to go to that one to find out about the rest of his journey. Inside he receives presents such as pipe, a bow and arrow, and a medicine bag. The final picture includes the figures that have previously been drawn and the concluding moral: "Just as he went through trials and tribulations and got gifts for his reward, so people say that those who endure hardship in a manly way will enjoy the privileges of a good man" (Beckwith 1930:339–442).

    Simon J. Bronner

References

Beckwith, Martha. 1930. Mythology of the Oglala Dakota. *Journal of American Folklore* 43:339–442.

Bronner, Simon J. 1978. Pictorial Jokes: A Traditional Combination of Verbal and Graphic Processes. *Tennessee Folklore Society Bulletin* 44:189–196.

Brunvand, Jan Harold. 1971. *Folklore in Utah: A Guide for Collectors.* Salt Lake City: University of Utah Press, pp. 59–60.

———. 1986. *The Study of American Folklore: An Introduction.* 3d. ed. New York: W.W. Norton, pp. 198–200.

Early, Maud G. 1897. The Tale of the Wild Cat: A Child's Game. *Journal of American Folklore* 10:80.

Wilder, Laura Ingalls. [1937] 1971. *On the Banks of Plum Creek.* New York: Harper and Row, p. 318.

See also Folktale; Storytelling

Piedmont Region

Or "Carolina Cotton Piedmont," a region of the American Southeast. Geographically, the area extends from the central part of North Carolina through South Carolina into Georgia, and is bordered on the west by the Blue Ridge and to the east by the Sand Hills (remnant Cenozoic beaches). Physically, culturally, and linguistically blending into central North Carolina's tobacco area and central Georgia's Atlantan megalopolis, the region historically was the heart of textile production in the Southeast. In the late 20th century, the "Upstate," as the region is also called, consists of rolling hills with pastures and small farms, linked by an expanding Interstate corridor extending from Charlotte, North Carolina, to Atlanta.

    The earliest European settlers were Scots-Irish, some Germans, and British migrants from colonial areas farther north, along with some African American slaves. Their settlement pattern of small, independent "yeoman" farms contrasted with the English plantations along the coast, establishing a cultural and dialectical distinction that persists to this day. Following Reconstruction of the 1870s, the Piedmont sprouted numerous cotton mills, utilizing the area's inexpensive water power, White labor, and raw materials. Consequently, mill-town residents gradually became a recognized folk group.

    Simultaneously, stemming in part from the devastation of the Civil War, a system of tenant farming and sharecropping evolved, establishing a second category of landless Black and White farmers. Both of these groups interacted further with a developing small-town elite, created by old money saved from antebellum times and new capital generated by the mills and related enterprises. Through time, the traditions of these groups interwove, creating Carolina Piedmont folklife.

    The ongoing social relationship between Anglo American and African American Upstate residents has been complex. While racism, paternalism, and segregation guaranteed that Blacks and Whites worshipped, learned, and lived separately, Black cooks fed their traditions to White households, Black "nurses" or nannies passed oral traditions on to their White charges, and White and Black tenant farmers often worked side by side. This social interaction followed unspoken but quite rigid rules, regulating not only marriage partners and occupational categories, but even forms of greeting and methods of home entry. For example, Whites would always address a Black (regardless of class) by first name or "Uncle" or "Aunt"; to retain their dignity indirectly, African Americans disclosed their first names to friends, leaving only initials by which Whites might address them.

    Seen acutely in the political economy, segregation prevented African Americans from working in the textile industry, effectively restricting men to manual labor or some professions such as preaching, women to domestic duties and other professions such as teaching, or either gender to tenant farming. Black women, in effect, supported the stereotypical "Southern hospitality" and gentility of their White employers by washing and starching clothes, caring for children, and especially by preparing and serving formal dinners and teas. Desegregation in the area has opened minds and places, but traces of these earlier attitudes may still be felt, as Blacks and Whites maintain informal social separation within a larger context of formal integration.

    Besides African American and Anglo American social groups, others exist in the area both in reality and in stereotype. From the ubiquitous mill towns developed the mill workers, disparaged by both town and farm residents as "lint heads"; the latter resented these perceptions and formulated their own views of farmers and town dwellers. These groups and their positive and negative stereotypes persist. Some scholars have argued that the region's yeoman farmers of the 18th century (with the addition of some former mill hands) have evolved into "rednecks." Perceived by outsiders as somewhat coarse and conservative, rednecks see themselves as a step above the "White trash," the trailer-dwelling lowest class, which everyone recognizes but in which very few acknowledge membership. As they interact, all of these social groups follow stereotypical, traditional patterns.

    Attitudes shaped by the past explain and justify contemporary folklife and the groups that continue these customs. For example, people in the region describe the Upstate value system as consisting of family togetherness, Southern hospitality, religious conservatism, individuality, and a stereotypical slower pace of life. Many Anglo Americans (from urban elites to rural rednecks) also adhere to an idealistic image of the "old South," emphasizing gentility and loyalty to the "lost cause" of the War for Southern Independence (also known facetiously as the War of Northern Aggression). These qualities in turn guide, influence, and explain Upstate folklife.

    Verbal genres of contemporary folklife include what locals themselves describe as a slower pace of speaking and storytelling, particularly when contrasted with Northerners. Residents also express a general enjoyment of leisurely conversation, which often seeks first to elicit one's family ties, place of origin, and religious background. Distinctive vocabulary words enliven conversations. Examples include stove "eyes" for burners or "buggies" for grocery carts; one "mashes" buttons and admits that he or she "might could" (may be able to) do something. Sentimental verses, copied from written sources or composed by the author, appear in local newspapers on important anniversaries for deceased loved ones, demonstrating the persistence of family cohesiveness beyond death. Stories of ancestral anecdotes preserve family history as well as entertainment at family reunions, while folktales and rhymes of landowners cheating tenants exemplify the region's agricultural past. Ghost stories reflect interweavings of Scots-Irish and African traditions, while pranks and practical jokes solidify neighborhoods or cotton mill workers.

Additional oral traditions also reflect the centuries-old connections between Black and White beliefs. For example, some in both groups affirm the power of the moon to influence human events, such as determining the appropriate times for cutting hair or extracting teeth. The moon is also said to affect the growth of vegetables, for underground ones should be planted in the dark (waning) of the moon, while aboveground vegetables should be planted in the light of the moon. Charms (such as silver dimes around the neck or ankle) to ward off the "Booger Man" or general evil influences are acknowledged by a few African Americans, as are "root doctors," those with an ability to cure by using supernatural and herbal remedies (such as "yellow root," available in area flea markets). Other healers might possess the power to stop blood (relying to some degree on Ezekiel 16:6) or to "talk fire out of burns" by reciting some other mystical words. A few such healers continue to practice.

Throughout contemporary Upstate social activities, hints of traditional values invigorate and underlie daily life. For example, Sunday afternoons after church remain the private domain of family gatherings, although the custom in the late 20th century is tempered by television. Friends continue to exemplify traditional Southern hospitality by assisting neighbors who are ill or bereaved by donating food to the family. Family reunions are frequently held during the midsummer slow time of traditional cotton farming ("lay-by time"), often staged at the "home place" or the country church where ancestors once lived or now lie. Church homecomings and annual revivals continue long-standing practices as well, tying family and faith with threads of sacred music and tastes of favorite foods.

The social context of foods enhances their symbolic meaning, further linking the past and the present with families and faith in an effective association. Whether at family reunions, political gatherings, or Sunday dinners, various forms of pork (often barbecued but sometimes rendered into "cracklings"—remnants of fried skin from melted fat) have been widely consumed by both Anglo Americans and African Americans. Grits, biscuits and gravy, black-eyed peas, and pinto beans had long been staples of working-class and tenant families, and many still love these foods, flavored as they are with nostalgia. Most Upstate families still mark the New Year with black-eyed peas and collard greens for their continued good fortune; the former represent change and the latter stand for greenbacks. Collard greens and okra may be purchased in stores, bought at roadside stands, or grown in home gardens. Peanuts are often boiled in saltwater, which softens

them and alters their taste. Cornbread traditionally might be crumbled into milk or mixed with cracklings, but mostly today it is just eaten as bread. Piedmont sweets include scuppernongs and muscadines (wild grapes) as well as molasses. Washing all of this food down is sweetened iced tea, served with every afternoon and evening meal.

These traditional foods frequently appear at informal types of adult recreation, which also reflect hints of earlier, more rural times. For example, at country crossroads and at outdoor malls, merchants sell everything from boiled peanuts to clothes to automobile parts to farm animals. These ubiquitous flea markets are the direct descendants of informal swap meets at country stores or county fairs. Flea markets also reflect the region's emphasis on individuality—one can sell anything, anywhere, anytime (except when this conflicts with religious conservatism; hence no Sunday alcohol sales in many communities). Upstate fairs might feature various "womanless" activities such as "beauty pageants," in which local men dress in women's costumes in mock ceremonies for charity. Hunting remains a popular and serious pastime; bumper stickers proclaim "when the tailgate drops the bullshit stops," meaning that at the release of the dogs, talk ceases in order to appreciate the music of the hounds' baying. Auto racing equals other professional, collegiate, and high-school team sports in popularity. Although illegal, cockfighting and moonshining occur but are said to take place "across the state line."

In virtually all Piedmont residents' backgrounds are ancestors who worked either as mill hands or tenant farmers. The textile industry remains a significant (but declining) employer in the Upstate, but paternalistic company control has been replaced by more impersonal companies. Practical jokes (to socially level new employees) have faded due to corporate professionalism, and the isolation of mill towns and their residents has been shattered by mass communication, improved transportation, and better education. Likewise, the snowy fields of ripening cotton have virtually disappeared from the Upstate, but many middle-age and older residents, whether Anglo American or African American, male or female, will proudly relate tales of how much cotton each could pick in a day. Especially in the calculations of debits and credits at the end of the field season, racism guaranteed the continuation of class distinctions, as exemplified by the traditional folk rhyme: "Naught's a naught and a figger is a figger; all for the White man, none for the Nigger." No one wishes for those backbreaking, heat-intensive, and low-paying days to return.

While cotton has disappeared, the landscape still preserves Piedmont traditions, for vernacular architecture reflects elements of the past. Mill towns dot hillsides all over the region; landscaping and paint barely disguise the patterned buildings today owned primarily by retired couples in aging communities. Tenant houses, often overgrown with kudzu (a perennial creeping vine) but occasionally still occupied, also stand, frequently near the larger, ostentatious "big house" of the former (or current) landowner. Most Upstate residents feel an inexorable tug of nostalgia to the "home place," either an original dwelling, a modified improvement, or the traditional but now empty site. There families schedule annual reunions, linking their ancestral heritage, family unity, and physical point of "origin" by means of the smells, sights, and tastes of traditional foods.

Elements of material culture, too, continue earlier traditions while simultaneously representing innovations. In the past, for example, women would gather in the home of a friend to spend the day talking, eating, and quilting; older women fondly remember the first times, as young girls, when they were promoted from the yard with the children into the house with the adults. Responding to both art and necessity, quilters changed designs and shapes through time, and in the late 20th century their labors represent several threads to the past: as valuable antiques and as honored heirlooms. In contrast, the art of making baskets from wooden oak splits, which traditionally produced utilitarian objects from washtub-size cotton baskets to hand-size sewing baskets, has largely (but not completely) disappeared. Several regionally known pottery traditions, however, still produce items, though primarily for tourists and less for home and farm. In tombstone inscriptions, especially in older, segregated cemeteries, one may see permanently preserved indications of social inequities. Some markers, for example, were given by the White employers of faithful servants termed "Aunt" or "Uncle," reflecting the genuine care offset by paternalistic racism of the donors. Other old African American stones were formed of wet concrete, with the names of the deceased stenciled or lettered by hand.

The organization of space, the social groups that interact in it, the activities in which they engage, and the beliefs and values that explain that interaction and shape that space constitute the elements of Piedmont folklife that characterize the region today.

John M. Coggeshall

See also Appalachia; South

Plantlore

Traditions associated with the growth and use of plants. Traditional uses of plants in America vary both regionally and ethnically, but some general trends are discernible. Traditional categories of plants include edible-nonedible, useful-nonuseful ("weeds"), and beautiful-nonbeautiful. Overlapping these categories are customs relating to the care, use, and potential meaning (usually luckiness) associated with each.

Since the value of many plants is measured by their usefulness as food, the category edible-nonedible is frequently the first applied. Food plants may be a self-evident category, but considerable differences exist between regions and ethnicities on what is edible. Until the 1840s, tomatoes were considered poisonous by some Americans, and raw fruit was believed to be unhealthy for children; well into the 1940s, raw vegetables—unpickled cucumbers or uncooked cabbage—were considered by many to be dangerous. On the other hand, some plant foods were particularly auspicious (sauerkraut or black-eyed peas on New Year's) or healthy, such as the common belief that dandelion greens were the best plants for making spring tonics.

Plants are also used as medicine, and some plants do have real medicinal value: digitalis (foxglove) as a heart tonic, rauzide *(rauwulfia)* as a blood pressure medication, and catnip as an antispasmodic are well documented. Other folk cures contain traces of important active ingredients: the Native American use of willow bark as a general pain killer rests on the presence of salicins (aspirin), and traditional herbal cures such as slippery elm bark or horehound as cough supressants, aloe vera for burns, or jewelweed for poison ivy are documented. Some traditional medical cures are soothing but have modest pharmacological (though considerable psychological) value. Such cures as mint teas for colds, mustard, onion, or spice poultices for chest colds, or plantain leaves or lily petals soaked in whiskey as wound dressings fall into this category. Finally, there are cures of dubious value, such as the common American cure for anything, boneset tea, mostly noted for its terrible taste. The taste may have been its sole value, for many believed the worse the taste, the better the cure.

Beliefs and practices associated with plants form a major category in collections of traditional lore. Particularly important is the class of beliefs associated with planting customs. Among Euro-Americans, there are various days by which certain food plants must be planted in order to assure a successful crop: Potatoes must be planted by St. Patrick's Day; peas, by Good Friday; corn, when oak leaves are as big as squirrel's ears. Spring greens must be picked and eaten on Maundy Thursday to assure luck and health throughout the year. The prettiest flowers are those planted very early on the morning on May Day. Certain plants may not be planted near one another: Some Pennsylvania Germans would not plant the artemesias Wormwood and Southernwood (called "Old Man" and "Old Woman") near each other in the garden because it was believed they would fight too much and neither would grow. Nor do potatoes and tomatoes go well together. Other plants, like beans and greens, are considered good companions. Marigolds get along with everyone. There is evidence that suggests some of these traditional practices work well for scientific reasons. Other traditions may be largely symbolic: Pennsylvania German gardeners traditionally planted a sedum they called "thunder weed" at the entrance to their gardens to protect against bad weather. These same gardeners would often place a yucca plant (called "Our Lord's Sword") or rosemary (in honor of the Virgin Mary) at the center of their gardens. Chinese Americans continue the tradition of including peonies and peach trees, both exceptionally lucky plants, in their gardens.

Plants may also be unlucky or predict bad luck: Fruit trees blooming out of season are believed to predict a death; plants in a sick room are believed to steal oxygen from the ill person, especially at night, hence hindering recovery. Thanking someone for a gift of plant cutting or seeds will cause the plant to die. The gift of yellow flowers means money will follow, but a gift of sage is followed by a quarrel. Plants, especially flowers, have accrued symbolic meaning as well, so a gift of rosemary is for remembrance; rue, for sorrow; roses, for true love; and a four leafed clover, for luck. In America as in Europe, meaning is extended to the images of fertility and fruitfulness implied by certain plants. Flowers are virginal, not yet fruitful. Seeds are the potential for fertility and fruit. Hence brides throw away their bouquets of girlish flowers when they marry, and are in turn pelted with rice, grain, or birdseed, a wish for a fruitful life.

Probably the most interesting area of plantlore is that related to magical practices and astrology. Based largely on Ptolemaic astronomy and documents attributed to Hermes Trismegistus (reputed to have been Moses' teacher), the astrological significance of plants in both healing and luck was championed in the Renaissance by scholars such as Marsilio Ficino. While Cartesian science has supplanted Ficinian science, there is nonetheless significant continuation of belief in the Renaissance systems of correspondences and homeopathic magic (the belief that like things affect each other). Planting by the signs, a tradition honored throughout North America, depends upon an intimate knowledge of the moon's position and its effect on growth. On the simplest level, it means planting crops that bear above ground during the waxing of the moon, and planting those that bear below ground while the moon is waning. On a more sophisticated level, it means planting while the moon is in astrological signs that favor growth (earth, air, and water signs, each one appropriate for particular crops) and avoiding planting during the sterile, or fire, signs. No food crops should be planted in Virgo, for as a virgin she will not bear fruit, although it is an auspicious sign for planting flowers. Even more sophisticated is Ficino's system of herbal medicine, aspects of which continue in American beliefs even in the late 20th century. Ficino recommended drinking, inhaling, or massaging concoctions of herbs associated with the sun as a cure for melancholy or herbs associated with Venus as love charms.

Plant shape also plays a significant role in magical use. Ginseng roots, with their human-like shapes, are attributed with profound homeopathic qualities. African Americans use a similarly shaped plant called Adam and Eve root as a part of the best love charms. Homeopathic thinking also extends to the use of water from the washing of menstrual rags in watering red flowers (an African American belief) or the prohibition against menstruating women from planting flowers or walking through the cucumber patch.

Yvonne J. Milspaw

References

Hyatt, Harry M. 1965. *Folklore from Adams County, Illinois.* Hannibal, MO: Western Printing.

———. 1970. *Hoodoo, Conjuration, Witchcraft, Rootwork.* 5 vols. Hannibal, MO: Western Printing.

Millspaugh, Charles F. [1892] 1974. *American Medicinal Plants.* New York: Dover.

Roberts, Warren E. 1979. Were Tomatoes Considered Poisonous? *Pioneer America* 11:112–113.

Tantaquidgeon, Gladys. [1972] 1977. *Folk Medicine of the Delawares and Related Algonkian Indians.* Harrisburg: Pennsylvania Historical and Museum Commission.

Yates, Frances A. 1964. *Giordano Bruno and the Hermetic Tradition.* Chicago: University of Chicago Press.

See also Foodways; Medicine, Folk

Play-Party

A social dance for adults performed without instrumental music. In general, the first American folklorists who discovered and described the play-party defined it as a uniquely Anglo American recreation that flourished as a part of the expanding Western frontier, probably because of the opposition of the religions of the frontier to instrumental music. Early folklorists noted that the play-party included "a crude set of rhymes," and they assumed that it died with the passage of the historical-geographical conditions that created it, leaving few if any traces in Anglo American folk tradition.

Later field research and analysis indicated there were many local revivals of the play-party across America in places and times long after it was supposed to have died out; furthermore, instrumental accompaniments were frequently used in this later development of the genre, the poetry of the games was complex and well suited to the tunes and actions of the dances, and the play-party lives on in Anglo American folk games and music.

The play-party was first called to the attention of American folklorists in general by an article in the *Journal of American Folklore* in 1907 by George Lyman Kittredge who edited and annotated a collection of ballads and rhymes made in the mountains of Kentucky and submitted to him by Katherine Pettit. The article included six poems that were described simply as "play songs" and, as was typical of much folklore scholarship of the time, included only the words of the songs and no music or contextual information.

Most of the ballads in Pettit's collection—at least most of the ones Kittredge included when he edited the material for publication—were well-known British traditional ballads also found in Francis James Child's monumental five-volume compilation, *The English and Scottish Popular Ballads* ([1882–1898] 1965), but the six "play songs" were short, nonnarrative "rhymes" that clearly were designed to accompany dances or singing games. For example:

> We are marching down to old Quebec,
> Where the drums and the fifes are a-beating;
> Americans, they have gained the day,
> And the British are retreating.

> The war's all over and we'll turn back,
> Ne'er to be parted;
> We'll open the ring and take a couple in
> So release the broken-hearted

Mrs. L.D. Ames' seminal 1911 article "The Missouri Play-Party," which was also published in the *Journal of American Folklore*, went far beyond Kittredge's listing and was the first widely disseminated folklore publication that actually described the play-party as play, discussed its history, social, performance contexts, and included transcriptions of the tunes of the play-parties as well. Ames began with a statement that the Missouri play-party was at the height of its popularity "some thirty years ago" (approximately the late 1870s and early 1880s) but had almost completely died out; she continued with the significant

Playing a swing game at a play-party. McIntosh County, Oklahoma, 1940. Photo Russell Lee. Library of Congress.

statement that the games were preplanned adult recreational dances, describing them as "a dance without the music of instruments." She began an ongoing controversy by noting that the words of the songs were "a very crude lot of rhymes—crude in sense and in form," and by claiming that the events were held as an alternative to dances because of the opposition of frontier religion. This was not so much, she wrote, because of opposition to musical instruments per se on the part of churches and churchmen, but because "regular dances where the music was furnished by a 'fiddle' were held, for the most part, only in the homes of the rough element and were generally accompanied by drunkenness and fighting."

Ames described the actual play itself in general terms: "The playing consisted in keeping step to the singing, and at the same time going through various movements: as swinging partners by one hand or both; advancing, retreating, and bowing; dancing in circles of four or eight; promenading singly or in pairs, sometimes hand in hand, sometimes with crossed hands; weaving back and forth between two rows of people going in opposite directions, and clasping right and left hands alternately with those they meet; etc."

The next article in the *Journal of American Folklore* to deal with the play-party (Hamilton 1914) took exception to Ames' discussion of the passing of the play-party by claiming that "the play-party in northeast Missouri is anything but dead," introducing evidence that "in a certain class of sixteen studying rhetoric here [the Kirksville, Missouri, Normal School] there is one student who knows all the songs but two in Mrs. Ames' collection, and has heard them at play-parties," and telling of a girl of twelve years of age who "has been to nine play-parties this year." Hamilton included thirty-eight play-party texts apparently collected from her rhetoric class but concluded that "the indications are that in a few years the play-party in northern Missouri will be a thing of the past."

In succeeding years, there was a continuing number of other regional reports and collections of play-party songs and dances published in folklore journals. The pioneering book of play-parties, Leah Jackson Wolford's *The Play-Party in Indiana,* was published in 1916, but the single most widely distributed and widely accepted discussions of the genre were written by Benjamin A. Botkin. Botkin selected the play-party as the subject of his Ph.D. dissertation, published an article "The Play-Party in Oklahoma" in the Publications of the Texas Folklore Society Series in 1928, and expanded and developed his research into a book, *The American Play-Party Song* (1937). Botkin's publications served to codify the conclusions of the early play-party scholars and to make them even more widely known. Botkin in general accepted and seconded the description and analyses of the play-party done before him but placed particular stress upon the idea that the words that accompanied the dance were "crude poetry of a crude people."

By the mid-1940s, there were enough regional collections of play-party songs—often including music and descriptions of the dances—published or included in archives that Altha Lea McLendon was able to prepare and publish "A Finding List of Play-Party Games" referencing "302 versions and 315 variants" and demonstrating that play-party songs had been collected from Missouri, North Carolina, Connecticut, Idaho, Maine, Oklahoma, Indiana, Tennessee, Virginia, Georgia, South Carolina, Michigan, Ohio, Mississippi, Kentucky, Arkansas, Wisconsin, and Illinois (McLendon 1944). Her finding list quickly became the standard index to the play-party and seemed—in conjunction with Wolford and Botkin—the final word on the subject.

An essay by Keith Cunningham published in 1972 in the regional folklore journal *AFF* (Arizona Friends of Folklore) *word* reopened the subject of the play-party, included an analytical review of previous research, introduced evidence gathered from recent field research in Arizona, Illinois, and Missouri, and included an exhaustive structural analysis of the games' poetics. Cunningham applied John Ciardi's scansion and explication system of poetry to a quatrain from the widely reported play-party song "Miller Boy" and concluded that the verse followed a consistent pattern, all components of which serve to accelerate the verse. There were two major and two minor stresses per line, with a varied but relatively large number of unaccented syllables, six alliterations, two assonantal rhymes, three approximate rhymes, and two syllabic end rhymes; there was also a minor fulcrum in each line and a major fulcrum between the third and fourth lines. The study concluded that the extremely complex verse of the poetry of "Miller Boy" was a direct reflection of, and very well suited to, the music and actions of the dance as it was played. Cunningham introduced field evidence indicating that there were many local revivals of the play-party across America in places and times long after the frontier had passed and when the play-party was supposed to have died out, and that instrumental accompaniments were frequently a part of the performance of these later examples of the genre. Also presented was evidence that the play-party lives on, not only in American popular culture, as Botkin noted, but also in Anglo American children's tra-

ditional games such as "Farmer in the Dell," "Go in and out the Window," "London Bridge," and "Ring Around the Rosey" and—the fact is not without irony—in the form of tunes such as "Turkey in the Straw," "Old Joe Clark," "Sally Goodin," and "Shoot the Buffalo," which have been a major element in the repertoires of many Anglo American fiddlers, banjo players, and other folk instrumentalists whose traditions made them their own.

Keith Cunningham

References

Cunningham, Keith. 1972. Another Look at the Play-Party. *AFFword* 2:12–23.

Hamilton, Goldy M. 1914. The Play-Party in Northeast Missouri. *Journal of American Folklore* 27:266–288.

Kittredge, George Lyman. 1907. Ballads and Rhymes from Kentucky. *Journal of American Folklore* 20:251–277.

McLendon, Altha Lea. 1944. A Finding List of Play-Party Games. *Southern Folklore Quarterly* 8:201–235.

Wolford, Leah Jackson. [1916] 1959. *The Play-Party in Indiana.* Indianapolis: Indiana Historical Commission. rev. ed. by W. Edson Richmond and William Tillson. Indianapolis: Indiana Historical Society Publications. Vol. 20, no. 2.

See also Games

Poetry, Folk

A form of symbolic communication, using rhyme and/or rhythm, usually directed to a group or community, often local in origin and invariably vernacular in language, intended for reading and/or recitation.

Many forms of folklore have poetic elements, but those most often termed "folk poetry" include children's verses such as nursery and skipping rhymes, occupational verses such as peddler's cries and military cadences, written short verses such as graffiti and autograph-book rhymes, and more extended, often narrative verses such as African American toasts, parodies, and cowboy poetry. Folksongs, though they may be composed of rhymed stanzas, are usually considered a separate category, because music is basic to them.

Many folk poets see rhyme as absolutely essential, but a few are comfortable with free or blank verse. Though rhythmic qualities are evident in folk poetry, few folk poets consciously employ rhythm in their verse. They and their audiences often appreciate rhyming structure because it makes a text more striking and memorable. Rhythm also helps to give poetry these qualities, but some recitations (orally, dramatically performed folk poems) involve other memorable structures as well, as does this nonsense piece, popular in Ontario in the early 1960s:

> I come before you
> to stand behind you
> to tell you something
> I know nothing about.

This Monday
being Good Friday,
there will be a ladies' meeting
for men only.
Admission is free,
pay at the door,
pull up a chair
and sit on the floor.

I have a spelling checker,
It came with my PC;
It plainly marks four my revue
Mistakes I cannot sea.
I've run this poem threw it
I'm sure your please too no,
Its letter perfect in it's weight,
My checker tolled me sew.

The opposing parallels—before versus behind, something versus nothing, Monday versus Friday, ladies versus men, and so on—allow reciters to reconstruct the second element once they have recalled the first. So, this verse's form contributes to its humorous and oxymoronic meaning, but also makes it difficult for a performer to forget.

Folk poetry's formal structures, however, are usually a minor consideration at best for folk poets and their audiences. Unlike fine art poetry, folk poetry is read and recited not because of its beautiful language, or because of its author's uniquely insightful sentiments and striking points of view, but because it expresses something the poet or presenter believes will be useful to the community or group to which it is directed. An autograph verse, for example, is not intended to be read as a work of art; it is simply an appropriate expression of one child's or adolescent's feelings toward another in a clever yet conventional mode. Thus, though some might confuse folk poetry with doggerel, or simply call it bad poetry, it must be evaluated in terms of its context instead of its aesthetic qualities.

Some folk poetry is communicated orally. For example, most children's rhymes and games are not written down until folklorists or other scholars record them; children circulate them by saying them to one another. Other examples, like nursery rhymes, may be transmitted both orally and in written form; parents may gather nursery rhymes from books to tell children orally, and children may retell them back to their parents or other children. Some folk poems are performed orally—at least on some occasions—but were originally composed in writing, such as the verses recited at wedding showers or anniversary celebrations to make fun of—and thus honor—a couple. Some folk poems are prepared for private family or small-group circulation and may be read or said, depending upon the circumstances—those composed to mark a birthday, for example, might be enclosed in a card or declaimed at a party—while others find publication in more public venues like local newspapers and histories, especially poems composed in celebration of a town or of an important figure. For example, some poems about amputee Terry Fox, whose 1980 attempt to run across Canada to raise funds for cancer research moved many people, were sent to his family; some were sent as well, or instead, to community and national newspapers.

Some folk poems require a written format to get their message across. The following example's subtleties—indeed, its point—would be lost if it were recited. The poem derives from the unique context of computerized word processing:

Similarly, graffiti verse is necessarily communicated in written form. The writer can remain anonymous, while creating a memorable message with an impact that depends upon its being present and available to anyone who may see it.

Most writers of folk poetry are moved to communicate in this form because it is an expression of personal or collective views in a form that can be memorable for others. Thus, they avoid language that will exclude their readers. The more familiar the text and its contents are, the better a poem may be used to influence its audience. Thus, many folk poems are based on other rhymed or rhythmic forms, such as well known songs or biblical quotations. "A parable (in rhyme) for careless drivers," published in an Ontario weekly newspaper, parodies a familiar nursery rhyme. Its message is highly significant and, like that of most folk poetry, represents collective knowledge and wisdom:

10 little drivers, cruising down the line, one had a
    heavy foot and then there were nine;
9 little drivers, the hour was late, one dozed a moment
    and then there were eight;
8 little drivers, the evening felt like heaven, one
    showed off his driving skills and then there were
    seven;
7 little drivers, their lives were full of kicks, one
    bought a bottle and then there were six;
6 little drivers, impatient to arrive, one ran a stop sign
    and then there were five;
5 little drivers, wheeling near the shore, one viewed
    the scenery and then there were four;
4 little drivers, happy as could be, one passed upon a
    hill and then there were three;
3 little drivers were busy it was true, one neglected car
    repairs and then there were two;
2 little drivers, the day was nearly done, one did not
    dim his lights and then there was one;
1 little driver who is still alive today, by following the
    safety rules he hopes to stay that way! (Quoted in
    Greenhill 1989:145)

Familiar, vernacular language is the primary vehicle for folk poetry's expression because it is most likely to be accepted by the intended audience. Similarly, especially in the case of longer examples like the above, the audience pays attention to the message because it comes from a fellow community or group member. While remote others' actions may affect any individual's life, where folk poetry is used, one's fellows' evaluations are taken especially seriously. Thus, folk poets speak not as artists with special individualistic knowledge, but as peers—coworkers, family members, and so on. Folk poetry's local origins contribute to its significance and effectiveness.

Authorship—who originally created a folk poem—is fundamentally unimportant to some of its forms. For example, friends who recite a drinking toast before raising their beer glasses do not care who wrote it. But even though other folk poems' authors are community or group members, known to their audiences, these creators notoriously deflect attention, and their texts, away from themselves. Their main aim is to communicate with others, though they may at the same time say a great deal about themselves.

It is not unusual for people to append their names to works that they did not write. By so doing, they do not claim to have originated these poems; instead they indicate its local presenter and advocate. By putting her or his name to a poem in a local newspaper, the presenter submits it to the community's scrutiny as something she or he thinks is worth knowing, or knowing about. Thus, a poem like "The House by the Side of the Road" (Cunningham 1990:166–167) can be recited by a Navajo in the Southwestern United States, or presented by a local poetry collector in the Grand Valley, Ontario, newspaper; each presenter must put his name to the poem because he takes responsibility for its relevance.

The groups or communities to which folk poetry is directed are extremely diverse. They may be ethnic groups, rural communities, age groups, religious congregations, special populations like prisoners, friends, families, and so on. The poems often glorify that group, but they are always internally directed. Since agreed-upon, shared, collective sentiment is almost always folk poetry's focus, we usually find conventional, traditional ideas expressed in folk poetry, rather than unconventional, innovative ones. For example, the late Pennsylvanian folk poet Roscoe Solley's poem "The Bugs Won't Let Me Be" discusses his encounters with the various diseases of old age. It begins:

> When I was young I was sporty
> I was happy, go lucky and free
> Now that old age should be golden
> The bugs won't let me be.

> I'm frequently seeing my doctor
> And taking a lot of his drugs
> But I just don't seem to be able
> To drive off those pesky old bugs.

The poet concludes:

> Now all you good folks pay attention
> For most of this story is true
> So do what you can while you're able
> 'Cause those bugs'll be coming for you (quoted in "Folk Poetry" 1993:90)

This poem's topic is not controversial; instead it knits the audience together by presenting an elder's viewpoint in a humorous way so that other seniors can relate to it, while younger people may both appreciate an elder's perspective and perhaps foresee their own future.

Some folk poetry, like the above, may have implicitly argumentative elements. Solley may have composed his verse to counter what he saw as insufficient understanding, recognition, or valuing of elders' positions; his poem teaches the listener about age and its consequences. Much folk poetry would never be written if its composers thought that prevailing opinions were with them—persuasion of others would then be unnecessary—or if there was no danger that prevailing opinions would ignore, forget, or dismiss their point of view. The relationship between folk poets and their audiences is crucial to much folk poetry's creation and is the fulcrum for its performance.

When people who are not part of a community or group that uses folk poetry read it or hear it, however, it often becomes more controversial. For example, the images of women presented in much folk poetry could offend people who expect an authentic presentation of modern North American women's experiences. Not all folk poetry by men shows women negatively, but this presentation is not uncommon, as in Texas prisoner Johnny Barone's poem about his life experiences:

> Once in jail he came to know,
> Of his wife and best friend Joe,
> She told his sons that he was dead,
> Married Joe and shared his bed (quoted in "Folk Poetry" 1993:45)

Barone's poem makes his wife directly responsible for most of the evil in his life. However, other folk poets extol women's conventional virtues, as in the verses many compose to nurses as a thank you after a hospital visit, which praise their nurturance, kindness, and so on. Realistic folk poetic portraits of women may be composed by female poets; though women are folk poets as frequently as men, they less often present their works in public.

In such a diverse genre as folk poetry, it is difficult to locate a series of specific common qualities. However, folk poetry is generally both symbolic and communicative. Its use usually indicates something about the message being conveyed. For example, in Ontario newspapers, when the same topic or issue is discussed in a letter to the editor and in a poem, the former will usually be contentious and critical, whereas the latter is almost invariably agreeable and positive. In fact, similar opinions may be expressed, but people are likely to choose the poetic form when they wish to invoke common cause, or to suggest that their opinion is shared and positive. Thus, folk poetry's meaning is symbolic, going beyond what it literally says. Though folk poetry is used in only a few communal contexts, these locations and uses become inextricably linked with each poem's actual contents, making folk poetry's manifestations as infinitely variable as are its possible meanings.

Pauline Greenhill

References

Cunningham, Keith. 1990. *The Oral Tradition of the American West: Adventure Courtship, Family, and Place in Traditional Recitation.* Little Rock, AR: August House.

Folk Poetry. 1993. *Canadian Folklore canadien* (Special Issue) 15: (1)1–30.

Greenhill, Pauline. 1989. *True Poetry: Traditional and Popular Verse in Ontario.* Montreal: McGill-Queen's University Press.

Renwick, Roger deV. 1980. *English Folk Poetry: Structure and Meaning.* Philadelphia: University of Pennsylvania Press.

See also Cowboy Poetry; Mnemonic Devices; Parody in Folklore; Prayer; Recitations

Polish Americans

American ethnic group of immigrants from east Europe. Nine million Americans claim Polish descent, according to the 1990 U.S. Census. The vast majority of Polish Americans are descendants of two million landless peasant immigrants who became unskilled laborers for the New World's mines, mills, foundries, factories, and slaughterhouses. These representatives of the economic immigration of 1860–1929 arrived in greatest numbers during the opening decades of the 20th century. At mid century, a second political immigration of 150,000 World War II refugees entered under the Displaced Persons Act of 1948–1954. These were a more educated, urban, nationally conscious group of circumstance-driven emigres. Recently, a third wave of highly educated, urban immigrants—currently estimated at 200,000—appeared in an increasing number of post-Solidarity exiles who, since the former Polish government's imposition of martial law in 1981, seek economic opportunity, career advancement, and status improvement in America.

The first two generations of the economic immigration built the communities and established the institutional structures for the perpetuation of Polish American cultural traditions. The recorded evidence of Polish American folklore derives primarily from these peasant immigrant generations. In the late 20th century, their subsequent generations, along with those of World War II and Solidarity groups, play the leading role in the modification and transformation of tradition in Polish America.

While dispersed throughout the nation, Polish Americans are concentrated in their original 19th-century settlement areas in the Mid-Atlantic, New England, and Upper Midwestern states. Their largest active population centers are in the metropolitan areas of Chicago, New York, Detroit, Buffalo, Pittsburgh, Philadelphia, and Milwaukee. Significant but smaller concentrations appear in Boston, Baltimore, Cleveland, Toledo, South Bend, Minneapolis, Los Angeles, and cities of coastal Connecticut and Northeastern New Jersey. Remnants of rural communities, often secondary settlement areas, can be found throughout the Northeastern American quadrant, most noticeably in the farmlands of the Connecticut River Valley of Massachusetts, and in the central portions of Wisconsin. The earliest rural settlements in Panna Maria, Texas (1854), Polonia, Wisconsin (1856), and Parisville, Michigan (1857) have in the 1990s Polish Americans in their fifth and sixth generations, while the more representative urban centers are characteristically in their third and fourth generations.

Polish Americans use the term "Polonia" to designate their organized community. An intricate interaction of super-territorial organizations such as the Polish American Congress, the Polish National Alliance, the Polish Roman Catholic Union, and the Polish Women's Alliance, combined with informal social networks, maintain a Polonia on both local and national levels. Characteristic behavioral norms that place high value on status competition reinforce individual involvement in Polonia's community life long after its predicted demise.

On the immediate local level, community life centers around family, parish, and neighborhood. In the major urban settlement areas, these foundational community centers can be located by the dominant presence of their characteristically ornate, magnificent Roman Catholic churches. Chicago has forty-three Polish parishes; Detroit has thirty. The earliest inner-city, ethnic parishes have declined in membership since the 1960s as the upwardly mobile third and fourth generations have moved to outer-city fringes and suburban neighborhoods, where they have become members of nonethnic territorial parishes, have intermarried with members of other Catholic groups, and have dispensed with the Polish language. Inner-city parishes, many of which now serve African American and Latin American populations, continue to fulfill both the liturgical needs of recent Polish-speaking immigrants as well as the symbolic needs of English-speaking Polish Americans in connection with rites of passage and calendrical customs.

A Polish presence in America from 1608 to 1854 had no demographic consequences yet contributed a legacy of myth and legend of great importance for ethnic traditions and symbols. Polish glassmakers and soap makers, among the first colonists at Jamestown, were enfranchised after staging America's first organized industrial strike in 1619. Polish American tradition also credits the Jamestown Poles with playing the first game of baseball in the New World.

This early period provides Polish America with its two most celebrated legendary heroes, Thaddeus Kosciuszko and Casimir Pulaski, the eminent, aristocratic generals in the War of Independence. Kosciuszko, the father of West Point and fervent champion of democratic ideals, has both a more luminous international reputation and a greater appeal to recent Polish immigrants as well as later, American-born generations. Pulaski, the father of the American cavalry, who gave his life on the Revolutionary battlefield and whose name is more easily spelled and pronounced, remains the more prominent ethnic and national figure. The United States has seven counties and twenty towns named for Pulaski, one of each for Kosciuszko. In 1911 the U.S. Congress established the national observance of October 11 in memory of Pulaski's sacrificial death; in 1986 the state of Illinois recognized Pulaski's birthday, March 4, as a legal holiday. Major cities of Polonia me-

morialize both Pulaski and Kosciuszko through statues, monuments, and names of streets, bridges, and schools. Both are common patrons of organizations and clubs. Portraits of the two Revolutionary heroes are standard fixtures in meeting halls and business establishments. As meaningful focal points for parades, celebrations, festivals, banquets, and balls, both equip Polonia with potent symbols for expressing a simultaneous sense of ethnic particularism and broad national identity.

Other military exiles arrived after partitioned Poland's unsuccessful, Kosciuszko-inspired insurrection against czarist Russia in 1794 and those of 1830, 1848, and 1863. Kosciuszko's 1797 triumphal return visit to his second country, along with the increasing frequency of American exposure to rebellious and aristocratic Polish emigres, led to the construction of the nation's first Polish stereotype in the early 19th century. The familiar freedom-loving Pole became a fixed image of American admiration for all that was noble, chivalrous, passionate, cultivated, and high minded. Throughout the 19th century, American popular fiction, poetry, and theater perpetuated this romantic image, based on the Pulaski-Kosciuszko prototype, expressing a Polish national ideal that essentially corresponded with the American "Spirit of '76." The popular romantic stereotype endured, to a lesser degree, into the 20th century, where it remains alive as recently as 1983, in the pages of James Michener's best-selling novel *Poland.*

A second American stereotype of the 20th century depends upon an image of the more familiar Polish American as a member of an urban, working-class, ethnic minority group.

The primary vehicle for this stereotype is American folklore, particularly the ethnic riddle joke known as the "Polack" joke. The "Polack" in these jokes is characteristically poor, stupid, dirty, inept, and tasteless. Some of these joke texts show a familiarity with Polish history and custom. Some refer to Polish American ethnographic realities such as personal and geographic names. Most conform to the parent universal numskull type. Unlike its variant numskull traditions that remain localized, directed at other locally prominent, working-class, minority groups, the "Polack" joke has persisted in American tradition on a national level. The exoteric ethnic-slur term "Polack" can be converted to esoteric use among Polish Americans in restricted social contexts. Exoteric usage often confuses the slur term with the Polish word *Polak,* the singular form for Polish male. Polish speakers hear a distinct phonemic difference in the first syllable of the two words (based on the distinction of a Polish open o and the English closed o) and do not accept the slur term as a substitute for the Polish word. Popular culture, particularly film, continues to employ the "Polack" joke, its stereotype, and its slur term to the frustrated displeasure of the members of Polonia.

Polish American oral traditions collected from the first and second generations of the economic immigrants show a characteristic tendency to preserve the memory of peasant agricultural folklife traditions in village Poland. Some of the texts deal with sorrow of immigration and have America as a referent. The principal collections, Harriet Pawlowska's folksongs and Marion Moore Coleman's folktales, represent traditional texts that have clear analogs in the ethnographic materials assembled in sixty-six volumes by Kolberg in 19th-century Poland. Polish American proverb collections show that some forms remain unaltered on both sides of the Atlantic, for example, *Gosc w dom, Bog w dom* (Guest in the home, God in the home). Others show changes and inventions that derive from a New World context. The Polish American proverb *Musial ale nie chcial* (He had to, but he did not want to) has a totally American meaning, rendering it incomprehensible and unproverbial to a European Pole. For Polish Americans, familiar with both the heroic stature of baseball star Stan Musial and the national media broadcasters' inability to say "Musial" the Polish way (like English "Mooshaw"), the proverb's meaning involves commentary on both the undesirability and the inevitability of either anglicizing or mispronouncing a difficult Polish surname.

Polish American oral tradition also contains many English-language narratives featuring a common Polish word, phrase, or cultural detail that can be understood and transmitted by Polish Americans with little or no knowledge of the mother tongue. Many of these take the form of the immigrant epic, a series of comic incidents in which the humor derives from the misunderstanding of a word in the home or host language. Others playfully focus on satirical or parodic comment on wedding and funeral customs. Still others deal with questions of identity, group conflict, and ethnic discrimination. One such narrative attributes the invention of the Volkswagen to a Polish guy in Detroit whose genius remains unrecognized in Europe and America. Western injustice is corrected only in Japan, where, the tale playfully claims, the Volkswagen has been named with the Polish words—and Japanese sounds—*Jaka Ta Mala Car"* (What a tiny car!).

Polish American jokes sometimes follow the riddle-joke pattern but contain sufficient esoteric content to confine their transmission to insiders. "What's the sound of a Polish grandfather clock? —tock, tock." (Since "tock" is phonetically equivalent to Polish *tak,* the word for yes, its association with the word "grandfather" imparts an affirmative message about heritage to the ears of a Polish American.) Comparable oral traditions commonly appear in the narratives of the third and fourth generations.

Customs and rituals associated with the Catholic liturgical calendar and the life cycle remain popular among Polish Americans of all backgrounds. Those traditions dependent upon material culture for their production and performance show a practice pattern shifting from homemade, family-centered activity to a manufactured, commercialized, public sphere. This trend may be indicative of the increasing value of symbolic ethnicity for Polish Americans. The Easter customs associated with *swiecone,* the paraliturgical blessing of food baskets on Holy Saturday, also converts to elaborate parties and banquets. So, too, does the secular *Dyngus-Smigus* Day on the Monday after Easter, a gender-based ritual water dousing and reed switching, in which young males customarily sprinkle young females with water or perfume prior to, or alternatively to, switching them with reeds. On the following day, the girls reciprocate the favor. These events are often sponsored by either Polish American cultural and fraternal organizations or by entrepreneurs of Polish restaurants, specialty shops, and mass media. Public, commercial entertainment for

such symbolic affairs also occasions revival and transmission of traditional village dance and the rural arts of *pisanki* (egg painting) and *wycinanki* (cut-paper designs).

Polish American Christmas customs feature the religious folksong *(koleda)* primarily in family and church contexts. Here too, organized community events aid the revival of ancient folklore—for example, the production of medieval Nativity plays as miniature puppet theatricals *(szopka)*. Christmas Eve supper (*Wigilia)* involving ritual sharing of an unleavened bread wafer *(oplatek)* along with a fixed number of meatless dishes may become a public occasion replete with meat-filled traditional foods and orchestrated entertainment beyond the capacity of the family.

Life-cycle folkways manifest similar contemporary adaptation. The band leader or the church organist usually arranges and performs traditional singing at weddings and funerals. The customary meal and social gathering after the wedding *(poprawiny)* or funeral *(stypa)* now commonly falls under the care of restaurateurs and caterers. Ethnic foods prepared within the household show the lingering persistence of regional variation. Popular favorites include sausage (kielbasa), stuffed cabbage *(golabek),* dumpling (pierogi), crepe *(nalesnik),* duck's blood soup *(czarnina),* sauerkraut *(kapusta),* and jelly-filled pastry *(paczek).* Polish Americans in the 1990s can satisfy both their culinary tastes and their identificational needs through convenient purchases at the neighborhood store, the supermarket, or the expanding restaurant trade. A widespread Polish American custom of distributing the jelly doughnut to outsiders at the workplace on Shrove Tuesday, makes "Paczki Day" an eagerly anticipated event among the general American populace in the major urban settlement areas.

Polish American polka music hybridizes folk and popular traditions into a lively, subcultural entertainment complex sometimes labeled "polka culture" or "*Hupaj Siupaj* culture," from the nonsense words of a traditional Polish drinking song. The Polish American polka phenomenon emphasizes a participatory, dynamic song-and-dance experience, learned and perfected through personal imitation of friends, neighbors, and kin at weddings, picnics, festivals, and bars within the contexts of general frivolity, eating, drinking, and socializing. At special events, like "polkabrations," participants may wear handmade or commercial costumes with ethnically meaningful colors and designs, in addition to jackets, buttons, bumper stickers, posters, and other signs that proclaim ethnic identity in creative ways.

There are many different Polish American polka styles. An urban, Eastern style, dominant in the 1930s and 1940s, gave way to the now prevalent rural, Chicago style in the 1950s. Adherents of the Eastern style prefer fast-paced, highly orchestrated, fixed compositions of formally trained New York musicians. The Chicago style, originated after World War II by L'il Wally Jagiello, a self-taught, Chicago-born, child virtuoso, began as a revitalization of the Polish village polka. Its practitioners favor informality, improvisation, slower tempo, and vocals reliant upon Polish folksong. Soulful emotionalism and attachment to ethnic roots as much as their practicality for the dance, attract second- and third-generation musicians to this popular development. Recent variations of the nationally prevalent Chicago style incorporate the influences of rock, blues, and country-western music.

Polish Americans are likely to continue their superterritorial organizations well into the future. Their expressions of ethnicity can be expected to undergo continued adaptation, as well as unforeseen revival and revitalization as evidenced in the polka. Involvement of professional and commercial interests in the formerly private sphere lessens the folkloric dimension of folklife while it increases both the knowledge of ethnic content and the options for selective ethnic experience. As Polish American populations disperse along with upward mobility, the need to create self-identity through association with collective heritage may extend the domain of public ethnic celebration that depends upon the realities of folk tradition.

John A. Gutowski

References

Bukowczyk, John J. 1987. *And My Children Did Not Know Me: A History of the Polish Americans.* Bloomington: Indiana University Press.

Clements, William M. 1969. The Types of the Polack Joke. *Folklore Forum,* Bibliographic and Special Series, Vol. 3. November.

Coleman, Marion Moore. 1965. *A World Remembered: Tales and Lore of the Polish Land.* Cheshire, CT: Cherry Hill.

Gladsky, Thomas S. 1992. *Princes, Peasants, and Other Polish Selves: Ethnicity in American Literature.* Amherst: University of Massachusetts Press.

Knab, Sophie Hodorowicz. 1993. *Polish Customs, Traditions, and Folklore.* New York: Hippocrene.

Lopata, Helena Znaniecki. 1976. *Polish Americans: Status Competition in an Ethnic Community.* Englewood Cliffs, NJ: Prentice-Hall.

Obidinski, Eugene E., and Helen Stankiewicz Zand. 1987. *Polish Folkways in America.* Lanham, MD: University Press of America.

Pawlowska, Harriet. 1961. *Merrily We Sing: 105 Polish Folksongs.* Detroit: Wayne State University Press.

Thomas, William I., and Florian Znaniecki. 1918–1920. *The Polish Peasant in Europe and America.* 5 vols. Boston: Richard G. Badger.

Wrobel, Paul. 1979. *Our Way: Family, Parish, and Neighborhood in a Polish-American Community.* Notre Dame: University of Notre Dame Press.

Politics and Folklore

The study of power and creativity at the grass roots, a rubric under which fall seven distinct but interrelated areas of folklore and folklife research. When folklorists use the term, they refer to the relationship between political life and folk expression in the following ways: (1) *the folklore of politics,* meaning the folklore that emerges from the political process and political conflict; (2) *the politics of folklore,* meaning the impact on people's lives and well-being as a result of their culture, their folklore, and their creation and dissemination of that culture; (3) *the politics of folkloristics,* meaning the political implications of the study of folklore; (4) *the politics of applied folklore policy,* meaning the political implications of government, corporate, and other nongovernmental policies regarding the implementation of folklore and cultural programming; (5) *political interpretations of folklore* by scholars; (6) *folk political organization and alternative social institutions,* meaning how power relationships among individuals and classes are expressed and negotiated informally in society or within smaller groups, and how small groups relate to the larger society; and (7) *political belief as folklore,* what may be called the study of ideology from a belief-centered perspective.

North American folklorists have paid the most attention to protest songs, political and ethnic jokes, folklore in the labor movement, Communism, and most recently cultural conservation. Some hotly political topics have not been discussed within the framework of politics and folklore, such as war, slavery, genocide, and, to some extent, feminism, while other political issues of concern to folklorists elsewhere in the world have drawn less attention to North America—namely, nationalism, folklorismus, colonialism, Nazism, and revolution.

The Folklore of Politics

The Declaration of Independence states that "all men are created equal," but human social institutions, from the nation-state to the family, have never really treated people that way. As a result, that inequity has produced conflict, and from that conflict has sprung creative expression, whether it is (to paraphrase German playwright and poet Bertolt Brecht) a mirror to reflect reality or a hammer to shape it.

Significant periods in American history have been shaped by their political folklore. Even before the establishment of the United States, social conflict was part of the weave of the North American continent. The Pueblo Revolt of 1680, the only successful major uprising by Native Americans, which ejected the Spanish from the area, began in northern New Mexico on August 10, 1680, a day chosen because it was the feast day of San Lorenzo, patron saint of Picurís Pueblo. The rebellion not only generated support among the Pueblo Indian villages through word of mouth, but also has been understood and commemorated through the telling of its legend to this day. Similarly, before the Civil War, the abolition movement spread through public speeches by orators such as Frederick Douglass and others, and through orally circulated stories of atrocities against enslaved persons, underground and oppositional newspapers, and hand-circulated photographs depicting the horrors of slavery. In fact, some of the enslaved Africans in North America rebelled against slave owners by various forms of folk protest, including sabotage, work slowdowns and strikes, coded songs, the teaching of literacy, and literally survived by means of clandestine practices, including the shared knowledge of escape methods and routes. Many of these stories of the Underground Railroad, as the movement to help slaves escape became known, were collected orally in the years after the war by William Still, then the clerk of the Pennsylvania Anti-Slavery Society in Philadelphia (see Still [1872]

1970). Later, in the 1930s and 1940s, narratives of ex-slaves were collected as part of the Federal Writers' Project (FWP) of the Works Progress Administration (WPA), and an anthology, concentrating on the "human and imaginative aspects" of slavery was edited by Benjamin A. Botkin, head of the FWP Folklore Division (Botkin [1945] 1994).

The wars between the United States and the Native American nations in the 19th century had their own impact on Native American cultures and religious practices, but except for James Mooney, who collected narratives from survivors of the Cherokee Trail of Tears, the Wounded Knee massacre, and the Apache resistance, few folklorists conducted research on the human cost of the politics of Manifest Destiny.

Another aspect of American political history to attract attention was the labor movement of the early 20th century, which has been of special interest to folklorists because of the inclusion of music in labor organizing by the Industrial Workers of the World (IWW, or "Wobblies"), the United Mine Workers, and other unions. Strikes and demonstrations, in addition to their oppositional social organization and unique tactics (such as fasts and long marches by Cesar Chavez and the United Farm Workers), also included music, songbooks, banners, buttons, and other protest ephemera, and topical songs and poetry. Historian Philip S. Foner compiled *American Labor Songs of the Nineteenth Century* (1975), while folklorists George Korson and Archie Green collected union folklore (see Green 1993). Prominent artists to arise from labor struggles included Aunt Molly Jackson, Woody Guthrie, and groups such as the International Ladies Garment Workers' Union (ILGWU) Chorus. Notable texts from the labor movement include the songs "Which Side Are You On?" (from the mine workers); "Joe Hill"; "Solidarity Forever"; James Oppenheim's topical song "Bread and Roses," (whose title was inspired by a strike banner in Lowell, Massachusetts); and the topical poetry of Carlos Bulosan, whose poems were sometimes first printed on cannery workers' union leaflets in California.

Folklore of the Communist Party from 1920 to 1960 has received much more attention from folklorists than has the lore of any other American political party, despite its relatively small membership. Serge Denisoff and Richard A. Reuss provided overviews of the Almanac Singers, People's Songs, the development of *Sing Out!* magazine, and Communism in the labor movement, but they focused mostly on the programmatic nature of folklore policy in the party rather than the beliefs and expressions of everyday members and their response to party music and culture. Communist, and indeed Left culture in general in the mid-20th century, had a lasting impact on American musical culture, whether through the performances of Paul Robeson, Pete Seeger, or Phil Ochs, the collection and promotion of the blues by John and Alan Lomax, or the folksong revival of the 1950s and 1960s. While the revival topical-song movement was smaller than the original movement in the earlier parts of the century, more lasting has been the impact of African American music on American and world music in general; the role of the blues, spirituals, and early rhythm and blues in the development of rock and contemporary popular, or mass, music around the world cannot be underestimated.

The civil rights movement provided a heyday for the blend of folklore and politics, as songs, marches, and creative protests incorporating the first American mass folk usage of civil disobedience were woven into the fabric of the movement. The Highlander Folk School in Tennessee, which had helped to train union organizers, became a veritable training ground for civil rights activists and musicians both, and such prominent folklorists-performers as Myles Horton, Bernice Johnson Reagon, and Guy and Candie Carawan, as well as scores of organizers for the Congress of Industrial Organizations (CIO) and the Student Non-Violent Coordinating Committee (SNCC), incorporated lessons both political and musical in their work for social justice. There and in the context of the civil rights movement, songs of spiritual origin were adapted for political and spiritual uses, including "We Shall Overcome" and "We Shall Not Be Moved," which have remained part of American political folklore through the end of the 20th century.

Much of American political life has remained unexamined by folklorists, and such broad themes as party politics, war, the suffrage and feminist movements, and race and class relations demand more research. Much of what has been done focuses on political texts, especially songs and jokes, and contextual information has been lacking. Prison lore, noted in American literature as early as Henry David Thoreau in "Civil Disobedience" and more recently examined by Bruce Jackson, and military folklore have received some attention, but more research into these areas is needed.

The Politics of Folklore

Folkloric expression itself can be a political act, even without a necessarily political interpretation. Folk protest can take the form of street theater, Luddite sabotage, or other kinds of creative protest, an excellent catalog of which can be found in Gene Sharp's *The Politics of Nonviolent Action* (1973). American folklorists, such as Susan Davis, have looked at carnivalesque protest forms such as parades, shivarees, and satirical burlesques. In addition to events, political attitudes can also be expressed through symbols and other displays, including flags, buttons, badges, posters, bumper stickers, signs, window decorations, and ceremonial foods. The arrangement and use as well as the content can affect the meaning.

The enforcement of folk justice, which can include such actions as vendettas and lynchings, is another topic that has drawn some interest, and William Lynwood Montell has done the most thorough job of putting such violence in its full context. Américo Paredes' understated *With His Pistol in His Hand* (1958) concerns the history and politics of a Texas ballad. Much occupational folklore, such as that documented by Archie Green and Robert McCarl, raises issues of unequal power and social exploitation, whether expressed through strikes, songs, or accident narratives. When and where all of these forms are expressed—and where they are not, either forbidden or hidden—carries enormous weight in both their symbolic and their practical value.

Folklore emerging from social conflict is inherently political. Philosophically, the challenge for the field of folklore is to balance two sets of questions about folk protest and the folklore of social conflict and struggle: aesthetic questions, concerning form, structure, and expediency; and ethical questions, concerning what is just and moral.

The Politics of Folkloristics

The political beliefs of folklorists—that is, their personal ideologies—have shaped American folkloristics, as ideologies shape the formation and agenda of every discipline. Joel Chandler Harris used his Uncle Remus tales to promulgate his at best paternalistic (at worst racist) views of Southern plantation society, while Zora Neale Hurston took the opportunity in both scholarly and popular works to promote a more egalitarian view. In the late 20th century, whether Marxist (Communist, Socialist) or post-Enlightenment liberal (capitalist), in outlook, choices about what to study, the methodology of that study, and the outcomes and outlets for research are determined by political attitudes, often unarticulated. While James Mooney was traveling among Native American nations during the late 19th and 20th century, documenting religious practices that had been outlawed by the U.S. government and fighting with government agents to allow such traditional cultural practices to continue, Alice Fletcher and John Wesley Powell were promoting allotment and individual capitalism as paths to lead the Indians to Christianity and lobbying on behalf of such programs in Congress. Years later, the very different personal politics of Richard M. Dorson and Kenneth S. Goldstein, for example, resulted in academic departments at Indiana University and the University of Pennsylvania, respectively, with different orientations and different traditions for scholarly practice. Likewise, the ideological differences between Benjamin A. Botkin and Archie Green resulted in different blueprints for applied and public-sector folklore. Indeed, the kinds of choices made in the field in the 1990s, between "pure" and "applied" research, between academic and public-sector emphases, between detached and engaged investigation, reflect more than is acknowledged in a century-old debate about social action, which most prominently manifested itself in debates about popularization, advocacy, and anti-Communism. Late-20th-century folklorists are concerned with questions of multiculturalism and representation; they think about the kinds of critical questions that are raised in academic texts, exhibits, and public programs, as well as about those that are left unasked.

The Politics of Applied Folklore and Folklore Policy

Half of American folklore work takes place in the public sector, and the choices made concerning what programs and policies to develop are inevitably political. The Federal Writers' Project, begun in the 1930s as part of President Franklin D. Roosevelt's New Deal, was the first systematic government public-folklore program in America, though historically folklorists and social workers made attempts to wed folklore with the ideals of social betterment and a Romantic, Whitmanesque celebration of common genius, with mixed success. Lucy McKim Garrison, daughter-in-law of the abolitionist William Lloyd Garrison, collected and published slave songs in South Carolina; folklorist Heli Chatelain worked to improve conditions in Africa in the late 1800s; Stewart Culin advocated on behalf of Philadelphia's Chinese community; Olive Dame Campbell attempted to uplift Appalachian culture around the turn of the 20th century; and Jane Addams incorporated art and folk culture into her work with immigrants at Chicago's Hull House. Whether these well-intentioned activities were motivated by noblesse oblige, or by political commitment, or some combination of the two, they met with mixed success, arguably because they placed less faith in the ability of the people being "helped" to control their own culture and destiny. The tension between the programmatic and the collaborative nature of applied and public-sector work has been a dominant theme in American folkloristics for more than fifty years, particularly since the Nazi manipulation of folklore in the 1930s and 1940s made all such agendas suspect by association. David Whisnant's critique of early cultural programming in Appalachia in particular has brought issues of what he calls the "politics of culture" into the forefront of folklorists' consciousness, by investigating the often unintended impact of the Romantic impulses behind the discipline (Whisnant 1983).

The site where public- and applied-folklore work take place can determine some of the political considerations, as government offices and nongovernmental nonprofit groups will have different relationships with the political structures. The New Deal Federal Writers Project, the American Folklife Center—established in 1976 at the Library of Congress as a result of considerable lobbying and groundwork by folklorist Archie Green—and the Smithsonian Festival of American Folklife have been government, essentially political, programs with far-reaching impacts. On the other hand, urban nonprofit organizations, such as New York's City Lore and the Philadelphia Folklore Project, have used their independence to ask critical questions and investigate politicized topics that might be too risky for government agencies. That such groups, whether in the governmental or the nongovernmental sector, can help communities find funding and provide technical assistance for their cultural programming is but one example of the ways in which folklorists use political skills to facilitate cultural diversity and self-determination. These choices and strategies even within folklore agencies are, of course, political, since questions of inclusion, neglect, collaboration, reciprocity, empowerment, and social transformation are always at the fore.

Within the field, the paradigm of cultural conservation became dominant once public-sector folklore gained a foothold, though saving remnants of dying cultures has always been a part of American folklore's manifesto. Not just studying, but saving and protecting traditional cultures, be they immigrant, Native American, or occupational, has been a primary goal of public-sector folklorists from the outset. As folklorists develop an analysis of why such cultures traditionally fare poorly as they are swept up into the American mainstream, the work of cultural resistance becomes increasingly political. Yet, cultural conservation has been critiqued in two very significant ways.

First, as James Abrams, director of the Folklife Division of America's Industrial Heritage project (AIHP) in Johnstown, Pennsylvania, has commented, as public and state agencies interpret ethnic and occupational experience historically, folklorists rightly ask the question, Whose version of the story is being told, to what end, and to whose benefit? Are states and corporations retelling the history and conserving an interpretation of the past that legitimates, rather than critiques, social injustice and inequality?

Second, folklorists interested in dynamic and emergent culture and the experience of migration wonder whether a cultural-conservation paradigm (1) discriminates against those who adapt and change their cultural forms to fit new environments; and (2) ghettoizes traditional artists, preventing them from entering into debates over so-called mainstream culture on an equal footing and insisting that the only way they can obtain funding as artists is if they retain traditional, favored forms. Do cultural-conservation programs and blueprints favor long-term, settled, propertied residents of an area over migrant workers, recent immigrants, and, in the Northern states in particular, African Americans who came north during the Great Migration?

The cultural-conservation paradigm has, however, resulted in festival, museum, and archival documentation, as well as the promotion and funding of traditional arts through apprenticeships and other programs that have had long-lasting social, economic, psychological, and political impacts in a range of underserved communities.

This is not to imply that government policy is always beneficently envisioned or executed. The U.S. military, in the 1960s and 1970s during the war in Southeast Asia, employed folklore research as a means of counterinsurgency and pacifying the Vietnamese countryside, particularly the brilliant work of Major General Edward Lansdale, who had earlier used such techniques to combat insurgency in the Philippines (Fish 1989). Similarly, when the elected government of Chile was overthrown by a CIA-backed coup, the junta's torture and murder of popular topical folksinger Victor Jara was carried out in a method so graphic—according to the legend that still circulates in communities of human rights activists throughout the hemisphere, including the United States—that it had to have had symbolic as well as practical significance. Policy decisions about, and uses of, folklore and culture can thus serve to protect life and human cultural diversity or destroy it.

Political Interpretations of Folklore

In addition to political decisions about research and policy, some folklorists engage in a political analysis of folkloric events and texts, some of which have more overt political content than others. These interpretations, often Marxist, feminist, or Weberian in orientation, have ranged from asserting that all folklore is inherently oppositional to the powers-that-be, to claiming that folklore is virtually ineffectual and palliative. Prior to 1970, most of the political analysis concentrated on the content of folklore and on relatively simple oppositions between the oppressor and oppressed. The advent in the mid-1970s of performance theory not only shifted the focus away from content and toward the full social context, but also added a degree of agency, individuality, and responsibility for performance that in most cases had not previously been accorded narrators and "informants." Henry Glassie's *Passing the Time in Ballymenone* (1982) is a complex example of political-song and folk-historical narrative in full ethnographic context.

In American folkloristics of the 1990s, several currents of political analysis predominate, borrowing from other disciplines and countries and exerting an influence even over seemingly nonpolitical interpretations in the field. Some folklorists have followed trends in literary theory, practicing a social analysis drawing from the Frankfurt school of Marxist analysis and combining it with the ideas of Frederic Jameson or Jürgen Habermas. In some cases, these cultural studies have minimized the role of class, the means of production, and native voice, in favor of the more postmodern literary approach of Michel Foucault, Jacques Derrida, and postmodern social-anthropological theory. Another line of inquiry has built upon the writings of Italian Communist Antonio Gramsci and incorporated that with the social-historical focus of Raymond Williams and E.P. Thompson. Complementing this latter approach are writings of Third World theorists and activists, notably Frantz Fanon, Amílcar Cabral, and Paulo Freire, who are interested in questions of culture, colonialism, and human liberation. In the United States, these approaches have been expanded upon particularly by African American writers, especially Cornel West and bell hooks in their essays on theology, anthropology, and literature. The work of literary critic Edward Said spans both literary theory and anticolonialism and is also important to current folklorists. In addition, the analysis of feminism, particularly in its attention to subjugated voices, coding strategies, and social history, has been influential within the field. African American and Latino scholars, particularly John W. Roberts, Gerald Davis, Patricia Turner, Manuel Peña, and José Limón, have synthesized folklore theory, American history, and African American and chicano studies to critique politically the past century of American folklore scholarship on issues of race and ethnicity and to address questions of conflict and inequality in both the larger society and the discipline (see Limón 1983).

Folk Political Organization and Alternative Social Institutions

Class and economic life are a central part of European folklife scholarship but are seldom discussed in American folkloristics. The study of power relations, whether in larger social structures or within family relationships, is a part of folklife studies, and the ways in which people organize themselves, decide to rebel, negotiate power, or subvert it are part of the strategies of everyday life. In some cases in American history, as elsewhere, groups have set up alternative social institutions—some withdrawing from the world, some confronting it—that are folk societies, albeit intentional ones. Religious settlements and cooperative communities, from New Harmony to The Farm, are an important part of American sectarian and political life. Whether their ideologies are far Left or far Right, they are commentaries on existing in the face of a larger dominant culture and are creative ways to dispense with aspects of the dominant culture that are unacceptable to adherents. On a smaller scale, people establish alternative social institutions that may affect fewer people (such as squatter settlements and subway concourse shantytowns) or concern a less all-encompassing aspect of everyday life (such as food co-ops or community or organic gardens). Along these lines, belief scholars have engaged in a critique of the medical establishment and the notion of religious homogeneity that can only be called political in its reassertion of individual self-knowledge and dignity in the face of overwhelming mass social institutions. This includes the study of alternative medicine and oppositional religious sects, such as acupuncture or *santeria*, respectively. Some of these alternative institutions become expressly political issues when they are outlawed by the dominant legal system.

Power structures within smaller groups and the political organization of small communities, be they neighborhoods, congregations, or families, are also subjects of interest for the folklorist. The prevalence, for example, of domestic violence as a means of maintaining physical and economic control within families is an important, if unacknowledged, part of American folklife, as is police brutality in city neighborhoods.

Alternative economic arrangements, such as bartering and under-the-table employment, are likewise part of the fabric of American society. Both bartering and the cash economy are means of undermining the state economic system; the former asserts independence from the knowledge of the government, while the latter can be a way for either the employer or the worker to get around official regulations, but all too often becomes an instrument of social exploitation.

Political Belief as Folklore

American folklorists have begun to examine political belief itself as an aspect of folklife that transcends genres, not unlike religious or health belief, from proverbs to autobiographical narratives. Political beliefs include attitudes and understandings of power and justice issues and how they affect individuals and groups. Folklorist David Shuldiner has termed such personal analysis of political, economic, and social conditions "folk ideology" (Shuldiner 1991), but thus far there have been few ethnographic studies that investigate within a group or movement the range of the expression in such beliefs in their full context. Botkin, in his collection of edited narratives of former slaves (Botkin [1945] 1994), began the collection with excerpts from oral literature and popular belief, thus grounding the personal narratives that followed in the depiction of the wisdom and analysis of the narrators. Since folklore, unlike other disciplines, pays special attention to the words, expressions, and beliefs of the people being observed or studied, the study of belief reminds us that there can be no understanding of living people without asking.

William Westerman

References

Botkin, B.A., ed. [1945] 1994. *Lay My Burden Down: A Folk History of Slavery.* New York: Delta.

Carawan, Guy, and Candie Carawan. 1990. *Sing for Freedom: The Story of the Civil Rights Movement through Its Songs,* comp. and ed. by Guy Carawan and Candie Carawan. Bethlehem, PA: Sing Out Publications.

Fish, Lydia M. 1989. General Edward G. Lansdale and the Folksongs of Americans in the Vietnam War. *Journal of American Folklore* 102:390–411.

Fowke, Edith, and Joe Glazer. 1973. *Songs of Work and Protest.* New York: Dover.

Green, Archie. 1993. *Wobblies, Pile Butts, and Other Heroes: Laborlore Explorations.* Urbana: University of Illinois Press.

Lieberman, Robbie. 1989. *"My Song Is My Weapon": People's Songs, American Communism, and the Politics of Culture, 1930–1950.* Urbana: University of Illinois Press.

Limón, José E. 1983. Western Marxism and Folklore: A Critical Introduction. *Journal of American Folklore* 96:34–52.

Radner, Joan N., and Susan S. Lanser. 1987. The Feminist Voice: Strategies of Coding in Folklore and Literature. *Journal of American Folklore* 100:412–425.

Shuldiner, David. 1991. The Celebration of Passover among Jewish Radicals. In *Creative Ethnicity,* ed. Stephen Stern and John Allan Cicala. Logan: Utah State University Press, pp. 159–170.

Still, William. [1872] 1970. *The Underground Railroad Records.* Chicago: Lincoln Press.

Whisnant, David E. 1983. *All That Is Native and Fine: The Politics of Culture in an American Region.* Chapel Hill: University of North Carolina Press.

See also Applied Folklore; Coding in American Folk Culture; Cultural Conservation; Cultural Studies; Feminist Approaches to Folklore; Marxist Approach; Military Folklore; Occupational Folklore; Postmodernism; Prison Folklore; Public Folklore; Social Protest in Folklore

Polka

A dance; a generic modifier for an entire musical complex. The word has been attributed variously to three Czech sources: *pulka* (half-step), perhaps because of the dance's footwork; *pole* (field), perhaps alluding to an outdoor village dance "floor"; and *polska* (Polish woman), perhaps in reference to the Bohemian adaptation of the Polish *krakowiak* dance-songs into polkas.

Performed by a couple executing a hop-step close-step pattern in 2/4 time, the dance emerged around 1830 in an appropriately eclectic Germanized Czech region near the Polish border. Although it draws upon earlier ethnically diverse forms, the polka's oft-printed origin legend, suffused with the era's Romantic nationalism, suggests that Anna Slezak, a Bohemian peasant girl in the village of Elbeteinetz, improvised a tune and steps one summer afternoon. The local schoolmaster noticed Slezak's invention, taught it to his students, and

Did they play a polka at the Polish Constitution Day Parade? Chicago, 1977. Photo Jonas Dovydenas. American Folklife Center.

inadvertently started an international dance craze. By the mid-1830s, the polka had entered the genteel ballrooms of Prague; by the mid-1840s, it had been introduced to Vienna, Paris, and London by Czech brass bands and dancing masters; and by the mid-19th century, the polka had conquered Europe's elite, swept the salons of urban America, and claimed the allegiance of rural dancers on both sides of the Atlantic.

After a few decades of popularity, the polka was gradually abandoned by upper-class American aficionados. It persisted, however, as a residual form among many rural Americans, and it never lost its power among northern and central European immigrants and their offspring. Indeed, "polka's" broader application as a generic term emerged in the early 20th century.

The international prominence of the polka was paralleled by the broad diffusion of such other central European dances as the waltz and the schottische. In the United States, these dances and the German accordion entered the repertoires of French, African, and Mexican Americans, thus contributing to the development of Cajun, zydeco, and *conjunto* styles. Meanwhile, the polka and related forms served as musical common denominators for many European newcomers, particularly those of Germanic, Scandinavian, and Slavic heritage. When second-generation ethnic band leaders began recording, performing over the radio, and touring in the 1920s, they sought increasingly broader audiences. Beyond a core ethnic repertoire, they played the favorites of their "foreign" neighbors, as well as Anglo American folk and popular tunes. The incipient genre's commercial promoters encouraged this "crossover" strategy.

The career of polka music's first "star," Hans Wilfahrt

(1893–1961) is instructive. Wilfahrt began playing old country tunes at the age of fifteen for house dances south of New Ulm, Minnesota, in an enclave of ethnic German immigrants from Bohemia. His first recordings, made in Minneapolis in 1927, were mostly Czech and German polkas, waltzes, and schottisches, but they also included waltzes of Polish and Swedish origin. Wilfahrt's Okeh label sought a still wider pan-ethnic audience by marketing the band variously as Hans Wilfahrt's Concertina Orchestra, Hans Wilfahrts Kapelle, Ceská Tanecni Hudba, Orkiestra Wiejska, L'Orchestre Chartier, and Orquesta De Concertina Juan Wilfahrt. By the mid-1930s, the band was known simply as Whoopee John Wilfahrt and His Orchestra, and all of its titles, whatever their origin, were issued in English. Whoopee John was no longer an esoteric ethnic musician; he was the noted leader of an American "polka band."

During the 1930s, the term "polka music" entered public and music-industry parlance in reference to a range of ethnically derived American dance traditions that all included some variation of the polka. The genre's popularity was boosted near the decade's end by a massive jukebox hit, "The Beer Barrel Polka." Written by a Czech, Jaromir Vejvoda (b. 1902), and originally titled "Skoda Lásky," the tune was also known in Germany as "Rosamunde." The initial American recording by Will Glahe's Musette Orchestra was soon "covered" by the Andrews Sisters, whose beckoning "Roll out the barrel, we'll have a barrel of fun" contributed mightily to polka music's enduring association with beer and celebration.

While their activities were curtailed by World War II, polka musicians prospered in its aftermath. More Americans had become acquainted with Europe's vernacular music.

America's polka musicians, meanwhile, had jammed with fellow servicemen in jazz and hillbilly bands. Frankie Yankovic (b. 1915), for example, expanded his Slovenian repertoire while he was in the Army by playing in various bands. His polka-style rendering of a hillbilly duet, "Just Because," became a million-seller for Columbia Records in 1948.

In the 1950s, rock and roll ended polka's flirtation with national prominence. The music, however, has continued to thrive and evolve as an ethnic-regional phenomenon. Yankovic's alpine Slovenian style, with its interweaving virtuoso accordions, claims followers in northern Ohio, in Milwaukee, on Minnesota's Iron Range, and in Western mining towns. Whoopee John's "oompah" sound, propelled by concertina and tuba, inspires the "Dutchman" music that dominates the rural Upper Midwest. Czech bands—combining brass, reeds, and accordions—are prominent in Nebraska and Texas. "Eastern-style" Polish bands from southern New England and the industrialized Middle Atlantic states persist with their tightly arranged, rapid instrumentals, but they have been overtaken by Chicago's "honky" and "push" sounds, which emphasize improvisation, surging rhythms, bilingual vocals, and rock-influenced amplification.

Since the 1970s, these major styles, and other minor departures, have been supported by a loosely organized "polka industry" of record and video companies, radio stations, periodicals, dance halls, festivals, fan clubs, and associations. Their efforts, coupled with the accordion's resurgence in rock and country genres, have contributed to an increased awareness of polka music's prolonged and varied presence in American life. The American Society of Composers, Artists, and Performers (ASCAP) has awarded a polka Grammy since 1986. National and regional media offer occasional polka features, and folklorists have begun to include polka musicians in their public programs.

Scholarship remains scant, especially when compared with the efforts devoted to other forms of American folk and vernacular music. But a slow parade of discographies, reissed sound recordings, and writings has begun and is liable, like the music, to continue into the 21st century.

James P. Leary

References

Dolgan, Robert. 1977. *The Polka King: The Life of Frankie Yankovic.* Cleveland: Dillon/Liederbach.

Ethnic Recordings in America: A Neglected Heritage. 1982. Washington, DC: American Folklife Center.

Greene, Victor. 1992. *A Passion for Polka: Ethnic Old Time Music in America, 1880–1960.* Berkeley: University of California Press.

Keil, Charles. 1992. *Polka Happiness.* Philadelphia: Temple University Press.

Kleeman, Janice Ellen. 1982. *The Origins and Stylistic Development of Polish-American Polka Music.* Ph.D. diss., University of California, Berkeley.

Leary, James P. 1990. *Minnesota Polka: Dance Music from Four Traditions.* St. Paul: Minnesota Historical Society Press. Sound Recording and Booklet.

Leary, James P., and Richard March. 1993. *Down Home Dairyland: Traditional and Ethnic Music of Wisconsin and the Upper Midwest.* Madison: University of Wisconsin.

Machann, Clinton, ed. 1987. *Czech Music in Texas: A Sesquicentennial Symposium.* College Station, TX: Komensk.

Rippley, LaVern J. 1992. *The Whoopee John Wilfahrt Dance Band.* Northfield, MN: German Department, St. Olaf College.

Spottswood, Richard K. 1990. *Ethnic Music on Records: A Discography of Ethnic Recordings Produced in the United States, 1893–1942.* Urbana: University of Illinois Press.

Popular Culture and Folklore

Relationships of mass-mediated culture ("popular") and small-scale, unmediated artistic expression ("folklore"). Some scholars use the terms interchangeably, while others think the terms refer to materials that exist in polar opposition to each other. Still other scholars see the two concepts as different but continuous with each other. Both terms, however, indicate human activities that are stylized and expressive in nature.

Many definitions of folklore have tended to be enumerative, naming genres such as beliefs, customs, ballads, and proverbs as examples, thus assuming a self-evident inherent similarity among them. Sometimes such lists are tautological in that they repeat the modifier "folk" in the examples given; that is, folklore is said to be comprised of *folk*song, *folk* dance, and other *folk* genres. Generalizing from certain data and attempting to arrive at a consensus as to what constitutes these genres we speak of as folk, some scholars have suggested that folklore is that portion of a culture or society that is passed on orally or by imitation.

In 1972 Dan Ben-Amos defined folklore as artistic communication in small groups. In this formulation, the concept of "small group" replaces the "folk" termination, while the "lore" becomes identified as "artistic communication." This communication need not necessarily be verbal, but it will be stylized and expressive, thus calling attention to itself. Stories told in conversations, for instance, are readily distinguished from the surrounding speech by any number of means, including body language and voice timbre, and often by the use of introductory formulas that signal that a specific genre of speech is about to be uttered. "Once upon a time" tells us to expect a fairy tale, while, "Have you heard the one about . . ." indicates that the teller is about to tell a joke. Even everyday conversational narratives about one's own personal experiences are often introduced with the word "once." The joke may be years, even centuries, old, but each telling is unique. The concept of "small groups" referred to requires that the genre be performed in company few enough in numbers and close enough in proximity to be able to affect the performance and to contribute to it.

Popular culture, on the other hand, has often been equated with the mass media: products of film, television, recordings, and print that are widely disseminated in society, or at least created with widespread dissemination in mind. Thus, when a friend tells us a joke, this is, by the above definition, a folk event. When we watch a comedian on television tell a joke—even the same joke—we have entered the realm of popular culture. We can have only indirect influence on the products of mass media, while we can have direct effects on small–scale, interpersonal communications. American scholars often distinguish folklore, or folk culture, from popular culture along many lines, including the communicative nature of the materials themselves: Are they mediated or unmediated? In other words, do we hear the story, or listen to the music, or see the dance directly? Can we join in, or are we merely watching a film, listening to a recording, or looking at a videotape?

Like the term "folklore," the term "popular culture" is also used as the name of a scholarly discipline. Popular-culture studies is the scholarly investigation of expressive forms widely disseminated in society. These materials include, but are not restricted to, products of mass media such as television, film, print, and recording. Thus, popular-culture studies may focus on media genres such as situation comedies, film noir, best-selling novels, or rap music. Other, nonmediated aspects of popular culture would include such things as clothing styles, fads, holidays and celebrations, amusement parks, both amateur and professional sports, and so forth. Ideally, the study of these or any other popular materials should be done holistically, viewing them both aesthetically and within the social and cultural contexts in which the materials are created, disseminated, interpreted, and used. In this way, the study of popular culture, like the study of folklore, involves the use of methodologies from both the humanities and the social sciences in the effort to interpret expressive cultural forms, specifically those that are widely disseminated in a group (that is, that are popular) as part of dynamic social intercourse.

Folklore and popular culture meet in the popular use of the mass media or mass–produced goods. Examples of this phenomenon are many and include scratch djs, customized cars, self-embroidered articles of clothing, and so forth. In the United States, it seems to have fallen largely to folklorists to study this phenomenon, as well as other contemporary forms that, while not necessarily or entirely mass-mediated, are fully defensible as popular culture in that they are widely known and practiced. The study of contemporary holiday celebrations, for example, ideally should combine the study of folk traditions with an investigation of the festive uses of mass-media products (the ways certain films have become traditionally associated with holidays, for example).

Many of those who consider folklore as unmediated, small group, face-to-face expressive culture, and popular culture as large-scale, mass-mediated forms, view the two as antithetical. Simply put, they argue that folklore thrives where the mass media has not taken hold. Conversely, by this formulation, popular culture kills folklore; where once people entertained one another with storytelling, instead they now watch television. There is often felt to be a moral dimension here: Storytelling (or another genre of folklore) is seen as active and creative, while consuming mass-mediated forms is described as passive and numbing. Thus, the former is said to be superior to the latter. Other scholars might view the folk genres pejoratively, describing them as unsophisticated, primitive, or naive.

On the other hand, some scholars use the terms "folklore" and "popular culture" more or less interchangeably. Social historians, for instance, who have researched everyday life in medieval, late medieval, and early modern societies (frequently reconstructing popular rituals, festivals, and celebrations) generally prefer the term "popular culture" to that of "folk culture," possibly owing to romantic associations of the concept of "folk" that the scholars consider as pejorative. In these cases, culture and society are more likely to be viewed in dichotomous terms, with allowances for overlap, between the courtly culture of the socially elite and the popular culture of the masses. Some popular-culturalists accept this view, maintaining that only after the Industrial Revolution and its attendant urbanization and the development of a middle class does it make sense to speak of a tripartite model of culture that includes folk, popular, and elite. In this formulation, the folk represent peasant society; a semiautonomous group that depends on a nation-state for at least part of its subsistence.

To a large extent, definitions indicate methodologies: the definitions one works with influence both what is studied and how it is studied. Janice Radway's study of a group of women who read romance novels is an example of the application of social science and ethnographic techniques to an area that had been dominated by humanities approaches. In the past, popular genre fiction such as romances would be studied as texts only, and found lacking in aesthetic merit as defined by Western European high-art critics. Radway (and other cultural-studies scholars) expanded the area of study to transcend the written text and to include ethnographic considerations, such as who exactly was reading the novels, when, for what purposes, and what meanings and values did they derive from them? In order to determine such things, the readers were interviewed in order to ascertain their own perspective on, and understandings of, the materials. Instead of condemning a genre in which millions of people find something of value, Radway attempted to understand what aesthetic principles were at work and how readers of popular romances themselves understand the texts.

Radway's work and that of others has shown that people are not as passive as was once thought in their interactions with mass or popular forms. In addition, there are a great many areas of overlap between folk and popular culture. As terms that refer to social dynamics rather than things, the two feed off each other. The examples here are numerous, but two brief instances will suffice. Children's jump-rope rhymes, a folk genre, commonly use well-known celebrities, popular songs, and commercial jingles for their subject matter, while the converse is also true; many popular hit songs and commercial jingles are derived from the poetry and song of the streets. Another example would be the relationship of the so-called slasher or stalker films, such as *Nightmare on Elm Street*, and the modern legends in oral circulation that tell of similar horrific killings.

Celebrations of contemporary holidays, life passages, and other special occasions are an area in which many of the various aspects of culture are coterminous. The use of yellow ribbons publicly displayed during wartime is one such example. Holidays such as Halloween are good examples of contemporary phenomena that combine customary behaviors and traditions carried out on the personal level (for example, trick-or-treating, learning to carve a jack-o'-lantern). There is also a tremendous commercialization of contemporary holidays, including the marketing of cards, candies, and costumes; media products such as episodes of television programs with Halloween themes or specials such as *It's the Great Pumpkin, Charlie Brown;* church-sponsored events; and, in certain cases, condemnations by churches.

Both folklorists and popular-culture scholars study created, expressive, and artistic materials as their primary data, much as literary scholars take the novel or the sonnet as their primary data. In this way, they are both within the tradition of the humanities. However, the disciplines of folklore studies and popular-culture studies differ from traditional humanities studies in that they recognize the existence of alternative systems of aesthetics that guide the creation of popular materials and the evaluation of those materials by an audience. Albert Bates Lord, in his important work *The Singer of Tales* (1960), identified the ways singers of epics in eastern Europe learn their art orally and how they compose as they perform. He suggests that these performances and the poems themselves be judged according to the specific goals of the artists and the audiences and to an understanding of the problems unique to an oral poet. In other words, oral poetry is a different genre from written poetry. Each has its own aesthetic standards, and it is misguided to judge one by the standards of the other. Popular-culture scholars recognize this principle and extend it to the popular arts such as television programs, popular films, popular music, best-selling novels, and genre fiction such as mysteries or romances.

Each medium or genre has an audience that can and does make evaluations according to aesthetic criteria. These criteria are usually unarticulated, but they are no less real because of it. People regularly make choices as to which book to read or movie to see, and just as regularly evaluate the experience: This was a good thriller, this a great party song, and so forth. Because these aesthetic criteria are generally unarticulated, it is the task of the researcher to identify them through ethnographic methods such as interviews and participant observation, as well as humanities techniques such as textual analysis. The term "ethnography" refers to the cultural description of any event, producers, consumers, or users of the artifact, or members of the cultural group in question. After these insider (or native) perceptions and categories are documented, the researcher may undertake the scholarly analysis of the materials as components of a dynamic social and cultural field of behavior. These methods enable the scholar to situate the discussion of any aspect of folklore or popular culture within the larger context of the meanings and values of the society within which it exists; to determine, as Clifford Geertz has suggested, what we need to know in order to make sense of something (Geertz 1984).

Social-science methodologies enable the popular-culture scholar to root an expressive form in its social context and to uncover the aesthetic system upon which it is judged. Humanities approaches provide models for the appreciation of aesthetic forms and enable the scholar to apply theories of genre and make comparative analytical statements. As social-science and humanities methodologies are combined in the study of artistic forms of expression that are broadly based in society, scholars can begin to provide an understanding of the social and cultural significance of these artistic forms, and begin to determine the aesthetic, social, commercial, and technological considerations that underlie their creation, distribution, and reception. Rather than attempting to determine ultimate worth or meaning according to an imposed value system, scholars have begun investigating the ways in which meaning is created and creativity evaluated. This requires ethnographic research. It is in the ethnographic study of the everyday uses of mass-cultural forms that folklore and popular culture merge.

Jack Santino

References
Burke, Peter. 1978. *Popular Culture in Early Modern Europe.* New York: Harper and Row.
Gans, Herbert. 1974. *Popular Culture and High Culture.* New York: Basic Books.
Geertz, Clifford. 1984. *The Interpretation of Cultures.* New York: Basic Books.
Nye, Russell. 1970. *The Unembarrassed Muse: The Popular Arts in America.* New York: Dial.
Paredes, Américo, and Richard Bauman. 1972. *Towards New Perspectives in Folklore.* Austin: University of Texas Press.
Santino, Jack. 1994. *All around the Year: Holidays and Celebrations in American Life.* Urbana: University of Illinois Press.

See also Mass Media and Folklore; Recitation; Revivalism; Urban Legend

Portuguese Americans

A diverse group, having emigrated not only from mainland Portugal, but also from its island possessions in the Atlantic. More than two-thirds of Portuguese Americans are of Azorean lineage; one-quarter are descendants of immigrants from Madeira, and the rest come variously from the European mainland, the Cape Verde Islands, Brazil, and Portuguese enclaves in China.

According to Portuguese American scholar Francis Rogers, two waves of Portuguese immigration have formed two separate Portuguese groups "living in close juxtaposition but not close harmony." Rogers stresses the differences between all arrivals prior to 1958 and those who have come later. In regard to Portuguese American folklore, however, there are more accurately *three* separate groups. The earliest arrivals (1820–1870) largely immigrated through the whaling trade to New England, Long Island, and, to a lesser degree, to the Hawaiian Islands and San Francisco. These men, embarking from

Horta in the western Azores, were likely to have had as much as three years' indoctrination in American speech and custom aboard the whalers before landing in the United States. Some sent for women from the home islands, others married English-speaking Roman Catholics in their new country.

Living in smaller communities, often intermarrying, the early immigrants appear to have had more options to assimilate and prosper than the second wave (1870–1920), who took advantage of the development of scheduled steamship travel and likely employment in the New England textile industry to arrive as families, indeed, as whole communities. Steamship lines connected a different group of islands—the most easterly of the Azores, and Madeira—with the New England ports. This second, much larger, wave of Portuguese immigrants not only originated in the more heavily populated and economically poorer islands, but also settled into more enclaved communities in their new homeland.

The most recent arrivals (1958–) have benefited from better education in the homelands and report their goals for immigration as increased educational opportunities for their children and economic success for themselves. They are more likely to travel frequently between their new homes and their homeland, to take overt pride in their Portugueseness and to enter the American politics generally eschewed by older immigrants. In joining traditional Portuguese social and religious societies, they have infused these with contemporary versions of traditions as these are now practiced in the islands.

Of the three groups, immigrants of the second wave remain the principal repository of traditional practices. The earlier arrivals often identify with the societies that implement folkloric performances but are less frequently active members. The most recent arrivals are enthusiastic about their folklore but are likely to prefer the more polished contemporary performances of their homelands, which, in the late 20th century, are oriented to a growing Portuguese tourist industry.

As early as 1892, the folklore of Portuguese Americans was the subject of scholarly study. When Henry Lang recorded his observations for the *Journal of American Folklore* that year, the dominant group was the early wave of immigrants brought by the whaling industry. Lang acknowledged that a new and larger Portuguese population was arriving as he wrote, describing them as overtaxed and poverty-stricken workers escaping military service and depressed wages. Older members of the Portuguese American community, whom Lang characterized as wealthy and substantial, were thought to be fast losing their traditions. Superstitions based on fear of natural phenomena, particularly the frequent seismic activity in the islands, he supposed, would disappear rapidly in America because of a lack of natural causes and the "positive social medium."

In fact, many surviving Azorean American traditions are based on such superstitions. Kept alive by adverse conditions in the American workplace, as well as natural disasters inherent in the farming and fishing that have been alternatives to factory work, traditional devotions to saints involved in Portuguese-specific miracles persist, as does the gesture of tweaking the earlobe between thumb and forefinger to indicate praise or good wishes. The Chama Rita *(chambritza)* that Lang documented in 1892 is still danced, at least by older members of Portuguese American communities. In fact, in 1989, members of a local Portuguese Holy Ghost Society taught the *chambritza* to the Connecticut-based cast of *Mystic Pizza*, a film about the coming of age of young Portuguese American women.

Most Portuguese Americans consider the *fado* of the Lisbon working class as an icon of their heritage, and some Portuguese American restaurants feature performers singing the sad and fatalistic songs as an attraction for their regular customers. Otherwise, noticeable differences in performance of Portuguese folk music and dance occur from one island or chain of islands to another, and these are reflected in the preferred music in various Portuguese American communities. An Azorean musician from Lowell, Massachusetts, characterized Madeiran music as "upbeat" and Azorean as slow and sad. But then, Azorean Americans claim a special state of mind called *soldad* (a longing, particularly for the other side of the ocean). In America, they say, they have *soldad* for their islands; in the Azores, they had *soldad* for the mainland that was their cultural home. Expressions of *soldad* for home and for loved ones is a pervading theme in Azorean song.

The *pezinho* (an Azorean serenade honoring benefactors of a feast) consists of extemporaneous verses, sometimes humorous, composed anew at each performance. Two or more singers take turns vying to do honor to the saint and to the benefactor, with lyrics specific to the situation and to the verses that have just been sung. In contemporary Lowell, and elsewhere in New England, Portuguese American singers use the *pezhino*, which they translate as "little feet," to compose their own extemporaneous verses, often ribald or insulting, but always skillfully referring to the immediate situation.

Portuguese folktales appear to have disappeared from the Portuguese American traditional repertoire, but saints' legends concerning divine intervention on behalf of Portuguese people are popular. Many of these are centuries old, like Queen Isabela's ability to cure the sick by placing her crown on the head of the afflicted; others are as contemporary as the story of an aged couple who survived a 1957 earthquake in Portugal because they held on to the Holy Ghost crown.

Personal narratives about overcoming hardships in America are told by older immigrants and their children. The value the Portuguese place on hard work and frugality is often at the heart of these narratives. A factory worker in Lowell told of "hiring" her invalid mother as an assistant spinner, then doing the work of both so that her mother would receive a paycheck. Most narratives tell of families in which every able-bodied member works, contributing their wages toward the purchase of a house and the rapid payoff of the mortgage. Portuguese urban communities have earned a reputation for restoring blighted neighborhoods through their industrious occupancy.

In Portuguese American neighborhoods, social and benevolent organizations serve a variety of functions. For the men, they are a substitute for the wine cellars and gardens of their homeland: a male social space for evening and weekend recreation. For the women, they are a center of devotional life beyond the reach of the clergy. Because the Portuguese Roman Catholic Church has historically conspired with the government to strengthen its control over the peasantry, these secular societies, like the Portuguese Holy Ghost Society, have taken over the observances of saints' days, including the organizing of processions and the building of altars to honor the saints.

Portuguese American feast days sponsored by these social organizations include the Feast of the Holy Ghost, an Azorean celebration based on legends involving Queen Isabela (not to be confused with the Spanish Isabella of Castile) and her *promessa* (promise) to the Holy Ghost that ended a famine; and the Madeiran Feasts of the Blessed Sacrament (Corpus Christi) and of Our Lady of Loreto. In New Bedford, Massachusetts, the San Miguelense (Azorean) community observes the Festa do Senhor da Pedra, celebrating a particular image of Christ seated on a rock. Also important in the Portuguese American calendar is the Feast of Our Lady of Fatima, commemorating the appearance of the Virgin to a group of peasant children in mainland Portugal. The Virgin's message to the children—to pray for the conversion of the ungodly—has been understood by Portuguese Americans as referring to Communism, and they have chosen to express their American patriotism through devotion to Fatima.

Feasts *(festas)* are opportunities for non-Portuguese Americans to sample the national cuisine, including *massa cevada* (Portuguese sweet bread), linguica sausage baked in a roll, chorizo sausage cooked with pepper and tomato, and "Holy Ghost" soup *(sopas)*, a rich beef and vegetable broth flavored with mint. Sweets include meringue cookies (called *suspiros,* or "sighs") and *malassadas* (fried sweet-bread dough topped with sugar or honey). In Portuguese American homes, and in the increasing number of Portuguese restaurants engendered by the late-20th-century interest in ethnic foods, many variations on the peasant dish of salt cod and potatoes are favorite offerings, along with the ubiquitous pork with clams *a alentejana.*

Portuguese American Christmas is celebrated with roast pork marinated in white wine (or in some homes, flavored vinegar) or with marinated salt cod and vegetables. Traditionally minded Portuguese Americans often eschew Christmas trees in favor of a "manger": A hilly landscape is constructed and covered with moss on which miniature figures are placed, all oriented toward the Holy Family occupying a stable at the pinnacle. Basins of water are artfully transformed into miniature lakes on which float flocks of miniature ducks. Herds of sheep and cows graze in fenced-off pastures. The manger in the Portuguese church in Lowell is large enough to hide the altar and require the removal of several rows of pews. Family mangers similarly dominate parlors; the moss covering is carefully stored and preserved from year to year.

The role of women in Portuguese American culture is central to the maintaining of these traditions. Women cook the feasts, construct and decorate the mangers, arrange the altars, and take responsibility for religious observances. (The Portuguese collusion between church and state often made it politically unwise for men to attend services.) In traditional Portuguese families, women did not work outside the home; they took care to behave modestly and to obey husband and father. In Portuguese American families, women have always worked outside the home. In the heyday of the textile industry, Portuguese women were surrounded by their peers, and decorum was maintained, but late-20th-century opportunities in education and a variety of workplaces have disturbed the equilibrium in traditional Portuguese American households. Younger women seek to escape the traditional domination of men even as they express concern over the possible loss of their ethnic heritage.

Barbara C. Fertig

References

Cabral, Stephen Leonard. 1992. *Tradition and Transformation: Portuguese Feasting in New Bedford.* New York: AMS.

Cook, Mary Alice. 1983. *Traditional Portuguese Recipes from Provincetown.* Provincetown, MA: Shank Painter.

Leder, Hans Howard. 1980. *Cultural Persistence in a Portuguese-American Community.* New York: Arno.

Pap, Leo. 1976. *The Portuguese in the United States: A Bibliography.* Staten Island, NY: Center for Migration Studies.

———. 1981. *The Portuguese Americans.* Boston: Twayne.

Rogers, Francis M. 1974. *Americans of Portuguese Descent: A Lesson in Differentiation.* Beverly Hills, CA: Sage.

Salvador, Mari Lyn. 1981. *Festas Acoreanas: Portuguese Religious Celebrations in California and the Azores.* Oakland, CA: The Oakland Museum.

Postmodernism

A controversial term, both in the confusing range of its application and in its obvious trendiness. Some would charge that the term "postmodernism" has been invoked so widely and loosely as to render it useless as either a descriptive or an analytical category. In some of its more restricted meanings, however, the term provides a tag for certain qualities of late-20th-century American culture that have no other good designation.

To sort out some of these meanings, one may usefully distinguish between postmodern*ism* and postmodern*ity* (Connor 1989:27). The former, which may appropriately be used in the plural, designates a whole array of cultural phenomena, especially in the arts, in which significant departures from modernist sensibilities or styles may be detected. Many of these shifts can be roughly dated to the 1960s, though attempts at periodization are open to debate. And, in fact, the very impulse to periodize is inconsistent with the postmodern sensibility, as, for that matter, are attempts at essentialist identifications of postmodernism's "qualities."

These dilemmas of definition notwithstanding, we may speak with some assurance about general properties shared by the various postmodernisms in the arts, in academic theory, and in mass-cultural forms. Foremost among these is a wholesale destabilization and fragmentation of cultural meaning, an insistence on the provisional status of historical understanding, and an acknowledgment that all representations of reality, from the most empirical to the most fantastic, are equally the result of textual construction. The various theoretical schools usually lumped together as "poststructuralism," a term often and inappropriately equated with postmodernism, have in common this basic assumption that all meaning, all representation, and even human subjectivity itself are textual effects, or, to use different terms, are traces of an infinite play of signifiers.

The philosophical implications of these premises are obviously immense, and troubling to many. If no meaning is fixed and no representation of reality immune from deconstruction (the most common name for poststructuralism's method of reading cultural texts "against themselves"), then moral judgment, coherent political action, and even personal identities can only be provisional and partial, always subject to repeal or displacement. On the other hand, for many of its theorists and its practitioners in the arts, postmodernism is inherently a liberating denial of the very possibility of absolute authority and a rejection of restrictive programs that appeal to some form of eternal truth. The tone and style of much self-conscious postmodern practice, particularly in the arts, are characterized by playfulness, surprising juxtapositions, and *not* violation of conventions (this could be said of early modernism), but reflexive citation of conventions so as to highlight their artifice.

The various postmodernisms that share these qualities can be thought of as manifestations or symptoms of an embracing cultural-historical moment that we might call postmodernity. Used in the singular, postmodernity refers to the whole complex of formations, institutions, and discourses that constitute our advanced consumer society. In a classic essay on the subject, Frederic Jameson uses postmodernity as the name for the "cultural logic" of the current phase of the capitalist mode of production (Jameson 1984). This "late" capitalism is characterized by advanced consumer social relations, the commodification of virtually all spheres of material life, a global economic order dominated by multinational corporations, and a technological order devoted to the production and rapid exchange of information.

Jameson identifies the signature characteristic of this cultural logic as a subtly pervasive "depthlessness," evident in such things as our collective fascination with detached, glossy surface images, the proliferation of flattened "historicist" images of past periods, and a pervasive but unfocused emotional register that might best be thought of as a blankly ironic stance toward all discourses.

Whatever version one fixes on, and whether one takes a positive or a negative position toward it, the phenomenon of postmodernism-postmodernity has some important implications for the study of contemporary American folklore. Although theorists of postmodernity have paid little attention to vernacular culture, their views on mass and elite cultural forms suggest the need to rethink the status of folk expression in the current historical context.

For one thing, the concept of postmodernity undercuts many received ideas about the relationship between mass and folk cultures. Under the regime of postmodernity, the old model according to which mass culture is seen simply as a

threat to, and supplanter of, folk forms no longer suffices. A basic tenet of postmodern theory is that the old stratified categories—elite, popular, mass, folk—do not any longer make much sense. The boundaries between these domains are now so constantly violated that one is hard pressed to decide whether, for example, jokes exchanged through fiber-optic computer nets are properly thought of as existing in the social space of vernacular or mass communication. Analogous examples are the folkloric performances staged at folk festivals, the oral narratives generated by the growing numbers of professional storytellers, and the New Age therapeutic programs inspired by forms of tradition healing and folk ritual (Warshaver 1991).

Another feature of postmodernity relevant to folklorists is its rejection of the grand narratives of modernist culture—that is, the ostensibly universal explanatory narratives of science, economics, psychoanalysis, and the like (Lyotard [1979] 1984). In their place, postmodernity emphasizes the provisional stories of more immediate and localized application—in short, the sort of stories that have always been of most concern to folklorists. Sensitivity to the multiplicity and situational variability of cultural identities is a similar point of connection between theories of postmodernity and the late-20th-century concerns of many folklorists.

Folklore studies stand, then, in an ambiguous relationship to the postmodern. On the one hand, the denial of the specificity and separateness of the folk domain implied by postmodernity would seem to be a challenge to the field. On the other hand, theories of postmodernity give, in concept if not much in practice, a special prominence to the sorts of local, partial, immediate cultural forms and expressions that folklorists are trained to document and analyze. This sort of paradox, some would say, is itself indicative of the postmodern moment.

John D. Dorst

References

Connor, Steven. 1989. *Postmodern Culture: An Introduction to Theories of the Contemporary.* New York: Basil Blackwell.

Dorst, John D. 1988. Postmodernism vs. Postmodernity: Implications for Folklore Studies. *Folklore Forum* 21:216–220.

Jameson, Frederic. 1984. The Cultural Logic of Late Capitalism. *New Left Review* 144:53–92.

Lyotard, Jean-Francois. [1979] 1984. *The Postmodern Condition: A Report on Knowledge.* Minneapolis: University of Minnesota Press.

Warshaver, Gerald E. 1991. On Postmodern Folklore. *Western Folklore* 50:219–229.

See also Cultural Studies

Pottery

The creation of useful and attractive vessels from fired clay. For thousands of years, the skilled hands of the potter have nurtured civilizations. From digging clays and grinding glazes, to

The pottery shop of Robert Ritchie (r.), Catawba County, North Carolina, ca. 1914. To the left rear is the groundhog kiln, at the back center is the log shop, and to the right is the pug mill for grinding the clay. Photo courtesy Clara Ritchie Wiggs.

throwing myriad forms on the wheel and firing them in their kilns, potters have sustained life in the most essential ways. Their jars and jugs, bowls and beanpots, churns and pitchers ensured that families would have sufficient foods to survive frozen winters or scorching droughts. And often, a graceful form, or a colorful glaze, or a rich texture would add an element of beauty to otherwise prosaic lives.

From Jamestown, Virginia, to Charlestown, Massachusetts, potters were among the earliest settlers. Through the late 18th century, their primary product was lead-glazed earthenware, a type of pottery that dates back to the ancient Near East. American potters used lead in many forms—raw ore (galena), oxides (red lead and litharge), even Civil War bullets—generally combining it with water, clay, and a silica source (flint, sand) to produce a creamy mixture into which each pot was dipped. The glaze served to seal the porous earthenware clay body and ensure that each container was impermeable.

Many of the early potters came from mature ceramic traditions in Great Britain and later, the German regions of central Europe. However, they quickly found it necessary to produce plainer, more utilitarian wares; colonists had little time or money to spend on decorative effects when survival was often their key concern. The one exception was the German earthenware potters, who began arriving in the late 17th century and encountered relatively settled conditions along the Eastern seaboard. Notably in eastern Pennsylvania, the Shenandoah Valley of Virginia, and the Moravian communities of North Carolina, they produced an extraordinary body of sophisticated,

brightly colored wares using multicolored slips (mixtures of clay, water, and other materials), graffito (decoration produced by scratching through a coating of slip to reveal the clay body beneath it), and molded forms.

By the late 18th century, potters and consumers alike were becoming aware that the lead glaze could be dangerously toxic, even lethal. Moreover, the earthenware clay body, which is fired to only about 1800°F, remains porous and easily breakable. Thus, between roughly the 1780s and 1830s, potters first in the North, and then later the South and Midwest, began switching over to stoneware clay and a series of new glazes. Unlike earthenware clays, which are widespread and occur near the Earth's surface, stoneware clays are a sedimentary type usually found in deep veins near rivers or bottom land. When fired to temperatures of 2300°F or more, they become extremely hard and vitreous—hence, very durable and easy to clean. All of the associated glazes are nontoxic.

The predominant glaze for this high-fired clay body was ordinary salt. Here there is no need to concoct a glaze solution. The potter simply sets his greenware (dried, unfired pottery) in the kiln, slowly raises it to full heat, and then introduces the salt through the firebox or the openings in the arch. The salt instantly vaporizes, and the sodium fluxes the surface of the pots, melting the silica in the clay and producing a hard, glassy coating. The salt glaze originated in Germany no later than the 15th century; it spread across Europe and reached England toward the end of the 17th century. Because large quantities of Continental and English stonewares were imported into America, it was not until the early 18th century that a native industry began to develop in the Mid-Atlantic region, based on the discovery of large stoneware clay deposits in New York and New Jersey. The salt glaze gradually spread north into New England (where potters had to import the new clay), south to Tennessee and North Carolina, and into the Midwest.

The characteristic Southern glaze for stoneware is the alkaline glaze, so-called because the flux—wood ashes or lime—contains alkaline compounds of calcium, sodium, and potassium. Having originated in China 2,000 years ago, it reappeared in the Carolinas—most likely, the Edgefield District of South Carolina—during the first quarter of the 19th century. It then spread south to Florida and west as far as Texas. Drawing on readily available materials, the potter combined his flux with water and some local silica source (clay, sand, feldspar, iron cinders, or crushed glass). The resulting glazes are characteristically dark brown or green and frequently flow down the sides of the pots in thick veins.

The third major stoneware glaze is Albany slip, a simple combination of water and a powdered clay mined near Albany, New York. Discovered in the early 19th century, it was widely used on the interiors of the Northern salt-glazed wares, particularly as the kilns became larger, preventing the salt fumes from getting inside the stacked pots. In the Midwest, potters applied it to the exteriors as well, creating a glossy, chocolate brown surface. Albany slip occurs sporadically in the South, where potters sometimes combined it with the salt glaze to produce a yellow-green hue known locally as frogskin.

The foregoing account only begins to suggest the intensely regional nature of American folk pottery. Migration patterns, local resources, and the needs and preferences of developing communities all combined to ensure that a deep sense of place was embedded in every pot. The potters themselves rarely signed their wares. They were craftsmen, not artists, and regarded the act of signing as an empty gesture, a waste of time in an already long and arduous process. Perhaps they also recognized that their "signatures" were there, even without their specific names, whether in a bulbous form, the hue of the glaze, or a neatly applied strap handle.

As practiced over the centuries, the craft of pottery was innately conservative, in that the knowledge and skills were transmitted through an informal oral tradition and on-the-job imitation with relatively slight change. Young men continued to follow their fathers' methods—this was entirely a man's world—because they were familiar, efficient, and right. Some young boys signed formal indentures of apprenticeship in which they pledged to faithfully serve until they reached a designated age. In turn, the master potter agreed to provide proper food, lodging, and apparel, and, most importantly, to teach "the art & mystery of a potter." Outside urban areas or tight-knit groups like the Moravians, such contracts were rare. Most young men simply went to work for the family or a neighbor.

Training often began at a very early age. Boys helped dig the clays, operate the animal-powered pug mill to grind the clay, and wedged balls of clay for the wheel. They also ground the glazes, cut and dried wood for the kiln, and lugged the wares in and out of the shop through all phases of manufacture. All of these repetitive tasks provided superb training for the future potter, instructing him in the nature of clays and glazes and the operation of the kiln.

Having mastered the basics and grown into his early teenage years, the aspiring potter next turned to the wheel. There he received little formal instruction. Instead, he carefully watched others and then seized the opportunity to use the wheel when his mentor was elsewhere. He usually began by throwing ("turning" in the South) small "toys," miniature forms perhaps 2 inches to 6 inches high. Fathers naturally encouraged this activity, occasionally constructing smaller wheels for their children to practice on. Gradually, the youths moved to full-size wares, and there, too, was a powerful underlying pattern to their progress. They began with simple, open forms like bowls, milk crocks, or flowerpots. Next came more complex and closed wares—jars, churns, or pitchers—that also required turned-out rims, flanges, and handles. Finally, the young man was ready to tackle a jug, a real challenge because of the difficulty of pulling up enough clay to close the shoulder and shape the narrow spout. As he learned the full repertoire of forms, he also moved on to larger sizes. A competent potter produced wares up to 5 gallons, but on occasion he might have to answer the call for jars holding 10 to 20 gallons.

Once he had mastered the essential skills, the young man might work for a number of years as a journeyman, throwing pots at other shops and helping fire ("burn" in the South) the kiln. This work extended his competence and exposed him to alternative techniques. Some never passed beyond this stage, but many others ultimately inherited, constructed, or purchased a shop of their own. Then, as "masters," they set the cycle into motion once again by training their children or neighbors.

The folk potter's business was very modest in scale. It included a log or frame shop containing the wheels, wedging benches (wooden surfaces on which the potter kneads the clay), a stove, and a storage area; a pug mill to grind the clay; a kiln; and one or two additional sheds for tasks like glazing. Each of these components was logically situated so that the clay moved efficiently and quickly from pug mill to wheel to glazing and drying area to kiln. There was little wasted motion.

Normally, the potter also farmed and worked at other crafts and occupations. Thus, pottery making was rarely a full-time business; it was a seasonal activity that dovetailed neatly with the natural cycle of planting and harvesting. The main period of demand was the fall, when people sought containers to put up their crops. Overall, output was quite small. According to the manufacturing census, the typical pottery shop in 19th-century North Carolina had a capital investment of about $200, employed two workers (plus available children), operated nine months of the year, and turned out 6,000 gallons of pottery at 12.5 cents per gallons for a gross of $750. In effect, pottery was a cash crop like corn or cotton or tobacco, one that provided the extra income to purchase what could not be grown or made at home.

If folk pottery is pervasively regional and conservative, it is also relentlessly utilitarian. As the statistics above reveal, it was valued for its usefulness (its capacity), not its appearance. The function of each pot was foremost—storing sauerkraut, making butter, watering chickens, even marking graves. Unquestionably, the preservation of food was critical. Jars, jugs, milk crocks (pans), and churns were essential and constituted more than half of the potter's output. Without an ample supply of jars ranging from 0.5 to 5 gallons, a rural family found it a long, hard winter indeed.

Wares intended for food preparation are far less numerous and may be subdivided into two categories: general preparation (bowls, strainers, funnels) and cooking (dishes, bean pots). Potters continued making earthenware cooking vessels into the 20th century, because the porous, open, clay body better withstands thermal shock than does the tight, vitreous stoneware. Pots designed for food consumption—cups, mugs, plates, teapots, coffeepots, sugars and creamers—are less common than might be expected, largely because American households contained ample quantities of pewter, wood, and tin vessels, as well as imported ceramics. Perhaps the most common form of tableware was the pitcher, in part because it doubled as a storage vessel.

While the major forms were most closely connected to the local foodways, the potter also maintained a sideline of implements and horticultural wares. In the late 20th century, most of his ceramic tools have been superseded by more efficient forms or superior materials. There was a time, however, when his grease lamps and candlesticks, chamber pots and spittoons, birdhouses and chicken waterers, pipes and inkwells were widely used in the home, farm, and community. Flowerpots appear as early as the 17th century in Virginia and provided an often overlooked aesthetic dimension to everyday life. With the growth of the tourist market in the late 19th century, potters began producing large quantities of vases, urns, and strawberry planters.

As potters mastered the technical aspects of their trade and learned what forms would sell, they also absorbed the hard realities of their world. Two criteria were foremost. First, each pot had to hold its stated capacity. Buyers paid by the gallon and wanted to be sure that when they spent a hard-earned 25 cents for a two-gallon jar, they were getting their full money's worth. Second, next to proper volume, a smooth, even, well-fired glaze was essential. If the glaze was too thin, uneven, or underfired, the pot was difficult to clean and likely to leak. Such work had no value in this pragmatic world.

Each new generation of folk potters, then, acquired the fundamental wisdom of their forebears: Their wares sold if they were useful. Fifty one-gallon jugs from the same kiln all fetched exactly the same price (provided none was defective). Granted, purchasers sometimes admired a well-turned form or a richly colored glaze, but they were rarely willing or able to pay a premium for such virtues. Thus, the potter knew that there was usually little point in adding superfluous decoration, in creating "art," when the jar or churn already did what it had to do.

Aesthetic flourishes represented wasted motions, a squandering of time and labor, the potter's most valuable assets.

Still, there was beauty in this austere world. In varied, sometimes subtle ways, the potter found the means to go beyond necessity, to transcend the purely functional demands on his abilities. The most common form of decoration was simple incising. Before cutting a freshly thrown form off the wheel, the potter might use his fingernail, trimming chip, a coggle wheel, even a fork or a comb to cut one or more bands or wavy lines in the neck, shoulder, or belly of the pot. The prime virtue of this technique was speed; one or more rotations of the wheel, and the job was done. Such rings helped accentuate the different sections of the pot, emphasizing its proportions. Much more rare is freehand pictorial incising of birds, fish, floral patterns, ships, homesteads, even humans. Sometimes cartoonish but often executed with remarkable skill, this technique required considerable time and is most common on the Northern stonewares before the mid-19th century.

Just as they drew, potters also painted. The low-fired earthenwares offered the greatest range of chromatic possibilities. Particularly in the German areas, the potters created multihued designs using the yellow-to-red earthenware clays, white clays, and a variety of metallic oxides that produced green (copper), brown to black (iron), and brown to purple (manganese). On stonewares made from Virginia to New England, potters brushed on all manner of flora and fauna with cobalt oxide. The deep blue stands out from the grey clay body and shines under the clear salt glaze. In the South, the dark and unpredictable alkaline glaze offered fewer decorative possibilities. However, during the mid-19th century, potters from the Edgefield District of South Carolina created a clear, lime-based glaze under which they painted swags, tassels, floral patterns and likenesses of roosters, snakes, pigs, and ladies in hoop skirts.

Clay is one of the most malleable substances, but only rarely did the potter turn sculptor and create three-dimensional ornamentation. In general, the earthenware potters did the bulk of the modeling, sometimes applying molded animals, flowers, and even human forms to their pitchers, coolers, bowls, and vases. They also molded whole pieces, such as tiles, picture frames, Bundt pans, toys, and bottles in the shape of fish, chickens, turtles, and other small animals. For the stoneware potters, the principal outlets for sculpturing were flowerpots, gravemarkers, and face vessels, forms that were less restricted by function and allowed a greater sense of play. In general, elaborately decorated, one-of-a-kind pieces were made to commemorate specific events or for presentation to family and friends.

The great age of the folk potter was the 19th century, when his work was essential to communities across the country, but even by mid-century there were clear signs of change. Large stoneware factories appeared in Vermont, New York, New Jersey, Pennsylvania, and Ohio. With annual capacities measured in the hundreds of thousands of gallons, these businesses differed radically from that of the folk potter. The wares were increasingly cylindrical and standardized; they were mass produced along assembly-line methods. No longer did a single craftsman control the process and mark the product with his unique hand. Instead, different individuals specialized in clay preparation, throwing, decorating, glazing, firing, and sales. Finally, marketing was far more extensive and sophisticated, with elaborate advertising and long-range transportation via canal, rail, and river.

By the beginning of the 20th century, most of the folk potters had closed the doors of their shops for the last time. The temperance movement and Prohibition destroyed the demand for jugs; cheap metal and glass containers replaced the storage jar; commercial dairies and better refrigeration made churns and milk crocks obsolete; and in general, improved transportation and the growth of large markets ended the self-sufficient foodways earlier generations had known. In the South, however, the demand for the old utilitarian wares persisted through World War II. Particularly in North Carolina and Georgia, a number of the old clay clans found ways to respond to changing times. They did so by adapting new forms and glazes from other ceramic traditions; by turning smaller, more colorful wares that are made to be seen as well as used; by employing newer, more efficient technologies; and by marketing their wares to a new clientele: middle-class homeowners, tourists, and collectors.

In the 1990s, the largest concentration of folk potters occurs around Seagrove, North Carolina. Other groups may be found near Sanford, Vale, and Asheville, North Carolina, and Cleveland, Georgia; individual potters work throughout the Southeast (Sweezy 1984). These remaining folk potters are flourishing, because they have adopted new operating principles. Eclectic inspiration has gradually replaced the old regionalism; a willingness to innovate, the old conservatism; and a conscious artistry, the once pervasive utilitarianism. Still, many elements of earlier days remain. Most of the potters learned their skills at an early age working alongside family members or neighbors. The dig and process their own clays and retain many old forms and glazes. They remain primarily craftsmen—production potters who replicate large numbers of useful (if no longer necessary) forms at reasonable prices. Most important, the shops remain firmly under family control. In effect, they have developed a healthy new hybrid tradition, one that remains deeply rooted in the old folk tradition but is also infused with contemporary ceramic tastes and needs.

Charles G. Zug III

References

Bivins, John, Jr. 1972. *The Moravian Potters in North Carolina*. Chapel Hill: University of North Carolina Press.
Burrison, John A. 1983. *Brothers in Clay: The Story of Georgia Folk Pottery*. Athens: University of Georgia Press.
Greer, Georgeanna H. 1981. *American Stonewares: The Art and Craft of Utilitarian Potters*. Exton, PA: Schiffer.
Guilland, Harold F. 1971. *Early American Folk Pottery*. Philadelphia: Chilton.
Lasansky, Jeannette. 1975. *Central Pennsylvania Redware Pottery, 1780–1904*. Lewisburg, PA: Oral Traditions Projects.
Rinzler, Ralph, and Robert Sayers. 1980. *The Meaders Family: North Georgia Potters*. Washington: Smithsonian Institution.
Spargo, John. 1974. *Early American Pottery and China*. Rutland, VT: Charles E. Tuttle.
Sweezy, Nancy. 1984. *Raised in Clay: The Southern Pottery Tradition*. Washington: Smithsonian Institution.
Watkins, Lura Woodside. 1968. *Early New England Potters and Their Wares*. Hamden, CT: Archon.
Zug, Charles G., III. 1986. *Turners and Burners: The Folk Potters of North Carolina*. Chapel Hill: University of North Carolina Press.

Pound, Louise (1872–1958)

Collector of folksongs and Nebraska folklore; ballad scholar. Pound, the daughter of Nebraska settlers, devoted her career to preserving her native state's folklore. After graduating from the University of Nebraska, Pound received a Ph.D. at the University of Heidelberg.

Returning to Lincoln as an English professor in 1900, Pound pioneered studies in philology and folklore. She introduced innovative studies of American speech, instead of continuing British-language scholarship, which linguists considered a more respectable scholarly field. Pound explored word origins, uses, and euphemisms. Deriving a methodology from her undergraduate biology courses, Pound stated that linguists should realize that language was constantly evolving. She was one of the first professors in the United States to teach American literature, and she also taught as a visiting professor during summer sessions at major institutions, including the Yale Linguistics Institute.

Unlike her colleagues, she promoted the collection and analysis of regional folklore, including Nebraska dialect, colloquialisms, and customs. Her *Folk-Song of Nebraska and the Central West: A Syllabus* (1915) was the first state collection of folksongs. In her most controversial work, *Poetic Origins and the Ballad* (1921), Pound refuted theories that ballads originated communally. She proved that ballads were individual compositions not communal improvisations, noting structure and historical derivation.

Working without sabbaticals and grants, Pound prolifically penned articles for diverse publications and earned international acclaim. She edited university publications at Nebraska and served on the advisory board of *Southern Folklore Quarterly*. Pound founded and edited *American Speech*. She was president of the American Folklore Society (1925–1927) and the American Dialect Society. In 1955 she was the first woman elected president of the Modern Language Association of America.

Considering teaching her most important work, Pound influenced such graduate students as Benjamin A. Botkin. She also was an accomplished athlete, being the first woman elected to the Nebraska Sports Hall of Fame. Her final work, *Nebraska Folklore* (1959), was published posthumously, and the July 1959 issue of *Western Folklore* was designated the Louise Pound Memorial Number.

Elizabeth D. Schafer

References

Botkin, B.A. 1959. Louise Pound, 1872–1958. *Western
    Folklore* 18:63–65.
Pound, Louise. 1913. The Southwestern Cowboy Songs
    and English and Scottish Popular Ballads. *Modern
    Philology* 11:195–207.
———. 1922. *American Ballads and Songs.* New York:
    Scribner.
———. 1949. *Selected Writings of Louise Pound.* Lincoln:
    University of Nebraska Press.
Turner, Elizabeth A. 1992. Legacy Profile: Louise Pound,
    1872–1958. *Legacy* 9:59–64.

Powwow

A contemporary intertribal Native American social dance
based primarily on the dance styles of the Plains Indians. Earlier, the term was used by European Americans to denote any
Native American ceremony, especially those believed to feature magic or sorcery. From the latter usage, the term was
borrowed by the Pennsylvania Dutch as a euphemism for
magical healing practices brought from Europe.

Like many other Algonquian words (for example,
"squaw" and "papoose"), powwow has been used by non-In-
dians principally as a pejorative, humorous term. The original word, *pauwaw* or *po'wah* or *pow'waw,* was used in the
Narragansett and Natick dialects to mean "one who uses divination" and probably referred to a native doctor. Since healing ceremonies featured dancing, singing, and the gathering
of large groups, such an event became for early settlers a metaphor for any Indian ceremony, and it eventually was used to
refer to any noisy gathering. In more recent times, probably
since the early 1900s, Native Americans have taken back the
word and have used it as a reference to the intertribal social
dances that have become extremely popular across the United
States and Canada among tribes who might have considered
each other enemies in years past but who now have political,
social, economic, and cultural interests in common.

Powwow music is provided by singers gathered around
large drums in an indoor or outdoor arena. Each group of five
to ten singers is called "a drum," and each drum alternates with
others in producing the variety of dance rhythms demanded
by powwow tradition. Singing may be in English, in various
Native American languages, and in chanted syllables without
lexical meaning. Dances range from "round dances," in which
participants form large circles doing a side-step, to energetic
"war dances," to spectacular "grass dances," "jingle dances,"
"fancy dances," and "shawl dances."

Usually, the dancers form a large circle that moves sun-
wise (clockwise), whether the steps are done together by everyone (as in the round dance, the Owl Dance, or the Oklahoma Two-Step) or separately (as in the war dances). In a "war
dance"—which has nothing to do with war—each person
dances according to his or her own style, using steps and gestures picked up from watching other dancers over the years.
Friends often dance near each other in small groups, but there
is no attempt to match each other's movements. "Fancy dancers" dress in materials that exaggerate their movements: long
feather bustles and shoulder pieces, feathered headdresses, and
noisemakers that accentuate the rhythm (shell rattles, sleigh
bells). "Traditional dancers" tend to dress more simply, and
their motions more closely resemble the gestures and postures
of hunters. While the male dancers use heavy foot movements,
women usually portray delicacy and grace by limiting arm
movements and stooping and by using a very light foot movement that makes them seem to float.

Since the 1930s, many new powwow traditions have

developed: rituals of the grand entry (which include the use of national and tribal flags as well as a staff of eagle feathers to commemorate all Native American people who have fallen in battle), rituals for recovering a feather dropped accidentally to the ground during the dancing (it can be retrieved only by a war veteran), customs about color, deportment, appropriate dress, "giveaways" (a public ceremony during which a family gives gifts to those assembled in the name of their relative who is being honored), as well as beliefs about the health of drums and the reintroduction into the powwow circle of dance "outfits" previously worn by deceased dancers. These and other customs growing out of intertribal associations over time have created a powwow society whose traditions have spread to tribes like the Hopi and the Navajo, who previously had no such customs. The contemporary powwow is a vivid example of folklore used selectively to foreground some older traditions by reincorporating them into modern contexts for cultural enjoyment and ethnic identity.

Barre Toelken

References

Brown, Vanessa, and Barre Toelken. 1988. American Indian Powwow. *Folklife Annual 1987*. Washington, DC: American Folklife Center, pp. 46–68.

Cronk, Michael Sam, et al. 1988. Celebrations: Native Events in Eastern Canada. *Folklife Annual 1987*. Washington, DC: American Folklife Center, pp. 70–85.

Horse Capture, George P. 1989. *Pow Wow*. Cody, WY: Buffalo Bill Historical Center.

Parfit, Michael. 1994. Powwow: A Gathering of the Tribes. *National Geographic* 185 (6):87–113.

Roberts, Chris. 1992. *Powwow Country*. Helena, MT: American and World Geographic Publishing.

Toelken, Barre. 1991. Ethnic Selection and Intensification in the Native American Powwow. In *Creative Ethnicity: Symbols and Strategies of Contemporary Ethnic Life*, ed. Stephen Stern and John Allan Cicala. Logan: Utah State University Press, pp. 137–156.

See also Social Protest in Folklore

Prank

A play activity in which one party (the trickster) attempts to cause another party (the target) to believe in and act upon a fabrication, which is usually discredited soon afterward at a time chosen by the trickster. Practical jokes are based upon the creation or exploitation of a situation in which participants have differential access to information about what is going on. Thus, those involved in a practical joke are divided into two opposed groups: those who know what is going on, and those who have a false idea of what is going on. Both groups may consist of one or many people. Those in the know may include not only the trickster(s) who claim at least partial responsibility for constructing the situation that the target group is in, but sometimes also collusive spectators who watch the practical joke unfold but do not participate in its construction beyond agreeing to keep it hidden from the target.

The terms "practical joke" and "prank" are largely interchangeable. There is some evidence that the latter term is reserved for deceptions that are either relatively malicious and/or less complex and less subtle, but this distinction is by no means hard and fast. "Hoax," a closely related term, tends to denote relatively complex and large-scale fabrications, especially those that target larger groups of people in a more or less public context. "Hoax," however, like the "confidence game," includes deceits that go beyond the merely expressive and playful and cause material loss or harm to the victims. The term "jape" (a device to deceive or cheat) is largely obsolete, while "sell" (a planned deception) is confined to slang.

Practical jokes are associated with calendar events, notably April Fools' Day, the Feast of the Holy Innocents (December 28)—in Catholic countries—and Halloween. Rites of passage are also popular excuses for pranks, especially birthdays and weddings. The hazing of initiation rites often includes practical jokes as well as more overt forms of physical horseplay and degradation of the initiate (Henningsen 1961).

At one end of the spectrum of practical jokes we may include simple acts of victimization such as goosing. College students are known for subjecting each other, their professors, and sometimes the general public to highly elaborate fabrications, including, for example, removing the contents of a dorm room into the quad. Many of these take place between traditional rivals, such as freshmen and seniors, the Harvard Lampoon versus the Harvard Crimson, or the rivalry between UCLA and USC. At MIT, "hacks" are practical jokes that combine publicity and ingenious uses of technology. Actors and radio and television announcers subject their fellows to pranks that test their composure while on stage or on the air, by, for example, modifying props or setting fire to an announcer's copy. These pranks are out of the view of the audience but test the actor's ability to remain in character.

The folklorist can rarely investigate practical jokes as they unfold without extensive immersion in the field community. Folklore archives and publications often contain prank recipes—generic instructions for particular practical jokes. Most often, data about this genre are found in personal narratives, folktales (lies), and occasionally legends. "The Shaggy Dog Story" is not a narrative account of a practical joke, but is itself a practical joke in that it leads its audience to expect a punchline ending.

Many practical jokes are traditional, as indicated by the assignment of the motif numbers between J2300 and J2349 ("gullible fools"). Motif J2346 (Type 1296) refers to the fool's errand: an apprentice, newcomer, or ignorant person is sent for an absurd, misleading, or nonexistent object, or on a ridiculous quest. Victims are sent for sky hooks, striped paint, left-handed tools, a device to stretch objects that are too small or a compressor for objects that are too large. Occupational fool's errands exploit the newcomer's ignorance of the jargon and tools of the trade: Novices in aviation search for a bucket of prop wash, while apprentice printers look for type lice and have their faces splashed with water. In a snipe hunt (Motif J2349.6*), the target is taken into the woods at night and is left holding a bag in which to catch the snipe, while the tricksters leave, allegedly to beat the prey toward him; instead they return home, leaving the dupe alone to work out what really happened. While the snipe hunt is known in virtually every part of the United States, the description of the prey varies: It may be described as a type of bird, a snake, or a small furry animal. In one version, the snipe is a type of deer with a distinctive call; the dupe is left kneeling and imitating the snipe call while holding the bag to catch it. Another traditional prank (J2349.8*) plays upon the target's lust; he is taken to visit an allegedly sex-starved local woman ("the widow," "the brakeman's wife," and the like), who is in on the joke; then accomplices playing the role of jealous husband or father chase him off with rifle shots.

Motif J2349.10*, convincing a newcomer of the existence of a wonderful animal, is closely related to the lie and the tall tale. The exotic flora and fauna of the New World that greeted European colonists, frontiersmen, and travelers gave rise to tall tales; to the uninitiated, the distinction between an amazing but true narrative, an exaggerated description, and a completely fictitious one would be difficult to discern. This characteristic of the New World leads to the common assertion that hoaxing is a typically American form of humor. Hoaxes have been attributed to well-known American historical and literary figures. John James Audubon, for instance, fooled a visiting naturalist with his description of the fictitious Devil Jack Diamond fish, whose scales were shaped like cut diamonds and were hard enough to resist rifle bullets; when dried, they could strike fire from steel. An English travel writer repeated the story, conferring on the fabulous fish the scientific name *litholepis adamantinus*. Fabrications of this sort were especially common in the colonial and frontier periods.

Outstanding practical jokers, who achieve fame beyond the confines of their particular folk group, may have apocryphal hoaxes attributed to them. The noted illustrator Hugh Troy (1906–1964) is one such; hoaxes attributed to him include starting a stream of bogus flypaper reports while in the Army, and posing as a workman with a group of conspirators to actually dig up a section of the pavement on Fifth Avenue.

In terms of their operation, practical jokes may be divided into three broad groups. The first method is to fabricate an event that is extraordinary enough to provoke the target to react. By reacting to, or acting upon, a fabrication, the targets reveal that they have been fooled. For example, the target is told that she has just won the lottery but that she must answer some revealing personal questions in order to claim the prize. The booby-trap method, on the other hand, requires that the target have no inkling that anything out of the ordinary is afoot; thus he walks into the trap and is left with some messy predicament to cope with. Exploding cigars, grease in a toolbox, and assembling a car on a roof are all examples of this technique. The final category is represented by the fake pizza delivery; the trickster fools one party, often a business, to interact with a second party. This person, the trickster's real target, is put in the predicament of dealing with the deceived person.

Folklorists are interested in the social context of practical jokes—the relationships between tricksters and targets, and the ways in which practical-joking patterns reflect and contribute to the maintenance of social identities. But the question of whether practical jokes are benign or aggressive cannot be answered in general terms; this evaluation is made by those directly involved in each trick event, especially the victim. In deciding whether to treat the event as a joke and whether to judge the trickster's motives as friendly or hostile, the previous relationship between them is the most important deciding factor. Thus, practical jokes cannot be fully understood outside of their social contexts.

We can construct a consistent typology of practical jokes based upon the relationships between tricksters and targets. Based on this criterion, practical jokes fall into three categories: esoteric, exoteric, and initiatory. Esoteric jokes involve tricksters and targets who belong to the same personal group. While it is not necessary for the two parties to have identical status, the social gap between them is not great. Esoteric joking is often reciprocal (the victim today is likely to be the trickster tomorrow) and relatively benign—in the sense that the trickster will try to keep the joke within the boundaries of play and ensure that the victim will be able to laugh along when the joke is revealed. Jokers avoid topics that they believe the intended recipient will not find amusing; they typically own up to their fabrications; and they assist the victim in dealing with whatever consequences the joke has left behind. By the same token, victims of esoteric jokes will make efforts to laugh along, suppressing any negative feelings they may have about the prank. April Fools' Day jokes are in this category. Exoteric jokes, in contrast, are played on outsiders. They are not typically reciprocal, and jokers in these situations may take pains to conceal their identities from the victims even after the deception has concluded. Rather than making sure it is play, jokers are interested only with "getting away with" the joke—that is, not being caught. The targets' response to the news of their deception is relatively unimportant; sometimes an angry response is what is desired. These jokes, of which Halloween pranks and telephone pranks are good examples, take place across status and identity lines and are expressive of those lines.

Initiatory jokes are played on outsiders with the possible outcome of transforming them into insiders, where they are included in the ongoing cycle of reciprocal esoteric jokes. Alternatively, some newcomers are denied full membership in the in-group, and such people may become permanent targets of nonreciprocal, aggressive joking, which expresses and maintains their outsider status. Initiation pranks, like other forms of hazing, function as a kind of test; the initiate's response to this victimization may determine whether he or she is admitted to full insider status.

Practical jokes, both esoteric and exoteric, are often customized to fit the idiosyncrasies of their targets. The joke enactment serves as an unfavorable comment on an alleged personality flaw of the victim. When someone annoys his fellow workers by boasting too much about a new car's gas mileage, they may exploit this point by surreptitiously adding gas to the tank, thus fooling the owner into boasting about absurd miles per gallon; they then reverse the procedure. Folk opinion holds that the target would not have been fooled were it not for a defect of character (in this case, excessive pride in the new car); in other words, he contributed to his own victimization.

Moira Smith

References

Bauman, Richard. 1986. We Were Always Pullin' Jokes. In *Story, Performance, and Event: Contextual Studies of Oral Narrative.* New York: Cambridge University Press, pp. 33–53.

Bowman, J.R. 1982. On Getting Even: Notes on the Organization of Practical Jokes. In *The Paradoxes of Play,* ed. J. Loy. West Point, NY: Leisure Press, pp. 65–75.

Henningsen, Hennig. 1961. *Crossing the Equator: Sailors' Baptism and Other Initiation Rites.* Copenhagen: Munksgaard.

Leary, James P. 1979. Adolescent Pranks in Bloomington, Indiana. *Indiana Folklore* 12:55–64.

MacDougall, Curtis D. 1940. *Hoaxes.* New York: Macmillan.

Santino, Jack. 1986. A Servant and a Man, a Hostess or a Woman: A Study of Expressive Culture in Two Transportation Occupations. *Journal of American Folklore* 99:304–319.

Smith, H. Allen. 1980. *The Compleat Practical Joker.* New York: William Morrow.

Steinberg, Neil. 1992. *If at All Possible, Involve a Cow: The Book of College Pranks.* New York: St. Martin's Press.

Tallman, Richard. 1974. A Generic Approach to the Practical Joke. *Southern Folklore Quarterly* (Special Issue) 38:259–274.

See also April Fools' Day; Cow Tipping; Halloween

Prayer

The process of individuals petitioning, praising, or thanking someone in hopes of achieving a desired end. Individuals and groups often address prayers to a deity (God, Goddess, Great Spirit), but also can intend the words spoken to be noted predominantly by human listeners. Across space, time, and ideologies, these petitions have typically concerned egocentric ends, such as that the weather may suit our local needs, that we may conquer our enemies, and that we may have health and prosperity.

Common formula prayers include the "Serenity Prayer," the "Lord's Prayer" from the New Testament, the prayer-like Psalm 23 from the Old Testament, and the popular bedtime prayer "Now I lay me down to sleep." Several parodies of these common texts exist, indicating a solid knowledge of the originals. For example:

> God grant me the senility to forget the things I cannot change. . . .

and

> The Ford is my auto, I shall not want another. It maketh me to lie down in mud puddles. . . .

A popular country-western song from 1993, "My Broken Heart," toys with the basics of the bedtime prayer demonstrating its continued popularity:

> Last night I prayed the Lord my soul to keep,
> Then I cried myself to sleep. . . .

Offering a prayer before eating is a common practice in some households. It is a way of expressing thanks for the food and for those who provided and prepared it. During this time of "saying grace," "asking a blessing," "returning thanks," or "giving a blessing on the food," family members can also pray for wants and needs. One California family, meaning to thank and praise God, holds hands while seated around the table and sings in round-fashion:

> For health and strength and daily bread we praise thy name, oh Lord.

Some "blessings" contain comments directed more toward those sitting around the table than to any deity, such as the parody "Good bread, good meat / Good God, let's eat."

Some tales contain verse prayers that are integral to the story. The verse contained in these cantefables depicts the resolution of a conflict in which a subordinate, for the moment, achieves the upper hand. Individuals praying these prayers definitely hope that their words will have the greatest impact on those seated around the table. This tale collected in Pennsylvania—one variant of a widely known story—serves as a good example:

> There was a little boy one time that had t' dig the potatoes, and he didn't like t' do it. So when the preacher come t' visit, they always had potatoes, an' it made him mad that he had' a dig potatoes fer the preacher t' eat. So they all set up t' the table, and his daddy asked him to say the blessing, so he said:

> > "Dear Lord above, send down a dove,
> > With teeth as sharp as razors,
> > To cut the throats of these damn goats
> > That eats my daddy's taters."

Public prayer at gatherings aside from church is on the decline in the United States. Congress still invites Christian ministers to offer prayer, but public prayer at sporting events, concerts, or conventions is the exception; not the rule. However, the tendency to publicly invite a blessing from God still exists. One common pronouncement on any individual sneezing in public is still often "(God) bless you."

S. Spencer Cannon

References

Barrick, Mac E. 1981. The Competitive Element in the Cante Fable. *Southern Folklore Quarterly* 45:123–134.

Hampton, Wade G. 1990. Culinary Prefaces: North Carolina Folk Blessings. *North Carolina Folklore Journal*

"The Angel of Prayer." Lithograph, Currier & Ives, 1875. Library of Congress.

37:88–96.

Janssen, Jaques, Joep de Hart, and Christine denDraak. 1990. Praying as an Individualized Ritual. In *Current Studies on Rituals: Perspectives for the Psychology of Religion.* Amsterdam: Rodopi, pp. 71–85.

Monteiro, George. 1964. Parodies of Scriptures, Prayer, and Hymn. *Journal of American Folklore* 77:45–52.

Porter, Kenneth W. 1965. Humor, Blasphemy, and Criticism in the Grace before Meat. *New York Folklore Quarterly* 21:3–18.

Pregnancy and Birth

Culturally patterned medical and socio-religious beliefs practiced to regulate the birth cycle and ensure successful delivery. Early folklorists took a simple approach to pregnancy and birth. They collected beliefs about prenatal marking and dietary intake and gathered traditional practices associated with pregnancy, delivery, and early infancy. Marie Campbell's *Folks Do Get Born* (Campbell 1946) and material in Volume 6 of the *Frank C. Brown Collection of North Caroline Folklore* (Hand 1961) are representative of this approach. Such collections cataloged and preserved knowledge concerning beliefs and represent the bulk of folkloristic materials concerning pregnancy and birth. These works, however, often treated individual examples as isolated and unrelated and reflected earlier definitions of folk medicine, which was seen as resting ". . . between official, scientific medicine (the top layer) and primitive medicine (the bottom layer)" (Hufford 1988:229). This definition was cultural evolutionary in nature and represented an understanding of folk medicine as ". . . having developed from its crudest, most primitive form into its modern, Western, highly sophisticated state" (Hufford 1988:228). This approach obscured or ignored entirely the dynamic interrelationship between birthlore, societal attitudes, changes in medical knowledge and practice, and the role of women within the community.

Many writers in the fields of anthropology, folklore, sociology, women's studies, history, and professional medicine have attempted more comprehensive studies of pregnancy and birth. Some (see Hoffert 1989; Leavitt 1986; and Scholten 1985; Wertz and Wertz 1989) employed a tripartite categorization, presenting a chronological progression of the history from a time when birth was a social project through a period of transition when medical authority assumed influence, and culminating in an era when the medical profession consolidated its hold on the process of pregnancy and birth. This approach attempted to move beyond mere categorization and listing by addressing changes in practice in relation to changes in cultural attitude and belief as well as advances in medical science. This categorization, however, created an image of birth traditions as characteristic of only limited periods of history that faded out of practice in response to the pressure and development of modern obstetrics.

The folklore of pregnancy and birth does not reflect the earlier ideas of "primitive" medicine versus "official" medicine, nor does it characterize a period of American history before the advent of professional obstetrics. Instead, traditional practices of pregnancy and birth are still practiced alongside, and in conjunction with, standard obstetrical technique and care, although they are frequently practiced without the knowledge or consent of obstetricians. Likewise, the contemporary alternative-birth movement utilizes and employs many so-called traditional or folk medical approaches to pregnancy and birth in a highly structured atmosphere. The presence of midwives, family and community involvement, herbal remedies, "natural" birth, and the revival of birth chairs are characteristic of this. However, like other forms of alternative health practices and folk medicine, the alternative-birth movement and the use of traditional pregnancy and delivery practices exist in tension with official attitudes and is often condemned as dangerous, primitive, and marginal.

There are three interrelated subjects of traditional beliefs and practices: conception, pregnancy, and delivery. Such practices and beliefs sought to ensure conception, guard against miscarriage or bring about abortion, protect the mother and child during gestation, determine the sex of the child, regulate diet and activity, and bring about a safe birth. The most detailed and rigorously employed practices were those that dealt with the actual approach to delivery and techniques to effect it.

Specific examples of traditional American beliefs associated with conception include these: that rubbing one's stomach against a pregnant woman's or ingesting large quantities of eggs would bring about conception; that vinegar-and-water douches would result in the birth of a boy, and eating salty food prior to conception would bring about the birth of a daughter; and that paint fumes, strenuous horseback riding, or drinking turpentine would produce an abortion, while swallowing fruit seeds would prevent miscarriage.

Many pregnancy practices are related to food taboos. These practices resulted from the "doctrine of maternal impression," the notion that certain foods would contaminate the milk supply, cause a difficult birth, bring about an abortion, grow a strong or a weak child, or "mark" a child with either a birthmark, a physical deformity, or an emotional disposition. Perhaps the best example of dietary practice during pregnancy is the widespread cultural symptom of pregnancy: cravings. The practice of "pica"—the desire for, and ingestion of, nonfood items—is a significant element of pregnancy folklore. Pica includes the eating of dirt or clay (a practice called geophagy), and/or the ingestion of laundry starch, matches, ice, or hair. Pica has a long association with pregnancy in the United States, with numerous examples and accounts in folklore materials and medical journals, as well as mention in popular American novels such as Toni Morrison's *Song of Solomon* and John Steinbeck's *The Grapes of Wrath*. The traditions associated with food intake during pregnancy, like other forms of pregnancy folklore, are widespread and are not culturally and ethnically specific. Mexican Americans, African Americans, those of European decent, Asian Americans, and others all have beliefs concerning various forms of food taboo and regulation as well as forms of pica during pregnancy.

Practices associated with delivery are concerned with ensuring a successful delivery for both mother and child and were the product of participation in neighboring women's births and the dissemination of knowledge from mother to daughter, from midwife to assistant, and from woman to woman. The practices are predicated on an understanding of birth as a natural consequence of nature, and they respond to and react to the event of birth. Delivery practices, therefore, serve to assist the mother as she delivers, intervening only in the event of difficulty or danger. Such practices include the choice of midwives and female members of the community as birth attendants, methods to alleviate the pain and apprehension associated with delivery, and, significantly, the use of birth chairs or an attendant's lap to assist in the preferred upright posture of delivery. Once delivery is completed other beliefs govern divining the future of the child based on the incidents and time of its birth. For example, in the United States it was traditionally believed that a child born with a caul would have some ability to foresee the future, a child born during a storm would have a stormy personality, or a child born with clenched fists would be greedy and selfish.

The folklore of pregnancy and birth in the United States incorporates many different ethnic and cultural approaches. The practices are cultural constructions—responding to the attitudes and beliefs within the context of society. As society changed its attitudes and beliefs, the practices and beliefs associated with pregnancy and birth likewise altered. All reflected a philosophy of birth as natural and were similar in their quality of responding to the event as opposed to manipulating or directing the process.

Amanda Carson Banks

References

Campbell, Marie. 1946. *Folks Do Get Born*. New York: Rhinehart.

Hand, Wayland D., ed. 1961. *The Frank C. Brown Collection of North Carolina Folklore*. Vol. 6. Durham, NC: Duke University Press.

Hochstein, G. 1968. Pica: A Study in Medical and Anthropological Explanations. In *Essays on Medical Anthropology*, ed. T. Weaver. Athens: University of Georgia Press.

Hoffert, Sylvia. 1989. *Private Matters: Attitudes toward Childbearing and Infant Nurture in Early Nineteenth-Century America*. Urbana: University of Illinois Press.

Hufford, David. 1988. Contemporary Folk Medicine. In *Other Healers: Unorthodox Medicine in America*, ed. Norman Gevitz. Baltimore: Johns Hopkins University Press.

Leavitt, Judith. 1986. *Brought to Bed: Childbearing in America, 1750–1950*. New York: Oxford University Press.

Scholten, Catherine. 1985. *Childbearing in American Society, 1650–1850*. New York: New York University Press.

Wertz, Richard, and Dorothy Wertz. 1989. *Lying-In: A History of Childbirth in America*. New Haven, CT: Yale University Press.

See also Medicine, Folk; Midwifery

Printers, Journeymen

Highly regarded group of skilled tradesmen and tradeswomen identified by their typesetting and printing skills, observance of historical customs, long apprenticeships, initiation rites, and use of peculiar trade jargon. The heyday of the journeymen printer ended in the 1960s when the craft all but ceased to center around metal type. By the 1970s, computer-generated type had become the norm. The technological transition from the physical production of metal-cast type to the electronic world of computer-mediated type displaced countless journeymen printers from their trade.

Hot-metal printers (compositors, stonehands, linotype operators) were craftspeople, engaged in the physical composition of the printed word. Their occupation dated back to the mid-15th century when Johannes Gutenberg perfected the use of movable type. As wordsmiths, the printers' command of language made them unique among labor craftspeople. Membership in an intellectual craft was a point of pride. Many renowned writers began their careers as printers' apprentices—Walt Whitman, Mark Twain, Erskine Caldwell, Joel Chandler Harris, Sherwood Anderson, and Benjamin Franklin, among others. The latter is the personage most often cited by printers, proud of the literary lineage associated wtih their trade.

Printers customarily entered the trade by completing a six-year apprenticeship. Formally serving an apprenticeship qualified one to work at the printing trade as a journeyman. The apprenticeship served as a practical education. Horace Greeley was known to have said that "a Printer's case is a better education than a high school or college." An apprentice was expected to learn by doing. In addition to gaining technical knowledge under the wing of an experienced journeyman, the apprentice was indoctrinated into the social traditions and customs of the trade.

As is commonplace in occupational life, journeyman printers observed the custom of playing initiation pranks on gullible apprentices, also known as printer's devils. One such prank involved a search for "type lice." A seasoned journeyman instructed an unsuspecting apprentice to look for these nonexistent critters. The apprentice leaned over a galley of loosely composed type, into which water had been poured. Not seeing anything unusual, the apprentice attempted to get a closer look. Once his scrutinizing eye was inches away from the galley, the journeyman printer slapped the lines of type together, splashing water all over the apprentice's face. The prank has been adapted to the cold type world of late-20th-century printing. In place of type lice, apprentices have been asked to look for halftone dots.

Itinerant printers were known as tramp printers. A traveling card, issued by the International Typographical Union, was their only credential. Tramp printers found temporary work setting type throughout the United States and Canada until the 1960s, when a decline in union membership put an end to tramp printing. Tramp printers epitomized the journeyman printers' jointly held values of respectability, reciprocity, and independence.

Though the freedom of the traveling printer's life is romanticized in oral and written tradition, the working conditions of both the itinerant and the stationary printer were harsh—excessive heat, noise, and the presence of burning lead took their toll on printers. Stories abound about missing limbs, varicose veins, and tuberculosis.

Many phrases that have entered the mainstream of everyday speech have their source in printer's hot-metal terminology. For example, the phrase "out of sorts" derives from the printer's term for individual pieces of metal type, including those bought individually to supplement a font. A font is a family of type in one single size and style. The quantity of each letter varies with frequency of use. A font will come equipped with more A's than X's. Even so, a particular job might require more A's, in which case the printer could supplement his font by purchasing "sorts." If he came up short, he was literally out of sorts, not to mention at his wits' end.

Other hot-metal terms, such as leading (the metal slugs that form the space between lines of metal type) have survived the transition into the computer type age, even though leads no longer exist in the physical sense. Galleys no longer mean the brass or wooden trays that held lines of composed type; they are the paper proofs of those lines, printed. In printer's terms, "30" means the end. A 30-point slug was used at the bottom of a galley to indicate the end of an article. The only time one would see "30" in print was when a newspaper folded and it ran its last issue. For printers who worked in hot metal, the symbol "30" is coterminous with "the end." But for the increasing majority of typesetters working in a coldtype environment, "30" is just a number.

At one time, a newspaper editor had to rely on journeymen printers to read inked lines of cast type, as they lay upside down and backward in the galley. Now, editors key in their own copy, completely bypassing the composing room, where linotype operators once composed the copy.

In just two decades, the craft of setting type was transformed from an age-old handicraft to semiskilled labor. Just as printers attained mastery of their craft, computer technology made hands-on application of their skills superfluous.

Maggie Holtzberg-Call

References

Brevier, Linafont (pseudonym). 1954. *Trampography: Reminiscences of a Rovin' Printer, 1913 to 1917.* Glendale: n.p.

Holtzberg-Call, Maggie. 1992. *The Lost World of the Craft Printer.* Urbana: University of Illinois Press.

Kelber, Harry, and Carl Schlesinger. 1967. *Union Printers and Controlled Automation.* New York: Free Press.

Moxon, Joseph. [1683–1684] 1958. *Mechanick Exercises on the Whole Art of Printing,* ed. Herbert Davis and Harry Carter. Oxford: Oxford University Press.

Savage, William. [1841] 1967. *A Dictionary of the Art of Printing.* New York: Burt Franklin.

Prison Folklore

Traditions of groups of people incarcerated for crimes. The folklore of prisons, like that of most residential communities determined by both setting and occupation (such as hospitals for the chronically ill, military bases, and cloistered religious institutions), is complex and multifaceted. We should probably speak of prison *folklores* rather than prison folklore.

All prisoners and staff bring to the prison community folklore from their noncriminal and noninstitutional lives: stories, toasts, foodways, medicine, speech, religious practices, and so forth. Some of this finds immediate and direct use and applicability within the prison situation; some may be adapted to fit; and some is of little or no use and appears only occasionally, if at all. Prisoners may, for example, maintain ethnic food preferences while in prison, but most will have far less opportunity to indulge those preferences than they did in the free world. On the other hand, nothing impedes maintenance and articulation of folk superstition and belief: Prison walls and fences do not influence the efficacy of charms or the accuracy of omens.

Some free-world genres exist longer or more vigorously in prison than in the free world. Because of brutality and maintenance of a 19th-century plantation system, Black convict worksongs survived in Southern prison farms well into the 1960s, long after they had disappeared outside. Because of the great amount of enforced free time in prisons and jails, Black toasts likewise survived behind the walls when they were all but extinct beyond them.

All prisoners have had experiences with police, courts, and jails (jails are city and county facilities where people serve short sentences, usually for misdemeanors, and await felony trials; prisons are where people serve state and federal felony sentences). Many prisoners have had extensive experience in criminal activity, other prisons, and in the parole system. Technical discussions of, and personal narratives about, these experiences are common in prisoner discourse.

Folklore indigenous to the prison itself—folkways and narratives told and learned within the institution—may exist in both staff and prisoner cultures, but most is specific to one or the other, and little of either travels to the free world. Both guards and prisoners, for example, may tell stories about notable prison characters or events, but neither prisoners nor guards are likely to tell the other stories in which the others' foolishness or cupidity is the point of the humor. Likewise, guards don't initiate prisoners in traditional methods of crowd control, and prisoners don't initiate guards in traditional methods of manufacturing and hiding bootleg alcohol.

Prisoners' language is rich in slang from the streets, from the world of crime, and from the prison community. All but the first-timers know most of the argot terms, but not all prisoners use them, and not all prisoners who use them use them all of the time. A Midwestern inmate who committed more than 150 armed robberies said, "I don't use slang. You want people to think I'm a crook?" Some argot terms carry multiple meanings; which meaning applies at any moment can only be inferred from the context. The word "joint," for example, can mean marijuana cigarette, penis, paraphernalia for injecting heroin, or the prison itself. To officials, "jacket" means a prisoner's official records; to prisoners, it usually means a person's reputation. If the warden says, "Smith has a fat jacket," he is saying that Smith's file is thick, hence he has been arrested many times, in prison many times, or has been in the warden's prison for a very long time. If a prisoner says, "Smith's got a snitch jacket on him," he is saying that Smith is known as an informer. "Jacket" is also an article of clothing worn on cool days, just like outside.

Slang is often particular to a prison system or an area, and to a specific point in time. Texas prisoners forced to do agricultural work had terms like "sideline" (working up one side of a row of crops), "flatweed" (working with a hoe), "catch up tight" (work closely together), and "don't leave a comeback" (get everything out of a row in one pass so that it is not necessary to come through a second time). Prisoners are aware of their argot and of its restricted venue, as is indicated by this joke from Texas: A man got out of prison and went to the barbershop for his first free-world haircut. Well, when he sat down in the barber's chair, the barber, after looking this fellow's head over, asked him if he had been in prison. This fellow said "No, I haven't. Why do you ask that?" The barber said, "No reason in particular. Just wondered." The barber then asked this fellow how he wanted his hair cut. The fellow said, "Sideline the sides, flatweed the top, catch up tight, and don't leave a comeback."

Much folklore specific to prison has to do with ways of doing things or material for doing or making things provided for by other means in the community outside prison, which is to say, much prison folklore is adaptive and transient, done or used only when the free-world alternatives are not available. At one time, for example, Indiana inmates were permitted to purchase jars of instant coffee from the commissary but not allowed to own devices with which to heat the water. Tap water was tepid at best, so they fashioned a device they called a hotstick out of a foot or two of lamp wire with a male plug at one end and a short stripped loop of wire at the other. It would boil a cup-water in a few seconds, but there was a problem: The hotstick produced so much heat it would boil the water completely away in a few minutes, so if one were left untended it would blow the cellblock's fuses or start a fire. When commercial water heaters were made available in the prison commissary, the hotsticks disappeared. Other adaptations are more complex. Staff can get alcoholic beverages in liquor stores; the only aspect of alcohol manufacture in staff folklore has to do with stories about inmates making it, getting caught having it, or behaving egregiously while intoxicated with it. Prisoners cannot get alcohol in liquor stores; their folklore consists not only of stories, but techniques: obtaining the makings (yeast, fruit), finding places for safe fermentation (it's not just a matter of finding unused tubs, toilet bowls, or rubber boots for fermenting, but having those operations take place where guards won't detect the pungent odor), and finding places to hide the product and drink it in safety.

Many prisoners have long experience with possessing and sometimes using weapons; being in prison changes the kinds of weapons used, but not the perceived need for them. Commercial knives are rarely found in prison, but substitutes can be made from many easily found objects. A 6-inch piece of stiff wire can pierce an eye or a throat. Knives are fashioned differently depending on the intended use. An all-purpose knife can be made from a hammered and filed spoon. Knives for slashing can be made in metal shops by shearing sheet steel at a diagonal; in prisons where license plates are made, this is particularly easy. A double-edged razor blade with one edge melted into a toothbrush handle is good for slashing a face or cutting a throat. Knives for inflicting puncture wounds can be made from pitchfork tines or rattail files. Knives are shaped and sized differently if they are to be hidden in jacket linings, taped to a leg, carried in a pocket or up a sleeve.

There may be different ethnic and regional patterns in use of knives. A Texas warden said: "In my experience, Black convicts want knives that slash; the Latin convicts knives that puncture; and Whites go either way, depending where they grew up. The Blacks want to hurt or scare somebody so they use slashers; the Latins, they aren't interested in scaring. When they use a knife they want to kill you so they go after these long thin things that get between the ribs." A man who had done a good deal of felony time in New York prisons read that statement and said: "When that warden says 'Latins' he means Mexican Americans. Up here in the East, the Latins are Puerto Ricans and they're not stabbers, they're slashers. Blacks are the stabbers. And Whites—well, up here, Whites aren't into knives."

Prison folklore is rich in stories about local characters, escapes, stupid guards and clever convicts, and how it was in the old days. These tales are rarely migratory. Inmates in Texas told of "Bullin Jack O'Diamonds," the meanest guard on Central Farm, a man so mean he had to be chained down to die. "If he catch you," one inmate said, "a dark cloud would go over." One story has him telling Satan, "Stand aside, I'm gonna rule old Hell myself!" Massachusetts inmates told of a stupid deputy warden nicknamed "Alligator" who "looked like a retired hit man." He decided inmates were abusing the pharmacy so he stopped all medication, no matter what the illness. One inmate had been receiving Doriden, a narcotic. He said he had to have his medication. The deputy refused. "But I've been getting heart palpitations," the inmate said. "Keep on taking those," Alligator said, "they're better for you than Doridens, believe me."

As in the free world, a good deal of prison folklore has to do with sexual roles and activities. Staff can leave the prison after their shift and engage in ordinary sexual activities. Prisoners are limited in partners, in opportunity, and they often suffer institutional punishments (isolation, loss of privileges, loss of good time) when officials catch them doing it. Prison sex parodies sex in the free world. In men's prisons, there are three primary roles, often designated by the argot terms "punks," "queens," and "studs." Studs are men who occupy the inserter role; punks and queens are insertees, but punks occupy that role only in prison while queens occupy that role wherever they are. Queens generally have much higher social status in the prison community than punks because punks are seen as accepting their sexual roles out of weakness while queens are "man enough to admit what they are." Sex in women's prison seems primarily grounded in continuing relationships; sex in men's prisons seems primarily focused on genital acts.

There are many jokes and anecdotes in prisons about prison sex roles, few of which travel outside. There is no point telling jokes about punks and queens and studs to people with no prison experience because those people don't know the difference between a punk and a queen, and by the time it is explained to them the momentum of the joke is gone. These are two typical sex-role jokes:

> Jesse James was robbin' a passenger train. Jesse James taken up all the money. He say, "I'm gonna rob this train. I'm gonna fuck all the men." This lady got up, said, "Mister Jesse James: you mean all the women." And there's this punk on there, and he got up and said, "Hey, lady, who robbin' this train, you or Mister Jesse James?" There was another captain, over on the Central [prison farm], every time you asked for a lay-in [time off because of sickness], you know, say 'My head hurts," he said, "I do, too. Mine, too; me, too," you know. "I got a . . . my arm hurts, my leg hurts, my stomach hurts, I got a stomach ache," and he'll say, "Me, too." So one day a guy says, "I'm gonna get me a lay-in." So he said, "Captain, I want to lay-in." "What's wrong with you?" He said, "I got the claps in the ass." He start to say—he said, "Lay in!"

Some Black prisoners in all of the Southern agricultural prison systems sang worksongs during the years the prisons were segregated and the work routines brutal. Worksongs were used to cut and chop trees, work fields, and pick cotton. Some songs were like blues—individual and private. Others were communal. White and Latin inmates did not sing these songs, nor did they have any body of metrically functional songs of their own used in similar fashion. By mid-20th century, the only place in North America the songs could be found were Southern plantation-type prison farms. The songs and the style of utilizing them were the property of Black inmates exclusively, and they were in a clear tradition going back beyond the importation of the first slaves to the Virginia Colony in 1631. Some of those songs could be found in prisons across the Deep South; others were found only in one prison or one prison system. The Texas convict songs "Midnight Special," about a train near Darrington prison farm, and "Grizzly Bear," reportedly about a warden, didn't travel to prisons in Louisiana or Mississippi. Indeed, none of the agricultural folklore common in Southern prisons traveled to prisons in the industrial North and Far West, where that kind of work and those work conditions did not exist.

As in any large institution, members of the prison community form subcommunities that provide their primary social identification. In states with extensive free-world gang culture, such as Texas and California, gangs often become the basis for subcommunities within the prison community. Gang folkways—including rivalries—are maintained within the institution. Sometimes the subcommunities are based on origin. New York prisons, for example, have "courts," areas in the yard maintained by people from a certain neighborhood or part of the state. Men will hang around the court, cook food, tell stories, share resources, and protect one another from men in other courts. One man who had lived much of his life in Manhattan and then in Buffalo was a member of two courts until a group from one of the courts said to him, "You got to choose. You're either upstate or downstate. You can't be both."

Bruce Jackson

References

Burke, Carole. 1992. *Vision Narratives of Women in Prison.* Knoxville: University of Tennessee Press.

Jackson, Bruce. 1965. Prison Folklore. *Journal of American Folklore* 78:317–325.

———. 1972a. *In the Life: Versions of the Criminal Experience.* New York: Holt, Rinehart, and Winston.

———. 1972b. *Wake up Dead Man: Afro-American Worksongs from Texas Prisons.* Cambridge: Harvard University Press.

Proffitt, Frank Noah (1913–1965)

Folk musician, instrument maker, folksong collector from northwestern North Carolina. Proffitt was perhaps best known as the source of the Kingston Trio's 1958 recording of the native American ballad "Tom Dooley," named by one scholar as "the best-known folksong in America."

When the New York–based folksong enthusiasts Anne and Frank Warner conducted fieldwork in Watauga County, North Carolina, in 1939, they collected several tunes from Proffitt, one of which was a ballad about the hanging in 1868 of a man named Tom Dula (pronounced "Dooley" in the Appalachian dialect) in nearby Wilkes County. Proffitt had learned the song from his father, Wiley, whose mother, Adeline Perdue, knew both Dula and his victim, Laura Foster. Proffitt's son, Frank, Jr., has written that his great-grandfather learned the song directly from Dula as he lingered about his jail cell shortly before the hanging. Frank Warner, himself a performer, dropped some verses, rearranged others, reshaped the melody, and sang the song for several years, recording it in 1950 for Elektra records. In 1947 the folklorist Alan Lomax published Warner's version of the ballad in *Folk Song U.S.A.,* crediting Warner, but not Proffitt. It was this text that was recorded in 1958 by the Kingston Trio. The song reached the top of the popular music "Hit Parade" and went on to sell over three million copies, playing a major role in the rediscovery and popularization of authentic American folk music during the late 1950s and early 1960s. In 1962, well after the period of its greatest popularity, arrangements were made for Proffitt to enjoy a share of the song's royalties.

Proffitt was born in Laurel Bloomery, Tennessee, his family moving shortly after his birth to the Beaver Dam section of Watauga County, a few miles away. He grew up immersed in folk traditions, learning folksongs from his father and aunt, Nancy Prather. The Warners sparked his interest in folk music further, and he became a dedicated student of Appalachian musical traditions, collecting what he called "the old songs from his people" from his neighbors and family. His family on his wife's side was indeed a rich source of folklore; she was

Anne Warner records Frank Proffitt's singing and playing, while neighbors listen. Pick Britches Valley, Watauga County, North Carolina, 1941. Photo Frank Warner. American Folklife Center.

Bessie Hicks, the sister of the world-famous storyteller Ray Hicks. Proffitt's repertoire of folksongs was prodigious; he performed Child ballads (some quite rare), broadsides, and native American ballads; original pieces; religious tunes; and numerous lyrical songs in his soft, relaxed baritone voice, accompanying himself with guitar, dulcimer, or banjo played in a gentle thumb-lead, two-finger up-picking style. Having also learned instrument making from his father, Proffitt supplemented his often meager income from tobacco farming and part-time carpentry work with the sale of his homemade dulcimers and five-string, fretless wooden banjos.

During the last few years of his life, Proffitt became an ambassador of Appalachian folk music, performing at numerous colleges and universities, including the University of Chicago and the Newport and National Folk festivals, always minimizing his own abilities, preferring to direct attention to the traditions that he championed.

William E. Lightfoot

References

Proffitt, Frank. 1962. *Frank Proffitt of Reese, North Carolina.* Folk–Legacy Records. FSA 1.

———. 1962. Frank Proffitt Sings Folk Songs. Folkways Records FA 2360.

———. 1968. *Frank Proffitt: Memorial Album.* Folk–Legacy Records. FSA 36.

Warner, Anne, and Frank Warner. 1973. Frank Noah Proffitt: Good Times and Hard Times on the Beaver Dam Road. *Appalachian Journal* 1:162–198.

Proverbs

Concise traditional statements of apparent truths with currency among the folk. More elaborately stated, proverbs are short, generally known sentences of the folk that contain wisdom, truths, morals, and traditional views in a metaphorical, fixed, and memorizable form and that are handed down orally from generation to generation. Many scholars have attempted to formulate *the* proverb definition, ranging from abstract formulations based on symbolic logic to Archer Taylor's almost proverbial statement that "an incommunicable quality tells us this sentence is proverbial and that one is not" (Taylor [1913] 1985:3). Two major ingredients of what constitutes proverbiality should be part of any definition, but they cannot be ascertained from the proverb texts themselves: The aspects of traditionality and currency will always have to be established before a particular text can, in fact, be called a proverb. This situation is particularly acute when the question arises whether such new formulaic statements like "garbage in, garbage out" or "it takes two to tango" have reached a proverbial status in the United States. However, some definite "markers" are helpful in identifying short sentences of wisdom or common sense as folk proverbs. These markers are also instrumental in assuring the memorability and recognizability of the texts as traditional wisdom. In addition to their fixed (and often oppositional) structure, their relative shortness, and their use of metaphors, proverbs usually exhibit at least some, if not all, of the following poetic or stylistic features: alliteration: "Money makes the mare go"; rhyme: "Man proposes, God disposes"; parallelism: "Easy come, easy go"; ellipsis: "Out of sight, out of mind"; personification: "Misery loves company"; hyperbole: "It is easier for a camel to go through a needle's eye, than for a rich man to enter the kingdom of God" (Matthew 19:24); and paradox: "The nearer the church, the farther from God."

While proverbs per se are complete thoughts that can stand by themselves, there are such subgenres as proverbial expressions, proverbial comparisons, proverbial exaggerations, and twin (binary) formulas, which are but fragmentary metaphorical phrases that must be integrated into a sentence. Proverbial expressions are usually verbal phrases as, for example, "To pay through the nose" or "To put someone through the wringer." Proverbial comparisons can be divided into two major groups. The first follows the structure of "as X as Y"—for example, "as black as a crow" and "as white as a sheet." The second group is based on a verbal comparison with "like"—for example, "to grin like a Cheshire cat" and "to leak like a sieve." Proverbial exaggerations describe the extraordinary degree to which someone or something possesses a certain characteristic. Many of them are based on the structural pattern "so . . . (that)," clearly illustrated in such texts as "She is so thin you have to shake the sheets to find her" and "He is so narrow-minded that he can see through a keyhole with both eyes." Twin formulas, finally, are traditional word pairs that are molded together by alliteration and/or rhyme—for example, "slowly but surely" or "to go through thick and thin." None of these proverbial phrases ("phraseological units," as linguists call them) contains any complete thought or wisdom. They are proverbial in that they are traditional, metaphorical, and even more frequently used than true proverbs. While they add color and expressiveness to oral and written communication, they cannot stand alone due to their fragmentary structure. Nevertheless, much of what is described about proverbs below, such as their origin and content, is also applicable to these subgenres.

Proverbs in actual use are verbal strategies for dealing with social situations. To understand the meaning of proverbs in actual speech acts, they must be viewed as part of the entire communicative performance. This is true for proverbs used in oral speech, but also in their frequent employment in literary works, the mass media, advertising, popular songs, cartoons, and the like. Only the analysis of the use and function of proverbs within particular contexts will determine their specific meanings. In fact, proverbs in collections are almost meaningless or dead, but they become significant and alive once they are employed as a strategic statement that carries the weight of traditional wisdom. Proverbs thus exhibit different semantic possibilities due to their various functions and situations. Yet, it is exactly this intangible nature of proverbs that leads to their continued and effective use in all modes of communication.

It is customary to group proverbs according to their content, some major groups being legal proverbs, medical proverbs, and weather proverbs. It should be noted, however, that while a text like "Make hay while the sun shines" is, indeed, a metaphorical proverb, such commonly heard sayings like

"Red sky at night, sailor's delight" are merely superstitious weather signs couched in proverbial language. Other groups that are based just on content would include all of the proverbs dealing with the body, love, work, friendship, and death. Such groupings have their limitations, for while the proverb "Two heads are better than one" clearly deals with the body, it might actually serve as a metaphorical statement to express the fact that two people working together (pooling their intelligence) might be more successful than an individual doing things alone.

Based on structural and semiotic considerations, scholars have begun to group proverbs more systematically according to linguistic and logical types. This methodology has the advantage that proverbs of the same structure (like "Where there is X, there is Y") or of the same logical thought pattern (such as texts based on such oppositions as one:two or small:large) can be grouped and analyzed together. While they might have completely different metaphors, such proverbial signs express fundamental human thought patterns. Grigorii L'vovich Permiakov in Russia, Matti Kuusi in Finland, and Alan Dundes in the United States have been particularly interested in fitting all proverbs into a limited number of universal types. This research will facilitate the work of scholars interested in comparative and international paremiology (study of proverbs) and paremiography (collection of proverbs).

Much has been written about the origin of proverbs, some of which goes back as far as texts carved on Sumerian cuneiform tablets from 3000 B.C. Many proverbs still in use, like "Big fish eat little fish" and "A sound mind in a sound body," date back to Greek and Latin antiquity. Another major source of proverbs is ancient-wisdom literature contained in such religious works as the Talmud or the Bible, as, for example "Pride goes before the fall" (Solomon 16:18) or "It is better to give than to receive" (Apostles 20:35). But the vernacular languages also developed their own proverbs, and the Anglo American world is rich in proverbs from the Middle Ages. Geoffrey Chaucer in particular used many early English proverbs in his works, and the same is true for William Shakespeare in the 16th century. All over Europe, the 16th and 17th centuries are considered the Golden Age of the proverb. They permeate all written records, from literary works and religious treatises to folk narratives. This is also the time when major proverb collections were put together, as, for example, John Heywood, *A Dialogue Conteinyng the Number in Effect of all the Prouerbes in the Englishe Tongue* (1549), George Herbert, *Outlandish Proverbs* (1640), and John Ray, *A Collection of English Proverbs* (1670).

Are proverbs still coined in such a modern technological society as the United States? Of course they are, and it might even be argued that modern-day America represents yet another "heyday" of the proverb. Proverbs are still "invented" by individuals, and if a particular statement exhibits at least one of the proverb markers mentioned above it might just catch on—it might gain currency in a family setting, a village, a city, a state, the entire nation, and eventually even the world. In a technological world connected globally by computer networks and the ever-present mass media of newspapers, radio, and television, short and witty utterances can become almost instantaneous quotations known throughout the land. The speed in which new and possible proverbial wisdom can be disseminated today is truly mind-boggling. While it might have taken decades in earlier times for a precise statement and its variants to become proverbial, this general currency might now be accomplished in a few days. Just think of a quip by a major public figure, an advertising slogan, a film or song title. Of course, the test of time still needs to be applied to such proverbial neologisms; the elements of traditionality and general currency must come into play in order for such a "pithy" statement to be considered as a bona fide proverb. One thing for sure, the time of "proverb making" is by no means over, and there are dozens of modern American proverbs to prove it.

The rich American proverb stock is to a large extent made up of classical, biblical, and English sayings, but besides the early English settlers many other groups of immigrants brought their own proverbs with them. Many of these texts were translated into English in due time, and thus there are plenty of Americanized foreign proverbs current in this nation of immigrants. These proverbs also continue to be in use in their original languages among the many ethnic groups in this country. The Spanish language in particular is gaining much ground in the Southwestern states due to their Mexican American population. French is still spoken in New Orleans, northern Vermont, and in the province of Quebec in Canada. There are also many Jewish citizens who speak Yiddish, a language that includes numerous metaphorical proverbs. The same is true for Chinese, German, Greek, Haitian, Irish, Italian, Polish, Russian, Scandinavian, Vietnamese, and many other immigrant minorities and their native proverbs. As cultural and ethnic diversity plays an ever greater role in American society, these foreign-language proverbs will continue to thrive, and some of them will also gain general currency in the form of American loan translations. Such a dual linguistic existence might be seen in the German proverb *"Man muß das Kind nicht mit dem Bade ausschütten"* (Don't throw the baby out with the bath water). German immigrants (especially the Pennsylvania Dutch) still cite this 16th-century proverb in German, while Americans in general have been using it in English translation since the early 20th century.

Very little is known about the indigenous proverbs of the Native Americans. In fact, anthropologists, folklorists, and linguists have repeatedly pointed out that they have hardly any proverbs at all, a unique phenomenon since proverbs are common throughout the world's populations. It is known, however, that Native Americans do communicate with metaphors, and some proverbs have been collected from the Crow Indians of Montana, the Kwakiutls of Vancouver Island, the Tsimshians of British Columbia, and the Tzotzils of southern Mexico. Among the few known authentic texts are "A deer, though toothless, may accomplish something," "What will you eat when the snow is on the north side of the tree?" and "The road is still open, but it will close." Further and concerted field research will surely bring to light additional texts of the neglected proverbial treasure of the Native American languages.

Much more information is available about African American proverbs. While some of them can be traced to African origins, others definitely have been coined in the United States. Joel Chandler Harris included a section of "Plantation Proverbs" in his classic book *Uncle Remus: His Songs and Sayings* (1881). Many of these texts, like "De proudness un a man don't count w'en his head's cold" and "Dem w'at eats kin say grace," reflect the early slave existence of African Americans. But more modern texts also refer to social concerns of the Black population that lives in inner-city ghettos, as, for example, "What goes around comes around," "Black is beautiful," and "If you don't know much, you can't do much."

It is obviously difficult to establish which English-language proverbs current in the United States were actually coined in this country. Each individual proverb would require its own researched history, but this has been done for only very few texts. Major and minor proverb collections that claim in their title that they contain "American" proverbs should, in fact, state that their registered texts represent proverbs *current* in the United States. The same is true for small regional collections of proverbs from various states. When such books use titles that speak of Michigan or Vermont proverbs, they actually mean that they contain proverbs that were collected in those states. For most texts, it would be very difficult or impossible to ascertain their specific origins. But there are some proverbs that are proven to be of American coinage, among them "It pays to advertise," "Paddle your own canoe," and the quintessential American proverb, "Different strokes for different folks." The latter was coined in the early 1950s among the African American population in the South, and it can be considered to express the general worldview of most Americans. Here is a truly liberating proverb that for once does not tell people what or what not to do. This is freedom and democracy translated into proverbial wisdom, using most of the structural and poetic markers discussed above, and thus having had no problem at all gaining proverbial status.

The worldview of the colonial period and the early years of this nation was expressed in the many proverbs that Benjamin Franklin included in his *Poor Richard's Almanacks* published between 1733 and 1758. The last issue of this popular publication included his famous essay entitled "The Way to Wealth" (1758), which in its few pages contains 105 proverbs culled from the almanacs. They add much traditional wisdom to this masterful treatise on virtue, prosperity, prudence, and, above all, economic common sense. Most of the proverbs had long been in use in England, but Franklin also included his own inventions that have over time become proverbial, such as "Industry pays debts, while despair increases them" and "There will be sleeping enough in the grave." Many Americans believe that Franklin coined most of the proverbs in this essay, but nothing could be further from the truth. Not even the popular proverb "Early to bed, early to rise, makes a man healthy, wealthy, and wise" stems from him. Earlier variants date back to the late 15th century, and the proverb in this precise wording was recorded for the first time in 1639 in England.

A century later, Ralph Waldo Emerson had a similarly high esteem for proverbial folk wisdom. This prolific American preacher, rhetorician, essayist, transcendentalist, philosopher, pragmatist, and humanist was also an early paremiologist of sorts. He included proverbs in all of his writings, at times also explaining more theoretically that they are the "language of experience," that they express "practical wisdom," that they teach "worldly prudence," and that they are "metaphors of the human mind." Many American literary figures shared this positive feeling about proverbs, integrating them with relative frequency in their novels, dramas, and poems. Some of the more "proverbial" authors are Edward Taylor, Cotton Mather, Henry David Thoreau, Herman Melville, Alice Cary, Emily Dickinson, Mark Twain, Rowland Robinson, William Faulkner, John O 'Hara, Arthur Guiterman, W.H. Auden, Eudora Welty, and Susan Fromberg Schaeffer. Robert Frost's famous poem "Mending Wall" (1914) includes one of America's favorite proverbs, which often is thought to have been coined by Frost himself. But "Good fences make good neighbors" in this precise wording found its way into an early farmer's almanac in 1850. Mention must also be made of Carl Sandburg's long poem "Good Morning, America" (1928), which includes a whole section on proverbial language that begins with the proclamation "A code arrives; language; lingo; slang; / behold the proverbs of a people, a nation."

Popular songs, from traditional folksongs and ballads to modern rock and roll and country-western hits, also do much to keep traditional proverbs alive or to disseminate new texts. Thus, the solidly American proverb "Root, hog, or die" appears at the end of each of the eight stanzas of an early-19th-century bull-whackers' song with the same title. The same independent and pragmatic approach to life during the pioneer days is expressed in the "proverb song" titled "Paddle Your Own Canoe" (ca. 1871). Proverbs are also popular in the musicals of Gilbert and Sullivan, and there are many modern "hits" with proverbial titles by major stars, such as "Takes Two to Tango" (1952) by Pearl Bailey, "Can't Buy Me Love" (1964) by the Beatles, "Like a Rolling Stone" (1965) by Bob Dylan, "Easy Come, Easy Go" (1967) by Elvis Presley, and "Apples Don't Fall Far from the Tree" (1973) by Cher. The proverbs cited in these songs are usually interpreted seriously: They are valued expressions of general human behavior and feelings.

Proverbs are not always taken at their face value. People have always been aware of the existence of contradictory proverbs. Such proverb pairs as "Absence makes the heart grow fonder" and "Out of sight, out of mind" are ample proof that proverbs do not express universal truths. Their truth value is actually quite limited and always dependent on the particular context in which they are used. Realizing that proverbs often are too rigorous in their moral or ethical message, and due to the fact that they have been quoted too often as ultimate wisdom, people have parodied and twisted them to get some humorous relief. There is even a special proverbial subgenre of "wellerisms," which are based on the triadic structure of (1) a statement (often a proverb), (2) an identification of the speaker, and (3) a phrase that puts the statement into an unexpected situation resulting in a satirical, ironic or humorous comment. Well-known examples include "'Everyone to his taste,' said the farmer and kissed the cow" and "'All's well that ends well,' said the peacock when he looked at his tail." Some wellerisms are quite old and rather internationally disseminated, but America experienced a particular "craze" for wellerisms in 19th-century magazines and newspapers. These "invented" texts followed the pattern of those that Charles Dickens placed into the mouth of his character Sam Weller (hence the term "wellerism") in his novel *Pickwick Papers* (1836).

While wellerisms are a unique proverbial subgenre that dates back to classical times, there also exists a long tradition of proverb parodies based only on the actual texts. The folk have never considered proverbs to be sacrosanct, and while they express rigid precepts on the one hand, their very rigidity also leads to parody and punning. Often it is a matter of a short addition to the traditional proverb, as in "New brooms sweep clean, but the old one knows the corner." This text has actually become proverbial in its own right over time. More common are small changes (a mere letter or word) within the short proverb text that changes it into an "anti-proverb" with an entirely new meaning: "A man's best friend is his dogma," "Money is the root of all wealth," "Better mate than never," "No body is perfect," "Beauty is only fur deep," "Chaste makes waste," "One man's meat is another man's cholesterol." Some of the more sexual examples are found as proverbial graffiti on bathroom walls, but so are such liberating new proverbs as "A woman without a man is like a fish without a bicycle" and "You have to kiss a lot of toads before you find your prince," the latter being a proverbial allusion to the fairy tale "The Frog Prince."

Advertising agencies have also discovered that proverbs in their traditional wording or cited with innovative twists can serve as effective attention getters. Realizing that most readers look only at the picture and the headline of an advertisement, it is not surprising that the slogans are often based on proverbs or at least on proverbial structures. They add a certain traditional authority to the slogan, especially in the case of biblical proverbs, and they also assure the recognizability and memorability of the slogan so that consumers will, in fact, think of it at the time of making a purchasing choice. Thus, a Vermont bank might simply use the headline "A penny saved is a penny earned" to proclaim its solid management of saving accounts, but a car company will use the altered proverb "A drive is worth a thousand words" to support its claim of a comfortable ride. Some slogans have attained proverbial status in their own right. Perhaps the best-known example is the slogan "When it rains it pours" by the Morton Salt Company, which most likely was based on the proverb "It never rains but it pours." Even slogans that are not based on proverbs usually use proverbial markers, making clear that advertising is at least in part both popular culture and folklore.

Many advertisements also include iconographical representations of proverbs in the form of glossy and glamorous pictures. But this, too, is nothing new. Proverbs and their metaphors have been translated into woodcuts, emblems, and oil paintings since the Middle Ages. The Dutch artist Pieter Bruegel even illustrated more than 100 proverbs and proverbial expressions in his painting *Netherlandic Proverbs* (1559). There were also broadsheets depicting up to thirty-six individually framed proverbs, and perhaps one can look at these as precursors of sorts to the modern cartoons, caricatures, and comic strips that are frequently based on proverbs. As American society tends ever more toward the visualization of the world, it is to be expected that metaphorical proverbs will also be transposed into pictures. Many young Americans do not learn proverbs any longer in school or through reading, but they pick them up from the comic pages or the political cartoons in newspapers and magazines. Proverbs and their pictorizations are still very suitable devices to communicate humorously or seriously about the social and human concerns that occupy modern Americans.

Proverbs, thus, are very much alive in modern society. While such other verbal folklore genres as the fable are declining, proverbs continue to play a considerable role in oral and printed communication. They even prolong the life of fables by reducing their longer texts to mere proverbial expressions, such as "sour grapes." Older proverbs that use archaic words or whose ideas are no longer appropriate tend to disappear; other old standbys continue to be frequently used; and there are also those new proverbs that express the social worldview of the modern age. The future looks good for proverbs, for proverbs are never out of season.

Wolfgang Mieder

References

Arora, Shirley L. 1977. *Proverbial Comparisons and Related Expressions in Spanish Recorded in Los Angeles, California*. Berkeley: University of California Press.

Brunvand, Jan Harold. 1961. *A Dictionary of Proverbs and Proverbial Phrases from Books Published by Indiana Authors before 1890*. Bloomington: Indiana University Press.

Bryant, Margaret M. 1945. *Proverbs and How to Collect Them*. Greensboro, NC: American Dialect Society.

De Caro, Francis A., and William K. McNeil. 1971. *American Proverb Literature: A Bibliography*. A Folklore Forum Publication. Bloomington: Indiana University.

Dundes, Alan, and Claudia A. Stibbe. 1981. *The Art of Mixing Metaphors: A Folkloristic Interpretation of the "Netherlandish Proverbs" by Pieter Bruegel the Elder*. Helsinki: Suomalainen Tiedeakatemia.

Fogel, Edwin Miller. 1929. *Proverbs of the Pennsylvania Germans*. Lancaster: Pennsylvania German Society.

Mieder, Wolfgang, ed. 1975. *Selected Writings on Proverbs by Archer Taylor*. Helsinki: Suomalainen Tiedeakatemia.

———. 1987. *Tradition and Innovation in Folk Literature*. Hanover, NH: University Press of New England.

———. 1989. *American Proverbs: A Study of Texts and Contexts*. New York: Peter Lang.

———. 1993. *Proverbs Are Never Out of Season: Popular Wisdom in the Modern Age*. New York: Oxford University Press.

———, ed. 1993. *Wise Words: Essays on the Proverb.* New York: Garland.

Mieder, Wolfgang, and Alan Dundes, ed. 1981. *The Wisdom of Many: Essays on the Proverb.* New York: Garland.

Mieder, Wolfgang, and Stewart A. Kingsbury, eds. 1993. *A Dictionary of Wellerisms.* New York: Oxford University Press.

Mieder, Wolfgang, Stewart A. Kingsbury, and Kelsie B. Harder, eds. 1992. *A Dictionary of American Proverbs.* New York: Oxford University Press.

Simpson, John A. 1982. *The Concise Oxford Dictionary of Proverbs.* 2d ed. 1992. Oxford: Oxford University Press.

Taylor, Archer. [1913] 1985. *The Proverb* with an Introduction and Bibliography by Wolfgang Mieder. Bern: Peter Lang.

Taylor, Archer, and Bartlett Jere Whiting. 1958. *A Dictionary of American Proverbs and Proverbial Phrases, 1820–1880.* Cambridge: Harvard University Press.

Whiting, Bartlett Jere. 1977. *Early American Proverbs and Proverbial Phrases.* Cambridge: Harvard University Press.

———. 1989. *Modern Proverbs and Proverbial Sayings.* Cambridge: Harvard University Press.

Wilson, F.P. 1970. *The Oxford Dictionary of English Proverbs.* 3d. ed. Oxford: Oxford University Press (1st ed. [1935] by William George Smith).

See also Fable; Franklin, Benjamin

Psychology and Folklore

The dynamic relationship between ideas in the two intellectual disciplines. Psychological theory has come to help some folklorists interpret the meanings of their materials, and some psychologists have turned to folklore for texts to help illuminate concepts in psychology. As the intellectual discipline that takes as its realm the understanding of the workings of the human mind, psychology addresses a number of concepts, such as "personality" and "identity," that are of central interest to folklorists. When folklorists and other culture critics write of the "psychological functions" of a folklore text or a performance, they are making the assumption that human beings have certain biological and, possibly, socially constructed needs that folklore helps meet. Psychology addresses collective as well as individual needs, so folklorists can speak both of the individual psychological functions of folklore and of the ways folklore operates in the psychology of the group.

It was only near the end of the 19th century that scientific psychology emerged as a discipline separate from philosophy or theology, and the professionalization of the two intellectual disciplines in the United States occurred at almost the same time (the American Folklore Society was founded in 1888; the American Psychological Association, in 1892). Sigmund Freud's work laid out the first understanding of the relations between psychology and folklore. Freud saw jokes, folktales, art, and other expressive behaviors as symptoms of the unconscious processes and contents of the mind. Just as the symptoms of an individual patient represented repressed thoughts displaced into more acceptable forms, so Freud saw collective expressive behaviors as clues to the thoughts society repressed in order for people to live together. Thus, the depth psychologies of Freud and others offer folklorists a theory to account for the symbolism present in the folklore (stories, jokes, riddles, proverbs, song lyrics, rituals, games, and material culture) of a group. Carl Jung and his followers, notably Joseph Campbell, went beyond Freud to posit universal archetypes in the collective human consciousness and looked to mythologies for evidence of these archetypes.

Despite the early popular reception of Freud's ideas in the United States (he lectured in the United States in 1910) and despite the development of a psychoanalytical school of anthropological theory and practice in the 1930s and 1940s (represented in the late 20th century, for example, by the *Journal of Psychoanalytic Anthropology),* psychoanalytic approaches have not become common in American folklore studies. Alan Dundes is the leading proponent of the psychoanalytic approach, sometimes combining it with the structural approach he has also helped promote in folklore studies, but most folklorists have not followed his lead. Some folklorists have been openly hostile to psychoanalytic approaches, complaining that the theory posits an unacceptable universalism and that the method relies so much upon the analyst's idiosyncratic interpretive performance that the interpretation is not reproducible. Dundes' own practices attempt to refute these charges, but he and other psychoanalytic folklorists cannot deny the fundamental disagreement they have with some other folklorists over the ability of the folk to help the folklorist interpret their own folklore. For Dundes and others ascribing to the psychoanalytic approach, the folk can show us the meanings of their folklore texts only indirectly, as those texts reflect the unconscious and serve their psychological functions only to the extent that the folk do not bring the repressed thoughts and anxieties (about sex, death, or racial hatred, for example) to consciousness. For other folklorists, the folk's interpretations of the meanings of their lore are valuable contributions to our understanding the multiple meanings of texts in their performance contexts.

Folklorist David Hufford has urged folklorists to expand their interdisciplinary cooperation with psychologists beyond the psychoanalysts, and he demonstrates the fruits of psychological approaches in his own work on the folkloric dimensions of medical beliefs and practices. But, again, few folklorists have accepted Hufford's invitation.

Psychological approaches lend themselves quite well to the study of children's folklore, as developmental psychology has a long history of theorizing and practice. Martha Wolfenstein wrote a classic psychoanalytic study of children's humor, and Brian Sutton-Smith has combined developmental psychology with folklore methods to study the structures and functions of children's storytelling and joking. The notion of "competence" in folklore performance studies (for example, narrative competence) intersects with developmental psychology in studies in which folklorists have determined at what ages and at what stages of cognitive development children are capable of understanding and telling stories, jokes, riddles, and so on.

Feminist folklorists have turned to some of the work done by feminist psychologists for ideas to bring back to the study of women's folklore. Carol Gilligan and others attempting to create a "new psychology of women" since the 1970s provide concepts and vocabularies for understanding the very different functions of communication and identity within women's small groups, but feminist folklorists have been reluctant to adopt even the feminist revisions of Freud offered by Juliett Michell, Nancy Chodorow, and others. Still another area awaiting the applications of feminist psychology is the folklore of male folk groups. One version of the new "men's studies" emerging in the 1990s brings two decades' worth of feminist theory to bear upon the creation and expressive performance of masculinities, and feminist psychology could shed new light on men's folklore.

Those folklorists who have written on the relation between folklore and psychology—notably, Dundes, Fine, and Hufford—generally bemoan the fact that there is so little interdisciplinary cross-fertilization between these two intellectual disciplines, which share a common interest in questions of meaning and identity. This lack became all the more pronounced in the 1980s, as senior scholars (such as Jerome Bruner) in social psychology, child psychology, and other specialties within psychology turned increasingly from experimental approaches toward a "narrative paradigm" that would be familiar to folklorists. Folklorists and psychologists have a great deal to learn from one another, but as of this writing (1995) the possibilities of this interdisciplinary cooperation have yet to be fulfilled.

Jay Mechling

References

Bruner, Jerome. 1986. *Actual Minds, Possible Worlds.* Cambridge: Harvard University Press.

Dundes, Alan. 1971. On the Psychology of Legend. In *American Folk Legend,* ed. Wayland D. Hand. Los Angeles: University of California Press, pp. 21–36.

———. 1980. *Interpreting Folklore.* Bloomington: Indiana University Press.

———. 1991. The Psychological Studies of Folklore in the United States, 1880–1980. *Southern Folklore* 48:97–120.

Fine, Gary Alan. 1992. Evaluating Psychoanalytic Folklore: Are Freudians Ever Right? In *Manufacturing Tales: Sex and Money in Contemporary Legends.* Knoxville: University of Tennessee Press, pp. 45–58.

Hufford, David. 1974. Psychology, Psychoanalysis, and Folklore. *Southern Folklore Quarterly* 38:187–197.

Mechling, Jay. 1984. High Kybo Floater: Food and Feces in the Speech Play at a Boy Scout Camp. *Journal of Psychoanalytic Anthropology* 7:256–268.

Oring, Elliott. 1992. *Jokes and Their Relations.* Lexington: University Press of Kentucky.

Sutton-Smith, Brian. 1981. *The Folkstories of Children.* Philadelphia: University of Pennsylvania Press.

Wolfenstein, Martha. [1954] 1978. *Children's Humor: A Psychological Analysis.* Bloomington: Indiana University Press.

See also Feminist Approaches to Folklore; Performance Approach; Sociological Approach

Public Folklore

The representation and application of folklore within new contexts, accomplished through the actions of folklorists or other cultural specialists, frequently through collaboration with concerned community members. A public-folklore activity may be directed toward a community within which a tradition is customarily practiced or may cross cultural boundaries through presentation to a general audience. Public folklorists may represent and interpret the traditions of their own or of different communities. They generally strive to collaborate with tradition bearers and community members to enable them to represent, preserve, and perpetuate their own traditions. Through public-folklore activities, folklorists "intervene" (see Whisnant 1983) in communities to achieve specific purposes, such as the conservation or revitalization of traditional cultural practices, reinforcement of group identities, or the amelioration of social problems.

Most contemporary public-folklore activity in the United States involves traditional-arts programming. Since these activities generally occur in new contexts removed from their customary settings within communities, much of the creative challenge in public folk-arts programming lies in the reframing of traditions (see Sheehy 1992). Through reframing, a tradition receives special attention as an art form singled out from everyday life. When presenting reframed folk arts, public folklorists strive to appropriately represent how traditions are practiced in the traditional settings and sociable occasions where they live and breathe in daily life—such as dance halls, duck blinds, kitchens, or schoolyards and during weddings, tall-tale "lying" sessions, quilting bees, or at a *quinceanera.*

The "representation" of folklore through public programming requires special artifice to recapture such traditional contexts as well as interpretive strategies to help audiences understand how tradition bearers infuse meaning, symbolism, order, and aesthetic sensibilities within their folk arts. These techniques are employed within a wide variety of genres of representation, including exhibitions, festivals, concerts, artists' residencies in schools and community arts organizations, film and media productions, lecture-demonstrations, and recordings. All of these types of public programming rely heavily upon original field research among traditional artists.

The folklife festival is an especially complex mode of presentation. Growing out of approaches developed by the Smithsonian Institution's Festival of American Folklife in the late 1960s and early 1970s, folklife festivals in the 1990s utilize multiple techniques of recontextualization and interpretation. In these festivals, traditions are often presented within contexts that evoke or replicate the places and events where folk arts are found in the artists' own communities. Storytellers may swap tales on a porch of a vernacular house, musicians play for a dance party, craftspersons make crafts in a setting like their workshop at home, carnival reenactors process about the festival grounds. Festivalgoers are encouraged to interact with artists as they dance to a traditional-music ensemble or ask questions of crafts demonstrators.

The interpretation of traditions at festivals is also carried out through signage, program booklets, and workshops. Festival workshops explore issues relating to featured traditional cultures and delve in depth into stylistic elements of traditional art forms. They combine artistic performances, demonstrations, and discussion among tradition bearers.

The use of such diverse media of interpretation reflects a strong emphasis on public education in contemporary folk-arts programming. Interpretation helps dispel stereotypic distortions of folk arts as simple, unsophisticated, and resistant to change while providing bridges to understanding other cultures when traditions are presented outside of their communities of origin. Folklorists often collaborate with tradition bearers to prepare them to interpret their folk arts without the folklorist's mediation. Academically trained public folklorists also work with "community scholars," lay folklorists who document, interpret, and present the traditions of their own communities. During the late 1980s and early 1990s, institutes to train community scholars were established by folklorists. These institutes equip community members to effectively assume primary responsibility for local folk-arts presentation and perpetuation.

Museums serve as venues for the exhibition and public performance of both contemporary and historical folk traditions. While elitist resistance to folk culture persists in some museums, many history and art museums find that folklife can provide palpable links between past and present and open up new relationships with previously underserved cultural communities. History museums provide opportunities for representation of many different kinds of folklife. Ongoing presentations of traditional work practices and recreational activities are key interpretive activities in "living history" museums made up of reconstructed cultural landscapes of particular periods in the past. In other history museums, public folklorists have curated exhibitions dealing with such topics as urban play, local ethnic festivals, county fairs, and maritime traditions.

Two sharply contrasting approaches to exhibiting folk art are used in American art museums. Exhibitions curated by public folklorists view folk art as embodying the aesthetics and values of particular cultures. They stress contextualized interpretation of the historical and social circumstances of the production of visual folk-arts. Objects in these exhibitions are chosen as both representative and aesthetically exemplary examples of the visual traditions of a culture. In contrast, folk-art specialists (as opposed to public folklorists) choose objects for exhibitions on the basis of putatively universal aesthetic values and their own sense of connoisseurship (see Baron [1981] 1987:14–15). They often consider folk art within the same framework as "outsider" or "naive" art, all said to be expressions of the individual genius of artists who lack formal training. Folk-art specialists are not associated with the field of folklore studies. They carry out their research independently or in association with galleries and museums supportive of their approach.

Exhibitions of contemporary folk art curated by public folklorists are based upon documentation of living folk artists. Many of these exhibitions result from surveys of the folk arts of particular states and regions within states. Interpretive programming organized by public folklorists for folk-art exhibitions often involves demonstrations by artists, ideally in galleries alongside their works on display.

Although many American museums contain collections of historical folk artifacts, relatively few actively collect the works of living tradition bearers. Outstanding exceptions to this pattern include the Museum of International Folk Art in Santa Fe, New Mexico, the Roberson Center of Binghamton, New York, and the Michigan State University Museum in East Lansing. All of these museums have curatorial departments devoted to folk art or folklife.

Folk-arts-in-education programs utilize the indigenous traditions of local communities to provide alternative learning experiences for young people. Through these programs, students encounter tradition bearers teaching about their traditional knowledge and demonstrating their artistry. These interactions occur in classrooms, in auditoriums, and in student research projects guided by folklorists. They provide validation for the living cultural heritage of students, thus building self-esteem and forging a stronger sense of community. By enabling young people to experience the diverse cultural traditions represented within a school population, folk-arts-in-education programs contribute to intercultural understanding.

Curricula designed for folk-arts-in-education programs integrate traditional systems of knowledge and art with other school subjects. Art is viewed expansively as ubiquitous among human cultures and accessible to the experience of a young person in his or her own home and neighborhood. In social-studies classes, students are equipped to learn about the cultures they inhabit as well as those distant in time and space. Mathematical learning is enhanced as students learn about pattern, order, and the uses of numbers in folk arts. Communication skills are developed through the participation of young people in school programs involving local oral traditions and through student writing about the folk arts they have researched and observed.

Through documentary film, video, and audio productions, the reach of public folklore extends far beyond the communities where traditions are practiced. They are frequently broadcast through the Public Broadcasting System, National Public Radio, and local public-radio stations. The form, length, and orientation of public-folklore productions are strongly influenced by the interests of these broadcasting outlets.

The creation of documentary film and video productions is shaped by what Gerald L. Davis calls the "cultural eye," which selects out and "illustrate[s] significant elements of expressive, aesthetic performance in contexts a mature community recognizes and values as traditional" (Davis 1992:115). Comparable selectivity is exercised in radio productions by what might be called the "cultural ear," where context is evoked through the use of ambient sound and excerpts from fieldwork interviews. Extensive editing occurs in creating these productions, as the public folklorist creates a "story" that offers native and folkloristic perspectives upon traditions and their contexts (see Spitzer 1992:88).

Recordings produced through public-folklore programs tend to deal with traditions ignored or underrepresented in commercially issued recordings. They generally include notes that provide detailed information about a music's cultural and historical contexts, its stylistic features, and the performers featured in the recording. Such recordings are issued through independent record companies or by private not-for-profit and government folklife programs.

Public folklore is viewed by some folklorists as part of a larger enterprise of "cultural conservation." Nonartistic dimensions of traditional culture are especially apt to be considered within the domain of culture conservation. As cultural conservationists, folklorists join with specialists from other disciplines concerned with "heritage protection" in an "integrated approach based on grass-roots cultural concerns and guided by ethnographic perspectives" (Hufford 1994:3). The efforts of cultural conservationists are often directed toward research and advocacy about environmental protection and historic preservation. Folkloristic interests in cultural conservation include the preservation of traditional land-use and work practices within environmental planning, incorporation of traditional cultural activities within economic development schemes, mitigation of the effects of highway construction and other public works upon traditional community life, and planning for cultural tourism that allows for the perspectives and directions desired by local traditional cultures. Challenging dominant standards for designating places of historic and cultural significance, folklorists argue for official recognition of places of local, vernacular significance.

Public folklore has been known by several names in postwar America. Each term reflects the concerns of folklorists of particular periods. During the late 1940s and early 1950s, "the utilization of folklore" referred to activities that put folklore materials to use within new contexts. In referring to folklore as "materials," this term reflected the text-centered orientation of folklorists at the time. Folklorists expressed considerable concern about the authenticity of adaptations of folklore to new audiences, accuracy of sources, and appropriateness of altering folklore in new contexts.

"Applied folklore" supplanted "the utilization of folklore" as the term of choice in the 1950s and was used with increasing frequency over the next two decades. The practice of applied folklore entailed the application of folkloristic knowledge for socially useful and ameliorative purposes as well as traditional arts programming. Folklore was "applied" in such arenas as health care, urban planning, education, and the fostering of intercultural understanding (see Botkin 1953; Sweterlitsch 1971). During the 1960s and 1970s, the term "applied folk-

lore" addressed concerns of social relevance, advocacy, and activism.

In the late 1970s, the term "public-sector folklore" came into use. The use of this term reflected the dominant role assumed by folklife programs in the government "sector" at the time. As government folklife programs spawned new programs by nongovernment entities in the late 1980s, the term "public folklore" was adopted. Both "public-sector folklore" and "public folklore" encompass activities covered by "the utilization of folklore" and "applied folklore" earlier in the postwar period.

The establishment of the Smithsonian Institution's Festival of American Folklife in 1967 signaled a renewal of federal folk-cultural initiatives, which had previously included the Bureau of American Ethnology, established in 1879; the Archive of American Folk-Song of the Library of Congress, founded in 1928, and the folklore program of the Works Progress Administration, which was in operation during the 1930s. Major federal-government folk-cultural programs were established at the National Endowment for the Arts (NEA) in 1974 and the American Folklife Center of the Library of Congress in 1976. Under the leadership of Bess Lomax Hawes in the late 1970s and into the 1980s, the NEA's folk arts program developed a national infrastructure for folk-arts programming. It provided initial funding for folk-arts coordinators at state agencies in virtually every state and jurisdiction. These coordinators survey and document traditions, produce folk-arts presentations, assist artists to promote and market their traditions, and provide financial support and technical assistance to local organizations interested in developing folk-arts programs. Beginning in the mid-1980s, public-folklore programs spread beyond government agencies to museums, regional arts organizations, local arts councils, and, with increasing frequency, private not-for-profit organizations devoted exclusively to folk-cultural programming.

American public-folklore activities undertaken by government and nongovernment programs are informed by ideologies, even if they tend not to be explicitly stated. In contrast, the "ideological" manipulation of folklore for Romantic nationalist and authoritarian purposes in other countries is easier to adduce. American public-folklore programs are characterized by a culturally relativistic approach to cultural difference, regarding each group as possessing worth and value and subject to evaluation on its own terms. American culture is considered to consist of multiple group identities within a pluralistic nation. "Cultural equity" is often viewed as a fundamental tenet of public-folklore work. First formulated by Alan Lomax, it refers to the global defense of cultural and stylistic diversity against the hegemonic, homogenizing forces of mass culture and electronic media (Lomax [1972] 1985).

The ideologies informing American public folklore can be evaluated as part of a cultural critique. For Barbara Kirshenblatt-Gimblett, a public-folklore ideology that celebrates diversity and affirms unity in diversity may "mask inequity and conflict" and uncritically embrace "received notions of ethnicity and ethnic group, of heritage and traditions." She believes that academic folklorists have a special responsibility to contribute to critical discourse about these matters (Kirshenblatt-Gimblett [1988] 1992:33, 42). Since American public-folklore programming tends to celebrate traditions and defers to the stated interests of the communities whose traditions are presented, critical discourse about ethnicity, heritage, tradition, and social inequity usually does not occur in public programs. However, public folklorists are mindful of these issues as they choose who and what to present and develop interpretive approaches for presentations in collaboration with community members.

Much of contemporary critical scholarship about public folklore assesses the impact of the intervention of folklorists upon traditional communities. David Whisnant contends that "the public sector folklore enterprise is unavoidably interventionist," impacting upon "the lives of individuals and in the institutions that embody their collective will and vision" (Whisnant 1983:234). Public folklorists often reflect upon how their involvement with tradition bearers changes the forms and contents of art forms and the relationships of artists to their communities. Artists who formerly created only for friends, family members, and neighbors redirect their work to new markets opened up by public-folklore presentations. Their work may become commodified, created for a cash economy, and changed in its cultural significance and formal qualities. The changes resulting from a folklorist's intervention can also be beneficial, resulting in new sources of income for low-income tradition bearers, validation of devalued art forms, creative stylistic innovations, and new personal horizons for artists enjoying travel and enhanced recognition.

Critical scholarship about public folklore also analyzes the power relationship of folklorists to traditional communities. By choosing to present certain aspects of traditional cultures to the public, the folklorist is said to act as the authenticator of traditions deemed worthy of preservation and presentation. Folklorists may "invent" traditions in selecting out particular dimensions of a culture as embodying continuity with the past. The folklorist thus exercises power to define a culture and objectify artists (see Kirshenblatt-Gimblett [1988] 1992). Others writing critically about public folklore stress the dialogical character of transactions between the folklorist and the tradition bearer. Within such a relationship, the representation of traditions is a collaborative, mutually defined undertaking rather than a starkly contrastive subject-object encounter. Through equipping community members to document and present their own culture and by training community scholars, public folklorists engage in the empowerment of traditional communities (Baron and Spitzer 1992).

Public folklorists tend to place special emphasis upon the preservation, presentation, and perpetuation of traditions no longer widely practiced. However, their rhetoric of presentation stresses that folk arts are "living traditions" rather than residual remnants of past practices. The act of public presentation may be intended to revitalize traditions that are endangered within their communities of origin. Newer, emergent folk arts rooted in older traditional forms are also presented in public-folklore programs. For example, community-based African American hip hop may be presented in programs that provide information about its antecedents in older Black musical and movement styles.

The choice of traditions to present to the public involves a kind of curatorial decision making. The folklorist selects traditions that can be made accessible to the public and meet criteria of skill or artistic excellence. Through the exercise of such selectivity, some aspects of culture are necessarily excluded. The traditions represented may appear to audiences as normative, although differences may exist within a community with regard to traditional cultural practices associated with gender, age, sexual orientation, or social class. As Mary Hufford indicates, reliance of folklife projects upon funding from arts agencies beginning in the 1970s led to an emphasis upon traditions that could be justified as aesthetic in order to obtain support (Hufford 1994:3). This situation began to change by the early 1990s, as a diversification of funding sources and broadening interests of public folklorists engendered representation of a wider spectrum of folklore traditions to the public.

Robert Baron

References

Baron, Robert. [1981] 1987. Folklife and the American Museum. In *Folklife and Museums: Selected Readings,* ed. Patricia Hall and Charles Seeman. Nashville: American Association for State and Local History, pp. 12–26.

Baron, Robert, and Nicholas R. Spitzer. 1992. Introduction. In *Public Folklore*. Washington: Smithsonian Institution, pp. 1–14.

Botkin, Benjamin. 1953. Applied Folklore: Creating Understanding through Folklore. *Southern Folklore Quarterly* 17:199–206.

Davis, Gerald L. 1992. "So Correct for the Photograph": "Fixing" the Ineffable, Ineluctable African American. In *Public Folklore,* ed. Robert Baron and Nicholas R. Spitzer. Washington, DC: Smithsonian Institution, pp. 105–118.

Hufford, Mary. 1994. *Conserving Culture: A New Discourse on Heritage.* Urbana: University of Illinois Press.

Kirshenblatt-Gimblett, Barbara. [1988] 1992. Mistaken Dichotomies. In *Public Folklore,* ed. Robert Baron and Nicholas R. Spitzer. Washington, DC. Smithsonian Institution, pp. 29–48.

Lomax, Alan. [1972] 1985. Appeal for Cultural Equity. In *1985 Smithsonian Festival of American Folklife Program Book,* ed. Thomas Vennom Jr. Washington, DC: Smithsonian Institution, pp. 40–46.

Sheehy, Daniel. 1992. Crossover Dreams: The Folklorist and the Folk Arrival. In *Public Folklore,* ed. Robert Baron and Nicholas R. Spitzer. Washington, DC: Smithsonian Institution, pp. 217–229.

Spitzer, Nicholas R. 1992. Cultural Conversation: Metaphors and Methods in Public Folklore. In *Public Folklore,* ed. Robert Baron and Nicholas R. Spitzer. Washington, DC: Smithsonian Institution, pp. 77–103.

Sweterlitsch, Dick., ed. 1971. Papers on Applied Folklore. *Folklore Forum*, Bibliographic and Special Series, No. 8. Bloomington, IN.

Whisnant, David. 1983. *All That Is Native and Fine: The Politics of Culture in an American Region.* Chapel Hill: University of North Carolina Press.

See also Applied Folklore; Cultural Conservation; Education, Folklife in; Folk Museums; New Deal and Folk Culture; Outsider Art

Puckett, Newbell Niles "Barry" (1897–1967)

Sociologist and folklorist noted for his studies of the American Southern Black and his extensive collection of popular beliefs and superstitions from Ohio. As a young man working for his bricklayer father, Puckett (nicknamed "Barry") became fascinated with the stories of his Black coworkers. This experience later helped shape the focus of his research. Deciding to seek a career in sociology and folklore, he enrolled at Yale University, receiving his Ph.D. in 1925. During his course of study, he began recording and classifying the folk beliefs and traditions of the American Black. He published the results of this research in *Folk Beliefs of the Southern Negro* (1926). His findings also allowed him to contribute to the study of onomastics, producing the articles "Names of American Negro Slaves" (1937), and "American Negro Names" (1938).

Throughout his career, Puckett was active in the Ohio and Cleveland folklore societies, ultimately being honored as a Fellow of the American Folklore Society. In his tireless search for early superstitions remembered by the natives of Ohio, he traveled thousands of miles, collecting more than 10,000 different superstitions. At times, in order to obtain beliefs from informants, he would even pose as a conjurer. Wayland D. Hand presided over the posthumous publication of a compendium containing this information, titled *Popular Beliefs and Superstitions* (1981) from Ohio. Hand noted that Puckett regarded this work as a companion piece to his *Folk Beliefs of the Southern Negro*.

S. Spencer Cannon

References

Kummer, George. 1967. In Memoriam: Newbell N. Puckett, 1889 [*sic*]–1967. *Journal of the Ohio Folklore Society* 2 (1):42–44.

——— 1981. Newbell Niles Puckett (Barry), 1897–1967: An Appreciation. In *Popular Beliefs and Superstitions: A Compendium of American Folklore from the Ohio Collection of Newbell Niles Puckett.* 3 vols. ed. Wayland D. Hand, Anna Casetta, and Sondra B. Thiederman. Boston: G.K. Hall, pp. 1533–1536.

Utley, Francis Lee. 1968. In Memoriam: Newbell Niles Puckett, 1897–1967. *Names* 16 (1):68–69.

Quilt Making

Processes and customs involved in the construction of three-layered textile bedcoverings. Quilts typically consist of a decorated top, a soft filler, and a plain lining. Quilts may include a number of different practical or decorative needlework processes, among the most common of which are piecework, in which cloth pieces are seamed together; appliqué, in which cloth pieces are sewn directly to a background fabric; embroidery, in which the surface is decorated with plain or colored yarns, and the actual quilting stitches that fasten the layers together.

Quilt making is a domestic activity traditionally performed by women, either singly or in groups. While ostensibly seen as practical bedcovers, quilts function in a variety of symbolic roles within families or communities. The complexity of quilt making within American society means that not only folklorists, but also scholars in many other fields study aspects of the subject, including scholars in textile, social, and art history; women's studies; communications; American studies; and popular culture.

In various American communities, particularly during the 19th century, the making of quilts was often associated with marriage and preparation for setting up a household. The number and quality of the quilts prepared by a young woman might have served as an indication of her suitability for marriage. Special quilts were typically the property of women and were often given or bequeathed to female relatives or friends.

One of the primary functions of quilts has always been to demonstrate the creativity, artistry, originality, or technical expertise of their makers. Other forms of needlework, such as samplers, also served this function, although, while samplers were displayed within the family home, the display function of quilts operated within the larger community. Quilt competitions in local fairs served as arenas in which women vied for public acclaim for their accomplishments in womanly spheres, and quilts were the most significant of the items entered. At times when women's opportunities for public recognition were limited, excellence in quilt making provided such recognition.

Beginning during the Civil War era, women's groups have used quilts to raise funds for churches, community groups, and other causes. During the late 19th and early 20th centuries, these fund-raiser quilts typically included embroidered names of persons or businesses who paid a few cents to have them included. The finished quilt was usually auctioned or raffled, depending upon the group's attitudes toward gambling. Church groups often used the money for mission work or to provide furnishings for their church building.

The sharing of quilt patterns and techniques has served as a basis for communication and interaction among women, not only in the 19th century when such exchanges were face to face, but later through quilt-pattern columns regularly printed by local, regional, and national periodicals.

Historic evidence suggests that while both quilting and patchwork (a term that often includes both piecework and appliqué) are ancient techniques, they were not combined in the making of bedcovers until, perhaps, the 17th or 18th century in Europe. A major influence for quilt making in Europe was the influx of Asian goods resulting from the Crusades and, later, sea trade with India: Among the goods brought from India to Europe were block-printed and dyed cotton fabrics, a novelty to Europeans limited largely to wool and linen textiles. Imported cottons were popular for clothing, bedcoverings, and bed curtains. An 18th-century English ban on the importation and use of imported cottons, intended to aid the domestic wool industry, was largely ineffective, although resulting shortages may have contributed to the practice of cutting out and appliquéing individual printed motifs on bedcovers and bed hangings. These appliquéd bedding textiles replaced an earlier and more time-consuming English tradition of embroidered textiles. Appliquéd, embroidered, and whole-cloth quilts (those without patchwork) represented the valued possessions of well-to-do families.

European settlers in the American colonies brought with them a variety of bedding textiles, including quilts and woven bed "ruggs" (sometimes spelled "rugs," this coarse, shagged textile is not to be confused with floor carpets), coverlets, and

A QUILTING PARTY IN WESTERN VIRGINIA.   [For description, see page 252.]

blankets. In colonial household inventories, quilts were always less numerous and more highly valued than other bedding. The popularity of quilts expanded in the late 18th century, aided by improvements in textile and printing technologies.

The earliest American quilts resemble their counterparts in Europe: They tended to be large (often more than 100 inches per side), square, and the designs generally included a central motif surrounded by one or more concentric borders. In the Northern colonies, households made glazed, solid-colored, whole-cloth, or simply pieced wool quilts, called "calimancoes" (sometimes inaccurately called linsey-woolseys). In the Southern colonies, quilt makers favored lightweight, white whole-cloth quilts, which were sometimes decorated with embroidery or stuffed work (small bits of filling inserted into the quilted design to add dimension). Because they served a decorative, not a utilitarian, function, early quilts generally have little or no filler and are typically highly embellished with quilting designs.

During the first half of the 19th century, block-style quilts gradually supplanted the European framed-center style in America. Recent evidence suggests that the development of early block patterns may have originated in the major folk-cultural area of southeastern Pennsylvania. As German immigrants had no tradition of patchwork bedcovers, the new American designs appear to be a result of a combination of English traditions of making patchwork quilts and German design elements and color choices.

The 1840s mark the beginning of an era of development

and expansion in American quilt making. New developments in domestic textile technology provided quilt makers with more fabric options at less cost, and, at the same time, westward migration contributed to the dissemination of patterns and styles.

A number of quilt styles went in and out of fashion during the 19th century. A method of piecing fabric over small paper templates developed in Great Britain and became popular in mid-century in American cities that traded with Britain, such as Charleston, South Carolina.

In the Mid-Atlantic cultural area adjoining the Chesapeake Bay, a local tradition developed of making sampler album appliqué quilts (in which each block represents a different pattern). The style, which has become known as the Baltimore Album quilt, is characterized by highly elaborate appliqué motifs, typically floral but sometimes depicting other designs such as birds, buildings, or "cut-paper" abstractions. Typically, each block is signed or inscribed by the maker, donor, or other designee. The album style spread throughout settled areas of the United States between 1840 and 1860.

The late 19th century represents the era of most widespread involvement in American quilt making. A large number of pieced and appliquéd patterns developed and were disseminated during this period. Domestic fabrics were inexpensive and plentiful so that, for the first time, quilts were made by all social classes, for utilitarian as well as decorative uses.

Perhaps the first nationwide quilt fad occurred between 1880 and 1900, as quilt makers everywhere made crazy quilts. While the impetus for this movement is unclear, possible contributing factors include Japanese decorative arts and English needlework, both of which were introduced to American audiences at the Centennial Exposition in Philadelphia in 1876. Crazy quilts are typically formed of irregular pieces of cloth attached to a cloth foundation and embellished with decorative embroidery. Late-19th-century crazy quilts generally included a large variety of silk remnants, which were available by mail order. Crazy quilts originated, not from economy or need, but from the late Victorian love of embellishment and excess.

After 1900, crazy quilts were no longer popular among urban quilt makers, but rural women made them from recycled wool and cotton clothing. Even the 20th-century folk versions of crazy quilts, however, usually include some embroidery. The production of utilitarian crazy quilts in the early 20th century led some writers of the period to conclude, incorrectly, that crazy quilts were the original, utilitarian form from which other quilts had developed.

The subject of quilts made by African American women is a controversial one. Surviving African American quilts from the 19th century are rare and are usually indistinguishable from those made by non–Black quilt makers. Art historians have pointed out compelling visual similarities between both historic and contemporary African textiles and late-20th-century African American quilts, but the absence of intervening evidence prevents the establishment of more definitive links.

The most famous African American quilter of the 19th century was Harriet Powers, whose two known extant quilts represent scenes of biblical and local history. These pictorial quilts, evidence of significant individual artistry, may also represent a larger African American tradition, of which little other documentation survives.

Generally, African American quilt makers who have lived in proximity to White quilt makers have produced similar quilts, while Black quilt makers who worked in comparative isolation from outside influences, including publications, developed their own intuitive, eclectic styles, techniques, and design traditions.

Many Native American groups adopted quilt making as contact with White settlers gave them access to woven cloth. Plains tribes in particular found that quilts substituted easily for decorated buffalo robes, and that certain patterns, especially the Rising Sun (later called Lone Star), were similar to traditional Native American designs. Contemporary Native American powwows include quilts as important elements in their gift-giving rituals.

American quilt making during the 20th century was influenced by two major factors. First, the Colonial Revival movement in the decorative arts encouraged women to make quilts like those of their ancestors. With the availability of inexpensive blankets, only the very poor had continued to make utilitarian quilts, so women's magazines suggested quilt making as a new hobby for middle-class women.

The second factor was the dissemination of quilt patterns through popular magazines and "story papers," inexpensive or free publications that included advertising, articles, and needlework columns, including syndicated quilt patterns. These two

factors created a climate for a renewed interest in quilt making during the period 1925–1940.

Quilts made during this period typically feature pastel colors, in both solids and small-figured prints. While occasional quilt makers employed favorite patterns from the 19th century, such as the Log Cabin and the Rising Sun, they more often used some of the new patterns shown in periodicals. The most popular patterns of the early 20th century include Double Wedding Ring, Little Dutch Girl (also called Sunbonnet Sue), Dresden Plate, and Grandmother's Flower Garden.

This period is also characterized by the development of a class of professional designers, collectors, and quilt entrepreneurs. Marie Webster designed quilts for *Ladies' Home Journal* beginning in 1911, and her book *Quilts: Their Story and How to Make Them* appeared in 1915, the first monograph on the subject of quilts. Anne Orr authored a regular needlework column in *Good Housekeeping* magazine in the 1920s that launched a design and mail-order pattern business.

During the 1940s and 1950s, interest in quilt making declined generally, although patterns and kits were still available. In addition to quilt makers, there were other individuals who began to collect patterns and quilt-related ephemera. Beginning in the late 1960s and early 1970s, a renewed interest in quilts and quilt making emerged. By the 1980s, hundreds of thousands of quilt makers had formed guilds throughout the United States, in order to share their interests, provide mutual support, sponsor competitions, and raise

money for charitable causes. A second generation of "quilt professionals," including authors, designers, and teachers, developed to serve the needs of these groups.

An interest in American-style quilt making spread internationally during the 1980s, particularly in Europe, Japan, Australia, and New Zealand, where American techniques have been adapted and merged with local needlework and design traditions by contemporary quilt makers.

Another important movement in the late 20th century has been the development of state and regional quilt projects. These projects originated in response to the desire to better understand quilt making traditions, both local and national. In the knowledge that hundreds of thousands, perhaps millions, of quilts exist but are generally not available to public view, quilt makers and interested others designed public "quilt days," during which the quilts in a local area could be brought out to be examined and photographed. As of 1993, each of the United States had begun at least one such project. Typically, the projects result in an archive of photographic and written documents, one or more exhibitions, and a book. The accumulated data from the projects are beginning to reveal important regional and local traditions within American quilt making.

In addition to a new generation of quilt makers who make quilts as art, to hang on walls, there remains a large number of traditional quilt makers, who, while not making quilts from necessity, make them for use, or potential use, on beds. Traditional quilt makers typically have grown up with a knowledge of quilts, prefer using familiar patterns, and make quilts as gifts for family and friends.

In the late 20th century, national groups have used quilts collectively to make political statements, including the Peace Ribbon, the combined quilt panels of thousands of contributors that was wrapped around the Pentagon; and the NAMES Project, which collects and displays quilt panels commemorating persons who have died from AIDS (acquired immune deficiency syndrome).

Laurel Horton

References

American Quilt Study Group. 1980–. *Uncoverings.* Vols. 1–. San Francisco: American Quilt Study Group.

Benberry, Cuesta. 1992. *Always There: The African-American Presence in American Quilts.* Louisville: Kentucky Quilt Project.

Brackman, Barbara, et al. 1993. *Kansas Quilts and Quilters.* Lawrence: University Press of Kansas.

Clark, Ricky, et al. 1991. *Quilts in Community: Ohio's Traditions.* Nashville: Rutledge Hill.

Ferrero, Pat, et al. 1987. *Hearts and Hands: The Influence of Women and Quilts on American Society.* San Francisco: Quilt Digest.

Heritage Quilt Project of New Jersey. 1992. *New Jersey Quilts, 1777 to 1950: Contributions to an American Tradition.* Paducah, KY: American Quilter's Society.

Horton, Laurel, ed. 1994. *Quilt Making in America: Beyond Mythology.* Nashville: Rutledge Hill.

Ice, Joyce. 1989. Splendid Companionship and Practical Assistance. In *Quilted Together: Women, Quilts, and Communities.* Delhi, NY: Delaware County Historical Association, pp. 6–32.

Lasansky, Jeannette. 1991. *Bits and Pieces: Textile Traditions.* Lewisburg, PA: Oral Traditions Project.

Williams, Clover. 1992. Tradition and Art: Two Layers of Meaning in the Bloomington Quilt Guild. In *Uncoverings 1991.* Vol. 12 of the *Research Papers of the American Quilt Study Group.* San Francisco: American Quilt Study Group, pp 118–141.

See also Needlework; Social Protest in Folklore

R

Radio, Amateur

A government-licensed, noncommercial radio service found throughout the world. Amateur radio is *not* citizens band (CB), an unlicensed and (in the United States) rather undisciplined radio service some countries permit for short-distance communication. An international transmission medium for folklore found in society at large, amateur radio also possesses its own body of lore and custom.

Radio amateurs, known as "hams," transmit folklore by two principal means. One, obviously, is over the radio, using frequencies assigned to the amateur-radio service. The other is via the radio-club newsletter.

Some of the radio frequencies available to amateurs support worldwide communications. It is possible for a joke originated in San Francisco to be known in Tel Aviv in a matter of hours. Although much folklore transmitted via amateur radio passes in real-time personal conversations, much is also circulated using computer-based bulletin board stations where items are posted for many other hams to read. These stations automatically relay messages over the air to one another internationally, posting those designated as public on each intermediary station. Although most of the material thus circulated is humorous, urban legends have also appeared.

Radio-club newsletters often use traditional filler items, depending for their humor on the reader's technical knowledge. Newsletter editors exchange copies of their papers and reprint these items as needed. For example, "a reward of 500 micro-Farads is offered for information leading to the arrest and conviction of Hopalong Capacity. He is charged with the induction of an 18-turn coil, Milli Henry, who was found choked and robbed of her Joules. He was last seen riding a kilocycle. . . ." Another example states that "for years it has been believed that electric bulbs emitted light. However, recent information has proven otherwise. Electric bulbs don't emit light, they suck dark." The complete items develop their mock-serious subjects with puns and examples.

Club newsletters also reprint urban legendary material such as "Little Buddy," the story of a terminally ill child who wanted to amass the world's largest postcard collection. Hams were encouraged to send him postcards showing their amateur radio station call signs; these colorful "QSL cards" are normally exchanged by hams who have had a conversation on the air. In the early 1980s, newsletters circulated a cautionary tale claiming that contact lenses could be cooked onto one's eyeballs during the use of heat-producing workbench tools. Several legends, all quite unverifiable and unreliable, circulate through newsletters concerning the origin of the nickname "ham" for amateur radio.

Amateur radio also has its own body of lore and custom, including a traditional vocabulary heavily indebted to early telegraphers' jargon. Not found in any government's rules or any electronics textbook, this terminology underscores the importance of custom in a future-oriented, technological hobby.

For example, a "lid" is someone who ignorantly or wilfully violates rules and customs, a poor operator. Conversations are commonly ended with "73," signifying "best regards." Under appropriate circumstances, "88," meaning "love and kisses," may be used in place of, or in addition to, "73." An "Elmer" is someone who mentors a newcomer in how to become licensed and how not to become a lid. "Band cops" are self-appointed guardians who rudely correct others' operating errors, real and imagined. "Homebrew" radio equipment is built by hams themselves from electronic components; the equivalent term in model railroading is "scratch-built," along the lines of baking a cake "from scratch" using basic ingredients rather than a cake mix. A "hamfest" is a combination trade show and flea market at which hams sell or trade components, new equipment, and used gear. Hamfests are like village market days, in which social interaction is at least as important as economic activity.

Radio amateurs take pride in having to pass licensing examinations and in rules that keep ham radio free of commercial activity and foul language. Esprit de corps is carefully maintained through indoctrination of new licensees in customs and values, over and above the government's formal rules.

Considerable effort is expended, for example, to teach newcomers never to use CB slang, such as "ten codes" ("Ten-four, good buddy"). Inevitably, some language from CB has crept into common usage. For example, it is now generally acceptable to refer to one's given name as a "handle," but one should still never call it a "personal." Club newsletters frequently editorialize against both the use of CB slang and the incorrect use of ham slang. There is, in other words, a conscious emphasis on purity of folk speech.

Mastering the technical material and formal rules is only the first step toward becoming a radio amateur. A person must also learn customs and folk speech to be accepted as an insider.

Kay Cothran Craigie

References

Dunnehoo, Donna M. 1991. Amateur Radio QSL Cards: Their Design and Exchange. *North Carolina Folklore Journal* 38:21–44.

Ford, Steve, ed. 1991a. *The ARRL Operating Manual.* Newington, CT: American Radio Relay League.

———. 1991b. *Your VHF Companion.* Newington, CT: American Radio Relay League.

Wolfgang, Larry D., Jim Kearman, and Joel P. Kleinman, eds. 1993. *Now You're Talking.* Newington, CT: American Radio Relay League.

Railroaders

Workers of the nation's railroads possessing rich occupational folk traditions and a pervasive occupational identity. Railroading inspired songs, tales, poems, legends, and also stories by nonrailroaders, as well as railroad-related place names.

Among the folk genres railroaders shared were personal-experience narratives, nicknames, slang, stories of railroad characters, esoteric codes and attitudes, worksongs and chants, union lore, poems, jokes, initiation pranks, tricks, food and lodging lore, stories of drinking, of gambling, and of womanizing, cautionary tales, and occupational techniques passed on by word and example (to supplement, or subvert, the industry's tradition of extensive written rules).

Railroading, which reached its last peak in the 1940s, developed several occupational crafts, foremost in folklore being the locomotive engineers. These men saw themselves as the most important workers, while other railroaders envied and resented their arrogance and their place in the popular mind. Discussions abounded about whether the conductor or the engineer was the most important person on a train. An engineer might be called a "hoghead" or defined as "a fireman with his brains baked out," while a conductor might be referred to as "the big ox" or defined as "a man, with or without brains, displaying pencils."

Other crafts on the moving trains were those practiced by the fireman and the brakeman. The conductor was in charge of the train and its contents but not the engine. Engineers often talked of "hauling" a certain conductor. Firemen worked on the engine and kept coal in the firebox to heat the steam to drive the engine; they worked for the engineer and were promoted to engineer. Among the slang names for them were "bakehead" and "clinker mechanic." Their stories concern having to deal with the engineer and having to shovel prodigious amounts of coal, perhaps because of a heavy train or because of the amount of steam wasted by an unskillful engineer.

Brakemen did the track switching, the coupling of cars, and the braking of individual cars. They were promoted to conductors. In early days, brakemen had to climb along the tops of cars and set and release hand brakes, a dangerous activity, especially in bad weather. Stories tell of brakemen being killed or having fingers or limbs amputated in accidents. When a brakeman hired out, the trainmaster would reputedly ask to see his hands. If he had a finger or two missing, the trainmaster knew he was experienced. Brakemen were often drifters in the early days and were called "boomers." Railroaders tell stories about such men either because they were interesting to talk to, were notorious drinkers, gamblers, and womanizers, or were unscrupulous characters. A few railroaders handled trains in the yard, putting trains together. Many boomers were hired during peak seasons to work in the yard.

Railroad lore also concerned telegraphers, dispatchers, signalmen, machine shop or roundhouse workers, section hands (track-repair workers), and passenger-train chefs and porters. Telegraphers, or operators, manned the stations along the road. They received messages by telegraph or telephone, including train orders instructing various trains as to when they were to take to a side track to let another train pass. They were called "brass pounders" or "lightning slingers." One of their jobs was handing up written train orders on a forked stick or hoop to passing trains, a dangerous and harrowing task. Stories about telegraphers deal with men who could send and receive messages by American Morse code very rapidly, and about their mistakes, sometimes resulting in train disasters.

Telegraphers sometimes became train dispatchers, whose job was (and is) to control train traffic efficiently without causing train collisions. Dispatcher errors could result in train wrecks, and legends persist of dispatchers who committed suicide, knowing that two trains were soon to collide and there was no way to stop them in time (they had no radio contact in the past). Women often worked as telegraphers and dispatchers, the only crafts in which they were allowed until recent decades.

Section crews, sometimes called "gandy dancers," are known in folklore for the work chants that they used to line track by hand. One man would sing out a two-line rhyme followed by such words as, "Hey, boys, won't you line 'em [push, push] / Hey, boys, won't you line 'em [push, push]," as a way of keeping everyone moving in unison. The folk singer Huddie Ledbetter (Lead Belly) recorded some of these chants.

The Black men who worked on Pullman sleepers developed a lore of their own, including "George" stories (a porter was often called by that name), stories about treatment by passengers and conductors, about long hours of work at low pay, about labor organizing (they had their own union), and about activities in the civil rights movement. Jack Santino reported that porters generally had good relationships with their wealthy, elite passengers, although they did encounter some abuse (Santino 1989). Their main source of abuse came from tyrant, racist conductors under whom they were forced to work; their jobs could be in jeopardy if they gave the conductor the least amount of trouble. Much of their lore deals with maintaining personal dignity and solidarity while suffering from racist stereotyping. In the civil rights movement, porters carried messages from city to city and served as a conduit among Black organizers and Black communities.

Folk ballads deal with train wrecks, usually centered on the engineer. The legendary engineer John Luther "Casey" Jones inspired several folk ballads and blues because of the 1900 train wreck in which he died. Beside "Casey Jones," "The Wreck of the Old 97" is the best-known wreck ballad. Another legendary figure is John Henry, who was involved in the building of railroad tunnel and the digging out of rock manually by drill and hammer in competition with a steam drill. In modern legendry, Jan Harold Brunvand collected versions of a story, "The Baby Train," in which the whistling of an early morning train at a crossing awakens sleeping couples. Since they cannot go back to sleep and it is too early to get up, the couples end up having sex, thus increasing the incidence of births in that vicinity.

Railroaders tell stories of characters they met whose adventures are akin to local-character anecdotes told in communities. They mention dirty men who seldom washed themselves or their work clothes, and eccentrics, such as a man who wore his overcoat in winter and summer. A legendary character on the Baltimore and Ohio Railroad in Ohio was an engineer named "Peg" Clary, who had a wooden leg below the knee as a result of a railroad accident. One of his tricks was to complain of his leg and then stab it with a knife in front of a stranger for the effect it would have.

Nicknames are a prevalent form of folklore among railroaders. Sometimes it was a man's physical or behavioral characteristic that yielded names like "Baloney Nose," "Bounce," or "the Whispering Hope." Often the name came from the work, including an error made by the man: "Silo Bill" because he mistook a silo for a water tower, "Hobby Horse" because he spotted a carload of hobby horses at the stock chute, or "Bone Crusher" because he was a rough handler.

Place names often relate to railroading. Helper, Utah, was so named because that was the point at which helper engines were attached. Chicago Junction, Ohio, started as a railroad town; later they changed its name to Willard, in honor of Daniel Willard, a president of the Baltimore and Ohio Railroad. When the Denver and Rio Grande Railroad built a remote track, they named the starting point Dotsero, for "dot zero" on the map.

Terry L. Long

References

Botkin, B.A., and Alvin F. Harlow, eds. 1953. *A Treasury of Railroad Folklore*. New York: Crown.

Cohen, Norm. 1981. *Long Steel Rail: The Railroad in American Folk Song*. Urbana: University of Illinois Press.

Gamst, Frederick C. 1980. *The Hoghead: An Industrial Ethnology of the Locomotive Engineer*. New York: Holt,

Rinehart and Winston.

Long, Terry L. 1992. Occupational and Individual Identity among Ohio Railroad Workers of the Steam Era. *Western Folklore* 51:219–236.

Santino, Jack. 1989. *Miles of Smiles, Years of Struggle: Stories of Black Pullman Porters*. Urbana: University of Illinois Press.

See also Henry, John; Jones, John Luther "Casey"

Rainey, Gertrude ("Ma") (1886–1939)

First significant female blues singer in America, known as "The Mother of the Blues." Beginning her professional singing career as a child in 1902, she matured into an exceptional vocalist and popular recording artist of the 1920s, with ninety-two existing recordings, one-third of which were her own compositions. A hybrid of the popular culture of show-business minstrelsy and the folk legacy of country blues, Ma Rainey moved back and forth between the two traditions throughout her career. She performed both rural blues and popular songs with equal proficiency and was also skilled as a dancer and a comedian, sometimes accompanying her songs with humorous skits. Instrumental backing on Ma Rainey's recordings includes jazz bands, piano, guitar, banjo, fiddle, bass jug, musical saw, and slide-whistle (or kazoo). Her singing style—characterized by masterful use of slurs, moans, and blue notes—was the paradigm for the classic blues technique of Bessie Smith, Alberta Hunter, Ida Cox, Sippie Wallace, and Victoria Spivey. While Bessie Smith refined the style and made it well-known, Ma Rainey was its earliest practitioner and perhaps its creator. Like the most eloquent of the classic blues, her songs compellingly expressed anger, sexual jealousy, revenge, despair, exhaustion, strength, and hope from a female point of view.

During the Depression era, when the classic blues lost its popularity owing to the increasing ascendance of swing music, she stopped appearing professionally, although still a robust performer. She is memorialized in Memphis Minnie McCoy's biographical ballad "Ma Rainey," recorded in 1940, six months after Ma Rainey died.

Ruth E. Andersen

References

Lieb, Sandra. 1981. *Mother of the Blues: A Study of Ma Rainey*. Cambridge: MIT Press.

Randolph, Vance (1892–1980)

Ozark folklorist. Born into a middle-class family in Pittsburg, Kansas—his father was an attorney and a Republican politician, and his mother was a librarian and a member of the DAR (Daughters of the American Revolution)—Randolph was attracted early on to the ethnic diversity and radical politics of the surrounding mining camps, and later devoted a long lifetime to the collection and documentation in print of the traditional folkways of the nearby Ozark Mountains.

After dropping out of high-school, working briefly for the *Socialist Appeal to Reason*, graduating from the local college and completing an M.A. in psychology at Clark University, teaching high school biology, and spending most of a brief stint in the U.S. Army in the hospital, Randolph moved in 1920 to Pineville, Missouri, where he spent the next sixty years earning a living as a self-described "hack writer" while he collected and published very nearly the entire traditional culture of his adopted regional home.

Randolph's first scholarly efforts were 1920s studies of dialect in *Dialect Notes* and *American Speech,* and studies of Ozark folk beliefs and play-parties in the *Journal of American Folklore.* His first books, *The Ozarks* (1931) and *Ozark Mountain Folks* (1932), went virtually unnoticed by academic reviewers and were sometimes resented by local residents sensitive to the region's reputation for "backwardness," but they are recognized in the late 20th century as early instances of what are now called folklife studies.

The 1940s saw the first publication of Randolph's work by a university press, when Columbia brought out *Ozark Superstitions* (later reprinted in 1964 as *Ozark Magic and Folklore*) in 1947. His four-volume *Ozark Folksongs* was also printed at this time (1946–1950). Randolph's folktale collections were published in the 1950s— *We Always Lie to Strangers* (1951), *Who Blowed up the Church House?* (1952), *The Devil's Pretty Daughter* (1955), *The Talking Turtle* (1957), and *Sticks in the Knapsack* (1958). His book-length study of Ozark speech, *Down in the Holler,* appeared in 1953.

Hot Springs and Hell, a collection of nearly 500 jokes and anecdotes praised by one reviewer as the first "fully annotated jokebook" in American folklore scholarship, appeared in 1965, three years after Randolph's marriage to Mary Celestia Parler, an English professor and folklore collector at the University of Arkansas. With the publication in 1972 of *Ozark Folklore: A Bibliography,* a massive work featuring 2,500 annotated entries, and the 1976 appearance of *Pissing in the Snow,* another folktale collection, which became the only portion of his bawdy materials to be published in his lifetime, Randolph completed his long lifetime's work in collecting and preserving in print the songs, stories, beliefs, and speech of the Ozark region. Through most of this period he also wrote, entirely for money and mostly under a variety of pseudonyms, everything from an etiquette book and adventure tales for young readers to science booklets and soft-core pornography.

Randolph was elected a Fellow of the American Folklore Society in 1978, two years before his death. A second volume of his bibliography appeared in 1987, followed in 1992 by the remaining bawdy materials in two large volumes, *Roll Me in Your Arms* and *Blow the Candle Out.*

Robert Cochran

References

Cochran, Robert. 1985. *Vance Randolph: An Ozark Life.* Urbana: University of Illinois Press.

Cochran, Robert, and Michael Luster. 1979. *For Love and for Money: The Writings of Vance Randolph.* Arkansas College Folklore Monograph Series No. 2. Batesville, AR: Arkansas College.

See also Ozarks

Rap

A term used by African Americans to define a stylized way of speaking. Salient features of a rap are braggadocio, double entendre, formulaic expressions, signifyin', and "playing the dozens." Folklorists trace the popularity of this speech genre to 1960s Black nationalist H. "Rap" Brown, whose praise name (nickname) depicted his style of speaking, called rappin'. Although Brown is credited for the name of this genre, elements of rap can be traced from African epic bardic traditions to rural southern-based expressions of African Americans such as toasts, folktales, sermons, blues, and game songs (such as the hambone).

African Americans transported Southern traditions during massive migrations to Northern urban centers between the 1920s and the 1950s. In the new milieu, Southern traditions were transformed and modified to reflect urban life. This new context also fostered a style of speaking known as jive talk, a metaphorical way of speaking that uses word and phrases from American mainstream English, but reinterpreted from an African American perspective (for example, man becomes "cat"; or house becomes "crib"). The art of jive is predicated on its ability to remain witty and original—hence its constant fluctuation in vocabulary over the years.

Between the 1930s and the 1950s, jive gained prominence in the performances and speech culture of jazz musicians like Cab Calloway, Louis Jordan, and Dizzy Gillespie and comedians like Redd Fox, Pigmeat Markham, Jackie "Moms" Mabley, and Rudy Ray Moore, who was known for popularizing toasts like "The Signifying Monkey" via audio recordings. In addition, Black radio disc jockeys—namely, Al Benson and Holmes "Daddy-O" Daylie—introduced jive talking to music (in rhyme) via the airwaves.

By the mid-1960s, jive was redefined and given newer meaning by H. "Rap" Brown, who adorned his political speeches with signifyin', rhyme, and double entendre. Although his way of speaking inaugurated the shift from jive to rap, Brown's stylized speech soon gained popular acceptance among young urban admirers as rappin'. It was not, however, until the late 1960s that Brown's speaking style was set to a musical accompaniment by political poets such as the Last Poets of Harlem and Gil-Scott-Heron, who recited rhyming couplets over an African percussion accompaniment.

In the late 1960s and the 1970s, the concept of rappin' over music emerged among Black music artists as two distinct song styles: the love rap (as in the music of Isaac Hayes) and funk rap (for example, George Clinton and his group Parliament). Unlike rappin' performed by early entertainers, these raps were loosely chanted over a repetitive instrumental accompaniment.

Rap as a distinct musical genre evolved in the Bronx, New York, during 1972 with itinerant disc jockeys called "mobile djs," who mixed prerecorded hits alternately on two turntables while reciting party phrases to the crowd in a microphone. Because deejaying became a demanding art, party-styled emcees teamed with deejays, thus giving rise to rap's 1990s form.

Rap music artists include Kool Moe Dee, Queen Latifah, Public Enemy, and Arrested Development, among others.
Cheryl L. Keyes

References

Keyes, Cheryl L. 1992. *Rappin to the Beat: Rap Music as Street Culture among African Americans.* Ann Arbor, MI: UMI Research Press.

Smitherman, Geneva. [1977] 1986. *Talkin and Testifyin: The Language of Black America.* Detroit: Wayne State University Press.

Toop, David. 1991. *Rap Attack 2: African Rap to Global Hip-Hop.* rev. ed. New York: Serpent Tail.

Recitation

Dramatic, solo, oral performance of prose or poetry spoken from memory or read from manuscript. Recitation is a major Anglo American folk and popular tradition that traces back to the British Isles. Many of the items performed derive from written sources; other recitation texts were composed by their performers and are known only to a small group. Perhaps for these reasons, there are no indexes to American (or British) recitations, and the widespread distribution of recitations in Anglo American tradition, their status as traditional performance, and the value they share with other folklore as a source of information for understanding people and cultures were seldom recognized by folklore research until recently.

Recitation was frequently encountered and occasionally noted in the British Isles from at least the 17th century; the *Oxford English Dictionary* indicates that the word "recitation" in the sense of spoken oral performance of memorized or read material was in use in England in the mid-17th century.

The popular-culture history of recitation in the British Isles is intertwined with its popularity in folk culture. The Irish poet and dramatist William Butler Yeats described the career of a "gleeman" who recited as well as sang in Dublin during the late 18th and early 19th centuries, and the clear implication was that the gleeman was part of a widespread, ancient tradition. Recitation was an important aspect of the music-hall and pub performance traditions of the British Isles, and it is still very much a part of popular entertainment there. Stanley Holloway is well known in Britain for his many years of professional recitation performance; books of recitation texts made famous by his performances are widely distributed, and recordings of his—and a number of other well known, cherished performers'—recitation performances are still occasionally broadcast over radio and provide a major source of inspiration, and parody, for British folk and popular entertainers.

The recitation-performance tradition was part of the oral tradition that the early British settlers brought to America, and the status and interactions of recitation in folk and popular culture in America are similar to the role it fills in Britain.

Although the folk recitation-performance tradition was seldom accorded the same stature or attention as folksongs or ballads, it was frequently noted by travelers, local historians, and folklorists. Many references to recitations were made more or less in passing by early American folklorists. John Lomax, in fact, not only observed recitation while he was collecting cowboy songs, but also learned the classic cowboy recitation "Lasca," written by the English popular poet Frank Desprez, and performed it at the 1911 Modern Language Society of America convention. From similar scattered evidence, it seems clear that recitation has long been a part of Anglo American folklore.

The importance of recitation in American popular culture is much more easily and completely documented. In the early years of the 20th century, a series of pamphlets titled *Werner's Readings and Recitations* were sold in great numbers to provide texts for reciters. Recitations constituted a relatively high percentage of the total record sales in the United States during the first quarter-century of the medium. The popular entertainer Cal Stewart, who billed himself as "The Talking Machine Storyteller," recorded thousands of recitations during the 1890s and the early decades of the 20th century. Hank Williams, Johnny Cash, Perry Como, Tex Ritter, Joan Baez, Tom Mix, and Andy Griffith are among the many American recording artists who have made records featuring recitation.

Popular-culture recitation fed and reinforced the folk recitation tradition. Folk and popular reciters alike relied upon Werner's collection, and many of the recitations recorded by Stewart—or, for that matter, Cash—passed into oral tradition and underwent the same sort of variations and reworkings as other folk forms such as ballads and tales. Still, recitation was largely ignored by folklorists until well after World War II.

Even an incomplete history of Johnny Cash's recitation "The Stars and Stripes" demonstrates the complex interaction between popular culture and folk culture. The original version of Cash's poem—using the flag as a symbol for the nation in lines such as: You see, that flag / Got a hole right there, / When Washington carried it / Across the Delaware—was disseminated primarily by television and ended in the Vietnam War period. But a recent public performance by St. Johns, Arizona, reciter Delbert Lambson included a new stanza he had added that brought the poem up to date by mentioning Operation Desert Storm.

The first major folklore collection and analysis of recitation in America dealt not with Anglo American forms, but with the related African American form, the "toast." With the exception of scattered research and occasional mentions in folksong and ballad collections—particularly those of Henry W. Shoemaker, (see Shoemaker 1919)—there was almost no significant scholarly work directed toward the Anglo American recitation until the 1970s. A description of a recitation, a reciter, and a recitation performance was published in a regional American folklore journal, *(AFF)Word* [Arizona Friends of Folklore], in 1972 and was followed a year later by more description in a *Journal of American Folklore* article. A session of the 1974 American Folklore Society annual convention was devoted to the topic. Revised versions of the session papers, along with four others, were published in a special issue of *Southern Folklore Quarterly* in 1976. These seminal articles were in turn followed in 1978 by a special sixty-three-page issue of *Southwest Folklore*, which served as extended liner notes for a documentary record, *Uncle Horace's Recitations* (1987 AFF [Arizona Friends of Folklore] Flagstaff, Arizona), featuring twelve recitations by one performer and transcriptions of the rest of his repertoire. Yet another article on recitation, concerning a bawdy text (Baker 1987), appeared in the *Journal of American Folklore* in 1987, and in 1990 the first book devoted completely to the subject of Anglo American recitation was published (Cunningham 1990). With this research, a picture of Anglo American recitation and its place in folklore is beginning to emerge.

It is clear that the oral tradition of America and the British Isles has long included individuals, families, and communities for whom the dramatic oral performance of poems and stories is as natural as speaking. Programs as varied as the *ceilidh* held at Bunratty Folk Park in Shannon, Ireland, and the Old West Show at Mesa, Arizona, continue to feature recitations in the 1990s. These performances utilize stories and poems from a variety of written and oral sources circumscribed by a broad range of performance conventions that govern their scripted, fixed-form, nonextemporaneous performances. The same sort of performances also take place as a part of the folklore of both groups. Some performers memorize their recitations, others read their's. In either case, both the reciters and their audiences have a clear concept of a script, a correct form of what is being performed. The reciters recite and the audiences provide the attention essential to the form's survival because that which they create and that which they adopt and adapt alike embody their values and beliefs while entertaining and fulfilling expectations and emotional needs.

Texts recited in the 1990s may be taken from traditional ballads or popular poetry (Ernest Lawrence Thayer's "Casey at the Bat" is probably the single most popular and most widely distributed such text in America, and "The Green Eye of the Little Yellow God," by J. Milton Hayes, holds the same position in Britain), or they may be written by performers themselves in the manner and form of traditional ballads or popular poetry; what makes recitation a folk genre is that it is a traditional oral performance. Elements of performance run through all presentations of recitation texts. Most of them are actually performed before an audience, and those that are not (such as those collected by folklorists outside of normal contexts) adhere to performance characteristics of the genre and *could* be so presented. The size of the audience ranges from a few family members to fairly large groups that are a part of family or community gatherings; they all share a basic familiarity with the conventions of recitation performance, which are introduced, indicated, and communicated in various subtle or more obvious ways. Performers are frequently formally introduced to their audience by a "master of ceremonies," or, in less formal situations, performers introduce themselves. Reciters stand while their audiences remain seated. By their performances, the reciters create and command an invisible stage so that their audiences recognize recitation in progress, enter the performance, and play their roles, too. A theatrical or a subtle gesture, a twinkle in the eye, words that tumble over each other, a shout, a whisper, the rising or falling of pitch, sometimes the tinkling of a piano or the sobbing of a violin, and even silence—all call into being a world of imagination wherein the audience becomes a part of the performance and shares the performers' evocation and evincing of joy and sorrow, laughter and tears.

Recitation is not as common in popular or folk entertainment in either the British Isles or America in the 1990s as it was in the 1890s, but wherever there are opportunities for reciters to perform, and wherever their performances are valued by their audiences, the tradition of recitation continues.

Keith Cunningham

References

Baker, Ronald L. 1987. Lady Lil and Pisspot Pete. *Journal of American Folklore* 100:191–199.

Cunningham, Keith, ed. 1990. *The Oral Tradition of the American West: Adventure, Courtship, Family, and Place in Traditional Recitation,* with an Introduction by W.K. McNeil. Little Rock, AR: August House.

Shoemaker, Henry W. 1919. *North Pennsylvania Minstrelsy.* Altoona, PA: Times Tribune.

See also Cowboy Poetry

Regional Folklore

Folklore generated or circulated within a particular region of the country and that reflects peculiar features or aspects of life in that region. Regional folklore may be indigenous to a particular place or it may be "regionalized" as people move from one part of the country to another and adapt their folklore to their new home.

In the history of American folklore scholarship, regional folklore has been a constant, if relatively minor, theme. Articles on folklore collected in various regional settings appeared more or less regularly in the *Journal of American Folklore* from its initial issues in 1888 through the 1940s. During that same period, the establishment of state and regional folklore societies and their journals both reflected and stimulated interest in regional folklore. The focus in these journals, and in the work of regional folklorists in general, was almost exclusively on the collection and publication of texts. Some regional folklore collectors concentrated on particular genres. Cecil Sharp, for instance, was interested in English ballads in the Appalachians. But the first half of the 20th century also saw multigenre collections within specific regions or states. Frank C. Brown, for instance, gathered exhaustively in North Carolina, while Vance Randolph was doing the same in the Ozarks. Underlying these collections of regional folklore seems to have been a conception of folklore as items that remained relatively unchanged during their transmission through generations of tradition bearers, rather than as the creative expression of people as shaped to some degree by their experiences, of and in, a particular place.

An exception to this view was promulgated by Benjamin A. Botkin, who was interested in the indigenous folk products of regional experience. Botkin's chief vehicle for his ideas about regional folklore was his own periodical, *Folk-Say*, initiated in 1929. Although Botkin's views had little direct impact on other folklorists at the time, he was part of a cadre of American historians, literary scholars, geographers, and sociologists who evinced a growing interest in regionalism and regional culture during the 1930s—an interest that culminated in the conference on "Regionalism in America" held at the University of Wisconsin at Madison in 1949.

Mid-century, in fact, seems to mark a turning point in folklorists' conceptions of regional folklore, as foreshadowed in Richard M. Dorson's *Bloodstoppers and Bearwalkers: Folk Traditions of the Upper Peninsula* (1952). When Dorson suggests in this book that the Upper Peninsula of Michigan is a "seedbed for folk culture," he is proffering, albeit implicitly, the notion that regional folklore can be understood as a response to UPers' (who sometimes call themselves "Yoopers") local experiences. Dorson's ideas about regional folklore appear more fully in *American Folklore* (1959) and *Buying the Wind: Regional Folklore in the United States* (1964), in which he samples folk materials from several distinctive cultural regions.

Where Dorson hinted at the possibilities of studying the folklore that is generated within a region rather than merely collecting the folk materials that happen to circulate within it, Américo Paredes presented a full-blown study of that very process in *"With His Pistol in His Hand": A Border Ballad and Its Hero* (1958). Paredes argued that the *corrido,* the native ballad form of the border country on the Lower Rio Grande Valley, was a product of historical and cultural forces in that region.

In the 1960s, folklorists' fundamental conceptions of the nature of folklore underwent a powerful transformation from the idea of folklore as static item to the notion of folklore as dynamic process. In the wake of this revolution, Suzi Jones argued in a 1976 article in the *Journal of the Folklore Institute* that the changes effected in folklore as people move from one place to another reflect adaptations to local regional environments. Regionalization, therefore, is the process by which folklore is transformed through people's response to place. Jones went on to suggest that regional folklore becomes a mark of regional identity and sense of place, as a rhetorical strategy for demonstrating familiarity with the local environment. According to this view, a regional folk group exists where people share a body of folklore by virtue of living in a certain geographical area that forms the basis for a shared identity as consciously expressed in their lore.

The relationship between regional folklore and local experience can be seen in three ways. First, imported forms of cultural expression can be adapted to regional conditions. Second, folklore can emerge from particular regional conditions and experiences. Third, folklore can be used to express a sense of identity with a place.

Adaptation of folklore occurs when people move into a place, bringing with them the traditional forms of expressions from their former homes, and alter those forms in response to the new setting. The dogtrot house in the Southern United States, with its characteristic breezeway, seems to have developed as a response to the summer heat and humidity of the place. Similarly, the hymn "Beulah Land" was parodied by homesteaders on the Great Plains in the 1870s, and in other parts of the arid and semiarid West after the turn of the century, in response to the region's harsh environmental conditions.

Regional folklore also emerges from specific local conditions and expresses the critical elements of the regional experience from the resident's point of view. In Mormon Utah, for instance, an area marked by low rainfall, an elaborate body of custom, belief, and narrative about water has developed. Often regional folklore evolves from particular historical or economic factors, such as dominant ethnic or occupational groups. The folklore of southern Louisiana is shaped nearly equally by the influence of the Cajuns and by its characteristic waterways, which provide many of its residents with their livelihood.

Finally, as Jones suggested, regional folklore can be used as a means of expressing identity. Within each American region, residents have devised ways of distinguishing between insiders and outsiders, and they often tell stories detailing the differences. The "Arkansaw Traveler" is perhaps the best-known example, "but is paralleled in a wide variety of other stories from Maine Down Easters' accounts of 'summer folks' to westerners' anecdotes of 'dudes.'" Also declaring pride in regional identity are aphorisms about drinking from a local water source or wearing out a pair of shoes in a place as a warranty that one will be become a permanent resident.

At the end of the 20th century, regional folklore seems to be holding its own in the face of mass-produced goods and the dominance of popular media. A number of academic regional-studies centers have been established since the mid-1970s, and public interest in local and regional forms of cultural expression has been stimulated by the activities of public-sector folklorists and other cultural conservationists who draw attention to those forms through museum exhibits, festivals, and other forms of programming.

Barbara Allen

References

Allen, Barbara. 1990. Regional Studies in American Folklore Scholarship. In *Sense of Place: American Regional Cultures,* ed. Barbara Allen and Thomas J. Schlereth. Lexington: University Press of Kentucky, pp. 1–13.

Jones, Suzi. 1976. Regionalization: A Rhetorical Strategy. *Journal of the Folklore Institute* 13:105–120.

Paredes, Américo. 1958. *"With His Pistol in His Hand": A Border Ballad and Its Hero.* Austin: University of Texas Press.

Whisnant, David. 1983. *All That Is Native and Fine: The Politics of Culture in an American Region.* Chapel Hill: University of North Carolina Press.

See also Great Basin; Great Plains; Middle Atlantic Region; Midwest; Northwest Coast and Alaska; Ozarks; Pennsylvania Culture Region; Piedmont Region; South; Southwest

"The Savior." Paper cutting, 25 x 20 cm. Ohio, probably 1860s. Collection J. W. Love.

Religion, Folk

A term covering a wide range of religious phenomena that have interested folklorists, anthropologists, and other scholars. Folklorist Don Yoder, who has done a great deal of research in the area of religion, provided the definition other folklorists turn to most often: "Folk religion is the totality of all those views and practices of religion that exist among the people apart from and alongside the strictly theological and liturgical forms of the official religion" (Yoder 1974:14). The study of folk religion often overlaps with the study of folk medicine and folk beliefs.

Folklorists and others have approached the study of folk religion in North America in many ways; this entry describes seven of the most prevalent and important approaches. In many instances, there can be significant overlap among these heuristic categories.

The seven categories are: (1) religion of the "folk society"; (2) religious practices of "the folk"; (3) religion of dissenters from orthodoxy; (4) religion as lived and experienced; (5) syncretistic religious practices and beliefs; (6) religious folklore; and (7) religious practices of the group to which the folklorist belongs or once belonged.

Religion of the "Folk Society"

Most conceptions of folklore, including Yoder's, rely on an (often unstated) assumption that folk culture exists in opposition to "mainstream" or "modern" culture. The concept of "the folk society," best known from Robert Redfield's article of that name makes this contrast explicit. The folk society exists in isolation from the mainstream society, retaining old practices and beliefs long after mainstream society has aban-

doned them, passing on its wisdom orally rather than through writing, and maintaining traditions in the face of change.

Folk religion, from this perspective, would include oral, traditional, residual, and informal religious beliefs and practices no longer recognized or active in mainstream society. The classic example of religion of the folk society would include the religious practices of any peasant people living alongside, but largely isolated from, a relatively more modern, urbanized society.

Religious Practices of "the Folk"

Related to, and often influenced by, the folk-society model are many folklorists' studies of the religion of people who might be said to "look like folk." This would include the rural and urban poor, as well as groups isolated from the mainstream by geography, culture, class, or preference. What makes a group of people "look folk" can vary from time to time, situation to situation, and folklorist to folklorist, but generally speaking any religious group or practice that seems nonmainstream, exotic, or marginal (from the folklorist's point of view) might well be labeled folk religion. Good examples include groups that maintain an older lifestyle, such as the Old Order Amish or the Pennsylvania Dutch; groups that are marginal in their society, such as Pentecostals; and groups made up of ethnic or racial minorities with their own distinctive practices, such as Black Baptists and Latino Catholics.

William M. Clements' discussion of the "folk church" in American society also fits in this category (Clements 1978). Clements defines as "folk churches" Protestant groups that exist apart from mainline denominations and on the margins of mainstream society.

Religion of Dissenters from Orthodoxy

Another conception of folk culture useful for the study of religion is the image of folk culture as a "culture of contestation," in the phrase originated by Luigi Lombardi-Satriani in 1974. From this point of view, folk culture is not merely in the shadow of mainstream culture, but is in an active state of conflict with popular or elite culture. Folklorists are often interested in subgroups within major religions that are distinct from the majority by virtue of gender, sexual preference, race, or other personal characteristics or philosophical stances, and who explicitly or tacitly protest or challenge some of their religion's tenets and/or practices.

Religion as Lived and Experienced

Another way of understanding the "folk" does not relegate them to a separate folk society, or to the status of a dissenting minority, but includes all of us as we live our lives day by day. Leonard Norman Primiano's formulation of "vernacular religion" draws attention to religious beliefs, practices, and experiences as they are understood, undertaken, and expressed by all people, modern and traditional, urban and rural (Primiano 1993). The opposition here is between an ideal of religion—the institutional, codified, set form of religion—and religion as experienced. While a distinction is maintained between institutional religion and vernacular

In front of the courthouse on court day, people listen to an itinerant preacher. Campton, Kentucky, 1940. Photo Marion Post Wolcott. Library of Congress.

religion, this conception of folk religion draws attention to that which all people, no matter what their background or social standing, have in common by way of religious experience. Urban sophisticates as well as rural rustics partake of vernacular religion.

Syncretistic Religious Practices and Beliefs

Syncretistic religions are sometimes considered folk largely because they are thought of as "hybrid" rather than "pure." Syncretistic religions, created through a blending of two or more religions, are especially common where world religions (Christianity, Islam) encroach on local religions through the efforts of missionaries. Most studies of North American folk religion in this sense have focused on blends of African, Native American, and Catholic religious beliefs and practices, such as *vodun* and *santeria*.

Religious Folklore

There are a large number of folk genres, such as legends, jokes, verbal art (including sermons—see Lawless 1988; Rosenberg 1989), foodways, family traditions, material culture, and the like, that can be found both in and outside of religious settings. The study of any such "ordinary folklore" that happens to have religious aspects or sacred overtones can well be described as religious folklore (Danielson 1986). Well-known examples would include Mormon saints' legends and ethnic religious holiday traditions.

Religious Practices of the Group to which the Folklorist Belongs or Once Belonged

There are a large number of studies by folklorists of the religion to which the folklorist adheres or once adhered. Examples would include studies of Mormons by William Wilson or the husband-and-wife team of Austin E. and Alta S. Fife; the Amish by John A. Hostetler; and Catholics by Primiano. This type of study is related to the tendency of folklorists to study their own region (Vance Randolph in the Ozarks) or ethnic group (Américo Paredes' work with Texas Mexicans).

The term "folk religion" is increasingly controversial as well as generally imprecise. Both the controversy and the lack of precision are exacerbated by the vagueness of the constituent terms "folk" and "religion," which are in their own right difficult to define. Elaine Lawless, a prominent scholar of religious folklife, begins her 1988 book, *God's Peculiar People,* by discussing definitions of folk religion, but in her 1993 work, *Holy Women, Wholly Women,* she does not use the term at all. Many scholars prefer to avoid the term "folk religion," substituting such terms as popular religion, unofficial religion, vernacular religion, and religious folklore and folklife.

Jennifer E. Livesay
Kenneth D. Pimple

References

Clements, William M. 1978. The American Folk Church in Northeast Arkansas. *Journal of the Folklore Institute* 15:161–180.

Danielson, Larry. 1986. Religious Folklore. *In Folk Groups and Folklore Genres: An Introduction,* ed. Elliott Oring. Logan: Utah State University Press, pp. 45–69.

Lawless, Elaine J. 1988. *Handmaidens of the Lord: Pentecostal Women Preachers and Traditional Religion.* Philadelphia: University of Pennsylvania Press.

Lombardi–Satriani, Luigi. 1974. Folklore as Culture of Contestation. *Journal of the Folklore Institute* 11:99–121.

Primiano, Leonard Norman. 1993. *Intrinsically Catholic: Vernacular Religion and Philadelphia's "Dignity."* Ph.D. diss., University of Pennsylvania.

Redfield, Robert. 1947. The Folk Society. *American Journal of Sociology* 52:293–308.

Rosenberg, Bruce A. 1989. *Can These Bones Live.* Urbana: University of Illinois Press.

Yoder, Don. 1974. Toward a Definition of Folk Religion. *Western Folklore* 33:2–15.

See also Christmas; Easter; Gospel Music; Jewish Americans; Mormon Folklore; Passover; Pennsylvania Germans ("Dutch"); Prayer; Sermon, Folk; Shout; Spirituals, African American

Reuss, Richard August (1940–1986)

Folklorist primarily remembered for his work on the folk-revival movement and on politics and American folklore. Reuss was a native of New York City, did his undergraduate work at Ohio Wesleyan University and his graduate work in folklore at Indiana University. He taught for several years at Wayne State University in Detroit until budget cuts resulted in his position being terminated. He then taught at several schools, including Indiana University, until he decided to shift vocations. In 1981 he received a master of social work degree from the University of Michigan, and thereafter he worked in that field.

Although Reuss published many articles, his most important work, *American Folklore and Left-Wing Politics, 1927–1957,* remains unpublished. Shortly after finishing this work as his Ph.D. dissertation in 1971, he submitted it to a university press that accepted it, providing that certain extensive revisions were made. Having just undergone the rigors of writing the dissertation, Reuss decided not to undertake this revision immediately; as a result, the manuscript became something of an underground classic. This dissertation reflected his long-standing interest that began when, as a teenager, Reuss participated in the folk-revival movement of the late 1950s. Later he worked as a volunteer for *Sing Out!* and *Broadside,* two important revival magazines; he also acquired an impressive personal library that included many revival publications. Reuss became interested in the history of the movement in which he had participated, and he wrote papers on the subject both for his undergraduate and graduate classes. This was at a time (during the late 1960s to 1970s), when most professional folklorists considered the folk-revival movement irrelevant to their academic discipline.

Reuss had a number of other passions, including the history of folklore studies, as evidenced by his establishing a journal, *Folklore Historian* (1983). Concurrent with this was a strong interest in the role of women in American folklore scholarship. He also founded the Michigan chapter of the Committee to Combat Huntington's Disease and became a member of that organization's national board. The apparent lack of records concerning the history of his own family and that of his wife led Reuss into extensive genealogical work as well. A long-time hobby of collecting baseball cards gained him such national attention that in 1971 he was featured in a front-page story in the *Wall Street Journal.*

In 1987, the year after Reuss' death, the Folklore and History Section of the American Folklore Society established a prize in his name for the best student paper dealing with the history of folklore studies.

W.K. McNeil

References

Green, Archie, ed. 1993. *Songs about Work: Essays in Occupational Culture for Richard A. Reuss.* Special Publication of the Folklore Institute No. 3. Bloomington: University of Indiana Press.

Reuss, Richard A. 1983. *Songs of American Labor, Industrialization, and the Urban Work Experience: A Discography.* Ann Arbor: Institute of Labor and Industrial Relations, University of Michigan.

Revivalism

A term used by folklorists to describe the conscious use of folklore to express or represent ideas about identity and/or art. The term has been used most frequently to describe practitioners of folk music particularly during the 1960s (Rosenberg 1993), and storytellers, starting in the 1970s (Sobol 1992). "Revivalism" is sometimes used by folklorists as a straightforward descriptive term to describe certain kinds of social movements, but it has more frequently carried with it meanings of judgment about authenticity. It is one of those terms, like "fakelore" (Dorson 1969), "folklorism" (Bendix 1988), "folksay" (Hirsch 1987), and "folkery" (Dean-Smith 1968) that has the potential to draw attention to often overlooked reflexive dimensions of thinking—be they academic, intellectual, or casual—about folklore.

An early appearance of the term "revival" in connection with folklore came in the writings of English folksong collector Cecil Sharp, who in 1907 called for a revival of English folk music. Following his lead, the English Folk Dance and Song Society became the center of the social movement called the first British folksong revival—although the strong interest in the ballad during the 18th century has also been characterized in retrospect as a revival—and this led indirectly to later-20th-century folksong revivals in Britain and elsewhere. Sharp, however, was using the term metaphorically (its oldest sense) to describe the refurbishment of a repertoire or genre, as when we speak of the revival of a Shakespeare play or some other historical work of art. "Revival" has also been used as a metaphor for the awakening of religious spirit since at least the time of Cotton Mather; during the 1970s to 1980s, folklorists have grown more interested in religious revivalism as a social phenomenon with folkloric aspects. This area of inquiry has, however, been considered by folklorists to be essentially different from that of secular revivalism and is generally treated as an aspect of the folk-organized religion continuum.

By the 1960s, when folklore emerged as a professionalized discipline, folklorists tended to read the term "revival" literally rather than metaphorically and, having shifted their focus outward from cultural products to include cultural producers and contexts, tended to see the term as referring to the resuscitation of "living" traditions in these new terms. Consequently, they used it to describe the uses of insiders' cultural products by outsiders, individuals from "other" cultural contexts. This perspective coincided with the apogee of the commercial folk-music boom of the 1960s. "Revivalism" thus became a pejorative or judgmental term for folklorists, referring to the contextually inauthentic or spurious, used, characteristically, to describe situations in which individuals or groups perform texts, enact customs, or create objects that are based on traditions from outside their own personal historical and/or cultural experience.

Revival—whether referred to literally or metaphorically—has been problematic to folklorists for another reason. While folklorists have typically defined their materials as emerging from a matrix of "unselfconscious" cultural production or enactment, any attempt to revive such materials implies some degree of self-consciousness. Those most interested in the revival of folklore tend to have, like Sharp, conscious (and articulated) political, artistic, or cultural agendas that extend far beyond the original contexts of production. Ironically, then, given their pejorative use of the term, folklorists have been among the principal folklore revivalists.

When folklorists analyze situations in which differing degrees of awareness about such matters are manifest, they tend to create categories of classification that differentiate on the basis of awareness and agendas. Ellen Stekert, writing in 1966 about the urban folksong movement, spoke of four groups: "traditional singers," "imitators" (she later altered this to "emulators"), "utilizers," and "new aesthetic" singers. For Stekert, traditional singers are those who "have learned their songs and their style of presentation from oral tradition as they grew up" (Stekert 1993:96). Joe Wilson and Lee Udall, in their 1982 book addressing folk-festival organizers and managers, present a somewhat similar, though more detailed, set of categories. They first separate performers into two categories: Those "reared in the culture from which the performed materials are drawn" are distinguished from those "who adopt elements of style and materials from cultures into which they were not reared." This allows them to split what is in essence Stekert's first category three ways: "traditional folk performer," "aware traditional performer," and "evolved traditional performer" (Wilson and Udall 1982:20–23). These subdivisions allow for the idea that traditional performers might lose the unselfconscious quality in their performance; they also split the second, nonreared, category into subdivisions that resemble Stekert's last three.

This is good as far as it goes in that it admits the possibility of nonunselfconsciousness, but what is usually left unsaid is that there is often collaboration among the reared and the nonreared with a revivalist or revitalizationist goal in mind. Examples abound within the domain of music: Since the 1960s, for example, the growth of old-time fiddle music associations in North America has been characterized by the participation of individuals who grew up hearing and performing fiddle music together with those who did not. They share a perception of this music culture as being threatened by outside forces, and they collaborate to protect and promote the tradition. Similarly, the late-20th-century storytelling revival brings together those who learned Jack tales from their family and friends and those who first encountered such *Märchen* through the Grimm brothers or Walt Disney. In a more general way, collaboration between insiders and outsiders occurs whenever folklorists conduct research into a tradition. Today folklorists recognize the intellectual necessity and ethical imperative for dialogue with their informants in the process of research and publication. As scholars become "aware" and "evolved" in their attitudes about the traditions they study, so, too, do the tradition bearers. Consequently, the possibility of revivalism always exists whenever anyone identifies something as folklore.

Neil V. Rosenberg

References

Bendix, Regina. 1988. Folklorism: The Challenge of a Concept. *International Folklore Review* 6:5–14.

Dean-Smith, Margaret. 1968. The Pre-Disposition to Folkery. *Folklore* 79:161–175.

Dorson, Richard M. 1969. Fakelore. *Zeitschrift für Volkskunde* 65:56–64. Reprinted in *American Folklore and the Historian*. Chicago: University of Chicago Press. 1971 pp. 3–14.

Hirsch, Jerrold. 1987. Folklore in the Making: B.A. Botkin. *Journal of American Folklore* 100:3–38.

Rosenberg, Neil V. 1993. *Transforming Tradition*. Urbana: University of Illinois Press.

Sobol, Joseph D. 1992. Innervision and Innertext: Oral and Interpretive Modes of Storytelling Performance. *Oral Tradition* 7:66–86.

Stekert, Ellen J. 1993. Cents and Nonsense in the Urban Folksong Movement: 1930–1966. In *Transforming Tradition*, ed. Neil V. Rosenberg. Urbana: University of Illinois Press, pp. 84–106.

Wilson, Joe, and Lee Udall. 1982. *Folk Festivals*. Knoxville: University of Tennessee Press.

See also Storytelling

Revolutionary War

American War for Independence from British rule. Any war creates a semifolk occupation—that is, an occupation with its own lore into which members come for a set period of time before returning to another part of society. This differs from a genuine folk occupation in that its members are from heterogeneous backgrounds and are made homogeneous only by the temporary situation. In such an occupation, the lore may be either brought from the outside and adapted to fit the new situation, created by the homogeneity of the semifolk occupation, or may be popular lore created by educated persons associated with, or looking back on, the occupation.

Three examples from the American Revolution will illustrate. The tale of the scout Tim Murphy shooting an enemy Indian hiding behind a rock by bending his rifle and firing the bullet in a curve is an old European folktale (Type 1890E in the Aarne-Thompson *Type-Index*). The story simply attached itself to the reputation of this famous rifleman. On the other hand, the New York legend that Murphy's shooting of Scottish General Simon Frazer from a tree was the turning point in one of the battles at Saratoga is a genuine bit of lore rising out of the Revolutionary experience. But stories like those about Nathan Hale and his famous last words, or Paul Revere's ride to Concord, are dramatizations that have been made part of Revolutionary lore after gaining popularity at the literary level.

Soldiers joining the armies or shipping aboard the privateers brought their own legends, songs, beliefs, and folkways with them. These were genuine bits of the lore of the colonial farmers, sailors, lumbermen, and villagers who came from Massachusetts, Pennsylvania, and Virginia to make up the troops. The traditions were adapted and melded into a body of material to serve the fighters. Genuine Revolutionary folk

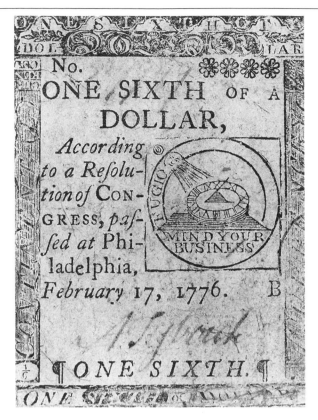

No.

ONE SIXTH OF A DOLLAR,

According to a Resolution of CONGRESS, passed at Philadelphia, February 17, 1776.   B

ONE SIXTH.

heroes like Murphy and the better-known Ethan Allen had their reputations salted with anecdotes and motifs common to this Anglo-colonial lore. They are bitten by snakes who get drunk on their alcohol-laden blood; they run deer into the ground because it is more fun that shooting them; and they grab their rifles and knock flies out of the air.

A major example of lore brought to the war from the communities that provided the troops is *The Green Mountain Songster*, printed in 1823 by "An Old Revolutionary Soldier" calling himself "a follower of Gen. Washington." It is a collection of British and colonial American songs and ballads—some old, some recent—that must have been sung around the campfires forty-five or so years before at Aquidneck or Valley Forge. Although the book contains no music, most of the songs are well enough known that scholars can make a good guess as to their tunes.

One piece in the *Songster*, "The Plymouth Colony," uses the phrase "yankee doodle dandy." "Yankee Doodle" was, of course, the best-known folksong of the Revolution. Originally a ballad-like song written during the French and Indian Wars by a British Army surgeon, George Shuckburgh, it set an old British refrain to an even older European melody. Popularized by the British in the early days of the Revolution as a means of mocking the shabby colonial troops, it was taken over by the colonials with many variations. Even today, the refrain beginning "Yankee Doodle went to town" and its tune are known to every American, although Shuckburgh's full text and the dozens of variations have been forgotten.

Also popular was "Chester," a hymn written by one of the Boston patriots, music master William Billings. Given fresh lyrics to fit the political situation, it was sung through-

out the war. In the 1990s, the hymn is still known to the shape-note singers of the South. "The World Turned Upside Down," the song played at Cornwallis' surrender, was another favorite.

To the soldiers fighting the war, the names most Americans associate with the Revolution—Paul Revere, Nathan Hale, John Paul Jones, Benedict Arnold, British Major John André, and the like—were everyday participants, however remote they may have seemed. They were certainly not folk heroes like Murphy and Allen. They owe their "legends" to publicity and literary endeavors fostered in the 19th century as our country began to establish cultural, as well as political, independence. Nor have the flag-waving fathers of these stories been bothered by presenting distorted pictures of these heroes who fought in a war in which loyalties and purposes were often confused.

Most Americans do not know or care that Paul Revere was a "mechanic" (part of the Underground) in Boston whose ride to warn of the British raids ended with his capture near Lexington before he got to Concord, and that his efforts were shared by William Dawes and Samuel Prescott; that Nathan Hale was an ill-prepared spy who almost certainly never said "I only regret that I have but one life to lose for my country"; that John Paul Jones was a hero to pro-colonial sympathizers in Europe and even England; that Benedict Arnold was not alone in thinking it would be best if the conflict were ended to British advantage; and that young, handsome Major André, besides being a fool to get captured, was sympathetically treated by many colonials.

Nonetheless, these figures have replaced the real folk heroes—the Murphys, the Allens, the Enoch Crosbys (a spy who was probably the model for James Fenimore Cooper's Harvey Birch), and the John Champes (the soldier assigned to kidnap Arnold after his treasonous act at West Point). These, too, have been eclipsed, this time by frontier and Western figures, the shapers of what we regard as our "manifest destiny." Somehow Davy Crockett seems more national, less colonial, than Murphy or Allen.

Tristram Potter Coffin

References

Alden, John Richard. 1954. *The American Revolution*. New York: Harper.

Browne, Ray B. 1961. Superstitions Used as Propaganda in the American Revolution. *New York Folklore Quarterly* 17:202–211.

Coffin, Tristram Potter. 1971. *Uncertain Glory: Folklore and the American Revolution*. Detroit: Gale.

Gephart, Ronald M. 1984. *Revolutionary America, 1963–1789: A Bibliography*. Washington, DC: Library of Congress.

Smith, Dwight L., ed. 1975. *Era of the American Revolution: A Bibliography*. Santa Barbara, CA: ABC-Clio.

Richmond, W. Edson (1916–1994)

Folklorist, literary scholar, professor emeritus of English literature and of folklore at Indiana University. Richmond was born and raised in Nashua, New Hampshire. He earned B.A. and M.A. degrees from Miami University of Ohio and his Ph.D. from Ohio State University, where he studied under Francis Lee Utley. Initially an instructor at Ohio State, in 1945 he took a position at Indiana University and remained there until his retirement in 1986. He was acting chairman of freshman literature in 1955–1956 and acting chairman of the folklore program in 1956–1957.

Richmond received an ACLS (American Council of Learned Societies) grant to attend the Linguistics Institute at the University of Michigan. In 1952–1953, he was vice-president of the American Folklore Society. In 1953–1954, he held a Fulbright Research Professorship at Oslo, Norway, and during that time he also lectured in folklore in Salzburg, Austria. In July 1954, he was a lecturer in American culture at Oslo, and in the fall of that year he was the Indiana University delegate to the Congress of Modern Languages and Literatures in Oxford, England. He was Fulbright visiting professor of English at the University of Helsinki, Finland, in 1959–1960, and in September 1959 he was the American Folklore Society delegate to the Scandinavian Folklife and Folklore Society Research Association. He also chaired the awards committee of the Chicago Folklore Prize, and for many years he compiled the annual bibliography published by the American Folklore Society.

Richmond served as editor of *Hoosier Folklore*, later renamed *Midwest Folklore*, and of the *Journal of Folklore Research*. He also edited *Studies in Honor of Professor Stith Thompson* in 1957. His specialty was the ballad, a subject on which he compiled a major bibliography (Richmond 1989) and wrote more than twenty-five essays and nearly 100 reviews. He sustained a lifelong interest in Scandinavian ballads and folklore, and spent a great deal of his life in Sweden and Norway, studying and lecturing. In 1977 Richmond was admitted to the Norwegian Academy of Science and Letters.

In 1985 a festschrift dedicated to Edson Richmond was published, reflecting the devotion his students and colleagues felt for him. By his friends, Richmond was admired for his warmth, his charm, and his courtliness. In his private life, Richmond was a skilled yachtsman, and he served in several capacities with the Bloomington (Indiana) Yacht Club, ultimately as commodore of the club. He died on August 11, 1994, in Bloomington Hospital at age 78.

Bruce A. Rosenberg

References

Edwards, Carol L., and Kathleen E.B. Manley, eds. 1985. *Narrative Folksong: New Directions: Essays in Appreciation of W. Edson Richmond.* Boulder, CO: Westview Press.

Richmond, W. Edson. 1989. *Ballad Scholarship: An Annotated Bibliography.* New York: Garland.

Rickaby, Franz (1889–1925)

Pioneering scholar of occupational folksong. Born in Rogers, Arkansas, Rickaby was raised in Springfield, Illinois, where he distinguished himself as a poet and a musician. He received a B.A. from Knox College in Galesburg, Illinois, in 1916 and an M.A. in English literature from Harvard University in 1917. From 1917 through spring 1923, Rickaby was an instructor at the University of North Dakota. He taught subsequently at Pomona College, Claremont, California, from 1923 until 1925, when he died at thirty-five of heart failure—a consequence of rheumatic fever.

Rickaby did not study the ballad at Harvard under Francis James Child's disciple George Lyman Kittredge. Rather, work with regional arts in North Dakota and a summer job in Charlevoix, Michigan, brought familiarity with what he called a "cultural frontier" wherein ballads flourished. He developed a "comparative balladry" course in 1919 and began collecting ballads on field trips and through students. His papers reveal 243 folksongs gathered, with variants from singers in North Dakota, Minnesota, Wisconsin, and Michigan.

Rickaby's posthumous *Ballads and Songs of the Shanty-Boy*, published in 1926, includes fifty-one texts, most accompanied by tunes. His "Introduction" and notes provide our first rich glimpse of lumber-camp singers, their performance style, their ethnic diversity, and the social meaning of their songs. Rickaby's book also mentions his critical reliance on three untrained logger-folklorists (William C. Bartlett, Michael Cassius Dean, and Otto Rindlisbacher) and offers a fine sketch of ballad-maker William N. Allen (alias "Shan T. Boy"), many of whose woods poems were published in *The Hodag*.

James P. Leary

References

Bartlett, William C. 1929. *History, Tradition, and Adventure in the Chippewa Valley.* Chippewa Falls, WI: Chippewa Printery.

Dean, Michael Cassius. 1922. *The Flying Cloud, and One Hundred and Fifty Other Old Time Songs and Ballads.* Virginia, MI: Quickprint.

Greene, Daniel W. 1968. "Fiddle and I": The Story of Franz Rickaby. *Journal of American Folklore* 82:316–336.

Kearney, Lake Shore. 1928. *The Hodag and Other Tales of the Logging Camps.* Wausau, WI: Democrat Printing.

Rickaby, Franz. ca. 1925. Ballads collected by Franz Rickaby. 7 vols. In Wisconsin Music Archives, Mills Music Library, University of Wisconsin, Madison.

———. 1926. *Ballads and Songs of the Shanty-Boy.* Cambridge: Harvard University Press.

———. 1977. 1919: Franz Rickaby in the Field. In *Folksongs Out of Wisconsin,* ed. Harry Peters. Madison: State Historical Society of Wisconsin, pp. 17–22.

Rindlisbacher, Otto. 1931. *Twenty Original Reels, Jigs, and Hornpipes.* Rice Lake, WI: Rice Lake Chrontopye.

Riddle, Almeda (1898–1986)

One of the most famous Ozark folksingers of the 20th century. Riddle's widespread acclaim was largely a result of her appearance at folk festivals, a number of her commercially released recordings, and her book written in collaboration with folklorist Roger D. Abrahams. An articulate woman with an excellent memory, Riddle learned her first song, "The Blind Child's Prayer," when she was seven years old. Her father, J. L. James, was a major influence and the source of many of her songs. There were, however, other influences, the most important of whom was an uncle, John Wilkerson. Her mother and other family members and friends also contributed to her repertoire, which she estimated eventually grew to more than 600 songs. Ninety percent of these Riddle learned by age eighteen.

In 1916 Almeda married Price Riddle, and she subsequently had four children by him. A cyclone that passed through her home near Heber Springs, Arkansas, on November 25, 1926, claimed the life of her husband and youngest child. Almeda was also seriously injured, but she survived to face the rigors of raising three young children by herself during the Depression. During these trying times, she continued to sing, as she said, just to keep her sanity, and occasionally she learned new songs. This activity brought her to the attention of folksong collector John Quincy Wolf Jr., who in 1952 recorded some of her songs. A few years later, Wolf brought her to the attention of the folksong-revival audience, enabling Riddle to begin a career as a singer at folk festivals throughout the United States. During the 1960s and the early 1970s, she maintained a heavy performing schedule, but health problems eventually forced her to quit touring.

In 1970 Abrahams produced the book *A Singer and Her Songs: Almeda Riddle's Book of Ballads* based on several hours of interviews with Riddle. This volume challenged the popular stereotype of folksingers as inarticulate and illiterate rustics. The book's six chapters contain a wealth of Riddle's comments on her songs and their sources. Her repertoire ranged from Child ballads to sentimental pop songs of Tin Pan Alley. Riddle considered the Child items the classics, but this view may reflect a recognition that folklorists considered such material the most important as well. A new edition of *A Singer and Her Songs,* titled *Preserving Even the Scraps,* focusing on a broader range of Riddle's folklore genres, was compiled by Abrahams and Deborah Kodish, but to date (1995) has yet to be published. In 1983 a video, *Now Let's Talk about Singing,* dealing with Riddle's life was produced by George West. The following year, in 1984, West and W.K. McNeil issued Riddle's final album, *How Firm a Foundation and Other Traditional Hymns.* Shortly thereafter, Riddle moved into a nursing home in Heber Springs, where she died on June 30, 1986.

W.K. McNeil

Riddle Joke

Type of riddle whose *proposition* (question) serves as a setup for the punch-line answer. Some riddle jokes draw on the resources of the *riddle conundrum* in that they depend on word play (for example, "What would happen if a girl ate bullets?—She would grow *bangs*") or on sound play ("What happened when the cow jumped over the barbed wire fence?—*Utter* [udder] destruction"). *Parody riddle jokes* extend the nature of riddle-joke humor into absurdity and nonsense. Typically, they violate mainstream assumptions of what can happen in the everyday, "real" world ("What's black, sits in a tree, and is dangerous?—A crow with a machine gun"). In addition,

riddle jokes can attempt to extend the durational impact of the humor through the use of the *riddle chain*—that is, a series of two or more interactionally sequential and topically related riddles in which subsequently given riddles build upon previously given ones. An example of a riddle joke chain is: "What's red and white and sits in a corner?—A baby chewing on razor blades. What's red and green and sits in a corner?—The same baby, two weeks later."

Riddle jokes often occur in topical cycles—that is, riddle jokes exploring a single topic develop as a fad; eventually, interest in that set of jokes declines, and the set is subordinated to, or replaced by, the next (and newer) joke fad. For instance, *little moron jokes* became popular in the 1940s and 1950s ("Why did the little moron tiptoe past the medicine cabinet?—He didn't want to wake the sleeping pills"). After World War II, *Polack jokes* surfaced. In their initial versions, they served as satiric commentary on the Polish army's ineffective defense of its homeland against invading Nazi forces in 1939 ("How do you tell a veteran Polish soldier from a rookie?—By the bullet holes"). By the 1960s, Polack-joke topics had broadened beyond the historical and had come to replace little moron jokes. Polack jokes then became the most frequently employed riddle-joke means for portraying stereotypically inept characters.

Various joke cycles have developed over the years. One cycle, popular during the 1970s, considered the nonsensical activities of fruits. There were, for instance, *banana jokes* ("What's yellow and goes click-click?—A ballpoint banana") as well as *grape jokes* ("What's purple and conquers continents?—Alexander the Grape"). Some of the cycles current in recent years have focused on *celebrities* such as the popular singer Dolly Parton, who is also known for her well-endowed bustline ("Why are Dolly Parton's feet so small?—Nothing grows in the shade"), on natural as well as human-made *disasters* ("What's 12–8–12?—The measurements of Miss Ethiopia" [referring to the 1980s Ethiopian drought and resulting famine], and "Have you heard the weather forecast for Kiev?—A high of 9,000 degrees and cloudy" [referring to the 1986 nuclear plant disaster in the Chernobyl-Kiev region of the USSR]), and on incurable *medical conditions* ("Do you know why all the alligators in Florida are dying?—They've got gator–AIDS" or "What's one advantage of [having] Alzheimer's? [The condition eventually results in severe memory loss and disorientation.]—You keep on meeting new people").

Typically, *ethnic riddle jokes* attribute a ludicrous and socially inappropriate trait to the ethnic group allegedly about whom the joke is told. The word "allegedly" is important because with many ethnic joke formulas—for instance, "How do you tell the bride at a(n) ——— wedding?"—the ethnic name "slot" in the riddle question can be filled with a reference to any one of a number of different ethnic groups ("How do you tell the bride at an Irish wedding?" or "How do you tell the bride at a Polack wedding?"). In each case, the answer—"She's the one in the maternity dress"—remains the same. Ethnic riddle jokes may accuse the target group of, for instance, physical dirtiness ("Why don't they allow Italians to swim in the Hudson River?—They would leave a [dirty] ring on the shoreline"), the inappropriate management of body apertures ("How do you break a Polack's finger?—Hit him in the nose"), spousal abuse ("What's an Irish theater party?—Watching a neighbor beat up his wife") or "uncivilized" food practices ("What happens to the garbage in Italian restaurants?—They serve it in Puerto Rican restaurants").

Christie Davies has reported that, around the world, the most frequently told type of ethnic joke is that which attributes the qualities of stupidity, ineptness, and/or ignorance to some target group (Davies 1990). An example is: "How many Polacks does it take to pull off a kidnapping?—Six. One to kidnap the kid and five to write the note." According to Davies, the 20th century's emphasis on the acquisition of information (particularly of specialized knowledge), coupled with conditions of rapid social and economic change, have fostered people's anxieties concerning what they do not know about the world around them. Jokes emphasizing *other people's* stupidity, Davies has suggested, may reflect and partly assuage those anxieties. Furthermore, feelings of superiority or of concern regarding others' ineptness may become especially focused if an allegedly inept group leader or group is viewed as having considerable influence on people's lives. This is illustrated in *Polish Pope jokes* told about a supposedly simpleminded Pope John Paul II ("What does TGIF on the Pope's slippers mean?—Toes Go in First") and in jokes about NASA's technological failings with respect to the *Challenger space shuttle* (which exploded in flight in January 1986, killing all seven aboard) ("What does NASA stand for?—Need Another Seven Astronauts"). Within the *Challenger* cycle, some jokes allege teacher and crew member Christa McAuliffe's incompetence as an astronaut. This incompetence was presumably due to her naiveté as a civilian and to her supposedly inherent weaknesses as a woman ("What were the last words of the [shuttle's] commander?—'Not that button, bitch!'"). Regional riddle jokes can also attribute to targeted groups the qualities of stupidity ("What happened when the smart Okies [residents of Oklahoma] moved to California?—It lowered the IQ of both states") or of cultural backwardness ("Do you know why they had to drop the teaching of drivers' education at Tech [Virginia Polytechnic Institute] this year?—The mule died").

The United States is not the only country whose citizens tell ethnic riddle jokes. For example, the following was told by Belgians about the Flemish (an ethnic group in Belgium): "Why did the Americans have the Negroes and the Belgians have the Flemish?—Because the Americans had first choice." Related to the ethnic joke is the *international slur (blason populaire)*, a derisive joke (or other insult) that the citizens of one country tell about the citizens of another country. One example is the Belgian joke given above. In addition to poking fun at the ethnic Flemish, it also manages to insult the residents of another country (African Americans). Another example is a joke that Americans have told about the residents of Mexico, allegedly all of whom want to enter the United States as illegal immigrants: "Why aren't there any swimming pools in Mexico?—Because everyone who could swim [across the river separating the two countries] is in the United States."

Simon J. Bronner has summarized various folklorists' hypotheses as to why certain riddle-joke cycles developed in particular sociopolitical and/or socioeconomic environments (Bronner 1988). Roger D. Abrahams and Alan Dundes (in Dundes 1987) have speculated, for example, that the *elephant riddles* of the 1960s developed among European Americans as a tension–releasing response to African Americans' involvement in the civil rights movement. Abrahams and Dundes point to the metaphoric awkwardness of a large, powerful, dark-colored animal from the jungle—that is, the riddle-joke elephant (representing African Americans)—as it tries to fit into "civilized" society (that is, a society dominated by European Americans). An example emphasizing the idea of "fitting in" is: "What is harder than getting a pregnant elephant into a Volkswagon?—Getting an elephant pregnant in a Volkswagon." In addition, such jokes can suggest defensive measures to be taken against the elephant: "How do you keep an elephant from charging?—Take away his credit card."

Secondly, one hypothesis about the *dead-baby jokes* of the 1960s and 1970s suggests that they arose as a response to the brutality of the Vietnam War, during which assumptions about the sanctity of life were severely tested. Typically, dead-baby jokes consider ways in which babies can die ("What's blue and sits in the corner?—A baby in a [plastic, food-storage] Baggie") as well as ways in which the bodies can be disposed of ("What is easier to unload: a truckload of dead babies or a truckload of bowling balls?—A truckload of dead babies because you can use a pitchfork"). A related hypothesis emphasizing the sanctity-of-life theme associates dead-baby jokes with concern over contraception and the abortion rights movement.

Thirdly, the proliferation of *lightbulb jokes,* from the late 1960s into the 1980s, has been associated with that era's increasing reliance on technology, with people's growing concern over energy shortages, and with people's increased awareness of (and sometimes lack of patience concerning) the special interests claimed by a variety of regional-, ethnic-, and gender-based groups as well as by foreign groups whose activities have impacted upon Americans. Examples of lightbulb jokes that comment humorously on special-interest groups include the following:

> How many Californians does it take to change a lightbulb?—Six. One to screw the bulb in, and five to share the experience.

> How many JAPs (Jewish American Princesses) does it take to change a lightbulb?—Two. One to call her father, and the other to open a can of Diet Pepsi.

> How many gay men does it take to change a lightbulb?—Five. One to screw in the Art Deco lightbulb, and four to stand back and yell, "Fabulous!"

> How many Iranians does it take to change a lightbulb?—One hundred. One to screw the bulb in, and ninety-nine

to hold the house hostage [referring to the period in 1979–1980 during which Americans were held hostage in the American Embassy in Iran].

Finally, some folklorists have linked riddle jokes about sensational murders and disasters to people's possible disgust with media reports of those events. In Willie Smyth's opinion, media presentations exploit viewers' emotional reactions to such events while, at the same time, promoting the media's and corporate America's own interests through product commericals (Smyth 1986). The folk response to this manipulation, it seems, comes in the form of riddle jokes that propose their own uncomfortable connections between death, disaster, and commercialized product, for example:

Why should (assassinated Prime Minister of India) Indira Gandhi have changed her deodorant?—Because her Right Guard couldn't protect her.

Why do they drink Pepsi at NASA?—Because they can't get 7-Up (that is, seven astronauts up).

Danielle M. Roemer

References

Bronner, Simon J., comp. and ed. 1988. *American Children's Folklore.* annotated ed. Little Rock, AR: August House.

Davies, Christie. 1990. *Ethnic Humor around the World: A Comparative Analysis.* Bloomington: Indiana University Press.

Dundes, Alan. 1987. *Cracking Jokes: Studies of Sick Humor Cycles and Stereotypes.* Berkeley: Ten Speed.

Smyth, Willie. 1986. Challenger Jokes and the Humor of Disaster. *Western Folklore* 45:243–260.

See also Disaster Folklore; Humor; Jokes

Riddles and Puzzles

Riddle: A type of enigmatic interrogative routine characterized by a *proposition* (that is, an implied or stated question), posed by the *riddler* (the initiating participant). The proposition is intended to call forth a reply from the *respondent* (the riddler's coparticipant). The respondent's reply is verbal and is oriented toward the proposition's solution. Roger D. Abrahams and Alan Dundes have noted that riddles are "framed with the purpose of confusing or testing the wits of those who do not know the answer" (Abrahams and Dundes 1972:130). The basic interactional unit of riddling is the *riddle act*, which consists of all of the interactional moves involved in posing, responding to, and providing the answer to a riddle proposition. Riddle-act organization can vary depending on the traditions of the culture or group involved as well as on the situational circumstances of the particular riddling encounter. However, the following sequence of moves appears to be typical: (1) the riddle-act invitation (for example, "I've got one"); (2) the riddler's proposition ("What goes up when the rain comes down?"); (3) the

respondent's initial response (offering a guess); (4) any riddler–respondent interaction during the contemplation period (requests for, and the supplying of, hints), and (5) the riddle answer sequence (which includes the supplying of an answer [such as "Your umbrella"] and confirmations of, or challenges to, that answer as the "correct" solution).

Riddles of various kinds are widespread across the world and throughout history. Generally speaking, they are traditional within the cultural group in which they are used. Charles Francis Potter has discussed riddles from historical and comparativist perspectives (Potter 1972). The present discussion surveys some of the situational and interactional contexts of riddling, common rhetorical strategies found in English-language riddles, some of the types of riddles, and some of the ways in which riddles have been studied.

Situational and interactional contexts as well as the appropriate personnel of riddling vary according to cultural and group values. However, the social situations in which riddles are told often develop as *riddle sessions* (a type of social interaction consisting of a series of riddles, possibly interspersed with other performative and/or conversational material). Some riddle sessions are restricted to adult riddlers and respondents (though it does appear that adult riddling is relatively rare in mainstream American society). In "The Turtles'" initiation rite, which is often conducted in bars and other public drinking areas, a previously initiated Turtle member (often male) asks a potential respondent (often female): "Are you a Turtle?" If the respondent does not give the appropriate ritual response (which is "You bet your sweet ass I am!"), the respondent is expected either to buy the riddler a drink or to submit to the asking of four potentially embarrassing riddles: (1) "What is it a man can do standing, a woman sitting down, and a dog on three legs?—Shake hands"; (2) "What is it a cow has four of and a woman has only two of?—Legs"; (3) "What is a four-letter word ending in *K* that means the same as intercourse?—Talk"; and (4) "What is it on a man that is round, hard, and sticks so far out of his pajamas you can hang a hat on it?—His head." In contrast, riddling in other types of session can involve both adults and youngsters.

In *pedagogic riddling,* the adult takes on the role of teacher; the child, the role of student. For example, in some Ozark mountain homes of the 1930s, parents regarded children's "workin' out [the answers to] riddles" as an appropriate intellectual discipline. For its part, adult-child *leisure-time riddling* (during which riddling is pursued primarily or ostensibly for entertainment) can develop between parents and youngsters as a way of relieving monotony—for instance, during long car trips or in the home during the joint execution of household chores. Finally, leisure-time sessions can be restricted to children only. This may be the most frequently occurring type of riddling interaction in the United States in the late 20th century. Children's riddling can develop on the playground during recess, in the cafeteria at lunchtime, on the school bus, or in neighborhood backyards. Because adult supervision in these areas is typically distant enough to permit children's peer-group interests to hold sway, youngsters often engage in what

John Holmes McDowell has called *contentious riddling*—that is, riddling in which participants are verbally aggressive, take liberties with one another, and repeatedly test each other's social competence (McDowell 1979). These sessions can be organizationally diffuse as the children variously engage in riddling per se, knock-knock routines, narratives, songs, name-calling, obscenities, and a variety of victimization procedures.

In their phrasing, riddles point to some of the interpretive work the respondent is expected to do. At a basic level, this work involves the respondent's coping with a riddle's use of one or more common rhetorical strategies. *Verbal riddles* employing *description* present information about the appearance, qualities, activities, or nature of some entity, phenomenon, or event ("What has teeth but no mouth?—A comb"). Descriptive propositions are also found in the *word charade,* a riddle whose proposition divides the answer *as a word* into syllables and gives a description of each:

> My first drives a horse,
> My second is needy,
> My third is a nickname,
> My whole is a bird.
> Answer—Whip-poor-will.

As a second strategy, riddles can depend on the use of either *comparison* ("Why is an alligator like a sheet of music?—Because they both have scales") or *contrast* ("What's the difference between a flea and an elephant?—An elephant can have fleas, but a flea can't have elephants"). A third strategy is that of *narration.* In the following, the riddle proposition and its answer each tell small stories:

> Whitey saw Whitey in Whitey.
> Whitey sent Whitey to drive Whitey out of Whitey.
> Answer—Mr. White sent a white dog to drive a white
>   cow out of his cotton field.

Fourth, riddles using definition fall into at least three groups: (1) riddles that ask for a definition ("What's the definition of a skeleton?—A striptease gone too far"); (2) riddles that involve negative definition—that is, the proposition identifies a category (such as doors, but then immediately indicates that category's inefficiency relative to a particular member ("When is a door not a door?—When it's a jar [ajar]"; and (3) riddles whose proposition provides a definition and asks for the defined term ("What kind of bow can you never tie?— A rainbow"). The two *nonverbal riddle* types summarized here rely on the strategy of description. *Gestural riddles* often depend on gestural description as part of their proposition: ("Hold your hands over your head, wriggle your fingers, and ask, 'What's this?'— A midget playing a piano").

Visual descriptive riddles (called droodles in the 1950s) use a hand-drawn sketch as the descriptive segment of their proposition. For example, consider this sketch, which would be accompanied by the riddler's asking, "What is it?":

The answer is "A ship arriving too late to save a drowning witch."

Riddle types have also been distinguished in terms of expectations about their difficulty of solution. Generally speaking, folklorists have called riddles "true" if their answers can be reasoned out, based on information supplied in the riddle proposition and on the respondent's adequate experience with, and recall of, tropes, symbols, and other relevant conventions shared within the particular culture. In terms of rhetorical strategies, the *true riddle* employs description and comparison. In the following true riddle, the proposition describes a stronghold containing gold. The answer makes possible a comparison between the stronghold, the gold, and an egg:

> In marble walls as white as milk,
> Lined with skin as soft as silk,
> Within a crystal fountain clear,
> A golden apple doth appear.
> No doors there are to this stronghold
> Yet thieves break in to steal the gold.
> Answer—An egg.

True riddles have garnered extensive attention in literature (for example, Taylor 1951). In contrast, the answers to other types of riddle are usually regarded as somewhat to very arbitrary. At the "somewhat arbitrary" end of the spectrum is the *conundrum*—that is, a riddle based on punning or on other word play. The punning may occur in the proposition ("What has four wheels and *flies?*—A garbage truck") or in the answer ("What kind of money do people eat?—*Dough*"). In the relatively arbitrary *riddle joke,* the proposition serves as a setup for the punch-line answer ("What's tall and says 'eef eif eof muf'?—A backward giant" or "How do you confuse a Polack?—Put him in a round room and ask him to stand in the corner"). Riddle jokes often run in topical cycles (such as *dead-baby jokes* or *dumb-blond jokes)* and, through stereotyping, may poke fun at a specific ethnic group (as in *Polack jokes)* or at a group with a particular medical condition (as in *AIDS jokes* or *Alzheimer's disease jokes). Parody riddle jokes* extend the humor and arbitrariness of riddle jokes into absurdity and nonsense. What marks them as extensions is the degree of violence they do to mainstream assumptions of what can happen in the everyday, "real" world ("Why do elephants have flat feet?—From jumping out of palm trees").

In *catch riddles,* the proposition sets up the respondent for some sort of victimization. For example, the catch riddle:

> A: What's red, purple, green, yellow, gray, sky-blue, and green?
> B: I don't know.
> A: I don't know either, that's why I'm asking you.

tries to "catch" the respondent in the conventional assumption that riddlers already know the answer to the riddle propositions they pose. In the type of catch riddle known as the *pretended obscene riddle,* the riddler tries to prompt the respondent into saying (or at least thinking) about something sexual or otherwise risqué ("What word starts with *F* and ends with *CK*?—Firetruck"). For their part, the answers to gestural riddles and to visual descriptive riddles are usually difficult to guess. Because there exist no widely accepted systems for interpreting either gestures or individual graphic lines, squiggles, or dots, answers in both of these riddle types are typically quite arbitrary. For example, in addition to the answer ("A ship arriving too late to save a drowning witch") given with the visual riddle sketch presented above, that sketch can also be described by the answer "A woman sitting down with her legs crossed."

Riddles can be studied in a variety of ways. Some studies have considered riddles' use of the *riddle block*—that is, those aspects of the riddle that interfere with the flow of information, thereby complicating the respondent's attempts to figure out the answer. Abrahams (as summarized in Abrahams and Dundes 1972) has given four techniques by which the image (or *Gestalt*) offered by the proposition can be impaired:

1. Opposition: The component parts of the presented image do not harmonize ("What has eyes but cannot see?—A potato").
2. Incomplete detail: Not enough information is given for the provided image parts to fit together in a recognizable image ("What is white, then green, then red?—A berry growing").
3. Too much detail: Inconsequential details bury the important traits, or misleading information diverts attention from them ("As I was crossing London Bridge, I met a man who tipped his hat and drew his cane, and now I gave you his name. What is it?—Andrew Cane").
4. False image: The details provided suggest an obvious answer; however, that answer is not only "wrong" but is also possibly "off-color" and, therefore, embarrassing (as in pretended obscene riddles such as "What's long and hard and contains semen [seamen]?—A submarine").

W.J. Pepicello and Thomas A. Green have considered various riddle blocks that foster different kinds of ambiguity (Pepicello and Green 1984), including *linguistic ambiguity* and *metaphoric ambiguity.* Linguistic ambiguity yields multiple linguistically based meanings for an utterance. An example, based on aspects of phonology (the intonational stress and pauses between words) is found in the riddle "What bird is lowest in spirits?—A bluebird," which exploits the meaning of "bluebird" (a species of bird) and the meaning of a "*blue* bird" (an emotionally sad bird). Metaphoric ambiguity fosters multiple metaphorically based frames of reference. An example is found in the riddle "There is something with a heart in its head.—A peach" in that the primary metaphor *heart* refers both to the bodily organ known as a heart and to a fruit pit that is shaped like the bodily organ.

Riddling has been considered in terms of its structure of context, which David Evans (in Köngäs-Maranda 1976) has discussed as the structuring of a session not only in terms of the interactional relationships emergent among its participants, but also in terms of the developed interrelationships obtaining among the riddles presented (as in riddle sequencing). Riddling has also been approached in terms of the functions it serves for its participants. McDowell, for example, has pointed to various socialization functions served in children's riddling (such as youngsters' acquisition of an artistic competence, their augmentation of sociability and interactional skills, and their exercise of skills concerning the assertion of self) (McDowell 1979). The final area of research to be mentioned here concerns children's developmental acquisition of competence in riddling. Richard Bauman and McDowell provide useful analyses of acquisition parameters, including discussions of children's made-up riddle routines (Bauman 1977; McDowell 1979).

Puzzle: A type of enigmatic interrogative routine characterized by a *proposition* (consisting of, or including, a question) that describes a problem. The *puzzler* (the initiating participant) offers the proposition, which is intended to call forth a reply from the *respondent.* This reply, which may be verbal or behavioral, is oriented toward the problem's solution. Puzzles tend to be traditional within the culture or group in which they are used. Unfortunately, there has been little analytic work done on puzzles, particularly in either distinguishing them from riddles or in arguing in detail that they are indeed a subset of riddles. As treated here, puzzles are interactional forms. As such, *puzzle-act* organization is analogous to riddle-act organization.

Abrahams and Dundes have suggested that there are two major teleological categories of puzzle: (1) puzzles whose proposition presents a problem and then asks for its solution, and (2) puzzles whose proposition presents a problem *as well as* its solution and then asks how that solution was derived (Abrahams and Dundes 1972). An example of the first category—puzzles that offer a problem and request its solution—is the following *narrative puzzle:*

> Two boys, each weighing 100 pounds, and their father, weighing 200 pounds, wanted to cross the river in a boat that could carry only 200 pounds at a time. How did they accomplish this? Answer—The two boys go across and one boy brings back the boat to his father. The father goes

across, and the boy that was left brings back the boat to the boy on the other side. Then both boys cross over and join their father.

Another member of this category is the *genealogical puzzle:*

> Brothers and sisters have I none,
> But that man's father is my father's son.
> Who is he?
> Answer—The speaker's [I's] son.

Also included are various *pencil-and-paper puzzles.* In this example, the proposition is verbal, but the solution is to be rendered graphically:

> How can you get ten horses into nine stalls in a barn? (You can't squeeze two horses into one stall.)

| T | E | N | H | O | R | S | E | S |

Another type of pencil-and-paper puzzle is the *rebus,* a graphically rendered puzzle that, according to a dictionary definition, represents "words or syllables by pictures of objects or by symbols whose names resemble the intended words or syllables in sound" (cited in Preston 1982:110). Rebus inscriptions may also indicate meaning through the strategic use of spatial relationships as well as through type styles and sizes and occasionally through color graphics. The puzzler presents the respondent with an inscription and asks a question such as "What does it say?" The respondent's task is to "read" the inscription. *Literal rebuses* emphasize the use of conventional graphic symbols for the rendering of language (such as the letters of the alphabet):

SOMEWHERE
RAINBOW

"Somewhere over the rainbow"

WOWOLFOL

"A wolf in sheeps clothing"

Pictorial rebuses emphasize the use of pictures:

"Read (reed) between the lines"

"Pointer Sisters"

Rebuses often challenge the conventions of written language by finding alternate ways of representing meaning. For example, three of the rebuses given above employ spatial relationships to suggest the meaning of prepositions: the word "somewhere" is placed over the word "rainbow"; the word "wolf" is located with*in* the word "wool"; and a picture of a reed is placed *between* two vertical lines. The puzzle "Pointer Sisters" is a hybrid of literal and pictorial rebus traits in that the word "sisters" is rendered alphabetically but in a typographic style with varying letter sizes that suggests the pictorial shape of an arrow (that is, a pointer). Some rebuses are based in special knowledge. Recognizing that the chemical symbols $HCCl_3$ stands for chloroform, for instance, facilitates one's figuring out that the answer "Maidenform" goes with this inscription:

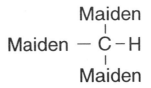

As mentioned above, the second major category of puzzles involves those whose proposition gives both a problem and its solution and then asks how that solution was derived. An example is the *coin puzzle* (a puzzle based on a knowledge of currency values) ("How can you change a dollar into exactly fifty coins?—Forty pennies, eight nickels, two dimes"). Here, the proposition gives the solution in that it indicates "that some combination of coins makes a total of fifty possible, the [challenge] being which coins?" (Abrahams and Dundes 1972:138). Another example is the *detective-story puzzle,* whose proposition describes the conclusion of a murder mystery and then asks how it was solved—specifically in the case below, how the man behind the counter knew whom to tell the police to arrest:

> A man standing behind a counter reads in the newspaper that some woman has been killed in Switzerland in a fall down a mountain. He immediately calls up the police and tells them to arrest the husband. Why?—He is an airline agent. The week before, he had sold this man two tickets to Switzerland, one one-way and one round-trip.

Finally, folklorists have identified certain types of puzzles in terms of the particular knowledge frame on which the puzzles draw. Such *special-knowledge puzzles* include genealogical and coin puzzles as well as chemical rebuses (all illustrated above). Another type is the *geographical puzzle:*

> A family built a big square house with each side facing south. A big bear wandered by. What color was the bear?—The house was built at the North Pole. That is the only place on Earth where each side would face south. The only bears in that region are polar bears. So the bear was white.

Still another is the *arithmetic puzzle* ("If a chicken and a half

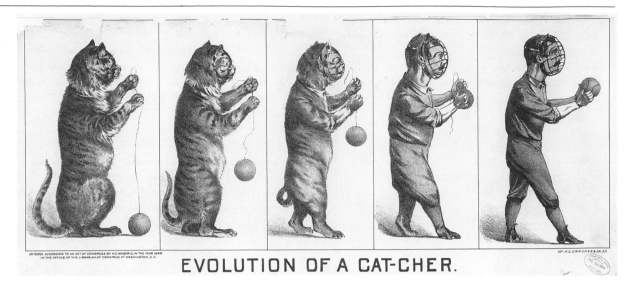

EVOLUTION OF A CAT-CHER.

could lay an egg and a half in a day and a half, how long would it take five chickens to lay five eggs?—One day." As might be the case with puzzles of any sort, the arithmetic puzzle is vulnerable to reframing as a *puzzle catch*.

> A: If it takes a woodpecker eight months to peck a 4-inch hole in a tree, how long would it take a grasshopper to kick all of the seeds out of a pickle 7 inches long and 3 inches thick?
> B: I don't know.
> A: I don't know either, that's why I'm asking you.

Danielle M. Roemer

References

Abrahams, Roger D., and Alan Dundes. 1972. Riddles. In *Folklore and Folklife,* ed. Richard M. Dorson. Chicago, IL: University of Chicago Press, pp. 129–143.

Bauman, Richard. 1977. Linguistics, Anthropology, and Verbal Art, with a Special Discussion of Children's Folklore. In *Linguistics and Anthropology,* ed. Muriel Saville-Troike. Washington, DC: Georgetown University Press, pp. 13–36.

Köngäs-Maranda, Elli, ed. 1976. *Riddles and Riddling. Journal of American Folklore.* (Special Issue) 89:127–265.

McDowell, John Holmes. 1979. *Children's Riddling.* Bloomington: Indiana University Press.

Pepicello, W.J., and Thomas A. Green. 1984. *The Language of Riddles.* Columbus: Ohio State University Press.

Potter, Charles Francis. [1949] 1972. Riddles. In *Funk and Wagnalls Standard Dictionary of Folklore, Mythology, and Legend,* ed. Maria Leach. New York: Funk and Wagnalls, pp. 938–944.

Preston, Michael J. 1982. The English Literal Rebus and the Graphic Riddle Tradition. *Western Folklore.* 41:104–1381.

Taylor, Archer. 1951. *English Riddles from Oral Tradition.* Berkeley: University of California Press.

See also Riddle Joke

Rinzler, Ralph Carter (1934–1994)

Musician; producer of concerts, recordings, and documentary films; a scholar, patron of traditional crafts, and the founding director of the Smithsonian Institution's Festival of American Folklife. Rinzler also founded the Office of Folklife programs and served as an assistant secretary at the Smithsonian.

Rinzler came to the Smithsonian to develop his plan for a living cultural presentation of folk and working-class community-based culture under then Secretary S. Dillon Ripley and James Morris. The Festival of American Folklife on the National Mall was largely Rinzler's creation in 1967, and its immediate success established a national commitment to the public presentation of folk cultural traditions. The popular festival grew to become the centerpiece of the 1976 U.S. Bicentennial and continues into the present. Rinzler's work on the festival involved hundreds of scholars, community artists, and cultural exemplars of every background from across the nation and the globe and inspired many to research and present their cultures in public settings. Alan Lomax, Bess Lomax Hawes, Roger D. Abrahams, Bernice Reagon, Henry Glassie, and Archie Green were some of the many activist, academic, and artistic colleagues in this effort.

As the Smithsonian's assistant secretary for public service from 1983 to 1990, Rinzler encouraged the cultural diversification of the Smithsonian in staffing, collections, exhibits, and programs. He established the Cultural Education Committee and the Committee for a Wider Audience, and he continued to bring into the Smithsonian many professionals from minority communities. Rinzler was also an innovator in the use of sophisticated technology to disseminate information from the Smithsonian collections. He founded the National Demonstration Laboratory and encouraged the development of digital media products that could reach a broad public.

Rinzler first explored the study of culture at Swarthmore College and later at the Sorbonne in Paris. His interest in folk music grew from exposure to Library of Congress recordings and the work of the Lomaxes, Charles Seeger, and Albert Lloyd. Rinzler traveled to many university folk festivals and mastered folk styles on several stringed instruments, including the mandolin. He was a member of the Greenbrier Boys, a bluegrass group of the folk revival with whom he toured and recorded. Rinzler was one of many musician-scholars at the time who were attracted to Woody Guthrie, and who worked on Folkways Records. He worked closely with Bob Dylan, Joan Baez, and Mary Travers in a variety of roles. As he became more knowledgeable about the roots of folk music, he recorded and then for some time managed the careers of Arthel "Doc" Watson and Bill Monroe. During the 1960s, he did considerable fieldwork on traditional folk music, traversing the country, recording numerous musicians, including Cajun fiddler Dewey Balfa, and bringing them to the Newport Folk Festival. It was during this time that Rinzler developed the model of a research-based presentation of culture and saw the positive effect of exposing traditional music to broader audiences. Though he himself stopped performing professionally once he was at the Smithsonian, Rinzler played the mandolin and banjo at home or at his beloved Naushon, Massachusetts, island retreat with Pete Seeger, Charlie Sayles, Mike Seeger, Hazel Dickens, David Grisman, Johnny Hartford, and numerous others.

Rinzler led the Smithsonian to acquire Folkways Records from Moses Asch in 1987, a move that enabled not only the preservation of the collection, but also the continued production of new recordings. The viability of Smithsonian/Folkways and a dynamic approach to the distribution of a museum collection was assured with the financial and critical success of *Folkways: A Vision Shared,* an album for which Rinzler won a Grammy Award in 1988 as coproducer. He also performed with Taj Mahal on the album and in a video of the same name which was nominated for an Ace Award in 1989. Rinzler produced several other recordings on the new Smithsonian/Folkways label, including the Grammy-nominated *Roots of Rhythm and Blues* (jointly with Columbia Records) that was based on a program he cocurated at the 1991 Festival of American Folklife with Worth Long. Other releases included a documentary compact disc (CD) on the Watson family, two CDs of his 1956–1969 recordings of Bill Monroe, and a two-volume CD that expands the Folkways release of recordings he made at the home of old-time musician Clarence Ashley. The latter includes the first recordings made of Doc Watson. At his death, Rinzler was working on a three-volume expansion of Harry Smith's seminal *Anthology of American Folk Music,* first published in 1952. Rinzler also produced a five-part series of Folkways instructional videos on folk music taught by master traditional musicians.

Rinzler's interest in contemporary traditional crafts led him to a long-term association with American potters in the Southeast. Through scholarship, museum exhibition, and other forms of support, he strove to help them continue to practice their craft. He led efforts to make *Raised in Clay* a successful Smithsonian Institution exhibition that toured the United States. With Nancy Sweezy and John Kenneth Galbraith, he helped revitalize the Jugtown pottery in Seagrove, North Carolina, which was still in production in 1995. He produced a film titled *The Meaders Family, North Georgia Potters,* and, in collaboration with Robert Sayers, he wrote a monograph of the same title. The same collaboration produced a monograph and Cine Golden Award-winning film on *The Korean Onggi Potter.*

Rinzler was a member of several professional societies, a lifelong member and a Fellow of the American Folklore Society. He also served on the White House Task Force for Music in Education. He was an active member (1976–1981) and vice chair of the U.S. National Commission to UNESCO (United Nations Educational, Scientific, and Cultural Organization). Rinzler maintained collegial relationships with scholars, administrators, and cultural activists in many parts of the world, and he was a longtime board member of many organizations, including the Highlander Center.

Rinzler won many awards, including Washingtonian of the Year. He was awarded the Smithsonian Secretary's Gold Medal in 1993 for developing the Festival of American Folklife as a paradigm of modern museum practice, which combines humanistic scholarship, community service, grass-roots arts advocacy, and high-quality public education.

Richard Kurin

Ritchie, Jean (1922–)

Folksinger, folksong collector, and composer. The youngest of fourteen children in a farming family near Viper, Kentucky, Ritchie was educated like the others at the Hindman Settlement School. There educators collected and taught ballads as part of primary education. Her older sister Edna had, in fact, sung ballads for Cecil Sharp during his 1916 visit to the school. Moving later to the Viper public high school and then to Cumberland College, Jean Ritchie became a social worker and used ballads as part of her work in New York City's Henry Street Settlement.

Her singing came to folklorists' attention in 1946, when she attended the Renfro Valley Folk Festival in Kentucky and met Artus Moser, then on a collecting trip for the Library of Congress. He recorded her versions of "Father Grumble" and "Lord Bateman," among others, and when these ballads were released the following year on 78-rpm records she found herself in demand for folk concerts at New York University. By 1950 she had recorded her first LP, and in 1952 she won a Fulbright grant to collect folksongs in the British Isles. Her well-known autobiography and song anthology, *Singing Family of the Cumberlands* (1955), appeared soon after.

Her upbringing and Hindman education made Ritchie familiar with the performance style of the unaccompanied ballad, but because she trained her voice during her college days she was able to modify the hard-edged native-ballad sound to a sweeter style more acceptable to urban audiences. Between her family's store and her own fieldwork, she developed a huge repertoire, and by the start of the 1960s folk-revival movement she was acknowledged to be one of the foremost, and most authentic, interpreters of folk ballads.

The wife of filmmaker George Pickow, she participated in many films and sound recordings documenting Appalachian ballads, folksongs, and singing folk games. She also composed a number of original songs, of which "Black Waters," a protest of water pollution caused by strip mining, is the best known.

Bill Ellis

References

Bronson, Bertrand H., ed. 1960. *Child Ballads Traditional in the United States.* AAFS L57. Washington DC: Library of Congress. Sound Recording.

Emrich, Duncan, ed. 1947. *Anglo-American Songs and Ballads.* AAFS L21. Washington DC: Library of Congress. Sound Recording.

Ritchie, Jean. 1958. *The Ritchie Family of Kentucky.* Folkways Records FA 2316.

———. 1961. *British Traditional Ballads [Child Ballads] in the Southern Mountains,* ed. Kenneth A. Goldstein. Folkways Records. FA 2301–02.

———. 1965. *Folk Songs of the Southern Appalachians.* New York: Oak Publications.

———. 1977. *None But One.* ABC Records. SK7530.

Whisnant, David E. 1983. *All That Is Native and Fine: The Politics of Culture in an American Region.* Chapel Hill: University of North Carolina Press.

Robb, John Donald (1892–1989)

Composer, educator, and student of folk music who contributed substantively to support for folkloristics in New Mexico. Born in Minneapolis in 1892, Robb attended Yale University, graduating in 1915. After teaching in China and serving in the armed forces during World War I, he attended Harvard Law School. While practicing law in New York from 1922 to 1941, he continued his studies in musical composition. Robb left the law to become professor of music and chair of the music department at the University of New Mexico in 1941. He was named acting dean of the College of Fine Arts in 1942 and dean in 1946, a position he held until his retirement in 1957. His musical mentors included Roy Harris, Paul Hindemith, Darius Milhaud, and Horatio Parker. His more than 200 compositions include solo instrumental, vocal, chamber, and symphonic works in addition to operas, musicals, dances, and electronic recordings. A number of his compositions are based on folk music. Robb received numerous awards for his compositions and scholarship.

Upon his arrival in New Mexico, Robb was fascinated by Native American, Hispanic, and Anglo American folk music. Moved by romantic notions of the "disappearance" of such traditions, he conducted extensive fieldwork throughout the state, initially using wire recorders. He also recorded folk music during his travels to Latin America, Nepal, Japan, and elsewhere. His collection, which contains more than 3,000 items, is housed in the John Donald Robb Archive of Southwestern Music in the Fine Arts Library at the University of New Mexico in Albuquerque; it has been used extensively by scholars. While his writings include articles that focus on a wide range of New Mexican music and dance forms, his two books are centered on Hispanic folksong. While *Hispanic Folk Songs of New Mexico* (1954) is a short collection of songs with commentary, his *Hispanic Folk Music of New Mexico and the Southwest: A Self Portrait of a People* (1980) is a monumental work that provides systematic documentation and analysis of a wide range of musical genres.

Robb was an early and tireless promoter of the study of folklore in New Mexico. In addition to his efforts to secure institutional support for folklore research and teaching at the University of New Mexico, he was founding member and president of the New Mexico Folklore Society, and he played a key role in organizing annual meetings and in the publication of the *New Mexico Folklore Record.*

Charles L. Briggs

Roberts, Leonard Ward (1912–1983)

Collector of Appalachian tales, ballads, legends, and family traditions. Roberts was born in a log house on Toler Creek, Floyd County, Kentucky, the seventh of eleven children. At the age of eighteen, when he enlisted in the U.S. Army, he had completed one year of high school. He returned home from three years in Hawaii, completed high school in two years, and enrolled at Berea College, where he set a state record for the javelin throw. Eager to become a novelist like Jesse Stuart, he accepted an unsolicited scholarship to the Iowa Writer's Workshop, offered apparently upon the recommendation of his college roommate Lawrence Edward Bowling, already enrolled in the program. His M.A. thesis was a novel with autobiographical elements, about a teacher in eastern Kentucky. At Iowa he studied Shakespeare and Milton under Visiting Professor Hardin Craig, who invited him to the University of North Carolina, an invitation he was able to accept when his teaching for the Army took him to Chapel Hill in 1944. There he seems to have met Stith Thompson and William Hugh Jansen, both then at Indiana University.

He enrolled at Indiana in 1948 and followed Jansen to Kentucky the next year. His 1953 dissertation, published in 1955 as *South from Hell-fer-Sartin: Kentucky Mountain Folktales,* established him as the leading American *Märchen* (fairy tale) and folktale collector. This book was followed by *Old Greasybeard: Tales from the Cumberland Gap* (1969), his collection of ballads and folksongs titled *In the Pine* (1978), and the monumental *Sang Branch Settlers: Folksongs and Tales of a Kentucky Mountain Family* (1974). In the latter work, which documented the oral history, folklife, and interconnected traditions of the Couch family of Hardin County, Roberts anticipated the focus on acquisition, performance, and context found in the next generation of American folklife scholars. His massive legend collection, unpublished because he had not yet decided how to organize the material and he hoped that a definitive typology might be forthcoming from the work of Wayland D. Hand, resides with his other papers in the Southern Appalachian Archive at Hitchins Library at Berea College, Berea, Kentucky.

Roberts taught at secondary schools, including Pine Mountain, and at small mountain colleges—Brevard, Piedmont, Union, Morehead, West Virginia Wesleyan, and finally Pikeville College, less than 10 miles from his birthplace. There he established the Appalachian Studies Center and the Pikeville College Press—both dismantled after his death—and he devoted his attention to genealogical studies, to the work of the Kentucky Place Name Survey, and to publishing local historians. Roberts served from 1964 to 1968 as vice president and then president of the National Folk Festival Association. All of his life he functioned as musician, dance caller, and storyteller. He developed his signature story, "Raglif Jaglif Tetartlif Pole," from the version of his Aunt Columbia Roberts, learned while he was collecting for his dissertation in 1950.

Roberts died in the Floyd County in which he was born. A coal company gravel truck hit his pickup as he was pulling onto Route 23 from the Mare Creek road on which he lived, killing him instantly.

William Bernard McCarthy

References
Leonard Ward Roberts. 1987. *Appalachian Heritage* (Special Memorial Issue) (15) 2.
McCarthy, William. 1994. What Jack Learned at School: Leonard Roberts. In *Jack in Two Worlds: Contemporary North American Tales and Their Tellers*. Chapel Hill: University of North Carolina Press, pp. 168–202.

Robinson, Rowland E. (1833–1900)

Vermont farmer-sportsman and author. With little formal education, Robinson did not begin to write until after middle age when his sight began failing, and he wrote most of his realistic stories and nature essays after he was totally blind. Except for a few years spent in New York City as an illustrator of magazines when he was a young man, Robinson never left his area of Vermont. He had a lifelong interest in the folklore and history of his region; and hiking, hunting, fishing, trapping, and sketching around his Ferrisburgh farm enabled him to come in direct contact with the oral traditions and material culture of his neighbors.

In realistic stories like those in *Uncle Lisha's Shop* (1887), *Sam Lovel's Camps* (1889), *Uncle Lisha's Outing* (1897), *A Hero of Ticonderoga* (1898), and *A Danvis Pioneer* (1900), Robinson drew upon nearly every form of folklore, including speech, proverbs, riddles, rhymes, games, beliefs, cures, songs, tales, customs, arts, crafts, and architecture, and, utilizing the frame device, he presented this lore in authentically reconstructed social and physical contexts. Among his writings, most of which were collected in a seven-volume centennial edition (Robinson 1934–1938), are a history, *Vermont: A Study of Independence* (1892), and collections of essays on nature and folklife, including *In New England Fields and Woods* (1896) and *Silver Fields and Other Sketches of a Farmer-Sportsman* (1921).

In his Author's Note preceding the text of his fourth book of fiction, *Danvis Folks* (1894), Robinson pointed out that he paid less attention to narration than to depiction of Vermont folklife in the early part of the 19th century: "It [*Danvis Folks*] was written with less purpose of telling any story than of recording the manners, customs, and speech in vogue fifty or sixty years ago in certain parts of New England." Since his main purpose for writing stories was to preserve folklore, his writings offer a literary ethnography of 19th-century Vermont folklife. As Richard M. Dorson observed, in a "carefully wrought series of vignettes portraying the folkways of a Vermont pioneer community," Robinson "harmonized form and material with results unequaled, in this genre, anywhere else in American literature" (Dorson 1946:221–222).

Ronald L. Baker

References
Baker, Ronald L. 1973. *Folklore in the Writings of Rowland E. Robinson*. Bowling Green, OH: Bowling Green University State Popular Press.
Dorson, Richard M. 1946. *Jonathan Draws the Long Bow*. Cambridge: Harvard University Press, pp. 221–230.
Martin, Terence. 1955. Rowland Evans Robinson: Realist of the Outdoors. *Vermont History* 23:3–15.
Robinson, Rowland E. 1934–1938. *Works of Rowland E. Robinson*, ed. Llewellyn R. Perkins. 7 vols. Rutland, VT: Tuttle.

Rocky Mountains

A giant geographical and psychological folk region stretching from Canada to Mexico between the West Coast and the Midwest excepting metropolitan areas. The location of this area was perhaps most pervasively and dramatically expressed by Bernard DeVoto in his alternately lyrical, moving, and funny Foreword to Benjamin A. Botkins' 1951 compilation, *A Treasury of Western Folklore*. DeVoto began by defining the folk West very precisely and scientifically in terms of climate, placing the beginning of the West where the annual rainfall drops below 20 inches, roughly the 100th meridian. "East of 100 degrees is something else," he wrote, "but west of it is assuredly West." After this very exact description, however, he added that there were some places included by his description—primarily urban and suburban areas—that should *not* be, and some areas outside of his mechanical definition that *should* be within it.

In 1980, twenty-eight members of the Rocky Mountain Folklife Caucus of the American Folklore Society identified the Rocky Mountain folk region very much as DeVoto had earlier defined the entire West. The region as drawn by the members of the caucus rarely followed state lines. Portions of Arizona, Colorado, Idaho, Montana, New Mexico, Utah, and Wyoming were included as a part of the region by twenty-five or more of the twenty-eight folklorists; areas of Nevada, Oregon, and Washington were included by ten to seventeen; and sections of California (six), Kansas (two), North Dakota (five), South Dakota (seven), and Texas (nine) were also included by some of the professional folklorists answering the survey. Those surveyed had as many exceptions as DeVoto did. Some specifically excluded areas that others specifically included. Minor differences aside, however, the survey indicated that the essence of the Rocky Mountain folk region is its unique geography and geology and its low population density.

Cultural geographers use the term "ecumene" to describe that portion of the Earth controlled and civilized—divided by roads and fields into right angles, a favorite design of man

A tourist from back East prepares to ascend Pike's Peak. Colorado, 1905. Collection J. W. Love.

precisely because they are rare in nature. The single most important geographical fact about the Rocky Mountain area is that most of it is not a part of Earth's ecumene in this sense. Its immense canyons, interconnected mountain ranges, forests, deserts, wild rivers, big skies, and sudden, fierce "natural" disasters are the reality through which all things come in the folklore of and about the Rocky Mountains. Perhaps it is the sheer size of the Rocky Mountain area that has caused there to be such extensive folklores both of the area and about the various groups in the area. DeVoto said that the Westerner feels "his personality shrunk to miniature size by the enormousness in which he lives."

There are many ethnic, occupational, hobby, and religious folk groups that are, or have been, a part of the Rocky Mountain folk culture through its long recorded history and prehistory. Many of them and their traditions are a part of both the folklore of the area and the folklore about the area. The "old ones," the Native Americans of prehistory, are regularly recalled in the area through their pervasive legacies. The old ones' descendants are many, and they are parts of many living tribes and vital cultures. "Coronado's children," as well, still live in the Rocky Mountain area and militantly trace their lineage to Spain. Mexican Americans from different sections of the area speak similar but different Spanish dialects reflecting the fact that they are a part of similar but different subcultures. Men called *vaqueros*, "cowboys," and "buckaroos" all work with stock, but each word refers to a related but different subculture of the Rocky Mountain area. Rocky Mountain Mormons, ranchers, miners, sheepherders, Basques, and loggers have all been recognized as regional folk groups. Mountain men and ring-tailed roarers (braggers and fighters) have

been widely investigated by, respectively, scholars in American history and American literature. Hunting, fishing, trapping, hiking, rock hunting, mountain climbing, skiing, river running, horseback riding, and bird-watching are all popular hobbies of Rocky Mountain folk, and there is a core few in each group who have made their hobbies their lives and their primary cultural identification. The folklore of some of these groups of the Rocky Mountain area has been collected, but the folklore of many has not, and there has been little research concerning the widespread American folklore *about* either category of groups.

The folk-cultural Rocky Mountain area is a way of thinking on the part of a great diversity of folk groups who have lived with and, to some extent at least, become a part of this land. There is great diversity of folk cultures of the Rocky Mountain region, and there are some major differences between general American folklore about these groups and their own traditions, but there are also some general regional characteristics of the folklore of, and the folklore about, Rocky Mountain folk. Living with enormousness DeVoto noted has produced a cross-cultural Rocky Mountain lore that emphasizes humor, is eclectically mystical, and supports an unwritten code stressing freedom, egalitarianism, and aesthetics.

Rocky Mountain folk place great emphasis upon laughter and talking well. Humor and the artistic dimension of communication are positive values shared by many groups in the region. From colorful folk speech to complex narrative traditions, and from practical jokes to stories of practical jokes, Rocky Mountain folk enjoy performing.

Many Rocky Mountain folk also seem to have as a part of their lives a kind of cross-cultural mysticism or natural religion in addition to, or in place of, their official religious faith. While many are active members of formal, organized religions, many more are not, although most of both groups profess an awareness of the supermundane and acknowledge it with a fascinating blend of eclectic belief, ancient ritual, and perhaps New Age ceremony.

Freedom is one of the most important values in the Rocky Mountain area, romanticized and avidly sought in both the folklore of, and, the folklore about, the region. While cowboys in American popular culture wore either black or white hats in keeping with their assigned roles, cowboys and other Rocky Mountain Anglo Americans at the end of the 20th century dress in full, ethnographically accurate, 1880s buckaroo regalia or contemporary blue jeans and sweat shirts. "Don't Fence Me In" is an old, traditional, frequently collected Rocky Mountain ballad. The fact that the song was originally written by Robert H. Fletcher, a cowboy poet, rewritten by Cole Porter, featured in a Roy Rogers movie, and passed into Rocky Mountain oral tradition says a lot about the ideals that cut across the cultures past and present. Most Rocky Mountain folk relate to that old cowboy ballad Cole Porter rewrote and celebrate and practice individual freedom—just like the folklore about them says that they do. In the land of the "Tumbling Tumbleweeds," lots of folk have made the kind of freedom extolled by the folklore about these weeds a part of their lives. (That song, too, is popular culture, but the weeds are still real, they do tumble, and Rocky Mountain folks catch them crawling over their fences, dip them in white wash or spray paint them, and use them as Christmas trees—as well as chuckle when a set blows by at eye level.) What the folk most often say is that the enormousness of the land shows what a minuscule and minor part of creation is man, and that this knowledge is liberating so that anyone who has known the land and his own insignificance can never be anything but free.

Egalitarianism is also a valued part of the Rocky Mountain folk code. Botkin noted that, "things being transient and conditions changing, it is the man that counts, judged not by what he says but by what he is and does." Women very early established their importance as coequals with men in the Rocky Mountain folk area. Nowhere else in America does a woman at the folk level so naturally enjoy the equality and power rightly due her as a member of the human race as she does in the folk culture of the Rocky Mountains. For example, Martha Arriol, a teenage German immigrant, who had read about the derring-do of the great fictional Westerner "Old Shatter Hand" in popular German Western novels, came to Nevada and became a ranch cook during the first quarter of the 20th century. Many years later, she vividly recalled the equality of a land where there were not enough ranch hands to go around. "I even helped on horseback," she said. "We had to help hold cattle and do things." The clear Rocky Mountain folk ideal, like all ideals in all cultures sometimes honored by its breach, is that people should be judged by what they do rather than by who they are—or, by extension, regardless of their gender.

A natural outgrowth of these dual emphases upon freedom and egalitarianism is an extreme emphasis upon artistic expression. Many Rocky Mountain folk accessorize their clothing with Native American traditional jewelry—and know its history and aesthetics—and an unusually high number have tried their hand at making it themselves, or painting pictures, or writing, or other arts and crafts. Other Rocky Mountain folklore forms and values, also, stress a strong sense of, and concern with, aesthetics. Just as the Rocky Mountain woman, in general, has a greater degree of social freedom than women in other American folk areas, so the Rocky Mountain man is more free to be concerned with color, form, and design than men in most other American folk regions. This emphasis upon aesthetics coupled with an appreciation of performance has led to a long tradition of performance art best described as leg pulling. The chief complaint made by the folklore about the Rocky Mountain folks' lives, tall tales, clothing, cedar smudges, and Indian jewelry is not so much that they dress informally, are concerned with aesthetics, and are aware of, and perhaps to some extent more accepting of, alternate realities than other Anglo Americans, but rather that mentally and physically they are always costumed and posturing and, as DeVoto noted, knowing at some level that they are getting away with something—and enjoying it.

The folklore of the Anglo American Rocky Mountain folk-cultural area was called into being partly by dichotomous metaphors that were a part of the folklore about the area: garden and wilderness, noble savage and child of nature, boom and bust. In folklore about their area, Rocky Mountain folk found international narrative themes, motifs, and characters to develop and localize and to use to entertain themselves and others. Rocky Mountain folk took the folklore about themselves and developed a richly diverse, flourishing folklore of the area stressing reality and humor through an emphasis upon accurately presented geographic, cultural, and human detail. Rocky Mountain folklore was further developed by the addition of local characters and local settings, gaining—even in parody forms such as tall tales—verisimilitude by grounding folklore in ethnographic and personal terms. Folklore about the Rocky Mountain area, in turn, continued to view the area and its inhabitants as dichotomous metaphorical referents and adopted and adapted the areas' folklore to the same end, in the process creating a new folklore about it by eliminating much of the emphasis upon accuracy and replacing living persons with stock characters. Folklore of the Rocky Mountains took these stereotypes, again, and revitalized them with realism and both folklore *of*, and folklore *about*, the Rocky Mountain folk area have lives of their own with far-ranging consequences. Ring-tailed roarers, Native Americans, cowboys, and the land itself all underwent a similar process in their movement from folklore *of* to folklore *about*. In each of these cases, folklore of the Rocky Mountains began as generalized stereotyped dichotomous themes and values. These values and themes helped shape the developing folklore of the Rocky Mountain folk-cultural area grounded in persons and places and then—so transformed—were carried forward in images and ideas in new folklore about the Rocky Mountain folk area again once more in terms of types. The interaction continues.

In effect, both the folklore of the Rocky Mountain area and the folklore about the Rocky Mountain folk area exist simultaneously as mountains of the imagination. The former serves as a broad, general metaphor, while the latter provides an experiential account of reality. Like a whirling, three-dimensional universe of moons, planets, and suns moving in their interrelated and interactive courses, the two Rocky Mountain folklores (of and about) intertwine stories, objects, customs, thoughts, and unconscious integrative principles, and shape and reshape them and each other in terms of freedom, egalitarianism, and aesthetics.

Keith Cunningham

References

Attebery, Louie W., ed. 1985. *Idaho Folklife: Homesteads to Headstones.* Salt Lake City: University of Utah Press.

Botkin, Benjamin A., ed. 1951. *A Treasury of Western Folklore,* with Introduction by Bernard DeVoto. New York: Crown.

See also Basque Americans; Cowboys; Great Basin; Great Plains; Mexican Americans; Mormon Folklore; Sheepherder

Rodeo

A sport deriving from the 19th-century folk games of the American cowboy, particularly as those games involved the work skills of roping and riding. Possessing the characteristics

At a rodeo. Cheyenne, Wyoming, 1905. Collection J.W. Love.

of community involvement, celebration, and ritual, rodeo is perhaps the only true folk festival to have sprung entirely from North American roots. While Wild West shows were instrumental in its popularization, rodeo is unique among American sports in having developed from the daily work of a manual-laboring occupation into a major spectator and participant sport.

Just as much of the cowboy's working methods and equipment derived from the Spanish *vaquero,* so, too, rodeo-like activities are first recorded, as early as 1792, in Spanish North America. By the 1860s, and particularly following the onset of the great Texas-to-Kansas cattle drives that followed the Civil War, exhibitions and competitions of steer roping and bronc riding, the two most difficult and dangerous parts of a cowboy's job, became a common feature of range-country celebrations. The first modern rodeo was held at Prescott, Arizona, in 1888, a Fourth of July event that featured cash prizes for steer-roping and bronc-riding contests, engraved trophies for the winners, and an admission charge for spectators. Canadian rodeo, developed around the turn of the 20th century largely through American influences, is interchangeable with the American version. The earliest Canadian "stampede," as the sport is usually termed there, was at Raymond, Alberta, in 1902; the largest rodeo in Canada is the Calgary Stampede. Two of the largest, most important rodeos in the United States are the Pendleton, Oregon, Roundup and the Cheyenne, Wyoming, Frontier Days. The most prestigious rodeo, however, is the National Finals Rodeo of the Professional Rodeo Cowboys Association, held annually since 1959 and featuring the top fifteen contestants in each event.

A contemporary rodeo is generally composed of three rough-stock events and up to five timed events. In bareback bronc riding, saddle bronc riding, and bull riding, contestants must ride for eight seconds, with equal points being given for both the quality of the ride and the bucking ability of the animal. Bareback riders use a surcingle called a bucking rig; saddle bronc riders, an association-approved saddle; and bull riders, a loose rope that is pulled tightly around the back of the bull; when released it is pulled off by a bell, whose clanging adds to the spectacle of the ride. In the two standard timed events (calf roping and steer wrestling, also called bulldogging) and the three optional timed events (team roping, single-steer roping, and cowgirls' barrel racing), winners are determined by speed. A calf must be roped, thrown by hand, and three legs tied, while a single-steer roper must rope and trip the steer from horseback, then tie the animal before he regains his feet. Team roping consists of a "header," who ropes the horns, and a "heeler," who ropes the two hind feet. Contestants must "dally"—that is, wrap the tail of the rope around the saddle horn after catching the animal—rather than tie the rope hard and fast before roping. Barrel racers run a cloverleaf pattern around three barrels set to form a triangle in the arena. Of these eight events, only saddle bronc riding and the three roping events are derived from actual ranch work.

Early-day rodeos often featured a dozen or more contest events, many of them directly related to ranch work: wild horse racing, wild cow milking, calf branding, relay racing, and chuck wagon racing. Trick and fancy roping and riding, at one time contest events, are now staged strictly as exhibitions. Earlier competitions for men and women were separate, as they are in the 1990s, but until the time of World War II women's events at regular rodeos included bronc and steer riding, relay races, roping events, and bulldogging. Today cowgirls compete primarily against one another in barrel races or in roping and rough-stock events at all-women rodeos.

A feature of nearly all rodeos is the clown. In the early years of rodeo, when cows or steers were ridden, clowns provided humor, but since the 1930s, when bulls were first introduced to the sport, rodeo clowns have also performed a pragmatic function: distracting bulls from fallen riders. This serious function differentiates the rodeo clown from the clown figure in other folk groups or festivals.

As are many athletes, rodeo cowboys are subject to a number of superstitions. The color yellow, for instance, is unlucky, as is eating peanuts at a rodeo or placing a hat on a bed. Spitting in a hat just before a ride, on the other hand, is said to bring good luck. The customs and language of rodeo are also distinctive. A "go-round" is one complete cycle of competition at a particular rodeo, while the "average" is won by the cowboy with the best combined score in all go-rounds. "Two wraps and a hooey" describes the tie made on a calf's legs, while "missed him out" means that a bronc rider has been disqualified because he failed to spur the horse in the shoulders on the first jump out of the chute. "There's never a horse that can't be rode and never a man that can't be throwed" is a traditional saying illustrating the spirit that led to the development of rodeo, a spirit depicted in the story line of the folksong "The Strawberry Roan."

As rodeo has become more and more slick and professional, there has been a movement, which began in the Southern and Central Plains, to return, through "ranch rodeos," to the type of cowboy folk games from which rodeo originally sprang. Contestants (usually four to a team rather than individual competitors) are working cowboys competing under the sponsorship of the ranch they work for and riding their own horses or those of the ranch. The events, which vary from locale to locale depending upon the ranching practices of that particular area, often include such things as calf branding, wild horse racing, cattle sorting and penning, bronc riding (using a stock saddle and both hands), cattle doctoring, and trailer loading.

James F. Hoy

References

Clayton, Lawrence. 1990. Ranch Rodeo: An Expansion of Ranch Life Ritual. *Western Folklore* 49:292–293.

Fredriksson, Kristine. 1985. *American Rodeo: From Buffalo Bill to Big Business.* College Station: Texas A&M University Press.

Hall, Douglas Kent. 1973. *Let 'Er Buck!* New York: Dutton.

Hoy, James F. 1978. The Origins and Originality of Rodeo. *Journal of the West* 17:16–33.

LeCompte, Mary Lou. 1989. Champion Cowgirls of Rodeo's Golden Age. *Journal of the West* 28:88–94.

Stoeltje, Beverly J. 1989. Rodeo: From Custom to Ritual. *Western Folklore* 48:244–255.

Westermeier, Clifford P. 1947. *Man, Beast, Dust: The Story of Rodeo.* Denver: World Press.

See also Cowboys

Rodgers, James Charles ("Jimmie") (1897–1933)

Known professionally as "The Singing Brakeman" and "America's Blue Yodeler," generally considered "The Father of Country Music." Largely ignored for many years by folksong collectors because of his identity as a popular entertainer on commercial records and radio, more recently Rodgers has been recognized as an important link with a valuable body of older traditional music, especially the country blues of Black musicians, which he heard growing up in the Deep South and drew on heavily for his famous "Blue Yodels" and other blues-related songs. He was, as John Greenway pointed out as early as 1957, "a folksong catalyst" who "had a most pervasive if not profound effect on American folksong" (Greenway 1957:231).

Born in Meridian, Mississippi, the son of a railroad section foreman, Rodgers developed show business aspirations early in life. At the age of thirteen, he won an amateur talent contest in his hometown and shortly afterward ran away to join a traveling medicine show. When those efforts came to nothing, he was put to work on the railroad by his father and spent the next dozen years or so at a variety of jobs on "the high iron"—as call boy, flagman, baggage master, brakeman— which took him far and wide across the nation. Throughout the period prior to World War I and into the 1920s, Rodgers made repeated attempts to earn a living as an entertainer but without success. After developing tuberculosis in 1924, he found the physical demands of railroading increasingly difficult and began to turn his attention full-time to his music, organizing amateur bands, playing on street corners, taking any small entertainment job he could find. Again, the results were meager and discouraging.

Rodgers's first big break came in August 1927. By this time he had located in Asheville, North Carolina, where he fronted a string band known as the Jimmie Rodgers Entertainers and broadcast briefly on the local radio station, WWNC. Learning that Ralph Sylvester Peer, an agent for the Victor Talking Machine Company, was making field recordings of area entertainers in nearby Bristol, Tennessee, he impulsively loaded up the band and went there with the hope of gaining an audition. Before they could record, however, the band broke up, and Rodgers convinced Peer to let him make his first recordings solo, accompanied only by his own guitar.

Within a year, he was fast becoming a star of national stature. Billed as "The Singing Brakeman" and "America's Blue Yodeler," Rodgers played first-run theaters in major cities, broadcast on radio stations throughout the country, and embarked on an extensive vaudeville tour through the South on the prestigious Loew Circuit. In the ensuing five years, he traveled to numerous cities across the nation, including New York and Hollywood, to record for Victor, and eventually recorded 110 titles, including such classics as "Blue Yodel No. 1" ("T for Texas"), "Waiting for a Train," "In the Jailhouse Now," "Frankie and Johnny," "Treasures Untold," "My Old Pal," "T.B. Blues," "My Little Lady," "My Blue-Eyed Jane," "The One Rose," "Miss the Mississippi and You," and the series of twelve sequels to "Blue Yodel" for which he was most famous. In the course of his brief career, Rodgers recorded with numerous other musicians of the time, including such "hillbilly" or country-music names as the Carter Family and Clayton Mc-Michen, and in at least one instance with a star of major national prominence—Louis Armstrong, who appears with him on "Blue Yodel No. 9." In 1931 he toured with a Red Cross benefit show headed by Will Rogers, who jokingly called him "my distant son."

During the years from 1928 to 1932, Rodgers' career was at its pinnacle. By late 1932, the Depression and his failing health had begun to take their toll. Audiences for live entertainment shrank, record sales plummeted, and Rodgers was too ill to undertake the ambitious film projects and international tours he had planned. After a sporadic effort to book theater dates in the spring of 1933, he went to New York to fulfill a contract with Victor for twelve recordings. Scarcely able to stand before the microphone, he rested between takes on a cot set up in a rehearsal room across the hall. On May 26, two days after finishing the sessions, he collapsed on the street and died a few hours later in his room at the Hotel Taft.

Although Rodgers' career and resulting fame derived largely from his commercial recordings, the roots of his art were in the traditional melodies and folk music of his Southern upbringing. As a boy, he was exposed to a vast body of musical influences typical of that time and place: down-home fiddling, the banjo ditties of medicine show minstrels, the old standard church hymns absorbed by almost every Southern consciousness, even the light classics and maudlin tearjerkers of the Victorian stage favored by the maiden aunt who raised him. Later, in his teens and early twenties, roaming the country as a railroad brakeman, he was drawn to the rhythmic work chants and keening country blues of the Black section-crew laborers, "gandy-dancers" who sang as they set new rail ties or hung about the roundhouse.

From these diverse strains, Rodgers fashioned songs that somehow retained their fine old homespun flavor yet were strikingly fresh and original. At least a third of his 110 recorded titles are variants of traditional songs or contain elements that can be traced back to folksong origins. In turn, many of those Rodgers recordings—"T for Texas," "Waiting for a Train," "Frankie and Johnny," "In the Jailhouse Now"—carried the tradition forward, not merely as the "country classics" of music-industry hyperbole but as familiar standards in the consciousness of a broad segment of the population. Although Rodgers often altered and rearranged the anonymous folk material he had absorbed as a youngster, in adapting it to the new technology of the 20th century—for wider audiences reached by phonograph record and radio—he performed a key role in preserving, transmitting, and disseminating vital elements of American musical culture.

The folk-like process of altering sources and recombining scattered elements can be seen in Rodgers' first recording. For "The Soldier's Sweetheart," he drew on variants dating back to the Spanish-American War, borrowed the tune to "Where the River Shannon Flows," and, in memory of a friend killed in the Argonne Forest, updated the setting to World War I. A similar instance is "Waiting for a Train," which, in fact, can be traced back to a stage recitation of the mid-1800s but which had

passed through any number of "folk" variants before it reached Rodgers, including "Danville Girl," "Wild and Reckless Hobo," "Ten Thousand Miles from Home," and others now authoritatively collected as genuine folksongs.

The thirteen "Blue Yodels" display a panoply of the maverick phrases and vagrant stanzas common in African American blues; through the years, several have been collected as "authentic Negro songs" by folksong scholars to whom Rodgers was unknown. The Blue Yodels are, in the words of country-music historian Bill C. Malone, Rodgers' "unique contribution to American folksong" (Malone 1985: 86). Other songs made popular by Rodgers but not written by him have also been admitted to the canon. So eminent an authority as Frank C. Brown thought that "Away Out on the Mountain," composed for Rodgers by Kelly Harrell, bore clear internal evidence of being a folksong and might even be "a relic of the days of Davy Crockett" (Belden and Hudson 1952:371).

Rodgers' popularity was such that he himself became a folkloristic icon of sorts as the subject of numerous folktales about his life and adventures. Bits of folk-say involved titles of songs he had made popular, and there were several versions of how he had "invented" the yodel when he eyed some attractive woman (whose occupation varied from story to story) and sang out, "I see your legs-o-lady-dee-hee." Anthropologist Hugh Tracey, working among the Kipsigi tribe of East Africa in the 1950s, reported a female puberty rite in which the young maidens chanted seductively before a centaur-god, half man and half antelope, known as "Chemirocha"—Kipsigi pronunciation of "Jimmie Rodgers," whose magnetic appeal on old records had moved them to elevate him to the status of a demigod (Oliver 1959:10).

Nolan Porterfield

References

Belden, Henry M., and Arthur Palmer Hudson, eds. 1952. *The Frank C. Brown Collection of North Carolina Folklore.* Vol. 3. Durham, NC: Duke University Press.

Greenway, John. 1957. Jimmie Rodgers: A Folksong Catalyst. *Journal of American Folklore* 70:231–234.

Malone, Bill C. 1985. *Country Music U.S.A.* Austin: University of Texas Press.

Oliver, Paul. 1959. Jimmy [*sic*] Rodgers. *Recorded Folk Music* 2:10.

Porterfield, Nolan. 1979. *Jimmie Rodgers: The Life and Times of America's Blue Yodeler.* Urbana: University of Illinois Press.

Romanian Americans

Romanian-speaking immigrants and their descendants. The vast majority of ethnic Romanians who settled in the United States came from the Austrian-Hungarian Empire in the late 19th and early 20th centuries. Along with Serbs, Hungarians, Saxons, ethnic Jews, and Gypsies, all of whom shared some folkways, Romanians (also identified as Rumanians or Roumanians), established enclaves in America closely tied to village and region in the old country. Few came from the "Old

Kingdom" of Romania (Moldavia and Wallachia). After World War II, the then borders of Romania incorporated much of the territory from which the immigrant Romanians came: Banat (adjacent to, and including, parts of northern Serbia), Bukovina (including much of the ethnically Romanian former Soviet state of Moldova), and especially Transylvania (those formerly Hungarian-dominated lands north of the Carpathian Mountains).

Spurred by visions of quick cash to be made in America that is graphically captured in the folk proverb of this era, *Mia di dolar si ban de drum inapoi* (A thousand dollars and money for the trip home), thousands of Romanians joined other immigrants of the "new wave" coming to urban industrial centers from farms of southern and eastern Europe. By the end of World War I, immigrants identified as Romanians numbered more than 100,000, and some Romanians were documented as Austrian or Hungarian. Even though thousands of the "birds of passage," as they were called, had returned to the old country with their hard-earned dollars, many young men stayed, sending for wives and sweethearts to join them as they were able to move out of boarding houses, supporting families on more or less steady pay from mills and factories.

The experience of immigration itself was incorporated into traditional folk expression. The earliest immigrants, often young men only in their teens, composed songs about their experiences. These were sung and written down aboard steamships or in cramped quarters of boarding houses. These folksongs followed the formulaic traditions of the "blues-like" *doina*, particularly the *doina de duca* (leaving songs) or *cintece di strain* (songs of estrangement), traditionally sung in Romanian villages when young men left home or were conscripted into the Army. Describing the difficulty of earning a dollar, the poor living conditions of the unskilled workers, and homesickness, these "America songs" were often sent back home as bitter, sarcastic commentary on the American Dream. Still found in folksong repertoires in parts of modern-day Romania (especially Transylvania), these songs were not transmitted beyond the first immigrant generation in America.

Folktales have been widely collected and studied in Romania, but this important folk tradition has not remained vital among Romanian Americans any more than among other 20th-century immigrant groups. The great *basme* (wonder tales) are known through translations of 19th-century collections, if at all. Several immigrant *povestitori* (storytellers) in America have been recorded, but their *Märchen* (fairy tale) traditions have not taken hold in America. Among many American-born Romanians, however, there is an awareness of folktale stereotypes of certain characters described in Romanian humorous tales, such as Pacala (a famous trickster), the *prost* (generic fool), priests and priest wives, and especially *tigani* (Gypsies). While few remember specific anecdotes about these Old World stereotypes, many people share the traditional attitudes toward them, as memories of stereotypical traits have become part of an ethnic sensibility.

As a result of a regional diversity in the old country, the American Romanian folk culture had from the beginning distinctive regional characteristics, although much of this intragroup diversity has been gradually diffused during the 20th century. Always a relatively small ethnic presence in America, Romanian American communities are based increasingly on formal religious organizations (including the Romanian Orthodox Church in America) and various cultural organizations devoted primarily to pan-Romanian "folklore revival" activities among the younger generations. Ethnic-neighborhood contexts of folklife, a coalescence of regional styles, repertoires, and dialects, have declined dramatically in the last two generations. Some Old World regional distinctions in foodways and music persist in a few settlement cities, such as Detroit, Cleveland, Philadelphia, and Gary, Indiana, that are based on the regional migration patterns of the early 20th century.

In communities where the American-born Romanians are active in ethnic affairs, different churches at Christmastime sponsor groups of *colindatori* (carolers), who visit houses of parish members. Also, about six weeks before Christmas, congregations of various Romanian Orthodox and Roman Byzantine Rite Catholic churches sing some *colinde* (carols) at the Sunday worship service after liturgy. Sometimes, on Christmas Eve, casually organized groups travel in cars to other parish members' homes. These *colindatori* will be invited inside to sing and be offered refreshments. Sometimes the host is expected to make a donation to the carolers, who in turn give the money to the church. In Romanian villages *colindatori* are always groups of young men and boys who will be ritually offered refreshments. The donation to the church is an American innovation. Also, American *colindatori* are not limited by age or gender. In south Florida, where some immigrants still live, groups have been mainly composed of elderly people. In the Cleveland and Detroit areas, however, where there are more active American-born people, groups may be largely composed of high-school students or young people returned from college for the holidays.

Songs most commonly sung are the *colinde* not usually limited to a local village in the old country. *"Trei Pastori," "O Ce Veste,"* and *"Florile d'Albe"* are the three most popular songs passed down to younger generations. While there once were known regional variations of these songs, nowadays the words are standardized and learned partly (and increasingly phonetically) from mimeographed sheets with words from homemade songbooks.

Romanian folk dances and dance music have also been adapted to a multiethnic environment in America, not always by ethnic Romanian Americans. Eastern European and Balkan dance bands may play Romanian dance music as a part of the mixed repertoires required by such multiethnic bands, who perform at weddings and other festive occasions, including bar mitzvahs, for different ethnic communities. From the beginnings of immigration, Romanian dance music was adapted to American opportunities. Manufactured brass and woodwind instruments, known to a certain extent in the Old World, replaced the traditional handmade folk instruments as soon as musicians could afford them. Romanian and Gypsy orchestras recorded dance tunes in the 1920s on RCA Victor and Columbia Phonograph Company labels, performing numbers that reflected regional sensibilities: *"Memorii din Banat," "Invartita dela Chicago," "Doina din America,"* and *"Doina din Seliste,"* to name a few. Dance music and dance styles became associated with a specific settlement community dominated by immigrants from specific Romanian regions: The Cleveland folk-dance style was identified as Transylvanian; the Chicago and Philadelphia style, as Banatian; and a Gary–East Chicago style, also as Transylvanian.

Although some specialty folk-dance groups consciously try to preserve Old World regional authenticity in their dancing, most younger generations who still perform Romanian folk dances have adapted a greatly simplified American style that shows little or none of the variation that marked village or regional dances for the immigrants. The dances most often performed as Romanian folk dances are performed generically throughout Europe as well as America: *the hora unirea,* (basic circle dance), and the *sarba* (snake dance), done in a long winding line with arms placed on adjacent dancers' shoulders, are the most popular. Some people still remember the *strigaturi,* or traditional shouts, that traditionally accompany many Romanian dances.

Foodways remain as an important ethnic social marker. Romanian American foods, basically peasant fare adapted to Americanized tastes and ingredients, may be served in honor of the standard American "heritage holidays" celebrated by multiethnic Americans of Romanian ancestry: Thanksgiving, Christmas, and Easter (although Romanian Orthodox celebrate *Craciun* [Christmas] and *Pas* [Easter] according to the Byzantine calendar). On these occasions, people might eat *mamaliga* (stiff corn mush) and *sarmale* (stuffed cabbage on sauerkraut) along with turkey and dressing or ham and potatoes. *Clatita* (a crepe or pancake) and *cozonac* (a cake) would also be appropriate to celebrate a festive occasion with an ethnic touch.

People in the late 20th century tend to disassociate themselves from Old World folk belief. Third and fourth generations remember that their grandparents believed in the evil eye *(deochi),* but dismiss this once widespread tradition as "just folklore." Likewise, the stories of *strigoi* (witches) and of the appearance of *dracul* (the devil) that have been passed down are now told for amusement, set in a time and place long ago and far away. One complication in the folklore of belief is the belief by Americans in general that Romanians, especially those of Transylvanian ancestry, have something to do with Dracula. Folk custom and belief in Romania in the 1990s do have some interesting parallels to the literary creation of Bram Stoker, but the obsessive connection devoted by American popular culture to this aspect of Transylvania has had impact on ethnic identity of Romanian Americans, leaving some insulted and some amused.

Members of a recent generation of immigrants, those who defected from the communist regimes after World War II, have energized some traditional Romanian American communities in important ways. Because they mostly are not from peasant or rural village backgrounds, the "newcomers" have tended to focus more on political and intellectual pursuits than on maintaining and reviving the Old World folkways.
Kenneth A. Thigpen

References

Galitzi, Christine A. 1929. *A Study of Assimilation among the Romanians in the United States.* New York: Columbia University Press.

Thigpen, Kenneth A. 1974. Romanian-American Folklore in Detroit. In *Ethnic Studies Reader,* ed. David W. Hartman, pp. 189–201.

———. 1980. *Folklore and the Ethnicity Factor in the Lives of Romanian-Americans.* New York: Arno.

———. 1986. European-American Music: Romanian. In *The New Grove Dictionary of Music in the United States.* Vol. 3. London: Macmillan, pp. 82–86.

See also Vampires

Rumor

Unverified information of uncertain origin often spread by the oral tradition, as well as by phone, fax, broadcasting, or computer. Although rumors may be malicious or idle, they thrive in most societies worldwide, in both urban and rural settings. Rumors affect all facets of human experience, and almost every person has participated at one time in either the simple form of rumor (gossip) or the more complex form that is closely akin to the legend.

Rumor topics circulate around sex, love and marriage, murder, war, illness, religion, crime, race, politics, and so on. In the United States, rumors thrive about California falling into the sea, about Chinese restaurants serving chopped cat, and about President John F. Kennedy's assassination in 1963. Whatever the subject, once a potentially dangerous or embarrassing rumor enters oral tradition, it gains powerfully in strength and dominance. The more intriguing the subject or deed, the stronger the paths of dissemination. While some rumors tend to remain extremely simplified in their re-creations, many tend to grow until they reach proportional dimensions that are almost unrecognizable to earlier renditions of the lore. Both creativity and exaggeration account for the endless versions in this field. The creative energies of the tellers allow for a type of subjectifying that reflects personal perception and remembrance and local geographical and physical setting. Exaggeration, a common characteristic of rumor, often takes the form of multiplication: One person becomes five; one incident becomes ten; $100.00 becomes $1,000.00; and the midget becomes the giant.

Rumors are legitimate folkloric items, whether the contents of the rumor narrative are true or contrived. Rumors almost always suggest to the folk that there must be some truth involved: "Where there's smoke there's fire!" Folk members can readily point to cases wherein initial rumors prove to be accurate. On the other hand, history teaches that the most powerful and tragic rumors may be utterly baseless. The thousand-fold repetition of the scapegoat rumor that Adolf Hitler invented against the Jews of Germany proved to be groundless but, nonetheless, highly effective in his campaign of Hebraic genocide. The stories in ancient Greece that Socrates was destroying the minds of the youth and causing them to turn to violence resulted in his death. During the early 20th century, rape rumors (the sexual assault of Whites by African Americans) triggered numerous race riots in American cities.

While relatively little research has been done on rumor, folklorists, psychologists, sociologists, political scientists, and anthropologists continue to probe this phenomenon in an effort to understand better the origins, the dissemination process, and the effects that rumor has had and continues to have on communities throughout the world.

Elon A. Kulii

References

Allport, Gordon W., and Leo Postman. 1947. *The Psychology of Rumor.* New York: H. Holt.

Knopf, Terry Ann. 1975. *Rumors, Race, and Riots.* New Brunswick, NJ: Transaction.

Rosnow, Ralph L., and Gary Alan Fine. 1976. *Rumor and Gossip: The Social Psychology of Hearsay.* New York: Elsevier.

Shibutani, Tamotsu. 1966. *Improvised News: A Sociological Study of Rumor.* New York: Bobbs-Merrill.

See also Gossip; Legend

S

Saint's Day

Christian holy day and holiday. Since the 2nd century, Christians have established special days in honor of martyrs and models of holiness. Usually observed on the reputed date of the saint's death, these holy days originally involved worshipful veneration at his or her tomb and, consequently, were quite localized. Later, local church calendars began to include feast days honoring saints from other churches. By the Middle Ages virtually every day of the year had become part of the sanctoral cycle, the annual round of holy days devoted to venerating particular saints. Moreover, many saints' days had become civic holidays as well as occasions for piety.

Though almost every day is a saint's day, an individual Christian observes only a few of them. These may include the feast of his or her patron saint, the holy person under whose special guardianship the person was placed when baptized. Often the person shares the saint's name. In some American ethnic groups with a strong Catholic heritage, the saint's day replaces a birthday celebration.

During the course of the year, Christians may also participate in the feast of the patron saint of the parish church, civic community, occupation, or some other group to which they belong. Moreover, since entire countries or regions may enjoy the special care of a particular saint, Americans whose ancestors came therefrom may observe that saint's day. For example, an Irish American seaman named Michael who attends St. Anne's Church might acknowledge at least with prayer the feast days of Sts. Patrick (March 17), Nicholas, patron of sailors (December 6), Michael (September 29), and Anne (July 26).

Though community observances of saints' days often assume specific ethnic dimensions and may, in fact, become expressions of ethnicity as much as of religious devotion, certain features are relatively consistent. Almost always, churchmen will carry the saint's statue through the community, usually arriving at the church for a Mass, which may be celebrated by a priest representing the community's ethnic heritage. Since in the late 20th century the festivities are frequently held on weekends instead of the traditional dates for feasts, several days may be given over to celebratory activities evincing little overt religiosity. Food booths and carnival-like games raise funds for the organization in charge of the celebration. Music, including that of the relevant ethnic folk heritage and contemporary popular music, provides accompaniment for dancing. A festival king and queen, often young children, may be crowned.

Though community saints' days flourish in virtually every American ethnic group with religious roots in Catholicism, no group has continued to observe such a variety of saints' feasts (*feste*) as Italian Americans, who use these occasions to demonstrate their enduring *campanilismo* (a sense of identity with their specific ancestral village). Consequently, Italian communities in the United States hold *feste* honoring Sts. Gennaro (Neapolitans), Rossilia (Palermitans), Paulinus (Nolani), Giusseppe (southern Italians, especially Sicilians), and many others.

Each saint's day celebration has its distinctive qualities, but they all remind the participants of who they are religiously, ethnically, and sometimes occupationally.

William M. Clements

References

Cohen, Hennig, and Tristram Potter Coffin, eds. 1991. *The Folklore of American Holidays.* 2d. ed. Detroit: Gale.

Orsi, Robert Anthony. 1985. *The Madonna of 115th Street: Faith and Community in Italian Harlem, 1880–1950.* New Haven, CT: Yale University Press.

Riis, Jacob. 1899. Feast Days in Little Italy. *Century* 58:491–499.

Sciorra, Joseph. 1985. Religious Processions in Italian Williamsburg. *Drama Review* 29:65–81.

Swiderski, Richard. 1987. *Voices: An Anthropologist's Dialogue with an Italian-American Festival.* Bowling Green, OH: Bowling Green State University Popular Press.

See also Festival; Religion, Folk

In a procession for the feast of Our Lady of Loreto, members of St. Anthony's Roman Catholic Church carry a decorated effigy of Saint Mary and the baby Jesus. Lowell, Massachusetts, 1988. Photo Tom Rankin. American Folklife Center.

Sandburg, Carl (1878–1967)

American author and collector of folksongs. Sandburg, the son of Swedish immigrants, was born in Galesburg, Illinois. He is best known for his six-volume biography of Abraham Lincoln, which was published between 1926 and 1939 and won him the Pulitzer Prize in 1939, and for his poetry, which earned him a second Pulitzer Prize for *Complete Poems* (1950).

While a teenager, Sandburg was possesssed of a restless wanderlust that drove him to travel as a self-styled "Eternal Hobo." Riding freight trains across the country to industrial centers and working odd jobs, such as delivering milk and washing dishes, during the 1890s depression, Sandburg recorded folksongs in his pocket journals. In the American heartland, Sandburg listened to hoboes, railroad workers, and harvest hands sing about their frustrations and hopes. Returning to Illinois, Sandburg learned more songs while selling stereographs door to door. He also served as district organizer for the Social Democratic Party in Wisconsin and was secretary for Milwaukee's Socialist Mayor Emil Seidel, from 1910 to 1912. The job he held the longest, from 1917 to 1932, was newspaper reporter for the *Chicago Daily News*.

After establishing himself as a writer, Sandburg embarked on a multivolume biography of Lincoln. When he traveled on research trips, he also collected regional folksongs. Presenting lectures and poetry readings to raise research funds for his Lincoln biography, Sandburg concluded each session, playing his guitar and crooning ballads, especially his favorite, "Hallelujah, I'm a Bum." Audience members provided him new variations of lyrics and tunes.

As a folksinger, Sandburg preserved the American vernacular voice. Enchanted with folk music, Sandburg collected new songs from labor organizers, folklorists, strangers, and famous friends, including poet Robert Frost and journalist H.L. Mencken. He traced versions' origins and studied America's history through its music, believing that songs reflected average peoples' life stories and feelings.

In 1926, at the same time that his two-volume *Abraham Lincoln: The Prairie Years* was released—the first part of the Lincoln-biography series—Sandburg recorded an album of songs from Lincoln's era. Inspired to publish a collection of his folksongs, he compiled 280 songs in the well-received *American Songbag* (1927), one of the first books of authentic American folksongs.

Sandburg introduced each song with a description of how

he collected it. The songs represented America's diverse regional, socioeconomic, and ethnic characteristics. Spirituals, railroad ballads, prison and work-gang blues, ditties, and military songs depicted America from colonial days to the 20th century.

While preparing another Lincoln-biography volume, this one on the Civil War, Sandburg collected American folk sayings, slang, and proverbs in *The People, Yes* (1936). Sandburg's *New American Songbag* (1950) offered additional folksongs that he had collected during his travels. Sandburg concentrated the remainder of his literary work on poetry and prose, enjoying folk music as entertainment on his Flat Rock, North Carolina, goat-farm retreat, Connemara, where he died in July 1967 at age 89.

Elizabeth D. Schafer

References

D'Alessio, Gregory. 1987. *Old Troubadour: Carl Sandburg with His Guitar Friends.* New York: Walker.

Niven, Penelope. 1991. *Carl Sandburg: A Biography.* New York: Charles Scribner's Sons.

Salwak, Dale. 1988. *Carl Sandburg: A Reference Guide.* Boston: G.K. Hall.

Sandburg, Helga. 1963. *Sweet Music: A Book of Family Reminiscence and Song.* New York: Dial.

Saxon, Lyle (1891–1946)

Writer and public-sector folklorist. Though born in Bellingham, Washington, Saxon grew up in Baton Rouge and was greatly attached to Louisiana as a place. Though he lived in New York for several years, he spent most of his adult life in New Orleans and in the Cane River country near Natchitoches.

Saxon worked as a journalist for much of his life and used his columns to promote restoration of the French Quarter and to encourage people to wear elaborate costumes for Mardi Gras. Though his desire was to write fiction, he became famous as a popular historian of Louisiana with such books as *Fabulous New Orleans* (1928), *Old Louisiana* (1929), and a biography of pirate Jean Lafitte, which was made into a movie by Cecil B. De Mille.

Though he included folklore in his books, it was primarily because he was recognized as an interpreter of Louisiana that he was asked in 1935 to head the Federal Writers' Project in the state. This project was part of the Works Progress Administration and had as its purpose providing employment for white collar workers during the Depression, who would undertake useful research and writing. Collecting folklore was a central undertaking. Saxon supervised this collecting, which resulted in *Gumbo Ya-Ya: A Collection of Louisiana Folk Tales* (1945), the book he coedited with Edward Dryer and Robert Tallant, and which stands as an end result of early government-sponsored folklore research.

Saxon's view of folklore was not sophisticated, and *Gumbo Ya-Ya,* though very readable and containing much information on Louisiana folklore, is primarily journalistic and limited in scope.

Frank de Caro

References

De Caro, F.A. 1985. A History of Folklife Research in Louisiana. In *Louisiana Folklife: A Guide to the State,* ed. Nicholas R. Spitzer. Baton Rouge: Louisiana Folklife Program and Center for Gulf South History and Culture, pp. 11–34.

Harvey, Cathy Chance. 1980. *Lyle Saxon: A Portrait in Letters, 1917–1945.* Ph.D. diss., Tulane University.

Scandinavian Americans

Immigrants to North America who came primarily from Norway, Denmark, Sweden and their descendants. Dorothy Burton Skaardal and others use the term "Scandinavia" to refer only to these three countries, arguing for the exclusion of Iceland and Finland primarily on the basis of language familiarity among contemporary speakers of Norwegian, Danish, and Swedish. This argument notwithstanding, Iceland is included here because of the similarity of language (Icelandic being an old form of Norwegian) and ethnic origin, and because of historical ties between Iceland and the development of Scandinavia. Iceland was an important link to the other three countries during the Viking Period and continued thereafter. The Icelandic Sagas are uniquely tied to the Norwegian Sagas, and during the period of Norwegian exploration Iceland was geographically an important link on the North Atlantic sailing and settlement route.

The term "Nordic" is also used to describe this group of five countries in northern Europe and is the term employed by the Nordic Council. In general, Finland is thought of as being one of the "Nordic" countries. Finnish peoples in Finland and North America do not, however, customarily identify themselves as Scandinavian. The term "Scandinavian" also takes into account some aspects, including folklore, of the people from Greenland and the Faeroe Islands (both part of Denmark), Aaland, a self-governing island province belonging to Finland and located between Sweden and Finland, and several other substantial island populations belonging to one of the primary Scandinavian countries.

Scandinavian American folkloric materials generally derive from the periods of immigration and settlement to North America and encompass the oral folklore of the group (folktales, legends, beliefs, sayings, and other forms of traditional oral lore) and the material folk culture of the group (the material objects made by Scandinavian Americans after their arrival in North America). In addition, much of the folklore carried on by Scandinavian Americans in the 1990s is the result of relearning Scandinavian traditions by the succeeding generations living in North America. Taken together, the oral and material forms of folklore represent the substantial body of traditional materials identified with, and perpetuated by, Scandinavian Americans. As an identifiable ethnic group, the descendants of the three primary Scandinavian American populations—the Norwegian Americans, the Danish Americans, and the Swedish Americans—and, to a lesser extent, the Icelandic Americans, make up a significant and highly visible immigrant influence in North American culture. The Icelandic American influence is more vis-

Selma Jacobson demonstrates Swedish strawcraft (halmslojd). Chicago, 1977. Photo Jonas Dovydenas. American Folklife Center.

ible in Canada than it is in the United States.

The folklore of American immigrant groups in general, and of Scandinavian Americans specifically, follows two lines of development. First, ethnic groups migrating to America brought specific traditions that were alive in their home country at the time they decided to immigrate. This is particularly true of Scandinavian Americans inasmuch as Norwegian, Danish, Swedish, and Icelandic cultures exhibit a strong attachment to their national traditional folk culture and to the historic events of their countries. Second, each ethnic group developed a hyphenated-American folk culture, retaining a portion or segment of their Old World home culture in the New World while creating new folklore in the host culture. The development of new forms of folklore enables the immigrants to maintain a tie to the Old World culture while living in the New World culture and describes for the immigrant groups their new lives.

The folklore of modern-day Scandinavian Americans evolved from language, habits, and customs that the groups brought with them and was limited to forms of oral and material folk culture that could be transported to North America. Hence, many oral pieces of folklore that could not survive translation into English also vanished once the speakers of original languages had disappeared. The disappearance of many language-based forms of folklore among Scandinavians, particularly Norwegian, Danish, and Swedish immigrants,

was due in part to the speed with which Scandinavians adopted the English language and North American forms of daily life. As a consequence, the folklore collector would not expect to find long narrative classic Scandinavian folktales such as those collected in Denmark in the mid-19th century by Hans Christian Andersen or in Norway by Peter Christen Asbjørnsen and Jørgen Moe. As an ethnic group, Scandinavian Americans joined the mainstream of North American culture within one or two generations, and, as a result, the longer, more complicated forms of folklore disappeared.

Some forms of traditional Scandinavian material folk culture, such as architecture, also disappeared; however, many forms of material folk culture persisted in North America. The folklore of Scandinavian Americans that is collected and studied in the 1990s is largely made up of the materials that survived from the first and second generation of Scandinavian immigrants. There are a number of Scandinavian American museum collections that contain folkloric materials, most notably Vesterheim: Norwegian American Museum (Decorah, Iowa); the Danish Immigrant Museum (Elk Horn, Iowa); the Swedish American Museum (Chicago); and the Nordic Heritage Museum (Seattle). Each of these collections contains significant historical, oral-historical, and material forms of traditional Scandinavian-American folklore, including textiles and weavings, furniture, wood carvings, boatbuilding, costumes, and other material items related to daily life in America. Many of the items of material folk culture, such as the immigrant painted chest or trunk, were brought from the immigrant's country of origin to the New World. Of the collections mentioned, the Vesterheim Collection, which is said to be the largest immigrant ethnic collection in North America, contains the most significant and well-documented body of materials.

Scandinavian Americans immigrated to North America throughout the history of the Americas. Early immigration of Norwegians, Danes, and Swedes dates back to the 17th and 18th centuries; however, by far the greatest numbers of immigrants from Scandinavia came during the last quarter of the 19th century and the first quarter of the 20th century. The emigration from Norway, Denmark, and Sweden exhibited characteristics similar to the overseas movement from Europe in general. Following a large movement of immigrants to North America during the period from the 1870s to the early 1890s, there was a decline of immigrants due to the economic depression of the early 1890s. Immigration returned to predepression numbers during the first two decades of the 20th century.

The numbers of Scandinavians immigrating to North America were very high in proportion to the total numbers of each country's population. Norway experienced the highest immigration intensity of the Scandinavian countries to North America. Between 1880 and the end of 1893, an average of ten of every thousand Norwegians immigrated, for a total of 256,068, and nearly all—99.25 percent—came to the United States. Between 1900 and 1915, another 235,410 Norwegians immigrated to the United States. The Norwegian Bureau of Statistics, using the U.S. Census of 1920, calculated that 1.2

million people of unmixed Norwegian descent, almost half the population of Norway, were living in the United States. Also by 1920, there were another 700,000 persons in the United States of mixed Norwegian descent.

The numbers of immigrants were almost as high for the other Scandinavian countries. For example, according to Varick A. Chittenden, between 1881 and 1930 more than 278,000 Danes immigrated to the United States. When Scandinavian Americans began to build their own communities in North America, they tended to settle near one another, enhancing the overall impact of the group. In the Midwestern United States, ethnic Scandinavians dominated some geographical regions in both the rural and urban areas. In Chicago, for example, Norwegians, Danes, and Swedes tended to congregate in the same areas of the city. In the countryside, in Wisconsin, Iowa, Illinois, Minnesota, and the Dakotas, Norwegian, Danish, and Swedish communities were often located close to one another. As a consequence, Scandinavian Americans reinforced their Old World traditions, even if they married a Scandinavian from a country other than their own. Still, by 1920, the Norwegian Bureau of Statistics estimated, 90 percent of the Norwegian-born immigrants married people who were either Norwegian or part Norwegian.

The oral folklore of ethnic Scandinavian Americans collected during the late 19th century and throughout the 20th century has been primarily minor and more modern types of folklore genres. Jan Harold Brunvand notes in his study of Norwegian folklore in Alberta, Canada, that the mode of folk expression that best endured is the brief oral narrative, either an anecdote or a traditional joke form (Brunvand 1974). For the three primary countries under discussion, the impact of immigration was unsettling for the immigrants and their families both at home and in their new home. Such large numbers leaving small countries, coupled with the immigrants' natural fidelity to their ethnic identity, led the immigrant populations to maintain their ethnic customs perhaps even more than they might have otherwise. Among the genres of folklore that were strongest during the settlement period were those that reflected the difficulty of immigration to a new country. Naming towns, villages, and farms reflected the immigrants' ethnic heritage. Hence, the names of settlements such as Norway, Michigan, Norway, Iowa, or New Norway, Alberta, announced to the immigrants and their neighbors the country of origin of the newly landed immigrant. "Dane Town," an informal name of a settlement in Iowa south of Council Bluffs across the Missouri River from Omaha, Nebraska, was never a formal designation, but it lasted through the first and second generations of Danish settler—after which it faded into memory. A similar fate befell "Swedetown," a section of northwest Salt Lake City, Utah. The process of naming was an important link to life in the Old World.

By far the largest body of oral-folklore materials that exists among Scandinavian Americans has to do with the actual process of settlement. Oral accounts and early newspapers abound with folkloric narratives that contain the recurring themes of settlement, including farm building, urban settlements, church building, famous characters in the settlement, and, of course, stories of neighbors who may or may not have been Scandinavian in origin. Chittenden, in his study of the folklore of a Danish community in New York, also notes that the oral folklore of ethnic Danes clearly depended upon the continued use of the language of the group (Chittenden 1985). During the second and third generation, when the language was used less frequently, traditional proverbs, sayings, riddles, rhymes, folktales, and folksongs faded from use and were largely forgotten among the folk. The fact of language currency is also evidenced in the older studies of Scandinavian folklore. Einar Haugen published his studies of early Norwegian ballads and songs in the 1930s and 1940s and Ella Valborg Rolvaag published her study of Norwegian American folk narrative in the 1940s.

Perhaps the strongest evidence of Scandinavian American folklore lay in the material folk culture produced by the group. It is not surprising, even in an ethnic group in which the original language was quickly disappearing, that the things produced by the group would continue to reflect their strong northern European heritage. Buildings, fishing boats, churches and church furniture, and many smaller handmade items designed for daily use continued to be part of the active Scandinavian American heritage. Possibly the first great monument to their Nordic heritage is the massive altar carved for the Seaman's Lutheran Church in Brooklyn, New York, and now housed at the Vesterheim Museum. Bay Ridge, a small Norwegian community located near the shipping docks in New York, was the site of a Norwegian immigrant community, and the altar served immigrants and Norwegian sailors alike for many years.

Among the finest examples of Scandinavian American folklore are the material-culture objects related to wood carving and wood painting. Wood carving among Norwegian Americans is documented by Marion J. Nelson, past director of the Norwegian-American Museum, who notes that the strongest traditions of carvings represented in North America come from the Gudbrandsdal and Telemark regions of Norway. Nelson points out that the strongest tradition of Norwegian carving represented in North America is acanthus carving, in which carvers exhibit a mastery of scroll design and intricate carving technique (Henning, Nelson, and Welsch 1978). The tradition of rosemaling (rose painting), primarily among Norwegian Americans, is a tradition that had its roots in Norway but was largely unpracticed in North America for several decades before experiencing a revival during the 1930s. Rosemaling styles, often named for different provinces in Norway from which a specific tradition originates, also display a mastery of painting small, intricate, natural patterns.

Two of the nearly 150 National Heritage Awards from the National Endowment for the Arts have gone to Norwegian Americans representing the traditions of wood carving and rosemaling. Leif Melgaard, who immigrated in 1920 to Minnesota, was recognized in 1985 for his expertise in wood carving. Known for the intricate detail in his wood carving, Melgaard learned his art at the Craft School of the Museum of Industrial Arts in Dakka, Norway, a school that had its origins in the Norwegian government's attempt to foster the indigenous folk crafts of the country. Ethel Kvalheim, who grew up in Wisconsin among Norwegian American neighbors, was recognized in 1989 for her expertise in traditional Norwegian rosemaling, which she learned from a neighbor as well as from classes offered at the Vesterheim Museum in Iowa. Melgaard and Kvalheim represent both the immigrant generation and the succeeding generation of Scandinavian Americans who express their culture through artifacts.

Perhaps as frequently as any other immigrant group to North America, Scandinavian Americans retained and created material-culture objects that expressed cultural values. Carved wooden spoons, painted drinking bowls, elaborately decorated silver jewelry, carved pieces of furniture, skis with heads of supernatural beings carved on the tips, flat woven rugs or tapestries, and traditional regional costumes are some of the items Scandinavian Americans use to display their heritage. Many artifacts reflected life in the old country, while handmade items were comments on life in the new country. For example, the well-known Norwegian American carver Ole Olson (1882–1966), known as "Ole the Hermit," carved small caricatures of the Norwegian immigrant types he knew from his native Valley City, North Dakota (Nelson 1989).

The folk arts and material culture among Scandinavian Americans were generally closely linked to the production of functional items related to daily life, a tradition that was carried from the old country to the New World. Farm buildings and boatbuilding provide two good examples of this phenomenon. While Scandinavians infrequently made buildings that were exactly like those made in their homeland, their American buildings were similar in general appearance to the Scandinavian archetype, but also expressed the immigrant's relatively quick assimilation in the new country. This assessment was noted by Norwegian folklorist Reidar Bakken in his fieldwork documentation of a granary from an Iowa farm. The granary, which was subsequently moved to the Norwegian Emigrant Museum in Hamar, Norway, was built in 1874 by a Norwegian immigrant who had come to the United States ten years earlier and exhibited qualities that more closely resembled traditional American Midwestern log buildings. It is documented that Norwegian American boatbuilders in Puget Sound in the Pacific Northwest continue to build boats using traditional styles inherited from the west coast of Norway as well as techniques from Denmark and the Faeroe Islands.

Most studies of contemporary folklore, and especially immigrant folklore, note that the tendency is for folklore to be expressed in shorter, more compact folklore genres such as the short joke or folk saying. This is certainly true of the development of forms of Scandinavian American folklore. Chittenden and Brunvand comment on this phenomenon and early immigrant novels illustrate this development (Brunvand 1974; Chittenden 1985). One reason for the decline of longer folklore genres is the disappearance of the immigrant language. Scandinavian Americans in the second and third generation will customarily be able to repeat counting rhymes and numbers in the original language while not being able to speak the language. Also, during celebrations such as birthdays and

holidays such as Christmas it is likely that Scandinavian Americans will know prayers or songs in the original Scandinavian language while not knowing exactly the meaning of the specific Scandinavian words. One rhyme often repeated by Danish Americans involves an adult naming in Danish a child's forehead, eyes, nose, mouth, and chin as he touches each part of the face, ending with a tickle under the chin. The rhyme serves to teach the child the names of the facial parts in Danish as well as to entertain. Today the Danish words are repeated even when the teller cannot speak the language.

Celebrations and holidays offer contemporary Scandinavian Americans an opportunity to express their ethnic heritage. Holidays observed in Scandinavian countries are popularly recognized in North America. Two examples are the Danish Constitution Day on June 5 *(Grundlovs Dag)* and Norwegian Independence Day on May 17 *(Syttende Mai)*. On these days, Danes and Norwegians in North America engage in an intense celebration of their ethnic heritage with traditional songs, foodways, national flags and ribbons, dance, and speech. Christmas, New Year's Day, and Midsummer Day (the summer solstice, around June 21) are also days that allow Scandinavian Americans the opportunity to celebrate their ethnic heritage. For example, Danes will make *aebleskiver* (Danish pancakes), *rullepolse* (pressed meat), *frikadeller* (meat balls), and *kleiner* (pastries) for holidays, while Swedes and Norwegians will prepare ethnic foods and build all-night fires for Midsummer, the longest day of the year. A standard foodway for Scandinavian Americans is coffee and tea with *smørrebrod* (butter and bread), an open-face sandwich of cheese or meat for any occasion. Among Swedish Americans, the celebration of St. Lucia (December 13), the ritual initiation of the Christmas season, is an important expression of their ethnic culture. Larry Danielson's study of this celebration in Lindsborg, Kansas, notes that among Swedish Americans the festivities are a public celebration performed each year as an expression of Swedish ethnic identity (Danielson 1991). In a similar way, Oakland, Nebraska, the self-proclaimed "Swede Capital of Nebraska," celebrates its Swedish identity with a festival held early in the summer.

One of the most important sources of Scandinavian American folklore is the rich body of immigrant literature. Immigrant Scandinavians and first-generation Scandinavian Americans produced a vast number of novels, short stories, and chronicles that related their lives in North America. Even though Scandinavian Americans assimilated into the population perhaps more easily than many other immigrant groups, they produced a literature that reflected, and commented on, their values and lives as a result of immigration. Perhaps the best example of the immigrant writer is Ole Edvart Rolvaag (1876–1931). In the novels *Giants in the Earth* (1927) and *The Third Life of Per Smevik* (1912), Rolvaag drew on the motifs of Norwegian folklore to describe the plight of the immigrants in their new country. An excellent account written by the grandchild of an immigrant is Kathryn Forbes' *Mama's Bank Account* (1943), in which the author uses folklore to describe the Americanization of a Norwegian family in California. Some of the best accounts of immigration were written by

Scandinavians who researched and interviewed immigrants to North America. Two classic works in this genre are Johan Bøjer's *The Emigrants* (1925), an account of Norwegian families in North Dakota, and Vilhelm Moberg's *Unto a Good Land* (1954), the chronicle of a Swedish immigrant family and their travel to Minnesota. Scandinavians in North America also produced a body of cultural and historical writing, the purpose of which was to instruct Scandinavian Americans about the old countries. Berner Loftfield's *Norge: Det Norske Folks Historie* (1900), published in Minneapolis, was an effort to teach Norwegians born in America about Norway.

In general, Scandinavian Americans are conscious and proud of their European heritage. The oral and material-culture folklore of the group reflects their particular history and settlement in North America. Like the literature, the collected oral narratives provide significant information and insight into Scandinavian American folkways. An example of the oral narratives that describe the process of settlement comes from a Danish woman born in Iowa of Danish-born parents. She told of growing up in "Dane Town." "It was always called Dane Town," she said, referring to the period from the 1880s to the 1920s, "I suppose because we were all Danes and there were new ones moving in all the time. People coming from Denmark could tell that the place was full of Danes." When she concluded the interview, she commented directly on Scandinavian heritage. "I always add a little cardamon to a lot of my food. It gives it a 'Danish' flavor, especially to the *aebleskiver*." Foodways, rhymes, songs, stories, artifacts, and house decoration used in the 1990s exhibit Scandinavian American folk traditions brought from the old countries and also developed in North America. Many of the traditions carried on in North America are believed by Scandinavian Americans to add a special "Norwegian, Danish or Swedish" flavor to their lives.

John F. Moe

References

Anderson, Philip J., and Dag Blanck. 1992. *Swedish-American Life in Chicago: Cultural and Urban Aspects of an Immigrant People, 1850–1930*. Urbana: University of Illinois Press.

Brunvand, Jan Harold. 1974. *Norwegian Settlers in Alberta*. Canadian Centre for Folk Culture Series Paper No. 8. Ottawa: National Museum of Man.

Chittenden, Varick A. 1985. *The Danes of Yates County: The History and Traditional Arts of an Ethnic Community in the Finger Lakes Region of New York State*. Penn Van, NY: Yates County Arts Council.

Danielson, Larry. 1991. St. Lucia in Lindsborg, Kansas. In *Creative Ethnicity: Symbols and Strategies of Contemporary Ethnic Life*, ed. Stephen Stern and John Allan Cicala. Logan: Utah State University Press, pp. 187–203.

Henning, Darrell D., Marion J. Nelson, and Roger L. Welsch. 1978. *Norwegian-American Wood Carving of the Upper Midwest*. Decorah, IA: Vesterheim: Norwegian-American Museum.

Jenner, Lars. 1992. Norwegian Maritime Traditions in the Pacific Northwest Halibut Industry. *Northwest Folklore* 10:43–52.

Klein, Barbro Sklute. 1980. *Legends and Folk Beliefs in a Swedish American Community*. New York: Arno.

Martin, Philip. 1989. *Rosemaling in the Upper Midwest: A Story of Region and Revival*. Mount Horeb: Wisconsin Folk Museum.

Nelson, Marion. 1989. *Norway in America*. Decorah, IA: Vesterheim: Norwegian-American Museum.

Paulsen, Frank M. 1974. *Danish Settlements on the Canadian Prairies: Folk Traditions, Immigrant Experiences, and Local History*. Canadian Centre for Folk Culture Series Paper No. 11. Ottawa: National Museum of Man.

Skaardal, Dorothy Burton. 1974. *The Divided Heart: Scandinavian Immigrant Experiences through Literary Sources*. Lincoln: University of Nebraska Press; Oslo: Universitetsforlaget.

Scarborough, Emily Dorothy (1878–1935)

Folklorist, novelist, and teacher. Scarborough, who used Dorothy as her first name and was known affectionately as "Miss Dottie" or "Aunt Dot," was a distinguished scholar and writer whose brief professional career spanned only seventeen years. While working as a teacher of creative writing at Columbia University in New York City, she wrote five novels, including *The Wind* (1925), which is regarded as a minor classic, and published two major folksong collections, *On the Trail of Negro Folksongs* (1925) and *A Song Catcher in the Southern Mountains* (1937). She also wrote and edited various other books, poems, short stories, reviews, and essays.

Scarborough was unusually well educated for her day, receiving a B.A. from Baylor University in 1896, an M.A. there in 1899, and a Ph.D. from Columbia University in 1917. She also studied at Oxford University in 1910, before that university awarded degrees to women.

She was elected president of the Texas Folklore Society in 1914, and her presidential address, "Negro Ballads and Reels," was the first public statement of her interest and expertise in folklore. Recognizing the blues as an original, indigenous American art form, she also interviewed W.C. Handy and published the first known scholarly article about him and his music in 1923.

Scarborough was squarely in the tradition of the literary approach to folklore materials, but she was not exclusively an "armchair scholar." She gathered the texts and tunes of many of the folksongs in her collections directly from the informants and then conducted extensive research and developed voluminous correspondence to annotate her materials thoroughly and place the materials in the context of other scholarly findings. She was well known by all of the leading ballad and folksong scholars of her generation, both in America and abroad. Her collections are exceptional not only for the extensive contextual data she provided about her informants, but also for her descriptions of her collecting methods and experiences.

Sylvia Ann Grider

References

Scarborough, Dorothy. 1917. *The Supernatural in Modern English Fiction.* New York: G.P. Putnam's Sons.

———. 1923. The "Blues" as Folk-Songs. *Publications of the Texas Folklore Society* 2:52–66.

Schoolcraft, Henry Rowe (1793–1864)

The first person to collect and analyze a large body of American Indian folklore. While serving as an Indian agent at Sault Ste. Marie, Michigan, Schoolcraft married into a Scots-Irish and Ojibwa family, the members of which served as an invaluable key to the culture.

The import of Schoolcraft's study of Indian folklore came from his use of native informants, his attempt to maintain at least some of their oral style in the translations, and his efforts to make a thorough collection of oral narratives. In his two-volume *Algic Researches* (1839), Schoolcraft published the narrative folklore he had collected among the Ojibwa. At a time that predated the establishment of folklore as a discipline, Schoolcraft emphasized the importance of understanding the language and of rendering exact translations. He discussed the Ojibwa narratives as reflectors of cultural values, religious beliefs, cosmology, history, child-rearing practices, and political perspective. As A. Irving Hallowell remarked: "Historically viewed, Schoolcraft was a pioneer in the collection of the folklore of any nonliterate people anywhere in the world. No other material of any comparable scope, obtained directly from American Indian informants, was published until several decades after *Algic Researches*" (Hallowell 1946:137). Schoolcraft's work was, Hallowell added, the first comprehensive collection of the myths and folktales of any Algonquian speakers. Thus, Schoolcraft provided a stimulus for subsequent collections of American Indian folklore.

Rosemary Lévy Zumwalt

References

Freeman, John Finley. 1959. Pirated Editions of Schoolcraft's Oneota. *Bibliographical Society of America Papers* 53 (3):252–254.

———. 1965. Religion and Personality in the Anthropology of Henry Schoolcraft. *Journal of the History of the Behavioral Sciences* 1 (4):301–303.

Hallowell, A. Irving. 1946. Concordance of Ojibwa Narratives in the Published Works of Henry R. Schoolcraft. *Journal of American Folklore* 59:136–153.

Zumwalt, Rosemary. 1978. Henry Rowe Schoolcraft, 1793–1864: His Collection and Analysis of the Oral Narratives of American Indians. *Kroeber Anthropological Society Papers* 53–59:44–57.

Scottish Americans

Major contributors to American social and cultural life since the earliest days of British settlement. A Scot named Thomas Henderson was one of the original settlers of Jamestown, Virginia, in 1607 (Donaldson 1980:909). Altogether about 1.5 million migrants have come to America from Scotland, which currently has a population of roughly five million.

During the 17th and 18th centuries, tens of thousands of Scots were transported and voluntarily migrated to British America, settling first along the Eastern seaboard, concentrating in greatest numbers in the Southern colonies. When the first U.S. Census was taken in 1790, at least 6 percent of the population was of Scottish or Scotch-Irish background (descendants of English-speaking Lowland Scottish Protestants who began colonizing the Northern Irish province of Ulster at the behest of James VI of Scotland and I of England in 1610). Between 1715 and 1775, roughly 250,000 Ulster Scots Presbyterians came to America, most landing in the middle colonies and gravitating to the colonial frontier. Nearly 2.5 percent of Americans claim some degree of Scottish ancestry, while approximately 3.3 percent identify themselves as Scotch-Irish, a term originating in America, not in Britain, where the terms "Ulster Scots" or "Scots-Irish" are preferred.

Scottish Americans and their Scotch-Irish cousins have not been clannish from a demographic perspective. Instead, American Scots have intermarried more than any other single European-American ethnic group, contributing to the general cultural mix of English-speaking America on many levels. Scottish influences pervade American folk music. Alexander Campbell "Eck" Robertson, Bill Monroe, Jim and Jesse McReynolds, Howdy Forrester, Jim Buchanan, Fiddling Cowan Powers, John Cowan Hartford, and Stuart Ian Duncan are a few notable 20th-century American fiddlers and bluegrass musicians with Scots ancestors. Folksinger Jean Ritchie and her family, and Woody Guthrie and his son Arlo, also have Scottish roots. Perhaps 40 percent of the Child ballads are distinctly Scottish rather than English in origin; most ballads found in Appalachia in the 1990s are still current in Northern Ireland and Lowland Scotland. Scottish singing styles have influenced various American regional ballad traditions. Many American fiddle tunes were originally Scottish, such as "Hop High Ladies" ("McLeod's Reel") "Leather Britches" ("Lord McDonald's Reel,") and "Too Young to Marry" (the tune of Robert Burns' "My Love Is But a Lassie-o"). Upland Southern American cabins, settlement patterns, and farming practices reflect Lowland Scottish and Ulster Scots prototypes. Scots influences are evident in American New Year's and Halloween celebrations, particularly in the South.

American regional dialects and folk speech are filled with Scottish and Scotch-Irish retentions. The hard postvocalic *r* that characterizes inland and Western American regional pronunciation patterns originated in north Britain, particularly Ulster and Lowland Scotland. The soft postvocalic *r* of America's Eastern coastal dialects from Maine down to Louisiana agrees with modern standard British usage, which emanates from metropolitan southern England. Nonstandard expressions like "used to could" for "used to be able to" and "done gone" for already gone" still commonly used by Southerners have been traced to north British sources. Scottish words in American folk speech are as localized as "bonnyclabber" for clabbered milk in eastern Massachusetts and as widely distributed as "pinky" for little finger and the exclamation "wow!" Golfing terms like "caddie," "birdie," and "bogie" have become as familiar to most Americans as Campbell's soup, McDonald's hamburgers, or Lassie, the canny collie who was perhaps America's favorite canine television celebrity.

Other Scottish contributions to American folklife are less obvious, less innocuous. Throughout its history, Scotland has been complex and conflict ridden. The successive waves of Scots who migrated to America included Gaelic-speaking Highlanders and English-speaking Lowlanders; Catholics versus Episcopalians versus Presbyterians versus Nonconformists and Dissenters; Tory royalists versus Whig republicans; repressive Calvinist fundamentalists and liberal secular humanists; Americanized pragmatists and nostalgic Romantics. Long-standing differences in language, religion, ethnicity, and regional politics carried over from the British Isles contributed to the tensions leading to the American Revolution and still affect the cultural politics of the United States (see Fischer 1989). Most Highland Scots in the colonies remained loyal to the Crown and removed to Canada following the Revolution. So many Lowlanders and Ulster Presbyterians supported colonial independence that many Tories were convinced the American Revolution was at heart a Scotch-Irish insurrection (Jackson 1993:121).

The anti-Catholic Lowland Scottish Calvinists who subjugated Ulster envisioned themselves as a righteous minority in a wicked world, a Church Militant justifying its violence against demonized infidels through a covenant with God transcending corrupt worldly authority. Their descendants on the American frontier carried on traditions of severely plain church architecture, rejection of a paid clergy, and insistence upon moralistic, repressive church discipline. Early Calvinist reformers in Scotland burned bagpipes, smashed fiddles, flogged fornicators, and hanged witches (Farmer [1947] 1970:117–158). Camp meetings, singing in unison, "lining out" of hymns, banning of musical accompaniment in church, and violent opposition to sinful secular amusements like fiddling, dancing, and ballad singing are all part of the legacy of militant covenanters and seceders who left the Presbyterian Church in America to join more radically evangelistic denominations. Historians note bickering between contending Scottish sects; the high degree of individualism and fragmentation of American Protestantism, especially in the South, is an extension of this schismatic tradition.

By the time most Ulster Scots arrived in America, the traditional system of clans (families bound by feudal ties between chiefs and their retainers) had largely disappeared in the Lowlands. Clans survived in the Highlands, however, well into the 18th century and were reorganized and revitalized following the series of Jacobite rebellions that failed to restore the Stuart dynasty to the British throne. Some Scots in America quickly came to think of themselves as Americans; others found ways of expressing their sense of Scottishness that did not conflict with their identities as Americans. Even as Scots played leading roles in British and American industry, medicine, the military, education, and politics, many still were deeply attached to the idea of Scotland.

The disintegration of the Jacobite cause gave rise to Scottish romantic nationalism, which survives in various forms even in the late-20th century. The Disarming Act of 1747, which followed Bonnie Prince Charlie's defeat at Culloden, specifically prohibited displays of Scottish national symbols, including kilts, tartans, plaids, and Highland bagpipes. Loyalist Highland regiments, however, were exempted from the bans on the kilt and pipes. Their officers refined modern Scottish martial music and costume, inventing regimental tartans, which in turn inspired the clan tartans we know today. In 1778 a group of Scottish gentlemen dwelling in London founded the Highland Society, so that they could periodically gather together ". . . in that garb so celebrated as having been the dress of their Celtic ancestors, and on such occasions at least to speak the emphatic language, to listen to the delightful music, to recite the ancient poetry, and to observe the peculiar customs of their country" (Trevor-Roper 1983:26). This group successfully petitioned the House of Commons in 1782 to repeal the ban on Highland dress and other strictures of the Disarming Act. By this time, a flourishing Scottish Romantic nationalist movement engaged artists and intellectuals like Robert Burns, who championed traditional Scottish music and the Lowlands Scots dialect during his brief, brilliant career.

Long before the 1745 Uprising or the American Revolution, Scottish immigrants in the New World were forming special-interest groups preserving the social and cultural traditions of their homeland. In 1657 a Scots Charitable Society was established in Boston, possibly the first organization of its kind anywhere (Donaldson 1966:44). Increased Scottish migration to America during the 18th century saw the establishment of St. Andrew's Societies in Charleston (1729), Philadelphia (1749), New York (1756), and Savannah (ca. 1750). Then as now, these societies provided periodic opportunities for the celebration of Scottishness. Some Scots in America were apparently engaged in the Scottish romantic movement before the American Revolution or the repeal of the Disarming Act, as Donaldson noted: "It is, however, curious that so early as 1765 George Bartram, a native of Scotland who had become a cloth merchant in Philadelphia, was advertising 'best Scotch Plaids for gentlemen's gowns and boy's Highland dress'" (Donaldson 1966:128).

The continued expansion of British industrialism and imperialism led to the establishment of more Scottish immigrant organizations and revivalistic institutions in the late 18th and 19th centuries. The state visit of George IV to Edinburgh in 1822 orchestrated by Sir Walter Scott inspired another wave of newly invented clan tartans. The patronage of the Balmoral Highland Games by Victoria and Albert established the prototype for modern Highland games, reaffirming the ties of the Scottish clans through their chiefs to the British royalty: "British national and imperial identity chimed quite nicely with a powerful strand of Scottish national identity, reinforced by Protestantism, Unionism, and militarism" (McCrone 1992:209). It seems ironic that the British aristocracy and the Lowland Scots came to romanticize the Highland Gaels and to expropriate selected features of their culture, after having struggled for centuries to subdue and disperse them (see Chapman 1992).

Roughly two million people left Scotland between 1830 and 1914; nearly half went to America. Burns' birthday was celebrated in New York as early as 1820; by 1836 the Highland Club of New York held its first annual Highland Games. Within a very short time, Caledonian Games including most of the sports and performing-arts competitions featured in the contemporary Highland Games were being held in major Scottish settlements in the United States, Canada, and New Zealand (see Redmond 1971). Though initially organized to celebrate Scottish culture, the Caledonian Games were soon open to the general public, regardless of national origin. During their peak years, the Caledonian Games attracted tens of thousands of spectators and participants. The same period also saw the formation of modern clan societies, which reorganized the traditional Scottish system of hereditary chiefs and retainers as formally chartered special-interest associations with elected officers and dues-paying members.

By the turn of the 20th century, most aspects of modern Scottish cultural revivalism were already in existence. Highland Games, Burns Suppers, and clan societies continue to flourish in the United States, Canada, and other Scottish diaspora communities. The magnitude of this interest can be gleaned from the annual listings of Scottish American organizations and events compiled by Angus Ray of Barrington, Illinois, publisher of *The Highlander: The Magazine of Scottish Heritage,* which reports a circulation of over 40,000. *The Highlander's* 1993 Directory Issue lists 255 clan societies, 172 Scottish societies, such as Saint Andrew's and Caledonian societies, 227 bagpipe bands, 179 vendors, 171 clan chiefs, 53 miscellaneous Scottish organizations, and 64 Highland Games and Gatherings. These figures only begin to suggest the actual number of Scottish American special-interest organizations. Emily Ann Donaldson's *The Scottish Highland Games in America* lists a minimum of 80 Highland Games held during 1985–1986 across the United States from Maine to Maui, featuring not only athletic events, but also competitions for Highland solo dancing and Scottish country dancing, solo piping and pipe bands, fiddling, Celtic harp, and sheepdog trials (Donaldson 1986).

Within the Scottish American heritage community there are many special-interest groups, part of a complex of Scottish social and cultural organizations that has been developing since colonial times. These organizations thrive because Scottishness is still meaningful to many people, regardless of the fact that Scotland ceased to be a sovereign state nearly 400 years ago. The idea of Scotland is still very much alive in Scotland in the 1990s. According to Scottish sociologist David McCrone, seven out of ten modern Scots consider themselves Scottish, not British, and an additional 19 percent consider themselves Scottish *and* British (McCrone 1992:198).

Many Americans consider themselves Scottish in spirit, though American by birth. Even though their ancestors might have left Scotland because their lairds displaced them to make way for sheep, there are Scottish Americans who thrill to Burns' often quoted lines: "My heart's in the highlands, my heart is not here. / My heart's in the highlands, a chasing the deer." Not all Scots share or appreciate that Romantic, nostalgic vision. In fact, debunkers have challenged the historical authenticity of the icons of Scottish Romantic nationalism for more than 200 years. James MacPherson, who claimed to have recovered gems of ancient Scots Gaelic poetry, was called a forger, yet his *Ossian* poems (1760–1763) contributed to the rise of romantic nationalism and the academic study of folklore in the 18th and 19th centuries. Modern Scottish antiroyalists have little love for tartans, kilts, and bagpipes, which they perceive as symbols of dependency and complicity in British colonialism. Their efforts to unravel the cult of the kilt, to expose it as a recent, spurious fabrication, have not changed the feelings of those Scots at home and abroad who do find positive value in the kilt and other emblems of Scottish identity. (The modern pleated kilt is quite literally a fabrication of the early industrial age, the product of the collaboration of an English foundryman, Thomas Rawlinson, and a Scottish chief, Ian McDonnell of Glengarry, who employed a regimental tailor in Inverness to fashion a garment less clumsy and bothersome in the workplace than the toga-like belted plaids still commonly worn by Highland Scots) (see Trevor-Roper 1983).

Alan Dundes has said that folklorists cannot prevent the folk from believing fakelore is folklore. If a group of people like Scottish Americans identifies with a set of cultural symbols, then it matters little whether these symbols are ancient or recently invented. As McCrone says: "Traditions may be invented; symbols of national identity re-manufactured. Perhaps there is a suggestion in the word 'invented' that myths and traditions are fabricated; what seems to happen is that the cultural raw materials are refashioned in a manner that gives coherence and meaning to action. The task is not to debunk these inventions, but to show how and why they are put to such telling use" (McCrone 1992:30).

Richard J. Blaustein

References

Chapman, Malcolm. 1992. *The Celts: The Making of a Myth.* London: Routledge.

Donaldson, Emily Ann. 1986. *The Scottish Highland Games in America.* Gretna, La: Pelican.

Donaldson, Gordon. 1966. *The Scots Overseas.* Westport, CT: Greenwood.

———. 1980. Scots. In *Encyclopedia of American Ethnic Groups.* Cambridge: Harvard University Press, pp. 908–916.

Farmer, Henry George. [1947] 1970. *A History of Music in Scotland.* New York: Da Capo.

Fischer, David Hackett. 1989. *Albion's Seed: Four British Folkways in America.* New York: Oxford University Press.

Jackson, Clayton. 1993. *A Social History of the Scotch Irish.* Lanham, MD: Madison Books.

Jones, Maldwyn A. 1980. Scotch Irish. In *Encyclopedia of American Ethnic Groups.* Cambridge: Harvard University Press, pp. 895–908.

McCrone, David. 1992. *Understanding Scotland: The Sociology of a Stateless Nation.* London and New York: Routledge.

Redmond, Gerald. 1971. *The Caledonian Games in Nineteenth Century America.* Rutherford, NJ: Fairleigh Dickenson University Press.

Trevor-Roper, Hugh. 1983. The Invention of Tradition: The Highland Tradition of Scotland. In *The Invention of Tradition,* ed. Eric Hobsbawm and Terence Ranger. Cambridge: Cambridge University Press.

Seeger, Charles Louis (1886–1979)

Outstanding musicologist of the 20th century. Seeger worked in virtually every facet of music, including composition, teaching, education, theory, ethnomusicology, and the relationship between music and society and between music and language. He was instrumental in the founding of many learned societies, including the American Musicological Society and the Society for Ethnomusicology.

Seeger was born in Mexico City and divided his youth between Mexico and Staten Island, New York. After graduating from Harvard University in 1908, he spent two and a half years in Europe preparing for a career in composition.

In 1912 he joined the faculty of the University of California, Berkeley. During his six years there, he developed a curriculum that included exposure to other musical cultures; he also immersed himself in the study of philosophy and history, which influenced much of his later writing.

In the early 1930s, Seeger realized the importance of folk music as a complement to fine-art music. Beginning in 1935, he headed cultural programs within President Franklin D. Roosevelt's Resettlement Administration and later the Works Progress Administration. These appointments gave him the opportunity to apply his theoretical notions to solving social problems. He used vernacular music to help heal social tensions and foster community goals. From 1941 to 1953, Seeger worked with the Pan American Union to bring close ties between musicians throughout the Americas.

From 1961 to 1971, Seeger was associated with UCLA's Institute of Ethnomusicology. During these years, he wrote many theoretical articles. He spent his final years in Bridgewater, Connecticut, where he continued to write.

Despite his considerable contributions to the field of musicology, he will undoubtedly be best remembered as father to a number of children, including Pete, Michael, and Peggy, all of whom made their mark as performers of folk and folk-like music.

Ed Kahn

References

Pescatello, Ann M. 1992. *Charles Seeger: A Life in American Music.* Pittsburgh: University of Pittsburgh Press.

Reuss, Richard A. 1979. Folk Music and Social Conscience: The Musical Odyssey of Charles Seeger. *Western Folklore* 38:221–238.

Seeger, Charles. 1977. *Studies in Musicology, 1935–1975.* Berkeley: University of California Press.

Seeger, Pete (1919–)

Folksinger, songwriter, and social activist. Seeger was a major figure in America's folk-music revival. He sought to link music with social change, doing so by popularizing traditional folksongs, then changing the words to address social issues: workers' rights in the 1940s, the role of government in the 1950s, civil rights and the peace movement in the 1960s, environmental issues in the 1970s and 1980s, and the role of technology in the 1990s. Seeger served as a bridge between traditional folksingers of the 1930s and 1940s and the popular folk performers of the 1960s and later.

Seeger was born in New York City, the son of musicologist and activist Charles Seeger, who left his son a legacy of musical theory and political radicalism. Pete entered Harvard University intending to go into journalism, but when he was unable to find employment after he left Harvard, he began playing his four-string banjo for schools and camps. Later he learned the five-string banjo, an almost extinct instrument, which he adapted to many different kinds of music. His elongated instrument, emblazoned with the credo "This machine surrounds hate and forces it to surrender," became the symbol of the tall, lanky performer.

Pete Seeger was fortunate to be living on the East Coast, where Huddie Ledbetter (Lead Belly), Woody Guthrie, Alan Lomax, Aunt Molly Jackson, and Moses Asch were laying the groundwork for the folk revival. They shared their vision, musical skills, and songs with him. In 1940 he traveled with Guthrie, playing to and learning the songs of American farmers and workers.

With Lee Hays, Seeger organized his first performing group, the Almanac Singers, in 1941. The members of the group—Seeger, Lee Hays, Millard Lampell, then Guthrie, and later others—played primarily to union groups. During this period, Seeger joined the Communist Party, believing in its program.

After World War II, during which Seeger served for three and a half years in the U.S. Army, he and Lee Hays joined with Ronnie Gilbert and Fred Hellerman to form the Weavers, a more professional singing group that, while still political, appealed to a larger audience. Among the group's biggest recorded hits were "Wasn't That a Time," "Kisses Sweeter Than Wine," "Wimoweh," "Tzena, Tzena," "Michael Row the Boat Ashore," and scores of their own versions of traditional folksongs. Although the Weavers were blacklisted in 1952 because of Seeger's earlier Communist Party affiliation, Seeger was in 1962 acquitted of contempt of Congress. The Weavers directly influenced many folksingers of the 1960s, including the Limelighters, the Kingston Trio, Arlo Guthrie, and Peter, Paul, and Mary. Seeger left the Weavers in 1957 in order to spend more time with his growing family.

They settled in Beacon, New York, overlooking the Hudson River, where Seeger built a cabin, continued to write songs and to perform, and became involved in environmental issues. Among the many songs, either composed or sung by Seeger and closely associated with his name, are "We Shall Overcome," "Turn! Turn! Turn!" "Waist Deep in the Big Muddy," and especially "Where Have All the Flowers Gone?"

In 1969 Seeger helped launch the sloop *Clearwater* as a vehicle to educate children and Hudson River inhabitants about the dangers of pollution, and in the 1990s he continues to worry about the destructive potential of technology. An uncompromising idealist, Seeger hopes to pull the world together with music. He has performed for somewhere between four million and five million people in forty countries, and he has released in excess of fifty albums, recording more than 300 songs.

Although Seeger's main contribution has been entering some types of folk music into mainstream American music, he is concerned that the role of many kinds of the traditional American folk performers has been minimalized.

Deirdre Paulsen

References

Dunaway, David King. 1981. *How Can I Keep from Singing: Pete Seeger.* New York: McGraw–Hill.

Seeger, Pete. 1962. *How to Play the Five String Banjo.* 3d rev. ed. New York: Oak Publications.

Seeger, Pete. 1993. *Where Have All the Flowers Gone: A Singer's Stories, Songs, Seeds, Robberies.* Bethlehem, PA: Sing Out Publications.

Seeger, Pete, Bud Schultz, and Ruth Schultz, eds. 1989. Thou Shall Not Sing. In *It Did Happen Here: Recollections of Political Repression in America.* Berkeley: University of California Press.

Seeger, Pete, and Jo Metcalf Schwartz, eds. 1972. *The Incompleat Folksinger.* New York: Simon and Schuster.

Semiotic Approach

Semiotics—the study of signs and sign systems. A "sign" is something present that stands for something absent, as a cross represents Christianity; a "sign system" is a set of signs and rules for their use. Semiotics is both a discipline and an approach used by other disciplines, including folklore.

While there have been recent attempts to document early theorizing that can belatedly be described as contributing to semiotics, there are two major early theorists who clearly intended to establish a new field of study: Ferdinand de Saussure (1857–1913), a Swiss linguist, and Charles Sanders Peirce (1839–1914), an American philosopher. Saussure thought there was something missing in the study of linguistics and introduced "semiology" as the science to "study the life of signs within society" (1916/1969, p. 16). Peirce wanted to expand the study of logic to include the study of signs and proposed calling the new field "semiotics" (1931–1958). It has become common in the United States to use the term semiotics to refer to all of the work of Saussure and Peirce and the followers of both (rather than semiology, a term more in favor in Europe) in deference to the fact that Peirce devoted the greatest amount of time and effort toward developing the groundwork of the discipline and in an attempt to consolidate rather than draw fine distinctions between areas of related research. Within folklore, Saussure has clearly had the greatest influence.

Part of what is interesting about semiotics is the breadth of topics covered (Sebeok 1986). At the least, everything that is granted meaning by humans can be included; a few scholars also include animals and even plants. What is important is not merely that semiotics encompasses many things that are rarely grouped together, but that it explains how they are similar. In each case, whether the topic is food, painting, or poetic imagery, something (the sign) conveys meaning—meaning that would not otherwise be obvious, or that we could not otherwise present in such a condensed form. It is not breadth of scope for its own sake that is significant, but breadth of scope for the surprising fact that so many different actions, objects, and behaviors, in so many different contexts, all appear to operate in a similar fashion that warrants attention.

Largely due to Saussure's role as a linguist, his early statements about semiotics are generally understood to imply that language should be taken as the model for other semiotic systems and that linguistics serve as the model for how to study all semiotic systems. There has been considerable discussion about the appropriateness of this presumptive role of language as the preeminent semiotic system and about whether linguistics is always the best model for semiotic analysis. Such discussion does not change the fact that language has, to date (1995), usefully served as the model for much work within semiotics.

As proposed by Saussure, each sign has two parts, termed the "signifier" and the "signified." The signifier is visible or in some other way present (for example, a flag is visible, and the word "flag" is audible); the signified is invisible but referred to (the country that verbal and material flags represent). In other words, the signifier is the explicit aspect of a sign, a material presence of some sort; the signified is the tacit element of a sign, something literally absent yet functionally present because it has been invoked.

In addition to designating the component parts of any sign, semioticians commonly sort the class of signs into different groups or types. Of the sixty-six potential varieties Peirce originally identified, three have gained wide acceptance. In each case, the relationship between the signifier and signified serves as focus of attention. An "icon" has the relationship of similarity (a photograph of someone is an icon since the signifier—the photograph—resembles the signified—the person it represents). An "index" has the relationship of contiguity (the top of the wedding cake kept for the first anniversary is an index since it served as a physical piece of the original event). A "symbol" has the relationship of arbitrariness (a white bridal gown is a symbol of innocence, standing for something it neither resembles nor was taken from).

Semioticians have touted the concept of the sign as the basic building block used in the construction of human meaning. The following quotation is from Charles Morris, but the sentiment is fairly common: "Indeed, it does not seem fantastic to believe that the concept of sign may prove as fundamental to the sciences of man as the concept of atom has been for the physical sciences or the concept of cell for the biological sciences" (Morris 1938:42). As with literal building blocks, signs function by being combined into larger sets; technically, the term for a set of signs is a "code." Yet the concept of code includes more than "groupness"; it also includes rules governing the use of signs. All codes share the same characteristics. Among these, two are critical. First, each code has a set of signs arranged into what are called "paradigms," and it is from each set of possibilities that a single one is chosen for a given purpose. For example, in the clothing code, all shoes are a single paradigm; it is from this set that each of us chooses one possible pair of shoes to wear each day.

Second, individual signs are chosen from paradigms and combined into new sets termed *syntagms*. For example, to go with the particular shoes I chose to wear today, I chose one shirt from the paradigm of shirts, and one pair of pants from the paradigm of pants; taken together they form a new group termed a syntagm. Meaning arises from the combination of two things: the choice of a particular sign from the range of possibilities (paradigms) and the combination of individual signs into new meaning sets (syntagms).

There are three main types of codes: (1) logical (those used by science, such as mathematics or Morse code); (2) aesthetic (those used by art, such as architecture or photography); and (3) social (those used by groups of people during interaction, such as language or clothing). It is primarily social codes that are of interest to folklorists, although aesthetic codes may also become a focus of attention. Most study of material culture and verbal art could appropriately use semiotics as an analytic tool. Some examples of scholars who have applied a semiotic approach to material aspects of culture are Roland Barthes (1967), Petr Bogatyrev (1971), and Bela Gunda (1973); some who have applied a semiotic approach to verbal art are Vladimir J. Propp ([1928] 1968), John H. McDowell (1981), and Danielle M. Roemer (1982).

Just as a single sign does not convey meaning alone but only as part of a larger system (a code), so also a single code does not stand alone but functions as one part of a system of codes. This system of codes does not yet have a name that everyone has agreed upon, but the most likely term is "culture" for, as Umberto Eco suggests, "to communicate is to use the entire world as a semiotic apparatus. I believe that culture is that, and nothing else" (Eco 1973:57; see Leeds-Hurwitz, 1993:155–176 for elaboration). Just as some aspects of meaning are determined from the (larger) code rather than the (smaller) sign, so are some drawn from the largest level of all, the entire set of codes utilized within a single culture. Presumably, one reason there has been so little focus at this level to date (1995) is the difficulty of such study; however, it is the logical next step in semiotic analysis.

Wendy Leeds-Hurwitz

References

Barthes, Roland. 1967. *Elements of Semiology*, trans. A. Lavers and C. Smith. New York: Hill and Wang.

Bogatyrev, Petr. 1971. *The Function of Folk Costume in Moravian Slovakia*, trans. R.G. Crum. The Hague: Mouton.

Eco, Umberto. 1973. Social Life as a Sign System. In *Structuralism: An Introduction*, ed. D. Bobey. Oxford: Clarendon, pp. 57–72.

Gunda, Bela. 1973. Sex and Semiotics. *Journal of American Folklore* 86:143–151.

Leeds-Hurwitz, Wendy. 1993. *Semiotics and Communication: Signs, Codes, Cultures*. Hillsdale, NJ: Lawrence Erlbaum Associates.

McDowell, John H. 1981. Toward a Semiotics of Nicknaming: The Kamsa Example. *Journal of American Folklore* 94:1–18.

Morris, Charles. 1938. *Foundations of the Theory of Signs*. Chicago: University of Chicago Press.

Propp, Vladimir J. [1928] 1968. *Morphology of the Folktale*. Austin: University of Texas Press.

Roemer, Danielle M. 1982. In the Eye of the Beholder: A Semiotic Analysis of the Visual Descriptive Riddle. *Journal of American Folklore* 95:173–199.

Sebeok, Thomas A., ed. 1986. *Encyclopedic Dictionary of Semiotics*. 3 vols. Berlin: Mouton de Gruyter.

See also Coding in American Folk Culture

Sermon, Folk

A sacred, hortatory oration, thematically based on Scripture, usually orally performed and transmitted. These performances are, to an extensive degree, spontaneously composed. Folk preachers may have been formally educated—many have not been—but their mode of preaching and the sermon's content are not decisively determined by their education. Scriptural support for oral preaching and for the irrelevance of formal education is found in Luke 24:49; the preacher does nothing to prepare himself for his mission, but rather waits—tarries—until the Spirit descends:

> And, behold, I send the promise of my Father upon you: but tarry ye in the city of Jerusalem, until ye be endued with power from on high.

The only fit sermon subject is the kingdom of God, as prescribed by Luke 16:16:

> The law and the prophets were until John: since that time the kingdom of God is preached, and every man presseth into it.

A few of the elements characteristic of folk sermons—oral performance and transmission, belief in the necessity of such spontaneity—are found in learned, conventional sermons as well, as preached by a very wide spectrum of priests, rabbis, and ministers. Most folk sermons in the United States are preached by Baptists, Methodists, and Pentecostals, and by a host of divines who are not squarely in the mainstream of American religious expression. More commonly, American preachers deliver sacred messages from a manuscript, prepared in advance, one that may actually have been reworked over months, even years. In a literate society, this mode of sermon preparation and transmission is the norm. Oral composition is with many preachers actually an article of dogma, deriving from the New Testament. For many folk preachers, it is not merely unnecessary to be educated, it is also probably a de-

"Jacob at the Well." Paper cutting, 15 x 21.5 cm. Ohio, probably 1860s. Collection J. W. Love.

terrent.

This form of preaching, and the resultant product, has been difficult to locate precisely in history. It may have been the product of marginal New England religious experiences; from there (if of American origin) it moved south, where it was found in colonial days among the Quakers and Shakers in the Middle South. Observers of Baptist sermons noted that emotions were expressed freely, and consequently these sermons were attacked by Anglicans for their "vehement pathos" and their "histrionics." Traditional divines belittled this unorthodox preaching style as the "Baptist whine." This style of 18th- and 19th-century sermon delivery was notable for its emotionalism, its free expression, and the musical tone of the preachers; it sounds much like the performance of the chanted folk sermon of the late 20th century.

African Americans are the most prolific and the most skilled practitioners of this form. Historically, the basic skills of oral sermon performance may have been acquired at the many camp meetings held throughout the colonies and the early states. Both Blacks and Whites attended these open-air services, and though the races were usually seated separately, the preaching could be heard by everyone. Yet, certain characteristics of these performances—for instance, the call-and-response style of performances found even in the 1990s—probably derived from Africa. So it is possible that what has become known as the American folk sermon came from Africa along with slaves shipped forceably to the New World. It is possible also that the modern-day form is the product of a blending of Black and White sacred cultures.

This style of preaching orally performed, spontaneously composed, and characterized by free emotional expression,

became popular during that religious movement of the early 19th century, the Second Great Awakening. During this period, a large number of African Americans were proselytized and converted. The "barking" and "jerking" of the Baptists and the Methodists, contemptuously derided by conventional New England divines, were first recorded during this period. The outdoor camp meetings, such as the one at Cane Ridge, Kentucky, attended by 20,000 people, were thought to be further examples of "primitive" behavior.

Chanting and other dramatic vocal modes liven the sermon, avoiding monotony, which in an oral performance could be especially deadly. The chanted folk sermon is dramatic, and its performer is a sacred actor, using many of the techniques of the stage performer to make the sermon more effective: gesture, facial expression, eye contact, and alteration of voice pitch. Many folk preachers, and others, believe that emotion expressed in church—the greater the abandonment the better—is appropriate. Frenzy, passion, and glossolalia (speaking in tongues) are signs of the presence of the Lord. If church services are not emotional, the minister (or priest or rabbi) is thought to have failed to evoke the Spirit of God.

Chanting builds the emotional tension of the performance; the preacher's tone of voice, increasing pace of delivery, and mounting emotional content move toward an emotional climax. The emotional curve of the entire performance is not significantly different from an audience's aesthetic response to well-written theatrical drama. In these important ways, the chanted folk sermon is an analogue of the secular aesthetic work embodying the catharsis of classical drama.

For these reasons, the spoken sermon is livelier and more dramatic than conventional performances, even for the uninitiated, to hear. The conventional text-based sermon, prepared in writing, is appropriate for the belief that God should be apprehended through intellectual exertion. The folk sermon appeals more directly to the emotions; a quiet, thoughtful congregation indicates to the folk preacher that God is not present. An outsider may think of such services as "emotional," but the preacher and the congregation view the performance as spiritual.

This delivery style establishes an intimacy between preacher and congregation, similar to the close relationship between the preacher and his or her God. The folk preacher is likely to say, "Jesus said to me the other day . . ." or "St. Paul said. . . ." The folk preacher may advise St. Peter not to worry about his children, or the leader of the Jews may be referred to as "Old man Moses." God and his saints are existential, living, and close at hand, not distant, or aloof, or abstract. The preacher addresses that God and his saints directly and immediately, a face-to-face confrontation with the divine presence in a meaningful world.

Oral recitation of spontaneous material allows the preacher a great deal of flexibility in performance. The sermon can be lengthened or abridged depending upon the preacher's inclination, and that may be decided by several personal factors, including a response to the congregation. If they are listless, the preacher can choose to enliven the performance or to abbreviate it. Conversely, an excited congregation may stimulate the preacher to further performative heights.

The folk sermon's structure is potentially fluid. While

many ministers strive for the conventional "text-context-application" format, during actual performance that form can vary considerably. The "text" for the day, and its scriptural "context" take only a short time to deliver. The "application" is the major portion of the sermon and may be composed of any of several generic components: exemplars, anecdotes, biblical narratives, first-person accounts. Seldom do these elements have to occur in a specific order; the preacher is free to insert them in the sermon as necessary or expedient. Thus, the folk sermon's form is fluid, its constituent elements are variable, and the order of their occurrence variable. Generic delineations are difficult to formulate.

Folk sermons in the United States are more often chanted than spoken formally. The preacher begins the performance in a conventional oratorical mode, gradually increasing the pace of delivery and the voice's emotional tension. Shortly into the sermon, the preacher of chanted performances is partly singing the message; by the end, he or she may break into song, spiritual or popular. The method of composition is approximately that described by Milman Parry and Albert Bates Lord in their several works on oral-formulaic composition and performance. The preacher's professional skills must be at the same level of the Yugoslavian *guslari* (traditional epic singers): Having mastered the material and the music of the delivered line, he or she can then improvise. But the basics must first be mastered, just as with jazz musicians, who must know their material intimately before being able to creatively depart from it. The preacher's utterance in the chanted-sung sermon is a metrically consistent line, of a regularly employed length, that induces frequent repetition of word and phrase. Thus, the formula of the Parry-Lord oral-formulaic theory is created. Composition by manipulation of oral formulas—those words and word groups that occur regularly in certain metrical situations—is common. The performances of some preachers are heavily formulaic: Up to 17 percent of their uttered lines are repetitions of other lines within the same performance. Most, however, are not nearly so repetitious.

The themes observed by Parry and Lord also occur. In the sermons, these take the forms of set scenes or episodes, often from the Bible. The preacher may have mentally formulated a description of the four horsemen of the apocalypse, or of Ezekiel preaching in the valley of dry bones. These themes are composed of several (sometimes more than two-score) formulas, not memorized but loosely structured, and which can be used in performance as a unit. Such employment eases the preacher's compositional task, enabling him or her to concentrate on the material ahead and, over several performances, facilitates honing the style and the message of the retained passage.

The folk character of the folk sermon derives from the content of the text, principly the origin of the materials from which the sermon is constructed. What differentiates the folk sermon from its literate, strictly biblical-based, kin is the preacher's use of folk materials.

Several kinds of materials may be found. Depending upon the preacher's background and musical competence, fragments of popular music—not gospels or church-sanctioned hymns—occur. Popular songs, not usually thought of as belonging to a sacred service, are used, particularly if the preacher feels confident in his or her singing ability.

Certain favored locutions and metaphors are also used, often derived from secular sources. The preacher may exclaim, "Hark Haleujah," or "God from Zion," or "Ain't God all right?" Folk preachers rephrase Scripture colloquially: "Now hear the word of the Lord" instead of the original "Thus *saith* the Lord God unto these bones." Or a homespun portrait of one of the four horsemen: "Dressed in raiment / White as driven as the snow." He wore a "rainbow 'round his shoulder."

Unconventional as these devices are, they are received with understanding by the congregation. The message always gets through. The congregation in the churches described here usually participate actively in the service, calling out individualized responses *ad libitim.* Their participation can influence the preacher's lexical choice, even in the form the message of the day will take.

This antiphonal call-and-response is not prepared in any way, except what tradition and custom directs. Both parties—preacher and congregation—are expressing their individual addresses to God.

The metrical folk sermon, chanted or sung and making heavy use of conventional, popular materials, is also used in ostensibly secular contexts. The most notable examples are the sermons of the Reverend Martin Luther King Jr. (especially his "I Have a Dream" speech) and the Reverend Jesse Jackson (perhaps most famously his address to the Democratic National Convention in 1988).

Yet, these contexts are not entirely secular. Certainly the civil rights march in Washington, DC, was in large measure religious, as was Jackson's address to the 1988 convention. If there was any doubt about the seriousness of the speaker, or of the message, that misunderstanding would be dispelled by the nature and style of the speaker-preacher.

When delivered by inspired preachers, the folk sermon has proven to exert a potent influence over a very wide range of congregations and audiences, literate and sophisticated (and jaded), as well as folk groups.

Bruce A. Rosenberg

References

Davis, Gerald. 1987. *I Got the Word in Me, and I Can Sing It, You Know.* Philadelphia: University of Pennsylvania Press.

Lawless, Elaine J. 1990. *Handmaidens of the Lord.* Philadelphia: University of Pennsylvania Press.

Rosenberg, Bruce A. 1989. *Can These Bones Live?* Urbana: University of Illinois Press.

Shape-Note Singing

A style of sacred choral performance, popular almost exclusively in the Southern United States. It is based on religious songbooks employing a nonstandard method of musical notation in which rectangular, circular or half-circular, triangular, or diamond-shaped characters are correlated with the traditional naming (solmization) of pitches in the major diatonic

"Amazing Grace" as it appears in shape-note notation in The Sacred Harp, *3rd edition (1859). The melody is in the middle part.*

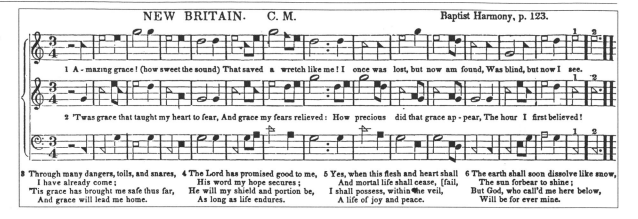

scale—that is, fa sol la fa sol la mi fa or do re mi fa sol la ti do. These "shape notes" (also known as "patent," "character," or "buckwheat notes") accordingly lent their name to the style, sometimes also described as "fasola," "dorayme," or "Sacred Harp singing," this last after the most popular of the shape-note hymnals, *The Sacred Harp,* by B.F. White and E.J. King, first published in 1844. Part of an organized movement to improve rural- and small-town hymnody, the shape-note method enabled individuals unacquainted with the rudiments of formal composition to sight-read. It was disseminated and perpetuated through "singing schools"—usually held in the summer and lasting for around two weeks—taught for a nominal fee by itinerant "masters"; through community "singings" (described in the traditional advertisement as "all day with dinner on the grounds"); or through county, state, or national conventions.

American singing schools first appeared in 18th-century New England with efforts to reform congregational singing in colonial churches, and they were rapidly carried to the rural South by singing-school teachers and songbooks employing various systems of nonstandard notation. The four-shape method, still in use, first appeared in 1801, and by the second decade of the 19th century it had spread south through Pennsylvania and the Shenandoah Valley of Virginia and west to Kentucky. Around mid-century, a seven-shape scheme was also introduced and gained wide popularity, though the four-shape system retained its adherents, supported in large part because of extraordinarily successful four-shape songbooks such as *The Sacred Harp* and William Walker's *The Southern Harmony and Musical Companion,* first published in 1835.

Soon disappearing in the urban Northeast, shape-note singing and its attendant institutions perfectly suited the social conditions and cultural climate of the South, abetted by the region's numerous and energetic singing-school masters, composers, and songbook compilers. From its hearth in the Deep and Upper South, the practice eventually spread as far west as east Texas, in the 1990s the site of some of the most active shape-note singing circles. Aside from their role in religious observance and musical expression, singing schools and similar gatherings constituted important social occasions in areas where such opportunities were otherwise limited. Indeed, while shape-note hymnody was especially associated

with denominations or sects that prohibited many of the secular entertainments and musical traditions of their less devout neighbors, the style gradually assimilated much of the general character of Southern folksong. Written in three or four parts with the melody in the tenor, the songs typically employ the gapped scales found in much folk music, often even borrowing specific melodic or textual elements directly from secular folksongs; such is the case, for example, with the popular hymn "Wondrous Love," set to the air of the older British ballad "Captain Kidd" (Laws K 35); or "The Old-Fashioned Bible," whose melody is a variant of the fiddle tune "Fisher's Hornpipe," its text a parody of "The Old Oaken Bucket." Harmonies often rely on nonstandard intervals that are nonetheless common among Southern folksingers (such as harmonic progressions in parallel octaves or fifths, frequently lacking the third), while the style as a whole offers individual singers considerable latitude to vary or ornament parts in actual performance.

More specifically, there have developed within the shape-note repertoire a number of distinct song types or styles representing different traditions or historical periods. In addition to "folk hymns"—that is, religious texts set to existing folk melodies harmonized in the traditional manner—"psalm tunes" have perpetuated the large corpus of northern European hymnody formally transmitted via the church. Another commonplace type is the "fuguing tune," an inheritance from the New England composers that is characterized by a distinctive counterpoint in which the lead shifts between the registers. Originating with the religious revivals of the early 1800s, "camp-meeting songs" are similar in their sources and structure to the folk hymns, distinguished mainly by their lively tempos, syncopation, and use of refrains. Still another parallel to secular folk tradition is the religious ballad, some instances of which (such as "Wicked Polly" [Laws H 6] or "The Romish Lady" [Laws Q 32]) have rivaled their secular counterparts in popularity. Though primarily a White tradition, shape-note singing also gained some currency among Blacks, whose songbooks and singing style more overtly reflect African American traditions and musical traits (here as in other aspects of Southern folksong, however, it is often nearly impossible precisely to distinguish the interrelated strands of Black and White tradition). In the early 20th century, there also arose a quartet style more typical of the modern gospel idiom, a trend promoted by professional touring groups sponsored by large songbook publishers. Moreover, while shape-note singing has remained primarily associated with the print medium, alternative channels such as records and radio have in the 20th century exercised a growing influence.

Like many older singing traditions, shape-note hymnody has suffered somewhat in popularity of late, especially in the years since World War II. However, the style appears to be experiencing something of a revival in the 1990s, as Southerners, sustained through the years by state and local organizations and now often encouraged by the interest of folklorists, increasingly recognize shape-note singing as an important aspect of their musical and cultural heritage.

John Minton

References

Eskew, Harry. 1980. Shape-Note Hymnody: An Inheritance from the New England Composers. In *The New Grove Dictionary of Music and Musicians,* ed. Stanley Sadie. London: Macmillan.

———. 1989. Sacred Harp. In *Encyclopedia of Southern Culture,* ed. Charles Reagan Wilson and William Ferris. Chapel Hill: University of North Carolina Press.

Jackson, George Pullen. [1933] 1965. *White Spirituals in the Southern Uplands: The Story of the Fasola Folk, Their Songs, Singings, and "Buckwheat Notes."* New York: Dover.

Lomax, Alan. 1977. Liner notes for *White Spirituals from the Sacred Harp: The Alabama Sacred Harp Convention.* New World Records LP NW 205.

Steel, David Warren. 1989. Shape-Note Singing Schools. In *Encyclopedia of Southern Culture,* ed. Charles Reagan Wilson and William Ferris. Chapel Hill: University of North Carolina Press.

Walker, William. [1854] 1939. (rev. ed.) *The Southern Harmony and Musical Companion.* New York: Hastings House.

White, B.F., and E.J. King. [1859 (3d. ed.)]. *The Sacred Harp,* with Introduction by George Pullen Jackson. Nashville: Broadman.

Sharp, Cecil James (1859–1924)

English folksong collector, musician, and educator. Sharp was born November 22, 1859. Though largely self-taught as a musician, he was formally employed in that capacity for much of his life. In 1903, motivated by a series of chance encounters with traditional music, Sharp embarked on an unparalleled career as a collector of English and Anglo American folksong and dance. He was instrumental in reviving the English Folk-Song Society and in founding the English Folk-Dance Society with which the Folk-Song Society later merged. Apart from his scholarly work, he helped popularize traditional music among the middle class through his arrangements of folksongs for home and school. Between 1916 and 1918, he and his assistant, Maud Karpeles, spent forty-six weeks in the Southern Appalachians, amassing a landmark collection of Anglo American material. A tireless fieldworker despite his poor health, Sharp had by the time of his death on June 23, 1924, personally noted nearly 5,000 tunes from traditional singers and musicians on both sides of the Atlantic.

In his American fieldwork, Sharp's focus on English "survivals" caused him to neglect many equally important musical forms. He thus failed to record religious material, derivations of popular compositions, or local or migratory American songs, even when these were offered by his informants; except for noting a few fiddle tunes, he claimed to have encountered virtually no instrumental music. Nevertheless, the authoritative edition of Sharp's American collection, published posthumously as *English Folk Songs from the Southern Appalachians* (1932), can only with considerable qualification be characterized as overly narrow, containing as it does 968 tunes for 274 individual ballads and songs.

In 1930 Cecil Sharp House was established in London as the permanent home of the English Folk Song and Dance Society. While there is no comparable monument to Sharp's contributions to American folklore, he indisputably remains one of the founders of serious folksong scholarship in both Great Britain and the United States.

John Minton

References

Karpeles, Maud. 1967. *Cecil Sharp: His Life and Work.* Chicago: University of Chicago Press.

———, ed. 1974. *Cecil Sharp's Collection of English Folk Songs.* 2 vols. London: Oxford University Press.

Sharp, Cecil. 1907. *English Folk Song: Some Conclusions,* ed. Maud Karpeles. 4th rev. ed. 1965. Belmont, CA: Wadsworth.

Sheep Camp

A covered wagon in which sheep herders live. The wagon is entered through a split (Dutch) door in the front from which draft animals can be reined as they pull the camp. The interior arrangement of wood or gas cook stove on the right (as the camp is entered), cabinets on the left, and bed spanning the rear is almost ubiquitous. A table either folds up or slides underneath the bed frame, and there are bench seats along the walls with storage beneath them on either side of the central table. The top of the older camps is canvas stretched across wooden bows, but in the 1990s most are aluminum-topped. The running gear used to be wooden wagon frames, but more recent, homemade camps use old truck chassis, axles, and wheels with rubber tires, and they are pulled by pickup trucks. The largest sheep camps of this design are about 7 feet wide and 16 feet long and are found throughout the Intermountain West. Larger camp wagons of a completely different design are found in the San Joaquin Valley of California. These are large, rolling wooden boxes with movable, rather than built-in, furniture. They have large shutters that span the wagon's length on both sides and swing up to provide ventilation through screened, full-length openings.

In the Intermountain West, sheep camps are used by some herders all year long, and by others mostly in the winter months, depending on the range where they tend their flocks. In steep, mountainous country, during the summer when sheep prefer the high mountain meadows to the hot, brushy valley floors, herders often pack their camp on pack horses or mules and sleep in canvas "teepee tents" (pyramidal, one- or two-man tents suspended from two poles that form an A-frame). In the winter, the sheep are moved to the lower reaches and the herders live in a sheep wagon. Whether living in teepee tents or sheep wagons, herders are regularly supplied by a camp tender, often the sheep boss for the ranch who owns the sheep and who hires the herders. A small "commissary wagon," containing mostly feed for the horses and dogs, is often trailed behind the main camp.

James Candlish, a blacksmith in Rawlins, Wyoming, is often credited as being the inventor of the sheep camp. In 1884, however, the same year Candlish reportedly built his first camp, an account of an almost identical contrivance appeared in a London publication, *Prairie Experiences in Handling Cattle and Sheep*, by Major W. Shepperd. The fact that sheep camp is so simple and obvious, and the fact that wagons of similar, if not identical, design were being built in several places at the same time, are strong indicators that there were probably several inventors; the sheep camp was in all likelihood a polygenetic creation. The Gypsy caravan of Europe is similar in form and use to the more modern sheep camp, but proving any direct connection in the development of one from the other has proved fruitless.

The first sheep camps were undoubtedly homemade, but by about 1892 the Schulte Hardware Company of Casper, Wyoming, was commissioned to construct a sheep wagon based on the older, traditional form. The first major manufacturer of such wagons was the Ahlander Company of Provo, Utah, which started production in 1918. Between 1920 and 1976, their last year in business, Ahlander produced more than 3,000 of their famous "Home on the Range" model, many of which are still in use in the 1990s. Other commercial manufacturers were the Studebaker Company, the Consolidated Wagon and Machine Works, Madsen, and Eddy. All but Studebaker were located in Utah. In 1995 there were two commercial builders still advertising in the *National Wool Grower:* the Wilson Brother's company in Midway, Utah, and Western Wagons in Ten Sleep, Wyoming.

In addition to its practical use, the sheep camp has become a traditional symbol for the Western sheep industry. The nostalgic icon of an old sheep wagon and a grizzled herder appears as the logo for the National Wool Growers Association Memorial Fund and Heritage Foundation, as well as in cartoons targeted for people in the wool-growing business.

The traditional form of the Intermountain sheep camp, whether homemade or commercially manufactured, has remained essentially unchanged for more than 100 years. Its use on the range continues, and its evolution as a traditional symbol of the Western sheep industry continues to grow.

Blanton Owen

References
Lane, Richard, and William A. Douglass. 1985. *Basque Sheep Herders of the American West: A Photographic Documentary*. Reno: University of Nevada Press.
Shepperd, Major W. 1884. *Prairie Experiences in Handling Cattle and Sheep*. London: Chapman and Hall.
Tanner, Ogden. 1977. Candlish's Moveable Home on the Range. In *The Ranchers*. Alexandria, VA: Time-Life Books, pp. 96–97.

Sheepherder

One whose job requires months of isolation on the Western landscape, overseeing the welfare of a band of sheep in a transhumant way of life. A sheepherder is required to keep an accurate count of his charges, take note of their health, and move them over their grazing area in such a way as to prevent the abuse of soil and vegetation. Regardless of how modern his outfit is, the sheepherder's work is permeated with tradition, with folk culture.

From the late spring until early fall, he will live in a tent or a sheep wagon as his sheep graze on summer range, often Bureau of Land Management range or U.S. Forest Service lands. From late fall until late winter, he lives in a sheepherder's wagon, an insulated and portable home, while he looks after his charges on their winter pastures or feeding grounds. Almost without exception in the Euro-American tradition of sheep raising, sheepherders are male.

In the American West, herding sheep is at, or very near, the bottom of the success scale. It is a job for those who, for whatever reason, can do little else. The immigrant is a good candidate for a job as sheepherder because he does not have to know English, he does not have to be elaborately trained, and he does not need to own special tools or equipment. Remuneration is low, but that fact is misleading. Sheepherders are provided tobacco, room and board, and they eat well, making legendary the hospitality that sheep camps provide their occasional visitors.

The numbers of sheep making up a band will vary from time to time and from season to season, depending upon the purposes for which a band is put together. Sheep may be banded together on the basis of age, by grade of wool, or for any reason that a sheepman might wish homogeneity. When pregnant ewes and short yearling ewe lambs (those not quite a year old) are trailed from winter ranges or feeding grounds prior to lambing and shearing, they often make up bands numbering 3,000. For the lambing itself, ewe bands typically number 1,000 individuals; if they all produce a living offspring, the band numbers 2,000, although the birth of many twins might cause the size of the band to be reduced to keep it at the optimum size of 2,000. Each band has one herder; for every two bands, a camp tender is customarily provided whose duty is to move the herders' tents or wagons from location to location, perhaps bake some bread for the herders, restock the supply of food, and do for both of his herders whatever is necessary to enable each herder to concentrate on his sheep.

The customary preparation of a sheepherder is a fairly simple process: The neophyte is placed with an old-timer. If

Shearing sheep. Rosebud County, Montana, 1939. Library of Congress.

there is any basic sensitivity to animal nature and a corresponding sense of responsibility, the newcomer becomes a sheepherder.

Seldom if ever is a sheepherder called a "shepherd" in the American West, and it is the West, of course, that developed large-scale range sheep operations. Although the two words denote the same thing, connotatively they are quite different.

In the British Isles, more particularly along the borders where Scots and English have shed and mingled their blood for centuries, one of the world's great livestock hearths developed. There, where sheep thrive on the bent grasses and heather of the Cheviot Hills, those who tend flocks are shepherds. But to Americans, whose sheep eat the native bunch grasses and shrubs, that word suggests the Christian Church with Jesus the

Good Shepherd and with the tradition of the pastor. Even the shepherd's crook, which in churches with an episcopate has become stylized as the crozier, is different in the American West. The European crook, or staff, has a wide hook for catching sheep by the neck. Sheepherders, by contrast, use sheep hooks with a small crook for catching sheep by the leg. Further comparisons could be made, but the point is secure that there is a semantic fracture between these two words.

Such a linguistic dislocation is a bit surprising in view of the prominence of folk of British ancestry in the development of large-scale American livestock enterprises. In many parts of the West—the Southwest may be an exception—those involved with cattle and sheep raising were mostly from the British Isles and Ireland. From ownership and management down to the herders themselves, folk with names identified with Wales, England, Scotland, and Ireland are prominent if not predominant. In the sheep business of Oregon and Idaho, for example, Scots by way of Appalachia (the Scotch-Irish), by way of emigration via Canada, and by way of direct removal from Scotland to America were prominent. However, since herding sheep was a job anyone could do regardless of language skills or previous training, many different linguistic groups were represented in sheep camps throughout the West. Greece contributed men from the Peloponnese, veritable Arcadia, for instance. But the linguistic group often incorrectly presumed to be the founders of sheep ranching in the West is the Basques. These enterprising folk, seldom sheepmen in their homeland, learned to be sheepherders in the American West following the precepts and examples of their British-descended teachers.

Whether from Tennessee or Visaya, the herders shared a routine that was traditional, varying according to local circumstances of rangeland and such other variables as the price of lamb and wool and the fiscal strategies of the sheepman. That routine is best exemplified when the sheepherder is out on the range in late spring, summer, and early fall.

He has trailed his sheep from the lambing area to the late-spring pasture, which may be at a fairly low elevation, perhaps 3,500 feet above sea level. His tent will have been set up by his camp tender, who leaves him a supply of drinking water, wood for his camp stove, food for the dogs, and food for the herder, which might include a fresh loaf of sourdough bread. He will remain at this campsite as many days as the supply of grass and water allows.

His day begins early, because his sheep will begin to graze at first light, and he does not want them to scatter too widely. If he ate a sandwich before he left the tent, he can stay with his sheep until the middle of the morning, when they tend to seek shade, lie down, ruminate, and nap until the middle of the afternoon. During their repose, the herder returns to his tent, cooks a meal, feeds the dogs, and, if necessary, waters them. If the camp tender is still with him, the noon meal will have been prepared. Then the herder returns to the bedded-down sheep before they begin to graze, gradually moving them in the direction of the camp in order to be near there by sundown. He fixes his supper, feeds the dogs again if they have worked especially hard, and after he eats he may fix a sandwich to eat just before he leaves camp in the morning. He counts his markers—customarily one black sheep for every 200 ewes—at least once a day. If he is a light sleeper, he may be wakened several times by noises that could presage problems for his band in the form of predators, electric storms, or any other source of trouble.

At the appropriate time, the sheep move ever upward to new grazing areas, the herder and the dogs leading and urging them along and keeping the flanks controlled lest the band expand and separate. By the time the sheep have moved to their subalpine pastures, both lambs and ewes have gained weight. If feed is good and all has gone well, the lambs will be ready for shipment by the middle of September.

With the total number of sheep reduced by the number of fat lambs shipped, the herders reconstitute the remaining ewes and any lambs that need fattening into new bands and return to the lowlands to fall and winter grazing areas, where tents are replaced by sheep wagons. The sheepman must reduce his work force, for the reduced numbers of sheep require fewer herders.

Many traditional stories circulate about how the laid-off herders spent their enforced winter vacations in an earlier time when Tennesseans and Basques made up much of the sheepherder population. Winter was a time when the unemployed herders checked in at hotels or boarding houses and, if so inclined, went on monumental drinking binges and kept company with prostitutes. By the end of winter, the savings were gone, and the herders were eager to return to work, which began with lambing. Herders do not wince when, after lambing, they castrate in the traditional way by using their pocket knives to open the scrotum and their teeth to pull out the testicles and spermatic cords.

Sheepherders are the subject of many other traditional narratives. In some of these stories, the herder goes insane from trying to make up his bedroll day after day, frustrated because he cannot discover the long axis of his soogan, the quilt or tarpaulin-covered blanket that is very nearly square. There is also the herder whose mind snaps under the strain of the constant counting of sheep. Loneliness, too, destroyed the mental equilibrium of more than one legended sheepherder. Some herders on whose hands time hung heavily fought the waves of depression by stacking rocks, creating monuments to aging intellect, by placing rocks in circles or other geometric shapes, and by carving on aspen trees. And it is true that homesickness, isolation, and loneliness did conspire against some of these sheepherders. An anonymous song puts the matter well in its lament for this difficult life:

> A tear runs down his wind-tanned cheek,
> And a sob that shakes his frame,
> For he's just a poor sheepherder
> And has sheep on his brain.

But is also true that for some the lowest rung on the success ladder was a temporary condition. The herder who let the owner hold his wages, who proved himself reliable by not losing any sheep, who was kept on the payroll over the winter because of the first two facts could, after five years or so, collect enough back wages to make a good down payment on an outfit of his own. More than one Scotsman, Irishman, Welshman, Basque, or mountaineer from Appalachia connected with the American Dream of upward mobility by this route.

Louie W. Attebery

References

Attebery, Louie W. 1984. Celts and Other Folk in the Regional Livestock Industry. *Idaho Yesterdays* 28 (2):20–19.

———. 1993. *Sheep May Safely Graze: A Personal Essay on Tradition and a Modern Ranch.* Moscow: University of Idaho Press.

Gilfillan, Archer B. [1929] 1993. *Sheep: Life on the South Dakota Range.* Minneapolis: Minnesota Historical Society Press.

McGregor, Alexander Campbell. 1982. *Counting Sheep: From Open Range to Agribusiness on the Columbia Plateau.* Seattle: University of Washington Press.

See also Basque Americans; Sheep Camp

Shine

Fictional Black hero of the *Titanic* toasts or songs who, after having his warnings about the ship's sinking ignored by its White captain, escapes through amazing physical feats and common sense while ignoring the pleas and bribes of the White passengers. In this well-known toast, Shine, the stoker and only Black person aboard the ship, initially warns the captain that the ship is taking on water. His warning is ignored as the captain relies on the ship's pumps to save them. Realizing that the ship is sinking, Shine jumps overboard and swims to safety. Various toasts present different passengers begging for his help and offering, in exchange, money, sex, or other rewards, all of which he turns down so that he can save himself:

> Here come the captain.
> Say, "Shine, Shine, please save me,
> I make you rich as any shine can be."
> Shine said, "Captain, to save you would be very fine,
> But I got to first save this black ass of mine."

Shine and the *Titanic* toast appear throughout Black folklore in various forms. The Shine character appeared occasionally in 19th-century minstrelsy, but he generally is found in later toasts that focus on the sinking of the *Titanic.* Although various suggestions as to the origin of his name exist, it probably derives from Black slang referring to a very dark-skinned person (Levine 1977:428). The *Titanic*-related character probably originated as a result of the denial of passage by the ship's company for Black boxer Jack Johnson. Langston Hughes notes that while Black people were denied passage on the ship, "folk versifiers insist that there was one Negro aboard" (Hughes 1959:367). Ironically, although no Blacks were aboard the ship, this toast is found primarily in Black folklore (Jackson 1974:35).

While the toast was first collected in the 1930s and early 1940s, it probably appeared much earlier in Black folk legend (Levine 1977:428). It continues to appear in the 20th century, and it has even been adopted and modified by White toast-tellers (Johnson 1981).

The importance of Shine in Black narrative is often seen in his representation of the entire race. His words and actions demonstrate personal empowerment as well as a challenge to White authority (Jackson 1974:37). Additionally, while he crosses accepted class and race boundaries in his profane and direct replies to the White passengers' requests that he save them, his responses also demonstrate the transparency of such boundaries as well as a practical focus on surviving. He also is able to accomplish this triumph through rebellion and a rejection of established social rules while, at the same time, remaining within legal boundaries, thus "defeat[ing] [W]hite society on *its* own territory and by *its* own rules" (Levine 1977:420).

Sandra G. Hancock

References

Hughes, Langston, and Arna Bontemps, eds. 1959. *The Book of Negro Folklore.* New York: Dodd, Mead.

Jackson, Bruce. 1974. *"Get Your Ass in the Water and Swim Like Me": Narrative Poetry from Black Oral Tradition.* Cambridge: Harvard University Press.

Johnson, James D. 1981. An Instance of Toasts among Southern Whites. *Western Folklore* 40:329–336.

Levine, Lawrence W. 1977. *Black Culture and Black Consciousness.* New York: Oxford University Press.

Shivaree

A noisy mock serenade given to newlyweds. It consists of noise made outside the couple's home in the evening with anomalous instruments, especially pots, pans, kettles, and other metal implements, bells, guns, and musical instruments played out of tune or in other than the normal fashion. The band may include traditional improvised noisemakers such as tick-tacks, horse fiddles (a plank sawed against the edge of a large box), or devil's fiddles (consisting of a rosined string passed through the bottom of a tin can). The noise does not cease until the shivaree band is offered money or invited into the house for food and drink. At this stage, they may play practical jokes on the couple, such as rearranging the contents of the kitchen and booby trapping the bed. Either the bride or the groom may be subjected to physical hazing, such as being carried out of the house, covered with messy substances, and dumped in a pond.

The term "shivaree" is derived from the French *charivari,* which designates the same custom. "Shivaree" is the term known all over Canada and most of the United States; less-common names for the custom include "serenade," "belling," "horning," "callathump," "bullbanding," "warming," and "skimmelton."

In addition to its function as a benign rite of passage for newlyweds, the shivaree was used as an extralegal ritualized expression of disapproval that enforced community morality by publicly shaming transgressors. Common targets for this folk justice were widows and widowers who remarried quickly, couples mismatched in age or rank, adulterers, and spouse beaters. These punitive rituals ranged from mild satire to extreme violence, sometimes ending with death or injury. In French Canadian areas and in New Orleans, remarriages were the most common target: The noise was kept up, sometimes for days, until the target paid a fine that was often given to charity.

Charivari (rough music) was a widespread popular custom in Europe, where it was primarily an expression of community disapproval or derision, and is now rare. In North America, the function of the shivaree expanded from an expression of public disapproval to a benign well-wishing extended to all newlyweds. The predominance of the term "shivaree" and its derivation from the French *charivari* have led to the assumption that the custom was brought to America by French settlers, but the existence of *charivari* customs throughout Europe suggests that other immigrants also brought their versions of the custom.

Because of social changes and a long tradition of official opposition—it was frequently outlawed as a danger to law and order and a challenge to authority—the popular-justice shivaree is rare in North America after the 1890s. Since World War II, the benign shivaree has been reported sporadically in rural areas of the United States. In some Canadian rural communities, however, the practice still thrives.

Moira Smith

References

Greenhill, Pauline. 1989. Welcome and Unwelcome Visitors: Shivarees and the Political Economy of Rural-Urban Interactions in Southern Ontario. *Journal of Ritual Studies* 3:45–67.

Morrison, Monica. 1974. Wedding Night Pranks in Western New Brunswick. *Southern Folklore Quarterly* 38 (4):285–297.

Palmer, Bryan D. 1978. Discordant Music: Charivaris and Whitecapping in Nineteenth-Century North America. *Labour, Le Travailleur* 3:5–62.

Shoemaker, Alfred L. (1913–?)

Founder of the first college department of folklore in the United States, cofounder of the Pennsylvania Folklife Society, and influential American folklife scholar. Shoemaker became assistant professor of American folklore in 1948 at Franklin and Marshall College in Lancaster, Pennsylvania, where he became head of the new Department of American Folklore. The department adopted an innovative folk-cultural model emphasizing the ethnological study of American regional-ethnic groups and their material and intellectual culture.

Shoemaker was particularly influential in introducing folklife and material-culture studies into American folklore studies. He offered groundbreaking courses on folk art and Pennsylvania German folk culture. Along with the department, Shoemaker established with Don Yoder and J. William Frey the Pennsylvania Dutch Folklore Center, which added a public-outreach component to the college's folklore research activities. Under Shoemaker's leadership, the Center produced a newspaper called *Pennsylvania Dutchman* (later the journal *Pennsylvania Folklife*), which claimed the largest circulation (more than 10,000) of any folklore serial in America, and it published more than twenty pamphlets and books on folklife topics. The Center established the Pennsylvania Dutch Folk Festival (later the Kutztown Folk Festival), which grew to be America's largest folk festival; seminars on folklife studies; cultural study tours to Europe; and a folklife museum and archives.

Shoemaker was eminently qualified for the task of introducing European folklife approaches into American academe. Born in the Pennsylvania "Dutch" country in Lehigh County in 1913, he received his A.B. in 1934 from Muhlenberg College followed by ethnological studies at universities in Munich, Heidelberg, Uppsala, and Lund. He returned to the United States and in 1940 received his Ph.D. in German at the University of Illinois. After World War II, he studied at the Irish Folklore Commission and the Folklore Institute in Basel, Switzerland. In addition to teaching German at Lafayette and Muhlenberg Colleges before going to Franklin and Marshall, he also served as curator of the Berks County Historical Society in Reading, Pennsylvania.

After 1952 Shoemaker resigned his teaching position to devote himself to the Center, and the department was dissolved. In 1956 he incorporated the Center and moved it from Lancaster to Kutztown. In 1958 the Center changed the title of its serial to *Pennsylvania Folklife*, still under Shoemaker's editorship, and expanded its scope from the study of Pennsylvania Germans to the full range of regional-ethnic groups in and around Pennsylvania. It was the first American journal to carry the folklife banner. Reflecting the broadening scope of Shoemaker's activities, the center became the Pennsylvania Folklife Society in 1959. In 1959 and 1960, Shoemaker published important studies of the Pennsylvania barn, Christmas, and Easter, under the imprint of the Pennsylvania Folklife Society. The society had a financial setback in 1963 and was reorganized without Shoemaker in its management.

After being institutionalized with mental illness during the mid-1960s, Shoemaker reportedly became homeless. He occasionally took up shelter in New York City at the home of a former folklife associate, but his whereabouts became unknown after 1970.

Simon J. Bronner

References

Bronner, Simon J. 1991. A Prophetic Vision of Public and Academic Folklife: Alfred Shoemaker and America's First Department of Folklore. *Folklore Historian* 8:38–55.

Shoemaker, Alfred L. 1959. *Christmas in Pennsylvania: A Folk Cultural Study.* Kutztown: Pennsylvania Folklife Society.

———, ed. 1959. *The Pennsylvania Barn.* Kutztown: Pennsylvania Folklife Society.

———. 1960. *Eastertide in Pennsylvania: A Folk Cultural Study.* Kutztown: Pennsylvania Folklife Society.

Shoemaker, Henry Wharton (1882–1958)

Pioneer collector of folklore in the central Pennsylvania mountain region and first official state folklorist in the United States (1948–1956), serving the state of Pennsylvania. As a journalist after 1898, he reported legends from Pennsylvania mountain residents and workers in lumber and hunting camps and coalfields, which he first published in central Pennsylvania newspapers and then more widely in the book *Pennsylvania Mountain Stories* (1908). This was the first of twelve volumes in the Pennsylvania Folklore Series (1908–1924) that promoted the culture and landscape of central Pennsylvania. From his home near Lock Haven, Pennsylvania, Shoemaker devoted much of his energy to environmental conservation and considered folklore associated with the endangered landscape deserving of preservation along with the state's forests and wildlife.

Praised for drawing attention to the traditions of the Pennsylvania "mountaineers," Shoemaker nonetheless drew criticism for his alteration and occasional fabrication of legends. A prolific writer, he produced more than 100 books and pamphlets and hundreds of articles. In addition to his books of legends, for which he is best known (and most criticized), he published reliable collections of songs and ballads *(Mountain Minstrelsy of Pennsylvania* [1931]), folk speech *(Scotch-Irish and English Proverbs and Sayings of the West Branch Valley of Central Pennsylvania* [1927]), and crafts *(Early Potters of Clinton County* [1916]).

Shoemaker became a prominent newspaper publisher in Pennsylvania after World War I and published many folkloristic pamphlets and books by himself and others. In 1924 he cofounded the Pennsylvania Folklore Society with Bishop J.H. Darlington, and he was its president from 1930 until 1957. From 1924 to 1932, he published a series of monographs for the society. He held several appointments to state government commissions and was particularly active in public-history activities: He was chair of the Pennsylvania Historical Commission (1923–1930) and president of the Pennsylvania Federation of Historical Societies (1925–1926). In 1930 President Herbert Hoover appointed him minister to Bulgaria, a post he held until 1933. While he was minister, he took notice of Bulgaria's official efforts to preserve its folklore. In 1935 he began a daily column for the *Altoona Tribune* in which he covered regional folklore and history and called for cultural conservation efforts. He had an opportunity to develop his plans when he was appointed state archivist of Pennsylvania from 1937 to 1948 and director of the State Museum in Harrisburg from 1939 to 1940. In the posts, he called for the state to sponsor collection and preservation of folklore.

After the archives, museum, and historical commission merged to form the Pennsylvania Historical and Museum Commission following World War II, he oversaw the creation of the Division of Folklore in the commission in 1948 and took the position of first state folklorist. In that post, he sponsored publications, meetings, festivals, and exhibits now common in public-folklore programming, although he entered into bitter disputes with academic folklorists in Pennsylvania over his popularized presentations of folklore. Shoemaker left the post in 1956, and a similar state folklore program was not established until 1966, again with the Pennsylvania Historical and Museum Commission. Shoemaker died near his McElhattan, Pennsylvania, home in 1958.

Simon J. Bronner

References

Bronner, Simon J. 1995. *Popularizing Pennsylvania: Henry Shoemaker and the Progressive Uses of Folklore and History.* University Park: Pennsylvania State University Press.

Hoffmann, Frank A. 1959. Henry W. Shoemaker, 1882–1958. *Journal of American Folklore* 72:345–346.

Shoemaker, Henry W. [1914] 1991. *Black Forest Souvenirs Collected in Northern Pennsylvania.* Baltimore: Gateway Press for the Pine Creek Historian.

———. [1915] 1992. *Tales of the Bald Eagle Mountains in Central Pennsylvania.* Baltimore: Gateway Press for the Lycoming County Historical Society.

Shout

A dance-like form of group worship in the African American community. The shout consists of singing, polyrhythmic clapping, and foot stomping, and is generally performed in a ring formation. A syncretism of West and Central African rituals with Christianity, the shout expresses intense religious devotion. Shouting is practiced by men and women, young and old, all over the Southern United States and also in Northern cities where Black migrants have settled. The shout was first recorded by White observers in the mid-19th century and is still in evidence in the late 20th century.

Shouting is akin to spirit possession in African and African Caribbean religious practices, but its imagery and language are those of Christianity. Its name may be derived from the Islamic word *saut,* which means to walk or run around the *Kaaba,* a cube-shaped building in the Great Mosque of Mecca. The African antecedents of the ring shout were probably the Bakongo and other cultures' ring dances honoring ancestors. The counterclockwise motion of the ring imitated the movement of the sun across the sky.

The shout is not considered a dance by most practitioners, and shouters are careful not to cross their feet. This distinction is made because dancing is frowned upon by the Baptist and Methodist faiths to which most shouters belong. Shouts are generally held in churches, smaller "Praise Houses," or the homes of elders. If possible, benches or chairs are pushed to the wall to make room for the shouters. Ring shouts usually take place in the evening and can follow a weekday prayer meeting or Sunday service. Christmas Eve traditionally provided an opportunity for slaves and their descendants to hold an all-night shout.

A shout may sometimes be accompanied by musical instruments, but the most vital music comes from the voices, hands, and feet of the participants. The songs that carry the shout are usually African American spirituals that allow for improvisation. A strong singer or dancer starts the shout with his or her song and movement and the inspiration of the Holy

Spirit. Four or five others stand back and act as "basers," singing refrains over and over, clapping, and stomping their feet to the beat. As others join in, the circular movement begins, with shuffling feet, and increases in intensity and motion. Dancers may retreat to the outskirts of the circle or outside the building to rest, rejoining the ring later.

Fluidity and flexibility characterize the expression of the shout, with room for each shouter to improvise and alternate among the various roles that keep the shout moving. Participants and those on the sidelines can make comments such as "Sister Rosa can shout!" and exhortations such as "Join, shouters!" The shout is an event that involves the whole person and community in vigorous physical exercise, spiritual communion, and artistic expression.

Monica M. Tetzlaff

References

Carawan, Guy, and Candie Carawan. 1989. *"Ain't You Got a Right to the Tree of Life?"* Rev. ed. Athens: University of Georgia Press, pp. 64–74.

Christensen, Abigail M. Holmes. 1894. Spirituals and "Shouts" of Southern Negroes. *Journal of American Folklore* 7:154–155.

David, Jonathan, and Michael Schlesinger, eds. 1992. *"On One Accord": The Singing and Praying Bands of Tidewater Maryland and Delaware.* Global Village Music.

Epstein, Dena. 1977. *Sinful Tunes and Spirituals: Black Folk Music to the Civil War.* Urbana: University of Illinois Press, pp. 232–234.

Federal Writers' Project, Georgia. [1940] 1986. *Drums and Shadows.* Athens: University of Georgia Press, pp. 10–11.

Raboteau, Albert. 1978. *Slave Religion: "The Invisible Institution" in the Antebellum South.* New York: Oxford University Press, pp. 66–73, 339–340.

Simpson, Robert. 1985. The Shout and Shouting in Slave Religion of the United States. *Southern Quarterly* 23:34–37.

Stuckey, Sterling. 1987. *Slave Culture: Nationalist Theory and the Foundations of Black America.* New York: Oxford University Press, pp. 3–97.

Skinner, Charles M. (1852–1907)

Author of popular myth and legend collections. Raised in Cambridge, Massachusetts, in a family dominated by Universalist clergy, Skinner migrated to Brooklyn, New York, to pursue a career in journalism. For many years a writer for the *Brooklyn Daily Eagle,* he took an unusual interest in myths and legends, compiling several popular collections mostly from written sources.

As a journalist, Skinner devoted much of his attention to nature writing and the outdoors movement. Beginning in 1890, he contributed to *Century* magazine, *Outlook, Atlantic Monthly,* and other magazines, articles on sky gazing, insects, urban gardening, hiking, and the Brooklyn electric trolleys. Permeating these was a concern for the social and economic ills of unrestrained urbanization and an effort to bring the principles of American Transcendentalism to bear on turn-of-the-century life.

In 1896 Skinner turned to folklore, publishing a two-volume compilation of *Myths and Legends of Our Own Land.* The book achieved strong sales and was influential in shaping popular tastes in folklore. Principally, it included local legends, organized by region, and suggested a national folk culture that assimilated materials from European Americans with other native and immigrant ethnicities. Using this basic plan, Skinner followed this collection with *Myths and Legends beyond Our Borders* (1898), *Myths and Legends of Our New Possessions and Protectorates* (1900), *American Myths and Legends* (1903), and *Myths and Legends of Flowers, Trees, Fruits, and Plants, in All Ages and in All Climes,* which was published posthumously in 1911.

Skinner's work was largely ignored by folklorists until Richard M. Dorson resurrected him as an exemplar of unprofessional practices, citing Skinner's dependence on unreliable and unidentified sources and his rewriting of texts to cater to popular tastes. But Skinner was never guided by these standards, instead using principles derived from nature writing and Transcendentalism to develop through local legend a rejuvenated American sense of place.

John Bealle

References

Bealle, John. 1994. Another Look at Charles M. Skinner. *Western Folklore* 53:99–123.

Dorson, Richard M. 1971. How Shall We Rewrite Charles M. Skinner Today? In *American Folk Legend: A Symposium,* ed. Wayland D. Hand. Berkeley: University of California Press, pp. 69–95.

Slavic Americans

A disparate group of varied nationalities who share ancestral mother tongues belonging to the Slavic family of languages. There is no historical evidence that Slavs ever constituted a single unified group. Despite politically motivated claims by adherents of pan-Slavism, millenia of separate development has led to distinctly differing Slavic cultures.

Scholars generally divide the main Slavic nationalities into three groups: (1) Eastern Slavs, including the Russians, White Russians, and Ukrainians; (2) Western Slavs, Poles, Czechs, and Slovaks; and (3) South Slavs, Slovenes, Croats, Serbs, Bosnians, Macedonians, and Bulgarians. Within these categories, there is a fair degree of linguistic mutual intelligibility, which markedly decreases across the divisions.

Mass migration of Slavic immigrants to North America occurred for the most part in the second half of the 19th century and the early decades of the 20th, although significant numbers of Slavic immigrants also arrived earlier than, and subsequent to, this period. The majority of Slavic immigrants were peasants in their homelands with relatively little formal education and few resources beyond their willingness to labor. Therefore, the greater portion of arriving Slavic immigrants found a livelihood in North America's rapidly developing heavy industries. The largest concentrations of Slavic Americans still are to be found in industrial cities and mining areas,

First-generation immigrants at Russian Sunday school. Potrero Hill, San Francisco, California, 1940. Note the inscription in Cyrillic letters. American Folklife Center, Cowell Collection (WPA).

although increased geographic and social mobility has diminished this concentration, especially in the decades since World War II.

There are significant communities of nearly every Slavic group in the cities of the Eastern U.S. megalopolis from Baltimore to Boston, in the mill and mining towns of western Pennsylvania, in all of the larger Great Lakes industrial cities, in Midwestern meat-packing centers, in Western mining towns, and in the Pacific Coast cities to which many Midwesterners and Easterners migrated. It is well known that Slavic Americans have labored in industries such as steel, meat packing, and coal, copper, and iron mining, but there are also significant Slavic rural farming communities, some established as early as the mid-19th century: of Czechs in eastern and central Wisconsin, southern Minnesota, eastern Nebraska, southern and central Texas, and Oklahoma; of Croatians in California's Pajaro and San Joaquin Valleys; of Poles in the onion-growing area of south–central New York state, in the potato-growing region of central Wisconsin, and intermingled with the Czech farmers and ranchers in Texas.

In the 20th century, other Slavic Americans managed to fulfill their dream of land ownership after earning a nest egg through toiling in the mines and mills. Often they had to settle for marginal farmland in regions with a short growing season. For example, in Wisconsin, the Slovaks of Moquah, the Poles of Pulaski, the Ukrainians of Clayton, and the Slovenes of Willard fit this pattern.

Slavs with a seafaring tradition, especially the Croatians from Dalmatia, settled in coastal communities, on New York's Long Island, and in New Orleans, Los Angeles, San Francisco, and Seattle, where they follow nautical pursuits: in all aspects of the shipping business, in shipbuilding, and notably in fishing. Dalmatians have fished off the Alaska coast from Washington ports, dominated tuna fishing in San Pedro, California, and have been the predominant oystermen in Buras and Empire, Louisiana, at the mouth of the Mississippi River.

Like other southern and eastern European immigrants, most Slavic American communities have been the victims of both overt and subtle forms of discrimination and prejudice. Pejorative terms such as "Polack," "Hunky," "Bohunk" and "Rusky" have been directed at Slavic Americans, usually designating a stereotype of the Slav as a dim-witted, coarse laborer. While most Slavic Americans acknowledge that prejudicial attitudes toward them have decreased, a legacy of this experience is a preoccupation with a type of ethnic boosterism that seeks to emphasize the length of time that some members of their nationality have been present in America and to point out prominent co-ethnics who have had notable achievements or attained celebrity.

For example, Croatians argue that the Croatian Indians who once inhabited the Carolina coast were the descendants of shipwrecked Croatian sailors from 16th-century Dubrovnik who intermarried with the local native people. Croatians are proud that monumental works by sculptor Ivan Mestrovic adorn the grounds of the United Nations building in New York and loom up along the Michigan Avenue lakefront in Chicago. Poles emphasize the important roles of Thaddeus Kosciuszko and Casimir Pulaski in the American Revolutionary War and are also eager to point out that McDonald's hamburger magnate Ray Kroc was Polish American. Russians mention their 19th-century California colony at Fort Ross; Serbs point to the scientific contributions of Nikola Tesla and to the pitching prowess of Pete Vuckovich. Slovenes note that U.S. Senator Frank Lausche was one of theirs as is polka king Frankie Yankovic; Ukrainians are proud of their macho movie star Jack Palance. Narratives affirming the significance of their group's contributions to America are a tradition readily found in most Slavic American communities.

It is important to remember that Slavic American ethnic communities are not homogeneous. There are class and educational differences stemming from divisions in their Old World society. These differences became especially apparent with the arrival of large numbers of urbanites as displaced persons after World War II. The culture, experience, and outlook of these middle-class political refugees tended to differ considerably from those of the peasant economic immigrants and their American-born progeny.

Also, there are regional differences within the ethnic groups, stemming either from their origins in a particular section of the homeland or from American regional differences. For example, the Hutzuli ethnic group from the Carpathian region of western Ukraine differs considerably from the lowland Ukrainians while they share many cultural traits with the Polish Gorali of the Tatras Mountains. The Gorali, in turn, are distinct from the Poles of the Vistula River Valley. Many Polish Americans are very conscious of distinctive traits owing to their origins in either the Prussian, Russian, or Austrian sections of the partitioned Poland of the 19th century.

The Czechs provide a good example of regional differences that have developed in North America. It is easy to distinguish the ethnic musical style of Czechs from Wisconsin from that of Czechs of Texas or Nebraska. Moreover, all of these are distinct from the music of urban Czech Americans from Cleveland or Chicago.

Some of the Slavic nationalities are relatively homogeneous when it comes to religion. The Bulgarians, Macedonians, Russians, and Serbs are all predominantly followers of Eastern Orthodox churches. Most Croatians, Poles, Slovenians, and Slovaks are Roman Catholics. The Ukrainians, however, are divided three ways among Eastern Orthodox churches, Eastern Rite churches (which follow liturgical practices similar to the Orthodox but profess allegiance to the Vatican), and Roman Catholicism. Most Czechs are Catholic, but there also are significant numbers of Protestants among them. Bosnians are a largely Islamic Slavic nationality, but there is considerable disagreement over whether the term "Bosnian" applies also to the numerous Orthodox Serbs and Catholic Croats from that troubled country.

Despite their considerable differences, it is possible to mention some common traditional forms emphasized by nearly all of the Slavic American ethnic groups. Church choirs, which perform liturgical music, are strong in both Orthodox and Catholic Slavic communities. Most larger Slavic American communities also support secular choirs, orchestras of folk-derived instruments, and ensembles that perform choreographed folk dances in peasant costume.

The model for these activities, which are self-consciously organized with the purpose of foregrounding positive symbols of ethnic identity both for internal and external consumption, stems from a convergence of the folk-based symbols from 19th-century national movements in the homelands and efforts since the 1920s by American social workers and ethnic-diversity enthusiasts to assist immigrants' adaption to, and acceptance in, American society through public events and festivals involving the sharing of performing arts, crafts, and foodways.

Many textile traditions, especially forms of embroidery, have been retained in Slavic American communities owing in part to the needs of folk-dance ensembles for replicas of peasant garb from the past. Other crafts traditions, often involving woodworking, musical instrument making, or the creation of elaborately decorated Easter eggs, have been invigorated by the symbolic meaning ascribed to them as manifestations of ethnic identity.

Richard March

See also Polish Americans; Tamburitza; Ukrainian Americans

Smith, Abraham ("Oregon") (1796–1893)

Legendary raconteur and folk doctor. Born in Tennessee, Smith migrated first to the Midwest (Illinois and Indiana) in 1821, then to Oregon in 1852; in 1859 he returned to Indiana, and finally moved to Chrisman, Illinois, where he died at age 97, having established a legendary reputation as a folk doctor (earning him one nickname "Sassafras Smith") and a storyteller. His fame lasted for more than a century, and may still exist in oral tradition.

Smith was the subject of one of the first exhaustive scholarly folklore studies of an American hero; William Hugh Jansen in his 1949 doctoral dissertation researched Smith's life to analyze the process by which a folk hero generates legends and the extent to which the legendary details correlate with historical fact. Smith's acclaim derived largely from his storytelling abilities, and his known repertoire of more than seventy tales included legends, tall tales, jokes, and lengthy traditional folktales. His stories about Oregon earned him his better-known nickname.

Jansen also analyzed Smith's storytelling and repertoire; Jansen's delineation of Smith's performer-audience relationships and how these were intertwined with performance style, genre, and context marked a seminal analytic approach now commonly employed in folkloristics.

Although "Oregon" Smith's reputation was limited to a confined area in the Midwest, that it lasted so long is testimony to the tenacity of folk-historical data, no matter how distorted they may become. Smith's legendary existence is an excellent example of the Swedish folklorist Carl Wilhelm Von

Sydow's notion of the "oikotype," a distinctive geographically limited and persistent form of oral narrative.

R. Gerald Alvey

References
Jansen, William Hugh. 1977. *Abraham "Oregon" Smith: Pioneer, Folk Hero, and Tale-Teller.* New York: Arno.

Smith, Bessie (1894–1937)

Known as "the Empress of the Blues." Smith was born in Chattanooga, Tennessee. By 1902 both of her parents were dead, and shortly thereafter the young girl was singing on the streets. Even then she reportedly possessed a fine voice; in 1903, at age nine, she made her professional debut at Chattanooga's Ivory Theater. A few years later, she met Gertrude "Ma" Rainey, an important blues recording artist of the 1920s and eight years Smith's senior. Smith toured with Rainey in the Rabbit Foot Minstrels, in which the older singer was given star billing. Because of this connection, Rainey is often called Smith's teacher, but it is more accurate to cite Rainey as simply an important influence on Smith.

Smith's first recordings came in 1921, but these sides, made for the Emerson label, were never released. Her first issued sides, "Downhearted Blues"/"Gulf Coast Blues," were cut for Columbia on February 16, 1921, and sold approximately 800,000 copies. The sales figure was phenomenal, since "Downhearted Blues" had been a previous year's hit for Alberta Hunter, and Smith's recording included uninspired accompaniment. Smith's achievement established her as a star, and over the next ten years she recorded more than 150 sides, mostly for Columbia.

Bessie Smith lived only four years after her final recordings, and her last days were unhappy. She continued singing in nightclubs and theaters, but her work was usually limited to renditions of popular songs such as "Smoke Gets in Your Eyes." Audiences occasionally demanded blues, but most people considered her earlier work old-fashioned. In fact, Smith might have passed out of public view altogether except for a controversy about her death. On September 26, 1937, she died of injuries suffered in an auto accident at Coahoma, Mississippi. An account first printed in a *Downbeat* article, later popularized by Edward Albee in his play *The Death of Bessie Smith,* said that she had bled to death after being refused admittance to a hospital because of her race. Another report claims that she died of exposure while awaiting attention in a hospital waiting room. The most likely account is that she was taken to the Black hospital in Clarksdale, Mississippi, where she died of her injuries. A week later, she was buried in Sharon Hill, Pennsylvania, but her grave remained unmarked until 1970 when a *Philadelphia Inquirer* reporter conducted a successful fund-raising campaign to buy a stone.

A majority of Smith's 160 issued sides are of very high quality, and they include many definitive versions of blues songs. Her repertoire ranged from traditional songs like "Careless Love" to double-entendre numbers like "I'm Wild about That Thing," to ragtime pieces like "Cake Walking Babies," to original compositions like "Poor Man's Blues." Her songs spoke of privation, bad luck, bad women, and both good and bad men, but it was Smith's voice that ultimately made each piece distinctive. Her rich contralto was a subtly controlled instrument. By skillfully using timing and phrasing, she gave fresh value to almost every song, providing nuances of feeling that the casual listener could miss. Her habit of holding over a word or a syllable into the next bar was widely copied. Highly influential, both in her own time and later, Smith's recordings still sell well.

Smith's performance style is often called "classic blues," but is perhaps more accurately labeled "city blues" or "jazz blues." It is distinguished by a jazz accompaniment, often consisting of instrumental responses and an orchestral, or "stride," style of piano in which a single instrument may fill the function of an entire band. The pianist makes rich harmonies with the right hand, while the left hand supplies a powerful bass line and emphasizes the strong beats with low-register octaves or tenths and the weak beats with mid-keyboard chords. The style also has a formulaic structure, standardized beginnings and endings, and a notable absence of any string instruments.

W.K. McNeil

References

Albertson, Chris. 1970. *Bessie.* New York: Stein and Day.
Steward-Baxter, Derrick. 1970. *Ma Rainey and the Classic Blues Singers.*

Smith, Grace Partridge (1869–1959)

Collector of folklore from the area of southern Illinois known as "Egypt." A folklorist by avocation rather than profession, Smith did most of her work after retiring in 1938 from the University of Iowa, where she had worked as a teacher, editor, and writer.

In 1946 Smith helped organize the Carbondale-based Illinois Folklore Society, which remained active until 1962. She was the society's president, a member of its board of directors, and a contributor to its newsletter. She was also active in the American Folklore Society, serving as a councilor from 1952 through 1957.

Smith's published works include short articles on proverbs, folksongs, children's folklore, narratives, beliefs, and folk speech. She had a special fondness for supernatural materials, tall tales, humorous anecdotes, and slang. In addition to studies of Illinois folklore, Smith researched the traditions of her own New England family and published studies of folk motifs in literature. She contributed forty-three short entries on folk belief and superstition to *Funk and Wagnalls Standard Dictionary of Folklore, Mythology, and Legend* (1949–1950).

Although known as a regionalist, Smith took a comparative approach, tracing the history and origins of the materials she collected. She was influenced in part by her son-in-law, Alexander Haggerty Krappe, and her work is typical of the then current literary approach to folklore. Smith was one of the first folklorists to note the appearance of folktale elements in modern comics. Her work with her own family's traditions anticipated later interest in family folklore.

Anne Burson-Tolpin

References

Burson-Tolpin, Anne. Forthcoming. Grace Partridge Smith. In *Notable Women in American Folklore,* ed. Susan Kalcik and W.K. McNeil. American Folklore Centennial Volume. Knoxville: University of Tennessee Press.
Leach, MacEdward. 1960. Grace Partridge Smith: Obituary. *Journal of American Folklore* 73:154.
Smith, Grace Partridge. 1952. The Plight of the Folktale in the Comics. *Southern Folklore Quarterly* 16:124–127.

Smithsonian Institution Center for Folklife Programs and Cultural Studies

A unit of the Smithsonian Institution in Washington, DC, that promotes the understanding and continuity of contemporary grass-roots cultures in the United States and abroad. The Smithsonian Institution is a unique public trust founded in 1846 and dedicated to the "increase and diffusion of knowledge" among humankind. The Smithsonian has a staff of 6,000 employees and includes sixteen national museums, a zoological park, research institutes for astrophysics and tropical biology, a press, two national magazines, various membership organizations, a traveling exhibition service, and a variety of other programs.

The Smithsonian Center for Folklife Programs and Cultural Studies produces the Festival of American Folklife, Smithsonian-Folkways Recordings, exhibitions, documentary films and videos, symposiums, and educational materials. The Center conducts ethnographic- and cultural-policy-oriented research, maintains a documentary archival collection, and provides educational and research opportunities. The Center works with other Smithsonian museums and programs, has a scholarly and technical staff, and relies upon hundreds of contract scholars, temporary employees, and volunteers. Activities are funded through federal appropriations, Smithsonian trust funds, grants and contracts, donations, and product and concessions sales. Center projects have received scholarly, public, and critical acclaim; its work on issues and methods of cultural representation has provided a model for other organizations and activities in the United States and internationally.

Prior to 1992, the Center was known as the Office of Folklife Programs. The office, established in 1976 with Ralph Rinzler as director, grew out of the Festival of American Folklife unit of the Smithsonian's Division of Performing Arts. Peter Seitel was director from 1982–1988, and Richard Kurin became acting director and then director in 1990.

The Festival of American Folklife is a research-based living cultural exhibition, held annually since 1967 outdoors on the National Mall of the United States for two weeks around the Fourth of July holiday. Over the years, it has brought more than 16,000 musicians, artists, performers, craftspeople, workers, cooks, storytellers, and others from fifty-three nations, every region of the United States, scores of ethnic groups, more than 100 American Indian groups, and more than sixty occupational groups to the National Mall to demonstrate their skills, knowledge, and artistry. The festival has energized local and regional tradition bearers, provided a training ground for two generations of public folklorists, and inspired many other cultural programs.

In 1987 the Smithsonian acquired Folkways Records, founded and operated by Moses Asch for four decades. Folkways activities are coordinated by the center as a "museum of sound," a business, and an archive under the direction of Anthony Seeger. The archive includes the Moses and Francis Asch Collection; documentation from the festival, its research, and special projects; and the Cook and Paradon record collections. Every one of the more than 2,000 Folkways titles is available on audio cassette through a mail-order archival service.

Smithsonian/Folkways produces new releases and reissues on CD, LP, and cassette. New releases grow out of festival and research projects, such as a multivolume set on Indonesia done in collaboration with the Indonesia Performing Arts Society sponsored by the Ford Foundation, and recent recordings on U.S.-Mexico Borderlands, New Mexico, Hawaii, and the former Soviet Union. Special recordings based on festival programs—*Rhythm and Blues* and *Musics of Struggle*—have been jointly produced with Columbia Records. A benefit album to support the acquisition of Folkways Recordings, *Folkways: A Vision Shared,* produced with Columbia Records, won a 1988 Grammy Award. Other products include audio recordings to accompany scholarly books, booklets for a thirty-volume *Video Anthology of World Music and Dance,* a children's series of recordings and videos, a folk-music instructional video series, CD-I, and CD-ROM educational materials.

The Center produces Smithsonian museum and traveling folklife exhibits—*Southern Pottery; Celebrations; Aditi: A Celebration of Life; Stand by Me: African American Expressive Culture in Philadelphia; Grand Generation;* and *Workers at the White House.* The Center produces Smithsonian Folklife Studies, a series of documentary films and monographs. It sponsors symposiums on key cultural issues with collaborating institutions—for example, *Other Orients: Soviet and American Views of Muslim Society,* and *Seeds of the Past, Seeds of Commerce, and Seeds of Industry*—held for the Columbus Quincentenary. The Center has also coproduced television and radio programs, documentary films like Marjorie Hunt and Paul Wagner's Academy Award-winning *The Stone Carvers* (1985), and popular books like the *Smithsonian Folklife Cookbook* (1991). The Center provides curatorial and production assistance for special projects, among them the U.S. Bicentennial in 1976, concerts for the Jimmy Carter and Ronald Reagan presidential inaugurals, and America's Reunion on the Mall, a festival for the inauguration of President Bill Clinton.

Center programs and research focus on issues of cultural representation, conservation, and creativity. The Center's most distinctive contribution has been the development of a dialogue and collaboration with the people whose traditions and aspirations are represented. Current collaborative research projects on the African diaspora, cognate American and Eurasian cultures, and the cultural landscape of Jerusalem are indicative of interest and range. Scholarly staff draw upon folklore, cultural anthropology, ethnomusicology, social history, ethnic and area studies, and cover various American and world regions. Recent examples of scholarship include Thomas Vennum's monographs on *Wild Rice among the Ojibway* and *Lacrosse: Little Brother of War* and Olivia Cadaval's exhibit on *Tirarlo al la Calle* (Taking to the Streets). Several scholars serve as faculty at local universities. Some have won prestigious recognition, such as Anthony Seeger, winner of the American Musicological Society's prize for best monograph, former president of the Society for Ethnomusicology, and 1993 inductee into the American Academy of Arts and Sciences. The Center is a vehicle for increased staff diversity in the Smithsonian, as former staff head important other offices and programs; it also has a distinguished outside advisory group.

The Center offers a variety of educational programs. Fellowships allow predoctoral, postdoctoral and senior postdoctoral scholars to work at the Center. One recent Fellow completed a textbook on American folk music; another completed a new Smithsonian/Folkways Recording. The Center's projects annually involve hundreds of volunteers and about a dozen or so college interns. A community-scholars program, initiated as a Summer Folklore Institute, brings lay scholars to Washington, DC, to discuss their work, meet with public officials, increase skills, and learn about other cultural organizations. Educational programs for primary and secondary schools include curriculum kits on folklife, teacher-training materials and courses, and cooperative instructional programming with selected schools.

Richard Kurin

Social Protest in Folklore

Traditional forms of expression used as vehicles for responding to social injustice. Members of social groups constituted by ethnicity, nationality, religion, class, ideology, gender, sexual preference, occupation, region, and other aspects of common identity have drawn upon shared expressive traditions to voice dissatisfaction with social, economic, or political conditions. Social protest through traditional expressive behavior may be individual (graffiti) or collective (parades), and may assume a variety of forms, both verbal and nonverbal. The message may be explicit, or it may be "coded," with hidden meanings understood largely by the subject group.

Indigenous peoples of the Americas have responded to their subjugation by Europeans through such vehicles as traditional oratory (for example, Tecumseh, a Shawnee chief, on the fate of Indians of the Northeast: "They have vanished before the avarice of the White Man, as snow before a summer sun") and ritual (such as the Ghost Dance of Plains Indians, both a revitalization movement and a form of passive resistance against genocide). In recent decades, powwows—festivals featuring ritual dance, craft, and native foods—have been held throughout North America to promote unity among Native Americans and to present a collective response to the continued adverse treatment of indigenous peoples.

The American Indian Movement (AIM), an activist group formed in the 1970s, has adapted and applied traditional spiritual teachings and practices in the pursuit of social justice. Leonard Peltier, an AIM leader in prison as the result of a confrontation with FBI agents at Wounded Knee, South Dakota, in the 1970s, has a symbolic presence at many powwows, where his guiding spirit and message of unity and re-sistance are publicly acknowledged (a portrait of him is often seen hanging over the drummers' tent during performances).

African Americans have a tradition of social protest reaching back to their initial forced migration to the Americas. In the Old World, musician-bards, such as the West African *griots,* offered praise but also sharp social criticism; even drummers injected biting commentary into their rhythmic messages. Prohibited from such overt cultural practices, slaves developed new forms of expression, such as Christian sermons drawing liberally from the biblical account of the Exodus and the sayings of the prophets, and spirituals, which similarly carried covert messages of social protest such as "Let My People Go." Later on, these songs formed the basis for more direct exhortation during the civil rights movement that began in the late 1950s. The lyrics to such spirituals as "We Shall Not Be Moved" and "We Shall Overcome" were adapted, with topical verses sung for particular occasions.

In some African American communities, parades and festivals commemorating the Emancipation Proclamation (such as Juneteenth, celebrating June 19, 1865, the day the Proclamation was announced in Texas) have been, and still are, conducted, both celebrating enfranchisement and protesting its incomplete realization.

Trade-union and political movements in North America have a well-documented history of enlisting traditional expressive forms, especially song, in the service of social protest. King George III's restive colonists broadsided the loyal troops of the mother country by throwing back a popular British army tune to them in the form of the satirical "Yankee Doodle." This parody appeared in countless incarnations, serving collectively as a weapon of protest against the Tories, as well as a vehicle for verbal attacks among competing factions of the Revolutionists.

The broadside, or topical folksong, dating back at least to the 16th century in England, has been one of the most popular vehicles for social protest among labor song-poets of the 19th and early 20th centuries, and peace activists in more recent times, who produced songsheets and booklets of lyrics, with instructions "to be sung to the tune of" a well-known song. The IWW (Industrial Workers of the World, or "Wobblies") *Little Red Song Book,* first issued in 1910, achieved among the widest circulation of such collections.

One of the most popular bards of social protest in the 20th century, Woody Guthrie, commonly penned topical lyrics and set them to well-known traditional tunes, a practice followed by his spiritual protégé Pete Seeger, who continues to employ folk music as an instrument for social change. An informal periodical titled *The Broadside,* started by activists in the early 1960s, was published for nearly three decades. The magazine *Sing Out!,* a successor to the *People's Songbook* of the 1950s, began as a vehicle for disseminating topical and protest folksongs; while no longer primarily political, it still occasionally publishes songs of civil rights, peace, environmental, and other activists for whom folk music remains an important vehicle for social protest.

In the "internationalist" spirit of the political Left, many songs of one group were adapted in form and content to become universal odes to social justice. One of the best-known instances of this crossover is that of African American spirituals, such as "We Shall Overcome," which has become an anthem not only for the civil rights activists, but for trade-union, women's, peace, environmental, and other groups as well (Spanish-speaking farmworkers sing it as "Nosotros Venceremos").

Forms of social protest among working people in North America have reflected both the diversity of occupational cultures and the multiethnic character of many workplaces. The vast body of labor lore has included veiled criticisms of management communicated in songs, drama, occupational jargon, ritual slowdowns (creative modification of the work process by stylized movements, gestures, and the like engaged collectively in a workplace to slow down the pace of production, often in response to a "speed-up" ordered by management) or sabotage of the work process.

Festivals and parades have often served as stages for labor and political protest. In Europe, tradespeople have for centuries organized such public events, both to display pride in their craft and to protest their treatment in the workplace. Such public demonstrations often involved rituals adapted from ethnic and religious practices of the groups to which the artisans belonged. These traditions were carried over into the New World, where artisanal processions were conducted as early as the 17th century. Workers' parades often parodied local customs, as in Philadelphia, where the popular mummers' processions provided part of the inspiration for the costumes and ritual antics of strike parades.

Song-poems have been among the most popular mediums of labor protest. In form and content, they have reflected both the class and the cultural background of their composers. Commonly set to traditional tunes, they were recited at the workplace and performed by workers' choruses. These choruses were organized not only by trade, but often within ethnic sections of trade unions and political organizations.

Traditional ethnic and religious rituals have also been transformed by workers into expressions of social protest. As an instance, members of the Jewish labor movement adapted the Passover Seder, which commemorates the Exodus, and to also pay tribute to contemporary struggles for liberation.

In the fields and orchards of the Southwestern United States, migrant workers have used traditional expressive forms in the service of the farm workers' movement, which was long headed by the legendary labor leader Cesar Chavez. Farm workers of Mexican ancestry have chronicled their plight, as well as efforts to unionize agricultural workers, in *corridos,* sung newspapers whose form may be traced back to the medieval Spanish ballads or romances. *El Teatro Campesino* (farm workers' theater) has employed the folk drama and song of rural Mexicans and chicanos to portray the lives and struggles of migrant farm workers.

The "unfinished revolution" of women for full equality has been reflected in direct and indirect forms of protest. Sometimes a contrary voice may appear as a subversive message in traditional expressive forms. Women have historically carried on a covert protest against inequity through their activity in the socially assigned realm of the "domestic" arts. A primary example of this is quilt making. Designs stitched into quilts have not only represented traditional patterns, but have sometimes reflected a "quiet protest," as in the crazy-quilt "epidemic" of the late 19th century. Partly a rebellion against rigid design standards, it was also, by extension, a protest against constricting social codes for women.

Another way that quilts have provided a social voice for women is through their use as commemorative documents. Historical scenes and commentary were often sewn into the fabric of these decorative, yet functional, artifacts. As North American women took part in social movements in the late 19th and early 20th centuries—such as abolition, temperance, and suffrage—they employed their traditional skills in making quilts that raised consciousness (and funds) around issues of social injustice. The tradition of "protest quilts" has been updated by such projects as the "Peace Quilt" and the "AIDS Quilt." The NAMES Project has enlisted relatives and friends of people who died of AIDS to sew memory patches, which are then stitched into large sections that are often presented at gay and lesbian civil rights demonstrations; the AIDS Quilt, when displayed in its entirety, has covered several acres. Within the nuclear disarmament movement, images and messages of peace have been sewn into sections by women and men from throughout North America and displayed at various public actions; as an instance, in the 1980s pieces of the Peace Quilt were held up by members of a human chain encircling the Pentagon in Washington, DC.

David Shuldiner

References

Carawan, Guy, and Candie Carwan, eds. 1990. *Sing for Freedom: The Story of the Civil Rights Movement through Its Songs*. Bethlehem, PA: Sing Out Publications.

Davis, Susan G. 1985. *Parades and Power: Street Theatre in Nineteenth-Century Philadelphia*. Philadelphia: Temple University Press.

Ferrero, Pat, Elaine Hedges, and Julie Silber. 1987. *Hearts and Hands: The Influence of Women and Quilts on American Society*. San Francisco: Quilt Digest Press.

Greenway, John. 1953. *American Folksongs of Protest*. Philadelphia: University of Pennsylvania Press.

Halker, Clark D. 1991. *For Democracy, Workers, and God: Labor Song-Poems and Labor Protest, 1865–1895*. Urbana: University of Illinois Press.

Kornbluh, Joyce L., ed. 1988. *Rebel Voices: An IWW Anthology*. Rev. ed. Chicago: Charles H. Kerr.

Wiggins, William. 1987. *O Freedom! Afro-American Emancipation Celebrations*. Knoxville: University of Tennessee Press.

Sociological Approach

Emphasizes the interrelationships of folk culture, social structure, and human interaction. Since sociology is the study of human groups and social organization, it is hard to imagine any folkloristic research, except perhaps the most formal literary analysis, that is not in some way sociological. As many disciplines in the humanities now recognize that human artistic products are inevitably connected to the sociopolitical context in which they were produced, a sociological perspective to folklore has become essential. In essence, the sociological approach investigates how biography and history are linked.

There have actually been numerous sociological approaches to folklore, although relatively few professional sociologists have explicitly addressed folkloric issues. Folklorists who examine community life (for example, Linda Dégh and Henry Glassie), the interplay of techno-industrial order and traditional culture (Hermann Bausinger, Lauri Honko, and Simon J. Bronner), and the role of context and performance features in creativity (Robert Georges, Roger D. Abrahams, and Richard Bauman) might each be considered a "sociological folklorist." Yet, such an approach is so inclusive that one might merely classify folklore as a corner of the sociological enterprise. In contrast, problems also arise from considering in the sociological domain only that which is published by a trained sociologist, leaving the approach too narrow and idiosyncratic. Still, one can echo Kenneth Thompson's surprise that sociology and folklore have not had closer linkages (Thompson 1980).

While boundaries of truly sociological approaches are inevitably hazy, a sociological perspective emphasizes the central position of social structure or interaction processes. The question "What does a text mean?" can only be answered through an examination of the broader contexts in which narrators and audiences operate. To distinguish a sociological approach from an anthropological one requires a primary focus on contemporary, Western, industrial societies, although this is by no means a perfect division.

Sociological approaches to folklore were not foreign to early folklorists or sociologists. William Graham Sumner, professor of sociology at Yale University, made the important distinction between stateways (laws or rules of a social system) and folkways (traditional ways of doing things). Joseph Jacobs, one of the Victorian English folklorists, had a distinctly sociological appreciation for the interpersonal dynamics of diffusion and the role of a folk group as a bounded behavior community, a point later emphasized by Alan Dundes. Howard W. Odum and his colleagues at the University of North Carolina, including Guy Benton Johnson and Newbell Niles Puckett, maintained a vigorous interest in folk culture, and much important collecting of African American traditions and music arose from this interest (see Odum 1953). Emile Durkheim, one of the "fathers" of sociology, and his student Marcel Mauss shared a profound interest in folk culture, particularly in the role of religion in providing a cohesive force for social order. Indeed, near the turn of the 20th century both sociological and folklore journals published articles linking the two disciplines.

Subsequently, several empirical areas have generated important studies that might be labeled a sociological approach to culture: (1) impression management and performance, (2) group dynamics and the creation of folk groups, (3) social control and social conflict, and (4) nation building and social change. Each approach produced considerable research tradition, but can only be summarized briefly here.

Impression Management and Performance

Performance theory, which did much to revitalize folklore theory in the late 1960s and 1970s, owed much of its own vitality to the insight of sociological analysts, such as Erving Goffman in his *Presentation of Self in Everyday Life* (1959), and other dramaturgical theorists, who tirelessly pointed out the existence of demands for impression management and effective presentation of self. The sociological argument claimed that individuals desired to act in such a way as to maximize the esteem that they received from those with whom they interacted. All social life could be analyzed from a theoretical metaphor grounded in actors, props, settings, and backstage preparation. Folkloristics, with its emphasis on the act of narration, proved to be a fertile ground for this metaphor, and researchers examined the art of narration in light of the immediate contextual constraints, often examining the collaborative qualities of narration, the effects of audience response on the content of narration, and the use of discursive practice to achieve behavioral dominance or social status. Further, the presentation of identity operates on a community level, as recent examinations of touristic traditions have indicated. One of the most exemplary works in this genre is Michael Bell's *The World from Brown's Lounge* (1983), a study of a west Philadelphia bar. Bell demonstrates how the employers and customers use narrative strategies to achieve important ends. Performance is, or can be, goal directed, in this case promoting sociability and supporting the organization by creating an environment in which clients will spend money. The fundamental goal of narrative, from this point of view, is to allow individuals to have others respond in ways that they consider socially desirable.

Group Dynamics and the Creation of Folk Groups

The recognition of the importance of folk groups (as they are called by folklorists) or subcultures (as sociologists usually refer to them) indicates a set of similar concerns. How do groups of various sizes create shared meanings, and what is the nature of the culture that is created. Louise Pound reminded folklorists in 1945 that folklore was simply traditional lore found among homogeneous groups. Gary Alan Fine speaks of a phenomenon he labels "idioculture"—referring to the collective traditions of a small group (Fine 1982). This model has been pursued both by folklorists who examine groups of ever-smaller size and by sociologists who expand the model of small-group culture to other substantive venues.

Sociologists argue persuasively that group culture serves a "boundary–maintenance" function: excluding outsiders from participation and also providing justification for internal cohesion by recognizing external threats. Everyone who has just joined an ongoing group recognizes how difficult it is to understand the humor and gossip swirling around. Family culture perhaps provides the most dramatic instance of this process by which tradition is localized: an intimate group, whose members are separated legally and/or biologically from those outside and whose traditions emphasize these boundaries.

Social Control and Social Conflict

One of the traditional areas for sociological study is the tension between domination and control in a society and protests against this domination and control. Social organization sometimes seems like a minuet between the forces of social control and those who wish to contest that. Often this rivalry takes place within the cultural domain, and cultural tradition can be used as a means of reacting to the power structure (Calhoun 1982).

The cultural challenge is met by attempts by elites to control those dominated through folk stories and beliefs—whether these are children, women, or those of a dominated race. From the standpoint of elites, collective and political ritual is often an essential means by which community is created and continually solidified. On whatever level—the individual or the societal—folk traditions can serve as a means of socialization and education.

Organizations frequently attempt to again authority by means of a collective ideology—an approach that has come to be known as organizational culture (Martin 1992). This identity serves to cement individuals to the larger unit, although it is possible that individuals construct traditions to counter organizational hegemony through the establishment of counter-cultures.

Groups and individuals also create, spread, and manipulate tradition in order to improve their status position within a hierarchy. This is perhaps most evident in folklore denigrating racial and ethnic groups, of which, tragically, there is much. Ethnic humor is a powerful motivating force (Davies 1990). Some folklore creates social deviants, such as the lore about threats to children from Halloween sadists (Best 1990) or kidnappers (Carroll 1987).

In other words, folklore is created to achieve ends that influence the relationship among groups and the relationship between individuals and organizations.

Nation Building and Social Change

Sociologists study the organization of society on both the level of social interaction and the level of the nation state (and the world system). Nations use folklore to justify their legitimacy (Hobsbawm and Ranger 1983). Within folkloristics, perhaps the most compelling study of the uses of national tradition is William A. Wilson's *Folklore and Nationalism in Modern Finland* (1976), which examines the use of the *Kalevala*, the Finnish national epic, by Finnish nationalists to provide legitimacy for their nation. In sociology there has been considerable interest in the process of commemoration of events and political leaders. Barry Schwartz demonstrates in *George Washington: The Making of an American Symbol* (1987) that Americans constructed the image of George Washington as a heroic and moral leader to capture some of the virtues that they believed were important for the creation of a new nation; the legends that surround Washington reflect these virtues. *What* we remember and *how* we remember explains something critical about the nature of the social order.

Sociologists and folklorists also agree that folklore is responsive to social and technological change. As the structure of a social system changes, so, too, do its traditions. Without this recognition, we would be left with a static model of culture, instead of the recognition that culture is dynamic. Culture changes with other alterations in the social structure: occasionally ahead of structural change and sometimes as part of a cultural lag (Ogburn 1937).

The disciplines of folklore and sociology have numerous points of fruitful contact. It is a shame that these similarities have not previously been better articulated. We should avoid the mistake of claiming that folklore is only a branch of the larger discipline of sociology—that is self-evidently not true. Still, one cannot help think that many of the most central issues of folklore are the ones that find their mirror in the concerns of sociologists. For the two disciplines to recognize their common concerns would enrich each.

Gary Alan Fine

References

Best, Joel. 1990. *Threatened Children: Rhetoric and Concern about Child Victims.* Chicago: University of Chicago Press.

Calhoun, Craig. 1982. *The Quest of Class Struggle.* Chicago: University of Chicago Press.

Carroll, Michael P. 1987. "The Castrated Boy": Another Contribution to the Psychoanalytic Study of Urban Legends. *Folklore* 98:216–225.

Davies, Christie. 1990. *Ethnic Humor around the World.* Bloomington: Indiana University Press.

Fine, Gary Alan. 1982. The Manson Family: The Folklore Traditions of a Small Group. *Journal of the Folklore Institute* 19:47–60.

Hobsbawn, Eric, and Terrence Ranger, eds. 1983. *The Invention of Tradition.* Cambridge: Cambridge University Press.

Martin, Joanne. 1992. *Cultures in Organizations: Three Perspectives.* New York: Oxford University Press.

Odum, Howard. 1953. Folk Sociology as a Subject Field for the Historical Study of Total Human Society and the Empirical Study of Group Behavior. *Social Forces* 31:193–223.

Ogburn, William F. 1937. Culture and Sociology. *Social Forces* 16:161–169.

Thompson, Kenneth. 1980. Folklore and Sociology. *Sociological Review* 28:249–275.

Solstices, Summer and Winter

The dates on which the sun's ecliptic reaches its extreme northern and southern latitudes. In the Northern Hemisphere, these fall around June 21 and December 22, which are known, respectively, as Midsummer and Midwinter Day. The celestial turning points have been celebrated for millennia with rituals designed to ensure the progress of the sun. In both pagan Europe and pre-Columbian North America, fire making and dancing were common practices. The Sioux Sun Dance, for example, was a summer solstice rite; Pueblo kachina dancing was a winter counterpart.

In Europe, Christianity absorbed pagan solstice customs, and in the case of the winter solstice virtually effaced them. The Catholic Church's early growth may be credited partly to the skill with which it conflated Roman and Persian solstice festivals (the Saturnalia and Mithra's birthday) to the birthday of the Christ Child, the "light of the world." Christmas gradually obscured other December rites, although the lighting of a "new fire" was preserved vestigially in the northern European custom of burning a Yule log.

Midsummer festivals, too, were Christianized, although the traces of sun worship remained more visible. When the liturgical calendar established June 24 as the Feast of John the Baptist, the bonfires that traditionally had honored the sun came to be associated with the saint whom Jesus called "a burning and shining light" (John 5:35). In parts of Europe, they are still called St. John's fires, although the attendant revelry has been muted. Traditional amusements included nocturnal dancing and leaping through, or over, the bonfire flames.

St. John's Day was introduced to North America by European immigrants, especially those from sun-poor Scandinavia, who transplanted not only the bonfires and the dancing, but also the belief—probably a pagan survival—that Midsummer's Eve was suited to divination. Midwestern folklore is rich in midsummer spells, many of which, like Halloween divinations, enable girls to identify future husbands. Fortune-telling and love were also linked, although more erotically, in the snake-dance ritual established for June 23 by New Orleans "voodoo queen" Sanite Dede (Anderson 1960).

Water, appropriately, also figures in beliefs surrounding the Baptist's feast day. In Latin areas, including Mexico and Puerto Rico, public bathing was a St. John's tradition, while Slavic families forbade their children from swimming until the saint had "blessed the water" on June 24 (Cohen and Coffin 1987:218). In one divination, a girl seeks her betrothed by reading the shape of an egg white in a glass of water; in another, the index is a wreath floated on a stream.

In the 1990s, such devotions are less visible than civic festivals. In Minneapolis, *Svenskarnas Dag* (Swede's Day) draws tens of thousands of tourists to a midsummer folk fest. Seattle's Vasa Day celebrates folk traditions in honor of Sweden's first king, Gustavus Vasa. At the *Fyr-Bal Fest* in Ephraim, Wisconsin, business leaders elect a "Viking chieftain" who consigns a "winter witch" effigy to a bonfire. A number of Alaskan communities hold midsummer festivals that celebrate both the memories of the Yukon gold rush and the late June arrival of the midnight sun.

Tad Tuleja

References

Anderson, John Q. 1960. The New Orleans Voodoo Ritual Dance and Its Twentieth-Century Survivals. *Southern Folklore Quarterly* 24:135–143.

Cohen, Hennig, and Tristram Potter Coffin, eds. 1987. *The Folklore of American Holidays*. Detroit: Gale.

Hatch, Jane M., ed. 1978. *The American Book of Days*. 3d. ed. New York: H.W. Wilson.

See also Christmas

South

A region rich in folklore, but one so stereotyped that it is difficult to approach objectively. Hoop-skirted belles vie with barefoot hillbillies and cotton-picking sharecroppers in the popular imagination. These distortions ignore the substantial middle-class population, dubbed "the plain folk of the Old South" by historian Frank Owsley. Yet they do reflect an important reality: the role of the land—both as terrain and as the basis for an agrarian way of life—in shaping the culture.

How do we define the region geographically? Where does the South begin and end? Although the Civil War and its aftermath certainly heightened the region's separateness, a historical approach based on membership in the Confederacy is not entirely satisfactory, for Kentucky would be left out, as would border states such as Maryland and Missouri that are, in part, culturally Southern. Central to the formation of a distinctly Southern culture was the plantation system with its enslaved labor force; the large African American presence has been a major shaper of the region's character. Defined in this way, it could be argued that the South extends as far west as east Texas, beyond which the Southwest is more Western than Southern.

Within this relatively homogeneous region there exists topographically and ethnically based diversity. The Upland South (the Appalachian and Ozark Mountains), which hardly participated in the plantation system, is nevertheless Southern in its own way and shares certain features with the Lowlands; the Cajun and Creole cultures of southern Louisiana, with their French roots, are clearly different from the more typical northern part of the state, yet still recognizably Southern. This dynamic tension between a unified Southern identity and affiliation with smaller communities is crucial to understanding the region's folklore.

Not all of the traditions practiced in the South are exclusive to the region. So what is Southern about Southern folklore? A group of folk-cultural traits helps distinguish the South from the North and West, while at the same time acknowledging subregional differences. As it is for people, much of a region's folk-cultural "personality" can be attributed to a combination of heredity (cultural rather than genetic, of course) and environment. The regional "stew" developed its unique flavor as settlers of varying Old World backgrounds exchanged traditions and responded to conditions in their New World locale, such as climate and natural resources. This process is particularly evident in the genres of material folk culture, wherein basic survival needs are channeled into culturally preferred patterns.

Southern folk architecture emphasizes wood construction, with walls of horizontal logs (a continental European trait introduced via the Mid-Atlantic) or a framework cov-

A sugarcane farmer rolls a cigarette. Near Morganza, Louisiana, 1938. Photo Russell Lee.

ered with weatherboards, and wood-shingle roofs. In the Deep South, external chimney placement is typical, a carryover from southern England as well as a function of the warm climate; the raised pier-and-sill foundation (which allows air to circulate under the floor) is drier and less labor-intensive than the underpinning of the North. Other features reinforced by the climate are galleried porches (possibly an African influence via the West Indies) and detached kitchens. Certain building types, such as the narrow, gable-fronted shotgun house (introduced from Haiti), are also regional. The bare-swept yard as a landscape tradition may have African origins.

No realm of folklife is more evocative of a region than its foodways. Greens, such as turnip and collard, loom large as a Southern vegetable, boiled for hours with fatty pork and the residual liquid ("potlikker") also eaten like soup. Pork was the everyday meat until the rise of the poultry industry, reaching its pinnacle of preparation in barbeque; hog lard was the medium for deep-fat frying. Corn remains a staple grain, manifested in such bread types as skillet-cooked pone, molded sticks and muffins, deep-fried hush puppies, and pudding-like spoon bread. The distilling of corn into moonshine and bourbon can be traced to Ireland (where other grains were used). Homemade cane syrup was the chief sweetener for those unable to afford sugar. Plant foods introduced from Africa via the slave trade—the peanut (its folk name, "goober," derived from the West African *nguba*) and okra (its African name, *gumbo,* applied to the coastal stew in which it is often an ingredient), among others—have made their culinary contributions. The peculiar habit of clay-eating as a mineral supplement also may have been brought from Africa. Coffee was the hot drink of choice (even in the late 1990s, tea is understood as iced), with buttermilk, a by-product of churning, a favorite cool drink (as in Ireland).

The folk craft of pottery has a number of regional features. Green or brown woodash- and lime-based alkaline glazes, used on stoneware of the Deep South since the early 19th century, are found nowhere else in the country and probably derive from China via printed descriptions. Rectangular cross-draft kilns and treadle wheels with ball-opener levers are key elements in the regional production technology. Large jugs for storing cane syrup, jugs with applied faces (first made by slave potters in South Carolina), and pottery gravemarkers (alternatives to more expensive stone) are ceramic types concentrated in the South.

There are also characteristic furniture types. Tall-legged case pieces—the huntboard (a variety of sideboard or buffet) and the smaller cellarette (for storing wine bottles) and sugar chest (for keeping solid sugar cones)—discouraged vermin and echo the pier-and-sill foundation of buildings. The round lazy-Susan table with its smaller turntable (another possible Chinese inspiration) could serve several courses at once with a minimum of passing. The meal bin with two lidded compartments, commonly found in Upland cabins, is an idea undoubtedly brought from Ireland. "Mule-ear" chairs, with their backward-curving rear posts, lean comfortably against a porch wall, and the springy "joggling board" on plantation porches was a pre-trampoline delight for children.

Regional characteristics of Southern folk textiles are less apparent. The predominant filling material for quilts (before the recent availability of polyester) was cotton, an obvious result of its availability as a crop. Hand-woven bedcoverlets typically are of the overshot type in mixed cotton and wool, lighter than their all-wool Northern counterparts. Such distinctive basketry traditions as the work in dyed river cane by Cherokee and Choctaw Indians and in coiled grass by Blacks of the Atlantic Coast tend to be localized or ethnically based, rather than panregional.

Such tangible traditions were not accepted as part of the American folklorist's research domain until the 1960s, whereas oral and musical traditions, which serve to enhance a people's quality of life and transmit community values, have been studied since the late 19th century and are what will first leap to the minds of many readers when thinking of Southern folklore.

Folk music and song have always been major vehicles of aesthetic expression in the South. Several of America's most important musical gifts to the world—Negro spirituals, blues, jazz, and bluegrass—arose as Southern folk idioms, the African American presence dominating the first three and influencing the fourth (which Bill Monroe and others developed mainly out of the White old-time string-band tradition, beginning in the 1940s). Commercial broadcasting and recording of American folk music was concentrated in the South, with record companies issuing blues and old-time performances in the 1920s and paving the way for the popular sounds of rhythm and blues and country and western. More old British ballads have been found in the South than in any other region, and the South also leads in the number of ballads created in the United States.

The most significant folk-musical instrument the South has produced is the banjo, originally a slave instrument with West African forerunners that became a mainstay of mountain music. The Appalachian dulcimer appears to have evolved from the *scheitholt,* a type of German zither transplanted in Pennsylvania. Southern fiddling features a drone or chorded sound reminiscent of bagpipes of the British Isles, from whence the instrument was brought. The French accordion is central to the pulsating sound of Cajun dance music and its Black counterpart, zydeco. The South contributed to the development of the American square dance, while producing such distinctive forms as buck, or flatfoot, and clog dancing (both having roots in the British Isles).

What could be called an oratorical aesthetic—emphasis on skill with the spoken word—permeates Southern life and is manifested in legal and political oratory. In folklore this love of entertaining talk is channeled into traditional preaching and storytelling. Several distinctive groups of folktales hark back to the Old World, such as the mountain Jack tales (popularized by Richard Chase) and African American animal tales (popularized by Joel Chandler Harris), while others, like the "Old Master and John" tales told by Blacks, grew out of Southern experience. Riddling was popular in the Uplands, and Southern speech is often creatively punctuated with colorful proverbial usages.

Southernisms also can be found in the realms of folk belief and custom. Witchcraft once was prevalent in the mountains and among African Americans, who often called it "hoodoo" and gained from it some sense of control as an oppressed minority. Voodoo, a folk religion emphasizing spirit possession, was imported from Haiti to New Orleans; more recently it was introduced to Miami, as was its similarly African-derived but Catholic-influenced Cuban counterpart, *santeria.* A southern folk sect that also involves spirit possession—in this case, by the Holy Ghost—and that is part of the White Pentecostal movement—is serpent handling.

A Southern custom illustrating the centrality of the family is Decoration Day, when members of a community come together in the summer to clean up their local cemetery and decorate their ancestors' graves with flowers. "Turnouts," in which children barred their teacher from the schoolhouse until they were granted a holiday, was a curious frontier custom brought from Britain; the frontier "sport" of "gander-pulling," in which horseback riders vied to yank off the greased head of a live male goose, was no more cruel than modern-day cock and dog fighting. Early Southern Christmas customs supplanted by the modern American observance include shooting off firecrackers, the ritual shouting of "Christmas gift" first thing on Christmas morning, and costumed teenagers known as "fantastic riders" or "surnaters" who sometimes played pranks as they made the rounds of their community (a survival of British "mumming" or "guising," and similar to Mardi Gras as celebrated in rural Louisiana; in both cases, the luck-bringing visits were institutionalized as parades in urban areas).

While this catalog certainly is not complete, it at least suggests the regional character of Southern folklore as an overlay to the historical, sociological, and linguistic approaches emphasized elsewhere in defining the region. Another distinguishing feature as important as any of the foregoing is that the South is a region of retentions, where traditions once shared with other parts of the country have been maintained after disappearing elsewhere. This can be attributed to the isolation of the dispersed farming population from centers of change, poverty following the Civil War, and a conservative tendency to cling to the old ways.

An example from the realm of traditional clothing is the sunbonnet, which passed out of fashion in less sunny climes (except for "plain" sects such as the Amish) but remained a common part of women's apparel in the rural South (especially the Uplands) until recently. In the food domain, grits (coarsely ground corn stirred into boiling water and eaten like mashed potatoes with butter or gravy) are still routinely served—even in fast-food chains—as part of the Southern breakfast, while their Northern equivalents—hasty pudding and mush (eaten as hot cereal with milk and sweetening)—are all but extinct. The White spiritual, an early type of religious folksong once quite widespread, survives as a continuous tradition only in the South. The South also is the only region where Euro-American folk pottery is still made, with the Meaders, Brown, Hewell, and other families working with elements of a preindustrial technology. A handcraft revival, begun about the turn of the 20th century and focused in Appalachia, stimulated crafts by providing classroom instruction and creating outside markets.

Rural-based Southern folk traditions remain vital; more than a third of the 143 outstanding American folklore practitioners awarded National Heritage Fellowships by the National Endowment for the Arts through 1991 are Southerners. But the South is rapidly becoming more like the rest of the country as urbanization, mass culture, and shifts in the economic base have their impact. Some of the characteristics that give the region its distinctiveness are destined to yield to modernization; but at the same time, incomers from other regions and countries (as exemplified by south Florida) are transplanting "new" traditions in a process akin to that of the early settlement period. The regional folk-cultural "stew" is still cooking.

John A. Burrison

References

Burrison, John A., ed. 1989. *Storytellers: Folktales and Legends from the South.* Athens: University of Georgia Press.

Egerton, John. 1987. *Southern Food.* New York: Alfred Knopf.

Kane, Harnett T. 1958. *The Southern Christmas Book.* New York: David McKay.

Tullos, Allen, ed. 1977. *Long Journey Home: Folklife in the South.* Chapel Hill, NC: Southern Exposure.

Wilson, Charles R., and William Ferris, eds. 1989. *Encyclopedia of Southern Culture.* Chapel Hill: University of North Carolina Press.

See also African Americans; Appalachia; Cajuns; Ozarks; Piedmont Region; Talking Trash

Southern Arts Federation Folk-Arts Program

Regional folk-arts program serving a nine-state area in the South. The Atlanta-based Southern Arts Federation (SAF) established its folk-arts program in 1989 to serve the traditional artists and arts presenters of Alabama, Florida, Georgia, Kentucky, Louisiana, Mississippi, North Carolina, South Carolina, and Tennessee. The program was the first to be based at one of the seven regional arts organizations in the United States and was funded initially by a grant from the National Endowment for the Arts folk-arts program. Building upon the work accomplished by state folk-arts programs, the SAF goals are to create networks, provide leadership, and effect positive change in the folk-arts communities of the South.

The first regional-arts service organization to be formed in the South was the Southern States Arts League. The league was established in 1921 in Charleston, South Carolina, to assist visual artists reach a wider regional audience. Exhibitions were sponsored by the league in a number of Southern cities, the most successful being the 1935 exhibition mounted in Nashville, which was attended by a reported 12,000 visitors. The Southern States Arts League also sponsored an annual conference and published a monthly newsletter in an effort to further arts education in the South and to help the public develop a "sense of art values." Due to internal conflicts and other factors, the league was dissolved in 1950, leaving a void in regional-arts services for a period of twenty-five years.

The Southern Arts Federation, incorporated in 1975 through the Southern Growth Policies Board, was established to share, enrich, and preserve the diverse artistic expression of its nine-state Southern region. The SAF is a nonprofit organization supported by its nine member states' arts agencies, the National Endowment for the Arts, and corporate and foundation partners. From its inception, the SAF and its member-state arts agencies have addressed the fundamental and advanced needs of the artists and arts institutions that inhabit this region of rich cultural diversity and rapid cultural transition.

Recognizing the vast, underserved constituencies of traditional artists and arts presenters in its region, the SAF convened a meeting of Southern folklorists in 1987 to provide guidance on how the agency might best address the needs of Southern folk artists. From this meeting, a proposal was developed and submitted to the National Endowment for the Arts folk-arts program to establish the position of regional folk-arts coordinator. The SAF folk-arts program works closely with Southern state folk-arts programs to bring local and state initiatives into a regional network. The program disseminates information, creates opportunities to collaborate across state lines, provides performing and visual-arts touring programs, artist fellowships, and educational programs, produces publications and media products, and lends technical assistance to locally-based folk-arts projects in the region.

Peggy A. Bulger

Southwest

Arid region with Arizona and New Mexico at its core, featuring native cultures, a strong Hispanic and Mexican presence, and an Anglo presence since the 1840s. The American Southwest is not an easy area to define. Most scholars will agree on the states of Arizona and New Mexico, the southern parts of Colorado and Utah, and west Texas around El Paso. However, the differences start there. Does one include the Mojave Desert of California? How far into Texas does one go? How far into Utah and Colorado? Does one define the area on the basis of physical characteristics, shared life forms, cultural characteristics, or a combination of all three? This vagueness of boundaries appears to be one of the characteristics of the region.

However one sets its boundaries, the Southwest is a dry land in comparison with the rest of the United States. This dryness, while very real, did not prevent indigenous cultures from developing there, more or less influenced by developments in Mesoamerica. The native cultures vary widely, from the village-building pueblo peoples of the north to the desert-dwelling O'odham of southern Arizona, to the Navajo and Apache peoples, probably relatively recent arrivals in the region.

The first Europeans in the American Southwest were Spaniards, with a history of exploration dating from Cabeza de Vaca's journey through the region in 1535–1536, and a history of settlement dating from the arrival in northern New Mexico of Oñate's colonists in 1598. By the 1840s, there were Mexican (previously Spanish) settlements in northern and southern New Mexico, El Paso, and southern Arizona. In 1848 much of the region became part of the United States through the Treaty of Guadalupe Hidalgo ending the war with Mexico; southern Arizona was added in 1853 through the Gadsden Purchase. Since that time, the region has been subject to increasingly intense immigration, both from the rest of the United States and from Mexico.

Culturally speaking, the Southwest has been defined mostly from the outside. Santa Fe, Tucson, and El Paso may resemble one another when seen from New York or New England, but from within the region one sees the differences as much as the similarities. Most of the writers who have fixed the images of the region in literature have come from elsewhere.

From the beginning, with Coronado's quest for a rich native civilization, Europeans have come to this region in search of something. Minerals, land for cattle raising, and native souls to bring into the fold of the Catholic Church were important objectives during Spanish times. Those three goals remained important through much of the 19th and 20th centuries as well, with business opportunities and, increasingly, a place to lead the good life eventually supplanting them. The lure of the Other seems to remain as strong as it was in Coronado's time.

In order to understand the region fully, one must remember that it has been "the Southwest" only since the 1840s and 1850s. Before that it was northwestern Mexico; before that, stretching back in time to the early 16th century, it was northwestern New Spain. Before that, if some archaeologists are to be believed, the region was the northernmost extension of the high cultures of the Valley of Mexico. Paradoxically, the cultural features that most distinguish the 1990s Southwest as a tourist destination—the features that comprise its identification with the Other—result from its historic character as a northern or northwestern frontier.

It is a cliché that there are three cultures in the Southwest: Native American, Hispanic, and Anglo. This is, of course, an oversimplification. Native American cultures in the region differ from one another in every way imaginable. Hispanics vary from the descendants of 18th-century settlers in northern New Mexico to late-20th-century from Mexico, Central and South America, and even Spain itself. Anglos include Anglo Americans, African Americans, Asian Americans—everyone, in fact, who is neither Hispanic nor Native American.

Hispanic cultures may be best discussed under two headings: the Hispanos of northern New Mexico and southern Colorado, and Mexican Americans everywhere else. Younger, more politically active members of both groups often prefer the term "chicanos." New Mexican Hispano culture has its roots in the 17th- and 18th-century colonial settlements in the region. It is traditionally pastoral, agricultural, and Catholic in nature. Religious arts include *alabados* (hymns), carved and painted *santos* (sacred Catholic images), and such ritual music and dance clusters as *los Matachines* (a ritual contra dance spread throughout much of former New Spain). The Penitente Brotherhood, a religious organization devoted to emulating some of the sufferings of Jesus Christ and providing community social welfare, permeated many of the villages, intensifying the ritual life. Secular forms include *romances* and their descendants, *corridos* (ballads), traditional tales in a wide variety, and a rich store of proverbs, riddles, and other forms. Secular folklife includes a repertoire of instrumental dance music (fiddle and guitar), a distinctive regional architecture based on adobe construction, and agricultural techniques including the organization of irrigation water.

Mexican American culture is much more widely distributed in the Southwest than is the northern village culture. There has always been passage to and fro across the border; a major wave of immigration accompanied the Mexican Revolution of 1910–1928. Other waves have succeeded this first one, and the Mexican Americans of the late-20th-century Southwest come from all parts of Mexico, bringing with them a variety of regional traditions.

Religious traditions include some that are similar to those of the New Mexico Hispanos. *Los Matachines,* for instance, is danced all over the region. Belief clusters involving the saints, death, and ghosts also have a wide distribution throughout the area. Tales of the devil appearing at a social dance have been collected in southern Colorado, northern New Mexico, and southern Arizona. *La Llorona,* the wailing woman who haunts watercourses and threatens to carry off children, is present in the Southwest as she is all over the Mexican American world. Tales of buried treasure are told and believed all through the Southwest as they are in much of rural Mexico.

Traditional music of the region ranges from unaccompanied *alabado* and *corrido* singing, to guitar-accompanied singing, to full orchestral styles. The latter include the *norteño* style with accordion lead, developed along the Texas-Mexican border, and the relatively recent import of mariachi music, once the regional folk music of the Mexican state of Jalisco and now the national musical symbol of Mexico.

Traditional foods vary within the region, but all are based on corn, beans, and chile peppers. In southern Arizona, wheat and beef gain importance; in northern New Mexico, pork is more common. Common all over are the tortilla and its derivatives, the enchilada and the taco; the tamale, a native Mexican dish often served on holiday occasions; and soups and stews using meats, beans, hominy, and other vegetables.

Traditional material culture includes the creation of several classes of ephemeral folk art. *Piñatas* are containers made of clay, or molded out of papier mache, and covered with cut and fringed colored tissue paper. They may take many different shapes: animals, clowns, and such popular culture figures as Superman and the Teenage Mutant Ninja Turtles. They are filled with candies and broken by children at birthday parties and other festive occasions.

Cascarones are eggshells that have been filled with confetti and decorated and that are broken over partygoers' heads. Paper flowers are traditionally made for weddings, to decorate home altars, and for floral offerings on the family graves at All Souls' Day.

All of these art forms have been taken over by Anglo Americans and used, not for their original purposes, but as interior decorations. The dominant society of the Southwest has a long history of co-opting elements of culture from both Hispanics and Native Americans and using them to give a regional flavor to their lives. This has happened with architectural forms, with foods (especially corn chips and salsa), and with such selected items of dress as the *guayavera* shirt of tropical Mexico.

This is not to say that Anglo American culture in the Southwest is simply derivative of Mexican and Native American cultures. Many traditions found elsewhere in the country—Mormonism and cowboy culture among others—flourish in the Southwest in their own regional variants, but much of Anglo folklore that is distinctive to the region reflects in one way or another the presence of Native American and Hispanic traditions. Some of this lore is prejudicial and stereotypic in nature. Beliefs, stories, and jokes hinging on negative stereotypes of Mexicans and Indians abound.

Paradoxically enough, the same Anglo society that produces this negative lore uses Hispanic and Native American images in its construction and marketing of the Southwest as a tourist and retirement region, which is the way the Southwest has been marketed since the turn of the 20th century, when the Fred Harvey Company sought to lure tourists to stop at its hotels while traveling by train across the continent. The marketing of the region by Anglos to other Anglos continues with such 1980s concepts as the "Santa Fe Style."

James S. Griffith

References

Byrkit, James W., ed. 1992. Land, Sky, and People: The Southwest Defined. *Journal of the Southwest* (Special Issue) 34:(3).

Griffith, James S. 1992. *Beliefs and Holy Places: A Spiritual Geography of the Pimería Alta.* Tucson: University of Arizona Press.

Weigle, Marta, and Peter White. 1988. *The Lore of New Mexico.* Albuquerque: University of New Mexico Press.

Wilder, Joseph C., ed. 1990. Inventing the Southwest. *Journal of the Southwest.* (Special Issue.) 32:(4).

See also Mexican Americans

Spirituals, African American

Religious folksongs by African Americans. Along with folktales, spirituals and their kindred folk-cry-derived genres—worksongs, field hollers, and the blues—form the bedrock of African American culture. Composed mostly during the period of American enslavement of the African, spirituals are a synthesis of African and Christian religious values and symbolism and of African and European musical aesthetics. Characterized often by an extraordinarily rhythmic lyricism, they have made homes for themselves in the plantation field as well as in the concert hall.

Spirituals in their thematic aspects tell the story of an embattled people and stand at the core of traditional African American Christian theology. They function as antidotes to the distorted Christianity disseminated by the slave masters for the purpose of indoctrinating the enslaved into submission. Fugitive Harriet Jacobs (alias Linda Brent) wrote in *Incidents in the Life of a Slave Girl* (1861) that slaves often reacted to the hypocritical teachings of the "Christian" slave masters by singing lines like "Ole Satan's church is here below; / Up to God's free church I wish to go." Spirituals comment on the chaotic aspects of the slave's existence and constitute a formidable corrective to slavery's chaos.

Spirituals function also to help this new, African-descended people construct a sense of selfhood. Spirituals propose three distinct localities of refuge where one might find or forge a new identity: the wilderness, the mountaintop, and the lonesome valley. They spell out the religious and secular dimensions of conversion, giving specific guidance for the preservation of the soul.

Placing the spirituals into categories helps demonstrate

their range and richness. Nine useful groupings are:

Lyrics of Sorrow, Alienation, and Desolation. Marked by despair and weariness, this category emphasizes experiences of unhappiness, abuse, disappointment, longing, yearning, exile, loss, beleagueredness, and disillusionment with humanity. Songs in this group reflect the slaves' identification with the crucified Christ and focus heavily on their confusion about their loss of birthright, identity, and place in the universal order.

Lyrics of Consolation and Faith. Noted for their arduous attempt to maintain spiritual wholeness, these songs provide fortification against bewilderment. Uniting joy and sorrow, hope and despair, these songs testify to the transforming power of the spirit. Starkly affirming that healing balms do exist, they speak of healing agents available to those who have experienced the insufferable. They address both personal and communal uplift and express concern and compassion for the tragic circumstances of humanity.

Lyrics of Resistance and Defiance. Defining the slave's reality as a condition of war, these songs demonstrate the will of the enslaved not to be overcome by the brutal aspects of their physical, political, psychological, and social reality. They convey one fundamental message: Continue to struggle. Emphasizing unity and organization and marked by dogged determination, their tone is audacious and valiant.

Lyrics of Deliverance. These songs speak of deliverance through means of physical escape, death, and resurrection. They appeal for release from all forms of obstacles and victimization and look forward to reunion with persons lost from the community. These songs proclaim the need for spiritual preparation in order to move to a better life. Much attention is given to alerting others to opportunities for escape. This category in particular consists of many songs that are reputed to have been used to signal captives of the feasibility of running away.

Lyrics of Jubilation and Triumph. Proclaiming the moral reordering of the New World, the enslaved nurtured and savored the word "jubilee," making it central to their sacred and ceremonial consciousness. Almost any form of triumph against the force of slavery becomes the subject of a spiritual, but, somewhat ironically, these spirituals express a resistance to stoicism and pessimism in the face of a harsh world. They celebrate affirmative psychology and spiritual resilience and serve as rituals of invigoration and exultation.

Lyrics of Judgment and Reckoning. These songs focus on the disharmony in the world and on the fact that correction or justice is needed. They refuse to accept that life in its present form is the norm of existence. Retribution will be meted out to this unnatural ordering. The time for the Reckoning Day seems well overdue, but each individual, free and slave, must stand ready to his or her moral account at the bar of judgment.

Lyrics of Regeneration. Confronted with constant attempts to render them degenerate, the captives created many songs about how to keep themselves charged with the life force. Thus, there are numerous songs about the electrifying, invigorating, and purifying baptism rituals.

Lyrics of Spiritual Progress. This category of songs dwells on the migratory experience of the human to a greater realm of existence. The progress of the soul is achieved by degrees. One must learn to interpret the signs along the way. True movement begins with humility, faith, steadfastness, and honest confession. The personal journey may be lonely; yet, it has no ultimate meaning without consideration for one's community.

Lyrics of Transcendence. This category of songs insists on creating a place and time beyond the historical moment and, indeed, beyond history itself. This transcendent capability reveals the vanity of earthly life by emphasizing that which is not bound by human definition. These songs show how the enslaved often merged the future with the present to create for themselves a sense of inner peace regarding their sojourn in the American wilderness.

Seen from the perspective of their formal aspects, both utilitarian and aesthetic dimensions are dominant in the spirituals. Thus, they can be called the sacred vernacular poetry of the African American experience. Sophisticated, though not erudite, in their employment of structural and semantic features, the spirituals demonstrate the American musical genius at its best. Essentially choral in origin (as opposed to solo), the musical style features unique breaks, syllabic quavers, off-tones and tone glides, and rare balancing and manipulation of principles of melody, rhythm, and harmony.

In their adept mixing of naiveté, dignity, and sophistication—qualities of the tragic and the epic—the semantics of the spirituals run the gamut from the magnificently simple, to the ambiguous, to the utterly confounding. As a result, the spirituals establish themselves as a prototypic layering from which later modes of African American musical and poetic arts could expand.

More specifically, the spirituals utilize a number of stylistic and rhetorical features. One is an assertion or reaction to a philosophical truth, often made emphatic by beginning the song with the chorus (For example, "Oh, the land I am bound for, / Sweet Canaan's happy land / I am bound for"). Another is clear, sharp phrasing through the vigorous use of Anglo-Saxon words (for example, "I looked over Jordan / And what did I see / Coming for to carry me home?").

Spirituals also employ maximal exploitation of repetition via individual words, refrains, and choruses ("I'm going to tell you about the coming of the Savior; / Fare you well, fare you well. / I'm going to tell you about the coming of the Savior; / Fare you well, fare you well. / There's a better day a-coming, / Fare you well, fare you well").

There is a predominance of familial and communal pronouns ("I met my mother the other day, / I gave her my right hand, / . . . I met my brother the other day; / I met my deacon the other day; / I met my elder the other day, / I gave him my right hand, / And jus' as soon as ever my back was turned, / He scandalize' my name. . . ."); a partiality toward call-and-response prompted by emphatic use of the vocative (a call or appeal) ("Mammy, is massa going to sell us tomorrow? / Yes, yes, yes! / Mammy, is massa going to sell us tomorrow? / Yes, yes, yes!").

Spirituals also make use of the easy interchange of phrases, verses, and stanzas. Thus, segments of one song may float easily into another song, as with the blues. Spirituals also feature the pervasive use of iambic tetrameter alternating with iambic trimeter, a variable but rudimentary beat or rhythm, and the predominance of the *abcb* rhyme scheme.

Frequent use is made of the listener as a creative device ("Believer, O, shall I die? / O, my army, shall I die? / Jesus died, shall I die? / Died on the cross, shall I die?"), of figures of speech ("My brother sittin' on the tree of life, / And he heard when Jordan roll"), and of the antiphonal structure, in which the verse and the refrain are sung alternately ("I have a leader over there, / I have a leader over there, / I have a leader over there. / Play on your harp, little David, / Play on your harp, little David, / Play on your harp, little David. / I have a Savior over there, / I have a Savior over there, / I have a Savior over there. / Play on your harp, little David, / Play on your harp little David, / Play on your harp, little David").

The meaning of the spirituals has been disputed by some who claim that the songs have no political intent, only a religious one, and others have argued that people of African and African-descended cultures were incapable of producing such artistic treasures, claiming, therefore, that the spirituals are grounded in European culture and are derived mainly from the so-called "White spirituals."

Erskine Peters

References

Allen, William Francis, et al. 1971. *Slave Songs of the United States.* New York: Books for Libraries.

Cone, James. 1972. *The Spirituals and the Blues.* New York: Seabury.

Courlander, Harold. 1963. *Negro Folk Music U.S.A.* New York: Columbia University Press.

Epstein, Dena J. 1977. *Sinful Tunes and Spirituals.* Urbana: University of Illinois Press.

James, Willis Laurence. 1955. The Romance of the Negro Folk Cry in America. *Phylon* 1:24–25.

Johnson, James Weldon. 1969. *The Book of American Negro Spirituals.* New York: Viking, pp. 19–30.

Krehbiel, Henry Edward. 1968. *Afro–American Folksongs.* New York: Frederick Ungar.

Lovell, James. 1972. *Black Song: The Forge and the Flame.* New York: Collier-Macmillan, pp. 204–214.

Peters, Erskine. 1993. *Lyrics of the Afro-American Spiritual.* Westport, CT: Greenwood.

Southern, Eileen. 1971. *The Music of Black Americans: A History.* New York: W.W. Norton.

See also Gospel Music; Jackson, George Pullen; Lyric Song

St. Patrick's Day

March 17, the feast day of St. Patrick, patron saint of Ireland, who brought Christianity to Ireland and reputedly chased away all of the country's snakes in the 5th century. People associate the shamrock with St. Patrick, as he used it to explain the concept of the divine trinity (Father, Son, and Holy Ghost).

Primarily a religious holiday in Ireland, St. Patrick's Day has become a time to demonstrate pride in Irish heritage for those living in the United States. In the mid- to late 1800s, lavish St. Patrick's Day parades became common in large American cities. Parades still provide the focal point of many St. Patrick's Day celebrations. In Washington, DC, members of the Ancient Order of Hibernians lay a wreath on the grave of John F. Kennedy. People of both Irish and non-Irish descent wear green on this holiday; children who do not wear green may get pinches from their classmates. Shamrocks and shamrock–shaped pins often appear on this day. It is traditional for many bars to offer green beer and for bakeries to sell green-iced cakes. Dinners of corned beef and cabbage abound on St. Patrick's Day; one can also find "green eggs and ham" breakfasts. One original ethnic hybrid is the green "leprecohen bagel," sold in New York City.

Various planting traditions connected with St. Patrick's Day indicate that this is a good day to begin sowing crops. Potatoes, peas, cabbage, or tomatoes planted on March 17 will make their owner prosperous. And, of course, a four-leafed clover discovered on St. Patrick's Day will bring good luck all year.

Elizabeth Tucker

References

Cohen, Hennig, and Tristram Coffin, eds. 1987. *The Folklore of American Holidays.* Detroit: Gale, pp. 109–112.

Dorson, Richard M. 1964 *Buying the Wind: Regional Folklore in the United States.* Chicago: University of Chicago Press, p. 123.

Gilbert, Elizabeth Rees. 1982. *Fairs and Festivals,* ed. Peter Seitel. Washington, DC: Smithsonian Institution, pp. 44–45.

See also Irish Americans

Stagolee

African American badman folk hero, also known as Stackerlee, Stackalee, Stacker Lee, or Stagalee, whose outrageous behavior, specifically the murder of Billy (or Bully) Lyon (also Lyons, Lion, Lions, O'Lyons, or Galion) over a magical Stetson hat, has been the subject of folksongs, legends, and toasts since the 1890s. According to oral tradition, Stagolee was supposedly born in Missouri with a veil over his face and consequently had supernatural powers, which he sought to increase by selling his soul to the devil. In some versions, Stagolee was intoxicated as the devil lured him into the pact. For payment, the devil gave him the hat, which enabled the protagonist to accomplish even more extraordinary feats, such as eating fire and changing his size and shape.

Some say he went west, and in April 1906 he blew San Francisco down in response to a bartender who was too slow in serving him; others say that Stagolee jerked out the bar and pulled out its pipes—along with the rest of the town's water pipes connected to it—causing the San Francisco earthquake. The song's beginning introduces some of the more typical characteristics of the badman. The following lines come from Southern Black prisoners and appear as examples in Roger Abrahams, *Deep Down in the Jungle: Negro Narrative Folklore from the Streets of Philadelphia*:

> Stagolee, he was a bad man, an' ev'body know,
> He toted a stack-barreled blow gun an' a blue steel
>   forty-four.

> Stackerlee, he was a bad man,
> He wanted the whole world to know
> He toted a thirty-two twenty
> And a smokeless forty-four (quoted in Abrahams
>   1970a:131)

Finally growing intolerant of Stagolee's obnoxious behavior, the devil removed the hat and its magical powers by using a professional gambler, Billy Lyon. The events leading to Lyon's death include a barroom brawl, which ensued in Memphis, St. Louis, or elsewhere (depending on the version) following Billy Lyon's theft of Stagolee's hat; consequently, Stagolee shot and killed him. Most versions of the ballad include Lyon begging for his life, crying that he has two or three children and an innocent wife, whereupon Stagolee typically responds:

> Damn your children,
> And damn your lovin' wife.
> You stole my good old Stetson hat,
> And now I'm goin' to have your life (quoted in
>   Courlander 1963:178)

Other versions focus on Stagolee's capture, his remorse, and his sentencing, or perhaps even have the devil climbing out of hell and shouting, "Come and get this bad Stagolee before he kills us all" (Courlander 1963:179). The following are the last nine of seventeen stanzas of a chain-gang worksong text that comes from Black prisoners in the Mississippi Penitentiary. This text includes the arrest, conviction, and sentencing of Stagolee and a final encounter with the devil:

> The high sheriff told the deputies,
> "Get your pistols and come with me.
> We got to go 'rest that
> Bad man Stagolee."

> The deputies took their pistols
> And they laid them on the shelf—
> "If you want that bad man Stagolee,
> Go 'rest him by yourself."

> High sheriff ask the bartender,
> "Who can that bad man be?"
> "Speak softly," said the bartender,
> "It's that bad man Stagolee."

> He touch Stack on the shoulder,
> Say, "Stack, why don't you run?"
> "I don't run, white folks,
> When I got my forty-one."

> The hangman put the mask on,
> Tied his hands behind his back,
> Sprung the trap on Stagolee
> But his neck refuse to crack.

> Hangman, he got frightened,
> Said, "Chief, you see how it be—
> I can't hang this man,
> Better set him free."

> Three hundred dollar funeral,
> Thousand dollar hearse,
> Satisfaction undertaker
> Put Stack six feet in the earth.

> Stagolee, he told the devil,
> Says, "Come on and have some fun—
> You stick me with your pitchfork,
> I'll shoot you with my forty-one."

> Stagolee took the pitchfork,
> And he laid it on the shelf.
> Says, "Stand back, Tom Devil,
> I'm gonna rule Hell by myself" (quoted in Lomax
>   1960:571–572)

Some scholars place the character, either real or imaginary, as a roustabout who gained his notoriety during the late 19th century's steamboating days along the Ohio River, until a murder conviction ended his career. Many claim the ballad "Stacker Lee" was composed on the levees, where it was most popular. Versions of the story on which the ballad in Black oral tradition is based include one that claims Stagolee actually existed and that his mother was a chambermaid on one of the many steamboats that carried the name of *Lee* and that plied the river between Memphis and Cincinnati, St. Louis and Vicksburg. Another story suggests he was born while his mother was a cook on board the *Stacker Lee*, on which he became a roustabout or a stoker; however, Stagolee allegedly murdered his arch-enemy, Billy Lyon, before the *Stacker Lee* was built, so the first account seems more compelling. One of the most convincing arguments that identifies the 1890s in St. Louis as the time and place for events informing the ballad of "Stackerlee," comes from John David's doctoral dissertation, *Tragedy in Ragtime: Black Folktales from St. Louis* (David 1976).

Besides appearing as the subject of the ballad and prose

narrative tradition, Stagolee has also emerged as a main character in toasts. "Stackolee," wrote Bruce Jackson in his book on Black prison toasts, *"Get Your Ass in the Water and Swim Like Me": Narrative Poetry from Black Oral Tradition*, "Is about an irrational badman who engages in gratuitous violence and joyless sexuality, a man who fires his gun a lot but is almost totally nonverbal. He is the archetypal bully blindly striking out [at] any passing object or person. His sheer strength and big pistol bring him fame, but there are for him no solutions. . . ." (Jackson 1974:13). Versions of the Stagolee toast emerge among males in military and other settings such as prisons, street corners, parties, and bars. While the bully ballad focuses primarily on Stagolee's motives for killing Billy Lyons, the toast concerns itself more with which of the two badmen is the meaner, and it usually has Stagolee sexually violating Billy's woman. In toasts Stagolee exercises his virility in direct rejection of women and femininity, such as in a confrontation with a woman who approaches the hero after he has murdered Billy's brother, the bartender. The woman attempts to keep him there until Billy arrives:

> "Hi there, baby, where's the bartender, if you please?"
> I said, "Look behind the bar, he's with his mind at
>   ease."
> So she peeped at her watch, it was seven of eight.
> She said, "Come upstairs, baby, let me set you
>   straight."
> Now, we went upstairs, the springs gave a twistle,
> I throwed nine inches of dick into that bitch before
>   she could move her gristle.
> Now we come downstairs big and bold.
> They was fucking on the bar, sucking on the floor.
> Then you could hear a pin drop. Benny Long [Billy
>   Lyon] come in (quoted in Abrahams 1970a:76)

And of course, Stagolee also demonstrates his powers in battle:

> And out went the lights.
> And Benny Long was in both of my thirty-eight
>   sights.
> Now the lights came on and all the best.
> I sent that sucker to eternal rest,
> With thirteen thirty-eight-bullet holes 'cross his mother-
>   fucking chest (quoted in Abrahams 1970a:77)

Abrahams has offered an interesting interpretation of the badman in Black oral traditions: "Where the trickster is a perpetual child, the badman is a perpetual adolescent. His is a world of overt rebellion. He commits acts against taboos and mores in full knowledge of what he is doing. In fact he glories in this knowledge of revolt" (Abrahams 1970a:65). In his subsequent work, *Positively Black*, Abrahams examines more closely the use of such stock characters in folklore, demonstrating that "a stereotype will always exhibit the bias of the group that fashions it" (Abrahams 1970b:11). Stagolee's actions in the toast form exhibit the importance of bravery as well as words, as the above story's ending attests:

> I was raised in the backwoods, where my pa raised a
>   bear,
> And I got three sets of jawbone teeth and an extra layer
>   of hair.
> When I was three I sat in a barrel of knives.
> Then a rattlesnake bit me, crawled off and died.
> So when I come in here, I'm no stranger.
> 'Cause when I leave, my asshole print leaves "danger"
>   (quoted in Abrahams 1970a:77)

As Abrahams observes, "the endings of many texts [of toasts] are conventional boasts which may have traveled from the river with the stories of Stack." The Black heroic conceptions of Stagolee, as the genres in which the figure appears demonstrate, have also remained intact, although some versions of the earliest ballads describe Stagolee's killing of Billy Lyon as simply a "good man's" response to a bully:

> Stack-O-Lee was a good man
> One everybody did love.
> Everybody swore by Stack,
> Just like the lovin' stars above.
> Oh, that Stack—that Stack-O-Lee (quoted in Roberts
>   1989:208)

In short, Stagolee epitomizes the Black badman folk hero, whose interpretation demands a genre- and culture-specific approach. He may exist as the dramatis persona in song, such as those ballads Howard Odum collected in the early 1900s; he may exist in both song and tale, such as those that Mississippi John Hurt told and sung in which the badman was White (Jackson 1974:4); and he may exist in both Black and White toasts (Evans 1977; Jackson 1974:44–54; Wepman, Newman, and Binderman 1976).

Richard Allen Burns

References

Abrahams, Roger. [1963] 1970a. *Deep Down in the Jungle: Negro Narrative Folklore from the Streets of Philadelphia.* Chicago: Aldine.

———. 1970b. *Positively Black.* Englewood Cliffs, NJ: Prentice-Hall.

Botkin, B.A. 1946. *The American People: In Their Stories, Legends, Tall Tales, Traditions, Ballads, and Songs.* London: Pilot.

Courlander, Harold. 1963. *Negro Folk Music U.S.A.* New York: Columbia University Press.

David, John. 1976. *Tragedy in Ragtime: Black Folktales from St. Louis.* Ph.D. diss., St. Louis University.

Evans, David. 1977. The Toast in Context. *Journal of American Folklore* 90:129–148.

Jackson, Bruce. 1965. Stagolee Stories: A Badman Goes Gentle. *Southern Folklore Quarterly* 29 (3):188–194.

———. 1974. *"Get Your Ass in the Water and Swim Like Me": Narrative Poetry from Black Oral Tradition.* Cambridge: Harvard University Press.

Labov, William, Paul Cohen, Clarence Robbins, and John Lewis. [1968] 1990. Toasts. In *Mother Wit from the Laughing Barrel: Readings in the Interpretation of Afro-American Folklore*, ed. Alan Dundes. Jackson: University of Mississippi Press, pp. 329–347.

Levine, Lawrence. [1977] 1980. *Black Culture and Black Consciousness: Afro-American Folk Thought from Slavery to Freedom.* New York: Oxford University Press.

Lomax, Alan. 1960. *The Folk Songs of North America.* Garden City, NY: Doubleday.

Roberts, John W. 1989. *From Trickster to Badman: The Black Folk Hero in Slavery and Freedom.* Philadelphia: University of Pennsylvania Press.

Wepman, Dennis, Ronald B. Newman, and Murray B. Binderman. 1976. *The Life: The Lore and Folk Poetry of the Black Hustler.* Philadelphia: University of Pennsylvania Press.

Wheeler, Mary. [1944] 1969. *Steamboatin' Days: Folk Songs of the River Packet Era.* Freeport, NY: Books for Libraries.

Steelworkers

Laborers in the nation's steel mills. The stories, music, and visual lore of steel towns speak of the harsh working conditions in the industry, the long struggle for labor unionization, the close connection between work and cultural background (ethnicity, religion, race), and the strong sense of pride among workers and their families in the mill communities during the heyday of steel.

Since the mid-1870s, the term "steelworker" has carried with it an aura of toughness and strength. For more than 100 years, steel built the industrialized nations. The center of steel production in the United States was southwestern Pennsylvania, due to the availability there of natural resources, river transportation, and a long tradition of mechanical and engineering inventiveness. Pittsburgh became known as "The Steel Capital of the World." It was there that Andrew Carnegie and Henry Clay Frick, with the help of financiers such as R.K. Mellon, established the industrial empire that became U.S. Steel Corporation, in a miles-long chain of Monongahela River Valley towns—Homestead, Braddock, Duquesne, McKeesport, Clairton, and others. Their rivals, Jones and Laughlin and others, built mills at Aliquippa and elsewhere along the Upper Ohio and Allegheny Rivers in the Pittsburgh industrial district.

From about 1880 to 1920, southwest Pennsylvania's steel mills burgeoned through intensive capitalization and technological innovation, generating a complex network of interrelated manufacturing in the region that became known as the site of "America's Second Industrial Revolution." With this impetus, steel quickly replaced iron as the preferred structural material throughout the United States. "Big Steel" and "Little Steel" companies established new steel mills all over the Northeast and Midwest (Ohio, West Virginia, Illinois, Indiana), and in the South (Alabama). The transportation and construction industries, based on steel, flourished from coast to coast.

In response to the rise of these huge corporations, the Pittsburgh region also became the crucible of industrial unionism, where both the American Federation of Labor (AF of L) and the Congress of Industrial Organizations (CIO), as well as the United Steelworkers of America (USWA), began. Watershed events in labor history occurred in the region and still resonate in community memory: the Pennsylvania Railroad strike of 1877, the Homestead strike and battle in 1892, the great steel Strike of 1919, and the struggles in the late 1930s that resulted in passage of the Wagner Act and protection of workers' rights.

In the mill towns of Pennsylvania, Ohio, and West Virginia, at first both labor and management were primarily of northern European stock. Soon, the demand for labor attracted waves of immigrants from eastern and southern Europe, along with African Americans from the South. In the Deep South, most steelwork was done by African Americans, under the management of the predominant Scotch-Irish. Except for during wartime, women did not work on the shop floor in the steel industry until the equal-opportunity and affirmative-action laws of the 1970s.

After World War II, the "Big Steel" corporations stopped investing in their older American plants, opting instead to begin new operations overseas. As suddenly as they had arisen a century earlier, the vast steel mills began to close in the 1980s, laying off hundreds of thousands of workers virtually overnight and dimming the economic future of once booming industrial towns. In the 1990s, these towns, including those in the former "Steel Capital" Pittsburgh region, have realized they must retrain their workers, reclaim their environments, and restructure their economies to include steel making where possible, but never again to depend upon it solely.

Systematic documentation of steelworker lore began in the 1940s, when George Korson asked Jacob Evanson, a talented public-school choral director in Pittsburgh, to collect folk music from mill workers in the area for a chapter in Korson's book on Pennsylvania lore. Evanson's chapter still stands as one of the most comprehensive and thoughtful field studies on the folklore of steel (Evanson 1949). His published versions of songs such as "The Twenty-Inch Mill" and "The Homestead Strike" drew national recognition through performances and recordings by singers such as Pete Seeger and Vivien Richman (see Richman 1959).

From the 1950s to the 1970s, collecting and analysis of steelworker lore continued with work by folklorist Hyman Richman and journalist George Swetnam, although no major projects were undertaken. Then, in the late 1980s, the precipitous decline of steel in the Pittsburgh area reignited documentation efforts. The regional nonprofit Steel Industry Heritage Corporation (SIHC), together with the Pennsylvania Heritage Affairs Commission, conducted a three-year ethnographic study of the traditions of steel and steel-related communities in six counties of southwestern Pennsylvania, to generate a variety of oral history and folklife programming. The SIHC is working in the 1990s with state and federal agencies to establish a heritage-park program and a Steel Heritage Center in the region. The Historical Society of Western Pennsylvania produced an exhibit on Homestead's history and is developing a worker's-house museum in Pittsburgh. Elsewhere in the country, the city of Birmingham, Alabama, has developed the Sloss Blast Furnace national historic site and conducted oral-history projects in the Birmingham steel district.

The largest steel mills often employed thousands of workers at one site, in dozens of hierarchically organized departments. The process of steel making requires working with molten metals at temperatures of 3000°F and more. Over the years, the work has often involved severe physical discomfort (noise leading to permanent hearing loss, extremes of heat and cold, air laden with chemicals and fine metal dust, floors soaked with water and grease, long hours of double and even triple "turns" to earn much-needed overtime pay—or to avoid losing one's job). Early on, there were virtually no safety rules or procedures to protect workers, and, though working conditions continue to improve, health and safety are still issues in the 1990s. The oral histories collected from workers often describe accidents and disasters (furnace explosions, crane-operating miscalculations), along with narratives of how problems were averted by quick thinking and action. Songs created by early-20th-century Slovak immigrant workers describe their efforts to adapt to the harsh conditions of the mills in the new land and the effects of accidents on workers' families. There are tales of ghosts in mills where workers died on the job, and stories of accidental "burials" of workers in ladles of molten steel or of their interment in unmarked graves within the mill complex (ascribed to management's attempts to suppress knowledge of the deaths).

The fifty-year struggle to unionize the steel industry was as much about working conditions and injury compensation as about wages. Songs and stories tell of strikes and battles and of repression by the company's "cossacks" (the Iron and Coal Police) and their hired Pinkerton guards. Among the most famous songs was "The Homestead Strike Ballad," one of several recounting the events of the strike and lockout at the Homestead Works in 1892. In 1993 folklorist Archie Green published his analysis of the long-term influence in American industrial folklore of the songs from the Homestead strike.

The ever-present danger, the need for dependable teamwork, and the solidarity forged through unionization efforts often have prompted intense camaraderie among steelworkers. "Reunion committees" of former employees at the Homestead Works, the Duquesne Works, and the mills at Aliquippa still meet annually, years after shutdown.

Ethnicity has also been an important factor in the steel workplace, especially during the early years of the industry. Signs showing plant regulations were often printed in a half-dozen languages. Foremen could hire and fire at will; ethnic tensions ran high between labor and management, and often among workers themselves, as they struggled to keep their jobs. Promotion was often denied to eastern and southern Europeans and to African Americans. English-speaking mill managers coined insulting names such as "garlic snapper" and "Hunkie" to refer to immigrant workers; the workers, for their part, called managers "cake-eaters," "Johnny Bulls," and "Irish." (The 1919 steel strike was dubbed the "Hunkie Strike," because so many foreign-born laborers took part in it.) Workers also gave each other nicknames based on cultural background, appearance, work habits, or other characteristics, a practice that continues ("Babe," "Lefty," "Kentucky Mike"). Interethnic practical jokes were part of mill life, as was the sharing of skills and games from the old country. Because of linguistic barriers and the high noise level in the mills, a supplementary communication system of gestures and sign language evolved.

Until college education became more widespread after World War II, much of the knowledge of iron and steel technology was passed down through semi-oral tradition from veteran workers to new ones. Although there were blueprints and manuals for equipment operation, workers often devised more efficient techniques on their own and invented modifications to the equipment. Production terminology and descriptions of work processes have found their way into workers' songs such as the late-19th-century "The Twenty-Inch Mill" and the late-20th-century "Steel Mill Scat."

In steelworkers' stories, strength of body, manual skill and dexterity, quick reactions in a crisis, and care for the safety of others are the most valued traits. Many mills have had local worker heroes embodying these characteristics about whose exploits stories and tall tales are related. Hyman Richman was told about Henny Palm in McKeesport, "Armstrong Joe" at the Edgar Thomson Works in Braddock, and Mike Lesnovich at the Duquesne Works. There are stories of antiheroes, too—clumsy or loutish workers, harsh or villainous foremen. Perhaps the best-known popular image is Joe Magarac, the Paul Bunyanesque steelworker superhero (Richman 1953).

In steelworking towns, the mill and the community were usually closely interrelated. Often the company had built much of the worker housing, and then controlled the town by putting company managers into political office. In southwestern Pennsylvania mill towns, immigrant workers usually lived in the flat areas close to the river and adjacent to the plant gates, while managers lived on slopes overlooking the mill (where the air was cleaner). Sometimes the company would give land or a building for a parish church, to encourage worker loyalty and indebtedness. A well-known example of industrial corporate paternalism was Andrew Carnegie's nationwide gifts of public libraries (actually community centers), a practice he started in Braddock and Homestead. The companies often built ballfields and sponsored baseball and football teams, encouraging rivalries between mill workers from neighboring towns. (At one time, the town of Duquesne had twenty baseball teams!) People's continued identification with these sports is reflected in their strong loyalty for the region's professional teams, the Pittsburgh Steelers and the Pittsburgh Pirates.

The liminal areas between the workplace and the community for most workers were the mill bars, which were (and in some cases still are) the worker's first stop after receiving a paycheck at the plant gate, before heading home. Located along streets just outside the gates, these establishments served large quantities of alcohol day or night. Among the most famous drinks is the "boilermaker" (named for one of the toughest jobs in a steel mill), which, in Pittsburgh, is also known as a "shot 'n' a beer" or an "Imp 'n' Iron" (Imperial whiskey with an Iron City Beer chaser). Mill bars, along with ethnic halls and "sportsmen's clubs," still function as male workers' social centers. Mill workers' wives belong to ladies' auxiliaries of ethnic fraternal societies, and Christian Mothers' organizations in their church parishes.

In Pittsburgh in the 1990s, there are still large neighborhoods with concentrations of specific ethnic groups: Italians in Bloomfield, Germans in Troy Hill, Jewish and Asian groups in Squirrel Hill, Ukrainians on the South Side, Polish people in Lawrenceville, and eastern Europeans followed by African Americans in the Hill District. In the nearby mill towns, ethnicity was less differentiated geographically: eastern and southern European immigrants grouped together in the worker-housing areas, while those of British and German background lived "up the hill." Nowadays ethnicity is more a matter of choice than proximity: The suburbanization of the 1950s and 1960s has diluted the original ethnic neighborhoods, but new forms and contexts of cultural expression allow people to maintain their sense of ethnic identity.

Religious denominations in the region still include, among others, Roman Catholic, Byzantine Catholic, Maronite Catholic, Russian Orthodox, Antiochian Orthodox, Serbian Orthodox, as well as Protestant groups (Presbyterian, Episcopalian, Methodist, Lutheran, Mennonite, Society of Friends, Holiness/Pentecostal) and the branches of Judaism. Newcomers to the region since World War II have introduced Hinduism, Islam, Baha'i, and other religions as well. When the 19th-century immigrants established their religious institutions, they further subdivided the denominations by nationality, so that some people would go to "the German church," others to "the Polish church," and still others to "the Lithuanian church" or "the Croatian church"—all Roman Catholic. (Even Jews in Pittsburgh identified their synagogues by nationality.) Some of this ethnic-religious linking persists, with special services still conducted in the old-country language, Saint's-Day parades, and church-sponsored old-country food and craft sales.

Some of the many ethnic-based social clubs and insurance associations still remain in the mill towns of Pennsylvania and Ohio, with Croatian, Slovenian, and other fraternal organizations continuing to sponsor music and dance ensembles and youth groups. *Kolo*, polka, and *czardas* dancing, tamburitza combos and *ballabale* bands, and German singing societies continue as a living legacy of the steelworking era.

In their homes, churches, and clubs, workers and their families also continue to express their cultural heritage through visual means. Men use metalwork skills they learned in the mill to craft sculptures or invent small machines during leisure hours at home, recycling scraps of steel that would otherwise have been thrown away by the company. Working families create shrine-like home displays of gear, tools, and metal test-samples from the mills, or of ethnic family heirlooms. Icon and egg "writing," mural painting and stenciling are still practiced; the murals at St. Nicholas Croatian Catholic Church in Millvale (near Pittsburgh), for example, combine ethnic, occupational, and religious symbolism.

In the 1940s, Pittsburgh schoolchildren regularly performed steelworking folksongs and folk-like songs arranged by Choral Director Jacob Evanson. In the 1970s, two Pittsburgh playwrights produced "Steel City," a documentary drama that incorporated narratives collected from steelworkers in Aliquippa. Local interest in, and promotion of, the legendary folklore (or fakelore) hero Joe Magarac have continued unabated, in spite of folklorists' attempts over the years to quash the Magarac stories as inauthentic. The Duquesne University Tamburitzans (founded in the 1930s), the Pittsburgh Folk Festival (started in the 1950s), and the Pittsburgh International Folk Theatre (begun in the 1990s) present highly stylized arrangements of eastern and southern European folk dance, and encourage mill-town children's participation in "junior tamburitzans" and other folklore-based performing groups sponsored by local ethnic churches and clubs.

Doris J. Dyen

References

Dorson, Richard M. 1981. *Land of the Millrats.* Cambridge: Harvard University Press.

Dyen, Doris J., and Randolph Harris. 1991. Aids to Adaptation: Southeast European Mural Paintings in Pittsburgh. In *Folklife Annual* 1990, ed. James Hardin. Washington, DC: American Folklife Center, pp. 10–29.

Evanson, Jacob A. 1949. Folk Songs of an Industrial City. In *Pennsylvania Songs and Legends*, ed. George Korson. Philadelphia: University of Pennsylvania Press, pp. 423–466.

Green, Archie. 1993. Homestead's Strike Songs. In *Wobblies, Pile Butts, and Other Heroes: Laborlore Explorations.* Urbana: University of Illinois Press, pp. 228–272.

Historical Society of Western Pennsylvania. 1991. *Homestead: Story of a Steel Town.* Exhibit Catalog. Pittsburgh.

Hoerr, John. 1991. *And the Wolf Finally Came.* Pittsburgh: University of Pittsburgh Press.

Richman, Hyman. 1953. The Saga of Joe Magarac. *New York Folklore Quarterly* 9:282–293.

Richman, Vivien. 1959. *Vivien Richman Sings Folk Songs of Western Pennsylvania.* Folkways Records FG 3568.

Steel Industry Heritage Corporation. 1994. *Ethnographic Survey of the Steel Heritage Region.* Homestead, PA: SIHC.

Swetnam, George. 1988. Slag Pile Annie. In *Devils, Ghosts, Witches: Occult Folklore of the Upper Ohio Valley.* Greensburg, PA: McDonald/Sward, p. 41.

United Steelworkers of America. Undated (late 1970s). *Songs of Steel and Struggle.* LP recording, with booklet, including Introduction, by Archie Green and liner notes by Joe Glazer.

See also Magarac, Joe

Stepping

A dynamic performance tradition among African American fraternities and sororities involving various combinations of dancing, singing, chanting, and speaking. This complex performance event and ritual draws on African American folk traditions and communication patterns, such as call-and-response, rapping, the dozens, signifying, marking, spirituals, handclap games, and military cadence chants. Stepping routines also incorporate material from popular culture, such as advertising jingles, television theme songs, and Top-40 hits. Fundamentally, stepping is a ritual performance of group identity. It expresses an organization's spirit, style, icons, and unity.

Like any other kind of folklore, step routines are transmitted orally and by example, but they are also transmitted by videotape and copied texts. Chapters of Greek organizations from nearby schools frequently visit each other and exchange steps, and national meetings provide the opportunity for steps to circulate widely. Since each fraternity and sorority has common symbols and history, each group has a core of material in common. For example, each fraternity and sorority has "trade steps," by which each group is known. Kappa Alpha Psi performs a trade step called "Yo Baby Yo." The oldest Black fraternity, Alpha Phi Alpha, founded in 1906, has a trade step called "The Grand-Daddy Step." And the oldest Black sorority, Alpha Kappa Alpha, founded in 1908, performs a trade step known as "It's a Serious Matter." Each of these trade steps has a recognizable rhythm, set phrases, and set movements that remain fairly constant, yet each can also be varied in innovative ways.

To establish and maintain a unique Greek identity, each fraternity and sorority must define itself with symbols and styles that distinguish it from any other group. Members first learn to step as part of their initiation process, and they are expected to perform publicly as a sign of their new status. Stepping performances have become a key way for displaying and asserting group identity, as well as for negotiating the status of each group within the social order. Members of Kappa Alpha Psi, for example, are noted for their dexterous use of canes, while Alpha Phi Alpha members pride themselves on the vigor of their stepping.

Stepping is a form of ritual communication that employs at least three distinct types of acts: cracking or cutting, freaking, and saluting. In the crack or cut, one group makes fun of another group, either verbally, nonverbally, or both. Freaking refers to a member who breaks the norm of synchronization and unity, in an attempt to get greater audience response. The freaker, or show dog, as he or she is sometimes called, is a crowd pleaser. Saluting is a ritualized greeting in which a fraternity or sorority greets another Greek organization by imitating the steps, style, or symbols of that organization.

The Black Greek organizations step in order to get publicity, promote unity and identity, raise money, and express a competitive spirit among the various fraternities and sororities.

Elizabeth C. Fine

References

Fine, Elizabeth C. 1991. Stepping, Saluting, Cracking, and Freaking: The Cultural Politics of African-American Step Shows. *Drama Review* 35 (2):39–59.

Freeman, Marilyn, and Tina Witcher. 1988. Stepping into Black Power. *Rolling Stone.* March 24:143–148.

Nomani, Asra Q. 1989. Steeped in Tradition, "Step Dance" Unites Blacks on Campus. *Wall Street Journal.* July 10, pp. A1, A4.

Storytelling

Solo performance of an oral narrative. The ancient art of storytelling endures as a recreational and educational activity in both rural and urban settings. Parents continue to tell bedtime tales. Other tellers share jokes, personal stories, legends and urban legends in social and educational contexts. Religious teachers tell stories to transmit spiritual history and values. Naturalists tell stories to teach about the environment. Frightening stories, a specialty at Halloween, are commonplace at slumber parties and summer camps. In fact, most people can identify someone in their family or community as "a natural born" storyteller.

A new development since the 1970s has been the mushrooming of "nontraditional," "contemporary," "revivalist," or "professional" storytellers. Unlike a traditional storyteller, who typically learns stories from, and tell stories to, populations who share a cultural heritage, a nontraditional teller may appropriate stories found in published texts, from cultures with which neither the teller nor the audience have firsthand experience. Performance oriented, story interpretation is shaped by the individual teller's personal taste. A story heard at a festival, even from a traditional teller, may go through idiosyncratic transformations.

Nontraditional storytelling was stimulated in the late 19th century when library schools began training librarians to tell stories. "Story hours" were offered in U.S. libraries as early as 1896, and in 1909 the American Library Association sponsored a story-hour symposium.

The popularity of nontraditional storytelling in the 1990s is documented by the hundreds of storytelling festivals, classes, conferences, and publications. National and regional storytelling directories list more than 1,000 storytellers in the United States performing in schools, libraries, museums, coffeehouses, theaters, and festivals. Magazine and newspaper articles have further demonstrated public awareness and appreciation of the art of storytelling. It is not uncommon for thousands of people to attend regional storytelling festivals.

The National Association for the Preservation and Perpetuation of Storytelling (NAPPS), founded by Jimmy Neil Smith in 1973, has played a major role in promoting both traditional and nontraditional storytelling through its festivals, conferences, and publications. NAPPS publishes a quarterly magazine, *Storytelling,* and sponsors an annual festival in Jonesborough, Tennessee, which more than 9,000 people attended in 1992.

The Black Storytelling Festival, an annual event since 1983, takes place in various urban settings around the country. The majority of the organizers, audience, and tellers at this festival are African American.

As modern technology becomes progressively impersonal, the face-to-face intimacy and simplicity of storytelling appears to be gaining personal and social appeal. Ironically, sales of storytelling audiocassettes and videotapes are also growing.

A newer trend is the telling of traditional oral narratives, especially by psychotherapists, to help people obtain insight and heal psychological wounds. Therapeutic storytelling has been popularized by storyteller-authors like Joseph Campbell, Robert Bly, and Jack Zipes. Conversely, telling traditional tales obtained from published texts by other nontraditional tellers is decreasing, supplanted by an increasing preference for telling original, personal, and family tales.

Despite theoretical and cultural differences between traditional and nontraditional storytellers, the *storytelling event* emerges as remarkably similar, and in some contexts, such as a Sunday-school classroom teacher telling stories, the line between traditional and nontraditional storytelling is, at best, fuzzy.

Ruth Stotter

References

Greene, Ellin, and George Shannon. 1986. *Storytelling: A Selected Annotated Bibliography*. New York: Garland.

National Association for the Preservation and Perpetuation of Storytelling (NAPPS), P.O. Box 309, Jonesborough, TN 37659. The NAPPS magazine, originally called the *National Storytelling Journal* (1984), changed to *Storytelling* in 1989.

Pellowski, Anne. 1990. *The World of Storytelling: A Practical Guide to the Origins, Development, and Applications of Storytelling*. New York H.W. Wilson.

See also Folktale; Revivalism; Yarn

Structural Approach

An approach whose goals are to discern and describe the basic structural components of a folklore genre or example and the interrelationships between or among them. The principal impetus for structural studies by American folklorists was the 1968 English translation of Vladimir Propp's 1928 *Morfológija skázki* (Morphology of the Folktale). Propp determined that fairy tales have a maximum number of thirty-one "functions" (actions of the dramatis personae), which always occur in a set sequence, unless they undergo a process of transformation. Obligatory functions in Propp's scheme are the pairs "lack" and "lack liquidated" or "villainy" and defeat of the villain ("victory"). Optional functions include such pairs as an "interdiction" and its subsequent "violation" and a difficult task and its eventual accomplishment, or "resolution."

Alan Dundes adapted Propp's scheme, identifying minimal structural units as "motifemes" instead of functions (Dundes 1962). In analyzing a set of North American Indian folktales structurally, Dundes discovered that functions (motifemes) that Propp had discerned in fairy tales are inherent in other kinds of traditional narratives and even in other folklore genres, including superstitions (Dundes 1964). Like Propp, Dundes demonstrated that while the content and style

of folklore examples may vary considerably over time, structural elements and their patternings do not. Dundes posited that motifemes—like phonemes and morphemes in language—are finite, stable, and recurrent. But each also has multiple "allomotifs" because of content variations. In North American Indian folktales, for instance, allomotifs of the motifeme "lack" include a lack of water, food, or fire and an inability to bear children or to remove and juggle one's eyes. The motifeme "interdiction" may have as its allomotifs the warning not to face the west wind while digging for roots, not to remove and juggle one's eyes more than a specified number of times (usually four), and not to open a particular box or other container because its contents (such as darkness or pestilence) will be exposed or escape. Because these motifemes (functions) occur in pairs in North American Indian oral narratives, just as they do in Euro-American fairy tales, lacks are predictably liquidated, and interdictions are always violated.

Since its objective is to uncover the fundamental framework of folklore forms and examples, the structural approach is reductionist in nature. Dundes' structural analysis of a corpus of superstitions he recorded in Brown County, Indiana, led him to offer this definition: "Superstitions are traditional expressions of one or more conditions and one or more results with some of the conditions signs and others causes" (Dundes 1961). Dundes noted that when the conditions are signs, the superstitions can be called "sign superstitions" ("If there's a ring around the moon, it's going to rain" or "When you hear a dog howling, somebody is going to die"). Human beings cannot or do not intentionally produce signs, but instead merely perceive and interpret them. The basic structural components (conditions and results) in sign superstitions are related temporally, since the results follow in time the appearance of the conditions. When the relationship between conditions and results is causal, the superstitions can be termed "magic superstitions" ("Turn a dead snake's belly up to bring about rain" or "Wear a blue bead around your neck to protect yourself from the evil eye"). In magic superstitions, human action is intentional and is assumed to bring about (cause) a predetermined result. A third (hybrid) category, that Dundes calls "conversion superstitions," combines the other two, with intentional human actions neutralizing or reversing results that signs foreshadow— for example, "If you spill salt, you'll have bad luck, unless you throw some over your left shoulder" or "If you drop a comb, you'll have bad luck, unless you step on it, turn around three times, and make a wish" (this conversion resulting in one's not only averting bad luck, but also having a wish come true). These three kinds of superstitions, note Elli Köngäs-Maranda, and Pierre Maranda, are structurally identical and therefore can be represented by a single formula: "If A, then B, unless C" (Köngäs-Maranda and Maranda 1962: 178).

Structural analyses of other folklore genres similarly illustrate the reductionist preoccupation of the approach. The structure of many proverbs can be described formulaically as A = B, as in such examples as "Business is business," "Enough is enough," and "Boys will be boys." Other proverbs exemplify an A ≠ B (A is the opposite of B) patterning, as in "Service is no heritage" and "A fair exchange is no robbery." Inequality rather than nonequality is expressed in still other proverbs— for example, "Half a loaf is better than no bread" and "A tale-teller is worse than a thief," which can be said to have an A > B (A is greater than B) and an A < B (A is less than B) structure, respectively (Dundes 1975:103–118; Köngäs-Maranda and Maranda 1962:176–177).

Material objects such as traditional crafts and buildings have also been subjected to structural analyses. For his 1975 study, *Folk Housing in Middle Virginia: A Structural Analysis of Historical Artifacts,* Henry Glassie analyzed 338 dwellings structurally. He hypothesized from his data that the houses he investigated were constructed according to a single set of rules that builders generated sequentially. Planning for all of the houses under scrutiny began with a square as the basic geometric entity. The square was then often transformed, the result being the creation of up to two different classes of shapes and up to three shapes allowable in any given whole. Working from a single set of generative and transformational rules, one could construct houses in such variations as single or double story and with from one to four chimneys. The transformations and such dependent forms as porches and sheds accounted for the existence of a set of dwellings that shared a basic structure but also varied and exhibited readily perceivable differences. Inferring and then describing precisely the set of structural rules followed in creating such houses is analogous to the linguist's discovery and description of the grammar of a language, notes Glassie, and such rules in both cases are both generative and transformational in nature.

Robert A. Georges

References

Dundes, Alan. 1961. Brown County Superstitions. *Midwest Folklore* 11:25–33; reprinted as The Structure of Superstition in *Analytic Essays in Folklore,* ed. Alan Dundes. Mouton: The Hague, 1975, pp. 88–94.

———. 1962. From Etic to Emic Units in the Structural Study of Folktales. *Journal of American Folklore* 75:95–105. Reprinted in *Analytic Essays in Folklore,* ed. Alan Dundes. Mouton: The Hague, 1975, pp. 61–72.

———. 1964. *The Morphology of North American Indian Folktales.* Folklore Fellows Communications No. 195. Helsinki: Soumalainen Tiedeakatemia.

———. 1975. On the Structure of the Proverb. In *Analytical Essays in Folklore,* ed. Alan Dundes. Mouton: The Hague, pp. 103–118.

Köngäs-Maranda, Elli, and Pierre Maranda. 1962. Structural Models in Folklore. *Midwest Folklore* 12:133–192.

Stubblefield, Blaine ("Stub") (1896–1960)

Riverman, singer of traditional songs, publicist, Chamber of Commerce executive. Stubblefield was born and reared in Enterprise, Oregon, and in this setting he absorbed materials identifiable with the history and traditional lore of Hell's Canyon, North America's deepest gorge.

After graduating from the University of Idaho, where he had been president of the student body, he worked for the Spokane, Washington, Chamber of Commerce and for the American Automobile Association, publicizing Idaho's newly completed north-South highway (US 95) from Weiser to Lewiston. He became publicity manager for Varney Air Lines, the predecessor of United Air Lines, with head offices in San Francisco. For many years, he was aviation editor in Washington, DC, for McGraw-Hill. He returned to the West in 1949 and began operating a fleet of boats and barges through the Snake River Canyon, serving at the same time as secretary of the Weiser Chamber of Commerce.

Drawing upon his broad acquaintance with traditional music, both instrumental and vocal, he obtained $150.00 from the Chamber for the establishment of the Northwest Mountain Fiddlers' Contest, an annual function that by 1963 had evolved into the present National Old-Time Fiddlers' Contest. Held the third full week each June in Weiser, it is one of the noteworthy festivities in Idaho, drawing participants quite literally from coast to coast and border to border, with some performers coming from Canada.

While in Washington, DC, Stubblefield recorded sixteen songs for Alan Lomax in the recording laboratory of the Library of Congress. Rae Korson, head of the Archive of American Folk-Song there, reported that in April 1938, "Stub" recorded eleven songs, including "Nelly at the Wake," "The Farmer's Curst Wife," and "Way Out in Idaho," all accompanied with guitar. In January 1939, he recorded two unaccompanied songs, "Bryan O'Lynn" and "Poor Miner," and three songs accompanied with guitar: "It's Hard Times, Boys," "Taji Buggeroo," and "The Lowlands Low," the last one in two versions.

Stubblefield died of cancer December 18, 1960.

Louie W. Attebery

Superstition

Also called folk belief, the lore of the supernatural, magic, and omens. In common parlance, the word "superstition" is loaded with pejorative connotations. Thought by many to be rooted in the pagan traditions of earlier, more primitive stages of human culture, superstition is conceived of as the irrational belief of the naive, uneducated, and the ignorant in superhuman powers. The fact that the term is, in the minds of the popular masses, so loaded with negative preconceptions would, in itself, reduce its value as a scholarly concept. But this problem is exacerbated to a considerable degree by the fact that prominent scholars, in attempting to define the term, have themselves been greatly influenced by the popular notions handed down by Western tradition.

The process by which "superstition" became a loaded term was delineated in a study of the term from its first recorded use in ancient Rome to modern times (Harmening 1979). Although the precise etymology of the word eludes classical scholars, there is no doubt that its first recorded use was in the term *homo superstitiosus,* meaning "seer" or "prophet." Cicero later associated the term with *superstes,* a thing "left over" or a "survival," an etymology that was characteristically seized upon by both Jacob Grimm and E.B. Tylor.

For a time used as a synonym for *religio*, the term later became a pejorative synonym for excessive religious fervor that characterized the intrusive mystery cults from the Orient that plagued Rome in pre-Christian times. The Roman Catholic Church fathers stressed this pejorative meaning when they sought to contrast the fatal moral depravity of pagan religions and cultures to the moral harmony of Christian faith. Augustine in so doing used *superstitio* in the sense of a false faith, a meaning that is still evident in such terms as German *Aberglaube,* Dutch *overgeloof,* Danish *overtro,* and in a now obsolete English term used by the 14th-century theologian John Bromyard to condemn "this blyndnesse of old misbelive" (quoted in Opie and Tatem 1989:viii).

This legacy of associations was adopted first by the clergy of Western nations and later became a focal issue for all of the philosophers and writers in the so-called Age of Reason during the 18th century, when superstition was reviled as the depraved wallowing of the unenlightened in the irrational ignorance of the "Dark Ages." Edmund Burke (1729–1797) in 1790, even declared superstition to be "the religion of feeble minds."

Nineteenth-century Romanticism saw a momentary respite in the centuries-old rejection of superstition as scholars like the Grimm brothers sought in these "survivals" fragments of the glorious myths and religions of the pagan past (Ward 1981, Vol. 2:534–553). However, in the Age of Positivism that dominated the succeeding century, these survivals were viewed by Tylor and his contemporaries as part of the excess baggage from primitive times that exerted a retarding force on the inexorable progress of cultural evolution.

It is apparent that the term "superstition" has become in its long cultural history burdened with increments of pejorative associations to the degree that its use as a scholarly construct has been called into question. Some have sought to solve the problem by eliminating the term from the scholarly lexicon and replacing it with "folk belief," "popular belief," "folk science," and even "conventional wisdom." Each of these terms, however, has its own drawback that introduces new problems. Folk belief for example, shares the same negative connotations that the word "folk" has in popular usage, and because the word "popular" connotes for many the lore of the broad masses as opposed to the world of scholars and the intellectually elite, such terms as "popular belief" are not satisfactory. The term "belief" is also problematic because it implies an element of faith in the efficacy of a given proposition or prescription. There are, however, specific superstitions that have become traditional and are cited even by those who do not believe in them. For example, most Americans in the late 20th century know that "to break a mirror means seven years' bad luck." When someone in an American household breaks a mirror, the notion is likely invoked by a household member. But the fact that individuals know and cite this "belief" does not necessarily imply that they believe it. For such items that persist in tradition, even when belief is absent, the term "superstition" remains useful (Ward 1993:xviii-xix).

American folklorists demonstrate a growing tendency, if not a consensus, to see folk belief as an element of tradition that makes its presence felt in a variety of forms of folklore (such as amulets and charms, folktale, legend, ballad, proverb, custom, ritual, and folk religion), while restricting the term "superstition" to the verbal utterances in which "beliefs" are framed (see Dundes 1961). Wayland D. Hand, America's most distinguished student of belief and superstition, insisted on using both "popular belief" and "superstition," and both words are evident in the titles of the collections of belief materials that Hand edited in his lifetime. Moreover, *The Encyclopedia of American Popular Belief and Superstition,* founded by Hand and being edited in the 1990s retains both words in its title (Hand and Ward 1993). Hand found justification for using both terms in the somewhat questionable distinction he drew between "superstitions" as being "patently false" and potentially harmful and "popular belief" as "faiths and foibles" of "a negligible or frivolous kind" (Hand 1961–1964, Vol. 6:xxi).

In spite of the fact that generations of scholars have inherited the legacy of negative associations invoked by the word "superstition," there remains the need for a term that refers to the long history of these notions in popular tradition without necessarily implying belief; and because the English language does not provide us with any other term for this purpose, "superstition" remains a valuable, if somewhat flawed, scholarly construct.

The popular notions of Americans about the nature of superstition were greatly influenced by the British Anthropological school, which included such renowned scholars as Herbert Spencer (1820–1902) and E.B. Tylor (1832–1917). Spawned by the Age of Positivism, which championed the scientific method with its stress on laws of natural causality and nurtured by the doctrine of "cultural evolution" that emerged from Darwin's discovery, this school culminated in the figure of Sir James Frazer (1854–1941) and his monumental twelve-volume work, *The Golden Bough.* In the first volume, and especially in the famous chapter on "Sympathetic Magic," Frazer analyzed the "magical" thinking that underlies superstition and, in so doing, identified mental processes that were supposed to characterize superstitious behavior everywhere.

In keeping with the tenets of positivism, Frazer saw magical thought processes as natural laws. The basic principle of what Frazer called "magic" was the perceived affinity linking individual items in a sympathetic relationship. In identifying the two basic principles of sympathetic magic, Frazer wrote: "Practices based on the Law of Similarity may be termed Homeopathic Magic; those based on the Law of Contact or Contagion, Contagious Magic." Homeopathic magic assumes that "like produces like, effect resembling cause," while contagious magic implies that "things once in contact continue even afterwards to act on each other." The principles of homeopathy thus are premised on the perceived bond between things or actions that resemble one another. For example, the belief that "If you drink all the bubbles on the surface of your cup of coffee, you will soon have lots of money" is based on the recognition that the shiny round bubbles look somewhat like coins. Thus, bubbles and money are symbolically linked to each other. Another example, "Eating walnuts will help intelligence," is based upon the perceived similarity of the brain with the two hemispheres of a shelled walnut. The principles of contagion, by contrast, imply not so much contact as notions of contiguity. Human imagination infers a permanent and contiguous relationship between items that once were either in contact or were parts of a whole that later became separated. The dairy farmer's fear that if someone boils milk, he or she will injure the cow that produced it exemplifies this principle. The fact that the milk has been completely separated from the cow does not diminish the perceived bond between the two (Ward 1993:xxi).

In spite of the fact that they have been discredited by modern anthropologists, Frazer's basic analysis and his implicit theories are irrefutable, and they continue to be cited by those who seek to understand the essence of traditions of belief. This fact, however, does not mean that Frazer's work can go completely unchallenged. For Frazer, like all scholars, was a product of the time in which he lived and worked. His choice of the word "magic" to describe the mental processes of superstitious behavior reveals a great deal about his own assumptions and preconceptions. In keeping with the principles of cultural evolution, Frazer was convinced that all human culture evolved from the simple and primitive to the complex and civilized along a unilinear route. Thus, the same "laws" that governed the evolution of the simple forms of life ultimately into *Homo sapiens* were also seen as operative in all cultural spheres, including those of a spiritual nature. At the bottom of the evolutionary scale—that is, at its most primitive stage—was a faith in "magic." At the top of the scale, toward which there is an inexorable drive, lies monotheistic religion. According to this model of human history, those of us who now live in a high civilization and worship one god are the end result of a development that began with primitive savages who practiced magic. Superstition was thus seen by Frazer and his contemporaries as the modern survival of humankind's most primitive impulse. It was, therefore, inferred that anyone who remained superstitious in the modern age was guilty of primitive and even "savage" thinking. Frazer evidences this attitude when he calls upon his readers to recognize "the spurious system behind the bastard art" of magic. "Homeopathic magic," he writes, "commits the *mistake* of assuming that things which resemble each other are the same; contagious magic commits the *mistake* of assuming that things which have once been in contact with each other are always in contact" (writer's emphasis). He further suggests giving "the name of magic to the whole erroneous system," that he considers "one great disastrous folly."

One of the first scholars to question the Frazerian paradigm was the Austrian philosopher and Cambridge professor Ludwig Wittgenstein (1889–1951). In a number of aphoristic writings between 1927 and 1945, Wittgenstein questioned the evolutionary model that separated the various levels of "savagery" from "civilization." He further insisted that "magic" was a vitally essential aspect of human life and that human beings suffer because people like Frazer have helped deprive us of its benefits. "Frazer," wrote Wittgenstein in 1967, "is much more savage than most of his savages, for they would not be so far removed from the understanding of a spiritual matter as an Englishman of the twentieth century."

The recognition that beliefs and superstitions are vital to humanity has come slowly to the scholars of the 20th century, but the signposts have been there for many decades. In 1819 the German poet Johann Wolfgang von Goethe, in a collection of aphoristic observations, stated that "Der Aberglaube ist die Poesie des Lebens" (Superstition is the poetry of life). Although Goethe did not explicate precisely what he meant by these words, it is evident that he recognized the affinity of superstition, which Frazer later decried as "sympathetic magic," with the splendid metaphors of the world's most gifted poets. Thus, when a priest sprinkles the naked body of a maiden with water in the attempt to ensure both rain and the fertile productivity of the earth, it is, to be sure, an example of the principles of homeopathic magic at work, but it is also much more than that. It is a vivid drama that demonstrates to divine powers the needs of the supplicants while using the dramatic and powerful metaphors that one finds in the best of the world's poetry. Indeed, one could argue that the ability to engage in metaphoric and analogous thinking that is evidenced in "sympathetic magic" was a highly significant milestone in the development of the brain of *Homo sapiens*.

There are similar poetic uses of metaphor in many thousands of the beliefs stored in the UCLA archive. There is, for example, a belief that an empty bird's nest should hang in the loft of a cabin where a woman is about to give birth (Hand and Ward, Forthcoming, Vol. 2: entry titled "Empty"). The fact that people equate the woman's womb to the empty nest is, again, a valid case of homeopathic magic. However, instead of debasing this belief as an example of primitive and naive ignorance or as "faulty reasoning," one should rather acknowledge the poetic value of its metaphoric dimension. One can, furthermore, imagine the potential benefits from such a belief in the days on the frontier when expectant mothers were days removed from any access to medical aid. One can envision the father's act of finding an empty nest and his placing it in the loft providing at least a modicum of solace and comfort for the woman in labor.

Other scholars who took Frazer to task included the Swedish folklorist Carl Wilhelm von Sydow and his student Albert Nilsson (later known as Albert Eskeröd). Drawing on the work of the German scholar Wilhelm Mannhardt, Frazer had discussed the widespread European agricultural custom of taking the last sheaf of the harvest, shaping it anthropomorphically, decorating it with colored fabrics and trinkets, and then using it as the centerpiece of the harvest festival. Frazer adopted Mannhardt's inference that the honoring of the sheaf represented the survival of the early pagan worship of a Spirit-of-the-Grain" *(Korndämon)*. Frazer also saw survivals of this heathen divinity in the beliefs and legends surrounding the Rye-Wolf and the Rye-Witch, frightening demons that were thought to inhabit grain fields.

Von Sydow objected strenuously to these inferences of pagan survivals and instead suggested universal emotional needs and the play instincts of human beings (Von Sydow 1934). He pointed out that the first and last in a sequence of items or events invariably attract attention to themselves solely by virtue of the fact that they stand out from others. Writing in German, he labeled these elements *externe Dominante* (external dominating elements); he contrasted these with the emotional needs and instincts of humans that he called *interne Dominante* (internal dominating concerns). He also took Frazer and his contemporaries to task for their having missed the essence of belief traditions when they assumed faulty reasoning behind the thought processes that they labeled "post hoc, ergo propter hoc" (after this, therefore caused by this)—that is, the tendency of the naive mind to assume causality when two events occur in a temporal sequence (B occurs after A, therefore B was caused by A). It was, von Sydow insisted, the scholar who was being naive when he assumed that any two events could be so linked. With highly convincing examples, von Sydow demonstrated that the chronological sequence of two arbitrary events was in itself not the occasion for inferring causality. Instead, it was only when the two events linked an *externe Dominante* with an *interne Dominante* that an individual assumed a causal sequence between the two. Von Sydow's student Albert Eskeröd later expanded these terms into three categories: *Milieudominanzen, Interessendominanzen,* and *Traditionsdominanzen.*

Von Sydow also criticized Mannhardt for his insistence in seeing traditions of the Rye-Wolf and the Rye-Witch as survivals of ancient heathen agricultural divinities. They were, he argued, a product of the playful spirit of humans and, above all, a means of frightening children so that they would not play in the grain and trample it before the harvest. He considered such traditional behavior not as ancient pagan beliefs, but rather as "fictions"—that is, free inventions created either for pragmatic reasons or from the human play instinct. The tradition of the "demon in the well" was, for example, not a creature of ancient folk beliefs, but rather a "cautionary fiction" a bogeyman created so that children would not lean over the well and thus be in danger of falling in. In addition to cautionary fictions, von Sydow also saw "jocular fictions," "pedagogical fictions," "etiological fictions," and "taboo fictions" underlying many traditional customs and beliefs. He further argued that both the emotional needs and the play instinct were there from the beginning. In other words, he saw—as Magne Velure has put it—play and jesting as perpetual factors that are equally as primordial as magic and cults. "Said in another way, *Homo ludens* is not necessarily a degenerate *Homo religiosus*" (Velure 1983:113). Donald Ward has also demonstrated the central role that play occupies in traditional beliefs and customs (Ward 1993:xxvi–xxviii).

One chapter in the history of the term "superstition" that we have not yet surveyed occurred when Christian missionaries sought to convert the peoples of Europe to the new faith. Seeking to eliminate recalcitrant pockets of paganism, medieval theologians and clergy began to conduct a more or less systematic study of the pagan superstitions they were fighting. In so doing, they divided superstition into three main categories: *superstitio observationis, superstitio divinationis,* and *superstitio artis magicae* (Harmening 1979:1–42 and passim). The first two categories deal with attempts of individuals to read signs in order to determine future events. They differ in that

superstitio observationis involves the passive attempt to identify and read the signs provided in nature or elsewhere in one's environment, while *superstitio divinationis* designates the active attempt, usually in the form of a divinatory ritual, to produce signs that the specialist (priest, shaman, sorcerer, and the like) then interprets as auguries of the future. The third category, *superstitio artis magicae,* by contrast, refers to the "magic arts," the specific rites of sorcerers to enlist superhuman forces to achieve desired ends. These magic practices, which were either malevolent or beneficent in their goals, were characterized by the use of magic books, symbols, and other implements as well as herbs, verbal charms, incantations, and the like.

There have been in recent decades new attempts to categorize superstition. Curiously, these later efforts have repeated the observations of medieval clergy without necessarily improving upon them. Swedish folklorist Eskeröd, for example, distinguished between omens that betoken various events and human acts that are thought to achieve desired effects. He saw superstitions, above all, as structured utterances consisting of a stated condition and an anticipated result, with some of the conditions being signs and others being causal actions. To designate these two kinds of sequences, Eskeröd used the actional and perfective Latin participles, *ominant-ominat* and *causant-causat.* Thus, "If geese fly south early" (*ominant*), "there will be an early winter" (*ominat*). But, "If you whistle on board a ship" (*causant*), "you will whistle up a storm" (*causat*).

The American folklorist Alan Dundes made essentially the same distinction when he classified superstitions into three categories. "Sign superstitions," wrote Dundes, "consist of one or more signs that are thought to indicate a result." Thus, "if one notes a ring around the moon, one can predict rain" (Dundes 1961:29). Contrasted to this are "magic superstitions" that "often consist of multiple conditions [that] . . . serve as a means of production and prescription rather than prediction. In contrast to sign superstitions, human activity in magic superstitions is intentional rather than accidental" (Dundes 1961:30). Dundes added a third category that he labeled "conversion superstitions, . . . a hybrid category in which, for the most part, sign superstitions are converted into magic superstitions, often in the attempt to neutralize the unwanted result of a sign superstition."

Dundes' observations have been challenged by several scholars of folklore. Ward noted that, in divinatory rites, human activity is never "accidental," as Dundes insists (Ward 1968), and a causal sequence of events need not be intentional, as, for example, when someone unwittingly "whistles up a storm" aboard a ship. Ward, moreover, notes that there is a vast body of beliefs in which it is not possible to distinguish between the passive reading of omens and the active use of magic to achieve a result. For example, a woman in Virginia maintains that "if in handling a loaf of bread you accidentally break it into two parts, it is a sign that there will be wet weather for a whole week" (Virginia: UCLA Archive). Does the use of the expression "it is a sign" indicate the absence of the notion of causality in this belief? Here the distinction between omens and causal agents seems to disappear. Ward suggests that it is likely that the woman is oblivious to this difference because she associates the two phenomena without necessarily seeing a direct linear relationship between them. Ward adduces a number of examples from the UCLA Archive in which the informant's choice of either a causal or an ominal verb seems to be highly arbitrary. There are, for example, countless variants of a belief documented throughout the United States that shows a perceived link between the call of a crow and an approaching storm. In many of the variants, one detects an *ominant-ominat* sequence: "If a rain crow calls": "you can expect rain," "it indicates rain," "it is a sign of rain," "it is a sure sign of rain," and "it foretells rain." Other variants of the belief, however, indicate a *causant-causat* sequence: "If the rain crow calls": "it is calling for rain," "it brings rain," ". . . causes rain," and ". . . is sure to bring rain." It is doubtful if the tradition bearers in these cases perceive any essential differences between supposed ominal and causal agents. Ward infers from these observations that folk belief often sees related phenomena existing in configurations other than that of linear causality, resulting in beliefs in which it is impossible to distinguish between a "sign" and a "cause." An example: A student has a dart board in his study where he is preparing for an important examination. He interrupts his study, picks up three darts and says to himself: "If one of these darts strikes the bull's-eye, I will get an 'A' on my exam." Although the dart's striking the bull's-eye is related to the good grade, it is not perceived as the direct cause of it. The two events exist in an associative relationship that is nonlinear.

Dundes was also taken to task by Michael Owen Jones for having treated superstitions as "superorganic" entities divorced from the human beings who are the bearers of the tradition (Jones 1967). For Jones, the people who make the utterances in living contexts are more important than the utterances themselves, and he suggests a modification of Dundes' categories that better represents the manner in which individuals invoke superstitions in their daily lives.

By observing carefully the manner in which living humans invoke superstitions, folklorists could discover significant aspects of human behavior. One can, for example, note how people, when invoking folk beliefs, invariably draw a firm dividing line between knowledge and belief. The former is accepted as fact, while the latter is accepted or rejected on faith. Thus, one farmer may plant his corn with the onset of the waxing moon because he "knows" it is most auspicious to do so, while the second farmer "believes" it to be so. The distinction is not mere academic hocus-pocus. People are aware that certain things can be known while others have to be accepted on faith. One will ask if you believe in ghosts, UFOs (unidentified flying objects), guardian angels, and Santa Claus, but they will not ask if you believe in the Empire State Building. The very question "Do you believe?" implies both the recognition of the need for faith and, more important, the possibility of doubt. A hunter will not say, "I believe in whitetail deer," but he might very well say, "I believe in Bigfoot." When he does so, he communicates that the latter does not belong to everyday reality and that its existence must be accepted or rejected as a matter of faith. He furthermore acknowledges that doubt is present. Indeed, belief in supernatural entitites thrives on a degree of doubt, for without it the encounters with them would not result in the numinousness central to supernatural experiences. Theoretically, if one accepted ghosts completely as part of everyday reality, seeing one would be no more significant than seeing one's spouse at the breakfast table. The point is, however, that people do not accept ghosts as everyday reality, nor do they "know" that ghosts exist; they occupy a dimension that is separate from daily reality, and they exist, above all, in human faith.

Anyone interested in studying belief and superstition must acknowledge the great work accomplished by one man, Wayland D. Hand. Hand assembled a massive archive of more than one million belief items (located at the University of California, Los Angeles), and he developed a classification system for these materials that serves as the model for all such collections worldwide. This system also has been applied by Hand to the regional collections of American beliefs that he edited (Hand 1961–1964, Hand, Casetta, and Thiederman 1981; Hand and Talley 1984). We also owe Hand a debt of gratitude for his analysis of superstitions that has contributed immeasurably to our understanding of belief as it has been, and continues to be, practiced by humans everywhere. That we now understand the processes of magical transference and divestment, plugging, pulling-through, measuring, and so forth is largely due to the published books and essays of Hand.

One more item from Hand's archive can serve as an exemplary model for the thought processes upon which the idea of transference is founded. "To cure a child of bedwetting, take him to a cemetery at midnight and have him urinate into an open grave." When the grave is later filled with the coffin of the deceased and covered over with earth, the affliction is thought to be transferred to the beyond, a realm from which there can be no return. When we consider that the UCLA Archive contains more than a million such items, we begin to grasp its potential for helping us understand the human condition. For such beliefs are not (to use Hand's own words) mere "mental errors" and "abberations of the human mind," they are pure artistry. It is obvious that Goethe was correct when he asserted that superstition is poetry.

Donald J. Ward

References

Dundes, Alan. 1961. Brown County Superstitions. *Midwest Folklore* 11:25–33.

Hand, Wayland D., ed. 1961–1964. *Popular Beliefs and Superstitions from North Carolina.* Vols. 6–7 of *The Frank C. Brown Collection of North Carolina Folklore.* Durham, NC: Duke University Press.

Hand, Wayland D., Anna Casetta, and Sondra Thiederman, eds. 1981. *Popular Beliefs and Superstitions: A Compendium of American Folklore from the Ohio Collection of Newbell Niles Puckett.* 3 vols. Boston: G.K. Hall.

Hand, Wayland D., and Jeannine E. Talley, eds. 1984. *Popular Beliefs and Superstitions from Utah,* coll. Anthon S. Cannon and others. Salt Lake City: University of Utah Press.

Hand, Wayland D., and Donald J. Ward. 1994–. *Encyclopedia of American Popular Belief and Superstition.* Vol. 1–. Berkeley: University of California Press.

Harmening, Dieter. 1979. *Superstitio: Überlieferungs- und theoriegeschichtliche Untersuchung zur kirchlich-theologischen Aberglaubensliteratur des Mittelalters.* Berlin: Erich Schmidt Verlag.

Jones, Michael Owen. 1967. Folk Belief: Knowledge and Action. *Southern Folklore Quarterly* 31:304–309.

Opie, Iona, and Moira Tatem. 1989. *Dictionary of Superstitions.* New York: Oxford University Press.

Tylor, E.B. 1871. *Primitive Culture.* 2 vols. London: John Murray.

Velure, Magne. 1983. Nordic Folk Belief Research: Schools and Approaches. In *Trends in Nordic Tradition Research. Studia Fennica,* ed. Lauri Honko and Pekka Laaksonen. Review of Finnish Linguistics and Ethnology No. 27. Helsinki: Finnish Literary Society.

Von Sydow, Carl Wilhelm. 1934. The Mannhardtian Theories about the Last Sheaf and the Fertility Demons from a Modern Critical Viewpoint. *Folk-Lore* 45:291–309.

Ward, Donald. 1968. Weather Signs and Weather Magic: Some Ideas on Causality in Popular Belief. *Pacific Coast Philology* 3:67–72.

———. 1981. *The German Legends of the Brothers Grimm.* 2 vols. Philadelphia: ISHI.

———. 1993. Introduction. In *Encyclopedia of American Popular Belief and Superstition,* by Wayland D. Hand and Donald Ward. Vol. 1. Berkeley: University of California Press, pp. xv–xxxi.

See also Animals; Dowsing; Medicine, Folk; Plantlore; Pregnancy and Birth; Weatherlore; Weddings

T

Talking Trash

A Southern male leisure activity involving several genres of folk speech and folklore; also, insulting, self-aggrandizing speech, often in a sports context. The kinds of talk in "talking trash" in the rural and small-town South are linked by performance context and by thematic threads of humor and aggressiveness. Roughly equivalent terms for "talking trash" are "shooting the breeze," "telling lies," "bullshitting," and "talking garbage."

Trash ranges from casual small talk about favorite activities such as hunting and fishing, to teasing, joke telling, and formal yarn spinning. Participants exchange whoppers, traditional tall tales, and stories of exaggerated personal experience. Whoppers, or exaggerated descriptions, may occur alone, in series, or in a story about telling a whopper. For example, the whopper "It got so hot last summer my hens laid hard-boiled eggs," may occur by itself or in series with other weather-related whoppers. It may also appear in a story showing how the shrewd country fellow makes a fool of the visiting city dweller.

Traditional tall tales, another important component of talking trash, have been studied in many folk cultures and are one of the roots of the humor of the old Southwest in American literature.

While stories of personal experience may not "go into folk tradition," the custom of narrating personal experience is deeply traditional. When men are talking trash, it may be difficult, and sometimes not especially relevant, to know how much these stories are based upon fact. The "fish story" in the context of talking trash does not depend on mere fact for its meaning. This is because when men talk trash, their speech is not so much "about" the events narrated as it is about the sociable event in which the talking trash event occurs.

Talking trash with other men increases mutual good feelings among participants, even when one man's narrative talents lift him above his fellows. The term "master narrator" was applied by Richard M. Dorson to the expert yarn spinner, or trash talker, who makes a conscious effort to improve his craft. He is recognized for his large repertoire of tales and admired as an unusually skillful narrator by his fellows, who enjoy talking trash with him and telling tales to others about his verbal feats. To support his reputation, gained from being a character in his own stories, the master narrator cultivates a personal style and an air of eccentricity. He thrives on the praise of others.

However, master narrators are not typical of trash talkers. All properly sociable men are expected to be able to contribute a clever experience story or wisecrack to the conversation. Through talking trash, men make characters of themselves and promote good humor within the group. However good it is, though, the humor found in talking trash is not gentle. By 1990s mainstream-culture standards, it is rough and violent. It is the humor of an America that laughed at physical humor in popular knockabout film comedies—people slipping on banana peels, having pianos fall on them, and being stuck in the bottom with pitchforks. It is the kind of humor found in old Southwestern humor.

For example, an African American from Georgia narrated the story of a dispute in a turpentine camp, in which a White supervisor angrily chased a Black worker. The strong Black man bent a pine sapling until his pursuer came close and then let it snap back, knocking the White man down hard. The narrator said this was very funny. With or without racial components, talking trash among both Blacks and Whites in the rural South demonstrates the participants' relish in such stories for "cartoon violence."

In recent years, a second sense of the term "talking trash" has emerged. Related to the aggressiveness and rough humor of trash talking in the rural South, this is insulting speech that "trashes" (derides, degrades, hurts) the listener. Examples from the popular press illustrate this sense of "talking trash." In a 1993 newspaper article, in North Carolina, the *Charlotte Observer* reported: "The South Carolina Supreme Court dealt chivalry another blow. Talking trash to women and girls is no longer a crime. The court . . . threw out a 50-year-old law, saying it's old-fashioned to think women . . . need special protection—in this case, from cuss words, obscenities, or suggestive remarks."

And the national news magazine *Newsweek,* also in 1993, commented: "[Baseball's] strength is also its weakness: It has a corner on the market for nostalgic, romantic sports hooey, but spectators increasingly favor basketball's fast-paced, trash-talking, macho hooey."

Kay Cothran Craigie

References

Cohen, Hennig, and William B. Dillingham, eds. 1964. *Humor of the Old Southwest.* Boston: Houghton Mifflin Riverside Editions.

Cothran, Kay L. 1979. Talking Trash in the Okefenokee Swamp Rim, Georgia. In *Readings in American Folklore,* ed. Jan Harold Brunvand. New York: W.W. Norton, pp. 215–235.

Dorson, Richard M. 1944. Maine Master-Narrator. *Southern Folklore Quarterly* 8:279–285.

Tall Tale

Humorous narrative, usually short, based on exaggeration. Tall tales are also known as "windies," "whoppers," "tales of lying" and, simply, "lies." To dismiss tall tales as lies, however, is to ignore the important creative and artistic dimension that characterizes their performance in those milieus where they have flourished.

Tall tales are usually told as factual accounts of real happenings, with the audience encouraging the narrator to spin out his yarns (there seem to be few or no female tall-tale tellers) while, in order to maintain a serious mien, listeners make that "willing suspension of disbelief" necessary to a successful session.

The subject matter of tall tales is certainly related to historically male-dominated occupations, with hunting and fishing narratives often dominating the tale teller's repertoire. Thus, a hunter will recount how, while using an old-time muzzle-loader, he was unable to take aim on more than a couple of birds amongst the hundreds lining the shore of a bay; he will tell how he judged the bay's curvature, then bent his gun barrel around a rock to suit the curve, with his resulting shot bagging dozens of birds.

Another will relate how, lacking shot, he loaded his gun with nails and was able to shoot a fox, nailing its tail to a tree; the fox jumped out of its skin, however. But the following year, the hunter shot the same fox, which he recognized, thereby gaining two skins from the same animal.

Fishermen in Newfoundland tell of the reef they hauled their dory onto in order to light a fire and boil their kettle, only to discover, as they are leaving, that the reef was, in fact, a whale. Others tell of a pond or river in which they were wading while playing a particularly large fish and how, on grabbing some tufts of grass to pull themselves out, they discover they have, in fact, caught a brace of hares; in addition, their hipwaders have filled with eels while they were struggling with their initial catch.

Many tales are told relating the remarkable qualities of certain individuals—about the great eaters and drinkers, the remarkable marksman, the extraordinary strong man, the remarkable spitter who could spit out a fire over which a steer was roasting.

Tall-tale tellers relate what they have seen or encountered in their travel—enormous fruits or vegetables, exceptionally thin or fat animals, or creatures able to pass on to their offspring various acquired traits; thus, the bitch whose hindlegs had been severed, and who had been provided with a little cart on which she could drag herself around, gives birth to a litter similarly endowed.

Extremes of weather are also the subject of tall tales. Rains so heavy it was impossible to tell where a lake ended and the sky began have been confirmed by sightings of fish flying in the air and birds swimming underwater; remarkable cold snaps in which conversations were frozen solid, to be heard in the spring thaw, are told by certain woodsmen.

Such themes, covering almost anything to be encountered in the natural world, have formed the stock-in-trade of the tall-tale narrator. In the 1990s, however, most people are likely to have encountered the tall-tale in its literary manifestations, such as in the published accounts of the doings of Paul Bunyan, but while Bunyan is widely held to be representative of American folklore, in actual fact there is little or no evidence such a character ever existed in folklore, or indeed that the stories attributed to him ever circulated in oral tradition.

The tall tale is generally transmitted in oral tradition in two ways: secondhand, as when a person attributes an exploit or an experience to another party who originally told the tale as a personal experience—this is how most tall tales have been recorded by collectors—and firsthand, as when the collector is fortunate enough to participate in a natural tall-tale-telling session.

There is ample evidence to suggest that a natural tall-tale-telling context—for example, the "liars' bench" in general stores, around a campfire, or any habitual gathering place—might include a good deal of swapping of yarns: one man might tell of a fishing exploit, with another man trying to cap it with one of his experiences—and the listeners doing their best to encourage such friendly competition, urging or provoking the participants to further narrations of their unlikely feats and taking pleasure both in the process and in the artistry of the narrators, who would begin with a detailed and plausible account of their experience, at the very end of which the exaggeration would be uttered, with the habitual poker-face expression.

The friendly rivalry typical of such yarn swapping seems, however, to have been absent entirely when audiences were faced with the kind of characters whose names have become synonymous with the tall tale in the regions where they flourished. These are the men whose reputations as "liars" spread beyond their immediate confines, and who brooked no competition in the matter of tall-tale telling. Indeed, their narrative style was such that prospective listeners sometimes had to be extremely careful in the way they broached the subject of the narrator's exploits. It was no good asking for a "tall tale," for example; to encourage a storyteller to begin a tale, the subject would have to be raised indirectly, with a passing ref-

erence to someone's recent fishing trip, for example. And woe betide the listener careless enough to make an uncharitable comment during the narration—the narrator might well stop dead and refuse to say another word, or stomp off in high dudgeon. Such "tall tale heroes" could be touchy individuals, but they were often so famous locally that their names and tales lingered long after their death.

These masters of exaggeration have only occasionally been brought to the attention of a wider public. The best known of these is undoubtedly Baron Münchhausen (Hieronymous Karl Friedrich, Freiherr von Münchhausen [1720–1797] of Bodenwerder, Brunswick, Germany), whose authentic yarns, documented by contemporaries, were taken up and published by Rudolph Erich Raspe, in the high-flown style of the late 18th century. Raspe's literary redaction became so popular that the baron's name became a byword for tall-tale heroes when folklorists began documenting them in the 20th century.

Some notable North American tall-tale heroes include Abraham "Oregon" Smith (1796–1893) from Indiana, whose exploits were first noted by Herbert Halpert in 1942 and then treated at length by William Hugh Jansen; Gib Morgan (1842–1909), who told his yarns in the context of the oil fields and was given a literary treatment in 1945 by Mody Boatright (1896–1970); and Jim Bridger (1804–1881), Western explorer and the man who was instrumental in opening up Yellowstone National Park. He was one of the earliest liars to come to more than local fame, since his tall tales, which he used to spin to greenhorn tourists, were included in early publications concerning Yellowstone.

John Darling (1809–1893) of New York state was first brought to public attention by Harold W. Thompson (1891–1963), but his yarns were, like those of Münchhausen and Morgan, also given a literary reworking, by Moritz Jagendorf. Darling was known to his contemporaries as "the damndest liar in seven states," and he used to tell his yarns at clambakes, elections, dances or "frolics," barnraisings, and the like.

"Captain" John Hance (ca. 1850–1919) of Arizona was, like Bridger, a guide who used to spin his tales to tourists, in his case while they visited the Grand Canyon. He once told a friend how he could convince a tenderfoot that frogs ate boiled eggs and make them believe the frogs would carry the eggs a mile to find a rock to crack them on.

A Canadian tall-tale hero was Dave McDougall (184?–1928) of Alberta. It was said that "the three biggest liars in Alberta were Dave McDougall; John McDougall [his brother] was the other two." Lorenzo "Len" Henry (1852–1946) of Idaho was described by Jan Harold Brunvand as "a Münchhausen," just as was Darling; other tall-tale tellers who have been documented include Daniel Stamps (1866–1950) of Illinois, Jones Tracy (1856–1939) of Maine, Ed Grant, also of Maine, Bill Greenfield of New York, Benjamin Franklin Finn of Oregon, and Moses Stocking of Nebraska; in New-foundland, Albert "Ding-Ding" Simon (188?–1968) possessed a nickname suggestive of another dimension to his character beyond that of a "liar."

While these men, and the many others whose tall tales have not been documented, owed their reputations to their narrative skills and often fertile imaginations, as often as not they were seen as somewhat marginal characters in the very societies that nurtured them. As explorers and guides, they were often solitary individuals; while admired for their narrative talent, they had to be treated with kid gloves in order to get them yarning; and they might be, as was Simon, mocked for eccentricities of behavior or any other observable peculiarity. They may or may not be a vanishing breed, but they have indubitably enriched the oral literature and verbal arts of America.

Gerald Thomas

References

Brown, Carolyn S. 1987. *The Tall Tale in American Folklore and Literature.* Knoxville: University of Tennessee Press.

Dorson, Richard M. 1982. *Man and Beast in American Comic Legend.* Bloomington: Indiana University Press.

Jansen, William Hugh. 1977. *Abraham "Oregon" Smith: Pioneer, Folk Hero, and Tale-Teller.* New York: Arno.

Lunt, C. Richard K. 1968. Jones Tracy: Tall Tale Teller from Mount Desert Island. *Northeast Folklore* 10.

Randolph, Vance. 1951. *We Always Lie to Strangers.* New York: Columbia University Press.

Thomas, Gerald. 1977. *The Tall Tale and Philippe d'Alcripe.* St. John's, Newfoundland: Memorial University of Newfoundland, in association with the American Folklore Society.

See also Bridger, Jim; Bunyan, Paul; Henry, Lorenzo "Len"; Jones, Hathaway; Loggers; Morgan, Gib; Smith, Abraham "Oregon"; Talking Trash; Yarn

Talley, Thomas Washington (1870–1952)

Folklore collector, teacher, writer. Though he was known for years in Nashville as a distinguished chemistry professor at Fisk University, Talley was also a pioneering gatherer of African American tales and songs. A native of middle Tennessee's rural Black culture, Talley was not only himself a product of the traditions he documented, but he was one of the first Black folklorists to do substantial fieldwork and publication. As a youth, he sang with a group from Fisk, the New Jubilee Singers, and by the early 1890s he was collecting songs and tales as he moved through various college teaching jobs in the South.

The year 1905 found him back at Fisk as a professor, and he soon came under the influence of colleague John Work II, who in 1915 had published *Folk Songs of the American Negro.* Challenged by Work's assertion that "Negro folk music is wholly religious," Talley compiled a collection of secular songs that he published in 1922, *Negro Folk Rhymes (Wise or Otherwise).* Predating more famous collections by Dorothy Scarborough and by Howard W. Odum and Guy Benton Johnson, Talley's book featured songs from the preblues rural Tennessee Black community and showed that this musical tradition was more complex and far-ranging than had been previously thought. In a long appendix, "A Study in Negro Folk Rhymes," Talley offered a richly detailed account of some of his collecting and described in great detail some elements of rural Black music. (In 1991 an expanded edition of the book was issued, incorporating newly found music notations that were not in the original.)

Negro Folk Rhymes was widely reviewed and well received, and Talley at once set about compiling a companion volume of middle Tennessee tales. This manuscript, *The Negro Traditions,* was finished in 1923 or 1924, but for some reason it could not find a publisher. By this time, Talley's work at Fisk was becoming more demanding, and he gradually put his folklore interests aside; upon his retirement in 1942, he did write a long article about his tales in the journal *Phylon* and made further attempts to get his work published. It was not until 1993, however, that Talley's large collection of tales was finally published.

Charles K. Wolfe

References

Talley, Thomas W. 1993. *The Negro Traditions,* ed. with Introduction by Charles Wolfe and Laura C. Jarmon. Knoxville: University of Tennessee Press.

———. 1942–1943. The Origin of Negro Traditions." *Phylon.* 1:371–77; pp. 30–38.

Wolfe, Charles K. 1991. *Thomas W. Talley's Negro Folk Rhymes: A New, Expanded Edition, with Music.* Knoxville: University of Tennessee Press.

Tamburitza

A family of fretted stringed instruments brought to the United States and Canada by immigrants from Croatia, Bosnia, and the Vojvodina section of Serbia. Tamburitza (the term also refers to the music played on these instruments) comprises an active American musical subculture with the core of musicians and audience members from the Croatian American and Serbian American ethnic communities. The tradition is strongest in western Pennsylvania and in Great Lakes industrial cities, where tamburitza combos regularly play for weddings and picnics and in taverns and restaurants. The activities of more than two-dozen youth tamburitza ensembles in the United States and Canada are supported and coordinated by the Junior Cultural Federation of the Croatian Fraternal Union. An acclaimed touring collegiate ensemble is based at Duquesne University in Pittsburgh. Thirty to forty professional combos assemble annually for the Tamburitza Extravaganza, an event sponsored by the Tamburitza Association of America.

There are five contemporary tamburitza instruments, from smallest to largest: *prima, brac, celo brac, bugarija,* and *berde.* They range in size from smaller than a mandolin to larger than a string bass, but the instruments have never been completely standardized. There are three competing "systems": Sremski, which most American players use; Farkas, an older system of instruments, now seldom played; and Jankovic, a newer system utilized by school orchestras in Croatia.

The modern tamburitza is a South Slavic adaption of the Middle Eastern long-necked lute with a small pear-shaped body. Precursors of the modern tamburitza were brought to the Balkans by the Ottomans as early as the late 14th century. Since then the Middle Eastern types of the instrument, such as *saz* and *baglama,* as well as such shepherd and peasant adaptations as *sargija, icitel, samica,* and *dangubica,* have been played, usually soloistically, by people of the various Balkan nationalities: Croatians, Serbians, Bosnians, Albanians, Macedonians, Bulgarians, and *Roma* (Gypsies).

From the second half of the 19th century until World War I, South Slavic musicians in the Hapsburg Empire, imbued with the spirit of the era's nationalist movements, developed tamburitza orchestras as a refined but folk-connected symbol of national identity. Such South Slavic musicians and composers as Pajo Kolaric and Miroslav Majer from Osijek and Milutin Farkas and Ivan Zajc from Zagreb used tamburitza performances as a form of opposition to Austrian and Hungarian political and cultural domination. To "ennoble" the folk instrument, artisans created tamburitzas in various sizes, like the members of the violin family. Unlike the earlier instruments, which played a Middle Eastern or a Western diatonic scale, by the end of the 19th century the newer tamburitzas were devised to play a Western chromatic scale. The new compositions included classical-influenced tamburitza symphonies and concerti as well as vocal pieces with lyrics in the then suppressed national languages. (Analogous nationalistic musical movements in the 19th century led to the creation of Italian mandolin orchestras, Ukrainian bandura orchestras and Russian balalaika orchestras).

The orchestral tamburitza efforts originated in such urban areas as Osijek and Zagreb but soon had an impact also upon villagers. Although some peasant players of the earlier forms of tamburitza have continued to make and play them, more have learned to play the more adaptable orchestral tamburitzas and have put them and the related orchestral musical concepts and skills to their own uses. By the last decades of the 19th century, small ensembles using orchestral tamburitzas became a fixture in village and small-town taverns and at rural celebrations of weddings, saints' days, and other festivities. Thus, the village tamburitza combos and the urban orchestras were well established in their homelands at the time of the greatest migration of South Slavs to North America.

Numerous reports and photographs from the beginning of the 20th century establish the presence of tamburitza groups in the mining and industrial communities where the bulk of the South Slavic peasant immigrants first settled: between 1900 and 1910, groups were active in industrial cities such as Buffalo; Johnstown, Pennsylvania; Milwaukee; Chicago; Pittsburgh; and in small mining towns like Chisholm, Minnesota; Centerville, Iowa; Rutland, Illinois; South Range, Michigan, and Bingham Canyon, Utah.

In the 1910s, record companies including Columbia, Edison, and Victor began to record tamburitzans. Columbia recordings made in March 1912 by Andras Tavic with singer Vlado Konstantinovic may be the earliest, while the influential tamburitza pioneer Vaso Bukvic recorded on Columbia in 1916 with his brother Mirko and on Victor in 1917 with Sandor Huszar. The number of commercial recordings of tamburitza artists by the major companies as well as by small ethnic labels such as Balkan in Chicago and Zora in Detroit increased through the 1920s, continuing until World War II. Some of the influential artists of this era included Stevan Zerbec, the Skertich brothers, the Kapudji brothers, Dusan Jovanovic, Milan Verni, the Crlenica brothers, Djoko Dokic, the Popovich brothers, and Dave Zupkovich, and the orchestras Zvonimir, Banat, Javor, Jorgovan, Zora, Balkan, and Balkan Serenaders.

Orchestras like Zvonimir and the Elias Serenaders toured nationally on the vaudeville and chatauqua circuits, exposing the music to a broader audience. Instruction manuals, original compositions, and orchestral arrangements of folk songs by Charles Elias Sr., his son Charles Jr., and Rudolf Crnkovic made it possible to establish the network of youth orchestras in North America.

The Duquesne University Tamburitzans, founded in 1937 by Matt Gouze and led by Walter Kolar from the 1950s through the 1980s, have provided college scholarships to outstanding young musicians and dancers. A majority of them come from the ranks of the junior tamburitza orchestras. Many of the veterans of the Duquesne or junior tamburitza ensembles have gone on to perform in professional combos such as Veseli, Cigani, Sinovi, and Slanina and to teach tamburitza to subsequent generations of young players in the youth groups.

Richard March

References

Kolar, Walter W. 1975. *A History of the Tambura*. Vol. 2. Pittsburgh: Tamburitzans Institute of Folk Arts, Duquesne University.

Tattooing

A traditional practice whereby pigment is introduced under the skin to form permanent designs for decorative or religious purposes, or as a means of identification. A tattoo often functions as an expressive form, people choosing specific designs to express loyalty, love, hate, mortality, and humor.

Tattooing in the Western world went through cycles of popularity, decline, and revival. The Picts, or "the painted ones," Teutons, Gauls, Scots, and Brits were tattooed. However, since the Bible forbids it (Leviticus 19:28), tattooing declined as Christianity spread through Europe. Subsequently, when European explorers in the 16th to 18th centuries discovered, and eventually brought back and exhibited, tattooed natives of North America and the South Seas, the practice was considered exotic; and in the late 1700s the Tahitian word tatau was adopted. European sailors who voyaged to the South Seas returned with tattoos as souvenirs of their journeys, and tattooing became an established tradition among sailors.

The beginnings of tattooing in the United States coincided with the beginnings of the American traveling circus. From the 1850s to the 1930s, heavily tattooed sideshow freaks were a popular attraction; also, itinerant tattooists traveled with the circuses.

At the turn of the 20th century, New York was a busy port catering to sailors, and Chatham Square became a center of tattooing. It was there that the electric tattoo "gun" was invented by Samuel O'Reilly and developed by his student Charlie Wagner. Besides a network of master tattooists, there was also an abundance of unskilled amateurs. Lewis Alberts saw much poor work done on, and by, shipmates when he served in the Spanish American War. When Alberts returned to the United States, he established himself in Chatham Square as tattooist "Lew the Jew" and endeavored to raise the level of artistry. His background as a wallpaper designer inspired him to distribute sheets of popular tattoo designs that tattooists could copy. Tattoo parlors, both in the United States and overseas, displayed Alberts' designs on their walls. Such wall charts, known as "flash," account for the widespread diffusion of tattoo designs; another factor in diffusion is the transience of many tattooees.

Although tattooing is practiced by a relatively small segment of the American population, tattoos record and reflect national experience. The first professional tattooist in the United States did a booming business during the Civil War, tattooing military emblems on both Yankee and Rebel soldiers. Tattooing flourished in both American and European navies during the World Wars, when military and national emblems and patriotic slogans became part of the standard flash. Characters from American popular culture like Popeye, Mickey Mouse, and Betty Boop entered circulation as well.

Although in the 1880s and again in the 1920s tattooing enjoyed short-lived popularity among American and European aristocracies, the art was generally associated with drunken sailors, circus freaks, and members of motorcycle gangs. After World War II, it became unfashionable, but in the late 1960s interest in tattooing was revived by hippies and others active in the peace movement. The West Coast became the new center of tattoo. Designs such as peace signs, astrological signs, and marijuana leaves reflected the spirit of the times. Singing stars like Janis Joplin, Joan Baez, and Cher got tattooed and subsequently so did many of their fans.

Until the 1970s, most people had gotten tattooed because it was a tradition of a group to which they belonged. Since the mid-1970s, an increasing number of unaffiliated individuals have been getting tattooed. In the 1980s, a new term for tattoo—"body art"—gained some currency. In the 1990s, standard flash is still the norm, but there is a trend toward personalized or even custom-made designs; Japanese and neotribal designs are increasingly popular as well. Also, although most tattooists apprentice with a master tattooist in order to learn the craft, traditionally practicing their skills by tattooing grapefruit, a small number of tattooists in the late 1900s are graduates of art school who have chosen the tattoo as their medium.

Ilana Harlow

References

Fried, Fred, and Mary Fried. 1978. Tattoos, In *America's Forgotten Folk Arts*. New York: Pantheon.

Governar, Alan. 1985. Tattooing in Texas. In *Folk Art in Texas*, ed. Francis Abernathy. Dallas: Southern Methodist University Press.

Hambley, W.D. [1925] 1974. *The History of Tattooing and Its Significance*. London: H.F. and G. Witherby.

Rubin, Arnold. 1988. *Marks of Civilization: Artistic Transformation of the Body*. Los Angeles: University of California Press.

Sanders, Clinton. 1989. *Customizing the Body: The Art and Culture of Tattooing*. Philadelphia: Temple University Press.

St. Clair, Leonard. 1981. *Stoney Knows How: Life as a Tattoo Artist*. Lexington: University Press of Kentucky.

Taylor, Archer (1890–1973)

One of the greatest folklorists of his generation. His scholarship enriched two disciplines, German and folklore. Taylor's bibliography through 1960 consists of nearly 500 items (Hand and Arlt 1960:356–374), many of them authoritative works of compilation and classification of various genres of folklore. His classification system for formula tales (see Taylor 1972: 369–394) was adopted in Stith Thompson's 1961 revision of *The Types of the Folktale*. Taylor wrote historic-geographic studies of folktales, including *The Black Ox* (1927) and "The Predestined Wife" (Taylor 1972:395–492), and of a ballad, *Edward and Sven i Rosengaard* (1931) (see also Taylor 1929). His favorite folklore genre was the proverb, on which subject he published more than 100 articles, reviews, and books, including *The Proverb* ([1931; index 1934] 1962). Many articles and several books on riddles culminated in *English Riddles from Oral Tradition* (1961), which provides comparative notes from all over the world.

While Taylor is usually described as a comparativist and not as an Americanist, he made both major and minor contributions to the study of American folklore. In addition to his *English Riddles* (with its Anglo American material), his notes on English and American riddle tales were the basis of a sequel, Roger D. Abrahams' *Between the Living and the Dead* (1980, FFC 225). Taylor collected oral proverbs in *Proverbial Comparisons and Similes from California* (1954) and literary ones, with B.J. Whiting, in *American Proverbs and Proverbial Phrases, 1820–1880* (1958). A technique he used in many of his articles was to give an American example of a traditional item and then explain its peculiarities by displaying its European antecedents. Many of his short notes comment on or ask for more information about purely American folklore (see Taylor 1947, 1959).

Taylor was educated at Swarthmore College and received his Ph.D. in German in 1915 from Harvard University, where he studied with many distinguished scholars, including George Lyman Kittredge (thus Taylor was part of the scholarly tradition of ballad scholar Francis James Child). In 1939 he became professor of German at the University of California, Berkeley, where he remained until his retirement in 1958. He was largely responsible for founding the California Folklore Society (Cattermole-Tally 1989), and he edited its journal, *California Folklore Quarterly* (later *Western Folklore*), from its inception in 1942 through 1954. He also edited *Proverbium* from 1965 until 1973.

Early in his career, Taylor cultivated European contacts, which led to the entry of European ideas, including exhaustive citations of parallels and the historic-geographic method, into American folklore scholarship. As evidenced in his incisive, sometimes caustic book reviews, he insisted on high standards in folklore scholarship. To Taylor folklore was the material that is handed on by tradition, either by word of mouth or by custom and practice, and, furthermore, "comparison is an essential and typical method in folklore" (Taylor 1964:116). He envisioned collections and indexes as tools that should be used to construct a firm foundation that would ultimately support the study of "the historical, social-historical, literary-historical, cultural, psychological, and methodological implications" (Taylor 1964:121) of the subject under scrutiny.

Christine Goldberg

References

Cattermole-Tally, Frances. 1989. From Proverb to Belief and Superstition: An Encyclopedic Vision. *Western Folklore* 48:3–14.

Hand, Wayland D. 1974. Archer Taylor, 1890–1973. *Journal of American Folklore* 87:2–9.

Hand, Wayland D., and Gustav O. Arlt, eds. 1960. *Humaniora: Essays in Literature, Folklore, and Bibliography Honoring Archer Taylor on His Seventieth Birthday.* Locust Valley, NY: J.J. Augustin.

Taylor, Archer. 1929. The English, Scottish, and American Versions of "The Twa Sisters." *Journal of American Folklore* 42:238–246.

———. 1947. Pedro! Pedro! *Western Folklore* 6:228–231.

———. 1959. One for the Cutworm. *Western Folklore* 17:52–53.

———. 1964. The Classics of Folklore. *Arv* 20:113–124. Reprinted in *Comparative Studies in Folklore.* Taiper: Orient Cultural Service, 1972, pp. 9–20.

———. 1972. *Comparative Studies in Folklore.* Taipei: Orient Cultural Service.

Terry, Sonny (Sanders Turell) (1911–1986)

Traditional blues vocalist and harmonica player. Terry was especially known for his longtime touring partnership with Piedmont blues guitarist Brownie McGhee. Terry's music was distinguished by smooth and rapid transitions from vocalizing to harmonica playing, interjecting wails, moans, whoops, and hollers, achieving a particularly closely knit rhythmic structure.

Born Sanders Turell near Greensboro, North Carolina, Terry learned to play the harmonica from his father when he was a young boy. Separate accidents at play, when he was eleven and sixteen years old, left Terry blind in both eyes. In the early 1930s, he toured with medicine shows and was a street musician in Durham, North Carolina, playing for tips with two blind guitarists, Gary Davis and Blind Boy Fuller. Terry and Fuller made several records together before Fuller's death in 1941.

In 1939 Terry appeared in a historic Carnegie Hall concert, "Spirituals to Swing," where he shared the stage with Big Bill Broonzy, the Golden Gate Quartet, Benny Goodman, Count Basie, and others. He settled in New York in the early 1940s and figured prominently in the folk-music revival in the following two decades, recording with such artists as Woody Guthrie, Pete Seeger, and Burl Ives, as well as McGhee.

For three years, beginning in 1946, Terry performed on Broadway in *Finian's Rainbow,* and in 1955 he was in *Cat on a Hot Tin Roof* with guitarist McGhee. The two appeared together in the Steve Martin film *The Jerk,* and Terry provided soundtrack music for *The Color Purple.*

Terry's partnership with McGhee began in the early 1940s. Together they recorded dozens of albums on such record labels as Savoy, Fantasy, Folkways, Verve, and Prestige. They were featured at the Newport Folk Festival and at coffee-houses across the country, and they toured Canada, India, Mexico, Japan, Australia, and New Zealand as well as the United States. In 1982 Terry received the prestigious National Heritage Fellowship from the National Endowment for the Arts.

Terry died in Mineola, New York, on March 11, 1986.

Henry Willett

Thanksgiving Day

Holiday observed on the fourth Thursday in November in the United States and the second Monday in October in Canada. Celebrations of thanksgiving and harvest festivals were known throughout Europe long before the Reformation and the coming of the Pilgrims to America. The Saxons and the Celts celebrated Harvest Home; the Romans observed Cerealia; the Israelites feasted during the Feast of Tabernacle, and all celebrated through communal eating. In America the first Thanksgiving was observed by the Popham colonists at Monkegon as part of the thanksgiving service of the Church of England; early churchmen referred derisively to Thanksgiving Day as St. Pompion's Day (Pumpkin Day). In a similar vein, modern Americans sometimes refer to the holiday as "Turkey Day." A second Thanksgiving took place in 1623 to give thanks for the end of a drought in July; the next recorded public Thanksgiving was celebrated in Boston by the Bay Colony in gratitude for the safe arrival of ships bearing food and friends. These early celebrations, more recreational than religious in nature, often lasted for several days and involved games of skill as well as eating.

Attitudes toward other holiday celebrations affected how Thanksgiving was celebrated. The Puritans were suspicious of the idolatry of the English Christmas celebration; however, over the years, their Thanksgiving holiday took on many aspects of English Christmas, including the reunion of family and friends and the serving of special foods. In time, turkey replaced beef roast, and pumpkin pie became an expected dessert.

In its early history, Thanksgiving was a moveable feast, not tied to any particular date. From 1631–1684 twenty-two public Thanksgivings were held; in 1742 there were two. Thanksgiving was celebrated on whatever day and in whatever season seemed appropriate. The idea of good harvest and a thanksgiving feast formed a natural connection.

Thanksgiving became a nationally recognized holiday during the American Revolution when Congress recommended a day be set aside for that purpose. However, after the General Thanksgiving for Peace in 1784, the custom was omitted until

HARPER'S WEEKLY.

CASTLE GARDEN—THEIR FIRST THANKSGIVING DINNER.—DRAWN BY ST. JOHN HARPER.

the adoption of the federal Constitution in 1789, when Washington and the Congress assigned Thursday, November 26, as a day for a national observance. Although the observance became uniform and traditional throughout New England, it was not recognized in the South until 1858 when eight governors sent forth proclamations much after the New England model, in spite of some opposition by their constituents to "Yankee ideas." President Abraham Lincoln recommended special days for Thanksgiving during the Civil War. Although few Americans had much to be thankful for, this symbolic idea began to heal the wounds. Credit for the permanent status of Thanksgiving Day as a national holiday must be given to Sarah Josepha Hale, editor of *Godey's Lady's Book,* who worked for years to promote this idea, petitioning congressmen and the president himself. Thanksgiving thus became a national institution, supported by the power and authority of the national government but based on an ancient agrarian tradition of giving thanks for bountiful harvests. In Canada a Thanksgiving holiday was first observed in 1879, but is celebrated in October.

The center of Thanksgiving is the dinner; the central symbol of that meal is the turkey. Although there is no evidence that turkeys were eaten at the first Thanksgiving, Governor William Bradford of Plymouth Colony himself mentioned that during that autumn wild turkeys were plentiful. The fowl suppliers in New Jersey and Pennsylvania began to push the idea of turkey for Thanksgiving in the mid-19th century, and by 1883 the American public adopted the Thanksgiving turkey. Historians, writers, and artists rendered not just contemporary Thanksgiving tables laden with turkey and pumpkin pies, but also the tables of times past.

In this same commercial vein, Thanksgiving has traditionally marked the official opening of the Christmas shopping season. In 1939 businessmen urged President Roosevelt to move the date of Thanksgiving from the last Thursday in November to the next-to-last in order to increase the number of shopping days before Christmas. Some Americans actually celebrated Thanksgiving twice that year, ordering twice as many turkeys. But in 1941, Congress officially mandated the last Thursday in November as the day of celebration, and so it has remained. Thus, a powerful set of historical memories reinforced by federal authority and the popular and commercial media created a Thanksgiving Day celebration more traditional and uniform today than in the past and the most uniformly celebrated of all of our national holidays, especially in terms of food.

Lin T. Humphrey

Thomas, Jeannette Bell (1881–1982)

Author of local-color stories pertaining to folklife in the Kentucky-West Virginia border region and director of the American Folk Song Festival, held annually near Ashland, Kentucky, from 1930 until 1972. Jean Thomas was widely known as "The Traipsin' Woman."

Born Jeannette Bell in Ashland, Kentucky, on November 14, 1881, she attended parochial school and won local acclaim as an artistic singer. Upon graduation from high school, she worked as a legal stenographer, attending circuit court sessions in the mountains of eastern Kentucky, and it was there she first encountered indigenous folk music.

Her marriage in 1913 to businessman Albert Hart Thomas ended in divorce a year later, and she never remarried. She attended Hunter College and the Pulitzer School of Journalism, and between 1913 and 1925 she maintained various secretarial positions in Kentucky, Ohio, and New York. Her friendships with Greenwich Village artists and socialites—and a brief stint as a script girl in Hollywood—gave rise to theatrical ambitions. Instead of becoming an actress, however, Thomas forged a successful career as a writer and a presenter of Appalachian folk culture.

Between 1925 and 1930, she supplemented her secretarial work with magazine and newspaper writing and also began to feel her way as an entrepreneur of folk culture. In 1928 she created a media stir by bringing to New York an aged Kentucky fiddler, J.W. Day, to perform at the elegant Roxy theater. She presented Day as the rustic "Jilson Setters," called him "the last minstrel," and made much of his repertoire of "Elizabethan" ballads and fiddle tunes.

Two articles inspired by her experiences in the Kentucky mountains appeared nationally in *American Magazine* in 1929 and 1930. One of these told an appealing tale of "Jilson Setters," while the other introduced Thomas herself as "The Traipsin' Woman," a moniker she eventually adopted as a legal part of her name. The two magazine stories were immensely popular and set the stage for Thomas' future success as a writer of books based on Appalachian history and folklife.

In 1930 she gathered a group of friends near Ashland, Kentucky, to hear a concert by local folk musicians. This "singin' gatherin'" evolved into the American Folk Song Festival, an annual event directed by Thomas that also became a thread of continuity through her long life. In conjunction with the festival, Thomas chartered an American Folk Song Society in 1931. This brought her into conflict with Robert Winslow Gordon of the Archive of American Folk Song at the Library of Congress, who founded an organization of the same name at roughly the same time.

Thomas' first book, published in 1931, was *Devil's Ditties,* a collection of mountain folksongs presented in an unusual descriptive format. This was followed by six other books within the decade, including Thomas' autobiographical *The Traipsin' Woman* (1933) and her most famous work, *The Singin' Fiddler of Lost Hope Hollow* (1938), which featured the half-imaginary "Jilson Setters" as its central character. Thomas' accounts of Kentucky mountain life interwove Appalachian regional history and folklife with supposed Elizabethan mannerisms, Chaucerian speech, and uplifting but sentimental plots.

She published no further books after 1942, but instead turned her attention to producing the American Folk Song Festival and to entertaining visitors at her museum home, "The Wee House in the Woods," a brick replica of a Tudor-style cottage built for her in Ashland. Her energy seemed boundless, and she continued to direct the festival until old age took her into a nursing home in 1972. She died there in 1982 at the age of 101.

In retrospect, although Thomas maintained an impressive roster of associates in American letters, entertainment, and business, her American Folk Song Festival was anathema to academic folklorists, who still tend to criticize its excessive Anglo-Saxon emphasis, its staged theatrical aspects, and its pseudo-historical presentation of Appalachian folk culture. While Thomas possessed a valuable awareness of folklife in Appalachia, she chose to ignore documentary modes of representation in favor of the theatrical-pageant tradition and the local–color story. Her failure to provide tangible sources for her findings undermined the validity of her work in the eyes of many folklorists. But while academicians have been less than positive about her contributions to the field, Thomas' books nevertheless found an enthusiastic readership, and her American Folk Song Festival remained popular with general audiences for more than four decades.

Stephen Green

References

Thomas, Jean. 1939. *Ballad Makin' in the Mountains of Kentucky.* New York: Holt.

———. 1940. *The Sun Shines Bright.* Englewood Cliffs, NJ: Prentice Hall.

Wolfe, Charles. 1982. *Kentucky Country.* Lexington: University Press of Kentucky, pp. 66–75.

Thompson, Harold W. (1891–1963)

Collector of New York state folklore. Thompson's collecting and devotion to that folklore spanned the years 1915 until his death in 1963. He was seminal in the formation of the New York Folklore Society in 1944 and served as its first president from 1945 to 1950.

Thompson had as his goal to make folklore materials accessible to the widest possible audience. To that end, he introduced folklore to his students at Albany State University (1915–1940) and at Cornell University (1940–1959), presented monthly radio broadcasts on folklore between 1935 and 1943, and encouraged the use of folklore by teachers. In addition to his work with the New York Folklore Society, Thompson served as president of the American Folklore society in 1942 and was elected a Fellow of the American Folklore Society in 1959. He was a Guggenheim Fellow in 1925 and was the first American to be named a Life Fellow of the Royal Society of Edinburgh and of the Society of Antiquaries of Scotland.

Because Thompson strove to present folklore in a manner accessible to a nonacademic audience, his work was criticized by some folklorists for being too popularist. However, the criticism pertained to presentational style rather than quality, as Thompson was a thorough and careful researcher. His collecting of oral literature from the various regions of New York state and his proactive stance toward folklore scholarship in New York was instrumental in laying the groundwork for future folkloristic study of New York state.

Ellen McHale

References

Thompson, Harold W. 1940. *Body, Boots, and Britches.* Philadelphia: Lippincott.

Thomsen, Fred C. 1993. Plowing It Back: Harold W. Thompson and the New York Folklore Society, 1945–1957. *Folklore Historian.* 10:57–75.

Thompson, Stith (1885–1976)

Many would agree, America's most important folklorist. The breadth and depth of his contributions speak for themselves.

Thompson was born near Springfield, Kentucky. After attending Butler University and the University of Wisconsin in Madison, he received his M.A. degree from the University of California, Berkeley, in 1912, and his Ph.D. degree from Harvard University in 1914. His dissertation, written under George Lyman Kittredge, was titled *European Borrowings and Parallels in North American Indian Tales.*

After teaching at several other universities, Thompson went to Indiana University in Bloomington in 1922. Over the years, he taught courses in English language and literature, and he wrote and edited several widely used textbooks. As early as 1922 he began offering courses in folklore—among the earliest such courses offered in the United States.

Thompson's efforts to promote folklore as a subject to be taught in colleges and universities culminated in his establishing at Indiana the first Ph.D-granting program in folklore in the country. The first doctorate in the program was awarded in 1953.

Thompson also supported and encouraged the establishment of folklore courses in other colleges and universities, and often these were taught by his former students. Hence, it can be said that one of his major contributions was that he was largely responsible for establishing folklore on a firm academic footing in the United States.

A second major contribution lies in his own research. He published a number of scholarly works that earned him recognition as one of the world's greatest folktale scholars. His fame rests largely on a group of indexes and surveys of the world's folktales, including *European Tales among the North American Indians* (1919), *The Types of the Folktale* (1928, a translation and expansion of a work by the Finn Antti Aarne), *Tales of the North American Indians* (1929), and *The Motif-Index of Folk-Literature* (1932–1936; rev. ed. 1955–1958). Other major works included *The Folktale* (1946), *Four Symposia on Folklore* (1953), and *One Hundred Favorite Folktales* (1968).

Thompson's final major contribution to folklore study is that he helped introduce European folklore methods and goals into the United States. During the late 19th and early 20th centuries, when British folklore scholarship was mainly concerned with identifying supposed ancient survivals in contemporary folklore, and when American folklore scholarship concentrated on ballads, few American folklorists knew of the research being done with folktales in Finland, Germany, and elsewhere in Europe. This research emphasized the comparative analysis of single, widely known stories to discover their original forms, places of origin, and paths of distribution. To facilitate this comparative analysis, scholars encouraged extensive collecting, classification, and archiving.

During the 1920s, through his travel and research, Thompson became acquainted with Finnish and other European scholars and their work. Through his publications and teaching, he helped make other American folklorists aware of European folktale research and its ramifications. He had, therefore, a marked influence on the direction of American folklore scholarship in the 20th century.

After he retired from teaching at Indiana University in 1955, Thompson continued his research, among other things by revising and enlarging his earlier indexes. He also taught at several other universities as a visiting professor.

Warren E. Roberts

Thorp, Nathan Howard ("Jack") (1867–1940)

First known collector of cowboy songs and first to edit and publish a cowboy songbook, *Songs of the Cowboy* (1908). Thorp was born in New York City and educated in New Hampshire, but he spent his summers on his brother's ranch in Nebraska. He loved the Western cowboy life, and in 1886 he moved to New Mexico to buy horses to be trained as polo ponies. There he learned the techniques of cowboying. In 1889, with his banjo-mandolin and on horseback, he rode to various cow camps in New Mexico, Texas, and Indian Territory collecting songs sung by cowboys. This was probably the first Anglo folksong field collecting in the United States.

In 1898, while trail herding cattle from New Mexico to Texas, Thorp wrote "Little Joe the Wrangler"; in 1908 he took twenty-three of his collected songs as well as songs he had written to a printer in Estancia, New Mexico, and had 2,000 paperback copies printed at six cents a copy. In 1921, angry that John A. Lomax, folksong collector, had used songs from his book without giving credit, he expanded his text to 101 songs and republished it. As a cowboy poet, Thorp had his poems published in *Poetry, Literary Digest,* and numerous cattlemen's publications. He was also a skillful raconteur; J. Frank Dobie credited Thorp as his source for many stories.

Thorp died in his home near Alameda, New Mexico, on June 4, 1940.

Guy Logsdon

References

Thorp, N. Howard "Jack" [1921] 1984. *Songs of the Cowboy,* with Introduction by Guy Logsdon. Lincoln: University of Nebraska Press.

———. 1926. *Tales of the Chuck Wagon.* Santa Fe: Privately Printed.

———. 1966. *Songs of the Cowboys.* Variants, Commentary, Notes, and Lexicon by Austin E. and Alta S. Fife. New York: Clarkson N. Potter.

Thorp, N. Howard "Jack," and Neil M. Clark. [1945] 1977. *Pardner of the Wind.* Lincoln: University of Nebraska Press.

Toast

A recitation or salute by an individual, sometimes with drink in hand. The following comes from one "Slim" of Jefferson City, Missouri, who recited it to Bruce Jackson in June 1964:

> Well here's to the crane that flew down the lane and lit upon the mast pole.
> Stretched his neck and shit a peck and sparks flew from his asshole. (quoted in Jackson 1977:229–230)

Scholars have most notably characterized toasts as a type of folk poetry and/or traditional prose narrative coming primarily from African American oral tradition, although folklorist David Evans reminds us that "such recitations have long been a standard part of men's gatherings, which usually involve drinking, among both Whites and Blacks" (Evans 1977:130). Folklorists concur that toasts circulating in black oral tradition are "usually long poetic recitations that tell a story or portray a situation" (Evans 1977:130). Performed toasts contain rhymed couplets coming from numerous sources. Roger Abrahams discusses the manner in which African Americans possibly appropriated the term in his seminal collection, *Deep Down in the Jungle: Negro Narrative Folklore from the Streets of Philadelphia* (Abrahams 1970:109–111), suggesting that on the one hand the minstrel show may have affected the tradition's early history but that on the other hand the form of toasts current in the late 20th century perhaps derived from the custom of verse toasts pledged with a drink (Abrahams 1970:109). Certainly the end of World War I and the subsequent Prohibition era must have had an effect on such a function; however, most of the informants who appear in 20th-century collections of toasts are male prisoners or minors unable to purchase liquor and who are often performing for a folklorist, with *no* drink in hand. Conversely, another published collection by Anthony M. Reynolds shows that liquor probably still plays an important role.

Reynolds includes in his collection a description of more natural settings among Black males in the free world: "The formal telling of toasts unrolls as the bottle of scotch is drained, and ends in laughter and discussion in much the same way it began" (Reynolds 1974:299). Reynolds recorded a representative body of toasts in South Central Los Angeles that he demonstrates come from a wide range of sources, including some locally well-known printed ones, such as George Milburn's *The Hobo's Hornbook* (1930). He distinguishes the "society toasts" from the bad man (for example, "Stackolee") and "contest" toasts ("The Signifying Monkey"), both of which have appeared in several collections. Society toasts, unlike the other types, lack obscenities, are fit for mixed company, have a greater frequency of internal rhyme, have a moralistic tone, and obtain close identification between the storyteller and the main characters (Reynolds 1974:273–274).

Perhaps one of the most popular toasts in Black oral tradition is the following version of a *Titanic* toast, which Bruce Jackson recorded in a southeast Texas prison farm in 1966. The protagonist, Shine, is a cross between the bad man and the trickster characters in African American folklore. This toast appears in Jackson's 1974 collection, *"Get Your Ass in the Water and Swim Like Me": Narrative Poetry from Black Oral Tradition:*

It was sad, indeed, it was sad in mind,
April the fourteenth of nineteen-twelve was a hell of a
  time,
When the news reached a seaport town
That the great *Titanic* was a sinking down.
Up popped Shine from the deck below,
Says, "Captain, captain," says, "you don't know."
Says, "There's about forty feet of water on the
  boilerroom floor."
He said, "Never mind, Shine, you go on back and
  keep stackin' them sacks,
I got forty-eight pumps to keep the water back."
Shine said, "Well, that seems damned funny, It may be
  damned fine,
But I'm gonna try to save this black ass of mine."
So Shine jumped overboard and begin to swim, and all
  the people were standin' on deck watchin' him.
Captain's daughter jumped on the deck with her dress
  above her head and her teddies below her knees
And said, "Shine, Shine," say, "won't you save poor
  me?"
Say, "I'll make you rich as any shine can be."
Shine said, "Miss, I know you is pretty and that is
  true,
But there's women on the shore can make a ass out a
  you."
Captain said, "Shine, Shine, you save poor me,

I make you as rich as any shine can be."
Shine say, "There's fish in the ocean, whales in the sea,
  captain, get your ass in the water and swim like
  me."
So Shine turned over and began to swim,
People on the deck were still watchin' him.
A whale jumped up in the middle of the sea,
Said, "Put a 'special delivery' on his black ass for me."
Shine said, "Your eyes may roll and your teeth may
  grit,
But if you're figurin' on eatin' me you can that shit."
Shine continued to swim, he looked back, he ducked
  his head, he showed his ass,
"Look out sharks and fishes and let me pass,"
He swimmed on till he came to a New York town, and
  people asked had the *Titanic* gone down.
Shine said, "Hell, yeah." They said, "How do you
  know?"
He said, "I left the big motherfucker sinkin' about
  thirty minutes ago" (quoted in Jackson,
  1974:185–186)

Jackson provides a brief discussion of some psychosocial functions of toasts as they occur in "certain kinds of parties, among youths hanging around street corners, [and] among inmates in jails and prisons" (Jackson 1972:123). Identifying themes and "culture hero" types characteristic of the genre, Wepman, Ronald B. Newman, and Murray B. Binderman compare and briefly discuss such culture heroes within toasts that Black prisoners performed during the 1950s and 1960s (Wepman, Newman, and Binderman 1976:1–15), while William Labov and colleagues give a linguistic treatment of toasts that also employ the trickster and the badman as protagonists (Lebov, Cohen, Robins, and Lewis [1968] 1994:329–347). Additionally, Wepman and colleagues identify the point of view in which performers typically narrated toasts; much of their own data contained third-person points of view, in contrast to the first-person point of view Reynolds reports. However, by assessing the collections of toasts from which folklorists draw conclusions when characterizing toasts in general (Jackson 1975; Wepman, Newman, and Binderman 1974), David Evans rightly identifies some folklorists' failure to print complete texts of the toasts they discuss" (Evans 1977:129). Nevertheless, Jackson, Labov, and other researchers have made available to the folklorist not only representations of folklore performances, but also, particularly with Reynolds' study, the contextual settings in which they typically emerge.

Finally, responding to Evans' request that folklorists attend to the genre as it appears among groups other than Black males, James D. Johnson documents the tradition among Southern Whites (Johnson 1981). Although Jackson never heard the *Titanic* from Whites (Jackson 1974:181), Johnson reports a version of the text among his informants, who, having learned it from other Whites, were surprised to hear that the protagonist was Black (1981:332)! Nevertheless, in Black oral tradition the *Titanic* toast proclaims the futility of earthly grandeur and riches, while taunting Whites for excluding

Blacks from the doomed vessel (including the Black heavy-weight champion of the world, Jack Johnson). This toast's relevance to racial tensions endures, even though the meaning such toasts have to those who perform and enjoy them will always be culturally specific. But the toast is more than a response to racial indignities. As Jackson observes: "[Shine] is the only one who has enough sense . . . to swim away from the sinking supership. . . . His power is total—body and mind—and so he alone gets home free, perfectly safe to fuck and signify as he wishes. That all this happens while a shipload of rich Whites drown is a gorgeous bonus."

Richard Allen Burns

References

Abrahams, Roger. [1963] 1970. *Deep Down in the Jungle: Negro Narrative Folklore from the Streets of Philadelphia.* Chicago: Aldine.

Evans, David. 1977. The Toast in Context. *Journal of American Folklore* 90:129–148.

Jackson, Bruce. 1972. Circus and Street: Psychosocial Aspects of the Black Toast. *Journal of American Folklore* 85:123–139.

———. 1974. *"Get Your Ass in the Water and Swim Like Me": Narrative Poetry from Black Oral Tradition.* Cambridge: Harvard University Press.

———. 1975. A Response to "Toasts: The Black Urban Poetry." *Journal of American Folklore* 88:178–182.

Johnson, James D. 1981. An Instance of Toasts among Southern Whites. *Western Folklore* 40:329–337.

Labov, William, Paul Cohen, Clarence Robins, and John Lewis. [1968] 1994. Toasts. In *Mother Wit from the Laughing Barrel: Readings in the Interpretation of Afro-American Folklore,* ed. Alan Dundes. Jackson: University of Mississippi Press, pp. 329–347.

Reynolds, Anthony M. 1974. Urban Toasts: A Hustler's Point of View from L.A. *Western Folklore* 33:267–300.

Wepman, Dennis, Ronald B. Newman, and Murray B. Binderman. 1974. Toasts: The Black Urban Folk Poetry. *Journal of American Folklore* 87:208–224.

———. 1975. A Rejoinder to Jackson. *Journal of American Folklore* 88:182–185.

———. 1976. *The Life: The Lore and Folk Poetry of the Black Hustler.* Philadelphia: University of Pennsylvania Press.

Tongue Twisters

Verbal puzzles perpetuating practical principles of plain and perfect pronunciation. Or, more scientifically defined, a tongue twister is ". . . a kind of speech play which has as its goal the correct pronunciation of combinations of words that are difficult to articulate rapidly and repeatedly" (Jorgensen 1981:67). The best-known example in English is the one beginning "Peter Piper picked a peck of pickled peppers . . ." which first appeared in print in 1674 as part of an entire alphabet comprising "a weird collection of characters, from Andrew Airpump to Walter Waddle" (Schwartz 1972:117).

Tongue twisters may be as short as two words—"toy boat," "truly rural," "Peggy Babcock," or "preshrunk shirts," for example—their difficulty lying in the challenge to repeat the same simple phrase several times rapidly without error. But most tongue twisters are complete sentences like "She sells sea shells by the sea shore"; "Around the rugged rock the ragged rascal ran"; and "How much wood could a woodchuck chuck if a woodchuck could chuck wood?" The latter example is often parodied, yielding such variations as "How many cans can a cannibal nibble, if a cannibal can nibble cans?"

Among the tongue-twister sentences that may lead one to uttering an impolite word are those beginning, "I slit a sheet a sheet I slit . . ." and "I'm not a fig plucker nor a fig plucker's son . . ." A similar challenge—not to slip into a risqué utterance—occurs in the tongue-twister song that starts "Sarah, Sarah, sitting in a shoe shine shop. / All day long she shines and sits . . ." Most tongue twisters, however, are innocent of such indecencies, or go no further in that direction than something like "He ran from the Indies to the Andes in his undies."

Besides tongue-twister songs, there are also tongue-tangling rhymes, such as the well-known limerick about the "tutor who tooted the flute" who "tried to tutor two tooters to toot. . . ." But a truly challenging tongue twister need not be lengthy or elaborate, since there is difficulty aplenty in trying to repeat several times without error something as deceptively simple as "Rubber baby buggy bumpers."

Tongue twisters, in general, function merely as entertainment, or (in the case of the off-color references) as pranks. However, some further functions have been documented, including to practice proper articulation for public speaking and singing, to test the fit of a new set of false teeth, to audition actors, and to train students in speaking foreign languages. A German class, for example, might struggle with this jaw breaker: *"Wir Wiener Waschweiber würden weisse Wäsche waschen wenn wir wüssten wo wärmes Wasser wäre"* (We washerwomen of Vienna would wash our washing white if we knew where some warm water was). Much simpler, but still a tough line to pronounce, is the Norwegian phrase *"fire ferske friske fiske"* (four fine fresh fish).

Tongue twisters are usually thought of as children's folklore, but they seem to be well remembered by people of all ages. When one writer mentioned his interest in this genre in a magazine circulated nationally, he received more than 13,000 tongue twisters from readers. Most contributors mentioned oral tradition via older friends and relatives as their sources (Potter 1972:1117). An experiment asking subjects to recite tongue twisters until a mistake was made revealed the kinds of errors most likely to occur and the sound combinations most frequently leading to mistakes. Confusion of similar morphemes was the most common kind of error, yielding garbled phrases such as "See shells she sells . . ." or "Rugger baby bubby gumpers . . ." Some subjects in the experiment, however, employed strategies for improving their performances, such as setting the texts to mental music, following a rhythmic beat in pronouncing them, grouping words together into patterns, or *not* thinking about the meaning of the words being said (Jorgensen 1981).

Jan Harold Brunvand

References

Emrich, Duncan. 1955. The Ancient Game of Tongue-Twisters. *American Heritage* 6 (February):119–120.

Jorgensen, Marilyn. 1981. The Tickled, Tangled, Tripped, and Twisted Tongue: A Linguistic Study of Factors Relating to Difficulty in the Performance of Tongue Twisters. *New York Folklore* 7:67–81.

Potter, Charles Francis. [1949] 1972. Tongue Twisters. In *Standard Dictionary of Folklore, Mythology, and Legend,* ed. Maria Leach and Jerome Fried. New York: Harper and Row, pp. 1117–1119.

Schwartz, Alvin. 1972. *A Twister of Twists, a Tangler of Tongues.* Philadelphia: Lippincott.

Tooth Fairy

Mythological sprite of childhood that magically appears at night to make an exchange, usually monetary, for a shed baby tooth. An acknowledged 20th-century popular-culture figure, the tooth fairy has roots in age-old rites of passage that mark the child's transition from infant to cognizant youngster. As such, the tooth fairy and the ritual of exchange (gift for tooth) tie in with superstitions and ancient ceremonies of life, death, and rebirth. Ancient folk methods to dispose of the shed baby tooth—throwing it to the sun or to a rodent, usually a mouse or some other animal; throwing it over or onto a roof; placing it in a tree, wall, or piece of furniture; salting, burning, or hiding it; or having someone or something swallow it—are practiced in the 1990s in European, African, and Asian countries, and in some isolated areas of the United States. However, in North America a singular tooth fairy takes precedence over these older rituals.

Variously known as an ubiquitous "good fairy" or "fairy godmother," one or more fairies appeared in the United States early in the 1900s to exchange a tooth for candy or money. Later, this "good fairy" became specialized, as shown in Lee Rogow's 1949 story, "The Tooth Fairy." Rosemary Wells' 1980 survey showed that the rate of exchange from 1900 to 1980 reflected the rising price index, that a singular tooth fairy was firmly entrenched in family life, and that parents voluntarily promoted the practice.

Economic affluence, emphasis on the child, an explosion of media fairies, and, more recently, commercial enterprises, helped change the tooth fairy from folk belief to national icon. In children's literature alone, this fairy appeared in six known stories in the 1960s, eleven in the 1970s, twenty-nine in the 1980s, and eighteen in the first two years of the 1990s, not to count the innumerable cartoons, jokes, and references in adult literature. The 1980s also saw the rise of commercial pillows, kits, jewelry, dolls, boxes, and banks. The late 1980s fairy became the "Expanded Duty Tooth Fairy," interested not only in children's good dental-health habits but in their social ones as well. The fairy, typically female and beneficent, always arrives at night while the child sleeps, generally looks under the pillow and absconds with the shed tooth after leaving a fair exchange. While this action is stereotyped, the reasons for the action vary, as does the image (adult, child, animal) and the tale involved.

This seemingly simple rite of passage is really complex and significant. It marks the physiological change in the child, the sociological one when the child shifts from home to school, and the psychological one when the child accepts an adult view and disbelieves in the fairy. It is a cultural event as well, promoted by parents to encourage imagination, but also to hold the child back from entering the harsh adult world too soon. The tooth-fairy period is voluntarily initiated twice, first in childhood, then in parenthood. It can last until all twenty baby teeth exfoliate, contrary to other cultures in which only the first shed tooth is honored, and it is enacted without a verbal charm or saying, again contrary to other cultures.

The tooth fairy's genealogy is obscure. England, Ireland, and Scotland have referenced fairies for centuries. However, these fairies were capable of evil as well as good, and any fairy could act on a child's behalf. The singular tooth fairy with a dedicated occupation was not documented by Iona Opie and Moira Tatem until a 1987 entry in the latest edition of *A Dictionary of Superstitions.* Current British children's stories of the late 20th century still place a tooth fairy in a large group of similar scavengers. Tad Tuleja has conjectured a possible relationship with the toothless Italian witch Marantega who functions as a tooth fairy, but by 1920, the referent source date, the fairy, not a witch, was well established in American folklore. More probable is the metamorphosis from tooth mouse, a much older and more widespread tradition, to tooth fairy through an 18th-century French fairy tale, "La Bonne Petite Souris," in which a mouse, changing into a fairy to help a good queen fight an evil king, hides under a pillow to heckle the king and punishes him by knocking out his teeth. Although Tuleja, William Carter, and colleagues think this is a "credible mechanism" to tie the two traditions of tooth mouse and tooth fairy together, no child, no exfoliated baby tooth, and no exchange of tooth with replacement gift are involved. The actual progenitor of the tooth fairy is still conjectural.

Rosemary Wells

References

Carter, William, Bernard Butterworth, Joseph Carter, and John Carter. 1987. *Ethnodentistry and Dental Folklore.* Overland Park, KA: Dental Folklore Books of Kansas City.

Hand, Wayland D. 1981. European Folklore in the New World. *Folklore* 92 (2).141–140.

Opie, Iona, and Moira Tatem. 1989. *A Dictionary of Superstitions.* Oxford: Oxford University Press.

Rogow, Lee. 1949. The Tooth Fairy. *Colliers* 124:26.

Rooth, Anna. 1982. *Offering of the First Tooth.* Uppsala: Ethnological Institute.

Tuleja, Tad. 1991. The Tooth Fairy: Perspectives on Money and Magic. In *The Good People: New Fairylore Essays,* ed. Peter Narváez. New York: Garland, pp. 406–425.

Wells, Rosemary. 1983. Tracking the Tooth Fairy. *Cal. Magazine* 46 (12):1–8, 47 (1):18–25, 47 (2):25–31.

———. 1991. The Making of an Icon: The Tooth Fairy in North American Folklore and Popular Culture. In *The Good People: New Fairylore Essays,* ed. Peter Narváez. New York: Garland, pp. 426–453.

Toys, Folk

Traditional handmade objects used by children at play. Folk toys are artifacts of the cultures that produce them, and as such they serve as one of many possible ways to begin investigating the traditions of a culture. They are especially important as one aspect of the study of children and play and as one form of material culture.

Traditions of toymaking have likely existed for thousands of years. Some of the miniature models of people, animals, and objects of clay or stone frequently found by archaeologists at sites around the world are thought to have been toys. In addition, some religious objects have a secondary use as toys once they have fulfilled their primary religious function (for example, Hopi kachina dolls). A small animal on wheels made of clay found in excavations of an early Mexican culture in which no other evidence of the wheel has been discovered is perhaps a toy; it is said to demonstrate the degree of creativity achieved by toymakers.

Folk toys can be made by children themselves, in which case they are often quite temporary ("cootie catchers" and paper folded into a specific form and used to tell fortunes). They can be made by adults for use by children, usually by parents or caretakers, in which case they are generally more permanent (cornhusk dolls), or they can be made by trained craftspeople for a larger clientele, in which case they are often not only more permanent but more elaborate (limberjacks, a jointed human figure that dances on a board).

Folk toys are made of any convenient materials, including wood, clay, plants, paper, fabric, metal, sand, or snow. If made by children, they most often utilize recycled or "found" materials (as when rubberbands are saved to make a "Chinese jump rope"). Adults, especially those who make toys for sale, are more likely to purchase new materials as needed. Folk toys come in many varieties: Dolls are common (often made of natural materials such as nuts, apples, or corncobs dressed in scraps of fabric), but there are also toys that move or require specific physical skills for their use (such as a ball and cup tied together by a string, in which the task is to get the ball into the cup), balance toys (such as a fisherman, pole, and fish, constructed so that he stands upright at the edge of a table and the fish swims under the table), puzzles (in which several pieces of wood or metal are combined in various ways and the puzzle is to assemble and reassemble them), and toys integral to various games (such as balls).

Folk toys have been most popular in places where there is little money to spare for store-bought toys. Thus, in the United States, Appalachia has been a major source of folk toys, made by parents for their children out of available materials, in lieu of spending money for commercially produced toys. In the 1990s, these same toys may be made for sale to outsiders, bringing money into the area. In places where folk toys have been usurped by mass-produced toys, they may still be found in attics and in boxes on back shelves, unused but functioning still as reminders of the family's past, or in museum collections where they serve as communal reminders of the past (Leeds-Hurwitz 1984).

In the modern urban United States, folk toys made by adults for their own children are becoming rare, as parents are often too busy to make toys, tending rather to purchase them. Anecdotal histories suggest that many folk toys were made by grandparents for their grandchildren as part of child-care responsibilities. Thus, it is to be expected that as more children are in day-care settings, separated from previous generations, some traditional folk toys will disappear. Also, the widespread increase of time spent watching television implies a decrease in the time children spend learning how to turn natural and discarded materials into toys. In addition, watching television generally includes watching ads for mass-produced toys, increasing interest in them.

However, there is simultaneous movement in the opposite direction: Folk toys are being rediscovered by craftspeople (Spotswood 1975) and are showing up at art and craft shows, there to be purchased by parents who have less time but more money to spend on their children's needs and desires. And, despite the fact that mass-produced toys are available to a majority of children in this country, most children still make some toys for their own use. A few questions to any group of children or parents quickly reveal that many of the same toys made a generation ago are still being made in the late 1990s, including slingshots, paper airplanes, and cat's cradles. Notwithstanding the widespread use of television and other media, children continue to pass a wide variety of traditions from one generation to the next, so it is unlikely that folk toys will ever completely disappear.

Folk toys fulfill too many uses to be eliminated merely because of the availability of commercial toys. As with any toys, folk toys encourage the growth of the child in a variety of ways, including physical, social, and cognitive development. In addition, toys created by children for their own use encourage creativity and a feeling of accomplishment. Wherever children manipulate the elements in their environment, whether that entails using leaves to represent family members in pretend play (Clavaud 1977) or combining a stick with a rubberband to make a slingshot, they can be said to have created folk toys. Wherever adults make toys by hand for children, whether they are trained specialists carving elaborate wooden vehicles or parents putting string through a button to make the moonspinner remembered from their own childhood, they also can be said to have created folk toys. Clearly, folk toys of some sort are to be found virtually everywhere there are children.

Despite their wide presence, folk toys have never become a major topic of interest in and of themselves in folklore (or any other field). In folklore, the strong historic emphasis on verbal art can be blamed for discouraging substantial attention to physical objects such as toys. Even with the growing current appreciation for studies of material culture, toys must overcome what has been termed the "triviality barrier" affecting all of children's folklore (Sutton-Smith 1970); that is, they don't seem to be highly significant. In addition, there is a practical constraint: Folk toys, especially those made by children for their own use, frequently have a short lifespan. Even once they have been noticed and granted stature as a potential research topic, it is difficult to study ephemeral objects—like

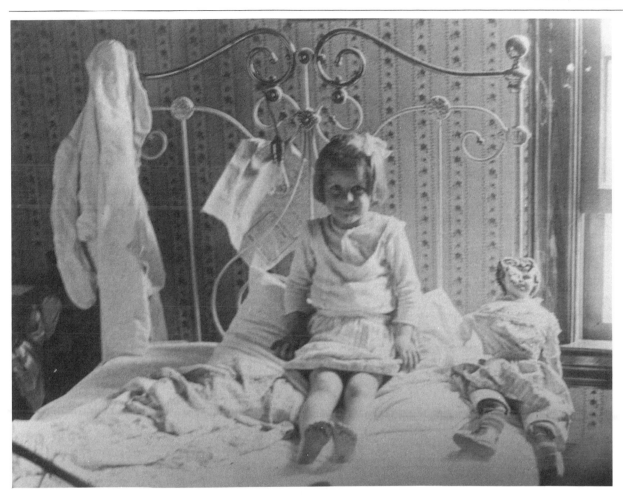

Ruth Webster and her doll. Ohio, 1905. Collection J. W. Love.

sand castles, snow sculptures, or string figures—that may be created and abandoned in the same day.

As a result of these influences, publications on folk toys are few. These tend to fall into several distinct categories: Some treat toys as a craft, providing detailed instructions mainly intended for parents wishing to make toys for their own children (Schnacke 1973); others treat toys as one of several expressive forms indigenous to an area, documenting them for future generations (Page and Smith 1985). Some brief descriptions of toys are included in works by anthropologists or folklorists primarily interested in children's play more generally (Bronner 1988:199–236; Dargan and Zeitlin 1990:11–120). Historically, the majority of the writing on folk toys has emphasized the objects themselves, much as early research on verbal art separated the forms of interest from their speakers and context, compiling lists of proverbs or jokes while ignoring the context from which they were drawn. As our ideas of how to study other forms of folklore change, the goal in studying folk toys is likely to change as well, moving from simple documentation of form to consideration of additional issues.

Theoretically, there are at least five major issues requiring investigation. The first concerns the definition of *folk:* What is it exactly that separates folk toys from other toys? How many children need to play with a toy, how long-standing does the tradition need to be, before it is defined as folk? How many changes are permitted to the original design? What of the means of passing on traditions: When an adult learns the design from a book, and then begins making similar toys, is that still traditional?

The second issue is one of *boundaries:* When commercial toy companies adopt designs for traditional toys and mass-produce them (as happened with the "clutch ball" for infants, now available from several manufacturers), is it still a folk toy? Where should the line between traditionally made toys and mass-produced toys be drawn? What are the critical elements: the design? the maker? the quantity available? the materials? the connection between the toymaker and the child given the toy?

The third issue is related to *community:* What is the community that should be studied as the appropriate environment for a folk toy? Traditionally, it was sufficient to assume a geographic region or an ethnic group as the obvious community, but in the heterogeneous world of the late 20th century, in which people move around and ethnic groups are far from the distinct homogeneous communities they once were, it is a more complex matter. When someone from Appalachia moves to the Midwest and gives new neighbors traditional toys, which they then pass on to their own children, what is the group within which the particular toy should be understood to exist?

The fourth issue concerns *context:* Serious thought needs to be given to what information must be included in a study of folk toys. To date (1995), the emphasis has been on the toy itself, but that is rather limited. At the minimum, information concerning three critical components—the toy, the maker, and the user (the functional roles of maker and user should be distinguished, even though the same person may fulfill both roles)—seems essential. This implies incorporating into a single study description of the particular objects used as toys (how they are made and of what materials, how they are used, the geographic region in which they are common), description of the maker and the role of toy making in his or her life (how the skill was acquired, how often toys are made, the reasons for making them—for their own use or for others, as gifts or for sale), and description of the larger social context (how the toys function for the children who play with them, what sort of games or play they encourage, what sorts of identity they express, how they serve to develop creativity).

The fifth issue is one of *creativity:* Folk toys are often said to require creativity on the part of their makers and to encourage the development of creativity on the part of the children who use them. This should be investigated. What do toy makers have to tell us? What other arts or crafts are toy makers involved in? What do studies of children making their own toys demonstrate? Are there, for example, any connections between early interest in toys demonstrating scientific principles (such as balance toys) and later interest in science?

Answering these and other related questions will provide a strong foundation for the study of folk toys as it develops in the future. Documenting what folk toys look like and how they are made is important, but it is only one part of what there is to understand. Discovering the roles folk toys play in the social world, for the children who use them as well as for everyone who makes them, should be the ultimate concern.

Wendy Leeds-Hurwitz

References

Abernathy, Francis Edward, ed. 1989. *Texas Toys and Games.* Publications of the Texas Folklore Society No. 48. Dallas: Southern Methodist University Press.

Bronner, Simon. 1988. *American Children's Folklore.* Little Rock, AR: August House.

Clavaud, Donna. 1977. Playing Leaves: A Study of a Traditional Kashaya Pomo Play Behavior. *Journal of California Anthropology* 4 (2):197–205.

Dargan, Amanda, and Steven Zeitlin. 1990. *City Play.* New Brunswick, NJ: Rutgers University Press.

Johnston, Kathryn. 1974. Anyone for a Whimmydiddle? *Smithsonian* 5 (9):54–57.

Leeds-Hurwitz, Wendy. 1984. Folk Toys in the Milwaukee Public Museum. *Wisconsin Academy Review* 30:19–21.

Page, Linda Garland, and Hilton Smith, eds. 1985. *The Foxfire Book of Toys and Games: Reminiscences and Instructions from Appalachia.* New York: E.P. Dutton.

Schnacke, Dick. 1973. *American Folk Toys: How to Make Them.* Harmondsworth, England: Penguin.

Spotswood, Beverly. 1975. Toys: A Portfolio of Magic. In *The Craftsman in America,* ed. National Geographic Society. Washington, DC: National Geographic Society, pp. 150–163.

Sutton-Smith, Brian. 1970. Psychology of Childlore: The Triviality Barrier. *Western Folklore* 29:1–8.

Trapping

The practice of capturing animals through the use of any mechanical device that kills or immobilizes the prey without requiring the presence of the trapper. The use of such devices is ancient: Egyptian tomb paintings depict the use of fish traps, but the practice undoubtedly has its roots in prehistory, with the earliest use of tools of any kind.

Fur provided a major economic incentive for European explorers of North America from the first, and all early accounts of the riches of the New World include descriptions of the abundance of valuable fur-bearing game. The development in the 15th and 16th centuries of a practical, reliable, and portable metal-spring trap that could be manufactured in quantity and packed into the wilderness with ease gave further impetus to the exploration of the American frontier. The Hudson Bay Company, founded in 1670 and still in existence, provided the foremost outlet for sales to the European market.

The dramatic and colorful role played by the professional trapper in American history has overshadowed the ongoing role of part-time practitioners—farmers and woodsmen with sufficient skill to put food on the table, rid their land of nuisance species, and supplement their income with fur sales. Most contemporary trappers belong to this part-time category, if only because state regulation of the activity in the United States limits the trapping of most species to an annual season of a few weeks or months. In the 1990s, the most frequently trapped mammals in the United States include beaver, opossum, skunk, muskrat, bobcat, mink, otter, raccoon, marten, bear, red and grey fox, nutria, and coyote.

Like hunting and fishing, trapping is an activity that must be learned by observation and experience. Many rural youngsters begin with simple homemade snares, pitfalls, deadfalls, and boxtraps, the designs for which are often centuries old or more. However, most serious would-be trappers eventually graduate to the steel-spring trap. To do so, they typically enter into an informal apprenticeship with a more expert individual who instructs the pupil in highly traditional aspects of the activity such as the habits and temperament of the target animals, the placement and construction of a trap set, the concoction and use of aromatic baits and lures, the responsible regular running (checking) of the trap line, humane dispatch of appropriate target animals, and techniques for release of accidental catches. In many rural communities, trapping under the guidance of a knowledgeable older man is considered an especially appropriate training for young boys, teaching them the virtues of patience, careful observation, hard work, and responsibility. Because some capital is tied up in the purchase of equipment, trapping is also understood to provide early training in financial management. Furthermore, successful implementation of educational and regulatory programs concerning animal population control at the state and local level since the 1930s has strongly reinforced the conviction among trappers that their work enhances the general health and strength of the fur-bearing species in their region. The predominant metaphor is agricultural: A trapper frequently speaks of "harvesting," and a female or young male of a target species that is released is "left for seed."

The activity thus carries for many participants a complex set of positive values and sentiments that go far beyond its practical utility. In addition, although few trappers trap purely "for the sport" in the same sense that American hunters hunt and fishermen fish, trapping affords its competent practitioners enormous personal satisfaction difficult to convey even to sympathetic nontrappers.

Historically, trapping has never shared the aristocratic traditional heritage that is a component in hunting—a heritage deriving from the deeply held classical and European belief that the hunt provided the best possible means for peacetime maintenance of military skills. Within the Anglo American tradition, the aristocratic youth George Washington hunted; Abe Lincoln, a backwoods boy, trapped. Among the general public, the romantic historical picture of the trapper on the frontier coexists uneasily with increasingly negative images of the contemporary trapper arising in part from the anti-fur stance of the animal rights movement, which gained momentum in the 1970s.

Trapper reaction to the "antis" has fundamentally altered the culture of trapping. Where once the communal aspect was limited to the dyads of the teacher-pupil relationship and the partnerships established between pairs of experienced trappers, trappers have now organized groups on the regional, state, local, and national levels for the purposes of educating the general public, neutralizing the political momentum of the animal rights lobby, and cooperating with state game agencies.

These organizations provide a forum for a great deal of informal interaction as well, adding substantially to the folklore of contemporary trapping. Meetings provide an opportunity to share narrative accounts of the adventures of the last season and to pass around the latest "anti" jokes and stories. (A whole cycle of humorous tales circulates concerning the animal rights activist Cleveland Amory, most of which turn on his putative ignorance of "real-life" animal behavior.) Snapshots of previous seasons' take are often brought out: Because the catch is sold, photographs provide the sole means of visual documentation. Pelts are arranged with a careful eye to pleasing and impressive composition. Garb at the meetings often includes items identifying the wearer as a proud trapper: Baseball caps, enamel pins, and T-shirts with the organization logos and slogans abound, although such clothing is less commonly used in the field, where the requirements are warmth and durability.

The meetings also provide an opportunity for participation by wives and girlfriends. Although women are seldom full participants in trapping itself, they are often very active in the local trapping organizations, providing support such as bookkeeping, food preparation, dues collection, and fund-raising through women's auxiliary organizations.

Trapping as a traditional activity has not been extensively explored by folklorists, with the exception of beliefs documented in the hunting sections of the major compendiums compiled by Wayland D. Hand and others. Most trappers are pessimistic about the future of the pursuit; it is possible that within a generation or two it may have passed completely from the roster of traditional American outdoor skills, with its latter years relatively undocumented.

Erika Brady

References

Bateman, James A. 1971. *Animals, Traps, and Trapping.* Harrisburg, PA: Stackpole Books.

Brady, Erika. 1990. Mankind's Thumb on Nature's Scale: Trapping and Regional Identity in the Missouri Ozarks. In *Sense of Place: American Regional Cultures,* ed. Barbara Allen and Thomas J. Schlereth. Lexington: University Press of Kentucky, pp. 58–73.

Hand, Wayland D. 1964. *Beliefs and Superstitions.* Vol. 7 of *The Frank C. Brown Collection of North Carolina Folklore.* Durham, NC: Duke University Press, pp. 483–490.

Hand, Wayland D., Anna Casetta, and Sondra B. Thiederman. 1981. *Popular Beliefs and Superstitions: A Compendium of American Folklore from the Ohio Collection of Newbell Niles Puckett.* Boston: G.K. Hall, pp. 1019–1023.

LaFleur, Normand. 1973. *La vie traditionelle du coureur de bois aux XIXe et XXe siecles.* Ottawa: Editions Lemeac.

Travis, Merle Robert (1917–1983)

Folk musician known for his distinctive guitar style, folk- and country-music vocal performances, and original compositions. Travis perfected and popularized the Muhlenberg County, Kentucky, guitar-playing technique known as the "thumb style" and, later, "Travis-picking," in which the thumb and index finger play simultaneously a song's melody with rhythmic, harmonic, and bass accompaniment. Although the paradigm of this method was introduced to the region in the 1920s by the African American folk musician Arnold Shultz, Travis learned it from White coal miners, Mose Rager and Ike Everly in particular. The technique was subsequently adopted by numerous musicians, including the master guitarist Chet Atkins, becoming a prominent instrumental element of the commercial country sound of the 1940s and 1950s.

Travis was also a folksinger, performing such pieces as "John Henry," "I Am a Pilgrim," and "Nine Pound Hammer" throughout his career, and a composer who wrote both folk-like and popular country-western songs. Many of the tunes in Travis' "folksong" mode dramatized and celebrated the lives and work of coal miners in his native region during the 1930s, some becoming popular nationally. "Dark as a Dungeon," for example, has been widely recorded, as has "Sixteen Tons," which was a No. 1 hit for Tennessee Ernie Ford in 1955.

In the mid-1940s, Travis became a major figure in the Los Angeles country-music scene, writing and recording several hit "honky tonk" songs in the Western Swing idiom, among them "No Vacancy," "Sweet Temptation," and "Divorce Me C.O.D."

Travis was given a Pioneer of Country Music Award in 1974 and was inducted into the Songwriters Hall of Fame in 1970 and the Country Music Hall of fame in 1977.

William E. Lightfoot

References

Green, Archie. 1972. *Only a Miner: Studies in Recorded Coal-Mining Songs.* Urbana: University of Illinois Press, pp. 279–367.

Humphrey, Mark. 1982–1984. Merle Travis Talking to Mark Humphrey. *Old-Time Music* 36:6–10, 37:20–24, 38:14–18, 39:22–25.

Travis, Merle. 1979. *The Merle Travis Story.* CMH Record 9018.

Wolfe, Charles K. 1982. *Kentucky Country: Folk and Country Music of Kentucky.* Lexington: University Press of Kentucky, pp. 109–118.

Trickster

Considered by scholars of religion as humanity's most ancient god. "Trickster" is a truly universal figure with many faces and roles. In North America, he is ubiquitous in Native American lore, where he takes the form of Coyote, Rabbit, Raven, and others. He is equally strong in African American traditions, where he is seen as Brer Rabbit, John, and Shine, among others. He appears in the traditions of yet other minority groups, such as the Latter-Day Saints and European immigrant groups. He lurks in European antiquity in the form of Hermes, Loki, and Christ, but—provocatively—it is now difficult to identify anything in the folklore of mainstream Euro-America that smacks of Trickster, unless the tall tale is rooted in that tradition.

Trickster is more likely to be discovered through roles and functions than through labels and appearances. As the scholarly name suggests, one of the characteristic activities of Trickster is the playing of tricks. Inordinately clever, he frequently lures others into humiliation, injury, or even death. He gives false hope of new skills and powers, but others are harmed by the attempt to emulate him. He betrays anyone who trusts him, and, in the venerable tradition of con artists everywhere, he reveals their venality and stupidity. Even in the grimmest of situations, as when he murders babies, he is likely to leave a propped-up smiling head as a final trick for the returning parent. As if to redress the balance, he reveals his own astounding ignorance of even the most basic realities, as in the story of his challenge of Rattlesnake to a biting contest, with fatal results to himself. In truth, Trickster is as much tricked as tricker in the countless stories about his dealings with others, often leaving the analyst to ponder who is the Trickster.

Especially notable in the Native American Trickster, but present in his alter egos in other traditions, is the trait of heedless self-gratification. For the Trickster, to feel a desire is to satisfy it. The impulse alone is adequate motivation, and there are no strictures of morality or rationality to impede him. This characteristic has led to major Freudian interpretations of some of the Trickster plots, for much of his behavior seems a clear illustration of the meaning of the id, neatly separated as it is from the ego and superego. In many texts, Trickster appears as a figure bent on self-gratification at any cost, and he is as heedless of personal consequences as he is of the cost to others. For him there is no past or future, only the present fulfillment. Paul Radin and others have pointed out his preconscious state, as seen in peculiarities such as his penis kept rolled up in a pack on his back, and his anus, which can be dealt with (and punished) as a separate person. As an alternate psychological viewpoint, C.G. Jung, in an essay included in a publication of Radin's study, approached the figure as a cultural expression of the archetype of the "Shadow," which exists in all humans. While there is not likely to be any sort of unanimity concerning psychological interpretations of folktale figures, both the Freudian and the Jungian perspectives offer helpful approaches to the complexities of the Trickster, which manages to confound all simple attempts at understanding.

In any case, his identification as the personification of the id makes Trickster the perfect antihero by almost any definition. He is the individual who is isolated from society and who has no concern for it. He is the one creature without goals for himself or others. He is a menace to society without being its enemy, and he brings disaster to others without any malevolence. He is the rule breaker par excellence: He mocks religious rituals, scorns the "proper way to do anything from cooking to war, has sex with his grandmother, and betrays all trusts." Since the Native American worldview stresses the ability of powerful people to do shape shifting, he even can transform himself into a woman and marry (temporarily) the son of a chief, thus mocking even sex, marriage, and family. Trickster is the breaker of taboos, and it does not take full Freudian analysis to see in that fact the source of his humor. There is something simultaneously horrifying and satisfying about his breaking the rules all humans in society chafe at. He does, it has been observed, what everyone would like to do, but cannot, whether because of fear, reason, or virtue. Trickster is the ultimate poor role model for living in community, and thus the opposite of the hero.

Despite his antiheroic role, however, he also manages sometimes to be the benefactor of society. In a fascinating set of Native American stories, he participates in the creation of the present order. In some cases, he creates good things just by accident or as a by-product of activities with other purposes. In other cases, as in the Iroquoian creation stories, he alters the creator's work to make it less perfect, as when he changes fruits to pine cones and makes the rivers run only in one direction, so humans will have to work hard to paddle upstream. In these myths, it is clear that Trickster is operating at some level of "divinity" and is connected with the primal forces of the universe. The scholarly label "Transformer" has thus been affixed to this form of Trickster as a way of warning people that something far beyond the playing of tricks is involved here.

The Trickster-Transformer is, somewhat confusingly, at least partly a heroic figure. He embodies powers that are legitimate goals for humans, and he does, in fact, accomplish good things for human society, which is worth emulating. He is thus to some extent a hero, after all. This heroic trait is seen much more clearly in African American Tricksters, where the trait of cleverness seems to rise to prominence in a way not seen in Native American traditions. The African antecedents were strongly embodied in American slave traditions, and the resulting tales of Uncle Remus have become a part of all Americans' lore. Br'er Rabbit, clever nemesis of the more physically powerful animals, does not stand alone, however, because the more human "John" is still outwitting "Old Marster" and other representatives of the dominant White society. The cleverness of the Trickster is probably the ancient characteristic that transformed the figure into a protest element for African Americans, for Trickster is the appropriate hero for the powerless—he is clever, glib, and extraordinarily intelligent; he understands his opponents much better than they understand him, uses their weaknesses against them, humiliates them repeatedly, and yet maintains his mask of submissiveness.

In Trickster traditions as in so many other aspects, North America became a melting pot. As alien versions of the figure came together, new syntheses arose. One of the most debated occurred in the Southeast, where European Tricksters vanished as African and Native American Tricksters merged. The Hare of the Eastern Woodlands met the Rabbit of Africa, and motifs were exchanged, leaving scholars to argue for the primacy of one over the other for more than a century. Aurelio M. Espinosa, in studying one single tale, argued that the complexities of the relationships of European and African folklore before reaching the New World have to be taken into account, and he found that the Spanish influence in the American Southeast was more powerful than is usually thought. It is unfortunate that the folklore of both groups was collected late, for if earlier data were available it might be possible to trace the changes in plot, form, and function of the Tricksters in the emerging South. It seems clear that the exchanges went in both directions, but it would have been of great interest to be able to follow the steps in the evolution of the new syntheses.

In view of the multiple roles and characteristics of the Tricksters in North America alone, it probably is a mistake to lump all of them together under the one categorical name "Trickster." Yet, there are unifying themes that make that act thought provoking, if not reasonable. As noted above, the psychological interpreters have found universal meaning in some aspects of the Trickster, and those discussions cannot be easily dismissed. One scholar, Mary Douglas, has offered a philosophical argument from another perspective. Focusing on African Tricksters, she suggests that the ultimate function of the figure is to remind people embedded in culture that their culture is itself an invention and is, therefore, limited. From that view, the Trickster is a god far beyond cultural gods, one whose awesome power is that he represents Reality beyond culture. There is some support for that interpretation in the Native American tradition of sacred clowns, which can be seen as a ritual-theatrical version of the Trickster in several ways. As commentators have pointed out, there is much to ponder in the fact of cultural institutionalization of ritual figures whose main function is to mock the rituals in which they appear.

It is clear that mainstream American culture does not permit mockery of the sacred, much less insist upon it, and Douglas' perspective at least gives some insight into why the obnoxious behavior of the Trickster-clown might be considered so important. That argument may help explain why the Trickster seems to have vanished from European American folklore, for mainstream American religion and philosophy seem to have little tolerance for prophetic critiques, tricksters, or sacred clowns. It may be that the contemporary Tricksters in mainstream American society will have to be sought not in folklore, but in popular culture, in such phenomena as comic strips and rock bands.

George E. Lankford

References

Dorson, Richard M. 1958. *American Negro Folktales.* Bloomington: Indiana University Press.

Douglas, Mary. 1968. The Social Control of Cognition: Some Factors in Joke Perception. *Man,* n.s., 3:361–376.

Dundes, Alan. 1965. African Tales among the North American Indians. *Southern Folklore Quarterly* 29:207–219.

Espinosa, Aurelio M. 1930. Notes on the Origin and History of the Tar-Baby Story. *Journal of American Folklore* 43:129–209.

Gerber, A. 1893. Uncle Remus Traced to the Old World. *Journal of American Folklore* 6:245–257.

Radin, Paul. 1956. *The Trickster.* New York: Schocken.

Thompson, Stith. 1946. The Trickster Cycle. In *The Folktale.* New York: Holt, Rinehart, and Winston, pp. 319–328.

Wilson, William A. 1983. Trickster Tales and the Location of Cultural Boundaries: A Mormon Example. *Journal of Folklore Research* 20:55–66.

See also Coyote; Local-Character Anecdote

Truckers' Folklore

Oral traditions shared by American truck drivers. Because they work in relative isolation and need timely information, truckers rely heavily on informal oral networks. Though handy and often entertaining, these networks encourage fantastic tales, both true and untrue. Tales of the small town—name forgotten—where one man served as patrolman, judge, jailer, banker, and telegraph employee may be safely discredited only because a trucker would never forget the name of such a town. Equally fantastic stories about a scalemaster extorting money from truckers (and that scale having been bombed) are true. The following riddle-joke (which has variations among other groups) illustrates the problem. "Q: What's the difference between a fairy tale and a trucker's story? A: The fairy tale starts out, 'Once upon a time,' and the trucker's story starts, 'This ain't no lie.'"

Truckers have unique versions of urban legends. Rumors of the truck in which a driver died (and literally exploded after several summer days) parallel the urban legend about a cheaply

available "Death Car" whose successive owners cannot rid it of its smell. In the trucking variant, the smell, which has resisted sandblasting, causes heart attacks and blackouts, and the death truck's number is said to be the "Beast's" number, 666.

Stories drawn from trucking tradition indicate that truckers may once have enjoyed their own versions of "The Vanishing Hitchhiker," though these are not in circulation in the 1990s. In those versions, it is the truck driver who vanishes mysteriously. In one version, a rescued rider conveys the driver's greetings to truck-stop employees and is told that years before, the trucker drove off a cliff to avoid a stalled school bus. His ghost now helps motorists. In another variant, the ghost adopts and trains a fledgling driver before disappearing, leaving the newcomer with his truck.

Two other genres are the cautionary tale and the Trickster tale. In most cautionary tales, a truck driver suffers for unconscientious or noncollegial behavior. Disasters (spilled, spoiled, or stolen loads, collisions, arrests, and so forth) follow shoddy work, failure to help colleagues, or refusing radio communication. Trickster tales, on the other hand, illustrate cleverness in fooling law-enforcement personnel, toll-road authorities, shippers, and occasionally even dispatchers. Tricks range from practical operating tips to the impractical tales of a man who avoided punishment by pouring coffee on his il-

legal log book and claiming that his urine bottle (to be used by truckers when they can't or won't stop; more a joke than a reality) had spilled. Both genres illustrate an ethic of personal responsibility: drivers who do not adhere to that ethic are punished, as are officials who challenge it.

CB (citizens band) radio use in the 1990s is more subtle than the flashy styles popularized in the 1970s. Numbered signals have faded, leaving only standards such as ten-four (agreement), and ten-twenty (location). Meanings of other words have shifted: the once-friendly address, "good buddy," is now considered an insult. And older terms (like "disco-lights" for the signal lights atop police cars) are being revived. Most surviving terms are practical metaphors, like "chicken coop" (scalehouse), "load of postholes" (empty trailer), or "bingo card" (permit stickers). Others compare trucks and humans: Driving is "running," the cab's front may be a "nose," an overturned vehicle is "belly-up," nontruckers are "four-wheelers," and prostitutes are often "commercial carriers." Because one shouldn't "walk" (overlap speaking) on someone else's transmission, many traditionalized speech patterns, like saying "come on" or "'four" after speaking, reflect etiquette shaped by the CB.

Handles (CB nicknames) are social overtures, as the names "Country Convert," "Rambling Rabbi," "Florida Boy," and possibly "Moonshine" indicate. "Salt Shaker," who collects salt and pepper shakers, is often hailed by "salt shakers" who salt winter roads. And the handle "Eightball" has been used by both a pool player and a balding African American trucker. Other CB names express images of trucking, as do "Lone Wolf" and "Midnight Runner." And since a shared sense of persecution can evoke community among truckers, most can identify with "Outlaw," "Trouble," and "Nobody." Because truckers use the CB for everyday communication, they are unlikely to use sexy names as their primary handles, though some adopt secondary handles in order to flirt or joke anonymously. Some truckers clown, pretending to be drivers for another company; when other drivers return the "favor," this creates a running gag.

Running gags are popular among truckers. For example, the straight line, "Be quiet so I can get some sleep," predictably elicits a chorus of "Turn your radio off!" Neither the straight man nor the respondents actually believe anyone would ask an entire truck stop to refrain from talking; they are mocking their own radio use. Some running gags convey social values by echoing belligerent speakers with a barrage of caricatured threats. Others are less didactic: Truckers caught in the same traffic jams have been known to experiment with limericks and animal imitations. Not surprisingly, running gags are most common in traffic jams, truck stops, and other situations where killing time is a shared goal.

One running gag is part of a cycle of jokes about a company we'll call Huge. A Huge truck in the act of parking elicits a chorus of "Watch out! Huge's backing up!" (In contrast, Huge drivers tell of a colleague who sports a striped cane and dark glasses as a gag.) In another joke, a Huge driver who is reprimanded for ignoring a crashed colleague responds, "Ha! We don't have wheels on top of our trucks." The jokes are also visual: Graffiti beside toilet-paper rolls sometimes reads "Huge job applications." In this and other cases, jokes are used to force collegiality: Huge drivers are snubbed or teased because their company is considered unethical.

All of these folklore forms help truckers discuss and share feelings about their work. Slang, jokes, and narrative traditions depict conditions and convey values important to professionalism, and CB handles allow truckers from diverse backgrounds to announce identity with a minimum of fuss. But shared culture does not mean homogeneity. Within the traditions outlined, new diversities have arisen; haulers of various commodities, drivers for each company, union men, and independents all have unique traditions. If specialization and diversity are tests of true cultures, then trucking delivers.

Clover Williams

Turnbo, Silas Claiborn (1844–1925)

Pioneer collector of Ozark folklore and oral history. Turnbo amassed one of the most important collections of Ozark material. He acted on his own without funding, working intuitively without prior guidelines and often without much encouragement. Turnbo's collecting began as early as 1866 and continued at least until 1913. His earliest interviews were, apparently, done incidentally; whenever he met someone with worthwhile information, he usually made notes and filed them away for later use. It was not until the 1890s that he started thinking in terms of a larger project, one in which he actively sought out old-time Ozarkers who would supply him with details about the past.

Turnbo's material was first published in numerous columns about "old-times" in several Arkansas and Missouri newspapers from 1898 to 1907. Two self–published books, both titled *Fireside Stories of the Early Days in the Ozarks,* appeared in 1905 and 1907 and registered disappointing sales. Attempts to convert his massive collection into profitable books were unsuccessful. In 1913 Turnbo sold his collection to William Elsey Connelley, secretary of the Kansas State Historical Society, for $27.50—the only money Turnbo ever received for his work. Portions of the Turnbo manuscripts made their way to various libraries in Arkansas and Missouri, and in 1987 six volumes of Turnbo's stories were printed without contextual commentary.

Turnbo's collectanea is still valuable because the data are very detailed and the documentation is good. It is strongest in the areas of material culture and folk narrative.

W.K. McNeil

References

Allen, Desmond Walls, ed. 1987. *Turnbo's Tales of the Ozarks.* 6 vols. Conway, AR: Arkansas Research.

Twain, Mark (1835–1910)

Pen name of Samuel Clemens, best known for works set on the Mississippi River, including *The Adventures of Tom Sawyer* (1876), *Life on the Mississippi* (1883), and *Adventures of Huckleberry Finn* (1885). Twain was an outstanding local-color writer, one whose skills lay in capturing the peculiar characters, humor, mannerisms, and settings of American regions.

Mark Twain in 1907. Photo Underwood & Underwood. Library of Congress.

Twain was born and grew up in Missouri, learning journalism and printing from his brother. He had a short-lived career as a riverboat pilot on the Mississippi River just before the Civil War. Then he accompanied his brother west to Nevada and California, working as a reporter and writer from 1861 to 1866. He eventually married and settled in Elmira, New York, and later in Hartford, Connecticut, although he traveled widely.

Twain was a charter member of the American Folklore Society in 1888, along with a few other American authors such as Edward Eggleston and Joel Chandler Harris. Twain was already aware of the popular interest in American folklore. In 1882 he had met Joel Chandler Harris and George Washington Cable in New Orleans and proposed a national tour, with each author speaking and reading from his own (folklore–based) works. Harris refused because he was too shy for stage appearances, but Twain and Cable did tour from November 1884 to February 1885. Like the other writers who helped form the American Folklore Society, however, Twain dropped out after only a few years, probably because the scientific interests of the society's ethnologists did not coincide with his own interests.

Many of Twain's publications are of interest to folklorists. He is widely known for his ability with tall tales (such as "The Notorious Jumping Frog of Calaveras County" and, in *Roughing It* (1872), "Grandfather's Old Ram") as well as humorous tales on himself (such as "The Private History of a Campaign that Failed" and "The Story of a Speech"). His works not only include examples of many forms of folklore, but also point out their value in regional cultures. The forms he recorded and commented on range widely, from folk speech to folk customs, from folk art to folk games. His masterpiece, *Adventures of Huckleberry Finn,* is a storehouse of folklore. The book's plot begins with a folk belief (Huck's flicking a spider into a candle, killing it, and, therefore, causing bad luck—and his feelings of helplessness in not knowing how to avoid the bad luck). Later chapters contain many other examples of folklore, from the "witch–riding" of Jim in Chapter 2 to a list of "signs" in Chapter 8. In fact, *Huckleberry Finn* is arguably a work *about* folklore, preferring it to Tom Sawyer's "book-learning."

Twain captured in his works the sense of humor, character types, and customs of the West and Mississippi River region. Twain's works gave folklore prominence and demonstrated how rich and significant folklore is in American culture.

Eric L. Montenyohl

References

Hoffman, Daniel. 1961. *Form and Fable in American Fiction.* New York: Oxford University Press.

Kaplan, Justin. 1966. *Mr. Clemens and Mark Twain: A Biography.* New York: Simon and Schuster.

LeMaster, J.R., and James D. Wilson. 1993. *The Mark Twain Encyclopedia.* New York: Garland.

U

UFO Lore

Narratives and beliefs concerning unidentified flying objects, supposed extraterrestrial spaceships visiting the Earth. Gallup Polls indicate that nearly all Americans have heard of UFOs, several million claim to have sighted one, and approximately half of the population believes they are real and not illusory. On this basis, UFOs qualify as perhaps the most vigorous paranormal belief of the modern age.

Pilot Kenneth Arnold watched nine silvery, disk-like objects fly in front of Mt. Rainier at supersonic speeds on June 24, 1947. The press summarized his description with the term "flying saucers," beginning a continuous symbiosis of UFO lore and the mass media. Hundreds of people throughout the country reported these disks over the next two weeks. Individual narratives of personal experience count as the basic unit of UFO lore, but several times since 1947 the occasional sighting has grown to a wave of hundreds, even thousands, of reports coming from wide areas over a short period of time, usually a few weeks to a month. Flying-saucer reports spread worldwide soon after Arnold's sighting.

The typical reported UFO experience is the unexpected observation of a mysterious aerial object by persons going about their everyday activities. It comes and goes, leaving behind only puzzlement and wonder. UFO reports range in complexity from descriptions of a distant light in the sky to close encounters, when witnesses observe the craft in detail or even glimpse its occupants. Strangest of all are abduction reports. Short aliens with bulbous heads and enormous eyes capture humans from cars or bedrooms, float the captives inside a UFO, and subject them to a bizarre and painful medical examination. It often includes the harvest of eggs and sperm to create hybrid alien-human children. These cases have burgeoned in number since the 1970s.

UFO beliefs have proved fertile for elaboration and extension. Some investigators speculate that "ancient astronauts" landed in the distant past, building such monuments as the Great Pyramid and inspiring ancient myths. Others attribute the disappearance of ships in the Bermuda Triangle and alleged mutilations of cattle in the West to UFO activity. A cosmic drama of good versus evil plays out in the conflicting opinions of "contactees," who claim to have met beautiful "Space Brothers" concerned with the salvation of mankind, and the abductees, who claim to have encountered dwarfish aliens bent on some exploitative and soulless project.

A rumor-legend persisting from 1947 in the 1990s concerns the crash of a UFO in New Mexico. The Air Force recovered the debris and several alien bodies, which have remained hidden ever after. A government conspiracy to hide the truth about alien visitation is an enduring theme of UFO lore. Sinister "Men in Black" intimidate witnesses to remain silent, and, according to an especially florid rumor, a government pact with aliens allowed them to build underground bases in the Southwest. The agreement went sour, and in the 1980s President Reagan ordered the "Star Wars" project not to defend against the Soviets, but to flush out the unwelcome invaders.

The folk of UFO lore divide into two camps—proponents and opponents—locked in spirited dispute over UFO reality. Proponents range from interested believers, to eccentric cranks, to serious "ufologists." The latter group investigates cases, writes about the phenomenon, and organizes societies to carry on ufological research. These societies publish periodicals that open the main channel of contact among the far-flung membership. Ufologists argue that once they separate hoaxes and misidentifications from the UFO record, a residue of detailed, well-documented cases stands as persuasive evidence that a genuinely mysterious phenomenon exists. It includes seemingly physical machines with capabilities surpassing any known aircraft, and occupants of unearthly appearance.

Opponents assert that all cases reduce to conventional causes with no residue left over. These skeptics point out media coverage and science fiction as sources of expectation, while the proneness to fantasy of some witnesses and leading questions from investigators seeking to confirm their personal beliefs suffice to realize even the most exotic tales. They also observe that UFO reports are simply not strange enough; they replicate the content of legends about ghost lights, demonic encounters, or fairy kidnap, preserving plot and function while transforming outmoded supernatural traditions into the up-to-date guise of extraterrestrial visitation.

Thomas E. Bullard

References

Bullard, Thomas E. 1989. UFO Abduction Reports: The Supernatural Kidnap Narrative Returns in Technological Guise. *Journal of American Folklore* 102:147–170.

Clark, Jerome. 1990. *UFOs in the 1980s.* Detroit: Apogee.

———. 1992. *The Emergence of a Phenomenon: UFOs from the Beginning through 1959.* Detroit: Omnigraphics.

Evans, Hilary, ed. 1987. *UFOs, 1947–1987: The Forty-Year Search for an Explanation.* London: Fortean Tomes.

Hynek, J. Allen. 1972. *The UFO Experience: A Scientific Inquiry.* Chicago: Henry Regnery.

Jacobs, David Michael. 1975. *The UFO Controversy in America.* Bloomington: Indiana University Press.

Peebles, Curtis. 1994. *Watch the Skies! A Chronicle of the Flying Saucer Myth.* Washington, DC: Smithsonian Institution.

Vallee, Jacques. 1969. *Passport to Matgonia: From Folklore to Flying Saucers.* Chicago: Henry Regnery.

See also Nuclear Lore

Ukrainian Americans

Immigrants to Canada and the United States and their descendants from a territory in eastern Europe now officially called Ukraine. This country borders with Romania, Hungary, Slovakia, Poland, Belarus, and Russia. When the first Ukrainians came to North America, their territories were part of the Austro-Hungarian and Russian Empires. Ukrainians arrived in three waves: 1870s–1914, 1920–1939, and 1947–1955.

Ukrainian immigrants during the first wave settled in Pennsylvania, where they found work in the mines, as well as in New York, New Jersey, Michigan, Ohio, Illinois, Connecticut, Massachusetts, and Rhode Island, usually being employed in factories there. A small number settled elsewhere and became farmers. In Canada the first wave of Ukrainian immigrants settled mainly on homesteads on the prairies, where a significant number are still involved in agriculture; others worked in mines and on railway gangs. In the 1990s, Ukrainian communities are found in major cities of both Canada and the United States.

Ukrainians who came to North America derived from a variety of dialectal regions. The majority of immigrants in the first wave had little or no education but a rich oral lore. The settlement patterns in the New World (either urban or with huge distances between farms) did not resemble the village or small-town life to which they had been accustomed. Also, the new settlers now found themselves in a foreign-language milieu. These factors weakened the traditional oral-lore processes among Ukrainians, especially among those born in North America. A form of bilingualism, sometimes termed "macaronism," developed among Ukrainian Americans in which English words became part of Ukrainian-language texts and vice versa. An example of this is found in the following lyrics (with English words italicized):

Skrypky hraly i tsymbaly; *Dzhoniz Meri* tantsiuvaly.
Tantsiuvaly *dyfrent* valets; *Dzhoni Meri* stav na palets.

[The violins were playing, and so was a hammered dulcimer; Johnny was dancing with Mary.
They were dancing a different waltz; Johnny stepped on Mary's toe.]

In many instances, Ukrainian names were Anglicized (Bill and Bob substituted for the Ukrainian given names Vasyl and Bohdan) or, North American place names were humorously Ukrainianized *(Derzhy syto* [hold the sieve] was used for Jersey City and *Mizerota* [poverty, wretchedness] for Minnesota).

Many examples of minor verbal genres—proverbs, proverbial sayings, riddles, and the like—are found in the speech of Ukrainian North Americans. Proverbs included "Not every pig comes on four feet" and "A good wife and health are the greatest treasures." Riddles are found in song texts or early childhood education material, for example: "There are no windows or doors yet the house is full of people"—Answer: Pumpkin or melon seeds, or "Who died yet was not born?"—Answer: Adam. Rhymes and folk poetry also were part of Ukrainian settlers' cultural baggage. A great number of these texts were produced in North America, and others were published in newspapers or in separate collections. One popular example is Fedyk's *Pisni imigrantiv pro Kanadu i Avstriiu* (Immigrant Songs about Canada and Austria) (1908).

North America as a land of milk and honey became the subject of myths and legends. After generations of Ukrainian settlement in America, stories appeared to "prove" that Ukrainians arrived in the New World much earlier than most people believed. (A certain Lavrentey Bohoon supposedly accompanied Captain John Smith to Jamestown.) Ukrainian folktales also made their way to the New World. Some were repeated with minimal variations. For example, an anecdote is told in which a husband on his way to town is instructed by his wife to buy her a pair of boots, " *bom bosa*" (because I go about barefoot). He returns home without them, saying that "Bombosa" boots are not sold in any of the stores. Other stories went through major transformations as with the following tale:

There, in Winnipeg, I was told about this Dowbush. That these big landowners had a big orchard in their village; well and right in the midst of it they would gather. Well and there was Dowbush.

A certain woman whose name was Zazulie [cuckoo bird] . . . Well and . . . "Crawl up there Zazulie!"

And she crawled up there on the fruit tree, and he shot her because she was Zazulie [a cuckoo bird]. Dowbush,

Easter eggs, painted by Maria Brama, using traditional Ukrainian motifs. Chicago, 1977. Photo Carl Fleischhauer. American Folklife Center.

he says, shot a cuckoo bird on a tree. (quoted in Rudnyc'kyj 1956:79)

In Ukrainian folk tradition, the real Dowbush was, in fact, a highwayman hero who robbed the rich and gave to the poor.

Folksong texts had greater staying power than narrative lore, partly because the melody, meter, and rhyme served as mnemonic devices. It is not unusual to hear third- or fourth-generation Ukrainians in North America singing folk or popular Ukrainian songs without understanding the lyrics. A great many Ukrainian folksongs are of a lyrical nature. For example,

[O] the cuckoo cooed,
The cuckoo cooed.
O my sweetheart is in the old country,
And I, poor one, am here.
And the cuckoo cooed
On the wide bridge,
"Do come, do come, my sweetheart,
At least visit me."
My head is aching so much
That I'm squinting my eyes.
There's no one to ask me
Why I'm worried.

Other folksongs are more historical, including the recitative epic *Duma* forms (performed in North America almost exclusively by professional singers often accompanied by the national Ukrainian instrument, the *bandura*). Folk music performed by North American Ukrainians has changed from traditional tunes to more popular ones, although polkas and waltzes are still common at Ukrainian weddings. Ukrainian folk music is performed by groups ranging from smaller bands with a traditional instrument, such as the *tsymbaly* (hammered dulcimer), to the more elitist and urban band. The hurdy-gurdy *(lira)*, which was popular at the turn of the 20th century when a great many Ukrainians came to North America, is in the 1990s almost unknown among Ukrainians in the New World. Other instruments, such as the *drymba* (Jew's harp) have become exotic.

Many of the customs practiced and believed in by Ukrainians in the old country survived in North America, at least in the first and second generations, and superstitions are not uncommon among Ukrainians. For example, Ukrainians may not greet guests or pass items to one another across a threshold for fear of bad luck. Black cats crossing a path bring bad luck just as they do with mainstream North Americans. Unmarried persons should not sit at a corner of the table during a meal, because then they won't get married for seven years. Some superstitions exhibit white magic, such as, for example, throwing knives and forks on the ground when storm clouds approach someone's farm to avoid hail damage.

Traditional calendar customs and rites of passage were much richer in the old country than in the New World. In North America, only Christmas (known for its meatless meal on the eve of the holiday and the mumming and caroling activities that go on almost to Epiphany) and Easter (preceded by ritual whipping on Palm Sunday and the decorating of special Easter eggs that make up part of the food basket blessed at the church service) are celebrated by the majority of the Ukrainian American population. Some communities visit with the dead and have their graves blessed either on the Sunday after Easter or on Whitsunday.

Parish feast days and weddings are occasions for community celebrations, as are the newer festivals that bring in visitors from several states or Canadian provinces. Ukrainian social dances performed in the old country on Sundays and at weddings to regional folk tunes survived to some degree in North America. A uniquely North American *kolomyika* or *hopak* evolved in the 1960s, combining the spontaneity of social dance with the spectacle of rehearsed acrobatic moves from a staged dance. Ukrainian dance on stage has become an extremely productive and visible symbol of Ukrainian culture in North America.

The once popular one-act plays have either disappeared or made room for more professional performances. Some common folk gestures used by Ukrainians include the *figa z makom,* performed with the thumb sticking out between the index and long finger signifying a big "nothing" for the recipient; the flipping of the long finger against one's throat signals a "drink" or "drinking." A gesture for a stupid act or stupidity is often made by slapping one's forehead or by pointing one's index finger to one's temple and rotating it back and forth. Hide-and-seek and other chasing games have been popular among children, and various traditional card games, such as *troyka* and *kaiser* among Ukrainian adults.

When Ukrainians moved into unsettled or uncultivated parts of North America, they tended to construct the traditional thatched-roof buildings with clay ovens or other structures they had possessed in eastern Europe. In some cases, temporary dugouts were constructed before a pioneer family could move into more comfortable housing. But Ukrainians soon adapted to mainstream framed-lumber construction, although the inside of the dwelling would often be decorated with religious icons or other important cultural symbols, such as portraits of the poets Shevchenko, Franko, or Lesia Ukrainka. Such decorations can also be found in modern city houses or apartments. Many Ukrainian churches were built in the first half of the 20th century, undergoing several unique architectural stages and producing many unmistakable rural and urban landmarks across the continent.

Folk arts and crafts have been maintained more than oral folklore expressions since the command of one's ancestral language is not necessary to produce these items. The best-known examples are the batik-decorated Easter eggs called *pysanky,* which are sold throughout the calendar year. The embroidery of shirts and other forms of clothing as well as ritual towels is another tradition retained in North America. Folk costumes are especially valued by members of Ukrainian dancing ensembles. The more ambitious a repertoire of an ensemble, the greater the likelihood of its members possessing a variety of folk costumes. In some families, during the main religious or community celebrations, the wearing of embroidered items of folk costumes is encouraged. Folk-medicine rituals persist, notably for healing victims of the evil eye.

Ritual foods were mentioned above as part of calendar customs. The meals prepared for Christmas (with twelve meatless dishes) and Easter (including sausage, eggs, butter, cheese, and *paska,* or Easter bread) tend to emphasize the Lenten and post–Lenten periods respectively. Other folk foods for which the Ukrainian kitchen is known include *holubtsi*

(stuffed cabbage rolls), *kapusniak* (sauerkraut soup), *pyrohy-varenyky* (dumplings), *studenets* (headcheese), *kovbasa* (garlic sausage), *oseledtsi* (herring), and in some cases *salo* (pork fat). Ukrainians in general do not shy away from alcoholic drinks. A well known Ukrainian proverb is: *De kovbasa i charka, mynet'sia i svarka* (When you have garlic sausage and a drinking cup, even an argument will cease). The lifestyle of Ukrainian settlers of east central Alberta from 1892 to the 1930s is represented at an outdoor museum named the Ukrainian Cultural Heritage Village, east of Edmonton, Alberta.

Bohdan Medwidsky

References

Canadian Museum of Civilization. 1989. *The Ukrainians in Canada, 1891–1991. Material History Bulletin* (Special Issue) 29.

———. 1991. *Art and Ethnicity: The Ukrainian Tradition in Canada.* Hull: Canadian Museum of Civilization.

Klymasz, Robert Bogdan. 1980. *Ukrainian Folklore in Canada.* New York: Arno.

Plaviuk, Volodymyr S. 1949. *Prypovidky, abo ukrains'ko-narodnia filosofiia* [Proverbs or Ukrainian Folk Philosophy]. Edmonton: Privately published.

Rudnyc'kyj, J.B. 1956. *Ukrainian-Canadian Folklore and Dialectological Texts.* Vol. 1. Winnipeg: Ukrainian Free Academy of Sciences.

Subtelny, Orest. 1991. *Ukrainians in North America: An Illustrated History.* Toronto: University of Toronto Press.

Uncle Remus

Fictional narrator of the 19th-century African American folklore compiled by Joel Chandler Harris. A Georgia journalist, Harris recorded the Uncle Remus stories depicting such characters as protagonist Brer Rabbit and his adversary Brer Fox. Folklorists consider Harris' interpretations, derived from internationally told folk motifs, to be the first compilation of authentic African American folklore.

While working on a Georgia plantation during the 1860s, Harris listened to slaves tell stories. In October 1876, as associate editor of the *Atlanta Constitution* newspaper, Harris created Uncle Remus, a composite of the slaves he knew, as the narrator of dialect sketches. The original Uncle Remus character was described as a freedman living in postbellum Atlanta who visited the *Atlanta Constitution* office to complain about Reconstruction politics.

Inspired by William Owens' article, "Folklore of the Southern Negroes," in the December 1877 *Lippincott's* magazine, outlining the story "Buh Rabbit and the Tar Baby," Harris molded Uncle Remus into a plantation storyteller of animal fables. "The Story of Mr. Rabbit and Mr. Fox as Told by Uncle Remus," appeared in the July 20, 1879, *Atlanta Constitution* under the heading "Negro Folklore."

Harris portrayed Uncle Remus telling his stories to a White boy. A humorous, wise narrator, Uncle Remus recited his allegories, using animals such as rabbits and turtles as heroes who outsmarted wolves and foxes. Brer Rabbit manipulated situations so that the weak triumphed over the strong. Brer Rabbit's nemesis, Brer Fox, countered traditional European animal tales in which fox, not a rabbit, usually played the role of the cunning hero. Explaining such themes as pride, revenge, and self-preservation, Uncle Remus justified Brer Rabbit's behavior no matter how cruel or violent.

When he recorded his stories, Harris was unaware that a body of scientific folklore scholarship existed or that parallels of his Uncle Remus tales circulated in other cultures. Receiving letters from folklorists and philologists, including John Wesley Powell of the Smithsonian Institution in Washington, DC, about the ethnological significance of his tales, Harris began to study folklore.

Folklorists reviewed his first book, *Uncle Remus: His Songs and His Sayings* (1880), as a valuable collection of southern black folklore previously unknown outside the region. In 1881 Thomas Frederick Crane wrote the first significant essay about Harris as a folklorist, noting parallels in other tales and encouraging more formal research of Black folklore. By 1888 Joseph Jacobs expressed a theory that Uncle Remus' origins were in India, where animal fables featured hares. An essay in the *Journal of American Folklore* initiated an ongoing debate among folklorists of whether Uncle Remus had African or Indian origins. Other folklorists focused on Harris' use of dialect.

Harris joined the American Folklore Society and read folklore theory, embracing a comparative approach. For his second book, *Nights with Uncle Remus* (1883), Harris researched in the Harvard University library's folklore collection and wrote a thirty-two-page, footnoted Introduction, defining his methodology for selecting tales. Harris emphasized oral collection, verification to ensure authenticity, and study of parallels and variations. He compared his stories to animal legends in other countries.

While some folklorists believed that Southern Blacks had appropriated stories from these societies, Harris argued that the Uncle Remus tales revealed unique aspects of African American culture; he noted that slaves in cotton-, tobacco-, and rice-growing areas of the South had developed differing versions of folktales. To provide examples, he created the character African Jack, a Sea Island slave who told Uncle Remus tales in a gullah dialect. Additional characters, the Virginia-born cook Aunt Tempy and house girl Tildy, recited their versions of each story.

By the 1890s, Harris shunned the study of folklore. David D. Wells, in his article "Evolution in Folklore" in the May 1892 *Popular Science Monthly*, suggested that Harris had incorporated aspects of White culture to alter the original Uncle Remus tales to make Blacks seem more civilized. An angry Harris realized that folklorists who promoted the theory of cultural evolution were using his tales to declare that Blacks were culturally inferior to Whites and to criticize Black folklore. Harris denounced their methods and abandoned the study of comparative folklore.

In his third Uncle Remus book, *Uncle Remus and His Friends* (1892), Harris described himself as a casual folklore collector with no systematic method of acquisition. He stated that his folktales were valuable merely for enjoyment and their insight into human nature and moral themes. He satirized folklorists in his 1898 story "The Late Mr. Watkins of Georgia: His Relation to Oriental Folk-Lore."

Harris focused on publishing plantation worksongs and hymns in national magazines and *The Tar-Baby and Other Rhymes of Uncle Remus* (1904). He collected his remaining local legends in *Told by Uncle Remus* (1905) and *Uncle Remus and Brer Rabbit* (1907) but, to prevent his stories from being misinterpreted, he removed all of the characteristics that folklorists had targeted. Brer Rabbit became more precocious and Uncle Remus more fallible. These works provided grist for Walt Disney's 1946 animated movie *Song of the South*, which distorted the original tales.

After Harris died in 1908, *Uncle Remus and the Little Boy* (1910), *Uncle Remus Returns* (1918), *The Witch Wolf: An Uncle Remus Story* (1921), and *Seven Tales of Uncle Remus* (1948) were published in addition to new editions and translations.

Numerous articles and two book-length studies (Bickley 1981; Brookes 1950) have analyzed Uncle Remus' value as folklore. Scholars have criticized the Uncle Remus tales for their racist and sentimental stereotypes. Folklorists were disappointed that Harris rarely named his informants or provided data about each tale's collection. They also wished that he had narrated the Uncle Remus tales in their original settings instead of relying on the artificial framework using the boy. Still, Harris and Uncle Remus have been most credited for inspiring collectors and scholars of African American folklore.

Elizabeth D. Schafer

References

Baer, Florence. 1980. *Sources and Analogues of the Uncle Remus Tales*. Helsinki: Academia Scientiarum Fennica.

Bickley, R. Bruce, Jr. 1981. *Critical Essays on Joel Chandler Harris*. Boston: G.K. Hall.

Brookes, Stella Brewer. 1950. *Joel Chandler Harris, Folklorist*. Athens: University of Georgia Press.

Walton, David A. 1966. Joel Chandler Harris as Folklorist: A Reassessment. *Keystone Folklore Quarterly* 11:21–26.

See also Harris, Joel Chandler

Urban Folklore

Traditions and creative expressions that reflect general conditions of urban life or the history and traditions of a particular city. Urban folklore is a combination of folklore brought with the city's inhabitants from their former homes, and of folklore that arises in response to life in the city.

Each city is unique, reflecting the peoples who have come there and the forces—geographic, political, economic—that have compelled its growth. Cities provide fertile grounds for cultural interaction and exchange, and cities inevitably force cultures and traditions to change, often in unexpected new directions. Bringing together diverse peoples, with many values, beliefs, and customs, creates the possibility of new cultural exchanges, the interaction of unlikely combinations of traditions, as well as the potential for conflict and misunderstandings. Folklore, a continually changing reflection of val-

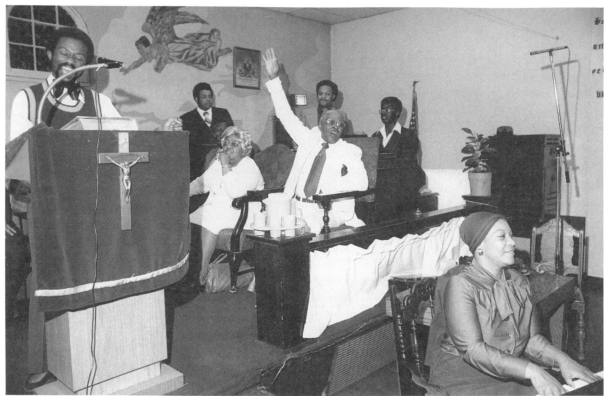

Friday-night service at McGee Temple, Church of God in Christ. Chicago, 1977. Photo Jonas Dovydenas. American Folklife Center.

ues and beliefs, helps explain how people make large and inhospitable cities into places small enough to nourish a human community.

Folklore that comes with new arrivals inevitably changes. Some things that do not speak to a community's new life in the city are "lost." Some musical instruments may no longer be played, and rural clothing styles are exchanged for the dress of the city. Children born in the city may not speak the language or dialect of their parents; they may speak English with an accent distinctive to that city, or even a particular part of a city. Other traditions, however, flourish, changing in response to the new place and growing stronger in their new homeland.

Folklore also arises in response to the life of the city, often in old forms but with new content. People have painted on walls for thousands of years; but in American cities of the 1960s, large mural paintings on buildings, reflecting Latino and African American experiences, became part of a unique grass-roots urban-art movement.

The study of folklore in Europe and the United States was originally focused on rural arts, traditions, and folklife. As recently as 1971, American folklorists were debating whether or not there was folklore in cities and, if so, what was it like? Beginning in the late 1960s and into the 1970s, folklorists and others began to pay more serious attention to the folklore of cities. Not-for-profit organizations directed by folklorists began to appear, the first in Memphis and New York City, later in Chicago, San Antonio, and elsewhere, to document, present, and support the arts and cultural expressions of the city and city dwellers. Lowell, Massachusetts, even be-

came, in the 1980s, the site of the first urban-industrial folklife heritage park, located in the city's textile mills.

Cities in the United States are centers of migration and immigration, reflecting the great movements of people off the land and into urban areas. Each city has a different mix of people who were searching for a better life, either economic or political. America's cities continue to draw immigrants from around the world. At the turn of the 20th century, urban areas reeled under the impact of thousands of immigrants from eastern and southern Europe and the Middle East. As the late 20th century's great wave of immigration continues, urban areas are growing even more diverse, bringing peoples of many different cultures and religions from Latin America and the Caribbean, Africa, and Asia.

Economic and political events around the world reverberate in American cities. Refugees from Laos, Ethiopia, and Guatemala declare their existence and concerns through cultural activities. In "port of entry" city neighborhoods, refugees and poor immigrants find themselves side by side. Vietnamese and Laotian New Year's celebrations, traditional dance groups (some professional, some for children), exhibitions and sales of crafts are important. These activities serve as sources of connection to their lost homes, help establish viable urban ethnic communities of support, and provide a source of income for some artists. As in the work of artists displaced from Eastern Europe after World War II who fled to the United States, themes of loss and longing for the homeland are often depicted in refugee artists' work.

The movement from rural areas to cities, one of the traditional sources of urban migration, continues. Urbanites with farming experience often become urban gardeners, growing the foods of their cuisine in vacant lots. In Philadelphia and Chicago, African American urban gardeners grow okra, mustard greens, and other necessities of Southern "soul food." "Hillbillies" worked in the automobile factories of Detroit. In New York City, Puerto Rican men build *casitas*, little houses in the traditional island style, on vacant lots. The *casitas* serve as clubhouses and reminders of home. *Vaqueros* transplanted from the *ranchos* of Mexico drive pickup trucks, wear Western hats and boots, teach their children to rope in city parks, and attend and participate in urban rodeos.

Verbal folklore flourishes in the city. "Urban legends," contemporary legendary stories, circulate in oral tradition in cities from coast to coast, telling of alligators in New York City sewers or of "The Vanishing Hitchhiker." Such legends are reported as fact in newspapers, or take on local reality: "The Vanishing Hitchhiker" appears in Chicago as "Resurrection Mary," who waits by Resurrection Cemetery on the city's southwest side.

Legends such as these help define a city's sense of itself as a particular place. Each city has its own ghost stories. New Orleans, for example, boasts a tour of haunted sites. Famous people can provide another good image for a city, such as Father Nelson Baker of Lackawanna, New York, who founded a famous orphanage that cared for generations of immigrant children. Stories of Father Baker have taken on miraculous overtones, with many of the themes of the stories of saints, such as the belief that his touch could heal the sick. In contrast, Al Capone and the image of the gangster have long dominated Chicago's image around the world.

Immigration to a city may change a community's stories. Mexican immigrant stories in Los Angeles, collected in the late 1960s, told of *La Llorona*, the weeping woman searching for her lost children. Some storytellers believed that *La Llorona* appeared only in Mexico; others thought that she could appear in Los Angeles. They also told stories of ghosts and religious tales of virgins and saints and recounted personal experiences, such as fighting with Pancho Villa. But, frequently, the legends and old stories are gradually forgotten. Storytelling continues, but people tell stories of their own lives, of immigration and struggle to make a new life, and of the events and everyday life while growing up in the city.

Southern cities, long dominated by the duality of White and Black residents, have a unique sense of tradition. Antebellum Charleston, South Carolina, was a cultural and economic center. One of the oldest cities in the United States, its communities of Orthodox Jews, French Huguenots, and African Americans are still important influences on the city's life. Throughout the older neighborhoods can be seen the beautiful tradition of fine wrought-iron fences created by African American craftsmen. The Charleston area is also home to an important community of African American sea-grass basket weavers, whose work can be traced back to the designs and techniques of African basketry.

Cities, where many people live close together, create urban stresses and strains. Graffiti art on subways, walls, and rooftops provides a way for young people without access to formal art resources to assert their presence in the urban scene. The owners of the property where the graffiti appears, however, feel threatened and must bear the cost of its removal. Transportation is an important theme. Modern ballads have immortalized the story of a passenger lost forever on the Boston subway and the notorious practice of towing cars to Chicago's city pounds—where cars are stripped of all usable parts before they can be reclaimed.

Urban crime victims tell true stories about their experiences, and fears about safety sometimes lead to frightening rumors. Police respond quickly, often with limited effect, to reassure the public when such rumors break out. Some rumors seem to erode the fabric of city life. One such rumor involved the courteous driving practice of a driver blinking headlights at cars driving at night without headlights on. A report circulated (often by fax) that drivers who blinked their headlights at another car would be shot as part of a gang initiation. Even when the story was debunked, many drivers stopped the practice. City dwellers felt betrayed by this rumor. In a place where neighbors often do not know one another, and a feeling of community is hard to create, this practice was a way to connect in a friendly fashion with an unknown "neighbor." Now, it was corrupted into a danger.

Cities may also concentrate feelings of distrust and misunderstanding. In urban African American communities, various rumors circulate widely reflecting beliefs that African Americans individually and as a group are being attacked physically and exploited financially. One rumor holds that the Ku Klux Klan owns the Church's Fried Chicken fast-food chain, and that "something" is put into the chicken to make Black men sterile. Another says that the Reebok company, which sells high-priced athletic footwear to young African Americans, is owned by South Africans. Given the history of atrocities against, and systematic exploitation of, African Americans, these rumors seem plausible to many members of that community. The legends reflect African American historical and contemporary experiences that provide grounds to fear that African Americans are not yet free of organized attempts on their rights to safety and freedom.

Urban dwellers often create their own sense of place and community through life in a particular neighborhood. Neighborhoods may draw a particular ethnic group together; "point of entry" neighborhoods may be multicultural. Some cities create new forms of segregation, as in Detroit, where the city is predominantly Black, and Chicago, where African Americans are clustered on the south and west sides of the city.

People develop varied mental maps of large cities. In heavily Roman Catholic cities, parish boundaries may serve as geographic identifications. Political wards and city-designated neighborhoods compete for space on inhabitants' mental maps with more local designations such as precincts, block-club areas, gang turf, or "the block." Children in some neighborhoods may never leave their neighborhood while they are growing up or may never go downtown.

In Baltimore paintings on screens brighten some neighborhoods with rural scenes, and they, too, express a sense of place. In many cities, block clubs announce their presence and agenda (often antigang violence) with signs at the end of each block. Shopping strips declare the communities they serve through the languages and signs and such advertisements as "We send packages to Poland."

In crowded cities, "the street" is often part of the city experience. People sit on their stoops, children play in the street, and young people gather to flirt or show off. In African American communities, tap dancing, doo-wop quartets and breakdancing started as street corner activities but became important influences in American popular culture. Street performers are part of a centuries-old tradition, one that cities have long sought to regulate. Street performers blow saxophones, pump accordions, pull together tight quartet harmonies, and even juggle and eat fire.

Crowded cities also treasure their open or green spaces. Venice Beach, next to Los Angeles, is famous for its boardwalk and beach that provides a colorful array of leisure-time activities for participation or observation. City dwellers take part in, or just watch, roller skating, weight lifting, volleyball, picnics, and fireworks on the Fourth of July. Central Park in New York City and the Lake Michigan beaches in Chicago provide similar crucial "green space" to people who live surrounded by concrete.

City dwellers personalize and beautify their environment in ways large and small. Many homes have carefully landscaped and decorated shrines to the Virgin Mary, from yards in San Antonio to windowsills in New York City. In Los Angeles, the sculpture of Watts Towers looms over South Central Los Angeles, a monument to its visionary creator, an Italian immigrant.

There is a folklore of work in the cities as well. Even white-collar businesses nurture the lore of office workers. Secretaries post images that circulate in photocopied form from desk to desk (now through faxes), such as the cartoon of laughing figures who ask, "You want it when?" Computer programmers and "hackers" have developed their own lore, which, with the exponential growth of computer use, reaches a wide audience. One example is the "smiley face," created using the colon, a hyphen, and the right parenthesis marks : -) and meant to be "read" sideways. It is used to give feeling or tone to written words exchanged over computer bulletin boards and dialogue groups that might otherwise be misinterpreted, playing the role of tone of voice or facial expression. There is a large lexicon of similar computer images.

City-style occupations spawn their own brand of occupational lore. Industrial work created new communities of people who worked in the mill, lived in its shadow, and drank in the tavern between. The meat-packing industry, the steel industry, the garment industry, and the automobile-manufacturing industry among others, all created their own traditions as sons followed fathers into the factories for several generations. Stories flourished, about work on the floor, or about legendary figures like Joe Magarac, or the apocryphal tale of smuggling out the components to build a new car, one piece at a time. Ironworkers, who are responsible for much of the dangerous work of riveting together steel high-rise buildings, "raise the tree," placing a newly cut tree on the top of completed skyscrapers. "Mom and pop" family-owned stores and businesses are often beloved in neighborhoods or become known even citywide. Chicago's Lou Mitchell's is famous as the breakfast place of politicans and politician-watchers. Traders on the great exchange trading floors, lawyers, stewardesses, and many others all develop their own stories.

Leisure in the city takes on particular urban forms. The streets and buildings of the city provide a special context for children's play. Children use the sidewalks, streets, and vacant lots of New York City as playgrounds for stickball and "skelly." Urban fishermen fish in the Pacific Ocean off the piers of Santa Monica, California, and wait for nighttime smelt runs each spring along Chicago's Lake Michigan beaches. New Yorkers fly pigeons from rooftops or take their ease on rooftop "tar beaches."

The sheer diversity of traditions found side by side in many cities is part of the excitement of urban life. Cities are the perfect theater for large-scale events such as parades. Parades sponsored by ethnic communities mark special ethnic holidays. The floats and marchers often provide a snapshot of an ethnic group's organizations and interests. The Doo-Dah parade in Pasadena, California, started as a light-hearted response to the Rose Bowl parade; Greenwich Village is the scene of an annual Halloween parade in which marchers may appear in such getups as "the intersection of Fifth Avenue and 59th Street."

The Vietnam Veterans parade of 1986, held in Chicago, was a national event marking the first-ever public event honoring Vietnam veterans. With the parade came a traveling version of the Vietnam War Memorial that stands in Washington, DC. As at the original wall, family and friends left moving and carefully constructed mementos, some almost shrines, by the name of a fallen loved one.

Art forms metamorphose and take on unique flavors in each city. Traditional music, for example, goes on in homes, churches, and community centers, but also in nightclubs, convention centers, and major concert halls.

African American music has influenced much of the development of typically "American" music. Jazz and the blues helped make New Orleans and Chicago famous, along with cities in between such as St. Louis and Kansas City, Missouri. Gospel music has flourished in urban centers, providing both diverse audiences and performers access to recording possibilities and contacts with publishers and other ways to "spread the good word." Gospel quartets flourish in some cities, such as Memphis, while elsewhere choirs dominate. Gospel music brings people to church on Sunday, enlivens official city or political celebrations, or enriches city coffers by attracting thousands of singers to national conventions. Rap music grew out of the life of urban inner-city youngsters, drawing on the rich musical traditions of their African American communities to create a new sound. In many ways, the music of young African Americans in the inner-city drives most of American popular music.

The music of immigrants has become part of the fabric of city life. Polka music is a national phenomenon with followers in both urban and rural areas, concentrated in cities with large Eastern European populations. Different cities and regions have their own styles, avid dancers, and fans, who congregate in urban nightclubs weekly, or in annual conventions at airport hotels to share their passion for polka with thousands of others.

Tamburitza music, a string-band sound played by Serbs and Croatians, also evolved a peculiarly American sound. In the 1920s and 1930s, American-born children of immigrants grew up listening to their parents' music at weddings and at home and to popular music and jazz in city nightclubs. Some of the American-born tamburitza musicians changed the irregular rhythms common in the Balkans (7/8 often became 3/4) and added subtle, jazz-influenced changes in rhythmic accompaniments. The bands continue to provide for many of the same musical needs in American cities that they fulfilled in Balkan villages. Musicians accompany brides to their wedding services and play for the reception as well as for other social events. But tamburitza orchestras are no longer very popular as dance bands.

In the 1970s, Los Angeles Japanese American musicians combined traditional Japanese drumming with jazz and other European sounds to create distinctively "American-style" *taiko* drum orchestras. More recent immigrant communities may present, side by side, rock bands and traditional orchestras for their audiences' listening pleasure.

Urban traditions continue, reenergized and transformed in each new generation. Traditions pass informally from older generations to the younger (often within the family) or from child to child. Communities also create their own educational institutions for young people, to help ensure that the children feel connected to particular symbols and aspects of their culture and religion. Ethnic-heritage schools teach language and history; church schools teach religion (and often language— whether Arabic for Islam, Greek for Greek Orthodoxy, or Hebrew for Judaism). Junior orchestras, dance groups, and Scout troops are also important teachers and conveyors of traditional forms of creativity.

Architecture reflects who is here as well. Particular skyscrapers come to be known as symbols of the city: the Empire State Building symbolizes New York City; the Renaissance Center is Detroit's attempt to revitalize its downtown. The architecture of homes reflects dominant periods in a city's history, from the adobe homes of Southwestern cities to San Francisco's Victorian gingerbread houses, known as "Painted Ladies" for their brightly painted decorations, often painstakingly restored.

Churches, synagogues, temples, and other houses of worship provide a culturally appropriate place for congregations to gather, and these become part of the urban landscape as well. Italian stone carvers worked for many years to complete the National Cathedral in Washington, DC, with its distinctive Gothic styling, complete with gargoyles. In Chicago, the Drehobl family has supplied stained-glass windows to houses of worship for three generations. Eastern Orthodox churches share older eastern European neighborhoods with Catholic parishes (of the Roman and Eastern rites). The churches' stonework, spires, and sometimes gilded golden domes are a continuing testament to the love, sacrifice, and often workmanship skills of the early congregations. Orthodox Jewish shuls (houses of worship) and yeshivas (schools) may be found in storefront buildings. More recent arrivals such as Buddhists and Hindus first take over older churches or storefronts; later they build their own, more suitable buildings, reflecting the architectural heritage of their religions.

The buildings echo the city's diverse religious beliefs and practices. On Ash Wednesday, the Wednesday before Lent begins, men and women in tailored business suits appear at work with a smudge of ash on their foreheads. In Boston, New York City, and Chicago, during Italian American *festas,* many strong men hoist platforms carrying a saint or the Madonna onto their shoulders for an annual procession. Worshipers kiss the statue, pinning on money, medallions, or other offerings. Eastern Orthodox cantors and choirs sing music with roots in Byzantine times. At the harvest festival of Sukkot, observant Jewish families raise a temporary structure, semi-open to the sky, in which to eat and remember the wandering of the Jews in the desert. Whether the sukkah is in the backyard, on a deck, or on a rooftop or fire escape, the meaning is the same. In Buddhist gatherings, monks with shaven heads and saffron robes chant and offer blessings. Among Hmong refugees from Laos, shamans remain important interlocutors with the spirit world.

Urban churches may also be the scenes of miracles. Icons in Eastern Orthodox churches have been reported to "cry" when moisture was seen trickling from the painting's eyes. Crowds of believers (of many faiths) gather at the church to see each miraculous occurrence.

Cities also offer a choice of healing traditions, both physical and psychic. "Readers and advisers," who read palms and use other methods of divination, are found in many urban neighborhoods. Many Mexican Americans seek out Mexican healers *(curanderas),* and buy their medication from a herbal pharmacy *(botanica),* in the neighorhood. Chinese herbal medicine remains popular among Chinese immigrants and has found new support among the New Age community. In the city, these healing systems mix and intermingle in many new ways, sometimes confusing, but often inventive and helpful.

Traditional practices and beliefs reflect each religion's roots in ancient times, and new transformations show continuing vitality in a vastly different place and era. What is new at the end of the 20th century, perhaps, is the broad mix of cultures and peoples. U.S. cities are becoming a meeting ground for cultures, languages, traditions, and religions with roots around the globe, not just in Europe.

Margy McClain

References

Allen, Ray, and Nancy Groce, eds. 1988. Folk and Traditional Music in New York State. *New York Folklore* (Special Issue) 14:3–4.

Dyen, Doris. 1991. Aids to Adaptation: Southeast European Mural Painters in Pittsburgh. *Folklife Annual 90.* Washington, DC: American Folklife Center.

Harrison-Pepper, Sally. 1990. *Drawing a Circle in the Square: Street Performing in New York's Washington Square Park.* Jackson: University of Mississippi Press.

McClain, Margy. 1988. *A Feeling for Life: Cultural Identity, Community, and the Arts.* Chicago: Urban Traditions.

Miller, Elaine K. 1973. *Mexican Folk Narratives from the Los Angeles Area.* Publications of the American Folklore Society Memoirs Vol. 56. Austin: University of Texas Press.

Paredes, Américo, and Ellen Stekert, eds. 1971. *The Urban Experience and Folk Tradition.* Publications of the American Folklore Society. Austin: University of Texas Press.

See also City Lore; Crimelore; Festival; Graffiti; Immigrant Folklore, Study of; Jazz; Organizational Folklore; Public Folklore; Steelworkers; Tamburitza

Urban Legend

An apocryphal contemporary story, told as true but incorporating traditional motifs, and usually attributed to a friend of a friend (FOAF). Such stories were formerly termed "urban belief tales" and are also called "contemporary legends," "modern legends," and "modern urban legends." While neither the subject matter nor the circulation of urban legends is necessarily "urban," the stories usually reflect themes of modern life in cities or suburbs. They concern such topics as crime, technology, current events, sex, academe, professions, government, and celebrities. Some modern urban legends are clearly *not* modern, *not* urban, and *not* always told as true, but at least *some* variants of the stories thus classified must fit these criteria, although other versions of modern urban legends may have ancient and/or rural prototypes and may sometimes be told merely for entertainment, usually in the form of jokes. Still, the term "urban legend" is used by many folklorists, and has become the generic usage among members of the public and journalists (who sometimes use the less accurate term "urban *myth*") to refer to many of the unverified odd "true" stories that circulate both orally and in the media in the modern world.

Although some folklorists in England and the United States collected and studied individual urban legends earlier, the American folklorist Richard M. Dorson focused attention on the whole genre in the last chapter ("Modern Folklore") of his 1959 textbook *American Folklore.* The widespread popularity of urban legends and some interpretations are suggested in the series of books by Jan Harold Brunvand, *The Vanishing Hitchhiker* (1981), *The Choking Doberman* (1984), *The Mexican Pet* (1986), *Curses! Broiled Again!* (1989), and *The Baby Train* (1993). Similar collections of urban legends have been published in England, Scandinavia, Germany, Holland, South Africa, Australia, and elsewhere. Growing from a series of annual seminars that began at the University of Sheffield, England, in 1982, the International Society for Contemporary Legend Research (ISCLR) was formed in 1988. The society publishes a newsletter, *FOAFtale News*, and an annual journal, *Contemporary Legend* (1991–).

The ten major headings of the "Type-Index of Urban Legends" included in Brunvand's 1993 book—along with a sample legend-title from each—suggest the range of stories to be found in this genre: Automobiles ("The Slasher under the Car"), Animals ("The Microwaved Pet"), Horrors ("The Babysitter and the Man Upstairs"), Accidents ("The Exploding Toilet"), Sex and Scandal ("The Girl on the Gearshift Lever"), Crime ("The Kidney Heist"), Business and Professions ("The Procter and Gamble Trademark"), Government ("The Wordy Memo"), Celebrities ("The Elevator Incident"), and Academe ("The One-Word Exam Question"). These and hundreds of other "true stories that are too good to be true" circulate by word of mouth among adolescents at slumber parties and bull sessions, among office and factory workers during breaks, and among just about everybody at car pools, parties, dinners, and other social gatherings.

Urban legends have invaded popular culture. Such legends appear regularly in the press, especially in tabloids, and they are further disseminated via photocopies, faxes, and computers. The stories are repeated on radio and television talk shows, and they have inspired sitcoms, films, and even serious literature. The New York City legend "Alligators in the Sewers" is depicted on a T-shirt sold by the New York City Department of Environmental Protection on which a cartoon allusion is captioned "The Legend Lives. . . ." The same story has been the subject of comic books, children's literature, and a Hollywood film (*Alligator* [1980]), and it was a major theme in Thomas Pynchon's 1963 novel titled *V.*

New urban rumors and legends regularly appear. For example, in late summer 1993 a warning about murderous gang initiations spread nationwide, mostly through faxes. A report in the Memphis, Tennessee, *Commercial Appeal* in mid-August described "heavily faxed" warnings, claiming to be official police bulletins, that warned of gang members driving at night with their car lights off. Supposedly, if someone blinked his own lights as a warning, the gang member would pursue the car and kill the occupants. As this anonymous rumor spread—via faxes and computers and by word of mouth—the story acquired details about claimed actual incidents of this kind, names of investigating authorities, and the supposed actual date of "Blood's [initiation] Weekend," said to be September 25–26, 1993. Police, journalists, and folklorists debunked the stories, and no such crimes were committed; by December 1993, the "Lights Out!" warnings had all but disappeared, but the première episode of a CBS-TV police drama, *Traps,* starring George C. Scott and broadcast in March 1994, mentioned a "Headlight Killer Taskforce" that was investigating "Lights Out!"-type crimes. Thus, in the space of about eight months an urban rumor emerged, developed some legendary features, made its way into contemporary popular culture, then apparently faded from popularity.

"The Mexican Pet" story illustrates how variations of an urban legend reflect different social or cultural themes. The first versions noted by folklorists described an American family vacationing in Mexico who adopts a stray Chihuahua dog and smuggles it home, only to learn from their veterinarian that the creature is a sewer rat, not a dog. This version depicts kind-hearted, if law-breaking, tourists traveling in a country with lower standards of public cleanliness. Later versions of the story claimed that the rat-dog was found at a major seaport (Baltimore, New York City, Los Angeles, and the like) and had come off a ship from a Third World country; thus, unclean conditions seemed to be invading the United States. In Europe the counterpart story was told about tourists from "clean" northern countries (such as Sweden, Holland, or England) who adopt the pet while traveling in a "dirty" southern or eastern country (such as Spain, Egypt, Thailand). In American versions in the mid-1990s, the "dog" is found floating on a piece of driftwood off the coast of Florida or Northern California, but it turns out to be a rat from either Haiti (Florida) or China (California); thus, the stray animal has become a symbol of refugees attempting to enter the United States illegally.

Rumors and legends have probably always been a feature of urban life, and sometimes virtually the same "modern" story can be documented from very early writings. For instance, a story about a supposed shopping-mall crime in which a boy is sexually mutilated, even killed, by members of a youth gang, has been traced to anti-Semitic analogues of Chaucer's "Prioress's Tale" and even earlier to anti-Christian stories documented in classical sources. "The Choking Doberman" legend, although including such modern aspects as a veterinarian, a telephone warning, and a modern crime situation, is actually a recent variation of an ancient fable that was first transmuted into a European legend and later adopted contemporary details as the story spread to the New World.

Most urban legends either originate from unknown sources or are updatings of older traditional legends, but occasionally one can be traced to an actual event. A good example is "The Unsolvable Math Problem," an account of how an undergraduate student mistakenly solved all three problems written on a classroom chalkboard, assuming they were all part of a test. In reality, the test had only *two* parts, and the third problem was given by the instructor as an example of an unsolved proposition that had baffled even Einstein. The instructor had written the problem on the chalkboard before the test began and was amazed that the student—unaware of the challenge and arriving late for the test—had naively found the solution that had long eluded the experts.

In the mid- to late-1980s, the story of the mathematics prodigy solving the Einstein-puzzler became a favorite pulpit anecdote as ministers retold the incident more-or-less as they had read it in the book *Robert Schuller: The Inside Story* (1983) or in newsletters containing inspiring anecdotes for ministers that had reprinted the Schuller version. The Reverend Robert H. Schuller, who hosts the weekly "Hour of Power" television worship service from the "Crystal Cathedral" in Garden Grove, California, attributed the story to "a meek little fellow" who told him, while sitting next to him on an airplane trip, the true story about solving an unsolvable problem. Schuller identified the teller as "George Danzig . . . [of] the Physics Department at Stanford University."

In oral tradition, "The Unsolvable Math Problem" had developed varying versions as it spread from person to person.

(For example, most people attributed the story to some particular university, and others claimed that the student had solved nine out of ten "unsolvable" problems.) But Schuller himself had modified the story as he heard it from Professor George B. *Dantzig*, who actually teaches in the Department of *Mathematics* at Stanford. In 1940, as a *graduate* student at the University of California, Berkeley, Dantzig had solved not one but *two* previously unsolved problems in *statistical analysis*, mistakenly thinking that the problems written on the classroom chalkboard were part of the class *homework*. Among the several changes (noted in italics above) Schuller made as he repeated the story as an example of successful "possibility thinking" was the reference to Einstein. After passing through the conduits of print, pulpit anecdote, and oral repetition, the story acquired a life and details of its own quite apart from Dantzig's actual experience.

When "The Unsolvable Math Problem" and its background appeared in an article on urban legends in the September 1990 issue of *Reader's Digest*, the story once again achieved widespread printed circulation, perhaps next to be re-seeded as an anonymous urban legend in "folk" circulation. As the *Digest* concluded, "[It] all goes to show that even when it comes to urban legends, truth *can* be stranger than fiction" (Jan Harold Brunvand "The Case of the Choking Doberman" pp. 129–132. Professor Dantzig himself, amused at the notoriety his feat has earned him among mathematicians and the general public alike, has suggested that the problem in the story should not accurately be called "unsolvable," since he (plus his anonymous counterpart in the legend) did, in fact, solve it, or in Dantzig's case, solved *them*.

Jan Harold Brunvand

References

Bennett, Gillian, and Paul Smith. 1993. *Contemporary Legend: A Folklore Bibliography*. New York: Garland.

Brunvand, Jan Harold. 1990. Dorson and the Urban Legend. *Folklore Historian* 7:16–22.

Gary Alan. 1992. *Manufacturing Tales: Sex and Money in Contemporary Legends*. Knoxville: University of Tennessee Press.

Turner, Patricia A. 1993. *I Heard It through the Grapevine: Rumor in African-American Culture*. Berkeley: University of California Press.

See also Academe, Folklore of; Legend; Mass Media and Folklore; Organizational Folklore; Rumor; Urban Folklore

Utley, Francis Lee (1907–1974)

Medievalist, folklorist, linguist, and teacher. A native of Wisconsin and a graduate of the University of Wisconsin, Utley earned his master's degree and doctorate from Harvard University. He joined the English department at Ohio State University in 1935 and introduced folklore studies there soon after. During Utley's thirty-nine years at Ohio State, he facilitated the creation of the Folklore Archives and fostered establishment of the Center for Medieval and Renaissance Studies.

Former students remember Utley as a gentle, book-loving man who gave generously of his time and guidance but demanded academic rigor in return. Many Utley students, including D.K. Wilgus, Bruce Rosenberg, and W. Edson Richmond, went on to distinguished careers in folklore. Both Utley's academic approach to folklore and his in-home seminars reflected the influences of his Harvard mentor, George Lyman Kittredge.

An avid reader and a prolific writer, Utley's major work, *The Crooked Rib*, examines medieval attitudes toward women. Many scholarly articles demonstrate Utley's eclectic interests, from medieval balladry to Ohio place names, as well as his extensive research on flood narratives. After his death, Ohio State acquired Utley's legendary, annotated, 21,000-volume personal library through the generosity of his widow, Ruth Scott Utley.

As president of the American Folklore Society (1951–1952), Utley decried disciplinary rivalries. He insisted that scientific rigor, aesthetic sensitivity, and holistic investigation were all essential to the collection, analysis, and documentation of folklore. An indefatigable scholar and promoter of folklore studies, Utley served in numerous organizations, including as president of the American Name Society (1966) and of the College English Association (1969).

Donna L. Wyckoff

References

Finnie, Bruce W. 1975. In Memoriam: Francis Lee Utley. *Names: Journal of the American Name Society* 23:127–129.

Utley, Francis Lee. 1944. *The Crooked Rib: An Analytical Index to the Argument about Women in English and Scots Literature to the End of the Year 1568.* Columbus: Ohio State University Press.

———. 1952. Conflict and Promise in Folklore. *Journal of American Folklore* 65:111–119.

———. 1953. Three Kinds of Honesty. *Journal of American Folklore* 66:189–199.

———. 1960. Noah, His Wife, and the Devil. In *Studies in Biblical and Jewish Folklore*, ed. Raphael Patai. Bloomington: Indiana University Press, pp. 59–91.

V

Valentine's Day

February 14, associated with love and courtship since medieval times. Two Christian martyrs, one a bishop and the other a priest, share the feast day of St. Valentine; legends tell of their good deeds. The Roman festival of Lupercalia, when young men drew the names of young women from an urn, is one of the earliest predecessors of Valentine's Day. Since the late Middle Ages, February 14 has been the day when people expect birds to begin their spring mating. It has also been a day to begin sowing particular crops, such as lettuce and onions.

In 19th-century America, young men pulled the names of prospective sweethearts from a hat at play-parties. Recognizing the "first-met" as a valentine sweetheart and seeking to dream of a future husband by sleeping on bay leaves sprinkled with rose water are among the Valentine's Day customs that came to America from the British Isles.

Printed valentine cards became common in America after 1860. Since then a great many people have exchanged valentines with serious or humorous wording. For adults the purchase or creation of cards and gifts can be an absorbing task. Children take delight in such comic parody verses as "Roses are red; they grow in this region. / If I had your face, I'd join the Foreign Legion." Valentine's Day parties for children may include heart-shaped cakes and other special refreshments; some children dress in red and white clothes.

With its commercial emphasis on the purchase of cards and gifts, Valentine's Day may seem to have lost some of its traditional essence. However, valentine verses still circulate orally, and local customs continue to develop.

Elizabeth Tucker

References

Cohen, Hennig, and Tristram Coffin, eds. 1987. *The Folklore of American Holidays*. Detroit: Gale, pp. 67–69.

Hand, Wayland D., ed. 1964. *The Frank C. Brown Collection of North Carolina Folklore*. Vol. 7. Durham, NC: Duke University Press, pp. 427, 530.

Knapp, Mary, and Herbert Knapp. 1976. *One Potato, Two Potato: The Secret Education of American Children*. New York: W.W. Norton, pp. 220–221.

Opie, Iona, and Peter Opie. 1959. *The Lore and Language of Schoolchildren*. Oxford: Oxford University Press, pp. 235–237.

Spicer, Dorothy. 1954. *Yearbook of English Festivals*. Westport, CT: Greenwood, pp. 36–38.

Vampires

Supernatural creatures thought to be humans who return from their graves to victimize the living. American vampires have widow's peaks and pale skin. Sensuous entities, they dress in black or tuxedos with black capes, sleep by day, and prowl by night seeking victims to suck their blood. They attack by sinking their fangs into the necks of their prey—often beautiful maidens. Once bitten, victims become vampires, but garlic, a crucifix, or daylight can prevent an attack. Staking the vampire through the heart will kill it and allow the vampire to rest in peace.

Contemporary American vampires differ sharply from European vampires. Movies have influenced popular ideas about vampires, particularly the 1931 portrayal of Count Dracula by Bela Lugosi, based on Bram Stoker's 1897 book *Dracula*. Although Stoker's creation was fictional, it was based in part on exploits of a real 15th-century Wallachian tyrant, Vlad Tepes, whose acts of cruelty included mass impalements of enemies, inspiring the nickname Vlad, the Impaler. Stoker's creation also drew upon widespread and ancient beliefs that undead spirits caused life's tragedies: barren fields, plague, milkless cows, malformed babies. Some Transylvanian villagers still believe that vampires prey upon unwed dead men or women. Dead single persons of marriageable age receive symbolic weddings at their funerals.

In New England, 19th-century newspaper accounts tell of bodies of tuberculosis victims being exhumed and hearts burned to prevent their taking the lives of other family members. That idea no longer prevails in America. Instead, the media version of vampires has become the standard—highly commercialized and trivialized. The vampire logo occurs on Count Chocula cereal boxes, hot-sauce bottles, and wine bottles. Advertisers use it for snail killer, pizza, batteries, light beer, and security systems. Adults as well as children popularize vampire costumes at Halloween, and youngsters learn to count by watching "The Count," a vampire on TV's *Sesame Street*.

Vampires inspire the creation of a continuous stream of books, short stories, films, television shows, plays, fan clubs, fan magazines, and conventions. Sexuality and power may account for their mass appeal. Some people identify themselves as vampires by wearing black and avoiding the light. Others go to the extreme imitation by drinking human blood. A 1989 survey of college and high school students found that 27 percent believed it possible for vampires to exist as real entities. Media bombardment of the symbol feeds this belief.

According to one explanation for its origin, need for a scapegoat for the plague fueled the creation of the vampire. The first victim who died became the most likely suspect. When survivors exhumed the body, they misunderstood and misinterpreted the stages of putrification. Expecting to find a dried up body, instead they found blood on the lips of a bloated corpse, a natural phenomenon of the decomposition process. Erroneously, they assumed that it fed upon the living. When the gaseous cadaver moaned or cried after being staked, this reinforced the idea that the body was still alive, thus a vampire.

Norine Dresser

References

Barber, Paul. 1988. *Vampires, Burial, and Death*. New Haven, CT: Yale University Press.

Dresser, Norine. 1989. *American Vampires: Fans, Victims, and Practitioners*. New York: W.W. Norton.

Kligman, Gail. 1988. *The Wedding of the Dead*. Berkeley: University of California Press.

McNally, Raymond T., and Radu Florescu. 1972. *In Search of Dracula*. Greenwich, CT: New York Graphic Society.

Vernacular

A potential synonym for "folk." The term "vernacular" has been used at least since the 17th century to indicate the rootedness of a given cultural expression within a particular nation, region, or province. Most often applied to language—specifically to dialect variations of received standard speech—"vernacular" is a word that signals indigenous character.

Having a Latinate origin, "vernacular" was never the term of choice among northern Europe's 19th-century Romantics, who pioneered the study of local custom and habit that came to be known as folklore. They opted instead for "folk," a term with a Teutonic pedigree that would both separate their scholarly ventures from classical Mediterranean learning and allow them to affiliate with the presumed nobility of newly emerging nations and empires. Moreover, since *verna*, the word's Latin root, describes specifically a home-born slave, "vernacular" carried for some the despicable con-

notations of misery, servitude, and failure. These unpleasant attributes obviously did little to enhance the term's overall popularity.

Contemporary associations for "vernacular," however, are considerably more positive. In the late 20th century the term signals authenticity, vigor, and independence. A vernacular building, for example, is presumed to naturally belong in its setting by virtue of its design, construction, and history. By contrast, an academic attempt to create a similar form will seem like an out-of-place affectation. Since the word "folk" has become freighted with contradictory and confusing meanings, "vernacular" is looked to more and more as a fresh alternative. Lacking, so far, a history of misuse, the word "vernacular" is now encountered frequently in folkloristic discussions.

To a great extent in the United States, the term owes its validity to the growth of material-culture research in the field of American studies in the 1950s. Folklorists seem to have encountered the term chiefly through their investigations of the sources of American folk buildings. It was British restoration architect Sir Gilbert George Scott who first used the word "vernacular" in connection with buildings in 1857 in his book *Remarks on Secular and Domestic Architecture*. Following almost a century's worth of publication on rural buildings of all types, an English scholarly organization calling itself the Vernacular Architecture Group (VAG) was founded in 1954, and in 1970 it began to publish an annual journal, *Vernacular Architecture*. By 1979 an American counterpart, the Vernacular Architecture Forum (VAF), was established to promote interdisciplinary dialogue on the topic, and soon, it too, began to publish not only a quarterly newsletter, but also occasional collections of papers from the organization's annual meetings titled *Perspectives in Vernacular Architecture*.

One by-product of VAF activities has been the further legitimization in American scholarly circles of the word "vernacular" as the preferred descriptor for architectural expressions that otherwise might be referred to as folk, traditional, native, indigenous, popular, ordinary, local, or customary. It may not be long before the term "vernacular" is regularly used to describe other genres like art, craft, food, medicine, music, and so forth. Henry Glassie already suggested this trajectory when he wrote: "Vernacular architecture is one area of folk art that has been accorded careful historical study and so supplies useful inspiration for the whole field" (Glassie 1989:264). One wonders then if the discipline of folklore might not eventually be re-named "vernacular studies." It was more than forty years ago that one scholar suggested that folk arts be dubbed "Vernacular Arts." However, given the fact that much that can be properly described as vernacular lies beyond the boundaries of folk culture, the word "folk" will probably never be completely supplanted.

John Michael Vlach

References

Glassie, Henry. 1989. *The Spirit of Folk Art: The Girard Collection at the Museum of International Folk Art*. New York: Harry N. Abrams.

De Zouche Hall, Sir Robert. 1974. Origins of the Vernacu-

Vernacular motifs of jack-o'-lantern and scarecrow decorate a porch. Pine Barrens, New Jersey, 1984. Photo Sue Samuelson. American Folklife Center.

lar Architecture Group. *Vernacular Architecture* 5:3–6.

Upton, Dell. 1990. Outside the Academy: A Century of Vernacular Architecture Studies, 1890–1990. In *The Architectural Historian in America,* ed. Elisabeth Blair MacDougall. Washington, DC: National Gallery of Art, pp. 199–213.

Upton, Dell, and John Michael Vlach. 1986. *Common Places: Readings in American Vernacular Architecture.* Athens: University of Georgia Press.

Vietnam War

The era from roughly 1965 to 1975. The folklore of the Vietnam War included both older ongoing traditions of the U.S. military and new folklore generated in the unique context of the war. Folk naming, slang and jargon, superstitions, jokes, songs, proverbs, graffiti, and narrative forms from the older stream of Army lore remained in active circulation, much of it learned in basic training as the informal education of new soldiers into the group. Terms like Jeep (from GP—general purpose vehicle), slang like "shit on a shingle" (creamed chipped beef on toast), beliefs like the "three on a match" taboo, sayings like "Military intelligence is a contradiction in terms," cadence calls like "I wanna be an airborne ranger" or those involving "Jodie," the civilian who in the soldier's absence gets his girl and/or car—all this older Army lore persisted into the Vietnam era.

As the war developed, new folklore emerged. Technical slang evolved, such as "lurp" (for LRRP, long-range reconnaissance patrols) and "huey" (for UH, utility helicopter). One famous term came from the radio alphabet letters for V and C—"Victor" and "Charlie"—the faceless Viet Cong enemy thus becoming the personalized "Charlie," while "dink" and "slope" evolved as racist epithets for all Vietnamese people. Vietnamese words and terms became part of the soldiers' slang as well—*sin loi* (sorry about that), *didi mau* (go away), *di wee* and *chum wee* (lieutenant and captain), and a pidgin scale of good and bad (number one and number ten respectively) were very common. "Taxi girl" became the generic term for a prostitute, though the Saigon-based reference didn't apply to "the bush," that is, to (rural areas). The slang term for the United States was "the world," as in "I'll be back in the world in fifty-four days."

The soldiers cycled into and out of the war individually in one-year assignments rather than as units. This created a great emphasis on their DEROS (date of estimated return from overseas) and on their "short" (as in a small number of days remaining) status, leading to quips like "I'm so short I trip over rugs." Xeroxed "count-down calendars," with one section to be colored in each day for 365 days, were ubiquitous. These depicted such things as maps of the United States, naked "round-eyed" [non-Oriental] women, or the word HOME. Superstitions surrounded "short" soldiers; it was considered good luck to be around anyone who was a "two-digit midget" or less.

A common form of verbal lore was a set of combat corollaries to Murphy's Law. The first was usually "Murphy was a 'grunt' (infantryman), and others were wry or cynical comments on combat, military bureaucracy, or the building frustration of being in a war with no clear mission. Some examples: "Remember, your weapon was made by the lowest bidder"; "The easy way is always mined"; "No inspection-ready unit ever passed combat"; "All five-second fuses last three seconds"; "The only thing more accurate than incoming fire is incoming friendly fire"; and "Peace is our profession—mass murder is just our hobby."

Traditional narratives circulated widely, often in the form of rumors—of large-scale confrontations with the NVA (the regular army of North Vietnam), of mass troop movements down the Ho Chi Minh Trail, of the entry of the Chinese into the war, of MIG aircraft in use by the enemy (a rare but deadly occurrence), or of large groups of defectors forming villages in Cambodia or Laos. Legends circulated too—about CIA (Central Intelligence Agency) operations, about the generals and politicians running the war (President Lyndon B. Johnson and General William Westmoreland were favorite topics), about the tunnel complexes under Cu Chi and the Black Virgin Mountain, Nui Ba Din. A common theme of folk anecdotes was the lucky wound or the self-inflicted wound that got a soldier out of combat.

As the body count grew, the 1960s counterculture emerged full blown, and opposition at home to the war became more vocal—especially after the January-February 1968 Tet Offensive in which 3,895 U.S. troops were killed—and graffiti, Xeroxlore, sayings, jokes, anecdotes, and folk narratives in Vietnam began to reflect these changes. Peace symbols on helmet liners, as tattoos, or as necklaces proliferated; anecdotes emerged of soldiers who stopped carrying weapons, even into combat; the elaborate embroidery done by Vietnamese "mama-sans" on fatigue jackets began to state new themes—"Another soldier for peace"; "Black man killing yellow man for white man"; and "Killing for peace is like fucking for virginity" all appeared beside the older motifs of "Proud American"; "I've been to Hell"; or "Semper Fi" *(Semper Fidelis,* always faithful, the Marine Corps' motto). Numerous belief tales about what protesters back in "the world" were doing to Vietnam vets found wide circulation.

A distinct folklore of the Vietnam vet also emerged as increasing numbers of soldiers returned to find themselves having great difficulty readjusting to civilian life. Jokes about vets cussing obsessively at dinner, much to grandma's dismay; anecdotes about vets strangling their wives when awakened without warning; and the use of the "crazed Vietnam vet" as villain in both folk and popular narratives—added to the extensive but deeply ambivalent folklore of America's longest and most confusing military venture. The novels of Tim O'Brien about the war give an accurate and detailed picture of the performance context of much of the folklore enumerated here.

Thomas E. Barden

References

Dewhurst, C. Kurt. 1988. Pleiku Jackets, Tour Jackets, and Working Jackets: "The Letter Sweaters of War." *Journal of American Folklore* 101:48–52.

O'Brien, Tim. 1973. *If I Die in a Combat Zone.* New York: Delta.

———. 1979. *Going after Cacciato.* New York: Delta.

———. 1990. *The Things They Carried.* New York: Penguin.

Vietnam. 1989. *Journal of American Folklore* (Special Issue) 102: No. 406.

Walton, Ivan (1893–1968)

Collector of Great Lakes folklore, with emphasis on sailors' songs. As a teenager in Ludington, Michigan, Walton visited the docks and listened to songs and stories of sailors. In the 1920s, he was already documenting these performances, and by 1932 he was spending summers on ships or around the lakes and on Beaver Island, Michigan, collecting the folklore of sailors, fishermen, and their families.

After receiving his B.A. in 1919 at the University of Michigan, Walton taught English literature while he continued graduate work for a time at the University of Chicago and the University of Illinois. In 1938 Walton and other Michigan folklorists, including Thelma James, E.C. Beck, and Emelyn Elizabeth Gardner, formed a folklore interest group, and in 1940 Walton founded the Michigan Folklore Society. In 1955 he established and taught the first folklore course at the University of Michigan.

Along with Beck, Walton participated in the song-collecting project of Alan Lomax, one result of which was the Library of Congress recording *Songs of Michigan Lumberjacks* (AFS L56).

When Walton died in 1968, he was one of the leading experts on Great Lakes folklore. Although he had not completed the manuscript of his life's work, he had presented papers at conferences and written articles based on his research. Walton's legacy, a vast collection of materials from more than thirty years of research, is housed at the Bentley Historical Library at the University of Michigan. An inventory compiled by Wil Rollman and Cheryl Baker was published by the library in 1979.

Yvonne R. Lockwood

References

McEwen, George M. 1970. Ivan H. Walton: A Pioneer Michigan Folklorist. *Michigan Academician* 2:73–74.

Walton, Ivan. 1941. Marine Lore. In *Michigan: A Guide to the Wolverine State.* Comp. Works Progress Administration. New York: Oxford University Press, pp. 113–134.

———. 1952. Folk Singing on Beaver Island. *Midwest Folklore* 2:243–250.

———. 1953. Sailor Lore of the Great Lakes. *Michigan History* 19:359–369.

———. 1955. Eugene O'Neill and the Folklore and Folkways of the Sea. *Midwest Folklore* 14:153–169.

See also Beck, Earl Clifton; Great Lakes

Ward, Marshall (1906–1981)

Traditional Appalachian storyteller who specialized in Jack tales. It was Ward who in 1935 acquainted the folklorist Richard Chase with the term "Jack tale" and introduced him to the many members of his family and community on Beech Mountain, North Carolina, who performed the stories—among them his father, Miles Ward and uncle Monroe Ward (grandsons of Council Harmon, the most immediate major conduit of the tradition), and the brothers Ben and Roby Hicks, also grandsons of "Old Counce." These four men were the primary sources of the stories published in Chase's *The Jack Tales* (1943).

Ward was himself an exceptional storyteller, having internalized twenty-five of his father's Jack tales before he entered primary school. He performed the stories throughout his life, especially enjoying telling them to his fifth-grade students at the Banner Elk Grade School, where he taught for thirty years. The folklorist Charlotte Paige Gutierrez believes that Ward's talents as a storyteller were directly related to his career as a schoolteacher. For example, Ward, unlike his fellow storytellers Ray and Stanley Hicks, inserted into the tales his personal advice about how best to conduct one's life, and he modified Jack's actions to the extent that they displayed much more ethical and less violent behavior. Further, Ward's performance style was much more animated than the Hickses', surely an adjustment undertaken to retain the attention of young schoolchildren. Other of Ward's important stylistic devices analyzed by Gutierrez include his use of voice changes and vocal dynamics, mimicry, facial expressions, and illustrative gestures.

Ward contributed greatly to the preservation and perpetuation of the Jack-tale tradition by performing them for seventy years for schools, festivals, and for his neighbors.

William E. Lightfoot

References

Gutierrez, Charlotte Paige. 1990. The Narrative Style of Marshall Ward, Jack-Tale Teller. In *Arts in Earnest: North Carolina Folklife*, ed. Daniel W. Patterson and Charles G. Zug III. Durham, NC: Duke University Press, pp. 147–163.

McGowan, Thomas. 1978. Marshall Ward: An Introduction to a Jack Tale. *North Carolina Folklore Journal* 26:51–74.

Oxford, Cheryl Lynne. 1987. *"They Call Him Lucky Jack": Three Performance-Centered Case Studies of Storytelling in Watauga County, North Carolina.* Ph.D. diss., Northwestern University, pp. 41–97.

See also Chase, Richard; Hicks-Harmon Families; Jack Tales

Warner, Frank (1903–1978) and Anne Locher Warner (1905–1991)

Collectors, performers, and interpreters of American folksong. In the late 1930s and early 1940s, at the same time that Richard Chase was investigating the Beech Mountain, North Carolina, story tradition, Frank and Anne Warner were discovering the parallel song tradition.

Their continued involvement in the folksong movement, especially in the Northeast, led to lectures and articles, to stints at the Pinewoods Folk Music Camp of the Country Dance and Song Society, to Frank's position as founding board member of the Newport Folk Festival in Rhode Island, and to Anne's publication of *Traditional American Folksongs from the Anne and Frank Warner Collection* (1984). The last, organized by repertoire and region, includes the important songs of New York's Yankee John Galusha, New Hampshire's Lena Bourne Fish, Frank Proffitt Sr. and other North Carolina singers, and many more.

Born in Selma, Alabama, Frank Warner at the age of six moved with his family to Jackson, Tennessee, home of railroad engineer John Luther "Casey" Jones. Six years later, the family moved to Durham, North Carolina, where Frank in time studied under Frank C. Brown at Duke University. In the early 1930s, he had a radio request program on WBIG, Greensboro. Son of a YMCA (Young Men's Christian Association) secretary, he, too, became a professional Y organizer and executive. In 1932, shortly after moving to New York City as program director of the Grand Central (now Vanderbilt) YMCA, he met Anne Locher. They were married in 1935 and had two sons, Jeff, an actor and folksinger, and Gerret, a filmmaker.

Anne Locher Warner, born in St. Louis, grew up in St. Paul, Minnesota, and in Chicago, where she attended Northwestern University. Leaving without a degree, she came to New York City in 1925. Her career included positions at the Council of Foreign Relations, the China Institute, and Hofstra University. Her last position was as executive secretary to the

county executive of Nassau County, New York.

In 1938 the Warners took their first trip to North Carolina to meet Nathan Hicks, who had made them a dulcimer. There, during an afternoon of music making, they met Frank Proffitt, who sang "Tom Dooley" for them. Thus began a lifetime of collecting, recording, and promoting American folksong. Frank recorded seven albums, carefully replicating the performance style appropriate to each piece. He appeared on TV and radio and in film, taught at Cooperstown, New York, and served as president of the New York Folklore Society, vice president of the Country Dance and Song Society, and program director of the society's Pinewoods camp. A 1963 series of lectures was published as *Folk Songs and Ballads of the Eastern Seaboard: From a Collector's Notebook* (1963). Anne, in addition to her book, published articles in *Appalachian Journal, North Carolina Folklore Quarterly, New York Folklore Quarterly, Sing Out!*, and elsewhere. Both served as trustees of the National Folk Arts Council.

The Warners pioneered the use of electronic recording devices in the field. Their work is characterized by rich documentation of context, attention to whole repertoires, and a sense of responsibility to singers, including returning royalties to them. (When a recording by the Kingston Trio turned "Tom Dooley" into an international hit, they helped negotiate the settlement to return at least some of the earnings to the Proffitt family.) Pursuing full careers while fitting collecting and writing into evenings, weekends, and vacations, Anne and Frank Warner were the last of the great amateurs in a field now fully professionalized.

William Bernard McCarthy

References

Baggelaar, Kristin, and Donald Milton. 1976. Frank Warner and Jeff Warner. In *Folk Music: More Than a Song.* New York: Thomas Y. Crowell, pp. 392–395.

Lawless, Ray M. 1968. *Folksingers and Folksongs in America.* new rev. ed. New York: Meredith, pp. 229–231, 672, 692–693, 705.

Rosenberg, Neil V. 1993. *Transforming Tradition: Folk Music Revivals Examined.* Urbana: University of Illinois Press, pp. 36–41.

Warner, Frank, and Anne Warner. 1973. Frank Noah Proffitt: A Retrospective. *Appalachian Journal* 1 (Autumn):163–193.

Warner, Jeff. 1990. Anne Warner. *North Carolina Folklore Journal* 37:67–70.

See also Revivalism

Watermen

Men whose economic survival depends upon the resources of inland waterways, bays, and (in a broader definition of the term) oceans and seas. Watermen's traditions include the material culture of their trade—small boats, traps, nets, hunting calls, decoys, floats, and the like—as well as stories and foodways, shad planking and seafood dishes. As with many working groups, there is often a level of social importance

Watermen's boats and houses. Edgartown, Massachusetts, 1910–20. Library of Congress.

recognized within the group that directly correlates to one's expertise in making the tools of the trade, such as nets or hunting calls. Watermen can often recognize one another's style of workmanship in the specific crafts, and an individual with a special talent may earn a few extra dollars from his colleagues for his more expert product.

The craft that watermen use in coastal waters tends to be a small shallow-water boat, like a skiff or a gunner boat. Sometimes small houseboats, called floating cabins, have been employed to make liveble the land too wet for conventional housing and to place the waterman as near to his source of income as possible. Seldom are these houseboats more than just practical places to eat and sleep, and they are almost always occupied only during the work season by working men.

Watermen, perhaps because of the time spent in self reliant, male-dominated work communities, sometimes develop carefully guarded recipes for traditional coastal fare, such as crab or turtle soups, fish specialties, and muskrat dishes. They also maintain secret preparation techniques, like the seven cuts it takes to completely debone the American shad—whose boniness earned it a Native American name that translates to "porcupine inside-out fish"—and the precooking used to rid muskrat of some of its gamey flavor. These techniques and recipes are almost never shared outside the community and sometimes die with older watermen.

In its broadest use, the term "watermen" is applied to all workers of the water, including those whose occupation is limited to the harvest of one specific product—for example, fishermen, oystermen, lobstermen, and crabbers. But in some regions, such as the East Coast of the United States, the term is reserved for men who spend their lives adapting to the many varied resources of the water and wetlands. Their activities tend to differ from season to season. Depending on his geographic location and the climate, a waterman may hunt waterfowl, fish, catch turtles, and trap small game, such as muskrats. He may also serve as a guide to amateur groups of hunters or freshwater fishermen. His survival is based on his ability to derive a living from whatever the wetlands and the adjacent waters have to offer him, and the changing market often determines where he places his greatest emphasis. Also, although a crabber or an oysterman may tolerate being identified as a waterman, the terms are not strictly synonymous, and he is just as likely to make the correction to a more specific descriptive term when identified this way.

The term is seldom, if ever, applied to women, although there are some rare cases of women who would fit the above definition. It is common for women to be seen by the watermen as an outsider group and to be treated with the same level of derogatory humor as are the government fish, game, and wildlife officials who impose regulations on the watermen. Watermen's stories are typically based on aspects of the work environment and, like the environment, the stories tend to be male specific. These stories also emphasize the close bonds within the community and may reflect an "us against them" mentality. Sometimes heroes are found in the watermen's stories and tall tales whose successes have to do with defeating nature, wildlife officials, or women.

Although many watermen are involved with conventional wildlife conservation groups, it is not uncommon to find a feeling of entitlement from the watermen when it comes to water and wetland resources. Their opinion that it is the sport fishermen and hunters, and industry, who do the most damage to natural resources adds to their sense of a closed "us against them" community.

Lifelong residents of coastal towns whose professions are not water oriented, but who enjoy water recreation, may also call themselves watermen, especially if their fathers or grandfathers were professional watermen. Usually, one does not adopt the term if one is not proficient in many of the same activities as the professional waterman.

William W. Warner, in his book *Beautiful Swimmers: Watermen, Crabs, and the Chesapeake Bay* (1987), charts the historical use of the term "watermen" back to Sir Thomas Malory's *Morte D'Arthur,* written in 1469–1470. According to Warner, the term has since then lost all but its archaic connotations in England and has migrated to the communities who work the waters on the East Coast of the United States. Warner offers further defining qualities of the term, such as that it is used "to separate those who had the resources to acquire land and those who didn't and went out on the water for subsistence." In the late-20th-century a waterman may or may not own land, and may or may not have a land residence, but he always goes "out on the water for subsistence."

Natalie Peters

References

Mullen, Patrick B. [1978] 1988. *I Heard the Old Fishermen Say: Folklore of the Texas Gulf Coast.* Logan: Utah State University Press.
Stutz, Bruce. 1992. *Natural Lives, Modern Times.* New York: Crown.

See also Fishing (Commercial)

Waters, Muddy (McKinley Morganfield) (1915–1983)

Chicago blues artist. The best-known transitional Mississippi Delta to Chicago bluesman, Muddy Waters was influenced by Son House and the recordings of Robert Johnson. While in his teens, he played with local string bands at house parties and country breakdowns. In the early 1940s, he ran his own juke joint in Mississippi and in 1941 he was field recorded by folklorist Alan Lomax. Moving to Chicago in 1943, he worked with other Delta musicians at rent parties and small taverns, where transplanted Southerners with a taste for downhome music supported Southern-born blues musicians. After an abortive test recording for Columbia Records in 1946, Waters began a productive thirty-year collaboration with Chess records. Initially recorded in a more-or-less solo format, Waters put together outstanding bands known for their "head hunting," or job-stealing, ability. Little Walter Jacobs, Jimmie Rodgers, Walter Horton, Junior Wells, James Cotton, Otis Spann, Willie Dixon, and countless others worked with, and were influenced by, Muddy Waters.

While his regional ethnic deep-blues style never appealed to the majority of African American record consumers, Southern Blacks and city folks with Southern roots supported his music. Through the 1960s and 1970s, however, his African American audience waned and he worked more and more for a revival audience. From down-home Delta folk artist, to Chicago ethnic star, to international superstar, Waters changed his music very little. A distinctive if limited instrumentalist, he was a great vocalist and a superb bandleader who recognized talent in others and had the strength to mold it into his own sound. His overall aesthetic remained keyed to the African American oral tradition, and his music has a timeless quality fueled by his personal charisma, the strength of his supporting musicians, and the quality of the Chess studios, which captured and polished the blues tradition at its best.

Barry Lee Pearson

References

Rooney, James. 1971. *Bossmen: Bill Monroe and Muddy Waters.* New York: Da Capo.
Palmer, Robert. 1982. *Deep Blues.* New York: Viking Penguin.

See also Blues

Watson, Arthel ("Doc") (1923–)

Virtuoso of the flat-picked acoustic guitar. From Deep Gap, North Carolina, Watson, with his vast repertoire of folk, country, and rockabilly songs, was one of the most commercially enduring instrumentalists to emerge from the folk revival. From his first New York concert in 1961 until his semiretirement in the late 1980s, Watson performed throughout the world, spending as many as 300 nights a year on the road and producing more than two dozen recordings.

Watson was born in Stoney Fork, North Carolina, the sixth of nine children born to Annie and General Dixon Watson. He contracted an eye disease as an infant that left him blind before he was two years old. His musical education began at home with a new harmonica in his holiday stocking each year and, at the age of eleven, a homemade banjo, built by his father. When he was twelve years old, Watson purchased a $12.00 Stella guitar and began to learn songs from the family's collection of 78-rpm recordings of the Skillet Lickers, the Carter Family, the Carolina Tar Heels, Jimmie Rodgers, Riley Puckett, and Mississippi John Hurt.

Watson acquired the nickname Doc when he was eighteen years old. While preparing to play for a remote radio broadcast at a furniture store, an announcer, deciding that Arthel was too cumbersome for the air, called him Doc. The name stuck.

It wasn't until 1953 that Watson became a successful working musician, teaming up with Tennessee piano player Jack Williams in a country-western-rockabilly band. It was during the 1950s that Watson, playing a Les Paul electric guitar, developed his skillful flat-picking style, often playing fiddle leads on the guitar.

In 1960 folklorist Ralph Rinzler, while researching traditional musicians in North Carolina, was introduced to

Watson by legendary banjo player Clarence Ashley. Impressed by Watson's skill, Rinzler arranged for him to play at Town Hall in New York City and at the Newport Folk Festival in Rhode Island in 1961. Soon after, Watson was much in demand at concert halls, coffeehouses and festivals across the country.

In 1946 Watson married Rosa Lee Carlton, the daughter of accomplished mountain fiddler Gaither Carlton. They had two children. Son Merle developed into an accomplished guitarist, and in 1964, at the age of fifteen, he joined his father as accompanist, road manager, and guide. For more than a decade, father and son were near-constant musical and personal companions until Merle's tragic death in a tractor accident in 1985.

To date (1995), Doc Watson has won four Grammy Awards, and in 1988 he was a recipient of a National Heritage Fellowship from the National Endowment for the Arts.

Henry Willett

See also Revivalism; Rinzler, Ralph Carter

Weatherlore

Beliefs and practices related to prediction, interpretation, and control of the weather. Most weather beliefs focus on signs of things to come, but many indicate magical causes and effects. Proverbs, tales, legends, rituals, and material culture extend the scope of weatherlore, which has regional variations but often covers large segments of the United States.

By far the largest corpus of weather customs and beliefs has to do with rain, a crucial ingredient in the growing of crops. People have scrutinized the sun, the moon, the stars, the sky, animals, birds, and insects to figure out when rain will come. For example, Illinois folklore states that a solar halo may indicate rain before night; a sun dog (parhelic halo) north of the sun means rain from the northwest, while a sun dog south of the sun means rain from the southwest. After an eclipse of the sun, one can expect five full days of rain. From New York folklore comes a proverb familiar to many Americans: "When there's a ring around the moon, rain is coming soon." A moon that has changed during the night may presage a wet season. Stars can also give clues about rain, as in this New York proverb about an upside-down Big Dipper: "If the stars are in a huddle, the world will be in a puddle." African American folklore states that if a circle around the moon encloses three stars, there will be rain in less than three days.

Colors of the sky and patterns of clouds are frequent indicators of rain. One popular mariners' proverb, also known by farmers, explains, "Red sky at night, sailors' delight. Red sky at morning, sailors take warning." Red skies generally signal rain, unless they follow gray. In New England tradition, a greenish tinge near the horizon means that rain will come soon, while a purple haze indicates a return to fine weather. Cloud patterns such as a "mackerel sky" (clouds in parallel bands) are widely recognized as rain indicators: "Mackerel sky, mackerel sky, three days wet and three days dry."

Animals, birds, and insects have a prominent role as weather forecasters throughout the United States. People say that cows will lie down, dogs and cats will become agitated, and ants will scurry to shelter as rain approaches. Seagulls will fly inland as a rainstorm builds; fish will begin to bite more readily, and bees or flies will sting harder. Even flowers can foretell rain's approach by the opening and closing of their buds.

Since flora and fauna can forecast rain, it is not surprising that people also can do this under certain circumstances. Rheumatism or a broken bone can make a person feel twinges before a rainstorm. Other sensations that presage rain include pains in corns, ringing in the ear, and a "lazy feeling." Itching on the heel or sole of the foot can mean either rain or snow; more specifically, if the nose itches three times in an hour, rain will come within twenty-four hours. An Illinois proverb states, "Curls that kink and cords that bind, sing of rain and heavy wind" (Hyatt 1965:30). Some people think that the elderly are better forecasters, because old bones feel rain more acutely than young ones.

Deliberate efforts to bring rain are fairly prominent in American folklore. The oldest practices come from Native American lore. For example, the Hopi snake-antelope dance calls upon the well-known power of snakes to invoke rain. Dancers wash the snakes in yucca suds, then release them toward the north, south, east, and west. Snake dances and other kinds of rain dances have occurred among numerous Native American peoples. Cross-culturally, snakes and other reptiles have a strong connection to rainmaking. According to both African American and general American folklore, one can bring rain by turning a dead snake belly-up or hanging it on a fence.

In the late 19th century in Nebraska, professional "rainmakers" sought to earn their pay by firing explosions from balloons, building large, smoky fires, or setting off gunpowder explosions from high peaks. More recent and lighthearted formulas for bringing rain include forgetting to carry an umbrella, opening an umbrella in the house, stopping a swing by dragging one's feet, and (probably most popular of all) washing and waxing a car.

Those who want to prevent rain may follow the Illinois adage, "Preparation for rain scares it away" (Hyatt 1965:32). One way to stop rain from coming is to turn upside down all buckets and other receptacles that are out in the yard. To keep rain from spoiling a picnic, some try to "fool" the weather by making no plans until the day the picnic will occur. In spite of people's best efforts, July 4 is likely to be rainy because—according to popular belief—ammunition and fireworks bring rain down from the sky.

On certain ceremonial occasions, rain has the onus of causing bad luck. A rainy wedding day may be a bad omen for the newly married pair; in North Carolina, rain (or snow) on the wedding day means that the groom will die first. On the other hand, some newlyweds who have married on rainy days have contended that rain brings especially good luck. Since rain is helpful for farmers, it may bring good things for the young couple. Nonetheless, rain on the traditional day for sweethearts, Valentine's Day, is a sign of trouble on the farm: Hens will stop laying.

Next to the many signs and results of rain, indicators of

the onset and severity of winter fill the annals of American weatherlore. Animals and birds can tell us if a winter will be harsh: Caterpillars will become very fuzzy; cats, dogs, foxes, and skunks will grow heavy coats; turkeys will roost high in a tree; and hogs will run around with straws in their mouths. In New England, oysters will burrow deep into their beds in the ocean. A popular New York proverb predicts winter's development: "As the days begin to lengthen, the cold begins to strengthen." Concern about heavy snow and fog ("A January fog will freeze a hog") emerges from folklore of the Northeast. Magic for stopping snow is somewhat rare; however, a Texas custom calls for striking a sputtering log in the fireplace to dislodge gas, break the spell of winter, and make the snow stop falling (Hendricks 1980:146).

Folklore across the United States chronicles many positive effects of winter. In North Carolina, a snowy winter means a good crop year, because the land is wet and insects are not numerous. Similarly, in Illinois snow at Christmas and wind on New Year's Day bring fruit in profusion. A "white Christmas" means health in New England: "When Christmas is white, the graveyard is lean; but fat is the graveyard when Christmas is green" (Botkin 1947:633).

Even though snow has these beneficial effects, people watch eagerly for signs of winter coming to a close. Groundhog Day or Candlemas Day, February 2, is the day when a groundhog, badger, or bear can foretell winter's end. If willows bud early and ducks lay ahead of schedule, one can expect winter to end early. And if a person sees baby squirrels in open nests in late February, an early spring is almost certain to arrive.

Since the 1950s, when the neopagan movement gathered force in England and North America, some individuals who identify themselves as neopagans or witches have accepted responsibility for causing severe winter weather, rainstorms, and winds. Using spells that date back to medieval European magic, neopagans have claimed to bring about dramatic weather changes, including blizzards and hurricanes. One medieval spell used in the 1990s involves knotting a cord while facing in a certain direction and whistling or spitting for wind or rain. When the spell setter releases the knots, the preset weather will come forth to surprise local inhabitants.

Just as medieval lore has influenced neopagan weather spells, ancient mariners' beliefs have had an impact upon relatively recent folklore of the sea. There are many stories and customs about buying the wind: throwing a nickel, a dime, or a quarter overboard to purchase a breeze for a sailing ship or small boat. This practice originates from efforts to buy the wind through human sacrifice in ancient times. One Texas narrative tells of a man who, in his greed for favorable weather, bought a dollar's worth of wind. His boat capsized, and his wife and children drowned (Mullin 1978:35–40).

Folklore about tornadoes, mainly from the Midwest and the Southwest, has to do with both prediction and prevention. Midwesterners say that a sky with a sickly, greenish cast tells you that a tornado is coming; Texans predict that a tornado follows the first thunder after the last snow. Those intrepid enough to try to deflect a tornado can turn it in another direction by driving a double-bit ax into the top of a stump, with the ax handle pointing in the direction desired. Deflection may not be necessary, though, if one relies on the belief that a tornado cannot strike a town located in a valley or between mountains or hills (Hendricks 1980:147).

Like tornadoes, lightning is something to deflect or avoid. "Lightning never strikes twice in the same place," a well-known proverb, helps to explain why people sometimes hide under burnt trees or logs. Methods for warding off lightning in Illinois include throwing an ax into the yard and burning blessed palm leaves. In Texas, people may cover mirrors and cross their suspenders. Some Americans believe that unplugging their television sets and wearing rubber shoes will decrease their chances of having lightning strike their homes. Lightning has connotations of divine punishment and diabolical presence, as in the African American belief that if lightning strikes while a man is dying, the devil has come for his soul. Some Native Americans on the North Pacific Coast have explained lightning as a flash of the Thunderbird's eye; others have perceived lightning as Thunder's wife or younger brother.

The precursor of lightning, thunder has many colorful explanations. Texans say thunder is the result of the devil's potato wagon turning over, while Native Americans on the North Pacific Coast say it comes from Thunderbirds flapping their wings or striking trees. Pueblo Native Americans sometimes call thunder by rolling two stone balls in front of a meal altar in their kiva. There are two Cherokee thunder boys, Tame Boy and Wild Boy. Some American children enjoy baking a "thundercake" when they first hear thunder and starting to eat it when the storm breaks (if the storm allows enough time for baking).

In addition to the rich array of verbal folklore, material culture shows a strong orientation toward the weather. Weathervanes featuring horses, arrows, and other figures are very popular. In Pennsylvania Dutch country, hex signs depict raindrops, thunderbolts, and other symbols of weather, either to propitiate or prevent. Even though meteorological science has taken over the official forecasting of American weather, folklore still offers a significant way for people to seek understanding and control of phenomena that often seem to defy rational analysis.

Elizabeth Tucker

References

Botkin, Ben A. 1947. *A Treasury of New England Folklore.* New York: Crown, pp. 630–635.

Brewer, J. Mason. 1968. *American Negro Folklore.* Chicago: Quadrangle Books, pp. 303–305.

Cutting, Edith. 1952. *Whistling Girls and Jumping Sheep.* Cooperstown: Farmer's Museum and New York Folklore Society, pp. 29–46.

Dorson, Richard M. 1964. *Buying the Wind: Regional Folklore in the U.S.* Chicago: University of Chicago Press, pp. 122–124.

Hand, Wayland D., ed. 1964. *The Frank C. Brown Collection of North Carolina Folklore.* Vol. 7. Durham, NC: Duke University Press, pp. 209–371, 510–511, 542, 577.

Hendricks, George D. 1980. *Roosters, Rhymes, and Railroad Tracks*. Dallas: Southern Methodist University Press, pp. 140–148.

Hyatt, Harry M. 1965. *Folklore from Adams County Illinois*. Hannibal, MO: Western Printing and Lithographing, pp. 1–35.

Mullin, Patrick B. 1978. *I Heard the Old Fishermen Say: Folklore of the Texas Gulf Coast*. Austin: University of Texas Press, pp. 35–40.

Pound, Louise. 1959. *Nebraska Folklore*. Lincoln: University of Nebraska Press, pp. 41–60.

See also Superstition

Weaving

The interlacing of two elements at right angles most often used in the construction of cloth. A loom is used in weaving to provide tension on the vertical, or warp, units while the horizontal, or weft, element is passed over and under the warp.

The weaving of cloth developed as one of the household arts and has been seen primarily as women's work in Western culture. However, when weaving evolved into the textile industry, males took over the occupation. In weaving, many currents exist simultaneously and intertwine. Woven textiles are either utilitarian or decorative and can be both. Weavers may use equipment as simple as a piece of cardboard and a stick or may employ complex looms and mechanisms. Weaving has been produced for personal, domestic use and manufactured for commercial sale. A weaver must have considerable skill to get a product at all, let alone be proficient at the craft. So, while other household arts have survived as popular hobbies, handweaving is practiced by relatively few when compared to the number of quilters or knitters.

Weaving encompasses a wide world from dish towels to huge narrative tapestries. Certainly weaving first began to supply functional items, but, like other crafts, embellishment made the use of these functional items more pleasing. Even the humble dish towel presents a wide range of options for the weaver. The weave structure may be the simple over-one-thread-and-under-the-next construction of a plain weave, or a diamond pattern created by varying the number of threads passed over and under in the repeated sequence. A waffle weave, the name indicative of the miniature indented grid created by the thread interlacement, combines function with design by increasing the absorbency of the towel. Desiring a greater visual effect, the weaver might choose a Damask structure, in which a warp-faced satin weave opposes weft-faced satin elements. Weave structures provide both decorative and functional qualities to the product.

Besides patterns created by combining the vertical warp elements with the horizontal weft elements, the weaver may employ color to enhance the towel. The towel can be a single color in both warp and weft, but decorative elements may be increased by weaving the body of the towel in a single color and switching to another color for a patterned border. Stripes of different colors in the warp produce striped towels if woven with a single color in the weft. When the striped warp is crossed with weft stripes, a plaid fabric is created. A checked towel results if uniform warp stripes, such as two light threads followed by two dark threads, are then woven with the same sequence of light and dark.

Fiber content and yarn size present other decisions to the weaver that will greatly affect the product. For the dish towel, the practical choice would be linen or cotton because of the absorbency of the fibers, wear potential, and reasonable cost. The function of the product, ease of construction, and decorative aspects all figure into the selection of yarn texture and size.

Continuing to use the dish towel as an example, this item would need a minimum of finishing after cutting from the loom. Most likely the towel would be woven vertically with selvages forming the two sides. A selvage is the edge of the fabric where the weft yarn reverses direction to combine with the warp in the next interlacement in the sequence. The resulting edge is firm and will not unravel. Hemming to a desired length or fringe completes the top and bottom of the towel. Warp left unwoven creates fringe, and the weft is secured with a locking stitch to prevent raveling.

Even for the very modest dish towel, a great number of decisions must be made in the production, with all affecting the usefulness and aesthetic qualities of the item. Other utilitarian weaving has at least as many functional and decorative considerations, and, most of the time, more. In your own home, walk from room to room and examine how and where textiles appear. Looking into the bedroom, you can catalog rugs on the floor, curtains at the window, and the bedcoverings—sheets, blankets, and spread. When you open the closet door you will see woven cloth in most of the garments. Textiles are so much a part of our daily lives and so easily and cheaply available that little thought is given to how they come to be. And since most of this fabric comes from machines in factories far away from sight, the significance and complexity of the process is not understood. The development of textiles coincides with the history of civilization at many important points. Domestication of animals for wool and the cultivation of crops for fibers led up to the Industrial Revolution, which began with the invention of the spinning jenny and continued with teaching machines to weave.

Very early in their histories, most cultures of the world discovered weaving independently and developed very complex structures for combining two elements. Carbon-dating of a piece of calcified fabric from near the headwaters of the Tigris River in what is now southern Turkey places the oldest cloth found at an age of 9,000 years. Archaeologists from the Oriental Institute of the University of Chicago identified the cloth as composed of linen fibers, but they also suspected that domesticated sheep and goats supplied wool.

Weaving is among the oldest crafts, predating even pottery. Baskets formed out of reeds probably represent the first weaving. While efficient for carrying multiple small items, baskets did not lend themselves to the transportation of water. Clay pressed inside the basket functioned better to contain liquids, as indentations of reeds in shards of prehistoric clay pots attest. A happy accident of civilization occurred when

Aldona Veselka,
Lithuanian-Ameri-
can weaver, at her
loom. Chicago,
1977. Photo Jonas
Dovydenas. Ameri-
can Folklife Center.

a clay-lined basket caught fire and burned away the reed, thus firing the clay into a vessel.

Before weaving can begin, the elements to weave have to be amassed. Reeds, grasses, vines, or other plant material constituted the earliest substances woven, used in baskets and mats. Twisting or spinning short fibers gathered from plant and animal sources produced a pliable element very suitable for weaving. Spinning can be accomplished with easily improvised equipment. A potato with a pencil stuck in it can function as a simple drop spindle. The weight assists in keeping the element turning, while the spinner feeds the fibers into the strand. A stick with a rock bound to the bottom served early spinners as a drop spindle. A spinning wheel speeds up the process. The actual twisting of the fibers occurs only at the very tip of the spindle, with the wheel simply being the mechanism for turning the spindle. In the United States, two major types of wheels have been used. The Great Wheel, or Walking Wheel, is a large wheel that the standing spinner keeps in motion with an occasional thrust from her hand. She draws out the fiber and lets it twist, taking three steps in the operation. The spinner sits on a stool for the smaller Flax Wheel and works a treadle with her foot, keeping the wheel turning to drive the spindle. Spinning is a time-consuming activity, taking many spinners to keep one weaver supplied with yarn. Unmarried women put to the task engendered the word "spinster," which although somewhat archaic still persists as a term for the unattached female.

The preparation of fibers for spinning depends on the source for the material. Natural fibers come in two basic types: cellulose from plants and protein derived from animals. While many other plants produce fibers that can be spun, cotton and flax have proven the most versatile and the easiest to grow. Linen or other long plant fibers draw directly from the distaff attached to the Flax Wheel in the spinning process. The term "distaff" to denote female lineage derives from this piece of spinning equipment.

Although the hair of most animals can be spun, wool from sheep is the favorite because of the early domestication of the animals and the rapidity with which the sheep grows a new coat. Carding prepares the wool fibers for spinning. Hand cards with rows of bent teeth comb the fibers in opposite directions to align them. Like wool, silk is also a protein fiber; it comes from the cocoon of a silkworm. Silk, although it can be spun, more often is unwound as a single filament from the cocoon after exterminating the worm inside. Rayon is a man-made fiber, of a cellulose base. Synthetic fibers, such as nylon, acrylic, and polyester, manufactured from combinations of chemicals, mimic properties of natural fibers. When spun, the synthetics reach the market under a variety of trade names like Orlon, Dacron, or Trevira.

Even though some fibers have color in their natural state, the tendency has been to add color. Dyestuffs to color yarn come from many natural sources, and throughout history the less accessible colors have had tremendous value. Royalty chose purple because of its scarcity, and brown fell to the common man because of the easy availability in many different tree barks. Most dyestuffs come from plants, although the red of cochineal derives from an insect, and the regal purple from a shellfish.

Specification of substance and time and temperature combine in natural dyeing formulas that passed down in families. The process first involves boiling yarn in a mordant, a chemical with a metal base. In the dye bath, the mordant unites with the dyestuff to form a tighter chemical bond than the dye alone would produce. Indigo does not require a mordant, because in this chemical process the indigo oxidizes when the fiber is exposed to air after being removed from the dye bath. Other than onion skins that give a golden brown color, most dyestuffs are very toxic. Pictures of dyeing for home use usually show a large iron kettle over a fire. The metal pot supplied the mordant while the open air dispersed the toxins. Since it is extremely difficult for large quantities of yarn to be dyed with natural dyes, the formulation of chemical dyes was of major significance to the textile world.

A loom may be a very large complex device or a small hand-held one such as the pronged metal, or now plastic, square that thousands of children have used to weave pot holders with cotton loopers. The function of a loom is to hold the warp, or vertical, threads at equal tension. Down through history some ingenious devices to do this have come into being. In ancient Greece, the vertically suspended warp was weighted with rocks. Several different peoples have come up with a loom in which the weaver is part of the warp tensioning. With various regional differentiations, the warp is stretched between two rods, with one end tied to an immovable object like a tree and the other rod secured around the waist of the weaver by a strap. With this back-strap loom, the weaver adjusted the tension by leaning back.

While the main purpose of the loom is to keep equal tension on warp threads, many other features contribute to the efficiency of the process and assist in pattern formation. The standard loom for the American handweaver is a foot-powered, four-harness jack type, constructed of maple and capable of weaving fabric 40 inches wide. The foot pedals, or treadles, activate the harnesses, which raise threads through a counterbalance, countermarch jack, or dobby mechanism. The number of harnesses determines the complexity of the weave structures possible on the loom. With more harnesses, more complex structures can be attempted, but more is not necessarily better; only different in kind. On a four-harness loom, thousands of patterns can be woven within four-harness weave structures. When combined with variations in color and yarn weight and texture, the possibilities are endless.

Before the weaver begins the actual weaving process, the loom must be dressed or warped. After planning the project, the weaver needs to put the exact number of warp threads needed to the same length. Winding threads in the desired

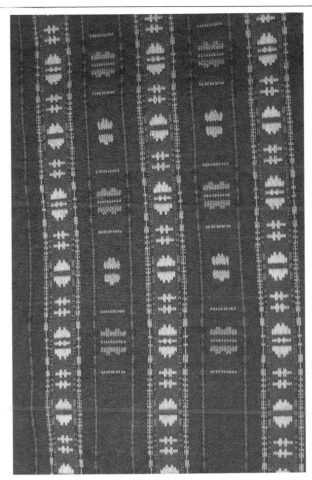

Cloth woven by Aldona Veselka, using traditional Lithuanian motifs. Chicago, 1977. Photo Jonas Dovydenas. American Folklife Center.

color sequence around pegs on a warping board or rotating them around a reel measures and arranges the threads. Although methods of putting the warp on the loom differ, all threads are separated through the reed, pass in the planned order through heddles on the harnesses, and are stored on the warp beam at the back of the loom. The long and tedious process of warping must be done accurately. A mistake will either make weaving impossible or show as a very visible defect throughout the entire fabric. A warp may be the length of a single project or long enough to accommodate many items. To return to the dish towel example, the threading of the loom takes the same time for one item as it does for 100. Because the weaver has options to vary the pattern and choose weft yarns of different kinds and colors, the resulting 100 towels may be identical or each one may be unique.

When the warp is finally tied to the cloth beam of the loom, the weaver is ready to begin the actual process of weaving. A treadle is depressed, bringing up threads and creating a shed; the shuttle with the weft yarn is thrown through the shed; and the weft is packed into place by the beater before advancing to the next shot or pick. The treadles activate the harnesses according to a desired sequence for the pattern.

Weavers save patterns in a system called a draft. Drafts from the early American years use long strips of paper that have lines drawn on them similar to a music staff. Tally marks denote the positioning of the warp threads on the harnesses

in the sequence in which the warp thread must be placed to achieve the pattern. Usually, the old draft rolls have tiny holes where generations of weavers have placed pins to keep their place during the warping.

The early American colonists led a frontier life, but the colonies were not intended from their inception to be self-sufficient. The parent country wanted raw materials from its satellites and also desired a market for finished goods. Unfortunately, a very large ocean lay between parent and child. And while this economic model worked well on paper, the practicality of transporting goods caused many problems, including increasing the cost of those goods. So one could assume that fabric production that could have been done in the home would have been. However, the colonists imported most of the textiles they used. Fashion, habit, and the extent of the skills required in home fabric production account for this. In some of the colonies, attempts to establish commercial textile manufacturing met with laws forbidding their establishment. When the Industrial Revolution advanced in the mid-18th century, with the invention of the spinning jenny followed by the automation of the loom, the secrets were jealously guarded and export of machinery forbidden. Although the colonial powers curtailed the development of a domestic commercial textile industry, methods for the construction of power looms found their way to America in the minds of immigrants. Although not of fine quality, local cloth manufacturing grew rapidly.

Individuals who came to the New World did know how to prepare fibers and weave. With an understanding of the weaving process, they were able to make spinning wheels and looms using simple woodworking tools. During the Revolutionary War, the wearing of "homespun" even gained fashion as a defiant and patriotic gesture. After the war, handweaving continued as a home art, most often in isolated areas where people had very little possibility of earning money to purchase necessities. Frontier life included weaving, but frontier settlers readily abandoned the tedious work when options to purchase textiles became available.

With increased migration to the United States in the 19th century, different peoples brought their skills in textile production with them. When ethnic groups concentrated in rural areas and farmed, the likelihood of continuing some weaving increased. Hispanic families wove rugs in the Southwest, and Scandinavian peoples brought their weaving to the Midwest. While household necessity played some role in the weaving, decorative and traditional cultural items proved more popular. Examples of weavers' work can be found in ethnic museums throughout the United States. While some of this has a traditional base, as seen in the folk costumes in the Lithuanian Museum in Chicago, most items defy specific cultural identity.

Since the rigidity of the weaving process imposes conditions on the product, and since the history of woven textiles is extremely long, the attribution of different weaving techniques to specific ethnic groups is very tricky. It is not even possible to trace to a specific European country the lineage of the most admired American woven item, the overshot coverlet. Found in hundreds of individualized patterns, coverlets, unlike totally utilitarian items, have been saved rather than discarded when signs of wear appeared. The older coverlets employ a linen warp, while the ones from early in the 20th century use a commercially spun bleached cotton yarn. Handspun and naturally dyed with the blue of indigo or red of madder, wool creates the pattern in the weft. Although coverlets can be found in many weave structures, overshot is by far the most common because it could be produced in the home on a four-harness loom. While some names like "Whig Rose" or "Lee's Surrender" refer to specific designs, others like "Pine Tree" or "Snowball" denote specific pattern figures. Weavers named patterns as they ordered design elements in new combinations, so similar patterns may have very different titles, or the variation may carry the same name as the original.

Besides handweaving items for home use, during the 1800s handweaving existed as a commercial venture, with the weaver producing commissioned items. Sometimes the customer would supply some of the material, such as handspun weft yarn. Primarily in the South, itinerant weavers traveled from plantation to plantation setting up looms and weaving with the help of slave labor. As in the Revolutionary War, the South considered it patriotic to wear homespun during the Civil War. Although the South produced cotton, the North owned the mills that turned it into cloth. By the mid-19th century, most fabric came from industrial looms. Although the names of some handweavers in the 1800s are known, many more worked outside the historical record with only an occasional product surviving to attest to their existence. Through her diary, we know that after her husband's death, Narcissa Erwin Black ran a thriving weaving business on the family plantation in McNairy County, Tennessee. An African American woman, Chany Scot Black, owned her own loom and assisted Narcissa Black in all phases of the weaving process both before and after Emancipation.

In the latter part of the 19th century, thousands of looms were sold to farm families in the Midwest, marketed as a vehicle for providing supplemental income. Many of these looms featured a fly-shuttle, a spring mechanism for propelling the shuttle through the open warp, or devices to control the raising of harnesses in set sequences. Rag rugs rolled off looms by the thousands and became quite fashionable as a floor covering in Colonial Revival interiors. Many customers salvaged fabric from used clothing and worn household items to supply their own rags cut into strips and sewn together ready for use as weft. The weaver calculated the cost by the inch for the weaving of the rug.

In Britain, in reaction to Victorian industrialization, John Ruskin and William Morris started the Arts and Crafts movement to promote handcrafted items. When these ideas traveled across the Atlantic, eager converts enlisted in most major American cities. As a leader in the Arts and Crafts movement with Tiffany and Stickley, Candace Wheeler promoted home decoration and the textile arts and established cooperatives for women. She first learned weaving as a household art during her childhood in upstate New York. Max West, in a 1904 Department of Labor bulletin details the activities of the many centers that promoted weaving as part of philanthropic efforts to help diverse populations. The Acadians of Louisiana, the Mothers and Daughters Industry of Plainfield, New Hampshire, the Southern-mountain weaving around Asheville, North Carolina, organized by the Presbyterian missionary Frances Louisa Goodrich, and several dozen other cooperatives received his notice. Jane Addams included spinning and weaving demonstrations as part of the Hull House Labor Museum designed to emphasize the dignity and importance of labor while providing links to the European cultures of the Chicago immigrants. The Shakers wove for their own use in their communities in New England, Ohio, and Kentucky and for commercial sale.

Late into the 19th century in some parts of the Appalachian Mountains, women continued weaving, supplying many of the textile needs of their homes as part of a subsistence lifestyle. In 1892, shortly after assuming the presidency of Berea College at the western edge of the Appalachian Mountains in Kentucky, William Goodell Frost received the gift of a coverlet. He believed that encouraging women to weave would have two major benefits as he promoted the college in the North. First, the beautiful designs would stand as testament to the worthiness of their creators, overcoming the negative stereotypes of mountain people as barely civilized and lazy. Second, the sale of the items would provide much

needed "cash money" to the weavers. When President Frost tried to commission half a dozen coverlets from a local woman, he received a detailed lesson on preparation of fibers and the dyeing and weaving process. The weaver estimated it would take twelve months to complete the work because many of the steps in the process could be performed only at a specific time of the year. In 1911 Berea hired Swedish-born Anna Ernberg to manage the Fireside Industry that provided part-time employment to women working in their own homes. Ernberg not only expanded the home-based production, but also developed weaving as one of the Berea College student industries. Hundreds of girls paid their tuition to high school and college by working in the log buildings that housed the weaving on the Berea campus.

During the early part of the 20th century, more than 150 settlement schools sprang up in the remote areas of the Appalachian Mountains, not only to educate children, but also to provide for the social and health needs of the families. While Protestant denominations sponsored most of these schools, women's organizations ran some of the most successful of the programs. Women of the Pi Beta Phi fraternity moved into Gatlinburg, Tennessee, in 1912, and by 1915 looms followed as part of the industrial program at their school. In 1925 Winogene Redding assumed management of the weaving, and the number of women working in the cottage industry grew rapidly. In the ten years between 1935 and 1945, no less than ninety weavers worked for Arrowcraft, the shop named for the Pi Beta Phi symbol. Hundreds of women learned to weave, many of them setting up shops of their own or working in others that appealed to the increasing tourist trade promoted by creation of the Great Smoky Mountains National Park.

Other early school-based weaving programs prospered at Hindman and Pine Mountain in Kentucky, Crossnore and John C. Campbell in North Carolina, and Tallulah Falls and Berry in Georgia. Although Lucy Morgan started the Penland Weavers and Potters as a Fireside Industry of the Appalachian School in North Carolina, it became independent of the school during the Depression. Edward F. Worst, the manual-arts coordinator for the Chicago public schools, demonstrated linen weaving to the Penland Weavers in 1928. Weavers around the country heard about the Worst visit through an article by Paul Bernat in the *Handicrafter* and requested to be included in the next workshop. The annual summer weaving institute expanded rapidly and, with the addition of other crafts, developed into the Penland School. Penland; the Arrowmont School of Arts and Crafts, which is still maintained by Pi Beta Phi in Gatlinburg; and the John C. Campbell Folk School at Brasstown, North Carolina, that grew out of the craft work of the settlement schools form the leaders in workshop-format craft education.

The women organizers who revived weaving in the Southern Highlands stated their two major goals as keeping alive a vanishing craft and supplying employment to local women. The weaving could be done at home while tending children, house, and farm. The settlement activity served as a model for other mountain craft businesses. In Berea, the Matheny Weavers and the Churchill Weavers; in Asheville, the Spinning Wheel; and at Russellville, Tennessee, the Shuttle-Crafters all began in the 1920s and turned out thousands of hand towels, placemats, and baby blankets, as well as the traditional coverlets.

The settlement workers met yearly in Knoxville, Tennessee, at the Conference of the Southern Mountain Workers and discovered that they shared similar problems in their craft-production activities. After an organizational meeting in 1929 at Penland, the schools and the craft-production centers joined together under the banner of the Southern Highland Handicraft Guild. The new organization addressed the common problems of publicizing work, marketing, quality control, and upgrading skills of workers.

Mary Meigs Atwater, often referred to as "The Dean of American Handweaving," published her first issue of the *Shuttle-Craft Guild Bulletin* in 1924. Through this subscription service for weavers, she shared her extensive research in weave structures and her pattern designs. Swedish weavers Margaret Bergman and Mama Valborg Gravander taught weaving and led the weaving community in their respective adopted homes of Seattle and San Francisco. Anni Albers brought the philosophy of the German art school, The Bauhaus, to this country. From her handweaving design studio in San Francisco, Dorothy Liebes produced fabrics that enlivened the use of color in weaving. Within a locality, the usual pattern was for there to be one principal teacher with guilds developing as groups of students desired contact and sharing with other weavers. Elsie Gubser led the handweaving community in Tulsa, Oklahoma. Lou Tate published the *Kentucky Weaver Newsletter* and taught weaving at her Little Loomhouse in Louisville. By the mid-20th century, most handweavers owned a copy of Marguerite Porter Davison's *A Handweaver's Pattern Book* and subscribed to Mary Alice Smith's quarterly *Handweaver and Craftsman.*

Within most cities of any size and quite a few rural areas, weavers have organized themselves into guilds. Weavers are by far the most organized of the crafter, and weavers, disproportionate to their numbers, assume leadership roles in craft organizations. Weavers Guilds hold regular meetings, sponsor workshops with weaving professionals, organize exhibitions, and engage in community-service education projects. Different parts of the country have either separate organizations or federations of guilds that sponsor regional conferences. On the national level the Handweavers Guild of America (HGA) sponsors Convergence, the major conference every two years that draws an average attendance of 2,000. The HGA, founded in 1969, offers many services to its members including the quarterly publication *Shuttle, Spindle, and Dyepot.*

The bimonthly *Handwoven* and the quarterly *Weavers* aim their full-color magazines exclusively at the handweaver. The magazines concentrate on techniques, improving skills, and how-to-do-it projects, with an occasional article on textile history. Interweave Press, Dos Tejedoras Fiber Arts Publications, and Lark Books publish textile books, many of them of a technical nature aimed at the experienced handweaver.

Handweaving is practiced throughout the United States primarily by women. The typical weaver is in her late forties, married to a professional man, mother of two children, holds a degree, and has done some graduate study, most often in the sciences. Her weaving may be the major focus of her life or may fill leisure hours. She may weave as a commercial venture or be a serious investigator of her craft. She may weave garments and functional projects for her home or use weaving for artistic expression. She may have learned to weave at a craft school, a professional art school, or a college, but most probably it was at a recreation program or from an experienced weaver. However the introduction to weaving occurred, she has an extensive library of weaving books and takes an occasional workshop.

Philis Alvic

References

Atwater, Mary Meigs. 1961. *The Shuttle Craft Book of American Handweaving.* New York: Macmillan.

Burnham, Harold B., and Dorothy K. Burnham. 1972. *"Keep Me Warm One Night": Early Handweaving in Eastern Canada.* Toronto: University of Toronto Press, in cooperation with the Royal Ontario Museum.

Eaton, Allen H. [1937] 1973. *Handicrafts of the Southern Highlands.* New York: Dover.

Goodrich, Frances Louisa. [1931] 1989. *Mountain Homespun.* Knoxville: University of Tennessee Press.

Gordon, Beverly. 1980. *Shaker Textile Arts.* Hanover, NH: University Press of New England, in cooperation with the Merrimack Valley Textile Museum and the Shaker Community Inc.

Meany, Janet, and Paula Pfaff. 1988. *Rag Rug Handbook.* St. Paul, MN: Dos Tejedoras Fiber Arts Publications.

Personal Stories: Handweaving in America between 1920 and 1960. 1990. *Handwoven* 11 (3).

Wilson, Sadye Tune, and Doris Finch Kennedy. 1983. *Of Coverlets: The Legacies, the Weavers.* Nashville: Tunstede.

Worst, Edward F. 1918. *Foot-Power Loom Weaving.* New York: Dover.

See also Folk Schools

Weddings

Tradition-regulated ceremonies joining couples in marriage. Weddings have generated rich folklore that crosses all cultures with variations and often contradictions. Symbolizing the transfer of a woman to her husband's family, weddings follow a prescribed set of rituals and superstitions that people believe will ensure happiness and safety for the couple.

Basic themes of folktales about weddings include the enchantment motif of marriages, with animals who transform into humans who had been held under spells, brides who marry a hero who saved their life, and grooms who undergo an initiation rite or solve riddles to win the bride.

Modern weddings have mythological and historical precedents. The wedding date is a crucial decision. Only certain months and days, depending on the couple's culture, are acceptable. When agriculture dominated daily life, winter weddings were considered to be best: "When December's showers fall fast,

At a Lithuanian-American wedding, the bride's mother adjusts the bride's costume. Chicago, 1977. Photo Jonas Dovydenas. American Folklife Center.

Marry and true love will last." Weddings coinciding with the new moon ensured fertility.

The site of the wedding also is important. Churches have replaced the older ceremonial location in the town square or near the tombstones of the couple's ancestors. Modern "church wedding" sites include the Las Vegas wed-

ding chapels that add eccentricities to traditional wedding lore. Once the couple establishes a date and a place, weather predicts the climate of their marriage: If a thunderstorm rages during the ceremony, for example, in one belief, the couple will be barren.

Superstitious taboos, such as the bride not baking her

wedding cake or making her gown, regulate prenuptial activity. The bride is also warned not to use her married surname or to wear her bridal gown before she is wed for fear of jinxing the ceremony. The participants' garb is also strictly regulated by custom. The well-known phrase "Something old, something new, something borrowed, something blue" dictates the basics of most bride's wardrobes. The wedding gown's color is especially crucial to depict chastity; popular rhymes note that "Married in white, you have chosen all right" but warn that "Married in pink, your fortunes will sink."

Brides also adorn their attire with trinkets and may wear a coin in a shoe in order to promise wealth. Some brides even carry sugar lumps in their gloves to ensure sweetness in their marriage, and many brides wear at least one item, often a veil, borrowed from a happily married woman.

Folk taboos about the bride include the warnings that she must not see the groom before the wedding, sometimes carried to the extreme of arranging for a proxy at the wedding rehearsal. This custom derives from protective customs to prevent brides from being abducted. Stories about the groom distinguishing his bride from a group of veiled women continues this theme and seems to be the basis for having several bridesmaids. The wedding procession must carefully approach the church, and if a toad hops across the couple's path, some say, they will have good luck. The opposite is true if they encounter a funeral procession.

The couple should begin walking toward the altar on their right foot to the strains of the traditional wedding march, and it is a common tradition that the marriage will be a happy one if the couple's feet point in the same direction as the floor boards of the church. Gold rings, symbolizing the nobility and continuity of the union, are placed on the hands according to the couple's cultural customs. The bride is advised to cry to banish sadness for the remainder of her marriage.

In some cultures, the couple jump forward, or backward, over a broom handle to seal their vows. An old custom, seldom observed, requires that an older unmarried sister of the bride must "dance in the pig trough" during the wedding.

The wedding reception provides more folklore, mostly concerning the wedding cake. One popular belief says that if the bride cuts the cake first, with the groom placing his hand over hers, their marriage will be cooperative. This ritual also ensures fertility. Some traditions urge the couple to fast, while others insist that they eat their entire meal for good luck. Trinkets in the shape of rings, horseshoes, and cupids are often baked inside the cake. Cages of doves promote a harmonious home. In the Jewish community, breaking a glass promises luck and a lasting marriage. The wedding dance validates the couple's union.

As the couple depart for the honeymoon, guests throw rice or seeds to ensure fertility and prosperity. Bells and fireworks blare as protective magic against any ill wishes cast against the couple. Whoever catches the bride's bouquet (tossed over her head while she is facing away from the unmarried women at the reception) is commonly believed to be the next who will marry.

Many newlyweds exit the church under arches—swords or rifles if the groom is a military man—symbolizing their completing the rite of passage. Guests frequently decorate the honeymoon car, retaining aspects of the *charivari* (shivaree) during which the couple were serenaded loudly by friends.

Elizabeth D. Schafer

References

Baker, Margaret. 1977. *Wedding Customs and Folklore.* Vancouver: David and Charles.

Dick, Ernst S. 1966. The Bridesman in the Indo-European Tradition: Ritual and Myth in Marriage Ceremonies. *Journal of American Folklore* 79:338–347.

Higgins, Rodney. 1984. The Plant-Lore of Courtship and Marriage. In *Plant-Lore Studies,* ed. Roy Vickery. London: Folklore Society, pp. 94–110.

Röhrich, Lutz. 1991. *Folktales and Reality,* trans. Peter Tokofsky. Bloomington: Indiana University Press.

Vickers, Carol. 1985. Something Old, Something New: Folklore in Matrimony. *Mississippi Folklore Register* 19:61–65.

See also Anniversaries; Shivaree

Wells, Evelyn Kendrick (1891–1979)

Educator, collector, author. *The Ballad Tree* (1950), an outgrowth of Wells' popular ballad class at Wellesley College, was the first comprehensive ballad study to enliven accurate library scholarship with astute field experience. Wells had supplemented her years of collecting while on the staff of Pine Mountain Settlement School in Kentucky (intermittently from 1915 to 1930) with fieldwork in the Northeast and in Britain. An anthology, history, and critique, the volume includes ballads well beyond the Child canon, highlights the American tradition, analyzes aesthetic issues, provides detailed data about singers, treats even-handedly the creation-memorization issue, and devotes an entire chapter to context. Its portrait of Cecil Sharp as field collector is based on firsthand observation.

Like Bertrand H. Bronson, Wells considered tune integral to the ballad. *The Ballad Tree* features carefully annotated tunes. And a 1958 review article in the *Journal of the English Folk Dance and Song Society* hails Joseph W. Hendren's analysis of the interdependence of text and tune in *Study of Ballad Rhythm* while lamenting the inaccuracy of Vance Randolph's transcriptions and the separation of texts and tunes in the Frank C. Brown collection.

At Pine Mountain, Wells discovered the singing Ritchie family, later bringing two of the daughters to study at Wellesley. Like Sharp and Olive Dame Campbell, she was interested in social and recreational uses of folk dance and folksong, and she taught them at Pine Mountain, during her tenure at Wellesley (1935–1956), and at the Country Dance Society camp at Pinewoods, Massachusetts. In 1961 she received the Gold Medal of the English Folk Dance and Song Society.

William Bernard McCarthy

Welsh Americans

Immigrants and their descendants from Wales (*Cymru,* in the Welsh language). The Welsh, or *Cymry* ("fellow countrymen"), were the original British, a Celtic people who occupied most of Britain until Anglo-Saxon invaders in the 6th and 7th centuries started pushing them back into the north and the west, eventually into present-day Wales. "Welsh" is a Saxon term for "foreigners." The Welsh have been entwined in American history from the earliest days of European exploration and settlement—colonizing Virginia in 1607, searching for the Northwest Passage, and helping establish the new nation through such an illustrious figure as Thomas Jefferson. Apart from the individual explorers, the Welsh came in several waves of migration, each with its own motivation—seeking religious freedom, political and cultural freedom, and economic improvement.

The first religious exiles were Welsh Baptists who settled on the Plymouth-Rhode Island border in 1667 at a healthy distance from the disapproving Puritans. In the 1680s, Welsh Quakers settled on land purchased from William Penn and were soon followed to Pennsylvania by Welsh Baptists who settled the area of Philadelphia, establishing their own Welsh barony before moving on to Delaware.

In the late 18th and the 19th centuries, driven by the economic pressures of an expanding population, poor crops, and rack-renting (extortionate rents, often equal to the full value of the land), emigrants from north Wales sought the farmlands of New York and then further west as they crossed the Alleghenies into western Pennsylvania, Ohio, Kentucky, Wisconsin, and beyond. In this period, the Welsh were also influenced by a new sense of nationalism and a desire to preserve their culture and language in the face of opposition from the English state and church. Their sense of being one people with their own language and culture had been forged in the period of the Anglo-Saxon invasions and had survived the loss of independence in 1282 and the Act of Union of 1536, but in the 19th century the Welsh faced yet more virulent assaults. Despairing of a future for their culture in their homeland, many were impelled to America by hopes of setting up Welsh communities, re-creating a Wales free of English interference (the impetus behind Welsh Patagonia in Argentina in 1865). Thus, Morgan John Rhys established Cambria with its townships of Beulah and Ebensburg in western Pennsylvania, and Ezeckiel Hughes led some of the settlers farther west to Paddy's Run in Ohio. A founder of the cooperative movement, Robert Owen, purchased the former religious community of New Harmony, Indiana, for his own attempt at a utopian society.

Nationalism also gave a new impetus to migration with revival of the story of Madog ab Owain Gwynedd, who reportedly discovered America in 1169 and settled among the Native Americans. Since he predated Columbus, his story had been important in the 16th century as a counterclaim for the English throne against Spanish claims on the New World. Anecdotal reports of White and of Welsh-speaking Indians combined with the revived legend to create a frenzy of interest. In the 1790s, John Evans' exploration of the Missouri

River was a by-product of his search for the Welsh Indians, and Lewis and Clark were given Evans' maps with the directive to continue the search. The search for the Welsh Indians became a strong incentive for both immigration and westward exploration, and the legend remains a topic of delight and debate.

The 19th century also saw major migration connected with industry, drawing mainly on the skilled workers in south Wales. In the first part of the century, these migrants were coal miners who resettled in Pennsylvania and lead miners who joined the Cornish in Wisconsin. As industry grew, the skilled Welsh ironworkers filled such towns as Scranton and Wilkes-Barre in Pennsylvania and helped establish the steel centers of Pittsburgh, Cleveland, and Chicago, while other artisans went to the copper works in Baltimore. In the 1890s, after the imposition of heavy duties on imports into the United States, the virtual Welsh monopoly on tin-plating moved to Ohio, Pennsylvania, West Virginia, and Indiana. Also in this period, slate quarriers from north Wales emigrated to Pennsylvania and Vermont.

Wherever the Welsh migrated, even in the rough gold-mining towns, they set up Welsh chapels. In Wales the Methodist revival played an important part in preserving and re-invigorating interest in Welsh culture; in America the chapel, or church as it became, continued as the focal point for community and language maintenance. Although English replaced Welsh as the language of worship in most communities by the early 1900s, so that only a few chapels in urban areas still hold services in Welsh, the churches continue to provide structure for expression of Welsh ethnicity. The immigrants also established immigrant-aid societies, often called St. David's Society, which also provided, and in some places continue to provide, institutional concern for tradition, preserving, cultivating, and disseminating information on Welsh culture.

Two 19th-century cultural developments in Wales were carried by the immigrants to their new homes—the *eisteddfod* and the *gymanfa ganu*. The *eisteddfod* (a medieval bardic competition) was revived by nationalist sentiment as a competitive festival celebrating Welsh literature, music, and other arts. *Eisteddfodau*, complete with chairing of the bard, were very popular in the last century in both mining and farming communities. However, while they have increased in importance in Wales, occurring on both the local and the national level and within special-interest organizations, they are held in only a few locations in the United States, where the stress on poetic composition has, moreover, almost disappeared. Following a contrary pattern, the *gymanfa ganu*, whose importance has declined in Wales, is probably the most clearly established form of Welsh ethnic celebration in the States; it is carried out on local, state, and national levels. The *gymanfa ganu* (a hymn-singing service in the Welsh style of part-singing, developed as a product of Nonconformist worship in the 1830s. In both Wales and the United States, it has become a form of community celebration with congregations visiting each other to share the event. The *eisteddfod* and the *gymanfa ganu* are both of necessity carried out on a public, community level. Celebrations of St. David's Day, March 1, are also usually organized at an institutional level, with a church or a Welsh heritage society holding a special service or dinner to honor the patron saint of Wales. Individuals, however, may mark the day by following the Welsh custom of wearing a daffodil or a leek, but more commonly with a bouquet of daffodils and foods made with leeks.

According to legend, the leek has been a symbol of Wales ever since a successful battle against the Saxons when the Welsh, at St. David's instigation, wore leeks in their hats as their fighting colors. Other traditions set their first use as crests in the 14th century, at the battles of Poitiers or Crécy. The daffodil, with its similar image—green shoots rising out of a white bulb—has become an alternative symbol. At one more remove, green and white ribbons may be worn on St. David's Day. Green and white, along with red for the red dragon, are the colors of Wales. The red dragon has symbolized Wales at least since the 9th century, when it appeared in *Historia Britonum,* a history of the Britons. It has appeared on the coat of arms of various Welsh princes, and it flies against a background of green and white on the Welsh flag. The Welsh language itself is known as *Tafod y Ddraig* (the dragon's tongue).

The Welsh are noted for their nicknaming practices, necessitated by the notorious dearth of surnames, which were first required with the Act of Union. Most people, following the earlier system of identification, *ap* (son of), simply took the father's name with an additional genitive *s*, creating a limited field of names such as Davies, Evans, Hughes, Jones, Roberts, and Williams. Other names were formed by allowing *ap* to combine with the father's name (for example, ap Hugh evolved into the name Pugh), resulting in such names as Parry, Powell, Price, and Pritchard. However, because there were so few available first name and surname combinations, and one community could easily have, for example, several men named Dafydd Jones, community custom assigned nicknames, identifying people by their profession, appearance, or habits (Dai Llaeth [Milk] might deliver milk, while Dai Goch [Red] might have red hair). This custom continued in the United States where Welsh Americans settled together, but it has mostly faded as Welsh Americans have integrated into American society, and the names within the communities have become more diverse.

Relatively little scholarly attention has been given to Welsh American folklore, partly because of a general failure to recognize Wales as separate and distinct from England, and partly because, after years of cultural contact, most folk traditions reveal little to distinguish Welsh Americans from their Anglo American neighbors. The few collections that have been made show that as the language disappeared so did much of the lore, with the older members of individual families retaining just a few songs or verses in Welsh or an occasional folk belief, such as that a wild bird in the house portends death. Individual Welsh Americans who choose to mark their ethnicity generally do so with certain symbols of Wales—the red dragon, the daffodil, the leek—or by preparing foods such as Welsh cakes for special occasions.

Elissa R. Henken

References

Ashton, Elwyn T. 1984. *The Welsh in the United States.* Hove, England: Caldra House.

Hartmann, Edward George. 1967. *Americans from Wales.* Boston: Christopher Publishing House.

Holmes, Fred L. 1944. *Old World Wisconsin.* Minocqua, WI: Heartland.

Korson, George. 1949. *Pennsylvania Songs and Legends.* Philadelphia: University of Pennsylvania Press.

Thomas, Islyn. 1972. *Our Welsh Heritage.* New York: St. David's Society of the State of New York.

Williams, David. 1946. *Cymru ac America* [Wales and America]. Caerdydd: Gwasg Prifysgol Cymru.

Williams, Gwyn A. 1987. *Madoc.* Oxford: Oxford University Press.

Wends (Sorbs) in the United States

West Slavic ethnic group, settled in central Texas in 1854. Wendish folklore is a blend of Germanic and Slavic folklore. Not surprisingly, Wendish folk traditions and beliefs in the United States have suffered the fate of those of other immigrant cultures. Wendish folklore in the late 20th century, to the extent that it exists at all, is found among the older generation. Motifs found in Texas as late as 1986 include the *wódny muz* (water sprite) and the *zmij* (kobold, or house spirit). An example of the latter is in the following tale:

> A farm boy finds a baby chicken in the pasture shivering in the cold. He puts it behind the stove in the house to let it get warm and gives it some feed. The next morning a large pile of feed has mysteriously appeared. When the boy's father sees it, he realizes that the baby chicken is really a kobold. He tells his son to take it back to the pasture. (The moral is that it is wrong to make use of the demonic powers of the kobold.)

The Wends are the only group of Slavs who are primarily Protestant. In 1854, because of differences with the state church, a group of 500 conservative Wendish Lutherans under the leadership of Reverand Jan Kilian emigrated from Germany. Having disembarked in Galveston, they founded the farming community of Serbin (between Austin and Houston). The descendants of this immigration call themselves "Wends," although the preferred academic term is "Sorbs."

The Texas Wendish Heritage Society in Serbin has attempted in recent years to increase an awareness among Texas Wends of their cultural and folkloric heritage. The society does this via folk festivals, guest speakers at society meetings, and a museum.

Charles Wukasch

References

Nielsen, George. 1961. Folklore of the German-Wends of Texas. In *Singers and Storytellers,* eds. Mody C. Boatright, Wilson M. Hudson, Allen Maxwell. Publications of the Texas Folklore Society No. 30, pp. 244–259.

———. 1989. *In Search of a Home: Nineteenth Century Wendish Migration.* College Station: Texas A&M University Press.

Wukasch, Charles. 1987. "Dragons" and Other Supernatural Tales of the Texas Wends. *Tennessee Folklore Society Bulletin* 52:1–5.

White, John I. (1902–1992)

Collector and performer of cowboy songs, author of a book on cowboy-song origins. White was born into a musical family in Washington, DC. In 1924 he summered in Arizona, where he met Wickenburg dude rancher and cowboy singer Romaine Loudermilk. Inspired by Loudermilk, White learned the rudiments of guitar playing and acquired a taste for cowboy songs. In 1926, while attending graduate school at Columbia University in New York City, he landed a weekly, non-paying, fifteen-minute radio spot singing cowboy songs on WEAF. In 1929 he published a song folio, and between 1929 and 1931 he recorded twenty songs, five of them cowboy songs. From 1930 until 1936 White appeared as the Lonesome Cowboy in the weekly *Death Valley Days* program. In 1936, he left radio in order to pursue his career as a mapmaker.

Retiring from that career in 1965, White returned to the extensive files on cowboy songs and their authors that he had compiled during his years as a singer of cowboy songs. Soon he began to write articles on D.J. O'Malley, Gail Gardner, Will Barnes, and other cowboy poets and songwriters. These articles and other essays were later gathered into book form and published by the University of Illinois Press in 1975 as *Git Along Little Dogies: Songs and Songmakers of the American West.* It has proven to be one of the best books written on the origins of cowboy and Western songs.

White occasionally lectured and performed in his later years. His collections were donated to Utah State University in Logan, Utah.

James S. Griffith

White, Newman Ivey (1892–1948)

Collector of African American and North Carolina regional folklore. A native of North Carolina, White graduated from Trinity College (Duke University) and received a Ph.D. in English from Harvard University.

While working on his doctorate, he taught English at the Alabama Polytechnic Institute. At Auburn University, he collected African American songs from students, citizens, and local Black singers, a compilation that is still preserved in the Auburn University Library's Special Collections. White published his first article on methods of folklore collection in 1916 and accumulated a substantial number of songs, reflecting the rural Alabama culture, before he returned to teach at Trinity College in 1919.

At Trinity with colleague Walter Clinton Jackson, White compiled and edited *An Anthology of Verse by American Negroes* (1924). A pioneering treatise, it included detailed bibliographical notes by White. He hoped the text would educate Whites about Black perspectives and provide Blacks a literary heritage, thus establishing a basis for racial cooperation.

White resumed collecting African American songs from his students in North Carolina and compiled a seminal book, *American Negro Folk-Songs* (1928), his major contribution to folklore scholarship. This tome gave permanency to part of the African American oral tradition and earned White recognition as a folklore authority.

White's primary scholarship focused on the English poet Percy Bysshe Shelley. He chaired the Trinity English Department, abandoning his folklore studies for almost a decade until 1943, when he accepted the general editorship of the *Frank C. Brown Collection of North Carolina Folklore*. White, who served two terms as president of the North Carolina Folklore Society, completed only the first volume before his death.

Elizabeth D. Schafer

References

Cannon, James, III, and Lewis Patton. 1950. In Memoriam: Newman Ivey White, Scholar and Humanitarian, February 3, 1892–December 6, 1948. *Duke University Library Bulletin:* (Newman Ivey White Memorial Issue). 24.

White, Newman Ivey. 1916. The Collection of Folk–Lore. *Proceedings of the Alabama Educational Association* 35:119–126.

———. 1946. Organization of the Frank C. Brown Collection of North Carolina Folklore. *Yearbook of the American Philosophical Society 1945*. Philadelphia: American Philosophical Society, pp. 218–219.

———. ed. 1952. *The Frank C. Brown Collection of North Carolina Folklore*. Vol. 1. Durham, NC: Duke University Press.

Whittier, John Greenleaf (1807–1892)

Author and amateur folklorist. Known primarily for such poetic efforts as *Snow-Bound* (1866), a recollection of winter evenings in his family home, Whittier is often unrecognized for his pioneering work in folklore. Yet, as one of the first American folklore collectors to gather oral traditions intentionally and as one of the first collectors to regard the data he obtained as source material for creative literature, he is a significant figure in the history of American folklore scholarship.

Whittier's work in folklore was an attempt to perform important salvage work by rescuing examples of New England's "traditionary lore" from oblivion. Much of the folklore Whittier presented came from printed sources, but the two books produced near the outset of his career, *Legends of New England in Prose and Verse* (1831) and *The Supernaturalism of New England* (1847), also contain items clearly taken from oral tradition. Whittier is vague in identifying informants, perhaps from a desire to protect his sources from ridicule because they believed in the supernatural. He has also been criticized, somewhat unfairly, for "improving" texts; but he was dealing with folklore as a creative writer rather than as a folklorist. His concept of folklore as consisting solely of

John Greenleaf Whittier in old age. Library of Congress.

daring, romantic, ancient, rustic stories is narrow, but, when judged against the standards of the 1830s and 1840s, Whittier's two volumes are well-done collections of local legendry. In their focus on traditions of White residents, they are virtually unique for their time.

W.K. McNeil

References

Whittier, John Greenleaf. 1831. *Legends of New England*. Hartford: Hammer and Phelps.

———. 1833. New England Superstitions. *New England Magazine* (July). Reprinted in *The Supernaturalism of New England,* by John Greenleaf Whittier. Norman: University of Oklahoma Press, 1969, pp. 119–129.

———. 1847. *The Supernaturalism of New England*. London: Wiley and Putnam.

Wilgus, D.K. (1918–1989)

American folksong scholar and academician. Wilgus was born December 1, 1918, at West Mansfield, Ohio, not far from Columbus, where he later earned his B.A., M.A., and Ph.D.degrees at Ohio State University. His M.A. thesis (1947) was the first academic study of commercially recorded country music, and his doctoral dissertation (1954) was the recipient of the 1956 Chicago Folklore Prize and the basis for his authoritative history of *Anglo-American Folksong*

Scholarship since 1898 (1959), still the definitive work on the subject. Joining the faculty of Western Kentucky State College (now Western Kentucky University) in 1950, Wilgus moved in 1963 to the University of California at Los Angeles, where he helped establish the UCLA folklore program and acted for seventeen years as its chair. Wilgus was elected a Fellow of the American Folklore Society (AFS) in 1960, and was president of the AFS in 1971 and 1972. He served as Professor of English and music at UCLA until his retirement in June 1989. Wilgus died in Los Angeles on Christmas Day, 1989.

As a student of folksong, Wilgus was remarkable both for the depth of his scholarship and the breadth of his interests. His eclectic, empiricist outlook is best summed up by his own credo: "I have yet to find an approach to folklore from which I have learned nothing; I have yet to find one whose dominance is not dangerous" (Wilgus 1973:252; see Wilgus 1964:237). In addition to championing the comparative method, he conducted extensive fieldwork in the American South and in Ireland, simultaneously tackling monumental problems in ballad classification (Wilgus 1970; Wilgus and Long 1985). Through his research on "hillbilly" records, he was a pioneer in the study of folklore and mass media (see Wilgus 1965, 1971). Primarily a student of music and song, he nonetheless worked with other genres as well, most notably, the legend. In fact, the impossibility of neatly summarizing or characterizing Wilgus' accomplishments may constitute the most fitting commentary of all on his wide-ranging contributions to the study of American folklore.

John Minton

References

Montell, William Lynwood. 1991. D.K. Wilgus, 1918–1989. *Journal of American Folklore* 104:72–73.

Wilgus, D.K. 1964. Folksong and Folksong Scholarship: Changing Approaches and Attitudes. IV: The Rationalistic Approach. In *A Good Tale and a Bonnie Tune,* ed. Mody C. Boatright, Wilson M. Hudson, and Allen Maxwell. Publications of the Texas Folklore Society No. 32. Dallas: Southern Methodist University Press, pp. 227–237, 268.

———. 1965. An Introduction to the Study of Hillbilly Music. *Journal of American Folklore* 78:195–203.

———. 1970. A Type-Index of Anglo-American Traditional Narrative Songs. *Journal of the Folklore Institute* 7:161–170.

———. [1970] 1971. Country-Western Music and the Urban Hillbilly. In *The Urban Experience and Folk Tradition,* ed. Américo Paredes and Ellen J. Stekert. American Folklore Society Bibliographical and Special Series Vol. 22. Austin: University of Texas Press, pp. 137–159.

———. 1973. The Text Is the Thing. *Journal of American Folklore* 86:241–252.

———. 1986. The Comparative Approach. In *The Ballad and the Scholars: Approaches to Ballad Study,* ed. D.K. Wilgus and Barre Toelken. Papers presented at a Clark Library Seminar, October 22, 1983. Los Angeles: William Andrews Clark Memorial Library, University of California, pp. 3–28.

Wilgus, D.K., and Eleanor R. Long. 1985. The Blues Ballad and the Genesis of Style in Traditional Narrative Song. In *Narrative Folksong, New Directions: Essays in Appreciation of W. Edson Richmond,* ed. Carol L. Edwards and Kathleen E.B. Manley. Boulder, CO: Westview, pp. 435–482

Wills, Bob (1905–1975)

"King of Western Swing." Wills is often credited with creating this musical form, but it seems more accurate to say that helped define the style, and he was its most famous proponent. Born near Kosse, Texas, into a family with rich musical traditions on both sides, it was expected that Wills would show some musical inclinations. Families of both of his parents included some of the best fiddlers in that part of Texas, and young Wills followed in their footsteps by also becoming a fiddler. He frequently performed for ranch dances until he moved to Fort Worth in 1929, where he came in closer contact with urban musical styles that played an important role in the music that he helped popularize. Wills' first recordings, both unissued, were made that year; the two titles, "Gulf Coast Blues" and "Wills Breakdown," were a portent of things to come. They combined blues and traditional fiddle music, a distinctive feature of Western Swing.

Eventually, Wills recorded more than 550 sides, most with his Texas Playboys, organized in 1933. His music was a combination of traditional fiddle tunes, popular music, African American blues, and small-band jazz. Wills knew the bulk of this material from records, radio broadcasts, and other commercial sources, although many of the fiddle tunes were acquired from folk tradition. He resented the term "hillbilly," and he deliberately sought to distance himself from that tradition by providing a type of string-band music that would appeal to both rural and urban audiences while simultaneously avoiding what he thought of as the hayseed connotations of country music. Wills did accept the term "Western" as an accurate description of his music, and he was also agreeable to the term "Western Swing," first used in 1946 to describe the music of Spade Cooley. Wills and the Texas Playboys emphasized their Western identity not only by some of the tunes they played, but also by appearing in Western movies and by wearing conservative Western-style clothing.

In 1964 health problems forced Wills to give up the Texas Playboys; later he fronted other bands, and a special recording session in December 1973 reunited him with several former Playboys. Unfortunately, Wills suffered a stroke and could not complete the session; appropriately, the resulting album was titled *For the Last Time.* For his contributions to music, Wills was inducted into the Country Music Hall of Fame, and for his popularization of the cowboy image he was voted into the National Cowboy Hall of Fame as one of only two performers (the other was Gene Autry) to be honored by induction into both institutions.

W.K. McNeil

References

Malone, Bill C. 1985. *Country Music U.S.A.* rev. ed. Austin: University of Texas Press.

———. 1993. *Singing Cowboys and Musical Mountaineers: Southern Culture and the Roots of Country Music.* Athens: University of Georgia Press.

Townsend, Charles R. 1975. Bob Wills. In *Stars of Country Music: Uncle Dave Macon to Johnny Rodriguez,* ed. Bill C. Malone and Judith McCulloh. Urbana: University of Illinois Press.

———. 1976. *San Antonio Rose: The Life and Music of Bob Wills.* Urbana: University of Illinois Press.

Wiseman, Lulu Belle (1913–) and Scotty Wiseman (1909–1981)

Folk and country musicians, among the first to introduce Appalachian folk music to national audiences in the early 1930s. Known as "The Hayloft Sweethearts" and "The Sweethearts of Country Music," Lulu Belle and Scotty were for almost twenty-five years mainstays of "The National Barn Dance," broadcast coast-to-coast over the Chicago radio station WLS. With Scotty on banjo and Lulu Belle on guitar, the duet sang folksongs, gospel pieces, sentimental "heart" tunes, and mainstream country songs in exquisite two-part harmonies, interspersing the music with cheerful patter and cornball comedy routines. Extremely popular throughout their career, Lulu Belle and Scotty became the longest-lasting, most successful, and best-loved husband-wife duet in the history of country music, despite never having been part of the Nashville music industry.

Scott grew up in the Blue Ridge Mountains of North Carolina, absorbing the songs and instrumental styles of his family and neighbors. Influenced by Bascom Lamar Lunsford and Bradley Kincaid, he became both an accomplished performer and an industrious folksong collector, joining WLS in 1933 as "Skyland Scotty." Wiseman was also a prolific composer, writing such country-music classics as "Remember Me" and "Have I Told You Lately That I Love You?"

Lulu Belle (Myrtle Cooper) also spent her early years in Appalachia, learning the songs of her parents. Perhaps the first female country-music "superstar," she joined WLS at the age of eighteen in 1932, becoming known as "The Belle of the Barn Dance." In 1936 she was named "Radio Queen," the most popular woman on radio, legitimizing her "mountain girl" image.

After marrying in 1934, Lulu Belle and Scotty recorded extensively, made innumerable radio broadcasts and personal appearances, and were featured in seven Hollywood films before retiring in 1958.

William E. Lightfoot

References

Lightfoot, William E. 1987. Belle of the Barn Dance: Reminiscing with Lulu Belle Wiseman Stamey. *Journal of Country Music* 12:2–5.

———. 1989. From Radio Queen to Raleigh: Conversations with Lulu Belle. *Old Time Country* 6 (2):4–10; 6 (3):3–9.

Wiseman, Lulu Belle, and Scotty Wiseman. 1985. *Lulu Belle and Scotty: Early and Great.* Vol. 1. Old Homestead Records 168.

Wiseman, Scott G. 1985–1986. Wiseman's View: The Autobiography of Skyland Scotty Wiseman. *North Carolina Folklore Journal* 33:1–90.

Witchcraft

The use of magic to cause harm; more broadly, the practice of magic. The words "sorcery" and "witchcraft" usually connote evil intent. Magic, however, can he helpful as well as harmful. Before the advent of the scientific method, people all over the world believed that an action performed on one thing could cause a similar effect on another thing. According to the British anthropologist Edward B. Tylor, this "sincere but fallacious" belief came from the confusion of the ideal (imaginary) and the real. James George Frazer, also a British anthropologist, coined the term "sympathetic magic" for this notion, because the two disparate things—which had once been in contact or consisted of one thing meant to represent the other—were expected to act in sympathy with each other. Frazer differentiated magic from religion on the principle that magic is thought to work directly, rather like technology, while in religion spirits are invoked to mediate the process. This can, however, be a difficult distinction to make.

It follows from Frazer's analysis that the practice of magic ought to be democratic: It should work for anyone. And, in fact, many people experiment with do-it-yourself magic. Whether or not a person has ever done so, everyone at least recognizes the purpose of image magic, in which a doll, representing an enemy, is attacked with a pin, or a picture of the enemy is torn or burned, because the symbolism is both obvious and vivid. Evidence of such practices is to be found in most collections of American superstitions, and knowledge of them is also conveyed through the media of popular culture.

Such malicious rituals, fortunately, often fail in their intended purpose. However, in America, as in other parts of the world, it is believed that certain individuals who specialize in magic are better able than the rest of us to make it work. After the Middle Ages in early-modern Europe, the Catholic Church equated the practice of magic with the power of the devil—taking what has bccn magic, according to Frazer's definition, and turning it into something that corresponded to his idea of religion. A layer of beliefs in accordance with those of the Catholic Church's position was superimposed on the existing strata of folklore, and, with time, these religious ideas became part of the popular tradition. In Catholic countries, witches were considered heretics and were persecuted by the Inquisition in a craze that lasted from the 15th through the 17th centuries.

In Britain and in New England, heresy was not an issue, and witches had to be convicted of particular crimes such as theft and assault. The notion that a mark on a witch's body confirms a (private) association with the devil was more common in British than in European tradition. Toward the end of the witch craze (1692–1693), accusations in Danvers, Massachusetts led to the infamous Salem Witch Trials (see

Demos 1982). As George Lyman Kittredge has shown (Kittredge 1972; see Leventhal 1976), belief in witchcraft was then an integral part of a prescientific worldview that included belief in such occult practices as divination and astrology. Accusations of witchcraft continued in the American colonies during the 18th century and sporadically thereafter.

In addition to witches, colonial America harbored several other kinds of practitioners of magic (Leventhal 1976: 107–125). Among the Germans in Pennsylvania were a few *magi,* men in the Renaissance scholarly tradition who sought to understand "natural magic," and many more *brauchers,* or "powwow doctors," who used incantations and other magical practices for divination, to treat sickness, and to ward off evil. This tradition, which relies on such books as John Hohman's *The Long-Lost Friend (The Sixth and Seventh Books of Moses,* in contrast, are considered diabolical), still exists. The British counterpart of *brauchers,* called "cunning-folk" or "white witches," consisted of men and women who claimed to be able to ward off and cast spells, find lost or stolen property, and tell fortunes. They generally claimed not to *be* witches, but rather that they *worked against* witchcraft. Slaves brought with them African magical practices (one of the Salem witches was an African from Jamaica) and conjure doctors who sought, on behalf of their patients, to combat them.

The most important characteristic of witches in traditional beliefs is the damage that is attributed to them: A witch can be blamed when people or animals sicken or die, when crops fail, or for any other sort of bad luck, including a faithless lover and inclement weather. They are thought to steal milk from cows and to prevent the butter in the churn from "coming." Evidence such as mysterious balls of hair, and feather crowns in the pillow of the bewitched, point to witchcraft, as do fits (convulsions) that seem to result from the beating or pinching of an invisible attacker.

Traditional remedies for these problems include identifying and harming (often magically) the witch and protecting the victim or the house, stable, or churn with an amulet. Iron knives, horseshoes, and silver coins are popular amulets. A pin in a chair is supposed to immobilize any witch who sits there. Objects such as sieves with their many holes, and brooms with their many straws, are thought to keep the witch busy counting (it may be significant, though, that European witches fly on brooms, and those of central Africa fly in winnowing baskets that look very much like sieves, so counting may not the the whole explanation). Both salt and mustard seeds are numerous and are also irritants. The Bible invokes divine protection and, in addition, has too many words to count. Turning one's clothes inside-out is thought to thwart witchcraft. Bottles are used to ward off and also to trap witches. Witches are believed to be impervious to ordinary bullets, but they can be shot—killed or banished, both in person and in effigy— with silver ones.

It is difficult to restrict the idea of witchcraft to harmful magic because the same principles apply to helpful magic: As in many other arenas, one person's help is another person's harm. Witches are thought to use sympathetic magic against their victims, and the victims—or their representatives—use the same methods both to counteract the witchcraft and to attack the witch. Witches are sometimes identified, in accordance with the principles of contagious magic, by means of their victims—for example, enclosing the victim's urine in a bottle inflicts strangury on the witch, and burning a bewitched animal also burns the witch.

As noted above, it is generally recognized that the religious, demonological aspects of witchcraft represent a layer of beliefs that has been superimposed on popular traditions of sympathetic magic. What has not been noticed is that the popular tradition itself consists of two strands: one of sympathetic magical practices, which is used by witches and also by cunning folk and witch doctors, and another of bizarre narrative motifs. Witches in Europe and America are the subject of persistent legends, undoubtedly based on ancient beliefs, that credit them with peculiar powers. In the night, a sleeper is saddled, bridled, and ridden by the witch. This phenomenon is the origin of the word "nightmare" (this "mare" originally meant a goblin, not a horse) and is also the source of the phrases "witches' stirrups" and "mare's nests" for tangles in the hair. In one legend, the victim is able to bridle the witch, thus turning her into a horse, which he has shod; the witch-woman is discovered, with horseshoes nailed to her feet, in the morning.

In addition to riding on sleepers, witches are thought to fly not only up chimneys but also through keyholes. They are said to travel in eggshells, causing storms and other mischief (so it is a good idea to crush all eggshells). The ability to fly and the ability to change shape into an animal are points that witches share with shamans. In one popular legend, a witch or a pair of witches smear themselves with salve and fly out into the night. They are witnessed by a man who tries to copy them but makes a mistake and gets into trouble. Witches are supposed to be able to change themselves into animals, and if they are harmed in their animal form, the injury appears on the human. After the paw of a certain cat is cut off, a woman's hand is found to be missing. A man shoots a hare that stole milk from his cow and then discovers a neighbor with a similar wound. Especially in New Mexico, witches *(brujos)* take the form of owls. Especially cats, but also hares and owls, have been cast in the role of witches' familiars, demons that associate with them.

In contrast to the Inquisition's notion that witches meet together in covens, traditional American witches are usually portrayed as loners. The idea that they are allied with the devil is evident in oral tradition primarily in instructions for becoming a witch, which often include cursing God in rituals involving sunrise, crossroads, circles, threefold repetitions, and the like. Knowledge of white witchcraft is passed from one practitioner to another, sometimes only between those of opposite sexes, sometimes from parent to child.

The devil as a religious figure is less of a presence in African American witchcraft (called "conjury" and "hoodoo"). Instead, this tradition focuses on the power of the dead as manifested in such evocative things as graveyard dirt, bones (especially bones of ritually killed black cats), and rabbits' feet. In an American witch legend with African antecedents, the witch takes off her skin before she flies away. When a man, observing this, rubs the skin with salt and pepper, the witch cannot put it back on and either sickens or makes a bargain with the man so he will wash the skin.

Nevertheless, in the American South it can be difficult to distinguish European witchcraft from African conjury: They were similar to start with, and each has borrowed from the other. Native Americans also have traditions of witchcraft, with witches that fly, take on animal forms, cause various kinds of trouble, and have to be ritually overcome. The same is true of Latin American witches and, although the evidence is scant, probably also of Asian ones—for example, Japanese foxes are thought to be able to bewitch and also to change into human form. This unanimity may be the product of an ancient set of beliefs about supernatural powers, which crystalized into a rather stereotyped pattern in Europe and into other patterns, unaffected by the Inquisition and its Protestant counterpart, elsewhere.

Today, while no "rational" person would admit to believing in the efficacy of witchcraft, there are still amateur and professional spell casters. Moreover, there is considerable interest in cults, particularly in satanism, which, whether practiced or only imagined, continues to be publicized by tabloids and horror films and even by respectable news media. Most of its motifs derive not from folklore, but rather from the Inquisition and other formal proceedings against witches.

The image of a witch as an ugly crone, which goes back to the 14th century, is immortalized in well-known films, such as *Snow White* (1937) and *The Wizard of Oz* (1939), and it is revived every year in Halloween costumes and decorations, so all children know that witches are scary. More recently, the image is the witch as a beautiful woman—for example, in the play and film *Bell Book and Candle* (by John van Druten, [1951]) and in the television series *Bewitched* (1964–1972). Fictional books about witchcraft are popular, especially with girls aged eight to twelve; their appeal seems to be the idea of having the power to do what one wants and to revenge the wrongs one has suffered. Girls, who also tell fortunes and entice spirits at slumber parties, are much more exposed to folklore of the supernatural than boys are. This difference in levels of awareness promises to prolong the stereotype that witches are usually women.

Feminists have responded to the flagrantly misogynistic idea of the Euro-American witch by insisting that witches were falsely condemned: They were wise women (white witches) persecuted by hostile agencies. Feminism is also prominent in the goddess-worshiping religion of self-proclaimed witches, founded by Gerald Gardner and called Wicca after the Old English word for witch. Wiccans and other New Age pagans are highly social, meeting regularly for celebrations, and most are conscientious, loath to use magic to do harm. In that respect, they resemble the cunning folk more than the stereotypical witch.

The idea, so attractive to feminists, that witches were part of a secret pre-Christian fertility cult has been around since the middle of the 19th century. Until quite recently, the evidence for it was entirely fabricated. For example, Charles Godfrey Leland's *Aradia, The Gospel of Witches* (1899) is based on material from a single informant who was determined to tell the author what he wanted to hear. The evidence in Margaret Murray's book *The Witch Cult in Western Europe* (1921) has long been known to be inadequate. Nevertheless, Murray's entry on witchcraft, which popularized her belief in the fertility cult, was printed in the *Encyclopedia Britannica* from 1929 until 1969, influencing a great many people, including such scholars as Robert Graves and Aldous Huxley. The historian Carlo Ginzburg has recently brought the idea of a fertility cult, this time directed *against* witches, into the realm of scholarly respectability (Simpson 1994).

Christine Goldberg

References

Demos, John. 1982. *Entertaining Satan: Witchcraft and the Culture of Early New England.* Oxford: Oxford University Press.

Goldberg, Christine. 1974. Traditional American Witch Legends: A Catalog. *Indiana Folklore* 7:77–108.

Hand, Wayland. 1980. *Magical Medicine.* Berkeley: University of California Press, pp. 215–237.

Kittredge, George Lyman. [1929] 1972. *Witchcraft in Old and New England.* New York: Atheneum.

Leventhal, Herbert. 1976. *In the Shadow of the Enlightenment: Occultism and Renaissance Science in Eighteenth-Century America.* New York: New York University Press.

Puckett, Newbell Niles. [1926] 1975. *Folk Beliefs of the Southern Negro.* New York: Negro Universities Press.

Russell, Jeffrey B. 1980. *A History of Witchcraft: Sorcerers, Heretics, and Pagans.* London: Thames and Hudson.

Simpson, Jacqueline. 1994. Margaret Murray: Who Believed Her, and Why? *Folklore* 105:89–96.

See also Curanderos; Halloween; Mojo; Superstition

Wolf, John Quincy, Jr. (1901–1972)

Collector of folk music in the Ozarks. Descended from pioneer Arkansas families, Wolf was reared in Batesville, Arkansas, where his father was a bank official and self-taught writer. He became a successful teacher and academician as chair of the English Department at Rhodes College.

He attended, then taught English at, Arkansas College in Batesville, where he met his wife, Bess Millen, a classical musician. Wolf earned his Ph.D. in English literature at Johns Hopkins University, then returned to Batesville briefly before moving to Southwestern at Memphis (now Rhodes College), where he spent the rest of his life.

His academic interest in ballads merged with his enthusiasm for his Ozark heritage, and beginning in 1941 he and his wife began to record the music they heard at festivals in the southeastern Ozarks. Through the years, his interests expanded to include Black folk music in north Mississippi and shape-note singing throughout the region.

As his taped collection grew, Wolf expanded his teaching to include folklore of various types, and student collections were added to the corpus. His academic attention began increasingly to be directed to issues in folklore, and he published a number of articles in professional journals in the field. At the time of his death in 1972, he was vice president of the Tennessee Folklore Society. His widow returned to Batesville and entrusted the tape collection to Arkansas College, where it is permanently archived.

George E. Lankford

References

Lankford, George E. 1985. John Quincy Wolf Jr.: An Appreciation. *Mid-America Folklore* 13:2–8.

Wolf, John Quincy, Jr. 1963. Three Spring Pilgrimages. *Tennessee Folklore Society Bulletin* 9:103–106.

———. 1965. A Country Dance in the Ozarks in 1874. *Southern Folklore Quarterly* 9:319–322.

———. The Sacred Days in Mississippi. *American Folklore* 81:337–341.

———. 1969a. Aunt Caroline Dye: The Gypsy in the "St. Louis Blues." *Southern Folklore Quarterly* 33:339–346.

———. 1969b. Two Folk Scientists in Action. *Tennessee Folklore Society Bulletin* 35:6–10.

———. 1970a. Folksingers and the Re-Creation of Folksong. *Western Folklore* 26:101–111.

———. 1970b. Who Wrote "Joe Bowers"? *Western Folklore* 29:77–89.

Wood Carving

Making an object or a design in wood while manifesting traditional behaviors and working within traditional contexts. Traditional wood carving in the United States embraces a wide range of forms that accompany human beings throughout their lives.

In childhood, limberjacks, dolls, puzzles, and other toys entertain people. Adulthood's days of work and worship bring spoons, butter and maple-sugar molds, door handles, knife handles, and other utensils; decorated shelves, cupboards, and other furniture; chains, balls-in-cages, fans and fan towers, and books made to hold chewable spruce-gum balls; decoys and decoy helmets for hunting; signs; religious figurines, amulets, objects, and decorated surfaces; masks and totem poles. In old age, people make their memories tangible with human and animal figurines; miniature tools (pliers, plows, spinning wheels, crosscut saws, and the like); miniature traditional boats; transformed objects—cigar boxes turned into highly decorated picture frames, and peach pits carved into baskets; assemblages of human, animal, and object figurines made into scenes of farm, lumbering, and family life; and walking canes. Finally, in death, people have been remembered with carved wooden gravemarkers and other mortuary sculptures.

Traditional carvers differ from people who learn to carve from hobby books alone and from people who attend art academies. Traditional wood-carvers learn to carve informally, often by customary example; they watch others, especially relatives and friends who belong to the same regional, occupational, religious, racial, and ethnic communities. They usually produce forms that have been produced before; their emphasis is not so much on creating an object that no one has

Decorative wood carvings by Antanas Poskočimas, using traditional Lithuanian motifs. Chicago, 1977. Photo Jonas Dovydenas. American Folklife Center.

ever seen as it is on producing a good version—or their own version—of some artifact that embodies meaning to people in their communities. Traditional wood-carvers keep in touch with the communities that inspire them, constantly dipping into the community's wellspring of knowledge, and they receive suggestions and criticism from community members.

Many traditional craftspeople who make objects from wood refer to themselves as "whittlers." Some use the term "carver," and some use both terms. Dictionaries present "whittling" as cutting or paring thin shavings from wood with a knife, a definition that emphasizes the use of one tool and stresses a casual, almost unintentional mode of production rather than an object itself. "Carving" conveys the use of chisels and other tools in addition to jackknives, as well as a more intentional mode of production of an object. Both terms refer to the creation of three-dimensional objects and surface decoration.

"Sculpture," dictionaries indicate, refers to the "art" of carving wood into three-dimensional representations. Such a definition would clearly include academically trained artists such as Henry Moore and Constantin Brancuşi, sculptors in wood and other materials. Instead of claiming an exclusive plane for sculpture in the world of art production, however, folklore study argues that whittlings, carvings, and sculptures are all art, and that traditional artists may whittle, carve, or sculpt. All are aesthetic experiences, the results of play, of need, and of the shaping of deeply felt values into meaningful forms. One could say that there is a great deal of interplay among the three words: "whittling" refers to the production of three-dimensional objects and surface decoration using jackknives only; "carving" refers to the use of many tools, such as jack-knives, chisels, and chainsaws, in making three-dimensional objects and surface decoration; and "sculpting" refers to the use of many tools in the production of three-dimensional objects.

Traditional wood-carvers learn their skills in a community where certain occupational, religious, regional, ethnic, and racial contexts overlap. Their learning also takes place in a particular historical moment when market pressures and attitudes toward collecting other people's cultural goods influence production. Before about 1910, for example, most traditional wood-carvers rarely sold their work for money; instead, they gave pieces away or exchanged them for other goods with family and friends. With the increased interest in what the fine-art world called "folk art," carvings were sought after for collections, both private and public. Also, the Arts and Crafts movement in urban centers and the southern Appalachians saw many Northern social workers encouraging recent immigrants and mountain people to carve for pleasure and profit and to sell their works through cooperatives. Since the mid-1960s, increased numbers of folklife festivals throughout the United States taught wood-carvers the possibilities of selling. Now many traditional wood-carvers make some or all of their living, especially as they approach retirement, from their carving. A detailed discussion of three wood-carving families will illustrate how traditional carvers learn their skills, how carving operates in their lives, and how market influences affect their work.

Beginning in the early 19th century, as lumbering concerns sent groups of men into the forests of Maine and then onto the North Central and Northwestern states, their traditional artwork traveled with them. Evenings in the "barroom" (bunkhouse) of a logging camp often found men singing, telling tales, playing cards, knitting socks, and carving wood. Especially men of Scandinavian, Russian, French, and Native American backgrounds decorated the frames and handles that they made for their bucksaws, knives, axes, and crosscut saws. Using one piece of pine and a knife, men fashioned books with a spine or a face that slid open; men climbed up spruce trees, cut "gum" (sap) balls from the limbs, and placed them in the books as gifts of chewing gum for mothers, sisters, and sweethearts. These gum books were often highly decorated with designs such as crosses, initials, and trees, and with row after row of carefully cut triangular chips. From a piece of white cedar, woodsmen also made hand fans and fan towers (vertical towers with a fan or two made to slip part way down the tower) as gifts or to while the time away with and then feed to the fire. Men less skilled in carving paid others to carve gifts for them. With the closing of many of the logging camps by the mid-20th century, the contexts for much of the lumbermen's art is now the families and town communities of independent loggers, retired loggers, or descendants of loggers—people such as the Christiansens of Oakridge, Oregon, the VanAntwerps of Lansing, Michigan, and the Richards of Rangeley, Maine.

William Richard (1900–1993) of Phillips, Maine, a French Acadian logger who emigrated from New Brunswick, learned double-fan-tower carving from Raymond Bolduc, a fellow logger. As a child, William carved all of his toys and watched as his brother made a fiddle and as neighbors built and decorated homes, furniture, and tools. He passed on his logging and wood carving skills to his son and grandson, Rodney (1929) and Rodney Jr. (1955), who, as loggers and mill workers, also whittled toys and now carve chains, animals and birds, loggers with old-time woods tools, and other human figures from local basswood and pine, using jackknives, chisels, and chainsaws. Although no women in the family carve, Rodney's wife, Lucille, comments on the carvings and often affects the final shape of a form.

After attending several festivals in the late 1970s, the Richards began to sell their carvings. As the years passed, they created new versions of earlier carvings, often in response to customers' requests or dares. "Anything I can see in my mind," Rodney explains, "I can put in the wood." Rodney's work has been exhibited internationally, and, with a group of local supporters, he founded the Rangeley Lakes Region Logging Museum for the preservation and celebration of the logging heritage of western Maine.

To the southwest, in the mountains of northern New Mexico, the López family carves *bultos* (images of saints, also called *santos de bultos*), *coronitas* (crowns), animals, trees with birds and animals, manger scenes and other religious scenes and stories ("Flight into Egypt," "Death Riding in a Cart"). All are carved in the round from local aspen, cedar, cottonwood, and pine. Folklorist Charles Briggs writes in his study of the family that Nasario López (1821–1891) was an image maker who, like others, used many colors of paint to decorate his images. Though all of his sons were carpenters, his youngest, José Dolores (1868–1937), was propelled into carving by a personal hardship when, in 1917, he worried continuously over his son who had left to serve in World War I. He began to decorate picture frames, clock shelves, and lamp stands with chip carvings and then turned to images, animals, and trees.

Further encouraged by folk-art collectors in the 1920s and pressed by rapidly changing economic conditions, José Dolores began to carve for a living, creating new forms and, at the request of patrons, leaving his carvings free of paint. His creativity lives on in the many carvers of Córdova, including his children George (1900–1993), Nicudemos, Raphael, Ricardo, and Liria and their spouses Silvanita, Precídez, and Benita and several of his grandchildren and their spouses. Unlike the 19th-century carvings made by Nasario for the chapels and worshipers in nearby communities, contemporary carvings are purchased largely by persons of a different social class, cultural background, and religion. Where the carvings once mediated between Hispanic Catholics and their God, they now create bridges between people of dissimilar traditions.

Religious impulses have also inspired wood carving in African American communities. From the 1920s, Elijah Pierce (1892–1974), barber, preacher, and Mason spoke through wood to members of his Columbus, Ohio, community. "Everything I carve," he said, "I want it to tell some kind of a story." Pierce was raised on a farm near Baldwyn, Mississippi, and began carving as a boy, cutting names and designs into bark of trees on his father's farm, then carving small animals and hickory walking sticks. His mother's brother, Lewis Wallace, taught him how to work in wood. "Anything that I could picture that I could carve, I used to carve it. Horses, cows, dogs, chickens. . . . I just naturally loved the knife when I was a kid."

Because of several childhood events, his Baptist family and community believed he had a God-given gift of prophecy and preaching. But Elijah, drawn to barbering and desirous of an independent trade, answered God's call through his carvings. He drew on the aesthetics of everyday living constantly performed within his African American community, transforming the sermons and stories he heard into wood. From the 1930s on, he created reliefs, sculptures, and assemblages of moral lessons and sacred stories—"Monday Morning Gossip," the "Grim Reaper," "Samson," "Christ Entering Jerusalem," and the "Crucifixion." His preaching stick, a walking stick made from a cue stick, is topped with a man, a barber chair, and a comb and decorated all over with secular, religious, and Masonic motifs. After a customer would enter his barbershop, Elijah would ask him his trade and then carve an emblem of it into a stick.

Elijah also carved secular pieces that featured African American heroes as well as community perspectives on national events and political figures—"Martin Luther King Jr. and the Kennedy Brothers" and "Pearl Harbor and the African Queen." His favorite carving, "The Book of Wood," consists of four two-sided panels of wood, each 27 1/8 inches by 30 3/4 inches carved with figures representing the seven great churches of Asia Minor and the thirty-three years of Christ's life on Earth. "Let's make a book," his wife, Cornelia, had suggested, "a book of wood." During summer vacations, Elijah and Cornelia packed their car with carvings and traveled to revivals and churches in a number of states, where they staged informal programs and explained the iconographic and moral implications of each carving.

He also gave carvings to members of his congregation, usually bestowing a sermonette at the same time. Recipients often commented on Elijah's powers of divination, as if the artist knew just who needed what story-carving. He and Cornelia also opened their home to people who wanted to see their "unique Biblical and Educational Art exhibit." In 1969 Pierce began to hang his carvings on the wall of his barbershop, and in 1971, a year after his first interview with an art student, his work was exhibited outside his community. Pierce's wood carvings have been shown internationally. "I dream things the way they ought to be," Elijah explained "I can see them in my mind and I know what they are going to look like."

Traditional wood carvings, whether whittled, carved, or sculpted, proceed from the talent of an individual whose work is informed by communally based aesthetics and performances. Influenced by the marketplace to differing degrees, traditional carvers also carve because they want to memorialize—and pass on—some aspect of their communities' wisdom and heritage. With a knife and some wood, carvers reach for the world and, sometimes, beyond.

Margaret R. Yocom

References

Becker, Jane S., and Barbara Franco. 1988. *Folk Roots: New Roots; Folklore in American Life.* Lexington, MA: Museum of Our National Heritage.

Briggs, Charles L. 1980. *The Wood Carvers of Córdova, New Mexico: Social Dimensions of an Artistic "Revival."* Knoxville: University of Tennessee Press.

Bronner, Simon. 1985. *Chain Carvers: Old Men Crafting Meaning.* Lexington: University Press of Kentucky.

Dewhurst, C. Kurt, and Marsha MacDowell. 1987. A Fantastic Tradition: Cedar Fan Carving in Michigan. In *Michigan Folklife Reader*, ed. C. Kurt Dewhurst and Yvonne R. Lockwood. East Lansing: Michigan State University Press, pp. 47–56.

Fair, Susan W., ed. 1985. *Alaska Native Arts and Crafts.* Publications of the Alaska Geographic Society. Vol. 12, No. 3. Anchorage: Alaska Geographic Society.

Hufford, Mary, Marjorie Hunt, and Steven Zeitlin. 1987. *The Grand Generation: Memory, Mastery, and Legacy.* Washington, DC: Smithsonian Institution; Seattle: University of Washington Press.

Jones, Suzi. 1977. *Oregon Folklore.* Eugene: University of Oregon Press.

Ohrn, Steven, ed. 1984. *Passing Time and Traditions: Contemporary Iowa Folk Artists.* Des Moines: Iowa Arts Council; Ames: Iowa State University Press.

Quimby, Ian M.G., and Scott T. Swank. 1980. *Perspectives on American Folk Art.* Winterthur, DE: Henry Francis du Pont Winterthur Museum; New York: W.W. Norton.

Roberts, Norma, ed. 1992. *Elijah Pierce, Woodcarver.* Columbus, OH: Columbus Museum of Art; Seattle: University of Washington Press.

Yocom, Margaret R. 1994. "Cut My Teeth on a Spud!" Rodney Richard, Mad Whittler from Rangeley, Maine. *Chip Chats* 41 (1):17–19.

Worksong

A song performed by an individual or a group at work to relieve the tedium, express thoughts or emotions, or facilitate the task by coordinating actions or movements; conversely, such performances are sometimes addressed not to the workers alone but to potential customers (as in auctioneers' chants or street vendors' cries), to draft animals or livestock (as in mule skinners' calls or cowboys' night-herding songs), even to supernatural forces or beings deemed capable of hindering or helping in a task's completion (as in the butter charms for hastening the milk's turning). While many such songs may be identified by content alone, it is this work context that most fundamentally defines worksong, distinguishing it from "occupational song," which simply describes or derives from work processes or occupations or trades, or "labor song," associated with labor unions, their ideologies, and the pursuit of their goals and agendas. Admittedly, there is, as one would expect, considerable overlap among these categories, so that a given item might at different times fall under any one or all three headings. Moreover, songs of quite various origin whose contents evince no relation whatsoever to laboring are frequently performed by persons at work. Again, then, the laboring context is the ultimate determinant of worksong status, even if folklorists have concentrated on materials whose contents overtly reflect this function—understandably so, since so much of our evidence dates from an earlier time when folksong collectors were less concerned with contexts than texts.

Worksongs are relatively rare among Native Americans, with some notable exceptions, such as the corn-grinding songs of the Navajo and Pueblos or the paddle songs found among some tribes in the Pacific Northwest. On the whole, however, this practice is best documented among Americans of African or European descent. (Given the importance of worksongs in Asia, one might anticipate their prevalence among Asian Americans, but documentation is in this case, unfortunately, lacking. So, for example, while railroad workers have been an especially rich source of worksongs, none seem to have been collected from the Chinese employed in building the Central Pacific during the late 19th century.)

Not surprisingly, the best-documented worksongs among American Whites are English-language performances often derived from the Anglo-Celtic traditions of Great Britain and Ireland. While there is considerable evidence of such singing among other European American groups, these traditions appear generally consistent in type, content, and context with the more extensively noted English-language examples.

Like their transatlantic counterparts, Anglo American women have sung at various tasks—washing, weaving, spinning, milking, and churning—in many instances the same or similar items as their British and Irish compatriots, such as, the ubiquitous "Come, Butter, Come." Outside the domestic context, the shearing songs occasionally collected in the United States perpetuate the rich pastoral traditions of the Old World, where shepherds have been a source not merely of worksongs, but also of a large body of instrumental music (typically played on pipes, flutes, or whistles) fulfilling a similar function. While American pastoralists have produced no comparable instrumental traditions, the songs of the cowboy do provide a uniquely American parallel to the repertoire of European shepherds. The trail-driving songs intended to pace a herd's progress while relieving the monotony of that arduous process often reveal themselves not only through their descriptions of life in the cattle camp or on the trail, but also by their jogging gait and the nonsense refrains built around the yips, hoops, and hollers with which the cowhands drove and directed the cattle; like many, "The Old Chisum Trail" is composed of floating stanzas that can be extended almost indefinitely:

> Oh come along, boys, and listen to my tale,
> I'll tell you my troubles on the old Chisum trail.
> Come a-ti yi youpy youpy ya youpy ya,
> Come a-ti yi youpy youpy ya.

However, the largest body of cowboy worksongs were the lullaby-like night-herding songs, ostensibly employed to calm the bedded-down herd, more likely (at least in greater part) inspired by the boredom or loneliness of the rider on watch. Like many worksongs, night-herding songs appear to have been drawn mainly from existing traditions, Western or otherwise (thus, one commonly finds popular items such as "I'll Remember Your Love in My Prayers," a 19th-century "hit" by Tin Pan Alley composer William Shakespeare Hays, traditionally sung as night-herding songs), though a few items—for example, "Doney Gal," or "Lay Down, Little Dogies"—may have originated in this context.

Given the available documentation, however, the most vigorous traditions of American worksong are without question those of African Americans. Partly an inheritance from Africa, where worksongs are especially prominent, often even closely resembling, in content and context, those of New World Blacks, partly a reflection of social and economic conditions in the Americas, the extensive African American worksong repertoire encompasses a myriad of subtypes, most conveniently divided between individual and gang songs. The former are epitomized by the "field hollers" (sometimes particularized as "cornfield" or "cotton field" hollers) or "arhoolies"—an onomatopoeic term evoking these mournful, almost ethereal performances—in some regions also called "whooping" or "loud mouthing." Although field hollers defy neat characterization or transcription, they are typified by relaxed meters (or even a seeming total lack thereof), irregular intervals or microtonality (that is, pitches falling between the standard half-steps of Western art music), and an especially high degree of improvisation and ornamentation, including glissandi and "bends," slides between notes or shifts in register suggestive of yodeling, quavers or sudden changes in dynamics, and so forth. Frequently wordless, the holler's verbal components, when present, may alternate between traditional commonplaces and the momentary thoughts or feelings of the worker. The following text from Alabama typifies such performances, simultaneously obscuring their usual vocal embellishments:

> Ay-oh-hoh!
> I'm goin' up the river!
> Oh, couldn't stay here!
> For I'm goin' home!

Though sometimes directed toward others, as in the various calls addressed to "waterboys," "bossmen," plough horses or mules, field hollers are primarily vehicles of self-expression. Black gang songs, on the other hand, coordinate the movements of groups at work, at one time or another documented for virtually any activity—hoeing and harvesting, tree cutting, rail laying and tie tamping, rowing, lifting, and loading—requiring work gangs. In many African worksongs, as in much if not most African and African American vocal music per se, such pieces invariably assume an antiphonal (call-and-response) structure, linking the vocal interplay between leader and chorus to the rhythms of work, which may themselves become part of the song "texts," manifested in the ringing of hammers, the falling of hoes, the chopping of axes, the stroke of oars, and the like. Workers may also conspicuously draw and expel breaths to the beat of the song or rhythmically punctuate the performance with grunts of exertion. Typical is the following from a group of Mississippi convicts "chopping out" weeds (the italicized words coincide with the beat of their hoes):

Leader: I'll *be* so glad *when*
Group: Uh huh!
Leader: the *sun* goes down.
Group: When the *sun* goes down.
Leader: I'll *be* so glad *when*
Group: Uh huh!
Leader: the *sun* goes down.
Group: When the *sun* goes down.
Leader: I ain't *all* that sleepy *but*
Group: Uh huh!
Leader: I *want* to lie down.
Group: But I *want* to lie down.
Leader: I *ain't* all that sleepy *but*
Group: Uh huh!
Leader: I *want* to lie down.
Group: But I *want* to lie down.

Even more than field hollers, Black gang songs are often, as in the foregoing example, vehicles of social protest or personal complaint, reflecting the oppressive or exploitative conditions with which African American workers have so often contended.

Ironically, the sea chantey, conventionally viewed as the quintessential Anglo-Celtic worksong type, may be largely a borrowing from Black tradition, a debt partly revealed by its identical coordination of group movements through antiphonal singing. In the following excerpt from a "short-haul" chantey, noted at Staten Island in the 1930s, the gang would heave together on the rope at the word "haul" ending each refrain:

Haul the bowline, the long-tailed bowline,
Refrain: Haul the bowline, the bowline haul.
Haul the bowline, Kitty, oh, my darling,
Refrain: Haul the bowline, the bowline haul.
Haul the bowline, we'll haul and haul together,
Refrain: Haul the bowline, the bowline haul.

While collectors of American maritime traditions have overwhelmingly concentrated on White singers, chanteying appears to have been every bit as common among African American seamen and dock workers. And although it has been suggested, such traditions may have been current among European sailors as early as the 15th century (the evidence is inconclusive), the sea chantey is indisputably best documented in 19th-century America, by which time Black and White crews had for centuries labored together along the Gulf and Atlantic Coasts and in the West Indies. Given the extreme rarity of such antiphonal worksongs in European and other European American traditions, coupled with their virtual universality among African and African American groups, it seems most likely that this custom is largely a Black innovation, even if many or perhaps most of the particular items in the chantying repertoire were created by Whites. (In fact, a 15th-century origin for the sea chanty would by no means disprove this hypothesis, since this in itself might simply reflect the well-documented interactions of Black and White crews along the West African Coast during this era.)

While most of the preceding examples derive from agrarian, or pastoral, or at least nonindustrial groups, worksongs are by no means unknown in the urban environment. The cries, chants, patters, and pitches of various occupations—peddlers, vendors, junk dealers, ragmen, shoeshine operators, grinders, and others—were until recently a common feature of many large cities; Baltimore, Charleston, South Carolina, and New Orleans have been especially renowned for such traditions. Although most of these forms have virtually vanished, the auctioneer's chant still enjoys a living tradition, and one may hear similar performances from carnival barkers or roving concessionaires at sporting events.

On the whole, however, the contemporary urban context, the growth of technology, and the consequent mechanization of most occupations have been no kinder to worksong than to most other older forms of traditional music. Rather, worksong traditions survive in the late 20th century almost exclusively in settings where manual labor or physical activity serves an institutionalized function, as in the marching cadences of American servicemen and women. In fact, most of the foregoing traditions were moribund by the time folklorists began systematically recording them during the early to mid-20th century. Not coincidentally, the most extensive collections of African American gang songs were amassed between 1930 and the late 1960s in Southern prison farms, where forced agricultural labor was exacted as a penal sentence—in some cases, long after the mechanization of farm work had obliterated these traditions in the general population. One can hardly, then, mourn the passing of these remnants of the venerable Black worksong tradition.

In the 1990s, the average American is most likely to encounter traditional worksong at one remove—that is, through popular or art music, often reflecting professional composers' self-conscious appropriation of folk materials (to cite only two instances, the backing vocalists on Sam Cooke's 1960 hit, "Chain Gang," evoke the wordless antiphony of a Black work crew, while George Gershwin re-created the Black street cries of Charleston in his 1935 opera *Porgy and Bess)*. More significant, however, are the less obvious, though more pervasive, imprints that some worksong traditions have left on popular idioms; again, the case is strongest for the African American strain, which substantially influenced the development of 20th-century genres such as the blues and gospel and, through these, contemporary world popular music.

John Minton

References

Cohen, Norm. 1993. Worksongs: A Demonstration Collection of Examples. In *Songs about Work: Essays in Occupational Culture for Richard A. Reuss,* ed. Archie Green. Special Publications of the Folklore Institute No. 3. Bloomington: Indiana University Press, pp. 332–355.

World Wars I and II

The two major 20th-century conflicts, sources of folklore among both military and civilian groups. Emphasizing drama, misery, and historical significance, World Wars folklore continued a tradition established in the American Revolution and strengthened by the Civil War and other 19th-century engagements.

A rich folklore of the common soldier exists, but both enlisted men and officers shape the basic themes of military folklore. Enlisted men created folk customs to cope with military demands and to bond with fellow soldiers, while officers encouraged folk patterns to reinforce comradeship and commitment to the military life.

Humor about rations, boredom, and cold provided cohesiveness and relief in the trenches and foxholes. Soldiers coined witticisms about such atrocities as gas attacks as well as such pleasures as leave time. In their leisure hours, troops told jokes in the canteen and created cartoons for camp newspapers, often depicting officers as bumbling incompetents who were less courageous than enlisted men.

Folk vocabulary described the war and its participants. Soldiers became commonly known as "doughboys" (from the biscuit flour they cooked) or GIs, and slang was created to cope with aspects of the wars, such as "cooties" (lice), "Jerry" and "Krauts" (Germans), "meat wagon" (ambulance), "Tommie" (British soldier), "Sammy" and "Yank" (American troops). Phrases such as "Stars and Stripes," "The Great War," "Keep the home fires burning," and "The War to End All Wars" also circulated.

Wartime folklore, especially songs, expressed soldiers' dissatisfaction and disillusionment with military life. Ballad scholar G. Malcolm Law argues that no true American folk ballads originated from World War I, only nonnarrative folk songs—such as drill songs and cadence chants—that reveal the voice of the composite soldiers and their culture. Soldiers yearned for adventure but usually encountered boredom. Their songs empowered the powerless who must succumb to military discipline. Traditional and popular military tunes also reaffirmed military values, purpose, and commitment as the World War I lyric that emphasized: "We won't be back till it's over, over there."

Most war songs patriotically memorialized a major battle and fleeing Huns, expressed hopes for returning to civilian life, or described mothers and sweethearts back home. Others were off-color rhymes, depicting local women's immorality and the taverns frequented or else complaining about superior officers, army life, and the ever-present mud. Parodies of songs were also common, such as substituting "Underwear" for "Over There."

World War I ditties, particularly the "Hinkie Dinkie Parlezvous" cycle, were constantly revised into new versions through communal composition as bored soldiers talked and sang at hospitals and over poker games. One typical stanza went: "John McGregor our top sarge—Parlezvous. / A nice little chap, but his head's too large." Another song criticized boxer Jack Dempsey, who avoided the draft by working in a shipyard: "Dempsey helped to build a ship, / But couldn't see the ocean trip." Some homefront lyrics even suggested women join military ranks: "If they should ever send a suffrage regiment I'd hurry to enlist."

Both American and Allied soldiers disseminated rumors and legends about battlefield occurrences, often embellishing the stories as they passed them by word of mouth. British troops told that they saw the ghost of a famous soccer player, kicking a ball as he led troops on an attack mission. Other stories described enemy officers appearing, then disappearing, in the Allied lines.

Some soldiers told of a deserter army that lived underneath no man's land, or that the German dead were rendered to fat at a tallow works, or that a giant German named "Joe the Lamplighter" placed the rocket glares and mortars in the sky, or that German Amazons manned machine guns and piloted planes. Others claimed that an Indian soldier, "The Gurkha with the Silver Knife," terrorized German trenches, disemboweling the enemy.

Assigning nicknames to units, such as the Wildcat Division, was another popular custom. Some nicknames were derisive, such as the Sightseeing Sixth, a unit that allegedly arrived late to every battle. Shoulder patches worn by troops indicated their division through symbolic patterns and phrases.

Apparitions are a well-known motif in military oral narratives. In both wars, soldiers claimed to see the crucifixion or rainbows (providing the name for the Rainbow Division) in the sky before battles or above the enemy during encounters. Troops considered this a sign of divine favor and a good omen for victory.

Legends about folk saints defending soldiers and citizens abounded. Variations include the saint appearing as an old man before or during battle, prayers by the soldier or a family member resulting in miracles, the saint healing injuries and aiding prisoners of war to survive or escape, or the saint appearing in a dream. Saints were also credited with disabling enemy weapons and altering the direction of enemy planes and missiles.

Many soldiers wore protective amulets. In World War I, a black cat sewn on a uniform was considered good luck. Mistletoe, shells etched with the soldier's name, Bibles, and the 91st Psalm were pinned over hearts to keep soldiers from being wounded. Soldiers also considered wearing a heroes' clothing lucky and believed that carrying a loved one's possessions ensured good fortune. Aviators wore mismatched socks and shoes from successful missions, but they avoided apparel from fliers who had been shot down.

World War II soldiers, fighting for the symbolic Four Freedoms listed by President Franklin D. Roosevelt, served "for the duration." These troops contributed new jargon, jokes, and jingles to war folklore. The terms included "SOP" (standard operating procedure), "deuce and a half" (a two-and-one-half ton truck), and "GI" (government issue). Kilroy was a familiar name found in soldiers' graffiti.

Women participated in World War II as auxiliary troops, adapting popular songs such as "Gee, Mom I Wanna Go Home" with verses unique to women's experiences and frustrations with military life: "The stockings in the Army they're

During the Great War (1914–18), soldiers rest at a canteen staffed by women of the Red Cross. Cincinnati, Ohio. Library of Congress.

made of binder twine" and "WAC [Women's Army Corps] days, WAC days, dear old break your back days." GI stories also belittled women at the front, describing the supposed promiscuity of USO entertainers who might, for example, misunderstand the military meaning of the word "mess."

Soldiers spread tall tales in their barracks. Many military anecdotes, pivoting on absurdities and lies, embellished and exaggerated events and personages to emphasize the superiority of one military branch over the other. A popular tale about the "USS NeverSail," really the *Tuscarora,* described a giant naval vessel manned by a monkey crew that sailed the Seven Seas.

Other tall stories depicted alcoholic mice, bent rifles that fired around hills to kill hidden Japanese soldiers, and the Ghost Dog of Florida Island near Guadalcanal that brought death or disaster to whoever saw it. Ghost ships and planes were common motifs of war folklore. Other tall tales known as "snow jobs" were perpetuated by drill instructors; these detailed severe punishments for minor infractions and functioned to scare recruits into conformity.

Soldiers circulated superstitions about how to be discharged or to flunk medical examinations, including eating a large stack of pancakes or sleeping with soap under both armpits. Soldiers believed that they had to eat all of the food on their plate to survive, and aviators threw glasses into fireplaces for good luck.

World War II folk imagery included bombers named for women and heroes and often decorated with erotic paintings and military symbols. Gestures, such as the traditional military salute learned by every enlisted man to express respect, or its derisive variation that involved thumbing the nose, and the two-finger "V for Victory" gesture popularized by British Prime Minister Winston Churchill boosted morale. In addition, political leaders used proverbs in their speeches to appeal to crowds.

On the homefront, wives were advised not to see their husband off to service or to talk about missions, past or future, in order to avoid bad luck. Schoolchildren stepped on cracks, believing that action killed Nazi soldiers. Rumors circulated about the possibility of men reported killed or missing in action unexpectedly returning home. The homefront also spread stories about Japanese and German invaders and saboteurs or domestic conspirators and traitors harming civilians.

Jokes about stupid civilians reinforced troops on the front. One story about a small Ohio town stated that when the citizens read the headlines "Americans fight with Axis," they assumed the Allies were doing so poorly they had to fight with axes not rifles. Terms such as "Rosie the Riveter" acquired everyday usage, and gold stars symbolized sons and husbands sacrificed to war. Rationing, flour-sack dresses, and care packages also joined mainstream folk culture.

Other folklore themes of World War II include stories about soldiers still fighting the war on deserted Pacific islands decades after the war ended. Rumors also circulated about the atomic bomb, its monstrous effects on the Japanese people, and the possibility of the Germans almost detonating an atomic weapon before the Americans. Other tales concerned the Holocaust and the fate of surviving European Jews. Stories abounded about Adolf Hitler and other prominent Nazis escaping the command bunker and safely moving to South America.

American traditions still glorify heroes of the two World Wars with patriotic motifs that incorporate Uncle Sam, the national colors, statues and memorials, commemorative items celebrating the anniversary of battles, and the observation of Decoration Day, Memorial Day, and Veterans Day with flags, parades, and red poppies to remember those who did not return.

Elizabeth D. Schafer

References

Ben-Ami, Issacher. 1978. Miraculous Legends of Wartime. In *Folklore Studies in the Twentieth Century,* ed. Venetia J. Newall. Woodbridge: Rowman and Littlefield, pp. 123–127.

Blum, John Morton. 1976. *V Was for Victory: Politics and American Culture during World War II.* New York: Harcourt Brace Jovanovich.

Burke, Carol. 1992. "If You're Nervous in the Service . . .": Training Songs of Female Soldiers in the 1940s. In *Visions of War: World War II Popular Literature and Culture,* ed. M. Paul Holsinger and Mary Anne Schofield. Bowling Green, OH: Bowling Green State University Popular Press, pp. 127–137.

Hench, Atcheson L. 1924. Communal Composition of Ballads in the A.E.F. *Journal of American Folklore* 34:386–389.

Miller, William Marion. 1946. Two Stories from World War II. *Journal of American Folklore* 59:198.

Sandels, Robert. 1983. The Doughboy: The Formation of a Military Folk. *American Studies* 24:69–88.

Yates, Norris. 1949. Some "Whoppers" from the Armed Forces. *Journal of American Folklore* 62:173–180.

X

Xeroxlore

Also known as "photocopylore," signifies traditional items reproduced by xerographic or analogous means that subvert the primary intentions of those in ostensible control of those higher-level technologies; the ubiquitous photocopier has replaced older technologies used for making copies, such as carbon paper, and its name is accordingly used to describe the phenomenon. Examples of other devices used similarly include printing presses, photographic printing, mimeograph machines, computer printers, computer networks, fax machines, and coin-minting presses. The themes of Xeroxlore are similarly various: current events and contemporary concerns (recent scandals, specific politicians, feminism, taxes, health care, and popular culture generally, but also one's circumstances of employment) as well as traditional concerns (sex and sexuality, humor at the expense of every conceivable group, and so forth). Here is a sample text:

> Heaven is where the police are British, the cooks French, the mechanics German, the lovers Italian, and it is all organized by the Swiss.

> Hell is where the chefs are British, the mechanics French, the lovers Swiss, the police German, and it is all organized by the Italians.

Any device that reproduces an item or transmits alphanumeric data may be employed in this folk practice, and most such devices are known to have been so employed.

Because Xeroxlore is the product of the unofficial use of technology, it reflects the customary practices of those who use it rather than the intentions of the institutions that own or control it. It is also affected by its host technology and often reflects folk attitudes to its institutional context: "Tell me again how lucky I am to work here. . . . I keep forgetting." Xeroxlore usually contains a visual component— "The Last Great Act of Defiance" depicts an eagle swooping down upon a mouse who presents it the *digitus impudicus*

This fractured-German warning became a classic example of xeroxlore. Photo courtesy of Judith Gray.

("the finger")—and Xeroxlore is often parodic of the values of the host institution through fake memos and of the values of dominant culture more generally through obscene Christmas cards and the like. An example of Xeroxlore, reproduced by photocopy machines on paper, by coin-elongating machines on U.S. cents, and by private mints on one-ounce silver ingots, reads:

> Big cats are dangerous,
> [representation of a tiger]
> but a little pussy never hurt anyone.

Although the technology often serves seemingly innocuous ends, such as the circulation of favorite recipes, chain letters, and favorite published cartoons, even these are reproduced despite managerial restrictions on what may be copied and often in violation of copyright; their circulation may violate postal regulations. It is a small step from such transgressive uses of the technology to the photocopying of body parts.

Just as the technology is an extension of human faculties, so also Xeroxlore is an extension of traditional joking practices and of the making of items of material culture, novelty items in particular, whether printed and pictorially represented or materially constructed. Thus, the genres of Xeroxlore (parody letters, memos, and glossaries, folk poetry, folk cartoons, parodies of comic strips, and so forth) and its forms (fold-up novelty cards, Rorschach tests, and the like) are as significant as its themes. The folk make their own uses of technological innovations as they become available, just as they always have. The fragmentary record of printed and graphic folklore of the past includes typeset folk verse and World War II-era blueprints of female nudes with their body parts labeled as if they were airplanes. The practice in the 1990s includes use of facsimile machines to transmit photocopied materials, with an increasing proportion of pictorial material that that technology permits, and wholesale circulation of alphanumeric Xeroxlore by means of the Internet.

Although Xeroxlore is an international phenomenon, the product of whatever technology is available for its duplication and dissemination, all items of Xeroxlore are not equally widespread. Xeroxlore is frequently adapted to different cultural contexts, but many items are of interest to specific groups of people only, whether employees of a particular corporation, the citizens of a particular country, or the speakers of a particular language or dialect. Early Xeroxlore was largely male centered, but an increasing percentage shows a female perspective: "Twenty-five reasons why cucumbers are better than men." Xeroxlore represents age-old human practices carried out by means of, and influenced by, modern inventions, but, despite the international availability of the same technologies, the same kind (and perhaps degree) of variation is to be found in it—based on race, color, creed, gender, sexual orientation, politi-cal ideology, and so forth—as in any other traditional practice.

Michael J. Preston

References

Bell, Louis Michael, Cathy Makin Orr (Preston), and Michael James Preston, eds. 1976. *Urban Folklore from Colorado: Photocopy Cartoons.* Research Monographs LD00079. Ann Arbor, MI: Xerox University Microfilms.

Dundes, Alan, and Carl R. Pagter, eds. 1978. *Work Hard and You Shall Be Rewarded: Urban Folklore from the Paperwork Empire.* Bloomington: Indiana University Press.

———. 1987. *When You're up to Your Ass in Alligators . . .: More Urban Folklore from the Paperwork Empire.* Detroit: Wayne State University Press.

———. 1991. *Never Try to Teach a Pig to Sing: Still More Urban Folklore from the Paperwork Empire.* Detroit: Wayne State University Press.

Orr (Preston), Cathy Makin, and Michael James Preston, eds. 1976. *Urban Folklore from Colorado: Typescript Broadsides.* Research Monographs LD00069. Ann Arbor. MI: Xerox University Microfilms.

Preston, Cathy Lynn, and Michael J. Preston, eds. 1994. *Photocopylore from Colorado: Folk Collections.* Boulder, CO: Janus Academic Press.

Preston, Michael J. 1994. Traditional Humor from the Fax Machine. *Western Folklore* 53:147–170.

Yarn

Narrative discourse or a narrative that is loquacious in style, usually picaresque in development, prone to hyperbole, and variable in form and length. The themes of the yarn typically deal with adventures and escapades in a manner either humorous or miraculous. Good "yarn spinners" (storytellers) are reputed to have had some experience of which they speak, especially if the narrative is first person, and they speak convincingly, although their listeners may or may not believe them. The term "yarn" lacks the analytical status of a folk-narrative-genre term, such as "folktale," "legend," or "tall tale." Instead, folkloristic usage of the term is casual and reflects local usage and classification. Richard M. Dorson, for instance, used the term in his essays on "Esthetic Form" and "Oral Styles" of American folk narrative but conceded that the terms of several such prose narrative traditions are imprecise and not sharply defined (Dorson 1972).

A yarn is defined by style, theme, and the scene of its telling more than by stability of content and form. Benjamin A. Botkin, in attempting a definition, followed the distinction Mark Twain made between "comic and witty stories," on the one hand, and the "humorous story," on the other. The former are concise, goal oriented, and display a more stable and transparent form than the latter, which "may be spun out to great length." Unlike the anecdote or comic, witty story, yarns are more conducive to garrulousness and not constrained by any expectation to reach a conclusion or achieve self-containment. It is in this sense that "yarning" (or, "to yarn") is sometimes used as a verb for conversation and conversational storytelling. Tellers spin yarns wherever the conditions for casual talk prevail, typically at the so-called "liars bench," but this context does not exclude serious talk or hybrid narratives recognizable in other respects as legend or tale.

Although "yarn" resists any clear generic classification and can serve as a catchall classification for a usually humorous and rambling narrative, it is often treated as a form of tall tale or "lie," possibly because of its association with the liars' bench or because of the liberties a narrator may be expected to take with the presumed ignorance of his or her audience. In the sense in which *"yarn"* is a species of tall tale, it is a narrative that promotes an untruth as true, but it does so in language that focuses attention on accumulating detail and in a style that is loquacious, and it progresses with narrative development intended to betray the "lie" of the narrative. It is accepted by listeners as a good-natured deception.

While the place of yarn spinning may commonly be the liars' bench, the term and occasion is traditionally applied to sailors and refers to their discourse and the stories they customarily tell during the leisure hours aboard ship. It is probable that the term "yarn" as denoting a narrative arose in this context. The *Oxford English Dictionary* cites an 1812 text as a first example of "yarn" in its narrative sense. A subsequent text from 1835 cites Captain Marryat, a popular writer of sea fiction. But in seafaring, "yarn," "rope yarn," or "spun yarn" as terms referring not to narrative, but to the intertwining strands of yarn or rope yarn from which rope is made, date at least to the 17th century with the publication of *A Sea Grammar* by Captain John Smith; an earlier (1535) citation linked the term to fishermen's nets. A contemporary of Marryat's in a book titled *An Old Sailor's Yarns* (1835) included the term "long yarn" among the terms "narratio," "apostrophe," "approsiopesis," "obtestasis," "invocatio," and "simile" in a brief exposition on the rhetoric of sailors. Whatever the origin of the term for a narrative, folk etymologies combined the two meanings of an intertwining strand in the making of rope and of a narrative discourse loosely held together by a single theme.

The term is still in use among seamen and may be used interchangeably with the increasingly more popular term "sea story," perhaps to distinguish true personal narratives from the ambiguous sense of "lie" inherent in the term "yarn."

Thomas Walker

References
Beck, Horace. 1973. *Folklore and the Sea*. Middletown, CT: Wesleyan University Press.

Botkin, B.A. 1944. *A Treasury of American Folklore.* New York: Crown.

Dorson, Richard M. 1972. *Folklore: Selected Essays.* Bloomington: Indiana University Press.

Henningsen, Gustav. 1962. The Art of Perpendicular Lying. *Journal of the Folklore Institute* 2:180–219.

See also Storytelling

Z

Zydeco

The accordion-based dance music of Gulf Coast Creoles, the French-speaking Blacks of southwest Louisiana and southeast Texas. Often described by non-Creoles as a combination of Black urban blues and Cajun accordion music, zydeco actually represents a more complex hybrid whose roots predate, and whose development instead parallels, these cognate African American and Louisiana French musical styles. Conversely, while "zydeco" is now sometimes applied, especially by outsiders, to any or all varieties of Creole music, both past and present, Creoles themselves usually restrict the term to the bluesy, highly amplified dance music that developed in cities just after World War II. Much like urban blues and contemporary Cajun music, then, zydeco is actually a relatively youthful popular style whose ultimate origins nonetheless reach to the folk traditions of the late 18th and early 19th centuries, the formative era in Gulf Coast Creole culture.

It was during the Caribbean slave rebellions of the late 1700s that large numbers of *gens libres de coulour,* the forebears of the contemporary Creoles, arrived in southwest Louisiana from Saint Domingue (present-day Haiti), settling the bayous, prairies, and marshlands west of New Orleans. Originally subsisting as small farmers or ranchers, trappers and fishermen, even as slave-owning planters, these "free persons of color" intermingled in subsequent generations with other French- or English-speaking African Americans; with the descendants of the colonial French and Spanish of pre-1803 Louisiana; with later European émigrés (notably Germans, Italians, and Irish); with the *Américains* who arrived from the Deep or Upper South after the Louisiana Purchase; even with the remnants of the region's Native American populations. However, the Creoles' most important neighbors from that early period to the present have been the Acadians, or Cajuns, whom the French colonists exiled to southwest Louisiana from Nova Scotia (Acadia) during the French and Indian War.

Given that cultural context, Creole music predictably reflects an extraordinary range of influences; however, three particular musical strains assumed special importance in the early development of zydeco: the instrumental traditions, originally dominated by the violin and later the accordion, shared by the Creoles and Cajuns; the dance songs known locally as "*juré* singing," a regional variant of the African and African American "ring shout"; and the rhythmic traditions of the Creole's Caribbean homeland. When, in the 1940s and 1950s, the social music derived from these various subcurrents further assimilated the instrumentation and idioms of Black urban blues—the fourth major influence in modern zydeco—the *style,* as it's now known, came into being.

The drumming of Creole slaves in south Louisiana was routinely remarked by 18th- and 19th-century observers; besides providing zydeco's rhythmic foundations, these percussive traditions also contributed one of the genre's most distinctive elements, the *frottoir* (rub board), a vest of corrugated metal that is rhythmically scraped and tapped with keys or spoons. Notwithstanding its unique form, the *frottoir* is actually only a regional variant of the ubiquitous African and African American "scraper." Thus, among the most frequently noted instruments of 19th-century Creoles was the jawbone, the mandible of a large draft animal, played by scraping the teeth with a bone, key, or stick (notched gourds or sticks were put to similar use). This rhythmic principle was later transferred to washboards of the household variety and, after the 20th-century industrialization of the Gulf Coast provided the materials and means, to the rub board metallic vests.

These 19th-century polyrhythmic traditions were clearly compatible, and often coincided with the subspecies of the African American "ring shout" known as *juré* singing, a circular dance accompanied by the antiphonal (call-and-response) singing and the shuffling, stamping, clapping, or patting of the dancers. As among ring shouts generally, these highly expressive, often extemporaneous, songs might be either secular or sacred—the Creole *juré* translates as "testify," a term with both personal and religious connotations in Black culture—thereby anticipating in form and content many 20th-century popular styles (such as the blues or gospel, besides, of course, zydeco itself). Significantly, Creole folk etymology traces the term "zydeco" to a lyric commonplace first documented among *juré* singers in the 1930s, "*les haricots sont pas salés*" (the snap beans aren't salted), a metaphor for hard times. (The basic idea is that the singer hasn't even a scrap of salt meat to season this meager diet, a trope symbolically linked to various other hardships, including romantic difficulties.) The orthography of "zydeco" or its many variants—"zodico," "zotico," "zordico," "zadeco," "zarico," and so forth—is thus said to be a phonetic representation of *s'haricots* (the elision of the final syllable of the plural article *les* with the noun *haricots*). Recent research suggests, however, that this idiom may also reflect a coincidental phonological similarity between the French word for beans and various West African terms for music and dance. Indeed, in late-20th-century Creole usage, "zydeco" functions much like the English word "dance," referring, as a noun, to a social occasion involving music, dance, and drink, to the music played at such a function, to a particular dance step or to the tune that accompanies it—specifically, in the last two cases, to a fast, syncopated two-step; in other instances, "zydeco" acts as a verb, signifying participation in these activities.

The term's possible origins aside, however, all available evidence suggests that the late-20th-century usage of "zydeco" postdates World War II, before which the dance music played on fiddles and, later, accordions at Creole house parties, picnics, or the like was most commonly called "La La," "French La La," or simply "French music," a tradition that, in conjunction with Afro-Caribbean rhythms and *juré* singing, constitutes a third seminal influence in zydeco. Derived in part from the Celtic fiddle tunes brought to Louisiana by the Acadians, this repertoire was both modified and enlarged in Creole tradition, especially after the arrival in the mid-19th century of the diatonic button accordion, an instrument gradually supplanting the fiddle among Cajuns, but especially Creoles.

At least from the date of the earliest aural evidence (the sound recordings made in the 1920s), there has been such a considerable overlap between Cajun and Creole instrumental styles that, for practical purposes, these have often constituted a single tradition. This was especially so before World War II. For example, the playing of Amadé Ardoin, the legendary Creole accordionist who recorded extensively in the 1920s and 1930s, often with Cajun fiddler Dennis McGee, is virtually indistinguishable from that of his Cajun counterparts. As time passed, however, Creole tradition increasingly reflected its African American provenance—for instance, through a greater emphasis on rhythmic complexity at the expense of melodic development. These qualities were accentuated during or just after the war, as large numbers of Creoles migrated to Louisiana cities like Lafayette and Lake Charles, or, in Texas, to Beaumont, Port Arthur, and especially Houston. Granting Black French music's longstanding affinity to the blues–partly a result of direct influence, partly a reflection of a common African and African American origin—it was during this period that Creole musicians fully assimilated the urban rhythm-and-blues (R&B) style, an adaptation signaling the emergence of zydeco proper.

During its early urban phase, Creole dance music maintained the basic instrumentation of accordion and rub board, occasionally (though with decreasing frequency) supplemented by fiddle. For a time, too, the most typical performance settings were house parties or similar gatherings likewise recalling the rural tradition. Soon, however, Creole musicians were performing in cafes, taverns, and dance halls, adding the amplification and amplified instruments—electric guitar and bass, drums, even keyboards and horns—characteristic of the postwar blues band, in the process absorbing much of that genre's style and repertoire. Around the same time, many accordionists discarded the diatonic button accordion for the chromatic piano instrument better suited to the blues or popular items now added to the traditional repertoire of two-steps and waltzes, while lyrics in English were now interspersed with Creole French folksongs. Two concurrent developments conclusively mark the maturation of zydeco: the increased interaction between Creole music and electronic media, and the appearance of professional or semiprofessional "stars."

Tellingly, the term "zydeco" itself first appears in its present sense on commercial recordings from the late 1940s and early 1950s, including among them the first records of the performer who more than any other shaped the genre, Clifton Chenier. Born at Opelousas, Louisiana, in 1925, Chenier learned to play the accordion from family and neighbors. In the late 1940s, he moved first to Port Arthur then eventually Houston, working as a truck driver by day, playing accordion at night with his brother Cleveland on rub board. By the early 1950s, however, Chenier was touring and recording with an expanded ensemble, scoring occasional regional or even national "hits" in the R&B vein. By the end of the decade, his recording career had come to a standstill, though he remained in demand as a regional performer, and in the early 1960s, he struck up a relationship with California record producer Chris Strachwitz. The recordings Chenier made over the next two decades for Strachwitz's Arhoolie label would largely define modern zydeco, not only solidifying Chenier's reputation within the Creole community but also earning him international acclaim. Besides drawing on French tradition and blues, Chenier continually expanded zydeco's boundaries by incorporating elements of other ethnic and popular styles—rock, soul, country-and-western, jazz, and swing. By the time of his death in 1987, he had appeared with his Red Hot Louisiana Band throughout Europe and the United States, serving as the subject of television and film documentaries, articles, and books, even winning a Grammy Award as well as a Heritage Fellowship from the National Endowment for the Arts.

Following Chenier's example, Creole musicians have continued to test the limits of zydeco, encouraged by the growth of ethnic pride within the Creole community, by the growing interest of outsiders in Creole culture and music, and by the ever-increasing role of media formats such as tapes, CDs, and videos. Like many contemporary ethnic styles, zydeco in the 1990s leads something of a dual existence: valued within the Creole community as a symbol of cultural identity, simultaneously consumed by outside enthusiasts as a musical commodity. Zydeco reaches a global audience through the performances of Creole artists and through the work of popular musicians who have recently begun to experiment with this distinctive Black sound. Even within the Creole community, the trend is toward larger, more commercialized, and self-conscious venues like festivals and trail rides; among the most important of these are the enormously popular dances regularly held by most Catholic parishes with large Creole memberships. Moreover, while many African American styles such as the blues have suffered because of the changing musical tastes of young Black performers and audiences, zydeco, in the 1990s at least, continues to attract young Creoles, albeit with concomitant modifications, as witnessed by the influences from funk, disco, and rap. One of the most vital and viable of all African American musical traditions, zydeco appears destined to remain so for some time to come.

John Minton

References

Ancelet, Barry Jean. 1988. Zydeco/Zarico: Beans, Blues, and Beyond. *Black Music Research Journal* 8:33–49.

Ancelet, Barry Jean, and Elemore Morgan Jr. 1984. *The Makers of Cajun Music: Musiciens cadiens et créoles.* Austin: University of Texas Press.

Broven, John. [1983] 1987. *South to Louisiana: The Music of the Cajun Bayous.* Gretna: Pelican.

Savoy, Ann Allen, ed. 1984. *Cajun Music: A Reflection of a People.* Vol. 1. Eunice: Bluebird Press.

Spitzer, Nick. 1979. Booklet for *Zodico: Louisiana Créole Music.* Rounder LP 6009.

Strachwitz, Chris. 1989. Booklet for *Zydeco. Volume One: The Early Years, 1961–1962.* Arhoolie CD 307. Compact Disc.

———. [1987] 1992 . Booklet for Clifton Chenier, *Clifton Sings the Blues.* Arhoolie CD 351. Compact Disc.

See also Cajuns

Index

Aarne, Antti, 177
Abbott, O. J., 118
Abduction reports, UFO, 721
Abrahams, Roger D., 25–26, 206–207, 228, 625–626, 627, 628, 675, 685, 686, 708
Abrams, James, 573
Academe, folklore of, 3–4
Academic programs in folklore, 4–6
Acadia, 305
Acadian Archives, 312
Acadians, 109
Acrostics, 489
Acuff, Roy, 165
Adams, James Taylor, 399
Addams, Jane, 572, 749
Addington, Maybelle, 128
Adirondacks, 6–8
Adler, Guido, 231, 233
Adorno, Theodor, 183
"Adventure" computer game, 155
Aesop, 239
Aesthetics, 53
Afikomen, 545
African American dance, 194–195
African American folk language, 280
African American folklore, 18
African American hairstyling, 163
African American house types, 11
African American music, 9
African American quilts, 11, 609
African American spirituals, 682–684
African American Vernacular English (AAVE), 86–87
African Americans, 8–11, see also Black entries; Negro entries
African Canadians, 116
AFS, see American Folklore Society
Age, food and, 301
Aging, folklore and, 12–14
Agricultural fairs, 242
Agriculture, rural, 246
AIDS, 325

AIDS Quilt, 675
Airplane, paper, 138
Alabama folklore, 126
Alaska, 514–516
Albany slip, 583
Albee, Edward, 671
Albers, Anni, 750
Alberts, Lewis, 703–704
Alcock, F. J., 66
Alkaline glaze, 583
All Fools' Day, 40
All Hallow's Eve, 359–361
Allen, David, 223
Allen, Ethan, 624
Allen, Raye Virginia, 317
Allen, Robert E., 103
Allen, William Francis, 18
Allen, William N., 625
Alley, Maurice, 437
Almanac, 14–15
Alpha Kappa Alpha, 690
Alpha Phi Alpha, 690
Alsberg, Henry G., 509
Altars, home, 327
Althusser, Louis, 183
Amateur radio, 613–614
Amber, 64
America, see United States
American anthropologists, 34
American Birding Association, 84
American body, 98–100
American Civil War, 145–146
American Design, Index of, 176, 389–390, 508
American dialect, 22–23
American Dialect Society, 22
American Federation of Labor (AF of L), 687
American festivals, 249–251
American folk culture, coding in, 147–148
American Folk Song Festival, 707
American Folklife, Festival of, 40, 250–251, 252–253, 672

American Folklife Center, 16–17
American Folklife Preservation Act, 16, 284, 286
American folklore scholarship, 17–23
American Folklore Society (AFS), 8–9, 19, 23–24, 77, 284, 286, 287, 509, 513
    Applied Folklore Section within, 38
American Folklore Society Newsletter, 23
American funeral, 134
American Indian folklore, 18, 20
American Indian Movement (AIM), 673–674
American Indian music, 21–22
American Indians, 170–171, see also Native American entries
American literature, folklore and, 287–290
American Motorcyclist Association, 81
American Sign Language (ASL), 198
American studies and folklore, 24–27
American vernacular houses, 41
Americans of English descent, 28–32
    list of ethnicities of, 388
Ames, Mrs. L. D., 562–563
Amiot, Father, 232
Amish farmers, 246
Amish migration, 553
Amory, Cleveland, 715
Anansi, 27–28, 69
Ancelet, Barry Jean, 111, 112
Andersen, Hans Christian, 648
Anderson, Bob, 487
André, Major, 624
Anecdote, 28
    local-character, 443–445
Angel-helper stories, 484
Angle smith, 89
Anglo American ballad, 57
Anglo American folksongs, 32
Anglo Americans, 28–32
Anglo Canadians, 121
Animals, 32–33

Anniversaries, 33–34
Anthropological approach to folklore, 34–35
Anthropologists, American, 34
Anti-legend, 35
Apocalyptism, 517
Appalachia, 31, 35–38, 80, 175–176, 279, 537
Appalachian folk music, 37
Apple Computer, 154
Appleseed, Johnny, 412
Applied folklore, 38–40, 509, 604
Applied Folklore Section within American Folklore Society, 38
Appliqué, 607
Appropriation strategy of expression, 147
April Fools' Day, 40
Archaic folklore, 63
Architecture, 729
    vernacular, 41–44
Archive of American Folk Song, 36
Archive of Folk Culture, 16, 44, 45
Archives, folklore, 45–46
Archuleta, Eppie, 504
Ardoin, Amadé, 111, 774
Arewa, E. Ojo, 555
Argots, 281
    of prisoners, 593–594
Arhoolies, 764
Arithmetic puzzle, 631–632
Armed services folklore, 484–485
Armstrong, Howard, 504
Armstrong, Louis, 406, 640
Armstrong, Z. B., 536
Arnold, Benedict, 624
Arnold, Kenneth, 721
Arnow, Harriet Simpson, 132
Arny, W. F. M., 162
Arriol, Martha, 637
Arsenault, Georges, 308
Art
    body, 704
    folk, see Folk art
    outsider, 535–536
Arts and Crafts movement, 73, 749
Asbjørnsen, Peter Christen, 648
Asch, Moses, 53, 298, 355, 633
Ash Wednesday, 729
Ashabranner, Brent, 547
Ashley, Clarence, 633, 743
Asian American Art Centre in New York, 141
Astrology, 15, 562
Atkins, Chet, 715
Atlas, folk, 465
Atomic Age folklore, 517–518
Atomic bombs, 148
Atwater, Mary Meigs, 750
Au, Dennis, 310, 311
Aubert de Gaspé, Philippe, 306
Auction process, verbal artistry of, 54
Auctions, 53–55
Audience-response theory, 463
Audio recorders, 259
Audubon, John James, 588

Austin, Mary Hunter, 55
Autobiography, 13
Autoharp, 55–56

Babcock, Barbara A., 248
Baby, Stanley, 118
Bachelor party, 98
Back-country, see Appalachia
Back spins, 101
Bait fishermen, 274–275
Baker, Cheryl, 739
Baker, Kenny, 504
Baker, Nelson, 727
Baker, Ron, 310, 311
Baker, Theodor, 21
Bakhtin, Mikhail, 543
Bakken, Reidar, 650
Balfa, Dewey, 111, 504, 633
Ballad, 57–61, 67–68, 292–293
    Anglo American, 57
    blues, 60–61, 293
    British, 60
    broadside, 293
    canal, 125
    Child, 57–58, 293
    crime, 178
    medieval, 57–58, 293
    Mexican American folk, 160
    parlor, 60–61, 293, 294
    religious, 660
Ballad singing, 158
Baltic peoples in United States, 61–64
Baltic socialists, 62
Baltimore Album quilt, 608
Balys, Jonas, 63
Bambaataa, Afrika, 101
Banjo, 64–65, 679
Banjo songs, 65
Banks, Ann, 508
Bar mitzvah, 410
Barbeau, Marius, 66, 115, 121, 123, 233, 306, 308, 432
Barkan, Elliott, 313
Barn, Cajun, 111
Barn dance, 512
Barn types, 41
Barnicle, Mary Elizabeth, 66–67
Barone, Johnny, 566
Barrick, Mac E., 67
Barry, Phillips, 67–68, 275–276, 443
Barth, Fredrik, 228
Bartlett, John Russell, 22
Bartlett, William C., 625
Bartók, Béla, 233
Bartram, George, 653
Bascom, William R., 69, 158, 316
Baseball, 69–71
Basketmaking, 71–72
Baskets, Native American, 52, 71
Basque Americans, 74–77
Basque festival cycle, 76
Bass fishermen, 275
Bassett, Fletcher S., 20–21, 77
Bateson, Gregory, 555
Baughman, Ernest Warren, 77–78, 547

Bauman, Richard, 25–26, 228, 554–555, 557, 630, 675
Bausinger, Hermann, 675
Bayes, Coy, 129
Beaches, 728
Bebop, 407
Beck, Earl Clifton, 78
Beckwith, Martha Warren, 24, 78–79, 464
Bedcoverings, textile, 607–611
Beiderbecke, Bix, 407
Belden, Henry Marvin, 79, 536
Belief legend, 438
Bell, Michael, 676
Belsnickel, 551
Ben-Amos, Dan, 228, 286, 555, 576
Benedict, Ruth, 34–35, 79–80
Bénéteau, Marcel, 310
Benfield, Neriah, 56
Benoit, Emile, 117
Benson, John, 512
Berea College, 80
Beregovski, Moshe, 233
Beresin, Ann Richman, 322
Bergman, Margaret, 750
Berlin Wall, 149
Berlin work, 506
Bernat, Paul, 749
Berra, Yogi, 71
Berthiaume, Roméo, 312
Bharata Natyam, 196
Bigfoot, 80–81, 445–446, 491
Bikel, Theodore, 423
Bikers, 81–83
Billings, William, 624
Billy the Kid, 83–84
Binderman, Murray B., 709
Bird, Michael, 119
Birders, 84–85
Birth, 591–592
Birthday anniversaries, 34
Birthdays, 85–86
Birthing practices, 113
Birthstones, 85
Bøjer, Johan, 651
Black, Chany Scot, 749
Black, Narcissa Erwin, 749
Black Americans, see also African American entries; Negro entries
Black English, 86–87
Black gang songs, 765
Black gospel music, 337
Black Storytelling Festival, 690
Blacking, John, 234
Blackley, Becky, 56
Blacksmithing, 87–89
Blair, Hugh, 635, 637
Blank, Les, 264
Blason populaire, 627
Blasphemy, 186
Blessing of the Fleet, 512
Blood Libel, 181
Blue cat (catfish), 131–132
Blue laws, 331
Blue notes, 91
Blue Ridge Folklife Festival, 251

Bluebird record label, 104
Bluegrass, 89–90, 165, 491
Bluegrass banjo, 65
Blues, 90–94, 203, 362–363, 546, 615
Blues ballad, 60–61, 293
Bly, Robert, 691
Boas, Franz, 19–20, 94–95, 120, 381, 513
Boast, 95–96
Boatbuilding, 96–97
Boatright, Mody Coggin, 97, 526, 528, 547, 701
Body art, 704
Bodylore, 98–100, 164
Bogatyrev, Petr, 555
Boggs, Ralph Steele, 100
Bogoras, Waldemar, 463
Bohoon, Lavrentey, 722
Boilermaker, 688
Bolduc, Raymond, 762
Bolton, Henry C., 138
Bon-odori, 405
Bon odori dance, 196
Bond, Elijah J., 534
Bondurant, Bill, 487
Bonney, William H., 83
Bontemps, Arna, 157
Boone, Lalia Phipps, 526
Borden, Lizzie, 178
Botanicals, 469
Botkin, Benjamin A., 44, 101, 290–291, 509, 520, 564, 571, 572, 618–619, 771
Bowers, Bryan, 56
Bowing fiddles, 254
Bowling, Lawrence Edward, 634
Boyle, David, 122–123
Boys' games, 322
Bradbury, John, 537
Bradford, William, 706
Brady, Margaret K., 138
Brady, Matthew, 392
Brag, 95–96
Brakemen, 614
Brandwine, Naftule, 423
Brasseaux, Carl A., 110
Brassieur, C. Ray, 310, 313
Breakdancing, 101–102
Breakdown, 371
Breckinridge, Mary, 483
Brendle, Thomas R., 552
Brent, Linda, 682
Brett, Katherine B., 119
Brewer, John Mason, 102–103
Brewster, Paul G., 103, 138, 319
Brewster, W. Herbert, 337
Bridger, Jim, 103–104, 701
Briggs, Charles, 762
Brinton, Daniel Garrison, 17
Bristol, Elisabeth, 116
British ballad, 60
British Folk-Lore Society, 286
Broadside, 674
Broadside ballad, 293
Broadside ballad style, 57, 58–60
Broadsides, 57, 58

Brockman, Polk, 127
Bromyard, John, 693
Bronner, Simon J., 138, 627, 675
Bronson, Bertrand Harris, 104, 753
Brooks, Garth, 165
Brooks, John Lee, 528
Broonzy, Big Bill, 104
Brother Jonathan, 104–105
Brown, Frank Clyde, 105, 618, 640, 740
Brown, George, 276
Brown, H. "Rap," 206, 616
Brown, James, 94, 101
Brown, Milton, 164
Brown, Sterling, 509
Bruegel, Pieter, 600
Brunvand, Jan Harold, 25, 284, 286, 649, 701, 730
Bryant, Pearl, 178
Bua Xou Mua, 504
Buffington, Albert F., 551–552
Bukvic, Vaso, 703
Bullhead fishing, 130
Bulosan, Carlos, 571
Bunyan, Paul, 105–107, 345, 445, 528, 700
Bureau of Land Management (BLM), 74
Burial sites, 132–134
Burke, Edmund, 693
Burke, John, 115
Burke, Kenneth, 555
Burlin, Natalie Curtis, 21–22
Burnett, Matt, 54
Burnham, Dorothy and Harold, 119
Burns, Robert, 653
Burns, Walter Noble, 83
Butch-femme era, 440–441
Butler, Gary, 117
Butler, Margaret, 279
Byington, Robert H., 522

Cable, George Washington, 18, 289, 720
Cadaval, Olivia, 673
Cadence chant, 109
Cadle, Tillman, 66
Cadman, Charles Wakefield, 22
Cahill, Holger, 47, 507–508
Cajuns, 109–112
Caledonian Games, 654
Calendar holidays, 186–187
Calf roping, 638
California, University of, 5
California Folklore Society, 361
Call-and-response singing style, 134–135
Calvanism, 653
Cameras, 258–259
Camitta, Miriam, 248
Camp, 324
    sheep, 661–662
Camp, Charles, 251
Camp-meeting songs, 660
Camp meetings, 658
Camp wagons, 661
Campa, Arthur Leon, 112–113
Campbell, Hector, 117
Campbell, John C., 36, 37, 113, 114

Campbell, Joseph, 113, 691
Campbell, Marie Alice, 113
Campbell, Olive Dame, 36, 37, 113–114, 279, 572
Campfire programs, 115
Camplore, 114–115
Campus, slang on, 3–4
Canada
    folklore programs in, 5–6
    Quebec and, 124
Canada First movement, 122
Canadian Centre for Folk Culture Studies (CCFCS), 121
Canadian Folk-Lore Society, 123
Canadian Folk Song Society, 120
Canadian folklore, 115–122
Canadian folklore scholarship, 120–122
Canadian Museum of Civilization, 119
Canadian Society for Music Traditions (CSMT), 120
Canadian songs, 118
Canadian studies and folklore, 122–124
Canadians
    African, 116
    Anglo, 121
    Finnish, 267–268
    French, 8, 115, 305–309
Canal ballad, 125
Canal lore, 124–125
Candle-blowing rite, 85
Candlish, James, 662
Cansler, Loman D., 125–126
Canvaswork, 505
Capitalism, folklore of, 148
Capone, Al, 178, 727
Cardinal, Roger, 536
Carding, 746
Carey, George G., 109
Carignan, Jean, 117
Carlton, Rosa Lee, 743
Carmer, Carl Lamson, 126
Carnegie, Andrew, 688
Carnival midway, 242
Carolina Cotton Piedmont, 559–561
Carolling, Christmas, 31
Carpenter, Carole H., 119, 124
Carpenter, Inta Gale, 63
Carpenter, James, 443
Carrière, Joseph Médard, 126–127, 310
Carson, Fiddlin' John, 127, 548
Carter, A. P., 128–129
Carter, Isabel Gordon, 368, 399
Carter, Maybelle, 56, 128–129
Carter, Sara, 56, 128–129
Carter, William, 711
Carter Family, 127–130, 164
Carver, Cynthia May, 418
Carver, George, 458
Cash, Johnny, 617
Casitas, 727
Casos, 477
Cass-Beggs, Barbara, 119
Cassidy, Butch, 130
Catalog songs, 58, 292
Catch riddles, 630

Catch tale, 414
Catfish, 130–132
Catholic Church, 392, 758
Cattle guard, 347
Cattlemen, 169
Cautionary tales, 718
Cecil Sharp House, 661
Cemeteries, 132–134
Center for Folklife Programs and Cultural
    Studies, 672–673
Center for the Study of Southern Culture,
    134
Central Pacific Railroad, 139
Centre d'etudes acadiennes (Cea), 308
Centre d'études sur la langue, les arts et les
    traditions populaires des
    francophones en Amérique du
    Nord (CELAT), 122, 307
Challenger space shuttle jokes, 627
Chambers, Robert, 119
Champ, 491
Champe, John, 624
Chant, cadence, 109
Chanted folk sermon, 658–659
Chantefables, 140
Chanteys, 134–135, 765
Chaos, 498
Chapayeka, 335
Chapelle, Howard I., 97
Chapman, John, 412
Chaps, 171
Charivari, 666
Charles, Ray, 94
Charters, Samuel, 94
Chase, Richard, 135–136, 295, 399, 739
Chatelain, Heli, 572
Chaucer, Geoffrey, 598
Chavez, Cesar, 674
Cheek, Florence, 49
Chenier, Clifton, 774
Chernobyl nuclear disaster, 517
Chiasson, Anselme, 308
Chicago Folk-Lore Society, 20–21, 77
Chicago Folklore Prize, 77
Chicanos, 476
Child, Francis James, 22, 57, 104, 136,
    152, 374
Child ballad, 57–58, 293
Childbirth, 482–483, 591–592
Children, 136–138
Children's folklore, 137–138
Children's literature, 33
Chinatown History Museum, 141–142
Chinatowns, 139
Chinese Americans, 138–142
Chinese geomancy, 140
Chinese seasonal festivals, 140–142
Chittenden, Varick A., 649
Chittendon, Lawrence, 168
Christensen, Abigail Mandana ("Abbie")
    Holmes, 142
Christeson, Robert Perry, 142–143, 371
Christian holy days and holidays, 645
Christiansen, Reidar, 387
Christmas, 143–145

Christmas Bird Count, 84, 85
Christmas carolling, 31
Christmas concert, 208
Christmas presents
    labels for, 143
    wrappings for, 144
Christmas tree, 144
    artificial, 243
Churches, 729
Cinéma vérité, 264
Citizens band radio, 613, 718–719
City lore, 145
Civil rights movement, 571
Civil War, 145–146
Civil War reenacting, 146
Clark, LaRena, 118
Clark, Leon "Peck," 51
Classification, narrative, 45
Clayton, Paul, 197
Clements, William M., 620
Clements, William P., 420
Clifton, Roy, 118
Clinton, Bill, 673
Clog, 254
Cloggers, 192
Clothing, secondhand, 162
Coal-mining folklore, 428
Code, 656–657
Coding in American folk culture, 147–148
Coffin, Tristram Potter, 25, 152, 276
Cohan, George M., 392
Cohen, Hennig, 25
Cohen, John, 264
Coiling baskets, 73
Coin puzzle, 631
Cold War, 148–149
Coleman, Joseph Ben, 126
Coleman, Marion Moore, 568
Coleman, William, 299
Colindatori, 641
Collage paper cutting, 541
Collecting, 45
College students, folk lore of, 3–4
Coltrane, John, 407
Columbus Day, 149–150, 397
Combs, Josiah H., 151
Comeaux, Malcolm, 111
Coming-out stories, 441
Comiskey, Charles, 392
Commercial fishing, 271–273
Communal re-creation, 68
Communism, 157
Communist Party, 571
Community-based museums, 277, 278
Community medicine, 468
Comparative approach to folklore studies,
    151–153
    in America, 152–153
Comparative musicology, 231
Complicit coding, 147
Computer folklore, 154–155
Computer viruses, 155
Con artist, 155–156
Conception, 591
Congress of Industrial Organizations

(CIO), 687
Conjunto music, 156
Conjure system, 11
Conn, Billy, 393
Connelley, William Elsey, 719
Conroy, Jack, 156–157
Conservation, cultural, 182
Conspiracy theories, 157–158
Contagious magic, 470
Contemporary legends, 730
Contentious riddling, 629
Context, 159
Contextual approach to folklore, 158–159
Contra dancing, 193–194
Conundrum, 629
    riddle, 626
Conversion superstitions, 691
Cooke, Sam, 765
Cooley, Spade, 757
Cooper, Myrtle, 758
Corbett, Jim, 393
Cordero, Helen, 248, 504
Cormier, Joseph, 504
Cornhusk mats, 174
Corporate fisheries, 273
Corridos, 160
Corroborative evidence, 289
Cortez, Gregorio, 160, 161
Cortéz, Hernan, 431
Cosbey, Robert, 119
Costumes, 463
    butch-femme, 441
    folk, 161–164
Couch, W. T., 509
Council for the Development of French in
    Louisiana (CODOFIL), 112
Countermagic, 470
Counting-out rhymes, 137
Country Dance and Song Society, 193
Country music, 164–166
Country Music Foundation, 166
Courlander, Harold, 166–167
Cousin Jack stories, 167
Coventry, Alexander, 213
Cow tipping, 167
Cowboy poetry, 167–169
Cowboys, 169–172, 343, 346
    rodeo, 639
Cox, John Harrington, 36, 172
Coyote, 172–173
Crafts, 173–176, 218
Craig, Burlon, 504
Craig, Hardin, 634
Crane, Thomas Frederick, 19, 177, 725
Crazy quilts, 609
Crazywork, 506
Creighton, Helen, 116, 121, 177
Creole music, 773–775
Creolization, 111
Crevecoeur, Michel Guillaume de, 331
Crevecoeur, Michel Guillaume de, 331
Crewelwork, 505–506
Crime ballad, 178
Crime-victim stories, 179
Crime victims, urban, 727
Crimelore, 177–179

Crissman, Maxine "Lefty Lou," 355
Crnkovic, Rudolf, 703
Croatians, 670
Crockett, Davy, 15, 95, 179–180, 266, 624
Crosby, Enoch, 624
Crossdressing, 327
"Crossing the line" ceremonies, 459, 484
Cryptozoology, 491
Culin, Stewart, 138, 181, 319, 464, 572
Cults, 181, 440
Cultural conservation, 182
Cultural displays, ethnic traditions and, 64
Cultural equity, 604
Cultural hearths, 465
Cultural landscape, 182
Cultural patterns, emphasis on, 35
Cultural studies, 183–184
Culture
    context of, 159
    democratization of, 222
    family, 243, 676
    folk, see Folk culture
    food and, 299–302
    group, 676
    material, see Material culture entries
    memory, 385
    Mexican American, 681–682
    organizational, 676
    popular, folklore and, 576–578
    preliterate, oral tradition of, 153
Culture makers, elderly as, 13–14
Cunningham, Keith, 564
Curanderismo, 471
Curanderos, 185
Curran, Pearl, 534
Cursing, 185–186
Curtin, Jeremiah, 23
Customary folklore, 137
Customs, 186–189
    student, 3–4
Cut-paper figures, 541–542
Czechs, 670

Dahmer, Jeffrey, 535
Dahu, 400
Dalhart, Vernon, 164
Dalmatians, 670
Daly, Marcus, 486
Dance
    African American, 194–195
    folk, 191–196
    French, 195
    instrumental music and, 254
    Spanish American, 195–196
    square, 193, 194
Danielson, Larry, 650
Danish Americans, 647–651
Danish Constitution Day, 650
Danish Immigrant Museum, 648
Dantzig, George B., 731
Dargan, Amanda, 323
Darling, John, 701
Darlington, J. H., 667
Darnell, Regna, 94

Davenport, Clyde, 504
David, John, 685
Davidson, Levette Jay, 113, 197
Davies, Christie, 627
Davis, Arthur Kyle, Jr., 197
Davis, Asa, 276
Davis, Gerald L., 603
Davis, Susan, 571
Davis-Floyd, Robbie E., 248, 483
Davison, Marguerite Porter, 750
Dawes, William, 624
Day, J. W., 706
De Caro, Francis, 450
Dead-baby jokes, 627
Deaf folklore, 197–200
Dean, Michael Cassius, 625
Death anniversaries, 34
DeBerger, Jean, 307
Declaration of Independence, 388
Decoration Day, 134, 679
Decorative needlework, 504
Deejaying, 616
Dégh, Linda, 35, 228, 675
Deitz, John F., 535
Delivery, 591–592
Delmore, Alton and Rabon, 418
Democratization of culture, 222
Dempsey, Jack, 766
Dendroglyphs, 77
Denisoff, R. Serge, 521, 571
Densmore, Frances, 21, 200, 201, 542
Deprogramming, 181
Desprez, Frank, 168, 617
Detective-story puzzle, 631
Devil, 759
Devil's fiddles, 665
DeVoto, Bernard, 635–637
Dial, Thornton, 536
Dialect
    American, 22–23
    eye, 281
    social, 281
Dialect story, 200–201
Dibblee, Randall and Dorothy, 117
Dickens, Charles, 600
Dietary rules, 302
Disaster folklore, 202–203
Disorder, 498
Distler, Marian, 298
Distraction strategy of expression, 147
Divination, 729
Divinatory rituals, 359–361
Divining rod, 205
Dixieland, 406
Dixon, Willie, 203
Dobie, J. Frank, 97, 102, 203–204, 708
Doctors, 467–468
Documentary materials, 259
Dolan, Ramblin' Jimmie, 528
Dollard, John, 206, 207
Dolores, José, 762
Domsch, Sonia, 504
Doomsday Button, 517
Dormon, James, 110
Dorn, Arthur, 416

Dorsey, Thomas A., 93–94, 337
Dorson, Richard M., 19, 25, 39, 69, 107, 153, 201, 204, 227–228, 242, 256, 266, 269, 286, 289, 291, 304, 374, 382, 387, 412, 437, 443, 473, 528, 557, 572, 619, 668, 699, 730, 771
Doucet, Alain, 308
Dougherty, Sara Elizabeth, 128
Douglas, Mary, 717
Dowsing, 205–206
Doyle, Gerald S., 116
Doyle, Sam, 536
Doyon-Ferland, Madeleine, 307
Dozens, 206–207
Dracula, 642, 733
Drafts of weaving, 747
Drag, 324
Drama, folk, 115, 208–210
Drinking songs, 328
Driver, Bill, 143
Droodles, 558, 629
Dryler, Edward, 647
Dubois, Rachel Davis, 220
Dugaw, Dianne, 248
Dula, Tom, 595
Dulcimer, 210–212
Dunden, Gottfried, 538
Dundes, Alan, 19, 25, 107, 228, 276–277, 287, 339, 375, 388, 475, 555, 598, 601, 627, 628, 654, 675, 691, 695–696
Dunham, Katherine, 195
Dunin, Elsie, 196
Dunn, Charles W., 117
Dupont, Jean-Claude, 307, 308
Durkheim, Emile, 315, 675
Dusenbury, Emma Hays, 212
"Dutch," 549
Dutch Americans, 212–214
"Dutch Country," 549
Dutch folksongs, 213
Dyestuffs, 747
Dzobko, J., 119

Earthenware clay body, 582
Easter, 217–218
Easter eggs, 217–218, 723
Easter pageants, 208
Eaton, Allen, 36, 175, 218
Eckstorm, Fannie Hardy, 218–219
Eco, Umberto, 657
Economic immigrants, 61
Ecumene, term, 635–636
Eddy, Mary O., 219
Education, folklife in, 219–220
Edwards, John, 412
Egg decorating, 217–218, 723
Eileschpiggel, 552
Eisteddfod, 754
Elbedritsche, 552
Elderly, as culture makers, 13–14
Election Day, 510, 512
Electric boogie, 102
Elephant riddles, 627

Elias, Charles, Sr., 703
Elijah, 545
Ellison, Ralph, 9
Elvis, 220–222
Emancipation Proclamation, 420, 674
Embraces, 334
Embroidery, 505–506, 607
Emerson, Ralph Waldo, 599
Empowerment, 222–223
Emrich, Duncan B. M., 25, 44, 223, 496
Enclave, ethnic, 378
Encounter stories, 33
English, Black, 86–87
English and Scottish Popular Ballads, The,
     22, 57, 136
English descent, Americans of, 28–32
English-language folklore of Canada, 115–
     122
Environmentalism, 55
Epic songs, 57
Epiphany, 144
Epitaph, 223–224, 340
Epithets, 186
Erie Canal, 124
Ernberg, Anna, 749
Eskeröd, Albert, 694, 695
Esoteric-exoteric factor in folklore, 224–
     225
Espinosa, Aurelio Macedonio, 225, 717
Estonian Americans, 61–64
Ethics in folklore research, 225–226
Ethnic cemeteries, 134
Ethnic costume, 161–164
Ethnic enclave, 378
Ethnic folklore, 226–229
Ethnic foods, 63
Ethnic-racial slurs, 186
Ethnic riddle jokes, 626–627
Ethnic stereotypes, 229–230
Ethnic traditions, cultural displays and, 64
Ethnicity, 387
     food and, 301
Ethnochoreology, 429–430
Ethnography, term, 578
Ethnography of speaking, 555–556
Ethnomusicology, 230–236, 367
Etymology, folk, 238
European Seminar in Ethnomusicology
     (ESEM), 235
Evangeline, 109–110
Evans, David, 630, 708, 709
Evans, John, 753–754
Evanson, Jacob, 687, 689
Events, 159
Everly, Ike, 715
Evil, 498
Evil eye, 349
Exaggerated imagery, 58
Exaggeration, 642
     hyperbolic, 95–96
Examinations, beliefs about, 3
Exclusion Act of 1882, 139
Exhibitions, 241–242
Exoteric folklore, 224
Explicit coding, 147

Eye dialect, 281
Eyewitness history, 369

Fable, 239
Face painting, 100
Faculty folklore, 4
Fahey, John, 546
Fairies, 239–240
Fairs, 241–242
Fairy tale, 57, 294
Fakelore, 204, 242
Family culture, 243, 676
Family folklore, 242–244
Family narratives, 146
Family saga, 97
Fancywork, 506
Farkas, Milutin, 703
Farmers, 244–246
Farmer's Almanac, 15
Farmhouse, 245
Farming songs, 347
Farrer, Clair R., 247
Farrier, 89
Farwell, Arthur, 22
Fauset, Arthur Huff, 116
Federal Arts Project (FAP), 507
Federal Music Project (FMP), 507, 508
Federal One, 507
Federal Theater Project (FTP), 507
Federal Writers' Project (FWP), 291, 448,
     507, 508–509
Feidman, Giora, 423
Feldman, Walter Zev, 423
Femaleness, 326–329
Feminism, 246–247, 760
Feminist approaches to folklore, 246–249
Femme-butch era, 440–441
Feng-shui, 140
Fergusson, Donald A., 117
Fernandez, James, 381
Ferris, William R., 134, 264
Feste, 645
Festival cycle, Basque, 76
Festival of American Folklife, 40, 250–
     251, 252–253, 672
Festivals, 249–251
     Chinese seasonal, 140–142
     folk, 188, 277
     folklife, 602–603
     monocultural, 250
Fewkes, Jesse Walter, 21, 233
Fiddle music, 253–256
Fiddle tradition, Scots-Irish, 65
Fiddlers (catfish), 131
Field hollers, 92, 764
Fieldwork, 19, 256–259, 387
     basis of, 26
Fiesta, 260
Fife, Austin E., 261
Filipino Americans, 261–263
Filk music, 263
Fillmore, John Comfort, 21, 200
Film
     folklore and, 263–265
Western, 164–165

Fine, Gary Alan, 322, 531, 676
Fink, Mike, 95, 265–266, 481
Finn, Benjamin Franklin, 701
Finnemore, Charles, 276
FinnFest USA, 270
Finnish Americans, 266–271
Finnish Canadians, 267–268
Finnish steam bath, 270
Finster, Howard, 536
Fireplace, 42
Firsthand history, 369
Fischer, David Hackett, 38
Fish, folk taxonomies of, 275
Fish, Lena Bourne, 276, 740
Fishing
     commercial, 271–273
     sport, 271, 274–275
     subsistence, 272
Fishing craft, 96
Flanders, Helen Hartness, 275–276
Flatheads (catfish), 131
Flatley, Michael, 504
Flatt, Lester, 89
Flea markets, 560
Fletcher, Alice Cunningham, 21, 200, 572
Fletcher, Robert H., 636
Floating cabins, 741
Floyd, Pretty Boy, 535
Fly fishermen, 274
Flying Dutchman, 459
Fo'c'sle songs, 474
Foley, Tom, 392
Folk architecture, 41
     Southern, 678
Folk art, 46–53
     exhibiting, 603
     religious, 478
Folk-art coordinators, state, 51
Folk-arts-in-education programs, 603
Folk atlas, 465
Folk beliefs, 137, 692–696
Folk blues, 91
Folk churches, 620
Folk costume, 161–164
Folk Culture, Fund for, 317
Folk culture, New Deal and, 507–509
Folk-culture research, 283
Folk dance, 191–196
Folk drama, 115, 208–210
Folk etymology, 238
Folk festivals, 188, 277
Folk games, 103
Folk groups, 676
Folk heroes, 107
Folk-heroes, 25
Folk history, 369–370
Folk hymns, 660
Folk ideas, 32, 276–277
Folk ideology, 574
Folk justice, 571
Folk language of African Americans, 280
Folk medicine, 468–472
     Mexican American, 185
Folk museums, 277–278
Folk music

Appalachian, 37
Greek, 348–349
Folk names, 501–502
Folk outlaw, 534–535
Folk poetry, 564–566
Folk regions, 465
Folk religion, 620–621
Folk rhythm, used in military, 109
Folk saints, 766
Folk-Say, 101
Folk-say, 71, 101, 290–291
Folk schools, 278–279
Folk sermon, 657–659
Folk society, religion of, 620
Folk-Song Society of the Northeast, 219
Folk-Songs of the South, 172
Folk speech, 279–281
Folk stereotypes, 277
Folk technical culture, 463
Folk toys, 712–714
Folklife
concept of, 522
in education, 219–220
Folklife Annual, 16
Folklife Center News, 16
Folklife festivals, 602–603
Folklife movement, 282–285
Folklife Reading Room, 17
Folklife research, 284–285
Folklife Source Book, 45–46
Folklife study, 26
Folklore, 285–287
of academe, 3–4
academic programs in, 4–6
African American, 18
aging and, 12–14
Alabama, 126
American Indian, 18, 20
American literature and, 287–290
American scholarship on, 17–23
American studies and, 24–27
anthropological approach to, 34–35
applied, 38–40, 509, 604
archaic, 63
Canadian, 115–122
Canadian studies and, 122–124
of capitalism, 148
children's, 137–138
coal-mining, 128
computer, 154–155
contextual approach to, 158–159
deaf, 197–200
defined, 576
disaster, 202–203
esoteric-exoteric factor in, 224–225
ethnic, 226–229
exoteric, 224
family, 242–244
feminist approaches to, 246–249
film and, 263–265
gender and, 326–329
immigrant, 204
immigration, study of, 385–388
Jamaican, 79
maritime, 458–460

Marxist approach to, 461
mass media and, 462–463
military, 484–485
Mormon, 493–496
Native American, 227
negro, 9
occupational, 519–523
oral, 288
organizational, 531–533
parody in, 543
Pennsylvania, 67
performance approach to, 554–556
politics and, 570–574
popular culture and, 576–578
prison, 593–595
psychology and, 601–602
public, 602–605
regional, 618–619
religious, 621
semiotic approach to, 656–657
social protest in, 673–675
sociological approach to, 675–677
transplanted, 497
of truckers, 717–719
urban, 725–729
Vermont, 635
wartime, 766–768
of work, 728
Folklore Americas, 100
Folklore archives, 45–46
Folklore research, ethics in, 225–226
Folklore studies, comparative approach to,
151–153
Folklore Studies Association of Canada
(FSAC), 120, 122, 123–124
Folklorism, 64
"Folklorismus," 242
Folkloristics, 676
Folklorists in New England (FINE), 512
Folklure, 242, 462
Folksongs, 26, 292–294
Anglo American, 32
Dutch, 213
Irish, 68
Kentucky, 151
Folktales, 294–295
West African, 10
Folkways, 295–298
term, 186
Folkways Records, 53, 298–299, 673
Foner, Philip S., 571
Font, 593
Fontenot, Canray, 504
Food fights, 114
Food plants, 561
Foods
Cajun, 111
culture and, 299–302
ethnic, 63
Irish, 393
Portuguese American, 580
preservation of, 584
Foodways, 298, 299–302, 327
Jewish, 411
Korean, 426

Mexican American, 478
Southern, 678–679
Foodways research, 300–301
Fool's errand, 40, 587–588
Forbes, Kathryn, 650
Formulaic systems, 530
Fort, Charles Hoy, 491
Fort Bridger, 103
Fortier, Alcée, 302–303
Foster, Stephen, 390
Fourth of July, 388–389
Fowke, Edith, 118
Fox, Terry, 565
Foxfire, 303–305
Foxfire Project, 37, 220
Fraktur, 550
Francis, Owen, 458
Franco-American identity issues, 313
Franklin, Benjamin, 15, 305, 331, 599
Franklin and Marshall University, 4
Fraser, Grace, 118
Fraser, Mary L., 116
Frazer, James George, 693–694, 758
Freaking, 690
Freedom, 636
Freeman, Bud, 407
Freemasons, 209
French, in United States, 309–313
French Canadians, 8, 115, 305–309
French dance, 195
Freud, Sigmund, 374, 601
Friday the Thirteenth, 314–315
Frost, Robert, 599
Frost, William Goodell, 175, 749
Fruit jokes, 626
Fuguing tune, 660
Fuld, William, 534
Fuller, Blind Boy (Fulton Allen), 315, 705
Functional analysis, 158
Functionalism, 315–316
Fund for Folk Culture (FFC), 317
Funeral
American, 134
Chinese, 141
Funk rap, 616

Gagnon, Ernest, 115, 306
Galbraith, John Kenneth, 633
Galleys, 593
Galusha, John, 740
Gambling, 343
Game animals, 379–381
Games, 181, 319–323
folk, 103
Gandy-dancers, 640
Gang songs, Black, 765
Gangsta music, 179
Gard, Robert, 119
Garden-of-Eden tree, 47
Gardner, Emelyn Elizabeth, 323, 403
Gardner, Gail I., 323
Gardner, Gerald, 760
Garrett, Pat, 83
Garrido de Boggs, Edna, 100
Garrison, Lucy McKim, 572

Gates, Bill, 154
Gay community, 328–329
Gay men, 324–325
Gayton, Anna Hadwick, 325–326
Geechee dialect, 9
Geertz, Clifford, 578
Gender, 247
    folklore and, 326–329
    food and, 301
Genealogical puzzle, 631
Genesee Valley, 51
Genres, 152
Gentry, Jane, 368
Geographical puzzle, 631
Geomancy, Chinese, 140
George, Elmer, 276
George, Robert A., 228, 286
Georges, Robert, 675
German Americans, 329–333
Gerontologists, 12
Gerould, Gordon Hall, 333
Gershwin, George, 765
Gery, Aldis, 56
Gestalt, 489
Gestural riddles, 629
Gestures, 100, 333–335
Ghost-dance movement, 492
Ghost stories, 137, 335–336
Ghosts, 98
Ghosts Festival, 141
Gibbon, J. Murray, 123
Gibbons, Phebe Earle, 283
Gifts
    anniversary, 34
    birthday, 86
Gilbert, Ronnie, 655
Gillespie, Dizzy, 407
Gilligan, Carol, 602
Gilmore, Janet, 522
Ginzburg, Carlo, 760
Girls' games, 322
Glass, Joseph W., 548
Glassie, Henry, 284, 479, 522, 548, 573,
    675, 692, 734
Glossolalia, 658
Gluckman, Max, 338
Godreau, Jane, 311
Goethe, Johann Wolfgang von, 694
Goffman, Erving, 555, 676
Goldstein, Kenneth S., 116, 159, 322,
    496, 572
Goliath effect, 532
Gomez, Lefty, 70
Gomme, Alice B., 319
Gonzales, Alicia, 522
Goodwin, Majorie H., 322
Gordon, John Wesley, 524
Gordon, Robert Winslow, 36, 336–337,
    707
Gospel music, 337, 728
Gossip, 338, 642
Gouze, Matt, 703
Graceland, 222
Graffiti, 338–340, 565, 727
Graffito decoration on pottery, 582

Grainger, Percy, 233
Gramsci, Antonio, 183, 573
Grand Ole Opry, 165, 457
Granger, Gordon, 420
Grant, Ed, 701
Grass-roots festivals, 249
Gravander, Mama Valborg, 750
Gravemarkers, 132–134, 340–341
    inscribed, 223–224
Great Basin, 342–344
Great Depression, 157
Great Lakes, 344–345
Great Plains, 345–348
Greek Americans, 348–350
Greek folk music, 348–349
Greely, Andrew M., 385
Green, Archie, 317, 486, 520, 572, 688
Green, Thomas A., 630
Greenfield, Bill, 701
Greenhill, Pauline, 118
Greenleaf, Elisabeth, 116
Greenway, John, 113, 350–351, 521, 639
Greetings, 334
Grimm, Jacob, 295, 374, 437, 693
Grimm, Wilhelm, 295, 374
Gringo, 238
Grits, 680
Groundhog Day, 351
Group culture, 676
Grover, Carrie, 116, 443
Grundtvig, Nikolaj Frederik Severin, 278
Grundtvig, Svend, 136
Guan Gung, 140
Gubser, Elsie, 750
Guillonée, 351
Guinchard, Rufus, 117
Guinness Stout, 390
Guiteau, Charles, 178
Gulf War, 352–353
Gullah dialect, 9, 86, 87
Gum books, 762
Gummere, Francis Barton, 67, 79, 353
Gunness, Belle, 178
Guthrie, Arlo, 356
Guthrie, Marjorie, 356
Guthrie, Woody, 353–356, 528, 674
Gutierrez, Charlotte Paige, 739
Gutter, Karl August, 55
Gymanfa ganu, 754
Gypsies, 356–357

Haberl, Rosalia, 504
Habitants, 310
Haggadah, 544
Hagopian, Richard, 504
Hairstyling, African American, 163
Hale, Horatio Emmons, 17
Hale, Nathan, 623, 624
Hale, Sarah Josepha, 706
Haley, Alex, 166
Hall, Benjamin Homer, 22
Halle, David, 526
Halloween, 163, 359–361
Hallowell, A. Irving, 652
Halpert, Edith, 48, 49

Halpert, Herbert, 117, 119, 124, 152,
    507, 539, 701
Hamfests, 613
Hamlin, M. C. W., 310
Hance, "Captain" John, 701
Hand, Wayland D., 361–362, 520–521,
    606, 634, 693, 696, 715
Handcox, John L., 362
Handles, 718–719
Handlin, Oscar, 385
Handshakes, 334
Handweavers Guild of America (HGA),
    750
Handweaving, 745
Handy, W. C., 93, 94, 362–363, 651
Handy, Walter, 72
Hanukkah, 410
"Happy Birthday to You," 85
Harley-Davidson bikers, 81–82
Harmon, Andrew, 368
Harmon, Council, 295, 368, 739
Harris, Joel Chandler, 9, 18–19, 363–364,
    572, 720, 724–725
Harvard University, 5
Harvey, Bessie, 536
Hasidic communities, 409
Haugen, Einar, 649
Haunted houses, 336
Hawaiian hula gestures, 335
Hawaiian mythology, 78
Hawes, Bess Lomax, 321–322, 604
Hayes, J. Milton, 618
Hays, Lee, 655
Hazelius, Artur, 277
Head spins, 101
Health-care professionals, 467–468
Hearn, Lafcadio, 23, 299–300
Hebrew, 410
Helen Hartness Flanders Folk Music
    Collection, 275–276
Hellerman, Fred, 655
Hell's Angels, 81
Hemphill, Herbert, 49, 50
Henderson, Thomas, 652
Hendren, Joseph W., 753
Henry, John, 364–365, 615
Henry, Lorenzo ("Len"), 365, 515, 701
Henry, Mellinger Edward, 366
Herbal medicine, Chinese, 141
Herbalism, 469, 470
Herkimer, Nicholas, 331
Hermann, George, 368
Herrera-Sobek, Maria, 248
Herskovits, Frances S., 367
Herskovits, Melville Jean, 69, 79, 153,
    227, 366–367
Herzog, George, 367
Heuvelmans, Bernard, 491
Hex signs, 550
Hickerson, Joseph C., 44
Hicks, Fanny, 368
Hicks, Nathan, 740
Hicks, Orville, 368–369
Hicks, Ray, 504
Hicks, Roby Monroe, 65

Hicks-Harmon families, 367–369, 399
Highland Games, 654
Highlander Folk School, 40, 279
Higinbotham, John C., 119
Higonnet, Patrice, 313
Hill, Joe, 369
Hillbilly, 390
Hindman Settlement School of
	Kentucky, 279
Hip hop, 207
Hippies, 162
Hispano culture, 681
Historias, 477
Historic anniversaries, 34
Historic-geographic method, 151–152,
	153
History, folk, 369–370
Hitler, Adolf, 643
Hix, David, 367
Hoax, 414, 587
Hobos, 339
Hodja, Nastradin, 350
Hoedown, 371–372
Hoerburger, Felix, 191–192
Hoffman, Walter James, 283
Holidays, calendar, 186–187
Holler, 372–373, 764
	field, 92
Holloway, Stanley, 617
Holtzberg-Call, Maggie, 522
Hom, Marlon K., 140
Home altars, 327
Home remedies, 469
Homeopathic magic, 694
Homespun, 748
Homespun Fair, 80
Homosexual men, 324–325
Honko, Lauri, 675
Hood, Mantle, 234
Hoodoo collection, 382
Hoodoo doctor, 489
Hoodoo system, 11
Hooker, John Lee, 92
hooks, bell, 573
Hoosier Folklore Society, 103
Hornpipe, 254
Horse fiddles, 665
Hot-metal printers, 592
Hotsfields, 594
Houseboats, 741
Household medicine, 469
Houses
	African American, 11
	American vernacular, 41
	haunted, 336
	Pennsylvania, 550–551
	sod, 347
Houston, David F., 447
Howard, Dorothy Mills, 319, 373
Hoy, Dummy, 199
Hudson, Arthur Palmer, 373
Hufford, David, 40, 601
Hufford, Mary, 605
Hughes, Ezeckiel, 753
Hughes, Langston, 9, 665

Hughes, Linda, 322
Hula gestures, Hawaiian, 335
Humor, 374–375
	legends and, 35
	Mormon, 495–496
Hungarian Americans, 376–379
Hunt, Marjorie, 673
Hunter, Alberta, 671
Hunting, 379–381
Hurston, Zora Neale, 9, 381–382, 418,
	572
Hussein, Saddam, 352
Huszar, Sandor, 703
Hutchison, Rosemary, 117
Hyatt, Harry M., 382
Hyer, Charles, 347
Hylton, James M., 399
Hymes, Dell, 555–556
Hymnody, Protestant, 337
Hyperbolic exaggeration, 95–96

Icelandic Americans, 647–651
Icelandic Sagas, 647
Icon, 656
Ideas, folk, 276–277
Idioculture, 676
Iditarod, 516
Illinois Folklore Society, 672
Illiteracy, 68
Ilmonen, Salamon, 269
Imagery, exaggerated, 58
Immigrant folklore, 204
Immigration, peasant, 386
Immigration folklore, study of, 385–388
Implicit coding, 147
Impression management, 676
Incompetence strategy of expression, 148
Independence Day, 388–389
Index, 656
Index of American Design, 176, 389–390,
	508
Index of American Design, The, 49–50
Indexing archives, 45
Indiana University, 5
Indirection strategy of expression, 147–
	148
Industrial Workers of the World (IWW),
	369
Initiatory jokes, 588
Insixiengmai, Khamvong, 504
Institute of Social and Economic Research
	(ISER), 117
Institutional Development and Economic
	Affairs Service (IDEAS), 303
Instrumental music, dance and, 254
Insults, 186
Intercontinental missiles, 148
Intergenerational ties, 14
Intermountain sheep camp, 662
Internal evidence, 289
International Business Machines (IBM)
	Corporation folklore, 532
International Council for Traditional
	Music (ICTM), 230
International Folk-Lore Congress of 1893, 21

International slur, 627
International Society for Contemporary
	Legend Research (ISCLR), 730
International Society of Cryptozoology
	(ISC), 491
Internet, 155
Interviews, 226, 442
Irish Americans, 390–393
Irish folksongs, 68
Iron Curtain, 148
Iron working, 88
Irrigation projects, 343
Irving, Washington, 213, 393–394
Issei, 404
Italian Americans, 394–398
Ives, Burl, 398
Ives, Edward, 117

Jabbour, Alan, 44, 317
Jack tales, 135–136, 399
Jackalope, 400
Jackson, Andrew, 390
Jackson, Bruce, 686, 708, 709, 710
Jackson, George Pullen, 400
Jackson, Jesse, 659
Jackson, Mary Magdalene (Garland; "Aunt
	Molly"), 401
Jacobs, Harriet, 682
Jacobs, Joseph, 675, 725
Jagendorf, Mortiz, 701
Jairazbhoy, Nazir, 235
Jakobson, Roman, 555
Jamaican folklore, 79
James, Frank, 401–402
James, J. L., 626
James, Jesse Woodson, 178, 401–403
James, Thelma Grey, 403
Jameson, Frederic, 581
Jameson, R. D., 403
Jansen, William Hugh, 224, 228, 404,
	671, 701
Japanese Americans, 404–405
Jara, Victor, 573
Jarrell, Tommy, 504
Jazz, 90, 91, 405–407, 423
Jefferson, Blind Lemon, 407–408, 436
Jefferson, Thomas, 28
Jersey Devil, 408
Jewish Americans, 409–411
Jig, 254
Jody (folk character), 109
John Birch Society, 157
John C. Campbell Folk School, 114, 279
John Edwards Memorial Foundation
	(JEMF), 166, 412
Johnny Appleseed, 412
Johnson, Clifton, 412–413
Johnson, Guy Benton, 413, 523, 675
Johnson, Jack, 665, 710
Johnson, James D., 709
Johnson, Jerry, 312
Johnson, Paula, 522
Johnson, Robert, 413–414
Johnson, Tommy, 414
Johnston, Richard, 118

Joke cycles, 375, 463
Jokes, 153, 414–416, 438
    deaf, 198–200
    initiatory, 588
    Polack, 568, 626
    practical, 587–589
    riddle, 137, 558, 626–628, 629
Jolicoeur, Catherine, 307, 308
Jolson, Al, 488
Jonathan, Brother, 104–105
Jones, Bessie, 321–322
Jones, Clyde, 536
Jones, Hathaway, 416, 515
Jones, John Luther ("Casey"), 417
Jones, John Paul, 624
Jones, Louis Clark, 284, 417
Jones, Louis Marshall ("Grandpa"), 417–
    418
Jones, Michael Owen, 284, 696
Jones, Rebecca King, 30
Jones, Suzi, 516, 619
Jones, William, 151, 232
Jordan, Brigitte, 483
Jordan, Terry, 479
Journal of American Folklore (JAF), 19, 23
Journeymen printers, 592–593
Juba, 371
Jukebox, 419
July Fourth, 388–389
Juneteenth, 146, 420, 674
Jung, C. G., 113, 716
Juré, 773–774
Justice, folk, 571
Juxtaposition strategy of expression, 147

Kalcik, Susan J., 25–26, 247
Kandel, Harry, 423
Karenga, Maulana "Ron," 430
Karpeles, Maud, 114, 116, 661
Kealiinohomoku, Joann Wheeler, 191
Kennedy, John F., 149, 157
Kentucky folksongs, 151
Kernel story, 247
Kibei, 404
Kilgore, Gaines, 399
Kilian, Jan, 755
Kilrain, Jake, 393
Kilroy, 339
Kilt, 654
Kimball, J. Golden, 495
Kincaid, Bradley, 418
King, Martin Luther, Jr., 659
King, Riley "B. B.," 504
Kirkland, Edwin Capers, 421, 496
Kirshenblatt-Gimblett, Barbara, 120, 145,
    228, 604
Kiskaddon, Bruce, 168
Kisses, 334
Kittredge, George Lyman, 151, 421–422,
    447, 562, 759
Klezmer music, 422–423
Klymasz, Robert B., 119, 228
Knapp, Mary and Herbert, 138
Knights of Columbus, 149
Knives, 594

Knortz, Karl, 283, 423–424
Knots, fishing, 272
Knott, Sarah Gertrude, 249, 251, 424,
    502, 503
Knox, George, 424–425
Kodály, Zoltán, 233
Kodish, Deborah, 626
Kolar, Walter, 703
Kolaric, Pajo, 703
Kolberg, Oskar, 233
Köngäs-Maranda, Elli, 228, 425
Konstantinovic, Vlado, 703
Kordish, Debora, 248
Korean Americans, 425–427
Korean War, 427–428
Korson, George, 428–429, 485, 519, 687
Korson, Rae Rosenblatt, 44, 429, 692
Kosciuszko, Thaddeus, 567–568, 670
Kosher, 411
Krappe, Alexander Haggerty, 429, 539,
    672
Krauss, Alison, 90
Kroc, Ray, 670
Krohn, Julius, 152
Krohn, Kaarle, 152
Ku Klux Klan, 158
Kunst, Jaap, 233–234
Kurath, Gertrude Prokosch, 191, 429–
    430
Kurath, Hans, 479, 548
Kurin, Richard, 672
Kutztown Folk Festival, 250, 549
Kuusi, Matti, 598
Kvalheim, Ethel, 504, 650
Kvitka, K., 233
Kwanzaa, 430

La Lechuza, 477
La Llorona, 431, 477, 727
Labanotation, 192
Labelle, Ronald, 308
Labor Day, 432
Laborlore, 486, 674
Labov, William, 709
L'Acadie, 109
Lacourcière, Luc, 66, 115, 306–307, 308,
    432–433
Laestadians, 271
Laine, Jack, 406
Lambson, Delbert, 617
Landscape, cultural, 182
Lane, Brigitte, 312, 313
Lang, Henry, 579
Language retention, Cajun, 112
Lansdale, Edward, 573
Lanser, Susan S., 248
Larkin, Margaret, 433
Larson, Gary, 462
Latvian Americans, 61–64
Laughead, William B., 106–107
Lausche, Frank, 670
Law, G. Malcolm, 60, 766
Lawless, Elaine J., 247–248, 621
Lawyers, 433–434
Laxalt, Robert, 75

Lay midwifery, 483
Le Gente, 113
Leach, MacEdward, 116, 434
Leading, 593
"Leaping and lingering" technique, 58
LeBlanc, Dudley, 110
Leblanc, Joseph-Thomas, 308
Ledbetter, Huddie ("Lead Belly"), 435–
    436, 448
Lee, Hector H., 436–437
Leeds, Jane, 408
Leeks, 754
Legend, 437–439
    urban, 439, 531, 730–731
Legend conduit, 35
Legend trip, 439–440
Léger, Lauraine, 308
Lehr, Genevieve, 116
Leisure-time riddling, 628
LeJeune, Iry, 111
Leland, Charles Godfrey, 23, 536, 760
Lemieux, Germain, 309
Lent, 217
Lesbian community, 328–329
Lesbians, 440–442
Lesnovich, Mike, 688
Liebes, Dorothy, 750
Life, stages of, 12
Life history, 442
Life list, birder, 84
Life review projects, 13
Lightbulb jokes, 627–628
Lightning, 744
Lila Wallace-Reader's Digest Fund, 317
Limón, José, 522
Lincoln, Abraham, 157, 199, 706, 715
Line dancing, 193
Linguistic ambiguity, 630
*Linguistic Atlas of the United States and
    Canada,* 280, 281
Linscott, Eloise Hubbard, 68, 442–443
Lipman, Jean, 48
Lippmann, Walter, 229
Literal rebuses, 631
Literature, 288
    American, folklore and, 287–290
    children's, 33
Lithuanian Americans, 61–64
Little Canadas, 311
Little moron jokes, 626
Little Peter, 397
Livesay, Florence R., 119
Livestock enterprises, 664
Local-character anecdote, 443–445
Loftfield, Berner, 651
Log construction, 516
Loggers, 344–345, 445–447
Logging traditions, 8
Lomax, Alan, 44, 234, 448, 604, 739
Lomax, John Avery, 94, 105, 168, 171,
    212, 436, 447–449, 509, 518,
    519, 617, 708
Lombardi-Satriani, Luigi, 620
Long, Eleanor, 152
Long, Maud, 368, 496

Long, Reub, 515
Long, Stephen H., 537
Long, Worth, 633
Longabaugh, Harry, 130
Longfellow, Henry Wadsworth, 109, 289
Longoria, Valerio, 504
Lönnrot, Elias, 152, 269
Loom, 747
Loomis, C. Grant, 449
Lopez, George, 51
López, Nasario, 762
Lord, Albert Bates, 449–450, 530, 578, 659
Loudermilk, Romaine, 755
Louis, Joe, 393
Louisiana, 306
Louisiana Association of the American Folklore Society, 303
Louisiana Cajuns, 110–112
Love rap, 616
Lovers' leaps, 450
Lowell Folk Festival, 251
Lucas, Charlie, 536
Lullaby, 450–451
Lumberjacks, 8, 78, 189, 445–447
Lunsford, Bascom Lamar, 451–452
Luomala, Katherine, 452–453
Lyon, Billy, 685, 686
Lyric song, 292, 453–456
Lyrics, rap and street-music, 96

Macaronism, 722
MacDonnell, Margaret, 117, 118
Mackenzie, W. Roy, 116, 121
MacLeod, Calum, 117
Macmillan, Ernest, 123
MacNeil, Joe Neil, 117
Macon, David Harrison ("Uncle Dave"), 457–458
MacPherson, James, 654
Magarac, Joe, 458, 688, 689
Magic, 694, 758
Magic superstitions, 691
Magical medicine, 469
Magyars, 376–379
Majer, Miroslav, 703
Maleness, 326–329
Malinowski, Bronislaw, 159, 315, 316
Malone, Bill C., 640
Maltz, Albert, 433
Manetta, Fess, 406
Mannhardt, Wilhelm, 694, 695
Manny, Louise, 116
Mansfield, Grace, 116
March, 254
Marchalonis, Shirley, 437
Märchen, 135, 289–290, 294
Mardi Gras, 111–112, 163, 188
Maritime folklore, 458–460
Maritime songs, 460
Marryat, Captain, 771
Martin, Elizabeth K., 526
Marxist approach to folklore, 461
Mason, Otis Tufton, 461–462, 464
Mass media, folklore and, 462–463

Material culture, 138, 463–466
Material-culture studies, 245
Material-culture traditions, 121
Material folklore, 137
Material History Bulletin, 121
Materials, documentary, 259
Mathias, Elizabeth, 39
Matsos, 545
Mauss, Marcel, 675
Mazzei, Filippo, 395
McAllester, David, 234
McAuliffe, Christa, 627
McCarl, Robert, 522, 523
McCarran, Patrick, 74
McCarthy, Joseph, 157
McCarty, Henry, 83
McCoy, Minnie ("Memphis Minnie"), 466
McCrone, David, 654
McCurdy, Ed, 118
McDonnell, Ian, 654
McDougall, Dave, 701
McDowell, John Holmes, 138, 629, 630
McEwen, Grant, 119
McGee, Dennis, 111, 774
McGhee, Brownie, 705
McGillivray, James, 106
McGuire, Peter J., 432
McKim, Lucy, 18
McLendon, Altha Lea, 564
McNeil, W. K., 626
McTell, Blind Willie, 466–467
Mead, Margaret, 300
Mechling, Jay, 184
Medical professionals, 467–468
Medicine, folk, 468–472
Medieval ballad, 57–58, 293
Meillet, Antoine, 530, 544
Melgaard, Leif, 649–650
Melograph, 234
Memorate, 472–473
Memorial park, 133
Memorial University of Newfoundland Folklore and Language Archive (MUNFLA), 117
Memory culture, 385
Memory projects, 13–14
Mender, Joseph, 63
Mercer, Henry Chapman, 473–474
Merchant seamen, 474–475
Merriam, Alan, 234
Mestrovic, Ivan, 670
Metafolklore, 475
Metaphor, 95
    myth as, 498
Metaphoric ambiguity, 630
Métis, 311
Mexican American culture, 681–682
Mexican American folk ballad, 160
Mexican American folk medicine, 185
Mexican Americans, 161, 475–478
Michigan Folk Art Show, 51
Michigan Folklore Society, 739
Michigan Lumberjacks, 78
Middle Atlantic region, 479–480
Midsummer and Midwinter Day, 677

Midwest, 480–482
Midwifery, 482–483
Miguels, Jose, 298
Milberg, Alan, 138
Milburn, George, 709
Miles, Emma Bell, 36
Military, folk rhythm used in, 109
Military folklore, 484–485
Mills, Alan, 118
Mills, Margaret, 249
Miners, 485–487
Miners' tools, 521
Minimalization strategy of expression, 148
Mining, 342
Minstrel shows, 64, 487–488
Miramichi Folk Festival, 116
Missiles, intercontinental, 148
Missouri Folk-Lore Society, 79
Mitchell, George, 392
Mnemonic devices, 467, 488–489
Moberg, Vilhelm, 651
Modern Language Association of America, 287
Modern legends, 730
Moe, Jørgen, 648
Mojo, 489
Moloney, Mick, 503
Monocultural festivals, 250
Monroe, Bill, 89, 165, 490–491, 633, 679
Monroe, Roby, 368
Monsters, 491–492
Montell, William Lynwood, 38, 571
Moody, Mart, 7
Moon Festival, 142
Moon walks, 102
Mooney, James, 492, 571, 572
Moore, Thomas, 390
Morgan, Gib, 492–493, 528, 701
Morgan, Kemp, 528
Morgan, Lucy, 749
Morganfield, McKinley, 742
Mormon folklore, 493–496
Morph, 632
Morra, 396
Morris, Robert, 178
Morris, William, 174, 749
Moser, Artus M., 496, 633
Motifemes, 691
Motorcycling, 81–83
Mourning scenes, 506
Moyers, Bill, 113
Mudras, 335
Muk-yu chantefable, 140
Mullen, Patrick B., 38, 316, 444
Müller, Max, 17
Multiculturalism, 386
Mummers, 359, 497
Münchhausen, Baron, 701
Münchhausen narrators, 365
Mural paintings on buildings, 726
Murko, Matija, 530, 544
Murphy, James, 115
Murphy, Mabel, 504
Murphy, Tim, 623
Murray, Margaret, 760

Museums, 603
    folk, 277–278
Music
    African American, 9
    American Indian, 21–22
    Cajun, 111
    conjunto, 156
    country, 164–166
    Creole, 773–775
    ethnomusicology, 230–236
    fiddle, 253–256
    filk, 263
    folk, *see* Folk music
    gospel, 337, 728
    instrumental, dance and, 254
    klezmer, 422–423
    powwow, 586
    rap, 179, 616–617
    vernacular, 164–166
    Western, 231
Musick, Ruth Ann, 497
Musicology, comparative, 231
Mussel-shell fiddle, 538
Myths, 94, 424, 497–498
    animals in, 33
    Hawaiian, 78
    science and, 113
    solar, 17

Name calling, 186
Name magic, 502
Namelore, 501–502
NAMES Project, 611, 675
Narrative, oral, 33
Narrative classification, 45
Narrative jokes, 414–416
Narrative puzzle, 630–631
Nashville, Tennessee, 165
Nast, William, 332
National Association for the Preservation
    and Perpetuation of Storytelling
    (NAPPS), 690
National Council for the Traditional Arts
    (NCTA), 502–503
National Endowment for the Arts (NEA),
    504
National Folk Festival, 249, 424, 502, 503
National Heritage Fellows, 504
Native American, *see also* American Indian
    entries
Native American baskets, 52, 71
Native American folklore, 227
Native American Grave Protection and
    Repatriation Act, 278
Native American performance rituals, 33
Nativity scenes, 144
Natural-conservation movements, 114
Natural phenomena, 498
Naturopathic cures, 469
Neckerchief, 171
Needlework, 504–507, 607
Neff, Pat, 436
Negro, *see also* African American entries;
    Black entries
Negro folklore, 9

Negro jig, 254
Nelson, Marion J., 649
Neopagans, 744
Nestle, Joan, 440
Nevin, Arthur, 22
New Deal, 507–509
    folk culture and, 507–509
New England, 510–512
New France, 310
New Jersey Folk Festival, 251
New Mexico Folklore Society, 634
New Year's dragon, 140
New York Center for Urban Folk Culture,
    145
New York Folklore Society, 707
Newell, William Wells, 19, 77, 138, 319,
    513
Newfoundland songs, 116
Newman, Ronald B., 709
Newport Folk Festival, 250
Newton, Eddie, 417
Nickerson, Bruce, 522
Nicknames, 501–502
Nicolaisen, W. F. H., 438
"Niggerlippers" (catfish), 132
Night-sky tree, 48
Niles, John Jacob, 94, 513–514
Nilsson, Albert, 694
Nisei, 404
Nixon, Richard M., 149
Nketia, J. H. K., 230
Noce, Angelo, 150
Nontraditional storytelling, 690–691
Nonverbal riddles, 629
Nordic, term, 647
Nordic Heritage Museum, 648
North American Basque Organizations,
    Inc. (NABO), 76
North Carolina, University of, 4, 100
North Carolina Folklore, 100
North Carolina Folklore Society, 105
Northeast Folklore, 68
Northrup, Clark S., 525
Northwest Coast, 514–516
Norwegian American Museum, 648
Norwegian Americans, 647–651
Norwegian Independence Day, 650
Norwegian Sagas, 647
Notre Dame, 392
Nova Scotia, 109
Nova Scotia songs, 116
Nuclear-arms race, 148–149
Nuclear-family model, 244
Nuclear lore, 517–518
Numskull tales, 415
Nursery rhymes, 565
Nurses, 467–468
Nye, Pearl R., 518
Nye, Russell, 25

Obon, 405
O'Brien, Tim, 737
Obscene-photocopy lore, 98, 100
Obscenity, 186
Occupation, food and, 302

Occupational folklore, 519–523
O'Donnell, John C., 117–118
Odum, Howard Washington, 94, 413,
    509, 523–524, 675, 686
Ohio Canal, 518
Ohrlin, Glenn, 524
Oikotypes, 437
Oilworkers, 524–528
Olien, Roger M. and Diana Davids, 526
Oliver, Paul, 94, 418
Olivier, Julien, 312
Olney, Marguerite, 276
Olsen, Bernard, 277
Olson, Ole, 650
Omens, 485
Ontario Heritage Policy Review (OHPR),
    124
Open-air museum, 277
Opera, Chinese, 141
Opie, Iona, 138, 319–320, 373, 711
Opie, Peter, 138, 319–320, 373
Opossum, 529
Oral folklore, 137, 288
Oral-formulaic theory, 449–450, 529–
    531, 544, 659
Oral historical traditions, 369–370
Oral narrative, 33
Oral performance, 375
Oral tradition of preliterate cultures, 153
O'Reilly, Edward, 546
O'Reilly, Samuel, 703
Organizational culture, 676
Organizational folklore, 531–533
Organology, 235
Oring, Elliott, 286
Ornamental ironworker, 89
Ornstein, Lisa, 312
Orr, Anne, 610
Ortega y Gassett, Jose, 380
Ory, Kid, 406
Ouija, 534
Out-of-body experiences, 98
Outlaw, 534–535
Outsider art, 535–536
Owen, Blanton, 46
Owen, Mary Alicia, 79, 536
Owen, Robert, 753
Owens, William A., 526, 753
Ownership, 288
    question of, 226
Owsley, Frank, 678
Ozarks, 537–539

Pacific Northwest, 514–516
Paddlefish (catfish), 132
Paige, Satchel, 70
Palance, Jack, 670
Palm, Henny, 688
Pane, Ramon, 17
Paper airplane, 138
Paper cutting, 541–542
Parade-dance, 194
Parades, 728
Paradigms, 657
Paradis, Roger, 312, 313

Parallel texts, 151
Paredes, Américo, 228, 522, 619
Parent, Michael, 312
Parker, Charlie, 407
Parker, Diana, 253
Parker, James, 313
Parker, Robert LeRoy, 130
Parler, Mary Celestia, 542
Parlor ballad, 60–61, 293, 294
Parlor songs, 455–456
Parody, in folklore, 543
Parody riddle jokes, 626, 629
Parry, Milman, 529–530, 544, 659
Parry-Lord theory, 449–450, 529–531,
    544, 659
Parsons, Elsie Clews, 248, 544
Passage, rites of, *see* Rites of passage
Passover, 217, 410–411, 544–545
Pastourelles, 416
Patchwork, 607
Patterson, George, 115
Patterson, Mary-Lou, 119
Patton, Charlie (Charley), 545–546
Pawlowska, Harriet, 568
Peace Ribbon, 611
Peacock, Kenneth, 116, 119
Peasant immigration, 386
Pecos Bill, 546–547
Pedagogic riddling, 628
Peddlers, 547
Peddler's cry, 547
Peer, Ralph Sylvester, 129, 547–548, 639
Peirce, Charles Sanders, 656
Peltier, Leonard, 535, 673–674
Pencil-and-paper puzzles, 631
Pennsylvania, University of, 5
Pennsylvania Culture Region, 548–549
Pennsylvania Dutch, 71–72, 212, 549–
    554
Pennsylvania Folk Festival, 249–250
Pennsylvania Folklife, 666
Pennsylvania folklore, 67
Pennsylvania-German Society, 548
Pensylvania Germans ("Dutch"), 71–72,
    212, 549–554
Pentecost, 214
Pentecostalism, 326
Pepicello, W. J., 630
Performance, oral, 373
Performance approach to folklore, 554–
    556
Performance rituals, Native American, 33
Performance theory, 676
Permiakov, Grigorii L'vovich, 598
Perrow, Eber Carle, 556
Perry, Ben Edwin, 239
Perry, Gaylord, 71
Persian Gulf War, 352–353
Personal-experience story, 556–558
Pesach, 545
Peterson, Meg, 56
Petits Canadas, 311
Petroleum industry, 524–528
Pettit, Katherine, 151, 562
Philippines, 261–262

Photocopylore, 154, 533, 769–770
Pica, 591
Pichette, Jean-Pierre, 307, 309
Pickering, John, 22
Pickering, M. J., 503
Picnic menus, 389
Pictorial rebuses, 631
Pictorial tale, 558–559
Piedmont region, 559–561
Pierce, Elijah, 762–763
Pieri, Pete, 395
"Pigeon drop," 155
Piñatas, 682
Pinkster, 214
Pipkin, Mr. and Mrs. Frank, 59
Pitt-Rivers, A. Lane-Fox, 463
Pittsburgh region, 687
Pitzer College, 5
Place, Etta, 130
Place names, 501–502
Plaiting baskets, 73
Plantlore, 561–562
Plavnieks, Janis, 63
Play-party, 562–564
Playing the dozens, 206–207
Plimoth Plantation, 246
Plugging, 470
Pocius, Gerald L., 117
Poetry
    cowboy, 167–169
    folk, 564–566
Poke plant, 469
Polack jokes, 568, 626
Polish Americans, 567–570
Polish Pope jokes, 627
Political humor, 415–416
Political refugees, 62
Politics and folklore, 570–574
Polka, 196, 254, 569, 574–576, 728–729
Polonia, 567
Polygamy, 494
Polygenesis, 151
Popping, 102
Popular culture, folklore and, 576–578
Porter, Cole, 636
Portuguese Americans, 578–580
Posen, Sheldon, 118
Possum, 529
Post vérité, 264
Postmodernism, 555, 580–581
Postmodernity, 581
Poststructuralism, 183, 581
Postures, 100
Potter, Charles Francis, 628
Pottery, 581–585, 679
Pound, Louise, 79, 450, 585, 676
POW-MIA bracelets, 149
Powell, John Wesley, 18, 175, 492, 572
Powers, Harriet, 609
Powwow, 586–587
Powwow music, 586
Powwowing, 551
Practical jokes, 587–589
Prank, 4, 587–589
Prayer, 589–590

Preachers, 657–659
Pregnancy, 591–592
Preliterate cultures, oral tradition of, 153
Premillennialism, 517
Prescott, Samuel, 624
Preservation, 45
    of food, 584
Presley, Elvis Aron, 220–222
Presnell, Lee Monroe, 368
Pretended obscene riddle, 630
Preternatural topics, 497–498
Primiano, Leonard Norman, 620
Prince Edward Island, 117
Print media, 462
Printers, journeymen, 592–593
Printer's devils, 592
Printwork, 506
Prison folklore, 593–595
Prisons, sexual roles in, 594–595
Profanity, 186
Professors, waiting period for, 3
Proffitt, Frank, Sr., 597, 740
Proffitt, Frank Noah, 368, 595–597
Prohibition, 331
Pronoun forms, 280
Pronunciations, vernacular, 279–281
Propp, Vladimir, 691
Prosterman, Leslie, 40
Protest, social, in folklore, 673–675
Protest songs, 521
Protestant hymnody, 337
Protestant Reformation, 329
Proverbs, 158, 597–600
Psalm tunes, 660
Pseudonyms, 226
Psychodrama, 209
Psychology, folklore and, 601–602
Public folklore, 602–605
Public-folklore movement, 223
Public prayer, 589
*Publications of the American Folklife
    Center,* 16
Puckett, Newbell Niles "Barry," 606, 675
Pueblo Revolt, 570
Pulaski, Casimir, 567–568, 670
Purim, 208
Puritans, 157
Puzzle catch, 632
Puzzles, 630–632

Quadrille, 371, 511
Quebec, Canada and, 124
Queer Nation, 325
Questing ritual, 351
Quilt making, 607–611
Quilts, 52, 679
    African American, 11, 609
Radcliffe-Brown, A. R., 315
Radin, Paul, 35, 716
Radio, amateur, 613–614
Radner, Joan N., 248
Radway, Janice, 577
Rager, Mose, 715
Ragtime, 254
Railroaders, 614–615

Railroads, 343
Rain, 743
Rain dances, 743
Rainey, Gertrude ("Ma"), 615, 671
Ramsay, Sterling, 117
Randolph, Vance, 20, 22, 539, 542, 615–616, 618, 753
Rap, 179, 616–617
Rap lyrics, 96
Rap themes, 102
Rapping, West Indian, 101
Raspe, Rudolph Erich, 701
Rautanen, Viljami, 269
Rawlinson, Thomas, 654
Read, Allen Walker, 339
Realm-shift, 98
Reaman, George Elsmore, 118
Rebus, 631
Recitation, 617–618
Record industry, 164
Recording devices, 257–258
Recreational craft, 96
Redding, Winogene, 749
Redemption rumors, 532
Redfield, Robert, 620
Reel, 254
Reenactment
        Civil War, 146
        in folk drama, 208–210
Refinery workers, 525
Regional costume, Western, 162
Regional folklore, 618–619
Regional foodways, 301–302
Regional riddle jokes, 627
Regionalization, 619
Regions of United States, list of, 619
Reid, Margaret, 483
Religion
        folk, 620–621
        food and, 302
Religious ballad, 660
Religious folk art, 478
Religious jokes, 415
Religious persecution, 62
Reminiscing, 12–13
Rent parties, 406
Research
        folk-culture, 283
        folklife, 284–285
        folklore, ethics in, 225–226
        foodways, 300–301
        team, 285
Residential summer camps, 114
Reuss, Richard August, 521, 571, 622
Revere, Paul, 624
Revivalism, 622–623
Revolutionary War, 623–624
Revson, Charles, 532
Reynolds, Anthony M., 709
Reynolds, Ralph, 304
Rheumatism cures, 469
Rhymes
        counting-out, 137
        nursery, 565
Rhys, Morgan John, 753

Rhythm, 564
        folk, used in military, 109
Rice, Thomas D., 487
Richard, William, 762
Richman, Hyman, 687, 688
Richmond, W. Edson, 624–625
Rickaby, Franz, 625
Riddle, Almeda, 625–626
Riddle act, 628
Riddle block, 630
Riddle joke chain, 626
Riddle jokes, 137, 558, 626–628, 629
Riddle sessions, 628
Riddles, 153, 158, 628–630
Rietl, Barbara, 117
Riffs, 91
Riggs, Lynn, 433
Riley, Steve, 110
Rindlisbacher, Otto, 625
Ring shouts, 667
Ring-tailed roarers, 636, 637
Rinzler, Ralph Carter, 252, 299, 632–633, 672, 742–743
Ritchie, Jean, 496, 633–634
Rites of passage, 12, 187–188
        annual, 33–34
        calendrical, 40
        Jewish, 410
        organizational, 533
        ritual drama in, 209
Ritual, 188
Roach, Hal, 392
Robb, John Donald, 634
Roberts, John M., 321
Roberts, Leonard Ward, 36, 80, 152, 399, 634–635
Roberts, Warren, 284, 300, 522
Robertson, Mrs. Sidney, 212
Robertson, Royal, 536
Robin Hood, 535
Robinson, Rowland E., 635
Rock and roll, 165
Rockefeller, Abby Aldrich, 49
Rocky Mountains, 635–637
Rodeo, 637–639
Rodeo cowboys, 639
Rodgers, James Charles ("Jimmie"), 93, 164, 639–640
Rogers, Francis, 578
Rogers, Will, 640
Rogow, Lee, 711
Role-playing, 226
Rollman, Wil, 739
Rolvaag, Ella Valborg, 649
Rolvaag, Ole Edvart, 650
Romani, 356–357
Romanian Americans, 640–642
Root medicine, 471
Roping events, 638
Rourke, Constance, 24, 266, 374, 390
Roy, Carmen, 308
Royce, Morton, 508
Rudnye'kyj, J. B., 119
Rumor, 438, 642–643, 727
Running gags, 719

Rural agriculture, 246
Rural Handicrafts movement, 73
Ruskin, John, 174, 749
Ruth, George Herman "Babe," 70
Ryan, Paddy, 393
Ryan, Shannon, 116

Sabael, 7
Sabattis, Mitchell, 7
Sachs, Curt, 233
Sacred lyric songs, 453
Said, Edward, 573
Sailing lugger, 111
Sailors, 474–475
St. David's Day, 754
St. John's Day, 677
St. Joseph's Day, 395, 397
St. Nicholas, 214, 332
St. Patrick's Day, 393, 684
St. Pierre, Simon, 504
St. Urho, 271
Saint-Gaudens, Augustus, 392
Saints, folk, 766
Saint's day, 645–646
Salt glaze, 582–583
Samhain, 359
Samplers, 505–506
Sandburg, Carl, 599, 646–647
Sansei, 404
Santa Claus, 145
Santana, Carlos, 92
Santino, Jack, 522, 533, 614
Sapoznik, Henry, 423
Saravino, Zulay, 264
Sasquatch, 81
Satanic cults, 181
Satanism, 760
Sauna, 270
Saussure, Ferdinand de, 656
Saxon, Lyle, 647
Sayers, Robert, 633
Scarborough, Emily Dorothy, 651
Scarecrow, 464
Scatology, 186
Schantz, F. J. F., 283
Scheiber, Larry, 557
Schmitz, Nancy, 307
Schneider, Marius, 233
Schoolcraft, Henry Rowe, 17, 184, 537, 652
Schools, folk, 278–279
Schottische, 254
Schuller, Robert H., 731
Schwartz, Abe, 423
Schwartz, Barry, 676
Schwoefferman, Catherine, 523
Science, mythology and, 113
Scots-Irish fiddle tradition, 65
Scott, Gilbert George, 734
Scott, Walter, 394
Scottish Americans, 652–654
Scruggs, Earl, 89, 504
Sculpture, 761
Sea chantey, 134–135, 765
Seamen, merchant, 474–475

Seasons, passage of, 498
Seaweed, 391
Second Great Awakening, 658
Secondhand clothing, 162
Secondhand folk history, 369
Secular lyric songs, 453–455
Seder, 544–545
Seeger, Anthony, 673
Seeger, Charles Louis, 234, 508, 655
Seeger, Mike, 56
Seeger, Pete, 298, 356, 655–656, 674
Séguin, Robert-Lionel, 307
Seibert, T. Lawrence, 417
Seitel, Peter, 672
Self-comparisons, 95
Self-empowerment, 223
Selvage, 745
Semiotic approach to folklore, 656–657
Semiotics, 236, 656
        of lyric songs, 454–455
Sennett, Mack, 392
Sephardic Jews, 409, 410
Sermon, folk, 657–659
Serpent handling, 679
Serrif, Suzanne, 522
Settlement-school idea, 278
Sexual roles in prisons, 594–595
Sexuality, 98
Shaggy-dog story, 414
Shakers, 71
Shakespeare, William, 598
Shamanism, 426
Shango, 69
Shantys, 135
Shape-note singing, 659–661
Sharp, Cecil James, 22, 36, 80, 114, 116,
        387, 618, 622, 661
Shaw, John, 117
Shaw, Lloyd, 194
Sheep camp, 661–662
Sheepherder, 662–665
Sheepherder Laws, 74
Shelburne Museum, 49
Shepherds, 663–664
Shepperd, W., 662
Shine, 665, 709, 710
Shivaree, 665–666
Shoemaker, Alfred L., 283, 464, 551, 666
Shoemaker, Henry Wharton, 266, 627,
        667
Shout, 667–668
Shrove Tuesday, 111–112, 214
Shuckburgh, George, 624
Shuldiner, David, 574
Shultz, Arnold, 490, 715
Sick jokes, 415
Sidle, Kenny, 504
Sign, 656
Sign superstitions, 691
Signifier and signified, 656
Signifying, 206
Silhouettes, 541
Simard, Jean, 307
Similes, 95
Simmons, Philip, 89

Simon, Albert "Ding-Ding," 701–702
Simpson, Jimmy, 528
Singing, shape-note, 659–661
Singing schools, 660
Singleton, Ann, 80
Sirka Finns, 267
Situation, context of, 159
Situational construction, 159
Skaardal, Dorothy Burton, 647
Skaggs, Ricky, 391
Skinner, Charles M., 668
Skits, 115, 209
Slang, 281
Slave Songs of the United States, 18
Slavic Americans, 668–671
Slezak, Anna, 574
Slip jig, 254
Sluckin, Andy, 322
Small, Larry, 116
Smile, 334
Smith, Abraham ("Oregon"), 671, 701
Smith, Ada B., 114
Smith, Bessie, 615, 671–672
Smith, C. Alphonso, 197
Smith, Grace Partridge, 672
Smith, Harry, 633
Smith, Henry Nash, 24–25
Smith, Jimmy Neil, 690
Smith, Joseph, 493
Smith, Mamie, 93, 548
Smith, Mary Alice, 750
Smith, Mary T., 536
Smithsonian Institution, 387
Smithsonian Institution Center for Folklife
        Programs and Cultural Studies,
        672–673
Smyth, Willie, 67, 628
Snider, C. H. J., 118
Snipe Hunt, 115
Snyder, Jib, 345
Social conflict, 676
Social control, 316, 676
Social dances, 191
Social dialect, 281
Social protest in folklore, 673–675
Social-welfare societies, 62
Socialists, Baltic, 62
Society toasts, 709
Sociological approach to folklore, 675–677
Socrates, 643
Sod houses, 347
Solar myths, 17, 424
Solley, Roscoe, 566
Solstices, summer and winter, 677
Song-poems, 674
Songs
        banjo, 65
        Canadian, 118
        catalog, 58, 292
        Civil War, 145–146
        drinking, 328
        epic, 57
        farming, 347
        fo'c'sle, 474
        lyric, 292, 453–456

maritime, 460
Newfoundland, 116
Nova Scotia, 116
parlor, 455–456
protest, 521
traditional, 68
Sorbs in United States, 755
Sorcery, 758
Sounding, 95–96, 206
South, 678–680
Southern Arts Federation, 680
Southern Arts Federation Folk-Arts
        Program, 680–681
Southern folk architecture, 678
Southern Folklife Collection, 373
Southern Folklore Quarterly, 100
Southern Highland Handicraft Guild, 175
Southern Highlands, see Appalachia
Southern States Arts League, 680
Southern Tenant Farmers Union
        (STFU), 362
Southwest, 681–682
Space Age, 149
Spanish American dance, 195–196
Speaking, ethnography of, 555–556
Special-knowledge puzzles, 631
Speck, Frank, 434
Speech, folk, 279–281
Spencer, Herbert, 315, 693
Spider trickster, 27–28
Spier, Leslie, 325
Spinning, 746
Spirit bodies, 98
Spirituals, 400
        African American, 682–684
Spivak, Gayatri Chakravorty, 249
Spoonbill (catfish), 132
Sports, 319
Sports fishing, 271, 274–275
Sportsmen, 380
Spray, Carole, 117
Square dance, 193, 194
Staebler, Edna, 119
Stages of life, 12
Stagolee, 684–686
Stahl, Sandra K. D., 443
Stampede, 638
Stamps, Daniel, 701
Staples, Roebuck "Pops," 546
Starr, Mary Agnes, 310
Statman, Andy, 423
Staub, Shalom, 229
Steam bath, Finnish, 270
Steel Industry Heritage Corporation
        (SIHC), 687
Steelworkers, 687–689
Stekert, Ellen, 623
Stepping, 689–690
Stereotypes
        ethnic, 229–230
        folk, 277
Stern, Stephen, 387–388
Stewart, Cal, 617
Still, William, 570
"Sting," 156

Stocking, Moses, 701
Stoeltje, Beverly J., 248
Stoker, Bram, 642, 733
Stone, Kay, 119, 248
Stoneman, Ernest, 56
Stories
    coming-out, 441
    Cousin Jack, 167
    dialect, 200–201
    ghost, 335–336
    kernel, 247
Story-patterns, 450, 530
Storytellers, 771
Storytelling, 295, 577, 690–691
    Cajun, 112
Storytelling traditions, 295
Street cry, 547
Street-music lyrics, 96
Street performers, 728
Stride piano, 672
Strongmen, 99
Structural analysis, 425
Stubblefield, Blaine ("Stub"), 692
Student customs, 3–4
Studies in American Folklife, 16
Stump, Dwight, 73
Stumpf, Carl, 233
Sturgis, Edith, 68
Subcultures, 676
Subsistence fishing, 272
Sukkot, 729
Sulkkonen, Elias, 269
Sullivan, John L., 393
Summer camps, lore of, 114–115
Summer solstices, 677
Sumner, William Graham, 295–296, 675
Sun dog, 743
Sunbonnet, 680
Sunbonnet Sue, 147
Sundance, 346
Superstitions, 459, 475, 691, 692–696
Sutton-Smith, Brian, 319–321, 601
Swearing, 185–186
Swede's Day, 677
Swedish American Museum, 648
Swedish Americans, 647–651
Sweeney, Joel, 65
Sweezy, Nancy, 633
Swetnam, George, 458, 687
Symbol, 656
Syncretistic religions, 621
Syntagms, 657

Taché, Joseph-Charles, 306
Taft, Michael, 119
Tagging, 339
Talismans, 532
Talking trash, 699–700
Tall tales, 95, 125, 381, 699, 700–702
Tallant, Robert, 647
Tallas, 477
Talley, Thomas Washington, 702
Tally, 488
Talmadge, Gene, 127
Tamburitza, 702–703, 729

Tap dance, 195
Taras, Dave, 423
Tartt, Ruby Pickens, 126
Tate, Lou, 750
Tatem, Moira, 711
Tattooing, 100, 703–704
Tavic, Andras, 703
Taylor, Archer, 79, 152–153, 597, 704–705
Taylor, David A., 313
Team research, 285
Team roping, 638
Technical culture, folk, 463
Tecumseh, 673
Teepee tents, 662
Telegraphers, 614
Tenor banjo, 65
Tepes, Vlad, 733
Terry, Sonny (Sanders Turell), 705
Tesla, Nikola, 670
Texas Folklore Society, 97
Textile bedcoverings, 607–611
Thanksgiving Day, 186–187, 705–706
Thayer, Ernest Lawrence, 618
Themes, 450
Theories, conspiracy, 157–158
Theriot, Roy, 110
Third World products, 532
Thirteen, number, 314
Thlunaut, Jennie, 504
Thomas, Gerald, 308
Thomas, Jeannette Bell, 706–707
Thomas, Philip J., 119
Thomas, Rosemary Hyde, 127
Thompson, Harold W., 701, 707
Thompson, Kenneth, 675
Thompson, Stith, 152, 509, 707–708
Thoms, William J., 285–286
Thorp, Nathan Howard ("Jack"), 171, 519, 546, 708
Three Mile Island Nuclear Power Plant accident, 517
Three Nephites, 494–495
Thunder, 744
Thurber, James, 239
Titanic, 665, 709
Toad Suck, Arkansas, 132
Toast, 153, 665, 708–710
Toelken, Barre, 173, 286
Tolliver, Moses, 536
Tolman, Albert H., 219
Tombstones, inscribed, 223–224
Tongue twisters, 710
Tonti, Enrico, 394–395
Toolmaker, 89
Tooth fairy, 187–188, 239, 711
Tornadoes, 347, 744
Totem pole, 52
Tough, Dave, 407
Tourist camps, 114
Town meeting, 510
Toys, folk, 712–714
Tracy, Jones, 701
Traditional architecture, 41
Traditional-arts programming, 602

Traditional medicine, 468
Traditional songs, 68
Trail-driving songs, 764
Train dispatchers, 614
Train wrecks, 615
Tramp printers, 592
Transplanted folklore, 497
Transylvania, 642
Trapping, 714–715
Trash, talking, 699–700
Travis, Merle Robert, 418, 715–716
Travis, William B., 179
Trickster, 415, 444, 716–717
    spider, 27–28
Trickster Coyote, 172–173
Trickster tales, 9, 718
Trickster-Transformer, 716
Triskaidekaphobia, 314
Trivialization strategy of expression, 148
Troxell, William S., 552
Troy, Hugh, 588
Truckers' folklore, 717–719
True riddles, 629
Truman, Harry, 428
Tsimouris, Nikitas, 504
Tuleja, Tad, 711
Turell, Sanders, 705
Turnbo, Silas Claiborn, 719
Turner, Frederick Jackson, 374
Turner societies, 331, 332
Turnvereine, 331, 332
Twain, Mark, 95, 131, 289, 290, 481, 719–720, 771
Tye, Diane, 444
Tyler, Royall, 105
Tylor, Edward B., 319, 693, 758

Udall, Lee, 623
UFO lore, 491, 517, 721–722
Ukranian Americans, 670, 722–724
Uncle Remus, 724–725
Uncle Sam, 104
Underground Railroad, 570
United States, *see also* American entries
    Baltic peoples in, 61–64
    comparative approach to folklore studies in, 152–153
    folklore programs in, 4–6
    French in, 309–313
    list of regions of, 619
United Steelworkers of America (USWA), 687
University students, folk lore of, 3–4
Upland South, *see* Appalachia
Urban folklore, 725–729
Urban legend, 439, 531, 730–731
Utley, Francis Lee, 731–732

Vachon, Jingo Viitala, 270
Valentine's Day, 733
Validation, 316
Vampires, 733–734
Vandalism, cemetery, 134
Vandiver, Pendleton, 490
Vaqueros, 162, 170, 478, 727

Vasa Day, 677
Vejvoda, Jaromir, 575
Velure, Magne, 695
Vennum, Thomas, 673
Verb forms, nonstandard, 280
Verbal artistry of auction process, 54
Verbal magic, 469
Verbal mnemonics, 488–489
Verbal riddles, 629
Vermont folklore, 635
Vernacular, term, 734
Vernacular architecture, 41–44
Vernacular Architecture Forum (VAF), 734
Vernacular Black English, 86–87
Vernacular boats, 96–97
Vernacular medicine, 468
Vernacular motifs, 735
Vernacular music, 164–166
Vernacular pronunciations, 279–281
Vernacular religion, 620–621
Verse, Child-ballad, 58
Vesekla, Aldona, 746, 747, 748
Vesterheim Collection, 648
Video, 263
Video cameras, 258–259
Vietnam Veterans Memorial, 736
Vietnam War, 484–485, 736–737
Vigil, Cleofes, 504
Villoteau, Guillaume-André, 232
Violin, 253
Viruses, computer, 155
Visiting Day, 188
Visual descriptive riddles, 629
Vocals, bluegrass, 90
Vocational gestures, 334
Von Sydow, Carl Wilhelm, 437, 438, 472–473, 671, 694–695
Voodoo, 11, 679
Voorhies, Felix, 110
Voyageurs, 310
Voyer, Simone, 307
Vuckovich, Pete, 670

Waddell, Rube, 70
Wagner, Charlie, 703
Wagner, Honus, 70–71
Wagner, Paul, 673
Wainwright, 89
Waiting period for professors, 3
Walker, Alice, 418
Wall, Ron, 56
Walton, Ivan, 739
Waltz, 254
Ward, Donald, 695–696
Ward, Lem, 52
Ward, Marshall, 739–740
Ware, Charles Pickard, 18
Warner, Anne Locher, 740
Warner, Frank, 595, 740
Warner, William W., 742
Warping, 747
Wartime folklore, 766–768
Washington, George, 676–677, 715
Wasserberger, George, 532
Water witching, 205

Watercraft, 96–97
Watergate, 149
Watermen, 740–742
Waters, Muddy (McKinley Morganfield), 742
Watson, Arthel ("Doc"), 504, 633, 742–743
Watson, Thomas, Jr., 532
Watterson, Bill, 462
Watts, Howard, 89
Watts Towers, 728
Wayne State University (WSU) Folklore Archive, 403
Weather extremes, 700
Weatherlore, 459, 743–744
Weathervanes, 744
Weavers, 655
Weaving, 745–750
Weaving baskets, 73
Webster, Marie, 610
Wedding anniversaries, 33–34
Wedding reception, 752
Weddings, 750–753
Weigle, Marta, 247
Weir, Charles, 138
Weiser, Fred, 554
Weiss, Richard, 282
Wellerisms, 600
Wells, David D., 725
Wells, Evelyn Kendrick, 753
Wells, Rosemary, 711
Wells, William, 513
Welsh Americans, 753–754
Wendell, Barrett, 447, 448
Wends in United States, 755
Wepman, Dennis, 709
Werner, Abraham Gootlob, 537
West, Cornel, 573
West, George, 626
West, Max, 749
West African folktales, 10
West Indian rapping, 101
West Virginia Folk-Lore Society, 172
West Virginia folklore, 497
Western film, 164–165
Western music, 231
Western Range Association, 74–75
Western regional costume, 162
Wetmore, Alphonso, 266
Weygandt, Cornelius, 434
Whaling tradition, 510
Wheeler, Candace, 749
Wheelwright, 89
Whisnant, David, 572, 605
White, John I., 755
White, Newman Ivey, 105, 755–756
White-collar crime, 178
White witches, 760
Whitman, Walt, 289–290
Whitney, Gertrude Vanderbilt, 49
Whitsunday, 214
Whittier, John Greenleaf, 756
Whittlers, 761
Whoppers, 699
Wicca, 760

Widdowson, J. D. A., 117
Wiggins, Ella Mae, 433
Wigginton, B. Eliot, 220, 303–304
Wild animals, 32–33
Wild Bunch, 130
Wild West shows, 638
Wilfahrt, Hans, 575
Wilgus, D. K., 151, 756–757
Wilkerson, John, 626
Williams, George W., 450
Williams, Hank, 165
Williams, Jack, 742
Williams, Michael Ann, 38
Williamsburg, Virginia, 41
Wills, Bob, 111, 164, 757
Wilson, Joe, 623
Wilson, Joseph T., 317, 503
Wilson, William A., 676
Winchester, Alice, 48
Wintemberg, W. J., 118
Winter, 744
Winter solstices, 677
Winterthur Museum, 49
Wiora, Walter, 233, 235
Wise, Chubby, 89
Wiseman, Lulu Belle, 758
Wiseman, Scotty, 758
Witchcraft, 758–760
Wittgenstein, Ludwig, 694
Wobblies, 369
Wolf, Howlin', 546
Wolf, John Quincy, Jr., 626, 760–761
Wolfenstein, Martha, 138, 601
Wolford, Leah Jackson, 564
Wolofs, 64, 135
Wolpertinger, 400
Wood carving, 761–763
Wooden boats, 97
Word charade, 629
Work, folklore of, 728
Work, John, II, 702
Workplace folklore, 531–533
Works Progress Administration (WPA), 9, 49
Worksong, 595, 763–765
World Series of Birding, 84, 85
World Wars I and II, 766–768
Worldview, 276
Worst, Edward F., 749
Wright, Joseph, 22

Xeroxlore, 154, 155, 769–770

Yankee, 510
Yankee Doodle, 104, 624
Yankovic, Frankie, 576, 670
Yarn, 474, 771
Yarrow, Grace, 116
Yava, Albert, 166
Yeats, William Butler, 617
Yiddish, 409–410
Yiddish theater, 422
Yodel, 640
Yoder, Don, 282–283, 300, 522, 551, 554, 620

Yonsei, 404
Yoopers, 201
Yoruba, 69
Young, Katharine, 98
Young, Lester, 407
Young, M. Jane, 248

Yule log, 677

Zajc, Ivan, 703
Zanetis, Alex, 528
Zeitlin, Steven, 145, 323, 523
Zelinsky, Wilbur, 479, 548

Zerbec, Stevan, 703
Zhushan Chinese Opera Institute, 142
Zimmerman, Charles F., 55
Zipes, Jack, 461, 691
Zulu Nation, 101
Zydeco, 94, 773–775